THE
ALL ENGLAND
LAW REPORTS

1989

Volume 1

Editor
PETER HUTCHESSON LLM
Barrister, New Zealand

Assistant Editor
BROOK WATSON
of Lincoln's Inn, Barrister
and of the New South Wales Bar

Consulting Editor
WENDY SHOCKETT
of Gray's Inn, Barrister

London
BUTTERWORTHS

UNITED KINGDOM	Butterworth & Co (Publishers) Ltd, 88 Kingsway, **London** WC2B 6AB and 4 Hill Street, **Edinburgh** EH2 3JZ
AUSTRALIA	Butterworths Pty Ltd, **Sydney, Melbourne, Brisbane, Adelaide, Perth, Canberra** and **Hobart**
CANADA	Butterworths Canada Ltd, **Toronto** and **Vancouver**
IRELAND	Butterworth (Ireland) Ltd, **Dublin**
MALAYSIA	Malayan Law Journal Pte Ltd, **Kuala Lumpur**
NEW ZEALAND	Butterworths of New Zealand Ltd, **Wellington** and **Auckland**
SINGAPORE	Butterworth & Co (Asia) Pte Ltd, **Singapore**
USA	Butterworth Legal Publishers, **St Paul**, Minnesota, **Seattle**, Washington, **Boston**, Massachusetts, **Austin**, Texas and D & S Publishers, **Clearwater**, Florida

ISBN 0 406 85167 0

Butterworths

 PART OF REED INTERNATIONAL P.L.C.

REPORTERS

House of Lords

Mary Rose Plummer Barrister

Privy Council

Mary Rose Plummer Barrister

Court of Appeal, Civil Division

Mary Rose Plummer Barrister
Frances Rustin Barrister
Carolyn Toulmin Barrister
Wendy Shockett Barrister
Sophie Craven Barrister
Dilys Tausz Barrister
Celia Fox Barrister

Court of Appeal, Criminal Division

N P Metcalfe Esq Barrister
Raina Levy Barrister
Dilys Tausz Barrister
Kate O'Hanlon Barrister

Chancery Division

Jacqueline Metcalfe Barrister
Evelyn M C Budd Barrister
Hazel Hartman Barrister
Celia Fox Barrister

Queen's Bench Division

M Denise Chorlton Barrister
K Mydeen Esq Barrister
J M Collins Esq Barrister

Family Division

Bebe Chua Barrister

Admiralty

N P Metcalfe Esq Barrister

Revenue Cases

Rengan Krishnan Esq Barrister
Heather Whicher Barrister

Courts-Martial Appeals

N P Metcalfe Esq Barrister

SUB-EDITOR

Caroline Vandridge-Ames

MANAGER

Eric W Spalding Esq

EDITORIAL STAFF

Audrey Trattell
Margaret Froome

House of Lords

The Lord High Chancellor: Lord Mackay of Clashfern

Lords of Appeal in Ordinary

Lord Keith of Kinkel
Lord Bridge of Harwich
Lord Brandon of Oakbrook
Lord Templeman
Lord Griffiths

Lord Ackner
Lord Oliver of Aylmerton
Lord Goff of Chieveley
Lord Jauncey of Tullichettle
Lord Lowry

Court of Appeal

The Lord High Chancellor

The Lord Chief Justice of England: Lord Lane
(President of the Criminal Division)

The Master of the Rolls: Lord Donaldson of Lymington
(President of the Civil Division)

The President of the Family Division: Sir Stephen Brown

The Vice-Chancellor: Sir Nicolas Christopher Henry Browne-Wilkinson

Lords Justices of Appeal

Sir Tasker Watkins VC
  (Deputy Chief Justice)
Sir Patrick McCarthy O'Connor
Sir Michael John Fox
Sir Michael Robert Emanuel Kerr
Sir John Douglas May
Sir Christopher John Slade
Sir Francis Brooks Purchas
Sir George Brian Hugh Dillon
Sir Roger Jocelyn Parker
Sir David Powell Croom-Johnson
Sir Anthony John Leslie Lloyd
Sir Brian Thomas Neill
Sir Michael John Mustill
Sir Martin Charles Nourse

Sir Iain Derek Laing Glidewell
Sir Alfred John Balcombe
Sir Ralph Brian Gibson
Sir John Dexter Stocker
Sir Harry Kenneth Woolf
Sir Donald James Nicholls
Sir Thomas Henry Bingham
Sir Thomas Patrick Russell
Dame Ann Elizabeth Oldfield Butler-Sloss
Sir Peter Murray Taylor
Sir Murray Stuart-Smith
Sir Christopher Stephen Thomas Jonathan
  Thayer Staughton
Sir Michael Mann

Chancery Division

The Lord High Chancellor

The Vice-Chancellor

Sir John Evelyn Vinelott
Sir Douglas William Falconer
Sir Jean-Pierre Frank Eugene Warner
Sir Peter Leslie Gibson
Sir David Herbert Mervyn Davies
Sir Jeremiah LeRoy Harman

Sir Richard Rashleigh Folliott Scott
(Vice-Chancellor of the County Palatine
of Lancaster)
Sir Leonard Hubert Hoffmann
Sir John Leonard Knox
Sir Peter Julian Millett
Sir Robert Andrew Morritt
Sir William Aldous

Queen's Bench Division

The Lord Chief Justice of England

Sir Bernard Caulfield
  (retired 24 April 1989)
Sir William Lloyd Mars-Jones
Sir Leslie Kenneth Edward Boreham
Sir Alfred William Michael Davies
Sir Kenneth George Illtyd Jones
  (retired 10 January 1989)
Sir Haydn Tudor Evans
Sir Kenneth Graham Jupp
Sir Walter Derek Thornley Hodgson
Sir Ronald Gough Waterhouse
Sir Frederick Maurice Drake
Sir Barry Cross Sheen
Sir David Bruce McNeill
Sir Christopher James Saunders French
Sir Peter Edlin Webster
Sir Donald Henry Farquharson
Sir Anthony James Denys McCowan
Sir Iain Charles Robert McCullough
Sir Hamilton John Leonard
Sir Alexander Roy Asplan Beldam
Sir David Cozens-Hardy Hirst
Sir John Stewart Hobhouse
Sir Andrew Peter Leggatt
Sir Michael Patrick Nolan
Sir Oliver Bury Popplewell
Sir William Alan Macpherson
Sir Philip Howard Otton

Sir Paul Joseph Morrow Kennedy
Sir Michael Hutchison
Sir Simon Denis Brown
Sir Anthony Howell Meurig Evans
Sir Mark Oliver Saville
Sir Johan Steyn
Sir Christopher Dudley Roger Rose
Sir Richard Howard Tucker
Sir Robert Alexander Gatehouse
Sir Patrick Neville Garland
Sir John Ormond Roch
Sir Michael John Turner
Sir Harry Henry Ognall
Sir John Downes Alliott
Sir Konrad Hermann Theodor Schiemann
Sir John Arthur Dalziel Owen
Sir Denis Robert Maurice Henry
Sir Francis Humphrey Potts
Sir Richard George Rougier
Sir Ian Alexander Kennedy
Sir Nicholas Addison Phillips
Sir Robin Ernest Auld
Sir Malcolm Thomas Pill
Sir Stuart Neill McKinnon
Sir Mark Howard Potter
Sir Henry Brooke
Sir Igor Judge
Sir Edwin Frank Jowitt

Family Division

The President of the Family Division

Sir John Brinsmead Latey
  (retired 10 January 1989)
Sir Alfred Kenneth Hollings
Sir Brian Drex Bush
  (died 3 April 1989)
Sir John Kember Wood
Sir Thomas Michael Eastham
Dame Margaret Myfanwy Wood Booth
Sir Anthony Leslie Julian Lincoln
Sir Anthony Bruce Ewbank
Sir John Douglas Waite

Sir Anthony Barnard Hollis
Sir Swinton Barclay Thomas
Sir Mathew Alexander Thorpe
Sir Edward Stephen Cazalet
Sir Thomas Scott Gillespie Baker
Sir Alan Hylton Ward
Sir Robert Lionel Johnson
  (appointed 18 January 1989)
Sir Douglas Dunlop Brown
  (appointed 19 January 1989)

CITATION

These reports are cited thus:

[1989] 1 All ER

REFERENCES

These reports contain references to the following major works of legal reference described in the manner indicated below.

Halsbury's Laws of England

The reference 26 Halsbury's Laws (4th edn) para 577 refers to paragraph 577 on page 296 of volume 26 of the fourth edition of Halsbury's Laws of England.

The reference 7(1) Halsbury's Laws (4th edn reissue) para 267 refers to paragraph 267 on page 177 of reissue volume 7(1) of the fourth edition of Halsbury's Laws of England.

Halsbury's Statutes of England and Wales

The reference 27 Halsbury's Statutes (4th edn) 208 refers to page 208 of volume 27 of the fourth edition of Halsbury's Statutes of England and Wales.

The reference 4 Halsbury's Statutes (4th edn) (1987 reissue) 953 refers to page 953 of the 1987 reissue of volume 4 of the fourth edition of Halsbury's Statutes of England and Wales.

The reference 28 Halsbury's Statutes (3rd edn) 751 refers to page 751 of volume 28 of the third edition of Halsbury's Statutes of England.

The Digest

References are to the green band reissue volumes of The Digest (formerly the English and Empire Digest).

The reference 36(2) Digest (Reissue) 764, 1398 refers to case number 1398 on page 764 of Digest Green Band Reissue Volume 36(2).

The reference 27(1) Digest (2nd reissue) 330, 2849 refers to case number 2849 on page 330 of Digest Green Band Second Reissue Volume 27(1).

Halsbury's Statutory Instruments

The reference 1 Halsbury's Statutory Instruments (Grey Volume) 278 refers to page 278 of Grey Volume 1 of Halsbury's Statutory Instruments.

The reference 17 Halsbury's Statutory Instruments (4th reissue) 256 refers to page 256 of the fourth reissue of volume 17 of Halsbury's Statutory Instruments.

Cases reported in volume 1

Digest of cases reported in volume 1

House of Lords petitions

This list, which covers the period 17 December 1988 to 21 April 1989, sets out all cases which have formed the subject of a report in the All England Law Reports in which an Appeal Committee of the House of Lords has, subsequent to the publication of that report, dismissed a petition or refused leave to appeal on a perusal of the papers or after an oral hearing. Where the result of a petition for leave to appeal was known prior to the publication of the relevant report a note of that result appears at the end of the report.

Carne v Debono [1988] 3 All ER 485, CA. Petition refused 20 December 1988 (Lord Bridge, Lord Brandon and Lord Goff) (perusal of papers)

Evpo Agnic, The [1988] 3 All ER 810, CA. Leave to appeal refused 19 January 1989 (Lord Bridge, Lord Templeman and Lord Oliver) (oral hearing)

Hilton v Plustitle Ltd [1988] 3 All ER 1051, CA. Leave to appeal refused 27 February 1989 (Lord Bridge, Lord Griffiths and Lord Goff) (oral hearing)

R v Anderson [1988] 2 All ER 549, CA. Leave to appeal refused 13 April 1989 (Lord Keith, Lord Griffiths and Lord Lowry) (perusal of papers)

T and ors (minors) (wardship: jurisdiction), Re [1989] 1 All ER 297, CA. Petition refused 28 February 1989 (Lord Keith, Lord Goff and Lord Jauncey) (perusal of papers)

United Bank of Kuwait v Hammoud [1988] 3 All ER 418, CA. Petition refused 20 December 1988 (Lord Bridge, Lord Brandon and Lord Goff) (perusal of papers)

b # Inglewood Investment Co Ltd v Forestry Commission

COURT OF APPEAL, CIVIL DIVISION
DILLON, BUTLER-SLOSS AND STAUGHTON LJJ
18 OCTOBER 1988

c

Game – Shooting and sporting rights – Reservation of shooting and sporting rights – Appointment of land in 1921 reserving to appointors 'hunting shooting fishing coursing and sporting rights' over and on land in respect of 'all game woodcocks snipe and other wild fowl hares rabbits and fish' – Whether 'game' including deer – Whether taking of deer reserved to appointors.

d

By an indenture made in 1921 certain lands in Staffordshire comprising some 1,200 acres were appointed by the plaintiffs' predecessors in title to the Forestry Commissioners for a term of 999 years subject to a reservation whereby the appointors reserved to themselves the exclusive right of 'hunting shooting fishing coursing and sporting over and on' the appointed land in respect of 'all game woodcocks snipe and other wild fowl hares rabbits and fish'. When deer on the land started to cause damage to the trees the commissioners

e shot them to protect the trees. The plaintiffs sought a declaration that the commissioners were not entitled to hunt or shoot any deer on the land, contending that deer were 'game' and had been reserved under the indenture to the original appointors and their successors. The judge held that the reservation of game did not include deer and that the commissioners were entitled to shoot them. The plaintiffs appealed.

f

Held – There was no established meaning of 'game' which included deer and therefore 'game' was to be construed in the context of the indenture. Having regard to the context of the reservation, since 'game' has been used in collocation with 'woodcocks snipe and other wild fowl hares rabbits and fish', which might not be clearly covered by the word 'game', 'game' could not be construed as including deer. Furthermore, the reservation of

g the right to hunt etc was merely the corollary of the reservation of game etc to the appointors and did not expand or grant additional rights in respect of animals or birds other than those reserved under the indenture to the appointors. The appeal would therefore be dismissed (see p 3 *h*, p 4 *b e h* and p 5 *b c*, post).

Decision of Harman J [1988] 1 All ER 783 affirmed.

h

Notes
For the meaning of 'game' and the reservation of game rights, see 2 Halsbury's laws (4th edn) paras 211, 245–247, and for cases on the subject, see 25 Digest (Reissue) 392, 394–399, 3536–3542, 3556–3588.

j **Case referred to in judgments**
Jeffryes v Evans (1865) 19 CBNS 246, 144 ER 781.

Case also cited
Blades v Higgs (1865) 11 HL Cas 621, 11 ER 1474.

Appeal

The plaintiffs, Inglewood Investment Co Ltd, appealed against the judgment of Harman   *a*
J ([1988] 1 All ER 783, [1988] 1 WLR 959) given on 17 November 1987 dismissing the
plaintiffs' action against the defendants, the Forestry Commission, for, inter alia, a
declaration that on the true construction of an indenture made on 17 August 1921
between (1) the Rt Hon Edward George Percy Third Baron Hatherton and the Hon
Edward Charles Rowley Littleton and (2) the Forestry Commissioners, the commission
was not entitled to any deer and was not entitled to hunt or shoot or sport after or take   *b*
any deer on or from land situate in the parishes of Cannock, Huntington, Teddesley Hay,
Bednall and Brereton, Staffordshire. The facts are set out in the judgment of Dillon LJ.

Nigel Davis for the plaintiffs.
John Mummery for the commission was not called on.

                                                                                                   c

DILLON LJ. The plaintiffs in this action, Inglewood Investment Co Ltd, appeal against
a decision of Harman J given on 17 November 1987 whereby their action was dismissed
with costs. Harman J's decision has been reported (see [1988] 1 All ER 783, [1988] 1
WLR 959), but I take the view that the decision is concerned only with the construction
and effect of a particular document and does not raise questions of general importance at
all.   *d*

That document is an indenture of 17 August 1921 made between the third Baron
Hatherton and his eldest son of Hatherton Hall in the county of Stafford of the one part
and the respondents to this appeal, the Forestry Commissioners (the commission), of the
other part. The document is in form an appointment, but its effect is the grant of a lease
to the commission for a term of 999 years of certain lands in Staffordshire, particularly in
the area of Cannock Chase, which are more particularly described in a schedule and by   *e*
reference to a plan. They comprise some 1,200 acres. What is in issue in the present
appeal, as before the judge, is the true construction and effect of a reservation to the
grantors, the former owners, of sporting rights which is contained in para 2 of the second
schedule to the indenture. The plaintiffs are the successors in title to Lord Hatherton and
his son, the original grantors.

The question of the true construction and effect of this reservation of sporting rights   *f*
depends on the wording used and I should read the clause as a whole. It is as follows:

> 'SUBJECT to the provisions of the Ground Game Act 1880 the Ground Game
> Amendment Act 1906 and the Forestry Act 1919 all game woodcocks snipe and
> other wild fowl hares rabbits and fish with the exclusive right (but subject as
> aforesaid) for the Appointors and all persons authorised by them at all times of   *g*
> preserving the same (except rabbits) and of hunting shooting fishing coursing and
> sporting over and on the appointed hereditaments and premises *Provided always*
> that as regards rabbits the Commission shall have an equal right with the Appointors
> to kill the same and the Appointors shall not keep or permit to be kept any rabbit
> warren in or in the immediate vicinity of the appointed lands.'

                                                                                                   h
There is an obligation imposed on the appointors by the lease to pay the rates on the
sporting rights excepted and reserved. That does not, however, give any indication of the
scope of the exception and reservation of sporting rights. What is in question is whether
the exception and reservation reserves to the grantors, the appointors, all fallow deer on
the land and the exclusive right to shoot deer.

It appears that at the time of the grant there were deer on the land and for some years   *j*
before the date of the grant it was apparently the practice of Lord Hatherton to require
his keepers to shoot two deer with shotguns each Saturday morning during the winter
months from October to March to provide Lord Hatherton and farm tenants and staff
with meat. That is the evidence of a Mr Samuel Price, who knew the land at the time
and whose father had been head keeper to the then Lord Hatherton from 1915 onwards.

It is not suggested that the shooting of the deer, as I have described it, was carried out for
a sport in the sense that gentlemen may form shooting syndicates to shoot various birds or
animals, or landowners and their friends may go out sporting over the land. It was an
operation under the instructions of Lord Hatherton for providing meat for the family
and staff on a regular basis during the winters.

It appears that that practice continued to some extent after the date of the grant, but I
cannot think, nor has this been contended for the plaintiffs, that such continuation can
b provide guidance to control of construction of the wording used in the reservation in the
indenture.

Subsequently, the deer have multiplied on the land and, as they were found by the
commission to be causing damage to trees, the commission started shooting the deer to
protect the trees. What is in question is whether they were entitled to do so. If there has
been effectively reserved to the original grantors the deer and the right to shoot the deer,
c then the commission were not entitled to shoot deer but, if the exception and reservation
does not extend to deer or to the right to shoot deer, then the commission, as the lessees
in occupation of the land, were entitled to shoot deer. That is what the judge held was
the effect of the reservation, that is to say the commission succeeded and therefore the
plaintiffs now appeal.

It is not in doubt that the Ground Game Act 1880 and the Ground Game Amendment
d Act 1906 gave the commission as occupier the right to kill hares and rabbits on the land.
Furthermore, the Forestry Act 1919, subject to which the reservation took effect, gave
the commission the right to kill on any land hares and rabbits and vermin, including
squirrels; but none of those Acts mentioned deer and it is not suggested that deer are
vermin, even if to the commission they may be a cause of trouble.

The case is put by counsel for the plaintiffs on two grounds. First, he says that, in the
e context of this particular document, the word 'game' in the collocation of nouns 'all game
woodcocks snipe and other wild fowl hares rabbits and fish' includes deer. It includes, he
says, all animals ferae naturae which are fit for the food of man and are usually sported
after. Second, he says that in the collocation of what the judge called participles and what
have been mentioned in argument as gerunds the words used 'hunting shooting fishing
coursing and sporting over and on the appointed hereditaments and premises', and, in
f particular, 'shooting', are not limited to shooting game, woodcock, snipe etc, but extend
to shooting anything which is usually sported after. Reference in that connection is made
to the decision in *Jeffryes v Evans* (1865) 19 CBNS 246 at 265–266 144 ER 781 at 789,
where Willes J regarded the words used in that case, 'the exclusive right of shooting,
fishing, and sporting [a] farm', as to be understood generally as including shooting etc
anything that is usually hunted, shot for and sported after, and regarded the expression
g 'game' as not limited to what had in Acts of Parliament been from time to time called
game, but extending to such things as were usually sported after 'excluding small birds
and vermin which are beneath the notice of a sportsman'.

We have, however, to construe the words in the context of this particular document.
As to the general background, it is quite clear that there is no established meaning to the
h word 'game' as including deer. There are various Acts of Parliament in which the word
'game' has been used in contexts which do not include deer. For instance, in s 13 of the
Night Poaching Act 1828 it was provided that for the purposes of that Act the word
'game' should be deemed to include 'hares, pheasants, partridges, grouse, heath or moor
game, black game and bustards'. The Act itself related to the unlawful taking or
destruction of any game or rabbits by night. The original definition of 'game' in the
j Game Act 1831, s 2 was the same: 'hares, pheasants, partridges, grouse, heath or moor
game, black game, and bustards'; and where in various Acts of Parliament it was intended
to refer to deer in contexts where game were also referred to, as in s 4 and, for that
matter, also s 2 of the Game Licences Act 1860, deer were expressly mentioned. The
same can be said of the Agricultural Holdings Act 1908, s 10. It would not be wholly
inappropriate to list deer among the animals and birds which are intended to be covered

by the particular clause including game, but is is not something which is the natural primary meaning of the word; the word 'game' is without comprehensive basic definition.

Looking at it in the context of the present case, what is immediately apparent is that the word 'game' has been used in collocation with woodcocks, snipe and other wild fowl, hares, rabbits and fish. Had deer been in the mind of the draftsman of the clause I have no doubt that it would have been mentioned. It is conspicuous by its absence. I find it, therefore, impossible to construe the word 'game' as including deer in this context where the draftsman has set out to list various other birds and animals to which the clause is to apply and which it might not be clear were definitely covered by the word 'game', that is to say woodcock, snipe and other wildfowl, hares, rabbits and fish. The clause has obviously been professionally drawn but it has not been identified as coming from any particular established precedent book. It is a clause which may have served its purpose reasonably well for many years but it has not been able to pass without criticism on all sides when it became necessary to apply it in circumstances which, as it seems to me, were outside the contemplation of the draftsman.

The other limb of the argument of counsel for the plaintiffs is that the reference to shooting covers shooting anything usually sported after which has not been specifically included in the catalogue of game, woodcock, snipe and other wild fowl, hares, rabbits and fish. It is not suggested that the shooting of vermin is expressly reserved; it must be shooting in a context of sporting rights. Again, if the words 'hunting, shooting, fishing, coursing and sporting over' stood alone without the earlier reference to a variety of targets, the words might well include the shooting of anything usually sported after. But, in my judgment, in the context of this clause the reference by way of reservation to 'hunting shooting fishing coursing and sporting over and on the appointed hereditaments and premises' is merely the corollary of the first part of the clause which reserved the game etc to the grantors and is only concerned with the hunting, shooting, fishing, coursing and sporting over and on the appointed hereditaments and premises in respect of the game, woodcock, snipe and other wild fowl, hares, rabbits and fish mentioned in the clause.

I do not regard it as of any materiality to the case that fish are expressly mentioned whereas there do not appear, so far as the evidence goes, to have been fish to be sported after on or in the area granted at the time of the indenture. Equally, I do not find it of much significance to consider whether or not it is appropriate to attach the word 'hunting' to deer. It is capable of being attached to hares which can be destroyed by hunting or shooting as well as by coursing. Again, I do not attach great importance in the context of this case to the words 'sporting over and on the appointed hereditaments' because no particular form of sporting other than shooting is in question. It is not suggested that the words 'sporting over' import any form of sport which does not involve the quest for animals by way of sport; field sports is the phrase that has been used. This was, on this latter point, the view taken by Harman J where he said ([1988] 1 All ER 783 at 786, [1988] 1 WLR 959 at 962):

'. . . I consider that the reservation of rights to hunt etc are exclusively to hunt etc after those things which are expressly included in the list of nouns earlier. It does not to my mind expend or grant additional rights beyond those granted in respect of the animals and birds listed above.'

I agree.

Counsel for the plaintiffs says, 'Oh well, the owners who in 1921 would have wanted to reserve sporting rights would have wanted to reserve sporting rights in respect of anything that could be sported after; and likewise they would not have wished their tenants to disturb the game on the land by shooting other animals or birds save that the owners would have been constrained to accept the rights of the occupiers under the Ground Game Act 1880 and the Ground Game Amendment Act 1906 to destroy rabbits

and hares and the right of the commission to destroy vermin as well'. That is, no doubt,
a consideration which can, to some extent, be taken into account, but it comes back at
the end of the argument to a question of the construction of this particular clause and, as
I have indicated, I am unable to construe the word 'game' in this context as against the
general usage of the word up to 1921 as including deer; and I am unable to construe the
participles 'hunting shooting fishing coursing and sporting over and on the appointed
hereditaments and premises' as extending to other animals or birds than those which
have been earlier by the clause reserved to the grantors. The latter part of the clause is
merely the counterpart of the earlier part and not an extension.

Accordingly, I agree with the result reached by the judge. I would uphold his order
and dismiss this appeal.

BUTLER-SLOSS LJ. I agree.

STAUGHTON LJ. I also agree.

Appeal dismissed.

Solicitors: *Pickering & Butters*, Stafford (for the plaintiffs); *Treasury Solicitor*.

Mary Rose Plummer   Barrister.

Gumbley v Cunningham

HOUSE OF LORDS
LORD BRIDGE OF HARWICH, LORD TEMPLEMAN, LORD GRIFFITHS, LORD ACKNER AND LORD LOWRY
10 NOVEMBER, 8 DECEMBER 1988

*Road traffic – Driving while unfit to drive through drink or drugs – Evidence – Back-calculation
– Specimen to determine driver's blood-alcohol level taken some hours after driving – Specimen
showing blood-alcohol level below prescribed limit – Whether evidence of calculation of amount of
alcohol eliminated between driving and providing specimen admissible – Road Traffic Act 1972,
s 6(1).*

Where a person is charged under s 6(1)[a] of the Road Traffic Act 1972 with driving,
attempting to drive or being in charge of a motor vehicle after consuming so much
alcohol that the proportion of it in his breath, blood or urine exceeds the prescribed limit
and the specimen provided by the person after a lapse of time shows an alcohol level
below the prescribed limit, the prosecution may adduce evidence to show, by means of
'back-calculation', ie by calculation of the amount of alcohol eliminated in the period
between driving and providing the specimen, that the proportion of alcohol in the
person's breath or blood was above the prescribed limit when he was driving. However,
the prosecution should not seek to rely on evidence of back-calculation unless it is both
easily understood and clearly establishes the presence of excess alcohol at the time when
the defendant was driving (see p 6 f to h and p 9 e to g, post).

Decision of the Divisional Court of the Queen's Bench Division [1987] 3 All ER 733
affirmed.

---

a   Section 6(1) is set out at p 8 g, post

Notes

For driving a vehicle with excess alcohol, see 40 Halsbury's Laws (4th edn) para 496, and   *a*
for cases on the subject, see 39(1) Digest (Reissue) 507–509, 3740–3748.

For the Road Traffic Act 1972, s 6 (as substituted by the Transport Act 1981, s 25(3),
Sch 8), see 51 Halsbury's Statutes (3rd edn) 1427, 1434.

Case referred to in opinions

Rowlands v Hamilton [1971] 1 All ER 1089, [1971] 1 WLR 647, HL.   *b*

Appeal

Stephen Gary Gumbley appealed with leave of the Appeal Committee of the House of
Lords given on 5 May 1988 against the decision of the Divisional Court of the Queen's
Bench Division (Watkins LJ and Mann J) ([1987] 3 All ER 733, [1988] QB 170) on 28
July 1987 dismissing the appellant's appeal by way of case stated by the Crown Court at   *c*
Birmingham (his Honour Judge Ross QC and two justices) in respect of its adjudication
on 18 November 1986 whereby it dismissed his appeal from the decision of justices
sitting at Birmingham on 25 June 1986 convicting him of driving a motor vehicle on a
road with excess alcohol concentration in his blood, contrary to s 6(1) of the Road Traffic
Act 1972, on an information laid by the respondent, Thomas Joseph Cunningham. The
Divisional Court had refused the appellant leave to appeal to the House of Lords but had   *d*
certified, under s 1(2) of the Administration of Justice Act 1960, that a point of law of
general public importance (set out at p 7 *f g*, post) was involved in the decision. The facts
are set out in the opinion of Lord Ackner.

John Morris QC and *Dominic Roberts* for the appellant.
Martin Wilson QC and *Roger D H Smith* for the respondent.   *e*

Their Lordships took time for consideration.

8 December. The following opinions were delivered.

                                                                                              f
LORD BRIDGE OF HARWICH. My Lords, I have had the advantage of reading in
draft the speech of my noble and learned friend Lord Ackner. I agree with it and, for the
reasons he gives, I would dismiss the appeal.

LORD TEMPLEMAN. My Lords, for the reasons to be given by my noble and learned
friend Lord Ackner, I would dismiss this appeal and answer the certified question in the   *g*
affirmative.

LORD GRIFFITHS. My Lords, for the reasons given by my noble and learned friend
Lord Ackner, I would dismiss the appeal.

LORD ACKNER. My Lords,   *h*

The facts

At about 8.30 pm on 7 May 1985 the appellant, Stephen Gary Gumbley, and his
brother Gordon arrived at a public house in the Northfield area of Birmingham called
The Dingle. At about 10.45 pm the appellant left with his brother and began to drive
his car to Erdington, which is on the other side of the city. He drove erratically for about *j*
six miles and at about 11.15 pm he collided at high speed with the wall of an underpass
in the city centre, thereby killing his brother.

The police arrived at about 11.35 pm. They found no evidence of braking. They
required the appellant to provide a specimen of his breath; he refused and was arrested
and taken to the police station arriving at about 11.45 pm. At the police station he

complained that he felt ill. Between 11.50 pm and 12.20 pm he vomited and was
a thereafter taken to a nearby general hospital. At 3.35 am at the general hospital, and
with the consent of the doctor in charge, the appellant provided a specimen of blood for
analysis. This analysis revealed a concentration of not less than 59 mg of alcohol per
100 ml of blood.

Although this analysis showed a concentration below the prescribed limit of 80 mg,
the specimen had been obtained over four hours after the accident. The respondent, the
b prosecution, accordingly sought to establish that the appellant's blood-alcohol concentration must have been in excess of the prescribed limit at the time of the collision.
Accordingly, medical evidence was called, it was unchallenged, and it established: (i) that
the appellant, who at the material time was 34 years old and of average height and
muscular build weighing some 11 stone, was in good physical condition; (ii) that such a
person would eliminate alcohol from his bloodstream at between 10 and 25 mg per
c 100 ml per hour; that the most likely elimination rate was in the region of 15 mg per
100 ml per hour and that the concentration of alcohol in his body four hours and twenty
minutes before the specimen was collected would have been in the region of 120 to 130
mg per 100 ml; (iii) that even in the most unheard of event of an elimination rate of six
mg per 100 ml per hour, the appellant's blood-alcohol concentration would have been in
excess of the prescribed limit at the time of the collision.
d

The issue

It was not nor could it have been disputed that this evidence was *relevant* to establishing
that the appellant, immediately before the accident, was driving his car after consuming
so much alcohol that the proportion of it in his blood exceeded the prescribed limit. The
appellant's contention was that the evidence although admissible was excluded by statute.
e This submission was rejected by the justices sitting on 25 June 1986 at Birmingham, by
the Crown Court sitting at Birmingham on 18 November 1986, and by the Divisional
Court on 28 July 1987, when the appellant's appeal was heard by way of case stated (see
[1987] 3 All ER 733, [1988] QB 170).

The following question was certified by the Divisional Court as a point of general
f importance:

'Whether on a true construction of Section 6(1) and Section 10(2) of the Road
Traffic Act 1972, as amended, the prosecutor is entitled to adduce evidence other
than by way of the specimen of breath or blood provided by the accused in order to
prove the proportion of alcohol in the accused's breath or blood at the material
time.'

g Your Lordships gave leave to appeal to your Lordships' House.

The relevant legislation

Section 1(1) of the Road Safety Act 1967 provided:

'If a person drives or attempts to drive a motor vehicle on a road or other public
h place, having consumed alcohol in such a quantity that the proportion thereof in his
blood, *as ascertained from a laboratory test* for which he subsequently provides a
specimen under section 3 of this Act, exceeds the prescribed limit at the time he
provides the specimen, he shall be liable . . .'

In *Rowlands v Hamilton* [1971] 1 All ER 1089, [1971] 1 WLR 647 your Lordships'
j House had to consider what was known as the 'hip-flask defence', which arose when the
defendant claimed that, although the analysis of his blood-alcohol concentration
established that it exceeded the prescribed limit, he had however drunk alcohol since
ceasing to drive, and accordingly the analysis could not be relied on. To meet such a
defence the prosecution sought to call evidence to establish that, after making the
appropriate adjustment to eliminate the post-driving alcohol, the defendant's blood-

alcohol concentration still exceeded the prescribed limit. However, it was the presence
of the words 'as ascertained from a laboratory test' which I have emphasised when setting   *a*
out the terms of s 1(1) of the 1967 Act which prevented the prosecution from leading
such evidence.

In his speech Lord Guest said ([1971] 1 All ER 1089 at 1091, [1971] 1 WLR 647 at
653–654):

> 'For the appellant to succeed it is, therefore, necessary for him to show that the   *b*
> adjustment made to eliminate the post-driving alcohol content could legitimately
> be made under the section. It is at this point that the words in s 1(1) "as ascertained
> from a laboratory test" become important. Detailed provisions are made in s 3
> regarding laboratory tests and "the prescribed limit" referred to in s 1(1) is given as
> the arithmetical proportion of 80 milligrammes of alcohol per 100 millilitres of
> blood. These provisions make it clear, to my mind, that the Act intended an   *c*
> automatic calculation to be made by means of a chemical analysis as to whether an
> offence had been committed. It is against the background of the disputes in the
> courts under the previous Road Traffic Acts as to the effect of alcohol on an
> individual's capacity to drive that Parliament has in the 1967 Act provided for
> automatic proof of guilt by the analysis. For Dr Dolan to make the adjustment of
> the proportions it would be necessary to go outside the "laboratory test" provided in   *d*
> s 1(1) and make calculations based on certain assumptions as to the individual
> concerned and the time factor. It would ultimately depend on the expert opinion of
> the doctor or chemist. I am convinced that Parliament never intended such
> calculations to be made and that these calculations would not be justified by the
> terms of the section. I am not satisfied that the section is ambiguous, but if it were I
> should unhesitatingly take the construction most favourable to the subject.'   *e*

In *Rowlands*'s case your Lordships pointed out that it was for Parliament and not for
the courts to close the loophole in the 1967 Act through which the hip-flask driver was
able to escape.

Section 1(1) of the 1967 Act was substantially re-enacted in s 6(1) of the 1972 Act. It
was not until some ten years after *Rowlands*'s case that specific statutory provision was   *f*
made to close this loophole. By virtue of the provisions of Sch 8 to the Transport Act
1981, s 6(1) of the 1972 Act now provides:

> 'If a person—(a) drives or attempts to drive a motor vehicle on a road or other
> public place; or (b) is in charge of a motor vehicle on a road or other public place;
> after consuming so much alcohol that the proportion of it in his breath, blood or
> urine exceeds the prescribed limit he shall be guilty of an offence.'   *g*

It will be noted that the words 'as ascertained from a laboratory test for which he
subsequently provides a specimen under section 3 of this Act' have been excised.

Further by the same schedule to the 1981 Act a new s 10 of the 1972 Act is substituted
for the old s 10, the material terms of which are as follows:

> '(1) The following provisions apply with respect to proceedings for an offence   *h*
> under section 5 or section 6 of this Act.
> (2) Evidence of the proportion of alcohol or any drug in a specimen of breath,
> blood or urine provided by the accused shall, in all cases, be taken into account, and
> it shall be assumed that the proportion of alcohol in the accused's breath, blood or
> urine at the time of the alleged offence was not less than in the specimen; but if the
> proceedings are for an offence under section 6 of this Act, or for an offence under   *j*
> section 5 of this Act in a case where the accused is alleged to have been unfit through
> drink, the assumption shall not be made if the accused proves—(a) that he consumed
> alcohol after he had ceased to drive, attempt to drive or be in charge of a motor
> vehicle on a road or other public place and before he provided the specimen; and

(b) that had he not done so the proportion of alcohol in his breath, blood or urine
a   would not have exceeded the prescribed limit and, if the proceedings are for an
      offence under section 5 of this Act, would not have been such as to impair his ability
      to drive properly . . .'

Counsel for the appellant has submitted that all that Parliament was seeking to achieve
by these new provisions was to close the loophole disclosed in *Rowlands's* case and that
b they can have no wider effect. It is his contention that evidence which is clearly relevant
must nevertheless be excluded from the court's consideration, because by statute it has
been rendered inadmissible. He, however, frankly concedes, as concede he must, that he
can point to no express statutory provision to that effect, nor has he submitted that your
Lordships should imply words into either s 6(1) or s 10(2) which make such provision.
His submission in essence is that Parliament would have expressly provided for the
c admissibility of 'back-tracking evidence' as this is now conveniently called, if it had
intended that such evidence, although undoubtedly relevant, should be considered by
the courts. However, Parliament's intention has to be ascertained by properly construing
the terms of the relevant legislation. Although I am prepared to accept that it may well
have been the primary intention of Parliament when enacting these provisions to deal
with the problem highlighted in *Rowlands's* case, it would in my judgment be quite
d wrong to interpret the new statutory provisions as continuing to exclude evidence which
is relevant to establishing the blood-alcohol concentration at a time when the defendant
was driving.

I therefore agree with the conclusion reached by the Divisional Court that those who
drive whilst above the prescribed limits cannot necessarily escape punishment because of
the lapse of time. Because back-calculations involve a number of factors, eg the
e individual's personal physiology, the amount, if any, which he has eaten and the nature
of the alcohol which he has drunk, I would indorse the advice given by the Divisional
Court that the prosecution should not seek to rely on evidence of back-calculations save
where the evidence is both easily understood and clearly establishes the presence of excess
alcohol at the time when the accused was driving. The Divisional Court was clearly right
to emphasise that justices must be very careful, especially where there is conflicting
f evidence, not to convict unless on the scientific and other evidence, which they find it
safe to rely on, they are sure that an excess of alcohol was in the defendant's body when
he was actually driving as charged.

I would accordingly dismiss this appeal.

LORD LOWRY. My Lords, I entirely agree with the speech of my noble and learned
g friend Lord Ackner, whose speech I have had the opportunity of reading in draft. I would
therefore dismiss this appeal.

Appeal dismissed.

Solicitors: *Cremin Small & Co* (for the appellant); *Crown Prosecution Service.*

Mary Rose Plummer   Barrister.

Barclays Bank plc v Bemister and another
Pryke and others v Gibbs Hartley Cooper Ltd

COURT OF APPEAL, CIVIL DIVISION
SIR JOHN DONALDSON MR, GLIDEWELL LJ AND SIR DENYS BUCKLEY
11 DECEMBER 1987

Practice – Transfer of proceedings between divisions of High Court – Transfer sought to obtain speedier trial – Procedure – What claimant for transfer must show – How transfer should be effected.

A party to an action should not apply for a transfer of the action from one division of the High Court to another merely in order to obtain a speedier trial unless the action has been begun in a division which, in accordance with the Rules of the Supreme Court or generally accepted practice, is inappropriate. If any party considers he has a claim for special expedition of his action he should apply for an expedited hearing in the existing division, which he will then have to justify. If the judge considers that a transfer is the appropriate course, he may of his own motion, after making inquiries of the head of the other division, direct a transfer to that division with the consent of his own head of division and that of the division to which the case is to be transferred (see p 13 *b* to *d h*, post).

Notes
For transfer of proceedings between and within divisions of the High Court, see 37 Halsbury's Laws (4th edn) para 64, and for cases on the subject, see 37(2) Digest (Reissue) 223–229, 1459–1497.

Case referred to in judgments
Zakhem International Construction Ltd v Nippon Kokkan KK (1987) 137 NLJ 641.

Interlocutory appeals

Barclays Bank plc v Bemister and anor
The plaintiff, Barclays Bank plc, appealed with leave of the Court of Appeal against so much of the order of Mr Raymond Kidwell QC sitting as a deputy judge of the High Court in the Queen's Bench Division dated 13 March 1987 as refused the plaintiff's application to transfer to the Chancery Division an action brought by the plaintiff against the defendants, Walter John Bemister and Edna May Bemister, on a guarantee given by them to the plaintiff in 1974. The facts are set out in the judgment of Sir John Donaldson MR.

Pryke and ors v Gibbs Hartley Cooper Ltd
The plaintiffs, John William Pryke and others, who were Lloyds underwriters, appealed with leave of the Court of Appeal against the order of Staughton J in the Queen's Bench Division (Commercial Court) dated 24 July 1987 whereby he refused the plaintiffs' application that the trial of the preliminary issues in an action brought by the plaintiffs against the defendants, Gibbs Hartley Cooper Ltd, who were Lloyds brokers, claiming damages for breach of contract or negligence be expedited or, alternatively, that the action be transferred to the Chancery Division. The facts are set out in the judgment of Sir John Lord Donaldson MR.

The appeals were heard successively.

a
Richard Salter for the bank in the first appeal.
Michael Supperstone for Mr and Mrs Bemister.
Roger Toulson QC and *Mark Cannon* for the plaintiffs in the second appeal.
Jeremy Cooke for the brokers.

SIR JOHN DONALDSON MR. In both these matters we are concerned with refusals to transfer actions from the Queen's Bench Division to the Chancery Division.

b   In the first action, Barclays Bank plc have sued Mr and Mrs Bemister on a guarantee given by them to the bank in 1974 in relation to the indebtedness of United Grange (Services) Ltd, a company owned and operated by their son. The defence is a familiar one of undue influence, lack of independent advice and negligence. The claim is for £76,278·41 with additional interest from 25 March 1985. Mr Bemister is aged 82 and his wife is 70.

c   The case came before Mr Raymond Kidwell QC sitting as a deputy judge of the High Court on 13 March 1987 on an appeal by the bank from an order of Master Turner setting aside a judgment obtained in default of defence. The appeal was dismissed and that decision is now accepted. The bank then applied for an order that the action be transferred to the Chancery Division, where, it was said, the action could have been heard within not more than six months after setting down, whereas if it remained in the
d   Queen's Bench Division it appeared unlikely that a hearing date could be obtained in less than 18 months after setting down. That of course produced a differential in speed of hearing of 12 months. The figures have been updated, and the differential is now probably nine months.

That application was refused by the judge, who also refused leave to appeal to this court. However, we have given leave. [His Lordship summarised the arguments
e   advanced by the bank for a transfer and the judge's reasons for refusing a transfer, and continued:]

In the second action Mr Pryke and other Lloyds underwriters sued Lloyds brokers for a sum in the region of $US1,275,000. The issues are complicated, but for present purposes they can, I think, be summarised as follows. The plaintiff underwriters gave binding authority (a binder) to Atlas Underwriting Ltd, a company incorporated in Virginia, to
f   write defined risks on behalf of underwriters. The brokers were responsible for administering the binder. Atlas, it is alleged, wrote risks which were outside the scope of the binder, but underwriters have been compelled to settle claims in respect of those risks. They seek to recover these sums from the brokers as damages for breach of contract or negligence.

g   The action was begun in June 1986 and discovery was ordered on 19 December of that year. On 27 March 1987 Hirst J ordered the trial of a preliminary issue relating to liability and causation, and counsel agreed that the probable length of that hearing would be six weeks. In June 1987 the parties were told that the earliest available date in the Commercial Court was 30 March 1990. In July 1987 the plaintiffs applied for an order that the trial of the preliminary issue be expedited or, alternatively, that the action be
h   transferred to the Chancery Division. [His Lordship summarised the submissions of the parties on whether the action should be transferred, referred to the judge's reasons for dismissing the application and also to *Zakhem International Construction Ltd v Nippon Kokkan KK* (1987) 137 NLJ 641 at 642, and continued:]

In very broad terms delay in hearing actions is determined by (a) the number of actions, (b) their weight and (c) the availability of judges and ancillary resources such as
j   courtrooms. Given the divisional structure of the High Court, which creates more or less watertight compartments, it is inevitable that the interplay of these factors will lead to actions in one division coming on for hearing more quickly than in others. At the present time, other things being equal, actions are heard more quickly in the Chancery Division than in the Queen's Bench Division and more quickly in the general list of the

Queen's Bench Division than in the Commercial Court. This was not always the case. Only a few years ago the longest delays were in the Chancery Division and by far the *a* least in the Commercial Court.

The Commercial Court is, of course, a special problem. Its raison d'être is to supply a speedy and expert service in support of national and international trade. Until recently, and over a period of nearly 90 years, it has been supremely successful, but it is now foundering under the pressure of business generated by its own success. If nothing is done, market forces in the form of consumer dissatisfaction may well restore the balance, *b* but that would be a policy of despair and contrary to the national commercial interest.

On appointment High Court judges are assigned to one or other of the three divisions: the Queen's Bench, Chancery and Family. Similarly, some types of actions are assigned to specific divisions, although, family matters apart, the majority of actions could be set down in either the Queen's Bench or the Chancery Divisions. In practice there is a generally accepted notion of what is appropriate to the Queeen's Bench and what to the *c* Chancery Divisions, although there remains a relatively small category which may well be started in either division; landlord and tenant disputes are perhaps a typical example.

The purpose underlying the creation of divisions and the allocation of work between the divisions was to ensure that disputes are resolved by High Court judges of the relevant expertise. In fact, with the possible exception of very specialised actions, such as patent disputes, all High Court work should be capable of being undertaken by all High Court *d* judges, but the hearing takes longer if the judge is unfamiliar with the territory. In other words, the system of divisions was designed to achieve judicial horses for judicial courses.

However, in recent years it has become apparent that the frontiers of the divisions are much too rigid. Leading members of the Bar, from whom the judges are appointed, no longer practice only in one division of the High Court. On appointment to the Bench they therefore have experience relevant to more than one division and it is inefficient *e* that, as judges, they should be confined to sitting in one division. No doubt other examples could be given, but for present purposes it is only necessary to draw attention to the overlap in experience of the 'commercial' judges of the Queen's Bench Division and the judges of the Chancery Division in relation to commercial disputes which do not arise in the context of shipping. The existence of divisions in the High Court, once *f* created as an aid to efficiency, is now an obstacle.

In this situation consideration will no doubt be given to the abolition of the divisions, thereby creating a unified High Court or to their redefinition. Consideration will also no doubt be given to centrally co-ordinated listing throughout the divisions. This would enable the court, not only to allocate judicial horses to judicial courses, but also to take account of any disparity in the weight being carried by some of those judicial horses.

However, that is not the present position. Where there is a choice of divisions or, in *g* the case of the Commercial Court, a subdivision, it is for the plaintiff to exercise that choice. In doing so, he or his legal advisers will or should have some regard to how his claim can be most speedily and satisfactorily determined. But mistakes can be made. Those mistakes may take the form of beginning an action in a division other than that to which that type of action is assigned, or to which, in terms of its subject matter, it is *h* appropriate. This can and would be remedied by ordering a transfer. However, they can also take the form of backing the wrong horse. The judges concerned may be running well at the time the action is begun, but, due to an excess weight of actions, may seem to be flagging long before the date for hearing is reached. Again the mistake can be remedied by transfer, but in this instance the court is faced with rather greater problems.

It is an understandable fact of life that plaintiffs will want to see their claims dealt with *j* as soon as possible and that defendants will usually wish to postpone the day of judgment. This is illustrated in the present action where it is the plaintiff underwriters and the bank who seek expedition, whilst the brokers and Mr and Mrs Bemister advance cogent arguments for the status quo.

a
The decisive factor is not of course the inconsistent wishes of the parties, but the objective need for speed if justice is not to be denied. This objective need is not an absolute. It is relative to the needs of other actions in the same and other divisions or subdivisions of the High Court, matters which will be unknown to individual litigants.

b
The practical approach in my judgment is therefore somewhat different from that adopted by the parties in the instant case. If an action has been begun in a division (or subdivision in the case of the Commercial Court, for example) to which, in accordance with the rules, or generally accepted practice, it is inappropriate, either party can and should apply for a transfer to the appropriate division. Subject to that qualification, no party should apply for a transfer to another division. If any party considers that he has a claim for special expedition (and I do not mean by that merely a certificate for a speedy trial, but a claim for special expedition), he should apply for an expedited hearing. It will then be for the judge concerned to consider the need alleged and whether an appropriate

c
degree of expedition can be achieved without transfer. If in his judgment it cannot, he should himself make inquiries of the head of another division with a view to ascertaining whether that division can afford the parties of speedier hearing without unduly prejudicing the legitimate needs and expectations of parties to actions which are already the concern of that division. If the result of those inquiries is that a transfer is the appropriate course, it would be for the judge of his own motion to direct a transfer with

d
the consent of his own head of division and that of the division to which the case would be transferred.

This approach would not in any way impede regular consultation between heads of divisions to see whether the disparity in lead times was such that in the general interests of the administration of justice some transfers should be made. By 'lead times' I mean the time between setting down, or applying for a date for trial, and hearing. Such

e
consultation is highly desirable and can no doubt be instituted. If the conclusion was that transfers were desirable, it is to be expected that criteria for selecting actions for transfer would be agreed between head of divisions, and it would then be for the judge in charge of the transferor list to identify the particularly actions to be transferred. An alternative and simpler approach, which is sometimes adopted, is for a judge from one division to sit as an additional judge of another division. But, however the matter is dealt with, it is

f
a problem of general judicial management and not something with which the parties to a particular action are in a position to concern themselves.

In the instant cases, Staughton J expressly and Mr Raymond Kidwell QC impliedly held that no *exceptional* case for expedition had been made out. This is essentially a discretionary decision with which this court should be slow to interfere. The more

g
general problem of ensuring that actions with like claims to expedition are heard as quickly in one division as in another and the particular problem of the Commercial Court, which should, by definition, be a court of expedition, are matters for consideration by the three heads of the trial divisions and the Lord Chancellor and not for this court.

Accordingly, I would dismiss both appeals.

h
GLIDEWELL LJ. I agree.

SIR DENYS BUCKLEY. I also agree.

Appeals dismissed.

j
Solicitors: *Durrant Piesse* (for the bank in the first appeal); *Glenn Evans & Co*, Twyford (for Mr and Mrs Bemister); *Fishburn Boxer* (for the plaintiffs in the second appeal); *Hewitt Woollacott & Chown* (for the brokers).

Mary Rose Plummer   Barrister.

Re Atkins

CHICHESTER CONSISTORY COURT
CHANCELLOR HIS HONOUR JUDGE QUENTIN EDWARDS QC
29 JULY, 9 NOVEMBER 1987

Ecclesiastical law – Faculty – Jurisdiction – Faculty for exhumation and reinterment of human remains – Principles to be applied in exercising jurisdiction – Burden on petitioner.

Ecclesiastical law – Burial of the dead – Corpse or ashes – Whether any distinction in canon law between corpse and ashes of cremated body.

In exercising its jurisdiction to grant a faculty authorising the exhumation of human remains from consecrated ground, the consistory court should bear in mind that the canonical intention, as represented in the rites and ceremonies of the Church of England, of those who committed the body or ashes of the deceased to the ground was committal into the safe custody of the Church, although in the nature of things that does not mean that the Church will ensure that the remains will be forever undisturbed. Furthermore, although the court's jurisdiction to grant or refuse such a faculty is quite unfettered, it is to be exercised reasonably, according to the circumstances of each case, taking into account changes in human affairs and ways of thought but always mindful that consecrated ground and human remains committed to it should, in principle, remain undisturbed. There is therefore a burden on a petitioner seeking leave to disinter remains to show that the presumed intention of those who committed the body or ashes to a last resting place is to be disregarded or overborne. Moreover the length of time since the interment is a matter to be considered, and a prompt application is stronger than one made where remains have been undisturbed for many months or years. In every case the arguments for the grant of a faculty must be weighed against the foregoing general principles and the desirability of maintaining a churchyard or a place set aside for the interment of cremated remains undisturbed, as a place of peace, for prayer and for the recollection of the departed (see p 16 *h*, p 17 *c d*, p 19 *e f j* to p 20 *b*, post).

The Church of England makes no distinction in canon law between a corpse and the ashes of a cremated body; both should be treated with the same reverence and decency and accorded the same dignity in interment. Although the physical difference cannot be ignored where any question of exhumation arises, the consistory court should make no distinction between a body and ashes and should be careful not to give undue weight to the fact that the disinterment and removal of ashes buried in a casket is simpler and less expensive than the disinterment of a body and is unlikely to give rise to any risk to health. Nor should the court ever regard ashes as less worthy of its protection or their disturbance as a lighter matter than the disturbance of a corpse and it should resist any trend towards regarding the remains of loved relatives and spouses as portable, to be taken from place to place so that the grave or place of interment of ashes may be the more easily visited (see p 16 *g h* and p 19 *g h*, post).

Notes

For faculties for the exhumation of human remains from consecrated ground, see 10 Halsbury's Laws (4th edn) para 1198 and 14 ibid paras 1315, 1323.

For ecclesiastical law as to the burial of the dead, see 14 ibid paras 1041–1043.

Cases referred to in judgment

Dixon, Re [1892] P 386, Con Ct.
Foster v Dodd (1867) LR 3 QB 67, Ex Ch.
Matheson (decd), Re [1958] 1 All ER 202, [1958] 1 WLR 246, Con Ct.
Pope, Re (1851) 15 Jur 614, Con Ct.

a   St Botolph without Aldgate (vicar and one of the churchwardens) v Parishioners [1892] P 161,
    Con Ct.
    St Helen's, Bishopsgate, with St Mary Outwich (rector and churchwardens) v Parishioners
    (M'Dougal intervening) [1892] P 259, Con Ct.
    St Mary-at-Hill with St Andrew Hubbard (rector and churchwardens) v Parishioners [1892] P
    394, Con Ct.
    St Michael Bassishaw (rector and churchwardens) v Parishioners (Braikenridge intervening)
b   [1893] P 233, Con Ct.
    Talbot, Re [1901] P 1, Con Ct.

Petition for faculty

By a petition dated 25 April 1987 Mrs Gladys May Atkins sought a faculty authorising
and empowering the proposed removal of the cremated remains of her late husband,
c Ernest Hart Atkins, which had been interred in a casket in Church Norton Churchyard
in the parish of Selsey on 14 January 1976 and their reinterment in a grave in
Twickenham cemetery in the London Borough of Richmond upon Thames, where the
remains of Mrs Atkins's father and sister were interred and where it was intended that
Mrs Atkins's remains would eventually be interred and where permanent arrangements
were in existence for the maintenance of such grave. The consent of the Rector of Selsey,
d the Rev Victor Reginald Cassam, to the proposed removal from Church Norton
Churchyard and the consent of the Richmond upon Thames London Borought Council,
the burial authority responsible for Twickenham cemetery, to the proposed reinterment
had both been obtained. The petition was unopposed. The facts are set out in the
judgment.

e   Mr Paul Bodkin, solicitor, for Mrs Atkins.

Cur adv vult

9 November. The following judgment was delivered.

f   **THE CHANCELLOR.** In this case the petitioner, Mrs Gladys May Atkins, prays for a
faculty authorising her to remove the cremated remains of her late husband, Ernest Hart
Atkins, from consecrated ground in this diocese to the consecrated part of Twickenham
cemetery in the London Borough of Richmond upon Thames. The petition is unopposed.
    There has, in my experience, and, I understand, in the experiences of other chancellors,
been an increase in the number of petitions of this nature in recent years. By petitions of
g this nature I mean petitions for the disinterment of bodies and of cremated remains and
their reinterment in other places, whether near to, or far from, the first place of sepulture.
I have in this diocese and in the diocese of Blackburn, of which I am also chancellor,
refused to grant the faculties sought under some of the petitions of this nature which
have been presented to me. I have learnt that these refusals have caused distress, not only
because of the frustration of sincerely held hopes, but also because, in some instances, the
h petitioners have been led to believe, wittingly or unwittingly, that the grant is no more
than a formality, that the faculty is, if all is in order, a licence to which a petitioner is
entitled as a matter of right. For this reason and as the petition of Mrs Gladys Atkins
appeared to me, on first examination, to be a petition which I should not grant, on
grounds which appear below, I directed that it should be heard in open court. I also
intimated to the petitioner and her solicitors that I should, in any event, reserve judgment
j as I wished to consider fully, and then state, the principles which, in my judgment,
should guide the consistory court in the exercise of its discretion in petitions of this
description.
    It is well established that the consistory court has jurisdiction to grant a faculty
authorising the exhumation of human remains from consecrated ground. Indeed, it is
unlawful to remove any body or the remains of any body which has or have been interred

in a place of burial without the authority of a faculty, in the case of consecrated ground, or, in other cases, a licence from the Home Secretary: see s 25 of the Burial Act 1857. *a* Certain statutory exceptions have been made to this rule, eg where there has been acquisition of a burial ground under planning legislation or where a pastoral order has been made, but even in those cases there are prescribed requirements to ensure that all is decently done. Where it is proposed to reinter the remains in consecrated ground no more authority than the faculty is required; where the proposal is to reinter the remains elsewhere or otherwise dispose of them a licence from the Home Secretary is also *b* required.

There are two reasons why a faculty is required at all. The first is that there may be no disturbance or alteration of consecrated ground or building on it at the whim or desire of any individual but only by lawful authority or well-established right. The parish priest who buries a parishioner has the right at common law to open the soil of the churchyard for that purpose; no one has a corresponding right of disinterment, though a coroner, *c* where there has been a violent death, may order exhumation if the body has been interred before he view it (see 2 Hawk PC c 9, s 23). The second reason given in former times was that, since the buried carcase belonged to no one and was, therefore, under the protection of the public, the ecclesiastical law would, if it lay in consecrated ground, interpose for its protection, just as it had the protection of the temporal law of burial elsewhere: per Byles J in *Foster v Dodd* (1867) LR 3 QB 67 at 77. While legislation in the *d* last century and this and changes in the disciplinary jurisdiction of consistory courts have taken away much of the force of this reason, nevertheless, as mentioned above it remains, residually, in the statutory necessity for a faculty where the exhumation is to be from consecrated ground.

The proposition that the consistory court has jurisdiction to grant a faculty involves necessarily the proposition that in English canon law burial is not absolutely final. Two *e* questions then arise. First, what, if any, distinction should at the present time be made between a corpse and the ashes of a corpse remaining after cremation? Second, what should a consistory court hold to have been the canonical intention of those burying, with due rite and ceremony, the body or ashes?

The first question is answered, in my judgment, by the Revised Canons Ecclesiastical, Canon B38 (Of the burial of the dead). Paragraph 2 of the Canon deals with the *f* obligations of parochial clergy with regard to burial and, in enjoining a minister to bury, in accordance with the rites of the Church of England, 'the corpse or ashes' of a person brought to him, no distinction is made between the two. Cremation is, by para 3, stated to be lawful in connection with Christian burial and para 4(b) states that, save for good and sufficient reason, the ashes of a cremated body should be interred or deposited, by a minister, in consecrated ground. I hold that, at the present time, the Church makes no *g* distinction in canon law between a corpse and the ashes of a cremated body; both should be treated with the same reverence and decency and accorded the same dignity in interment. The physical difference between the two cannot be ignored where any question of exhumation arises but I consider that the court should never regard ashes as less worthy of its protection or that their disturbance is a lighter matter than the *h* disturbance of a corpse.

The answer to the second question must be found in the rites and ceremonies of the Church of England, for what is said and done, in accordance with the authorised forms of worship, must be taken to represent the intention of the Church and its members. The relevant passages from the Book of Common Prayer and the Alternative Service Book are as follows. Book of Common Prayer (The Order for the Burial of the Dead): *j*

'. . . FORASMUCH as it hath pleased Almighty God of his great mercy to take unto himself the soul of our dear *brother* here departed: we therefore commit *his* body to the ground; earth to earth, ashes to ashes, dust to dust; in sure and certain hope of the Resurrection to eternal life, through our Lord Jesus Christ . . .'

Alternative Service Book (Funeral Services: The Committal):

a
' We have entrusted our *brother* N to God's merciful keeping, and we now commit *his* body to the ground (*or* to be cremated): *[earth to earth, ashes to ashes, dust to dust:] in sure and certain hope of the resurrection to eternal life through our Lord Jesus Christ, who died, was buried, and rose again for us.
* The words in square brackets may be omitted.'

In the section entitled 'A Form which may be used at the Interment of the Ashes' the word 'ashes' is substituted for the word 'body'.

b
'We . . . commit his body to the ground': these are the critical words and I cannot do better than quote from *Wheatly on the Book of Common Prayer* (1858 edn) p 586:

'The phrase of *commit his body to the ground* implies that we deliver it into safe custody and into such hands as will safely restore it again. We do not cast it away as a lost and perished carcass; but carefully lay it in the ground, as having in it a seed
c
of eternity *and in sure and certain hope of the resurrection to eternal life . . .*'

The court should, then, approach the exercise of its discretion in the knowledge that the canonical intention of those who committed the body or ashes of the deceased to the ground was committal into the safe custody of the Church. In the nature of things this cannot, and has never been held to, mean that the Church will ensure that the remains
d
will be for ever undisturbed. The changes and chances of this mortal world may make some disturbance necessary or expedient.

I have examined the reported cases on the exercise of this discretion over the last century and a half in order to discover, if I can, whether any, and if so what, general principles may be deduced which should govern its exercise by me. The authorities, in so far as I have been able to find them, begin with *Re Pope* (1851) 15 Jur 614. Dr
e
Lushington, as Chancellor of the Diocese of London, granted a faculty for the exhumation of the body of an adult female which had been buried for some three weeks for the purpose of identifying the deceased. In the course of a brief judgment he said: 'Faculties for the removal of bodies are of very frequent occurrence, and are decreed to gratify the wishes of relations.' This suggests a greater readiness in Dr Lushington to grant faculties of this description than is to be found in the reported decisions of Dr Tristram QC, a later
f
but equally distinguished ecclesiastical judge. In the volumes for 1892, 1893 and 1901 of the Law Reports, Probate Division, there are six reports of decisions of his, as Chancellor of the Diocese of London, concerning exhumation of bodies. Four of these cases arose out of the unhealthy and overcrowded state of certain crypts and churchyards in the City of London and of the desire to widen roads, construct sewers and otherwise to develop land in the City. These are, citing the names of the churches concerned only, *St Botolph*
g
without Aldgate [1892] P 161, *St Helen's, Bishopsgate* [1892] P 259, *St Mary-at-Hill* [1892] P 394 and *St Michael Bassishaw* [1893] P 233. The following passage may be cited from *St Botolph without Aldgate* [1892] P 161 at 167, as showing Dr Tristram's approach to the exercise of his discretion in cases where public convenience is concerned:

h
'In churchyards there are certain alterations, which by practice and in accordance with precedent, the Ecclesiastical Courts have from early times been accustomed to authorize by faculty, such as the enlarging of a church, the erection or enlargement of a vestry, the making of footways in or through a churchyard for public convenience, the making of a carriage drive up to the church door, and the construction of necessary drains. To enable such alterations to be made, it is frequently necessary to remove the remains of persons buried in vaults or graves
j
situated in the ground required for the alterations. And upon the Court being satisfied, that such an alteration is desirable, and that it cannot be made without the removal of a vault and the remains in it, or without the removal of remains in a common grave, it invariably orders the removal of the vault and remains in it, or of the remains in a common grave to another part of the churchyard, after citing and giving notice to the families interested in the vault or common grave of the proposed removal. And the practice of the Court is to give effect to their wishes, as far as is

practicable, in the selection of the site for the new vault or grave, and to afford them an opportunity of superintending the removal.'

a

In relation to the question whether part of a churchyard might be used for the purpose of widening a public thoroughfare Dr Tristram said (at 169):

'The principle upon which the Court holds, that it has jurisdiction to grant such faculties, is, that there is a discretionary power vested in it as to making orders relating to churchyards; and that it is the duty of the Court to exercise this discretion b reasonably, and, as Sir John Nicholls [sic][1] observes, "to vary the exercise of it according to the change of times and circumstances;"...'

He went on to say that the change of circumstances in the City, viz the great increase of traffic, warranted the grant of such faculties 'for the convenience of those who attend church, as well as for that of the general public' (at 170).

c

In *Re Dixon* [1892] P 386 the petitioner, the widow of Lieut-Col John Dixon, sought a petition authorising the exhumation of her husband's body, buried some 18 years previously in a mausoleum in the consecrated part of a cemetery, in order that the body might be cremated and the ashes returned to the mausoleum. Dr Tristram refused to grant this strange request on the grounds that cremation should precede and not follow burial. In dealing with the argument that a court would ordinarily grant a faculty for d the removal of remains from one part to another of a churchyard, or from one churchyard to another churchyard, in deference to the wishes of members of the family, unless the deceased had left contrary directions in his will he said (at 391):

'Where the deceased has left no testamentary or clear directions as to the place of his burial, the practice of the Court is to grant a faculty to proper parties, on reasonable grounds shewn and subject to proper precautions, to remove the remains e to another grave or vault in the same or in another churchyard; but where the deceased has himself expressed a wish to be buried in that or in any other churchyard, the invariable practice of the Court is by a faculty to give effect to such wish.'

He summed up the exercise of the discretion thus (at 393–394):

f

'... one result of being buried in consecrated ground is, that the site is under the exclusive control of the Ecclesiastical Courts, and no body there buried can be moved from its place of interment without the sanction of a faculty to be granted upon the application of the executors or members of the family, for reasons approved of by the Court, or upon the application of other parties upon the ground of necessity or of proved public convenience, and then only for reinterment in other g consecrated ground.'

In *Re Talbot* [1901] P 1 Dr Tristram granted a faculty for the exhumation of a body, buried in consecrated ground, in order that it might be reinterred in ground which was, in law, unconsecrated, though was, in fact, below a Roman Catholic church. In the course of his judgment he amended his dictum, just quoted, that there was a limitation on the h exercise of the discretion. He said that the former practice to refuse a faculty where it was proposed to reinter the remains in unconsecrated ground, viz to a place under the protection of no court, need no longer be followed now that Parliament had made it unlawful to remove any body or the remains of any body interred in *any* place of burial, and he cited s 25 of the Burial Act 1857, which is still in force. Dr Tristram added that the court might, in the exercise of its discretion, have regard to all the circumstances of j the case.

In this century there are other reported cases concerning the use of part of a churchyard,

1   Sir John Nicholl (1759–1838) was Dean of the Arches from 1809 to 1834. The quotation appears to be an adaptation of a passage in Sir John's judgment in *Butt v Jones* (1829) 2 Hag Ecc 417 at 424, 162 ER 909 at 911.

a and the consequent disinterment of bodies buried in that part and their reinterment in another part, for the purposes of highway improvement, but they require no special mention here since, it appears to me, in each case the general principles propounded by Dr Tristram and referred to in the passages quoted above were followed.

In *Re Matheson (decd)* [1958] 1 All ER 202, [1958] 1 WLR 246 Chancellor Steel, sitting in the Liverpool Consistory Court, considered a petition for a faculty for a disinterment for reasons almost identical with those in *Re Dixon* [1892] P 386. Chancellor Steel held

b that Dr Tristram did not reach his decision in that case on the ground that he was precluded from granting the petition as a matter of law but did so in the exercise of his discretion. Chancellor Steel granted the faculty sought and said ([1958] 1 All ER 202 at 204, [1958] 1 WLR 246 at 248):

c 'From the earliest times it has been the natural desire of most men that after death their bodies should be decently and reverently interred and should remain undisturbed. Burial in consecrated ground secured this natural desire, because no body so buried could lawfully be disturbed except in accordance with a faculty obtained from the church court. As all sorts of circumstances which cannot be foreseen may arise which make it desirable or imperative that a body should be disinterred, I feel that the court should be slow to place any fetter on its discretionary

d power or to hold that such fetter already exists. In my view there is no such fetter, each case must be considered on its merits and the chancellor must decide, as a matter of judicial discretion, whether a particular application should be granted or refused.'

I propose, in the light of these authorities, to state the principles which, in my judgment, should guide me, as chancellor, in the exercise of my discretion in granting

e or refusing faculties of this description. The discretion has undoubtedly been expressed to be quite unfettered. It is to be exercised reasonably, according to the circumstances of each case, taking into account changes in human affairs and ways of thought but always mindful that consecrated ground and human remains committed to it should, in principle, remain undisturbed.

The court then should begin with the presumption that, since the body or ashes have

f been interred in consecrated ground and are therefore in the court's protection or, in *Wheatly*'s words, 'safe custody', there should be no disturbance of that ground except for good reason. There is a burden on the petitioner to show that the presumed intention of those who committed the body or ashes to a last resting place is to be disregarded or overborne. The finality of Christian burial must be respected even though it may not be absolutely maintained in all cases. The court should make no distinction in this between

g a body and ashes and should be careful not to give undue weight to the undoubted fact that where ashes have been buried in a casket their disinterment and removal is simpler and less expensive than the disinterment of a body and is unlikely to give rise to any risk to health.

The court must take account of changes in the incidence of cremation in the last two

h generations. More than two-thirds of those dying in England are now cremated. There are also grounds for believing that society has become more mobile. The court should resist a possible trend towards regarding the remains of loved relatives and spouses as portable, to be taken from place to place so that the grave or place of interment of ashes may be the more easily visited.

Notwithstanding these general principles cases occur in which the discretion to grant

j a faculty should be exercised. It is impossible, and I should be wrong in attempting, to give, or even foreshadow, a list of classes into which such cases may fall. Some instances may, nevertheless, be mentioned. Errors occur and bodies and ashes are placed in the wrong grave. Interment of both bodies and ashes are sometimes, for understandable reasons, conducted before all relevant considerations are weighed. A family mausoleum or group of graves may be overlooked; the wishes of the deceased may not be known at the time of burial or fully taken into account. In all such cases the length of time which has elapsed since the interment is a matter to be considered; a prompt application must

be stronger than one which seeks leave to disinter remains which have been undisturbed
for many months or years.

The wish of the personal representatives or next of kin of the deceased to remove the
body or ashes from one part of a churchyard to another or from one churchyard to
another for reasons which appear to the court to be well founded and sufficient is, on the
authorities, a ground for the grant of a faculty. So is public necessity or even convenience,
as for example the extension of a church, provision of heating facilities for church or
parish room, the widening of a hazardous road. In a proper case even the laying out
afresh of the churchyard to enable it to be better maintained may be a ground. In every
case the arguments for the grant of a faculty must be weighed against the general
principles already mentioned and the desirability of maintaining a churchyard, or a place
set aside for the interment of cremated remains, undisturbed, as a place of peace, for
prayer and for the recollection of the departed. Deep offence may be given to those who
cherish the memory of a loved one buried in a churchyard, or tend a grave there, if
disinterments are lightly or frequently allowed.

Having expressed the general principles by which I hold the court should be guided I
turn to the evidence adduced and arguments addressed to me in support of the petition
of the present petitioner Gladys May Atkins. The evidence shows that Ernest Hart Atkins,
her late husband, died aged 66, in the parish of Selsey in this diocese on 29 November
1975, after an illness of two or three months. His body was cremated and the ashes
remaining were placed in a box or casket made, so I was informed, of oak. The casket
containing the ashes was, on 14 January 1976, interred in a part of Church Norton
churchyard which was then set aside for the burial of cremated remains. Church Norton
churchyard is the churchyard of the old church of the parish (the new parish church
having been built about 120 years ago) but is still open for burials. The place where the
late Ernest Atkins's ashes were interred was marked with a stone plaque about 12 inches
by 8 inches suitably inscribed. Other similar memorial stones, recording the interment
of ashes, are nearby.

Mrs Atkins says that her decision to bury her husband's ashes in Church Norton
churchyard was taken in haste, under the stress of bereavement and without due
reflection. She wishes now, and has wished for many years, that she had decided to bury
the ashes in the consecrated part of Twickenham cemetery where other members of her
family are buried and where she hopes her own mortal remains will lie. Mr Ernest
Atkins never said where he wished his body, or ashes, to be buried.

Mrs Atkins said that although she regretted the decision nevertheless she abided by it.
She was able to visit the grave by walking through the fields from her house in Selsey
although the journey took one and a half hours each way. She is now 77 and is unable to
undertake the journey on foot; the journey by omnibus is inconvenient and she finds it
difficult to make her former weekly visit.

Church Norton churchyard is very large and the parochial church council of the parish
has found, as have many others in recent times, increasing difficulty in maintaining it in
good order. Mrs Atkins said that she used to keep the grass down round her husband's
grave but she was finding it almost impossible, because of her advancing years, to
continue to do so and she complained, though without attaching blame, that that part of
the churchyard where her husband's ashes rested was becoming very neglected. Her
evidence as to the state of the churchyard was confirmed by the rector of Selsey, the Rev
V R Cassam. He explained that the ashes of Mr Atkins were buried in a plot of land set
aside for the interment of cremated remains and that since 1985, when a new plot,
authorised by faculty, had been brought into use, no interment had taken place in the
former plot. In the new plot the places of interment were not identified and interments
were recorded otherwise. He was confident that the new plot would be much easier to
keep in order. He agreed that the old plot was rather neglected, that the arrangement
there of small plaques recording the interment of ashes made maintenance difficult and
that it was likely that within a generation a petition would be presented for a faculty to
authorise, after due notice to all concerned, the clearing of memorials from, and the
returfing of, the old plot.

Some further facts which appeared to me relevant should be mentioned. Mrs Atkins
a lived in the house which, before she owned it, had belonged to, and been the home of,
her grandparents and parents and she lived there for the whole of her life until, at the
age of 65, she moved, with her husband, to Selsey. On her marriage, in about 1935, her
husband had come to live with her in that house. There were no children of the marriage.
Mrs Atkins said her husband had no family of his own and became a devoted son-in-law
and cared for her mother, who was afflicted by a stroke, in her declining years. Mrs
b Atkins's paternal grandparents, her parents, her sister and a cousin were all buried in two
graves in the same plot in the consecrated part of Twickenham cemetery before she
moved with her husband to Selsey. Mrs Atkins intends to return to live in Twickenham,
where she has friends and relatives, and wishes, as I have already said, that, on her death,
her cremated remains may be interred in one of those graves. I am satisfied, from
documentary evidence, that there is space in those graves for that interment and for the
c interment of her husband's ashes.

Having heard the evidence and Mr Bodkin's submissions and those of the Archdeacon
of Chichester, to whom I am obliged for their help, I have come to the conclusion that I
should grant this petition. When I read the papers in chambers I considered that the
lapse of time since the interment of the ashes in 1976 was so great that, for that reason
alone, the petition should be refused. I have been persuaded that, while that is an
d important fact, it has to be viewed against the rest of the evidence, including Mrs Atkins's
continued residence in Selsey from 1976. The petition is supported by the incumbent
and the parochial church council. As the ashes are contained in a stout casket they may
be removed and transported without difficulty. There is what amounts to a family grave,
or graves, in Twickenham and I accept that Mrs Atkins would, if she had thought the
matter over fully at the time of her husband's death, have buried his ashes there and not
e at Selsey. The late Mr Atkins was, for 40 years, a resident of Twickenham. The strongest
feature of the case, however, is the likely future of the plot in which Mr Atkins's ashes
presently lie. There are serious difficulties in maintaining it as it is; it is no longer in use
for the interment of cremated remains; the parochial church council will be able to
present a strong case should it file a petition for clearing and returfing it. Should such a
petition be presented then Mrs Atkins would, on the authorities (see, for example, *St*
f *Helen's, Bishopsgate* [1892] P 259 at 260), have an equally strong case for objecting to the
grant unless the petition contained provisions authorising her to remove her husband's
ashes and memorial stone to another part of the churchyard or to another consecrated
burial ground.

Accordingly I direct that a faculty should pass the seal, authorising the removal of the
cremated remains of the late Ernest Hart Atkins from Church Norton churchyard and
g their reinterment in grave no 165, plot E, class A in Twickenham cemetery and the
removal of the memorial stone relating to the said remains and its re-erection on or
beside the said grave. The consent of the London Borough of Richmond upon Thames,
to whom Twickenham cemetery belongs, has been obtained to the removal of the ashes;
its consent to the re-erection of the stone in the cemetery must also be obtained before
h the stone is placed in the cemetery. If the London Borough of Richmond upon Thames
so requires the approval of the borough's medical officer must be obtained before the
ashes are removed.

The costs of the petition are to be paid by the petitioner. As I sat for one half-day and
the time of the court was also occupied by the hearing of another petition and I have
made an order that the petitioner in that case should pay the fee incurred through the
j sitting of the court for one half-day no fee is to be payable by Mrs Atkins in respect of the
sitting of the court.

Petition granted.

Solicitors: *Chamberlain Martin & Spurgeon*, Selsey (for Mrs Atkins).

N P Metcalfe Esq   Barrister.

R v Bellman

HOUSE OF LORDS

LORD MACKAY OF CLASHFERN LC, LORD FRASER OF TULLYBELTON, LORD BRIDGE OF HARWICH,
LORD GRIFFITHS AND LORD JAUNCEY OF TULLICHETTLE

2, 3 NOVEMBER, 8 DECEMBER 1988

*Indictment – Joinder of charges – Charges founded on same facts – Mutually contradictory counts
– Defendant charged with obtaining property by deception or conspiracy to import controlled
drugs illegally – Counts mutually contradictory and mutually destructive – Whether judge
entitled to leave both counts to jury – Whether prosecution required to elect on which count it
intends to proceed.*

Where an indictment contains mutually exclusive counts which are factually
contradictory and which will entail an acquittal on one charge if there is a conviction on
the other it is nevertheless permissible for the trial judge to leave both counts to the jury
if the evidence establishes a prima facie case on both counts, without requiring the
prosecution to elect during the course of the trial on which count they wish to proceed
(see p 23 *b* to *d*, p 26 *f* and p 29 *e* to *h*, post).

Notes

For joinder of offences in an indictment, see 11 Halsbury's Laws (4th edn) para 213, and
for cases on the subject, see 14(1) Digest (Reissue) 294–304, 2245–2326.

Cases referred to in opinions

Connolly v DPP [1962] 2 All ER 401, [1964] AC 1254, [1964] 2 WLR 1145, HL.
Ludlow v Metropolitan Police Comr [1970] 1 All ER 567, [1971] AC 29, [1970] 2 WLR 521,
    HL.
R v Ailes (1918) 13 Cr App R 173, CCA.
R v Barnes (1985) 83 Cr App R 38, CA.
R v Barrell (1979) 69 Cr App R 250, CA.
R v Harris (1822) 5 B & Ald 926, 106 ER 1430.
R v Kray [1969] 3 All ER 941, [1970] 1 QB 125, [1969] 3 WLR 831, CA.
R v Lane (1985) 82 Cr App R 5, CA.
R v Shelton (1986) 83 Cr App R 379, CA.
R v Smith (1926) 19 Cr App R 151, CCA.
R v Taylor (1924) 18 Cr App R 25, CCA.
R v Tyreman (1925) 19 Cr App R 4, CCA.
Tsang Ping-nam v R [1981] 1 WLR 1462, PC.

Appeal

The Crown appealed with leave of the Appeal Committee of the House of Lords given
on 10 December 1987 against the decision of the Court of Appeal, Criminal Division
(Neill LJ, Bush and Ian Kennedy JJ) (86 Cr App R 40) on 22 May 1987 allowing the appeal
of the respondent, André Patrick Bellman, against his convictions on 13 October 1986 at
the Central Criminal Court before his Honour Judge Machin QC and a jury on three
counts of dishonestly obtaining money by deception contrary to s 15(1) of the Theft Act
1968. On 4 June 1987 the Court of Appeal (Neill LJ, Potts and Ian Kennedy JJ) refused
the Crown leave to appeal to the House of Lords but certified, under s 33(2) of the
Criminal Appeal Act 1968, that a point of law of general public importance (set out at
p 23 *e f*, post) was involved in the decision. The facts are set out in the opinion of Lord
Griffiths.

Stephen Mitchell QC and *David Fisher* for the Crown.
a *Nicholas Purnell QC* and *Lesley Orme* for Bellman.

Their Lordships took time for consideration.

8 December. The following opinions were delivered.

b **LORD MACKAY OF CLASHFERN LC.** My Lords, I have had the privilege of reading in draft the speech of my noble and learned friend Lord Griffiths. I entirely agree with his reasoning and that this appeal should be disposed of as he suggests.

LORD FRASER OF TULLYBELTON. My Lords, I have had the advantage of reading in draft the speech of my noble and learned friend Lord Griffiths. I agree with it c and, for the reasons given by him, I would allow the appeal and answer the certified question in the way he has proposed.

LORD BRIDGE OF HARWICH. My Lords, I have had the advantage of reading in draft the speech of my noble and learned friend Lord Griffiths. I agree with it and, for the reasons he gives, I would allow the appeal.
d

LORD GRIFFITHS. My Lords, this is an appeal by the Crown from the decision of the Court of Appeal, Criminal Division ((1987) 86 Cr App R 40) quashing the conviction of the respondent, Bellman, on three counts of obtaining property by deception contrary to s 15(1) of the Theft Act 1968. At the request of the Crown, the Court of Appeal certified the following point of law of general public importance:
e
'Is it proper when an indictment contains mutually exclusive counts for both counts to be left to the jury for them to decide which, if either, count has been proven, or should the prosecution be obliged to elect during the course of the trial upon which count they wish to proceed?'

f The expression 'mutually exclusive' is used in the question to mean counts which are factually contradictory so that a conviction on one count necessarily involves an acquittal on the other count.
    Bellman was originally charged with two co-accused, MacAlesher and Ford, on an indictment containing 22 counts. MacAlesher and Ford pleaded guilty to a number of the counts and the court ordered that the remaining counts against them should not be proceeded with without the leave of the Court of Appeal, Criminal Division. The g indictment was redrawn and Bellman faced trial on an indictment containing ten counts.
    The broad outline of the prosecution case against Bellman was that he and MacAlesher were two conmen who, between May 1982 and June 1983, had either attempted to obtain or succeeded in obtaining large sums of money from individuals by various false pretences. In the case of the attempt and in three of the instances of obtaining money by h deception, the false pretence had been that the money would be used to buy drugs in the United States which would be smuggled into this country and sold at a vast profit. As an alternative to the counts alleging that the false pretence related to drugs, the prosecution said that if Bellman and MacAlesher had not been deceiving these individuals and had in fact been intending to buy drugs in the United States, then they were guilty of a conspiracy to evade the prohibition on the importation of controlled drugs. The j prosecution therefore included in the indictment three counts of conspiracy to contravene s 170(2) of the Customs and Excise Management Act 1979, contrary to s 1(1) of the Criminal Law Act 1977. The prosecution put forward these counts of conspiracy as alternatives to the counts in which the false deception related to the purchase and importation of drugs.

The judge, in his summing up, pointed out to the jury that the conspiracy counts were alternatives to the counts alleging obtaining by deception and instructed the jury, first to consider the conspiracy counts, and only if they acquitted on the conspiracy counts would it be necessary for them to consider the counts of deception.

One of the counts of obtaining by deception, count 5, had no alternative conspiracy count and the jury were instructed to consider this separately.

The jury acquitted on the three conspiracy counts but convicted Bellman on four counts of obtaining money by deception, namely counts 5, 6, 7 and 8. The judge sentenced Bellman to serve a term of 2½ years' imprisonment on each of the counts, the sentences to run concurrently.

Bellman appealed against his conviction. The Court of Appeal allowed his appeal against conviction on counts 6, 7 and 8, but dismissed his appeal against conviction on count 5. Count 5 alleged that Bellman had dishonestly obtained £12,000 from one Childs by falsely pretending that he was concluding a real estate transaction in the United States, that the money would be used to conclude the transaction and that Mr Childs would double his money. Mr Childs in fact lost all his money. There was no alternative conspiracy count in respect of count 5, nor was there any evidence pointing to a connection between this count and any drug dealing. There was ample evidence to support the count, and the Court of Appeal accordingly dismissed the appeal against the conviction in respect of count 5 and it need not be further considered.

Counts 6, 7 and 8 all concerned money obtained from a man by the name of Cannon in June 1983. The false deception alleged in counts 6 and 7, by which Bellman obtained sums of £10,000 and £5,000 from Cannon, was that the money would be used to purchase luxury cars in the United States which would then be illegally imported into this country and sold at a great profit. The false deception alleged in count 8, by which £3,000 was obtained from Cannon, was that the money would be used to facilitate the importation of controlled drugs from the United States to this country and that Cannon's investment of £15,000 would be lost unless he invested this further sum of £3,000 but that if he did so the return on his investment, which had in fact been used for the purchase of drugs, would be very great. The judge treated these three counts together as alternative to count 10 which was one of the conspiracy counts. Counts 6 and 7 were not strictly alternatives to the conspiracy count but there can be no doubt that count 8 was a true alternative. Because of the way in which they had been treated by the judge the Court of Appeal decided that they must treat them similarly.

The prosecution case in respect of these four counts depended primarily on the evidence of Cannon and a man by the name of Short. Short himself had been named as the loser in counts 3 and 4 which alleged that money had been obtained from him by the false deception that it was to be used to buy drugs in the United States. Short and Cannon, who were both treated as accomplices, gave evidence to the following effect. Short said that he believed that he was putting up money to buy drugs and that he had introduced Cannon to MacAlesher and Bellman in order to provide further funds for this purpose. He said, however, that the story told to Cannon to induce him to part with the first two sums was that the money was to be used to buy cars in the United States which would then be smuggled into this country without paying any import duty and thereby sold at a great profit. After the money had been obtained from Cannon for this purpose, Short had gone to the United States with Bellman and MacAlesher. They flew to Tampa in Florida. On the following day, Short said, MacAlesher and Bellman went to a bank and emerged with a bag which they said contained the money and then told him that they were going off to buy the drugs. When they returned they told him they had bought the drugs and that they were in the bag. He said the bag was always kept padlocked and in the custody of MacAlesher and Bellman. Short said that in his presence Bellman had then telephoned Cannon in England and told him that his money had been used to purchase drugs which had proved more expensive than they thought and they needed another £3,000 or Cannon would lose his money, and it was as a result of that

telephone conversation that Cannon telexed out the further £3,000 that formed the basis
a of count 8. Later, he said, it was decided that this bag would be put in the car for safe
keeping because the hotel cleaners may have become suspicious about it. Short said he
put the bag in the boot of the car and locked it. Later, he said, when he went to fetch the
car, he looked in the locked boot and discovered that the bag was no longer there. It is
clear from the judge's summing up that Short gave somewhat confused evidence about
when the bag was put in the boot and when it was last seen before he discovered that it
b was missing.

Cannon in evidence described how he was invited by Short to meet Bellman and
MacAlesher to discuss the purchase of cars in the United States and bringing them in
without paying customs duty and thereby making a large profit on resale in this country.
He described how he raised the money and handed it over. He then described being
telephoned by Bellman from the United States and being told that it was not cars that
c were purchased but drugs and that £3,000 more was needed. If the £3,000 was not
forthcoming, he was told, he would have lost his investment of £15,000. As a result of
that conversation he said he raised a further £3,000 and telexed it to the United States.

Cannon said that shortly thereafter he met Bellman and MacAlesher, after they had
returned from the United States, and they repeated the story about the stolen drugs
saying that they had lost much more than he had.

d   Bellman did not make a statement to the police and he did not give evidence.

This is but a bare outline of the evidence extracted from the summing up of the judge
after a trial that lasted many days but it is sufficient to show that the jury would have to
decide whether what had taken place in America and what had been told to Cannon
about the drugs was all an elaborate charade to deceive Cannon and possibly also Short,
or whether, in fact, this had been an attempt to purchase drugs which had come to grief
e when the drugs were stolen.

It was conceded in argument before your Lordships that if the prosecution had elected
to present this case solely as a conspiracy to import drugs, there was, by the end of the
prosecution evidence, a prima facie case to be considered by the jury on that charge. It
was of course also conceded that there was a prima facie case to be considered on the
charges of deception on which the jury convicted. But it was submitted that because
f these two charges were mutually contradictory neither should have been left to the jury.

The Court of Appeal, in giving its reasons for allowing the appeal on counts 6, 7, and
8, said (86 Cr App R 40 at 46):

> 'Having considered with care the course of the trial, the submissions made to the
> trial judge and the summing-up it seems to us to be clear that the prosecution were
g > putting before the jury counts which were not merely mutually exclusive but were
> mutually destructive; they were seeking to satisfy the jury by means of the deception
> counts that the representations as to the importation of drugs were false while at the
> same time seeking to satisfy them by means of the conspiracy counts that there were
> in fact conspiracies to import drugs and that accordingly the representations were
> true. We see the force of the argument by counsel for the Crown that the issue for
h > the jury concerned the state of mind of the appellant rather than the overt acts of
> the other persons involved, but it is plain that on the conspiracy counts the jury
> were being asked to draw inferences of fact which were diametrically opposed to
> the inferences they were asked to draw on the deception counts. We therefore
> consider that on the facts of this case the prosecution should have been required to
> make an election at the close of their case and to decide whether to proceed on the
j > deception counts or on the conspiracy counts in so far as they were alternatives. . . .
> Accordingly, the convictions on counts 6, 7 and 8 must be quashed.'

As to count 5, the Court of Appeal, in dismissing the appeal on that count, said:

> 'The false representations alleged in count 5 were quite separate from those in the

other counts and the person who was deprived of money was different. Moreover it
was not alleged by the prosecution that any mention of drugs was made on this   *a*
occasion. The appeal against conviction in relation to count 5 is therefore dismissed.'

Bellman has already served his sentence on count 5 and as all his sentences were
concurrent he will not have to serve any further term of imprisonment if this appeal is
allowed.

Counsel for Bellman did not seek to support the Court of Appeal's decision on the
ground that the prosecution should have been put to their election at the end of the   *b*
prosecution case. If the prosecution have put before a jury evidence which, if believed, is
capable of supporting a conviction, it is for the jury and not the judge to evaluate the
evidence and decide the question of guilt; still less is it the function of the prosecution to
elect which interpretation to place on the evidence, for that is to usurp the function of
the jury. The outcome of this case turned primarily on the jury's assessment of Short and
Cannon and whether they believed that the visit to the United States, which was   *c*
supported by other evidence, was all part of an elaborate charade or whether, in truth, an
attempt had been made to obtain drugs. The evidence was capable of supporting either
view of the facts and it was the jury's task to determine where the truth lay.

Counsel for Bellman argued this appeal on the more fundamental proposition that
under our adversarial procedure of trial in which the burden of establishing the guilt of   *d*
the accused is placed on the prosecution, it can never be right for mutually contradictory
counts to be contained in one indictment. He submitted that to do so would be contrary
to the prosecution's duty of proving the case, unfair to the accused and an embarrassment
for the jury.

My Lords, I am sure that it will only be comparatively rarely that the prosecution will
wish to charge counts which are factually mutually contradictory in the sense that proof   *e*
of one charge destroys the other. The very fact that offences are being charged in the
alternative obviously weakens the prosecution case and enables the defence to invite the
jury to say that as the prosecution cannot make their mind up which crime the accused
committed they, the jury, cannot be sure of his guilt. But equally, I have no doubt that
in certain circumstances justice requires that an accused should face mutually
contradictory counts. To take a simple example. Suppose the police were keeping watch   *f*
in Soho because they had evidence that a drug pedlar was regularly selling heroin on the
streets. The police see the drug pedlar handing over a packet of white powder to an
addict and receiving a large sum in bank notes. They arrest the pedlar but the addict
disposes of the packet down a grating in the road so that its contents are lost and cannot
be analysed. The addict is prepared to give evidence that he believed he was buying
heroin and had bought heroin before from the same drug pedlar, and there is other   *g*
evidence to support the belief that the packet contained heroin. The drug pedlar,
however, says that the packet did not contain heroin but only a mixture of chalk and
some other harmless substance, but admits that he received a £1,000 for it because he
told the addict it was heroin. In such circumstances I can see no injustice in requiring the
accused to face the alternative counts of supplying a controlled drug, and obtaining
£1,000 by deception. Whichever be the true explanation, he has committed a crime and   *h*
the prosecution, lacking the positive evidence of an analysis of the drug because it was
dropped down the grating, might not be wholly confident that the jury would draw the
inference that the drug was heroin on this occasion and might fear that the jury would
accept the accused's explanation. Of course, there is the possibility that the prosecution
might fail to establish either charge because the jury would be directed first to consider
the count of supplying a controlled drug, and only if they acquitted on that count, to   *j*
proceed to consider if they were sure that the accused's explanation that he sold a harmless
substance as heroin was true, in which case they would convict on the second count; but
if they were left in doubt then they would have no alternative but to acquit on the second
count also. However, it seems to me unlikely that, looking at the evidence as a whole, a
jury would not feel able to be sure which was the true explanation of the transaction.

a   There are, of course, rare situations in which it is clear that the accused has committed a crime but the state of the evidence is such that it is impossible to say which crime he has committed. In such circumstances no prima facie case can be established to support either crime and neither crime can be left to the jury. The classic example arises where a man has given contradictory evidence on oath on two occasions. It is obvious that one statement must be false but in the absence of any evidence to indicate which statement was false it cannot be proved on which occasion the perjury was committed: see *R v*
b   *Harris* (1822) 5 B & Ald 926, 106 ER 1430.

A modern example of this dilemma arose in *Tsang Ping-nam v R* [1981] 1 WLR 1462. A police officer had made contradictory statements in the course of an investigation into corruption in the police force and at the trial of his police colleagues on charges of corruption. His statement implicated his colleagues but his evidence at the trial exonerated them. The police officer was charged with and convicted of an attempt to
c   pervert the course of justice. The following passage from the judgment of the Judicial Committee delivered by Lord Roskill gives the reasons for allowing the appeal (at 1465):

'It will be observed that no particulars of this count were ever asked for ... Had particulars been sought and ordered, the Crown's dilemma must at once have emerged. The Crown conceded that perjury could not be proved against the
d   defendant for there was no affirmative evidence that the defendant had lied in court let alone any corroboration of any such affirmative evidence. The Crown also conceded that it could not be affirmatively proved that the defendant had given false information to the investigating officers to whom the several statements had been given. But the Crown averred that it was clear that either the defendant had committed perjury or had given false information to the investigating officers and
e   that, whichever was the case, he was guilty of an attempt to pervert the course of public justice by his conduct ... Had the particulars been asked for, the Crown must have given alternative and mutually inconsistent particulars which could not have been allowed to stand as particulars under the same count. If that pleading difficulty had been surmounted by adding in the case of each of the three officers an
f   additional count, their Lordships are of the clear opinion that, at the close of the case for the prosecution, a submission of no case to answer on both of each pair of counts must have succeeded on the ground that the Crown had wholly failed to prove the relevant facts averred in either count.'

The reference to the Crown wholly failing to prove the relevant facts must, of course,
g   be read as a failure by the Crown to establish a prima facie case on either count, for it is the duty of the prosecution to establish a prima facie case of guilt, and it is the function of the jury to say whether the evidence which supports the prima facie case is sufficient to prove guilt.

An accused is always entitled to have the counts in the indictment considered separately by the judge at the end of the prosecution's evidence and, if there is insufficient evidence
h   to provide a prima facie case on any count, to have that count withdrawn from the jury. This was the evidential difficulty that faced the prosecution in *Tsang Ping-nam v R*, but it does not deal with the problem in a case such as the present where the evidence is sufficient to support a prima facie case on either of the two alternative hypotheses and it is for the jury to say on their assessment of the witnesses and the inferences that they are prepared to draw from the evidence as a whole whether they are sure that either
j   hypothesis is correct.

It, of course, goes without saying that if the evidence shows that one of two accused must have committed a crime but it is impossible to go further and say which of them committed it, both must be acquitted: see *R v Lane* (1985) 82 Cr App R 5.

As I have said, the submission of counsel for Bellman was that contradictory counts can never be properly joined in the same indictment. He concedes that no support for his argument can be gained from a consideration of the Indictments Act 1915 and the Indictment Rules 1971, SI 1971/1253, made thereunder. The counts of conspiracy and *a* false deception in the present case would clearly be based on the same facts within the meaning of r 9 of the 1971 rules, which provides:

> 'Charges for any offences may be joined in the same indictment if those charges are founded on the same facts, or form or are a part of a series of offences of the same or a similar character.'
b

Nor was he able to cite any authority in which joinder had been refused on the ground that the facts of the two counts were mutually self-destructive.

The Crown, on the other hand, were able to point to the long-established practice of charging counts of larceny and receiving as alternatives and to the present practice since the passing of the Theft Act 1968 of charging robbery or theft and handling as alternatives in separate counts and the express approval of this practice by the Court of Appeal in *R v* *c* *Shelton* (1986) 83 Cr App R 379.

Perhaps the most striking example of the joinder of mutually contradictory counts in recent times is *R v Barnes* (1985) 83 Cr App R 38. Barnes had given evidence at the trial of his brother on a charge of wounding with intent that it was he, Barnes, who had attacked and wounded the victim and not his brother. The brother was acquitted. Barnes was then tried on an indictment that charged him with committing perjury at his *d* brother's trial and, alternatively, with wounding with intent. Barnes was convicted of perjury and appealed on the ground that the two counts should not have been joined in the same indictment as they were not 'founded on the same facts' within the meaning of r 9. The Court of Appeal dismissed the appeal by the application of the proviso to s 2(1) of the Criminal Appeal Act 1968 on the ground that there had been no miscarriage of justice and found it unnecessary to decide whether the two counts had been properly *e* joined.

My Lords, I entertain no doubt that the two counts were properly joined in the indictment. In *Ludlow v Metropolitan Police Comr* [1970] 1 All ER 567 at 574, [1971] AC 29 at 40 Lord Pearson, in a speech with which the rest of their Lordships agreed, when dealing with r 3 contained in Sch 1 of the Indictments Act 1915 (which had identical *f* wording to the present r 9 of the Indictment Rules 1971) approved the following passage in the judgment of the Court of Appeal in *R v Kray* [1969] 3 All ER 941 at 944, [1970] 1 QB 125 at 131:

> 'It is not desirable, in the view of this court, that r 3 should be given an unduly restricted meaning, since any risk of injustice can be avoided by the exercise of the judge's discretion to sever the indictment. All that is necessary to satisfy the rule is *g* that the offences should exhibit such similar features as to establish a prima facie case that can properly and conveniently be tried together.'

Lord Pearson added:

> 'That last sentence is not a construction of the rule, but I think it is helpful practical advice for those applying the rule. The view that r 3 should not be given *h* an unduly restricted meaning derives support from authority: *R v Ailes* (1918) 13 Cr App R 173. When it is available, it should be used: *R v Taylor* (1924) 18 Cr App R 25; *R v Tyreman* (1925) 19 Cr App R 4; *R v Smith* (1926) 19 Cr App R 151; and *Connelly v Director of Public Prosecutions* [1964] 2 All ER 401 at 406, 416–417, 440, 451, [1964] AC 1254 at 1296, 1312–1313, 1351, 1367.'
j

In *R v Barrell* (1979) 69 Cr App R 250 at 252–253 Shaw LJ said:

> 'This contention rests on too narrow a construction of the language of the statute and the relevant rule. The phrase "founded on the same facts" does not mean that for charges to be properly joined in the same indictment, the facts in relation to the

respective charges must be identical in substance or virtually contemporaneous. The
test is whether the charges have a common factual origin. If the charge described by
counsel as a subsidiary charge is one that could not have been alleged but for the
facts which give rise to what he calls the primary charge, then it is true to say that
for the purposes of rule 9 that those charges are founded, that is to say have their
origin, in the same facts and can legitimately be joined in the same indictment.'

The case against Barnes of wounding with intent was founded on the evidence he gave at
his brother's trial and which the prosecution maintained as their primary case was in fact
perjured evidence. The factual origin of both offences was the attack on the victim. If
the prosecution had been forced to proceed against Barnes in separate trials and Barnes
had been acquitted of perjury in the first trial, it would have enabled Barnes on the
second trial for wounding with intent to give evidence that what he had said in the
witness box at his brother's trial was, in fact, untrue and perjury, in the knowledge that
he would be protected from any further prosecution for perjury by a plea of autrefois
acquit. This manifest manipulation and abuse of the judicial process is only to be avoided
by joinder of both counts in one indictment so that the whole of the facts can be
adjudicated on by one jury.

It is also to be observed that in *Tsang Ping-nam v R* Lord Roskill did not apparently
consider that it would have been fundamentally wrong to include separate but
contradictory counts in the indictment. He used the example of charging the offences in
separate counts to illustrate the evidential difficulties of the prosecution on the particular
facts of that case. If the Judicial Committee had considered that the joinder of such
counts was fundamentally wrong the judgment would surely have been differently
expressed.

My Lords, for these reasons I find no support in law for the submission that mutually
contradictory counts can never be joined in one indictment. I can find no overriding
reason why justice requires there should be such a rule nor was it suggested that Bellman
suffered injustice in the present case. As I have endeavoured to point out, there will be
rare occasions when I think justice positively requires there should be such joinder.

I would therefore allow this appeal and restore the convictions on counts 6, 7 and 8,
but as I have already pointed out this will not affect Bellman as he has already served his
sentence.

I would answer the certified question by saying that there is no rule of law that
prevents the inclusion in one indictment of mutually exclusive counts and that if, at the
end of the prosecution case, the evidence establishes a prima facie case on both counts,
the matter should be left to the jury to determine the question of guilt, and the
prosecution should not be put to their election on which count to proceed.

LORD JAUNCEY OF TULLICHETTLE. My Lords, I have had the advantage of
reading in draft the speech prepared by my noble and learned friend Lord Griffiths. I
agree with it, and would allow this appeal.

Appeal allowed.

Solicitors: *Crown Prosecution Service*; *Offenbach & Co* (for Bellman).

Mary Rose Plummer   Barrister.

R v East Sussex Coroner, ex parte Healy and   *a*
another

QUEEN'S BENCH DIVISION
WOOLF LJ AND HUTCHISON J
6 MAY 1988
                                                                                b

Coroner – Jurisdiction – Inquest – Death occurring 'in or near' area of jurisdiction – Death occurring eight or nine miles off coast – Whether death occurring 'in or near' area of coroner's jurisdiction – Coroners Amendment Act 1926, s 18.

The deceased disappeared while diving from a vessel some eight or nine miles off the Sussex coast. His body was never recovered. The coroner for the county nearest the scene   *c* of the accident refused to hold an inquest and expressed the view that he had no jurisdiction to do so because the death had not occurred 'in or near' the area of his jurisdiction for the purposes of s 18[a] of the Coroners Amendment Act 1926. The deceased's parents applied for judicial review of the coroner's refusal to hold an inquest.

Held – Although the question of whether a coroner had jurisdiction under s 18 of the   *d* 1926 Act to hold an inquest if there was no body was primarily a matter for his belief and assessment as to whether the death had occurred 'in or near' the area of his jurisdiction, a distance of eight or nine miles off the coast could not be described as 'in or near' the area of his jurisdiction. The coroner had accordingly been right to decline to hold an inquest into the deceased's death. The application would therefore be refused (see p 35 *d* to *h j* and p 36 *f g*, post).   *e*

Notes
For death occurring 'in or near' the area of a coroner's jurisdiction, see 9 Halsbury's Laws (4th edn) para 1056.
    For the Coroners Amendment Act 1926, s 18, see 11 Halsbury's Statutes (4th edn) 378.

Case referred to in judgments   *f*
Tyne River Keelmen v Davison (1864) 16 CBNS 612, 143 ER 1267.

Cases also cited
R v Shrewsbury Coroner's Court, ex p British Parachute Association (1987) Times, 21 September, DC.
R v West Yorkshire Coroner, ex p Smith [1982] 3 All ER 1098, [1983] QB 335, CA.   *g*

Application for judicial review
Marian Healy and Peter Healy, the parents of Trevor Healy deceased, applied, with the leave of McCullough J given on 16 February 1988, for judicial review by way of (i) certiorari to quash the refusal by Dr Donald Gooding, HM Coroner for the western district of East Sussex, to hold an inquest into the death of the deceased and (ii) mandamus   *h* requiring the coroner to hold an inquest. The facts are set out in the judgment of Woolf LJ.

Jeremy Carey for the applicants.
Giles Kavanagh for the coroner.
David Pannick for the Secretary of State for the Home Department.
                                                                                j

WOOLF LJ. This is an application for judicial review. It is an application made by Mr and Mrs Peter Healy and it arises out of the tragic death of their 17-year-old son on 9 August 1986. The reason for the application is that there has not been any coroner's

_____
a   Section 18 is set out at p 31 *e* to *g*, post

inquest into the death of their son, Trevor, and the applicants, not unnaturally in the
a circumstances, feel that there should be an inquest, not so much for their own personal
satisfaction, though that is no doubt a factor which they have in mind as well, but
because they feel that an inquest could result in steps being taken to avoid further tragic
fatalities of this sort.

The circumstances of Trevor's death do not have to be gone into in detail for the
purposes of this application. It is sufficient if I recite the barest outline of the facts. On 9
b August 1986 Trevor, together with other people, went out on a diving expedition. They
went to the scene of two wrecks very approximately eight or nine miles offshore and
Trevor descended into the sea in that position with another diver, who was much more
experienced than Trevor, and that was the last that was seen of Trevor. His body has
never been recovered. Precisely what went wrong has never been discovered, albeit, as I
will indicate hereafter, there was an inquiry under the Merchant Shipping Acts 1970 and
c 1979 into his death.

The jurisdiction which it is alleged that the coroner has in these circumstances is an
unusual one. It is unusual because the jurisdiction of the coroner is normally founded on
the presence of the body of the deceased within his area of jurisdiction. In this case the
respondent coroner, Dr Donald Gooding, is the coroner of the western district of East
Sussex but as the coroner makes clear in his evidence in fact his jurisdiction extends to
d the whole of East Sussex, and he is normally required to inquire into deaths where they
occur in circumstances warranting an inquest when the body is within his area of
jurisdiction.

However, because there are occasions where a body is destroyed or never recovered, a
special jurisdiction was introduced, as I understand the position, for the first time by the
Coroners (Amendment) Act 1926, s 18. That section provides:
e
'Where a coroner has reason to believe that a death has occurred in or near the
area within which he has jurisdiction in such circumstances that an inquest ought
to be held, and that owing to the destruction of the body by fire or otherwise or to
the fact that the body is lying in a place from which it cannot be recovered, an
inquest cannot be held except by virtue of the provisions of this section, he may
f report the facts to the Secretary of State, and the Secretary of State may, if he
considers it desirable so to do, direct an inquest to be held touching the death, and
an inquest shall be held accordingly by the coroner making the report or such other
coroner as the Secretary of State may direct, and the law relating to coroners and
coroners' inquests shall apply with such modifications as may be necessary in
consequence of the inquest being one into the death of a person whose body does
g not lie within the coroner's jurisdiction.'

It will be noted immediately from the terms of s 18 that the basis of jurisdiction in
cases where there is no body available is the coroner having 'reason to believe that a death
has occurred in or near the area within which he has jurisdiction'. It is also to be noted
that the death need not in fact have occurred in or near the area within the coroner's
h jurisdiction as long as the coroner has reason to believe that the death did in fact occur in
or near the area within his jurisdiction.

When the circumstances of Trevor's death were drawn to the coroner's attention he
naturally was concerned to do what he could to assist the parents of Trevor, the present
applicants. He took the view initially that he had no jurisdiction and wrote indicating
that was so. He also communicated with the Home Office and the Home Office advised
j him that there was no jurisdiction in these circumstances, the Home Office taking the
view, based on their practice, that a distance of seven or eight miles offshore was not near
the coroner's area of jurisdiction, that is to say the county of East Sussex.

The matter did not rest there because a member of Parliament raised the matter with
the Home Office and in consequence a letter was written from the Home Office by Mr
Douglas Hogg, the Parliamentary Under-Secretary of State, and another letter was written

on 4 February 1987 on behalf of the Prime Minister. In those letters it was set out that
'in or near his jurisdiction', that is the coroner's jurisdiction, in s 18 of the Act is to be   a
construed to be a matter of yards, not miles and accordingly a death seven or eight miles
out to sea could not fall within the terms of the section. It is right to say that in coming
to his conclusion that there was not jurisdiction, Dr Gooding, the coroner, acted on the
advice of the Home Office which he had received which was to the effect that seven or
eight miles was beyond the parameters of nearness. He did, however, draw the attention
of those who were advising the applicants to the provisions of the Merchant Shipping   b
Acts 1970 and 1979. Although the applicants could not themselves institute an inquiry
under the provisions of those Acts, to which I must now turn, they did in fact make
representations indicating their support for an inquiry to take place (under those Acts).
The provisions of the 1970 Act as amended which are relevant are contained in s 61,
which provides:
                                                                                                  c
  '(1) Subject to subsection (4) of this section, where—(a) any person dies in a ship
  registered in the United Kingdom; or in a boat or life-raft from such a ship; or
  (b) the master of or a seaman employed in such a ship dies in a country outside
  the United Kingdom; an inquiry into the cause of the death shall be held
  by a superintendent or proper officer at the next port where the ship calls after the
  death . . .   d
  (1B) Subject to subsection (4) of this section, where it appears to the Secretary of
  State that a person may—(a) have died in a ship registered in the United Kingdom
  or in a boat or life-raft from such a ship; or (b) have been lost from such a ship, boat
  or life-raft and have died in consequence of having been so lost, the Secretary of
  State may arrange for an inquiry to be held by a superintendent or proper officer
  into whether the person died as aforesaid and, if the superintendent or other officer   e
  finds that he did, into the cause of death . . .'

Pursuant to those provisions the Secretary of State arranged that there should be an
inquiry held by a superintendent into the death of Trevor, the view being taken that he
had been lost from a ship, boat or life-raft, the definition of ship being extremely wide
and covering certainly the vessel from which Trevor descended on his dive.   f
An inquiry was held in accordance with the provisions of s 61 on 18 June 1987 by a
marine superintendent at the Department of Transport. At the outset of that inquiry, he
made it clear that the purpose of the inquiry was, firstly, to establish the fact that death
had occurred, and secondly, so far as possible, to establish the physical cause of that death.
His jurisdiction to inquire was limited. However, witnesses were called before him who
could give relevant evidence. The way the evidence was given was for the statement   g
which the witnesses had previously made to be read out; then the witness was asked if he
agreed with the statement; and then there was an opportunity for counsel for the
applicants who has appeared before this court, and for whose argument we are indebted,
and who appeared before the superintendent, to ask questions. It is right to say that
although counsel for the applicants conducted his examination with great circumspection
and precision, there were times where the chairman felt it necessary to confine the   h
examination that was being conducted by counsel. Having heard the evidence, the
superintendent found that Trevor was lost whilst sports diving from the vessel concerned
and that he believed him to be asphyxiated or drowned. He added:

  'Part of the attraction of many sports is that there is an element of risk involved;
  be it mountaineering or potholing, hang-gliding or sports diving. The pitting of   j
  one's skills and experience against the forces of nature is all part of the challenge . . .'

He indicated that the circumstances here were tragic and that it was important in that
situation for 'everybody involved in organising such events to minimise the risks
involved as far as is humanly possible.' He went on to say:

'The greatest care should be taken when planning these activities and thought
a   should be given in that planning, as to whether it is really practical to mix deep
dives for the experienced with shallow dives for the novices. Perhaps serious
consideration too, should be given to the possibility that a pair of experienced divers
should forego taking part in the programme, but remain kitted up whilst diving is
in progress, in order to be ready to mount an immediate search and rescue or
recovery operation should an emergency arise. Let us all learn something from
b   Trevor's tragic death. May it be that lesson will teach us that the sea is not an element
to be trifled with; it must be respected. The professional seaman recognises this,
although even he may be caught unawares. How much more, therefore, that the
casual recreational users who, such as the sports diver or sea fishing enthusiast,
consider that the sea is just a means to an end, should recognise it also.'

c   He then closed the inquiry.
    Although evidence was given by those most closely involved in this tragic accident,
the applicants felt that the inquiry was not satisfactory. In his submissions before this
court, counsel for the applicants was careful to point out that he did not make any
personal criticism of the way the inquiry was conducted. He was submitting that the
shortcomings were because of the extent of the jurisdiction of the inquiry and he submits
d   that notwithstanding that inquiry a coroner's inquest would serve a useful purpose
because the extent of the jurisdiction of the coroner is wider than that of the
superintendent. It is right to say that there is substance in counsel's submission. The
jurisdiction of a coroner is wider. However, it also must be recognised that the coroner's
jurisdiction is restricted. The nature of the restriction is indicated by the terms of the
Coroners Rules 1984, SI 1984/552, and in particular r 36(1) and (2), which provides:

e   '(1) The proceedings and evidence at an inquest shall be directed solely [I
        emphasise the word 'solely'] to ascertaining the following matters, namely—(a) who
        the deceased was; (b) how, when and where the deceased came by his death; (c) the
        particulars for the time being required by the Registration Acts to be registered
        concerning the death.
        (2) Neither the coroner nor the jury shall express any opinion on any other
f   matters.'

    Rule 36 indicates the limits of the jurisdiction of the coroner but it does indicate also
that one of the matters that the coroner is entitled to investigate is how the deceased
came by his death. 'How the deceased came by his death' are wider terms than those
contained in the Merchant Shipping Act 1970, to which I have made reference, but the
g   ability of the coroner to express any opinion is extremely limited because of the terms of
para (2), and it is to be noted that the importance of that rule is underlined by r 41, which
provides:

        'Where the coroner sits with a jury, he shall sum up the evidence to the jury and
        direct them as to the law before they consider their verdict and shall draw their
h   attention to Rules 36(2) and 42.'

Rule 42 provides:

        'No verdict shall be framed in such a way as to appear to determine any question
        of—(a) criminal liability on the part of a named person, or (b) civil liability.'

    However, counsel for the applicants drew attention to a limited power of the coroner
j   which is contained in r 43. The rule provides:

        'A coroner who believes that action should be taken to prevent the recurrence of
        fatalities similar to that in respect of which the inquest is being held may announce
        at the inquest that he is reporting the matter in writing to the person or authority
        who may have power to take such action and he may report the matter accordingly.'

So there is that power in the coroner to report. The applicants feel here that if there was an inquest this might be a case where the coroner would wish to avail himself of that power.

The first matter that this court has to decide, is bearing in mind that the clear indications here are that Trevor met his death eight or nine miles offshore, is whether there jurisdiction. For the purposes of the argument, counsel for the applicants accepts, as is contended on behalf of the respondents, that the normal limit to the coroner's jurisdiction is the point of low tide but he submits that eight or nine miles from that point is well within the provisions of s 18 of the 1926 Act. He refers, with regard to the term 'near', to a decision of the court decided as long ago as 1864, when methods of transport were not as advanced as they are today, in which consideration was given to the meaning of the term 'near' in a different context, namely *Tyne River Keelmen v Davison* (1864) 16 CBNS 612, 143 ER 1267. In that case consideration was given as to when payments were due in respect of the export of coal. The provision of the Act in question referred to the right to make a levy in respect of the export of coal near the River Tyne. Erle CJ said 16 CBNS 612 at 621, 143 ER 1267 at 1271):

'. . . I think a colliery which is ten miles off is "near the river Tyne," within the meaning of the act.'

Williams J was of the same view and added (16 CBNS 612 at 621–622, 143 ER 1267 at 1271):

'. . . every colliery or coal-mine whence coals are exported by the river Tyne is "near," within the meaning of this statute. A colliery which is ten miles off may well be considered near, within the words used. The word must necessarily be construed in different senses according to the subject-matter.'

Willes J was of the same view. Byles J said (16 CBNS 612 at 622, 143 ER 1267 at 1271):

'. . . the word "near" is not a restraining, but an expanding word,— to be extended so far as to give effect to the intention of the legislature. Railways have brought places in one sense near to each other which were not so before the discovery of that rapid mode of transit. It is enough to say that I agree with the rest of the court in thinking that this colliery is near the river Tyne within the meaning of the act.'

It is clear from that case that there are circumstances where ten miles can be regarded as near, never mind eight or nine miles. However, it is important to bear in mind in coming to the conclusion as to what is the meaning of 'near' in this Act, the intent and purpose of the legislation with which we are dealing and, as was recognised in the decision to which I have just made reference, the context in which the word 'near' is used can be of particular significance.

The first point that has to be made with regard to s 18 is that it is primarily concerned with situations where there could be a conflict of jurisdiction between adjoining jurisdictions of two coroners where there is a situation where it cannot be said whether the death had occurred within the boundaries of one coroner or without those boundaries. That is made clear by the discretion which the Secretary of State has, not only to order that an inquest should be held by the coroner making the report but by such other coroner as the Secretary of State may direct. The section, however, and this is not disputed, also applies to cases where there is no conflict of jurisdiction between two coroners. It can apply in situations where someone dies off the shore of the district of a coroner whose ordinary jurisdiction extends to that shore. In my view there is no reason to construe the section in a way which prevents the coroner investigating a death where there is no body and the death has some real connection with his jurisdiction. Here I adopt a submission helpfully made by counsel for the coroner who referred to the jurisdiction as being normally land-based and submitted that the sort of event in the present circumstances which falls within the section is one which has some nexus with

the land over which the coroner has jurisdiction. He gave as an example the situation
a where somebody goes out swimming from the shore and is never seen again. Another
example he gave was somebody who goes out in a rowing boat from the shore. He also
drew attention to s 61(4) of the Merchant Shipping Act 1970 which makes it clear that
where there is a coroner's inquest there should not then be an inquiry under the 1970
Act.

However, it does not follow that there is an implication that there should not be an
b inquest when there has been an inquiry under that Act. First of all, of course we are
dealing here with a jurisdiction under the 1926 Act whereas the Merchant Shipping Act
which I have just been considering is a 1970 Act, albeit a 1970 Act which replaced earlier
legislation. Secondly, it could be equally argued that the absence of any similar provision
in s 18 of the 1926 Act which is equivalent to s 61(4) points the other way. It is, however,
fair to say that if there is some other suitable form of inquiry which can take place this is
c relevant as it is less likely that Parliament intended there to be an overlap between the
two jurisdictions. Here, counsel for the coroner submits that this was clearly a marine
accident whereas the section is referring to a land-based jurisdiction.

I regard as being most important in deciding on the proper approach to s 18 the fact
that it refers to situations where the coroner has reason to believe that a death has
occurred in or near the area within which he has jurisdiction. Having regard to those
d words, it seems to me that in the first instance the question of whether or not a coroner
has jurisdiction is to be judged by the coroner's belief and his assessment as to whether or
not the death occurred in or near the area within which he has jurisdiction. The word
'near', being an ordinary word of the English language indicating a short distance or at
close proximity, is to be applied by the coroner in a commonsense manner and as long as
the coroner approaches the matter in a way which is not wholly unreasonable it seems to
e me that it is not for the courts to define precisely what is meant by the word 'near'. It is a
matter to be judged initially by the coroner. It seems to me also that there can be differing
circumstances which can cause a different effect to be given to the word 'near' by a
coroner. It will not always have exactly the same application in yards, feet, inches or
longer distances than that.

The role of the court, it seems to me, is confined to laying down what are the
f parameters of what is capable of being regarded as within his jurisdiction by a coroner.
The court does that on the basis of particular cases that come before the court. So far as
this case is concerned, I consider it is right that I should indicate that I would not accept
the Home Office approach as to 'a matter of yards'. That seems to me to be far too
constrained. If the coroner had applied that limited approach indicated by the Home
Office he would be wrong. If yards is too short an approach to indicate the limits of the
g jurisdiction under s 18, what is the maximum extent of that jurisdiction? In particular,
having regard to this case, is eight or nine miles beyond that maximum? Notwithstanding
the authority on by counsel for the applicants and to which I have already made reference
relied, I have come unhesitatingly to the conclusion that eight or nine miles is beyond
the jurisdiction of the coroner under s 18 and the coroner accordingly had no jurisdiction,
h whatever he may have believed to be the position, in this particular case. In saying that,
I am bearing in mind in particular that this was a death at sea, on the high seas. At the
time, and I do not regard this as being critical, the jurisdiction, so far as sovereignty was
concerned, of this country's territorial boundaries was three miles from the shore. It has
now been extended to twelve miles. The fact that it was at the time of Trevor's death
three miles makes clear in my view that it was not intended by Parliament by using the
j word 'near' in relation to a death in these circumstances that the coroner should be given
jurisdiction.

Approaching the matter in the way I have indicated, and limiting the court's role to
that which I have indicated, I have come to the conclusion that while the Home Office's
approach can be criticised, equally it is not possible to regard the coroner's jurisdiction as
extending to eight or nine miles. That is enough to determine this case.

I feel it is right that I should say a few words about the question of discretion. I do so while stressing that I fully understand and accept the basis of this application by the *a* parents. I equally do not in any way criticise the parents for adopting the course they did. They thought it was right not to rush to the courts, which is understandable, but to see what happened at the Merchant Shipping Act inquiry and only when they knew the result of that inquiry did they ultimately decide they should come to this court. Once they decided to come to this court, they moved as expeditiously as was possible as is indicated by the fact that the application for leave was made on 25 January 1988 and *b* leave was obtained on 16 February 1988, but this is a long time after the tragic death of Trevor. The position is that this jurisdiction of the court is normally to be exercised promptly though the court has power to extend time. In considering whether to extend the time for making an application, as the court would have to do in this case, what the court has to consider even if it was possible otherwise to grant leave, is whether an inquest now would serve any purpose. It is also necessary to have in mind the fact that if *c* there were now to be an inquest it would bear hard on those who were closely involved in the death of Trevor and who have already had to go through the harrowing experience of giving evidence in one inquiry. Bearing in mind the period of time which has elapsed and above all the statement of the coroner in his affidavit, which is before this court, that a further inquiry into the death of Trevor might well serve no useful purpose and that in effect the inquiry that has already taken place, albeit more limited, has established the *d* cause of death, the conclusion I would come to as a matter of discretion is that it would not be right for this court to intervene. Therefore, notwithstanding that the court appreciates the feelings of the parents, the court would have come to the conclusion that enough is enough and that so far as proceedings of this nature and inquest are concerned there should be an end. I emphasise the fact that even if the court's conclusion had been different, it would have been up to the coroner whether or not to make an application to *e* the Secretary of State, and having regard to the sentiments which he expressed and the arguments which were advanced on his behalf, clearly he would not have made such an application. If he had made such an application it appears extremely unlikely that the Secretary of State would ever have contemplated ordering or directing an inquest in this case.

Accordingly, in these circumstances I would refuse this application. *f*

HUTCHISON J. I agree with the judgment Woolf LJ has given and I agree that the application should be refused for the reasons which he has mentioned. I would add only two observations on my own part. Nobody who has heard the facts of this tragic accident could feel other than the greatest sympathy for Mr and Mrs Healy, not only in the loss that they sustained as a result of it but in the motives that understandably have made *g* them feel that they must seek to pursue this application in order that every possible investigation may take place into the circumstances of the death. However, like Woolf LJ, I am quite satisfied, first, that there is no power in this court to direct the coroner to take any further steps because he himself would have had no jurisdiction; and second, that as a matter of discretion, even had that not been so, it would not have been right to *h* compel an inquest at this stage. I would add in that connection that though I perfectly appreciate the distinction that there is under the statutes between the nature of the inquiry under the Merchant Shipping Act 1970 and the nature of a coroner's inquiry, it did seem to me, when I read last night the full note of the inquiry under the Merchant Shipping Act 1970, that there had been a very full inquiry on that occasion. In particular, it occurred to me that whatever were the theoretical limits which might have inhibited *j* counsel for the applicants from pursuing those matters which he wished on behalf of the parents to investigate, in practice he was not much, if at all, curtailed in the questions he was allowed to ask and he contrived, and I think those instructing him can be grateful for what he achieved, to investigate matters very fully; and I am sure the superintendent conducting that inquiry was indebted to him for that achievement. That is all I wish to say about the facts of this matter.

a   I would just add one observation on the question of territorial limits. The matter was raised really in the first instance when counsel for the Secretary of State was addressing us. He indicated that he relied on the point no further than this, to submit that it would be extremely improbable that Parliament was intending to provide that the coroner could assume jurisdiction outside the sovereign limits as laid down at the time. The point was not explored any further in argument. I would wish to reserve the question which was not investigated, namely whether quite apart from s 18 and the matters which *b* we have had argued before us there would have been any jurisdiction in the coroner to embark upon an inquiry where there was within his jurisdiction no body and where it was clear that the death had occurred outside the limits of territorial jurisdiction. I express no opinion one way or the other on that. I simply say what I have said in order to make it clear that the matter has not been argued and we have not decided it.

c *Application dismissed.*

Solicitors: *Linnells,* Newport Pagnell (for the applicants); *Sharpe Pritchard* (for the coroner); *Treasury Solicitor.*

Sophie Craven   Barrister.

d

Esso Petroleum Co Ltd v Hall Russell & Co
e # Ltd (Shetland Islands Council, third party)
The Esso Bernicia
and conjoined appeal

f HOUSE OF LORDS
LORD KEITH OF KINKEL, LORD BRANDON OF OAKBROOK, LORD TEMPLEMAN, LORD GOFF OF CHIEVELEY AND LORD JAUNCEY OF TULLICHETTLE
27, 28, 29, 30 JUNE, 4, 5, 6 JULY, 6 OCTOBER 1988

Shipping – Negligence in collision cases – Subrogation – Collision with jetty – Berthing of oil tanker *g* *at oil terminal – Tanker colliding with jetty and escaping oil polluting foreshore – Shipowners making payments to occupiers of foreshore in respect of pollution damage under voluntary agreement between major oil companies – Shipowners also making payments under arbitration award to operators of oil terminal for work done to clear up pollution – Whether shipowners entitled to sue tortfeasor in own name – Whether shipowners entitled to recover sums paid from tortfeasor as economic loss directly resulting from damage to their tanker.*

h
Harbour – Pilotage district – Compulsory pilot – Loss or damage caused by and to vessel when under compulsory pilotage – Collision of oil tanker with jetty while being berthed at oil terminal — Collision damaging tanker and jetty and allowing oil to escape causing foreshore to be polluted – Collision allegedly due to pilot's negligence – Whether harbour authority vicariously liable for pilot's negligence – Pilotage Act 1913, s 15(1).

j
While an oil tanker owned by the shipowners was being berthed at a jetty at an oil terminal in the Shetland Islands one of the three tugs in attendance caught fire and the tow line from the tug to the tanker was cast off. The tanker, being no longer under the full control of the remaining tugs, crashed into the jetty causing damage to her hull and to the jetty and also causing bunker oil to escape in large quantities which polluted the foreshore. The fire on the tug was caused by a coupling blowing out of a hydraulic pipe

and the escaping hydraulic oil coming into contact with an engine exhaust. At the time
of the accident a compulsory pilot employed by the harbour authority was aboard the *a*
tanker. The shipowners, who were were parties to the Tanker Owners Voluntary
Agreement Concerning Liability for Oil Pollution (TOVALOP), made payments under
that agreement to crofters on the Islands in respect of harm caused to sheep by the
pollution of the foreshore. Following arbitration the shipowners also made payments
under TOVALOP to the operators of the terminal to compensate them for work done to
clear up the pollution. The shipowners brought an action against the builders of the tug, *b*
averring that the accident to the tanker was caused by the negligence of the tug's builders
in designing and building the tug and they claimed (i) damages in respect of the damage
caused to the tanker and consequential loss and (ii) by subrogation, reimbursement of
payments made by them under TOVALOP to the crofters and the terminal operators.
The tugbuilders averred that the accident was caused, inter alia, by the fault of the
compulsory pilot, for whose acts or omissions the harbour authority were vicariously *c*
responsible and the harbour authority were brought in as one of the third parties. The
shipowners also sought a declarator that if they were compelled to pay for the damage to
the jetty they were entitled to be reimbursed by the tugbuilders and the third parties.
On the trial of preliminary pleas the First Division of the Inner House of the Court of
Session, on appeal from the Lord Ordinary, rejected the tugbuilders' submission that the
damage to the tanker, the jetty and the foreshore were not a reasonable and probable *d*
consequence of their alleged negligence and excluded their averments relating to the
vicarious responsibility of the harbour authority for the acts or omissions of the pilot.
The First Division also excluded averments by the shipowners in support of their claims
to recover the sums paid by them to the crofters and the terminal operators under
TOVALOP and for payment by the tugbuilders and the third parties of sums relating to
the value of the bunker oil lost, the costs of repairs to the tanker and consequential loss. *e*
The shipowners appealed and the tugbuilders appealed and cross-appealed to the House
of Lords.

Held – (1) It was clearly arguable that the damage suffered by the tanker and resultant
damage to others caused by oil spillage were reasonable and probable consequences of the *f*
tugbuilders' alleged negligence and therefore the shipowners' averments of negligence
were of sufficient relevance to go to inquiry. Accordingly, the tugbuilders' cross-appeal
would be dismissed (see p 41 *f* to *h*, p 44 *e* to *h* and p 47 *j* to p 48 *c*, post).
(2) The general rule that if an indemnifier was subrogated to the rights of someone
whom he had indemnified he could only pursue those rights in the name of that person
and not in his own name applied even where the indemnifier also had a claim for damage *g*
to property arising out of the same act which gave rise to the indemnification. It followed
that the shipowners were not entitled to sue the tugbuilders in their own name for the
amounts paid to the crofters and the terminal operators (see p 41 *f* to *h*, p 43 *e*, p 44 *b* to
d, p 51 *h* to p 52 *a* and p 53 *d* to *f*, post); *Simpson & Co v Thomson* (1877) 3 App Cas 279
and *Castellain v Preston* [1881–5] All ER Rep 493 applied; *Cattle v Stockton Waterworks Co*
[1874–80] All ER Rep 220 considered. *h*
(3) Furthermore, the shipowners' obligation under TOVALOP to indemnify persons
affected by oil spillage was entirely gratuitous and therefore the payments made to the
crofters and the terminal operators by the shipowners were made under a voluntary
obligation and were not recoverable from the tugbuilders as economic loss directly
resulting from the damage to their tanker, notwithstanding that the event which gave
rise to the payments was the physical damage to their tanker (see p 41 *f* to *h*, p 44 *j* to *j*
p 45 *a* and p 54 *f* to p 55 *a*, post).
(4) The shipowners' statutory liability to the harbour authority (under s 74*a* of the

---

a   Section 74 provides: 'The owner of every Vessel or Float of Timber shall be answerable to the
     Undertakers for any Damage done by such Vessel or Float of Timber, or by any Person employed
     about the same, to the Harbour, Dock, or Pier, or the Quays or Works connected therewith, and
     the Master or Person having the Charge of such Vessel or Float of Timber through whose wilful
     (Continued on p 39)

Harbours, Docks and Piers Clauses Act 1847) for the damage to the jetty was prima facie
a a valid head of damage in their action against the tugbuilders rather than being merely a
claim for relief which could be postponed until after liability for payment of the repairs
to the jetty had been determined. Accordingly, since all claims arising out of a single act
of negligence had to be pursued in the same action and since the shipowners could be
substantially prejudiced if they were disabled from pursuing their claim, the claim was
rightly included in the action and the shipowners' appeal against the decision of the First
b Division striking it out would be allowed (see p 41 *f* to *h*, p 45 *j*, p 56 *c* to *e h j* and p 57 *c*,
post); *Dunlop v M'Gowans* 1980 SC (HL) 73, dicta of the Lord President (Inglis) in *Stevenson
v Pontifex & Wood* (1887) 15 R 125 at 129, of the Lord President (Emslie) in *British Rlys
Board v Ross and Cromarty CC* 1974 SC 27 at 37 and of the Lord President (Cooper) in
Central SMT Co Ltd v Lanarkshire CC 1949 SC 450 at 458 applied.

(5) The tugbuilders' appeal against the exclusion of their averments that the harbour
c authority were vicariously liable for the acts or omissions of the compulsory pilot would
be dismissed because, as a general rule, a pilot was an independent professional man who
navigated the ship as a principal and not as a servant of his general employer.
Furthermore, s 15(1)*ᵇ* of the Pilotage Act 1913 made a pilot the servant of the shipowner
for all purposes connected with navigation and therefore the employer of a qualified
licensed pilot was not responsible to the owner of a ship damaged by the pilot's negligence
d while under pilotage. On the facts, the general rule applied and therefore the shipbuilders'
averments that the harbour authority were vicariously responsible for the pilot's acts or
omissions had been rightly excluded (see p 41 *f* to *h*, p 45 *j*, p 60 *f* and p 64 *d e*, post);
Workington Harbour and Dock Board v Towerfield (owners) [1950] 2 All ER 414 and *Clark
(or Thom) v J & P Hutchison Ltd* 1925 SC 386 applied; *Fowles v Eastern and Australian
Steamship Co Ltd* [1916] 2 AC 556 and *Oceanic Crest Shipping Co v Pilbara Harbour Services
e* *Pty Ltd* (1986) 160 CLR 626 adopted; *Holman v Irvine Harbour Trustees* (1877) 4 R 406 and
dictum of Denning LJ in *Cassidy v Ministry of Health (Fahrni, third party)* [1951] 1 All ER
574 at 586–587 considered.

Notes

For remoteness of damage and causation in tort, see 12 Halsbury's Laws (4th edn) paras
f 1138–1141, and for cases on the subject, see 17 Digest (Reissue) 135–150, 312–412.

For the doctrine of subrogation, see 16 Halsbury's Laws (4th edn) para 1438, and for
cases on the subject, see 20 Digest (Reissue) 890–891, 6652–6653.

For a shipowner's liability where a ship is under pilotage and for a shipowner's liability
for damage done to a harbour, see 43 Halsbury's Laws (4th edn) para 868 and 36 ibid
para 543.

g For vicarious liability of a harbour authority for acts of its employees, see 36 ibid para
535, and for cases on the subject, see 43 Digest (Reissue) 734–736, 12375–12388.

For the Harbours, Docks, and Piers Clauses Act 1847, s 74, see 34 Halsbury's Statutes
(4th edn) 42.

As from 9 August 1983 s 15(1) of the Pilotage Act 1913 was replaced by s 35 of the
Pilotage Act 1983, which in turn was replaced as from 1 October 1988 by s 16 of the
h Pilotage Act 1987. For s 16 of the 1987 Act, see 39 Halsbury's Statutes (4th edn) 1123.

Cases referred to in opinions

Arabert, The, A R Appelqvist A/B v Tyne-Tees Steam Shipping Co Ltd [1961] 2 All ER 385,
[1963] P 102, [1961] 3 WLR 215.
'Beechgrove' Steamship Co Ltd v Akt 'Fjord' of Kristiana [1916] 1 AC 364, HL.
j

(Continued from p 38)

Act or Negligence any such Damage is done shall also be liable to make good the same; and the
Undertaker may detain any such Vessel or Float of Timber until sufficient Security has been given
for the Amount of Damage done by the same: Provided always, that nothing herein contained
shall extend to impose any Liability for any such Damage upon the Owner of any Vessel, where
such Vessel shall at the Time when such Damage is caused be in Charge of a duly licensed Pilot,
whom such Owner or Master is bound by Law to employ and put his Vessel in charge of.'
b Section 15(1) is set out at p 58 *b*, post

British Rlys Board v Ross and Cromarty CC 1974 SC 27, Ct of Sess.
Candlewood Navigation Corp Ltd v Mitsui OSK Lines Ltd, The Mineral Transporter, The Ibaraki
 Maru [1985] 2 All ER 935, [1986] AC 1, [1985] 3 WLR 381, PC.
Cassidy v Ministry of Health (Fahrni, third party) [1951] 1 All ER 574, [1951] 2 KB 343, CA.
Castellain v Preston (1883) 11 QBD 380, [1881–5] All ER Rep 493, CA.
Cattle v Stockton Waterworks Co (1875) LR 10 QB 453, [1874–80] All ER Rep 220.
Central SMT Co Ltd v Lanarkshire CC 1949 SC 450, Ct of Sess.
Cia Colombiana de Seguros v Pacific Steam Navigation Co [1964] 1 All ER 216, [1965] 1 QB
 101, [1964] 2 WLR 484.
Clark (or Thom) v J & P Hutchison Ltd 1925 SC 386, Ct of Sess.
Dunlop v M'Gowans 1980 SC (HL) 73.
Edwards (John) & Co v Motor Union Insurance Co Ltd [1922] 2 KB 249.
Fowles v Eastern and Australian Steamship Co Ltd [1916] 2 AC 556, PC.
Gold v Essex CC [1942] 2 All ER 237, [1942] 2 KB 293, CA.
Holman v Irvine Harbour Trustees (1877) 4 R 406, Ct of Sess.
King v Victoria Insurance Co Ltd [1896] AC 250, PC.
Leigh & Sillavan Ltd v Aliakmon Shipping Co Ltd, The Aliakmon [1986] 2 All ER 145, [1986]
 AC 785, [1986] 2 WLR 902, HL.
Lister v Romford Ice and Cold Storage Co Ltd [1957] 1 All ER 125, [1957] AC 555, [1957] 2
 WLR 158, HL.
London Assurance Co v Sainsbury (1783) 3 Doug KB 245, 99 ER 636.
Lumley v Gye (1853) 2 E & B 216, [1843–60] All ER Rep 208, 118 ER 749.
Malcolm (or Macdonald) v Glasgow Western Hospitals Board of Management 1954 SC 453, Ct
 of Sess.
Maria, The (1839) 1 Wm Rob 95, 166 ER 508.
Nacap Ltd v Moffat Plant Ltd 1987 SLT 221, Ct of Sess.
Neptune the Second, The (1814) 1 Dods 46, 165 ER 1380.
Oceanic Crest Shipping Co v Pilbara Harbour Services Pty Ltd (1986) 160 CLR 626, Aust HC.
Ogilvie v Edinburgh Magistrates (1821) 1 S 24, Ct of Sess.
Orakpo v Manson Investments Ltd [1977] 3 All ER 1, [1978] AC 95, [1977] 3 WLR 229,
 HL.
Parker v North British Rly Co (1898) 25 R 1059, Ct of Sess.
Payne (David) & Co Ltd, Re [1904] 2 Ch 608, CA.
Rylands v Fletcher (1868) LR 3 HL 330, [1861–73] All ER Rep 1; affg (1866) LR 1 Exch
 265, [1861–73] All ER Rep 1, Ex Ch.
Simpson & Co v Thomson (1877) 3 App Cas 279, HL.
Stevenson v Pontifex & Wood (1887) 15 R 125, Ct of Sess.
Thom v J & P Hutchison Ltd 1925 SC 386, Ct of Sess.
Workington Harbour and Dock Board v Towerfield (owners) [1950] 2 All ER 414, [1951] AC
 112, HL.
Yorkshire Insurance Co Ltd v Nisbet Shipping Co Ltd [1961] 2 All ER 487, [1962] 2 QB 330.

Conjoined interlocutory appeals and cross-appeal

The defenders, Hall Russell & Co Ltd (Hall Russell), appealed with leave of the First
Division of the Inner House of the Court of Session against two interlocutors of the First
Division (the Lord President (Lord Emslie), Lord Grieve and Lord Brand) (1988 SLT 33)
dated 10 July allowing in part reclaiming motions from the decision of the Lord Ordinary
(Wylie) contained in three interlocutors dated 11 and 20 December 1985 pronounced in
an action by the pursuers, Esso Petroleum Co Ltd (Esso), the owners of the oil tanker Esso
Bernicia which collided with the no 2 jetty at Sullom Voe, Shetlands on 30 December
1978 while being berthed, against Hall Russell and four third parties, (1) Donkin & Co
Ltd, an engineering company specialising in, inter alia, hydraulic towing winches, and
its liquidator, Gordon Christopher Horsefield, (2) Shetland Towage Ltd, a tug operator,
(3) Royal Bank Leasing Ltd, the owner of the tugs operated by the latter and (4) the
Shetland Islands Council (SIC), the employers of the pilot on board the oil tanker, in

respect of loss resulting to Esso from the collision. The issue raised by the appeal was
a whether SIC were vicariously liable for the pilot's negligence in navigating the tanker. In
the second appeal, Esso appealed against three interlocutors of the First Division of the
Court of Session (the Lord President (Lord Emslie), Lord Grieve and Lord Brand) (1988
SLT 33) dated 10 July 1987 and preceding interlocutors of the Lord Ordinary (Wylie)
dated 11 and 20 December 1985 and 14 March 1986 pronounced in an action by Esso
against Hall Russell and the above-named third parties which excluded from probation
b certain averments of loss made in support of Esso's claim to be entitled to recover
payments made by them pursuant to the Tanker Owners Voluntary Agreement
Concerning Liability for Oil Pollution (TOVALOP) from Hall Russell and the third
parties. The questions raised in the appeal were whether Esso were entitled to
reimbursement in respect of various payments made by them under TOVALOP and
whether the averments made in support of their conclusion for declarator that they were
c entitled to be reimbursed by Hall Russell and the third parties should any party recover
from Esso the cost of repairing the jetty were premature and irrelevant. The First
Division and the Lord Ordinary held that they were not so entitled. Hall Russell cross-
appealed against those parts of the interlocutor which allowed Esso a proof of their
averments of negligence against them. The issue raised by the cross-appeal was whether
Hall Russell was liable for the damage sustained to the tanker. The appeals were
d conjoined. The facts are set out in the opinion of Lord Jauncey.

Alastair Cameron QC (Vice-Dean of Faculty), *Bruce Kerr QC* and *Marion Caldwell* (both of
   the Scottish Bar) for Esso.
Michael Bruce QC (of the Scottish Bar), *Robert Webb QC* and *Patrick Hodge* (of the Scottish
   Bar) for Hall Russell.
e *Alan Rodger QC* and *J Gordon Reid* (both of the Scottish Bar) for SIC.
Joseph O'Neill for the second and third named third parties.

Their Lordships took time for consideration.

f 6 October. The following opinions were delivered.

LORD KEITH OF KINKEL. My Lords, I have had the opportunity of considering in
draft the speech prepared by my noble and learned friend Lord Jauncey. I agree with it
and for the reasons he gives would allow Esso's appeal only to the extent which he
proposes and dismiss Hall Russell's appeal and cross-appeal.

g **LORD BRANDON OF OAKBROOK.** My Lords, I have had the advantage of
reading in draft the speech prepared by my noble and learned friend Lord Jauncey. I
agree with it and for the reasons which he gives I would allow Esso's appeal so far as it
related to the declaratory conclusion but no further and dismiss Hall Russell's appeal and
cross-appeal.

h **LORD TEMPLEMAN.** My Lords, for the reasons given by my noble and learned
friends Lord Jauncey and Lord Goff I would allow Esso's appeal so far as it is related to
the declaratory conclusion but no further and dismiss Hall Russell's appeal and cross-
appeal.

j **LORD GOFF OF CHIEVELEY.** My Lords, the course which the proceedings have
taken, and the relevant facts, are set out in the speech of my noble and learned friend
Lord Jauncey; his account I gratefully accept.
   The first issue in these appeals is whether the averments of Esso Petroleum Co Ltd
(Esso) in support of the second conclusion are irrelevant to the loss claimed. The Lord
Ordinary held that they were irrelevant, and excluded them from probation. Before the
First Division it was common ground betweeen the parties that, on the Lord Ordinary's

approach, he should also have excluded from probation the averments in support of
Esso's third conclusion. Both conclusions were designed to lay the ground for the *a*
recovery by Esso from Hall Russell & Co Ltd (Hall Russell) of sums paid out by Esso in
satisfaction of claims in respect of oil pollution damage (or the removal of the threat of
such damage) which Esso claimed they were bound to pay under the Tanker Owners
Voluntary Agreement Concerning Liability for Oil Pollution (TOVALOP). The First
Division affirmed the judgment of the Lord Ordinary which excluded the averments in
support of the second conclusion, and they further excluded from probation the *b*
averments in support of the third conclusion. Against that decision, Esso now appeal to
your Lordships' House.

These conclusions relate to two substantial sums paid by Esso in respect of oil pollution
damage (or expenditure incurred in preventing or removing oil pollution damage). The
first sum, amounting so far to £480,935·06 (there being a further sum of £46,343 still
in dispute) was paid largely through the Shetland Islands Council, either in direct *c*
reimbursement of costs incurred by the council, or to the council as representing other
bodies or persons in the islands, in particular crofters. The second sum, amounting in all
to £3,466,160·55 (including interest) plus expenses in the sum of £160,000, was paid by
Esso to BP Petroleum Development Ltd (BP) pursuant to an arbitration award dated 15
October 1985. All these sums have been paid under TOVALOP.

Before the First Division, Esso advanced their claim against Hall Russell in respect of *d*
these sums on three grounds: (1) that by virtue of express provisions of TOVALOP Esso
were subrogated to the rights of the parties indemnified by them against Hall Russell;
(2) that in any event Esso were entitled to a right of recourse, whether or not called
subrogation, against Hall Russell; and (3) that the sums paid by Esso fell to be considered
as losses incurred by Esso caused by the alleged negligence of Hall Russell. All these
submissions were rejected by the First Division. The last two of these submissions have *e*
been renewed before your Lordships; the first is no longer pursued.

In order to consider these submissions, it is necessary first to consider the legal effect of
TOVALOP. I need only refer to the salient features of that agreement, which was before
your Lordships in its amended form dated 1 June 1978.

First, the parties to the agreement are expressed to be tanker owners and bareboat *f*
charterers. Consistently with that statement, it is provided that the parties 'in
consideration of their mutual promises, have agreed with one another and do hereby
agree as follows'; there then follow 11 clauses, under the last of which it is provided that
the agreement shall be governed by the laws of England. From this, it is plain that the
agreement is essentially an agreement as between the tanker owners and bareboat
charterers (described as participating owners) who are parties to it. Under cl IV: *g*

'(A) Subject to the terms and conditions of this Agreement, the Participating
Owner of a Tanker involved in an incident agrees to assume liability for Pollution
Damage caused by Oil which has escaped or which has been discharged from the
Tanker, and the cost of Threat Removal Measures taken as a result of the incident.'

The expressions 'Pollution Damage', 'Oil' and 'Threat Removal Measures' are all defined *h*
in cl 1, which is concerned with definitions. Certain exceptions to the agreed liability
under cl IV(A) are set out in cl IV(B). It is further provided, in cl VIII(D):

'Persons making claims hereunder may, in the event of a dispute with a
Participating Owner concerning same, commence arbitration proceedings . . .
within two years of the date of the incident, and these proceedings shall be the *j*
exclusive means for enforcing a Participating Owner's liability hereunder. Each
Participating Owner by becoming a Party to this Agreement, and so long as he
remains bound hereby, shall be deemed irrevocably to have offered to any such
Person to submit all such disputes to arbitration . . .'

It was pursuant to such arbitration proceedings that BP obtained the award against Esso
to which I have already referred. Clause VIII further provides, in para (E):

a
'Unless otherwise agreed in writing, any payment to a Person by or on behalf of a Participating Owner shall be in full settlement of all said Person's claims against the Participating Owner, the Tanker involved, its charterer, their officers, agents, employees and underwriters, which arise out of the incident.'

By cl III(B) it is provided:

b
'A party may withdraw from this Agreement . . . by giving at least six months prior written notice of withdrawal to the Federation . . .'

No provision is made in the agreement that a participating owner, on making a payment to a claimant, shall be entitled to require, as a condition of making such payment, an assignation of the claimant's rights of action against any third party who may be liable to the claimant in respect of any relevant loss or damage suffered by him, or indeed authority from such a claimant to proceed against any such third party in the name of the claimant.

c
There can, in my opinion, be no doubt that TOVALOP constitutes an agreement binding inter se on those participating owners who are, at the relevant time, parties to it. Counsel for Esso submitted that the agreement created rights enforceable by third parties expressed to be entitled to claim under it, both under English law (the governing law of the agreement) and under Scots law. Like the Lord President, I do not find it necessary to decide this point; for, in my opinion, Esso's submissions under this head must in any event fail, substantially for the reasons given by the Lord President.

d
I take the example of the crofters' claims, since these were the claims concentrated on in agrument, although BP's claim, the subject of the arbitration award, is in fact very much more substantial. The primary submission of counsel for Esso was that Esso were entitled to be subrogated to the crofters' claims in tort against Hall Russell, and further that Esso were entitled to pursue such claims against Hall Russell in their own name. In my opinion, this submission is not well founded.

e
In considering this submission, I proceed on the basis (which appears to have been common ground throughout the case) that there is for present purposes no material distinction between Scots law and English law. Now, let it be assumed that the effect of Esso's payment to the crofters was to indemnify the crofters in respect of loss or damage suffered by them by reason of the wrongdoing of Hall Russell. If such a payment was made under a contract of indemnity between Esso and the crofters, there can be no doubt that Esso would on payment be subrogated to the crofters' claims against Hall Russell. This would enable Esso to proceed against Hall Russell in the names of the crofters; but it would not enable Esso to proceed, without more, to enforce the crofters' claims by an action in their own name against Hall Russell.

f

g
The reason for this is plain. It is that Esso's payment to the crofters does not have the effect of discharging Hall Russell's liability to them. That being so, I do not see how Esso can have a direct claim against Hall Russell in respect of their payment. I put on one side Esso's claim against Hall Russell in negligence; that I will consider in a moment. There can of course be no direct claim by Esso against Hall Russell in restitution, if only because Esso have not by their payment discharged the liability of Hall Russell, and so have not enriched Hall Russell; if anybody has been enriched, it is the crofters, to the extent that they have been indemnified by Esso and yet continue to have vested in them rights of action against Hall Russell in respect of the loss or damage which was the subject matter of Esso's payment to them. All that is left is the fact that the crofters' rights of action against Hall Russell continued to exist (until the expiry of the relevant limitation period), and that it might have been inequitable to deny Esso the opportunity to take advantage of them, which is the classic basis of the doctrine of subrogation in the case of contracts of indemnity (see *Castellain v Preston* (1883) 11 QBD 380, [1881–5] All ER Rep 493). In normal cases, as for example under contracts of insurance, the insurer will on payment request the assured to sign a letter of subrogation, authorising the insurer to proceed in the name of the assured against any wrongdoer who has caused the relevant damage to the assured. If the assured refuses to give such authority, in theory the insurer can bring

h

j

proceedings to compel him to do so. But nowadays the insurer can short-circuit this cumbrous process by bringing an action against both the assured and the third party, in which (1) he claims an order that the assured shall authorise him to proceed against the third party in the name of the assured and (2) he seeks to proceed (so authorised) against the third party. But it must not be thought that, because this convenient method of proceeding now exists, the insurer can without more proceed in his own name against the third party. He has no right to do so, so long as the right of action he is seeking to enforce is the right of action of the assured. Only if that right of action is assigned to him by the assured can he proceed directly against the third party in his own name (see e g *Cia Colombiana de Seguros v Pacific Steam Navigation Co* [1964] 1 All ER 216, [1965] 1 QB 101). I have no doubt that the like principles apply in the present case. It follows that Esso could only proceed directly in their own name against Hall Russell in respect of the crofters' claims against Hall Russell if, on paying the crofters, they received from them a valid and effective assignation of their claims. I cannot think that, in practice, Esso would have met with difficulty if they had, at the time of payment to the crofters, asked each of them for a receipt which operated either as an assignation or as an authority to proceed against the third party in the name of the crofters concerned; if any such practical difficulty should exist, it could surely be overcome in future by an appropriate amendment to TOVALOP.

For these reasons, which are substantially the same as those expressed by the Lord President in his judgment, I would reject Esso's claim based on subrogation. I would only add that, in agreement with my noble and learned friend Lord Jauncey, I do not consider that *Cattle v Stockton Waterworks Co* (1875) LR 10 QB 453, [1874–80] All ER Rep 220 has any relevance to this aspect of Esso's appeal.

There remains however Esso's claim in negligence. Their claim under this head can be summarised as follows. By reason of Hall Russell's negligence, physical damage has been caused to Esso's property, ie to the tanker. It follows that, on ordinary principles, Esso are entitled to recover not only damages in respect of such physical damage, but also damages in respect of any financial loss suffered by Esso by reason of such physical damage. It is into the latter category that Esso seek to place the sums paid or payable by them under TOVALOP.

Hall Russell's first answer to this claim was that the only damage which could arguably be held to have been caused in law by their alleged negligence was the damage to the tanker herself. Any further damage must be excluded as being too remote from their alleged negligence to be held to be caused by it. However, like the Lord President, I find it impossible to accept any such argument. Let it be supposed that, Hall Russell having negligently caused damage to the tanker, the tanker in consequence immediately ran into some physical object, the property of a third party, and damaged it. It is inconceivable that, as a matter of simple causation, Hall Russell's responsibility should be held to stop at damage to the tanker. The principle of causation cannot be so rigidly confined. There is, in such a case, no supervening cause independent of Hall Russell's wrong to which the damage to the physical object can be attributed; and I cannot see how, in such circumstances, the negligence of Hall Russell should be held to have ceased to constitute a sufficiently potent cause for such damage to be legally attributed to it.

Even so, there is a formidable difficulty in the way of Esso's claim to recover from Hall Russell, in negligence, their payments to BP and the crofters under TOVALOP. It is that TOVALOP appears on its face, and indeed in its name, to be no more than an agreement voluntarily entered into between a large number of tanker owners and bareboat charterers, whereby each participating owner has agreed with the others that, in the event of oil escaping from his tanker and causing oil pollution damage to a third party or expense being incurred by a third party in removing the threat of oil pollution damage, the participating owner in question will compensate the third party under the terms of TOVALOP, irrespective of any negligence on his part. In such circumstances, as it seems to me, Esso cannot claim the sums paid by them under TOVALOP as financial loss attributable to the physical damage to the ship caused by Hall Russell's alleged negligence.

a   The damage to the ship did no more than trigger off the event which led to the pollution
in respect of which Esso became bound under the terms of TOVALOP to make the
payments which are the subject matter of their claim. In truth, Esso's claim to damages
falls under two separate heads: (1) damages in respect of the physical damage to the
tanker, and any financial loss (eg loss of use) flowing from such physical damage; and (2)
damages in respect of the sums paid out by Esso under TOVALOP. But, as the Lord
President pointed out in his judgment, damages of the type claimed under the second
b   head are irrecoverable in negligence, as has been established for over 100 years, ever since
the decision of your Lordships' House in *Simpson & Co v Thomson* (1877) 3 App Cas 279.

Like the Lord President, I can see no injustice in this conclusion. It was suggested by
counsel for Esso, in the course of argument, that, in so far as *Simpson & Co v Thomson*
provided no more than an example of the general principle that damages are not
recoverable in negligence in respect of pure economic loss, your Lordships should not
c   hesitate to make an exception to that principle in relation to cases such as the present,
because to allow recovery in such cases would not open the floodgates to other claims.
But so to do would effectively contradict *Simpson & Co v Thomson* itself; and I can see no
injustice in denying a direct claim in negligence to a claimant such as Esso in a case such
as the present, where, quite apart from any question of subrogation, the necessary
arrangements can be made to ensure that, on payment, an assignation is taken of the
d   payee's (here the crofters') claims against third parties.

Esso's final response to this apparently insuperable difficulty was to seek leave from
your Lordships' House to amend their averments by adding the following passage:

'At the time of said incident on 30 December 1978 it was a practical necessity for
the owner of a tanker in order to trade internationally to be a participating owner in
e   TOVALOP. It was in particular a necessity for the owner of a tanker in order to use
the facilities at Sullom Voe to be a participating owner in TOVALOP.'

The purpose of the proposed amendment was apparently to attempt to equate the
position of Esso in the present case to that of a shipowner who has been compelled by
law (for example, under the provisions of the Merchant Shipping (Oil Pollution) Act
f   1971) to indemnify a third party against the consequences of oil pollution arising from
an escape of oil from the ship. However, quite apart from any other difficulties in the
way of the allegation raised by the proposed amendment (and a number of these were
adumbrated by counsel in his able argument on behalf of Hall Russell), it seems to me
that it must in any event be irrelevant for the following very simple reason. The proposed
amendment does not allege that it was by reason of the practical necessity so averred that
g   Esso entered into TOVALOP, nor even that it was by reason of such practical necessity
that Esso had not taken advantage of their rights under cl III(B) to withdraw from
TOVALOP. I must confess that I am not in the least surprised. As appears from a copy of
TOVALOP before your Lordships, Esso were (with the other major oil companies) a
founder-member of TOVALOP. It is obvious that Esso cannot have become a member
of TOVALOP by reason of the practical necessity averred in the proposed amendment.
h   Plainly they must have done so voluntarily, no doubt for very good commercial reasons.
Likewise it is inconceivable that Esso should have been deterred from withdrawing from
TOVALOP by reason of such practical necessity. But, this being so, the mere existence of
the practical necessity, as averred in the proposed amendment, is of no materiality; and
the amendment would provide, therefore, no answer to the point that Esso are seeking
to claim from Hall Russell, as a separate head of damage, sums paid by them under a
j   voluntary agreement whereby they undertook to indemnify persons in the position of
BP and the crofters. For this reason alone I, for my part, would refuse Esso's application
for leave to amend. It follows that I would dismiss Esso's appeal on this issue.

For the reasons given by my noble and learned friend Lord Jauncey, I would allow
Esso's appeal on the issue of the prematurity of the declaratory conclusion, and I would
dismiss Hall Russell's appeal, as against the Shetland Islands Council, on the issue of
compulsory pilotage.

LORD JAUNCEY OF TULLICHETTLE. My Lords, these appeals arise out of an unusual incident at the oil terminal in Sullom Voe in the Mainland of Shetland on 30 *a* December 1978 when a tanker Esso Bernicia (the Bernicia) came in contact with a number of mooring dolphins whereby a large quantity of bunker oil escaped from her. The case comes before your Lordships at the stage of debate as to the relevancy of certain pleadings, no proof having yet taken place.

The salient facts which are a matter of admission between the three parties to these appeals are as follows. (1) Late on the above date the Bernicia was being berthed at no 2 *b* jetty with three tugs in attendance. One of these tugs, the Stanechakker, had a towing line secured to the stern of the Bernicia. At about 2333 hrs the coupling blew out of a hydraulic pipe above the starboard engine exhaust of the tug, the escaped hydraulic oil caught fire and the towing line was cast off. The Bernicia was then no longer under the full control of the remaining two tugs and she came in contact with a number of dolphins whereby she and the dolphins sustained damage and bunker oil escaped in large *c* quantities. (2) At the time of the incident there was on board a pilot, Captain Hemingway, Sullom Voe being a compulsory pilotage area. (3) The Stanechakker was designed and built by Hall Russell & Co Ltd (Hall Russell) for the purpose of berthing tankers at the Sullom Voe oil terminal.

On 23 November 1981 Esso Petroleum Co Ltd (Esso), the owners of the Bernicia, raised an action against Hall Russell and two other defenders who, for reasons which are *d* not relevant to these appeals, are no longer in the process. As a result of the averments by Hall Russell four different third parties were brought into the process. Only the fourth third parties, Shetland Islands Council (SIC), took an active part in these appeals and I therefore say nothing more about the other three. It will be convenient to refer to the parties to these appeals as Esso, Hall Russell and SIC. The pleadings have been amended on various occasions both before and after the hearing in the First Division but in the *e* form in which they reach this House Esso conclude:

(1) for payment to them by the defenders and third parties of the sums (a) £170,086·39, (b) £527,278·06, (c) £3,727,589·02, together with interest. The first of these sums relates to the value of the bunker oil lost and to the cost of repair of the Bernicia and the loss to Esso consequential thereon. The second of these sums relates to sums paid to crofters in *f* respect of damage to sheep due to pollution of the foreshore. These sums were paid under and in terms of an agreement dated 7 January 1969 between the major oil companies of the western world known as the Tanker Owners Voluntary Agreement Concerning Liability for Oil Pollution (TOVALOP), to which I shall have occasion to refer in more detail later. The third of these sums relates to (i) sums paid by Esso to BP Petroleum Development Ltd (BP) as the operators of the Sullom Voe oil terminal in *g* respect of operations carried out by BP to deal with the pollution caused by the Bernicia bunker oil (those sums were paid in terms of an award by an arbitrator in contested preceedings brought by BP against Esso under and in terms of TOVALOP) and (ii) expenses incurred by Esso in those arbitration proceedings.

'(2) For (1) declarator that in the event of any body or person recovering from the pursuers by or in consequence of any process in any Court of Law the costs of *h* repairing and reinstating the No. 2 Jetty at Sullom Voe Harbour in the Shetlands incurred in consequence of damage inflicted on said Jetty when the pursuers' tanker "ESSO BERNICIA" came in contact therewith on or about 30th December, 1978 then the pursuers will in that event be entitled to be paid *et separatim* reimbursed by the defenders and the first, second, third and fourth named third parties jointly and severally or severally to the extent of the whole amount of any such repair and *j* reinstatement costs recovered from them as a result of any such Court proceedings together with any expenses paid or incurred by the pursuers in consequence of any such proceedings or such other sum or sums as to the Court may seem proper and (2) decree in the event of decree of declarator being pronounced in the foregoing terms ordaining payment to the pursuers by the defenders and the first, second,

a third and fourth-named third parties jointly and severally or severally of (first) the
sum of TWO HUNDRED AND SEVENTY THOUSAND FOUR HUNDRED AND TWENTY THREE
POUNDS AND TWO PENCE (£270,423·02) Sterling or such other sum or sums as shall
have been recovered from the pursuers or incurred as expenses by them in
consequence of any such Court proceedings or such other sum or sums as to the
Court may seem proper with interest thereon at the rate of Fifteen *per centum per
annum* from the date of any payment made by the pursuers in respect of any such

b recovery until payment, and (second) the sum of ONE THOUSAND ONE HUNDRED AND
THREE POUNDS AND SIXTY FIVE PENCE (£1,103·65) Sterling with interest at the rate of
Fifteen *per centum per annum* from 30th June, 1979 until payment.'

Esso aver that the accident to the Bernicia was due to the negligence of Hall Russell in
designing and building the tug. Hall Russell aver that the accident was caused by the
fault of a number of persons including that of the pilot for whose actings SIC were

c responsible. The pleadings of all three parties contain preliminary pleas which were
debated before the Lord Ordinary and First Division of the Inner House of the Court of
Session over a total period of 16 days (see 1988 SLT 33). Many issues were raised but I
think that it is sufficient at this stage to summarise the result of the First Division's
decision. The court held: (1) agreeing with the Lord Ordinary, that there was no

d substance in a submission by Hall Russell that on the averments the damage suffered by
the tanker and the resultant damage to others due to oil spillage was not a reasonable and
probable consequence of their alleged negligence; (2) agreeing with the Lord Ordinary,
that the averments of Esso in support of their claim to recover the sums paid by them to
the crofters and to BP under and in terms of TOVALOP were irrelevant; (3) differing
from the Lord Ordinary, that Esso's averments in support of the declaratory conclusion

e were irrelevant; (4) agreeing with the Lord Ordinary, that Hall Russell's averments anent
the vicarious responsibility of SIC for the acts and omissions of the pilot were irrelevant.

The practical effect of this decision was that Esso's claim was restricted to the
£170,086·39 first concluded for in conclusion (1) and SIC ceased to be parties to the
action. Esso appealed to this House against that part of the interlocutor of the First
Division which excluded from probation their averments (i) in support of the sums in

f conclusion (1) which were paid under and in terms of TOVALOP, and (ii) in support of
the declaratory conclusion. Hall Russell cross-appealed against those parts of the
interlocutor which allowed Esso a proof of their averments of negligence against them,
and appealed against the exclusion from probation of their averments anent the vicarious
responsibility of SIC for the acts of the pilot.

Five separate issues were raised in these appeals: (1) whether the doctrine of subrogation

g entitled Esso to recover in their own name sums paid out by them in terms of TOVALOP;
(2) whether Esso were entitled to recover such sums directly as a head of damage suffered
by them; (3) whether the declarator sought in conclusion (2) was premature and in any
event couched in terms too wide; (4) whether Esso had relevantly averred a causative
connection between the alleged negligence of Hall Russell and damage to the Bernicia;
and (5) whether Hall Russell had relevantly averred that SIC were vicariously responsible

h for the acts and omissions of the pilot.

I have set out the foregoing issues in the order in which they were raised in this House.
By agreement of parties Esso argued their appeal before that of Hall Russell but logically
Hall Russell's attack on Esso's averments of negligence should be considered first since
success in that attack would involve dismissal of the whole action and would elide
consideration of all other issues.

j

(4) *Relevance of Esso's averments of negligence*
Hall Russell's argument that damage to the Bernicia and damage due to the spillage of
bunker oil were not reasonable and probable consequences of their alleged negligence
was decisively rejected by both the Lord Ordinary and the First Division. In this House
it was argued that the single true and effective cause of the casualty was the disablement

of the tug and that it was unrealistic to look back and see what caused that disablement. Put another way, the damage complained of was not a direct result of the alleged negligence. To this argument your Lordships did not require Esso to reply.

My Lords, when it is remembered that it is matter of admission that the Stanechakker was designed and built for the purpose of berthing tankers in Sullom Voe, I do not see how it could possibly be said that in no circumstances could Hall Russell have reasonably foreseen the consequences of the tug catching fire during the course of a berthing manoeuvre. Equally, to ignore the reason for the Stanechakker becoming disabled is to put one's head in the sand. A reparation action will only be dismissed as irrelevant if it is clear that proof by the pursuer of all his averments would establish no liability in law on the part of the defender. Such is not the case here. The Lord President has dealt with Hall Russell's argument in some detail and I do not think that I could improve on or usefully add to what he has said. Esso's averments of negligence on the part of Hall Russell are of sufficient relevance to go to inquiry.

(1) *TOVALOP: subrogation*

Esso incorporate the TOVALOP agreement into their pleadings and it is therefore appropriate to set out some of the provisions thereof in detail.

The foreword includes the following paragraph relevant to the background of TOVALOP:

> 'TOVALOP originated from the determination of certain tanker owners to take constructive action to mitigate and to provide compensation for damage by oil pollution from tankers. TOVALOP came into effect on October 6, 1969 at which time owners of 50 per cent. of the world's tanker tonnage (excluding government-owned tonnage and the tonnage of tankers under 3,000 grt), as measured by gross registered tonnage, became parties. By October 6, 1971 the owners of over 80 per cent. of the world's tanker tonnage had become parties and at the present time the parties to TOVALOP are owners of almost 99 per cent. of the world's tanker tonnage.'

It is stated in the preamble that the parties to the agreement are tanker owners and bareboat charterers. Clause I contains the following, inter alia, definitions:

> '(*f*) "Participating Owner" means the Owner of a Tanker who is a Party.
> (*o*) The "Federation" means the International Tanker Owners Pollution Federation, a Company limited by guarantee and formed pursuant to the laws of England for the purpose of administering the Agreement.'

Clause II(B)(3) provides that each party shall 'dispose of all valid claims against him arising under this Agreement as promptly as is practicable'. Clause III provides for a party withdrawing from the agreement on giving certain specified periods of notice. Clause IV, which is headed 'Liability', provides, inter alia:

> '(A) Subject to the terms and conditions of this Agreement, the Participating Owner of a Tanker involved in an Incident agrees to assume liability for Pollution Damage caused by Oil which has escaped or which has been discharged from the Tanker, and the cost of Threat Removal Measures taken as a result of the Incident.'

Clause VII(A) limits the liability of a participating owner in respect of an incident. Clause VIII provides, inter alia:

> '(D) Persons making claims hereunder may, in the event of a dispute with a Participating Owner concerning same, commence arbitration proceedings, in accordance with Paragraph (I) hereof, within two years of the date of the incident, and these proceedings shall be the exclusive means for enforcing a Participating Owner's liability thereunder. Each Participating Owner by becoming a Party to this Agreement, and so long as he remains bound hereby, shall be deemed irrevocably

a   to have offered to any such Person to submit all such disputes to arbitration as
provided in said Paragraph (I).

(E) Unless otherwise agreed in writing, any payment to a Person by or on behalf
of a Participating Owner shall be in full settlement of all said Person's claims against
the Participating Owner, the Tanker involved, its charterer, their officers, agents,
employees and underwriters, which arise out of the incident . . .

b   (J) No payment made hereunder shall be deemed (i) an admission of, or evidence
of liability on the part of the Participating Owner in any other proceeding or to any
other claimant, or (ii) submission to any jurisdiction on the part of the Participating
Owner for any purpose whatsoever, other than as provided in Clause VIII.

(K) Nothing in this Agreement shall prejudice the right of recourse of a
Participating Owner against third persons or vessels.'

c   Clause XI provides that the agreement shall be governed by the laws of England. Then
exhibit 'A' which is appended to the agreement is in, inter alia, the following terms:

'To: THE INTERNATIONAL TANKER OWNERS POLLUTION FEDERATION LIMITED The
undersigned hereby: (A) Applies to become a Party to the Tanker Owners Voluntary
Agreement Concerning Liability for Oil Pollution dated as of the Seventh day of
January, 1969, as amended from time to time, and agrees, if this application is
d   accepted, to assume and perform all of the obligations of a Party thereto . . .'

The agreement contains no provision whereby a participating owner can require from
a claimant to whom he has made payment an assignation of the claimant's rights of
action against third parties responsible in law for the relevant damage.

Esso appear as one of the seven original signatories to the agreement.

e   Esso's general submission was that, having indemnified the crofters and BP in terms
of TOVALOP, they were subrogated to their rights against Hall Russell and were entitled
to sue that company in their own name. Six propositions were advanced in support of
that submission. (1) In cases of subrogation such as the present, there is a transfer to the
indemnifier of all the rights which the person indemnified has or had against the third
party to the extent that it is necessary to reimburse the indemnifier in the sum paid by
f   him. (2) It therefore follows that the right of the indemnified person to sue the third
party is also transferred. (3) The reason why a further equitable provision is normally
required to enable the indemnifier to sue in his own name is the long-established rule
enunciated in *Cattle v Stockton Waterworks Co* (1875) LR 10 QB 453, [1874–80] All ER
Rep 220 that a person claiming in delict for loss resulting from damage to property must
have had a proprietary or possessory interest in the property damaged at the relevant
g   times. (4) If, contrary to proposition (2), there is only an equitable assignation by the
indemnified person to the indemnifier, the latter can deal with the problem in England
since the Supreme Court of Judicature Act 1873 by joining those with the legal right to
sue as co-defendants in the action and in Scotland by convening them as parties if the
defender tables a plea of 'all parties not called'. (5) Esso have undoubted title to sue Hall
Russell in respect of the damage to and loss of oil from the Bernicia, from which it
h   follows that the reasons which prevent most indemnifiers suing in their own name are
not here present. (6) The principle enunciated in *Cattle v Stockton Waterworks Co* has, on
occasion, given way to pragmatic considerations and it is appropriate that it should do so
in this case.

Although these propositions were all advanced under the broad umbrella of
subrogation they involve two separate questions of law, namely (1) the nature and
j   enforceability of the rights to which an indemnifier is subrogated and (2) the right, if
any, to sue for economic loss occasioned by damage to the property of another. These
questions are quite distinct because in the first case the subrogated pursuer is enforcing
the rights of another which have been transferred to him, whereas in the second case the
pursuer is seeking to enforce a right of his own to recover loss which he has suffered.

In his classic definition of subrogation in *Castellain v Preston* (1883) 11 QBD 380 at

388–389, [1881–5] All ER Rep 493 at 496 Brett LJ, having stated that the fundamental
principle of insurance was that the contract of insurance contained in a marine or fire
policy was a contract of indemnity whereby the assured should be fully indemnified but
never more than fully indemnified (see 11 QBD 380 at 386, [1881–5] All ER Rep 493 at
495), said:

> 'Now it seems to me that in order to carry out the fundamental rule of insurance
> law, this doctrine of subrogation must be carried to the extent which I am now
> about to endeavour to express, namely, that as between the underwriter and the
> assured the underwriter is entitled to the advantage of every right of the assured,
> whether such right consists in contract, fulfilled or unfulfilled, or in remedy for tort
> capable of being insisted on or already insisted on, or in any other right, whether by
> way of condition or otherwise, legal or equitable, which can be, or has been exercised
> or has accrued, and whether such right could or could not be enforced by the insurer
> in the name of the assured by the exercise or acquiring of which right or condition
> the loss against which the assured is insured, can be, or has been diminished. That
> seems to me to put this doctrine of subrogation in the largest possible form, and if
> in that form, large as it is, it is short of fulfilling that which is the fundamental
> condition, I must have omitted to state something which ought to have been stated.
> But it will be observed that I use the words "of every right of the assured." I think
> that the rule does require that limit.'

A few years earlier in *Simpson & Co v Thomson* (1877) 3 App Cas 279 at 284 Lord Cairns
LC referred to the well-known principle of law that the indemnifier—

> 'will, on making good the indemnity, be entitled to succeed to all the ways and
> means by which the person indemnified might have protected himself or
> reimbursed himself for the loss.'

Although these two cases related to insurance the doctrine of subrogation is not
restricted to the law of insurance (see per Diplock J in *Yorkshire Insurance Co Ltd v Nisbet
Shipping Co Ltd* [1961] 2 All ER 487 at 490, [1962] 2 QB 330 at 339, Lord Diplock in
Orakpo v Manson Investments Ltd [1977] 3 All ER 1 at 7, [1978] AC 95 at 104). It
undoubtedly extends to other contracts of indemnity and to cautionary obligations such
as guarantees given to a creditor on behalf of a debtor, although in the former case the
indemnifier is subrogated to the rights and remedies of the assured or other person
indemnified whereas in the latter he is subrogated to the rights of the creditor. What is,
however, absolutely clear from the authorities is that the rights and remedies to which
the indemnifier is subrogated are those which were vested in the person to whom
payment has been made, no more and no less, and that rights and liabilities of third
parties unconnected with the contract are not affected.

How then is the indemnifier to enforce the rights to which he is subrogated? In
Simpson & Co v Thomson 3 App Cas 279 at 284 Lord Cairns LC, after the passage to which
I have already referred, continued:

> 'It is on this principle that the underwriters of a ship that has been lost are entitled
> to the ship in specie if they can find and recover it; and it is on the same principle
> that they can assert any right which the owner of the ship might have asserted
> against a wrongdoer for damage for the act which has caused the loss. But this right
> of action for damages they must assert, not in their own name, but in the name of
> the person insured, and if the person insured be the person who has caused the
> damage I am unable to see how the right can be asserted at all.'

Lord Penzance said (at 290):

> 'But the ground upon which I will ask your Lordships to reject this contention of
> the Respondents' counsel is this—that upon the cases cited no precedent or authority

has been found or produced to the House for an action against the wrongdoer except
in the name, and therefore, in point of law, on the part of one who had either some
property in, or possession of, the chattel injured. On the other hand, the existence
of authorities in which the suit has been brought in the name of the owner, though
for the benefit of persons having a collateral interest, is somewhat strong to shew
that such persons had no right of action in themselves. For it is to be presumed that
a person having such a right would pursue it directly, and not indirectly through
the name of another.'

Lord Blackburn similarly stated the position (at 293):

'In *England*, the action must be in the name of the shipowner, not of the
underwriters. I think this material, as shewing that it is the personal right of action
of the shipowner, the benefit of which is transferred to the underwriters.'

In *King v Victoria Insurance Co Ltd* [1896] AC 250 at 256 Lord Hobhouse in delivering the
advice of the Board stated:

'It is true that subrogation by act of law would not give the insurer a right to sue
in a court of law in his own name. But that difficulty is got over by force of the
express assignment of the bank's claim, and of the Judicature Act . . .'

In *John Edwards & Co v Motor Union Insurance Co Ltd* [1922] 2 KB 249 at 253–254
McCardie J, in a detailed consideration of the doctrine of subrogation, said:

'If once the claim be paid then as a matter of equity the rights to recover against
third persons pass from the assured to the insurer although the legal right to
compensation remains in the assured and although actions at law must be brought
in the name of the assured and not of the insurer: see *London Assurance Co.* v.
Sainsbury ((1783) 3 Doug KB 245 at 253–254, 99 ER 636 at 640); *King* v. *Victoria
Insurance Co.* As pointed out in MacGillivray [*Insurance* (1st edn, 1912) p 740], it
follows from this equity that if the assured upon tender of a proper indemnity as to
costs refuses the use of his name the insurer can by proceedings in equity compel
him to give the use of his hame. This has long been settled law.'

In *Yorkshire Insurance Co Ltd v Nisbet Shipping Co Ltd* [1961] 2 All ER 487 at 490, [1962] 2
QB 330 at 339 Diplock J observed in relation to the doctrine of subrogation:

'Although often referred to as an "equity" it is not an exclusively equitable
doctrine. It was applied by the common law courts in insurance cases long before
the fusion of law and equity, although the powers of the common law courts might
in some cases require to be supplemented by those of a court of equity in order to
give full effect to the doctrine; for example, by compelling an assured to allow his
name to be used by the insurer for the purpose of enforcing the assured's remedies
against third parties in respect of the subject-matter of the loss.'

My Lords, the foregoing authorities leave me in no doubt as to the existence of a
general rule in both English and Scots law that where an indemnifier is subrogated to the
rights of someone whom he has indemnified he can only pursue those rights in name of
that person. It follows that I reject Esso's second proposition.

Esso sought to get round the general rule by arguing that since they had suffered
physical damage as a result of Hall Russell's negligence they were entitled to pursue the
subrogated rights in their own name. In short the general rule does not apply where
both the indemnifier and the person indemnified suffer physical damage as a result of
the relevant act of negligence. My Lords, it is at this stage important to remember the
distinction between the two questions of law to which I have already referred. Esso
maintain that it is the rule in *Cattle v Stockton Waterworks Co* (1875) LR 10 QB 453,
[1874–80] All ER Rep 220 which necessitates the further equitable provision normally

required to enable the indemnifier to sue in his own name and that this rule will not
apply where a pursuer has suffered physical damage as well as economic loss due to *a*
damage to the property of another.

In *Cattle v Stockton Waterworks Co* the plaintiff was a contractor working on the land of
Knight which was damaged by the negligence of the defendants. Blackburn J put the
question thus (LR 10 QB 453 at 457, [1874–80] All ER Rep 220 at 223):

> 'can Cattle sue in his own name for the loss which he has in fact sustained, in   *b*
> consequence of the damage, which the defendants have done to the property of
> Knight, causing him, Cattle, to lose money under his contract? We think he cannot.'

He then went on to justify his conclusion by reference to the floodgates argument in the
following terms (LR 10 QB 453 at 457–458, [1874–80] All ER Rep 220 at 223):

> 'In the present case the objection is technical and against the merits, and we   *c*
> should be glad to avoid giving it effect. But if we did so, we should establish an
> authority for saying that, in such a case as that of *Rylands* v. *Fletcher* ((1866) LR 1
> Exch 265, [1861–73] All ER Rep 1, Exch; *affd* (1868) LR 3 HL 330, [1861–73] All
> ER Rep 1) the defendant would be liable, not only to an action by the owner of the
> drowned mine, and by such of his workmen as had their tools or clothes destroyed,
> but also an action by every workman and person employed in the mine, who in   *d*
> consequence of its stoppage made less wages than he would otherwise have done.
> And many similar cases to which this would apply might be suggested. It may be
> said that it is just that all such persons should have compensation for such a loss, and
> that, if the law does not give them redress, it is imperfect. Perhaps it may be so. But,
> as was pointed out by Coleridge, J., in *Lumley* v. *Gye* ((1853) 2 E & B 216 at 252,
> [1843–60] All ER Rep 208 at 221), Courts of justice should not allow themselves, in   *e*
> the pursuit of perfectly complete remedies for all wrongful acts, to transgress the
> bounds, which our law, in a wise consciousness as I conceive of its limited powers,
> has imposed on itself, of redressing only the proximate and direct consequences of
> wrongful acts." In this we quite agree. No authority in favour of the plaintiff's right
> to sue was cited, and, as far as our knowledge goes, there was none that could have
> been cited.'   *f*

Blackburn J concluded (LR 10 QB 453 at 458, [1874–80] All ER Rep 220 at 224):

> 'In the present case there is no pretence for saying that the defendants were
> malicious or had any intention to injure anyone. They were, at most, guilty of a
> neglect of duty, which occasioned injury to the property of Knight, but which did
> not injure any property of the plaintiff. The plaintiff's claim is to recover the damage   *g*
> which he has sustained by his contract with Knight becoming less profitable, or, it
> may be, a losing contract, in consequence of this injury to Knight's property. We
> think this does not give him any right of action.'

That was a case in which the plaintiff was seeking to recover the loss directly sustained by
him as a result of damage to Knight's property rendering his contract less profitable. He   *h*
was not seeking to recover in his own name the loss which Knight had sustained, which
loss would no doubt have been very different in character. *Cattle's* case has been cited
with approval in many subsequent cases both in England and in Scotland. Suffice it to
mention three. In *Candlewood Navigation Corp Ltd v Mitsui OSK Lines Ltd, The Mineral
Transporter, The Ibaraki Maru* [1985] 2 All ER 935, [1986] AC 1 it was held that a time
charterer was not entitled to recover damages for pecuniary loss resulting from damage   *j*
caused to the chartered vessel by a third party. In delivering the advice of the Board Lord
Fraser said ([1985] 2 All ER 935 at 939–940, [1986] AC 1 at 17):

> 'These two cases of *Cattle* and *Simpson* have stood for over a hundred years and
> have frequently been cited with approval in later cases, both in the United Kingdom

a   and elsewhere. They show, in their Lordships' opinion, that the justification for denying a right of action to a person who has suffered economic damage through injury to the property of another is that for reasons of practical policy it is considered to be inexpedient to admit his claim.'

In *Leigh & Sillavan Ltd v Aliakmon Shipping Co Ltd, The Aliakmon* [1986] 2 All ER 145 at 149, [1986] AC 785 at 809 Lord Brandon said:

b   'My Lords, there is a long line of authority for a principle of law that, in order to enable a person to claim in negligence for loss caused to him by reason of loss of or damage to property, he must have had either the legal ownership of or a possessory title to the property concerned at the time when the loss or damage occurred, and it is not enough for him to have only had contractual rights in relation to such property which have been adversely affected by the loss of or damage to it. The line c   of authority to which I have referred includes the following cases: *Cattle v Stockton Waterworks Co . . . Simpson & Co v Thomson . . .*'

Finally, in *Nacap Ltd v Moffat Plant Ltd* 1987 SLT 221 the Lord Justice Clerk (Ross) in delivering the opinion of the First Division cited with approval and applied the dicta of Lord Fraser and Lord Brandon to which I have just referred.

d   My Lords, I very much doubt whether the rule in *Cattle's* case has any relevance to a claim to pursue subrogated rights. Although there may be cases in which the measure of a subrogated claim may be the same as a claim for economic loss arising from damage to a third party's property, the legal character of each claim is essentially different. So far as subrogation is concerned, the only question is whether the general rule laid down in *Simpson & Co v Thomson* and the subsequent cases admits of an exception when the e   indemnifier has also a claim for damage to property arising out of the same act which gave rise to the indemnification. No authority was cited in which such an exception had been admitted and in principle it is not easy to see what basis could exist. The reason for the rule is to prevent a wrongdoer or debtor being subjected to double claims. A successful action by an indemnifier in his own name against a wrongdoer or debtor would not relieve the latter of his liability to the person indemnified. Such liability f   would only be extinguished by an action brought in the name of the person indemnified or in the name of the indemnifier suing as assignee of the rights of the person indemnified. The fact that the indemnifier also has a claim for damage to his property does not in any way affect the liability of the wrongdoer to the person indemnified.

It was urged on your Lordships that to recognise such an exception would not be to open the floodgates since there could be relatively few cases where the indemnifier would g   be in a position in which he, as well as the person indemnified, were both likely to suffer damage to their respective property. My Lords, given the reason for the rule and the fact that it has stood for over 100 years, much more than the above consideration would be needed to convince me that there exists an exception thereto such as Esso contend for. The damage to the tanker allows Esso to sue Hall Russell for such loss as they have sustained as a result thereof but it in no way affects their inability to pursue in their own h   name the crofters' subrogated rights.

Esso also maintain that they could have convened the crofters as defenders, that any claims which the crofters might have had against Hall Russell were now time-barred and that accordingly no prejudice would result to Hall Russell if they were allowed to pursue in their own name the rights to which they were subrogated. My Lords, the fact that Esso might have brought the crofters into the action or might indeed have obtained j   from them assignations of their claims against Hall Russell is nothing to the point. They have not chosen to do so and they cannot complain if the case is decided on what was done rather than on what might have been done. All in all I reject Esso's argument on subrogation and in so doing express my agreement with the reasoning of the Lord President and with that of my noble and learned friend Lord Goff.

(2) *TOVALOP: a direct head of damage*

Esso maintained that they had suffered physical damage to their tanker as a result of *a* the negligence of Hall Russell from which it followed that they could recover not only the cost of repairing such damage but also the financial loss which they had incurred as a result of the damage, which loss included the sums paid by them under TOVALOP. The Lord President rejected this contention on two grounds, namely (1) that Hall Russell and the pilot were not said to have known of the existence of TOVALOP and (2) that in any event it was well established by authority that an indemnifier could not sue for reparation *b* by reason of his contractual liability to the person indemnified for damage to his property. Following on the hearing in the First Division Esso amended their pleadings to make averments imputing to Hall Russell knowledge of the existence of TOVALOP and of the likely liability of Esso thereunder in respect of damage from oil pollution. Esso also sought to amend further during the hearing by making the following additional averments: *c*

> 'At the time of said incident on 30th December 1978 it was a practical necessity for the owner of a tanker in order to trade internationally to be a participating owner in TOVALOP. It was in particular a necessity for the owner of a tanker in order to use the facilities at Sullom Voe to be a participating owner in TOVALOP.'

I propose to deal first with the second and general ground on which the Lord President *d* rejected Esso's contentions. The authorities to which the Lord President referred were *Simpson & Co v Thomson, Candlewood Navigation Corp Ltd v Mitsui OSK Lines Ltd, Leigh & Sillavan Ltd v Aliakman Shipping Co Ltd* and *Nacap Ltd v Moffat Plant Ltd.* Esso sought to distinguish these authorities for the purposes of this case as they had sought to get round the general rule as to the name in which an indemnifier must sue, namely by relying on the damage suffered by the Bernicia. *e*

If the circumstances of the casualty had been such that Esso had been liable to pay compensation to the crofters under s 1(1) of the Merchant Shipping (Oil Pollution) Act 1971 in respect of an escape of oil I do not doubt that the sums payable would have been a proper head of damage in Esso's claim against the wrongdoers. In such an event Esso's liability would have been unavoidably imposed on them by statute. A claim of a similar *f* nature was admitted to be good in *The Arabert, A R Appelqvist A/B v Tyne-Tees Steam Shipping Co Ltd* [1961] 2 All ER 385, [1963] P 102, to which I shall refer in more detail later. Equally, Esso could have claimed for loss of hire occasioned by a period of necessary repair consequent on damage to the tanker. The present case is, however, in a different position. Esso chose to enter into and remain a party to TOVALOP for what were no doubt sound policy and commercial reasons but under no compulsitor of law so to do. They agreed voluntarily to indemnify persons affected by oil spillage. They were under *g* no general duty in law to the crofters and as far as they were concerned the payments which they received were entirely gratuitous. Indeed, having received payments from Esso the crofters could have sued Hall Russell, arguing that what they had received was no more than gratuities from a disaster fund. TOVALOP is and remains a gratuitous contract of indemnity notwithstanding that the event which gave rise to the payments *h* thereunder was damage to the Bernicia. Esso cannot pray in aid the latter event to convert their claim to repayment of sums paid under that indemnity into a claim for economic loss resulting directly from the damage. The matter can be tested in this way. Assume in the first place that the spillage of bunker oil was entirely due to the negligence of Hall Russell and that Esso had not entered into TOVALOP. In that event Esso would have been liable to the crofters neither in delict nor by virtue of statute and would have made *j* no payments to them. Assume in the second place the same facts but that Esso had entered into TOVALOP and had made payments thereunder to the crofters. What has caused these payments to be made? In my view they were made because Esso has chosen, by entering into and remaining a party to TOVALOP, to assume a voluntary obligation to the crofters and not because of any alleged negligence on the part of Hall Russell. It

follows that Esso are not entitled to claim the sums second and third concluded for in
a conclusion (1) as direct heads of damage.

In view of the conclusion which I have reached in relation to the Lord President's
second ground for rejecting Esso's contention it is not necessary to consider further the
effect of the amendments which were made before the hearing in this House and those
which were proffered at the bar. Suffice it to say that neither of these amendments go so
far as to suggest that there was any legal requirement on Esso to be a party to TOVALOP
b at the relevant time. I would only add in relation to this branch of the case that the
conclusion which I have reached does not mean that Esso never had a remedy in respect
of the sums paid by them under TOVALOP. They could either have obtained from the
crofters and BP assignations of their claims against Hall Russell and sued that company
in their own name or they could have obtained from those persons permission to sue in
their names.

c

(3) *Prematurity of declarator*

The First Division upheld Hall Russell's contentions that the declaratory conclusion
was premature inasmuch as the claim, being one for relief, could competently be brought
without the impediment of prescription after Esso's liability for payment of the repairs
d to the jetty had been determined.

Esso's averments disclose a somewhat curious situation. As the pleadings stood before
the First Division Esso averred (1) that by Court of Session summons signetted on 20
December 1983 SIC raised an action against Esso for payment of £270,423, being the
cost of repair to no 2 jetty with which the Bernicia came in contact, and (2) that by Court
of Session summons signetted on 19 December 1983 BP and Shell UK Ltd raised an
e action against Esso claiming payment of the same sum. Those pleadings made no
reference to the basis of either action. However, prior to the hearing of these appeals Esso
amended their pleadings to aver (1) that the basis of SIC's action was a claim under s 74
of the Harbours, Docks and Piers Clauses Act 1847 and s 4 of the Zetland County Council
Act 1974 (c viii) and, alternatively, a claim in respect of negligence of the master and
crew of the Bernicia, and (2) that the basis of the claim by BP and Shell was that they
f were bound by agreement to provide SIC with funds to repair the jetty and that having
paid the sum of £270,423 they sought relief from Esso who were primarily liable under
s 74 of the 1847 Act. Thus, Esso's pleadings on the matter are now in a form materially
different from that in which they were before the First Division.

Prima facie Esso's liability to SIC under s 74 of the 1847 Act is undeniable. It is equally
certain that Esso cannot be rendered liable twice over for the same damage to the jetty.
g It does therefore seem most unfortunate that time should have been spent both in the
First Division and in this House arguing on the basis that both actions will proceed. I
cannot help feeling that some consultation between Esso and the pursuers in the two
actions could have resolved the position and obviated the need for Esso to seek protection
in the form in which they have done in the declaratory conclusion. However, that being
said, it is necessary to look at that conclusion and pleadings as they now stand.
h   The primary question is whether Esso's liability to SIC under s 74 of the 1847 Act is a
good head of damage in this action against Hall Russell. If it is, then it must be included
in this action, since it is trite law that all claims arising out of a single act of negligence
must be pursued in the same action. In *Stevenson v Pontifex & Wood* (1887) 15 R 125 at
129 the Lord President (Inglis) enunciated the rule of practice as follows:

j   '. . . I am of opinion that a single act amounting either to delict or a breach of
contract cannot be made the ground of two or more actions, for the purpose of
recovering damages arising within different periods but caused by the same act. On
the contrary, I hold the true rule of practice based on sound principle to be, that
though the delict or breach of contract be of such nature that it will necessarily be
followed by injurious consequences in the future, and though it may for this reason

be impossible to ascertain with precise accuracy at the date of the action or of the
verdict the amount of loss which will result, yet the whole damage must be   *a*
recovered in one action, because there is but one cause of action. The most familiar
illustration of this rule is to be found in actions for injury to the person, in which
the practice is invariable.'

The foregoing rule has been consistently followed. It was restated in this House in
Dunlop v M'Gowans 1980 SC (HL) 73, where it was held that an obligation to make   *b*
reparation for loss, injury and damage was a single and indivisible obligation and that
only one action could be prosecuted for enforcing it. Furthermore, even if as a head of
damage the matter could otherwise competently be raised in future proceedings, time-
bar would operate to defeat the claim.

In *British Rlys Board v Ross and Cromarty CC* 1974 SC 27 the county council, who were
constructing a new road alongside the railway to Kyle of Lochalsh, were obliged by   *c*
private Act to pay on demand to the railways board compensation for any loss which
they might sustain by reason of damage to railway property. In considering the conduct
of the county council in defending an action by the board claiming compensation under
the private Act in the context of a proposed action by the county council against their
consultant engineers, the Lord President (Emslie) said (at 37):

'. . . and although the action proposed by these defenders is of a kind sometimes   *d*
quite improperly described as one of "relief," it is nothing more than an action of
damages in which the liability of the third parties will in character and origin be
wholly different from that under which the defenders have been required to satisfy
the claim of the pursuers in this action.'

Although the Lord President's observations were not essential to his decision in that case   *e*
I have no doubt that they correctly stated the law and are equally applicable to any claim
by Esso to recover from Hall Russell such sums as they have been or will be obliged to
pay to third parties in terms of s 74 of the 1847 Act. Although counsel were unable to
find any case in which sums paid by a pursuer under an absolute statutory liability had
been held to be a good head of damage, I understand that in Admiralty practice in   *f*
England it is accepted that sums paid under statute by an innocent ship in respect of
damage to jetties or raising of wrecks are recoverable as a head of damage from a
wrongdoing ship. In *The Arabert, A R Appelqvist A/B v Tyne-Tees Steam Shipping Co Ltd*
[1961] 2 All ER 385, [1963] P 102 Lord Merriman P held that the owners of a wrongdoing
vessel were entitled to include the expense of raising the wreck of the innocent vessel in
their claim for limitation against the owners of the latter vessel. It was admitted in that   *g*
case that the expenses incurred by the port authority in raising the vessel, for which her
owners were by statute liable, were recoverable as damages against the owners of the
wrongdoing vessel. With very experienced Admiralty counsel appearing before a judge
so well versed in Admiralty matters it seems most unlikely that such a claim could have
passed unchallenged and without judicial comment if it had not accorded with what was
understood to be the true position in law.   *h*

However, although I consider that Esso's statutory liability is a good head of damage,
it is not necessary at this stage to reach a concluded view on the matter. It is sufficient to
entitle Esso to a declaratory conclusion that they 'have a plain interest to protect
themselves against a possibility of prejudice which is by no means fanciful or unreal'
(*Central SMT Co Ltd v Lanarkshire CC* 1949 SC 450 at 458 per the Lord President (Cooper)).
For the reasons which I have already stated there could be substantial prejudice to Esso if   *j*
they were disabled from pursuing their claim to what is at least prima facie a good head
of damage.

The next question is whether the terms of the declarator sought are too wide. They
are undoubtedly framed to cover all eventualities and I see no prospect of a Lord Ordinary
pronouncing an order precisely as sought. However, I do not consider that this is fatal

for Esso. A pursuer may in petitory action conclude for what is patently a grossly
a extravagant sum. The result is not that the conclusion is struck out at the stage of
considering relevancy but rather that at the end of the day a Lord Ordinary will grant
decree, if at all, for a much reduced sum. In this case if the Lord Ordinary after proof
determines liability in favour of Esso he will, in relation to the declaratory conclusion,
have two alternatives, namely (1) if Esso's position vis-à-vis SIC on the one hand and BP
and Shell on the other is then clarified, to pronounce a declarator which conforms to the
b established fact or (2) if the position is not clarified, to make no order in hoc statu in
relation to the declarator and to continue consideration of the matter until clarification
has taken place.

I do not consider that any prejudice would result by allowing the declaratory conclusion
to stand whereas substantial prejudice could result to Esso if it were struck out. For the
foregoing reasons, I would allow Esso's appeal in relation to this conclusion. I would only
c add that in differing from the First Division on this matter I have been much influenced
by the averments anent s 74 of the 1847 Act which were added in this House. I doubt
whether your Lordships would have taken a different view from the First Division in
relation to the averments which were before that court.

d
(5) *Vicarious responsibility for acts of pilot*
   Section 6 of the Zetland County Council Act 1974 provided that the county council
should exercise jurisdiction as harbour authority within a defined area which included
the whole of Sullom Voe. On the coming into operation of the Local Government
(Scotland) Act 1973, SIC replaced the county council as the local authority and assumed
all the functions of harbour authority under s 154. By the Sullom Voe, Shetland, Pilotage
Order 1976, SI 1976/1541, which was made under s 7(1) of the Pilotage Act 1913, there
e was created a pilotage district which included the whole of Sullom Voe and for which
SIC were the pilotage authority. In terms of the order pilotage became compulsory
within the district from 1 February 1978.

Hall Russell aver that the pilot was 'an employee of [SIC] . . . acting in the course of his
employment with them'. SIC answer this averment as follows: 'Admitted that he was
f employed as a Marine Officer with [them].' Hall Russell aver negligence on the part of
the pilot in a number of respects which it is unnecessary to detail. For the purposes of the
present issue the relevant averments are to the effect that SIC employed the pilot in their
capacity as port authority and that they are responsible 'for his actings and omissions in
the course of his employment with them'. In their case, Hall Russell intimated that they
were prepared, if necessary, to make the following amendment in amplification of the
g foregoing averments:

   'The fourth third party had been contacted by the vessel with a request for
   pilotage. The harbour master had instructed the said pilot that he was at liberty to
   delay the entry of "Esso Bernicia" to Sullom Voe if he had doubts concerning the
   manoeuvre but that he must inform the harbour-master if he so decided. The
   pursuers duly paid the pilotage dues to the fourth third party. It was in the interests
h   of the fourth third party, both as harbour authority and as pilotage authority, that
   vessels entering and berthing at Sullom Voe be safely navigated by the said pilot.
   Further, it was within the powers of the fourth third party to stipulate in advance
   the number and disposition of tugs which should be used for bringing vessels to
   berth in varying weather conditions. In these circumstances it is believed and
   averred that the fourth third party accepted responsibility for ensuring the safe
j   pilotage of "Esso Bernicia" into Sullom Voe and are vicariously liable for the actings
   of the said pilot in the course of his employment with them.'

SIC are the fourth third party.
   Before turning to consider the arguments presented by Hall Russell it may be
convenient to consider the relationship which has existed historically between shipowner

and pilot. At common law a shipowner was liable for the negligence of a pilot voluntarily
engaged just as he was for the negligence of the master. Such a pilot was treated as the   *a*
servant of the owner. However, a shipowner was not responsible for the negligence of a
compulsory pilot, who was not deemed to be his servant or agent. Express provision to
this effect was contained in s 633 of the Merchant Shipping Act 1894. The position of a
compulsory pilot was equiparated to that of a voluntary pilot at common law by s 15(1)
of the 1913 Act, which is in the following terms: *b*

> 'Notwithstanding anything in any public or local Act, the owner or master of a
> vessel navigating under circumstances in which pilotage is compulsory shall be
> answerable for any loss or damage caused by the vessel or by any fault of the
> navigation of the vessel in the same manner as he would if pilotage were not
> compulsory.'

Section 15 came into operation on 1 January 1918.   *c*
    Hall Russell advanced two reasons for their contention that they had relevantly averred
vicarious responsibility on the part of SIC for the negligence of the pilot. *In the first place*
it was said that although earlier authorities had appeared to impose liability on a
shipowner for the negligence of a voluntary pilot on the basis of a master and servant
relationship this rationale was no longer correct. The true position was that the shipowner
owed a non-delegable duty to third parties to have his ship navigated carefully and that   *d*
he could not discharge that duty by delegating it to an independent contractor in the
shape of a pilot. When s 15(1) was looked at against that background there was nothing
in it which altered the common law position obtaining between the shipowner and pilot,
which remained that of employer and independent contractor. It followed that quoad
the shipowner the pilot remained the servant of SIC. *In the second place* it was said that
SIC were the principals in carrying out the business of pilotage and that the pilot was   *e*
merely carrying out those functions on their behalf, from which it followed that SIC, as
the independent contractor, were responsible for acts of negligent pilotage. Similar
arguments were presented to the First Division and rejected by the Lord President in his
carefully reasoned judgment.
    A long line of authority establishes that a shipowner is liable to third parties for the   *f*
negligent navigation of a voluntary pilot and, since 1 January 1918, he has been similarly
liable for negligent acts of compulsory pilots. The basis of this liability is that the pilot is
treated as the servant of the owner. Dr Lushington so stated in *The Maria* (1839) 1 Wm
Rob 95 at 103, 166 ER 508 at 511–512. In *'Beechgrove' Steamship Co Ltd v Akt 'Fjord' of
Kristiania* [1916] 1 AC 364 it was held that a pilot navigating outwith a compulsory
pilotage district was de jure the servant of the onwers and a defence that they were not   *g*
responsible for his actions was repelled. In *Thom v J & P Hutchison Ltd* 1925 SC 386 it was
held that s 15 of the 1913 Act operated to make a pilot a servant of the owners for the
purposes of the doctrine of collaborateur in an action at the instance of the widow of a
deceased member of the crew. The pursuer sought to traverse the defence of collaborateur
by arguing that the pilot was an agent to whom the business of navigation was deputed
and not a servant. The Lord President (Clyde), after remarking that it was impossible to   *h*
conceive of the pilot in relation to his duties as other than a constituent member for the
time being of the crew, said (at 392):

> 'These considerations point to service, not to agency, as the foundation on which
> the relations between a licensed pilot, voluntarily employed, and the owners rest.
> There is nothing inconsistent with this in the fact that a licensed pilot who is taken
> on board in a compulsory area is held not to be the servant of the owners. In that   *j*
> case there is no room for contract of any kind.'

The Lord President later observed:

> '. . . though I rather think it is true that there is no case in which the true nature
> of the legal relation of a pilot (voluntarily engaged) to the owners has been

canvassed—it has never been doubted throughout a long series of cases that it is that
a   of service.'

Lord Cullen said (at 393):

b
'Now, it is well settled that an owner is liable for loss or damage caused by fault in
navigation on the part of a pilot voluntarily employed by him. And the ratio of this
liability has always been stated to be that such a pilot is the servant of the owner. He
is employed to take up *pro tempore* the captain's function of navigator in
circumstances where special local knowledge is required. It is true that he is not a
kind of servant of whom it can be said that he is bound to obey his employer's
orders, not only as to work to be done, but also as to how he shall do it. But the same
thing applies to the captain.'

c   In *Workington Harbour and Dock Board v Towerfield (owners)* [1950] 2 All ER 414, [1951]
AC 112 a ship went aground due partly to the negligence of a harbour authority and
partly to that of a compulsory pilot. It was held that s 15 of the 1913 Act had the effect of
rendering the owner responsible so that he was both liable for the loss and damage caused
to others and debarred from recovering any damage which he had suffered. The events
d   in question took place before the coming into operation of the Law Reform (Contributory
Negligence) Act 1945. Lord Porter, in construing the words 'answerable for any loss or
damage caused . . . by any fault of the navigation of the vessel', said ([1950] 2 All ER 414
at 425, [1951] AC 112 at 133–134):

'"Answerable", as I think, simply means "responsible," and a shipowner who
through a compulsory pilot is responsible for faulty navigation is responsible for
e   damage to his own ship as well as for injury to the property of another. It follows
that [he] neither pays for the damage which has been done to the other nor can
recover his own damage from the other who is implicated.'

Lord Normand expressly approved the decision and the reasoning of the Lord President
and Lord Cullen in *Thom v J & P Hutchison Ltd* 1925 SC 386 that s 15 created the relation
f   of a master and servant between the shipowner and the pilot (see [1950] 2 All ER 414 at
433, [1951] AC 112 at 145). In the recent case of *Oceanic Crest Shipping Co v Pilbara
Harbour Services Pty Ltd* (1986) 160 CLR 626 the majority of the High Court of Australia
considered that a shipowner was responsible for the negligence of a pilot on the basis that
the latter became the servant of the former (see per Gibbs CJ, Wilson and Dawson JJ (at
640, 644, 683)).

g
In the face of these powerful authorities it might be thought that there was little scope
for arguing that a compulsory pilot could be treated as anything other than a servant of
the owner for all purposes. Counsel for Hall Russell, however, was not to be deterred.
Although the rejection by the Lord President (Clyde) of agency as the basis of the owner-
pilot relationship was approved by Lord Normand in the *Towerfield* case, counsel did not
shrink from arguing that the Lord President was wrong. The basis of his submission that
h   the pilot remained an independent contractor quoad the owner was the following
observation by Denning LJ in *Cassidy v Ministry of Health (Fahrni, third party)* [1951] 1 All
ER 574 at 586–587, [1951] 2 KB 343 at 363:

'I take it to be clear law, as well as good sense, that, where a person is himself
under a duty to use care, he cannot get rid of his responsibility by delegating the
performance of it to someone else, no matter whether the delegation be to a servant
j   under a contract of service or to an independent contractor under a contract for
services . . . All those cases give good illustrations of the principle, but I would add
two others. One is the case of a shipowner who is under a duty to navigate his ship
with reasonable care. He cannot escape that duty by delegating the handling of the
ship to someone else, no matter whether it be a ship's captain under a contract of
service or to a pilot under a contract for services; and that is so even though the pilot

is in control and the captain acts throughout under his directions: see *The Neptune the Second* ((1814) 1 Dods 467, 165 ER 1380).   *a*

Relying on these observations, counsel maintained that while the owner was responsible throughout to third parties for the acts and omissions of the pilot, he was not the master of the pilot for the purposes of any damage which the pilot caused to him. Therefore he could sue both the pilot (*Lister v Romford Ice and Cold Storage Co Ltd* [1957] 1 All ER 125, [1957] AC 555) and, if he was employed by an authority, his employer. Thus, so far as the pilot is concerned it matters not whether he falls to be treated as the servant of the *b* owner or an independent contractor for the purposes of a negligent act. In either event the owner can recover from him subject always to any statutory limitation of liability. The critical question is whether the owner can recover from a general employer of the pilot. My Lords, I do not consider that the observations of Denning LJ warrant the proposition which counsel sought to derive therefrom. *Cassidy v Ministry of Health* was a *c* case of negligent medical treatment in which Denning LJ made passing reference to a pilot 'under a contract for services'. There is no doubt that a pilot was in many cases an independent contractor to the extent that he made his services available to a shipowner and received not a salary but pilotage dues payable in respect of his services under such deductions as the pilotage authority had determined by byelaw made under s 17 of the 1913 Act. However, the fact that he was an independent contractor did not alter the *d* common law rule that when he had been engaged voluntarily by a shipowner he was, so far as any acts or omissions on his part were concerned, the servant of the shipowner. The rule operated whether he was in the general employment of a pilotage authority or whether he was an independent contractor. Denning LJ neither referred nor had occasion to refer to the foregoing rule or to the line of authority which I have mentioned above. In these circumstances his observations cannot be taken as in any way qualifying the *e* general statement of Lord Porter in *Workington Harbour and Dock Board v Towerfield (owners)* [1950] 2 All ER 414 at 425, [1951] AC 112 at 133–134 that in terms of s 15 of the 1913 Act an owner is responsible for damage to his own ship due to faulty navigation of a compulsory pilot.

My Lords, nothing that has been said on behalf of Hall Russell persuades me that the rationale of the line of authority to which I have referred was wrong or that there is any *f* exception to the general application of s 15 of the 1913 Act to damage suffered by a ship under pilotage. Subject only to what I have to say in the context of Hall Russell's second submission, the pilot is to be considered for all purposes as the servant of the owner. I would only add that if Hall Russell's argument were correct there would follow the curious result that the doctrine of respondeat superior would apply to two different masters in respect of two different claims of damage arising out of a single act of *g* negligence. It is a well-recognised principle, exemplified in cases involving crane-drivers, that a servant in the general employment of A may, for a particular purpose, be treated as in the pro hac vice employment of B. However, there is no principle which permits a servant to be in the de jure employment of two separate masters at one and the same time. As the Lord President (Lord Emslie) said in this case (1988 SLT 33 at 48): '... no man can serve two masters.' For all these reasons I reject Hall Russell's first argument as *h* unsound.

Hall Russell's second argument involved the proposition that SIC had held themselves out as undertaking pilotage services as principals and that the pilot was merely carrying out those services on their behalf. It was said that the position of SIC was indistinguishable from that of hospital authorities, inasmuch as both assumed obligations to others which they performed through professional staff in their employment. The critical question is *j* whether SIC had assumed the obligation of piloting ships in Sullom Voe, in which event they would bear responsibility for any negligence in navigation by a pilot in their employ, or whether they had merely assumed the obligation to provide the services of a qualified pilot, in which event he would be the principal in the pilotage and SIC would not be liable for his negligence.

In *Gold v Essex CC* [1942] 2 All ER 237, [1942] 2 KB 293 a local authority was held
a liable to a patient injured by the negligence of a competent radiographer who was a
whole-time employee of the hospital. Lord Greene MR said ([1942] 2 All ER 237 at 242,
[1942] 2 KB 237 at 301):

b

'Apart from any express term governing the relationship of the parties, the extent
of the obligation which one person assumes towards another is to be inferred from
the circumstances of the case ... but in each case the first task is to discover the
extent of the obligation assumed by the person whom it is sought to make liable.
Once this is discovered, it follows of necessity that the person accused of a breach of
the obligation cannot escape liability because he has employed another person,
whether a servant or agent, to discharge it on his behalf; and this is equally true
whether or not the obligation involves the use of skill.'

c   And he observed ([1942] 2 All ER 237 at 243, [1942] 2 KB 237 at 304):

'It is clear, therefore, that the powers of the respondents include the power of
treating patients, and that they are entitled and indeed bound in a proper case to
recover the just expense of doing so. If they exercise that power, the obligation
which they undertake is an obligation to treat, and they are liable if the persons
d   employed by them to perform the obligation on their behalf act without due care. I
am unable to see how a body invested with such a power and to all appearance
exercising it, can be said to be assuming no greater obligation than to provide a
skilled person and proper appliances.'

In *Cassidy v Ministry of Health* [1951] 1 All ER 574 at 585, [1951] 2 QB 343 at 360
Denning LJ observed that whenever hospital authorities 'accept a patient for treatment,
e they must use reasonable care and skill to cure him of his ailment'. He later said: 'Once
they undertake the task, they come under a duty to use care in the doing of it ...' Finally,
in *Macdonald v Glasgow Western Hospitals Board of Management* 1954 SC 453 at 485 Lord
Carmont said:

f

'If A bargained with B to do a piece of work, did it matter, if the work was
inadequate, whether the agent employed to do the work was a servant or a
contractor? Surely not! If there was a failure adequately to fulfil the undertaking, it
was no excuse to blame either the one or the other where A was sued for breach. If
then a hospital board proposes or holds out an offer to the public to nurse, it seems
no answer to one who has not been adequately nursed to refer to the failings of the
agent selected to carry out the work for A.'

g

These cases are undoubted authority for the proposition that if A assumes an obligation
towards B he cannot avoid responsibility for a failure of performance due to lack of care
on the part of persons whom he has employed to perform on his behalf. They do not,
however, assist in determining whether in any particular case A has assumed an
obligation to B. That, as Lord Greene MR said in *Gold*'s case, is a matter to be inferred
h from the circumstances of the case.

Hall Russell could point to no statutory provision which either obliged or empowered
SIC to undertake the pilotage of ships in Sullom Voe. Section 16 of the 1913 Act
empowers pilotage authorities to license pilots for their district, and s 19 provides that
the grant of a pilot's licence does not impose any liability on the authority for any loss
occasioned by the pilot's fault. The Act contains no provision empowering a pilotage
j authority to employ pilots or undertake pilotage. The Zetland County Council Act 1974
contains no reference to pilotage and the 1976 order empowers SIC by art 10 to acquire
and own work vessels for the purposes of the order but contains provision relating neither
to their employment of pilots nor to performance of pilotage duties. However, Hall
Russell argued that the averment that the pilot was acting in the course of his employment
with them must be taken as meaning that he, as pilot, was carrying out on behalf of SIC

the obligation of pilotage towards shipowners which they had assumed. I do not consider that this is a legitimate inference from these bare averments, even as expanded by the *a* proffered amendments in the case, but it is not necessary to decide this point on the pleadings alone, since authority is uniformly against it.

Hall Russell sought to derive support from *Holman v Irvine Harbour Trustees* (1877) 4 R 406, in which the defenders were held liable to the owners of a ship damaged by the negligence of an unlicensed pilot in their employment. Lord Ormidale said (at 416):

> 'A duly qualified or licensed pilot is a public officer who obtains his certificate *b* only after a careful examination of his qualifications by parties competent to judge of them. On being licensed he occupies an independent position, very much as a notary-public or messenger-at-arms does. The public constitute his master, and he is the servant of the public, like these and other public functionaries; and the usual consequences and responsibilities arising from the ordinary relation of master and servant do not arise. It was for this reason—a reason which has no application to the circumstances of the present case—that the harbour and pilotage authorities were assoilzied from liability in the case of Ogilvie and Others v. The Magistrates of Edinburgh ((1821) 1 S 24) relied on so much by the Lord Ordinary.'

Lord Gifford summarised the matter as follows (at 417):

d

> 'The short ground upon which I rest my opinion may be stated almost in a single sentence. I think, upon the evidence, and looking to the whole circumstances of the case, including the terms of the various statutes under which the harbour trustees acted, that Jeremiah M'Gill, on the occasion in question, was not acting as an independent pilot employed by the shipmaster or captain of the "Gertrude," and merely licensed or authorised by the defenders, but was acting solely and simply as *e* the servant of the defenders, employed by them alone, and paid by them alone, and acting within the limits of the defenders' harbour in discharging a duty which the defenders themselves had undertaken to perform.'

The Lord Justice Clerk (Moncreiff) said (at 422):

> 'No doubt, if the harbour commissioners had sent out a licensed pilot they would *f* have done all that could have been required of them, for it is certain that a pilotage authority, having duly licensed a pilot, is not responsible for any fault he may commit.'

The basis of that decision was that an unlicensed pilot working about the harbour remained the servant of the harbour authority in contradistinction to a licensed pilot who occupied an independent position. Thus, far from assisting Hall Russell, the case is *g* against them as there is no challenge to the licensing or general competence of Captain Hemingway. In *Parker v North British Rly Co* (1898) 25 R 1059 at 1067 the Lord Justice Clerk (Macdonald), in the context of a harbour authority's liability to the owner of a damaged ship, observed, obiter:

> 'But I cannot hold that if any vessel was picked up by one of these pilots the *h* company were responsible for him as their servant, because they had an arrangement with him that, in respect of their providing him with a boat and a fixed weekly payment, he agreed to hand them the fees he drew from ships which he boarded and piloted in.'

Lord Moncreiff expressed tentative views to the same effect.

j

In *Fowles v Eastern and Australian Steamship Co Ltd* [1916] 2 AC 556 it was held that a shipowner's claim to recover damages caused by the negligence of a compulsory pilot was not maintainable against the government of Queensland, who owed no duty to manage or control ships but merely a duty to license and appoint duly qualified pilots,

which latter duty was not alleged to have been breached. In delivering the advice of the
a Board, Earl Loreburn said (at 560–561):

> 'In examining the statutes, it is well to bear in mind the condition of things in
> regard to pilots before Parliament interposed. Originally the business was simply a
> matter of private enterprise; seamen of local experience made their own bargains
> with masters of ships. The acting Chief Justice (Barton J. traces the sequel in his
> judgment. A licence was required, in the interests of public safety; then pilotage
> *b* fees were turned by statute into pilotage rates, no doubt for public reasons, but still
> the rates were paid to the men for their private emolument. Then the Treasury took
> the rates and empowered the Government to fix the remuneration of pilots. "The
> statutes also provided for constitution of a Marine Board acting in the execution of
> its powers and functions under the control of the Crown. The same statutes
> *c* regulated the pilots in their duties after the manner of public servants and provided
> for a pilotage service, and, indeed, as was admitted, the Government supplied the
> port pilots with the instruments of their calling in the shape of boats maintained
> and crews paid, at Government cost, while the admissions and the regulations show
> that, on the other hand, the coast pilots were allowed to receive fees for themselves,
> and had to find their own boats and crews. The port pilots were made regular
> *d* officers of the Government service, paid from the public funds, though the
> department called the Marine Board managed the pilot service under the immediate
> control of the Government. The port pilots were classified under the public service
> laws, according to salary, as professional servants of the Government." To this it
> may be added that pilotage in prescribed ports was made compulsory.'

After posing the question of whether or not the government were bound to navigate the
e ship and employed the pilot to do for them the work which they were bound to do, Earl
Loreburn continued (at 562–563):

> 'In their Lordships' opinion these Acts of Parliament did not alter the original
> status of a pilot, which is, in effect, that he must be regarded as an independent
> professional man in discharging his skilled duties. If it had been intended to alter
> *f* this old and familiar status, it is to be supposed that the Legislature would have done
> it more explicitly. What it has done is more consistent with a different and limited
> purpose, namely, to secure a proper selection, a proper supply, a proper supervision,
> and a proper remuneration of men to whose skill life and property is committed,
> whether the shipowner likes it or not. For this purpose they become servants of the
> Government. For the purpose of navigating ships they remain what they were, and
> *g* the duty which the State or Government owes to a shipowner, exercised, it is true,
> by various authorities, is to provide a qualified man in the terms of the statutes, but
> not to take the conduct or management of the ship. It is not said that they have
> failed in this duty of providing a qualified man.'

The statutory provisions in this case certainly do no more to alter the original status of a
h pilot or to impose a duty of navigation on SIC than did the provisions to which Earl
Loreburn referred. However, counsel argued that *Fowles's* case was distinguishable from
the present case inasmuch as it was here to be inferred from facts averred that SIC had
accepted responsibility for ensuring the safe pilotage of the Bernicia.

Fowles's case was applied by the majority of the High Court of Australia in *Oceanic
Crest Shipping Co v Pilbara Harbour Services Pty Ltd* (1986) 160 CLR 626, who held that a
j port authority was not vicariously liable for the negligence of a pilot because such liability
was impliedly excluded by statute and also because the pilot was a public officer executing
an independent duty which the law cast on him. The relevant statutory provision was
s 410B(2) of the Navigation Act 1912 (Aust), which was, for practical purposes, in terms
identical to s 15(1) of the 1913 Act. Gibbs CJ pointed out that *Fowles's* case had since been

understood in the High Court of Australia as depending on the circumstance that the pilot was executing an independent duty which the law cast on him (at 637). After considering a number of authorities involving tortfeasors who were acting in the performance of a duty imposed by law he rejected an argument that the principles on which Fowles's case depended no longer accorded with modern principles of vicarious responsibility. He further concluded that the provisions of s 410B(2) of the 1912 Act excluded any liability of the general employer of a pilot thus providing what would have been an additional reason for the conclusion in Fowles's (at 641), case had the provision then been in force. Wilson and Dawson JJ both reached a similar conclusion as to the effect of s 410B(2). In their dissenting judgments, Brennan and Dean JJ both considered that the reasoning in Fowles's case should not be applied to a trading corporation empowered to employ licensed pilots for reward. Brennan J expressed the further view that s 410B(2) did not affect the relationship between the master of the ship and the pilot in connection with the conduct of the ship by the pilot and that the owner of the ship and the general employer of the compulsory pilot were both liable to a plaintiff whose damage was caused by the negligence of the pilot in the conduct of the ship. I would respectfully agree with the reasoning and conclusions of the majority of the judges of the High Court and I decline Hall Russell's invitation to adopt the reasoning of Brennan J in relation to s 410B(2).

My Lords, it may be stated as a general rule that the employer of a qualified licensed pilot is not vicariously responsible to the owner of a ship damaged by his negligence while under pilotage. All the authorities support such a rule and none appear to controvert it. The basis of the rule is twofold, namely (1) the pilot is an independent professional man who navigates the ship as a principal and not as a servant of his general employer and (2) s 15(1) makes him the servant of the shipowner for all purposes connected with navigation.

In stating this rule I am not going so far as to say that an employer of a licensed pilot could never be responsible for his negligent navigation. It is theoretically possible that such an employer could himself assume the obligation of safe pilotage, although at the moment I have very great difficulty in envisaging a situation in which such an event could occur. However, it is unnecessary to speculate further since there is nothing in the present case to take it out of the general rule. It follows that I would reject Hall Russell's second argument on this branch of the case.

On the whole matter I would allow Esso's appeal so far as it relates to the declaratory conclusion and quoad ultra dismiss their appeal and the appeal and cross-appeal of Hall Russell.

Interlocutors of Inner House of 10 July 1987 varied and, as varied, affirmed. First appeal and cross-appeal in second appeal dismissed.

Solicitors: *Thomas Cooper & Stibbard*, agents for *Boyd Jameson & Young WS*, Edinburgh (for Esso); *S J Berwin & Co*, agents for *Morton Fraser & Milligan WS*, Edinburgh (for Hall Russell); *Elborne Mitchell*, agents for *Dundas & Wilson CS*, Edinburgh (for SIC); *Ingledew Brown Bennison & Garrett*, agents for *Maclay Murray & Spens*, Edinburgh (for the second and third named third parties).

Mary Rose Plummer   Barrister.

Greenwich London Borough Council v Powell and another

a

HOUSE OF LORDS

LORD BRIDGE OF HARWICH, LORD TEMPLEMAN, LORD GRIFFITHS, LORD ACKNER AND LORD LOWRY

7, 8 NOVEMBER, 8 DECEMBER 1988

b

Local authority – Caravan sites – Provision of caravan sites – Duty of local authority – Duty to provide accommodation for gipsies – Gipsies occupying caravans on site seasonally as main or only residence – Whether sites 'protected sites' – Whether occupants entitled to security of tenure – Caravan Sites Act 1968, s 6 – Mobile Homes Act 1983, s 5(1).

c A caravan site provided by a local authority in the discharge of its duty under s 6[a] of the Caravan Sites Act 1968 to accommodate those whom it bona fide believes to be gipsies because they are nomadic for part of the year is not a 'protected site' within s 5(1)[b] of the Mobile Homes Act 1983 thereby entitling the occupants to security of tenure under that Act, notwithstanding that they may occupy the caravans as their main or only residence and may establish a permanent residence on the site by returning from year to year.

d Moreover, even if the occupants give up their erstwhile nomadic way of life entirely such a site will still not become a protected site unless the local authority adopts a policy of offering vacancies on the site to static residents who have fixed full-time employment (see p 69 *j* to p 70 *a d e* and p 71 *b c f* to *h*, post).

Notes

e For the powers of local authorities with respect to the provisions of caravan sites, see 29 Halsbury's Laws (4th edn) para 118.

For the Caravan Sites Act 1968, s 6, see 32 Halsbury's Statutes (4th edn) 503.

For the Mobile Homes Act 1983, s 5, see ibid 517.

Cases referred to in opinions

f *Mills v Cooper* [1967] 2 All ER 100, [1967] 2 QB 459, [1967] 2 WLR 1343, DC.

West Glamorgan CC v Rafferty, R v Secretary of State for Wales, ex p Gilhaney [1987] 1 All ER 1005, [1987] 1 WLR 457, CA.

Appeal

g Greenwich London Borough Council appealed with leave of the Appeal Committee of the House of Lords given on 9 June 1988 against the decision of the Court of Appeal (Purchas LJ and Heilbron J) on 23 February 1988 allowing an appeal by the defendants, George Powell and Harriett Powell, against the order of his Honour Judge James sitting in the Woolwich County Court on 3 November 1988 whereby, on the application of the council under CCR Ord 24, he ordered that the Powells give up possession of pad J1 at

h the Thistlebrook Caravan Site, Harrow Manorway, London SE2, owned by the council. The facts are set out in the opinion of Lord Bridge.

John R Macdonald QC and *C P L Braham* for the council.

Nigel Pascoe QC and *David Wade* for the Powells.

j **LORD BRIDGE OF HARWICH.** My Lords, the appellants are the local authority for the London borough of Greenwich. I shall refer to them as 'the council'. The respondents are Mr and Mrs Powell. I shall refer to them as 'the Powells'. The council own a caravan

---

a   Section 6, so far as material, is set out at p 67 *a b*, post

b   Section 5(1), so far as material, is set out at p 68 *b*, post

site known as the Thistlebrook Caravan Site at Abbey Wood, London SE2. The Powells occupy part of the site known as pad J1, on which they are permitted to station two *a* caravans pursuant to the terms of an agreement with the council. In October 1986 the council gave the Powells four weeks' notice to quit and in November 1986 they instituted proceedings for possession. The Powells pleaded in defence that the Thistlebrook site was a 'protected site' as defined by s 5(1) of the Mobile Homes Act 1983. An agreement under which a person is entitled to station a caravan on a protected site and to occupy it as his only or main residence may only be terminated as provided by Sch 1 to the 1983 Act. *b* The Powells' agreement has never been so terminated and there is no dispute that they occupy the caravans as their only or main residence. Hence the only issue in the case is whether the Thistlebrook site is a 'protected site' as defined by s 5(1). On 3 November 1987 his Honour Judge James at the Woolwich County Court held that it was not and made an order for possession. On 23 February 1988 the Court of Appeal (Purchas LJ and Heilbron J) held that it was and allowed the Powells' appeal. The council now appeal by *c* leave of your Lordships' House.

The issue raised is one of great importance for local authorities. It can only be understood in the context of the historical development of the legislation governing caravan sites.

In the 1950s the mushrooming of residential caravan sites to alleviate the acute shortage of conventional housing presented many problems to local planning authorities *d* which their powers under the Town and Country Planning Acts were inadequate to resolve. The first direct statutory control over caravan sites as such was imposed by the Caravan Sites and Control of Development Act 1960. This established a system of licensing of caravan sites by local authorities which gave effective control over both the establishment of new sites and the conditions under which sites were required to be operated. Section 24 of the Act gave power to local authorities themselves to provide *e* both residential and holiday sites within their areas and to acquire land compulsorily for the purpose. Sites provided by local authorities, since they were themselves the licensing authorities, were not required to be licensed: see para 11 of Sch 1.

Part I of the Caravan Sites Act 1968 introduced for the first time a very limited form of statutory security of tenure for the occupier of a residential caravan on a 'protected site' *f* as defined by s 1(2), either as licensee of a pitch on which to station his own caravan or as occupier of a caravan belonging to the site owner. In each case his contractual right could only be determined by four weeks' notice and he could only be evicted by court order. The court was given power to suspend enforcement of an eviction order 'for such period not exceeding 12 months from the date of the order as the court thinks reasonable' and from time to time to extend the period of suspension for not more than 12 months at a *g* time: see s 4. This limited protection I shall refer to as 'the 1968 security of tenure'. A 'protected site' is defined by s 1(2), which provides:

'For the purposes of this Part of this Act a protected site is any land in respect of which a site licence is required under Part I of the Caravan Sites and Control of Development Act 1960 or would be so required if paragraph 11 of Schedule 1 to that Act (exemption of land occupied by local authorities) were omitted, not being *h* land in respect of which the relevant planning permission or site licence—(*a*) is expressed to be granted for holiday use only; or (*b*) is otherwise so expressed or subject to such conditions that there are times of the year when no caravan may be stationed on the land for human habitation.'

The effect of this definition is that the 1968 security of tenure is available to all occupiers *j* of residential caravans on local authority sites as well as on privately owned sites.

Part II of the 1968 Act, which came into force on 1 April 1970, attempted to resolve the problem of providing orderly caravan sites to accommodate the gipsy community and of controlling unauthorised gipsy encampments. By the definition in s 16—

'"gipsies" means persons of nomadic habit of life, whatever their race or origin, *a* but does not include members of an organised group of travelling showmen, or of persons engaged in travelling circuses, travelling together as such.'

Section 6 imposes a duty on local authorities—

'to exercise their powers under section 24 of the Caravan Sites and Control of Development Act 1960 (provision of caravan sites) so far as may be necessary to provide adequate accommodation for gipsies residing in or resorting to their area.'

b
Sections 10 to 12 impose a system of control of the unauthorised stationing of gipsies' caravans in the area of any local authority which is dependent on the designation of that area by the minister under s 12 as an area to which s 10 applies. The condition to justify designation under s 12 is that it must appear to the minister—

c 'either that adequate provision is made in the area for the accommodation of gipsies residing in or resorting to the area, or that in all the circumstances it is not necessary or expedient to make any such provision.'

(See s 12(3).)

Within a designated area it is an offence under s 10 for a gipsy to station a caravan on land within the boundaries of a highway, on other unoccupied land or on occupied land
d without the consent of the occupier. Section 11 provides machinery for the expeditious removal by order of a magistrates' court of unauthorised gipsy caravans stationed in a designated area.

The policy underlying Pt II of the 1968 Act is, if I may say so, admirably described by Ralph Gibson LJ in *West Glamorgan CC v Rafferty* [1987] 1 All ER 1005 at 1010, [1987] 1 WLR 457 at 463:

e 'First, adequate accommodation is to be provided for gipsies in the area of the local authority in the interest of the gipsies themselves, giving them sites to which they can lawfully go and which will be supplied with facilities and supervised so that the sites will be maintained in decent order. Given some security of accommodation their children are more likely to get effective instruction in school.
f Any gipsies not complying with the regulations of the site may be ejected. Such sites will be better both for the travelling people who use them and for those who live near the sites. The second purpose of the legislation is plain from ss 10 and 12 of the 1968 Act.'

Ralph Gibson LJ then summarised the effect of ss 10 to 12 and continued ([1987] 1 All ER 1005 at 1010–1011, [1987] 1 WLR 457 at 463):
g
'The rest of the community is thus to an extent protected from visitation by gipsies trespassing on land, and camping on unregulated sites so as to cause nuisance, and sometimes damage, to those areas in which they trespass and the people living there.'

h The Mobile Homes Act 1975 gave greatly enhanced security of tenure to a person stationing his own caravan on a licensed caravan site for occupation as his only or main residence. The detailed provisions are elaborate and have now been superseded. It is sufficient, therefore, to say that, in substance, they gave the occupier statutory security of tenure for five years, renewable for a further three years. This I will call 'the 1975 security of tenure'. The 1975 Act, however, by its own definition of 'protected site', which I need not set out, deliberately excluded from the benefit of the 1975 security of tenure
j occupiers of caravans on all local authority sites.

The Mobile Homes Act 1983 replaced the main provisions of the 1975 Act and still further enhanced the security of tenure enjoyed by a person stationing his own caravan on an authorised site for occupation as his only or main residence. Subject to exceptions which are immaterial for present purposes, this security (the 1983 security of tenure) in substance continues indefinitely and is transmissible by sale or gift of the caravan. The

occupier cannot be evicted except by court order which may only be made on the
grounds, put shortly, (1) that the occupier is in breach of agreement and that it is *a*
reasonable for the agreement to be terminated, (2) that the occupier is not occupying the
caravan as his only or main residence, (3) that the condition of the caravan is detrimental
to the amenity of the site (see Sch 1, Pt I, paras 4, 5 and 6). For present purposes, the all-
important change effected by the 1983 Act, as compared with the 1975 Act, is to extend
the 1983 security of tenure to caravans stationed on all local authority sites except gipsy
sites. This change is effected by the definition in s 5(1) of the 1983 Act, which reads: *b*

> '"protected site" does not include any land occupied by a local authority as a
> caravan site providing accommodation for gipsies . . . but, subject to that, has the
> same meaning as in Part I of the Caravan Sites Act 1968.'

The question on which this case turns is whether the Thistlebrook site is occupied by the
council 'as a caravan site providing accommodation for gipsies'. It is common ground *c*
that the question must be answered by reference to the site as a whole, not by reference
to individual pads or pitches.

The facts may not have been investigated at the trial as fully as they might have been
if the issues canvassed in the Court of Appeal and before your Lordships had been fully
anticipated. But the essential primary facts are not, I think, in dispute. The Thistlebrook
site was acquired by the council by compulsory purchase in 1967 under s 24 of the 1960 *d*
Act. Before acquisition the site was occupied by a number of caravan dwellers who may
or may not have been persons of nomadic habit of life. The trial judge gave an interesting
account of the historical background leading to the compulsory purchase, but treated it,
as I think rightly, as irrelevant to the issues. In the Court of Appeal there was produced
for the first time the report of the inspector who held an inquiry into objections to the
council's compulsory purchase order and this report was admitted without objection as *e*
additional evidence. The Court of Appeal seem to have attached some importance to it,
but there are two reasons why I find it difficult to draw any relevant inferences from the
case made for the council in support of the compulsory purchase order as reported by the
inspector. First, the acquisition was effected long before the council had any statutory
duty to provide accommodation for gipsies. Second, the evidence is silent as to what *f*
happened to the site between 1967 and 1972. The most the inspector's report proved of
possible relevance was that a few of the caravan dwellers now resident on the site had
been there before 1967 and objected to the compulsory purchase order.

The evidence of the principal witness for the council, which the judge accepted, was
that the site was opened in three stages between October 1972 and December 1973 as a
site to provide accommodation for gipsies in discharge of the council's duty under s 6 of *g*
the 1968 Act. The Powells were among the first to come on the site after it was opened.
The site had 54 pads, of which some, like that occupied by the Powells, accommodated
more than one caravan. In May 1974 the Secretary of State for the Environment made
the Gipsy Encampments (Designation of the London Borough of Greenwich) Order
1974, SI 1974/920. The order recites that it appears to the Secretary of State that adequate
provision is made in the London borough of Greenwich for the accommodation of *h*
gipsies residing in or resorting to that area and designates it as an area to which s 10 of
the 1968 Act applies. The order must necessarily be read as referring to the Thistlebrook
site as this was the only caravan site provided for by the council, and hence the only site
in the borough purporting to provide accommodation for gipsies.

The Powells both gave evidence which the judge accepted. Mr Powell said that he was
a gipsy by race and proud of it. Their evidence was that they did seasonal work fruit- *j*
picking away from the Thistlebrook site which had usually been for four to five months
a year. In 1987 they had been absent for three months. They had one residential caravan
(presumably left permanently at Thistlebrook) and one mobile caravan (presumably used
on their travels). Their pattern of life was typical of many others resident on the

Thistlebrook site. They and all the other occupants of the site had their permanent
a residence there and many others, like the Powells, had been there for many years.

The council's principal witness produced in evidence a helpful schedule, again accepted
by the judge, showing absences from the site in 1986 and 1987. A substantial number of
occupants of pads on the site had been absent from the site for periods up to five months
in each year and for longer than could reasonably be accounted for as holiday absences.
The clear inference from this evidence taken together with the Powells' evidence was
b that these occupiers were seasonal workers like the Powells who went on their travels in
their caravans for substantial periods of the year moving from place to place to find work.
It is not without significance that the site rules which were incorporated in occupiers'
agreements with the council allowed occupiers to be absent from the site for up to 20
weeks in any one year (or for longer if agreed in writing with the council) and to retain
their right to return by paying for the weeks of absence half the fixed weekly payments
c provided for in their agreements. This appears to have been designed to make provision
for persons following just such a pattern of life as the Powells.

The judge held that the character of the site was determined by the purpose of the
council to occupy it as a site providing accommodation for gipsies and that this was
affirmed by the order made by the Secretary of State for the Environment in 1974 under
s 12 of the 1968 Act designating the London borough of Greenwich as an area to which
d s 10 applies. He had no material to indicate any subsequent change in the council's
purpose. On this view he did not find it necessary to decide whether those presently
occupying the site were persons of nomadic habit of life. On the evidence, in particular
the schedule of absences in 1986 and 1987, he indicated that 'it would if applicable have
been my conclusion that none of those now occupying Thistlebrook are at the present
time of nomadic habit of life'. The Court of Appeal held that the status of the site was
e determined by the character of those presently occupying the site and that none were
persons of nomadic habit of life. Hence the site was a 'protected site' as defined by s 5(1)
of the 1983 Act and the Powells' agreement giving them the right to occupy had never
been determined.

In *Mills v Cooper* [1967] 2 All ER 100, [1967] 2 QB 459 the Divisional Court had to
consider the meaning of the word 'gipsy' in s 127 of the Highways Act 1959 without the
f aid of any statutory definition. The section provides:

'If, without lawful authority or excuse . . . (*c*) . . . a gipsy pitches a booth, stall or
stand, or encamps, on a highway, he shall be guilty of an offence . . .'

Lord Parker CJ said ([1967] 2 All ER 100 at 103, [1967] 2 QB 459 at 467):

g 'I think that, in this context, "gipsy" means no more than a person leading a
nomadic life with no, or no fixed, employment and with no fixed abode.'

Diplock LJ indicated his view that 'gipsy' in the section bore—

'its popular meaning, which I would define as a person without fixed abode who
leads a nomadic life, dwelling in tents or other shelters, or in caravans or other
h vehicles.'

(See [1967] 2 All ER 100 at 104, [1967] 2 QB 459 at 468.)

Both Lord Parker CJ and Diplock LJ rejected the argument that 'gipsy' in the context
referred only to a person of Romany race.

It is difficult to think that the draftsman of the 1968 Act did not have these passages in
j mind when he provided the definition of 'gipsies' in s 16. He could have defined them as
'persons of nomadic habit of life and of no fixed abode', but he did not. Moreover, the
duty imposed by s 6(1) is to provide accommodation 'for gipsies *residing in* or resorting to
their area'. I am inclined to conclude from these indications alone that a person may be
within the definition if he leads a nomadic life only seasonally and notwithstanding that

he regularly returns for part of the year to the same place where he may be said to have a
fixed abode or permanent residence.

But we are only concerned with the definition of 'gipsies' in s 16 of the 1968 Act, so to
speak, at one remove. What we have directly to construe is the definition of 'protected
site' in the 1983 Act. It was for this reason that I thought it necessary to trace the
legislative history in some detail. This made it clear that from 1968 to 1983 the only
security of tenure enjoyed by a caravan resident on any local authority site was the 1968
security of tenure. Meanwhile, from 1970 to 1983 local authorities up and down the
country, and in particular London boroughs, were doing their best to discharge their
duty under s 6 of the 1968 Act to provide sites for gipsies in accordance with policy
guidance issued to them by the Department of the Environment. Likewise, local
authority areas were being designated under s 12 of the 1968 Act, in order to make
available the important powers of control over unauthorised gipsy caravans under ss 10
and 11, in accordance with the view then taken as to what could amount to 'adequate
provision ... for the accommodation of gipsies residing in or resorting to' the local
authority area.

It was only when the 1983 Act came into force that it became important to distinguish
between local authority sites 'providing accommodation for gipsies' and other local
authority sites, because it was then for the first time that the crucial distinction between
the security of tenure enjoyed by caravan residents on the two classes of site was
introduced. The Bill which became the 1983 Act was a government Bill and it would be
quite unrealistic not to recognise that the distinction between the two classes of site made
in the statute must have been made with full knowledge of the policy which had been
followed since 1970 with regard to the performance by local authorities of their duty
under s 6 of the 1968 Act. That policy, whilst technically inadmissible as an aid to the
construction of the definition of 'gipsies' in s 16 of the 1968 Act, is, in my opinion, fully
cognisable as a powerful pointer to the intention of the legislature in excluding local
authority sites 'providing accommodation for gipsies' from the definition of 'protected
site' in the 1983 Act.

The available indications of the relevant policy are twofold. First, your Lordships have
had the advantage of seeing Department of Environment circular 28/77 issued to local
authorities in England on 25 March 1977. The appendix to that circular is headed 'Gipsy
Caravan Sites. Notes for the Guidance of Local Authorities in the Implementation of Part
II of the Caravan Sites Act 1968'. Paragraph 5 of the notes observes perspicaciously:

> 'The criterion "nomadic habit of life" leads to a certain ambiguity, especially in
> relation to gipsies who settle for lengthy periods on authorised sites.'

But later passages in the notes firmly grasp the nettle of this ambiguity and encourage
local authorities to provide sites to accommodate gipsies in four categories as follows: (1)
emergency stopping places (paras 55 and 56); (2) transit or short-stay sites (para 57); (3)
residential sites (paras 58–60); (4) permanent sites for long-term residential use (paras 61–
65). The last of these categories can only have had in contemplation sites such as that at
Thistlebrook to which gipsies return year after year as their permanent residence but
from which they set forth at certain seasons to pursue their traditional nomadic way of
life.

Second, there is ample evidence that the policy advocated in the circular with regard
to permanent sites for long-term residential use had been recognised by the Secretary of
State as an appropriate criterion before 1977 for application under s 12 of the 1968 Act
in deciding whether adequate provision had been made in a local authority area for the
accommodation of gipsies to justify designation of the area. The undisputed evidence of
the council's principal witness at the trial, which the judge accepted, was that 17 other
London boroughs besides Greenwich had been designated under s 12 on the basis that
they had made adequate provision for the accommodation of gipsies on sites which were
operated on similar lines to the Thistlebrook site, ie by providing permanent

accommodation for gipsies as a home base from which they pursued their nomadic habit
a of life only seasonally. At least eight of these designation orders were made by statutory
instruments dated between 1973 and 1975.

These considerations confirm me in the opinion that, even if there is an ambiguity in
the definition of 'gipsies' in s 16 of the 1968 Act, the intention of the legislature in the
1983 Act was clearly to exclude from the definition of 'protected site' sites such as that at
Thistlebrook provided by local authorities in discharge of their duty under s 6 of the
b 1968 Act to accommodate those whom they bona fide believe to be gipsies because they
are nomadic for part of the year, notwithstanding that they may establish a permanent
residence on the site by returning from year to year. Such a site will not become a
'protected site' even if some of the erstwhile nomads, as well they may, give up their
nomadic way of life entirely. It would be different, of course, if the local authority
adopted a policy of offering vacancies on the site to static residents with fixed full-time
c employment, but this is hardly ever likely to happen.

Any other construction of 'protected site' in s 5(1) of the 1983 Act would, it seems to
me, cause great difficulties both for local authorities and for most of the gipsy community
and would undo much of the good work which has been done in this difficult field.
Those already established on sites like Thistlebrook would, of course, enjoy full 1983
security of tenure. But local authorities in the position of the council would need to start
d de novo to discharge their duty under s 6 of the 1968 Act. Many existing designations
under s 12 would have to be revoked or would perhaps be automatically invalidated.
Your Lordships were told that, on the strength of the Court of Appeal's decision, some
proceedings had already been instituted seeking judicial review of existing orders made
under s 12. For the future, local authorities establishing new sites providing
accommodation for gipsies would have to be vigilant to prevent their residence acquiring
e any degree of permanency. This, I think, they could in practice only do by applying a
short rule-of-thumb limit of stay, which would be quite contrary to the interests of the
gipsy community.

I would accordingly allow the appeal, set aside the order of the Court of Appeal and
restore the order of the Woolwich County Court.

f **LORD TEMPLEMAN.** My Lords, for the reasons given by my noble and learned
friend Lord Bridge, I would allow this appeal.

LORD GRIFFITHS. My Lords, I agree that this appeal should be allowed for the
reasons given in the speech of my noble and learned friend Lord Bridge.

g **LORD ACKNER.** My Lords, I have had the advantage of reading the speech of my
noble and learned friend Lord Bridge, and I would allow this appeal.

LORD LOWRY. My Lords, I have had the advantage of reading in draft the speech of
my noble and learned friend Lord Bridge. I respectfully agree with it and for the reasons
h given by him I would allow the appeal.

Appeal allowed.

Solicitors: *Colin Roberts* (for the council); *Thos Boyd Whyte*, Bexleyheath (for the Powells).

Mary Rose Plummer   Barrister.

R v Inner South London Coroner, ex parte Kendall

QUEEN'S BENCH DIVISION

PARKER LJ AND SIMON BROWN J

19, 20, 27 MAY 1988

Coroner – Inquest – Verdict – Solvent abuse – Death occurring as result of casual glue sniffing – Whether death by drug abuse appropriate verdict.

Where death is caused by casual glue sniffing the appropriate verdict is death by solvent abuse or a similar verdict, rather than death by drug abuse (see p 76 *g* to p 77 *d* and p 78 *b c*, post).

Notes

For the coroner's verdict, see 9 Halsbury's Laws (4th edn) paras 1120, 1122, and for cases on the subject, see 13 Digest (Reissue) 180–182, *1544–1563*.

Cases referred to in judgments

Bradford v Wilson [1984] RTR 116, DC.

R v Inner West London Coroner, ex p De Luca [1988] 3 All ER 414, [1988] 3 WLR 286, DC.

R v Portsmouth Coroner, ex p Anderson [1988] 2 All ER 604, [1987] 1 WLR 1640, DC.

Cases also cited

Rapier (decd), Re [1986] 3 All ER 726, [1988] QB 26, DC.

R v West London Coroner, ex p Gray [1987] 2 All ER 129, [1988] QB 467, DC.

Application for judicial review

Maria Kendall, the mother of Graham Kendall deceased, applied, with the leave of Henry J given on 22 January 1988, for, inter alia, judicial review by way of (i) an order of certiorari to quash the verdict of acute abuse of drugs recorded by HM Coroner for Inner South London sitting at Southwark Coroner's Court on 11 February 1987 at an inquest into the death of the deceased and (ii) an order of mandamus requiring a fresh inquest to be held by another coroner. The facts are set out in the judgment of Simon Brown J.

Edward Fitzgerald for the applicant.

Terence Coghlan for the coroner.

Cur adv vult

27 May. The following judgments were delivered.

SIMON BROWN J (giving the first judgment at the invitation of Parker LJ). On Friday, 8 August 1986 Lee Kendall, a boy just turned 14, died tragically in a Bermondsey park after inhaling the solvent trichloroethane, better known as Tipp-Ex thinning fluid. It was a much publicised case. The shopkeeper who supplied the boy was prosecuted and sent to prison for three months, a sentence which was then increased to four months when he imprudently appealed to the Crown Court.

On 11 February 1987 an inquest was held. It was conducted by the then coroner for Southwark sitting alone without a jury. At the end of the hearing, having found the cause of death to be trichloroethane over-dosage, the coroner recorded his verdict thus: 'Acute abuse of a drug.' This verdict has greatly distressed Lee's family. They are deeply upset by the stigma which understandably they believe to attach to it. Lee's mother now seeks to quash this offending part of the inquisition and to ensure that no further verdict

shall make any reference whatever to drugs. The proceedings consist of both an
a application under s 6 of the Coroners Act 1887 brought with the Attorney General's fiat
and an application for judicial review pursuant to leave. For the purposes of this
judgment we are proceeding solely under this latter jurisdiction. Under the statute,
indeed, as matters presently stand, the Divisional Court, as opposed to a single judge, is
not empowered to make an order. More fundamentally than that, however, this court
has wider powers at common law as to the relief which can be granted. In particular, we
b are entitled to grant relief short of an order for a fresh inquest, something that could not
be done under the statute.

The essential grounds of challenge are these. First, even if the coroner was entitled to
arrive at the disputed verdict, he was certainly not bound to do so and thus he misdirected
himself in law and improperly fettered his discretion in regarding himself as having no
alternative here but to enter this particular verdict. Second, and yet more fundamentally,
c it is argued that trichloroethane is not a drug, so that this particular verdict was simply
not open to the coroner. At an earlier stage of these proceedings other grounds were
advanced. In particular it was contended that the coroner failed to make full inquiry or
to call evidence sufficient to satisfy himself beyond reasonable doubt that Lee inhaled
this volatile substance voluntarily and intentionally, the necessary precondition of any
verdict of abuse, whether of a drug or a solvent. Very sensibly, however, counsel for the
d applicant on instructions did not pursue these additional grounds before the court. They
must inevitably have failed: the evidence supporting the coroner's conclusions on the
basic circumstances of this tragic death is overwhelming and irrefutable. It accordingly
becomes unnecessary to relate the underlying facts in any great detail. Shortly they are as
follows. On 22 July 1986, just over a fortnight before he died, Lee's parents found him
inhaling Tipp-Ex thinners in his sister's bedroom at home. They sought to impress on
e him the dangers of solvent abuse, glue sniffing as it is colloquially known, and they
confined him to the house as a punishment. Plainly, however, this could not continue
indefinitely, and after Lee's birthday on 3 August he again became free to join his friends.
The evidence clearly established that he was one of a group of boys who used to meet
together in a den formed by a clump of bushes in a public park hear where they lived.
f On Thursday, 7 August, the day before he died, it is clear that Lee was again affected by
this solvent. Although the statement of one of the group, a boy of 12, suggested that Lee
was on that occasion forced to swallow it, the other four vehemently denied any such
thing. Whatever may have been the true position as to this, it is really now of no
significance either way. Certain it is that, at about midday on the Friday, Lee returned to
the park entirely of his own volition and again voluntarily inhaled this lethal solvent. All
g the medical evidence points irresistibly to this conclusion. At 1.15 pm Lee was found by
a member of the public lying next to an empty Tipp-Ex bottle. Efforts were made to
resuscitate him both there in the park and again when he was taken by ambulance to
Guy's Hospital. Sadly they failed. Lee had paid with his life for a euphoric high lasting
but a few seconds. The mechanics of death were described by the pathologist at the
inquest as follows:

h
> 'Normally the thinners are taken by sniffing. They can be taken by ingestion, but
> by far the commonest way is to sniff or inhale the drug. It is rapidly absorbed
> through the nasal lining, it entered the brain extremely rapidly, and one normally
> finds that where acute deaths occur they occur because of an effect on the heart, or
> an effect on the heart combined with an effect on the brain, and that this effect is
> rapid.'

j
As I have said, the coroner's basic conclusions on the facts were inevitable and, indeed,
so much is not now in issue. But immediately having reached those conclusions and after
stating that he would record that Lee had died from trichloroethane over-dosage the
coroner continued thus: '. . . and his death was, I have to put I am afraid, due to acute
dependence on drugs.'

That unfortunate slip of the tongue, as the coroner deposes and clearly it was in referring to drug dependence rather than abuse, precipitated the family's outraged intervention in the inquest proceedings. They protested that Lee had not been a drug addict. The coroner thereupon corrected his verdict to one of 'acute abuse of drug'. The family remained dissatisfied. Their protests to the coroner continued. I need not recite the exchange in its entirety. Suffice to relate two of the coroner's closing observations: 'I am afraid if it was only done on one occasion and he died from it then it would have had to have been that verdict,' and, finally, 'I am afraid the verdict is laid down by law.'

During this final period of the inquest there were in fact a total of five passages in the coroner's remarks which in my judgment establish conclusively that he regarded himself as bound to enter the verdict which finally he announced. In such view, however, he was plainly wrong. It is necessary at this stage to refer to the legislation. First the governing statute, the Coroners Act 1887, as amended. By s 4(3) it is provided:

> 'After hearing the evidence the jury [here the coroner alone] shall give their verdict, and certify it by an inquisition in writing, setting forth, so far as such particulars have been proved to them, who the deceased was, and how, when, and where the deceased came by his death.'

Section 4(4) requires there also to be found certain particulars required for the Registration Acts. By s 18(2) of the 1887 Act an inquisition is enabled to be made in such form as is from time to time prescribed 'or to the like effect, and the statements therein may be made in concise and ordinary language'.

I come next to the Coroners Rules 1984, SI 1984/552, those currently in force. Rule 36, under the heading 'Matters to be ascertained at inquest', provides as follows:

> '(1) The proceedings and evidence at an inquest shall be directed solely to ascertaining the following matters, namely—(a) who the deceased was; (b) how, when and where the deceased came by his death; (c) the particulars for the time being required by the Registration Acts to be registered concerning the death.
> (2) Neither the coroner nor the jury shall express any opinion on any other matters.'

Rule 42 reads:

> 'No verdict shall be framed in such a way as to appear to determine any question of—(a) criminal liability on the part of a named person, or (b) civil liability.'

More relevant still is r 60, which provides:

> 'The forms set out in Schedule 4, with such modifications as circumstances may require, may be used for the purposes for which they are expressed to be applicable.'

Form 22 in Schedule 4 is entitled 'Inquisition'. So far as relevant it provides for findings on the following matters:

> '1. Name of the deceased (if known):
> 2. Injury or disease causing death:
> 3. Time, place and circumstances at or in which injury was sustained:
> 4. Conclusion of the jury/coroner as to the death:
> 5. [Registration Acts particulars].'

The scheduled form then contains certain notes. Note 2 reads:

> 'In the case of a death from natural causes or from industrial disease, want of attention at birth, or dependence on, or non-dependent abuse of, drugs insert the immediate cause of death . . .'

Note 4 reads:

a
'(a) Where the cause of death is one to which Note 2 applies, it is *suggested* that one of the following forms be adopted . . . [The deceased] died from dependence on drugs/non-dependent abuse of drugs . . .' (My emphasis.)

It may be observed that the suggested verdict 'non-dependent abuse of drugs' made its first appearance in those 1984 rules. The equivalent notes to the predecessor rules in 1953 (the Coroners Rules 1953, SI 1953/205, Sch 3, Form 18, note 5(a)) suggested instead

b
possible verdicts of 'chronic alcoholism/addiction to drugs'. As to those verdicts, moreover, contemporary commentaries in *Jervis on Coroners* (9th edn, 1957) and Home Office circular 68/1955, App 4, para 3, emphasised that they referred only to the deaths of confirmed alcoholics or drug addicts; deaths due to poisoning resulting from an excess of alcohol or drugs were recommended to be treated as accidental.

In short, as counsel for the coroner rightly recognises, even assuming that this

c
particular verdict is appropriate, there was certainly no compulsion whatever on the coroner to enter it. Rule 60 merely introduces a particular form which 'with such modifications as circumstances may require, *may* be used', and note 2 to the form merely 'suggests' a particular form of words.

It inevitably follows that the applicant succeeds on her first ground: this verdict must be quashed so that a proper discretion may be exercised. But such a limited order would

d
still leave it open to the coroner to return the same verdict as before. It is therefore necessary to turn to the applicant's more fundamental contention, that not only was a verdict of drug abuse not forced on the coroner but rather it was not even open to him. Put shortly, counsel for the applicant argues that, even if in any circumstances trichloroethane can reasonably be characterised as a drug, it certainly cannot be so described for the purposes of a coroner's verdict.

e
There is before the court a great deal of evidence on this issue. It includes opposing views from highly qualified experts. In support of the coroner's approach Professor Griffith Edwards, the professor of addictive behaviour at the University of London, whose many qualifications well justify his description as an expert of the very greatest eminence, argues:

f
'It is fully in accord with medical and scientific usage to describe Lee's death as being due to acute abuse of a drug and such a statement also conveys an intelligible and correct meaning to the general public.'

I should mention that one of the grounds for Professor Edwards's opinion is the particular definition given to the term 'drug' by the World Health Organisation. Expressing the rival view, Dr Toseland, professor of clinical chemistry at Guy's Hospital,

g
prefers the definition of the word 'drug' in the *Concise Oxford Dictionary* as 'medicinal substance, used alone or as ingredient'. Because trichloroethane has never been used for therapeutic purposes and there is no general acceptance of the description of it as a drug, he asserts that it is not one. He further deposes to having dealt with 'literally hundreds of solvent abuse deaths and knows that they are generally described as accidental deaths', a contention which appears to be borne out by some of the statistical material before us as

h
to the type of verdicts returned in these cases, although this evidence is difficult to interpret given that the verdict now at issue was not introduced even as a suggestion until 1984. It is in my judgment wholly unnecessary, indeed unprofitable, to attempt any detailed analysis of all this evidence. It seems to me perfectly plain that in some contexts solvents can properly be described as drugs, in others not; as counsel for the coroner conceded, it is impossible to provide a definition for universal application. One

j
context where such a definition is appropriate is in relation to motoring offences, where there exists a plain social purpose for arriving at this construction. In *Bradford v Wilson* [1984] RTR 116, an appeal by case stated from a defendant's conviction for being in charge of a motor vehicle when unfit to drive through drugs, having inhaled solvent from a tin of Evo-Stik, Robert Goff LJ said:

'Accordingly, adopting a commonsense approach, I would say, without attempting to give a definition, that, as a general rule, a substance which is taken into the *a* human body by whatever means—for example by inhalation, or by injections, or by mouth—which does not fall within the description "drink" (because that is specifically mentioned in the subsection) and which is not taken as a food, but which does affect the control of the human body, may be regarded as a drug for the purposes of this section. A particular example of such a substance is one which has a narcotic effect on the human body. That provides, I hope, some guidance as to what *b* can properly be regarded as a drug for these purposes.'

The most crucial words in that passage are the last three: 'for these purposes.' It may further be noted that the only reason why drink fell to be excluded from that approach was 'because that is specifically mentioned in the subsection'. In my judgment, therefore, this authority provides not the least assistance to us in our task of determining whether *c* or not trichloroethane is properly capable of being described as a drug for the purposes of a coroner's verdict on drug abuse. Looking at the matter in the particular context in which it now arises for our decision, I have not the least doubt that it cannot. As it seems to me, two central considerations should be in mind when determining the proper approach to the various forms of verdict suggested in the notes to the scheduled form of inquisition.

d

The first such consideration is the application within the coroner's jurisdiction of a clearly established policy of avoiding so far as possible any necessary stigma to the memory of the deceased. It is a reflection of this policy that a verdict of suicide will only be entered if established beyond all reasonable doubt, if in truth there is no other possible conclusion to be drawn from the circumstances of the death. It was doubtless this same policy which occasioned the removal from the Coroners Rules 1984 of the suggested *e* verdict of 'chronic alcoholism', such a verdict being needlessly offensive and wounding to the memory of the deceased. Rules 36(2) and 42 are further indications of such a policy existing in this part of our law. The other crucial consideration is the actual purpose of these various suggested forms of verdict. The primary, if not indeed the sole, purpose of entering a verdict of the kind here in question must surely be to alert the public to certain specific dangers. It is this desirable social end which, on occasion, *f* outweighs the first consideration and justifies departure from the policy of not stigmatising the deceased.

Viewed in the light of those considerations, it seems to me plain that the verdict with which we are here concerned was both unnecessarily wounding to the deceased's family and positively misleading in so far as it was designed to warn the public against the dangers of solvent abuse. It is flawed by the twin vices of being both offensive and yet *g* uninformative. Its offensiveness is obvious: the very word 'drugs' evokes clear overtones of addiction and criminality. As to its being uninformative, I do not accept for a moment that the general public would recognise within the expression 'acute abuse of drug' this sort of casual glue-sniffing. Still less do I accept Professor Edwards's conclusion:

'It is in the public interest that inhalation of volatile solvents such as trichloroethane *h* should be recognised as a form of drug abuse which can have an acutely or immediately fatal outcome.'

Rather I believe the inclusion within that sentence of the word 'drug' to be not merely optional but unjustifiable. It is moreover difficult to reconcile with Professor Edwards's earlier comment under the heading 'Terminology' when he says the correct term for this *j* activity is 'volatile substance abuse', the term 'solvent abuse' being roughly synonymous, and the phrase 'glue sniffing' being often loosely employed. It really cannot be in the public interest to publish a verdict which, so far from alerting people to the highly dangerous nature of this particular activity, is instead likely to mislead them. A press report of death by drug abuse must inevitably convey to the general public the sordid

image of heroin or cocaine addiction rather than this boy's casual stupidity. In short,
a such a verdict in the instant case seems to me to produce the worst of all possible worlds
and I have not the least doubt that it should not stand.

Counsel for the coroner invited the court to give clear guidance whether solvents are
or are not drugs for the purposes of coroners' verdicts. He told us that in the past some
coroners have treated them as such, others have not. It is to be hoped that this judgment
will provide that guidance and ensure that henceforth solvent abuse deaths are not so
b designated. What verdict then should be entered on such a death? In my judgment the
lawful options are these.

(1) Accident, or just possibly misadventure. Although commentators have hitherto
suggested that these verdicts carry distinctive meanings, in which event misadventure
might be thought the more appropriate of the two in the circumstances of the present
case, Mann J in the recent case of *R v Portsmouth Coroner, ex p Anderson* [1988] 2 All ER
c 604 at 609, [1987] 1 WLR 1640 at 1646 suggests that the term misadventure 'should
now be given its quietus'. I wish to say nothing to encourage its resurrection.

(2) Any of the following expressions: 'Abuse of volatile substances', 'solvent abuse',
'sniffing Tipp-Ex thinners', 'inhalation of Tipp-Ex thinners'.

(3) Any of the above terms could properly be used in combination. Thus it would be
perfectly lawful to enter a verdict of 'accidental death resulting from the inhalation of
d Tipp-Ex thinners', or 'solvent abuse: inhalation of Tipp-Ex thinners'.

After all, the statutory obligation is merely to record 'in concise and ordinary language'
the coroner's verdict on 'how . . . the deceased came by his death', and this in the context
of a form of inquisition in which, before entering his 'Conclusion as to . . . the death', the
coroner has already recorded both 'Trichloroethane overdosage' as the 'Injury or disease
causing death' and also 'that the deceased sniffed Tippex thinners' as part of the entry
e under the heading 'Time, place and circumstances at or in which injury was sustained'.

One might indeed be forgiven for wondering whether anything further than that was
strictly required by way of verdict. Certainly no criticism could have been made of an
inquisition recording 'inhalation of trichloroethane' as the 'Injury . . . causing death' and
'solvent overdosage' as the coroner's conclusion: it seems to me that the two together
f really constitute the coroner's conclusion as to 'how . . . the deceased came by his death'
and thus the verdict properly so called. And, indeed, it may be noted that in the standard
form headed 'Coroner's Certificate after Inquest', attached to the form of inquisition
itself, there twice appears a space for insertion of the 'Cause of death', one of these
moreover under the general heading 'Part IV. Accident or Misadventure . . .', and the
coroner completed both thus: 'Trichloroethane overdosage—acute abuse of drugs.'

g With those thoughts in mind it therefore seems to me for consideration whether the
present draft form of inquisition and notes thereto are entirely sensible and satisfactory.
We, of course, do not know precisley what use the responsible authorities make of these
inquisitions, or indeed of the annexed coroner's certificates. But, in so far as these records
are intended as information for research, I for my part would have thought that they
could with advantage be redesigned. It should then be possible to secure both greater
h uniformity of approach by coroners up and down the country, and also information
better adapted to statistical analysis. If, for example, as I assume to be the case, it is useful
for the Home Office to monitor the incidence of death by solvent abuse, perhaps indeed
by reference to particular substances with a view to taking controlling measures, then
clearly this form, whilst helpful in parts, is for the reasons already stated misleading in
its conclusion.

j To return to this application. As I have said, this verdict cannot stand. Must we
therefore quash the inquisition in its entirety? Such a course would involve a fresh
hearing, further public expense and renewed distress to Lee's family. We conclude not.
And this despite our being told that coroner has retired, so that any further step must
now be taken by his successor. As stated, there can be no doubt as to the correctness of
the other conclusions recorded on this inquisition: the actual cause of death is not in

doubt. All therefore that remains is for a decision to be taken on an appropriate label to describe in general terms the character of this death. Thus the verdict alone should be *a* quashed. In my judgment such a course is clearly open to the court. Not only was this identical relief granted in the recent case of *R v Inner West London Coroner, ex p De Luca* [1988] 3 All ER 414, [1988] 3 WLR 286, but it is consistent also with this court's increasing flexibility of response and remedy in the ever-developing field of judicial review.

In the result I would quash the verdict of death by the abuse of a drug and remit the *b* inquisition to the new coroner for Inner South London to enter such verdict as he considers proper in the light of this judgment.

PARKER LJ. I agree.

Application granted. Verdict quashed. Case remitted for new verdict to be entered.   *c*

Solicitors: *Simons Muirhead & Burton* (for the applicant); *Hempsons* (for the coroner).

Sophie Craven   Barrister.

d

Leverton v Clwyd County Council

HOUSE OF LORDS

LORD BRIDGE OF HARWICH, LORD TEMPLEMAN, LORD GRIFFITHS, LORD ACKNER AND LORD GOFF OF CHIEVELEY   *e*

23, 24 NOVEMBER, 15 DECEMBER 1988

Employment – Equality of treatment of men and women – Same employment – Woman employed as nursery nurse by local authority under same collective agreement as male comparators – Comparators working in different establishments from woman – Woman enjoying longer holidays and working less hours than male comparators – Whether woman employed 'in the same ***f*** *employment' as comparators – Equal Pay Act 1970, s 1(6).*

Employment – Equality of treatment of men and women – Variation between woman's and man's contracts due to material difference other than sex – Material factor – Hours of work and holidays – Woman enjoying longer holidays and working less hours than male comparators – Whether difference in hours of work and holidays a material factor – Whether variation in woman's ***g*** *contract and contracts of male comparators genuinely due to material factor other than the difference of sex – Equal Pay Act 1970, s 1(3).*

The appellant, a woman, was employed by the respondent local authority as a qualified nursery nurse at a salary of £5,058 a year. Her hours of work were 32 hours a week and she was required to work only during school terms. She claimed to be doing work of *h* equal value to the work of male employees employed by the authority in other establishments under the same collective agreement for local authority administrative, professional, technical and clerical staff by which the appellant's salary was determined and claimed that she was entitled to equal pay by virtue of s 1(2)(c)ᵃ of the Equal Pay Act 1970. The male comparators were paid between £6,081 and £8,532 a year but worked longer hours and had less holidays. However, there was no substantial difference between *j* the appellant's salary and the salary of the comparators when the rates of pay and hours worked were translated into a notional hourly rate. The industrial tribunal dismissed her

---

a   Section 1(2), so far as material, is set out at p 87 *h j*, post

claim on the grounds that the appellant was not employed 'in the same employment' as
a the male comparators for the purposes of s 1(6)[b] of the 1970 Act and that the variation
between her pay and theirs was genuinely due to a material factor other than the
difference of sex, namely the difference in working hours and length of holidays, and
therefore under s 1(3)[c] of the 1970 Act the equality of pay provisions did not apply. The
appellant appealed to the Employment Appeal Tribunal, which affirmed the decision on
the ground that the appellant and the male comparators were not in the same
b employment although it rejected the industrial tribunal's finding that the variation
between the contracts of the appellant and the comparators was due to a material factor
other than the difference of sex. On appeal, the Court of Appeal affirmed the conclusion
of both tribunals that the appellant and the male comparators were not employed in the
same employment but rejected the conclusion of the Employment Appeal Tribunal that
the respondents had not established the material factor defence. The appellant appealed
c to the House of Lords.

Held – (1) In deciding whether a woman and a man employed by the same employer at
different establishments were 'in the same employment' for the purposes of s 1(6) of the
1970 Act the appropriate comparison was a comparison between the terms and conditions
of employment at both the establishment where the woman was employed and the
d establishment where the male comparator was employed and applicable either generally
(ie to all the employees at the relevant establishments) or to a particular class or classes of
employees to which both the man and woman belonged. Accordingly, where the terms
and conditions of employment observed at two or more establishments were governed
by the same collective agreement they were common terms and conditions as defined by
s 1(6). It followed that the appellant was employed 'in the same employment' as the
e comparators (see p 82 b c e to p 83 a and p 89 f to h, post).
(2) However, since there was no significant difference between the notional hourly
rates of pay of the appellant and the male comparators, the clear inference was that the
substantial difference in working hours and holidays between the appellant and the
comparators was a 'material factor' within s 1(3) of the 1970 Act which genuinely
accounted for the difference in their annual salaries, and that difference had nothing to
f do with the difference in sex. It followed that the appellant was not entitled to equality
of pay with the comparators and the appeal would therefore be dismissed (see p 86 g to j
and p 89 a b f to h, post); *Jenkins v Kingsgate (Clothing Productions) Ltd* [1981] 1 WLR 1485
and *Rainey v Greater Glasgow Health Board* [1987] 1 All ER 65 applied.

g **Notes**
For equal treatment of men and women regarding terms and conditions of employment,
see 16 Halsbury's Laws (4th edn) para 767 and 52 ibid paras 21.11–21.12, and for cases
on the subject, see 20 Digest (Reissue) 579–595, 4466–4523.
For the Equal Pay Act 1970, s 1, see 16 Halsbury's Statutes (4th edn) 188.

h **Cases referred to in opinions**
Bilka-Kaufhaus GmbH v Weber von Hartz Case 170/84 [1987] ICR 110, CJEC.
Bromley v H & J Quick Ltd [1988] ICR 623, CA.
Edwards (Inspector of Taxes) v Bairstow [1955] 3 All ER 48, [1956] AC 14, [1955] 3 WLR
410, HL.
Hayward v Cammell Laird Shipbuilders Ltd [1988] 2 All ER 257, [1988] AC 894, [1988] 2
j WLR 1134, HL.
Jenkins v Kingsgate (Clothing Productions) Ltd [1981] 1 WLR 1485, EAT.

---

b   Section 1(6), so far as material, is set out at p 81 b, post
c   Section 1(3) is set out at p 81 a, post

Macarthys Ltd v Smith Case 129/79 [1981] 1 All ER 111, [1981] QB 180, [1980] 3 WLR
  929, CJEC and CA.   *a*
National Coal Board v Sherwin [1978] ICR 700, EAT.
Rainey v Greater Glasgow Health Board [1987] 1 All ER 65, [1987] AC 224, [1986] 3 WLR
  1017, HL.

Appeal
Marion Leverton, who was employed as a nursery nurse by the respondents, Clwyd   *b*
County Council, appealed with leave of the Court of Appeal against the decision of that
court (May, Balcombe and Stocker LJJ) ([1988] IRLR 239) on 17 March 1988 dismissing
her appeal against the decision of the Employment Appeal Tribunal (French J, Mr J A
Powell and Mr G H Wright) ([1987] 1 WLR 65) on 11 June 1986 whereby it dismissed
her appeal against the decision of the industrial tribunal (chairman Mr J A O Shand)
sitting at Shrewsbury dated 12 July 1985 dismissing her application under s 1(2)(c) of the   *c*
Equal Pay Act 1970 as amended for equality of pay with male comparators who were not
nursery nurses but who like her were classified by the respondents as being in the
administrative, professional, technical or clerical services. The facts are set out in the
opinion of Lord Bridge.

Anthony Lester QC and *David Pannick* for the appellant.   *d*
G W Wingate-Saul QC and *Alistair Webster* for the respondents.

Their Lordships took time for consideration.

15 December. The following opinions were delivered.
                                                                                     e

LORD BRIDGE OF HARWICH. My Lords, the appellant is employed as a qualified
nursery nurse by the respondents at the Golftyn Infants' School, Connah's Quay, Clwyd.
On 4 September 1984 she applied to an industrial tribunal claiming under s 1(2)(c) of the
Equal Pay Act 1970, as inserted by the Equal Pay (Amendment) Regulations 1983, SI
1983/1794, that she was employed on work of equal value to that of male employees of   *f*
the respondents. The initial application was clearly defective in that it failed to name the
comparators. However, after obtaining on discovery particulars of the terms and
conditions of employment of some 200 men employed, as she is, in the administrative,
professional, technical and clerical (APT & C) services of the respondents, she nominated
11 male comparators by reference to whom the application proceeded. At the time of
the hearing by the industrial tribunal in June 1985 the appellant was in receipt of an   *g*
annual salary of £5,058. The annual salaries of the comparators ranged from £6,081 to
£8,532.
    By virtue of the equality clause deemed to be included in her contract of employment
under s 1(1) of the 1970 Act, the appellant, if she could establish that she was employed
on work of equal value to that of 'a man in the same employment', would prima facie be
entitled under s 1(2)(c) to have the terms of her contrtact treated as modified as provided   *h*
by the section to bring them into line with the terms of his contract. The far-reaching
scope of that modification appears from your Lordships' decision in *Hayward v Cammell
Laird Shipbuilders Ltd* [1988] 2 All ER 257, [1988] AC 894.
    The respondents resisted the appellant's claim, inter alia, on the grounds (1) that none
of the comparators was 'a man in the same employment' with the appellant, and (2) that
the variation between the appellant's contract and the contracts of the comparators was   *j*
'genuinely due to a material factor which is not the difference of sex'. These two grounds
relied on by the respondents, each, if well founded, sufficient to defeat the appellant's
claim, give rise to the two issues for decision in the present appeal. They depend on sub-
ss (6) and (3) respectively of s 1, which provides, so far as material, as follows:

'. . . (3) An equality clause shall not operate in relation to a variation between the
a   woman's contract and the man's contract if the employer proves that the variation
is genuinely due to a material factor which is not the difference of sex and that
factor—(a) in the case of an equality clause falling within subsection (2)(a) or (b)
above, must be a material difference between the woman's case and the man's; and
(b) in the case of an equality clause falling within subsection (2)(c) above, may be
such a material difference.
b   (6) . . . for purposes of this section . . . men shall be treated as in the same
employment with a woman if they are men employed by her employer or any
associated employer at the same establishment or at establishments in Great Britain
which include that one and at which common terms and conditions of employment
are observed either generally or for employees of the relevant classes.'

c   It will be necessary to examine some aspects of the facts in detail later, but it is
convenient at this point to summarise the facts which are of central importance. None of
the comparators works at the same establishment as the appellant. The appellant and all
the comparators, however, are employed on terms and conditions derived from the same
collective agreement known as the 'purple book', being a scheme agreed by the National
Joint Council for Local Authorities' APT & C Services. Under the terms of that agreement
d   the appellant's salary is on scale 1; the salaries of the comparators are at different points
on scales 3 and 4. The appellant's basic working week including paid lunch breaks is 32½
hours. Her holidays are coterminous with the school holidays. The comparators' basic
working week is 37 hours (in one case 39 hours). Their annual holiday entitlement is 20
days plus 8 statutory and 3 local holidays with increments after five years' service. The
effect of these differences is that each of the comparators works many more hours in the
e   year to earn his annual salary than the appellant works to earn hers. As one measure of
the extent of this differnce the respondents put forward for comparison at the hearing a
pro rata calculation of notional hourly income yielding figures of £4·42 for the appellant
and £4·40 for the comparator who works 37 hours a week and earns the maximum
salary under scale 4. Although rejecting this method of comparison as inappropriate, the
industrial tribunal appear to have accepted the accuracy of the arithmetical calculation.
f   The majority of the industrial tribunal held both that the appellant was not 'in the
same employment' with the comparators as that phrase is defined by s 1(6) and that the
respondents had established what it will be convenient to call 'the material factor defence'
under s 1(3) in that the variation between the appellant's contract and the comparators'
contracts was genuinely due to a material factor which was not the difference in sex, viz
the difference in working hours and length of holidays being a material difference
g   between her case and theirs. They accordingly dismissed the application. The minority
member dissented on both grounds. The Employment Appeal Tribunal affirmed the
decision of the industrial tribunal on the ground that the appellant and the comparators
were not in the same employment (see [1987] 1 WLR 65). They held, however, that the
industrial tribunal had erred in law in upholding the material factor defence on the
ground that there was no evidence capable of supporting a finding that the variation
h   between the appellant's contract and the comparators' contract was 'genuinely due' to a
material factor which was not the difference of sex. The Court of Appeal (May, Balcombe
and Stocker LJJ) ([1988] IRLR 239) affirmed by a majority (May LJ dissenting) the
conclusion of both tribunals that the appellant and the comparators were not in the same
employment and held by a majority (Balcome LJ dissenting) that there was evidence to
support the finding by the majority of the industrial tribunal that the respondents had
j   established the material factor defence and that there was accordingly no ground on
which the Employment Appeal Tribunal could reverse this finding as erroneous in law.
The appellant now appeals to your Lordships' House by leave of the Court of Appeal.
On the question of whether the appellant was in the same employment as the
comparators working at different establishments, the view which prevailed with the

majority of the industrial tribunal, the Employment Appeal Tribunal and the majority
of the Court of Appeal was that the comparison called for by s 1(6) was between the
terms and conditions of employment of the appellant on the one hand and of the
comparators on the other and that it was only if this comparison showed their terms and
conditions of employment to be 'broadly similar' that the test applied by the phrase
'common terms and conditions of employment' in s 1(6) was satisfied. The majority of
the industrial tribunal, affirmed by the Employment Appeal Tribunal and the majority
of the Court of Appeal, held that the difference in this case in working hours and holidays
was a radical difference in the 'core terms' of the respective contracts of employment
which prevented the comparison from satisfying the statutory test. The contrary view
embraced by the dissenting member of the industrial tribunal and by May LJ in the
Court of Appeal was that the comparison called for was much broader, viz a comparison
between the terms and conditions of employment observed at two or more establishments,
embracing both the establishment at which the woman is employed and the establishment
at which the men are employed, and applicable either generally, ie to all the employees
at the relevant establishments, or to a particular class or classes of employees to which
both the woman and the men belong. Basing himself implicitly on this view, the
dissenting member of the industrial tribunal expressed his conclusion in the matter
tersely. Having referred to the purple book, he said:

> '... 3 Within that agreement there are nine sections and numerous clauses. They
> do not apply, with few exceptions, to any particular grade. It is clearly a general
> agreement and not specific to any particular group or class of employee. 4 It is, in
> my opinion, beyond doubt that the [appellant] and the comparators are employed
> on common terms and conditions, ie the APT & C Agreement, and clearly it is
> within the provisions of section 1(6)...'

My Lords, this is an important difference in principle which depends on the true
construction of s 1(6). I have no hesitation in preferring the minority to the majority
view expressed in the courts below. It seems to me, first, that the language of the
subsection is clear and unambiguous. It poses the question whether the terms and
conditions of employment 'observed' at two or more establishments (at which the
relevant woman and the relevant men are employed) are 'common', being terms and
conditions of employment observed 'either generally or for employees of the relevant
classes'. The concept of common terms and conditions of employment observed generally
at different establishments necessarily contemplates terms and conditions applicable to a
wide range of employees whose individual terms will vary greatly inter se. On the
construction of the subsection adopted by the majority below the phrase 'observed either
generally or for employees of the relevant classes' is given no content. Terms and
conditions of employment governed by the same collective agreement seem to me to
represent the paradigm, though not necessarily the only example, of the common terms
and conditions of employment contemplated by the subsection.

But if, contrary to my view, there is any such ambiguity in the language of s 1(6) as to
permit the question whether a woman and men employed by the same employer in
different establishments are in the same employment to depend on a direct comparison
establishing a 'broad similarity' between the woman's terms and conditions of
employment and those of her claimed comparators, I should reject a construction of the
subsection in this sense on the ground that it frustrates rather than serves the manifest
purpose of the legislation. That purpose is to enable a woman to eliminate discriminatory
differences between the terms of her contract and those of any male fellow employee
doing like work, work rates as equivalent or work of equal value, whether he works in
the same establishment as her or in another establishment where terms and conditions
of employment common to both establishments are observed. With all respect to the
majority view which prevailed below, it cannot, in my opinion, possibly have been the
intention of Parliament to require a woman claiming equality with a man in another

establishment to prove an undefined substratum of similarity between the particular

a terms of her contract and his as the basis of her entitlement to eliminate any discriminatory differences between those terms.

On the construction of s 1(6) which I would adopt there is a sensible and rational explanation for the limitation of equality claims as between men and women employed at different establishments to establishments at which common terms and conditions of employment are observed. There may be perfectly good geographical or historical

b reasons why a single employer should operate essentially different employment regimes at different establishments. In such cases the limitation imposed by s 1(6) will operate to defeat claims under s 1 as between men and women at the different establishments. I take two examples by way of illustration. A single employer has two establishments, one in London and one in Newcastle. The rates of pay earned by persons of both sexes for the same work are substantially higher in London than in Newcastle. Looking at either the

c London establishment or the Newcastle establishment in isolation there is no sex discrimination. If the women in Newcastle could invoke s 1 of the 1970 Act to achieve equality with the men in London this would eliminate a differential in earnings which is due not to sex but to geography. Section 1(6) prevents them from doing so. An employer operates factory A where he has a long-standing collective agreement with the ABC union. The same employer takes over a company operating factory X and becomes

d an 'associated employer' of the persons working there. The previous owner of factory X had a long-standing collective agreement with XYZ union which the new employer continues to operate. The two collective agreements have produced quite different structures governing pay and other terms and conditions of employment at the two factories. Here again s 1(6) will operate to prevent women in factory A claiming equality with men in factory X and vice versa. These examples are not, of course, intended to be

e exhaustive. So long as industrial tribunals direct themselves correctly in law to make the appropriate broad comparison, it will always be a question of fact for them, in any particular case, to decide whether, as between two different establishments, 'common terms and conditions of employment are observed either generally or for employees of the relevant classes'. Here the majority of the industrial tribunal misdirected themselves

f in law and their conclusion on this point cannot be supported.

Before turning to the issue which arises directly for decision in relation to the material factor defence, it is appropriate to refer to certain wider considerations to which your Lordships' attention was drawn in the course of the argument. When considering an equal pay claim made by a woman under s 1(2)(c) of the 1970 Act with respect to any man who is in the same employment with her, subject to any material factor defence,

g which the industrial tribunal has a discretion to entertain at the preliminary stage, the industrial tribunal is obliged to refer the claim to an expert under s 2A(1) unless '(a) it is satisfied that there are no reasonable grounds for determining that the work is of equal value . . .' In this case the industrial tribunal was not so satisfied. Accordingly, the next step, if the material factor defence did not succeed at this stage, would be to refer the claim to an expert who would be required to carry out a job evaluation to determine, as

h between the applicant and each comparator, whether their work was of equal value. 'Job evaluation', a phrase derived from the language of s 1(5), is a term of art describing the highly sophisticated technique adopted by the English legislation to give effect to community law by measuring what, apart from 'like work' as defined by s 1(4), is to qualify as 'equal work' under art 119 of the EEC Treaty or 'work to which equal value is attributed' under art 1 of EC Council Directive 75/117. A general job evaluation study is

j a study undertaken of the jobs of all the employees, or of any group of employees, in an undertaking or group of undertakings which, as described in s 1(5), evaluates their jobs 'in terms of the demand made on a worker under various headings (for instance effort, skill, decision)'. Such a study may operate in two ways. If a woman's and a man's jobs are rated as equal by the study, she may claim the benefits of an equality clause in relation to him under s 1(2)(b). If a woman's and a man's jobs are rated as unequal by the study, the employer may rely on the study to defeat the woman's equal value claim under s 1(2)(c) in limine under s 2A(1) provided there are no reasonable grounds for determining that *a* the study itself discriminated on grounds of sex. Just how complex and sophisticated the process of job evaluation is required to be to satisfy the statutory criteria embodied in ss 1(5) and 2A(3) for eliminating sex discrimination will be appreciated by anyone who reads the judgments of the Court of Appeal in *Bromley v H & J Quick Ltd* [1988] ICR 623. Where, as here, there has been no relevant general job evaluation study, the expert, if the matter were referred to him, would have to apply the same technique of evaluation, as *b* required by the language of s 1(2)(c) 'work which . . . is, in terms of the demands made on her (for instance under such headings as effort, skill and decision), of equal value . . .', in carrying out what would be, in effect, an ad hoc job evaluation study as between the appellant and her comparators.

In the course of their very thorough examination of every aspect of this case, the industrial tribunal considered whether the differences in hours of work and holidays *c* between the appellant and the comparators might be a matter for assessment by the expert when considering the 'demands' made on them by their respective jobs. They concluded as follows:

> 'We are unanimously agreed that such an assessment would not fall within his expertise and experience of job evaluation studies and that the tribunal must address *d* itself to this fundamental difference.'

Your Lordships were assured by counsel appearing in the appeal, whose collective experience in this somewhat esoteric field of law must be unrivalled, that in job evaluation studies the demands made by different jobs have in practice always been assessed under whatever headings are adopted on a qualitative, not a quantitative, basis. That this is the correct basis, if English law is to conform to Community law, seems to *e* be amply borne out by the judgment of the Court of Justice of the European Communities in *Macarthys Ltd v Smith* Case 129/79 [1981] 1 All ER 111 at 118–119, [1981] QB 180 at 198; see also *National Coal Board v Sherwin* [1978] ICR 700. I have no doubt that demand in terms of hours worked is not only beyond the expertise of the job evaluator but is, on the true construction of s 1(2)(c) and (5), a factor which is outside the scope of job *f* evaluation.

It was suggested by counsel for the appellant, instructed not only by the appellant's union but also by the Equal Opportunities Commission, that in relation to the material factor defence the present appeal raised some great issue of principle which called for a general pronouncement by your Lordships' House in order to clarify the law as to the nature and scope of the burden which an employer must discharge when seeking to *g* justify a pay practice which has the effect, whether directly or indirectly, of differentiating between men and women. Since the decision of the industrial tribunal in the instant case there have been two judgments of first importance relevant to the consideration of a material factor defence: the judgment of the European Court in *Bilka-Kaufhaus GmbH v Weber von Hartz* Case 170/84 [1987] ICR 110 and the judgment of this House in *Rainey v Greater Glasgow Health Board* [1987] 1 All ER 65, [1987] AC 224. Although the industrial *h* tribunal did not have the advantage of the guidance afforded by those cases, they did consider and apply the principles which had been expressed in the judgment of Browne-Wilkinson J in *Jenkins v Kingsgate (Clothing Productions) Ltd* [1981] 1 WLR 1485 at 1492, to which the House in *Rainey*'s case gave its full approval. In the circumstances it does not appear to me that any new problem of law arises here for resolution. The speech of my noble and learned friend Lord Keith in *Rainey*'s case expressing the unanimous *j* opinion of the House, expounds the applicable principles, if I may say so, with admirable lucidity and it seems to me quite unnecessary for your Lordships in the instant case to traverse the same ground. The question which arises here is not what principles are applicable, but whether the applicable principles were correctly applied or, more accurately, whether there is any indication that the majority of the industrial tribunal

erred in principle or, to apply the well-known test in *Edwards (Inspector of Taxes) v*
a *Bairstow* [1955] 3 All ER 48 at 57, [1956] AC 14 at 36 per Lord Radcliffe, whether their
determination contradicted the 'true and only reasonable conclusion' to which the
evidence before them led.

I must now turn to examine in more detail the facts on which the material factor
defence depends. I have already referred to the notional calculation put forward by the
respondents to compare the appellant's salary with that of the comparators on an hourly
b rate basis. It is not wholly clear whether the respondents were advancing this in support
of a defence that the terms of the appellant's contract were not less favourable than those
of any of the comparators. If so, the industrial tribunal rightly rejected it as misconceived,
anticipating the decision of your Lordships' House in *Hayward v Cammell Laird Shipbuilders
Ltd* [1988] 2 All ER 257, [1988] AC 894. But the decision records that, if the method of
approach involved in this comparison were proper, the industrial tribunal would regard
c the respondents' point as 'well made'. It adds later that the comparison is viewed by the
majority as 'casting interesting light on the broader merits of the case'. The majority
must have had this comparison in mind, as they were entitled to, when considering the
material factor defence.

Between the date of the appellant's application to the industrial tribunal and the
hearing a difference between the staff side and the employers' side of the National Joint
d Council on rates of pay for the APT & C services of local authorities had been referred to
arbitration by the Central Arbitration Committee (the CAC) under s 3 of the Employment
Protection Act 1975. The arbitration resulted in an award which enhanced the pay of all
grades concerned, but also enhanced the pay of nursery nurses and nursing assistants
relative to other grades. The report of the CAC promulgating the award shows that the
relative remuneration of nursery nurses and nursing assistants, taking account of the
e difference in hours worked and holidays, was fully examined in the course of the
arbitration and the CAC report and award were naturally much relied on by the
respondents before the industrial tribunal. It is common ground, however, that an
arbitration under s 3 of the 1975 Act is not directly concerned with questions of sexual
discrimination.

f At the time of the hearing before the industrial tribunal a general job evaluation study
had been undertaken but not completed in relation to all the respondents' employees in
the APT & C services except nursery nurses and nursing assistants. These latter had been
excluded from the job evaluation study by agreement between the respondents and the
unions concerned on behalf of the nurses.

When the appellant appealed to the Employment Appeal Tribunal her case was taken
g up by the Equal Opportunities Commission. One of the grounds of appeal relied on was:

> '. . . the Industrial Tribunal failed to decide whether or not the pay difference was
> due to, that is caused by, the different working hours and holidays for the Appellant
> and the male comparables.'

Since it was to be argued that there was no evidence to establish the necessary causal link,
h the Equal Opportunities Commission wrote to the Employment Appeal Tribunal seeking
the chairman's notes of evidence and the request was passed on to the industrial tribunal.
A reply was written on behalf of the chairman dated 5 December 1988 enclosing certain
notes of evidence. The covering letter reads, so far as material:

> 'Further to your letter dated 26 November 1985, the Chairman directs me to say
> that his Notes of Submissions and Evidence cover 105 sides. He has refreshed his
j memory by going through the Notes. The question of causality raised at paragraph
> 3(ii)(d) of the Notice of Appeal was not raised at the Tribunal and not dealt with
> specifically in evidence. Any causal link can only be inferred from the evidence.
> The Chairman has extracted those passages that seem to him relevant . . .'

Although I have expressed my disagreement with the conclusion reached by the majority of the industrial tribunal on the issue which arose under s 1(6), I must express my admiration for the care, lucidity and thoroughness with which the majority examined *a* every issue in the case and explained the reasoning which led to their conclusions. In particular, they considered the implications of the differences in hours of work and holidays between the appellant and the comparators in great detail. They concluded that, though the appellant might in certain circumstances be required to work outside school hours, such work was of 'very limited significance'. Likewise hours worked outside the school term were 'extremely limited'.   *b*

In examining the effect of the CAC arbitration report and award, the majority directed themselves in the following terms:

> 'It is clear from the judgment of Mr Justice Browne-Wilkinson (as he then was) in
> *Jenkins v Kingsgate (Clothing Production) Ltd* ([1981] 1 WLR 1485 at 1495), that some
> parallel exists between the concept of material factor or material difference and the
> concept of justifiability of indirect sexual discrimination under the Sex Discrimina- *c*
> tion Act. It is for the respondents to show that the factor upon which they rely was
> reasonably necessary to achieve some objective other than an objective related to the
> sex of the worker.'

They concluded, in effect, that they could not safely rely on the CAC report and award per se and in advance of an expert job evaluation as necessarily having eliminated any *d* element of unintentional sex discrimination between the almost exclusively female nursery nurses and the male comparators employed in other APT & C services. It was suggested that there was some inconsistency between this conclusion and the conclusion that the difference in hours of work and holidays established the material factor defence. I see no such inconsistency. On the contrary the way in which the majority of the industrial tribunal dealt with the argument for the respondents based on the CAC report *e* and award leaves me in no doubt that they had the appropriate criteria of reasonable necessity and objective justifiability clearly in mind when they addressed the question whether, in their own judgment, the difference in hours of work and holidays as between the appellant and any comparator in receipt of the maximum salary on scale 4 established a material factor defence. In reciting the respondents' argument they clearly directed *f* themselves to the question whether 'the variation in pay is genuinely due to these different terms', sc the difference in hours of work and holidays, 'which constitute a material factor which is not the difference of sex'. They set out their conclusion in the following terms:

> 'The majority of the tribunal is satisfied at this stage on the evidence that we have
> heard that the differing contractual terms on hours and holidays are a genuine *g*
> material factor which make it reasonably necessary for the respondent to impose
> pay differentials between the applicant and the relevant comparators. We at this
> stage would dismiss the application upon the additional basis that the respondents
> have fully established that material factor defence.'

Looking no further, I should conclude that this was a finding of fact which was amply *h* justified by the evidence as a whole, but perhaps particularly by the comparison between the rates of pay and hours worked. Where a woman's and a man's regular annual working hours, unaffected by any significant additional hours of work, can be translated into a notional hourly rate which yields no significant difference, it is surely a legitimate, if not a necessary, inference that the difference in their annual salaries is both due to and justified by the difference in the hours they work in the course of a year and has nothing *j* to do with the difference in sex.

I cannot help thinking that the rejection of the material factor defence by the Employment Appeal Tribunal and by Balcombe LJ in his dissent on this point was due to the circumstance that they concentrated attention on the letter written on behalf of the chairman of the industrial tribunal six months after the hearing rather than on the

decision itself. It was this, I believe, which led them into error. I doubt if it was legitimate
a to attach any significance to the chairman's letter at all. But it certainly did not afford a
ground for impugning the decision if the decision itself was otherwise unassailable.
Equally, the enclosure with the letter of three pages of evidence which the chairman
presumably considered of immediate relevance could not justify confining attention to
that evidence alone, to the exclusion of all the other material summarised and examined
in the course of the decision, as the basis of any inference which the majority had drawn.
b   For these reasons I would dismiss the appeal.
    I cannot leave this case without adding a word about the procedure involved in equal
value claims under s 1(2)(c) of the 1970 Act. If such a claim is referred to an expert under
s 2A, the expert's job evaluation and the subsequent procedural steps which follow the
presentation of his report under the special rules of procedure governing equal value
claims in Sch 2 to the Industrial Tribunals (Rules of Procedure) Regulations 1985, SI
c 1985/16, will involve a lengthy, elaborate and, I apprehend, expensive process. The larger
the number of comparators whose jobs have to be evaluated, the more elaborate and
expensive the process is likely to be. Here, as already mentioned, the appellant spread her
net very widely by claiming equality with 11 comparators. But, by the time the case
reached the House, your Lordships were told that, if her appeal succeeded, she would
only seek a reference to an expert in relation to four of the original comparators. This
d only goes to show what a lot of time and money would have been wasted if the matter
had proceeded on a reference to an expert with respect to all the 11 comparators. I do not
in any way criticise the industrial tribunal in this case for deciding under s 2A(1)(a) that
they could not be satisfied that there were no reasonable grounds for determining her
work to be of equal value with any one of the comparators. But I think that industrial
tribunals should, so far as possible, be alert to prevent abuse of the equal value claims
e procedure by applicants who cast their net over too wide a spread of comparators. To
take an extreme case, an applicant who claimed equality with A who earns £X and also
with B who earns £2X could hardly complain if an industrial tribunal concluded that
her claim of equality with A itself demonstrated that there were no reasonable grounds
for her claim of equality with B. That said, however, it is right to point out that an
employer's most effective safeguard against oppressive equal vlaue claims is to initiate his
f own comprehensive job evaluation study under s 1(5), which, if properly carried out,
will afford him complete protection.

LORD TEMPLEMAN. My Lords, art 119 of the EEC Treaty requires and EC Council
Directive 75/117 (the Equal Pay Directive) reiterates that member states shall secure the
g elimination of all discrimination on grounds of sex in conformity with the principle of
equal pay for the same work or for work of equal value. The United Kingdom complied
with its Community obligations by the Equal Pay Act 1970 which was enacted, as its
title indicates, 'to prevent discrimination, as regards terms and conditions of employment,
between men and women'.
    By s 1(2)(c) of the 1970 Act (as inserted by the Equal Pay (Amendment) Regulations
h 1983, SI 1983/1794):

> 'where a woman is employed on work which . . . is, in terms of the demands
> made on her (for instance under such headings as effort, skill and decision), of equal
> value to that of a man in the same employment . . . (i) if . . . any term of the woman's
> contract is . . . less favourable to the woman than a term of a similar kind in the
> contract under which that man is employed, that term of the woman's contract shall
j > be treated as so modified as not to be less favourable . . .'

    In the present case the appellant, Mrs Leverton, claims under the 1970 Act salary
equality with men named by her and employed, like her, by the respondents, Clwyd
County Council. The appellant alleges that the men are paid more than her although her
work is equal in value to the work of the men. The respondents resist the appellant's

claim on the grounds, inter alia, that even if the work of appellant is equal in value to the work of the men, the difference in salary is not due to sex discrimination but is due to *a* the fact that the appellant enjoys a shorter working week and longer holidays than the men.

The appellant is employed as a nursery nurse at an infants school. Nursery nurses and the men with whom she claims salary equality are employed by the respondents in the administrative, professional, technical and clerical services of the council. The salary scales for men and women employed in such services are determined in default of *b* agreement by the Central Arbitration Committee (the CAC) appointed under s 10 of the Employment Protection Act 1975 to resolve trade disputes by arbitration. The CAC last made a relevant award in 1985 when special improvements were made to the salaries of nursery nurses. The respondents employ 400 nursery nurses, of whom all but one are women; they are paid salaries in accordance with scale 1 as determined and adjusted by the CAC in 1985. Other staff employed by the respondents include 205 paid on scale 3; *c* of these 148 are women. Other staff include 79 paid on scale 4; of these 42 are women. The difference between scale 1 and scale 3 salaries is roughly £1,000 per annum; the difference between scale 1 and scale 4 is roughly £1,500.

After initiating these present proceedings by making a general complaint that nursery nurses were unfairly paid, the appellant obtained discovery concerning over 200 employees of the council on scale 3 and scale 4. The appellant then complained of 11 *d* employees. The industrial tribunal found that of these 11, nos 6, 7 and 9 were the most obviously appropriate comparators. Number 6 is a library assistant employed in the library department of the council on scale 3. Number 7 is a driver/assistant employed in the library department on scale 3. Number 9 is a caretaker/supervisor employed in the administrative and legal department on scale 4. The appellant works 32½ hours a week against 37 hours worked by the men with whom she claims salary equality, apart from *e* one employee who works for 39 hours. The appellant enjoys 70 days holiday; the men are entitled to 20 days holiday plus increments after five years service. It has not been decided whether the work performed by the appellant is in fact equal in value to the work of one or more of the scale 3 and scale 4 men with whom she seeks salary equality. But even if work of equal value were established, the appellant is not entitled to equality *f* of salary unless the difference in salary is attributable to sex discrimination, conscious or unconscious. Article 119 of the EEC Treaty and the Equal Pay Directive and the 1970 Act are directed to the elimination of sex discrimination and not to the elimination of wage differences. Accordingly, s 1(3) of the 1970 Act (as amended) provides:

> 'An equality clause shall not operate in relation to a variation between the woman's contract and the man's contract if the employer proves that the variation *g* is genuinely due to a material factor which is not the difference of sex . . .'

The industrial tribunal found by a majority that the difference between the salary paid to the appellant and the salaries paid to the men she chose for comparison was not due to a difference of sex but to the difference between the hours worked and holidays enjoyed by the appellant, on the one hand, and her chosen comparators on the other hand. The *h* industrial tribunal decided that the difference in hours and holidays was a 'material factor' within the meaning of s 1(3) of the 1970 Act and that the difference in salaries was 'genuinely due' to that material factor. On behalf of the appellant it was said that there was no evidence that the difference in hours of work and holidays was a 'material factor'. But the difference between the hours and holidays of the appellant, on the one hand, and of the comparators on the other hand, is sufficiently striking to constitute prima facie *j* evidence of a material factor without calling any witness to say so. It was then said that there was no evidence that the difference between salaries corresponded exactly to the difference between hours and holidays. Exact correspondence is impossible to evaluate and unnecessary; s 1(3) only requires that the difference in salaries be 'genuinely due' to the difference in hours and holidays which constitutes the relevant 'material factor'. The

division of annual salary by hours worked attributed £4·42 for every hour worked by
a the appellant and £4·40 for every hour worked by the highest paid comparator. The
industrial tribunal rightly rejected the argument that this hourly calculation proved that
the appellant was paid as much as or more than the comparators. Nevertheless, the
calculation supported the respondents' contention that the difference in hours and
holidays was a material factor which genuinely accounted for the difference in annual
salary. The appellant did not produce any evidence to the contrary and did not produce
b any evidence which might have raised the suspicion that the difference in salary was due
to sex discrimination. In the course of this appeal it was said on behalf of the appellant
that for historical or other reasons the work of the CAC might be tainted, consciously or
unconsciously, by sex discrimination in favour of men and against women. The CAC
considered a submission that nursery nurses were underpaid and were informed on
behalf of local authorities that nursery nurses only worked a 32½ hour week. The CAC
c made its award in 1985 in the light of these and other submissions and must have been
fully cognisant of and desirous of giving effect to the principle of equal pay which formed
part of Community law when the United Kingdom joined the Community in 1972 and
which is embodied in the 1970 Act (as amended). The industrial tribunal by a majority
decided, on the evidence adduced, that the difference in hours and holidays was a material
factor which genuinely accounted for the difference in salary. The soundness of that
d decision is illuminated by a consideration of the results which might have followed a
finding in favour of the appellant. If she were entitled to an increase of £1,500 in her
annual salary, all scales 1, 3 and 4 employees could claim to be paid the same salary and
all scales 1, 3 and 4 employees could claim a 32½-hour working week and the enjoyment
of 70 days of holiday. Nursery nurses are not indispensable, and such a result could have
fatal consequences to the profession of nursery nurses and serious consequences for local
e authorities and all employees of local authorities. The elimination of sex discrimination
may produce results which are painful to employers and surprising to some employees.
But the industrial tribunal was not bound to assume sex discrimination against the
evidence or to tear up the CAC award in order to account for the difference between the
salary paid to nursing nurses and the salary paid to scale 3 and scale 4 employees, male
and female. The evidence entitled the industrial tribunal to conclude that the difference
f in salaries was genuinely due to the material factor that there was a substantial difference
in hours worked and holidays enjoyed.

For these reasons and for reasons given by my noble and learned friend Lord Bridge,
with whose speech I am in complete agreement, I would dismiss the appeal.

LORD GRIFFITHS. My Lords, I have had the advantage of reading in draft the speech
g of my noble and learned friend Lord Bridge. I agree with it and for the reasons he gives I
would dismiss this appeal.

LORD ACKNER. My Lords, I have had the advantage of reading in draft the speech
of my noble and learned friend Lord Bridge. I agree with it and for the reasons he gives I
h too would dismiss this appeal.

LORD GOFF OF CHIEVELEY. My Lords, for the reasons given by my noble and
learned friend Lord Bridge, I would dismiss this appeal.

Appeal dismissed.

j
Solicitors: *Pattinson & Brewer*, agents for *Nicola Jones*, Manchester (for the appellant);
Sharpe Pritchard, agents for *E R Ll Davies*, Mold (for the respondents).

Mary Rose Plummer   Barrister.

R v Manchester City Magistrates' Court, ex parte Davies

a

COURT OF APPEAL, CIVIL DIVISION
O'CONNOR, NEILL LJJ AND SIR ROGER ORMROD
22 JUNE, 29 JULY 1988

b

Magistrates – Civil liability – Limitation of damages – Magistrates acting without jurisdiction – Wrongful imprisonment – Magistrates committing applicant to prison for non-payment of rates – Non-payment not caused by applicant's wilful refusal or culpable neglect – Applicant granted certiorari quashing committal order – Applicant seeking damages against magistrates for unlawful imprisonment – Whether magistrates liable in damages – Whether damages limited to one penny – General Rate Act 1967, ss 96(1), 102, 103(1) – Justices of the Peace Act 1979, ss 45, 52.

c

The applicant received a rate demand for over £15,000 from the local authority in respect of his shop premises. When the applicant failed to pay, a distress warrant was issued on the council's application. The applicant paid off some £6,000 of the outstanding rates but the council applied for a warrant of committal in respect of the balance. His accountant advised him to close his business or go bankrupt but he decided not to follow that advice. At the hearing of the committal proceedings the magistrates decided that the applicant's failure to take his accountant's advice constituted 'culpable neglect' within s 103(1)*[d]* of the General Rate Act 1967 and committed him to prison, where he remained for almost eight weeks before being released on bail. He then sought judicial review of the committal warrant and damages. The judge found that the applicant's failure to pay the rates had not been caused by culpable neglect and he quashed the warrant but adjourned the claim for damages. When the claim came on for hearing the judge held that the applicant was entitled to damages to be assessed. The magistrates appealed, contending (i) that they had not acted outside or in excess of their jurisdiction when committing the applicant to prison, and therefore under s 45*[b]* of the Justices of the Peace Act 1979 were not liable at all in damages, and (ii) if they had, they were entitled to the protection of s 52*[c]* of the 1979 Act, which limited damages to one penny if, inter alia, the plaintiff 'had undergone no greater punishment than that assigned by law' for non-payment of the sum he was ordered to pay.

d

e

f

Held – The appeal would be dimissed for the following reasons—

g

(1) (Sir Roger Ormrod dissenting) Since by s 102*[d]* of the 1967 Act it was a statutory condition precedent to the issue of a committal warrant for non-payment of rates that the magistrates should conduct a proper inquiry, as required by s 103 of the 1967 Act, whether the defaulting ratepayer's failure to pay the rates had been caused by his wilful refusal or culpable neglect and since, on the facts, there was no connection between the applicant's decision not to follow his accountant's advice and his failure to pay the rates, the magistrates had failed to conduct such an inquiry and had acted outside or in excess of their jurisdiction when committing the applicant to prison. Accordingly, the magistrates were liable in damages under s 45 of the 1979 Act for acting outside or in excess of their jurisdiction when committing the applicant to prison (see p 93 g to j, p 94 d, p 95 a to c, p 98 g to p 99 a and p 101 a, post); *McC v Mullan* [1984] 3 All ER 908 considered.

h

j

<hr>

a   Section 103(1), so far as material, is set out at p 93 *de*, post
b   Section 45, so far as material, is set out at p 96 *d* to *f*, post
c   Section 52 is set out at p 92 *e* to *h*, post
d   Section 102, so far as material, is set out at p 93 *b c*, post

(2) Since the ordinary procedure provided by s 96(1)^e of the 1967 Act for non-payment
a of rates was the seizure and sale of the defaulting ratepayer's goods and chattels under a
distress warrant and since there was no provision for imprisonment for mere non-
payment of rates, the applicant had undergone a 'greater punishment than that assigned
by law' for non-payment of his rates and accordingly the damages to which he was
entitled were not limited to one penny under s 52 of the 1979 Act but were at large (see
p 95 *b c*, p 100 *h* to p 101 *a*, p 105 *g* to *j* and p 106 *a*, post); *R v Waltham Forest Justices,*
b *ex p Solanke* [1986] 2 All ER 981 considered.
   Decision of Simon Brown J [1988] 1 All ER 930 affirmed.

Notes
For the civil liability of magistrates, see 1 Halsbury's Laws (4th edn) paras 206–215 and
29 ibid paras 278–279, and for cases on the subject, see 1(1) Digest (Reissue) 183–195,
c 1091–1163.
   For the General Rate Act 1967, ss 96, 102, 103, see 36 Halsbury's Statutes (4th edn)
731, 736, 737.
   For the Justice of the Peace Act 1979, ss 45, 52, see 27 ibid 131, 135.

Cases referred to in judgments
d Anisminic Ltd v Foreign Compensation Commission [1969] 1 All ER 208, [1969] 2 AC 147,
   [1969] 2 WLR 163, HL.
Houlden v Smith (1850) 14 QB 841, 117 ER 323.
Liverpool Corp v Hope [1938] 1 All ER 492, [1938] 1 KB 751, CA.
McC v Mullan [1984] 3 All ER 908, [1985] AC 528, [1984] 3 WLR 1227, HL.
Marshalsea Case (1612) 10 Co Rep 68b, 77 ER 1027.
e O'Connor v Isaacs [1956] 2 All ER 417, [1956] 2 QB 288, [1956] 3 WLR 172, CA.
Polley v Fordham (No 2) (1904) 91 LT 525, [1904–7] All ER Rep 651, DC.
R v Waltham Forest Justices, ex p Solanke [1986] 2 All ER 981, [1986] QB 983, [1986] 3
   WLR 315, CA; affg [1985] 3 All ER 727, [1986] QB 479, [1985] 3 WLR 788.
R (ex p Vestry of St Mary, Islington) v Price (1880) 5 QBD 300, DC.
Willis v Maclachlan (1876) 1 Ex D 376, CA.
f

Case also cited
R v Birmingham Justices, ex p Turner (1971) 219 EG 585, DC.

Appeal
g The Manchester City Justices appealed against the decision of Simon Brown J ([1988]
1 All ER 930, [1988] 1 WLR 667) on 16 November 1987 whereby, on the hearing of the
issue of damages only and limited to certain agreed questions on a restored notice of
motion by the applicant, Barry Davies, for judicial review of an order of the justices on
16 July 1986 committing the applicant to prison for 90 days in respect of the non-
payment of rates of £9,303·83, the judge held that the justices were liable to the applicant
h for damages to be assessed for unlawful imprisonment of the applicant. The facts are set
out in the judgment of O'Connor LJ.

Mark Turner for the justices.
M P Sylvester for the applicant.

Cur adv vult
j
29 July. The following judgments were delivered.

O'CONNOR LJ. On 16 July 1986 the applicant was committed to prison for 90 days
for non-payment of rates by the Manchester City Magistrates. On 2 September 1986 he

---

e   Section 96(1) is set out at p 92 *j* to p 93 *a*, post

was given leave to move for judicial review of that order and on 5 September he was
released on bail. On 22 September 1987 Webster J quashed the decision of the magistrates   *a*
and adjourned the issue whether the applicant was entitled to recover damages against
them. On 16 November 1987 Simon Brown J gave judgment holding that the magistrates
had exceeded their jurisdiction and that the applicant was entitled to damages to be
assessed (see [1988] 1 All ER 930, [1988] 1 WLR 667). The respondents appeal against
that decision.

The appeal raises two important issues of law affecting the liability of justices sued for   *b*
damages for false imprisonment. Justices are afforded protection by statute under Pt V
of the Justices of the Peace Act 1979. The provisions with which we are concerned were
formerly contained in the Justices Protection Act 1848. Sections 44 and 45 have to be
read together. Section 44 protects a justice for an act done by him in the execution of his
duty with respect to any matter within his jurisdiction unless it is proved that the act was
done maliciously and without reasonable and probable cause. That protection is   *c*
withdrawn for acts done outside or in excess of jurisdiction by s 45, but if the act
complained of is done under any conviction or order no action lies unless the conviction
or order has been quashed. I must set out the relevant part of sub-s (1):

> 'This section applies—(*a*) to any act done by a justice of the peace in a matter in
> respect of which by law he does not have jurisdiction or in which he has exceeded   *d*
> his jurisdiction, and (*b*) to any act done under any conviction or order made or
> warrant issued by a justice of the peace in any such matter . . .'

The first issue is whether the justices acted outside or in excess of their jurisdiction in
committing the applicant to prison.

If that issue is decided in favour of the applicant the second issue arises under s 52,
which provides: *e*

> '(1) The provisions of this section shall have effect where, in any action brought
> against a justice of the peace for anything done by him in the execution of his office
> as such a justice, the plaintiff is (apart from this section) entitled to recover damages
> in respect of a conviction or order, and proves the levying or payment of a penalty
> or sum of money under the conviction or order as part of the damages which he   *f*
> seeks to recover, or proves that he was imprisoned under the conviction or order
> and seeks to recover damages for the imprisonment, but it is also proved—(*a*) that
> the plaintiff was actually guilty of the offence of which he was so convicted, or that
> he was liable by law to pay the sum he was so ordered to pay, and (*b*) where he was
> imprisoned, that he had undergone no greater punishment than that assigned by
> law for the offence of which he was so convicted or for non-payment of the sum he   *g*
> was so ordered to pay.
> (2) In the circumstances specified in subsection (1) above, the plaintiff shall not
> be entitled to recover the amount of the penalty or sum levied or paid as mentioned
> in that subsection or (as the case may be) to recover any sum beyond the sum of one
> penny as damages for the imprisonment, and shall not be entitled to any costs.'
>   *h*

The question is whether the justices are protected by sub-s (1)(*b*). I will consider these
issues in turn but, before I do so, I must consider the provisions of the General Rate Act
1967 which brought the applicant before the justices.

The statute provides a comprehensive code for the recovery of unpaid rates. No action
lies at the suit of a rating authority outside the provisions of the statute: see *Liverpool Corp
v Hope* [1938] 1 All ER 492, [1938] 1 KB 751. The prime provision is s 96, which   *j*
provides:

> '(1) Subject to section 62 of this Act and to subsection (2) of this section, if any
> person fails to pay any sum legally assessed on and due from him in respect of a rate
> for seven days after it has been legally demanded of him, the payment of that sum
> may, subject to and in accordance with the provisions of this Part of this Act, be

a   enforced by distress and sale of his goods and chattels under warrant issued by a magistrates' court; and, if there is insufficient distress, he may be liable to imprisonment under the provisions of this Part of this Act in that behalf . . .'

It will be seen that there is no power to imprison until after a properly issued distress warrant has been executed and a nil or insufficient return has been made. Sections 97 and 99 make detailed provision for the issue and execution of the distress warrant. Section 102 of the General Rate Act 1967 provides:

b

'*Imprisonment in default of sufficiency of distress.*—(1) If the person charged with the execution of a warrant of distress for levying a sum to which some other person has been rated makes a return to the magistrates' court that he could find no goods or chattels (or no sufficient goods or chattels) on which to levy the sums directed to be levied under the warrant on that other person's goods and chattels, a magistrates'

c   court may, if it thinks fit, and subject to the provisions of section 103 of this Act, (a) issue a warrant of commitment against that other person; or (b) fix a term of imprisonment and postpone the issue of the warrant until such time and on such conditions (if any) as the court thinks just . . .'

Section 103(1) is also relevant:

d

'*Inquiry as to means before issue of warrant of commitment.*—(1) Section 102 of this Act shall have effect subject to and in accordance with the following provisions:— (a) on the application for the issue of a warrant for the commitment of any person, the magistrates' court shall make inquiry in his presence as to whether his failure to pay the sum to which he was rated and in respect of which the warrant of distress was issued was due either to his wilful refusal or to his culpable neglect; (b) if the

e   magistrates' court is of opinion that the failure of the said person to pay the sum was not due either to his wilful refusal or to his culpable neglect, it shall not issue the warrant or fix a term of imprisonment . . .'

In the present case a distress warrant had been properly issued and a nil return made in 1985. For the proceedings in July 1986 proper notice had been given and the applicant

f   was before the court. It follows that the justices were entitled to embark on the s 103 inquiry as to means and were acting within their jurisdiction when they did so.

As Webster J has made clear in his judgment, that inquiry disclosed that there was no question of the applicant having wilfully refused to pay the rates. In the course of the hearing the applicant told the justices that in January 1986 his accountant had advised him to close down his business and to go bankrupt but that he had decided to see whether

g   he could weather the storm. The justices came to the conclusion that he had been guilty of culpable neglect in failing to take his accountant's advice, but again as Webster J pointed out that had nothing whatsoever to do with his failure to pay the rates. There was no causal connection between rejecting the advice of his acountant and the non-payment of the rates; for this reason Webster J quashed the decision. It follows that the only opinion open to the court was that failure to pay was not due either to wilful refusal

h   or to culpable neglect and in the result there was no power to imprison.

The very fact that the justices came to the conclusion that they did is strong evidence that they never carried out the inquiry required by s 103. An examination of the evidence filed on behalf of the justices demonstrates to my mind that they never did carry out the inquiry required by s 103. The affidavits of the three justices and that of their clerk show exactly what happened. I can summarise the proceedings as follows. (i)

j   The rating officer opened the case, told the court that £9,303·83 was owing, a portion of the 1985–86 rate. He gave the court the applicant's rating history and although the justices cannot remember the details they must have been told that in the previous 12 months the applicant had paid off £6,000. The rating officer then gave them details of the applicant's income and expenditure as given to him or his colleagues outside the courtroom and told the court that the applicant had made no offer as to how he could pay off the sum due. The applicant was asked if he agreed with what the rating officer had said and he said that he did. (ii) The applicant was asked what he wanted to say and he told the court what his domestic situation was, what his commitments were, how he had raised a loan on his house, sold his car and was waiting for the autumn when he expected a substantial revival of his business. In the course of what he said he told the court that his accountant had advised him in January 1986 and more than once since then that he should close down his business. (iii) The justices spent a considerable amount of time asking the applicant questions regarding his ability to pay, that is his ability as at that time. The court was told that he had received a further rates demand for the current year in the sum of £12,000, the applicant saying that he could pay nothing off the arrears for the next two or three months. (iv) The chairman sums up the matter in para 13 of his affidavit, which reads:

> 'My colleagues and I retired to consider and deliberate on the matter. We were of the opinion that the applicant had unreasonably failed to accept the professional advice given to him and as a result had unnecessarily worsened the financial position.'

This summary of the proceedings shows that what the court was doing was inquiring into the applicant's present means in order to ascertain what if anything he could reasonably be asked to pay off the arrears. I have some sympathy with the justices: they had 208 cases of rates defaults of one kind or another in their list with nine defaulters actually in court. Quite properly it is necessary to try and find out what the present financial position of a defaulter is and it seems to me that they overlooked the requirements of s 103 altogether.

I return to the issue under s 45 of the 1949 Act. This section was considered by the House of Lords in *McC v Mullan* [1984] 3 All ER 908, [1985] AC 528. That was a case from Northern Ireland but the relevant statutory provisions are the same. The justices had sentenced a juvenile offender to a custodial sentence in breach of art 15(1) of the Treatment of Offenders (Northern Ireland) Order 1976, SI 1976/226, which provides:

> 'A magistrates' court on summary conviction or a court of assize or county court on conviction on indictment shall not pass a sentence of imprisonment, Borstal training or detention in a young offenders centre on a person who is not legally represented in that court and has not been previously sentenced to that punishment by a court in any part of the United Kingdom, unless either—(a) he applied for legal aid and the application was refused on the ground that it did not appear his means were such that he required assistance; or (b) having been informed of his right to apply for legal aid and had the opportunity to do so, he refused or failed to apply.'

The defendant was unrepresented and had not been informed of his right to apply for legal aid. Lord Bridge reviewed the authorities, English and Irish, in great depth and concluded ([1984] 3 All ER 908 at 924, [1985] AC 528 at 552):

> 'Parliament plainly attached importance to ensuring that none of these custodial sentences should be imposed for the first time on a defendant not legally represented unless the defendant's lack of representation was of his own choice. The philosophy underlying the provision must be that no one should be liable to a first sentence of imprisonment, borstal training or detention, unless he has had the opportunity of having his case in mitigation presented to the court in the best possible light. For an inarticulate defendant, as so many are, such presentation may be crucial to his liberty. It is impossible to say in this or any other case that, if the requirements of art 15(1) had been satisfied, it would have made no difference to the result. For these reasons I am of opinion that the fulfilment of this statutory condition precedent to the imposition of such a sentence as the appellants here passed on the respondent is no less essential to support the justices' jurisdiction to pass such a sentence than, for

a   example, in the case of a sentence of immediate imprisonment, a prior conviction of an offence for which a sentence of imprisonment can lawfully be passed.'

Parliament plainly attached importance to ensuring that no one should be imprisoned for non-payment of rates unless it was established that his failure to pay was due to wilful refusal or culpable neglect. The inquiry required by s 103 is a statutory condition precedent to the imposition of a sentence of imprisonment and its fulfilment is essential
b   to support the justices' jurisdiction to impose it. In my judgment the first issue must be resolved in favour of the applicant.

It remains to consider the issue under s 52 of the Justices of the Peace Act 1979. Without deciding it I am prepared to accept that the judge was right in holding that the rate demand was sufficient to satisfy the requirement of para (a) but I am in no doubt that para (b) is not satisfied. The only punishment assigned by law for non-payment of
c   rates is the seizure and sale of goods and chattels under a distress warrant. It follows that the justices are not protected by s 52.

For these reasons I would dismiss this appeal.

NEILL LJ. In November 1984 the applicant entered into an underlease of shop premises at the Arndale Centre in Manchester. The underlease was for 20 years from 29 September
d   1984 at a rent of £14,250 per annum. According to the evidence of the applicant in later proceedings he understood at that time that the rates would be £2,700 per annum.

In December 1984, however, the applicant received a rate demand in the sum of £15,284·33. Believing that there was some mistake he immediately applied to the rating authority (the Manchester City Council) to have the rates reassessed. On 14 August 1985 a distress warrant was issued but there was insufficient distress on the premises to satisfy
e   the arrears. Between August 1985 and July 1986 the applicant managed to pay about £6,000 towards the rates demanded, but an unpaid balance of about £9,300 remained. No reduction had been made in the original demand for £15,284·33.

In July 1986 the rating authority applied to the justices for a committal order. On 16 July the matter came before the three justices who are the appellants in the present proceedings. The applicant appeared at the hearing. He was unrepresented. At the
f   conclusion of the hearing the justices made an order that the applicant be committed to prison for 90 days. He remained in prison until he was released on unconditional bail on 5 September 1986. Meanwhile on 2 September he was granted leave to challenge the warrant of commitment by way of proceedings for judicial review.

On 22 September 1987 the motion seeking an order to quash the committal order and a writ of habeas corpus came before Webster J. In addition the motion included a claim
g   for damages which had been added by leave of the court on 28 January 1987. Webster J had before him an affidavit sworn by the applicant and also affidavits sworn by each of the three justices and by the clerk of the court who had attended on 16 July 1986. On this occasion the applicant was represented by counsel. The justices were not represented. After hearing the submissions of counsel Webster J quashed the committal order and granted a writ of habeas corpus. At the same time he adjourned the claim for damages.
h   On 16 November 1987 the adjourned motion came before Simon Brown J. At that hearing both the applicant and the justices were represented. It was agreed between counsel that there were two questions for the decision of the court: (i) are the justices liable in damages for the applicant's unlawful imprisonment? (ii) if so, are such damages limited to one penny by s 52 of the Justices of the Peace Act 1979?

After hearing argument Simon Brown J answered both questions in favour of the
j   applicant, holding that the justices were liable in damages and that the damages were at large (see [1988] 1 All ER 930, [1988] 1 WLR 667). He ordered that the damages should be assessed by a master of the Queen's Bench Division pursuant to RSC Ord 37, r 1. The justices now appeal to this court.

The questions which were raised before Simon Brown J and which are now before this

court are of some general importance. In order to answer them it is necessary to consider
both the relevant legislation and the affidavit evidence. It is also necessary to have regard *a*
to the principles established in the decided cases and in particular to take account of the
guidance to be found in the speech of Lord Bridge in *McC v Mullan* [1984] 3 All ER 908,
[1985] AC 528.

I turn to the first question.

Are the justices liable in damages?   *b*

The applicant claims damages against the justices for unlawful imprisonment. In
order to succeed it will be necessary for him to satisfy the court that in making the order
for commitment the justices acted without jurisdiction or in excess of jurisdiction. The
applicant asserts that they did so act. The justices on the other hand, though they concede
that the order for commitment should not have been made, contend that it was an order
which was made within their jurisdiction.   *c*

It will be convenient to refer first to s 45 of the Justices of the Peace Act 1979, which,
so far as material, provides:

> '(1) This section applies—(*a*) to any act done by a justice of the peace in a matter
> in respect of which by law he does not have jurisdiction or in which he has exceeded
> his jurisdiction, and (*b*) to any act done under any conviction or order made or *d*
> warrant issued by a justice of the peace in any such matter; and in the following
> provisions of this section "the justice", in relation to any act falling within paragraph
> (*a*) above, means the justice of the peace by whom it is done, and, in relation to a
> conviction, order or warrant falling within paragraph (*b*) above, means the justice of
> the peace by whom the conviction or order is made or the warrant is issued.
> (2) Any person injured by an act to which this section applies may maintain an *e*
> action against the justice without making any allegation in his statement or
> particulars of claim that the act complained of was done maliciously and without
> reasonable and probable cause.
> (3) In respect of any act done under such conviction or order as is mentioned in
> subsection (1)(*b*) above no action shall be brought against the justice until the
> conviction or order has been quashed, either on appeal or upon application to the *f*
> High Court . . .'

It is therefore necessary to consider the meaning of the word 'jurisdiction' in s 45(1).

In *McC v Mullan* [1984] 3 All ER 908 at 912, [1985] AC 528 at 536 Lord Bridge drew
attention to the problem posed by the use of the word 'jurisdiction':

> 'There are many words in common usage in the law which have no precise or *g*
> constant meaning. But few, I think, have been used with so many different shades
> of meaning in different contexts or have so freely acquired new meanings with the
> development of the law as the word "jurisdiction".'

It is to be noted that in *Anisminic Ltd v Foreign Compensation Commission* [1969] 1 All ER
208 at 213, [1969] 2 AC 147 at 171 Lord Reid expressed the opinion that it is better not *h*
to use the term 'except in the narrow and original sense of the tribunal being entitled to
enter on the enquiry in question'. It is plain, however, that in s 45(1) 'jurisdiction' has a
wider meaning than this original meaning.

In his judgment in the present case Simon Brown J concluded that it was established
by the decision of the House of Lords in *McC v Mullan* that there were three categories of
case in which justices would be regarded as either not having jurisdiction or having *j*
exceeded their jurisdiction. I do not find it necessary to decide in the present case whether
these three categories are all-embracing, but I am content for the purposes of the present
case gratefully to adopt the judge's analysis.

In the first category are cases where the justices do not have 'jurisdiction of the cause'
to use the phrase of Coke CJ in *Marshalsea Case* (1612) 10 Co Rep 68b at 76a, 77 ER 1027

at 1038. A simple example of a case in this category is provided by *Houlden v Smith* (1850)
a 14 QB 841, 117 ER 323, where the plaintiff recovered damages because he had been
imprisoned by the order of a county court judge whose jurisdiction was limited to a
geographical area which did not include the town where the plaintiff lived and carried
on his business.

   In the second category are cases where the justices have properly entered on a summary
trial of a matter within their jurisdiction but where 'something quite exceptional' has
b occurred in the course of the proceedings so as to oust their jurisdiction. Lord Bridge
gave as an example of such an exceptional event a case where a justice absented himself
for part of the hearing and then relied on another justice to tell him what had happened
during his absence (see [1984] 3 All ER 908 at 920, [1985] AC 528 at 546–547). Lord
Bridge expressed the opinion that in such a case, because of the gross and obvious
irregularity of the procedure, the justices would have acted without jurisdiction or in
c excess of jurisdiction.

   As will appear when I come to consider the relevant legislation and the facts, the third
category of cases is the one which has particular relevance in the present appeal. In this
third category are cases where, though the justices have 'jurisdiction of the cause' and
may have conducted the trial impeccably, they may nevertheless be liable in damages on
the ground of acting in excess of jurisdiction if their conviction of the defendant or other
d determination does not provide a proper foundation in law for the sentence or order
made against him.

   In *McC v Mullan* the respondent to the appeal had earlier been convicted of a criminal
offence by a juvenile court and had been ordered to attend an attendance centre. He
failed to attend regularly and was then tried and convicted by the appellant magistrates
of the offence of failing to attend the attendance centre. For that offence the respondent
e was ordered to be detained at a training school. It was common ground that the
magistrates' court which sentenced the respondent to detention was properly constituted
and convened and that the proceedings were properly instituted. It was also common
ground that the respondent was properly tried and convicted. The magistrates were
nevertheless held to have acted without jurisdiction or in excess of jurisdiction because
f the respondent was not represented at the hearing and had not been informed of his
right to apply for legal aid. It was therefore held that a statutory condition precedent (as
provided in art 15(1) of the Treatment of Offenders (Northern Ireland) Order 1976, SI
1976/226) had not been observed, that the detention order was unlawful and that the
magistrates were liable to damages though they had a right to an indemnity.

   I come now to the relevant provisions of the legislation relating to the imprisonment
of a ratepayer for non-payment of rates.
g
   Section 102 of the General Rate Act 1967 (so far as material) provides:

   '(1) If the person charged with the execution of a warrant of distress for levying a
   sum to which some other person has been rated makes a return to the magistrates'
   court that he could find no goods or chattels (or no sufficient goods or chattels) on
   which to levy the sums directed to be levied under the warrant on that other person's
h goods and chattels, a magistrates' court may, if it thinks fit, and subject to the
   provisions of section 103 of this Act, (a) issue a warrant of commitment against that
   other person ...
   (5) The order in the warrant of commitment shall be that the said person be
   imprisoned for a time therein specified but not exceeding three months, unless the
   sums mentioned in the warrant shall be sooner paid ...'
j
   I come next to s 103(1) of the 1967 Act. This subsection provides:

   'Section 102 of this Act shall have effect subject to and in accordance with the
   following provisions—(a) on the application for the issue of a warrant for the
   commitment of any person, the magistrates' court shall make inquiry in his presence
   as to whether his failure to pay the sum to which he was rated and in respect of

which the warrant of distress was issued was due either to his wilful refusal or to his culpable neglect; (b) if the magistrates' court is of opinion that the failure of the said person to pay the said sum was not due either to his wilful refusal or to his culpable neglect, it shall not issue the warrant . . .'

It seems to me to be quite clear that the making of an inquiry under s 103(1)(a) is a statutory condition precedent to the issue of a warrant of commitment. In other words, if the justices failed to hold any inquiry at all as required by the section they would have no jurisdiction to issue a warrant. Nor would they have any jurisdiction if they were 'of opinion that the failure . . . to pay the . . . sum was not due either to his wilful refusal or to his culpable neglect'.

If the justices reached such a conclusion they would be deprived of jurisdiction to issue a warrant. It is also clear, though the point does not arise in the present case, that the justices would have no jurisdiction to issue a warrant of commitment which provided for a period of imprisonment in excess of three months.

In the present case the position is less clear cut because some inquiry about the applicant's finances was made. It therefore becomes necessary to consider the nature of the inquiry which the justices did carry out on 16 July 1986 and to assess the legal consequences of the defects in that inquiry.

In his judgment on 22 September 1987 Webster J set out the relevant passages in the affidavits of the three justices and in the affidavit of the clerk of the court. The judge summarised the matter in these terms:

'They appear to have paid no regard to the necessity of it being established, before they have a power to commit anyone to prison, that the failure to pay the rates demanded was due to that culpable neglect and none of the evidence is evidence of a conclusion, which was a necessary precondition of a committal order, that the applicant's failure to pay the rates due was due to his culpable neglect in failing to take his accountant's advice. Indeed, without a much more extensive inquiry as to his financial position than actually occurred, it would have been impossible to have made such a finding and any such finding would have been unsustainable in law. For instance, if the applicant had taken the accountant's advice, as one of the justices expresses it, and had gone bankrupt, it is improbable in the extreme that the rates would have been paid in full and quite possible, I imagine, that less would have been recovered from the bankruptcy than was in fact paid and, for these reasons alone, the committal order must be quashed.'

I understand this passage in the judgment of Webster J to amount to a finding by the judge that the inquiry which was carried out by the justices on 16 July 1986 was directed to finding an answer to the wrong question and that accordingly it did not constitute a sufficient inquiry as required by s 103(1)(a) of the 1967 Act.

It seems to me to follow that a statutory condition precedent to the exercise by the justices of their power to issue a warrant under s 102 was not satisfied. It may be that there will be cases under other statutes where a statutory inquiry is provided for and where the inquiry which is in fact carried out does not comply with the requirements in every particular but where the defects are of little importance or can be treated as purely procedural.

In the present case, however, it seems to me that a clear and crucial distinction can be drawn between the inquiry required by the statute and the inquiry which was in fact carried out. The justices never examined the question whether *failure to pay* was due to culpable neglect.

I do not find it possible to take the view that this was merely a procedural irregularity. The discretion to issue a warrant which is given by s 102 is limited and circumscribed by the provisions of s 103. The statutory inquiry has to be held before the discretion can be exercised. In my judgment the statutory inquiry was not held in the present case.

For these reasons I would answer the first question in the same way as the judge. I
a consider that the justices are liable in damages.

I turn to the second question.

Are the damages limited to one penny?

Section 52 of the Justices of the Peace Act 1979 (so far as material) provides:

> *b* '(1) The provisions of this section shall have effect where, in any action brought
> against a justice of the peace for anything done by him in the execution of his office
> as such a justice, the plaintiff is (apart from this section) entitled to recover damages
> in respect of a conviction or order, and . . . proves that he was imprisoned under the
> conviction or order and seeks to recover damages for the imprisonment, but it is
> also proved—(*a*) that the plaintiff was actually guilty of the offence of which he was
> *c* so convicted, or that he was liable by law to pay the sum he was so ordered to pay,
> and (*b*) where he was imprisoned, that he had undergone no greater punishment
> than that assigned by law for the offence of which he was so convicted or for non-
> payment of the sum he was so ordered to pay.
> (2) In the circumstances specified in subsection (1) above, the plaintiff shall not
> be entitled . . . to recover any sum beyond the sum of one penny as damages for the
> *d* imprisonment, and shall not be entitled to any costs.'

In this court certain concessions were made on behalf of the applicant. In the first place
it was conceded that the issue of the unlawful warrant of commitment was an act done
by the the justices in the execution of their office: see *R v Waltham Forest Justices, ex p
Solanke* [1986] 2 All ER 981 at 983, [1986] QB 983 at 987 per Sir John Donaldson MR.

It was also conceded that for the purpose of the present proceedings a proper rate had
e been levied against the applicant and that he had failed to pay the full amount of that
rate. It is apparent from s 102(3) of the 1967 Act that where a warrant of commitment is
made it is to be made not only for non-payment of the sum alleged to be due for rates
but also for certain specified costs and charges.

The argument on behalf of the applicant was therefore concentrated on s 52(1)(*b*).

f   It was submitted that he had suffered a greater punishment than that 'assigned by law
. . . for the non-payment of the sum he was so ordered to pay', because the law does not
provide for the imposition of any term of imprisonment for *mere* non-payment of rates
but only where the non-payment is due to wilful refusal or culpable neglect.

On behalf of the justices reliance was placed on the decision of Woolf J in *Ex p Solanke*
[1985] 3 All ER 727, [1986] QB 479. In that case the plaintiff was ordered by the High
g Court to make weekly periodical payments to his former wife for four of his children.
She applied to have the order registered in a magistrates' court but due to an oversight it
was not so registered. When the plaintiff defaulted in payment the wife brought the
matter before the justices who, finding that they were not satisfied that the default was
not due to the plaintiff's wilful refusal or culpable neglect, issued a warrant of
commitment. The warrant was later quashed on the basis that the justices had no
h jurisdiction because the High Court order had not been registered.

The plaintiff claimed damages against the justices who relied on the provisions of s 52.
Woolf J considered the ambit of s 52(1)(*b*) ([1985] 3 All ER 727 at 732–733, [1986] QB
479 at 489):

> 'Then counsel for the applicant submits that this is a case where it would not be
> possible to rely on s 52 of the 1979 Act because the applicant has undergone a greater
> *j* punishment than assigned by law for the offence of which he was convicted. The
> six weeks is the maximum period of imprisonment which justices can now impose
> under s 93 of the Magistrates' Courts Act 1980 (which at the relevant time was s 74
> of the Magistrates' Courts Act 1952). However, before such a sentence can be
> imposed the magistrates' court has to comply with s 93(6), which provides: "A

magistrates' court shall not impose imprisonment in respect of a default to which a
complaint under this section relates unless the court has inquired in the presence of *a*
the defendant whether the default was due to the defendant's wilful refusal or
culpable neglect, and shall not impose imprisonment as aforesaid if it is of the
opinion that the default was not so due . . .'' On the facts as I find them, and as I
have indicated already, I regard this as a case where the justices had complied with
the terms of s 93(6) of the 1980 Act. However, on my interpretation of s 52 of the
1979 Act that is an unnecessary finding for the purposes of my conclusion with *b*
relation to this submission of counsel for the applicant because as I read s 52(1)(b), in
order to avail themselves of the limitation of damages [defence], the justices have
only to be in a position to show that they have not imprisoned the applicant for a
period longer than that assigned by law for the offence. The period assigned by law
was six weeks. They imposed six weeks. It is true that before they could impose that
sentence there were certain steps that had to be taken, and it could well be, having *c*
regard to the House of Lords decision in *McC v Mullan*, that if the justices did not
take those steps, as I find they did in this case, they would be acting without
jurisdiction. None the less, as I read s 52(1)(b), the section would still be available to
the justices in those circumstances, it being the intention of the provision that it
should apply even though the justices have been in error in other respects and those
errors go to jurisdiction. The reason for this is that if that were not the situation s 52 *d*
could never apply when the justices imprison and in doing so go outside their
jurisdiction, because whenever they do that they cannot have any power to impose
the punishment which they did.'

Mr Solanke then appealed to the Court of Appeal, where the argument took rather a
different turn. In that court the effect of s 52(1)(b) was considered quite shortly by Sir *e*
John Donaldson MR. In his judgment he said ([1986] 2 All ER 981 at 984, [1986] QB
983 at 987–988):

'That leaves para (b). It has not been argued in front of us, but I think it was
argued before Woolf J, that Mr Solanke had undergone a greater punishment than
that assigned by law for the non-payment of the sum he was ordered to pay. I think
that that argument got a little mixed up with the whole question of whether the *f*
High Court order was valid; but, as the judge pointed out, if Mr Solanke was liable
to pay the sum which arose under the High Court order and the order had been
registered, then six weeks was the maximum period of imprisonment. So there is
nothing in that point either.'

In my judgment this court is not bound by the decision in *Ex p Solanke* as to the effect *g*
of the analogous provision in s 93(6) of the Magistrates' Courts Act 1980, because the
argument on this point was not developed in the Court of Appeal. I therefore feel free to
consider the matter afresh and, in so far as it is necessary to do so, to differ from the
approach of Woolf J in *Ex p Solanke*.

The ordinary procedure provided for the non-payment of rates is by way of distress
and the sale of the ratepayer's goods and chattels under a warrant. It is to be noted, *h*
however, that s 96(1) of the 1967 Act provides in terms that 'if there is insufficient
distress' the ratepayer may be liable to imprisonment under the provisions of Pt VI of the
Act. Imprisonment is therefore a penalty contemplated by the Act.

Nevertheless it seems to me to be clear that the combined effect of ss 102 and 103 is
that imprisonment can *only* be imposed where the non-payment is due to wilful refusal
or culpable neglect. In the absence of a finding that the non-payment was blameworthy *j*
in the way specified in s 103 imprisonment cannot be imposed as a punishment for non-
payment.

In the present case the non-payment was not due to wilful refusal or culpable neglect
and imprisonment for any period could not be imposed.

a
In my judgment therefore the applicant has undergone a greater punishment than that assigned by law for the non-payment of the sum he was ordered to pay.

I would dismiss the appeal.

SIR ROGER ORMROD. This is an appeal by the three justices concerned against an order made by Simon Brown J on 16 November 1987 on a claim for damages in proceedings for judicial review, pursuant to RSC Ord 53, r 7 (see [1988] 1 All ER 930,

b
[1988] 1 WLR 667). The judges decided two preliminary points in favour of the applicant, namely that the justices were liable in damages to him and that they were not entitled to claim the benefit of the limitation provisions of s 52 of the Justices of the Peace Act 1979. The matter was referred to a master for assessment of damages. On appeal the justices contend that they are entitled to the benefit of s 44 of the 1979 Act or, alternatively, of s 52.

c
The facts are surprising but apparently not in dispute. The appellant is a skilled glass blower who had been carrying on his craft in Blackpool for some years, seemingly successfully. In November 1984, however, he took a lease of a shop or unit in Halle Mall, Arndale Centre, in Manchester at a rent of £14,250 a year. Arndale Centre is said to be a very expensive area. A month later he received a rate demand for some £15,000. He at once applied for a reduction but quickly got into arrears.

d
In August 1985 the rating authority applied to the magistrates' court for and obtained a distress warrant. There was insufficient distress on the premises to satisfy the outstanding arrears of rates. However, the applicant managed to pay off some £6,000. There are still substantial arrears, approximately £9,300 outstanding.

On 16 July 1986 the rating authority took the next step, that is of applying to the court for a warrant of commitment under s 102 of the General Rate Act 1967. This application

e
came before Mr Alan Frost, Dr Elizabeth Marcuson and Mr Kenneth McKeon. The applicant appeared in person. At the conclusion these justices granted a warrant of commitment against the applicant for 90 days' imprisonment. It is this committal which is the basis of the applicant's claim for damages.

At the hearing evidence was given, partly through the rating officer who had made inquiries and partly by the applicant himself, as to his financial position. From this it

f
appeared that the applicant had not made any offer to pay the amount owing. He was married with three children and had an overdraft at the bank of £22,000. His earnings had decreased but he expected them to increase greatly towards Christmas time. He also said that he had been advised by his accountant to stop trading and go bankrupt, as the only way of escape from his impossible financial predicament, but he had not taken this advice.

g
He was in prison from 16 July to 5 September 1986, when he was let out on bail, having started proceedings for judicial review with a view to getting an order quashing the warrant of commitment. On 22 September 1987 Webster J quashed the warrant on the ground that the justices had not complied with the requirements of ss 102 and 103 of the General Rate Act 1967, which provide:

h
'**102.**—(1) If the person charged with the execution of a warrant of distress for levying a sum to which some other person has been rated makes a return to the magistrates' court that he could find no goods or chattels (or no sufficient goods or chattels) on which to levy the sums directed to be levied under the warrant on that other persons' goods and chattels, a magistrates court may, if it thinks fit, and subject to the provisions of section 103 of this Act, (a) issue a warrant of commitment

j
against that other person . . .

(5) The order in the warrant of commitment shall be that the said person be imprisoned for a time therein specified but not exceeding three months, unless the sums mentioned in the warrant shall be sooner paid . . .

103.—(1) Section 102 of this Act shall have effect subject to and in accordance with the following provisions:—(*a*) on the application for the issue of a warrant for the commitment of any person, the magistrates' court shall make inquiry in his presence as to whether his failure to pay the sum to which he was rated and in respect of which the warrant of distress was issued was due either to his wilful refusal or to his culpable neglect; (*b*) if the magistrates' court is of opinion that the failure of the said person to pay the said sum was not due either to his wilful refusal or to his culpable neglect, it shall not issue the warrant . . .'

In the light of those provisions the decision of the justices to issue a warrant was clearly insupportable, and so it was quashed. The applicant's claim for damages was adjourned to give the justices an opportunity to be heard.

All three of them have filed affidavits and there is also before us an affidavit by the clerk, Mr Jeffrey Wills. From this evidence it is quite clear that the justices carried out an inquiry as to means carefully and in detail and spent a considerable time considering the matter in their retiring room. It is equally plain that they misdirected themselves completely as to the terms and meaning of s 103(1). They 'made inquiry in his presence' but failed to realise that the question they had to decide was whether the applicant's failure to pay his rates was '*due* either to his wilful refusal or to his culpable neglect'. They seem to have treated the question as disjunctive, ie was there a failure to pay and was the defendant guilty of culpable neglect? They considered his failure to take the advice of his accountant amounted to 'culpable neglect'.

Clearly the justices had no answer to the application to quash the warrant of commitment but whether at the same time they are exposed to an action for damages for trespass is another and difficult question.

The answer depends on the true construction of ss 44 and 45 of the Justices of the Peace Act 1979. Section 44 provides:

'*Acts done within jurisdiction.* If apart from this section any action lies against a justice of the peace for an act done by him in the execution of his duty as such a justice, with respect to any matter within his jurisdiction as such a justice, the action shall be as for a tort, in the nature of an action on the case; and—(*a*) in the statement of particulars of claim it shall be expressly alleged that the act in question was done maliciously and without reasonable and probable cause, and (*b*) if that allegation is not proved at the trial of the action, judgment shall be given for the defendant, if it is in the High Court, or, if it is in the county court, the plaintiff shall be non-suited or judgment shall be given for the defendant.'

Section 45 provides:

'(1) This section applies—(*a*) to any act done by a justice of the peace in a matter in respect of which by law he does not have jurisdiction or in which he has exceeded his jurisdiction, and (*b*) to any act done under any conviction or order made or warrant issued by a justice of the peace in any such matter; and in the following provisions of this section "the justice", in relation to any act falling within paragraph (*a*) above, means the justice of the peace by whom it is done, and, in relation to a conviction, order or warrant falling within paragraph (*b*) above, means the justice of the peace by whom the conviction or order is made or the warrant issued.

(2) Any person injured by an act to which this section applies may maintain an action against the justice without making any allegation in his statement or particulars of claim that the act complained of was done maliciously and without reasonable and probable cause.

(3) In respect of any act done under any such conviction or order as is mentioned in subsection (1)(*b*) above no action shall be brought against the justice until the conviction or order has been quashed, either on appeal or upon application to the High Court . . .'

The crucial question is the meaning to be given to the word 'jurisdiction' in this context. It is a notoriously difficult word to construe and is often used by lawyers as a

synonym for 'power'. In the course of his speech in *McC v Mullan* [1984] 3 All ER 908 at
a 912, [1985] AC 528 at 536 Lord Bridge said:

> 'There are many words in common usage in the law which have no precise or
> constant meaning. But few, I think, have been used with so many different shades
> of meaning in different contexts or have so freely acquired new meanings with the
> development of the law as the word "jurisdiction".'

b
Our task is not made any easier by the fact that the crucial expressions in the 1979 Act
are taken verbatim from the corresponding sections of the Justices Protection Act 1848,
the title of which is significant. It was the culmination of a number of Acts designed to
protect justices from civil litigation arising out of their functions as justices which, as
Blackstone observed, was a serious detriment to recruitment.

c Some assistance as to the meaning of the word 'jurisdiction' in the 1848 Act can be
obtained from examining the cases reported since it was passed. (There are remarkably
few of them, which suggests that the protection was effective). They are conveniently
summarised by Lord Bridge in *McC v Mullan*.

In *Houlden v Smith* (1850) 14 QB 841, 117 ER 323 the want of jurisdiction was
geographical. As judge of the Spilsby County Court, the defendant had no jurisdiction
d over the plaintiff, who lived and carried on business in Cambridge and so was not
amenable to the jurisdiction of the Spilsby County Court.

In *Willis v Maclachlan* (1876) 1 Ex D 376 the revising barrister had no jurisdiction to
order the removal of the plaintiff from his court except for interrupting his business. All
the plaintiff had done was to have wrongfully withheld documents in a previous case.

In *Polley v Fordham (No 2)* (1904) 91 LT 525, [1904–7] All ER Rep 651 the summons
e on which the plaintiff was fined and later sent to prison for non-payment was bad on its
face and, therefore, a nullity. It related to failure to have a child vaccinated but the
Vaccination Acts 1867 to 1898 required this to be done before the child was six months
old and the summons to be issued within 12 months of the failure. But on the face of the
summons the child's age was then over 18 months. There was, therefore, no jurisdiction
at all.

f In *O'Connor v Isaacs* [1956] 2 All ER 417, [1956] 2 QB 288 the plaintiff was committed
to prison for non-payment of maintenance to his wife, purportedly under the Summary
Jurisdiction (Married Women) Act 1895, but the order recited that the justices had found
that persistent cruelty was *not* proved but that the parties had consented to an order.
There was, therefore, no jurisdiction to make any order for maintenance since proof of a
matrimonial offence was a prerequisite. Consequently, this order was bad on its face and
g a nullity and the subsequent committal order was made without jurisdiction.

A similar want of jurisdiction was found in *R v Waltham Forest Justices, ex p Solanke*
[1985] 3 All ER 727, [1986] QB 479; *affd* [1986] 2 All ER 981, [1986] QB 983, CA. In
that case proceedings were taken by the wife in the magistrates' court for enforcement of
arrears of maintenance which resulted in Mr Solanke's committal to prison for six weeks.
It was then discovered that the arrears were due under an order of the High Court which
h had not been registered in the magistrates' court, which therefore had no jurisdiction.

In all these cases (with the possible exception of the revising barrister) the act
complained of was done by judge or magistrate 'in a matter in respect of which by law
he does not have jurisdiction'.

In the present case the justices had jurisdiction 'in the matter', that is the proceedings
to recover arrears of rates, and had power to issue a warrant of committal if the conditions
j of s 103(1) of the 1967 Act were satisfied. The distress warrant had been properly issued
and a return of no or no sufficient goods and chattels had been made. The mistake which
the justices made, and which made the committal unlawful, was to apply the wrong test.

So, if the case law had stopped there, I would have had no doubt that, given the then
accepted meaning of the word 'jurisdiction', the justices in the present case where entitled
to the benefit of s 44 of the 1979 Act. In other words, their act was an error of law in a
matter within their jurisdiction, not an error going to jurisdiction.

But the law has not stood still. It can fairly be said that the word has acquired a new
meaning with the development of the law by the House of Lords in *McC v Mullan*. This
was an appeal from the Court of Appeal in Northern Ireland and it was held that a
magistrate in Belfast who made a training order (ie an order that the juvenile defendant
be sent to a training school) without first informing the defendant of his right to apply
for legal aid had acted without jurisdiction or in excess of jurisdiction and was
consequently deprived of the protection of s 15 of the Magistrates' Courts (Northern
Ireland) Act 1964, and so liable to be sued for damages.

Article 15(1) of the Treatment of Offenders (Northern Ireland) Order 1976, SI 1976/
226, provides:

> 'A magistrates' court on summary conviction ... shall not pass a sentence of
> imprisonment, Borstal training or detention in a young offenders centre on a person
> who is not legally represented ... unless ... (b) having been informed of his right to
> apply for legal aid and had the opportunity to do so, he refused or failed to apply.'

Section 15 of the 1964 Act provides:

> 'No action shall succeed against any person by reason of any matter arising in the
> execution or purported execution of his office of resident magistrate or justice of the
> peace, unless the court before which the action is brought is satisfied that he acted
> without jurisdiction or in excess of jurisdiction.'

The language is different from that used in ss 44 and 45 of the 1979 English Act in which
the word 'jurisdiction' appears to be used in relation to 'the matter', whereas in the
Northern Ireland Act it appears to refer to 'acted', though it seems unlikely that any
different meaning was intended. Section 15 has its own problem: when and how is an
act done in purported execution of a justice's duty within his jurisdiction?

I do not think that there can be any doubt but that the decision in this case has
substantially eroded the protection which since 1848 it has been thought the justices
enjoyed. The difficult question in this appeal is to determine how far the erosion has
gone. If Simon Brown J's judgment stands, it will further reduce the justices' protection
and it will become increasingly difficult to distinguish between errors of law which are
amenable to correction on appeal or judicial review only, and errors of law which destroy
the protection of s 44.

If one may respectfully say so, it is evident from Lord Bridge's speech that he was
conscious that he was moving into unchartered waters. In *McC v Mullan* [1984] 3 All ER
908 at 913, [1985] AC 528 at 536–537 he spoke of the very wide spectrum of meaning
which the word jurisdiction covers and said:

> 'Your Lordships' task is to try to discern somewhere within this wide spectrum a
> sensible line to be drawn by which to determine whether or not justices are acting
> "without jurisdiction or in excess of jurisdiction" ...'

He concluded that that case fell clearly on the side of liability, the ratio decidendi being,
I think, that the magistrate had ignored an express statutory prohibition, ie against
making detention orders against unrepresented offenders unless and until they had had
an opportunity of obtaining legal aid.

Moreover, it is important to note that Lord Bridge expressly disagreed with the
'equiperation' by Lord Lowry LCJ in the Court of Appeal of an excess of jurisdiction
which will afford a sufficient ground to quash an order by certiorari with an excess of
jurisdiction sufficient to deprive the justices of their statutory protection (see [1984] 3 All
ER 908 at 917, [1985] AC 528 at 543). Again he said ([1984] 3 All ER 908 at 920, [1985]
AC 528 at 546):

> 'But once justices have duly entered on the summary trial of a matter within their
> jurisdiction, only something quite exceptional occurring in the course of their
> proceeding to a determination can oust their jurisdiction so as to deprive them of

a   protection from civil liability in a subsequent trespass . . . It is clear, in my opinion, that no error of law committed in reaching a finding of guilt would suffice, even if it arose from a misconstruction of the particular legislative provision to be applied, so that it could be said that the justices had asked themselves the wrong question.'

Our task, and in the absence of guidelines it is a difficult one, is to determine the position which this case occupies on the spectrum. There is no express statutory
b   prohibition in s 103 of the 1967 Act as in *McC v Mullan*; instead, there is a rather odd inversion in s 103(1)(*b*) which provides that if the magistrates' court is of opinion that the failure to pay was *not* due to wilful refusal or culpable neglect 'it shall *not* issue the warrant'. In all other respects the situation in this case, for reasons set out above, seems to correspond closely to the class of case described by Lord Bridge (see [1984] 3 All ER 908 at 920, [1985] AC 528 at 546). On the other hand, in other parts of his speech Lord
c   Bridge referred to a 'statutory condition precedent' which had not been complied with by the magistrates. If this is the test, the justices in this case plainly had not complied with the statutory condition precedent in s 103(1)(*a*) because, although they made a financial inquiry in the defendant's presence, as a result of misconstruing or misunderstanding the section they directed it to the wrong question.

However, in my judgment, the statutory condition precedent test is not a sufficiently
d   sensitive criterion to discriminate between the class of case which is amenable to certiorari only and the class which is caught by s 45 of the 1979 Act and exposes justices to civil liability. If applied, it will lead I think inevitably to Lord Lowry LCJ's 'equiperation'.

One approach which may be helpful is to consider what would have been the situation in this case had the justices not given evidence, or stated in some other way their reasons for issuing the warrant of commitment. Their decision would have been open to
e   challenge on judicial review on the ground either that there was no evidence on which they could have found that the requirements of s 103(1)(*a*) were satisfied or that no reasonable bench of magistrates, properly directing themselves, could have come to the conclusion that the failure to pay the rates was 'due either to his wilful refusal or to his culpable neglect'. It could be said that in one sense the justices had acted 'without jurisdiction or in excess of jurisdiction' but, in my judgment this is not the sense in
f   which 'jurisdiction' was used in either the 1848 Act or the 1979 Act. If I am wrong, s 44 of the 1979 Act affords much less protection than has hitherto been supposed. I would therefore allow the appeal on this part of the case.

I now turn to the alternative ground of appeal, namely that Simon Brown J was wrong in holding that the justices could not invoke the provisions of s 52 of the 1979 Act to limit the damages to one penny. I have come to the conclusion that the judge was right
g   on this part of the case although my reasons are different.

The section is dealing with a plaintiff who is entitled to recover damages against a justice of the peace 'in respect of a conviction or order'. There is no conviction in this case but there was an order, namely to issue the warrant of commitment. But is this an order within the meaning of the section? I do not think so. Paragraphs (*a*) and (*b*) which follow on refer to 'the sum he was so ordered to pay'. 'So ordered' must refer back to 'conviction
h   or order'. 'Order' must, therefore, mean an order to pay a sum of money, e g a fine or maintenance on an instalment order. In this case there was no order to pay, merely a debt due to the rating authority. So there can be no question of the plaintiff's liability to pay the sum 'so ordered to be paid' or of his having undergone no greater punishment than that assigned by law for non-payment because no punishment is assigned by law.

So I do not think the present case can be brought within the terms of this section at all,
j   however ingenious a construction is suggested. (With respect to the judge, to adopt Cockburn CJ's view in *R (ex p Vestry of St Mary, Islington) v Price* (1880) 5 QBD 300 at 301 that 'The rate itself is the order' is to open the door to an ever-deepening morass of construction difficulties.) The judge thought, understandably, that this point was covered by the decision of this court in *Ex p Solanke*, but in fact the point was not argued since it was assumed that there was an order within the meaning of the section, i e the High

Court order to pay maintenance. But whether such an order is within the section was not considered and need not be decided in this case.

    Accordingly, in my judgment, the justices are not entitled to the benefit of s 52, and I would dismiss this part of the appeal.

Appeal dismissed. Leave to appeal to House of Lords refused.

12 December. *The Appeal Committee of the House of Lords (Lord Brandon of Oakbrook, Lord Ackner and Lord Oliver of Aylmerton) refused a petition for leave to appeal.*

Solicitors: *Philip K Dodd*, Manchester (for the justices); *Linder Myers*, Manchester (for the applicant).

Raina Levy   Barrister.

Kelly v Shulman

QUEEN'S BENCH DIVISION
WOOLF LJ AND HUTCHISON J
28 APRIL, 6 MAY 1988

Road traffic – Goods vehicle – Limitation of driver's time on duty – Breaks and rest periods – Weekly rest period – Day – Whether 'day' meaning any 24-hour period commencing at midnight – Whether driver guilty of breaking weekly rest period requirement if he works six consecutive driving periods in less than six days – Transport Act 1968, s 96(11A) – EC Council Regulation 3820/85, arts 6(1), 8(3).

For the purposes of calculating the mandatory rest periods for drivers of commercial vehicles under art $6(1)^a$ of EC Council Regulation 3820/85, the term 'day' means successive periods of 24 hours commencing with the resumption of driving after the last weekly rest period and not any 24-hour period commencing at midnight. Accordingly, where a driver works six consecutive driving periods in less than six days he will not necessarily be guilty under s $96(11A)^b$ of the Transport Act 1968 of a breach of the weekly rest period requirement under art $8(3)^c$ of Regulation 3820/85, since art 6(1) states that the weekly rest period may be postponed until the end of the sixth day and the driver may be permitted to continue driving during the period of postponement provided that in so doing he does not exceed the maximum number of hours permitted by the regulations in six consecutive daily driving periods (see p 110 e to p 111 a j to p 112 a h to p 113 a, post).

Notes

For drivers' hours on goods vehicles and rest periods, see 40 Halsbury's Laws (4th edn) paras 827–828 and 52 ibid paras 18·140–18·142, and for cases on the subject, see 39(1) Digest (Reissue) 568, 4069 and 21 ibid 273, 1765.

For the Transport Act 1968, s 96(11A) (as inserted by the European Communities Act 1972, s 4(1), Sch 4, para 9(2)(a), see 42 Halsbury's Statutes (3rd edn) 1907.

Case stated

Patrick Joseph Kelly appealed by way of case stated by the justices for West Yorkshire

---

a   Article 6(1), so far as material, is set out at p 108 c d, post
b   Section 96(11A), so far as material, is set out at p 108 a, post
c   Article 8(3) is set out at p 108 g h, post

a acting in and for the petty sessional division of Bradford in respect of their adjudication
as a magistrates' court sitting at Bradford on 28 September 1987 whereby they convicted
the appellant of four charges brought by the respondent, Jeremy I Shulman, on behalf of
the licensing authority for the north eastern traffic area, that on 10, 11, 12 and 13 January
1987 on four separate journeys he drove a goods vehicle the use of which was subject to
the applicable Community rules as prescribed by s 96 of the Transport Act 1968, so that
he did not have 45 consecutive hours off after six daily driving periods, contrary to
b s 96(11A) of the 1968 Act as amended. The question for the court was whether, on the
evidence before it, a reasonable bench of magistrates could come to the conclusion that
the appellant could be found guilty of the offences. The facts are set out in the judgment
of the court.

c Paul F Worsley for the appellant.
Andrew Woolman for the respondent.

Cur adv vult

6 May. The following judgment of the court was delivered.

d **HUTCHISON J.** This is an appeal by Patrick Joseph Kelly by way of case stated by the
Bradford justices in respect of his conviction before them on 27 September 1987 of four
offences involving allegations of driving without observing the statutory requirements
as to rest periods. We were informed that the problems to which this case gives rise have
not previously been considered by the courts, and that the present is regarded as a test
case. Both sides expressed the hope that our judgment would provide assistance to
e haulage contractors and magistrates, for both of whom, as Woolf LJ observed during the
argument, one feels considerable sympathy.

The charges
The first of the four informations charged the appellant, who is employed as a goods
vehicle driver, with driving a lorry on 10 January 1987 the use of which was subject to
f the applicable Community rules as prescribed by s 96 of the Transport Act 1968 so that
he did not have 45 consecutive hours off after six daily driving periods, contrary to
s 96(11A) of the Transport Act 1968. The other three informations alleged identical
offences on 11, 12 and 13 January 1987.

g *The material facts*
The appellant (who, though he is a driver, also undertakes other work for his
employers) began the particular sequence of work and rest periods with which this case
is concerned on Sunday, 4 January 1987 at 1515 hrs. From then until 1300 hrs on
Saturday, 10 January he both worked and enjoyed rest periods, but all of the rest periods
were of less than 24 hours duration. His work consisted both of driving and of other
h types of work, and it is implicit in the findings of fact in the case that he undertook a
period of driving on each of the days 4 to 9 January inclusive. His driving hours were
recorded on the tachograph and in the course of the hearing we were told that before the
magistrates it had been common ground between the parties that none of the individual
periods of driving prior to 10 January had infringed the regulations. We were also told
something which was not contained in the case, but which was not disputed by the
j respondent, namely that in the period between 1515 hrs on 4 January and 1300 hrs on
10 January the appellant had driven for a total of 32 hours. From 1300 hrs on 10 January
until 1315 hrs on 11 January the appellant enjoyed a rest period. He was then at Greenore.
His and the vehicle's base is Bradford. At 1315 hrs on 11 January he resumed working
and thereafter continued to work and drive enjoying rest periods of less than 24 hours,
over the next few days.

The statutory provisions

Section 96(11A) of the Transport Act 1968, as inserted by s 4 of and para 9(2) of Sch 4 *a*
to the European Communities Act 1972 and amended by the Community Drivers'
Hours and Recording Equipment Regulations 1986, SI 1986/1457, reg 2, provides:

> 'Where, in the case of a driver of a motor vehicle, there is in Great Britain a
> contravention of any requirement of [the applicable Community rules] as to periods
> of driving, or . . . periods on or off duty, then the offender . . . shall be liable . . . to a
> fine . . .' *b*

The relevant provision of the Community rules is EC Council Regulation 3820/85. It
is necessary to quote extensively from this regulation. What it does, in the area with
which this case is concerned, is to lay down rules as to driving hours and rest periods, in
particular in arts 6, 7 and 8:

c

'Driving periods

Article 6

> 1. The driving period between any two daily rest periods or between a daily rest
> period and a weekly rest period, hereinafter called "daily driving period", shall not
> exceed nine hours. It may be extended twice in any one week to 10 hours.
> A driver must, after no more than six daily driving periods, take a weekly rest *d*
> period as defined in Article 8(3).
> The weekly rest period may be postponed until the end of the sixth day if the
> total driving time over the six days does not exceed the maximum corresponding to
> six daily driving periods . . .
> 2. The total period of driving in any one fortnight shall not exceed 90 hours . . .

Breaks and rest periods   *e*

Article 7

> 1. After four-and-a-half hours' driving, the driver shall observe a break of at least
> 45 minutes, unless he begins a rest period. [There follow some qualifications and
> exceptions, not at present material.]
> 4. During these breaks, the driver may not carry out any other work . . .
> 5. The breaks observed under this Article may not be regarded as daily rest *f*
> periods.

Article 8

> 1. In each period of 24 hours, the driver shall have a daily rest period of at least
> 11 consecutive hours, which may be reduced to a minimum of nine consecutive
> hours not more than three times in any one week, on condition that an equivalent *g*
> period of rest be granted as compensation before the end of the following week.
> On days when the rest is not reduced in accordance with the first subparagraphs,
> it may be taken in two or three separate periods during the 24-hour period . . .
> 3. The course of each week, one of the rest periods referred to in paragraphs 1
> and 2 shall be extended, by way of weekly rest, to a total of 45 consecutive hours.
> This rest period may be reduced to a minimum of 36 consecutive hours if taken at *h*
> the place where the vehicle is normally based or where the driver is based, or to a
> minimum of 24 consecutive hours if taken elsewhere. Each reduction shall be
> compensated by an equivalent rest taken *en bloc* before the end of the third week
> following the week in question.
> 4. A weekly rest period which begins in one week and continues into the *j*
> following week may be attached to either of these weeks . . .'

We mention at this stage that it seems to us that the key to understanding the
interaction between art 6 and art 8 is to appreciate that, whereas *restrictions* on daily
driving are expressed in terms of the maximum length of driving periods between daily
rests (the 'daily driving period'), the *requirements* as to daily rests are expressed in terms of
minimum daily rest periods in 24 hours (the ('daily rest period'). This explains why it was

a   common ground between the parties to this appeal that it was perfectly possible lawfully
    to fit six daily driving periods into fewer than six days.
        Article 1 contains some definitions, and those that are material are:

        '3. "driver" means any person who drives the vehicle even for a short period, or
    who is carried in the vehicle in order to be available for driving if necessary;
        4. "week" means the period between 00.00 hours on Monday and 24.00 hours on
    Sunday;
b   5. "rest" means any uninterrupted period of at least one hour during which the
    driver may freely dispose of his time.'

    There is no definition of 'day'.

The basis of the convictions
c   The magistrates concluded that 'day' in the regulations meant not (as the prosecutor
    contended before them and as both parties submitted to us) the period of 24 hours
    beginning with the moment when driving was resumed following the conclusion of a
    weekly rest period, but any period of 24 hours commencing at midnight. It follows, if
    their view be correct, that the first day of the period under consideration ended not at
    1515 hrs on Monday, 5 January but at 2400 hrs on Sunday, and the sixth day not at
d   1515 hrs on Saturday, 10 January but at 2400 hrs on Friday, 9 January. They found that
    the appellant's sixth daily driving period ended on 10 January at 0050 hrs at Greenore,
    and that he thereupon became obliged to take a minimum rest period of 24 hours.
    Accordingly, they held that by resuming work and driving at 0845 hrs on 10 January he
    broke his rest period and was therefore guilty on the first information. As to the second,
    third and fourth informations, they were of the view that by failing to complete his 24-
e   hour rest period on 10 January he became obliged, before driving on 11, 12 and 13
    January, to take a 45-hour break; and that, not having done so, he was guilty on these
    informations also.
        The question posed for this court is, in effect, whether as a matter of law they were
    right to convict on any one or more of the charges. It was conceded by counsel for the
    respondent that the convictions on the second, third and fourth informations could not
f   stand, for reasons which we shall explain at the end of this judgment. The discussion of
    the regulations which follows is in the context of the first information only.

The appellant's argument
    Counsel for the appellant advanced the following propositions.
g   (1) 'Day' means successive periods of 24 hours beginning at whatever time the driver
    resumes driving after a weekly rest period, what counsel for the appellant described as a
    rolling period of 24 hours. In each 24 hours a driver must have a rest period of at least 11
    consecutive hours which may, if appropriate compensatory rest is taken, be reduced to
    nine consecutive hours three times in any one week (art 8(1)).
        (2) As to driving periods, the basic rule under art 6(1) is that after no more than six
h   daily driving periods (however short each of those periods may be) a driver is to have a
    weekly rest of 45, 36 or 24 hours, the duration depending on where he is when he ends
    the sixth period. This basic rule is, however, subject to an important (and in this case
    crucial) qualification, set out in the next paragraph.
        (3) Even where six daily driving periods have been undertaken without an intervening
    weekly rest, the driver may continue to drive until (at the latest) the end of the sixth day
j   from the time when after his last weekly rest he resumed driving, provided that the total
    number of hours driven between weekly rests does not exceed the maximum that the
    driver would have been lawfully entitled to drive in six weekly periods, ie ordinarily 56
    hours. (In fact, as we shall show, the theoretical maximum is 58 hours, but that is a
    refinement.) This, it is argued, is the correct interpretation of art 6(1).
        (4) Quite independently of the last mentioned limitation, there is an obligation on
    every driver to take a weekly rest of 45 consecutive hours (which may in appropriate

circumstances be reduced to 36 or 24 hours subject to compensation) once in every period
of seven days beginning at 0000 hrs on Monday. This is the effect of art 8(3) standing   *a*
alone; it will be remembered that, by virtue of the provisions of art 6(1), the operation of
art 8(3) may in certain circumstances be made more restrictive.

Counsel, applying his interpretation of the regulations to the facts of this case, pointed
out that, while it was perfectly true that the appellant had by 0050 hrs on Saturday, 10
January undertaken six daily driving periods since 1515 hrs on Sunday, 4 January, he
was at that moment only 9 hours and 35 minutes into the sixth day, that day having   *b*
begun at 1515 hrs on Friday, 9 January. His next working period, in the case of which
he admittedly undertook a seventh driving period, ended at 1300 hrs on Saturday, 10
January, ie 2 hours and 15 minutes before the end of the sixth day, brought his total
driving hours in that six day period to 32 hours, was followed by a 24-hour rest period,
and therefore did not infringe the regulations.

c

The respondent's argument

Counsel for the respondent conceded the correctness of the 'rolling day' argument, and
therefore accepted that the sixth day ended at 1515 hrs on Saturday, 10 January. His
submissions in support of the conviction involved construing art 6(1) as permitting (in
the circumstances defined) postponement of the rest period, but not allowing driving,
merely other kinds of work, during the extension resulting from the postponement.   *d*
Article 6(1) says that a driver must take a weekly rest after no more than six daily driving
periods; and while the qualification in the next paragraph permits postponement of the
rest period, it does not say that further driving is permitted, and therefore it is not.
Counsel conceded that the words 'total driving time over the six days does not exceed the
maximum' presented a problem, because on his construction it was difficult to give them
any sensible meaning. It does, we think, no injustice to counsel's helpful argument if we   *e*
say that, as it seemed to us, the more these matters were explored in argument, the
readier he was to recognise the difficulties posed by these words.

Conclusions

1. We consider that the magistrates were wrong and that the view advanced by both   *f*
counsel, namely that a day is any period of 24 hours beginning with the resumption of
driving after the last weekly rest period, is correct. The magistrates justified their
conclusion, that it was a 24-hour period beginning at midnight, by reference to the
definition of a week (cited above), but we find no support for their view in that definition.
As it seems to us, the fact that the regulations are dealing with an activity which proceeds
by day and night, and lay down certain driving and rest periods, militates in favour of   *g*
the rolling day construction, which should be adopted unless there is in the regulations
some clear indication to the contrary. It is true that the use in art 8(1) of the words 'In
each period of 24 hours' might at first sight be thought to suggest that 'day' in art 6 bears
some different meaning. However, in the very next paragraph of art 8(1) appear the
words 'On days when the rest is not reduced in accordance with the first subparagraph, it
may be taken in two or three separate periods during the 24-hour period . . .' This, in our *h*
opinion, supports the rolling day construction; and we find nothing in the regulations to
compel us to adopt what, for reasons we have briefly mentioned, appears to us to be an
inappropriate and practically inconvenient alternative.

2. We consider that the appellant's construction of art 6(1) is correct for the following
reasons.

(a) We begin with the reflection that, as one sees in a number of the regulations, the   *j*
draftsman's approach is to impose a limitation and then by subsequent qualifications
relax it in defined circumstances. We see no reason for thinking that the relaxation in art
6 is not intended to relate to driving rather than merely to postponement of the rest
period. There is nothing in the article which amounts to a prohibition of driving during
the period of postponement.

(b) The decisive consideration, however, is to be found in the words 'if the total
driving time over the six days does not exceed the maximum corresponding to six daily

driving periods'. The qualification to the basic restriction is contemplating a situation
a when six daily driving periods have taken place in less than six days, and is defining the
circumstances in which the weekly rest period, prima facie due as soon as the sixth
driving period ends, may be postponed to the end of the sixth day. At the moment when
the sixth daily driving period ends the total number of hours that the driver has driven
in the six periods will necessarily be known. The respondent's construction involves that,
if at that moment the total hours driven in the six periods amounts to 56 hours or less,
b then the rest period may be postponed, but if it exceeds 56 hours (which could only occur
if the driver had breached other provisions of the regulations, an assumption hardly to
be attributed to the draftsmen) it may not. (It will be osberved that, for simplicity's sake,
we are for the moment assuming that 56 is the theoretical maximum; we have yet to
explain why it is in fact 58.) What possible logic is there in such a provision?

Moreover, this approach reads the words 'driving time over the six days' as though
c they were 'driving time over the six driving periods'. That the qualification is framed in
terms which involve (i) that at the end of the sixth driving period the aggregate hours
driven will not exceed 56, and (ii) that postponement of the rest period to a time beyond
the end of the sixth period depends on the aggregate driving hours in that extended
period not exceeding 56, necessarily involves that it is contemplated that the driver may
drive in the period between the conclusion of the sixth driving period and the end of the
d sixth day.

(c) In this connection we have considered an argument that was not canvassed in the
course of the hearing of the appeal. In rereading art 6(1) while preparing this judgment
it occurred to us that there is, strictly speaking, no warrant for the assumption (implicit
in the appellant's argument and in all we have said so far assumed to be correct) that the
right to a postponement of the weekly rest period to the end of the sixth day is dependent
e on the driver's having driven for less than the legally permitted maximum in the course
of the six daily driving periods. It could be argued that, in the absence of express
provision to this effect, the right to postponement is always available, save where the
driver has in the six daily periods already exceeded (thereby breaking the law) the
aggregate hours permitted. In the case of a driver who has already equalled his maximum,
the condition of the right to postpone is that he should not drive at all during the period
f of postponement; in the case of any other driver, that he should during the postponement
drive only as many hours as will bring him up to the aggregate maximum permitted in
six driving periods.

We have, however, felt impelled to reject this argument on the basis that, if it be
correct, it is impossible to understand why art 6(1) was drafted as it was. It is surely not
to be contemplated that a regulation would be drafted on the premise that the only
g circumstance in which one of its primary provisions will be operative is where those
affected by the regulation have broken its provisions. We pose this question because, if
the argument rehearsed in the previous paragraph be correct, only those who are already
in breach at the end of the sixth driving period will be precluded from taking advantage
of postponement.

h The conclusion we have reached is that, looking at art 6(1) as a whole, it must be a
matter of implication that the right to postpone arises only where, at the end of the sixth
daily driving period, the permitted aggregate has not yet been equalled (or exceeded). In
saying this we are conscious that it can be said that there seems little logic in distinctions
which have the arbitrary result that postponement is available where $55\frac{3}{4}$ hours, but not
where 56 hours, have been driven. But that seems to us to be a consideration less
j compelling than the difficulty that, in the absence of such an implication as we suggest,
the basic rule is, in the case of law-abiding drivers, never operative.

(d) Putting the matter simply, and for that purpose still taking 56 as the theoretical
maximum, what art 6 is laying down is this. A driver who, with only daily rest periods
between them, has driven six consecutive daily periods amounting in the aggregate to
56 hours' driving (or more) must immediately on the conclusion of the sixth period
begin a weekly rest period. But in any case where the aggregate hours in the six daily
driving periods amount to less than 56 hours he may postpone the commencement of

his weekly rest period to the end of the sixth day, and may in the interval between the conclusion of the sixth period and the end of the sixth day undertake further driving *a* periods provided the hours driven in those periods do not bring the total hours driven since the beginning of the six day period to more than 56. For completeness, it is appropriate to emphasise here that all drivers, even those who have driven fewer than six driving periods since the conclusion of their last weekly rest, are in any event obliged to have a weekly rest in the course of each week. This is the effect of art 8(3) construed independently of art 6 rather than in conjunction with it. However, a weekly rest period *b* begun in one week and ended in another may be attached to either (art 8(4)).

3. The reason the theoretical 'maximum corresponding to six daily driving periods' (art 6(1)) is 58 rather than 56 is this. A week in the regulations means the period from the beginning of Monday to the end of Sunday. Article 6(1) allows the daily driving period of nine hours to be extended to ten hours 'twice in any one week'. If, therefore, one envisages a driver who, following his weekly rest, begins a period of driving towards *c* the end of a week in which he has not previously driven any period of more than nine hours, who, between then and the end of Sunday, drives two periods of ten hours, who on Monday and Tuesday drives two further periods of ten hours, and who concludes with two further periods of nine hours, all six periods taking place in less than six days, he will lawfully have driven 58 hours in the six driving periods. A driver who starts on Monday morning will be confined to 56 hours. *d*

The second, third and fourth informations

The magistrates' reasons for convicting (that since the 24-hour break after the daily driving period came, on the view they took of the case, a day too late, the only break that could be accepted before driving on the 11, 12 and 13 January was one of 45 hours) was not supported by the respondent. Nor did the respondent feel able to support the *e* contention underlying this approach, namely that since the 24-hour rest (while appropriate in length for a weekly rest break at Greenore) came a day late, any subsequent driving was illegal. The simple fact is that if, as the magistrates held, the appellant was obliged to start a weekly rest after concluding work at 0050 hrs on 10 January, then by driving on that day he was in breach of the requirements of the regulations as to rest periods. However, when a day or so later he took a weekly rest appropriate in length to *f* the place where he was, that was an effective rest period for the purpose of the regulations. We see no warrant for saying that the entitlement to have a weekly rest shorter than 45 hours is conditional on its being taken not only at the appropriate place but also at the appropriate time; and it cannot be right that a driver who in breach of the regulations starts his weekly rest late is precluded from ever driving thereafter.

It follows that, even had the conviction on the first information been sustainable, the *g* appeals in relation to the other three would have succeeded. As it is, the fact that the appeal on the first information succeeds eliminates even the argument for upholding the other three.

Summary of conclusions

1. The term 'day' in art 6(1) means successive periods of 24 hours beginning with the *h* driver's resumption of driving after his last weekly rest period. 2. Every driver must have a weekly rest period, as defined by art 8, once in every week, ie in the period between midnight on Sunday and midnight on the following Sunday. 3. In certain circumstances the weekly rest period falls to be taken earlier. Thus: (a) any driver who in the course of six consecutive driving periods since his last weekly rest has driven in the aggregate not less than the maximum number of hours permitted by the regulations in *j* six such periods must begin a weekly rest immediately on the conclusion of the sixth period; but (b) any such driver who in those six driving periods has driven for an aggregate of less than the maximum number of hours permitted by the regulations may (i) postpone the commencement of his weekly rest period until the end of the sixth day and (ii) drive during the period of postponement provided he does not by so doing increase the aggregate of the hours driven since his last weekly rest to a figure exceeding

the maximum number of hours permitted by the regulations in six consecutive daily
a driving periods.

The question posed by the magistrates was, in effect, whether it was open to them on
the basis of the facts found to convict the appellant on any of the four informations. We
would answer that question by saying that, for the reasons we have given, it was not.
Accordingly, the convictions and sentences must be quashed.

We should add, in the form of a postscript to this judgment, that it appears to us that
b in one respect the appellant was in breach of the regulations. It will be remembered that
he began a daily rest period at 0050 hrs on Saturday, 10 January and resumed work again
at 0845 hrs the same day. This rest period was therefore of only 8 hours and 50 minutes
duration. It should have lasted for a minimum of nine hours. However, the offence
alleged in the first information was of failing at this stage to take a weekly rest, and the
wording of the information was not apt to cover this comparatively venial lapse.

c

Appeal allowed.

Solicitors: *Ford & Warren*, Leeds (for the appellant); *Shulmans*, Leeds (for the respondent).

N P Metcalfe Esq   Barrister.
d

Nurse v Morganite Crucible Ltd

HOUSE OF LORDS
e LORD BRIDGE OF HARWICH, LORD TEMPLEMAN, LORD GRIFFITHS, LORD ACKNER AND LORD LOWRY
9, 10 NOVEMBER, 15 DECEMBER 1988

*Factory – Process – Demolition of disused equipment – Escape of asbestos dust in course of
demolition – Duty to provide approved respiratory protective equipment where asbestos dust
f from factory 'process' liable to escape – Duty to store asbestos waste in suitable sealed containers
– Duty to keep internal surfaces clear of asbestos waste and dust – Demolition of driers over
period of nine days – Whether demolition of driers amounting to 'process' – Whether occupier of
factory required to provide approved respiratory protective equipment during demolition, store
waste in sealed containers and keep internal surfaces clear of asbestos waste and dust – Factories
Act 1961, ss 76, 155(2) – Asbestos Regulations 1969, regs 3, 5, 8(1), 9, 15.*

g The defendants were the occupiers of a factory which manufactured crucibles. Asbestos
was not used in the crucible manufacturing process. In 1984, over a period of about nine
days, the defendants demolished a number of large brick driers within the factory. The
roof panels of two of the driers contained asbestos and in the course of breaking up and
removing the panels asbestos dust escaped. The defendants were charged with failing to
h provide its employees with approved respiratory protective equipment where asbestos
dust from 'a process' was liable to escape, failing to store asbestos waste from a process in
suitable sealed containers and failing to keep internal surfaces clear of asbestos dust and
waste from a process, contrary to s 155(2)[a] of the Factories Act 1961 and regs 8(1)[b], 15[c]

---

a   Section 155(2), so far as material, provides: 'In the event of a contravention by any person of any
j   regulation . . . made under this Act which expressly imposes any duty upon him, that person shall
         be guilty of an offence . . .'
b   Regulation 8(1), so far as material, provides: '. . . there shall be provided for the use of each person
         employed in any part of the factory, being a part into which asbestos dust from a process to which
         these Regulations apply is liable to escape—(a) approved respiratory protective equipment . . .'
c   Regulation 15 provides: 'All loose asbestos in a factory shall when not in use be kept in suitable
         closed receptacles which prevent the escape of asbestos dust therefrom, and all asbestos waste in a
         factory shall, when stored, be kept in such receptacles.'

and 9[d] of the Asbestos Regulations 1969 made under s 76[e] of the 1961 Act. Regulation 3[f]
applied the regulations to premises and places in which a process involving asbestos was   a
carried on and reg 5[g] required every employer or occupier of a factory where such a
process was carried on to comply with the requirements of the regulations. The
defendants were convicted. They appealed, contending that for the purposes of the 1961
Act and the 1969 regulations a 'process' meant a manufacturing process or other regular
activity carried on at a factory and that the demolition of the driers did not constitute
such a process. The Crown Court dismissed the defendants' appeal and the defendants   b
appealed to the Divisional Court, which allowed the appeal. The prosecutor appealed to
the House of Lords.

Held – In the context of s 76 of the 1961 Act and 1969 regulations the word 'process' was
used in the broad sense of meaning any operation or series of operations and included an
activity of more than a minimal duration which had some degree of continuity or   c
repetition of a series of acts. Since the demolition of the driers was carried out by the
defendants over a period of days, it was a process involving materials containing asbestos
within the meaning of the regulations. The defendants were therefore rightly convicted
of the offences and the prosecutor's appeal would be allowed (see p 115 d e, p 117 e to g j,
p 118 d and p 119 a to f; to p 120 a d to f, post).
    R v AI Industrial Products plc [1987] 2 All ER 368 overruled.   d

Notes

For protection of employees from dust or fumes, see 20 Halsbury's Laws (4th edn) para
640, and for cases on the subject, see 26 Digest (Reissue) 383–386, 2696–2705.
    For the meaning of 'process', see 20 Halsbury's Laws (4th edn) para 411, and for a case
on the subject, see 26 Digest (Reissue) 386, 2710.   e
    For the Factories Act 1961, ss 76, 155, see 19 Halsbury's Statutes (4th edn) 479, 535.
    For the Asbestos Regulations 1969, regs 3, 5, 8, 9, 15, see 8 Halsbury's Statutory
Instruments (4th reissue) 282–284, 286.
    Section 76 of the 1961 Act was repealed with savings as to regulations made thereunder
by the Factories Act 1961 etc (Repeals and Modifications) Regulations 1974, SI 1974/
1941. Power to make health and safety regulations is now conferred by s 15 of the Health   f
and Safety at Work etc Act 1974.
    As from 1 March 1988 the 1969 regulations were revoked and replaced avoiding the
use of the word 'process' by the Control of Asbestos at Work Regulations 1987, SI 1987/
2115.

Cases referred to in opinions

R v AI Industrial Products plc [1987] 2 All ER 368, CA.
Vibroplant Ltd v Holland (Inspector of Taxes) [1981] 1 All ER 526; *affd* [1982] 1 All ER 792,
    CA.

Appeal

The prosecutor, Michael Godfrey Nurse, one of Her Majesty's inspectors of factories,   h
appealed with the leave of the Divisional Court of the Queen's Bench Division against

d   Regulation 9, so far as material, provides: 'All . . . plant and equipment used in any factory for the
    purposes of any process to which these Regulations apply . . . all floors, inside walls, ceilings, ledges
    and other internal surfaces of any part of a building . . . being a part in which any process to which
    these Regulations apply is carried on or into which asbestos dust from any such process carried on   j
    in the factory is liable to escape, shall, so far as is practicable, be kept in a clean state and free from
    asbestos waste and dust in accordance with the provisions of this Part of these Regulations.'
e   Section 76, so far as material, is set out at p 117 h, post
f   Regulation 3, so far as material, is set out at p 117 j to p 118 b, post
g   Regulation 5, so far as material, is set out at p 118 e to j, post

a   the decision of that court (Woolf LJ and Hutchison J) on 29 April 1988 allowing an appeal
    by the defendants, Morganite Crucible Ltd, by way of a case stated by the Crown Court
    at Hereford (his Honour Judge Roy Ward QC and two justices) in respect of its decision
    on 14 February 1985 dismissing the defendants' appeal against their conviction by the
    justices for the petty sessional division of Worcester (county) sitting as a magistrates'
    court at Worcester on 22 November 1984 on three informations preferred by the
    prosecutor alleging offences contrary to s 155(2) of the Factories Act 1961 and regs 8(1),
b   9 and 15 of the Asbestos Regulations 1969, SI 1969/690. The Divisional Court had
    certified under s 12(1) of the Administration of Justice Act 1969 that its decision involved
    a point of law of general public importance (set out at p 119 h, post). The facts are set out
    in the opinion of Lord Griffiths.

    John F M Maxwell and *Carmel Wall* for the prosecutor.
c   *John Saunders* and *Alison Lockwood* for the defendants.

    Their Lordships took time for consideration.

    15 December. The following opinions were delivered.

d   **LORD BRIDGE OF HARWICH.** My Lords, I have had the advantage of reading in
    draft the speech of my noble and learned friend Lord Griffiths. I agree with it and, for
    the reasons he gives, I would allow the appeal.

    LORD TEMPLEMAN. My Lords, for the reasons to be given by my noble and learned
    friend Lord Griffiths, I would allow this appeal.
e

    LORD GRIFFITHS. My Lords, this is an appeal by the prosecutor from the decision
    of the Divisional Court who, on a case stated by the Crown Court at Hereford, allowed
    the appeal of the respondent defendants against their conviction on three summonses
    alleging breaches of the Asbestos Regulations 1969, SI 1969/690. It is clear from the
    judgment of the Divisional Court that it only allowed the appeal of the defendants
f   because it rightly held itself bound by the decision of the Court of Appeal, Criminal
    Division in *R v AI Industrial Products plc* [1987] 2 All ER 368. It is I think manifest from
    the wording of the judgment of Woolf LJ in the Divisional Court that but for the
    decision in *R v AI Industrial Products plc* it would have dismissed the appeal. This appeal
    then is in effect an appeal from the decision of the Court of Appeal in that case.
        The case stated by the Crown Court is a model of its kind and it states all relevant
g   matters so succinctly that I reproduce it almost in its entirety:

        '1. The [prosecutor] is one of H.M. Inspectors of Factories appointed by the
        Health and Safety Executive.
        2. On 6th August 1984 the [prosecutor] preferred three informations against the
h   [defendants] alleging offences contrary to Section 155(2) of the Factories Act 1961
        namely: (i) that the [defendants] being occupiers of a certain factory within the
        meaning of the Factories Act 1961 to which the Asbestos Regulations 1969 applied
        did contravene Regulation 8(1) of the said Regulations in that they failed to provide
        for the use of persons employed approved respiratory protective equipment in that
        part of the factory into which asbestos dust from a process namely the breaking up
j   and removal of Marinite panels from the roofs of the two larger driers in the Cut
        Block 380 Department was liable to escape. (ii) that the [defendants] being occupiers
        of a Factory within the meaning of the Factories Act to which the Asbestos
        Regulations 1969 applied did contravene Regulation 15 of the said Regulations in
        that asbestos waste from a process to which these Regulations applied namely
        broken Marinite panels forming part of a pile close to the Concaste building in the

said factory was not stored in suitable closed receptacles which would prevent the
escape of asbestos dust. (iii) that the [defendants] being occupiers of a Factory within   *a*
the meaning of the Factories Act 1961 to which the Asbestos Regulations 1969
applied did contravene Regulation 9 of the said Regulations in that all floors, ledges
and other internal surfaces of the Cut Block 380 Department being parts of a
building in which a process to which these Regulations applied namely the breaking
up and removal of the Marinite panels forming the roofs of the two larger driers
was carried on were not, so far as was reasonably practicable kept in a clean state and   *b*
free from asbestos waste and dust.

3. On 22nd November 1984 the [defendants] were convicted of the said offences
by Justices for the Petty Sessional Division of Worcester County.

4. An appeal against these said convictions was made by the [defendants] which
appeal we heard on 14th February 1985. We were given written statements of all
prosecution witnesses and photographs and a "Schedule of Main Facts and Expert   *c*
Evidence". We heard oral evidence from Mr Duggan a director of the [defendants]
and called on their behalf. All the facts were agreed and we found the following.

FACTS

(1) The [defendants] occupied premises at Woodbury Lane, Norton, Worcester
which were a factory within the meaning of the Factories Act 1961. (2) At these
premises the [defendants] manufactured crucibles. (3) Asbestos was not used in the   *d*
course of the manufacture of the crucibles. (4) On dates between 25th April and
2nd May 1984 the [defendants] demolished a number of brick driers within 380
Cut Block Department of the Factory. (5) Two large driers were 40 feet by 12 feet
and 8 feet high. The walls were of brick construction. The roof was constructed of
1 inch Marinite panels (containing asbestos) bolted to steel frames. Approximately   *e*
10 to 12·5 tons of rubble was removed during demolition before the intervention
of the Factory Inspector and much remained on site thereafter as shown in the
photographs. The driers were themselves buildings. (6) Driers had never been
demolished at the factory before. (7) In the course of the demolition the [defendants]
failed to comply with the requirements of the Asbestos Regulations 1969 as set out
in the informations.   *f*

5. It was contended by the [defendants] that the Asbestos Regulations 1969 did
not apply because the demolition of the driers was not a process carried on in their
factory.

6. The [defendants] further contended that "process" meant a manufacturer's
process or other regular activity carried on at the factory and did not include the
demolition of a drier.   *g*

7. The [prosecutor] contended that "process" should be widely interpreted and
included demolition of the driers . . .

11 . . . we accepted the contention of the [prosecutor] that the word "process" in
the Regulations meant any activity or operation of some duration. Accordingly, we
found that the Asbestos Regulations 1969 did apply to the [defendants'] premises.
This being the only issue raised on the appeal, accordingly we dismissed the appeal.   *h*

QUESTION

The question for the opinion of the High Court is whether we were correct in
ruling that the Asbestos Regulations 1969 at the material time applied to the
demolition of the driers in this factory.'

The defendants' appeal was dismissed by the Crown Court on 14 February 1985. There   *j*
matters rested until the decision in *R v AI Industrial Products plc* [1987] 2 All ER 368 was
given by the Court of Appeal a year later. On the strength of that decision the defendants
were given leave to appeal out of time and the case was accordingly stated by the Crown
Court at Hereford.

I turn straight away to *R v AI Industrial Products plc.* The facts in that case were
a virtually indistinguishable from the present. They were that between Friday, 22 February
1985 and Monday, 25 February 1985 the occupier of a factory demolished a kiln within
his factory which resulted in releasing considerable quantities of asbestos dust into the
atmosphere. The defence was that the demolition of the kiln was not a 'process' to which
the 1969 regulations applied. In the Crown Court Mr Recorder Stuart Shields QC ruled
that the demolition of the kiln was a process within the meaning of the regulations and
b the appellants accordingly changed their plea to guilty and were fined. They appealed to
the Court of Appeal with the leave of the recorder on the ground that his ruling was in
error and that the demolition of the kiln was not a process in a factory within the
regulations as it was unconnected with the manufacturing processes undertaken in the
factory and was an isolated incident. The Court of Appeal accepted this argument and
said ([1987] 2 All ER 368 at 370–371):
c
> '. . . the word "process" must be construed according to the meaning to be given
> it under [the Factories Act 1961] . . . In our judgment, the word "process" as used in
> this section [s 175] and elsewhere in the 1961 Act connotes some continuous activity
> regularly carried on within a factory, and does not include a single operation such as
> the demolition and removal of a disused piece of machinery or a kiln.'

d Later, it said:

> '. . . it is wrong to extend the meaning of "process" in the 1961 Act beyond some
> manufacturing process or continuous and regular activity carried on as a normal
> part of the operation of a factory.'

In arriving at its conclusion the Court of Appeal focused primarily on the meaning to
e be attached to the word "process" where it appears in the definition of a factory in s 175(1)
of the Factories Act 1961. I think, with all respect, that this led it into error. 'Process' is a
word of very wide general meaning and must take colour from its context. When used
in the context of defining a factory it is natural to think of the word 'process' in the
context of the operations carried on within the factory. The 1969 regulations, however,
are not confined to operations carried on within a factory and, in particular, they apply
f to building operations to which the Court of Appeal's attention does not appear to have
been drawn in *R v AI Industrial Products plc.* If the Court of Appeal decision is correct it
will gravely limit the protection of the regulations. It is difficult to see how they could
be applied to normal building operations and it is also difficult to see how they would
apply to what is one of the primary risks from asbestos dust, namely the use of asbestos
g lagging material either for pipes or for furnace repairs.

The regulations were made pursuant to powers contained in ss 62, 76 and 180(6) and
(7) of the 1961 Act. Section 76(1) provided:

> 'Where the Minister is satisfied that any manufacture, machinery, plant,
> equipment, appliance, process or description of manual labour is of such a nature as
> to cause risk of bodily injury to the persons employed or any class of those persons,
h > he may, subject to the provisions of this Act, make such special regulations as appear
> to him to be reasonably practicable and to meet the necessity of the case.'

It is immediately to be observed that the word 'process' in the enabling section is used in
apposition to manufacture and would appear to be used in a wide sense.

I turn now to the regulations themselves:

j
> '*Application of Regulations*
> **3.**—(1) These Regulations shall apply to the following premises and places in
> which any process to which these Regulations apply is carried on, that is to say,
> factories and all premises and places to which the provisions of Part IV of the
> principal Act with respect to special regulations for safety and health are applied by

the following provisions of that Act, namely, section 123 (which relates to electrical
stations), section 124 (which relates to institutions), so much of section 125 as relates
to warehouses other than warehouses within any dock or forming part of any wharf
or quay, section 126 (which relates to ships) and section 127 (which relates to
building operations and works of engineering construction).

(2) These Regulations apply to every process involving absestos or any article
composed wholly or partly of asbestos, except a process in connection with which
asbestos dust cannot be given off . . .'

By reg 3(1) the regulations are to apply to any such process carried on in a factory or a
deemed factory and it also applies the regulations to building operations and works of
engineering construction. Counsel for the defendants in a most able argument sought to
persuade your Lordships that 'process' should be given a different meaning when used in
reference to a process carried on in a factory or deemed factory, in which case, he submits,
it should bear the restricted meaning given to it by the Court of Appeal, and in the case
of building operations or works of engineering construction, in which case a wider
meaning should be given to the word so that it covers all activities involving the use of
asbestos in building operations and works of engineering construction. This construction
of the regulations would involve not only construing the word 'process' as having two
different meanings when used in reg 3(1) but also giving two different meanings to it in
reg 3(2). Regulation 3(2) is framed in simple language and I can find no indication that
the word 'process' is to have other than the single broad meaning of 'any activity'. I am
satisfied that the same word 'process' is used in the same sense in reg 3(1) as it is in reg
3(2) and that it is not permissible to attach two different meanings to it.

Regulation 5 is of importance and is in the following terms:

'*Obligations under Regulations*
    5.—(1) Except in the case of any place where building operations or works of
engineering construction are carried on it shall be the duty—(a) of every employer
(whether or not an occupier) who is undertaking in a factory any process to which
these Regulations apply to comply with the requirements of these Regulations in
relation to any person employed by him, any plant or material under his control,
and any part of the factory in which he is carrying on the process or into which
asbestos dust in connection with that process is liable to escape; (b) of every occupier
of any factory (whether or not such an employer as aforesaid) where any such process
is being carried on to comply with the requirements of Regulations 8, 18 and 19 in
relation to any person employed in the factory (other than any person employed by
an employer who is undertaking in the factory any process to which these
Regulations apply) and with the requirements of Part III of these Regulations; and
(c) of every person who is undertaking in a factory any process to which these
Regulations apply and who employs no other person in the carrying on of that
process to comply for the protection of employed persons working there, with the
requirements of these Regulations (other than Regulations 8, 14 and 18 to 20) with
which he would have to comply if he were the employer of a person doing there the
work which he does himself.
    (2) In the case of places where building operations or works of engineering
construction are carried on it shall be the duty of every contractor and of every
employer who is undertaking any process to which these Regulations apply to
comply with the requirements of these Regulations in relation to any person
employed by him and any person employed there who is liable to be exposed to
asbestos dust in connection with any process carried on by the contractor or
employer (as the case may be), and in relation to any plant or material under his
control and any part of the site where he is carrying on the process or where asbestos
dust in connection with that process is liable to escape . . .'

There are, I think, two powerful indications from the wording of this regulation that
a 'process' cannot have the restricted meaning attached to it by the Court of Appeal. In the
first place, if a process is construed as a 'manufacturing process or continuous and regular
activity carried on as a normal part of the operation of a factory' (see [1987] 2 All ER 368
at 371), it is difficult to see how the regulations can apply either to a building operation
or to a work of engineering construction.

Second, reg 5(1)(*b*) is clearly drafted to cover the situation in which the factory occupier
b calls in an independent contractor to carry out a process to which the regulations apply,
in which case the occupier has to comply with certain parts of the regulations to protect
any person employed in the factory, except the employees of the independent contractor
who are protected by reg 5(1)(*a*) which puts the duty of compliance with the regulations
on their employer, the independent contractor. Now an occupier of a factory is not going
to call in an independent contractor to carry out the 'manufacturing process' in the
c factory or to perform some 'continuous and regular activity carried on as a normal part
of the operation' of the factory, for those are the very operations carried on by the
occupier of the factory, for which he has no need of the services of an independent
contractor. The occupier of the factory is going to call in the independent contractor to
carry out some specialist work of maintenance or repair such as lagging or furnace
repairs, and it is clearly this situation that is covered by reg 5(1)(*b*) and, to my mind,
d indicates quite clearly that 'process' must be given a broad meaning so that if the work
involves risk from asbestos dust it is covered by the regulations. If the word is given the
narrow meaning it is difficult to see in what circumstances reg 5(1)(*b*) would ever be
likely to apply.

The foregoing considerations which depend on the words of the 1961 Act and the
1969 regulations themselves satisfy me that the word 'process' is not used in the limited
e sense in which it was construed by the Court of Appeal, but in the broader sense of
including any activity of a more than minimal duration involving the use of asbestos.
Some common sense has to be introduced into the definition of 'process'. Obviously the
single act of knocking a nail into an asbestos panel cannot be considered a process. There
has to be some degree of continuity and repetition of a series of acts in order to constitute
a process. On the facts of *R v AI Industrial Products plc* [1987] 2 All ER 368 and of the
f present case the activity went on over a period of days involving materials containing
asbestos and in both cases was a 'process' within the meaning of the regulations.

We were referred to a number of authorities in which the meaning of the word
'process' was considered in other contexts and particularly in the context of the extended
definition of a factory within the meaning of s 175 of the 1961 Act. I do not wish to cast
any doubt on the correctness of these decisions but I do not derive any assistance from
g them because the word 'process' is used in an entirely different context. Still less do I
derive any assistance from *Vibroplant Ltd v Holland (Inspector of Taxes)* [1981] 1 All ER
526, in which the word 'process' was considered in its context in the Capital Allowances
Act 1968.

The Divisional Court in giving leave to appeal to your Lordships' House certified the
h following point of law of general public importance:

> 'Whether for the purposes of the Factories Act 1961 and Regulations thereunder
> "process" carried on in a factory means a manufacturing process or other continuous
> and regular activity carried on as a normal part of the operation of the factory.'

My Lords, I am not prepared to answer the question in this form because the word
j 'process' is scattered throughout many sections of the 1961 Act, and it appears in many
regulations made thereunder. Your Lordships have not had the opportunity to consider
the meaning to be attached to 'process' wherever it appears and it is possible that it has
different meanings in different contexts. I would confine my opinion to the meaning of
the word 'process' where it is used in the 1969 regulations and I would answer the

certified question by saying that where the word 'process' is used in the regulations it means any operation or series of operations being an activity of more than a minimal duration. *a*

I would add this rider. The Crown Court found that the driers being demolished by the defendants were a building. But the defendants were not charged with the offences in their capacity as persons carrying out an operation to which the Building Regulations applied. Counsel for the defendants conceded that on the construction for which he argued the defendants would have had no defence if they had been charged as persons *b* carrying out building operations. However, as matters stood under the decision in R v AI Industrial Products plc, the Court of Appeal had applied a narrow construction to the meaning of 'process' in the 1969 regulations which would have provided a defence even if the defendants had been charged as carrying out a building operation. The prosecution was brought against the defendants in their capacity as occupiers demolishing a plant within their factory. This was the basis on which the case was dealt with in the courts *c* below, and the reason why it was identical to R v AI Industrial Products plc. It is on this basis that the case was argued and dealt with before your Lordships, although naturally in argument counsel for the prosecutor drew attention to the impact of the Court of Appeal's construction on building operations and works of engineering construction.

I would therefore allow this appeal and restore the convictions of the defendants. It was a condition on which leave was given to appeal to your Lordships' House that the *d* prosecutor would indemnify the defendants in respect of their reasonable costs in the House of Lords; I would therefore order that the prosecutor pay to the defendants their costs in your Lordships' House.

LORD ACKNER. My Lords, I have had the advantage of reading in draft the speech prepared by my noble and learned friend Lord Griffiths. I agree with it, and I too would *e* allow this appeal. I also agree with the order that the prosecutor pay to the defendants their costs in your Lordships' House.

LORD LOWRY. My Lords, I have had the advantage of reading in draft the speech of my noble and learned friend Lord Griffiths. I agree with it and accordingly I, too, would allow this appeal and restore the defendants' convictions. I also agree with the order as to *f* costs which my noble and learned friend proposes.

Appeal allowed. Convictions retored.

Solicitors: *Treasury Solicitor*; *Pinsent & Co*, Birmingham (for the defendants).
g

Mary Rose Plummer   Barrister.

a
R v Johnson

COURT OF APPEAL, CRIMINAL DIVISION
WATKINS LJ, McNEILL AND McCOWAN JJ
22, 29 JULY 1988

b *Criminal evidence – Prosecution evidence – Disclosure of sources of information – Confidentiality of sources – Police observation posts in private premises – Protection of occupiers of premises used as police observation posts – Guidance on requirements for excluding evidence which would reveal address and identity of occupiers of private premises used as police observation posts.*

The appellant was seen to be selling drugs by police officers watching from private c premises which were used by the police as observation posts in a known drug-dealing locality. The appellant was charged with possessing and supplying controlled drugs. At his trial the only evidence that the appellant had been supplying drugs was that given by the police officers stationed in the observation posts and the appellant's counsel applied to be permitted to cross-examine the police officers on the exact location of the observation posts so that he could test the police evidence by reference to their distance from the d alleged transactions, their angle of vision and possible obstructions in their line of sight. The Crown contended that the police officers should not be required to reveal the exact location of the observation posts because it would put at risk occupiers who had permitted their premises to be used by the police as observation posts. The judge ruled that the exact location of the observation posts need not be revealed. The appellant was convicted. He appealed, contending that his defence had been so hampered by the judge's ruling e that there had been a miscarriage of justice.

Held – A trial judge could exclude evidence which would reveal the address and identity of occupiers of private premises which were used by the police as observation posts provided that there was a proper evidential basis for the exclusion of such evidence and that he was satisfied that the defendant would nevertheless receive a fair trial and that the f desirability of protecting from reprisals those who assisted the police outweighed the principle that there should be full disclosure of all the material facts. In order that the judge should be in a position to make such an evaluation a senior police officer should be able to testify, from visits made by him both before the observation commenced and immediately prior to the trial, as to the attitude of the occupiers towards the possible disclosure of their addresses and identities. Since on the facts the appellant had not g received an unfair trial, because the judge had given the jury directions which safeguarded his position in the light of the judge's ruling to exclude evidence of the exact location of the police observation posts, the jury's verdict was not unsafe or unsatisfactory and the appeal would therefore be dismissed (see p 127 *e* to *h* and p 128 *b* to *g*, post).

Notes
h For the exclusion of evidence of sources of police information, see 11 Halsbury's Laws (4th edn) para 464.

Cases referred to in judgment
D v National Society for the Prevention of Cruelty to Children [1977] 1 All ER 589, [1978] AC j 171, [1977] 2 WLR 201, HL.
Marks v Beyfus (1890) 25 QBD 494, CA.
R v Brown (1988) 87 Cr App R 52, CA.
R v Hennessey (1978) 68 Cr App R 419, CA.
R v Rankine [1986] 2 All ER 566, [1986] QB 861, [1986] 2 WLR 1075, CA.
R v Turnbull [1976] 3 All ER 549, [1977] QB 224, [1976] 3 WLR 445, CA.

Cases also cited

Ellis v Home Office [1953] 2 All ER 149, [1953] 2 QB 135, CA.   *a*
Hehir v Comr of Police of the Metropolis [1982] 2 All ER 335, [1982] 1 WLR 715, CA.
Rogers v Secretary of State for the Home Dept [1972] 2 All ER 1057, [1973] AC 388, HL.
Webb v Catchlove (1886) 3 TLR 159, DC.

Appeal

Kenneth Johnson appealed against his conviction on 19 May 1988 before his Honour   *b*
Judge Pownall QC and a jury in the Crown Court of Knightsbridge on three counts of
possessing a class B controlled drug, three counts of supplying a class A controlled drug,
and one count of possessing a class A controlled drug, for which he was sentenced to two
years' imprisonment, to run concurrently, on the charges of supplying and 12 months'
imprisonment, to run concurrently, on the possession charge, both sentences suspended
for two years. The facts are set out in the judgment of the court.   *c*

Patrick M J O'Connor (assigned by the Registrar of Criminal Appeals) for the appellant.
Jeremy Benson for the Crown.

Cur adv vult *d*

29 July. The following judgment of the court was delivered.

WATKINS LJ. On 19 May 1988 in the Crown Court at Knightsbridge before his
Honour Judge Pownall QC, after a second retrial, the appellant was convicted of a number   *e*
of offences by a majority verdict (ten to two). On the following day he was sentenced for
supplying a controlled class B drug to another (three counts), and for supplying a
controlled class A drug to another (three counts), to concurrent terms of two years'
imprisonment, suspended for two years, and for possessing a class A drug to a concurrent
term of 12 months' imprisonment, suspended for two years. A supervision order for two
years was also made.   *f*

   The appellant appeals against conviction on the certificate of the trial judge, which is
in the following terms:

   'I ruled that on the evidence before me, the police officers should not reveal the
   location of their observation points or answer questions, the answers to which would
   or might reveal those observation points. I further ruled that there was not likely to   *g*
   be a miscarriage of justice.'

The judge added this footnote: 'There are 18 other such cases awaiting trial at this court.'
He conducted all the trials about to be referred to.

   The Crown alleged that in June 1987 the appellant was selling cannabis and cocaine on
the street in the vicinity of All Saints Road, Ladbroke Grove. He had been observed by
police officers during the course of an operation known as 'Trident'. They were stationed   *h*
at several points in buildings in the locality. There was no evidence but theirs that the
appellant was a supplier of these dangerous drugs.

   The first of three trials of the appellant was aborted. The jury in the second trial,
having failed to agree, were discharged.

   The evidence of the police officers emanated from observations kept on 20, 26 and 27
June 1987. Altogether six separate sales of drugs to persons, who included a teenager and   *j*
a woman, were observed. Packets were handed over by the appellant to those persons in
exchange for money. In most instances the packets were taken from the purchasers on
arrest by the police afterwards. Those packets contained either cannabis resin or cocaine
hydrochloride in relatively small amounts.

a The appellant was arrested on 30 June at his home in Westbourne Park Grove. Police found equipment there consistent with the use of cocaine. There were several folds of paper, but only one contained a small amount of cocaine. The appellant denied that he had at any time been involved in selling drugs in or near All Saints Road. He did not give evidence but his mother was called to do so. She told the jury that the appellant was always short of money and from time to time she gave him some. She stopped doing that when she learnt that he spent it on drugs which he was taking and which were doing *b* him no good.

Counsel suggested on his behalf that what the police had seen were not sales but purchases of drugs by the appellant. It was also suggested, rather more faintly, that the police officers had fabricated their logs of observations. And it was submitted that, by not having to reveal the nature of their locations when keeping observations, those officers were able successfully to cover up inconsistencies in their evidence. It was alleged *c* that there was no love lost between the appellant and the Notting Hill police because the appellant was known to have assaulted one of the officers stationed there when that officer was endeavouring to arrest the appellant for a suspected driving offence.

During the course of the trial the Crown argued that the police officers should not be compelled to reveal the location of the places from which they had kept observation. If evidence of that kind had to be given it would, it was said, do considerable harm to the *d* discovery of crime and the apprehension of criminals in an area where policing problems are acute. So, it was contended, it was in the interests of the public that police officers should keep observation from buildings neither the address nor the identity of occupiers of which should be revealed. The evidence which the Crown should be compelled to give should go no further than revealing that all the observation points were within a given maximum distance.

e Counsel for the appellant argued strongly against these propositions. He maintained that to uphold them would gravely embarrass him in endeavouring to test in cross-examination the evidence of the police officers as to what it was from here and there they actually could see, having regard to the layout of the street and the various objects in it, including trees.

f The judge was referred to authority. He had listened to similar arguments in the trial (the second trial) in which the jury had failed to agree. He heard evidence then (in the absence of the jury) from police officers about how difficult it was to obtain assistance from the public for the purpose of keeping observation. There was a need, it was claimed, to protect people who assisted the police for that purpose.

The judge ruled in that trial as follows:

g 'First of all, I am indebted to both counsel for the very careful argument each has addressed to me. [Counsel for the Crown] wants to adduce evidence of observation by a number of police officers without their disclosing the precise spot from which the observations were made. This is a case involving, allegedly, the possession and supplying of drugs and is one of a number of such cases to be heard at this court which are the result of police observations called "Operation Trident" in April, May *h* and June of last year in the All Saints Road, a road which is not altogether unknown to this court. Superintendent Hart has explained how it is not easy, indeed it is extremely difficult, to get assistance for the police in those circumstances, and he has explained, too, that there is every possibility that these premises that were used on these occasions will be used in the future. Sergeant Jacklyn has explained, and explained in detail, the need for protection. There is, of course, a long-recognised *j* rule of law that investigating police officers cannot be required to disclose the sources of their information. That rule has been held recently to apply equally to protect the identity of a person or persons who have allowed his or their premises to be used as observation points. The precise location of these premises is therefore protected by that rule. The rule is subject to a duty on me to admit such evidence if that is necessary in order to prevent a miscarriage of justice, and [counsel for the defendant] submits that there will be such a miscarriage of justice if I do not allow *a* him to put certain questions, the answers to which will, in the end, identify to those with the meanest of intelligence precisely the various observation points, and therefore the identity of the occupiers during this period. He says that his defence is that, at worst, the observing police officers have fabricated their evidence or, at best, have mistakenly identified this defendant. It is vital that observations of this sort should take place. They plainly cannot take place without the full co-operation *b* of members of the public, and it is very likely in most cases that co-operation would be lost if those members of the public thought they ran the risk of their co-operation being made known by being disclosed in court. It is equally plain that it is in the public interest that such people should not be discouraged from giving their co-operation. As Lawton LJ said in *R v Hennessey* (1979) 68 Cr App R 419 at 426: ". . . but cases may occur when for good reason the need to protect the liberty of the *c* subject should prevail over the need to protect informers. It will be for the accused to show that there is good reason." Putting it another way, as [counsel for the defendant] does put it to me, "If you rule in favour of the Crown the testing by me of their evidence will be so limited that justice for this defendant will be at risk." I have had the opportunity of considering this question very carefully, and have had the advantage, as I have said, of hearing careful argument on both sides. I have come *d* to the firm conclusion that it would be quite wrong to order, and therefore I will not order, that the police officers disclose the precise observation points, though some approximate details may be given. Nor will I order at which level the officers were, not will I order them to give details of the angles of their views, or exact distances; and I stress the word "exact" and I stress the word "precise". As a result of that ruling there are, of course, bound to be some limitations on the various cross- *e* examinations of witnesses by [counsel for the defendant] but in my view they are not so limiting that there is a risk of a miscarriage of justice.'

That ruling he maintained after further argument in the present trial (the third), having heard one of the police officers, namely Sergeant Jacklyn, give evidence to the effect that he had caused recent inquiries to be made of the occupiers of the premises *f* used for observation. All of them were the occupiers at the material times and none of them was, he said, happy for their names and addresses to be disclosed because they feared for their safety.

In summing up to the jury the judge dealt with this matter at some length. What he said needs to be fully stated. He said:

'You may think that those verdicts will, to a very large extent, depend on what *g* you make of those police witnesses who have told you what they saw as part of this larger Operation Trident, as it was called, in the All Saints Road. You have not only heard and seen all of them give evidence, how they gave it and how [it was] sought to have that evidence tested, so far as it could be, by way of cross-examination. Normally of course many, if not all, of the questions that [counsel for the defendant] *h* sought to ask, and did very properly ask, would have been answered. In this case, and it is not unique by any means, you have heard all of these police officers decline to answer a number of the questions, a number of important questions, that [counsel] asked of them and so it is important perhaps that I give you a brief outline why that came about and, indeed, [counsel] is anxious that you should know and it is right that you should. This case started originally in front of another jury. Before *j* long it became quite clear, I think during Pc Mayhew's evidence, that there ought to be some guidelines given to him and to others of the observing officers who were going to give evidence, there ought to be some guidelines which they had not as yet been given, as to how far they could go in giving their evidence, and so I brought that trial to an end I think, if my memory serves me right, during Pc Mayhew's evidence; the precise moment does not matter. After that a meeting was held with senior officers at which none of the observing officers were present and that meeting was called to decide how far all the various witnesses could go when giving their evidence. The problem was this: should police officers be ordered to give, if asked, details of where their observation point was, how high it was, at what level it was, what angle their view was from, which side of the road it was, or give exact distances from any point to their observation point, or say whether they were looking through net curtains or not, when to do so would, or might, identify the precise location of their observation point, especially when the answer of any particular police officer was to be added to answers given by other police officers in this case? You would no doubt readily understand that it is obviously important that police officers should not have to disclose the source, for instance, of their information, because surveillance and observation are a vital part of criminal intelligence and as a result it has been a long-standing rule that they should not be required to give the source of their information, and that rule has been extended to protect the identity of a person, or persons, who have allowed their premises to be used for such surveillance or observation and that came about, which must go without saying you may think, because people would not be half so keen to give their permission and co-operation for their premises to be used if they thought for a moment that their names and addresses would be disclosed in public for all to hear, and [counsel for the defendant] naturally accepts that as being a very real and proper fear, and, indeed, Mrs Johnson may not be crystal clear you may think [but] she said that, if she has an informer in the area and lets her premises be used by the police as an observation point, the whole area would be against her and maybe if she was walking down the road home to Shepherd's Bush she would get a gun or a knife in her back and she simply would not be able to do it, namely allow her premises to be so used, and so it is accepted that this is a very proper position for the police to take and an equally proper, clear and firm rule in the public interest and it is subject only to this: that the evidence should be allowed to be given, and indeed ordered to be given, if there is no likelihood of a miscarriage of justice taking place. That was gone into in some detail in the first retrial, by that I mean proceedings subsequent to the one I have just told you about, where I broke it off at the end of Pc Mayhew's evidence. I took the view that there was not likely to be a miscarriage of justice despite the fact that there would naturally be no answers given to some, even many, of the questions that [counsel] would quite properly seek to ask. One recognises, anybody would, that that puts something of an extra burden on you to consider particularly carefully all the evidence so as to ensure that a miscarriage of justice does not take place. It was decided at that meeting that the furthest the police officers could safely go was to say that observation points 1, 3 and 4 were within 100 yards south of the junction of the All Saints Road and St Luke's Mews and that observation point 2 was between 100 and 150 yards down St Luke's Mews and the east side. The trial took place and was completed, but at the end of it it stalled, the jury were unable to agree. That is something you have not heard put till now, but [counsel] wished you to hear it and so I have told you and so of course there had to be a retrial and this is it and you are trying it. The defence here you may think is twofold and in the alternative. Firstly, these deals that the police officers have told you about may well have taken place; did the officers make a dreadful mistake in their identification of this defendant as being the person conducting those deals with customers? and secondly, in the alternative, that the deals may well have taken place but the officers have quite deliberately burnished it, as [counsel] put it, fabricated their evidence that it was this defendant conducting them, and have done that thoroughly dishonestly. You of course will decide whether you are sure that these officers are right on the one hand, in which case your verdict would no doubt be one of guilty, or, on the other hand whether it may be put that they have fabricated their evidence, or are

dreadfully mistaken in their identification, either of this defendant, or as to nature
of the transactions. If that may be sensibly put, then your verdict no doubt would   *a*
be one of not guilty.'

The judge also directed the jury, impeccably in our view, on the issue of identification,
with the well-known case of *R v Turnbull* [1976] 3 All ER 549, [1977] QB 224 in mind.

The grounds of appeal are, first, that the judge was wrong to rule that neither the
observation points nor angles of views and so forth should be disclosed and he wrongly   *b*
concluded that this would not result in a miscarriage of justice. Second, the observation
evidence was unreliable and vulnerable to challenge and was unsupported by observation
from a different point or points. There was no supporting evidence whatsoever. Third,
the judge was wrong to prohibit cross-examination as to any existing restrictions on a
clear view of the appellant's alleged transactions. And, fourth, there were inconsistencies
in the evidence which made some, if not much, of it unreliable.   *c*

Counsel for the appellant began his submissions to us in support of these grounds by
contending that the judge's ruling was wrong in law, that there was insufficient material
given to him to raise a public interest immunity and accordingly the principle of a
miscarriage of justice applies. The very severe restrictions place on him, counsel said,
were unjustified in law. If such restrictions were necessary, that illustrates how inevitable
a miscarriage of justice became. It is simply not enough for counsel for the Crown, he   *d*
argued, merely to assert that restrictions were necesssary, there must be specific evidence
going to the need for the imposition of them. The Crown sought an unusual indulgence
and the judge in allowing it took an extraordinary course.

We were referred by him and by counsel for the Crown to a number of authorities,
some of which deal with what is known as the exclusionary rule. That the application of
this is warily regarded by the courts there is no doubt. The following observations of   *e*
Lord Edmund-Davies in *D v National Society of the Prevention of Cruelty to Children* [1977]
1 All ER 589 at 615, [1978] AC 171 at 242 testify to that:

> 'My Lords, it is a truism that, while irrelevant facts are inadmissible in legal
> proceedings in this country, not all inadmissible facts are irrelevant. To be received
> in evidence, facts must be both relevant and admissible, and under our law relevant
> facts may nevertheless be inadmissible. It is a serious step to exclude evidence   *f*
> relevant to an issue, for it is in the public interest that the search for truth should, in
> general, be unfettered. Accordingly, any hindrance to its seeker needs to be justified
> by a convincing demonstration that an even higher public interest requires that
> only part of the truth should be told.'

The rationale of that rule was explained by Lord Diplock in that very case. He said   *g*
([1977] 1 All ER 589 at 595, [1978] AC 171 at 218):

> 'The rationale of the rule as it applies to police informers is plain. If their identity
> were liable to be disclosed in a court of law, these sources of information would dry
> up and the police would be hindered in their duty of preventing and detecting
> crime. So the public interest in preserving the anonymity of police informers had   *h*
> to be weighed against the public interest that information which might assist a
> judicial tribunal to ascertain facts relevant to an issue on which it is required to
> adjudicate should be withheld from that tribunal. By the uniform practice of the
> judges which by the time of *Marks v Beyfus* (1890) 25 QBD 494 had already hardened
> into a rule of law, the balance has fallen on the side of non-disclosure except where
> on the trial of a defendant for a criminal offence, disclosure of the identity of the   *j*
> informer could help to show that the defendant was innocent of the offence. In that
> case, and in that case only, the balance falls on the side of disclosure.'

In *R v Rankine* [1986] 2 All ER 566, [1986] QB 861 this court held that that rule was
capable of being extended to this effect: its extension always having covered the sources

of information, it was also apt to cover points from which there was observation or
a surveillance of the commission of offences.

In *R v Brown* (1988) 87 Cr App R 52, a decision of this court, the authorities to which I
have referred were referred to in the context of a review of the exclusionary rule. In the
course of giving the judgment of the court Hodgson J said (at 59–60):

'We have been referred to no authority where a Court has held that the making
public of police methods or techniques was a public policy ground which would
b justify a judge in refusing to admit relevant evidence. Even if there is, or there
becomes, such a rule in the future, it would not, and could not, apply, we think, to
this particular case. We do not rule out the possibility that with the advent of no
doubt sophisticated methods of criminal investigation, there may be cases where
the public interest immunity may be successfully invoked in criminal proceedings
c to justify the exclusion of evidence as to police techniques and methods. But if and
when such an argument is to be raised, it must, in the judgment of this Court, be
done properly. The Crown Prosecution Service must at least ensure that counsel is
properly instructed to make the application and to identify with precision the
evidence sought to be excluded and the reasons for its exclusion. It would seem clear
that if such a contention is put forward the judge must be given as much information
d as possible and the application will have to be supported, not by the instructions of
the junior officer in charge of the case, but by the independent evidence of senior
officers.'

These citations suffice to show that it has been regarded as part of the exclusionary rule
that, provided there is a proper evidential basis for it, a trial judge may on application
exclude evidence which, if given, would reveal not only where the police have kept
e observation from but also, if they have kept that observation at premises, especially
dwellings, the identity of the occupiers.

The paramount consideration here is of course whether the appellant had an unfair
trial which led to a verdict which is either unsafe or unsatisfactory. Although the conduct
of the defence was to some extent affected by the restraints placed on it by the judge's
f rulings, which were in our view properly made, we are not persuaded that this led to any
injustice. The jury were well aware of these restraints and most carefully directed about
the very special care they had to give to any disadvantage they may have brought to the
defence. It was a summing up which was as a whole, we think, favourable to the defence
and which contained safeguarding directions which could have left the jury in no doubt
as to the nature of their task.

g The judge was not, of course, acquainted with the guidance we are about to give and
did not receive evidence which conformed to it before making the rulings complained
of. But he heard some evidence going part of the way to meet that guidance and he had
knowledge from previous trials conducted by him of the difficulties police encounter in
obtaining help from the public in the area where the appellant's offence was found to be
committed. He was, we think, in a sound enough position to balance the competing
h interests between the principle of full disclosure of material facts on the one hand and
the need, in the interests of justice, to in some degree conduct a trial without conforming
with it. It is risking condescension to say of him that he knew well the legal principles
involved. Moreover, we cannot agree that his rulings went too far to meet the needs of
the protection sought. We cannot accept that there was unfairness in this trial, or that
the verdict was either unsafe or unsatisfactory.

j While the judge, who is, as has already been indicated, so very experienced in handling
criminal trials, took infinite care to satisfy himself that there was in his opinion a
satisfactory evidential basis in the circumstances of this case for ruling that there be non-
disclosure by the police of information which could lead to identification of places used
for the purpose of observing the suspected commission of criminal offences, we accept
that, for the benefit of the police, counsel and judges who will have to face in the future

a similar problem to that which confronted this judge, some guidance from this court on basic evidential requirements would be found helpful. The submissions as to that, *a* from counsel for the appellant in particular, we have found valuable in considering what that guidance should be.

Clearly a trial judge must be placed by the Crown, when it seeks to exclude evidence of the identification of places of observation and occupiers of premises, in the best possible position to enable him properly in the interests of justice, which includes of course providing a defendant with a fair trial, to determine whether he will afford to the police *b* the protection sought. At the heart of this problem is the desirability, as far as that can properly be given, of reassuring people who are asked to help the police that their identities will never be disclosed lest they become the victims of reprisals by wrongdoers for performing a public service.

The minimum evidential requirements seem to us to be the following. (a) The police officer in charge of the observations to be conducted, and no one of lower rank than a *c* sergeant should usually be acceptable for this purpose, must be able to testify that beforehand he visited all observation places to be used and ascertained the attitude of occupiers of premises, not only to the use to be made of them but also to the possible disclosure thereafter of the use made and facts which could lead to the identification of the premises thereafter and of the occupiers. He may, of course, in addition inform the court of difficulties, if any, usually encountered in the particular locality of obtaining *d* assistance from the public. (b) A police officer of no lower rank than a chief inspector must be able to testify that immediately prior to the trial he visited the places used for observation, the results of which it is proposed to give in evidence, and ascertained whether the occupiers are the same as when the observations took place and, whether they are or are not, what the attitude of those occupiers is to the possible disclosure of the use previously made of the premises and of facts which could lead at the trial to *e* identification of premises and occupiers.

Such evidence will of course be given in the absence of the jury when the application to exclude the material evidence is made. The judge should explain to the jury, as this judge did, when summing up or at some appropriate time before that, the effect of his ruling to exclude, if he so rules.

There are trials waiting to be held, where we have to suppose the requirements of (a) *f* cannot be satisfied or wholly satisfied, because the guidance of this judgment was not available at the material time or times. In that event we think a judge may, according to the quality of the evidence before him under (b), and possibly in part satisfaction of (a), be able properly and safely to exclude evidence of facts sought to be protected.

For the reasons we have given, this appeal is dismissed.

g

Appeal dismissed.

Solicitors: *Crown Prosecution Service.*

N P Metcalfe Esq   Barrister.

a
Somasundaram v M Julius Melchior & Co (a firm)

COURT OF APPEAL, CIVIL DIVISION
MAY, STOCKER AND STUART-SMITH LJJ
4, 5, 6 MAY, 12 JULY 1988

b
Counsel – Negligence – Immunity – Conduct of criminal or civil proceedings – Impugning decision of court of competent jurisdiction – Whether action against barrister or solicitor in respect of conduct of criminal or civil proceedings an abuse of process if it involves attack on decision of court of competent jurisdiction.

c *Counsel – Negligence – Immunity – Conduct of criminal or civil proceedings – Advice as to plea in criminal proceedings – Barrister's immunity.*

Solicitor – Negligence – Immunity – Immunity when acting as an advocate – Advice as to plea in criminal proceedings – Extent of immunity.

d Following an incident in which he stabbed his wife during an argument, the plaintiff was charged with unlawful and malicious wounding. He instructed his solicitors that he intended to plead not guilty but later changed his story. The solicitors arranged a conference with counsel, who advised the plaintiff that on the basis of his revised story he had no defence and that he ought to plead guilty, which he did. He was sentenced to two years' imprisonment, which was reduced on appeal to 18 months. The plaintiff
e brought an action for damages for negligence against his solicitors alleging, inter alia, that he had been overpersuaded by them to change his story by suggestions that a guilty plea would improve his position in matrimonial proceedings between him and his wife. The master ordered the plaintiff's action to be struck out on the ground that it disclosed no reasonable cause of action and was frivolous and vexatious and an abuse of process.
f On appeal the master's decision was upheld by the judge. The plaintiff appealed to the Court of Appeal.

Held – An action for negligence against a barrister or solicitor in respect of the conduct of either criminal or civil proceedings would be struck out if it involved an attack on the decision of a court of competent jurisdiction. Accordingly, the plaintiff's action against
g his solicitors was an abuse of process since it necessarily involved an attack on the conviction in the Crown Court which was upheld by the Court of Appeal. The appeal would therefore be dismissed (see p 133 c d, p 136 b to d and p 137 b, post); *Hunter v Chief Constable of West Midlands* [1981] 3 All ER 727 applied; dicta of Lord Reid and Lord Morris in *Rondel v Worsley* [1967] 3 All ER 993 at 1000, 1012–1013 and *Saif Ali v Sydney Mitchell & Co (a firm)* [1978] 3 All ER 1033 considered.

h   Per curiam. Immunity from suit in respect of advice given to a client as to his plea in criminal proceedings is so intimately connected with the conduct of the cause in court that it is covered by the immunity applying to the conduct of litigation and such immunity extends not only to barristers but also to solicitors when acting as advocates, but it does not apply to solicitors when a barrister has also been engaged to advise, although in practice a solicitor's advice on plea which results in a decision of the court or
j which is subsequently confirmed by counsel could not give rise to liability on the part of the solicitor (see p 136 e f and p 137 a b, post).

Notes

For immunity from suit in the conduct of litigation, see 3 Halsbury's Laws (4th edn) para 1194, and for cases on the subject, see 3 Digest (Reissue) 786–787, 4875–4879.

For a solicitor's liability to a client for negligence, see 44 Halsbury's Laws (4th edn) paras 135–137, and for cases on the subject, see 44 Digest (Reissue) 132–135, *1306–1361*. a

Cases referred to in judgment

Hunter v Chief Constable of West Midlands [1981] 3 All ER 727, [1982] AC 529, [1981] 3 WLR 906, HL; *affg* sub nom *McIlkenny v Chief Constable of West Midlands Police Force* [1980] 2 All ER 227, [1980] QB 283, [1980] 2 WLR 689, CA.

Ladd v Marshall [1954] 3 All ER 745, [1954] 1 WLR 1489, CA. b

Rees v Sinclair [1974] 1 NZLR 180, NZ CA.

Reichel v Magrath (1889) 14 App Cas 665, HL.

Rondel v Worsley [1967] 3 All ER 993, [1969] 1 AC 191, [1967] 3 WLR 1666, HL; *affg* [1966] 3 All ER 657, [1967] 1 QB 443, [1966] 3 WLR 950, CA.

Saif Ali v Sydney Mitchell & Co (a firm) [1978] 3 All ER 1033, [1980] AC 198, [1978] 3 WLR 849, HL. c

Stephenson v Garnett [1898] 1 QB 677, CA.

Cases also cited

Evans v London Hospital Medical College [1981] 1 All ER 715, [1981] 1 WLR 184.

Hill v Chief Constable of West Yorkshire [1987] 1 All ER 1173, [1988] QB 60, CA; *affd* [1988] 2 All ER 238, [1988] 2 WLR 1049, HL. d

Jones v Dept of Employment [1988] 1 All ER 725, [1988] 2 WLR 493, CA.

Meah v McCreamer [1985] 1 All ER 367.

R v Foster [1984] 2 All ER 679, [1985] QB 115, CA.

R v Lee [1984] 1 All ER 1080, [1984] 1 WLR 578, CA.

R v Smith (Martin) [1974] 1 All ER 651, [1975] QB 531, CA.

S (an infant) v Manchester City Recorder [1969] 3 All ER 1230, [1971] AC 481, HL. e

Scudder v Prothero & Prothero (1966) 110 SJ 248.

Stupple (J W) v Royal Insurance Co Ltd [1970] 3 All ER 230, [1971] 1 QB 50, CA.

Appeal

The plaintiff, Harischandra Christian Thanjan Somasundaram, appealed against the decision of Sir Douglas Frank QC, sitting as a deputy judge of the High Court on f
12 November 1986, dismissing his appeal against the decision of Master Hodgson on 21 March 1986 to strike out his writ and statement of claim in his action against the respondents, M Julius Melchior & Co, a firm of solicitors, claiming damages for negligence while acting as his solicitors, on the ground that the claim disclosed no reasonable cause of action and was frivolous and vexatious and an abuse of process. The facts are set out in the judgment of the court. g

The appellant appeared in person.
Rupert Jackson QC and *Iain Hughes* for the respondents.
George Pulman as amicus curiae.

h

Cur adv vult

12 July. The following judgment of the court was delivered.

MAY LJ. This judgment which has been prepared principally by Stuart-Smith LJ is the judgment of the court. j
In April 1982 the appellant was arrested and charged following an incident in which he stabbed his wife during an argument. At his subsequent trial on 5 November 1982 he was indicted on alternative counts of causing grievous bodily harm with intent and unlawful and malicious wounding. He pleaded guilty to the latter count and was sentenced to two years' imprisonment. On 24 October 1983 his application for leave to

appeal against conviction was dismissed but his sentence was reduced to one of 18
a months' imprisonment. Throughout these matters the respondents, who are a firm of
solicitors, were instructed by and acted for the appellant.

On 4 May 1984 the appellant, acting in person, issued a writ against the respondents
for damages for their alleged negligence in acting for him in the matters to which we
have referred between April 1982 and February 1984.

On 21 March 1986, on the respondents' application to Master Hodgson, the latter
b struck out the appellant's statement of claim on the ground that it disclosed no reasonable
cause of action and that it was frivolous and vexatious and an abuse of the process of the
court. The appellant appealed against the master's order and his appeal came before Sir
Douglas Frank QC, sitting as a deputy judge of the High Court in the Queen's Bench
Division, on 12 November 1986. The deputy judge dismissed that appeal. The appellant
now appeals to this court asking that the order of the judge should be reversed and that
c he should be at liberty to continue with this litigation.

As the appellant before us was in person and the points raised by this appeal were
potentially important, the court asked for the appointment of an amicus curiae. Mr
Pulman of counsel was instructed so to act and we are grateful for the arguments which
he presented and for the assistance which he gave to us in the course of the appeal,
particularly as he did not consider himself able to support all the arguments addressed to
d us by counsel for the respondents.

Apart from two other substantial grounds relied on by the respondents both before us
and before the judge below, to which we refer later in this judgment, counsel submitted
in the first place that the appellant's claim in this action was clearly frivolous and
vexatious on its facts. The original version of the events which he gave to his solicitors,
the respondents, was that he had no recollection of picking up the knife with which his
e wife was stabbed; the incident must either have been an accident or at least the injury
caused by him acting in self-defence. On this basis the appellant originally instructed his
solicitors that he intended to plead not guilty and to defend the allegations against him
on this basis. He subsequently told his solicitors that he wished to change his story;
having spoken further to his wife and to his minister he remembered getting the knife
himself and hitting his wife on the head with it. In these circumstances the respondents
f arranged a conference with counsel attended by the appellant. At this, despite considerable
questioning by counsel, the appellant stuck to his revised story. Counsel consequently
advised him that he had no defence and the appellant decided that he would plead guilty,
which in the event he did.

It seems at least possible from the material we have that the appellant changed his
story to his solicitors in this way in the hope of achieving some reconciliation with his
g wife. There were at the time serious matrimonial difficulties and part of the appellant's
case before us, as we were able to understand it, was that as the respondents were acting
as his solicitors in the matrimonial proceedings between him and his wife, they were
able to exert pressure on him by pointing out, and indeed threatening, what might be
the result in the matrimonial proceedings, particularly in so far as the children were
h concerned, if he, the appellant, did not take their advice. It was in these circumstances,
the appellant suggested, that he had been overpersuaded to change his story and plead
guilty. It is sufficient to say that there is absolutely no evidence to support such a
contention and indeed all the relevant material in our papers is clearly to the contrary.

The appellant has also suggested that his solicitors and counsel failed to put forward
various matters of mitigation on his behalf. There is nothing in the papers to suggest
j that this is so; indeed it is apparent that the respondents did obtain a psychiatric report
on the appellant to see if this would be of assistance, but it clearly was not.

In these circumstances we have no doubt that this appellant has no reasonable chance
of success in this action on the facts alone and that consequently his claim is truly
frivolous and vexatious and should be struck out.

This would be sufficient to dispose of the appeal, but as two other important arguments

were raised by counsel for the respondents, and dealt with by counsel as amicus curiae,
we think that we too should deal with them in this judgment.   *a*

The first of these was that this action is an abuse of the process of the court in that the
plaintiff is seeking to attack in civil proceedings the final decision of a criminal court of
competent jurisdiction. In *Hunter v Chief Constable of West Midlands* [1981] 3 All ER 727
at 733–734, [1982] AC 529 at 541–542 Lord Diplock, with whose speech the other Law
Lords agreed, said:

b

'The abuse of process which the instant case exemplifies is the initiation of
proceedings in a court of justice for the purpose of mounting a collateral attack on a
final decision against the intending plaintiff which has been made by another court
of competent jurisdiction in previous proceedings in which the intending plaintiff
had a full opportunity of contesting the decision in the court by which it was made.
The proper method of attacking the decision by Bridge J in the murder trial that   *c*
Hunter was not assaulted by the police before his oral confession was obtained
would have been to make the contention that the judge's ruling that the confession
was admissible had been erroneous a ground of his appeal against his conviction to
the Criminal Division of the Court of Appeal. This Hunter did not do. Had he or
any of his fellow murderers done so, application could have been made on that
appeal to tender to the court as "fresh evidence" all material on which Hunter would   *d*
now seek to rely in his civil action against the police for damages for assault, if it
were allowed to continue. But since, quite apart from the tenuous character of such
evidence, it is not now seriously disputed that it was available to the defendants at
the time of the murder trial itself and could have been adduced then had those who
were acting for him or any of the other Birmingham bombers at the trial thought
that to do so would help their case, any application for its admission on the appeal   *e*
to the Court of Appeal, Criminal Division, would have been doomed to failure . . .
My Lords, collateral attack on a final decision of a court of competent jurisdiction
may take a variety of forms. It is not surprising that no reported case is to be found
in which the facts present a precise parallel with those of the instant case. But the
principle applicable is, in my view, simply and clearly stated in those passages from   *f*
the judgment of A L Smith LJ in *Stephenson v Garnett* [1898] 1 QB 677 and the
speech of Lord Halsbury LC in *Reichel v Magrath* (1889) 14 App Cas 665 which are
cited by Goff LJ in his judgment in the instant case. I need only repeat an extract
from the passage which he cited from the judgment of A L Smith LJ in *Stephenson v
Garnett* [1898] 1 QB 677 at 680–681: ". . . the Court ought to be slow to strike out a
statement of claim or defence, and to dismiss an action as frivolous and vexatious,   *g*
yet it ought to do so when, as here, it has been shewn that the identical question
sought to be raised has been already decided by a competent court." The passage
from Lord Halsbury LC's speech in *Reichel v Magrath* 14 App Cas 665 at 668 deserves
repetition here in full: ". . . I think it would be a scandal to the administration of
justice if, the same question having been disposed of by one case, the litigant were
to be permitted by changing the form of the proceedings to set up the same case   *h*
again."'

On the face of it that statement of the law appears to be directly in point. But counsel
as amicus curiae submits that it is inconsistent with the law as laid down in the House of
Lords in *Saif Ali v Sydney Mitchell & Co (a firm)* [1978] 3 All ER 1033, [1980] AC 198. In
that case it was held that the barrister's immunity from suit for negligence was not total   *j*
but only extended so far as was absolutely necessary in the interests of the administration
of justice. It was not confined to what was done in court but extended to pre-trial work—

'where the particular work is so intimately connected with the conduct of the
cause in Court that it can fairly be said to be a preliminary decision affecting the
way that cause is to be conducted when it comes to a hearing.'

The quotation is from the judgment of McCarthy P in *Rees v Sinclair* [1974] 1 NZLR 180
a at 187 and was approved by the majority of their Lordships' House.

In some cases where the barrister gives advice that is not immune from suit under this
principle there may be a judgment of a competent court against the plaintiff who wishes
to sue the negligent barrister. Counsel as amicus curiae submits that the House of Lords
cannot have intended in *Hunter's* case to say that such claims were an abuse of the process
of the court. He therefore invites this court to deal with the matter solely on the basis of
b immunity, so that the reconciliation of these difficulties can be left for resolution to the
House of Lords. But in our judgment the two decisions are not unreconcilable. In *Saif
Ali's* case the alleged negligence was failure to sue the correct defendant before the claim
was statute-barred. The claims against the allegedly negligent drivers were never
considered on their merits. The situation is akin to that which all too commonly occurs
where through negligence a writ is not issued in time or proceedings are struck out for
c want of prosecution. In such cases there is no question of there being a direct or indirect
attack on the decision of a court of competent jurisdiction.

It is perfectly possible to reconcile the two decisions on the basis that even if a barrister
is not immune from suit, where there has in fact been a decision on the merits by a court
of competent jurisdiction public policy requires that that decision should not be
impugned either directly or indirectly.
d Moreover we find it impossible to accept that Lord Diplock overlooked the implications
of the decision in *Saif Ali*. Not only was the case cited in argument in *Hunter's* case but a
passage from the speech of Lord Diplock was cited by Goff LJ in the Court of Appeal (see
McIlkenny v Chief Constable of West Midlands Police Force [1980] 2 All ER 227 at 250, [1980]
QB 283 at 337) on the abuse of the powers of the court. Goff LJ's judgment was approved
in the House of Lords (see [1981] 3 All ER 727 at 736, [1982] AC 529 at 545 per Lord
e Diplock). The passage cited by Goff LJ was as follows ([1978] 3 All ER 1033 at 1045,
[1980] AC 198 at 222–223):

'Under the English system of administration of justice, the appropriate method
of correcting a wrong decision of a court of justice reached after a contested hearing
is by appeal against a judgment to a superior court. This is not based solely on
f technical doctrines of res judicata but on principles of public policy, which also
discourage collateral attack on the correctness of a subsisting judgment of a court of
trial on a contested issue by retrial of the same issue, either directly or indirectly in
a court of co-ordinate jurisdiction ... My Lords, it seems to me that to require a
court of co-ordinate jurisdiction to try the question whether another court reached
a wrong decision and, if so, to enquire into the causes of its doing so is calculated to
g bring the administration of justice into disrepute.'

Counsel as amicus curiae submitted that it would be an anomaly amounting to an
absurdity if a barrister or solicitor could be sued for work in respect of which he is not
immune under the principle of *Saif Ali*, where no decision of a court on the merits was
involved, but could not where there was such a decision and the claim involved reopening
h that decision. But this is no more than saying that the rule involves hardship on the
plaintiff in the latter case who cannot sue in respect of the negligence. All decisions that
a suit, which would otherwise lie, cannot be brought on the grounds of public policy,
involve hardship.

It may be objected that abuse of the process on the basis of a collateral attack on the
judgment of another court would have been the short answer to the claim in *Rondel v
j Worsley* [1967] 3 All ER 993, [1969] 1 AC 191, whereas in fact it was merely one of the
bases on which the barrister's immunity was founded. Lord Reid put it shortly ([1967] 3
All ER 993 at 1000, [1969] 1 AC 191 at 230):

'So after the plaintiff's appeal against conviction had been dismissed by the Court
of Criminal Appeal, the whole case would in effect have to be retried in a civil court
where the standard of proof is different. That is something one would not
contemplate with equanimity unless there is a real need for it.'

But Lord Morris dealt with it at length ([1967] 3 All ER 993 at 1012–1013, [1969] 1 AC
191 at 248–251):

> 'Is it, as a matter of public policy, expedient that actions which involve a searching
> review almost amounting to a re-trial in different actions of previous actions or cases
> already concluded should not be allowed? Is the administration of justice (which is
> so much the concern of the community) better promoted if such actions are not
> countenanced? If it is recognised that there could be some cases where negligence
> (as opposed to errors of judgment) could be established, is it nevertheless on a
> balance of desirabilities wise to disallow the bringing of such cases? In my view, the
> answer to these questions is that it is in the public interest that such actions should
> not be brought. In this, as in other aspects of the present case, I find myself in
> general accord with the judgment of SALMON, L.J. ([1966] 3 All ER 657 at 673,
> [1967] 1 QB 443 at 514). It will be useful to consider some of the circumstances that
> would arise if such actions were permitted. If someone has been tried on a criminal
> charge and has been convicted, it would not be of any purpose for him to assert that
> his counsel had been unskilful, unless he could prove that he would have been
> acquitted had his counsel conducted the case with due care and skill. He would have
> to prove that on a balance of probability. He would, however, only have been
> convicted if the jury had been sure that his guilt had been established. If he asserts
> that, had his counsel asked some more questions than he did ask, the jury in the
> criminal case or the magistrates would have acquitted him, would he be entitled in
> his negligence action to call as witnesses the members of the jury or the members of
> the bench of magistrates who had convicted him? I have no doubt that it would be
> against public policy to permit any such course. If there were a conviction by a
> majority verdict of ten to two, could one of the ten be called to say that had there
> been further questions put to some witness he would have agreed with the two
> jurors? Again, that, in my view, would be procedure that ought not to be permitted.
> If there were a jury in the civil action for negligence they would have to decide
> whether, on the assumption that the additional questions had been put, there
> probably would have been an acquittal. Presumably they would have to review all
> the evidence that had been given in the criminal case. They would either need to
> have a transcript of it or they would have to hear the witnesses who had previously
> given evidence. After a period of time the witnesses might not be available. The
> transcript might not be obtainable. If obtainable it might relate to a trial that had
> taken not days but weeks to try. Assuming, however, that all the necessary evidence
> was available and assuming that memories were not dimmed by the passing of time,
> the civil jury would in effect be required to be engaged in a re-trial of the criminal
> case. That would be highly undesirable. And supposing that after a criminal trial a
> person was convicted and then appealed unsuccessfully against his conviction and
> later brought a civil action against his counsel alleging negligence: if he succeeded,
> would any procedure have to be devised to consider whether or not it would be
> desirable to set aside the conviction. The conviction (as in the present case) might
> have taken place years before. Any sentence of imprisonment imposed might have
> been served (as in the present case) long before. If in the civil action the suggestion
> was made that, had there been further evidence called or further questions put in
> the criminal case, there might have been a disagreement rather than a conviction,
> this only serves to demonstrate how difficult it would be for a court to decide on a
> balance of probabilities what the jury in the criminal case would have done had
> there been different material before them. A trial on a trial would raise speculation
> on speculation. It may be said that these considerations merely point to the
> difficulties that would lie in the way of success by a convicted person who brought
> an action. (The difficulties would be greater in the case of a private prosecutor who,
> being disappointed by the acquittal of someone who had been prosecuted, brought
> an action for negligence against prosecuting counsel. Apart from the difficulties of

proving damage, it would surely be highly undesirable that an issue whether
a someone was guilty of an offence should be tried in proceedings to which he was
not a party.) In my view, the considerations to which I have referred are of deeper
and more fundamental significance. The procedure regulating criminal trials and
the machinery for appeals in criminal cases is part of the structure of the law. Much
of it is statutory. In practice the judges who preside at criminal trials do what they
can to ensure that the case of an accused person, whether he is represented or
b whether he is not, is fairly and adequately presented. If there is an appeal there are
rules which regulate the approach of the appeal court, and which apply to such
matters as whether evidence will be heard on appeal or whether a new trial will be
ordered. In practice it is unlikely that, owing to some want of care, counsel would
refrain from calling at the trial a witness who was thought to be dependable and
whose testimony would certainly secure an acquittal. It is to be remembered also
c that an accused person is at liberty to give evidence on his own behalf. A system
which is devised so as to provide adequate and reasonable safeguards against the
conviction of innocent persons and to provide for appeals must nevertheless aim at
some measure of finality. If the system is found not to be adequate then it can be
altered and modified: it can be kept continually under review. I cannot think,
however, that it would be in the public interest to permit a sort of unseemly
d excrescence on the legal system whereby someone who has been convicted and has,
without success, exhausted all the procedures for appeal open to him should seek to
establish his innocence (and to get damages) by asserting that he would not have
been convicted at all but for the fact that his advocate failed to exercise due care and
skill. Many of these considerations have parallel validity in regard to complaints of
lack of care and skill in a civil action. It is true that courts must not avoid reaching
e decisions merely because there are difficulties involved in reaching them. It may
not be impossible in certain circumstances for one civil court to decide that an
earlier case in a civil court (one, for example, tried by a judge alone) would have had
a different result had some different course been pursued, though in most cases
there would be likely to be various difficulties in the way of reaching such a
conclusion. It would, in my view, be undesirable in the interests of the fair and
f efficient administration of justice to tolerate a system under which, as a sort of by-
product after the trial of an action and after any appeal or appeals, there were
litigation on litigation with the possibility of a recurring chain-like course of
litigation.'

In *Rondel v Worsley* the case seems to have turned on the barrister's immunity, but it
g seems to us that these principles of public policy enunciated by Lord Morris stand in
their own right and might be applied to a case where no immunity existed.

Counsel as amicus curiae suggested that it might be impossible to argue that a different
rule applied to civil and criminal cases, though his submission was that there should be
no difference. It may be said that there is a greater public interest in preventing collateral
attacks on decisions of criminal courts, than there is in civil cases, since the former
h involve the public at large, whereas the latter involve only the parties. But this is not so
in applications for judicial review and many civil actions have repercussions on those
who are not directly parties. There is a greater public interest that a person should not be
wrongly convicted of a criminal offence, than that there should be a wrong decision in a
civil case. This is reflected in the differing standard of proof and the greater scope for the
admission of fresh evidence in a criminal case than in a civil case. Under s 23(1) of the
j Criminal Appeal Act 1968 the court has a wide discretion to admit further evidence if
they 'think it necessary or expedient in the interests of justice'. In a civil court, the Court
of Appeal will only grant leave to adduce further evidence if it is shown that the evidence
could not have been obtained with reasonable diligence for use at the trial, that it would
probably have an important influence on the result of the case and is credible: *Ladd v
Marshall* [1954] 3 All ER 745, [1954] 1 WLR 1489. These requirements broadly

correspond to the provisions of s 23(2) of the 1968 Act, which if satisfied require the
court to admit the evidence. Thus in a criminal case it may well be easier for an appellant   *a*
to persuade the Court of Appeal, Criminal Division to quash a conviction on the ground
that the verdict is unsafe and unsatisfactory, or to grant a retrial because through the
negligence of the appellant's solicitor important evidence was not available at the trial,
than it would be for an appellant in a civil appeal, who would not normally be able to
surmount the hurdle in *Ladd v Marshall* of showing that the evidence could not have
been obtained with the exercise of reasonable diligence. This would involve hardship   *b*
and injustice on the civil litigant if he could not sue his solicitor. Both *Hunter's* case
[1981] 3 All ER 727, [1982] AC 529 and the present involve an attack on the decision of
a criminal court and therefore any opinion in relation to the decision of a civil court is
not strictly necessary. But we cannot read Lord Diplock's speech in *Hunter* as confined to
criminal cases, especially as the authorities to which he refers are both civil cases. We
agree with counsel that it is difficult in principle to draw any distinction between the   *c*
decision of a criminal court and a civil court.

For these reasons it is in our judgment an abuse of the process of the court for the
appellant to bring this action which necessarily involves an attack on the conviction and
sentence imposed by the Crown Court and upheld in the Court of Appeal, Criminal
Division, subject to the reduction in sentence.

The remaining ground on which counsel for the respondents submits that the action   *d*
should be struck out is on the ground that the respondents are immune from suit in
respect of the allegations in the statement of claim and the action is therefore bound to
fail. This submission was supported by counsel as amicus curiae. Both counsel submit,
rightly in our judgment, that advice as to a plea is something which is so intimately
connected with the conduct of the cause in court that it can fairly be said to be a
preliminary decision affecting the way that the cause is to be conducted when it comes   *e*
to a hearing, within the test proposed by McCarthy P in *Rees v Sinclair* [1974] 1 NZLR
180 and approved by the House of Lords in *Saif Ali's* case [1978] 3 All ER 1033, [1980]
AC 198. Indeed it is difficult to think of any decision more closely so connected. Counsel
submitted that such immunity must therefore extend to solicitors and he relied on
passages in the speeches of their Lordships in *Rondel v Worsley* [1967] 3 All ER 993,   *f*
[1969] 1 AC 191 to this effect. But to our minds it is clear that in extending the immunity
to solicitors, their Lordships limited it to the occasions when they were acting as
advocates, as of course they frequently do in the magistrates' courts and county courts
and occasionally in those Crown Courts where they have rights of audience. Lord Reid
said ([1967] 3 All ER 993 at 1001, [1969] 1 AC 191 at 232):

> 'There are differences between the position of barristers and solicitors; not all the   *g*
> arguments which I have adduced apply to solicitors. But the case for immunity of
> counsel appears to me to be so strong that I would find it difficult to regard those
> differences as sufficient to justify a different rule for solicitors. I have already shown
> that solicitors have the same absolute privilege as counsel when conducting a case.
> So my present view is that the public interest does require that a solicitor should not
> be liable to be sued for negligence in carrying out work in litigation which would   *h*
> have been carried out by counsel if counsel had been engaged in the case.'

(See also [1967] 3 All ER 993 at 1024, 1035, [1969] 1 AC 191 at 267, 284 per Lord Pearce
and Lord Upjohn.)

Counsel as amicus curiae submitted that in a case where there was both solicitor and
barrister, it would be anomalous if the immunity in relation to advising on plea extended   *j*
to the barrister, but not to the solicitor. That may be so; but we would not be willing to
extend the immunity that protects barristers and solicitors qua advocates any further
than is necessary in the interests of justice and public policy. Thus we are not persuaded
in this case that the action should be struck out on the grounds of immunity from suit,
in so far as this is a separate heading from the first ground.

a   In practice of course it makes no difference, because in a criminal case advice on plea is likely to result in a decision of the court, which would first have to be upset by the proper appeal process before any action for damages could be sustained. Moreover where, as here, the advice as to plea was later confirmed by counsel, any action against the solicitor would almost certainly be bound to fail either on the ground that the solicitor has also been advised by counsel and was not negligent or, as a matter of causation, counsel's intervention broke any link between the solicitor's advice and the eventual plea.

b   For these reasons we think that the judge was right in the conclusion he reached and this appeal is dismissed.

Appeal dismissed. Leave to appeal to House of Lords refused.

Solicitors: *Reynolds Porter Chamberlain* (for the respondents); *Treasury Solicitor.*

c
                                                              Carolyn Toulmin   Barrister.

d

Public Disclosure Commission v Isaacs

PRIVY COUNCIL
LORD BRIDGE OF HARWICH, LORD BRANDON OF OAKBROOK, LORD BRIGHTMAN, LORD GRIFFITHS AND LORD ACKNER
e   16 MAY, 20 JUNE 1988

Natural justice – Hearing – Duty to hear parties etc – Bahamas Public Disclosure Commission – Complaint as to incomplete declarations of financial affairs – Whether complainant entitled to be given opportunity to rebut finding of commission – Public Disclosure Act 1976 (Bahamas).

f   The complainant, the Leader of the Opposition in the Bahamas, made a complaint to the Bahamas Public Disclosure Commission that the Prime Minister of the Bahamas had made incomplete declarations as to his financial affairs for the years 1977 to 1982, contrary to the Public Disclosure Act 1976. The commission investigated the complaint and held that it had not been substantiated. The complainant sought an order of certiorari to quash the commission's decision but his application was dismissed. On appeal the
g   Bahamas Court of Appeal granted the application on the ground that the complainant had not been given an opportunity of rebutting the commission's finding before it announced its decision. The commission appealed to the Privy Council. The complainant contended that once the commission formed the opinion under the Act that a complaint should be investigated it was obliged to give the complainant the opportunity not only
h   to lay before it whatever factual material he relied on, but also to controvert, refute or rebut any case made to the commission by the declarant in answer to the complaint.

Held—Since the commission's procedure under the 1976 Act was inquisitorial rather than adversarial the commission was not required by the rules of natural justice to give a
j   complainant the opportunity of rebutting a finding that the complaint made against the declarant had not been made out before the commission reached its decision. It followed that the commission was entitled to find that the complaint had not been substantiated. The appeal would accordingly be allowed (see p 141 *e f* and p 141 *h* to p 142 *a h*, post).

Dictum of Lord Denning MR in *Selvarajan v Race Relations Board* [1976] 1 All ER 12 at 19 considered.

Notes
For the right to a hearing, see 1 Halsbury's Laws (4th edn) para 76, and for cases on the   *a*
subject, see 1(1) Digest (Reissue) 200–201, *1172–1176*.

Case referred to in opinion
Selvarajan v Race Relations Board [1976] 1 All ER 12, [1975] 1 WLR 1686, CA.

Appeal   *b*
The Public Disclosure Commission appealed with leave of the Court of Appeal of the
Bahamas against the judgment of the Court of Appeal (Luckhoo P, Henry and Smith JJA)
given on 27 February 1986 allowing an appeal by the respondent, Kendal G L Isaacs QC,
from the judgment of Georges CJ dated 5 July 1985 in the Supreme Court whereby he
dismissed the respondent's application for an order of certiorari to quash the decision of
the commission made on 20 December 1984 and published in the Official Gazette dated   *c*
18 January 1984 that the complaint made by the respondent on 2 October 1984 that the
Prime Minister of the Bahamas, the Rt Hon Sir Lynden Pindling KCMG, had failed to
declare various payments made to him in declarations under the Public Disclosure Act
1976 was unsubstantiated, and for an order of mandamus directed to the commission to
rehear the complaint. The facts are set out in the judgment of the Board.
                                                                                              d
Mark Littman QC and *Michael Hamilton* (of the Bahamas Bar) for the commission.
Robin Potts QC and *David Mabb* for the respondent.

20 June. The following judgment of the Board was delivered.

LORD BRIDGE. The Public Disclosure Act 1976 requires senators and the members   *e*
of Parliament in the Commonwealth of the Bahamas to make disclosure to the Public
Disclosure Commission (the Commission) of their financial affairs. In October 1984 the
respondent to the present appeal, Mr Kendal Isaacs QC, the Leader of the Opposition,
made a formal complaint to the commission that for each of the years 1977 to 1982 the
declarations made under the Act by the Prime Minister, Sir Lynden Pindling, relating to
his financial affairs had been incomplete. The commission investigated the complaint   *f*
and on 20 December 1984 reached the conclusion that it was not substantiated. A notice
to that effect was in due course published in the Official Gazette.
    In April 1985 the respondent instituted proceedings for judicial review, applying for
orders of certiorari to quash the commission's decision and mandamus to require it to
hear his complaint according to law. The application was dismissed by Georges CJ on
5 July 1985. This decision was unanimously reversed by the Court of Appeal (Luckhoo   *g*
P, Henry and Smith JJA) on 27 February 1986, who granted the orders of certiorari and
mandamus sought. The commission now appeals to Her Majesty in Council pursuant to
leave granted by the Court of Appeal on 21 October 1986.
    It appears from the affidavit of the respondent sworn in support of his application that
in November 1983 the Governor General of the Commonwealth of the Bahamas   *h*
appointed a commission of inquiry to inquire into drug trafficking between the Bahamas
and the United States of America and other ancillary matters. It is important to emphasise
that their Lordships know nothing of the proceedings of that commission of inquiry and
are in no way concerned with its subject matter. The only relevance of the commission
of inquiry is that the factual basis of the complaint made to the commission by the
respondent was a statement by one Inspector Richter relating to the financial affairs of Sir   *j*
Lynden Pindling which was exhibited to the respondent's affidavit as representing the
evidence given by Inspector Richter to the commission of inquiry. Again it must be
noted that the issues which arise for determination in this appeal do not require their
Lordships to examine the factual material contained in Inspector Richter's statement,
still less to pass any judgment on it. The fact that the present proceedings arise from a

a dispute between the Prime Minister and the Leader of the Opposition in the Commonwealth of the Bahamas of a somewhat dramatic character is of no relevance to the appeal and their Lordships are certainly not required, nor are they in any position, to pronounce on the merits of that dispute. The only issues their Lordships have to decide are whether the procedure followed by the commission in investigating the respondent's complaint contravened in any way the provisions of the Act or can otherwise be impugned as failing to conform to procedural standards applicable in accordance with

b established principles of public law.

It is common ground that the object of the Act is the maintenance of probity in public life. Sections 4 and 5 require every senator and member of Parliament to make an annual declaration to the commission in a prescribed form disclosing the assets, income and liabilities of himself and his family. The critical sections on which the issues in the appeal primarily depend are ss 6, 7 and 8 which provide as follows:

c

'**6.**—(1) The Commission shall examine every declaration furnished to it and may request from a Senator or Member of Parliament any information or explanation relevant to a declaration made by him, which in its opinion, would assist it in its examination.

(2) Where upon an examination under subsection (1) the Commission is satisfied
d that a declaration has been fully made, it shall publish a summary of that declaration in the Gazette in the form prescribed by Form B in the Second Schedule.

(3) Where the Commission publishes a summary of a declaration under section (2) any person may make a written complaint to the Commission in relation to that summary.

7.—(1) Where—(a) upon an examination under section 6(1) the Commission is
e not satisfied that a declaration has been fully made and is of the opinion that further investigation is necessary; or (b) after a summary of a declaration has been published in the Gazette under section 6(2) and any person makes a written complaint to the Commission in relation to that summary and the Commission, after consideration of the complaint, is of the opinion that the complaint should be investigated, the Commission may—(i) in writing request the Senator or Member of Parliament
f concerned or the complainant to furnish such further information or documents as it may require, within such time as it may specify; (ii) in writing require the Senator or Member of Parliament concerned to attend on the Commission at such time as may be specified by the Commission; (iii) make such independent inquiries and investigation relating to the declaration or complaint as it thinks necessary; (iv) summon witnesses, require the production of documents and do all such things as
g it considers necessary or expedient for the purpose of carrying out its functions; and (v) in respect of paragraph (b), in addition, summon the complainant, hear the complainant, (who may be represented by a counsel and attorney), and any witnesses of the complainant in support of the complaint.

(2) Where a Senator or Member of Parliament is required to attend on the
h Commission pursuant to subsection (1), he shall have the right to be accompanied, and represented by a counsel and attorney for the purpose of such enquiry, and may require the Commission to summon such witnesses as he thinks necessary.

8.—(1) Where—(a) any person fails to furnish the Commission with a declaration which he is required to furnish in accordance with this Act; or (b) the Commission examines a declaration and any related information or documents, or conducts an
j enquiry into any such declaration or into a complaint made in respect of any summary of a declaration and is not satisfied with any aspect thereof, the Commission shall report the matter (setting out such details and particulars as the Commission in its discretion thinks fit) to the Prime Minister and the Leader of the Opposition.

(2) The Prime Minister or the Leader of the Opposition, when a report is made pursuant to subsection (1), may—(a) publish by way of communication to the

House of Assembly any information furnished to him by the Commission; (b) cause
to be published to the Senate any information furnished to him by the Commission; **a**
(c) authorise the furnishing of any information furnished to him by the Commission
to the Attorney-General or the Commissioner of Police.

(3) Where the Commission after conducting an enquiry in accordance with
section 7(1) into any complaint made under section 6(3) is satisfied that the
complaint is groundless or has not been substantiated it shall publish a statement in
the Gazette to that effect, and in addition, where the complaint is groundless, the **b**
Commission shall report the matter to the Attorney-General.'

Section 10 imposes a duty on the commission and its staff to treat all documents and
information relating to a declaration as secret and confidential and prohibits their
disclosure otherwise than as authorised by or for the purposes of the Act. Section 13
makes it a criminal offence, inter alia, to make 'any frivolous, vexatious or groundless
complaint to the Commission in relation to a summary of a declaration'.   **c**

As already indicated, the respondent, in making his complaint to the commission,
relied on the factual material contained in the statement of Inspector Richter as showing
that the Prime Minister had failed to make proper disclosure in his statutory declarations
under s 4 of the Act for the years 1977 to 1982. He did not then suggest, nor has it at any
time been suggested in the course of the proceedings, that he had any additional relevant **d**
factual material which he was in a position to put before the commission in support of
his complaint.

The procedure of the commission in investigating the complaint is described by the
chairman of the commission in an affidavit as follows:

'4. On 27th November, 1984 the Commission of which I was a member and the
Chairman commenced consideration of the complaint pursuant to our duty under **e**
section 7 of the Public Disclosure Act, 1976.

5. On considering the complaint we enquired into the matters complained of
and on November 29th, 1984 we called upon Sir Lynden Pindling for clarification
and explanation as to particular aspects of his declaration to the Commission for the
years 1977 to 1983 inclusive.   **f**

6. On December 13th, 1984 the Commission received explanations and answers
from Sir Lynden Pindling, and the Commission continued its consideration of and
enquiry into the complaint.

7. On December 20th, 1984 the Commission concluded its consideration and
enquiry. The decision of the Commission was that the complaint had not been
substantiated.'   **g**

The deponent to this affidavit was not cross-examined.

No issue was raised in argument before the board turning on the construction of any
of the detailed provisions of the statute and, in particular, it was common ground that
the several powers conferred on the commission by s 7(1)(i) to (v) of the Act are
discretionary. The essence of the attack on the procedure of the commission mounted on **h**
behalf of the respondent was in the submission that, either as a matter of construction
arising from a consideration of the underlying purpose of the Act or as a matter of
procedural fairness to a complainant, once the commission formed the opinion under
s 7(1)(b) that a complaint should be investigated, it was obliged to give the complainant
the opportunity not only to lay before it whatever factual material he relied on, but also
to controvert, refute or rebut any case made to the commission by the declarant in answer **j**
to the complaint.

At the outset, their Lordships express their agreement with Georges CJ that if the
commission was provisionally minded to find a complaint frivolous, vexatious or
groundless and, in so reporting to the Attorney General under s 8(3), to expose the
complainant to the risk of prosecution for an offence under s 13, it would have to indicate

a to the complainant the reasons for their provisional view and give him a fair opportunity, at an oral hearing if he so wished, to demonstrate that its provisional view was unfounded and that he had at least good grounds for making the complaint. But such a question would ordinarily arise before the commission ever called on the declarant to meet or answer the complaint and in any event does not arise in this case.

It is important, in their Lordships' judgment, to appreciate the implications of the case made for the respondent. Counsel for the respondent, in presenting the argument,
b appeared reluctant to go further than saying that the commission, having received from a declarant his answer to a complaint, must reveal to the complainant the gist of that answer. Their Lordships find it difficult to understand how this would significantly advance the matter or how merely being told the gist of the declarant's answer would assist a complainant in making good his complaint. In their Lordships' judgment there can really be no half-way house in this matter. Once the complainant has laid before the
c commission all the material on which he relies in support of the complaint, the ensuing procedure must take one of two courses. One alternative is that the commission should conduct its investigation of the complaint wholly in private as a purely inquisitorial body making whatever further inquiry it thinks necessary into the material furnished by the complainant, calling for any answers and explanations it requires from the declarant and reaching its own conclusions. The other alternative is that the procedure on investigation
d of a complaint should take on a fully adversarial character treating the complainant and the declarant as parties to a lis, each having an equal opportunity to challenge and comment on the cases made by the other, with the commission simply adjudicating between them.

Their Lordships think that there are clear indications in the statute that it was the inquisitorial, not the adversarial, procedure which the legislature contemplated. First, it
e is to be noted that a full investigation into the declaration made by a senator or member of Parliament may be undertaken by the commission either of its own motion under s 7(1)(a) before it publishes any summary or after publication of the summary on receipt of a complaint under s 7(1)(b). The discretionary powers available to it in either case, save those expressly referring to the complainant, are the same. It is difficult to see why the
f procedure should be fundamentally different in the one case than in the other. If evidence casting doubt on the sufficiency of a declaration comes to the attention of the commission before it publishes any summary, it may investigate it fully itself and reach the conclusion that the declaration is nevertheless satisfactory. If then, after publication of the commission's summary, exactly the same evidence is submitted to them in support of a complaint, it may properly form the opinion under s 7(1)(b) that, the matter having already been investigated, no further investigation is necessary. This was rightly conceded
g by counsel for the respondent in argument. It underlines the difficulty of construing the statute as requiring fundamentally different procedures to be followed by the commission in investigating the selfsame material according to whether it reaches it before it publishes any summary or after publication by way of complaint.

But a second and perhaps even more formidable obstacle to a construction which
h would require the commission to afford to every complainant the rights of a party litigant is that this would necessarily undermine the provisions protecting the secrecy and confidentiality of information which senators and members of Parliament may have to disclose to the commission in relation to their private affairs. The publication of the summary for which s 6(2) and Sch 2 to the Act make provision is already a substantial and no doubt necessary invasion of privacy. But the legislature have provided by s 10
j that the possibly intimate and more far reaching information relating to the private affairs of a declarant and his family which he may have to disclose to the commission in the course of an investigation under s 7 shall be protected from public scrutiny. An adversarial procedure would destroy that protection by making such information available to a complainant who could not then be prevented from disseminating it further.

Accordingly, so far from supporting the respondent's contention, a construction of the Act in the light of its underlying purpose appears to their Lordships to weigh heavily *a* against it.

The respondent succeeded in the Court of Appeal on the alternative ground that the so-called audi alteram partem rule applied. The principle underlying the rule is clearly expressed in the judgment of Lord Denning MR in *Selvarajan v Race Relations Board* [1976] 1 All ER 12 at 19, [1975] 1 WLR 1686 at 1693–1694, where he said:

> 'In recent years we have had to consider the procedure of many bodies who are *b* required to make an investigation and form an opinion . . . In all these cases it has been held that the investigating body is under a duty to act fairly; but that which fairness requires depends on the nature of the investigation and the consequences which it may have on persons affected by it. The fundamental rule is that, if a person may be subjected to pains or penalties, or be exposed to prosecution or *c* proceedings, or deprived of remedies or redress, or in some such way adversely afflicted by the investigation and report, then he should be told the case made against him and be afforded a fair opportunity of answering it.'

With respect to the Court of Appeal, their Lordships do not think that this principle has any application to a complainant under the Act, save in the case already considered and not here applicable where the commission is minded to report to the Attorney *d* General under s 8(3) that the complaint was groundless. In any other case the complainant is not liable to be subjected to any pains or penalties or exposed to prosecution. He is not seeking to enforce any private right, so there is no question of depriving him of any remedies or redress to which he may be entitled. He is acting as a public spirited citizen in giving information to the commission to assist it in the performance of its public duty. Any personal or political interest he may have in the outcome is irrelevant. He *e* cannot be 'told the case made against him and afforded a fair opportunity of answering it' because no case is made against him; it is he who makes a case against the declarant. It was submitted for the respondent that he was adversely affected by the publication in the gazette of the commission's conclusion that his complaint was not substantiated. Their Lordships cannot accept that this is a matter of sufficient weight to prevail against the *f* countervailing considerations to which attention has already been directed. The language used in the statute distinguishing between complaints which are frivolous, vexatious or groundless on the one hand and complaints which are not substantiated on the other may be open to misunderstanding by uninformed members of the public. But on the true construction of the statute a finding that a complaint has not been substantiated connotes no more than that, when investigated and considered in the light of all available *g* evidence, the complaint was not made out. Such a finding casts no adverse reflection on the complainant. Any person making a complaint under s 7(1)(b) must be presumed to know that, although made in good faith and on sufficient grounds, his complaint may fail because it can be successfully rebutted and that this will lead to a published statement by the commission that it was not substantiated.

For these reasons their Lordships will humbly advise Her Majesty that the appeal *h* should be allowed, the order of the Court of Appeal set aside and the order of Georges CJ restored. The respondent must pay the commission's costs in the Court of Appeal and before the Board.

Appeal allowed.

Solicitors: *Charles Russell Williams & James* (for the commission); *Simmons & Simmons* (for *j* the respondent).

Mary Rose Plummer   Barrister.

a
R v North Yorkshire County Council, ex parte M

QUEEN'S BENCH DIVISION (CROWN OFFICE LIST)

EWBANK J

b
1, 2 SEPTEMBER 1988

Children and young persons – Care proceedings in juvenile court – Guardian ad litem – Local authority's duty to disclose changes in child's circumstances to guardian ad litem – Local authority deciding to place child for adoption without informing guardian ad litem – Whether local authority under duty to disclose changes in child's circumstances to guardian ad litem – Whether
c *local authority's decision should be quashed – Magistrates' Courts (Children and Young Persons) Rules 1970, r 14A(6).*

Care of a little girl aged seven who had been indecently assaulted by her father was granted to the local authority by the juvenile court pursuant to s 1 of the Children and
d Young Persons Act 1969. The local authority took the view that the child should never be returned to the care of the parents and decided that it was in the best interests of the child for her to be adopted, initially with the parents having access. The parents applied for the care order to be discharged and the juvenile court appointed a guardian ad litem to act for the child in those proceedings. Before the application to discharge the order was heard the local authority, without informing the guardian ad litem, decided to
e implement a proposal to place the child for adoption without access to the parents. The parents applied for judicial review of the local authority's decision on the ground that it pre-empted the juvenile court's decision on the parents' application to discharge the care order.

f **Held** – The prejudice caused to the parents by the local authority's decision and the influence it would have on the juvenile court's decision was not sufficiently serious to merit setting aside the local authority's decision. However, arising out of the guardian ad litem's duty under r 14A(6)[a] of the Magistrates' Courts (Children and Young Persons) Rules 1970 to safeguard the interests of the child and to investigate the circumstances of the case, there was implied on the local authority a corresponding and reciprocal duty to
g disclose to the guardian ad litem any proposed major changes in the child's circumstances and to consider the guardian ad litem's views before implementing those changes, and since the local authority had failed to inform the guardian ad litem of their decision that failure had flawed the local authority's decision. The application for judicial review would therefore be granted (see p 146 d to f h j, post).

Dictum of Sir Stephen Brown P in *R v Birmingham Juvenile Court, ex p G and ors (minors)*
h [1988] 3 All ER 726 at 732 applied.

Notes

For the procedure in care proceedings, see 24 Halsbury's Laws (4th edn) paras 764–765, and for cases on the subject, see 28(2) Digest (Reissue) 944–945, 2447–2451.
j For the Children and Young Persons Act 1969, s 1, see 6 Halsbury's Statutes (4th edn) 229.

For the Magistrates' Courts (Children and Young Persons) Rules, r 14A, see 4 Halsbury's Statutory Instruments (Grey Volume) 238.

---

a   Rule 14A(6) so far as material, is set out at p 145 *d*, post

Cases referred to in judgment

R v Birmingham Juvenile Court, ex p G and ors (minors) [1988] 3 All ER 726, [1988] 1 WLR *a*
950.
R v Newham London Borough, ex p McL [1988] 1 FLR 416.

Case also cited

Associated Provincial Picture Houses Ltd v Wednesbury Corp [1947] 2 All ER 680, [1948] 1
KB 223, CA.   *b*

Application for judicial review

The parents of a child, BM, applied, with the leave of Hollings J given on 16 August
1988, for judicial review by way of an order of certiorari to quash the decision of the
North Yorkshire County Council to place BM with long-term foster parents with a view
to adoption, on the grounds that the manner in which the decision had been made had *c*
been unfair and/or irrational. Hollings J also granted an injunction restraining the local
authority from implementing their decision pending the hearing of the applicants'
application to discharge a care order granted on 31 March 1987. The facts are set out in
the judgment.

Brian Jubb for the applicants.   *d*
Allan Levy for the guardian ad litem.
Caroline Budden for the local authority.

EWBANK J. This is an application for judicial review of a decision made by a local
authority to place a child, BM (whom I shall call 'B'), for adoption during the course of
juvenile court proceedings relating to that child. Leave was sought to issue the application *e*
for judicial review. That came before Hollings J on 16 August 1988. He granted leave.
He granted an injunction restraining the local authority from implementing their
decision for the time being, and he recommended the local authority to consider taking
wardship proceedings. This recommendation follows the suggestion made by Latey J in
R v Newham London Borough, ex p McL [1988] 1 FLR 416. The local authority have *f*
declined to start wardship proceedings, and so the juvenile court proceedings will
continue.

B was born on 15 February 1981. She is now seven and a half. Her father is now 47
and her mother is 50. They were married in 1978. The father had a conviction in 1970
for indecency with children. In November of 1985 he was again charged with an
indecent assault on two little girls. B was put on the 'at risk' register of the local authority. *g*
The father was convicted of the offence on 12 December 1985 and put on probation with
a condition for psychiatric treatment.

Concern was felt about B over the ensuing months. The father was eventually charged
with an offence against her. A place of safety order was made in relation to the child on
5 December 1986, and on 8 December 1986 B was moved to a foster placement. On 27
January 1987 the father was convicted of an offence of indecency with B. Care proceedings *h*
were started. Various interim care orders were made in favour of the local authority.
The case came for hearing on 31 March 1987. A care order was made in favour of the
local authority. The local authority's plan at that time was that B should remain in long-
term care with foster parents, with access to the parents. It was the local authority's view
that, in the circumstances, there could be no reunion of B with the parents.

On 4 December 1987 the local authority decided that adoption would be appropriate *j*
for B. They had already come to the conclusion that it would never be safe to return her
to the care of her parents. They proposed to look for a family who would accept B having
access to her parents.

The parents were informed of the local authority's decision on 7 January 1988. It was
implicit in the decision that circumstances might arise when access would have to stop.

It was in those circumstances that the parents, on 18 January 1988, applied for the
a discharge of the care order. That is an application which is made under s 21 of the
Children and Young Persons Act 1969. The ground on which a care order can be
discharged is if the juvenile court is satisfied that it is appropriate to do so. Having regard
to the father's history as a child sexual molester, the proposal that the care order should
be discharged must have sounded somewhat unpromising, but the father and mother
are entitled in law to make the application.

b   In the spring of 1988, the local authority became concerned about the foster placement.
On 6 May 1988 B was moved to a second foster home. On 24 July 1988 she was moved
to a third foster home. This was a short-term foster placement.

When the application for discharge of the care order was made, the juvenile court
ordered that a guardian ad litem should act for B. The order was made under s 32A of
the Children and Young Persons Act 1969. The duties of the guardian ad litem are set
c out in s 32B. This provides that a guardian ad litem shall be under a duty to safeguard
the interests of the child in the manner prescribed by rules of court. The rules of court
are the Magistrates' Courts (Children and Young Persons) Rules 1970, SI 1970/1792, as
amended. The relevant rule is r 14A(6)(a) and (b), which provides:

> 'The guardian . . . shall—(a) so far as it is reasonably practicable, investigate all
d   circumstances relevant to the proceedings and for that purpose shall interview such
>   persons, inspect such records and obtain such professional assistance as the guardian
>   *ad litem* thinks appropriate; (b) regard as the first and paramount consideration the
>   need to safeguard and promote the infant's best interests until he achieves adulthood,
>   and shall take into account the wishes and feelings of the infant . . .'

Mrs Wakefield was the guardian duly appointed.
e   On 20 May 1988 the question of B came to be considered by the adoption panel of the
local authority. The local authority had not found it possible to find a permanent family
on the basis·of access to the parents. The panel decided to recommend that access to the
parents should be phased out with a view to termination, and that B should be placed for
adoption. It is submitted on behalf of the parents that that decision is amenable to
f judicial review. In fact there was no decision to implement that recommendation until
later. I am of the view that the decision itself is unobjectionable.

The local authority knew that the guardian ad litem took a different view. They
decided to take the opinion of Dr Wollkind who is the consultant child psychiatrist at
the Maudsley Hospital. His report was prepared some time in July 1988. He agreed, in
effect, with the decision of the local authority.

g   B's case came before the adoption panel again on 5 August 1988. On this occasion the
panel decided to implement the original decision and to start the process of introductions
preceding the placement. The decision was indorsed and made final by the director of
social services on 8 August.

Meanwhile, the application to discharge the care order had been trundling along in
the juvenile court with various adjournments asked for by the guardian ad litem, agreed
h to by the other parties and ordered by the court. The final hearing is due on 21 September
1988. So, the decision to implement the proposal that B should be placed for adoption
was taken only six weeks away from the hearing which was due. The parents say that
this decision was unreasonable and improperly made. They say that the local authority,
in coming to that decision, did not take into account the effect of that decision on the
forthcoming juvenile court hearing. The parents say that if the local authority had taken
j account of the forthcoming hearing, they would have seen that instead of presenting the
juvenile court with a child being with short-term foster parents, they will be presenting
the court with a child being in a placement which was intended to be permanent even
though it could be cut short. The parents say that their case before the juvenile court
would be seriously prejudiced. They say that the local authority intended to leave the
juvenile court with no realistic alternative but to dismiss their application. They also say

that it is wrong that the local authority should try to tip the scales of justice even further in their favour, and it is as if the local authority could not trust the court to come to the *a* right decision without a little extra help.

The local authority say that the forthcoming hearing was taken into account, and that the decision was made despite the forthcoming hearing because, in the opinion of the local authority, that decision was in the best interests of the child. The local authority point to their duty under s 18 of the Child Care Act 1980, where the local authority are given the duty in reaching any decision relating to a child in their care to give 'first *b* consideration to the need to safeguard and promote the welfare of the child throughout his childhood'.

On behalf of the parents, it is said that the local authority only had to wait six weeks for the hearing, but the local authority point out that B had already been moved on several occasions and in the intersts of B it was time that a potentially secure placement should be found for her. Moreover, they say that the idea that the hearing on 21 *c* September is going to be the end of the line is unrealistic. There has certainly been a hint to the local authority, so I am told, that an appeal will be mounted by the parents if the application fails. So, the local authority say that it is by no means clear when the position will be such that they can be sure that proceedings are at an end.

The move of B to this new placement will, of course, influence the juvenile court because the circumstances will be different from the circumstances that exist at the *d* moment. However, I have come to the conclusion that the local authority are right in thinking that prejudice to the parents is not so serious as to merit their decision being set aside, and that the local authority's decision to act in accordance with the best interests of the child cannot be faulted.

The matter, however, does not rest there because, on behalf of the parents and on behalf of the guardian ad litem, a further criticism is made of the decision-making *e* process of the local authority. I have already read out the rules governing the duties of a guardian ad litem. The guardian has to investigate all the circumstances and interview such persons as she thinks appropriate. This implies, in my judgment, a corresponding and reciprocal duty on the part of the local authority to disclose to the guardian ad litem any major changes in the circumstances of the child which are proposed. In *R v* *f* *Birmingham Juvenile Court, ex p G and ors (minors)* [1988] 3 All ER 726, [1988] 1 WLR 950 Sir Stephen Brown P had to deal with the responsibilities of local authorities and guardians ad litem. The circumstances were very different. The local authority in that case had withdrawn an application against the wishes of a guardian ad litem. Sir Stephen Brown P said ([1988] 3 All ER 726 at 732, [1988] 1 WLR 950 at 957):

> 'The local authority has a grave responsibility in the matter of children. It should *g* never have applied to withdraw the proceedings without full consultation with the guardian ad litem who represented the children.'

In my view, the remarks of Sir Stephen Brown P in that case constitute an example of a more general duty. In my judgment, there is a reciprocal duty on the part of the local authority not only to disclose proposals for change in relation to the child, but also to *h* listen to the views of the guardian ad litem. I am not in any way suggesting that the guardian ad litem makes the decisions or in any way is a party to the decisions, but the guardian ad litem is appointed, in accordance with the statute, to safeguard the interests of the child. While a case is in train, the local authority ought not to take any major decisions without informing the guardian ad litem before the decision is made of the proposal and listening to her views. That the local authority have failed to do in this case. *j* They failed to do it on 20 May when the initial decision was made. They failed to do it on 5 August when the decision to implement the proposal was made. In my view, the failure to do this flaws the decision-making of the local authority.

I accordingly come to the conclusion that for that reason the decision must be quashed. An order for certiorari will lie. The application for judicial review succeeds. The *a* injunction will continue until such time as the local authority have informed the guardian, so far as it is neccessary for any further information to be given, and heard the guardian's views and taken them into account.

Certiorari granted. Injunction continued.

b Solicitors: *Wilford McBain*, agents for *Jenkinson & Nott*, York (for the applicants); *Stamp Jackson & Procter, Selby* (for the guardian ad litem); *Gillings Walker & Keen*, York (for the local authority).

Bebe Chua   Barrister.

Birmingham City Council v Anvil Fairs (a
c firm) and others

CHANCERY DIVISION
SIR NICOLAS BROWNE-WILKINSON V-C
5, 6 OCTOBER 1988

d *Markets and fairs – Disturbance – Levying of rival market – Rival market within common law distance – Measurement of common law distance – Whether distance to be measured from place where lawful market held or from boundary of area over which monopoly granted.*

The owner of market rights, whether arising under a franchise or under statute, is entitled to protection from disturbance occasioned by the levying of a rival market
e within the common law distance of $6\frac{2}{3}$ miles measured from the place where one of the owner's markets is actually being conducted and not from the boundary of the area within which the owner is authorised to hold markets (see p 149 *e f h j* and p 150 *h*, post).
    Halton BC v Cawley [1985] 1 All ER 278 and *Manchester City Council v Walsh* (1985) 84 LGR 1 applied.
f   Dicta of Earl Selborne LC in *Great Eastern Rly Co v Goldsmid* (1884) 9 App Cas 927 at 936 and of Griffiths LJ in *Manchester City Council v Walsh* (1985) 84 LGR 1 at 10 not followed.

Notes
For levying of a rival market within the common law distance, see 29 Halsbury's Laws
g (4th edn) para 653, and for cases on the subject, see 33 Digest (Reissue) 227–232, 1890–1936.

Cases referred to in judgment
Birmingham Corp v Perry Barr Stadium Ltd [1972] 1 All ER 725.
Great Eastern Rly Co v Goldsmid (1884) 9 App Cas 927, HL.
h *Halton BC v Cawley* [1985] 1 All ER 278, [1985] 1 WLR 15.
Islington Market Bill, Re (1835) 3 Cl & Fin 513, [1835–42] All ER Rep 323, 6 ER 1530, HL.
Manchester City Council v Walsh (1985) 84 LGR 1, CA.
Stoke-on-Trent City Council v W & J Wass Ltd [1988] 3 All ER 394, CA; *rvsg* (4 March 1987, unreported), Ch D.

j **Case also cited**
Yard v Ford (1670) 2 Saund 172, 85 ER 922.

Preliminary issue
By a writ and statement of claim dated 1 December 1986 the plaintiffs, Birmingham City Council, sought an injunction restraining the defendants, Anvil Fairs (a firm),

T Morris Jones, Roger John Smith and Terence O'Connor, from holding a rival market.
On 11 February 1988 Master Barratt ordered the trial of a preliminary issue, namely   *a*
whether the levying of a market by the defendants at the Black Boy Inn, Heronfield,
Knowle, Solihull which was within 6⅔ miles of the Birmingham City boundary
constituted or would constitute an actionable disturbance of the plaintiffs' market rights
within the City of Birmingham notwithstanding that the premises were situate more
than 6⅔ miles from the markets held at Northfield and Cotteridge or any of the other
markets held or licensed by the plaintiff within the City of Birmingham. The facts are   *b*
set out in the judgment.

Nicholas Patten QC for the plaintiffs.
The defendants did not appear.

SIR NICOLAS BROWNE-WILKINSON V-C. This is a preliminary issue directed   *c*
to be tried in an action brought by the Birmingham City Council as owner of statutory
rights of market against four defendants, who, they allege, have interfered with the
plaintiffs' rights by holding a rival market.

A right of market, whether arising under a franchise or under statute, confers on the
owner a monopoly right, that is to say the exclusive right to hold markets within a
limited area. In the case of a franchise market, rival markets cannot be held within a   *d*
distance of 6⅔ miles. It appears that the same distance applies in the case of statutory
markets. The question I have to determine is whether that distance of 6⅔ miles has to be
measured from the place at which the plaintiffs' market or markets are held or from the
boundary of the area within which the plaintiffs are authorised to hold markets.

The plaintiffs enjoy an exclusive statutory right to hold markets within the City of
Birmingham under s 89 of the Birmingham Corporation (Consolidation) Act 1883 (46 &   *e*
47 Vict c lxx). The area of the City of Birmingham is defined by statute. The plaintiffs
themselves conduct certain markets within the city boundaries and have licensed many
others to conduct markets at various points within the city. By the statement of claim it
is alleged that the defendants have conducted rival markets on land at the Black Boy Inn,
Heronfield, Solihull. The Black Boy Inn is more than 6⅔ miles from the nearest market   *f*
conducted within the City of Birmingham under the statutory powers. On the other
hand, the Black Boy Inn is less than 6⅔ miles from the boundary of the City of
Birmingham, ie from the boundary of the area within which the plaintiffs have power
to establish markets.

It is in those circumstances that a preliminary issue was directed to be tried in these
terms: *g*

'Whether upon the facts and matters set out in the Statement of Claim herein the
levying of a market by the Defendants at the Black Boy Inn Heronfield Knowle
Solihull which is within 6⅔ of the Birmingham City boundary has constituted or
would upon proof of special damage constitute an actionable disturbance of the
plaintiff's market rights within the City of Birmingham notwithstanding that the
said premises are situate more than 6⅔ miles from the markets held at Northfield   *h*
and Cotteridge or any of the other markets held or licensed by the plaintiff within
the City of Birmingham . . .'

Only the third defendant has served a defence; none of the defendants has appeared
before me to argue their case. In the circumstances, counsel for the plaintiffs has had the
difficult task of presenting not only his clients' case, but also any points which might   *j*
assist the defendants. Needless to say, he has performed this function with his usual skill,
balance and learning. I am very grateful to him.

Section 89 of the 1883 Act provides as follows, so far as relevant:

'The market undertaking of the Corporation as it exists at the commencement of
this Act including all property rights powers and privileges of the Corporation in

a relation to markets and fairs shall continue vested in and may be held exercised and enjoyed by the Corporation subject to the provisions of this Act and the Corporation shall have the following powers (namely) . . . (III.) They may continue the markets and fairs held at the commencement of this Act and may from time to time alter the days on which and the places at which the same respectively are or may be held and may establish and hold new markets and cattle fairs but not within the Parish of Edgbaston . . .'

b There is no doubt that under this section the plaintiffs have the right to establish markets anywhere within the city boundaries. Moreover, it is clear that once a market has been established the plaintiffs have the right to prevent persons from holding rival markets within the protected area. Pennycuick V-C so held in *Birmingham Corp v Perry Barr Stadium Ltd* [1972] 1 All ER 725, a case in which the defendants had levied a rival market within the City of Birmingham itself.

c I will also assume, but without deciding, that the protected area of the statutory market enjoyed by the plaintiffs is the same as in the case of a franchise market, ie that the radius of 6⅔ miles applies (see *Manchester City Council v Walsh* (1985) 84 LGR 1). I will further assume, again without deciding, that even if this radius of 6⅔ miles extends outside the boundaries of the city, a rival market conducted outside the city limits but within 6⅔

d miles of any market can be restrained (see *Halton BC v Cawley* [1985] 1 All ER 278, [1985] 1 WLR 15).

The question remains: from what point should the distance of 6⅔ miles be measured, from the place where one of the plaintiffs' markets is actually established and conducted, or from the boundary of the area within which the plaintiffs are entitled to establish markets?

e There is no decision directly on the point, although there are some obiter dicta to which I must later refer. As a matter of principle it seems to me that the distance falls to be measured from the place at which a market is actually being conducted. Both at common law and under statute the right to establish and conduct a market authorises the market to be established in a defined place or within a defined area, in the present case the City of Birmingham. In addition to the area within which the market may be

f established, the market owner is given further protection over a wider area, that is to say over an area having a radius of 6⅔ miles. The purpose of this wider protection is to protect the market owner from competition for customers who would normally use his market. The source of the 6⅔ miles distance appears to be in the writings of Bracton. Bracton treated 6⅔ miles as being one-third of the Roman 'dieta', a day's journey (Bract (1640 edn) bk IV ch 46 fo 235a–b). A man going to market should have one third of a day to get to

g market, one third to attend the market and another third to return home (see Pease 'Some Early Cases on Disturbance of Market' (1916) 32 LQR 199 at 203). If the rival market was within 6⅔ miles, it would attract customers who might otherwise come to the authorised market. If the authorised market was given a wider protection than 6⅔ miles, users of markets would have to spend too long getting to the nearest market. Hence the limit of 6⅔ miles.

h The whole basis of that rule, unbelievably archaic as it is, is therefore linked to the distance from an actual market, the customers of that market and their ability to get to it. I can see no basis in principle why protection should be afforded to persons who could establish a market in a particular place but have not done so. Unless and until the market is established, they are not losing customers, nor is there any actionable disturbance of the market owner's rights by holding a rival market (see Nicholls LJ in *Stoke-on-Trent City*

j *Council v W & J Wass Ltd* [1988] 3 All ER 394 at 404). Moreover, if and when the plaintiffs do elect to establish a market within the city boundaries which is within 6⅔ miles of the Black Boy Inn, on the assumptions that I have made they will be entitled to restrain the holding of any further markets at the Black Boy Inn (see Peter Gibson J in the *Stoke-on-Trent City Council* case at first instance (4 March 1987, unreported)).

It has been said many times recently that the statutory monopoly of a market owner is anomalous. In my judgment, it should not be extended save if the law compels that conclusion.

What then of the authorities? The latest edition of Pease and Chitty's *Law of Markets and Fairs* (3rd edn, 1984) suggests that the 6⅔ miles is to be measured from the boundary of the area within which the plaintiffs' market can be established. The only authority cited for this proposition is very dubious. In *Great Eastern Rly Co v Goldsmid* (1884) 9 App Cas 927 at 936 Earl Selborne LC said:

'. . . market rights according to the general presumption of law would be entitled to a certain amount of protection, primâ facie extending to a distance of nearly seven miles from the places in which they might be exercised . . .'

That dictum plainly indicates that it is the distance from the area in which a market is authorised rather than the position in which the market is held. But in that case nothing turned on the point from which the distance should be measured, and I can attach little importance to the formulation that he there uses.

More to the point is the recent Court of Appeal decision in *Manchester City Council v Walsh* (1985) 84 LGR 1. In that case the defendants were conducting a rival market within the City of Manchester and within 6⅔ miles of many markets conducted by the plaintiff corporation. The defendants submitted that the owner of a statutory market did not enjoy any rights of protection other than those conferred by the statute; that is to say, submitted that the 6⅔ rule did not apply. In giving the judgment of the Court of Appeal Griffiths LJ said (at 10):

'In our judgment, this weight of authority must prevail over the view of Pickford L.J. and establish that a statutory market, whether established under a private or public Act, enjoys as a part of the market rights protection from disturbance by a rival market set up within six and two-thirds miles of the boundaries, unless the wording of the relevant statute modifies that right.'

It is clear from that quotation that the Court of Appeal was saying that the distance extended from the boundaries of the area within which the market can be established.

But again, in that case, nothing turned on the point as to the point from which the 6⅔ miles fell to be measured, since the rival market was within the city limits and within 6⅔ miles of the plaintiffs' markets. Nor can I recollect any argument being directed to the point in that case.

On the other side, one of the answers given by the judges to the House of Lords in *Re Islington Market Bill* (1835) 3 Cl & Fin 513 at 515, [1835–42] All ER Rep 323 at 324 expresses the distance to be measured from the site of the old market. Again, nothing turned on the point from which the measurement was to be made in answering the questions put by the House of Lords in the first instance. Subsequent questions did raise the point much more directly, but unfortunately the judges did not choose to answer the further questions.

Accordingly, there is no authority which persuades me that my own view is wrong. I therefore give the answer 'No' to the question raised in the preliminary issue, and hold that the distance of 6⅔ miles has to be measured, not from the boundaries of the City of Birmingham, but from a market actually being conducted under the statutory powers within those boundaries.

Order accordingly.

Solicitors: *Sharpe Pritchard*, agents for *G W T Pitt*, Birmingham (for the plaintiffs).

Celia Fox   Barrister.

R v Chief Metropolitan Stipendiary Magistrate, ex parte Secretary of State for the Home Department

QUEEN'S BENCH DIVISION
STUART-SMITH LJ AND FARQUHARSON J
16, 17, 18, 27 MAY 1988

Extradition – Committal – Extradition crime – Offence arising out of tax evasion – Whether ordinary offence arising out of tax evasion an extradition crime – Extradition Act 1870, s 10.

N was convicted in Norway of 11 offences of theft, attempted theft, deception, false accounting and forgery for which he was sentenced to a single sentence of five years imprisonment. He escaped from prison and fled to England where he was arrested. The Norwegian government applied for his extradition and the magistrate made an order under s 10ᵃ of the Extradition Act 1870 that he be held in custody to await extradition on six of the charges but not on the other five because they were concerned with tax evasion. The Secretary of State applied for judicial review of the magistrate's decision refusing to commit N on the tax related charges.

Held – Although the courts would not enforce a claim by a foreign state to recover a tax, that did not prevent the courts from extraditing a person for an ordinary offence arising out of tax evasion if that offence was an extradition crime under the 1870 Act. Since the five offences were extradition crimes albeit they arose out of tax evasion the case would be remitted to the magistrate for him to consider whether N should be extradited on those crimes (see p 155 e, p 159 d, p 160 j and p 163 c d f to h).

R v Governor of Pentonville Prison, ex p Khubchandani (1980) 71 Cr App R 241 not followed.

Notes
For extradition crimes, see 18 Halsbury's Laws (4th edn) paras 213–215, and for cases on the subject, see 24 Digest (Reissue) 1125–1129, 11946–11979.

For the Extradition Act 1870, s 10, see 17 Halsbury's Statutes (4th edn) 488.

Cases referred to in judgment
Becke v Smith (1836) 2 M & W 191, 150 ER 724.
Brokaw v Seatrain UK Ltd [1971] 2 All ER 98, [1971] 2 QB 476, [1971] 2 WLR 791, CA.
Buchanan (Peter) Ltd v McVey (1951) [1955] AC 516n, Eire HC and SC.
Cia Naviera Vascongada v Cristina [1938] 1 All ER 719, [1938] AC 485, HL.
Denmark (Government) v Nielsen [1984] 2 All ER 81, [1984] AC 606, [1984] 2 WLR 737, HL.
Hellenes (King) v Brostrom (1923) 16 Ll L Rep 167.
Huddersfield Police Authority v Watson [1947] 2 All ER 193, [1947] KB 842, DC.
Huntington v Attrill [1893] AC 150, PC.
India (Government) Ministry of Finance (Revenue Division) v Taylor [1955] 1 All ER 292, [1955] AC 491, [1955] 2 WLR 303, HL.
R v Governor of Pentonville Prison, ex p Khubchandani (1980) 71 Cr App R 241, DC.
R v Greater Manchester Coroner, ex p Tal [1984] 3 All ER 240, [1985] QB 67, [1984] 3 WLR 643, DC.
R v Harden [1962] 1 All ER 296, [1963] 1 QB 8, [1962] 2 WLR 553, CCA.

---

a   Section 10 is set out at p 155 h j, post

Rees v Secretary of State for the Home Dept [1986] 2 All ER 321, [1986] AC 937, [1986] 2
WLR 1024, HL.
Request for International Judicial Assistance, Re (1979) 102 DLR (3d) 18, Alta QB.
Rossano v Manufacturers Life Insurance Co Ltd [1962] 2 All ER 214, [1963] 2 QB 352,
[1962] 3 WLR 157.
Schemmer v Property Resources Ltd [1974] 3 All ER 451, [1975] Ch 273, [1974] 3 WLR
406.
Sydney Municipal Council v Bull [1909] 1 KB 7, [1908–10] All ER Rep 616.
Thompson v Goold & Co [1910] AC 409, HL.
Tzu-Tsai Cheng v Governor of Pentonville Prison [1973] 2 All ER 204, [1973] AC 931, [1973]
2 WLR 746, HL.
Visser, Re, Queen of Holland v Drukker [1928] Ch 877, [1928] All ER Rep 305.
Williams & Humbert Ltd v W & H Trade Marks (Jersey) Ltd [1986] 1 All ER 129, [1986]
AC 368, [1986] 2 WLR 24, CA.

Cases also cited
Athanassiadis v Government of Greece [1969] 3 All ER 293, [1971] AC 282, HL.
Atkinson v US Government [1969] 3 All ER 1317, [1971] AC 197, HL.
Chung Chi Cheung v R [1938] 4 All ER 786, [1939] AC 160, PC.
Cohen (a bankrupt), Re, ex p the bankrupt v IRC [1950] 2 All ER 36, CA.
Cotton v R [1914] AC 176, PC.
Garland v British Rail Engineering Ltd [1982] 2 All ER 402, [1983] 2 AC 751, HL.
Greece (Royal Government) v Brixton Prison Governor [1969] 3 All ER 1337, [1971] AC 250,
HL.
Indian and General Investment Trust Ltd v Borax Consolidated Ltd [1920] 1 KB 539, [1918–
19] All ER Rep 346.
R v Governor of Brixton Prison [1911] 2 KB 82, DC.
R v Governor of Pentonville Prison, ex p Budlong [1980] 1 All ER 701, [1980] 1 WLR 1110,
DC.
R v Wilson (1877) 3 QBD 42, DC.
Regazzoni v K C Sethia (1944) Ltd [1956] 2 All ER 487, [1956] 2 QB 490, CA; *affd* [1957] 3
All ER 286, [1958] AC 301, HL.
Thakrar v Secretary of State for the Home Dept [1974] 2 All ER 261, [1974] QB 684, CA.
US Government v McCaffery [1984] 2 All ER 570, [1984] 1 WLR 867, HL.

Application for judicial review
The Secretary of State for the Home Department applied, with the leave of McNeill J
given on 22 March 1988, for judicial review by way of an order of certiorari to quash the
refusal of the Chief Metropolitan Magistrate on 27 January 1988 to commit Tore Kjell
Nuland to prison under s 10 of the Extradition Act 1870 to await extradition to Norway
on six offences for which he had been sentenced in Norway to imprisonment. The facts
are set out in the judgment of the court.

David Pannick for the Secretary of State.
Clive Nicholls QC and *Robert Rhodes* as amicus curiae.
Mr Nuland did not appear.

Cur adv vult

27 May. the following judgment of the court was delivered.

STUART-SMITH LJ. This is an application for judicial review of a decision of the
Chief Metropolitan Magistrate made on 27 January 1988. On that date he committed
Tore Kjell Nuland to custody pursuant to s 10 of the Extradition Act 1870 (the Act) to
await directions of the Secretary of State on six charges of theft, attempted theft and
inducing a creditor by deception to wait for payment. But he refused to commit him on

five further charges involving false accounting, forgery and theft. It is in respect of that
a refusal that the Secretary of State seeks judicial review.

On 9 August 1985 Nuland was convicted in the Sandnes District Court in Norway of
11 offences under the Norwegian criminal code. He was sentenced to five years'
imprisonment, subject to remission for the time spent in custody. On appeal to the
Supreme Court his sentence was confirmed on 18 June 1987. For reasons which do not
appear Nuland came to this country. In September 1987 a request was duly made by the
b Royal Norwegian Embassy to the Foreign and Commonwealth Office for his extradition
pursuant to the extradition treaty between Norway and the United Kingdom (Stockholm,
26 June 1873; 63 BFSP 175, C 900). The request was transmitted to the Home Office;
and on 13 November 1987 the Secretary of State for the Home Department signed an
order addressed to the Chief Metropolitan Stipendiary Magistrate or other metropolitan
stipendiary magistrate sitting at Bow Street, requiring him to issue a warrant for Nuland's
c apprehension. In due course, he was arrested and brought before the court.

As we have indicated, he was committed to custody under s 10 of the 1870 Act to
await the order of the Secretary of State on six of the charges on which he was convicted,
but not on the remaining five. The magistrate explained in a letter to the Secretary of
State dated 28 June 1988 why he declined to commit Nuland on these five charges. The
reason is that he considered that the charges were in various ways connected with tax
d evasion, and he considered himself bound by the decision of this court in *R v Governor of
Pentonville Prison, ex p Khubchandani* (1980) 71 Cr App R 241 to decline on that ground to
commit him.

This creates a problem for the Norwegian authorities because the sentence is a global
one, passed in respect of all 11 offences and not concurrently on each offence or
consecutively amounting in total to five years.
e It is accepted by counsel for the Secretary of State that the magistrate was bound by the
decision in *Khubchandani* to act as he did, and there is no criticism of him in any way. But
the submission is that that case was wrongly decided on this point and that we should
not follow it. Although we pay great regard to the decision and we should follow it as a
matter of judicial comity unless we are convinced that it is wrong, we are not bound by
it.
f In *R v Greater Manchester Coroner, ex p Tal* [1984] 3 All ER 240 at 248, [1985] QB 67 at
81 Robert Goff LJ said:

'If a judge of the High Court sits exercising the supervisory jurisdiction of the
High Court then it is, in our judgment, plain that the relevant principle of stare
decisis is the principle applicable in the case of a judge of first instance exercising
g the jurisdiction of the High Court, viz that he will follow a decision of another
judge of first instance, unless he is convinced that that judgment is wrong, as a
matter of judicial comity; but he is not bound to follow the decision of a judge of
equal jurisdiction (see *Huddersfield Police Authority v Watson* [1947] 2 All ER 193 at
196, [1947] KB 842 at 848 per Lord Goddard CJ), for either the judge exercising
such supervisory jurisdiction is (as we think) sitting as a judge of first instance, or
h his position is so closely analogous that the principle of stare decisis applicable in the
case of a judge of first instance is applicable to him. In our judgment, the same
principle is applicable when the supervisory jurisdiction of the High Court is
exercised not by a single judge but by a Divisional Court, where two or three judges
are exercising precisely the same jurisdiction as the single judge. We have no doubt
that it will be only in rare cases that a Divisional Court will think it fit to depart
j from a decision of another Divisional Court exercising this jurisdiction. Furthermore,
we find it difficult to imagine that a single judge exercising this jurisdiction would
ever depart from a decision of a Divisional Court. If any question of such a departure
should arise before a single judge, a direction can be made under RSC Ord 53, r 5(2)
that the relevant application should be made before a Divisional Court. These are,
therefore, the principles which we propose to apply in the present case.'

The relevant part of the judgment in *Khubchandani*'s case is in the final ground on which the court granted the writ of habeas corpus. Kilner Brown J, giving a judgment   *a* with which Shaw LJ agreed, said (71 Cr App Rep 241 at 248):

'Finally [counsel for the applicant] submitted that whatever view might ultimately be taken about the application of and the correctness of the decision in HARDEN's case ([1962] 1 All ER 286, [1963] 1 QB 68), there still remained an insuperable barrier in the way of extradition. The alleged offences were in substance and in reality breaches of the Ghanaian laws relating to exchange control and embargo   *b* upon the removal of currency outside the jurisdiction. Claims on behalf of a foreign State to recover taxes due under its fiscal laws are unenforceable in English courts and there is no valid distinction between foreign States and States which are members of the British Commonwealth—see GOVERNMENT OF INDIA, MINISTRY OF FINANCE v. TAYLOR ([1955] 1 All ER 292, [1955] AC 491). Nor does it make any   *c* difference that the breaches were founded upon fraud or dishonest deception. For this latter proposition persuasive support is to be found in the case of SCHEMMER v. PROPERTY RESOURCES LTD. ([1974] 3 All ER 451, [1975] Ch 273), to the effect that even if the breaches of a foreign country's fiscal laws were perpetrated through fraud, the English courts will not act to enforce the public law of that other country. In answer to the contention of the respondents that there could and should be spelt   *d* out from the words of item 18 in Schedule 1 to the Fugitive Offenders Act 1967 an inference that breaches of fiscal laws would be covered if fraud or dishonesty were resorted to it was argued that this would be doing that which Lord Simon of Glaisdale roundly condemned in CHENG v. GOVERNOR OF PENTONVILLE PRISON ([1973] 2 All ER 204, [1973] AC 931). In cases where extradition is sought, words in the relevant act must be strictly construed and no gloss be put upon them. In my   *e* opinion this argument on behalf of the applicant also succeeds. I would allow this application.'

Counsel for the Secretary of State submits that the reasoning and decision is inconsistent with the reasoning of the House of Lords in *Government of Denmark v Nielsen* [1984] 2 All ER 81, [1984] AC 606. This case, he submits, makes it clear that what the magistrate has   *f* to do in a conviction case, such as this, is to consider whether the conduct and state of mind proved in the foreign court amounts, as a matter of English law, to one of the offences listed in the schedules to the Extradition Acts and contained in the relevant treaties. If it does, then unless the offence falls within the statutory exception where the offence is political (see s 3 of the Act) he must commit the offender under s 10.

It is necessary to refer to some of the provisions of the 1870 Act. Section 2 provides: *g*

'Where an arrangement has been made with any foreign state with respect to the surrender to such state of any fugitive criminals, Her Majesty may, by Order in Council, direct that this Act shall apply in the case of such foreign state. [There is then provision for limitation or restriction of the order. It continues:] Every such order shall recite or embody the terms of the arrangement, and shall not remain in force for any longer period than the arrangement.'   *h*

Orders must be laid before Parliament and published in the London Gazette.

Section 3 provides for restrictions on the surrender of fugitive criminals. The precise wording of this section is important, and must be set out in full:

'The following restrictions shall be observed with respect to the surrender of fugitive criminals: (1) A fugitive criminal shall not be surrendered if the offence in   *j* respect of which his surrender is demanded is one of a political character, or if he proves to the satisfaction of the police magistrate or the court before whom he is brought on habeas corpus, or to the Secretary of State, that the requisition for his surrender has in fact been made with a view to try or punish him for an offence of a

a
political character: (2) A fugitive criminal shall not be surrendered to a foreign state unless provision is made by the law of that state, or by arrangement, that the fugitive criminal shall not, until he has been restored or had an opportunity of returning to Her Majesty's dominions, be detained or tried in that foreign state for any offence committed prior to his surrender other than the extradition crime proved by the facts on which the surrender is grounded: (3) A fugitive criminal who has been accused of some offence within English jurisdiction not being the offence for which

b
his surrender is asked, or is undergoing sentence under any conviction in the United Kingdom, shall not be surrendered until after he has been discharged, whether by acquittal or on expiration of his sentence or otherwise: (4) A fugitive criminal shall not be surrendered until the expiration of fifteen days from the date of his being committed to prison to await his surrender.'

c
Section 5 provides:

'When an order applying this Act in the case of any foreign state has been published in the London Gazette, this Act (after the date specified in the order, or if no date is specified, after the date of the publication,) shall, so long as the order remains in force, but subject to the limitations, restrictions, conditions, exceptions, and qualifications, if any, contained in the order, apply in the case of such foreign

d
state . . .'

Section 6 is concerned with the liability for apprehension and surrender of a fugitive criminal, who is defined as a person accused or convicted of an extradition crime committed within the jurisdiction of a foreign state and who is in or suspected of being in the United Kingdom.

e
An 'extradition crime' means a crime which if committed in England or within English jurisdiction would be one of the crimes described in Sch 1 to the 1870 Act (see s 26). Further offences have been added by the schedule to the Extradition Act 1873. There is no dispute that the offences covered in charges 6 to 11 are offences covered by the expression 'extradition crime', unless the exception in *Khubchandani*'s case applies.

f
Section 7 deals with the requisition by the foreign state to the Secretary of State and the order by him to the police magistrate to issue a warrant for the arrest of the fugitive criminal, unless the offence is of a political character. Section 8 deals with the issue of warrants and provisional warrants for apprehension.

Section 9 provides:

g
'When a fugitive criminal is brought before the police magistrate, the police magistrate shall hear the case in the same manner, and have the same jurisdiction and powers, as near as may be, as if the prisoner were brought before him charged with an indictable offence committed in England. The police magistrate shall receive any evidence which may be tendered to show that the crime of which the prisoner is accused or alleged to have been convicted is an offence of a political character or is not an extradition crime.'

h
Section 10 deals with committal. So far as it relates to convicted fugitives it provides:

'. . . In the case of a fugitive criminal alleged to have been convicted of an extradition crime, if such evidence is produced as (subject to the provisions of this Act) would, according to the law of England, prove that the prisoner was convicted of such crime, the police magistrate shall commit him to prison, but otherwise shall

j
order him to be discharged. If he commits such criminal to prison, he shall commit him . . . there to await the warrant of a Secretary of State for his surrender, and shall forthwith send to a Secretary of State a certificate of the committal, and such report upon the case as he may think fit.'

Section 11 deals with surrender of the fugitive and provides:

'If the police magistrate commits a fugitive criminal to prison, he shall inform
such criminal that he will not be surrendered until after the expiration of fifteen
days, and that he has a right to apply for a writ of Habeas corpus. Upon the   *a*
expiration of the said fifteen days, or, if a writ of Habeas corpus is issued, after the
decision of the court upon the return to the writ, as the case may be, or after such
further period as may be allowed in either case by a Secretary of State, it shall be
lawful for a Secretary of State, by warrant under his hand and seal, to order the
fugitive criminal (if not delivered on the decision of the court) to be surrendered to   *b*
such person as may in his opinion be duly authorised to receive the fugitive criminal
by the foreign state from which the requisition for the surrender proceeded, and
such fugitive criminal shall be surrendered accordingly . . .'

This then is the structure of the Act.
It is now necessary for us to set out at some length passages from the speech of Lord   *c*
Diplock in *Government of Denmark v Nielsen* [1984] 2 All ER 81 at 84, 91, [1984] AC 606
at 615, 624–625, with which the other Law Lords agreed:

'The introductory words to both the 1870 list and the later list provide that the
list of crimes is to be construed according to the law existing in England at the date
of the alleged crime. So in order to determine whether conduct constitutes an   *d*
'extradition crime' within the meaning of the Extradition Acts 1870 to 1935, and
thus a *potential* ground for extradition if that conduct had taken place in a foreign
state, one can start by inquiring whether the conduct if it had taken place in England
would have fallen within one of the 19 generic descriptions of crimes in the 1870
list. If it would have so fallen the inquiry need proceed no further where, as in the
case of the principal treaty with Denmark, the extradition treaty with the foreign   *e*
state demanding the surrender of a person as a fugitive criminal incorporates the
whole of the 1870 list in the descriptions of crimes for which surrender may be
required and makes no modification to those descriptions . . . The jurisdiction of
the magistrate is derived exclusively from the statute. It arises when a person who
is accused of conduct in a foreign state which if he had committed it in England
would be one described in the 1870 list (as added to and amended by later   *f*
Extradition Acts) has been apprehended and brought before the magistrate under a
warrant issued pursuant to an order made by the Secretary of State under s 7 or
confirmed by him under the last paragraph of s 8. At the hearing, ss 9 and 10
require that the magistrate must first be satisfied that a foreign warrant (within the
definition in s 26 that I have already cited) has been issued for the accused person's
arrest and is duly authenticated in a manner for which s 15 provides. Except where   *g*
there is a claim that the arrest was for a political offence or the case is an exceptional
accusation case, the magistrate is not concerned with what provision of foreign
criminal law (if any) is stated in the warrant to be the offence which the person was
suspected of having committed and in respect of which his arrest was ordered in the
foreign state. The magistrate must then hear such evidence, including evidence   *h*
made admissible by ss 14 and 15, as may be produced on behalf of the requisitioning
foreign government, and by the accused if he wishes to do so; and at the conclusion
of the evidence the magistrate must decide whether such evidence would, *according
to the law of England*, justify the committal for trial of the accused for an offence that
is described in the 1870 list (as added to or amended by subsequent Extradition
Acts) provided that such offence is also included in the extraditable crimes listed in   *j*
the English language version of the extradition treaty. In making this decision it is
English law alone that is relevant. The requirement that he shall make it does not
give him any jurisdiction to inquire into or receive evidence of the substantive
criminal law of the foreign state in which the conduct was in fact committed.' (Lord
Diplock's emphasis.)

a   Counsel for the Secretary of State submits that if the magistrate's jurisdiction derives exclusively from the statute, he must look only to that and any treaty provisions, which are in effect incorporated under s 5 of the Act, for any limitation and restriction on that jurisdiction. The issue before the court is therefore one of construction of the 1870 Act. On the construction of the statute there is no room to incorporate the limitations.

   It is common ground that the House of Lords in *Nielsen's* case did not have in mind the particular problem that confronts us; had they done so their decision would of course
b   be binding on us and no problem would arise. But counsel for the Secretary of State submits that the decision on this point in *R v Governor of Pentonville Prison, ex p Khubchandani* (1980) 71 Cr App R 241 is quite inconsistent with the reasoning of the House of Lords.

   We have had the advantage of submissions on this matter by counsel appearing as amicus. He has submitted that Lord Diplock's statement of the law in the last passage to
c   which we have referred is too narrow, in that it does not take into account limitations imposed by the specific treaties in question. For example, as was quite common in earlier treaties, there was provision that nationals of this country could not be extradited. This is a fetter or restriction on the magistrate's jurisdiction. We agree, but it seems to us that Lord Diplock makes this plain (see [1984] 2 All ER 81 at 85, [1984] AC 606 at 616). Such limitations therefore are nothing to the point.

d   Secondly, counsel appearing as amicus submitted that there were issues such as abuse of the process of the court and pleas of autrefois convict or acquit which it is accepted that the magistrate has jurisdiction to consider, though they do not fall expressly within the limitations found in s 3 of the Act. As to abuse of process, in *Rees v Secretary of State for the Home Department* [1986] 2 All ER 321, [1986] AC 937 the House of Lords left open the question whether the magistrates did have jurisdiction to prevent abuse of the process
e   in respect of proceedings under the Act; and it is equally unnecessary in this court to decide that question, because it is clear, as it seems to us, and counsel appearing as amicus accepted, that such a matter could properly be considered under the provisions of s 9 of the Act. So too with questions of autrefois convict and acquit. Sometimes these matters are specifically dealt with in the treaty in question, but if they are not, and if the magistrate has jurisdiction to consider them, as to which we express no opinion, he could
f   do so under that section, without going outside the ambit of the Act.

   But that is not so with the restriction in relation to revenue offences; and this, as counsel appearing as amicus concedes, is the only limitation that is relevant, that is not expressly dealt with in the Act or treaty or may not fall within the powers of the magistrate conferred by s 9 of the Act.

   His main submission is as follows: (1) as a matter of construction it requires clear and
g   express language in a statute to derogate from the common law or to take away common law rights; (2) it is a rule of international custom and practice that states will not directly or indirectly enforce revenue or penal laws of another state; (3) the rule of international custom and practice has become part of the common law; (4) the 1870 Act does not specifically take away this limitation.

   In support of the first proposition counsel appearing as amicus relied on the dissenting
h   speech of Lord Simon in *Tzu-Tsai Cheng v Governor of Pentonville Prison* [1973] 2 All ER 204 at 216–218, [1973] AC 931 at 954–955. Lord Wilberforce agreed with Lord Simon, and it matters not for these statements of principle that they were in the minority. Lord Simon said:

j   'Presumption against changes in the common law

   "Few principles of statutory interpretation are applied as frequently as the presumption against alterations in the common law. It is presumed that the legislature does not intend to make any change in the existing law beyond that which is expressly stated in, or follows by necessary implication from, the language of the statute in question. It is thought to be in the highest degree improbable that Parliament would depart from the general system of law without expressing its *a* intention with irresistible clearness." (Maxwell (*Interpretation of Statutes* (12th edn, 1969) p 116)). International lawyers were not unanimous whether comity required a state to extradite offenders against the criminal law of a foreign state, Grotius and Pufendorf being ranged on opposite sides of the argument; but the overwhelming modern view is that any international obligation to extradite is imperfect, needing treaty to perfect it (Wheaton (*International Law* (6th edn, 1929) vol 1, p 212)). There *b* can be no question, though, what answer the English common law returned: no English authority had the right to extradite (Clarke on Extradition (4th edn, 1903), pp 6–7), citing Coke (3 Co Inst (1644) ch 84, p 180); Wheaton (pp 213–214) citing Lord Denman (see Forsyth *Cases and Opinions on Constitutional Law* (1869) p 369) speaking in your Lordships' House). This was indeed the inevitable result of the following fundamental principles of English common law: (1) no one can be *c* deprived of his liberty except for an offence against English law; (2) this liberty is vindicated by the writ of habeas corpus, statute in this respect merely embodying the common law; (3) criminal law being (other than exceptionally) territorial, an offence against a foreign criminal code is no offence against English law; (4) therefore anyone taken into custody for the purpose of delivery to a foreign state in respect of an offence against the criminal code of that foreign state could secure his release by *d* habeas corpus proceedings. A fugitive offender against the criminal law of a foreign state being thus protected by the common law from arrest for the purpose of extradition, the Extradition Act 1870 and the orders in council implementing it were necessarily in derogation from the common law. It follows that the positive powers under the Act should be given a restrictive construction and the exceptions from those positive powers a liberal construction. Even if it were otherwise *e* permissible to read s 3(1) as allowing the implication that "offence ... of a political character" refers only to an offence which is of a political character as regards the state seeking extradition, the presumption against changes in the common law would preclude such an implication and demand the construction proposed by the appellant. The construction proposed by the respondent cannot possibly be said to *f* be a "necessary" implication from the language of the statute, nor can it possibly be said that Parliament has expressed "with irresistible clearness" the intention that the political character of the offence should be limited to the politics of the state seeking extradition. Since the common law, as so often, favours the freedom of the individual, the rules enjoining strict construction of a penal statute or of a provision in derogation of liberty (Maxwell (p 238)) merely reinforce the presumption against change in the common law. *g*

Presumption in favour of conformity with international law

"... every statute is interpreted, so far as its language permits, so as not to be inconsistent with ... the established rules of international law, and the court will avoid a construction which would give rise to such inconsistency unless compelled *h* to adopt it by plain and unambiguous language." (Maxwell (p 183).) I have already cited Oppenheim (*International Law* (8th edn, 1955) vol 1, ch 3(x), p 704) and Wheaton (vol 1, p 217) as showing the general consensus that political crimes are not the subjects of extradition, though both indicate the difficulties of definition.'

But these cannons of construction only apply subject to the primary rule that Lord *j* Simon had already quoted, and is to be held as an aid to construction in the event of ambiguity. He said ([1973] 2 All ER 204 at 212–213, [1973] AC 931 at 950):

'What Maxwell (*Interpretation of Statutes* (12th edn, 1969) p 28) calls "The first and most elementary rule of construction" is that (except in technical legislation) it is to

be assumed the words and phrases are used in their ordinary and natural meaning.
Moreover (at p 33): "It is a corollary to the general rule of literal construction that
nothing is to be added to . . . a statute unless there are adequate grounds to justify
the inference that the legislature intended something which it omitted to express."
"It is a strong thing to read into an Act of Parliament words which are not there and
in the absence of clear necessity it is a wrong thing to do." (Lord Mersey in *Thompson
v Goold & Co* [1910] AC 409 at 420.) If Parliament had intended to say "offence . . .
of a political character *against* (or *in respect of*) *the foreign state demanding such
surrender*", nothing would have been easier than to have inserted such words. Since
they are not there, it is not for the courts to supply them. This primary rule of
construction is so fundamental that it is sometimes called "the golden rule". It was
so stated by Parke B in *Becke v Smith* (1836) 2 M & W 191 at 195, 150 ER 724 at 726:
"It is a very useful rule, in the construction of a statute, to adhere to the ordinary
meaning of the words used . . . unless that is at variance with the intention of the
legislature, to be collected from the statute itself, or tends to any manifest absurdity
or repugnance, in which case the language may be varied or modified, so as to avoid
such inconvenience, but no further."' (Lord Simon's emphasis.)

To our minds the language of the 1870 Act is clear, that provided the conduct amounts
to an extradition crime, then subject to the specific limitations in the Act, the magistrate
must commit.

Section 3 of the Act deals with two situations which existed under international
custom and practice and were adopted as part of the common law, namely the non-
extradition of those whose offence was of a political character (s 3(1)) and specialty, that
is to say that there will be no extradition unless there is provision in the law of the
requesting state that the offender will not be tried for offences other than those in respect
of which he has been extradited (s 3(2)).

We find it very difficult to accept the argument that these provisions were otiose, and
could have been left to the common law to ensure that extradition would not occur in
such cases. Moreover, where Parliament has dealt with two of the alleged three common
law restrictions expressly in the Act, it is difficult to suppose that the third, relating to
revenue offences, was to be left intact and unaffected.

If the construction of counsel appearing as amicus is correct it involves reading into
the 1870 Act a similar provision to that found in the Extradition Act 1965 of the Republic
of Ireland. Section 13 of the Irish Act provides: 'Extradition shall not be granted for
revenue offences'. Since revenue offences as such are not extraditable crimes within the
1870 Act, but only specific offences such as forgery or false accounting that may be
committed in a revenue context, revenue offences would have to be defined more widely,
as is done in the Irish Act. Section 3(1) of the Irish Act provides:

'. . . "Revenue offence" in relation to any country or place outside the State, means
an offence in connection with taxes, duties or exchange control but does not include
an offence involving the use or threat of force or perjury or the forging of a
document issued under statutory authority or an offence alleged to have been
committed by an officer of the revenue of that country or place in his capacity as
such officer.'

The limitations in the latter part of this definition are of course necessary, otherwise
murder of a revenue officer might amount to a revenue offence.

In our judgment, the language of the 1870 Act is clear and admits of no ambiguity; it
would be extremely surprising if Parliament expressly incorporated into the statute two
common law limitations but omitted a third, which was nevertheless intended to co-
exist unabated. This approach to the construction of the Act appears to us to accord with
the guidance laid down in *Government of Denmark v Nielsen* [1984] 2 All ER 81, [1984] AC

606. And as counsel for the Secretary of State pointed out, the question of construction of the 1870 Act never seems to have been considered by the Divisional Court in *R v Governor of Pentonville Prison, ex p Khubchandani* (1980) 71 Cr App R 241.

As to the second proposition put forward by counsel appearing as amicus, we have found considerable difficulty in determining the extent of the supposed rule of international custom and practice. In *Khubchandani*'s case the court relied on the decision of *Government of India, Ministry of Finance (Revenue Division) v Taylor* [1955] 1 All ER 292 at 295, [1955] AC 491 at 503–504, where Viscount Simonds said:

> 'My Lords, I will admit that I was greatly surprised to hear it suggested that the courts of this country would, and should, entertain a suit by a foreign state to recover a tax. For at any time since I have had any acquaintance with the law I should have said, as Rowlatt, J., said in *King of the Hellenes* v. *Brostrom* ((1923) 16 Ll L Rep 167): "It is perfectly elementary that a foreign government cannot come here—nor will the courts of other countries allow our government to go there—and sue a person found in that jurisdiction for taxes levied and which he is declared to be liable to by the country to which he belongs." That was in 1923. In 1928, Tomlin, J., in *Re Visser* [*Queen of Holland v Drukker* [1928] Ch 877 at 884, [1928] All ER Rep 305 at 307], after referring to *Sydney Municipal Council* v. *Bull* ([1909] 1 KB 7, [1908–10] All ER Rep 616), in which the same proposition had been unequivocally stated by Grantham, J., and saying that he was bound to follow it, added: "My own opinion is that there is a well recognised rule, which has been enforced for at least two hundred years or thereabouts, under which these courts will not collect the taxes of foreign states for the benefit of the sovereigns of those foreign states; and this is one of those actions which these courts will not entertain." My Lords, it is not seemly to weigh the pronouncements of living judges, but it is, I think, permissible to say that the opinions of few, if any, judges of the past, command greater respect than those of Lord Tomlin and Sir Sydney Rowlatt, and what appeared to one of them to be a "well recognised rule" and to the other "elementary" law cannot easily be displaced.'

But the limited extent of this proposition was stated by Lord Mackay, with whose speech Lord Scarman, Lord Bridge and Lord Brandon agreed. In *Williams & Humbert v W & H Trade Marks (Jersey) Ltd* [1986] 1 All ER 129 at 143, [1986] AC 368 at 440–441 he said:

> 'Having regard to the questions before this House in *Government of India v Taylor* I consider that it cannot be said that any approval was given by the House to the decision in the *Buchanan* case [*Peter Buchanan Ltd v McVey* (1951) [1955] AC 516] except to the extent that it held that there is a rule of law which precludes a state from suing in another state for taxes due under the law of the first state. No countenance was given in *Government of India v Taylor*, in *Rossano*'s case [1962] 2 All ER 214, [1963] 2 QB 352 or in *Brokaw v Seatrain UK Ltd* [1971] 2 All ER 98, [1971] 2 QB 476 to the suggestion that an action in this country could be properly described as the indirect enforcement of a penal or revenue law in another country when no claim under that law remained unsatisfied. The existence of such unsatisfied claim to the satisfaction of which the proceeds of the action will be applied appears to me to be an essential feature of the principle enunciated in the *Buchanan* case for refusing to allow the action to succeed.'

It is one thing to say that the courts of this country will not entertain a suit by a foreign state to recover a tax; it is another to say that criminal offences which stand independently of revenue offences, albeit in a revenue connection, are within the rule. This distinction is made clear, as it seems to us, in the Backing of Warrants (Republic of Ireland) Act 1965. Section 2(2) provides:

a '. . . nor shall such an order be made if it is shown to the satisfaction of the court—
(a) that the offence specified in the warrant is an offence of a political character . . .
or an offence under an enactment relating to taxes, duties or exchange control . . .'

Two points may be made. First, that Parliament is specifically referring to revenue
offences, which it does not do in the 1870 Act, save that revenue offences in the sense
here defined of offences under enactments relating to taxes are not offences to be found
in Sch 1 as amended. The second is that the limitation is restricted to offences under
b enactments relating to taxes, and does not extend to the wide definition of revenue
offences in the Irish Extradition Act of 1965.

A similar distinction was drawn in the judgment of Miller J in *Re Request for
International Judicial Assistance* (1979) 102 DLR (3d) 18 at 38:

c 'In my opinion, that line of cases does not assist [the defendants] in this application.
While it is perhaps true that the ultimate consequences of guilty findings in the tax
evasion charges against the defendants will be a civil liability to pay additional
income tax, it is my view that the pith and substance of the charges are criminal in
nature and the assistance of our Court is sought primarily to enable a full hearing to
be held on the criminal charges rather than to help the United States collect alleged
arrears of income tax. I do not think it is particularly relevant that most of the
d charges arise out of alleged offences under the Internal Revenue Code in the United
States. The fact is that they are charges which are criminal in nature and which can
attract severe monetary and incarceration penalties. In any event, clearly the
conspiracy charges against Sedlmayr and Andrews do not fall within any impediment
regarding tax collections in a foreign jurisdiction. I do not feel that any compliance
with the request in this case runs contrary to the rule against assisting a foreign
e jurisdiction to collect taxes owing.'

The high water mark of the submission of counsel appearing as amicus is to be found
in the European Convention on Extradition 1957 (ETS 24). The United Kingdom took
part in the preparation of this convention, but so far has neither signed nor ratified it.
Article 5 provides:

f 'Fiscal offences—Extradition shall be granted, in accordance with the provisions of
this Convention, for offences in connection with taxes, duties, customs and exchange
only if the Contracting Parties have so decided in respect of any such offence or
category of offences.'

Here, too, there is to our minds doubt whether this provision relates to offences under
g enactments relating to taxes, as in the Backing of Warrants (Republic of Warrants) Act
1965 or the wider meaning given in the Irish Extradition Act 1965. But assuming that it
is the latter, counsel for the respondent submits that it amounts to good evidence of the
international rule of custom and practice.

We were at one time impressed by this argument. But quite apart from the difficulty
that the convention has not been ratified or signed by the United Kingdom, though it
h has by Norway, and the ambiguity to which we have referred, it is not an absolute rule
like that in relation to political offences, but may be modified in the treaties between
states. And in any event, the article has now been altered by art 2 of the Second Additional
Protocol to the European Convention on Extradition 1978 (ETS 98) as follows:

'Fiscal offences. 1. For offences in connection with taxes, duties, customs and
j exchange extradition shall take place between the Contracting Parties in accordance
with the provisions of the Convention if the offence, under the law of the requested
Party, corresponds to an offence of the same nature.
2. Extradition may not be refused on the ground that the law of the requested
Party does not impose the same kind of tax or duty or does not contain a tax, duty,
customs or exchange regulation of the same kind as the law of the requesting Party.'

In *Khubchandani*'s case the Divisional Court relied on *Schemmer v Property Resources Ltd* [1974] 3 All ER 451, [1975] Ch 273 for the proposition that foreign fiscal laws are *a* unenforceable in the English courts even when the breaches concerned were founded on fraud or dishonest deception. But *Schemmer*'s case was in an entirely different context and was not concerned with extradition. It is true that the relevant rule, r 5, made by the United States Securities and Exchange Commission under § 10(b) of the Securities Exchange Act 1934 (15 USC § 78j(b)), did involve fraud. Rule 5 provides:

'It shall be unlawful for any person directly or indirectly by the use of any means *b* or instrumentality of interstate commerce, or of the mails, or of any facility of any national securities exchange, (1) to employ any device, scheme, or artifice to defraud, (2) to make any untrue statement of a material fact or to omit to state a material fact necessary in order to make the statements made, or in the light of the circumstances under which they were made, not misleading, or (3) to engage in any act, practice, *c* or course of business which operates or would operate as a fraud or deceit upon any person, in connection with the purchase or sale of any security.'

But the matter is dealt with in the judgment of Goulding J ([1974] 3 All ER 451 at 458–459, [1975] Ch 273 at 288):

'I am naturally led on to a different and alternative ground for denying Mr *d* Schemmer's alleged cause of action. The 1934 Act is, in my judgment, a penal law of the United States of America and, as such, unenforceable in our courts. I have read enough of it to show that it was passed for public ends and that its purpose is to prevent and punish specified acts and omissions which it declares to be unlawful. It was, of course, enacted not merely in the interest of the nation as an abstract or political entity, but to protect a class of the public. In that it resembles the greater *e* part of the criminal law of any country. Like many other penal laws, the 1934 Act also provides in some cases a private remedy available to the victims of the offences which it forbids, and it may possibly be that a private plaintiff who recovers a judgment in a federal court under the 1934 Act can enforce it by action here. As Lord Watson said in *Huntingdon v Attrill* [1893] AC 150 at 161: "... a delict may give rise to a purely civil remedy, as well as to criminal punishment. Although a *f* right of action is given to the party aggrieved, it does not follow that the law of nations must regard his action as a suit in favour of the State." Here, however, I have nothing of that sort. Mr Schemmer comes before this court, in effect, as a public officer charged to reduce the London funds into possession in order to prevent the commission or continuation of offences against federal law. In my judgment, and in the absence of specific legislation founded on treaties, preventive criminal justice *g* is no more a proper subject of international enforcement than retributive criminal justice. The point would be obvious if the plaintiff here were the plaintiff in the District Court, namely, the commission (in effect the financial police of the American Union) and its character is not altered by the substitution of Mr Schemmer, the receiver appointed on the commission's application.'

h

This is an application of the rule that our courts will not enforce foreign penal statutes in the absence of treaty or specific legislation; but the Extradition Acts and the extradition treaties are precisely the means by which in-roads into that principle are made. With all respect, therefore, we fail to see how this case supports the proposition for which it is cited in *Khubchandani*'s case.

In Dicey and Morris *The Conflict of Laws* (11th edn, 1987) pp 100–101 the rule is stated *j* as follows:

'English courts have no jurisdiction to entertain an action: (1) for the enforcement, either directly or indirectly, of a penal, revenue or other public law of a foreign State. [It is said in the comment (at 101)] There is a well-established and almost universal principle that the courts of one country will not enforce the penal and revenue laws of another country. Although the theoretical basis for the Rule is a matter of some controversy, the best explanation, it is submitted, is that suggested by Lord Keith of Avonholm in *Government of India v Taylor*, that enforcement of such claims is an extension of the sovereign power which imposed the taxes, and "an assertion of sovereign authority by one state within the territory of another, as distinct from a patrimonial claim by a foreign sovereign, is (treaty and convention apart) contrary to all concepts of independent sovereignties".'

This plainly relates to civil proceedings, since criminal jurisdiction in this country depends on the crime being committed within the jurisdiction. It is treaty and convention, as given effect to in the Extradition Acts, that enable foreign penal laws to be enforced to the extent that they are extradition crimes, and offences under enactments relating to tax are not extradition crimes.

It does not appear to us therefore, that there is any clear statements, other than in *Khubchandani*'s case and possibly in the original version of art 5 of the European Convention, putting the rule as widely as counsel appearing as amicus contends, namely, that it extends to any offence in connection with revenue matters even though the offence itself falls clearly within the definition of extradition crime.

Even if there were such a rule of international custom and practice, it has to be incorporated into our municipal law before it becomes part of the common law. In *Cia Naviera Vascongada v Cristina* [1938] 1 All ER 719 at 725, [1938] AC 485 at 497 Lord Macmillan said:

'It is a recognised prerequisite of the adoption in our municipal law of a doctrine of public international law that it shall have attained the position of general acceptance by civilised nations as a rule of international conduct, evidenced by international treaties and conventions, authoritative text-books, practice and judicial decisions. It is manifestly of the highest importance that the courts of this country, before they give the force of law within this realm to any doctrine of international law, should be satisfied that it has the hall-marks of general assent and reciprocity.'

It seems to us, in the light of the 1870 Act, that it is impossible to say that the rule in its wide interpretation has been incorporated into our municipal law. In the narrow construction found in the Backing of Warrants Act 1965, of course, it has, since offences under enactments relating to tax are not extraditable offences.

For all these reasons, we are convinced that the decision in *Khubchandani* on this point was wrong, and in our view it is not without significance that neither the point as to construction of the statute nor the question whether the supposed rule of international custom and practice was adopted into the common law appear to have been considered by the court in that case.

In the result, the application will be granted and the case referred back to the Chief Metropolitan Magistrate with a direction to commit on the remaining five charges, if he is satisfied, as it appears that he is, that the conduct complained of in these charges amounts to extradition crimes.

Application granted. Case referred back to Chief Metropolitan Magistrate.

Solicitors: *Treasury Solicitor.*

Dilys Tausz   Barrister.

Seven Seas Properties Ltd v Al-Essa and another

CHANCERY DIVISION
HOFFMANN J
24, 25, 27 MAY 1988

Specific performance – Sale of land – Mareva injunction – Specific performance order combined with Mareva injunction – Whether jurisdiction to make combined order.

Sale of land – Damages for breach of contract – Vendor's inability to show good title – Limitation on damages if vendor's inability to show good title not attributable to his default – Sale and sub-sale – Vendor failing to complete in sale to purchaser – Purchaser unable to complete sub-sale to sub-purchaser – Sub-purchaser rescinding contract on day notice to complete sale expired – Sub-purchaser bringing action against purchaser for breach of contract of sub-sale – Purchaser given no chance to use best endeavours to obtain good title – Whether sub-purchaser's damages limited to its expenses.

The plaintiff agreed to purchase a leasehold property from the defendants for £1·5m and on the same day contracted to sell the property to a sub-purchaser for £1,635,000. Both contracts provided for completion on the same day. The defendants failed to complete on time and the sub-purchaser rescinded its contract on the day notice to complete expired. The sub-purchaser later brought an action against the plaintiff claiming over £600,000 damages for breach of contract. The plaintiff brought an action against the defendants seeking specific performance and applied for an inquiry as to damages and an order that £650,000, representing the sub-purchaser's claim and the plaintiff's costs in defending that claim, be retained in an account in the joint names of the parties' solicitors and not paid out to the defendants when the specific performance order was enforced. The master made the order sought. The defendants appealed against that part of the order preventing the £650,000 from being paid out to them, contending that the court had no jurisdiction to include such a provision in an order for specific performance and that in any event the amount to be retained was excessive.

Held—(1) Since in an appropriate case the court could, when making an order for specific performance, make a separate Mareva injunction restraining the vendor from dealing with the purchase money, it was convenient to combine the two orders into one. The master had therefore had jurisdiction to include the retention order in the specific performance order (see p 166 *e* to *g*, post).

(2) Since the sub-purchaser's claim would be limited to its conveyancing expenses, under the rule limiting a purchaser's damages to his expenses if the vendor failed to make good title, and because the plaintiff had been given no chance by the sub-purchaser to use its best endeavours to obtain a good title, the amount representing the sub-purchaser's claim would be excluded from the amount retained. Instead, the amount retained would be limited to the plaintiff's loss of profit on the sub-sale and other matters in respect of which the plaintiff had a good arguable claim (see p 167 *b* to *d* and p 168 *h j*, post); *Bain v Fothergill* [1874–80] All ER Rep 83 applied.

Notes

For proceedings for summary judgment in actions for specific performance, see 44 Halsbury's Laws (4th edn) para 526, and for cases on the subject, see Digest (Reissue) 173–174, 1543–1546.

For Mareva injunctions, see 37 Halsbury's Laws (4th edn) para 362, and for cases on the subject, see 37(2) Digest (Reissue) 474–476, 2947–2962.

Cases referred to in judgment

a *Bain v Fothergill* (1874) LR 7 HL 158, [1874–80] All ER Rep 83.
   Day v Singleton [1899] 2 Ch 320, CA.
   Engell v Fitch (1869) LR 4 QB 659, Ex Ch.
   Flureau v Thornhill (1776) 2 Wm Bl 1078, [1775–1802] All ER Rep 91, 96 ER 635.
   Hadley v Baxendale (1854) 9 Exch 341, [1843–60] All ER Rep 461, 156 ER 145.
   Sharneyford Supplies Ltd v Edge (Barrington Black Austin & Co (a firm), third party) [1987]
b   1 All ER 588, [1987] Ch 305, [1987] 2 WLR 363, CA.

Case also cited

Seligman Bros v Brown Shipley & Co (1916) 32 TLR 549.

Appeal

c The defendants, Fatima Al-Essa and Sheika Sabaha Al Sabah, appealed against that part of
   an order made by Master Cholmondeley Clarke on 17 February 1988 when making an
   order for specific performance of a contract dated 26 June 1987 for the sale of a leasehold
   property at 27–29 Sloane Gardens, London SW1, to the plaintiff, Seven Seas Properties
   Ltd, whereby the master ordered that the sum of £650,000 be retained in an account in
   the joint names of the parties' solicitors and not paid out to the defendants when the
d specific performance order was enforced. The appeal was heard and judgment was given
   in chambers. The case is reported by permission of Hoffmann J. The facts are set out in
   the judgment.

David H J G Powell for the defendants.
Benjamin Levy for the plaintiff.
e

Cur adv vult

27 May. The following judgment was delivered.

f **HOFFMANN J.** This is an appeal against part of an order for specific performance
   made by Master Cholmondeley Clarke under RSC Ord 86. On 26 June 1987 the
   defendants, who are two ladies resident in Kuwait, agreed in writing to sell the leasehold
   property known as 27–29 Sloane Gardens, London SW1 to the plaintiff for £1,500,000.
   A deposit of £150,000 was paid. The property consists of two houses which have been
   converted into a number of self-contained flats. On the same date the plaintiff entered
   into a contract to sub-sell the property to a Panamanian corporation called Grangeville
g Marketing Co Inc (Grangeville) for £1,635,000. Both contracts provided for completion
   on 7 September.
       The first defendant's husband, who acted on behalf of the vendors in negotiating the
   sale, says that he knew nothing of the sub-sale until the plaintiff's solicitors submitted a
   draft of a transfer to Grangeville on 25 August. He says on information from the
h defendants that they knew no more. The defendants' solicitor has also sworn an affidavit
   in which he says that he knew of the sub-sale after 2 September. I observe that in their
   letter on 26 June confirming that contracts had been exchanged by agreement on the
   telephone, the plaintiff's solicitors asked for an additional authority to inspect the register
   in favour of another firm of solicitors who were in fact acting for the sub-purchasers.
   This might have provided an earlier clue, but there is nothing to contradict the evidence
j that neither the defendants nor their agents knew anything of the sub-sale at the time
   when contracts were exchanged.
       There were some delays on obtaining a consent to assignment of the lease from the
   Cadogan Estate as landlords and the parties twice agreed to postpone completion. It was
   eventually set for 21 October. On that date the defendants failed to complete. Notices to
   complete were served by both the plaintiff and Grangeville on 22 October and expired
   on 13 November. On that date Grangeville rescinded its contract but the plaintiff did

not. On 2 December it issued a writ claiming specific performance and damages, including '. . . damages caused by delay leading to the breach by the Plaintiff of its contract of sub-sale'.

A summons for summary judgment under RSC Ord 86 was supported by an affidavit sworn by the plaintiff's solicitor. He said that Grangeville had put forward a very substantial claim for breach of contract, totalling more than £600,000 and that the plaintiff was therefore likely to be involved in 'a major contested action' in which the legal costs were likely to be not less than £50,000. The defendants were resident outside the jurisdiction and there was 'a substantial risk that any award of damages against them [would] not be met unless it [was] secured by payment into a joint account or into Court . . .' The plaintiff therefore asked for an inquiry into damages and a provision in the specific performance order that £650,000 of the purchase price should not be released to the defendants but be retained in the joint names of the parties' solicitors pending the outcome of the inquiry. The master made an order in those terms.

In this appeal counsel for the defendants does not challenge the order for specific performance, which was carried into effect by completion on 21 April 1988, or the order for an inquiry as to damages. But he challenges the provision for retention of the £650,000 in joint names. First, he submits that the court has no jurisdiction to include such a provision in an order for specific performance. The essence of specific performance is mutuality and the party seeking the order must be ready, willing and able to perform his obligations under the contract. In the case of a purchaser, he must be willing to pay the full purchase price to the vendor. Payment into joint names is not payment to the vendor.

Counsel for the plaintiff did not in principle challenge this analysis of a specific performance order in its pure form, though he did refer to the power to make an order with abatement of the price as an example of the court's power to adapt its orders to meet the justice of the case. Instead, he said that this was not a pure specific performance order but a convenient marriage of the specific performance and Mareva jurisdiction. Counsel for the defendants did not dispute that in an appropriate case, a court which had made an order for specific performance in the pure form for which he was contending could also, by a separate Mareva injunction, restrain the vendor from dealing with all or some part of the purchase money. If that is right, I think that it would be excessively formalistic to require this result to be achieved by two orders rather than one. It is true that in theory the provision for retention in joint names gives the plaintiff better protection against other creditors of the defendants than it would have under a Mareva order, but counsel for the defendants took no point on this difference. He wanted the defendants to have unrestricted access to the whole of the purchase price. There was no challenge to the allegation that they are resident out of the jurisdiction and no evidence that they have any other assets within. Accordingly, it seems to me that provided the other grounds for a Mareva order were satisfied, the master was right to make the order he did.

Counsel for the defendants' alternative submission was that even as an exercise of the Mareva injunction, the provision for retention of so large a sum of £650,000 could not possibly be justified. The sole basis on which the claim was put in the supporting affidavit was that the plaintiff was faced with a £600,000 claim for damages from the sub-purchaser. But such a claim against the plaintiff was excluded by the rule in *Bain v Fothergill* (1874) LR 7 HL 158, [1874–80] All ER Rep 83, and even if sustainable against the plaintiff, would be too remote a head of damage to claim against the defendants.

There seems to me much force in the *Bain v Fothergill* point. There has been much criticism of the rule (see the 1987 report of the Law Commission on *Transfer of Land: The Rule in Bain v Fothergill* (Law Com no 166) and *Sharneyford Supplies Ltd v Edge (Barrington Black Austin & Co (a firm), third party)* [1987] 1 All ER 588, [1987] Ch 305) but it remains the law and not the basis on which vendors contract to sell land which they do not own. (The Law Commission recommended that the rule should be abolished only in relation to contracts made after the commencement of the proposed statute).

In *Flureau v Thornhill* (1776) 2 Wm Bl 1078, [1775–1802] All ER Rep 91 at 91–92 De
a Grey CJ stated the rule in the following terms:

> 'Upon a contract for a purchase, if the title proves bad, and the vendor is (without
> fraud) incapable of making a good one, I do not think that the purchaser can be
> entitled to any damages for the fancied goodness of the bargain, which he supposes
> he has lost.'

b   The rule is subject to various qualifications and counsel for the plaintiff drew attention
to the line of authority based on *Day v Singleton* [1899] 2 Ch 320 which requires a vendor
to have used his best endeavours to obtain a good title before being able to rely on the
rule. In this case, however, there was no question of the plaintiff having failed to use its
best endeavours. It was given no chance to do so because Grangeville rescinded the
contract on the very day that its notice to complete expired. Nor would the plaintiff,
c which stood to make a profit of £135,000, have had any motive for failing to do its
utmost to obtain a title. The result is that in my judgment this was a straightforward
case of a sub-seller who, despite his good faith and best endeavours, was unable to obtain
a title to convey before the sub-purchaser elected to rescind the contract. It falls squarely
within the rule in *Bain v Fothergill*. The evidence before the master therefore did not
justify a retention of more than the damages recoverable under that rule. These are
d traditionally said to be confined to wasted conveyancing expenses and costs. The sub-
purchaser appears also to have paid a facility fee to the bank from which it intended to
borrow and to have employed architects and surveyors in connection with proposed
works on the premises and the application for the landlord's consent. Whether a
purchaser can recover these costs under the rule appears to be a matter of controversy (see
Law Com, no 166 para 2.19).
e   After the master made his order, the purchase was, as I have mentioned, completed on
21 April. The order had provided for the defendants to execute a transfer in favour of
the plaintiff, but on 6 April the plaintiff wrote to the defendants' solicitors saying that it
now proposed to sell to Grangeville for £1,375,000 and asked for a transfer direct to
Grangeville. The defendants did not do so and the completion took place by two separate
transfers from the defendants to the plaintiff and from the plaintiff to Grangeville. There
f was no formal contract between the plaintiff and Grangeville for the sale at £1,375,000,
but there was an exchange of correspondence which included a term that the sale and
completion was not to 'effect [sic] or prejudice [Granville's] rights and remedies arising
directly or indirectly from [the previous contract] . . .'
   In view of the completion of the sale to Grangeville, counsel for the plaintiff submitted
a different method of calculating his claim for damages. First, the plaintiff claims
g £135,000 as loss of profit on the original sub-sale to Grangeville. Second, it claims
£125,000 as loss incurred on the eventual sub-sale to Grangeville. Then there is a claim
for £20,000 in respect of the costs of Grangeville's action arising out of the first contract,
£30,000 for interest on Grangeville's original deposit which had to be repaid, £15,000
for additional stamp duty payable on the two-stage completion on 21 April and £40,000
h for some missing fixtures and fittings to which I shall return later.
   Counsel for the defendants submits that for Mareva purposes there is no good arguable
case for the recovery of any of these heads of claim. All except the last two arise out of
the sub-sale to Grangeville and are therefore, he says, not recoverable under the rule in
Hadley v Baxendale (1854) 9 Exch 341, [1843–60] All ER Rep 461. I shall consider this
point first and return later to the last two items.
j   This is not a case of total failure to complete or 'loss of the bargain' but a case of delayed
completion. Was it within the contemplation of the parties at the time of the contract
that such delay might result in the loss by the purchaser of a profit on a sub-sale? The
cases suggest that one cannot answer this question by reference to a general rule. In *Engell
v Fitch* (1869) LR 4 QB 659 at 668 Kelly CB declined to say that 'in all cases parties to the
sale of real estate must be taken to have contemplated a resale', but does not suggest that

such contemplation cannot be held to have existed in an appropriate case. Counsel for the plaintiff submits that in the case of the sale of an investment property such as this, it would be contemplated as 'not unlikely' that the purchaser was buying for immediate resale. I think that this must be a matter for evidence and that there must be a good arguable case that damage arising from such a resale is not too remote.

There is a separate point about the claim for the loss incurred by the abatement of the price on the eventual sale to Grangeville. At that stage, the plaintiff would, notwithstanding the order for specific performance, have been entitled to rescind the contract with the defendants. If it had done so, then apart from the loss of profit on the original sub-sale and any liability within the rule in *Bain v Fothergill*, it would have suffered no loss. Instead, it chose to complete the purchase subject to an immediate sub-sale at a loss of £125,000. This loss would appear to be entirely a consequence of the plaintiff's own choice. Why should it be laid at the door of the defendants?

Counsel for the plaintiff said that the plaintiff agreed to sell at a loss in order to mitigate Grangeville's claim for damages under the first contract. If this was so, it was never communicated to either of the other parties and Grangeville, as I have noted, extracted an agreement that the completion was to be without prejudice to its claims under the first contract. In any case, given the position under *Bain v Fothergill*, I doubt whether it was a reasonable thing to do. I find the circumstances of the second sale to Grangeville extremely puzzling and the plaintiff's case for recovering the loss thereby arising is in my judgment a weak one. On the other hand, the plaintiff may, if it overcomes the hurdle or remoteness, be able to recover the damages which it would have had to pay, or may still have to pay, to Grangeville on account of the first contract. I think that a generous estimate for this claim would be £50,000.

On the claim for stamp duty, I think that counsel for the defendants is right in his objection. The judgment under RSC Ord 86 defined the obligations of the parties. No doubt the plaintiff could have applied to have it varied but while it stood the defendants could not in my view be obliged to execute a transfer in different terms from those prescribed by the order.

That brings me finally to the claim for the missing fixtures and fittings. It is alleged that shortly before completion the defendants caused to be removed from the premises fixtures such as washing machines, cookers, sink units and fitted cupboards. The cost of replacing these items is said to be £40,000. The contract says nothing about the fixtures and fittings and the answers to preliminary inquires are ambiguous but tend, I think, to suggest that everything which could be so described was included. It appears to me that the plaintiff has at least an arguable case that the items were included in the sale. Counsel for the defendants submitted that £40,000 was grossly excessive but I have very little material on which to judge this question. As I am dealing only with a retention pending a full hearing on the claim I must approach the question with a very broad brush indeed.

Adding up the items for which the plaintiff appears to have a good arguable case, they appear to me to be as following:

Loss of profit	£135,000
Loss of interest	£30,000
Fixtures and fittings	£40,000
Grangeville action	£50,000
Plaintiff's costs	£20,000
Total	£275,000

I shall therefore vary the master's order by reducing the sum ordered to be retained in joint names to £275,000.

Appeal allowed in part.

Solicitors: *Jepson Goff* (for the defendants); *Allan Jay & Co* (for the plaintiff).

Evelyn M C Budd   Barrister.

Practice Direction

FAMILY DIVISION

Adoption – Practice – Prospective adoption – Ward placed with long-term foster parents with view to adoption – Disclosure of wardship papers to prospective adopters – Leave to disclose wardship file to be made to judge in main wardship proceedings.

Ward of court – Practice – Application in wardship proceedings – Ex parte application – Applications for routine leave or directions where court has authorised placement of ward with view to adoption – Notice to other parties not normally necessary – Consultation with Official Solicitor when acting as guardian ad litem.

1. *Advance authority for disclosure of wardship papers to prospective adopters*

Prospective adopters with whom a ward of court has been placed, with the court's authority, as long-term foster parents with a view to adoption require the further authority of the court before they can be granted access to the documents in the wardship proceedings. Requests for such authority have commonly been made, until now, at a separate and subsequent appointment before the registrar or district registrar.

In the opinion of the judges of the Family Division it will in most cases be a more suitable and convenient course for the relevant authority to be sought from the judge at the main wardship hearing, on application by the local authority for an advance authorisation permitting disclosure of the wardship file (subject to conditions safeguarding confidentiality) to the prospective adopters and their legal advisers.

Leave to disclose the wardship file should therefore normally be sought from the judge at the main wardship hearing, subject to such terms and conditions (including the exception from disclosures of any particular document or category of documents) as the judge may think fit. It will be desirable for the judge's order to indicate the stage at which disclosure is to be allowed to take place; and normally this will either be before the placement is made or when leave to commence adoption proceedings is about to be sought.

2. *Procedure for obtaining any necessary leave or directions from the court following authorisation of a placement*

Although it continues to be the general rule in wardship that ex parte applications are permitted only in cases of urgent necessity (*Re H (a minor)* [1985] 3 All ER 1, [1985] 1 WLR 1164, CA), applications for routine leave or directions (eg for medical attention or holidays outside the jurisdiction), in cases where the court has already made an order authorising the placement of the minor with a view to adoption, by the person or authority having the care of the minor may be made ex parte and without notice to any other party (but subject to consultation with the Official Solicitor in cases where he is acting as guardian ad litem).

Issued with the concurrence of the Lord Chancellor.

C F TURNER
Senior Registrar.

5 December 1988

Re St Thomas à Becket, Framfield

CHICHESTER CONSISTORY COURT

CHANCELLOR HIS HONOUR JUDGE QUENTIN EDWARDS QC

29 JULY, 17 SEPTEMBER 1987

Ecclesiastical law – Parochial church council – Member – Liability – Personal liability – Liability for works executed to church without due authority – Extent of liability.

Ecclesiastical law – Church – Repairs and maintenance – Authority for execution of works to consecrated buildings – Duty of architect – Duty to be satisfied of existence of faculty, interim order of consistory court or archdeacon's certificate – Duty in cases of urgent works.

Since a parochial church council is a body corporate, no individual member of such a council is personally liable for any debt or other liability of the council which has been lawfully incurred, but if works to a church are executed without due authority, and so unlawfully, by the direction of a churchwarden or other member of the council that protection is lost. Accordingly if a churchwarden, acting alone or with others, directs works to a church without the authority of an archdeacon's certificate or a faculty he may expose himself to grave financial liability and loss, and may be ordered personally to pay the costs incurred in obtaining a confirmatory faculty and further, if the archdeacon himself seeks and is granted a faculty authorising the undoing or alteration of the works, may be ordered to pay all the archdeacon's costs and expenses, viz both his legal costs and the costs of the remedial works (see p 173 *e* to *h*, post).

Architects who accept retainers for the execution of works to consecrated buildings over which a consistory court has jurisdiction have a duty to satisfy themselves before the works are begun that there is due ecclesiastical authority for the execution of those works, ie the authority of a faculty, an interim order of the consistory court or an archdeacon's certificate or, in cases of extreme urgency, the authority of necessity, to which is coupled an obligation to seek directions concerning the urgent works from the chancellor, the registrar or the archdeacon as soon as practicable (see p 174 *a* to *c*, post).

Notes

For parochial church councils as bodies corporate, see 14 Halsbury's Laws (4th edn) paras 569, 1256.

For faculties relating to church buildings, see ibid para 1312, and for cases on the subject, see 19 Digest (Reissue) 445–452, 3529–3563.

For an archdeacon's certificate authorising repairs or maintenance to a church, see 14 Halsbury's Laws (4th edn) paras 1098, 1331.

Cases referred to in judgment

Atkins, Re [1989] 1 All ER 14, Con Ct.

Hawkes v Jones and Ruscoe (1888) Trist 222, Con Ct.

Petition for confirmatory faculty

By an application dated 6 April 1987 under r 3(1) of the Faculty Jurisdiction Rules 1967, SI 1967/1002, for an archdeacon's certificate, which on 12 April 1987 was directed by the Archdeacon of Lewes and Hastings, the Ven Max Leon Godden, pursuant to s 12(4) of the Faculty Jurisdiction Measure 1964 to be treated as an application for a faculty, the vicar of the parish of Framfield in the Diocese of Chichester, the Rev Jeremy Cross, and two of the churchwardens, Peter Berry and Betty Gillies, sought authority for the carrying out of certain works of internal repair and decoration to the parish church of St Thomas à Becket. Because of doubts as to the materials and colours to be used in the proposed a works the chancellor directed that there should be citation stating precisely what was proposed, and when it was learnt that the works in question had already been executed the chancellor countermanded the direction for citation and directed that the petitioners should apply for a confirmatory faculty. The application was unopposed. The facts are set out in the judgment.

The petitioners did not appear.

b

Cur adv vult

17 September. The following judgment was delivered.

THE CHANCELLOR. The church of St Thomas à Becket is the parish church of
c Framfield in this diocese. The church dates from the early sixteenth century, most of it having been constructed after a fire in 1509, though the western tower was rebuilt in 1892. In recent times the parishioners have undertaken several works of repair and improvement to the building; others have been proposed and are under consideration.

The present case arises out of repairs to the internal wall plaster in all parts of the church and redecoration of the plaster surfaces, once repaired, and the plaster ceilings
d within the church. On the instructions of the first petitioner, the Rev Jeremy Cross, the parish priest, and the parochial church council Wells-Thorpe & Suppel Ltd, architects and project managers, prepared, in February 1987, a specification of the necessary works. By a unanimous resolution, passed on 16 February 1987, the parochial church council resolved to apply for an archdeacon's certificate for authority to execute these works. Estimates from three builders for the works described in the specification were obtained
e and the estimate of Press & Banks Ltd, which was for approximately £5,500 exclusive of value added tax, was accepted. In fact the parochial church council itself did not apply for an archdeacon's certificate; the application was made, in the form prescribed by the Faculty Jurisdiction Rules 1967, SI 1967/1002, by the above-named petitioners, viz the incumbent and the two churchwardens, on 6 April 1987.

f This application was by no means the first application for an archdeacon's certificate in recent times made by the parochial church council or by the incumbent and churchwardens. Applications were made in 1985 and 1986 and in more than one instance the Archdeacon of Lewes directed, pursuant to his power to do so under s 12(4) of the Faculty Jurisdiction Measure 1964, that the application should be treated as an application for a faculty. For reasons not germane to this case there was a meeting between the archdeacon and the incumbent and parochial church council at the beginning of this
g year in which the archdeacon emphasised the importance of observing the law and procedure relating to the faculty jurisdiction. Finally, it is material to mention at this stage that last year the parochial church council complained to the diocesan authorities of delay by the diocesan advisory committee in dealing with an application relating to the stonework of the church. The complaint was referred to me and I examined the
h relevant papers and correspondence and reported, through the registrar, that I was satisfied that the diocesan advisory committee had not been guilty of delay or unreasonable conduct.

In the instant case the application of 6 April 1987 was referred to the archdeacon and, as is required by the Measure, to the diocesan advisory committee. The archdeacon, on 12 April 1987, directed that application should be made to the court for a faculty
j authorising the proposed works. The diocesan advisory committee considered the proposals at its meeting on 7 May and reported to the registrar on 11 May.

In giving its advice the diocesan advisory committee was not able to recommend, without qualification, the execution of the works. The architects specified that the decoration to the plaster wall and ceiling surfaces should be with a water-based masonry paint, approved by the architects. The application of 6 April stated that the proposal was to use 'Crown Covermatt Emulsion', 'because an emulsion was used on some of the walls, about 20 years ago, and consequently those areas will not take lime wash'. The diocesan advisory committee, in its advice to me, pointed out the apparent discrepancy between the specification and application and said that the committee considered 'this church to be worthy of a limewash application following rubbing down of the old emulsion and would advise that this be investigated and carried out if possible'.

Following the archdeacon's direction the papers, and the diocesan advisory committee's observations, were referred to me and I gave certain directions which, with the diocesan advisory committee's advice, were given to the petitioners by the registrar by letter dated 11 June. As there was some doubt as to the material and colour proposed to be applied to the walls and ceilings I directed that there should be citation and that the citation should state precisely what was proposed. The registrar also, in accordance with my directions, asked the petitioners to 'bear in mind the strong recommendation of the [diocesan advisory committee] concerning lime wash' and to provide a report from the church's architect on this issue.

I interpolate here that I have, as chancellor of this and of another diocese, learnt of the firmly held view of many architects experienced in ecclesiastical work of the merit of using lime wash in old churches. The reason is, as I understand it, that the moisture which inevitably occurs in old rubble, stone and cob walls can pass through lime wash, whereas it cannot pass through emulsion or oil paint. This barrier to natural evaporation may cause condensation which is likely to have deleterious consequences on main timbers and other parts of the structure.

The petitioners replied to the registrar's letter of 11 June on 23 June by a letter stating that the redecoration of the church had been completed using emulsion. Their letter made it clear that all three were aware there was neither the authority of an archdeacon's certificate nor of a faculty for the execution of the work and that the work was done under the direction and supervision of Wells-Thorpe & Suppel Ltd. The letter adds that 'the architect, Mr Matthews of Wells-Thorpe and Suppel . . . was unaware that we were proceeding without an Archdeacon's Certificate'. Briefly stated the reasons the petitioners gave for proceeding with the works were that they had already considered and rejected the use of lime wash on the ground of expense, that savings were to be made by the immediate execution of the works, that the congregation had been meeting in the village hall 'since January' and that there had been past delays in the making of decisions.

As the works in question had already been executed I countermanded the direction that there should be citation and, instead, directed that the application for a confirmatory faculty (as it had become) should be heard at a sitting of this consistory court which had already been fixed for 29 July 1987. The petitioners and the architects were given notice of the hearing and warned that I was likely to be critical of them and that if they wished to answer any criticism which might be made they should attend the hearing. The petitioners did not attend, nor did the architects, though Mr Matthews sent a letter stating that he was 'not aware that a Faculty or Archdeacon's Certificate had not been issued for the work'.

The case was called on; I perused the correspondence and relevant papers and said that I would deliver judgment in writing in due course, which I now do.

In my judgment none of the reasons given by the petitioners, whether taken singly or in combination, justify their action in executing a major work to an ancient church without due authority. The application for authority was made only two months before the work was put in hand. No inquiry was made of the registry as to its progress. No inquiry was made of the diocesan advisory committee as to its views by the petitioners or their architects. Because the work was put in hand without notice the diocesan advisory committee could not make any useful inspection of the church or undertake any other investigation. The consequence is that a chance has been lost to undo that which was ill done a generation ago. It may be that for good economic or other reasons

the chance could not practicably have been taken. The petitioners' actions have deprived
a the court and its advisers from making a decision on the matter.

Having said this I recognise, in the light of a report by the architects made after the
works were completed, that, on full inquiry and investigation, the diocesan advisory
committee may well have withdrawn its suggestion to me that lime wash should be
used. I shall, for this reason, grant a faculty confirming the works described in the
application of 6 April. In the light of the recent history of this parish and the terms of
b the petitioners' letter of 23 June 1987 I am not, however, prepared to pass this matter
over and I therefore make the order as to costs and the observations to the Rev Mr Cross,
the churchwardens and the architects which follow.

The order as to costs is that the petitioners pay the costs of the application, which is to
be treated as a petition for a major faculty. They must pay the costs appropriate to a half-
day hearing in court. (No costs of the hearing in court were ordered to be paid by the
c other petitioner whose case was heard on that day, Mrs G M Atkins, for reasons which
are given in my judgment in that case: see *Re Atkins* [1989] 1 All ER 14 at 21). The
petitioners must also pay the registrar's correspondence fee, which fee will, in due course,
be submitted to me for my approval.

As appears from what I have already stated the Rev Mr Cross, with the churchwardens,
directed the execution of major works to the ancient and fine church in his care without
d due authority and in the knowledge that he had no authority. In my judgment this was
a serious breach of his obligation of canonical obedience. He should appreciate that if he
should ever again execute works to the church of St Thomas à Becket which require the
authority of an archdeacon's certificate or a faculty, but without having that authority,
he may, in the light of my above findings, have to face proceedings under the Ecclesiastical
Jurisdiction Measure 1963.
e The churchwardens, and their successors in that office, are not, as lay men and women,
liable to such proceedings. They, however, should appreciate the pecuniary risks which
they will run should they ever again execute such works without authority. A parochial
church council is a body corporate (see s 3 of the Parochial Church Councils (Powers)
Measure 1956), and therefore no individual member of a council is personally liable for
f any debt or other liability of the body corporate which has been lawfully incurred. If,
however, works to a church are executed without due authority, and so unlawfully, by
the direction of a churchwarden or other member of the council that protection is lost.
If, therefore, a churchwarden, acting alone or with others, directs works to a church
without the authority of an archdeacon's certificate or a faculty he may expose himself to
grave financial liability and loss. He may be ordered, personally, to pay the costs incurred
in obtaining a confirmatory faculty. The archdeacon may himself seek a faculty
g authorising the undoing or alteration of the works and if such a faculty be granted to the
archdeacon the churchwarden may be ordered to pay all the archdeacon's costs and
expenses, viz both his legal costs and the costs of the remedial works. Finally I should
repeat the warning given by Chancellor Dr Tristram QC in the Hereford Consistory
Court in 1888 that if a settlement or other damage were to result from alterations done
h to the fabric without a faculty the churchwarden would be personally liable to make
good the damage: see *Hawkes v Jones and Ruscoe* Trist 222 at 226.

The individual who acted throughout for the petitioners and the parochial church
council on behalf of their architects, Wells-Thorpe & Suppel Ltd., was, as I have stated,
Mr J G Matthews. He is an employee of that company and, though no doubt appropriately
qualified for the work for which he is employed, is not an architect. He says, and the
j petitioners support him in this, that he was not aware that there was neither an
archdeacon's certificate nor a faculty authorising the works which he, in the name and
on behalf of his employers, specified and supervised in their execution. It is well
established that it is part of the professional duty of an architect to comply with the
requirements of all relevant public and local statutes, and all subsidiary legislation, such

as bye-laws and the building regulations, affecting works on which he is engaged. An architect is, for example, under a professional obligation to ensure that any necessary planning consents and consents under the building regulations have been obtained before directing the execution of any works. In my judgment architects who undertake ecclesiastical commissions, and particularly those on a diocesan panel maintained under the Inspection of Churches Measure 1955, are under a like obligation with regard to the faculty jurisdiction. In plain words architects who accept retainers for the execution of works to consecrated buildings over which a consistory court has jurisdiction have a duty to satisfy themselves that there is due ecclesiastical authority for the execution of those works before the works are begun. By due ecclesiastical authority I mean the authority of a faculty or interim order of the consistory court, or of an archdeacon's certificate, or, in cases of extreme urgency, the authority of necessity, to which is coupled an obligation to seek directions concerning the urgent works from the chancellor, the registrar or the archdeacon as soon as practicable.

The company, Wells-Thorpe & Suppel Ltd, regularly undertakes ecclesiastical work in the diocese. Mr J A Wells-Thorpe, a director, and Mr Z A Suppel, a consultant, are on the diocesan panel of architects. In my judgment the company, acting through Mr Matthews, should not have supervised the execution of the works specified in the application of 6 April 1987 without first satisfying itself that there was a faculty or archdeacon's certificate authorising their execution.

The court, in the exercise of its faculty jurisdiction, relies a good deal on the professional integrity and care of architects. It is the practice of this court (and, I understand, of most other consistory courts) when granting faculties for works affecting the fabric of churches to require that the works should be carried out under the supervision of an architect. The court has power to make a faculty subject to such a condition: see s 10(a) of the Faculty Jurisdiction Measure 1964. To my mind this practice is of great value to the Church's courts. They have neither sheriffs nor tipstaffs; the enforcement and monitoring of their orders rests, in the main, on informed consent and exhortation. The court knows that it may rely on architects, of standing in the diocese, on whom the duty of supervision has by such a condition been placed, to ensure that works are not executed without authority and that there is no deviation from the terms of the faculty authorising the works.

In the light of these considerations I have had to decide whether to state, in this judgment, that I am not prepared henceforward to make it a condition of any faculty which may hereafter issue that Wells-Thorpe & Suppel Ltd should supervise any works authorised by that faculty. If I did so state and a case arose in which that company had been retained to design and carry through works to a church I should have to make it a condition that the works might not be executed unless they were carried out under the supervision of another architect.

I shall not take that step because I realise the hardship it might cause but I give due warning that such a step is in my power. As it is the direction I give is that in any case henceforward in which Wells-Thorpe & Suppel Ltd are the architects retained and in which, following the ordinary practice of the court, I would grant a faculty, subject to the condition that the carrying out of the works is to be supervised by that company, I shall require a personal undertaking to the court from an architect who is a director of, or employed by, the company that the works will be executed in accordance with the terms of the faculty and that no work will be executed without the court's authority.

Faculty granted. Costs to be paid by petitioners in terms appearing in judgment.

N P Metcalfe Esq   Barrister.

R v Licensing Authority, ex parte Smith Kline & French Laboratories Ltd (Generics (UK) Ltd and another intervening)

COURT OF APPEAL, CIVIL DIVISION

DILLON, BALCOMBE AND STAUGHTON LJJ

12, 13, 16, 17, 18, 19 MAY, 29 JUNE 1988

Medicine – Product licence – Generic product – Essential similarity – Demonstrating essential similarity – Use of originator's confidential information – Originator supplying details of research and testing in development of drug when applying to licensing authority for product licence – Generic companies subsequently applying for product licence for similar generic product – Whether licensing authority entitled to use information supplied by originator when considering subsequent applications for product licences – Whether information supplied by originator forming part of licensing authority's general store of scientific knowledge – EEC Council Directive 65/65, art 4(8)(a)(iii) – EC Council Directive 87/21.

The applicant pharmaceutical company applied in 1972 for a product licence in respect of a drug developed by it for controlling the secretion of gastric acid and treating peptic ulcers. The applicant supplied the licensing authority with details of its research and testing in the development of the drug and was duly granted a licence. Under EC Council Directive 87/21 other pharmaceutical companies were entitled to apply to the licensing authority for a product licence for a similar generic product after the lapse of ten years from the grant of a licence to the applicant. In 1987 two firms (the generic companies) applied for product licences to market generic forms of the applicant's drug. Under art 4(8)(a)(iii) of EEC Council Directive 65/65 (as replaced by Directive 87/21) an applicant for a product licence in a member state was not required to supply results of tests on his drug if he could 'demonstrate' that his product was essentially similar to a product which had been authorised within the Community for ten years and was marketed in the member state. The generic companies claimed that the essential similarity could be demonstrated by reference to the research and testing details supplied by the applicant in support of its application for a product licence. The applicant opposed the use by the licensing authority of the information supplied by it to determine the essential similarity of the generic companies' drugs, on the ground that the applicant's information was confidential, and was granted an injunction restraining the authority from so using the information. The licensing authority appealed to the Court of Appeal.

Held – Applying a purposive construction to Directives 65/65 and 87/21 (which declared that the purpose of the rules regulating the production and distribution of proprietary medicinal products was the protection of public health, the harmonisation of trade within the Community by the removal of disparities in licensing procedures and the prevention of unnecessary repetitive tests on humans or animals) the essential similarity of a generic product did not have to be demonstrated by a generic company from the results of its own tests when applying for a product licence. Instead, although the licensing authority was not entitled to make the originator's confidential information gratuitously available to its rivals, it was entitled to use that information as part of its general store of scientific knowledge when considering subsequent applications for product licences. Accordingly, the applicant was not entitled to an injunction restraining the licensing authority from using confidential information supplied by it when considering the generic companies' applications for product licences. The appeal would therefore be allowed (see p 181 *d e g h*, p 182 *a b*, p 183 *f*, p 185 *g h*, p 186 *a b e f*, p 187 *g*, p 188 *j*, p 190 *d e* and p 191 *j* to p 192 *a*, post).

Notes

For factors relevant to the determination of product licence applications, see 30 Halsbury's *a* Laws (4th edn) para 654.

For EEC policy on importation and marketing of medicinal products, see 51 ibid, paras 6·73, 8·74.

Cases referred to in judgments

Allen & Hanburys Ltd's (Salbutamol) Patent, Re [1987] RPC 327, CA. *b*

Burroughs-Delplanque Decision 72/25 OJ 1972 L13, p 50, [1972] CMLR D67, EC Commission.

Castrol Australia Pty Ltd v Emtech Associates Pty Ltd (1980) 33 ALR 31, NSW SC.

de Peijper, Re Case 104/75 [1976] ECR 613.

Frans-Nederlandse Maatschappij voor Biologische Producten BV, Re criminal proceedings against Case 272/80 [1981] ECR 3277. *c*

Kabelmetal-Luchaire Decision 75/494 OJ 1975 L222, p 34, [1975] CMLR D40, EC Commission.

Procureur du Roi v Debauve Case 52/79 [1980] ECR 833.

Cases also cited

A-G v Newspaper Publishing plc [1987] 3 All ER 276, [1988] Ch 333, Ch D and CA. *d*

Albert (Prince) v Strange (1849) 1 Mac & G 25, 41 ER 1171, LC.

Allied Mills Industries Pty Ltd v Trade Practices Commission (1981) 34 ALR 105, Aust Fed Ct.

Burmah Oil Co v Bank of England (A-G intervening) [1979] 3 All ER 700, [1980] AC 1090, HL; affg [1979] 2 All ER 461, [1979] 1 WLR 473, CA.

Bushell v Secretary of State for the Environment [1980] 2 All ER 608, [1981] AC 75, HL. *e*

BV Industrie Diensten Groep v J A Beele Handelmaatschappij BV Case 6/81 [1982] ECR 707.

Church of Scientology of California v Kaufman [1973] RPC 627.

Coca-Cola Co's Applications, Re [1986] 2 All ER 274, [1986] 1 WLR 695, HL.

Coco v A N Clark (Engineers) Ltd [1969] RPC 41.

Comrs of Crown Lands v Page [1960] 2 All ER 726, [1960] 2 QB 274, CA.

Corrs Pavey Whiting & Byrne v Collector of Customs (Vic) (1987) 74 ALR 428, Aust Fed Ct. *f*

Crofton Investment Trust v Greater London Rent Assessment Committee [1967] 2 All ER 1103, [1967] 2 QB 955, DC.

Hauer v Land Rheinland-Pfalz Case 44/79 [1979] ECR 3727.

I G Farbenindustrie AG Agreement, Re [1943] 2 All ER 525, [1944] Ch 41, CA.

Johnson (B) & Co (Builders) Ltd v Minister of Health [1947] 2 All ER 395, CA.

Keurkoop BV Rotterdam v Nancy Kean Gifts BV Case 141/81 [1982] ECR 2853. *g*

Löwenbrau München v Grünhalle Lager International Ltd [1974] RPC 492.

Marshall (Thomas) (Exports) Ltd v Guinle [1978] 3 All ER 193, [1979] Ch 227.

Norwich Pharmacal Co v Customs and Excise Comrs [1973] 2 All ER 943, [1974] AC 133, HL.

Padfield v Minister of Agriculture Fisheries and Food [1968] 1 All ER 694, [1968] AC 997, *h* HL.

Pioneer Aggregates (UK) Ltd v Secretary of State for the Environment [1984] 2 All ER 358, [1985] AC 132, HL.

R v Deputy Industrial Injuries Comr, ex p Moore [1965] 1 All ER 81, [1965] 1 QB 456, CA.

R v Goldstein [1983] 1 All ER 434, [1983] 1 WLR 151, HL; affg [1982] 3 All ER 53, [1982] 1 WLR 804, CA. *j*

R v Monopolies and Mergers Commission, ex p Elders IXL Ltd [1987] 1 All ER 451, [1987] 1 WLR 1221.

R v Secretary of State for Social Services, ex p Wellcome Foundation Ltd [1987] 2 All ER 1025, [1987] 1 WLR 1166, CA.

Ruckdeschel (Albert) & Co and Hansa-Lagerhaus Ströh & Co v Hauptzollamt Hamburg-St Annen, Diamalt AG v Hauptzollamt Itzehoe Joined Cases 117/76 and 16/77 [1977] ECR 1753.

Appeal

a The licensing authority under the Medicines Act 1968 appealed from the decision of Henry J on 21 December 1987 whereby on an application for judicial review by the applicant, Smith Kline & French Laboratories Ltd (SKF), he declared that the licensing authority, when considering an application under the abridged procedure set out in item 8(a)(iii) of the second paragraph of art 4 of EEC Council Directive 65/65, as replaced by EC Council Directive 87/21, for product licences by third parties in respect of generic
b versions of the pharmaceutical product cimetidine originated by the applicant, was not permitted to use, refer to or have recourse to any confidential information supplied by the applicant except with the applicant's express consent. At the hearing of the appeal leave was given to Generics (UK) Ltd and Harris Pharmaceuticals Ltd to intervene. The facts are set out in the judgment of Dillon LJ.

c *Andrew Collins QC* and *Helen Rogers* for the licensing authority.
Jonathan Sumption QC and *Thomas Sharpe* for the first intervener.
Henry Carr for the second intervener.
Jeremy F Lever QC and *Derrick Turriff* for SKF.

d
Cur adv vult

29 June. The following judgments were delivered.

e **DILLON LJ.** The licensing authority under the Medicines Act 1968, in fact, the Minister of Health, appeals against a decision of Henry J of 21 December 1987 whereby, on an application for judicial review by Smith Kline & French Laboratories Ltd (SKF) the judge made a declaration that in considering an application for a product licence in respect of a medicinal product containing cimetidine made pursuant to the abridged procedure provided for by point 8(a)(iii) of the second paragraph of art 4 of EEC Council
f Directive 65/65 as amended the licensing authority may not for the purpose of such application use, refer to or have recourse to any confidential information supplied to it by SKF in connection with any application by SKF for a product licence in respect of such a product except with the express consent of SKF.

Cimetidine is, as the judge said, a drug which has proved useful and popular because of its capacity for controlling gastric acid secretion and healing peptic ulceration. It is
g marketed by SKF in Britain under the brand name Tagamet. It is also covered by UK patents belonging to SKF. These patents were originally granted in 1972 for a period of 16 years, which was due to expire on 9 March 1988. By the Patents Act 1977, however, which was enacted to give effect to the Convention on the Grant of European Patents (Munich, 5 October 1973; TS 20 (1978); Cmnd 7090), which in turn had been concerned
h to harmonise national patent laws throughout the EEC, the duration of the patents was extended from 16 to 20 years on the basis that during the extra four years the patents would be treated as endorsed 'licences of right'.

There have consequently been several applications for licences of right under SKF's cimetidine patents. The terms of such licences fall to be settled by the comptroller, subject to appeal. But before he can market his product, which would be a generic form
j of cimetidine, in Britain, an applicant will need, in addition to the licence under the Patents Act 1977, a product licence under the Medicines Act 1968 as amended. It is with the applications, by present or prospective licensees of right under the Patents Act, for product licences under the 1968 Act that the declaration made by Henry J is concerned; in fact the same issues will arise after the full 20 years of extended patent protection have expired and the patented products and processes are in the public domain, if others than SKF then desire to market cimetidine products.

The issue involved can of course equally apply to generic versions of valuable drugs other than cimetidine.

In the court below, two of the applicants for licences of right, Generics (UK) Ltd and Harris Pharmaceuticals Ltd, were heard as interveners in opposition to SKF's application for judicial review. This was allowed under RSC Ord 53, r 9 on the basis that they desired to be heard in opposition and appeared to the court to be proper persons to be heard. On this appeal, this court has allowed the two interveners to be heard in this court in support of the licensing authority's appeal.

The product licence is necessary in respect of any medicinal product, whether patented or not, because it is provided by s 7(2) and (3) of the 1968 Act that:

'(2) Except in accordance with a licence granted for the purposes of this section (in this Act referred to as a "product licence") no person shall, in the course of a business carried on by him, and in circumstances to which this subsection applies,— (a) sell, supply or export any medicinal product, or (b) procure the sale, supply or exportation of any medicinal product, or (c) procure the manufacture or assembly of any medicinal product for sale, supply or exportation.

(3) No person shall import any medicinal product except in accordance with a product licence.'

Each formulation of the product, eg each strength of tablet or liquid or other form of dosage, requires a separate product licence, and each licensee, whether voluntary or as of right, of the originator of the product also requires a separate product licence for each formulation.

The 1968 Act contains provisions requiring any application for a product licence to be in the prescribed form and to be supported by the prescribed information, but it is unnecessary to refer to these provisions since for many years the procedure and requirements for obtaining a product licence for a medicinal product have been governed by European Community law embodied in a succession of directives of the EEC Council. This is a field in which the Community has, for obvious reasons, been concerned to harmonise the practice in all member states. The 1968 Act has been amended to require regard to be had to Community obligations and the EEC Council directives have direct effect as part of English law.

There are, however, certain provisions of the 1968 Act which I should summarise now, before I turn to the EEC law, as I shall have occasion to refer to them later. In particular, s 21(1) provides that, if the appropriate committee established under the 1968 Act or the Medicines Commission have reason to think on grounds of safety, quality or efficacy of the medicinal product in question that they may be unable to advise the licensing authority to grant a licence for the product in accordance with the application, the applicant is to be notified and is to be afforded an opportunity of appearing before and being heard by them, or of making representations in writing with respect to those grounds. Furthermore by sub-s (3) of the same section if the appropriate committee or the commission advise the licensing authority that the licence ought on any such grounds to be refused, or ought if granted to contain special provisions, the applicant is to be given a notice stating that advice and the reasons for it.

Section 28 empowers the licensing authority to suspend, revoke or vary the provisions of a licence on a variety of grounds, including that the medicinal products as sold fail to a material extent to correspond to the characteristics by reference to which the licence was granted, that the products can no longer be regarded as safe or efficacious for the purposes indicated in the licence and that the specification and standards to which the products are manufactured can no longer be regarded as satisfactory.

Section 118(1) makes it an offence for any person to disclose, save in the performance of his duty, any information obtained by or furnished to him in pursuance of the 1968 Act.

Section 133(2) provides that except in so far as the 1968 Act otherwise expressly
a provides the provisions of the Act are not to be construed as derogating from any right
of action or other remedy (whether civil or criminal) in proceedings instituted otherwise
than under the Act.

So far as EEC law is concerned, the main directive in relation to the licensing of
medicinal products in the member states is EEC Council Directive 65/65. This was
adopted in January 1965, but it has been several times amended. The latest amendment
b was effected by EC Council Directive 87/21 and it is Directive 87/21 that is at the heart
of the present appeal, since it laid down in its present form the abridged procedure
referred to in the declaration made by the judge.

Counsel for SKF rightly points out that Directive 87/21 merely amended Directive 65/
65 and the amendments have to be construed in their context in Directive 65/65 read as
a whole. For present purposes however, it is, in my judgment, sufficient to say that
c Directive 65/65 prescribes by art 3 that no proprietary medicinal product may be placed
on the market in a member state unless an authorisation has been issued by the competent
authority of that state, and the directive then sets out in numbered points 1 to 11 of the
second paragraph of art 4 the general information which an applicant for a product
licence in respect of a medicinal product has to supply to the relevant licensing authority
to get such an authorisation. What is required by way of information to satisfy art 4, and
d particularly point 8, is then spelt out in much greater detail in the Annex, which is
mandatory and binding on all member states, to a later directive, EC Council Directive
75/318. The information so required includes a great deal of scientific information,
which will embody the results of the extensive research and testing which will, in the
case of a new medicinal product, have been carried out by the originator before there
could be any question of that product being licensed for marketing.
e It is not in doubt that any research-orientated pharmaceutical company such as SKF
incurs a great deal of expense on research and testing for any new medicinal product
which is successful and proves valuable, and incurs also incidentally a great deal of
expense on research and testing in following up other possible lines of inquiry which in
the event are found to lead nowhere. It is also not in doubt that in order to obtain its
f product licences for its various formulations of cimetidine, and particularly the earliest
formulations, SKF had to supply the licensing authority, either under Directive 65/65 or
under previous regulations, with a great deal of scientific information, on the results of
its research and tests, which it rightly regards as highly confidential and which it would
be most reluctant to make available for the benefit of any competitor.

It is SKF's contention that this confidential information, supplied by SKF to the
g licensing authority in support of SKF's own applications for product licences for SKF's
cimetidine formulations, cannot be used at all by the licensing authority, without SKF's
consent, when the licensing authority considers other companies' applications, and
particularly the applications of those who hold or seek licences of right under the SKF
patents, for product licences in respect of cimetidine. Such applications have been made
under the abridged procedure now in force, which is set out in Directive 87/21, the
h relevant provisions of which are as follows:

'Whereas point 8 of the second paragraph of Article 4 of Council Directive 65/65/
EEC, as last amended by Directive 83/570/EEC, provides that various types of proof
of the safety and efficacy of a proprietary medicinal product may be put forward in
an application for marketing authorization depending upon the objective situation
of the proprietary medicinal product in question; Whereas experience has shown
j that it is advisable to stipulate more precisely the cases in which the results of
pharmacological and toxicological tests or clinical trials do not have to be provided
with a view to obtaining authorization for a proprietary medicinal product which is
essentially similar to an authorized product, while ensuring that innovative firms
are not placed at a disadvantage; Whereas additional details were provided in respect

of the application of the abovementioned provision by Council Directive 75/318/
EEC of 20 May 1975 on the approximation of the laws of the Member States relating   *a*
to analytical, pharmaco-toxicological and clinical standards and protocols in respect
of the testing of proprietary medicinal products, as last amended by Directive 87/
19/EEC; Whereas, however, there are reasons of public policy for not conducting
repetitive tests on humans or animals without over-riding cause . . . [The Council of
the European Communities] HAS ADOPTED THIS DIRECTIVE:

Article 1   *b*

Directive 65/65/EEC is hereby amended as follows: 1. Point 8 of the second
paragraph of Article 4 shall be replaced by the following text:
    "8. Results of: —physico-chemical, biological or microbiological tests, —
pharmacological and toxicological tests, —clinical trials. However, and without
prejudice to the law relating to the protection of industrial and commercial property:
(a) the applicant shall not be required to provide the results of pharmacological and   *c*
toxicological tests or the results of clinical trials if he can demonstrate: (i) either that
the proprietary medicinal product is essentially similar to a product authorized in
the country concerned by the application and that the person responsible for the
marketing of the original proprietary medicinal product has consented to the
pharmacological, toxicological or clinical references contained in the file on the   *d*
original proprietary medicinal product being used for the purposes of examining
the application in question; (ii) or by detailed references to published scientific
literature presented in accordance with the second paragraph of Article 1 of Directive
75/318/EEC that the constituent or constituents of the proprietary medicinal
product have a well established medicinal use, with recognized efficacy and an
acceptable level of safety; (iii) or that the proprietary medicinal product is essentially   *e*
similar to a product which has been authorized within the Community, in
accordance with Community provisions in force, for not less than [in the present
case ten] years and is marketed in the Member State for which the application is
made . . ." . . .'

The products in question have been on the market for over ten years, and the   *f*
applicants, lacking any consent from SKF, have relied on para (a)(iii).
    Henry J upheld the contention of SKF that the licensing authority could not use SKF's
confidential information at all, and he consequently made the declaration which I have
set out at the outset of this judgment. His primary ground for his decision was that he
construed the word 'demonstrate' in Directive 87/21 as imposing an obligation that an
application under the abridged procedure under that directive must, save in so far as the
consent of SKF as the originator is available, depend solely and exclusively on material   *g*
supplied by the applicant. He also, however, considered that as a matter of English law
the licensing authority owed an obligation of confidence to SKF, in respect of the
technical information supplied by SKF to the licensing authority in support of SKF's own
past applications to the licensing authority for product licences, and that it would be a
breach of that duty of confidence if the licensing authority were to make use of that   *h*
confidential information when considering any other companies' applications for product
licences in respect of cimetidine.
    The general attitude of the licensing authority is that it accepts that it does owe a duty
of confidence to SKF in respect of SKF's confidential information, in the sense that it is
not entitled to make that information gratuitously available to SKF's rivals. But it claims
to be entitled to use the information for the purpose of discharging its statutory and EEC   *j*
functions, particularly in relation to cimetidine, and as part of its general store of scientific
knowledge in considering applications for product licences. The sort of phrase that has
been used in the evidence is that the licensing authority does not seek to use the
information to supplement or reinforce or help out an application for a product licence
which appears to be defective, but to assess and compare the application and to check on

the validity of claims that an applicant's product and a product of SKF are indeed
a 'essentially similar' within the meaning of Directive 87/21. There is, however,
considerable practical difficulty in discerning any workable hard-and-fast line between
these concepts, not least because those charged with the examination and assessment of
product licences on behalf of the licensing authority will be scientists and not lawyers.
There have been several occasions in the recent past on which statements of its current
practice made on behalf of the licensing authority, including a statement by Lady
b Trumpington in answer to a question by Lord Hacking in the House of Lords, have had
to be corrected because, through failures of communication between those doing the
work and those trying to explain it, the statements turned out to be inaccurate.
Furthermore the duties of the licensing authority under sub-ss (1) and (2) of s 21 of the
1968 Act, summarised above, may well result in an applicant having to be notified of
grounds of objection, or reasons for advice against the grant of a product licence, which
c are founded on SKF confidential information, if the licensing authority is entitled to have
regard to that information in considering an application for a product licence; the
difficulty might perhaps then arise that the authority could not fairly discharge its duties
under those subsections without disclosing enough to give the applicant some inkling of
the confidential information involved. In these circumstances, it seems to me that the
court has got to adopt a practical approach to the problems set by this case, and to eschew
d sophisticated distinctions as to what is or is not permissible for the licensing authority.

These problems depend, in my judgment, essentially on questions of Community law,
and not of domestic law. The Community directives apply to member states whose
systems of law are not founded on the common law, as well as to this country. Those
directives must be construed by an appropriately purposive approach, and not by the
somewhat rigidly linguistic approach sometimes considered appropriate by English
e courts for the construction of documents. The first step is, however, to define the position
of the directives in the scheme of Community law and to discern their purpose.

The relevant articles of the EEC Treaty on which the directives are founded are arts 30
and 36. Article 30 is concerned with the elimination of quantitative restrictions on the
import and export of goods and of all other measures having the equivalent effect; by
f contrast art 36 provides that art 30 shall not preclude prohibitions or restrictions on
imports, exports or goods in transit justified, inter alia, on grounds of the protection of
health and life or the protection of industrial and commercial property.

Against this background, the purposes of the directives are indicated in the recitals in
the directives. In particular Directive 65/65 declares that the primary purpose of any
rules concerning the production and distribution of proprietary medicinal products must
g be to safeguard public health, and that this objective must be obtained by means which
will not hinder the development of the pharmaceutical industry or trade in medicinal
products within the Community. It then declares that trade in proprietary medicinal
products within the Community is hindered by disparities between national provisions
and that such hindrances must accordingly be removed.

Directive 75/318 then provides by its recitals that standards and protocols for the
h performance of tests and trials on proprietary medicinal products are an effective means
of control of these products and hence of protecting public health and can facilitate the
movement of these products by laying down uniform rules applicable to tests and trials,
the compilation of dossiers and the examination of applications, and that the adoption of
the same standards and protocols by all the member states will enable the competent
authorities to arrive at their decision on the basis of uniform tests and by reference to
j uniform criteria and will therefore help to avoid differences in evaluation. The recitals
further indicate that the particulars and documents which must accompany an application
for authorisation to place a proprietary medicinal product on the market must
'demonstrate' that potential risks are outweighed by the therapeutic efficacy of the
product; but I do not regard this fairly ordinary use of the word 'demonstrate' as casting
any special burden of proof on the applicant, or as restricting what a licensing authority

may consider in deciding whether it has been 'demonstrated' in a particular case that
potential risks are outweighed by therapeutic efficacy.   *a*

I come then to the recitals in Directive 87/21 which are set out above. Certain points
are obvious, viz: (i) it is considered undesirable, for reasons of public policy, to conduct
repetitive tests on humans or animals without overriding cause. Pharmacological and
toxicological tests involve, often, tests on animals, and clinical trials involve tests on
humans. The undesirability of repeating such tests unnecessarily must therefore be the
reason for the distinction drawn by the directive between physico-chemical, biological or   *b*
microbiological tests on the one hand and pharmacological and toxicological tests and
clinical trials on the other hand. That distinction.does not, however, necessarily define
what is required to determine whether one proprietary medicinal product is essentially
similar to another. Essential similarity does not depend only on physico-chemical,
biological and microbiological tests and does not merely involve equivalence in physico-
chemical, biological or microbiological factors: it also involves bio-equivalance, viz   *c*
equivalence of the two products in the way they are absorbed by the human body, and
this would often, possibly ordinarily, involve clinical trials on humans. Additionally,
essential similarity would involve similarity of impurity profile, which could well
involve toxicological tests on animals, to test the significance of the amounts of particular
impurities. (ii) The directive is concerned that innovative firms are not to be placed at a
disadvantage. This is more fully explained in para 15 of the explanatory memorandum   *d*
from the EC Commission to the Council. It is the reason why under the directive no
application for a product licence can be made on the grounds of essential similarity to
another product, without consent of the orginator of that other product within ten years
of first authorisation of that other product in the Community. The originator of the
other product is thus given lead time, but, with consent of the originator, essential
similarity can warrant the grant of a product licence for a generic product within the ten   *e*
years.

A further point which emerges from para 14 of the explanatory memorandum from
the Commission is that the previous requirement of a 'bibliography' had led to problems
over the completeness or appropriateness of references to published literature. No one
has suggested, however, that this point casts any relevant light on the aspects of the
construction of the new point 8 in the second paragraph of art 4 in Directive 87/21 with   *f*
which this case is concerned.

Certain further relevant points in community law can be seen in decisions of the Court
of Justice of the European Communities.

Re de Peijper Case 104/75 [1976] ECR 613 was concerned with parallel imports. An
importer desired to market in Holland by its generic name a product manufactured in
the UK under a product licence there which was identical (because from the same source)   *g*
with the product marketed by the originator in Holland under a Dutch product licence.
The Dutch authorities insisted that the importer's product could under the Dutch
regulations only be marketed in Holland if various documents and consents were
provided by the originator which the originator was not prepared to provide for a
competitor. The court held that in the circumstances the enforcement of these regulations   *h*
was incompatible with the EEC Treaty. The court had to consider the interplay of arts 30
and 36 of the Treaty, and it held that national rules or practices which restrict imports of
pharmaceutical products or are capable of doing so are only compatible with the Treaty
to the extent to which they are necessary for the effective protection of the health and life
of humans, and that national rules or practices do not fall within the exception specified
in art 36 if the health and life of humans can be as effectively protected by measures   *j*
which do not restrict intra-Community trade so much (see [1976] ECR 613 at 636 (paras
16–17)). The court stated that health and the life of humans rank first among the
property or interests protected by art 36, and it considered that parallel imports should
not be placed at a disadvantage, since the effective protection of health and the life of
humans demanded that medicinal preparations should be sold at reasonable prices (at

635 (para 15), 637 (para 25)). The court considered, as I read its decision, that the public
a health authorities of the member state where the product was to be imported should use
the materials they already had on file from the originator's applications, in order to check
the import (at 636–637 (para 21, 23)). The court also envisaged that simple co-operation
between the authorities of the member states would enable them to obtain on a reciprocal
basis the documents necessary for checking certain largely standardised and widely
distributed products (at 637 (para 27)).

b   It was not suggested in *Re de Peijper* that the information on the files of the public
health authorities of the member states, and in particular of the member state where the
product was to be imported, was confidential to the originator and could not be looked
at without the originator's consent and that that information was itself protected by
art 36 of the Treaty as being industrial or commercial property. Had the suggestion been
made, however, it is plain, in my judgment, that the court would have rejected it, in
c view of the overriding importance of the protection of the health and life of humans and
the consequent requirement that medicinal preparations should be sold at reasonable
prices. The necessity from the point of view of public health and the free movement of
medicinal products for the competent authorities in the member states to have at their
disposal all useful information on authorised proprietary products, based in particular on
summaries adopted in the other member states of the characteristics of the products, was
d recorded in EC Directive 83/570. It is obviously implicit that the authorities will be free
to use the information at their disposal, though in fact the information in the particular
summaries envisaged may not be in any sense confidential.

There is then *Re criminal proceedings against Frans-Nederlandse Maatschappij voor
Biologische Producten BV* Case 272/80 [1981] ECR 3277, where the European Court laid
down in very clear terms that the licensing authorities of a member state are not entitled
e unnecessarily to require technical or chemical analyses or laboratory tests in respect of a
fungicide where those analyses and tests have already been carried out in another member
state and their results are available to those authorities or may at their request be placed
at their disposal. It must be a fortiori if the analyses and tests have already been carried
out in the same member state.

Against that background of Community law, I am unable to attach the same weight
f as Henry J did to the word 'demonstrate' in Directive 87/21. In my judgment, the word
is used in the same ordinary sense as in the recital in Directive 75/318 to which I have
already referred, or as the word 'proves' is used in art 5 of Directive 65/65, without
restricting the licensing authority to looking only at material produced by the applicant.
Such a passive role for a licensing authority is not incidentally consistent with the general
view that the court has taken of the role a licensing authority should play: see *Re de
g Peijper* Case 104/75 [1976] ECR 613 at 637 (para 24) ('instead of waiting passively for the
desired evidence to be produced to them') and the *Frans-Nederlandse* case [1981] ECR
3277 at 3291 (para 14) ('the authorities of the Member States are nevertheless required to
assist') (although these cases were of course decided before Directive 87/21 was adopted
and not in relation to that directive.)

h   In addition, in my judgment, if there is any right under English law (as opposed to
Community law) for SKF to restrain the licensing authority from making any use of
SKF's confidential information without SKF's consent when considering someone else's
application for a product licence, that right under domestic law is, in my judgment,
overridden by the requirements of Community law. Counsel for SKF referred, in support
of his arguments on English law, to s 133(2), summarised above, of the 1968 Act, but he
j accepted that that section could not override the requirements of Community law.

On this part of the case the judge placed importance on the state of the evidence in the
court below, and he commented (i) that there was no assertion that there would be any
public health risk resulting from the licensing authority not having recourse to SKF's
confidential information for the limited purposes for which it claimed to desire recourse
to it, (ii) that the licensing authority's evidence did not identify any difficulties or dangers

that would follow if the authority was not to enjoy the recourse to that information which the authority claimed without the consent of SKF, and (iii) that the licensing authority's chief scientific witness, Dr Jones, had nowhere said that such recourse to the information was 'essential' for the proper consideration of an application. *a*

As to (i), it is of course unlikely that there would be a public health risk, because SKF will continue to supply Tagamet and the licensing authority will not grant an applicant a product licence unless the authority is satisfied that there is no public health risk. What is more likely to happen, whether with cimetidine or with other drugs, is that some *b* applicants, whose applications ought to succeed, will have their applications refused, because the authority will not be prepared to take the chance of approving without checking against the SKF (or other originator's) information, or some applicants will be required to carry out additional tests, and in particular pharmacological and toxicological tests and clinical trials, duplicating unnecessarily the tests carried out by SKF (or other originator). Thus there would be restrictions on the movement of goods in contravention *c* of art 30.

Moreover the judge's choice of the word 'essential' in the passage I have referred to in (iii) above puts any burden on the licensing authority far too high, in my judgment; in essence, the judge has, in my respectful view, got the balance the wrong way round, probably because he has overlooked the importance of art 30.

It is next necessary to consider the passage in point 8 as replaced by Directive 87/21, *d* 'However, and without prejudice to the law relating to the protection of industrial and commercial property: (*a*) The applicant shall not be required to provide' etc. It appears that the phrase 'industrial and commercial property', which also appears in art 36 of the Treaty as already mentioned, has not been comprehensively defined by the Community. It is therefore necessary to look to the national law to see what right exists under the national law, and then to consider whether a right of that nature falls within the *e* Community law concept of 'industrial and commercial property'. That has been done, for instance, with copyright. For present purposes, I would be prepared to assume, without deciding, that the English law concept of confidential information is, if the information relates to technical or scientific matters, within the concept of 'industrial and commercial property' in Community law. Even so, however, the passage 'However, and without prejudice' etc does not, in my judgment, bear on the present case, because *f* in its context in Directive 87/21, and in the context of the amendment effected by that directive to Directive 65/65, the passage is only concerned with the position of the applicant, and with what the applicant may or may not do, and not with the position of the licensing authority. To put it very briefly, if one looks at art 4 of Directive 65/65 as amended, the words do not bear on the licensing authority at all. They are not an injunction to the licensing authority not, when exercising its functions under Directive *g* 65/65, to interfere with industrial or commercial property.

On grounds of Community law, therefore, I would, for the reasons which I have endeavoured to explain, allow this appeal.

An alternative approach is to consider the position solely under English law, the national law. In the circumstances of this case, has SKF a right, founded on breach of *h* confidence and the law relating to confidential information, to object to the licensing authority using SKF's confidential information without SKF's consent when considering any other applicant's application for a product licence in respect of cimetidine? Essentially SKF has to win on both limbs of the case, both on English law and on Community law, and to show (a) that it has a right under English law and (b) that that right is not overridden by Community law. *j*

There is no doubt that SKF supplied confidential information to the licensing authority. There is no doubt also that in an appropriate context unauthorised use of confidential information by the recipient can be restrained as much as unauthorised disclosure to a third party. It does not, however, follow that use of information will necessarily be restrained just because disclosure of it would be restrained; the two are not necessarily

the same and whether and how far use is authorised must depend on the context. The
a crucial question is therefore whether the use to which the authority proposes to put the
information would be an unauthorised use, to the detriment of SKF as the party who
communicated the information. The court must therefore consider, on an objective view
of the facts, what use SKF must be taken to have authorised the authority to make of the
information. Since the authority is a public authority exercising important functions in
the public interest, it does not follow that the answer to the question will be the same as
b it might have been in a wholly commercial context, eg if one commercial body had
supplied confidential information to another commercial body in the course of
negotiations for a purely commercial joint venture.

The judge appears to have taken the view that the confidential information supplied
by SKF to the licensing authority could only be used by the authority for the limited
purpose for which SKF originally supplied it, viz the purpose of considering and granting
c (or presumably if the facts had warranted it refusing) SKF's application for a product
licence for its own medicinal product. Counsel for SKF concedes, however, that the
implied authority must go further than that, and must extend to enabling the authority
to use the information for the purpose of policing any licence granted to SKF, ie
suspending, revoking or varying the provisions of the licence under s 28 of the 1968 Act.
The concession is inevitable on the wording of s 28 and in particular on the wording of
d grounds in paras (c), (g) and (h) (summarised earlier in this judgment) of sub-s (3). But it
indicates that the matters in relation to which the information can be used extend to
matters where the use of it is in the public interest, albeit against the private, or purely
personal, interest of SKF.

Counsel for SKF seemed also to concede that the confidential information might be
used by the licensing authority, without SKF's consent, to avoid a potential danger to
e health. Thus, in appropriate circumstances, if not in general, it might be used to defeat a
competitor's application for a product licence. Whether or not this is conceded by
counsel, I have no doubt that it is right: in the context of a licensing scheme set up in the
public interest for the protection of health and life, it must be clear that all information
supplied to the licensing authority by any applicants must be available to the authority
f as a general fund of knowledge to avoid dangers to health and life. One can imagine the
public outcry if it were not so. Counsel founds this on the proposition that use of the
information to avoid a danger to health or to defeat an application which ought not to
succeed could not be to the detriment of SKF, and so could not found an action in breach
of confidence as damage, or apprehended damage, is an essential ingredient of the cause
of action. For my part, however, I would put it on a much wider basis. The protection of
g public health is the fundamental purpose of the licensing system under the 1968 Act. It
is a purpose of great public importance, and I find it inconceivable that anyone could
have supposed that the licensing authority was not free to have regard to any information
in its possession, if that information might be relevant to avoiding a danger to health.

I assume that SKF and other research pharmaceutical companies act in good faith and
after careful investigation when they make application for product licences for medicinal
h products. None the less, a question of revocation of a licence, not necessarily SKF's licence,
may arise in the light of subsequent experience and there may then be a suspicion that
the product may have side effects which had not been appreciated when the licence was
granted. Any such question of revocation of a licence is likely to be difficult, and to be
grave in its implications whichever way it is decided. I cannot believe that where any
question of public health is concerned the licensing authority is only to be entitled to use
j SKF's confidential information in so far as SKF specifically consents or the use turns out
not to be detrimental to SKF.

Because of the importance of the protection of public health, the licensing procedure
under the 1968 Act has since then become linked to Community law. The harmonising
of the national laws of the member states into a uniform procedure is in itself an
important purpose where matters of public health are concerned. Again, I do not see that

that can be read as subject to a qualification that no detriment to the interests of SKF is
involved.   *a*

In my judgment SKF when it supplied confidential information to the licensing
authority was bound by the overriding public purposes of the 1968 Act in its context in
Community law, viz the purposes of the protection of public health and of harmonising
practice throughout the Community and removing obstacles to trade between member
states of the Community. The licensing authority is, in my judgment, as a matter of
English law, entitled to use that information, without further consent from SKF, at its   *b*
discretion in performing any of its functions as licensing authority under the 1968 Act
and Community law. Accordingly on English law also, I would allow this appeal.   *

I should mention in passing that counsel for the licensing authority and the interveners
sought to support their arguments on English law by reference to s 118(1) of the 1968
Act. I have been unable, however, to derive assistance from that section since it seems to
me that the argument is circular: to say that a person cannot disclose information   *c*
obtained under the 1968 Act save in the performance of his duty does not per se show
what his duty is, and casts no light at all on whether or not his duty permits him to use
particular information in considering someone else's application for a product licence.

Finally, there has been reference in the course of the argument to the possibility that
this court might direct a reference to the European Court. No party has, however, invited
this court to direct a reference and in my judgment it is better that this court should   *d*
express its views on the issues involved, in the hope of clarifying those issues, and should
leave it to others to direct a reference if a reference be considered necessary.

As indicated, I would allow this appeal.

BALCOMBE LJ. I have had the advantage of reading in draft the judgments of Dillon
and Staughton LJJ, and I agree with them that this appeal should be allowed. Although *e*
we are differing from the judge below, I propose to deal with the matter quite shortly.

I propose to consider EEC law first since, even if SKF would otherwise have a right
under English law, it is common ground that that right will be overridden by
Community law, if applicable. The question of Community law in turn depends
primarily on the meaning and effect of EC Council Directive 87/21. I agree with Dillon   *f*
LJ that the directive should be construed by an appropriately purposive approach and I
therefore turn first to the report (explanatory memorandum) from the Commission to
the Council which explained the necessity for the replacement of point 8 of the second
paragraph of art 4 of EEC Council Directive 65/65 which was effected by Directive 87/
21. I set out below the relevant extracts from paras 14 and 15 of this report:

'14. When certain applications for marketing authorization submitted to the   *g*
Committee for Proprietary Medicinal Products were being examined, it became
clear that not all the Member States interpreted Article 4(8) of Directive 65/65/EEC
in the same way. Paragraph 8 provides that the person responsible for placing the
product on the market shall submit in support of his application not only the results
of analytical tests but also those of: —pharmacological and toxicological tests (on
laboratory animals and sometimes in vitro tests) —clinical trials (in humans,   *h*
whether patients or healthy volunteers). By way of exception, another company
may submit an application for marketing authorization in respect of a proprietary
product which is similar to a medicine already authorized, by submitting a summary
dossier consisting of bibliographical information. However the manufacturing
dossier and the results of the analytical tests (physico-chemical, biological and microbiological) must be submitted in every case. It has nevertheless been found that the *j*
published literature is, in fact, often incomplete or inappropriate. Confronted by
this problem, certain national authorities have tended not to be too demanding as
regards the bibliographical evidence submitted by the second applicant. This
practice seriously penalizes the innovatory firm which has [had] to meet the high

a cost of clinical trials and animal experiments, while its product can be copied at lower cost and sometimes within a very short period. Protection of a medicinal innovation by means of a patent is not in fact always possible or effective, as for example in the case of a natural substance or of a substance which is already known but on which additional research has been carried out with a view to a new therapeutic use.

b 15. The proposed amendment of Article 4(8) of Directive 65/65/EEC is intended to reestablish the normal principle for exemption, i.e. that according to which the innovating firm consents to the second applicant referring to the tests described in the dossier of the original medicine. The second applicant is also the beneficiary of the exemption as it now stands in Article 4(8), i.e. the right to use published literature. This possibility is, in practice, very limited, since, in accordance with the second paragraph of Article 1 of Directive 75/318/EEC, this bibliographical evidence

c must be submitted in order to correspond "in like manner" to the criteria of safety and efficacy in the Annex to that Directive. Where the innovatory producer does not give its consent or if the bibliographical evidence cannot be adduced, it appeared advisable to insert a clause not permitting the second applicant to submit an application in simplified form in respect of a copy of a medicine until ten years have elapsed following the authorization of the original medicinal product in the country

d concerned by the application. This ten-year period will enable the partial recovery of the research investment, which might not be protected otherwise, for example by a patent . . .'

When this report is read in full, in conjunction with the two principal recitals to Directive 87/21, viz:

e 'Whereas experience has shown that it is advisable to stipulate more precisely the cases in which the results of pharmacological and toxicological tests or clinical trials do not have to be provided with a view to obtaining authorization for a proprietary medicinal product which is essentially similar to an authorized product, while ensuring that innovative firms are not placed at a disadvantage . . . Whereas,

f however, there are reasons of public policy for not conducting repetitive tests on humans or animals without over-riding cause'

it seems to me that the purpose of the directive is clear. It is to achieve a balance between the interests of the public, and in particular their interest to prevent unnecessary tests on humans and animals, and the interests of the innovative firm in its confidential data (OCD) so far as that relates to the results of pharmacological and toxicological tests and

g clinical trials. The pattern of the directive then becomes obvious. During the protected period, in the present case ten years, the applicant for a generic product licence under the abridged procedure must produce its own pharmacological, toxicological and clinical data, unless (a) the originator consents to the use of its OCD for the purpose of examining the application, (para (a)(i) of point 8 of the second paragraph of art 4); or (b) the necessary material is contained in published scientific literature (para (a)(ii) of point 8).

h However, after the expiry of the ten-year period, which will have given the innovator the necessary degree of protection for his research investment (and it is to be recalled that in many cases, as in the present, the innovator will retain the benefit of patent protection so that he will receive a royalty even if a licence of right is granted to the generic applicant, which will take into account his research expenditure: see Re Allen & Hanburys

j Ltd's (Salbutamol) Patent [1987] RPC 327), the balance swings towards the public interest, and the licensing authority will be entitled to use the OCD without the originator's consent, thus preventing further unnecessary tests on animals and humans.

If one approaches Directive 87/21 in this manner, then it becomes clear that the approach of SKF, which commended itself to the judge, effectively destroys the object of the directive. Counsel for SKF submitted that a literal construction of the directive requires a two-stage approach. (i) The general applicant must first demonstrate the essential similarity of his product to that of the originator's product. It was common *a* ground that essential similarity is not confined to the physical and chemical properties of the two products. It extends to such matters as bio-equivalence and purity profile, which, as counsel conceded, might well need to be established by the tests on humans and animals which it is the avowed policy of the directive to minimise. (ii) It is only when the generic applicant has demonstrated the essential similarity of the two products that the licensing authority is entitled to use the OCD.   *b*

The fallacy in this literal approach is readily apparent. If the generic applicant must first demonstrate the essential similarity of the two products without reliance on the OCD, this must apply as much to the procedure under para (*a*)(i) of point 8 of the second paragraph of art 4, where the innovator has consented to the use of the OCD for the purpose of examining the application, as it does to the procedure under para (*a*)(iii), where there has been no consent but the ten-year period has elapsed. But it makes a *c* nonsense of the directive if, notwithstanding that the innovator has consented to the use of his OCD, the licensing authority cannot use it because the applicant must *first* demonstrate the essential similarity of his product, which he may not be able to do without either using the OCD or conducting further animal and human tests, which it is the avowed object of the directive to avoid.

There remains the question of the effect of the proviso in the introductory words to *d* para (*a*) of point 8: '. . . without prejudice to the law relating to the protection of industrial and commercial property.' Like Dillon and Staughton LJJ, I am prepared to assume that confidential information can be industrial or commercial property under Community law, although I have considerable doubts whether that assumption is justified: see *Re Burroughs-Delplanque* Decision 72/75 [1972] CMLR D67 at D70 and *Kabelmetal-Luchaire* Decision 75/494 OJ 1975 L222, p 34 at p 38. But, even on that assumption, in my *e* judgment the proviso does no more than make it plain that the grant of a product licence to the generic applicant does not override any rights (eg patent rights) to which the originator of the product may be entitled.

On the view which I have taken of Community law, it becomes unnecessary to consider the English law relating to confidential information. However, on this point, *f* the question comes down to this: what was the purpose for which SKF provided the OCD to the licensing authority? Counsel for SKF would limit that purpose to that of SKF, the specific purpose of obtaining a product licence. That submission found favour with the judge. But, as Dillon LJ has pointed out and as counsel was constrained to concede, the purpose must go further than that: it must at least enable the authority to use OCD for the purpose of the exercise of its powers to suspend, revoke or vary the original product licence under s 28 of the Medicines Act 1968. Like Dillon and Staughton *g* LJJ, I can see no reason why the purpose should be other than the purpose of the licensing authority to enable it to perform its statutory functions under the 1968 Act and under Community law. That is sufficient to distinguish this case from *Castrol Australia Pty Ltd v Emtech Associates Pty Ltd* (1980) 33 ALR 31 and I say no more about this and certain other Australian cases to which we were referred, save to say that I do not find them of *h* any help in answering the question which I have posed above.

Having regard to the way in which this case has developed, and was argued both before us and below, and since no party has invited us to direct a reference to the Court of Justice of the European Communities at this time, I too would not be minded to direct a reference at the present stage.

For these reasons, and for those given at greater length by Dillon and Staughton LJJ, I *j* too would allow this appeal.

STAUGHTON LJ.
1 *The meaning of the Council directives*
    The first and principal ground on which Henry J allowed this application for judicial

review was based on the language of EEC Council Directive 65/65, as amended by EC
a Council Directive 87/21. This now provides that an applicant need not supply results of
certain tests 'if he can demonstrate' that his product is essentially similar to a produce which
has been authorised within the Community for ten years and is marketed in this country.
This suggests that he, the applicant, must produce proof of essential similarity.

The argument is strengthened when that provision in Directive 87/21 is inserted in its
proper place, which is art 4 of Directive 65/65. That article provides:

b
        'The application shall be accompanied by the following particulars and documents
        . . .'

There is then a list of information and documents to be supplied. Article 5 provides that
the application shall be refused—

c
        'if the particulars and documents submitted in support of the application do not
        comply with Article 4.'

Consequently it is said that, if the applicant fails to supply proof of essential similarity
from his own resources, he is not excused from conducting the tests in question. Either
d he must provide test results or else his application will fail.

That argument has force, and the judge accepted it. However, there are powerful
arguments to the contrary. Firstly, if the words 'he can demonstrate' exclude any reliance
on material already in the possession of the licensing authority, then an applicant cannot
establish essential similarity by referring the authority either to (i) a drug master file
which it holds, or (ii) the originator's confidential data (OCD) when the owner of the
e information consents to or even supports the application. That is not a fanciful possibility:
it could arise when the applicant is a licensee, whom the owner does not wish to have
direct access to his information. Counsel for SKF accepts that in such a case information
in the possession of the authority can be used to establish essential similarity by reference.

Secondly, counsel accepts (subject, I think, to his separate argument on confidentiality)
that the authority can and should have regard to information already in its possession for
f the purpose of considering the safety, efficacy and quality of the new applicant's product.
It seems to me very proper that the authority should do so. Of course it may still be the
law that essential similarity must first be established by independent evidence before that
stage is reached. But I should not be inclined to believe that the Council directives
intended such a complicated process, unless they plainly say so.

Thirdly, although the evidence is by no means clear, it emerges that with some
g products it simply will not be possible to demonstrate essential similarity without
reference to the OCD, the very word 'similarity' implies comparison, and 'essential' that
there is no difference which is of material importance. The judge considered that
reference to the data was 'a matter of convenience rather than a necessity'. I cannot regard
that conclusion as justified by the evidence. Indeed before this court it was conceded that
with some products reference to the data was a necessity if essential similarity was to be
h established.

The answer of counsel for SKF to this point was, in effect: too bad, the new applicant
must then conduct his own tests, or else abandon his application. But one of the objects
of Council Directive 87/21 was the avoidance of unnecessary tests. That is shown by the
recital:

j   'Whereas, however, there are reasons of public policy for not conducting repetitive
        tests on humans or animals without over-riding cause.'

It scarcely promotes that objective to hold that unnecessary tests must be conducted, if
the new applicant is to obtain a licence, in a case where essential similarity could be
demonstrated by reference to the OCD but not otherwise.

Fourthly, there is provision in ss 20 and 21 of the 1968 Act for a form of appeal against
the refusal of a licence, and for the giving of reasons when a licence is refused. Similar *a*
provisions apply to the suspension, revocation or variation of a licence under s 28. I
would suppose that the authority can and should have regard to the OCD in exercising
any of those powers, although no doubt care is taken to avoid unnecessary disclosure of
it to the new applicant or licence-holder when reasons are given.

We were referred to art 9 of Council Directive 65/65, and to s 133(1)(c) of the 1968
Act. Those, broadly speaking, are saving provisions for civil and criminal liability arising *b*
apart from the legislation in question. In my judgment they have no bearing on the
point. I agree with counsel for SKF that the directives are at pains to achieve a balance
between the reward due to innovators for their enterprise and labour on the one hand
and freedom of trade on the other. But innovators have the benefit of patent rights,
where their invention can be patented, and those are wholly unaffected by the directives.
It must be of much less importance to them whether, after their product has been *c*
licensed for ten years, their confidential data can be used without their consent in
establishing the essential similarity of a new applicant's product. I can see no presumption
that the reward to innovators should include the right to prevent their data being used
for that purpose.

In the result I conclude that too much emphasis is placed on the words 'he can
demonstrate', and particularly the word 'he', if it is held that the new applicant must *d*
establish essential similarity wholly by his own efforts, and may not refer the authority
for this purpose to the OCD which is already in its possession. It might perhaps have
been better to say 'if it can be demonstrated that' or 'if it is proved that'.

But we are not to adopt a narrow, semantic approach to the interpretation of
Community legislation. In my judgment that is the true meaning of the directive: the
new applicant is not confined to evidence which comes from his own possession and his *e*
own researches.

2 *The proviso*
This occurs in the revised point 8 of the second paragraph of art 4, and reads:

'. . . without prejudice to the law relating to the protection of industrial and *f*
commercial property . . .'

In *Procureur du Roi v Debauve* Case 52/79 [1980] ECR 833 at 878 Mr Advocate-General
Warner said that 'industrial and commercial property' was not a term of art in English
law. However, it is the meaning of the phrase in Community law which has to be
considered; and there it appears in art 36 of the EEC Treaty itself.

It is not clear to me whether the right to protection of confidential information is or is *g*
not industrial or commercial property in Community law. But I can assume for the
purposes of this judgment that it is. What the proviso then says, so far as that particular
topic is concerned, is at most that the amendment to Council Directive 65/65 shall not
alter or affect any rights or liabilities concerned with the protection of confidential
information. If that is the right view, I would not dissent from the opinion of Dillon LJ *h*
that it is with the rights of the new applicant that the proviso is concerned. But if that is
wrong one then has to inquire whether any such right of SKF is altered or affected by the
terms of the amendment. For the reasons given in section 3 of this judgment, I am of
opinion that none is altered or affected.

I have said that this is the most which the proviso achieves. But I am inclined to doubt
whether, on a true view, it achieves even that. My doubt arises because I have difficulty *j*
in seeing how the terms of the amendment ever could alter or affect rights or liabilities
relating to the protection of industrial and commercial property. Perhaps then the
proviso is unnecessary, introduced from an abundance of caution. Alternatively, counsel
for the first intervener, Generics (UK) Ltd, may be right in an argument which I can
fairly describe as arcane. This was that the amendment, when it mentioned in para 8(*a*)(i)

of point 8 the person responsible for the marketing of the original proprietary medical
a product, might be said to be touching for the first time in this field on the law relating
to the protection of industrial and commercial property; it might also be said to be a
measure for the harmonisation of national laws within the Community; and if it
answered that description, it could be held to replace the saving for such protection in
art 36 of the Treaty. That, according to counsel, was the result which it was desired to
avoid.
b

3 Confidential information

The second ground on which Henry J allowed the application for judicial review was
that it would be a breach of the authority's duty of confidence if it were to use the OCD
in considering whether a new applicant's product was essentially similar.

It is not said that SKF has any contractual right to confidence against the authority, or
c that such use of the data would be tortious. The case is that equity would grant an
injunction to restrain it. That being the law, in judicial review proceedings the court can
hold that such use of the data would be improper.

There has been no contest as to that analysis of the legal problem as it arises in this case.
Nor has it been disputed that the OCD is, by its nature, confidential. It is agreed that
equity would restrain disclosure of the data to others, save for certain limited purposes.
d That view is fortified by s 118(1) of the 1968 Act:

'If any person discloses to any other person . . . (b) any information obtained by or
furnished to him in pursuance of this Act, he shall, unless the disclosure was made
in the performance of his duty, be guilty of an offence.'

e There are instances of disclosure which would plainly be permissible, such as to the
committees or the commission established by the Act, if indeed that could be regarded
as disclosure to another person.

Although the statute deals only with disclosure, it is agreed on all sides that it would
also be wrongful in certain circumstances to use the OCD. Equally it is argued that use
for some purposes is both the right and the duty of the authority. Thus the authority
f must use the data in considering the original application by those who provided the data;
but it would plainly be wrong for the authority or one of its employees to use the data so
as to manufacture its or his own medicinal products. The problem is to find the line that
divides those extremes.

Counsel for SKF argues, and this argument found favour with the judge, that one
must ascertain the purpose for which the information was provided to the authority.
g This, he says, was specifically in order that SKF should obtain a licence for its own
product; consequently the authority may only use the information in connection with
that application.

In my judgment that argument plainly goes too far. It would preclude the authority
from using the data in considering, for example, the safety of a new applicant's product.
Counsel's answer to that is (i) that the data could be used to show that the new product
h was unsafe, which would not be to the originator's detriment, or (ii) that use in connection
with safety could be justified by higher public interest. For my part, I do not accept that
use to demonstrate the safety of the new product, as opposed to lack of safety, would be
wrongful. One of the objects of the system is, as I have said, to avoid unnecessary and
repetitive tests. Nor do I think that safety, which lies at the heart of the system, should
only be considered in the context of the exception of higher public interest.

j I prefer the view put forward by counsel for Generics that use, like disclosure, is
authorised if it occurs in the course of the authority's duties. In reality that is no different
from saying that use is permitted if it is within the purpose for which the information
was entrusted to the authority. No doubt the purpose of SKF was to obtain a licence for
its own product. But I do not see why the purpose of SKF alone should be relevant, and
the purpose of the authority disregarded. As between two private parties it may be

possible to discern a common purpose for entrusing information. But the purpose is less likely to be common to both when one is a body with statutory functions. The purpose of the authority in acquiring the information was to use it for all or any of its duties as might be appropriate. I would hold that the authority is not in breach of confidence if it uses the originator's data in any such manner. That makes it unnecessary to consider whether any countervailing public interest would excuse a breach of confidence in this case.

4 *Reference to the Court of Justice of the European Communities*
    No party invited us to refer this case to the European Court. But counsel for SKF drew our attention to the discretion we have to refer it of our own motion. He also submitted that, if the case reaches the House of Lords, there might then be an obligation to refer it under art 177 of the EEC Treaty.
    The issue as to the meaning of the Council directives is, of course, a question of Community law. But if SKF fails on that issue, it may still succeed on the ground of breach of confidence. Indeed the full width of the declaration granted by Henry J could only be justified, if at all, on that ground. That is, initially at any rate, an issue of the national law of England and Wales. In theory, if this were a case of breach of confidence by our national law, that could be sanctioned by Community law. But I am not wholly convinced that it would be. For the reasons given by Dillon LJ I do not consider that we should refer the case to the European Court at this stage.

Appeal allowed. Leave to appeal to House of Lords refused.

10 October. *The Appeal Committee of the House of Lords (Lord Bridge of Harwich, Lord Ackner and Lord Oliver of Aylmerton) gave SKF leave to appeal.*

Solicitors: *Treasury Solicitor*; *S J Berwin & Co* (for the first intervener); *Roiter Zucker* (for the second intervener); *Simmons & Simmons* (for SKF).

                                                        Carolyn Toulmin Barrister.

a
Barclays Bank of Swaziland Ltd v Hahn

COURT OF APPEAL, CIVIL DIVISION
FOX, PARKER AND CROOM-JOHNSON LJJ
2, 3 AUGUST 1988

b
Practice – Service – Service by post – Writ for service on defendant within jurisdiction – Whether defendant required to be physically present within jurisdiction at time when service is effected by post – RSC Ord 10, r 1(2).

It is not a condition of valid service under RSC Ord 10, r 1(2)[a], which provides for 'A writ for service on a defendant within the jurisdiction' to be served by post instead of being served personally, that the defendant be physically present within the jurisdiction at the time when service is so effected, since 'within the jurisdiction' refers to the writ and service of it rather than to the defendant (see p 195 *e f h j*, p 196 *f g* and p 197 *b h j*, post).

Notes
For service of process by post, see 37 Halsbury's Laws (4th edn) paras 151–152, and for cases on the subject, see 37(2) Digest (Reissue) 263, *1711–1714*.

Interlocutory appeal
The plaintiff, Barclays Bank of Swaziland Ltd, a company incorporated under the laws of Swaziland, appealed against the order made by Sir Neil Lawson sitting as a judge of the High Court in the Queen's Bench Division in chambers on 28 January 1988 whereby he dismissed the plaintiff's appeal from the order made by Deputy Master Ashton on 7 October 1987 declaring that a writ issued on 16 December 1986 by the plaintiff against the defendant, John Aneck Hahn, had not been duly served on the defendant and that therefore the court had no jurisdiction to hear the plaintiff's claim. The facts are set out in the judgment of Fox LJ.

f
Conrad Dehn QC and *Michael Brindle* for the plaintiff.
Winston Roddick QC and *Michael Soole* for the defendant.

FOX LJ. This is an appeal by the plaintiff from an order of Sir Neil Lawson sitting as a judge of the High Court in the Queen's Bench Division, whereby he dismissed the appeal of the plaintiff from a decision of Deputy Master Ashton, declaring that the plaintiff's writ in the action had not been duly served on the defendant, Mr Hahn.

The plaintiff, which is a Swaziland bank, claims that the defendant owes it some £12m under a guarantee executed in Swaziland in 1982.

The defendant, who is retired, lives with his wife in various places. For some part of the year they visit their family in South Africa. For another part of the year, amounting, according to the defendant's wife's evidence, to more than four weeks but seldom more than twelve weeks in aggregate, at a flat rented by the wife at a house called Shardeloes, near Amersham in Buckinghamshire. The flat is known as apartment 7. The defendant's evidence is that his wife has a right to occupy the flat for not more than six months in a year. For the remainder of the year they travel, mostly on the continent of Europe. The defendant's evidence is that generally on average they spend no more than three months a year in England, though in some years he stays for considerably longer than that.

The plaintiff originally sought to sue the defendant in South Africa in 1986, but those proceedings were abandoned because the defendant could not be served. On 6 November 1986, in the course of the proceedings in South Africa, the defendant's son swore an affidavit that the defendant was permanently resident in England.

---

a   Rule 1(2) is set out at p 194 *c*, post

The next thing that happened was that on 6 December 1986 the plaintiff instituted the present proceedings in England. On 26 January 1987 leave was obtained to serve the defendant out of the jurisdiction, namely in South Africa. Leave to serve out of the jurisdiction was made on the basis of an affidavit, on behalf of the plaintiff, that the defendant was domiciled in England. No application was made to set that order aside. However, the order did not avail the plaintiff since it did not prove possible to serve the defendant in South Africa.

On 14 April 1987 the plaintiff sought to effect service in England. At this point I refer to RSC Ord 10, under r 1 of which service was sought to be effected. Rule 1 is as follows:

'(1) A writ must be served personally on each defendant by the plaintiff or his agent.

(2) A writ for service on a defendant within the jurisdiction may, instead of being served personally on him, be served—(a) by sending a copy of the writ by ordinary first-class post to the defendant as his usual or last known address, or (b) if there is a letter box for that address, by inserting through the letter box a copy of the writ enclosed in a sealed envelope addressed to the defendant. In sub-paragraph (a) "first-class post" means first-class post which has been pre-paid or in respect of which prepayment is not required.

(3) Where a writ is served in accordance with paragraph (2)—(a) the date of service shall, unless the contrary is shown, be deemed to be the seventh day (ignoring Order 3, rule 2(5)) after the date on which the copy was sent to or, as the case may be, instead through the letter box for the address in question; (b) any affidavit proving due service of the writ must contain a statement to the effect that—(i) in the opinion of the deponent (or, if the deponent is the plaintiff's solicitor or an employee of that solicitor, in the opinion of the plaintiff) the copy of the writ, if sent to, or, as the case may be inserted through the letter box for, the address in question, will have come to the knowledge of the defendant within 7 days thereafter; and (ii) in the case of service by post, the copy of the writ has not been returned to the plaintiff through the post undelivered to the addressee.

(4) Where a defendant's solicitor indorses on the writ a statement that he accepts service of the writ on behalf of that defendant, the writ shall be deemed to have been duly served on that defendant and to have been so served on the date on which the indorsement was made.

(5) Subject to Order 12, rule 7, where a writ is not duly served on a defendant but he acknowledges service of it, the writ shall be deemed, unless the contrary is shown, to have been duly served on him and to have been so served on the date on which he acknowledges services.

(6) Every copy of a writ for service on a defendant shall be sealed with the seal of the office of the Supreme Court out of which the writ was issued and shall be accompanied by a form of acknowledgment of service in Form No. 14 in Appendix A in which the title of the action and its number have been entered.

(7) This rule shall have effect subject to the provisions of any Act and these rules and in particular to any enactment which provides for the manner in which documents may be served on bodies corporate.'

On 14 April 1987, at about 1530 hrs, believing that the defendant was at apartment 7 at Shardeloes, Amersham, or would be there on that day, the plaintiff's agent inserted a copy of the writ in a sealed envelope (addressed to the defendant) through the letter box of apartment 7. On the same day the defendant and his wife had left Geneva on a British Airways flight to Heathrow. The flight took off from Geneva at about 1540 hrs British time. It landed at Heathrow at 1727 hrs and it crossed the French coast en route for London at about 1705 hrs.

At Heathrow the defendant was met by the caretaker of apartment 7, who told him that a brown envelope addressed to him had been put through the letter box at apartment

7 that day by a man who had asked whether the defendant was present. The defendant
a then instructed the caretaker to drive him to a hotel in Beaconsfield. That was done. Mrs
Hahn, the defendant's wife, was however driven to apartment 7 and was shown the
envelope, which contained a copy writ. She did not open it. She then drove to the hotel
in Beaconsfield and joined the defendant.

The defendant stayed in England for the rest of that day (14 April) and he and his wife
stayed that night at an hotel at Heathrow. On the next day the defendant returned by air
b to Geneva. Mrs Hahn stayed a further night at Heathrow and then drove to Geneva,
arriving there on 17 April.

The defendant's contention is that since he was not within the jurisdiction when the
copy writ was put through the letter box at apartment 7 at about 1530 hrs on 14 April
(he did not arrive in England until some time after 1700 hrs) the writ was not duly
served on him. It is the defendant's case that the methods of service permitted by Ord
c 10, r 1(2) are only available if the defendant is within the jurisdiction when the service is
effected under that order. The judge accepted that. The plaintiff appeals.

Order 10, r 1(2) opens with the words: 'A writ for service on a defendant within the
jurisdiction may, instead of being served personally on him, be served . . .' There then
follow paras (a) and (b) specifying (a) posting by first-class post to the defendant at his
usual or last-known address, or (b) if there is a letter box for that address, by inserting
d through the letter box a copy of the writ enclosed in a sealed envelope addressed to the
defendant.

The defendant contends that, in terms, Ord 10, r 1(2) only applies to service on a
defendant who is within the jurisdiction. That, it is said, is the consequence of the words
'A writ for service on a defendant within the jurisdiction'. The words 'within the
jurisdiction', it is said, relate to the defendant.
e I am unable to accept that. It seems to me that the words 'A writ for service on a
defendant within the jurisdiction' are descriptive of the writ and its service and not of
the defendant. In my opinion they are directed at the distinction between a writ for
service within the jurisdiction and one for service out of the jurisdiction. Thus, for
example, RSC Ord 6, r 6(2) provides:
f
> '. . . a writ for service within the jurisdiction may be issued as a concurrent writ
> with one which is to be served out of the jurisdiction and a writ which is to be
> served out of the jurisdiction may be issued as a concurrent writ with one for service
> within the jurisdiction'.

g I agree that the rules provide for one form of writ only, but the distinction between the
two kinds of writ which I have mentioned is, it seems to me, clear. A writ for service out
of the jurisdiction must (subject to other provisions in the rules) be served personally; a
writ for service within the jurisdiction may be served personally, or by one of the
methods specified in Ord 10. Thus Ord 10, r 1(1) provides in general terms that a writ
must be served personally on each defendant. Rule 1(2) relaxes that requirement in the
h case of a writ to be served within the jurisdiction. A writ for service within the
jurisdiction will give the defendant's address as one which is within the jurisdiction. The
result, in my opinion, is that the language of Ord 10 does not require the presence of the
defendant within the jurisdiction when the envelope containing a copy writ is put
through the letter box or is posted.

Should such a provision be implied? I do not think so. I do not disregard the
j importance which, historically, has been attached to the physical presence of a defendant
within the jurisdiciton. But Ord 10 in its present form has introduced great changes in
methods of service. Certainly it much diminishes the importance of personal service.
But at the same time, however, it gives protection to defendants. It is important to
observe that we are not dealing with a situation in which service is effectively permissible
on persons having no real connection with this country. In that respect I am not troubled

by the example of service through the letter box at the last-known address of a person who has not entered this country for, say, 20 years. Thus, under para (3)(*b*) of Ord 10, r 1: *a*

'any affidavit proving due service of the writ must contain a statement to the effect that—(i) in the opinion of the deponent (or, if the deponent is the plaintiff's solicitor or an employee of that solicitor, in the opinion of the plaintiff) the copy of the writ, if sent to, or as the case may be inserted through the letter box for, the address in question, will have come to the knowledge of the defendant within 7 days thereafter; and (ii) in the case of service by post, the copy of the writ has not *b* been returned to the plaintiff through the post undelivered to the addressee.'

These provisions, it seems to me, protect the person who has ceased to have any real connection with the address at which the service is made. The opinion that is required to be sworn to on behalf of the plaintiff involving, as it does, the likelihood that the writ will come to the knowledge of the defendant within seven days, assumes a substantial *c* degree of contact with this country on the part of the defendant served. Further, if the draftsman had contemplated presence within the jurisdiction as being essential to effective service, it is difficult to see why he did not stipulate for it to be sworn to in the affidavit to which I have just referred.

It seems to me that within the framework of Ord 10 it would be little more than a formality to insist on the physical presence of the defendant within the jurisdiction in *d* order to achieve effective service under Ord 10, r 1(2). The important matter, for practical purposes, is not the presence of the defendant within the jurisdiction, but that service of the process should come to the attention of the defendant speedily. Order 10, r 1(3) assumes that for the making of effective service a significant degree of association with this country will exist because it requires evidence that the writ will come to the knowledge of the defendant within seven days. On the other hand there is a significant *e* disadvantage in requiring the presence of the defendant in the jurisdiction in that if the defendant happens to have left the jurisdiction even for only 24 hours or less the service will fail. Moreover the service of process should be as simple and as certain as possible. It is not desirable that it should depend, for example, on calculations as to the time that an aircraft enters English air space.

In my opinion there is nothing in Ord 10 which requires the assumption that the *f* presence of the defendant within the jurisdiction is necessary for effective service under Ord 10, r 1(2). The order is self-contained and neither expresses nor imports such a requirement. I should add that the matter appears to me to be purely one of construction. Nobody suggests there is any question of ultra vires. In my judgment the writ was validly served and I would allow the appeal accordingly.

g

PARKER LJ. I agree. I add only a few words as we are differing from the judge.

It is in my opinion significant that the possibilities of service are service at the usual, or at the last-known, address. The rule thus expressly contemplates that the plaintiff desiring to serve a writ may well not know where the defendant is. Furthermore, if one had a defendant living in the northern part of Cumbria, who was regularly in the habit of crossing the border for his lunch, it appears to me to make a complete nonsense of the *h* whole matter if he is able to say service was bad because at the time the letter was put through the letter box or at the time it was posted he happened to be in the southern part of Scotland for no more than an hour. That is one example. There are many others. People go in droves from southern ports to Calais for day trips in order to replenish supplies of alcoholic liquor. Is it to be said that it was really the intention of the draftsman *j* that although he had lived, and continued to live permanently in this country for years and years, he could say that he had not been served because the vessel on which he had gone to Calais was just outside the territorial limits at the time of posting or at the time the letter came through the letter box. It appears to me that to attribute that sort of intention to the draftsman simply because of the presence of the words 'of a defendant'

in the rule is to impute to him a mischievousness which, for my part, I am not prepared
a to accept. If the draftsman had so intended, he would as it seems to me have made it a
requirement that the affidavit of service, without which no default judgment can be
obtained, should include a statement that the deponent verily believed the defendant to
be in the jurisdiction at the time of posting or putting through the letter box as the case
may be.

In my view also, the wording of this rule is plain and the service was good.
b

CROOM-JOHNSON LJ. I agree. RSC Order 10, although it is headed 'Service of
Originating Process: General Provisions', deals in fact throughout with service which
takes place within the jurisdiction. This is emphasised by the other provisions of the
order, in particular by r 3(2), which says that service made in accordance with the special
c provisions contained in the contract shall not be effective if the writ is served out of the
jurisdiction, unless such service is permitted by RSC Ord 11. Order 11, by distinction,
deals entirely with service out of the jurisdiction.

I agree that this is a matter of construction. The words which require interpretation in
Ord 10, r 1(2) are: 'A writ for service on a defendant within the jurisdiction may, instead
of being served personally on him, be served . . .' by posting or inserting through the
d letter box. That short phrase contains three nouns, writ, service and defendant, although
the noun 'service' is used adjectivally. The plaintiff says that this describes the type of
writ. The defendant, on the other hand, says that 'within the jurisdiction' describes the
whereabouts of the defendant when he is to be served. If the words describe where the
service is to take place, that is consistent with the general wording of Ord 10 and assists
the plaintiff's construction as being a description of the writ.
e   It has been suggested to us that the only way of interpreting this provision is in effect
by rewriting it, but in my view it is possible to construe the sentence without resorting
to rewriting the sentence, or making any deletion such as omitting the reference to the
defendant altogether, or leaving out the words 'on him'. It is therefore helpful in
construing the words, by seeing what was the object of putting in Ord 10, r 1(2) the
f provisions relating to service by post or service through the letter box. This was done to
make service more easy, compared with the previous restriction on service, which
required it to be done personally.

In the course of the argument both parties to this appeal adopted the attitude that the
addition in Ord 10, r 1(2) was not made with the object of enlarging the jurisdiction of
the court. It was only concerned with adding a means of asserting what jurisdiction it
already had, which is another way of getting before the court the defendant over whom
g the court has jurisdiction in any event. The purpose of the addition was simplicity.

I do not think that in making these provisions, the rule is concerned with building in
complications such as having to ensure that the proposed defendant was personally
present inside the jurisdiction of the court at the moment when the writ was sent, by
being put in a postal box, or whether that was so at the moment when the postman
h delivered it at his address. The defendant might be anywhere out of the jurisdiction,
even temporarily. Nor was the rule designed to make the plaintiff find out where he was
when the alternative method was used by the process server of putting it through the
letter box, which is, after all, only another way of achieving the same result.

In my view the correct interpretation of the phrase is that put on it by the plaintiff,
that the words 'within the jurisdiction' describe the writ and its service within the
j jurisdiction and not the physical whereabouts of the defendant, which would lead to all
kinds of problems.

Counsel for the defendant has called our attention to various passages and texts which
he says support his interpretation. An example is the note in *The Supreme Court Practice
1988*, vol 1, para 10/1/2 (sub-para (3)), which I need not read but which only repeats the
wording of the rule. I do not regard that note, or any of the other passages to which he

referred, as doing any more than simply repeating with prudence the actual words used
in Ord 10, r 1(2) which themselves have required interpretation.

I too would allow this appeal.

Appeal allowed. Leave to appeal to the House of Lords refused.

16 January 1989. The Appeal Committee of the House of Lords gave leave to appeal.

Solicitors: *Lovell White Durrant* (for the plaintiff); *Kingsford Dorman & Routh Stacey*, agents
for *Hart Brown & Co*, Guildford (for the defendant).

Wendy Shockett   Barrister.

The Powstaniec Wielkopolski

QUEEN'S BENCH DIVISION (ADMIRALTY COURT)
SHEEN J
28 JUNE, 12 JULY 1988

*Admiralty – Jurisdiction – Action in rem – Claim in nature of salvage – Tidal waters – Salvage
services rendered to ship and cargo within tidal reach of estuary or navigable river – Whether
services provided within 'harbour' – Whether person rendering services entitled to claim salvage
– Merchant Shipping Act 1894, ss 546, 742.*

The entitlement to remuneration for salvage services under s 546[a] of the Merchant
Shipping Act 1894 extends to services rendered in any tidal water within the limits of
the United Kingdom, which, by virtue of the definition of 'tidal water' in s 742[b] of that
Act, is 'any part of the sea and any part of a river within the ebb and flow of the tide . . .
not being a harbour', where 'harbour' has its ordinary and natural meaning of a pier or
jetty at which ships can ship or unship goods or passengers, and not the wider meaning
assigned to the definition of 'harbour' in s 742 as including estuaries and navigable rivers
in which ships can obtain shelter. Accordingly, salvage is payable for services rendered
in a tidal reach of an estuary or navigable river provided the vessel is not berthed at a pier
or jetty (see p 202 *e g* to p 203 *a*, post)

Notes

For the Admiralty jurisdiction of the High Court in respect of salvage claims, see 1
Halsbury's Laws (4th edn) paras 323–335, and for cases on the subject, see 1(1) Digest
(Reissue) 279–281, 1648–1668.

For the Merchant Shipping Act 1894, ss 546, 742, see 39 Halsbury's Statutes (4th edn)
553, 606.

As from 4 July 1988 s 456 of the 1894 Act was amended by the Merchant Shipping
Act 1988, s 48, Sch 5, para 3, which added thereto a sub-s (2) defining 'tidal water' in that
section as meaning '(*a*) any waters within the ebb and flow of the tide at ordinary spring
tides; or (*b*) the waters of any dock which is directly, or (by means of one or more other
docks) indirectly, connected with any such waters'.

Cases referred to in judgment

Beatsa, The (1937) 58 Ll LR 85.
Conifer, The (1924) 19 Ll LR 116.
Gamecock Steam Towing Co v 'Sif' Cargo and Freight (1921) 6 Ll LR 116.
Goring, The [1988] 1 All ER 641, [1988] AC 831, [1988] 2 WLR 460, HL.

---

a   Section 546 is set out at p 200 *c d*, post
b   Section 742, so far as material, is set out at p 200 *e*, post

Hudson Light, The [1970] 1 Lloyd's Rep 166.

a *Mitchell v Simpson* (1890) 25 QBD 183, CA.

Tees, The, The Pentucket (1862) Lush 505, 167 ER 230.

Zeta, The (1875) LR 4 A & E 460.

Cases also cited

Atsuta Maru, The (1926) 26 Ll LR 151.

Gorsefield, The (1937) 60 Ll LR 6.

b *Gregerso, The* [1971] 1 All ER 961, [1973] QB 274.

Mount Cynthos, The (1937) 58 Ll LR 18.

Mud Hopper No 4, The (1879) 4 Asp MLC 103.

Trask v Maddox, The Carrier Dove (1863) 2 Moo PCCNS 243, 15 ER 893, PC.

Preliminary issue

c The plaintiffs, the owners, masters, officers and crews of the motor tugs Sun London, Hibernia and Ionia, brought an Admiralty action in rem against the first and second defendants, the owners of the ship Powstaniec Wielkopolski and the cargo shipped thereon (the shipowners and cargo owners), claiming remuneration for salvage services rendered to the Powstaniec Wielkopolski in Gravesend Reach on 23 April 1985. The shipowners denied that the services rendered were salvage services. The following points

d of law were ordered to be tried as a preliminary issue: (i) whether the plaintiffs' right to claim salvage was governed by the provisions of s 546 of the Merchant Shipping Act 1894 which, as construed in accordance with s 742 of the Act, excluded services performed in harbours; and (ii) whether the plaintiffs' services were performed in a harbour, namely the Port of London, and therefore the plaintiffs were not entitled to claim salvage in respect of them. The facts are set out in the judgment.

e

Nigel Teare for the plaintiffs.

Belinda Bucknall QC for the shipowners and cargo owners.

Cur adv vult

f 12 July. The following judgment was delivered.

SHEEN J. In this action the plaintiffs claim salvage remuneration for services rendered to the property of the first and second defendants, the shipowners and cargo owners, in Gravesend Reach of the river Thames on 23 April 1985. By their defence the shipowners denied that such services as were rendered by the plaintiffs were salvaged services. On 20 June 1988 the shipowners applied for and obtained leave to amend their defence by the

g addition of the two following paragraphs:

'3a. Further or alternatively the Plaintiffs' right to claim salvage is governed by the provisions of Section 546 of the Merchant Shipping Act 1894 which, as construed in accordance with Section 742 of the said Act excludes services performed in harbours.

h 3b. The Plaintiffs' services were performed within a harbour, namely the Port of London. In the premises the Plaintiffs are not entitled to claim salvage in respect of them.'

When leave to introduce this amendment was given the court ordered the point of law raised by those paragraphs to be tried as a preliminary issue. This judgment relates

j solely to that issue.

The following facts were agreed. The Powstaniec Wielkopolski is a bulk carrier of 20,593 tons gross. At the material time she was laden with a cargo of 30,560 metric tons of wheat. The value of the ship, her bunkers, stores and cargo was nearly £7m. The claim for salvage is brought by the owners, masters and crews of three tugs, the Sun London, Ionia and Hibernia. On 23 April 1985 the ship was in Gravesend Reach, within the limits of the Port of London as defined by the Port of London Act 1968 (c xxxii),

lying moored fore and aft at buoys on the southern side of the river off Imperial Paper
Mills while waiting for a berth at the Tilbury Grain Terminal. The bunkering barge   *a*
Varsseveld was moored alongside the ship. At about 1800 hours the wind was north-
easterly about force 6 and the tide was ebbing. Low water was predicted for 2207 hours
(BST). The ship's bow moorings began to part. At a later stage the stern moorings also
parted. Thereafter the ship drifted to the north side of the river. The tugs, which were
lying further down Gravesend Reach, heard a report on VHF channel 12 from the
Varsseveld that the ship was breaking adrift. They set off up river. There was no call for *b*
assistance from the ship.

There is a dispute between the parties as to whether the ship was in danger when the
tugs arrived and as to what action (if any) was taken by the tugs on their arrival. Without
prejudice to the contention of the defendants that the true facts do not give rise to a claim
for salvage, I must assume, for the purposes of the issue before the court, that services in
the nature of salvage services were rendered by the plaintiffs on this occasion.   *c*

Section 546 of the Merchant Shipping Act 1894 provides:

> 'Where any vessel is wrecked, stranded, or in distress at any place on or near the
> coasts of the United Kingdom or any tidal water within the limits of the United
> Kingdom, and services are rendered by any person in assisting that vessel or saving
> the cargo or apparel of that vessel or any part thereof, and where services are   *d*
> rendered by any person other than a receiver in saving any wreck, there shall be
> payable to the salvor by the owner of the vessel, cargo, apparel, or wreck, a reasonable
> amount of salvage to be determined in case of dispute in the manner herein-after
> mentioned.'

Section 742 of the 1894 Act provides:
                                                                                           e
> 'In this Act, unless the context otherwise requires the following expressions have
> the meanings hereby assigned to them; (that is to say,) ... "HARBOUR" includes
> harbours properly so called, whether natural or artificial, estuaries, navigable rivers,
> piers, jetties, and other works in or at which ships can obtain shelter, or ship and
> unship goods or passengers; "TIDAL WATER" means any part of the sea and any part
> of a river within the ebb and flow of the tide at ordinary spring tides, and not being *f*
> a harbour ...'

In relation to those definitions Lord Brandon said in *The Goring* [1988] 1 All ER 641 at
645, [1988] AC 831 at 849–850:

> 'The definitions of the expressions "harbour" and "tidal water" in s 742 create a
> problem when applied to ascertain the meaning of the expression "tidal water" in *g*
> s 546. The result of applying the very wide definition of "harbour" to the definition
> of "tidal water" and then applying the definition of "tidal water" so produced to
> interpret [s 546], is to exclude from the meaning of "tidal water" in that section
> numerous localities which might be expected to be included in it. It is fortunately
> not necessary to solve this problem in this appeal. The significance of s 546 is the
> same as that of s 458 of the [Merchant Shipping Act 1854]. It prescribes the places *h*
> in which services must be rendered in order to qualify as salvage services in the
> United Kingdom ...'

On this preliminary issue the problem has to be solved.

Section 458 of the Merchant Shipping Act 1854 was the equivalent of s 546 of the
1894 Act. It did not give rise to the present problem because there was no definition of *j*
the words 'tidal water'. Section 476 of the 1854 Act provided that:

> '... the High Court of Admiralty shall have jurisdiction to decide upon all claims
> whatsoever relating to salvage, whether the services in respect of which salvage is
> claimed were performed upon the High Seas, or within the Body of a County ...'

My attention was drawn to examples of the exercise of this jurisdiction in relation to
salvage services rendered 'within the Body of a County'. The first was a decision of Dr

Lushington in *The Tees, The Pentucket* (1862) Lush 505, 167 ER 230 in which case the
a steamship Tees was in danger in a dock near London Bridge when a serious fire broke
out in warehouses surrounding the dock and the fire spread to the upper sails of the Tees
and another vessel in the dock. The Tees was towed to a place of safety in the river
Thames, for which services an award of salvage was made. As a second example of a
claim for salvage for services rendered to a barge adrift in the river Thames, my attention
was drawn to *The Zeta* (1875) LR 4 A & E 460.

b   The question raised by the amended defence is whether by the enactment of the 1894
Act Parliament changed the substantive law of salvage by enacting indirectly that after
that Act came into force salvage would not be payable for services rendered in certain
tidal waters within the limits of the United Kingdom in which before the passing of the
1894 Act similar services would have attracted a salvage reward.

If the submissions made by counsel for the defendants are valid that unexpected and
c unseen result would follow. It is unexpected for two reasons. First, because the 1894 Act
is a consolidation statute. As such it 'does not profess to amend or alter the provisions of
the Acts consolidated. Prima facie, therefore, the same effect ought to be given to its
provisions as was given to those of the Acts for which it was substituted' (per Fry LJ in
Mitchell v Simpson (1890) 25 QBD 183 at 190). Second, because it would be a construction
of the 1894 Act which is contrary to the public interest. When construing an Act of
d Parliament it is to be presumed that Parliament intended to legislate in the public
interest. My view as to what is in the public interest is based on two factors, namely (1)
that one of the reasons for awarding salvage is to encourage mariners to go voluntarily to
the assistance of ships in distress, and it is in the public interest that they should be so
encouraged, and (2) the speed with which Parliament has taken steps to remove any
possibility of argument as to the meaning of s 546 of the 1894 Act by the provisions of
e para 3 of Sch 5 to the Merchant Shipping Act 1988 suggests that the construction for
which the defendants contend is not in the public interest. It is also surprising that the
construction of the 1894 Act for which counsel contends was unseen by many eminent
counsel and judges for 94 years. There have been innumerable successful claims for
salvage in respect of services rendered in harbours as defined by s 742 of the 1894 Act
and many cases in which an award of salvage has been made for services rendered in the
f river Thames within the Port of London. Some of those claims arose out of services
rendered in Gravesend Reach: see *Gamecock Steam Towing Co v 'Sif' Cargo and Frieght*
(1921) 6 Ll LR 116, *The Conifer* (1924) 19 Ll LR 116, *The Beatsa* (1937) 58 Ll LR 85 and
The Hudson Light [1970] 1 Lloyd's Rep 166.

In *The Goring* [1988] 1 All ER 641, [1988] AC 831 Lord Brandon reviewed the statutory
g provisions enacted between 1840 and 1982 which dealt with the substantive law of
salvage and the jurisdiction of the Admiralty Court over claims for salvage. It is
unnecessary for me to repeat that review. However, counsel for the plaintiffs submitted
that it is unnecessary to bear in mind the historical statutory background when applying
one's mind to the relevant meanings assigned to certain expressions by s 742 of the 1894
Act. Section 742 introduces those meanings with the words 'unless the context otherwise
h requires'. He submitted that s 546 of the 1894 Act plainly requires that the words 'tidal
water' should not be given the extended meaning which would result from the definition
of harbour being incorporated into it. Counsel relied on the following points. First, prior
to the 1894 Act there was a cause of action for salvage on tidal waters within the limits of
the United Kingdom whether or not the place of the services was a harbour (see the
speech of Lord Brandon in *The Goring* [1988] 1 All ER 641 at 643, [1988] AC 831 at 846–
j 847). Second, there is no reason to infer from the 1894 Act that Parliament intended to
narrow the substantive law of salvage. Lord Brandon pointed out that the 1840 Act did
not affect the substantive law of salvage (see [1988] 1 All ER 641 at 643, [1988] AC 831
at 847). Then Lord Brandon said ([1988] 1 All ER 641 at 644–645, [1988] AC 831 at
848):

'Section 458 [of the 1854 Act] is important because in it the legislature for the
first time prescribed the places in which it was necessary for services to a ship, her

cargo, or her apparel to have been rendered in order to qualify as salvage services within the United Kingdom. It was necessary that they should have been rendered on the shore of any sea or tidal water in the United Kingdom. If the legislature had intended that services rendered in non-tidal inland waters of the United Kingdom should also qualify as salvage services, it would surely have expressly so provided. It did not do so, however, and the inference which I draw is that the legislature did not have that intention.'

Counsel for the plaintiffs submitted that, if express terms are required for the purpose of extending the substantive law of salvage, then a fortiori, if the legislature intended to change the law of salvage by excluding from the places in which services to ships in distress qualified as salvage services a large number of places which had only 54 years earlier been brought within the jurisdiction of the High Court of Admiralty, it would have done so expressly. Furthermore, it would not have made such an important change in the law in a consolidating statute.

I turn now to consider the relevant provisions of the 1894 Act. The relevant words of s 546 are:

> 'Where any vessel is . . . in distress in any place on . . . any tidal water within the limits of the United Kingdom, and services are rendered by any person in assisting that vessel . . . there shall be payable to the salvor . . . a reasonable amount of salvage . . .'

The definition of 'tidal water' in s 742, quoted earlier, ends with the word 'harbour'. Therefore the first question to be answered is whether it is possible in that context to give the word 'harbour' the meaning assigned to it by s 742. Bearing in mind that the definition of 'harbour' immediately precedes the definition of 'tidal water' it would be surprising if the context required some other meaning.

But if the definition of 'harbour' is incorporated into the definition of 'tidal water' it reads as follows:

> '"TIDAL WATER" means any part of the sea and any part of a river within the ebb and flow of the tide at ordinary spring tides, and not being a harbour properly so called, whether natural or artificial, estuaries, navigable rivers, piers, jetties, and other works in or at which ships can obtain shelter, or ship and unship goods or passengers.'

That definition of tidal water incorporating the definition of 'harbour' only has to be set out to expose its absurdity. The only rivers on which ships can proceed are 'navigable rivers'. It seems to me that it would, therefore, be absurd to enact that salvage is payable to the salvor of a ship in distress in any part of a river within the ebb and flow of the tide within the limits of the United Kingdom so long as those waters are not an estuary or a navigable river. Where else could a ship be found on tidal water within the United Kingdom? For this reason the context does require that the word 'harbour' in the definition of 'tidal water' should not be given the meaning assigned to it in s 742.

The word 'harbour', where it appears in the definition of 'tidal water', must be given its ordinary and natural meaning. The ship Powstaniec Wielkopolski was in a reach of the river Thames. She was not in a harbour, if that word is given its ordinary and natural meaning. Gravesend Reach may on occasions provide some shelter for ships in weather conditions which would cause distress in the open sea, but no mariner would ordinarily or naturally describe Gravesend Reach as a 'harbour'.

I agree with the submission of counsel for the plaintiffs that it is a misuse of language to say that the whole of that part of the river Thames which forms the Port of London is a harbour; it is more accurate to say that there are many harbours along the river Thames and within the Port of London.

For these reasons I hold that the place where the services of the plaintiffs were rendered

is tidal and is not a harbour. That is sufficient to dispose of the defence raised by paras 3a
a and 3b of the amended defence.

Counsel for the plaintiffs invited me to hold that the special meaning assigned to 'tidal
water' by s 742 should not be applied when construing s 546 of the 1894 Act. Counsel
was correct when he pointed out that Lloyd's Law Reports have reported many cases
involving salvage services in harbours. For 94 years the special meaning assigned to 'tidal
water' has either been overlooked or the court has taken the view that the context of
b s 546 does require the words 'tidal waters' to have their ordinary meaning. It is
unnecessary for me to decide this point, and the provisions of the Merchant Shipping Act
1988 may make it unnecessary for the point to be decided hereafter.

Order accordingly.

c Solicitors: *Thomas Cooper & Stibbard* (for the plaintiffs); *Elborne Mitchell* (for the
shipowners); *Waltons & Morse* and *Clyde & Co*, Guildford (for the cargo owners).

N P Metcalfe Esq   Barrister.

d
C E Heath plc v Ceram Holding Co and others

COURT OF APPEAL, CIVIL DIVISION
KERR AND NEILL LJJ
1, 5 JULY 1988

e

*Practice – Summary judgment – Counterclaim against co-defendant – Whether defendant entitled
to summary judgment against co-defendant – RSC Ord 16, rr 4(3), 8(1)(2)(3).*

A defendant who has counterclaimed against both the plaintiff and a co-defendant is not
entitled to obtain summary judgment against the co-defendant under RSC Ord 16, r 4(3)[a]
f by using the procedure set out in Ord 16, r 8(3)[b] because, having made his claim against
the co-defendant by means of a counterclaim, he is precluded by Ord 16, r 8(2) from
serving the 'notice containing a statement of the nature and grounds of his claim' referred
to in r 8(1), as required by r 8(3) when it refers to service of 'such a notice'. Furthermore,
there is no residual or inherent jurisdiction by which the court can give summary
judgment against the co-defendant (see p 210 *e f* and p 212 *a* to *d*, post).

g

Notes
For claims between co-defendants, see 37 Halsbury's Laws (4th edn) paras 257, 261–262,
and for cases on the subject, see 37(2) Digest (Reissue) 413–414, 2533–2541.

h
Case referred to in judgments
Gloucestershire Banking Co Ltd v Phillipps (Creagh, third party) (1884) 12 QBD 533, DC.

Cases also cited
Felix v Shiva [1982] 3 All ER 263, [1983] QB 82, CA.
Moore v Assignment Courier Ltd [1977] 2 All ER 842, [1977] 1 WLR 638, CA.
Official Custodian for Charities v Parway Estates Developments Ltd [1984] 3 All ER 679,
j [1985] Ch 151, CA.
Tiverton Estates Ltd v Wearwell Ltd [1974] 1 All ER 209, [1975] Ch 146, CA.

---

a   Rule 4(3), so far as material, is set out at p 209 *d*, post
b   Rule 8, so far as material, is set out at p 211 *a* to *e*, post

Interlocutory appeal

The second defendants, Knoxville Investments Ltd, in an action brought by the plaintiffs, *a*
C E Heath plc, against the first defendants, Ceram Holding Co, an unlimited company
incorporated in Gibraltar, to which the second defendants were joined as a party,
counterclaimed against both the plaintiffs and the first defendants. An accommodation
was reached between the second defendants and the plaintiffs, although the counterclaim
against the plaintiffs remained in being. The second defendants issued a summons
applying for summary judgment on the counterclaim as against the first defendants *b*
under either RSC Ord 16, rr 4, 8(3) and 11, or under s 49(2) of the Supreme Court Act
1981 or under the court's inherent jurisdiction. The first defendants applied to strike out
the summons on the ground that there was no procedural basis for it. On 26 May 1988
Hirst J dismissed the first defendants' application to strike out the second defendants'
summons and held that where a defendant counterclaimed against both the plaintiff and
his co-defendant he could obtain summary judgment against his co-defendant. The first *c*
defendants appealed from Hirst J's order. The plaintiffs were not a party to the appeal.
The facts are set out in the judgment of Neill LJ.

Gavin Lightman QC and *Michael Briggs* for the first defendants.
J M Chadwick QC and *John Mummery* for the second defendants.

Cur adv vult *d*

5 July. The following judgments were delivered.

NEILL LJ (giving the first judgment at the invitation of Kerr LJ). This is an appeal
from an order of Hirst J dated 26 May 1988 whereby he dismissed the application by the
first defendants to strike out the summons by the second defendants for summary *e*
judgment against the first defendants. It is now clear from the amended respondents'
notice and from the amended summons that the second defendants seek summary
judgment, first, under RSC Ord 16, rr 4, 8(3) and 11, second, under the Supreme Court
Act 1981 and, third, under the inherent jurisdiction of the court.

The question which arises for decision in this case is whether one of two defendants
who makes a counterclaim against the plaintiff and the other defendant can obtain *f*
summary judgment against that other defendant. At this stage the merits of the action,
and, indeed, of the summons for summary judgment, do not require investigation.

I can outline the facts very shortly. The specially indorsed writ was issued on 2 January
1986. The plaintiffs claimed against the first defendants, an unlimited company
incorporated in Gibraltar, to be entitled to a sum in excess of £6·2m provided by the first
defendants by way of security. On 5 February 1987 the first defendants served points of *g*
defence alleging that the sum in fact represented the deferred purchase price for the sale
in 1982 by the plaintiffs of their then subsidiary the second defendants, at that time
known as Motolease, and that the sum was irrecoverable because the sale agreement was
illegal as being a fraud on the creditors of the second defendants, including the Revenue,
and also involved a breach of s 42 of the Companies Act 1981.

On 24 July 1987 the second defendants applied to be joined as a party. In support of *h*
their application they exhibited a draft defence and counterclaim. On 18 September
1987 the second defendants were joined; the counterclaim was against both the plaintiffs
and the first defendants. I understand that it was served in October 1987. The relief
sought against the plaintiffs and the first defendants was as follows:

'(1) A declaration that the Plaintiff and the First Defendant are jointly and *j*
severally liable as constructive trustees to account for and pay to the Second
Defendant the sum of money now standing in the joint account in their names at
Mercantile Credit Company Limited in London and that the said sum is held upon
trust by them for the Second Defendant.

a

(2) A declaration that the sum standing in the said joint account in the joint names of the Plaintiff and the First Defendant at Mercantile Credit Company Limited in London is an asset of the Second Defendant.

(3) An order under s. 172 of the Law of Property Act 1925 setting aside the transfer or transfers of money out of the account of the Second Defendant with Handels Kredit, Zurich on the ground that such transfer or transfers of money were made with intent to defraud the creditors of the Second Defendant.

b

(4) An account of all moneys directly or indirectly received by or on behalf of the Plaintiff and the First Defendant in respect of the sale by the Second Defendant of its leasing contracts and payment to the Second Defendant of all sums found due from them to the Second Defendant on the taking of such account'

and further and other relief including necessary consequential accounts and directions.

c

On 30 October 1987 the second defendants issued a summons for judgment. This summons has now been amended with the leave of this court and without objection. The application is now for the following directions under RSC Ord 16, rr 4, 8(3) and 11 and/or the Supreme Court Act 1981 and/or the inherent jurisdiction of the court—

d

'1. That final judgment be entered in favour of the Second Defendants against the First Defendants in the terms of the declarations and other relief sought in the Points of Counterclaim served herein. 2. That such other judgment or order be made as the nature of the case requires. 3. That the costs of the Second Defendants' claim against the First Defendants including the costs of this application be taxed and paid by the First Defendants.'

e

It seems that some accommodation has now been reached between the second defendants and the plaintiffs, but the action by the plaintiffs and the counterclaim against the plaintiffs remain in being.

On 2 December 1987 the first defendants issued the summons which is the subject of the present appeal.

The argument for the first defendants can be stated in three propositions. (1) The power to grant summary judgment without a full trial is a power conferred by statute

f

and by the rules. (2) The court has no residual or inherent power to grant summary judgments. (3) The rules do not confer any power to grant summary judgment against a co-defendant where there is a counterclaim, or could be a counterclaim.

The first defendants recognise that there is an apparent lacuna in the rules and that the situation is anomalous. But they submit that this is a matter for the rules committee and that the court should not be tempted to place a strained interpretation on the plain words

g

of Ord 16, r 8.

In support of this argument we were referred to Ord 14, r 5(1) and to Ord 16, r 8, and in particular to Ord 16, r 8(2). I should start by reading these provisions in their present form. Ord 14, r 5 provides as follows:

h

'(1) Where a defendant to an action in the Queen's Bench Division (including the Admiralty Court) or Chancery Division, begun by writ, has served a counterclaim on the plaintiff, then, subject to paragraph (3) the defendant may, on the ground that the plaintiff has no defence to a claim made in the counterclaim, or to a particular part of such a claim, apply to the Court for judgment against the plaintiff on that claim or part . . .'

j

The next two paragraphs of the rules deal with consequential provisions. Paragraph (3) provides that the rule shall not apply to a counterclaim which includes any such claim as is referred to in r 1(2); those are the well-known exclusions of claims such as claims for libel, false imprisonment and where there is an allegation based on fraud.

In order to examine the argument presented on behalf of the first defendants it is necessary to make some reference to the history and development of the rules of court governing four separate forms of procedure: first, summary judgment under Ord 14; second, counterclaims; third, third party proceedings and summary judgments against third parties; and finally, proceedings between co-defendants and summary judgment against a co-defendant. Before turning to these specific forms of procedure, however, it will be convenient to remind oneself of the framework within which the individual rules of court are set.

For the purposes of the present appeal it is unnecessary to consider the forms of procedure in existence before the Supreme Court of Judicature Act 1873. Thus, it was common ground at the hearing before us that before 1873: (a) that, save as provided by the Summary Procedure on Bills of Exchange Act 1855, there was no power to grant summary judgment on the lines now covered by Ord 14; (b) that a defendant who wished to make a counterclaim against a plaintiff had to bring a separate action against the plaintiff and could not introduce a counterclaim into the plaintiff's action; (c) that a defendant who wished to obtain an indemnity or other relief against a third party had to bring a separate action against that third party.

In 1873 the Supreme Court of Judicature was created by the Supreme Court of Judicature Act of that year. At the same time it was provided by s 24 of the 1873 Act that law and equity should be concurrently administered. We were referred in particular to s 24(3) and (7); I should read those provisions. I read the opening words of s 24:

'In every civil cause or matter commenced in the High Court of Justice law and equity shall be administered by the High Court of Justice and the Court of Appeal respectively according to the Rules following . . .'

Then, in sub-s (3):

'The said Courts respectively, and every Judge thereof, shall also have power to grant to any defendant in respect of any equitable estate or right, or other matter of equity, and also in respect of any legal estate, right, or title claimed or asserted by him, all such relief against any plaintiff or petitioner as such defendant shall have properly claimed by his pleading, and as the said Courts respectively, or any Judge thereof, might have granted in any suit instituted for that purpose by the same defendant against the same plaintiff or petitioner; and also all such relief relating to or connected with the original subject of the cause or matter, and in like manner claimed against any other person, whether already a party to the same cause or matter or not, who shall have been duly served with notice in writing of such claim pursuant to any Rule of Court or any Order of the Court, as might properly have been granted against such person if he had been made a defendant to a cause duly instituted by the same defendant for the like purpose; and every person served with any such notice shall thenceforth be deemed a party to such cause or matter, with the same rights in respect of his defence against such claim, as if he had been duly sued in the ordinary way by such defendant.'

Then, in sub-s (7):

'The High Court of Justice and the Court of Appeal respectively, in the exercise of the jurisdiction vested in them by this Act in every cause or matter pending before them respectively, shall have power to grant, and shall grant, either absolutely or on such reasonable terms and conditions as to them shall seem just, all such remedies whatsoever as any of the parties thereto may appear to be entitled to in respect of any and every legal or equitable claim properly brought forward by them respectively in such cause or matter; so that, as far as possible, all matters so in controversy between the said parties respectively may be completely and finally determined, and all multiplicity of legal proceedings concerning any of such matters avoided.'

In the schedule to the 1873 Act were set out some rules of procedure, but I do not

consider that it is necesary to refer to them specifically because they were soon superseded
a by the detailed rules of court set out in Sch 1 to the Supreme Court of Judicature Act
1875. These rules were in turn superseded by the Rules of the Supreme Court 1883,
which came into force on 24 October 1883. The 1883 rules, though much added to and
amended, remained in force for about 80 years until they were partially revised and
superseded in 1962 and then wholly revised and superseded by the Rules of the Supreme
Court 1965, which came into operation on 1 October 1966. The 1965 rules (as amended)
b are the rules currently in force.

With this general introduction I turn to the first of the specific forms of procedure to
which I referred earlier.

Summary judgment under Ord 14
c Schedule 1 to the Supreme Court of Judicature Act 1875 contained rules of court set
out in numbered orders. Order XIV was in these terms:

> 'Where the defendant appears on a writ of summons specially indorsed, under
> Order III, Rule 6, the plaintiff may, on affidavit verifying the cause of action, and
> swearing that in his belief there is no defence to the action, call on the defendant to
> show cause, before the Court or a Judge why the plaintiff should not be at liberty to
d > sign final judgment for the amount so indorsed, together with interest, if any, and
> costs; and the Court or Judge may, unless the defendant, by affidavit or otherwise,
> satisfy the Court or Judge that he has a good defence to the action on the merits, or
> disclose such facts as the Court or Judge may think sufficient to entitle him to be
> permitted to defend the action, make an order empowering the plaintiff to sign
> judgment accordingly.'
e

As time passed the scope of Ord 14 increased because further types of claim were added
to those which could be specially indorsed in accordance with Ord 3, r 6. Later the
reference to Ord 3, r 6 was abolished and today the scope of Ord 14 is very wide. At no
time before the 1962 revision, however, was it possible for a defendant to obtain
judgment under Ord 14 against a plaintiff.
f In the 1962 revision, however, a new Ord 14, r 5 was introduced. In its amended form
its provisions are in the terms to which I have already made specific reference.

I need say no more about summary judgment under Ord 14, because it is not suggested
that the second defendants can make use of Ord 14 in the present case against the first
defendants.

g
Counterclaims
Order XIX, r 3 of the rules of court set out in Sch 1 to the Supreme Court of Judicature
Act 1875 gave a defendant the right to make a counterclaim against the plaintiff in the
plaintiff's action. The 1883 rules contained a similar provision. The present equivalent
rule is Ord 15, r 2(1).
h Order XXII, r 5 of the 1875 rules provided for a counterclaim against the plaintiff and
any other person or persons. This rule later became Ord 21, r 11 and is now, in a
somewhat different form, Ord 15, r 3(1). This paragraph is the paragraph which the
second defendants used to make their counterclaim in this case. It is in the following
terms:

j > 'Where a defendant to an action who makes a counterclaim against the plaintiff
> alleges that any other person (whether or not a party to the action) is liable to him
> along with the plaintiff in respect of the subject-matter of the counterclaim, or
> claims against such other person any relief related to or connected with the original
> subject-matter of the action, then, subject to rule 5(2) he may join that other person
> as a party against whom the counterclaim is made.'

It is not suggested, however, that any right to obtain summary judgment is to be found in Ord 15, r 3.

Third party proceedings and summary judgment against third parties

It may be remembered that s 24(3) of the 1873 Act contained what were in effect three separate provisions; I should refer again to the second limb of the subsection, reading also the opening words:

'The said Courts respectively, and every Judge thereof, shall also have power to grant to any defendant [and then I turn to what I have described as the second limb] . . . all such relief relating to or connected with the original subject of the cause or matter, and in like manner claimed against any other person, whether already a party to the same cause or matter or not, who shall have been duly served with notice in writing of such claim pursuant to any Rule of Court or any Order of the Court, as might properly have been granted against such person if he had been made a defendant to a cause duly instituted by the same defendant for the like purpose . . .'

It will be seen that this part of the subsection was expressed in wide terms. Moreover, Ord XVI, r 18 of the 1875 rules referred to a claim by a defendant 'to be entitled to contribution, indemnity, or other remedy or relief over against any person not a party to the action'. But the words 'other remedy or relief' were omitted from the 1883 rules and third party proceedings were confined by the 1883 rules to claims by a defendant 'to contribution or indemnity'. That is set out in Ord 16, r 48, as appears in *The Annual Practice 1924* p 281. It is to be noted, however, that Ord 16, r 52 of the 1883 rules gave the court power to order summary judgment if the court was not satisfied that there was a question to be tried as to the liability of the third party. In *Gloucestershire Banking Co Ltd v Phillipps (Creagh, third party)* (1884) 12 QBD 533 the Divisional Court rejected an argument that Ord 16, r 52 was ultra vires, and held that it was consistent with s 24(3) of the 1873 Act and s 24 of the 1875 Act.

Section 39 of the Supreme Court Judicature (Consolidation) Act 1925 re-enacted, in somewhat different language, the earlier provisions relating to counterclaims and third parties. That section provided as follows:

'The court or judge shall have power to grant to any defendant in respect of any equitable estate or right or other matter or equity, and also in respect of any legal estate, right or title claimed or asserted by him—(a) all such relief against any plaintiff or petitioner as the defendant has properly claimed by his pleading, and as the court or judge might have granted in any suit instituted for that purpose by that defendant against the same plaintiff or petitioner; and (b) all such relief relating to or connected with the original subject of the cause of matter, claimed in like manner against any other person, whether already a party to the cause or matter or not, who has been duly served with notice in writing of the claim pursuant to rules of court or any order of the court, as might properly have been granted against that person if he had been made a defendant to a cause duly instituted by the same defendant for the like purpose.'

Following the 1925 Act the scope of third party procedure was extended in, I think, 1929 by the introduction of a new Ord 16A. It is sufficient to refer to Ord 16A, r 1 as set out in *The Annual Practice 1952* p 290. That was in these terms:

'(1) Where in any action a defendant claims as against any other person not already a party to the action (in this Order called the third party) (a) that he is entitled to contribution or indemnity, or (b) that he is entitled to any relief or remedy relating to or connected with the original subject-matter of the action and substantially the same as some relief or remedy claimed by the plaintiff, or (c) that any question or issue relating to or connected with the said subject-matter is substantially the same a as some question or issue arising between the plaintiff and the defendant and should properly be determined not only as between the plaintiff and the defendant but as between the plaintiff and defendant and the third party or between any or either of them, the Court or Judge may give leave to the defendant to issue and serve a "third party notice".'

It is to be noted, therefore, that sub-paras (b) and (c) of Ord 16A, r 1(1) were new and an extension of what the law had been previously.

b However, the right to seek summary judgment on the summons for directions remained and Ord 16A, r 7(1) provided as follows:

'If the third party enters an appearance the defendant giving notice may, after serving notice of the intended application upon the plaintiff, the third party and any other defendant, apply to the Court or Judge for directions, and the Court or Judge

c may—(a) where the liability of the third party to the defendant giving the notice is established on the hearing of the application, order such judgment as the nature of the case may require to be entered against the third party in favour of the defendant giving the notice . . .'

The modern counterpart of Ord 16A, r 7 is of course, Ord 16, r 4, which provides for

d third party directions. It is sufficient to refer to Ord 16, r 4(3)(a), which is in these terms:

'On an application for directions under this rule the Court may—(a) If the liability of the third party to the defendant who issued the third party notice is established on the hearing, order such judgment as the nature of the case may require to be entered against the third party in favour of the defendant . . .'

e *Proceedings between co-defendants and summary judgment against a co-defendant*
Order XVI, r 18 of the 1875 rules referred to claims against any person not a party to the action. Order XVI, r 17 was expressed more generally; it was in these terms:

'Where a defendant is or claims to be entitled to contribution or indemnity, or any remedy or relief over against any other person, or where from any other cause

f it appears to the Court or a Judge that the question in the action should be determined not only as between plaintiff and defendant, but as between the plaintiff, defendant, and any other person, or between any or either of them, the Court or a Judge may on notice being given to such later-mentioned person, make such order as may be proper for having the question so determined.'

g The 1883 rules, however, limited claims between co-defendants, as it limited claims between a defendant and a third party, to claims to an indemnity or contribution. Order 16, r 55 of the 1883 rules, as set out in *The Annual Practice 1924* p 296, was in these terms:

'Where a defendant claims to be entitled to contribution or indemnity against any other defendant to the action, a notice may be issued and the same procedure

h shall be adopted, for the determination of such questions between the defendants, as would be issued and taken against such other defendant, if such last-mentioned defendant were a third party: but nothing herein contained shall prejudice the rights of the plaintiff against any defendant in the action.'

The effect of Ord 16, r 55 was that a co-defendant who had given the appropriate notice could apply for directions and could take advantage of the summary procedure available

j under Ord 16, r 52. When the scope of third party proceedings was increased in 1929 the rights of one defendant against another were also increased. It is sufficient to refer to Ord 16A, r 12 in *The Annual Practice 1952* p 306, in which it is set out as follows:

'(1) Where a defendant claims against another defendant (a) that he is entitled to contribution or indemnity, or (b) that he is entitled to any relief or remedy relating to or connected with the original subject-matter of the action and substantially the same as some relief or remedy claimed by the plaintiff, or (c) that any question or issue relating to or connected with the said subject-matter is substantially the same as some question or issue arising between the plaintiff and the defendant making the claim and should properly be determined not only as between the plaintiff and the defendant making the claim but as between the plaintiff and that defendant and another defendant or between any or either of them, the defendant making the claim may without any leave issue and serve on such other defendant a notice making such claim or specifying such question or issue.

(2) No appearance to such notice shall be necessary and the same procedure shall be adopted for the determination of such claim, question or issue between the defendants as would be appropriate under this Order if he were a third party . . .'

It is clear by reason of para (2) that a defendant, having served a notice, could take advantage of the summary procedure available under Ord 16A, r 7. The modern equivalent of Ord 16A, r 12 is Ord 16, r 8.

It is necessary now to pause and take stock. It seems clear (1) that the procedure under Ord 14 has never applied to a claim by a defendant against a third party or to a claim by one defendant against another. It has only applied to a counterclaim by a defendant against a plaintiff since the 1962 revision. (2) That a different form of summary procedure has been available since 1883 for claims by a defendant against a third party or a co-defendant. Until 1929 the claims by a defendant, and thus the summary procedure, were restricted to claims for a contribution or indemnity. Since 1929 the scope of third party proceedings and of claims by one defendant against another has been extended on the lines I have already indicated. (3) That, notwithstanding the wide language used in s 24(3) of the 1873 Act, the actual scope of third party proceedings and proceedings between defendants has been determined at all times by the rules of court. Similarly, the scope of Ord 14 proceedings has been a matter which has been determined by the rules. There would therefore appear to be little, if any, room for an argument that the court has some wider powers in these fields than that conferred by the rules, or that it has some residual or inherent jurisdiction to grant relief where it is just to do so, or that the wide language of the statute confers some additional powers to act outside and beyond the rules. Nevertheless, it is relevant to bear in mind that the old powers, whatever they are, are preserved by s 49(2) of the Supreme Court Act 1981, which is in these terms:

'Every such court shall give the same effect as hitherto—(a) to all equitable estates, titles, rights, reliefs, defences and counterclaims, and to all equitable duties and liabilities; and (b) subject thereto, to all legal claims and demands and all estates, titles, rights, duties, obligations and liabilities existing by the common law or by any custom or created by any statute, and, subject to the provisions of this or any other Act, shall so exercise its jurisdiction in every cause or matter before it as to secure that, as far as possible, all matters in dispute between the parties are completely and finally determined, and all multiplicity of legal proceedings with respect to any of those matters is avoided.'

(4) That the general direction of any additions and amendments to the rules in the last 100 years has been towards achieving the fundamental objectives of the 1873 and 1875 Judicature Acts. These are conveniently stated in *The Supreme Court Practice 1988* vol 2, para 5187, p 1396 as follows:

'(a) to bring about the concurrent jurisdiction of law and equity in all civil causes and matters in all civil courts on the basis that in any matter where there is a conflict or variance between the rules of equity and the rules of the common law, the rules of equity shall prevail; and at the same time (b) to secure that the Court will be empowered to determine finally all matters in dispute between the parties and to avoid all multiplicity of proceedings.'

It is against this background that I return to Ord 16, r 8, which I must now read:

a

'(1) Where in any action a defendant who has given notice of intention to defend—(*a*) claims against a person who is already a party to the action any contribution or indemnity; or (*b*) claims against such a person any relief or remedy relating to or connected with the original subject-matter of the action and substantially the same as some relief or remedy claimed by the plaintiff; or (*c*)

b   requires that any question or issue relating to or connected with the original subject-matter of the action should be determined not only as between the plaintiff and himself but also as between either or both of them and some other person who is already a party to the action; then, subject to paragraph (2) the defendant may, without leave, issue and serve on that person a notice containing a statement of the nature and grounds of his claim or, as the case may be, of the question or issue

c   required to be determined.

(2) Where a defendant makes such a claim as is mentioned in paragraph (1) and that claim could be made by him by counterclaim in the action, paragraph (1) shall not apply in relation to the claim.

(3) No acknowledgment of service of such a notice shall be necessary if the person on whom it is served has acknowledged service of the writ or originating summons

d   in the action or is a plaintiff therein, and the same procedure shall be adopted for the determination between the defendant by whom, and the person on whom, such a notice is served of the claim, question or issue stated in the notice as would be appropriate under this Order if the person served with the notice were a third party and (where he has given notice of intention to defend the action or is a plaintiff) had given notice of intention to defend the claim, question or issue . . .'

e
It is first to be noticed that Ord 16, r 8(1) corresponds with Ord 16, r 1(1), just as Ord 16A, r 12 corresponded with Ord 16A, r 1.

It is next to be noticed that in Ord 16, r 8(2) reference is made to 'such a claim as is mentioned in para (1)', and that the word 'claim' does not appear in sub-para (*c*) of Ord 16, r 8(1). It may therefore be arguable that Ord 16, r 8(2) apples only to claims under

f sub-paras (*a*) and (*b*) of Ord 16, r 8(1). I feel bound to reject this argument, however, because it seems to me to be implicit in sub-para (*c*) that if the defendant requires 'a question or issue' to be determined he may also want some consequential relief which would amount to a claim. I can see no satisfactory basis for distinguishing between the three sub-paragraphs of r 8(1). Furthermore, in the present case the second defendant is clearly making a claim.

g   Prima facie, therefore, r 8(2) applies to the claim by the second defendants against the first defendants. The claim not only 'could have been made' by counterclaim, but was in fact so made by the second defendants.

There is no doubt that if the claim by the second defendants had been against the first defendants alone, they could have taken advantage of the procedure available under Ord 16, r 4. This right to seek summary judgment against a co-defendant has been available

h for over 100 years. Moreover, it was accepted on behalf of the first defendants that, in the absence of Ord 16, r 8(2), the second defendants could, if they had wished, sought summary judgment against the plaintiffs under Ord 14, r 5(1) and against the first defendants under Ord 16, rr 8 and 4.

It has to be recognised, however, that the rights to claim summary judgment against a plaintiff on the one hand and against a co-defendant on the other hand depend on the

j availability of a different code or set of rules. These codes or sets of rules are contained in delegated legisation, though it is legitimate to construe them in the light of the objectives which the primary legislation is seeking to achieve.

I come now to Ord 16, r 8(3); I read again the relevant words:

'. . . the same procedure shall be adopted for the determination between the defendant by whom, and the person on whom, such a notice is served of the claim,

question or issue stated in the notice as would be appropriate under this Order if the
person served with the notice were a third party . . .'　　　　　　　　　　　　　　　　*a*

Hirst J felt able to construe the crucial words 'such a notice' as meaning merely a notice
containing 'a statement of the nature and grounds of his claim or, as the case may be, of
the question or issue required to be determined', and the counterclaim in the action
amounted to such a notice. I cannot agree with this construction.

The central question is whether the procedure set out in Ord 16, r 4 can be used for　*b*
the determination of the claim by the second defendants against the first defendants.
This procedure can only be used if a notice falling within the description 'such a notice'
in Ord 16, r 8(3) has been served. 'Such a notice' in r 8(3) must mean, in my view, a
notice served in accordance with r 8(1). But by the express words of r 8(2), para (1) of r 8
does not apply, and therefore a notice under it cannot be served, where the claim by the
defendant 'could be made' by counterclaim. Rule 8(2) would seem to apply a fortiori　*c*
where a claim *has been made* by counterclaim.

I see no escape from the express words of Ord 16, r 8(2). The route to summary
judgment by rr 8(3) and 4(3) of Ord 16 is closed. No other route is open.

Accordingly, and not without regret, I feel bound to say that the appeal should be
allowed. In my opinion the anomaly merits the attention of the Supreme Court
Procedure Committee.　　　　　　　　　　　　　　　　　　　　　　　　　　　　　*d*

KERR LJ. I agree entirely with the judgment which Neill LJ has delivered. I share his
regret and I hope, with him, that this anomaly may be considered and remedied. I agree
that the appeal must be allowed.

Appeal allowed. Second defendants' summons struck out.　　　　　　　　　　　　　　*e*

Solicitors: *John Wood & Co* (for the first defendants); *Booth & Blackwell* (for the second
defendants).

Wendy Shockett　Barrister.

a

National Bank of Greece SA v Pinios Shipping Co No 1 and another
The Maira

b
COURT OF APPEAL, CIVIL DIVISION
O'CONNOR, LLOYD AND NICHOLLS LJJ
19, 20, 21, 25 JANUARY, 2 MARCH 1988

Bank – Duty of care – Duty of care implied by law – Mortgage of vessel – Mortgagor defaulting under mortgage – Bank entering into agreement relating to management of vessel – Management of vessel entrusted exclusively to management agent subject to bank's directions – Total loss of vessel – Management agent appointed by bank failing to carry out obligation to keep vessel fully insured – Whether bank under duty to ensure that management agent kept vessel fully insured.

c

Interest – Compound interest – Mortgage – Mortgage securing bank's guarantee of payment of instalments of purchase price of vessel – No express provision in mortgage entitling bank to charge compound interest – Bank issuing written demand for repayment under mortgage – Whether relationship of banker and customer terminated following demand for repayment – Whether bank entitled to charge compound interest following demand for repayment.

d

The owners of a vessel built in Japan deferred payment of part of its purchase price by securing the relevant amount by a first preferred mortgage in favour of the builders and by 14 promissory notes payable at six-monthly intervals. The plaintiff bank guaranteed the first six promissory notes under a letter of guarantee, having secured the shipowners' liability by a second preferred mortgage and a personal guarantee given by T. When the shipowners failed to honour the first promissory note the bank paid the amount due and debited the shipowners. Instead of declaring the shipowners in default under the second mortgage, the bank entered into a tripartite agreement with the shipowners and a management agent, G, under which the exclusive management of the vessel, including responsibility for its insurance, was transferred to G, subject to the bank's directions. The vessel was subsequently lost and at the time of her loss the insurance proceeds were insufficient even to discharge the shipowners' indebtedness under the second mortgage. The insurance was payable under a policy which had been renewed by G for less than 130% of the outstanding indebtedness, contrary to the terms of the management agreement and the two mortgages. The shipowners claimed damages against G for under-insurance in breach of its duty under the management agreement. The claim was successful, but G failed or refused to pay and the bank made a written demand to the shipowners and T for repayment of the second mortgage and when the shipowners and T failed to pay the bank issued a writ against the shipowners and T claiming the amount owing under the mortgage plus interest. The judge awarded the bank the amount owing under the mortgage and compound interest to the date of judgment. The shipowners and T appealed, contending (i) that the bank was under a duty of care to see that G did not under-insure the vessel, such a duty arising either under an implied term of the contract or in tort, and (ii) that the judge had erred in awarding compound interest to the date of the judgment since the second mortgage contained no provision entitling the bank to charge compound interest and, if by implication or bankers' practice it did, that entitlement ended when the bank made its demand for repayment and consequently terminated the relationship of banker and customer.

e

f

g

h

j

Held – (1) The court would impose neither a contractual duty of care nor a duty in tort on the bank to ensure that the management agent, G, carried out its obligation to keep the vessel fully insured, since it was not possible to establish either a generalised duty of care applying to all contracts of a defined type into which the management contract

could be fitted or a duty arising from the particular facts of the case, given that the
management contract was a one-off agreement carefully drawn for a specific purpose in   *a*
special circumstances which did not fit into any defined type or category of contract and
that the bank was entitled to leave all decisions about the management and operation of
the vessel, including the renewal of insurance, to G. Accordingly, the appeal on the duty
of care issue would be dismissed (see p 219 *e* to *g*, p 221 *h j*, p 222 *f g*, p 223 *j*, p 230 *f g*,
p 231 *h* to p 232 *c* and p 234 *j*, post); dictum of Lord Cross in *Liverpool City Council v Irwin*
[1976] 2 All ER 39 at 46–47 and *Tai Hing Cotton Mill Ltd v Liu Chong Hing Bank Ltd* [1985]   *b*
2 All ER 947 applied.

(2) Once a bank had unequivocally demanded immediate payment of outstanding
sums due on account with the intention of being paid in full, thereby closing the account,
the relationship of banker and customer was replaced by one of creditor and debtor, and
compound interest ceased to be payable in the absence of an express or implied agreement
on the part of the customer to pay, or a binding custom entitling the bank to charge,   *c*
compound interest. Since there was no such agreement between the parties and the bank
had not sought to establish any such custom, the bank was only entitled to recover simple
interest from the date of the demand for repayment to the date of judgment. Accordingly,
the appeal on the compound interest issue would be allowed (see p 225 *a b*, p 229 *h* to
p 230 *c f g*, p 234 *b* to *d j* and p 235 *f*, post); *Ex p Bevan* (1803) 9 Ves 223, *Lord Clancarty v
Latouche* (1810) 1 Ball & B 420, *Fergusson v Fyffe* [1835–42] All ER Rep 48, dictum of   *d*
Romilly MR in *Crosskill v Bower* (1863) 32 Beav 86 at 93 and *Deutsche Bank und Disconto-
Gesellschaft v Banque des Marchands de Moscou* (1931) 4 Legal Decisions Affecting Bankers
293 applied.

Per O'Connor LJ. It cannot be said that, where a bank enters a contract of guarantee as
surety, the contract of itself creates between the bank and the principal the banker/
customer relationship which would be needed to enable the bank to recover from the   *e*
principal, in the event of a default, compound interest where no express provision in that
behalf has been made (see p 235 *e*, post).

Notes

For contractual terms implied by law, see 9 Halsbury's Laws (4th edn) para 354, and for   *f*
cases on the subject, see 12 Digest (Reissue) 746–754, 5371–5410.

For a bank's right to charge interest, see 3 Halsbury's Laws (4th edn) para 160, and for
cases on the subject, see 3 Digest (Reissue) 686–687, 4210–4219.

Cases referred to in judgments

American Express International Banking Corp v Hurley [1985] 3 All ER 564.
Anns v Merton London Borough [1977] 2 All ER 492, [1978] AC 728, [1977] 2 WLR 1024,   *g*
   HL.
Bevan, Ex p (1803) 9 Ves 223, 32 ER 588, LC.
Brown v Boorman (1844) 11 Cl & Fin 1, 8 ER 1003, HL; *affg* (1842) 3 QB 511, 114 ER 603,
   Ex Ch.
Clancarty (Lord) v Latouche (1810) 1 Ball & B 420, LC.   *h*
Crosskill v Bower (1863) 32 Beav 86, 55 ER 34.
Cuckmere Brick Co Ltd v Mutual Finance Ltd [1971] 2 All ER 633, [1971] Ch 949, [1971] 2
   WLR 1207, CA.
Deutsche Bank und Disconto-Gesellschaft v Banque des Marchands de Moscou (1931) 4 Legal
   Decisions Affecting Bankers 293, CA.
Eaton v Bell (1821) 5 B & Ald 34, 106 ER 1106.   *j*
Economic Life Assurance Society v Usborne [1902] AC 147, HL.
Esso Petroleum v Mardon [1976] 2 All ER 5, [1976] QB 801, [1976] 2 WLR 583, CA.
Fergusson v Fyffe (1841) 8 Cl & Fin 121, [1835–42] All ER Rep 48, 8 ER 49, HL.
Glafki Shipping Co SA v Pinios Shipping Co No 1, The Maira (No 2) [1986] 2 Lloyd's Rep 12,
   HL; *affg* [1985] 1 Lloyd's Rep 300, CA; *rvsg* [1984] 1 Lloyd's Rep 660.

Greenwood v Martins Bank Ltd [1933] AC 51, [1932] All ER Rep 318, HL.

a *Home Office v Dorset Yacht Co Ltd* [1970] 2 All ER 294, [1970] AC 1004, [1970] 2 WLR
     1140, HL.

Lister v Romford Ice and Cold Storage Co Ltd [1957] 1 All ER 125, [1957] AC 555, [1957] 2
     WLR 158, HL.

Liverpool City Council v Irwin [1976] 2 All ER 39, [1977] AC 239, [1976] 2 WLR 562, HL;
     affg in part [1975] 3 All ER 658, [1976] QB 319, [1975] 3 WLR 663, CA.

b *London Joint Stock Bank Ltd v Macmillan* [1918] AC 777, [1918–19] All ER Rep 30, HL.

Paton v IRC [1938] 1 All ER 786, [1938] AC 341, HL.

Smith v Littlewoods Organisation Ltd (Chief Constable, Fife Constabulary, third party) [1987] 1
     All ER 710, [1987] AC 241, [1987] 2 WLR 480, HL.

Standard Chartered Bank Ltd v Walker [1982] 3 All ER 938, [1982] 1 WLR 1410, CA.

Tai Hing Cotton Mill Ltd v Liu Chong Hing Bank Ltd [1985] 2 All ER 947, [1986] AC 80,

c   [1985] 3 WLR 317, PC.

Williamson v Williamson (1869) LR 7 Eq 542.

Yourell v Hibernian Bank Ltd [1918] AC 372, HL.

Cases also cited

Banque Keyser Ullmann SA v Skandia (UK) Insurance Co Ltd [1987] 2 All ER 923, [1987] 2
d   WLR 1300.

Corinthian Securities Ltd v Cato [1969] 3 All ER 1168, [1970] 1 QB 377, CA.

Great Western Rly v London and County Banking Co Ltd [1901] AC 414, [1900–3] All ER
     Rep 1004, HL.

IRC v Holder [1931] 2 KB 81, CA; *affd* [1932] AC 624, [1932] All ER Rep 265, HL.

IRC v Lawrence Graham & Co [1937] 2 All ER 1, [1937] 2 KB 179, CA.

e *IRC v Oswald* [1945] 1 All ER 641, [1945] AC 360, HL.

Mosse v Salt (1863) 32 Beav 269, 55 ER 106.

Panchand Frères SA v Ets General Grain Co [1970] 1 Lloyd's Rep 53, CA.

Peabody Donation Fund (Governors) v Sir Lindsay Parkinson & Co Ltd [1984] 3 All ER 529,
     [1985] AC 210, HL.

f *Rufford v Bishop* (1829) 5 Russ 346, 38 ER 1058.

Shell International Petroleum Co Ltd v Transnor (Bermuda) Ltd [1987] 1 Lloyd's Rep 363, CA.

Yuen Kun-yeu v A-G of Hong Kong [1987] 2 All ER 705, [1988] AC 175, PC.

Appeal

The first defendant, Pinios Shipping Co No 1 (Pinios) of Monrovia in the Republic of
Liberia, owner and mortgagor of the vessel Maira, and the second defendant, George
g Dionysios Tsitsilianis, the guarantor of the Pinios's liabilities, appealed against the
decision of Leggatt J made on 29 January 1987 giving judgment for the plaintiff, National
Bank of Greece SA (the bank), a foreign corporation registered in England under the
Companies Act 1948, s 412 and carrying on business in London, in its claim for
repayment under a second preferred mortgage taken by the bank in support of its
guarantee of payment of the first six instalments of the purchase price of the vessel, in
h the sum of $US2,118,213·03 which included a sum for compound interest to the date of
judgment, and ruling that the bank owed the defendants no duty of care to ensure that
Glafki Shipping Co SA carried out its obligation under a tripartite agreement relating to
the management and operation of the vessel to keep it fully insured. The facts are set out
in the judgment of Lloyd LJ.

j
   Adrian Hamilton QC and *Geraldine Andrews* for the defendants.
   Murray Pickering QC and *David Owen* for the bank.

                                                                    Cur adv vult

2 March. The following judgments were delivered.

LLOYD LJ (giving the first judgment at the invitation of O'Connor LJ). This is another chapter in the protracted litigation arising out of the total loss of the Maira nearly ten years ago on 10 April 1978. At the time of her loss the vessel was insured for $US10m. The proceeds of insurance, when paid, were insufficient to enable the vessel's owner, Pinios Shipping Co No 1 (Pinios), to repay the National Bank of Greece SA (the bank) under an agreement dated 8 February 1977. On 13 November 1978 the bank wrote to Pinios demanding payment of the amount then due under the agreement. By a letter before action dated 28 January 1980 the bank calculated the amount due at 29 January 1980 as $US894,224 including interest. A statement of account was enclosed with the letter. On 8 July 1980 the bank issued a writ. The writ was amended by leave on 30 June 1983. By its points of claim indorsed on the amended writ, the bank claimed $US598,107·70 plus interest to 30 June 1983 amounting to $US734,979·46. Although the interest is not described as such, it was in fact compound interest, calculated with quarterly rests. On 29 January 1987 Leggatt J gave judgment in favour of the bank. The amount for which he gave judgment, including compound interest to the date of his judgment, amounts to $US2,118,213·03. There is now an appeal to this court. One of the two questions in the appeal is whether the judge was right to award compound interest to the date of judgment.

The second question in the case arises as follows. The Maira was built in Japan, under a shipbuilding contract dated 28 July 1975. The price was payable in yen. 30% of the price was payable on or before delivery. 70% of the price was deferred. It was secured by a first preferred mortgage, in favour of the builders, and by 14 promissory notes signed by Pinios payable at six-monthly intervals. The first six promissory notes were guaranteed by the bank under a letter of guarantee. The bank was secured by a second preferred mortgage, and by a personal guarantee given by Mr Tsitsilianis, the second defendant in the action.

The ship was delivered on 19 February 1977. The first promissory note fell due on 9 August 1977. It was dishonoured. The bank thereupon paid the amount of the promissory note under its letter of guarantee, and debited Pinios.

The bank, on payment under the letter of guarantee, could have declared Pinios in default under art II(18)(B) of the second preferred mortgage. But instead of exercising its rights under that clause, the bank entered into a tripartite agreement dated 6 September 1977 with Pinios and a company called Glafki Shipping Co SA (Glafki). By virtue of that agreement Glafki was appointed sole and exclusive agent to manage and conduct the activities of the vessel. Under cl 2 of the agreement Glafki was obliged to manage the vessel in the best interests of Pinios and the bank. Under cl 3 Glafki was obliged to exercise due diligence to protect and safeguard the interests of Pinios and the bank in various specific respects. The effect of the management agreement was to transfer the entire management of the vessel to Glafki, subject to the directions of the bank under cl 13.

Under art I(15) of the second preferred mortgage, it was Pinios's obligation to insure the vessel for not less than 130% of the total amount secured by the mortgage. There was a similar, though not identical, provision in the first preferred mortgage. Under cl 3(g) of the management agreement, it became Glafki's duty to place all insurances 'in accordance with the respective Insurances Clauses of this Mortgage'. When the vessel was delivered on 9 February 1977 she was insured by Pinios for $US10m. This was then sufficient to comply with Pinios's obligations under both mortgages. But as time went on, and the dollar depreciated against the yen, the margin narrowed. The insurance was renewed on the instructions of Glafki on 9 February 1988 and again on 1 April 1988. The April renewal worked out at less than 130% of the total amount due under both mortgages, with the consequence that Pinios was unable to repay the bank. Accordingly, Pinios brought a claim against Glafki for damages for breach of duty under the management agreement. The claim was referred to arbitration. On 9 February 1982 the

arbitrator issued his award in favour of Pinios. His award was reversed by Hobhouse J:
a see *Glafki Shipping Co SA v Pinios Shipping Co No 1, The Maira (No 2)* [1984] 1 Lloyd's Rep
660. But Pinios was successful in the Court of Appeal ([1985] 1 Lloyd's Rep 300) and in
the House of Lords ([1986] 2 Lloyd's Rep 12). Unfortunately its success has proved
fruitless. Glafki has failed or refused to pay. So Pinios now seeks to recover by
counterclaim from the bank what it has failed to recover from Glafki.

The case is put in a number of different ways. But in essence Pinios says that the bank
b was under a duty of care to see to it that Glafki did not under-insure the vessel. It says
that that duty arose either as an implied term of the contract or in tort. The judge has
decided, on orthodox lines, that the bank was under no such duty. The second question
in the appeal is whether he was right.

We were told that the first question is one of considerable general importance to
bankers. But it is logical, and convenient, to consider the second question first, as did the
c judge.

At the end of his speech in *Smith v Littlewoods Organisation Ltd (Chief Constable, Fife
Constabulary, third party)* [1987] 1 All ER 710 at 736, [1987] AC 241 at 280 Lord Goff
epitomised the judicial function as an educated reflex to facts. I have to confess that in
the present case my immediate reflex was that the bank must succeed. I could see no
ground for implying a contractual duty of care in favour of Pinios. At the conclusion of
d the argument, my reflex, though much better educated, remains the same. The judge
dealt with the question shortly as follows:

'Since in this matter the parties have expressly provided for the insurance of the
ship, it is not necessary to imply any further duty of supervision. Had the officious
bystander inquired whether the bank was under a duty to see to it in the interests of
e Pinios that Glafki insured the ship for the full sum required under the mortgages, it
is by no means obvious that all the parties would have acknowledged that they were.
No doubt it was commercially prudent for the bank to ensure that the insurance
was sufficient to cover its own interest, but it does not follow that it was bound to
go further and determine whether Pinios's interest too was properly protected. It
would in the circumstances be unreasonable to impose on the bank a duty to
f reinforce the obligation which Glafki assumed under the agency agreement.'

From this it would appear that the argument in the court below was that the implication
of a term in favour of Pinios was necessary in order to give the contract business efficacy.
Both parties, it must have been argued, would readily have agreed to such a term had
they been asked.

g The notice of appeal and the defendants' skeleton argument reflect this approach. Thus
in para 8(2) of the skeleton argument it is said:

'The existence of Glafki's obligations did not in itself make it unreasonable or
unnecessary for there to be an independent duty on the Bank to take steps to prevent
Glafki from under-insuring the vessel and thereby causing damage to Pinios.'

h The basis for the implication is set out in para 8(6):

'The learned Judge gave insufficient weight to the fact that the Bank, by insisting
on a Management Agreement which deprived Pinios of all rights to safeguard its
own interests and which required the managers, Glafki, to regard the Bank's interests
as paramount, had arrogated to themselves the exclusive power to intervene with
j the managers in the protection of the respective interests of the Bank and Pinios in
the insurance monies.'

The conclusion is set out in para 8(8):

'The implication of the term that the Bank did owe such a duty to Pinios is
necessary to give effect to the intentions of the parties and the duty is both fair and
reasonable.'

The argument was put concisely and forcefully by counsel for the defendants at the outset of his submissions as follows: 'There was nobody to look after Pinios's interests, *a* once the management agreement had been entered into. The bank owed a duty of care to those that it had deprived of the opportunity of protecting themselves.' But in the course of developing his submissions, counsel shied away from the 'officious bystander' test. In this he was wise. For, so far from it being obvious that the bank would have agreed to the suggested implied term, it seems to me quite obvious that it would not. Why should it? *b*

Counsel for the defendants made much of the fact that the management agreement was forced on Pinios. He relied on the observation of Lord Brandon in *Glafki Shipping Co SA v Pinios Shipping Co No 1, The Maira (No 2)* [1986] 2 Lloyd's Rep 12 at 14 that the bank had 'insisted' on Pinios entering into the management agreement, an observation which Leggatt J has adopted as a finding of fact. It is true that the bank had every reason not to exercise its power of sale under art II(18) of the second preferred mortgage, since the *c* market value of the vessel was already far less than the amount due under the combined mortgages. But Pinios also had much to gain from entering into the management agreement. For so long as it remained the owner of the vessel, even if only in name, there was always the possibility that the market would improve and its fortunes recover. Why, in those circumstances, should the bank have agreed to exercise care on Pinios's behalf? If the bystander had asked, 'What happens if Glafki fails or refuses to insure for the full *d* 130%?', the bank's answer would have been simple and straightforward. If Glafki were to refuse to insure for the full sum, Pinios could arrange its own insurance for the balance. It would make no difference to its pocket whether Glafki insured for 100% and Pinios for 30% or Glafki for the full 130%. If, on the other hand, Pinios were only to learn of the under-insurance too late, as in the present case, Pinios could recover its loss as damages from Glafki. It would hardly have entered into the parties' consideration that *e* Glafki might refuse to honour an award. In those circumstances the judge was, if anything, understating the position when he said that it was by no means obvious that the bank would have agreed to act as 'guarantor' for Glafki, more especially as Glafki was Pinios's own nominee to act as manager. To my mind it is obvious that it would not. So counsel for the defendants was, as I say, wise to abandon the officious bystander. No term *f* can be implied on that ground.

But that is by no means the end of the story. Counsel for the defendants submits that this is a case where the law imposes a duty of care, irrespective of what the parties must have intended or agreed. To adopt the terminology of Treitel *Law of Contract* (7th edn, 1987) p 158, counsel relies on a term implied by law as distinct from a term implied in fact. He puts the case in two ways. It is important to keep them separate. In the first *g* place he submits that the relationship between the parties is such that the law imposes on the bank a generalised duty of care towards Pinios. Secondly, he submits that the law imposes a duty of care arising out of the particular facts, namely that the bank actively intervened in the process of arranging the insurance. I will take each of these two ways of putting the case in turn.

That there is a distinction between a term implied in a contract because it is what the *h* parties must have agreed and a term implied by law is now well established, even if, as Lord Wilberforce preferred to put it in *Liverpool City Council v Irwin* [1976] 2 All ER 39 at 43, [1977] AC 239 at 254, the distinction only represents two ends of a 'continuous spectrum'. When *Liverpool City Council v Irwin* was before the Court of Appeal, Lord Denning MR, in a dissenting judgment, said that it was time to get rid of the old clichés about 'necessary to give business efficacy' and the 'officious bystander' (see [1975] 3 All *j* ER 658 at 664, [1976] QB 319 at 329). The law, he said, implies a term whenever it is reasonable to do so, and that is an end of it. He gave, as examples, terms implied in a contract for the sale of goods and many others. Nobody asks in such cases whether the term is one which the parties must have intended or agreed. When the case reached the

House of Lords the decision of the Court of Appeal was reversed. But there was no
a support for the broad principle stated by Lord Denning MR in the Court of Appeal. Lord
Wilberforce described Lord Denning MR's principle as going a long way beyond sound
authority. The point is put very clearly by Lord Cross ([1976] 2 All ER 39 at 46–47,
[1977] AC 239 at 257–258):

> 'When it implies a term in a contract the court is sometimes laying down a
b > general rule that in all contracts of a certain type—sale of goods, master and servant,
> landlord and tenant, and so on—some provision is to be implied unless the parties
> have expressly excluded it. In deciding whether or not to lay down such a prima
> facie rule the court will naturally ask itself whether in the general run of such cases
> the term in question would be one which it would be reasonable to insert.
> Sometimes, however, there is no question of laying down any prima facie rule
c > applicable to all cases of a defined type but what the court is being in effect asked to
> do is to rectify a particular—often a very detailed—contract by inserting in it a term
> which the parties have not expressed. Here it is not enough for the court to say that
> the suggested term is a reasonable one the presence of which would make the
> contract a better or fairer one; it must be able to say that the insertion of the term is
> necessary to give—as it is put—"business efficacy" to the contract and that if its
d > absence had been pointed out at the time both parties—assuming them to have
> been reasonable men—would have agreed without hesitation to its insertion. The
> distinction between the two types of case was pointed out by Viscount Simonds and
> Lord Tucker in their speeches in *Lister v Romford Ice and Cold Storage Co Ltd* [1957] 1
> All ER 125 at 134, 143, [1957] AC 555 at 579, 594, but I think that Lord Denning
> MR in proceeding—albeit with some trepidation—to "kill off" Mackinnon LJ's
e > "officious bystander" must have overlooked it.'

So there is no doubt that there are, in the words of Lord Cross, contracts of a defined
type in which the law will imply a term unless the parties have expressly excluded it.
Can the present case be brought within any defined type? If we were concerned in the
present case with the ordinary relationship of banker and customer, the law would imply
certain obligations on the part of the bank, and a limited duty of care on the part of the
f customer (see *Tai Hing Cotton Mill Ltd v Liu Chong Hing Bank Ltd* [1985] 2 All ER 947,
[1986] AC 80). But we are not here concerned with the ordinary relationship of banker
and customer. We are concerned with a carefully drawn 'one-off' contract between three
parties, made for a particular purpose in special circumstances, and apparently making
full provision for that purpose. I cannot imagine a contract which it would be more
difficult to fit into a 'defined type'.
g But there is a further difficulty. Even if one could conjure up and define a type of
contract into which the present contract could be fitted, there would remain the question
whether the term on which counsel for the defendants seeks to rely should be implied.
In the passage I have quoted from Lord Cross's speech in *Liverpool City Council v Irwin*, he
appears to have accepted that where the court is laying down a general rule for all
contracts of a certain type (sale of goods, master and servant, landlord and tenant and so
h on), the court asks whether the term is one which it would be *reasonable* to insert in the
general run of such cases. But Lord Wilberforce took a rather different line. In his view
only such obligations should be read into the contract 'as the nature of the contract itself
implicitly requires, no more, no less; a test in other words of necessity' (see [1976] 2 All
ER 39 at 44, [1977] AC 239 at 254). It was Lord Wilberforce's test that the Privy Council
j adopted in *Tai Hing Cotton Mill Ltd v Liu Chong Hing Bank Ltd*. If, in that case, the Privy
Council found it unnecessary to imply into an ordinary contract between banker and
customer a duty wider than the duties recognised in *London Joint Stock Bank Ltd v
Macmillan* [1918] AC 777, [1918–19] All ER Rep 30 and *Greenwood v Martins Bank Ltd*
[1933] AC 51, [1932] All ER Rep 318, I can see no necessity for implying any duty of

care on the part of the bank in the present case. For if we were to imply a duty of care on the part of the bank to see that Glafki did not under-insure the vessel, should we not also *a* have to imply a duty of care to see that Glafki fulfilled its other specific duties under cl 3 of the management agreement? Should we not have to imply a duty to see that Glafki purchased all necessary stores and bunkers at the best price? Should we not have to imply a duty in relation to the supervision of repairs? Clearly not. Such an implication would not only be unnecessary, but wholly unreasonable. So I see no necessity to imply a duty of care in relation to the procuring of insurance, assuming, contrary to my view, that this *b* is the type of case in which the court would imply a term irrespective of the parties' presumed intentions.

Counsel for the defendants returned over and over again in the course of his argument to the close relationship which existed between the bank and Pinios. But the closeness of the relationship does not in itself justify the implication of a contractual term.

So I turn to the second way in which the case is put. It is said that the bank owed Pinios *c* a duty of care because it actively intervened in the procuring of the insurance. Here counsel is on firmer legal ground. But he is in difficulty on the facts.

The authorities on which counsel relies for this part of his argument are *Cuckmere Brick Co Ltd v Mutual Finance Ltd* [1971] 2 All ER 633, [1971] Ch 949, *Standard Chartered Bank Ltd v Walker* [1982] 3 All ER 938, [1982] 1 WLR 1410 and *American Express International Banking Corp v Hurley* [1985] 3 All ER 564. In the *Cuckmere Brick Co* case it was held that *d* a mortgagee, in exercising his power of sale, owes a duty of care to the mortgagor to obtain the best or 'proper' price. In the *Standard Chartered Bank* case it was held, in interlocutory proceedings, that a receiver, realising assets under a debenture, owes a duty of care to the borrower to obtain the best price that circumstances permit. In the *American Express* case it was submitted that the decision in the *Standard Chartered Bank* case established no more than that the point was arguable. Mann J refused to accept that *e* submission. After quoting extensive passages from the *Cuckmere Brick Co* case and the *Standard Chartered Bank* case, he summarised the law as follows ([1985] 3 All ER 564 at 571):

> '(i) The mortgagee when selling mortgaged property is under a duty to a guarantor of the mortgagor's debt to take reasonable care in all the circumstances of the case to *f* obtain the true market value of that property. (ii) A receiver is under a like duty. (iii) The mortgagee is not responsible for what a receiver does whilst he is the mortgagor's agent unless the mortgagee directs or interferes with the receiver's activities. (iv) The mortgagee is responsible for what a receiver does whilst he is the mortgagee's agent and acting as such.'

Counsel for the bank does not dispute these propositions. He accepts that if, in the *g* words of Mann J, the bank had directed or interfered with Glafki's activities in relation to the insurance the bank would have owed Pinios a duty of care. Similar language to that used by Mann J is to be found in the *Standard Chartered Bank* case [1982] 3 All ER 938 at 942, [1982] 1 WLR 1410 at 1416, where Lord Denning MR said:

> 'The debenture holder, the bank, is not responsible for what the receiver does *h* except in so far as it gives him directions or interferes with his conduct of the realisation. If it does so, then it too is under a duty to use reasonable care towards the company and the guarantor.'

So the question is whether the bank directed or interfered with Glafki's activities when arranging the insurance. That the bank was *entitled* to direct or interfere is clear enough. *j* Clause 13 of the management agreement provides:

> '*Directions and Approvals*—In acting under this Agreement the Agent must insofar as this proves possible or realisable accept and rely upon directions instructions consent or approvals made or given on behalf of with the consent of the Bank after

having received written notice from the Bank by any Officer of the Bank or by any other person designated in writing by the Bank to give such directions approvals or consent . . .'

But whether the bank *in fact* directed or interfered is less clear. Neither side is appealing on fact, so we are bound by the findings of the judge in the court below. Owing to the way in which the case was argued before him, his findings are rather less precise on this point than they might be. He says:

'Although for its own protection it would no doubt have been prudent for the bank to check whether the amount of the insurance continued to cover [Pinios's] debt, they [the officers of the bank] did not regard their responsibility as going further than that. All decisions about the management and operation of the ship were left to Glafki, including the renewal of the insurance.'

The reference to 'renewal of the insurance' presumably includes the renewal in April 1978.

Later on in his judgment the judge refers to the evidence of Mr Theodoropoulos, the manager of the London branch of the bank. On 16 July 1980 Mr Theodoropoulos signed a statement which was intended for use by Glafki in the arbitration proceedings between Glafki and Pinios. In para 4 he said:

'I was fully aware and approved of the continuation of the insurance of the Maira at a total of £10 million in February and April 1978.'

In a subsequent statement, prepared for the present proceedings, Mr Theodoropoulos said that he never discussed the amount of the insurance cover with anybody. He had asked for para 4 of his earlier statement to be deleted, as it was not true. But this had not been done.

Mr Theodoropoulos gave evidence at the trial. The judge disbelieved him. But the only finding that the judge makes is in terms of para 4 of the earlier statement, namely that 'when the insurance was renewed Mr Theodoropoulos on behalf of the bank knew and approved of what was done'.

This finding places us in some difficulty, since it was common ground before us that Mr Theodoropoulos left the London branch of the bank very shortly after the renewal of the insurance in February, to take up a new position as general manager of an associated insurance company in Athens. It seems unlikely that he would have been asked to approve the April insurance in that capacity. That would have been a task for his successor in London. Moreover it was never pleaded by Pinios that Pinios would rely on para 4 of Mr Theodoropoulos's earlier statement in relation to the *April* renewal. It was relied on in relation to the *February* renewal only. Counsel for the defendants tells us that that was a simple oversight on the part of the pleader.

So the position on the facts is not altogether satisfactory. But since neither side is appealing on the facts, we need only concern ourselves with the findings made by the judge. What is meant when it is said that Mr Theodoropoulos, on behalf of the bank, 'knew and approved' of what was done? Does it mean that the bank actively intervened? Does it mean that the bank 'directed and interfered' with Glafki's activities, so as to give rise to a duty of care, which, if that is the meaning, counsel for the bank concedes? Or does it mean simply that the bank did not object?

In my view it means the latter. I form that view for two reasons. First, it is more consistent with the judge's earlier finding that 'all decisions about the management and operation of the ship were left to Glafki, including the renewal of the insurance'. Second it is more consistent with the contemporary correspondence. Both parties were content that we should look at the correspondence, presumably as some sort of aid to construing the judge's findings.

Starting with the February renewal, the previous cover was due to expire on 8 February 1978. The first the bank heard of the matter was a telex dated 9 February from Messrs *a* Frank B Hall, the New York brokers, confirming that they had already placed 10% of the insurance in New York. When the bank inquired about the remaining 90%, it was informed that this had already been placed by Messrs Colburn French & Kneen in London. So the correspondence does not support any suggestion of *prior* intervention by the bank. As for the April renewal, the first reference in the correspondence is a letter from the bank dated 12 April to the two brokers asking whether the insurance had been *b* renewed. This was not only long after the renewal date, it was also after the vessel had become a total loss. No doubt the bank was relieved to hear that the insurances had indeed been renewed. Again the correspondence does not suggest that there had been any active intervention before the April renewal.

The only support which counsel for the defendants could derive from the correspondence is a letter from the brokers to the bank dated 10 February 1978 *c* confirming that the insurances had been effected, and undertaking, inter alia—

> 'to advise you immediately of any material changes which are proposed to be made in the terms of the insurances and following an application received from you not later than 1st March, 1978 . . .'

But at best this letter points only to advance knowledge on the part of the bank of the *d* proposed terms of renewal, coupled with an opportunity to intervene. There is a world of difference between an opportunity to intervene and active intervention. As Lord Goff pointed out in *Smith v Littlewoods Organisation Ltd* [1987] 1 All ER 710 at 729, [1987] AC 241 at 271, the law is always slow to impose liability for what he called a pure omission. In that case he was concerned with tort, but the same must apply when the court is considering whether to imply a term in a contract. *e*

There is one further small pointer as to what the judge had in mind when he used the phrase 'knew and approved of what was done'. When stating his conclusion, in the passage which I have already cited, the judge said that it was not necessary to imply any further duty of supervision. If the judge had already found as a fact that there had been active intervention by the bank, then 'supervision' is surely not the word he would have *f* used to describe the alleged duty.

So I would hold that, in finding that the bank 'knew and approved', the judge meant no more than that the bank did not disapprove, or, in other words, that the bank acquiesced. The words fall short of a finding of active intervention, which is the finding which counsel for the defendants needs if he is to succeed on this part of his argument. In the absence of that finding, I would hold that Pinios has failed to establish a duty of care arising on the particular facts of the case, just as it has failed to establish a generalised *g* duty applying to all contracts of this 'type'.

For completeness I should add one last point. Counsel for the defendants did not seek to argue that the bank is vicariously liable for the shortcomings of Glafki. In the *American Express* case [1985] 3 All ER 564 Mann J held that the receiver became the bank's agent after the company had gone into liquidation. He therefore held the bank liable for the *h* receiver's negligence on ordinary agency principles. Such an argument would not have been open here.

Turning from contract to tort, counsel for the defendants argues strenuously that even if he fails in contract he is entitled to succeed in tort. He relies on *Home Office v Dorset Yacht Co Ltd* [1970] 2 All ER 294, [1970] AC 1004, and the much discussed and increasingly precarious dictum of Lord Wilberforce in *Anns v Merton London Borough* *j* [1977] 2 All ER 492 at 498, [1978] AC 728 at 751. But those were cases where there was no contract between the parties. So it was tort, or nothing. Here there is a contract, and a most elaborate contract at that.

Now I accept that in a large class of cases it always was, and maybe still is, possible for the plaintiff to sue either in contract or in tort. The obvious example would be actions

against innkeepers and the like, and those exercising a common calling. In *Brown v*
a *Boorman* (1842) 3 QB 511 at 525–526, 114 ER 603 at 608–609 Tindall CJ, delivering the
judgment of the Court of Exchequer Chamber, said:

> 'That there is a large class of cases in which the foundation of the action springs
> out of privity of contract between the parties, but in which, nevertheless, the
> remedy for the breach, or non-performance, is indifferently either assumpsit or case
> upon tort, is not disputed. Such are actions against attorneys, surgeons and other
b > professional men, for want of competent skill or proper care in the service they
> undertake to render ... The principle in all these cases would seem to be that the
> contract creates a duty, and the neglect to perform that duty, or the nonfeasance is a
> ground of action upon a tort.'

In the House of Lords Lord Campbell said (1844) 11 Cl & Fin 1 at 44, 8 ER 1003 at 1018–
c 1019:

> '... wherever there is a contract, and something to be done in the course of the
> employment which is the subject of that contract, if there is a breach of a duty in
> the course of that employment, the plaintiff may either recover in tort or in
> contract.'

d See also *Esso Petroleum Co Ltd* [1976] 2 All ER 5 at 15, [1976] QB 801 at 819 per Lord
Denning MR.

But so far as I know it has never been the law that a plaintiff who has the choice of
suing in contract or tort can fail in contract yet nevertheless succeed in tort; and, if it ever
was the law, it has ceased to be the law since *Tai Hing Cotton Mill Ltd v Liu Chong Hing Bank
Ltd* [1985] 2 All ER 947, [1986] AC 80. In that case the bank advanced very much the
e same argument as has been advanced by counsel for the defendants. But the argument
was rejected. Lord Scarman said ([1985] 2 All ER 947 at 957, [1986] 1 AC 80 at 107):

> 'Their Lordships do not believe that there is anything to the advantage of the
> law's development in searching for a liability in tort where the parties are in a
> contractual relationship. This is particularly so in a commercial relationship.
f > Though it is possible as a matter of legal semantics to conduct an analysis of the
> rights and duties inherent in some contractual relationships including that of banker
> and customer either as a matter of contract law when the question will be what, if
> any, terms are to be implied or as a matter of tort law when the task will be to
> identify a duty arising from the proximity and character of the relationship between
> the parties, their Lordships believe it to be correct in principle and necessary for the
g > avoidance of confusion in the law to adhere to the contractual analysis: on principle
> because it is a relationship in which the parties have, subject to a few exceptions, the
> right to determine their obligations to each other, and for the avoidance of confusion
> because different consequences do follow according to whether liability arises from
> contract or tort, eg in the limitation of action ... Their Lordships do not, therefore,
> embark on an investigation whether in the relationship of banker and customer it
h > is possible to identify tort as well as contract as a source of the obligations owed by
> the one to the other. Their Lordships do not, however, accept that the parties'
> mutual obligations in tort can be any greater than those to be found expressly or by
> necessary implication in their contract.'

Nothing in the subsequent cases at first instance on which counsel for the defendants
j relied throws any doubt on the appropriateness of Lord Scarman's observations to the
present case. I would hold without hesitation that if, in a case such as the present, the
plaintiff fails in contract he must necessarily fail in tort.

The position would be different if the contract and the tort lay in different fields. Thus,
if, to take a simple example, I give my employee a lift home and injure him by my
careless driving, then obviously he will not be prevented from recovering from me in

tort because of the existence between us of a contract of employment. But that is not this case.

I return now to consider the bank's claim for compound interest. I start by setting out the relevant provisions of the loan agreement between Pinios and the bank dated 8 February 1977. The agreement provides that, in consideration of the bank agreeing to issue a letter of credit in favour of the builders, Pinios would execute a second preferred mortgage as security for the payment on demand of all sums which the bank might be called on to pay under the letter of guarantee. Clause (8) provides:

> '(A) We shall pay interest on the amount payable and paid by you under your said Letter of Guarantee at the rate (hereinafter called "the agreed interest rate") of two per cent (2%) per annum above the rate at which three (3) or six (6) months deposits of amounts in United States Dollars equivalent to the amount of each Promissory Note payable under the said Letter of Guarantee are offered to you by first class Banks in the London Interbank Eurodollar Market with a minimum rate of interest of eight per cent (8%) per annum.
>
> (B) If you shall at any time determine that by reason of changes affecting the London Inter Bank Euro Dollar Market adequate and fair means do not exist for ascertaining the agreed interest rate you may give notice of such fact to us and we shall discuss with you an alternative basis for securing the amount paid under the said Letter of Guarantee on the basis that the return to you shall be the same as that provided for in this agreement. If no agreement is reached upon an alternative basis for securing the amount paid under the said Letter of Guarantee before the next succeeding interest payment date after such notice shall have been given, then the amount paid by you under the said Letter of Guarantee shall become repayable and if not repaid shall bear interest at the amount provided in sub-clause (C) below for interest in default.
>
> (C) If any interest shall be due and unpaid four working days after the relevant interest payment date the amount of interest shall be recalculated from the interest payment date until the date of payment at the rate of two per cent (2%) per annum above the agreed interest rate.
>
> (D) Each determination under this clause shall be conclusive.'

The second preferred mortgage provides for the vessel to stand as security—

> 'for the payment by [Pinios] on demand of the total amount of its said liability ... and also the payment of interest thereon at the rate of Two per cent (2%) above the current London Euro Dollar Market rate in respect of three (3) or six (6) months deposits whichever be the higher rate for the time being with a minimum of Eight per cent (8%)...'

A little later the mortgage provides:

> 'In case of default in paying any amount due hereunder within four (4) days of the same having been demanded [Pinios] will pay interest after the expiration of the aforesaid period of four (4) days at the rate of Two per cent (2%) per annum above the rate hereinbefore provided until repayment to the Mortgagee in full.'

It will be noticed that, although the mortgage is annexed to the agreement, there are some differences in the language of the two interest provisions. Thus in the mortgage it is provided that the rate of interest should be the higher of the three or six months' deposit rate, plus 2%, whereas in the agreement the words 'whichever be the higher' are omitted. Another difference is that the default rate of interest in the mortgage applies when an amount due has not been paid within four days of the same having been demanded; whereas by cl (8)(C) of the agreement the default rate is payable if any interest remains unpaid four working days after 'the relevant interest payment date'. There is a further reference to 'interest payment date' in cl (8)(B).

Leggatt J regarded the compound interest question as simple. Having set out the terms
a of the mortgage which I have just quoted, he continued:

> 'The effect of this was to entitle the bank to charge compound interest on the
> outstanding debt. The relationship governed by the mortgage never came to an
> end; but, even if it were not so and the right to charge compound interest is to be
> founded on implied agreement, the conclusion would be the same.'

b I find this hard to follow. The judge seems to have thought that there was an express
provision in the mortgage entitling the bank to charge compound interest. But I can find
no such provision. There is a provision for an increase in the rate of interest in the event
of default. But there is no reference anywhere to compound interest; nor is there any
provision for periodic rests. Counsel for the bank submitted that the reference to the
three- or six-month deposit rate whichever be the higher imports periodic rests. But why
c should it? It fixes the *rate* of interest, not the frequency with which interest is capitalised.

Counsel for the bank relies also on the reference to 'interest payment date' in cl (8)(B)
and (C). But again it is impossible to spell out from these references any right to capitalise
the interest. So I would reject the submission that there is any express agreement to pay
compound interest.

Then, was there an implied agreement to pay compound interest? Counsel for the
d defendants concedes that the bank was entitled to charge compound interest with
quarterly rests during the currency of the banker/customer relationship. But once the
account was closed the banker/customer relationship ceased. According to counsel that
occurred on 13 November 1978 when the bank demanded payment. Thereafter the
bank was in the same position as any other creditor, and became entitled to simple
interest only.

e Counsel for the bank on the other hand says that the account was never closed, and the
banker/customer relationship never ceased. It continued until judgment. On that view
the bank was entitled, he says, to continue to charge compound interest, and the judge
was right to give judgment on that basis.

That being the issue between the parties, it is unnecessary to consider whether counsel
f for the defendants was right to concede that the bank was entitled to charge compound
interest up to 13 November 1978. It could be said, as O'Connor LJ has pointed out, that
the relationship between the parties was not the ordinary relationship of banker and
customer, and that in any event the express right to charge a higher rate of interest in the
event of default, and the provision for recalculating the interest 'until the date of
payment', is fundamentally inconsistent with any implied right to charge compound
g interest. Be that as it may, I am content to assume that the bank was entitled to charge
compound interest up to 13 November 1978. On what basis was it so entitled? Why
should the law imply a right to charge compound interest in favour of the bank, when
the parties have abstained from expressing any such right for themselves?

As with so much else in our law, the explanation is historical. A convenient point to
start is the beginning of the nineteenth century when the Usury Acts were still in force.
h An Act of Henry VIII had fixed the maximum rate of interest which could lawfully be
charged on money lent at 10% pa (37 Hen 8 c 9 (1545)). The rate of interest was gradually
reduced in successive reigns because, as is stated in the preamble to a 1713 Act (12 Anne
Stat 2 c 16 (1713)), 'the Reducing of Interest to ten, and from thence to eight, and thence
to six in the Hundred, hath, from Time to Time, by Experience been found very
beneficial to the Advancement of Trade . . .' By the beginning of the nineteenth century
j the maximum lawful rate of interest stood at 5% pa. Any contract reserving a higher
rate of interest was 'utterly void'. If therefore a contract between banker and customer
provided for compound interest at 5% pa with half-yearly rests, the contract was void;
for the true rate of interest would be more than 5%. But bankers found a way round this
difficulty. At the end of six months the parties were presumed to settle their account,
without any previous agreement. Instead of the customer paying the amount of interest

then due, it was added to the principal. The banker forbore to sue for principal and interest, since he was content to charge interest on the new principal over the next six *a* months.

This practice was upheld as lawful by Lord Eldon LC in *Ex p Bevan* (1803) 9 Ves 223 at 224, 32 ER 588:

'So this is legal between merchants; where there is no agreement to lend to either; but they stipulate for mutual transactions; each making advances; and that, if at the *b* end of six months the balance is with A., he will lend to B.; and *vice versa.*'

The principle was restated by the House of Lords in *Fergusson v Fyffe* (1841) 8 Cl & Fin 121 at 140, [1835–42] All ER Rep 48 at 50 as follows:

'Generally a contract or promise for compound interest is not available in England, as was decided in *Ex parte Bevan* except perhaps as to mercantile accounts current *c* for mutual transactions . . .'

Counsel for the bank argued that once the Usury Acts had been repealed, as they were by the Usury Laws Repeal Act 1854, *Fergusson v Fyffe* ceased to have any relevance: cessante ratione legis, cessat lex ipsa. But, with respect, that argument was hopeless. It is only necessary to refer to the decision of a strong Court of Appeal in *Deutsche Bank und Disconto-Gesellschaft v Banque des Marchands de Moscou* (1931) 4 Legal Decisions Affecting *d* Bankers 293. Scrutton LJ clearly regarded *Fergusson v Fyffe* as being good law when he said (at 295):

'The House of Lords in *Fergusson* v. *Fyffe* treated compound interest as not payable, except perhaps on mercantile accounts current for mutual transactions.'

Greer LJ said (at 295–296): *e*

'I regard the law as stated in *Ex parte Bevan*, and *Fergusson* v. *Fyffe* as laying down two propositions, first, that there can be no title to compound interest without a contract expressed or implied between the debtor and creditor; and, secondly, that it is never implied except as to mercantile accounts current for mutual transactions.' *f*

The corollary of the rule in *Fergusson v Fyffe* is that once the account has ceased to be 'a mercantile account current for mutual transactions' (in other words, once the account has been closed and the relationship of banker and customer brought to an end) the bank is entitled to simple interest only. This is clear from *Fergusson v Fyffe* itself, where, as it happens, the balance of account was in favour of the customer. It was held that the bank was liable for compound interest up to the date of the customer's death but not thereafter. *g* Lord Cottenham LC said (8 Cl & Fin 121 at 139, [1835–42] All ER Rep 48 at 50):

'From that time there was no party with whom any account current could be carried on, there not having been any representative of [the customer] for many years afterwards.'

The point was put very clearly, long after the Usury Acts had been repealed, by James *h* V-C in *Williamson v Williamson* (1869) LR 7 Eq 542 at 546. That was another case of banker and customer. It was held that the bank was entitled to charge compound interest up to the date of the customer's death, but not thereafter:

'With regard to the interest accruing after the testator's death, I should take some time before assenting to the proposition that the account did not bear simple *j* interest, but I have not to decide this point. I am bound, however, by the authority of the House of Lords to hold that compound interest is incidental to the continuance of the relation of banker and customer. From the testator's death therefore, only simple interest at 5 per cent. will be allowed on the account.'

a But the death of the customer is not the only event which will bring the relationship of banker and customer to an end. In *Crosskill v Bower* (1863) 32 Beav 86, 55 ER 34 the customer, who was heavily overdrawn, executed two deeds whereby he assigned his entire estate to trustees for the benefit of his creditors. Thereafter he ceased to carry on business. He neither paid into nor drew on his bank account, and 'the account was virtually closed'. Romilly MR said (32 Beav 86 at 93, 55 ER 34 at 37):

b 'But this stoppage of interest is not confined to the case of death; a customer may say to his banker "I close my account with you, and I shall have no further dealings with you from this day," thereupon the balance of the account, whichever way it may be, would have to be ascertained at that period, and then all interest would cease. It depends on the pleasure of the bankers, either to enforce payment of the balance due to them or to abstain from doing so, or to obtain such security for it as c they may be able. If the last course were adopted, a new contract would be entered into, which would regulate the matter of interest.'

In the *Deutsche Bank* case (1931) 4 Legal Decisions Affecting Bankers 293, to which I have already referred, the plaintiff bank advanced over £100,000 to the defendant bank before the 1914–18 war. In 1930 the plaintiffs issued a writ for the recovery of the sum lent together with compound interest. Rowlatt J held that the relation of banker and d customer continued despite the war. After referring to *Fergusson v Fyffe*, he said (at 294–295):

e 'I cannot see why the mere allowing an account to become dormant, as opposed to an active account, affects it as from the moment of the last transaction. The account does not become dormant to-morrow, because you have had a transaction to-day ... It seems to me I must find something analogous to the death of the party to effect a termination of the relationship or contract, of whatever you like, which governs this matter ... What am I to lay my finger on for saying when they stopped the currency of this system of half-yearly rests? I do not find anything that stopped it, and therefore I must hold it has gone on ...'

f But Rowlatt J's decision on compound interest was reversed in the Court of Appeal. Scrutton LJ, after referring to *Fergusson v Fyffe* in the sentence I have already quoted, continued (at 295):

g 'In my opinion, after December 31st, 1914, this was not such an account; Germany was at war with Russia, and there were no mutual dealings between the Deutsche Bank and the Moscow Merchants Bank, only debits of interest and credits for securities sold by the English Government. I should be of the opinion, if it were necessary to decide the question, that compound interest should stop after the account of December 31st, 1914; or that, at any rate, it should stop after the order for winding up in 1918 ...'

Greer LJ said (at 296):

h 'It seems to me that upon the facts stated in the case there was a contract implied from the transactions between the parties that compound interest would be allowed on one side or the other on the current account so long as it was a current account; but that when War broke out, and it became impossible for the Russian Bank to keep the account going by payments into it to set off against withdrawals, it ceased to be a current account, and the fact that the amount due on the loan account and j interest was transferred to current account is not sufficient to show that by not objecting to the interest then due being added to the principal, the defendants agreed that when placed in the current account it should carry further compound interest. In my opinion, though it appeared in the bank's books as a current account, there was nothing proved in the case sufficient to found a decision that the Russian

Bank agreed that once it was placed in the current account it should carry compound interest, whether that account continued to be in reality a current account or not.'   *a*

Romer LJ said (at 297):

'In these circumstances it seems plain that the defendants must be taken to have agreed to be charged with compound interest. It is, however, established by several authorities that this implied agreement must be taken to be limited in its operation to the time during which the relation of banker and customer existed between the *b* parties. The plaintiffs cannot justify the charge of compound interest after the mercantile account current for mutual transactions had been closed and the relations between the parties had become merely that of creditor and debtor (see *Fergusson* v. *Fyffe*; *Crosskill* v. *Bowe*; *Williamson* v. *Williamson* ((1869) LR 7 Eq 542).'

The law is well summarised in *Paget on Banking* (9th edn, 1982) p 116 as follows: *c*

'The indorsement of a statement of claim must show how the claim is based. Where the customer has acquiesced in the charging of interest, that would justify the claim. Such acquiescence will justify the charging compound interest or interest with periodical rests, so long as the relation of banker and customer exists, and the relationship is not changed into that of mortgagee and mortgagor.'
                                                                                    d
Counsel for the bank relied on certain tax cases which are cited on the following page of *Paget*, and on the decision of the House of Lords in an Irish case, *Yourell v Hibernian Bank Ltd* [1918] AC 372. That decision appeared, at first sight, to lend some assistance to his argument. The case is complicated on the facts. But the key to understanding the case is that the account remained, in the words of Lord Atkinson, a 'living mercantile account' right down to and, indeed, beyond the issue of the writ in 1913 (at 389); see also the *e* observations of Lord Finlay LC (at 380). The bank was in truth seeking to 'rewrite' the account, as counsel for the defendants submitted, in order to maximise its security. This it was not entitled to do.

With that brief resumé of the law, I turn to the point for decision. Counsel for the defendants conceded, as I have said, that the bank is entitled to compound interest down to 13 November 1978, when the bank demanded repayment. The point for decision is *f* whether, once the bank had demanded repayment, the relation of banker and customer ceased. Did the relationship change into that of mortgagee and mortgagor, as counsel for the defendants submits, in which case the bank would be entitled to simple interest only? Or did it remain a relationship of banker and customer?

The judge dealt with the matter as follows:
                                                                                    g
'The relationship governed by the mortgage never came to an end; but, even if it were not so and the right to charge compound interest is to be founded on implied agreement, the conclusion would be the same. The account on which the bank is suing is indisputably a mercantile account. There is no evidence that the account was closed nor that it had ceased to be current for mutual transactions. The fact that Pinios has not used the account does not mean that it is not current. Both Pinios and *h* the account have continued in being, as has the bank. Nothing has occurred to render the operation of the account impossible. The relationship between the parties is unchanged. Neither the mortgage nor any ancillary agreement relating to the account was ever superseded or supplanted by any subsequent agreement between the parties. The bank's right to charge compound interest has therefore remained unimpaired.'   *j*

The difficulty with this passage is that it treats the relationship created by the mortgage as the crucial relationship for determining whether the bank is entitled to compound interest. This with respect was erroneous. It goes without saying that the mortgage, as a security, has not been determined or affected in any way. But the mortgage is not 'an

account current for mutual transactions' as that phrase has been understood since
a *Fergusson v Fyffe.* The only account which could perhaps be regarded as an 'account
current for mutual transactions' is the bank account. The question is whether the bank
account remained open, or, in other words, whether the relationship of banker and
customer continued after the demand for repayment. That question is not answered by
asking whether the mortgage continued as the bank's security. It obviously did. So, with
great respect, the judge's findings in the passage I have quoted seem to be based on the
b wrong premise.

But that is only the start of our difficulties. For the judge only allowed the compound
interest point to be taken at all on the footing that it could be argued as a point of law.
His reason was that the point was only taken by Pinios at a late stage before him, and had
not been pleaded. That may be so. But it is the bank who ought to have pleaded the basis
of its claim for compound interest in the first place. That it never did. So I do not think
c that the failure to take the point until a late stage can be blamed entirely on Pinios.

But, wherever the blame may lie, the fact remains that we are required to determine
whether the relationship of banker and customer continued, as a question of law, with
very few facts to go on. Almost all we have is the account submitted with the letter
before action, and the final account submitted shortly before the trial.

These show that interest was charged, with value date 15 September 1977, on the
d amount of the first promissory note paid by the bank under its letter of guarantee on 16
August 1977. Thereafter interest was charged at quarterly intervals, with value dates of
15 December 1977, 15 March, 15 June and 15 September 1978. We do not know how
often Pinios received bank statements during the currency of the account. But, in the
light of the quarterly interest charges to which I have referred, counsel for the defendants
was sensible to concede that Pinios had 'acquiesced' in the charging of compound interest.
e   If so, then an agreement to pay compound interest can be implied. As Lord Manners
LC said in the Irish case of *Lord Clancarty v Latouche* (1810) 1 Ball & B 420 at 429–430:

> 'From the Acquiescence of Mr. *Conolly* I ought to presume an Agreement at the
> End of every Year, that the interest then due, should become Principal and carry
> Interest, which according to *Ex parte Bevan* ((1803) 9 Ves 223, 32 ER 558), this Court
f > will admit of, and that was a Case of Half yearly Rests.'

But did the acquiescence continue beyond 13 November 1978 when the bank demanded
repayment? There is nothing in the letter itself which indicates that the bank would go
on charging compound interest, assuming that that would be sufficient to establish a
continuing entitlement; and we were told that once the bank demanded repayment it
ceased to send bank statements. True there is no evidence to that effect. But it would
g have been odd if the bank had continued to send statements once it had called in the
loan, and even odder once it had commenced proceedings. Pinios only learnt for certain
that the bank had continued to charge compound interest when it received the bank's
final account shortly before the trial commenced in 1987. So far as we know there were
no statements in the intervening eight years. In those circumstances it could not be right
h to infer that Pinios knew it was being charged compound interest, and without
knowledge there could be no continuing acquiescence.

Then can the bank rely on *prior* acquiescence to justify a claim for compound interest
continuing after 13 November 1978? I do not think so. It is difficult to see how the
relationship of banker and customer could be said to have continued after the bank had
commenced proceedings. But I would go further. In my judgment the correct inference
j and, indeed, the only possible inference is that the relationship ceased when the bank
demanded repayment. The account was then closed. A line was drawn. Instead of banker
and customer, the relationship became that of creditor and debtor, without the
superadded rights and obligations imported by the banker/customer relationship. It is
true that certain payments are shown as having been made into the account after the
bank had demanded repayment. I need not go into details. They are equally consistent

with payments having been made in reduction of the mortgage debt. They do not show
a continuing relationship of banker and customer in any true sense.

For the reasons I have given, I would hold that the bank is entitled to simple interest
only after 13 November 1978. I would summarise those reasons as follows: (i) there is no
right to compound interest save by agreement, express or implied, or custom binding on
the parties; (ii) there was no express agreement to pay compound interest in the present
case; (iii) an agreement to pay compound interest may be implied by virtue of
acquiescence (see *Lord Clancarty v Latouche* (1810) 1 Ball & B 420 at 429–430); but (iv) such
an agreement is not normally implied except as to 'mercantile accounts current for
mutual transactions' (see the *Deutsche Bank* case (1931) 4 Legal Decisions Affecting Bankers
293 at 295–286 per Greer LJ; (v) it is open to question whether the agreement between
the bank and Pinios dated 8 February 1977 was an account current for mutual
transactions; but, even if it was, it ceased to be such an account when the bank closed the
account and demanded repayment on 13 November 1978; and (vi) the bank never
pleaded or proved a custom entitling it to continue to charge compound interest after
the account had been closed, or, a fortiori, after it had issued proceedings for the recovery
of debt.

We were told by counsel for the bank that a decision to the above effect would cause
dismay and consternation among bankers. If so, the remedy lies in their own hands.
They should make express provision for compound interest in their contracts. Since the
repeal of the Usury Acts there has been nothing to stop them. Why they have not done
so I do not know. But it may be that the explanation is to be found in the mordant
observations of Lord Atkin in *Paton v IRC* [1938] 1 All ER 786 at 788, [1938] AC 341 at
347:

> 'It is obvious that the system adopted by banks, which seems to have been
> common practice in the time of LORD ELDON, L.C., is for the purpose of giving them
> compound interest without perhaps flaunting that fact before their customers.'

As for the rate of simple interest, counsel for the defendants argued that interest is
recoverable under s 35A of the Supreme Court Act 1981. But I see no reason why the
bank should not receive simple interest at the rate stipulated in the agreement dated 8
February 1977, which provides, as does the mortgage, for interest to continue until
payment.

So I would allow the appeal on the compound interest point, but dismiss it on all other
points.

NICHOLLS LJ. I agree that an order should be made in the terms proposed by
Lloyd LJ. I add some observations of my own because we are differing from Leggatt J on
one point of general importance, and out of deference to the arguments of counsel.

The bank's duty

Neither the National Bank of Greece SA (the bank) nor Pinios Shipping Co No 1
(Pinios) sought to challenge any of the judge's conclusions of fact. So I consider first what
were the judge's relevant conclusions of fact. This is necessary, because counsel put
different interpretations on the judge's finding that 'when the insurance was renewed Mr
Theodoropoulos on behalf of the bank knew and approved of what was done'.

We were referred to some of the evidential material which was before the judge, so as
to enable us the better to appreciate the setting against which the judge reached his
conclusions. In my view, read in its context in the judgment, the phrase 'knew and
approved' does not mean that before renewing the insurance in April 1978 Glafki
Shipping Co SA (Glafki) was given instructions by the bank on the amount of the
insurance which the bank required or wished to be effected, nor does it mean even that
at the time the bank's approval of the amount was communicated to Glafki. In the
crucial sentence the judge made a finding as to Mr Theodoropoulos's state of mind: he

knew what was being done by Glafki regarding the insurance and, for his part, he
a approved of what was being done. We have been shown nothing which would justify
giving to the word 'approved' in the judge's finding any wider meaning than that.

Of course, the pattern of dealings between two parties may be such that the failure of
one to object to a course proposed by the other is fairly to be understood by the other as
assent. But there is no finding of fact to this effect by the judge in the present case.

The second factual point to be noted is this. The judge said that both Mr
b Demetracopoulos, the bank's loan officer, and Mr Theodoropoulos, the manager of the
bank's main London branch, would have known 'if they had thought about it' that the
1978 insurance was likely to have been a breach of the obligation to keep the ship insured
for not less than 130% of the amount secured by the mortgage (which must be a reference
to both mortgages). The judge also found that they (the officers of the bank) did not
regard their responsibility as going further 'than that', namely checking, for the bank's
c own protection, that the amount of the insurance continued to cover the bank's debt.
The judge's findings, thus, do not go so far as to find that, at the time when the bank
through Mr Theodoropoulos approved of the April 1978 insurance, he or any other
officer in the bank appreciated that, or even considered whether, the amount of the cover
fell short of the 130% figure.

The third point to be noted is the judge's finding that 'all decisions about the
d management and operation of the ship were left to Glafki, including the renewal of the
insurance'.

Those being the facts as found, it follows that this is not a case where the bank
intervened in the carrying out by Glafki of its duties in the way it considered fit. The
bank did not instruct Glafki on the amount of insurance cover to be effected. Had it done
so, I think that (depending on the particular facts) there might well have been a liability
e on the bank in respect of the under-insurance. Glafki's obligations under cll 1 and 2 of
the management agreement required it to insure for the 130% figure. Take, therefore,
by way of hypothetical example, a case where without reference to Pinios and without
the knowledge of Pinios the bank intervenes and exercises its powers under the
management agreement by directing Glafki to insure for a much lower sum than 130%,
f or not to insure at all, even though such an instruction is not in accordance with the way
in which any reasonably prudent shipowner would operate, and even though (depending
on the amount of the insurance) that might be an event of default under the first
mortgage and under the bank's own mortgage. I would have no doubt that such an
instruction would be a breach of the duty of care which in my view this agreement
implicitly requires shall be exercised by the bank in giving instructions to Glafki
g regarding insurance. I confine my observation to insurance, because the field over which
the bank might give directions is so wide that generalisation in respect of all directions
would be unwise and, in my view, unjustified. I am not persuaded that either there is a
duty of care in respect of all directions given by the bank or there is a duty of care in
respect of none. There may be matters where there would be a conflict between the
interest of the bank and the owners, and in respect of which the bank would not owe a
h duty of care to the owners when giving instructions to Glafki. However, it is not
necessary to explore these points further, because this is not a case in which the bank
actively intervened at all.

What the bank did was that, knowing of the amount of the 1978 insurance, it failed
to object. Its officers were content to leave unaltered the amount of the insurance Glafki
had effected or was effecting, because that amount was thought sufficient to cover the
j bank's indebtedness. Thus to succeed in this appeal Pinios has to go much further than
establishing an obligation on the bank to use reasonable care in the exercise of its powers
under the management agreement. To succeed, Pinios must show that under this
agreement there was imposed on the bank an obligation positively to take action to check
that Glafki was not committing a breach of its duty under the management agreement
regarding insurance.

I do not think that there was any such obligation on the bank. In the absence, at any rate, of actual knowledge or suspicion by the bank of misconduct on the part of Glafki, I consider that the bank was entitled to do what it did, viz leave to Glafki, the appointed agent, all decisions about the management and operation of the ship, including renewal of the insurance. By the agreement the bank was expressly given wide powers to override Glafki, and conversely Pinios was expressly excluded from interfering with the ship. But I do not think that these two elements in the parties' relationship lead to the conclusion that the management agreement of its nature implicitly required the imposition on the bank of an obligation to the effect I have mentioned. I take the test of 'implicitly required' from the speech of Lord Wilberforce in *Liverpool City Council v Irwin* [1976] 2 All ER 39 at 44, [1977] AC 239 at 254. The bank is a bank, not a shipowner or operator. The management of the vessel had been put in the hands of a mutually agreed agent. The agent was required to report monthly to the bank and Pinios. The agent, Glafki, and not the bank, was the party required to insure. If (as here) the agent was in breach of one of its duties, Pinios would have a remedy against it. I see no good reason for impliedly importing into this relationship an obligation on the bank, even in respect of insurance, to check that Glafki was duly performing its obligations.

We heard much learned argument in support of a submission that Pinios has a cause of action in tort, as distinct from a cause of action based on the breach of an implied term of the management agreement. In my view this argument is misconceived. If the nature of the management agreement between the parties is not such as implicitly to require that the bank should be under an obligation to the effect I have mentioned, I do not see how it can be right none the less for the law of tort to impose such a requirement. Pinios entered into a written agreement with the bank and, echoing the words of Lord Scarman in *Tai Hing Cotton Mill Ltd v Liu Chong Hing Bank Ltd* [1985] 2 All ER 947 at 957, [1986] AC 80 at 107, Pinios cannot rely on the law of tort to provide it with a greater protection against the bank than that for which, expressly or impliedly, it has contracted with the bank.

Compound interest

The bank sought to establish an entitlement to compound interest in two ways. First, it relied on the terms of the documents. As to that, neither the loan agreement nor the mortgage contains an express provision authorising the bank to charge compound interest. Nor is such a provision implicit in the documents. Clause (8)(A) of the loan agreement and the corresponding provision in the mortgage are concerned only to fix a rate of interest, 'the agreed interest rate', as it is described in the agreement. Clause (8)(C), with its reference to 'interest payment date', does contemplate that the interest will be due and payable from time to time whilst the principal is still outstanding. But this does not assist the bank because, if anything, this provision is inconsistent with the charging of compound interest. The provision does not envisage that unpaid interest will be capitalised and itself bear interest along with the principal. What it seems to envisage (the drafting is not wholly clear) is that the effect of non-payment of interest will be that the interest will remain payable but, from the date when it ought to have been paid until the date when it is actually paid, interest on the principal sum will be payable at a higher rate.

Second, the bank relied on the practice or custom of bankers. Counsel for the defendants did not challenge the bank's entitlement to charge compound interest on this footing until payment was demanded in November 1978, but he disputed its right to do so thereafter.

I confess that when the argument was first advanced I found it surprising. Interest on a debt, of course, ceases to accrue after the principal sum has been repaid. And there is the familiar principle that on judgment being given an agreement to pay interest which is merely incidental to the agreement to pay the principal sum will merge in the judgment to pay the principal sum (see the Earl of Halsbury LC in *Economic Life Assurance*

Society v Usborne [1902] AC 147 at 149). But, if the arrangement between two parties is
a such that, impliedly, compound interest *is* agreed to be payable on a loan of money, it
seemed to me at first sight very odd if compound interest should cease to be payable as
soon as the creditor asks for his money back, even though it may be months or years
before he gets the money. Unassisted by authority I would not have expected to find that
the law today was that, if a bank is, by implication, entitled to charge compound interest
on an overdraft, its entitlement continues only so long as it is prepared to leave the
b money outstanding and that its entitlement ceases when it demands immediate
repayment. So that, so far as interest is concerned, the customer's position improves
when the bank makes such a demand; thenceforth, unlike previously, interest which is
due but not paid does not itself bear interest.

    I turn to the authorities. These establish clearly that the practice relied on by the bank
in this case is one of long standing. To facilitate the use of compound interest by banks
c despite the usury laws, which were not finally repealed until the Usury Laws Repeal Act
1854, the courts resorted to the fiction that a fresh agreement for the payment of interest
was made on the occasion of each rest in a customer's account. An agreement, express or
implied, to pay compound interest made when a customer opened an account with a
bank would have been unlawful. But, if on each occasion when a bank charged or
credited interest to an account the parties were to enter into a new agreement that the
d balance then struck would bear interest, that agreement would be lawful because it
would provide only for the payment of simple interest on an agreed sum. Thus, on this
analysis, over a period of years there would be a series of separate agreements between
banker and customer, made at intervals of one year or six months or whenever,
depending on the manner in which the bank kept its accounts. That notion, of each
debiting or crediting of interest being the subject of a separate, fresh agreement, was
e fundamental to the lawfulness of this practice. There was a succession of agreements,
implied from the customer's acquiescence in the practice of the bank regarding the
debiting and crediting of interest.

    Thus Lord Eldon LC in *Ex p Bevan* (1803) 9 Ves 223 at 224, 32 ER 588 said:

f   '... it is clear, you cannot *a priori* agree to let a man have money for twelve
        months, settling the balance at the end of six months; and that the interest shall
        carry interest for the subsequent six months: that is, you cannot contract for more
        than 5 *per cent.*; agreeing to forbear for six months. But, if you agree to settled
        accounts at the end of six months, that not being part of the prior contract, and then
        stipulate, that you will forbear for six months upon those terms, that is legal.'

    In *Paton v IRC* [1938] 1 All ER 786 at 795, [1938] AC 341 at 357 Lord Macmillan
g commented on that principle and its survival despite the repeal of the usury laws:

        'On this principle it was held in *Eaton v. Bell* ((1821) 5 B & Ald 34, 106 ER 1106)
        that the bankers who, with the knowledge of, and without objection by, their
        customers, debited them with interest with half-yearly rests in accordance with
        their general practice did not offend against the usury laws. This method of dealing
h   with loan accounts, which became common form among bankers, survived the
        abolition of the usury laws and is well-established as the ordinary usage prevailing
        between bankers and customers who borrow from them and do not pay the interest
        as it accrues.'

    Although this rationale of the arrangements between banker and customer, with a
j succession of separate agreements, was (as it seems to me) essentially fictitious, the courts
did not apply the artificiality beyond the point at which, on the facts in a particular case,
it was possible to spell out from the parties' relationship the necessary fresh agreement
for the payment of interest on an agreed balance. Thus compound interest ceased to be
payable, by virtue of this practice, on the death of a customer (*Fergusson v Fyffe* (1841) 8
Cl & Fin 121, [1835–42] All ER Rep 48) or of the banker (*Crosskill v Bower* (1863) 32 Beav

86 at 93, 55 ER 34 at 37), on the bankruptcy of either (*Crosskill v Bower*); on the winding
up of the banker (*Deutsche Bank und Disconto-Gesellschaft v Banque des Marchands de Moscou*   *a*
(1931) 4 Legal Decisions Affecting Bankers 293) and on the customer's announcement to
a banker that he is closing his account and having no further dealings with him (per
Romilly MR in *Crosskill v Bower* (1863) 32 Beav 86 at 93, 55 ER 34 at 37).

This being the underlying principle it follows, in my view, that once a banker or
customer has unequivocally demanded immediate payment of what is due to him from
the other, with the intention of being paid in full and ending their relationship,   *b*
compound interest normally will cease to be payable. The usual formal letter, written by
a bank before proceedings are started, would be typical of such a demand. Compound
interest will cease to be payable in that event because there will no longer be the factual
basis on which to found the implication of a fresh agreement to pay interest on an agreed
balance. Such a demand, as much as the other events I have mentioned, will end the
relationship in which alone the making of a fresh agreement to pay interest on an agreed   *c*
balance is to be implied. This relationship, that of banker and customer, is to be
contrasted with the position after an account has been closed 'and the relations between
the parties . . . become merely that of creditor and debtor' (see the *Deutsche Bank* case
(1931) 4 Legal Decisions Affecting Bankers 293 at 297 per Romer LJ).

In the present case the bank's letter to Pinios of 13 November 1978, sent by registered
post, was such a demand. The letter read as follows: *d*

'Dear Sirs,

"MAIRA"

Your Account No. 322392/2

We refer to your account showing the amount of US$.784,959·11 due to us, being
the balance of the amount paid by us to the Dai Ichi Kangyo Bank Ltd., Tokyo in   *e*
accordance with the terms of our Letter of Guarantee No: 926335 dated 9th
February, 1977. We now write to demand payment of the amount due to us. A
Statement of Account will follow in due course.

Yours faithfully . . .'

It may be thought anachronistic that the law in this field is still shaped by a fiction   *f*
adopted to circumvent laws that were repealed in the middle of the last century. But the
banks are not without a remedy. Express intimation to all their customers of the manner
in which interest will be charged on overdrafts and loans, and that this will continue
until payment, would not seem to be impractical or particularly expensive nowadays.

Before us some argument was directed at how expressions such as 'mercantile accounts
current for mutual transactions' (*Fergusson v Fyffe* (1841) 8 Cl & Fin 121 at 140, [1835–   *g*
42] All ER Rep 48 at 50) and 'a living mercantile account' (per Lord Atkinson in *Yourell v
Hibernian Bank Ltd* [1918] AC 372 at 389) are to be understood today and whether they
exclude deposit accounts or loan accounts from the ambit of the bankers' practice.
However, those questions, and the further question of what was the true nature of the
bank's account with Pinios, do not call for determination on this appeal, because (as I
have said) counsel for the defendants expressly did not challenge the bank's right to   *h*
charge compound interest until payment was demanded in November 1978.

For these reasons, I agree that the bank was not entitled to charge compound interest
after making that demand.

O'CONNOR LJ. I agree with the order proposed by Lloyd LJ for the reasons given by
him.   *j*

On the issue of compound interest I add a few words of my own. Lloyd LJ has traced
the history of the way in which capitalisation of interest was permitted at periodical rests
in order to achieve a payment of compound interest which would otherwise have been
illegal by virtue of the usury laws. In my judgment cl (8) of the loan agreement is in
clear terms: it provides for payment of interest at an agreed rate. By its terms it envisages

that interest is to be charged periodically: see the reference to an 'interest payment date'.

a In sub-cl (C) express provision is made for what is to happen if interest is not paid on a 'relevant interest payment date'. For convenience I set out that paragraph:

> 'If any interest shall be due and unpaid four working days after the relevant interest payment date the amount of interest shall be recalculated from the interest payment date until the date of payment at the rate of two per cent (2%) per annum above the agreed interest rate.'

b

For my part I see no ambiguity in this provision. If interest due on a payment date remains unpaid for four days then as from that payment date the rate of interest is to be increased by 2%. That is a clear simple interest provision.

By reason of the authorities considered by Lloyd and Nicholls LJJ in their judgments Pinios Shipping Co No 1 has accepted throughout that it was liable to pay compound

c interest after the first default. I must not be taken as agreeing that the cases required that concession to be made. The bank account in this case does not seem to me to qualify as a 'mercantile account current for mutual transactions' (see *Ex p Bevan* (1803) 9 Ves 223, 32 ER 588). I am very doubtful that the requisite banker/customer relationship was created by either the guarantee agreement or the second mortgage. I see no reason why a bank should be in any different category to any other surety. The account was not opened

d until the bank made the first payment under the guarantee on 16 August 1977. From that time down to the demand letter of 13 November 1978 the account records interest at quarterly rests from 15 September 1977, the payment of the second bill under the guarantee and the receipt of insurance moneys in 1978 after the loss of the ship. There is one payment to the management agent, Glafki Shipping Co SA, $US12,116·82 in September 1977 when the agency agreement was made.

e However, in view of the concession, we heard no argument on the matter and I express my doubt so that bankers do not take this decision as authority for saying that a contract of guarantee of itself creates the banker/customer relationship needed to enable them to recover compound interest where no express provision in that behalf has been made.

For the reasons given by Lloyd LJ I agree that the bank is entitled to recover simple

f interest at the contracted rate from 13 November 1978.

Appeal allowed in part.

Solicitors: *Elborne Mitchell* (for the defendants); *Thomas Cooper & Stibbard* (for the bank).

Dilys Tausz   Barrister.

g

Braithwaite v Thomas Cook Travellers Cheques Ltd

h

QUEEN'S BENCH DIVISION
SCHIEMANN J
4, 5, 6, 13 JULY 1988

Bank – Cheque – Traveller's cheque – Loss or theft – Reimbursement – Conditions of purchase –

j *Purchaser required to safeguard cheques properly against loss or theft – Test of proper safeguarding of cheques.*

The plaintiff wished to transfer £50,000-worth of traveller's cheques from Jersey to London. He got up at 4 am, flew to Jersey, collected the traveller's cheques, put them in a brown envelope, which he placed in a transparent plastic bag, and flew back to London the same day. The conditions of purchase of the cheques stated that the issuer would replace or refund the face value of any traveller's cheques lost or stolen provided the *a* purchaser had 'properly safeguarded each cheque against loss or theft'. When the plaintiff arrived in London he spent the evening drinking with friends and then took the Underground home. In the course of the Underground journey he fell asleep and when he got off the Underground he realised that he no longer had the plastic bag. He made a claim to the issuer of the cheques for reimbursement of their value on the ground that they had been lost or stolen but the issuer refused to pay. The plaintiff brought an action *b* to recover the value.

Held – Where an agreement for the purchase of traveller's cheques contained an express condition that the purchaser should properly safeguard the cheques against loss or theft, the whole of the purchaser's behaviour had to be considered when determining whether he had in fact properly safeguarded them. Taking into account the facts that the plaintiff *c* had carried the cheques in a transparent bag instead of concealing them about his person and that he had fallen asleep because he was tired and had been drinking, the plaintiff could not be said to have properly safeguarded the cheques and therefore he was not entitled to reimbursement of their face value. The action would accordingly be dismissed (see p 240 *j* to p 241 *e*, post).

d

Notes
For traveller's cheques, see 3 Halsbury's Laws (4th edn) para 122.

Cases referred to in judgment
British and Foreign Marine Insurance Co Ltd v Gaunt [1921] 2 AC 41, [1921] All ER Rep 447, HL. *e*
Fellus v National Westminster Bank plc (1983) 133 NLJ 766.

Action
The plaintiff, Charles James Braithwaite, brought an action against the defendants, Thomas Cook Travellers Cheques Ltd, claiming reimbursement of lost traveller's cheques worth £50,000 which he had purchased from the defendants. The facts are set out in the *f* judgment.

Frederic Reynold QC and *Charles Howard* for Mr Braithwaite.
Murray Pickering QC and *David Etherington* for the defendants.

Cur adv vult *g*

13 July. The following judgment was delivered.

SCHIEMANN J. This case is concerned with traveller's cheques and the circumstances in which someone who has purchased them and subsequently parts with possession of *h* them, without having received value therefor, can reclaim the purchase price from the issuer. The matter arises in this way. Mr Braithwaite purchased £50,000-worth of traveller's cheques from Thomas Cook Travellers Cheques Ltd in Jersey on 12 February 1987. Within 24 hours he claimed that they had all been lost or stolen on the London Underground and asked Thomas Cook for reimbursement of the purchase price. They refused to pay because they were suspicious of him and put him to proof of his claim. *j* Hence his appearance as a plaintiff in this court.

Two witnesses gave evidence on behalf of Mr Braithwaite: James Halliday, who was a customer of the Midland Bank plc (a chartered accountant and a director of various property companies) and the plaintiff himself, who was employed by the Midland Bank in their securities department.

Mr Halliday told me that at the end of January and in early February 1987, after
a having met Mr Braithwaite on a few occasions socially, he asked him if he was interested
in investing £50,000 in a property development scheme to be carried out by Fenwick
Securities Ltd, a company over which Mr Halliday had control. Mr Braithwaite agreed
to do so. Mr Halliday told him that Fenwick Securities intended to purchase some
property in Sutton and convert it into flats. The vendor wished to complete quickly. In
consequence Fenwick Securities needed the money by mid February. Mr Braithwaite
b told him there would be no problem. On 13 February Mr Halliday rang Mr Braithwaite
asking for the money. Mr Braithwaite told him that he had lost it. A cheque for £30,000
was provided on or about 18 February. Contracts were exchanged on 20 February. I
accept Mr Halliday's evidence.

Mr Braithwaite verified the foregoing. He had an account with Barclays Finance Co in
Jersey where £50,000 was available. He did not wish to arrange for a bank transfer of
c that £50,000 to his account in England because he feared this would be brought to the
attention of the tax authorities which he feared might expose him to demands for tax on
the interest which he had earned on his Jersey account. In consequence the practical
choices available to him were transferring the money physically from Jersey to London
either in cash or by way of traveller's cheques. He chose the latter course. The reasoning
behind the, on the face of it, strange course of not using a bank transfer was not revealed
d to the defendants' inspector investigating this claim or to the court in RSC Ord 14
proceedings because, said Mr Braithwaite, he did not wish to put his head into a noose.

I accept his evidence on this point. It reflects little credit on him and it leads me to
view his remaining evidence with suspicion. There are a number of other factors which
also cause me to view his evidence with suspicion. However, although as I say I have
approached his evidence with considerable scepticism, I am persuaded, having seen him
e in the witness box, where he made a very good impression, and having considered all the
circumstances, that his evidence is honest and, with two exceptions (which relate
respectively to the layout of the Underground and to the availability of traveller's cheques
in very large denominations) reliable.

What then is his evidence? It is essentially this. He purchased 400 traveller's cheques,
being 100 of a £200 denomination and 300 of a £100 denomination. The paperwork
f relating to these took longer than he had anticipated and thus, since he had a plane to
catch and since the issuers were anxious to get on with other work, he was permitted to
leave the bank where he had purchased them without having signed more than 50 of
them. He realised that this made them peculiarly attractive to the dishonest. He signed
another 50 at Jersey Airport; a few on the plane; a few more at a café at Heathrow; the
vast majority on the Underground between Heathrow and King's Cross, and the
g remaining ones at a café near King's Cross. I am satisfied that all the cheques were signed
by 6 pm, and that, in all probability, others (during the course of this signing process)
had observed that he had an unusual number of cheques about him. He carried them in
a brown envelope which, in turn, was in a plastic bag supplied at Jersey Airport and
containing 200 cigarettes which were visible through the bag. He did not put them in
h the pockets of his clothing preferring to fill these with cigarettes and other material.

Having arrived at King's Cross he then spent the evening socialising with his friends
which, in his case, took the form of drinking several pints of beer. All this against a
background of having risen at 4 am, having eaten only a few snacks, and having also
taken alcohol at lunch and on the plane. He himself summed up the situation in an
interview as follows: 'I was not sober but I don't consider I was drunk'.

j At one of the public houses he told Mr Halliday's brother that he had Mr Halliday's
money there. It is possible that he was overheard. At closing time he left the last public
house with the bag. I find, on the balance of probability, that the bag then still contained
the envelope and the cheques.

He then caught the Underground train at Baker Street, put the bag on his lap but fell
asleep promptly. Sometime later he was nudged by a fellow passenger. He woke up. He

realised that he had overshot his destination, namely King's Cross. He leapt out of the
train. He caught another one back to King's Cross. He changed trains to Oakwood, on   *a*
the Piccadilly Line, and reached there shortly after midnight. He stepped off the train
and as it moved away he realised that he no longer had the bag although he still had the
newspaper which originally had concealed it. He looked around for London Transport
staff but could find none. He walked home, a five minute journey. He then took his car
to Cockfosters at the end of the Piccadilly Line, found the stationmaster and explained
his predicament. Thereafter he did all that could be done to recover the situation. No   *b*
one suggests that he could have done more at that stage.

The purchase of the traveller's cheques was made subject to the following purchase
conditions:

> 'These travellers cheques are sold to you on the following conditions

> *Refund* The issuer will replace or refund the face value of any travellers cheques   *c*
> which are lost or stolen from you, provided that [1] you have signed each (at the
> bottom) in permanent ink immediately upon receipt and you have not countersigned
> the cheques (at the top) [2] you notify the issuer within 24 hours of the loss or theft
> of any cheques, and the local police if requested, reporting the circumstances of such
> loss or theft in reasonable detail [3] when making your refund claim, you present
> the purchaser's copy of hte Sales Advice and provide serial numbers of the missing   *d*
> cheques and the place and date of their purchase [4] you complete and sign the
> appropriate refund document and provide acceptable proof of your identity [5] you
> will cooperate in the investigation and any prosecution resulting from such loss or
> theft [6] you have not parted with the cheques voluntarily or in connection with a
> game of chance, a wager or an illegal transaction, nor given them to any party as
> collateral, and you have properly safeguarded each cheque against loss or theft [7]   *e*
> the cheques have not been seized or confiscated by governmental action

> *Stop Payment* The issuer shall not be obliged to stop payment of travellers
> cheques for any reason whatsoever.'

No point is taken by the defendants on non-fulfilment of conditions 1 to 5. Counsel
for the defendants submitted that (1) Mr Braithwaite must prove that the traveller's   *f*
cheques were lost or stolen, (2) Mr Braithwaite must prove that he has properly
safeguarded each cheque against loss or theft, (3) 'loss' in this context does not cover a
certainty, or a loss which the plaintiff brings about by his own act and (4) Mr Braithwaite
has not discharged the burden of proof.

Counsel on behalf of Mr Braithwaite accepts submissions (1) and (2). He does not
accept submission (3) and submits that his client had discharged the burden of proof.   *g*

The basis of the third submission, dealing with the meaning of 'loss', was an analogy
with the learning on all risks policies, as exemplified in the following passage from the
speech of Lord Sumner in *British and Foreign Marine Insurance Co Ltd v Gaunt* [1921] 2 AC
41 at 57, [1921] All ER Rep 447 at 455:

> 'There are . . . limits to "all risks". They are risks and risks insured against.   *h*
> Accordingly the expression does not cover inherent vice or mere wear and tear . . .
> It covers a risk, not a certainty . . . Nor is it a loss which the assured brings about by
> his own act, for then he has not merely exposed the goods to the chance of injury,
> he has injured them himself.'

If one accepts, as I do, Mr Braithwaite's account, then it seems to me that it follows that   *j*
the traveller's cheques were lost or stolen, as those words would be understood by a
purchaser of a traveller's cheque. Of course, if the loser's conduct is such that he, in effect,
ensures that he will lose the traveller's cheques, then he will not have proved that he has
'properly safeguarded each cheque against loss or theft'. Conversely, if he proves that he
has properly safeguarded each cheque against loss or theft, then, even if the third

submission be right in law, its application to the facts of this case would not prevent Mr
a Braithwaite from recovering, in that he would not have brought about the loss by his
own act. Thus, in the context of this case, a decision in favour of counsel for the
defendants on his third submission would put him in no stronger position than the one
in which he finds himself by reason of the acceptance of his second submission. I,
therefore, say no more about the third submission.

I come, therefore, to what I regard as the crucial question in this case: has Mr
b Braithwaite shown that he has properly safeguarded each cheque? Let me first clear away
some brushwood.

1. Although each side made submissions about the extent of what they referred to as
the purchaser's duty, we are not, strictly speaking, concerned with a duty at all. We are
concerned with a condition precedent which must be fulfilled by a purchaser if he wishes
to recover.

c 2. The primary obligation of an issuer of traveller's cheques is to pay the presenter of
the cheque. In so far as the purchaser retains the cheque or recovers it prior to encashment
and wishes to encash it, he can present it.

3. Apart from contract, the purchaser is not entitled to any refund of the face value of
the traveller's cheques which he has lost or which have been stolen from him.

4. Although on a literal reading of condition 6 any failure to safeguard would disentitle
d the purchaser from claiming a refund, where there is no causal link between that failure
and the ultimate loss, counsel for the defendants was, rightly in my judgment, not
inclined to argue that in those circumstances there would be such a disentitlement. For
example, let us suppose that, having purchased the cheques in England on day one, the
purchaser, in order to demonstrate his wealth to the world at large, deliberately left them
behind on his restaurant table when he left the table. That would clearly be a failure to
e safeguard. However, he comes back and they are still there. A few days later, in Peru, he
is in a hotel and there is a fire in the middle of the night. He is rescued by firemen from
his hotel bedroom and has no time to collect his belongings. The fire is put out, he
returns to his room and finds the cheques gone. If, in those circumstances, it were held
that he had not failed to safeguard the cheques in Peru but he had so failed in England,
f in my judgment he would nevertheless, be entitled to recover.

5. Although it could be argued that any loss inevitably involves a failure to safeguard,
such a construction would be at odds with the primary undertaking by the issuer to
refund the face value of the cheques which are lost, and counsel for the defendants did
not argue in favour of such a construction. Mere momentary inadvertence cannot
disentitle the purchaser from a refund. It was so decided by Stuart-Smith J in *Fellus v*
National Westminster Bank plc (1983) 133 NLJ 766. In that case the relevant clause read,
g and I quote: 'A refund will be made upon completion of our form of application,
providing the cheques were signed but not countersigned and there has been no undue
negligence.'

6. Although in his case Stuart-Smith J opined that it was for the bank to establish the
matters set out in the proviso if they wished to avoid payment, in the present case it is
h conceded on behalf of Mr Braithwaite that the burden of providing that he had properly
safeguarded the cheques is on him. In my judgment that concession is rightly made.
One must bear in mind that in these cases all the relevant facts are within the knowledge
of the purchaser. If he refused to answer any questions, the bank would find it practically
impossible to prove lack of due care on his part.

7. Further, in my judgment, once the purchaser has failed to establish that he has
j properly safeguarded the cheques, if he wishes none the less to recover on the basis that
there is no causal link between his lack of care and the ultimate loss, as in my example of
the fire in Peru, the burden of satisfying the court that there was no such causal link is
on the purchaser.

Counsel for the defendants argues that Mr Braithwaite has failed properly to safeguard
the cheques against loss or theft. He relies on two groups of factors: (1) by signing the
cheques in the presence of strangers, Mr Braithwaite made it clear to numerous persons

that he was in possession of a considerable amount of traveller's cheques and was keeping
them in a plastic bag; and (2) Mr Braithwaite, by his course of conduct in staying awake   *a*
for 20 hours, drinking too much, travelling on the Underground, which is known to
attract dishonest people, keeping the cheques in a plastic bag and falling asleep, disabled
himself from properly safeguarding the cheques and did not properly safeguard them.

Counsel for Mr Braithwaite submits, as to the first of these points, that the probability
is that the cheques were not, in fact, taken by anyone who had seen Mr Braithwaite
signing them earlier in the day. Had he been robbed earlier on in the day the position   *b*
might have been different, but it seems improbable that he was shadowed until he fell
asleep. After some hesitation, I have come to the view that this submission is well
founded. Mr Braithwaite may have been shadowed but, on the balance of probability, I
find that he was not. In consequence there is no causal nexus shown between the
carelessness and the loss or theft, and the position is similar to carelessness in England
followed by theft in Peru.   *c*

So far as the second submission is concerned, counsel for Mr Braithwaite helpfully, at
my suggestion, reduced his submission to writing under two heads, and I quote from the
document:

> '1. *Meaning of "properly safeguard"*. The expression only contemplates and
> encompasses steps taken and/or arrangements made in regard to the custody of the   *d*
> cheques, viz conscious and deliberate acts: (a) Because this would be a logical ejusdem
> generis construction, having regard to the other contingencies specified in clause 6.
> (b) Because to construe the expression as covering forms of *inadvertence*—eg
> momentary inattention, absent-mindedness, forgetfulness, whether arising from
> fatigue, drink or otherwise—would be to construe it in a manner inconsistent with
> the vendor's primary obligation to refund the face value of cheques which the   *e*
> purchaser has lost. The promise to refund would be virtually illusory since—apart
> from the exceptional case of eg a fire or serious accident—loss invariably involves
> some element of fault on the part of the loser. Furthermore, such a construction
> would be inconsistent with one of the objective aims of the transaction, viz, a
> convenient form of insurance against one's own fallibility, having regard to the
> normal incidents and hazards of travel, or of being on holiday. The expression is *not*   *f*
> to be construed as imposing an obligation on the purchaser to exercise reasonable
> care at all material times—this is not a contract of bailment. The words "negligent"
> or "negligence" do not appear.
>
> (2) The *only* circumstances which are relevant are those immediately surrounding
> the loss. The Plaintiff's conduct at an earlier moment of time is not material unless
> it is causative of the ultimate loss. The steps taken in regard to the safeguarding of   *g*
> the cheques on the homeward tube journey were perfectly reasonable. They were
> concealed from view, being in a brown envelope and inside a carrier bag. The
> Plaintiff was unencumbered by other luggage, and it was clear that he envisaged
> that throughout his journey he would be either holding the bag in his hand or it
> would be resting on his lap. In the context of what is or is not a reasonable
> arrangement, there is a crucial distinction between carrying £50,000 in cash and   *h*
> carrying such a sum in travellers' cheques. The loss occurred as a result of the
> Plaintiff's fatigue, probably aggravated by drink, momentary absent-mindedness
> and inattention. These are typical lapses not encompassed by the expression
> "properly safeguard".'

And that is the end of counsel's submission. What makes this submission attractive is   *j*
the way it identifies various aspects of Mr Braithwaite's behaviour and then goes on to
look at each of those aspects in turn and in isolation. However, in my judgment, this is
not permissible. Mr Braithwaite's conduct that evening involved the following:
(1) carrying £50,000 in traveller's cheques around London in a plastic bag, with a carton
of cigarettes, visible to the outside world. This was an attractive target for the dishonest;

a more attractive than if he had concealed the cheques about his person; (2) failing to go home when he had made no arrangements to meet the intended recipient; (3) instead he socialised, notwithstanding that he had got up at 4 am and had been on two aeroplane flights and must have been feeling increasingly tired. His socialising took the form of drinking more and more alcohol, notwithstanding that he was tired and had not eaten properly all day; (4) finishing the evening, when he was dog tired and not sober, by making a long journey on the Underground at night rather than taking a taxi home;

b (5) falling asleep on the Underground within minutes of taking his seat; and (6) failing even to notice that he had dropped or had had stolen from him the bag containing the cheques and cigarettes.

It may well be that some of these factors can be present without the plaintiff failing properly to safeguard. But in the present case they were all present and, in my judgment, all contributed to the ultimate loss and, between them, were causative of it. The reason

c he fell asleep and did not notice the loss was because he was dead tired and not sober. Falling asleep, and the subsequent loss or theft, could and should have been foreseen as the not unlikely conclusion to that evening following that day. In my judgment, if an ordinary member of the travelling public was asked: 'Has Mr Braithwaite properly safeguarded these traveller's cheques?', he would answer: 'Of course he has not.'

Let me quote from an interview which Mr Braithwaite had with the defendants'
d investigating officer. Mr Braithwaite said this: 'I fell asleep on the train. I mean, obviously. I had been up at 4 o'clock in the morning. I have also had a couple of drinks.' Then, in another passage, Mr Braithwaite said: 'I had a look at a leaflet. It says you have to properly safeguard them.' The investigating officer said: 'Right, and have you?' 'No', Mr Braithwaite replied.

I give the same answer. In my judgment, the defendants have proved that he failed
e properly to safeguard the cheques. As I indicated earlier in this judgment, the burden of proof in fact is on him and not on the defendants. It is clear that he has not discharged it. In those circumstances, he has no claim in contract against them.

The defendants have indicated that they have recovered some of the cheques before any money was paid out against them. They are, of course, willing to refund Mr Braithwaite the face value of those, which amounts to £2,000.

f There is another group of cheques where, although they were presented and paid, the payer has not so far recovered from the defendants, who appear to have successfully argued that the payer was negligent in making the payment. They amount to £7,400, and I understand that the defendants are prepared to reimburse Mr Braithwaite with their face value unconditionally.

g There is a third category, amounting to £6,000, where the traveller's cheques are still outstanding, and no attempt has been made to encash them. In relation to this category the defendants are prepared to reimburse Mr Braithwaite, subject to a condition that he agrees to indemnify them should they be successfully sued by the payer.

Finally, there is a group of cheques in respect of which the defendants have paid out £34,000 to outside institutions who have paid the persons who presented them. On the
h pleadings as they stand Mr Braithwaite has, in the light of my findings, no claim in respect of any of them.

Judgment for Mr Braithwaite for £16,000 with interest on certain undertakings by Mr Braithwaite to indemnify the defendants.

j Solicitors: *Philip Ross & Co* (for Mr Braithwaite); *Beachcroft Stanleys* (for the defendants).

K Mydeen Esq   Barrister.

Elawadi v Bank of Credit and Commerce International SA

a

QUEEN'S BENCH DIVISION
HUTCHISON J
18 JULY, 5 SEPTEMBER 1988

b

Bank – Cheque – Traveller's cheque – Loss or theft – Reimbursement – Conditions of purchase – Purchase agreement providing that any claim for refund of lost or stolen cheques subject to appoval by bank – Cheques stolen due to purchaser's own negligence – Whether contract containing express or implied obligation to refund – Whether obligation subject to discretion or implied term not to refund where loss resulting from purchaser's negligence.

c

The plaintiff purchased £50,000-worth of traveller's cheques in £100 denominations from the defendant bank. The agreement covering the purchase contained a clause which stated that 'Any claim for a refund of a lost or stolen cheque shall be subject to approval by the Issuer and to presentation to the Issuer of the Purchaser's copy of this Agreement'. The plaintiff signed the cheques before taking them away, having been informed by the bank that if the cheques were taken away unsigned he would not be covered in the event of their loss. A few days later the cheques were stolen from the plaintiff's car, largely as a result of his own negligence, and £40,700-worth were subsequently encashed. The bank refused to refund to the plaintiff the full value of the stolen cheques, agreeing only to refund the sum of £9,300 in respect of those cheques which had not been encashed. The plaintiff brought an action against the bank claiming, inter alia, a refund of £40,700 on the ground that the bank's statement that it would not refund on unsigned cheques together with the provision in the purchase agreement regarding claims for refunds constituted an express term of the contract obliging the bank to refund lost or stolen cheques. The bank contended that it was under no such obligation since that provision conferred an unfettered disrection on the bank whether to make a refund. Alternatively, the bank contended that, even if there was an obligation to make a refund, it was an implied term of the purchase agreement that the plaintiff would take reasonable care of the cheques and that a refund would not be made where the plaintiff had been negligent or reckless.

d

e

f

Held – Where a contract for the sale and purchase of traveller's cheques contained an express term obliging the issuing bank to refund the value of lost or stolen cheques, that obligation was subject to a discretion not to pay where the purchaser had broken one of his contractual obligations, but it was not (in the absence of any express provision) subject to an implied term precluding recovery by the purchaser where the loss resulted from his own negligence or recklessness. Where the contract contained no express term obliging the bank to refund the value of lost or stolen cheques, there would, of necessity, be an implied obligation to refund but subject to a discretionary right to resist a refund. On the true construction of the contract entered into by the parties, it contained an express obligation on the part of the bank to refund lost or stolen cheques regardless of the plaintiff's own negligence or recklessness in safeguarding the cheques. The bank would therefore be ordered to pay the £40,700 claimed (see p 248 *g h*, p 249 *c*, p 250 *c d*, p 255 *g* and p 256 *b* to *d g*, post).

g

h

Dictum of Schiemann J in *Braithwaite v Thomas Cook Travellers Cheques Ltd* [1989] 1 All ER 235 at 239 doubted.

i

Notes
For traveller's cheques, see 3 Halsbury's Laws (4th edn) para 122.

Cases referred to in judgment

a   *Braithwaite v Thomas Cook Travellers Cheques Ltd* [1989] 1 All ER 235.
Fellus v National Westminster Bank plc (1983) 133 NLJ 766.
Greenwood v Martins Bank Ltd [1933] AC 51, [1932] All ER Rep 318, HL.
Lister v Romford Ice and Cold Storage Co Ltd [1957] 1 All ER 125, [1957] AC 555, [1957] 2
WLR 158, HL.
Liverpool City Council v Irwin [1976] 2 All ER 39, [1977] AC 239, [1976] 2 WLR 562, HL;

b   *affg in part* [1975] 3 All ER 658, [1976] QB 319, [1975] 3 WLR 3 WLR 663, CA.
London Joint Stock Bank Ltd v Macmillan [1918] AC 777, [1918–19] All ER Rep 30, HL.
National Bank of Greece SA v Pinios Shipping Co No 1, The Maira [1989] 1 All ER 213, CA.
Sullivan v Knauth (1917) 220 NY 216, NY Ct of Apps; *affg* (1914) 146 NYS 583, NY SC.
Tai Hing Cotton Mill Ltd v Liu Chong Hing Bank Ltd [1985] 2 All ER 947, [1986] AC 80,
[1985] 3 WLR 317, PC.

c

Action
The plaintiff, Moshen Elawadi, by a writ issued on 18 December 1985 and an amended
statement of claim re-served on 15 June 1988, brought an action against the defendants,
Bank of Credit and Commerce International SA (sued as Bank of Credit and Commerce
International SA Ltd), who were licensed deposit takers, a declaration that the plaintiff

d   was entitled to reimbursement in the sum of £40,700 as the outstanding balance of
£50,000 in Visa traveller's cheques which he had purchased from the bank in August
1985 and which had been stolen on or about 17 August 1985 and subsequently encashed,
(ii) payment to the plaintiff of £40,700, alternatively damages, and (iii) interest pursuant
to s 35A of the Supreme Court Act 1981. The facts are set out in the judgment.

e   *Peter Cresswell QC* and *Stephen Hockman* for the plaintiff.
Nicholas Stadlen for the bank.

Cur adv vult

f   5 September. The following judgment was delivered.

HUTCHISON J. This case is to do with an alleged theft of traveller's cheques. It gives
rise to numerous difficult and interesting issues of fact and law which I shall have to
consider in some detail, but of which I give a foretaste by saying that they include the
following questions. (1) Were the cheques stolen at all? (2) If they were, is there some
express or implied contractual right in the plaintiff to have them replaced or to be

g   reimbursed by the issuing bank? (3) If there is, is that right itself subject to an implied
term that the plaintiff's right to recover is dependent on his having exercised care in the
custody of the cheques and, if so, what degree of care? (4) Is the bank liable in conversion
for those cheques which ultimately found their way into its possession, but which it has
not restored to the plaintiff and, if so, what is the measure of damage?

h   The history of the pleadings is a tortuous one, and even their final state does not reflect
all that was at one stage proposed. In the course of the hearing I rejected an application
by the plaintiff to plead reliance on the Unfair Contract Terms Act 1977; and the bank
flirted with the idea of pleading fraud (a flirtation which at one stage turned into a
proposal when it sought leave to amend to raise it) but was refused leave because of the
total lack of particularity in its draft amendment. In the circumstances I think I should

j   begin with a careful review of the pleadings in their final form.
By his amended statement of claim the plaintiff, Mr Moshen Elawadi, asserts that in
August 1985 he purchased from the defendants, Bank of Credit and Commerce
International SA (the bank), who are licensed deposit takers, £50,000-worth of Visa
traveller's cheques in £100 denominations; that it was an express or alternatively an

implied term of the purchase agreement that should the cheques be stolen from or lost
by him the bank would refund to him their full value; that on about 17 August they *a*
were stolen; and that the bank, despite requests to do so, has refused to refund their
value, apart from £9,300, being the value of those stolen cheques which were not
encashed. By amendment made during the trial the plaintiff claims, in the alternative,
that following presentation of cheques to the value of £40,700 to the bank for payment
it converted them, as a result of which he has suffered damage equal to their face value.
There is also a conventional alternative claim for money had and received. So the plaintiff *b*
is claiming reimbursement of £40,700 in contract, and in the alternative the same sum
as damages for conversion and/or as money had and received.

The defence, amended twice during the hearing, is to the following effect.

1. The purchase of the cheques is admitted to have taken place on 2 August, and is
alleged to have been subject to the purchase agreement form which the plaintiff signed
that day. The point is made that the issuer was not the bank but the Bank of Credit and *c*
Commerce International (Overseas) Ltd (BCCI Overseas); but in a letter from the bank's
solicitors it is made clear that no point is taken as to parties. Provisions of the purchase
agreement (to which I shall have to refer in detail) are pleaded, the purport of which (so
it is alleged) was that the bank was under no liability to refund the value of lost or stolen
cheques. Particular reliance is placed on these words in the purchase agreement: 'Any
claim for a refund of a lost or stolen cheque shall be subject to approval by the Issuer and *d*
to presentation to the Issuer of the Purchaser's copy of this Agreement.'

2. Alternatively it is said that if by the purchase agreement or otherwise the bank
undertook to refund lost or stolen cheques, then it was an implied term of the purchase
agreement that the plaintiff should take reasonable care of the cheques to ensure that
they were not lost or stolen and further that he owed the bank such a duty, independently
of contract. There follow allegations, to which I shall need to refer, detailing the *e*
circumstances of the theft, said to constitute a breach by the plaintiff of this implied term
and/or duty.

3. The theft had originally been the subject of a 'not admitted' plea. The only part of
the proposed amendment to plead fraud that I allowed was the substitution for those
words of a denial. I did this because it became clear, in the course of the argument about
the proposed amendment, that the bank's predicament was that, while it was highly *f*
suspicious about the veracity (because of its supposed improbability) of the plaintiff's
account of the loss of the cheques, it had no positive case of fraud which it could put
forward; and it seemed to me that in the circumstances the modest amendment I did
allow was appropriate.

4. The second of the amendments raised a plea that if there was an implied term
obliging the bank to refund the value of lost or stolen cheques, it was part of that implied *g*
term that the bank was not obliged to make a refund in circumstances where it had
reasonable grounds for believing that the plaintiff had been, or alternatively he had in
fact been, dishonest and/or reckless and/or grossly negligent and/or negligent. The
pleading goes on to allege (i) that the plaintiff had been reckless etc (relying on the case
originally pleaded, to which I have already made passing reference) and (ii) that the bank *h*
had reasonable grounds for believing that the plaintiff's account was untrue or that he
had been reckless etc.

5. In answer to the claim in conversion or for money had and received, the bank
pleads that the plaintiff is, by reason of his negligence, estopped from asserting the claim
in conversion and, in support of that plea, relies on the implied term and/or duty to take
care of the cheques, the breach of that term and/or duty which resulted in the theft and *j*
subsequent forging of the counter-signature, and go on to allege that, in the result, 'they
were obliged to make payment to the cashing agents with whom the traveller's cheques
had been encashed'. I have cited these words particularly because, as I shall show, counsel
for the plaintiff argued that on undisputed evidence it was established that such payments
as the bank made were made without legal obligation.

6. The bank pleads alternative answers to the claim in conversion, on the following

a lines: (a) it denies that any loss suffered by the plaintiff was caused by conversion of the cheques; (b) it says that any loss suffered by the plaintiff was caused by his carelessness, negligence, breach of contract or breach of duty; and (c) it relies on the provision in the purchase agreement which, it says, gives it a discretion to refuse a refund of stolen cheques, and the absence in that agreement of any express obligation to make a refund, and says that those are inconsistent with the alleged claim in conversion, and that

b therefore it was an implied term of the agreement between the parties that the bank would not be liable in conversion in circumstances where it was entitled to withhold its approval to the making of a refund.

By his amended reply the plaintiff asserts that the purchase agreement was partly oral, and relies on a conversation alleged to have occurred with the manager when, in response to an inquiry, the manager told him that if he took the cheques away before signing

c them, the bank would not be liable in the event of loss. He contends that the provision in the purchase agreement as to approval is of no legal effect, or at most is confined to the question whether he had countersigned the cheques.

The rejoinder, though maybe not strictly necessary, serves the useful purpose of making clear the bank's stance as to the effect of the refund provision in the purchase agreement. What it contends is (i) that it gives the bank an absolute discretion to make

d or refuse a refund and, alternatively, (ii) that, if there is any fetter, it amounts to no more than a requirement that it should act honestly in making its decision or alternatively that it should exercise the discretion bona fide and/or reasonably. It asserts that on the facts it did so exercise it.

I propose next to consider the evidence in relation to the purchase of the cheques, and to make some findings of fact that will be material to the crucial questions as to express

e or implied terms in the contract. It will be appreciated that, while the circumstances of the alleged loss of the cheques were the subject of controversy, there was much less room for dispute as to the facts to do with their purchase.

The plaintiff, who is an Egyptian, was a customer of the bank of considerable standing. He maintained his own and his company's accounts there and his brother also banked

f there. He is a man of some means, and on occasions his account had substantial credit balances. An indication of the bank's regard for him is that overdraft facilities of the order of £250,000 and £100,000 were permitted on the company's and his own accounts. He was an important customer and the relationship was valued by the bank. He normally dealt with Mr Musafer Chowdry, the deputy manager, but he also knew the recently appointed manager, Mr Baakza.

g On 2 August 1985, the plaintiff told me, he went to the bank, saw Mr Chowdry and indicated that he wished to purchase traveller's cheques to the value of £50,000, the cost to be debited to his brother's account, in respect of which he had a mandate. His evidence was that he told Mr Chowdry that he wanted the cheques because he was intending to purchase a factory in Egypt. Mr Chowdry recalled that the plaintiff had first telephoned to arrange the purchase, and said that he was going to Cairo and needed the cheques for

h some business commitment. Mr Chowdry said that he asked why a transfer of funds would not do, and the plaintiff said that it would not because the cheques gave him a better exchange rate. I shall return to this aspect of the matter, which is of relevance to the question of his credit and the issue of the loss of the cheques, but of no materiality to the contract.

The cheques, each for £100, were produced, and each was signed by the plaintiff

j before he left the bank. That much is common ground. The plaintiff said that when Mr Chowdry asked him to sign them he, because he was in a hurry, asked if he could take them away and sign them elsewhere, and that Mr Chowdry said that he could, but if he did the bank would not pay if they were lost. The plaintiff did not profess to remember the precise words, but was clear that the purport of what was said was that if he chose to take the cheques away unsigned he was not covered in the event of their loss. He therefore sat down, in a back room made available to him, and signed all 500 cheques.

Mr Chowdry's evidence was to the following effect. He said that he could not recall *a* any specific conversation on 2 August, though he did remember that all 500 cheques were signed at the bank. However, Mr Chowdry did say that if he had been asked about taking the cheques away unsigned he would have said words to this effect: 'As I've told you before, if you do that you're not entitled to claim for loss.' That this should be Mr Chowdry's position is hardly surprising, for the bank has a standard form of waiver of liability for cheques issued in blank (one such form was signed by the plaintiff in *b* connection with a further purchase of cheques in January 1986), which provides that:

> 'neither the issuer nor selling agent shall be liable to . . . the purchaser with respect to any claims arising out of this transaction including the loss or theft of Travellers' Cheques until [the cheques have been signed by the purchaser].'

Bearing in mind that Mr Chowdry did not deny (merely did not recall) this *c* conversation and that the plaintiff's account is in my view inherently probable, I accept that a conversation such as he describes did take place.

The plaintiff also, of course, signed the purchase agreement, the relevant provisions of which are as follows:

> 'The Issuer and the Purchaser agree as follows: 1. Using the same signature used *d* for signing this Purchase Agreement, the Purchaser shall sign each cheque in permanent ink at the time of purchase and countersign each cheque in the presence of the person cashing the cheque. 2. The purchaser shall report immediately the loss or theft of any cheque to the local police and to the Visa Refund Referral service at the telephone and telex numbers indicated. 3. Any claim for a refund of a lost or stolen cheque shall be subject to approval by the Issuer and to presentation to the *e* Issuer of the Purchaser's copy of this Agreement.'

On the plaintiff's copy of the agreement there also appeared: 'Safeguard cheques as cash.'

The relevant part of the cheques themselves, which of course contain the usual spaces for signature and countersignature, is the statement: 'Issuer pay this cheque to   or order in the above amount in accordance with terms on reverse.' The terms referred to are: *f*

> 'When countersigned by the purchaser whose signature appears on the face in the presence of the person cashing, the issuer will pay in the United Kingdom one hundred pounds Sterling. Elsewhere negotiable at current rates of exchange. Valid in all countries of the world unless otherwise endorsed.'

These are the material matters which go to the issue of what was the contract between *g* the bank and the plaintiff. However, I shall postpone stating my conclusions as to the contractual effect of what I have found took place until I have dealt with the loss of the cheques and the legal arguments.

[His Lordship considered the evidence and found that the plaintiff had put the cheques in his office safe and had then decided to take them to Amsterdam to give to a client to *h* take them to Cairo. On the evening of Friday, 16 August the plaintiff had put the cheques in a plastic bag which he put in his car. He had then made a number of business calls, during which he left the plastic bag unattended in the car. When he returned home that evening he had parked the car in an open parking space adjoining his home and had left the plastic bag in it overnight. The following morning he drove to his shop and parked his car. Some time later during the day he remembered the cheques but when he looked *j* for them in his car they were missing. He had then contacted the police. His Lordship continued:] It is convenient at this stage that I should express my conclusions whether the plaintiff was negligent in his dealings with the cheques. The onus in that regard is, of course, on the bank, though questions on onus are unimportant in the circumstances of this case. I have no hesitation at all in saying that in my view the plaintiff was guilty

of the most serious negligence. He is and was at the time an experienced businessman
a accustomed to dealing with large sums of money. On any view, £50,000 is a large sum.
He plainly appreciated that traveller's cheques require to be carefully and safely kept;
presumably that is why he put them straight into his safe on 2 August. When he took
them from the safe preparatory to departing for Amsterdam, he should at all times have
been alive to the fact that he was carrying a very valuable, readily stealable and highly
negotiable commodity. He put them in his car in a plastic bag, in full view of any casual
b passer-by. I am satisfied that on the occasion when they were stolen he must, on the
balance of probabilities, have left the car unlocked, an act of gross carelessness in the
circumstances. A measure of his carelessness is the fact that he did not even have this
valuable packet of traveller's cheques sufficiently in mind to remember its presence in
the car until after six o'clock on the Saturday evening. It seems to me that it is an
inescapable conclusion that, in his dealing with these cheques, he was guilty of the most
c serious negligence and that it was that singular want of care that led to their being stolen.
  In the light of these findings, I must now consider the remaining and crucial issues in
the case. These, it seems to me, can broadly be summarised as follows. (1) Was the bank
under any contractual obligation to refund the value of lost or stolen cheques? (2) If it
was, was that obligation absolute or was it in some way qualified by (a) a discretion of
some sort to refuse a refund or (b) an implied right to resist payment where the customer
d had been guilty of negligence, alternatively, gross negligence leading to the loss or (c) an
implied right to resist payment where the bank believed that the customer had been
dishonest and/or negligent and/or grossly negligent, whether or not that belief was
justified? (3) Did the bank convert the cheques on which it paid out? If so, did that
conversion give rise to any damage suffered by the plaintiff? If so, has the bank made
good its plea of estoppel and/or can it resist the claim in conversion on the basis that the
e plaintiff was careless etc and/or is there an implied term in the contract exempting the
bank from liability in conversion in those cases where it is not liable in contract?
  Traveller's cheques are and have now for many years been widely used in the United
Kingdom. It is, therefore, surprising that there are hardly any decisions of English courts
dealing with the crucial question of the rights and liabilities of the purchaser and the
f issuer of such instruments. Two cases were cited to me, in both of which the contracts
contained express terms in relation to the right to a refund and the obligation to use care.
In the first, a decision of Stuart-Smith J in *Fellus v National Westminster Bank plc* (1983)
133 NLJ 766, the question was whether there had been 'undue negligence' by the
plaintiffs. In the course of giving judgment (in which he found that there had not)
Stuart-Smith J said (and I read from the transcript of his decision):

g
  'There is a considerable advantage over cash so far as the public are concerned
  because of the refund provisions. This is a matter which is advertised by issuing
  banks in general, including the defendant bank.'

That observation, in so far as it was intended to be of general application rather than to
h be confined to the facts of the case he was considering, where there was an express
obligation to refund, was, of course, obiter. However, it summarises succinctly that
quality which makes traveller's cheques attractive, viz the security they give which cash
does not, and I would suppose that members of the public who buy them assume without
question that they are getting such an advantage. In this case it is suggested that any such
assumption is misplaced.
j   The other English decision of which I am aware is that of Schiemann J in *Braithwaite v
Thomas Cook Travellers Cheques Ltd* [1989] 1 All ER 235. In that case too there was a
specific obligation to refund, subject to a specific qualification in relation to negligence.
However, in the course of his judgment Schiemann J made an observation which showed
that he considered it to be clear law that it was not one of the ordinary incidents of a
contract for the sale and purchase of traveller's cheques that the purchaser should be

entitled to a refund of the face value in the event of loss. He said ([1989] 1 All ER 235 at 239):

> 'Apart from contract, the purchaser is not entitled to any refund of the face value of the traveller's cheques which he has lost or which have been stolen from him.'

That observation, while of course also obiter, provides support for the contention of counsel for the bank to the like effect and certainly shows that, despite what I have ventured to suggest would be the understanding of ordinary purchasers of traveller's cheques, the contention that there is no liability to refund in the absence of particular contractual provisions is not a startling or outrageous one.

There are, of course, cases in other jurisdictions (particularly America, where traveller's cheques have been in use for very much longer) which do afford some guidance on the law applying to them. The matter is also treated in a number of textbooks, particularly fully and helpfully in Cowen *Law of Negotiable Instruments in South Africa* (5th edn, 1985) vol 1, pp 295–313. However, it will only be necessary for me to embark on a general review of the law in relation to traveller's cheques if I conclude that the present is a case in which there is no express term obliging the bank to make a refund and I have only said as much as I have about the law relating to traveller's cheques to show why it was that counsel for the plaintiff invited me to begin by considering the question of whether he had made good his plea that there was an express term in the present case.

Neither counsel sought, in the course of the argument, to analyse precisely when the contract was concluded; and certainly counsel for the bank did not argue that, if there was a conversation such as I have found that there was between the plaintiff and Mr Chowdry, that could not have contractual effect because it followed rather than preceded the conclusion of the contract. If it is necessary to express to a view about it, I should have thought that in the ordinary case the contract is concluded when the purchaser pays for the cheques and takes possession of them or, in the case of a customer of the issuing bank, takes possession of the cheques and signs the form authorising the debiting of his account. In the present case there is no evidence as to precisely in what order things occurred, but as I have indicated I can properly regard the conversation as being a contractual exchange. I reach that conclusion the more readily since, having regard to its content, it was clearly intended by Mr Chowdry that should the plaintiff, notwithstanding the warning he had been given, take the cheques away unsigned, his rights would be affected.

The express term contended for is that the bank will refund lost or stolen cheques. The material said to give rise to such a term is (1) the statement by Mr Chowdry that, if the cheques were taken away unsigned, the plaintiff would not be entitled to claim for their loss and (2) the words of para 3 of the purchase agreement, 'Any claim for a refund of a lost or stolen cheque shall be subject to approval by the Issuer . . .' Counsel for the plaintiff argues that either the conversation or the terms of para 3 or the two together constitute an express term obliging the bank to make a refund of lost or stolen cheques. It seems to me that these submissions are justified for reasons which I shall briefly explain.

It is convenient to begin with the argument of counsel for the bank as to the meaning and significance of para 3. He concedes, as he must, that it is an express term of the contract. However, he contends that all it does is to confer on the issuer an absolutely unfettered discretion whether to pay or not and he argues that neither in this paragraph nor anywhere else in the contract is there any obligation to pay.

The difficulty about that argument, and it is one which counsel never succeeded in resolving to my satisfaction, is that it makes no sense to talk of a discretion that is entirely divorced from any kind of obligation or duty in regard to which the discretion is exercisable. For me to stipulate that I have an absolutely unfettered discretion whether to make good the loss of a £5 note which is blown into the Thames from the hand of the old lady queuing for a bus in front of me is a true but pointless assertion. Accordingly,

either this paragraph is mere surplusage (an unnecessary and therefore, in the context, a
a meaningless stipulation in the contract) or it contains within it an obligation on which
the reserved discretion is to operate. I lean against holding that it is mere surplusage: it is
part of what is plainly a carefully drawn, though briefly expressed, contract and obviously
regarded by the bank as having significance. I would only hold that it has none if I could
not find in it words capable of supporting an express obligation to refund.

The paragraph begins with the words: 'Any *claim* for a refund of a lost or stolen cheque
b . . .' The word 'claim', it seems to me, is most naturally to be construed as referring to a
right. In my judgment a legitimate construction of these words is that they import an
obligation (subject of course to what follows) to refund lost or stolen cheques. The issuer
is recognising expressly an entitlement in the purchaser to have lost or stolen cheques
refunded, and making a reservation cutting down the extent of that entitlement. I find
further support for this construction in paras 1 and 2. If there is no obligation to make a
c refund the issuer has, strictly, no interest in the safeguarding of the cheques or the
reporting of their loss. It may be said, with reason, that he has a commercial interest and
also an interest in trying to minimise crime. However, the fact remains that looking at
the three paragraphs together reinforces the argument for an express obligation to
refund.

The next question is: what is the nature of the discretion? The words are: 'Any claim
d for a refund of a lost or stolen cheque shall be subject to approval by the Issuer and to
presentation to the Issuer of the Purchaser's copy of this Agreement.' Plainly it cannot be
a wholly unfettered discretion, because then there would be no obligation. Counsel for
the plaintiff argues that the words 'subject to approval by the Issuer' are of no legal effect,
or, if that be wrong, that they are confined to the question whether there has been a
breach by the purchaser of the terms imposed in paras 1 and 2 and perhaps to the
e question whether there has or has not been a loss or theft. Alternatively, he submits that
the bank cannot withhold approval on grounds not covered by the terms of the contract.
Finally, he reserved, but did not press, an argument to the effect that the issuer was not
in fact the bank, but BCCI Overseas. I shall say nothing about that since my understanding
of the concession made by the bank and accepted by the plaintiff's advisers is that,
f whereas strictly the defendants should have been BCCI Overseas, no point is taken as to
parties, which means that the action is proceeding as if BCCI Overseas had been sued.

Counsel for the bank advanced a number of alternative propositions. He suggested
that perhaps all that was required was that the bank should act honestly, or that the bank
had a right to withhold approval of a claim if it would be reasonable for a reasonable
issuer to do so. It would be reasonable, he submitted, if the purchaser had acted
negligently and certainly if he had been guilty of gross negligence or recklessness leading
g to the loss or theft. Further, he argued that approval could be withheld if the bank
believed on reasonable grounds that the purchaser had given an untrue account of the
loss or had been negligent etc.

I can dispose of some of these submissions quite shortly. The concept of the right to
reject being dependent on the bank's acting honestly is altogether too vague. On the
h other hand, I can see no justification for the plaintiff's contention that the words do not
confer any discretion at all nor for his submission that the discretion is confined to the
question of whether there has been a breach of paras 1 and 2 or whether there has or has
not been a theft. As to the first, from one point of view, any claim to a refund must
always be subject to the issuer's approval, because the issuer has to pay. By stipulating for
the right to approve, the issuer is reserving some sort of discretion and to hold otherwise
j involves that the words are surplusage. However, while plainly the right to withhold
approval exists where there has been no loss or theft, I see no basis for saying that the
only other factor entitling the issuer to refuse a refund is whether paras 1 and 2 have
been complied with.

There are difficulties about any of the suggested resolutions of the question as to the
nature of the discretion to withhold approval. They stem, in part, from the fact that the

contractual provisions are so sparse. However, the solution which I consider to be preferred is that which ties the discretion firmly to the provisions of the contract, namely *a* the formulation of counsel for the plaintiff that the issuer cannot withhold approval on grounds not covered by the contract. If the contract includes an implied obligation of care on the purchaser's part (which I have still to decide) this solution may be closer to one of the suggested alternatives of counsel for the bank than at first sight appears.

The other basis for the contention of counsel for the plaintiff that there was an express term that lost or stolen cheques would be refunded was the conversation with Mr *b* Chowdry. I have found that he said words to the effect that if the plaintiff took the cheques away unsigned, he would not be entitled to claim for loss and that this is to be regarded as of contractual significance. For reasons similar to those I have given for holding that para 3 of the purchase agreement imports an express obligation to refund lost or stolen cheques, I consider that these words also have that effect. However, the obligation is subject to the para 3 discretion.   *c*

I should add that, in so far as my conclusion that para 3 and the conversation with Mr Chowdry individually support the contention that there is an express entitlement to a refund is open to challenge, I would support my finding of an express term by reference to those two features collectively.

If I am wrong in finding an express obligation to refund lost or stolen cheques, is such an obligation to be implied? This is a question which, for a variety of reasons, it is not *d* easy to resolve.

I was referred to the passages dealing with implied terms in the standard textbooks: Treitel *Law of Contract* (7th edn, 1987) pp 158–162 and *Chitty on Contracts* (25th edn, 1983) vol 1, paras 841–848. I was also referred to, and found very helpful, passages from the judgment of Lloyd LJ in *National Bank of Greece SA v Pinios Shipping Co No 1, The Maira* [1989] 1 All ER 213. The issue with which the part of the judgment I am about to *e* cite was concerned was whether a term should be implied in a tripartite contract between a bank (the mortgagee of a ship which, in due course, was lost), Pinios (the owners of the ship who had defaulted in making an instalment payment of the price, which had therefore been paid by the bank pursuant to its guarantee of payment of Pinios's promissory note for that instalment) and Glafki (the agents appointed by the bank to manage and control the ship). The term contended for by Pinios was an implied term *f* obliging the bank to see that Glafki (who under the agreement were contractually obliged to insure the vessel for 130% of the amount secured by the mortgage, but had not fully complied with that obligation at the date of the loss of the vessel) did not under-insure the vessel; in effect, to supervise the carrying out by Glafki of their obligation in relation to insurance. I cite at some length from the judgment of Lloyd LJ ([1989] 1 All ER 213 at 218–220):   *g*

> '... in the course of developing his submissions, counsel [for the defendants, Pinios and its guarantor] shied away from the "officious bystander" test. In this he was wise. For, so far from it being obvious that the bank would have agreed to the suggested implied term, it seems to me quite obvious that it would not. Why should it? ... But that is by no means the end of the story. Counsel for the defendants *h* submits that this is a case where the law imposes a duty of care, irrespective of what the parties must have intended or agreed. To adopt the terminology of Treitel *Law of Contract* (7th edn, 1987) p 158, counsel relies on a term implied by law as distinct from a term implied in fact ... That there is a distinction between a term implied in a contract because it is what the parties must have agreed and a term implied by law is now well established, even if, as Lord Wilberforce preferred to put it in *j* *Liverpool City Council v Irwin* [1976] 2 All ER 39 at 43, [1977] AC 239 at 254, the distinction only represents two ends of a "continuous spectrum". When *Liverpool City Council v Irwin* was before the Court of Appeal, Lord Denning MR, in a dissenting judgment, said that it was time to get rid of the old clichés about "necessary to give business efficacy" and the "officious bystander" (see [1975] 3 All

ER 658 at 664, [1976] QB 319 at 329). The law, he said, implies a term whenever it is reasonable to do so, and that is an end of it. He gave, as examples, terms implied in a contract for the sale of goods and many others. Nobody asks in such cases whether the term is one which the parties must have intended or agreed. When the case reached the House of Lords the decision of the Court of Appeal was reversed. But there was no support for the broad principle stated by Lord Denning MR in the Court of Appeal. Lord Wilberforce described Lord Denning MR's principle as going a long way beyond sound authority. The point is put very clearly by Lord Cross ([1976] 2 All ER 39 at 46–47, [1977] AC 239 at 257–258): "When it implies a term in a contract the court is sometimes laying down a general rule that in all contracts of a certain type—sale of goods, master and servant, landlord and tenant, and so on—some provision is to be implied unless the parties have expressly excluded it. In deciding whether or not to lay down such a prima facie rule the court will naturally ask itself whether in the general run of such cases the term in question would be one which it would be reasonable to insert. Sometimes, however, there is no question of laying down any prima facie rule applicable to all cases of a defined type but what the court is being in effect asked to do is to rectify a particular—often a very detailed—contract by inserting in it a term which the parties have not expressed. Here it is not enough for the court to say that the suggested term is a reasonable one the presence of which would make the contract a better or fairer one; it must be able to say that the insertion of the term is necessary to give—as it is put—'business efficacy' to the contract and that if its absence had been pointed out at the time both parties—assuming them to have been reasonable men—would have agreed without hesitation to its insertion. The distinction between the two types of case was pointed out by Viscount Simonds and Lord Tucker in their speeches in *Lister v Romford Ice and Cold Storage Co Ltd* [1957] 1 All ER 125 at 134, 143, [1957] AC 555 at 579, 594, but I think that Lord Denning MR in proceeding— albeit with some trepidation—to 'kill off' Mackinnon LJ's 'officious bystander' must have overlooked it." So there is no doubt that there are, in the words of Lord Cross, contracts of a defined type in which the law will imply a term unless the parties have expressly excluded it. Can the present case be brought within any defined type? If we were concerned in the present case with the ordinary relationship of banker and customer, the law would imply certain obligations on the part of the bank, and a limited duty of care on the part of the customer (see *Tai Hing Cotton Mill Ltd v Liu Chong Hing Bank Ltd* [1985] 2 All ER 947, [1986] AC 80). But we are not here concerned with the ordinary relationship of banker and customer. We are concerned with a carefully drawn "one-off" contract between three parties, made for a particular purpose in special circumstances, and apparently making full provision for that purpose. I cannot imagine a contract which it would be more difficult to fit into a "defined type". But there is a further difficulty. Even if one could conjure up and define a type of contract into which the present contract could be fitted, there would remain the question whether the term on which counsel for the defendants seeks to rely should be implied. In the passage I have quoted from Lord Cross's speech in *Liverpool City Council v Irwin*, he appears to have accepted that where the court is laying down a general rule for all contracts of a certain type (sale of goods, master and servant, landlord and tenant and so on), the court asks whether the term is one which it would be *reasonable* to insert in the general run of such cases. But Lord Wilberforce took a rather different line. In his view only such obligations should be read into the contract "as the nature of the contract itself implicitly requires, no more, no less; a test in other words of necessity" (see [1976] 2 All ER 39 at 44, [1977] AC 239 at 254). It was Lord Wilberforce's test that the Privy Council adopted in *Tai Hing Cotton Mill Ltd v Liu Chong Hing Bank Ltd*. If, in that case, the Privy Council found it unnecessary to imply into an ordinary contract between banker and customer a duty wider than the duties recognised in *London Joint Stock*

Bank Ltd v Macmillan [1918] AC 777, [1918–19] All ER Rep 30 and *Greenwood v Martins Bank Ltd* [1933] AC 51, [1932] All ER Rep 318, I can see no necessity for *a* implying any duty of care on the part of the bank in the present case. For if we were to imply a duty of care on the part of the bank to see that Glafki did not under-insure the vessel, should we not also have to imply a duty of care to see that Glafki fulfilled its other specific duties under cl 3 of the management agreement? Should we not have to imply a duty to see that Glafki purchased all necessary stores and bunkers at the best price? Should we not have to imply a duty in relation to the *b* supervision of repairs? Clearly not. Such an implication would not only be unnecessary, but wholly unreasonable. So I see no necessity to imply a duty of care in relation to the procuring of insurance, assuming, contrary to my view, that this is the type of case in which the court would imply a term irrespective of the parties' presumed intentions. Counsel for the defendants returned over and over again in the course of his argument to the close relationship which existed between the bank *c* and Pinios. But the closeness of the relationship does not in itself justify the implication of a contractual term.' (Lloyd LJ's emphasis)

In the course of the hearing I more than once suggested that the term that issuers and purchasers might reasonably wish to include in their contract was a term along the following lines: that the issuer should be liable to replace or refund the value of lost or *d* stolen cheques provided that the purchaser had not breached his obligation in relation to counter-signature and had not been reckless or grossly negligent in caring for the cheques, so bringing about their loss or theft. For this suggestion there was, in the evidence, a considerable body of support. Mr Strange, who is employed by the bank as manager of its security and investigation department, made it clear that (assuming that the purchaser had not breached the countersigning obligations) he regarded the bank as being under *e* an obligation to refund the value of lost or stolen cheques save where the loss or theft had been occasioned by the gross negligence of the purchaser. Mr Baakza said that there was an obvious obligation on the bank to refund in all cases where there was no negligence and in the context I have no doubt that he meant by negligence something more than ordinary carelessness, something akin to recklessness or gross negligence. The general purport of the evidence of Mr Chowdry and Mr Krishnan (the man in charge of the *f* bank's traveller's cheque operations worldwide and an adviser to Visa) was to the same effect. In the case of Mr Krishnan, he may have been speaking essentially of practice rather than obligation, but he did say that there were only six or seven occasions in all his experience when a claim had been rejected and that the present case was exceptional.

Despite this evidence, counsel for the parties rejected any such implication. The primary contention of counsel for the bank was that there is no obligation to refund at *g* all, but that, if there is an obligation, there goes hand in hand with it an obligation on the purchaser to take care and/or to refrain from gross negligence, and breach of that precludes recovery. Counsel for the plaintiff was at the other end of the spectrum: there is an absolute obligation to refund, however negligent the customer had been.

If I approach the matter, as I must, not on the basis of what the parties might reasonably have agreed, but of what the law entitles me to regard as implied in their contract, I must *h* reject the argument of counsel for the plaintiff in so far as it is based on the officious bystander test. If I pose the question, would both parties readily have agreed, had they been asked, that the bank was obliged to replace lost or stolen travellers' cheques, however reckless or negligent the plaintiff had been in their custody? the answer must be that the bank would certainly not have agreed (see the evidence of the witnesses I have mentioned).

Counsel for the plaintiff, arguing for a favourable answer, sought to rely on those *j* witnesses' evidence, but overlooked the qualification that they attached to their ready assent to the bank's liability; and he did not seek to pose the question in terms which reflected the qualifications attached by the bank's witnesses. Perhaps that was because he recognised that an implied term so qualified would not avail him, or perhaps it was

because he anticipated that it was difficult for him to do so consistently with his strongly
a maintained position that there was no basis for confidently asserting that the plaintiff
would have assented to a term imposing an obligation to refund, but conditional on his
taking a degree of care.

However, so far as I recall and my note records, the plaintiff was not asked what would
have been his response to a suggestion that the bank's obligation to refund was subject to
an exception excusing it from doing so where he had been grossly negligent or reckless
b in the custody of the cheques and that conduct on his part had brought about the theft.
Can I be satisfied that the plaintiff would, as a reasonable man, have agreed to a term so
qualified had it been suggested to him? I would be glad if I could be persuaded to give
an affirmative answer to this question because it seems at first sight so obviously sensible
to accept that a purchaser should take at least some care of his traveller's cheques.
However, further reflection has convinced me that I cannot be confident that the plaintiff
c would have given such an answer. He probably would readily have assented to the
proposition that he must, as a matter of common sense, take proper care of the cheques;
but, if it had been suggested that failure to do so, at least if amounting to reckless want
of care, precluded him from recovering, I think that he would, as a reasonable man, have
hesitated, wanting to reflect on what would be the consequences to the bank of such
conduct on his part. Such reflection would have led him to the conclusion that, since if
d (as he would expect to do) he promptly notified the loss of the cheques in accordance
with the express obligation placed on him by the contract the bank would know, by the
time any cheques were presented to it for payment, that they were not 'countersigned by
the purchaser whose signature appears on the face in the presence of the person cashing'
and that, therefore, the condition on which the bank undertook to pay would to its
knowledge not have been complied with, the bank would not be out of pocket. This in
e turn might well have led him to reject the suggested qualification to the bank's liability.
He, of course, would not have known of the arrangements that existed between the bank
and Visa to accept such traveller's cheques in certain circumstances to which I shall make
reference later.

I conclude, therefore, that approaching the matter on the basis of the officious
f bystander test, while it can confidently be predicted that each of the parties would have
regarded it as going without saying that some term was to be implied, it can by no means
be confidently predicted that they would have had in mind the same term.

Turning, then, to the alternative approach to implied terms, is this a case in which
irrespective of the intention of the parties, the law imposes an obligation to refund, and,
if so, is it unqualified or subject to some such qualification as that for which counsel for
g the bank contends? As I understand the decisions of the House of Lords and the Privy
Council in *Liverpool City Council v Irwin* [1976] 2 All ER 39, [1977] AC 239 and *Tai Hing
Cotton Mill Ltd v Liu Chong Hing Bank Ltd* [1985] 2 All ER 947, [1986] 1 AC 80, cited by
Lloyd LJ in the passage I have quoted from his judgment in *National Bank of Greece SA v
Pinios Shipping Co No 1, The Maira* [1989] 1 All ER 213 at 218–220, the first requirement
is that the contract in question should be a contract of a defined type. That poses no
h difficulty because the issue and purchase of traveller's cheques is self-evidently such a
contract. The second requirement is that the implication of the term should be necessary:
in the words of Lord Wilberforce, 'such obligation should be read into the contract as the
nature of the contract itself implicitly requires, no more, no less; a test in other words of
necessity' (see *Liverpool City Council v Irwin* [1976] 2 All ER 39 at 44, [1977] AC 239 at
254). It must be remembered of course that this type of implied term can be excluded
j by express stipulation: see Lord Cross's speech in *Liverpool City Council v Irwin* [1976] 2
All ER 39 at 48, [1977] AC 239 at 259. It can also be so modified.

Here, it seems to me, counsel for the plaintiff is on much firmer ground. As I have
already pointed out, Stuart-Smith J in *Fellus v National Westminster Bank plc* said:

'There is a considerable advantage over cash as far as the public are concerned

because of the refund provisions. This is a matter which is advertised by issuing
banks in general . . .'

a

I have so far refrained from mentioning, but in this context it is relevant, that the bank
in this case was shown to have included in some of its advertising material (not seen by
the plaintiff) the words, 'If lost, worldwide refund service is provided at 60,000 locations
including banks' branches and major hotels'.

In Cowen *Law of Negotiable Instruments in South Africa* (5th edn, 1985) vol 1, p 295 I find
this statement:

b

> 'They [traveller's cheques] offer the great advantage, compared with carrying
> foreign currency, that if they are lost or stolen before the traveller has countersigned
> them, he may claim a refund from the issuer, or replacements, with comparative
> ease.'

Later in the same work is this passage (at 309):

c

> 'The main problem [in the relations between issuer and traveller] concerns the
> traveller's legal rights against the issuer in the event of the instruments being lost or
> stolen. In dealing with this problem it must again be emphasised that the point of
> departure is the particular contract entered into between the issuer and the traveller.
> The American Express "purchase agreement" makes express provision for prompt
> refunds or the issue of substitutes in the event of loss, provided that the traveller had
> not signed the instruments before loss. However, in the case of some other issuers
> (e.g. Visa travellers' cheques), claims for a refund are made "subject to approval by
> the issuer", though it is understood in practice the Amexco procedure is followed.
> Under the Amexco "purchase agreement" if the loss or theft occurs at a time when
> the instruments have not yet been countersigned by the traveller, then the traveller
> is entitled as of right to obtain a refund of the face value of the instruments, or to
> have them replaced.'

d

e

In *Chitty on Contracts* (25th edn, 1983) vol 2, para 2557 is the following statement:

> 'If the loss of the instruments occurs while they do not bear a countersignature,
> the traveller is entitled to obtain their face value from the issuing banker, provided
> he agrees to sign an indemnity. Such an indemnity would protect the banker if it
> turned out that, despite the traveller's statement, the cheques had been countersigned
> before they were lost. In such cases the banker would have to honour them when
> presented by a holder in due course, and the indemnity would enable him to recover
> the amount so paid from the traveller. The indemnity does not, however, enable
> the banker to recover from the traveller an amount paid to a holder who was not
> entitled to payment.'

f

g

For this last statement, the authors cite *Sullivan v Knauth* (1914) 146 NYS 583; *affd*
(1917) 220 NY 216. The basis of the decision was that the relationship was one equivalent
to banker and customer, and that the bank, having paid, albeit in good faith, on a forged
counter-signature, the purchaser was entitled to reimbursement. In his judgment at first
instance Clarke J said (146 NYS 583 at 585–586):

h

> 'In my opinion a relation cognate to that of depositor and banker should be
> considered to have been established between the plaintiff and these defendants. If
> that is not the effect of the transaction, the traveler obtains little advantage from
> these so-called travelers' checks and might as well carry bills or gold. The basis of his
> purchase is protection by reason of the double signature. Safety is the thing
> impressed upon him.'

j

In Chorley *Law of Banking* (6th edn, 1974) p 261 are statements distinctly pointing the
other way:

'A traveller who has lost cheques, or even had them stolen from him, is not
unlikely to claim to have them replaced, and it is believed that issuing banks
normally adopt a generous policy in such cases, but their legal obligation to do so
seems doubtful.'

A footnote extends the argument:

'In law it is difficult to see any valid ground on which such a traveller could base
a claim. He has bought the instrument, and if he loses it, how can he claim to be
indemnified? Such a right could, of course, arise out of the contract between the
parties, and it would seem possible that the advertisements of the American Express
Company amount to such an offer which the traveller accepts by the purchase of the
cheques. But the position is not the same with the British banks, and although it is
believed that the policy pursued by them is a generous one, it is not considered that
any usage to replace lost cheques could be proved.'

Again, in Sheldon and Fidler *Practice and Law of Banking* (11th edn, 1982) p 263 appears
the following statement:

'If travellers' cheques are lost, the loss may technically be the traveller's, but most
major banks now undertake to replace lost or stolen cheques provided the local
police have been informed.'

Assisted by these authorities and statements of opinion, I must address the question: is
it a necessary incident of contracts for the purchase and sale of traveller's cheques that the
issuing bank should be under an obligation to refund the value of lost or stolen cheques?
The following features of the transaction seem to be of particular importance.

1. The object of the transaction is security, otherwise, as Clarke J observed, the traveller
might as well carry cash (and save himself the commission ordinarily charged on such
cheques).

2. The issuing bank has had the traveller's money, and has contracted with the
traveller to pay the cheque when countersigned with the travellers' signature.

3. I believe I am justified in inferring that the issuing bank invariably requires prompt
notification of loss, so that ordinarily, if the traveller has complied (and, if he has not, the
bank anyway has grounds for resisting a refund) the bank will know before any cheque
is presented that the countersignature is a forgery.

It seems to me that, in these circumstances, it is necessary to imply an obligation of
some sort on the part of issuing banks to refund the value of lost or stolen cheques.

I can see no reason for qualifying that obligation by confining it to cases where the loss
has occurred without negligence or without gross negligence or recklessness. Such
deficiencies on the part of the traveller do not determine whether he or the issuer is out
of pocket. An argument may exist for a qualification of a different sort, but for reasons
which I shall explain I need not, in this case, reach a final conclusion about that. What I
have in mind is that, as I learnt in this case, there do exist between issuers and Visa (and
no doubt other organisations who furnish cheques) agreements as to the circumstances
in which issuers may refuse to honour cheques known to be forged. In the present case,
there is a provision that final payment may not be refused on a cheque reported lost or
stolen, unless the signature and counter-signature do not compare favourably, or the
original signature has been obviously altered or the cheque has been altered in a manner
which should have been obvious to the acceptor.

Such agreements are dictated by good commercial considerations: forgeries are
widespread and often skilful; the intermediate party, who cashes the cheque, does not
know the signature of the traveller and a too ready refusal to pay wholly innocent and
careful intermediaries could soon lead to a refusal by them to accept that brand of cheque
and a consequent decline in its use.

It may well be, therefore, that the obligation, which I do consider necessity requires to be implied in contracts between issuers and purchasers, ought to be subject to some qualification to take account of commercial realities. It can be argued, on the other hand, *a* that if, without modifying the contractual provisions as to payment that are made between the issuer and purchaser, issuers choose to bind themselves to such extraneous contracts they must suffer the loss.

The reason I need not decide in the present case whether any such qualification is necessary is that the evidence establishes that none of the forged signatures compared favourably, but the bank nevertheless, for what it conceived to be good commercial *b* reasons, paid most of them. Accordingly, any such qualification would not avail them.

It is appropriate at this stage to summarise the conclusions I have reached in relation to express and implied terms. (1) I consider that the contract contained an express term obliging the bank to refund the value of lost or stolen cheques. (2) That term was subject to a discretion not to pay where the purchaser had broken one of his contractual obligations. (3) There was no implied term precluding recovery by the purchaser where *c* the loss of the cheques had resulted from his want of care or recklessness. It follows that neither the fact of want of care or recklessness nor the bank's belief in their existence offered the bank grounds for refusing, in its discretion, to make refunds. (4) If I am wrong in holding that there was an express term entitling the purchaser to a refund, I hold that there was an implied term. That term is subject to the same qualifications afforded by the discretionary right to resist a refund.   *d*

There remains the alternative claim in conversion and/or for money had and received. In the light of the conclusions I have reached, I do not propose to rehearse the arguments or state my conclusions in any detail. It does, however, seem to me distinctly arguable that the bank, by honouring cheques which it had agreed with the plaintiff not to pay unless they were countersigned by him and in the knowledge that they were not countersigned by him (and I would added for good measure, without any contractual *e* obligation as between itself and the intermediate parties), did convert the cheques. They belonged to the plaintiff, and had he repossessed himself of them, he would, by adding his counter-signature, have been able to require the bank to pay their face value. As it is, the bank has precluded him from doing so.

The plea of estoppel fails, if only because plainly the bank was not 'obliged to make *f* payments to cashing agents'. The plea that the plaintiff's loss was not caused by the conversion fails for the same reason. The suggested defences based on the claim in conversion being inconsistent with the bank's discretion and/or contrary to an implied term, likewise fail both in principle (I cannot see how they could be justified even apart from my conclusions on the extent of the discretion and the issue of implied terms) and because, on the view I take, there would be nothing inconsistent between the claim for *g* conversion and the provisions of the contract.

There will accordingly be judgment for the plaintiff for the sum claimed, with appropriate interest, as to which, no doubt, counsel can agree.

Judgment for the plaintiff.

h

Solicitors: *L B Marks & Co* (for the plaintiff); *Stephenson Harwood* (for the bank).

K Mydeen Esq   Barrister.

a
Gibson or Scoullar or Archibald v Archibald

HOUSE OF LORDS
LORD KEITH OF KINKEL, LORD BRANDON OF OAKBROOK, LORD TEMPLEMAN, LORD OLIVER OF
AYLMERTON AND LORD GOFF OF CHIEVELEY
5 DECEMBER 1988, 19 JANUARY 1989

b
Divorce – Financial provision – Lump sum order – Deferment of payment – Deferment of payment of capital sum for lengthy period – Husband's conduct causing breakdown of marriage – Husband's only asset was matrimonial home – Husband living in matrimonial home with three children of marriage – Whether appropriate to award substantial capital sum to wife while postponing payment for six years until youngest child attaining 16 years – Divorce (Scotland)
c
Act 1976, s 5.

The husband and wife were married in 1973 and had three children. In 1983 the wife was granted a decree of divorce in the Court of Session in Scotland on the ground that the marriage had irretrievably broken down as the result of the husband's conduct. The husband was awarded custody of the three children. In ancillary proceedings the wife sought payment by the husband of a capital sum of £25,000 under s 5[a] of the Divorce
d
(Scotland) Act 1976. At the date of proof before the Lord Ordinary the husband and the wife were aged 58 and 49 respectively. The husband's only asset was the matrimonial home, valued at £42,000, in which he resided with the children. The husband had bought the house before his marriage to the wife when he was married to another woman. The wife did not seek immediate payment of the capital sum but payment in six years' time (by which time the youngest child would have attained the age of 16) so
e
that disturbance to the children would be avoided. The Lord Ordinary considered that it would be inappropriate to defer payment for such a long period and he awarded the wife a capital sum of £500, which the husband would be able to realise without selling the house. The Second Division of the Inner House of the Court of Session, even though it considered a payment of £500 to be inequitable, affirmed that decision on the ground
f
that there were too many imponderables, namely uncertain and speculative future events, in deferring payment for more than six years. The wife appealed to the House of Lords.

Held – Since at the time of making an order under s 5 of the 1976 Act it was not open to a spouse to return to the court later to seek revision of the order if there was a change of circumstances, it was appropriate for the court when considering the equitable order to
g
make to take account of future changes of circumstances which were foreseeable as being likely to occur, rather than those which were merely speculative. Since it was foreseeable that the three children would, in the ordinary course of events, become self-supporting or marry and leave home the court was not debarred, in arriving at an equitable result, from awarding a substantial capital sum and deferring payment for a lengthy period.
h
The appropriate course in the circumstances was to award the wife a capital sum of £15,000 and postpone enforcement of the order until the sixteenth birthday of the

---

a   Section 5, so far as material, provides:
       '(1) In an action for divorce ... either party to the marriage may, at any time prior to decree
j
    being granted, apply to the court for any one or more of the following orders ... (b) an order for
    the payment to him or for his benefit by the other party to the marriage of a capital sum ...
       (2) Where an application under the foregoing subsection has been made in an action, the court,
    on granting decree in that action, shall make with respect to the application such order, if any, as
    it thinks fit, having regard to the respective means of the parties to the marriage and to all the
    circumstances of the case, including any settlement or other arrangements made for financial
    provision for any child of the marriage ...'

youngest child in December 1991. Accordingly, the appeal would be allowed (see p 259 *g* to p 260 *h*, post).

a

Notes

For power to order lump sum payments, see 13 Halsbury's Laws (4th edn) para 1105, and for cases on the subject, see 27(3) Digest (2nd reissue) 243–256, 10634–10698.

As from 1 September 1986 the Family Law (Scotland) Act 1985 made fresh provision regarding financial or other consequences of decrees of divorce in place of, inter alia, s 5 *b* of the Divorce (Scotland) Act 1976. By s 12(2) of the 1985 Act the court may stipulate that an order for financial provision may come into effect at a specified future time. Section 12(2) of the Family Law (Scotland) Act 1985 corresponds to s 24A(4) of the Matrimonial Causes Act 1973. For s 24A(4) of the 1973 Act, see 27 Halsbury's Statutes (4th edn) 729.

c

Cases referred to in opinions

Crooks v Crooks 1986 SLT 500, Ct of Sess.
Gray v Gray 1968 SC 185, Ct of Sess.

Appeal

Mrs Iris Gibson or Scoullar or Archibald (the wife) appealed against an interlocutor of the *d* Second Division of the Inner House of the Court of Session, Scotland (the Lord Justice Clerk (Ross), Lord Dunpark and Lord McDonald) dated 24 February 1988 refusing a reclaiming motion for the wife for review of an interlocutor of the Lord Ordinary (Lord Kincraig) dated 21 November 1985 whereby he ordered the respondent, Leonard Cecil Charles Archibald (the husband), to pay the wife a capital sum of £500 with extract superseded for six months following the grant of a decree of divorce to the wife. The *e* facts are set out in the opinion of Lord Keith.

Donald Macauley QC and *Clive Shenton* (both of the Scottish Bar) for the wife.
W M Campbell QC and *R A Dunlop* (both of the Scottish Bar) for the husband.

Their Lordships took time for consideration.

f

19 January. The following opinions were delivered.

LORD KEITH OF KINKEL. My Lords, this appeal arises out of an action of divorce, at the instance of the appellant (the wife) against the respondent (the husband). The parties were married at Glasgow on 13 April 1973, and there are three children of the *g* marriage, two daughters and a son, born respectively on 13 January 1971, 27 November 1973 and 15 December 1975. The marriage finally broke down in August 1983 and on 15 August the wife started proceedings for divorce on the grounds of irretrievable breakdown of the marriage occasioned by the husband's behaviour. The Lord Ordinary (Lord Kincraig) granted a decree of divorce on that ground on 21 November 1985. *h* Custody of the three children was awarded to the husband.

The wife claimed against the husband payment of a capital sum of £25,000. In the conclusions of the summons she also claimed a periodical allowance for herself, but at the proof she in effect abandoned that claim in respect that at the time the husband was unemployed and subsisting on social security payments. By a separate interlocutor of 21 November 1985 the Lord Ordinary awarded the wife a capital sum of £500. The wife *j* reclaimed, but on 24 February 1988 the Second Division affirmed that interlocutor, the opinion of the court being delivered by Lord Dunpark. The wife now appeals to your Lordships' House.

At the date of the proof before the Lord Ordinary the husband and the wife were aged respectively 58 years and 49 years. The husband's only capital asset was the former

matrimonial home, valued at £42,000, in which he resided with the three children. He
a had bought it in 1960 for £3,000 with the aid of a mortgage, since paid off. At the time
he was married to another woman. In the course of her evidence at the proof, the wife
stated that in order that disturbance to the children might be avoided she did not seek
immediate payment of a capital sum. Funds to meet it could only be raised by selling the
house. She did, however, wish to be paid a capital sum after the youngest child had
attained the age of 16 or 17 years.
b   In these circumstances the Lord Ordinary, in his words—

> 'gave to the parties an opportunity of coming to an agreement with regard to the
> disposal of the house in the event of my finding [the wife] entitled to payment of a
> substantial capital sum, since I did not consider it appropriate to grant decree now
> for any substantial sum and supersede extract for six years.'

c In the event, the parties did not reach any agreement. Thereupon the Lord Ordinary
decided not to award the wife a substantial capital sum, because to do so would in his
view be contrary to the interests of the children in respect that the husband would have
to sell the house and move with them to other accommodation. He expressed himself as
satisfied, however, that the husband would be able to realise a sum of £500 without
selling the house, and he accordingly awarded the wife a capital sum of that amount,
d with extract superseded for six months.
    In the course of delivering the opinion of the Second Division Lord Dunpark said:

> 'It is certainly not equitable that the husband whose conduct was solely responsible
> for the breakdown of the marriage should be left with a house worth £42,000,
> while the wife's contribution to the organisation of the home and the care of the
e > children for a period of 12 years is only marked by a capital award of £500 ... We
> do not consider that the Lord Ordinary can be faulted in deciding that it was
> inappropriate to supersede extract for what would have been more than six years ...
> There are too many imponderables in superseding extract for a period of six years,
> and the Lord Ordinary was entitled to conclude that superseding extract for so long
> a period was not appropriate.'

f   The principle to be applied in considering whether the decision of a Lord Ordinary on
a financial claim arising on divorce is open to successful challenge was thus stated by
Lord Guthrie in Gray v Gray 1968 SC 185 at 193:

> 'The Inner House would be entitled to interfere with the amount of his award if
> he had misdirected himself in law, or had failed to take into account a relevant and
g > material factor, or had reached a result which was manifestly inequitable.'

    Under the legislation relating to financial provision for spouses and children on divorce
which was in force at the time of the proof in this case, namely s 5 of the Divorce
(Scotland) Act 1976, a decision about payment of a capital sum had to be made finally on
decree of divorce being granted. It was not open to a spouse to return to the court later
h and seek revision of the decision in the light of a change of circumstances. In that
situation it was, in my opinion, entirely appropriate in making the decision to take into
account future changes of circumstances which were foreseeable. In the present case it
was foreseeable that in the ordinary course of events the three children of the marriage
would eventually become self-supporting or marry and would leave home. It is true that
this result, although likely to happen in the ordinary course of events, might be frustrated
j by circumstances not foreseeable. But in considering what is the equitable order to make,
it is those changes of circumstances which are likely, not those which are merely
speculative, which are proper to be taken into account, or at least which are deserving of
being given greater weight. It is not correct to be distracted from arriving at a just and
equitable result on the ground of 'imponderables', which simply means uncertain and
speculative future events.

It appears that both the Lord Ordinary and the Second Division took the view that in general it would never be appropriate to award a substantial capital sum and postpone *a* extract of the decree for so long as six years. In my opinion that view involves placing an unwarranted fetter on the discretion of the court in the exercise of its function of arriving at an equitable result, and amounts to a misdirection in law. Lord Dunpark described the outcome as regards payment of a capital sum to the wife in this case as 'certainly not equitable' which would appear to mean much the same as 'manifestly inequitable', the words used by Lord Guthrie in *Gray v Gray*. He went on to suggest that the provisions of *b* s 5 of the 1976 Act necessarily led to inequity in a considerable number of cases, a situation which had been alleviated by the wider provisions contained in s 8 of the Family Law (Scotland) Act 1985. The latter provisions have indeed introduced an enhanced and welcome degree of flexibility to the powers of the court to do justice in property matters arising on divorce. In so far, however, as it was open to the court to use its available powers to enable the provisions of the 1976 Act to operate as equitably as *c* possible, it was surely its duty to do so. In certain cases the award of a substantial sum with supersession of extract for a lengthy period may have been capable of achieving that result. *Crooks v Crooks* 1986 SLT 500 was such a case and the present, in my opinion, is another.

My Lords, I would allow the appeal on the ground that both the Lord Ordinary and the Second Division misdirected themselves in law by placing an unwarranted fetter on *d* their discretion so as to disable themselves from arriving at an equitable result, and so arrived at a manifestly inequitable one. It is for consideration whether the appropriate course in the circumstances is to remit the case back to the Court of Session to assess the substantial capital sum which should properly be awarded to the wife, subject to extract being superseded, or whether your Lordships should undertake that exercise. I am of opinion that considering that over three years have passed since the decision of the Lord *e* Ordinary and in the interest of saving further expense the right course is for this House to assess the capital sum payable to the wife by the husband at £15,000, extract of the decree therefor being superseded until 15 December 1991, the sixteenth birthday of the youngest child.

LORD BRANDON OF OAKBROOK. My Lords, for the reasons given by my noble *f* and learned friend Lord Keith, I would allow the appeal and make the order which he proposes.

LORD TEMPLEMAN. My Lords, for the reasons given by my noble and learned friend Lord Keith, I would allow the appeal and make the order which he proposes.

g

LORD OLIVER OF AYLMERTON. My Lords, I have had the advantage of reading in draft the speech delivered by my noble and learned friend Lord Keith. I agree that this appeal should be allowed for the reasons which he has given. I also agree with the order which he has proposed.

h

LORD GOFF OF CHIEVELEY. My Lords, I have had the advantage of reading in draft the speech delivered by my noble and learned friend Lord Keith and, for the reasons he gives, I would allow the appeal and make the order which he proposes.

Appeal allowed.

j

Solicitors: *Baileys Shaw & Gillett*, agents for *John G Gray & Co*, Edinburgh, agents for *Robertson & Ross*, Paisley (for the wife); *Gasters*, agents for *Pairman Miller & Murray WS*, Edinburgh, agents for *Armstrong & Co*, Glasgow (for the husband).

Mary Rose Plummer　Barrister.

a
Gomba Holdings UK Ltd and others v Minories Finance Ltd and others

COURT OF APPEAL, CIVIL DIVISION
FOX, STOCKER AND BUTLER-SLOSS LJJ
12, 13, 29 JULY 1988

b

Company – Receiver – Appointment by debenture holder – Document created by receiver during receivership – Termination of receivership – Mortgagor companies seeking delivery up of documents relating to companies' affairs created for or on behalf of receivers – Mortgagor companies asserting ownership of documents – Whether fact that documents were created for or on behalf of receivers sufficient to confer ownership of the documents on the companies.

c

Two partners in a firm of accountants were appointed by the debenture holder to be receivers and managers of a group of companies which included the plaintiff companies. Following the discharge of the receiverships the plaintiff companies obtained an order requiring the receivers to deliver up all documents relating to the plaintiff companies' affairs. In pursuance of that order the receivers delivered up a number of files of

d documents belonging to the plaintiff companies but refused to deliver up various categories of documents comprising, inter alia, documents created by the receivers to advise and inform the debenture holder on the conduct of the receiverships and the draft accounts and working papers which had been prepared as part of the final audit of the plaintiff companies' books. The receivers claimed that such documents, although they related to the plaintiff companies' affairs, did not belong to the plaintiff companies. The

e plaintiff companies' subsequent motion for the delivery up of the remaining documents was based on a claim to ownership, namely that during the receivership the receivers were the agents of the plaintiff companies and that, as between principal and agent, all documents concerning the principal's affairs which had been prepared or received by the agent belonged to the principal. The judge dismissed the motion and the plaintiff

f companies appealed.

Held – The ownership of documents in the tripartite situation of a receivership of a company depended on whether the documents were brought into being in discharge of the receiver's duties to the mortgagor or the debenture holder or neither. The receiver had a duty to advise and inform the debenture holder regarding the conduct of the

g receivership and, consequently, documents created for that purpose, such as those in dispute, could not be the property of the company even though they could be said to relate to the company's affairs. The fact that the documents were created for or on behalf of the receiver who was, technically, the agent of the company was not sufficient to confer ownership of the documents on the company. Accordingly, the judge's decision rejecting the plaintiffs companies' claim to ownership of the documents in dispute was

h correct and the appeal would therefore be dismissed (see p 263 *b* to *d e* to p 264 *b e j*, p 265 *b c e* to *g* and p 266 *b c e*, post).
Chantrey Martin & Co v Martin [1953] 2 All ER 691 applied.

Notes
For an order against a receiver to give discovery of documents belonging to a company,

j see 7(2) Halsbury's Laws (4th edn reissue) para 1166, and for a case on the subject, see 10 Digest (Reissue) 887, 5143.

Cases referred to in judgments
Chantrey Martin & Co v Martin [1953] 2 All ER 691, [1953] 2 QB 286, [1953] 3 WLR 459, CA.

Magadi Soda Co Ltd, Re (1925) 41 TLR 297.
North and South Trust Co v Berkeley [1971] 1 All ER 980, [1971] 1 WLR 470.

Cases also cited
Gomba Holdings UK Ltd v Homan [1986] 3 All ER 94, [1986] 1 WLR 1301.
Leicestershire CC v Michael Faraday & Partners Ltd [1941] 2 All ER 483, [1941] 2 KB 205, CA.

Appeal
The plaintiffs, Gomba Holdings UK Ltd and seven other companies belonging to the Gomba group of companies, appealed against the decision of Hoffmann J ([1988] BCLC 60) made on 9 October 1987 dismissing the plaintiffs' motion for delivery up of various categories of documents relating to the plaintiffs' affairs which had been created by or on behalf of the second and third defendants, Andrew Mark Homan and Colin Graham Bird, who were accountants and partners in the firm of Messrs Price Waterhouse and had been appointed to be receivers and managers of the Gomba group by its debenture holder, the first defendants, Minories Finance Ltd, on the ground that the documents did not belong to the plaintiffs. The facts are set out in the judgment of Fox LJ.

T L G Cullen QC and *Anthony Trace* for the plaintiffs.
Robin Potts QC and *Richard Adkins* for the defendants.

Cur adv vult

29 July. The following judgments were delivered.

FOX LJ. This is an appeal by the plaintiffs from a decision of Hoffmann J on a motion for the delivery up by the defendants of certain documents (see [1988] BCLC 60).

In 1985 the second and third defendants, Mr Homan and Mr Bird, who were accountants and partners in the firm of Messrs Price Waterhouse, were appointed by the first defendants, Minories Finance Ltd (MFL), as debenture holder to be receivers and managers of certain companies known as the Gomba group (the companies) and which included the plaintiffs. The receiverships were discharged about the end of 1986 or early 1987.

By an order of 13 April 1987 the receivers were ordered by Hoffmann J to deliver up to the plaintiffs or their solicitors within two months—

'all other documents of title books records accounts and other documentation of whatsoever description belonging to the plaintiffs and all other companies within the group of companies of which the plaintiffs form part in the possession of [the receivers] . . .'

In pursuance of that order the receivers delivered up some 268 files of documents belonging to the companies. At the same time, Price Waterhouse on behalf of the receivers, by a letter of 12 June 1987 to the plaintiffs' solicitors, set forth various categories of documents relating to the affairs of the companies which came into existence or were received by or on behalf of the receivers during the receivership but which the receivers declined to deliver up on the grounds that such documents were not the property of the companies. By the present motion, the plaintiffs asserted their ownership of these documents or some of them. Hoffmann J dismissed the motion and the plaintiffs now appeal.

The plaintiffs' case is put forward on the basis of title: they claim ownership of the documents. Thus we are not concerned with any issue as to relevance (this is not a claim for discovery). And we are not concerned with the ownership of information.

The basis of the claim to ownership is that the receivers were, during the receivership,

a the agents of the companies and were paid by the companies. It is said that, as between principal and agent, all documents concerning the principal's affairs which have been prepared or received by the agent belong to the principal and have to be delivered up on the termination of the agency.

In general terms that is a correct statement of principle but it cannot be applied mechanically to the somewhat complex position of a receivership. The agency of a

b receiver is not an ordinary agency. It is primarily a device to protect the mortgagee or debenture holder. Thus, the receiver acts as agent for the mortgagor in that he has power to affect the mortgagor's position by acts which, though done for the benefit of the debenture holder, are treated as if they were the acts of the mortgagor. The relationship set up by the debenture, and the appointment of the receiver, however, is not simply between the mortgagor and the receiver. It is tripartite and involves the mortgagor, the

c receiver and the debenture holder. The receiver is appointed by the debenture holder, on the happening of specified events, and becomes the mortgagor's agent whether the mortgagor likes it or not. And, as a matter of contract between the mortgagor and the debenture holder, the mortgagor will have to pay the receiver's fees. Further, the mortgagor cannot dismiss the receiver since that power is reserved to the debenture holder as another of the contractual terms of the loan. It is to be noted also that the

d mortgagor cannot instruct the receiver how to act in the conduct of the receivership.

All this is far removed from the ordinary principal and agent situation so far as the mortgagor and the receiver are concerned. Whilst the receiver is the agent of the mortgagor he is the appointee of the debenture holder and, in practical terms, has a close association with him. Moreover, he owes fiduciary duties to the debenture holder who has a right, as against the receiver, to be put in possession of all the information

e concerning the receivership available to the receiver: see *Re Magadi Soda Co Ltd* (1925) 41 TLR 297.

The result is that the receiver, in the course of the receivership, performs duties on behalf of the debenture holder as well as the mortgagor. And these duties may relate closely to the affairs of the entity which is the subject of the receivership. It is, therefore, not satisfactory to approach the problem of the ownership of documents which come

f into existence in the course of the receivership on the basis that ownership depends on whether the documents relate to the affairs of (in this case) the companies.

I agree with Hoffmann J that the ownership of the documents in the tripartite situation of a receivership depends on whether the documents were brought into being in discharge of the receiver's duties to the mortgagor or to the debenture holder or neither. The fact that a document relates to the mortgagor's affairs cannot be determinative. All

g sorts of documents may relate to the mortgagor's affairs but to which the mortgagor cannot possibly have any proprietary claim.

It is said that the judge's approach is unworkable because the receivers owed a duty both to MFL and the companies. No doubt they did owe duties to both, but they were quite separate duties. The existence of the two duties does not entitle the court to ignore

h the fact that the ownership of documents created pursuant to one cannot determine the ownership of documents created pursuant to the other. It is also said that the receivers have a duty to maintain the records of the companies. But that does not help one to decide what *are* the records of the companies, ie whether a document belongs to the companies or someone else.

The receivers in the present case plainly had a duty to manage the affairs of the

j companies. All documents which were created or received in pursuance of that duty must be the property of the companies. That would include, for example, the ordinary correspondence sent and received by the companies in the conduct of their affairs.

On the other hand (and this is the second group), the receivers had to advise and inform the debenture holders regarding the conduct of the receivership. Documents created for that purpose, while they can certainly be said to relate to the affairs of the companies, cannot be the property of the companies. They were not brought into being for the purpose of the companies' business or affairs and the fact that they were created by or on behalf of persons who are, technically, the agents of the companies cannot be sufficient to create ownership in the companies.

Thirdly, there are documents prepared by, or on behalf of, the receivers not in pursuance of any duty to prepare them but simply to enable the receivers to prepare such documents or perform such duties as they were required to prepare or perform for the purposes of their professional duties to the debenture holders or the companies. Such papers are, I think, the property of the receivers. Thus, in *Chantrey Martin & Co v Martin* [1953] 2 All ER 691, [1953] 2 QB 286 it was held by the Court of Appeal that working accounts and the papers which are brought into existence by chartered accountants in the preparation of a final audit of a client's books are the property of the accountants.

Against that background I come to the documents which have been in dispute and which are set out in Price Waterhouse's letter of 12 June 1987. They are as follows:

'*List A*
    (i) advice to [MFL] by Price Waterhouse prior to the appointment of the receivers.'

As I understand it, there is no longer any issue as to these. In any event I see no basis for any claim by the companies to ownership of documents created for the purpose of enabling professional advisers of MFL to give such advice.

    '(ii) formal reports to MFL by the Receivers, notes of any meetings whose purpose was to report on the current situation with regard to the receivership and letters written by the Receivers to MFL updating them on the current situation with regard to the receivership.'

All these are to a greater or lesser extent concerned with the affairs of the companies. But that, as I have indicated, does not advance the companies' claims to ownership.

The test cannot be whether a document relates to the companies' affairs (as the judge said, this is not a claim for discovery) but must depend on the capacity in which the receivers were acting when they brought the documents into existence. Thus, in *North and South Trust Co v Berkeley* [1971] 1 All ER 980, [1971] 1 WLR 470 a Lloyds broker also acted as agent for the underwriters in instructing an assessor to deal with a claim by the assured. It was held that he was not obliged to disclose the report to his principal. Donaldson J said ([1971] 1 All ER 980 at 993, [1971] 1 WLR 470 at 486):

    'However, I think that the fallacy underlying the plaintiffs' claim may be even simpler and more basic. Lamberts [the broker] in acting for the defendant, were undertaking duties which inhibited the proper performance of their duties towards the plaintiffs, but insofar as they acted for the defendant they were not acting in the discharge of any duty towards the plaintiffs. Lamberts wore the plaintiffs' hat and the underwriter's hat side by side, and in consequence, as was only to be expected, neither hat fitted properly. The plaintiffs had a legitimate complaint on this account and can claim damages if and to the extent that the partial dislodgment of their hat has caused them loss or damage. But what the plaintiffs ask in these proceedings is to be allowed to see what Lamberts were keeping under the underwriter's hat, and for that there is no warrant.'

Thus, the information in the report directly concerned the affairs of the assured but it did not belong to him because the brokers had, albeit wrongly, received it in the capacity of agents for the underwriters. There is no question of breach of duty in the present case. The only issue is were the documents brought into being in discharge of a duty to the debenture holders or to the companies?

It seems to me that all the documents in this category were prepared in discharge of the receivers' duties to the debenture holders and are not the property of the companies. I do not disregard the fact that the receivers are remunerated by the companies. But I do a not think that is any indication of ownership in a case where professional advisers owed duties to two separate persons and are paid by one of those persons in pursuance of a contract entered into with the other of them.

'(iii) memoranda to the file written by MFL personnel and copied to the receivers.'

b The judge, in my view rightly, concluded that those were documents created by MFL for its own purposes (ie as MFL records) and that the receivers were merely sent copies as advisers to MFL. The receivers were not sent them as agents for the companies. The documents are the property of MFL.

'(iv) any documents relating to advice given by [Price Waterhouse] to MFL in connection with assets of the Plaintiffs charged to MFL.'

c These are documents produced by professional advisers to MFL for MFL's own purposes, ie advice regarding MFL's security. They do not belong to the companies.

'(v) documentation belonging to us [the receivers] in our personal capacities, including legal advice . . . press releases and other partnership documents belonging to Price Waterhouse.'

d As I understand it, production of these documents is not now being sought.

'(vi) documentation relating to our advice to MFL in connection with the several attempts by the plaintiffs to redeem the security.'

e Documents prepared for the purpose of giving advice to MFL relating to their own property (ie the security) cannot, in my view, be the property of the companies. They were prepared solely by reference to a relationship between the receivers and MFL in which the receivers were acting as agents for, or personal advisers to, MFL.

'(vii) copy court documentation (ie pleadings, affidavits etc) relating to the various actions in the High Court by the Plaintiffs against the receivers and MFL, including records of information received relating directly to the challenge to our appointment and of conversations with our solicitors in connection therewith.'

f These documents were prepared not by the receivers as receivers but simply as agents for MFL. The companies, accordingly, have no property in them.

'(viii) notes with an exclusively internal circulation prepared by the receivers or their staff relating to the receivership, and other working papers and drafts.'

g On the evidence filed in these proceedings it is clear that the reference to internal circulation is intended to indicate documents prepared for the receivers for their own purposes to enable them to discharge their professional obligations to MFL and the companies. On that basis, they must belong to the receivers.

h '(ix) hybrid documents, to the extent that they arise primarily in connection with one or more of the excluded categories listed under (i) to (viii) above. In respect of hybrid documents primarily of a disclosable nature photocopies are supplied with other sections blanked out.'

There is no longer an issue as to these.

j The List A documents are in the possession of the receivers. There is also List B, of documents which is in the possession of Messrs Freshfields, the receivers' solicitors. The List B documents are, strictly, not within the scope of the order of 13 April 1987 since they are not documents in the possession of the receivers. But putting that aside, the position is as follows. The dispute has related to items (iii), (iv), (v), (vii) and (viii) in Price Waterhouse's letter of 12 June 1987. I deal with these in turn.

'(iii) letters and documents from third parties which were also copied to the receivers.'

These have now been given up.

'(iv) working papers and working drafts: notes with an exclusively internal circulation.'

These are not the property of the companies. They are working papers within the principle of the *Chantrey Martin* case [1953] 2 All ER 691, [1953] 2 QB 286 and belong to Freshfields.

'(v) attendances.'

These are attendance notes made by Freshfields for their own assistance in advising the receivers and are really working papers. They therefore belong to Freshfields, and their content is irrelevant.

'(vii) documents relating to advice given in connection with points (i) to (x) of List A above.'

'(viii) hybrid documents, to the extent that they arise primarily in connection with matters other than the role as solicitors to the receivers. In respect of hybrid documents which arise primarily from this role, photocopies are supplied with other sections blanked out.'

There is no longer an issue as to these.

The result, in my view, is that the decision of Hoffmann J was correct and this appeal fails.

STOCKER LJ. I agree.

BUTLER-SLOSS LJ. I also agree.

Appeal dismissed. Leave to appeal to the House of Lords refused.

Solicitors: *Holman Fenwick & Willan* (for the plaintiffs); *Freshfields* (for the defendants).

Frances Rustin   Barrister.

R v Tandy

a

COURT OF APPEAL, CRIMINAL DIVISION
WATKINS LJ, ROSE AND ROCH JJ
2 NOVEMBER, 21 DECEMBER 1987

b *Criminal law – Murder – Diminished responsibility – Abnormality of mind induced by disease –
Abnormality of mind induced by alcohol – Alcoholic's first drink of day not involuntary – Judge's
direction to jury ruling out defence of diminished responsibility – Whether direction wrongly
removing from jury issue of whether alcoholic's craving for drink had in itself produced
abnormality of mind – Whether judge misdirecting jury – Homicide Act 1957, s 2(1).*

c The appellant was an alcoholic who strangled her 11-year-old daughter after drinking
almost a whole bottle of vodka rather than her customary drink of vermouth or barley
wine. She was subsequently charged with the daughter's murder and at her trial sought
to establish the defence of diminished responsibility under s 2(1)[a] of the Homicide Act
1957. The judged directed the jury that the issue they had to decide was whether, at the
moment of strangling her daughter, the appellant was suffering from an abnormality of
d mind in the form of grossly impaired judgment and emotional responses as a direct
result of her condition of alcoholism, over which she had no immediate control, or
whether, as the Crown contended, the appellant's abnormal state of mind at that time
was due merely to the fact that she was drunk on vodka, having chosen to drink vodka
as her first drink of the day in preference to her customary drink, in which case it could
not be said that her resultant abnormality of mind was involuntarily induced by
e alcoholism. The appellant was convicted. She appealed on the ground, inter alia, that the
judge's direction had wrongly removed from the jury any consideration of the issue
whether she had proved that she had such a craving for drink as in itself to produce an
abnormality of mind within s 2(1).

Held – For a craving for drink, in itself, to produce an 'abnormality of mind' induced by
f the disease of alcoholism, within s 2(1) of the 1957 Act, the alcoholism had to have
reached such a level that the accused's brain was damaged so that there was gross
impairment of his judgment and emotional responses or the craving had to be such as to
render the accused's use of drink involuntary because he was no longer able to resist the
impulse to drink. On the other hand, if the accused had simply not resisted an impulse
to drink he could not rely on the defence of diminished responsibility. The judge's
g direction to the jury was therefore correct in stating that if the appellant's taking of her
first drink of the day was not involuntary then the whole of her drinking on that day was
not involuntary, since it clearly explained how great the craving for drink had to be
before it could in itself produce an abnormality of mind. Accordingly, since there had
been no material misdirection the appeal would be dismissed (see p 272 d to j and p 273
a to d, post).

h

Notes
For the defence of diminished responsibility to a charge of murder, see 11 Halsbury's
Laws (4th edn) paras 1165–1166, and for cases on the subject, see 15 Digest (Reissue)
1128–1131, 9490–9506.
    For the Homicide Act 1957, s 2, see 12 Halsbury's Statutes (4th edn) 311.

j

Cases referred to in judgment
R v Byrne [1960] 3 All ER 1, [1960] 2 QB 396, [1960] 3 WLR 440, CCA.
R v Fenton (1975) 61 Cr App R 261, CA.
R v Gittens [1984] 3 All ER 252, [1984] QB 698, [1984] 3 WLR 327, CA.

---

a   Section 2(1), so far as material, is set out at p 271 f, post

Appeal

Linda Mary Tandy appealed with the leave of the single judge against her conviction for **a**
murder on 29 January 1987 in the Crown Court at Leeds before Kennedy J and a jury on
the ground, inter alia, that the judge's direction to the jury had wrongly removed from
the jury consideration of the defence of diminished responsibility, within s 2(1) of the
Homicide Act 1957. The facts are set out in the judgment of the court.

James Stewart QC and *Thomas Bayliss,* (assigned by the Registrar of Criminal Appeals) for **b**
the appellant.
Robert Smith QC and *Andrea Addleman* for the Crown.

Cur adv vult

21 December. The following judgment of the court was delivered.   **c**

WATKINS LJ. The appellant was convicted of the murder of her 11-year-old daughter,
Amanda, in the Crown Court at Leeds on 29 January 1987 in a trial before Kennedy J
and sentenced to life imprisonment.

The appellant, to whom the single judge gave leave to appeal against conviction, did
not at the trial dispute that she had caused Amanda's death on Wednesday, 5 March 1986 **d**
in a bedroom at the home of the appellant and her second husband, Martin Tandy.
Amanda and her brother were the children of the first marriage. Death was caused by
strangulation with a scarf; the act of strangulation took place at approximately 8 pm.
Death followed at 9.30 the following morning after Amanda had been admitted to
hospital. She did not at any time recover consciousness.

The evidence at the trial indicated that the relationship between the appellant and her **e**
daughter was a good one: that they were like sisters.

On 5 March the appellant telephoned the police at 5.45 pm, because Amanda,
according to her, had not returned home at the expected time. She searched for her, she
said, but could not find her. That call was tape recorded by the police, to whom the
appellant sounded as though she had been drinking.

At 6.45 pm a woman police constable went to the appellant's home. By this time **f**
Amanda had returned, had gone to her bedroom and was refusing to leave it. The
constable saw Amanda there. She maintained that the appellant had known where she
was. The constable reported that the appellant looked and smelt as though she had been
drinking; she was dirty, unkempt, nervous and shaking.

After the constable had left the house at about 7.50 pm, the appellant went to speak to **g**
Amanda in her bedroom. Martin Tandy was still in the house at that time. Whilst the
appellant was speaking to Amanda he left. Amanda told her mother that she wanted to
go and live with her grandmother. When asked why, she said that she had been sexually
interfered with but she would not name the person responsible. The appellant asked
Amanda whether it was her stepfather who had been interfering with her. The appellant's
evidence as to that was: **h**

'I said to the child on the bed, is it that bastard just gone out? And then after a
long while there was a scream and that was it. I thought that she meant that Martin
had been at her. I just saw her there in the bed blue and lifeless. That was when I
went to the neighbours. I accept that I must have been responsible, but I have no
recollection of having killed her. I don't know where the scarf came from or
anything. I don't remember what I said to the police or Mrs Hemmingway. I **j**
remember the ambulance going and I remember going to the police station and
being arrested.'

In fact, having strangled her daughter, the appellant went to a neighbour and asked

her to go to the appellant's house, because she, the appellant, thought Amanda was dead.
a Later the appellant claimed that Amanda had tried to kill herself.

A post-mortem performed on the Thursday afternoon showed that Amanda's death
had been caused by the application of a ligature for tens of seconds. It also revealed that
she had been sexually abused over a period of weeks or months in that there was dilation
of the anus consistent only with a number of acts of intercourse per anum; in the
pathologist's view, more than 12 such acts. In addition Amanda's pubic hairs had been
b shaved.

Evidence at the trial established that it was not the appellant who had interfered with
Amanda. The appellant claimed (there was no evidence to contradict this) that until the
Wednesday evening she had had no idea that her daughter was being sexually abused.

At the trial the appellant's intention at the time of the killing was put in issue. No
complaint has been raised in regard to the trial judge's directions to the jury on the
c requisite intent for murder and no ground of appeal arises out of this issue.

The second issue raised at the trial was the defence of diminished responsibility under
s 2(1) of the Homicide Act 1957.

It was raised in this way. The appellant was at all material times an alcoholic. According
to her first husband she had been in that condition by 1980. Her own evidence was that
she had been drinking heavily for a number of years, her drinking being due to loneliness
d and two unhappy marriages. She told the doctors who examined her, and the jury, that
she normally drank either barley wine or Cinzano, but that on Monday, 3 March, she
had purchased a bottle of vodka. She had not opened this until the morning of the
Wednesday, but having opened and started the bottle of vodka, she had consumed 90%
of it during the course of that day. She had had her last drink at about 6.30 pm. She had
not previously drunk vodka. Vodka contains more alcohol than Cinzano which the
e appellant said she had drunk on Monday, 3 March. She could not recall whether or not
she had had a drink on the Tuesday.

Forensic evidence showed that her blood-alcohol level at midnight on Wednesday,
5 March, when a sample of blood was taken from her by Dr Stoker, was 240 mg of
alcohol per 100 ml of blood. The opinion of Dr Wood, a consultant forensic psychiatrist
f called by the defence, was that at the time of the act of strangulation the level of alcohol
in the appellant's blood would have been not less than 330 mg of alcohol per 100 ml of
blood and could have been anything up to 400 mg of alcohol per 100 ml of blood.

Dr Lawson, who gave evidence for the Crown, said that in his view the appellant's
blood at the time of the strangulation would have contained approximately 300 mg of
alcohol per 100 ml of blood. The medical evidence indicated that this level of alcohol
g would be a lethal intake of intoxicants for a normal person, but that alcoholics, because
of their persistent abuse of alcohol, become able to tolerate such levels of alcohol in their
bloodstreams and to dissipate alcohol from their bloodstreams more quickly than non-
alcoholics are able to. Indeed in this case the evidence of Dr Stoker, who examined the
appellant when at midnight he obtained the sample of blood from her, was that her
movements were co-ordinated, her speech was all right and the appellant displayed no
h clinical evidence of intoxication. Dr Stoker had observed her walking up two flights of
stairs.

There were three principal areas of conflict between the medical witnesses called at the
trial on behalf of the appellant and the medical witness called by the Crown. The first
was whether alcoholism is or is not a disease. Dr Wood and Dr Milne (a consultant
psychiatrist) both expressed the view that alcohol dependence syndrome, or alcoholism
j in the severity manifested in the appellant's case, constituted a disease. Dr Lawson, who
accepted that the appellant was an alcoholic, expressed the opinion that alcoholism, even
chronic alcoholism, is not a disease.

In summing up the judge told the jury with regard to that:

'... it is totally unnecessary for you to involve yourselves in that medical

controversy about labelling. You have to apply the words of the Act of Parliament
in a commonsense way and those words are reflected in the wording on that sheet   *a*
before you. [Here the judge was referring to a document headed 'Questions for the
jury' which he had prepared and provided to the jury.] If you find that a woman is
suffering from an abnormality of mind in the form of grossly impaired judgment
and emotional responses and if you find that she is so suffering as a direct result of a
condition over which she had, and I emphasise the words, *no immediate control*, then
you can say that the second element in this defence is proved because her abnormality   *b*
of mind is induced by disease or injury.'

The judge was there telling the jury that the issue they had to decide was not whether
alcoholism is or is not a disease, but whether the appellant was suffering from an
abnormality of mind, in the form of grossly impaired judgment and emotional responses,
as a direct result of her alcoholism, or whether, as the Crown on the evidence of
Dr Lawson contended, her abnormal state of mind at the moment of the act of   *c*
strangulation was due to the fact that she was drunk on vodka.

The second area of conflict between the doctors was whether the appellant's drinking
on the Wednesday was voluntary or involuntary. Dr Wood said of this that he thought
it would have been very difficult for her to resist the temptation of drink on that day.
She was under some pressure to continue drinking to stave off the shakiness and other
symptoms of withdrawal affecting her. He also said he would argue that drinking to that   *d*
extent (that is to say most of the bottle of vodka) was an inherent part of the disease. He
considered that compulsion was certainly partly causative of her drinking as she did on
that day in that the choice to do so was not a free choice. Compulsion stemmed from her
being an alcoholic and her experience that to deny herself drink would lead her to being
severely uncomfortable, if not ill. When asked if the appellant, in his view, at that time   *e*
had control over her drinking habits, he replied, 'No, none whatsoever.' Dr Milne said
that he believed the appellant drank involuntarily, because she was an alcoholic.
Dr Lawson agreed that a person who is an alcoholic has a craving for alcohol and a
compulsion to drink. His view was that the appellant had control over whether she had
the first drink of the day, but once she had had the first drink she was no longer in
control.   *f*

The third area of conflict in the medical evidence was on the question whether, if the
appellant had not taken drink that day, she would have strangled her daughter.

Dr Lawson put his view in one short answer: 'I could not see her killing the child if
she were sober.' Dr Milne, when asked whether he went as far as to say that if the
appellant had not consumed any drink that day she would have still committed this
offence, answered, 'No.' Dr Wood agreed that an alcoholic may do something which he   *g*
or she would not otherwise do but for the intake of alcohol. When asked whether, if the
appellant had not consumed any drink that day, she would have still done what she did
to her daughter, he said: 'I do not know. I think had she not consumed drink on that day
she would have been quite seriously ill in another fashion by 8 o'clock that evening.' He
amplified that answer by saying that the appellant's problem on 5 March was serious
alcoholism and until she was withdrawn from alcohol, whether or not she was   *h*
intoxicated, she would have suffered from seriously disturbed judgment and emotional
control. He thought that her judgment and emotional control would have continued to
be severely disturbed on the Wednesday, even had she not drunk the vodka which she
did drink that day.

The ground of appeal is that there was a material misdirection of the jury in regard to
the defence of diminished responsibility. The relevant passages in the summing up are   *j*
where the judge said:

'The choice [of the appellant whether to drink or not to drink on Wednesday,
5 March 1986] may not have been easy but . . . if it were there at all it is fatal to this
defence, because the law simply will not allow a drug user, whether the drug be

a   alcohol or any other, to shelter behind the toxic effects of the drug which he or she need not have used.'

And where he stated earlier:

b
> 'If she had taken no drink on 5 March 1986, or if you were satisfied that Dr Wood is right in saying that her judgment and emotional response would have been grossly impaired even if no drink had been taken, then the answer would be easy, but clearly she did take drink on 5 March and if she did that as a matter of choice, she cannot say in law or in common sense that the abnormality of mind which resulted was induced by disease.'

c
Counsel for the appellant submits that these are misdirections, because: (1) the medical evidence had been unanimous that there might be compulsion to drink at least after the first drink of the day; that it was the cumulative effect of the consumption of 90% of the bottle of vodka which caused her to be in the state of intoxication she was in at the time of the killing. By his directions the judge removed the question of compulsion after the taking of the first drink from the jury's consideration; (2) the directions removed from the jury's consideration Dr Wood's evidence that the alcoholism alone produced an abnormal state of mind which substantially impaired her mental responsibility for her
d   acts; (3) the directions removed from the jury the issue which this court in *R v Fenton* (1975) 61 Cr App R 261 at 263 recognised could arise when an accused person proves such a craving for drink as to produce in itself an abnormality of mind. Lord Widgery CJ's actual words were:

e
> '... cases may arise hereafter where the accused proves such a craving for drink or drugs as to produce in itself an abnormality of mind; but that is not proved in this case. The appellant did not give evidence and we do not see how self-induced intoxication can of itself produce an abnormality of mind due to inherent causes.'

The jury, he went on to say, had been rightly told to ignore the effect of alcohol.

Section 2(1) of the Homicide Act 1957 provides:

f
> 'Where a person kills ... another, he shall not be convicted of murder if he was suffering from such abnormality of mind (whether arising from a condition of arrested or retarded development of mind or any inherent causes or induced by disease or injury) as substantially impaired his mental responsibility for his acts and omissions in doing ... the killing.'

g   *R v Byrne* [1960] 3 All ER 1 at 4, [1960] 2 QB 396 at 403 established that the phrase 'abnormality of mind' was wide enough to cover the mind's activities in all its aspects, including the ability to exercise will power to control physical acts in accordance with rational judgment. But 'abnormality of mind' means a state of mind so different from that of ordinary human beings that a reasonable man would term it abnormal.

h   The defence of diminished responsibility was derived from the law of Scotland, in which one of the colloquial names for the defence was 'partial insanity'. Normal human beings frequently drink to excess and when drunk do not suffer from abnormality of mind, within the meaning of that phrase in s 2(1) of the 1957 Act.

Whether an accused person was at the time of the act which results in the victim's death suffering from any abnormality of mind is a question for the jury; and, as this
i   court stated in *R v Byrne*, although medical evidence is important on this question, the jury are not bound to accept medical evidence if there is other material before them from which in their judgment a different conclusion may be drawn.

The Court of Appeal in *R v Gittens* [1984] 3 All ER 252, [1984] QB 698 said that it was a misdirection to invite the jury to decide whether it was inherent causes on the one hand or drink or pills on the other hand which were the main factor in causing the appellant in that case to act as he did. The correct direction in that case was to tell the jury that they had to decide whether the abnormality arising from the inherent causes substantially impaired the appellant's responsibility for his actions. Lord Lane CJ said ([1984] 3 All ER 252 at 256, [1984] QB 698 at 703):

a

'Where alcohol or drugs are factors to be considered ... the best approach is that ... approved by this court in *R v Fenton* (1975) 61 Cr App R 261. The jury should be directed to disregard what, in their view, the effect of the alcohol or drugs on the defendant was, since abnormality of mind induced by alcohol or drugs is not, generally speaking, due to inherent causes ... Then the jury should consider whether the combined effect of the other matters which do fall within the section amounted to such abnormality of mind as substantially impaired the defendant's mental responsibility ...'

b

c

In his summing up and in the document headed 'Questions for the jury', the judge set out the three matters which the defence had to establish on the balance of probability for the defence of diminished responsibility to succeed. No criticism of that part of the summing up or that part of the 'Questions for the jury' has been made nor could it have been.

So in this case it was for the appellant to show (1) that she was suffering from an abnormality of mind at the time of the act of strangulation, (2) that that abnormality of mind was induced by disease, namely the disease of alcoholism, and (3) that the abnormality of mind induced by the disease of alcoholism was such as substantially impaired her mental responsibility for her act of strangling her daughter.

d

The principles involved in seeking answers to these questions are, in our view, as follows. The appellant would not establish the second element of the defence unless the evidence showed that the abnormality of mind at the time of the killing was due to the fact that she was a chronic alcoholic. If the alcoholism had reached the level at which her brain had been injured by the repeated insult from intoxicants so that there was gross impairment of her judgment and emotional responses, then the defence of diminished responsibility was available to her, provided that she satisfied the jury that the third element of the defence existed. Further, if the appellant were able to establish that the alcoholism had reached the level where although the brain had not been damaged to the extent just stated, the appellant's drinking had become involuntary, that is to say she was no longer able to resist the impulse to drink, then the defence of diminished responsibility would be available to her, subject to her establishing the first and third elements, because, if her drinking was involuntary, then her abnormality of mind at the time of the act of strangulation was induced by her condition of alcoholism.

e

f

g

On the other hand, if the appellant had simply not resisted an impulse to drink and it was the drink taken on the Wednesday which brought about the impairment of judgment and emotional response, then the defence of diminished responsibility was not available to the defendant.

In our judgment the direction which the judge gave the jury accurately reflected these principles. There was evidence on which the jury, directed as they were, could reach their verdict. The appellant had chosen to drink vodka on the Wednesday rather than her customary drink of Cinzano. Her evidence was that she might not have had a drink at all on the Tuesday. She certainly did not tell the jury that she must have taken drink on the Tuesday or Wednesday because she could not help herself. She had been able to stop drinking at 6.30 pm on the Wednesday evening although her supply of vodka was not exhausted. Thus her own evidence indicated that she was able to exercise some control even after she had taken the first drink, contrary to the view of the doctors. There was the evidence of Dr Lawson that the appellant would have had the ability on that Wednesday to abstain from taking the first drink of the day.

h

j

Counsel for the Crown pointed out in his submissions that the abnormality of mind

described by Dr Wood and Dr Milne was of grossly impaired judgment and emotional
a responses and it did not include an irresistible craving for alcohol.

The three matters on which the appellant relies in the perfected grounds of appeal for
saying that there was a misdirection can be dealt with shortly. As to the first, in our
judgment the judge was correct in telling the jury that, if the taking of the first drink
was not involuntary, then the whole of the drinking on the Wednesday was not
involuntary. Further, as we have pointed out, the appellant's own evidence indicated that
b she still had control over her drinking on that Wednesday after she had taken the first
drink.

As to the second, the jury were told correctly that the abnormality of mind with which
they were concerned was the abnormality of mind at the time of the act of strangulation
and as a matter of fact by that time on that Wednesday the appellant had drunk 90% of a
bottle of vodka.

c On the third point, we conclude that for a craving for drinks or drugs in itself to
produce an abnormality of mind within the meaning of s 2(1) of the 1957 Act the
craving must be such as to render the accused's use of drink or drugs involuntary.
Therefore in our judgment the judge correctly defined how great the craving for drink
had to be before it could in itself produce an abnormality of mind. In any event, it was
not the evidence of the doctors called on behalf of the appellant that her abnormality of
d mind included, let alone consisted solely, of a craving for alcohol.

For those reasons we find that there was no material misdirection of the jury and we
dismiss this appeal.

Appeal dismissed.

e Solicitors: *Crown Prosecution Service*, Leeds.

N P Metcalfe Esq   Barrister.

Van Oppen v Clerk to the Bedford Charity Trustees
f

QUEEN'S BENCH DIVISION
BOREHAM J
14–18, 21–25, 28–30 MARCH, 12–15, 18–22, 25–28 APRIL, 22 JULY 1988

g *Negligence – School – Duty of care – Sport – Injury to pupil – Pupil injured during rugby match
at school – Whether school under duty to insure pupils against injuries received while playing
sport – Whether school under duty to advise parents to take out personal accident insurance.*

The plaintiff was seriously injured in 1980 when he tackled another pupil in a game of
h rugby at school. In the previous year the school had received a report from the school
medical officers' association recommending that schools take out accident insurance for
pupils playing rugby, but at the time of the plaintiff's accident the school had not decided
on what sort of insurance was required and how it was to be obtained. The plaintiff
brought an action against the school's trustees alleging that the school had been negligent
in failing (i) to take reasonable care for the plaintiff's safety on the rugby field, in that the
j school had failed to coach or instruct the plaintiff in proper tackling techniques, (ii) to
insure the plaintiff against accidental injury and (iii) to advise the plaintiff's father of the
risk of serious injury in rugby, of the need for personal accident insurance for the plaintiff
and of the fact that the school had not arranged such insurance. The plaintiff claimed
damages for pain, suffering and loss of amenity, loss of earnings and the cost of future
assistance.

Held – The plaintiff's claim would be dismissed for the following reasons—

(1) On the facts, the school was not negligent in its coaching or teaching of rugby and *a*
it was not liable for the plaintiff's injuries, since they were the result of an accident rather
than negligence on anyone's part (see p 277 *c d*, post).

(2) There was no general duty arising simply from the relationship between a school
and its pupils requiring the school to insure its pupils against accidental injury or to
protect the pupils' economic welfare by insuring them, because such a duty would be in
excess of the school's obligations to educate and care for the pupils and would be wider *b*
than the duty imposed on a school in its position in loco parentis. Similarly, a school was
under no duty to advise a parent of the dangers of rugby football or of the need for
personal accident insurance, just as a parent was under no duty to insure if he was advised
to do so. Furthermore, the plaintiff's school had never assumed legal responsibility for
advising on the need for insurance or for insuring its pupils, since it did not hold itself
out as having the expertise to advise parents on insurance or to deal with insurance itself, *c*
and there was no evidence that the plaintiff's father had relied on the school for such
advice (see p 291 *c* to *f*, p 292 *b* to *d*, p 293 *c* to p 294 *a* and p 295 *h* to p 296 *f*, post)

Notes
For the duty of care owed by a schoolteacher to the pupils in his charge, see 15 Halsbury's
Laws (4th edn) paras 122, 124, and for cases on the subject, see 19 Digest (Reissue) 526– *d*
534, 4010–4052.

Cases referred to in judgment
Anns v Merton London Borough [1977] 2 All ER 492, [1978] AC 728, [1977] 2 WLR 1024,
HL.
Donoghue (or M'Alister) v Stevenson [1932] AC 562, [1932] All ER Rep 1, HL.   *e*
Hedley Byrne & Co Ltd v Heller & Partners Ltd [1963] 2 All ER 575, [1964] AC 465, [1963]
3 WLR 101, HL.
Home Office v Dorset Yacht Co Ltd [1970] 2 All ER 294, [1970] AC 1004, [1970] 2 WLR
1140, HL.
Junior Books Ltd v Veitchi Co Ltd [1982] 3 All ER 201, [1983] 1 AC 520, [1982] 3 WLR 477, *f*
HL.
Moorgate Mercantile Co Ltd v Twitchings [1976] 2 All ER 641, [1977] AC 890, [1976] 3
WLR 66, HL.
Mutual Life and Citizens' Assurance Co Ltd v Evatt [1971] 1 All ER 150, [1971] AC 793,
[1971] 2 WLR 23, PC.
Peabody Donation Fund (Governors) v Sir Lindsay Parkinson & Co Ltd [1984] 3 All ER 529, *g*
[1985] AC 210, [1984] 3 WLR 953, HL.
Ross v Caunters (a firm) [1979] 3 All ER 580, [1980] Ch 297, [1979] 3 WLR 605.
Seale v Perry [1982] VR 193, Vic Full Ct.
Weller & Co v Foot and Mouth Disease Research Institute [1965] 3 All ER 560, [1966] 1 QB
569, [1965] 3 WLR 1082.
Wilkinson v Coverdale (1793) 1 Esp 75, [1775–1802] All ER Rep 339, 170 ER 284, NP.   *h*
Yuen Kun-yeu v A-G of Hong Kong [1987] 2 All ER 705, [1988] AC 175, [1987] 3 WLR 776,
PC.

Action
By writ and statement of claim served on 13 June 1984 the plaintiff, Simon Richard Van
Oppen, claimed against the defendant, the clerk to the trustees of the Bedford Charity, *j*
sued in a representative capacity on behalf of the Harpur Trust which was responsible for
the administration of Bedford School, damages for a spinal injury sustained by the
plaintiff when playing rugby at the school while a pupil there. The plaintiff alleged, inter
alia, that the school was negligent in (i) failing to instruct the plaintiff in proper tackling
techniques, (ii) failing to ensure that the plaintiff was insured against accidental injury

a and (iii) failing to advise the plaintiff's father (a) of the need for accident insurance or (b) that the school had not arranged such insurance. The facts are set out in the judgment.

Christopher Wilson-Smith QC and *David Westcott* for the plaintiff.
Charles Aldous QC and *Christopher Symons* for the defendant.

Cur adv vult

b 22 July. The following judgment was delivered.

BOREHAM J. The plaintiff, Simon Van Oppen, claims damages for severe personal injury sustained on the rugby football field at Bedford School on 4 November 1980. He was then aged 16½ years and had been a pupil at the school for nearly three years. The
c defendant represents the trustees of the Bedford Charity, who were and are responsible for administering and running the school, and to whom I shall refer hereafter as 'the defendants'.

What happened, in short, was this. The plaintiff was playing in a senior league game at centre three-quarter for Bromham House against Crescent House. Within the last three minutes of the game an opposing three-quarter, William Grant, had the ball and
d was running for the Bromham try line. The plaintiff launched himself at Grant (whether from an acute angle from the front or an obtuse angle from the side is in dispute) in a flying tackle. Unfortunately his forehead and nose came into contact with Grant's left hip or thigh, with the result that he sustained injury to the cervical spine, causing an incomplete tetraplega.

Because his injuries and subsequent progress are well documented and because the
e general and special damages have been agreed subject to liability, it is unnecessary to give more than an outline of the plaintiff's injuries, his progress and his present condition. At first he was totally paralysed in all four limbs, though there was some appreciation of sensation in his legs. On arrival at hospital he was found to have a severe tetraparesis, though there was some sensation particularly on the right side. X-ray examination
f disclosed a severe compression fracture of the fifth cervical vertebra. There followed a gradual recovery in the left foot and left leg and then in the right leg and right arm. By Christmas of 1980 there was power and sensation in the bladder, which was emptying automatically. There was moderate power in the muscles of the left arm and the muscles of the left hand were improving; there was near normal power in the left leg.

On 15 January 1981 he was transferred to the National Spinal Injuries Centre at Stoke
g Mandeville. He continued to improve and was discharged home at the end of May. His progress thereafter is well documented and need not be repeated here.

By the time he appeared at the trial the left hand and arm showed very little weakness, but he had very little function in the right hand and only some power in the right arm. There was generalised weakness of both lower limbs, the right being weaker than the left, with some spasticity. The right foot had virtually no power and was flail. He walked
h without a stick, but dragged his right leg. He is unable to walk very far and, because of the condition of his right leg, is liable to lose his balance and fall. He experiences severe and uncomfortable spasms, mainly in the right leg, but occasionally spreading to the left. There is pain in the left leg of a burning nature and a different kind of pain in the right foot. This pain is sufficient to keep him awake at night. His bladder function is to a degree impaired, but provided he is strict about his liquid intake during the evening he
j is not incontinent during the night.

He has, of course, been deprived of his sporting activities on which he was so keen, though he is still able to enjoy sailing, provided he has a crew. Prior to the accident it had been the plaintiff's hope to join the Royal Navy and to enter Dartmouth. That of course has had to be abandoned. He is now in the second year of a three-year degree course in estate management, his aim being to become a chartered surveyor.

He has lodgings at Roehampton and a maisonette in Devon. He manages to look after
himself, even doing his own cooking. But he finds that the domestic chores take rather *a*
longer than they would have done. He also finds it difficult to get about on rough ground
doing professional surveys and in scrambling about in roof spaces. He has learnt to write
with his left hand. His writing is slower, but, as he said in an answer to a question from
me, it is as legible now as it was when he wrote with his right hand. The plaintiff showed
not the slightest inclination to exaggerate his disabilities; on the contrary, I was left with
a clear impression of a young man who was determined to make the best of his physical *b*
abilities and to get the best out of life. There is no reason to think that he will not have a
successful and satisfying career as a chartered surveyor.

He now alleges that those injuries were caused by the negligence of the school.

In the statement of claim a number of particulars of negligence are alleged, many of
which are no longer relied on. The plaintiff's case before the court can be summarised as
follows. The school, which was, or ought to have been, aware of the risk of serious injury *c*
to players of rugby football and of the serious risk of injury from unorthodox tackling,
particularly from the front, was negligent in: (i) failing to take reasonable care for the
plaintiff's safety on the rugby field by failing to coach or instruct the plaintiff in proper
tackling techniques and in particular in the technique of the head-on tackle. The
consequence, it is alleged, was that the plaintiff adopted a dangerous technique in tackling
William Grant and so was seriously injured; (ii) failing to advise the plaintiff's father (a) *d*
of the inherent risk of serious injury in the game of rugby, (b) of the consequent need
for personal accident insurance for the plaintiff, (c) that the school had not arranged such
insurance; (iii) failing to ensure that the plaintiff was insured against accidental injury at
the time of his accident on 4 November 1980.

It is alleged that by reason of such negligence, the plaintiff has suffered damage. The
heads of damage, and the sums recoverable under each head if liability is established, *e*
have been agreed by counsel as follows. *General damages*: (a) for pain and suffering and
loss of amenity, £38,000; (b) future losses including loss of earnings and handicap on the
labour market and cost of future assistance, £58,295. *Special damages*: £2,330. That is a
total of £98,625. In addition it has been agreed that, had the school in November 1980
had the personal accident insurance policy which they had in June 1981, the plaintiff *f*
would have been entitled to receive on account of his disability the sum of £55,000.

So far as the court and counsel are aware, the claims under (ii) and (iii) above are
entirely novel; their validity turns on interesting questions of law as well as on disputed
issues of fact. They provide for a head of compensation which is quite separate from and
additional to the claim under (i).

I deal now with the circumstances and cause of the plaintiff's injury. [His Lordship *g*
then described the circumstances in which the plaintiff was injured and continued:]

I am satisfied that the plaintiff made a flying tackle from a wide angle from Grant's
left, that he aimed to get his head behind Grant's left buttock or thigh and that in so
doing he was applying or attempting to apply the correct technique. In the event, the
tackle was mistimed, most probably because, once the plaintiff was committed, Grant
checked in his stride and so the plaintiff's head crashed into, instead of passing behind, *h*
Grant's left hip.

It was almost an exact replica of the tackle which produced such disastrous results for
an English international, Mr Danny Hearne. It is said that at first the plaintiff blamed no
one but himself. I venture to doubt whether it can properly be said that anyone at all was
to blame. The plaintiff made a bold bid at speed to stop Grant. His technique was correct.
The tackle went wrong because Grant was sufficiently skilful and agile to check his stride *j*
at the crucial moment when the plaintiff was already launched. It was no more and no
less than a tragic accident.

Strictly, therefore, it may be thought unnecessary for me to consider the defendants'
duty to the plaintiff as a player of rugby football at Bedford School or whether the
defendants were in breach of that duty. However, a great deal of time has been occupied

in adducing evidence and in presenting submissions on these two issues. It seems to me
a therefore only fair to the parties that I should make my findings on them known.

It is accepted on all sides that Bedford School, being in loco parentis, owed a general
duty to the plaintiff and to all pupils to exercise reasonable care for his and their safety
both in the classroom and on the games field. It is also accepted that rugby football is a
game in which injury may be sustained. It is further accepted that injury is more likely
if the correct techniques are not followed by the players, particularly in tackling. It
b follows therefore that it was the school's duty by teaching or by coaching or by correction
to take reasonable care to ensure that the plaintiff in playing the game of rugby football
applied correct techniques when tackling.

Then comes the question: were the defendants in breach of that duty? [His Lordship
then described the organisation and supervision of rugby football at the school and
continued:]
c I am satisfied that the defendants, through the staff 'taking' rugby, were well aware of
the inherent risks in playing rugby football and of the need for the application of correct
techniques and the correction of potentially dangerous errors and lapses. I am also
satisfied that the standard of supervision was high, that the refereeing was vigilant and
strict and that, as one of the plaintiff's contemporaries put it, there was at the school an
emphasis on discipline, which meant playing the game correctly. There is therefore no
d substance in the allegations of negligence so far as they relate to the playing of rugby
football at Bedford School.

With that I turn to the question of personal accident insurance. In the course of the
hearing much time has, understandably, been devoted to oral evidence relevant to this
question and to the perusal of reports, articles and other documents dealing with the
incidence of injuries to the cervical spine of rugby players and the need for personal
e accident insurance. To review all those documents would lead to a tedious and unhelpful
extension of this judgment. They are available should they be required in the future. In
the main, therefore, reference to and identification of particular documents will suffice.
There are, as will appear, one or two notable exceptions.

During the later 1970s there was a growing general awareness of the incidence of
f spinal cord injuries to rugby players. [His Lordship described the efforts of various
doctors to draw attention to injuries occurring to schoolboys while playing rugby
football. His Lordship continued:]

At the end of a special meeting of the Medical Officers of Schools Association (MOSA)
held on 22 March 1979 certain conclusions were reached and a number of
recommendations were made. These conclusions and recommendations were set out in
a document (the MOSA document), signed by those present, which was prepared for
g publication in May. So far as it is directly relevant to the issues now under discussion it
read as follows:

'At a General Meeting of the Association called on 22nd March 1979 the
undersigned spoke on the increase in rugby injuries to the cervical spine in
schoolboys. Our most urgent recommendation is that schools *must* take out accident
h insurance for all their rugby players before the beginning of the 1979–80 season, so
that schoolboys who become permanently disabled should receive a substantial sum
to help supply their life-long needs. It is not generally realised that English
schoolboys are seldom insured against sports injuries, whereas all rugby clubs
affiliated to the RFU are obliged to carry insurance, and permanent disablement
from spinal injuries due to negligence or road accidents usually attracts compensation
j of over £100,000.' (MOSA's emphasis.)

There followed recommendations as to the instruction, supervision and playing of
rugby in schools. These had been culled from a discussion document circulated on a date
unknown by the headmaster of a school in Northern Ireland. It is not necessary for me
to refer to them in detail here.

The recommendation of personal accident insurance had been made by Dr Silver, a consultant physician at the Spinal Injury Centre at Stoke Mandeville, and was adopted by the meeting without opposition. There was in his mind a conflict between his love of the game and his concern for the youngsters he had treated for spinal injuries. As appears from the document itself, he was concerned that, whereas the Rugby Football Union (RFU) insisted that all adults playing for affiliated clubs be insured, there was no such provision for schoolboys. I should add, however, that such insurance provided cover for permanent disablement in a sum far below that recommended by MOSA. He, Dr Silver, had tried to obtain personal accident insurance for his own rugby-playing sons. It had proved difficult and, in any event, he was reluctant, as he put it, to make them the odd men out.

The MOSA document was sent to all rugby-playing schools and to other interested parties. It made a very considerable impact. [His Lordship then described the reaction of the school's headmaster, Mr Jones, and bursar, Major Mantell, to the MOSA document. His Lordship continued:]

The position therefore at the end of 1979 was this.

1. The MOSA document had caused a great furore, particularly its insurance recommendation.

2. There were some, such as the RFU and the Public Schools Bursars' Association (PSBA), who were advising caution in accepting the MOSA recommendations. The RFU seem to have left the matter of insurance to the schools' governing bodies.

3. There were differences of opinion within the school on the subject of insurance: (a) Mr Thorpe, the master in charge of rugby, was strongly in favour of cover for rugby alone. He seems to have had the support of the rugby staff; (b) the bursar, supported by others, was strongly of the view (i) that insurance was a matter for the parents, of whom he was one, (ii) that if the school were to assume responsibility then it should be compulsory for all pupils and should cover all activities.

4. The headmaster had great sympathy for the views of Mr Thorpe; he wished to put the minds of his staff at rest. He thought they might lose some of their enthusiasm because of the risk of their being accused of negligence. On the other hand (a) he agreed with the bursar as to the responsibility for insurance and as to the comprehensiveness of the cover, (b) he hoped for guidance from the Headmasters' Conference (HMC) and from other responsible bodies who were considering the matter, (c) he knew of no other schools who had warned parents of the risks inherent in some of the school's activities or had urged parents to take out personal accident insurance. He had made no personal inquiries, but the bursar had and the headmaster knew this to be true of Felstead, where his own son was a rugby-playing pupil. Moreover, there had been no serious injury at Bedford, where rugby was well supervised both under Mr Murray Fletcher, the former master in charge of rugby, and Mr Thorpe. In the course of cross-examination Mr Jones agreed that by the end of 1979 there was a consensus of opinion that personal accident insurance was desirable. There was, however, a debate as to the scope of the cover, as to whether or not it should be compulsory and as to who should pay. He also agreed, in retrospect, that it would have been better if in his letter to the parents he had disclosed these views, though he doubted whether that would have made any difference.

In 1980 things moved more slowly than the headmaster had hoped. It was put to him in cross-examination that from the end of 1979 he did nothing. In other words, he had taken the bursar's words literally and had suspended further action. For the only time in a very long cross-examination that allegation appeared to hurt. He accepted that he did not canvass the parents but that would, he thought, have been unwise until he had obtained the support of the governing body. For the moment he knew that there were differences of opinion there. The school was not, he said, deliberately marking time; it was just that there was a disappointing lack of information from bodies he had hoped would advise. For instance, the RFU's definitive statement had been expected at the end of 1979 and had not been forthcoming. There was still resentment in some quarters that MOSA should, without prior consultation with any other interested parties, have advised so categorically on the need for insurance. That was not Mr Jones's attitude, but it was

a known to exist. He agreed with the Times Educational Supplement of 25 January 1980 that there was confusion about insurance. He agreed that, had he been disposed to do so, he could have arranged an optional scheme without reference to his governors. For the reasons already give, he was not disposed to promote or to support such a scheme.

I consider the criticism of stagnation to be unjustified. The school had taken their own inquiries as far as they could and with commendable dispatch. There were problems,

b still under serious debate, to be resolved. Finally, there was the outcome of the deliberations of interested and influential bodies to be considered when available, in particular the views of the HMC, the PSBA and the RFU. Mr Jones had been persuaded that the school had ample cover if negligence were established and that the legal responsibility for effecting personal accident insurance rested on the parents rather than the school. He had advised the parents of the school's insurance cover and of the lack of

c cover for personal accident. He had confidence in the rugby staff, who had responded to the rugby recommendations of MOSA. He agreed there always remained a risk of injury but he rejected the suggestion that every time a boy took the field he risked breaking his neck. It these circumstances he considered that matters were not so urgent that he could not await the views of those other responsible advisory bodies. I accept his evidence.

By March 1980 the PSBA had negotiated a policy which was adopted and recommended

d by the Independent Schools Joint Council (ISJC). This appears to have been referred to wrongly on occasions as the ISIS scheme. In his letter to schools publicising the scheme the secretary of the ISJC wrote as follows:

'I am writing to announce to schools the details of a Personal Accident Insurance Scheme for pupils which is recommended by ISJC and which can be offered to the

e parents on an optional basis. The need for such a scheme has been tragically emphasised by certain serious injuries which have occurred. These have involved permanent disability, not occasioned by negligence and therefore ineligible for compensation. A Personal Accident Insurance Scheme would produce a guaranteed scale of benefits for specific disabilities, irrespective of any legal liability. To make this available to parents at the low cost which can be achieved through common

f participation would be a valuable extension of the service which an independent school provides.'

The letter then set out in broad terms the benefits which could be achieved and the premium rate. It was also pointed out that it was intended that, were it to be promoted immediately, the scheme should be in operation from the beginning of Michaelmas

g term 1980. In April 1980 Mr Wood, the chairman of the school's games committee, expressed the view to Mr Thorpe that 'all-in' cover arranged for the school but paid for by the parents within the fees was worth further consideration. There is no doubt that the staff were anxious to have cover and to remove the responsibility for insurance from the parents. In early June the school received the ISJC proposals. They were studied by the headmaster and by Major Mantell. The latter compared them with those which had

h been offered by the school's own brokers at the end of the previous year. He came to the conclusion that, so far as the extent of cover and the premiums were concerned, the two schemes were comparable. The essential and, to him, worrying difference between the two was that the ISJC scheme was voluntary whereas their own brokers' scheme had been compulsory. The disadvantage of a voluntary scheme was, in his view, that it would impose on the school an unacceptable administrative burden. In a letter to the headmaster

j dated 9 June he concluded:

'My thoughts on this have not changed since the matter first came up last year and I still believe that our two alternatives are: a) We advise parents that we have no cover (except Public Liability) and they must make their own arrangements if they think it necessary. b) We go in for a scheme which offers the least administrative load and this will be one where all boys have to be included, we pay a single long term per capita premium, and this premium is included in the Tuition Fee. You will realise from this that my view is to opt for (b) but only if we think this sort of *a* cover is essential.'

Major Mantell still held the view that insurance was the responsibility of the parents.

In cross-examination the headmaster accepted that there was no reason why he could not then have gone to the governors and said, in effect: 'I want this ISJC scheme at the school.' He also agreed, as he put it, in retrospect, that he could have circulated the *b* scheme to parents at the end of the summer term and left the decision to them. Had he done so and had they expressed a wish to join the ISJC scheme, it being a voluntary scheme, there would have been no need to obtain the governors' approval. Alternatively, he could have written to the parents saying: 'We are going to arrange cover but it will take some time. Meanwhile I suggest you insure.' That again was something which he accepted in retrospect. At the time he did not think that it was something that he should *c* do.

He had by now reached the conclusion that a scheme of personal accident insurance was desirable for the boys as well as to placate the staff. It was now necessary to seek the best value for both school and pupils. He still thought that any scheme embarked on by the school should be compulsory and should embrace all activities, not just rugby. He was anxious to avoid the situation where, if two boys were injured, one was covered and *d* one was not. To him that was unacceptable.

He had no doubt that it was his responsibility to get as much advice as he could. He clearly felt somewhat uncomfortable about insurance policies: he thought that they were not always as advantageous in all respects as they sounded. In this he spoke with recent experience of problems concerning insurance after a serious fire at the school. He was still awaiting the views of the RFU. He agreed that that might be regarded by some *e* people as an abdication of his own responsibility. He regarded the brokers' advice as important and that was being sought.

There was a further problem. He still saw advantage in the school taking insurance cover, but there were some who took the view that the parents would then appear to be abdicating their responsibility. Mr Abrahams, for instance, one of the governors, held the view that it was the parents' responsibility. If a comprehensive scheme with *f* premiums added to the school fees were adopted, it would be necessary to win over the governing body. This was one of the reasons for his seeking as much backing from responsible, interested bodies as he could obtain. In particular the governors would expect him to await the RFU definitive statement. In any event, the fees for a whole year were set in the spring of each year and became effective at the commencement of the summer term. Thus, any addition to fees could only be made effective in the summer of *g* 1981. In theory it was possible for him to approach the governors as an emergency but that was something which he said would have caused surprise, to say the least. In any event, as I have indicated, they would expect him to await the advice of the RFU. I accept his evidence.

Meanwhile, as appears from the minutes of their meetings, the HMC were in touch *h* with the RFU and since early February had been expecting the RFU to circulate details of a scheme to cover all schoolchildren in all extracurricular activities. They maintained a correspondence and dialogue with Mr Kendall Carpenter the headmaster of Wellington School, senior vice-president of the RFU and an ex-rugby captain of England, still hoping for an insurance scheme. In mid-June 1980 the London branch of the HMC took the view that the ISJC scheme should be recommended to parents. *j*

In July 1980 there was published the long-awaited definitive statement of the RFU. This was received by the headmaster probably towards the beginning of the Christmas term. He was surprised and disappointed to find that it made no mention of insurance. He had by now made up his mind on what he wanted to do, and support from the RFU would have been helpful.

Having received the RFU definitive statement, though deriving little benefit from it,
a Mr Jones was in a position to make a final decision. He had decided that the school should
take out personal accident insurance, though it was still open to debate whether the
responsibility was that of the parents or of the school, and despite the fact that at the
meeting of HMC on 27 September 1980 there was still a debate as to the need for
insurance.

In cross-examination he agreed that the school was in a better position to decide if
b insurance was necessary for rugby and for all activities. The school would not wish to see
one boy covered and another not. They were in a better position to see that this did not
happen because they could probably compel the reluctant parent. Moreover, the school
had a better chance of appreciating the risks and had more ready access to expert advice.
However, he considered it premature to inform the parents of this decision until the
governors had made theirs. If it were to be decided ultimately that it was the parents'
c responsibility, he was not sure that it was his responsibility to give the parents information
as to the risks involved in various activities or the need for or desirability of personal
accident insurance, though he conceded that it might have been helpful for them to have
such information. He certainly did not consider it necessary to circulate the MOSA
document.

Towards the end of September there came news of another tragic accident to a
d schoolboy on the rugby field. A pupil at Sedburgh had been badly injured and
permanently paralysed. The news came from a doctor who had a son in the upper sixth
at Bedford in a telephone message to the bursar's secretary. The injured boy was his
partner's son. He disclosed that Sedburgh had insurance for that type of accident and he
considered that it would be a good idea if Bedford School arranged similar cover. Other
parents made inquiries of the bursar about the school having personal accident cover and
e one criticised the school for not having it.

News of this unfortunate incident increased the headmaster's concern and, coupled
with the continuing lobbying of Mr Thorpe, persuaded the bursar to think again. In a
letter to the headmaster on 29 September he had this to say:

f 'I have not heard of the Sedburgh accident but it seems sadly apparent that
accidents such as this are becoming more frequent and that we should think again.
Maybe you were able to assess views on this at the HMC last week? If we do change
our minds and opt for a Personal Accident Insurance Scheme then may I plead that
it is one which causes the least administrative load on the School. This means, as I
argued in my letter of 9th June 1980, the Scheme offered through our Brokers
whereby all boys (and Staff although we may have to draw the line carefully for this
g category) are IN the scheme with no option to contract out and the charge, about
£4·50 per head, is another charge to the Tuition Fee. I do not know whether any
answer was ever received to your letter to the Clerk of 12th June, but would you
like me to seek the up to date views of our Brokers?'

Major Mantell in evidence said that he still thought that insurance was the parents'
h responsibility, but he had subordinated his views to those of the majority in the school.
In cross-examination he denied that in September 1980 the parents were entitled to
assume that the school had arranged insurance. On the other hand, he agreed that if the
school had decided to suspend action on insurance, the parents should have been
informed. The school had not then decided not to take out insurance: they were still
considering the various possibilities.

j The headmaster's response to the bursar's letter was positive. For reasons which he
gave tersely in a note on the letter, he thought that the school should, as he put it, opt in.
He added, 'Let us therefore proceed'; this despite the division of opinion on the topic of
insurance which had been apparent in the HMC. He, like the bursar, wanted the views
of the trust's brokers on the respective merits of their scheme and the ISJC scheme. And
so the bursar and the trust's officers made further inquiries of the brokers. It was

suggested in cross-examination that the bursar in writing to the brokers and stating that
attitudes had changed over the past year was unfair. This the headmaster refuted; I agree *a*
with him. The views of the bursar and the headmaster had changed over the past year.
They had both initially taken the view that the provision of personal accident insurance
was not the school's legal liability: it was the responsibility of the parent. The bursar
adhered to that view but he had subordinated his opinion to that of the majority in the
school. The headmaster's view now was that, whatever the legal position, the school
should now take a lead.   *b*

It was now necessary for the headmaster and the bursar to decide which policy to
recommend to the governing body. In this they would be assisted by the advice of the
school's brokers. Once the appropriate policy was identified it would then be necessary
for the bursar to prepare the figures for inclusion in the estimates for 1981–82. These
figures would be prepared towards Christmas 1980.

In November 1980 there came the accident to the plaintiff. This strengthened the *c*
view of the headmaster that personal accident insurance should be effected. In December
1980 he sent his end-of-term letter to the parents. He again referred to personal accident
insurance in terms very similar to those employed in 1979, but he added that Mr Raynor,
the representative of the parents of day boys on the school's governing body, had been
asked to co-ordinate their views. He thought that he could not be more definite about
the provision of insurance cover, because the governors had yet to agree. He hoped that *d*
they would agree but he expected a debate on the subject of responsibility. He wanted
Mr Raynor to attend the committee meetings to give the parents' views in the hope that,
with their support, his recommendation would be accepted. He thought that the parents
were aware of the need for or desirability of personal accident insurance. He did not
consider it necessary therefore to warn them that risks were involved in some school
activities or to alert them to the need for insurance. In cross-examination he agreed, in *e*
retrospect, that it would have been better to have done so. The plaintiff's accident was in
the forefront of his mind. At the end of 1980 MOSA recorded that by the end of the year
many schools had joined one or other of the schemes for personal accident insurance, but
even more had not done so. This was confirmed by the insurance broker called on behalf
of the plaintiff.

On 22 January 1981 the headmaster persuaded the school committee of governors to *f*
recommend to the trust that they consider effecting personal accident insurance for the
pupils at Bedford School, though Mr Abrahams reiterated his views that it was the
parents' responsibility to effect such insurance. It was still his view that the school's duty
was to insure well against negligence and that they had done. Having regard to the
decision of the committee, it now remained for Mr Jones and its chairman to put the
committee's recommendation before the trust's committees. With this in mind the *g*
headmasters of Bedford School and Bedford Modern School combined to produce a
memorandum setting out their case. They were agreed on what should be done.

It was a document which evoked unqualified approval during the course of the hearing
and was given close attention in the course of these proceedings. It represented a powerful
plea supported by cogent arguments. As Mr Jones said, it was strongly worded because *h*
he and his colleague felt strongly. It reflected views more strongly held in 1980 than in
1979. No doubt those views had been strengthened by the news from Sedburgh and the
injury to the plaintiff. The memorandum ended with a summary and recommendations
in these terms:

'*Summary*   *j*
   1. There is a growing general concern over injuries and their consequences.
   2. There is a constant debate over responsibilities between parents and School.
   3. Authoritative bodies are suggesting Schools should offer some form of insurance
to provide cover in cases other than negligence. 4. The cover offered represents an
excellent buy for the parents.

Recommendations

a   The Harpur Trust, through the Schools, should offer Personal Accident Insurance for all pupils, and extend this to cover selected staff, and the cost of this should be absorbed within the Tuition Fee. It is also proposed that the Bursar be authorised to continue negotiations with the Trust's brokers and recommend the most suitable policy. In this connection a copy of the outline details of a scheme already in discussion with Bowring Scholfield (Eastern) Ltd is attached. It must be emphasised

b   that the proposed scheme only gives benefit in the case of death, dismemberment or permanent disablement as discussed. It does not cover disfigurement or temporary disablement or hospital or medical expenses.'

Meanwhile Mr Raynor, armed with the recommendations of the school committee, had sought the views of parents. There was now apparently a strong tide of feeling

c   among the parents, including Mr Raynor, that a comprehensive accident insurance policy should be arranged. This was a very different reaction from that which he had experienced in 1979. He communicated this information by letter dated 28 February to the headmaster. The latter now felt that he was in a strong position for his meeting with the relevant committees and finally the governing body of the trust. This view was bolstered to a degree by the receipt on 20 February of the school's brokers' proposals. They were in

d   line with their previous proposals. Their scheme was preferable to that of the ISJC.

The education committee considered these matters on 5 March. There was still a strong body of opinion that prudent parents would make their own insurance arrangements rather than rely on the schools. However, it was felt by the committee that each school should decide whether to invite parents to take part in an appropriate insurance scheme. It was resolved:

e   '(a) That the Trust should not make any general arrangement to provide personal accident insurance automatically for all pupils at the 4 schools. (b) That each School should determine whether to arrange this insurance on the basis of parent voluntary participation.'

This resolution was substantially indorsed on 12 March by the finance and policy

f   committee. It was later indorsed by the governing body of the trust.

It appears that the two boys' schools administered by the trust had been strongly in favour of a compulsory comprehensive insurance cover; the two girls' schools did not share that view. Mr Jones was very unhappy. A voluntary scheme was not what he wanted, for the reasons that he had made clear on many occasions. He was determined to seek reconsideration by the committees and the governing body of the trust.

g   First, however, he made known to the parents in a letter of 19 March the governors' decision that the responsibility for taking personal accident insurance should be continued to be left to the parents' own judgment. He pointed out, however, that, because of the inquiries made of the schools' brokers, the school could probably assist by introducing parents to a group scheme. With each letter was enclosed a pro forma by means of which each parent could indicate to the school whether or not he or she was interested in joining

h   a scheme of personal accident insurance limited to permanent disability.

He was cross-examined at very considerable length as to the respective merits of this letter and a draft which was prepared by Mr Squires, the headmaster of Bedford Modern. Mr Jones acknowledged that his colleague's draft was a very good one, and so it was. However, there is no evidence that it was sent, nor is there any evidence as to Mr Squires's attitude towards the relative merits of optional and compulsory insurance. To judge

j   from his draft letter alone, it might appear that he was telling parents to look to their own insurances and consider whether they ought not to take personal accident cover for their sons. This, however, might not be the correct conclusion.

The same might be said of Mr Jones, to judge from his letter alone, whereas I accept that he was concerned about a voluntary scheme: he wanted a compulsory scheme and he wanted the governors of the trust to change their minds. As he put it, he would have been very unhappy to face another rugby term without insurance or even with insurance limited to rugby alone.

At about the same time Mr Abrahams produced a memorandum for the heads of all four schools to consider, as the governors wished, he said, for clarification of the personal accident insurance issue. That memorandum pointed out that the issues arose because the heads and some staff felt that parents were not covering their children at present against personal accident either through ignorance or indolence. The memorandum went on to point out the options that were available for consideration. It seems unnecessary for me to repeat those here.

Meanwhile, the bursar commenced inquiries of the trust's brokers of the terms on which the brokers would be able to offer cover to parents if they indicated a willingness to participate in a voluntary scheme. Inquiries were also directed in similar terms to the brokers of the ISJC scheme.

On 6 May the school's games committee strongly recommended that the school should introduce a personal accident insurance policy to cover all members of the school (boys and staff). This was clearly intended to add weight to the renewed plea to the governors. The headmaster's letter of 19 March did not receive an encouraging response. This was particularly disappointing to the headmaster and the bursar, especially after what they had been told by Mr Raynor of the parents' interest in such a scheme. 1,146 questionnaires had been sent out; only 528 were returned. Of these, only 370 were interested at all in a personal accident scheme. In a memorandum to the Bedford School committee for its meeting scheduled for 14 May, the headmaster set out those results and recommended that the school should take part in a personal accident scheme, preferably through the trust's brokers if they would agree to administer it, but, if suitable terms could not be agreed, then the school should participate in the ISJC scheme. At the meeting on 14 May Mr Abrahams, while disagreeing with the headmaster's view, conceded that, despite his personal convictions, it might be more generally acceptable for the school to take part in that sort of scheme. It was therefore resolved that:

> '(a) In the best interest of the School all pupils should be compulsorily covered by a Personal Accident Insurance Scheme and the cost included in the Tuition Fee.
> (b) The Finance and Policy Committee be asked to reconsider the need for a Personal Accident Insurance (Permanent Disability) Scheme for pupils only. (c) The Trust's Brokers be asked by the Clerk to arrange urgent temporary cover for all pupils for a period of three months. (d) In the event that any obligatory scheme is not accepted by the Governors the Bursar may continue to negotiate a voluntary Scheme through the Trust's brokers.'

Mr Abrahams had been persuaded. It now remained to persuade the relevant committees and governing body of the trust.

On 21 May the bursar wrote to the clerk to the trust asking him to arrange urgent temporary cover for all pupils for three months. This request was passed on in urgent terms by the clerk to the trust finance officer. It was becoming clear that some at least of the senior governors were revising their views and that the appropriate committees would probably be persuaded to do the same. Temporary cover was in fact arranged through the trust's brokers to be effective from 16 June. On 23 June the finance and policy committee discussed this question of insurance again and were reminded of the advantages of a compulsory scheme, namely that the heavy responsibilities of the staff when dealing with insured and uninsured pupils would thus be removed. The committee recommended (a) that the trust enter forthwith into the scheme offered through the trust's own brokers covering all pupils at the four schools, (b) that supplementary estimates be granted to cover the expenditure for the two girls' schools, since the budget provision had only been made for the two boys' schools.

In his end-of-term letter to parents the headmaster was able to advise them in the following terms:

a   'Since I took soundings of parents about pupils' Personal Accident Insurance, the Governors have been re-examining this matter. A recommendation is now going forward for consideration by the full Governing body, at their meeting on 9th July, that the Trust should enter into an Insurance Scheme for this purpose, on lines matching the arrangements which very many other independent Schools have now made. The Scheme would cover pupils for all activities, world wide and throughout the year in terms and holidays until a pupil left School, and would provide

b   substantial financial compensation in respect of specific and total disabilities arising from accidental injuries. If the Trust decides to participate in the Scheme, it would extend to all the pupils at the four Schools and the premiums would be covered within tuition fees. Subject to the Governors' decision, full details of the Insurance Scheme will be sent to parents early next term, or I shall advise parents again concerning independent arrangements which they could make.'

c

On 9 July the trust's governing body resolved that the trust enter forthwith a scheme offered through the trust's brokers, covering all pupils at the four schools. Mr Jones had succeeded in obtaining what he had set out to do. Two years later the RFU was still complaining that all schools were still not covered; the Department of Education and the local authorities were still not arranging insurance cover for pupils in their schools. The

d   RFU had concluded, somewhat despairingly, that if insurance were left to parents nothing would ever be done.

Before leaving this aspect of the matter, I should say that I found Mr Jones a careful and reliable witness who was anxious to do what was in the interests of the boys and who was receptive of ideas to promote those interests. He was equally concerned for his staff. Comment has been made of an expression which he used several times in the course of a

e   long cross-examination, 'on reflection'. It is said that this meant 'after further consideration'. I regard that as fair comment: that was what he meant, but that was not all. It was said when he was agreeing with suggestions as to what he might have done or said in 1979 and 1980. It was much to his credit that he accepted these suggestions, but he did so with hindsight, with the grim experience of the plaintiff's accident and the daunting experience of this trial and the allegations of negligence made against him. In

f   1979 he was undergoing a novel experience; in 1988 the novelty has gone. In between, I have no doubt, he had given the matter of personal accident insurance and his part in introducing it to Bedford School a great deal of thought.

Major Mantell, the bursar, has been criticised as obdurate and intent on seeing his own views prevail. I think this is a harsh criticism. He is a man of strong views; he adhered to

g   his view of parental responsibility until he was persuaded to give way to the majority view. Whether he was right or wrong remains to be seen, but, whatever the answer, I am satisfied that his views were born of reason and not of prejudice and that they were shared by others in authority.

Finally, in my judgment, neither the headmaster nor the bursar should be criticised for seeking as much information and as many opinions from well-informed sources as

h   were available. They would have been open to criticism had they communed together and acted in a vacuum.

It is in these circumstances that the plaintiff alleges that the defendants were in breach of their duty to him. By his statement of claim he alleges that the defendants were negligent in: (1) failing to ensure that the plaintiff was insured against accidental injury at the time of his accident on 4 November 1980. One might have been forgiven for

j   thinking that the allegation was that the defendants were in breach of a general duty arising from the relationship of school and pupil. If that was the case, it is now (as will appear) somewhat refined; (2) failing to advise the plaintiff's father (a) of the inherent risk of serious injury in the game of rugby, (b) of the need of personal accident insurance and (c) that the school had not arranged such insurance. It is alleged that, had the school thus advised his father, the latter would have arranged insurance cover for him.

In his final submissions counsel for the plaintiff made it clear that he did not contend
for a general duty to insure arising from the relationship of school and pupil. There was   *a*
no general duty, he said, to protect the plaintiff from economic loss. He accepts that the
economic welfare of the child is the responsibility, or probably no more than the
prerogative, of the parent and, if the parent makes a judgment or decision, it would be
difficult to hold him liable. The school's duty, he submits, was to take such care as, in all
the circumstances, a reasonably prudent parent would have taken for the plaintiff's
welfare: a duty to protect from physical harm and *to have regard to* the plaintiff's   *b*
economic welfare. This latter duty includes a duty to inform the parent of matters of
which the school was aware and the parent was not, and which were material to the
parents' judgment as to what ought to be done for the boy's economic welfare.

Finally he submits that, if in fact the school assumed responsibility for a particular area
of a child's economic welfare, then they had a duty to act with reasonable care and were
liable for the loss which they ought to have foreseen would be consequent on their   *c*
careless acts or omissions. This duty arose from the relationship of school and pupil and
from the assumption by the school of a particular responsibility; it is wide enough to
cover economic loss. The plaintiff's case is that the school did undertake the following:
(1) the responsibility of deciding on the need for personal accident insurance and of
advising parents of that need; (2) the responsibility of insuring. Thus they were under a
duty to effect personal accident insurance within a reasonable time. In this respect the   *d*
school's duty, he submits, was wider than that of the parent.

Counsel for the defendants submits that, in the light of current authority, the plaintiff
cannot succeed unless he establishes either (1) a general duty on all parents and on all
those in loco parentis to take reasonable care to protect boys from economic loss or (2) a
duty to advise the parent of (a) the risk of serious injury in rugby football and/or (b) the
need for personal accident insurance or (3) a duty arising in the particular circumstances   *e*
of this case to insure against personal accident. He contends that the plaintiff cannot
establish any of these duties. Finally he submits that the plaintiff has not suffered damage
which is recognised by the law.

Counsel for the plaintiff submits that, if the defendants are correct (namely that there
was no duty at all) and that the defendants having investigated the need for personal   *f*
accident insurance and found that there was one, it means that the school could put away
their files and forget all about them. This, it is submitted, would not only be morally
reprehensible, it would defy common sense and, by inference, would contravene what is
fair and reasonable in the relationship between school and pupil and the duty of the
former to the latter.

In the course of these submissions, which extended over many days, counsel have
helpfully referred me to many authorities. I take this opportunity to express my gratitude   *g*
to them for their industry, their submissions and their efforts to point me in the right
direction, albeit that the directions that they suggested were diametrically opposed. It is
with no disrespect to them or to the high authorities whose judgments and opinions
have been cited to me, that I refrain from a detailed review of all those authorities.

It is accepted that this case breaks new ground: it cannot be brought precisely within   *h*
the categories so far identified and recognised by authority. The plaintiff relies on the
well-known dictum of Lord Macmillan in *Donoghue v Stevenson* [1932] AC 562 at 619,
[1932] All ER Rep 1 at 30 that the categories of negligence are never closed. His
submission is that this case establishes a category which is within, or is based on,
principles already well established. The defendants' case is that the plaintiff's submissions
fly in the face of true principle. They are both agreed therefore that the claim must be   *j*
judged according to principle. It is because I have come to the conclusion that the basic
principles at least are clear that I consider an elaborate review of the authorities to be
unnecessary. Reference to one or two, of course, will be necessary. The following basic
propositions are accepted by both sides.

1. The defendants, being in loco parentis, clearly owed the plaintiff a duty to take

reasonable care of his person and of his property and to prevent damage from foreseeable
a injury both in school and on the playing fields. So far as sport was concerned, that duty
may be further particularised as a duty (a) not to require the boys to participate in any
activity which a reasonable parent would consider carried an unacceptable risk of injury.
Rugby football is not within this category nor is it alleged to be, (b) to take reasonable
care to ensure that the game was properly organised and supervised so as to be reasonably
safe for the participants, (c) to take reasonable care to ensure that the boys were taught
b and applied the basic skills and proper techniques so that they could play the game with
reasonable safety. It is said that the standard of care expected of the defendants is that of
a reasonably careful and prudent parent, while taking into account the fact that the
conditions of school life are different from the conditions of home life, and that a larger
number of pupils are in the care of a particular teacher than are likely to be in the care of
any one parent. I also think that account should be taken of the fact that there will be
c occasions when the school will have greater relevant knowledge than a parent, and vice
versa. For instance, the chemistry master will, or at least should, have a better
understanding of the properties of the various substances he calls on his charges to handle
than many prudent and careful parents will have. This special knowledge does not
enlarge the chemistry master's duty; it does bring into account an important, in some
cases an essential, consideration in deciding whether or not he has discharged that duty.
d At the same time the parent is more likely to be aware of any idiosyncratic reaction of
his child. I doubt therefore whether it is always helpful to define the standard of care
further than to say it is the degree of care which is reasonable in all the circumstances,
including, among other things, any special knowledge which the school actually had or
ought reasonably to have had. This, however, is not to say that special knowledge enlarges
the ambit of the duty.
e 2. For breach of that duty the defendants may be liable not only for damages for
personal injury or damage to property, but also for economic loss directly flowing from
such injury or damage.
3. There are circumstances in which a defendant may be liable for economic loss
which is not consequent on personal injury or damage to property (hereafter referred to
f as pure economic loss): see *Hedley Byrne & Co Ltd v Heller & Partners Ltd* [1963] 2 All ER
575, [1964] AC 465. It is conceded that the plaintiff's claim in respect of personal accident
insurance is for pure economic loss.
4. So far the circumstances in which pure economic loss has been recovered have been
limited. The following are examples: (a) where the defendant has undertaken a voluntary
act and the plaintiff has, as the defendant knows, relied on his doing it with care and he
g does it carelessly: see *Wilkinson v Coverdale* (1793) 1 Esp 75, [1775–1802] All ER Rep 339;
(b) where the defendant has gratuitously performed a service by giving advice, knowing
that the plaintiff will rely on it and will suffer financial loss if it is negligently given: see
Hedley Byrne & Co Ltd v Heller & Partners Ltd [1963] 1 All ER 575, [1964] AC 465. It has
been said that this category is limited to those who engage in a calling or profession
requiring special knowledge or skill or who hold themselves out as having special
h knowledge or skill. Counsel for the defendants relies on that proposition: see *Mutual Life
and Citizens' Assurance Co Ltd v Evatt* [1971] 1 All ER 150, [1971] AC 793. That was a
decision of the Privy Council. Thus, while it is of high persuasive authority, it is not
strictly binding on this court. Moreover, there was a powerful dissenting opinion of Lord
Reid and Lord Morris, who were parties to the unanimous decision in the *Hedley Byrne*
case, which would extend this category to advice given on business occasions or in the
j course of business activities, whether or not the party giving the advice was engaged in a
calling or profession requiring special knowledge or skill or held himself out as having
special knowledge or skill. In the light of these opinions the limitation by the majority
in *Evatt's* case may still be open to agument. Moreover, in the *Hedley Byrne* case [1963] 2
All ER 575 at 612, [1964] AC 465 at 531 Lord Devlin referred to such a limitation in
these terms:

'Since the essence of the matter in the present case and in others of the same type is the acceptance of responsibility, I should like to guard against the imposition of *a* restrictive terms notwithstanding that the essential condition is fulfilled. If a defendant says to a plaintiff:—"Let me do this for you, do not waste your money in employing a professional, I will do it for nothing and you can rely on me", I do not think that he could escape liability simply because he belonged to no profession or calling, had no qualifications or special skill and did not hold himself out as having any. The relevance of these factors is to show the unlikelihood of a defendant in *b* such circumstances assuming a legal responsibility and as such they may often be decisive. But they are not theoretically conclusive, and so cannot be the subject of definition. It would be unfortunate if they were.'

(c) there may be cases where the plaintiff's reliance on the defendant's acts, omissions or utterances is not a necessary link in the chain of causation of loss, some cases even where *c* the plaintiff has been unaware of the defendant's intervention, where economic loss may be recovered: see *Anns v Merton London Borough* [1977] 2 All ER 492, [1978] AC 728. As Lord Salmon said in that case, in some cases reliance by the plaintiff may be important (see [1977] 2 All ER 492 at 513, [1978] AC 728 at 769). In this case it is not even relevant (see also *Ross v Caunters (a firm)* [1979] 3 All ER 580, [1980] Ch 297); (d) where the defendant has carried out carelessly a contractual duty which he owed to a third person *d* and has thus caused foreseeable economic loss to the plaintiff; (e) where the defendant has actually carried out a public duty and by performing it carelessly has caused the plaintiff foreseeable damage.

These examples cover a wide range of factual situations. Only in *Wilkinson v Coverdale* and in *Hedley Byrne & Co Ltd v Heller & Partners Ltd* were the circumstances at all analogous to the present. In each of these examples the plaintiff succeeded only because *e* the court found a sufficiently proximate relationship between the parties and a duty of care sufficiently wide in its ambit to cover pure economic loss. I respectfully adopt what Widgery J had to say in *Weller & Co v Foot and Mouth Disease Research Institute* [1965] 3 All ER 560 at 570, [1966] 1 QB 569 at 587:

'The decision in *Hedley Byrne & Co., Ltd.* v. *Heller & Partners, Ltd.* does not depart *f* in any way from the fundamental that there can be no claim for negligence in the absence of a duty of care owed to the plaintiff. It recognises that a duty of care may arise in the giving of advice even though no contract or fiduciary relationship exists between the giver of the advice and the person who may act on it, and having recognised the existence of the duty it goes on to recognise that indirect or economic loss will suffice to support the plaintiff's claim. What the case does not decide is that *g* an ability to foresee indirect or economic loss to another as a result of one's conduct automatically imposes a duty to take care to avoid that loss. In my judgment there is nothing in *Hedley Byrne & Co., Ltd.* v. *Heller & Partners, Ltd.* to affect the common law principle that a duty of care which arises from a risk of direct injury to person or property is owed only to those whose person or property may foreseeably be injured by a failure to take care. If the plaintiff can show that the duty was owed to *h* him, he can recover both direct and consequential loss which is reasonably foreseeable, and for myself I see no reason for saying that proof of direct loss is an essential part of his claim. He must, however, show that he was within the scope of the defendant's duty to take care.'

For a time it was thought that a wider, more general principle imposing a duty of care in a wider range of cases had been laid down by Lord Wilberforce in *Anns v Merton* *j* *London Borough* [1977] 2 All ER 492, [1978] AC 728. In an oft-quoted dictum he said ([1977] 2 All ER 492 at 498–499, [1978] AC 728 at 751–752):

'Through the trilogy of cases in this House, *Donoghue v Stevenson* [1932] AC 562, [1932] All ER Rep 1, *Hedley Byrne & Co Ltd v Heller & Partners Ltd* [1963] 2 All ER

a
575, [1964] AC 465 and *Home Office v Dorset Yacht Co Ltd* [1970] 2 All ER 294, [1970] AC 1004 the position has now been reached that in order to establish that a duty of care arises in a particular situation, it is not necessary to bring the facts of that situation within those of previous situations in which a duty of care has been held to exist. Rather the question has to be approached in two stages. First one has to ask whether, as between the alleged wrongdoer and the person who has suffered damage there is a sufficient relationship of proximity or neighbourhood such that, in the

b
reasonable contemplation of the former, carelessness on his part may be likely to cause damage to the latter, in which case a prima facie duty of care arises. Secondly, if the first question is answered affirmatively, it is necessary to consider whether there are any considerations which ought to negative, or to reduce or limit the scope of the duty or the class of person to whom it is owed or the damages to which a breach of it may give rise (see the *Dorset Yacht* case [1970] 2 All ER 294 at 297–298,

c
[1970] AC 1004 at 1027, per Lord Reid). Examples of this are *Hedley Byrne & Co Ltd v Heller & Partners Ltd* where the class of potential plaintiffs was reduced to those shown to have relied on the correctness of statements made, and *Weller & Co v Foot and Mouth Disease Research Institute* [1965] 3 All ER 560, [1966] 1 QB 569.'

It appears that this passage was applied literally in a number of subsequent decisions,
d
including *Ross v Caunters (a firm)* [1979] 3 All ER 580, [1980] Ch 297 and *Junior Books Ltd v Veitchi Co Ltd* [1982] 3 All ER 201, [1983] 1 AC 520. Both these decisions have been regarded as turning on their own special facts, and *Ross v Caunters* has been criticised in the Supreme Court of Victoria in *Seale v Perry* [1982] VR 193. I am relieved of the task of deciding whether or not they should be followed because they were decided on facts which are so different from the present as to be of no assistance and because, save for the
e
literal application of Lord Wilberforce's dictum, they lay down no new principle. Of course, as Lord Wilberforce emphasised, there must be a relationship of sufficient proximity between the parties before a duty of care can possibly arise. But mere proximity is not enough, as Lord Wilberforce was at pains to point out. By his second question he imposed limitations dictated by policy.

This whole approach has been considered by their Lordships in two recent decisions.
f
In the first, *Governors of the Peabody Donation Fund v Sir Lindsay Parkinson & Co Ltd* [1984] 3 All ER 529, [1985] AC 210, the facts are so far removed from the present as not to be material. Lord Keith, having considered Lord Wilberforce's approach in *Anns*'s case, said ([1984] 3 All ER 529 at 534, [1985] AC 210 at 240–241):

g
'The true question in each case is whether the particular defendant owed to the particular plaintiff a duty of care having the scope which is contended for and whether he was in breach of that duty with consequent loss to the plaintiff. A relationship of proximity . . . must exist before any duty of care can arise, but the scope of the duty must depend on all the circumstances of the case . . . So in determining whether or not a duty of care of particular scope was incumbent on a defendant it is material to take into consideration whether it is just and reasonable
h
that it should be so.'

Lord Keith returned to the same question again in *Yuen Kun-yeu v A-G of Hong Kong* [1987] 2 All ER 705 at 710, [1988] AC 175 at 191–192, where he said:

'Their Lordships venture to think that the two-stage test formulated by Lord Wilberforce for determining the existence of a duty of care in negligence has been
j
elevated to a degree of importance greater than it merits, and greater perhaps than its author intended. Further, the expression of the first stage of the test carries with it a risk of misinterpretation . . . The truth is that the trilogy of cases referred to by Lord Wilberforce each demonstrate particular sets of circumstances, differing in character, which were adjudged to have the effect of bringing into being a relationship apt to give rise to a duty of care. Foreseeability of harm is a necessary

ingredient of such a relationship, but it is not the only one. Otherwise there would be liability in negligence on the part of one who sees another about to walk over a cliff with his head in the air, and forbears to shout a warning.'

I am relieved to be guided by these principles. I share the feelings of Murphy J in the Victorian case of *Seale v Perry* [1982] VR 193 at 225, that courts of last resort are more accustomed and better situated to engage in policy decisions than this court is.

It seems to me that the crucial question in this case is that which was posed by Lord Devlin in *Hedley Byrne & Co Ltd v Heller & Partners Ltd* [1963] 2 All ER 575 at 608, [1964] AC 465 at 525:

'Is the relationship between the parties in this case such that it can be brought within a category giving rise to a special duty? As always in English law the first step in such an inquiry is to see how far the authorities have gone, for new categories in the law do not spring into existence overnight.'

I have attempted so far to take that first step. The question which now has to be answered is whether, in the various circumstances postulated on behalf of the plaintiff, the scope of the duty owed by the school to the plaintiff was wide enough to take account of (or, as the plaintiff submits, *to have regard to*) his economic welfare. In answering that question it is material to take into consideration all the circumstances, in particular the relationship between the parties and what was reasonably to be expected of that relationship and whether it is just and reasonable that it should be so. I shall assume for the moment that failure to insure has caused what the law recognises as economic loss to the plaintiff.

Although it is conceded by counsel for the plaintiff that there is no general duty arising simply from the relationship of school and pupil to ensure that the plaintiff was insured against accidental injury, it will, I think, be helpful to examine why this should be so. Counsel for the defendants submits a number of reasons. First, there is no such duty on parents. A parent has the prerogative of deciding whether or not to insure his offspring, and, whatever decision he makes, none shall complain. A parent is under no duty to insure; he cannot be compelled to do so, nor can he be sued if he carelessly fails. His duty extends to maintaining his child, not to insuring him. If there is no such duty on the parent, it is submitted, there can be no duty on those in loco parentis. Even the duty to maintian does not extend to the school. Thus, even if the parent were under a duty to insure, it would not follow that the school, being in loco parentis, is under a similar duty. It is, he submits, fallacious to contend that the school's duty is to act in all respects as a careful parent should act towards the child. That is the standard of care to be applied where there is a duty; it does not define the duty itself.

The school's duty is more limited than that of the parent. It relates to matters over which the school has control and to no other matters. What is a matter of choice or discretion for the parent is outside the ambit of the duty of the school. A duty is not established merely because a prudent headmaster or a prudent parent might think that in certain circumstances it was desirable to have personal accident insurance. Schools are under a duty to protect their pupils from harm. This involves taking reasonable care to ensure, inter alia, that the school's activities are reasonably safe and well organised. The taking out of personal accident insurance could not justify relaxation of that duty and in particular would not justify allowing the boys to participate in any activity which, because of inherent dangers, should not be undertaken. No one has seriously suggested that rugby football is such an activity.

It is submitted that, if this duty were to be imposed, then we are getting very close to no fault liability. That has never been part of our law. Even the statutory duty imposed in respect of road traffic accidents and the duty imposed by the Employers' Liability (Compulsory Insurance) Act 1969 is to take out cover for death or injury caused by negligence. If such a duty as the plaintiff contends for is imposed, it really opens the gates to a flood of claims. Moreover, it would apply to many other relationships where

inherent risks have to be faced, for instance the builder and his employees, the window
a cleaner and his employees, the car driver and many others.

This, therefore, is a novel claim, it is submitted. That is not conclusive against its
validity but it gives cause for pause and serious reflection. Further cause for pause, he
submits, lies in the reluctance shown by the courts to extend the duty of care to protect
against economic loss.

I approach the matter in this way. It is fundamental to the relationship between school
b and pupil that the school undertakes to educate him in as wide a sense as it reasonably
can. This involves the school having the pupils in its care and it involves the pupils in
various activities in the classroom, in the chapel, in the gymnasium, on the sports field
and so on. There are risks of injury inherent in many human activities, even of serious
injury in some. Because of this, the school, having the pupils in its care, is under a duty
to exercise reasonable care for their health and safety. Provided due care is exercised in
c this sphere, it seems to me that the school's duty is fulfilled. The law expects no more,
nor, I venture to think, do reasonably prudent parents. In particular, there is no general
duty to insure, not even against negligence. No doubt it is prudent for a school to insure
against negligence but that is in its own interests; it is under no duty to the pupils to do
so.

It could hardly be said, therefore, that a school is under a duty to insure against personal
d accident. Such a duty would, in my judgment, be in excess of the obligations it has
undertaken to educate and care for the pupils. The duties imposed on the school must
bear a fair and reasonable relationship to the activities carried on at the school. The
school's activities are not designed, nor are they intended (save in an indirect manner), to
promote or protect the pupil's economic welfare. A duty to insure is not a necessary
adjunct to its primary undertaking to educate; a duty to take reasonable care of person
e and property while the pupils are in its charge clearly is.

The same duty rests on the parent, who, in addition, is bound to maintain his child.
But even the parent has no duty to insure. It has often been said that the standard of care
required to discharge the school's duty is that of the reasonably careful parent. While this
does not, of course, define the scope of the duty, it does seem somewhat remarkable if
f the school is to be judged by a standard which the parent is bound neither to adopt nor
even to consider. It would be neither fair nor reasonable to place a wider duty on the
school, which stands in loco parentis, than is imposed on the parent. Moreover, it is
necessary to consider in what respects the plaintiff had a right to have care taken. It was
put by Lord Macmillan in *Donoghue v Stevenson* [1932] AC 562 at 619, [1932] All ER Rep
1 at 30 in this way:

g
'The grounds of action may be as various and manifold as human errancy; and
the conception of legal responsibility may develop in adaptation to altering social
conditions and standards. The criterion of judgment must adjust and adapt itself to
the changing circumstances of life. The categories of negligence are never closed [I
interpose to say that that is usually the only sentence quoted] . . . Where there is
h room for diversity of view, it is in determining what circumstances will establish
such a relationship between the parties as to give rise, on the one side, to a duty to
take care, and on the other side to a right to have care taken.'

Here the plaintiff clearly had a right to have his person and his property protected
from careless acts or omissions of those for whom the defendants were vicariously liable.
j He had no right to protection from purely accidental injury or from the consequences of
such injury.

It is true that on climbing holidays Mr Pleuger, the referee of the game in which this
plaintiff was injured and a master at the school, insisted that all boys who participated
were insured. That was no doubt a prudent precaution taken primarily, not to protect
the boys from economic loss, but to protect their parents from heavy claims for medical
and rescue expenses. The personal accident element, which might be said to be for the

benefit of the boy, was trivial when considered in relation to serious injury. In any event, this merely begs the question whether Mr Pleuger was under a duty to do what he did. *a* In my view, he was not.

Finally, it seems pertinent to consider what would be the results of the imposition of a duty to insure. What level of cover would be necessary to discharge the school's duty of reasonable care in these circumstances? Would cover up to, say, £10,000 suffice for permanent disability? That would be a derisory sum by way of compensation in such circumstances. Would it be necessary to obtain cover for all the school's activities or *b* would it suffice to cover only those where those in authority in the school considered the greater inherent risks obtained? Should it cover only permanent disability of a substantial kind? Or should it cover all injuries?

All these matters convince me that the relationship of proximity which existed between the school and its pupils did not of itself give rise to a duty to insure or to protect the plaintiff's economic welfare. That was beyond what either party to that relationship *c* contemplated. Viewed more objectively, it was beyond what is reasonable and fair. The school's duty has been identified on many occasions. In my judgment, there is no warrant either in principle or in authority for extending it to the provision of personal accident insurance. It follows therefore that the concession of counsel for the plaintiff was very well founded.

It was in these circumstances that he refined the duty which he alleges was owed by *d* the school to the plaintiff to a duty to take reasonable care for the plaintiff's welfare in general. In this context 'welfare' includes a duty to protect his person and property from physical harm and *to have regard to his economic welfare*. Consistent with that duty the plaintiff was entitled as against the school to have his parent informed of material matters which might induce the latter, as a prudent parent, to insure against personal accident. In the end the discretion would be that of the parent and, however he exercised it, no *e* one, not even the plaintiff, could complain. But, it is submitted, the plaintiff was entitled to have his parent apprised of the warning given by the MOSA document in May 1979. By then the school had been made aware of the dangers inherent in the game of rugby football, even when it was properly supervised and played correctly. It was, therefore, it is submitted, the school's duty to keep the plaintiff's father abreast of this information in *f* case he might wish to take personal accident insurance cover for his son.

Counsel for the defendants submits that there was no such duty. If there was no duty to insure, then there could be no duty to advise either directly or indirectly on the subject of insurance. There was no area, save that relating to health or physical welfare, or perhaps to purely educational matters, where the defendants were under a duty to advise. Moreover, in his submission, such a duty could only arise if: (a) the defendants were in *g* fact qualified to give such advice or held themselves out as so qualified. There was no evidence that they did hold themselves out in this way; (b) the parents actually relied on the advice so given. There is no evidence, he submits, that parents did rely on the defendants for advice.

I think the answer to the plaintiff's submission lies in the main in the reasons already given for not finding the more general duty of care. It is not open to doctors, however, *h* eminent, to enlarge the school's duty. The duty has to be one recognised and enforced by the law. It is, of course, conceivable that information provided by doctors might sound such a warning that, consistent with the school's duty to protect the plaintiff from harm, they ought not to have allowed him to play rugby football. It is not suggested that this situation arose here. It may very well be, indeed I hold, that the school should take such additional information into account in ensuring, so far as it reasonably can, by proper *j* supervision and coaching and by vigilant and strict refereeing, that the consequences referred to in the MOSA document did not occur. To this extent the information would impose additional burdens on the school, not by widening the scope of the duty but by making more onerous the discharge of that duty.

But that is not the question. The question is: did that additional information, coupled

with the relationship of school and pupil, enlarge the scope of the duty resting on the
a school to take account of the plaintiff's economic welfare and, as a consequence, to advise
on the dangers of rugby football? I accept that a duty to advise may arise. For instance, if
the chemistry master were to allow a pupil to conduct experiments at home and for that
purpose provided him with a dangerous substance, it would clearly be his duty to warn
the parent of the danger and to advise on safety precautions. That would be consistent
with the school's well-established general duty to protect its pupils from harm. The duty
b to advise would, in those circumstances, not extend the duty of care.

It is not suggested in this case that the advice was necessary for such a purpose. There
is no suggestion that the advice would have enabled the plaintiff's father to protect his
son from harm. Here, it is contended, it was part of a wider duty to protect by insurance
from the economic consequences of accidental injury. Thus it inevitably throws up the
basic question: was there such a wider duty? If there was not, there was no obligation to
c advise. In my view there was no wider duty for the following reasons.

(a) If the parent who is given such information is under no duty to act on it, it is
difficult to see how the school can be under any duty to the pupil. A duty to the parent
might be more acceptable and fair because serious injury leading to incapacity might
very well increase the parent's burden of maintaining his child. It is not suggested,
however, that such a duty arose. It seems to me that if a duty were to arise it must stem
d from the relationship between the parties and the attendant circumstances and not
merely from the fact that information was available to one and not to the other.

(b) The MOSA recommendation regarding personal accident insurance was restricted
to rugby football. But, if there was a duty in respect of rugby football, what of other
activities on the sports field such as cricket or in the gymnasium such as gymnastics or in
the squash court? It may be that it is in playing rugby football that the cervical spine is
e most at risk (though it may be that gymnastics will run it close), but what of the cricket
ball hit high in the air and lost in the sun and striking the fielder on the head? The effect
could be devastating. What of the squash ball in the eye? What of the gymnast who slips
and lands on his head through nobody's fault? These are mere instances of the sort of
accidents which have occurred. Indeed, what of the science master who must realise that
in the best regulated circumstances accidents may occur in the laboratory? Is he under a
f duty to warn parents so that they might consider exercising a discretion to insure their
sons? In my judgment, the answer is a clear No. His duty is to take care to protect his
pupils from harm. Provided he exercises due care in that regard his duty is fulfilled. The
law expects no more of him.

(c) If, as I consider to be the case, the plaintiff had no right to protection from purely
accidental injury or its consequences, how can it be said that he had a right to have his
g father informed of matters which might induce the father to exercise a discretion to
insure against personal accident? It is accepted that he could not compel his father to
insure, or sue him if he failed.

(d) In the circumstances of this case there could only be a duty of the kind contended
for if the plaintiff's father relied on the school to give him advice. If it were otherwise
h there would be no causal link between the breach and the damage. Indeed, that is the
plaintiff's case. Mr Van Oppen senior has said that, had he been apprised of the dangers
of rugby and of the need of insurance, he would have sought insurance cover. In other
words, he would have heeded the advice if it had been forthcoming. There is no reason
to doubt his evidence. But that is a different matter. In fact he did not rely, nor is there
any evidence that any parent relied, on the school to advise him on the question of
j insurance. That question did not cross his or their minds.

(e) The most I think that could be said is that it would have been prudent and careful
so to advise the parents. But as Lord Edmund-Davies said in Moorgate Mercantile Co Ltd v
Twitchings [1976] 2 All ER 641 at 659, [1977] AC 890 at 919: 'In most situations it is
better to be careful than careless, but it is quite another thing to elevate all carelessness
into a tort'. Liability only arises when there is a legal duty not to be careless. In my

judgment, for the reasons I have attempted to give, there was no such duty as is contended for in the circumstances which have been postulated. I should add that, in giving the *a* reasons as I have, it is not to be assumed that I regard the school as having been careless or lacking in prudence. That is not so.

Next it is contended that the school actually had assumed the following responsibilities:

(a) For assessing, and advising the plaintiff's father of, the need for personal accident insurance from December 1979. It failed to give such advice and so was in breach of its duty.   *b*

(b) Later for effecting personal accident insurance to cover the plaintiff. That being so, it had imposed on it, in accordance with the decisions in *Hedley Byrne & Co Ltd v Heller & Parters Ltd* [1963] 2 All ER 575, [1964] AC 465 and *Wilkinson v Coverdale* (1793) 1 Esp 75, [1775–1802] All ER Rep 339, a duty to exercise reasonable care and in particular a duty to act with reasonable dispatch, namely to effect insurance cover within a reasonable time. The foreseeable result of any breach of duty was that the plaintiff, if injured, would *c* or might suffer economic loss.

Counsel for the plaintiff submits that the headmaster's letter of December 1979 bears the following interpretations: (a) if insurance is necessary, we will effect it; (b) if we do not effect it, it is not necessary; (c) if we do not tell you we have effected cover, it is either unnecessary or you may assume that we have done it. The school, he says, foresaw the risk of serious injury which was ever present and, having reached the conclusion, as it *d* did, that personal accident insurance was necessary, it ought not to have relied on its own cumbersome internal procedures but should have acted with reasonable dispatch.

It is submitted that the responsibility for effecting personal accident insurance had been assumed by the school by June 1980 or, at the latest, September 1980. Whatever genuine doubts there might have been as to the extent of the cover, emergency cover for rugby alone should by then have been taken. The fact that the school at that time opted *e* for a compulsory comprehensive policy covering all pupils in all activities is the clearest evidence that it accepted responsibility for this particular economic loss. Had cover been effected, the plaintiff would have received a substantial sum by way of compensation. It was not done and so he has been deprived.

Counsel for the defendants submits that in order to found such duties it would be *f* necessary for the plaintiff to prove that the school did in fact undertake these respective obligations. This it never did. The headmaster's letters of Christmas 1979 and 1980, the only relevant communications to parents, did not purport to advise; they were merely informative and they were factual and accurate; no more.

If there was such a duty, then the question must arise: at what level of cover would the school be absolved from liability for negligence? Let it be supposed, it is said, that the school took out cover for £1,000 for permanent disability. Would the school then be *g* held negligent if the injuries were so catastrophic that £1,000 was derisory by way of compensation?

In addition it is submitted it would be necessary for the plaintiff to prove that the parents relied on the defendants to insure or to advise on insurance. There is no evidence, it is said, that any parent, not even the plaintiff's father, did rely on the school to provide *h* either of these services.

I accept the defendants' submissions that the school did not in fact undertake to advise the parents nor, prior to early 1981, did it undertake to effect insurance. In particular I accept that the plaintiff's interpretation of the headmaster's letter of December 1979 is too strained. It was not intended to be, nor do I think it would have been read by any parent as being, any more than a factual account of the situation so far as personal *j* accident insurance was concerned. The fact is that the school never intended to advise the parents of the need for taking personal accident insurance, nor did it undertake to do so. As for effecting insurance, while the headmaster concluded at quite an early stage that accident insurance would be desirable, there was a continuing debate, both within the school and among the representative bodies to whom he properly looked for advice,

on a number of issues: who was responsible for providing insurance cover; should the
a cover be restricted to rugby or should it embrace all activities; should it be compulsory
or optional; which policy was the most suitable? There were many people to be looked
to for advice and others to persuade. This was a novel experience and new ground for Mr
Jones and his staff. They were not insurance advisers or brokers. They moved with
understandable and proper caution and it might be said that day by day they had more
important duties to perform. Even by September 1980 there was still uncertainty in
b some areas, particularly as to who was legally responsible and which policy was the best
buy. The school had not undertaken to insure. There is no doubt that news from Sedburh
and the plaintiff's accident helped to resolve many of the doubts. But, for whatever
reason, it was not until early in 1981 that the school decided to go ahead with insurance.
Not until then could it be said that it undertook to insure.

In any event, it seems to me that the plaintiff's argument is fatally flawed in two
c respects. First, a person who undertakes to perform a voluntary act is or may be liable if
he performs it improperly but not if he neglects to perform it at all: see *Hedley Byrne &
Co Ltd v Heller & Partners Ltd* [1963] 2 All ER 575 at 588–589, 609, [1964] AC 465 at
494–495, 526–527 per Lord Morris and Lord Devlin. A voluntary undertaking to advise
or to act of itself gives rise to no duty of care; it gives rise to no legal obligation at all. In
support of this part of his submission, counsel for the plaintiff relies on *Wilkinson v
d Coverdale* (1793) 1 Esp 75, [1775–1802] All ER Rep 339. That was a case where the
defendant undertook to effect a policy of insurance on the plaintiff's house and where
the plaintiff relied on him to do so. The defendant carried out that undertaking so
carelessly that the insurance was wholly ineffective. In those circumstances, the defendant
was held to owe a duty of care to the plaintiff. He was in breach of that duty and was
therefore liable.
e Here the plaintiff's case is not that the school was careless in giving advice or in
effecting insurance. In reality his case is that the school failed to advise on the need for
insurance and failed to insure within a reasonable time, namely by the time the plaintiff
was injured. It is accepted that when, later, the school did insure, it acted reasonably in
the terms of the policy effected, the premiums agreed and in terms of the activities and
the pupils covered. So far as the plaintiff is concerned, his case is that it failed to insure at
f all. It follows therefore that, even if the school had voluntarily undertaken to advise or to
insure, it would have been under no legal duty to do either, nor could there have been
any duty of care cast on it.

Secondly, and in any event, the question is not simply whether the defendants
undertook to advise on the need for or to effect insurance. The question is whether by
such undertaking they should be held by the court to have assumed a legal responsibility
g to the plaintiff, whether they must be taken, in the circumstances, to have assumed a
duty to exercise reasonable care, a duty which was of sufficient scope to include protection
against economic loss. The answer to that question must depend on a consideration of all
the relevant circumstances, including, of course, the relationship between the parties.

There are a number of matters which are material. First, particularly so far as advice
h was concerned, whether or not the plaintiff relied on the school to give advice or to be
careful in advising. As I have already said, the plaintiff's father said that, had the school
given him advice on the need for insurance, he would have heeded it. I do not doubt
that. But that is not to say that he or any other parent relied on the school for advice.
Indeed there is no evidence that any parent did rely on the school either to advise or to
insure.
j Next it is material to consider whether or not the school held itself out as having the
expertise to advise on or deal with insurance. As Lord Devlin said in *Hedley Byrne & Co
Ltd v Heller & Partners Ltd* [1963] 2 All ER 575 at 612, [1964] AC 465 at 531, this may
not be invariably conclusive, but it is clearly an important consideration in deciding
whether or not the defendants accepted a legal responsibility. Here it is not even
suggested that the school held itself out in this way. Certainly there is no evidence to

support such a suggestion. Moreover, unlike *Wilkinson v Coverdale* (1773) 1 Esp 75, [1775–1802] All ER Rep 339, there was here no representation, either express or implied, *a* to the plaintiff or to his father that the school accepted responsibility either to advise or to act. Nor, unlike the plaintiff in the *Hedley Byrne* case, had the plaintiff or his father sought the advice of the school or sought the school's assistance in effecting insurance. This is not surprising when one considers that the school had no expertise in insurance matters and thus would not be expected by the parents either to advise or to act.

The very nature of the relationship between the parties militated against any *b* expectation that the school would assume an obligation to advise on the need for or to effect insurance or indeed any other business. I have no doubt that, if, in September 1980, either party (that is either the school or the plaintiff's father) had been asked whether or not the defendants had undertaken any legal responsibility for advising or insuring, the answer would have been an emphatic No.

In short, nothing had occurred, in my judgment, to alter the normal relationship of *c* school and pupil. The school never assumed any legal responsibility. It sought to provide an additional service for its pupils. There was therefore, in my judgment, nothing to enlarge the duty normally owed by the school to the plaintiff. A duty to advise or to insure could only have arisen if there had been a more fundamental duty to act positively to protect the plaintiff's economic interest. I have already given my reasons for concluding that there was no such duty.   *d*

Finally, to revert to Lord Keith's observations in *Governors of the Peabody Donation Fund v Sir Lindsay Parkinson & Co Ltd* [1984] 3 All ER 529 at 534, [1985] AC 210 at 240–241 and *Yuen Kun-yeu v A-G of Hong Kong* [1987] 2 All ER 705 at 710, [1988] AC 175 at 191–192, it seems to me unfair and unreasonable that a school should stand in peril of a finding of negligence at the suit of a pupil for failing to do, either expeditiously or at all, something which the parent could avoid doing or could do carelessly with complete *e* impunity. Moreover, it would be remarkable, to say the least, if the plaintiff, who had no right to expect anyone to insure him, should acquire such a right simply because a caring school considered it desirable that its pupils should have the advantage of personal accident insurance and should have taken steps to effect it.

Before leaving this aspect of the case, I ought to deal shortly with the submission made *f* by counsel for the defendants that, in any event, the plaintiff has suffered no damage which is recognised by the law. He contends that the plaintiff has been deprived of nothing to which he was entitled or of which he was possessed or of any benefit of which he was assured or had reason to expect. Nor had he ventured anything in reliance on the defendants' skill and judgment. This argument might be more appropriate to demonstrate that the plaintiff had no recognisable interest which he was entitled to have protected. Thus there was no duty on the school. Had there been a duty to insure and had the *g* defendants failed in that duty, then, in my judgment, the result must have been a loss to the plaintiff which would have been recoverable in the courts (see, for instance, *Wilkinson's* case (1773) 1 Esp 75, [1775–1802] All ER Rep 339).

For the reasons that I have attempted to give I am driven to conclude that the plaintiff's claim must fail.   *h*

Action dismissed.

Solicitors: *Clarke Willmott & Clarke* (for the plaintiff); *Herbert Smith* (for the defendant).

K Mydeen   Barrister.   *j*

a
Re T and others (minors) (wardship: jurisdiction)

COURT OF APPEAL, CIVIL DIVISION
SIR STEPHEN BROWN P AND PURCHAS LJ
5 SEPTEMBER, 27 OCTOBER 1988

b
Child – Care – Local authority – Wardship proceedings – Interim care orders made in respect of four children of same family – Care orders made in two juvenile courts for different children on the application of two different local authorities – Same guardian ad litem appointed for children – Guardian ad litem applying to High Court to make children wards of court to enable one court to exercise jurisdiction over whole family – Whether guardian ad litem having locus standi to
c *issue wardship summons – Children and Young Persons Act 1969, s 3 2B(1) – Magistrates' Courts (Children and Young Persons) Rules 1970, r 14A(1)(6).*

A mother had three children by her first marriage, namely G, a boy aged 16, S, a girl aged 15, and L, a girl aged 13. She also had one child, R, a boy aged 9, by her second
d marriage. Following allegations by S that her stepfather had sexually abused her, a place of safety order was obtained in respect of her and she was placed in the interim care of the local authority. The mother, the stepfather and the three other children moved to the area of another local authority and following further allegations by S of sexual abuse within the family the three remaining children were placed in the interim care of that local authority. In proceedings in the juvenile court for each area the same guardian ad litem was appointed to act for all four children. Because of the difficulties of dealing with
e two separate sets of proceedings in two different juvenile courts the guardian ad litem issued an originating summons for the children to be made wards of court so that one court could exercise jurisdiction over the whole family. Both local authorities applied to the High court to discharge the wardship in respect of the children but their applications were refused. The local authority having the interim care of G, S and L appealed,
f contending, inter alia, that the guardian ad litem had no locus standi to issue the wardship proceedings in the High Court because under s 32B(1)[a] of the Children and Young Persons Act 1969 and r 14A(1)[b] and (6)[c] of the Magistrates' Courts (Children and Young Persons) Rules 1970 the guardian was appointed solely 'for the purpose of the proceedings' in the juvenile court to safeguard the interests of the relevant infant before the court and had no role outside or beyond those proceedings and therefore had no authority to
g embark on wardship proceedings.

Held – The appointment of a guardian ad litem pursuant to s 32B(1) of the 1969 Act did not give the guardian any additional status or authority beyond or outside the proceedings before the juvenile court. Accordingly, the guardian ad litem had no locus standi to issue an originating summons initiating wardship proceedings in the High Court and the
h summons was therefore procedurally defective. Moreover, even if the summons had been procedurally valid, the wardship would not have been confirmed because the two sets of care proceedings under the 1969 Act had been properly commenced in the

_____

a Section 32B(1), so far as material, provides: 'Where the court makes an order under section 32A(2) of this Act the court, unless satisfied that to do so is not necessary for safeguarding the interests of the child or young person, shall in accordance with rules of court appoint a guardian ad litem of
j   the child or young person for the purposes of the proceedings...'
b Rule 14A(1) provides: 'In any proceedings to which an order under section 32A(1) of the [Children and Young Persons Act 1969] relates (not being an order under section 32A(2)) the court shall appoint a guardian *ad litem* of the relevant infant for the purposes of the proceedings if it appears to the court that it is in his interests to do so.'
c Rule 14A(6), so far as material, is set out at p 305 f, post

appropriate juvenile courts and neither local authority envisaged any problem in seeking
to protect each of the children concerned. It followed therefore that the appeal would be *a*
allowed (see pp 302 *j* to p 303 *b*, p 304 *b c*, p 305 *j* and p 306 *a b* post).

Notes
For the appointment and duties of a guardian ad litem, see 24 Halsbury's Laws (4th edn)
paras 738, 765, 796.
    For the wardship jurisdiction, see ibid paras 576–583, and for cases on the subject, see *b*
28(2) Digest (Reissue) 911–916, 2220–2247.
    For the Children and Young Persons Act 1969, s 32B, see 6 Halsbury's Statutes (4th
edn) 277.
    For the Magistrates' Courts (Children and Young Persons) Rules 1970, r 14A, see 4
Halsbury's Statutory Instruments (Grey Volume) 238.

c
Cases referred to in judgments
A v Berkshire CC (1988) Times, 10 June; affd (1988) Times, 24 October, CA.
A v Liverpool City Council [1981] 2 All ER 385, [1982] AC 363, [1981] 2 WLR 948, HL.
D (a minor) (wardship: sterilisation), Re [1976] 1 All ER 326, [1976] Fam 185, [1976] 2
    WLR 279.
H (a minor) (wardship: jurisdiction), Re [1978] 2 All ER 903, [1978] Fam 65, [1978] 2 WLR *d*
    608, CA.
P (infants), Re [1967] 2 All ER 229, [1967] 1 WLR 818.
W v Hertfordshire CC [1985] 2 All ER 301, [1985] AC 791, [1985] 2 WLR 892, HL.

Cases also cited
A, B, C and D (minors), Re (20 April 1988, unreported), Fam Div.   *e*
E (minors) (wardship: jurisdiction), Re [1984] 1 All ER 21, [1983] 1 WLR 541, CA.
J (a minor) (wardship: jurisdiction), Re [1984] 1 All ER 29, [1984] 1 WLR 81, CA.
Surrey CC v S [1973] 3 All ER 1074, [1974] QB 124, [1973] 3 WLR 579, CA.

Interlocutory appeal
On 7 April 1988 the plaintiff child S, by her guardian ad litem Mrs Jane Elizabeth Booth, *f*
who was also the guardian ad litem of the minors G, L and R, issued an originating
summons to make the four minors wards of court. The respondents to the summons
were (1) the Bradford Metropolitan City Council (Bradford council), which had interim
care of S, (2) the mother of the children, (3) Mr T, the father of S, G and L, (4) Kirklees
Metropolitan Borough Council (Kirklees council), which had interim care of G, L and R,
and (5) Mr M, the father of R and stepfather of the other children. G was subsequently *g*
joined as a separate respondent. On 20 April 1988 Kirklees council issued a summons to
discharge the wardship in respect of G, L and R and on 16 May 1988 Bradford council
made a similar application in respect of S. On 16 June 1988 Booth J ([1988] 3 WLR 713),
in a judgment delivered in open court after a hearing in chambers, refused the
applications. Kirklees council appealed. Bradford council did not appeal. The facts are set *h*
out in the judgment of Sir Stephen Brown P.

Hugh Bennett QC and *Eleanor Hamilton* for Kirklees council.
R M Harrison QC and *Rebecca Thornton* for S.
Anita M Ryan QC and *Stephen Glover* for G.
James Goss for the mother.   *j*

                                                                    Cur adv vult

27 October. The following judgments were delivered.

SIR STEPHEN BROWN P. On 16 June Booth J decided as a preliminary issue that

the High Court should exercise its wardship jurisdiction in respect of four children of
a one family who individually are the subjects of two sets of care proceedings brought by
two different local authorities in two different juvenile courts. After hearing argument
she ordered that the wardship should be confirmed (see [1988] 3 WLR 713). Kirklees
Metropolitan Borough Council (Kirklees council) as the local authority concerned with
three of the children now appeals against that order. The other local authority concerned,
Bradford Metropolitan City Council (Bradford council), whilst not abandoning the
b position which it adopted before the judge, nevertheless does not wish to pursue an
appeal in this court.

The facts which gave rise to the hearing before the judge are succinctly set out in her
judgment. The four children are G, a boy of 16, S, a girl of 15, L, a girl of 13, and R, a
boy of 9 years of age. G, S and L are the children of the mother by her first husband, Mr
T. The fourth child, R, is the child of the mother by her second husband, Mr M. In May
c 1987 the mother with Mr M and all her four children were living in Bradford. The girl
S made an allegation that she had been raped. She did not at that stage identify the
alleged perpetrator. However, in November 1987 she alleged that her stepfather Mr M,
the mother's second husband, had sexually abused her. As a result of her disclosures a
place of safety order was obtained by Bradford Social Services Department, and on 8
December 1987 the Bradford Juvenile Court made an interim care order placing S in the
d care of Bradford council. At the end of November 1987 the mother with Mr M and her
three other children moved from Bradford to Huddersfield. They thereupon came
within the area of Kirklees council. As a result of the order made in Bradford in relation
to S Kirklees social services department was informed of the situation. They got in touch
with the family but at that stage decided to take no action. By this stage Mr M, the
stepfather of S, had been charged with an offence of indecent assault on S and was no
e longer living in the family home. At the hearing of this appeal this court has been told
that Mr M has been convicted of indecent assault and has been sentenced to a term of
imprisonment. Meanwhile, S resided in a children's home in Bradford pursuant to the
interim care order of the Bradford Juvenile Court. She then made an allegation that Mr
M had also sexually abused her elder brother, G, and she made yet a further allegation
that the maternal grandfather had sexually abused L. As a result of these further
f allegations Kirklees social services department obtained a place of safety order in respect
of L and she was taken from the mother's home in Huddersfield and interviewed. She
did not herself make any allegations when seen, and was permitted to return home. In
March 1988 S made further allegations of sexual activity within the family which
prompted Kirklees council to obtain place of safety orders in respect of the three children,
G, L and R, who then resided in their area.
g Police interviews, it is said, disclose that R has apparently admitted having had sexual
intercourse with the two girls when he was aged seven but G had always contended that
the allegations concerning him are a complete fabrication. On 3 March 1988 the Bradford
Juvenile Court made a further interim care order in respect of S in favour of Bradford
council. After making a short visit to her mother's home in Huddersfield S returned to
h reside in the children's home in Bradford. On 31 March 1988 the Huddersfield Juvenile
Court, on the application of Kirklees council, made interim care orders in respect of the
three children G, L and R. L and R are presently residing in two different children's
homes. G is currently at an assessment centre.

In the proceedings in each juvenile court a Mrs Jane Elizabeth Booth was appointed to
act as guardian ad litem to all the children. In two affidavits which she has sworn she has
j made known her concern as to the difficulty which she feels she faces in dealing with
two separate sets of proceedings in two different courts. It is apparent that there is a sharp
conflict of interest in particular between the child S and the child G. Indeed, G has since
been ordered to be separately represented. In consequence of this he was separately
represented at the hearing of this appeal. On 7 April 1988, as a result of the difficulties
which she felt she encountered, Mrs Booth, acting on her own initiative, took the step of
issuing an originating summons in wardship. Her stated purpose was to enable one court

to exercise jurisdiction over the whole family. The originating summons is entitled 'In the matter of S—— G—— L—— & R—— [I give the initials in order to preserve their *a* anonymity] . . . *Between* S—— [plaintiff] (by her Guardian Ad Litem JANE BOOTH) *and* CITY OF BRADFORD METROPOLITAN COUNCIL' and the mother, the father of S, Kirklees council and Mr M, the mother's second husband, are all named as defendants. The form of the summons then reads:

'By this summons, which is issued on the application of the plaintiff [S] (by her *b* Guardian Ad Litem Jane Booth) . . . the plaintiff claims against the defendant 1. That the children [and all are named] be made Wards of this Honourable Court during their minority 2. That the Court do make orders regarding care and control and access regarding these children.'

On 16 May 1988 Bradford council issued a summons seeking the discharge of the wardship in respect of S, and Kirklees council also applied to discharge the wardship in *c* respect of G, L and R. At the hearing before the judge they relied on the principles established in *A v Liverpool City Council* [1981] 2 All ER 385, [1982] AC 363 and in *W v Hertfordshire CC* [1985] 2 All ER 301, [1985] AC 791, each submitting that both local authorities concerned had acted in accordance with the statutory code relating to children in trouble or need and that in the light of those decisions it was neither necessary nor appropriate for there to be a review of the councils' actions by the High Court. The cases *d* could and should be dealt with in accordance with the statutory code. For the guardian ad litem it was submitted that the court could and should exercise its wide jurisdiction to entertain the originating summons and to decide the issues relating to all the children. It was argued that the Children and Young Persons Act 1969 did not provide any means whereby one court could entertain care proceedings relating to children of the same family if they happened individually to reside in different areas. It was claimed that this *e* constituted a lacuna in the statutory powers of juvenile courts which the High Court could and should fill by the exercise of its wardship jurisdiction.

The two authorities submitted that as 'guardian ad litem' appointed under the 1969 Act Mrs Booth had no remit or authority to embark on wardship proceedings. They pointed out that the summons was issued in the name of the child S as plaintiff 'by her *f* guardian ad litem'. The child was then in fact in the statutory care of Bradford council. The district registrar in due course ordered that she should be referred to as 'next friend'. Nevertheless, the judge decided that in the circumstances of this case the court did have power to exercise its wardship jurisdiction and that the circumstances of the case required that it should do so. The judge said ([1988] 3 WLR 713 at 722–723):

'Neither juvenile court has jurisdiction to transfer the case before it to the other *g* court and neither court has jurisdiction to transfer a case to the High Court. Therefore the only means by which the guardian ad litem could achieve a hearing before one tribunal was to invoke the wardship proceedings.'

The judge then ordered that the wardship should be confirmed.

Counsel for Kirklees council, in a careful argument, submitted that the judge was in *h* error in deciding that there was a lacuna in the powers of the juvenile courts under the provisions of the 1969 Act. He reviewed the structure of the Act, pointing out that s 2(2) required a local authority to bring care proceedings in respect of a child residing in its area if it should appear to it that there were grounds for bringing care proceedings. He acknowledged that by virtue of s 2(11) the juvenile court in which care proceedings were to be initiated must be the court for the area in which the child resided. He accepted that *j* the Act contained no provision for the transfer of care proceedings from one juvenile court to another juvenile court. However, he said that a juvenile court is obliged to act in the best interests of the child. He challenged the assertion that it would not be possible or practicable to do justice to each of the children if the proceedings were to continue in separate courts. Mere apparent inconvenience, he submitted, was not a ground for removing the proceedings from the jurisdiction of the juvenile courts to the High Court.

a Mrs Booth, as guardian ad litem, was under a duty to seek the views of the juvenile court in the event of encountering difficulty. In this case it might well be that she would find it difficult to continue to act as guardian to G whilst acting as guardian to the other children, in particular to S, having regard to the conflict between S and G. If, as seemed highly probable, the Bradford Juvenile Court were to find the ground for making a care order made out in the case of S, then it could and probably would make a care order in

b her case. In the area of Kirklees the Huddersfield Juvenile Court would by virtue of the provisions of s 1(2)(b) of the Act be able to take into consideration the finding of the Bradford Juvenile Court in respect of S when considering the cases of the other three children. Should it be considered necessary for S to give evidence in relation to the allegations which she had made concerning the other children then there would appear to be no procedural impediment to prevent her being called to give evidence in

c Huddersfield. However, it might prove unnecessary or undesirable for her to be called. Accordingly, he submitted that there was no justificiation for the High Court to be called on to exercise its wardship jurisdiction in relation to these children. The proceedings under the Children and Young Persons Act 1969 had been properly set in train and the relevant courts were fully competent to decide the relevant issues in respect of each of the children.

d   Counsel for Kirklees council further submitted that Mrs Booth as guardian ad litem in the juvenile court proceedings had no locus standi to enable her to institute wardship proceedings in the High Court in these cases. Her appointment as guardian ad litem had been made under the provisions of s 32B(1) of the 1969 Act for the purpose 'of these proceedings'. The proceedings are those in the juvenile court. Rule 14A(1) of the Magistrates' Courts (Children and Young Persons) Rules 1970, SI 1970/1792, provided

e that the court should appoint a guardian ad litem 'for the purpose of the proceedings'. Rule 14A(6) sets out the duties of the guardian ad litem 'with a view to safeguarding the interests of the relevant infant before the court'. He therefore contended that as guardian ad litem she had no role outside or beyond the proceedings in the juvenile court. He acknowledged that the availability of wardship is very wide and that it would appear that

f any person, including a local authority and indeed the child himself acting by his 'next friend', may apply for the child to be made a ward of court. In this instance, however, the application was not in reality that of the child S herself, although it was so expressed. It was in fact the application of the guardian ad litem as the summons itself indicated. The registrar's direction that she should be referred to as 'next friend' was not valid. It could not alter the nature or status of the proceedings. He argued that there was therefore a fundamental procedural defect in these wardship proceedings. He said that Mrs Booth

g was apparently seeking an opportunity to transfer the proceedings from the jurisdiction of the juvenile courts when there was no authority for her to do so. Counsel for Kirklees council compared her role with that of the Official Solicitor. He pointed out that it is settled law that the Official Solicitor cannot initiate and then pursue wardship proceedings by purporting to act on the infant's behalf as his 'next friend'. He cited Re D (a minor)

h (wardship: sterilisation) [1976] 1 All ER 326 at 335–336, [1976] Fam 185 at 196–198. He also referred to A v Berkshire CC (1988) Times, 10 June. He placed a transcript of the judgment before this court. It is a case which I decided at first instance on the application of Berkshire County Council to discharge a wardship summons relating to a boy who was the subject of care proceedings in a juvenile court. The substantive facts were different from the facts of this case. In that case the guardian ad litem had become

j dissatisfied with proposals to be put before a juvenile court by the county council at the substantive hearing of care proceedings in relation to the minor. As a result she took the step of issuing a summons in wardship. It was said that she wished to be able to obtain a further medical report from a doctor of her own choice and then to put forward alternative detailed proposals for the care of the minor, although by her summons she sought a care order under the Family Law Reform Act 1969 in favour of the same county council. The court held that her action was in direct conflict with the principles expressed by the House of Lords in *A v Liverpool City Council* [1981] 2 All ER 385, [1982] AC 363 **a** and *W v Hertfordshire CC* [1985] 2 All ER 301, [1985] AC 791 and, furthermore, that she had no locus standi in the High Court as a guardian ad litem appointed by the juvenile court.

Counsel for S submitted that there was a lacuna in the juvenile court code. He claimed that the effect of s 2(11) of the 1969 Act was that no single juvenile court was able to consider the cases of all children from one family if the children happened to reside in **b** different petty sessional areas at the material time. He claimed that there was nothing in the decisions in *A v Liverpool City Council* or *W v Hertfordshire CC* to prevent the High Court from assuming wardship jurisdiction in order to bring all such cases before the same tribunal. He submitted that the judge had properly exercised her discretion to confirm the wardships in order to supplement the powers of the juvenile courts. He further submitted that a guardian ad litem appointed by a juvenile court under s 32B of **c** the 1969 Act was entitled in that capacity to initiate wardship proceedings if she considered that the welfare of the minor required her to do so. He argued that her authority arose either from the statute itself or, alternatively, at common law by reason of the fact that she was a person having an interest in the welfare of the minor.

The judge took the view that the likely conflict between S and G would make it difficult not only for the guardian ad litem but also for each juvenile court to make **d** orders which were in the interests of each child, bearing in mind that they were the children of one family. The judge said ([1988] 3 WLR 713 at 719):

> 'I am of the view that the guardian ad litem is justified in her fears that in the particular circumstances of this case neither juvenile court has the necessary statutory power to safeguard and protect the welfare of these children having regard to the **e** fact that they are of one family and that their respective interests cannot properly be considered in isolation one from another. Since it is not open to either court to transfer its jurisdiction to the other so that the interests of all the children may be considered by one tribunal the question is whether it is open to this court to exercise its wardship jurisdiction despite the fact that the two local authorities concerned wish to proceed in accordance with the statutory code.' **f**

The judge cited *Re P (infants)* [1967] 2 All ER 229, [1967] 1 WLR 818, where Stamp J held that despite the fact that a custody order had already been made in a magistrates' court the High Court could nevertheless exercise its wardship jurisdiction where relief was genuinely sought which the magistrates were not empowered to give. The judge also cited *Re H (a minor) (wardship: jurisdiction)* [1978] 2 All ER 903, [1978] Fam 65. However, that case received criticism from the House of Lords in *A v Liverpool City* **g** *Council*. It is also to be noted that *Re P (infants)* was decided before the 1969 Act. The judge further took the view that in *W v Hertfordshire CC* [1985] 2 All ER 301, [1985] AC 791 the House of Lords did not express any view which might appear to derogate from the principle that the High Court may exercise its wardship jurisdiction wherever it is necessary to do so in order to supplement the inadequate statutory powers of the **h** magistrates. The judge said ([1988] 3 WLR 713 at 722):

> 'I am therefore satisfied that in this case the High Court can and should exercise its wardship jurisdiction to supplement the powers of the justices and to ensure that one tribunal may consider the future welfare of all the children of this family and make such orders as are found to be in their best interests.'

Whilst it might be thought to be more convenient for the cases of all these children to **j** be decided by one tribunal I am unable to take the view that these sets of proceedings are exceptional. In each case the local authority concerned acted properly in the discharge of its duties under the 1969 Act. The proceedings were commenced in the appropriate courts and appropriate interim care orders were made. Neither authority considered that

it was inhibited in any way in seeking to protect each of the children concerned. In
a neither case has the juvenile court indicated that it experienced any difficulty in
considering and dealing with the cases before it. The judge said in her judgment that
under the Magistrates' Courts (Children and Young Persons) Rules 1970 the guardian ad
litem has an obligation to seek the views of the court in any case where difficulties arise
in relation to the performance of her duties. In this case she did not do so. However, the
judge said ([1988] 3 WLR 713 at 722): '. . . it seems to me that in the circumstances of
b this case to do so would have been of no avail.'

The position is, however, that neither of the local authorities concerned has suggested
that it envisages any problem in pursuing the proceedings which it has initiated under
the statute. Indeed, the contrary is the case. Neither juvenile court has expressed concern
at the lack of any powers that it may possess.

From the facts recited in the judgment of the judge it would appear that there is a
c clear division between the case of S and the cases of the other children involved. The
guardian ad litem as guardian for all the children may face a conflict of interest personally.
This court has been led to believe that in the case of G there is in any event to be a separate
guardian. It would appear that the difficulty in this case therefore arises from the position
of the guardian herself, having regard to her dual appointment. It does not appear to me
that that of itself affects the powers of the courts or their ability to make appropriate
d decisions in the individual cases. Perhaps if she had brought her problem to the notice of
the courts concerned her position might have been regularised by giving up the
appointment to one or other of these positions. This wardship summons was issued
before either court had approached any determination of the matter before it, although
each had made interim orders. The guardian's action was clearly designed to remove
these matters from the jurisdiction of these juvenile courts. I believe that this action is in
e conflict with the ratio of the judgments of the House of Lords in *A v Liverpool City Council*
and *W v Hertfordshire CC*. In his speech in the *Hertfordshire* case [1985] 2 All ER 301 at
303, [1985] AC 791 at 796 Lord Scarman referred to the speech of Lord Wilberforce in
the *Liverpool* case. He said:

'In the *Liverpool* case [1981] 2 All ER 385 at 388, [1982] AC 363 at 372, Lord
f Wilberforce put the point succinctly: "Parliament has by statute entrusted to the
local authority the power and duty to make decisions as to the welfare of children
without any reservation of a reviewing power to the court." He indicated where the
line had to be drawn between the wardship jurisdiction of the High Court and the
statutory responsibilities of the local authority ([1981] 2 All ER 385 at 388–389,
[1982] AC 363 at 373): "This is not to say that the inherent jurisdiction of the High
g Court is taken away. Any child, whether under care or not, can be made a ward of
court by the procedure of s 9(2) of the Law Reform (Miscellaneous Provisions) Act
1949. In cases (and the present is an example) where the court perceives that the
action sought of it is within the sphere of discretion of the local authority, it will
make no order and the wardship will lapse. But in some instances, there may be an
area of concern to which the powers of the local authority, limited as they are by
h statute, do not extend. Sometimes the local authority itself may invite the
supplementary assistance of the court. Then the wardship may be continued with a
view to action by the court. The court's general inherent power is always available
to fill gaps or to supplement the powers of the local authority: what it will not do
(except by way of judicial review where appropriate) is to supervise the exercise of
discretion within the field committed by statute to the local authority."'

j
In this case neither local authority has indicated that it feels any difficulty in dealing
under the statutory procedure with the case of the child or children within its area.
Nevertheless, the guardian, doubtless in good faith, has without reference to either of the
courts which appointed her taken it on herself to issue wardship proceedings.

When she made the order confirming the wardship the judge directed that the Official

Solicitor should be invited to act as guardian ad litem for all these children. This court
has been informed that the Official Solicitor has declined that invitation. Now that the *a*
child G is separately represented it does not appear to me that there is likely to be any
insuperable difficulty in dealing with this matter through the normal statutory procedure.

Despite the wide ambit of s 9(2) of the Law Reform (Miscellaneous Provisions) Act
1949 I do not consider that the originating summons was regularly or properly issued in
this case. The position of the guardian ad litem is a statutory role pursuant to the
provisions of s 32B(1) of the Children and Young Persons Act 1969. The appointment *b*
pursuant to that section does not in my judgment give any additional status or authority
to the guardian beyond or outside the proceedings before the juvenile court. I do not,
therefore, consider that Mrs Booth had any locus standi to issue this wardship summons.

In the result I have come to the conclusion, first, that the wardship summons was
procedurally defective but, second, even if it was procedurally valid so as to initiate
wardship proceedings it should not have been confirmed. In the circumstances I would *c*
have to say that in doing so the judge erred in exercising her discretion.

PURCHAS LJ. I agree.

In view of the fact that we are differing from a judge of great experience in these
matters I will add a few words of my own. The full history and circumstances have
already been set out in the judgment just delivered and need not be repeated. The family *d*
involved consisted of children ranging from the age of 16 down to the age of 9. The
allegations which were to be investigated by the two juvenile courts concerned are both
serious and complex. Moreover, they involve nearly all, if not all, of the children and the
mother, stepfather and the maternal grandfather. There is a serious conflict of testimony
to be anticipated between S and G, both of whom are of an age to appreciate the impact
and significance of allegations of this kind and, in the case of G, on the unestablished *e*
assumption that the allegations are true, the desirability of making a false denial.
Similarly, S on the other hand is of an age where it is not unknown for young girls to
fabricate allegations of a sensational nature. There is considerable force in the suggestion
that one court ought to resolve these conflicts of testimony where they are relevant to the
determination of the future of the members of the family. However, this is not
necessarily the same thing as one court having to resolve the future of the whole family. *f*
The possibility, if it is necessary, of S being called in the proceedings in the Bradford
Juvenile Court have already been considered by Sir Stephen Brown P. I agree that whilst
it is clear that Mrs Booth, the guardian ad litem, must find herself in a position of
conflicting interest as between G and S, this of itself is not a cause for removing the
matter from the jurisdiction of the juvenile courts. As the guardian ad litem in one
court, namely the wardship court, she would still suffer a conflict of interest between G *g*
and S. The central point is whether there is any case to be made based on the proper
disposition of the various members of this family being only capable of achievement in
one court in wardship proceedings.

S's future, which would appear likely to be one of remaining in the care of the Bradford
City Council, can clearly be determined by the Bradford Juvenile Court. Her future does *h*
not depend on any conflict of testimony which could be relevant. On the other hand, the
future of G, L and R must depend to a material extent on the veracity of the testimony
of S. This problem can clearly be resolved in accordance with their function within the
statutory code by the Huddersfield Juvenile Court. The so-called 'lacuna' passage in the
speech of Lord Wilberforce in *A v Liverpool City Council* [1981] 2 All ER 385 at 388–389,
[1982] AC 363 at 373 has been a haven of resort in many cases sought by persons wishing *j*
to invoke the wardship jurisdiction. In *W v Hertfordshire CC* [1985] 2 All ER 301 at 304,
[1985] AC 791 at 797 Lord Scarman, after referring to the passages from the speech of
Lord Wilberforce in the *Liverpool* case, said:

'The High Court cannot exercise its powers, however wide they may be, so as to
intervene on the merits in an area of concern entrusted by Parliament to another

a public authority. It matters not that the chosen public authority is one which acts administratively whereas the court, if seised of the same matter, would act judicially. If Parliament in an area of concern defined by statute (the area in this case being the care of children in need or trouble) prefers power to be exercised administratively instead of judicially, so be it. The courts must be careful in that area to avoid assuming a supervisory role or reviewing power over the merits of decisions taken administratively by the selected public authority.'

b
This passage can be adapted to the problem in the present case. By the statutory code Parliament has decreed that the welfare of any particular child resident within the area of the local authority concerned shall be dealt with administratively by that authority subject only to the powers to grant or withhold care orders etc vested in the first instance in the juvenile court for the area concerned. The fact that the statutory code is framed in *c* such a way that the care of the individual child is the object of attention and supervision rather than the family as a whole is not a matter in which the wardship court should intervene. Intervention in this area is no different from the intervention which was held to be wrongful in *A v Liverpool City Council* and *W v Hertfordshire CC*.

Finally, in the course of his argument counsel for Kirklees council referred to *A v Berkshire CC* (1988) Times, 10 June, in which the judgment at first instance was delivered *d* by Sir Stephen Brown P. Since the argument in the present case was heard that case has been before the Court of Appeal when the appeal was dismissed ((1988) Times, 24 October). It is sufficient for the purposes of this judgment to record that on appeal the Court of Appeal considered submissions relating to the locus standi of the guardian ad litem in that case. The judgments confirmed that the guardian ad litem appointed under s 32B and r 14A of the Magistrates' Courts (Children and Young Persons) Rules 1970, SI *e* 1970/1792, was appointed 'for the purposes of the proceedings in the juvenile court'. With the determination of those proceedings the guardian ad litem becomes functus officio. Reference was made to r 14A(6), which provides:

'The guardian *ad litem* appointed under this rule or section 32B(1) of the [Children and Young Persons Act 1969], with a view to safeguarding the interests of the *f* relevant infant before the court shall—(a) so far as it is reasonably practicable, investigate all circumstances relevant to the proceedings and for that purpose shall interview such persons, inspect such records and obtain such professional assistance as the guardian *ad litem* thinks appropriate . . .'

As has been set out in the judgment just delivered, in that case the guardian ad litem, holding professional views as to the proper treatment of the child which conflicted with *g* reports in the hand of the local authority, sought an adjournment in order to obtain a psychiatric report from an independent specialist. In the context of an indication from the local authority that they would oppose the adjournment or even if such a report were obtained would not alter their views, the guardian ad litem issued an originating summons in wardship. In the event the local authority at a late stage did not oppose the adjournment and after the hearing before Sir Stephen Brown P a report from the *h* specialist concerned was obtained. The decision to dismiss the wardship summons and deward the child was in those circumstances upheld and the judgments confirmed that the powers given to the guardian ad litem were confined within the ambit of the 1969 Act and the 1970 rules, particularly r 14A. The guardian's appointment as guardian ad litem is and can only be for the purposes of the proceedings in the juvenile court and she cannot enjoy a similar status until a subsequent appointment has been made in her *j* favour by the High Court in the wardship proceedings. For different reasons, as already indicated, this would be unlikely although not impossible. On the other hand, as an ordinary member of the public especially concerned with the welfare of the child involved, anyone may apply to make that child a ward of court or act as next friend. The fact that the applicant had previously been appointed as guardian ad litem in the juvenile proceedings would not be a cause for restricting the rights available to any individual in appropriate circumstances to apply to the wardship court. This, however, is the limit of her locus standi before the court. As has already been said, the real purpose of the application in wardship in this case is to usurp the execution by the two local authorities and the respective juvenile courts of their functions under the statutory code.

For these reasons and for the reasons already given by Sir Stephen Brown P I agree that this appeal must be allowed and that the order he proposes should be made.

Appeal allowed. Leave to appeal to the House of Lords refused.

Solicitors: *Sharpe Pritchard*, agents for M R G *Vause*, Huddersfield (for Kirklees council); *Williscroft & Co*, Bradford (for S); *Parker Bird*, Huddersfield (for G); *Ramsdens*, Huddersfield (for the mother).

Mary Rose Plummer   Barrister.

Commission for Racial Equality v Dutton

COURT OF APPEAL, CIVIL DIVISION
STOCKER, NICHOLLS AND TAYLOR LJJ
18, 19, 20 MAY, 27 JULY 1988

Race relations – Discrimination – Discrimination against racial group – Gipsies – Racial group defined by reference to colour, race, nationality or ethnic or national origins – Ethnic origins – Travellers – Publican refusing to admit 'travellers' to public house – Whether unlawful discrimination against gipsies – Whether gipsies a racial group – Race Relations Act 1976, ss 1(1)(a)(b), 3(1), 29.

The defendant, who was the licensee of a public house, refused to serve a person who was living in an illegally parked caravan nearby and an unpleasant incident ensued. The licensee, as he had done at his previous licensed premises, then put up a sign saying 'Sorry, no travellers'. Following a complaint the Commission for Racial Equality sought a (i) declaration that the sign contravened s 29[a] of the Race Relations Act 1976 on the grounds that it was an advertisement indicating that the defendant intended to discriminate against gipsies and (ii) an injunction restraining the defendant from displaying the sign. The judge, sitting with assessors in the county court, dismissed the action. The commission appealed, contending that the defendant had either directly discriminated against gipsies on racial grounds for the purposes of s 1(1)(a)[b] of the 1976 Act because 'traveller' was synonymous with gipsies or had indirectly discriminated against gipsies for the purposes of s 1(1)(b) because he had applied to a gipsy who wished to have a drink at his public house a condition, viz that he was not a traveller, which he applied to persons not of the same 'racial group' when the proportion of gipsies who could comply with it was considerably smaller than the proportion of other racial groups who could comply with it.

Held – (1) The term 'traveller' was not synonymous with gipsies but referred to all persons leading a nomadic way of life. Accordingly, the defendant's sign prohibiting the entry of 'travellers' to his public house could not reasonably be understood as indicating an intention by the defendant to discriminate against gipsies as a racial group and therefore there had been no direct discrimination under s 1(1)(a) of the 1976 Act (see p 309 d, p 311 c to f, p 315 h and p 318 c d, post).

---

a   Section 29, so far as material, is set out at p 308 *h*, post
b   Section 1(1), so far as material, is set out at p 308 *j* and p 311 *g h*, post

(2) For the purposes of race relations and the 1976 Act gipsies were capable of being a
a separate 'racial group' as defined by s 3(1)^c of that Act because, despite their long presence
in England and the fact that they were no longer derived from common racial stock,
they had not merged wholly with the population but remained an identifiable group
defined by reference to their 'ethnic ... origins'. Since the proportion of gipsies who
could comply with the defendant's 'no travellers' condition was considerably smaller than
the proportion of non-gipsies who could comply with it, because a much higher
b proportion of gipsies were travellers, and since the condition operated to the detriment
of nomadic gipsies, the defendant's 'no travellers' condition amounted to indirect
discrimination against gipsies under s 1(1)(*b*) of the 1976 Act unless the defendant could
show that it was justified. Since the judge had not decided that issue the appeal would be
allowed and the case remitted to the county court to determine the justification issue (see
p 313 *e f j* to p 314 *a g h*, p 315 *d* to *g*, p 317 *j* to p 318 *c* and p 320 *g h*, post); *Mandla v*
c *Dowell Lee* [1983] 1 All ER 1062 applied.

Notes
For unlawful discrimination on grounds of ethnic or national origins, see 4 Halsbury's
Laws (4th edn) para 1035, and for cases on the subject, see 2 Digest (Reissue) 316–317,
d 1783–1786.
    For the Race Relations Act 1976, ss 1, 3, 29, see 6 Halsbury's Statutes (4th edn) 767,
769, 788.

Cases referred to in judgments
Clarke v Eley (IMI) Kynoch Ltd [1983] ICR 165, EAT.
King-Ansell v Police [1979] 2 NZLR 531, NZ CA.
e *Mandla v Dowell Lee* [1983] 1 All ER 1062, [1983] 2 AC 548, [1983] 2 WLR 620, HL.
Mills v Cooper [1967] 2 All ER 100, [1967] 2 QB 459, [1967] 2 WLR 1343, DC.

Cases also cited
Brutus v Cozens [1972] 2 All ER 1297, [1973] AC 854, HL.
f *Commission for Racial Equality v Associated Newspapers Group Ltd* [1978] 1 WLR 905, CA.
Ealing London Borough v Race Relations Board [1972] 1 All ER 105, [1972] AC 342, HL.
Greenwich London BC v Powell (1988) 20 HLR 411, CA; *rvsd* [1989] 1 All ER 65, HL.
Patel v Mehtab (1980) 5 HLR 80, DC.
West Glamorgan CC v Rafferty [1987] 1 All ER 1005, [1987] 1 WLR 457, CA.

g **Appeal**
The Commission for Racial Equality appealed from the decision of his Honour Judge
Harris QC, sitting with assessors at the Westminster County Court at the trial of the
action on 29 June 1987, whereby he dismissed the commission's claim for a declaration
that the defendant, Patrick Dutton, the licensee of the Cat and Mutton public house,
London Fields, Hackney, by displaying a sign stating 'Sorry, no travellers' outside his
h public house had contravened s 29 of the Race Relations Act 1976 and an injunction
restraining the defendant from displaying the sign or any sign bearing the same words
or words to similar effect. The facts are set out in the judgment of Nicholls LJ.

Stephen Sedley QC and *Keith Hornby* for the commission.
John E A Samuels QC and *Roger McCarthy* for Mr Dutton.
j
                                                                    Cur adv vult

c   Section 3(1), so far as material, provides: '... "racial group" means a group of persons defined by
     reference to colour, race, nationality or ethnic or national origins, and references to a person's racial
     group refer to any racial group into which he falls.'

27 July. The following judgments were delivered.

NICHOLLS LJ (giving the first judgment at the invitation of Stocker LJ). This case concerns gipsies, and whether they are a racial group within the Race Relations Act 1976. Mr Patrick Dutton has been the licensee of the Cat and Mutton public house, at Broadway Market, London Fields, London E8 for four years. Previously he was the licensee for a year at the Earl of Beaconsfield in Southwark, and before that he was at the Lord Cecil in Clapton from 1978. At both those houses Mr Dutton had unpleasant experiences with people who came from caravans which were parked illegally on nearby sites. They caused damage. They threatened Mr Dutton and terrorised his wife. They behaved generally in such a way as to upset Mr Dutton's regular customers. So much so that, after such incidents, he put up a sign in the windows of the Earl of Beaconsfield and, subsequently, the Lord Cecil, which read 'No travellers'. By that he meant, as he said in evidence, a person who travels around in a caravan and parks on illegal sites and gives him 'hassle'. He wanted only to stop such people coming into his public house. Had the incidents continued he would have lost all his customers. After he put up the signs he had no more problems with such people.

One weekend, after Mr Dutton had been at the Cat and Mutton for about 18 months, some 15 or so caravans parked opposite the public house on London Fields, illegally, about 150 yards away. On Sunday morning some of these 'travellers' came into the Cat and Mutton. Mr Dutton refused to serve one of them on the ground he was from the site. There was an incident. Mr Dutton then put up handwritten signs in the windows of the Cat and Mutton: 'Sorry, no travellers.' Since then Mr Dutton has had no more trouble with travellers.

In June 1985 a local resident, who does not use the Cat and Mutton, brought these signs to the attention of the Commission for Racial Equality. The commission took the view that the signs discriminated against gipsies. After correspondence this action was brought by the commission, in the exercise of its functions under s 63 of the 1976 Act. The commission seeks a declaration that by displaying the signs Mr Dutton has contravened s 29 of the 1976 Act and an injunction restraining him from continuing to display the signs. The action was heard by his Honour Judge Harris QC at the Westminster County Court. He sat with two assessors appointed from the list maintained by the Secretary of State under s 67(4) of persons who appear to him to have special knowledge and experience of problems connected with relations between persons of different racial groups. On 29 June 1987 the judge dismissed the action. The commission has appealed from that decision.

The statute

Section 29(1) of the 1976 Act provides:

> 'It is unlawful to publish or to cause to be published an advertisement which indicates, or might reasonably be understood as indicating, an intention by a person to do an act of discrimination, whether the doing of that act by him would be lawful or, by virtue of Part II or III, unlawful.'

Discrimination for the purposes relevant in the present case is defined in s 1(1). Two types of conduct are within the definition. Paragraph (a) defines what is generally known as 'direct' discrimination, although not so called in the Act, as follows:

> '(1) A person discriminates against another in any circumstances relevant for the purposes of any provision of this Act if—(a) on racial grounds he treats that other less favourably than he treats or would treat other persons . . .'

Section 3(1) defines 'racial grounds' as meaning 'any of the following grounds, namely colour, race, nationality or ethnic or national origins'.

Mr Dutton's notices are advertisements within the definition in s 78(1). Further, they *a* indicate an intention by him to treat travellers less favourably than he treats other persons, in circumstances relevant for the purposes of the 1976 Act. By the notices he is informing would-be customers that he will not serve any who are travellers. They cannot use the Cat and Mutton. That is discrimination in the provision of goods, facilities or services (see s 20). Thus arises the question on this part of the case: is that discrimination 'on racial grounds'? On this, the first issue to be considered is the meaning of the expression 'travellers' in the context in which the signs are being displayed.

b The commission's case was that in these notices 'travellers' is synonymous with gipsies. Before the judge there was material supporting the contention that, in recent years, the two expressions are sometimes used interchangeably. For example *Chambers 20th Century Dictionary* (1983) includes under the word 'travel' the sub-heading 'traveller': 'travelling folk, people the name by which itinerant people often call themselves, in preference to the derogatory names gipsies or tinkers.' Again, the *Supplement to the Oxford English*

c *Dictionary* (1986) added a further meaning to the word 'traveller': 'Also, a gypsy.' There was also evidence to the same effect from two expert witnesses, Dr Donald Kenrick and Dr Thomas Acton.

The meaning of 'gipsy'

Notwithstanding this material the judge rejected the view that the words are

d synonymous. I agree with him. But before proceeding further it is necessary for me to comment on the word 'gipsy'. One of the difficulties in the present case, in my view, is that the word 'gipsy' has itself more than one meaning. The classic dictionary meaning can be found as the primary meaning given in the *Oxford English Dictionary* (1933):

e 'A member of a wandering race (by themselves called *Romany*), of Hindu origin, which first appeared in England about the beginning of the 16th c. and was then believed to have come from Egypt.'

Hence the word 'gipsy', also spelt as 'gypsy'. It is a corruption of the word 'Egyptian'. We find this usage in Shakespeare, where Othello says to Desdemona (*Othello* III. iv. 56–59):

'That handkerchief
f   Did an Egyptian to my mother give;
She was a charmer, and could almost read
The thoughts of people . . .'

Alongside this meaning, the word 'gipsy' also has a more colloquial, looser meaning. This is expressed in the *Longman Dictionary of Contemporary English* (1984), where two meanings are attributed to 'gipsy'. The first meaning is along the lines I have already

g quoted. The second is: 'a person who habitually wanders or who has the habits of someone who does not stay for long in one place'; in short, a nomad.

I can anticipate here by noting that if the word 'gipsy' is used in this second, colloquial sense it is not definitive of a racial group within the 1976 Act. To discriminate against such a group would not be on racial grounds, namely on the ground of ethnic origins.

h As the judge observed, there are many people who travel around the country in caravans, vans, converted buses, trailers, lorries and motor vehicles, leading a peripatetic or nomadic way of life. They include didicois, mumpers, peace people, new age travellers, hippies, tinkers, hawkers, self-styled 'anarchists', and others, as well as Romany gipsies. They may all be loosely referred to as 'gipsies', but as a group they do not have the characteristics requisite of a racial group within the Act.

j I give two further illustrations of this point. First, an extract from a report of the Greater London Conciliation Committee, set out in the Report of the Race Relations Board for 1967–68 (HC Paper (1967–68) no 262) App III, which refers neatly to a difficulty arising in this field from the two meanings I have mentioned:

'There are the pubs which discriminate against Gipsies. In tackling this problem the Committee has been hampered by two ambiguities. There is, first, some doubt as to the status of Gipsies under the Act. The Committee feels that there is little or no justification for this doubt, but equally believes that it persists and that it does so largely because of the second ambiguity. This second ambiguity arises out of common parlance, for it seems that the word "Gipsy" is used to designate wanderers generally as opposed to ethnic Gipsies. The Committee is, therefore, trying to prevent discrimination against Gipsies in the one (proper) sense while being aware that it may not interfere with discrimination against Gipsies in the other (vulgar) sense, and it is in a weak position in any argument with a publican about which way he uses the word.'

Second, the decision of the Queen's Bench Divisional Court in Mills v Cooper [1967] 2 All ER 100, [1967] 2 QB 459. The court was there concerned with the meaning of the word 'gipsy' in s 127 of the Highways Act 1959. So far as material the section provides:

'If, without lawful authority or excuse . . . (c) a hawker or other itinerant trader or a gipsy pitches a booth, stall or stand, or encamps, on a highway, he shall be guilty of an offence . . .'

In Mills v Cooper [1967] 2 All ER 100 at 103, [1967] 2 QB 459 at 466 it was argued that the word 'gipsy' should be 'given its dictionary meaning, as being a member of the Romany race . . .' Lord Parker CJ said ([1967] 2 All ER 100 at 103, [1967] 2 QB 459 at 467):

'That a man is of the Romany race is, as it seems to me, something which is really too vague of ascertainment, and impossible to prove; moreover, it is, I think, difficult to think that Parliament intended to subject a man to a penalty in the context of causing litter and obstruction on the highway merely by reason of his race. I think that, in this context, "gipsy" means no more than a person leading a nomadic life with no, or no fixed, employment and with no fixed abode. In saying that, I am hoping that those words will not be considered as the words of a statute, but merely as conveying the general colloquial idea of a gipsy.'

Likewise Diplock LJ said ([1967] 2 All ER 100 at 104, [1967] 2 QB 459 at 467–468):

'I agree that the word "gipsy" as used in s. 127(c) of the Highways Act, 1959, cannot bear its dictionary meaning of a member of a wandering race (by themselves called Romany) of Hindu origin. If it did, it would mean that Parliament in 1959 had amended the corresponding section of the Highway Act, 1935, which referred to "gipsy or other person" so as to discriminate against persons by reason of their racial origin alone.'

In the context provided by this difficulty, and the impossibility of ever being able to prove pure Romany origin, Diplock LJ preferred what he described as the popular meaning of the word 'gipsy' ([1967] 2 All ER 100 at 104, [1967] 2 QB 459 at 468):

'. . . a person without fixed abode who leads a nomadic life, dwelling in tents or other shelters, or in caravans or other vehicles.'

The substance of that definition was then adopted by Parliament in the Caravan Sites Act 1968. Section 6 of that Act imposed on local authorities a duty to exercise their powers, under the Caravan Sites and Control of Development Act 1960, to provide caravan sites 'so far as may be necessary to provide adequate accommodation for gipsies residing in or resorting to their area'. Section 16 provides:

'. . ."gipsies" means persons of nomadic habit of life, whatever their race or origin, but does not include members of an organised group of travelling showmen, or of persons engaged in travelling circuses, travelling together as such . . .'

I shall return at a later stage to the relevance of those statutory provisions. For the moment it is sufficient to note that there is ambiguity in the word 'gipsy', and when a considering reports and other material about gipsies it is essential therefore to identify what is the meaning with which the author is using the word 'gipsy'. In this judgment, save where I indicate otherwise, I shall henceforth use the word 'gipsy' in the narrower sense of the first of the two meanings mentioned above.

'No travellers'

b I can now state my reasons for agreeing with the judge's conclusion on the 'direct' discrimination issue. Like most English words, the meaning of the word 'traveller' depends on the context in which it is being used. It has one meaning when seen on a railway station. For some time now the refreshment service provided at railway stations and on trains has been styled 'Travellers Fare'. The word has a different meaning when in its context it is directed at travelling salesmen. In my view, in the windows of the Cat and Mutton 'No travellers' will be understood by those to whom it is directed, namely c potential customers, as meaning persons who are currently leading a nomadic way of life, living in tents or caravans or other vehicles. Thus the notices embrace gipsies who are living in that way. But the class of persons excluded from the Cat and Mutton is not confined to gipsies. The prohibited class includes all those of a nomadic way of life mentioned above. As the judge said, they all come under the umbrella expression 'travellers', as this accurately describes their way of life.

d It is estimated that nowadays between one-half and two-thirds of gipsies in this country have wholly or largely abandoned a nomadic way of life in favour of living in houses. I do not think that the notices could reasonably be understood as applying to them, that is, to gipsies who are currently living in houses. Gipsies may prefer to be described as 'travellers' as they believe this is a less derogatory expression. But, in the context of a notice displayed in the windows of a public house near a common on which nomads e encamp from time to time, I do not think 'no travellers' can reasonably be understood as other than 'no nomads'. It would not embrace house-dwellers, of any race or origin.

For this reason I cannot accept that Mr Dutton's notices indicate, or might reasonably be understood as indicating, an intention by him to do an act of discrimination within s 1(1)(a). Excluded from the Cat and Mutton are all 'travellers', whether or not they are gipsies. All 'travellers', all nomads, are treated equally, whatever their race. They are not f being discriminated against on racial grounds.

Indirect discrimination: a racial group

That suffices to dispose of the claim based on s 1(1)(a) of the 1976 Act, but that is not the end of the action. I must now turn to consider s 1(1)(b), which is in the following g terms:

'(1) A person discriminates against another in any circumstances relevant for the purposes of any provision of this Act if . . . (b) he applies to that other a requirement or condition which he applies or would apply equally to persons not of the same racial group as that other but—(i) which is such that the proportion of persons of the same racial group as that other who can comply with it is considerably smaller h than the proportion of persons not of that racial group who can comply with it; and (ii) which he cannot show to be justifiable irrespective of the colour, race, nationality or ethnic or national origins of the person to whom it is applied; and (iii) which is to the detriment of that other because he cannot comply with it.'

On this the first question which arises is whether gipsies are a racial group. If they are j not, para (b) cannot apply to Mr Dutton's notices. Mr Dutton cannot apply to a gipsy who wishes to have a drink at the Cat and Mutton a condition (in this case, of not being a traveller) which he applies equally to persons 'not of the same racial group' unless gipsies are a racial group within the Act. Indeed, if gipsies are not a racial group, a notice saying 'No gipsies' would be lawful.

The definition of 'racial group' in s 3(1) includes a group of persons defined by

reference to 'ethnic . . . origins'. This definition was considered by the House of Lords in
Mandla v Dowell Lee [1983] 1 All ER 1062, [1983] 2 AC 548. There the context was   *a*
whether Sikhs constituted a group defined by reference to ethnic origins. Lord Fraser
observed that the word 'ethnic' in the Act should be construed relatively widely, in a
broad cultural/historic sense. He approved the following passage from the judgment of
Richardson J sitting in the New Zealand Court of Appeal in *King-Ansell v Police* [1979] 2
NZLR 531 at 543:

> '. . . a group is identifiable in terms of its ethnic origins if it is a segment of the   *b*
> population distinguished from others by a sufficient combination of shared customs,
> beliefs, traditions and characteristics derived from a common or presumed common
> past, even if not drawn from what in biological terms is a common racial stock. It is
> that combination which gives them an historically determined social identity in
> their own eyes and in the eyes of those outside the group. They have a distinct social   *c*
> identity based not simply on group cohesion and solidarity but also on their belief
> as to their historical antecedents.'

Lord Fraser summarised his opinion on the construction of the Act in his own words
([1983] 1 All ER 1062 at 1066–1067, [1983] 2 AC 548 at 562–563):

> 'For a group to constitute an ethnic group in the sense of the 1976 Act, it must, in   *d*
> my opinion, regard itself, and be regarded by others, as a distinct community by
> virtue of certain characteristics. Some of these characteristics are essential; others are
> not essential but one or more of them will commonly be found and will help to
> distinguish the group from the surrounding community. The conditions which
> appear to me to be essential are these: (1) a long shared history, of which the group
> is conscious as distinguishing it from other groups, and the memory of which it   *e*
> keeps alive; (2) a cultural tradition of its own, including family and social customs
> and manners, often but not necessarily associated with religious observance. In
> addition to those two essential characteristics the following characteristics are, in my
> opinion, relevant: (3) either a common geographical origin, or descent from a small
> number of common ancestors; (4) a common language, not necessarily peculiar to
> the group; (5) a common literature peculiar to the group; (6) a common religion   *f*
> different from that of neighbouring groups or from the general community
> surrounding it; (7) being a minority or being an oppressed or a dominant group
> within a larger community, for example a conquered people (say, the inhabitants of
> England shortly after the Norman conquest) and their conquerors might both be
> ethnic groups. A group defined by reference to enough of these characteristics
> would be capable of including converts, for example, persons who marry into the   *g*
> group, and of excluding apostates. Provided a person who joins the group feels
> himself or herself to be a member of it, and is accepted by other members, then he
> is, for the purpose of the 1976 Act, a member. That appears to be consistent with
> the words at the end of sub-s (1) of s 3: 'references to a person's racial group refer to
> any racial group into which he falls.' In my opinion, it is possible for a person to fall
> into a particular racial group either by birth or by adherence, and it makes no   *h*
> difference, so far as the 1976 Act is concerned, by which route he finds his way into
> the group.'

In the present case the judge expressed his conclusion on the conditions enunciated by
Lord Fraser in this way:

> 'It may well be, as I have said, that there is a small number of travelling people   *j*
> who can claim either by looks or characteristics to be true gipsies but these people
> have been absorbed into a larger group. Some have abandoned the nomadic way of
> life and some are indistinguishable from any ordinary member of the public. The
> larger group of travellers or gipsies forming a part of a larger group cannot in my
> judgment, on the evidence before the court, satisfy those two essential conditions

a   and can satisfy barely any of the other five conditions. Although there may be a Romany language, some may be able to trace their ancestry back to people who came to England many hundreds of years ago, the language does not seem to be in general use. There is no common religion, they have no literature. Although it was urged on the court that there should be some relevance in the fact that they have what was described as oral literature passing on myths and other old stories I do not think that was what Lord Fraser was referring to.'

b   He decided that gipsies were not a group defined by reference to ethnic origins.
     I come here to a further difficulty about the present case. The evidence on this part of the case consisted principally of evidence called by the commission: the two experts I have mentioned, and a Mr Peter Mercer, who is a gipsy. No expert evidence was led by Mr Dutton. But although there was no contrary evidence called by Mr Dutton, the judge was not impressed by either of the commission's expert witnesses. He approached their
c   evidence with much caution and doubt. Counsel for the commission criticised the judge's comments in this regard, but on this the judge's advantage, of having seen and heard the witnesses is obviously of paramount importance. We are not in a position to conclude that the judge erred in his assessment of the reliability of these witnesses.
     Nevertheless, taking the judge's assessment of the witnesses fully into account, and
d   with all respect to the judge, I am unable to agree with his conclusion on what have been called the Mandla conditions when applied, not to the larger amorphous group of 'travellers' or 'gipsies' (colloquially so-called), but to 'gipsies' in the primary, narrower sense of that word. On the evidence it is clear that such gipsies are a minority, with a long shared history and a common geographical origin. They are a people who originated in northern India. They migrated thence to Europe through Persia in medieval times.
e   They have certain, albeit limited, customs of their own regarding cooking and the manner of washing. They have a distinctive traditional style of dressing, with heavy jewellery worn by the women, although this dress is not worn all the time. They also furnish their caravans in a distinctive manner. They have a language or dialect, known as 'pogadi chib', spoken by English gipsies (Romany chals) and Welsh gipsies (Kale) which consists of up to one-fifth of Romany words in place of English words. They do not have
f   a common religion, nor a peculiar, common literature of their own, but they have a repertoire of folk-tales and music passed on from one generation to the next. No doubt, after all the centuries which have passed since the first gipsies left the Punjab, gipsies are no longer derived from what, in biological terms, is a common racial stock, but that of itself does not prevent them from being a racial group as widely defined in the 1976 Act.
     I come now to the part of the case which has caused me most difficulty. Gipsies prefer
g   to be called 'travellers' as they think that term is less derogatory. This might suggest a wish to lose their separate distinctive identity so far as the general public is concerned. Half or more of them now live in houses, like most other people. Have gipsies now lost their separate, group identity so that they are no longer a community recognisable by ethnic groups within the meaning of the Act? The judge held that they had. This is a finding of fact.
h   Nevertheless, with respect to the judge, I do not think that there was before him any evidence justifying his conclusion that gipsies have been absorbed into a larger group, if by that he meant that substantially all gipsies have been so absorbed. The fact that some have been so absorbed and are indistinguishable from any ordinary member of the public, is not sufficient in itself to establish loss of what Richardson J in the King-Ansell
j   case [1979] 2 NZLR 531 at 543 referred to as 'an historically determined social identity in [the group's] own eyes and in the eyes of those outside the group'. There was some evidence to the contrary from Mr Mercer, on whose testimony the judge expressed no adverse comment. He gave evidence that 'we know who are members of our community' and that 'we know we are different'. In my view the evidence was sufficient to establish that, despite their long presence in England, gipsies have not merged wholly in the population, as have the Saxons and the Danes, and altogether lost their separate identity.

They, or many of them, have retained a separateness, a self-awareness, of still being gipsies.

I feel less constrained than otherwise I would to depart from the judge's conclusions on this point because of the importance attached by him to the meaning borne by the word 'gipsy' in the Highways Act 1959 and the Caravan Sites Act 1968. He said:

> 'Although the Highways Act 1959 and the Caravan Sites Act 1968 are statutory examples of the use of the word "gipsy" the meaning given to the word in those Acts does have great weight in my mind. If you find a word defined in a definition section of one Act of Parliament and defined by the Divisional Court on another use of the same word in another statute it would be difficult to say: well when you are looking at the Race Relations Act 1976 you must have a wholly and totally different meaning attached to it. I consider, agreeing as I do with the Divisional Court in *Mills v Cooper* [1967] 2 All ER 100, [1967] 2 QB 459, that it would be impossible to discover if any person or any body of persons were members of the Romany race or true gipsies. It is not difficult to discover whether they are leading a nomadic life, whether they are travelling from place to place with no fixed abode and no fixed employment. But having ascertained these matters one might justifiably come to the conclusion that they being travellers were not clearly gipsies. As I say I do not think one can be a gipsy or a non-gipsy in one statute and not in another.'

In my view those two statutes do not materially assist in the present case, and the judge misdirected himself on this point. The present case is quite different from *Mills v Cooper*. In the present case the issue is not which of two or more meanings of the word 'gipsy' is to be preferred in the context of a particular statute or document. The question is whether there is an identifiable group of persons, traditionally called 'gipsies', who are defined by reference to ethnic origins. That is essentially a question of fact, to be determined on the evidence, applying the approach set out in *Mandla's* case [1983] 1 All ER 1062, [1983] 2 AC 548. On that question the definition of 'gipsy' used in the Caravan Sites Act 1968, and the meaning of the word 'gipsy' in the Highways Act 1959 as interpreted in *Mills v Cooper*, are of little assistance, if any. Furthermore, the difficulty, mentioned in *Mills v Cooper* [1967] 2 All ER 100 at 103–104, [1967] 2 QB 459 at 467–468, of determining today whether a person is of 'the Romany race' or is of 'pure Romany descent' or 'Romany origin', seems to have led the judge into thinking that that difficulty constituted an obstacle to the commission's success in the present case. But that is not so. The material provision in the 1976 Act is concerned with ethnic origins, and 'ethnic' is not used in that Act in a strictly biological or racial sense. That was decided in *Mandla's* case.

In my view, accepting the judge's doubts about the evidence of Dr Kenrick and Dr Acton, the evidence was still sufficient to establish that gipsies are an identifiable group of persons defined by reference to ethnic origins within the meaning of the 1976 Act.

Indirect discrimination: adverse impact

Having concluded that gipsies are a racial group, each of sub-paras (i) to (iii) in s 1(1)(b) of the 1976 Act must be satisfied before the conduct complained of amounts to discrimination within the meaning of the Act. I shall consider the three sub-paragraphs one by one, starting with sub-para (i).

Clearly the proportion of gipsies who will satisfy the 'no travellers' condition is considerably smaller than the proportion of non-gipsies. Of the estimated gipsy population in the United Kingdom of some 80,000, between one-half and two-thirds, now live in houses. But this still means that a far higher proportion of gipsies are leading a nomadic way of life than the rest of the population in general or, more narrowly, than the rest of the population who might wish to resort to the Cat and Mutton.

Counsel for Mr Dutton submitted that the word 'can' in the expression 'can comply' in sub-para (i) means 'can comply without giving up the distinctive customs and cultural

rules of gipsies'. He submitted that gipsies can cease to be nomadic, and become house-
a dwellers, and comply with the 'no travellers' condition, without giving up their customs
and cultures and that, therefore, sub-para (i) is not satisfied in this case. I do not accept
this. Lord Fraser's words in *Mandla*'s case [1983] 1 All ER 1062 at 1069, [1983] 2 AC 548
at 565 which counsel embraced in this submission, were used in the context of a 'no
turban' condition being applied in relation to a Sikh. Lord Fraser was rejecting the
submission that 'can' meant 'can physically'. But that does not assist the solution of the
b present case. Indeed, gipsies can and do cease to be nomadic, but that will be of little use
to a particlar nomadic gipsy when he chances on the Cat and Mutton and wishes to go in
for a drink. At that stage he is, in practice, unable to comply. In the present case the
problem is a different one: at what moment of time does ability to comply fall to be
judged? Is it when the condition is invoked (in this case, when the gipsy is outside the
public house wishing to enter) or is it at some earlier date (which would give the gipsy
c sufficient opportunity to acquire housing accommodation for himself before turning up
at the Cat and Mutton)?

A similar question was considered by the Employment Appeal Tribunal in *Clarke v
Eley (IMI) Kynoch Ltd* [1983] ICR 165 with regard to s 1(1) of the Sex Discrimination Act
1975, the wording of which does not differ materially from s 1(1)(b) of the 1976 Act.
Browne-Wilkinson J delivered the judgment of the tribunal to the effect that the relevant
d point of time at which the ability or inability to comply has to be shown is the date at
which the requirement or condition has to be fulfilled. I find his reasoning compelling,
and I agree with his conclusion (see [1983] ICR 165 at 171–172).

In my view, therefore, sub-para (i) is satisfied in the present case.

Indirect discrimination: detriment
e Sub-paragraph (iii) requires the applied condition to be to the relevant person's
detriment because he cannot comply with it. Rightly, it was not disputed that sub-para
(iii) is satisfied in the present case, by the hypothetical nomad gipsy being excluded from
the Cat and Mutton (I say hypothetical, because there was no evidence that there were
any gipsies among the travellers on the nearby sites).

f *Indirect discrimination: justification*
I have left sub-para (ii) to the end for this reason. On the admitted or proved facts it is
possible for this court to decide whether sub-paras (i) and (iii) are satisfied, even though
the judge himself did not decide these points. Sub-paragraph (ii) is different. On the facts
before us it would not be satisfactory for this court to attempt to decide this point, which
the judge expressly left open.
g In these circumstances for my part I would remit the action to the county court for
the judge to determine whether s 1(1)(b)(ii) is satisfied in the present case and, if it is, for
him to make such order as he considers appropriate. I would allow this appeal accordingly.

TAYLOR LJ. I agree. The commisson's case under s 1(1)(a) of the Race Relations Act
h 1976 must fail for the reasons given by Nicholls LJ. The word 'traveller' is not
synonymous with the word 'gypsy'.

The case under s 1(1)(b) turns essentially on whether gipsies are a racial group within
the meaning of the 1976 Act. It is only on that issue that I wish to add some observations.

The judge considered four different approaches to the issue. First he said he would
consider the evidence of the two expert witnesses called on behalf of the commission and
j its gipsy witness, Mr Mercer. In fact, he made no reference to Mr Mercer in dealing with
this first approach. Clearly, the two experts made an unfavourable impression on the
judge who described their views as wholly obsessive, biased and totally preconceived. In
particular, he found Dr Acton to be a very bad witness in that he could not be contained
within the ordinary question and answer routine. The judge summarised his conclusions
on this approach (ie via the commission's witnesses) by saying merely that he approached

the experts 'with much caution and doubt' and did not consider 'that their evidence overrides or displaces the views' he later set out. But, however difficult or partisan the *a* experts may have been, it was surely an excessive reaction to reject their evidence altogether. The historical account they gave of gipsies, their origins and customs was not contradicted by any other evidence. Furthermore, Mr Mercer gave firsthand evidence confirming much of what they said and the judge made no finding adverse to his qualities as a witness.

The second approach was headed by the judge 'Statutes and statements in government *b* reports on the legal interpretation of the word "Gipsy"'.

It is clear that the word gipsy bears at least two broad meanings. Historically it referred to:

> 'A member of a wandering race (by themselves called Romany), of Hindu origin, which first appeared in England about the beginning of the 16th c. and was then *c* believed to have come from Egypt.'

(See *Oxford English Dictionary* (1933).)

More recently it has come to mean 'a nomad'. The latter meaning has been adopted in certain statutes. Thus, as the trial judge noted, the word 'gipsy' in s 127 of the Highway Act 1959 was held to have the colloquial meaning of 'a person leading a nomadic life with no, or no fixed, employment and with no fixed abode' (see *Mills v Cooper* [1967] 2 *d* All ER 100 at 103, [1967] 2 QB 459 at 467). Again, s 16 of the Caravan Sites Act 1968 defines gipsies as meaning:

> 'persons of nomadic life, whatever their race or origin, but does not include members of an organised group of travelling showmen, or of persons engaged in travelling circuses, travelling together as such.' *e*

Those statutes, however, have nothing whatsoever to do with race relations or discrimination. They are concerned with highways and the provision and regulation of caravan sites. The statutory adoption of the second broad meaning of gipsy in those contexts cannot be taken to consign a racial group called gipsies to oblivion if it still exists in fact. I therefore agree that the trial judge misdirected himself in relying on the *f* statutory meaning of 'gipsy' in contexts quite different from that of the present case. In his judgment he said:

> 'Although the Highways Act 1959 and the Caravan Sites Act 1968 are statutory examples of the use of the word "gipsy" the meaning given to the word in those Acts does have great weight in my mind. If you find a word defined in a definition section of one Act of Parliament and defined by the Divisional Court on another use *g* of the same word in another statute it would be difficult to say: well when you are looking at the Race Relations Act 1976 you must have a wholly and totally different meaning attached to it . . . As I say I do not think one can be a gipsy or a non-gipsy in one statute and not in another.'

That approach assumes 'gipsy' must have the same meaning in all contexts and fails to *h* identify the two different meanings mentioned above. In fact, the word 'gipsy' does not occur in s 1 of the 1976 Act. The phrase which has to be construed is a 'racial group' as defined in s 3(1) and as interpreted in *Mandla v Dowell Lee* [1983] 1 All ER 1062, [1983] 2 AC 548.

Confusion of the two meanings of gipsy continued when the judge came to refer to certain reports which had been put before him. He quoted from a report of the Greater *j* London Conciliation Committee (the passage referred to in Nicholls LJ's judgment). He went on to cite *Accommodation for Gypsies*, A report on the Working of the Caravan Sites Act 1968 by Sir John Cripps for the Department of the Environment and the Welsh Office. However, they were not dealing with the same subject matter. The first report was concerned with the type of problem presented by the present case. The second was

clearly made in the context of provision of caravan sites and defined the word 'gipsy' in
a that context as, in effect, a person of 'nomadic habit of life' (see para 1.5).

The third approach was to examine dictionary definitions. Here, the judge expressed
the view that one could pick and choose the meaning one wished to find. He cited six
definitions ranging from 'A member of a dark-haired race which may be of Indian origin
...' through the broader meaning of 'A person who habitually wanders...' to the merely
abusive 'Cunning rogue'. Having set out those definitions the judge said:

b
> 'Accordingly in my judgment the [commission] cannot really derive any assistance
> from dictionary definitions. People obtaining the meaning from the dictionary
> could not think that a gipsy was a member of a racial group or had basic ethnic
> origins.'

Here, I do not follow the judge's reasoning. The fact that dictionaries give more than one
c meaning for the word 'gipsy' does not prevent the work from having, at any rate in some
contexts, the meaning given in four out of six of the definitions.

Finally the judge considered the approach laid down in *Mandla v Dowell Lee* [1983] 1
All ER 1062 at 1066, [1983] 2 AC 548 at 561–562. It is important first to emphasise that
ethnic origin is not now limited to or to be equated with strict racial or biological origins.
d Lord Fraser said:

> 'My Lords, I recognise that "ethnic" conveys a flavour of race but it cannot, in my
> opinion, have been used in the 1976 Act in a strict racial or biological sense. For one
> thing it would be absurd to suppose that Parliament can have intended that
> membership of a particular racial group should depend on scientific proof that a
> person possessed the relevant distinctive biological characteristics (assuming that
e > such characteristics exist). The practical difficulties of such proof would be
> prohibitive, and it is clear that Parliament must have used the word in some more
> popular sense ... In my opinion, the word "ethnic" still retains a racial flavour but
> it is used nowadays in an extended sense to include other characteristics which may
> be commonly thought of as being associated with common racial origin.'

f Lord Fraser then set out what he described as the two essential conditions followed by
five other relevant characteristics (see [1983] 1 All ER 1062 at 1067, [1983] 2 AC 548 at
562). The passage has already been cited in full by Nicholls LJ. The judge's application of
the *Mandla* tests is as follows:

> 'It may well be, as I have said, that there is a small number of travelling people
> who can claim either by looks or characteristics to be true gipsies but these people
g > have been absorbed into a large group. Some have abandoned the nomadic way of
> life and some are indistinguishable from any ordinary member of the public. The
> larger group of travellers or gipsies forming a part of a larger group cannot in my
> judgment on the evidence before the court satisfy those two essential conditions and
> can satisfy barely any of the other five conditions.'

h With respect to him, the fact that some gipsies, even a substantial proportion, have
abandoned the nomadic way of life or have become assimilated in the general public is
not decisive of the issue. There are no doubt other religious, racial or ethnic groups
whose numbers diminish due to inter-marriage, lack of adherence to the group or lapsed
observance. But if there remains a discernible minority which does adhere it may still be
a racial group within Lord Fraser's criteria.

j On the evidence, and perhaps that of Mr Mercer in particular, there is still a discernible
group of gipsies with 'a long shared history, of which the group is conscious as
distinguishing it from other groups, and the memory of which it keeps alive' (see [1983]
1 All ER 1062 at 1067, [1983] 2 AC 548 at 562 per Lord Fraser). There may well be
individuals on the borderline between membership and assimilation whom it might be
difficult to classify, but that does not deny the existence of the group. Likewise, the fact

that some of those within the group prefer to call themselves travellers rather than gipsies is not indicative of whether a discrete racial group has ceased to exist.

As to Lord Fraser's second essential characteristic, I agree that the evidence summarised *a* by Nicholls LJ does show gipsies have a cultural tradition of their own including family and social customs and manners.

Accordingly, I conclude that the four approaches rightly identified by the judge, ought to have led him to a different conclusion from the one he reached.

I too would remit the action to the county court for the judge to determine whether *b* s 1(1)(*b*)(ii) is satisfied and to make the appropriate order. I would allow this appeal.

STOCKER LJ. I have had the benefit of reading in draft the judgments of Nicholls and Taylor LJJ. I agree with their conclusions that the matter should be remitted for determination under s 1(1)(*b*)(ii) of the Race Relations Act 1976, though for my part I have entertained considerable doubt on one aspect of this matter in the light of some of *c* the findings of fact made by the judge.

I agree that in order to succeed under s 1(1)(*a*), direct discrimination, the commission had to prove that the words 'traveller' and 'gipsy' were synonymous. For the reasons given by Nicholls LJ, they plainly are not and the claim under this subsection must fail.

So far as indirect discrimination is concerned the judge dealt with the question whether or not gipsies were of 'ethnic origin' and thus a racial group in general terms in his *d* consideration of direct discrimination and applied his findings that they were not to indirect discrimination and dismissed the claim under s 1(1)(*b*) in a single paragraph. There is no reason why he should not have adopted this approach but it seems to me that it may have concealed the problem that 'gipsy' is used in two different senses. On the one hand it is used to embrace the category which may be described as 'true gipsies', ie one who is, or believes he is, of Romany descent, or by long established adherence is a *e* member of that class. On the other, it embraces all those of nomadic habit and disposition.

I agree that the judge's reasoning whereby he concluded that gipsies, in the strict sense, are not an ethnic group was in many respects flawed. I say nothing of his rejection of the evidence of the expert witnesses (he saw and heard them and was entitled to regard their evidence with doubt and caution) though their evidence on the historical migration, settlement and customs of gipsies was not the subject of any evidence to the contrary. I *f* also agree with Nicholls and Taylor LJJ that dictionary definitions can support a conclusion either way on the essential question of the ethnic origins of gipsies where the word is capable of the two distinct meanings referred to, but this fact does not itself resolve the problem raised on this appeal. I further agree that contrary to the judge's finding no assistance is to be derived from the meaning of the word 'gipsy' for the purpose of s 127 of the Highways Act 1959 or the Caravan Sites Act 1968, since both statutes would be *g* unworkable in practice if 'gipsy' for the purposes of those Acts were to be defined in the strict sense. The definition accorded to the word for the purpose of the 1959 Act in *Mills v Cooper* [1967] 2 All ER 100, [1967] 2 QB 459 and the definition in the Caravan Sites Act 1968 do not assist at all when the issue under the 1976 Act is whether or not the word 'gipsy' for the purpose of that Act imports the conception of 'ethnic origin'. I refer *h* hereunder to the dicta of Lord Parker CJ in that case in a different context. Before considering the fourth basis of the judge's reasoning, his application of the decision of the House of Lords in *Mandla v Dowell Lee* [1983] 1 All ER 1062, [1983] 2 AC 548, I think it convenient to refer to four passages in his judgment which are findings of fact made by the judge. He said:

'There is, in my judgment, no easily identifiable group of gipsies as there were *j* Sikhs. The evidence is that persons who had hitherto regarded themselves as true gipsies or Romanies no longer wish to be known as gipsies because they think that is perjorative and they wish to adhere to a larger amorphous group known apparently as travellers ... Gipsies may as I have said be a part of a group of travelling people, they may well be accurately called 'travellers' but they themselves do not in my

judgment form any clearly identifiable group . . . It may well be, as I have said, that
a   there is a small number of travelling people who can claim either by looks or
characteristics to be true gipsies but these people have been absorbed into a larger
group. Some have abandoned the nomadic way of life and some are indistinguishable
from any ordinary member of the public. The larger group of travellers or gipsies
forming a part of a larger group cannot in my judgment on the evidence before the
court satisfy those two essential conditions and can satisfy barely any of the other
b   five conditions . . . I am wholly satisfied that the group, whether you call them
gipsies or travellers, are not a group forming a racial group referred to by reference
to their ethnic origins as provided by s 3(1) of the 1976 Act.'

If the reference in the earlier passage to the larger group is a reference to the wide
meaning of the word 'gipsy' and the small number to the word in its strict sense then
c   this conclusion may beg the question rather than answering it. Finally the judge adopted
as a finding of fact in the instant case the dicta of Lord Parker CJ in *Mills v Cooper* [1976]
2 All ER 100 at 103, [1967] 2 QB 459 at 467:

'That a man is of the Romany race is, as it seems to me, something which is really
too vague of ascertainment, and impossible to prove . . .'

d   My hesitation arises from the conclusion to be drawn from these findings, if justified
on the facts, in the context of *Mandla's* case read in its full context. It seems to me clear
from the speeches of Lord Fraser and Lord Templeman that the fact alone that a group
may comply with all or most of the relevant criteria does not itself establish that such a
group is of ethnic origin. Examples of such groups which might comply with the criteria
but which would not be of ethnic origin was cited by the respondent in *Mandla's* case
e   [1983] 2 AC 548 at 555. Indeed, such groups might themselves be of multi-racial
composition where no question of racial discrimination on the grounds of ethnic origin
could possibly arise though many of the criteria could apply to them. No doubt there are
many other examples. Lord Fraser said ([1983] 1 All ER 1062 at 1066–1067, [1983] 2 AC
548 at 561–562):

f   '. . . I recognise that "ethnic" conveys a flavour of race but it cannot, in my
opinion, have been used in the 1976 Act in a strict racial or biological sense . . . the
word "ethnic" still retains a racial flavour but it is used nowadays in an extended
sense to include other characteristics which may be commonly thought of as being
associated with common racial origin. For a group to constitute an ethnic group in
the sense of the 1976 Act, it must, in my opinion, regard itself, and be regarded by
others, as a distinct community by virtue of certain characteristics.'
g
It is in this context that he sets out the criteria which in his opinion were essential or
helpful to 'distinguish the group from the surrounding community'. Lord Templeman
said ([1983] 1 All ER 1062 at 1072, [1983] 2 AC 548 at 569):

'In my opinion, for the purposes of the 1976 Act a group of persons defined by
h   reference to ethnic origins must possess some of the characteristics of a race, namely
group descent, a group of geographical origin and a group history. The evidence
shows that the Sikhs satisfy these tests. They are more than a religious sect, they are
almost a race and almost a nation.'

It is in the context of these comments that the House considered the question whether or
not the Sikh community complied with the relevant criteria. It seems to me relevant to
j   observe that the main issue before the House was not so much whether the Sikh
community did or did not comply with the criteria but what was the correct test to apply
in deciding the question of ethnic origin. The question whether or not the Sikh
community complied with the criteria seems to me to have been one which was almost
self-evident once the appropriate criteria were established and for my part I doubt very
much whether an ordinary member of the public would have had any doubts about this.

Most people would regard Sikhs as a 'race' even if they falsely believed that their race was
'biologically derived'. Many, if not all, of the general public would know that there had   *a*
been two Sikh wars and would know that for generations regiments of Sikhs formed a
part of the Indian Army and were often a symbol, through their presence on guard at
British embassies and establishments, of British Imperial power based on the Indian army
and the British army in India. They would know that they fought in two World Wars as
distinctive units. They would know of their distinctive dress and probably some of their
customs regarding hair and the wearing of turbans. They would know that the Sikhs had   *b*
a distinct religion or would at least have heard of the Golden Temple at Amritsar. The
question whether or not Sikhs were of ethnic origin within the criteria was, in my view,
a simple and obvious one and would have been regarded as such by the general public
once the appropriate criteria for the phrase 'ethnic origin' were established. A Sikh would
certainly have so regarded himself and his fellow Sikhs. The same does not necessarily
apply to gipsies and if the judge's findings of fact were justified by the evidence I would,   *c*
for my part, be inclined to agree that even if individual gipsies fall within many of the
Mandla criteria they were not an ethnic group because on the judge's finding such a
group was not in any true sense identifiable as a group even by the gipsies themselves or
by others, and no sufficient racial flavour existed. If the judge's findings were justified by
the evidence, the fact that the conclusion was reached by a process of flawed reasoning
would not necessarily be fatal to the decision.   *d*

Was the finding justified on the evidence? Accepting that the judge was entitled,
having heard them, to form an unfavourable view of the experts and to regard their
evidence with caution, it is not easy to understand how he can have wholly rejected their
historical discourse nor their evidence with regard to the customs and traditions and
traditional way of life peculiar to gipsies since no evidence to controvert this was
tendered. The evidence of Mr Mercer, who described himself as 'a gipsy by birth' and   *e*
whose people 'were gipsies back in 1888', was to the effect that he would identify 'our
own people'. However, the evidence of the continued separate identity of gipsies as
people 'who regarded themselves and who were regarded by others as a distinct
community' (see *Mandla v Dowell Lee* [1983] 1 All ER 1062 at 1066, [1983] 2 AC 548 at
562 per Lord Fraser) was scant and it is for this reason I have hesitated whether or not it   *f*
could be said that the ethnic identity of gipsies in the strict sense was established. The
validity of the judge's finding above recited 'that there is a small number of travelling
people who can claim either by looks or characteristics to be true gipsies but these people
have been absorbed into a larger group' must depend on whether or not there is sufficient
evidence that such absorption has occurred. There was, at least, some evidence that it has
not and for these reasons I do not feel I can properly dissent from the conclusions of   *g*
Nicholls and Taylor LJJ. I reach this conclusion with some regret. I doubt whether if the
claim for breach of the Act is finally established, benefit rather than detriment will result
to either side.

For the reasons I have given I agree with the conclusion of Nicholls and Taylor LJJ and
would allow this appeal. I agree with the directions proposed.
    h

Appeal allowed. Case remitted to county court for further consideration.

Solicitors: *Bindman & Partners* (for the Commission); *Edward Fail Bradshaw & Waterson*
(for Mr Dutton).

                                                        Frances Rustin   Barrister.

a # Attorney General's Reference (No 1 of 1988)

COURT OF APPEAL, CRIMINAL DIVISION
LORD LANE CJ, HUTCHISON AND TUCKER JJ
26 SEPTEMBER, 18 OCTOBER 1988

b

Company – Insider dealing – Prohibition on stock exchange deals by insiders etc – Person who obtains insider information – Obtain – Whether 'obtains' restricted to acquiring by purpose and effort – Whether person who receives unsolicited inside information prohibited from dealing in company's securities – Company Securities (Insider Dealing) Act 1985, s 1(3)(4)(a).

c The respondent was interested in purchasing a publicly-quoted company and had discussions with the company's merchant bankers. Shortly afterwards, the company's chairman agreed to the company being taken over by another company. The merchant bankers informed the respondent of the proposed take-over and told him that a public announcement would be made shortly but that until then the information was price d sensitive and highly confidential. Ten minutes later the respondent purchased 6,000 shares in the company. The next day the take-over of the company was announced and five weeks later the respondent sold the shares at a substantial profit. He was charged with two offences of dealing in the securities of a company as a prohibited person, contrary to s 1(3) and (4)(a)^a of the Company Securities (Insider Dealing) Act 1985. The respondent contended that he had not 'obtained' the information since it had been given e to him unsolicited and had not been acquired by purpose and effort on his part. The trial judge upheld that contention and directed the respondent's acquittal. The Attorney General referred the question of the meaning of 'obtained' in s 1(3) of the 1985 Act to the Court of Appeal for its opinion.

Held – A recipient of inside information about a company who dealt in the company's f securities committed an offence under s 1(3) and (4) of the 1985 Act whether he procured that information from the primary insider by purpose and effort or came by it without any positive action on his part (see p 327 c to e, post).

Notes

For insider dealing, see 7(1) Halsbury's Laws (4th edn reissue) paras 1060–1068.

g   For the Company Securities (Insider Dealing) Act 1985, s 1, see 8 Halsbury's Statutes (4th edn) 829.

Cases referred to in opinion

Black-Clawson International Ltd v Papierwerke Waldhof-Aschaffenburg AG [1975] 1 All ER 810, [1975] AC 591, [1975] 2 WLR 513, HL.
h *DPP v Ottewell* [1968] 3 All ER 153, [1970] AC 642, [1968] 3 WLR 621, HL.
   R v Fisher [1963] 1 All ER 744, [1964] AC 210, [1963] 2 WLR 1137, CCA; *rvsd in part sub nom Fisher v Raven* [1963] 2 All ER 389, [1964] AC 210, [1963] 2 WLR 1137, HL.
   R v Hayat (1976) 63 Cr App R 181, CA.

Cases also cited

j *Brighton Parish Guardians v Strand Union Guardians* [1891] 2 QB 156, CA.
   London and Country Commercial Property Investments Ltd v A-G [1953] 1 All ER 436, [1953] 1 WLR 312.
   New Plymouth BC v Taranaki Electric-Power Board [1933] AC 680, PC.
   R v Dones [1987] Crim LR 682, CCC.

a   Section 1, so far as material, is set out at p 323 c d, post

R v Munks [1963] 3 All ER 757, [1964] 1 QB 304, CCA.
Spillers Ltd v Cardiff (Borough) Assessment Committee [1931] 2 KB 21, [1931] All ER Rep   *a*
   524, DC.
Tait v Bonnice [1975] VR 102, Vic SC.
Woods (decd), Re, Woods v Woods [1941] St RQ 129, Qld Full Ct.

Reference
The Attorney General referred to the Court of Appeal, Criminal Division, pursuant to   *b*
s 36 of the Criminal Justice Act 1972, the following points of law for its consideration:
(a) whether or not the word 'obtained' in s 1(3) of the Company Securities (Insider
Dealing) Act 1985 had the restricted meaning of 'acquired by purpose and effort' or
whether it had a wider meaning, and (b) whether or not any individual who had, from
another, information within the scope of the prohibitions contained in ss 1(4) and (6) and
2 of the 1985 Act, might be an individual who had 'obtained' within the terms of ss 1(3)   *c*
and (6) and 2 of that Act. The facts are set out in the opinion of the court.

The Attorney General (Rt Hon Sir Patrick Mayhew QC), Nicholas Purnell QC and *Timothy Nash*
   with him, in his own behalf.
Richard Ferguson QC and *Antony White* for the respondent.
                                                                              d

Cur adv vult

18 October. The following opinion of the court was delivered.

LORD LANE CJ. On 11 April 1988 the respondent appeared in the Crown Court at
Southwark and pleaded not guilty to two offences of dealing in the securities of a   *e*
company as a prohibited person, contrary to s 1(3) and (4)(a) of the Company Securities
(Insider Dealing) Act 1985.
   The material facts were as follows. In the autumn of 1985 the respondent held himself
out as a possible purchaser of company A. He was put in touch with Miss M, an employee
of the company's merchant bankers. He asked her to provide him with financial
information about the company. In the event the type of information envisaged did not   *f*
reach the respondent until after the date of the offences alleged.
   On the morning of 5 December 1985 the chairman of the company agreed with
representatives of company B for their take-over of company A. The merchant bank took
no part in the negotiation of this agreement.
   Miss M, on hearing of the agreed take-over and with the chairman's blessing, informed
the respondent of the agreement and that an announcement would be made shortly. She   *g*
told the respondent that the information she was imparting to him was sensitive and
highly confidential and that as a result of what she was saying to him he would be an
'insider'. Ten minutes later the respondent telephoned to his stockbroker and placed an
order for 10,000 shares in company A. In the event he actually purchased two blocks of
shares, 5,000 shares at one price and 1,000 shares at another price.
   The next day a public announcement of the take-over was made. The share price rose   *h*
quickly and five weeks later he sold his two blocks of shares at a handsome profit.
   The prosecution conceded that the respondent had taken no step directly or indirectly
to secure, procure or acquire the information given to him by Miss M. Whether that
concession was wisely made it is not our task to inquire.
   The two counts in the indictment reflected the purchase by the respondent of the two   *j*
blocks of shares and charged him in the following terms:

   'For that he on or about the 5th December 1985, having information which he
   knowingly obtained from [Miss M] who was connected with the company and
   whom he knew or had reasonable cause to believe held the information by virtue of

a   being so connected, and Knowing or having reasonable cause to believe that because
    of the said [Miss M's] connection and position it would be reasonable to expect her
    not to disclose that information except for the proper performance of the functions
    attaching to that position, and Knowing that the information was unpublished price
    sensitive information in relation to the securities of [the company] purchased 5,000
    (1,000) ordinary shares in [the company] on a recognised stock exchange, namely
    the Stock Exchange.'

b
    The wording of that indictment followed the wording of the material sections in the
    1985 Act, which provide as follows. Section 1:

    '... (3) The next subsection applies where—(a) an individual has information
    which he knowingly obtained (directly or indirectly) from another individual
    who—(i) is connected with a particular company, or was at any time in the 6 months
c   preceding the obtaining of the information so connected, and (ii) the former
    individual knows or has reasonable cause to believe held the information by virtue
    of being so connected, and (b) the former individual knows or has reasonable cause
    to believe that, because of the latter's connection and position, it would be reasonable
    to expect him not to disclose the information except for the proper performance of
    the functions attaching to that position.

d   (4) Subject to section 3, the former individual in that case—(a) shall not himself
    deal on a recognised stock exchange in securities of that company if he knows that
    the information is unpublished price sensitive information in relation to those
    securities...'

    Section 3(1)(a) exempts a person acting otherwise than with a view to making a profit
e   or the avoidance of a loss. Section 3(1)(b) exempts an individual entering into a transaction
    in good faith as a liquidator, receiver or trustee in bankruptcy. Section 3(1)(c) exempts an
    individual acting in the course of a business of a jobber if the information was obtained
    by him in that capacity. Section 174 of the Financial Services Act 1986 provides a further
    exception in relation to market makers.
    Counsel for the respondent at the close of the prosecution case submitted, inter alia,
f   that there was no evidence that the respondent 'obtained' information from the connected
    individual (ie Miss M), that he merely received it, that the prohibition contained in s 1(4)
    of the 1985 Act did not therefore operate against the respondent since the proper
    construction of the word 'obtained' in s 1(3) of the Act connoted active conduct on the
    part of the respondent.
    The trial judge upheld the respondent's submissions and in the light of the concession
g   made by the prosecution had no option but to direct the respondent's acquittal, which he
    did.
    The Attorney General now refers the following points of law to this court for our
    consideration:

    '(a) Whether or not the word "obtained" in section 1(3) of the Company Securities
h   (Insider Dealing) Act 1985 has the restricted meaning of "acquired by purpose and
    effort" or whether it has a wider meaning.
    (b) Whether or not any individual who has, from another, information within
    the scope of the Act and is otherwise within the scope of the prohibitions contained
    in sections 1(4), 1(6) and 2 of the Act, may be an individual who has "obtained"
    within the terms of sections 1(3), 1(6) and 2 of the Act.'

j   The first task in these circumstances is to discover the ordinary meaning of the word
    'obtained'. As Lord Diplock observed in Black-Clawson International Ltd v Papierwerke
    Waldhof-Aschaffenburg AG [1975] 1 All ER 810 at 836, [1975] AC 591 at 638: '... the
    court must give effect to what the words of the statute would be reasonably understood
    to mean by those whose conduct it regulates.'

There are, it is clear from the lexicographers and one's own experience, two such
meanings. The definition in the *Shorter Oxford English Dictionary* is: 'To procure or gain, *a*
as the result of purpose and effort; hence, generally, to acquire, get.' *Black's Law Dictionary*
(5th edn, 1979) is not dissimilar: 'to get hold of by effort; to get possession of; to procure;
to acquire, in any way.' Thus the word is capable of supporting the contention of either
party: that of the Attorney General, who argues that it means to 'acquire in any way', and
that of the respondent that it means to 'procure as the result of purpose or effort'.

The Attorney General, to support his submission that it is the latter, broader, meaning *b*
which the draftsman was intending to adopt, draws our attention to the scheme of the
1985 Act. This shows that potential offenders are divided into classes. The first target of
s 1 is the primary insider. Broadly speaking, subject to the defences in s 3, any individual
who is or at any time in the preceding six months has been knowingly connected with a
company may not deal on a recognised stock exchange in securities of that company if
he is in possession of inside information as defined in the section. It is not necessary for *c*
the prosecution to establish that the inside information was actually used by the person
in reaching his decision to deal.

The other class is the secondary insider. It was to this class that the respondent was
alleged to have belonged. As already indicated, to succeed against such a defendant the
prosecution must prove that he had information which he knowingly obtained directly
or indirectly from another individual who was connected with a particular company, or *d*
who was so connected at any time during the preceding six months, who the defendant
knew or had reasonable cause to believe, held the information by virtue of being so
connected; that the information was, in short, confidential and that it was price sensitive.
As with the primary insider, the offence is committed when he deals in the securities of
that company.

Thus, in the case of each type of insider, the offence is not one of using information *e*
but of dealing in the securities while being in possession of the relevant information.

The Attorney General submits that, looking at the Act as a whole, as one is entitled to
do in construing the relevant word, one should conclude that the vice aimed at is the
exploitation of an unfairly privileged advantage gained from a particular source. If so,
why, he asked rhetorically, should the unsoliciting 'tippee' (to adopt the inelegant but
convenient expression used by the editors of *Gore-Brown on Companies* (44th edn, 1986)) *f*
be any less culpable than the person who has deliberately sought out the information?
The vice lies in the way the information is used, not in the method of its receipt.

Moreover, picking up the words of Lord Diplock already cited and making the not
unreasonable assumption that the editors of *Gore-Brown on Companies* are comparable to
those whose conduct the Act regulates, it is clear from para 12.21 of that publication that
they assume that the broader interpretation of the word 'obtain' is intended. Indeed, one *g*
notes from his admirably clear ruling on the submission of no case that the intial reaction
of the judge was the same as that of those editors, when he said: 'Let me admit at once
that my initial reaction to this [sc the respondent's] submission was that it could not be
right; indeed that it might even be described as jejune.'

We had our attention drawn to the history of the 1985 Act. Its effect was to consolidate *h*
earlier enactments, including the provisions of the Companies Act 1980, and was itself
the subject of amendments by the provisions of the Financial Services Act 1986 which
by s 174 thereof adds a further exception as already explained.

Preceding the 1980 Act was a White Paper on *The Conduct of Company Directors* (Cmnd
7037), which dealt, inter alia, with the subject of insider dealing. That type of conduct
was not then subject to any legal sanctions, although it was causing serious concern not *j*
only in business circles.

We are invited to look at the contents of that paper in order to see the mischief which
it was desired by Parliament to remedy. As Lord Diplock pointed out in the *Black-Clawson*
case [1975] 1 All ER 810 at 836, [1975] AC 591 at 638, such papers—

'may be used to resolve the ambiguity in favour of a meaning which will result
a   in correcting those deficiencies in preference to some alternative meaning that will
leave the deficiencies uncorrected. The justification of this use of such reports . . . is
that knowledge of their contents may be taken to be shared by those whose conduct
the statute regulates and would influence their understanding of the meaning of
ambiguous enacting words.'

b   Paragraph 22 of the paper contains the following passage:

'Insider dealing is understood broadly to cover situations where a person buys or
sells securities when he, but not the other party to the transaction, is in possession of
confidential information which affects the value to be placed on those securities.
Furthermore the confidential information in question will generally be in his
possession because of some connection which he has with the company whose
c   securities are to be dealt in (e g he may be a director, employee or professional
adviser of that company) or because someone in such a position has provided him,
directly or indirectly, with the information. Public confidence in directors and
others closely associated with companies requires that such people should not use
inside information to further their own interests. Furthermore, if they were to do
so, they would frequently be in breach of their obligations to the companies, and
d   could be held to be taking an unfair advantage of the people with whom they were
dealing.'

Our attention was drawn particularly to the expressions 'the . . . information . . . will
generally be in his possession' and 'someone in such a position has provided him . . . with
the information', as indicative of the broad rather than the narrow approach to the
e   problem which we have to decide. What is in our view much more significant is the
obvious and understandable concern which the paper shows about the damage to public
confidence which insider dealing is likely to cause and the clear intention to prevent so
far as possible what amounts to cheating when those with inside knowledge use that
knowledge to make a profit in their dealing with others.

That is the reason for the proposals in para 25 of the paper:

f   '. . . that it shall be a criminal offence for an insider to deal on the market . . . in
certain circumstances where he has inside information . . . The prosecution will
need to show that the insider knew or had reasonable grounds to believe that the
information was not generally known and was price sensitive and that he dealt
nevertheless. Also, it will be possible for a person to offer as a defence that his
purpose in dealing was not to make a profit or avoid a loss by the use of his inside
g   information.'

Now, so far as gaining an unfair advantage of or, put bluntly, cheating the other party
to a transaction is concerned, it makes no difference to the person cheated whether the
information on which the 'tippee' is basing the cheating was sought out by him or came
his way by unsolicited gift. Against the background of public and government concern
h   it would indeed have been surprising if Parliament had intended that persons such as, for
example, the respondent in the instant case should be free to make a profit from their
insider information simply because of the way in which they came by the information.
It would do nothing to increase the confidence of the public in the probity of the business
world if behaviour such as that of the respondent were to be free from sanction. The
wording of para 25 is consistent with that approach. In other words, if one construes the
j   key word 'obtained' in the light of the purpose behind the Act, the conclusion must, in
our judgment, be that it means no more than 'received'.

Counsel for the respondent, however, submits that this broad construction of the word
provides inadequate protection for the involuntary recipient of information. We disagree.
The involuntary recipient does not, in our view, require protection. There is no crime in

receiving information. He can protect himself from prosecution by the simple expedient of not dealing in the relevant securities.

Perhaps more cogent is the submission that since the word 'obtain' has already been the subject of interpretation by this court, and since that interpretation adopts the narrower meaning, that is the meaning which the word must have been intended to bear in the 1985 Act.

In *R v Fisher* [1963] 1 All ER 744, [1964] AC 210 the appellant had been convicted of obtaining credit by fraud other than false pretences contrary to s 13(1) of the Debtors Act 1869 and of obtaining credit when an undischarged bankrupt contrary to s 155(a) of the Bankruptcy Act 1914. The case was largely concerned with the meaning of 'credit', but Winn J had this to say ([1963] 1 All ER 744 at 747, [1964] AC 210 at 215):

> '"Obtaining" a thing means that one person A has secured from another B, normally by some active process, what A did not already possess, e.g., by purchase, exchange, force or deceit. For present purposes, it suffices to note that the word is not synonymous with accepting or receiving; for this reason, none of the various criminal offences of obtaining by fraud would be established by mere proof of a payment of money or transfer of goods to a fraudulent person in the absence of further proof that such payment or transfer was induced by, and so obtained by a fraudulent pretence or other fraud.'

It is to be noted that the judgment is careful to confine the definition to the purposes of case under consideration.

R v Hayat (1976) 63 Cr App R 181 was another case under s 155(a) of the Bankruptcy Act 1914. James LJ, delivering the judgment of the court, said (at 186):

> 'We are of the view that in order to establish the offence of obtaining credit within the meaning of section 155(a) of the Bankruptcy Act 1914, not only must the Crown prove that it is "credit" which is obtained, but they must also prove the "obtaining" of the credit and in order to do that some conduct, either by words or otherwise, must be proved to have taken place on the part of the accused person which amounts to an obtaining.'

In that case the credit which the appellant was alleged to have obtained consisted of an overdraft at his bank. The reason for his overdrawing was that, unknown to him, a cheque drawn in his favour had been stopped by the drawer. Thus the credit he had unwittingly received in the shape of the overdraft was due to nothing which he himself had done. In such a case, brought under the provisions of the Bankruptcy Act 1914, the actus reus is the obtaining, and the mischief aimed at by the Act is that the bankrupt, without disclosing his status, procures credit for himself. It is perhaps not surprising that in those circumstances the court concluded that Parliament intended to adopt the narrow meaning of 'obtain'. As already explained, the situation here is quite different. The crucial element is the dealing. The obtaining on its own is of no import. We do not consider that in those circumstances it is either necessary or proper to adopt the meaning ascribed to the word in the judgment of James LJ in the 1985 Act.

Finally, it is submitted on behalf of the respondent that this being a penal enactment any ambiguity should be resolved in favour of the defence.

This principle of construction is of limited application. As stated in 44 Halsbury's Laws (4th edn) para 910, it—

> 'means no more than that if, after the ordinary rules of construction have first been applied, as they must be, there remains any doubt or ambiguity, the person against whom the penalty is sought to be enforced is entitled to the benefit of the doubt.'

As Lord Reid stated in *DPP v Ottewell* [1968] 3 All ER 153 at 157, [1970] AC 642 at 649:

'I would never seek to diminish in any way the importance of that principle
a   within its proper sphere; but it only applies where after full enquiry and
consideration one is left in real doubt. It is not enough that the provision is
ambiguous in the sense that it is capable of having two meanings. The imprecision
of the English language (and, so far as I am aware, of any other language) is such
that it is extremely difficult to draft any provision which is not ambiguous in that
sense. This section is clearly ambiguous in that sense; the Court of Appeal (Criminal
b   Division) attach one meaning to it, and your lordships are attaching a different
meaning to it. But if, after full consideration, your lordships are satisfied, as I am,
that the latter is the meaning which Parliament must have intended the words to
convey, then this principle does not prevent us from giving effect to our conclusion.'

We have not found the decision easy, but taking all these matters into account, we
c have reached the conclusion that Parliament intended to penalise the recipient of inside
information who deals in the relevant securities, whether he procures the information
from the primary insider by purpose and effort or comes by it without any positive
action on his part.

This conclusion will have the advantage of avoiding the fine distinctions which would
otherwise have to be drawn between what is and what is not a sufficient purpose or effort
d to satisfy the narrow meaning of 'obtain'. These would have been distinctions so fine as
to be almost imperceptible, and would have done nothing to enhance the reputation of
the business world for honesty or of the criminal law for clarity.

The answers to the two questions posed are therefore as follows: (a) the word 'obtained'
in s 1(3) of the Company Securities (Insider Dealing) Act 1985 has a wider meaning than
'acquired by purpose and effort'; (b) any individual who has, from another, information
e within the scope of the 1985 Act and is otherwise within the scope of the prohibition
contained in ss 1(4) and (6) and 2 of that Act may be an individual who has 'obtained'
within the terms of those sections.

*Reference answered accordingly. In pursuance of an application by the respondent in that behalf
the court referred the point to the House of Lords under s 36(3) of the Criminal Justice Act 1972.*
f

Solicitors: *Solicitor to the Department of Trade and Industry; Offenbach & Co* (for the
respondent).

Sophie Craven   Barrister.

R v HM Treasury and others ex parte Daily Mail and General Trust plc

(Case 81/87)

COURT OF JUSTICE OF THE EUROPEAN COMMUNITIES

JUDGES LORD MACKENZIE STUART (PRESIDENT), BOSCO, DUE, RODRIGUEZ IGLESIAS (PRESIDENTS OF CHAMBERS), KOOPMANS, EVERLING, BAHLMANN, GALMOT, JOLIET, O'HIGGINS AND SCHOCKWEILER

ADVOCATE GENERAL M DARMON

22 MARCH, 7 JUNE, 27 SEPTEMBER 1988

European Economic Community – Freedom of establishment – Beneficiaries – Companies and firms – Movement within Community – Transfer of activities or of central management and control – National provision requiring consent to transfer – United Kingdom tax legislation requiring Treasury consent for body corporate resident in United Kingdom to cease to be so resident or to transfer its trade or business to person not so resident – Whether Treaty provisions guaranteeing freedom of establishment applying to companies or firms – Whether Treaty provisions conferring right on company incorporated in one member state to transfer central management and administration to another member state while retaining status as company incorporated in first member state – Whether United Kingdom legislation restricting freedom of establishment – Income and Corporation Taxes Act 1970, s 482(1) – EEC Treaty, arts 52, 58 – EC Council Directive 73/148.

Income tax – Corporation tax – Migration etc of companies – Treasury consent – Consent for body corporate resident in the United Kingdom to cease to be so resident or to transfer trade or business to person not so resident – Whether requirement of Treasury consent restricting freedom of establishment guaranteed to nationals of member states of European Economic Community – Income and Corporation Taxes Act 1970, s 482(1) – EEC Treaty, arts 52, 58 – EC Council Directive 73/148.

The applicant, which was an investment holding company, applied to the Treasury for consent under s 482(1)[a] of the Income and Corporation Taxes Act 1970 to transfer its central management and control to the Netherlands. It was common ground that the principal reason for the proposed transfer was to enable the applicant, after establishing its residence in the Netherlands for tax purposes, to sell a significant part of its non-permanent assets and to use the proceeds of that sale to buy its own shares, without having to pay the capital gains tax and advance corporation tax to which it would be liable under United Kingdom tax laws. After establishing its central management and control in the Netherlands the applicant would be subject to Netherlands corporation tax, but the transactions envisaged would be taxed only on the basis of any capital gains which accrued after the transfer of its residence. Following negotiations with the Treasury, which proposed that it should sell at least part of the assets before transferring its residence out of the United Kingdom, the applicant brought proceedings in the High Court seeking a declaration that it was entitled under art 52[b] of the EEC Treaty to transfer its residence to the Netherlands without Treasury consent or that it was entitled under art 52 to the unconditional consent of the Treasury. The High Court referred to the

---

a Section 482(1), so far as material, is set out at p 331 *d*, post

b Article 52, so far as material, provides: '. . . restrictions on the freedom of establishment of nationals of a Member State in the territory of another Member State shall be abolished by progressive stages in the course of the transitional period. Such progressive abolition shall also apply to restrictions on the setting up of agencies, branches or subsidiaries by nationals of any Member State established in the territory of any Member State. Freedom of establishment shall include the right . . . to set up and manage undertakings, in particular companies or firms within the meaning of the second paragraph of Article 58, under the conditions laid down for its own nationals by the law of the country where such establishment is effected, subject to the provisions of the Chapter relating to capital.'

Court of Justice of the European Communities for a preliminary ruling the questions (1)
a whether arts 52 and 58ᶜ of the EEC Treaty gave a company, incorporated under the
legislation of a member state and having its registered office there, the right to transfer
its central management and control to another member state, and, if so, whether the
member state of origin could make that right subject to the consent of national
authorities, and (2) whether EC Council Directive 73/148 on the abolition on restrictions
on movement and residence within the Community for nationals of member states with
b regard to establishment and the provision of services conferred that right on a company.

Held – (1) Freedom of establishment constituted one of the fundamental principles of
the Community, and the provisions of the EEC Treaty guaranteeing that freedom
secured the right of establishment in another member state not merely for nationals but
also for companies or firms formed in accordance with the law of a member state and
c having their registered office, central administration or principal place of business within
the Community. Even though those provisions of the Treaty were directed mainly to
ensuring that foreign nationals and companies were treated in the host member state in
the same way as nationals of that state, they also prohibited the member state of origin
from hindering the establishment in another member state of one of its nationals or of a
company incorporated under its legislation and having its registered office, central
d administration or principal place of business within the Community (see p 348 d to f,
post).
  (2) Section 482(1) of the 1970 Act imposed no restriction on the setting up of agencies,
branches or subsidiaries nor on the taking part in the incorporation of a company in
another member state. Furthermore, s 482(1) did not stand in the way of a partial or total
transfer of the activities of a company incorporated in the United Kingdom to a company
e newly incorporated in another member state, if necessary after winding up and,
consequently, the settlement of the tax position of the United Kingdom company; it
only required Treasury consent where such a company sought to transfer its central
management and control out of the United Kingdom while maintaining its legal
personality and status as a United Kingdom company (see p 348 h j, post).
f   (3) Companies, unlike natural persons, were creatures of law and, in the present state
of Community law, were creatures of national law, and none of the directives on the co-
ordination of company law adopted under art 54(3)(g) of the EEC Treaty dealt with the
differences in national law in issue. In those circumstances arts 52 and 58 of the Treaty
could not be interpreted as conferring on companies incorporated under the law of a
member state a right to transfer their central management and control and their central
g administration to another member state while retaining their status as companies
incorporated under the legislation of the first member state (see p 348 j to p 349 a e to g
and p 350 d, post).
  (4) Since the title and provisions of EC Council Directive 73/148 referred solely to the
movement and residence of natural persons, it was clear that those provisions could not,
by their nature, be applied by analogy to legal persons. It followed therefore that the
h directive conferred no right on a company to transfer its central management and control
to another member state (see p 349 j to p 350 a e, post).

Notes
For the right of establishment and freedom to provide services under EEC law, see 52

---

j c   Article 58 provides:
       'Companies or firms formed in accordance with the law of a Member State and having their
       registered office, central administration or principal place of business within the Community shall,
       for the purposes of this Chapter, be treated in the same way as natural persons who are nationals
       of Member States.
       "Companies or firms" means companies or firms constituted under civil or commercial law,
       including cooperative societies, and other legal persons governed by public or private law, save for
       those which are non-profit-making.'

Halsbury's Laws (4th edn) paras 16·01–16·05, 16·12–16·15, and for cases on the subject, see 21 Digest (Reissue) 267–271, 1743–1758.

For Treasury consent to the removal abroad of the residence of a company, see 23 Halsbury's Laws (4th edn) paras 1488–1491.

In relation to companies' accounting periods ending after 5 April 1988 s 482(1) to (4) of the Income and Corporation Taxes Act 1970 were replaced by s 765 of the Income and Corporation Taxes Act 1988. For s 765 of the 1988 Act, see 44 Halsbury's Statutes (4th edn) 895.

For the EEC Treaty, arts 52, 58, see 50 ibid 285, 287.

Cases cited

Association des Centres distributeurs Édouard Leclerc v Sàrl 'Au blé vert' Case 229/83 [1985] ECR 1.

EC Commission v French Republic Case 270/83 [1986] ECR 273.

EC Commission v French Republic Case 96/85 [1986] ECR 1475.

EC Commission v Hellenic Republic Case 192/84 [1985] ECR 3967.

EC Commission v Italian Republic Case 95/81 [1982] ECR 2187.

Fabriek voor Hoogwaardige Voedingsprodukten Kelderman BV, Re criminal proceedings against Case 130/80 [1981] ECR 527.

Insurance Services, Re, EC Commission v Germany Case 205/84 [1987] 2 CMLR 69, CJEC.

Knoors v Secretary of State for Economic Affairs Case 115/78 [1979] ECR 399.

Levin v Staatssecretaris van Justitie Case 53/81 [1982] ECR 1035.

NV International Fruit Co v EC Commission Joined Cases 41 to 44/70 [1971] ECR 411.

R v Pieck Case 157/79 [1980] ECR 2171.

Rewe-Zentral AG v Bundesmonopolverwaltung für Branntwein Case 120/78 [1979] ECR 649.

Royer, Re Case 48/75 [1976] ECR 497.

Steinhauser v City of Biarritz Case 197/84 [1985] ECR 1819.

van Bennekom, Re criminal proceedings against Case 227/82 [1983] ECR 3883.

van Binsbergen v Bestuur van de Bedrijfsvereniging voor de Metaalnijverheid Case 33/74 [1974] ECR 1299.

Walrave and Koch v Association Union Cycliste Internationale Case 36/74 [1974] ECR 1405.

Reference

By order dated 6 February 1987 the High Court of Justice, Queen's Bench Division referred to the Court of Justice of the European Communities for a preliminary ruling under art 177 of the EEC Treaty four questions (set out at p 347 c to f, post) on the interpretation of arts 52 and 58 of the Treaty and the provisions of EC Council Directive 73/148 of 21 May 1973 on the abolition of restrictions on movement and residence within the Community for nationals of member states with regard to establishment and the provision of services. The questions arose in the course of an action brought by Daily Mail and General Trust plc against HM Treasury for a declaration that it was entitled under art 52 of the Treaty to transfer its residence to the Netherlands without the consent provided for under s 482(1) of the Income and Corporation Taxes Act 1970 or, alternatively, that it was entitled under art 52 of the Treaty to the unconditional consent of the Treasury. The Commission of the European Communities, Daily Mail and General Trust plc and the government of the United Kingdom submitted written observations to the court. The language of the case was English. The facts are set out in the report for the hearing presented by the Judge Rapporteur.

The Judge Rapporteur (O Due) presented the following report for the hearing.

I—FACTS AND PROCEDURE

1. The Income and Corporation Taxes Act 1970 makes companies resident in the United Kingdom subject to corporation tax. That tax consists mainly of: income tax levied, in principle, on all income wherever accruing; a tax on capital gains made on the disposal of investments; advance corporation tax on all payments of dividends or other

distributions made by a company; the amount may be deducted by the company (solely)
a from income tax and corresponds to a tax credit in favour of the beneficiary.

Under the above Act companies which are resident outside the United Kingdom, even
those incorporated under its legislation and having their registered office there, are as a
rule liable to tax only on income arising in the United Kingdom.

For the purposes of corporation tax, s 482(7) defines residence in the United Kingdom
as follows:
b
'A body corporate shall be deemed . . . to be resident or not to be resident in the
United Kingdom according as the central management and control of its trade or
business is or is not exercised in the United Kingdom . . .'

The same section also regulates the transfer of a company's residence out of the United
Kingdom.
c   Section 482(1) provides:

'Subject to the provisions of this section, all transactions of the following classes
shall be unlawful unless carried out with the consent of the Treasury, that is to say—
(a) for a body corporate resident in the United Kingdom to cease to be so resident
. . .'

d   According to s 482(4), the consent referred to in sub-s (1)—

'(a) may be given either specially (that is to say, so as to apply to specified
transactions . . .) or generally (that is to say, so as not only to apply as aforesaid); and
(b) may, if given generally, be revoked by the Treasury; and (c) may in any case be
absolute or conditional . . .'

e   Section 482(5) provides that any infringement of the provisions of s 482(1) is a criminal
offence; under sub-s (6) that offence is punishable by imprisonment for not more than
two years or a fine not exceeding £10,000 or both or, in the case of a company, a fine
three times the tax to which the company was liable in the 36 months immediately
preceding the commission of the offence or £10,000, whichever is the greater.
f   2. Daily Mail and General Trust plc, the applicant in the main proceedings, is a limited
company incorporated under English law whose registered office is in London. In the
sense in which the term is used here, the company is also resident in London.

The company is an investment company. It has a substantial holding in the share
capital of two companies, Associated Newspaper Holdings plc and Bristol United Press
Ltd, assets which the company regards as permanent and whose value at the end of 1986
was estimated at approximately £275m. It also holds a portfolio of investments quoted
g on the London Stock Exchange, which are regarded as assets of a non-permanent nature
and whose value at the end of 1986 was estimated at approximately £73m.

3. On 1 March 1984 the applicant in the main proceedings submitted to the tax
authorities an application for consent under s 482(1) of the above-mentioned Act with a
view to transferring its residence to the Netherlands.
h   In order to make that transfer, the company states in its application that it proposes to
take the following steps. All board meetings will be held in the Netherlands and the
applicant's articles of association will be amended to require this. Two persons resident
in the Netherlands will be appointed directors of the company in place of two existing
directors resident in the United Kingdom, with the result that of the eight directors only
two will have their residence in the United Kingdom. An office will be rented on a
j permanent basis in the Netherlands and as much as possible of the applicant's bookkeeping
and administration will be transferred there. The applicant will open a bank account
with a bank resident in the Netherlands and register with the Netherlands Chamber of
Commerce.

According to the application, if the transfer of residence were permitted the result for
tax purposes would be that the company would be liable to Netherlands corporation tax,
as a company resident in the Netherlands, but would no longer be liable to capital gains

tax and advance corporation tax in the United Kingdom. The company would remain liable, substantially to the same extent as previously, to income tax in the United Kingdom.

The application also states that the purpose of the transfer of residence is to correct a significant discount in the price of the company's shares compared to the real value of its assets, in the light of capital gains on the shares constituting those assets. That discount, of about 31·3% (on 30 April 1986), reflects the substantial liability to capital gains tax to which disposal of those shares would give rise, since the value of the permanent assets at the end of 1986 was more than £256m greater than their book cost and the value of the non-permanent assets at the end of 1986 was £60m greater than their acquisition cost. After a transfer of residence, those capital gains would no longer be taxable in the United Kingdom and the company would be liable in the Netherlands to tax only on the capital gains accruing after the change of residence.

It may also be seen from the application that the company considers that the tax charge to which its non-permanent assets would be subject in the event of disposal interferes with its ability to dispose freely of those assets, and it intends, after transferring its residence to the Netherlands, to sell a substantial part of that portfolio and to use the money thereby raised to repurchase some of its own shares, thus further reducing the discount at which the remaining shares stand in relation to the real value of the company's assets.

The application also states that after transferring its residence to the Netherlands the company intends, so as to avoid prejudicing the tax position of its shareholders who are resident in the United Kingdom and would otherwise lose the benefit of the tax credit, to set up a subsidiary resident in the United Kingdom and transfer to it the shares constituting its permanent assets; shareholders in the parent company would then be issued dividend-bearing shares in the subsidiary, thus permitting them to receive a large part of their dividends from a United Kingdom source.

Finally, the application states that the two directors who constitute the applicant's investment committee are resident outside the United Kingdom (in Paris and in Jersey) and it would be easier for them to meet if the company's main office were in the Netherlands rather than in London.

4. In a letter of 13 March 1984 the tax authorities asked the applicant company to provide an estimate of the tax that would be payable on the transactions which it proposed to carry out if the company remained resident in the United Kingdom. The company provided that information in a letter of 19 April 1984. It shows that, with the figures updated to 31 December 1986, the loss of tax revenue as a result of a transfer of residence, leaving aside income tax revenue, estimated by the tax authorities at £500,000 per year, may be calculated as follows:

Tax on capital gains in respect of non-permanent assets:

Total value	£73,094,493	
Acquisition cost	£12,380,000	
Total capital gains	£60,714,493	
Tax at 30%		£18,214,348
Tax on the proposed sale of shares to the amount of £53,094,493		£13,230,567
Advance corporation tax (levied on the purchase of the company's shares with the money obtained from the sale):		
Amount available	£53,094,493	
	−£13,230,567	
	£39,863,926	

a

Tax at a rate of 29/71	£11,560,538
(of which only a very small part may be deducted from income tax)	
TOTAL	£24,791,105

b In a letter of 9 July 1984 the tax authorities asked the company, inter alia, for its comments on the suggestion that prior to its intended migration it should liquidate a significant proportion of its portfolio. The applicant's solicitors replied in a letter dated 19 November 1984 that the possibility of the company's agreeing to such a sale would depend on the amounts involved.

After further negotiations and exchanges of letters, the company informed the tax authorities in a letter of 1 April 1986 that it had decided, even in advance of transferring
c the residence of the company to the Netherlands, to establish a branch there through which it could, inter alia, provide services to third parties. In the same letter the company stated that it was entitled under art 52 of the EEC Treaty to transfer its residence to the Netherlands without securing the consent of the Treasury and it asked the latter to confirm that proposition or give unconditional consent before 31 May 1986.

5. On 24 June 1986 the applicant in the main proceedings brought an action before
d the Queen's Bench Division of the High Court of Justice essentially for a declaration that it is entitled under art 52 of the EEC Treaty to transfer its residence to the Netherlands without the consent provided for under s 482(1) of the Income and Corporation Taxes Act 1970 or, in the alternative, that it is entitled under art 52 of the EEC Treaty to the unconditional consent of the Treasury.

By order of 6 February 1987 the national court decided to stay proceedings until the
e Court of Justice had given a preliminary ruling on the following questions:

f '1. Do Articles 52 and 58 of the EEC Treaty preclude a Member State from prohibiting a body corporate with its central management and control in that Member State from transferring without prior consent or approval that central management and control to another Member State in one or both of the following circumstances, namely where: (i) payment of tax upon profits or gains which have already arisen may be avoided; (ii) were the company to transfer its central management and control, tax that might have become chargeable had the company retained its central management and control in that Member State would be avoided?

g 2. Does Council Directive 73/148/EEC give a right to a corporate body with its central management and control in a Member State to transfer without prior consent or approval its central management and control to another Member State in the conditions set out in Question 1? If so, are the relevant provisions directly applicable in this case?

3. If such prior consent or approval may be required, is a Member State entitled
h to refuse consent on the grounds set out in Question 1?

4. What difference does it make, if any, that under the relevant law of the Member State no consent is required in the case of a change of residence to another Member State of an individual or firm?'

6. The order of the High Court of Justice, Queen's Bench Division was lodged at the
j court registry on 19 March 1987.

7. Pursuant to art 20 of the Protocol on the Statute of the Court of Justice, written observations were submitted on 12 June 1987 by the Commission of the European Communities, represented by its legal adviser, D R Gilmour, on 20 July 1987 by Daily Mail and General Trust plc, the applicant in the main proceedings, represented by David Vaughan QC and Derrick Wyatt, Barrister, and on 21 July 1987 by the United Kingdom, represented by S J Hay, Treasury Solicitor, acting as agent.

8. On hearing the report of the Judge Rapporteur and the views of the Advocate General, the court decided to open the oral procedure without any preparatory inquiry. *a*

II—OBSERVATIONS SUBMITTED TO THE COURT

1. *Observations of the applicant in the main proceedings*

The applicant in the main proceedings claims first of all that arts 52 and 58 of the EEC Treaty grant to natural and legal persons a right of exit from their own member states, as *b* well as a right of entry to other member states for the purposes of establishment.

Under art 52 nationals of one member state wishing to establish themselves in another member state are entitled to challenge not only restrictions on entry and establishment imposed by the other member state but also restrictions on emigration imposed by the member state of which they are nationals. That restrictions on emigration are caught by art 52 is confirmed by EC Council Directive 73/148 of 21 May 1973 on the abolition of *c* restrictions on movement and residence within the Community for nationals of member states with regard to establishment and the provision of services. According to art 1, the directive is concerned, inter alia, with nationals of a member state who wish to establish themselves in another member state, and under art 2(1) and (4) member states must grant such persons the right to leave their territory and may not demand from them any exit visa or equivalent requirement. In its judgment in *Re Royer* Case 48/75 [1976] ECR *d* 497 the court decided that the directive gives rise to no new rights in favour of persons protected by Community law, but simply lays down the scope and detailed rules for the exercise of rights conferred directly by the Treaty. To deny a right of exit would render nugatory the right of establishment in another member state.

Article 52 itself thus bestows a right of exit from a member state, and it follows that the same right is enjoyed by legal persons since, under the first paragraph of art 58, such *e* persons are to be treated in the same way as natural persons for the purposes, in particular, of the implementation of art 52.

It cannot be argued that that right is not enjoyed by legal persons since they do not need to transfer their residence in order to exercise their right of establishment but may do so by setting up branches and agencies. In its judgment in *EC Commission v French* *f* *Republic* Case 270/83 [1986] ECR 273 the court decided that art 52 expressly leaves traders free to choose the appropriate legal form in which to pursue their activities in another member state and that freedom of choice may not be limited by national provisions discriminating against branches and agencies in relation to subsidiaries of foreign companies. As art 52 leaves companies the freedom to choose between the different modes of secondary establishment, it would follow that they are equally free to make the initial choice as between primary establishment on the one hand and secondary *g* establishment on the other.

The applicant in the main proceedings claims, second, that the transfer of a company's central management and control to another member state amounts to establishment in that state.

Article 52 of the Treaty grants a right of primary establishment (first paragraph, first *h* sentence) and a right of secondary establishment (first paragraph, second sentence). In regard to companies, guidance as to the content of the right of primary establishment may be found in the General Programme for the abolition of restrictions of freedom of establishment (OJ 1962, p 36 (S Edn (2nd Series) IX, p 7)), on which the court has relied on several occasions. According to Title I of the programme (Beneficiaries), companies and firms formed under the law of a member state and having the seat prescribed by *j* their statutes, their centre of administration or their main establishment situated within the Community are equivalent to 'nationals of Member States'. Furthermore, companies so defined are equivalent to 'nationals of Member States established in a Member State' provided that, where only the seat prescribed by their statutes is situated within the

Community, their activity shows a real and continuous link with the economy of a
a member state. The court has held with regard to companies that it is their prescribed
seat or registered office that serves as the connecting factor with the legal system of a
particular state, corresponding to nationality in the case of natural persons (cf *EC
Commission v French Republic* Case 270/83 cited above); it follows that a company must be
regarded as established in a member state if its central administration is situated in a
member state, its main establishment is situated in a member state or, in the absence of
b either of the above links, the activity of the company shows a real and continuous link
with the economy of that member state. The decisive factor is therefore the real and
continuous link with the economy of a member state, and the presence of the central
administration or the main establishment is presumed to constitute such a link.

A transfer of the central management and control of a company such as that
contemplated by the applicant in the main proceedings would amount to a transfer of its
c central administration within the meaning of the General Programme. The central
administration is located where the company organs take the decisions that are essential
for the company's operation.

Such a transfer of central management and control a fortiori constitutes establishment
when that transfer is accompanied, as in this case, by the opening of an investment
management office with a view to the provision of financial services to third parties. It
d clearly amounts to an effective and genuine economic activity (see, in regard to the free
movement of workers, the judgment in *Levin v Staatssecretaris van Justitie* Case 53/81
[1982] ECR 1035). Article 52 of the Treaty must be given a broad interpretation in that
regard, as the court stressed in its judgment in *Steinhauser v City of Biarritz* Case 197/84
[1985] ECR 1819 at 1825 (para 10).

The applicant in the main proceedings claims, in the third place, that the motives of a
e company seeking to change the place in which its central management and control is
located do not affect its rights under art 52 of the Treaty.

It emphasises that the primary concern of an investment company must be to manage
its assets in the most commercial way and that it is natural for it to take account of the
incidence of taxation and to seek to make its activities subject to the least onerous tax
f system.

In the area of freedom of movement for workers, the court has accepted that the
intentions of the person seeking to benefit from the rights conferred by the Treaty are of
no account in the eyes of Community law. In *Levin's* case cited above, which was
concerned with a part-time worker, the court decided that the advantages which
Community law confers may be relied on only by persons who actually pursue or
g seriously wish to pursue activities as employed persons but that the enjoyment of this
freedom may not be made to depend on the aims pursued by the worker, as long as he
pursues or wishes to pursue an effective and genuine activity as an employed person. The
court decided that, once that condition is satisfied, the motives which may have prompted
the worker to seek employment in another member state are of no account and must not
be taken into consideration.

h The situation is identical in this case, in which the applicant company wishes to
establish itself in another member state with every prospect of permanence and to pursue
effective and genuine economic activity both in and from that member state, and for
that reason the motives of those controlling the company are of no account.

However, that does not imply that recourse may be had to the provisions of
Community law in a temporary and perfunctory manner solely in order to avoid the
j application of national law. In its judgment in *Association des Centres distributeurs Édouard
Leclerc v Sàrl 'Au blé vert'* Case 229/83 [1985] ECR 1 the court held that reimports of
books exported for the sole purpose of reimportation so as to avoid national rules on
price-fixing for books did not fall within the scope of art 30 of the Treaty. The situation
is very different in this case, in which the transfer of central management and control

produces real effects in the economy of the member state in which establishment is to take place. It should be noted that in this case the national authorities do not contest the fact that the applicant company wishes to establish a real and effective presence in the Netherlands.

Fourth, the applicant in the main proceedings claims that a national rule such as s 482 of the Income and Corporation Taxes Act 1970 which subjects all transfers of corporate residence to other member states to the consent of the national authorities and to compliance with national conditions is incompatible with arts 52 and 58 of the Treaty.

A provision of national law may not make the exercise of a right conferred by Community law subject to such a procedure or to compliance with such conditions.

In the area of free movement of goods, the court has established the principle that the enjoyment of such a right may not be made dependent on a discretionary power or a concession granted by the national authorities and that a requirement to obtain import or export licences constitutes an unlawful hindrance to trade even where such licences are granted as of right (see the judgments in Re criminal proceedings against Fabriek voor Hoogwaardige Voedingsprodukten Kelderman BV Case 130/80 [1981] ECR 527 and NV International Fruit Co v EC Commission Joined Cases 41 to 44/70 [1971] ECR 411).

That principle is equally applicable with regard to the free movement of persons. In its judgment in R v Pieck Case 157/79 [1980] ECR 2171 the court decided that the right of workers under Community law to enter the territory of a member state may not be made subject to clearance by the authorities of that member state. The same principle should also apply to the right to leave a member state, a right also conferred by Community law, and with regard to legal persons, which Community law treats in the same way as natural persons for these purposes.

In the fifth place, the applicant in the main proceedings claims that a national rule such as that at issue is inconsistent with arts 52 and 58 of the Treaty where transfers of corporate residence may, at the discretion of the national authorities, be treated as taxable events.

The applicant emphasises that under United Kingdom tax law emigration is not an event giving rise to liability to capital gains tax.

A provision which permits the national authorities, at their discretion, to treat emigration as a taxable event, as seems to have been the case here, constitutes an obstacle to freedom of establishment because it creates an ambiguous and uncertain situation calculated to deter the potential emigrant (see, in regard to free movement of goods, the judgment in EC Commission v Hellenic Republic Case 192/84 [1985] ECR 3967).

In the sixth place, the applicant in the main proceedings claims that a national rule such as that at issue is incompatible with arts 52 and 58 of the Treaty since it places restrictions on the right of exit of corporate bodies where no such restrictions are placed on the right of exit of individuals.

Article 58 of the Treaty treats companies in the same way as natural persons for the purposes of the provisions concerning freedom of establishment. Consequently, a member state may not impede the right of establishment by drawing unjustifiable distinctions between the activities of individuals on the one hand and the 'companies and firms' referred to in art 58 of the Treaty on the other. Member states must permit the establishment of companies on the same basis as they permit the establishment of natural persons. The same principle applies to the right to leave a member state in order to become established in another.

In the seventh place, the applicant in the main proceedings claims that the fact that a transfer of residence by a corporate body may lead to a loss of future tax revenue to a member state cannot justify derogation from the principle of freedom of establishment.

According to art 56(1) of the Treaty, the provisions of Community law on freedom of establishment may not prejudice the applicability of national provisions providing for special treatment for foreign nationals on grounds of public policy, public security or public health. That article, which must be construed strictly, is not applicable to this

case, which is concerned with a measure restrictive of emigration invoked by a member
a state against one of its own nationals, not against a foreign national. In any event, the
derogations referred to in that article cannot be construed as extending to the protection
of the economic or fiscal interests of the member state (see, in regard to similar concepts
in art 36 of the Treaty, the judgment in *EC Commission v Italian Republic* Case 95/81 [1982]
ECR 2187).

However, the applicant in the main proceedings accepts that art 52 may in principle
b be subject to such exceptions as are recognised by the Court of Justice, but such exceptions
must be narrowly defined, applied without discrimination and be proportionate. As the
court has held, the protection of the fiscal interests of a member state cannot justify
derogation from the requirements of art 52 of the Treaty. In its judgment in *EC
Commission v French Republic* Case 270/83 [1986] ECR 273 cited above the court stated
expressly that the risk of tax evasion cannot justify any derogation from the fundamental
c principle of freedom of establishment laid down in art 52 of the Treaty. In this case there
is no question of tax evasion or any improper motive. Almost every emigration of a
natural or legal person involves a loss of revenue to a member state and to justify
restrictions on emigration on that ground alone would seriously undermine the scope of
art 52 of the Treaty.

If there were any exception to art 52 on fiscal grounds, it could only justify measures
d to secure the payment of a tax liability already accrued or to prevent fraudulent or
improper practices. Such an exception could not in any circumstances justify measures
to secure the payment of tax for which there was not yet any liability and to which
liability would probably not arise if emigration did not take place.

Finally, in its eighth submission the applicant in the main proceedings claims that
even if derogation from the right of emigration under art 52 may be justified in specific
e cases, a general restriction such as the one contained in the national rule at issue is
disproportionate.

As the court has consistently held, exceptions to the free movement of persons must
be construed strictly. National measures derogating from art 52 must not go beyond
what is necessary to achieve the ends justifying the derogation (see the judgment in *EC
Commission v French Republic* Case 96/85 [1986] ECR 1475). Furthermore, the burden of
f proof in establishing exceptions to fundamental Treaty provisions lies on the party
relying on the exception (see *Re criminal proceedings against van Bennekom* Case 227/82
[1983] ECR 3883).

It is thus not open to a member state to impose restrictions on all companies seeking
to emigrate and to impose on them the burden of demonstrating that an exception to
the free movement provisions is not applicable in their case. At most, the member states
g may require generally that those contemplating emigration notify the national authorities
of their identity and their intentions. National legislation making the transfer of
residence of companies a criminal offence in the absence of the consent of the national
authorities is in any event excessive and disproportionate.

In conclusion, the applicant in the main proceedings suggests that the questions asked
h by the national court should be answered as follows:

'1. Where under the law of a member state unrealised profits or gains have
accrued, but no tax liability in respect thereof has arisen, and where the transfer of
central management and control of a corporate body from the member state to
another member state does not amount to a taxable event, arts 52 and 58 of the EEC
j Treaty preclude the former member state from prohibiting a body corporate with
its central management and control in that state from transferring, without prior
consent or approval, its central management and control to another member state,
notwithstanding the fact that no tax on unrealised gains will be payable to the first
member state as a result of such transfer. Furthermore, where the tax liabilities of
bodies corporate accrue from time to time under the law of a member state by

virtue of the presence in that state of the central management and control of such
bodies corporate, arts 52 to 58 of the EEC Treaty preclude that member state from
prohibiting a body corporate from transferring its central management and control
to another member state in order to ensure continued liability to tax under the law
of the former member state.

2. Article 2(1) and (4) of EC Council Directive 73/148, in conjunction with
arts 52 to 58 of the EEC Treaty, gives a right to a corporate body with its central
management and control in a member state to transfer without prior consent or
approval its central management and control to another member state in the
circumstances referred to in the first question referred by the Divisional Court.

3. Since no consent or approval is required, a member state is not entitled to
refuse consent in the circumstances set out in the first question referred by the
Divisional Court.

4. Since arts 52 to 58 of the EEC Treaty give expression to the principle that
natural and legal persons must be free to choose the appropriate legal form in which
to pursue their activities in other member states, it is incompatible with arts 52 to
58 to subject a transfer of corporate residence to another member state to prior
consent or approval, where no such prior consent or approval is required in the case
of a change of residence to another member state of an individual or a firm.'

2. Observations of the United Kingdom

The United Kingdom observes first of all that the transfer of 'residence' at issue in the
main proceedings, which concerns an investment company, is not intended to entail and
will not be accompanied by any alteration in the nature of the principal business activity
of the company, in the location of its registered office or in the proportion of the
company's business that is transacted on the Stock Exchange in the United Kingdom.
The transfer is not intended to integrate the company into the Netherlands economy but
is solely intended to permit it to avoid United Kingdom corporation tax.

The United Kingdom argues principally that a change of a company's residence does
not, by itself, amount to 'establishment' under art 52 of the EEC Treaty. If Community
law protected such changes of residence, in the absence of harmonisation of national
corporate tax systems capital movements and the internal structure of the Community
market could be seriously distorted.

In the alternative, if that submission is not accepted, the United Kingdom considers
that any right granted to companies by art 52 of the Treaty to transfer their residence
may not be relied on when the sole or main purpose of asserting that right is to avoid the
operation of national fiscal laws.

With regard to its principal submission, the United Kingdom contends that art 52 of
the Treaty does not create any general right for a company to change its residence, that
such a right is not expressly conferred by other Community legislation and that it may
not be inferred from the freedoms granted by arts 52 to 58 of the Treaty.

Article 52 is concerned with establishment in the sense of location in a member state
in order to conduct economic activity there. Like the free movement of workers and the
freedom to provide and obtain services, also covered by Title III of Pt II of the Treaty, it is
not a simple freedom of movement but rather a freedom of movement created in order
to promote the economic integration of the Community. In its judgment in *Walrave
and Koch v Association Union Cycliste Internationale* Case 36/74 [1974] ECR 1405 the court
decided that freedom of movement for workers does not affect the composition of sports
teams, in particular national teams, since that has nothing to do with economic activities.
That decision was confirmed in *Levin v Staatssecretaris van Justitie* Case 53/81 [1982] ECR
1035, concerning the right of residence of a part-time worker, in which the court stated
that the employment must be effective and genuine.

However, fixing the residence of a company in a member state does not by itself
necessarily involve an effective and genuine economic activity in the host state. The

'residence' of a company corresponds, according to the definition contained in s 482(7) of
a the Income and Corporation Taxes Act 1970, to the place in which the 'central
management and control' of the company is located. That is the place where the ultimate
directing authority of the company is exercised. In order to change residence, all that
United Kingdom law requires is that the place in which overall decisions about the
conduct of the activities of the company (in this case the place in which the board adopts
its decisions) should be changed. It is not necessary that the actual activities of the
b company should be changed, and in this case the transfer of the applicant company's
residence to the Netherlands would in no way alter the economic activities at present
carried on by the company.

Nor is such a right on the part of a company to change its residence expressly provided
for by other provisions of Community law. A right to change one's residence is expressly
provided for in EC Council Directive 73/148 on the abolition of restrictions on movement
c and residence within the Community for nationals of member states with regard to
establishment and the provision of services, on which the applicant company relies.
However, the express terms of the directive apply only to individuals. Article 2 thus
makes the exercise of the right to leave the territory of a member state subject to the
holding of an identity card or passport, which is manifestly inappropriate in the case of a
corporate body.

d The only relevance of that directive is in considering whether the recognition in the
directive of a right to leave a member state merely determines the scope of a right
conferred directly by the Treaty and the manner in which it may be exercised (see the
judgment in Re Royer Case 48/75 [1976] ECR 497). The question is whether the right to
transfer residence or to leave the territory of a member state is a right inherent in art 52
of the Treaty and extends to all persons covered by that article, both individuals and
e companies, on the ground that it is essential to the exercise of the right of establishment.

The United Kingdom considers that that right is inherent in the right of establishment
granted to individuals by the Treaty. It would be difficult, if not impossible, for
individuals to exercise genuine and effective economic activity in a particular member
state without residing there. However, a company can extend its international locus by
the establishment of agencies, branches or subsidiaries without being obliged to transfer
f its residence. It thus cannot be assumed in the case of a company that a right of
establishment necessarily entails a right of residence. The irrelevance of the location of a
company's residence to the exercise of the freedoms conferred by art 52 of the Treaty is
demonstrated by the facts of the present case. A transfer of residence would make no
difference to the applicant's ability to carry out effective and genuine economic activity
in the Netherlands. Indeed, it is its intention to carry out such activity whether or not it
g is able to transfer its residence there. Moreover, it does not intend to cease to be
established in the United Kingdom.

The conclusion that the right to transfer residence is not inherent in the exercise of the
rights conferred on legal persons by art 52 of the Treaty is not contrary to the judgment
of the court in EC Commission v French Republic Case 270/83 [1986] ECR 273. The court
h decided in that case that the freedom for companies to choose the appropriate legal form
in which to pursue their activities in another member state, expressly conferred on them
by art 52 of the Treaty, must not be limited by discriminatory tax provisions. The
judgment was concerned with discrimination on grounds of nationality between
branches and agencies on the one hand and subsidiaries on the other, contrary to the
express provisions of art 52, and not the question whether a rule not expressly laid down
j in art 52 was necessarily to be inferred from freedoms expressly conferred by that article.

With regard to its alternative submission, the United Kingdom contends that, if art 2
of the Treaty gives a company a right to change its residence, that right must be subject
to an exception in the case where the sole or main object of the change of residence is the
avoidance of the tax laws of the state where the company previously resided.

In its case law the court has recognised a principle preventing individuals from using

Community freedoms in order to avoid the application of legitimate national rules. In regard to freedom to provide services, the court decided in *van Binsbergen v Bestuur van de* **a** *Bedrijfsvereniging voor de Metaalnijverheid* Case 33/74 [1974] ECR 1299 that specific requirements imposed on the person providing a service cannot be considered incompatible with the Treaty where they have as their purpose the general good and are binding on any person established in the member state in question, where the person providing the service would escape from the ambit of those rules by being established in another member state. In regard to freedom of establishment, the court decided in *Knoors* **b** *v Secretary of State for Economic Affairs* Case 115/78 [1979] ECR 399 that it is not possible to disregard the legitimate interest which a member state may have in preventing certain of its nationals, by means of facilities created under the Treaty, from attempting wrongly to evade the application of their national legislation as regards training for a trade.

The above principle is not the same as that enunciated in *Rewe-Zentral AG v Bundesmonopolverwaltung für Branntwein* Case 120/78 [1979] ECR 649, which recognised **c** the possibility of limited derogations from general Community rules in order to promote a restricted number of public policy interests. Whether the principle being discussed here applies or not depends on the conduct and purpose of the subject who seeks to assert in his own favour the prima facie directly effective rights granted by Community law. The principle provides that a subject cannot rely on such rights where his sole or main purpose in asserting those rights is to avoid the application to him of legitimate national **d** rules.

That principle should be applied in the present case. The freedom to alter one's residence cannot be relied on where the sole or main purpose of that change of residence is to avoid the application of national fiscal rules.

That submission is fully in accordance with Community policy on the prevention of tax avoidance, which must be distinguished from tax evasion, the latter usually involving **e** elements of dishonesty. In the absence of harmonisation of the tax systems relating to companies, the Community institutions have recognised that there is a direct Community interest in preventing tax evasion and avoidance. As is stated in the preamble to EC Council Directive 77/799 of 19 December 1977 concerning mutual assistance by the competent authorities of the member states in the field of direct taxation, practices of tax evasion and tax avoidance extending across the frontiers of member states lead to budget **f** losses and violations of the principle of fair taxation and are liable to bring about distortions of capital movements and of conditions of competition, thus affecting the operation of the common market.

This case therefore concerns the protection not merely of a national interest but also of a Community interest.

According to the United Kingdom, the above-mentioned principle justifies a national **g** provision such as that at issue in the main proceedings since it enables the authorities to control a change of company residence in any case where the sole or main objective of that change is the avoidance of liability for United Kingdom taxation.

Finally, the United Kingdom observes that there are sound practical reasons for a difference of treatment between individuals and companies inasmuch as only the latter **h** are subject to the obligation to obtain the approval of the authorities for a transfer of residence. Article 58 treats companies in the same way as individuals for the purposes of the provisions of the Treaty on freedom of establishment but does not require the member states to apply in every case the same rules of domestic law to companies as to individuals.

The United Kingdom therefore submits that the questions posed by the national court **j** should be answered as follows:

'1. Articles 52 to 58 of the EEC Treaty do not preclude the member state from prohibiting the transfer of central management and control in either of the stated circumstances.

a

2. EC Council Directive 73/148 gives no rights to corporate bodies. The second part of the question accordingly does not arise.

3. The prior consent or approval referred to may be required, and the member state is entitled to refuse consent on either of the grounds set out in question 1.

4. The provisions of the domestic law of the member state referred to make no difference to the above replies.'

b

3. Observations of the Commission

The Commission points out first of all that the questions referred by the national court concerning the right of exit by a legal person from its home state raise for the first time the question of the right of exit from a member state in order to take advantage of the provisions of the EEC Treaty.

c

The Commission goes on to observe that although under art 58 of the Treaty a company established in conformity with the law of one member state is treated in the same way as a natural person, who has the right under art 52 to establish himself in another member state, there is a significant difference in the legal framework affecting natural and legal persons. A natural person can decide of his own volition to remove himself from one state and establish himself in another. A legal person cannot necessarily

d

act in the same way or, at least, with the same degree of freedom. Legal persons depend for their existence on their law of incorporation and the extent to which, inter alia, they can change their residence, moving from one state to another, depends on the law of the state of incorporation and on that of the host state. In some countries a change in the location of the central management and control of the company is possible and implies a change in residence. In others, if the central management and control emigrates, it is

e

equivalent to winding up the company. In these respects the law is not harmonised. However, all Community legal systems appear to have one point in common: any company can be wound up in one state and reincorporated in another. Short of that solution, how far a company can migrate remains a matter of national law. In this case the question to be resolved is whether, where national company law bestows the right to alter residence, a company may rely on art 52 of the Treaty in a situation where the

f

national authorities seek to impede emigration.

Under United Kingdom company law there is a distinction between the registered office and the location of the central management and control. While nationality of a company is dependent on the location of the registered office, its residence is dependent on the location of central management and control. The latter can emigrate without any consequences for the nationality of the company. Dutch law allows a company to

g

establish itself in the Netherlands by locating its central management and control there without however acquiring Netherlands nationality. In this respect, United Kingdom and Dutch law are compatible.

There is no doubt, as far as individuals are concerned, that Community law recognises a right of exit from the member state of origin. That point has been expressly dealt with by art 2 of EC Council Directive 73/148 of 21 May 1973 on the abolition of restrictions on movement and residence within the Community for nationals of member states with

h

regard to establishment and the provision of services. The Commission considers that that directive cannot apply to legal persons since the terms in which it is drafted are such as to make it clear that it applies only to natural persons. However, in the view of the Commission, whether one is dealing with natural or legal persons, the rights conferred under art 52ff of the Treaty would be rendered meaningless if the state of nationality could actually prevent emigration. Any legal person may be wound up and reincorporated

j

in another member state, and a legal person has the right to change its residence, where that possibility is provided for under national company law. The Commission therefore considers that where national company law draws a distinction between nationality and residence, and provides for the retention of nationality by companies which decide to establish residence abroad, art 52 of the Treaty confers on a company the right to exercise that choice without being dependent on an authorisation from national fiscal authorities. However, there would appear to be no objection to a requirement that notice be given.

a

With regard to whether tax considerations can modify that solution, the Commission considers that the member state of origin may not impose conditions on emigration in order to secure potential revenue. In its judgment in *EC Commission v French Republic* Case 270/83 [1986] ECR 273 the court decided that art 52 of the Treaty does not permit any derogation from the fundamental principle of freedom of establishment on the ground that there is a risk of tax evasion.

b

This case is concerned not with tax evasion but only with a maximisation of lawful fiscal possibilities. The real problem in this case arises under United Kingdom law and from the absence of appropriate provisions in the Netherland–United Kingdom double tax convention.

The Commission concludes by proposing that the Court of Justice should give the following answers to the questions submitted by the national court:

c

'1. Articles 52 and 58 of the EEC Treaty preclude a member state from prohibiting a body corporate with its central management and control in that member state from transferring without prior consent or approval that central management and control to another member state in one or both of the following circumstances, namely where: (i) payment of tax on profits or gains which have already arisen may be avoided; (ii) were the company to transfer its central management and control tax that might have become chargeable had the company retained its central management and control in that member state would be avoided.

d

2. EC Council Directive 73/148 confers no rights on bodies corporate.

3. In the light of the answer given to question 1, this question is not applicable.

e

4. The answer to question 1 is not affected by the legal situation attaching to an individual or firm.'

David Vaughan QC and *Derrick Wyatt* for Daily Mail and General Trust plc.
Richard Buxton QC, Alan Moses and *Nicholas Green* for the United Kingdom.
D R Gilmour for the EC Commission.

f

7 June. **The Advocate General (M Darmon)** delivered the following opinion[1]. Mr President, Members of the Court,

1. The issue in the main proceedings lies at the point where company law meets tax law. In the United Kingdom the connecting factors governing the application to a legal person of those branches of law are not necessarily the same. The concept of incorporation, as it is understood in English law, makes it possible to dissociate a company's domicile, expressed through its registered office, and its nationality, on the one hand, from its residence, which largely determines the tax rules applicable to it, on the other. The proceedings pending before the national court arise from the possibility of such a separation.

g

2. In that regard, the legislation of the member states is very diverse, and that situation is aggravated by differences in the content of the relevant concepts. In order to overcome the resulting difficulties recourse must be had to harmonisation at Community level or agreements concluded by the member states. In any event, the function of the Court of Justice is to interpret Community law as it now stands. Thus the context of the case in which the Queen's Bench Division of the High Court has referred questions to the court for a preliminary ruling, as it appears from the file, calls for certain general observations in order to attempt to reply to the questions. Those questions raise delicate problems concerning the interpretation of the Community provisions in regard to the right of

h

j

1　Translated from the French

establishment which have not until now been considered by the court. What is involved
a in this case is the claim by a company to exercise the right of establishment and, in
particular, the conditions to which the member state of origin in which its registered
office is situated may make subject the transfer of its central management and control to
another member state.

3. Does such a transfer come within the scope of the right of establishment guaranteed
by the EEC Treaty? Establishment 'means integration into a national economy' (see
b Schapira, Le Tallec and Blaise *Droit Européen des Affaires* (1984) p 534). Thus, it is not
contested that establishment within the meaning of the Treaty involves two factors:
physical location and the exercise of an economic activity, both, if not on a permanent
basis, at least on a durable one (see, for example, Renauld *Droit Européen des Sociétés* (1969)
p 2.08, Colomès *Le Droit de l'Etablissement et des Investissements dans la CEE* (1977) p 78 and
Burrows *Free Movement in European Community Law* (1987) p 187).
c   4. Let me point out that the right of establishment, as laid down in arts 52 to 58 of
the Treaty, applies to 'Companies or firms formed in accordance with the law of a
Member State and having their registered office, central administration or principal place
of business within the Community' (see art 58, first paragraph). The right of establishment
can manifest itself in two different ways (see, for example, Temple Lang 'The right of
establishment of companies and free movement of capital in the European Economic
d Community', in Lafave and Hey (eds) *International Trade, Investment and Organization*
(1967) esp pp 302–303). On the one hand, subsidiaries, branches or agencies may be set
up. That is known as secondary establishment. The court, in *Re Insurance Services, EC
Commission v Germany* Case 205/84 [1987] 2 CMLR 69 at 100 (para 21), stated that an
undertaking is established in a member state as soon as it has a permanent presence there
even if that presence consists merely of—
e
'an office managed by the undertaking's own staff or by a person who is
independent but authorised to act on a permanent basis for the undertaking, as
would be the case with an agency.'

Establishment may also take the form of the setting up of a new company or the
f transfer of the central management and control of the company, often regarded as its real
head office. That is called 'primary establishment'. It has been said in that regard that
'central management and control is not a legal concept but an economic one' (see
Schwartz *Le droit d'établissement des sociétés commerciales dans le traité instituant la
Communauté économique européene* (1963) p 61) and that it 'is located where the company
organs take the decisions that are essential for the company's operations' (see Everling *The
right of establishment in the Common Market* (1964) p 75).
g
5. The concept of establishment itself is essentially an economic one (see Renauld
Droit Européen des Sociétés pp 2.19, 2.35). It always implies a genuine economic link (see
Harding 'Freedom of establishment and the rights of companies' [1963] CLP 162 at 163).
The transfer of the central management and control of a company, understood by
reference to 'criteria which are more economic than legal' (see *Renauld* p2.43), is covered
h by the right of establishment in so far as it is necessary to determine in concrete terms
'the economic centre of gravity of the undertaking' (see *Renauld* p 2.44). Thus 'the
concept of central management and control . . . corresponds . . . not merely to the
physical location of the principal administration services but also, and perhaps principally,
to the place from which the company is actually run' (see *Renauld* p 2.31). The real head
office is normally the place where the company's central management and administration
j is located, since that is 'the place in which the decisions concerning the company's
independent activity are made and from which that activity is set in motion; in other
words, it is the centre from which that activity is exercised . . .' (see Goldman and Lyon-
Caen *Droit commercial européen* (4th edn, 1983) p 357).
6. The parties to the main proceedings take entirely opposite views on the question
whether the transfer of the management of a company constitutes 'establishment' within

the meaning of the EEC Treaty. According to Daily Mail and General Trust, such a transfer comes within the scope of the right of establishment. Arguing on the basis of art 52 to 58 of the Treaty and the General Programme for the abolition of restrictions on freedom of establishment (see OJ 1962, p 36 (S Edn (2nd Series) IX, p 7)), the applicant in the main proceedings considers that the location in a member state of the central management and control of a company is sufficient to permit the existence of a 'real and continuous link' (expression borrowed from the General Programme, Title I) with the economy of that state to be presumed, and thus constitutes 'establishment' within the meaning of the Treaty. Conversely, the United Kingdom takes the view that a change of residence by a company does not constitute establishment. It does not necessarily imply a change in the company's economic activities, especially since a company wishing to conduct economic activity in another member state can do so through secondary establishments. Finally, the Commission is of the opinion that it is for national law to determine whether a company may transfer its residence without being wound up. It considers that art 52 applies where national legislation permits a company to transfer its residence without losing its nationality.

7. In my view, the problem should be expressed in different terms. The concept of central management is difficult to pin down. Even where it designates the place at which the board of directors meets, it is not sufficient to provide a satisfactory connecting factor. As has been noted—

'owing to the progress made by means of communication, it is no longer necessary to arrange formal board meetings. The telephone, telex and telecopier enable each director to state his point of view and to take part in the decision-making without being physically present in a given place. The board meetings each director will attend via television will soon form part of company's everyday life. The board of directors can meet in a place chosen arbitrarily, which bears no real relation with the decision centre of the company.'

(See Rivier 'General Report: The Fiscal Residence of Companies' LXXIIa *Studies on International Fiscal Law* 75.)

The place in which the board of directors meets cannot, therefore, constitute the sole criterion making it possible to designate with certainty in each case the place in which the central management is located. That designation cannot be arrived at by means of a formal legal assessment which does not take account of a number of factual elements the respective scope of which may vary according to the type of company involved.

8. In order to determine whether the transfer of the central management and control of a company constitutes establishment within the meaning of the Treaty it is therefore necessary to take into consideration a range of factors. The place at which the management of the company meets is undoubtedly one of the foremost of those factors, as is the place, normally the same, at which general policy decisions are made. However, in certain circumstances those factors may be neither exclusive nor even decisive. It might be necessary to take account of the residence of the principal managers, the place at which general meetings are held, the place at which administrative and accounting documents are kept and the place at which the company's principal financial activities are carried on, in particular, the place at which it operates a bank account. That list cannot be regarded as exhaustive. Moreover, those factors may have to be given different weight according to whether, for example, the company is engaged in production or investment. In the latter case, it may be perfectly legitimate to take account of the market on which the company's commercial or stock exchange transactions are mainly carried out and the scale of those transactions.

9. In the light of the judgment in *Association des Centres distributeurs Édouard Leclerc v Sàrl 'Au blé vert'* Case 229/83 [1985] ECR 1 it is clear that Community law offers no assistance where 'objective factors' show that a particular activity was carried out 'in order to circumvent' national legislation: see *Leclerc*'s case (at 35 (para 27)). The fact that the

essential activities of a company take place on the territory of a member state other than
a that to which it intends to transfer its central management may not be ignored. Such
circumstances may, in certain cases, constitute an indication that what is involved is not
genuine establishment, in particular when the effect of the transfer of the central
management is to cause the company to cease to be subject to legislation which would
otherwise apply to it. I believe that that conclusion can be drawn from the judgments of
the court in *van Binsbergen v Bestuur van de Bedrijfsvereniging voor de Metaalnijverheid* Case
b 33/74 [1974] ECR 1299 and *Knoors v Secretary of State for Economic Affairs* Case 115/78
[1979] ECR 399. As a general rule it appears that the national court may assess whether,
in a specific case and having regard to the circumstances, there is a suggestion of abuse of
a right or circumvention of the law and whether it should decide not to apply Community
law.

10. However, when the proper conclusion to be drawn from the circumstances is that
c the transfer of the central management genuinely constitutes establishment within the
meaning of the Treaty, the question then arises whether the right to make such a transfer
may be made subject to the authorisation of the national authorities and whether those
authorities may object to the transfer for fiscal reasons.

11. Generally, in most of the member states, the transfer of the central management
of a company, in the sense of its real head office, may take place only through the
d winding up of the company and its reconstruction in the host member state. That
solution, the 'legal death' of the company, involves the settlement of its tax position,
determined on the day of the winding up, both in regard to the existing debt and in
regard to matters in respect of which the event normally giving rise to tax liability has
not yet occurred. Capital gains are thus taxed even though no disposition of assets has
taken place. In regard to the member states referred to above, the transfer of the central
e management of a company without loss of legal personality or nationality may take place
under agreements between member states of the kind provided for in art 220 of the
Treaty.

12. No prior authorisation may be required for the exercise of a fundamental freedom
laid down in the Treaty. Similarly, a member state cannot prevent a company from
f exercising its right of establishment on the ground that such exercise entails a loss of
revenue in respect of taxes which would have been due on the basis of the company's
future activities if it had remained subject to the tax laws of that state.

13. However, I consider that, as Community law now stands, member states are not
prevented from requiring a company to settle its fiscal position on any transfer of its
central management, even where winding up is not required. It is generally accepted
that the winding up required by national legislation as a condition for the emigration of
g a company is not contrary to Community law (see *Renauld* p 2.47). It would be
paradoxical if a member state not requiring winding up were to find itself placed by
Community law in a less favourable fiscal position precisely because its legislation on
companies is more consistent with Community objectives in regard to establishment. A
company set up under the legislation of a member state in which 'fiscal allegiance' (this
h expression comes from *Rivier* p 15) is determined in the light of the location of the
central administration will maintain its registered office in that country and continue to
have that country's nationality even after transferring its residence, or, more precisely,
the seat of its management, to another member state. However, for the reasons indicated
above, that does not seem to me, in the present state of Community law, to preclude
national authorities from attaching to such a transfer fiscal consequences similar to those
j of winding up.

14. The guidelines which I propose should enable the court to reply to the first and
third questions referred to it by the Queen's Bench Division of the High Court. They
make a reply to the fourth question unnecessary. The remaining question does not
require any long discussion. Although the first paragraph of art 58 provides that
companies or firms are, for the purposes of the provisions of the Treaty on freedom of

establishment, to be treated in the same way as natural persons who are nationals of
member states, they clearly cannot be placed entirely on the same footing; along with   *a*
the United Kingdom and the Commission, therefore, I consider that EC Council Directive
72/148 does not apply to legal persons.

15. Consequently, I propose that the court should rule that: (1) the transfer to another
member state of the central management of a company may constitute a form of exercise
of the right of establishment, subject to the assessment by the national court of any
elements of fact showing whether or not such a transfer reflects a genuine integration of   *b*
the said company into the economic life of the host member state; (2) under Community
law a member state may not require a company wishing to establish itself in another
member state, by transferring its central management there, to obtain prior authorisation
for such transfer; (3) however, Community law does not prohibit a member state from
requiring a company established on its territory, on establishing itself in another member
state by transferring its central management there, to settle its tax position in regard to   *c*
the part of its assets affected by the transfer, the value of which is to be determined at the
date of transfer; (4) EC Council Directive 73/148 is applicable only to natural persons.

27 September. **THE COURT OF JUSTICE** delivered the following judgment.

1. By an order of 6 February 1987, which was received at the court on 19 March 1987,
the High Court of Justice, Queen's Bench Division, referred to the court for a preliminary   *d*
ruling under art 177 of the EEC Treaty four questions on the interpretation of arts 52
and 58 of the Treaty and EC Council Directive 73/148 of 21 May 1973 on the abolition
of restrictions on movement and residence within the Community for nationals of
member states with regard to establishment and the provision of services.

2. Those questions arose in proceedings between Daily Mail and General Trust plc, the
applicant in the main proceedings (hereinafter referred to as 'the applicant'), and HM   *e*
Treasury for a declaration, inter alia, that the applicant is not required to obtain consent
under United Kingdom tax legislation in order to cease to be resident in the United
Kingdom for the purpose of establishing its residence in the Netherlands.

3. It is apparent from the documents before the court that under United Kingdom
company legislation a company such as the applicant, incorporated under that legislation
and having its registered office in the United Kingdom, may establish its central   *f*
management and control outside the United Kingdom without losing legal personality
or ceasing to be a company incorporated in the United Kingdom.

4. According to the relevant United Kingdom tax legislation, only companies which
are resident for tax purposes in the United Kingdom are as a rule liable to United
Kingdom corporation tax. A company is resident for tax purposes in the place in which
its central management and control is located.   *g*

5. Section 482(1)(a) of the Income and Corporation Taxes Act 1970 prohibits companies
resident for tax purposes in the United Kingdom from ceasing to be so resident without
the consent of the Treasury.

6. In 1984 the applicant, which is an investment holding company, applied for
consent under the above-mentioned national provision in order to transfer its central   *h*
management and control to the Netherlands, whose legislation does not prevent foreign
companies from establishing their central management there; the company proposed, in
particular, to hold board meetings and to rent offices for its management in the
Netherlands. Without waiting for that consent, it subsequently decided to open an
investment management office in the Netherlands with a view to providing services to
third parties.   *j*

7. It is common ground that the principal reason for the proposed transfer of central
management and control was to enable the applicant, after establishing its residence for
tax purposes in the Netherlands, to sell a significant part of its non-permanent assets and
to use the proceeds of that sale to buy its own shares, without having to pay the tax to
which such transactions would make it liable under United Kingdom tax law, in regard

a in particular to the substantial capital gains on the assets which the applicant proposed to sell. After establishing its central management and control in the Netherlands the applicant would be subject to Netherlands corporation tax, but the transactions envisaged would be taxed only on the basis of any capital gains which accrued after the transfer of its residence for tax purposes.

8. After a long period of negotiations with the Treasury, which proposed that it should sell at least part of the assets before transferring its residence for tax purposes out of the *b* United Kingdom, the applicant initiated proceedings before the High Court of Justice, Queen's Bench Division, in 1986. Before that court, it claimed that arts 52 and 58 of the EEC Treaty gave it the right to transfer its central management and control to another member state without prior consent or the right to obtain such consent unconditionally.

9. In order to resolve that dispute, the national court stayed the proceedings and referred the following questions to the Court of Justice:

c
'1. Do Articles 52 and 58 of the EEC Treaty preclude a Member State from prohibiting a body corporate with its central management and control in that Member State from transferring without prior consent or approval that central management and control to another Member State in one or both of the following circumstances, namely where: (i) payment of tax upon profits or gains which have *d* already arisen may be avoided; (ii) were the company to transfer its central management and control, tax that might have become chargeable had the company retained its central management and control in that Member State would be avoided?

2. Does Council Directive 73/148/EEC give a right to a corporate body with its central management and control in a Member State to transfer without prior consent *e* or approval its central management and control to another Member State in the conditions set out in Question 1? If so, are the relevant provisions directly applicable in this case?

3. If such prior consent or approval may be required, is a Member State entitled to refuse consent on the grounds set out in Question 1?

4. What difference does it make, if any, that under the relevant law of the *f* Member State no consent is required in the case of a change of residence to another Member State of an individual or firm?'

10. Reference is made to the report for the hearing for a fuller account of the facts and the background to the main proceedings, the provisions of national legislation at issue and the observations submitted to the court, which are mentioned or discussed hereinafter only in so far as is necessary for the reasoning of the court.
g

First question

11. The first question seeks in essence to determine whether arts 52 and 58 of the Treaty give a company incorporated under the legislation of a member state and having its registered office there the right to transfer its central management and control to *h* another member state. If that is so, the national court goes on to ask whether the member state of origin can make that right subject to the consent of national authorities, the grant of which is linked to the company's tax position.

12. With regard to the first part of the question, the applicant claims essentially that art 58 of the Treaty expressly confers on the companies to which it applies the same right of primary establishment in another member state as is conferred on natural persons by *j* art 52. The transfer of the central management and control of a company to another member state amounts to the establishment of the company in that member state because the company is locating its centre of decision-making there, which constitutes genuine and effective economic activity.

13. The United Kingdom argues essentially that the provisions of the Treaty do not give companies a general right to move their central management and control from one

member state to another. The fact that the central management and control of a company
is located in a member state does not itself necessarily imply any genuine and effective *a*
economic activity on the territory of that member state and cannot therefore be regarded
as establishment within the meaning of art 52 of the Treaty.

14. The Commission emphasises, first of all, that in the present state of Community
law, the conditions under which a company may transfer its central management and
control from one member state to another are still governed by the national law of the
state in which it is incorporated and of the state to which it wishes to move. In that *b*
regard the Commission refers to the differences between the national systems of company
law. Some of them permit the transfer of the central management and control of a
company and, among those, certain attach no legal consequences to such a transfer, even
in regard to taxation. Under other systems the transfer of the management or the centre
of decision-making of a company out of the member state in which it is incorporated
results in the loss of legal personality. However, all the systems permit the winding up *c*
of a company in one member state and its reincorporation in another. The Commission
considers that, where the transfer of central management and control is possible under
national legislation, the right to transfer it to another member state is a right protected
by art 52 of the Treaty.

15. Faced with those diverging opinions, the court must first point out, as it has done
on numerous occasions, that freedom of establishment constitutes one of the fundamental *d*
principles of the Community and that the provisions of the Treaty guaranteeing that
freedom have been directly applicable since the end of the transitional period. Those
provisions secure the right of establishment in another member state not merely for
Community nationals but also for the companies referred to in art 58.

16. Even though those provisions are directed mainly to ensuring that foreign
nationals and companies are treated in the host member state in the same way as nationals *e*
of that state, they also prohibit the member state of origin from hindering the
establishment in another member state of one of its nationals or of a company
incorporated under its legislation which comes within the definition contained in art 58.
As the Commission rightly observed, the rights guaranteed by art 52 ff would be
rendered meaningless if the member state of origin could prohibit undertakings from *f*
leaving in order to establish themselves in another member state. In regard to natural
persons, the right to leave their territory for that purpose is expressly provided for EC
Council Directive 73/148, which is the subject of the second question referred to the
court.

17. In the case of a company, the right of establishment is generally exercised by the
setting up of agencies, branches or subsidiaries, as is expressly provided for in the second *g*
sentence of the first paragraph of art 52. Indeed, that is the form of establishment in
which the applicant engaged in this case by opening an investment management office
in the Netherlands. A company may also exercise its right of establishment by taking
part in the incorporation of a company in another member state, and in that regard
art 221 of the Treaty ensures that it will receive the same treatment as nationals of that
member state as regards participation in the capital of the new company. *h*

18. The provision of United Kingdom law at issue in the main proceedings imposes
no restriction on transactions such as those described above. Nor does it stand in the way
of a partial or total transfer of the activities of a company incorporated in the United
Kingdom to a company newly incorporated in another member state, if necessary after
winding up and, consequently, the settlement of the tax position of the United Kingdom
company. It requires Treasury consent only where such a company seeks to transfer its *j*
central management and control out of the United Kingdom while maintaining its legal
personality and its status as a United Kingdom company.

19. In that regard it should be borne in mind that, unlike natural persons, companies
are creatures of the law and, in the present state of Community law, creatures of national

law. They exist only by virtue of the varying national legislation which determines their
a incorporation and functioning.

20. As the Commission has emphasised, the legislation of the member states varies
widely in regard to both the factor providing a connection to the national territory
required for the incorporation of a company and the question whether a company
incorporated under the legislation of a member state may subsequently modify that
connecting factor. Certain states require that not merely the registered office but also the
b real head office, that is to say the central administration of the company, should be
situated on their territory, and the removal of the central administration from that
territory thus presupposes the winding up of the company with all the consequences that
winding up entails in company law and tax law. The legislation of other states permits
companies to transfer their central administration to a foreign country but certain of
them, such as the United Kingdom, make that right subject to certain restrictions, and
c the legal consequences of a transfer, particularly in regard to taxation, vary from one
member state to another.

21. The Treaty has taken account of that variety in national legislation. In defining, in
art 58, the companies which enjoy the right of establishment, the Treaty places on the
same footing, as connecting factors, the registered office, central administration and
principal place of business of a company. Moreover, art 220 of the Treaty provides for
d the conclusion, so far as is necessary, of agreements between the member states with a
view to securing, inter alia, the retention of legal personality in the event of transfer of
the registered office of companies from one country to another. No convention in this
area has yet come into force.

22. It should be added that none of the directives on the co-ordination of company
law adopted under art 54(3)(g) of the Treaty deal with the differences at issue here.
e 23. It must therefore be held that the Treaty regards the differences in national
legislation concerning the required connecting factor and the question whether, and if
so how, the registered office or real head office of a company incorporated under national
law may be transferred from one member state to another as problems which are not
resolved by the rules concerning the right of establishment but must be dealt with by
f future legislation or conventions.

24. Under those circumstances, arts 52 and 58 of the Treaty cannot be interpreted as
conferring on companies incorporated under the law of a member state a right to transfer
their central management and control and their central administration to another
member state while retaining their status as companies incorporated under the legislation
of the first member state.

g 25. The answer to the first part of the first question must therefore be that in the
present state of Community law arts 52 and 58 of the Treaty, properly construed, confer
no right on a company incorporated under the legislation of a member state and having
its registered office there to transfer its central management and control to another
member state.

26. Having regard to that answer, there is no need to reply to the second part of the
h first question.

Second question

27. In its second question, the national court asks whether the provisions of EC
Council Directive 73/148 of 21 May 1973 on the abolition of restrictions on movement
and residence within the Community for nationals of member states with regard to
j establishment and the provision of services give a company a right to transfer its central
management and control to another member state.

28. It need merely be pointed out in that regard that the title and provisions of that
directive refer solely to the movement and residence of natural persons and that the
provisions of the directive cannot, by their nature, be applied by analogy to legal persons.

29. The answer to the second question must therefore be that EC Council Directive
73/148, properly construed, confers no right on a company to transfer its central *a*
management and control to another member state.

Third and fourth questions

30. Having regard to the answers given to the first two questions referred by the
national court, there is no need to reply to the third and fourth questions.

b

Costs

31. The costs incurred by the United Kingdom and the Commission of the European
Communities, which have submitted observations to the court, are not recoverable.
Since these proceedings are, in so far as the parties to the main proceedings are concerned,
in the nature of a step in the action pending before the national court, the decision on
costs is a matter for that court.

c

On those grounds, the court, in answer to the questions referred to it by the High
Court of Justice, Queen's Bench Division, by order of 6 February 1987, hereby rules: (1)
in the present state of Community law, arts 52 and 58 of the EEC Treaty, properly
construed, confer no right on a company incorporated under the legislation of a member
state and having its registered office there to transfer its central management and control *d*
to another member state; (2) EC Council Directive 73/148 of 21 May 1973 on the
abolition of restrictions on movement and residence within the Community for nationals
of member states with regard to establishment and the provision of services, properly
construed, confers no right on a company to transfer its central management and control
to another member state.

e

Agents: *Freshfields* (for Daily Mail and General Trust plc); *Susan Hay*, Treasury Solicitor's
Department (for the United Kingdom); *D R Gilmour*, Legal Adviser, EC Commission (for
the Commission).

Rengan Krishnan Esq   Barrister.

a

Barrett v Lounova (1982) Ltd

COURT OF APPEAL, CIVIL DIVISION
KERR LJ AND SWINTON THOMAS J
20, 22 JUNE 1988

b *Landlord and tenant – Repair – Landlord's covenant – Implication of repairing covenant – Implication necessary to give business efficacy to tenancy agreement – Express covenant by tenant to repair inside of premises – Agreement silent on obligation to repair outside – Whether covenant by landlord to repair outside correlative to tenant's obligation to repair inside should be implied.*

c *Negligence – Defective premises – Landlord's duty of care by virtue of obligation to repair – Enforcement of duty – Injunction requiring landlord to repair premises – Defective Premises Act 1972, s 4(1).*

The tenancy agreement of a terrace house contained a covenant by the tenant to keep the inside of the premises in good repair. The agreement did not contain any covenant by either the landlord or the tenant to keep the outside of the premises in repair. Over the d years the outside of the house fell into a bad state of disrepair, and the tenant alleged that as a result of that disrepair there was extensive water penetration causing damage to the interior of the house. The tenant brought an action against the landlord claiming damages and specific performance of the agreed repairs, on the grounds (i) that there was an implied covenant by the landlord to keep the outside of the house in repair or alternatively, (ii) that the landlord was in breach of the duty of care owed to her under e s 4(1)[a] of the Defective Premises Act 1972. The judge held that a covenant by the landlord to repair the outside of the premises was to be implied into the agreement and, accordingly, he awarded the tenant agreed damages for breach of that covenant and specific performance by the landlord of an agreed schedule of dilapidations. The landlord appealed.

f **Held** – An obligation on a landlord to repair the outside of premises could be implied into a tenancy agreement where it was necessary to do so to give business efficacy to the agreement. Accordingly, where a tenancy agreement contained an express covenant by the tenant to keep the inside of the premises in repair but was silent as to any obligation to repair the outside, and the tenant's covenant was intended to be enforceable throughout the tenancy and could not be properly performed unless the outside was kept in repair, g an obligation by the landlord to repair the outside, correlative to the tenant's obligation to repair the inside, could be implied in order to give business efficacy to the agreement. In all the circumstances, such a term would be implied. The appeal would therefore be dismissed (see p 356 j to p 357 e g and p 358 g h, post).
Dicta of Ormerod and Willmer LJJ in *Sleafer v Lambeth Metropolitan BC* [1959] 3 All ER 378 at 386, 388 and of Slade LJ in *Duke of Westminster v Guild* [1984] 3 All ER 144 at 149 h applied.
Hart v Windsor [1843–60] All ER Rep 681 considered.
Dictum of Bankes LJ in *Cockburn v Smith* [1924] All ER Rep 59 at 62 disapproved.
Per Kerr LJ. There is no reason why an injunction should not issue to enforce a landlord's duty under s 4(1) of the 1972 Act where there is appropriate evidence to support such an injunction (see p 358 d h, post).

j

Notes
For a landlord's liability to repair apart from express covenant, see 27 Halsbury's Laws

---

a   Section 4, so far as material, is set out at p 357 h j, post

(4th edn) para 264, and for cases on the subject, see 31(2) Digest (Reissue) 596–599, 4863–
4876.   a
    For the Defective Premises Act 1972, s 4, see 31 Halsbury's Statutes (4th edn) 199.

Cases referred to in judgments
Cockburn v Smith [1924] 2 KB 119, [1924] All ER Rep 59, CA.
De Falco v Crawley BC [1980] 1 All ER 913, [1980] QB 460, [1980] 2 WLR 664, CA.
Hart v Windsor (1844) 12 M & W 68, [1843–60] All ER Rep 681, 152 ER 1114.   b
Liverpool City Council v Irwin [1976] 2 All ER 39, [1977] AC 239, [1976] 2 WLR 562, HL.
Sleafer v Lambeth Metropolitan BC [1959] 3 All ER 378, [1960] 1 QB 43, [1959] 3 WLR
    485, CA.
Smith v Bradford Metropolitan Council (1982) 44 P & CR 171, CA.
Warren v Keen [1953] 2 All ER 1118, [1954] 1 QB 15, [1959] 3 WLR 702, CA.
Westminster (Duke) v Guild [1984] 3 All ER 144, [1985] QB 688, [1984] 3 WLR 630, CA.   c
Wilchick v Marks and Silverstone (Silverstone, third party) [1934] 2 KB 56, [1934] All ER
    Rep 73.

Appeal
The defendant, Lounova (1982) Ltd (the landlord), appealed against the decision of Mr
Recorder Desmond Keane QC on 10 December 1987 in the Shoreditch County Court   d
whereby, in an action brought by the plaintiff, Elsie Mary Barrett (the tenant), claiming
by recommended particulars of claim dated 10 December 1987 damages limited to
£2,000, interest thereon and an order of specific performance compelling the landlord to
execute such works as were necessary to remedy specified defects or damages in lieu
thereof limited to the cast of executing and supervising the works, he held that there was
to be implied in the tenancy agreement between the landlord and the tenant, a term that   e
the landlord was bound to keep the outside of the tenant's premises at 70 Lansdowne
Drive, London E8 in reasonable repair and gave judgment for the tenant for the agreed
sum of £1,250 damages, inclusive of interest, and ordered the landlord to carry out the
repairs itemised in an agreed schedule of repairs within six months from 10 December
1987. The facts are set out in the judgment of Kerr LJ.   f

Robert Pryor QC and Simon Monty for the landlord.
Derek Wood QC and Martin Seaward for the tenant.

KERR LJ. This is an appeal from a decision of Mr Recorder Desmond Keane QC in the
Shoreditch County Court given on 10 December 1987. The case concerns an end of   g
terrace house in the East End of London in the borough of Hackney, 70 Lansdowne
Drive, London E8, which has been occupied under the Rent Acts since 1941. The outside
of the premises is in a bad state of repair and dilapidated; probably no work has been
done to it for decades.
    The issue is whether the landlord is bound to repair the outside. The tenancy contained
a covenant that the tenant should keep the inside in good repair and it gives the landlord   h
access for any reasonable purpose. But there is no express obligation on anyone to keep
the outside in repair. The recorder held that a term was to be implied, correlative to the
tenant's obligation, to the effect that the landlord would keep the outside in a reasonable
state of repair. There is also, in the alternative, an issue under s 4 of the Defective
Premises Act 1972, but the main issue on this appeal has been whether a term can be
implied as the recorder has held.   j
    I turn to the tenancy agreement. This was made on 5 April 1941 between a Mr Frank
Hayllar of Brighton, described as a solicitor, as 'the landlord', and a Mr Albert Edward
Arbon of Dalston, described as a bread baker, as 'the tenant'. It demised the house
together with the landlord's fixtures in and about the premises—

    'From the twelfth day of April [1941] for the term of One year certain and *a*   thereafter on a monthly tenancy At the yearly rent of Seventy eight pounds such rent to be payable weekly in advance on Monday in each week the first payment of One pound ten shillings to be made on the signing hereof.'

There followed the covenant to pay the rent; I need not read that. But I must read the following one:

b   'THE Tenant hereby agrees . . . To do all inside repairs (if any) now required and to keep and at the expiration of the tenancy to leave the inside of the said premises and fixtures in good repair order and condition but fair wear and tear to be allowed at the end of the tenancy.'

Next the tenant agreed:

c   'TO permit the Landlord and his agents to enter at all reasonable times upon the said premises and for all reasonable purposes.'

Then I can go on to the tenant's agreement:

'NOT without . . . consent . . . to make any alterations in or addition to the said premises [and] NOT to carry on any trade or business upon the said premises or use the same otherwise than as a private dwellinghouse.'

d
The only relevant agreement on the part of the landlord was that the tenant should be entitled to quiet possession in the usual way and that the landlord would pay all rates and taxes payable in respect of the premises so long as the tenant performed his part of the agreement and paid all moneys due from him punctually.

The whole agreement must of course be construed by reference to the circumstances *e* as they existed at the conclusion of the contract. The recorder referred to some allowances in the early rent books in evidence, which had evidently been made by the landlord for minor external work done by the tenant, as being consistent with his conclusion that the landlord was under an obligation to repair, though rightly not as any aid to the construction of the agreement. I put that matter out of my mind.

The plaintiff (the tenant) occupies the house as the result of two transmissions under *f* the Rent Acts. After the death of the original tenant the tenancy was transmitted to his widow and I understand that the plaintiff is her daughter. So far as the landlord company is concerned, it is not known when it acquired this freehold. To complete the history, more for historical than for any other purposes, the rent has now gone up to £15 per week.

Complaints from the tenant about the state of disrepair of this property began in May *g* 1985, and proceeded with a solicitors' letter in August 1985. There was then a surveyors' report with further chasers which were sent more or less throughout 1986. Ultimately there was some response from the landlord and an inspection was carried out on its behalf. But recently the landlord changed its mind and claimed that on the true construction of the agreement there was no obligation to repair.

The particulars of claim were issued on 20 March 1987. Under the heading 'PARTICULARS *h* OF DEFECTS' they include the following:

'The structure and exterior, including the drains and gutters, of the premises is in such poor condition as to cause extensive water penetration and damage to the internal plaster and timbers.'

j   Then there is reference to a survey report which sets out the defects in detail.

There was also (by the amended particulars of claim) a claim in the alternative under the Defective Premises Act 1972, to which I shall come later.

The defence was simply a denial of liability on all counts.

In the course of the hearing it was agreed that the tenant was entitled to damages in the sum of £1,250 subject to liability. These were to cover special as well as general damages, damages for inconvenience, damage caused to the contents by damp and so forth.   *a*

A fairly comprehensive schedule of dilapidations was also agreed, on the basis of what a repairing covenant by the landlord, if one were to be implied, would require to be done to the premises. The cost was estimated at about £10,000.

As I have mentioned, the recorder took the view that such a covenant should be implied. He accordingly gave judgment for the sum of £1,250 and ordered specific performance of the terms of the schedule agreed between the surveyors, to be carried out   *b* within six months from 10 December 1987, the date of his order. He granted a stay of 21 days for the purposes of an appeal, but only subject to the payment of £5,000 into court within seven days.

Apart from giving notice of appeal, the landlord did nothing at all in relation to that order and it was rightly conceded on its behalf that the company was clearly in contempt of court.   *c*

When the time for the hearing of this appeal approached, a few days after the expiry of the six-month period on 10 June, it appears that a builder was sent to the premises, but without any prior notice, and not surprisingly he was not admitted by the tenant in those circumstances. Moreover, the sum of £5,000 was not brought into court. Accordingly, we declined to proceed with the appeal unless and until £5,000 was brought into court. That was done last Monday, the day on which we heard this appeal, and the   *d* sum was duly paid into the Shoreditch County Court.

Against that background I turn to the issue whether or not there is to be implied a term to the effect that the landlord was bound to keep the outside in reasonable repair, as the recorder decided. In that regard it is common ground that he directed himself correctly when he said:
                                                                                              e
> 'Clearly on the authorities the law does not permit the court to imply terms
> merely on the basis that implication would seem to be reasonable or fair. In essence,
> what is required before such implication is made is either a situation where the
> parties to the agreement, if asked about the suggested implied term, would have
> said words such as, "Oh yes, of course we both agree. Is there any need to mention
> it?" or where it is not merely desirable but necessary to imply such a term to give   *f*
> business efficacy or in other words necessary to make the contract workable, which
> amounts to the same thing.'

Those two ways of putting the test whether or not a term should be implied, sometimes referred to as 'the officious bystander test' and the 'business efficacy test', are of course correct. But whether or not, on applying those tests, the implication falls to be made is not easy, and the authorities are of no direct assistance.   *g*

The landlord relied strongly on a well-known passage in *Woodfall on Landlord and Tenant* (28th edn, 1978) para 1–1465, in the following terms:

> 'In general, there is no implied covenant by the lessor of an unfurnished house or
> flat, or of land, that it is or shall be reasonably fit for habitation, occupation or
> cultivation; or for any other purpose for which it is let. No covenant is implied that   *h*
> the lessor will do any repairs whatever . . .'

The first authority cited was the old case of *Hart v Windsor* (1844) 12 M & W 68, [1843–60] All ER Rep 681. There there was a full tenant's repairing covenant of a house, but he declined to pay the rent because the house was bug-infested to such an extent that he said it was unfit for human habitation. That plea was rejected. Parke B, giving the judgment   *j* of the court, said (12 M & W 68 at 87–88, [1843–60] All ER Rep 681 at 685):

> 'We are all of opinion . . . that there is no contract, still less a condition, implied
> by law on the demise of real property only, that it is fit for the purpose for which it
> is let. The principles of the common law do not warrant such a position; and
> though, in the case of a dwelling-house taken for habitation, there is no apparent

a injustice in inferring a contract of this nature, the same rule must apply to land taken for other purposes—for building upon, or for cultivation; and there would be no limit to the inconvenience which would ensue. It is much better to leave the parties in every case to protect their interests themselves, by proper stipulations, and if they really mean a lease to be void by reason of any unfitness in the subject for the purpose intended, they should express that meaning.'

b Secondly, there is an even stronger passage in a dictum of Bankes J in *Cockburn v Smith* [1924] 2 KB 119, [1924] All ER Rep 59, a decision of this court. The owner of a block of flats had let one of the top flats but had kept the roof of the building and the guttering in his own possession and control. The guttering became defective, water escaped and wetted the tenant's outside wall and so caused damage to the inside. Not surprisingly, it was held that since the landlord had retained control of the guttering he was under a *c* duty to take reasonable care to remedy any defects in it of which he had notice and which were a source of damage. Those facts, of course, do not apply here, but in an obiter dictum Bankes LJ said ([1924] 2 KB 119 at 128, [1924] All ER Rep 59 at 62):

'I want to make it plain at the outset that this is not a letting of the whole house where, without an express covenant or a statutory obligation to repair, the landlords *d* would clearly be under no liability to repair any part of the demised premises whether the required repairs were structural or internal and whether they had or had not notice of the want of repair.'

That statement was not only obiter, but if it purported to lay down any general rule that no repairing covenant could arise by implication then, with all respect, it clearly went *e* too far, as shown by later cases.

Finally in this context the landlord relied on the decision of Goddard J in *Wilchick v Marks and Silverstone (Silverstone, third party)* [1934] 2 KB 56, [1934] All ER Rep 73. But implication derived from the true construction of the terms of the letting was not raised in argument in that case. It was also not dealt with by the judge since no relevant implication could have been derived from the terms of that particular instrument.

f I turn now to the more recent cases. They show that there is no rule of law against the implication of any repairing covenant against landlords and that the ordinary principles of construction concerning implied terms apply to leases in that context as they apply generally in the law of contract. That is illustrated, but in a very different context, by the decision of the House of Lords in *Liverpool City Council v Irwin* [1976] 2 All ER 39, [1977] AC 239. I need not refer to that case, but I should mention two other cases, both decisions *g* of this court, which show that implication of a landlord's repairing covenant is a permissible approach if the terms of the agreement and circumstances justify it.

The first is *Sleafer v Lambeth Metropolitan BC* [1959] 3 All ER 378, [1960] 1 QB 43. That was an extraordinary case, in which the tenant found that he was unable to open his front door due to a minor defect which caused it to jam. So he pulled hard on the only external handle, the letterbox knocker. That came off, and he fell backwards against an iron *h* balustrade and suffered injury to his back. He sued the landlord for allowing the door to get into that state. Perhaps not surprisingly, it was held that in relation to a minor defect of that kind no question of any obligation on the landlord could arise. It is also to be noted that the lease provided, by cl 2, that the tenant was to reside in the dwelling, that is to say, in the same way as here, that it was not to be used for any business purposes, and by cl 9 the tenant was not to do, or to allow to be done, any decorateve or other work *j* without the landlord's consent in writing. In rejecting the tenant's claim against the landlord, Morris LJ, who gave the first judgment, quoted the passages in *Hart v Windsor* and *Cockburn v Smith* which I have already set out (see [1959] 3 All ER 378 at 383, [1960] 1 QB 43 at 55). But I do not think that he said anything about the possibility of implying a term dealing with repairs. However, that was dealt with by Ormerod LJ in a passage which I must read ([1959] 3 All ER 378 at 386, [1960] 1 QB 43 at 60):

'When this matter was argued before the learned judge, it was contended by
counsel for the landlords that in no circumstances could a condition be implied that   *a*
the landlords should be under an obligation to repair. The learned judge dealt with
that in this way: "Although I cannot follow counsel for the tenant in saying that the
mere fact that the landlords have reserved the right to do repairs means that an
obligation is imposed on them, I cannot agree with counsel for the landlords when
he says that the absence of some express term in the tenancy, whether oral or in
writing, means that a contractual duty on the landlords to do the repairs can never   *b*
arise—in other words, that such term can never be implied. I am not sure that that
is right; I am not prepared to say that circumstances may not arise in which a court
could find itself impelled to imply such terms in a tenancy agreement." Without
having to decide that question, as at present advised, I should certainly agree with
the learned judge. A tenancy agreement, like any other agreement, must be read as
a whole, and it may very well be that in construing the agreement it is possible to   *c*
imply an obligation on the landlords to do repairs, but the question for the learned
judge and for this court to decide was whether such an obligation could be implied
in this particular agreement.'

That is equally the issue which arises on the present appeal.

Wilmer LJ said ([1959] 3 All ER 378 at 388, [1960] 1 QB 43 at 63):   *d*

'There is much to be said for the view that cl. 2 of the agreement, which requires
the tenant to reside in the dwelling-house, does by implication require the landlords
to do such repairs as may make it possible for the tenant to carry out that obligation.
At least it seems to me that that is a possible view.'

Then he said that, even if that view be right, in his judgment the obligation would not   *e*
extend to cover the type of repairs which fell to be considered in that case, which was no
more than easing the bottom of the jammed door. He said in that regard ([1959] 3 All
ER 378 at 388, [1960] 1 QB 43 at 63):

'Wherever the line is drawn, even assuming that counsel for the tenant is right in
saying that some obligation on the part of the landlords to execute repairs must be
implied, I should have thought that that line must be drawn well short of including   *f*
responsibility for such a trivial repair as the unsticking of this door.'

Finally, there is a recent decision of this court in *Duke of Westminster v Guild* [1984] 3
All ER 144, [1985] QB 688, in which the judgment was delivered by Slade LJ. He
referred to two decisions in which an obligation on landlords had been implied to do
certain work, in the first case the cleaning of the common parts of the premises and in   *g*
the second painting the premises (see [1984] 3 All ER 144 at 149, [1985] QB 688, 696–
697). These obligations were implied from terms imposed on the tenants to pay for the
cost of a cleaner in the first case and for the cost of the necessary paint in the second. The
position in those cases was of course far stronger than here. Before quoting the general
proposition from *Woodfall on Landlord and Tenant* (28th edn, 1978) para 1–1465, which I
have already set out, Slade LJ said ([1984] 3 All ER 144 at 149, [1985] QB 688 at 697):   *h*

'We do not question the correctness of these two decisions on their particular
facts, or doubt that in some instances it will be proper for the court to imply an
obligation against a landlord, on whom an obligation is not in terms imposed by the
relevant lease, to match a correlative obligation thereby expressly imposed on the
other party. Nevertheless we think that only rather limited assistance is to be derived   *j*
from these earlier cases where obligations have been implied.'

Then he referred to the proposition in *Woodfall* which I have read.

So it follows that a repairing obligation on the landlord can clearly arise as a matter of
implication. But that leaves the question already mentioned, which I find difficult and

on the borderline, whether the terms and circumstances of this particular lease enable
a such an implication to be made. As to that, although I have not found this an easy case, I
agree with the conclusion of the recorder. In my view the clue lies in what Slade LJ
referred to as a 'correlative obligation', in this case one which is correlative to the express
covenant by the tenant to keep the inside and fixtures in good repair, order and condition.

The considerations which lead me to that conclusion are the following. It is obvious,
as shown by this case itself, that sooner or later the covenant imposed on the tenant in
b respect of the inside can no longer be complied with unless the outside has been kept in
repair. Moreover, it is also clear that the covenant imposed on the tenant was intended to
be enforceable throughout the tenancy. For instance, it could not possibly be contended
that it would cease to be enforceable if the outside fell into disrepair. In my view it is
therefore necessary, as a matter of business efficacy to make this agreement workable,
that an obligation to keep the outside in repair must be imposed on someone. For myself,
c I would reject the persuasive submission of counsel for the landlord that both parties
may have thought that in practice the landlord (or possibly the tenant) would do the
necessary repairs, so that no problem would arise. In my view that is not a businesslike
construction of a tenancy agreement. Accordingly, on the basis that an obligation to keep
the outside in a proper state of repair must be imposed on someone, three answers are
possible.

d   First, that the tenant is obliged to keep the outside in repair as well as the inside, at any
rate to such extent as may be necessary to enable him to perform his covenant. I would
reject that as being unbusinesslike and unrealistic. In the case of a tenancy of this nature,
which was to become a monthly tenancy after one year, the rent being paid weekly, it is
clearly unrealistic to conclude that this could have been the common intention. In that
context it is to be noted that in *Warren v Keen* [1953] 2 All ER 1118, [1954] 1 QB 15 this
e court held that a weekly tenant was under no implied obligation to do any repairs to the
structure of the premises due to wear and tear or lapse of time or otherwise and that it
was doubtful whether he was even obliged to ensure that the premises remained wind
and watertight. Any construction which casts on the tenant the obligation to keep the
outside in proper repair must in my view be rejected for these reasons, and also because
there is an express tenant's covenant relating to the inside, so that it would be wrong, as a
f matter of elementary construction, to imply a covenant relating to the outside as well.

The second solution would be the implication of a joint obligation on both parties to
keep the outside in good repair. I reject that as being obviously unworkable and I do not
think that counsel for the landlord really suggested the contrary.

That leaves one with the third solution, an implied obligation on the landlord. In my
view this is the only solution which makes business sense. The recorder reached the same
g conclusion by following much the same route, and I agree with him. Accordingly I
would dismiss this appeal.

However, for the sake of completeness I should also refer briefly to the alternative
claim under s 4 of the Defective Premises Act 1972, with which the recorder also dealt.
Section 4 is in the following terms:

h   '(1) Where premises are let under a tenancy which puts on the landlord an
obligation to the tenant for the maintenance or repair of the premises, the landlord
owes to all persons who might reasonably be expected to be affected by defects in
the state of the premises a duty to take such care as is reasonable in all the
circumstances to see that they are reasonably safe from personal injury or from
damage to their property caused by a relevant defect . . .

j   (4) Where premises are let under a tenancy which expressly or impliedly gives
the landlord the right to enter the premises to carry out any description of
maintenance or repair of the premises, then, as from the time when he first is, or by
notice or otherwise can put himself, in a position to exercise the right and so long as
he is or can put himself in that position, he shall be treated for the purposes of

subsections (1) to (3) above (but for no other purpose) as if he were under an
obligation to the tenant for that description of maintenance or repair of the *a*
premises . . .'

The recorder held that the effect of sub-s (4) read together with sub-s (1) of s 4 and, in
the present case, with the express right of entry for any reasonable purpose granted to
the landlord was that the landlord owed a duty of care under s 4(1) and was in breach of
it, and that this enured to the benefit of the tenant as well as third parties.

Originally the landlord had appealed against that conclusion. But that was rightly *b*
dropped, having regard in particular to the decision of this court in *Smith v Bradford
Metropolitan Council* (1982) 44 P & CR 171, where it was held that the reference to 'any
person' in s 4(1) could include the tenant himself.

The sum of £1,250 by way of damages, which I have already mentioned, had been
agreed also to cover any liability, as is now conceded, owed to the tenant under the 1972 *c*
Act. But the schedule of dilapidations had not been agreed with reference to the limited
scope of the statutory duty. In those circumstances it was conceded below by counsel for
the tenant (not Mr Derek Wood QC who appeared on this appeal) that no injunction
could issue under the Act compelling the landlord to carry out any repairs. On the
present state of the evidence that is clearly right. But on proper evidence and proper
considerations whether or not an injunction should issue there is no reason, of principle *d*
or jurisdiction, why an injunction to enforce obligations under s 4(1) of the 1972 Act
should not issue in appropriate circumstances. In that context there was a brief reference
to the decision of this court in *De Falco v Crawley BC* [1980] 1 All ER 913, [1980] QB 460.

If this appeal had been allowed instead of being dismissed, we would accordingly have
remitted the matter to the Shoreditch County Court to deal with the alternative claim
under the 1972 Act for the purpose, not of recovering damages, which are already *e*
covered by the agreement which was made, but to enable the tenant to apply for an
injunction under the 1972 Act if so advised. However, since we are agreed that this
appeal fails, that aspect falls away.

It follows that in my view the tenant is entitled to the agreed damages and to an
injunction, once again in mandatory terms, to compel the landlord to carry out the work
in the agreed schedule of dilapidations. In relation to that we shall have to hear counsel *f*
as to a timetable which, having regard to the lamentable history, should be stringent.

For those reasons I would dismiss this appeal.

SWINTON THOMAS J. I confess that my mind has waivered in the course of the
extremely persuasive submissions that have been presented to us on this appeal. Like the
judge below I do not find the central point that arises in the appeal easy, but in the end I *g*
have been wholly persuaded that in order to give business efficacy to this tenancy
agreement it is necessary to imply the term set out by Kerr LJ in his judgment.

I am also persuaded that if the parties had been asked, in April 1941, whether such a
term should be included in this particular tenancy agreement, which provides that the
tenant shall be responsible for internal repairs, they would immediately and without
hesitation have agreed that it should be so included. *h*

Accordingly, and for the reasons that have been given by Kerr LJ, I too would dismiss
this appeal.

*Appeal dismissed. Injunction to continue for work to be completed within four months from 22
June 1988. £5,000 to remain in court until order complied with. Leave to appeal to House of
Lords refused.* *j*

Solicitors: *Bernstein & Co* (for the landlord); *Geo J Dowse & Co* (for the tenant).

Wendy Shockett   Barrister.

Lui Mei-lin v R

PRIVY COUNCIL
LORD KEITH OF KINKEL, LORD ROSKILL, LORD TEMPLEMAN, LORD ACKNER AND LORD JAUNCEY OF
TULLICHETTLE
25 JULY, 24 OCTOBER 1988

Criminal evidence – Co-accused – Cross-examination – Previous inconsistent statement – Co-accused's inconsistent statement excluded – Whether defendant having right to cross-examine co-accused on excluded statement.

A witness may be cross-examined as to any previous inconsistent statement made by him in writing or which is reduced to writing subject, where the inconsistent statement is said to be in writing, to his attention first being called to those parts of the written statement which are to be used to contradict him. Where a co-accused wishes to cross-examine another co-accused on a previously excluded statement, he has an unfettered right to do so and the only limit on that right is relevancy (se p 362 *c* to *e* and p 363 *c d*, post).

Dicta of Devlin J in *R v Miller* [1952] 2 All ER 667 at 668–669, of Lord Donovan in *Murdoch v Taylor* [1965] 1 All ER 406 at 416 and *R v Rowson* [1985] 2 All ER 539 adopted.
Dictum of Humphreys J in *R v Treacy* [1944] 2 All ER 229 at 236 explained.
Yu Tit-hoi v R [1983] HKLR 7 overruled.

Notes
For evidence by a defendant as to the character of a co-defendant, see 11 Halsbury's Laws (4th edn) para 371, and for a case on the subject, see 14(2) Digest (Reissue) 502, *4113*.

Cases referred to in judgment
Murdoch v Taylor [1965] 1 All ER 406, [1965] AC 574, [1965] 2 WLR 425, HL.
R v Miller [1952] 2 All ER 667, Assizes.
R v Rice [1963] 1 All ER 832, [1963] 1 QB 857, [1963] 2 WLR 585, CCA.
R v Rowson [1985] 2 All ER 539, [1986] QB 174, [1985] 3 WLR 99, CA.
R v Treacy [1944] 2 All ER 229, CCA.
Yu Tit-hoi v R [1983] HKLR 7, Hong Kong CA.

Appeal
Lui Mei-lin appealed with the special leave of the Judicial Committee of the Privy Council granted by an Order in Council dated 18 December 1987 against the decision of the Court of Appeal of Hong Kong (Yang ACJ, Kempster and Power JJA) on 25 June 1987 dismissing her application for leave to appeal against her conviction on 23 January 1987 in the High Court of Hong Kong before Deputy Judge Ryan and a jury on two counts of forgery. The facts are set out in the judgment of the Board.

Desmond Keane QC and *Paul Storey* for the appellant.
The Director of Public Prosecutions of Hong Kong (J K Findlay QC) and *Ross Dalgleish* (of the Hong Kong Bar) for the Crown.

At the conclusion of the argument the Board announced that the appeal should be allowed and the conviction quashed for reasons to be given later.

24 October. The following judgment of the Board was delivered.

LORD ROSKILL. At the conclusion of the hearing of this appeal on 25 July 1988 their Lordships stated that they would humbly advise Her Majesty that the appellant's appeal should be allowed and her conviction on 23 January 1987 in the High Court of Hong Kong on two counts of forgery quashed and that their Lordships' reasons for that advice would be given in due course. Their Lordships now give those reasons.

The appellant was one of three defendants jointly charged on two counts (the first and second counts in the indictment), one of having forged dies with intent to defraud, the other of having forged valuable securities. The first defendant was named Liu Kan-por. The appellant was the third defendant. Yick Hak-kan was the second defendant. Yick Wai-ming was the fourth defendant. The third and fourth counts in the indictment were against the second defendant alone, while a fifth count was against the first defendant alone. The first defendant, the appellant and the fourth defendant were all convicted on counts one and two. The second defendant was acquitted on counts three and four. The first defendant was also convicted on the fifth count. Substantial prison sentences were imposed on all three defendants so convicted. Subsequent appeals to the Court of Appeal by the first and fourth defendants against their convictions on counts one and two succeeded on the ground of misdirection by the trial judge. Retrials were ordered. The appellant's appeal against her convictions was dismissed.

The issue involved in the appellant's appeal to the Court of Appeal and now to this Board is entirely different from the issues involved in the appeals by the other defendants. On 11 June 1986 the first defendant was interviewed by and made a statement to the police. That statement, which their Lordships have read, beyond doubt incriminated the appellant. The prosecution sought to adduce that statement in evidence against its maker, the first defendant. The admissibility of the statement was challenged. At the outset of the trial a voir dire was held to determine whether or not the statement had been made voluntarily. The trial judge held that the statement was made as a result of inducements by a police officer. He accordingly excluded the statement on the ground that it was not made voluntarily. The first defendant in due course gave evidence in his own defence. He admitted that he had taken part in the arrangements for printing stamps, but had done so innocently, having been misled by the appellant. He was cross-examined on behalf of the second and fourth defendants. There is no doubt that his oral evidence differed in a number of material respects (the details do not now matter), from what he had said in the excluded statement. The appellant's counsel naturally cross-examined the first defendant on the basis that the oral evidence was false. He sought the leave of the trial judge further to cross-examine the first defendant on the excluded statement as being an inconsistent statement previously made by the first defendant. Counsel for the Crown opposed the application, relying on a previous decision of the Court of Appeal in *Yu Tit-hoi v R* [1983] HKLR 7. The trial judge was of course bound by that decision and refused the application for leave to cross-examine the first defendant on his statement. A further application on behalf of the appellant for a separate trial was also refused.

When the appellant appealed to the Court of Appeal that court also held that the appeal must fail because it too was bound by the decision in *Yu Tit-hoi v R* and indeed by later decisions following that decision. Power JA in a separate judgment, while accepting that the court was so bound, expressed the view that it was 'unfortunate that [the court was] not free to consider the [appellant's] arguments . . .' On 18 December 1987 special leave to appeal to the Board was given.

Since the Hong Kong decisions to which their Lordships have just referred were given, the same issue arose for decision in England in *R v Rowson* [1985] 2 All ER 539, [1986] QB 174. In that case the trial judge had ruled that a statement made by one co-accused was inadmissible in that the relevant rule of the Judges' Rules (see *Practice Note* [1964] 1 All ER 237, [1964] 1 WLR 152) had been broken. Counsel for other co-accused in due course sought to cross-examine the maker of that statement on its content when he gave evidence. The trial judge allowed the facts alleged in the statement to be put to the maker of the statement but declined to allow the jury to be told that the facts emanated from the statement which he had already excluded. All the accused were convicted but the two co-accused appealed on the ground that their counsel had an unfettered right to a cross-examine on the statement and had been prevented from exercising that right. The Court of Appeal, Criminal Division in a judgment delivered by Robert Goff LJ, held that the submission was well founded though the court applied the proviso and dismissed the appeals (see [1985] 2 All ER 539 at 542, [1986] QB 1974 at 180). The attention of the court was not, it seems, drawn to the relevant Hong Kong decisions. It is therefore clear that there has been a divergence of view between the Court of Appeal in Hong Kong on the one hand and in England on the other which their Lordships must now resolve.

b   The decision in *Yu Tit-hoi v R* was founded on the decisions of the Court of Criminal Appeal in *R v Treacy* [1944] 2 All ER 229 and *R v Rice* [1963] 1 All ER 832, [1963] 1 QB 857. In the former case the Crown had not sought to put in evidence, as part of the prosecution case, a statement made by a defendant charged with murder (there was no co-accused in that case) but when the defendant gave evidence in his own defence he was allowed to be cross-examined on that statement. This, as the Court of Criminal Appeal

c held, was plainly wrong and the conviction for murder was quashed. Much reliance was placed by the Court of Appeal in *Yu Tit-hoi v R* on the statement in the judgment of the Court of Criminal Appeal delivered by Humphreys J that a statement made by a person under arrest was either admissible or not admissible. The judge went on ([1944] 2 All ER 229 at 236):

d   'If it is admissible, the proper course for the prosecution is to prove it, give it in evidence, let the statement if it is in writing be made an exhibit, so that everybody knows what it is and everybody can inquire into it and do what they think right about it. If it is not admissible, nothing more ought to be heard of it, and it is quite a mistake to think that a document can be made admissible in evidence which is otherwise inadmissible simply because it is put to a person in cross-examination.'

e In *R v Rice* the same principle was applied to the use by the prosecution of a statement made by one co-accused against another co-accused. But their Lordships emphasise that neither case was concerned, as the present case is concerned and as *Yu Tit-hoi v R* and *R v Rowson* were concerned, with the attempted use by a co-accused of an excluded statement made by another co-accused.

f   Counsel for the appellant placed great reliance on the decision of the House of Lords in *Murdoch v Taylor* [1965] 1 All ER 406, [1965] AC 574. The question there arose under s 1(*f*)(iii) of the Criminal Evidence Act 1898. The House decided that, once a co-accused had 'given evidence against' another co-accused, the latter was under the statute entitled without restriction to cross-examine the former as to character and to put his previous convictions to him. Lord Donovan emphasised the difference between the position of the prosecution and the position of a co-accused in this respect ([1965] 1 All ER 406 at

g 416, [1965] AC 574 at 593):

        '... but when it is the co-accused who seeks to exercise the right conferred by proviso (*f*)(iii) different considerations come into play. He seeks to defend himself; to say to the jury that the man who is giving evidence against him is unworthy of belief; and to support that assertion by proof of bad character. The right to do this

h   cannot, in my opinion, be fettered in any way.'

A similar view had earlier been expressed by Devlin J in an interlocutory ruling given in *R v Miller* [1952] 2 All ER 667 at 668–669. Their Lordships think it right to quote the relevant passage in full:

j   'The fundamental principle, equally applicable to any question that is asked by the defence as to any question that is asked by the prosecution, is that it is not normally relevant to inquire into a man's previous character, and, particularly, to ask questions which tend to show that he has previously committed some criminal offence. It is not relevant because the fact that he has committed an offence on one occasion does not in any way show that he is likely to commit an offence on any subsequent occasion. Accordingly, such questions are, in general, inadmissible, not primarily for the reasons that they are prejudicial, but because they are irrelevant. There is, however, this difference in the application of the principle. In the case of the prosecution, a question of this sort may be relevant and at the same time be prejudicial, and, if the court is of the opinion that the prejudicial effect outweighs its relevance, then it has the power, and, indeed, the duty, to exclude the question. Therefore, counsel for the prosecution rarely asks such a question. No such limitation applies to a question asked by counsel for the defence. His duty is to adduce any evidence which is relevant to his own case and assists his client, whether or not it prejudices anyone else.'

Counsel for the Crown invited their Lordships to distinguish *Murdoch v Taylor* on the ground that the rights there in question arose under a statute and that what was there allowed to be put in cross-examination were the previous convictions of the co-accused. Their Lordships agree that this is so but find no sufficient ground of distinction in that fact. Ever since s 5 of the Criminal Procedure Act 1865 (Mr Denman's Act) was enacted (this section is exactly reproduced in s 14 of the Evidence Ordinance (Cap 8) of Hong Kong) it has been permissible in every criminal and indeed in every civil trial to cross-examine a witness as to any previous inconsistent statement made by him in writing or reduced into writing subject, where the inconsistent statement is said to be in writing, to his attention first being called to those parts of any writing which were to be used in order to contradict him. The only limit on the right of a co-accused to cross-examine another co-accused in these circumstances is, in their Lordships' opinion, relevancy. If one co-accused has given evidence incriminating another it must be relevant for the latter to show, if he can, that the former has on some other occasion given inconsistent evidence and thus is unworthy of belief.

Counsel for the Crown also argued before their Lordships that *R v Rowson* was wrongly decided and should not be followed. With respect their Lordships disagree. That decision is entirely in line with the principles which their Lordships have endeavoured to enunciate and is clearly consistent with the decisions in *R v Miller* and *Murdoch v Taylor*. Their Lordships respectfully agree with the distinction which the Court of Appeal, Criminal Division drew in *R v Rowson* between *R v Treacy* and *R v Rice* on the one hand and the case then before that court where it was, as already stated, counsel for one co-accused who sought to cross-examine another co-accused on his excluded statement. When Humphreys J said in *R v Treacy* that 'nothing more ought to be heard of it' he clearly meant that nothing more ought to be heard of the excluded statement, as between the prosecution and the defendant. The judge plainly did not have in mind the possibility of a co-accused subsequently seeking to make use of the excluded statement, for in that case there was no co-accused. It follows that their Lordships have also reached the conclusion, with great respect to the Court of Appeal, that *Yu Tit-hoi v R* and the later Hong Kong cases following it were wrongly decided and should not be followed. As already pointed out, their Lordships have noted that in the present case Power JA clearly had reservations as to the correctness of those decisions.

Counsel for the Crown pressed on their Lordships the submission that to allow a co-accused complete freedom to cross-examine on an excluded statement could give rise to difficult questions how far, if at all, a trial judge should explain to a jury why it was that they were suddenly hearing of this statement and perhaps even seeing it for the first time at a comparatively late stage of the trial. This question was touched on by the Court of Appeal, Criminal Division in *R v Rowson* [1985] 2 All ER 539 at 543, [1986] QB 174 at 182. Their Lordships doubt if it is possible to state general principles which should be uniformly applied in every case where the question arises. But, in agreement with the judgment of Robert Goff LJ in the passage just referred to, they are clearly of the view that the trial judge should warn the jury that they must not use the statement in any way as evidence in support of the prosecution's case and that its only relevance is to test the

credibility of the evidence which the maker of the statement has given against his co-
a accused. Their Lordships consider that as a general rule the trial judge should briefly tell
the jury why the statement had previously been excluded and cannot therefore be relied
on by the prosecution to prove its case, as for example that it was or may well have been
procured by inducement. It should be remembered that in cross-examination as to credit
the cross-examiner is bound by the answers which he receives and that it is not legitimate
to reopen all the circumstances in which the excluded statement was taken. In many
b cases, as in the present, the trial judge may well think it right to remind the jury that the
maker of the statement may well have a motive for incriminating a co-accused and that
his or her evidence should be approached with extreme caution.

It was also suggested on behalf of the Crown that, if cross-examination on the excluded
statement were to be permitted, the trial judge might have to carry out what was
described as a balancing exercise, balancing the interests of the maker of the statement
c against the interests of the co-accused on whose behalf it was sought to cross-examine,
before deciding whether or not to permit the proposed cross-examination. Their
Lordships disagree. In their view the right to cross-examine is, as Lord Donovan stated
in *Murdoch v Taylor* [1965] 1 All ER 406 at 416, [1965] AC 574 at 593, unfettered, the
only limit being relevancy. If the statement contains irrelevant matter the trial judge
would no doubt insist that that irrelevant matter should not be referred to and, if
d necessary, excised from any copies of the statement which the jury might be allowed to
see.

Their Lordships were told that the practice in Hong Kong is to hold the voir dire at
the beginning of the trial, as was done in the present case. If at the conclusion of the voir
dire the trial judge decides to exclude the statement, their Lordships see no reason why
he should not at that time ask counsel for any co-accused whether they will thereafter
e seek to make any use of the excluded statement. In the present case, after leave to cross-
examine on the statement in the appeal had been refused, there was an application for a
separate trial of the appellant which the trial judge also rejected. For the reasons given by
Devlin J in *R v Miller* [1952] 2 All ER 667 at 669, cases of this type, where it is right to
grant separate trials, are indeed rare but, if that possibility is to be envisaged at all, that
will normally be the right moment to consider that issue and not at a much later stage
f when, for the first time, the statement is referred to and perhaps produced before the
jury.

Counsel for the prosecution informed their Lordships that, in the event of their
Lordships humbly advising Her Majesty that the appellant's appeal should be allowed
and her conviction quashed, as their Lordships have now done, the prosecution would
neither seek the application of the proviso nor an order for the appellant to be retried.
g Unlike her co-accused, whose convictions were quashed but who were ordered to be
retried (their Lordships were told that the first defendant was convicted but the fourth
defendant acquitted on the retrial), the appellant in common with the fourth defendant
stands acquitted.

h *Appeal allowed. Conviction quashed.*

Solicitors: *Philip Conway Thomas & Co* (for the appellant); *Macfarlanes* (for the Crown).

Mary Rose Plummer   Barrister.

EC Commission v United Kingdom

a

(Case 416/85)

COURT OF JUSTICE OF THE EUROPEAN COMMUNITIES
JUDGES LORD MACKENZIE STUART (PRESIDENT), BOSCO, DUE, MOITINHO DE ALMEIDA, RODRIGUEZ
IGLESIAS (PRESIDENTS OF CHAMBERS), KOOPMANS, EVERLING, BAHLMANN, GALMOT, KAKOURIS, *b*
JOLIET, O'HIGGINS AND SCHOCKWEILER
ADVOCATE GENERAL M DARMON
15 SEPTEMBER 1987, 2 DECEMBER 1987, 21 JUNE 1988

*European Economic Community – Value added tax – Exemptions – Public interest exemptions –
Measures taken for clearly defined social reasons and for benefit of final consumer – Clearly* *c*
*defined social reasons – Benefit of final consumer – Final consumer – Identification of social
reasons – Whether identification of social reasons a matter of political choice for member states –
Whether identification of social reasons subject to supervision at Community level – Whether 'final
consumer' restricted to persons not using goods or services in course of economic activity –
Whether United Kingdom in breach of obligations in respect of exemptions from value added tax
– Value Added Tax Act 1983, Sch 5 – EC Council Directive 67/228, art 17 – EC Council* *d*
Directive 77/388, art 28(2).

*European Economic Community – Treaty provisions – Obligations under treaty – Failure to fulfil
obligation – Matters to be considered by court – Whether court entitled to consider objectives
pursued by Commission in bringing action against member state for failing to fulfil treaty
obligations – EEC Treaty, art 169.* *e*

The Commission of the European Communities sought a declaration that by continuing
in Sch 5[a] to the Value Added Tax Act 1983 the exemption from value added tax of items
yielding or used to produce food for human consumption, fuel and similar public utility
supplies to industry, news services supplied for business use, the construction of industrial
and commercial buildings and community and civil engineering works and the sale of *f*
protective boots and helmets to employers, the United Kingdom had contravened art
28(2)[b] of EC Council Directive 77/388 (the Sixth Directive). The Commission submitted
that although art 28(2), in conjunction with the last indent of art 17[c] of EC Council
Directive 67/228 (the Second Directive), permitted the retention by member states of
reduced rates and exemptions 'with refund of the tax paid at the preceding stage' in force
on 31 December 1975, the exemptions granted by the United Kingdom did not meet the *g*
requirement of art 17 of the Second Directive that an exemption should only be granted
'for clearly defined social reasons and for the benefit of the final consumer', where the
final consumer was to be construed as the person who acquired goods or services, the
benefit of which was to be direct, without having any right to deduct value added tax.
The United Kingdom contended, inter alia, that the final consumer was the person at the
end of a production or distribution chain and that it was sufficient if he acquired an *h*
indirect benefit from the supply, ie where reduced production costs resulting from the
application of exemptions to items used in the production process of an item which was
itself exempt were then passed on to the consumer in the form of lower prices.

Held – (1) The identification of social reasons was in principle a matter of political choice
for the member states and could be the subject matter of supervision at the Community *j*
level only in so far as it led to measures which because of their effects and true objectives
were outside its scope (see p 381 *c*, post).

---

a Schedule 5, so far as material, is set out at p 367 *g* to p 368 *g, post*
b Article 28(2) is set out at p 379 *g h, post*
c Article 17, so far as material, is set out at p 379 *j* to p 380 *a, post*

(2) Under the general scheme of value added tax the final consumer was the person
a who acquired goods or services for personal use, rather than for economic activity, and
thus bore the tax. However, the provision of goods or services at a stage higher in the
production or distribution chain which was nevertheless sufficiently close to the
consumer to be advantageous to him could also be for the benefit of the final consumer
(see p 381 *f g*, post).

(3) It followed that—

b (a) since animal feeding stuffs, seeds and live animals used as, or yielding or producing,
food for human consumption contributed to the production of substances intended for
human consumption, those supplies were sufficiently close to the final consumer to be of
advantage to him, and, since the negative effects of any taxation of those products on
food prices could not be neglected, the alleged failure of the United Kingdom to fulfil its
obligations had not been established in respect of those supplies (see p 311 *j* to p 312 *a*
c and p 384 *a* to *c*, post);

(b) since the provision of sewerage services, water, fuel and power to industry, the
provision of news services to undertakings such as banks and insurance companies, the
construction of industrial and commercial buildings and community and civil
engineering works and the sale of protective clothing to employers could not be
considered to be for the benefit of the final consumer, the United Kingdom had failed to
d fulfil its obligations under art 28 of the Sixth Directive in continuing to exempt those
goods and services from value added tax (see p 382 *b* to *h j*, p 383 *a f* to *h* and p 384 *a* to *c*,
post);

(c) since the measures adopted by the United Kingdom in order to implement its
social policy of facilitating home ownership for the whole population fell within the
purview of 'social reasons' for the purposes of art 17 of the Second Directive, in exempting
e housing constructed by local authorities and the private sector from value added tax the
United Kingdom had not failed to fulfil its obligations in respect of those measures (see
p 383 *e* and p 384 *a* to *c*, post).

Per curiam. In the context of the balance of powers between the institutions laid down
in the EEC Treaty, it is not for the court to consider what objectives are pursued by the
Commission in an action brought under art 169[d] of the Treaty, but simply to decide
f whether the member state in question had failed to fulfil its obligation as alleged (see
p 380 *g*, post).

Notes

For public interest exemptions in relation to value added tax, see 52 Halsbury's Laws (4th
edn) para 20.27.
g For the Value Added Tax Act 1983, Sch 5, see 48 Halsbury's Statutes (4th edn) 666.
For the EEC Treaty, art 169, see 50 ibid 323.

Cases cited

EC Commission v Italian Republic Case 7/68 [1968] ECR 423.
h *EC Commission v Germany* Case 107/84 [1985] ECR 2655.
European Parliament v EC Council Case 13/83 [1985] ECR 1513.
R v Henn, R v Darby Case 34/79 [1980] 2 All ER 166, [1981] AC 850, [1980] 2 WLR 597,
[1979] ECR 3795, CJEC.
Staatssecretaris van Financiën v Hong Kong Trade Development Council Case 89/81 [1982]
ECR 1277.

j ────────────────────────────

d   Article 169 provides:
    'If the Commission considers that a Member State has failed to fulfil an obligation under this
Treaty, it shall deliver a reasoned opinion on the matter after giving the State concerned the
opportunity to submit its observations.
    If the State concerned does not comply with the opinion within the period laid down by the
Commission, the latter may bring the matter before the Court of Justice.'

Verbond van Nederlandse Ondernemingen v Inspecteur der Invoerrechten en Accijnzen Case 51/
76 [1977] ECR 113.

Application

The Commission of the European Communities brought an action under art 169 of the
EEC Treaty for a declaration from the Court of Justice of the European Communities
that by exempting from value added tax certain categories of goods and services, namely
food (animal feeding stuffs, seeds and live animals of a kind generally used as, or yielding
or producing, food for human consumption), sewerage services and water supplied to
industry, new services supplied for business use, fuel and power supplied to industry, the
construction of industrial/commercial buildings and community/civil engineering works
and the sale of protective boots and helmets to employers pursuant to Groups 1, 2, 6, 7, 8
and 17 of Sch 5 to the Value Added Tax Act 1983, contrary to the provisions of art 28(2)
of EC Council Directive 77/388 of 17 May 1977 on the harmonisation of the laws of the
member states relating to turnover taxes, the United Kingdom had failed to fulfil its
obligations under the EEC Treaty. The language of the case was English. The facts are
set out in the report for the hearing presented by the Judge Rapporteur.

The Judge Rapporteur (Giacinto Bosco) presented the following report for the
hearing.

I—SUMMARY OF THE FACTS

Article 28(2) of EC Council Directive 77/388 of 17 May 1977 (on the harmonisation of
the laws of the member states relating to turnover taxes: common system of value added
tax: uniform basis of assessment) (the Sixth Directive) provides as follows:

> 'Reduced rates and exemptions with refund of the tax paid at the preceding stage
> which are in force on 31 December 1975, and which satisfy the conditions stated in
> the last indent of Article 17 of the Second Council Directive of 11 April 1967, may
> be maintained until a date which shall be fixed by the Council, acting unanimously
> on a proposal from the Commission, but which shall not be later than that on which
> the charging of tax on imports and the remission of tax on exports in trade between
> the Member States are abolished. Member States shall adopt the measures necessary
> to ensure that taxable persons declare the data required to determine own resources
> relating to these operations. On the basis of a report from the Commission, the
> Council shall review the above-mentioned reduced rates and exemptions every five
> years and, acting unanimously on a proposal from the Commission, shall where
> appropriate adopt the measures required to ensure the progressive abolition thereof.'

The last indent of art 17 of EC Council Directive 67/228 of 11 April 1967 (on the
harmonisation of legislation of member states concerning turnover taxes) (the Second
Directive), to which art 28 of the Sixth Directive refers, provides:

> '... Member States may ... provide for reduced rates or even exemptions with
> refund, if appropriate, of the tax paid at the preceding stage, where the total
> incidence of such measures does not exceed that of the reliefs applied under the
> present system. Such measures may only be taken for clearly defined social reasons
> and for the benefit of the final consumer, and may not remain in force after the
> abolition of the imposition of tax on importation and the remission of tax on
> exportation in trade between Member States.'

Article 28 of the Sixth Directive therefore provides for exemption from value added
tax (VAT) with refund of the tax paid at the preceding stage. Under that system VAT is
paid at all stages of the distribution chain except the retail stage. At that stage the
consumer is not required to pay VAT and the retailer receives a refund of the input tax
paid.

a The United Kingdom used the possibilities of exemption provided for in art 28 to retain a system known as 'zero-rating', now governed by Sch 5 to the Value Added Tax Act 1983 (which re-enacted almost in its entirety Sch 4 to the Finance Act 1972). The system of zero-rating applies to the supplies specified in a list comprising 17 groups of goods and services and, according to the Commission, covers some 35% of private consumption in the United Kingdom, whereas (again according to the Commission) in other member states such as Italy, Belgium and Denmark similar systems of relief only

b apply to a relatively small part of the VAT base (see Report from the Commission to the Council annexed to the reply; extracts reproduced in its reply).

Consequently, VAT coverage in the United Kingdom is limited to 44% of private consumption as compared with 90% in most other member states (see extracts from the White Paper from the Commission to the Council 'Completing the Internal Market' (June 1985) on the completion of the internal market reproduced by the Commission in

c its reply).

Zero-rating differs from the system of exemption with refund inasmuch as no VAT is charged on zero-rated goods and services at the various stages of the marketing chain. Consequently, at the retail stage there is no VAT to refund.

Despite that difference, the Commission accepts that, as far as the fiscal result is concerned, the system of zero-rating as applied by the United Kingdom is equivalent to

d the system of exemption with refund of the VAT paid at the preceding stage provided for by art 28(2) of the Sixth Directive.

The Commission also accepts that the system of zero-rating does not affect the Community's own resources and that it was already in force on 31 December 1975, the material date for the purposes of the Sixth Directive.

However, the Commission contests the application ratione materiae of the zero-rates

e in the United Kingdom. In its letter of 19 October 1981 to the United Kingdom government, the Commission maintained that certain of the zero-rates provided for by the Value Added Tax Act 1983 were not in conformity with the requirements laid down by art 28(2) of the Sixth Directive. Consequently, it requested the United Kingdom, pursuant to art 169 of the EEC Treaty, to submit its observations on the matter.

f In its reply of 25 February 1982 the United Kingdom government defended the zero-rates in question and proposed that discussions on the matter be opened. Following those discussions the Commission withdrew its objections to the zero-rating of some of the categories of goods and services mentioned in its letter of 19 October 1981. However, it adhered to the observations which it had made concerning the following groups of goods and services which are set out in Sch 5 to the 1983 Act:

g   'GROUP 1—FOOD
...
General items
Item No.
...
2. Animal feeding stuffs.

h 3. Seeds or other means of propagation of plants comprised in item 1 or 2.
4. Live animals of a kind generally used as, or yielding or producing, food for human consumption ...

                  GROUP 2—SEWERAGE SERVICES AND WATER
Item No.

j 1. Services of—(a) reception, disposal or treatment of foul water or sewage in bulk; and (b) emptying of cesspools, septic tanks or similar receptacles.
2. Water other than—(a) distilled water, deionised water and water of similar purity, and (b) water comprised in any of the excepted items set out in Group 1.

[In so far as supplies to industry are concerned]
...

GROUP 6—NEWS SERVICES

Item No.

1. The supply to newspapers or to the public of information of a kind published in newspapers . . .

GROUP 7—FUEL AND POWER

Item No.

1. Supplies of coal, coke and other solid substances, being supplies held out for sale solely as fuel.
2. Coal gas, water gas, producer gases and similar gases.
3. Petroleum gases, and other gaseous hydrocarbons, whether in gaseous or liquid state.
4. Fuel oil, gas oil and kerosene.
5. Electricity, heat and air-conditioning . . .

[All items in so far as not supplied to the final consumer.]

GROUP 8—CONSTRUCTION OF BUILDINGS, ETC.

Item No.

1. The granting by a person constructing a building of a major interest in, or in any part of, the building or its site.
2. The supply—(a) in the course of the construction . . . or demolition of . . . any building or any civil engineering work, of any services other than the services of an architect, surveyor or any person acting as consultant or in a supervisory capacity.
3. The supply, by a person supplying services within item 2 and in connection with those services, of—(a) materials or of builder's hardware, sanitary ware or other articles of a kind ordinarily installed by builders as fixtures; or (b) in respect of such goods, services described in paragraph 1(1) of Schedule 2 to this Act . . .

[All items in so far as the zero-rate is not restricted to buildings by and for the final consumer within a social policy.]

. . .

GROUP 17—CLOTHING AND FOOTWEAR

Item No.

. . .

2. Protective boots and helmets for industrial use [in so far as sold to employers] . . .'

Consequently, on 4 September 1984 the Commission sent to the United Kingdom government a reasoned opinion as provided for by art 169. By a letter of 6 November 1984 the United Kingdom government asked the Commission for further clarification on certain points. However, the discussions which followed produced no result. Consequently, the Commission lodged the present application, which was registered at the court on 10 December 1985.

II—WRITTEN PROCEDURE AND CONCLUSIONS OF THE PARTIES

The written procedure followed its normal course. On hearing the report of the Judge Rapporteur and the views of the Advocate General, the court decided to open the oral procedure without any preparatory inquiry.

The Commission claims that the court should declare that, by maintaining in force the application of the zero-rate of value added tax on the items set out above, the United Kingdom of Great Britain and Northern Ireland has contravened the provisions of the Sixth Directive and has therefore failed to fulfil the obligations incumbent on it under the Treaty establishing the European Economic Community; and that the United Kingdom is liable in costs.

The United Kingdom contends that the application should be dismissed; and that the
a Commission should be ordered to pay the United Kingdom's costs.

III—SUBMISSIONS AND ARGUMENTS OF THE PARTIES

A *General observations*
The Commission maintains, first, that the method used by the United Kingdom in
b applying zero-rates goes far beyond anything contemplated in the Sixth Directive. It
accepts that the system of zero-rating does not affect the Community's own resources and
that, at national level, it produces the same fiscal results as a system of exemption with
refund as envisaged by art 28(2) of the Sixth Directive; however, the Commission
considers that when used on such a large scale this form of tax relief is liable to undermine
the process of the progressive harmonisation of VAT. The use of zero-rates should
c therefore be limited to the transactions which meet the criteria laid down in art 28(2) of
the Sixth Directive and the last indent of art 17 of the Second Directive.
By permitting the member states to retain certain exemptions, those provisions
constitute a major exception to the general principle that all supplies of goods and services
are to be taxed and must therefore, in the Commission's view, be interpreted strictly.
The Commission then considers the conditions laid down in the last indent of art 17
d of the Second Directive. That article provides that exemptions may be granted only
(a) 'for clearly defined social reasons' and (b) 'for the benefit of the final consumer'.
As regards 'social reasons', the Commission accepts that the member states have a
margin of discretion in determining the social reasons which justify tax relief. In its
reply the Commission concedes that it may not challenge measures taken by a member
state in pursuance of a social policy unless it can be shown that the social policy is not
e sufficiently clearly defined or that the measures in question are either not justified or
disproportionate.
Further, the Commission accepts that an exemption which is justified for social reasons
may not be called in question because it may *incidentally* benefit a category of consumer
which does not require the social benefit. However, in its view the fact that, in the case
of a product or service which may be put to a variety of uses, certain uses may be zero-
f rated does not mean that the other uses which do not fulfil the conditions laid down by
the directives may also be zero-rated.
As regards the requirement that the exemption must be granted for the benefit of the
final consumer, the Commission first of all defines the term 'final consumer' and
distinguishes it from the term 'taxable person' in art 4 of the Sixth Directive. The final
consumer is the person who acquires the goods or services without having any right of
g deduction (see *Staatssecretaris van Financiën v Hong Kong Trade Development Council* Case
89/81 [1982] ECR 1277). Taxable persons, on the other hand, are always entitled to
deduct their input tax from the output tax for which they are liable.
According to the Commission, in referring to the final consumer art 17 of the Second
Directive means persons who are at the final stage in the distribution chain and have no
h right to deduct VAT.
Moreover, it is inherent in the exemption with refund mechanism provided for by
the Sixth Directive that the benefit only goes to the final consumer. It was therefore
designed to be of *direct and immediate* benefit to persons at the final stage of a production
or distribution chain. Consequently, exemptions which are only of indirect benefit to
the final consumer are not in conformity with art 28.
j The Commission accepts that the system of zero-rating applied in the United Kingdom
is equivalent to the system of exemption with refund provided for by the Sixth Directive.
However, it points out that, unlike exemptions, zero-rates apply not only at the final
stage but at all stages of the commercial chain.
Consequently, it is necessary to determine how far up the commercial chain zero-
rating can go and still fulfil the requirements laid down in art 28. In general terms, the

Commission considers that zero-rates may be applied to transactions which would qualify for deduction of VAT under a system of exemptions with refunds. In other words, only products which are bona fide inputs for a product which is itself zero-rated may be zero-rated. As an illustration of this the Commission states that it would not accept that farmers' boots could be zero-rated simply because food is zero-rated.

The United Kingdom contests the Commission's restrictive interpretation of art 28(2) of the Sixth Directive and the last indent of art 17 of the Second Directive.

As a general point the United Kingdom observes that in the Sixth Directive the Council placed great stress on the vital need to provide for a transitional period to allow national laws to be gradually adapted. At the time when the Sixth Directive was adopted it was clearly envisaged that measures allowing the retention of reduced rates and exemptions would continue in force for many years.

The United Kingdom emphasises that art 28 lays down a procedure for the progressive abolition of reduced rates and exemptions (on the basis of reports submitted by the Commission to the Council 'every five years') and that as yet the Commission has made no specific proposals in that regard. It claims therefore that the Commission's motive is to bypass the procedural requirements of the Sixth Directive in the hope of achieving a result which it has not yet even proposed to the Council. In order to do so the Commission is stretching the interpretation of the Community rules in question.

According to the United Kingdom, art 17 does not constitute an exception but forms part of a general rule, in relation to which the need for 'transitional' provisions was seen to be 'vital'.

The United Kingdom maintains that in *Verbond van Nederlandse Ondernemingen v Inspecteur der Invoerrechten en Accijnzen* Case 51/76 [1977] ECR 113 and *EC Commission v Germany* Case 107/84, [1985] ECR 2655 the court did not accept that art 17 constituted an exception or that it should be interpreted strictly.

As regards more particularly the requirements for tax relief laid down by art 17, the United Kingdom maintains, first of all, that the member states enjoy a margin of discretion in determining their own social policies and hence in determining what measures are justified by social reasons. Such a measure cannot be challenged unless the social reason is not sufficiently clearly defined or unless the measure is unjustified or disproportionate.

However, where there is a social reason for the introduction of tax relief, that reason cannot be negated by the existence of some other reason, whether primary or secondary or subsidiary.

As regards the requirement that the exemption should benefit the 'final consumer', the United Kingdom defines that term as meaning the person at the end of a particular distribution chain rather than a person who has no right to deduct VAT.

The United Kingdom further observes that art 17 does not require that it should 'only' or 'solely' be the final consumer who benefits. On the contrary, it is sufficient for the purposes of that provision if the final consumer gains an *indirect* benefit, for example by way of lower prices.

The restrictive interpretation proposed by the Commission is in conformity neither with the letter nor with the spirit of the articles in question and would be liable to render ineffective rules which were considered to be 'vital' within the context of the Sixth Directive.

As regards the question of inputs, the United Kingdom observes that the Commission seems to have misunderstood the operation of zero-rates in the United Kingdom. The United Kingdom does not, as a matter of course, zero-rate *all* inputs which go towards the production of a zero-rated supply.

B *Specific observations*

Group 1—Food

The Commission considers that the contested items in this group are too remote to

form part of the direct production and distribution chain of food (which is zero-rated)
a and hence do not fulfil the requirement of benefiting the final consumer. The
Commission also questions whether the use of zero-rating in this manner for social
purposes is proportionate to the end sought.

The United Kingdom, on the other hand, observes that the zero-rating of the items in
question plays an essential role in preventing the increase in food prices which would
occur as a result of the input VAT paid being passed on to the final consumer. Moreover,
b it does not accept the 'remoteness' test advanced by the Commission and argues, for
example, that an animal awaiting slaughter (which the Commission does not accept as
correctly zero-rated) is equally proximate or remote from the 'final consumer' as a potato
awaiting harvesting (which the Commission accepts to be correctly zero-rated).

c *Group 2—Sewerage services and water*
As regards the disposal of sewage, it should be noted that in the United Kingdom this
service is normally paid for by a rate based on property values. Services are provided on a
commercial basis and hence fall within the scope of VAT only where premises are too
remote to be connected to the main drainage systems and sewage enters into cesspools,
septic tanks and the like.
d The Commission challenges the zero-rating of such services in so far as they are
supplied to industry. There is no social justification for such relief.

The United Kingdom observes that it would be inequitable to tax such services while
rate-funded services did not bear tax. It adds that it is most unlikely that there are many
industrial concerns which rely on cesspits.

The Commission replies that, in view of this limited use, there should be no difficulty
e in repealing the offending provisions.
As regards supplies of water, the Commission does not accept that either of the criteria
laid down by art 17 are met. Supplies of water to industry are zero-rated, yet the United
Kingdom has not specified the social reasons for this.

According to the United Kingdom, it is principally the individual who benefits from
supplies of potable water, even where it is supplied to industry. Moreover, the
f Commission accepts, in relation to Luxembourg, a member state which exempts water
from VAT, that water as a basic necessity warrants special tax treatment (see the answer
to written question 1243/85, OJ 1986 C87, p 6).

With respect to that specific point, the Commission replies that the exemption of
water in Luxembourg is based on another paragraph of art 28, namely para 3(b).

g *Group 6—News services*
The Commission accepts that the requirements of art 28 are fulfilled in the case of
services supplied directly to the public and of supplies to undertakings which themselves
have zero-rated outputs. On the other hand, the Commission contests the zero-rating of
the supply of news services to producers of positively rated services.
h According to the United Kingdom, the function of news services is broadly equivalent
to that of newspapers, which are zero-rated. Services supplied to undertakings whose
supplies are positively rated may be regarded as an 'incidental benefit', since the main
beneficiaries of such services are newspapers; that incidental benefit cannot negate the
social reasons which justify generally the zero-rating of this type of supply.

j *Group 7—Fuel and power*
The Commission contests the zero-rating of fuel and power which is not supplied to
the final consumer. It observes that as a result of the zero-rating of such supplies the
largest consumers of fuel and power, namely industrial users, do not pay VAT. Such
relief is not in conformity with art 28 because such inputs are too remote to form part of
the production chain of products which are correctly zero-rated.

The Commission adds that administrative difficulties alone cannot justify the total
exclusion of inputs of fuel and power to the whole of industry from the scope of VAT.   *a*

According to the United Kingdom, the administrative difficulties involved in limiting
the application of zero-rates to final consumers alone would probably be insurmountable.

Moreover, in sectors which at present are partly exempt, in particular schools and
hospitals, the imposition of VAT at the full rate would have undesirable social effects.

Group 8—Construction of buildings etc   *b*

The Commission emphasises that it does not seek to enter into a discussion concerning
the validity of the United Kingdom's social policy in the area of housing. However, the
Commission considers that, with the exception of local authority housing, the
indiscriminate zero-rating of the housing sector is disproportionate to the objectives
pursued.

According to the United Kingdom, there can be no simple distinction for VAT   *c*
purposes between private and public sector housing. All housing fulfils a social need,
particularly since it is now the private sector which provides an increasing proportion of
housing for the needier section of the community.

Moreover, the Commission wholly disregards the social reasons for building schools
and hospitals or other civil engineering works and the resultant benefit to the consumer.
          d

Group 17—Protective boots and helmets

In the Commission's view, protective clothing sold to employers does not constitute
an input forming part of the production chain of zero-rated products. Consequently,
such clothing cannot qualify for relief under art 28(2).

According to the United Kingdom, this relief is intended to promote industrial safety,
since the imposition of a positive rate of VAT would have the effect of discouraging   *e*
employers from providing protective clothing for their employees. Moreover, such
clothing must be considered separately and not as an input in the production process.
The employer is the final consumer of the goods concerned.

D R Gilmour for the EC Commission.
David Vaughan QC for the United Kingdom.   *f*

2 December. **The Advocate General (M Darmon)** delivered the following opinion[1].
Mr President, Members of the Court,

1. This action against the United Kingdom for failure to fulfil its obligations concerns
the criteria for the application of art 28(2) of EC Council Directive 77/388 of 17 May
1977 (on the harmonisation of the laws of the member states relating to turnover taxes: *g*
common system of value added tax: uniform basis of assessment) (the Sixth Directive).
The essence of the claim is that the United Kingdom applies to a number of goods and
services a 'zero rate' which is not justified for 'clearly defined social reasons and for the
benefit of the final consumer', as required by the last indent of art 17 of EC Council
Directive 67/228 of 11 April 1967 (on the structure and procedures for application of the   *h*
common system of value added tax) (the Second Directive), to which art 28(2) of the
Sixth Directive refers.

2. That provision was adopted as part of a process initiated in 1967, when the first two
directives on the harmonisation of legislation concerning turnover taxes were adopted
(ie EC Council Directive 67/227 of 11 April 1967 (the First Directive) and the Second
Directive); it should be noted that in the United Kingdom these taxes have never been as   *j*
important as they were in the original member states of the Community, nor have they
taken the same form, that of a cumulative multi-stage tax (see J C Scholsem, 'La TVA
impôt européen' in *Mélanges Fernand Dehousse* vol II, p 305). Although 'the rates and

---

1   Translated from the French

exemptions [were] not harmonised at the same time' (see the eighth recital in the
a preamble to the First Directive), the result was the establishment of a 'general tax on
consumption' (art 2 of the First Directive). The Sixth Directive (the Third, Fourth and
Fifth Directives merely delayed the introduction of the common VAT system), adopted
ten years later, had as its aim an essential objective, the creation of 'own resources' for the
Communities, which were to include 'those accruing from value added tax and obtained
by applying a common rate of tax on a *basis of assessment determined in a uniform manner*
b according to Community rules' (see the second recital in the preamble to the directive).

3. 'So that the Communities' own resources may be collected in a uniform manner in
all the Member States' (see the eleventh recital in the preamble to the Sixth Directive),
arts 13 to 16 of the directive lay down a list of exemptions common to all the member
states. However, on a transitional basis art 28 of the Sixth Directive allows them to retain,
under certain conditions, inter alia, the reduced rates and exemptions which were in
c force on 31 December 1975 and satisfy the criteria set out in the last indent of art 17 of
the Second Directive. That possibility was left open on the ground that it was '*vital* to
provide for a *transitional period* to allow national laws in *specified fields* to be *gradually
adapted*' (see the nineteenth (last) recital in the preamble to the directive).

4. Although it was adopted on the basis of art 28(2), the system of zero-rating at issue
differs from the exemption mechanism provided for in that article. That is to say, art 28
d provides for exemption 'with refund of the tax paid at the preceding stage' which takes
effect at the retail stage. At earlier stages every taxable person as defined in art 4 of the
Sixth Directive must apply the tax. Only a retailer who sells an exempted product to a
'final consumer' does not pass on the VAT which he has paid but obtains a refund from
the tax authorities. The zero-rating system takes a different approach. A list of goods and
services designated by the national legislature is subject to purely notional taxation,
e under which no VAT is actually charged either on delivery or at earlier stages in the
marketing chain. Naturally, there is nothing to refund to the retailer. According to the
Commission, some 35% of the private consumption of households is zero-rated in the
United Kingdom and 33% in Ireland; Ireland disputes that percentage and states that the
real figure is 25%. The zero-rating technique exists in three other states, but they operate
f it only on a very small scale, largely in favour of the press.

5. Let me state right away that the *system itself* is not challenged by the Commission,
which considers it to be equivalent to the system of exemption and refund. However,
the Commission disputes the *application* of zero-rating to certain categories of goods and
services in the list contained in the Value Added Tax Act 1983 (disputed zero rates:
Group 1: food (animal feeding stuffs, seeds and live animals of a kind generally used as,
g or yielding or producing, food for human consumption); *Group 2*: sewerage services and
water (supplies to industry); *Group 6*: news services (supplies to industry); *Group 7*: fuel
and power (supplies to industry); *Group 8*: construction of buildings, etc other than by
or for the final consumer within a social policy; *Group 17*: clothing and footwear
(protective boots and helmets sold to employers)). It considers that those provisions do
not comply with the criteria laid down in art 17. While it admits that zero-rating has no
h effect on own resources, it states that 'in the context of the completion of the internal
market, of the abolition of fiscal frontiers and of the drive towards a standardisation of
the rate of VAT' its aim is to 'limit the use of zero-rates to those transactions which meet
the criteria laid down in art 28(2) of the Sixth Directive and this as part of its overall fiscal
policy of working towards the total phasing out of all zero-rates or exemptions with
refunds'.

j 6. According to the Commission, in determining how far up the commercial chain
zero-rating may be applied if it is to *benefit the final consumer*, only stages corresponding to
'bona fide inputs' in the production or distribution of a final product which may be
exempted in accordance with the criteria laid down in art 28(2) may be taken into
account. The Commission further argues that only the person who acquires the goods or
services without having any right of deduction may be regarded as the final consumer.

7. The United Kingdom disagrees with that definition, and submits that the final consumer is the person at the end of a production or distribution chain. Moreover, it is *a* not necessary that it should 'only' be the final consumer who benefits, or that he should benefit directly. It is sufficient if he gains an indirect benefit from the transaction, in particular by way of a lower end price. The United Kingdom points out that it enjoys considerable discretion in determining its own social policies and hence in deciding on the national measures to be taken for 'clearly-defined social reasons'. The Commission does not deny that such a prerogative exists, but it submits that the court, exercising its *b* supervisory power, should hold that in this case those measures are unjustified or disproportionate in relation to the social reasons relied on, and that the meaning of that concept for Community purposes must be defined by the court.

8. The United Kingdom complains more generally, however, that what the Commission is really doing is using an action against it for alleged failure to fulfil its obligations in an endeavour to evade the provisions of art 28, according to which it is for *c* the Council, acting unanimously, to decide to abolish the exemptions permitted by that article. That analysis, it says, is illustrated by the terms used by the Commission, from which it appears that the application of zero-rates constitutes one of the 'stumbling blocks' on the path towards a uniform rate of VAT. The United Kingdom considers that its assessment of the Commission's real motive is supported by the fact that the Commission accepts that the zero-rating in question has no bearing on own resources *d* because of the mechanism established by the last sentence of the first sub-paragraph of art 28(2), which requires that 'taxable persons declare the data required to determine own resources' relating to exempted operations. The United Kingdom also argues that when it instituted these proceedings the Commission had not yet submitted to the Council a proposal for progressive abolition as provided for in that article. It may be noted in that regard that such a proposal was submitted while these proceedings were in *e* progress (see OJ 1987 C250, p 2).

9. Let me say right away that these objections concerning the Commission's possible motives for bringing the action do not seem relevant to the role of the court. It scarcely needs pointing out that the decision whether or not to bring an action against a member state for failure to fulfil its obligations is in any event in the entire discretion of the Commission, as the custodian of the Treaties, and that it is for the Commission 'to judge *f* at what time it shall bring an action before the Court' (see *EC Commission v Italian Republic* Case 7/68 [1968] ECR 423). Moreover, the role of the court in proceedings of this kind is to determine whether or not a member state has failed to fulfil its obligations towards the Community as defined by the law in force. It should be recalled in that regard that in *European Parliament v EC Council* Case 13/83 [1985] ECR 1513 at 1588 (para 17), where the Council contended that the Parliament was using the action for failure to act as a *g* means of furthering political objectives, the court held:

'... it is not possible to restrict the exercise of that right [to bring an action for failure to act] by one of them [the Community institutions] without adversely affecting its status as an institution under the Treaty ...'

h

Rejecting the objection of inadmissibility raised in that respect by the Council, the court followed the opinion of the Advocate General (C O Lenz), who had stated (at 1518 (para 1)):

'It is not for this Court to decide whether the action has political objectives. An action is being prosecuted before the Court according to the rules of procedure on a question of law, namely the scope of the duties of a Community institution. The *j* action will be decided according to the relevant provisions, namely those of the Treaty establishing the European Economic Community of 25 March 1957. It is prosecuted in the interests of the Community and its legal system which will be given a binding ruling on the scope of the rights and obligations of the parties.'

Such statements of principle, emphasising the objective nature of actions brought before
a the court, make possible a correct assessment of the weight of the arguments submitted
in that respect by the United Kingdom. Although the Commission did refer in rather
general terms to the interests which it considered to be at issue in this case, the fact
remains that its action is directed unambiguously at a failure to comply with art 28 of
the Sixth Directive in conjunction with art 17 of the Second Directive. It is obviously on
the basis of those provisions alone that the court can determine whether or not the United
b Kingdom has failed to fulfil its obligations, since although the Sixth Directive states
expressly that it is for the Council to *abolish* the exemptions established under art 28,
their retention until such abolition depends on their conformity with that provision.
The next step must therefore be to examine that issue.

c I—MEASURES TAKEN FOR CLEARLY DEFINED SOCIAL REASONS AND FOR THE BENEFIT OF THE FINAL
CONSUMER
    10. Let me emphasise right away that 'clearly defined social reasons' and 'benefit of
the final consumer' are not alternative conditions. One of them concerns the *objective* of
the measures in question, the other its *beneficiaries*. They are therefore cumulative.
Moreover, a provision creating an exception to the rules on the uniform basis of
d assessment for VAT cannot be construed liberally.

A *'Clearly defined social reasons'*
    11. The parties are agreed that the determination of their own social policy is a matter
for the discretion of the member states. The Commission considers, however, that it is
for the court to lay down a definition for Community purposes of the phrase 'clearly
e defined social reasons' and that the court should hold that in this case the measures
adopted are not sufficiently well-defined or are unjustified or disproportionate in relation
to the reasons relied on.
    12. The application of zero-rating may result in a reduction of the tax burden on the
least well-off segments of society. It is equally conceivable, however, that the member
states should also use fiscal instruments in order better to satisfy the needs of the great
f majority of the population. With regard to the concept at issue, moreover, I do not think
that it is the role of the court to review the expediency of choices made by the member
states. With reference to the 'public morality' exception to the rules on the free
movement of goods, the court has held in *R v Henn, R v Darby* Case 34/79 [1980] 2 All
ER 166 at 191, [1981] AC 850 at 898:

g   'In principle, it is for each member state to determine in accordance with its own
    scale of values and in the form selected by it the requirements of public morality in
    its territory.'

I propose that the court take the same approach in this case. That is to say, if it is accepted
that the member states can restrict that fundamental freedom in the manner described,
it must be possible to accord them, without thereby endangering to any greater extent
h the consistency of the Community legal system, a similar latitude with regard to
provisional exceptions to rules establishing a uniform basis of assessment for VAT.
    13. However, compliance with the directive in question requires that the court should
be able to intervene in the event that the exercise by the member states of their powers
in the matter, where it has no relation to the field at issue, might frustrate the Community
provision itself. I therefore suggest that the court should declare measures contrary to
j Community law only where their objective is clearly unrelated to the satisfaction of the
fundamental needs, be they individual or collective, of the population of the member state.

B *The final consumer*
    14. In my view the final consumer must be defined as the person who acquires goods

or services for his personal use, as opposed to an economic activity, which art 4 of the Sixth Directive uses as the criterion for determining who is a taxable person. The *a* distinction between a taxable person and a final consumer lies in the fact that a taxable person carries out transactions for consideration, while a final consumer is one who *acquires* goods or services for his own use. That distinction has fundamental consequences for tax purposes; in principle a taxable person deducts VAT, whereas a final consumer must bear that tax 'unless there is a further transaction in which a price is paid' (see *Staatssecretaris van Financiën v Hong Kong Trade Development Council* Case 89/81 [1982] *b* ECR 1277 at 1286 (para 9)). That consequence cannot be ignored in the case of a zero-rate. In such a case the final consumer is the person who would have to bear a positive tax and would not be able to deduct it. That definition is not, I think, based on a narrow approach; it corresponds strictly to a fiscal interpretation, the only one which, in the context of provisions on VAT, is appropriate to the categories relevant to such taxation. It is, moreover, that which appears in art 3 of the proposal for a sixteenth VAT directive *c* (OJ 1984 C226, p 2):

'For the purposes of this directive: (a) "final consumer" means: 1. any person who, with regard to the importation of goods referred to in Article 2, is not deemed to be a taxable person within the meaning of Article 4 of Council Directive 77/388/EEC, 2. a taxable person who was not entitled to deduct value added tax when purchasing *d* goods.'

C '*For the benefit*' *of the final consumer: the concept of a benefit*
15. It remains for me to consider the concept of a 'benefit' as used in art 17 of the Second Directive, where it speaks of exemptions 'for the *benefit* of the final consumer'. In the case of a 'normal' exemption, such a benefit results from the non-application of VAT *e* at the retail stage. In essence, the benefit is entirely identical under the zero-rating system; the consumer pays no VAT. The application of zero-rating at earlier stages of distribution results in no additional fiscal benefit for the consumer since he does not pay the tax in any event. However, as the Commission says, zero-rating may be accepted higher in the commercial chain in so far as it is applied to the *product itself* which is zero-rated on purchase by the final consumer. *f*
16. Can we go further and take into account the indirect benefit which, according to the United Kingdom, results from the application of zero-rating to *inputs* used to produce goods which are themselves zero-rated? It should be emphasised that from the fiscal point of view such a benefit does not exist once a zero-rate is applied on purchase by the final consumer. That is to say the extension of a zero-rating higher up the commercial chain has no effect on the fiscal burden on the consumer, who in any event benefits from *g* a zero-rate. The only benefit for him, therefore, lies in a possible reduction in the cost of the product resulting from a reduction in cash outlays and overheads in the absence of positive rates of tax on the inputs concerned. I think, however, that these consequences, which are revealed by an economic analysis, should be regarded with prudence in so far as they vary according to the time limits for deductions, the size and structure of the *h* producers or dealers in question, credit arrangements between them etc. The complexity of such effects requires, in my opinion, a degree of caution in that respect in considering the notion of a 'benefit' for the final consumer for the purposes of art 17. However, in so far as the very existence of a reduction in production costs is likely to result in a benefit, albeit variable, for the final consumer, I propose that the court should not reject, as a matter of principle, the zero-rating of inputs which are *directly and exclusively* used in a *j* product which itself is properly zero-rated.
17. Now that the conditions laid down in the provision at issue have been defined, we may determine whether or not the contested measures comply with them.

II—THE CONTESTED ZERO RATES

a A *Group 1 of the list set out in Sch 5 to the Value Added Tax Act 1983: food*

18. At issue is the application of zero-rates to animal feeding stuffs, seeds or other means of propagation of plants, and live animals used as, or yielding or producing, food for human consumption. These are all *inputs* used in the production of food for human consumption, and there is no dispute as to the application of zero-rates to food. The United Kingdom argues that the application to them of zero-rates is of direct benefit to

b final consumers who themselves use those inputs to produce food. It refers more generally to the reduced burden on farmers' cash-flow and its possible effects on food prices.

19. Although this last consideration must be approached with caution, as I have already stated, the negative effects of any taxation of those products on food prices, increases in which are particularly 'sensitive' at the level of the final consumer, cannot be

c ignored. It should be observed that all the supplies referred to contribute directly and exclusively to the production of food for the final consumer. Moreover, persons using such supplies to produce their own food and farmers keeping part of their production for the use of their family receive a direct benefit from the application of the zero-rates at issue. I therefore propose that the court hold that the United Kingdom has not failed to fulfil its obligations in this respect.

d

B *Group 2: sewerage services and water*

20. Sewerage services (reception, disposal or treatment of sewage and emptying of cesspools, septic tanks etc) are normally financed by a rate which is not subject to VAT. Consequently, taxable commercial services are provided only in respect of cesspools or septic tanks which are made necessary by the absence of any main drainage system. The

e United Kingdom justifies the application of zero-rates to such services essentially for reasons of equity between town-dwellers and isolated farmers, who are generally the beneficiaries of the measure in question. There are also, it maintains, domestic considerations justifying exemption. The Commission, in any event, disputes only the supply of such services to industry. Since the United Kingdom states that it is highly unlikely that industrial concerns would make use of such services, I agree with the

f Commission that the repeal of the disputed provision (since industrial concerns cannot be regarded as final consumers) should not present any difficulty.

21. With regard to the supply of water, only supplies to industry are in dispute; while the United Kingdom admits that the industrial sector is the largest consumer, it argues that in certain cases water is used principally for the benefit of the individual in the preparation of food and drink. In its view there is, moreover, no practical reason for

g attempting to identify the status of the final consumer, since water is connected in the public mind with food and should be treated in the same way by analogy.

22. That argument cannot be upheld. Industrial uses of water are important enough to preclude, so it seems to me, the application of zero-rates, in the light of the fact that the users are taxable persons. All I would allow, following the Commission's view, is the

h application of a zero-rate for the industrial production of finished food products. The United Kingdom did point out that there is an exemption for supplies of water in another member state. The Commission observed that that exemption was based on art 28(3)(b) of the Sixth Directive, under which member states may, during the transitional period, continue to exempt the activities set out in Annex F, inter alia 'the supply of water by public authorities' (item 12 of the annex). The United Kingdom, which based its

j contentions expressly on art 28(2), has not argued that it could rely on art 28(3) (which to my mind is strictly alternative to art 28(2)) or even asserted that it met the conditions laid down in the latter. I therefore think that the United Kingdom has failed to fulfil its obligations in this respect.

C *Group 6: news services*

23. Since the Commission has accepted that zero-rates may be applied in respect of *a*
the supply of information directly to the public or to undertakings which use that
information in the production of products such as newspapers, it seems that it is only the
application of zero-rates to the supply of information, essentially by electronic means, for
other business uses that remains at issue. Such beneficiaries of zero-rating (banks,
insurance companies etc) cannot be regarded as final consumers.
                                                                                  b
D *Group 7: fuel and power*

24. The Commission contests the exemption of supplies other than to final consumers.
The United Kingdom argues, first of all, that in the case of mixed users it is difficult to
distinguish between business uses and private uses. Such an objection is unconvincing,
and it is for the member states to find appropriate technical solutions to what does not
appear to be an insurmountable difficulty. Second, it argues that the taxation of such *c*
supplies in the education and health sectors would have undesirable social effects. Having
regard to the very large energy consumption of the industrial sector it is clear that zero-
rates do not benefit the final consumer in this area. The Commission's claim must
therefore, in my opinion, be upheld in this respect.

E *Group 8: construction of buildings*   *d*

25. This is certainly the most important group of exemptions from the economic
point of view since it covers the housing sector, industrial and commercial buildings,
and the community and civil engineering sector. The Commission considers that the
failure to distinguish according to the type of housing concerned is disproportionate
having regard to the objectives pursued. The United Kingdom argues that it is very
difficult to distinguish, as the Commission suggests, between housing constructed by *e*
local authorities, which unquestionably qualify for exemption, and other housing,
especially since it is now the private sector which, because of the steps taken to encourage
home ownership, provides an increasing proportion of housing for the most disadvantaged
segments of the community.

26. If it was for the court to consider whether or not the decision to apply a zero rate *f*
in respect of the construction of *all* private housing was well-founded, it could
undoubtedly hold that measures of such an indiscriminate nature reflect a very wide
view of the social reasons relied on. As I have already said, however, the exercise of such
a supervisory role would impinge on the powers of the member states. In any event, the
approach adopted by the United Kingdom, that is to say, facilitating home ownership for
the whole population, clearly does not go beyond the discretion which it undoubtedly
retains in this field.   *g*

27. In the industrial and commercial sector zero-rating is used by the United Kingdom
as a means of encouraging renewal of infrastructure and construction, especially from
the point of view of employment. I do not share the Commission's reserves with regard
to the social reasons put forward. The improvement of industrial infrastructure, the
development of residential areas and, above all, the quantitative and qualitative effects of *h*
such development for employment are clearly important social reasons. However, I must
propose that the court hold that the United Kingdom has failed to fulfil its obligations in
so far as the zero-rates at issue, although undoubtedly benefiting workers, users and
citizens, cannot be regarded as benefiting the *final consumer* as defined in the directive.
To treat the entire population as the final consumer does not seem to me to be compatible
with a provision which clearly concerns a person who *acquires* goods or services for his *j*
own use. Moreover, such a wide interpretation of the term 'final consumer' would
amount to the de facto removal of the condition laid down in that respect by the relevant
provision, and allow any exemption based on social reasons.

28. With regard to community works and civil engineering, I am inclined, for reasons
similar to those I have just set out, to adopt the same approach. Here again, despite the

a social aspect of the reasons put forward, it is hard to see any distinction between the final consumer and the population as a whole.

F *Group 17: protective boots and helmets*

29. The zero-rating of purchases of such supplies by employers is said to be justified by the fear that taxation would discourage them from providing such equipment for their staff. I need simply point out that the beneficiary cannot be regarded as a final
b consumer according to the definition I have adopted. It may be added that it appears from the United Kingdom's pleadings themselves that many employers should be able to recover the tax on such supplies.

I therefore propose that the court (1) hold that by applying zero-rates of VAT to supplies to industry of water and sewerage services, to information services other than those intended directly for the public or for the production of zero-rated products such
c as newspapers, to the construction of buildings for industrial and commercial use and in the community and civil engineering sector, to supplies of fuel and power and of protective boots and helmets in so far as they are not supplied to the final consumer, the United Kingdom has failed to fulfil its obligations under the EEC Treaty and under art 28(2) of the Sixth Directive of 17 May 1977, (2) dismiss the remainder of the
d application and (3) order the United Kingdom to pay the costs.

21 June. **THE COURT OF JUSTICE** delivered the following judgment.

1. By an application lodged at the court registry on 13 December 1985 the Commission of the European Communities brought an action pursuant to art 169 of the EEC Treaty for a declaration that by continuing to apply a zero-rate of value added tax to certain
e groups of goods and services the United Kingdom of Great Britain and Northern Ireland has contravened the provisions of EC Council Directive 77/388 of 17 May 1977 (on the harmonisation of the laws of the member states relating to turnover taxes: common system of value added tax: uniform basis of assessment) (the Sixth Directive) and has therefore failed to fulfil its obligations under the EEC Treaty.

2. Article 28 of the Sixth Directive lays down transitional provisions for the progressive
f adaptation of national legislation in certain respects. Article 28(2) provides as follows:

'Reduced rates and exemptions with refund of the tax paid at the preceding stage which are in force on 31 December 1975, and which satisfy the conditions stated in the last indent of Article 17 of the second Council Directive of 11 April 1967, may be maintained until a date which shall be fixed by the Council, acting unanimously on a proposal from the Commission, but which shall not be later than that on which
g the charging of tax on imports and the remission of tax on exports in trade between the Member States are abolished. Member States shall adopt the measures necessary to ensure that taxable persons declare the data required to determine own resources relating to these operations. On the basis of a report from the Commission, the Council shall review the above-mentioned reduced rates and exemptions every five
h years and, acting unanimously on a proposal from the Commission, shall where appropriate, adopt the measures required to ensure the progressive abolition thereof.'

3. The last indent of art 17 of EC Council Directive 67/228 of 11 April 1967 (on the harmonisation of legislation of member states concerning turnover taxes: structure and procedures for application of the common system of value added tax) (the Second Directive), to which art 28 of the Sixth Directive refers, provides that member states
j may—

'provide for reduced rates or even exemptions with refund, if appropriate, of the tax paid at the preceding stage, where the total incidence of such measures does not exceed that of the reliefs applied under the present system. Such measures may only be taken for clearly defined social reasons and for the benefit of the final consumer, and may not remain in force after the abolition of the imposition of tax on importation and the remission of tax on exportation in trade between Member States.'

4. On the basis of art 28(2) of the Sixth Directive, the United Kingdom has continued to apply a system called 'zero-rating'. Originally Sch 4 to the Finance Act 1972 contained a list of 17 groups of goods or services which were zero-rated. That list was incorporated almost in its entirety into Sch 5 to the Value Added Tax Act 1983.

5. The Commission considered that certain of the zero-rates provided for by the United Kingdom legislation did not comply with the criteria contained in the last indent of art 17 of the Second Directive; by a letter of 19 October 1981 it therefore called on the United Kingdom to submit its observations in accordance with the first paragraph of art 169 of the EEC Treaty.

6. The United Kingdom did not agree that it had failed to fulfil its obligations under the Treaty, and on 4 September 1984 the Commission therefore delivered a reasoned opinion. Since the United Kingdom did not comply with that opinion, the Commission brought these proceedings.

7. Reference is made to the report for the hearing for a fuller account of the facts of the case, the course of the procedure and the submissions and arguments of the parties, which are mentioned or discussed hereinafter only in so far as is necessary for the reasoning of the court.

The jurisdiction of the court

8. The United Kingdom contends that there is a political motive behind the Commission's application to the court and that such a motive is not a proper basis for an action pursuant to art 169 of the EEC Treaty. The Commission's action is intended in fact to attain by means of judicial proceedings an objective which can be achieved only by a decision of the Community legislature. It is clear from the Commission's reply that its intention in bringing these proceedings is to bypass the procedural requirements of art 28 of the Sixth Directive, under which it is for the Council, acting unanimously, to decide to abolish the exemptions permitted by that article. The United Kingdom therefore submits that it is not the task of the court 'to substitute itself for the political procedures envisaged by art 28 of the Sixth Directive and to substitute an immediate obligation on a member state for the progressive compliance envisaged by art 28'.

9. That argument cannot be upheld. In the context of the balance of powers between the institutions laid down in the Treaty, it is not for the court to consider what objectives are pursued in an action brought under art 169 of the Treaty. Its role is to decide whether or not the member state in question has failed to fulfil its obligation as alleged. As the court held in *EC Commission v Italian Republic* Case 7/68 [1968] ECR 423, an action against a member state for failure to fulfil its obligations, the bringing of which is a matter for the Commission in its entire discretion, is objective in nature.

Substance

10. It should be pointed out first of all that the Commission does not dispute the legality of the zero-rating system in general; it considers that system to be essentially equivalent to the exemptions provided for by art 28 of the Sixth Directive, as it expressly stated in its proposal for a Sixth Directive submitted to the Council on 29 June 1973. It submits, however, that the requirements laid down in the last indent of art 17 of the Second Directive, which provides that exemptions may be made only 'for clearly defined social reasons and for the benefit of the final consumer', are not met with regard to certain groups of goods and services included in Sch 5 to the 1983 Act.

11. It must therefore be determined whether the zero-rating of the goods and services at issue complies with the conditions laid down in those provisions.

The concept of 'clearly defined social reasons'

a   12. With regard to the first condition, that is to say that exemption may be granted only for clearly defined social reasons, the parties are agreed that the determination of their own social policy is a matter for the discretion of the member states. They accept, however, that that discretion may be subject to supervision at the Community level.

13. In particular, the United Kingdom accepts that the Commission may challenge a measure where the social reason cannot be said to be sufficiently 'clearly defined', where

b   the social reason advanced cannot justify the measure or if the measure lacks all proportionality. The Commission states that by 'social reasons' it understands measures which are introduced primarily for general social purposes and not principally for industrial, sectoral or fiscal reasons; it accepts, however, that it may not challenge measures taken in pursuance of a member state's social policy unless it can be shown that the social policy is not sufficiently clearly defined or that the measures in question either

c   are not justified by or are disproportionate to the social reasons advanced.

14. The identification of social reasons is in principle a matter of political choice for the member states and can be the subject matter of supervision at the Community level only in so far as, by distorting that concept, it leads to measures which because of their effects and their true objectives lie outside its scope.

d   *The phrase 'for the benefit of the final consumer'*

15. The Commission regards as 'final consumers' those persons who stand at the final stage in the manufacturing and commercial chain and have no right to deduct VAT, that is to say non-taxable persons.

16. The United Kingdom considers that there is nothing in the general scheme of VAT to indicate that the term 'final consumer' should be treated as synonymous with the

e   term 'non-taxable person'. On the contrary, the final consumer must be taken to be the natural or legal person at the end of a particular production or distribution chain for a particular product or service, even where that product or service is used in the production of other products or the provision of other services, regardless of whether or not the person is a taxable person.

17. Under the general scheme of VAT the final consumer is the person who acquires

f   goods or services for personal use, as opposed to an economic activity, and thus bears the tax. It follows that having regard to the social purpose of art 17 the term 'final consumer' can be applied only to a person who does not use exempted goods or services in the course of an economic activity. The provision of goods or services at a stage higher in the production or distribution chain which is nevertheless sufficiently close to the consumer to be of advantage to him must also be considered to be for the benefit of the final

g   consumer as so defined.

The zero rates at issue

A *Group 1: food* (animal feeding stuffs, seeds or other means of propagation of plants comprised in food for human consumption or animal feeding stuffs, live animals of a kind generally used as, or yielding or producing, food for human consumption)

h   18. The Commission's allegation is essentially that the zero-rating of these products does not comply with the second condition laid down in the last indent of art 17 of the Second Directive. It submits that transactions in these products are too remote from the final zero-rated food product to fulfil the criterion of benefit to the final consumer.

19. The United Kingdom argues that the application of a positive rate of VAT to these

j   products would entail an increase in food prices and thus jeopardise the achievement of the social objectives which it is pursuing. It also disputes the Commission's argument concerning remoteness from the final product.

20. All the supplies at issue contribute to the production of substances intended for human consumption and are sufficiently close to the final consumer to be of advantage

to him. Moreover, the negative effects of any taxation of those products on food prices, increases in which are particularly sensitive for the final consumer, who himself enjoys *a* zero-rating, cannot be neglected.

21. It follows that with regard to the products of this group at issue the alleged failure of the United Kingdom to fulfil its obligations has not been established.

B *Group 2: sewerage services and water*

22. The Commission's submission in this respect concerns services provided to *b* industry regarding the emptying of cesspools and septic tanks made necessary by the absence of a mains drainage system, on the one hand, and the supply of water to industry, on the other.

23. In neither of these cases can the provision of services to industry be regarded as fulfilling the second criterion laid down in art 17 of the Second Directive, since industrial users cannot be regarded as final consumers.   *c*

24. With regard in particular to the supply of water to industry, the United Kingdom pointed out that such supplies are exempted in another member state. In the course of the proceedings the Commission explained that that exemption is based on art 28(3)(*b*) of the Sixth Directive, according to which the member states may, during the transitional period, continue to exempt the activities set out in Annex F, in this instance 'the supply of water by public authorities'. The United Kingdom has not sought to rely on that *d* provision.

25. The failure of the United Kingdom to fulfil its obligations in respect of these products and services is therefore established.

C. *Group 6: news services provided to certain undertakings*

26. The Commission's submissions concern the supply of news services to undertakings *e* which themselves provide services which are not zero-rated, such as banks or insurance companies.

27. The United Kingdom argues that the services in question can be included as an 'incidental benefit' and that the intrinsic characteristics of news services remain the same whether they are supplied to a bank or to a newspaper, the latter being zero-rated.

28. Leaving aside the fact that an incidental benefit such as that relied on by the *f* United Kingdom has no place in the concept of a benefit to the final consumer for the purposes of art 28 of the Sixth Directive, it is clear that since the undertakings to which the news services in question are provided, such as banks and insurance companies, cannot be regarded as final consumers, the second criterion laid down in art 17 of the Second Directive is not fulfilled.

29. The failure of the United Kingdom to fulfil its obligations in respect of these *g* services is therefore established.

D *Group 7: fuel and power* (coal, coke, coal gas, water gas, petroleum gases, fuel oil, gas oil, electricity etc)

30. The Commission challenges the zero-rating of supplies of fuel and power other *h* than to final consumers.

31. In its defence the United Kingdom relies essentially on the negative effects from the social point of view of any taxation of supplies of fuel and power, in particular to schools and hospitals.

32. Whilst the court does not call in question the social reasons underlying that policy, it must point out that the services in question cannot be considered to have been provided *j* for the benefit of final consumers, since final consumers as defined above derive only very indirect advantages from zero-rating. They therefore do not fulfil the second criterion of art 17 of the Second Directive.

33. With regard to the United Kingdom's alternative argument to the effect that the difficulties in administering the tax if only supplies to final consumers were zero-rated

would probably be insurmountable, it must be observed that where a member state
a wishes to make use of the derogations in question it must take all the practical measures
necessary for the correct application of those provisions. If it considers that such measures
cannot be implemented, it must refrain from applying zero-rates.

34. The alleged failure of the United Kingdom to fulfil its obligations is therefore
established.

b E *Group 8: construction of buildings* (including in particular the initial sale of new
  buildings, the services provided by a contractor constructing a new building for a
  client who owns the site, the construction of commercial and industrial buildings,
  civil engineering works, the construction of roads, railways and airports)

35. The Commission challenges the zero-rating of all the items in Group 8 with the
exception of housing constructed by local authorities. With regard to the housing sector,
c the Commission argues that the indiscriminate application of a zero-rate to the whole
sector, regardless of the nature of the dwellings concerned, is contrary to the first criterion
laid down in the last indent of art 17 of the Second Directive inasmuch as it is
disproportionate in relation to the objectives of the United Kingdom's social policy in
housing matters. With regard to commercial and industrial buildings and to community
and civil engineering works the Commission considers that any benefit to the final
d consumer is too remote to meet the second criterion laid down in the last indent of
art 17.

36. With regard to buildings intended for housing, the Commission's arguments
cannot be upheld. The measures adopted by the United Kingdom in order to implement
its social policy in housing matters, that is to say facilitating home ownership for the
whole population, fall within the purview of 'social reasons' for the purposes of the last
e indent of art 17.

37. By applying a zero rate to the activities comprised in Group 8 with regard to
housing constructed both by local authorities and by the private sector, the United
Kingdom has not, therefore, contravened the last indent of art 17.

38. However, activities included in Group 8 in relation to the construction of industrial
f and commercial buildings and to community and civil engineering works cannot be
considered to be for the benefit of the final consumer.

39. It follows that the United Kingdom has failed to fulfil its obligations, as alleged by
the Commission, in so far as it applies a zero-rate to services in relation to the construction
of industrial and commercial buildings and to community and civil engineering works.

g F *Group 17: protective boots and helmets*
40. The Commission submits that the supply of these products to employers for the
use of their employees cannot benefit from zero-rating because they cannot be regarded
as inputs in the chain of production of products which are zero-rated.

41. The United Kingdom argues that protective boots and helmets must be considered
in their own right, not as part of a production process. The employer must, it says, be
h regarded as the final consumer of these goods.

42. In the light of the considerations set out above, it must be held that the persons to
whom these goods are supplied cannot be regarded as final consumers.

43. The alleged failure of the United Kingdom to fulfil its obligations in this respect
is therefore established.

44. It follows from all the foregoing that by continuing to apply a zero-rate of value
j added tax to the groups of goods and services specified above, the United Kingdom has
contravened the provisions of EC Council Directive 77/388 and has therefore failed to
fulfil its obligations under the EEC Treaty.

Costs
45. Under art 69(2) of the Rules of Procedure, the unsuccessful party is to be ordered

to pay the costs. Since the United Kingdom has failed in most of its submissions, it must
be ordered to pay the costs.

    a

    On those grounds, the court hereby (1) declares that, by continuing to apply a zero-
rate of value added tax to supplies to industry of water and sewerage services (emptying
of cesspools and septic tanks) included in Group 2 of Sch 5 to the Value Added Tax Act
1983, in so far as they are not supplied to final consumers; to news services included in
Group 6, in so far as they are not provided to final consumers; to supplies of fuel and   *b*
power included in Group 7 and to protective boots and helmets included in Group 17, in
so far as they are not supplied to final consumers; to the provision of goods and services
included in Group 8 in relation to the construction of industrial and commercial
buildings and to community and civil engineering works, in so far as they are not
provided to final consumers, the United Kingdom of Great Britain and Northern Ireland
has contravened the provisions of EC Council Directive 77/388 of 17 May 1977 and has   *c*
therefore failed to fulfil its obligations under the EEC Treaty; (2) for the rest, dismisses
the application; (3) orders the United Kingdom to pay the costs.

Agents: *D R Gilmour*, Legal Adviser, EC Commission (for the Commission); *Susan Hay*,
Treasury Solicitor's Department (for the United Kingdom).

Mary Rose Plummer   Barrister

a

Singh v Atombrook Ltd

COURT OF APPEAL, CIVIL DIVISION
KERR LJ AND SIR JOHN MEGAW
17 JUNE 1988

b
Writ – Amendment – Amendment to correct party's name – Amendment after judgment – Whether court having jurisdiction to allow amendment of writ after final judgment in proceedings – RSC Ord 2, r 1(2), Ord 20, r 5.

Writ – Service on company – Service at company's registered office – Failure to serve writ on company at its registered office – Whether failure nullifying proceedings – Whether failure a mere irregularity capable of remedy – Companies Act 1985, s 725(1) – RSC Ord 2, r 1.

c

The court can in principle allow a plaintiff to amend his writ even after final judgment in the proceedings has been entered (eg for the purpose of substituting the defendant's correct name for the incorrect name in which he was sued), since the court has wide general powers under RSC Ord 2, r 1(2)[d] to allow amendments and there is no rule which precludes the court from exercising its power under Ord 20, r 5[b] to allow amendments

d
to the writ or pleadings at any stage of the proceedings after final judgment has been entered (see p 390 c d and p 393 g, post); *Whittam v W J Daniel & Co Ltd* [1961] 3 All ER 796 applied; *Davies v Elsby Bros Ltd* [1960] 3 All ER 672 distinguished; *Midland Bank Trust Co Ltd v Green (No 2)* [1979] 1 All ER 726 considered.

Having regard to the wide terms of Ord 2, r 1 and its purpose of abolishing the distinction between non-compliance with procedural rules which renders proceedings a

e
nullity and non-compliance which merely renders proceedings irregular, failure to comply with s 725(1)[c] of the Companies Act 1985, which provides that a writ may be served on a company by leaving it at, or sending it by post to, the company's registered office, does not, even on the basis that the provision is mandatory, constitute such an irregularity in the proceedings as to render them a nullity and entitle the defendant to have them set aside ex debito justitiae; instead, non-compliance with s 725(1) is a mere

f
irregularity within Ord 2, r 1(1) and as such does not nullify the proceedings (see p 391 h j, p 392 b, p 393 g and p 394 g h, post); *Vignes v Stephen Smith & Co Ltd* (1909) 53 SJ 716 distinguished.

Notes

For non-compliance with rules of court, see 37 Halsbury's Laws (4th edn) paras 36–39,

g
and for cases on the subject, see 37(2) Digest (Reissue) 205–217, 1355–1412.

For amendment of a writ, see 36 Halsbury's Laws (4th edn) paras 68–71 and 37 ibid para 271, and for cases on the subject, see 37(1) Digest (Reissue) 255–272, 1696–1781.

For the Companies Act 1985, s 725, see 8 Halsbury's Statutes (4th edn) 664.

---

h
a   Rule 1, so far as material, is set out at p 388 d, post
b   Rule 5, so far as material, provides:
    '(1) ... the Court may at any stage of the proceedings allow the plaintiff to amend his writ, or any party to amend his pleading, on such terms as to costs or otherwise as may be just and in such manner (if any) as it may direct.
    (2) Where an application to the Court for leave to make the amendment mentioned in paragraph (3) ... is made after any relevant period of limitation current at the date of issue of the

j
writ has expired, the Court may nevertheless grant such leave in the circumstances mentioned in that paragraph if it thinks it just to do so ...
    (3) An amendment to correct the name of a party may be allowed under paragraph (2) notwithstanding that it is alleged that the effect of the amendment will be to substitute a new party if the Court is satisfied that the mistake sought to be corrected was a genuine mistake and was not misleading or such as to cause any reasonable doubt as to the identity of the person intending to sue or, as the case may be, intended to be sued ...'
c   Section 725(1) is set out at p 390 g, post.

Cases referred to in judgments

Davies v Elsby Bros Ltd [1960] 3 All ER 672, [1961] 1 WLR 170, CA.

Harkness v Bell's Asbestos and Engineering Ltd [1966] 3 All ER 843, [1967] 2 QB 729, [1967] 2 WLR 29, CA.

Midland Bank Trust Co Ltd v Green (No 2) [1979] 1 All ER 726, [1979] 1 WLR 460.

Pritchard (decd), Re [1963] 1 All ER 873, [1963] Ch 502, [1963] 2 WLR 685, CA.

Sharpley and Manby's Arbitration, Re [1942] 1 All ER 66, [1942] 1 KB 217, CA.

Stylo Shoes Ltd v Prices Tailors Ltd [1959] 3 All ER 901, [1960] Ch 396, [1960] 2 WLR 8.

Tennant v London CC (1957) 121 JP 428, CA.

Vignes v Stephen Smith & Co Ltd (1909) 53 SJ 716.

White v Weston [1968] 2 All ER 842, [1968] 2 QB 647, [1968] 2 WLR 1459, CA.

Whittam v W J Daniel & Co Ltd [1961] 3 All ER 796, [1962] 1 QB 271, [1961] 3 WLR 1123, CA.

Interlocutory appeal

By a writ issued on 4 June 1987 the plaintiff, Mrs Santosh Kumari Singh, suing as administratrix of the estate of her deceased husband Mr Ranjit Singh, claimed against 'Sterling Travel (a firm)' as defendant the return of money paid by Mr Singh to Sterling Travel Ltd for three airline tickets which, following Mr Singh's death, the plaintiff returned to Sterling Travel, which agreed to arrange for a refund of the price of the tickets. In default of any appearance by Sterling Travel the plaintiff obtained a default judgment on 21 July 1987. On 25 November 1987 the defendant, Atombrook Ltd (trading as Sterling Travel), applied to have the default judgment set aside for irregularity, because of the misnomer of the defendant in the writ on the grounds that the defendant should have been named as 'Atombrook Ltd trading as Sterling Travel', and the failure to serve the writ on Atombrook Ltd at its registered office. On 22 December 1987 Mr District Registrar Bailey-Cox set aside the default judgment on condition that the defendant pay into court the full sum claimed by the plaintiff. On appeal by the defendant, Hutchison J, sitting in the High Court at Winchester on 29 January 1988, affirmed the registrar's order, and also directed that the writ be amended to name the defendant as Atombrook Ltd trading as Sterling Travel. The defendant appealed, seeking to have the orders of the district registrar and Hutchison J set aside and the default judgment of 21 July 1987 set aside unconditionally. The facts are set out in the judgment of Kerr LJ.

Thomas Weitzman for the defendant.
David Bartlett for the plaintiff.

KERR LJ. This is an appeal by the defendant from an order made by Hutchison J sitting at Winchester on 29 January 1988, whereby he affirmed an order of Mr District Registrar Bailey-Cox made in the Southampton District Registry on 22 December 1987. Both orders set aside at the request of the defendant a judgment which had been obtained by the plaintiff against the defendant in an incorrect name, but in each case on terms that the defendant bring into court the full sum claimed, about £1,300, on the ground that the indicated defence was shadowy. The appeal is on the ground that this was an irregular judgment, irregular to the point of being a nullity, with the result that notwithstanding the far-reaching changes introduced by the new RSC Ord 2, the defendant was entitled to have it set aside as of right, or ex debito justitiae, to use the phrase used in a number of the authorities, and accordingly without the imposition of the condition that it brings the amount claimed into court. The defendant also submits that both the district registrar and the judge were wrong in allowing the writ to be amended so as to substitute the defendant's correct name for the name in which it had been sued.

The claim arises in sad circumstances. The plaintiff is the widow and administratrix of the estate of her late husband, Mr Ranjit Singh. On or about 6 June 1984 Mr Singh, in

the company of the plaintiff and another member of the family, went to the premises of
a   travel agents trading under the name 'Sterling Travel', or at least displaying that name,
in Rupert Street, London W1. They bought three airline tickets for a flight to the United
States for Mrs Singh and her two children on 25 July 1984. Sadly, on 27 June 1984 Mr
Singh died and his wife and the two children were therefore unable to travel to the
United States. The daughter took the tickets back to Sterling Travel on or about 10 July
1984 and, as she said, was assured that the agents would obtain a refund of the price of
b   the tickets for the plaintiff. She never obtained such a refund, although the tickets were
never returned to her or not for a long time.

After the tickets had been taken back to Sterling Travel, without any further response
from them, repeated inquiries were made and letters were written by the plaintiff and
her solicitors, who have done everything possible to try to obtain some satisfaction for
her. In the early stages there were some telephone calls in response to these letters to
c   Sterling Travel in Rupert Street. So they were being received. Various temporising
assurances were given; but no satisfaction was obtained. As it transpires, Sterling Travel,
or whoever was trading in the name of Sterling Travel, then moved away from Rupert
Street, and by the time these proceedings had been started they were no longer trading
there. The writ was issued on 4 June 1987 addressed to 'Sterling Travel (a firm)' at the
Rupert Street address. It was posted to Rupert Street on 5 June 1987. Nothing was heard
d   from the defendant and some six weeks later, on 21 July 1987, judgment was entered in
default.

Steps were than taken to try to execute the judgment. But on 24 August 1987 a
company called United Air Travel Services Ltd sent a telex to the plaintiff's solicitors
saying that they had just received the writ. They said that there was no firm called
Sterling Travel; there was a company called Atombrook Ltd who were, as they said, an
e   associated company of United Air Travel Services Ltd, and Atombrook Ltd was the
proprietor of Sterling Travel. One can see from the notepaper of this company that
although it is prominently headed 'Sterling Travel' there is a very small note at the
bottom saying 'Proprietors, Atombrook Limited', whose registered address is stated to be
in Goswell Road, London E1. Although in certain circumstances it is possible for a
f   limited company to have an interest in a firm in a way which would appropriately
describe them as proprietors of the firm, it is not suggested that this is the present
situation. It is accepted that the correct name of the defendant whom the plaintiff
intended to sue, and who obviously realised that they were the parties whom the plaintiff
intended to sue, should have been 'Atombrook Limited, T/a Sterling Travel'. One can see
immediately that this line of defence by the defendant, unlike the name Sterling Travel
in which they chose to trade, no doubt because they thought it sounded and would sell
g   better, is utterly without merit.

The response to the telex from United Air Travel was that the plaintiff's solicitors
wrote on 26 August 1987 inviting an application to have the judgment set aside. There
were then abortive execution proceedings because the sheriff could not find anybody still
trading in the name of Sterling Travel in Rupert Street. Ultimately, on 25 November
h   1987 the defendant applied to have the judgment set aside on the ground that it had
been 'irregularly obtained'. Accordingly there had been a delay of several months from
the time when United Air Travel Services Ltd knew about the writ and from the time
when the defendant, through United Air Travel Services Ltd, had been advised to have
the judgment set aside if it wished to do so. In the view of the judge, which is not open
to criticism, that was an unreasonably long time in the circumstances.

j   I should add that the evidence filed on behalf of the defendant is significantly silent on
the question as to when anybody concerned with the defendant first became aware of the
writ and the judgment. That may well have been substantially before the telex of
24 August. That telex may only have been sent because those associated with Atombrook
Ltd, and previously with Sterling Travel, or whatever may have been the position, were
becoming uncomfortable because of the attempts to enforce this judgment.

There then followed the orders which I have already mentioned. Both the registrar and the judge took the view that the defendant should have the opportunity of raising a defence which it claimed to have, but only on terms of bringing the money into court. The effective issue today is whether the defendant is bound to bring that amount into court if it wishes to resist the plaintiff's claim, now amended by describing the defendant in its full correct name.

To see the issues which arise I must refer to a number of provisions of the Rules of the Supreme Court. Order 2, r 1(1) and (2) is as follows:

'(1) Where, in beginning or purporting to begin any proceedings or at any stage in the course of or in connection with any proceedings, there has, by reason of any thing done or left undone, been a failure to comply with the requirements of these rules, whether in respect of time, place, manner, form or content or in any other respect, the failure shall be treated as an irregularity and shall not nullify the proceedings, any step taken in the proceedings, or any document, judgment or order therein.

(2) Subject to paragraph (3) the Court may, on the ground that there has been such a failure as is mentioned in paragraph (1) and on such terms as to costs or otherwise as it thinks just, set aside either wholly or in part the proceedings in which the failure occurred, any step taken in those proceedings or any document, judgment or order therein or exercise its powers under these rules to allow such amendments (if any) to be made and to make such order (if any) dealing with the proceedings generally as it thinks fit.'

The first two paragraphs of the notes to that rule in *The Supreme Court Practice 1988* vol 1, para 2/1/1 are in the following terms:

'*Effect of rule*—The predecessor of this rule (O.59 of R.S.C. 1875; O.70, r. 1, of R.S.C. 1883) sought to provide that non-compliance with any of the rules should not of itself render any proceedings void unless the Court should so direct, but that they might be set aside wholly or in part as irregular or amended on such terms as the Court might think fit. Nevertheless the decisions under the rule preserved a distinction between a non-compliance such as rendered the proceedings a nullity (in which case the Court had no discretion but to treat them as a nullity and set them aside) and a non-compliance which merely rendered the proceedings irregular (in which case they remained valid and the Court had a discretion what order to make in the circumstances). It was held, indeed, that the Order did not apply to the former class of case but only the latter.

As a result of the decision of the Court of Appeal in *Re Pritchard decd.* ([1963] 1 All ER 873, [1963] Ch 502) the present rule was by R.S.C. 1964 substituted for rr. 1 and 2 of the previous O.2 and under it the above distinction between nullity and mere irregularity disappears (see *Harkness* v. *Bell's Asbestos & Engineering Ltd* ([1966] 3 All ER 843 at 845, [1967] 2 QB 729 at 735)) at any rate in regard to "a failure to comply with the requirements of these rules", though it may still be that there are other failures to comply with statutory requirements or other improprieties so serious as to render the proceedings in which they occur, and any order made therein, a nullity . . .'

I must then quote Ord 2, r 2:

'(1) An application to set aside for irregularity any proceedings, any step taken in any proceedings or any document, judgment or order therein shall not be allowed unless it is made within a reasonable time and before the party applying has taken any fresh step after becoming aware of the irregularity.

(2) An application under this rule may be made by summons or motion and the grounds of objection must be stated in the summons or notice of motion.'

a It will be noted that under Ord 2, r 2(1) the grant of an application to set aside for irregularity is only permissible if it is made 'within a reasonable time'. As already mentioned, the judge rightly took the view that the summons to set this judgment aside had not been issued within a reasonable time. Accordingly, as he held, the defendant was not entitled to have the judgment set aside under Ord 2 as a matter of right. He accepted, and I shall have to deal with this in a moment, that the judgment had been obtained irregularly in two respects. First, there was no firm called Sterling Travel; the only

b relevant entity was 'Atombrook Limited, trading as Sterling Travel'. Second, the writ and subsequent proceedings had not been served at the registered address of Atombrook Ltd in Goswell Road but at an address in Rupert Street. However, he held that while the defendant could accordingly not rely on Ord 2, r 2, the was willing in the circumstances to set aside the judgment under Ord 13, r 9, which provides that the court may set aside any judgment on such terms as it thinks just, which would include the default judgment

c in the present case. In the same way as the district registrar, the judge considered that it was just in this case that the defendant should bring the full amount claimed into court. At the same time, and in my view it does not matter precisely in which order he did so, he exercised his discretion to give leave to amend the writ by substituting for 'Sterling Travel', 'Atombrook Limited, T/a Serling Travel'. In doing that, he may have been purporting to exercise his powers under Ord 20, r 5(3) by correcting the name of a party

d in the circumstances there set out. Or perhaps (but it does not matter for present purposes) he was proceeding under Ord 2, r 1(2), which includes a general power of amendment.

In connection with Ord 20, r 5(3), it is at least to be said in favour of the defendant that it has conceded throughout that the plaintiff acted under a mistake which was entirely genuine, that they (I am referring throughout to the individuals who were in

e fact concerned as 'the defendant') had no doubt that these proceedings were directed to them and that they were never misled by the fact that the defendant was named 'Sterling Travel' and not 'Atombrook Limited, T/a Sterling Travel'. Indeed, the mistake was not only genuine but entirely understandable, since this entity, Atombrook Ltd, was clearly purporting to trade as Sterling Travel, giving the impression in every way that there was a firm of travel agents called Sterling Travel. It was that which induced this mistake. In

f these circumstances it would be a case of regret, if not for shame, if the change in the rule under Ord 2, r 1, which had been designed to achieve the purposes set out in the note to it which I have read, was unable to deal with this situation. It would be a blemish on the law if the judge did not have power to do what he did.

Counsel for the defendant submits, nevertheless, that that is the position. He has taken two points, of which the second falls into two parts.

g The point which I take first is that since this was a final judgment, albeit a default judgment, there was no power to amend the writ once judgment had been entered. Therefore, he said, as I followed his submission, that even if the judge was correct in setting the judgment aside as he did, nevertheless there was no power to amend the writ thereafter. Accordingly the writ falls away, the judgment having been set aside; and if

h the plaintiff wishes to start again the ordinary rules would apply, enabling the defendant to defend unconditionally.

Counsel for the defendant bases that on a summary of three authorities referred to in a note to Ord 20, r 5 (which I have mentioned) in *The Supreme Court Practice 1988* vol 1, para 20/5–8/14 which is somewhat cautiously worded. Having referred in the first paragraph to interlocutory judgments and decrees in Admiralty actions leaving damages

j to be assessed, the second paragraph states: 'But after final decree or judgment the Judge of first instance cannot, or at all events will not, amend the pleadings or add new parties . . .' Then there is a reference to three cases, of which the latest, was in 1907. Counsel for the defendant offered to refer us to them but he described them as 'gnomic' and was conscious, at any rate to some extent, of the passage of time and of the importance that counsel must be selective in their submissions. We have therefore not seen those cases;

but counsel for the defendant did not suggest that they were any more definite than the note.

However, he was right to refer us to a decision of Oliver J in *Midland Bank Trust Co Ltd v Green (No 2)* [1979] 1 All ER 726 at 733, [1979] 1 WLR 460 at 468, where there are remarks on the power to amend after judgment. I do not propose to read what Oliver J there said. It is perhaps not entirely clear whether he took the view that the general jurisdiction of the court to give leave to amend pleadings 'even after judgment', the phrase which he used, was intended to cover the position where the judgment is final but execution and enforcement proceedings are still pending, as in the present case. I think his language is capable of being construed in that way, that pending enforcement there is still power to amend the proceedings even after final judgment. But he was admittedly dealing with a different situation. However, no case having been cited which precludes the court from amending the pleadings under Ord 20, r 5 after final judgment, and having regard to the cautious way in which the note in *The Supreme Court Practice* is expressed, I would hold that there is no reason in principle, particularly given the width of the new Ord 2, r 1, which precludes the court in appropriate cases from amending the pleadings and proceedings even after final judgment. There being no clear authority to the contrary, and having regard to Ord 2, r 1(1) and (2), I reject the first submission of counsel for the defendant as being contrary to that provision.

I then come to the two matters which counsel for the defendant put in the forefront. He said that the defendant was entitled to have this judgment set aside ex debito justitiae on the ground that it was a total nullity and not merely one which had been obtained irregularly, even though his own summons had applied to have it set aside on the ground that it had been obtained irregularly. This is a somewhat complex argument, since counsel for the defendant cannot challenge the judge's conclusion under Ord 2, r 2(1), to that extent clearly unappealable, that the application to set aside was not made within a reasonable time. But counsel for the defendant submits, as I understand it, that that does not matter, because the judgment was not merely one which has been obtained irregularly, but a nullity. In that context he relied on the remarks of Diplock LJ in *Harkness v Bell's Asbestos and Engineering Ltd* [1966] 3 All ER 843 at 846, [1967] 2 QB 729 at 736.

Counsel for the defendant claims that it was a nullity on two grounds. First, and this is the order which he adopted, the writ was served on the defendant at an address other than its registered address. In that regard he relied on s 725(1) of the Companies Act 1985, which provides:

'A document may be served on a company by leaving it at, or sending it by post to, the company's registered office.'

That provision is echoed in Ord 10, r 1(2) and (7) and Ord 65, r 3(2), but I do not think it is necessary to refer to those rules, which do not go further than s 725. Counsel for the defendant submits that a writ served on a body corporate elsewhere than at its registered address is simply a nullity and that although the word in the section is 'may' it is to be read as 'must'. For that purpose he relies on a decision of Eve J in *Vignes v Stephen Smith & Co Ltd* (1909) 53 SJ 716, in which a writ had been served on a company elsewhere than at its registered office and Eve J held that that writ could not stand. He said in relation to the predecessor of s 725:

'Now counsel for the plaintiff points out that the words in the section and in the rule are "may be served" and not "must be served," and he says that the court may look at the surrounding circumstances and say whether the fact that the writ has been issued has been brought home to the company, and whether the company have not done all that is necessary for that purpose, and he cited cases where the writ was not set aside, though the rule had not been strictly adhered to. Those cases were mostly cases of foreign companies, and are not really germane to the present case. Here the question is whether it is competent to serve a company with a writ except

in the prescribed form. I am precluded by the decisions cited by the defendants'
a counsel from holding that the writ has been properly served. The rule and the
section clearly indicate that the only way in which a writ can be served on a company
is by leaving it at or sending it by post to the registered office. There will therefore
be an order setting aside the writ.'

There are a number of things to be said about that decision, apart from the fact that it
b does not appear to have been referred to in any subsequent case, at any rate not one which
has been cited to us. First, the judge was not concerned with any application for
amendment of the address for service, or of the process, or of anything which would
have been in the previous Ord 70 or the predecessor of what is now Ord 2, r 1. That
simply did not arise. The only question was whether the writ could stand or whether it
should be set aside.

c   Second, the strictness of that interpretation of the word 'may' in legislation which deals
with service by various means is not borne out by two subsequent decisions. The first
was a decision of this court in *Re Sharpley and Manby's Abitration* [1942] 1 All ER 66,
[1942] KB 217, in which the relevant statutory provision stated that one of the ways of
serving process might be by registered post. But it was held that sending it by ordinary
post was a sufficient compliance with the word 'may' in that provision. It is true that the
d result of that case can also be justified by reference to another provision which rendered
it sufficient if the process had been brought to the attention of the defendants.
    That was pointed out in the second of these cases by Wynn-Parry J in *Stylo Shoes Ltd v
Prices Tailors Ltd* [1959] 3 All ER 901 at 905, [1960] Ch 396 at 405. He dealt with *Re
Sharpley and Manby's Arbitration* and pointed out that the decision could be explained on
the basis that another part of that provision was satisfied, and that it was not necessarily
e based on the interpretation of the word 'may'. But he went on:

    'But there is another point which to my mind was fatal to the tenants in this case.
    On the reasoning of the members of the Court of Appeal in *Tennant* v. *London County
    Council* ((1957) 121 JP 428) I feel constrained to construe s. 23(1) as being permissive
    so far as the mode of service is concerned. It is perfectly true, as was pointed out by
f   counsel for the tenants, that the requirement that the notice etc. is to be in writing
    is imperative—"Any notice, request, demand or other instrument under this Act
    shall be in writing"; but then when the subsection goes on to deal with service the
    permissive verb "may" is used, and that is in clear contradistinction to the imperative
    "shall". I can see no canon of construction which would entitle me to qualify the
    nature of the verb "may" by anything that has gone before in the subsection.'
g
It is true, of course, that that was an entirely different provision from s 725 of the 1985
Act and it may well be that the decision of Eve J is still good law so far as what is now
s 725 is concerned, viewed in isolation.
    But even if that is so, and I must say that I have some doubts as to why 'may' must be
construed as 'must' in that provision, it appears to me quite clear that even if there were
h an irregularity under the statute to that extent, and therefore also under the rules which
contain provisions to the same effect, it would nevertheless be insufficient to render the
proceedings a nullity so as to entitle the defendant to have them set aside ex debito
justitiae. Any other view would produce an extraordinary result in the face of Ord 2, r 1
and the note to it which I have read. Accordingly I would reject that submission.
    I should add that, among other cases, we were referred to the decision of this court in
j *White v Weston* [1968] 2 All ER 842, [1968] 2 QB 647. Russell and Sachs LJJ held that a
judgment should be set aside unconditionally ex debito justitiae without referring to the
new rule because it was a plain case of the defendant being totally unaware of the
proceedings from the beginning to the end of the history. Both Russell and Sachs LJJ
thought that one did not get much assistance from considering whether a judgment is to
be described as having been obtained irregularly or whether it was a nullity. In a passage

with which Sachs LJ agreed (see [1968] 2 All ER 842 at 848, [1968] 2 QB 647 at 662),
Russell LJ said ([1968] 2 All ER 842 at 846, [1968] 2 QB 647 at 659):   *a*

> 'I do not myself attach importance to the question whether it is proper to label a
> judgment obtained in circumstances such as this as "irregular" or "a nullity". The
> defect is in my judgment so fundamental as to entitle the defendant as of right, ex
> debito justitiae, to have the judgment avoided and set aside.'

In my view there can be no question of the present case involving any defect of a *b*
fundamental nature, let alone one as fundamental as in *White v Weston.*

I come to the second point raised by counsel for the defendant, which at first sight
appears to be more fundamental. He says that this was a writ issued against a non-existent
person, since there was no firm called Sterling Travel. That is conceded. But it leaves
open the question whether this is a proceeding issued against someone who can properly
be described as non-existent, or merely against a defendant who has been misnamed or *c*
misdescribed. If it is the latter, then Ord 2, r 1 clearly applies, and Ord 20, r 5(3) probably
as well. There are two helpful decisions of this court in that connection. The first was
Davies v Elsby Bros Ltd [1960] 3 All ER 672, [1961] 1 WLR 170. A writ had been issued
against 'Elsby Brothers (a firm)' and then amended by striking out '(a firm)' and adding
the word 'Ltd.' after the limitation period had expired. It concerned an accident sustained
by the plaintiff, who had been an employee both of the firm, Elsby Bros, and of the *d*
limited company which it subsequently became. The writ did not state on what date the
accident occurred, so that it was impossible to ascertain from the writ whether the
plaintiff had intended to sue one legal entity, the firm, or another legal entity, the
company. In the view of the court that was fatal to the power to amend the writ. Devlin
LJ dealt with the matter by saying that whether a writ was addressed to a non-existent
party or whether it was a case of misnomer or misdescription must be decided on the *e*
basis of what a reasonable reader in the position of the defendant would conclude on
receiving the writ. He said ([1960] 3 All ER 672 at 676, [1961] 1 WLR 170 at 176):

> 'The test must be: How would a reasonable person receiving the document take
> it? If, in all the circumstances of the case and looking at the document as a whole,
> he would say to himself: "Of course it must mean me, but they have got my name *f*
> wrong", then there is a case of mere misnomer. If, on the other hand, he would say:
> "I cannot tell from the document itself whether they mean me or not and I shall
> have to make inquiries", then it seems to me that one is getting beyond the realm
> of misnomer. One of the factors which must operate on the mind of the recipient
> of a document, and which operates in this case, is whether there is or is not another
> entity to whom the description on the writ might refer.'   *g*

Then he dealt with the facts of that case as an example. As one can see, given the absence
of the date of the accident sued on, it would be impossible for any objective reader to
know, or to be sure, from the writ whether the plaintiff intended to sue the firm or the
company; he would have to make inquiries as to when the alleged accident took place
and so forth.   *h*

Of course, in the present case there was never the slightest doubt in the mind of the
defendant that the plaintiff intended to sue it and that it was the person with whom this
case was concerned. From start to finish it knew that perfectly well, and in my judgment
it was taking steps throughout to avoid the pursuit of this claim against it. Undaunted,
however, counsel for the defendant said that this still left it open for an objective person
to have construed the writ in a different way. He was suggesting, though I find it *j*
impossible to follow the argument in full or to accept it, that an objective person,
although knowing all the facts which the defendant knew, might still have thought that
this plaintiff intended to sue a firm called Sterling Travel which might be an existing
entity, or something of that kind. That is fanciful and I reject it. The matter is put
beyond doubt by a further decision of this court in *Whittam v W J Daniel & Co Ltd* [1961]
3 All ER 796, [1962] 1 QB 271. In that case a limited company was sued within the

limitation period but without adding the word 'Limited', and therefore appeared to have
a been sued in the name of a firm. The court allowed the word 'Limited' to be added after
the limitation period had expired, and distinguished *Davies v Elsby Bros Ltd* [1960] 3 All
ER 672, [1961] 1 WLR 170. Donovan LJ quoted the test of Devlin LJ to which I have
referred and said ([1961] 3 All ER 796 at 799, [1962] 1 QB 271 at 277):

> 'Applying that test, there could have been no doubt in the mind of the defendants
> when they got the writ that it was they whom the plaintiff intended to sue and that
b > she had simply got the name wrong.'

Danckwerts LJ said that the case was plainly distinguishable from *Davies v Elsby Bros
Ltd* because:

> '... in the present case, there is no other entity to which the description in the
> writ could be taken to refer.'
c
(See [1961] 3 All ER 796 at 802, [1962] 1 QB 271 at 282.)
He went on:

> 'On the other hand, counsel for the defendants' argument is that it is a description
> which describes nothing and, therefore, is an action against nobody, and, therefore,
d > it would be improper and against the rules to put in the defendants in place of a
> person which did not exist. I cannot accept that argument. It seems to me that this
> is a case in which the description could only refer to the defendants and would not
> be taken by any reasonable person to refer to anybody but the defendants.'

That authority applies precisely to the present case. Although at first sight a more
fundamental point, one can therefore see why counsel for the defendant put it second to
e the point which he took on service. In my view it is simply untenable in the face of the
authorities. This is a case which falls plainly within the scope of the new Ord 2, r 1. The
judgment had been obtained irregularly in the two respects to which I have referred. But
it could still be amended, although it was a final judgment, both under Ord 2, r 1(2) and
Ord 20, r 5. The defendant was not entitled to have it set aside as of right. It was only
entitled to have it set aside, as it was, under Ord 13, r 9. Proceeding under that provision
f the judge was entirely right to impose the condition that the defendant should bring the
amount claimed into court, and he was also entitled to amend the name of the defendant
in the writ as he did.
I would dismiss this appeal.

g **SIR JOHN MEGAW.** I agree that the appeal should be dismissed for the reasons that
have been given by Kerr LJ.
I would add a few paragraphs. First, I would like to express my sympathy with counsel
for the defendant for the fact that he had an extremely difficult row to hoe because, to
carry on the metaphor, the ground which he had to plough was far from fertile. But I
would pay tribute to the thoroughness of the research and the diligence with which he
h has put forward the points which, I should also say, were expressed with admirable
fullness and clarity in his skeleton argument.
The only issues on which I desire to add anything to what Kerr LJ has said (it may be
nothing more than repetition) is in relation to what appears to me to be the only issue in
this case which can really be said to involve an important question of principle. That is
dealt with by counsel for the defendant in his skeleton argument under the heading
j 'Scope and operation of the Rules of the Supreme Court O.2'.
He sets out the relevant part of RSC Ord 2, r 1(1), including the provision that any
'failure to comply with [the Rules of the Supreme Court] ... shall be treated as an
irregularity and shall not nullify the proceedings, any step taken in the proceedings, or
any document, judgment or order therein'. Counsel for the defendant goes on to submit
that there are certain failures, nevertheless, which fall outside the scope of that part of the
order and which will render proceedings, or any subsequent steps in the proceedings,

nullities. In other words, he submits that, as the position was on the authorities before
the amendment was made bringing in the present Ord 2 in 1964, there is a distinction *a*
between things that go wrong procedurally which constitute invalidity so as to make the
whole of the proceedings invalid as a matter of course on the one hand and irregularities
in procedure on the other.

I do not propose to go into the submission that, in spite of the way in which Ord 2, r 1
is now framed, there still remain failures, which presumably mean failures in compliance
with some part of the Rules of the Supreme Court, which will render proceedings *b*
nullities. The two 'failures' which appear to me to be of possible significance, as set out
in the skeleton argument of counsel for the defendant, are, first, the bringing of
proceedings against a non-existent party and, second, the failure to comply with a
statutory requirement. He also sets out a third, with which I do not think it is necessary
to deal.

If indeed there were in this case nullities in the sense of rendering the proceedings *c*
invalid, whether by virtue of proceedings having been brought against a non-existent
party, or by virtue of failure to comply with a statutory requirement, then, while the
judge would properly have set aside the judgment at the instance of the defendant, he
would not have been entitled to make such setting aside conditional. But the judge did
not regard the irregularities as being other than irregularities coming within Ord 2, r 1.

So far as there is a suggestion that invalidity is caused by the bringing of proceedings *d*
against a non-existent party, the simple answer on the facts of this case is that the
proceedings here are not properly to be treated as against a non-existent party. There was
merely a misnomer. Once you get from persons representing the defendant what appears
in the telex which United Air Travel Services Ltd sent on 24 August 1987, it becomes
quite impossible to believe that the defendant itself regarded these proceedings as being
against a non-existent party. It is to be assumed, as the defendant would wish us to *e*
assume, that that telex was sent on behalf of, and with the authority of, the proper
defendant, Atombrook Ltd.

It is perhaps theoretically possible in some circumstances that, though the defendant
itself did not regard the proceedings as being against a non-existent party, some person
with the same knowledge as the defendant might have so regarded them, that is to say
such a person might have taken a different view from that which the defendant itself *f*
took. But in the circumstances of this case that is not a probable, nor, I think, a
conceivable, hypothesis.

With regard to the second of the alleged nullities or invalidities, the failure to comply
with the statutory requirement, as Kerr LJ has pointed out, the statutory requirement
which is asserted here is s 725 of the Companies Act 1985. Subsection (1) says that a
document may be served on a company by leaving it at, or sending it by post to, the *g*
company's registered office. This document, for reasons which are apparent and which
really cannot be put as being in any serious way the fault of the plaintiff, was not
addressed to Atombrook Ltd's registered office, but in my view that does not, in the
circumstances, by itself result in invalidity: it is merely an irregularity. How serious an
irregularity a failure to state a company's address accurately may be will of course depend *h*
on the circumstances. It may well be that it would in some cases be an irregularity that
would justify the court, without more, in setting aside unconditionally any judgment
that had been entered. But it would be absurd to suggest that any failure to send the writ
to the correct address, as for example some minor error in the address which caused no
conceivable prejudice to the defendant, could result in the whole of the proceedings
being invalid; and in this case I see no basis whatever for suggesting that there was a *j*
failure to comply with the statutory requirement such as to invalidate the proceedings.

The judge thought it right to set aside the judgment on the basis that there was at least
a possibility that the defendant had not had the opportunity to appear in court and put
its case before judgment was entered, because it may not have had notice of the writ and
of the proceedings by that time. If that is a possibility, then it could be an injustice that
it should not have the judgment set aside and the opportunity to be heard and to put its

a defence. But in the present case, having regard to all the relevant circumstances, I see no basis for saying that the judge, in setting aside the judgment, was wrong in making that order conditional on the payment into court, having regard to the basis on which he reached that decision, namely that the defence, as put forward in the documents that were before him (and here of course I am not speaking about what may be the defence in the ultimate trial but the defence as it appeared in the documents before the judge) was indeed shadowy.

b   I agree that the appeal should be dismissed.

Appeal dismissed. Payment into court to be within 14 days of judgment in Court of Appeal. Defence to be served within 14 days of same date.

c Solicitors: *Brutton & Co*, Fareham (for the defendant); *Lamport Bassitt*, Southampton (for the plaintiff).

Wendy Shockett   Barrister.

d
Re C and another (minors) (wardship: adoption)

COURT OF APPEAL, CIVIL DIVISION
PURCHAS LJ AND SIR DENYS BUCKLEY
e 4 OCTOBER 1988

Adoption – Removal of child outside Great Britain – Removal by relative – Relative – Great-uncle – Whether great-uncle a 'relative' – Whether great-uncle permitted to remove child outside Great Britain for adoption – Adoption Act 1976, ss 56(1), 72(1).

f
Adoption – Ward of court – Guardianship order – Removal of child outside Great Britain – Removal by guardian – Wards' great-uncle and great-aunt wishing to adopt wards and remove them to Australia – Whether court having inherent jurisdiction to make guardianship order in respect of wards of court – Whether court should exercise jurisdiction to make guardianship order which derogates from wardship jurisdiction.

g
Following the breakdown of their parents' marriage the two young children of the marriage were made wards of court and committed to the care of the local authority, which was given leave to place them with foster parents with a view to adoption. The childrens' paternal great-uncle and great-aunt, who were domiciled in Australia, wished to adopt the children and were regarded as suitable adopters by the local authority, which h applied to the court for leave to remove the children from the jurisdiction and place them with the great-uncle and great-aunt in Australia as prospective adopters. Under s 56(1)[a] of the Adoption Act 1976 the removal of children for adoption outside Great Britain by any person who was not 'a parent or guardian or relative of the child' was prohibited. The local authority accordingly made an interim application for a declaration that the great-uncle was a 'relative' for the purposes of s 56(1) or alternatively an order j making the great-uncle and great-aunt 'guardians' of the children. The judge held that for the purposes of the 1976 Act a great-uncle was not a 'relative' and he refused to make a declaration to that effect but with a view to leaving open the possibility of adoption by the great-uncle and great-aunt as 'guardians' he appointed them guardians of the children pending the hearing of the application for leave to remove the children from the

---

a Section 56(1), so far as material, is set out at p 398 *f g*, post

jurisdiction. The mother, who was opposed to the adoption by the great-uncle and great-aunt, appealed against the order and the local authority cross-appealed against the judge's   *a*
ruling that a great-uncle was not a 'relative'.

Held – (1) Having regard to the clear and precise definition of 'relative' in s 72(1)^b of the 1976 Act, which included 'uncle' but not 'great-uncle', a great-uncle was not a 'relative' for the purposes of s 56(1) of that Act. The local authority's cross-appeal would therefore be dismissed (see p 399 *d e* and p 401 *h*, post).   *b*

(2) It was doubtful whether the court had inherent jurisdiction to make a guardianship order when there was an existing wardship, but, even if there was, it was a wrong exercise of that jurisdiction to make a guardianship order which derogated from the wardship jurisdiction being exercised by the court itself and the local authority's statutory powers arising out of the children being in their care. The mother's appeal against the interim guardianship order would therefore be allowed (see p 400 *f* and p 401 *h*, post); *Re M (a*   *c*
minor) (adoption: removal from jurisdiction) [1973] 1 All ER 852 distinguished.

Notes
For restrictions on the removal of children for adoption abroad and for who is a relative for the purposes of adoption, see 24 Halsbury's Laws (4th edn) paras 640, 653.

For the Adoption Act 1976, ss 56, 72, see 6 Halsbury's Statutes (4th edn) 488, 501.   *d*

Cases referred to in judgments
M *(a minor) (adoption: removal from jurisdiction)*, Re [1973] 1 All ER 852, [1973] Fam 66, [1973] 2 WLR 515.
M*'Cullochs (minors)*, Re (1844) 6 I Eq R 393, LC.
McGrath (infants), Re [1893] 1 Ch 143, CA.   *e*

Interlocutory appeal
The mother of two infant children, who were wards of court, appealed against the order of his Honour Judge Aglionby, sitting as a judge of the High Court in wardship on 8 September 1988, making the wards' paternal great-uncle and great-aunt guardians of the wards within the jurisdiction pending the hearing of an application by Kent County   *f*
Council, to whom the care of the wards had been committed, for leave to remove the wards from the jurisdiction. The local authority cross-appealed against a ruling by the judge that a great-uncle was not a 'relative' for the purpose of the application to remove the wards from the jurisdiction. The facts are set out in the judgment of Purchas LJ.

Jean Adele Williams for the mother.   *g*
Caroline Budden for the council.

PURCHAS LJ. The appellant in this case is the mother. She appeals from an order of his Honour Judge Aglionby, sitting as a judge of the High Court in wardship, made on 8 September 1988. The first respondents to the appeal are the Kent County Council (to   *h*
whom I shall refer as 'the council'). There is before the court not only the notice of appeal but a respondent's notice by which the council challenge part of the judge's order.

The wards involved are Sara, who was born on 16 November 1985, and Julie, who was born on 1 January 1987. They were made wards of court on the council's originating summons as plaintiff, dated 28 February 1987. The defendants to that summons were the mother, the father and the maternal grandparents. Apart from the mother, the other   *j*
defendants have taken no part in this appeal.

The history can be shortly stated. The parents are still very young. They had a stormy marriage with a number of breakdowns, but it finally broke down in August 1988. It is,

---

b   Section 72(1), so far as material, is set out at p 398 *h*, post

however, quite apparent that serious difficulties affecting the children had arisen before
that causing the council to issue the summons, to which I have referred, in February
1986. There is an elder daughter who at all material times has been living with the
maternal grandparents, and the court is not concerned with her.

Sara and Julie have been in the care of the council, who placed them with foster
parents, granting access to the family, ie the mother, the father and the maternal
grandparents.

On 15 January the summons came before Wood J. He made the following interim
orders. There were two orders, one in respect of each of the wards, which are in the same
terms. It was ordered that each of the children should remain a ward of court during her
minority or until further order, that they should be committed to the care of the council
under s 7(2) of the Family Law Reform Act 1969, that the council should have leave to
place each of the wards with long-term foster parents with a view to adoption and that
there should be one more period of access by the first, second, third and fourth defendants,
ie the mother, the father and the maternal grandparents, within the following four
weeks and thereafter there should be no more access to any member of the family. Leave
was given to persons named as the prospective adopters, ie the persons referred to in the
earlier part of the order, unidentified, to issue adoption proceedings in the county court.
Apart from costs, the final provision in each order was that the matter should be brought
back to court if adoption proceedings had not been issued within nine months.

The whole purpose and tenor of those orders is quite clear. There was to be a final
separation between the family and the two wards and the council should proceed in
proper order to achieve the adoption of these two young girls.

The history of the matter did not turn out as envisaged. As a result of a summons, to
which I must come in a moment, the main wardship issues will once again be before the
court on 10 October, that is next Monday.

After the orders had been made by Wood J, the council set about looking for suitable
adopters. Whilst they were doing this, they were contacted by a paternal great-uncle of
the wards, Mr H and his wife, who gave to the council every appearance of being suitable
adopters. They are domiciled in Queensland, Australia, and have had no contact with the
wards although each of them originated in this country.

The mother, who had accepted the orders of Wood J in the sense that she made no
appeal against them, which meant that her contact with the two children would be
determined, now objects to an adoption in Australia on two grounds. The first is that the
children will be brought up as Australians and the second is that she objects to the
influence, however remote, of her husband's family in their upbringing. Those are
matters with which this court is not concerned and are clearly matters which, if
appropriate, will be considered on the restored hearing of the summons.

Becoming aware of the interest of the paternal great-uncle and his wife (to whom I
shall for convenience refer as 'the prospective adopters'), the council issued summonses
in respect of both wards. On 11 August they issued summonses in equivalent terms to
this effect:

'... to show cause why an order should not be made that the Plaintiff do have
leave to remove the above-named minor from the jurisdiction and place the said
minor with [the prospective adopters] both of [an address in Queensland] to the
intent that the said [prospective adopters] should adopt the said minor in Australia.'

So that was a straightforward summons in the wardship proceedings in each case.

Five days later, however, the council issued two more summonses. These sought in
each case the following:

'(1) [A declaration] that for the purposes of the Adoption Act 1976 "relative"
includes a great uncle. (2) Alternatively that [the proposed adopters] be appointed
guardians to the above named Minor. (3) That the Plaintiff [ie the council] do have

leave to place the [minor] with the [prospective adopters] [and these words are important] within the jurisdiction as foster parents pending the hearing of the Plaintiff's summons herein dated 11 August 1988.'

There is also an application for leave to apply for passports and visas for Australia.

That summons on its face only sought interim relief pending the hearing of the main summons. Although the perspective may have been distorted by the passage of time, the return date for the second summons was 8 September whereas, of course, the return date for the earlier summons is next month. So the period for this order to run was about a month.

The summonses, we have been told, very properly were issued because the council were anxious not to offend against the provisions of the Adoption Act 1976 relating to adoption by persons not domiciled in this country, and it is convenient at this stage to refer shortly to the relevant provisions of that Act. Section 55 of the 1976 Act deals with the adoption of children abroad, and reads as follows:

'(1) Where on an application made in relation to a child by a person who is not domiciled in England and Wales or Scotland an authorised court is satisfied that he intends to adopt the child under the law of or within the country in which the applicant is domiciled, the court may, subject to the following provisions of this section, make an order vesting in him the parental rights and duties relating to the child.

(2) The provisions of Part II relating to adoption orders [except for the various sections there enumerated which are not relevant] shall apply in relation to orders under this section as they apply in relation to adoption orders subject to the modification that in section 13(1) for "19" and "13" there are substituted "32" and "26" respectively.'

Those two periods of time, which are both extended, relate to periods of time over which the child should have resided with the prospective adopter.

I need not refer to sub-ss (3) and (4) of s 55. I pass to s 56, which deals with the restriction on removal of children for adoption outside Great Britain. Subsection (1) provides:

'Except under the authority of an order under section 55 . . . it shall not be lawful for any person to take or send a child who is a British subject or a citizen of the Republic of Ireland out of Great Britain to any place outside the British Islands with a view to the adoption of the child by any person not being a parent or guardian or relative of the child . . .'

Then the section provides that any person who does so is guilty of an offence.

'Relative' is one category of person who is not caught by s 56(1). The definition of 'relative' is to be found in s 72(1), and reads as follows:

'"relative" in relation to a child means a grandparent, brother, sister, uncle or aunt, whether of the full blood or half-blood or by affinity and includes, where the child is illegitimate, the father of the child and any person who would be a relative within the meaning of this definition if the child were the legitimate child of his mother and father.'

Whilst referring to statutory provisions I want to mention only one other: that is s 17(1) of the Guardianship of Minors Act 1971, which provides:

'Nothing in this Act shall restrict or affect the jurisdiction of the High Court to appoint or remove guardians or otherwise in respect of minors.'

The matter came before Judge Aglionby, who declined to declare that 'relative' included a great-uncle but appointed the prospective adopters as guardians of the two

wards. The mother appeals, asserting that it was wrong of the judge to have appointed
the prospective adopters as guardians. Counsel for the mother, in her submissions in
support of the appeal, has submitted that, where there is a full provision to deal with the
question of adoption by persons not domiciled within the country and the dealings with
the wards of court are already under the wardship jurisdiction of the court, it was a
wrong exercise of jurisdiction to appoint guardians whether that be under the inherent
jurisdiction of the court to appoint guardians or otherwise.

Counsel for the council supports the course taken by the judge, but by her respondent's
notice asserts that he was wrong to decline to make a declaration that 'relative' includes
'great-uncle'. Counsel submits further that he was right to act within the inherent
jurisdiction of the court to appoint the prospective adopters as guardians even if she is
wrong in her assertion that the definition of 'relative' extends to 'great-uncle'.

The judge, in an admirable judgment, has recognised the problems and has accurately
and carefully set out the factual background, to which it is not necessary for me to refer
in any greater detail.

The appeal raises two very short points. I take them in the order in which they appear
in the judge's judgment. One is whether he was right to decline to make the declaration
sought, and I turn to the passage in his judgment:

> 'I declare that for the purposes of the Adoption Act 1976 relative does not include
> great-uncle. The definition in s 72 is clear and precise and it would not be right to
> judicially interpret uncle to include great-uncle. Although grandparent is included,
> if Parliament had wished to include great-uncle it could have done so and the
> [council] must have realised this was the likely outcome because the second part of
> their application is that the [prospective adopters] be appointed guardians.'

I express my gratitude to both counsel for the helpful submissions they have made
both on this and the second point. I find it impossible to fault the approach made by the
judge on this first aspect of the case. If one needed any further assurance, it would come
from the realisation that this definition applies throughout the whole of the 1976 Act
where it refers to children. That includes s 13(1), where these particular periods of
qualification are laid down:

> 'Where—(a) the applicant, or one of the applicants, is a parent, step-parent or
> relative of the child, or (b) the child was placed with the applicants by an adoption
> agency or in pursuance of an order of the High Court, an adoption order shall not
> be made unless the child is at least 19 weeks old and at all times during the preceding
> 13 weeks had his home with the applicants or one of them.'

It is those two periods of '19 weeks old' and '13 weeks' which are enlarged to '32' and '26'
respectively in s 55(2). In s 13 the category of persons involved under sub-s (1)(a) is 'a
parent, step-parent or relative of the child'.

'Parent' and 'step-parent' are quite precise, and 'relative', in my judgment, ought to be
construed in the same sense. Therefore, if a wider definition of 'uncle' than 'uncle'
without qualification was adopted, it would strike at the efficacy of the provision under s
13(1) just as it would strike at the protection in respect of s 56 as regards persons who act
in relation to adoption outside the jurisdiction, which in my judgment it would be
wrong to distort.

For those reasons and the reasons given by the judge, I have come to the conclusion
that his judgment on this aspect of the case was correct, and I would not disturb it.

Turning now to the second point, the judge recognised the purposes of s 55 in these
terms:

> 'This provides a restriction and requires where the applicant is seeking an order
> that the child is of certain age and has lived with the applicant for a period of time
> which these children have not.'

Then the judge referred to a case in the Family Division, *Re M (a minor) (adoption: removal from jurisdiction)* [1973] 1 All ER 852, [1973] Fam 66, which concerned a purported *a* adoption by two Danish people resident and domiciled in Denmark of a child in the care of the local authority and placed with foster parents in this country. The judge referred to part of the judgment of Brandon J in which the judge indicated that, if the applicants had been made guardians, they would have escaped the prohibitions in the sections to which I have referred (see [1973] 1 All ER 852 at 856, [1973] Fam 66 at 71).

The judge was referred to a passage in Lowe and White *Wards of Court* (2nd edn, 1986) *b* p 246 for the proposition that he was entitled to make guardianship orders notwithstanding the existence of the wardship proceedings and, indeed, was making them within those same wardship proceedings. The authors refer to *Re McGrath (infants)* [1893] 1 Ch 143 as indicating that there was residing in the court an inherent power to appoint guardians notwithstanding the provisions of the Guardianship of Minors Act 1971, because s 17(1) of that Act specifically provides for the preservation of the inherent *c* jurisdiction.

Re McGrath (infants) was dealing with the dismissal and reappointment of another guardian in very special circumstances. In that case mention is made of the 'jurisdiction of the Court of Chancery [regarding children] who had no property' (see [1893] 1 Ch 143 at 147). It was a different issue that was being considered from that which is being considered in the present case. It related to the doubt at one time, now well settled to be *d* unfounded, whether the old Court of Chancery had, and the present Family Division has, an inherent jurisdiction to interfere with and deal with the guardianship of children even though there are no issues as to property, which was the basis of the old wardship jurisdiction.

That, in my judgment, does not take the matter very much further; nor, indeed, does the other case to which we were referred by counsel for the respondent, which was again *e* a case of some venerability, *Re M'Cullochs (minors)* (1844) 6 I Eq R 393. In that case, during argument, counsel for the petitioner withdrew the part of the prayer which was seeking the substitution of one testamentary guardian by another or others and merely sought an order making the minors wards of court. Sugden LC held that it was not inconsistent with the testamentary guardianship to make the children also wards of *f* court. As counsel for the mother submitted, that is the obverse side of the coin. Here the position is quite different. There is an existing jurisdiction being exercised in accordance with the statutory powers now granted to the court by Parliament.

I agree with the submission of counsel for the mother that, whether or not there may be a residue of inherent jurisdiction which could in special circumstances be brought into play where there is a statutory lacuna, there is no statutory lacuna here and the *g* welfare of these wards can be fully provided for under the existing wardship proceedings.

Now to return to the judgment of Judge Aglionby. Having considered the submission made by counsel on the same basis, the judge acknowledged the difficulty, having recognised that it was unusual, to say the least, to appoint as guardians persons who had never actually seen the children. He held that that was not, however, an absolute bar. I do not find it necessary to decide that as a point of law, because it does not really arise in *h* this case. But I look to the reasons which motivated the judge to exercise such a jurisdiction as he might have had in the terms that he quite properly relates. I emphasise that, when I describe the motivation of the judgment as a device, I am in no way being opprobrious about it. It was a perfectly proper approach if it was a correct one in law. The judge said:

> 'Introducing the [prospective adopters] to the children would not constitute the *j* making or taking part in transferring the actual custody of any person for that purpose.'

That is dealing with the anxiety of the council not to offend against s 56. The judge continued:

a   'Of course the [council] do, however, wish to go further than merely introducing the [prospective adopters] to the children and in my judgment bearing in mind what is best for the children I ought to make the order if I can properly do so. At the main hearing it will allow the court to consider the main proposals for the future of the children. Whether the court approves is a different matter however. In making such an option available I do not take the view that appointing the [prospective adopters] as guardians breaks any statutory provisions. Brandon J would

b   not have mentioned the possibility if it involved a clear breach of the statute. In my view although the [council] had the power given to them by Wood J to place with foster parents with a view to adoption it may well be that if the [council] placed the children with the [prospective adopters] then they could fall foul of the provision of s 56(1). In my opinion it is not an improper exercise for the court's discretion and it may be helpful to the children that the option should be assessed. It is always open

c   to the court to remove the [prospective adopters] as guardians and this can be considered by the court at the main hearing.'

   I understand the judge's reasoning and approach, but with great regret I have come to the conclusion that it was a wrong approach. I have come to this conclusion for a number of reasons. Going back for a moment to the summonses, the summons of 16 August

d   1988 requests that the council have leave to place the minor with the prospective adopters within the jurisdiction as foster parents pending the hearing of the council's summons herein. That provision of the summons would have provided the council with the power within the jurisdiction to take all the steps necessary pending the hearing next week to make an introduction, albeit with a view to adoption if those steps proved fruitful.

   I do not, with respect, share the anxieties expressed, which were apparently accepted

e   by the judge, that, if that order had merely been acceded to by the judge, the whole process in the interests of these children would not have taken place during the four weeks with which we are concerned, and that the whole matter could remain in wardship to be dealt with on the next hearing. I have come to the conclusion, whether there is jurisdiction or not (and I have very grave doubts whether there is any inherent jurisdiction to make a guardianship order in the presence of an existing wardship), that, with respect

f   to the judge, it was a wrong exercise of that jurisdiction to make the guardianship orders which are a derogation of the wardship jurisdiction being exercised by the court itself and, although not exactly the same but similar, the powers which had been given to the council under the care order made in the wardship proceedings.

   Sympathising, as I do, with the judge, I have come to the conclusion that the part of his order which relates to the prospective adopters as guardians to either of these two

g   minors was an order which he should not have made. I would therefore allow the appeal to the extent that that part of each of the two orders should be deleted, and dismiss the cross-appeal.

SIR DENYS BUCKLEY. I agree, and I do not think that I can usefully add anything to what Purchas LJ has already said.

h

Appeal allowed. Cross-appeal dismissed.

Solicitors: *E A Morling & Sons*, Maidstone (for the mother); *W G Hopkin*, Maidstone (for the council).

Bebe Chua   Barrister.

Forsikringsaktieselskapet Vesta v Butcher and others (No 1)

HOUSE OF LORDS

LORD BRIDGE OF HARWICH, LORD TEMPLEMAN, LORD GRIFFITHS, LORD ACKNER AND LORD LOWRY

14, 15, 16, 17 NOVEMBER 1988, 26 JANUARY 1989

Insurance – Reinsurance – Risk insured – Breach of condition – Livestock insurance for Norwegian fish farm – Original insurance policy governed by Norwegian law – Reinsurance policy made in England covering 90% of liability – Both policies containing condition that 24-hour watch be kept on fish farm – Breach of 24-hour watch condition not rendering original policy null and void under Norwegian law if breach irrelevant to loss – Breach of condition rendering reinsurance policy null and void under English law irrespective of whether breach relevant to loss – Fish stock destroyed by storm – Insured in breach of 24-hour watch condition but breach irrelevant to loss – Norwegian insurers paying loss – Whether reinsurer liable to make good loss under resinsurance policy.

The plaintiffs, a Norwegian insurance company, insured the owners of a Norwegian fish farm against loss of fish and reinsured 90% of the risk with London underwriters. The insurance and the reinsurance policies each incorporated an identical condition that a 24-hour watch be kept on the farm and further provided that 'failure to comply' with any of the conditions would render the policy null and void. Following the loss of fish stocks in a storm the plaintiffs settled the owners' claim and sought indemnity under the reinsurance policy from the defendant underwriters. A 24-hour watch would not have prevented the loss but the underwriters repudiated liability on the ground, inter alia, that there had been a breach of the 24-hour watch condition. The plaintiffs brought an action against the underwriters to recover the 90% indemnity. Under Norwegian law, which governed the insurance policy, the breach of the 24-hour watch condition did not render the policy null and void, despite the express words of the policy, because the breach was not relevant to nor causative of the loss. However, under English law, which governed the reinsurance policy, the breach of the 24-hour watch condition, whether relevant to the loss or not, rendered the reinsurance policy null and void. The judge held that, although the reinsurance policy itself was governed by English law, relevant clauses such as the 24-hour watch condition were to be construed according to Norwegian law because the reinsurance policy had been made back-to-back with the original policy, which was governed by Norwegian law, and, since under Norwegian law breach of the 24-hour watch condition did not provide a valid defence to the plaintiffs' claim, the plaintiffs were entitled to judgment against the underwriters. The underwriters appealed to the Court of Appeal, which dismissed their appeal. The underwriters appealed to the House of Lords.

Held – Since on the true construction of the reinsurance policy the underwriters had agreed to indemnify the plaintiffs against the risks covered by the original insurance policy, the risks covered by the reinsurance policy were to be interpreted by reference to Norwegian law. The underwriters were therefore liable to indemnify the Norwegian insurers for 90% of the loss which was, under Norwegian law, a risk covered by the reinsurance policy, since once the word 'failure', in the phrase 'failure to comply', was incorporated from the original insurance policy into the reinsurance policy it meant 'relevant' or 'causative' failure in the English contract of reinsurance. It followed that since breach of the 24-hour watch condition was irrelevant to the loss it did not render the reinsurance policy null and void. The appeal would therefore be dismissed (see p 403 j, p 404 j to p 405 a c to f j, p 406 g, p 409 e f h, p 419 h to p 420 b and p 422 a b, post).

25th March 1991

Margaret from the Accrington office rang. She wants to know if you can fax her a
copy of a case - 1989 - Singh -v- Atombrook. It is for Peter Dugdale.

Please fax the copy of the case to
Margaret at the Accrington Office.

a   Per Lord Bridge and Lord Griffiths. It is desirable that the Lloyd's standard form of reinsurance be redrafted in grammatical, intelligible and unambiguous language (see p 404 *a* and p 409 *f*, post).

Decision of the Court of Appeal [1988] 2 All ER 43 affirmed.

Notes

For contracts of reinsurance, see 25 Halsbury's Laws (4th edn) paras 209–215.

b
Cases referred to in opinions

Amin Rasheed Shipping Corp v Kuwait Insurance Co, The Al Wahab [1983] 2 All ER 884, [1984] AC 50, [1983] 3 WLR 241, HL.
Charrington & Co Ltd v Wooder [1914] AC 71, HL.
Gwyn v Neath Canal Navigation Co (1868) LR 3 Exch 209.

c   *Hamlyn & Co v Talisker Distillery* [1894] AC 202, [1891–4] All ER Rep 849, HL.
Helbert Wagg & Co Ltd, Re [1956] 1 All ER 129, [1956] Ch 323, [1956] 2 WLR 183.
Home Insurance Co of New York v Victoria-Montreal Fire Insurance Co [1907] AC 59, PC.
Insurance Co of South Africa v Scor (UK) Reinsurance Co Ltd [1985] 1 Lloyd's Rep 312, CA.
Njegos, The [1936] P 30, [1935] All ER Rep 863.
Pine Top Insurance Co Ltd v Unione Italiana Anglo Saxon Reinsurance Co Ltd [1987] 1 Lloyd's
d   Rep 476.
Prenn v Simmonds [1971] 3 All ER 237, [1971] 1 WLR 1381, HL.
Reardon Smith Line Ltd v Hansen-Tangen, Hansen-Tangen v Sanko Steamship Co [1976] 3 All ER 570, [1976] 1 WLR 989, HL.
Royal Exchange Assurance Corp v Sjorforsakrings Aktiebolaget Vega [1901] 2 KB 567.
Schuler (L) AG v Wickman Machine Tool Sales Ltd [1973] 2 All ER 39, [1974] AC 235, [1973]
e   2 WLR 683, HL.
Wear (River) Comrs v Adamson (1877) 2 App Cas 743, [1974–80] All ER Rep 1, HL.

Appeal

The first defendant, James Neil Eric Butcher, a nominated Lloyd's underwriter acting on behalf of himself and other underwriters (the underwriters), appealed with leave of the
f   Appeal Committee of the House of Lords given on 3 March 1988 against that part of the judgment and order of the Court of Appeal (O'Connor, Neill LJJ and Sir Roger Ormrod) ([1988] 2 All ER 43, [1988] 3 WLR 565) given 30 October 1987 dismissing the underwriters' appeal against the judgment of Hobhouse J ([1986] 2 All ER 488) given on 20 December 1985 whereby it was adjudged, inter alia, that the underwriters should pay the first respondent plaintiffs, Forsikringsaktieselskapet Vesta (Vesta), Nkr 1,223,243·64,
g   being Nkr 611,638·59 as damages for breach of a reinsurance contract under which the underwriters had contracted to indemnify the plaintiffs for 90% of the risk covered in Vesta's insurance policy with Fjordlaks Tafjord SA and Nkr 611,605·05 agreed interest thereon. The second and third defendants, Bain Dawes Ltd and its subsidiary Aquacultural Insurance Service Ltd (the brokers), sought affirmation of the order of the Court of Appeal. The facts are set out in the opinion of Lord Lowry.

h
Timothy Walker QC and *Andrew Smith* for the underwriters.
Andrew Longmore QC and *Adam Fenton* for Vesta.
Michael Ogden QC and *Christopher Purchas* for the brokers.

Their Lordships took time for consideration.

j
26 January. The following opinions were delivered.

LORD BRIDGE OF HARWICH. My Lords, I have had the advantage of reading in draft the speeches of my noble and learned friends Lord Templeman and Lord Lowry. For the reasons they give I would dismiss the appeal.

I wish also to record my concurrence in the views expressed by my noble and learned friend Lord Griffiths regarding the relationship normally to be found between contracts   *a*
of insurance and contracts of reinsurance. I entirely agree with him as to the desirability of the Lloyd's standard form of reinsurance being redrafted in grammatical, intelligible and unambiguous language. The only people who can expect to profit from the obscurities of the present Form J1 are the lawyers.

LORD TEMPLEMAN. My Lords, the business of the respondent Norwegian   *b*
company, Vesta, comprises or includes the issue of insurance policies against the risk of loss from storm damage and other catastrophe being suffered by Norwegian fish farmers. The business of the appellant underwriters includes the issue of reinsurance policies against the risk of loss being suffered by insurers of fish farmers in many parts of the world. Vesta insured a Norwegian fish farmer. Vesta effected reinsurance with the underwriters for 90% of the liability of Vesta to the fish farmer. The fish farmer suffered   *c*
loss as a result of storm damage and Vesta paid the loss. In these proceedings Vesta seek to recover 90% of the loss from the underwriters. The trial judge (Hobhouse J) ([1986] 2 All ER 488) and the Court of Appeal (O'Connor, Neill LJJ and Sir Roger Ormrod) ([1988] 2 All ER 43, [1988] 3 WLR 565) found in favour of Vesta. The underwriters appeal.

When both the insurance policy by Vesta in favour of the fish farmer and the reinsurance policy by the underwriters in favour of Vesta were under negotiation the   *d*
brokers required both policies to incorporate the following terms:

'SPECIAL CONDITIONS AND WARRANTIES
It is warranted that a 24-hour watch be kept over the site.

CLAIMS CONTROL CLAUSE
In the event of loss hereunder, no payment, offer or compromise shall be made   *e*
without the consent of underwriters who shall have sole control of all negotiations. Failure to comply with any of the warranties outlined hereunder will render this policy null and void. All warranties to be completed at the assured's expense.'

A 24-hour watch was not kept on the fish farm so that there was a breach of warranty in each policy. Under Norwegian law, which governed the insurance policy issued by   *f*
Vesta to the fish farmer, the breach of warranty did not render the policy null and void, despite the express words of the policy, because the breach was irrelevant to the loss. A 24-hour watch could not have prevented the loss of fish caused by the storm. Under English law, which governed the reinsurance policy issued by the underwriters to Vesta, the breach of warranty, whether relevant to the loss or not, rendered the reinsurance policy null and void. Therefore, say the underwriters, they are not liable to pay Vesta   *g*
under the reinsurance policy although Vesta were liable to pay the fish farmer under the insurance policy.

The question is whether the reinsurance policy, on its true construction, insured 90% of the liability of Vesta under the insurance policy or 90% of the liability which would have been incurred by Vesta if the insurance policy had been governed by English law.

By the reinsurance policy, in terms both inelegant and ungrammatical—   *h*

'the Underwriters hereby agree to reinsure against loss to the extent and in the manner hereinafter provided. Being a reinsurance of and warranted same gross rate, terms and conditions as and to follow the settlements of the Company [Vesta] and that the Company retains during the currency of this Policy at least the amount stated in the Schedule as the retention on the identical subject matter and risk and in identically the same proportion on each separate part thereof but, in the event of   *j*
the retention being less than that stated in the Schedule, the Underwriters' lines to be proportionately reduced.'

The reinsurance policy thus emphasised that the two policies were on identical terms, that the risks of the underwriters and Vesta were identical and that a claim settled under

the insurance policy would be a claim payable under the reinsurance policy. By the
a operative parts of the reinsurance policy—

> 'the Underwriters ... hereby bind ourselves ... to pay or make-good to the
> Company all such loss as herein provided, such payment to be made after such loss
> is proved ...'

The schedule defined the reinsured as Vesta and the original assured as the fish farmer.
b Retention was 10%. The sum reinsured was 90% of Nkr 750,000, the amount insured by
Vesta. The period of reinsurance was expressed to commence and expire at the hour
expressed in the original policy. 'The perils and interest reinsured hereunder' were
expressed to be 'LIVESTOCK REINSURANCE Rainbow Trout and Salmon only, the property of
[the fish farmer] only as more fully set forth in the original policy'.

By the reinsurance policy, the underwriters promised that, if Vesta became liable for a
c loss under the insurance policy, then the underwriters would make good 90% of the loss.
Vesta became liable for a loss under the insurance policy and the underwriters must
perform and observe their promise in the reinsurance policy. The provision incorporated
in the reinsurance policy that on a breach of warranty the reinsurance policy shall become
null and void is identical with the provision in the insurance policy that on a breach of
warranty the insurance policy shall become null and void. In my opinion, in the absence
d of any express declaration to the contrary in the reinsurance policy, a warranty must
produce the same effect in each policy. The effect of a warranty in the reinsurance policy
is governed by the effect of the warranty in the insurance policy because the reinsurance
policy is a contract by the underwriters to indemnify Vesta against liability under the
insurance policy. The reinsurance policy could have provided expressly that the
warranties were to have different effects in the two policies. The reinsurance policy could
e have limited the liability of the underwriters by providing that a breach of warranty by
Vesta would absolve the underwriters even if an identical breach of warranty by the fish
farmer did not absolve Vesta. Any such limitation would, however, have been
inconsistent with the concept of reinsurance, unacceptable as a basis for the business
relationships between brokers, insurers and reinsurers and contrary to the language of
f the reinsurance policy which insists on the identity of terms, subject matter and risk
involved in both the reinsurance policy and the insurance policy.

Counsel, in the course of a painstaking and forceful address on behalf of the
underwriters, submitted that the 'follow settlements' clause, which provided for the
reinsurance 'to follow the settlements' of Vesta, was emasculated by the incorporated
'claims control clause' which provided that no payment, offer or compromise should be
made without the consent of underwriters who should have sole control of all
g negotiations. For this purpose, he cited the judgment of Robert Goff LJ in *Insurance Co of
South Africa v Scor (UK) Reinsurance Co Ltd* [1985] 1 Lloyd's Rep 312 at 331. In deciding
this appeal I decline to follow counsel down the trail of insurance jargon in a reinsurance
policy and incorporated documents littered with language which is ungrammatical and
contradictory.

h The 'follow-settlements clause' shows that a compromise of Norwegian proceedings
brought by the fish farmer against Vesta was intended to bind the English underwriters.
The 'claims control clause' shows that the underwriters were entitled to negotiate a
settlement of Norwegian proceedings brought by the fish farmer against Vesta. Neither
the settlements clause nor the claims control clause indicates that if Vesta, or underwriters
on behalf of Vesta, unsuccessfully defend proceedings brought by the fish farmer in
j Norway on the grounds that the fish farmer has committed a breach of warranty,
nevertheless the underwriters may successfully defend proceedings brought by Vesta in
England on the grounds that an identical breach of warranty was committed by Vesta.

In my opinion the reinsurance policy in the present case, on its true construction,
insures 90% of the liability of Vesta under the insurance policy and I would dismiss the
appeal of the underwriters.

LORD GRIFFITHS. My Lords, it is commonplace for an insurer to wish to lay off in the reinsurance market part of the risk he has accepted on a policy of insurance. This litigation arises out of that everyday situation in the insurance market. I find it disturbing that the underlying document, Form J1, used in the Lloyd's market to effect reinsurance should be framed in terms which are inelegant and ungrammatical, to quote Lord Templeman, and, in my view, obscure. I also regret that so little thought was apparently given to the difference between a primary insurance contract and a reinsurance contract at the time the reinsurance was placed with Lloyd's.

The essential facts are simple. Lloyd's brokers produced a policy of insurance to cover fish farms. The brokers interested Vesta, a Norwegian insurance company, in accepting insurance of fish farms on the terms of this policy on the understanding that the brokers would be able to obtain reinsurance of 90% of Vesta's risk under the policy in the Lloyd's reinsurance market in London. Vesta insured a Norwegian fish farm on the terms of the policy and the brokers effected reinsurance with Lloyd's. In fact the reinsurance was placed before the insurance; the details are fully set out in the speech of Lord Lowry and I will not repeat them. In my view no importance attaches to the fact that the reinsurance antedated the insurance.

The policy of insurance contained a warranty that a 24-hour watch would be kept over the fish stocks and a further clause in the following terms:

'Failure to comply with any of the warranties outlined hereunder will render this policy null and void. All warranties to be completed at the assured's expense.'

The fish stocks were destroyed in a storm. A 24-hour watch was not kept over the stock but even if it had been kept it could not have prevented the storm damage. Under Norwegian law a breach of warranty cannot be relied on by an insurer to avoid liability unless there is a causal link between the breach and the damage. There was no causal link in this case and Vesta were therefore liable under the policy.

Vesta therefore turned to their reinsurers to recover 90% of the claim that they had had to meet under the policy. The reinsurers refused to pay. They said that the terms of the reinsurance contract were the same as the terms of the original insurance contract and therefore contained the 24-hour watch warranty and the clause rendering the policy null and void in breach of the warranty. It is one of the less attractive features of English insurance law that breach of a warranty in an insurance policy can be relied on to defeat a claim under the policy even if there is no causal connection between the breach and the loss. The reinsurance policy is undoubtedly governed by English law and the reinsurers claim that they are entitled to rely on the breach of the 24-hour watch clause to refuse to pay under the reinsurance policy.

This litigation has been conducted on the basis that the same terms were terms of both the insurance policy and the reinsurance policy. In so far as I must accept this assumption, I agree that this appeal fails for the reasons given in the speeches of Lord Templeman and Lord Lowry. However, at the trial the brokers sought to challenge this assumption and to argue that the 24-hour watch clause, the stock control clause and other clauses in the original insurance policy were not terms of the reinsurance policy. They would have required to obtain leave to amend their pleading to raise this issue and the judge, Hobhouse J, after hearing argument, gave the following reasons for refusing leave to amend ([1986] 2 All ER 488 at 496–497):

'Because of the way in which they sought to raise this argument the brokers had to ask for leave to amend their pleadings to do so. If this leave had been given certain other consequential amendments raising further issues would have had to have been allowed for other parties. Therefore, I permitted the brokers to develop their argument (which was purely one of law and based on English law) to establish whether the argument had any substance in it. It did not and was plainly demurrable and I therefore refused the brokers leave to amend. The brokers' argument was

a
unsustainable for a number of reasons but three will suffice. First it overlooked that policy Form J1 was to be used; this meant that any term of the original insurance was also to be a term of the reinsurance. Second, it is not sound to argue that because a provision relates to an act to be done by another the contracting party is not promising that that other will do that act. For example, a warranty of seaworthiness may be given in a charterparty by a disponent owner or, under the Marine Insurance Act 1906, by a cargo owner insured under a policy of marine insurance. In any such

b
case the contracting party is dependent on another to perform the obligation and, if he is wise, has a back-to-back contract with another to give him a like remedy for non-performance. Third, even on the reinsurance slip itself the document annexed is not one which refers to the original insurance but to the 90% reinsurance. It follows that each of the stock control and 24-hour watch clauses as well as the claims control clause are terms of the reinsurance contract between plaintiffs and the

c
reinsurers.'

Whilst I fully appreciate the reluctance of the judge to allow an amendment at such a late stage which altered the basis on which the case had been pleaded and prepared for trial, I myself regret that it has not been possible to examine the issues in this case in the light of such an amendment.

d
I am not myself persuaded that on its true construction Form J1 does make the terms of the original policy of insurance terms of the policy of reinsurance, but if it does have that effect it is, I think, a highly unsatisfactory way of conducting reinsurance business and likely to lead to many unnecessary disputes.

An insurer who has accepted a risk by issuing a policy of insurance goes to reinsurers to lay off part of that risk. Before the reinsurer accepts part of the insurer's risk, he will

e
wish to assess the risk for himself. The reinsurer can only assess the risk if he is shown the terms on which the insurer has accepted the risk, in other words if the reinsurer is shown the policy that has been or is to be issued by the insurer. When the reinsurer has assessed the risk covered by the policy he can then decide whether or not he will reinsure the risk. In the ordinary course of business reinsurance is referred to as 'back-to-back' with the insurance, which means that the reinsurer agrees that if the insurer is liable

f
under the policy the reinsurer will accept liability to pay whatever percentage of the claim he has agreed to reinsure. A reinsurer could, of course, make a special contract with an insurer and agree only to reinsure some of the risks covered by the policy of insurance, leaving the insurer to bear the full cost of the other risks. Such a contract would, I believe, be wholly exceptional, a departure from the normal understanding of the back-to-back nature of reinsurance and would require to be spelt out in clear terms. I

g
doubt if there is any market for such a reinsurance.

With these general considerations in mind I turn to consider the slip, and Form J1. The contract of reinsurance is contained in the slip which incorporates Form J1:

'TYPE   Livestock Reinsurance.

FORM   J.1

h
ASSURED   R/I Forsikringsaktieselskapet Vesta a/c Fjordlaks, Tafjord A/S. [Then it states the period covered.]

INTEREST   Rainbow Trout and Salmon only, the property of Fjordlaks Tafjord A/S only as more fully set forth in the original policy. [Then it gives the sum insured as 90% of the relevant Kroner figure. It also gives the situation of the cages in Tafjord.]

j
CONDITIONS Being a reinsurance of Forsikringsaktieselskapet Vesta who retain 10% of Full R.I. Clause. PREMIUM [The Kroner deposit premium is stated.]

BRKGE   25%.

INFN   Original policy of Forsikringsaktieselskapet Vesta as attached hereto.'

Form J1 is the standard form of reinsurance policy used in the Lloyd's market. The material parts read:

'LLOYD'S REINSURANCE POLICY

Whereas the Reinsured named in the Schedule herein (hereinafter called "the   *a*
Company") has paid the premium specified in the Schedule to the Underwriting
Members of Lloyd's who have hereunto subscribed their names (hereinafter called
"the underwriters"). *Now We the Underwriters* hereby agree to reinsure against loss
to the extent and in the manner hereinafter provided. Being a Reinsurance of and
warranted same gross rate, terms and conditions as and to follow the settlements of
the Company and that the Company retains during the currency of this Policy at   *b*
least the amount stated in the Schedule as the retention on the identical subject
matter and risk and in identically the same proportion on each separate part thereof
but, in the event of the retention being less than that stated in the Schedule, the
Underwriters' lines to be proportionately reduced. If the Company shall make any
claim knowing the same to be false or fraudulent, as regards amount or otherwise,
this Policy shall become void and all claim hereunder shall be forfeited.'   *c*

For my part, I would be reluctant to read these contractual documents as making the
terms of the contract of insurance terms of the contract of reinsurance. Although the
wording is archaic and difficult to comprehend I understand the phrase 'warranted same
gross rate terms and conditions' as a warranty given by the company, ie the insurer, that
he has placed the risk on the same terms that he has disclosed to the reinsurers. This view   *d*
is I think strongly supported by the fact that the policy is attached to the slip against the
heading 'INFN' which is clearly an abbreviation of the word 'Information' and shows that
at the time the slip is completed the policy terms are available to the reinsurer to show
the nature of the risk that he is accepting. The warranty in the reinsurance is that the
policy has been or will be written in those terms.

A contract of insurance will almost inevitably contain terms that are wholly   *e*
inappropriate in a contract of reinsurance. The two contracts are dealing with entirely
different subject matter. The original policy is concerned to define the risk that the
insurer is prepared to accept. The contract of reinsurance is concerned with the degree of
that risk as defined in the policy that the reinsurer is prepared to accept.

I accept that this view of the documents faces the difficulty that the brokers altered the
schedule of the policy attached to the slip to show the name of the assured as Vesta and   *f*
not the fish farmer and referred to the 90% reinsurance, and that the policy of insurance
contained a claims control clause which is only relevant to a reinsurance policy. But I
would prefer to regard this as indicative of thoughtless confusion rather than an intention
to introduce into a contract of reinsurance terms which were wholly inappropriate. To
take but one example, the stock control clause provides:

'In the event of a claim under this policy, Underwriters reserve the right to replace   *g*
the stock lost, for which the claim is made, with similar stock of a like species.'

Is it seriously to be supposed that it was the intention of the parties that London
underwriters were to have the option of discharging their liability to Vesta by delivering
a load of live fish to them?

The fact is that all the terms of the policy attached 'for information' to the slip (apart   *h*
from the reference to the reinsurance in the schedule and the claims control clause) are
sensible terms in a policy of insurance on a fish farm but many of them are wholly
inappropriate in a policy of reinsurance, and I find it difficult to conceive that sensible
and skilled reinsurers, brokers or insurers should have intended them to apply to the
contract of reinsurance.

In *Home Insurance Co of New York v Victoria-Montreal Fire Insurance Co* [1907] AC 59 the   *j*
Privy Council were faced with a problem in many ways similar to that presented by the
present case. Reinsurers denied liability to meet a reinsurance claim arising out of a fire
policy on the ground that a condition in the original fire policy had been incorporated
into the reinsurance policy and resulted in the reinsurance claim being time barred. The
reinsurance contract had been created by attaching to the printed form of the original

fire policy a reinsurance slip and amending the original fire policy by insertion of the
a word 're' before the word 'insure' thus substituting the expression 'does reinsure' for 'does
insure' (which is an echo of the way in which the brokers amended the schedule to the
policy attached to the slip in this case). Reinsurers argued that all the terms of the original
policy were thus terms of the reinsurance and that they were entitled to repudiate
because a breach of the time clause in the original policy. That clause provided that no
claim could be brought unless commenced within 12 months of the fire. The insurance
b claim had taken time to investigate and settle and therefore the claim against the
reinsurers was not made until more than 12 months after the fire. In rejecting this
defence Lord Macnaghten said (at 64–65):

> 'It is difficult to suppose that the contract of re-insurance was engrafted on an
> ordinary printed form of policy for any purpose beyond the purpose of indicating
> the origin of the direct liability on which the indirect liability, the subject of the re-
> *c* insurance, would depend, and setting forth the conditions attached to it. In the
> result their Lordships have come to the conclusion that according to the true
> construction of this instrument, so awkwardly patched and so carelessly put together,
> the condition in question is not to be regarded as applying to the contract of re-
> insurance. To hold otherwise would, in their opinion, be to adhere to the letter
> *d* without paying due attention to the spirit and intention of the contract.'

The opinion expressed in the first sentence of this passage accords closely with my own
approach to the case. I appreciate that I have not heard full argument but, if I am right,
it provides a simple answer to the problem posed by this case. Vesta did place the
insurance on the terms they disclosed to the reinsurers and thus fulfilled the warranty in
Form J1. The policy took effect in Norway on Norwegian fish stocks and therefore the
e risks covered by the policy fell to be judged by Norwegian law. Reinsurers had agreed to
indemnify against the risks covered by the policy and therefore are liable to indemnify
Vesta for 90% of the claim which was, under Norwegian law, a risk covered by the policy.

I have ventured to set out these views because I am satisfied that the Lloyd's market,
perhaps the largest reinsurance market in the world, would be well advised to give
urgent consideration to the desirability of redrafting their standard form of reinsurance
f policy.

At present, whatever it is intended to mean, it is obscure. If it means what I have
suggested it should be redrafted to make that clear. If, on the other hand, it is really
intended to mean that the terms of the original policy of insurance are to be terms of the
reinsurance contract then, again, the policy should be redrafted to spell this out. If that is
done, however, Lloyd's must face the difficulties that will inevitably follow when trying
g to construe and apply terms in reinsurance contracts which serve no useful purpose and
are appropriate only to the original policy of insurance.

LORD ACKNER. My Lords, I have had the advantage of reading in draft the speeches
of my noble and learned friends Lord Templeman and Lord Lowry. For the reasons they
h give I would dismiss the appeal.

LORD LOWRY. My Lords, the appellant, who is the nominated representative of a
group of Lloyd's underwriters, seeks in this appeal to reverse the judgment of the Court
of Appeal (O'Connor, Neill LJJ and Sir Roger Ormrod) ([1988] 2 All ER 43, [1988] 3
WLR 565), which, affirming the decision of Hobhouse J ([1986] 2 All ER 488), held that
j the underwriters, as reinsurers, were liable to indemnify the plaintiff and first respondent,
Forsikringsaktieselskapet Vesta (Vesta), a leading Norwegian insurance company, as to
90% (the reinsured proportion of the risk borne by Vesta) of a sum of Nkr 2·75m properly
paid by Vesta to Fjordlaks Tafjord A/S, the owner of a Norwegian fish farm (the insured)
in settlement of its claim under an insurance policy in respect of loss and damage caused
to the fish farm by a storm. The contracts of insurance and reinsurance each expressly

incorporated identical wording, known as 'Aquacultural Wording No V', which contained
a warranty that a 24-hour watch would be kept over the site, and also the following   *a*
statement:

> 'Failure to comply with any of the warranties outlined hereunder will render this
> policy null and void. All warranties to be completed at the assured's expense.'

A 24-hour watch was not kept but the failure to keep watch was not a cause of the loss
and, accordingly, by virtue of s 51 of the Norwegian Insurance Contracts Act 1930 (out   *b*
of which the parties may not contract), Vesta was fully liable to the insured despite the
breach. On the other hand, if considered exclusively under English insurance law, the
breach of a warranty renders the insurance policy null and void, even if, as in the present
case, the breach has not caused any part of the loss sustained by the insured. The question
for decision, as between Vesta and the underwriters, is whether the 24-hour watch
warranty should, as the courts below have held, be given, in spite of the principles in   *c*
English law, the same meaning and effect in the contract of reinsurance as it had in the
Norwegian contract of insurance. If Yes, the appeal fails and the underwriters are liable
on their contract with Vesta; if No, the appeal succeeds, the underwriters escape liability
and further questions fall to be decided between Vesta and Aquacultural Insurance
Services Ltd (the brokers), who were co-defendants in the action and are also respondents
in this appeal.   *d*

The facts of the case are fully set out in the judgment of the trial judge (see [1986] 2
All ER 488 at 490). For present purposes I am content to say that in 1977 the insured set
up at Tafjord in Norway a fish farm consisting of about 14 large net cages moored in the
water and containing trout and some small salmon, which are fed and allowed to grow
with a view to slaughter and sale. On 17 September 1978 a violent storm broke the
moorings and broke open about ten of the cages so that most of the fish escaped. Some   *e*
were recaptured but a serious loss occurred and the insured claimed under its contract
with Vesta, which was by necessary implication governed by Norwegian law. It is now
agreed that Vesta was fully liable on the contract and that the sum of NKr 2·75m, for
which it settled the claim on 27 October 1978, was a fair figure. Vesta had covered the
insured for 12 months from 26 October 1977 against loss of living fish from any cause   *f*
and were through the brokers reinsured for 90% of the loss. The underwriters, however,
repudiated liability and declined to consent to any settlement of the insured's claim.
Then Vesta sued the underwriters on the reinsurance contract and, in the alternative,
claimed damages from the brokers for negligence and breach of contract, while in a
separate action the underwriters (in the event of their being found liable to Vesta) have
claimed damages against the brokers.   *g*

Before this particular insurance or reinsurance had been effected or contemplated the
brokers, as part of a scheme for insuring fish farms which they were promoting
worldwide, had prepared a set of clauses considered suitable for this kind of insurance
and known as the Aquacultural no V wording. As their name implies, the brokers, a
subsidiary of Bain Dawes Ltd, the second defendants, had been set up to cater for this
type of business, which might accrue not only in Norway but in other countries, such as   *h*
Canada, France and the United States. They issued brochures in different languages,
claiming to provide 'a comprehensive world-wide facility for fish farmers, their insurance
brokers and agents ... and solely concerned with solving the insurance problems of
aquaculture' and they prepared insurance schemes of which the no V wording was one.
As Hobhouse J put it (at 492):   *j*

> 'Bain Dawes and London underwriters wished to promote and share in this
> business either by way of direct insurance or by way of reinsuring local insurance
> companies carrying on business in the relevant foreign countries.'

In March 1977 the brokers' manager visited Vesta in Norway, partly at Vesta's expense,

and discussed the possibility of selling insurance to Norwegian fish farmers. Vesta then
a began to get orders for fish farm insurance which it passed on to the brokers for
reinsurance. The brokers provided the documentation which, as they and Vesta
recognised, had to be translated into Norwegian and, while it was difficult to be certain,
the judge considered it more likely that it was the brokers' translations which were used.

In London the brokers had obtained from the underwriters in June 1977 a slip (C/792)
in the form of 12 months' open cover worldwide on all risks to aquatic creatures, terms
b of cover to be agreed with leading underwriters in each case. The special conditions,
which gave the brokers a profit commission and authority to bind the underwriters,
granted permission to issue cover notes showing the terms, conditions and wordings for
each risk, to cancel policies and to bind risks up to £100,000 or equivalent subject to
confirmation within seven days. Translations, where required, of wordings, terms and
conditions were to be carried out by translators specified by the Lloyd's Policy Signing
c Office and policies and cover notes would be issued accordingly. The slip was in the form
of a binder given by all underwriters to the brokers to give limited temporary cover and
by the following underwriters to the leading underwriters to write risks on their behalf,
and all underwriters authorised the brokers to issue cover notes on their behalf and to
cancel the cover. The slip was accordingly referred to as 'the binder slip'.

The terms of the insurance and reinsurance and the circumstances in which they came
d about are important and I cannot describe what follows more succinctly than did the trial
judge ([1986] 2 All ER 488 at 493–494):

'When on 26 October 1977 the plaintiffs telexed the brokers asking for cover in
respect of Fjordlaks, Mr Secretan made use of the authority given by the binder slip
to hold the plaintiffs covered for seven days, obtaining the confirmation of the
e leading underwriters for a further thirty days on 2 November. This was subject to
the completion of a proposal form within thirty days and a marine survey. However,
by the beginning of December the plaintiffs had still not forwarded either of these
documents, so the brokers sent them a reminder and repeated the process of
themselves first giving and then obtaining from the leading underwriters a further
held covered note. In fact the proposal form arrived shortly afterwards and no one
f seems to have insisted on the marine survey. The specific slip under which the
plaintiffs were reinsured was prepared by Bain Dawes and was, on 30 December
1977, initialled by the three leading underwriters on behalf of all the underwriters
who had underwritten the open cover together with an indorsement which
increased the sum insured to Nkr 8 m. It is now agreed that this slip and indorsement
is the actual contract under which the plaintiffs were reinsured and that no further
g problem of rectification arises. The slip provides:

"TYPE   Livestock Reinsurance.
FORM   J.1
ASSURED   R/I Forsikringsaktieselskapet Vesta a/c Fjordlaks, Tafjord A/S. [Then
              it states the period covered.]
h INTEREST   Rainbow Trout and Salmon only, the property of Fjordlaks Tafjord
              A/S only as more fully set forth in the original policy. [Then it gives
              the sum insured as 90% of the relevant Kroner figure. It also gives
              the situation of the cages in Tafjord.]
CONDITIONS   Being a reinsurance of Forsikringsaktieselskapet Vesta who retain
              10% of Full R.I. Clause. PREMIUM [The Kroner deposit premium is
j   stated.]
BRKGE   25%.
INFN   Original policy of Forsikringsaktieselskapet Vesta as attached hereto."

Form J1 is a standard form of Lloyd's reinsurance policy which contains the words
(printed in red) "being a reinsurance of and warranted same gross rate and terms

and conditions as and to follow the settlements of the [reassured]". It is thus an
express term of this form that the reinsurance shall be on the same terms and
conditions as the original insurance. It also includes an express follow-settlements
provision. The document attached to the slip was not in fact the original insurance
policy but was a document headed "The Aquacultural Insurance Service Ltd.
Aquacultural wording No. V. General purpose wording. Monthly reporting of
values. Schedule". There then follow various particulars of the contract which start
with "ASSURED: R/L Forsikringsaktieselskapet Vesta a/c Fjordlaks Tafjord A/S" and
the sum assured is again given as 90% of the full Norwegian kroner sum. Then
there follow some six pages of unnumbered clauses which make up the Aquacultural
no v wording. It is only necessary to make limited quotations from the wording.
The scheme is that of an insurance on wide terms with a few warranties and
exclusions in favour of the insurer, and among other provisions, an indemnity
clause which provides for agreed values (in Norwegian kroner) of fish lost depending
on the average weight of the individual fish concerned, a differential franchise clause
and premium adjustment clause. The clauses on which the defendants particularly
rely are as follows:

> "STOCK CONTROL CLAUSE The assured will maintain regular written stock control
> records which records will, at all times, be available to Underwriters or their
> representatives for their inspection . . .
> SPECIAL CONDITIONS AND WARRANTIES It is warranted that a 24 hour watch be kept
> over the site.
> CLAIMS CONTROL CLAUSE In the event of loss hereunder, no payment off or
> compromise shall be made without the consent of Underwriters who shall have
> sole control of all negotiations. Failure to comply with any of the warranties
> outlined hereunder will render this policy null and void. All warranties to be
> completed at the assured's expense."

Having obtained the signatures of the leading underwriters on the slip, the brokers
on 4 January 1978 sent to the plaintiff a letter enclosing a cover note. This letter
said:

> "Fjordlaks Tafjord A/S
> Please find enclosed the bills, Cover Note and a copy of the Policy Wording No.
> V in respect of the above client. You will note from the Wording that the sum
> insured is shown in NKr. 750,000. The increase of the sum insured to NKr.
> 8,000,000 from 8th December 1977 will be dealt with by endorsement and the
> relevant document will be forwarded to you together with the policy document
> when it is received from the Lloyd's Policy Signing Office. You will further note
> that the increased sum insured has been noted on the Cover Note. We would ask
> that the assured reads his policy wording carefully in order that there are no
> misunderstandings. We trust that the enclosed documents are in order."

The enclosed cover note had a first sheet which was similar to the schedule attached
to the slip but it also included the heading "COVER NOTE THE AQUACULTURAL INSURANCE
SERVICE LIMITED. Subscribed by Lloyd's and Company Underwriters under Cover
Number C792/7" and the words:

> "This is to certify that insurance has been arranged with Lloyd's and Company
> Underwriters in accordance with the terms, conditions and limitations provided
> by The Aquacultural Insurance Service Limited Wording Number V under
> Cover Number C792/7 subject to the attached special conditions and loss
> reporting clause, as more fully set forth in the policy document to be issued on
> receipt of the stipulated premium . . ."

and then below the signature of Mr Hewitt of the brokers the words "Specially

empowered by Underwriters to issue this temporary Cover Note." The attached no
v wording was the same, save for some minor and irrelevant differences, as that
attached to the slip.'

Having received the cover note, Vesta issued its policy to the insured, with a request to
read through the terms and stressing their importance. Mr Pedersen, the 'alter ago' of
the insured, on reading the 24-hour watch clause, appreciated that he could not comply
with it and so informed the local branch of Vesta by telephone. Mr Kolbeinsen of Vesta
then passed this information to the brokers, but nothing more happened. By doing
nothing Vesta can be taken, as the judge held, to have waived this condition, but the
position of the underwriters was not affected by what happened and, for the purpose of
the question now before your Lordships, this complication can be disregarded.

The reinsurance policy was issued on 7 February 1978. It was on the J1 form mentioned
in the slip, specified the 10% retention and referred in a number of places to the original
policy or policies. In the relevant box in the schedule it stated: 'The peril and interest
reinsured hereunder LIVESTOCK REINSURANCE Rainbow Trout and Salmon only, the
property of Fjordlaks Tafjord A/S only as more fully set forth in the original policy.'

The underwriters raised three defences against Vesta's claim: (1) that a 24-hour watch
had not been kept; (2) that stock control records had not been kept or produced; (3) that
the underwriters had not consented to Vesta's settlement with the insured. The judge
rejected the second and third defences for reasons which I need not recall, since the
arguments which he dismissed were not revived.

Turning to the 24-hour watch clause, he noted the effect under English law of failure
to comply and, in the course of what Sir Roger Ormrod rightly described as a meticulously
careful judgment, stated his conclusion on this part of the case. Vesta had contended that
the reinsurance contract was governed by Norwegian law. Its alternative submission,
'pursued with only lukewarm enthusiasm' but supported by the brokers, was that the no
V wording incorporated in both contracts was so governed. The underwriters had
contended that the contract was governed by English law and that English law alone was
relevant. The judge said ([1986] 2 All ER 488 at 504–505):

'I consider that there is a solution to the problem of the choice of law in the
present case which does give a satisfactory answer. It is the almost invariable rule
that there is only a single proper law of a contract which governs all aspects of the
contract. This is conceptually sound as the primary function of the proper law is to
give effect to the parties' intention not merely to agree but also to make a legal
contract, ie to create a legal relationship. This presupposes a legal system since a
legal contract cannot be made without a reference to a legal system which is to give
it its legal effect. As Lord Diplock said in *Amin Rasheed Shipping Corp v Kuwait
Insurance Co, The Al Wahab* [1983] 2 All ER 884 at 891, [1984] AC 50 at 65: ". . .
contracts are incapable of existing in a legal vacuum. They are mere pieces of paper
and void of all legal effect unless they were made by reference to some system of
private law . . ." In the present case one would prima facie assume that this
underlying legal system was English law. But by the same logic the choice of law is
a matter for the actual or imputed choice of the parties and it has been recognised
for a long time that parties may choose that different parts of the contract should be
governed by different laws. This is stated in the current edition of Dicey and Morris
Conflicts of Laws (10th edn, 1980) p 749. In *Hamlyn & Co v Talisker Distillery* [1894]
AC 202 at 207, [1891–4] All ER Rep 849 at 852 Lord Herschell LC said: "Where a
contract is entered into between parties residing in different places, where different
systems of law prevail, it is a question, as it appears to me, in each case, with
reference to what law the parties contracted, and according to what law it was their
intention that their rights under the whole or any part of the contract should be
determined." In *Re Helbert Wagg & Co Ltd* [1956] 1 All ER 129 at 135, [1956] Ch

323 at 340 Upjohn J, considering a contract which in certain of of its areas of operation clearly contemplated that a foreign law would apply, said: "Those considerations are not conclusive of the question for the parties may well contemplate that different parts of their contract shall be governed by different law." In the present case there is an express provision for the terms and conditions of the reinsurance contract and those of the original insurance to be the same and the reinsurance is manifestly to be back-to-back with the original insurance. From this one should infer a contractual intent that the legal effect of the clauses which define and limit the scope of the cover should be the same in the reinsurance and in the original insurance. When one takes into account that the parties clearly must contemplate that the original insurance is governed by Norwegian law I infer as a matter of English law that the parties intended the construction and effect of the clauses of the Aquacultural wording shall be governed by Norwegian law. Whether one chooses to categorise this conclusion as an application of the English substantive law of construction of an English law contract or as the application of the English choice of law rules does not matter. They are in the present context essentially the same thing. The parties have on the true ascertainment of their contractual intention chosen that that part of the contract shall be governed by Norwegian, not English, law. It will be appreciated that it is a corollary of this particular conclusion that it is the law of Norway applicable to domestic contracts of original insurance which the parties intend shall govern, not the Norwegian law which may or may not apply to reinsurance contracts. The reinsurance contract itself is and remains an English law contract but it is one which is made with reference to, and on the terms of, the Norwegian law contract of original insurance. This view of the English law parallels that of Mr Rafen on the first point I discussed under the heading of Norwegian law and which I accepted. It follows from this that the dispute about the Norwegian law applicable to reinsurance contracts is really irrelevant and the plaintiffs could succeed even if that dispute had been decided against them. I therefore hold as a matter of English law that the proper law of the reinsurance contract is English law subject to the construction and effect of the clauses of the Aquacultural wording being determined in accordance with Norwegian law in the same manner as they are as part of the contract of original insurance. If I had not decided that this hybrid and admittedly somewhat unorthodox conclusion was open to me, I would have been compelled to the conclusion that the whole contract should be governed by Norwegian law, because any other conclusion would be contrary to the manifest intention of the parties to provide the plaintiffs with reinsurance cover in respect of a contract of original insurance on the same terms which is governed by Norwegian law.'

The judge rounded off this part of his judgment thus (at 505–506):

'I accordingly hold that the plaintiffs are entitled to judgment against the reinsurers. I would add that this conclusion is fully in accordance with the business nature of the transaction. London underwriters and brokers are seeking to market insurance contracts in foreign countries. As a matter of business they do not do this directly but make use of a local insurance company to obtain the business. The business reality is that the contract that is marketed is a local contract fronted by the local insurance company. The 90% reinsurance framework, like the profit commission and 25% brokerage payable to the brokers, is in reality only a mechanism to achieve this end. It is commercially unrealistic for reinsurers to rely on an English law consequence which forms no part of the scheme of insurance which is being provided and which, if they had stopped to think, they would have realised made the insurance package wholly unsaleable to the overseas insurers and assureds from whom they are seeking to acquire premium income. In subsequent years the package was expressly varied to take this into account.'

The reasoning of the Court of Appeal is well summarised by the learned reporter in
a her headnote ([1988] 2 All ER 43 at 44):

'(1) Although the reinsurance contract was in the main governed by English law
the 24-hour watch clause was to be construed in the same way as in the underlying
insurance contract because (a) that condition was to be performed locally and by the
insured, (b) the insurance and the reinsurance were in essence back-to-back, (c) the
follow-settlements clause, however much it was affected by the claims control clause,
b could not be ignored, (d) if the underwriters had exercised their right under the
claims control clause to negotiate with the insured they would have had to have
done so on the basis that the insurance policy was governed by Norwegian law and
(e) the only construction that made commercial sence was that the 24-hour watch
clause in the reinsurance contract was to be given the same effect as it had in the
c underlying insurance contract. Since the breach of the 24-hour watch condition did
not provide a valid defence in Norwegian law to the owners' claim under the
underlying insurance contract, the reinsurers could not rely on that breach as a
defence to the plaintiffs' claim under the reinsurance policy . . .'

O'Connor LJ devoted his judgment to Vesta's claim against brokers. As to the case
against the underwriters, he agreed with Neill LJ for the reasons given by him. Neill LJ,
d having pointed out that the brokers were formed for the specific task of providing
specialised insurance cover for fish farms throughout the world and that they considered
with Vesta the possibilities of selling insurance cover to groups of Norwegian fish farmers
(see [1988] 2 All ER 43 at 56, [1988] 3 WLR 565 at 583), expressed his view on this part
of the case as follows ([1988] 2 All ER 43 at 58, [1988] 3 WLR 565 at 585):

e 'What effect then should be given to the watch clause? I have found this to be a
difficult question to answer and the arguments put forward so attractively on behalf
of the underwriters very formidable. There are, it would appear, three possible
solutions. (a) The reinsurance contract, like the insurance contract, is governed by
Norwegian law. (b) The reinsurance contract in its entirety is governed by English
law. (c) Though the reinsurance contract is in the main governed by English law,
f the watch clause is to be construed in the same way as in the underlying insurance
contract. The first solution, though it was pressed by Vesta before the judge and was
kept alive as an alternative in this court, appears to me to be quite unrealistic. The
reinsurance was placed in London on the London market and the documents which
were used stongly support the argument that the contract was prima facie governed
by English law. It follows therefore that the second solution has much to commend
g it. In the end, however, I find myself compelled, as was the judge, to reject it. The
relevant term was one to be performed locally and by the insured. The contract of
insurance itself was in a form devised by the brokers and was part of an operation in
which the underwriters themselves were clearly keenly interested. Both the history
of the negotiations and the form of the documents shows that in essence the
insurance and the reinsurance were back-to-back. The follow-settlements clause,
h however much emasculated by the claims control clause, cannot be ignored.
Furthermore, the rights given to the underwriters by the claims control clause
included the right to negotiate with the insured with reference to an insurance
policy, which was indubitably governed by Norwegian law. In my judgment the
word "hybrid" may itself be a source of confusion. I would prefer to say that as a
matter of construction of the reinsurance contract and by seeking to ascertain the
j presumed intention of the parties the watch clause has to be given the same effect as
it is given in the underlying insurance contract. In the context of the present case
this solution is to my mind the only one that makes commercial sense.

Sir Roger Ormrod began his judgment with a trenchant introduction ([1988] 2 All ER
43 at 59, [1988] 3 WLR 565 at 586):

'The main issue in this appeal, stated bluntly but fairly, is whether underwriters under a contract of reinsurance with the plaintiffs (Vesta), a Norwegian insurance company, can avoid liability to reimburse them for losses sustained by them under a policy with their insured (Fjordlaks) on the ground of breach of a warranty which is wholly irrelevant to the cause or size of the loss, when they themselves, whose policy with the insured contained a warranty in identical terms, are precluded by Norwegian law from relying on it.'

He also attributed some of the difficulties in the case to the way in which the business was conducted in London by the brokers, Bain Dawes Ltd, whom he described as the prime movers through their subsidiaries ([1988] 2 All ER 43 at 59, [1988] 3 WLR 565 at 586–587):

'They designed the form of words (form V) to be used in contracts for the insurance of fish farms. They negotiated with underwriters and obtained their approval to this form of words and arranged that the business would be done in the form of reinsurance at a time when they had no actual clients and no "original" insurance contracts to be reinsured. In this case the terms of the reinsurance contracts were copied into the original insurance contracts. Finally, it was the brokers' expressed intention to market this form of insurance "worldwide" for fish farms wherever situated.'

Noting the general principle stated in *The Njegos* [1936] P 90, [1935] All ER Rep 863 that interrelated contracts should prima facie be governed by the same law, Sir Roger did not consider that principle, 'which is after all one of common sense', powerful enough to take the whole of the reinsurance contract into Norwegian law, but he saw a strong argument for saying that it was not governed entirely by English law. He said ([1988] 2 All ER 43 at 60, [1988] 3 WLR 565 at 587):

'Whereas the risk insured by the original policy . . . was financial loss arising from damage to or loss of the fish, the risk insured by the reinsurance policy was loss to the reinsured arising out of their liability under the original policy. Liability under the original policy and the quantum of the loss are governed by Norwegian law. Therefore, liability under the reinsurance policy is governed de facto by Norwegian law.'

He continued ([1988] 2 All ER 43 at 60–61, [1988] 3 WLR 565 at 588):

'Finally, and perhaps most cogent, is the fact that it was the intention of all parties that the terms of the reinsurance contract governing liability should be the same as the terms governing liability under the original contract. The reinsurance policy expressly says so; the brokers insisted on the form V wording being incorporated in both the reinsurance and the original policies; and Vesta clearly expected to be covered up to 90% of anything they would be called on to pay under their policy with Fjordlaks. In fact, all concerned were agreed that the two policies were to be back-to-back. Faced with this problem Hobhouse J held—"as a matter of English law that the proper law of the reinsurance contract is English law subject to the construction and effect of the clauses of the Aquacultural wording being determined in accordance with Norwegian law in the same manner as they are as part of the contract of original insurance." (See [1986] 2 All ER 488 at 505.) Had he not gone on to refer to his conclusion as "hybrid and admittedly somewhat unorthodox", the matter might have been left as a question of construction of an English contract on English principles. Notwithstanding counsel's powerful argument for the reinsurers, I think that Hobhouse J's conclusion was correct. There is no other way in which the intention of the parties that liability of Vesta should be matched by liability of the reinsurers on a back-to-back basis can be achieved.'

Sir Roger concluded his judgment on this part of the case with a passage which views the
a problem differently and which I wish to cite and comment on, partly because it was
criticised by the appellant as being inconsistent with what had gone before ([1988] 2 All
ER 43 at 61, [1988] 3 WLR 565 at 588–589):

'Turning to the warranty, both the reinsurance contract and the original insurance
contract contain a warranty that a 24-hour watch shall be kept over the site. Both
b contracts also contain a claims control clause to which there appears to be attached a
provision, which has no connection with it, providing that failure to comply with
any of the warranties will "render this policy null and void". The claims control
clause itself was, of course, wholly inapposite and ineffectual in the original insurance
contract. Although there is no evidence that the 24-hour watch warranty was
included in the reinsurance contract by a similar mistake and it is accepted that it
c formed part of it, it is obviously much more appropriate to the original contract. By
s 51 of the Norwegian Insurance Contracts Act 1930 breach of a safety regulation
(anglice warranty) gives no defence to an insurer unless the breach caused the loss.
In English law causation is still irrelevant. This introduced a major difference
between the two contracts and, if the English version prevails, effectively destroys
the basis of the reinsurance policy. So there is a direct conflict between the terms of
d the Lloyd's reinsurance policy which contains a warranty that its terms are the same
as those in the original contract, and the warranty provision. It is also plainly
inconsistent with the intention of the parties when they entered into the reinsurance
contract. In my judgment the only way to resolve this problem is to imply into the
reinsurance contract a term to the effect that breach of warranty will only avoid, or
permit reinsurers to repudiate, the policy if breach of the same warranty would
e permit the reinsured to avoid the original policy with their clients. Some such term
is necessary to give business efficacy to the reinsurance contract and to give effect to
the real intention of the parties.'

The words to which exception is taken are 'the only way to resolve this problem', having
f regard to what Sir Roger had said when agreeing with Hobhouse J, namely: 'There is no
other way in which the intention of the parties . . . can be achieved.' I do not, with due
respect to the argument of counsel for the underwriters (which at every other point was
extremely clear, well marshalled and persuasive), detect here an inconsistency because I
have understood 'this problem' to be the one mentioned in the immediately preceding
paragraph of the judgment. Sir Roger had found a clear intention that the terms of the
g two contracts should be the same and that Vesta should be insured against its own
liability to the fish farmer. At the same time he had found a term in the reinsurance
contract which, if read literally according to English insurance law, would have a
different effect from that of the same term in the insurance contract, thereby nullifying
that intention and depriving Vesta of what it had contracted for; hence the problem.
This passage in the judgment clearly illustrates the legal problem that, given the joint
h intention found to exist by all the judges, a way must, if possible, be found of giving
effect to it. I readily concede counsel's point that one ought not to imply a term in a
contract which contradicts an express term of the same contract. Moreover, neither the
proposed nor any other implied term had been pleaded by Vesta or relied on in argument.
Reinsurance is prima facie a contract of indemnity, as the many examples in the
Vesta's printed case effectively illustrate, under which the reinsurer indemnifies the
j original insurer against the whole or against a specific amount or proportion (in this case
90%) of the risk which the latter has himself insured. This, my Lords, is the situation one
expects to find on turning to look at the reinsurance contract. The judge has mentioned
the slip and indorsement under which Vesta was reinsured. The slip incorporated Lloyd's
Form J1, a standard form of reinsurance policy, which was incorporated by reference in

the slip and became the reinsurance policy here. It was 'a reinsurance of and warranted same gross rate, terms and conditions as and to follow the settlements of the Company' (Vesta) under which the underwriters 'hereby bind ourselves . . . to pay or make good to the Company all such loss as herein provided'. The no V wording was also incorporated in the contracts of insurance and reinsurance. I am of the opinion, like all the judges in the courts below, that the intention of the underwriters and Vesta to enter into a legally binding contract of indemnity (up to 90% of the risk) is absolutely clear. Because, however, the underwriters have contended that the contracts are not, in insurance jargon, 'back-to-back', I shall consider, as the courts below have done, the surrounding circumstances which I have already referred to. The propriety of doing this in order to ascertain and give effect to the intention of the parties is amply illustrated by authority. A basic rule is stated by Kelly CB in *Gwyn v Neath Canal Navigation Co* (1868) LR 3 Exch 209 at 215, where he said:

> 'The result of all the authorities is, that when a court of law can clearly collect from the language within the four corners of a deed, or instrument in writing, the real intention of the parties, they are bound to give effect to it by supplying anything necessarily to be inferred from the terms used, and by rejecting as superfluous whatever is repugnant to the intention so discerned.'

I would also refer to *Prenn v Simmonds* [1971] 3 All ER 237 at 239–240, [1971] 1 WLR 1381 at 1383, where Lord Wilberforce observed:

> 'The time has long passed when agreements, even those under seal, were isolated from the matrix of facts in which they were set and interpreted purely on internal linguistic considerations. There is no need to appeal here to any modern, anti-literal tendencies, for Lord Blackburn's well-known judgment in *River Wear Comrs v Adamson* (1877) 2 App Cas 743 at 763, [1874–8] All ER Rep 1 at 11 provides ample warrant for a liberal approach. We must, as he said, enquire beyond the language and see what the circumstances were with reference to which the words were used and the object, appearing from those circumstances, which the person using them had in view.'

In *Reardon Smith Line Ltd v Hansen-Tangen* [1976] 3 All ER 570 at 574, [1976] 1 WLR 989 at 995–996 again Lord Wilberforce stated:

> 'In a commercial contract it is certainly right that the court should know the commercial purpose of the contract and this in turn presupposes knowledge of the genesis of the transaction, the background, the context, the market in which the parties are operating.'

His speech also made reference to an apt quotation from the speech of Lord Dunedin in *Charrington & Co Ltd v Wooder* [1914] AC 71 at 82:

> '. . . in order to construe a contract the Court is always entitled to be so far instructed by evidence as to be able to place itself in thought in the same position as the parties to the contract were placed, in fact, when they made it—or, as it is sometimes phrased, to be informed as to the surrounding circumstances.'

(See [1976] 3 All ER 570 at 575, [1976] 1 WLR 989 at 997.) Finally, the observation of Lord Reid in *L Schuler AG v Wickman Machine Tool Sales Ltd* [1973] 2 All ER 39 at 45, [1974] AC 235 at 251 may be thought particularly apposite in this case:

> 'The fact that a particular construction leads to a very unreasonable result must be a relevant consideration. The more unreasonable the result the more unlikely it is that the parties can have intended it, and if they do intend it the more necessary it is that they shall make that intention abundantly clear.'

a   I consider that all the surrounding circumstances to which I have already referred provide strong confirmation that the intention of the parties was to provide an indemnity for Vesta. Assuredly, they furnish no support for the opposite view.

The main thrust of the argument of counsel for the underwriters was as follows: (1) the proper law of the reinsurance contract is English law; (2) that contract contained a warranty by Vesta that a 24-hour watch would be kept, accompanied by the words, 'Failure to comply with any of the warranties outlined hereunder will render the policy b   null and void'; (3) there was failure to comply; (4) that failure, even though not a cause of damage, rendered the policy null and void according to English law; (5) therefore the underwriters are not liable.

Put like that, nothing could be simpler and no logical conclusion more inevitable. But, the real intention of the parties having, as I, like every judge who has considered the case, believe, been found within the four corners of the contract, effect should if legally c   possible, be given to it.

As your Lordships will recall, so clear was Hobhouse J about the intention of the parties and the need to give effect to it that he would, if compelled, have held Norwegian law to be the proper law of the reinsurance contract. He did not, however, adopt that unlikely solution, described by Neill LJ as 'quite unrealistic', but said ([1986] 2 All ER 488 at 505):

d   '... I infer as a matter of English law that the parties intended the construction and effect of the clauses of the Aquacultural wording shall be governed by Norwegian law. Whether one chooses to categorise this conclusion as an application of the English substantive law of construction of an English law contract or as the application of the English choice of law rules does not matter. They are in the present context essentially the same thing. The parties have on the true ascertainment e   of their contractual intention chosen that that part of the contract shall be governed by Norwegian, not English, law.'

The judge described his conclusion as 'hybrid and somewhat unorthodox'. As to this, Neill LJ, having rejected the underwriters' argument that the contract was in its entirety governed by English law, said ([1988] 2 All ER 43 at 58, [1988] 3 WLR 565 at 585):

f   'In my judgment the word "hybrid" may itself be a source of confusion. I would prefer to say that as a matter of construction of the reinsurance contract and by seeking to ascertain the presumed intention of the parties the watch clause has to be given the same effect as it is given in the underlying insurance contract. In the context of the present case this solution is to my mind the only one that makes commercial sense.'

g   On this point Sir Roger Ormrod said ([1988] 2 All ER 43 at 60, [1988] 3 WLR 565 at 588):

'Had he not gone on to refer to his conclusion as "hybrid and admittedly somewhat unorthodox", the matter might have been left as a question of construction of an English contract on English principles. Notwithstanding counsel's powerful h   argument for the reinsurers, I think that Hobhouse J's conclusion was correct.'

My Lords, I respectfully consider the problem to be one of construing the words in the reinsurance contract and not one involving an imputed choice of law. The words 'It is warranted that a 24-hour watch be kept over the site' are clear in any language and mean what they say. The important words (italicised) are in the next sentence:

j   'Failure to comply with any of the warranties outlined hereunder will render this policy null and void.'

The original insurance contract was governed by Norwegian law. Consequently the word 'failure' in the phrase 'failure to comply', once the no V wording was incorporated in the

Norwegian contract, meant 'relevant failure', that is 'causative failure' because that contract was governed by Norwegian law. 'Failure to comply' had, despite the general rule of English law, the same meaning and effect in what I shall without compromise call the English contract of reinsurance. The parties to that contract are deemed to have used the same dictionary, in this case a Norwegian legal dictionary, to ascertain the meaning of the terms and conditions in wording no V, including the conditions relating to the 24-hour watch and the words 'failure to comply'. There is, in my view, no need to treat the reinsurance contract as partly governed by Norwegian law, except in the special sense that one must resort to Norwegian law in order to interpret and understand the meaning and effect of the no V wording in both contracts. That is a different concept from 'the proper law of the contract' (or of part of the contract) which is discussed in the authorities on that subject.

I do not, having regard to my conclusion, consider that it would be helpful to me to discuss those authories. The ascertainment of the parties' intention (including imputed intention) with regard to the choice of law is, however, often related (and must be subservient) to their contractual intention as deduced from the instrument and the surrounding circumstances, because an imputed choice of law for the whole or part of a contract will sometimes be determined by the court by reference to what it finds the parties were trying to achieve. As Bigham J said in *Royal Exchange Assurance Corp v Sjorforsakrings Aktiebolaget Vega* [1901] 2 KB 576 at 574:

'Now, no doubt, as a rule, the law to be applied in construing and enforcing a contract is the law of the country where the contract is made; but this is only because, in the absence of other circumstances, our Courts assume that such was the intention of the parties. If it should appear clearly from other circumstances that the parties intended that the rights should be ascertained and determined by some other law, our Courts will give effect to such intention.'

There is another possible approach which I would briefly examine. The no V wording was included in both contracts in toto, with the strange result, among others, that not only Vesta but the underwriters appear to claim the benefit of the following provision:

'In the event of a claim under this policy, Underwriters [the term must be generic] reserve the right to replace the stock lost, for which the claim is made, with similar stock of a like species.'

Sir Roger Ormrod has already pointed out that the claims control clause was 'wholly inapposite and ineffectual in the original contract'. It is tempting to say that different parts of the no V wording ought to be rejected in each contract as superfluous or, alternatively, that in the reinsurance contract Vesta is simply telling the underwriters the terms on which it has signed its original insurance. The 24-hour watch clause, like the stock control clause, could very well with a different method of drafting have been confined to the insurance contract, leaving the reinsurance contract to function as a straightforward indemnity incorporating further settlements and claims control clauses. But both the underwriters and Vesta have throughout regarded the entire no V wording as part of both contracts and have presented their arguments on this basis. Accordingly, I have not felt able to adopt this solution, which was briefly canvassed during the argument before your Lordships. Indeed, in view of the way in which the contracts were formed, it is doubtful whether Vesta could ever have adopted this approach.

Since the hearing, and after reaching my own conclusion, I have read an instructive article by Mr Robert Merkin, 'Reinsurance, Brokers and the Conflict of Laws' [1988] Lloyd's MCLQ 5, in which the author criticised the drafting of the contracts as having failed to distinguish between insurance and reinsurance and cited two cases, *Home Insurance Co of New York v Victoria-Montreal Fire Insurance Co* [1907] AC 59 and *Pine Top Insurance Co Ltd v Unione Italiana Anglo Saxon Reinsurance Co Ltd* [1987] 1 Lloyd's Rep 476, as authority for the proposition that the courts will not permit the incorporation of

inappropriate terms from an insurance agreement into a reinsurance agreement. The
a way in which the reinsurance contract was formed in those cases is interesting, but it is
now impossible to say how far Vesta could have succeeded with the argument which
prevailed there or whether its advisers would have risked the attempt when the case
which they actually made depended on showing that the terms of the two contracts were
the same.

My Lords, the parties devoted considerable time at every stage of these proceedings to
b arguing about the effect of the follow-settlements clause and the claims control clause. I
have not found in those clauses any real help for either side, but ought to mention them,
starting with the observations of the judge where he said ([1986] 2 All ER 488 at 497):

'Where a reinsurance contract contains a provision requiring the reinsurers to
follow the settlements of the reassured, a consent and control of the negotiations
clause is a qualification of that provision. Thus reinsurers are not under an obligation
c to follow settlements if made without their consent. If the consent has not been
obtained then the reassured must prove his loss, that is to say, prove his legal liability
under the policy of original insurance to the original assured. If he fails to do so, he
fails to prove his right [to] an indemnity under the reinsurance contract; if he
succeeds, he has proved his loss and may, subject to other defences, recover under
d the reinsurance contract. As Robert Goff LJ said in *Insurance Co of Africa v Scor (UK)
Reinsurance Co Ltd* [1985] 1 Lloyd's Rep 312 at 331: "In my judgment the
undertaking by the insurers not to make a settlement without the approval of
reinsurers must have been intended to circumscribe the power of insurers to make
settlements binding upon reinsurers, so that reinsurers would only be bound to
follow a settlement when it had received their approval. In other words, the follow
e settlements clause must be construed in its context in the policy, containing as it
does a claims co-operation clause in this form, as only requiring reinsurers to follow
settlements which are authorised by the policy, i.e., those which have received their
approval, though presumably reinsurers can, if they wish, waive that requirement.
This effectively emasculates the follow settlements clause; but it is nevertheless, in
my judgment, what the parties to a policy in this form have agreed." See also per
f Fox LJ (at 334). Therefore under English law the presence of the consent clause has
only limited effect. This conclusion is not affected by its juxtaposition with the
breach of warranty provision which clearly deals with a different subject matter
altogether.'

The insurer, if he settles a claim without the reinsurer's consent, must prove his liability
by showing (1) that he was liable and (2) that the amount paid was correct. (I am not for
g present purposes concerned with compromise settlements.) The reinsurer must then pay
up, unless he has a good defence, as the underwriters have contended they have in this
case. Let me give an example. If the failure of the insured here to keep a 24-hour watch
has been a cause of the loss, Vesta, having waived the obligation, would still have been
liable to the insured for the proper amount of the claim, but the underwriters, not having
h waived it, would have had a good defence against Vesta.

It is idle for the underwriters to attack Vesta's case by pointing to the absurdity of
saying that the follow settlements clause is governed by English law and the claims
control clause, which qualifies it, by Norwegian law. In saying that I am not merely
relying on the 'construction of contract' solution but am pointing out the fallacy of
regarding the words 'Failure to comply with any of the warranties' etc as part of the
j claims control cause. As the judge said in the passage quoted above: '... the breach of
warranty provision ... clearly deals with a different subject matter altogether.'

I wish finally to mention another fallacious argument of the underwriters, who said
that if, contrary to their contention, the no V wording in the reinsurance contract is
governed by Norwegian law then it should be remembered that the need for the breach
to be causative expressly does not apply to *reinsurance* contracts under Norwegian law.

The answer to this point is that, according to the view taken in the courts below, with
which I respectfully agree, we are not here concerned with Norwegian reinsurance law
and that the meaning and effect of the failure to comply provision are the same in both
contracts.

For these reasons, my Lords, I would affirm the judgment of the Court of Appeal on
the question at issue and would dismiss the underwriters' appeal.

Appeal dismissed.

Solicitors: *Clyde & Co* (for the underwriters); *Richards Butler* (for Vesta); *Hewitt Woollacott
& Chown* (for the brokers).

Mary Rose Plummer   Barrister.

Dino Services Ltd v Prudential Assurance Co Ltd

COURT OF APPEAL, CIVIL DIVISION
KERR, MANN LJJ AND SIR DENYS BUCKLEY
31 OCTOBER, 1 NOVEMBER 1988

*Insurance – Property insurance – Perils insured against – Theft – Loss or damage from theft
involving 'forcible and violent' means of entry to premises – 'Violent' means of entry – Thieves
stealing keys to premises and entering premises by normal use of keys to unlock doors – No physical
damage caused to locks or doors – Whether entry by 'violent' means.*

A business insurance policy taken out by the plaintiff with the defendant insurers to
cover the plaintiff's business premises provided the plaintiff with cover against loss or
damage to property on the premises resulting from, inter alia, theft involving entry to
the premises 'by forcible and violent means'. Goods were stolen from the premises by
thieves who had stolen the keys to the premises from the plaintiff's car and then entered
the premises at night by simply using the keys in the normal way to unlock various
doors, without causing any physical damage to the locks or to the doors. The defendants
refused to indemnify the plaintiff under the policy on the ground that the thieves' entry
had not been 'by forcible and violent means' within the terms of the policy. The plaintiff
brought an action seeking a declaration that he was entitled to be indemnified under the
policy. The judge upheld his claim, on the ground that there had been entry to the
premises by both forcible and violent means within the policy. The defendants appealed.
On the basis that the opening of the doors with the stolen keys constituted 'forcible' entry
within the policy, the only issue was whether the entry had also been by 'violent' means.
The plaintiff contended that entry to premises was by 'violent' means where the entry
was unlawful or illegal because the word 'violent' characterised the unlawfulness of the
act of theft.

Held – In the context of a policy of insurance against theft from premises by 'forcible
and violent' means of entry, the word 'violent' was to be construed according to its
ordinary meaning and meant entry by the use of any force which was accentuated or
accompanied by a physical act which could properly be described as violent in nature and
character. In the context of such a policy the word 'violent' accordingly referred to the
physical character of the means of entry and not merely to its unlawful character. It
followed that the thieves, by gaining entry to the premises simply by using the proper
keys to unlock the doors of the premises, had not entered the premises by 'violent' means.

Accordingly, the plaintiff's loss was not covered by the policy. The appeal would
a therefore be allowed (see p 426 *d* to *j*, p 427 *a b* and p 432 *d f* to *h*, post).

Re George and Goldsmiths and General Burglary Insurance Association Ltd [1899] 1 QB 595,
and dictum of Atkin LJ in *Re Calf and Sun Insurance Office* [1920] 2 KB 366 at 383 applied.

Dictum of Bankes LJ in *Re Calf and Sun Insurance Office* [1920] 2 KB 366 at 378
considered.

b **Notes**
For the requirement in insurance against burglary that the entry is forcible and violent,
see 25 Halsbury's Laws (4th edn) para 672, and for cases on the subject, see 29 Digest
(Reissue) 557–558, 4991–4992.

Cases referred to in judgments
c *Calf and Sun Insurance Office, Re* [1920] 2 KB 366, CA.

George and Goldsmiths and General Burglary Insurance Association Ltd, Re [1899] 1 QB 595,
CA; rvsg [1898] 2 QB 136, DC.

Swales v Cox [1981] 1 All ER 1115, [1981] QB 849, [1981] 2 WLR 814, DC.

Appeal
d By a writ issued on 11 November 1985 the plaintiff, Dino Services Ltd, amended in place
of William Joseph Nash (trading as Dino Services Ltd), claimed as against the defendant,
Prudential Assurance Ltd, sued in error as Prudential Assurance Services Ltd, a declaration
that the plaintiff was entitled to be indemnified under a combined business policy
effected by Mr Nash with the defendant, in respect of loss sustained by the plaintiff in a
theft from the plaintiff's premises. By a judgment given on 10 November 1987 Peter
e Pain J held that the theft involved entry to and exit from the premises 'by forcible and
violent means' within the cover provided by the policy and declared that the plaintiff
was entitled to indemnity under the policy in respect of recoverable loss and damage
sustained in the theft. The defendant appealed. The facts are set out in the judgment of
Kerr LJ.

f *James Wadsworth QC* and *Michael Pooles* for the defendant.
John B Deby QC and *Q Tudor-Evans* for the plaintiff.

KERR LJ. This is an appeal by the defendant insurers from a judgment delivered by
Peter Pain J on 10 November 1987. The judge had to decide a number of points under a
combined business policy dated 11 November 1984 held by the plaintiff. The issues
g under the policy arose following a successful theft of valuable property from the
plaintiff's premises on the night of 4–5 October 1985.

The plaintiff company is effectively a one-man company of which Mr William Joseph
Nash is the moving spirit. It carries on business at unit 7, Endsleigh Industrial Estate,
Endsleigh Road, Norwood Green, Heston, Middlesex. Its business is in connection with
h Ferrari motorcars, particularly the older type of Ferraris, being the maintenance,
rebuilding and repair of such cars which can have a very considerable value.

Briefly, before I turn to the detailed facts, what happened is that on a Friday evening
Mr Nash locked up the premises. That involved using quite a number of keys. He then
drove away in his car, which I think was also a Ferrari, and which is equipped with every
kind of alarm and locking device to prevent theft. He parked the car outside a nearby
j public house where he often went at the end of the working week. He left the keys to
his premises in the glove compartment and later on made his way home, leaving the car
parked where it was. In the morning the car was gone and when he then went to his
premises he discovered that during the night they had been entered unlawfully by means
of his own keys taken from the car. So, for the purposes of the interpretation of the
policy, they were stolen keys which were used to open the various locks of the premises

to carry out the theft. The physical operation of opening the doors was normal, but of course the entry was unlawful and criminal.

We are solely concerned with that part of the cover which is headed 'Theft Section', of which I read the first clause although it is only para (a) which is relevant to the present facts. The cover provides as follows:

> 'In the event of 1 any of the Property Insured described in the Appendix to this Section contained within the Premises being lost or damaged as the result of theft or attempted theft involving a) entry to or exit from the Premises by forcible and violent means or b) actual or threatened assault or violence or use of force at the premises against the Insured or any director partner or employee of the Insured or any other person lawfully on the Premises ... during the Period of Insurance the Company will indemnify the Insured by at their option repairing replacing or paying the amount of the loss or damage.'

The judge was also concerned with another provision of the policy, on which a great deal of time was spent both in evidence and argument. That was the Reasonable Precautions Conditions, whereby the insured was to take all reasonable precautions to safeguard the property, to secure the premises and so forth. That issue no longer arises before us. I must say, although of course we have heard no argument on it, that I am somewhat surprised to find that the judge took the view in passing that Mr Nash was not to be equated with the insured for the purposes of that provision. But nothing turns on it at this stage. The main point on that part of the case was that the judge held that in all the circumstances, and after a careful review of the facts, that condition had been satisfied even if Mr Nash was included in the persons to whom it applied. That has not been challenged on this appeal. We are solely concerned with the meaning of the words 'by forcible and violent means' in cl 1(a).

I come now to the description of the premises, which I can take from the judgment. I add the identification of the various doors referred to, which are numbered on an agreed plan. The judge said:

> 'I have the benefit of a plan and a number of photographs. The premises are a comparatively small unit in an industrial estate, rectangular in shape; the major part being a workshop which has a sliding door [7] coming to the front and then, beside that, an entrance door [2], which opens and leads into a small vestibule. A door to the right [3] leads into the office; a door to the left [5] leads into the wc, and a door straight ahead leads into the workshop [6]. There is in addition, a door at the back of the workshop which leads into an alley [9]. Those doors are numbered on the plan which I have, and I shall be referring to them in the course of my judgment, by the numbers which appear on the plan.'

Before turning to the judge's findings, it is of some interest to see how the matter was pleaded in the face of the phrase 'entry by forcible and violent means'. I need only refer to the further and better particulars which were given in reply to an allegation that force and violence had been applied to effect entry. The answer was:

> 'The office lobby to workshop door [6] was secured by means of four locks. At the top and the bottom were two Chubb security locks ...'

and then it refers to further locks and then to marks which were found on the wooden door frame immediately below the five-lever Chubb lock. It is said that portions of wood were missing from the door frame—

> 'possibly caused by the use of a screwdriver or similar object [therefore] the Plaintiff will contend that force and violence was used on that door [6].'

As regards door 5 it was said that similar marks were found in a similar position on that door and that the wood was dented and that the paint had been damaged and removed and that there were signs of forcing that door.

Finally, in relation to door 9, it was said, and this was accepted by the judge, that the
a upper hinge of the rear door had been partially levered out by means of a tool or tools,
and that that constituted forcible and violent entry or exit through that door. The judge
did not accept any of these allegations, save to the extent of the physical damage to door
9, and his findings are now accepted by both parties to this appeal.

In his judgment, in dealing with what in his view had happened, he said:

b   'One has to proceed by inference as to what the thieves must have done, but I
        think by the conclusion of the evidence both parties were agreed that the thieves
        must have found the keys in the car in the car park, have also noticed (if they did
        not already know) some documents which he had in the car which showed where
        the business was, then driven there, let themselves in at door 2 (the front door) and
        then gone in quickly through door 3 and switched the alarm off within the 45-
c   second period. It is common ground, as agreed evidence, that the alarm had not
        been activated on that evening. Then they went through door 6, they went to door
        9 (the door at the back) and I think it right to infer that that door was opened by
        them. The reason I infer that is that there was evidence, both from Mr Nash and
        from Mr Dann, who had more acquaintance, perhaps, with door 9, because his used
        to be the job to do the dirty work, washing down various parts near that door, and
d   he frequently had it open in order that fumes could escape and he could get fresh
        air. And they both told me that before this theft the door opened quite easily, but
        after the theft the door did not open easily, it required two men (because it is a
        heavy door) to lift it up into position in order to shut it, and this was because, in the
        way that doors so often have, the top hinge had come away from the framework
        (not completely come away but was loose) and the effect of that of course is that the
e   door drops.'

Then he dealt with the steps which were taken to put that right, and he went on:

        'But, on the basis of that, I think it right to draw the inference that the thieves
        went to the back of the workshop and opened the door, as indeed any competent
        thief would because he would want to see where it led, in case he was surprised in
f   the middle of his depredations, and, having opened the door (and opened it for some
        reason somewhat roughly), it may well be the hinge was already a little bit loose and
        they loosened it considerably more, which led to this difficulty in shutting the door.
        It is I think quite clear that they did not use that door in order to evacuate what they
        were stealing, because it was so much easier to load up from the front, where they
        could operate by bringing the material out through the sliding door. I ought also to
g   mention that it is suggested that door 6 had been damaged in the course of the theft,
        but the only evidence as to that was that Mr Nash noticed, after the locksmith had
        been, that it was sticking slightly. It seems to me that is very slender evidence on
        which to base anything (doors often will start sticking a bit) and there is certainly no
        physical evidence of any damage of any substance having been done to that door or
        the frame. Accordingly, I hold that the thieves went straight in through door 6 and
h   that in this burglary no damage was done to door 6. The thieves then having got in,
        opened the sliding door (door 7) and then proceeded to evacuate a considerable
        number of tools and parts.'

Mr Nash referred to a press of some 3 cwt, which would have had to be carried some
60 ft from the back of the workshop in order to load it on some conveyance which must
j have been parked outside the sliding doors in the front of the premises. Those findings
are now accepted, and against that background I turn to consider the relevant terms of
the cover.

In that regard certain matters were agreed. Counsel for the defendant agreed that, on
the authorities, the opening of various doors by means of the stolen keys satisfied the
word 'forcible'. The defendant accepts that force in this context means the application of
energy to an obstacle with a view to its removal, as Donaldson LJ said in a quite different

context in *Swales v Cox* [1981] 1 All ER 1115 at 1119, [1981] QB 849 at 854. However, I think the reason why the defendant, understandably, accepts that an application of *a* minimal force is sufficient to satisfy the word 'forcible' derives from the later of two decisions of this court given as long ago as 1899 and 1920 (see *Re George and Goldsmiths and General Burglary Insurance Association Ltd* [1899] 1 QB 595 and *Re Calf and Sun Insurance Office* [1920] 2 KB 366), to which I shall come in a moment.

In itself, this technical interpretation of the word 'forcible' appears surprising. Until I saw the 1920 decision it certainly surprised me. It seems to imply that if I use my own *b* house key to let myself into my house, I effect an entry by forcible means. From the first of those two cases it is clear that Lord Russell CJ would not have accepted that as having been the meaning of the word 'forcible' in a similar context. But it is equally clear, at any rate as from 1920, that by reason of the later decision, and in particular of what Atkin LJ said in that case, the ordinary action of turning the knob of a door, or turning a key so as to open a lock, has been taken to satisfy the term 'forcible' in this context. So the issue in *c* the present case turns on the effect of the additonal word 'violent'.

As to that, counsel for the plaintiff concedes that that word must be given some meaning additional to the word 'forcible'. That again is a concession which he obviously had to make.

The word 'violent' is an ordinary English word, which here appears in a common commercial document. It seems to me that there is no reason why its meaning should be *d* in any way different from what any ordinary person would understand. At first sight I therefore conclude that there should be no need to resort either to a dictionary, or to authorities, to interpret this work; nor to the rule that, this being an insurers' document, it must be construed against them. On that basis I would take the ordinary meaning of the word 'violent' in this context to be that it is intended to convey that the use of *some* force to effect entry, which may be minimal, such as the turning of a key in a lock or the *e* turning of a door handle, if accentuated or accompanied by some physical act which can properly be described as violent in its nature or character. An obvious picture that springs to mind is the breaking down of a door or the forcing open of a window, which would be acts of violence directed to the fabric of the premises to effect entry. Or there might be violence to a person, such as knocking down someone who seeks to prevent entry, *f* irrespective of whatever may be contained within para (b) of that part of the cover.

Accordingly, on that basis I would not consider for one moment that the ordinary meaning of the phrase 'entry to premises by forcible and violent means' can be applied to the action of moving the lever of a lock into its open position by means of its proper key and then turning a knob or pushing the door open to go inside. That would be 'forcible' in the sense which I have explained, as is conceded on the authorities. But there would be nothing violent about it at all. That would be my impression. *g*

However, counsel for the plaintiff, who has said everything that could possibly be said, does not accept that approach. He obviously cannot. He stresses the fact that the keys were stolen, and he says that 'violent' is a term which characterises the unlawfulness of the act, relying in particular on one short passage in one of the cases to which I shall come. So what he says in effect is that 'forcible and violent' is to be equated with 'forcible *h* and unlawful' in relation to the means of entry.

Unless constrained by authority, which I would be astonished to find, I cannot accept that submission for one moment. I say that for two reasons. First, 'violent' as an ordinary word obviously has a different meaning from 'unlawful' or any similar word such as 'illegal'. Violence is often unlawful, but not always or necessarily so. For instance, if I break down my own door because I have lost my key, I do something violent but nothing *j* unlawful. On the other hand, a forcible entry which is unlawful is not necessarily one which is effected by violent means. There may be unlawfulness in which violence plays a part (that is what is covered by this provision) or there may be unlawfulness without anything which can be described as violence, and in my view that would not be covered.

The second reason why I would not accept the submission of counsel for the plaintiff,

even if one dictionary meaning of 'violent' is 'unlawful' as referred to in the judgment to
a which I come later, is that 'unlawful' cannot have been the intended meaning here,
because the phrase 'by forcible and violent means' occurs in a context which assumes a
state of unlawfulness, since we are concerned with 'theft or attempted theft' involving
entry by the means referred to. Accordingly, I have no doubt that the valiant attempt of
counsel for the plaintiff to equate 'violent' with 'unlawfulness' must be rejected, unless
astonishingly there were to be any authority binding on this court which compels its
b acceptance.

Two decisions of this court have been cited in this connection, on which Peter Pain J
said that a good deal of time had been spent, but in my view neither has this effect.
Indeed, it seems to me that they support the natural construction of the word 'violent'
which I have sought to indicate. The first is Re George and Goldsmiths and General Burlgary
Insurance Association Ltd [1899] 1 QB 595. I read part of the headnote, which refers to a
c policy on stock in trade. It was insured against loss or damage by burglary or
housebreaking 'as hereinafter defined', and the definition was: 'by theft following upon
actual forcible and violent entry upon the premises . . .' The insured property was in a
shop in the Strand, the front door of which was shut but not locked or bolted, so that
access could be obtained by merely turning the handle of the door. The headnote goes
on:
d

'In the early morning before business hours, during the temporary absence of a
servant of the assured, some person opened the front door, entered the shop, and,
breaking open a locked-up compartment or show-case within, which formed a
portion of the shop, stole therefrom part of the insured property . . .'

This court reversed the judgment of the Divisional Court ([1898] 2 QB 136) and held
e that the loss was not covered by the policy.

In that connection two matters should be mentioned before referring to the judgments.
First, the word 'actual' has disappeared from the words of the cover in this policy, but it
clearly survived at least as long as 1920 as appears from the next case. However, counsel
for the plaintiff has not suggested, again, if I may so so, rightly, that that affects the
present position. It may be that 'actual forcible and violent means' was thought to be an
f unhappy phrase because 'actual' suggested something which is the opposite of constructive,
and it is difficult to see what can be meant by 'constructive violence' in this context.
Second, the reason why the judgment of the Divisional Court was reversed in that case
was because that court had concentrated on the technical meaning of 'burglary' and
'housebreaking' and had not, in the view of this court, paid sufficient attention to the
definition which followed and which is so similar to the words in the present case.
g
I should mention one part of the argument on behalf of the respondent plaintiff. This
is reported as follows ([1899] 1 QB 595 at 598–599):

'If the word "violent" means anything more than "forcible", it merely means
unlawful as being against the will of the owner of the premises. All that it imports
h is that the entry must be by unlawful force. Here the entry by turning the handle
of the door involved a certain amount of force, and it was unlawful; and it amounted
to housebreaking . . .'

Although not precisely the same as the argument which has been addressed to us on
behalf of the plaintiff in the present case, there is a distinct echo of it there.
j The leading judgment was given by Lord Russell CJ. He said that he wished to say
that the case involved no question of principle or of general interest (see [1899] 1 QB 595
at 600). However, as so often happens, judges underestimate the importance of what
they are saying, since we have been asked to look at this case again and again as it were
through a microscope.
He said (at 602):

'Taking the language of the policy, namely, that the assured is to be protected against loss "by theft following upon actual forcible and violent entry upon the *a* premises", apart from technical considerations, could any one, as a matter of good sense, and, applying its ordinary meaning to ordinary language, suppose that an entry which is effected by turning the handle of the door and walking into the shop is an "actual forcible and violent entry" within the meaning of the policy? It appears to me that such a suggestion is repugnant to good sense.'

He added (at 603) that what was intended to be covered was an entry effected by real *b* violence in contrast to an entry effected by stealth without violence; and he then dealt with the word 'actual' in a passage which I need not read. But if one goes on, one can see that he would not have accepted the meaning of the word 'forcible' which is now conceded in this case. He said (at 603–604):

'Suppose that the door is closed, and in order to obtain entrance it is necessary to *c* turn the door-handle, that being the natural method by which every one is intended to go in and out of the shop; it is suggested that that is sufficient to constitute a forcible entry within the policy, and the Court cannot enter upon the question, if there be any force, whether a greater or less degree of force was used. But let us go a little further, and suppose that the door is ajar and is pushed open for the purpose of effecting an entry. It was argued that that would be sufficient force to constitute an *d* actual forcible and violent entry within this policy. But let us go a little further still, and suppose that the door is ajar, but so far open that a little boy or a lean person could enter without opening it further, but a stout person could not do so. Would it be a forcible entry within the policy, if such a person pushed it fully open and entered, but not so, if a small thief entered without pushing it open? It seems to me that such considerations shew that the line of reasoning on behalf of the respondent *e* is not sound. As I have said, I conceive that the policy was directed to securing the assured against the consequences of an entry effected by real "violence," as the word is commonly understood, in contradistinction to an entry effected by stealth without violence as I think the entry in this case was effected.'

Pausing there, one can see that that does not accord with the concession in this case. *f* The stout person in the example given by Lord Russell CJ who had to push the door a little to get in would, it appears, have entered forcibly, whereas the lean person or the little boy would not. Therefore it is rightly said by counsel for the plaintiff that between 1899, the date of that decision, and after the second case in 1920, it seems clear that the word 'forcible' acquired a new meaning in the insurance context.

Lord Russell CJ then dealt with that part of the argument which I have read and said, *g* referring to counsel for the respondent (at 604):

'His argument was this. He adopted the argument of his leader to the effect that the word "actual" was the really important word in the policy. He then proceeded to argue that it would be no unfair construction of the words "forcible and violent" to construe them as meaning "unlawful," and therefore, if there was an unlawful *h* entry, that was sufficient to satisfy the words of the policy. It seems to me that that view cannot be accepted, because it would follow from it that any man who in broad daylight entered a shop, the door being wide open, with the felonious purpose of committing a theft therein, if he got an opportunity of doing so, would have effected an unlawful entry within the meaning of that argument; and therefore that the words of the policy would cover the case of a man who enters a shop without *j* any impediment in his way at all, and, having done so, contrives to distract the attention of the shopman or get him on some pretext to go to another portion of the premises, and then proceeds to commit a theft. I think no one could say as a matter of good sense that such a case came within a policy which in express terms is confined to cases of "theft following on an actual forcible violent entry on the premises".'

A L Smith LJ agreed. He said (at 606):

> 'The first question is, Did this theft follow upon "actual forcible and violent entry upon the premises"? The answer to this certainly appears to me off-hand to be that it did not; for I ask, where is the force and where is the violence?'

Then, there is a passage in his judgment, which, speaking for myself, I find of the greatest assistance in explaining the meaning, or the general sense, of the word 'violent' in this context. He said (at 608):

> 'It is said that the word "violent" has no meaning other than that of the word "forcible" to which it is conjoined in the clause in question, and should therefore be ,discarded. [Pausing there, that is not what counsel for the plaintiff has argued here. A L Smith LJ went on:] I do not think so. In my opinion the word "violent" was used to accentuate and give point to the kind of force which was covered by the policy, and to prevent, if possible, it being argued, as argued it has been, that, as the mere act of turning the handle of a door is the exercise of some force, therefore such an act was covered by the policy. It is true the entry must be actual, but also with force and violence. These last works cannot be omitted.'

I do not think I need read anything from the judgment of Collins LJ in that case; he also agreed that the words of the cover had not been satisfied.

I come now to the second case, in which the words were again very similar. That arose out of an arbitration in *Re Calf and Sun Insurance Office* [1920] 2 KB 366. It concerned a burglary and housebreaking policy on business premises which covered property in the premises if it be—

> 'stolen by theft following upon an actual forcible and violent entry of the said premises by the person or persons committing such theft.'

This was a tailor's shop in the West End of London. The premises consisted of a shop on the ground floor, a fitting room on the first floor and a trimming room in the basement. It was admitted that all three of these were within the word 'shop' in the cover. There were then residential premises above these premises. As appears from the headnote, what happened was that:

> 'During the currency of the policy a person in the day-time entered the house in the normal way without any force or violence, and concealed himself in a coal cellar in the basement. At night, after the shop and trimming room had been locked up, he left the coal cellar and entered the trimming room from the passage, having by means of an instrument slid back the catch of the lock and so opened the door. He took a quantity of goods from the room and went up the stairs with the goods to the shop, which he entered by violently breaking open the door leading into the shop, and having taken more goods from the shop he left the house, with all the goods he had taken, by the front door.'

The arbitrator had concluded that entry had been made without any force or violence, but that if, contrary to that view, there had been some entry which satisfied the words of the cover, then the entry into the trimming room was not actual, forcible and violent entry (that was where the catch of the lock had been slid back by some instrument). On the other hand, the entry into the shop was obviously violent, since the shop door had been violently broken down. That was the view of Mr MacKinnon KC who stated a case for the opinion of the court. On these findings this court did not agree with him and decided that the insured was entitled to recover. The main issue was whether a forcible and violent entry on an inner door, a part of the premises, satisfied the cover, which referred to 'forcible and violent entry of the premises'. If the violent breaking down of the shop door was sufficient, then that decided the case, because it was conceded that the policy would then cover the goods which had previously been removed from the trimming room. The reason, of course, was that the theft would have taken place, as a matter of common sense, when all the goods were removed which had been taken from anywhere on the premises.

The first judgment was given by Bankes LJ. For present purposes the relevant part concerns the entry into the trimming room, although it was not strictly necessary for the decision. Describing this entry, Bankes LJ said that by means of an instrument the intruder, who had secreted himself in a cellar—

'forced back—I use those words deliberately—the latch of the Yale lock sufficiently to enable him to open the door, and so gained access to that room.'

(See [1920] 2 KB 366 at 376.)

He then dealt with the forcible and violent entry to the shop premises, and concluded that that was sufficient to decide the case. He went on to say that there had been considerable argument about the nature of the entry to the trimming room, and referred to George's case [1899] 1 QB 595. He said ([1920] 2 KB 366 at 378):

'The facts in that case were wholly different from those in the present case. No force was used in obtaining access to the premises covered by the policy. The thief simply turned the handle of the front door and walked in.'

Pausing there, one can see that Bankes LJ is apparently still taking the same view as that of Lord Russell CJ in 1899, that turning a door handle is not 'forcible'. He went on:

'In the present case the thief did something very different. Instead of finding a door through which persons were to pass by turning the handle, he found a locked door through which only an authorized person who had the key was intended to pass. To open the door he used sufficient force to force back the catch of the lock. All I need say about the words "forcible and violent entry" is that in my opinion they have reference to the character of the act by which an entry is obtained rather than the actual amount of force used in making the entry.'

That is the passage on which the judge principally relied and on which counsel for the plaintiff placed reliance on this appeal.

However, in referring to the character of the act, Bankes LJ was clearly referring to the forcing, having used that word deliberately in the passage already read, of a lock as opposed to opening it in the normal way with its key. In my view he was not referring to the unlawful nature of the act at all, but to its physical nature, the forcing of the lock.

Atkin LJ said a number of things which have no doubt considerably influenced the interpretation of the word 'forcible' since then (see [1920] 2 KB 366 at 382–383). He dealt with the shop and then came to the trimming room (at 383):

'As, however, the point has been argued and the arbitrator has expressed an opinion upon it, I desire to say that in my opinion there was an actual forcible and violent entry of that room. In ordinary language the lock was forced, and forced in such a sense that it could properly be said that the room was forcibly and violently entered.'

Then he referred to the old law dealing with indictments of persons who unlawfully enter on property, where the words 'by force and arms' in the Latin text occur; I need not read that. He then went on as follows:

'I think that the view taken by the learned judges in George's Case was this: that by the words "actual forcible and violent entry" it was intended to mean an entry effected by the exercise of force in a manner that was not customary in order to overcome the resistence of the usual fastenings and protections in the premises.'

In my view, that is a very important sentence. He went on:

'If a person turns a key he uses force but not violence. If he uses a skeleton key, he uses force but not violence. If on the other hand instead of using a key he uses a

a
pick-lock, or some other instrument, or a piece of wire, by which as a lever he forces back the lock, it appears to me that he uses force and violence, and in the present case both force and violence were used.'

Younger LJ agreed, and I need not read from his judgment.

I then come to the relevant passage in the judge's judgment in the present case. It begins:

b
'Now "violent" is defined in the *Oxford English Dictionary* in this way. Of things: "Having some quality or qualities in such a degree as to produce a very marked or powerful effect, especially in the way of injury or discomfort. Intense, vehement, very strong or severe." Of persons: "Acting with or using physical force or violence, especially in order to injure, control or intimidate others. Committing harm or destruction in this way. Acting illegally. Taking illegal possession." And, of actions:

c
"Characterised by the doing of harm or injury accompanied by the exercise of violence. Characterised by the exertion of great physical force or strength, done or performed with intense or unusual force and with some degree of rapidity. Not gentle or moderate." That is not the whole definition, but I think those are the parts which are helpful for the purpose of this case. So one arrives at the position that "violent" may, in certain circumstances, mean no more than "very forcible". But

d
commonly, it means "forcible" in some context where the force is being used in a way that is injurious or illegal. That it has in this context the latter meaning, is borne out partly by the fact that the word "forcible" is used as well as "violent", and one starts on the basis there would be no point in using "violent" if it simply meant the same thing, and, second, by the context in which it is used. It is used in the Theft Section in cl 1(a) of the cover, which couples theft involving "entry to or exit

e
from the Premises by forcible and violent means" with theft involving "actual or threatened assault or violence . . ."'

And he than quotes the words of cl 1(b) of the cover.

He then reviewed at length the judgments in the two cases to which I have referred, and states his conclusion in the following passage:

f
'In construing this clause, I have to bear in mind of course the contra proferentem principle. This was the defendant's document and in so far as there are ambiguities, those are to be resolved in favour of the plaintiff. Now the use of the key by the thieves was unlawful and the purpose of the use was to injure the plaintiff's rights in his property by depriving him of it, and I am quite happy to follow the phrase of Bankes LJ (in *Re Calf and Sun Insurance Office* [1920] 2 KB 366 at 378), that the words

g
to be construed have reference to the character of the act by which the entry is obtained. It seems, applying the definition in the *Oxford English Dictionary*, that the theft did involve entry to and exit from the premises by forcible and violent means.'

With great respect, I cannot accept that reasoning. We have not been referred to the dictionary, where one illustration of 'violent' is evidently equated with illegality or

h
unlawfulness in relation to persons. Presumably it would have been of no assistance to us. Whatever that illustration may be, that cannot be the meaning of the word here. I have also already indicated that in my view the judge misinterpreted the passage from the judgment of Bankes LJ on which he relied.

Counsel for the plaintiff also referred to another part of the cover, dealing with keys, as an aid to the construction of cl 1(a) of the theft section. It is in the 'Extensions' to the

j
theft section, cl 5, headed 'Keys', in the following terms:

'The company will in addition to the Limits of Liability pay to the Insured an amount not exceeding £500 incurred as a result of the necessary replacement of locks at the Premises following the loss of keys pertaining to the Premises . . . by theft involving entry or exit by forcible and violent means from the Premises or the home of any director partner . . .'

What counsel for the plaintiff submits, as I understand it, and I think I do understand it, is that given the words 'in addition to the Limits of Liability", this provision is based *a* on the assumption, or at any rate points to the assumption, that the keys and the changed locks which it covers in the two circumstances referred to, namely 'forcible and violent' entry to the premises or 'forcible and violent' entry to a relevant person's home, are covered in addition to the limits of liability comprised in the main part of the theft cover. So, says counsel for the plaintiff, in cases covered by cl 5 the keys and the changed locks are covered, but it is envisaged that that cover will be additional to the main cover. *b* Therefore, he says, you there have an illustration of a situation where, if for instance the keys were taken from one of the persons described by entry into his home by forcible and violent means, then they become stolen keys with whose assistance the business premises which are covered by the policy are then simply entered in the normal way and the main cover then applies. That is an ingenious argument. But in my view one cannot construe insurance policies in this overanalytical way, because they so often contain *c* words which on a strict analysis may be unnecessary but cannot properly be used to distort the ordinary meaning of the main part of the cover. What cl 5 was intended to do was merely to make it clear in what circumstances up to £500-worth of loss due to stolen keys and changed locks will be covered. It cannot be used as a means of affecting the ordinary sense of the words used in the main cover in cl 1(a).

The point is similar to another one made by counsel for the plaintiff. He asks *d* rhetorically: if 'violent' has its ordinary meaning, as I think it has, then why use the word 'forcible' at all, since 'violent' would include the concept of 'forcible'? I can see that would be so. The reason why the word 'forcible' is there is no doubt because it has an old history and one knows that insurance policies, like other standard business documents, very often do not have their wording changed even when it might be logical to do so. I regret that I cannot attach any weight to either of these submissions. *e*

Counsel for the plaintiff finally says, in my view entirely reasonably, that this is a business document which to the ordinary person would convey that cl 1(a) is intended to cover against burglary, and cl 1(b) against robbery, and that Mr Nash would be amazed to find that on the facts of this case he was uninsured. I agree and have every sympathy with Mr Nash. Since it is now accepted that he took reasonable precautions and this is an exceptional and novel point, and an important one for insurers generally, I would *f* personally hope that this might be regarded as a deserving case for an ex gratia payment. But, having to construe the policy as I must, I have no doubt that it cannot be construed in the way in which the judge construed it, and accordingly I would allow this appeal.

MANN LJ. I agree. Although we are differing from the judge below, there is nothing I can usefully add, except to say that it seems to me that this phrase, which has been in *g* currency now for nearly 100 years ought to be the subject of scrutiny.

SIR DENYS BUCKLEY. I also agree. I do not think I can usefully add anything to the very full judgment which Kerr LJ has delivered.

h

Appeal allowed.

Solicitors: *R J Hunter* (for the defendant); *Howard Kennedy* (for the plaintiff).

Wendy Shockett   Barrister.

a Babanaft International Co SA v Bassatne and another

COURT OF APPEAL, CIVIL DIVISION
KERR, NEILL AND NICHOLLS LJJ
12, 13, 18 MAY, 29 JUNE 1988

b

Practice – Pre-trial or post-judgment relief – Mareva injunction – Worldwide Mareva injunction – Post-judgment injunction – Extra-territorial effect of injunction – Protection of third parties – Foreign defendant having foreign assets – Defendant likely to attempt to frustrate execution of judgment against him – Whether court having jurisdiction to grant Mareva injunction over defendant's foreign assets before or after judgment – Whether worldwide injunction should be
c *qualified by express proviso protecting third parties.*

The plaintiffs obtained judgment for over $15m against the defendants, who were two brothers who were Lebanese nationals, one of whom lived mainly in Switzerland while the other lived mainly in Greece. They owned property in the United Kingdom and carried on shipping and oil-trading transactions worldwide. They had a peripatetic
d lifestyle and carried out their business transactions in a secretive manner through a network of family companies. When the defendants failed to satisfy the judgment the judge made an order for the examination of the defendants under RSC Ord 48 to determine what assets were available to meet the judgment debt. The judge also ordered the defendants to file an affidavit disclosing their assets wherever situated and, because he considered that they would be likely to take any step open to them to frustrate the
e execution of the judgment, he granted an injunction restraining the defendants from dealing with their assets outside the jurisdiction without giving the plaintiffs notice of their intention to do so. The defendants appealed against the injunction.

Held – Although the court had jurisdiction to grant a Mareva injunction over a
f defendant's foreign assets after judgment, had been given the court would not make an unqualified Mareva injunction covering assets abroad because it would involve an exorbitant and extra-territorial assertion of jurisdiction of an in rem nature over third parties outside the jurisdiction. Instead, such an injunction, if made, should be qualified by an express proviso making it clear that the injunction was directed to the defendant himself and did not affect the rights of third parties or seek to control their activities.
g Accordingly, the unconditional injunction made by the judge would be replaced by an injunction directed specifically to the defendants and to that extent the appeal would be allowed (see p 438 g h, p 440 h j, p 441 a to c, p 446 e to h p 447 d e, p 449 c, p 450 b to g j, p 452 d e and p 453 d e, post).

Dictum of Hoffmann J in *Bayer AG v Winter (No 3)* [1986] FSR 357 at 362 approved.
Ashtiani v Kashi [1986] 2 All ER 970 considered.

h   Per Kerr LJ. (1) The principles applying to the grant of a worldwide post-judgment Mareva injunction also apply to a pre-trial worldwide injunction (although the cases in which it is appropriate to grant such an injunction will be rare) (see p 441 e and p 447 j, post).

(2) A Mareva injunction covering assets abroad should provide that it does not affect the rights of third parties except to the extent that the order is enforced by the courts of
j states in which the defendant's assets are located (see p 441 c e f j to p 442 a and p 447 f g, post).

Notes
For Mareva injunctions, see 37 Halsbury's Laws (4th edn) 362, and for cases on the subject, see 37(2) Digest (Reissue) 474–476, 2947–2962.

Cases referred to in judgments

A-G v Newspaper Publishing plc [1987] 3 All ER 276, [1988] Ch 333, [1987] 3 WLR 942, *a*
 Ch D and CA.
Ashtiani v Kashi [1986] 2 All ER 970, [1987] QB 888, [1986] 3 WLR 647, CA.
Ballabil Holdings Pty Ltd v Hospital Products Ltd (1985) 1 NSWLR 155, NSW CA.
Bayer AG v Winter [1986] 1 All ER 733, [1986] 1 WLR 497, CA.
Bayer AG v Winter (No 3) sub nom *Bayer AG v Winter (No 2)* [1986] FSR 357.
Clunies-Ross, Re, ex p Totterdell (1987) 72 ALR 241, Aust Fed Ct.   *b*
Coombs & Barei Constructions Pty Ltd v Dynasty Pty Ltd (1986) 42 SASR 413, S Aust SC.
Crown Petroleum Corp v Ibrahim (27 April 1988, unreported), QBD.
de Cavel v de Cavel Case 143/78 [1979] ECR 1055.
Denilauler v Snc Couchet Frères Case 125/79 [1980] ECR 1553.
Faith Panton Property Plan Ltd v Hodgetts [1981] 2 All ER 877, [1981] 1 WLR 927, CA.
Home Office v Harman [1982] 1 All ER 532, [1983] 1 AC 280, [1982] 2 WLR 338, HL.   *c*
Interpool Ltd v Galani [1987] 2 All ER 981, [1988] QB 738, [1987] 3 WLR 1042, CA.
Iraqi Ministry of Defence v Arcepey Shipping Co SA (Gillespie Bros & Co Ltd intervening), The Angel Bell [1980] 1 All ER 480, [1981] QB 65, [1980] 2 WLR 488.
Maclaine Watson & Co Ltd v International Tin Council (No 2) [1988] 3 All ER 257, [1988] 3 WLR 1190, CA.
Mareva Cia Naviera SA v International Bulkcarriers SA, The Mareva (1975) [1980] 1 All ER *d*
 213, CA.
Penn v Lord Baltimore (1750) 1 Ves Sen 444, [1558–1774] All ER Rep 99, 27 ER 1132.
Portarlington (Lord) v Soulby (1834) 3 My & K 104, [1824–34] All ER Rep 610, 40 ER 40.
Reilly v Fryer (1987) 138 NLJ 134, CA.
Seaward v Paterson [1897] 1 Ch 545, [1895–9] All ER Rep 1127, CA.
Siskina (cargo owners) v Distos Cia Naviera SA, The Siskina [1977] 3 All ER 803, [1979] AC *e*
 210, [1977] 3 WLR 818, HL.
South Carolina Insurance Co v Assurantie Maatschappij 'De Zeven Provincien' NV [1986] 3 All ER 487, [1987] AC 24, [1986] 3 WLR 398, HL.
Toller v Carteret (1705) 2 Vern 494, 23 ER 916.
Yandil Holdings Pty Ltd v Insurance Co of North America (1986) 7 NSWLR 571, NSW SC.
Z Ltd v A [1982] 1 All ER 556, [1982] QB 558, [1982] 2 WLR 288, CA.   *f*

Appeals

The defendants, Bahaedine Bassatne and Walid Mohamed Bassatne, appealed against the decisions of Vinelott J whereby (i) on 19 April 1988 he granted, on the application of the plaintiffs, Babanaft International Co SA, a Mareva injunction precluding the defendants from dealing with any of their assets worldwide without giving five days' notice to the *g* plaintiffs' solicitors and (ii) on 20 April 1988 he refused the defendants' application to restrain the plaintiffs from giving notice of the injunction to persons who might hold the defendants' assets. The facts are set out in the judgment of Kerr LJ.

Gavin Lightman QC, Barbara Dohmann QC and *Hugo Page* for the defendants.   *h*
Anthony Clarke QC, Simon Mortimore and *Charles Haddon-Cave* for the plaintiffs.

At the conclusion of the argument the court announced that the appeals would be allowed, the injunction discharged and an injunction limited to the defendants personally substituted for reasons to be given later.

j

29 June. The following judgments were delivered.

KERR LJ. On 29 March 1988, after a trial which had lasted several weeks, Vinelott J gave judgment for the plaintiff company (Babanaft) against both defendants in a total sum which exceeded $15m inclusive of interest. On the following day, on an ex parte

application on notice, he made an order for the disclosure by the defendants of their
a assets worldwide pursuant to RSC Ord 48 and for the oral examination of the defendants
in relation to their assets. He also granted a Mareva injunction covering any assets of the
defendants in this country, but refused to extend this to assets outside the jurisdiction.
He said that he concluded, with some regret, that he was precluded from doing so by the
reasoning of the decision of this court in *Reilly v Fryer* (1987) 138 NLJ 134 in which
Mustill LJ had delivered the main judgment. The plaintiffs appealed against this refusal
b on the same day, the last day of the term, and sought a 'holding order' freezing the
defendants' assets worldwide pending a full hearing of their appeal after the Easter
vacation. A division of this court consisting of Slade, Mustill and Russell LJJ declined to
make any order to this effect and adjourned the plaintiffs' appeal. However, in the course
of the discussion, in particular as the result of comments from Mustill LJ, it became
apparent to the plaintiffs' advisers that neither the decision nor the reasoning in *Reilly v*
c *Fryer* would have precluded Vinelott J from granting the worldwide Mareva injunction
which they sought. They therefore renewed their application to him on 15 April 1988
to extend the injunction to assets outside the jurisdiction. That application was heard
inter partes. On seeing the notes of what had been said in the Court of Appeal on 30
March, Vinelott J agreed that *Reilly v Fryer* did not stand in the way of the order which
he had wanted to make, and it is now common ground that he was correct in this view.
d We have accordingly not been referred to *Reilly v Fryer* and I say no more about it.
Having heard the application, the judge then granted a Mareva injunction on 19 April
1988 precluding the defendants from dealing with any of their assets worldwide without
giving five days' notice to the plaintiffs' solicitors in every case. On the following day he
gave a further brief judgment in which he refused the defendants' application to restrain
the plaintiffs from giving notice of the injunction to persons such as banks or other
e institutions who might hold assets of the defendants. In pursuance of that judgment the
plaintiffs' solicitors notified some 47 entities in various countries of the terms of the
injunction, including some 24 banks and two international credit card companies.
    The defendants appealed against both of these judgments. We heard the appeals on 12
and 13 May. On 18 May we allowed the appeals, discharged the order of 19 April and
substituted an order limited to the defendants personally, as explained below, which
f expressly excluded any effect on any third party. We also ordered that all persons who
had been informed of the previous order should be notified that they should now
disregard it, since it had been discharged and replaced by an order which merely affected
the defendants personally. We announced that we would put our reasons in writing and
give them as soon as convenient. We adopted this course because of the urgency of the
situation and of pressures of time which would not have enabled us to give full judgments
g before the spring vacation and during the absence of two members of the court for some
weeks, also bearing in mind that the case obviously raises issues of general importance.
    Before giving my reasons for allowing the appeals to that extent I must summarise the
history. It is most unusual, and judgments of the order of $15m against individual
defendants are of course also not common. Although we all concluded that the orders
made by Vinelott J could not stand, one can readily see why he considered that drastic
h measures were necessary.
    The defendants are brothers, and I will refer to them as 'BB' and 'WB'. Babanaft is a
Panamanian company which was incorporated in 1976 but insolvent and in members'
voluntary liquidation since May 1985. Its incorporators, shareholders, directors and
officers were BB as the president and WB as secretary and treasurer respectively, together
j with a Mr Aladin Hassan Bahri as vice-president, who is believed to have died in August
1979 when travelling in a private jet which crashed in the desert on a flight to Jeddah.
These three persons had until then operated highly successfully in shipping and oil
transactions through a number of companies, and from about 1978 they decided to
combine their operations into a joint venture which was channelled through Babanaft.
But, after the death of Mr Bahri, the moving spirit in the shipping business, and also due

to trade recessions in oil, the business of the company deteriorated, and it was evidently
stripped of its assets, which had been very substantial. There was a lengthy and highly   *a*
complex history of BB and WB's dealings with the company's assets and of proceedings
concerning the estate of Mr Bahri, which were closely examined in the lengthy judgment
of Vinelott J in the action. But for present purposes it is only necessary to refer to the
matters which gave rise to the judgment against the defendants. In 1979 Babanaft had
entered into a long-term time charter for a new building, subsequently named the
'Eastern Venture', with Beeston Shipping Ltd, a Liberian company. The vessel was   *b*
delivered in December 1980, but in March 1982 Babanaft ceased to pay hire. In May
1982 Beeston treated the charterparty as repudiated and brought proceedings in the
Commercial Court. These resulted in a judgment for some $700,000 against Babanaft
for unpaid hire, and a reference to arbitration to assess the full damages to which Beeston
was entitled. This led to a default award against Babanaft for about $12m and an
additional sum of £41,000, and judgment in terms of the award was entered in March   *c*
1987.

A Mr C T E Hayward had meanwhile been appointed as receiver of Babanaft in
January 1985. He brought the present action in the name of Babanaft against BB and WB
in the Commercial Court, and the action was subsequently transferred to the Chancery
Division. The substance of the plaintiff's allegation was that, although BB, WB and Mr
Bahri had nominally merely been shareholders and directors of Babanaft, in truth they   *d*
had carried on a joint venture as partners which used Babanaft as a vehicle and as a screen
to protect them from personal liability, with the result that they were jointly and
severally liable to indemnify Babanaft in respect of, inter alia, the judgment debt owed
to Beeston. This is the allegation which Vinelott J found to be established and which
resulted in the judgment for over $15m against the defendants. We understand that the
defendants intend to appeal.   *e*

It is now necessary to say something about them. They are unusually peripatetic in
their lifestyle and elusive in the way they do business and hold assets. Both are Lebanese
nationals, but it is not clear whether they are still domiciled in the Lebanon. BB is mainly
resident in Switzerland and WB mainly in Greece. However, three substantial residential
properties are also available to BB in this country (which are comprised in the domestic   *f*
Mareva injunction) and the brothers are also joint owners of a number of properties in
the Lebanon. Both are described as oil traders in a very substantial way, and BB says that
he has an income from transactions and commissions of the order of $400,000 to
$500,000 a year. All 'their' assets appear to be held in the names of a large network of
companies incorporated in many countries in which they or members of their families
hold bearer shares. The properties available to BB in this country appear to be owned in
this way. He appears to spend considerable time here and was served with these   *g*
proceedings when he was here in hospital after an attack with a knife, following which
he says that both brothers received anonymous threats to their lives and demands for
money. WB has no apparent connection with this country but submitted to the
jurisdiction after the proceedings had been served on his brother. Thereafter both
defendants have complied with the orders made for the disclosure of their assets pursuant   *h*
to RSC Ord 48, but the true nature and location of their assets remains unclear, and they
are due to be cross-examined on their affidavits in the near future. In his judgment of 29
March 1988, when he granted the domestic Mareva injunction but at that stage refused
to extend it abroad, Vinelott J said:

'I should at the outset say that in the course of the hearing, extending over a long   *j*
period in which both defendants gave evidence and in the course of which I had to
go through a very large volume of documentary evidence, I reached the conclusion
that the defendants would be likely to take any step open to them to frustrate the
execution of the judgment.'

In the judgment of 19 April now under appeal, whereby he extended the Mareva
a injunction worldwide, he said about the defendants:

> 'They are businessmen who carry on their business activities in the field of,
> among other things, oil trading worldwide. WB has a settled home in Athens. BB
> has for some years had a house available to him in England. Indeed he has had the
> use of a house in the country and one in London, although both are owned by
> Panamanian companies, and some at least of his business affairs are conducted from
> *b* offices in London. He also has an address in Switzerland and offices elsewhere. BB
> and WB carry on their business activities through a large number of companies
> almost all incorporated in jurisdictions, Panama, Liberia, and the Dutch Antilles, in
> which it is difficult for outsiders to obtain information about their ownership,
> control and assets. The shares of these companies are for the most part bearer shares,
> and no annual returns or accounts are required to be filed in any registry in which
> *c* they can be inspected by the public. Babanaft is, therefore, likely to face considerable
> difficulties in ascertaining the extent of the assets available to meet the judgment it
> has obtained and in enforcing that judgment. Moreover, during the course of the
> hearing, I reached the conclusion that BB and WB would be likely to take any step
> open to them to frustrate or delay execution of the judgment.'

d The judge then considered the decisions of this court in *Faith Panton Property Plan Ltd
v Hodgetts* [1981] 2 All ER 877, [1981] 1 WLR 927, *Ashtiani v Kashi* [1986] 2 All ER 970,
[1987] QB 888 and *Reilly v Fryer* and concluded that he was—

> 'free to decide whether on the facts of this case an injunction should be granted to
> restrain BB and WB from disposing of their assets without as well as within the
> *e* jurisdiction.'

In considering this, he gave particular weight to the second reason given by Dillon LJ in
Ashtiani v Kashi [1986] 2 All ER 970 at 977, [1987] QB 888 at 901, namely the difficulty
for English courts to control or police enforcement proceedings in other countries, and
the problems liable to arise from notification of such orders to third parties in other
f countries. He then said:

> 'These are important practical considerations which must be borne in mind in
> deciding whether to grant an injunction affecting foreign assets. Their weight must
> be evaluated in the context of the particular facts and of the width of the order
> sought. In the instant case the injunction is sought in aid of the examination under
> Ord 48, that is, to ensure that BB and WB do not frustrate the purpose of the
> *g* examination by disposing of assets disclosed in the course of or before the
> examination until after Babanaft has had an opportunity of considering whether it
> can take effective steps to execute the judgment in the jurisdiction where those
> assets are situate. That purpose, it seems to me, will be fully answered by the grant
> of an injunction restraining BB and WB from dealing with their assets outside the
> jurisdiction without giving Babanaft reasonable notice of their intention to do so.
> *h* Once the existence of an asset with which BB and WB propose to deal has been
> disclosed, it will be open to Babanaft to take any steps available in the jurisdiction
> where the asset is situate to execute the judgment or to prevent BB and WB from
> disposing of it or, if appropriate, to make a further application to this court for, for
> instance, the appointment of a receiver. An injunction in those limited terms would
> not, it seems to me, create the difficulties developed by counsel for the defendants.'

j The order which he subsequently made was subject to an undertaking on behalf of
Babanaft to pay the reasonable costs and expenses of third parties served with notice of
the order and to indemnify them against liability arising from compliance with it. It was
pointed out on behalf of the defendants on this appeal that this was unsatisfactory, since

Babanaft was insolvent and there was no undertaking to pay damages. These matters were disposed of without opposition from the plaintiffs by a full undertaking in damages *a* given on behalf of Beeston's P & I club who had supported the litigation, the London Steamship Owners Association, and no more need be said about that aspect. The operative part of the order which is relevant for present purposes restrained the defendants until further order, whether by themselves, their servants or agents or otherwise howsoever from—

'(i) disposing of or transferring charging or diminishing or causing or procuring *b* or permitting the disposal transfer charging or diminution or in any way howsoever dealing with any of their respective assets money or goods without the jurisdiction whether such assets be in their own names or jointly with any other persons or in the names of nominees or trustees for them save in so far as the value of such assets money or goods within the jurisdiction exceeds the sum of $16,000,000 (Sixteen million United States Dollars), and (ii) Without prejudice to the generality of the *c* foregoing and save as aforesaid from disposing of transferring charging or diminishing or removing from their present locations or otherwise dealing with any bearer shares held by them or either of them or jointly with any other person or by agents or nominees for them in the capital of any company wherever such shares are situate and such company incorporated without first giving at least 5 clear *d* English working days' notice in writing or by telex to the Receiver's solicitors Messrs Holman Fenwick & Willan at their offices in London at Marlow House Lloyds Avenue London EC3N 3AL marked "For the urgent attention of Mr N Robinson and Mr T Jones" of their intention to do so identifying with particularity the precise value nature and whereabouts of such assets including but not limited to the number(s) of any bank account(s) where relevant.' *e*

This order was qualified by a proviso in the following terms:

'Nothing in this injunction shall prevent any bank or third party (not being a third party connected or associated in any way with the Defendants or either of them or any relative of the Defendants or either of them or any company or firm united or associated in any way with the Defendants or either of them or any relative *f* of the Defendants or either of them) from exercising any right of set off it may have in respect of facilities given to the Defendants or the said companies before the date of this injunction including any interest which has accrued or may hereafter accrue in respect of such facilities.'

We understand that this is nowadays a standard type of proviso to Mareva injunctions, and it is of course inserted for the benefit of third parties who may be affected by the *g* freezing order. My reason for quoting it is that it illustrates that, although Mareva injunctions are orders made in personam against defendants, they also have an in rem effect on third parties. It shows that, save to the extent of the proviso, the order is binding on third parties who have notice of the injunction. Although the passage in the judgment of Lord Denning MR in *Z Ltd v A* [1982] 1 All ER 556 at 562, [1982] QB 558 at 573 *h* headed '*Operation in rem*' may well go too far in a number of respects, there cannot be any doubt that Mareva injunctions have a direct effect on third parties who are notified of them and who hold assets comprised in the order.

This needs no elaboration and is demonstrated by the events which followed. I have already mentioned that, pursuant to leave granted by Vinelott J in general terms, some 47 entities in various countries were notified of the terms of the order by the plaintiff's *j* solicitors. This was done by telexes which quoted the order in full and then concluded as follows:

'We are giving you notice of this injunction because we believe that you may hold assets beneficially owned by either or both of the defendants. You will note a from paragraph 1 of the injunction that the defendants are bound to give at least 5 clear English working days notice to us before dealing with any of their assets. We strongly advise you to check with us at the following address or telex number that the requisite notice has been given before you allow the defendants to deal with any of their assets held by you.'

b We were also briefly referred to a number of the responses. Many of the replies were to the effect that the addressees held no assets of the defendants'. Others queried the meaning and effect of the order or its validity. In one case a foreign bank rejected it in strong terms, perhaps unnecessarily drawing the senders' attention to the fact that 'the decisions have been rendered by a British court'. In other cases further correspondence was necessary in an attempt to clarify the effect of the orders. In some cases the clarifications contained phrases such as 'We are sure that you, as their lawyers in France, will also be keen to ensure that your clients are not in breach of court orders'. And in the

c case of one international bank with a branch in England a telex to its Athens branch included the following:

'It is of course conceivable that officers of the bank within the English jurisdiction could be responsible for any breaches of the injunction by the bank in foreign jurisdictions, and it is possible that those breaches may be punishable by proceedings

d for contempt.'

This correspondence speaks for itself. The judge clearly had some misgivings about the implications of his order. In his short judgment of 20 April he said in this connection:

'These are inevitably, I think, rather tentative steps in a new situation. I do not think, so far as authority goes, that an injunction has been sought worldwide even

e after judgment in this wide form. I formulated provisions for notification and the five day moratorium with a view to mitigating, if possible, injury to third parties rather than to the defendants, who are, after all, indebted to the plaintiffs for a very substantial sum and are not in my view entitled to protection unless and until they can show that they have assets available on which they can give security. But I do not think that there would be any grave hardship to third parties if the full terms of

f the injunction are communicated to persons who are given notice of it and if reasonable restraint is exercised by the plaintiffs' solicitors in deciding the range of persons to be notified. The third parties will be free to deal with the assets of the defendants provided that they first satisfy themselves by communicating with Holman Fenwick that the requisite notice has been given and expired.'

g I then turn to the law.

The jurisdiction of the court to grant injunctions is now to be found in s 37 of the Supreme Court Act 1981:

'Powers of High Court with respect to injunctions and receivers.—(1) The High Court may by order (whether interlocutory or final) grant an injunction or appoint a

h receiver in all cases in which it appears to the court to be just and convenient to do so.

(2) Any such order may be made either unconditionally or on such terms and conditions as the court thinks just.

(3) The power of the High Court under subsection (1) to grant an interlocutory injunction restraining a party to any proceedings from removing from the

j jurisdiction of the High Court, or otherwise dealing with, assets located within that jurisdiction shall be exercisable in cases where that party is, as well as in cases where he is not, domiciled, resident or present within that jurisdiction . . .'

Subsection (3) is clearly directed specifically to Mareva injunctions covering assets located within the jurisdiction. In *Ashtiani v Kashi* [1986] 2 All ER 970 at 976, 979, [1987]

QB 888 at 900, 904 both Dillon and Neill LJ attached some importance to this provision in support of their conclusion that Mareva injunctions should be limited to assets located *a* within the jurisdiction, and Nicholls LJ agreed with both judgments. But it is clear from a reading of these judgments as a whole that the decisions were not founded on the construction of s 37 but on wider considerations of policy. The purpose of sub-s (3) was not to restrict the territorial ambit of Mareva injunctions but to ensure that there should be no discrimination against persons not domiciled, resident or present within the jurisdiction. Subsection (3) does not restrict the scope, geographical or otherwise, of *b* sub-s (1). And it is perhaps worth noting that the appointment of a receiver pursuant to sub-s (1). And it is perhaps worth noting that the appointment of a receiver pursuant to sub-s (1) may extend to assets outside the jurisdiction, whether movable or immovable (see 8 Halsbury's Laws (4th edn) para 648 (Conflict of Laws) and 39 ibid para 855 (Receivers).

And, in regard to the proper scope of the exercise of the court's discretion, the practice is *c* clearly still in a state of development which has moved on since then. Thus, the Australian courts have not followed the policy indicated in *Ashtiani v Kashi* by granting Mareva injunctions before judgment covering assets located in other Australian jurisdictions: see *Ballabil Holdings Pty Ltd v Hospital Products Ltd* (1985) 1 NSWLR 155 and *Coombs & Barei Constructions Pty Ltd v Dynasty Pty Ltd* (1986) 42 SASR 413; and the General Division of the Federal Court of Australia has granted an interim injunction *d* against a bankrupt living in Western Australia from dealing with real property in the Cocos (Keeling) Islands Territory pending the hearing of a substantive application: see *Re Clunies-Ross, ex p Totterdell* (1987) 72 ALR 241. Moreover, for the reasons mentioned hereafter it is in my view also necessary to consider the policy of the *Ashtiani v Kashi* decision in the context of international reciprocity as evidenced by the Convention on Jurisdiction and the Enforcement of Judgments in Civil and Commercial Matters *e* (Brussels, 27 September 1968; EC 46 (1978); Cmnd 7395), or, to give it its popular title, the European Judgments Convention, set out in Sch 1 to the Civil Jurisdiction and Judgments Act 1982.

The fact that the practice in this field is still in a state of development is also shown by recent decisions concerning orders for the *disclosure* of assets outside the jurisdiction. In *Ashtiani v Kashi*, albeit on the particular facts, this court took a restrictive view of an order *f* for the disclosure of assets situated abroad because, it was said, such a disclosure might enable the plaintiffs to use the disclosed information to obtain an attachment of the defendant's assets in other jurisdictions. That was a pre-judgment case, and the court was not referred to any of the relevant international jurisprudence discussed below. However, two more recent decisions of this court have held that the position is in any event different in principle once a judgment has been obtained. The first was *Interpool Ltd v* *g* *Galani* [1987] 2 All ER 981, [1988] QB 738, which decided that orders for the disclosure of assets after judgment pursuant to Ord 48 could properly extend to assets outside the jurisdiction. And in *Maclaine Watson & Co Ltd v International Tin Council (No 2)* [1988] 3 All ER 257, [1988] 3 WLR 1190 this court held that the defendants should make a full disclosure of their assets, both within and outside the jurisdiction, where the plaintiffs *h* had obtained judgment but were unable to rely on Ord 48. The order for extra-territorial disclosure was made pursuant to s 37(1) of the Supreme Court Act 1981.

I therefore proceed on the basis that in appropriate cases, though these may well be rare, there is nothing to preclude our courts from granting Mareva-type injunctions against defendants which extend to their assets outside the jurisdiction.

On that assumption three questions fall to be answered which did not arise or were *j* not raised in *Ashtiani v Kashi* but which now need to be considered in principle. To take them in the order in which they were raised in the present case, they are as follows. (1) Should we adopt a different policy in relation to applications made after judgment, in line with the authorities on post-judgment orders for the disclosure of assets, by granting unqualified Mareva injunctions over foreign assets after judgment in appropriate cases?

That was the conclusion of Vinelott J and the main issue argued on this appeal,
a distinguishing *Ashtiani v Kashi* on that ground. (2) If the answer to (1) is in the negative,
because this would involve an exorbitant assertion of extra-territorial jurisdiction over
third parties, should we restrict such orders expressly so as to bind only the defendant
personally by adding a proviso to make it clear that third parties shall not be affected by
the order? This was a fall-back position suggested on behalf of the defendants as a
compromise between upholding the unqualified Mareva injunction, which they
b submitted was clearly wrong in law, and declining to make any order affecting the
defendants' foreign assets, which they recognised to be more or less unacceptable on the
facts of this case. As explained below, on the basis of the oral arguments addressed to us,
this was the solution which we ultimately adopted in the order which we announced
after the hearing. (3) Alternatively to (2), should the terms of the order in such cases take
the form of a normal Mareva injunction, but with the qualification that the order shall
c not affect third parties unless and to the extent that it is enforced by the courts of the
state in which the assets are located? This appears to me to be the correct international
approach, stemming from the jurisprudence dealing with art 24 of convention entitled
'Provisional, including protective, measures', to which I come shortly. That aspect was
only raised by the court itself towards the end of the oral argument. After the conclusion
of the hearing counsel then referred us in writing to some of the relevant material,
d including the three Australian cases to which I have referred, and they also submitted
brief comments on one of the relevant decisions of the Court of Justice of the European
Communities mentioned below.

Three matters should be noted about solutions (2) and (3). First, both are in principle
equally relevant before and after judgment. Second, neither militates against the
reasoning of the judgments of this court in *Ashtiani v Kashi*. Third, it may be that in some
e foreign jurisdictions there would be no real difference between these solutions in their
practical effect. Thus, some foreign courts might enforce orders in terms of solution (2)
in ways which would affect third parties holding assets of the defendant, and to that
extent the proviso to such orders might in practice prove to be nugatory. This is an
additional reason, together with those set out hereafter, for the conclusion that in my
f view solution (3) is the correct approach in principle in those cases where a Mareva-type
injunction extending to foreign assets is considered to be appropriate.

However, before coming to these aspects, I must briefly refer to the reasons which led
Vinelott J to adopt solution (1).

The judge founded himself squarely on the consideration that in the present case the
order was sought after judgment and therefore in aid of execution. In that connection he
g dealt at length with the judgments in this court in *Faith Panton Property Plan Ltd v
Hodgetts* [1981] 2 All ER 877, [1981] 1 WLR 927, which had been an appeal from
himself. This court had there granted a Mareva injunction after judgment to protect an
order for costs in favour of the plaintiffs pending taxation, and the judgments emphasised
the difference in approach to orders of this kind when the plaintiff has already obtained
a judgment. That is of course understandable. The court is then no longer so concerned
h to protect the defendant, and there are good reasons for assisting judgment creditors, as
shown by *Interpool Ltd v Galani* and *Maclaine Watson & Co Ltd International Tin Council
(No 2)*. But the *Faith Panton* case had no foreign element of any kind and is no authority
for present purposes. In the context of orders which operate extra-territorially, wholly
different considerations arise, as discussed below. These show that unqualified Mareva-
type injunctions applying to foreign assets can never be justified, neither after nor before
j judgment. None of the counsel could recollect any order of any foreign court, however
'long-arm' the nature of the jurisdiction claimed, which had gone as far as the order made
in this case.

In my view, the key to the proper exercise of any extra-territorial jurisdiction must lie
in the question whether there is international reciprocity for the recognition and
enforcement of the type of order which is under consideration, in this case a Mareva

injunction or a variant of it purporting to operate on the defendants' assets abroad. In
that context one must have regard to the practice and jurisprudence concerning art 24 of *a*
the convention. This was concluded in 1968 between the original six members of the
European Economic Coummunity (the EEC) and extended to the United Kingdom,
among others, by the Convention on Accession of 9 October 1978 of the Kingdom of
Denmark, of Ireland and of the United Kingdom of Great Britain and Northern Ireland
to the Convention on Jurisdiction and Enforcement of Judgments in Civil and
Commercial Matters and to the Protocol on its Interpretation by the Court of Justice *b*
(Cmnd 7395, OJ L304/78 p 1), without any alteration to art 24. The convention requires
the recognition and enforcement of all judgments or orders which fall within its scope,
whether final or interlocutory, subject to limited exceptions which have no application
in the present case: see arts 1, 25, 26 to 28 and 31 of the convention and the comments of
Mr P Jenard on Title III of the convention (OJ 1979 C59, p 42ff). The convention
therefore applies prima facie to any order made on the plaintiffs' application in this case, *c*
ie both to the order made by Vinelott J and to the qualified order which we substituted
on this appeal.

But this is not the main reason for the importance of the convention in the present
context. The main reason lies in the fact that it contains the most extensive code
evidencing international reciprocity in the recognition and enforcement of judgments
and orders issued in foreign jurisdictions, and that it includes art 24 dealing with *d*
provisional and protective measures. The forerunner of the European Judgments
Convention had been a network of bilateral conventions, and among the original six
member states nearly all of these had included a provision corresponding to art 24: see
the comment on this article by Mr P Jenard (at 42). So the European Judgments
Convention is now the widest embodiment of international consensus in this field,
founded on decades of bilateral conventions. A parallel convention in similar terms to *e*
the Judgments Convention, including art 24 without alteration, between the EEC and
the European Free Trade Association (EFTA) states (Austria, Finland, Iceland, Norway,
Sweden and Switzerland) will be discussed at a diplomatic conference later this year. It
will probably result in the adoption of art 24 throughout virtually the whole of Western
Europe, and with it the decisions of the European Court concerning it. A discussion of
the relevant jurisprudence as it stood some years ago will be found in the valuable article *f*
by Mr Lawrence Collins, the editor of Dicey and Morris *The Conflict of Laws*, 'Provisional
Measures, the Conflict of Laws and the Brussels Convention' [1981] *Yearbook of European
Law* 249.

With apologies for this lengthy introduction, I then come to the text of art 24 which
is in the following terms:
                                                                                          g
'Application may be made to the courts of a Contracting State for such provisional,
including protective, measures as may be available under the law of that State, even
if, under this Convention, the courts of another Contracting State have jurisdiction
as to the substance of the matter.'

Without legislation this provision could not have been used by our courts to grant, for *h*
instance, Mareva injunctions over assets situated in this country in aid of substantive
proceedings pending in other EEC jurisdictions. To do so would have been contrary to
the decision of the House of Lords in *Siskina (cargo owners) v Distos Cia, The Siskina* [1977]
3 All ER 803, [1979] AC 210. This had held that, unless our courts were properly seised
of the substance of an action, there was no jurisdiction to grant a Mareva injunction over
assets in this country in aid of proceedings abroad. The reversal of *The Siskina* and *j*
adherence to art 24 was achieved by s 25 of the 1982 Act. It is unnecessary to set this out
for present purposes. However, its effect was to focus attention on only one aspect of
art 24: the power of a court in EEC state A, which is not seised of the substantive action,
to make some provisional or protective order in aid of a substantive action pending in
state B. I will refer to this as the primary effect of art 24. However, that leaves out of

account a secondary and entirely distinct effect of art 24, to take a corresponding example:
a the recognition and enforcement by the courts of state A, pursuant to the requirements
of the convention, of provisional or protective orders made by a court in state B pursuant
to art 24 in aid of a substantive action pending before it, which orders purport to have
effect in state A. It is this latter aspect which is material in the present context.

Two important decisions of the European Court on art 24 indicate that extra-territorial
orders akin to Mareva injunctions, made by the courts in one EEC state and purporting
b to operate on assets located in another EEC state, will be recognised and enforced by the
courts of the latter state if they fall within the scope of the European Judgments
Convention and satisfy certain requirements designed to protect the defendant against
whom the orders were made. They are *de Cavel v de Cavel* Case 143/78 [1979] ECR 1055
and *Denilauler v Snc Couchet Frères* Case 125/79 [1980] ECR 1553. Both cases concerned a
pre-judgment saisie conservatoire issued by a French court over assets of the defendants
c located in Germany. In the first case divorce proceedings were pending before a court in
France. On the application of the husband the court froze the furniture, effects and other
objects situated in the couple's flat in Frankfurt and in a safe hired in the wife's name in
a bank in Frankfurt, and the wife's account at that bank. The husband sought
enforcement of this order by proceedings in Germany pursuant to art 24 of the European
Judgments Convention. The German Federal Court of Justice referred his entitlement to
d enforcement to the European Court. The issue was whether art 24 applied to orders
made in divorce proceedings which involved the status of the parties and proprietary
legal relations resulting from the matrimonial relationship. Since these are not matters
falling within art 1 of the convention, the European Court held that the French order
was not entitled to recognition and enforcement in Germany under art 24. In *Denilauler
v Snc Couchet Frères* a French court was seised of a commercial action and in the course of
e it made an order authorising the freezing of the defendants' assets in a bank in Frankfurt
as security. The plaintiffs sought to enforce that order under art 24, but the German
court referred the case to Luxembourg on the ground that the German defendants had
had no notice of the order before it had been made. On that ground the European Court
held that the order was not entitled to recognition and enforcement by the German
courts under art 24. But there was no suggestion in the opinion of either Advocate-
f General in either case (who was Mr Advocate General J-P Warner in *de Cavel v de Cavel*),
or in the judgments of the court, that there was any basis for criticising the orders of the
French courts on the ground that, subject to their recognition and enforcement by the
German courts, they purported to operate extra-territorially. This is not at all surprising
when it is remembered that the object of the European Judgments Convention was to
create something analogous to a single law district for the whole of the EEC.
g I have expressed the outcome of these cases in Luxembourg in broad terms which may
well to some extent oversimplify the detailed grounds of the decisions. But that does not
matter for present purposes. What these cases show, if one transposes them by reference
to our courts, can be summarised as follows. A pre-judgment Mareva injunction granted
by an English court in aid of English proceedings, freezing specific assets of a defendant
h located in the territory of any EEC state, is entitled to recognition and enforcement by
the courts of that state if (i) the English proceedings fall within the scope of art 1 of the
Judgments Convention (civil and commercial matters) and do not fall within any of the
exceptions, in particular those in arts 27 and 28, and (ii) the order was made inter partes,
or at any rate after the defendant had had an opportunity to resist the plaintiff's
application for the order. Depending on the local law and practice, it may be that the
j same would apply to orders covering the defendant's assets generally, without specifying
their nature or location.

There are three important implications of these decisions.

(A) Viewed purely from the point of view of international comity, and indeed
reciprocity, there appears to be no reason why our courts should refrain from granting
inter partes pre-judgment Mareva injunctions in cases falling within the European

Judgments Convention in relation to assets situated in the territories of other EEC states; and the same may soon apply to the territories of all or most of the EFTA states.	*a*

(B) However, there can be no question of such orders operating directly on the foreign assets by way of attachment, or on third parties, such as banks, holding the assets. The effectiveness of such orders for these purposes can only derive from their recognition and enforcement by the local courts, as should be made clear in the terms of the orders to avoid any misunderstanding suggesting an unwarranted assumption of extra-territorial jurisdiction. However, if the orders fulfil the requirements of (i) and (ii) above, then the	*b* local courts will be bound to recognise and enforce them.

(C) Apart from any EEC or EFTA connection, there is in any event no jurisdictional (as opposed to discretionary) ground which would preclude an English court from granting a pre-judgment Mareva injunction over assets situated anywhere outside the jurisdiction, which are owned or controlled by a defendant who is subject to the jurisdiction of our courts, provided that the order makes it clear that it is not to have any	*c* direct effect on the assets or on any third parties outside the jurisdiction save to the extent that the order may be enforced by the local courts. Whether an order which is qualified in this way would be enforced by the courts of states where the defendant's assets are situated would of course depend on the local law, as would the question whether such orders would be recognised and enforced if they refer to the assets of the defendant generally or only if specified assets are mentioned in the order. As the European Court	*d* said in *Denilauler v Snc Couchet Frères* [1980] ECR 1553 at 1570 (para 16):

> 'The courts of the place ... where the assets subject to the measures sought are located, are those best able to assess the circumstances which may lead to the grant or refusal of the measures sought or to the laying down of procedures and conditions which the plaintiff must observe in order to guarantee the provisional and protective	*e* character of the measures ordered ...'

That comment applies equally to what I have referred to as the primary as well as to the secondary effect of art 24.

Before turning to post-judgment orders I would add two further comments on the decision of this court in *Ashtiani v Kashi* [1986] 2 All ER 970, [1987] QB 888, bearing in	*f* mind that none of this jurisprudence was brought to the court's attention in that case.

First Dillon LJ expressed the view that ([1986] 2 All ER 970 at 978, [1987] QB 888 at 903)—

> 'If in a future case disclosure of foreign assets is in a proper case ordered on special grounds, it does seem to me that prima facie at any rate the plaintiffs should be	*g* required to give an undertaking not to use any information disclosed without the consent of the defendant or the leave of the court.'

With all due respect, I do not think that as a general rule this comment can be correct, and it was regarded as 'somewhat surprising' by Rogers J hearing the Commercial List of the Common Law Division of the Supreme Court of New South Wales: see *Yandil*	*h* *Holdings Pty Ltd v Insurance Co of North America* (1986) 7 NSWLR 571 at 577. Its application would deny the intended effect, both primary and secondary, of art 24. No doubt, as emphasised by Nicholls LJ at the end of his judgment in the present case, any orders affecting foreign assets should always be considered with great care, since they may have unforeseen and unintended consequences for defendants. But it should also be said, with equal emphasis, that some situations, which are nowadays by no means	*j* uncommon, cry out, as a matter of justice to plaintiffs, for disclosure orders and Mareva-type injunctions covering foreign assets of defendants even before judgment. Indeed, that is precisely the philosophy which underlies art 24 and which has been applied by the development of the common law in Australia.

Second in *Ashtiani v Kashi* [1986] 2 All ER 970 at 975, [1987] QB 888 at 898 there is a
a lengthy citation of a passage from the judgment of Hoffmann J in *Bayer AG v Winter*
(No 3) [1986] FSR 357 at 362, which was also cited by Rogers J in the *Yandil Holdings* case
7 NSWLR 571 at 575. I do not propose to repeat it in full, but the passage concluded as
follows:

'There are territorial limits to the effectiveness of this court's own orders. If
b   however there is evidence that a foreign court would be willing to make orders
similar in effect to a *Mareva* injunction upon assets within its jurisdiction, it seems
to me that, other things being equal, this court should not restrict a plaintiff's ability
to obtain such a relief. It would be a pointless insularity for an English court to put
obstacles in the way of a plaintiff who wished, with the aid of foreign courts, to
enforce an English judgment against a defendant's assets wherever they might be.'

c Dillon LJ rejected the view expressed in this passage in favour of a contrary view which
had been expressed by Sir Neil Lawson at first instance (see [1986] 2 All ER 970 at 978,
[1987] QB 888 at 902). However, since none of the foregoing considerations had been
brought to the attention of the court in *Ashtiani v Kashi*, I feel entitled to suggest that,
viewed internationally, Hoffmann J was quite right in his approach, at any rate within
the scope of the decisions of the European Court on what I have referred to as the
d secondary effect of art 24. Indeed, I would respectfully go further by suggesting that this
approach, based as it is on international reciprocity, is in principle altogether correct.

I then turn to post-judgment Mareva injunctions purporting to freeze foreign assets.
Perhaps surprisingly from an English point of view, it appears at first sight to be more
difficult to justify such orders than pre-judgment Mareva injunctions. The reason is that
it can be suggested that they would not be regarded as provisional or protective measures
e within art 24. It seems that the jurisprudence of our continental partners may not
recognise provisional orders having the character of attachments or saisies conservatoires
after judgment. Thus, as was pointed out by Collins in 'Provisional Measures, the Conflict
of Laws and Brussels Convention' [1981] *Yearbook of European Law* 249 at 263, referred to
above:

f   '... the Hague Convention of February 1971 on recognition of judgments
excludes, in terms, judgments ordering provisional measures ...'

One can see the same approach in art 16(5) of the European Judgments Convention, on
which Miss Dohmann QC for the defendants relied in her argument. This provides that,
regardless of domicile, 'in proceedings concerned with the enforcement of judgments,
the courts of the Contracting State in which the judgment has been or is to be enforced'
g shall have 'exclusive jurisdiction'. In *Interpool Ltd v Galani* [1987] 2 All ER 981, [1988]
QB 738 this court ordered the defendant to make a full disclosure after judgment of his
assets abroad, clearly in order to enable the plaintiff to use the disclosure for the purpose
of enforcement proceedings in the jurisdictions where the disclosed assets were situated.
The court also held that an order for disclosure by the defendant of his assets worldwide
h pursuant to Ord 48 did not infringe art 16(5) of the European Judgments Convention
(see [1987] 2 All ER 981 at 984–985, [1988] QB 738 at 742–743). In my view, the
correctness of that decision is not open to doubt. However, there remains the question
whether an English court would be precluded by art 16(5) from granting a Mareva
injunction over assets situated elsewhere within the EEC. The commentary on this
article by Mr P Jenard, which is an admissible aid to the construction of the European
j Judgments Convention scheduled to the 1982 Act by virtue of s 3(3) of the Act, is in the
following terms (OJ 1979 C59, p 36):

'What meaning is to be given to the expression "proceedings concerned with the
enforcement of judgments"? It means those proceedings which can arise from
"recourse to force, constraint or distraint on movable or immovable property in

order to ensure the effective implementation of judgments of authentic instruments".
Problems arising out of such proceedings come within the exclusive jurisdiction of   *a*
the courts for the place of enforcement.'

Mr P Jenard adds: 'Provisions of this kind appear in the internal law of many Member
States, and cites the position in France, whereby:

> 'French courts have exclusive jurisdiction over measures for enforcement which
> is to take place in France (preventive measures, distress levied on tenant's chattels,   *b*
> writs of attachment and applications for enforcement of a foreign judgment); over
> distraint levied on immovable or movable property, and over proceedings concerned
> with the validity of measures for enforcement.'

Despite the apparent width of these comments I do not think that a 'holding order' in
the form of a post-judgment Mareva injunction, covering assets of a defendant in the   *c*
territory of an EEC state pending proceedings for the enforcement of the judgment in
accordance with the applicable provisions of the European Judgments Convention and
the national law of that state, would constitute any infringement of art 16(5). It seems
illogical, at any rate from an English point of view, that a post-judgment provisional
protective order should fall outside the scope of art 24. The better view would be that
after judgment 'the substance of the matter' referred to in art 24 consists of the   *d*
'proceedings concerned with the enforcement of judgments' referred to in art 16(5). The
latter are of course within the exclusive jurisdiction of the state where the assets are. But
I can see no reason why art 24 should not be available in the interim, pending enforcement
of the judgment there, to entitle our courts, if the judgment has been given here, to
grant a Mareva injunction over the foreign assets pending execution abroad.

I appreciate that in this discussion I have strayed a long way from the course which the   *e*
present appeal in fact took on the basis of the limited issues which were debated.
Unfortunately, the important international perspective was only touched on superficially
at the end of the hearing and briefly in the subsequent written submissions. But, if one
goes back to the suggested alternative solutions numbered (1), (2) and (3) to the problems
posed by extra-territorial Mareva-type injunctions which I have set out earlier, I think
that I have said enough to indicate my reasons for concluding that solution (1) is clearly   *f*
unacceptable, and that this appeal therefore had to be allowed to that extent in any event.
Unqualified Mareva injunctions covering assets abroad can never be justified, either
before or after judgment, because they involve an exorbitant assertion of jurisdiction of
an in rem nature over third parties outside the jurisdiction of our courts. They cannot be
controlled or policed by our courts, and they are not subjected to the control of the local
courts, as the European Court advised in *Denilauler v Snc Couchet Frères* [1980] ECR 1553   *g*
at 1570 (para 16) they should be. In consequence, as can be seen from the correspondence
between the plaintiffs' solicitors and the 47 or so third parties to whom the injunctions
were notified in the present case, any purported assertion of such jurisdiction is
unworkable and merely gives rise to problems and disputes.

Solution (3), which I believe to be the correct solution in principle, was never canvassed,   *h*
for the reasons which I have stated. It obviously binds the defendant personally, in
common with solution (2), but would go further and would therefore be more useful.
So that leaves our adoption of solution (2) in the present case. For the reasons set out in
the judgment of Nicholls LJ there is clearly no objection to making a personal order
binding on the defendant alone. That was the effect of the order made by Hobhouse J in
Crown Petroleum Corp v Ibrahim (27 April 1988, unreported), to which Nicholls LJ has   *j*
referred. The order which we made in the present case went further, and its terms
covered immovable as well as movable property of the defendants. Its crucial difference
from the order made by Vinelott J was that it was qualified by the following proviso:

> 'Provided always that no person other than the defendants themselves shall in any
> wise be affected by the terms of this order . . . or concerned to enquire whether any

a   instruction given by or on behalf of either defendant or by anyone else, or any other
act or omission of either defendant or anyone else, whether acting on behalf of
either defendant or otherwise, is or may be a breach of this order ... by either
defendant.'

In addition, to complete the history, we added a paragraph entitling each of the
defendants to draw living and other expenses which they claimed to be necessary and for
b   which no allowance had been made below. Since both defendants undertook that these
would come exclusively out of income to be generated by their business activities and
that they would not dispose of any capital assets, we agreed to the lavish amounts for
which they asked, £15,000 per month for BB and $17,000 for WB. In that connection
we bore in mind that the whole position will be reviewed in whatever way may appear
to be necessary in the light of the defendants' full evidence which they are required to
c   give pursuant to Ord 48. They undertook to supplement their present inadequate
affidavits by supplying full details of the nature, value and location of their assets, and
they will then be cross-examined on them.

Finally, it is perhaps hardly necessary to add an emphatic note of caution in relation to
those parts of this judgment which, as I have indicated, were not canvassed in the
arguments of counsel, either before Vinelott J or on this appeal. In these circumstances,
d   it is obviously particularly likely that there may be errors in what I have said. But, in
view of its great general importance, I feel that it is right to air this topic more fully,
albeit obiter, than was necessary for the purposes of this particular appeal. Viewed in that
way I can summarise my present views as follows. (A) An unqualified Mareva-type
injunction purporting to freeze assets situated outside the jurisdiction of our courts is
always inadmissible, both after and before judgment. (B) A Mareva-type injunction
e   (perhaps it should be called 'a personal Mareva' for identification) qualified by an express
proviso excluding any effect on third parties, which was the order which we made on the
present appeal, is clearly unobjectionable in principle. But it is not a satisfactory
formulation, because it disregards the realities which a Mareva injunction seeks to
achieve. Hobhouse J recognised this in *Crown Petroleum Corp v Ibrahim* when he said that
the order 'will be solely binding on the conscience of the defendant ...' (C) Subject to
f   the note of caution which I have sounded, if the arguments addressed to us had fully
deployed the considerations discussed in this judgment, then it would in my view have
been equally permissible, and the better course, to have allowed this appeal by making
an order in terms of my solution (3), viz an order in the form of a normal Mareva
injunction against both defendants with a qualification that the order should not affect
third parties unless and to the extent that it is enforced by the courts of the states in
g   which any of the defendants' assets are located. This would be the logical and
internationally appropriate course, and it would have taken the plaintiffs further than
the order which we made, without, so far as I can see, any basis for objection by the
defendants; nor in principle, for the reasons discussed. (D) Viewed purely jurisdictionally,
the comments in (B) and (C) above apply equally to orders made after, as well as before,
judgment. However, as a matter of discretion, such orders will in practice no doubt be
h   made much more readily after judgment. (E) The orders for the disclosure of the
defendants' assets abroad pursuant to RSC Ord 48 were not in issue on this appeal, and
their jurisdictional justification was not open to question in view of the decisions of this
court in *Interpool Ltd v Galani* [1987] 2 All ER 981, [1988] QB 738 and *Maclaine Watson
& Co Ltd v International Tin Council (No 2)* [1988] 3 All ER 257, [1988] 3 WLR 1190.
However, in my view there is equally no jurisdictional objection to such orders before
j   judgment. The cautionary comments in the judgments in *Ashtiani v Kashi* [1986] 2 All
ER 970, [1987] QB 888 should no doubt be borne in mind in this context. But in extreme
situations, which justify a pre-judgment Mareva injunction covering a defendant's assets
outside the jurisdiction, orders for the disclosure of the nature and location of such assets
must be equally justifiable. Prima facie, both types of orders should be considered in
parallel.

NEILL LJ. We are concerned in this appeal with a branch of the law which is in a stage
of development and where the court will be asked to exercise its discretion to grant *a*
injunctive relief in many differing sets of circumstances. It seems to me therefore that
any guidelines which are laid down by this court should be expressed in general terms.

The power of the High Court to grant injunctions is now a statutory power. It is
conferred by s 37(1) of the Supreme Court Act 1981, which is in similar terms to s 45(1)
of the Supreme Court of Judicature (Consolidation) Act 1925 and s 25(8) of the Supreme
Court of Judicature Act 1873. Section 37(1) of the 1981 Act provides: *b*

'The High Court may by order (whether interlocutory or final) grant an injunction
or appoint a receiver in all cases in which it appears to the court to be just and
covenient to do so.'

It will be seen that the power to grant injunctions is expressed in very wide terms. It *c*
contains no territorial limitation. Furthermore, there is abundant authority for the
proposition that, where a defendant is personally subject to the jurisdiction of the court,
an injunction may be granted in appropriate circumstances to control his activities
abroad. Thus, for example, a party to an action may be restrained from commencing or
continuing an action in a foreign court. Nevertheless, as Lord Brandon explained in *South
Carolina Insurance Co v Assurantie Maatschappij 'De Zeven Provincien' NV* [1986] 3 All ER *d*
487 at 495, [1987] AC 24 at 40, the wide power conferred by s 37(1) and its predecessors
has been circumscribed by judicial authority dating back for many years.

The decision of this court in *Ashtiani v Kashi* [1986] 2 All ER 970, [1987] QB 888 is
authority for the proposition that, where a Mareva injunction is granted before judgment,
the injunction should be limited to assets within the jurisdiction of the court. Dillon LJ
gave four reasons to explain this general rule ([1986] 2 All ER 970 at 977, [1987] QB 888 *e*
at 901–902):

'In my judgment there are valid reasons why the Mareva injunction should be
limited to the assets of the defendant within the jurisdiction of the court. Firstly, it
could very well be oppressive to the defendant that, as a result of an order of an *f*
English court, his assets everywhere should be frozen or he should be subjected to
applications for seizure orders in many other jurisdictions. Secondly, it is difficult
for the English court to control or police enforcement proceedings in other
jurisdictions. It is not very desirable that the English court should attempt to control
such foreign proceedings, and the difficulties are underlined where, as here, the
plaintiffs are not resident within the jurisdiction of the English court. Thirdly, as *g*
Lord Roskill pointed out in his speech in *Home Office v Harman* [1982] 1 All ER 532
at 552, [1983] 1 AC 280 at 323, our judicial process in requiring discovery involves
invasion of an otherwise absolute right to privacy. The particular form of discovery
he was concerned with there was the discovery in the course of an action and the
production of relevant documents with a view to the fair trial of the action, but his
comment that the order involves an invasion of privacy applies with the fullest force *h*
to an order on an individual or a company to disclose all his or its assets throughout
the world. Fourthly, it has been many times laid down that the object of a Mareva
injunction is not to give the plaintiff security for the amount of his claim in advance
of judgment in the action; but, if there is an order for disclosure of foreign assets,
that may lead to the plaintiff obtaining security in some foreign jurisdiction. For
instance, in the present case an order has been obtained in Belgium. We have *j*
evidence that under Belgian law the court will not make any order attaching assets
unless those assets are specifically identified. It would be necessary, for instance, in
order to attach a bank account to have particulars of that account and the branch
where it is kept. The defendant has been compelled by Hirst J's order to disclose and

identify his bank account in Belgium. The plaintiffs have thereby been enabled to
a obtain an order in Belgium. That order is described as a saisie-arrête conservatoire.
Prima facie its effect is not necessarily the same as a Mareva injunction, but the same
as a saisie-arrête conservatoire under Belgian law, whatever that may be. Whether
or not it does have that effect in Belgium, such an ancillary seizure attachment of a
debt may have the effect of giving the plaintiff much greater security than the
Mareva injunction gives him over English assets.'

b   I was a party to the decision in *Ashtiani v Kashi* and I remain of the opinion that it
accurately reflected the way in which the jurisdiction to grant Mareva injunctions had
been exercised and developed in England in the period between the original decision in
Mareva Cia Naviera SA v International Bulkcarriers SA, The Mareva (1975) [1980] 1 All ER
213 in June 1975 and June 1986.

c   I am satisfied, however, that the court has *jurisdiction* to grant a Mareva injunction over
foreign assets, and that in this developing branch of the law the decision in *Ashtiani v
Kashi* may require further consideration in a future case.

In the present case we are concerned with an injunction which has been granted
following a judgment. I therefore propose to restrict my comments on pre-trial
injunctions to the following matters to which our attention was drawn either in the
d course of or following the conclusion of the argument.

It is first to be noted that the Court of Justice of the European Communities has
recognised the right of a court of one state to grant 'provisional, including protective,
measures' within the meaning of art 24 of the European Judgments Convention of 1968
affecting assets situated in another state: see *Denilauler v Snc Couchet Frères* Case 125/79
[1980] ECR 1553.

e   It is also to be observed that several courts in Australia have granted interlocutory
injunctions of a Mareva type in relation to assets which were outside the jurisdiction of
the relevant court: see, for example, *Coombs & Barei Constructions Pty Ltd v Dynasty Pty
Ltd* (1986) 42 SASR 413, *Re Clunies-Ross, ex p Totterdell* (1987) 72 ALR 241 and *Yandil
Holdings Pty Ltd v Insurance Co of North America* (1986) 7 NSWLR 571.

At the same time it is to be remembered that art 24 of the 1968 convention is not the
f source of any power to grant protective measures. It is the relevant national law which
supplies the remedy. Furthermore, it is important to bear in mind the need for caution
where a court is minded to grant an injunction which may take effect outside the
territory of its own jurisdiction. In *Denilauler v Couchet Frères* [1980] ECR 1553 at 1570
(paras 15, 16) the European Court underlined the need for care:

g   'Whilst it is true that procedures of the type in question authorizing provisional
and protective measures may be found in the legal system of all the Contracting
States and may be regarded, where certain conditions are fulfilled, as not infringing
the rights of the defence, it should however be emphasized that the granting of this
type of measure requires particular care on the part of the court and detailed
knowledge of the actual circumstances in which the measure is to take effect.
h   Depending on each case and commercial practices in particular the court must be
able to place a time-limit on its order or, as regards the nature of the assets or goods
subject to the measures contemplated, require bank guarantees or nominate a
sequestrator and generally makes its authorization subject to all conditions
guaranteeing the provisional or protective character of the measure ordered. The
courts of the place or, in any event, of the Contracting State, where the assets subject
j   to the measures sought are located, are those best able to assess the circumstances
which may lead to the grant or refusal of the measures sought or to the laying down
of procedures and conditions which the plaintiff must observe in order to guarantee
the provisional and protective character of the measures ordered.'

I turn now to the present case.

It is clear that, after a judgment has been obtained, an order for the disclosure of assets can be made pursuant to RSC Ord 48: see *Interpool Ltd v Galani* [1987] 2 All ER 981, *a* [1988] QB 738. Leave to appeal against that decision was refused by the Appeal Committee of the House of Lords (see [1987] 3 All ER facing p 1, [1988] 1 WLR 134). It is further clear that an order for extra-territorial disclosure can be made pursuant to s 37(1) of the 1981 Act in a case where judgment has been obtained but where the applicants for disclosure cannot rely on Ord 48: see *Maclaine Watson & Co Ltd v International Tin Council (No 2)* [1988] 3 All ER 257, [1988] 3 WLR 1190. *b*

In my judgment, the arguments against granting a Mareva-type injunction extending to assets outside the jurisdiction are much weaker in a case where judgment has been obtained than in a case where an interlocutory order is sought before trial. Indeed, I am satisfied that there will be many cases, of which the present case is one, where justice requires that, once judgment has been obtained, the successful plaintiffs should be able to obtain the protection of an injunction extending to all the assets of the defendants *c* whether within or outside the jurisdiction of the court. It is always to be remembered, however, that a Mareva injunction is not a form of attachment but is a form of relief in personam which prohibits certain acts in relation to the assets in question: see *Iraqi Ministry of Defence v Arcepey Shipping Co SA, The Angel Bell* [1980] 1 All ER 480 at 486, [1981] QB 65 at 72. In other words, the injunction has its legal operation not on the property itself but on the person who is subject to the jurisdiction of the court. *d*

I have had the advantage of reading in draft the judgments of Kerr and Nicholls LJJ. Kerr LJ has explained the difficulties which arose in this case when notice of the judge's order was given to the 47 banks and other institutions who held or might have held assets of the defendants. I am satisfied that it is wrong in principle to make an order which, though intended merely to restrain and control the actions of a person who is subject to the jurisdiction of the court, may be understood to have some coercive effect *e* over persons who are resident abroad and who are in no sense subject to the court's jurisdiction. It was with these considerations in mind that I took the view that the following proviso should be added to the injunction:

'Provided always that no person other than the defendants themselves shall in any wise be affected by the terms of this order numbered (1) or concerned to enquire *f* whether any instruction given by or on behalf of either defendant or by anyone else, or any other act or omission of either defendant or anyone else, whether acting on behalf of either defendant or otherwise, is or may be a breach of this order numbered (1) by either defendant.'

The purpose of this proviso was to make it clear that the injunction was and was intended to be directed to the defendants themselves and did not affect the rights of third parties *g* or control their activities.

The present order is intended to hold the ring for the time being and to prevent the defendants from making dispositions in breach of the order. I envisage that in due course further orders may be required. The plaintiffs may require directions as to what steps they can take to obtain additional relief abroad in respect of specific assets. I also envisage *h* that in future orders of this type a less widely drafted proviso may be appropriate so as to limit the protection of third parties to acts by them outside the jurisdiction.

Like Nicholls LJ, however, I consider it to be important that the court should not abandon control of what use is made of the discovery which plaintiffs are able to obtain by means of orders of the kind made in this case.

For the reasons which I have endeavoured to outline I am satisfied that the *j* unconditional order which was made by the judge cannot be supported, though I can well understand the reasons which led him to make this order. In my view, it will take time before the courts will be able to work out, on a case-by-case basis, the most satisfactory way of controlling injunctions and discovery orders which relate to assets outside the jurisdiction. It will be necessary to take full account of the European

Judgments Convention, and also of the policy which underlines that convention. Thus it
a may be appropriate to seek to follow the policy of the convention even though in the
particular case the convention itself has no direct application. At the same time, however,
it will be necessary to remember that, where an English order relates to foreign assets,
the enforcement of the order may be under the control of a court which is unfamiliar
with a form of relief which takes effect in personam rather than in rem. A proviso in the
terms of that included in our order, or in similar terms, would, I think, go a long way
b towards explaining to the foreign court the limited and personal nature of the order
made by the English court. Nevertheless, in my view, an English court should remain
alert to the possibility that a foreign court might treat the injunction as though it were a
form of attachment in rem.

NICHOLLS LJ.

c *In personam*
    Equity acts in personam and an injunction is an equitable remedy. At first sight,
therefore, there would seem to be no reason why, faced with defendants who are
amenable to the court's jurisdiction and who, as the judge found, would be likely to take
any step open to them to frustrate or delay execution of the judgment, the court should
d not exercise its wide jurisdiction under s 37(1) of the Supreme Court Act 1981 by
granting against them a 'holding' injunction in respect of their overseas assets, to give the
plaintiff time to apply to the relevant foreign court for appropriate orders of attachment
or the like. The jurisdiction to make such an order would, of course, need to be exercised
with caution, and the terms of any injunction would need to be framed with care to
ensure that the injunction did not operate oppressively. In particular, as is usual in
e Mareva orders, the normal conduct of a defendant's business should not be impeded, and
provision should be made for his living expenses and payment of legal fees. Further, the
'holding' nature of the injunction might well be reflected in a provision to the effect that
the injunction would cease to apply to any specific asset or assets once the defendant has
given, with due particularity, a specified number of days' notice to the plaintiff regarding
that asset or those assets. But, in principle, the observations of Lord Brougham LC in
f *Lord Portarlington v Soulby* (1834) My & K 104 at 108, [1824–34] All ER Rep 610 at 612,
concerning an application for an injunction to restrain a defendant from taking
proceedings in Ireland on a bill of exchange, would be apt to the making of an order such
as I have described:

g 'In truth, nothing can be more unfounded than the doubts of the jurisdiction.
    That is grounded, like all other jurisdiction of the Court, not upon any pretension
    to the exercise of judicial and administrative rights abroad, but on the circumstance
    of the person of the party on whom this order is made being within the power of
    the Court. If the Court can command him to bring home goods from abroad, or to
    assign chattel interests, or to convey real property locally situate abroad if, for
    instance, as in *Penn* v. *Lord Baltimore* ((1750) 1 Ves Sen 444, [1558–1774] All ER Rep
h 99), it can decree the performance of an agreement touching the boundary of a
    province in North America; or, as in the case of *Toller* v. *Carteret* ((1705) 2 Vern 494,
    23 ER 916), can foreclose a mortgage in the isle of Sark, one of the channel islands;
    in precisely the like manner it can restrain the party being within the limits of its
    jurisdiction from doing anything abroad, whether the thing forbidden be a
    conveyance or other act in *pais*, or the instituting or prosecution of an action in a
j foreign Court.'

    I can see nothing in the decision of this court in *Ashtiani v Kashi* [1986] 2 All ER 970,
[1987] QB 888 inconsistent with this approach. That was a 'disclosure' case, concerned
with the position of a defendant before any judgment had been obtained against him.
There the court was troubled about the unsatisfactory, even oppressive, consequences

that might befall a defendant if he were compelled by an English court to disclose the
whereabouts of his overseas assets in advance of judgment. But after judgment has been   *a*
obtained the parties' positions are different in an important respect. Under English law,
unlike the position before judgment, after judgment a plaintiff is able to attach assets of
the defendant against whom he has obtained judgment. Thus it is now established that,
after judgment has been obtained, there is no objection in principle to the judgment
debtor being required to give disclosure of his assets worldwide under RSC Ord 48, r 1(1)
(*Interpool Ltd v Galani* [1987] 2 All ER 981, [1988] QB 738) or, in a case outside Ord 48,   *b*
under s 37 (*Maclaine Watson & Co Ltd v International Tin Council (No 2)* [1988] 3 All ER
257, [1988] 3 WLR 1190). The object of ordering such disclosure is to render the
judgment effective, by enabling the judgment creditor to discover whether, in the
absence of sufficient assets within the jurisdiction, there are assets elsewhere which may
be attached by him if he seeks to enforce his judgment overseas. But, in a given case, that
purpose, for which such worldwide disclosure is ordered, may itself be at real risk of   *c*
being defeated if an unscrupulous judgment debtor, after he has (truly) disclosed the
whereabouts of overseas assets, remains at liberty to move them from one country to
another before the judgment creditor has had an opportunity, however diligent he and
his advisers may be, to apply to the local court for an attachment of the assets. Many
assets, ranging from money in a bank through bearer shares to valuable postage stamps,
can be moved speedily and easily from country to country. That being so, such a case, in   *d*
principle, would be an eminently proper occasion for the court to exercise its ample
jurisdiction under s 37 by making a temporary 'holding' injunction against the judgment
debtor, requiring him not to move or deal with his assets without giving to the judgment
creditor the few days' notice which is the minimum reasonably required to enable the
judgment creditor to invoke any assistance which the local court may afford to him in
respect of his judgment debt. Such an injunction would be supplementary to the   *e*
worldwide disclosure order.

Third parties
      But there is a troublesome point here concerning third parties. An injunction, as an
order of the court, can affect the conduct of persons other than the defendant in the
proceedings against whom the order is made. This was a matter considered in the recent   *f*
Spycatcher litigation (*A-G v Newspaper Publishing plc* [1987] 3 All ER 276, [1988] Ch 333).
For the purposes of the present appeal it is sufficient to note that it is well established that
a person who knowingly assists in the breach of a court order is himself in contempt of
court: see, for example, *Seaward v Paterson* [1897] 1 Ch 545, [1895–9] All ER Rep 1127
and, in the context of a Mareva injunction, *Z Ltd v A* [1982] 1 All ER 556, [1982] QB 558.
This principle is one of the strengths of a Mareva order, but it is the application of this   *g*
principle to an injunction in respect of overseas assets such as I have described above that
causes difficulty.
      Take the present case. After the judge made the order under appeal on 19 April 1988,
the plaintiffs' solicitors gave notice of the order to numerous overseas banks and other
organisations. In some of their telexes the plaintiffs' solicitors strongly advised the   *h*
recipients that, before allowing the defendants to deal with any of the defendants' assets
held by them, they should check with the plaintiffs' solicitors directly to see that the
defendants had given the requisite notice. There is no question of the solicitors having
acted improperly in taking these steps. These matters were ventilated before the judge,
and on 20 April 1988 he declined to place any restraint on dissemination of notice of the
injunction by the plaintiffs' solicitors. In so doing the judge recognised that, inevitably,   *j*
he was having to feel his way in a new situation, no similar worldwide injunction having
been ordered previously even after judgment. But a consequence of the plaintiffs taking
these steps was that, so far as the English court was concerned, if a French or Swiss bank,
or other person to whom notice was given, thereafter parted with money or some other
asset of either defendant without proper advance warning having been given to the

plaintiffs' solicitors, the bank or other person would or might be in contempt of the
a English court. Indeed, it was precisely for this purpose that the notice of the injunction
was being given to third parties. By thus affording the plaintiffs a possible sanction
against third parties the plaintiffs' position was intended to be fortified.

This is not an acceptable situation. It would be wrong for an English court, by making
an order in respect of overseas assets against a defendant amenable to its jurisdiction, to
impose or attempt to impose obligations on persons not before the court in respect of
b acts to be done by them abroad regarding property outside the jurisdiction. That, self-
evidently, would be for the English court to claim an altogether exorbitant, extra-
territorial jurisdiction.

In *Crown Petroleum Corp v Ibrahim* (27 April 1988, unreported) Hobhouse J sought to
avoid this difficulty by accepting from the plaintiff an undertaking not to serve notice of
a post-judgment restraint order in respect of assets outside the jurisdiction on any person
c other than the defendant (and, in that case, another person who was a party to the action)
and his legal representatives. This, in practice, would go a long way towards resolving
the difficulty, but in my view it does not go far enough. This form of order is still
unsatisfactory in respect of a third party who may learn of the existence of the order
without being formally notified by the plaintiff's solicitors.

To meet this difficulty I can see no alternative but to grasp the nettle firmly, and write
d into the order, which applies only to property outside the jurisdiction, an express
provision to the effect that nothing in the relevant part of the order is to affect any person
other than the defendants personally. This will remove any extra-territorial vice which
otherwise the order might have, or be thought to have. The order will be binding only
on the conscience of the defendants.

I have considered anxiously whether an order in such a form would be wrong in
e principle. It is certainly unattractive to make an order which, contrary to the normal
position, third parties are bidden to ignore. But in this case the alternative is not to make
any temporary 'holding' order at all. Given that choice, I think that justice and
convenience require an order binding only on the defendants rather than no order at all.
The touching concern shown by the defendants on this appeal for the integrity of banks
and others overseas should not be allowed to obscure the judge's finding that these
f defendants would be likely to do whatever they can to frustrate execution of the
judgment.

This is a novel form of order, and in this developing field still further refinements may
be shown to be necessary. For instance, it may be that the proviso protecting third parties
should, in a given case, be confined to acts done by them outside the jurisdiction. This
was not a point explored in the present case, and so I say no more about it. But, as to the
g novelty, I echo the words of Fox LJ in *Bayer AG v Winter* [1986] 1 All ER 733 at 737,
[1986] 1 WLR 497 at 502:

'Bearing in mind we are exercising a jurisdiction which is statutory, and which is
expressed in terms of considerable width, it seems to me that the court should not
shrink, if it is of opinion that an injunction is necessary for the proper protection of
h a party to the action, from granting relief, notwithstanding it may, in its terms, be
of a novel character.'

To the above I add four comments. First, if an order is made in the terms just
mentioned, I do not see why land need be excluded. Second, the defendants will be
restrained from doing the prohibited acts by any means whatsoever, whether by their
j servants or agents or otherwise. In that respect the order will have the usual, wide ambit.
But the order should be confined in its *effect* to the defendants personally, thus excluding
everyone else, even the defendants' servants or agents. The defendants' servants or agents,
as much as banks and other third parties, may be acting outside the jurisdiction, so that
the problem of extra-territorial effect may be as much relevant to them as it is to banks
and others. Third, I do not think that it would be right to attempt to distinguish between

third parties who are resident or domiciled or present within the jurisdiction and those who are not. This could give rise, for instance, to a distinction between an overseas bank which has a branch in London and one which does not. More importantly, however, attempting to draw any such distinction is wrong in principle. If it is to be free from extra-territorial vice, the order must not attempt to regulate the conduct abroad of persons who are not duly-joined parties to the English action in respect of property outside the jurisdiction. The actual residence or domicile of such persons, or their presence within the jurisdiction, is essentially irrelevant. For instance, Banque Nationale de Paris should not be affected by this order in respect of any money it may hold for the defendants abroad. This should be so whether or not it has a branch in London. Likewise with Lloyds Bank. It is resident here, but it should not be affected by the order in respect of any money it holds for the defendants abroad.

Fourth, for the plaintiff it was submitted that banks and others not amenable to the jurisdiction of the English court who disregard an order freezing a defendant's assets overseas would not be in contempt of the English court. No authority was cited on this point, nor were the underlying principles analysed further. The point does not call for decision on this appeal, and it is preferable therefore not to express a view, necessarily obiter, on such an important point. For, even if giving notice to a third party abroad does not have the effect, so far as an English court is concerned, that the third party may be in contempt of court if he knowingly assists in a breach of the order of which he has been given notice, I consider that it is still not desirable to make an unqualified order freezing assets abroad. If, under English law, notice to a third party abroad has no effect on him, at any rate as to acts outside the jurisdiction, Vinelott J's order would seem, strictly, to be free of extra-territorial vice so far as such a party is concerned. Nevertheless, it would still be potentially misleading for a plaintiff to give notice of an English court order to an overseas third party without explaining that the third party was not affected by the order, and, even if such an explanation were given with the notice, there would remain a real risk of confusion. Moreover, there would remain a difficulty about overseas banks and others with branches in this country. The sensible course must be to include in the order itself a limiting provision as mentioned above, and thereby (a) ensure that the order does not purport to have an (unintended) extra-territorial operation and (b) remove the risk of third parties being confused about the effect of the order so far as they are concerned.

The European Judgments Convention

The defendants placed some reliance on the exclusive jursdiction provision in art 16(5) of the convention. I was not persuaded by these submissions. The order, binding the defendants only, albeit in respect of assets in other countries, is not an order made in proceedings in which the judgment is sought to be *enforced* in those countries. It is a provisional or protective measure within art 24, with a strictly limited objective and scope. The enforcement of the judgment in other countries, by attachment or like process, in respect of assets which are situated there is not affected by the order. The order does not attach those assets. It does not create, or purport to create, a charge on those assets, nor does it give the plaintiff any proprietary interest in them. The English court is not attempting in any way to interfere with or control the enforcement process in respect of those assets.

Addendum

Since writing the above I have had the advantage of reading a draft of Kerr LJ's judgment. He has raised a point on the making of Mareva orders with extra-territorial effect, both before and after judgment, in cases where such orders of an English court would be recognised and enforced by the court of the state in which the assets are located. I prefer to reserve my view on this interesting suggestion, which was not canvassed or explored in argument.

However, having considered Kerr LJ's observations on *Ashtiani v Kashi*, one point
a which strikes me forcefully is this. I say nothing concerning the circumstances in which
it will be proper for the court to make an order for the disclosure of information
regarding assets situated abroad, either before judgment or after judgment. That is not a
matter which arose, or was argued, on this appeal. But in all cases where such an order is
sought or made the court will need to be alive to the importance of exercising control
over the use of information disclosed compulsorily about assets situated overseas. It is
b obvious that such information can be used by a plaintiff in a manner that, in some
circumstances, would be unjust to the defendant who has been compelled to disclose it.
Dillon LJ gave some examples of this, in a pre-judgment case, in *Ashtiani v Kashi* [1986] 2
All ER 970 at 977–978, [1987] QB 888 at 901–902. I add the further example that,
apparently, in some countries the mere presence of assets within the country is regarded
as giving to the court of that country jurisdiction over the owner of the assets. As noted
c by Mr Lawrence Collins in his valuable article 'Provisional Measures, the Conflict of Laws
and the Brussels Convention', [1981] *Yearbook of European Law* 249, in some such instances
any judgment obtained is limited to the value of the locally-sited assets. In other instances
the jurisdiction assumed from the presence of assets is unlimited in its extent. Thus an
order for the disclosure of information, whether made before or after judgment, can
easily have results not foreseen or intended by an English court. Hence the need for the
d court to control strictly the use made of the information overseas. In some cases it may
be possible and proper, in advance of the disclosure of the information, for the court to
spell out with sufficient precision in the disclosure order one or more uses which the
plaintiff may make of the information in a particular country or countries. In other cases,
where in advance of disclosure little is known of what assets a defendant has overseas, the
court will need to have the information about the assets and be told of the overseas
e proceedings envisaged, before the court can decide what use it will permit to be made of
that information in foreign proceedings, either in countries which are parties to the 1968
convention or elsewhere. Hence the need for the undertaking mentioned by Dillon LJ
in *Ashtiani v Kashi* [1986] 2 All ER 970 at 978, [1987] QB 888 at 903.
    A second point follows from this. Once information has been disclosed it cannot be
recalled. The disclosure of information is an irreversible step. The only means available
f to the English court to control the use made abroad of information disclosed concerning
foreign assets is such control as the English court may have in the circumstances over the
plaintiff to whom it has compelled the defendant to make disclosure. Thus, before
making a disclosure order in respect of foreign assets, the court normally will need to be
satisfied that, by reason of the plaintiff's continuing connection with this country or
otherwise, the court has over the plaintiff a degree of control sufficient to ensure
g compliance with any orders it may make regarding the use of the information.

*Appeal allowed in part. Order of 19 April 1988 discharged and order substituted limited to
defendants personally.*

h Solicitors: *Theodore Goddard* (for the defendants); *Holman Fenwick & Willan* (for the
plaintiffs).

Dilys Tausz   Barrister.

Republic of Haiti and others v Duvalier and others

COURT OF APPEAL, CIVIL DIVISION
FOX, STOCKER AND STAUGHTON LJJ
4, 5, 6, 7, 22 JULY 1988

Practice – Pre-trial or post-judgment relief – Mareva injunction – Worldwide Mareva injunction – Pre-trial injunction – Extra-territorial effect of injunction – Protection of third parties – Foreign defendant having foreign assets – Proceedings brought by Republic of Haiti in French court to recover money embezzled by former president – Defendant likely to attempt to frustrate execution of judgment against him – Whether court having jurisdiction to grant Mareva injunction over defendant's foreign assets before judgment – Whether worldwide injunction should be qualified by express proviso protecting third parties – Civil Jurisdiction and Judgments Act 1982, s 25, Sch 1, art 24 – RSC Ord 11, r 1(2).

The Republic of Haiti commenced proceedings in France in July 1986 to recover from a former president of the republic and from his family and associates some $120m alleged to have been embezzled while the president was in power in Haiti. In June 1988 the republic issued a writ in England against the defendants, namely the former president, members of his family, his associates and a bank, and on the same day obtained ex parte a Mareva injunction (i) restraining the defendants from dealing with assets, wherever they might be, which represented the proceeds which were the subject of the French action, (ii) freezing their assets within the jurisdiction except to the extent that they exceeded $120m, (iii) ordering the defendants' solicitors to disclose the nature, location and value of the defendants' assets known to them and (iv) ordering the solicitors not to disclose the making of the order. The defendants, once they were served with the order, applied to have it set aside but the judge refused to do so. The defendants appealed to the Court of Appeal, where the questions arose, inter alia, (i) whether a writ claiming interim relief in aid of foreign proceedings pursuant to s 25[a] of the Civil Jurisdiction and Judgments Act 1982 could be served out of the jurisdiction pursuant to RSC Ord 11, r 1(2)[b] without leave, since under r 1(2) service of a writ out of the jurisdiction without leave was permissible only if the court had jurisdiction to hear and determine the 'claim' made by the writ and there were no proceedings between the parties concerning the same cause of action pending in the United Kingdom or in a state (including France) which was a party to the Convention on Jurisdiction and the Enforcement of Civil and Commercial Judgments 1968 (which had the force of law in the United Kingdom by virtue of s 2(1) of the 1982 Act), (ii) whether the court had jurisdiction to restrain a non-resident defendant from dealing with assets situated outside the jurisdiction (iii) if so, whether the court should exercise its discretion to grant such an injunction, and (iv) the nature of the protection to be accorded to third parties. The defendants contended, regarding the issue of the writ, that an application for interim relief was not a 'claim' and that the English proceedings concerned the same cause of action as the French proceedings and, regarding the issue of the Mareva injunction, that the court ought not to grant an injunction when it had no jurisdiction on the merits, the defendants were resident and the assets were situated outside the jurisdiction and the proper court to make the order was the French court.

Held – The appeal would be dismissed for the following reasons—
(1) RSC Ord 11, r 1(2) was to be construed as giving effect to the United Kingdom's obligation under art 24[c] of the 1968 convention (set out in Sch 1 to the 1982 Act) to make

---

a   Section 25, so far as material, is set out at p 462 *b*, post
b   Rule 1(2), so far as material, is set out at p 462 *e*, post
c   Article 24 is set out at p 463 *b*, post

a available in aid of the courts of other contracting states such provisional and protective measures as English domestic law would afford if an English court were seised of the substantive action. Accordingly, service of the republic's writ out of the jurisdiction without leave was permissible under Ord 11, r 1(2), since either a claim for interim relief was itself a cause of action or there could be proceedings and a claim without a cause of action. In either case the cause of action in the English proceedings was not the same as the cause of action in the French proceedings (see p 462 *f* to *j* p 463 *h*, p 464 *c* and

b p 469 *b*, post).

(2) The court had jurisdiction to grant a Mareva injunction pending trial over assets worldwide even where the relief was sought in aid of a foreign monetary claim and not a proprietary claim. However, such an injunction ought to be subject to a proviso protecting third parties except to the extent that the order was enforced by the courts of states in which the defendant's assets were situated, but such a proviso should only apply

c to assets and acts done outside England and Wales and not to individuals resident in England and Wales. Having regard to the plain and admitted intention of the defendants to move their assets out of the reach of courts of law and the vast amount of money involved, an injunction ought to be granted but subject to a suitable proviso to protect third parties (see p 466 *b*, p 467 *a* to *c* and p 468 *d e j* to p 469 *b*, post); *Babanaft International Co SA v Bassatne* [1989] 1 All ER 433 considered.

d

Notes

For Mareva injunctions, see 37 Halsbury's Laws (4th edn) para 362, and for cases on the subject, see 37(2) Digest (Reissue) 474–476, 2947–2962.

For the Civil Jurisdiction and Judgments Act 1982, ss 2, 25, Sch 1, art 24, see 11 Halsbury's Statutes (4th edn) 906, 911, 939.

e

Cases referred to in judgments

Ashtiani v Kashi [1986] 2 All ER 970, [1987] QB 888, [1986] 3 WLR 647, CA.
Babanaft International Co SA v Bassatne [1989] 1 All ER 433, CA.
Bankers Trust Co v Shapira [1980] 3 All ER 353, [1980] 1 WLR 1274, CA.

f *Denilauler v Snc Couchet Frères* Case 125/79 [1980] ECR 1553.
Garland v British Rail Engineering Ltd [1982] 2 All ER 402, [1983] 2 AC 751, [1982] 2 WLR 918, HL.
Joh Verhulst & Zn BV v PVBA Thovadec Plastics (1978) Eur Ct Dig (D series) 1-21–B2, 's-Hertogenbosch District Ct.
Liddell's Settlement Trusts, Re [1936] 1 All ER 239, [1936] Ch 365, CA.

g *MacKinnon v Donaldson Lufkin & Jenrette Securities Corp* [1986] 1 All ER 653, [1986] Ch 482, [1986] 2 WLR 453.
Siskina (cargo owners) v Distos Cia Naviera SA, The Siskina [1977] 3 All ER 803, [1979] AC 210, [1977] 3 WLR 818, HL.

Cases also cited

h *Bankers Trust International Ltd v Todd Shipyards Corp, The Halcyon Isle* [1980] 3 All ER 197, [1981] AC 221, PC.
Company, Re a [1985] BCLC 333, CA.
Cook Industries Inc v Galliher [1978] 3 All ER 945, [1979] Ch 439.
Fothergill v Monarch Airlines Ltd [1980] 2 All ER 696, [1981] AC 251, HL.
Hollandia, The [1982] 3 All ER 1141, [1983] 1 AC 565, HL.

j **Interlocutory appeal**

The defendants, Jean-Claude Duvalier, his wife, Michele Bennett Duvalier, and Simone Ovide, the widow of François Duvalier, who were the defendants together with others in proceedings brought in France and England by the plaintiffs, the Republic of Haiti and five of its agencies, La Minoterie d'Haiti, L'Office de l'Assurance des Vehicles contre Tiers,

La Loterie de L'Etat Haitien, La Commission de Controle des Jeux de Hasard, La Banque
Nationale de Crédit, appealed against the order of Leggatt J made on 22 June 1988   *a*
whereby he dismissed the defendants' application to set aside the English proceedings
under RSC Ord 12, r 8 and discharge the order made by Knox J on 3 June 1988
restraining the defendants from dealing with the assets which were the subject of the
French action and from removing from the jurisdiction or dealing with their assets
within the jurisdiction except to the extent that they exceeded $120m in value and
ordered the defendants, acting by their solicitors, Messrs Turner & Matlin, to disclose to   *b*
the plaintiffs' solicitors the nature, location and value of the defendants' assets. The facts
are set out in the judgment of Staughton LJ.

Steven Gee for the defendants.
Nicholas Strauss QC and *Michael Jones* for the plaintiffs.

c

Cur adv vult

22 July. The following judgments were delivered.

STAUGHTON LJ (giving the first judgment at the invitation of Fox LJ). Jean-Claude   *d*
Duvalier, the first defendant in these proceedings, was the President of the Republic of
Haiti from 1971 until 7 February 1986. The second defendant is his wife, Michele
Bennett Duvalier, and the sixth defendant his mother. She is the widow of François
Duvalier, who was the president from 1957 until his death in 1971. Those three members
of the family are the appellants in this court. All are now resident in France.

The Republic of Haiti started proceedings in the Tribunal de Grande Instance at Grasse   *e*
in July 1986; five of its agencies were later added as co-plaintiffs. Those proceedings were
against various members of the Duvalier family, including Jean-Claude Duvalier, his
wife and mother, and their associates. It is said that they were responsible for embezzling
sums totalling $120m from the Republic during the presidency of Jean-Claude Duvalier,
that is between 1971 and 1986. Indeed it is suggested that this is only the tip of the   *f*
iceberg and that very much larger sums were involved.

The defendants in the French action altogether deny liability. They observe that it has
been a tradition in Haiti for over 180 years for a new government to take legal proceedings
against those who were in charge under the previous regime. (One is reminded of the
Roman historian who noticed that it was the practice of the later emperors to bring to
justice the murderers of the previous emperor but one.) But this appeal is scarcely   *g*
concerned with the merits of the substantive claims made in France. It is acknowledged
that the plaintiffs' evidence demonstrates a prima facie case, or even a good arguable case.
Counsel for the plaintiffs goes further: he submits that there is a very strong case, to
which the defendants have offered no substantive or detailed answer, either in the French
proceedings or in the courts of this country.

Unless it is essential to do so, I do not feel that I should make any comment at this stage   *h*
on the strength of the plaintiff's case. It is enough that on the affidavit evidence there is
a case to answer, or a good arguable case, such as would justify the use of interim
protective measures in an English domestic case, and would also justify service out of the
jurisdiction if that is permitted by the Rules of the Supreme Court.

What is more striking, and less usual, is the evidence that the members of the Duvalier
family have been attempting to conceal their assets, or place them beyond the reach of   *j*
courts of law. It is unnecessary to set out this evidence in detail, since the conclusion
from it is admitted. In the affidavit of Professor Vaisse, a French lawyer acting for the
Duvalier family, there is this passage:

'9. The plaintiffs have drawn attention to the fact that assets in the control of the
defendants have, when threatened with legal attachment proceedings, been removed

from the jurisdictions concerned. It is my understanding that this has occurred.
a   This does not reflect any doubts that the defendants have about the merits of their
position. They are simply aware that there is a worldwide campaign being conducted
against them by the Haitian Government supported by the United States Government
to persecute them by seizing their assets wherever they can be found. This campaign
is assisted by the International Press which provokes prejudice against them
wherever they go and they have merely sought to frustrate this campaign which I
b   submit is a normal reaction in the circumstances . . .'

If those be the true facts, one would suppose that the Duvalier family would welcome
an early trial of the case against them by a just court in a country which has, by
international law, jurisdiction to try it.

It is, however, necessary to enlarge on that admission by referring to some features of
c the evidence which are striking. First, the plaintiffs' evidence exhibits extracts from a
book *Les Banques Suisses et l'Argent* written by a French lawyer, Maître J-P Carteron. This
is said to treat the concealment of funds within the Swiss banking system. It points to
the advantage of using a fiduciary as the legal owner of the assets to be concealed, rather
than the beneficial owner himself, and the added advantage of choosing a lawyer as the
fiduciary: 'Le secret de sa profession [translated 'his professional secrecy'] protegera
d totalement l'identité du client.'

There is evidence that Maître Carteron, between 1984 and 6 February 1986 (which
was when the Duvalier family left Haiti), received approximately $500,000 in Switzerland
from Haitian government funds. There is also evidence of 13 telexes or telephone calls
from the Ministry of Finance or the National Palace in Haiti to Maître Carteron's number
in Geneva, the last telephone call being on 6 February 1986.

e   Furthermore there is evidence that the Duvalier family made use of the idea, whether
or not derived from Maître Carteron's book, of employing a professional lawyer as
intermediary. Some documents have been disclosed pursuant to an order of Knox J (to
which I shall refer later) by Messrs Turner & Co, an English firm of solicitors in which
Paul Turner and John Stephen Matlin are partners. Among other things, Turner & Co
were asked to identify bank accounts—
f

> 'from which or to which any moneys which belong to any of the 1st to 10th
> defendants (whether directly or indirectly) or which are reasonably apparent or
> believed by Turner & Co. to be moneys in which one or more of the 1st to 10th
> defendants is or are beneficially interested or otherwise held by a nominee or trustee,
> have been transferred.'

g The answer listed 17 accounts, at eleven different banks, in seven different countries.
Eleven of the accounts were in the name of Turner & Co or the partners of the firm.

A second striking feature emerges from documents which the plaintiffs have obtained
by proceedings in Jersey. These tend to show that Mr Matlin arranged for the deposit
with the Hongkong and Shanghai Banking Corp (CI) Ltd, via their correspondent in
Toronto and for the credit of 'Messrs. Turner & Co No 2 Clients' Account' of Canadian
h treasury bills worth in excess of Can $40m. Turner & Co, in answer to the order for
disclosure of the first to tenth defendants' assets, wrote:

> 'Canadian Government Treasury Bills have been held by us on occasion. They
> have all been encashed.'

j   I should also refer to the evidence which tends to show, as Professor Vaisse admits, that
assets threatened with attachment have been removed from the jurisdictions concerned.
I can summarise that evidence by saying that it leads to one of three possible conclusions:
(1) the Duvalier family or their advisers have somehow obtained advance notice of the
plaintiffs' efforts at attachment, or (2) assets are moved so regularly and so frequently that
it is no coincidence if some have been moved just before attachment took effect, or (3) it
is coincidence.

It should be emphasised as to all this evidence that no wrongdoing on the part of Turner & Co or its partners is alleged on behalf of the plaintiffs. Furthermore Mr Matlin has said in an affidavit that he has never heard of Maître Carteron, or read his book; nor was he even aware of it until it was referred to in the plaintiffs' evidence. He says that he is not aware of any elaborate and co-ordinated scheme to conceal funds.

The English proceedings

On 3 June 1988 the Republic of Haiti and the five other plaintiffs in the French action made an ex parte application to Knox J, sitting as a vacation judge of the Commercial Court. In the writ issued that day they were named as plaintiffs, and the first to tenth defendants were members of the Duvalier family or their associates. None of those defendants had an address within the jurisdiction. The eleventh defendants were Barclays Bank plc of Lombard Street, London EC3.

The order made by Knox J can be summarised as follows, so far as is material: (1) the plaintiffs undertook to notify the defendants of the terms of the order by 4 pm on 6 June, and to notify Mr Matlin forthwith, (2) the first to tenth defendants were restrained from dealing with assets which represented the proceeds of the payments which are complained of in the French action, (3) the first to tenth defendants were restrained from removing from the jurisdiction or dealing with their assets within the jurisdiction save in so far as they exceed $120m in value, (4) the first to tenth defendants were ordered, acting by Messrs Turner & Matlin, to disclose to the plaintiffs' solicitors by 10 am on 6 June information known to Mr Turner or Mr Matlin as to the nature, location and value of those defendants' assets, (5) the defendants were ordered, in particular by Messrs Turner & Matlin, not to disclose the making of the order for the time being and (6) there was leave to serve out of the jurisdiction and substituted service.

Notice that not only was the order made in the absence of the defendants and without their knowledge; it was also not to be communicated to them until after their solicitors had complied with that part of it relating to disclosure of information. In those respects it was in line with current English practice. While there may not be much point in making an order that a defendant himself disclose documents or provide information ex parte, since he will have to know of the order before he complies with it, the situation is different where information or documents are sought from some third party (see *Bankers Trust Co v Shapira* [1980] 3 All ER 353, [1980] 1 WLR 1274) or even the solicitors as in this case, or when there is to be a compulsory search by an Anton Piller order. That is why particular caution is needed in making such orders.

On 6 June 1988 the solicitors applied to Knox J to vary or discharge his order. He declined to do so. The time limits for compliance with the order and notification of it to the defendants were extended. On 7 June the solicitors appealed to this court. Their appeal was heard in camera, and did not feature in the cause list. It would seem from the judgment of Lord Donaldson MR that the principal points argued were: (i) whether the relief sought was within s 25 of the Civil Jurisdiction and Judgments Act 1982, (ii) whether an English court should make an order for the disclosure of information about assets abroad, except in connection with a tracing claim, (iii) whether the plaintiffs' affidavits were sufficient in point of form and (iv) whether the solicitors could rely on legal professional privilege.

The Court of Appeal rejected the solicitors' arguments on all four grounds. I need say nothing about their reasons on grounds (i) and (iii), since those arguments were not repeated before us; nor need I consider ground (iv), since a further claim for legal professional privilege is, by agreement, to be remitted to a Commercial judge. (Counsel for the plaintiffs accepts that the affidavit on its face appears to assert a valid claim for privilege in respect of a limited class of information.) As to ground (ii), Lord Donaldson MR said in terms that he was not happy to accept the suggested limitation on the disclosure of information about assets abroad, viz that it should only be ordered in

connection with a tracing claim. But he found on the evidence before the court that the
a French action was in the nature of a tracing claim.

The appeal was allowed only to the extent that the time limits were again varied. In
all other respects it was dismissed.

On 7 and 8 June 1988 Phillips J made three orders permitting the plaintiffs to use
certain information provided by Turner & Co for the purpose of legal proceedings in
some other jurisdictions. This was necessary because the plaintiffs had given an
b undertaking to Knox J, although not recorded in his order, that they would not use the
information disclosed pursuant to his order without the leave of the court. Counsel
instructed by Turner & Co on behalf of the defendants appeared before Phillips J; it does
not seem that the defendants themselves were aware by then that the order of Knox J
had been made. That again would be in line with English practice and common sense,
since the intention was to obtain Mareva orders abroad, or information as to the new
c location of assets by order of foreign courts.

Thereafter the defendants were informed of the English proceedings. They were
served with a summons on behalf of the plaintiffs seeking disclosure of further
information and documents relating to the assets of the first to tenth defendants. That
was met by a summons on behalf of the first and second defendants to set aside the
proceedings under RSC Ord 12, r 8, in effect for want of jurisdiction. Those applications
d came before Leggatt J, inter partes but in chambers. On 22 June 1988 he made the order
from which this appeal is brought.

By that order Leggatt J, so far as is material for present purposes, (1) dismissed the
application to set aside the English proceedings under Ord 12, r 8, (2) upheld the order
of Knox J which restrained the first to tenth defendants from dealing with assets,
wherever they might be, which represented the proceeds of the payments complained of
e in the French action, (3) upheld the order of Knox J which restrained the first to tenth
defendants from removing from the jurisdiction or dealing with their assets within the
jurisdiction, up to a limit of $120m and (4) ordered that the first to tenth defendants
acting by Messrs Turner & Matlin do within 24 hours permit inspection of documents,
and disclose information, relating to their assets wherever they may be.

f *The issues*

These are as follows. (a) Can the writ be served without leave on the first to tenth
defendants out of the jurisdiction pursuant to RSC Ord 11, r 1(2)? (b) If not, can leave be
granted for service out of the jurisdiction pursuant to RSC Ord 11, r 1(1)(b)? (c) Should
there be a restraint on dealing with assets which are out of the jurisdiction? (d) Discretion.
g (e) The *Babanaft* proviso (see *Babanaft International Co SA v Bassatne* [1989] 1 All ER 433).
(f) Privilege. I shall consider those issues in turn.

(A) *Service without leave*

The crucial feature of this case is that the plaintiffs do not seek any substantive relief in
England. They seek only information as to where the assets of the Duvalier family are,
h and a temporary restraint on dealing with those assets. It is said that these remedies are
sought in aid of the French action; and so in a sense they are. But whether further
proceedings will be confined to France, and to the tribunal at Grasse, is at the very least
doubtful. To the extent that the information already disclosed, and to be disclosed under
the order of Leggatt J, reveals assets in other jurisdictions, there may well be other
proceedings of an interim nature, and possibly also seeking substantive relief.

j Until the Civil Jurisdiction and Judgments Act 1982 came into force, an English court
would not have entertained a claim of this limited nature. The plaintiffs would not have
had a cause of action: see *Siskina (cargo owners) v Distos Cia Naviera SA, The Siskina* [1977]
3 All ER 803 at 824, [1979] AC 210 at 256, where Lord Diplock said:

'A right to obtain an interlocutory injunction is not a cause of action. It cannot

stand on its own ... the High Court has no power to grant an interlocutory
injunction except in protection or assertion of some legal or equitable right which   *a*
it has jurisdiction to enforce by final judgment ...'

That conclusion is now superseded by s 25(1) of the Civil Jurisdiction and Judgments
Act 1982:

'The High Court in England and Wales or Northern Ireland shall have power to
grant interim relief where—(*a*) proceedings have been or are to be commenced in a   *b*
Contracting State other than the United Kingdom ...'

Counsel for the defendants does not dispute that there can now be English proceedings
in which only interim relief is sought, if the requirements of that subsection are met.
But he contends that there is no means of effecting service of such proceedings out of the
jurisdiction, should that be necessary. If right, this is a curious result, since s 25(2)   *c*
expressly confers a discretion to refuse that relief if—

'the fact that the court has no jurisdiction apart from this section in relation to
the subject-matter of the proceedings in question makes it inexpedient for the court
to grant it.'

Power to effect service out of the jurisdiction must be found in the Rules of the   *d*
Supreme Court: see Ord 6, r 7. The primary contention of counsel for the plaintiffs,
which the judge accepted, is that it is to be found in Ord 11, r 1(2):

'Service of a writ out of the jurisdiction is permissible without the leave of the
Court provided that each claim made by the writ is either:—(*a*) a claim which by
virtue of the Civil Jurisdiction and Judgments Act 1982 the Court has power to hear
and determine, made in proceedings to which the following conditions apply—   *e*
(i) no proceedings between the parties concerning the same cause of action are
pending in the courts of any other part of the United Kingdom or of any other
Convention territory, and (ii) either—the defendant is domiciled in any part of the
United Kingdom or in any other Convention territory ...'

Counsel for the defendants submits first that a 'claim' must mean a cause of action,   *f*
and that an application for interim relief only is therefore not a claim which the court
can 'hear and determine', by reason of *The Siskina*. I do not accept that argument. Since
the enactment of s 25, *either* a claim for interim relief is itself a cause of action *or* there
can be proceedings and a claim without a cause of action. Which solution one chooses is
merely a matter of semantics; there is no need to make such a sterile choice, and I do not
do so.   *g*

Second, counsel for the defendants submits that the condition in Ord 11, r 1(2)(*a*)(i) is
not satisfied because the English proceedings concern the same cause of action as the
French proceedings. Curiously, the Supreme Court Rule Committee used the word
'concerning' in that condition, in contrast to the word 'involving' in RSC Ord 6, r 7(1)(*b*)
and in art 21 of the Convention on Jurisdiction and the Enforcement of Judgments in
Civil and Commercial Matters (Brussels, 27 September 1968; EC 46 (1978); Cmnd 7395).   *h*
But I cannot see anything in the distinction.

The answer to counsel's second argument, so far as English domestic law is concerned,
emerges from what I have already said in connection with his first point. Either a claim
for interim relief does not involve or concern any cause of action, or it is based on a new
and distinct cause of action created by s 25. Whichever be right, the condition in Ord 11,
r 1(2)(*a*)(i) is satisfied because any cause of action with which the English proceedings are   *j*
concerned or involved is not the same as that with which the French action is concerned
or involved.

Taking a wider view, I must refer to arts 21 and 24 of the convention. Article 21 is in
Title II, section 8, headed 'Lis Pendens—Related Actions'. It reads:

a

'Where proceedings involving the same cause of action and between the same parties are brought in the courts of different Contracting States, any court other than the court first seised shall of its own motion decline jurisdiction in favour of that court ...'

Article 24 is in section 9, headed 'Provisional, including protective, measures':

b

'Application may be made to the courts of a Contracting State for such provisional, including protective, measures as may be available under the law of that State, even if, under this Convention, the courts of another Contracting State have jurisdiction as to the substance of the matter.'

c

It is plain as can be that RSC Ord 11, r 1(2)(a)(i) was intended to reflect art 21 of the convention, so that two contracting states should not simultaneously try a dispute between the same parties involving the same cause of action. It is equally plain that art 24 deals with provisional and protective measures as a different topic, not impinging on art 21: see the decision of the Dutch court in *Joh Verhulst & Zn BV v PVBA Thovadec Plastics* (1978) Eur Ct Dig (D series) 1-21–B2. Yet if the argument of counsel for the defendants is correct, RSC Ord 11, r 1(2)(a)(i) would prevent the United Kingdom giving full effect to art 24 in England and Wales if a substantive action has already been

d

commenced in another contracting state between the same parties.

Lord Diplock said in *The Siskina* [1977] 3 All ER 803 at 827, [1979] AC 210 at 260:

'... as art 24 of the convention indicates, this is a field of law in which it has not been considered necessary ... to embark on a policy of harmonisation.'

e

This is because art 24 expressly refers to 'measures ... available under the law of that State', and does not attempt to lay down what those measures must be. However, it seems to me that the convention *requires* each contracting state to make available, in aid of the courts of another contracting state, such provisional and protective measures as its own domestic law would afford if its courts were trying the substantive action. That would be harmonisation of jurisdiction, although not of remedies.

If that be the right construction of the convention, I refer to the words of Lord Diplock

f

in *Garland v British Rail Engineering Ltd* [1982] 2 All ER 402 at 415, [1983] 2 AC 751 at 771:

'... it is a principle of construction of United Kingdom statutes, now too well established to call for citation of authority, that the words of a statute passed after the treaty has been signed and dealing with the subject matter of the international obligation of the United Kingdom, are to be construed, if they are reasonably capable of bearing such a meaning, as intended to carry out the obligation and not to be inconsistent with it.'

g

Applying the same principle to the Rules of the Supreme Court, I would construe Ord 11, r 1(2) as giving effect to the obligation of the United Kingdom in England and Wales to make available in aid of the courts of other contracting states such provisional and

h

protective measures as our domestic law would afford if our courts were seised of the substantive action.

Accordingly, I agree with the judge that this was a case where service out of the jurisdiction without leave was authorised by Ord 11, r 1(2). It is agreed that the action, begun by writ, ought properly to have been begun by originating summons: see Ord 5, r 3. However, it is also agreed that nothing turns on that point in the present case. Order

j

11, r 9(1) provides that Ord 11, r 1 shall apply to the service out of the jurisdiction of an originating summons; consequently there may be service without leave where Ord 11, r 1(2) would allow a writ to be served without leave. Rule 9(5) provides that r 4(1)(b), which requires an affidavit that in the deponent's belief there is a good cause of action, 'shall, so far as applicable, apply in relation to an application for the grant of leave under

this Rule . . .' If, which I have refrained from deciding, that would otherwise be an
obstacle to a claim for interim relief only, it does not apply where no grant of leave is *a*
necessary.

(B) *Service out of the jurisdiction with leave*
This issue raises an alternative argument on behalf of the plaintiffs. It is said that leave
to serve out of the jurisdiction was properly given under Ord 11, r 1(1)(*b*) ('an injunction
is sought ordering the defendant to do or refrain from doing anything within the *b*
jurisdiction'). If the plaintiffs had succeeded only on this ground, there would have been
some necessary limitation on the orders sought; the injunctions which relate to dealing
with assets should at the least have been confined to acts done within the jurisdiction.
That might have been a severe impediment to the efficacy of the relief granted. Before
Leggatt J counsel for the plaintiffs conceded that the case was within r 1(1)(*b*). That
concession was withdrawn in this court.   *c*
In the event we do not need to decide the point. Rule 1(1) contains a provision that the
writ 'is not a writ to which paragraph (2) of this rule applies'. But I have held that para
(2) does apply, and that the writ can be served without leave.
Leggatt J, before whom the point was conceded, would if necessary have held that
there was power to grant leave under r 1(1)(*b*). That involves the conclusion that s 25 of
the 1982 Act has had a greater impact on *The Siskina* than I have so far accepted. In that *d*
case Lord Diplock rejected the submission that r 1(1)(*i*), the predecessor of r 1(1)(*b*),
comprehended a claim for an injunction that was interlocutory only (see [1977] 3 All ER
803 at 824, [1979] AC 210 at 256). For my part I would not express any view on the
question whether s 25 has superseded that aspect of the decision of the House of Lords.
It does not arise in this case.
                                                                                          e
(C) *Restraint on dealing with assets which are out of the jurisdiction*
In the light of recent authority, counsel for the defendants conceded that the court has
power to restrain a defendant who is not resident here from dealing with his assets which
are out of the jurisdiction. He desires only to keep the point open in case this dispute
goes further. Nevertheless, I consider that, as the issue goes to the jurisdiction of this
court and is of considerable general importance, we ought to examine it. In doing so it is *f*
necessary to travel over some ground which is also relevant to discretion.
It may be that the powers of the court are wider, and certainly discretion is more
readily exercised, if a plaintiff's claim is what is called a tracing claim. For my part, I
think that the true distinction lies between a proprietary claim on the one hand, and a
claim which seeks only a money judgment on the other. A proprietary claim is one by
which the plaintiff seeks the return of chattels or land which are his property, or claims *g*
that a specified debt is owed by a third party to him and not to the defendant.
Thus far there is no difficulty. A plaintiff who seeks to enforce a claim of that kind
will more readily be afforded interim remedies in order to preserve the asset which he is
seeking to recover, than one who merely seeks a judgment for debt or damages. But if
the asset has been converted into some other form of property, the question of tracing *h*
arises. If the defendant stole the plaintiff's peas, sold them and bought beans with the
proceeds, the plaintiff claims that the beans are his property. Or if the defendant
misappropriated the plaintiff's credit balance with bank X, and established a credit with
bank Y from the proceeds, the plaintiff claims that the debt due from bank Y is his
property. In that last case, if the proceedings are brought by the plaintiff against the
defendant only, the relief claimed can be no more than a declaration, and an injunction *j*
against interference with the plaintiff's property. Ultimately the right must be enforced
against the debtor, in my example bank Y.
With that introduction I turn to consider whether the claim which the plaintiffs seek
to enforce in France is a proprietary claim. New evidence has emerged since this dispute
was last before the Court of Appeal, when the proceedings were ex parte so far as the

defendants were concerned. In form the claim in the French action is for damages in
a tort. But process is available there to attach specific assets held by the defendants, which
would result in the plaintiffs having priority over other creditors. The plaintiffs have in
fact made use of that process in respect of two assets, a flat in Paris and a chateau in
France. They have not yet sought any proprietary remedy in respect of other assets of the
Duvalier family in the French proceedings, because they do not know what or where
those assets are. The very object of the English proceedings is to find out. When they are
b discovered, I do not doubt that the plaintiffs will seek to assert any proprietary remedy
that may be available, whether in France or some other jurisdiction.

In that state of affairs I would not go so far as to say that the action in France, in aid of
which these proceedings are said to be brought, is itself a proprietary or tracing claim. It
does not presently assert ownership of any of the assets expected to be revealed by orders
in the English proceedings. But I am confident that ownership will be asserted when and
c where the assets are found. This is then something of a hybrid situation; and one should
perhaps consider it on the basis that interim relief is sought in aid of a monetary claim
only, without any claim to ownership of the Duvaliers' assets.

The law on this topic has developed in recent years; and in particular a distinction has
emerged between pre-judgment and post-judgment restraint. Our courts are more
willing to restrain a defendant from dealing with his assets after, than before, judgment
d has been given against him. (In passing, I would say that an injunction granted after
judgment should normally, in my view, be of limited duration; the plaintiff should be
encouraged to proceed with proper methods of execution; perpetual injunctions
restraining a defendant from dealing with his assets until the crack of doom are
undesirable.) This, of course, is a pre-judgment case.

The decision of this court in *Ashtiani v Kashi* [1986] 2 All ER 970, [1987] QB 888 was
e concerned with a Mareva injunction, pre-judgment, over assets within the jurisdiction,
coupled with an order for disclosure of assets worldwide. The injunction was discharged.
Both Dillon and Neill LJJ considered that a Mareva injunction should be limited to assets
within the jurisdiction, if there is no proprietary or tracing claim. But I think that they
regarded this limitation as arising from settled practice, rather than from any restriction
on the powers of the court. There are indications in both judgments to that effect.
f Nicholls LJ agreed with both judgments.

The problem was extensively reviewed by this court in *Babanaft International Co SA v
Bassatne* [1989] 1 All ER 433. That was a post-judgment case, and what was said as to
injunctions before judgment was obiter. The court upheld a worldwide injunction on
dealing with assets, subject to a proviso which I shall consider later.

There were some features in the *Babanaft* case that are similar to those in the present
g case. The judgment was against two individuals, whom Kerr LJ described as 'unusually
peripatetic in their lifestyle and elusive in the way they do business and hold assets', for
$15m (at 436). He said (at 436):

> 'All "their" assets appear to be held in the names of a large network of companies
> incorporated in many countries in which they or members of their families hold
h > bearer shares.'

The judge below had found that they would be likely to take any step open to them to
frustrate the execution of the judgment.

I do not attempt to summarise the reasoning of Kerr LJ. He concluded (at 440):

> 'I therefore proceed on the basis that in appropriate cases, though these may well
j > be rare, there is nothing to preclude our courts from granting Mareva-type
> injunctions against defendants which extend to their assets outside the jurisdiction.'

Neill LJ said (at 449):

> 'I was a party to the decision in *Ashtiani v Kashi* and I remain of the opinion that it

accurately reflected the way in which the jurisdiction to grant Mareva injunctions had been exercised and developed in England . . . I am satisfied, however, that the court has *jurisdiction* to grant a Mareva injunction over foreign assets, and that in this developing branch of the law the decision in *Ashtiani v Kashi* may require further consideration in a future case.' (Neill LJ's emphasis.)

Nicholls LJ declined to express any opinion on the pre-judgment position.

For my part, if the point had not been conceded before us, I would have agreed with the view expressed by Kerr LJ, for the reasons given in his judgment, that there is jurisdiction to grant a Mareva injunction, pending trial, over assets worldwide; and that cases where it will be appropriate to grant such an injunction will be rare, if not very rare indeed.

(D) *Discretion*

This arises in two ways. First, the judge had to consider whether it was just and convenient to grant an injunction, in terms of s 37(1) of the Supreme Court Act 1981. Second, he ought to have refused interim relief under s 25(2) of the Civil Jurisdiction and Judgments Act 1982 if the fact that the court had no jurisdiction apart from that section made it 'inexpedient' to grant relief.

Counsel for the defendants advanced different arguments on discretion in relation to the order restraining dealings with assets abroad on the one hand, and the order for disclosure of information on the other. As to the first of those orders, he observes that the English courts have no jurisdiction on the merits, none of the first to tenth defendants are resident here, there is no judgment against them, the assets concerned are mainly if not wholly outside the jurisdiction, and the proper court to make such orders is either the French court at Grasse or the court(s) having jurisdiction where the assets are located.

I can see considerable force in that last point. It is supported by the judgment of the Court of Justice of the European Communities in *Denilauler v Snc Couchet Frères* Case 125/79 [1980] ECR 1553 at 1570 (para 16) where it was said:

> 'The courts of the place or, in any event, of the Contracting State, where the assets subject to the measures sought are located, are those best able to assess the circumstances which may lead to the grant or refusal of the measures sought . . .'

But the plaintiffs, when they launched the English proceedings, did not know where the assets were located. One of their objects was to find out. The proceedings were started here because it was here that the information is available. There is a case to be made for any injunction over assets abroad to be of limited duration. This would preserve the plaintiffs' position until there had been a reasonable opportunity, after discovering where the assets were, to apply for some interim relief in the jurisdiction(s) where the assets are. But although the question of a time limit was raised by the court in the course of the argument, no application was made that one should be imposed.

Counsel for the defendants also argued that it was wrong in principle to order persons not resident in this country as to what they should or should not do out of the jurisdiction, and relied on the judgment of Hoffmann J in *MacKinnon v Donaldson Lufkin & Jenrette Securities Corp* [1986] 1 All ER 653, [1986] Ch 482. That case was actually concerned with an order against a bank which was not a party to the action. There have been many cases where parties out of the jurisdiction have been subjected to an injunction as to their conduct abroad, for example as to commencing or continuing proceedings there, or bringing children back to this country: see *Re Liddell's Settlement Trusts* [1936] 1 All ER 239 at 248, [1936] Ch 365 at 374, where Romer LJ said:

> 'The moment that a person is properly served under the provisions of R.S.C. Ord. XI, that person, so far as the jurisdiction of a court is concerned, is in precisely the same position as a person who is in this country.'

a Counsel argues that even though substantive relief may be granted in such cases, interim relief should not be. I can see no ground for drawing that distinction.

It is beyond question that the injunction granted by Knox J and upheld by Leggatt J was a most unusual measure, such as should very rarely be granted. But this case is most unusual. It is not the nature or strength of the plaintiffs' cause of action which puts them in that category. What to my mind is determinative is the plain and admitted intention of the defendants to move their assets out of the reach of courts of law, coupled with the

b resources they have obtained and the skill they have hitherto shown in doing that, and the vast amount of money involved. This case demands international co-operation between all nations. As the judge said, if ever there was a case for the exercise of the court's powers, this must be it. Or to quote Kerr LJ in *Babanaft International Co SA v Bassatne* [1989] 1 All ER 433 at 444: '. . . some situations . . . cry out, as a matter of justice to plaintiffs, for disclosure orders and Mareva-type injunctions covering foreign assets of

c defendants even before judgment'; and I think that this is such a case. If the Duvalier family have a defence to the substantive claim, and feel that they are being persecuted, then their remedy as I have said is to co-operate in securing an early trial of the dispute. It is not to secrete their assets where even the most just decision in the world cannot reach them.

As to discretion in connection with the information order, the objection of counsel for

d the defendants is as to the use which the plaintiffs may make of the information obtained. It gave an undertaking to Knox J, as I have said, not to use the information without leave of the court; and it has three times applied for and obtained that leave. But it is said that the court would have no sanction which could be imposed if the plaintiffs were to break that undertaking in the future. This was not taken into account by the judge; but he can scarcely be blamed for that, as the point was not raised before him.

e Kerr LJ in the *Babanaft* case did not agree that, as a general rule, such an undertaking should be required. But Neill and Nicholls LJJ differed from Kerr LJ on that point; and Nicholls LJ said that normally the court will need to be satisfied that it has a sufficient degree of control over the plaintiff to secure compliance with the undertaking (see [1989] 1 All ER 433 at 455).

It is difficult to see how, as a matter of law, the court *could* ensure that it had that

f degree of control over the Republic of Haiti, short of requiring a bank guarantee in a very large sum which could be called on in the event that the undertaking was broken. But I doubt if the court should make such a demand on a foreign sovereign state, or assume that it would be at all likely to break an undertaking given to the court. The republic has complied scrupulously with its undertaking in the past. And if it were to come about that the undertaking were broken in the future, I would expect that foreign

g courts, particularly those in the European Community, would take that into account in exercising any discretion they may have in proceedings between the republic and the Duvalier family. I do not consider that, in this case, the discretion to order disclosure of information ought to have been exercised against the republic because it is not in law subject to the control of the English courts.

h
(E) *The Babanaft proviso*

This is, as Nicholls LJ said in the *Babanaft* case [1989] 1 All ER 433 at 452, a troublesome point. The proviso in fact imposed by the Court of Appeal on the injunction restraining dealing in assets was as follows:

j
'Provided always that no person other than the defendants themselves shall in any wise be affected by the terms of this order . . . or concerned to enquire whether any instruction given by or on behalf of either defendant or by anyone else, or any other act or omission of either defendant, or anyone else, whether acting on behalf of either defendant or otherwise, is or may be a breach of this order . . . by either defendant.'

It is plain from the judgments that the proviso was intended to apply (and may in fact have applied, for we do not have a full copy of the order) to dealing in assets abroad, not those within England and Wales.

Kerr LJ would have preferred to add 'unless . . . [the order] is enforced by the courts of the states in which any of the defendants' assets are located' (at 447). It is not clear to me precisely what benefit that addition will confer on the republic; until the order is so enforced it will not operate on third parties, and after the order is so enforced the addition may well not be needed. But it may encourage the courts of other countries to enforce the English order; and if it has that effect it is in my opinion desirable. I would add that I doubt if Kerr LJ was concerned about the formal drafting of his order. It ought to apply to each asset severally, if a court of the state in which *that* asset is located has enforced the English order.

Neill LJ acknowledged that in other cases 'a less widely-drafted proviso may be appropriate so as to limit the protection of third parties to acts by them outside the jurisdiction' (see at 450). Nicholls LJ expressed a similar view. But he did not think it right to attempt to distinguish between third parties who are resident or domiciled or present within the jurisdiction and those who are not (at 453–454).

We first have the question whether *any* proviso should be added to the order of Leggatt J. In my opinion there should be some proviso, firstly because counsel for the plaintiffs acknowledges that there should be, and secondly because we ought not to differ, even on a matter of discretion, from a recent and considered decision of another division of this court.

Secondly, I would include the addition proposed by Kerr LJ, with some alteration in the drafting.

Thirdly, I consider that the proviso should only apply to assets outside England and Wales, and to acts done outside England and Wales.

Fourthly, I regret that I differ from Nicholls LJ in the circumstances of this case, and consider that the proviso should not apply to individuals (ie natural persons) who are resident in England and Wales. If it so happens that there is a bank account in the Channel Islands or the Isle of Man, which can be operated on the signature of an English resident, whether a solicitor with Turner & Co or another firm, or anybody else, I would find it offensive that he should be free to cross the channel and sign away the money. I have some qualms about limiting this category to natural persons as opposed to corporations. But this should avoid one problem that troubled Nicholls LJ, which was whether the court should distinguish between an overseas bank which has a London branch and one that has not. And a corporation can only act by a natural person, unless its computer is programmed to take action without instructions from anybody.

I realise that these conclusions will involve formidable problems in drafting. The orders already made are long enough in all conscience; and as I have frequently observed in the past, Mareva injunctions are served on and have to be understood by persons who are not lawyers (in this case not even English-speaking), who must obey instantly on pain of imprisonment. It is to be hoped that counsel can prepare a draft order which is precise but intelligible. For example, as an aid to comprehension it might be preferable to replace 'out of the jurisdiction' with 'outside England and Wales'. One solution may be to prepare a separate order dealing with foreign assets, so that there is no need for it to contain a mass of material relating to disclosure and English assets.

(F) *Privilege*

It is agreed, as I have said, that the claim for privilege against disclosure of certain classes of documents and information should be remitted to a Commercial judge. The order should identify these classes, so that it will operate forthwith in all other respects.

Conclusion

I would vary the order of Leggatt J (i) by inserting the undertaking as to the use of information that was given to Knox J, (ii) by inserting a proviso in the order for disclosure

of assets outside England and Wales, of the kind which I have described, and (iii) by
a excepting disclosure of the material for which privilege is claimed. The order of Leggatt
J should remain in full force and effect until the variations have either been agreed and
approved by this court, or else settled by this court.

In all other respects I would dismiss this appeal.

STOCKER LJ. I agree and wish to add nothing further.

b

FOX LJ. I also agree.

Appeal dismissed subject to variation of order. Leave to appeal to the House of Lords refused.

Solicitors: *Watson Farley & Williams* (for the defendants); *Slaughter & May* (for the
c plaintiffs).

Sophie Craven   Barrister.

d Derby & Co Ltd and others v Weldon and others (No 1)

COURT OF APPEAL, CIVIL DIVISION

MAY, PARKER AND NICHOLLS LJJ

19, 22, 25, 26, 27, 28, 29 JULY 1988

e

*Practice – Pre-trial or post-judgment relief – Mareva injunction – Worldwide Mareva injunction
– Pre-trial injunction – Extra-territorial effect of injunction – Protection of third parties – Foreign
defendant having foreign assets – Proceedings brought by United States banking group against
former directors of subsidiary alleging breach of contract, conspiracy and fraudulent breach of
fiduciary duty over loans made to Far Eastern commodity dealer which collapsed owing over
f £35m to banking group – Defendants likely to attempt to frustrate execution of judgment against
them – Whether court having jurisdiction to grant Mareva injunction over defendants' foreign
assets before judgment – Whether worldwide injunction should be subject to undertakings by
plaintiffs not to enforce order overseas or use in foreign proceedings information about overseas
assets disclosed by defendants without leave of English court.*

g The plaintiffs were foreign companies which were all part of a United States banking
group. The first and second defendants were the directors of a London company, CML, a
commodity dealer which specialised in trading internationally in cocoa. CML was owned
by the third and fourth defendants. In 1981 the plaintiff group purchased CML, which
continued to be managed by the first and second defendants. While under their
h management CML offered very extensive credit to a Far Eastern commodity dealer
which in 1984 became insolvent owing over £35m to CML. The plaintiff group
recovered less than £1½m in the insolvency and brought an action against the defendants
alleging breach of contract, conspiracy and fraudulent breach of fiduciary duty. The
plaintiffs applied for, inter alia, a Mareva injunction restricting the first and second
defendants from dealing with their assets worldwide but the judge, although finding
j that there were grounds for supposing that the first and second defendants had acted
dishonestly and that there was a real risk that any judgment in favour of the plaintiffs
would remain unsatisfied because the first and second defendants had the ability to lock
away assets in inaccessible overseas companies, held that he only had jurisdiction to grant
a Mareva injunction over assets within the jurisdiction. He granted an injunction limited
accordingly. The plaintiffs appealed, seeking the grant of a worldwide Mareva injunction.

Held – Whether the court should grant a worldwide Mareva injunction pending trial depended on the particular facts in each case but, having regard to the drastic and *a* oppressive nature of the remedy, such an injunction should only be granted in exceptional cases and should (i) protect the defendant from oppression by exposure to a multiplicity of proceedings, (ii) protect the defendant against the misuse of information obtained by an order for disclosure made in aid of the Mareva injunction and (iii) protect the position of third parties. On the facts, the court would grant a worldwide Mareva injunction pending trial and make an ancillary order for disclosure by the defendants of their *b* overseas assets because the first and second defendants' English assets were wholly insufficient to afford protection to the plaintiffs and there were substantial foreign assets, but there was a high degree of risk that the first and second defendants would dispose of them in the face of an adverse judgment. However, the grant of the injunction would be conditional on the plaintiffs giving undertakings that they would neither apply to a foreign court to enforce the order to seek nor use in foreign proceedings any information *c* disclosed by the defendants about their overseas assets without first obtaining leave from the English court. The appeal would accordingly be allowed (see p 473 *c d f* to *h*, p 474 *a b d f g j* to p 475 *b*, p 476 *d g h*, p 477 *d f g j*, p 478 *c g h* and p 480 *e*, post).

Babanaft International Co SA v Bassatne [1989] 1 All ER 433 and *Republic of Haiti v Duvalier* [1989] 1 All ER 456 considered.

Per curiam. On an application for a Mareva injunction there are only three issues, *d* namely (i) whether the plaintiff has a good arguable case, (ii) whether the plaintiff can satisfy the court that there are assets within or, where an extra-territorial injunction is sought, outside the jurisdiction and (iii) whether there is a real risk that those assets will be dissipated or secreted so as to render any judgment which the plaintiff may obtain nugatory, and those issues should be decided on comparatively brief evidence. In particular, the court ought not to be asked either to resolve disputed questions of fact, *e* whether relating to the merits of the underlying claim or the Mareva jurisdiction, or to hear detailed argument on difficult points of law (see p 474 *f g*, p 475 *c d*, p 476 *c d* and p 480 *e f*, post); dictum of Lord Templeman in *Spiliada Maritime Corp v Cansulex Ltd, The Spiliada* [1986] 3 All ER 843 at 847 applied.

Notes *f*

For Mareva injunctions, see 37 Halsbury's Laws (4th edn) para 362, and for cases on the subject, see 37(2) Digest (Reissue) 474–476, 2947–2962.

Cases referred to in judgments

A v C [1980] 2 All ER 347, [1981] QB 956, [1981] 2 WLR 629.
American Cyanamid Co v Ethicon Ltd [1975] 1 All ER 504, [1975] AC 396, [1975] 2 WLR *g* 316, HL.
Ashtiani v Kashi [1986] 2 All ER 970, [1987] QB 888, [1986] 3 WLR 647, CA.
Babanaft International Co SA v Bassatne [1989] 1 All ER 433, CA.
Ballabil Holdings Pty Ltd v Hospital Products Ltd (1985) 1 NSWLR 155, NSW CA; *affg* [1984] 2 NSWLR 662, NSW SC. *h*
Bankers Trust Co v Shapira [1980] 3 All ER 353, [1980] 1 WLR 1274, CA.
Clunies-Ross, Re, ex p Totterdell (1987) 72 ALR 241, Aust Fed Ct.
Coombs & Barei Constructions Pty Ltd v Dynasty Pty Ltd (1986) 42 SASR 413, S Aust SC.
Guinness plc v Saunders [1988] 2 All ER 940, [1988] 1 WLR 863, CA; *affg* [1988] BCLC 43.
Hait (Republic) v Duvalier [1989] 1 All ER 456, CA.
Home Office v Harman [1982] 1 All ER 532, [1983] 1 AC 280, [1982] 2 WLR 338, HL. *j*
Interpool Ltd v Galani [1987] 2 All ER 981, [1988] QB 738, [1987] 3 WLR 1042, CA.
Lister & Co v Stubbs (1890) 45 Ch D 1, [1886–90] All ER Rep 797, CA.
Maclaine Watson & Co Ltd v International Tin Council (No 2) [1988] 3 All ER 257, [1988] 3 WLR 1190, CA.

a   *Spiliada Maritime Corp v Cansulex Ltd, The Spiliada* [1986] 3 All ER 843, [1987] AC 460, [1986] 3 WLR 972, HL.
    Wakefield v Duke of Buccleuch (1865) 12 LT 628; *subsequent proceedings* (1866) LR 4 Eq 613; *on appeal* (1870) LR 4 HL 377.

Cases also cited

    A-G's Reference (No 1 of 1985) [1986] 2 All ER 219, [1986] QB 491, CA.
b   *Allied Arab Bank Ltd v Hajjar* [1987] 3 All ER 739, [1988] QB 787.
    Avant Petroleum Inc v Gatoil Overseas Inc [1986] 2 Lloyd's Rep 236, CA.
    British Syphon Co Ltd v Homewood [1956] 2 All ER 897, [1956] 1 WLR 1190.
    Cook v Deeks [1916] 1 AC 554, [1916–17] All ER Rep 285, PC.
    Cook Industries Inc v Galliher [1978] 3 All ER 945, [1979] Ch 439.
    Denilauler v Snc Couchet Frères Case 125/79 [1980] ECR 1553.
c   *House of Spring Gardens Ltd v Waite* [1985] FSR 173, CA.
    London and Counties Securities Ltd v Caplan (26 May 1978, unreported), Ch D.
    Marshall (Thomas) (Exports) Ltd v Guinle [1978] 3 All ER 193, [1979] Ch 227.
    Mediterranean Raffineria Siciliana Petroli SpA v Mabanaft GmbH [1978] CA Transcript 816.
    Metropolitan Bank v Heiron (1880) 5 Ex D 319, CA.
    National Bank of Greece v Constantinos Dimitriou (1987) Times, 16 November, CA.
d   *Porzelack KG v Porzelack (UK) Ltd* [1987] 1 All ER 1074, [1987] 1 WLR 420.
    Shell-Mex and BP Ltd v Clayton (Valuation Officer) [1956] 3 All ER 185, [1956] 1 WLR 1198, HL.
    Space Investments Ltd v Canadian Imperial Bank of Commerce Trust Co (Bahamas) Ltd [1986] 3 All ER 75, [1986] 1 WLR 1072, PC.
    Sterling Engineering Co Ltd v Patchett [1955] 1 All ER 369, [1955] AC 534, HL.
e   *Thompson's Settlement, Re, Thompson v Thompson* [1985] 2 All ER 720, [1986] Ch 99.
    Yandil Holdings Pty Ltd v Insurance Co of North America (1986) 7 NSWLR 571, NSW SC.

Interlocutory appeal

The plaintiffs, Derby and Co Ltd, Cocoa Merchants Ltd (CML), Phibro-Salomon Finance AG, Phibro-Salomon Ltd, Philipp Bros Inc, Philipp Bros Ltd and Salomon Inc of the
f   United States of America (the holding company of the other plaintiff companies), by a writ issued on 25 June 1987 brought an action against the defendants, Anthony Henry David Weldon, Ian Jay, Milco Corp, a Panamanian company, and CML Holding SA of Luxembourg (CMI), claiming damages for breach of contract, misrepresentation, negligence, deceit, conspiracy to defraud and fraudulent breach of fiduciary duty arising out of the trading activities of CML between February 1981 and June 1984 while under
g   the management of the first and second defendants as executive directors of CML after it had been purchased by Salomons from the liquidator of a subsidiary of Milco, which was itself a subsidiary of CMI. In particular, the plaintiffs alleged that between June 1981 and February 1984 the first and second defendants caused CML to suffer losses of £35m on unauthorised advances and credit made available to the Allied Group of companies of Hong Kong when the first and second defendants were owed large sums in their personal
h   capacity by the persons who controlled Allied. The plaintiffs further alleged that when Allied collapsed in 1984 the plaintiffs were owed £35,580,424 of which they were only able to recover £1,485,148 in the insolvency. On 4 December 1987 the plaintiffs applied ex parte to Sir Nicolas Browne-Wilkinson V-C and were granted Mareva injunctions against the first and second defendants restraining them from removing their assets out
j   of the United Kingdom or those countries which were parties to the Convention on Jurisdiction and the Enforcement of Civil and Commercial Judgments 1968 or from dealing in any way with those assets except to the extent that they exceeded £25m and requiring the first and second defendants to file an affidavit disclosing the full value of their assets. By a notice of motion dated 8 December the plaintiffs sought an order freezing the first and second defendants' assets up to £25m wheresoever in the world

situated and disclosure of particulars of bank accounts, nominees etc. The motions were heard by Mervyn Davies J who on 27 June 1988 made a Mareva injunction restricted to *a* the first and second defendants' assets in the United Kingdom and further ordered, by para 6 of his order, that the first and second defendants file an affidavit disclosing what had become of all moneys paid by CML in respect of commodity and foreign exchange transactions with certain specified companies with particulars of accounts into which the moneys had been paid and the identity of the account holder or assets acquired with or representing those moneys. The plaintiffs appealed against the judge's refusal to grant a *b* worldwide Mareva injunction. The first and second defendants cross-appealed against para 6 of the judge's order. The facts are set out in the judgments.

Michael Lyndon-Stanford QC, Charles Purle and J Stephen Smith for the plaintiffs.
Philip Heslop QC, John Brisby and Robert Miles for the first and second defendants.
c

MAY LJ. We have before us an appeal and cross-appeals in respect of orders made in Mareva proceedings before Mervyn Davies J on 27 June 1988. The facts of the case are complicated: they were fully set out in the judge's judgment whose exposition of them I gratefully adopt. In brief, at material times the first two defendants were directors of the second plaintiffs. The latter were members of what I may call the Salomon Group of which the principal holding company was the seventh plaintiff. At such times the first *d* and second defendants were also directors of or had substantial interests in the fourth defendant.

The plaintiffs' various claims against the respondents rely on allegations of breach of contract, conspiracy, tort and fraudulent breach of fiduciary duty. They arose initially out of the insolvency of a group of companies known as the Allied Group in February 1984 owing the second plaintiffs £35,580,424. That sum, less £1,485,148 recovered *e* from Allied in Hong Kong, namely a net £34,095,276 is among other relief now claimed from the respondents.

In general terms the plaintiffs' complaints are that for their own ends, the defendants, and particularly the first and second defendants (a) were content to allow improper credit to Allied, (b) on their own account, through the medium of companies in which they *f* (the defendants) had influence or interest, engaged in transactions that were incompatible with their fiduciary duties to the plaintiffs. As to (b) the plaintiffs' case is that for their own interests and contrary to their obligations to the plaintiffs they and companies which they controlled carried out foreign exchange dealings and business transactions in cocoa (physical) and cocoa futures to a substantial extent.

In the course of his judgment, having considered the material put before him, the *g* judge made the following comments:

'. . . it seems to me that in the light of matters such as I have tried to summarise above, the refusal of a Mareva injunction "would involve a real risk that a judgment in favour of the plaintiffs would remain unsatisfied." I say that because there are grounds for supposing that the [defendants] may have acted dishonestly, coupled *h* with the fact that they have the ability to lock away assets in inaccessible overseas companies . . . there is no doubt in my mind that this is a very plain case for an ordinary Mareva order in that the two basic ingredients for the making of an order are present in a high degree. Although a different picture may emerge when oral evidence is given, the plaintiffs' case is highly arguable. As well there is, I think, a high risk that any assets the [defendants] have, whether here or overseas, will, if the *j* plaintiffs obtain judgment, be unavailable for execution . . . The [defendants] are well used to moving funds worldwide.'

Notwithstanding these findings the judge was only prepared to make a Mareva order in respect of assets within the jurisdiction, refusing any wider order on the basis of the decision of this court in *Ashtiani v Kashi* [1986] 2 All ER 970, [1987] QB 888. However,

as has been said in a number of decisions in Mareva proceedings, the jurisdiction is a
a developing one. In *Babanaft International Co SA v Bassatne* [1989] 1 All ER 433 this court
was prepared to make a post-judgment worldwide Mareva order subject to a proviso
preserving the personal effect of such an order on and to the particular defendants against
whom it was directed. The court in *Babanaft* indicated that in its view a pre-judgment
worldwide Mareva was legitimate, but of course that comment was then obiter. However,
in *Republic of Haiti v Duvalier* [1989] 1 All ER 456 decided during the hearing of the
b instant appeal, another division of this court made a pre-judgment worldwide Mareva,
again subject to the personal proviso to which I have already referred. The court
recognised that such an injunction was a most unusual measure, such as should very
rarely be granted. Nevertheless the court quoted the dictum of Kerr LJ in *Babanaft* [1989]
1 All ER 433 at 444: '... some situations ... cry out, as a matter of justice to plaintiffs,
for disclosure orders and Mareva-type injunctions covering foreign assets of defendants
c even before judgment.' Even though we are hearing this appeal almost simultaneously
with the delivery of the judgment in the *Duvalier* case, for my part I think that this case
also is one which cries out for a worldwide Mareva injunction even though it is being
sought before judgment. The amount involved and the findings of the judge about the
first two defendants, which I have already quoted in my judgment, make this clear.

In his submissions in the instant appeal, counsel for the defendants submitted that,
d other things apart, a worldwide Mareva should only be made where there was evidence
either that the defendant had in fact secreted or alternatively had attempted to secrete
assets of his outside the jurisdiction so as to render nugatory any judgment to which the
plaintiff might ultimately be entitled. Counsel based this submission not only on
Duvalier's case to which I have already referred, but also on *Ballabil Holdings Pty Ltd v
Hospital Products Ltd* [1984] 2 NSWLR 662; *affd* (1985) 1 NSWLR 155, *Coombs & Barei
e* *Constructions Pty Ltd v Dynasty Pty Ltd* (1986) 42 SASR 413 and *Re Clunies-Ross, ex p
Totterdell* (1987) 72 ALR 241. As counsel originally submitted, all these authorities show
that as wide an order as that sought in the instant case should only be made where there
is evidence of previous malpractice or nefarious intent. Counsel originally contended
that one could deduce this as a principle of law from the authorities; in his reply,
however, he accepted that the highest he could put it was that the cases demonstrated
f that at least evidence of this nature, or of equivalent persuasive effect, was needed before
the court was entitled to make so draconian an order as that sought in this case.

I entirely accept that it will only be in an exceptional case that the court will make
such an order. Nevertheless, each case must depend on its own facts. In the light of the
cases decided since the judge gave judgment herein, to which I have referred, I
respectfully think that he misdirected himself with relation to his approach to the facts
g which he found and which I have outlined. For the reasons given by Nicholls LJ in his
judgment, which I have had the benefit of reading in draft, I do not think that at this
stage any valid challenge can be sustained against those findings of fact made by the
judge on the vast amount of material before him.

Nevertheless, as the court in this type of case is exercising the widest jurisdiction,
h which may, unless precautions are taken, prove more oppressive to those against whom
the orders are made than beneficial to those whom they are intended to protect, I think
that these orders should normally be restricted even more than merely by the proviso to
which I have referred and suggested originally in *Babanaft*.

As the judge in the instant case pointed out, first, such a wide order can be severely
oppressive if the defendants, while preparing for a very complicated trial in England, at
j the same time find themselves engaged in courts overseas in further applications of a
Mareva nature, bearing in mind that plaintiffs with substantial resources may not be
slow to engage the respondents in as many courts throughout the world as possible.
Further, the judge, in referring to objections which had been voiced by Dillon LJ in
Ashtiani v Kashi [1986] 2 All ER 970, [1987] QB 888 also pointed out that if a worldwide
disclosure order is made simultaneously with a Mareva injunction, this may enable a

plaintiff to obtain security in some foreign jurisdiction. It is in addition, as Lord Roskill has pointed out, a substantial invasion of privacy (see *Home Office v Harman* [1982] 1 All ER 532 at 552, [1983] 1 AC 280 at 323). To obviate these very real difficulties, counsel on behalf of the plaintiffs undertook in the course of the argument in the instant case to leave any decision whether action should be taken by his clients in any foreign jurisdiction in respect of any of the assets of the two defendants to the English court. In my judgment such a term or undertaking should generally be part of any worldwide pre-judgment Mareva obtained in circumstances not dissimilar from those in this or the *Duvalier* case [1989] 1 All ER 456. It is worth making the point that if a worldwide Mareva is not obtained and the plaintiffs do from time to time discover the whereabouts of assets of the defendants, they may well be minded to take those steps in foreign jurisdictions which in totality might well be oppressive, whereas if a worldwide Mareva does contain a term giving the English court the general control over the litigation this would clearly obviate this potential difficulty.

I should add that the third particular reason which the judge gave for refusing a worldwide order was: 'No dishonesty is yet proved and may never be proved. I must assume that the respondents are honest. Furthermore, they are not in breach of any court order.' These comments do not lie easily alongside the earlier comments made by the judge in his judgment which I have already quoted, to support which there was certainly evidence before him.

In these circumstances my opinion is that it falls to us to decide whether the relief sought should be granted on the judge's findings of fact and in the light of the law as I understand this court has now stated it to be. For my part I have no doubt that with the appropriate safeguards to which I have referred, this is a case in which a worldwide Mareva injunction ought to be granted, with the concomitant disclosure.

As to the limited proprietary relief claimed by the plaintiffs, I have, as I have indicated, had the opportunity of reading the judgment of Nicholls LJ in draft. I respectfully agree with it and with the conclusion to which he comes.

I have also had the opportunity of reading the judgment of Parker LJ in draft and for my part would respectfully endorse the views he expresses therein.

Subject to the caveats I have expressed, therefore, I would allow the appeal and dismiss the cross-appeal.

PARKER LJ. I agree that this appeal should be allowed and I also agree with the judgments of May and Nicholls LJJ which I have had the opportunity to read in draft. I desire however to add some observations of my own on two matters.

(1) It was submitted for the defendants (i) that if a worldwide Mareva could be granted on no more than a good arguable case and a risk of dissipation of assets it would follow that such an order could be made in the vast majority of commercial cases in which material existed for the grant of an internal Mareva and (ii) that this would conflict with statements in *Ashtiani v Kashi* [1986] 2 All ER 970, [1987] QB 888, *Babanaft International Co SA v Bassatne* [1989] 1 All ER 433 and *Republic of Haiti v Duvalier* [1989] 1 All ER 456 that an extra-territorial Mareva, albeit effective only in personam would only rarely be granted and would require exceptional circumstances.

I do not accept the first of the above submissions. The mere fact that the plaintiff shows a good arguable case and a real risk of disposal or hiding of English assets, the requisites for an internal Mareva, clearly cannot by itself be sufficient to justify an extra-territorial Mareva either worldwide or at all. Such a Mareva would clearly be unjustified if, for example, there were sufficient English assets to cover the appropriate sum, or if the court were not satisfied that there were foreign assets or that there was a real risk of disposal of the same, or if it would in all the circumstances be oppressive to make the order.

Here, however, it is accepted that there are foreign assets. The judge has found, correctly in my view, that there is a high risk of disposal of such assets. The English assets

are wholly insufficient to afford protection. The defendants are clearly sophisticated
operators who have amply demonstrated their ability to render assets untraceable and a
determination not to reveal them.

In those circumstances it appears to me that there is every justification for a worldwide
Mareva, so long as, by undertaking or proviso or a combination of both, (a) oppression of
the defendants by way of exposure to a multiplicity of proceedings is avoided, (b) the
defendants are protected against the misuse of information gained from the ordinary
order for disclosure in aid of the Mareva, (c) the position of third parties is protected.

Whether, ultimately, the order in personam will be converted into an order attaching
some or all of the assets disclosed will of course depend on (i) the court here giving the
plaintiffs leave to proceed in a jurisdiction in which assets have been found and (ii) the
decision of the court in such jurisdiction whether to make an order.

(2) That the hearing of an application for interlocutory relief should take 26 days is,
in my view, entirely unwarranted, as is also the fact that the documents for an appeal
from the judge should comprise several thousand pages of affidavits and exhibits.

There are in essence only three issues: (i) has the plaintiff a good arguable case, (ii) has
the plaintiff satisfied the court that there are assets within and, where an extra-territorial
order is sought, without the jurisdiction, (iii) is there a real risk of dissipation or secretion
of assets so as to render any judgment which the plaintiff may obtain nugatory? Such
matters should be decided on comparatively brief evidence. In *American Cyanamid Co v
Ethicon Ltd* [1975] 1 All ER 504 at 510, [1975] AC 396 at 407–408 Lord Diplock, dealing
in that case with an application for an interlocutory injunction, said:

> 'It is no part of the court's function at this stage of the litigation to try to resolve
> conflicts of evidence on affidavit as to facts on which the claims of either party may
> ultimately depend nor to decide difficult questions of law which call for detailed
> argument and mature considerations. These are matters to be dealt with at the trial.
> One of the reasons for the introduction of the practice of requiring an undertaking
> as to damages on the grant of an interlocutory injunction was that "it aided the court
> in doing that which was its great object, viz abstaining from expressing any opinion
> on the merits of the case until the hearing" (*Wakefield v Duke of Buccleuch* (1865) 12
> LT 628 at 629.'

In my view the difference between an application for an ordinary injunction and
Mareva lies only in this: that in the former case the plaintiff need only establish that there
is a serious question to be tried, whereas in the latter the test is said to be whether the
plaintiff shows a good arguable case. This difference, which is incapable of definition,
does not however affect the applicability of Lord Diplock's observations to Mareva cases.

In the present case this seems to have been forgotten. It was not until the 18th day of
the hearing before the judge that the defendants accepted that there was a good arguable
case which, unless the many conflicts on the affidavit evidence are resolved in the
defendants' favour, there plainly is. Moreover, the defendants sought to go into and
obtain the court's view on questions of law, which the argument before us and the
judgment of the judge show clearly to be questions calling for detailed argument and
mature consideration. This is quite wrong.

More recently, in relation to an application under RSC Ord 12, r 8 to set aside service
of a writ outside the jurisdiction, Lord Templeman in *Spiliada Maritime Corp v Cansulex
Ltd, The Spiliada* [1986] 3 All ER 843 at 847, [1987] AC 460 at 465 said that such cases
should be measured in hours not days, that appeals should be rare and that this court
should be slow to interfere. These observations in my view also apply to cases such as the
present.

Counsel for the defendants has however sought to go yet again into large parts of the
evidence in order to persuade us that the judge's finding that there is a high risk of
dissipation of assets both here and overseas should be reversed in respect of overseas assets.
In essence he sought to persuade us to attempt to resolve conflicts of fact going to the

merits of the claim but which were also important on the question of risk of dissipation.
This is no part of this court's function any more than it is the function of the court at first   *a*
instance. He also sought to show that the plaintiffs in the present case have no proprietary
claim. His submissions in this behalf depended on the resolution both of disputed,
detailed and complex fact and of difficult questions of law requiring mature consideration.
The function of this court is again misappreciated.

It is to be hoped that in future the observations of Lord Diplock and Lord Templeman
will be borne in mind in applications for a Mareva injunction, that they will take hours   *b*
not days and that appeals will be rare. I do not mean by the foregoing to indicate that
argument as to the principles applying to the grant of a Mareva injunction should not be
fully argued. With a developing jurisdiction it is inevitable and desirable that they should
be. What, however, should not be allowed is (1) any attempt to persuade a court to
resolve disputed questions of fact whether relating to the merits of the underlying claim
in respect of which a Mareva is sought or relating to the elements of the Mareva   *c*
jurisdiction such as that of dissipation or (2) detailed argument on difficult points of law
on which the claim of either party may ultimately depend. If such attempts are made
they can and should be discouraged by appropriate orders as to costs.

NICHOLLS LJ. I agree that this appeal should be allowed.   *d*

It is now established that under s 37 of the Supreme Court Act 1981 the English court
has jurisdiction to make a Mareva 'restraint' order in respect of assets outside England
and Wales, both before judgment (*Republic of Haiti v Duvalier* [1989] 1 All ER 456 and
after judgment (*Babanaft International Co SA v Bassatne* [1989] 1 All ER 433). Likewise,
the English court has jurisdiction to make a 'disclosure' order in respect of assets outside
England and Wales, both before judgment (*Republic of Haiti v Duvalier*) and after   *e*
judgment (*Interpool Ltd v Galani* [1987] 2 All ER 981, [1988] QB 738 and *Maclaine Watson
& Co Ltd v International Tin Council (No 2)* [1988] 3 All ER 257, [1988] 3 WLR 1190).

The jurisdiction is established, but what is still being worked out, in this fast
developing area of law, is the manner in which, in practice, the court should exercise its
discretionary power under this wide jurisdiction. One important matter in this regard
concerns the limitations and safeguards normally appropriate to be built into restraint   *f*
and disclosure orders regarding overseas assets. As to restraint orders, some of the points
canvassed, but left open, in the judgments of this court in the *Babanaft* case were
subsequently considered in the very recent decision, also of this court, in *Republic of Haiti
v Duvalier*. In particular, in the *Duvalier* case the court engrafted onto what was there
described as the 'Babanaft proviso', whereby the order was expressed not to affect third
parties, the qualification 'unless and to the extent that it is enforced by the courts of the   *g*
states in which ... the ... assets are located'. This was the limitation suggested by Kerr
LJ in the *Babanaft* case [1989] 1 All ER 433 at 447. In the present case the plaintiffs
proposed that this point should be dealt with by the plaintiffs giving to the English court
an undertaking in terms which will preclude them from making any application to a
foreign court to enforce the order without first obtaining leave from the English court.
This seems to me to be a convenient course. If this undertaking is accepted, and an order   *h*
is made, it would then be for the judge of the English court to whom any application for
such leave might be made to consider, among other matters, whether the enforcement
of the order in the country (or countries) for which leave is sought will, under the law of
that country, result in the order having a substantially similar effect there to a Mareva,
restraint order in this country, as distinct from the order having there a more far-
reaching effect (such as the assets in the country being attached as a form of security for   *j*
the plaintiffs' claims, which is not the object of a Mareva, restraint order). On any
application for such leave, which normally would be inter partes, the judge can be
expected to have before him what we do not have, namely evidence of the law and
practice in the country or countries in which the order is sought to be enforced. The
undertaking, I add, is being offered by all the plaintiffs, which include among their

number English companies whose substance has not been questioned. So the undertaking
a is a worthwhile one.

As to extra-territoriality and the protection of third parties, the restraint order as
sought by the plaintiffs also embodies the restriction on the *Babanaft* proviso adopted in
the *Duvalier* case, to the effect that individuals who are resident in this country are to be
affected by the restraint order regarding overseas assets, even in respect of acts done by
them outside England and Wales. As Staughton LJ recognised in *Duvalier*, the distinction
b thus drawn between natural and other persons resident in this country is not satisfactory.
However, no argument was addressed to us on this point by counsel. This is not a suitable
case therefore to seek to take this particular point further.

As to the disclosure order in respect of overseas assets, in the present case this order is
intended to be ancillary to the worldwide restraint order. Disclosure is sought in order
to render that restraint order effective, or more effective. Here also the undertaking
c being offered by the plaintiffs is in terms which will preclude them from making any
use of information so disclosed in proceedings abroad against the first and second
defendants (to whom I shall refer simply as 'the defendants') without the leave of the
(English) court. Here again, therefore, reasonable protection for the defendants is being
built into the order to ensure that the information compulsorily disclosed is not misused
and that it does not lead to the defendants being harassed or oppressed by having to face
d litigation, brought by financially more powerful parties, in overseas courts throughout
the world.

I have referred to the safeguards being embodied in the order before considering
whether a worldwide restraint order, and an ancillary worldwide disclosure order, should
be made at all, because the extent and adequacy of the safeguards available are of
particular relevance in the present case having regard to the criticisms advanced by the
e plaintiffs of the factors which weighed with the judge when he exercised his discretion.
After a full exploration of voluminous, complex affidavit evidence for more than five
weeks, made with the assistance of submissions by leading counsel on both sides, the
judge's conclusions on the facts included the following. First, that there was a very real
risk that assets, here or abroad, presently owned by the defendants would, by the use of
foreign companies, nominee directors, bearer shares and the like, remain hidden or now
f be spirited away, so as to render any future judgment useless. Second, that that risk
would be reduced, if not eliminated, by a restraint order affecting overseas assets. Third,
in the circumstances of this case an order affecting only assets in England and Wales
might for practical purposes be virtually useless. Fourth, that the defendants had not
sought to help themselves by disclosing any details of their assets beyond saying that they
have some assets in England and that they have no assets elsewhere in the EEC countries.

g Despite this the judge declined to make a restraint order, with an ancillary disclosure
order, in respect of overseas assets (the defendants did not resist the making of such orders
in respect of assets in England and Wales). He declined, because of the importance he
attached to three considerations. He felt that these three considerations were of such
strength as to outweigh all the others. Two of those considerations concerned the
oppressiveness of the use which the plaintiffs might make of information regarding the
h defendants' overseas assets: the defendants could be made to engage in courts overseas in
applications of a Mareva nature, and the information could lead to the plaintiffs obtaining
security in some foreign jurisdiction. If making the disclosure order would be likely to
have those consequences in this case, I would agree with the judge on the weightiness of
these factors. As the judge rightly recognised, these were the considerations which
prompted this court to discharge an overseas disclosure order in *Ashtiani v Kashi* [1986] 2
j All ER 970, [1987] QB 888. But in the present case the undertaking offered by the
plaintiffs puts the matter into an altogether different light, by giving the defendants
reasonable protection. So I think that the judge, who did not have the benefit of the
subsequent decisions in *Babanaft* and *Duvalier*, fell into error in not taking the undertaking
proffered by the plaintiffs into account as providing an answer to his justifiable concern
on these two points.

The third point to which the judge attached overriding weight was that in previous cases where orders have been made regarding overseas assets there was a background of *a* proven misconduct by a defendant, but in the present case no dishonesty has yet been proved. The judge said that he must assume that the two individual defendants are honest. Of course, the outcome of the trial may be that the defendants are wholly innocent of all the charges, and are not liable under any of the claims made against them. But, if by what he said the judge meant that a restraint order in respect of overseas assets should not be made in the absence of proof of dishonesty on the part of the defendants *b* even though the action is only at a very early interlocutory stage, then I would feel bound to part company from him. However, I do not think that it is necessary to consider further whether this indeed is what the judge meant. Having regard to the misdirection already mentioned, the judge's exercise of his discretion cannot stand.

In these circumstances it is for this court to exercise its own discretion. As to that I am in no doubt that a restraint order in respect of overseas assets ought to be made pending *c* the trial or further order, with an ancillary disclosure order. Counsel for the defendants challenged the judge's conclusions about the very real risk of assets remaining hidden or being spirited away so as to render any judgment useless. Counsel drew our attention to certain passages in the evidence. These were lengthy but they still fell far short of the totality of evidence considered by the judge. Having considered those passages, and the submissions of counsel for the defendants, I am not persuaded that the judge can be *d* faulted in his conclusion on these points.

Counsel for the defendants further submitted that, even if these conclusions regarding the risk of assets being secreted or removed were to stand, no order should be made. He placed much emphasis on judicial observations that pre-judgment restraint orders regarding overseas assets will be granted only 'in extreme situations' (per Kerr LJ in *Babanaft* [1989] 1 All ER 433 at 447) and that cases where it will be appropriate to grant *e* such injunctions 'will be rare, if not very rare indeed' (per Staughton LJ in *Republic of Haiti v Duvalier* [1989] 1 All ER 456 at 466). He submitted that before an overseas restraint order is made more must be required than a good arguable case and a real risk that the overseas assets will be dissipated or secreted. He contended that if those were the only pre-requisites to a worldwide restraint order, the facts which would justify a restraint *f* order regarding assets in England and Wales would frequently, if not normally, also justify a restraint order regarding assets overseas. If that were so, a restraint order regarding overseas assets would become commonplace, because if a defendant is likely to dissipate or spirit away or secrete his UK assets, he is likely to behave similarly regarding his overseas assets.

In my view each case must depend on its own facts. An order restraining a defendant *g* from dealing with any of his assets overseas, and requiring him to disclose details of all his assets wherever located, is a draconian order. The risk of prejudice to which, in the absence of such an order, the plaintiff will be subject is that of the dissipation or secretion of assets *abroad*. This risk must, on the facts, be appropriately grave before it will be just and convenient for such a draconian order to be made. It goes without saying that before such an order is made the court will scrutinise the facts with particular care. In the *h* instant case there are present the special factors to which May and Parker LJJ have referred. I do not think that it is correct that, if an order is made in the present case regarding overseas assets, such an order will become, or should become, the norm in cases where a restraint order is made regarding assets within the jurisdiction.

For completeness I should add that in the present case nothing turns on the position regarding assets which are located abroad in countries which are parties to the Convention *j* on Jurisdiction and the Enforcement of Judgments in Civil and Commercial Matters (Brussels, 27 September 1968; EC 46 (1978); Cmnd 7395) as distinct from assets which are located elsewhere abroad. The defendants assert that they have no assets in convention countries. Quite rightly, time was not spent on what, in that circumstance, would have been arid argument. Counsel for the defendants accepted that his clients' position regarding convention countries should stand or fall with the fate of this appeal so far as it is related to other countries throughout the world: if a worldwide order should be made, that should embrace convention countries as well as non-convention countries. Conversely, if a worldwide order should not be made, there should be no special order regarding convention countries.

I turn to the defendants' cross-appeal in respect of para 6 in the judge's order. In my view it is clear that an order along these lines cannot be justified unless the plaintiffs have a seriously arguable claim to have a proprietary interest in the sums of money paid by or on behalf of Cocoa Merchants Ltd (CML) to Cocoa Merchants (Far East) Ltd (CMFE) in respect of profits from the foreign exchange transactions being attacked by the plaintiffs. The judge's order, indeed, goes wider than foreign exchange transactions entered into with CMFE, but before us counsel for the plaintiffs was content to confine the plaintiffs' claim to CMFE transactions. Counsel for the defendants presented a formidable argument to the effect that neither on the pleadings nor on the evidence is such a claim made out as a serious issue. I agree with him that the statement of claim leaves much to be desired on this point. But in a case of this complexity I do not think that the present state of the statement of claim, already once amended and likely, I suspect, to be amended more than once hereafter, should be decisive on an interlocutory application of the nature with which this appeal is concerned. I attach more importance to the state of the evidence. There will be ample opportunity for the statement of claim to be tidied up well before the trial so as to accord with the case being advanced against the defendants as deposed to in the affidavit evidence.

So I turn to the evidence. As to that, the defendants' liability to account, like all the other claims against the defendants, is strenuously resisted by the defendants. But counsel for the respondents, rightly in my view, accepted for the purposes of this appeal that on the evidence, much disputed though it is, the plaintiffs have an arguable case that the defendants are required in equity to account for the profits in question. Counsel's case on this point on this appeal was that this claim is not proprietary in nature. The plaintiffs' claim, he submitted, is one of obligation leading (if established at the trial) to a money judgment. The claim, however much the plaintiffs contend otherwise, is not an ownership claim under which specific property from the moment it reached CMFE was impressed with a trust in favour of CML. For this distinction counsel relied on such well-known cases as *Lister & Co v Stubbs* (1890) 45 Ch D 1, [1886–90] All ER Rep 797.

The plaintiffs sought to distinguish these cases on the basis that here the money being claimed as an unauthorised profit emanated from CML. Contrast *Lister & Co v Stubbs*, where the money received as a bribe came to the defendant from a third party. Reliance was placed on the very recent decision of this court in *Guinness plc v Saunders* [1988] 2 All ER 940, [1988] 1 WLR 863. That case concerned a sum of £5·2m paid by Guinness to a company on behalf of Mr Ward under a contract made in breach of Mr Ward's fiduciary duty as a director of Guinness. The Court of Appeal upheld Sir Nicolas Browne-Wilkinson V-C's decision ([1988] BCLC 43), which included a declaration that Guinness was entitled to an equitable charge over any bank account or other property to the extent to which the balance in the account, or the property, derived from the sum of £5·2m or any part of that sum.

In turn counsel for the defendants sought to deflect that line of attack. He submitted that the crucial question is whether the money paid over by the plaintiff to the defendant, and received by him as an unauthorised profit, was the property of the plaintiff *before* the alleged wrongful act. If it was not, then there is no proprietary claim. On the facts in the instant case, he submitted that the money paid by CML to CMFE which the plaintiffs are asserting was impressed with a trust in favour of CML was not money which belonged to CML prior to the acts of which complaint is being made. He relied on his clients' evidence that all the foreign exchange transactions by CML with CMFE were backed by corresponding transactions between CML and a bank. So that the source of the money which passed to CMFE as its profits was not CML but was the banks under the corresponding backing transactions. The money only came to CML, and passed through CML, as part and parcel of the transactions now being impugned.

In my view these rival contentions raise a seriously arguable point, of some general importance, which it is undesirable for the court to pursue and decide on this interlocutory application. The underlying facts are far from clear. There is a dispute on the evidence on the way in which the impugned foreign exchange transactions were conducted. This is not a satisfactory basis for the court to decide a point of law which, as presented to us, may turn on fine questions of fact, presently obscure, concerning what sums of money actually passed from whom and to whom and when and in respect of what.

If the plaintiffs have a seriously arguable case that they had a proprietary interest, under a constructive trust, in certain sums of money paid to CMFE, then in my view the court has jurisdiction, under the principles set out in *A v C* [1980] 2 All ER 347, [1981] QB 956 and *Bankers Trust Co v Shapira* [1980] 3 All ER 353, [1980] 1 WLR 1274, to require the defendants to provide information about what has happened to those sums. In the exercise of his discretion Mervyn Davies J considered that an order to that effect should be made in this case. I can see no ground entitling or requiring this court to interfere with that exercise of his discretion.

Counsel for the defendants challenged the form of the order in several respects. I agree that the order, so far as it related to the disclosure of copies of documents this should be limited to documents in the possession, custody or power of the defendants. But I am unable to accept counsel's other criticisms of the width of the order. In particular, for the disclosure obligation to cease once the money (running into millions of pounds) paid to CMFE has been mixed with the general assets of that company would fail to recognise that, if there is a trust claim here, the plaintiffs may be entitled to a charge on a mixed fund held by CMFE or on property derived therefrom.

With that one minor variation, and subject to confining the order to foreign exchange transactions entered into with CMFE, I would dismiss the defendants' cross-appeal. There will, of course, be an undertaking by the plaintiffs not to make any use of the information provided by the defendants without leave of the court.

In his judgment, which I have had the advantage of reading in draft, Parker LJ has commented on the nature of Mareva proceedings. Of course, whether or not a restraint or disclosure order should be made will often be a matter of great importance to one or both of the parties in an action. But this is equally true of applications for other forms of interlocutory injunctive relief. I wish to associate myself, therefore, with Parker LJ's observations on this point. It is devoutly to be hoped that never again will there be an application for Mareva relief which will occupy the court for over five weeks.

Appeal allowed. Cross-appeal dismissed.

Solicitors: *Lovell White Durrant* (for the plaintiffs); *Hopkins & Wood* (for the first and second defendants).

Carolyn Toulmin   Barrister.

a # Chloride Industrial Batteries Ltd and another v F & W Freight Ltd

QUEEN'S BENCH DIVISION
SHEEN J
6, 13 OCTOBER 1988

b *Carriers – Contract – Carriage of goods – International carriage of goods by road – International carriage – Carriage between different countries – Carriage of goods by road from north of England to Jersey – Whether Jersey a different country – Whether carriage from England to Jersey international carriage – Carriage of Goods by Road Act 1965, s 9, Sch, art 1, para 1.*

c The provisions of the Convention on the Contract for the International Carriage of Goods by Road 1956, which has the force of law in the United Kingdom by virtue of the Carriage of Goods by Road Act 1965, do not apply to a contract for the carriage of goods by road from the north of England to Jersey, since 'country' in para 1^a of art 1 of the convention (which is set out in the schedule to the 1965 Act) refers to a sovereign state which is competent to enter into an international convention on its own behalf and
d Jersey is not a 'different country' from the United Kingdom for the purposes of para 1 because under s 9^b of the 1965 Act the convention can only become applicable to Jersey by an Order in Council directing that the Act shall extend to Jersey (see p 484 *a b d e*, *post*).

Notes

e For the international carriage of goods by road, see 5 Halsbury's Laws (4th edn) paras 417–418.

    For the Carriage of Goods by Road Act 1965, s 9, Sch 1, art 1, see 28 Halsbury's Statutes (3rd edn) 440, 442.

Case referred to in judgment

f *Stag Line Ltd v Foscolo Mango & Co Ltd* [1932] AC 328, [1931] All ER Rep 666, HL.

Preliminary issue

The plaintiffs, Chloride Industrial Batteries Ltd and the States of Jersey Telecommunications Board, by a writ issued on 5 November 1986 in the District Registry of Liverpool, claimed against the defendant, F & W Frieght Ltd, damages for breach of contract or
g negligence and/or breach of duty in respect of the total loss of a consignment of batteries which the defendant had agreed to carry under contract, at the request of the first plaintiff in November 1985, from the first plaintiff's premises in Manchester to the second plaintiff's premises in Jersey. On 19 April 1988 Master Warren, by the consent of the parties, ordered that the question whether the provisions of the Convention on the Contract for the International Carriage of Goods by Road 1956, as enacted into English
h law by the Carriage of Goods by Road Act 1965, applied to goods carried by road from Manchester of Jersey be tried as a preliminary issue. The facts are set out in the judgment.

Nigel Meeson for the plaintiffs.
George Leggatt for the defendant.

j *Cur adv vult*

---

a   Paragraph 1 is set out at p 482 *e*, post
b   Section 9, so far as material, provides: 'Her Majesty may by Order in Council direct that this Act shall extend, subject to such exceptions, adaptations and modifications as may be specified in the Order, to . . . (*b*) any of the Channel Islands . . .'

13 October. The following judgment was delivered.

a

SHEEN J. The court has before it a preliminary issue to be tried by order of Master Warren made on 19 April 1988 by consent of the parties. The question of be tried is whether the Convention on the Contract for the International Carriage of Goods by Road (Geneva; 19 May 1956) as enacted into English law by the Carriage of Goods by Road Act 1965 applies to the carriage forming the subject matter in this action, being from Manchester in England to Jersey.

b

The plaintiffs' claim arises out of a contract made in November 1985, whereby the defendant agreed to carry a consignment of batteries by road from the first plaintiff in Manchester to the second plaintiff in Jersey.

Section 1 of the Carriage of Goods by Road Act 1965 provides:

> 'Subject to the following provisions of this Act, the provisions of the Convention on the Contract for the International Carriage of Goods by Road . . . as set out in the Schedule to this Act, shall have the force of law in the United Kingdom so far as they relate to the rights and liabilities of persons concerned in the carriage of goods by road under a contract to which the Convention applies.'

c

As appears in its preamble, the convention was signed on 19 May 1956 by nine European states which recognised the desirability of standardising the conditions governing the contract for the international carriage of goods by road. Article 1, para 1 of the convention provides:

d

> 'This Convention shall apply to every contract for the carriage of goods by road in vehicles for reward, when the place of taking over of the goods and the place designated for delivery, as specified in the contract, are situated in two different countries, of which at least one is a Contracting country, irrespective of the place of residence and the nationality of the parties.'

e

It follows that the convention applies to the contract of carriage on which this action is founded if, but only if, the first plaintiff's premises in Manchester and the second plaintiff's premises in Jersey are in different countries within the meaning to be attributed to the word 'country' in art 1 of the convention.

f

The defendant put in evidence an affidavit of Caroline Dorey, who is a member of the Bar of England and Wales and an Advocate of the Royal Court of the Island of Jersey, in which she dealt with the constitutional position of the Island of Jersey and its relationship with the United Kingdom in this way:

> 'The Channel Islands were part of the Duchy of Normandy before the Norman conquest but remained in allegiance to the King of England when continental Normandy was lost in 1204. When later the ducal title was surrendered the King of England continued to rule the Islands as though he were Duke of Normandy, observing their laws customs and liberties; those were later confirmed by charters of successive sovereigns which secured for them their own judiciaries and freedom from process of English Courts and other important privileges of which the Islands are justly proud and which have always been respected. Although expressed in somewhat different terms in different ages, this has remained the essence of the relationship between the Islands and the Crown to the present day. After the separation of the Islands from Normandy and Norman administration the local institutions were gradually moulded over time very largely on local initiative to meet changing circumstances until their present constitutional position evolved. This evolution, however, did not at any time involve amalgamation with, or subjection to, the government of the United Kingdom and even today the Islands' link with the United Kingdom and the remainder of the Commonwealth is through the Sovereign as latter-day successor of the Dukes of Normandy. The constitutional

g

h

j

a   position of the Channel Islands is thus unique. They enjoy wide powers of self-government. However, this must not blind the observer to the exact constitutional position. The main feature of the constitutional relationship between the United Kingdom and the Island of Jersey is that the Crown has ultimate responsibility for the good government of the Island. The Crown acts through the Privy Council. It is the practice at the beginning of each reign to appoint Committees to the Committee of the Privy Council to entertain petitions from the Channel Islands. It is, in fact,

b   the Home Secretary who is the member of the Council primarily concerned with the affairs of the Island and is the channel of communication between Jersey and the Crown and the United Kingdom government. The most important point to note in relation to the present case is that Jersey is not a Sovereign State and that the United Kingdom Government is responsible for the Island's international and external relations. The status of the Island is that of a dependent territory. This has always

c   been the case notwithstanding the Island's claim to various privileges and liberties previously granted to it. Those relate to fiscal and domestic matters and no more.'

On behalf of the plaintiffs counsel submitted first that Jersey is not part of the United Kingdom, which is the country in which Manchester is situated. Furthermore, counsel relied on the fact that in the past Parliament has treated Jersey as a country. Counsel drew

d   my attention to s 1(4) of the Evidence (Foreign, Dominion and Colonial Documents) Act 1933, which provides:

'In this section the expression "country" means a Dominion, the Isle of Man, any of the Channel Islands, a British colony or protectorate, a foreign country, a colony or protectorate of a foreign country, or any mandated territory . . .'

e   In answer to this point counsel for the defendant submitted that, although there are occasions on which it is permissible to look at an earlier statute which is in pari materia in order to resolve an ambiguity in the statute under consideration, the 1933 Act is of no assistance to the court when it is interpreting the convention. Counsel reinforced this submission by drawing my attention to the words of Lord Macmillan in *Stag Line Ltd v Foscolo Mango & Co Ltd* [1932] AC 328 at 350, [1931] All ER Rep 666 at 667:

f   'It is important to remember that the [Carriage of Goods by Sea Act 1924] was the outcome of an International Conference and that the rules in the Schedule have an international currency. As these rules must come under the consideration of foreign Courts it is desirable in the interests of uniformity that their interpretation should not be rigidly controlled by domestic precedents of antecedent date, but rather that the language of the rules should be construed on broad principles of general

g   acceptation.'

The task of the court is to interpret the word 'country' in its context in art 1 of the convention. That word occurs twice in para 1 of art 1. It must be given the same meaning on both occasions.

On the second occasion on which the word is used, it is in the phrase 'a Contracting

h   country'. Counsel for the defendants submitted that its use in that context shows that it can only mean a state, as that term is used internationally, which has the power to enter into a convention. Its most important characteristic is its capacity to make treaties or enter into negotiations which another country or state. Counsel drew my attention to O'Connell *International Law* (2nd edn, 1970) vol 1, p 284, in which the author deals with

j   the attributes of statehood and says:

'The fully sovereign State is one which is not subordinate in its capacity for international action to any other legal entity . . . it is an organised community and this implies a population occupying a defined territory which it asserts to be exclusive to it, and which it administers through governmental agencies competent

to deal with foreign States in the way accepted as normal by the international community.'
         a

Counsel submitted that Jersey does not have these attributes. Jersey is not competent to enter into an international contract or convention on its own behalf. This is apparent from s 9 of the 1965 Act, which provides that Her Majesty may by Order in Council direct that this Act shall extend to, amongst other territories, any of the Channel Islands.

It is equally clear from para 3 of art 31 of the convention that in the convention the words 'country' and 'state' are synonymous. In the French text the word 'pays' is used on both occasions.
    b

Counsel for the plaintiffs developed an argument that as a matter of logic Jersey must be a different country from the United Kingdom for the purposes of the convention, because the convention applies in the United Kingdom and does not apply in Jersey. It would follow that if there was a contract for the carriage of goods by road from the United Kingdom to Turkey, which is not a party to the convention, the convention would apply, because the convention applies in the United Kingdom, but if the contract was from Jersey to Turkey, the convention would not apply because the convention does not apply in Jersey. Counsel submitted that it follows from this that the United Kingdom and Jersey are treated as different countries for the purposes of the convention.
    c

In answer to this, counsel for the defendant pointed out that the law of Jersey is different from the law of England and that the convention is not part of the law of Jersey. But it does not follow that Jersey is a different 'country' within the meaning of art 1, para 1. Indeed, if one asks the question, 'How would the convention become applicable to Jersey?' the answer is by an Order in Council directing that the 1965 Act shall extend to Jersey. This demonstrates that Jersey is part of one contracting country.
    d

I have been left in no doubt that for the purposes of the convention Jersey is not a different country from the United Kingdom and that the contract of carriage is not in respect of international carriage. Accordingly the answer to the question posed for the court is No.
    e

Order accordingly.

    f

Solicitors: *Hill Dickinson & Co*, Liverpool (for the plaintiffs); *Clyde & Co* (for the defendant).

K Mydeen Esq   Barrister.

Re Calmex Ltd
Calmex Ltd and another v C Lila Ltd and others

CHANCERY DIVISION (COMPANIES COURT)
HOFFMANN J
11 AUGUST 1988

Company – Compulsory winding up – Winding up order – Rescission – Application for rescission – Court's jurisdiction to rescind order – Company wound up by mistake – Removal of winding-up order from register – Whether order should be removed from register – Insolvency Act 1986, s 130(1) – Insolvency Rules 1986, rr 4.3, 7.47(1)(4).

A company which has been wound up by mistake instead of an unconnected company with a similar name is entitled to rescission of the winding-up order under r 7.47(1) and (4)[a] of the Insolvency Rules 1986, which gives the court jurisdiction to rescind the order within seven days of it being made, which time limit can be extended under r 4.3[b] of those rules where appropriate. The company is also entitled to have the order removed from the register since on the true construction of s 130(1)[c] of the Insolvency Act 1986 the registrar cannot retain in his records a winding-up order which the court has declared to be a nullity (see p 487 a c and p 488 a e g to j, post).

Notes
For rescission of a winding-up order, see 7(2) Halsbury's Laws (4th edn reissue) para 2027.

For the Insolvency Act 1986, s 130, see 4 Halsbury's Statutes (4th edn) (1987 reissue) 811.

For the Insolvency Rules 1986, rr 4.3, 7.47, see 3 Halsbury's Statutory Instruments (Grey Volume) 285, 441.

Cases referred to in judgment
Craig v Kanseen [1943] 1 All ER 108, [1943] KB 256, CA.
Intermain Properties Ltd, Re [1986] BCLC 265.
R v Registrar of Companies, ex p Central Bank of India [1986] 1 All ER 105, [1986] QB 1114, [1986] 2 WLR 177, CA.

Application
By notice of application dated 26 July 1988 the applicants, Calmex Ltd (the company) and Anthony Hanley, a director of the company, applied for, inter alia, orders that (i) the compulsory winding-up order made in respect of the company by Mr Registrar Bradburn on 2 December 1987 be rescinded and (ii) all copies of and references to the winding-up order appearing in the company's file at Companies House be removed from the file and destroyed. The respondents to the application were C Lila Ltd, on whose petition the company had been wound up, the Official Receiver and the Registrar of Companies. The petitioner and the Official Receiver took no part in the proceedings. The facts are set out in the judgment.

---

a   Rule 7.47, so far as material, is set out at p 486 j, post
b   Rule 4.3 provides: 'Where by any provision of the Act or the Rules about winding up, the time for doing anything is limited, the court may extend the time, either before or after it has expired, on such terms, if any, as it thinks fit.'
c   Section 130(1) provides: 'On the making of a winding-up order, a copy of the order must forthwith be forwarded by the company (or otherwise as may be prescribed) to the registrar of companies, who shall enter it in his records relating to the company.'

William Trower for the applicants.
Kevin Garnett for the Registrar of Companies.   *a*

HOFFMANN J. Calmex Ltd has been trading since 1985 as a haulage contractor in
Lancashire. On 2 December 1987 it was wound up by mistake. The petitioner had not
intended to have it wound up and the company knew nothing about the proceedings.
The petitioner's solicitor has explained in an affidavit that it was the result of a series of   *b*
errors. His client was owed money by an entirely unconnected company called Calmex
Fashions Ltd. But the petition as presented and advertised named Calmex Ltd. The
affidavit of service said that the petition had been served at the registered office of Calmex
Ltd by being left pinned to a panel at the bottom of the staircase, but the registered office
was in fact at a different address. Not surprisingly, no one appeared for the company on
the hearing before Mr Registrar Bradburn and he made the usual compulsory order.   *c*
    Unusually, the order appears to have been drawn up before the mistake was discovered.
On 11 January 1988 an application was made by the petitioner's solicitors for a stay of
the winding up, purportedly in the name of Mr Anthony Hanley, a director and
contributory of the company. The order was made by Mervyn Davies J on 1 February
1988. Mr Hanley says that he knew no more about this application than he had about
the original order. It was made on the authority of his accountant, who presumably   *d*
learnt of the winding-up order via the true registered office and later told Mr Hanley that
he had assumed that the stay would put right the mistake and decided not to bother him
with the matter.
    The first that Mr Hanley knew of the winding up was at the end of March, when he
was arranging finance to buy a new tractor unit for the company's business. The finance
house told him that his bank reference and accounts were satisfactory but its credit   *e*
reference agency had told them that the company was in liquidation. It refused to
proceed with the transaction. In April there was a similar incident. A sub-contractor
failed to perform a haulage contract and said afterwards that the credit reference agency
had told him that Calmex Ltd had been blacklisted. As a result, the company lost the
main contract. Last month, the suppliers of a photocopier came to repossess the machine   *f*
because the finance house had turned down the company's application because of an
adverse report from a credit reference agency. This time the company's solicitors
managed to persuade the finance house that the winding-up order had been made in
error.
    Counsel for the company now moves for an order that the winding-up order be
rescinded and that the relevant documents be removed from the company's records at
Companies House. The respondents are the petitioning creditor and Official Receiver,   *g*
who have no interest in the matter and do not appear, and the Registrar of Companies
who is indifferent to whether or not the order is rescinded but says that the court has no
jurisdiction to order the removal of documents from the file and, even if it has, should
not do so.
    The first question is whether the winding-up order can be rescinded. Until the   *h*
Insolvency Rules 1986, SI 1986/1925, came into force, a winding-up order could not be
rescinded after it had been drawn up. The only remedy was to apply for a stay: see *Re
Intermain Properties Ltd* [1986] BCLC 265. But r 7.47(1) of the 1986 rules says:

    'Every court having jurisdiction under the Act to wind up companies may review,
    rescind or vary any order made by it in the exercise of that jurisdiction.'
                                                                          j
That power is expressed in completely general terms and in my judgment gives me
jurisdiction to rescind the order notwithstanding that it has already been drawn up and,
indeed, that proceedings have been stayed. Rule 7.47(4) says:

    'Any application for the rescission of a winding-up order shall be made within 7
    days after the date on which the order was made.'

This time limit will usually be sufficient to ensure that a rescission order is in fact made

before the order has been drawn up. But r 4.3 gives the court power to extend the time
a limit in an appropriate case. I think that in the exceptional circumstances of this case it
would be right to do so.

As for the grounds for exercising the jurisdiction, they are plain enough. As Lord
Greene MR said in *Craig v Kanseen* [1943] 1 All ER 108 at 113, [1943] KB 256 at 262:

> '. . . an order which can properly be described as a nullity is something which the
b > person affected by it is entitled *ex debito justitiae* to have set aside . . . Apart from
> proper *ex parte* proceedings, the idea that an order can validly be made against a
> man who has had no notification of any intention to apply for it is one which has
> never been adopted in England. To say that an order of that kind is to be treated as
> a mere irregularity, and not something which is affected by fundamental vice . . .
> cannot be sustained.'

c   The company is therefore entitled to have the order rescinded. I declare it to have been
a nullity and it follows that the order staying proceedings had nothing on which it could
fasten and was also a nullity.

The next question is whether anything can be done about the register. This is a serious
matter for the company because credit reference agencies can in good faith give reports
which cause great damage but are based on mistaken information or inferences. For
d example, inquiries by the company's solicitors from a number of credit reference agencies
showed that five of them had on their files copies of the winding-up order but no copy
of the stay order. Furthermore, the hire-purchase company concerned in the photocopier
transaction said that its usual policy was to refuse credit to a company against which a
winding-up order had been made even if the proceedings had been subsequently stayed.
This is not in the ordinary case an unreasonable attitude, because the usual reason for an
e order staying the winding up is that at the thirteenth hour a director or contributory has
paid off the debts due to the petitioning and supporting creditors and the costs of the
Official Receiver. The fact that a winding-up order was made is therefore still a black
mark against the company. It can however be very unfair in an exceptional case like the
present where the stay was ordered because the winding-up order should never have
been made. But credit reference agencies operate by using general criteria which can be
f programmed into a computer and they cannot be expected to inquire into the individual
circumstances of each case.

It is impossible to eliminate mistakes in searching official records or injustices caused
by applying generalisations to exceptional cases. But I think that one should try so far as
possible to minimise the risks. The question here is whether anything further can be
done which is consistent with the registrar's statutory duties and whether the court has
g power to order the registrar to do it.

The effect of s 130(1) of the Insolvency Act 1986 and r 4.21(3) of the 1986 rules is that
'On the making of a winding-up order' the Official Receiver is under a statutory duty to
forward a copy to the registrar, who 'shall enter it in his records relating to the company'.
Section 709(1) of the Companies Act 1985 entitles anyone to inspect a copy of 'any
h document kept by the registrar' and by s 711(1) the registrar must give notice in the
Gazette of his receipt of various classes of documents, including any winding-up order.
There are no provisions for the removal of any documents from the registrar's keeping
except by way of the removal to the Public Record Office of the records of dissolved
companies and the destruction of accounts and annual returns more than ten years old,
subject to the retention of copies.

j   Is the registrar under a duty to retain in his records a copy of a winding-up order which
the court has rescinded on the grounds that the company was never served and the entire
proceedings were a mistake? In *Craig v Kanseen* [1943] 1 All ER 108 at 113, [1943] KB
256 at 262 Lord Greene MR described an order made in such circumstances as a 'nullity'.
As I said in *Re Intermain Properties Ltd* [1986] BCLC 265 at 266 the word 'nullity' can be
rather slippery and Lord Greene MR's reference to the order being 'set aside' make it
difficult to know whether he regarded the order as incapable of having any legal
consequences whatever. But I need not explore the meaning of nullity at this level of

generality: the relevant question here is whether the order is a nullity for the purposes of s 130(1) of the 1986 Act. In my judgment it is. The present question could not have *a* arisen before the 1986 rules because the order could not have been rescinded after it had been drawn up and registered. But, now that it can be, I think that justice requires s 130(1) to be construed to give effect to the nullity principle stated by Lord Greene MR.

The registrar's view, as put to the court by counsel, is that the removal of the order would be a falsification of history. The indelible fact is that the order was made. But I do not think that the purpose of the register is simply to chronicle events. Anyone who *b* wants information about the minor fiasco which occurred in Mr Registrar Bradburn's court on 2 December 1987 will be able to find it in the records of the court. The companies register is to record information which may be useful to persons dealing with the company. I can see no purpose in recording the fact that the company was a victim of mistaken identity as a consequence of which the court purported to make an order which had no legal consequences and was afterwards declared to have been a nullity. On *c* the other hand, as we have seen, the existence of the record is a potential source of serious injustice to the company.

Counsel for the registrar expressed concern about the confusion which might be caused if a search of the register failed to disclose a document which had been present when a previous search had been made. He told me that in cases in which, by administrative error, a document had been wrongly placed in the file, the registrar's *d* practice was to remove it but to leave a note giving a brief description of the document and saying that it had been inserted by mistake and subsequently removed. In such cases the microfiche of the file which was made available to searchers would have to be reconstructed. This procedure seems to me entirely sensible and I see no reason why it cannot be followed in this case. The winding-up and stay orders can be removed and replaced by a note saying 'Winding-up order made in error and subsequent stay of that *e* order removed from the file' or words to that effect.

The registrar was also worried that the precedent set by this application might lead to many others which would add to the burdens of his office. I do not think that it would. Although cases of mistaken identity in the Companies Court are not rare, they are almost always discovered as soon as the Official Receiver notifies the company of the order and an application for rescission is made before the order has been drawn up. Cases like the *f* present are likely to be infrequent and I think that any administrative burdens placed on the registrar are outweighed by the prejudice which might otherwise be caused to the companies.

Finally, counsel for the registrar submitted that the court had no jurisdiction to tell the registrar to remove documents from the register. I would be surprised if a company had no remedy against the registrar if he chose to include in the file a document which *g* was prejudicial to the company and which he had no statutory duty to keep. And I have held that, on the true construction of s 130(1) of the 1986 Act, the registrar has no duty to retain entered in his records a winding-up order which the court has declared to be a nullity. I suspect that the remedy would be by way of judicial review, but counsel for the registrar said that the registrar did not wish to take any point on the procedure by *h* which the matter has been brought before the court, but contended that even by way of judicial review there was no jurisdiction. In my judgment the court does in principle have jurisdiction according to ordinary public law principles to control the way in which the registrar carries out his statutory duties, subject to any specific exclusions of that jurisdiction or the evidence on which it could be founded, as in *R v Registrar of Companies, ex p Central Bank of India* [1986] 1 All ER 105, [1986] QB 1114. I will therefore make an *j* order that the winding-up and stay orders be removed from the registrar's files, subject, if the registrar thinks it desirable, to their replacement by a note in terms on which I shall invite the views of counsel.

Order accordingly.

Solicitors: *Joynson-Hicks* (for the applicants); *Treasury Solicitor.*

Hazel Hartman   Barrister.

a

The Rosa S

QUEEN'S BENCH DIVISION (ADMIRALTY COURT)
HOBHOUSE J
7, 8, 21 JULY 1988

b *Shipping – Carriage by sea – Damages for breach of contract – Loss of or damage to goods – Limitation of liability – Liability determined by reference to gold value – Shipowners admitting liability in respect of damage to goods – Provisions of bill of lading limiting liability to £100 – Cargo owners claiming damages of £100 expressed as a gold value figure – Whether shipowners' liability limited to '£100' or '£100 sterling gold value' – Hague Rules, art IV, r 5, art IX.*

c The defendant shipowners shipped a complete aluminium continuous casting and rolling plant, consisting of a consignment of 222 cases, on board their vessel for carriage from Italy to Mombasa, Kenya. The bill of lading issued by the defendants was subject to the provisions of the Hague Rules. On discharge one of the cases and its contents was found to be damaged. The loss suffered by the plaintiffs exceeded £K100,000. The defendants admitted liability, but submitted that art IV, r 5[a] of the Hague Rules limited their
d liability to '£100 per package or unit, or the equivalent of that sum in other currency' and claimed that their liability was accordingly limited to £100 actual value. The plaintiff cargo owners submitted that r 5 was to be read in conjunction with art IX[b], which provided that 'The monetary units mentioned in [the Hague Rules] are to be taken to be gold value' so that '£100' was to be read as '£100 sterling gold value'. The plaintiffs claimed that the gold value of £stg100 was the value of 732·238 g of fine gold in
e accordance with the Coinage Act 1971 and that since the sterling value of 732·238 g of fine gold at the date of delivery of the cargo, which was the relevant date for assessment of the defendants' liability, was £6,630·50, that amount, converted into Kenyan pounds, was the correct limit of the defendants' liability.

Held – On its true construction art IV, r 5 of the Hague Rules was to be read in
f conjunction with art IX, which clearly provided that the gold value of sterling was to be used as a measure of value of the monetary units mentioned in the rules. Accordingly, '£100' in r 5 was to be understood as '£100 sterling gold value', and the correct limit of the defendants' liability in respect of the damaged cargo was therefore the sterling value of 732·238 g of fine gold at the date of delivery of the cargo, ie £6,630·50. It followed that the plaintiffs were entitled to recover £K6,491·25, being the equivalent sum in
g Kenyan currency (see p 494 *c*, p 496 *d*, p 497 *b h* and p 499 *d e*, *post*).

Feist v Société Intercommunale Belge d'Electricité [1933] All ER Rep 228 applied.
Dictum of Morris LJ in *Treseder-Griffin v Co-op Insurance Society Ltd* [1956] 2 All ER 33 at 41 distinguished.

Notes
h For limitation of the liability of a carrier of goods by sea, see 43 Halsbury's Laws (4th edn) para 786.
For the Hague Visby Rules (which revised the Hague Rules), see ibid paras 759–793.
For the Coinage Act 1971, see 10 Halsbury's Statutes (4th edn) 181.

Cases referred to in judgment
j *Adamastos Shipping Co Ltd v Anglo-Saxon Petroleum Co Ltd* [1958] 1 All ER 725, [1959] AC 133, [1958] 2 WLR 688, HL.

---

a   Rule 5, so far as material, is set out at p 492 *b*, post
b   Article IX is set out at p 492 *c d*, post

Adelaide Electric Supply Co Ltd v Prudential Assurance Co Ltd [1934] AC 122, [1933] All ER
     Rep 82, HL.

Agemar Srl v Siat [1979] Dir maritt 215, Corte d'appello di Trieste.

Air Cameroun v Cie Maritime des Chargeurs Révnis [1967] Jurisprudence Français 675, Cour
     d'appel de Rouen.

Brown Boveri (Australia) Pty Ltd v Baltic Shipping Co (31 July 1986, unreported), NSW SC.

Despina R, The [1979] 1 All ER 421, [1979] AC 685, [1978] 3 WLR 804, HL.

Dobell & Co v Steamship Rossmore Co Ltd [1895] 2 QB 408, [1895–9] All ER Rep 885, CA.

Doroty, The [1979] ETL 550, Can Fed Ct.

Feist v Société Intercommunale Belge d'Electricité [1934] AC 161, [1933] All ER Rep 228, HL.

Fiat Co v American Export Lines Inc [1965] AMC 384, Corte d'appello di Firenze.

Holyman (William) & Sons Pty Ltd v Foy & Gibson Pty Ltd (1945) 73 CLR 622, Aust HC.

Hussain v Great Eastern Shipping Co [1960] ILR Ker 1028, Kerala CA.

Miliangos v George Frank (Textiles) Ltd [1975] 3 All ER 801, [1976] AC 443, [1975] 3 WLR
     758, HL.

New Brunswick Rly Co v British and French Trust Corp [1938] 4 All ER 747, [1939] AC 1,
     HL.

Norway and Asia Lines v Adamjee Jute Mills Ltd [1981] Bangladesh LD 152, Bangladesh CA.

Pyrene Co Ltd v Scindia Steam Navigation Co Ltd [1954] 2 All ER 158, [1954] 2 QB 402,
     [1954] 2 WLR 1005.

SpA Carniti v SpA Comesmar [1979] Dirmaritt 90, Tribunale di Genova.

Treseder-Griffin v Co-op Insurance Society Ltd [1956] 2 All ER 33, [1956] 2 QB 127, [1956]
     2 WLR 866, CA.

Vishva Pratibha, The [1980] 2 MLJ 265, Singapore HC.

Cases also cited

Auckland Corp v Alliance Assurance Co Ltd [1937] 1 All ER 645, [1937] AC 587, PC.

Campos v Kentucky and Indiana Terminal Railroad Co [1962] 2 Lloyd's Rep 459.

De Bueger v J Ballantyne & Co Ltd [1938] 1 All ER 701, [1938] AC 452, PC.

Maurice v Goldsbrough Mort & Co Ltd [1939] 3 All ER 63, [1939] AC 452, PC.

Ottoman Bank of Nicosia v Chakarian [1937] 4 All ER 570, [1938] AC 260, PC.

Pendle & Rivett Ltd v Ellerman Lines Ltd (1927) 29 Ll L Rep 133.

Syndic in Bankruptcy of Nasrallah Khoury v Khayat [1943] 2 All ER 406, [1943] AC 507, PC.

Thomas (T W) & Co Ltd v Portsea Streamship Co Ltd [1912] AC 1, HL.

Woodhouse AC Israel Cocoa Ltd SA v Nigerian Produce Marketing Co Ltd [1972] 2 All ER 271,
     [1972] AC 741, HL.

Action

The plaintiffs, Kaluworks Ltd, the owners of a cargo shipped on board the vessel Rosa S,
by a writ issued on 21 November 1985, brought an Admiralty action in rem against the
defendants, the owners of the Rosa S, claiming damages for breach of contract and/or
duty in and about the loading, handling, custody, care and discharge of their cargo and
the carriage thereof from Leghorn, Italy to Mombasa, Kenya on board the Rosa S in 1984.
The carriage of the cargo was pursuant to the terms and conditions of a bill of lading
which was itself subject to the provisions of the Hague Rules. The issue which arose was
how the defendants' liability in respect of the damaged cargo was to be determined under
the Hague Rules. The facts are set out in the judgment.

Julian Malins for the plaintiffs.
A E Diamond QC for the defendants.

Cur adv vult

21 July. The following judgment was delivered.

a

HOBHOUSE J. On 9 April 1984 at Leghorn in Italy there was loaded by New Hunter Engineering SpA of Turin on board the defendants' vessel Rosa S a consignment of 222 cases consisting of one complete aluminium continuous casting and rolling plant together with related ancillaries for carriage to Mombasa in Kenya. The carriage was covered by a bill of lading in the English language issued on behalf of the defendants. The goods were

b consigned to a firm called Kaluworks Ltd of Mombasa who are the relevant plaintiffs in this action. When the consignment came to be discharged at Mombasa it was found that one of the cases, together with its contents, was badly damaged. The net loss suffered by the plaintiffs in respect of that damage was £K107,758·53. It is agreed by the parties that the carriage of the goods on board the Rosa S was subject to the provisions of the International Convention for the Unification of certain Rules of Law relating to Bills of

c Lading (the Hague Rules) (Brussels, 25 August 1924; TS 17 (1931); Cmd 3806). The defendants further admit that the damage was caused by their breach of their contractual duties as carriers under the bill of lading. The dispute between the parties is what is the limit of the defendants' liability to the plaintiffs in respect of such breach and damage. No value of the goods was declared by the shippers or inserted in the bill of lading.

Clause 2 of the bill of lading provided that:

d
> 'Any dispute arising out of this bill of lading shall be governed by English law and . . . the High Court of Justice in London shall have exclusive jurisdiction . . .'

Clause 1 of the bill of lading was a paramount clause, which read:

> 'It is mutually agreed that this bill of lading shall have effect subject to the
e provisions of the International convention relating to bills of lading dated Brussels 25th August 1924 hereafter called the Hague Rules except where legislation giving effect to the Hague Rules as amended by the protocol signed at Brussels on 23rd February 1968 (hereafter called the Hague Visby Rules) is compulsorily applicable, in which case this bill of lading shall have effect subject to such legislation. Neither the Hague Rules nor the Hague Visby Rules shall apply where the goods carried
f hereunder are live animals. Nothing in this bill of lading shall be deemed to be a surrender by the carrier of any of his rights or immunities or an increase of any of his responsibilities under the said rules or enactments and/or their protocols. If anything herein contained is inconsistent with the said legislation or Hague Rules or Hague Visby Rules it shall, to the extent and on the occasion of such inconsistency and no further, be null and void.'

g
At the material time Italy had not become a contracting party to the Hague-Visby Rules, hence the parties' agreement that this bill of lading was subject to the provisions of the 1924 convention, the Hague Rules.

Clause 28 of the bill of lading provided, inter alia:

h
> 'Neither the carrier nor the ship shall in any event be or become liable for any loss or damage to or in connection with goods in an amount exceeding pound sterling 100 per package or unit . . .'

The defendants before me somewhat faintly sought to rely on this clause as showing a contractual intention that, whatever might be the true effect of the Hague Rules, they
j were entitled to a limit of £stg100 and no more. This contention of course could not survive the concluding words of the clause paramount ('if anything herein contained is inconsistent with the . . . Hague Rules . . . it shall . . . be null and void') and art III, r 8 of the Hague Rules, which provides that any clause in a contract of carriage purporting to relieve the carrier from liability or lessening his liability otherwise than as provided in the rules is to be null and void and of no effect. Accordingly, the question of what is the

limit of the defendant's liability under this bill of lading must be ascertained by reference
to the provisions of the Hague Rules and those alone.

The only authorititive text of the Hague·Rules is the French text. The bureau of the
conference did however authorise an English translation. During the argument before
me the parties have been content to proceed on the basis of the English translation subject
to two points to which I will refer. In this translation art IV, r 5 reads:

> 'Neither the carrier nor the ship shall in any event be or become liable for any loss
> or damage to or in connection with goods in an amount exceeding £100 per package
> or unit, or the equivalent of that sum in other currency, unless the nature and value
> of such goods have been declared by the shipper before shipment and inserted in
> the bill of lading . . .'

Article IX provides:

> 'The monetary units mentioned in this Convention are to be taken to be gold
> value. Those contracting states in which the pound sterling is not a monetary unit
> reserve to themselves the right of translating the sums indicated in this convention
> in terms of pound sterling into terms of their own monetary system in round
> figures. The national laws may reserve to the debtor the right of discharging his
> debt in national currency according to the rate of exchange prevailing on the day of
> the arrival of the ship at the port of discharge of the goods concerned.'

In art IV, r 5 the French text reads '100 Livres sterling'; therefore a better translation
would be '£100 sterling'. In the third sentence of art IX the French phrase is 'réserver au
débiteur la faculté de se libérer' which perhaps has been too narrowly translated by using
the words 'debtor' and 'debt' as opposed to for example 'the party liable' and 'his liability'.
No submission was advanced before me by either party which depended on this
refinement of the precise meaning of the French text of art IX.

The plaintiffs submit that art IV, r 5 must be read with the first sentence of art IX so
that instead of saying '£100 sterling' it says '£100 sterling gold value'. They say that the
gold content of £stg100 was in 1924 defined as a matter of English law by the Coinage
Act 1870, and was at the date of this bill of lading, and is at today's date, defined by the
Coinage Act 1971, as being 798·805 g of gold of a millesimal fineness 916·66, which is
the same as 732·238 g of fine gold. They say that the gold value is therefore the value of
that quantity of gold. Taking the relevant date for the assessment of the defendants'
liability as being the date of the delivery of the goods, which the parties have agreed can
be treated as 1 June 1984, this gives a value of the gold expressed in sterling as being
£6,630·50. They therefore say that that is the value which expresses the relevant limit
applicable to their claim. Their claim is for a sum in Kenyan pounds. That sum of
sterling converted into Kenyan pounds at the same date gives a limit of liability expressed
in Kenyan pounds of £6,491·25. That is what the plaintiffs say is the correct limit of the
defendants' liability in respect of the plaintiffs' claim in the present action.

The defendants on the other hand say that the correct limit is £stg100 in today's
money or its nominal equivalent expressed in Kenyan currency. They say that all
considerations of gold value should be excluded. They say that art IV should be construed
on its own without recourse to art IX, that art IX is in any event too unclear and unspecific
to qualify the words of art IV. As a matter of English law a gold clause to be effective
must have a greater clarity and degree of definition than art IX contains. They sought to
rely on historical arguments to support the conclusion that the Hague Rules treated
sterling currency as a nominal money of account and not any gold value of sterling. They
finally argued that if any gold value was to be taken into account it was simply the
quantity of gold that £stg100 would at the date of the accrual of the cause of action have
bought and that its purpose was simply to provide stability in terms of sterling between
the date of the accrual of the cause of action and any date when judgment might
thereafter be given.

a Some preliminary observations need to be made. The court in the present case is concerned to construe a contract, the contract contained in this bill of lading. The parties to this bill of lading have choosen to refer to the provisions of an international convention. International conventions are agreements between states, not between private individuals, nor as a matter of English law do they of themselves have any legal effect in English law unless made law by some statute.

b Under the Carriage of Goods by Sea Act 1924, the substance of what were subsequently to become the Hague Rules were not made part of English law as such, but were compulsorily incorporated into bills of lading issued in this country. That Act was based on the draft Hague Rules; art IX of the final Hague Rules was not part of the draft rules yet the United Kingdom legislature chose to include in the draft rules as scheduled to the 1924 Act a sentence which corresponded to the first sentence of art IX of the Hague Rules as it was finally agreed to. The 1924 Act has been repealed by the Carriage of Goods by

c Sea Act 1971 and was not in force at the date of this bill of lading. I am not concerned in this case with any problem that there might have been of construing the 1924 Act. The way in which the gold value provision has been included in the schedule to the 1924 Act has been described in the leading text books on carriage of goods by sea, Scrutton on Charterparties (18th edn, 1974) p 449 and Carver on Carriage by Sea (12th edn, 1971) vol 1, para 307, as giving rise to 'difficult' or 'very difficult' questions. The editors of Scrutton

d resolved those questions in an way that is consistent with the submissions of the plaintiffs before me; the editor of Carver expressed a view which was more favourable to the defendants' approach but which the defendants were not able fully to adopt. Dr F A Mann in The Legal Aspect of Money (4th edn, 1982) p 154 has commented: 'It cannot be readily appreciated why the City of London found the Act of 1924 so mysterious.' Dr Mann clearly believes that the view expressed by Scrutton and the approach adopted by

e the plaintiffs before me are correct. I recognise that there may have been difficulties under the 1924 Act in precisely understanding the intentions of the draftsman. There could be an argument that the Act was stating what was the monetary limit for the purposes of English law and the reference to gold value was only appropriate and necessary where the limit had to be assessed in some other currency. In this connection it is relevant to note that, in their Hague Rules legislation, many other countries have

f chosen to exercise the liberty to express the limit in their own currencies in a fixed amount; for example in the United States Carriage of Goods by Sea Act 1936 it is $US500. But these considerations of domestic legislation do not arise in the present case. What the parties have chosen to refer to in their contract is not any domestic legislation but instead the provisions of an international convention.

g A second preliminary observation is that where a bill of lading is to have effect subject to the provisions of another document the parties must be taken to have intended to give effect to those provisions as contractual provisions between themselves and not as provisions having some separate or different validity and effect: see Dobell & Co v Steamship Rossmore Co Ltd [1895] 2 QB 408, [1895–9] All ER Rep 885 and Adamastos Shipping Co Ltd v Anglo-Saxon Petroleum Co Ltd [1958] 1 All ER 725, [1959] AC 133. The provisions which

h have no relevance to the contract between the parties to the bill of lading are not incorporated; the construction of the provisions must be a construction which is to be given to them as contractual provisions. Therefore I question the extent to which the defendants were right to advance before me arguments derived from the monetary history of the United Kingdom in the 1920s. However I do accept that one must take into account that the bill of lading expressly identifies the provisions as having originally

j formed part of and as deriving from the Hague Rules which were made in 1924 and which have as their purpose, both express and implicit, the furtherance of international uniformity in the rules governing bill of lading contracts. One must not expect, nor must one treat the parties to this bill of lading as if they expected, that the provisions of the rules were in all respects drafted as contractual provisions or provisions of domestic legislation. This is particularly the case with regard to art IX itself. Two of the sentences of art IX can solely have relevance in relation to the freedom of action of contracting states and the domestic legislation that they may pass. They will not themselves have *a* direct effect in relation to this bill of lading contract. But those two sentences, like the preamble to the rules, are part of the rules and are properly to be taken into account in construing the provisions to which the parties to this bill of lading have said that their ' contract is to be subject. If, for example, the parties had wished to incorporate as a matter of contract the United States Carriage of Goods by Sea Act 1936 they could have done so, in which case no question of gold values would have arisen. What they have chosen to *b* do is to incorporate the provisions of the Hague Rules which do make reference to gold values.

Turning now to the Hague Rules themselves, it seems to me clear beyond argument that the first sentence of art IX is intended to qualify the reference to '£100 sterling' in art IV, r 5. No other purpose for the inclusion in the rules of the relevant sentence of art IX has been suggested. There is no reason to suppose that those words were not *c* intended to have any effect. They were clearly intended to have the effect of expressing the sterling figure as a gold value figure. This, in respect of the 1924 Act, was regarded as too obvious for argument by Devlin J in *Pyrene Co Ltd v Scindia Steam Navigation Co Ltd* [1954] 2 All ER 158 at 160, [1954] 2 QB 402 at 413, where he said: 'The limit stated in that rule is £100, but this is subject to art. IX which prescribes that the figure is to be taken to be the gold value.' *d*

Whether one looks at the matter as at the date of the Hague Rules or as at the date of this bill of lading contract the provision that the limit in art IV, r 5 is to be treated as a gold value presents no problem. As previously stated the Coinage Acts of the United Kingdom define the gold content of the pound sterling. As Morris LJ put it in *Treseder-Griffin v Co-op Insurance Society Ltd* [1956] 2 All ER 33 at 40, [1956] 2 QB 127 at 151: 'I take the word "sterling" as referring to English currency. I consider that "gold sterling" *e* denotes gold coins.' The 1971 Act identifies various denominations of coin including gold coins (see also the Currency Act 1983). It specifies their weight and fineness. It is therefore still possible, as a matter of English law, to answer the question what is the gold content of £1 gold sterling. (It is also notable that the 1971 and 1983 Acts similarly preserve the concept of gold coins as currency; s 2(1) expressly provides that gold coins can be legal tender.) The provisions of the 1971 Act create no relevant conflict with those *f* of the 1870 Act; under both it is possible to identify the monetary unit that is being referred to. Therefore there is no uncertainty about, or inability to ascertain, what is the gold value which the parties were by their contract agreeing should be the limit of the carriers' liability.

In an attempt to undermine this conclusion the defendants referred me to what was said by Morris LJ in the *Treseder-Griffin* case [1956] 2 All ER 33 at 41, [1956] 2 QB 127 at *g* 152. That case involved a lease dated 30 December 1938 of two shops in Queen Street, Cardiff, for a period of 99 years from 1933. The lease provided for the payment 'yearly during the said term either in gold sterling or Bank of England notes to the equivalent value in gold sterling the rent of £1,900 ... by equal quarterly payments'. This was construed by the majority of the Court of Appeal as being a gold payment clause, not a *h* gold value clause and, in so far as it stipulated for payment in gold, as being illegal or ineffective. The judgments of the majority were strongly influenced by what they regarded as the public policy regarding such a provision. Morris LJ said:

'The lease is for a term which ends on June 24, 2029. It is clearly impossible to forecast whether within that period gold coins will be minted and re-introduced for *j* ordinary and general use. The Coinage Act, 1870, prescribed the standard of both gold and silver coins. No one can foresee whether, if before the year 2029 gold coins come back into use, they will be coins of the weight and fineness specified in the Act of 1870. It is I think of significance that the lease refers merely to "gold sterling". There is no provision that the gold sterling is to be of specified weight and fineness.

a   There is no wording comparable with that in *Feist* v. *Société Intercommunale Belge d'Electricité* ([1934] AC 161, [1933] All ER Rep 228); the obligation imposed by the bonds there in question was to pay "the sum of £100 in sterling in gold coin of the United Kingdom of or equal to the standard weight and fineness existing on Sept. 1, 1928.'"

b   I do not find that this passage assists me in the present case. Morris LJ was concerned with a situation where the defined obligation was going to have to continue until the year 2029 and was affected by what he regarded as a hiatus in the relevant legislation. On any view those problems do not affect the construction of this bill of lading contract. At the time the contract was made the gold content of the pound sterling was defined and ascertainable. It was in fact the same content as had existed in 1924. There is no element of uncertainty. There is no problem of having to look forward to some data far into the future. Further, there is no question of any illegality in the present case nor is there any
c   question of the infringement of any principle of public policy. In respect of this contract the parties were at liberty to fix the limit of liability of the carrier in any way they chose and by reference to any money account or any unit of value.

    The purpose of any gold clause must be to escape from the principle of nominalism. As stated in the *Feist* case [1934] AC 161, [1933] All ER Rep 228, which must be regarded
d   as the leading authority on this point, the gold clause if it is to be effective for this purpose must be a gold value clause, not merely a gold payment clause. The decision of their Lordships' House was given by Lord Russell, with whose speech all other members of the House agreed. He said ([1934] AC 161 at 172, [1933] All ER Rep 228 at 233):

    'In my opinion the purpose can be discerned from clause 4, in which the reference to gold coin of the United Kingdom is clearly not a reference to the mode of
e   payment but to the measure of the Company's obligation. So too, condition 6, which again is a clause not directed to mode of payment, but to describing and measuring liability, shows that the words are used as such a measure. In just the same way I think that in clauses 1 and 2 of the the bond the parties are referring to gold coin of the United Kingdom of a specific standard of weight and fineness not as being the mode in which the Company's indebtedness is to be discharged, but as
f   being the means by which the amount of that indebtedness is to measured and ascertained.'

    There can be no doubt into which category the provisions of the Hague Rules come. The function of art IV, r 5 is to provide the measure of the limit of liability of the carrier. The first sentence of art 9 expressly refers to gold value.
g   The defendants also sought to rely on *New Brunswick Rly Co v British and French Trust Corp* [1938] 4 All ER 747, [1939] AC 1. In that case the House of Lords followed and applied the *Feist* case. Lord Maugham LC said ([1938] 4 All ER 747 at 754, [1939] AC 1 at 18): '. . . I do not think that a construction on the lines of the *Feist* decision ought to be adopted unless the so-called gold clause obligation is expressed in clear language . . .' And Lord Wright said ([1938] 4 All ER 747 at 764, [1939] AC 1 at 35): 'If it had been intended
h   to apply the gold obligation to the interest, that should have been done by precise words, as was done in *Feist's* case . . .' There the House of Lords was concerned with the question whether the gold value provision should apply both to the liability in respect of principal and the liability in respect of interest. They held that as regards the former the intention of the document was clear but as regards the latter it was not.

    In the present case I consider that the intention of the parties is clear and sufficiently
j   precise. I am concerned with the construction of a commercial contract between a goods owner and a carrier and there is no reason why the ordinary rules of construction should not be applied to such a document; indeed, in so far as there is any rule of certainty applicable to such documents, it is that the carrier, if he wishes to exclude or limit his liability, must do so by clear terms. The argument of the defendants in the present case stands that principle on its head.

The defendants next sought to rely on a historical argument. They attempted to
suggest that in 1924, whilst the international community might have been concerned   *a*
about the stability of other currencies, there was no concern about the stability of the
pound sterling or any reason to suppose that they might be interested in referring to a
gold value for the pound sterling. I was taken by counsel for the defendants through a
series of English statutes starting with the Bank of England Act 1833 and ending with
the Coinage Act 1971; I was referred to various summaries of the historical development
of the relationship between the pound sterling and the value of gold given in speeches of   *b*
Lord Wright particularly that in *Adelaide Electric Supply Co Ltd v Prudential Assurance Co
Ltd* [1934] AC 122 at 153–155, [1933] All ER Rep 82 at 94, and the useful and authoritive
exposition in Mann *The Legal Aspect of Money* (4th edn, 1982) ch 2. As already indicated I
doubt whether such material has any relevance to the construction of the contract with
which I am concerned, but in any event it merely served to reinforce the plaintiffs'
submissions and undermine those of the defendants. In the 1920s a number of currencies   *c*
were under very strong inflationary pressures. The question of the gold standard and of
the gold backing of currencies was in the forefront of every economist's mind. The
degree to which the English paper currency was to be convertible into gold and the
extent to which the United Kingdom should adhere to the gold standard or to a bullion
standard were the subject of successive changes of policy until the United Kingdom
finally abandoned the gold standard in 1931. The material placed before me by counsel   *d*
for the defendants showed every reason why the draftsmen of the Hague Rules should
be concerned to include in it not merely a reference to the pound sterling but also a
reference to the gold value of that currency.

The radical arguments of the defendants accordingly fail. They also advanced certain
alternative arguments which were partly designed to answer the obvious question why
the first sentence of art IX was included if it was not intended to have the effect for which   *e*
the plaintiffs contend. Thus the defendants argued that the first sentence of art IX could
be given adequate effect to by construing it as a reference to the amount of gold that
could be bought with £stg100 at the date of the contract or at the date of the delivery of
the goods. I suppose that a clause could be drafted which would have this effect but that
is not the effect of the natural meaning of the words in the first sentence of art IX. What
is referred to in the Hague Rules is the gold value of £stg100. It is monetary gold that is   *f*
referred to, the expression being 'monetary units'. The relevant monetary unit is the £1
gold coin or sovereign which has a defined gold content and it is the value of that
quantity and fineness of gold that is the measure of value. Next it was argued that the
reference to gold value only becomes material when it is necessary to convert from
pounds sterling into some other currency. This argument has the support of the editor
of *Carver* and is also supported by the other sentences of art IX. The second sentence   *g*
enables contracting states which do not wish to pass domestic legislation referring to the
pound sterling to use a figure in art IV, r 5 expressed in their own currency. If they
choose to do this it is clear that it is their obligation to take the sum in their own currency
which corresponds to the gold value of sterling not some other nominal value. (It was of
course contemplated that such legislation might come to be passed some considerable   *h*
time after 1924). Similarly the last sentence contemplates that the domestic legislation
may give the carrier the right to discharge his liability in the local currency ascertained
at the rate of exchange prevailing on the day of the arrival of the ship at the port of
discharge. But again the Hague Rules clearly contemplate that it is to be the gold value
of sterling that is to be used as the measure of value against which the right to discharge
the liability in the local currency must be assessed.   *j*

These arguments therefore do not detract from the primary proposition of the
plaintiffs that the gold value referred to is the gold value of sterling. Indeed, it can be
commented that it would appear that this was the belief of the draftsman of the 1924
Act since the 1924 Act was of course domestic United Kingdom legislation. Since the

pound sterling was (and is) the monetary unit used in the United Kingdom and the gold
a sovereign was (and still is) legal tender in the United Kingdom, if the defendants be right
there was no need or justification to include any reference to gold value in the 1924 Act.
But as already remarked, a reference to gold value was specially inserted in the 1924 Act
even though it had not appeared in the draft Hague Rules. This can only have been to
underline as a matter of English law that what was being referred to in art IV, r 5 was
the gold value of the pound sterling, not its nominal or paper value.

b   Even if the defendants were correct to say that the reference to gold value in the first
sentence of art IX was solely to be referred to when there was a necessity for converting
to some other currency than sterling that argument would not assist them in the present
case. In the present case, as they are entitled to, the plaintiffs claim damages expressed in
Kenyan pounds. That is the currency in which they have suffered their damage. They
are entitled if they so choose to a judgment expressed in Kenyan pounds: see *The Despina*
c *R* [1979] 1 All ER 421, [1979] AC 685. Therefore, if the defendants are to avail themselves
of their right to limit their liability under art IV, r 5, they must convert that limit into
Kenyan pounds so as to establish that the limit is less than the amount for which the
plaintiffs are asking judgment. An expression of the value of that limit in terms of
Kenyan pounds is required; there has to be a translation from the gold value of sterling
into the nominal value of Kenyan pounds. Therefore even on this argument the
d defendants cannot escape from the consequences of the first sentence of art IX.

   The defendants further developed their argument by submitting that the purpose of
the first sentence of art IX was to guard against the devaluation of sterling currency
between the date when the goods owner's cause of action accrued, normally the date of
delivery of the goods, and the date when he was able to obtain either a judgment or an
arbitration award in his favour. Thus, counsel submitted that what was contemplated
e was that on, say, the date of discharge one would assess what quantity of gold could be
bought with £stg100 (nominal) and that one would then use that quantity of gold as the
basis for assessing the limit of the carrier's liability which was applicable at the date of
judgment or award. Thus if the judgment or award was to be given in, say, Kenyan
pounds one would ask what number of Kenyan pounds was necessary at that later date
to purchase that quantity of gold. This argument cannot be supported. Firstly, it depends
f on the erroneous approach of treating the gold value provision as requiring consideration
of how much gold a sterling pound would buy as opposed to what was the gold value of
the pound sterling. Secondly, it patently does not fit in with the scheme of the Hague
Rules. The purpose of the gold clause provision in art IX of the Hague Rules is clearly to
provide a single and constant measure of value by reference to gold, not a fluctuating
value. What would result on the defendants' submission is that that value would be
g constantly fluctuating up to the time of discharge. Further, it is unrealistic to suppose
that the parties to the Rules, or indeed the parties to this bill of lading, had in mind and
were making provision for the essentially procedural problems which existed under
English law prior to the decision in *Miliangos v George Frank (Textiles) Ltd* [1975] 3 All ER
801, [1976] AC 443 and *The Despina R.*

h   The defendants' arguments therefore fail. The gold value provision in art IX of the
Hague Rules is of sufficient clarity; it is effective. The defendants' submission how the
provision should be applied likewise fails.

   In evaluating the submissions of the parties I have not so far referred to the opinion or
decision of any overseas court. In fact since 1964 there have been a series of decisions in
which the gold value provision in the Hague Rules has been considered. With one
j exception, these have all to a greater or lesser extent supported the plaintiffs' submissions
before me. I must express my debt to those acting for the plaintiffs in collecting together
these various decisions. They are as follows: (1) *Fiat Co v American Export Lines Inc* [1965]
AMC 384, Corte d'appello di Firenze; (2) *Air Cameroun v Cie Maritime des Chargeurs Réunis*
[1967] Jurisprudence Français 675, Cour d'appel de Rouen; (3) *SpA Carniti v SpA Comesmar*

[1979] Dir maritt 90, Tribunale di Genova; (4) *Agemar Srl v Siat* [1979] Dir Maritt 215, Corte d'appello di Trieste; (5) *The Doroty* [1979] ETL 550, Can Fed Ct; (6) *Hussain v Great*   *a*
Eastern Shipping Co [1960] ILR Ker 1028, Kerala CA; (7) *Norway and Asia Lines v Adamjee Jute Mills Ltd* [1981] Bangladesh LD 152, Bangladesh CA; (8) *The Vishva Pratibha* [1980] 2 MLJ 265, Singapore HC (Sinnathuray J); (9) *Brown Boveri (Australia) Pty Ltd v Baltic Shipping Co* (31 July 1986, unreported), NSW SC (Yeldham J). The only decision at all favourable to the defendants is that in Singapore in 1980. This was fully considered by Yeldham J in the *Brown Boveri* case in New South Wales in 1986 in the course of a   *b*
judgment which upheld contentions similar to those advanced before me by the plaintiffs.

The *Fiat* case merely provides an illustration of the common assumption that art IX had the effect of introducing a gold value, that is to say the value of £100 gold stg. The parties had agreed that that was the position and the court simply had to give effect to that agreement. In the Court of Appeal at Rouen a similar decision was arrived at by the   *c*
court rejecting an argument to the contrary. The two Italian decisions in 1978 also appear to have been given in proceedings where the point was in dispute. The provision that the gold value of sterling should be taken as the measure of the limit of the carrier's liability was given effect to though of course in a context where it was necessary to convert that limit into the currency units of the court. The decision in Trieste particularly stresses that the carrier's argument for taking a paper value would have virtually nullified the   *d*
clause and would have contradicted its manifest intent which was to refer to a system of gold parity. The point was again in dispute in the Canadian case and was again decided in favour of the good's owners. The judge clearly treated the provision of art IX as too clear to admit any worthwhile debate. The cases from the Indian subcontinent were again decided against the carriers in the face of argument to the contrary. Each court considered that it had to have regard to the value in rupees of the gold content of 100   *e*
gold sovereigns. The judges in Bangladesh specifically followed and applied the decision in *Feist v Société Intercommunale Belge d'Electricité* [1934] AC 161, [1933] All ER Rep 228.

The judge in the Singapore case was of a contrary view. He was concerned to construe the Singapore Carriage of Goods by Sea Act, which was in all material respects in the same terms as the 1924 Act. He therefore had the potential difficulties of construction to which I have previously referred in relation to the 1924 Act and he furthermore had the   *f*
difficulty that he had no evidence before him of the value of a sovereign. He commented ([1980] 2 MLJ 265 at 267):

> 'Counsel for the plaintiffs assumed that the £100 in Article IV rule 5 means "£100 gold". It stems from the fact that the only reference to a monetary unit in the rules is in Article IV rule 5, and therefore the reference to gold value in Article   *g*
> IX must be "£100" in gold value. I am not satisfied that such an assumption is valid.'

He discussed the differing views in *Scrutton* and *Carver*. He preferred the view that art IX was only relevant when it was *necessary* to convert £100 into the equivalent of that sum in another currency, which he considered that he did not need to do. He concluded (at 268):   *h*

> 'I have also, I think, sufficiently demonstrated that neither "gold" nor "sovereign" is "currency". Therefore, either of them does not arise for consideration in the construction of Article IV rule 5. As regards Article IX, for the reasons I have given, it is otiose. Leaving aside the mystery of how it got into the municipal law in the form it is, I agree with *Carver* that it should not have been incorporated into it. I also agree with *Carver* that it should have been repealed. I hold that "£100" in   *j*
> Article IV rule 5 does not mean "£100 gold".'

Before Yeldham J in the Supreme Court of New South Wales, Admiralty Division, the relevant question appears to have been fully argued and the previous decision referred to. The case concerned goods which were damaged in the course of their carriage by sea

from Genoa in Italy to Sydney. The Hague Rules as in the 1924 convention had been
a incorporated into the bill of lading as a matter of contract. The judge was therefore
concerned with a question that was for practical purposes the same as that with which I
am concerned except that the currency in which the plaintiff had suffered his loss was
the currency of the forum. The carrier argued that the limit of his liability was $A200
per package or unit, being the nominal value in Australian dollars of a £stg100 paper.
The judge considered the effect of the Hague Rules and the principles governing
b contractual incorporation of such rules into a bill of lading. He was able to adopt dicta in
a previous decision of the High Court of Australia similar in effect to the dictum of
Devlin J in *Pyrene Co Ltd v Scindia Steam Navigation Co Ltd* [1954] 2 All ER 158 at 160,
[1954] 2 QB 402 at 413 (see *William Holyman & Sons Pty Ltd v Foy & Gibson Pty Ltd* (1945)
73 CLR 622). He adopted the definition of the gold content of the pound sterling in the
Coinage Act 1870 and followed and applied the *Fiest* case. He preferred the Indian and
c Bangladeshi decisions to that in Singapore. He recognised that the goods owner was
entitled to ask for his judgment in Australian currency and that on any view a translation
of the limit into Australian currency was necessary. He, rightly in my view, criticised
the 'confusion between the means of discharging the liability of the carrier on the one
hand and the measure of such liability on the other'.

In my judgment these decision of other courts strongly support the conclusion which
d I have reached. They rebut the argument that art IX lacks sufficient clarity to be effective.
They show that, with one unpersuasive exception, there has been a consistent international
practice of recognising and giving effect to art IX; and it does not need to be stressed that,
in connection with international conventions such as the Hague Rules, the court should
seek to give such conventions and the contracts into which they are incorporated an
interpretation which is consistent with the international practice and not overinfluenced
e by domestic prejudices.

The sum by way of damages that the plaintiffs are entitled to recover from the
defendants in this action is, accordingly, £K6,491·25.

Order accordingly.

f Solicitors: *Clyde & Co* (for the plaintiffs); *Lloyd & Co* (for the defendants).

                                                        N P Metcalfe Esq   Barrister.

R v Worcester City Juvenile Court, ex parte F

QUEEN'S BENCH DIVISION (CROWN OFFICE LIST)
SIR STEPHEN BROWN P
10 OCTOBER 1988

Children and young persons – Care proceedings in juvenile court – Care order – Application to discharge care order – Refusal of application – Whether juvenile court required to give reasons for refusal of application.

If asked to do so, a juvenile court is required to give its reasons if it decides to refuse an application to discharge a care order made in respect of a child (see p 501 e, post).

Notes
For applications to discharge care orders, see 24 Halsbury's Laws (4th edn) para 755.

Application for judicial review
F, the mother of two children taken into care by the Worcester City Council, applied with the leave of Mann LJ given on 1 December 1987 for judicial review by way of an order of mandamus requiring the justices for the petty sessional division of the City of Worcester to state a case following their decision as a juvenile court on 15 May 1987 to refuse an application by the applicant to discharge care orders made in respect of the children. The facts are set out in the judgment.

David Hershman for the applicant.
The justices and the local authority were not represented.

SIR STEPHEN BROWN P. This is an application by F for an order of mandamus directed to the justices of the peace for the petty sessional division of the City of Worcester requesting them to state a case for the opinion of this court, following their refusal as a juvenile court to discharge care orders made on 15 May 1987 in respect of two children of the applicant. The justices, by their clerk, have declined to state a case. They say, by their clerk, that no question of law or of mixed law and fact arises in the circumstances.

The brief history of the matter is that the two children in question were made the subject of care orders in November 1985 by the Worcester City Juvenile Court, as a result of injuries received by the younger child. The applicant is their mother. In her affidavit before this court, she states that the injury in question was caused by a man who was cohabiting with her at the time but that that relationship had now terminated. She therefore applied to the Worcester City Juvenile Court to discharge the care orders, contending that she was able to put forward proposals for her own parents to be the principal carers of the children in question.

It appears that her application to discharge the care orders was opposed by the county council, the local authority in whose favour the care orders had been made, and it was also opposed by the children's guardian ad litem. At the conclusion of what appears to have been a full hearing the magistrates announced that they did not propose to discharge the care orders. They did not give any reason for their decision. The mother is aggrieved by their decision and is anxious to discover on what basis they came to their conclusion.

At the time when the magistrates heard this matter there was no right of appeal on the part of a parent to the Crown Court. The guardian ad litem in this case did have a right of appeal but did not seek to exercise it, perhaps not surprisingly since the guardian had apparently opposed the application to discharge the care orders. The local authority did not take any step in the matter, presumably also because they had succeeded before the magistrates.

a Counsel for the applicant obtained leave to move for judicial review from Mann LJ, who granted leave—

> 'upon an undertaking by counsel on behalf of the applicant to reconsider the matter when the respondent's evidence is filed, and if he takes the view that further proceedings would be fruitless, then he will withdraw the application.'

b The justices have declined to divulge any reason or, indeed, to indicate the basis on which they came to their conclusion.

The applicant has amended the questions which it is desired to pose for the consideration of this court. The questions now suggested are: whether the evidence justified the following findings of fact that (1) it would not be appropriate for the care orders to be discharged, (2) the children would not receive the care and control they required after discharge, whether through the making of a supervision order or c otherwise. The phraseology is taken from the words of the statute. It is the first question which is principally relied on.

The justices, through their clerk, expressed the view that they did not consider that the questions so posed raised any question of law or mixed law and fact. It would seem that what the applicant is seeking to do is to overcome, by this route, the absence of any right of appeal against the refusal to discharge the care order since the legislation in force d at the time did not provide for any right of appeal.

Nevertheless it is, in my judgment, invidious that an applicant, such as this mother, should be kept in the dark and not know, even in the briefest terms, what evidence weighed with the justices in coming to their conclusion, having regard to the fact that it appears that a substantial body of evidence was adduced before them. There was clearly a conflict, having regard to the stance taken by the parties before the magistrates.

e I have come to the conclusion that the magistrates should be required to state a case. Accordingly, mandamus will go requiring them to state a case.

I should add at this stage that when the case is stated the matter will come for consideration on its merits. I would not, in the absence of any detailed information about the actual nature of the case which the justices heard, be minded to give any indication which might be optimistic for the applicant. In other words, the fact that this application f is allowed today does not in any sense bear on the final outcome of the matter. I think it wise to make those cautionary remarks. No doubt they were in Mann LJ's mind at the time when he gave what I would describe as conditional leave.

Order of mandamus granted.

g Solicitors: *Curtler & Hallmark*, Worcester (for the applicant).

Bebe Chua   Barrister.

Customs and Excise Commissioners v Fine Art Developments plc

HOUSE OF LORDS

LORD KEITH OF KINKEL, LORD TEMPLEMAN, LORD ACKNER AND LORD LOWRY

12, 13 DECEMBER 1988, 2 FEBRUARY 1989

Value added tax – Overpayment of tax – Deduction of overpayment – Deduction of overpayment from subsequent payment of tax – Overpayment occurring because of taxpayer's compliance with directions issued by commissioners subsequently ruled to be invalid – Taxpayer deducting overpayment from subsequent payment of tax – Whether taxpayer entitled to deduct overpayment – Value Added Tax Act 1983, s 14 – Value Added Tax (General) Regulations 1985, reg 58(1), Sch, Form 4.

The taxpayer company manufactured greeting cards which it sold at a wholesale price to retail customers for resale. The taxpayer company, in accordance with a direction issued by the Commissioners of Customs and Excise, paid value added tax on the retail value of the goods supplied to customers who were not registered for value added tax. The Court of Justice of the European Communities subsequently ruled, in unconnected proceedings, that the commissioners had no power to issue such a direction and the taxpayer company sought repayment of some £1·39m overpaid tax. When the commissioners refused to make any repayment the taxpayer company deducted that amount from a subsequent payment of value added tax. The commissioners brought an action against the taxpayer company claiming the £1·39m and the judge gave them leave to enter summary judgment for that amount. The taxpayer company appealed, contending that, although the Value Added Tax Act 1983 did not expressly permit an overpayment of tax to be deducted, reg 58(1)[a] of the Value Added Tax (General) Regulations 1985 and the form of return for value added tax set out in Form 4[b] in the schedule to those regulations envisaged overpayments of tax in previous periods being deducted from the amount of tax otherwise payable in the accounting period in which the overpayment was discovered. The Court of Appeal dismissed the taxpayer company's appeal and it appealed to the House of Lords.

Held – A taxpayer was entitled to deduct overpaid value added tax when computing his liability for a subsequent instalment of value added tax since, although s 14[c] of the 1983 Act contemplated that, in the ordinary case, liability to value added tax would fall to be established simply by deducting input from output tax in the current accounting period, that section had to be read with the 1985 regulations and, in particular, with the prescribed form for value added tax returns set out in Form 4 and the value added tax guide issued by the commissioners (both of which had the force of law), which, on their true construction, gave a legal right and imposed an obligation to make deductions from current liability to value added tax in respect of past overdeclarations made in error, irrespective of whether the error was one of law or of fact. It followed that the taxpayer company had been entitled to deduct the overpayment in computing its liability for a subsequent period. The appeal would therefore be allowed (see p 507 e to g and p 508 e to h, post).

Betterware Products Ltd v Customs and Excise Comrs (No 2) [1988] STC 6 approved.

Decision of the Court of Appeal [1988] 2 All ER 70 reversed.

---

a   Regulation 58(1), so far as material, is set out at p 505 *a b*, post
b   Form 4, so far as material, is set out at p 505 *c* to *g*, post
c   Section 14(2) is set out at p 507 *b*, post

Notes

a   For the deduction of input tax from output tax in general, see 12 Halsbury's Laws (4th edn) paras 935–938.

For the Value Added Tax Act 1983, s 14, see 48 Halsbury's Statutes (4th edn) 614.

Cases referred to in opinions

Betterware Products Ltd v Customs and Excise Comrs (No 2) [1988] STC 6.

b   *Direct Cosmetics Ltd v Customs and Excise Comrs* Case 5/84 [1985] STC 479, [1985] ECR 617, CJEC.

Appeal

Fine Art Developments plc (the taxpayer) appealed with leave of the Court of Appeal against the decision of the Court of Appeal (Glidewell and Taylor LJJ) ([1988] 2 All ER

c   70, [1988] QB 895) on 28 January 1988 dismissing the taxpayer's appeal from the decision of Sir Neil Lawson sitting as a judge of the High Court in chambers on 9 July 1987 whereby the judge allowed on terms an appeal by the Crown against an order of Deputy Master Rose dated 5 March 1987 dismissing the Crown's application for judgment under RSC Ord 14, r 2 in respect of alleged overpayments of value added tax which were deducted by the taxpayers from a subsequent payment of value added tax. The facts are

d   set out in the opinion of Lord Keith.

Andrew Park QC and *Robin Mathew* for the taxpayer.
John Laws and *Robert Jay* for the Crown.

Their Lordships took time for consideration.

e
2 February. The following opinions were delivered.

LORD KEITH OF KINKEL. My Lords, this appeal is concerned with the question whether, under the relevant statutory provisions relating to value added tax a taxpayer who by mistake has in a particular accounting period paid a greater amount of tax than

f   was properly due is entitled to deduct the amount of the excess in computing his liability for a later period.

The appellant taxpayer carries on the business of manufacturing and distributing greetings cards, and has at all material times been registered for purposes of value added tax. The statute which now governs that tax is the Value Added Tax Act 1983, a consolidating measure. Some of the events material to the present case took place before

g   the consolidation, but, as the terms of the enactments in force at the earlier time have not been altered by the 1983 Act, it will be convenient to refer throughout to that Act. The supply of cards by the taxpayer to its customers in the United Kingdom was a taxable supply, so it was liable to charge its customers with value added tax and to account for the tax so charged (output tax) to the Commissioners of Customs and Excise. However,

h   under s 14(2) of the 1983 Act it was entitled to take credit for the tax on the supply to it of goods or services (input tax). Some of the customers of the taxpayer were not registered for value added tax, so that they were not liable for output tax nor in a position to take credit for any input tax. The prices charged to these customers by the taxpayer for wholesale supplies of cards were lower than the prices charged by the customers on sale by retail. On 13 August 1981 the commissioners served on the taxpayer pursuant to

j   what is now para 3 of Sch 4 to the 1983 Act a notice of direction requiring it to calculate output tax on the open market value of the cards on sale by retail, which was of course more than the prices actually charged by the taxpayer company to the customers in question. The taxpayer duly complied. However, another taxpayer subject to a similar direction successfully challenged its validity under Community law in proceedings before the Court of Justice of the European Communities: see *Direct Cosmetics Ltd v*

Customs and Excise Comrs Case 5/84 [1985] STC 479, [1985] ECR 617. The invalidity
flowed from the failure of the United Kingdom government to notify the Commission   *a*
of the European Communities of the amendment, by s 14(1) of the Finance Act 1981, of
para 3 of Sch 3 to the Finance Act 1972. It is unnecessary to go into further detail. In the
result, all notices of direction issued after the amendment took effect, on 27 July 1981,
became null and void, including that issued to the taxpayer on 13 August 1981. So on
5 March 1985 the commissioners informed the taxpayer company that the notice was
withdrawn with effect from 14 February 1985 (the day after the decision of the European   *b*
Court), and that as from that date it should account for value added tax on the basis of
the prices actually charged by the taxpayer to its customers.

The taxpayer had accounted for value added tax in accordance with the notice of
direction from 13 August 1981 until 30 June 1983. Thereafter it had ceased to do so
because of doubts about the validity of the notice. The excess of what had been paid by
way of tax over what had been properly payable was £1,399,022. By letter dated 13 June   *c*
1985 the commissioners intimated to the taxpayer that they were prepared to consider
claims for repayment of value added tax paid under invalid notices but would not do so
in respect of payments made before 9 November 1983 unless the taxpayer in question
had queried the validity of the relevant notice at an earlier date. The significance of
9 November 1983 was that it was the date on which the London value added tax tribunal
had referred the *Direct Cosmetics* case to the European Court. On 22 July 1985 the   *d*
taxpayer requested the commissioners to refund to it the sum of £1,399,022, but this
was refused. Accordingly, the taxpayer in its value added tax return for the quarter ended
31 December 1985 deducted that sum from the net amount of value added tax then
otherwise due. By letter dated 3 March 1986 the commissioners contended that the
overpayment was irrecoverable as having been made under a mistake of law, and
requested payment of the £1,399,022 within seven days, failing which they would take   *e*
proceedings for recovery.

On 20 October 1986 the commissioners issued a writ in the High Court claiming
payment by the taxpayer of the sum of £1,399,657·67 (later reduced by amendment to
£1,399,022) as a debt due to the Crown. Later they applied for summary judgment
under RSC Ord 14, r 1, but the application was dismissed by Deputy Master Rose on
5 March 1987. The commissioners appealed, and on 9 July 1987 Sir Neil Lawson, sitting   *f*
as a judge of the High Court, allowed the appeal and gave the commissioners leave to
enter judgment for the sum claimed with interest to be assessed if not agreed. Execution
of the judgment was stayed on condition that the taxpayer issued by a specified date a
writ against the commissioners claiming restitution of the disputed sum. Sir Neil gave
no reasons for his decision. The taxpayer appealed to the Court of Appeal but on
28 January 1988 that court (Glidewell and Taylor LJJ) ([1988] 2 All ER 70, [1988] QB   *g*
895) dismissed the appeal, while giving leave to appeal to your Lordships' House, which
the taxpayer now does.

The taxpayer is not entitled to deduct past overpayments of value added tax from that
currently due unless there is some provision of primary or subordinate legislation which
authorises it to do so. It maintains that such authorisation is to be found in certain   *h*
provisions of the Value Added Tax (General) Regulations 1985, SI 1985/886, made by the
commissioners under various powers conferred on them by the 1983 Act. The powers
particularly relevant are those to be found in paras 2(1) and (4) of Sch 7 to the Act.
Paragraph 2(1), so far as material, provides:

'Regulations under this paragraph may require the keeping of accounts and the
making of returns in such form and manner as may be specified in the regulations   *j*
...'

Paragraph 2(4), omitting irrelevant words, reads:

'Regulations under this paragraph may make provision . . . (c) for the correction
of errors.'

Regulation 58(1) of the 1985 regulations provides:

'Save as the Commissioners may otherwise allow, every person who is registered or was or is required to be registered shall, in respect of every period of a quarter or in the case of a person who is registered every period of 3 months ending on the dates notified either in the certificate of registration issued to him or otherwise, furnish the Controller, not later than the last day of the month next following the end of the period to which it relates, with a return on the form numbered 4 in the Schedule to these Regulations showing the amount of tax payable by or to him and containing full information in respect of the other matters specified in the form and a declaration that the return is true and complete . . .'

There follow certain provisos not relevant for present purposes.

The Form 4 referred to in the regulation, as at the time of the relevant return by the taxpayer, set out the following table:

			£	p
'FOR OFFICIAL USE	VAT DUE in this period on OUTPUTS (sales, etc), certain postal imports and services received from abroad	1		
	Underdeclarations of VAT made on previous returns (but not those notified in writing by Customs and Excise)	2		
	TOTAL VAT DUE (box 1 + box 2)	3		
	VAT DEDUCTIBLE in this period on INPUTS (purchases, etc)	4		
	Overdeclarations of VAT made on previous returns (but not those notified in writing by Customs and Excise)	5		
	TOTAL VAT DEDUCTIBLE (box 4 + box 5)	6		
	NET VAT PAYABLE OR REPAYABLE (Difference between boxes 3 and 6)	7		

The form also contained the following section:

'Please tick only ONE of these boxes:

| box 3 greater than box 6 | payment by credit transfer | ☐ | payment enclosed | ☐ |
| box 6 greater than box 3 | repayment due | ☐ | | |

Regulation 64 provides:

'Correction of errors
64. If a person makes an error in accounting for tax or in any return furnished under these Regulations he shall correct it in such manner and within such time as the Commissioners may require.'

The commissioners have issued and revised from time to time a VAT Guide. The guide as revised on 1 January 1984 stated in para 2 that section VIII of it contained requirements made by the commissioners by virtue of their powers under Sch 7 of the 1983 Act and had legal force. Section VIII contained a para 63 dealing with adjustment of errors. Sub-paragraph (b) of para 63 provided:

'Other errors. Any others affecting tax due from you or repayable to you, which are discovered after you have sent in your return for the tax period in which they occurred, should be recorded separately as underdeclarations or overdeclarations of tax in previous periods. You should carry the totals to your VAT account for adjustment in your next return.'

The VAT account was thus described in para 64:

'For each tax period, you must keep a summary of the totals of your output tax and input tax. This is called your **VAT account**. You should keep it in a special book or ledger opening. You will find an example of a simple VAT account in **Keeping records and accounts** but any form of account containing the same information will be acceptable to Customs and Excise. If you are in doubt, ask your local VAT office for advice.

You make up your VAT account by adding up the VAT in your records at convenient intervals—for example, one a month, and putting the totals in your VAT account with separate headings for:

• **VAT DEDUCTIBLE**   • **VAT PAYABLE**

Under **VAT PAYABLE** itemise separately:

• output tax on goods or services supplied by you;	Taken from records referred to in paragraph 58(a)(i)
• tax due but not paid on imported goods, goods removed from bonded warehouse and on services listed in Appendix G received from abroad:	Taken from records referred to in paragraph 58(a)(v).
• any underdeclarations of VAT from previous periods, but not those notified in writing by Customs and Excise.	See paragraph 63(b)

Under **VAT DEDUCTIBLE** itemise separately:

• tax you have been charged on goods and services you have received	Taken from records referred to in paragraph 61(a)(i)
• tax due on imported goods and on goods removed from bonded warehouse, whether paid or postponed and on services listed in Appendix G received from abroad;	Taken from records referred to in paragraph 61(a)(ii).
• any overdeclarations of tax from previous periods, but not those notified in writing by Customs and Excise;	See paragraph 63(b)
• any relief allowed from VAT on bad debts	See paragraph 55

Add up separately the **VAT PAYABLE** and **VAT DEDUCTIBLE**, take the smaller amount from the larger and record the difference.

If the VAT payable is more than the VAT deductible, the difference is the amount that you must pay to Customs and Excise.

If the VAT deductible is more than the VAT payable, the difference is the amount that you should claim from Customs and Excise.'

The argument for the taxpayer is that the terms of Form 4 and the requirements of paras 63(b) and 64 of the VAT Guide, which have the force of law, incorporate arrangements for the correction of errors which the commissioners are authorised to make by para 2(4)(c) of Sch 7 to the 1983 Act. Regulation 64 of the 1985 regulations obliges the taxpayer to correct errors, including those arising from previous overdeclarations, in accordance with those arrangements. That is what the taxpayer did in its return for the quarter ended 31 December 1985.

The argument for the commissioners is primarily founded on s 14 of the 1983 Act,
a which has the cross-heading 'Credit for input tax against output tax', the relevant
subsections being:

'(1) A taxable person shall, in respect of supplies made by him, account for and
pay tax by reference to such periods (in this Act referred to as "prescribed accounting
periods"), at such time and in such manner as may be determined by or under
b regulations.
(2) Subject to the provisions of this section, he is entitled at the end of each such
period to credit for so much of his input tax as is allowable under section 15 below,
and then to deduct that amount from any output tax that is due from him . . .
(5) If either no input tax is due at the end of the period, or the amount of the
credit exceeds that of the tax, then, subject to subsections (6) and (7) below, the
c amount of the credit or, as the case may be, the amount of the excess shall be paid to
the taxable person by the Commissioners . . .'

The contention is that the effect of these provisions is that, for the purposes of
accounting for value added tax, the taxpayer is entitled to credit in any accounting period
only for input tax, and that any regulations made by the commissioners allowing credit
d for anything else, in particular for past overdeclarations, would be inconsistent with
those provisions and thus ultra vires. The purpose of boxes 2 and 5 in Form 4, to be filled
in in accordance with regs 58 and 64, is said to be merely the administrative convenience
of imparting information to the commissioners, who are at liberty to allow the deductions
if they think fit, and, if they do not do so, to disallow the deductions and leave the
taxpayer to any remedies he may have at law.
e   In my opinion, the terms of s 14 are not inconsistent with an intention on the part of
Parliament that the commissioners should have power to bring about that past errors
resulting, in whatever way, in overdeclarations or underdeclarations of tax should be
corrected in subsequent returns. No doubt in the ordinary case liability will fall to be
established simply by deducting input tax from output tax, or vice versa, in the current
accounting period, and that is what s 14 contemplates. But para 2(4)(c) of Sch 7 gives the
f commissioners specific power to make regulations for the correction of errors, and such
regulations, when made, take their place in the Act alongside the provisions of s 14. The
prescribed Form 4 and the requirements of paras 63(b) and 64 of the VAT Guide can only
be construed as giving a legal right, and indeed as imposing an obligation, to make
deductions from current liability to value added tax in respect of past overdeclarations
made in error. No differentiation is made between overdeclarations made through error
g of law and those made through error of fact. If the commissioners do not accept that a
deduction has been properly made, they can raise an assessment on the taxpayer under
para 4(1) of Sch 7, and the assessment will be subject to appeal to the value added tax
tribunal under s 40(1)(m) of the Act.
    In *Betterware Products Ltd v Customs and Excise Comrs (No 2)* [1988] STC 6 Simon
Brown J had occasion to deal with a case on facts indistinguishable from those of this
h case. He accepted the argument of the taxpayer and rejected that of the commissioners,
both being similar to those advanced before your Lordship's House. After summarising
the argument for the commissioners, he said (at 12):

'Persuasively as these submissions were advanced, I find myself quite unable to
accept them. The problems attendant upon them appear to me formidable. In the
j first place, it is a necessary corollary of the commissioners' argument that they have
in fact made no provision at all for the correction of errors, but only for their
notification. The difference is crucial. At the heart of their case lies the proposition
that it is entirely a matter for their discretion whether, once notified of errors, they
give effect to them by relieving the taxpayer of any part of his current liability. If
they choose, they may instead leave it to the taxpayer to sue them in the courts,
reserving their rights to invoke defences clearly beyond the contemplation of

Parliament when envisaging the correction of errors. That, indeed, is precisely the course the commissioners are following in this very case. Secondly, I find it quite impossible to construe and apply the statutory form of return other than as providing for the correction of errors in the full sense for which the company contends. It is in my judgment perfectly plain that the form requires previous errors to be declared so as to affect "the amount of tax payable by or to" the taxpayer as envisaged by reg 58(1). Putting it in the language of para 63(b) of the General Guide, any underdeclarations or overdeclarations are, by the very structure of the form "carried to your VAT account for adjustment in your next tax return". Both the form and the guide represent, in my judgment, the commissioners' requirements of the manner and time in which past errors should be corrected as contemplated by reg 64.'

Glidewell LJ giving his judgment in the present case, with which Taylor LJ agreed, quoted that passage and continued ([1988] 2 All ER 70 at 76, [1988] QB 895 at 906):

'That judgment is obviously most persuasive in the present taxpayer company's favour. The arguments that the form of return appears to envisage an overpayment in a previous period being deducted in the accounting period in which it comes to light, and that if necessary the issue can be decided by the commissioners' raising an assessment which can be the subject of an appeal to the value added tax tribunal, are strong. Nevertheless, with considerable reluctance, I have concluded that the submissions of counsel for the Crown are correct. In my view, the wording of ss 1, 2(1) and 14 of the 1983 Act compel us to hold that the tax for which a taxable person must account in any accounting period is calculated by deducting input tax from output tax. No other deduction is envisaged or permitted by the Act.'

My Lords, in my opinion the reasoning contained in the judgment of Simon Brown J in the *Betterware* case was entirely correct, and there is nothing in either ss 1 and 2(1) or s 14 of the 1983 Act which compels a contrary conclusion to that which he reached. I would accordingly allow this appeal. The result of that would technically be simply that the summary judgment in favour of the commissioners is set aside. Counsel for the Crown agreed, however, that if the appeal is allowed their action against the taxpayer should appropriately be dismissed, and I would make an order accordingly. The commissioners must pay the taxpayer's costs here and of the proceedings in the courts below.

LORD TEMPLEMAN. My Lords, for the reasons given by my noble and learned friend Lord Keith, I would allow this appeal.

LORD ACKNER. My Lords, I have had the advantage of reading in draft the speech of my noble and learned friend Lord Keith. I agree with it and, for the reasons which he gives, I, too, would allow the appeal, dismiss the action and make the order as to costs which my noble and learned friend proposes.

LORD LOWRY. My Lords, I have had the advantage of reading in draft the speech of my noble and learned friend Lord Keith. I agree with it and, for the reasons which he gives, I, too, would allow the appeal, dismiss the action and made the order as to costs which my noble and learned friend proposes.

Appeal allowed.

Solicitors: *Berrymans*, agents for *Shakespeare Duggan Lea & Co*, Birmingham (for the taxpayer); *Solicitor for the Customs and Excise.*

Mary Rose Plummer   Barrister.

R v Panel on Take-overs and Mergers, ex parte Guinness plc

COURT OF APPEAL, CIVIL DIVISION
LORD DONALDSON OF LYMINGTON MR, LLOYD AND WOOLF LJJ
13, 14, 18, 19, 20, 28 JULY 1988

Judicial review – Availability of remedy – Take-over Panel – Panel refusing to adjourn hearing held to determine whether company's take-over affected by operation of concert party in breach of Take-over Code – Company applying for judicial review of panel's decision to refuse adjournment – Company not exercising right of appeal to panel's appeal committee – Whether panel's refusal to grant adjournment causing injustice – Whether panel's decision subject to judicial review.

In the course of a contested take-over by two public companies, A and G, for a third public company, D, the purchase of a block of 3% of D's shares by a Swiss company, P, was investigated by the Panel on Take-overs and Mergers at the request of A. The panel decided not to take the matter any further when it received an assurance from G's finance director that G and P were not acting in concert. G's bid for D was successful but following the take-over the Department of Trade and Industry (the DTI) decided to investigate G's affairs and the panel decided to reopen its investigation into whether P had acted in concert with G during the take-over of D, contrary to the City Code on Take-overs and Mergers. The panel subsequently advised G that it would proceed to investigate the concert party issue without waiting for the outcome of the DTI inquiry, particularly since a copy of a letter purportedly from P to a director of G had come to light, the contents of which, if correct, showed that P had acted in concert with G. The panel also advised G that the two-stage investigation, which would not be disciplinary in nature, would (i) decide whether there had been a concert party and (ii) if so, consider the consequences. G objected, seeking an adjournment of the hearing until the DTI inspectors' report had been published and any resulting criminal or civil proceedings concluded. The panel nevertheless continued its inquiries and also received confirmation from the DTI of P's letter to G. At a preliminary hearing of the panel held to determine whether there should be an adjournment G again sought an adjournment on the grounds (i) that the panel's speedy and informal procedures, though appropriate in the context of a current bid, were ill-adapted to an inquiry after a take-over, which was to be equated with disciplinary proceedings, and (ii) that essential witnesses from Switzerland regarding P's letter to G should be called for examination. The panel refused the adjournment and further refused to vacate the date for the hearing of the concert party issue, because of its concern for the former shareholders in D to whom G would be liable for any breach of the code, and because of the fact that the panel had received no information from G which cast doubt on the strong evidence in favour of a concert party. Immediately before the hearing of the concert party issue the panel executive delivered to G the final version of its submissions to the panel, which contained a new and significant addition, namely a letter from the solicitors of P's Swiss bank amounting to an admission that P's purchase of shares in D had been a concert party operation. At that hearing G again sought an adjournment to enable it to respond to the executive's final submissions but that was refused by the panel. Without exercising its right of appeal to the panel's appeal committee, G then applied for judicial review of the panel's decisions refusing adjournments. The Divisional Court dismissed the application and G appealed to the Court of Appeal.

Held – The test of whether particular acts or decisions of a body, such as the Panel on Take-overs and Mergers, whose constitution, functions and powers were sui generis should be subject to judicial review was whether, considering the matter in the round,

something had gone wrong with that body's procedure such as to cause real injustice and
require the intervention of the court. However, a decision whether to adjourn a hearing   *a*
was essentially a matter for the exercise of judicial discretion by the court or tribunal
seised of the matter and, furthermore, where a right of appeal from the decision-making
body existed but was not exercised, the court would only grant relief by way of judicial
review in exceptional circumstances. Accordingly, although the panel's decision to refuse
to adjourn the hearing of the concert party issue even for a short period was open to
criticism, the panel's conduct of the investigation as a whole had been fair and had not   *b*
caused injustice to G. It followed that the court would not intervene and that G's appeal
would therefore be dismissed (see p 512 *j* to p 513 *c*, p 526 *g*, p 527 *c h j*, p 528 *a* to *e*,
p 529 *f g*, p 530 *e f*, p 534 *a* to *c*, p 537 *g* to *j*, p 538 *j* to p 539 *a*, p 541 *g j* and p 544 *c d g*,
post).

Notes   *c*
For the City Take-over Code and the Panel on Take-overs and Mergers, see 7 Halsbury's
Laws (4th edn) paras 790–794.

Cases referred to in judgments
Associated Provincial Picture Houses Ltd v Wednesbury Corp [1947] 2 All ER 680, [1948] 1
    KB 223, CA.
Chief Constable of the North Wales Police v Evans [1982] 3 All ER 141, [1982] 1 WLR 1155,   *d*
    HL.
Council of Civil Service Unions v Minister for the Civil Service [1984] 3 All ER 935, [1985] AC
    374, [1984] 3 WLR 1174, HL.
General Medical Council v Spackman [1943] 2 All ER 337, [1943] AC 627, HL.
Guinness plc v Saunders [1988] BCLC 43; *affd* [1988] BCLC 607, CA.   *e*
John v Rees [1969] 2 All ER 274, [1970] Ch 345, [1969] 2 WLR 1294.
R v Chief Constable of the Merseyside Police, ex p Calveley [1986] 1 All ER 257, [1986] QB
    424, [1986] 2 WLR 144, CA.
R v Hillingdon London Borough, ex p Royco Homes Ltd [1974] 2 All ER 643, [1974] QB 720,
    [1974] 2 WLR 805, DC.
R v Liverpool City Justices, ex p Lunt [1988] CA Transcript 675.   *f*
R v Monopolies and Mergers Commission, ex p Argyll Group plc [1986] 2 All ER 257, [1986]
    1 WLR 763, CA.
R v Panel on Take-overs and Mergers, ex p Datafin plc [1987] 1 All ER 564, [1987] QB 815,
    [1987] 2 WLR 699, CA.
R v Secretary of State for the Environment, ex p Brent London BC [1983] 3 All ER 321, [1982]
    QB 593, [1982] 2 WLR 693, DC.   *g*
R v Thames Magistrates' Courts, ex p Polemis [1974] 2 All ER 1219, [1974] 1 WLR 1371,
    DC.
Secretary of State for Education and Science v Thameside Metropolitan Borough [1976] 3 All ER
    665, [1977] AC 1014, [1976] 3 WLR 641, CA and HL.

Cases also cited   *h*
Findlay v Secretary of State for the Home Dept [1984] 3 All ER 801, [1985] AC 318, HL.
R v Board of Visitors of Hull Prison, ex p St Germain (No 2) [1979] 3 All ER 545, [1979] 1
    WLR 1401, DC.
R v Crown Court at Aylesbury, ex p Farrer (1988) Times, 9 March, CA.
R v Leyland Justices, ex p Hawthorn [1979] 1 All ER 209, [1979] QB 283, DC.
R v Monopolies and Mergers Commission, ex p Elders IXL Ltd [1987] 1 All ER 451, [1987] 1   *j*
    WLR 1221.
R v Monopolies and Mergers Commission, ex p Matthew Brown plc [1987] 1 All ER 463,
    [1987] 1 WLR 1235.
Sanko Steamship Co Ltd v Shipping Corp of India and Selwyn and Clark, The Jhansi Ki Rani
    [1980] 2 Lloyd's Rep 569.
Wiseman v Borneman [1969] 3 All ER 275, [1971] AC 297, HL.

Appeal

a Guinness plc appealed against the decision of the Divisional Court of the Queen's Bench
Division (Watkins, Russell LJJ and Tudor Evans J) on 29 March 1988 dismissing their
application for judicial review of two decisions of the Panel on Take-overs and Mergers
made on 25 August and 2 September 1987 refusing to adjourn a hearing of the panel
relating to the issue whether Guinness had acted in concert with a Swiss company,
Pipetec AG, during their take-over bid for Distillers Co plc, contrary to r 11 of the City
b Code on Take-overs and Mergers. The facts are set out in the judgment of Lord
Donaldson MR.

David Oliver QC, Richard Field QC and *Patrick Elias* for Guinness.
Roger Buckley QC and *Paul Walker* for the panel.

c   *Cur adv vult*

28 July. The following judgments were delivered.

LORD DONALDSON OF LYMINGTON MR. On 25 August 1987, and again on
d 2 September, the Panel on Take-overs and Mergers considered and rejected an application
by Guinness plc that it postpone a hearing concerned with one aspect of the April 1986
take-over bid by Guinness for Distillers Co plc. Guinness obtained leave to apply for
judicial review of these decisions, but on 29 March 1988 that application was refused by
a Divisional Court of the Queen's Bench Division consisting of Watkins, Russell LJJ and
Tudor Evans J. Guinness now appeal to this court.

e
The take-over panel
   The panel is a truly remarkable body, whose nature was considered by this court in *R
v Panel on Take-overs and Mergers, ex p Datafin plc* [1984] 1 All ER 564, [1987] QB 815.
Part legislator, part court of interpretation, part consultant, part referee, part disciplinary
tribunal, its self-imposed task is to regulate and police the conduct of take-overs and
f mergers in the financial markets of the United Kingdom.
   Lacking a statutory base, it has to determine and declare its own terms of reference
and the rules applicable in the markets, thus acting as a legislator. It has to give guidance
in situations in which those involved in take-overs and mergers may be in doubt how
they should act. These doubts may arise because the situation is one which is novel and
not covered by the rules. The panel then acts as the conscience of the markets. This is the
g consultancy role. Or they may arise out of difficulty in applying the rules literally, in
which case the panel interprets them in its capacity as a court of interpretation. I use the
word 'interpret' rather than 'construe' advisedly because, as noted in *Ex p Datafin plc*
[1987] 1 All ER 564 at 579, [1987] QB 815 at 841, the panel as legislator tends to lay
down general principles on the lines of EEC legislation rather than to promulgate specific
prohibitions, although such prohibitions do exist. Where it detects breaches of the rules
h during the course of a take-over, it acts as a whistle-blowing referee, ordering the party
concerned to stop and, where it considers it appropriate, requiring that party to take
action designed to nullify any advantage which it has obtained and to redress any
disadvantage to other parties. Finally, when the dust has settled, it can take disciplinary
action against those who are found to have broken the rules.
   In *Ex p Datafin plc* [1987] 1 All ER 564 at 579, [1987] QB 815 at 842 I said:
j
      '. . . I wish to make it clear beyond a peradventure that in the light of the special
      nature of the panel, its functions, the market in which it is operating, the time scales
      which are inherent in that market and the need to safeguard the position of third
      parties, who may be numbered in thousands, all of whom are entitled to continue
      to trade on an assumption of the validity of the panel's rules and decisions, unless
      and until they are quashed by the court, I should expect the relationship between

the panel and the court to be historic rather than contemporaneous. I should expect the court to allow contemporary decisions to take their course, considering the *a* complaint and intervening, if at all, later and in retrospect by declaratory orders which would enable the panel not to repeat any error and would relieve individuals of the disciplinary consequences of any erroneous finding of breach of the rules.'

This passage has, I think been misunderstood, at least by academic writers. When the take-over is in progress the time scales involved are so short and the need of the markets and those dealing in them to be able to rely on the rulings of the panel so great that *b* contemporary intervention by the court will usually either be impossible or contrary to the public interest. Furthermore, it is important that this should be known, as otherwise attempts would undoubtedly be made to undermine the authority of the panel by tactical applications for judicial review. On the other hand, once the immediate problem has been dealt with by the panel, no similar objections would apply to a retrospective review *c* of its actions designed to avoid the repetition of error, if error there has been. And when it comes to disciplinary action by the panel, which necessarily will be taken in retrospect and with all due deliberation, the court will find itself in its traditional position of protecting the individual from any abuse of power.

Until the present problem arose, I imagine that all concerned visualised a complete dichotomy between the contemporaneous refereeing function and the retrospective *d* disciplinary function. However in the instant case the panel, having failed for lack of evidence to blow the whistle whilst the take-over was in progress, thought it right over a year later to resume its refereeing function on the basis of an 'action replay'. I am far from saying that it was wrong to do so. Indeed Guinness does not complain of this course being adopted, although it strongly objects to the timing. But it is a novel situation and both the panel and the court are necessarily breaking new ground. *e*

The jurisdiction of the court

The court's jurisdiction and limitations on its exercise are established in *Ex p Datafin plc*. However the present appeal calls for a further review and, in particular, consideration of whether the *separate* grounds for granting relief (illegality, irrationality, procedural impropriety and, possibly, proportionality) are appropriate in all situations. Illegality *f* would certainly apply if the panel acted in breach of the general law, but it is more difficult to apply in the context of an alleged misinterpretation of its own rules by a body which under the scheme is both legislator and interpreter. Irrationality, at least in the sense of failing to take account of relevant factors or taking account of irrelevant factors, is a difficult concept in the context of a body which is itself charged with the duty of making a judgment on what is and what is not relevant, although clearly a theoretical *g* scenario could be constructed in which the panel acted on the basis of considerations which on any view must have been irrelevant or ignored something which on any view must have been relevant. And similar problems arise with procedural impropriety in the narrow sense of failing to follow accepted procedures, given the nature of the panel and of its functions and the lack of any statutory or other guidance as to its procedures which are intended to be of its own devising. Similarly, in the broad sense of breach of the rules *h* of natural justice, what is or is not fair may depend on underlying value judgments by the panel as to the time scale which is appropriate for decision, the consequences of delay and matters of that kind. Approaching the problem on the basis of separate grounds for relief may at once bring several interlocking and mutually inconsistent considerations into play. Were the underlying judgments tainted by illegality or irrationality? If not, accepting those judgments, was the action unfair? If the underlying judgments were so *j* tainted, was the action unfair on the basis of judgments which might reasonably have been made? The permutations, if not endless, are considerable and confusing.

It may be that the true view is that, in the context of a body whose constitution, functions and powers are sui generis, the court should review the panel's acts and omissions more in the round than might otherwise be the case and, whilst basing its

decision on familiar concepts, should eschew any formal categorisation. It was Lord
a Diplock who in *Council of Civil Service Unions v Minister for the Civil Service* [1984] 3 All ER
935, [1985] AC 374 formulated the currently accepted categorisations in an attempt to
rid the courts of shackles bred of the technicalities surrounding the old prerogative writs.
But he added that further development on a case-by-case basis might add further grounds
(see [1984] 3 All ER 935 at 950, [1985] AC 374 at 410). In the context of the present
appeal he might have considered an innominate ground formed of an amalgam of his
b own grounds with perhaps added elements, reflecting the unique nature of the panel, its
powers and duties and the environment in which it operates, for he would surely have
joined in deploring any use of his own categorisation as a fetter on the continuous
development of the new 'public law court'. In relation to such an innominate ground the
ultimate question would, as always, be whether something had gone wrong of a nature
and degree which required the intervention of the court and, if so, what form that
c intervention should take.

The background

The starting point is December 1985, when Argyll Group plc announced an offer for
the shares of Distillers and January 1986 when Guinness put forward a rival offer. The
d take-over rules set out in the City Code on Take-overs and Mergers applied and one such
rule, r 11, provided:

> '11.1 WHEN A CASH OFFER IS REQUIRED   Except with the consent of the Panel in
> cases falling under (a), where:—(a) the shares of any class under offer in the offeree
> company purchased for cash by the offeror and any person acting in concert with it
> during the offer period and within 12 months prior to its commencement carry
e > 15% or more of the voting rights currently exercisable at a class meeting of that
> class; or (b) in the view of the Panel there are circumstances which render such a
> course necessary in order to give effect to General Principle 1, then the offer for that
> class shall be in cash or accompanied by a cash alternative at not less than the highest
> price paid by the offeror or any person acting in concert with it for shares of that
> class during the offer period and within 12 months prior to its commencement.
f > 11.2 DISPENSATION FROM HIGHEST PRICE   If the offeror considers that the highest
> price (for the purposes of Rule 11.1) should not apply in a particular case, the offeror
> should consult the Panel, which has discretion to agree an adjusted price.'

The definition section of the rules provides that—

g > 'Persons acting in concert comprise persons who, pursuant to an agreement or
> understanding (whether formal or informal), actively co-operate, through the
> acquisition by any of them of shares in a company, to obtain or consolidate control
> ... of that company.'

General principle 1 reads: 'All shareholders of the same class of an offeree company must
be treated similarly by an offeror.'
h Guinness and those acting in concert with them, 'the Guinness concert party', at that
time held marginally less than 15% of the shares in Distillers and it followed that, under
the rules and subject to any dispensation by the panel under r 11.2, they could acquire
no more Distillers shares in the market without at the same time making an offer to buy
all Distillers shares of the same class at a price not less than that paid by them for any
Distillers shares during the offer period or within 12 months prior to its commencement.
j In terms of hard cash, this meant that whereas the cash offer contained in the bid was
630p per share, if the 15% limit was exceeded, Guinness would have to raise their offer
to 731p per share, that being the highest price at which the Guinness concert party had
acquired Distillers shares in the relevant period. This must have been an unwelcome
prospect when even Argyll, as the rival bidder, was at that stage only offering 660p per
share.

On 17 April 1986 Mercury Warburg Investment Management Ltd, which owned 3% of Distillers shares, decided that the time had come to sell and that it wished to do so by *a* cash settlement that day. This block constituted 10·6m shares. Professional opinion was that so large a block would be difficult to place quickly, but, rather surprisingly, a buyer was found in the shape of Pipetec AG, a Swiss company, the agreed price being 705p per share. The stockbrokers acting for Pipetec were Cazenove & Co, who also acted for Guinness. The voting rights attached to such a large block of shares could obviously have a significant influence on whether Guinness or the rival Argyll bid succeeded. When the *b* deal came to the knowledge of Samuel Montagu & Co Ltd, advisers to Argyll, they invited the panel to investigate the matter with a view to finding out whether Pipetec was acting in concert with Guinness with the consequences to which I have already referred.

At this stage I should perhaps explain how the panel works and, for this purpose, I do not think that I can do better than refer to the first affidavit of Mr John Walker-Haworth, *c* the then director general:

'4. *The Panel executive*
    4.1 The Panel executive staff comprise both permanent officials and a number of individuals seconded from City firms and institutions. The Director General is usually a senior merchant banker experienced in corporate finance; in my own case *d* I am a director of S.G. Warburg & Co. Limited and have been involved in corporate finance for many years. The other seconded staff include accountants, stockbrokers, solicitors, civil servants, clearing bankers and personnel from the Bank of England.
    4.2 The role of the Panel executive is dealt with in paragraph 1(c) of the introduction to the Code which states: "The Panel works on a day to day basis through its executive, headed by the Director General. The Director General, or one *e* of his Deputies, is available to give rulings on points of interpretation of the Code or for consultation before or during take-over or merger transactions. Companies and their advisers are encouraged to make full use of this service. Consultations are confidential." In connection with any take-over, particularly where it is contested by the board of the offeree company or where there are competing offerors (as in *f* the case of the take-over of Distillers), the Panel executive is usually in daily contact with the principals' advisers, operating through telephone conversations, submissions of written information where necessary and through meetings as required, often at a few minutes' notice.
    4.3 The Panel executive is involved daily in giving many rulings on the interpretation of the Code to parties involved in take-overs. In 1986 there were some 40 or 50 take-overs proceeding at any one time including perhaps 10–20 *g* contested take-overs. Most issues do not involve breaches of the Code, but rather clarifying the application of the Code in advance of action taken so that a breach does not occur. In the vast majority of cases the Panel executive's rulings are simply accepted.
    4.4 Thus on a day-to-day basis, as is stated in paragraph 1(c) in the introduction *h* to the Code set out above, the work of the Panel in giving rulings and advice is carried out by the Panel executive. However, where a party is dissatisfied with the decision of the Panel executive it may appeal to the Panel. Alternatively the Panel executive may refer a particularly difficult or important matter to the Panel without giving a ruling itself. These matters are dealt with in paragraph 5 of the introduction to the Code.
    4.5 In the course of its work—whether in the context of giving rulings or advice *j* at the request of a party or in the context of its own investigations—the Panel executive may consider that there has or may have been a breach of the Code. This will have consequences for two different aspects of the Panel's work.
    4.5.1. The Code itself contemplates that if certain events occur requisite action should be taken in order to ensure that the principles of fair dealing are upheld.

This will, for example, include the principle of equality of treatment for offeree company shareholders. In such circumstances the Panel executive may where appropriate give a ruling in line with the principles of the Code as to the action necessary to ensure that no unfair advantage is received by the person in breach and that any disadvantage, such as to offeree company shareholders, is rectified. A ruling of this kind is described as a ruling as to the "Code consequences" arising from the events which have taken place. As I indicated above, the Panel executive may, instead of giving a ruling itself, refer the matter to the Panel for a ruling.

4.5.2. A breach of the Code does not necessarily result in any disciplinary action. Where a breach of the Code is thought to warrant disciplinary action, the Panel executive invites the person concerned to appear before the Panel for a hearing. The procedure at that hearing and the action which may be taken by the Panel are dealt with in paragraphs 6 and 7 of the introduction to the Code.

5. *The procedures of the Panel executive*

5.1   The object of the Panel procedures is to produce the right answer in Code terms in the circumstances. Though the procedures adopted by the Panel executive and the Panel are flexible so as to accommodate, wherever possible, the timetable set in relation to a take-over offer, the need to reach a correct answer is not sacrificed under the Code for the sake of speed.

5.2 When an issue requires the Panel executive to give a ruling on the interpretation of the Code or on a question of fact, such as whether or not persons are acting in concert, it seeks to establish the position as soon as practicable. Its procedures in an investigation of concert parties would be:—

5.2.1 to contact the relevant identifiable parties and to describe the substance of the issues;

5.2.2 to interview them (where possible) and examine any written information that may be available, in order to establish the relationship between the persons who might be acting in concert;

5.2.3 to look at the surrounding facts to discover whether actions are consistent with acting in concert;

5.2.4 to relay to the interested parties relevant evidence and give the principals the opportunity to respond to the evidence (including written evidence if available, although this is unusual because persons who might be seeking to conceal that they are acting in concert are unlikely to have any written understanding);

5.2.5 to assess the evidence and interpret Code consequences arising;

5.2.6 if the Panel executive considers that it is necessary for the Panel to decide the question of acting in concert, or if the Panel executive decides the question and any party disagrees, a meeting of the Panel will be called, at such notice as is reasonably necessary: during a take-over that might mean one or two days notice;

5.2.7 the parties will be notified of the time and venue for the hearing and asked to produce written submissions of the information available to them and their views on the case. The Panel executive will do the same. In advance of the hearing, copies of all such submissions will be distributed to the parties. These submissions would also be distributed to the Panel in advance. In some cases new evidence may appear at a Panel hearing which was not previously available to the Panel executive; such evidence is normally dealt with ad hoc at the hearing;

5.2.8 in cases where the Panel executive does not find evidence either to conclude that persons are acting in concert or to justify referring the question to the Panel, it will not proceed to a decision or such referral (although the matter may be referred to the Panel on appeal).

5.3 The aims of the Panel are to ensure the right application of the Code in the circumstances of the case; its procedures are directed at achieving this aim. They have been operated in relation to over 5,000 take-overs over some twenty years, and been accepted by practitioners, investors, and companies subject to the Code as reasonable to produce a fair conclusion in the light of the principles of the Code.

6. *Hearings of the Panel*

6.1 The composition of the panel for any hearing depends on availability of *a* individuals and conflicts of interest (e.g. a representative of the Issuing Houses Association who is a director of the adviser to a party would be ineligible): an attempt is made to ensure that as many Panel members are present as possible; in cases of unavailability or conflict an alternative is appointed if possible.

6.2 Any hearing opens with the Chairman briefly describing the nature of Panel hearings: their confidentiality and informality, the ability of all parties to make such *b* statements and representations and call such witnesses as they wish, to question other persons present, to question written submissions and otherwise make such oral submissions as they see fit. The Panel executive will express its views and the reasons for them and can question and be questioned by the parties. All parties present express their own views and submit such information as they wish and are free to question each other. Panel members in turn will ask questions and make *c* such comments as they think appropriate.

6.3 As stated in the introduction to the Code, there are no rules of evidence. A tape recording will normally be taken only for the administrative assistance of the Panel in its deliberations and even for this purpose has very rarely to be consulted but no permanent record is maintained and transcripts are not normally made.

6.4 Once all submissions have been made, the parties and the Panel executive *d* withdraw whilst the Panel makes its decision. All parties then reconvene to hear the decision of the Panel; the full reasons may be written thereafter, and, depending on the nature of the issues and the decision, may be published in the form of a public statement, sight of which is given to the parties before publication.

6.5 The consequences of a Panel decision, for example a finding that persons are or were acting in concert, may be evident from the application of the Code's rules *e* themselves. Where this is not the case, the Panel seeks to find an equitable solution in accordance with the principles of the Code.'

The complaint or invitation to investigate by Samuel Montagu was received by the panel executive on 17 April 1986. In accordance with r 31.6 of the code, the last day for either the Guinness or the Argyll offers to be successful or to lapse was 18 April 1986. It *f* was therefore a matter of the utmost urgency to determine whether or not the purchase of the 10·6m shares by Pipetec was a concert party operation. What happened next I can take from a background paper prepared by the executive and submitted to the panel for the purposes of the hearing on 2 September 1987:

'5.3 (Note: paragraph 5.3 is verbatim from the executive's notes except for *g* depersonalising the individual at the executive and entitling names.) (a) The executive (Mr Hinton through this paragraph) spoke to Mr Mayhew of Cazenoves explaining the Argyll concern. Mr Mayhew said that the order had been received from Banque Leu in Switzerland. Cazenoves dealt from time to time with Banque Leu but felt that they were acting as agents rather than principal in this deal. According to Mr Mayhew, the block of shares which had come onto the market that *h* morning, had been offered to one of the advisers to Distillers and had subsequently been brought to his attention by advisers to Guinness. He had been able to find a purchaser for these shares who was prepared to pay cash for immediate delivery. Mr Mayhew gave the executive the name of his contact at Banque Leu. Accordingly, the executive spoke to Mr Baumann in Lausanne. Mr Baumann said that he had been contacted by his client Pipetec AG who had informed him that they were *j* prepared to pay £7 cash for a line of Distillers shares. The reason that Banque Leu had been brought into the deal was because Mr Mayhew wanted a bank confirmation that Pipetec had the resources available. Mr Baumann described Pipetec as an investment company. After speaking to his principal, he was able to give to the executive the name of Dr Frey, managing director of Pipetec. (b) On 18 April the executive spoke to Dr Frey who said that Pipetec had absolutely no connection with

a
either of the offeror companies or with the offeree company. He felt that the Distillers shares were a good investment which would enable him to get into Guinness, "a company with considerable prospects". The executive decided that there was little more that the executive could obtain in the way of information but, in the circumstances, it was decided that the executive should ask Guinness and Morgan Grenfell for written confirmation that there were no arrangements for any side deal between Guiness and Pipetec. The executive contacted Mr Seelig of Morgan

b
Grenfell to this effect and he was quite happy for Guinness to provide such confirmation.

5.4 That written confirmation was given in a letter of 17 April 1986 which the executive received on 18 April . . .

5.5 It was clear that, as the Guinness share price was some 330p (making the Guinness basic securities exchange offer somewhat above 705p per Distillers share),

c
it was possible that an investment decision could be made in the way indicated to the executive.

5.6 On 18 April [Mercury Warburg Investment Management Ltd] (the seller of the 10·6mn shares) made a disclosure of the sale to The Stock Exchange and to the Panel. In the event, the price was 705p per share, not £7.'

d
The letter of confirmation from Guiness signed by Mr Olivier Roux was in the following terms:

'GUINNESS PLC

39 PORTMAN SQUARE LONDON W1H 9HB TELEPHONE 01 486 0288

TELEX 23368 FAX 01 486 4968

e
Confidential

17 April 1986

Dear Sir,

Distillers

You have asked us to write to you with respect to the reported purchase today of approximately 10 million shares in Distillers through Cazenove & Co. We have

f
spoken to Cazenoves and can confirm that the purchaser is not a subsidiary or associated company of Guinness, that such shares were not bought for our account and that we have made no financial arrangements with the purchaser with respect to such shares (including any arrangement linked to the sale of Distillers' listed investments).

g
Yours faithfully,

Olivier Roux

For and on behalf of

Guinness PLC

h
The Director General

Panel on Take-overs and Mergers

PO Box No. 226

The Stock Exchange Building

London EC2P 2JX.'

The panel executive having concluded that, on the evidence available to it, it should take no action, Guinness were free to declare their unconditional and did so on 18 April

j
1986.

Nothing further which is material happened until on 1 December 1986 inspectors were appointed under ss 432 and 442 of the Companies Act 1985, with wide terms of reference calling for an investigation of the affairs of Guinness. This was followed on 7 January 1987 by Bank Leu AG writing to the non-executive directors of Guinness:

'During the closing stages of the Guinness bid, Guinness entered into letter

agreements with subsidiaries of the Bank whereby these subsidiaries agreed to
purchase Guinness shares up to the value of £50,000,000 and confirmed the　*a*
purchase of Distillers shares to the value of £75,612,149·38. Guinness, for its part,
agreed to repurchase these shares within 60 days. These letters set out the Bank's
fees and remuneration for effecting the purchase as well as Guinness's obligation to
repurchase. In the events which followed, and at the request of Guinness, this 60
day period was extended. Subsequently, on the 2nd June, one of the subsidiaries
purchased a further 23,630,000 ordinary shares of Guinness on the same basis and,　*b*
as part of the arrangements to extend the 60 day period, the Guinness subsidiary G.
& C. Moore deposited £50,000,000 with Bank Leu (Luxembourg) as security for
Guinness's obligations. The documents setting up the above arrangements were
signed variously by Olivier Roux and Tom Ward. We had always assumed that the
transactions were properly carried out and that any necessary formalities would
have been complied with. The Distiller shares purchased were accepted to the offer　*c*
in consideration of Guinness shares. Certain sales of the Group's total holding of
Guinness shares occurred in the second half of June 1986, leaving a balance of
41,080,599 shares now held by the Bank Leu Group. It was at one time proposed
that these shares should form part of an international placing operation.'

There followed a boardroom upheaval as a result of which Sir Norman Macfarlane was　*d*
appointed chairman of Guinness and their accountants were asked to go to Switzerland
and talk to Bank Leu. During that visit they were given a copy of a letter dated 18 April
1986 purporting to be signed by Dr F Burger on behalf of Pipetec and by Mr Thomas
Ward, a United States attorney and director of Guinness, on behalf of Guinness. The
letter was in the following terms:

'Dear Mr. Ward,　　　　　　　　　　　　　　　　　　　　　　　　　　　　*e*
We are pleased to confirm our yesterday's telephone conversation with Mr. W. Frey
as follows: We, Pipetec AG, Luzern/Switzerland, have upon respective instructions
received from yourself bought Distillers Shares on the London Stock Exchange in
an aggregate value of 75'612'149.38 pound sterling. Guinness Plc, London, on the
other hand undertakes to a) To pay to us an up front arrangement fee of 47'250.—
pound sterling b) Repurchase from us the shares bought as per above (or the　*f*
respective securities issued by Guinness Plc upon conversion, as the case may be)
within 60 days at a price determined by adding (I) the original purchase price, (II)
commissions, fees and other costs charged in London in connections with such
purchase, (III) the taxes levied in Switzerland for securities transactions of 0,33% flat
(i.e. 0,165% each for purchase and sale of the shares), (IV) our commission of 0,1%
flat calculated on the purchase price and (V) our refinancing cost for the period from　*g*
the purchase of the shares to their sale on the basis of our actual funding cost plus a
margin of ⅛% p.a. We ask you to kindly confirm your agreement with the above by
returning to us the enclosed duplicate of this letter duly signed on behalf of Guinness
Plc.

　　　　　　　　　　　　　　　　　　　　Yours faithfully,　　　　　　*h*
　　　　　　　　　　　　　　　　　　　　PIPETEC AG
　　　　　　　　　　　　　　　　　　　　[Signed]
　　　　　　　　　　　　　　　　　　　　Dr. F. Burger.'

If this letter, which was referred to in argument and which I will refer to as 'the Pipetec
letter' was either genuine *or* accurate, it followed that the purchase by Pipetec of 10·6m　*j*
Distillers shares had indeed been a concert party operation and on 16 January 1987 Sir
Norman Macfarlane wrote to all stockholders telling them of the boardroom changes
and of what the new board had been able to find out about a number of transactions
entered into by Guinness under their previous board. This letter included the following
passage:

a
'In the last two weeks, a number of serious disclosures have been made to the Board and I feel it is important that I inform you forthwith of their main substance. It has been alleged that, during and after the bid for Distillers, substantial funds of the Company were applied in a widespread series of transactions involving both the purchase of its own shares and the giving of financial assistance with a view to their purchase. In particular, it has been established that substantial purchases of both Guinness and Distillers shares were made by wholly-owned subsidiaries of Bank Leu

b
AG on the strength of Guinness's agreement, signed on its behalf by Mr. Ward or Mr. Roux, to repurchase the shares at cost plus carrying charges—an agreement which, at least as regards its own shares, Guinness could not lawfully have fulfilled. It is also alleged that these purchases may have been financed by lines of credit granted by Bank Leu AG. In connection with these purchases, and in apparent breach of Companies' Act requirements, a Guinness subsidiary made a deposit of

c
£50 million with a Luxembourg subsidiary of Bank Leu AG. The present position is that the £50 million deposit remains and a total of approximately 41 million Guinness shares are held by the Bank Leu group.'

This was followed by a statement from the panel in the following terms:

'GUINNESS PLC

d
The Panel naturally views the events relating to Guinness that have unfolded over recent weeks with the greatest concern. From the public statements made by the company it appears that there may have been breaches of the law during the take-over of Distillers by Guinness. It seems likely to the Panel from the information which has so far emerged that there was also material, and it could well be in some cases deliberate, breaches of the Take-over Code. These concern disclosures of

e
dealings which should have been made, but were not. Furthermore, if any of the persons who received a secret undertaking of support or benefit from Guinness or its agents, and so were working in concert with Guinness, purchased shares in Distillers at above the level of the cash offer by Guinness for Distillers that would have had significant Code consequences for the Guinness offer. Normally, following its own investigation in any Code case in order to determine what had happened,

f
and, if breaches of the Code had occurred, who was at fault and what should be done, the Panel would promptly set out its findings and decisions in detail in a public statement. In the present situation, however, because Inspectors have been appointed, and legal consequences may flow from their work, the Panel must await the outcome of the Inspectors' enquiries, before publishing any findings or judgments of its own.'

g
There matters rested until 1 May 1987, when Sir Norman Macfarlane again wrote to shareholders in Guinness. The letter included the following paragraph:

'You may recall that Bank Leu, through two of its subsidiary companies, made purchases of Guinness and Distillers shares, on the basis of purported agreements for Guinness to repurchase these shares within a given period. Guinness subsequently

h
deposited £50 million with a Bank Leu subsidiary, which the Bank regarded as security. Guinness maintains that the supposed agreements with the Bank Leu subsidiaries are null and void, and has sought the return of the deposit. Bank Leu disputes this interpretation, but both parties are currently discussing how best to resolve their differences.'

j
It will be noted that there was no direct challenge to the fact of the agreements, only to their validity, that validity being a matter which might be thought to be irrelevant to the existence of a concert party operation.

On 13 May 1987 the Financial Services (Disclosure of Information) (Designated Authorities No 2) Order 1987, SI 1987/859, constituted the panel a designated authority for the purposes of s 180 of the Financial Services Act 1986 and s 449 of the Companies Act 1985 in relation to all its functions. The practical effect of this was that the Secretary of State for Trade and Industry was thereby permitted, but not required, to disclose information to the panel which he had acquired from his inspectors and, if he decided to make such disclosures, could, in the exercise of his discretion, impose conditions on the use which the panel could make of such information.

The panel executives' investigation

On 17 June 1987 Lazard Bros & Co Ltd, advisers to Guinness, were invited to a meeting with the executive at which Lazards were informed that the panel proposed to investigate the Pipetec purchase. It was explained that the decision no longer to await the Department of Trade and Industry (the DTI) inspectors' report resulted from additional information coming into the hands of the panel and specific mention was made of comments during legal proceedings before Sir Nicolas Browne-Wilkinson V-C in *Guinness plc v Saunders* [1988] BCLC 43. The representative of the panel executive made it clear that, whilst it had come to no conclusion on the question of whether the Pipetec purchase was a concert party operation, it had information which led it to conclude that this was a real possibility and it would appreciate information from Guinness about the precise details of that purchase. It was also made clear that the panel executive contemplated an investigation in two phases, the first involving a judgment on whether or not there was a concert party and, if there was, a second phase when the panel would consider the consequences. Those consequences might involve Distillers shareholders who had accepted the Guinness cash offer, or who might have done so if it had been of the same amount as that at which Pipetec purchased, being given a further sum to make up the difference.

Lazards raised three objections on behalf of Guinness, namely: (i) such had been the exodus of senior personnel from Guinness that there were real problems in Guinness discovering what had happened; (ii) what did happen was the subject of litigation which inhibited the scope of Guinness's response to a panel investigation; (iii) no reserve had been made in the Guinness accounts for any such liability as that contemplated by the panel executive.

On 23 July 1987 Messrs Herbert Smith, solicitors for Guinness, informed the panel that in the light of legal advice it would be unlikely that Guinness would be ready to co-operate with the panel until (i) the report of the DTI inspectors had been published, (ii) all criminal proceedings arising out of the take-over had been completed and (iii) all civil claims against Guinness, threatened or pending, had been fully settled or determined.

The letter then elaborated on Guinness's objections to a panel investigation *at that stage*. It was a closely reasoned document of five pages which I do not feel justified in reproducing in full. However, it is relevant that it made clear that: (a) Guinness objected to an investigation of the Pipetec transaction in isolation from any other aspect of the take-over, unless it was clear that there would be no other such investigations; (b) Guinness feared that any information given to the panel and any conclusions of the panel might be used by others to their detriment in civil proceedings or, if Guinness themselves became involved in criminal proceedings, in those proceedings; (c) Guinness concluded that it was not only their actions, but those of other concert party members, which would be relevant to the consequences of any finding of a concert party operation and they wanted to be assured that the investigation would be wide enough to give effect to such a view; (d) Guinness doubted whether the panel could secure effective co-operation from all concerned at the present stage, bearing in mind their conflicting interests and the panel's lack of power to compel discovery and the attendance of witnesses and further doubted whether, in the absence of such voluntary co-operation, the truth could be expected to emerge; in particular Guinness sought an assurance that the panel executive was satisfied that Bank Leu would co-operate fully.

On 31 July 1987 the panel executive told Herbert Smith informally that it would be continuing with the investigation, unless prevented by court order, that it would be making inquiries of merchant bankers and brokers during the next week and that, if a

a hearing was needed, it would be held on 2 September 1987. This was formally confirmed by a letter dated 5 August 1987 which explained that a hearing date was being fixed at that time in order to cover the possibility that a meeting of the full panel might be necessary and that, in the absence of such advance notice, relevant people might be unavailable. The letter also contained these passages:

b   'We consider that it is incumbent on the Panel executive, in the present circumstances, to look further into whether the relevant purchase was made by a person acting in concert with Guinness. If that were so, the Code consequences which may flow from that fact may be of importance. In determining to establish this point now, we have had particular regard to the interests of Distillers shareholders at the relevant time. Although we are focussing on one specific Code

c   aspect of the take-over of Distillers, it may be that further investigations on other matters, and perhaps meetings of the Panel, will be necessary in the future. We will obviously review when those should occur in the light of circumstances as they unfold. In this particular investigation, and any other investigation, the outcome could include a public statement by the Panel, incorporating such comments as the Panel considers appropriate. The extent to which any proceedings take on a

d   disciplinary aspect must depend on the facts and the Panel's approach to them. We would envisage following our normal procedures with regard to inviting those parties whom we consider appropriate to provide us with such relevant information as they may have; as with all Panel matters, this process should be completed as quickly as possible. With regard to the extent to which parties are willing to provide information and attend any Panel hearing, that is for them to inform us. Persons

e   who attend any Panel hearing will of course be given the usual opportunity to state their views and ask questions on matters relevant to the issues before the Panel which may concern them.'

On 7 August the DTI wrote confirming a telephone conversation of 3 August in which it had revealed the existence of the Pipetec letter and added that it was understood that nothing in the evidence given to the inspectors up to that time contradicted that letter.

f The DTI asked for undertakings that the Pipetec letter would not be published or disclosed other than to Guinness, Pipetec and Bank Leu without the consent of the Secretary of State. These undertakings were given and the Pipetec letter was passed to the panel executive.

On 10 August the panel executive told Herbert Smith on behalf of Guinness that it had a copy of the Pipetec letter. As it happened, Guinness had had this since January

g 1987, but this fact had previously been unknown to the panel executive. Next day the panel executive wrote again to Herbert Smith saying that it had not yet completed its inquiries, but hoped to do so shortly. It expressed the view that there was a prima facie case for holding that there had been a concert party operation and confirmed its intention, which had previously been only tentative, to convene a meeting of the full panel for

h 2 September. The letter invited Guinness to submit in advance a written paper for circulation to the panel, asked for any further information to be provided as soon as possible and offered to discuss the matter generally.

Between 11 and 13 August 1987 there were a series of oral and written exchanges between the panel executive, Guinness, Herbert Smith and Lazards, in which Guinness disputed the authority and accuracy of the Pipetec letter and pressed that there should be

j no hearing on the grounds previously advanced and on the grounds of the commercial disruption which Guinness might experience. The panel executive felt unable to agree to a postponement of the hearing on 2 September, but proposed that there should be a preliminary meeting of the panel on 25 August which could consider and rule on the issue of adjournment. The panel executive said that it would itself prepare a paper for the panel setting out its reasons for believing that there had been a concert party

transaction and invited Guinness to prepare and submit a paper setting out why the
matter should not be investigated at this stage. The executive added that if, on commercial a
grounds, Guinness were minded to seek a two- or three-month adjournment, it must be
clearly understood that they could not later come back and ask for a further adjournment.

Thereafter there were exchanges between the panel executive and Guinness's solicitors,
but the next event of moment was the delivery by the panel executive of its submissions
for the 25 August hearing on the issue of adjournment and draft submissions for the
hearing on 2 September on the substantial issue. b

The hearing on 25 August 1987
Mr Edward Walker-Arnott of Herbert Smith appeared for Guinness. We had been
furnished with a shorthand note of the proceedings and it is clear that he put the case for
an adjournment forcefully and persuasively. For present purposes perhaps his most
significant submissions were the following. (i) The panel's speedy and informal c
procedures were appropriate and acceptable in the context of a current take-over bid, but,
as was accepted by the panel, inappropriate to disciplinary proceedings where less speed
and a much more sustained attempt to get at the full facts was appropriate and indeed
essential. The present investigation, whilst perhaps not disciplinary in character, did
involve very substantial issues for Guinness, was being conducted after the bid had been
concluded and, in terms of what procedure was appropriate, was to be equated with d
disciplinary proceedings. (ii) To do justice, it was essential that Mr Tom Ward (lately a
director of Guinness), Mr Baumann, Dr Frey and Mr Burger (all executives of Bank Leu),
Mr Mayhew of Cazenove (Guinness's stockbrokers) and Mr Hinton (the member of the
panel executive who took part in its investigations in April 1986) should be called to give
evidence and be cross-examined. In Guinness's view neither Mr Ward nor any of the
Bank Leu witnesses would be willing to attend at that time. In answer to an inquiry e
from the chairman (Mr Robert Alexander QC), Mr Walker-Arnott said that Guinness did
not know when would be the right time to hold an inquiry, but it was not then.

The contemporary note of the chairman's ruling on behalf of the panel refusing to
vacate the 2 September hearing date reads as follows:

Judgment f
When all the parties had re-assembled RA [the chairman] thanked the parties
especially EWA [Mr Walker-Arnott]. He said the clear issue is whether or not the
hearing fixed for 2nd September should go ahead. There are a number of points
relevant to this which he wishes to make clear:—1. The case brought before the
Panel is not as a disciplinary matter but whether the facts which have been brought
to light have Code consequences. 2. If there were a breach of the Code this is one g
which took place some 15 months ago. If the facts had been known at the time this
matter would probably have been dealt with in April 1986. 3. Any delay would be
one which would run at least until the DTI Report and that must be some time
ahead. The delay would require a cogent case. RA said that he recognised two
points:—(a) That EWA had pointed out that there are potential serious consequences
to Guinness. EWA emphasised that the Panel would have to be careful before h
making a finding against Guinness. It is wholly accepted by the Panel that the
current management of Guinness is doing all it can. Having said that the Panel has
to bear in mind that the concern is for former Distillers shareholders. If there was a
breach of the Code then Guinness is responsible. (b) EWA's chief submission was
that justice could not be done now. If the Panel had accepted that it would have
adjourned the hearing of 2nd September. The Panel Executive have laid information, j
including: (1) the Pipetec letter; (2) the money that went to Cazenoves overnight;
(3) the two shareholders letters; and (4) that the DTI have received no information
that contradicts. The Panel therefore do not accept that the case is based almost
exclusively on the Pipetec letter. The Panel have received no positive information
from Guinness to throw doubt on the Pipetec letter. EWA has said that without co-

operation from Ward and others it will not be easy to evaluate the transaction.

a However, the Panel has received no evidence as to why Guinness throws doubt on the facts. In the circumstances the Panel does not think that it would be fair to adjourn the 2nd September hearing. RA emphasised:—(1) That if during the course of the hearing on 2nd September it appears that injustice would be done to Guinness the Panel will reconsider, but the Panel hopes that it will receive the co-operation of Guinness and that they will alert the Panel to any injustice. (2) Under the Code there

b is an opportunity of appeal to the Appeal committee. RA said he thought it right to indicate here and now that if the Panel decides against Guinness at the 2nd September hearing it would give leave to Guinness to appeal and include the opportunity of arguing that the state of facts was such that that hearing could not justly have been heard. RA said that he had not dealt at length with the jeopardy point as this could be severe and would depend in particular on whether Guinness owed a duty to

c Argyll. In his view this does not constitute a reason for no hearing to take place. Finally at the end of his submission EWA said that if the hearing went against Guinness there could be a public row. He asked the Panel to decline to exercise short term muscularity, but instead to exercise long term wisdom. RA said that he hopes that in considering the Distillers shareholders' position the Panel is showing long term wisdom. RA said that he hopes that Guinness will participate in the

d 2nd September hearing. An alternative would be for Guinness to seek to take Court proceedings. The Panel cannot be deflected by suggestions that this may lead to a dispute even where the company involved is one of the most reputable in the country. RA made it clear that he was refusing leave to appeal as of now. *Note*: The hearing commenced shortly after 3·00 p.m. and ended around 6·00 p.m.)'

e *Events between the two hearings*

At about 3·00 pm on 28 August 1987, which was the Friday before the August bank holiday weekend, the panel executive gave Lazards (on behalf of Guinness) the final version of its submissions for the hearing on Wednesday, 2 September. On Tuesday, 1 September Herbert Smith wrote a letter again seeking an adjournment, this time on

f the additional ground of the late delivery of the panel executive's final submissions. It is noteworthy that the letter contained the sentence: 'This effectively left one working day (today) for consideration of the paper and, *if Guinness should decide to participate in tomorrow's hearing*, for the formulation of a written submission' (my emphasis). The letter also submitted that, even if the issue of concert party or no concert party was decided on 2 September, the panel should not at once proceed to consider consequences since, in Guinness's view, this question of consequences in the present context raised

g novel issues of great complication and difficulty.

The panel executive rejected this submission and complained that it had continually invited Guinness to play a full part in the investigation, but they had failed to do so.

It is a fact that the final submission of the panel executive differed from the draft in two respects. The first, to which counsel for Guinness drew attention, but was unable to

h suggest reasons why it was really significant, was an expansion of section 3, 'Further information and the Executive's views', from 2½ pages to just over 9 pages. The second, which was undoubtedly crucial, was the disclosure of a letter from Messrs Allen & Overy, solicitors to Bank Leu, dated 27 August 1987 in which they too protested at the refusal to adjourn the hearing on 2 September 1987. The letter continued:

j 'In all the circumstances our clients have decided to confine themselves to a short statement of what they believe to be the salient facts, so far as they are concerned, relating to the Distillers share purchase. This statement runs as follows:—"The question of Bank Leu buying Distillers shares was first raised on the morning of 17th April 1986 when Tom Ward, a Guinness director, telephoned Dr. Werner Frey (a senior vice president of the Bank and deputy head of its trading division) at the Bank's offices in Zurich. Mr. Ward explained that approximately £75m worth of

Distillers shares was being offered for sale and asked whether the Bank would be in a position to make an immediate purchase of these shares for cash settlement that *a* same day. After Dr. Frey had first consulted with members of the Bank's board of management and reverted to Mr. Ward, he spoke (at the suggestion of Mr. Ward) to David Mayhew of Cazenove, Guinness's brokers, and confirmed the purchase of a total of 10,598,826 shares for the account of Pipetec AG, an investment company which was a sub-subsidiary of the Bank. The price was £7·0544 per share (exclusive of commission and stamp duty). The Bank's efforts to secure the necessary funds at *b* short notice were successful and Cazenove duly received payment of the inclusive purchase price of £76,612,149·38 during the afternoon of 17th April. (The Bank has no knowledge whatever of any funds being advanced, temporarily or otherwise, by Guinness in connection with the transaction). Following the purchase, on 17/ 18th April, both Mr. Kurt Baumann (in charge of the foreign stock exchange department within the Bank's trading division and responsible to Dr. Frey for *c* processing the transaction) and Dr. Frey himself received telephone calls from Mr. Hinton of the Take-over Panel. Mr. Hinton was primarily concerned to know whether Pipetec had any connection with either Guinness, Distillers or Argyll. There being no shareholding relationship between Pipetec and any of those companies, Mr. Baumann and Dr. Frey confirmed in separate conversations that Pipetec had no such connection. The arrangements agreed between Mr. Ward and *d* Dr. Frey for the purchase of the Distillers shares were subsequently confirmed in a letter from Pipetec to Mr. Ward dated 18th April 1986, of which the Panel apparently has a copy, supplied (it is understood) by the DTI. This letter sets out the arrangements for an up-front fee and the repurchase of the shares (or the Guinness shares representing them) within a 60 day period. The fee was not in fact paid nor were the shares repurchased. The Distillers shares were purchased by Pipetec in non- *e* assented form and registered in the name of Cazenove Nominees. They were subsequently accepted to the Guinness offer for a mix of Guinness ordinary and convertible preference shares. The £50m was not deposited by Guinness with the Bank until some weeks after the Distillers share purchase: no such security was in contemplation at the time of the purchase. To the best of the Bank's knowledge, no *f* other Distillers shares were bought for the account of the Bank or any of its subsidiaries in connection with the Guinness bid, either before or after 17th April 1986." The Bank intends to rest on this statement for the purpose of the hearing on 2nd September. Accordingly it is not proposed that any of the Bank's officers should attend the hearing, indeed Dr. Frey will in any case be away on military service at the time. Representatives of this firm will however be entrusted with a watching *g* brief on the Bank's behalf. Finally, quite apart from our clients' objections to the principle of the Panel's enquiry at this particular juncture, may we say that we regard it as quite unjustifiable that our clients should be subjected to such a stringent timetable: we were given less than one month's notice to prepare for the hearing, the whole of which falls within the August holiday period when inevitably key people are unavailable for significant periods of time. As you will appreciate more *h* than 16 months has already elapsed since the transaction took place—why now the sudden urgency?'

The hearing on Wednesday, 2 September 1988

At this hearing Guinness again asked for an adjournment. Mr Walker-Arnott's main point was that the panel's submission was substantially different from the draft which *j* they had previously had and that they had been faced with dealing with it over the bank holiday weekend. Furthermore, it was only on the previous day that the Guinness directors had decided to attempt to put all the material which they had before the panel. He said:

'In this matter there has been pace and frenetic activity. This may be all right in a a   bid situation. Even accepting the principle of fairness to the Distillers shareholders does not justify this speed. Four days' notice of an articulated case of principles given the sums of money involved and the damage to Guinness is utterly unfair and unreasonable.'

Mr Walker-Arnott then asked for an adjournment of some weeks.

The panel refused this adjournment and proceeded to the first phase of the hearing,
b   dealing with the issue of whether or not there had been a concert party. In the course of that hearing Mr Walker-Arnott clarified a previous offer, made in the context of the application for an adjournment, to pay interest to Distillers shareholders on any 'top-up' award. He said:

'The present directors do not think that they can possibly assure the panel here and now and bind future directors to whatever the finding of the panel may be and
c   whenever it may be made. The Guinness directors can say that if they accept the panel finding and its consequences, they would accept a panel requirement for a compensatory interest uplift.'

This formulation reflects some reservations on the part of Guinness whether making payments in accordance with the direction or request by the panel would be intra vires
d   the company. The panel held that there had been a concert party operation.

When the panel moved on to phase 2, 'consequences', it became apparent that the problem was more complicated than it had at first appeared and, at the chairman's suggestion, this aspect was adjourned to enable talks to take place between the panel executive, Guinness and others.

e   *The panel's reasons*

At a later date the panel gave written reasons for its decisions not to adjourn and for its finding of a concert party. These are clearly of the greatest importance and I do not think that I can fairly summarise them. [His Lordship appended to his judgment the panel's reasons for its decisions, but they are not reproduced in this report.]

f   *The panel appeal committee*

The panel has established an appeal committee consisting of a chairman (at present Lord Roskill) and members of the panel who did not attend the panel hearing and are not disqualified from sitting by interest or involvement in the dispute. The introduction to the code provides at section A6:

'There is a right of appeal to the Appeal Committee in a case where the Panel
g   finds a breach of the Code and proposes to take disciplinary action; and also in a case where it is alleged that the Panel has acted outside its jurisdiction. An appeal may also lie, with leave of the Panel, against decisions which, although not strictly of a disciplinary nature, inflict in the view of the Panel serious hardship on an individual or company. No appeal, however, lies against a finding of fact or against a decision
h   of the Panel on the interpretation of the Code. A right of appeal to the Appeal Committee will also lie in respect of any refusal by the Panel to recognise, or any decision of the Panel to cease to recognise, a market-maker or fund manager as an exempt market-maker or exempt fund manager as the case may be. The Appeal Committee does not normally hear new evidence. If the Appeal Committee considers there may be material new evidence which could not have been presented
j   to the Panel, then it will normally remit the matter to the Panel for further consideration. If an appeal is upheld, the appellant is consulted on the form of statement (if any) which is to be published. If an appeal is dismissed, the findings of the Panel are published and any steps decided upon by way of penalty implemented. In either case the Appeal Committee may make any further comment it thinks fit.'

The panel took the view that it would be right to give Guinness leave to appeal to the appeal committee on all points, but to make this leave only operative after a decision has been reached on 'consequences'. There were two reasons given for this approach. First, it *a* was at that time thought that consequences could be resolved by agreement or otherwise within a relatively short time. Second, it was thought that the appeal committee should be enabled to view the matter 'in the round'. Guinness were dissatisfied with this decision, wishing to have the right, whether or not they would exercise it and whether or not they would in any event apply for judicial review, to take the issues of adjournment and concert party to the appeal committee before embarking on any consideration of *b* consequences.

Conclusion

I approach this appeal by reminding myself that the judicial review jurisdiction of the High Court, and of this court on appeal, is a supervisory or 'longstop' jurisdiction. It also has a large discretionary content, which contributes to its value. Thus, to take extremes, *c* in *R v Liverpool City Justices, ex p Lunt* [1988] CA Transcript 675 this court gave leave to apply for judicial review of an order of magistrates sentencing the applicant to 42 days' imprisonment for non-payment of rates, notwithstanding that he had served the sentence in August and September 1985 and that the normal time limit for such an application is three months. Suffice it to say that the circumstances were wholly exceptional. At the opposite end of the spectrum, and coincidentally in the context of the take-over battle for *d* Distillers, this court found that the chairman of the Monopolies Commission had acted wholly without jurisdiction, but refused to quash his order (see *R v Monopolies and Mergers Commission, ex p Argyll Group plc* [1986] 2 All ER 257, [1986] 1 WLR 763). I also remind myself that, consistently with this 'longstop' character, it is not the practice of the court to entertain an application for judicial review unless and until all avenues of appeal have been exhausted, at least in so far as the alleged cause for complaint could *e* thereby be remedied. The rationale for this self-imposed fetter on the exercise of the court's jurisdiction is twofold. First, the point usually arises in the context of statutory schemes and if Parliament directly or indirectly has provided for an appeals procedure it is not for the court to usurp the functions of the appellate body. Second, the public interest normally dictates that, if the judicial review jurisdiction is to be exercised, it *f* should be exercised very speedily and, given the constraints imposed by limited judicial resources, this necessarily involves limiting the number of cases in which leave to apply should be given.

I also remind myself, as a general proposition, that a decision whether or not to adjourn a hearing is par excellence a matter for the exercise of judicial discretion by the court or tribunal seised of the matter and that it is well settled that, on an appeal from such a decision, an appellate court will not intervene only on the ground that it thinks that it *g* would have reached a different decision. It must be satisfied that the first instance decision was wrong in principle or, which is usually the same thing, that it resulted from a self-misdirection. Where, therefore, a right of appeal exists but is not exercised, something more is required if relief is to be granted on judicial review. Quite how much or what more defies definition, if only because intervention by the court in such *h* circumstances is wholly exceptional, but an example is provided by *R v Chief Constable of the Merseyside Police, ex p Calveley* [1986] 1 All ER 257, [1986] QB 424 and, in particular, the judgment of May LJ. If the right of appeal has been exercised, a different situation arises, because the court will then be reviewing the decision of the appellate body and asking itself whether that body has fulfilled its proper function.

The application for judicial review which is the subject matter of this appeal is limited *j* to the panel's refusals to order an adjournment when requested to do so on 25 August 1987 and on 2 September 1987. Essentially the application on 25 August was for what might be described as a long adjournment, ie until after all proceedings, both civil and criminal, had been concluded and the report of the DTI inspectors had been published. This is not to say that the panel did not have to consider whether some shorter

adjournment, until, for example, the DTI inspectors had completed taking evidence,
a would have been appropriate. The panel also had to consider whether an adjournment
of whatever duration would enable it to be more sure that it had got at the truth of the
matter. Although this application was expressly or impliedly repeated on the occasion of
the 2 September hearing, the application on that occasion was essentially for a short
adjournment to enable Guinness to respond to the final submission of the panel executive,
which they had received only on Friday, 28 August 1987. Somewhat different
b considerations apply to the two applications, although there is an overlap, and I will
consider them separately.

The long adjournment

As I have already indicated, I think that, at least in the circumstances of this appeal, it
is more appropriate to consider whether something has gone wrong of a nature and
c degree which require the intervention of the court, rather than to approach the matter
on the basis of separate heads of *Wednesbury* unreasonableness and unfairness or breach
of the rules of natural justice (see *Associated Provincial Picture Houses Ltd v Wednesbury
Corp* [1947] 2 All ER 680, [1948] 1 KB 223). In passing I would, however, accept that
whether the rules of natural justice have been transgressed is not to be determined by a
Wednesbury test: could any reasonable tribunal be so unfair? On the other hand, fairness
d must depend in part on the tribunal's view of the general situation and a *Wednesbury*
approach to that view may well be justified. If the tribunal's view should be accepted,
then fairness or unfairness falls to be judged on the basis of that view rather than the
court's view of the general situation.

Counsel for Guinness has taken a number of points in support of his submission that
the court should intervene. His first is that the panel approached the matter very much
e as though it were an investigation taking place within the constraints of time imposed
when a bid is current, whereas the bid had been concluded 15 months earlier and there
were a number of unique features. In particular he drew attention to (a) the unenviable
and unavoidable state of ignorance of the present Guinness board as to what actually
happened, (b) the fact that DTI inspectors had been appointed and the panel had become
a designated body to which the Secretary of State could convey information derived from
f evidence given to the inspectors and (c) the fact that criminal and civil proceedings might
well inhibit candour on the part of those in a position to know the facts.

Counsel also criticised the distinction which, in his submission, the panel made
between investigations into a bid and disciplinary proceedings, treating these proceedings
as being in the former category, whereas he said that they were either sui generis or
should be equated with the latter category. He went on to criticise the weight which, in
g his submission, the panel gave to the fact that, if, in April 1986, it had been disclosed to
the panel that Guinness had attempted to assist in the purchase of the Pipetec shares by
providing £76m to Cazenove on an overnight basis, there would have been a
contemporaneous further investigation, the outcome of which could not be predicted.
Finally he submitted that former Distillers shareholders would be amply protected if
h they were told to keep evidence of their transactions and any 'top-up' award included
interest at commercial rates.

There is force in these criticisms in the sense that they have to be taken very seriously.
However, the conduct of the panel has to be judged in the light of the position as it saw
it, provided always that its assessment was a reasonable one.

In my judgment it was not unreasonable for the panel to regard the investigation as
j having some of the character of one which was contemporaneous with the bid, for at
least two reasons. First, it was concerned with precisely the same issue as had in fact
arisen during the bid: concert party or no concert party? Second, assuming that there
had been a concert party, and of course no problem arises on any other hypothesis, the
primary reason why it was not dealt with by the panel during the currency of the bid
was the fact that Mr Olivier Roux on behalf of Guinness had falsely confirmed in the

letter dated 17 April 1986 that Guinness had made no financial arrangements with
Pipetec.   *a*

Furthermore, in my judgment it was not unreasonable for the panel to regard these
proceedings as being essentially different from disciplinary proceedings. They were
inquisitorial in nature as well as procedure, being directed at finding out what happened,
rather than convicting anyone of an offence. It was, as it were, an inquiry in rem, rather
than an adversarial proceeding, whether or not conducted inquisitorially, in personam.
True it is that the panel's findings might give rise to financial consequences, favourable *b*
to former Distillers shareholders and unfavourable to others, notably Guinness, but not
necessarily limited to Guinness. However, financial consequences are inherent in all the
work of the panel and their existence does not, of itself, point to any particular activity of
the panel having a disciplinary character.

That said, the panel had to, and I am clear did, take account of the fact that, the bid
being an accomplished fact, it was not working to an imminent and defined deadline, *c*
but could investigate the facts more fully than would otherwise have been possible.

Given the fact that Guinness could put forward no grounds for believing that the panel
would be better informed in any respect directly relevant to the issue of whether the
purchase of the shares by Pipetec was a concert party operation before or even when all
proceedings had been concluded and the DTI inspectors' report published, months and
possibly years into the future, and the panel's assessment of the detriment to former *d*
Distillers shareholders which would flow from such a delay, I am quite unable to criticise
the panel for its decision. No doubt there is always a possibility that any trial or inquiry
will one day be shown by further evidence to have reached a wrong conclusion, but even
in the context of the trial of capital offences, this was never an argument for long
adjournments. Rather it was an argument for not having any such offences and therefore
trials relating to them, but Guinness does not suggest that the panel should not one day *e*
decide whether there was a concert party operation in April 1986.

This does not dispose of the question of whether the panel should not have granted a
shorter adjournment of, say, three months. Parties who open their mouths far too wide
may still be entitled to a cut off the joint, even if they are clearly not entitled to the joint
itself. Looking at the matter as it stood on 25 August 1987 I find this not an easy problem *f*
to resolve. Evidentially the position was that there were very powerful indications that
Pipetec had been involved in a concert party operation. Unless the panel itself were to
embark on some further and different methods of investigation, there was no realistic
basis for believing that an adjournment for even six months would provide it with other
or better evidence. No one was likely to volunteer information who had not already done
so and, whilst the DTI investigation was proceeding, nothing had emerged to contradict *g*
the accuracy (I leave on one side the authenticity) of the Pipetec letter and, I would add,
that remained the position when the appeal was heard in this court nearly 12 months
later.

And this brings me to what caused me the greatest anxiety in this appeal. Should the
panel not have sought to achieve the personal attendance of relevant witnesses from Bank
Leu as requested by Guinness? The difficulties in the way of securing the attendance of *h*
Mr Ward were obvious and virtually insurmountable, but personal evidence from Mr
Baumann, Dr Frey and Mr Burger might well have either put the matter beyond all
doubt or, perhaps, created real doubt.

Now it is quite true that the panel has no power to compel the attendance of witnesses,
still less witnesses from overseas. But this may be a somewhat narrow view. The panel
has no de jure power to do anything, but it wields immense de facto power and influence *j*
by means of the support of others who have the power to render untenable the position
in the market of those who do not choose to co-operate with the panel. Counsel for the
panel, said that the panel did not agree that it could have used indirect pressure to secure
the attendance of these gentlemen. I have to accept that the panel is in the best position
to know, but I find the answer surprising. I bear in mind that, possibly apocryphal, story

of the office boy who was invited to meet the chairman for a friendly discussion on the
a former's conduct. The dialogue ended with the chairman saying, 'Well Jones, it was only
a suggestion, but I am sure that you will remember who made it.' The Bank Leu
witnesses were very far from being office boys, but I should· have thought that they
might, for rather different reasons, have been susceptible to strongly worded suggestions.

My anxieties on this score, looking at the situation as it was on 25 August 1987, do not
exist looking at the situation as it had revealed itself by 2 September. The panel by then
b had the Allen & Overy letter containing the Bank Leu statement. This was a carefully
considered, indeed counsel for Guinness described it as 'negotiated', statement authorised
at the highest level and made with legal advice. It amounted to a complete admission
that the Pipetec purchase was indeed a concert party operation. True it is that it was short
on any detail as to why this occurred or what Bank Leu or those who took the decision
thought that they would get out of it, but it was unequivocal in relation to all matters
c with which the panel was concerned.

Any court or tribunal faced with such an admission will bear in mind the fact that,
however rarely, false admissions are sometimes made when the consequences of telling
the truth and the whole truth may be even more undesirable than those flowing from
the false admission. In this situation I pressed counsel for Guinness to advance any reason,
however fanciful, why Bank Leu should have made this admission if it was not true. The
d bank's conduct was, it appeared, under investigation by the Swiss banking authorities
who would get to know of it and were in a position to test its accuracy. In addition the
bank had given evidence to the DTI inspectors and that evidence must have been
consistent with their admission, since the panel had been told that the inspectors had no
evidence to contradict the contents of the Pipetec letter. All that counsel could suggest
was that the statement might be an attempt to explain away a hypothetical failure by the
e bank to maintain liquidity ratios. This suggestion was in fact touched on before the panel
and appears not to have made any impression on the members, although it was supremely
something which it, rather than the court, was in a position to evaluate.

In other such cases, if they ever occur and if the evidence is not so overwhelming, I
have no doubt that the panel should, and I hope would, give serious consideration to
whether, de facto, it may not be in a position to summon witnesses if there is time to do
f so.

In short, whilst I have reservations about the wisdom of the decision of 25 August in
refusing even a relatively short adjournment during which the panel might have made
more vigorous attempts to secure the attendance of the Bank Leu witnesses, I have no
doubt that the situation had changed by 2 September 1987.

g *The short adjournment*

By this I refer to the application on 2 September 1987 based on the later arrival of the
Bank Leu statement and the need for Guinness indeed to indulge in frenetic activity if
they were to prepare an adequate submission over the bank holiday weekend. At this
point it is necessary to give separate consideration to actual and apparent injustice to
h Guinness. Of actual injustice there is no trace. The essential evidence supporting a
finding of a concert party along the lines set out in the Pipetec letter, which incidentally
had been in the possession of Guinness for nine months, and the corroborative evidence,
apart from the Allen & Overy letter, had been in the possession of Guinness for ample
time to enable them to formulate submissions, as indeed they had been continually
urged to do. The Allen & Overy letter was the last nail in the coffin, and a substantial
j one, but it could not in any way affect what Guinness had to say and no one is suggesting
that it did. The reality is that their embarrassment stemmed from the eleventh hour
decision by the board of Guinness to co-operate in the panel's investigation. Even this
need not have created embarrassment, because contingency plans could have been laid.

As to the apparent injustice, counsel for Guinness relied on the attitude of the courts
as exemplified by *R v Thames Magistrates' Court, ex p Polemis* [1974] 2 All ER 1219, [1974]

1 WLR 1371, where the court quashed a conviction on the grounds that the defendant
had no reasonable opportunity of preparing and presenting his defence, even if, with   *a*
hindsight, it could be established that he had no defence to present. There is force in this
submission, but I think that it confuses the position of Guinness with that of a defendant.
Guinness were only witnesses at an inquiry, albeit with a substantial interest in the
outcome. In this they were not alone. The same could be said of others. But in any event
'apparent' injustice is concerned with the appearance of proceedings if the full facts are
known, not with injustice as it might appear to someone who knows only some of the   *b*
facts. If a disinterested observer had been told that, apart from the Allen & Overy letter,
Guinness had had ample time to prepare, but had chosen not to do so, and that it was
open to them to suggest any reason why the Allen & Overy letter was not conclusive of
the issue but they had been unable to do so, I do not think that he would have concluded
that there had been any injustice. Bank Leu were not surprise witnesses in the sense that
they arrived out of the blue. Guinness's accountants had been talking to officials of the   *c*
bank in the previous January and could have talked to them at any time thereafter. The
element of surprise was only that the bank should have made the statement at all and
done so at the eleventh hour.

That said, it is the experience of the courts that it is sometimes wiser to appear naive
and to grant unmeritorious applications for short adjournments, even when the full facts
reveal no injustice actual or apparent, provided always that it can be done without   *d*
creating insuperable difficulties to reaching an early decision. Such difficulties may well
have existed had a short adjournment been granted on 2 September and it had been
necessary to convene a further meeting of the panel. Suffice it to say that, whilst the
panel could never have been criticised if it had granted a short adjournment, I do not
find it possible to say that its decision not to do so was wrong.

This is sufficient to dispose of this appeal and to explain why I would dismiss it, but I   *e*
should also make brief mention of the failure on the part of Guinness to use the panel's
appeal machinery. The panel appeal committee had in many respects wider powers to
review the panel's decision and it is not apparent why the requirement that a decision
should first be reached on consequences should be an insuperable obstacle from the point
of view of Guinness. However, bearing in mind the novelty of the panel, its powers and
constitution and the unprecedented situation which had arisen, I do not regard this   *f*
failure as an absolute bar to the granting of relief. Nevertheless, I wish to make it clear
that, if such a case should recur, any applicant for relief on judicial review may well find
that such a failure is of itself treated as a bar.

I would dismiss the appeal.

LLOYD LJ. This is only the second case in which a decision of the Panel on Take-overs   *g*
and Mergers has been challenged in the courts. In the first, *R v Panel on Take-overs and
Mergers, ex p Datafin plc* [1987] 1 All ER 564 at 579, [1987] QB 815 at 842, Sir John
Donaldson MR said:

> 'The only circumstances in which I would anticipate the use of the remedies of
> certiorari and mandamus would be in the event, which I hope is unthinkable, of the   *h*
> panel acting in breach of the rules of natural justice, in other words, unfairly.'

Counsel for Guinness plc submits that the unthinkable has occurred in this case. His
central submission is that his clients have not had a fair opportunity of presenting their
case. If that were so, then whatever the nature of the proceedings before the panel,
whether they are properly characterised as adversarial, inquisitorial or somewhere in   *j*
between, we should not hesitate to intervene.

Counsel made it clear at the very outset of his submissions that he is not attacking the
substance of the panel's decision. He conceded that there was evidence on which the
panel could conclude that Pipetec AG was a concert party, and that the panel's decision
might well turn out to have been correct. Counsel's attack is not on the substance of the

panel's decision, but on its decision to go ahead with the hearing on 2 September 1987. I
a refer to 'decision' in the singular because, although there are two decisions under attack,
that of 25 August and that of 2 September, in the end it is the panel's conduct in the
round which is called in question.

So I emphasise again that we are not here concerned with the substantive decision on
the issue whether there was a concert party. It is the 'decision-making process', in Lord
Brightman's often repeated phrase, that we have to consider: see *Chief Constable of the*
b *North Wales Police v Evans* [1982] 3 All ER 141 at 154, [1982] 1 WLR 1155 at 1173. The
point is of a special importance in the present case for two reasons.

In the first place the question whether we are entitled to intervene at all is not to be
answered, as counsel for the panel argued, by reference to *Wednesbury* unreasonableness
(see *Associated Provincial Picture Houses Ltd v Wednesbury Corp* [1947] 2 All ER 680, [1948]
1 KB 223). It is not a question whether, in the language of Lord Diplock, quoted by
c Watkins LJ in the Divisional Court, the decision to hold the hearing on 2 September was
'so outrageous in its defiance of logic or of accepted moral standards that no sensible
person who had applied his mind to the question to be decided could have arrived at it'
(see *Council of Civil Service Unions v Minister for the Civil Service* [1984] 3 All ER 935 at 951,
[1985] AC 374 at 410). Rather, the question has to be decided in accordance with the
principles of fair procedure which have been developed over the years, and of which the
d courts are the author and sole judge. These principles, which apply as well to
administrative as judicial tribunals, are known compendiously (if misleadingly) as the
rules of natural justice.

Counsel for the panel argued that the correct test is *Wednesbury* unreasonableness,
because there could, he said, be no criticism of the way in which the panel reached its
decision on 25 August. It is the substance of that decision, viz the decision not to adjourn
e the hearing fixed for 2 September, which is in issue. I cannot accept that argument. It
confuses substance and procedure. If a tribunal adopts a procedure which is unfair, then
the court may, in the exercise of its discretion, seldom withheld, quash the resulting
decision by applying the rules of natural justice. The test cannot be different just because
the tribunal *decides* to adopt a procedure which is unfair. Of course the court will give
great weight to the tribunal's own view of what is fair, and will not lightly decide that a
f tribunal has adopted a procedure which is unfair, especially so distinguished and
experienced a tribunal as the panel. But in the last resort the court is the arbiter of what
is fair. I would therefore agree with counsel for Guinness that the decision to hold the
hearing on 2 September is not to be tested by whether it was one which no reasonable
tribunal could have reached.

The second reason why it is important to emphasise that we are not here concerned
g with the substance of the panel's decision is that it touches on another point, very faintly
argued by counsel for the panel, that the application for judicial review is premature.
Guinness should first, he says, have exhausted their remedies by way of appeal to the
appeal committee.

There is no doubt as to the general rule. It applies not only where Parliament has
h provided an avenue of appeal, as in *R v Chief Constable of the Merseyside Police, ex p Calveley*
[1986] 1 All ER 257, [1986] QB 424, though the rule was not applied on the special facts
of that case. It applies also where the appeal procedure is contractual, and indeed where
it is neither statutory nor contractual. The justification for the rule is convenience, by
which I mean not just the convenience of the court, but the public interest in abating
litigation.

j But, as *Ex p Calveley* itself shows, there are exceptions to the general rule. The present
case is exceptional, partly because the panel has refused leave to appeal until after there
has been a further hearing as to the consequences of its decision, and partly because when
the appeal takes place (if it does) it will not be in the nature of a complete rehearing.
When the substance of a decision is attacked by judicial review, on the ground of
Wednesbury unreasonableness or any other ground, the court will be very reluctant

indeed to intervene, if there is an immediate appeal open on the merits. However, the court will be less reluctant to intervene where the attack is based on procedural irregularity, and the substantive appeal has to be postponed for some reason or is limited in scope. So I would respectfully agree with the Divisional Court that it was fully open to Guinness to apply for judicial review in the present case.

There is one other matter which I should mention at the outset, since it featured prominently in the argument of counsel for the panel. Over and over again he stressed that the task which faced the panel, both on 25 August and 2 September, was a balancing task. By this he meant, I think, that the panel had to balance the need to give Guinness a fair hearing against the urgent need to compensate former Distillers shareholders, or perhaps, more accurately, the urgent need to ensure that they receive fair treatment in accordance with general principle 1 of the City Code on Take-overs and Mergers.

I would only comment at this stage that no amount of urgency in compensating former shareholders would justify depriving Guinness of a fair opportunity of presenting their case. It was said that the concept of fairness is flexible; and so in a sense it is. I would accept that what is required of a tribunal, if it is to be fair, must depend on the nature of the task in hand and the circumstances prevailing at the time in question. But it is certainly not flexible in the sense that, once what is fair has been ascertained, the tribunal can be allowed to fall short of that standard by so much as an iota.

Secondly, if, by his emphasis on the panel's balancing task, counsel was hinting that the decision as to what was fair in the present case was really one for the panel rather than the court, then I would disagree. One can understand the view that the panel, with its great experience of City affairs, is well equipped to decide what is fair by City standards. The court does not seek to match the panel's experience in that regard. But it does have long experience of other tribunals of all sorts, high and low. It would be failing in its duty if it did not enforce those principles of fair procedure which it has developed over many years. As the court pointed out in *Ex p Datafin* case [1987] 1 All ER 564, [1987] QB 815, the unique character of the panel should not, and does not, exclude it from the court's purview in this or any other respect.

The central submission counsel for Guinness, as I have said, is that Guinness did not have a fair opportunity of presenting their case. He supports that submission on two grounds. The first and main ground, known as the general adjournment point, was that the panel should not have proceeded with the hearing until after the Department of Trade and Industry (the DTI) inspectors had completed their taking of evidence. The request for a general adjournment was considered and rejected by the panel on 25 August. The second and subsidiary ground, known as the limited adjournment point, was that the panel should have adjourned for a matter of weeks or even days in order to enable Guinness to give proper consideration to the panel executive's case, the final version of which only came into Guinness's hands at 3·00 pm on Friday, 28 August. Since Monday, 31 August was a bank holiday and since the Guinness director dealing with the matter, Mr S C Dowling, only returned from holiday on the Monday night, Guinness had only one working day to consider the final version of the executive's case and decide what to do. The request for a limited adjournment, together with a renewal of the request for a general adjournment, was considered and rejected by the panel on 2 September.

Although the main weight of counsel's argument rested on the general adjournment point, it is convenient to consider the limited adjournment point first. The facts have been set out in the judgment of Lord Donaldson MR. I will not repeat them. Although Guinness had been in possession of the first version of the executive's case for some days, they did not know that Bank Leu's witnesses would not be available for cross-examination, and they did not see Bank Leu's written statement contained in Messrs Allen & Overy's letter of 27 August until they were sent the final version on 28 August. Moreover, the executive's views, as set out in section 3, had expanded from two and a half pages to just over nine pages. Guinness asked for a short adjournment to consider the position, and prepare a further answer if necessary, without prejudice to their request for a longer adjournment. Counsel for Guinness submitted that the panel's refusal of a short

a adjournment was, in the circumstances, quite simply incomprehensible.

Counsel for the panel, on the other hand, relied first and foremost on the fact that Guinness had been in possession of the Pipetec letter, which was the crucial piece of evidence against them (if so it can be called) since January. He submitted that Bank Leu's written statement added nothing of substance to the Pipetec letter other than to make clear where Bank Leu stood. It showed in effect that the executive had been deceived by

b Bank Leu when it was making its inquiries in April 1986. Secondly, counsel submitted that, even if the panel had granted a short adjournment for a matter of weeks or days, there was not anything much Guinness could usefully have done. They never said why they wanted a short adjournment. The panel was presented with nothing but a naked request.

I would unhesitatingly reject counsel's second argument. In *R v Thames Magistrates'*

c *Court, ex p Polemis* [1974] 2 All ER 1219, [1974] 1 WLR 1371 the master of a Greek vessel was served with a summons alleging a breach of the Prevention of Oil Pollution Act 1971. The summons was returnable at 2·00 pm that same day. The solicitors appearing for the master applied for an adjournment. But an adjournment was refused, no doubt because the vessel was due to sail at 9·00 pm that night. The hearing took place at 4·00 pm. The master was convicted. The Divisional Court quashed the conviction on

d the ground that the master had not had a reasonable opportunity of preparing his case. There had been a breach of natural justice. One of the arguments put forward in support of the conviction was that an adjournment would have served no purpose. There was no useful evidence which the master could have obtained. The result would have been the same. Lord Widgery CJ said ([1974] 2 All ER 1219 at 1223, [1974] 1 WLR 1371 at 1375)

e 'I reject that submission. It is again absolutely basic to our system that justice must not only be done but must manifestly be seen to be done. If justice was so clearly not seen to be done, as on the afternoon in question here, it seems to me that it is no answer to the applicant to say, "Well, even if the case had been properly conducted, the result would have been the same". That is mixing up doing justice with seeing that justice is done, so I reject that argument.'

f It was said that the principles on which *Ex p Polemis* was decided do not apply, or do not apply with the same force, to the sort of investigation being carried out by the panel. I do not agree. I do not find it helpful to draw any distinction, for present purposes, between the panel's disciplinary function and its investigatory function, or to characterise the proceedings as adversarial or inquisitorial. The bare facts of the matter are that the inquiry was being held some 16 months after completion of the take-over. The result of

g the inquiry may yet be that Guinness will have to compensate former Distillers shareholders with a sum which may be as much as £200m. These facts speak for themselves. Whatever the nature of the inquiry, and however unlikely it be that Guinness could have made good use of a short adjournment, by obtaining evidence or otherwise, the law requires, as it required of the magistrates in *Ex p Polemis*, that Guinness should be

h given a chance.

So I would reject counsel's second argument on the short adjournment point. There is, I think, much more to be said for his first argument that Guinness had already had time enough, since they had been in possession of the Pipetec letter since January (without disclosing the existence of that letter to the panel), and had known the substance of the case against them since June.

j What then would I have done if I had myself been in the position of the panel on 2 September and had to make up my own mind as to the limited adjournment point? I am fairly certain that I would have granted a short adjournment. For I can see hardly any reason for *not* granting a short adjournment, unless it be the convenience of the panel, by which I have in mind the difficulty of reconvening at short notice. Obviously this should not have weighed heavily against an adjournment, any more than did the imminent

departure of the vessel in *Ex p Polemis*. One need not quote the well-known dictum of
Lord Atkin in *General Medical Council v Spackman* [1943] 2 All ER 337 at 341, [1943] AC   *a*
627 at 638 that 'convenience and justice are often not on speaking terms'.

But the question is not what I would have done if I had been a member of the panel,
but whether the panel's refusal of a short adjournment was fair. After much hesitation I
have come to the conclusion that it was. Wise it was not, but fair it was, having regard to
what Guinness already knew of the case against them. So, if the limited adjournment
point had stood alone, I should have decided it in favour of the panel. However, even if I   *b*
had been against the panel on the limited adjournment point, I should not have been in
favour of quashing the panel's decision without considering the wider context. As I said
earlier, it is the panel's conduct of the inquiry as a whole which is called in question. The
limited adjournment point and the general adjournment point are interrelated, so much
so that they cannot, or at any rate should not, be considered in isolation. It is to the
general adjournment point, therefore, that I now turn.   *c*

The essence of the argument of counsel for Guinness, as I have already foreshadowed,
is that the panel ought to have waited until after the DTI inspectors had completed taking
evidence. This had been the panel's original intention, as appears clearly from the press
release dated 30 January 1987:

> 'Normally, following its own investigation in any Code case in order to determine   *d*
> what had happened, and, if breaches of the Code had occurred, who was at fault and
> what should be done, the Panel would promptly set out its findings and decisions in
> detail in a public statement. In the present situation, however, because Inspectors
> have been appointed, and legal consequences may flow from their work, the Panel
> must await the outcome of the Inspectors' enquiries before publishing any findings
> or judgments of its own.'   *e*

Nothing, according to counsel, had happened, or nothing that we know of had happened,
to make the panel change its mind save that it came into possession of the Pipetec letter
from the DTI. It was said on behalf of the panel that by May 1987 there was no
immediate prospect of the DTI inspectors publishing their findings. But I should be
surprised if the panel had thought there was any such immediate prospect in January   *f*
1987.

We do not know the reason for the panel's original view that it should wait until the
DTI inspectors had reported, or, save as appears from its reasons, why it continues to
think that disciplinary proceedings should be postponed. Guinness's reasons for seeking
an adjournment, as expounded by counsel can be summarised as follows.

(i) By August 1987 the Guinness directors who were most closely concerned at the
time of the bid were no longer in office. The new board was gravely handicapped. They   *g*
had no real alternative but to look to others to find out what had happened, not only on
the Guinness side of the disputed transaction, but still more on the Bank Leu side.

(ii) Whatever powers of persuasion the panel may have, it has no power to compel the
attendance of witnesses. The DTI inspectors have such powers and have already examined
under oath a number of Bank Leu witnesses. Other witnesses are still to be seen,   *h*
including Mr Ward, one of Guinness's directors, though this must remain highly
unlikely. At the conclusion of their investigation the DTI inspectors would be able to
review the case as a whole, not just one isolated aspect. It must therefore make sense to
wait at least until the inspectors have completed taking evidence, in case any further
evidence might throw light on the concert party issue, and even perhaps contradict the
panel's conclusion.   *j*

(iii) The crucial piece of 'evidence' against Guinness at the hearing on 25 August was
the Pipetec letter. The panel must have had at least some doubt about the genuineness of
that letter, in view of what the executive had been told by two Bank Leu executives, Dr
Frey and Mr Baumann, in April 1986. The original of the letter has never been produced.
Yet the panel decided to go ahead with the hearing on 2 September, although it knew

that Dr Frey would not be available to give evidence on that day and had no reason to
a suppose that Mr Baumann, Dr Fürer or Dr Burger, who signed the letter on behalf of
Bank Leu, would be available. By 2 September it had Allen & Overy's letter of 27 August,
including Bank Leu's written statement. The statement confirms the arrangement agreed
between Dr Frey and Mr Ward as set out in the Pipetec letter. But it leaves many relevant
questions unanswered.

(iv) The consequences of deciding against Guinness at a hearing on 2 September on
b the strength of the Pipetec letter, the Bank Leu statement and such other evidence as the
panel may have had would be very serious indeed. By contrast, the consequences of
adjourning the hearing would be that former Distillers shareholders would have to wait
a little longer to receive the cash they would have received if the bid had gone through
and they had exercised the cash option. Guinness had undertaken to pay interest at a full
commercial rate to all those who might ultimately be held entitled to compensation.
c More than 16 months had already elapsed. 'Why now,' in the words of Allen & Overy,
'the sudden urgency?'

The above arguments were all available to Guinness at the hearings on 25 August and
2 September. But since 2 September the attendance notes and correspondence passing
between the executive and Mrs S E Brown of the DTI and also between the executive and
those representing other potential witnesses, including in particular Allen & Overy
d representing Bank Leu, have been made available to Guinness on discovery. These
documents have enabled counsel for Guinness to advance a further argument as follows.
He submits that the steps taken by the executive in the course of its investigation and its
attempts to obtain the attendance of crucial witnesses were wholly inadequate. By way
of example, the executive seems to have accepted without question Mrs Brown's assurance
in a letter of 7 August that the Pipetec letter 'would give the Panel the evidence it needs
e to make progress with its enquiries' and that 'none of the other evidence given to the
Inspectors contradicts it'. We now know that there are transcripts of the evidence given
to the DTI inspectors by the Bank Leu witnesses. Even if there was some difficulty in
making these transcripts available to Guinness (a difficulty which, for my part, I do not
fully understand), the transcripts should surely, says counsel, have been scrutinised by
f the executive, if not by the panel, in case they opened up some further line of inquiry.

Another example taken by counsel for Guinness comes from the executive's first
meeting with Allen & Overy on 11 August. Mr Hewat of Allen & Overy explained that
Bank Leu were co-operating fully with the DTI and were also helping the Swiss Federal
Banking Commission. He was not sure how Bank Leu would regard yet another inquiry.
There then appears the following passage from the attendance note:

g   'Hewat asked how to proceed on the matter as he saw it there were three
      alternatives. Allen & Overy could write a reply on behalf of their client, or Allen &
      Overy and Bank Leu's in-house lawyer could come for a meeting, or the relevant
      parties could come for a meeting in our offices. *PRF* [Peter R Frazer, the deputy
      director general of the panel] *said we would be happy with any of those three approaches.*
      On the timing of our request, ADP [A D Paul, secretary of the panel] said that we
h   had investigated the purchase at the time and been given misleading information,
      we have been waiting for the DTI's interim report which is taking longer than
      expected, and we now felt that we had sufficient information to put the question of
      a breach of the Code to the Panel. Hewat said that he would explain this timing
      then on the basis of those facts.' (My emphasis.)

j   Surely, says counsel, it was the executive's duty to press harder for the attendance of
the relevant witnesses. It seems as if it was happy to rely on the contents of the Pipetec
letter, backed by Mrs Brown's hearsay evidence, without obtaining, or even apparently
seeking, the oral evidence of those directly concerned. Counsel submits with force that,
in the context of a major inquiry, with very serious consequences for Guinness and no
obvious pressure of time, such a lax approach was not good enough. When one adds the

further special feature that Guinness were handicapped in making their own inquiries, the result, says counsel, was patently unfair.

Counsel for Guinness had one final argument which I should mention. Rule 11.2 of the code makes clear that, in the event of a concert party being proved, the panel has a discretion whether or not to require Guinness to compensate former Distillers shareholders to the full extent. A consideration on which Guinness might wish to rely in mitigation (so to speak) would be that Mr Ward was engaged on a frolic of his own without the knowledge or consent of any of the Guinness directors. We were told that Mr Ward has indicated, in the course of very delicate negotiations with the current board of Guinness, that he sees no reason why Guinness should be liable to pay a penny piece. I attach no weight to that consideration. But I do attach weight to counsel's argument that if Guinness are to be in a position to mitigate they must be given the material with which to do so. It is said on behalf of the panel that, if Guinness feel themselves in a difficulty at the hearing as to consequences, they could always apply for an adjournment at that stage. To that counsel for Guinness replies that, if the hearing as to consequences is going to have to be adjourned, what possible benefit could there be to the former Distillers shareholders in knowing in advance that they have, as it were, succeeded on liability? Counsel for the panel ripostes that they are entitled to know where they are, and sooner rather than later. But the same would be true of any plaintiff in any litigation.

I have mentioned in passing a number of counsel's incidental arguments in support of the panel's decision to go ahead on 2 September. But I have left it to the end to summarise his main submissions as follows.

(i) Guinness never asked the panel to adjourn until after the DTI inspectors had completed taking evidence. They asked for an adjournment until the publication of their report at the earliest. That might be years away.

(ii) The strength of the evidence available to the panel is a material factor in deciding whether to postpone the hearing. Here the evidence in support of a concert party was overwhelming.

(iii) The panel has a public duty to perform in determining whether there was a concert party and, if so, in ensuring that the former Distillers shareholders receive fair treatment in accordance with general principle 1 of the code. The concert party issue is an isolated issue which does not impinge on other issues being investigated by the DTI inspectors. It is in the public interest that the concert party issue should be determined as soon as possible. The offer of interest is never adequate compensation.

(iv) The panel is an important City watchdog. It depends for its success on public confidence. To decide that the panel had acted unfairly would undermine public confidence in the panel and jeopardise its authority among City institutions.

In addition, counsel for the panel relied on the matters set out by the panel itself in paras 19 and 20 of its reasons, which largely overlap his own submissions.

As to the first of counsel's arguments, I accept that Guinness were asking for a longer adjournment than they now regard as a minimum. But they made it clear why they were asking for an adjournment. They wanted the evidence of the relevant witnesses to be available to the panel, and preferably the witnesses themselves available for cross-examination. It must have been obvious to the panel that for this purpose they would not necessarily have to wait until after publication of the DTI inspectors' report.

As for the second of the arguments, counsel for Guinness relied on the salutary warning of Megarry J in *John v Rees* [1969] 2 All ER 274 at 309, [1970] Ch 345 at 402, echoed by Ackner LJ in *R v Secretary of State for the Environment, ex p Brent London BC* [1983] 3 All ER 321 at 357, [1982] QB 593 at 646:

'As everybody who has anything to do with the law well knows, the path of the law is strewn with examples of open and shut cases which, somehow, were not; of unanswerable charges which, in the event, were completely answered; of inexplicable conduct which was fully explained; of fixed and unalterable determinations that, by discussion, suffered a change.'

Nevertheless there remains much force in the second argument of counsel for the panel,
a as in his third.

As for the reasons given by the panel itself, counsel for Guinness identified six reasons
in all. (i) The panel was not concerned with the taking of disciplinary action, but with
ensuring fair treatment for former Distillers shareholders. (ii) If there was a concert
party, this should have been disclosed by Guinness in April 1986. (iii) If Guinness had
disclosed the provision of £76m as temporary cover in April 1986, it would have led to
b immediate further investigation by the executive. (iv) Former Distillers shareholders
would be prejudiced by any further delay. (v) The concert party issue was a separate issue
which could conveniently be considered by the panel in isolation. (vi) Guinness had not
attempted to offer any explanation of the Pipetec letter.

Counsel subjected these reasons to detailed criticism. He argued that there is no logical
distinction between disciplinary proceedings and other proceedings. They both have, or
c may have, serious consequences. Nor can one justify hurrying the investigation in
September 1987 just because the panel would have had to act in a hurry in April 1986.
Guinness are not to be punished for having failed to disclose the concert party in 1986 by
depriving them of a proper opportunity of presenting their case 18 months later. Two
blacks do not make a white. As for the argument that the concert party issue is an isolated
issue, it would have been a strong reason for postponing the inquiry if it had *not* been an
d isolated issue. But the converse does not follow. The fact, if it be the fact, that the concert
party issue *is* an isolated issue affords no positive reasons for treating it in advance of all
other issues. According to counsel, only one of the reasons given by the panel for refusing
an adjournment can withstand scrutiny, and that is the fourth; but any prejudice to the
shareholders is, he says, far outweighed by the prejudice to Guinness.

Those were the arguments advanced before us. Like Watkins LJ in the Divisional
e Court, I have found my mind going one way and the other. At one stage of the hearing I
was all but persuaded that to press ahead on 2 September was unfair to Guinness. Just as
on the limited adjournment point I could see no good reason for *not* granting a short
adjournment, so on the general adjournment point I could see no good reason for *not*
waiting until the DTI inspectors had completed the taking of evidence. It could do little
harm to the shareholders for the panel to explore the origins of the Pipetec letter in
f greater depth, whereas the converse could do great and perhaps irreparable harm to
Guinness. We are constantly reminded that justice delayed is justice denied. This might,
I thought, be a case where justice was denied by being rushed.

But in the end I have come to the conclusion that we ought not to intervene. Despite
the very forceful arguments of counsel for Guinness, he has failed in the end to satisfy
g me that there has been any real injustice, or even any real risk of injustice, in this case.
My reasons are, first, that Guinness have been in possession of the crucial piece of evidence
against them, namely the Pipetec letter, since January 1987; and have known the broad
lines of the case they would have to meet since June 1987. Second, the combination of
the Pipetec letter and the Bank Leu statement adds up to a very strong case indeed. I bear
in mind Megarry J's warning in *John v Rees* [1969] 2 All ER 274 at 309, [1970] Ch 345 at
h 402. I accept that there may just possibly be some explanation for the Pipetec letter other
than the apparent one. But the chances of such an explanation emerging if the panel
were to wait until the DTI inspectors have completed taking evidence must be extremely
remote. Third, there is the public interest in the panel getting on with, and being seen
to get on with, its self-appointed task. I have applied the penetrating oil of natural justice
to the facts before us. I conclude that the procedure adopted by the panel in the instant
j case was not unfair. Accordingly I would dismiss the appeal.

WOOLF LJ. I would also dismiss this appeal. I have, however, reservations as to the
appropriateness of the actions of the Panel on Take-overs and Mergers and in these
circumstances I feel I should set out my own reasons for coming to the same conclusion
as the other members of the court.

It is not necessary for me to repeat the facts, which are fully set out in the judgment of
Lord Donaldson MR. I should however make it clear that I regard the unique qualities *a*
of the panel as being important in deciding what is the correct outcome of this appeal. I
have in mind two particular features of the panel. The first is that its authority is not
derived from any statutory power. Instead it derives its authority from the institutions
in the City of London who give it their support and nominate its members. The second
is that the scope of its activities are self-determined. Except in so far as the panel itself
decides to limit its jurisdiction and to set out its functions, as it has in the City Code on *b*
Take-overs and Mergers, the constraints on its powers are those dictated not by legal but
by practical considerations. The closest analogy to the panel is to be found in bodies set
up by the Crown under its prerogative powers, such as the Criminal Injuries
Compensation Board. Indeed, if it was appropriate to talk of the City of London having
prerogative powers, then it could be said that the panel has been set up under just such
powers. *c*

These qualities of the panel create constraints as to the circumstances and as to the
manner in which the courts can intervene which do not exist in the case of statutory
bodies. For example, in this case with some justification, it is suggested that the panel,
having deciding to adopt an inquisitorial role in conducting its investigations as to
whether or not Guinness plc had contravened the code, could have pressed home those
investigations more vigorously than it did. However, subject to what I have to say *d*
hereafter, the panel is under no duty to carry out its investigations in any particular way
and it must be for the panel to decide to what extent it is appropriate for it having regard
to its resources to engage in extensive investigations. Again in the case of a statutory
body it is possible to identify considerations which it is under a statutory obligation to
take into account or to ignore. Failure to comply with this statutory obligation can
invalidate a decision. However, there is no equivalent obligation in the case of the panel. *e*

The panel's ability to carry on its activities without being subject to legal constraint or
the intervention of the courts can however be limited by the nature of an activity which
it undertakes. If in the private law sphere an individual, as a volunteer, undertakes to
provide services which require professional standards of care, by undertaking those
activities the individual becomes under an obligation, enforceable in law, to exercise the
appropriate standard of care. So in the public law field, if the panel, without being under *f*
any enforceable duty to do so, engages on an activity which can have consequences to a
third party, then the panel by so doing can impose on itself legally enforceable obligations
of a similar nature to those to which it would be subject if it were carrying out that
activity pursuant to a statutory duty. However, this does not mean the obligations are
identical to those which would exist if it were under a statutory duty. In the normal case
a body such as the panel will retain a very wide discretion how it performs the task it sets *g*
itself and the court will regard its role as being one of last resort reserved for plain and
obvious cases.

In this case the function on which the panel embarked was to determine whether in
the circumstances Guinness had contravened the terms of its own code. Having set itself
this adjudicative objective, the panel placed itself under an obligation not to carry out *h*
this function in a manner which was inconsistent with that objective. If it reached a
result which was unjust, this would be in breach of this obligation. In the words of its
then own chief executive, the director general, Mr John Walker-Haworth, the object of
the panel's procedures is to produce the right answer in code terms in the circumstances.
If it goes about this role in a manner which manifestly creates a real and not theoretical
risk of injustice, then it would be abusing its power and, because it is performing a public *j*
function, on an application for judicial review the courts could intervene on behalf of the
public to protect those liable to be adversely affected by the exercise of the power.

On the application for judicial review it is appropriate for the court to focus on the
activities of the panel as a whole and ask with regard to those activities, in the words of
Lord Donaldson MR, 'whether something has gone wrong' in nature and degree which

requires the intervention of the courts. Nowadays it is more common to test decisions of
a the sort reached by the panel in this case by a standard of what is called 'fairness'. I
venture to suggest that in the present circumstances in answering the question which
Lord Donaldson MR has posed it is more appropriate to use the term which has fallen
from favour of 'natural justice'. In particular in considering whether something has gone
wrong the court is concerned whether what has happened has resulted in real injustice.
If it has, then the court has to intervene, since the panel is not entitled to confer on itself
b the power to inflict injustice on those who operate in the market which it supervises.

On the facts of this appeal we are principally concerned with three decisions of the
panel. They are: (1) the decision of 25 August 1987 to refuse an adjournment (the long-
term adjournment decision); (2) the decision of 2 September 1987 not to adjourn (the
short-term adjournment decision); and (3) the decision of the panel on 2 September 1987
to reach its decision that Guinness had acted in breach of the code on the material then
c before the panel and not to require further investigations to be carried out before it came
to its determination (the inadequate investigation issue).

It is convenient to consider separately Guinness's case on each of these decisions.
However, the outcome of Guinness's appeal does not necessarily depend on the result of
that separate consideration, since, although intervention by the court may not be justified
on an examination of any single decision, the intervention could be justified by the
d collective findings on the three decisions. Furthermore, the facts relating to one decision
affect the other decisions. Thus the alleged inadequacy of the investigations carried out
by the panel's executive, if established, strengthens Guinness's case for the grant of a
short- or long-term adjournment. It is because they form the background against which
the adjournment decisions are to be judged that I propose to consider first of all the
adequacy of the investigations carried out on behalf of the panel by its executive. In
e doing so, I do not propose to make any separate examination of the extent to which the
panel was aware of the limited nature of investigations carried out by its executive, since
on the general approach indicated above it seems to me that whether the default was that
of the executive or the panel would not affect the outcome of this appeal.

f *The inadequate investigation issue*
It is not disputed that when the panel decided to inquire into whether Guinness had
contravened r 11.1 of the code it was required to conduct that investigation properly.
This involved the panel taking reasonable steps to inform itself of the material facts. Like
the Secretary of State for Education and Science in *Secretary of State for Education and
Science v Thameside Metropolitan Borough* [1976] 3 All ER 665 at 696, [1977] AC 1014 at
g 1065 in Lord Diplock's words the panel had to 'take reasonable steps to acquaint [itself]
with the relevant information to enable [it] to answer [the question] correctly'. As long
as the party affected by its decision was given a reasonable opportunity to put forward
any facts it wished, normally it will be very much a matter for the judgment of the panel
and its executive as to what steps it should take. However, in this case the panel should
h have had in mind the fact that Guinness were labouring under a considerable disadvantage
in making any representations. The persons who were directors of Guinness at the
material time were now in dispute with Guinness. In particular Mr Ward, who was
abroad, would certainly not at that time co-operate with Guinness. In addition, Bank Leu
AG was in dispute with Guinness, so that information was not likely to be forthcoming
to Guinness from the bank or its officers who were involved in the critical transaction of
j 17 April 1986, namely Dr Burger, Mr Frey and Mr Baumann, all of whom Guinness
would have liked the opportunity to cross-examine. Furthermore, when on 13 May 1987
the panel became a designated body under the Financial Services (Disclosure of
Information) (Designated Authorities No 2) Order 1987, SI 1987/859, the panel was
entitled to seek information from a most important source which was not available to
Guinness.

In these circumstances it was desirable that the panel should conduct a full investigation within the limits of its resources. In carrying out that investigation, unlike the situation on a normal investigation, the panel was not under any pressing constraints as to time. Because of the delay which had already occurred, any reasonable period of extra time which the panel needed to complete its inquiries would not materially affect the Distillers shareholders, whose interests the panel was most anxious to protect.

Having carefully considered the documents which are now available but which were not available to Guinness until discovery in these proceedings, it is my impression that, whether or not there was any legal obligation to do so, it would have been preferable for the panel to carry out fuller inquiries than it did. Its failure to do so is probably explained by a natural tendency to conduct this investigation in the same way as investigations are normally conducted in the heat of a take-over battle, the fact that the date for the hearing had been provisionally arranged for 2 September and the fact that the executive regarded itself as already in possession of evidence which indicated a virtually irrefutable case against Guinness.

Having expressed my impression as to the adequacy of the investigation, I turn to consider the three sources of possible information which Guinness complain were inadequately investigated.

(1) *Mr Ward* Although the panel was content to accept a statement made by Mr Ward's solicitors that he would not attend a meeting on 2 September and did not inquire whether Mr Ward would be prepared to make himself available on a later date, I have no doubt that it was reasonable for the executive not to have pursued investigations further in relation to Mr Ward. It was most unlikely that he would be prepared to co-operate and the panel was not in a position to compel him to do so.

(2) *The Bank Leu witnesses* The bank has co-operated with the Department of Trade and Industry inspectors. The bank has a branch in this country and, bearing in mind that it is being investigated by the Swiss authorities with regard to its role, the bank is likely to be anxious to appear to be co-operating with the panel. At the same time its undisputed role in relation to the critical purchase of shares meant that the bank and its officers were going to be very cautious about being forthcoming as to precisely what happened. In this respect the timescale which the panel's executive had set for its investigations put the bank in the ideal position to confine what it was prepared to say to no more than was necessary so as not to be labelled as being unco-operative. As in the case of Mr Ward, the first approach was made on 4 August 1987. On 6 August there was a prompt response by Mr Hewat of Messrs Allen & Overy, the bank's solicitors, during which he indicated that 'the client was . . . not available for a meeting'. It is not clear from this statement whether or not Mr Hewat was saying that it was because his clients were abroad that they were not available or that he was indicating they would not attend the meeting. He himself, however, attended a meeting on 11 August with the executive when he indicated that his clients had co-operated fully to date with the Department of Trade and Industry (the DTI) and with the Swiss Federal Banking Commission, but that he was not sure 'what his client's stance would be on our enquiry. Similarly in response to our request for help, he could not answer for his client's reaction'. He went on to point out that a 'key individual (Mr Frey) was training with the Swiss Army at the moment'. Mr Hewat also indicated three alternative courses which were open to his client, one of which was to provide a reply by the letter from Allen & Overy, the second of which was for there to be a meeting with the panel by the bank's in-house lawyer and Allen & Overy, and the third of which was a meeting at the panel's offices with the 'relevant parties'. Complaint is made by counsel for Guinness about the response of the executive, which was that they 'would be happy with any of those three approaches'. However, it is right to note that later at the meeting Mr Hewat was told that it was expected 'that the meeting would follow the usual procedures and that relevant parties would be invited to submit papers in advance of the meeting and to attend the hearing on the 2nd September'.

What then happened was that the executive were informed that the bank would 'put

in' a written statement, and, no objection having been raised to that course, Allen &
a Overy delivered on 27 August 1987 a letter which contains the statement from the bank
as to the Pipetec transaction and a protest that the bank had been subject to such a
stringent timetable.

As counsel for Guinness fairly submits, this letter of 27 August bears the hallmark of
being carefully 'negotiated'. It does not answer a number of questions which Guinness
would like explaining, in particular why no fee was in fact paid to the bank, why the
b shares were not required to be repurchased and why there was delay in seeking to enforce
the obligations contained in the letter of 18 April 1986.

If there had been more time prior to the hearing on 2 September, it would have at
least been open to the executive to have raised further inquiries with the bank through
its solicitors by letter. It would also have been possible to clarify the position with regard
to the bank's officers being prepared to attend a hearing at a later date. However, the
c executive was content to rest on the contents of the letter of 27 August 1987. The nearest
the executive went to objecting to the bank's limited contribution was to suggest at one
stage that the bank's solicitors might not be entitled to attend the hearing if the bank's
contribution was confined to a response by letter.

d *The Department of Trade and Industry inspectors*
The DTI made available to the panel the critical letter of 18 April 1986. Through Mrs
Brown it also confirmed that it had no information which was inconsistent with the
contents of that letter. Counsel for Guinness submits that in not seeking further
information the executive showed to a remarkable degree 'a lack of curiosity' which
could not be supplemented by anyone else's activity: 'The executive were in a unique
e position to extract information and failed to do so.'

While I accept counsel's approach, I recognise that it is extremely unlikely that any
other information would have been made available to the executive which would have
had any direct bearing on the actual issue which was decided by the panel on 2 September.
Obviously Guinness would like to have seen any statements of witnesses which threw
f light on the context in which the Pipetec letter came into existence or the details of the
transactions as a result of which the critical shareholding was purchased. However,
because of the DTI's concern with the criminal proceedings, it is unlikely that anything
material would have resulted from further approaches to the department and the panel
was aware that the DTI inspectors did not have information which conflicted with the
contents of the Pipetec letter.

g Considering the executive's information-gathering process as a whole, I do not regard
its failure to press home its inquiries more forcefully as a justification for the court
intervening in these proceedings. As counsel for the panel pointed out, with regard to
the securing of the attendance of witnesses, at the hearing on 25 August 1987, Guinness
themselves accepted that, even if the witnesses agreed to come before the panel, they
would not agree to be cross-examined by Guinness, and that 'their consistent posture had
h been to hide behind lawyers'. This was a realistic assessment of the position and in
practice I have little doubt that without cross-examination nothing further would have
been revealed which was even of interest to Guinness, never mind directly relevant to
the sole issue which the panel had set itself to determine.

In the course of argument the question arose as to the extent to which the panel should
have taken advantage of its ability to bring pressure to bear on anyone operating in the
j City of London to co-operate. That it has such power I have little doubt. However, it
must be for the panel and the panel alone to decide whether, and if so how, it should use
such a power.

My conclusion under this head is therefore that, while the panel by the executive
could have been more energetic, this did not affect the outcome and the court would not
be justified in intervening on this ground.

The short adjournment decision

I regret that the panel did not feel able to accede to the submission that the hearing *a* should be adjourned for a few weeks. Such an adjournment could not possibly have caused prejudice to anyone, but it would clearly have caused inconvenience to the panel and difficulty in finding another date when the panel could reassemble. However, it should have been recognised that this administrative inconvenience was at least contributed to by the failure of the executive to realise the problems which would be caused to those involved in preparing for a hearing by the holiday period during the *b* preceding month. Although counsel for the panel eloquently sought to establish the limited nature of the new material contained in the final submissions of the executive as compared with its earlier submissions, the fact remains that the letter of 27 August from Allen & Overy setting out the bank's position did materially strengthen the case against Guinness, albeit this did not involve any change of stance on the part of the bank.

However, while making this criticism of the panel's decision, I wholly agree with the *c* view expressed by Watkins LJ in the Divisional Court that this amounted to no more than inconsideration on the part of the panel. Events since 2 September have clearly shown, as the panel was entitled to assume would be the position, that a limited period adjournment would not have enabled additional material to have been obtained by Guinness: it would merely have provided an opportunity to Guinness to reflect on the manner in which they would present their case, and could not in any way have affected *d* the final outcome.

The long adjournment

The argument on this aspect of the case has been advanced marginally differently at different stages. The original position of Guinness was that the adjournment should be until the DTI inspectors' report was available. This in practice could mean until after the *e* criminal proceedings were concluded. The alternative way in which the argument was advanced was that the adjournment should be until the inspectors had completed their investigations and presumably had made available to the panel the results of those investigations so far as they affected the issue before the panel. Both arguments, if accepted, would involve a substantial delay. In considering whether the panel was required to delay its investigations to this extent, it is important to first of all identify the *f* precise issue which the panel in fact determined on 2 September. I draw attention to this because I recognise that the position could be different with regard to a decision as to what should be the *consequences* of a determination by the panel that there had been a breach of the code.

The underlying reason why Guinness were anxious that the panel should adjourn, at *g* least until the DTI inspectors had heard evidence from all the witnesses, was because Guinness knew that the only prospect of avoiding an adverse decision, the relevant witnesses not being available for cross-examination, was if evidence was obtained from the inspectors which indicated that the letter of 18 April was manufactured by the bank, or Pipetec, with the connivance of Mr Ward and did not reflect a genuine transaction between the bank and/or Pipetec and Guinness. Guinness had reason to be suspicious of *h* the alleged agreement reflected in the letter and the DTI inspectors, through their powers, might be the means by which they could obtain confirmation of their suspicions. Their concern about the panel's refusal to allow the adjournment is underlined by the criticisms to which I have already referred which they are now in a position to make with regard to the investigations carried out by the executive. Guinness also submit that the attitude adopted by the panel is inconsistent because it had agreed to adjourn *j* disciplinary proceedings for the required period and there is no real distinction between proceedings for breach of the code and disciplinary proceedings, bearing in mind that the consequences of the adverse finding by the panel is that Guinness could be required to make compensatory payments of many millions of pounds.

The panel, on the other hand, submits that, notwithstanding the offer of Guinness to

pay interest, the delay would prejudice the shareholders in Distillers. I do not dismiss
a this suggestion of prejudice, but, bearing in mind the offer of interest, I do not myself
regard the degree of prejudice as a matter of very great substance. I do, however, accept
that lengthy delay in determining an issue as important as whether or not Guinness had
contravened the code is undesirable. The panel was clearly not in a position to act until it
had been provided with a copy of the 18 April 1986 letter. However, once it was in
receipt of that letter, I can well understand why the panel regarded it as its duty to
b proceed if this was practical. The significance of a decision whether or not Guinness were
in breach of the code was not confined to the former Distillers shareholders. It was also
important to Guinness's shareholders and the reputation and standing of the panel in the
City. I accept, therefore, that the panel was not required as a matter of law to adjourn for
what could be a very substantial period of time unless there was some real advantage to
be achieved by doing so or a real risk that justice could not be done without doing so.
c   The test which the panel posed for itself in deciding whether to adjourn the hearing
was to ask itself whether 'there was any substantial risk of injustice to Guinness' in not
doing so. If, as I assume is the case, by using the word 'substantial', the panel meant no
more than that there was a real as opposed to a fanciful risk of injustice, then this is a
perfectly appropriate test to apply. Furthermore, I cannot fault the conclusion of the
d panel that there was no such risk. This is emphasised by the panel pointing out in the
reasons given for its decision that, if in the course of the hearing on 2 September it should
appear that there was any such risk, the panel would reconsider the position.
       Although counsel for Guinness was able to canvass a possible motive for the letter of
18 April 1986 being manufactured, it is impossible to escape from the conclusion that
the case for concluding that there was a breach of the code was overwhelming. While I
e regard it as legitimate to contemplate that, in consequence of the DTI inspectors' greater
powers, more information could be revealed about the circumstances in which the
agreement, which is reflected in the letter of 18 April 1986, was made, I do not accept
that there was any realistic likelihood of anything being disclosed which would have
avoided a finding of a breach of the code. If previously there had been any doubt on this
subject, it was removed by Bank Leu's statement contained in the letter of Allen & Overy
f dated 27 August 1987. While, as Guinness submitted, that letter involved simply a
repetition by Bank Leu of an assertion previously made, the fact that the bank was
prepared to repeat its admission of involvement to the panel in the terms contained in
the statement in that letter is highly significant.
       I would, however, again emphasise that the views that I have expressed are confined to
the determination of the question of whether there was a breach of the code. It now
g appears that the determination of the consequences of that finding of breach may be
complex and involve wider considerations than was thought previously, and the panel
may well have to give anxious consideration whether it would be right to proceed to
determine this issue before the DTI inspectors' investigations are completed.
       However, I do not fault the decision of the panel on the present issue. Before leaving
the issue I should make reference to R v Thames Magistrates' Court, ex p Polemis [1974] 2
h All ER 1219, [1974] 1 WLR 1371, which relied on by counsel for Guinness. In his
judgment in that case Lord Widgery CJ emphasised the importance that not only should
justice be done, but it should also appear to be done (see [1974] 2 All ER 1219 at 1223,
[1974] 1 WLR 1371 at 1375). Both justice and the appearance of justice are important in
considering whether or not an adjournment can be properly refused. While the approach
adopted by Lord Widgery CJ in that case is important and one of general application, it
j must be remembered that it related to the trial of a defendant on a criminal charge and
not to an inquiry of the type on which the panel was engaged. This principle is
particularly important where, as sometimes happens in a case involving bias, the
applicant cannot discharge the onus of proving actual bias but can establish the appearance
of bias. I do not consider that Lord Widgery CJ's remarks should be treated as indicating
that if on a proper examination of the facts of a decision of this sort it appears that no

injustice has in fact been done then on an application for judicial review, for technical reasons, notwithstanding that the relief is discretionary, the decision of the panel would *a* have invariably to be quashed because of some appearance of injustice when a person aware of all the relevant facts would accept there was no actual injustice. To invariably quash a decision of the panel in such circumstances would be inconsistent with the use of the proviso in a criminal appeal and could result in injustice to the panel without remedying any legitimate complaint of Guinness. It could also be in conflict with the principle that the requirements of natural justice are not technical but requirements *b* relating to the substance and not the form of the proceedings.

It remains for me to consider whether, looking at the cumulative effect of the argument so ably advanced by counsel for Guinness, I consider this is a case in which the court is required to intervene, adopting the approach which I identified at the beginning of this judgment. The conclusion which I have come to, while in agreement with Lloyd LJ that many of the criticisms counsel makes of the panel's conduct are well founded, is *c* that the intervention would not be justified because no injustice has been caused and what was wrong was not of the nature or gravity which required the intervention of the court. The decisions were after all in the field of activities which the panel's combined experience and expertise make it peculiarly well qualified to determine and in this field as a matter of substance and discretion the court should only interfere to avoid injustice. Although I have come to this conclusion, I acknowledge, as I did earlier, that the appeal *d* none the less has caused me concern. I trust with hindsight the panel will understand the reasons for this concern and that this will enable the panel to avoid situations arising in the future where a body, the subject of its decision, can feel a genuine sense of grievance because of the way in which an inquiry has been conducted. In making this last comment I do, however, stress that I do not intend to deter the panel from acting with all due expedition where this is required. Here the situation was different from normal and this *e* case gave the panel scope to be more accommodating in the interests of Guinness than would usually be possible. In these circumstances to rush the investigation so as to obtain an early hearing while not unlawful was insensitive.

Having come to this conclusion, it is not necessary for me to deal with the argument that Guinness should in any event be deprived of relief because of their failure to resort *f* to the appeal procedures which were available. I do however conclude by pointing out that while normally it is preferable for an appeal procedure to be exhausted prior to application for judicial review, particularly where there is an appeal procedure prescribed by statute, there are always cases where this approach has no application, as was indicated as long ago as 1974 in *R v Hillingdon London Borough, ex p Royco Homes Ltd* [1974] 2 All ER 643, [1974] QB 720.

For the reasons given in the judgment of Lord Donaldson MR as well as in this *g* judgment I would dismiss this appeal.

Appeal dismissed. Leave to appeal to the House of Lords refused.

7 November. The Appeal Committee of the House of Lords (Lord Keith of Kinkel, Lord Templeman *h* *and Lord Goff of Chievely) refused leave to appeal.*

Solicitors: *Herbert Smith* (for Guinness); *Lovell White Durrant* (for the panel).

Frances Rustin   Barrister.

Bank of Boston Connecticut v European Grain and Shipping Ltd
The Dominique

HOUSE OF LORDS

LORD KEITH OF KINKEL, LORD BRANDON OF OAKBROOK, LORD OLIVER OF AYLMERTON, LORD GOFF OF CHIEVELEY AND LORD JAUNCEY OF TULLICHETTLE

8, 9, 10, 14, 15, 16 NOVEMBER 1988, 9 FEBRUARY 1989

Shipping – Freight – Claim for freight – Set-off – Shipowner's failure to complete contract – Failure to complete voyage – Damages for shipowner's repudiation – Voyage charterparty providing for payment of lump sum freight within five days of signing bills of lading – Freight assigned to bank – Vessel arrested and impounded during voyage because of owner's insolvency – Bank claiming payment of freight – Whether owner's right to freight accruing before termination of charterparty – Whether charterers entitled to set off claim for damages for owner's wrongful repudiation against claim for freight – Whether charterers entitled to maintain set-off against bank claiming as assignees – Law of Property Act 1925, s 136(1).

The owners chartered a vessel to the charterers on the Gencon form for a voyage from India to European ports at a lump sum freight. The vessel's earnings, including all freight, were assigned absolutely to a bank. Clause 16 of the charterparty provided that freight was to be pre-paid within five days of signing and surrender of final bills of lading and that full freight would be deemed to be earned on the signing of the bills. Bills of lading were signed before the vessel sailed for Europe via Colombo. When the vessel arrived at Colombo it was arrested by creditors, and, because of the owners' insolvency, it remained impounded. The charterers, as they were entitled to do, elected to treat the owners' conduct as a repudiation of the charterparty and arranged for the cargo to be discharged and shipped on in another vessel to the European ports of destination, thereby incurring costs which exceeded the amount of the advance freight payable under the charterparty. A claim by the bank for the advance freight and the charterers' cross-claim for damages for the owners' repudiation of the charterparty were referred to arbitration. The arbitrators held that the charterers' claim for damages for wrongful repudiation could be set off against the bank's claim for freight and dismissed the bank's claim because the charterers' claim exceeded the amount of the freight. On appeal, the judge set aside the award, on the grounds that the owners were entitled to recover the freight regardless of their repudiation and that the charterers' cross-claim did not provide a defence to, or set-off against, the claim for freight. The charterers appealed to the Court of Appeal, which allowed their appeal and restored the arbitrators' award, on the grounds that the owners, and the bank as assignees, could not recover the freight in full without regard to the damage caused by the owners' own wrongful repudiation of the charterparty. The bank appealed to the House of Lords, contending that the charterers would not have been entitled to set off their claim for damages as a defence to a claim by the owners for freight and were not entitled to such a set-off as against the bank claiming as assignees. The charterers contended that the charterparty had been terminated by the repudiation before the owners' right to advance freight accrued and that even if they could not set off their claim for damages as a defence to a claim by the owners for freight they were entitled to such a set-off as against the bank claiming as assignees, since under s 136(1)[a] of the Law of Property Act 1925 the assignment of freight, although conferring the legal right to the freight on the bank, was 'subject to equities having priority over the right of the assignee' and the charterers' claim for damages constituted such an equity.

a   Section 136(1), so far as material, is set out at p 558 *b c*, post

Held – (1) On the true construction of cl 16 of the charterparty the owners' right to
freight accrued on completion of the signing of all the bills of lading, which took place *a*
before the termination of the charterparty, and the postponement of payment until after
the termination of the charterparty did not render the owners' prior acquisition of the
right to the freight conditional, since the postponement of payment was an incident
attaching to the right acquired and was not a condition of its acquisition. It followed that
the owners' right to the freight had been unconditionally acquired before termination of
the charterparty and was not divested or discharged by the termination (see p 547 *f g*, *b*
p 549 *d* to *g*, p 550 *a* to *c* and p 559 *d e*, post); dictum of Dixon J in *McDonald v Dennys
Lascelles Ltd* (1933) 48 CLR 457 at 476–477 applied.

(2) The principle that there was no right to set off a claim for damages for breach of a
charterparty against a claim for freight applied to both a repudiatory and a non-
repudiatory breach of the charterparty. Accordingly, as between the owners and the
charterers, a defence by way of equitable set-off in respect of the damage suffered by the *c*
charterers as a result of the owners' repudiatory breach of the charterparty would not
have been available to the charterers in a claim by the owners for freight. Furthermore,
the charterers were not entitled to rely on their counterclaim as a defence as between
them and the bank because the fact that such counterclaim constituted an equity to
which the assignment of the freight was made subject under s 136(1) of the 1925 Act did
not avail the charterers, since the obligations giving rise to the counterclaim arose out of *d*
the same contract under which the freight was payable. It followed that the bank could
recover the freight in full without regard to the damage caused by the owners' wrongful
repudiation of the charterparty. The bank's appeal would therefore be allowed (see p 547
f g, p 556 *a* to *c*, p 557 *j* to p 558 *a* and p 559 *b* to *e*, post); *Newfoundland Government v
Newfoundland Rly Co* (1888) 13 App Cas 199 and *Aries Tanker Corp v Total Transport Ltd*
[1977] 1 All ER 398 considered.   *e*

Decision of the Court of Appeal sub nom *Colonial Bank v European Grain and Shipping
Ltd, The Dominique* [1988] 3 All ER 233 reversed.

Notes

For the effect of an assignment of freight, see 43 Halsbury's Laws (4th edn) paras 720–
721, and for cases on the subject, see 43 Digest (Reissue) 456–457, 9997–10013.   *f*

For the Law of Property Act 1925, s 136, see 37 Halsbury's Statutes (4th edn) 257.

Cases referred to in opinions

Allison v Bristol Marine Insurance Co Ltd (1876) 1 App Cas 209, [1874–80] All ER Rep 781,
HL.
Aries Tanker Corp v Total Transport Ltd, The Aries [1977] 1 All ER 398, [1977] 1 WLR 185, *g*
HL; *affg* [1976] 2 Lloyd's Rep 256, CA.
A/S Gunnstein & Co K/S v Jensen Krebs and Nielson, The Alfa Nord [1977] 2 Lloyd's Rep 434,
CA.
Beasley v D'Arcy (1800) 2 Sch & Lef 403.
Best v Hill (1872) LR 8 CP 10.   *h*
Cleobulos Shipping Co Ltd v Intertanker Ltd, The Cleon [1983] 1 Lloyd's Rep 586, CA.
Elena Shipping Ltd v Aidenfield Ltd, The Elena [1986] 1 Lloyd's Rep 425.
Fibrosa Spolka Akcyjna v Fairbairn Lawson Combe Barbour Ltd [1942] 2 All ER 122, [1943]
AC 32, HL.
Hanak v Green [1958] 2 All ER 141, [1958] 2 QB 9, [1958] 2 WLR 755, CA.
Henriksens Rederi A/S v P H Z Rolimpex, The Brede [1973] 3 All ER 589, [1974] QB 233, *j*
[1973] 3 WLR 556, CA.
Johnson v Agnew [1979] 1 All ER 883, [1980] AC 367, [1979] 2 WLR 487, HL.
McDonald v Dennys Lascelles Ltd (1933) 48 CLR 457, Aust HC.
Mondel v Steel (1841) 8 M & W 858B, [1835–42] All ER Rep 511, 151 ER 1288.
Newfoundland Government v Newfoundland Rly Co (1888) 13 App Cas 199, PC.

a
Piggott v Williams (1821) 6 Madd 95, 56 ER 1027.
Rawson v Samuel (1839) 1 Cr & Ph 161, 41 ER 451.
Smith v Parkes (1852) 16 Beav 115, 51 ER 720.
Stumore v Campbell & Co [1892] 1 QB 314, [1891–4] All ER Rep 785, CA.
Turnbull v Great Eastern and Peninsular Navigation Co (1885) Cab & El 595.
Vagres Cia Maritime SA v Nissho-Iwai American Corp, The Karin Vatis [1988] 2 Lloyd's Rep
    330, CA.

b

Appeal
The Bank of Boston Connecticut (formerly Colonial Bank) of Connecticut, USA (the bank) appealed with the leave of the Appeal Committee of the House of Lords given on 13 June 1988 against the order of the Court of Appeal (Fox, Croom-Johnson and Mustill LJJ) ([1988] 3 All ER 233, [1988] 3 WLR 60) dated 21 December 1987, as amended on
c 14 January and 11 April 1988, allowing an appeal by European Grain and Shipping Ltd (the charterers) from the order of Hobhouse J ([1987] 1 Lloyd's Rep 239) dated 24 October 1986 made on the hearing of an appeal by the bank against an arbitration award dated 12 February 1986 made by the arbitrators Clifford Clark, Alex Kazantzis and Andrew Longmore QC, whereby the judge held, inter alia, (i) that under cl 16 of a charterparty on the Gencon form dated 16 June 1982, by which Vilamoura Maritime Inc, the owners
d of the vessel Dominique, let her to the charterers at a lump sum freight of $US223,676 for a voyage from India to European ports, the charterers were liable to pay the bank, as assignee of the earnings of the vessel, the full amount of freight due notwithstanding the owners' wrongful repudiation of the charter and (ii) that the charterers were not entitled to set off a cross-claim for damages for wrongful repudiation of the charter against the bank's claim to freight. The facts are set out in the opinion of Lord Brandon.
e

Bernard Eder and *Steven Berry* for the bank.
Martin Moore-Bick QC and *Timothy Young* for the charterers.

Their Lordships took time for consideration.

f 9 February. The following opinions were delivered.

LORD KEITH OF KINKEL. My Lords, I have had the opportunity of considering in draft the speech to be delivered by my noble and learned friend Lord Brandon. I agree with it, and for the reasons he gives would allow the appeal.

g **LORD BRANDON OF OAKBROOK.** My Lords, the subject matter of this appeal is a claim by the appellants (the bank) as assignees of the owners of the mv Dominique (the owners) to recover from the respondents (the charterers) advance freight which the bank alleges became payable by the charterers under a voyage charterparty relating to that vessel made between the owners and the charterers in June 1982. The charterers
h dispute that any such freight became payable, but it is agreed between the parties that, if it did, the amount of it was $US233,676.
    The bank's claim was referred to arbitration by three arbitrators in London, who by a reasoned award made on 12 February 1986 decided in favour of the charterers and dismissed the claim. The bank appealed with leave to Hobhouse J in the Commercial Court ([1987] 1 Lloyd's Rep 239), who by an order dated 24 October 1986 allowed the
j appeal and awarded to the bank the full amount of their claim. The charterers appealed to the Court of Appeal (Fox, Croom-Johnson and Mustill LJJ) ([1988] 3 All ER 233, [1988] 3 WLR 60), which by an order dated 21 December 1987, as amended on 14 January and 11 April 1988, allowed the appeal, set aside the order of Hobhouse J and restored the arbitrators' award. The bank now brings a further appeal from the decision of the Court of Appeal with the leave of your Lordships' House.

The facts found by the arbitrators are as follows. By an assignment under seal dated 14 April 1982 the owners assigned absolutely to the bank all the earnings of the Dominique *a* including all freight. By a charterparty dated 16 June 1982 the owners chartered the Dominique to the charterers to proceed to Kakinada, in India, and there load a cargo of agricultural products in bulk for carriage to European ports. Under that charterparty the Dominique loaded at Kakinada between 28 June and 13 July 1982 various parcels of cargo, in respect of which bills of lading were signed between those dates and on 14 July 1982. On that date the Dominique left Kakinada bound for Colombo for bunkers. At *b* about the same time the bank received notice that the vessel's club entry would be cancelled with effect from 28 June 1982, and they accordingly gave to the charterers written notice of the assignment referred to earlier. On 19 July 1982 the Dominique arrived at Colombo and was arrested by previous suppliers of bunkers to her. The Dominique remained under arrest and it became apparent to both the charterers and the bank that the owners had no funds of their own with which to procure her release and *c* that the club would not assist them. By a telex from the charterers to the owners dated 22 July the charterers justifiably elected to treat the owners' conduct as a repudiation of the charterparty. By 26 July all the bills of lading previously signed had been surrendered, which I take to mean delivered, to the shippers. On 12 August the charterers obtained the leave of the court in Colombo to discharge the cargo from the Dominique. During September the cargo, following such discharge, was transhipped to another vessel. That *d* vessel then on-carried the cargo to European ports where it was discharged during November. The Dominique was later sold by order of the court in Colombo.

The cost to the charterers of discharging and transhipping the cargo at Colombo, and having it on-carried to European ports and discharged there, exceeded the amount of the advance freight claimed from them by the bank.

The charterparty was on the Gencon form with typed alterations, a series of additional *e* typed clauses and an addendum, and was governed by English law. The essential provision relating to the payment of advance freight was cl 16 of the additional typed clauses, which was in these terms:

> 'Freight shall be prepaid within 5 days of signing and surrender of final Bills of Lading, full freight deemed to be earned on signing Bills of Lading, discountless *f* and non-returnable, vessel and/or cargo lost or not lost and to be paid to [a named bank in Piraeus].'

The charterers disputed their liability to pay the advance freight claimed by the bank on two grounds. The first ground was that the charterers, by accepting the owners' repudiation of the charterparty, had lawfully brought the charterparty to an end before *g* the owners' right to be paid freight under cl 16 had accrued. The second ground was that, if, contrary to the first ground, the owners' right to be paid freight under cl 16 had accrued before the charterparty was brought to an end, the charterers were entitled to set off against the bank's claim to freight the damage suffered by them as a result of the owners' repudiation.

Hobhouse J considered, rightly in my view, that the grounds for disputing liability *h* relied on by the charterers raised four questions for decision. Using my own words I would formulate those four questions as follows. (1) Had the owners' right to advance freight accrued before the charterparty was terminated by the charterers' acceptance of the owners' repudiation of it? (2) If such right had so accrued, did it survive such termination? (3) If so, would the charterers, had the owners not assigned their right to freight to the bank, have been entitled to set off against such right the damage suffered *j* by the charterers as a result of the owners' repudiation of the charterparty? (4) If not, are the charterers nevertheless entitled to such set-off as against the bank claiming as assignees?

Question (1): accrual of owners' right to advance freight

a   The answer to this question depends on two matters. The first matter is the sequence of the relevant events as found by the arbitrators. The second matter is the true construction of cl 16 of the charterparty.

So far as the first matter is concerned the arbitrators found the sequence of the relevant events to have been as follows: (i) on 14 July 1982 the signing of the bills of lading was completed; (ii) on 22 July the charterparty was terminated by the charterers' acceptance

b   of the owners' repudiation of it; and (iii) by 26 July all the bills of lading had been surrendered to the shippers. The expression 'by 26 July', used by the arbitrators in relation to event (iii) above, is in a sense equivocal, in that, on a literal interpretation, it might refer to any date not later than 26 July, including a date earlier than 22 July. The inference which I would draw, however, is that, while the arbitrators were unable to fix the date with certainty, they were satisfied that it was later than 22 July. In any case, in

c   so far as it would be to the advantage of the bank to have had a finding that the surrender of the bills of lading was completed before the termination of the charterparty on 22 July, they failed to obtain such finding.

So far as the second matter is concerned, it was recognised by both courts below that cl 16 of the charterparty is confusingly drawn and because of that difficult to interpret. The main difficulty arises from the apparent conflict between the first phrase of the

d   clause, which reads 'Freight shall be prepaid within 5 days of signing and surrender of final Bills of Lading', and the second phrase, which reads 'full freight deemed to be earned on signing Bills of Lading'. For the bank it was contended that the effect of the two phrases taken together was that the owners' right to the freight accrued on completion of the signing of all the bills of lading, but payment was postponed until five days after the bills of lading, having been signed, were delivered to the shippers. On this

e   basis the owners' right to freight accrued on 14 July 1982, well before the termination of the charterparty on 22 July. For the charterers it was contended that their obligation to pay the freight and the corresponding right of the owners to be paid the freight were both governed, and governed only, by the first phrase. On that basis the owners' right to be paid the freight accrued after 22 July 1982.

f   While the matter is far from easy, I consider that the contention for the bank is to be preferred to that for the charterers. The reason why I take that view is that the contention for the charterers gives no effect to the second phrase of cl 16 'full freight deemed to be earned on signing Bills of Lading', whereas the contention for the bank does. This conclusion accords with the decision of the Court of Appeal on a different but comparable clause in a charterparty in *Vagres Cia Maritima SA v Nissho-Iwai American Corp, The Karin Vatis* [1988] 2 Lloyd's Rep 330.

g   I would therefore answer question (1) by saying that the owners' right to freight accrued before the termination of the charterparty.

Question (2): effect of charterparty being terminated

The principles of law applicable when a contract is terminated by the acceptance by

h   one party to it of a repudiation by the other party to it are not in doubt. They were clearly and simply stated by Dixon J in *McDonald v Dennys Lascelles Ltd* (1933) 48 CLR 457 at 476–477, where he said:

'When a party to a simple contract, upon a breach by the other contracting party of a condition of the contract, elects to treat the contract as no longer binding upon him, the contract is not rescinded as from the beginning. Both parties are discharged

j   from further performance of the contract, but rights are not divested or discharged which have already been unconditionally acquired. Rights and obligations which arise from the partial execution of the contract and causes of action which have accrued from its breach alike continue unaffected.'

That statement of the relevant principles was expressly approved and adopted by Lord
Wilberforce in *Johnson v Agnew* [1979] 1 All ER 883 at 892, [1980] AC 367 at 396. *a*
Applying those principles to the facts of the present case it is necessary to consider
whether the owners' right to the freight had been 'unconditionally acquired' by them
before the termination of the charterparty. The circumstance that, by reason of the first
phrase of cl 16, the charterers' obligation to pay the freight was postponed until after the
termination of the charterparty does not, in my view, mean that the owners' prior
acquisition of the right to the freight was conditional only. The postponement of *b*
payment was an incident attaching to the right acquired, but it was not a condition of its
acquisition. It follows that, in accordance with the principles of law referred to above,
the owners' right to the freight, having been unconditionally acquired before the
termination of the charterparty, was not divested or discharged by such termination.

I would therefore answer question (2) by saying that the owners' right to the freight
survived the termination of the charterparty. *c*

Question (3): set-off as between charterers and owners
Under a contract for the carriage of goods by sea, such as the voyage charterparty in
the present case, freight is the monetary consideration payable by the cargo owner to the
shipowner for the carriage of the goods. The time when the freight is payable depends *d*
on the terms of the contract. It may be payable on delivery of the goods at the port of
discharge, in which case it is called 'freight' without any qualifying epithet; or it may be
payable at an early stage of the voyage, such as on completion of the signing of bills of
lading, in which case it is called 'advance freight'; or part of it may be payable at an early
stage of the voyage and the balance on delivery.

It is a long-established rule of English law, dating at least from the early part of the *e*
nineteenth century, that a cargo owner is not entitled to set up, as a defence to a claim for
freight, damage suffered by him by reason of some breach of contract by the shipowner
in relation to the carriage, causing for instance partial loss of or damage to the goods, but
must enforce any right which he has in respect of such breach by a cross-claim. The effect
of the rule before the coming into force of the Supreme Court of Judicature Acts 1873
and 1875 was that a cargo owner sued by a shipowner for freight could only recover his *f*
damage by bringing a separate cross-action against the shipowner; the effect of the rule
since the coming into force of those Acts has been that the cargo owner, instead of having
to bring a separate cross-action, has been able (though not bound) to raise his cross-claim
by way of counterclaim in the shipowner's action. The rule applies equally to freight
payable on delivery of the goods and to advance freight payable at some earlier stage of
the voyage. *g*

The rule of law referred to differs from that prevailing in many other countries and
has been subjected to a considerable amount of criticism in various quarters from time
to time. The continued existence of the rule was, however, affirmed by the Court of
Appeal in *Henriksens Rederi A/S v P H Z Rolimpex, The Brede* [1973] 3 All ER 589, [1974]
QB 233, in which the earlier authorities were fully examined. That decision of the Court
of Appeal was unanimously approved by your Lordships' House in *Aries Tanker Corp v* *h*
Total Transport Ltd, The Aries [1977] 1 All ER 398, [1977] 1 WLR 185. It follows that the
rule concerned (which I shall from now on call 'the rule against deduction'), whatever its
merits or demerits may be, is not open to challenge.

In all the cases in which the rule against deduction has been applied, up to and
including *The Aries*, the breaches of contract by shipowners sought to be relied on as
defences to claims for freight have been non-repudiatory breaches resulting in partial loss *j*
of or damage to cargo or delay in its delivery. So in *A/S Gunnstein & Co K/S v Jensen Krebs*
and Nielsen, The Alfa Nord [1977] 2 Lloyd's Rep 434 at 436, a case in which charterers
claimed the right to deduct damage caused by delay from freight due to shipowners, we
find Roskill LJ applying the rule against deduction and saying:

a   'We have to apply the well-established principle that there is no right of set-off for claims for damages for breach of charter, whether for loss of or damage to goods or for alleged failure to prosecute a voyage with reasonable dispatch or otherwise, against a claim for freight.'

The words 'or otherwise' used by Roskill LJ in this passage might, if taken out of context, cover a claim for damage caused by an accepted repudiation. In my view, however, Roskill LJ did not have a claim of that kind in mind, but was referring to other breaches
b   of contract of a non-repudiatory character.

Since 1977 the rule against deduction has been applied to cases of non-repudiatory breaches of kinds different to those referred to above. In *Cleobulos Shipping Co Ltd v Intertanker Ltd, The Cleon* [1983] 1 Lloyd's Rep 586 the rule was applied by the Court of Appeal to a case in which the breach of contract relied on was inadequacy in the ship's cargo pumps, making it necessary for her to leave one port of discharge and proceed to
c   another. In *Elena Shipping Ltd v Aidenfield Ltd, The Elena* [1986] 1 Lloyd's Rep 425 the rule was applied by Steyn J to a case in which the breach of contract relied on was the unfitness of some cargo spaces because of lack of facilities for ventilation.

It does not appear that, in any of the nineteenth century cases in which the rule against deduction was applied, equitable principles were invoked in order to defeat such rule. In
d   *The Brede* [1973] 3 All ER 589, [1974] QB 233 a defence by way of equitable set-off, based on short delivery of and damage to cargo, was put forward and rejected by the Court of Appeal. In *The Aries* [1977] 1 All ER 398, [1977] 1 WLR 185 the same defence, based on short delivery, was again put forward and rejected by your Lordships' House. As is apparent, however, the breaches of contract relied on in both these cases were again of a non-repudiatory character. The present case, therefore, raises for the first time the
e   question whether, although a claim in respect of a non-repudiatory breach of a voyage charterparty cannot operate as a defence by way of set-off to a claim for freight, a claim in respect of repudiation of such contract, accepted as such, is capable of doing so.

In the present case it was contended for the bank that, as between the owners and the charterers, the owners were entitled to rely on the rule against deduction as precluding the charterers from setting up, as a defence to any claim by the owners for advance
f   freight, the damage suffered by them as a result of the owners' repudiation of the charterparty. For the charterers, on the other hand, it was contended that, while they could not, having regard to the decision in *The Aries*, set up their damage as a defence at common law by way of abatement or otherwise, they were entitled to set it up as a defence by way of equitable set-off. They accepted that an ordinary cross-claim in respect of loss of or damage to cargo amounting to no more than a breach of warranty, such as
g   was relied on in *The Aries*, could not give rise to a defence by way of equitable set-off; but they contended that, where there was a much more serious breach of contract by the owners in the form of a repudiation of the charterparty accepted by them, a defence by way of equitable set-off was available to them.

Before examining this contention for the charterers it is necessary to explain briefly the nature, origins and basis of a defence by way of equitable set-off. Until the coming
h   into force of the Supreme Court of Judicature Acts 1873 and 1875 courts of equity had the power to prohibit by injunction the enforcement of a common law claim where there was a cross-claim which they regarded as being of an appropriate character. Section 24 of the Supreme Court of Judicature Act 1873 took away that power and provided instead that such a cross-claim could be raised as a defence to the claim. Those provisions of the 1873 Act have since been replaced successively, without any difference in effect,
j   first by ss 36 to 41 of the Supreme Court of Judicature (Consolidation) Act 1925 and more recently by s 49 of the Supreme Court Act 1981. It therefore becomes necessary, in order to decide whether a party can rely on a particular cross-claim as giving him a defence by way of equitable set-off to a common law claim today, to see whether such cross-claim is of such a character that it would before the coming into force of the

Supreme Court of Judicature Acts 1873 and 1875 have led a court of equity to prohibit by injunction the enforcement of such common law claim.

The authority most relied on as providing the relevant test is *Rawson v Samuel* (1839) 1 Cr & Ph 161 at 179, 41 ER 451 at 458, in which Lord Cottenham LC said that a cross-claim, in order to give rise to a defence by way of equitable set-off, must be such as 'impeached the title to the legal demand'. He then gave examples of cross-claims of that character. One case referred to was *Beasley v D'Arcy* (1800) 2 Sch & Lef 403. There a tenant was entitled to redeem his lease on payment to his landlord of rent due. The landlord had previously caused damage to the land let and the tenant was held to be entitled to deduct from the rent due the amount of the damage so done. Another case referred to was *Piggott v Williams* (1821) 6 Madd 95, 56 ER 1027. There a solicitor brought a claim against a client for the costs of work done. The client cross-claimed on the ground that the incurrence of the costs had been caused by the solicitor's negligence. It was held that the client was entitled to rely on such cross-claim as a defence.

The concept of a cross-claim being such as to 'impeach the title to the legal demand' is not a familiar one today. A different version of the relevant test is to be found in the decision of the Judicial Committee of the Privy Council in *Newfoundland Government v Newfoundland Rly Co* (1888) 13 App Cas 199. In that case there was a contract between the Newfoundland Railway Co and the government of Newfoundland under which the company agreed to build a railway line some 340 miles in length in five years and, having done so, to maintain it and operate it continuously. In return the government agreed, inter alia, to pay the company an annual subsidy for 35 years, such subsidy to be paid in proportionate parts as and when each five-mile section of the line was completed and operated. The company built part of the line and, on completion of each five-mile section, was paid by the government a proportionate amount of the annual subsidy attributable to it. Subsequently, the company abandoned the building of the remaining part of the line, on which the government refused to make any further payments of subsidy. The company, together with certain assignees of its rights under the contract, brought a petition of right against the government claiming, inter alia, that the government was bound to continue payment of subsidy in respect of the five-mile sections of the line which had been completed for the full period of 35 years. It was held that the government was bound by the terms of the contract to continue the payments of subsidy as claimed, but that it was entitled, as against both the company and the assignees, to set off against that liability the damage suffered by it by reason of the failure of the company to complete the whole of the line. In this connection Lord Hobhouse, who delivered the judgment of the Board, said (at 212–213):

> 'There is no universal rule that claims arising out of the same contract may be set against one another in all circumstances. But their Lordships have no hesitation in saying that in this contract the claims for subsidy and for non-construction ought to be set against one another.'

Lord Hobhouse then referred to *Smith v Parkes* (1852) 16 Beav 115 at 119, 51 ER 720 at 722, and continued (at 213):

> 'That was a case of equitable set-off, and was decided in 1852, when unliquidated damages could not by law be the subject of set-off. That law was not found to be conducive to justice, and has been altered. Unliquidated damages may now be set off as between the original parties, and also against an assignee if flowing out of and inseparably connected with the dealings and transactions which also give rise to the subject of the assignment.'

It is to be inferred that the change of law there referred to by Lord Hobhouse had been brought about by legislation in what was then the colony of Newfoundland, which adopted the principles enacted in England by s 24 of the Supreme Court of Judicature Act 1873 to which I drew attention earlier. *Newfoundland Government v Newfoundland Rly*

a

b

c

d

e

f

g

h

j

Co was clearly a case of a defence by way of equitable set-off based on a cross-claim. It was treated as such by Sellers LJ in *Hanak v Green* [1958] 2 All ER 141 at 154, [1958] 2 QB 9 at 31, and by Hobhouse J in his judgment in the present case (see [1987] 1 Lloyd's Rep 239 at 255). It is to be observed, however, that the criterion which Lord Hobhouse applied in deciding whether the government's cross-claim for unliquidated damages could be set off against the company's claim was not that the cross-claim 'impeached the title to the legal demand', as in *Rawson v Samuel* (1841) 1 Cr & Ph 161, 41 ER 451, but rather that it was a cross-claim 'flowing out of and inseparably connected with the dealings and transactions which also give rise' to the claim (see 13 App Cas 199 at 213).

I turn now to examine, against the background of the origin and nature of a defence by way of equitable set-off which I have described, the manner in which your Lordships' House dealt with such a defence in *The Aries* [1977] 1 All ER 398, [1977] 1 WLR 185. That case arose out of a voyage charterparty under which the entire freight was payable on delivery. Delivery having been made, the charterers did not pay to the shipowners the full amount of freight due but deducted a substantial sum from that amount on the ground of short delivery of the cargo. The owners brought an action against the charterers in the Queen's Bench Division in which they claimed payment of the balance of freight so deducted. The charterers resisted the claim on the ground that they were entitled to set off against it the amount of the damage which they had suffered by reason of the short delivery. They also counterclaimed for the amount of that loss. The owners having applied for summary judgment under RSC Ord 14, Donaldson J refused leave to defend and gave judgment in favour of the owners for the full amount of their claim. The charterers, having appealed unsuccessfully to the Court of Appeal (see [1976] 2 Lloyd's Rep 256), brought a further appeal to your Lordships' House which was, as I indicated earlier, unanimously dismissed.

The primary ground on which the House dismissed the appeal was that the charterparty expressly incorporated art III, r 6 of the Hague Rules, which provides that any claim for loss of or damage to cargo shall be discharged unless suit is brought within one year from the date of delivery or the date on which the goods should have been delivered, that the charterers had failed to bring suit within that period of time and that their cross-claim in respect of short delivery had therefore become prescribed, so that it could not be relied on by way of either defence or counterclaim.

While this was the primary ground on which the appeal was dismissed, the House also rejected arguments put forward for the charterers that their cross-claim in respect of short delivery afforded them a defence to the owners' claim for the balance of the freight either by way of abatement at common law or by way of equitable set-off.

Lord Wilberforce emphasised four main points (see [1977] 1 All ER 398 at 403–404, [1977] 1 WLR 185 at 189–191): first, that it was a long-established rule of English law that a claim in respect of cargo could not be asserted by way of deduction from freight; second, that the status of the rule, as a rule of law, was not affected by the fact that the reason for it could not readily be ascertained; third, that the principle of abatement at common law was confined to contracts for the sale of goods and contracts for work and labour: it did not extend to contracts for the carriage of goods by sea and it would not be right for the courts so to extend it; fourth, that the parties had contracted on the basis of the rule, and it was not for the courts to alter that basis even if they were convinced that a different rule would have greater merit. Having dealt with these matters Lord Wilberforce turned to the question of equitable set-off, saying ([1977] 1 All ER 398 at 404–405, [1977] 1 WLR 185 at 191):

'My Lords, a yet further argument was developed, that the charterers' claim for short delivery might operate by way of equitable set-off—this, on the assumption as I understood it, that the right of deduction at law was not upheld. This contention was given more prominence in this House than perhaps it received in the Court of Appeal's judgments in *The Brede* [1973] 3 All ER 589, [1974] QB 233 though in fact

it seems to have been given adequate consideration in that case. It does not appear
to me to advance the charterers' case. One thing is certainly clear about the doctrine
of equitable set-off—complicated though it may have become from its involvement
with procedural matters—namely that for it to apply, there must be some equity,
some ground for equitable intervention, other than the mere existence of a cross-
claim: see *Rawson v Samuel* (1841) Cr & Ph 161 at 178, 41 ER 451 at 458, per Lord
Cottenham LC, *Best v Hill* (1872) LR 8 CP 10 at 15, and the modern case of *Hanak v
Green* [1958] 2 All ER 141 at 147, [1958] 2 QB 9 at 19, per Morris LJ. But in this
case counsel could not suggest, and I cannot detect, any such equity sufficient to
operate the mechanism, so as, in effect, to override a clear rule of the common law
on the basis of which the parties contracted. It is significant that in no case since the
Supreme Court of Judicature Act 1873 or at a time before that Act when equitable
jurisdiction was available to a court dealing with the claim, was any such equitable
set-off or equitable defence upheld or, until *The Brede*, suggested.'

Lord Simon also dealt with the question of equitable set-off, where he said ([1977] 1
All ER 398 at 406–407, [1977] 1 WLR 185 at 193):

> 'The argument from equity fails, in my respectful opinion, for a number of
> reasons. First, the mere existence of cross-claims per se did not give rise to equitable
> intervention: it was not enough that they arose from the same contract; the equity
> of the bill had to impeach the title to the legal demand: per Lord Cottenham LC in
> *Rawson v Samuel* (1841) Cr & Ph 161 at 178–179, 41 ER 451 at 458. The title to a
> claim for freight is not impeached by short delivery of cargo—unless, of course, the
> latter amounts to repudiation of the contract of carriage. Secondly, there is no record
> of equity having in fact intervened at any time before the Common Law Procedure
> Act 1854 ... Thirdly, there is no record of the alleged equitable defence having
> been essayed at any time since the Supreme Court of Judicature Act 1873. Equity
> did not bark at all at a claim for freight during this century-long night; to adopt
> Holmes, this would be a curious incident ... Fourthly, the cases of assignment like
> *Newfoundland Government v Newfoundland Railway Co* (1888) 13 App Cas 199, on
> which the charterers so greatly relied, are clearly distinguishable. You cannot
> equitably take the benefit of an assignment without also assuming its burdens; both
> flow out of and are inseparably connected with the same transaction ... Fifthly, at
> the time of *Mondel v Steel* (1841) 8 M & W 858, [1835–42] All ER Rep 511 the Court
> of Exchequer itself still had an equitable jurisdiction; but it seems to have occurred
> to no one that any rule of equitable set-off affected the situation.'

There are certain observations which I would make with regard to the passages from
the speeches of Lord Wilberforce and Lord Simon quoted above. First, the cross-claim of
the charterers which they held could not operate as a defence by way of legal set-off to a
claim for freight was, as I indicated earlier, a cross-claim based on a non-repudiatory
breach of contract, namely short delivery of cargo. Lord Wilberforce did not deal with
the question whether a cross-claim based on repudiation of a charterparty could or could
not operate as such a defence. He did not do so because the case before him did not raise
that question. Lord Simon did refer to repudiation when he said: 'The title to a claim for
freight is not impeached by short delivery of cargo—unless, of course, the latter amounts
to repudiation of the contract ...' It is not entirely clear to what kind of repudiation Lord
Simon was there referring. Since, however, he was dealing with a case in which freight
was only payable on delivery, it seems likely that he was referring to repudiation in the
form of total failure to deliver, a failure which would of itself prevent freight becoming
payable at all. In any case it is clear that he was not referring to a case like the present
one, in which, after the owners' right to advance freight had accrued, they then
repudiated the charterparty.

Second, both Lord Wilberforce and Lord Simon considered that the characteristic of a cross-claim necessary to enable it to operate as a defence by way of equitable set-off was the characteristic prescribed by Lord Cottenham LC in *Rawson v Samuel* (1841) Cr & Ph 161 at 179, 41 ER 451 at 458, namely that the cross-claim impeached the title to the legal demand. Lord Wilberforce added that it must create an equity sufficient to override a clear rule on the basis of which the parties contracted (see [1977] 1 All ER 398 at 404–405, [1977] 1 WLR 185 at 191).

Third, Lord Simon distinguished cases of assignment, such as *Newfoundland Government v Newfoundland Rly Co* (1888) 13 App Cas 199 on the basis that one cannot take the benefit of an assignment without assuming the burdens, because both flow out of and are inseparably connected with the same transaction. With great respect to Lord Simon, I believe him to have been in error on this point. The decision in the *Newfoundland* case was that the government's cross-claim for damage caused by the company's failure to complete the railway line could operate as a defence by way of equitable set-off against both the company and the assignees, no distinction in this respect being drawn between the two. It is essential to bear in mind, however, that the company's claim in that case was a claim for subsidy under the particular terms of what was in essence a building contract, so that the special character which the law attaches to a claim for freight under a contract for the carriage of goods by sea was in no way relevant.

My Lords, in *The Aries* [1977] 1 All ER 398 at 405, 410, [1977] 1 WLR 185 at 191, 197 Viscount Dilhorne and Lord Edmund-Davies agreed with Lord Wilberforce on all points. Lord Salmon delivered a separate speech, agreeing substantially with Lord Wilberforce, except on the question of the prescriptive effect of art III, r 6 of the Hague Rules, with regard to which he reserved his opinion.

The speeches of Lord Wilberforce and Lord Simon in *The Aries* make it clear that, when an owner's breach of charterparty is of a non-repudiatory character, such as partial loss of or damage to cargo, it does not give rise to an equity in favour of the charterers sufficient to override the established rule against deduction. The question for decision in the present case is whether, where an owner's breach of charterparty is of a repudiatory character, it does give rise to such an equity.

Various arguments can be advanced to support an affirmative answer to that question. First, it can be said that a repudiatory breach or breach of a voyage charterparty by an owner, occurring after the right to the payment to him of advance freight has accrued, satisfies the test for a defence by way of equitable set-off laid down in *Rawson v Samuel* of giving rise to an equity sufficient to 'impeach the legal title' to the claim for such advance freight. I find it difficult, however, to see how, when a charterparty expressly provides, in effect, that the legal title to advance freight is to be deemed to be complete on the signing of bills of lading, a subsequent breach of the charterparty, even one of a repudiatory character, can properly be regarded as impeaching that title.

Second and alternatively, it can be said that a claim based on a repudiatory breach of a voyage charterparty by an owner, occurring after the right to the payment to him of advance freight has accrued, satisfies the test for an equitable set-off laid down in *Newfoundland Government v Newfoundland Rly Co* of being a breach flowing out of and being inseparably connected with the transaction, namely the charterparty which gave rise to the claim for such advance freight. The same might be said, however, of claims with regard to non-repudiatory breaches, such as partial loss of or damage to cargo, in respect of which *The Aries* is conclusive authority that they do not give rise to a defence by way of equitable set-off.

Third, it can be said that the rule against deduction is in any case anomalous, that it has hitherto been applied only to cases of non-repudiatory breach and that the courts ought not to extend its application to cases of repudiatory breach. In my view, however, there is little force in this argument, because a case like the present one seems never to have arisen before, and it is unlikely, except very rarely, that it will arise again.

Once the three arguments discussed above are rejected, as I think on the grounds
which I have given that they should be, it is possible to state a number of good reasons   *a*
for holding that a repudiatory breach of a voyage charterparty is no more capable of
giving rise to a defence by way of equitable set-off than is a non-repudiatory breach. I
shall set out those reasons shortly first and then develop them. The first reason is that a
repudiatory breach of a charterparty by an owner does not necessarily cause more damage
to a charterer than a non-repudiatory breach; it may cause less. There is, therefore, no
justification based on quantum of damage for applying the rule against deduction to the   *b*
latter breach but not to the former. The second reason is that the application of the rule
against deduction only works to the ultimate disadvantage of a charterer when the
owner's financial situation makes it impossible for a counterclaim to be enforced against
him. That risk, however, exists whether the breach is repudiatory or non-repudiatory.
The third reason lies in the manner in which the legislation has treated the premature
termination of a voyage charterparty by frustration.   *c*

With regard to the first reason it is easy to visualise a case where partial loss of or
damage to a valuable cargo would cause greater loss to a charterer than a premature
termination of the voyage as a result of accepted repudiation, especially if the latter
occurred at a late stage of the voyage rather than an early one. Yet, if the contentions for
the charterers are right, the rule against deduction would apply to the former greater loss
but not to the latter lesser loss. It is difficult to see any justification for this.   *d*

With regard to the second reason, provided that an owner's financial situation is such
that a counterclaim for damages can be enforced against him, the charterer will not in
the end suffer from the application of the rule against deduction. A good illustration of
this is to be found in *Turnbull v Great Eastern and Peninsular Navigation Co* (1885) Cab &
El 595. In that case a steamer was chartered to carry a cargo of coal from Birkenhead to
Bombay. The charterparty provided that four-fifths of the freight was to be paid in cash   *e*
in one month from the ship's sailing from her last port in Great Britain, steamer lost or
not lost. The perils excluded by the charterparty did not include negligence of the master.
The ship sailed with her cargo on 12 July 1884 and was lost through the negligence of
the master on 19 July, the loss being known in England on 21 July. On 26 July the
charterers paid four-fifths of the freight to the owners. In an action subsequently brought
by the charterers against the owners for damages for breach of the charterparty resulting   *f*
in the loss of the cargo, it was held, first, that the expression 'steamer lost or not lost' did
not apply to a loss caused by the master's negligence and, second, that the charterers were
entitled to include in the damages recoverable by them the four-fifths of the freight
which they had paid in advance. The risk of a charterer's counterclaim being defeated by
insolvency of the owner can arise when such counterclaim is based on a non-repudiatory
breach as well as when it is based on a repudiatory breach, so that, since the rule against   *g*
deduction applies in the former case, there is no good reason, so far as that risk is
concerned, why it should not also do so in the latter case.

The third reason requires rather more elaboration. At common law frustration of a
contract did not cause it to be rescinded ab initio, but terminated it forthwith on the
occurrence of the frustrating event. The effect of such termination was to release both   *h*
parties from further performance of the contract, while leaving intact any payments
already made and any rights already acquired under it. Put shortly, the principle followed
by the common law was that, on a contract being frustrated, losses and gains lay where
they fell and no adjustment of the parties' rights could be made. So, in the case of a
voyage charterparty stipulating for the payment of freight in advance, if the charterparty
became frustrated after the date for such payment had passed, the result was this: if the   *j*
charterer had already paid the advance freight, he had no right to recover it, while, if he
had not already paid it, he remained obliged to do so. If authority for these propositions
is needed, it is to be found in the advice of Brett J to the House of Lords in *Allison v Bristol
Marine Insurance Co Ltd* (1876) 1 App Cas 209 at 226. One modification to the common

law of frustration as it had previously been understood to be was made by the decision of
a your Lordships' House in *Fibrosa Spolka Akcyjna v Fairbairn Lawson Combe Barbour Ltd*
[1942] 2 All ER 122, [1943] AC 32. That modification was that, when, as a result of a
contract being frustrated, there was a total failure of consideration for a payment already
made, the payment could be recovered by the payer as money had and received to his
use. This modification, however, was of a very limited effect, since it left untouched
payments in respect of which the consideration had failed partly but not wholly.

b   The law relating to the frustration of contracts as I have described it was radically
altered, soon after the decision in the *Fibrosa* case referred to above, by the passing of the
Law Reform (Frustrated Contracts) Act 1943. That Act, except in the case of a few
specified kinds of contract, got rid of the common law principle that, on a contract being
frustrated, losses and gains lay where they fell, and substituted for it an elaborate code by
which the rights of the parties could be readjusted in an equitable manner. It is not
c necessary to go into the details of this code of readjustment; it is sufficient to say that it
included, where appropriate, repayment in whole or in part of payments already made
by one party to the other, and the release of a party in whole or in part from obligations
to make payments already accrued due: see s 1(2) including the proviso to it.

          The significance of the 1943 Act for present purposes, however, lies in the fact that, as
I indicated earlier, certain specified contracts are excluded from its application. These
d contracts include 'any charterparty, except a time charterparty or a charterparty by way
of demise' and 'any contract (other than a charterparty) for the carriage of goods by sea':
see s 2(5)(a). The legislature must have had a reason for this exclusion and the only reason
which it seems to me that it could have had is an unwillingness to create a situation in
which, following the frustration of contracts of this kind, advance freight already due
could, if paid, be recovered back in whole or in part, or, if not paid, cease to be payable in
e whole or in part. In other words the legislature was preserving, in the context of the
premature termination of such contracts by frustration, the indefeasibility of an accrued
right to advance freight. The attitude of the legislature in this respect seems to me to
make it difficult to say that, when a voyage charterparty or other contract for the carriage
of goods by sea is prematurely terminated by the owner's repudiation of it, the
indefeasibility of an accrued right to advance freight should not be similarly preserved
f by applying the rule against deduction to the situation so created.

          It was argued for the charterers that, where a court had before it in the same action an
owner's claim for freight under a charterparty and a charterer's counterclaim for damages
for breach of that charterparty, it could by procedural means bring about a set-off of the
counterclaim against the claim, even though, under the substantive law governing the
rights of the parties, no such set-off was available. The court, it was said, could try and
g determine both the owner's claim for freight and the charterer's counterclaim for
damages, and then, supposing both to have succeeded in whole or in part, exercise its
power under RSC Ord 15, r 2(4), which provides: 'Where a defendant establishes a
counterclaim against the claim of a plaintiff and there is a balance in favour of one of the
parties, the Court may give judgment for the balance . . .' It was further argued that, if
h the court could act in this way, arbitrators could do the same thing. The practical result
would be a set-off, by procedural means, between the owner's claim for freight and the
charterer's counterclaim for damages.

          In my opinion, for the court to act in the manner suggested would constitute a wrong
exercise of its discretion, because it would involve using rules of procedure to bring about
a result contrary to the rights of the parties under the substantive law. That would be
j inconsistent with the principle that the Judicature Acts, while making important changes
in procedure, did not alter and were not intended to alter the rights of parties: see *Stumore*
v Campbell & Co [1892] 1 QB 314 at 316, 318, [1891–4] All ER Rep 785 at 787 per Lord
Esher MR and Lopes LJ.

          For the reasons which I have given I would answer question (3) by saying that, if the owners had not assigned their right to freight to the bank, the charterers would not have been entitled to set off against such right the damage suffered by them as a result of the *a* owners' repudiation of the charterparty.

Question (4): set-off as between charterers and bank

The bank's claim for freight against the charterers was brought by them as legal assignees of the owners. It follows that the bank's rights against the charterers are governed by s 136(1) of the Law of Property Act 1925, which provides: *b*

'Any absolute assignment by writing under the hand of the assignor (not purporting to be by way of charge only) of any debt or other legal thing in action, of which express notice in writing has been given to the debtor, trustee or other person from whom the assignor would have been entitled to claim such debt or thing in action, is effectual in law (subject to equities having priority over the right of the assignee) to pass and transfer from the date of such notice—(*a*) the legal right *c* to such debt or thing in action; (*b*) all legal and other remedies for the same; and (*c*) the power to give a good discharge for the same without the concurrence of the assignor . . .'

It was contended for the charterers that, even if, as I have held in answering question (3), they were not entitled to set up their counterclaim in respect of the damages suffered by *d* them as a result of the owners' repudiation of the charterparty as a defence by way of equitable set-off as between them and the owners, they were nevertheless entitled to rely on such counterclaim as a defence as between them and the bank, on the ground that it constituted an equity to which the assignment of the right to freight was made subject under s 136(1) above.

In support of this contention for the charterers reliance was placed on certain passages *e* in the judgment of the Privy Council delivered by Lord Hobhouse in *Newfoundland Government v Newfoundland Rly Co* (1888) 13 App Cas 199 and on passages from various textbooks which appear to be largely founded on that case. I discussed the *Newfoundland Rly* case in some detail in connection with question (3), and I also referred to what I respectfully suggested was a misunderstanding about its effect in the speech of Lord *f* Simon in *The Aries* [1977] 1 All ER 398 at 406–407, [1977] 1 WLR 185 at 193. The charterers relied particularly for present purposes on a passage in the speech of Lord Hobhouse immediately preceding the passage which I quoted earlier. In the passage so relied on by the charterers Lord Hobhouse, referring to the company's claim for subsidy on the one hand and the government's counterclaim for damages for the failure to complete the railway on the other, said (13 App Cas 199 at 212):   *g*

'The two claims under consideration have their origin in the same portion of the same contract, where the obligations which give rise to them are intertwined in the closest manner. The claim of the Governement does not arise from any fresh transaction freely entered into by it after notice of the assignment by the company. It was utterly powerless to prevent the company from inflicting injury on it by breaking the contract. It would be a lamentable thing if it were found to be the law *h* that a party to a contract may assign a portion of it, perhaps a beneficial portion, so that the assignee shall take the benefit, wholly discharged of any counterclaim by the other party in respect of the rest of the contract, which may be burdensome.'

Hobhouse J in his judgment in the present case made a very full and careful analysis of the *Newfoundland Rly* case (see [1987] 1 Lloyd's Rep 239 at 254–257). I respectfully agree *j* with that analysis, and in particular with two matters contained in it. The first matter is that the case was one of equitable set-off, in the sense that it was held that the government's counterclaim in respect of the company's breach of contract in failing to complete the railway, because it flowed out of and was inseparably connected with the contract between the parties, operated as a defence by way of equitable set-off to the

company's claim for subsidy. The second matter is that Lord Hobhouse drew no
a distinction in this respect between the rights of the government against the company on
the one hand and its rights against the company's assignees on the other. On the contrary
he made it clear that the government's counterclaim operated as a defence by way of
equitable set-off both against the company and against the assignees.

Having regard to these matters I do not consider that the *Newfoundland Rly* case affords
any support for the contention of the charterers presently under discussion. On the
b contrary, it seems to be inconsistent with it.

I would, therefore, answer question (4) by saying that the charterers are no more
entitled to rely on their counterclaim for damages as a defence by way of equitable set-
off against the bank than they would have been entitled to rely on it, but for the
assignment, against the owners.

Having regard to the answers which I have given to the four questions discussed above,
c I would allow the appeal, set aside the order of the Court of Appeal dated 21 December
1987 as later amended and restore the order of Hobhouse J dated 24 October 1986.

LORD OLIVER OF AYLMERTON. My Lords, I have had the advantage of reading
in draft the speech delivered by my noble and learned friend Lord Brandon. I agree that
the appeal should be allowed for the reasons which he has given.
d

LORD GOFF OF CHIEVELEY. My Lords, for the reasons given by my noble and
learned friend Lord Brandon, I would allow this appeal.

LORD JAUNCEY OF TULLICHETTLE. My Lords, I have had the opportunity of
considering in draft the speech to be delivered by my noble and learned friend Lord
e Brandon. I agree with it, and for the reasons he gives would allow the appeal.

Appeal allowed.

Solicitors: *Holman Fenwick & Willan* (for the bank); *Wilde Sapte* (for the charterers).

Mary Rose Plummer   Barrister.

Byng v London Life Association Ltd and another

COURT OF APPEAL, CIVIL DIVISION

SIR NICOLAS BROWNE-WILKINSON V-C, MUSTILL AND WOOLF LJJ

5, 6, 7, 21 DECEMBER 1988

Company – Meeting – Adjournment – Powers of chairman – Location notified for meeting proving too small to accommodate all members wishing to attend – Chairman of meeting adjourning meeting to another location in afternoon of same day – Whether chairman having power to adjourn meeting without its consent – Whether power to adjourn validly exercised – Test to be applied.

Notice was duly given of an extraordinary general meeting of a company to be held at a specified location at 12 noon on 19 October 1988. There was an assembly of members of the company at that time and place, but the location proved to be too small to accommodate all those members wishing to be present. D, the president of the company and chairman of the meeting, purported to adjourn the meeting and direct that it be resumed in the afternoon of the same day at another location. The reconvened meeting passed the sole resolution of which notice had been given. The plaintiff, a shareholder of the company, brought an action claiming that D had not validly adjourned the meeting in the morning and that accordingly all business conducted at the reconvened meeting in the afternoon had been invalidly conducted. The judge dismissed the plaintiff's claim. The plaintiff appealed to the Court of Appeal.

Held – (1) There was no rule of law that a meeting from which members were wrongly excluded was a nullity notwithstanding the fact that it was incapable of conducting any business. On the true construction of the company's articles of association an inquorate meeting of the company incapable of conducting any business was nevertheless a 'meeting' of the company which was capable of being adjourned. It followed that on the facts (Mustill LJ dissenting) there had been a meeting of the company on 19 October at the first location presided over by D as chairman (see p 565 *h* to p 566 *a*, p 567 *c d*, p 571 *j*, p 572 *a d e* and p 575 *h*, post).

(2) Where there was a meeting at which the views of the majority could not be validly ascertained, the chairman had a residual common law power to adjourn the meeting without its consent in order to give all persons entitled a reasonable opportunity of voting and speaking at the meeting (see p 567 *e*, p 568 *c* to *e h j*, p 569 *c*, p 573 *c* to *e* and p 575 *h*, post); *Jackson v Hamlyn* [1953] 1 All ER 887 applied.

(3) The test to be applied in deciding whether the chairman's decision to adjourn was lawful was the same as that applicable on judicial review in accordance with accepted principles relating to unreasonableness. However, since the chairman's power was only exercisable for the purpose of giving the members a reasonable opportunity to debate and vote on the resolution, there had to be very special circumstances to justify a decision to adjourn a meeting to a time and place where, to the chairman's knowledge, a number of members who had attended the original meeting would not only be unable to attend but also be unable to lodge a proxy vote. Accordingly, although D had acted in good faith, his decision to adjourn to another location on the same date was not valid, on the grounds either that he failed to take into account relevant factors or that the decision was unreasonable. The appeal would therefore be allowed (see p 569 *g* to *j*, p 570 *g j* to p 571 *c e* to *g*, p 573 *f* to p 574 *a* and p 575 *g h*, post); *Second Consolidated Trust Ltd v Ceylon Amalgamated Tea and Rubber Estates Ltd* [1943] 2 All ER 567 and *Associated Provincial Picture Houses Ltd v Wednesbury Corp* [1947] 2 All ER 680 applied.

Notes

a For powers of a chairman to adjourn a meeting, see 7(1) Halsbury's Laws (4th edn reissue) para 696, and for cases on the subject, see 9 Digest (Reissue) 627, 640, 3734, 3841.

Cases referred to in judgments

A-G v Edison Telephone Co of London Ltd (1880) 6 QBD 244.
Associated Provincial Picture Houses Ltd v Wednesbury Corp [1947] 2 All ER 680, [1948]

b   1 KB 223, CA.
Fletcher v New Zealand Glue Co Ltd (1911) 31 NZLR 129, NZ SC.
Harben v Phillips (1883) 23 Ch D 14, Ch D and CA.
Jackson v Hamlyn [1953] 1 All ER 887, [1953] Ch 577, [1953] 2 WLR 709.
John v Rees [1969] 2 All ER 274, [1970] Ch 345, [1969] 2 WLR 1294.
London Flats Ltd, Re [1969] 2 All ER 744, [1969] 1 WLR 711.

c *McLaren v Fisken* (1881) 28 Gr 352, Ont Ch Ct.
National Dwellings Society v Sykes [1894] 3 Ch 159.
Portuguese Consolidated Copper Mines Ltd, Re (1889) 42 Ch D 160, Ch D and CA.
R v D'Oyly (1840) 12 Ad & El 139, 113 ER 763.
Salisbury Gold Mining Co Ltd v Hathorn [1897] AC 268, PC.
Second Consolidated Trust Ltd v Ceylon Amalgamated Tea and Rubber Estates Ltd [1943] 2 All

d   ER 567.

Cases also cited

Associated Color Laboratories Ltd, Re (1970) 12 DLR (3d) 338, BC SC.
Cambrian Peat Fuel and Charcoal Co Ltd, Re, De La Mott's and Turner's Case (1875) 31 LT

e   773.
D'Arcy v Tamar Kit Hill and Callington Rly Co (1867) LR 2 Ex 158.
Musselwhite v C H Musselwhite & Son Ltd [1962] 1 All ER 201, [1962] Ch 964.
Newman (George) & Co, Re [1895] 1 Ch 674, CA.
Sharp v Dawes (1876) 2 QBD 26, CA.
Shaw v Tati Concessions Ltd [1913] 1 Ch 292, [1911–13] All ER Rep 694.

f **Appeal**

The plaintiff, Julian Michael Edmund Byng, appealed against the order of Vinelott J made on 14 November 1988 whereby he dismissed the plaintiff's claim that the second defendant, Oliver Dawson, the chairman of the extraordinary general meeting of the first defendant, London Life Association Ltd, convened to be held at Cinema 1, Barbican Centre, Barbican, London EC2 on Wednesday, 19 October 1988 at 12 noon, was not

g entitled to adjourn the meeting to the Café Royal, Regent Street, London W1 at 2.30 pm on the same day and that all business conducted at the purported adjourned meeting was invalid. The facts are set out in the judgment of Sir Nicolas Browne-Wilkinson V-C.

Robin Potts QC and *Nigel Davis* for the plaintiff.

h *David Oliver QC* and *Robert Hildyard* for the defendants.

At the conclusion of the argument the court announced that the appeal would be allowed for reasons to be given later.

21 December. The following judgments were delivered.

j **SIR NICOLAS BROWNE-WILKINSON V-C.** Notice of an extraordinary general meeting of the first defendant, London Life Association Ltd (London Life), to be held at Cinema 1, The Barbican, London EC2 at 12 noon on Wednesday, 19 October 1988 was duly given. There was an assembly of members of London Life at that time and place, but Cinema 1 proved too small to accommodate all those members wishing to be present.

The second defendant, Mr Dawson, purported to adjourn that meeting and direct that it   *a*
be resumed in the afternoon of the same day at the Café Royal. The meeting at the Café
Royal passed the sole resolution of which notice had been given. The plaintiff, a member
of London Life, brought this action claiming that the second defendant had not validly
adjourned the 'meeting' in the morning and that accordingly all business conducted at
the purported adjourned meeting in the afternoon was invalidly conducted. The action
was heard with great speed, and on 14 November 1988 Vinelott J dismissed the action.
The plaintiff appealed to this court and the appeal was heard by us on 5, 6 and 7 December   *b*
1988. At the end of the hearing we gave our decision to allow the appeal, stating that our
reasons would be given later. These are those reasons.

London Life is a mutual life assurance company. It has no share capital but is limited
by guarantee. The members are some, but not all, of its policyholders. Early in 1988
London Life started negotiations with another mutual life assurance company, Australian
Mutual Provident Society (AMP), for the merger of their long-term businesses. The   *c*
existence of these negotiations was disclosed at the annual general meeting of London
Life in May 1988.

Thereafter negotiations continued and agreement in principle was reached between
the two companies which is conditional on completion taking place by 31 March 1989.
The agreement required the London Life long-term fund to become a separate fund
administered by AMP. The view was taken that the scheme could not go ahead until the   *d*
memorandum of association of London Life had been amended to include a general
power to transfer the business of London Life. The sole business of the meeting convened
for 19 October 1988 was to pass the necessary special resolution so to amend the
memorandum of association. The scheme also has to be sanctioned by the court under
s 49 of the Insurance Companies Act 1982.

The proposed merger gave rise to some opposition and some adverse press comment.   *e*
It became apparent to the board that the meeting was likely to be far better attended than
the ordinary run of general meetings of London Life at which normally only
approximately 80 people attend. In the circumstances the board determined to hold the
meeting at Cinema 1 at the Barbican Centre which could seat 280 people but could, if
necessary, accommodate some 300.

Notice of the proposed extraordinary general meeting was given on 27 September   *f*
1988. Very shortly thereafter the board became anxious whether Cinema 1 would in fact
prove adequate. As a result arrangements were made with the Barbican Centre to book
two overflow rooms together with additional accommodation in the foyer to
accommodate those who could not fit into the cinema. The intention was that there
would be an audio-visual link between the overflow rooms, the foyer and the cinema.
The two overflow rooms could, at a maximum, hold 100 persons each.   *g*

As the date of the meeting approached the board continued to feel anxious lest Cinema
1 and the provisions for overflow at the Barbican Centre should themselves prove
inadequate for the number who attended. They accordingly booked another room at the
Café Royal (with a seating capacity of 800) between 1.30 and 5 pm on 19 October. The
judge found that those concerned with the organisation throughout thought that the   *h*
cinema together with the overflow provision at the Barbican Centre would accommodate
all those wishing to attend: the room at the Café Royal was booked merely as a precaution,
it not being thought that it would be necessary to have the meeting there.

The details of what occurred on 19 October are set out in the judge's judgment. For
my purposes I can summarise the events as follows. Those arriving for the meeting had
to register in order to be issued with voting cards. Such registration took place in the   *j*
foyer. Some of those arriving to attend the meeting were diverted to the overflow rooms
which were on the ninth floor but they were not told that there would be no facilities for
registration there. The cinema became overcrowded and members unable to gain access
to the cinema were diverted to both the overflow rooms and the foyer.

Under art 17 the president of London Life is made the chairman of any general

meeting. Mr Dawson is the president. At about 12 noon he and the directors took their
a places at a table at the end of the cinema facing the body of the room. They were
accompanied by their legal advisers. Since registration was not complete, Mr Dawson
announced that the start of the meeting would be delayed by 20 minutes. He later
delayed the start a further ten minutes until 12.30 pm. It emerged that many people
had gone to the overflow rooms without registering and they were unwilling to go down
to the foyer to register.

b   A small party went up to the overflow rooms to discover what the situation was. They
found that the audio-visual link was deficient; although the board could be seen and the
chairman could be heard, members speaking from the body of the cinema could not be
heard. There was no direct audio-visual link from the overflow rooms to the cinema.
This was contrary to expectations. To meet the position, a person with headphones and a
portable microphone had been stationed in each of the overflow rooms, in the foyer and
c in the cinema. These persons could communicate with each other and thereby a message
from someone in an overflow room or in the foyer could be passed to the person equipped
with headphones and a microphone in the cinema. He could then write down the
message and take it to the chairman.

The arrangements for the meeting were plainly unsatisfactory and before 12.30 pm
suggestions had been made from the floor of the cinema that the meeting should be
d adjourned. However, Mr Dawson decided to open the meeting at 12.30 pm. Registration
was not then complete. As soon as the meeting opened a member rose to object that it
was not fair to start the meeting while there were people outside trying to get in. Others
proposed that the meeting should be adjourned which was taken to mean dissolved or
abandoned. One member insisted that there should be a vote on this resolution, although
there was some opposition to an adjournment in the body of the cinema. Mr Dawson
e having pointed out that a vote would take a considerable time, the member who had
proposed an adjournment withdrew it. Mr Dawson then started to deliver his prepared
speech.

While this was going on, a number of messages had been received from the overflow
rooms and passed in note form to Mr Dawson. One in particular records that the plaintiff
had proposed an adjournment sine die. Mr Dawson said that he did not recollect reading
f this note.

The time was now about 12.45 pm or 12.50 pm. One of the doors of the cinema was
forced open letting in a 'muted roar' from the foyer. At that stage Mr Dawson said that
he proposed the adjournment of the meeting himself and proposed that it should adjourn
to alternative accommodation at the Café Royal where the meeting would resume at
2.30 pm. A policyholder objected that he had appointments for the afternoon and
g received support from the body of those in the cinema. The chairman repeated that he
proposed the adjournment to the Café Royal but said that he would like it to be done
with the majority consent of the members. Another policyholder suggested that such an
adjournment of the meeting would be invalid (which again received support) and
pointed out that the meeting could not continue if part of the membership was excluded.
h Another policyholder said words to the effect that such an adjournment would exclude
those who could not attend at 2.30 pm and that such an adjournment would prejudice
those who had appeared at the right time and in the right place. This again received
support from the floor. Another policyholder then proposed a vote of no confidence in
the board. The chairman then adjourned the meeting to the Café Royal at 2.30 pm.

At the meeting in the Café Royal in the afternoon Mr Dawson gave his prepared
j speech and there was an orderly debate. As the room had only been booked until 5 pm
Mr Dawson ruled that a vote would have to be taken on the resolution before 4.30 pm.
When the resolution was put, it was carried by a small majority and therefore failed as a
special resolution. However, Mr Dawson demanded a poll and the meeting was closed.
The result of the poll was announced the following day and the resolution was passed.

The judge found that there were approximately 800 people at the meeting in the morning of whom 468 were registered to vote. At the meeting at the Café Royal in the afternoon there were approximately 600 people present of whom 335 were registered to vote.

I must now mention the articles of London Life which are directly in question. Article 12 requires that 21 days' notice of an extraordinary general meeting convened to pass a special resolution must be given 'specifying the place, the day and the hour of the meeting . . .' Article 17 provides that the president is to preside as chairman at any general meeting. Article 18 provides:

> 'The Chairman may, with the consent of any meeting at which a quorum is present (and shall if so directed by the meeting) adjourn the meeting from time to time and from place to place, but no business shall be transacted at any adjourned meeting except business which might lawfully have been transacted at the meeting from which the adjournment took place. When a meeting is adjourned for thirty days or more, notice of the adjourned meeting shall be given as in the case of an original meeting. Save as aforesaid, it shall not be necessary to give any notice of an adjournment or of the business to be transacted at an adjourned meeting.'

Article 25 provides: 'The Chairman of the meeting shall regulate the proceedings thereat . . .'

It is common ground between the parties that, in the circumstances obtaining at the Barbican Centre on the morning of 19 October, no business could have been validly conducted at that meeting. Those who wished to be present in the cinema had been excluded from it and the audio-visual arrangements made for the overflow rooms and the foyer had broken down. The issue between the parties is whether Mr Dawson, as president of London Life, could and did validly adjourn anything which was a 'meeting' of London Life to the Café Royal. If there was no valid adjournment, the business purported to be done at the alleged adjourned meeting would have been wholly invalid.

The arguments put forward by counsel on behalf of the plaintiff both to the judge and to us were broadly the same. He made three submissions, each supported by a number of different arguments. First, he submitted that the assembly at the Barbican Centre was not a meeting of London Life at all. If this submission is correct, Mr Dawson could not claim to be chairman under art 17, since there was no meeting of London Life to which that article could apply. Therefore Mr Dawson could not adjourn the meeting. Moreover, if the assembly at the cinema was not a meeting of London Life, the meeting at the Café Royal in the afternoon could not be an adjourned meeting of London Life. Counsel's second submission for the plaintiff was that, even if there was a meeting of London Life of which Mr Dawson was the chairman, he had no power to adjourn it without the consent of the meeting since art 18 so provides. Counsel's third main submission was that, even if there was a meeting of London Life which Mr Dawson could, in certain circumstances, adjourn without the consent of the meeting, he did not validly exercise such power. I will consider these submissions in turn.

Was there a meeting?

The first difficulty is to identify what, if anything, was the meeting. Was it the assembly of the members in the cinema alone (from which all those in the overflow rooms and foyer were excluded) or was it the conglomerate assembly of those in the cinema plus those in the overflow rooms and foyer?

Counsel's first submission for the plaintiff under this head was made with a view to showing that the conglomerate assembly in the cinema, the overflow rooms and the foyer could not constitute a meeting. He submitted that for there to be a meeting at all everyone must be in the same place, face to face. If this submission were correct, even if the audio-visual links had worked perfectly, there would still have been no meeting at the Barbican on 19 October since all the members attending would not have been face to face but scattered between different rooms. In support of this submission counsel relied

on the definition of the word 'meet' in the *Shorter Oxford English Dictionary*, viz 'To come
a face to face with or into the company of [another person]'. He also relies on the fact that
the requirement in the Companies Act 1985, s 378 that an extraordinary resolution has
to be passed at a general meeting has a long statutory history dating back to times long
before the invention of audio-visual links. This, he submits, shows that a meeting for the
purpose of the Act requires that everyone shall be physically present in the same room or
space.

b   I do not accept this submission. The rationale behind the requirement for meetings in
the 1985 Act is that the members shall be able to attend in person so as to debate and vote
on matters affecting the company. Until recently this could only be achieved by everyone
being physically present in the same room face to face. Given modern technological
advances, the same result can now be achieved without all the members coming face to
face; without being physically in the same room they can be electronically in each other's
c presence so as to hear and be heard and to see and be seen. The fact that such a meeting
could not have been foreseen at the time the first statutory requirements for meetings
were laid down, does not require us to hold that such a meeting is not within the
meaning of the word 'meeting' in the 1985 Act. Thus, communication by telephone has
been held to be a 'telegraph' within the meaning of the Telegraph Acts 1863 and 1869,
notwithstanding that the telephone had not been invented or contemplated when those
d Acts were passed: see *A-G v Edison Telephone Co of London Ltd* (1880) 6 QBD 244.

I have no doubt therefore that, in cases where the original venue proves inadequate to
accommodate all those wishing to attend, valid general meetings of a company can be
properly held using overflow rooms provided, first, that all due steps are taken to direct
to the overflow rooms those unable to get into the main meeting and, second, that there
are adequate audio-visual links to enable those in all the rooms to see and hear what is
e going on in the other rooms. Were the law otherwise, with the present tendency towards
companies with very large numbers of shareholders and corresponding uncertainty as to
how many shareholders will attend meetings, the organisation of such meetings might
prove to be impossible.

In the event, counsel for the defendants did not contend that the conglomerate
f assembly was a meeting of the company. He submitted that the assembly in the cinema
was the meeting. I accept this submission. If there was a meeting at all it was the
assembly in the cinema, that being the venue specified in the notice convening the
meeting. Such meeting was incapable of proceeding to business, since all those members
unable to get into the cinema were excluded. For the reasons I have given, if proper
overflow facilities had in fact been provided, those in the overflow rooms and the foyer
would not have been excluded from that meeting but would, electronically, have been
g present at it. But since the audio-visual links did not work, those in the overflow rooms
and foyer were excluded and the meeting in the cinema was incapable of transacting any
business.

Does the fact that the assembly in the cinema was incapable of conducting any business
necessarily mean that it was not a 'meeting' at all? Counsel for the plaintiff submitted
h that it was an invalid meeting, a nullity. He said that, as in the case of a meeting of which
proper notice has not been given or at which there is no quorum, where members are
excluded from a meeting it is invalid and cannot be adjourned.

In my judgment the phrase 'invalid meeting', although useful as a shorthand
description of a meeting at which no business can be validly transacted, is capable of
giving rise to confusion. The fact that a meeting cannot pass a valid resolution in certain
j circumstances does not necessarily mean that there has been no meeting at all. Thus in
many cases (including the present) the articles of a company provide that, in the event of
there being no quorum present at a meeting, the meeting shall be adjourned for a fixed
period. In such a case it is clear that the inquorate meeting was a meeting notwithstanding
the fact that it could conduct no business.

In my judgment there is no absolute rule of law that a meeting from which members are wrongly excluded is a nullity. The meeting, as such, can conduct no business, but it is nevertheless a meeting. I can see no good reason why the law should shut its eyes to *a* the reality that, in response to a notice convening them, certain members of the company have assembled together at what, in ordinary usage, would be called a meeting. What that meeting can validly do is quite another matter.

In the present case the sole question is whether Mr Dawson was, within art 17, the chairman of a general meeting of London Life. The answer to that question must depend on the meaning of the word 'meeting' in the articles of London Life. Article 15 provides: *b*

'No business shall be transacted at any General Meeting unless a quorum is present when the meeting proceeds to business . . .'

Article 16 then provides:

'If within half an hour from the time appointed for the meeting a quorum is not *c* present, the meeting, if convened on the requisition of Members, shall be dissolved. In any other case it shall stand adjourned to the same day in the next week, at the same time and place . . .'

These two articles therefore proceed on the basis that an inquorate meeting incapable of conducting any business is still a 'meeting' of London Life, capable of being adjourned. *d* Similarly, under regs 40 and 41 of Table A in the Companies (Tables A to F) Regulations 1985, SI 1985/805, an inquorate meeting is treated as a meeting capable of adjournment. Therefore, the draftsman of the London Life articles and Parliament both plainly envisaged that the word 'meeting' covered an assembly which could conduct no business.

Counsel for the plaintiff relied on certain authorities to show that as a rule of law a meeting from which those entitled to be present were excluded is a nullity. In *Harben v* *e* *Phillips* (1883) 23 Ch D 14 four directors were wrongly excluded from a board meeting. The three directors present at the board meeting purported to adjourn it. The adjourned board meeting purported to take certain decisions. Chitty J said that the first meeting was 'an unlawful meeting, that it was not properly constituted, and that everything that was done at it is invalid' (at 26). In consequence he held that the adjourned board meeting could not validly transact the business it purported to transact. In the Court of Appeal *f* Cotton LJ expressed very grave doubt whether the first board meeting could be considered a proper meeting (at 34). The only question in that case was whether the first board meeting had been validly adjourned. The purported adjournment was the act of the meeting itself (ie of the three directors present). Therefore in that case it was being contended that the meeting itself (as opposed to the chairman of the meeting) could conduct business, notwithstanding the exclusion of some members entitled to be there *g* and to vote on the resolution. That, to my mind, is a wholly different case. In the present case the meeting at the cinema did not purport to transact business; the claim is that its ex officio chairman had power to adjourn it.

In *Re Portuguese Consolidated Copper Mines Ltd* (1889) 42 Ch D 160 there was a board meeting of which inadequate notice was given. Only two directors attended. They resolved that two directors should be a quorum, purported to allot certain shares and *h* adjourned the meeting. The adjourned meeting purported to ratify the allotment. The Court of Appeal held that, there having been no proper notice of the first meeting, it was 'no valid meeting, and being an invalid meeting could not adjourn itself . . .': per Lord Esher MR (at 167). The position, therefore, was the same as in *Harben v Phillips*, viz a meeting which had excluded (through lack of notice) persons entitled to attend. It therefore could not transact business and could not resolve to adjourn itself. Certainly *j* the language used by Lord Esher MR goes wider than that, but it must be read in the light of the question he was there considering.

The Canadian case of *McLaren v Fisken* (1881) 28 Gr 352 is the same. An inquorate meeting of a board purported to do business by adjourning itself, there being no article permitting them so to do. It was held that the purported adjournment was a nullity and *a* therefore no business could be validly transacted at the adjourned meeting. There again the question was not whether a meeting had been held but whether such meeting could validly adjourn itself.

On the other side there is one authority which lends some support to the view that there can be a general meeting even when that meeting is incapable of conducting business. In *Fletcher v New Zealand Glue Co Ltd* (1911) 31 NZLR 129 the company was bound to submit a return of the persons who were its members on the fourteenth day *b* after its annual general meeting. The company duly convened an annual general meeting which proved to be inquorate. Under its articles, an inquorate meeting was automatically adjourned sine die. The company made a return of the members 14 days after the date of the inquorate meeting. It was held that the return was proper since there was a valid general meeting but valid only for the purposes of adjournment. Although the circumstances there under consideration were very different, the case is some authority *c* for the proposition that there can be a meeting of a company even though such a meeting is incapable of conducting any business.

I can therefore see no reason why, as common sense suggests, the assembly at the cinema should not in law constitute a 'meeting' within the meaning of that word in the 1985 Act and the articles of London Life. It follows that I agree with Vinelott J that under art 17 Mr Dawson was the chairman of the meeting and had all the powers of the *d* chairman.

Did the chairman have power to adjourn?

Counsel for the plaintiff submits that since art 18 expressly provides that the chairman can only adjourn the meeting with its consent, Mr Dawson could have no power in any circumstances to adjourn without such consent. Vinelott J rejected this submission, to *e* my mind rightly.

I will first consider the powers of a chairman at common law, there being no document expressly regulating powers of adjournment. A chairman has no general right to adjourn a meeting at his own will and pleasure, there being no circumstance preventing the effective continuation of the proceedings: see *National Dwellings Society v Sykes* [1894] 3 *f* Ch 159 at 162. However, it is clearly established that a chairman has such power where unruly conduct prevents the continuation of business: see *John v Rees* [1969] 2 All ER 274 at 290–293, [1970] Ch 345 at 379–383. In my judgment it is also established that when in an orderly meeting a poll is demanded on a motion to adjourn and such poll cannot be taken forthwith, the chairman has power to suspend the meeting with a view to its continuance at a later date after the result of the poll is known: *Jackson v Hamlyn* [1953] 1 *g* All ER 887, [1953] Ch 577. In that case Upjohn J expressly held that the chairman was not 'adjourning' the meeting within the meaning of the article there in question (see [1953] 1 All ER 887 at 889, [1953] Ch 577 at 588). Even so, he held that the chairman had power to stand over the proceedings to another time, since some such power had to exist in order to give effect to the provisions as to polls in the articles. Therefore, although it may not have been an adjournment within the meaning of the articles there under *h* consideration, he held that there was a residual power in the chairman to take such steps as would, in the ordinary usage of the word, amount to an adjournment.

In my judgment the position at common law is correctly set out in *John v Rees* and in the two following passages. The first is from *R v D'Oyly* (1840) 12 Ad & El 139 at 159, 113 ER 763 at 771:

j 'Setting aside the invonvenience that might arise if a majority of the parishioners could determine the point of adjournment, we think that the person who presides at the meeting is the proper individual to decide this. It is on him that it devolves, both to preserve order in the meeting, and to regulate the proceedings *so as to give all persons entitled a reasonable opportunity of voting.* He is to do the acts *necessary for those purposes* on his own responsibility, and subject to being called upon to answer for his conduct if he has done anything improperly.' (My emphasis).

The second passage is from Rogers *A Practical Arrangement of Ecclesiastical Law* (1840) p 874 quoted in *John v Rees* [1969] 2 All ER 274 at 292, [1970] Ch 345 at 381. The passage　*a* says that a particular decision—

'by no means interferes with the right which every chairman has to make a bona fide adjournment, whilst a poll or other business is proceeding, if circumstances of violent interruption make it unsafe, or seriously difficult for the voters to tender their votes; nor of adjourning the place of polling, if the ordinary place used for that　*b* purpose be insufficient, or greatly inconvenient. In most of such cases, the question will turn upon the intention and effect of the adjournment, if the intention and effect were to interrupt and procrastinate the business, such an adjournment would be illegal; if, on the contrary, the intention and effect were to forward or facilitate it, *and no injurious effect were produced*, such an adjournment would, it is conceived, be generally supported.' (My emphasis).　　　　　　　　　　　　　　　　　　　*c*

In my judgment, were it not for art 18, Mr Dawson would at common law have had power to adjourn the meeting at the cinema since the inadequacy of the space available rendered it impossible for all those entitled to attend to take part in the debate and to vote. A motion for adjournment could not be put to the meeting as many who would be entitled to vote on the motion were excluded. Therefore, at common law it would have　*d* been the chairman's duty to regulate the proceedings so as to give all persons entitled a reasonable opportunity of debating and voting. This would have required him either to abandon the meeting or to adjourn it to a time and a place where the members could have a reasonable opportunity to debate or vote. I see no reason to hold that in all circumstances the meeting must be abandoned; in my judgment the chairman can, in a suitable case, merely adjourn such meeting.　　　　　　　　　　　　　　　　　　*e*

What then is the effect of art 18 which expressly confers on the chairman power to adjourn but only with the consent of a quorate meeting? Counsel for the plaintiff submits that the chairman's power to adjourn having been expressly laid down and expressly circumscribed, there is no room for the chairman to have any implied power at common law. He relies on the decision of the Privy Council in *Salisbury Gold Mining Co Ltd v Hathorn* [1897] AC 268. In that case the articles provided that the chairman could　*f* adjourn with the consent of the members; the articles did not provide (as does art 18 in the present case) that the chairman was bound to adjourn if so directed by the meeting. It was held that the chairman was not bound to put a motion for adjournment to the meeting but was entitled to insist in the meeting proceeding to business. Lord Herschell treated the express provision making it the chairman's decision whether or not to adjourn as ousting the general rule that a meeting can always adjourn itself. So, by analogy,　*g* counsel for the plaintiff argues that the express provision in art 18 requiring the chairman to obtain the consent of the meeting as a precondition to the exercise of his power to adjourn precludes the existence of any power in the chairman to adjourn without such consent.

Like the judge, I reject this submission. In my judgment art 18 regulates the　*h* chairman's powers of adjournment to the extent that its machinery is effective to cover the contingencies which occur. Therefore if the circumstances are such that it is possible to discover whether or not the meeting agrees to an adjournment, art 18 lays down a comprehensive code. But if the circumstances are such that the wishes of the meeting cannot be validly ascertained, why should art 18 be read as impairing the fundamental common law duty of the chairman to regulate proceedings so as to enable those entitled　*j* to be present and to vote to be heard and to vote? In my judgment *Jackson v Hamlyn* [1953] 1 All ER 887, [1953] Ch 577 is an authority in support of that view since in that case there was an article in much the same terms as art 18 in the present case.

As the judge pointed out, the contrary result would produce manifest absurdities. Say that there was a disturbance in a meeting which precluded the taking of any vote on a

motion to adjourn. Would this mean that the meeting had to be abandoned even though
a a short adjournment would have enabled peace to be restored and the meeting resumed?
Again, say that in the present case the adjoining Barbican theatre had been available on
19 October so that a short adjournment to the theatre would have enabled an effective
meeting of all members wishing to attend to be held that morning. Can it really be the
law that because a valid resolution for such an adjournment could not be passed in the
cinema (many members entitled to vote being excluded from the cinema) no such
b adjournment could take place?

I do not find that any principle of construction requires me to hold that an express
provision regulating adjournment when the views of the meeting can be ascertained
necessarily precludes the existence of implied powers when consent of the meeting
cannot be obtained. The *Salisbury Gold* case lays down no such proposition. Accordingly,
I reach the conclusion that in any circumstances where there is a meeting at which the
c view of the majority cannot be validly ascertained, the chairman has a residual common
law power to adjourn 'so as to give all persons entitled a reasonable opportunity of voting'
and, I would add, speaking at the meeting.

Was the power validly exercised?
Vinelott J held that Mr Dawson validly exercised the power to adjourn by adjourning
d the meeting to the Café Royal in the afternoon. This is the only point (though a decisive
one) on which I differ from the judge. As I understand his judgment, he took the view
that provided Mr Dawson acted in good faith (which it is accepted that he did) his
decision could not be impugned and in particular that it was irrelevant that the effect of
the adjournment to the Café Royal was that some 200 of those present in the morning
did not attend the meeting at the Café Royal in the afternoon and that 133 people (being
e over 25% of the total) who had registered at the Barbican did not register at the Café
Royal. I am unable to agree with this view.

The starting point is to consider the nature of the residual power to adjourn which in
my judgment remains vested in the chairman. It was a residual power exercisable only
when the machinery provided by the articles had broken down. This residual common
f law power is itself tightly circumscribed by reference to the objects for which it exists. I
quote again from the passages which I have emphasised above in the quotations from *R v
D'Oyly* and Mr Rogers's book. The power is to regulate proceedings 'so as to give all
persons entitled a reasonable opportunity of voting'. The chairman must 'do the acts
necessary for those purposes'. The power to adjourn is only validly exercised if 'no
injurious effect were produced'. I would add that at a company meeting a member is
entitled not only to vote but also to hear and be heard in the debate. Therefore it is the
g very purpose of the power to facilitate the presence of those entitled to debate and vote
on a resolution at a meeting where such debate and voting is possible. To my mind, this
is inconsistent with the view that the exercise of the power can only be impugned on the
grounds of lack of good faith. In my judgment the chairman's decision must also be
taken reasonably with a view to facilitating the purpose for which the power exists.
h Accordingly, the impact of the proposed adjournment on those seeking to attend the
original meeting and the other members must be a central factor in considering the
validity of the chairman's decision to adjourn.

The quotation from *Rogers* might suggest that if the chairman's decision proves in the
event to have an adverse effect on the members, that will render the decision invalid. In
my judgment that is not the correct test. The chairman's decision will not be declared
j invalid unless on the facts which he knew or ought to have known he failed to take into
account all the relevant factors, took into account irrelevant factors or reached a conclusion
which no reasonable chairman, properly directing himself as to his duties, could have
reached, ie the test is the same as that applicable on judicial review in accordance with
the principles of *Associated Provincial Picture Houses Ltd v Wednesbury Corp* [1947] 2 All
ER 680, [1948] 1 KB 223. This was the approach adopted by Uthwatt J in *Second*

Consolidated Trust Ltd v Ceylon Amalgamated Tea and Rubber Estates Ltd [1943] 2 All ER
567, where he held a chairman's decision invalid on the grounds that he had failed to   *a*
take into account a relevant factor.

I turn then to consider the position confronting Mr Dawson at the Barbican cinema
on the morning of 19 October. The principal factors were as follows: (1) the business
before the meeting was to amend the memorandum of association but the meeting was
also treated as being in the nature of a referendum to establish the attitude of the
members to the proposed merger of a large part of the business of London Life with   *b*
AMP, a matter of fundamental importance to the company and its members; (2) the last
date by which the merger had to be approved was 31 March 1989 (I note that this fact is
not mentioned in the judgment of Vinelott J and may well not have been brought to his
attention; (3) the merger would be much easier to put into operation if completed on 31
January 1989 being the end of the accounting years of both London Life and AMP. To
that end a date (5 December 1988) had been fixed for a hearing in court under the   *c*
Insurance Companies Act 1982; (4) the meeting at the cinema was incapable of either
debating or voting on the resolution to amend the memorandum of association; (5) there
was a substantial 'ginger group' opposing the merger, at least until alternative courses
had been considered; many of them were present at the Barbican; (6) there were repeated
attempts from the floor and the overflow rooms to obtain an adjournment of the meeting
sine die; (7) when the possibility of adjournment to the Café Royal in the afternoon was   *d*
first suggested, there were objections from the floor that some members present in the
cinema would not be able to attend such adjourned meeting; (8) there were present at
the meeting a number of members who had come from a distance and might not be able
to attend a further meeting on another date; (9) if the meeting were adjourned to the
Café Royal on the same day, those present at the Barbican but unable to be present at the
Café Royal in the afternoon would not only be unable to speak but also unable to vote.   *e*
Under art 30, proxies have to be deposited 48 hours before any adjourned meeting; and
(10) the chairman was advised by leading counsel that he could properly adjourn to the
Café Royal in the afternoon.

Mr Dawson gave evidence of the factors which most persuaded him to adjourn to the
Café Royal. These include all the factors mentioned above, except those which in my
view were of central importance, viz (2), (6), (7) and (9). It would not be fair or sensible   *f*
to find that, because he did not specifically mention that he took into account the desire
of certain members for an adjournment sine die and their inability to be at the Café
Royal in the afternoon, he did not have that well in mind; he was being bombarded with
this information at the time he took his decision. But I can see nothing to suggest that he
took into account the fact that there was no absolute necessity to obtain approval of the
merger until 31 March 1989, a date more than five months away. Nor is there anything   *g*
to suggest that he appreciated that those who could not be at the Café Royal would not
only be unable to speak but would be unable to vote even by proxy.

It was suggested in argument that those whose other arrangements precluded them
from attending the afternoon meeting at the Café Royal would probably not have been
able to stay long enough to vote even if the Barbican meeting had proceeded in the   *h*
ordinary way, since this would have lasted for a long time. This is a point which carried
weight with the judge. But, to my mind, it has only a limited impact. First, it is a
hypothesis, not a fact. Second, and more important, the purpose of members attending
meetings is to enable them not only to vote but also to take part in the debate. Those
present in the morning could in any event have been present and spoken in the debate if
it had continued at the Barbican, even if they could not have waited until the vote was   *j*
taken. By the adjournment to the Café Royal they were precluded from even taking part
in the debate.

In these circumstances, in my judgment, Mr Dawson's decision to adjourn to the Café
Royal in the same afternoon was not valid on the ground either that he failed to take into
account relevant factors or that the decision was *Wednesbury* unreasonable. The legal

advice tendered was in my judgment erroneous, probably because it failed to take
account of the very limited ambit of the chairman's residual power to adjourn. Since
such power is only exercisable for the purpose of giving the members a proper
opportunity to debate and vote on the resolution, there must in my judgment be very
special circumstances to justify a decision to adjourn the meeting to a time and place
where, to the knowledge of the chairman, it could not be attended by a number of the
members who had taken the trouble to attend the original meeting and could not even
lodge a proxy vote. To overlook this factor is to leave out of account a matter of central
importance. True it is that those who were available for the afternoon meeting would
have been inconvenienced by an adjournment to another date or the convening of a
wholly new meeting since they would either have to have attended at the fresh meeting
or to have lodged proxies. But in my judgment this could not outweigh the central point
that the form of the adjournment was such as undoubtedly to preclude certain members
from taking any part in the meeting either by way of debate or by way of vote.

If the time factor had been such that the merger proposal could not have been carried
through at all unless there was an immediate decision on the resolution before the
meeting (ie if the merger had to be approved within a period which rendered impossible
the convening of a further meeting on 21 days' notice or the adjournment of the original
meeting for a sufficient period to allow proxies to be lodged) the matter might have been
different. But in fact there was no compelling time factor in this case. True it is that
expenditure would have to be incurred in calling a further meeting. But if, instead of
adjourning to the detriment of certain members, the meeting at the Barbican had either
been abandoned or adjourned sine die, 21 days' notice could have been given of a fresh
meeting to be held, say, a month later, well before even the date fixed for the hearing in
court. If such fresh meeting had been called, all the members would have had an
opportunity to be present either in person or by proxy. There is no sign that Mr Dawson
ever appreciated this factor or took it into account in reaching his decision.

Accordingly, although Mr Dawson acted in complete good faith, his decision to
adjourn to the Café Royal on the same date was not one which, in my judgment, he
could reasonably have reached if he had properly apprehended the restricted nature and
purpose of his powers. Therefore in my judgment his decision was invalid.

I would therefore allow the appeal and declare first that the meeting at Cinema 1 on
the morning of 19 October was not validly adjourned and also that proceedings
purportedly conducted at the meeting at the Café Royal in the afternoon are invalid and
of no effect.

MUSTILL LJ. I agree that this appeal should be allowed, but since we differ from the
conclusion of the judge and since my reasons for doing so are not in every respect the
same as those expressed by Sir Nicolas Browne-Wilkinson V-C and Woolf LJ, I will add
some observations of my own.

My starting point is the proposition that a gathering of people may occupy an
intermediate status between a meeting which can validly effect the business which it was
convened to transact and a mere assembly which can do nothing at all. The intermediate
status involves that the gathering may have a chairman and that the chairman has powers
to dissolve the meeting and, subject to the points mentioned below, to adjourn it on his
own initiative, and to prorogue it; and yet the gathering cannot transact any real business,
including even a decision, qua meeting, to adjourn. I use the word 'prorogue', defined in
the *Oxford English Dictionary* as 'To discontinue the meetings of (a legislative or other
assembly) . . . without dissolving it', because it seems to come closest to the idea of
simultaneously bringing the meeting to an end and keeping it in existence. The concept
of such an impotent body having any true legal existence seems odd, but it does appear
to be implicit in arts 13, 16 and 19 of London Life's articles of association, and also in *Re
London Flats Ltd* [1969] 2 All ER 744 at 752, [1969] 1 WLR 711 at 719 and *Fletcher v New
Zealand Glue Co Ltd* (1911) 31 NZLR 129.

I also accept that it is possible to have a meeting, not all of whose members are present
in the same room. It is unnecessary to consider the extreme case where none of the   *a*
participants are face to face, but are linked by simultaneous audio-visual transmissions.
This would require consideration of whether it is possible to convene a meeting which
does not take place in any single location, and which consists only of the exchange of
electronic impulses. No such problem arises here. If the arrangements had gone according
to plan, and if the participants had first occupied Cinema 1 until it was full, and had then
all found a place in the adjacent rooms by the time the business had commenced, and if   *b*
they all had been able to see, hear and communicate with the other participants I would
have seen no intellectual and practical objection to regarding this as a 'meeting'.
Moreover, it would have been a meeting held at the place of which notice had been
given, namely Cinema 1, since this was where the centre of gravity of the meeting was
to be found.

In the event, however, this is not what happened at all. Those who found places in the   *c*
overflow rooms could not see or hear properly. The opportunity for an exchange of
views and arguments between one overflow room and another, and between each room
and those on the platform in Cinema 1 was virtually non-existent. Many of those in the
overflow rooms were unable to carry out the registration formalities, and did not know
whether and how to do so. Still others were milling around in the foyer and had not yet
achieved a place in any room. It is said for the company that this amounted to a meeting,   *d*
albeit not one which was capable of transacting any business, let alone the business which
it was summoned to transact. For this purpose, it was said, and rightly said, that one
must leave out of account the shouts, hubbub and general disturbance. A disorderly
meeting is none the less a meeting. I agree, but one must still inquire, where in this
chaotic scene was to be found the meeting of the members of London Life, of which Mr
Dawson is said to have acted as chairman?   *e*

As I understand it, the main thrust of the company's case is that there was a meeting
in Cinema 1; an ineffectual meeting, with many people shut out who should have been
there, but a meeting none the less. I can certainly understand the theory of this
proposition, in that the presence of all these members outside the cinema, who were
entitled to be inside it, is not conclusive against the existence of a meeting with just
sufficient substance in it to have a chairman. But, on the facts, is this what happened?   *f*
Reading through the partial transcript, partial because it only begins at 11.30 am, it
seems to me plain that Mr Dawson never conceived his meeting to consist only of those
who had managed to gain entry to Cinema 1 but, on the contrary, was trying to marshal
the scattered fragments of the intended meeting which but for the breakdown of the
communications which he was attempting to re-establish would have taken place in
three places simultaneously. I think it equally plain that on no view could these fragments   *g*
be regarded as a meeting of any kind, even one with the very limited capacity previously
described.

We were pressed in argument to give 'meeting' its ordinary meaning, and to avoid a
decision based on technicalities. As to the ordinary meaning, I believe that there may be
several. I doubt whether the characteristics of a meeting as understood by the law   *h*
correspond with those of an informal meeting in everyday life; but in any event (and the
matter is really one of impression) I would not myself have thought that the events at
the Barbican Centre on the morning of 19 October 1988 are what the man in the street
would have called a meeting. He would be more likely to describe it as a meeting which
London Life had tried to hold, but which had never got off the ground. As to
technicalities, I believe that an insistence on regular form is not the invention of lawyers   *j*
determined to find objections to what is really unobjectionable, but a recognition
founded on the practical experience over very many years of those who have been
concerned with meetings that if the forms are not observed there is an ever-present risk
of confusion, resentment and dispute, as the present case has clearly shown.

a On this ground alone, therefore, I would have been prepared to hold that the attempts made at the Barbican did not amount to any meeting which would have been capable of prorogation to the opinion at the Café Royal on the initiative of Mr Dawson. But since Sir Nicolas Browne-Wilkinson V-C and Woolf LJ in company with the judge are of a different opinion, I will go on to deal briefly with the remaining issues. The first is whether, in the absence of express contrary provisions in the articles or rules governing the conduct of the meeting, the chairman has power to prorogue where circumstances

b make it impossible for the conduct of business to continue. It is true that the earlier cases were concerned with polls which could not be completed within the time-span of the meeting, and it might be said that the conducting of a poll after the participants had dispersed never to reassemble is not in any real sense the continuance of the meeting, rather than the completion of unfinished business on behalf of the concluded meeting. Nevertheless, the power was addressed in much wider terms in *John v Rees* [1969] 2 All

c ER 274, [1970] Ch 345 and *Jackson v Hamlyn* [1953] 1 All ER 887, [1953] Ch 577, and I see no reason to differ from what is there stated.

Nor do I regard the presence of art 18 as a ground for concluding that a power to prorogue cannot in the present case be implied. The purpose of art 18 is to enable the meeting to validate, by a motion properly proposed and carried, a decision to adjourn. The powers under the article are capable of employment only if the meeting is in a

d condition to conduct its business in an orderly manner. This is just the situation in which the implied power to prorogue comes into existence, and I cannot see how the presence of art 18, which ex hypothesi is inoperable, can have any effect on the implication which would otherwise have been made.

It must, however, be borne in mind that prorogation is an emergency measure, to be employed only if the business of the meeting can be saved by no other method and only

e if saving the business does not cause incommensurate hardship on those who have attended to speak and vote, by comparison with the damage which would be done if the chairman adopted the alternative course of dissolving it and summoning another. That there was an emergency at the Barbican is, of course, undeniable. But did the chairman address himself appropriately to the choice which he had to make? If he had done so, we would not be entitled to intervene simply because in the light of hindsight it appeared

f that he had made the wrong choice. It would be necessary for the plaintiff to establish the degree of unreasonableness contemplated by the tests laid down in authorities too well known to require repetition and, speaking for myself, I would be slow to make such a finding, given the very difficult circumstances in which the chairman had to act. I do, however, agree with Sir Nicolas Browne-Wilkinson V-C that the chairman omitted from consideration certain important factors which bore on the exercise of this exceptional

g power, and thereby established the decision to prorogue on an insecure foundation. There is no need to set out my reasons for this conclusion, since they correspond exactly with those set out in the judgment of Sir Nicolas Browne-WilkinsonV-C. Accordingly, I would on this ground also hold that the plaintiff was entitled to the relief which he claimed.

h I would allow the appeal.

WOOLF LJ. I agree that in accordance with the judgment of Sir Nicolas Browne-Wilkinson V-C this appeal should be allowed. There is nothing that I can usefully add to his judgment on the first of the three issues which he identifies. I would, however, add a few comments on the second and third issues which I regard as being closely interrelated.

j In deciding whether Mr Dawson's decision to adjourn the meeting was lawful, the approach of the court is no different from that which it regularly adopts when reviewing the exercise of discretion by a public body under a statutory power. This is the position even though when acting as chairman of the meeting Mr Dawson is not performing a public function and he derives his powers either expressly or by implication from the

articles of the company. While the source of his power is different from that of a person
performing a public function, the well-established principles which determine whether   *a*
there has been a proper exercise of discretion by a public body apply to the exercise by
Mr Dawson of his powers. In particular he must have regard to the nature of the power
which he is exercising and use the power for the purpose for which it was given.

The general source of Mr Dawson's powers is to be found in art 25, which provides:
'The Chairman of the meeting shall regulate the proceedings thereat . . .' This power is
conferred on the chairman so as to enable the chairman to assist the meeting in achieving   *b*
the purpose for which the meeting was taking place. It is a general power which has to
be considered in the light of the specific provisions of the other relevant articles which
will, in so far as they are inconsistent with the general power, restrict it. In particular,
the chairman's power to regulate the meeting is subject to the express provisions of art 18
which make it clear that Mr Dawson as chairman has only an *express* power to adjourn a
meeting (1) if he is acting with the consent of a meeting at which a quorum is present,   *c*
and (2) subject to giving notice of the adjournment when the meeting is being adjourned
for more than 30 days.

Because of the conditions which existed on 19 October 1988 it was clearly impossible
to obtain the consent of the meeting which was then taking place at Cinema 1 in the
Barbican and it was only because of this inability to ascertain the wishes of the meeting
in accordance with art 18 that Mr Dawson had an exceptional and residual discretion to   *d*
adjourn without the consent of the meeting which would normally be required. If it had
been possible to obtain the views of the meeting then Mr Dawson could only have
adjourned the meeting if he complied with art 18.

The exceptional and residual nature of the power which Mr Dawson was exercising
placed constraints on the manner in which it was proper to exercise the power. The
power was not one which should be exercised as freely as it could be if it was exercised   *e*
under art 18.

In adjourning the meeting to the Café Royal Mr Dawson was adjourning to a different
location and to a different time from that of the meeting for which notice had been
given. He was therefore taking a step without the specific authority of a meeting which
could interfere with the rights of those who were entitled to receive notice of the time
and place of the meeting and he was doing so when he should have been aware and was   *f*
almost certainly in fact aware that there was a strong body of opinion which strongly
objected to his taking this course.

In deciding whether or not to adjourn to the Café Royal Mr Dawson was therefore
required, in my view, to give very great weight to the alternative course which was open
to him of abandoning the meeting so that it could be reconvened after proper notice had
been given on a subsequent date. This alternative course might have caused inconvenience   *g*
to some or indeed many of those who attended in the afternoon at the Café Royal but,
unlike the decision to adjourn, there could be no question of it interfering with the rights
of those entitled to attend the meeting to express their views either in person or by proxy.
The course of adjourning to the Café Royal could therefore, in my view, only be justified
if there was some ground such as an urgent need for decision because of which Mr   *h*
Dawson could properly come to the conclusion that it was not possible to adopt the
alternative of reconvening a fresh meeting.

I would emphasise that this was not a case of merely adjourning the meeting for a
short period so as to enable the meeting to reconvene at an adjoining location. While no
doubt those who were minded and able to do so could, without undue difficulty, travel
from the Barbican to the Café Royal in Regent Street for the meeting in the afternoon,   *j*
the fact is that the change of time and location would inevitably be inconvenient to a
number of those attending as is borne out by the substantially smaller number who
attended the adjourned meeting when compared with the number who were present in
the morning.

In his evidence Mr Dawson explains the factors which he took into account in deciding

to adjourn to the Café Royal. One of those factors is the advice which he received from
a leading counsel that—

> 'if it was [Mr Dawson's] view . . . that no sensible meeting could take place and
> that there was no practical means of conducting a show of hands or poll [Mr
> Dawson] was not only entitled to but should immediately adjourn of [his] own
> motion.'

b While I make no criticism of leading counsel for giving this advice in the confused
situation which existed that morning, with respect, the advice was not correct because it
made no mention of the fact that there was an alternative course which Mr Dawson was
required to consider which was whether it would be preferable to terminate the meeting
and have it reconvened on a later date and instead it suggested Mr Dawson was obliged
to adjourn to the Café Royal in accordance with the arrangements which had already
c been made.
   The whole approach of Mr Dawson's evidence, consistent with the advice which he
received, was that because of the conditions which existed that morning he had an
unfettered right to adjourn. As I have sought to show, he had no such unfettered right;
his discretion to adjourn was a limited and restricted discretion which ordinarily would
only be appropriately exercised by bringing the meeting to an end and by arranging at a
d later date for a new meeting to be reconvened. It is true that Mr Dawson indicates that
of the many factors which he relied on when coming to his decision one was the fact that
he regarded it—

> 'as of very great importance that the issues should be properly debated and
> resolved that day, given the carefully structured timetable.'

e   However, as Sir Nicolas Browne-Wilkinson V-C has pointed out, there was not that
degree of urgency as the language which Mr Dawson uses suggests; and, while he was
perfectly entitled to take into account as a factor the desirability of keeping to the planned
timetable, this certainly was not an overwhelming consideration in the context of the
exceptional and residual special power which he was purporting to exercise.
f   If Mr Dawson had recognised the limits on his discretion which I have sought to point
out, then I would like to think that he would not have adopted the course that he did.
However, he did not appreciate the limited nature of the power that he was exercising
and he did not take into account the considerations which favoured his taking the
alternative course. It is, therefore, my view that on the material before this court Mr
Dawson, in exercising his discretion, did not take into account considerations which he
g was required to take into account. It is for that reason that his decision was not a proper
one, with the result that the adjourned meeting was invalid. I would not myself
categorise Mr Dawson's conduct as *Wednesbury* unreasonable (see *Associated Provincial
Picture Houses Ltd v Wednesbury Corp* [1947] 2 All ER 680, [1948] 1 KB 223). A decision
had to be taken in a difficult situation relying on an ill-defined residual power and when
the consequences of that decision would not be as apparent as they are afterwards in a
h court of law.
   For those reasons, and in agreement with the other reasons of Sir Nicolas Browne-
Wilkinson V-C, I would allow the appeal.

Appeal allowed. Leave to appeal to the House of Lords refused.

Solicitors: *Farrer & Co* (for the plaintiff); *Herbert Smith* (for the defendants).

Celia Fox   Barrister.

Fairfield-Mabey Ltd v Shell UK Ltd (Metallurgical Testing Services (Scotland) Ltd, third party)

QUEEN'S BENCH DIVISION (OFFICIAL REFEREES' BUSINESS)
HIS HONOUR JUDGE BOWSHER QC
23 NOVEMBER 1988

Evidence – Exchange of witnesses' statements – Statements of oral evidence – Examination on statements which have been exchanged – Whether exchange of statements thereby putting them in evidence – Whether witness may be cross-examined by reference to statement of another witness who has not been called – Whether cross-examining counsel may put to opposing witness a statement taken on behalf of his own client – Whether putting part only of such statement entitling opposing counsel to re-examine his own witness on whole statement – RSC Ord 38, r 2A.

Witness statements which have been exchanged under RSC Ord 38, r 2A are not put in evidence by the fact of exchange but remain confidential until the witness makes the statement public by verifying it on oath in the witness box or the party who served the statement waives the privilege. It follows, therefore, that in opening counsel should not refer to such a statement, nor should a witness called by an opposing party be cross-examined by reference to a statement of another witness who might or might not be called by that opposing party or someone other than the party on whose behalf the cross-examination is being conducted. Cross-examining counsel may, however, put to an opposing witness a statement taken on behalf of the cross-examiner's own client, but by so doing he waives his client's privilege in the statement. Furthermore, if he puts to an opposing witness only a small part of his own client's statement, he will thereby entitle counsel who called the witness to re-examine that witness on the whole of the statement. The risk of promoting lengthy re-examination may, however, be avoided either by cross-examining counsel agreeing with opposing counsel that part only of a statement may be put to a witness without the whole being opened up for re-examination or by cross-examining counsel preparing written questions to be handed to the witness either in the witness box or several days previously (see p 577 *f g j* and p 578 *b c*, post).

Notes
For exchange of witnesses' statements, see Supplement to 37 Halsbury's Laws (4th edn) para 457A.

Ruling
By an originating summons dated 22 January 1985 and a statement of claim served on 29 July 1985 the plaintiff, Fairfield-Mabey Ltd, sought declarations as against the defendant, Shell UK Ltd (trading as Shell UK Exploration and Production), (i) that the CTOD tests carried out on certain specimens on 18 June 1984 were valid, that the specimen in each case passed the test and that the test results should have been approved and (ii) that the plaintiff was entitled to a variation order in respect of the defendant's oral amendments to specification ES.108 instructed between 8 June and 10 July 1984 and to the costs of the variation. By a counterclaim dated 29 August 1985 the defendant counterclaimed against the plaintiff damages for breach of contract, and by a third party notice dated 14 March 1986 issued pursuant to the order of his Honour Judge David Smout QC dated 24 February 1986 the plaintiff claimed against the third party, Metallurgical Testing Services (Scotland) Ltd, (i) an indemnity against the defendant's claim on the grounds that if the plaintiff was in breach of its contract with the defendant it was because the third party was in breach of an oral contract made on 12 June 1984 whereunder the third party undertook for reward to test certain of the plaintiff's welding

procedures and (ii) that the question whether the CTOD tests were valid and whether the
specimens passed the tests and should have been approved by the defendant should be
determined not only as between the plaintiff and the defendant but also as between either
or both of them and the third party. During the course of the trial a ruling was sought as
to the manner in which exchanged statements of witnesses of fact might be used during
the trial.

Desmond Wright QC and *Nicholas Baatz* for the plaintiff.
Colin Reese QC and *David Streatfield-James* for the defendant.
Michael Lewer QC and *Jeremy Nicholson* for the third party.

HIS HONOUR JUDGE BOWSHER QC. During the course of the trial of this action
I have been asked to give a ruling as to the manner in which exchanged statements of
witnesses of fact may be used during the trial so as to save time without causing any
injustice and without breach of any rule of law.

In 1981 official referees began making orders for the cross-service of statements of
witnesses of fact in cases where the parties gave their consent (in practice the majority of
cases before the official referees). The success of that practice led to its official approval in
1986 by RSC Ord 38, r 2A as regards the official referees and certain other parts of the
High Court. The practice has since been further extended. It is common for such
statements to be ordered to stand as the evidence-in-chief of the witness and for no oral
evidence-in-chief to be given except in relation to new matters which have arisen in the
course of the trial. The extent of oral examination-in-chief is a matter to be determined
by the trial judge in the circumstances of the particular case. There is however some
division of opinion amongst practitioners as to the use which may be made of statements
served under this practice in those parts of the trial falling outside evidence-in-chief.

Statements which have been so exchanged are clearly not put in evidence by the fact
of exchange. I take the view that such statements are served on a confidential basis and
that they remain confidential until *either* the witness makes the statement public by
verifying it on oath in the witness box *or* the party who served the statement waives the
privilege. The confidence in the statement is the confidence of the party on whose behalf
the statement was taken. That is not to say that there is any property in a witness. It may
be that more than one party will take a statement from one particular witness but each
statement will be confidential to the party taking it.

It follows that it would be quite wrong for counsel in opening to refer to any witness
statement. It would also be wrong to cross-examine a witness called by an opposing party
by reference to a statement of another witness who might (or might not) be called in the
future by that opposing party or by some other party other than the party on whose
behalf the cross-examination is being conducted. For example, counsel for the plaintiff
can put to the defendant any evidence which has already been given whether orally or in
writing, but it would be wrong to seek to put to the defendant the statement of a
proposed witness for the defendant or a third party who had not yet given evidence. The
decision might be taken not to call that further witness and meanwhile his evidence
remains confidential.

Counsel however may do what he could have done before the adoption of the new
procedure of cross-service of statements. Cross-examining counsel may put to an opposing
witness a statement taken on behalf of the cross-examiner's own client. By so doing the
cross-examiner waives his client's confidence in the statement. As a matter of courtesy,
counsel should give notice to other counsel in the case of his intention to take this course
so that they may take any appropriate objection. When this course is adopted, the judge
should direct himself that the unsworn statement being put to the witness is not evidence
and that the only evidence will be the answers of the witness in relation to it. If the
witness under cross-examination agrees with the whole of the statement, it may be that
it will be unnecessary to call the maker of the statement to give evidence.

A difficulty may arise when counsel wishes to put to a witness a small part only of his client's statement. Faced with the task of putting to an opposing witness an account of a *a* long conversation, counsel might wish to put to an opposing witness one page only of a very lengthy statement. I take the view that by so doing he would entitle counsel calling the witness to re-examine that witness on the whole of the statement. I regret that conclusion, since I believe that it is in the interests of all parties that cross-examination should be shortened by the questioning being done in documentary form during those parts of the cross-examination devoted to 'putting' matters or coldly eliciting information. *b*

Clearly the promotion of lengthy re-examination will not shorten trials. The difficulty may be avoided in one or both of two ways: first, cross-examining counsel may agree with opposing counsel that a part only of a statement may be put to a witness without the whole being opened up for re-examination; or second, cross-examining counsel may prepare written questions to be handed to the witness either in the witness box or some days previously. Such questions might be of the following nature: 'Do you agree the facts *c* set out in the attached schedule?', 'Do you agree that a conversation took place between you and X in the terms set out below?', 'Please mark on the attached plans all the welds which were required to be subjected to CTOD testing.'

I encourage both of these procedures, while recognising that they impose further burdens on counsel. To shorten time taken at trial, much work has to be done before trial. *d*

Ruling accordingly.

Solicitors: *Davies Arnold & Cooper* (for the plaintiff); *D H Roose* (for the defendant); *Berrymans* (for the third party).

K Mydeen Esq   Barrister. *e*

Smith Kline & French Laboratories Ltd v Licensing Authority (Generics (UK) Ltd and another intervening) *f*

HOUSE OF LORDS

LORD BRIDGE OF HARWICH, LORD TEMPLEMAN, LORD ACKNER, LORD OLIVER OF AYLMERTON AND LORD LOWRY

11, 12, 16, 17 JANUARY, 9 FEBRUARY 1989 *g*

Medicine – Product licence – Generic product – Essential similarity – Demonstrating essential similarity – Use of originator's confidential information – Originator supplying details of research and testing in development of drug when applying to licensing authority for product licence – Generic companies subsequently applying for product licence for similar generic product – Whether licensing authority entitled to use information supplied by originator when considering *h* *subsequent applications for product licences – EEC Council Directive 65/65, art 4(8)(a)(iii) – EC Council Directive 87/21.*

The appellant pharmaceutical company applied in 1972 for a product licence to manufacture and sell under a particular brand name a proprietary drug developed by them for the treatment of duodenal and gastric ulcers and other gastro-intestinal tract *j* disorders. As required by art 4 of EEC Council Directive 65/65 the appellants supplied the licensing authority under the Medicines Act 1968 with details of their research and testing in the development of the drug in order to show that the drug was safe and effective and could be produced to a consistently high quality. They were duly granted a licence in November 1976. Under EC Council Directive 87/21 other pharmaceutical companies were entitled to apply to the licensing authority for a product licence for a similar generic product after the elapse of ten years from the grant of a licence to the

appellants. In 1987 two firms (the generic companies) applied for product licences to
a market generic forms of the appellants' drug. Under art 4(8)(*a*)(iii)*ᵃ* of the 1965 directive
(as replaced by the 1987 directive) an applicant for a product licence in a member state
was not required to supply results of tests on his drug if he could 'demonstrate' that his
product was essentially similar to a product which had been authorised within the
Community for ten years and was marketed in a member state. The generic companies
claimed that the essential similarity could be demonstrated by reference to the research
b and testing details supplied by the appellants in support of their application for a product
licence. The appellants opposed the use by the licensing authority of the information
supplied to it by them to determine the essential similarity of the generic companies'
drugs, on the ground that the appellants' information was confidential, and they were
granted an injunction restraining the authority from so using the information. The
licensing authority appealed to the Court of Appeal, which allowed its appeal on the
c ground that, although the licensing authority was not entitled to make an originator's
confidential information gratuitously available to its rivals, it was entitled to use that
information as part of its general store of scientific knowledge when considering
subsequent applications for product licences. The appellants appealed to the House of
Lords.

d **Held** – The licensing authority had a duty to safeguard public health and ensure fairness
to all applicants for product licences and it could not discharge that duty without having
recourse to all the information available to it, whether confidential or not, which assisted
it in considering whether to grant any application for a product licence or which assisted
it in performing its other functions under the 1968 Act. Accordingly, the licensing
e authority had a right and duty to make use of all the information supplied by the
appellants when considering the generic companies' applications for product licences. It
followed that the appeal would be dismissed (see pp 580 *e* , p 586 *h j* p 587 *c* to *e* and
p 590 *e* to *h*, post).
     Per curiam. Not only may the licensing authority use but it may also disclose
information supplied to it by an applicant for a product licence if the disclosure is made
f in the performance of its duty under the 1968 Act (see p 580 *e*, p 588 *d* and p 590 *g h*,
post).
     Decision of the Court of Appeal sub nom *R v Licensing Authority, ex p Smith Kline &
French Laboratories Ltd (Generics (UK) Ltd intervening)* [1989] 1 All ER 175 affirmed.

Notes
g For the determination of applications for product licences, see 30 Halsbury's Laws (4th
edn) para 654.
     For EEC policy on importation and marketing of medicinal products, see 51 ibid, para
6.73, 8.74.

h **Cases referred to in opinions**
     Allen & Hanburys Ltd v Generics (UK) Ltd Case 434/85 [1988] 2 All ER 454, CJEC; *on
          reference from* sub nom *Beecham Group plc v Gist-Brocades NV* [1986] 1 WLR 51, HL.
     British Leyland Motor Corp Ltd v Armstrong Patents Co Ltd [1986] 1 All ER 850, [1986] AC
          577, [1986] 2 WLR 400, HL.
     Butler v Board of Trade [1970] 3 All ER 593, [1971] Ch 680, [1970] 3 WLR 822.
j *Castrol Australia Pty Ltd v Emtech Associates Pty Ltd* (1980) 33 ALR 31, NSW SC.
     Coca-Cola Co's Applications, Re [1986] 2 All ER 274, [1986] 1 WLR 695, HL.
     Interlego AG v Tyco Industries Inc [1988] 3 All ER 949, [1988] 3 WLR 678, PC.
     Keene, Re [1922] 2 Ch 475, [1922] All ER Rep 258.
     Metropolitan Asylum District Managers v Hill (1881) 6 App Cas 193, [1881–5] All ER Rep
          536, HL.

---

a   Article 4(8), so far as material, is set out at p 584 *h* to p 585 *c*, post

Appeal

Smith Kline & French Laboratories Ltd appealed with the leave of the Appeal Committee   *a*
of the House of Lords given on 10 October 1988 against the decision of the Court of
Appeal (Dillon, Balcombe and Staughton LJJ) ([1989] 1 All ER 175, [1988] 3 WLR 898)
on 29 June 1988 allowing the appeal of the licensing authority under the Medicines Act
1968 against the judgment of Henry J ([1988] 2 CMLR 883) hearing the Crown Office
list on 21 December 1987 and order dated 23 February 1988 whereby, on an application
by the appellants for judicial review, he declared that the licensing authority, when   *b*
considering an application under the abridged procedure set out in point 8(*a*)(iii) of the
second paragraph of art 4 of EEC Council Directive 65/65, as replaced by EC Council
Directive 87/21, for product licences by third parties in respect of generic versions of the
pharmaceutical product cimetidine originated by the appellants, was not permitted to
use, refer or have recourse to any confidential information supplied by the appellants
except with the appellants' express consent. At the hearing before the Court of Appeal,   *c*
Generics (UK) Ltd and Harris Pharmaceuticals Ltd were given leave to intervene. The
facts are set out in the opinion of Lord Templeman.

Jeremy F Lever QC, Derrick Turriff and *Vivien Rose* for the appellants.
Andrew Collins QC and *Helen Rogers* for the licensing authority.
Jonathan Sumption QC and *Thomas Sharpe* for the first intervener.   *d*
Henry Carr for the second intervener.

Their Lordships took time for consideration.

9 February. The following opinions were delivered.
                                                                                            e
LORD BRIDGE OF HARWICH. My Lords, I have had the advantage of reading in
draft the speech of my noble and learned friend Lord Templeman. I agree with it and,
for the reasons he gives, I would dismiss the appeal.

LORD TEMPLEMAN. My Lords, on 9 March 1972 the appellants, Smith Kline &   *f*
French Laboratories Ltd, filed a complete specification for the grant, subsequently made,
of an United Kingdom patent for the compound known as cimetidine, a medicinal
product. That patent and allied patents conferred on the appellants an effective monopoly
of the production, sale and importation of cimetidine for the period of 16 years expiring
on 9 March 1988. Cimetidine is a most valuable drug which heals duodenal and gastric
ulcers and treats and cures several other gastro-intestinal tract disorders. Cimetidine was
first marketed by the appellants in the United Kingdom in November 1976 under the   *g*
trade mark and brand name of Tagamet. The four-year delay between the filing of the
patent specification and the first marketing of Tagamet was largely due to the research
and development, detailed and expensive, which were required to prove, pursuant to the
Medicines Act 1968, that cimetidine was safe and effective and that Tagamet, a brand of
cimetidine, would be produced of a consistently high quality.
                                                                                            h
By s 7(2) of the 1968 Act, no person shall, in the course of a business, sell, manufacture
or import any medicinal product except in accordance with a product licence granted by
the appropriate licensing authority, in this case the Minister of Health. By s 18(1) of the
Act:

'Any application for the grant of a licence ... shall be made to the licensing
authority and shall be made in such form and manner, and shall contain, or be   *i*
accompanied by, such information, documents, samples and other material, as may
be prescribed.'

By s 19(1), in dealing with an application for a product licence, the licensing authority
shall in particular take into consideration—

'(*a*) the safety of medicinal products of each description to which the application relates; (*b*) the efficacy of medicinal products of each such description for the purposes for which the products are proposed to be administered; and (*c*) the quality of medicinal products of each such description, according to the specification and the method or proposed method of manufacture of the products, and the provisions proposed for securing that the products as sold or supplied will be of that quality.'

By s 20(1) of the 1968 Act, as amended by reg 4(3) of the Medicines (Medicines Act 1968 Amendment) Regulations 1977, SI 1977/1050, on any application to the licensing authority for a licence, the licensing authority—

'(*a*) may grant a licence containing such provisions as they consider appropriate, or (*b*) if, having regard to the provisions of this Act and any Community obligation, they consider it necessary or expedient to do so, may refuse to grant a licence.'

By sub-s (3):

'The licensing authority shall not refuse to grant such a licence on any grounds relating to the safety, quality or efficacy of medicinal products of any description, except after consultation with the appropriate committee or, if for the time being there is no such committee, with the Commission.'

The commission mentioned in s 20(3) is the Medicines Commission established by the minister pursuant to s 2 of the 1968 Act and comprising experts in the fields of medicine and pharmacy. The appropriate committee mentioned in s 20(3) is a committee established by the minister under s 4 of the Act to deal with any particular kind of medicinal product and charged under s 4(3) with—

'(*a*) giving advice with respect to safety, quality or efficacy, or with respect to all or any two of those matters; (*b*) promoting the collection and investigation of information relating to adverse reactions, for the purpose of enabling such advice to be given.'

On 1 January 1973 the United Kingdom became a member of the European Communities and, pursuant to the European Communities Act 1972, became subject to Community law. Article 100 of the EEC Treaty provides that the Council of the Community shall—

'issue directives for the approximation of such provisions laid down by law, regulation or administrative action in Member States as directly affect the establishment or functioning of the common market . . .'

On 26 January 1965 the Council promulgated EEC Council Directive 65/65 on the approximation of provisions laid down by law, regulation or administrative action relating to proprietary and medicinal products (the 1965 directive). The provisions of the 1965 directive, as amended and amplified from time to time by subsequent directives, became binding on the United Kingdom and must be performed and observed by the licensing authority. The 1965 directive recited, inter alia:

'. . . the primary purpose of any rules concerning the production and distribution of proprietary medicinal products must be to safeguard public health; . . . however, this objective must be attained by means which will not hinder the development of the pharmaceutical industry or trade in medicinal products within the Community; . . . trade in proprietary medicinal products within the Community is hindered by disparities between certain national provisions, in particular between provisions relating to medicinal products . . . and . . . such disparities directly affect the establishment and functioning of the common market: . . . such hindrances must accordingly be removed; and . . . this entails approximation of the relevant provisions . . .'

Article 3 of the directive directed:

'No proprietary medicinal product may be placed on the market in a Member
State unless an authorisation has been issued by the competent authority of that
Member State.'

In the United Kingdom the authorisation issued by the competent authority consists
of a product licence granted by the licensing authority pursuant to its powers under the
Medicines Act 1968.

Article 4 of the 1965 directive required an application for a product licence to be
accompanied by certain specified particulars and documents which were detailed under
11 numbered points, including the following:

'1. Name or corporate name and permanent address of the person responsible for
placing the proprietary product on the market and, where applicable, of the
manufacturer.

2. Name of the proprietary product . . .

3. Qualitative and quantitative particulars of all the constituents of the proprietary
product in usual terminology . . .

4. Brief description of the method of preparation.

5. Therapeutic indications, contra-indications and side-effects.

6. Posology, pharmaceutical form, method and route of administration and
expected shelf life if less than three years.

7. Control methods employed by the manufacturer (analysis and assay of the
constituents and of the finished product, special tests, e.g. sterility tests, tests for the
presence of pyrogenic substances, the presence of heavy metals, stability tests,
biological and toxicity tests).

8. Results of: —physico-chemical, biological or microbiological tests; —
pharmacological and toxicological tests; —clinical trials. However: (a) a List of
published references relating to the pharmacological tests, toxicological tests and
clinical trials may be substituted for the relevant test results in the case of: (i) a
proprietary product with an established use, which has been adequately tested on
human beings so that its effects, including side-effects, are already known and are
included in the published references; (ii) a new proprietary product, in which the
combination of active constituents is identical with that of a known proprietary
product with an established use; (iii) a new proprietary product consisting solely of
known constituents that have been used in combination in comparable proportions
in adequately tested medicinal products with an established use . . .'

Thus, in the case of an application for a new proprietary product 'identical' with that
of a known proprietary product with an established use, or in the case of a new
proprietary product consisting of known constituents that had been used in 'comparable
proportions' in medicinal products with an established use which had already been
adequately tested, the applicant was not compelled to carry out time consuming and
expensive tests and trials provided there was evidence in published references that tests
on and trials of the 'identical' or 'comparable' product had been carried out with
satisfactory results. It was for the licensing authority to determine whether two products
were or were not 'identical' or 'comparable' for the purposes of point 8 applying any
criteria laid down by the Council.

By EC Council Directive 75/318, dated 20 May 1975, the Council laid down uniform
rules applicable to tests and trials, the compilation of dossiers and the examination of
applications for product licences in every member state and specified the data to be
provided under point 8 of art 4 of the 1965 directive. The declared objects of the directive
were to protect public health and to prevent obstruction to the free movement of
medicinal products within the Community by different standards and evaluations in
different member states. By EC Council Directive 75/319, also dated 20 May 1975,

further rules were laid down in order to reduce or eliminate disparities between the
a practices of different member states and in order to facilitate the movement of proprietary
medicinal products.

The appellants applied to the licensing authority for a product licence to manufacture
and sell cimetidine under the brand name Tagamet. The appellants provided all the
particulars and documents specified in art 4 of the 1965 directive and in compliance with
the 1975 directives. There being no 'identical' or 'comparable' product, the appellants
b provided the results of tests and trials carried out by the appellants and complying with
point 8 of art 4. A product licence was granted in November 1976. The particulars and
documents provided by the appellants to the licensing authority disclosed information
acquired by the appellants in the course of their research into and development of
cimetidine and information concerning the manufacturing processes of Tagamet. This
information had been acquired by the appellants with much ingenuity, care, time and
c expense, and was, for the most part, unavailable to the public. The information was
invaluable to the appellants and would be valuable to any competitor seeking to exploit
cimetidine after the expiry of the appellants' patents. In these circumstances, the
confidential information supplied by the appellants to the licensing authority, that is to
say information which was not available to the public, could only be used by the licensing
authority for the purposes of carrying out their functions under the 1968 Act. Under
d English law, the courts applying equitable principles would consider that it was
unconscionable for the licensing authority to make use of the confidential information,
supplied by the appellants, otherwise than for the purpose of carrying out the functions
of the licensing authority under the 1968 Act.

By the Patents Act 1977 the term of a patent was increased from 16 to 20 years. A
patent granted after 1 June 1967, and before the passing of the 1977 Act, for a term of 16
e years, obtained the benefit of an extension from 16 to 20 years but at the end of the
sixteenth year the 1977 Act provided that such a patent should be subject to licence of
right provisions whereby any person might exploit the patent on terms to be settled by
the comptroller in default of agreement between the proprietor of the patent and the
licensee. The appellants' patents relating to cimetidine became subject to the exercise of
f licences of right powers between 10 March 1988 and 9 March 1992.

After the 1965 directive had been amplified and amended in 1975 and further
experience had been gathered, the European Commission reported to the Council and
recommended further amendments to point 8 of art 4 of the 1965 directive: report
(explanatory memorandum). Under the 1965 directive as originally promulgated, the
first applicant for a product licence relating to a medicinal product was bound to produce
g all the particulars and documents required by art 4 of the 1965 directive. In the present
case the appellants were bound to prove that cimetidine was safe and effective and that
Tagamet would be cimetidine of consistently high quality. A second applicant for a
product licence, for the same or a similar medicinal product, where the first applicant
was not protected by a patent or where the first applicant's patent had expired, was also
bound to produce all the particulars and documents required by art 4. Where, however,
h the second application related to a product which was 'identical' or 'comparable' and
fulfilled the requirements of point 8(*a*) of the 1965 directive, the second applicant was
not bound to carry out and repeat all the tests and trials specified in point 8 of art 4 of the
1965 directive, but could rely on published literature. The Commission reported, at
para 14, that where a licensing authority was satisfied that the products of the two
applicants were 'identical' or 'comparable' but the published literature was incomplete or
j inappropriate, then—

'certain national authorities have tended not to be too demanding as regards the
bibliographical evidence submitted by the second applicant. This practice seriously
penalizes the innovatory firm which has [had] to meet the high cost of clinical trials
and animal experiments, while its product can be copied at lower cost and sometimes

within a very short period. Protection of a medicinal innovation by means of a patent is not in fact always possible or effective, as for example in the case of a natural substance or of a substance which is already known but on which additional research has been carried out with a view to a new therapeutic use.'

It appears, therefore, that some member states were more willing than others on a second application to dispense with tests and trials by accepting published literature which other member states found to be inadequate. To achieve uniformity, the Commission proposed that the 1965 directive should be amended so that if the second applicant was, in effect, copying the product of the first applicant, he would not be obliged to carry out the tests and trials required by point 8 of art 4 of the 1965 directive, provided that ten years had elapsed since the grant of a product licence to the first applicant. The second applicant could rely on the tests and trials carried out by the first applicant, provided that the first applicant had been able to market his product for ten years. The Commission stated in para 15: 'This ten-year period will enable the partial recovery of the research investment, which might not be protected otherwise, for example by a patent.' In the present case, the appellants were protected by a patent and were able to recover their costs of research and investment during a period of 12 years between 1976, when the appellants obtained a product licence from the licensing authority to market cimetidine under the brand name of Tagamet, and 1988, when, for the first time, a second applicant became entitled under a patent licence of right to apply for a product licence to market cimetidine under some other brand name. The tests and trials carried out by the appellants, pursuant to art 4, point 8 of the 1965 directive together with the other particulars and documents furnished by the appellants, were sufficient to satisfy the licensing authority in 1976 that cimetidine was safe, effective and could be produced with a consistent high quality. Provided nothing had happened since 1976 to cast doubts on the results of these tests and trials, the Commission's proposals meant that a second applicant in 1988 would not have to prove by further tests and trials that cimetidine was safe and effective and could be produced of good quality. The second applicant must, however, satisfy all the other requirements of the 1965 directive in order to prove that his brand of cimetidine was as safe and effective as Tagamet and of comparable quality.

The Council by EC Council Directive 87/21, dated 22 December 1986, implemented some of the recommendations of the Commission's report. The directive recited:

'... experience has shown that it is advisable to stipulate more precisely the cases in which the results of pharmacological and toxicological tests or clinical trials do not have to be provided with a view to obtaining authorization for a proprietary medicinal produce which is essentially similar to an authorized product, while ensuring that innovative firms are not placed at a disadvantage ...'

The directive amended the 1965 directive by replacing point 8 so that it now reads as follows:

'Results of: —physico-chemical, biological or microbiological tests, —pharmacological and toxicological tests, —clinical trials. However, and without prejudice to the law relating to the protection of industrial and commercial property: (a) The applicant shall not be required to provide the results of pharmacological and toxicological tests or the results of clinical trials if he can demonstrate: (i) either that the proprietary medicinal product is essentially similar to a product authorized in the country concerned by the application and that the person responsible for the marketing of the original proprietary medicinal product has consented to the pharmacological, toxicological or clinical references contained in the file on the original proprietary medicinal product being used for the purpose of examining the application in question; (ii) or by detailed references to published scientific literature presented in accordance with the second paragraph of Article 1 of Directive 75/318/ EEC that the constituent or constituents of the proprietary medicinal product have

a   a well established medicinal use, with recognized efficacy and an acceptable level of
      safety; (iii) or that the proprietary medicinal product is essentially similar to a
      product which has been authorized within the Community, in accordance with
      Community provisions in force, for not less than six years and is marketed in the
      Member State for which the application is made; this period shall be extended to 10
      years in the case of high-technology medicinal products within the meaning of Part
      A in the Annex to Directive 87/22/EEC or of a medicinal product within the
b   meaning of Part B in the Annex to that Directive for which the procedure laid down
      in Article 2 thereof has been followed; furthermore, a Member State may also
      extend this period to 10 years by a single Decision covering all the products
      marketed on its territory where it considers this necessary in the interest of public
      health. Member States are at liberty not to apply the abovementioned six-year
      period beyond the date of expiry of a patent protecting the original product.
c   However, where the proprietary medicinal product is intended for a different
      therapeutic use from that of the other proprietary medicinal products marketed or
      is to be administered by different routes or in different doses, the results of
      appropriate pharmacological and toxicological tests and/or of appropriate clinical
      trials must be provided . . .'

d   In a written parliamentary answer, dated 30 June 1987, the government of the United
      Kingdom announced that the ten-year period allowed by point 8(a)(iii) of art 4 of the
      directive would be extended to all medicinal products marketed in its territory (see 118
      HC Official Report (6th series) written answers col 82). Thus, by the amended point 8 of
      art 4 of the 1965 directive, as applied in the United Kingdom, a second applicant for a
      product licence in respect of a product which is 'essentially similar' to a product licensed
e   less than ten years before the second application can only dispense with the tests and trials
      specified by point 8 if the first applicant consents to the pharmacological, toxicological
      and clinical references contained in the file on the first applicant's medicinal product
      being used for the purpose of examining the second application. This is the effect of the
      amended point 8(a)(i). But where the two products are 'essentially similar' and the first
      applicant has been in possession of a product licence for ten years or more, the second
f   applicant need not carry out and supply the results of pharmacological and toxicological
      tests and clinical trials. This is the effect of the amended point 8(a)(iii).
          Point 8(a) of art 4 of the 1965 directive, as amended, is expressed to be 'without
      prejudice to the law relating to the protection of industrial and commercial property'.
      These words cannot create a restriction where none existed. The quoted words suffice in
      the present case to preserve the English law of confidentiality which prevents the
g   licensing authority from using the appellants' confidential information for purposes
      other than the performance by the licensing authority of its functions under the 1968
      Act.
          On 16 January 1987 the first intervener, Generics (UK) Ltd (Generics), applied to the
      Comptroller General of Patents, Designs and Trade Marks to settle the terms of a licence
h   of right for Generics as from 9 March 1988 to make, import and sell cimetidine
      compound and its products defined as pharmaceutical formulations containing cimetidine
      as the sole active ingredient. The terms were settled by the comptroller on 15 March
      1988 and included payment to the appellants of a royalty of £178 per kilo of the
      compound manufactured or imported. On 10 June 1987 Generics applied to the licensing
      authority for a product licence in respect of cimetidine. That application was not
j   supported by the results of tests and trials pursuant to point 8 of art 4 of the 1965
      directive, as amended, such tests and trials being unnecessary in view of point 8(a)(iii).
      'Essential similarity' between Tagamet and Generics' brand will appear because both
      products will contain cimetidine as the sole active ingredient and a comparison between
      the information supplied by the appellants and the information supplied by Generics
      will demonstrate whether the two brands are similarly safe, effective and of good quality.

The second intervener, Harris Pharmaceuticals Ltd (Harris), in March 1987, applied to the comptroller to settle the terms of a licence of right for cimetidine and they were *a* settled on 8 April 1988 on terms identical with those decided in the case of Generics. There have been other applications for licences of right in respect of cimetidine. In July 1987 Harris applied to the licensing authority for a product licence in respect of cimetidine. That application also was not supported by the results of tests and trials pursuant to art 4, point 8 of the 1965 directive, as amended, in view of point 8(a)(iii).

On 2 October 1987 the appellants instituted judicial review proceedings against the *b* licensing authority claiming a number of declarations prohibiting the licensing authority from making use of any of the information contained in the appellants' 1976 application for a product licence without the consent of the appellants.

As a result of these proceedings the applications of Generics and Harris for product licences for their brands of cimetidine have not yet been granted or refused by the licensing authority.   *c*

On 23 February 1988 Henry J made a declaration that—

> 'in considering an application for a product licence in respect of a medicinal product containing cimetidine made pursuant to the abridged procedure provided for by Article 4(8)(a)(iii) of Council Directive 65/65/EEC as amended the [licensing authority] may not for the purpose of such application use refer or have recourse to *d* any confidential information supplied to it by the [appellants] in connection with any application by the [appellants] for a product licence in respect of such a product except with the express consent of the [appellants].'

Counsel for the appellants did not, on this appeal, seek to support this declaration in so far as it precluded the licensing authority from using information relevant to the protection of the public from unsafe medicinal products. Nevertheless, counsel submitted *e* that the appellants' file of information in the possession of the licensing authority should be sealed up and that no person concerned with the grant of a product licence relating to cimetidine to the appellants should deal with any application by Generics, Harris or anyone else for a product licence in case that person should recollect or be unconsciously influenced by anything which he had learned from the appellants' application. *f*

On 29 June 1988 the Court of Appeal (Dillon, Balcombe and Staughton LJJ) ([1989] 1 All ER 175, [1988] 3 WLR 896) set aside the order made by Henry J. The appellants now appeal to this House.

In my opinion the first and only question which requires to be answered on this appeal is whether English law prohibits the licensing authority from having recourse to the confidential information provided by the appellants in the course of their application for *g* a product licence relating to cimetidine for the purpose of considering whether to grant or reject an application by Generics or Harris or anyone else for a product licence in respect of cimetidine.

The licensing authority are advised by experts in the field of medicinal products. The information available to the licensing authority consists of the knowledge obtained by these experts based on long experience, the information available in published literature *h* and, over the years, the vast amount of information provided by large numbers of applicants for product licences, such information being partly confidential and partly available to the public. The principal task of the licensing authority is to protect the public. But in performing its functions, the licensing authority must treat all applicants fairly and equally. The standard which it requires from the first applicant for a product licence for cimetidine must be required of the second and subsequent applicants. If the *j* licensing authority sanctions the first application, notwithstanding the presence of certain impurities, the same deviations from purity must be allowed to second and subsequent applicants. If the information disclosed by a first applicant when compared with the information disclosed by the second applicant leads the licensing authority to conclude that the second application ought to be allowed, then the licensing authority must act accordingly. Conversely, if the information supplied by the second applicant casts doubt

a on some aspect of the product of the first applicant, then the licensing authority must consider whether to exercise the power conferred on the licensing authority by the 1968 Act to revoke the first applicant's product licence. It is for the licensing authority, comparing the information received from the first applicant and the information received from the second applicant, and taking into account all other information available to the licensing authority, from whatever source, and whether confidential or

b not confidential, to decide in the case of any particular application whether it shall be declined or granted. There may be, there will be, in the case of a popular medicinal product many applications by many different applicants. It is essential for the licensing authority to compare the applications of the first and subsequent applicants in order to satisfy themselves that both products are similar, safe, effective and reliable. The licensing authority cannot discharge its duty to safeguard the health of the nation and its duty to

c act fairly and equally between applicants without having recourse to all the information available to the licensing authority, confidential or otherwise. Indeed, it would not be practicable and it would be highly dangerous for the licensing authority to attempt to segregate in the case of each applicant the information which was confidential to that applicant and to forget or ignore that information when carrying out any function imposed on the licensing authority by the 1968 Act in the interests of the public.

d My Lords, I am satisfied that it is the right and duty of the licensing authority to make use of all the information supplied by any applicant for a product licence which assists the licensing authority in considering whether to grant or reject any other application, or which assists the licensing authority in performing any of its other functions under the 1968 Act. The use of such information should not harm the appellants and, even were it to do so, this is the price which the appellants must pay for co-operating in the

e regime designed by Parliament for the protection of the public and for the protection of the appellants and all manufacturers of medicinal products from the dangers inherent in the introduction and reproduction of modern drugs.

The appellants asserted that they had no intention of obstructing the licensing authority in its onerous task of protecting the public but their proceedings and the order made by Henry J would have that effect. The appellants relied on three English

f authorities and one Australian authority. In *Metropolitan Asylum District Managers v Hill* (1881) 6 App Cas 193, [1881–5] All ER Rep 536 this House determined that an Act of Parliament which authorised an asylum did not authorise the asylum to commit a nuisance. Lord Blackburn said (6 App Case 193 at 208, [1881–5] All ER Rep 536 at 543):

g 'It is clear that the burthen lies on those who seek to establish that the Legislature intended to take away the private rights of individuals, to shew that by express words, or by necessary implication, such an intention appears.'

In the present case the 1968 Act does not take away any private rights. If the appellants choose to apply for a product licence under the Act, they choose to provide information to the licensing authority for the purposes of the Act. It is not unconscionable for the

h licensing authority to make use of that information in the public interest for the purposes of the Act, although it would be unconscionable for the licensing authority to disclose that information to third parties for other purposes. In *Re Keene* [1922] 2 Ch 475, [1922] All ER Rep 258, a debtor was obliged to disclose to his trustee in bankruptcy secret formulas for the making of certain proprietary articles. In *Butler v Board of Trade* [1970] 3 All ER 593, [1971] Ch 680 the Board of Trade were not allowed in criminal proceedings

j to put in evidence the copy of a letter written by a solicitor to his client, the plaintiff, which was a privileged letter. I am unable to derive any assistance from these authorities in the present circumstances; the appellants have voluntarily provided information to the licensing authority for the purposes of the Act. In *Castrol Autralia Pty Ltd v Emtech Associates Pty Ltd* (1980) 33 ALR 31, in the Supreme Court of New South Wales, Rath J, perhaps surprisingly, held in interlocutory proceedings that a report furnished by Castrol to the Trade Practices Commission in order to persuade the commission that Castrol's advertisements were justified in claiming that tests on Castrol oil showed an improvement in fuel consumption could not be used by the commission in prosecuting Castrol for publishing misleading advertisements. In that case, however, the commission had expressly undertaken to Castrol to treat the report as confidential. The judge recognised that 'in some cases public interest in disclosure will prevail over public interests in the preservation of confidence' (at 52). But he concluded that 'the public interest does not require that the Commission, at this stage, should be excused from breaking the confidence that on the present evidence was reposed in it'. In the present case, the licensing authority gave no undertaking to the appellants and do not propose to break any confidences but only to make use of information supplied under the Act for the purposes of carrying out their duties under the Act.

Section 118(1) of the 1968 Act provides:

'If any person discloses to any other persons . . . (b) any information obtained by or furnished to him in pursuance of this Act, he shall, unless the disclosure was made in performance of his duty, be guilty of an offence.'

That subsection reinforces the view which I have formed that information obtained under the Act may be used by the licensing authority and that even disclosure is lawful if the disclosure is made in the performance by the licensing authority of its duty under the Act.

Accordingly, there is no principle of confidentiality in English law which prevents the licensing authority from making use of the information supplied by the appellants for any of the purposes for which the licensing authority was established. Article 30 of the EEC Treaty prohibited quantitative restrictions on imports and all measures having equivalent effect between member states, but by art 36, the provisions of art 30 do not preclude prohibitions or restrictions on imports justified on grounds, inter alia, of the protection of industrial and commercial property. Article 36 did not impose on member states any Community obligation of confidentiality. The directives to which we were referred did not impose on member states any Community obligation of confidentiality. Article 4, point 8 of the 1965 directive, as amended by the 1987 directive is expressed to operate 'without prejudice to the law relating to the protection of industrial and commercial property'. The only relevant law in the present case is English law and for the reasons which I have indicated, English law does not protect the appellants against the use by the licensing authority of confidential information supplied by the appellants to the licensing authority for the purposes of the 1968 Act. The appellants suggested that it was necessary or might be useful to refer to the Court of Justice of the European Communities for a ruling under art 177 of the EEC Treaty on questions concerning the ambit of the expression 'without prejudice to the law relating to the protection of industrial and commercial property'. In my opinion no question of Community law arises in connection with confidentiality or otherwise. The 1965 directive, as amended, authorises the licensing authority to grant a product licence to Generics and Harris without requiring Generics and Harris to produce the results of pharmacological and toxicological tests and clinical trials, provided that Generics and Harris furnish all the particulars and documents required by the 1965 directive with the exception of the results of such tests and trials and provided that the licensing authority, after comparing the applications of Generics and Harris with the earlier applications of the appellants and after considering all other information in their possession, is satisfied that the Generics and Harris products of cimetidine are essentially similar to Tagamet and are safe, efficient and reliable. Point 8(a) of art 4 of the 1965 directive, as amended and as applied to the United Kingdom, would have required a second applicant for a product licence of cimetidine to produce the results of the relevant tests and trials if the second application had been made before November 1986 unless the appellants consented to the use of their files which contained results of the relevant tests and trials. Point 8(a) does not require a

second applicant to produce the results of the relevant tests and trials after November
a 1986. Generics and Harris may, without the consent of the appellants, rely on the fact
that the appellants produced satisfactory results relating to cimetidine when the appellants
obtained a produce licence for Tagamet.

The argument most pressed by the appellants was that Generics and Harris cannot
comply with point 8 of art 4 of the 1965 directive, as amended, unless they 'demonstrate'
that the cimetidine, for which they seek produce licences, is 'essentially similar' to
b Tagamet by carrying out the very tests and trials which are expressly rendered
unnecessary by point 8(*a*)(iii). The applications of Generics and Harris must be in respect
of a formulation which contains cimetidine as the sole active ingredient. In support of
those applications Generics and Harris must supply all the information which they are
bound to supply under points 1 to 7 of art 4 of the 1965 directive, as amended, and any
other information required by the directive or by regulations made under the 1968 Act.
c It will be the duty of the licensing authority to compare the applications made by
Generics and Harris for product licences for their brands of cimetidine with the
application made by the appellants in 1976 for their Tagamet brand of cimetidine in
order to determine whether the licensing authority is satisfied that the Generics and
Harris brands are, in the opinion of the licensing authority, 'essentially similar' to
Tagamet. The declared objects of Generics and Harris are to copy Tagamet and to equal
d or improve on Tegamet. The licensing authority will decide whether Generics and Harris
succeed or fail without obliging Generics or Harris to demonstrate in 1988 (as the
appellants were perforce constrained to demonstrate in 1976), by the tests and trials
required by point 8 of art 4 of the 1965 directive, that cimetidine is capable of being
manufactured in a form which is safe, effective and of high quality.

The appellants object, understandably, to Tagamet being copied by Generics, Harris or
e anyone else. The appellants' submissions are, in essence, based on the proposition that if
a product is worth copying, the law should protect the product against being copied. My
Lords, that is not the law. In *British Leyland Motor Corp Ltd v Armstrong Patents Co Ltd*
[1986] 1 All ER 850, [1986] AC 577 this House declined to allow the law of copyright to
be exploited and rejected the argument that a motor car manufacturer was entitled to a
perpetual monopoly in spare parts and could prevent the copying of spare parts which
f were no longer protected by a patent. In *Re Coca-Cola Co's Applications* [1986] 2 All ER
274, [1986] 1 WLR 695 this House declined to allow trade mark law to be exploited and
rejected the argument that the manufacturer of a beverage sold under a trade name had
established a perpetual monopoly in and could prevent the copying of the shape of a
bottle which was no longer protected by the Registered Designs Act 1949. In *Interlego*
g *AG v Tyco Industries Inc* [1988] 3 All ER 949, [1988] 3 WLR 678 the Privy Council
declined to allow the law of copyright in Hong Kong to be exploited and rejected the
argument that a manufacturer of a toy was entitled to a perpetual monopoly in the toy
and could prevent the copying of the shape of the toy which was no longer protected by
the 1949 Act. In *Beecham Group plc v Gist-Brocades NV* [1986] 1 WLR 51 and in *Allen &*
Hanburys Ltd v Generics (UK) Ltd Case 434/85 [1988] 2 All ER 454 proprietors of patented
h drugs sought to obstruct and delay the settlement of terms of licences of right by the
comptroller and met with some success until the European Court ruled that the
comptroller had no power to prohibit imports from Community countries.

In the present case the appellants seek to enlist the law of confidentiality and to extend
their patent monopoly beyond the term granted. The appellants seek to harass and
obstruct the licensing authority in the determination of the applications by Generics and
j Harris and others of their applications for product licences in respect of cimetidine. The
campaign began with parliamentary questions and debate which sought to inhibit the
licensing authority from making use of information derived from product licence
applications. At the same time, lawyers' letters interrogated the licensing authority with
regard to its practice, refused to agree terms of licences of right, threatened Harris with
actions for breach of patent and threatened the licensing authority with judicial review

proceedings. The advisers of the Minister of Health, in his parliamentary role and in his role as licensing authority, were anxious to appease their critics and made statements some of which were inept and confusing and which wrongly accepted that the powers of the licensing authority were much more restricted than I hold them to be. The soothing attitude on the part of the licensing authority did not prevent the appellants from issuing judicial review proceedings, and obtaining interlocutory injunctions and undertakings. The practical effect has been that the applications of Generics and Harris and others for product licences have not yet been determined and one year of the licence of right term will shortly expire.

My Lords, the patent term of 14 years authorised by the Statute of Monopolies (1623) was increased in 1919 to 16 years and in 1977 to 20 years. The effective term of the patent monopoly afforded to the appellants in respect of cimetidine from 1976 when Tagamet was first sold until 1988 was 12 years and in addition the appellants are entitled to royalties under the licence of right provisions for a further four years. The appellants have been able, for 12 years, to establish their trade mark of Tagamet and to establish the reputation of their product with the medical profession and the public. The appellants still possess, and always will possess, advantages over other producers of cimetidine and will only suffer the hardship of competition from which they have hitherto been protected by their patent. The obstructions which the appellants now seek to place in the path of the licensing authority in the consideration by the licensing authority of other applications for product licences would apply not only during the period of licences of right but also after all patent protection has expired. The appellants are seeking to prolong their monopoly beyond the statutory term. Of course, the appellants and their supporters are entitled to amount campaigns in Parliament, in the press and elsewhere and they are entitled to institute such legal proceedings as they may be advised. But in my opinion the licensing authority should not be deterred from exercising its right and powers so as to ensure public safety and to ensure fairness to all applicants whether or not they resort to campaigns and litigation. The courts should be reluctant to criticise the practices of the licensing authority or to grant injunctions or orders or declarations against the licensing authority which is endeavouring reasonably and conscientiously to discharge the onerous duties imposed by Parliament and is acting in good faith. I would dismiss this appeal.

LORD ACKNER. My Lords, I have had the advantage of reading in draft the speech of my noble and learned friend Lord Templeman. I agree with it and, for the reasons given by my noble and learned friend, I, too, would dismiss this appeal.

LORD OLIVER OF AYLMERTON. My Lords, I have had the advantage of reading in draft the speech prepared by my noble and learned friend Lord Templeman, and would dismiss the appeal for the reasons which he has given.

LORD LOWRY. My Lords, I have had the advantage of reading in draft the speech of my noble and learned friend Lord Templeman. I entirely agree with it and, for the reasons given by my noble and learned friend, I, too, would dismiss this appeal.

Appeal dismissed.

Solicitors: *Simmons & Simmons* (for the appellants); *Treasury Solicitor*; *S J Berwin & Co* (for the first intervener); *Roiter Zucker* (for the second intervener).

Mary Rose Plummer   Barrister.

Re Berger (deceased)

COURT OF APPEAL, CIVIL DIVISION
MUSTILL, MANN LJJ AND SIR DENYS BUCKLEY
28, 29 MARCH, 21 JULY 1988

Probate – Document – Admission to probate – Testator's intention regarding admission to probate – Relevance of testator's intention – Zavah in Hebrew language – Testator executing zavah in Hebrew alongside English will – Zavah intended to be binding in Jewish law and enforceable in rabbinical court – Testator expressing no intention whether it was to be enforceable in English court – English will invalid – Whether zavah should be admitted to probate as testator's last will.

Probate – Document – Admission to probate – Will in foreign language – Whether authenticated translation or text in foreign language document admissible to probate.

Probate – Document – Admission to probate – Will in foreign language – Evidence of foreign law to ascertain testator's intention – Whether permissible for court to refer questions on meaning or effect of foreign law to foreign court.

The deceased was an orthodox Jew domiciled in England. From 1964 onwards he made dispositions of his estate to his family by executing two parallel series of documents. The first consisted of a succession of English wills drawn up by the deceased's legal adviser containing dispositions of his movable property which the deceased clearly intended should be given effect to, and be provable, in the English courts. The second series consisted of documents handwritten by the deceased in Hebrew and known as zavah. They contained religious exhortations to his family in terms which were alien to an English will but also contained dispositions of his movable property. The zavah were intended by the deceased to be binding in Jewish law and to be enforceable in the rabbinical court, but he did not indicate whether they were intended also to be enforceable in the English courts or what was to happen if his current English will failed. In 1975 the deceased executed a valid English will which revoked all former wills. On 6 August 1977 the deceased executed the last of his zavah, the document being executed in accordance with the Wills Act 1837. On 9 August the deceased purported to execute another English will but that will was invalid because it was improperly attested and did not comply with the 1837 Act. The deceased died on 20 September. The 1977 zavah contained testamentary dispositions of the deceased's movable property to his family, as well as religious exhortations addressed to them, and also contained provisions relating to matters over which the deceased had no testamentary powers of control. It concluded by stating that it was 'binding' on the deceased's family, that it was 'additional' to what was written in the 1977 English will and that if any clarification of that will was needed the 'present [Hebrew] will . . . is the definitive one'. On the deceased's death his executors claimed that, because the 1977 English will had failed, the 1977 zavah (with the terms of the 1977 English will incorporated into it) should be admitted to probate as the deceased's last will and testament. The defendants, who were the beneficiaries under the 1975 will, sought pronouncement in favour of that will, on the ground that the 1977 zavah was not a testamentary document in English law governing the disposition of the deceased's estate. The judge pronounced in favour of the 1977 zavah with the terms of the 1977 will incorporated into it. The defendants appealed.

Held – (1) For an instrument to be a provable will which would be admitted to probate in the English court, it was not necessary that the testator should have positively intended that the instrument should be provable in the English court. Provided the testator had not positively indicated the contrary, namely that the instrument should not be admitted

to probate in the English court, all that was necessary for the instrument to be admitted
to probate was that it should contain directions for the disposal of the testator's property
after his decease which were revocable during his lifetime. The fact that the testator had
not contemplated the possibility of the instrument being enforced in the English court
did not necessarily mean that it should not be so enforced (see p 599 *f* to *j*, p 600 *d e h* and
p 602 *a b*, post).

(2) Since the 1977 zavah had been executed in accordance with the 1837 Act, since it
contained dispositions of the deceased's movable property which were to take effect on
his death and which, having regard to the history of the series of zavah, were to be
revocable and capable of modification during his lifetime and since the deceased had
never positively indicated that he did not wish his zavah to be enforced in the English
court but (per Sir Denys Buckley) on the contrary, by referring to the 1977 English will
in the 1977 zavah, had expressed the intention that the 1977 zavah should take effect in
English law, it followed that the 1977 zavah, with the terms of the 1977 will incorporated
into it, should be admitted to probate as the deceased's last will on the basis that those
documents were intended by the deceased to be taken together as being his last will. The
appeal would therefore be dismissed (see p 600 *e* to *j*, p 601 *d f* to *h*, p 602 *e j* and p 603 *c
d f* to p 604 *a*, post).

Per curiam. (1) Where a will is in a foreign language the court must be furnished with
an authenticated translation, and it is the translation, not the text in the foreign language,
which will be admitted to probate (see p 600 *g h* and p 602 *b c*, post).

(2) Where the will of a testator domiciled in England is in a foreign language and uses
terms inappropriate to English law but appropriate to a foreign system of law, the
English court when administering the distribution of the testator's movable property in
accordance with English law can have recourse to evidence of the foreign system of law
for the purpose of ascertaining the testator's intention, but it cannot refer any questions
on the meaning or effect of the foreign law to the foreign court, even if the testator
expressly provided that any such question must be decided by the foreign court, because
for the English court to do so would conflict with the rule of English law that the
devolution and distribution of the movable property of a testator domiciled in England
shall be governed by the lex domicilii (see p 600 *g h* and p 602 *j* to p 603 *c*, post).

Notes

For the essential characteristics of a will, for evidence of testamentary character and for
testamentary form and testamentary intention, see 50 Halsbury's Laws (4th edn) paras
202, 206, 249–250.

For the Wills Act 1837, see 50 Halsbury's Statutes (4th edn) 150.

Cases referred to in judgments

Douglas-Menzies v Umphelby [1908] AC 224, PC.
Ferguson-Davie v Ferguson-Davie (1890) 15 PD 109.
Godman v Godman [1920] P 261, CA.
Guardhouse v Blackburn (1866) LR 1 P & D 109, [1861–73] All ER Rep 680.
Lemage v Goodban (1865) LR 1 P & D 57.
Lister v Smith (1863) 3 Sw & Tr 282, 164 ER 1282.
Meynell, Re, Meynell v Meynell [1949] WN 273.
Milnes v Foden (1890) 15 PD 105.
*Raven, Re, Spencer v National Association for the Prevention of Consumption and other forms of
Tuberculosis* [1915] 1 Ch 673, [1914–15] All ER Rep 353.
Whyte v Pollok (1882) 7 App Cas 400, HL.
Wynn's Will Trusts, Re, Public Trustee v Newborough (Baron) [1952] 1 All ER 341, [1952]
Ch 271.

Appeal

By a writ issued on 2 October 1984 the plaintiffs, Sarah Englander and Doris Feldman,
claimed, as two of the executors of the will of Gerson Berger deceased, for pronouncement

a and admission to probate as the deceased's last will and testament of a manuscript Hebrew will dated 6 August 1977, incorporating therein an invalid English will made by the deceased on 9 August 1977. The defendants, Sighismund Berger, Mendel Berger and Brucha Berger, two of the deceased's sons and his wife, and Gerson Berger Association Ltd, by their defence denied that the 1977 Hebrew will was the deceased's last will and testament. The first, second and fourth defendants, by a counterclaim, claimed for pronouncement and admission to probate of an English will made by the deceased in b 1975 as being his last valid will and testament. On 3 April 1987 Warner J pronounced for the 1977 Hebrew will with the 1977 English will incorporated into it. The fourth defendant appealed. The facts are set out in the judgment of Mustill LJ.

Michael Nield for the fourth defendant.
David Ritchie for the plaintiffs.

c
                                                                    Cur adv vult

21 July. The following judgments were delivered.

MUSTILL LJ. This case concerns the testamentary effect of an instrument executed by Mr Gerson Berger on 6 August 1977. This document was handwritten in the Hebrew d tongue, and there is no doubt that Mr Berger, who was a devout orthodox Jew, intended it to be a zavah. This term has for convenience been rendered as a 'Hebrew will', but I think it preferable to employ the technical expression, so as to avoid begging the question whether the document was a will at all. At first instance Warner J has pronounced for the zavah, holding also that it should take effect with the incorporation of a roughly contemporaneous document in the English language, which was undoubtedly intended e to take effect as a will, but which failed for want of proper execution. An appeal is now brought against this decision by certain beneficiaries under an English will made on 15 July 1975, the contention being that the zavah was not apt for admission to probate, either with or without the incorporation of the invalid English will of 1977, and that accordingly the 1975 will stands as the last valid testamentary disposition of Mr Berger.

f This appeal is concerned with two groups of documents. The first consists of a series of documents in the English language, plainly intended to take effect as wills to which effect would be given through the English law of probate. So far as is shown by the evidence now before us, there were seven such documents, executed in 1957, 1958, 1963, 1964, 1972, 1975 and 1977. Current at the same time was a series of documents in the shape of a zavah. The first was dated 1965. The second was executed on 18 December 1972, the same date as the fifth English will. The third was dated 11 February 1976, g between the sixth and seventh English wills. As will later appear, it was intended by Mr Berger and his solicitors that the fourth zavah should be executed at about the same time as the seventh English will, as had been the case with the pair of documents dated 18 December 1972. In fact the zavah was signed on 6 August 1977, three days before the seventh and last English will, and about six weeks before Mr Berger died.

h The present dispute arises from the fact, that although as planned the deceased appended his signature to the last English will within a few days of the last zavah, that will was not properly executed, and therefore has no direct testamentary effect. The question for decision is whether in consequence the estate should be distributed in accordance with the last of the valid English wills, namely the will of 15 July 1975, or whether the zavah of 6 August 1977 should be admitted to probate, as representing the j last of the deceased's valid testamentary dispositions. Warner J has held in favour of the latter alternative, and against this decision the beneficiaries under the 1975 will now appeal.

In order to form an impression of how the deceased envisaged that the two series of documents were to take effect concurrently it is convenient to look as briefly as possible at the dispositions which they contained. We may begin with the English will of 25 July 1964. As did all the English wills, this began with a revocation clause. It proceeded to

appoint executors and trustees, and then dealt specifically with the shares in Raymond
Sun Ltd, which were to go in unequal portions to two of the testator's sons. The residue *a*
of the estate was devised to the trustees, in trust for the testator's daughter Doris, with
liberty to apply capital to the benefit of the deceased's wife. The remainder of the will
consisted of various provisions in common form relating to the powers and rights of the
trustees. By a codicil dated 27 July 1964 the testator gave his personal effects to his
children, after the death of his wife.

Nine months later Mr Berger executed the first zavah. This document, which was of *b*
some length, began with words translated as follows: 'This is concerning the division of
the estate after 120 years', the last three words being a circumlocution for the death of
Mr Berger. The first clause stated that Raymond Sun Ltd 'is not included in the Trust',
and was to pass to the same sons in the same proportions as in the English will. The
remainder of the will consisted of: (1) directions as to the disposal of companies 'in the
Trust'; (2) a direction that various relatives should take stipulated sums from those *c*
companies, with a wide discretion as to the time at which this should be done; (3) a
stipulation that certain named 'companies from the Trust' which he had given to his
daughter should belong to her 'although they, too, are in the Trust'; (4) a command that
all the heirs should give Mr Berger's wife an income of £100 per week free of tax, as a
director's fee or in some other way; (5) a declaration that the shares in certain companies
which Mr Berger had given to his son-in-law during his lifetime were his property, 'Even *d*
the 25 per cent I have therein are his'; (6) a request 'In the matter of charity: from the
value of the Trust companies . . . and from the charitable company G.B. Association Ltd.'
a certain income should be given to a brother-in-law, and that marriage settlements
should be made for his sons and daughter; (7) the expression of a wish that from moneys
'from my Charity' and 'from the Charity funds that shall remain after me' various
dispositions should be made; (8) expressions of affection, and exhortations to good *e*
conduct, directed to various relatives.

Next, on 18 December 1972 there were executed, in unknown order, an English will
and a zavah. The English will contained specific legacies of £50,000 and £15,000 to the
Gerson Berger Association Ltd and to his wife respectively. As to the residue, the trustees
were to pay the income to the wife for life, and on her death were to hold the trust fund *f*
for the children in equal shares.

The contemporaneous zavah began with the words (in translation) 'Here are some
changes in my Will'. It is clear that the words translated as 'my will' were a reference to
the zavah of 25 May 1965. Paragraph 1 stated that, since Raymond Sun Ltd now
belonged to the charitable company Gerson Berger Association Ltd (the fourth defendant),
para 1 of the former zavah was now irrelevant, as were certain of the directions that
relatives should have sums from companies in the trust, as distributions had already been *g*
made. For the rest, the provisions of the former zavah were either stated to be unchanged,
or were varied in minor respects.

Next, there was the English will of 15 July 1975. This simply contained an absolute
gift of £100,000 to Gerson Berger Association Ltd, with the residue to the testator's wife.

On 11 February 1976 he made a further zavah. In brief, this was to the following *h*
effect. 1. Certain paragraphs of the two previous zavah were cancelled, as were some of
the specific directions for payments to named persons. 2. The provision for the wife was
increased to £200 per week free of tax. 3. Various new gifts were added. It may be noted
that nothing was said in this zavah about the sources from which those responsible for
administering it were to find the additional expenditure which it entailed.

Now we arrive at the pair of documents which the deceased executed during August *j*
1977. The circumstances were found by the judge to have been as follows:

'Mr Rabin [the solicitor of Mr Berger] took instructions for the English will at
two meetings which he had with the deceased at 8 Gilda Crescent at the end of July
1977. During the course of those meetings, the deceased told Mr Rabin that he was

a
going to write to his children a "zavah" (a Jewish will) and he instructed Mr Rabin to refer to it in the English will. Mr Rabin told me, and it is, I think, common ground, that if a zavah is to be morally binding only, it need not be witnessed, but that if it is to be binding in Jewish law it must have two witnesses. Mr Rabin assumed that the deceased's zavah would be of the former kind. Otherwise he would have asked the deceased for details of what he was going to put in it and taken steps to ensure that the two wills were consistent. Mr Rabin sent the

b
engrossment of the English will to the deceased by hand at 8 Gilda Crescent in the afternoon of 5 August 1977, with a covering letter. He had not previously submitted to the deceased a draft of it. 5 August 1977 was a Friday. The Jewish sabbath began at sunset on that day and ended at sunset on the following day. A man of the deceased's religious convictions would not have taken any step to execute a will during that period. After sunset on Saturday 6 August 1977 the deceased executed

c
the Hebrew will. He did so at 8 Gilda Crescent. Why he did not execute the English will at the same time is unknown. Possibly he had not had time to read it. Undoubtedly he was not well at the time. On the following Sunday or Monday he went to stay with one of his granddaughters at Margate. Mr Pinter described him as convalescing there. It was there that on Tuesday 9th he and Mr Pinter put their signatures to the English will.'

d
As to the invalid English will this purported to revoke 'all former Wills and Codicils', so that the prior gift of £100,000 to the charitable association and the absolute gift of the residue fell away, and in substitution (a) the wife was to have an income of £10,000 free of tax, (b) the wife was to have a home for life of a value equivalent to that of the existing matrimonial home and (c) the residue was to go to the testator's four children in equal

e
shares.

Paragraph 13 of the will read as follows:

'I wish my children to know that I have immediately prior to the making of this my Will written to them a letter expressing my wishes and requirements of them in the future. I request my children to comply with my wishes and desires with all

f
the authority which I as a father am entitled to require from them as religious Jews.'

We should mention that when the English will of 1977 came to be drawn the deceased's solicitor was unaware that English wills had previously been made in 1972 and 1975. Whether the deceased had forgotten them, we do not know.

Finally, as to the last zavah, which the judge has directed shall be admitted to probate. So that the flavour of this document may be understood it is best to set it out at length,

g
omitting only the signatures and other formal parts (the translator's notes are in square brackets):

'With the help of God

To my dear sons. Shalom Zvi, may his light shine, Aharon Menachem Mendl, may his light shine, Eli' and Sarah Englander, Chaim Moshe and Devorah Feldman,

h
may they live [long]. I hereby reiterate my decision, that the division I have made some time ago, i.e., the part of my property that I apportioned to each of you, is still in force (and there, my eldest son Shalom Zvi, may his light shine, received a larger portion). But regarding the part I have not divided, which is in my own name or in that of a Company or a Charity Company, or in another manner, both Companies the shares of which belong to me alone or in which I am partner with fifty per cent

j
of the shares, or less, and the like, [these] shall be divided equally among my four sons, may they live [long], and all the other appointments I have made, either in writing or orally, are null and void, and once again, I repeat and command— invoking the commandment "honour thy father"—my son Shalom Zvi, may he live [long], to take all the steps in order to fulfil my wishes expressed in this will. I also command all the previous appointees which are not my sons, to sign all manner

of resignations and all manner of documents that you ask of them either together
or each one of you separately, and you must make any excuse in the world to fulfil
my wish and should anybody whosoever hold on to my property in contravention
of my instructions in the present will, then these are strictly forbidden to him in
this [world] as well as the next one. With regard to the Charities, I hereby command
you to distribute to all the Charities as I used to do myself, out of the income from
my portion and the balance of the income shall be for distribution among my four
sons, may they live [long]. You are not obligated to sell capital in order to distribute
to charity and the distribution to charity shall be exclusively from future income.
As I have written, my property shall be divided equally among the four of you and,
if you wish, you may separate and you have no obligation to be in partnership.
    [Signatures and Attestations]
    I reiterate and command my son Shalom Zvi, may his light shine, to appoint my
son Aharon Menachem Mendl and my two sons-in-law or daughters governors,
directors or trustees of G.B. Association Ltd and any company or Charity company
[in which] which I have a share., or a trust I set up and, as I have written above,
dismiss all the other appointees who are not my sons. My ardent wish is that all my
four sons, may they live [long] will have equal say in each company, or Charity
company or trust or association and that every resolution shall be passed unanimously
and, if that prove impossible, by majority opinion. I reiterate and stress that all the
benefits due to me in any way whatsoever, either from companies or association or
the like, be equally divided among my four sons, may they live [long], and their
families. I command you to strictly honour your mother, that is, my dear spouse,
may she live [long] and, from my share, give her "free of tax", the sum of two
hundred pounds Sterling per week, according to today's rate and, should she need
more, give her more, according to need. Additionally, she has a right to a flat for
herself either at 1–2 Warwick Court or another flat, befitting her status, without the
expense of rent. Each of my sons, may they live [long], should know that what I
have written in this will is binding on you and additional to what was written in
the English language will, and should any clarification be needed, the present will
(in the Holy Tongue) [Hebrew] is the definitive one.
    [Signature and Attestation]'.

I have described the terms of the various documents in some detail, because they
represent almost the sum total of the evidence from which the court must form an
opinion on the crucial issue of Mr Berger's intentions when executing the zavah. To my
mind, this is most unfortunate. Much guidance could have been furnished by
information on the following topics.
    1. The nature and effect of a zavah under Jewish religious law. It was agreed that a
document of this kind bearing the signatures of two witnesses is enforceable through the
religious courts, but we know nothing about the mechanisms for such enforcement, or
of the sanctions available to the tribunal. Nor again were we informed whether the
enforcement would apply to all the provisions of the document, or only to those which
were expressed as dispositive, leaving the expressions of the writer's wishes to the good
conscience of the persons who were desired to carry them out. Equally, we do not know
what, if any, steps the religious tribunal would have taken regarding those instances, of
which there are several in the successive Hebrew documents, where Mr Gerber was
expressing instructions or desires for the disposition of property which no longer
belonged to him. Information on these and other relevant aspects of Jewish law is no
doubt readily to hand, but in the absence of expert evidence or agreement we cannot
properly make any assumptions about them.
    2. It was explained to us in the course of argument that Mr Berger had made
dispositions of a substantial part of his wealth in the course of his lifetime. It is possible
to glean from a letter written by Mr Rabin to Mr Berger while in the course of taking

instructions for the failed English will that Mr Berger had created and endowed certain
a charitable companies of which the shares were held in the family, that among these
endowments were some or all of the shares in various of Mr Berger's trading companies
and that Mr Berger had made gifts to his family of holdings in his companies. More than
this we do not know. This is a pity, for it is material to any attempt to reconstruct from
the Hebrew documents themselves what Mr Berger intended when he executed them to
consider whether the dispositions which they contain related to property which it was
b already beyond his power under English law to bequeath.

3. We were informed that, in the course of the extensive and bitter family dispute
which has followed the death of Mr Berger, an issue or issues concerning the zavah was
referred to a rabbinical court in New York, but counsel were unable to state the subject
matter of the reference, or anything about its outcome.

One thing does seem to me quite clear, namely that Mr Berger cannot have caused the
c documents to be produced with the conscious intention that the current zavah should be
admitted to probate together with the current English will. On their own, the revocation
clauses in the English wills would be enough to show this. If each zavah was conceived
by the testator to be a will, he must have intended that the 1972 English will would
revoke the 1965 zavah, which is impossible, since this was treated as subsisting by the
1972 zavah, which purported to amend it. Similarly, if the 1972 English will was
d executed after the 1972 zavah (which was the order of events contemplated in 1977) it
would have revoked both the 1965 and the 1972 zavah, which was plainly not intended.
Again, the 1975 English will would have revoked the 1965 and 1972 zavah, yet the latter
part of the 1976 zavah clearly contemplates that the 1972 zavah was subsisting, and Mr
Berger cannot have intended that the 1975 English will would operate to create a gap in
the succession of zavah.

e Moreover, the contrary proposition entails that the Hebrew documents of 1965, 1972
(possibly, depending on the order of execution) and 1976 were intended to operate as
codicils to the current English wills. This is unconvincing, first because the 1976 zavah
is expressed to amend the earlier Hebrew documents, not the 1975 English will, which
it does not mention, and second because Mr Berger was a successful and experienced
businessman, who knew what to do when he wished to make a will which would be
f enforced by the English court, namely he sought the advice of an English professional
adviser, gave him instructions on what he wanted and signed the resulting document.
That Mr Berger should have intended, by creating documents of his own composition,
written in the Hebrew tongue, and quite alien in tone and content to the instruments
which his lawyer had prepared for him, to bring about a variation in the effect which the
English court would be obliged to give to his current English wills seems quite impossible
g to conceive.

To my mind there is nothing in cl 13 of the failed English will, nor in the last clause
of the 1977 zavah, to demand any opposite conclusion. The former is if anything the
other way, for it speaks only of 'a letter', and 'wishes' and 'requirements'. It is conceivable
that there was some misunderstanding between Mr Rabin and Mr Berger, and that Mr
Rabin believed that Mr Berger had in mind an unattested zavah, binding in honour only.
h But is it possible that if Mr Berger had intended to execute, contemporaneously with the
document which he was instructing Mr Rabin to prepare, a home-made document
designed to rank with Mr Rabin's document as a testamentary disposition to be enforced
by the English court he would not at least have mentioned it? Or that if he had
mentioned it, Mr Rabin would not have insisted on a sight of it, and redrawn cl 13
j accordingly? Nor again, is it possible that Mr Berger would have executed a will
containing cl 13 if it contradicted his intentions? Granted, he was a sick man at the time,
but the zavah plainly contained instructions which were close to his heart, and if cl 13
entirely misrepresented their effect, he could hardly have failed to protest.

As for the last paragraph of the 1977 zavah, I find it hard indeed to understand this as
an intimation to the English courts of probate and construction that the zavah was to be

regarded as a definitive exposition of the contemporaneous English will. It seems to me
more consistent with the notion, to which I shall return, that the zavah was to operate in *a*
the shadow of the English will.

Accordingly, if the right question is whether Mr Berger intended that the series of
zavah in general, and the last one in particular, should operate in tandem with the
current effective English language wills, as documents which were to be read in
conjunction with them as dispositions to which the English court would give effect, I
would without hesitation answer in the negative. I am not convinced however, although *b*
the point achieved no prominence in argument, that this is indeed the right question.
We are not concerned here with any attempt to enforce the current valid English will
and the 1977 zavah at the same time. For the current English will was the 1975 will, and
neither party has contended that this should be admitted to probate along with the zavah.
This is not surprising, not only because the zavah is plainly referring to the 1977 will,
and not to some other document which would have been obsolete but for the error in *c*
execution, but also because there is reason to believe that Mr Berger had forgotten, and
Mr Rabin had never known, that he had made a will in 1975.

Thus, if one is to seek out the intention of Mr Berger, the right question is this: what
did he intend to be the status of the zavah as a document to be admitted to probate, on
the unforeseen contingency that the English will was ineffectual? To this question there
is no rational answer, for in reality Mr Berger had no intention at all, since the possibility *d*
that the English will might fail obviously never crossed his mind: and if it had done, he
would have looked into the matter, and the course of events would have been different.
But, whatever intention should be imputed to him, I see no reason to suppose that he
intended a document designed to be enforced by the rabbinical tribunal, and written in
the appropriate terms, to be enforced by a court to which its terminology and social
underpinnings were entirely alien, and still less that he would have wished a linguistic *e*
and intellectual hybrid between a valid zavah and an invalid English will to be enforced
by an English court, and this is what the plaintiffs' argument entails.

So far, the discussion has concerned the intentions of Mr Berger as to the enforcement
of the zavah in the English probate registry; and the answers, as suggested, seem to be all
in the negative. But it is also right to ask whether we can infer anything about what Mr
Berger positively did intend. Here we are much impeded by the lack of information to *f*
which I have already referred. Nevertheless, I think it legitimate to infer that the zavah
were intended to operate in the shadow of the English wills, in two respects. First, the
rights created by the English wills were alone to be those recognised by the mechanisms
of English law; but the persons who were beneficiaries of these rights were to hold them
subject to a further group of rights and duties as to the manner in which they were to be
enjoyed, the enforcement of which was to be the business of the rabbinical tribunal. In *g*
this respect, there might be seen a likeness to the way in which rights enforceable
through the courts of equity shadowed those conferred by the common law, before the
two systems were merged. Second, the zavah was designed to impose on various persons
obligations in regard to the disposition of assets which they did not derive from any
English will, but from the prior bounty of the deceased. So far as these obligations were *h*
enforceable at all, the only medium of enforcement was the rabbinical tribunal.

So the position in short seems to me as follows. Mr Berger intended that the wishes
expressed in the English wills should be obeyed, and enforced by the English court. He
also intended that the wishes expressed in the zavah should be obeyed, and enforced if
necessary by the rabbinical tribunal. He had no intention about what would happen if
the English will failed. *j*

If this is a fair reconstruction of what the testator desired, how does the matter stand
in law? Not surprisingly, there is no case in point. Litigation on facts such as the present
must surely be unique. It may not be unusual (for aught we know) that the same person
executes parallel series of English will and zavah, but it seems highly improbable that
the zavah (designed to be enforced by the rabbinical court) would ever be presented for

probate in the English court in preference to the English will (designed for enforcement
a in that court) otherwise than in the exceptional circumstances of the present case.
Furthermore, modern authority in this field is in short supply. Although there were
several cases (to which we have not been referred) before the Wills Act 1837 introduced
the requirements as to signature and attestation, there have been few since then. This is
not surprising. If a document which resembles a will bears the signature and attestation
required by the Act, the presumption that it was intended to be enforced by those judicial
b mechanisms to which compliance with the Act is a condition precedent will be hard to
rebut: see per Barnard J in *Re Meynell, Meynell v Meynell* [1949] WN 273. If on the other
hand the document is not signed and attested as required, it will not be admitted to
probate unless it falls into certain confined categories, such as soldiers' wills. Accordingly,
the problems raised by the kind of informal and ambiguous documents which were
formerly the subject of dispute as to their testamentary effect will now only infrequently
c arise.

Furthermore, I believe that care should be taken not to draw too readily on general
statements in the few reported cases, given the great dissimilarity of their subject matter
to the present. In particular, all the cases were concerned with an issue whether the
instrument was intended to be a will or something else, such as an immediate gift inter
vivos, or as a document which had no legal effect at all, such as a draft or an expression of
d intent. None had occasion to address the problem of the document which was meant to
be a testamentary disposition, but not one which would be enforced by the mechanisms
of probate.

Subject to these reservations, the following propositions may be derived from the
authorities, among which I include *Lister v Smith* (1863) 3 Sw & Tr 282, 164 ER 1282,
Guardhouse v Blackburn (1866) LR 1 PD 109, [1861–73] All ER Rep 680, *Milnes v Foden*
e (1890) 15 PD 105, *Whyte v Pollok* (1882) 7 App Cas 400, *Ferguson-Davie v Ferguson-Davie*
(1890) 15 PD 109, *Re Raven, Spencer v National Association for the Prevention of Consumption
and other forms of Tuberculosis* [1915] 1 Ch 673, [1914–15] All ER Rep 353, *Godman v
Godman* [1920] P 261, *Re Wynn's Will Trusts, Public Trustee v Newborough (Baron)* [1952] 1
All ER 341, [1952] Ch 271, *Jarman on Wills* (8th edn, 1951) vol 1, pp 6, 26, 32, 37 and 50
Halsbury's Laws (4th edn) paras 201–203, 250, 376.
f (1) An instrument cannot be a 'provable will' (by which expression I mean the type of
instrument which will be admitted to probate in the English courts) unless it contains a
revocable ambulatory disposition of the maker's property which is to take effect on death.

(2) An instrument cannot be a 'provable will' unless the maker had an 'animus
testandi'.

(3) This expression does not mean that a document cannot be a 'provable will' unless
g the maker has addressed his mind to the question whether the instrument will be capable
of admission to probate in the English court, and wishes that it shall be so. Rather, it
conveys only that the maker must intend that his document shall effect the kind of
disposition referred to under item 1 above.

(4) Thus, it is possible to make a 'provable will', whatever its form or appearance or
h mode of expression and irrespective of the language in which it is written, so long as it
combines the requirements above mentioned, the necessary intention and execution as
required by the 1837 Act (if the circumstances are such as to require execution).

(5) If the document has the necessary dispositive effect, and is duly executed, the
necessary animus will be presumed. This presumption is however rebuttable, either by
other terms of the document itself, such as the statement that the document is intended
j for guidance only, or by strong extrinsic evidence.

These propositions, if correct, will serve to illuminate the source of the present
problem, for they distinguish between the (necessary) intention to make a revocable
disposition which is to operate on death and the (unnecessary) intention to make a
'provable will'. At first they seem to disclose a contradiction. Imagine a document headed
with the words, 'This is not a will and is not intended to be admitted to probate'. To hold

that it could nevertheless be proved would seem to be not only absurd, and an unjustifiable thwarting of the testator's intentions, but would also contravene the rule *a* that internal evidence can negative animus; and yet the conclusion would seem to be justified by the distinction between animus testandi and the desire to make a 'provable will'. In my judgment there is no true contradiction here, for the heading would show that the maker did not intend the document to be enforced by the probate court, and in the absence of any other mode of enforcement he would thereby have demonstrated that he did not wish his dispositions to be enforced at all, and thus took away one of the *b* essential characteristics of a will.

The present case raises a different problem, which the authorities do not appear to touch at all. What if the zavah had been headed with the words: 'I solemnly declare that I wish this document, in case of dispute, to be construed and enforced by the rabbinical tribunal, and that it shall not be admitted to probate or otherwise pronounced on by the English court.' Could the court properly grant probate of such a document? Granted *c* that there was animus testandi in the shape of an intention to make a disposition on death, still there was no intention that it should make a disposition enforceable by the only mechanisms to which such animus testandi was relevant. To my mind the court should not grant probate in such a case: a testator who has made a will but has demonstrated that he did not wish it to be a 'provable will' has not made a 'provable will'.

This proposition, even if right, is not the end of the case, for Mr Berger did not write *d* anything in his will similar to the hypothetical heading which I have discussed. Nor does the fact he never contemplated the possibility of the zavah being enforced in the English court necessarily mean that he desired, that if all else failed, it should not be so enforced. In the event, it is impossible to conceive that he intended anything at all about the unforeseen combination of circumstances which has actually come to pass. One must therefore fall back on two undeniable facts, namely (i) he made a document containing *e* directions for the disposal of his property the language of which was dispositive and (ii) it was executed in a form sufficient to render it enforceable by the English court. This being so, I am driven to the conclusion that the document does amount to a will, and should be admitted to probate. This is not a result which I view with much enthusiasm. I believe that Mr Berger would have been startled to learn that the zavah was to be administered by the English court, rather than the tribunal to whose religious and *f* cultural norms it so plainly appealed. Moreover, the court of administration to which we now remit all further consideration of this document is likely to have an unenviable task in deciding what if any effect should be given to it. On the other hand, it is reassuring that at least a part of the arrangements made by Mr Berger in the 1977 documents should survive, rather than yielding place to an outdated will whose very existence he seems to have forgotten. *g*

At all events, I conclude in respectful agreement with the reasons to be stated by Sir Denys Buckley that the appeal should be dismissed.

MANN LJ. I have had the advantage of reading in draft the judgments of Mustill LJ and Sir Denys Buckley. I agree with them. I share the regret of Mustill LJ that the court *h* was not better informed. However, I entertain no doubt but that the zavah of 6 August 1977 should be admitted to probate. Having been so admitted, its effect will have subsequently to be determined. I would hope that the determination could be achieved without recourse to further litigation. I also would dismiss this appeal.

SIR DENYS BUCKLEY. By English law the devolution and distribution of the *j* movable property of anyone who dies domiciled in England is governed by the lex domicilii of that person, that is to say by English law: *Jarman on Wills* (8th edn, 1951) vol 1, p 4. The present action has proceeded on the assumption that Mr Gerson Berger (the deceased) died domiciled in England. The pleadings are silent about this, and we have been referred to no evidence on this aspect of the matter. It appears to be common

a ground. The correct forum for decision of any question relating to the devolution of the deceased's movable property is accordingly an English court.

Jarman p 25 further stated that 'in a general and comprehensive sense, a will consists of the aggregate of all the papers through which it is dispersed'. Sir J P Wilde said in *Lemage v Goodban* (1865) LR 1 P & D 57 at 62 that a will is the aggregate of a man's testamentary intentions so far as they are manifested in writing duly executed according

b to the Wills Act 1837. So, to discover what the deceased's testamentary intentions were when he died, we must identify whatever duly executed testamentary documents were made by him and were in operation at his death.

The relevant facts have already been fully stated and I need not repeat them.

Jarman p 26 describes a document qualified to be recognised as a will or testamentary instrument in this way:

c
> 'A will is an instrument by which a person makes a disposition of his property to take effect after his decease, and which is in its own nature ambulatory and revocable during his life.'

It must be manifest that the instrument is not to operate until the testator dies and is to be revocable meanwhile.

d   It is, to my mind, perfectly clear that the deceased intended to make certain dispositions of his property by the 1977 zavah. After referring in the second paragraph to certain 'apportionments' which he had made among his sons 'some time ago' he proceeds:

> 'But regarding the part I have not divided, which is in my own name or in that of a Company or of a Charity Company, or in another manner . . . [these] shall be
e   divided equally among my four sons . . .'

I need not pause to investigate the 'apportionments . . . made some time ago'. The following passage relating to 'the part I have not divided' clearly, in my judgment, discloses an intention to make a disposition of property which he had not theretofore disposed of. This is supported by the later passage: 'As I have written, my property shall be divided equally among the four of you . . .'

f   This, in my judgment, clearly discloses some dispositive intention, to take effect at the death of the deceased. Moreover, I think that clearly the document was intended to have an ambulatory effect and (particularly having regard to the history of the series of zavahs) to be revocable and capable of modification by the deceased.

Consequently, in my judgment, the 1977 zavah has, in at least some respects, the characteristics of a testamentary instrument. No special ground for excluding the

g document from probate, such as lack of testamentary capacity, fraud or undue influence is alleged. Consequently, in my judgment, the 1977 zavah should be admitted to probate as part of the deceased's will, unless it can be established either that it was not executed in accordance with the 1837 Act or that it was written without any intention that it should have any operation and effect as a testamentary disposition, that is without animus

h testandi.

The 1977 zavah consists of two sheets, each of which the deceased signed, and each signature was attested by two witnesses. The trial judge found as a fact that the 1977 zavah was duly executed in accordance with the Act. There is no appeal against that finding. He also found as a fact that the deceased had no positive intention that the zavah should not take effect in English law. The appellant contends that that finding was

j against the weight of the evidence and inconsistent with another finding of the judge that the deceased saw his English and Hebrew wills as being in separate and parallel streams, one to be enforced in the English courts and one in the rabbinical courts. The appellant contends that the judge ought to have held that the deceased did not intend that the 1977 zavah should have any effect *in English law*. I emphasise the last three words because I shall later consider whether a testamentary document can be excluded by the testator from consideration by a court of the forum in which the devolution of his property primarily falls to be regulated.   *a*

English law does not require a document which is intended to have testamentary effect to assume any particular form or to be couched in language technically appropriate to its testamentary character. It is, says *Jarman* p 32, sufficient that the instrument, however irregular in form or artificial in expression, discloses the intention of the maker respecting the posthumous destination of his property. It may be made in any language. If it is made in a foreign language, the court must be furnished with an authenticated translation made by a qualified translator. It is that translation, not the text in the foreign language, which is admitted to probate. It is from the document so admitted to probate together with any other relevant testamentary instruments that an English court will ascertain the testator's testamentary intentions and determine their effect and validity.   *b*

The 1977 zavah as translated contains the following passage: *c*

'Each of my sons . . . should know that what I have written in this will is binding on you and additional to what was written in the English language will, and should any clarification be needed, the present will (in the Holy Tongue) [Hebrew] is the definitive one.'

This seems to me to be irreconcilable with any suggestion that that zavah was not intended to have any testamentary force. On the contrary, the deceased's signature on it was attested by two witnesses which, according to the evidence, would render its provisions judicially enforceable in a rabbinical court.   *d*

I would therefore reject any argument to the effect that the 1977 zavah was intended only to have exhortatory or advisory effect but no legal effect under any system of law.

The function in English law of a probate court is to ascertain and determine what testamentary paper or papers is or are to be regarded as constituting the last will of the testator and who is entitled to be constituted his legal personal representative. However many testamentary documents a testator may leave—   *e*

'it is the aggregate or the net result that constitutes his will, or, in other words, the expression of his testamentary wishes . . . In this sense it is inaccurate to speak of a man leaving two wills; he does leave, and can leave, but one will.'   *f*

(See *Douglas-Menzies v Umphelby* [1908] AC 224 at 233.)

Having regard to the existing distribution of business between the various divisions of the High Court, under which contentious probate business is now allocated to the Chancery Division, it is important to distinghish between the jurisdiction of a judge of that division trying a probate action from the jurisdiction of a judge of that division trying an administration action. The probate jurisdiction extends to the function referred to in the preceding paragraph. A judge exercising that jurisdiction can, of course, receive all evidence and enterain all submissions relevant to the performance of that function. He has, however, no duty to construe any of the instruments sought to be proved except so far as to do so may be necessary for the performance of that function. The probate court has no role to play in the administration of the testator's estate in accordance with whatever valid testamentary disposition the testator may have made, nor in determining how far his intended dispositions are valid. Once the identity of the deceased's testamentary papers has been determined and they have been admitted to probate, all questions of construction arising in the administration of the estate concern only the court of administration.   *g*   *h*

I have already indicated why I, for my part, consider that the 1977 zavah contains at least some testamentary dispositions which were not intended to be merely precatory.   *j*

If a testator, who at all relevant times has been domiciled in England and whose movable property accordingly falls to be distributed in accordance with English law has

made a will which, or some part of which, is in a foreign language and perhaps uses
a technical terms inappropriate to English law but appropriate to a foreign system of law,
an English court administering his estate must ascertain what the testator intended by
ordinary processes of construction, including expert evidence of the meaning and effect
of those technical terms in the relevant foreign law and possibly of how a court within
that system of foreign law would give effect to that document. The English court in the
light of all the admissible evidence will determine what the testator intended and will
b give effect to that intention so far as it is valid and effectual by English law. In so doing
the English court is applying English law and has recourse to evidence of foreign law
merely for the purpose of ascertaining the testator's intention. The English court would
not refer any question arising on the meaning or effect of the foreign document for
decision by a court in the foreign jurisdiction. This would, I think, be the case even if the
testator were to provide expressly that any such question must be decided by a court of
c the foreign jurisdiction. To hold otherwise must, I think, conflict with the English law
that the devolution and distribution of the movable property of such a testator shall be
governed by the lex domicilii.

Moreover, Warner J in his judgment drew attention to the fact that there is in the
present case no evidence, let alone clear evidence, that the deceased positively intended
that his Hebrew wills should not have effect in English law. On the contrary, as it seems
d to me, the reference in the 1977 zavah to the 1977 English will, which I have already
mentioned, is to a precisely opposite effect.

I do not myself consider that any reliable conclusion can be drawn from the
circumstances that the deceased does not seem to have appreciated that the revocation
clauses in his various English wills, or indeed the terms of subsequent zavahs, may have
affected the continuance in force of earlier zavahs or parts of them. A failure on his part
e to realise this would in my view have little or no bearing on the question whether the
deceased's intentions, when writing the 1977 zavah, were of a testamentary character. I
think that the deceased may well have believed that the zavahs, written in Hebrew and
invoking certain religious rules or concepts, would have a more solemn and compelling
effect on his children than his English wills. In this respect it is not, I think, inappropriate
f to speak of the wills and the zavahs constituting parallel streams or to describe one series
as operating in the shadow of the other. But to use terms of that kind does not, to my
mind, help to solve the problem which confronts us.

The 1977 zavah and the 1977 English will (had it been duly executed) should, in my
opinion, have been regarded as mutually incorporated in one testamentary exercise, that
is to say as together constituting the deceased's last will. If that had been the case, the
g presence in the English will of a revocation clause would not, in my judgment, have
occasioned, as has been suggested, a revocation of the 1977 zavah.

For reasons which I hope I have sufficiently explained, I am of the opinion that the
1977 zavah, which unquestionably contains some provisions which seem to relate to
matters over which the deceased had no testamentary powers of control, nevertheless
equally unquestionably contains provisions which have all the indicia of being
h testamentary dispositions of property over which he had power to dispose by will.
Consequently, in my judgment, the judge was right in holding that the 1977 zavah
should be admitted to probate. The operation and effect of such provisions of the 1977
zavah as are capable of having testamentary effect and what that effect should be are
matters for the court charged with the duty of controlling the administration of the
deceased's estate.

j The judge's order pronounced in favour of the force and validity of the 1977 zavah
incorporating therein the defectively executed English will dated 9 August 1977. In my
opinion he was justified on the facts in treating the English will as incorporated in the
zavah by virtue of the reference to the English will contained in the zavah. It is clear on
the facts and from the language used in the zavah that the English will was a document

which was in existence when the zavah was signed and so was capable of incorporation in the zavah.

For these reasons I for my part would dismiss this appeal.

Appeal dismissed.

Solicitors: *Grangewoods* (for the fourth defendant); *Pickering Kenyon* (for the plaintiffs).

Wendy Shockett Barrister.

Attorney General v Associated Newspapers Group plc and others

QUEEN'S BENCH DIVISION

MANN LJ AND HENRY J

7, 8, 26 JULY, 20 OCTOBER 1988

Contempt of court – Publications concerning legal proceedings – Court – Inferior court – Mental health review tribunal – Plaintiffs bringing proceedings for contempt – Whether mental health review tribunal a 'court' – Contempt of Court Act 1981, s 19.

The respondents, who were the editors and publishers of two newspapers published articles about a mental health patient who had been sent to a secure hospital after pleading guilty to the manslaughter of a young girl. The articles appeared shortly before a mental health review tribunal was due to hear an application for the patient's release and stated that the Home Office would be opposing his release. The articles contained interviews which were critical of the hospital director for supporting the patient's release. The tribunal hearing was subsequently adjourned part heard because of the publicity that had been aroused. The Attorney General applied for an order that the two papers were guilty of contempt of court because the articles had tended 'to interfere with the course of justice in particular legal proceedings', within s 1[a] of the Contempt of Court Act 1981. The issue arose whether the proceedings of a mental health review tribunal were proceedings before a 'court' within s 19[b] of the 1981 Act, which defined a court as including 'any tribunal or body exercising the judicial power of the State'.

Held – A mental health review tribunal was not a 'court' for the purposes of the 1981 Act and therefore an article published in a newspaper prior to or during the hearing by such a tribunal of an application by a restricted patient for release from a secure hospital was not contempt of court under s 1 of that Act. In any event, on the facts any risk of prejudice to the tribunal's proceedings but had been remote. It followed that the Attorney General's application would be dismissed (see p 611 *d* and p 612 *f g*, post).

A-G v BBC [1980] 3 All ER 161 considered.

Notes

For what constitutes a court, see 10 Halsbury's Laws (4th edn) paras 701–702, and for cases on the subject, see 16 Digest (Reissue) 136–138, 1373–1392.

For the Contempt of Court Act 1981, ss 1, 19, see 11 Halsbury's Statutes (4th edn) 181, 196.

---

a Section 1 is set out at p 607 *j*, post
b Section 19, so far as material, is set out at p 608 *f*, post

Cases referred to in judgments

a *A-G v BBC* [1980] 3 All ER 161, [1981] AC 303, [1980] 3 WLR 109, HL; *rvsg* [1979] 3 All ER 45, [1981] AC 303, [1979] 3 WLR 312, CA.

A-G v English [1982] 2 All ER 903, [1983] 1 AC 116, [1982] 3 WLR 278, HL.

A-G v Leveller Magazine Ltd [1979] 1 All ER 745, [1979] AC 440, [1979] 2 WLR 247, HL.

De Wilde v Belgium (No 1) (1971) 1 EHRR 373, E Ct HR.

F (a minor) (publication of information), Re [1977] 1 All ER 114, [1977] Fam 58, [1976] 3
b WLR 813, CA.

R v Horsham Justices, ex p Farquharson [1982] 2 All ER 269, [1982] QB 762, [1982] 2 WLR 430, CA.

R v Oxford Regional Mental Health Review Tribunal, ex p Secretary of State for the Home Dept [1986] 3 All ER 239, [1986] 1 WLR 1180, CA; *affd* [1987] 3 All ER 8, [1988] AC 120, [1987] 3 WLR 522, HL.

c *R v St Mary Abbotts, Kensington Assessment Committee* [1891] 1 QB 378.

Royal Aquarium and Summer and Winter Garden Society Ltd v Parkinson [1892] 1 QB 431, [1891–4] All ER Rep 429, CA.

Sunday Times v UK (1979) 2 EHRR 245, E Ct HR.

X v UK (1981) 4 EHRR 188, E Ct HR.

d ## Case also cited

A-G v News Group Newspapers Ltd [1986] 2 All ER 833, [1987] QB 1, CA.

Application

The Attorney General applied with leave of the Divisional Court (Watkins LJ and
e Macpherson J) on 22 January 1987 for orders of committal in respect of contempts of court allegedly committed by (i) the first respondents, the editor of the Daily Mail newspaper, Sir David English, and the owners, Associated Newspapers Group plc, in respect of an article published in the Daily Mail newspaper on 2 November 1985 under the heading 'Storm over bid to free sex killer' and (ii) the second respondents, the editor of the Liverpool Echo newspaper, Christopher John Oakley, and the owners, Trinity
f International plc, in respect of an article published in the Liverpool Echo on 2 November 1985 under the heading 'Storm over sex killer'. The facts are set out in the judgment of Mann LJ.

John Mummery for the Attorney General.
John Mathew QC, Geoffrey Shaw and *Manuel Barca* for the first respondents.
g *Brian Leveson QC* and *John Corless* for the second respondents.

Cur adv vult

26 July. Mann LJ announced that the applications would be dismissed for reasons to be given later.

h
20 October. The following judgments were delivered.

MANN LJ. Her Majesty's Attorney General by these proceedings makes application in respect of two newspapers alleging that they have been guilty of contempt of court. The proceedings are brought under the 'strict liability' rule in the Contempt of Court Act
j 1981. It is accepted that the respondents and their editors acted in good faith and that there was no intent to prejudice.

The respondents are as follows: Sir David English, who is the editor of the Daily Mail; Associated Newspapers Group plc, which is the proprietor and publisher of the Daily Mail; Christopher John Oakley, who is the editor of the Liverpool Echo; and Trinity International plc, which is the proprietor and publisher of the Liverpool Echo.

In order to understand the way in which these proceedings have come to pass it is
necessary to recite a chronology. On 7 December 1972 Peter Pickering pleaded guilty to   *a*
the manslaughter of a young girl. He was sent to a secure hospital by means of an order
under s 60 of the Mental Heath Act 1959 and he was the subject of a restriction order
without limit of time made under s 65 of that Act. Those orders subsequently have effect
as if made under ss 37 and 41 of the Mental Health Act 1983. In December 1984
Pickering applied for his discharge. On 23 August 1985 a hearing date before a mental
health review tribunal was fixed. On 2 November 1985 there appeared the articles of   *b*
which complaint is now made. The hearing occurred on 11 November but on the second
day was adjourned part heard because of the publicity which the proceedings had
attracted. The proceedings were recommenced on 24 March 1986 and concluded on 26
March. The result was that Pickering was not discharged. On 27 January 1987 the
motions now before the court were initiated.

The articles of which complaint is made were both published on 2 November 1985.   *c*
They were respectively in the following terms. First, the Daily Mail:

'Ministers are battling to prevent a child killer being freed from a security
hospital, because they believe he is still dangerous. They are horrified at the
willingness of the hospital's chief, Dr Malcolm MacCulloch, to back rapist Peter
Pickering in his bid for release later this month. Pickering, 48, was convicted in   *d*
1972 of the brutal killing of a 14-year-old schoolgirl. He was sent to Broadmoor but
was transferred four years ago to Park Lane Hospital, Liverpool, "the Broadmoor of
the North" where Dr MacCulloch is medical director. Now Pickering will plead for
his freedom before a mental health review tribunal on November 11 and 12.

Confession

Dr MacCulloch, whose opinion is likely to be a key factor at the hearing, is   *e*
pushing for his release. But Home Office Ministers and MPs are determined to resist
the move. Some Tory MPs are also expected to call for the removal of Dr MacCulloch,
who became nationally known in 1981 during the trial of the Yorkshire Ripper,
Peter Sutcliffe. He decided Sutcliffe was mad within an hour of meeting him and
diagnosed the mass murderer as a paranoid schizophrenic without reading evidence   *f*
of what he had done or his voluntary confession to police. He argued that Sutcliffe
was unfit to plead. Ministers are now alarmed that Dr MacCulloch appears to be
more ready than Broadmoor's director, Dr John Hamilton, to believe that patients,
particularly sexual psychopaths, have made sufficient progress either to be released
from top security confinement or to be released into the community at large. One
Minister has been heard to say: "Pickering's release would terrify me." During his   *g*
trial, Pickering was said to have committed "sub-human acts" on his victim,
schoolgirl Shirley Ann Boldy. He grabbed her near her home in Barnsley, South
Yorkshire, raped her and held her prisoner in his car before finally stabbing her.
Five months earlier, he had come out of prison after a nine-year sentence for
indecency and assaulting a woman. He had spent a total of 15 years behind bars for
attacks on teenage girls. Ministers say there are too many warnings in the case files   *h*
about the potential risk to the public of releasing a man with his history. The Home
Office believes that had Pickering remained at Broadmoor—with its longer
experience of treating such cases—there would have been no question of him yet
being released into the community. Only six months ago another Park Lane inmate,
a convicted child killer, won a conditional discharge. He had been detained there
and in Broadmoor (from where he once escaped in 1981) as a restricted patient. He   *j*
is now accused of assault and unlawful wounding in two attacks on young women,
according to Home Office Under Secretary David Mellor who told MPs last week
that he and then Home Secretary Leon Brittan took a very serious view of the case
and had opposed the man's release in April. Dr MacCulloch last night admitted he
was "extremely anxious" about Pickering's release tribunal, following the arrest of

a the other man. "But if I am going to perform as a straightforward doctor, I am bound to give my professional opinion," he said. "I am not expected to get it right. I am expected to act competently." He refused to say if he would back Pickering's bid. At one time, the Home Secretary made the decision on any release. But Britain was forced to change its law following a ruling by the European Court of Human Rights, which said that some patients detained indefinitely were being denied their rights. Patients can now apply for a discharge every 12 months to a tribunal. The

b parents of Pickering's victim, Norman and Edna Boldy, have lived with the constant nightmare that he would be released. Mr Boldy, 58, who is a homeless families officer with Barnsley Council, said: "I find it horrific that this man could ever be let out." He and his wife, also 58, live quietly in Wood Walk, Wombwell, where they cannot bear to have pictures of their dead daughter in the room. The mother of the girl killed by the patient who was freed in April demanded to talk to Dr MacCulloch

c after learning of the man's release. By her side at the meeting in a police station, close to the spot where her daughter's body was found, was the patient's ex-wife. Together they quizzed Dr MacCulloch and warned him—despite his assurances— that the man was still dangerous and would strike again. The mother said yesterday: "Dr MacCulloch told us, 'I think we have got through to him—he will never ever do it again.'" Just six weeks later the man was arrested and charged with assault and

d wounding. The mother said: "Dr MacCulloch was sure that the man was totally cured and we did not understand him. He said he had made a good friend of the man and had gained his confidence. I told Dr MacCulloch: 'You are mistaken. You are wrong'." Clutching a colour photograph of her dead daughter, the woman described how the killer's ex-wife was terrified when he arrived at her home to speak to their teenage son after being released. "I feel disgusted this man was let out.

e After what happened to my daughter they promised me he would never be freed."'

Second, the Liverpool Echo:

'The Home Office pledged today to fight moves by Park Lane top security hospital to free a child killer. Ministers are furious at chiefs at the Maghull psychiatric hospital for trying to release rapist Paul Pickering, who was convicted in 1972 for

f the horrific killing of a 14-years-old girl. And some MPs may call for the sacking of Park Lane director Dr. Malcolm MacCulloch. One minister is reported to have told officials he would be "terrified" by Pickering's release. The Home Secretary no longer has the power to detain prisoners like Pickering. The issue will be decided by a mental health review tribunal on November 11–12, which will hear evidence from hospital chiefs and a barrister briefed by the Home Office. A Home Office

g spokesman said today: "We will continue to oppose the question of his release vigorously because we do not feel that he is fit for release into the community. We are concerned about the safety of the public." The row comes only four days after MPs were told that another killer who won his release from Park Lane in March— against Home Office advice—had now been charged following two attacks on

h young women. Pickering (48), was said at his trial to have committed "sub-human acts" on schoolgirl Shirley Ann Boldy from South Yorkshire, who was raped and held prisoner in his car before being stabbed. He had been released from prison five months earlier after a nine-year sentence for indecency and assaulting a woman, and had spent a total of 15 years in jail. Barnsley East Labour MP Terry Patchett, whose constituents include the dead girl's parents, said local people still remembered the

j terrible crime and would be horrified at his proposed release.'

The relevant provisions of the 1981 Act are as follows:

'**I.** *The strict liability rule.* In this Act "the strict liability rule" means the rule of law whereby conduct may be treated as a contempt of court as tending to interfere with the course of justice in particular legal proceedings regardless of intent to do so.

2. *Limitation of scope of strict liability.*—(1) The strict liability rule applies only in relation to publications, and for this purpose "publication" includes any speech, writing, broadcast or other communication in whatever form, which is addressed to the public at large or any section of the public.

(2) The strict liability rule applies only to a publication which creates a substantial risk that the course of justice in the proceedings in question will be seriously impeded or prejudiced.

(3) The strict liability rule applies to a publication only if the proceedings in question are active within the meaning of this section at the time of the publication.

(4) Schedule 1 applies for determining the times at which proceedings are to be treated as active within the meaning of this section.

3. *Defence of innocent publication or distribution.*—(1) A person is not guilty of contempt of court under the strict liability rule as the publisher of any matter to which that rule applies if at the time of publication (having taken all reasonable care) he does not know and has no reason to suspect that relevant proceedings are active.

(2) A person is not guilty of contempt of court under the strict liability rule as the distributor of a publication containing any such matter if at the time of distribution (having taken all reasonable care) he does not know that it contains such matter and has no reason to suspect that it is likely to do so.

(3) The burden of proof of any fact tending to establish a defence afforded by this section to any person lies upon that person . . .

5. *Discussion of public affairs.* A publication made as or as part of a discussion in good faith of public affairs or other matters of general public interest is not to be treated as a contempt of court under the strict liability rule if the risk of impediment or prejudice to particular legal proceedings is merely incidental to the discussion.

6. *Savings.* Nothing in the foregoing provisions of this Act . . . (b) implies that any publication is punishable as contempt of court under that rule which would not be so punishable apart from those provisions . . .

19. *Interpretation.* In this Act . . . "court" includes any tribunal or body exercising the judicial power of the State, and "legal proceedings" shall be construed accordingly . . .'

It may be observed that the draftsman of s 19 borrowed language used by Lord Fraser and Lord Scarman in *A-G v BBC* [1980] 3 All ER 161 at 177, 181, [1981] AC 303 at 353, 359.

It was common ground that the publication of the two newspaper articles were publications within s 2(1) of the Act. It was also common ground that proceedings were active at the time of publication (see s 2(3) of the Act). Once the common ground is left two questions were agitated before the court. First, is a mental health review tribunal a court for the purposes of the Act? If Yes, was there a substantial risk of prejudice? Third, in the Liverpool case there was discussed, but mutedly, the question of a defence under s 5.

In resolving the first question it is necessary to look at the history of mental health review tribunals. They were established under the Mental Health Act 1959. They had power to discharge certain categories of patient but they had no power to discharge a patient who was subject to a s 60 order and a restriction order under s 65 of the Act. In regard to such a patient they had an advisory function and a power of recommendation (see ss 65(3)(b) and 66(2)). It was conceded by the Attorney General if concession was necessary, that in discharging their advisory and recommendatory functions they were exercising an administrative function. The decision in regard to the discharge of a s 60 patient who was subject to a s 65 restriction order was for the Secretary of State. His act was essentially an executive act (see *R v Oxford Regional Mental Health Review Tribunal, ex p Secretary of State for the Home Dept* [1986] 3 All ER 239 at 244, [1986] 1 WLR 1180 at 1185). The legislative structure in so far as it related to patients subject to a restriction

order was criticised in *X v UK* (1981) 4 EHRR 188 at 207 as being contrary to art 5(4) of
a the Convention for the Protection of Human Rights and Fundamental Freedoms (Rome,
4 November 1950; TS 71 (1953); Cmd 8969). Article 5(4) provides:

'Everyone who is deprived of his liberty by arrest or detention shall be entitled to
take proceedings by which the lawfulness of his detention shall be decided speedily
by a court and his release ordered if his detention is not lawful.'

b In their judgment the court said:

'53. It is not within the province of the Court to enquire into what would be the
best or most appropriate system of judicial review in this sphere, for the Contracting
States are free to choose different methods of performing their obligations. Thus, in
Article 5(4) the word "court" is not necessarily to be understood as signifying a court
c of law of the classic kind, integrated within the standard judicial machinery of the
country. This term, as employed in several Articles of the Convention (including
Art. 5(4)), serves to denote—"bodies which exhibit not only common fundamental
features, of which the most important is independence of the executive and of the
parties to the case, but also the guarantees ('appropriate to the kind of deprivation of
liberty in question') of [a] judicial procedure", the forms of which may vary from
d one domain to another.'

(The words quoted in the above extract come from *De Wilde v Belgium (No 1)* (1971) 1
EHRR 373 at 408, 407 (paras 78, 76).)

It appears to me that the court was requiring some tribunal independent of the
executive. It does not seem to me that it was requiring a court in the strict sense of the
e term whatever that strict sense may be. There is however in my mind no doubt that the
decision of the European Court of Human Rights led to legislative changes which are
now embodied in the 1983 Act. Under that Act a restricted patient has a right of access
to a mental health review tribunal every 12 months. The tribunal has power to direct
absolute or conditional discharges (see ss 70 and 73). The giving of the direction as to the
discharge of any form is however subject to the tribunal being satisfied of the existence
f of certain criteria. I need not recite them for nothing turns on them.

There is no previous authority on whether a mental health review tribunal is a court
for the purposes of proceedings for contempt. The textbook writers are not in agreement.
Thus Arlidge and Ealy *Law of Contempt* (1982) p 293 suggests that it would be difficult to
classify the activities of a mental health tribunal as an administrative activity; however,
Borrie and Lowe *Law of Contempt* (2nd edn, 1983) p 336 submits that a mental health
g review tribunal does not satisfy the term 'court of law'. I approach the question on the
basis of caution. Such caution seems to me to be justified by reference to passages in the
speeches in *A-G v BBC*. Lord Salmon said ([1980] 3 All ER 161 at 168–169, [1981] AC 303
at 342):

'I agree, for the reasons given by counsel for the Attorney General, which I need
h not repeat, that a local valuation court has some of the attributes of the long-
established "inferior courts". There is today a plethora of such tribunals which may
well resemble the old "inferior courts". In my view, it does not by any means follow
that the modern inferior courts need the umbrella of contempt of court or that they
come under it. Indeed, in my opinion, public policy requires that most of the
principles relating to contempt of court which have for ages necessarily applied to
j the long-established inferior courts such as county courts, magistrates' courts, courts-
martial, coroners' courts and consistory courts shall not apply to valuation courts
and the host of other modern tribunals which may be regarded as inferior courts;
otherwise the scope of contempt of court would be unnecessarily extended and
accordingly freedom of speech and freedom of the press would be unnecessarily
contracted.'

Lord Edmund-Davies said ([1980] 3 All ER 161 at 172, [1981] AC 303 at 346):

> 'Equal clarity and certainty should prevail in relation to the question of *jurisdiction*   *a*
> to commit for contempt. It is unacceptable to leave it to the Attorney General
> ultimately to decide when and where contempt proceedings will lie for, as Sir
> Stanley Rees pertinently observed in the Court of Appeal ([1979] 3 All ER 45 at 57,
> [1981] AC 303 at 318): "... it is ... vital to ensure that freedom of expression in the
> press and in broadcasting should not be unwarrantably fettered. *It is equally important*
> *that the press and the broadcasting authorities should be able to know in advance what*   *b*
> *tribunals are inferior courts within the ambit of RSC Ord 52, r 1.*"' (Lord Edmund-
> Davies's emphasis.)

Lord Fraser said ([1980] 3 All ER 161 at 177, [1981] AC 303 at 353):

> 'Uncertainty is a serious objection because of the large number of tribunals set up   *c*
> by modern legislation, many of which might be on the borderline. It is undesirable
> that anyone intending to publish information in the newspapers or on radio or
> television relating to proceedings pending before a tribunal should have to examine
> in detail the functions and constitution of the tribunal in order to ascertain whether
> it is protected by the law against contempt.'

Lord Scarman said ([1980] 3 All ER 161 at 183, [1981] AC 303 at 362):   *d*

> 'Neither the meagre authorities available in the books nor the historical origins of
> contempt of court require the House to extend the doctrine to administrative courts
> and tribunals. Legal policy in today's world would be better served, in my judgment,
> if we refused so to extend it. If Parliament wishes to extend the doctrine to a specific
> institution which it establishes, it must say so explicitly in its enactment, as it has   *e*
> done on occasion, eg the Tribunals of Inquiry (Evidence) Act 1921. I would not
> think it desirable to extend the doctrine, which is unknown, and not apparently
> needed, in most civilised legal systems, beyond its historical scope, namely the
> proceedings of courts of judicature. If we are to make the extension, we have to ask
> ourselves, if the United Kingdom is to comply with its international obligations,
> whether the extension is necessary in our democratic society. Is there "a pressing   *f*
> social need" for the extension? For that, according to the European Court of Human
> Rights see *Sunday Times v United Kingdom* (1979) 2 EHRR 245 at 275. It has not been
> demonstrated to me that there is.'

It is axiomatic that a mental health review tribunal must act judicially in the discharge
of its functions otherwise it will be exposed to an application for judicial review. That
exposure is not however in any way indicative of whether the tribunal is a 'court'.   *g*
Viscount Dilhorne said in *A-G v BBC* ([1980] 3 All ER 161 at 167, [1981] AC 303 at 339–
340):

> 'I do not think that the Divisional Court's jurisdiction extends to all courts created
> by the state, for I think that a distinction has to be drawn between courts which   *h*
> discharge judicial functions and those which discharge administrative ones, between
> courts of law which form part of the judicial system of the country on the one hand
> and courts which are constituted to resolve problems which arise in the course of
> administration of the government of this country. In my opinion a local valuation
> court comes within the latter category. It discharges functions formerly performed
> by assessment committees. It has to resolve disputes as to the valuation of   *j*
> hereditaments. While its decisions will affect an occupier's liability for rates, it does
> not determine his liability. It is just part of the process of rating. It has to act
> judicially but that does not make it a court of law. The fact that it has to act judicially
> means, as Fry LJ said in *Royal Aquarium and Summer and Winter Garden Society Ltd v*
> *Parkinson* [1892] 1 QB 431 at 447, [1891–4] All ER Rep 429 at 434, that its

a proceedings must be "conducted with the fairness and impartiality which characterise proceedings in Courts of justice, and are proper to the functions of a judge" and not, though established by law, that it is a court of law and part of the judicial system of the country. In *R v St Mary Abbotts, Kensington Assessment Committee* [1891] 1 QB 378 Lord Esher MR said that an assessment committee was not a court or tribunal exercising judicial functions in the legal acceptation of the term. A local valuation court, as I have said, discharges the same functions as an assessment committee did

b and they have not changed their character. I hold that such a court's functions are administrative, not judicial. No case was cited to us of the law of contempt being applied to tribunals or courts discharging, albeit judicially, administrative functions and I for my part am not prepared to extend the law by applying it to such tribunals or courts.'

c Something of this passage is applicable here. In regard to restricted patients the mental health review tribunals are inheritors of an executive function and on a 12 monthly basis review a patient's position against specified criteria. Counsel for the Attorney General said that the tribunals deal with the liberty of the subject. However, the tribunals cannot deprive a person of liberty and a refusal to discharge is not final. The case is reviewable within a 12 month. Those seem to me to be powerful counter-indications against the

d suggestion that the tribunals are dealing with the liberty of the subject.

Bearing in mind the caution which the House of Lords has admonished the Divisional Court to observe (ie, in *A-G v BBC*), I have come to the conclusion that a mental health tribunal is not a 'court' for the purposes of the 1981 Act. For that self-sufficient reason these applications fail.

I must mention that there was much discussion about s 6(*b*) of the Act. Of the

e forerunner of that provision, s 12(4) of the Administration of Justice Act 1960, Scarman LJ in *Re F (a minor) (publication of information)* [1977] 1 All ER 114 at 131, [1977] Fam 58 at 99 said:

'... I think it likely that the subsection was enacted to ensure that no one would in future be found guilty of contempt who would not also under the pre-existing law have been found guilty. Certainly such a construction is consistent with the

f law's basic concern to protect freedom of speech and individual liberty ...'

That observation was indorsed by Lord Edmund-Davies in *A-G v Leveller Magazine Ltd* [1979] 1 All ER 745 at 761, [1979] AC 440 at 465 and by Lord Denning MR in *R v Horsham Justices, ex p Farquharson* [1982] 2 All ER 269 at 285, [1982] QB 762 at 791. Those observations are of course binding on me but I do not think they would have

g bitten in the present case had I taken a different view as to 'court'. It would not have been the 'foregoing provisions' which would have caused difficulty but it would have been the provisions of the 1983 Act conferring the new power on the mental health review tribunals.

Should I be wrong on the question of 'court' I must deal with the issue of 'substantial risk' under s 2(2). There was no dispute on the law. The court has to assess the risk created

h at the time when publication occurred and the risk which is only remote is alone to be excluded (see *A-G v English* [1982] 2 All ER 903 at 918–919, [1983] 1 AC 116 at 141).

No complaint was made by counsel appearing on behalf of Pickering before the tribunal about either the Daily Mail or the Liverpool Echo articles. The Liverpool Echo article was not mentioned throughout the hearing before the tribunal. The Daily Mail article was referred to once when Dr MacCulloch said: 'Reports in the Daily Mail compare

j me unfavourably with the medical director of Broadmoor Hospital, Dr John Hamilton and also similar other echoes have appeared in other papers.' True it was that the chairman of the tribunal, her Honour Judge Ebsworth, said:

'This case has been severely hampered by ill-informed media comment before and during its hearing. The coverage persisted after the tribunal had drawn attention

to the private nature of the proceedings. The content and persistence of the coverage
was calculated to put unreasonable pressure on the parties and the witnesses. It *a*
obviously and unfairly affected the RMO [regional medical officer] and placed
unnecessary strain on the patient.'

I do not know to what publication these remarks were addressed. It is however pertinent
to observe that there was discussion at the hearing about an article in the Guardian which
appeared on the second day of the hearing under the heading 'DHSS launches inquiry on
release of psychopaths'.   *b*

To what is it that the Attorney General wishes to draw the court's attention? In the
case of the Daily Mail it is the following:

'Dr MacCulloch, whose opinion is likely to be a key factor at the hearing, is
pushing for his [the patient's] release. But Home Office Ministers and MPs are
determined to resist the move. Some Tory MPs are also expected to call for the *c*
removal of Dr MacCulloch, who become nationally known in 1981 during the trial
of the Yorkshire Ripper . . .'

In the case of the Liverpool Echo it is this passage:

'Ministers are furious at chiefs at the Maghull psychiatric hospital for trying to
release rapist Paul Pickering . . . And some MPs may call for the sacking of Park *d*
Lane director Dr. Malcolm MacCulloch.'

I would not for one moment wish to encourage assaults on expert witnesses but Dr
MacCulloch is well used to controversy and cannot have been innocent of the attitude of
the Home Office and of members of Parliament. I think it unnecessary to rehearse in
detail the controversial activities of Dr MacCulloch but I should say that on 4 July 1985 *e*
Mr Mellor on behalf of the Secretary of State for the Home Department said in Parliament
that the Secretary of State 'continues to take the firm view that Mr Pickering is not fit for
release into the community'.

In my judgment, no suggestion of impact on the tribunal having been made, the risk
of prejudice by any effect on Dr MacCulloch is remote.

There remains s 5 in regard to the Liverpool Echo. The onus is on the Attorney *f*
General to show that the defence does not apply (see *A-G v English* [1982] 2 All ER 903 at
918, [1983] 1 AC 116 at 141). I think in the present case the Attorney General has
discharged the burden on him. The discussion in the Liverpool Echo seems to me to be
limited to the instant case and not to be a discussion of a matter of general public interest.

For the reasons which I have given I would dismiss these applications.

        g

HENRY J. I agree.

Applications dismissed.

*28 October. The court refused leave to appeal to the House of Lords but certified, under s 1(2) of
the Administration of Justice Act 1960, that the following point of law of general public importance* *h*
*was involved in the decision: Whether a mental health review tribunal is a 'tribunal . . . exercising
the judicial power of the State' and is therefore a court for the purposes of the Contempt of Court
Act 1981.'*

Solicitors: *Crown Prosecution Service*; *Swepstone Walsh & Son* (for the first respondents);
Lace Mawer, Liverpool (for the second respondents).   *j*

                                                Dilys Tausz   Barrister.

a
Richco International Ltd v International Industrial Food Co SAL
The Fayrouz III

b QUEEN'S BENCH DIVISION (COMMERCIAL COURT)
HIRST J
22, 23 JUNE, 4 JULY 1988

Arbitration – Practice – Securing amount in dispute – Failure to comply with order to bring amount in dispute into court – Jurisdiction of High Court to stay arbitration proceedings for
c *failure to comply with order – Whether court should stay further proceedings of arbitration – Arbitration Act 1950, s 12(6)(f) – RSC Ord 29, r 2.*

The plaintiff sellers sold 25,000 tonnes of wheat for Denmark or Germany, destination Syrian ports, for \$US2,342,896 on a GAFTA 64 contract which included normal GAFTA arbitration terms. Shortly after loading, the buyers rejected the cargo on the grounds of
d sub-standard quality and notified the sellers that the cargo would be kept at the sellers' disposal when the vessel arrived in Syria. The sellers denied the default but when they presented the sale documents to the buyers' bank they were rejected. The buyers notified the sellers that the sub-buyers, a Syrian state purchasing agency, had also rejected the cargo on the grounds of quality. The buyers sought to have the dispute referred to arbitration but before the arbitration commenced the buyers, without the sellers'
e knowledge, received payment from the sub-buyers for the wheat, less a discount for the lower quality, and the wheat was off-loaded at a Syrian port while the sellers continued to assert title to it. On an application by the sellers the judge ordered the buyers to pay into court the sum of \$US1,820,000. The buyers did not comply with the order and the sellers applied for an order that in default of paying the sum into court the sellers be
f debarred from contesting the arbitration.

Held – The court had power under s 12(6)(f)[a] of the Arbitration Act 1950 to secure the amount in dispute in an arbitration and under RSC Ord 29, r 2[b] could exercise that power by ordering a party to pay the amount in dispute into court on terms, and if that party failed to comply with such an order the court could order a permanent stay of his claims
g in the arbitration thereby debarring him from pursuing or defending his claims. Since on the facts the sellers had a virtually irrefutable case that the buyers had sold goods which remained the property of the sellers and had retained the proceeds and since the buyers had failed to pay the net proceeds into court as ordered, the court would order that the buyers be debarred from defending the sellers' claims in the arbitration unless they complied with the order for payment into court within four weeks (see p 618 f g,
h p 619 c to e h j and p 620 d e, post).
   Dorval Tankers Pty Ltd v Two Arrows Maritime and Port Services Ltd, The Argenpuma [1984] 2 Lloyd's Rep 563 applied.

Notes
j For the court's powers to secure amounts in dispute in a reference to arbitration, see 2 Halsbury's Laws (4th edn) para 595.
   For the Arbitration Act 1950, s 12, see 2 Halsbury's Statutes (4th edn) 547.

a   Section 12(6), so far as material, is set out at p 616 j to p 617 b, post
b   Rule 2, so far as material, is set out at p 617 d e, post

Cases referred to in judgment

Bremer Vulkan Schiffbau Und Maschinenfabrik v South India Shipping Corp [1981] 1 All ER *a*
    289, [1981] AC 909, [1981] 2 WLR 141, HL.
Dorval Tankers Pty Ltd v Two Arrows Maritime and Port Services Ltd, The Argenpuma [1984]
    2 Lloyd's Rep 563, CA.
Golden Trader, The, Danemar Scheepvaart Maatschappij BV v Golden Trader (owners) [1974]
    2 All ER 686, [1975] QB 348, [1974] 3 WLR 16.
Paal Wilson & Co A/S v Partenreederei Hannah Blumenthal, The Hannah Blumenthal [1983] 1 *b*
    All ER 34, [1983] 1 AC 854, [1982] 3 WLR 1149, HL.

Application

The plaintiffs, Richco International Ltd, a corporation with limited liability under the
law of Bermuda (the sellers), applied for an order that the defendants, International
Industrial Food Co SAL, a corporation established under the law of the Republic of *c*
Lebanon (the buyers), be debarred from defending the sellers' claim in an arbitration
between the parties in which the sellers were the respondents and the buyers were the
claimants, on the grounds that the buyers had failed to comply with an order made by
Hirst J on 25 May 1988 requiring them to pay into court within 14 days $US1,820,000,
being the fund in dispute in the arbitration, in default of which all of the buyers' claims
in the arbitration were to be stayed. The application was heard in chambers but judgment *d*
was given by Hirst J in open court. The facts are set out in the judgment.

L J West-Knights for the sellers.
Nigel Meeson for the buyers.

Cur adv vult *e*

4 July. The following judgment was delivered.

HIRST J.

Introduction *f*

    This case raises the question, on which there seems to be no decided authority, as to
the powers of the court to make an effective order to secure by payment into court a
specific fund of money where the right to that fund is in dispute in a pending arbitration.
I am giving this judgment in open court in response to a strong request by counsel for
the plaintiffs, Richco International Ltd (the sellers), who are the claimants for present
purposes in the arbitration. *g*
    This was not opposed by counsel for the defendants, International Industrial Food Co
SAL (the buyers), though he invited me to avoid naming the parties: such anonymity is
inconvenient, and in my view unnecessary in the present case.

Factual outline *h*

    By a contract on GAFTA 64 terms, including normal GAFTA arbitration, the sellers
sold to the buyers 25,000 tonnes of wheat fob Denmark or Germany, payment against
documents, destination Syrian ports, for a total price of $US2,342,896. A vessel called the
Fayrouz III was nominated, and loaded the cargo partly at Emden and partly at
Nordenham, completing the latter loading on 29 March 1988. There was then a dispute
as to the certification of quality and on 31 March the buyers rejected the cargo and *j*
confirmed such rejection by telex a week later stating they were holding the cargo at the
sellers' disposal, and that the vessel was proceeding to Tartous in Syria where the goods
would be kept at the sellers' disposal. The sellers' denied the default, and notified the
vessel that the cargo was still their property. Meantime the buyers notified the sellers
that their sub-buyers, a Syrian state purchasing body called l'Organisme Générale pour la

Commercialisation et l'Industrialisation des Céréales (OGCIC), had also rejected the
a goods. The vessel by this time was anchored off Crete. On 12 April the sellers presented
the documents to the buyers' bank, Union des Banques Arabes et Françaises (UBAF) at
Neuilly in France. These were rejected on the ground of a number of alleged documentary
defects. Avoiding all unnecessary detail, the essence of the buyers and sub-buyers'
complaint concerning the goods was that the 'falling number' was too low, showing too
high a proportion of germinated grains, and the essence of the complaint about the
b documents was that the attached certificates failed in numerous respects to comply with
the contractual requirements.

On 21 April the buyers and the sellers met in Paris and tried to thrash out their
difficulties. In the course of that meeting the buyers proposed a compromise which the
sellers rejected, insisting on strict compliance with the contractual terms of which they
denied any breach. On 25 April the buyers claimed arbitration and nominated a GAFTA
c arbitrator. Telex correspondence meantime continued in which each side maintained
their position, until on 28 April the sellers' Dutch lawyers offered a compromise on the
same lines as that put forward by the buyers in Paris a week earlier, while explicitly
maintaining their claim that they were still the owners of the cargo. This offer was not
accepted by the buyers, who in a series of telexes promised to revert with a detailed offer
from their side which was never forthcoming. (I mention these details because in the
d buyers' evidence it is suggested that the sellers' compromise offer on 28 April amounted
to a belated acceptance of the buyers' oral offer at the meeting in Paris a week earlier; but,
on the proper construction of this telex correspondence as a whole, such an interpretation
is completely unarguable, and indeed was not supported in argument by counsel for the
buyers.)

At about this juncture an extraordinary sequence of events ensued. On 25 April the
e buyers presented documents to OGCIC's bank in Syria, the Banque Centrale de Syrie, and
the following day UBAF notified the Syrian bank that in accordance with their
instructions they were debiting their current account with the sub-purchase price, and
had paid the buyers against presentation of the relevant documents. The exact date of
payment is unclear, but on the buyers' own evidence it was not later than 2 May. All this
f was completely unbeknown to the sellers, who were meantime maintaining their claim
to the title in the goods and attempting to forestall any discharge from the vessel. The
amount of this payment from the sub-buyers to the buyers was $US3,024,783 which, on
the buyers' own evidence, allowed for a discount on the sub-purchase contract price of
$20 per tonne to make allowance for the alleged quality defects which had been the
subject of complaint. The sub-contract purchase price was on a cif basis, and on the
g buyers' evidence the insurance and freight element amounted to a little short of $1m so
that, in round figures, the strict sub-purchase price amounted to about $2m.

On 6 May Leggatt J granted the sellers an ex parte order restraining the buyers from
instructing the vessel to enter Tartous. However, on the following day the vessel was
placed under restraint by the Syrian authorities. This came to the knowledge of the
sellers (who still did not know about the payment by the sub-buyers to the buyers of the
h sub-purchase price) and on 10 May the sellers sought confirmation from the buyers that
the cargo still belonged to the sellers. On 16 May a court in Syria ordered the vessel to
discharge, and on the following day discharge began in Tartous under the supervision of
armed Syrian officers. Discharge was finally completed on 24 May.

On 25 May the matter came before me on an inter partes summons, and I made an
order containing, inter alia, the following requirement:

j   'That the [buyers] do bring into Court within 14 days of the date hereof the sum
of US $1,820,000 being a fund in dispute between the parties in default of which all
of the [buyers'] claims in the arbitration between the parties do be stayed.'

The jurisdiction on which that order was based is the same as that relied on by the sellers
at the present hearing as described below. I refused leave to appeal and no attempt was

made by the buyers to make any necessary application to the Court of Appeal within the prescribed time limits. However the order has not been complied with.

The sellers' claim in the arbitration

The essence of the sellers' claim in the arbitration, in which of course they are for present purposes the effective claimants though technically respondents, is that the goods have at all times remained their property, both the goods and the documents having been rejected by the buyers, and that such rejection remains effective to this day, there having been no subsequent agreement by way of compromise or otherwise which could result in a transfer of the property in the goods from the sellers to the buyers. It is the sellers' contention that these goods are now represented by the purchase price paid by the Syrian sub-buyers to the buyers. Their principal claim in the arbitration is that the buyers sold to the sub-buyers as (in effect) self-appointed agents of the sellers and therefore owe the sellers the fiduciary duty to account for and pay over to the sellers the proceeds of the sale, less freight and insurance, and that such proceeds constitute a specific fund. The claim is also framed on a number of alternative bases, including a claim for the purchase price, but those other formulations are immaterial for present purposes.

Counsel for the buyers expressly concedes that for present purposes this purchase price received by the buyers from the sub-buyers does constitute a specific fund, and I do not therefore need to evaluate a piece of affidavit evidence from the buyers' commercial manager in Syria, Mr Daniel Fernandez-Diaz, that the money received has been spent to reimburse the bank, though I should have in any event found great difficulty in giving that evidence any weight since, notwithstanding his pivotal position on behalf of the buyers, it is given on no better basis than secondhand information.

Other contractual disputes

There are a number of other contracts for the sale of wheat between the sellers and the buyers which have also given rise to disputes, with assertions and counter-assertions of numerous breaches by each side against the other which I need not recite. All these are GAFTA contracts, and in each case separately the buyers have instituted a GAFTA arbitration. There is also pending litigation between the sellers and the buyers' French bankers in the Commercial Court in Nanterre in France concerning a claim under a performance bond.

In their evidence the buyers seek to rely on their various claims under these other contracts as validly constituting potential set-offs in the present arbitration. Let me say at once that I regard this as a completely untenable proposition. Each of these GAFTA arbitrations is contractually separate from each other, as indeed are the contracts themselves, and no claim in one of them can in my judgment possibly constitute a valid set-off against an opposite claim in another. I shall therefore entirely disregard in the present context all the pending claims in the other arbitrations under the other contracts.

The sellers' claim in the present summons

The sellers now seek an extension of the order which I made on 25 May, to provide that, in default of payment into court of the sum of $US1,820,000 by some appropriate future date, the buyers should be debarred from defending the sellers' claim in the arbitration. It is convenient to note at this juncture that the buyers explicitly accept that the sellers' fiduciary claim to the specific fund falls within the terms of the GAFTA arbitration clause, which is very widely drawn.

The legal framework

Section 12(6) of the Arbitration Act 1950 provides:

'The High Court shall have, for the purpose of and in relation to a reference, the same power of making orders in respect of—(*a*) security for costs . . . (*f*) securing the amount in dispute in the reference; (g) the detention, preservation or inspection of any property or thing which is the subject of the reference or as to which any question may arise therein, and authorising for any of the purposes aforesaid any persons to enter upon or into any land or building in the possession of any party to the reference, or authorising any samples to be taken or any observation to be made or experiment to be tried which may be necessary or expedient for the purpose of obtaining full information or evidence . . . as it has for the purpose of and in relation to an action or matter in the High Court . . .'

The immediately relevant paragraph is of course para (f) (with which para (g) is closely linked), but I have also quoted para (a) because it gives rise to a very close parallel on which there is decided authority. The court's general powers in relation to the detention, preservation or inspection of property and for the securing of a specific fund, are contained in RSC Ord 29, r 2, which provides so far as relevant as follows, paras (3) and (4) being those directly in point:

'*Detention, preservation, etc., of subject-matter of cause or matter.*—(1) On the application of any party to a cause or matter the Court may make an order for the detention, custody or preservation of any property which is the subject-matter of the cause or matter, or as to which any question may arise therein, or for the inspection of any such property in the possession of a party to the cause or matter.

(2) For the purpose of enabling any order under paragraph (1) to be carried out the Court may by the order authorise any person to enter upon any land or building in the possession of any party to the cause or matter.

(3) Where the right of any party to a specific fund is in dispute in a cause or matter, the Court may, on the application of a party to the cause or matter, order the fund to be paid into court or otherwise secured.

(4) An order under this rule may be made on such terms, if any, as the Court thinks just . . .'

The power to order security for costs which is contained in Ord 23 contains in r 2 an identical provision mutatis mutandis to that contained in Ord 29, r 2(4). In *Dorval Tankers Pty Ltd v Two Arrows Maritime and Port Services Ltd, The Argenpuma* [1984] 2 Lloyd's Rep 563 the Court of Appeal held that under s 12(6)(a) of the 1950 Act the court had statutory jurisdiction to order a permanent stay of a claim in an arbitration where the claimant had failed to comply with an order of the court to furnish security for costs, expressly distinguishing *Bremer Vulkan Schiffbau Und Maschinenfabrik v South India Shipping Corp* [1981] 1 All ER 289, [1981] AC 909, in which the House of Lords held that the court has no inherent jurisdiction to grant a stay of an arbitration for want of prosecution. The two leading judgments were given by Eveleigh and Kerr LJJ, with whom Fox LJ agreed. Eveleigh LJ stated ([1984] 2 Lloyd's Rep 563 at 566):

'It is said that the Court has no power to put an end to an arbitration. Reference was made to *Bremer Vulkan Schiffbau und Maschinenfabrik Corporation Ltd. v. South India Shipping Corporation Ltd.* ([1981] 1 All ER 289 at 296–297, [1981] A.C. 909 at 979–980). That case decided that the Court had no inherent jurisdiction to do so, but the jurisdiction that is invoked in this case is that which flows from s. 12(6) of the Arbitration Act, 1950. It has the effect of incorporating the Rules of Court, O. 23 into the Arbitration Act. Order 23, r. 2 provides: "Where an order is made requiring any party to give security for costs, the security shall be given in such manner, at such time, and on such terms (if any), as the Court may direct." Consequently, the Court has statutory jurisdiction in this matter to do what it considers just.'

Kerr LJ stated (at 567–568):

'The second issue is whether Mr. Justice Leggatt had jurisdiction to order a permanent stay of the arbitration. In my view, he did. *Bremer Vulkan Schiffbau und Maschinenfabrik Corporation Ltd. v. South India Shipping Corporation Ltd.* decided that *a* the Court has no power to dismiss an arbitration for want of prosecution ... The present case differs radically from the position in *Bremer Vulkan* and *The "Hannah Blumenthal"* [*Paal Wilson & Co A/S v Partenreederei Hannah Blumenthal* [1983] 1 All ER 34, [1983] 1 AC 854], since it turns on express powers of the Courts concerning arbitrations which are conferred by statute and under the Rules of Court. Part I of the Arbitration Act, 1950, confers a number of powers upon various parts of our *b* Court system to make orders in relation to arbitrations. The present case is concerned with s. 12(6)(*a*) which confers power upon the High Court to make orders for the security for the costs of arbitrations in the same way as in relation to actions in the High Court. Section 28 of the Act provides: "Any order made under this Part of this Act may be made on such terms as to costs or otherwise as the authority making the order thinks just." In relation to orders for security for costs R.S.C., O. 23, r. 2 *c* provides for a similar discretion to impose terms. A stay of the proceedings in relation to which an order for security is made, pending the provision of the security, is commonplace, if not invariable in the absence of consent, because further unsecured costs may be incurred in the interim. The power to impose a stay of the arbitration in this case, which was exercised ex parte on Feb. 5, 1982 and inter partes on Apr. 2, 1982, is therefore not open to doubt. Having ordered a stay of the *d* arbitration, it is equally within the power of the Court to decide whether the stay should be lifted or maintained if—as happened here—the security is not provided within the prescribed time ... Given the foregoing, I think that Mr. Justice Leggatt also had jurisdiction to order that the stay be permanent. In relation to proceedings in the Courts this can be achieved by an order striking out or dismissing the action for want of prosecution: see the note in the Annual Practice 23/1–3/23.' *e*

The Argenpuma demonstrates that Ord 23 is the counterpart of s 12(6)(*a*) of the 1950 Act; similarly Ord 29, r 2 is the counterpart of s 12(6)(*f*) and (*g*) of the Act: see *The Golden Trader, Danemar Scheepvaart Maatschappij BV v Golden Trader (owners)* [1974] 2 All ER 686 at 695, [1978] QB 348 at 359 per Brandon J.

f

Submissions and conclusions in law

The kernel of the submissions of counsel for the sellers is that the powers under paras (*a*) and (*f*) of s 12(6) of the 1950 Act are strictly comparable, and that, just as, on the authority of *The Argenpuma*, the court has statutory jurisdiction in appropriate circumstances to put a permanent stop on a plaintiff's claim in an arbitration where he is in default of an order for security for costs (on the basis of its wide power to impose terms *g* under Ord 23, r 2), so the court is statutorily entitled to debar a defendant from defending pursuant to its wide powers under Ord 29 if he is in default of complying with an order to secure a specific fund, or, where the situation arises, if he is in breach of an order for the custody or preservation of the property. He draws attention to the wide range of circumstances in which the court has power to order either the dismissal of claims or the debarring of defences where orders are not complied with, either under the express *h* terms of rules of court themselves, or under the inherent jurisdiction of the court; default in pleading or failure to give discovery under Ord 29 or Ord 24, r 16 respectively are examples of the former, and delay or default in drawing up an order or abuse of process are instances of the latter (see the full catalogue helpfully set out in *The Supreme Court Practice 1988* vol 2, paras 4624–4626).

Counsel for the buyers submits that there is no such jurisdiction, no specific authority *j* having been produced in support of such an order under s 12(6)(*f*) of the 1950 Act. Alternatively, he submits that it would be wholly unjust to impose such draconian terms on default under an order to secure a specific fund, since that might debar the defendant from establishing a valid defence, thus giving the plaintiff an unjust judgment. He

submits that the only cases where the defendant should be so debarred are those expressly
a   contained in the rules in relation to such matters as discovery and inspection, or default
in filing a defence, which are due to the defendant's own fault in the actual conduct of
the proceedings, where he has only himself to blame. The proper course, counsel submits,
would be for the plaintiff to invoke the powers of the court under Ord 45, r 1(2), which
provides:

b   'Subject to the provisions of these rules, a judgment or order for the payment of
money into court may be enforced by one or more of the following means, that is
to say—(a) the appointment of a receiver; (b) in a case in which rule 5 applies, an
order of committal; (c) in such a case, writ of sequestration.'

In my judgment, the submissions of counsel for the sellers are sound in principle. The
c   analogy of *The Argenpuma* [1984] 2 Lloyd's Rep 563 seems to me so close as to provide all
but binding authority in favour of his basic proposition, and certainly to give me a sound
foundation on which to uphold his basic argument. Counsel for the buyers' suggested
rationale for the cases where parties are debarred from suing or defending claims seems
to me inconsistent with the security for costs cases; in such cases there is no default by
the plaintiff in the actual conduct of the case, and he may indeed (and no doubt often
d   does) have a good sound claim, but because of his default in complying with an order for
security the court undoubtedly has powers to debar him from pursuing that claim, be
that claim just or unjust. This is the only sanction the court has for compliance with its
order and it is a sanction which the court in proper cases can and will impose.

A defendant who fails to comply with an order under s 12(6)(f) or Ord 29 for the
securing of a specific fund (or under para (g) for the custody or preservation of property)
e   is in no worse position than the plaintiff in the above-mentioned comparable
circumstances, when his defence, just or unjust, is debarred. In each case the sanction is
undoubtedly a severe one, and it goes without saying that the court will only impose it
in the exercise of its discretion if the circumstances fully warrant so stringent an order.

Order 45, r 1(2) provides other specific sanctions which the court may impose, not an
exhaustive catalogue of permissible remedies in the case of non-payment of a sum of
f   money into court. In the case of an English defendant an order appointing a receiver
might no doubt often be appropriate, and, in bad cases, an order for committal or a writ
of sequestration. But any such orders would be completely futile in the present case,
where the defendant buyers are a Lebanese company. Counsel for the buyers drew my
attention to a passage in *Kerr on Receivers* (16th edn, 1983) p 83 which shows that the
court may appoint a receiver over foreign property, but in the same paragraph the author
g   goes on to state, citing authority, that 'the court will not make such an order if it would
be useless'; this in my judgment is manifestly the situation here.

The exercise of my discretion
The relevant facts are as follows. (i) The sellers have a virtually cast-iron case that the
property in the goods always remained in their hands, so that the sub-sale by the buyers
h   was a sub-sale of goods belonging not to the buyers but to the sellers. (ii) These goods are
now represented in the buyers' hands by the specific fund amounting to approximately
$2m, ie the purchase price of just over $3m with a full allowance of $1m for freight and
insurance expenses. (iii) The buyers have received this money for the sellers' goods as
sub-sellers without paying so much as a cent to the sellers under the sale contract between
the sellers and the buyers.
j   On these facts alone, it seems to me that, if ever there was a strong case in favour of an
order for security under s 12(6)(f) and for tough sanctions in support of such an order,
this is that case.

I reach this conclusion without regard to other factors which might also be prayed in
aid, not least the somewhat surreptitious conduct of the buyers in receiving payment

from their sub-buyers without disclosing any inkling of this fact to the sellers but rather, on the contrary, continuing the desultory and eventually fruitless discussions in which *a* they promised but never provided alternative proposals for solving the problem.

None the less, to avoid any vestige of a warrantable sense of injustice in the minds of the buyers, I wish to be careful to exclude from the amount ordered to be secured any sum in respect of which the buyers might conceivably have a viable defence on the merits. The only heading in the present case for any such defence is the alleged quality defects, which, as is demonstrated by the buyers' own evidence, and as is common *b* ground between counsel, have already been fully taken into account in the computation of the price paid by the sub-buyers. There is therefore no need to make allowance under this head a second time over. It follows that the amount sought of $1,820,000 falls well short of the sum of $2m approximately to which the sellers are virtually certain to be entitled after making full allowance to the buyers for all possible defences on the merits.

The buyers are already several weeks in default of my previous order and it seems very *c* unlikely that they will comply with it, especially since their affidavit contains no mention of the order, let alone any explanation for their non-compliance. There is indeed no incentive for them to comply, since, having received the full price from their sub-buyers, there is no need for them to pursue any claim in the present arbitration, and therefore no hardship to them in their own claim being stayed.

It follows that in my judgment an order to secure the amount sought of $1,820,000 *d* remains fully justified, and that the additional sanction of debarring a defence in default of compliance with such an order is also fully justified in all the circumstances. I shall therefore in the exercise of my discretion make an order in these terms. However, to make sure the buyers have ample opportunity to reconsider their position in the light of this judgment, I shall give them until 4 pm on Friday, 29 July 1988 to make the payment into court, in default of which they will be debarred from defending the sellers' claims *e* in the arbitration.

Order accordingly.

Solicitors: *Richards Butler* (for the sellers); *Sinclair Roche & Temperley* (for the buyers). *f*

K Mydeen Esq   Barrister

Jobson v Johnson

COURT OF APPEAL, CIVIL DIVISION
KERR, DILLON AND NICHOLLS LJJ
20, 21, 22, 25 APRIL, 25 MAY 1988

Contract – Penalty – Forfeiture clause – Penalty for non-performance of contractual obligation – Penalty requiring transfer of property – Sale of shares by instalments – Clause in sale agreement requiring purchaser to transfer shares back to vendor for fixed sum if he defaulted in payment of instalments – Fixed sum for transfer back not reflecting true value of shares – Purchaser defaulting in payment of instalments – Whether retransfer clause a penalty – Whether clause should be struck out – Whether clause enforceable subject to equitable relief – Nature of relief available to vendor.

The defendant entered into an agreement with the vendors for the purchase of 62,566 shares in a football club for a total purchase price of £351,688 payable by an initial payment of £40,000 and six instalments of £51,948 payable half-yearly. The agreement contained a clause that if the defendant defaulted on the payment of the second or any subsequent instalment he was required to transfer the shares back to the vendors for the sum of £40,000. That sum was not a genuine pre-estimate of the vendors' loss in the event of the defendant's default and did not reflect the true value of the shares. The defendant paid £140,000 towards the purchase price and the shares were transferred to him. He then defaulted on payment of the instalments. The plaintiff, who was the assignee of the vendors, sought specific performance of the agreement for the retransfer of the shares. The defendant claimed that the retransfer agreement was a penalty and therefore unenforceable and counterclaimed for relief against forfeiture if the agreement was enforceable. At the trial the counterclaim was struck out because the defendant had not complied with an undertaking to disclose certain documents. The judge held that the retransfer agreement was a penalty but nevertheless enforceable unless the defendant was granted relief against forfeiture, which, because of the striking out of the defendant's counterclaim, was not possible. The judge accordingly ordered specific performance of the agreement for the retransfer of the shares for the sum of £40,000. The defendant appealed, contending that the agreement for the retransfer of the shares was unenforceable because it was a penalty.

Held – The appeal would be allowed for the following reasons—

(1) There was no distinction between a penalty for non-payment of money due under a contract and a penalty for the non-performance of some other obligation under the contract and, furthermore, there was no distinction between a penalty which required the payment of money and a penalty which required the transfer of property. In each case the consequences of a contractual term being identified as a penalty clause were the same, namely the clause remained a term of the contract and would not be struck out merely because it was a penalty but enforcement of the clause would be subject to equitable relief without the need for a specific claim in that behalf on the part of the defendant; accordingly, if the clause was sued on by the plaintiff it would not be enforced by the court beyond the amount of the plaintiff's actual loss (see p 627 *e*, p 628 *d* to *f*, p 630 *a*, p 631 *c d*, p 632 *e f*, p 633 *a b h j*, p 634 *j*, p 638 *e* to *h* and p 639 *c*, post); *Beckham v Drake* (1849) 2 HL Cas 579, *Craig v M'Beath* (1863) 1 M 1020, dictum of Lord Hatherley LC in *Thompson v Hudson* (1869) LR 4 HL 1 at 15, *Re Dagenham (Thames) Dock Co, ex p Hulse* (1873) LR 8 Ch App 1022, *Public Works Comr v Hills* [1904–7] All ER Rep 919, *Wall v Rederiaktiebolaget Luggude* [1915] 3 KB 66 and *Bridge v Campbell Discount Co Ltd* [1962] 1 All ER 385 applied.

(2) On its true construction the retransfer agreement was intended to provide the plaintiff with security for unpaid instalments and it gave the plaintiff the remedy of

repossession as an alternative to suing for recovery of any unpaid instalments. In those
circumstances (Kerr LJ dissenting) the court would make available to the plaintiff two   *a*
alternative forms of relief, namely (a) an order for the sale of the shares by the court and
payment to the plaintiff of the unpaid instalments and interest out of the proceeds of the
sale or (b) an inquiry as to the value of the shares and if the value of the shares did not
exceed the amount of the unpaid instalments and interest by £40,000 an order for
specific peformance of the agreement for the retransfer of the shares, with the choice of
relief being left to the plaintiff. If the plaintiff declined to accept either form of relief the   *b*
order for specific performance would be discharged since otherwise the court would be
enforcing a penalty and the plaintiff would be left to his remedy of suing to recover the
amount of the unpaid instalments in a fresh action (see p 630 *e* to *j* and p 635 *b f j* to
p 636 *a d g* to p 637 *d j*, post); *Peachy v Duke of Somerset* (1721) 1 Stra 447, *Re Dagenham*
(Thames) Dock Co, ex p Hulse (1873) LR 8 Ch App 1022 and dictum of Lord Wilberforce
in *Shiloh Spinners Ltd v Harding* [1973] 1 All ER 90 at 100 applied.   *c*

Notes
For equitable relief against penalties and forfeiture, see 16 Halsbury's Laws (4th edn)
paras 1444–1450, and for cases on the subject, see 20 Digest (Reissue) 892–899, 6656–
6703.   *d*

Cases referred to in judgments
Alder v Moore [1961] 1 All ER 1, [1961] 2 QB 57, [1961] 2 WLR 426, CA.
Astley v Weldon (1801) 2 Bos & P 346, [1775–1802] All ER Rep 606, 126 ER 1318.
Beckham v Drake (1849) 2 HL Cas 579, 9 ER 1213.
Bridge v Campbell Discount Co Ltd [1962] 1 All ER 385, [1962] AC 600, [1962] 2 WLR 439,   *e*
    HL.
Clydebank Engineering and Shipbuilding Co Ltd v Yzquierdo y Castaneda [1905] AC 6,
    [1904–7] All ER Rep 251, HL.
Cooden Engineering Co Ltd v Stanford [1952] 2 All ER 915, [1953] 1 QB 86, CA.
Craig v M'Beath (1863) 1 M 1020, Ct of Sess.
Dagenham (Thames) Dock Co, Re, ex p Hulse (1873) LR 8 Ch App 1022, LJJ.   *f*
Dixon, Re, Heynes v Dixon [1900] 2 Ch 561, CA.
Dunlop Pneumatic Tyre Co Ltd v New Garage and Motor Co Ltd [1915] AC 79, [1914–15] All
    ER Rep 333, HL.
Gerrard v Clowes [1892] 2 QB 11.
Kemble v Farren (1829) 6 Bing 141, [1824–34] All ER Rep 641, 130 ER 1234.
Kreglinger (G & C) v New Patagonia Meat and Cold Storage Co Ltd [1914] AC 25, [1911–13]   *g*
    All ER Rep 970, HL.
Peachy v Duke of Somerset (1721) 1 Stra 447, 93 ER 626, LC.
Photo Production Ltd v Securicor Transport Ltd [1980] 1 All ER 556, [1980] AC 827, [1980]
    2 WLR 283, HL.
Public Works Comr v Hills [1906] AC 368, [1904–7] All ER Rep 919, PC
Reynolds v Pitt (1812) 19 Ves 134, 34 ER 468, LC.   *h*
Roles v Rosewell (1794) 5 Term Rep 538, 101 ER 302.
Shiloh Spinners Ltd v Harding [1973] 1 All ER 90, [1973] AC 691, [1973] 2 WLR 28, HL.
Sloman v Walter (1783) 1 Bro CC 418, 28 ER 1213, LC.
Stockloser v Johnson [1954] 1 All ER 630, [1954] 1 QB 476, [1954] 2 WLR 439, CA.
Thompson v Hudson (1869) LR 4 HL 1.   *j*
Wall v Rederiaktiebolaget Luggude [1915] 3 KB 66.
Wallingford v Mutual Society (1880) 5 App Cas 685, HL.
Wallis v Smith (1882) 21 Ch D 243, CA.
Wyllie v Wilkes (1780) 2 Doug KB 519, 99 ER 331.

Cases also cited

a *Anglo-Auto Finance Co Ltd v James* [1963] 3 All ER 566, [1963] 1 WLR 1042, CA.
Barton Thompson & Co Ltd v Stapling Machines Co [1966] 2 All ER 222, [1966] Ch 499.
Preston v Dania (1872) LR 8 Exch 19.
United Dominion Trust (Commercial) Ltd v Ennis [1967] 2 All ER 345, [1968] 1 QB 54, CA.

Appeal

b By a writ issued on 5 August 1985 the plaintiff, Victor Thomas Jobson, sought, inter alia, specific performance of an agreement contained in or evidenced by a letter dated 12 August 1983 whereby, under cl 6(b) of the letter, the defendant, Anton Leslie Johnson, agreed to retransfer to the plaintiff 62,666, or alternatively 62,566 ordinary shares in Southend United Football Club Ltd for the sum of £40,000 in the event of the defendant defaulting on payment of instalments of the purchase price of £351,688 for the shares

c under a sale agreement made between the plaintiff's assignors and the defendant. By his defence the defendant pleaded that cl 6(b) of the letter was a penalty clause and as such was unenforceable, and counterclaimed for relief from forfeiture of the shares if, which he denied, cl 6(b) was a valid and enforceable provision. By an order made on 5 February 1987 Harman J, having struck out the defendant's counterclaim because of the defendant's

d default in complying with an undertaking given to the court, ordered that the agreement contained in cl 6(b) of the letter be specifically performed by the defendant. The defendant appealed. The facts are set out in the judgment of Dillon LJ.

Leslie Joseph QC and *Victor Levene* for the defendant.
James Munby QC and *Guy Newey* for the plaintiff.

e

Cur adv vult

25 May. The following judgments were delivered.

f **DILLON LJ** (giving the first judgment at the invitation of Kerr LJ). The defendant, Mr Johnson, appeals against an order of Harman J of 5 February 1987 whereby the judge ordered, in favour of the plaintiff Mr Jobson, as assignee of two brothers named Rubin (the Rubins), specific performance of an agreement in writing of 12 August 1983 whereby the defendant agreed, in the events which have happened, to sell 62,566 ordinary shares of 25p each in Southend United Football Club Ltd (the club) to the

g Rubins for a sum of £40,000. The appeal raises a narrow point of considerable difficulty, which only arises because of the unusual course these proceedings have taken.

Briefly the origin of this matter is that in August 1983 the Rubins were, by inheritance from their father, entitled to 62,666 ordinary shares in the club, which constituted 44·914% of the issued share capital of the club. By two documents, both dated 12 August

h 1983, which have to be read together to get the full terms of the contract, the Rubins contracted to sell the 62,666 shares to the defendant.

The first of these two documents was a sale agreement made between the Rubins and a Mr Machutchon who was a nominee for the defendant. It provided for the sale by the Rubins to Mr Machutchon of the 62,666 shares for a price of £40,000 in cash, and for completion to take place immediately after the signing of the agreement. The sale

j agreement contained many other provisions but none is relevant to this appeal.

The second of the two documents was a side-letter of the same date. It was written by the defendant to the Rubins and was countersigned by them and was expressed to be agreed in consideration of the Rubins entering into the sale agreement with Mr Machutchon.

Clause 2 of the side-letter provided for the Rubins, without extra consideration, to procure the transfer to Mr Machutchon of extra shares in the club to bring the total sold to over 50% of the share capital, but that did not happen and an option given to the defendant by cl 5 of the side-letter to require the Rubins to reacquire the shares for £40,000 if the extra shares were not acquired was never exercised. These provisions can therefore be ignored. What is important about the side-letter is however (1) that by cl 3 and the last three lines of cl 2 the defendant agreed to pay the Rubins, in addition to the £40,000 under the sale agreement, a sum of £311,688 by six equal half-yearly instalments of £51,948 commencing on 12 February 1984; the £311,688 represented £260,000 plus interest at 12½% per annum on a reducing balance, and (2) that by cl 6 there were alternative provisions for the retransfer to the Rubins of 44·9% of the issued share capital of the club in the event of default by the defendant, as follows:

'(a) In the event of any default by me in payment of the first instalment of the sum referred to in paragraph 3 of this letter for a period of 7 days from the due date of payment I shall transfer (or procure the transfer) of ordinary shares of 25p each in the Company amounting to not less than 44·9% of the issued share capital of the Company as at the due payment date to you jointly subject to the payment to me (or as I may direct) of £15,666·50. (b) In the event of any such default by me in respect of any subsequent instalment of the sum I shall transfer (or procure the transfer) of ordinary shares of 25p in the Company amounting to not less than 44·9% of the issued share capital of the Company at the due payment date to you jointly subject to the payment to me (or as I may direct) of £40,000.'

It is the retransfer under cl 6(b) that the plaintiff, as assignee of the Rubins, now claims to enforce. Because the number of shares comprised in the sale agreement represented, as indicated above, slightly more than 44·9% of the issued share capital of the club, the action has been about, and the judge's order relates to, the slightly smaller number of 62,566 shares. But nothing turns on precise numbers.

The defendant paid the £40,000 provided for by the sale agreement and the 62,666 shares were transferred to him or to his nominee. He defaulted, however, in paying the first instalment, due on 12 February 1984, under cl 3 of the side-letter. A variation agreement was accordingly entered into on 1 June 1984 between the Rubins and the defendant. This substituted a sum of £300,000 for the £311,688 specified in cl 3 of the side-letter and provided for that sum to be paid by instalments (a) as to £50,000 on the signing of the variation agreement, (b) as to a further £50,000 on 31 August 1984 and (c) as to the balance of £200,000 by 12 quarterly instalments of £15,000 each commencing on 31 March 1985 and a final instalment of £20,000 on 31 March 1988.

There were certain provisions included in the variation agreement for the protection of the Rubins, in that the defendant agreed that the freehold or leasehold properties of the club should not be sold without their consent; he agreed not to charge or encumber the shares and agreed to deposit the share certificate relating to the shares with his then solicitors with irrevocable instructions not to part with it. The defendant also agreed that until a certain level of payments has been reached (which has not yet happened) the Rubins should have the right to appoint one director to the board of the club.

The defendant paid the Rubins the first £100,000 under the variation agreement, in addition to the £40,000 already mentioned, but he has failed to make any payment at all in respect of the balance of £200,000. The rights of the Rubins against the defendant were assigned to the plaintiff for value in July 1985, and he now claims against the defendant to enforce the repurchase of 62,566 shares under cl 6(b) of the side-letter.

At the trial a great deal of time was devoted to claims by the defendant that the sale agreement and the side-letter were tainted with fraud and illegality, and so could not be enforced. The judge held that there was no sufficient evidence to support these claims, which he accordingly rejected, and as to that there is no appeal. Apart from that, however, the defendant pleaded in his defence that the provisions contained in cl 6 of the

side-letter constituted penalties and were accordingly unenforceable. He then counter-
a claimed that if, which he denied, cl 6 was valid and enforceable, he ought to be granted
relief, which was described as 'relief from the forfeiture of his said shares . . .'

In a reserved judgment delivered on 23 January 1987 after the trial of the action
Harman J held that cl 6(b) of the side-letter was indeed a penalty clause, but he held that
the effect of that was not that the clause was unenforceable or to be 'blue-pencilled out',
but that, all other things being equal, the defendant might in the discretion of the court
b be granted relief under his counterclaim. He then at the defendant's request adjourned
the hearing of the counterclaim to 9 February. It appeared, however, after Harman J had
given judgment on 23 January 1987, that the defendant was then in default in complying
with certain undertakings given to the court in November 1986 to disclose documents
relating to the defendant's own recent financial circumstances. Harman J accordingly
extended the defendant's time for compliance with those undertakings to the close of
c business on 30 January 1987, but as by that time the defendant still had not complied
with the undertakings, Harman J on 5 February struck out the counterclaim for relief.
There is no appeal against the striking out.

The defendant challenges by this appeal the judge's ruling that, although a penalty
clause, cl 6(b) of the side-letter creates an enforceable obligation from which the only
escape for the party bound would be by relief, akin to relief against forfeiture, granted to
d that party by the court in its discretion. The defendant submits that the true view is that
cl 6(b), being a penalty clause, is unenforceable. Thus the defendant relies on his defence
that the penalty clause is unenforceable, and says that he does not need to rely on his
counterclaim for relief, which has been struck out. The position on the record is that if
the defendant fails on this submission the appeal must fail because the striking out of the
counterclaim is not challenged.

e The plaintiff's submission is that the law as to penalty clauses is that a penalty clause
creates a binding obligation which the courts will enforce unless the courts see fit to grant
equitable relief. This view of the law Harman J accepted in his judgment of 23 January
1987, contrary, as he said, to his initial reaction when the proposition was first advanced.
The plaintiff submits that if this view of the law is correct, it must follow that, as the
counterclaim for relief was struck out, the court cannot give the defendant relief from
f the penalty clause, and must order specific performance of the defendant's obligation
under cl 6(b), as the judge did by his order of 5 February 1987.

In this court the plaintiff does not challenge the judge's ruling that cl 6(b) is a penalty
clause. That ruling was, in my judgment, plainly right for a combination of two reasons:
(1) the repurchase of the shares under cl 6(b) was to be at the fixed price of £40,000 if
there was default in payment of any instalment, without regard to how much the
g defendant had already paid; it would make no difference if the default was in the
payment of the second, the last, or an intermediate instalment, and (2) there was also
cl 6(a) of the side-letter providing for repurchase at an even lower price than £40,000 in
the event of default in the payment of the first instalment under the side-letter, ie default
when the defendant had only paid the £40,000 under the sale agreement. The plain
h reading of cl 6 is therefore that the defendant was to be punished for any default by
being bound to retransfer substantially all the shares to the Rubins at a fixed price which
was bound to be less, and could be very much less, than the defendant had paid. The
retransfer price under either part of cl 6 could not have been based on a genuine pre-
estimate either of the Rubins's loss or of the value of the shares.

The penal effect of cl 6(b) would of course be all the greater if, having enforced a
j retransfer of the shares for £40,000 under that paragraph, the plaintiff as assignee of the
Rubins would remain entitled to sue the defendant to recover additionally all the unpaid
instalments under the side-letter as varied by the variation agreement. For my part,
however, I would hold as a matter of construction of the side-letter that retransfer of the
shares under cl 6(b) was to be in lieu of all other remedies and would preclude the
plaintiff recovering any unpaid instalments, whether those unpaid at the date when the

retransfer was called for or those which would only have become payable subsequently.

We have therefore to consider what the basis is of the court's approach to penalty *a* clauses, and we have had the benefit of very interesting historical argument on each side.

The effect of the court's approach has been to establish what Lord Diplock in *Photo Production Ltd v Securicor Transport Ltd* [1980] 1 All ER 556 at 567, [1980] AC 827 at 850 referred to as 'the equitable rule against penalties'. He said that an agreement—

> 'must not offend against the equitable rule against penalties, that is to say, it must *b* not impose on the breaker of a primary obligation a general secondary obligation to pay to the other party a sum of money that is manifestly intended to be in excess of the amount which would fully compensate the other party for the loss sustained by him in consequence of the breach of the primary obligation.'

There is no doubt that the rule originated in equity, and is of long standing in equity. Thus, Lord Mansfield CJ tells us in *Wyllie v Wilkes* (1780) 2 Doug KB 519 at 523, 99 ER *c* 331 at 333 that Sir Thomas More, when Lord Chancellor, summoned the judges to a conference concerning the granting of relief at law, after the forfeiture of bonds, on payment of principal, interest and costs, 'and when they said they could not relieve against the penalty, he swore by the body of God, he would grant an injunction'.

The refusal of the court to sanction legal proceedings for penalties was thus, as Lord Radcliffe stated in *Bridge v Campbell Discount Co Ltd* [1962] 1 All ER 385 at 395, [1962] *d* AC 600 at 622:

> 'a rule of the court's own, produced and maintained for purposes of public policy (except where imposed by positive statutory enactment, as in [the Administration of Justice Act 1696 and the Administration of Justice Act 1705]).'

In *Clydebank Engineering and Shipbuilding Co Ltd v Yzquierdo y Castaneda* [1905] AC 6 at *e* 10, [1904–7] All ER Rep 251 at 253 Lord Halsbury LC held that the law as to penalties is now the same in England as in Scotland. He referred to the different form of the administration of the law in England as giving rise to the Administration of Justice Act 1696, and held also, more importantly in my judgment for present purposes, that what gave the jurisdiction to the courts in both countries to interfere at all in an agreement *f* between the parties was that an agreement to pay a penalty was regarded as 'unconscionable and extravagant, and one which no Court ought to allow to be enforced'. This is of course not saying that the courts claim a general power not to enforce any agreement which the courts regard as unconscionable and extravagant; as Lord Radcliffe also stated in *Bridge v Campbell Discount Co Ltd* [1962] 1 All ER 385 at 397, [1962] AC 600 at 626, the courts of equity never undertook to serve as a general adjuster of men's *g* bargains. But rules evolved as to the types of cases in which relief would be given, and one of those rules, now too entrenched to be challenged, is the equitable rule against penalties, based on the view, as stated by Lord Halsbury, that an agreement to pay a penalty was, for the reasons given, one that no court ought to allow to be enforced.

An explanation of the rule against penalties that leads to the same result is given by the Lord Justice Clerk (Inglis) in the Scots case of *Craig v M'Beath* (1863) 1 M 1020 at *h* 1022, where he put as the basis of the rule that parties cannot lawfully enter into an agreement that the one party shall be punished at the suit of the other. Consequently, the court was bound to modify the penalty to the actual loss 'if duly required by the defender to do so'.

One consequence of the attitude of the courts to penalty clauses is that the question whether a sum stipulated is penalty or liquidated damages is a question of construction *j* to be decided on the terms and inherent circumstances of each particular contract, judged as at the time of the making of the contract, not as at the time of the breach: see *Dunlop Pneumatic Tyre Co Ltd v New Garage and Motor Co Ltd* [1915] AC 79 at 86–87 per Lord Dunedin. This was interpreted, in my view correctly, by Somervell LJ in *Cooden Engineering Co Ltd v Stanford* [1952] 2 All ER 915 at 919, [1953] 1 QB 86 at 94 as meaning

that the question whether a sum was a penalty or a pre-estimate of damages, if it arose,
a had to be considered as at the date of the contract and having regard to its terms, and not
on the particular breach or breaches on which the claim was based. The approach makes
it less likely, in my view, that the enforcement of the penalty should depend on the
particular breach or breaches on which the claim was based, and on whether or not relief
in equity should be granted against those breaches.

It is also to be noted that a clause which was identified by the court of equity as a
b penalty clause as a matter of construction of the contract was not enforced, even though
the desired result could legitimately have been achieved if the clause had been drawn
differently. Thus in *Astley v Weldon* (1801) 2 Bos & P 346 at 353, [1775–1802] All ER
Rep 606 at 610 Heath J stated:

> 'It is a well known rule in equity, that if a mortgage covenant be to pay 5*l. per
c *cent.* and if the interest be paid on certain days then to be reduced to 4*l. per cent.* the
> Court of Chancery will not relieve if the early day be suffered to pass without
> payment; but if the covenant be to pay 4*l. per cent.* and if the party do not pay at a
> certain time it shall be raised to 5*l.* there the Court of Chancery will relieve.'

This concept was echoed by Lord Hatherley many years later in *Wallingford v Mutual
Society* (1880) 5 App Cas 685 at 702. It is clear to me that equity relieved by not enforcing
d the penal increased interest which only became payable on default, not by examining the
financial circumstances of the mortgagor at the time of breach and considering whether
his breach was wilful or culpable or whether he ought to be let off paying the increased
interest if he actually paid the arrears at the lower rate within a specified and reasonable
time.

All the cases to which I have referred were cases where the penalty was a sum of
e money. Now that the jurisdictional differences between the courts of common law and
equity no longer exist, any court, English or Scottish, when faced with a claim for a sum
of money payable on default which it identifies as a penalty, must refuse to enforce the
penal part of the sum and must give judgment for the claimant merely for the actual
damages suffered by the claimant, with, as appropriate, interest and costs. Where the
f penalty is a sum of money, the relief, once the penalty has been identified, does not
involve a consideration of the circumstances of the defendant, or of the factors which
might be appropriate to a grant of relief against forfeiture in such a case as *Shiloh Spinners
Ltd v Harding* [1973] 1 All ER 90, [1973] AC 691, where there was no question of penalty.
Giving judgment for the actual damage without further inquiry into the circumstances
was the course taken in *Cooden Engineering Co Ltd v Stanford* [1952] 2 All ER 915, [1953]
g 1 QB 86 and *Bridge v Campbell Discount Co Ltd* [1962] 1 All ER 385, [1962] AC 600 and in
my judgment it was the correct course.

Counsel for the plaintiff submits otherwise, in reliance in particular on s 8 of the 1696
Act. That rather lengthy section, which I do not propose to set out, applied to actions in
any of the King's courts of record on any bond or any penal sum for non-performance of
any covenant or agreement in any indenture deed or writing contained. The procedure
h under the section was that the plaintiff might sign judgment for the full amount of the
penalty claimed, but he could not enforce the judgment by execution or otherwise
without assigning or alleging the breaches of the agreement on which he relied and
proving his damage from those breaches, and he could only enforce the judgment to the
extent of the damage so proved. Parke B stated in *Beckham v Drake* (1849) 2 HL Cas 579
at 629, 9 ER 1213 at 1231 that the the statute in effect made the bond a security only for
j the damages really sustained.

It was held in *Roles v Rosewell* (1794) 5 Term Rep 538, 101 ER 302 that the procedure
under s 8 was mandatory even if the defendant did not appear to plead the Act, and
consequently the plaintiff could not levy a default judgment for the full amount of a
penalty without going to a jury to prove his actual loss. The result under the Act was
explained by Tindal CJ in *Kemble v Farren* (1829) 6 Bing 141 at 148, [1824–34] All ER

Rep 641 at 642 as follows:

'But that a very large sum should become immediately payable, in consequence *a*
of the nonpayment of a very small sum, and that the former should not be
considered as a penalty, appears to be a contradiction in terms; the case being
precisely that in which courts of equity have always relieved, and against which
courts of law have, in modern times, endeavoured to relieve, by directing juries to
assess the real damages sustained by the breach of the agreement.'
                                                                                b
The judgments of Lord Eldon CJ and Chambre J in *Astley v Weldon* (1801) 2 Bos & P 346,
[1775–1802] All ER Rep 606 are in my view, to the same effect.

I find nothing therefore in the 1696 Act or the procedure under it to change my view,
as indicated above, where the penalty is a sum of money.

The procedure in Scotland, as explained in *Craig v M'Beath* (1863) 1 M 1020, seems to
have been somewhat different from the procedure in England under the 1696 Act, and *c*
there seems to have been some difference of opinion among the Scottish judges in that
case as to where the onus of proving the extent of actual damage lay. Lord Benholme,
however, stated (at 1024):

'Where it is truly penal—where the parties have not had in view a mere statement
of liquidated damages—the penalty is to be modified and reduced to the amount of *d*
the damage actually sustained.'

Does it make any difference, then, that the penalty in the present case is not a sum of
money? In principle, a transaction must be just as objectionable and unconscionable in
the eyes of equity if it requires a transfer of property by way of penalty on a default in
paying money as if it requires a payment of an extra, or excessive, sum of money. There
is no distinction in principle between a clause which provides that if a person makes *e*
default in paying a sum of £100 on a certain day he shall pay a penalty of £1,000, and a
clause which provides that if a person makes default in paying a sum of £100 on a certain
day he shall by way of penalty transfer to the obligee 1000 shares in a certain company
for no consideration. Again, there should be no distinction in principle between a clause
which requires the defaulter, on making default in paying money, to transfer shares for
no consideration, and a clause which in like circumstances requires the defaulter to sell *f*
shares to the creditor at an undervalue. In each case the clause ought to be unenforceable
in equity in so far as it is a penalty clause.

Instances in the books of cases where the penalty has been other than a penalty in
money for non-payment of money are infrequent. Perhaps the closest on the facts is *Re
Dagenham (Thames) Dock Co, ex p Hulse* (1873) LR 8 Ch App 1022. In that case the *g*
company, incorporated by Act of Parliament, had contracted to purchase some land for
the purpose of making a dock in exercise of its statutory powers. The price was payable
by two instalments and on payment of the first instalment the company was let into
possession and began construction on the land. The contract included a clause that if the
company defaulted in paying the second instalment, the vendors could re-enter on the
land and repossess it as in their former estate, with the benefit of the company's *h*
expenditure on it, and eject the company without repaying any part of the price which
had been previously paid. There were successive agreements extending the time for
payment of the second instalment and interest, and in the latest agreement the power of
re-entry on default was again repeated, and the report records that the repossession was
to be of 'the lands and all works thereon' (at 1023). The right of repossession was to be
exercisable whether or not any conveyance of the land had been made to the company. *j*
In the event it seems that no conveyance had been made. The company failed to pay the
money, became insolvent and was put into compulsory liquidation. The vendors started
an action of ejectment, and, under a consent order in the winding up, they were given
liberty to sign judgment on an undertaking not to issue execution until further order,
and to abide by any order the court might make as to the property. The vendors then

applied to the court for an order that they might be at liberty to issue execution and for
a possession of the property free from all claims by the company.

That application came before Lord Romilly MR at first instance. It seems (from the
analysis of the record by Romer LJ in his judgment in *Stockloser v Johnson* [1954] 1 All ER
630 at 641, [1954] 1 QB 476 at 497) that there was before Lord Romilly MR an affidavit
in which it had been stated that the liquidator of the company had represented that, if
further time were allowed, the company would be able to come to some satisfactory
b arrangement. But it would seem that there was no immediate offer by the liquidator to
pay the unpaid balance and interest, let alone a tender of it. Lord Romilly MR offered
the vendors an order for sale of the property and payment out of the proceeds as in the
ordinary case of a vendor's lien, but on the vendors declining that offer he refused to
make any order on the application. The vendors appealed. James and Mellish LJJ did not
find it necessary to call on counsel for the liquidator, and agreed with Lord Romilly MR
c that the repossession clause was plainly a penalty. The way it was put, however, by James
LJ, at the end of his judgment was that it was a penalty 'from which the company are
entitled to be relieved on payment of the residue of the purchase-money with interest'
(see LR 8 Ch App 1022 at 1025).

It is to be observed that, on the facts of that case, time to pay was what the liquidator
needed, since he had to pay the balance of principal and interest to the vendors in full if
d he was to get a clear title to the lands so that he could realise them towards satisfaction of
the creditors. It is to be inferred that after the order of the Court of Appeal some
satisfactory arrangement was indeed come to between the parties, presumably by
payment by the liquidator. The court therefore never had to face up, as it might have
had to if the liquidator had again defaulted, to actually enforcing the penalty clause in
full, despite its penal nature. The case is an instance of the court refusing to enforce a
e penalty clause, in that Lord Romilly MR refused to make the possession order, but in a
context in which equitable relief on payment of the residue of the purchase money with
interest was still available.

In the context of the present case, relief by way of an extension of time for the
defendant to pay the unpaid purchase money and interest is just the relief which would
have been considered on the defendant's counterclaim if the counterclaim had not been
f struck out. Moreover, it is the sort of relief to which the documents which, in breach of
his undertaking, the defendant failed to disclose might have been marginally relevant,
in that they might have indicated what period he would realistically have required to
raise the necessary amount of money. Therefore in my judgment it is not open to this
court to grant that form of relief on this appeal. It does not necessarily follow, however,
in my judgment, that this court is therefore bound to enforce the penal clause, cl 6(b) of
g the side-letter, in all its rigour and without regard to its penal consequences.

There is one other penalty case to which I should refer: *Public Works Comr v Hills* [1906]
AC 368, [1904–7] All ER Rep 919. In that case there had been an agreement between the
government of the Cape of Good Hope and a contractor for the contractor to build a
railway between two places by a certain date. The agreement contained a clause that if
h the contractor failed to complete the railway in time (save for specified causes) certain
securities provided by the contractor for the due performance of the contractor's
obligations should be forfeit to the government; these included a security deposit paid
by the contractor to the government in relation to that particular contract and also
retention moneys held by the government for the contractor under two other contracts
in respect of other lengths of railway which the contractor had completed. The contractor
j defaulted under the contract in suit, the government declared the securities forfeit, and
the contractor's assignee sued for the return of the security moneys on the ground that
the forfeiture clause was a penalty clause. The Privy Council upheld a decision in the
court below that the forfeiture clause was a penalty clause and that the contractor was
entitled to repayment of the security moneys, but the Privy Council, in an opinion
delivered by Lord Dunedin, allowed the government an inquiry as to the actual damage

suffered by it as the result of the failure of the contractor to complete the railway on time
and the amount of such damage was to be deducted from the moneys payable. The case
is thus a further illustration that a clause identified by the courts as a penalty clause
cannot be enforced so as to enable a party to recover or retain more than his actual loss.

What then should the court do in the present case? It is not, in my judgment, open to
the court to decree specific performance of the sale of the shares to the plaintiff, but at a
higher price than the £40,000, so as to recoup to the defendant what he has actually paid
for the shares, since that would involve the court making a new contract between the
parties.

One possibility that might have been considered is that the court, while refusing
specific performance, should, as in the money penalty cases such as *Cooden Engineering Co
Ltd v Stanford* [1952] 2 All ER 915, [1953] 1 QB 86 and *Bridge v Campbell Discount Co Ltd*
[1962] 1 All ER 385, [1962] AC 600, enter immediate judgement for the plaintiff against
the defendant for the amount of the plaintiff's loss, viz all the unpaid instalments under
the variation agreement with interest from default in respect of each instalment until
judgment. That however is disclaimed by counsel for the plaintiff and has not been
sought at any earlier stage. Moreover, if cl 6(b) of the side-letter is wholly unenforceable,
the plaintiff could sue the defendant for the unpaid instalments and interest in a fresh
action and would be entitled to summary judgment under RSC Ord 14.

There remain two other alternatives. Counsel for the plaintiff concedes that in the
circumstances of this case the plaintiff is not entitled to any unpaid vendor's lien under
the general law on the shares which have been transferred to the defendant under the
sale agreement. If I am right, however, that the remedy of repurchase of the shares under
cl 6(b) of the side-letter is an alternative, and not in addition to, the recovery of the
unpaid instalments, the repurchase is in substance a security for the payment of the
unpaid instalments and interest.

Accordingly, the court could, I apprehend, follow the course taken by Lord Romilly
MR in *Re Dagenham (Thames) Dock Co* (1873) LR 8 Ch App 1022 and offer the plaintiff an
order for sale of the 62,566 shares by the court, and payment of the unpaid instalments
and interest out of the proceeds as in the ordinary case of a vendor's lien.

Alternatively, by analogy to the power which the court has had for a very long time to
direct an inquiry as to damages in a penalty case so as to ensure that there is no
enforcement beyond the plaintiff's actual loss, the court could, in my judgment, direct
inquiries to ascertain (i) the present value of the 62,566 shares, (ii) the present aggregate
of the unpaid instalments under the variation agreement with interest as above and (iii)
the present amount charged on the shares under the charging order obtained by
Chartered Standard Bank (C I) Ltd. The order for specific performance would then stand
if the present value of the shares as certified under (i) did not exceed by more than
£40,000 (the sale price under cl 6(b) of the side-letter) the aggregate of the unpaid
instalments and interest under (ii) and the amount, if any, by which the present amount
charged under the charging order as certified under (iii) exceeds the £40,000 (and so
cannot be paid off out of the purchase price under cl 6(b)). If, however, that condition is
not satisfied, the order for specific performance would have to be discharged, since its
enforcement would be the enforcement of a penalty.

These two alternatives should, in my judgment, be offered to the plaintiff, but they
cannot be forced on him. If neither is acceptable to him the appeal must, in my
judgment, be allowed and the order for specific performance must be discharged since
otherwise the court would be lending its machinery to the enforcement of the penal
effects of a clause which has been clearly identified as a penalty clause. But in that event,
as mentioned above the plaintiff will be free to bring a fresh action for payment.

NICHOLLS LJ. This case, as it has proceeded on appeal in this court, is a very unusual
one. Partly this is because the term in the contract, cl 6(b), of which the plaintiff is
seeking specific performance, is itself a somewhat unusual provision. More especially is

a
this case unusual because of two other matters. First, in the court below the judge struck out the defendant's counterclaim for relief, not after an investigation of its merits, but because of the defendant's failure to comply with an undertaking given by him to the court regarding discovery of documents considered material on the issues raised by his counterclaim for relief. Secondly, there has been no appeal from the striking out order. This has made it necessary to grapple with problems concerning the effect of an admittedly 'penal' provision in a case where there is no extant application for relief from

b
'forfeiture'.

Equitable relief

In considering this appeal it is right to have in mind that the legal principles applicable today regarding penalty clauses in contracts and those applicable regarding relief from forfeiture stem from a common origin. A penalty clause in a contract, as that expression

c
is normally used today, is a provision which, on breach of the contract, requires the party in default to make a payment to the innocent party of a sum of money which, however it may be labelled, is not a genuine pre-estimate of the damage likely to be sustained by the innocent party, but is a payment stipulated in terrorem of the party in default. For centuries equity has given relief against such provisions by not permitting the innocent party to recover under the penal provision more than his actual loss. In *Wyllie v Wilkes*

d
(1780) 2 Doug KB 519 at 522–523, 99 ER 331 at 333 Lord Mansfield observed that in the reign of Henry VIII Sir Thomas More had attempted unsuccessfully to persuade the judges to give relief in respect of money bonds:

'For he summoned them to a conference concerning the granting relief at law, after the forfeiture of bonds, upon payment of principal, interest, and costs; and

e
when they said they could not relieve against the penalty, he swore by the body of God, he would grant an injunction.'

Likewise with forfeiture. Take the simple case of a provision for forfeiture of a lease on non-payment of rent. That provision was regarded by equity as a security for the rent. So that, where conscience so required, equity relieved against the forfeiture on payment

f
of the rent with interest. Again with mortgages: if an estate was conveyed with a condition enabling the 'feoffor', to use the ancient terminology, to re-enter on payment by him of a given sum on a given date, and in substance the transaction was intended to be by way of security for payment of that sum, equity relieved against the condition by permitting the feoffor to redeem his estate on payment of principal, interest and costs within a reasonable time. Viscount Haldane LC observed in *Kreglinger v New Patagonia*

g
Meat and Cold Storage Co Ltd [1914] AC 25 at 35, [1911–13] All ER Rep 970 at 973 that the intervention of equity with regard to mortgages was 'merely a special application of a more general power to relieve against penalties and to mould them into mere securities'. In *Thompson v Hudson* (1869) LR 4 HL 1 at 15 Lord Hatherley LC summarised the underlying principle as follows:

h
'I take the law to be perfectly clear . . . namely, that where there is a debt actually due, and in respect of that debt a security is given, be it by way of mortgage or be it by way of stipulation that in case of its not being paid at the time appointed a larger sum shall become payable, and be paid, in either of those cases Equity regards the security that has been given as a mere pledge for the debt, and it will not allow either a forfeiture of the property pledged, or any augumentation of the debt as a

j
penal provision, on the ground that Equity regards the contemplated forfeiture which might take place at Law with reference to the estate as in the nature of a penal provision, against which Equity will relieve when the object in view, namely, the securing of the debt, is attained, and regarding also the stipulation for the payment of a larger sum of money, if the sum be not paid at the time it is due, as a penalty and a forfeiture against which Equity will relieve.'

Penalty clauses

The particular procedure by which the Court of Chancery prevented a party seeking *a* payment under a penalty clause in a contract, including a bond, from recovering more than his actual loss seems to have differed a little according to whether the penalty was intended to secure only a payment of money on a specified date or was intended to secure the performance of an obligation other than a payment of money. The details are not material for the purpose of this appeal. It suffices to say that an example of the latter type of case is to be found in *Sloman v Walter* (1783) 1 Bro CC 418, 28 ER 1213. The party *b* seeking payment of the penalty was prevented by injunction from recovering, by execution or otherwise, more from his judgment obtained at law on a bond than the amount of his loss as established by an issue of quantum damnificatus directed by the Court of Chancery. In the former case, of a bond securing only a money payment, the Court of Chancery proceeded on the principle that failure to pay the principal on a certain day could be compensated sufficiently by payment of principal, interest and costs *c* on a subsequent day. Thus it was unnecessary to direct an issue of quantum damnificatus. If necessary, the court referred the calculation to a master (see Rigby LJ in *Re Dixon, Heynes v Dixon* [1900] 2 Ch 561 at 576). Subsequently the common law courts became obliged to give effect to these equitable principles, under the Administration of Justice Act 1696 and the Administration of Justice Act 1705, ss 12 and 13. After the Supreme Court of Judicature Act 1873 came into force these two statutes ceased to be necessary, *d* and eventually they were repealed.

Thus today, when law and equity are administered concurrently in the same courts, and the rules of equity prevail whenever there is any conflict or variance between the rules of equity and the rules of the common law with reference to the same matter (s 49 of the Supreme Court Act 1981), a penalty clause in a contract is, in practice, a dead letter. An obligation to make a money payment stipulated in terrorem will not be enforced *e* beyond the sum which represents the actual loss of the party seeking payment, namely, principal, interest and, if appropriate, costs, in those cases where (to use modern terminology) the primary obligation is to pay money, or where the primary obligation is to perform some other obligation, beyond the sum recoverable as damages for breach of that obligation. (For convenience I shall hereafter refer to that sum as 'the actual loss of *f* the innocent party'.) Hence normally there is no advantage in suing on the penalty clause. In *Wall v Rederiaktiebolaget Luggude* [1915] 3 KB 66 at 73 Bailhache J concluded his examination of the history of this matter in the context of a penalty clause in a charterparty with these words:

'This being the state of the law as I understand it, one easily sees why in charterparty cases no one sues on the penalty clause now. You cannot under it *g* recover more than the proved damages, and if the proved damages exceed the penal sum you are restricted to the lower amount. As the penalty clause may be disregarded it always is disregarded and has become a dead letter, or from another point of view a "brutum fulmen" . . .'.

This accords with authoritative dicta in *Bridge v Campbell Discount Co Ltd* [1962] 1 All ER *h* 385, [1962] AC 600. In particular, Lord Morton observed that the result of the conclusion that the clause there in point was a penalty was that Bridge, the hirer, was 'entitled to relief in accordance with the principles laid down by LORD THURLOW L.C., in *Sloman v. Walter* ((1783) 1 Bro CC 418, 28 ER 1213)' (see [1962] 1 All ER 385 at 391, [1962] AC 600 at 616). Likewise Lord Radcliffe said ([1962] 1 All ER 385 at 397, [1962] AC 600 at 625): *j*

'In my opinion, a clause of this kind, when founded on in consequence of a contractual breach, comes within the range of the court's jurisdiction to relieve against penalties, and the respondents should be confined to the right of claiming from the appellant any damage that they can show themselves to have actually suffered from his falling down on the contract.'

Lord Denning's remarks on this are to the same effect (see [1962] 1 All ER 385 at 401,
a [1962] AC 600 at 632).

Although in practice a penalty clause in a contract as described above is effectively a
dead letter, it is important in the present case to note that, contrary to the submissions of
counsel for the defendant, the strict legal position is not that such a clause is simply
struck out of the contract, as though with a blue pencil, so that the contract takes effect
as if it had never been included therein. Strictly, the legal position is that the clause
b remains in the contract and can be sued on, but it will not be enforced by the court
beyond the sum which represents, in the events which have happened, the actual loss of
the party seeking payment. There are many cases which make this clear. I have already
referred to the decision of Bailhache J in *Wall's case* [1915] 3 KB 66. I mention only two
other decisions. In *Beckham v Drake* (1849) 2 HL Cas 579, 9 ER 1213 a contract of
employment provided for the payment of a penal sum of £500 in the event of default
c by the other party. As one of the judges advising the House of Lords, Maule J, said (2 HL
Cas 579 at 622, 9 ER 1213 at 1228–1229):

'The clause by which, in the event that has happened, the master agreed to pay
the servant 500*l.*, is certainly in its terms an agreement to pay money, and though
the construction which the law requires to be put upon it prevents the whole sum
d   from being payable when it would be more than a reasonable compensation for a
failure of performance, it is not thereby rendered wholly inoperative, but it retains
the effect of binding the failing party to pay such part of the sum as may be
reasonable in respect of the failure.'

Lord Campbell said (2 HL Cas 579 at 645, 9 ER 1213 at 1237):
e
'The [Administration of Justice Act 1696], although it prevents the party
recovering, as he might have done at Common Law, the whole of the penalty, does
not at all prevent that part of the penalty which is recovered being considered in the
nature of a debt; and so much is it a debt that an action of debt might be maintained
for it. Instead of an action of assumpsit upon damages, an action of debt might have
f   been maintained, and there would have been judgment for the amount of the debt.'

Consistently with this, in *Gerrard v Clowes* [1892] 2 QB 11 it was decided that a claim for
£500, the amount stated in a bond securing payment of £250, was not a claim for
damages but was a claim properly brought under RSC Ord 14 on the bond, judgment
being given for £250 as part of the claim to which there was no defence.
g   There is a further point to be mentioned here. As noted above, equity adopted the
attitude in relation to penalty clauses that non-payment of money is adequately
compensated by late payment with interest. This seems to have been established by the
time of Lord Eldon LC, although he was critical of the principle in *Reynolds v Pitt* (1812)
19 Ves Jun 134 at 140, 34 ER 468 at 470. Jessel MR was equally critical in *Wallis v Smith*
(1882) 21 Ch D 243 at 257, but he too accepted that the old decisions were binding.
h Accordingly, once a court becomes aware that the amount claimed by the plaintiff is a
penalty arising on default of payment of a specific sum of money the legal consequence
which follows, as day follows night, is that the amount claimed will be scaled down by
the court to a sum equal to the unpaid principal, with interest and costs. That
consequence, albeit having its historical origin in equity, is not dependent on the court
exercising a discretion to grant or withhold relief having regard to all the circumstances.
j It is a consequence which for many years has followed automatically, regardless of the
circumstances of the default.

In this respect, as the law has developed, a distinction has arisen between the
enforcement of penalty clauses in contracts and the enforcement of forfeiture clauses. A
penalty clause will not be enforced beyond the sum which equals the actual loss of the
innocent party. A forfeiture clause, of which a right of re-entry under a lease on non-

payment of rent is the classic example, may also be penal in its effect. Such a clause frequently subjects the defaulting party, in the event of non-payment of rent or breach *a* of some other obligation, to a sanction which damnifies the defaulting party, and benefits the other party, to an extent far greater than the actual loss of the innocent party. For instance, the lease may be exceedingly valuable and the amount of unpaid rent may be small. But in such a case the court will lend its aid in the enforcement of the forfeiture, by making an order for possession, subject to any relief which in its discretion the court may grant to the party in default. Normally the granting of such relief is made *b* conditional on the payment of the rent with interest and costs. If that condition is not complied with, and subject to any further application by the tenant or other person in default for yet more time, the forfeiture provision will be enforced. Thus the innocent party is in a better position when seeking to enforce a forfeiture clause than when seeking to enforce a penalty clause in a contract.

This is not the occasion to attempt to rationalise the distinction. One possible *c* explanation is that the distinction is rooted in the different forms which the relief takes. In the case of a penalty clause in a contract equity relieves by cutting down the extent to which the contractual obligation is enforceable: the 'scaling-down' exercise, as I have described it. In the case of forfeiture clauses equitable relief takes the form of relieving wholly against the contractual forfeiture provision, subject to compliance with conditions imposed by the court. Be that as it may, I see no reason why the court's ability to grant *d* discretionary relief against forfeiture should deprive a defendant of the relief automatically granted in respect of a penalty clause if, exceptionally, a contractual provision has characteristics which enable a defendant to pray in aid both heads of relief.

Property and not money

I return to penalty clauses. The scaling-down exercise which is carried out automatically *e* by equity is straightforward when the penalty clause provides for payment of a sum of money. More difficult, and more unusual, is the case where the penal obligation triggered by the breach is an obligation to transfer property to the party not in default, as under cl 6(b). Even in such a case there is no difficulty where the value of the property at the time when the court is making its order does not exceed the actual loss of the innocent party. In that event there can be no more objection to the court specifically enforcing the *f* obligation to transfer the property than there would be to the court making an order for the payment of a sum of money stipulated in a (pecuniary) penalty clause where, in the event, that sum does not exceed the actual loss of the innocent party. The difficulty arises where the value of the property agreed to be transferred exceeds the actual loss of the innocent party. A precisely comparable scaling-down exercise would not provide an acceptable solution, at any rate where the property consists of a single piece of land, or a *g* block of shares in a company such as Southend United Football Club Ltd, whose shares are not traded in one of the securities markets. It could not be right to order specific performance of cl 6(b) in part only, namely in respect of the reduced number of shares whose value does not exceed the actual loss of the plaintiff. That, indeed, would be to make a new bargain for the parties. *h*

In the present case we do not know what is the current value of the shares comprised in cl 6(b), even in approximate terms. I shall return later to the question of what, in that circumstance, can and should be done. For the moment it is sufficient to note that, apart from the difference between shares and money, cl 6(b) possesses all the essential characteristics of a penalty clause. In principle, and subject to the complication arising from the difficulty of 'scaling-down' an obligation to transfer shares, there can be no *j* difference between an obligation to pay a stipulated sum of money arising on a default and an obligation to transfer specified property arising on a default. The essential vice is the same in each case. In principle, so far as this can be achieved, the parties' respective positions should be no better, or worse, than they would be if cl 6(b) had stipulated for payment of money rather than a transfer of shares.

A forfeiture clause

a   Clause 6(b), however, is something of a hybrid. It possesses the essential characteristics of a penalty clause in a contract. It also possesses features which resemble those of a forfeiture provision. Clause 6(b) provided that if the purchaser failed to pay all the agreed instalments, he would retransfer to the vendors a slice (44·9%) of the issued share capital of the company equal to the slice the vendors had sold to him. In substance cl 6(b) is equivalent to a right to re-take the property being sold in default of payment of the full

b   price. Clause 6(b) was inserted as an attempt to give the vendors some 'security' over the property being sold if the purchaser failed to pay in full. This was sought to be buttressed by cl 7 of the side-letter. Although worded infelicitously, the object of cl 7 was to impose on the purchaser an obligation to keep a 44·9% stake in the company until the whole of the purchase price had been paid. The protection afforded to the vendors by cl 6(b) was strengthened further by the variation agreement. The purchaser was required to deposit

c   his certificate for his 62,666 shares with his solicitors with irrevocable instructions not to part with possession of it without the consent of the vendors. The purchaser agreed not to charge the shares. Until further instalments to a stated amount had been paid, which has not yet occurred, the vendors were to be entitled to appoint a director to the board of the company. Until all the further instalments had been paid the purchaser agreed that the company would not dispose of any land without the consent of the vendors.

d   The terms of the agreement between the parties were unusual in that, despite the presence of cl 6(b) and the elaborate terms just mentioned, after completion the vendors (and this is common ground between the parties) had no lien or charge over the shares sold. Clause 6(b) operated only as an unsecured personal obligation. Furthermore, under cl 6(b) the shares to be retransferred to the vendors need not be precisely the same shares as those sold by the vendors, nor did the 62,666 shares sold to the defendant comprise

e   exactly 44·9% of the then issued share capital of the company (62,666 shares represented just over 44·9%). Again, if the issued share capital were to be increased (or reduced) before cl 6(b) was invoked, the defendant would be required to transfer a correspondingly larger (or smaller) number of shares under that sub-clause than he had bought. But I do not regard these features as undermining the conclusion that the purpose of cl 6(b) was

f   to provide a form of security for payment in that the purchaser was obliged to restore to the vendors their former stake in the company if default occurred in payment, that stake not to be diminished by any further issues of shares made meanwhile.

So construed, cl 6(b) falls squarely within the words I have emphasised in the following extract from the speech of Lord Wilberforce in *Shiloh Spinners Ltd v Harding* [1973] 1 All ER 90 at 100, [1973] AC 691 at 722:

g   'There cannot be any doubt that from the earliest times courts of equity have
        . asserted the right to relieve against the forfeiture of property. The jurisdiction has
         not been confined to any particular type of case. The commonest instances concerned
         mortgages, giving rise to the equity of redemption, and leases, which commonly
         contained re-entry clauses; but other instances are found in relation to copyholds, or
         where the forfeiture was in the nature of a penalty. Although the principle is well

h   established, there has undoubtedly been some fluctuation of authority as to the self-
         limitation to be imposed or accepted on this power. There has not been much
         difficulty as regards two heads of jurisdiction. First, *where it is possible to state that the
         object of the transaction and of the insertion of the right to forfeit is essentially to secure the
         payment of money, equity has been willing to relieve on terms that the payment is made with
         interest, if appropriate, and also costs (Peachy v Duke of Somerset* (1721) 1 Stra 447, 93

j   ER 626 and cases there cited).'

In the present case cl 6(b) is a term intended to provide the unpaid vendors with some 'security' against non-payment by giving them an alternative remedy (repossession of their former slice in the company) in the event of default in payment of all the instalments. That is a situation in which, par excellence, equity in its discretion, and having regard to all the circumstances, may grant relief. Such relief would normally be on terms that the primary obligation for which this alternative remedy is 'security' is *a* performed within a reasonable time, albeit later than stipulated in the agreement.

In the present case legal and beneficial title to the 62,666 shares had passed to the purchaser before cl 6(b) was invoked. Thus, it was submitted, this case is different from one where the forfeiting party seeks merely to repossess property title to which, or a reversion in which, he has retained throughout. For example, where a landlord seeks to re-enter following forfeiture of a lease for non-payment of rent, or a vendor seeks to eject *b* a purchaser whom he has permitted to enter on the property being sold pending completion. I am unable to accept that this difference represents a crucial distinction in this case. I note that relief from forfeiture was held to be available in the *Shiloh Spinners* case [1973] 1 All ER 90, [1973] AC 691 even though the forfeiting party there had retained no legal or equitable interest, other than the right to re-enter, in the property in question. As the owner of adjoining land he had retained a live, practical interest in *c* seeing that the fencing and support obligations were performed, but the fact that the forfeiting party had this interest cannot by itself turn the case into one in which the defaulting party could have recourse to the equitable principles of relief from forfeiture if otherwise he could not have done so.

I think, therefore, that cl 6(b) is a clause in respect of which Harman J had jurisdiction to grant relief. The most obvious form which the relief might have taken was to relieve *d* the defendant from complying with cl 6(b) if he paid the balance of the price with interest and costs, as occurred in *Re Dagenham (Thames) Dock Co, ex p Hulse* (1873) LR 8 Ch App 1022 at 1025. The contrary conclusion, that the court had no jurisdiction to give relief, would mean that if the defendant's claim for relief had not been struck out at the trial, and if the defendant had been able and willing to pay the outstanding instalments with interest and costs at once in full, the court could still not have given him any relief *e* in respect of cl 6(b), however deserving his case. That is not an acceptable conclusion.

Procedurally it is established practice for a claim by a defendant for relief from forfeiture to be the subject of a counterclaim. Whether that is an issue which can be raised only in a counterclaim as distinct from in a defence is not a matter which calls for consideration in this case, because in the present case the claim for relief from forfeiture *f* was made, in the normal way, in a counterclaim and it was this counterclaim that was struck out by the judge. Thus the defendant's claim for relief from forfeiture was the issue which the judge barred the defendant from pursuing. Against that order of the judge there has been no appeal.

The consequence of no claim for relief

However, I am unable to accept that in the absence of a claim for discretionary relief *g* from forfeiture it follows that the court must or should now specifically enforce cl 6(b) in its entirety, whatever the value of the shares. As I have said, I see no reason why there should not be an order for specific performance of cl 6(b) if the shares do not exceed in value the actual loss of the plaintiff. What that loss comprises, in arithmetical terms, is set out with regard to the facts in the present case in the judgment of Dillon LJ. If, on *h* the other hand, the shares are now worth more than the amount of the plaintiff's loss, the court has available to it a means of ensuring that the purpose for which cl 6(b) was included in the main agreement is duly fulfilled without either party otherwise being prejudiced. Clause 6(b) was intended to provide the vendors with a form of 'security' if the purchaser defaulted in paying the full price. If the shares are now worth more than the actual loss of the plaintiff, ex hypothesi a sale of the shares will realise a sum which is *j* sufficient to put the plaintiff in the financial position he would have occupied if the defendant had not defaulted. If the shares are now sold and the plaintiff is duly paid the amount of his actual loss, with the surplus proceeds being paid to the defendant, the plaintiff will have obtained from cl 6(b) everything for which it was provided as 'security'.

In my view that is the course which the court can and should take. It is the equivalent

in the different circumstances of this case to the automatic scaling-down of a (pecuniary)
a penalty clause. Clause 6(b) is being enforced, in favour of the plaintiff and against the
defendant, but in a form modified to preclude it from operating penally. As I have said,
it would not be right to order the transfer to the defendant of a reduced number of
shares. Nor would it be right to order the transfer of all the shares, to the prejudice of the
defendant, or to refuse to grant any specific relief with regard to the shares, to the
prejudice of the plaintiff, when by ordering (if the plaintiff so requests) that the shares be
b sold, the court can enforce cl 6(b) to an extent, or in a manner, that would give the
plaintiff everything for which cl 6(b) was intended to be 'security' and yet still prevent
the clause operating punitively against the defendant. If the court orders a sale it will be
granting a limited form of specific relief in respect of the defendant's obligations under
cl 6(b). In an early leading case, *Peachy v Duke of Somerset* (1721) 1 Stra 447 at 453, 93 ER
626 at 630, Lord Macclesfield LC observed: 'The true ground of relief against penalties is
c from the original intent of the case, where the penalty is designed only to secure money,
and the Court gives him all that he expected or desired . . .' That will be achieved in this
case by ordering specific relief which stops short of an order for specific performance. A
similar course seems to have been adopted by Lord Romilly MR at first instance in the
Dagenham case. He offered to the applicant seeking leave to execute an order for possession
'an order for sale and payment, as in the ordinary case of vendor's lien' (see LR 8 Ch App
d 1022 at 1024).

Counsel for the plaintiff submitted that the plaintiff ought not to be worse off than he
would be if the defendant had made an application for relief which had succeeded on
terms that the defendant paid all the outstanding instalments with interest and costs
within a stated period. In such event, if the defendant had not complied with the
conditions on which relief was given, the court would have made an order for specific
e performance of cl 6(b). In this way the plaintiff would have obtained either the money
due to him or the shares. As to that, I will say only that the course proposed above will
result in the plaintiff obtaining either the shares (if they are worth less than the actual
amount of the plaintiff's loss) or the money (if the shares are worth more). Both parties
should be free to bid and buy the shares if there is a sale, so that if the plaintiff is anxious
f to acquire a stake in the company he will have the opportunity to do so.

Other defences
For completeness I should add that counsel for the defendant further submitted that
in any event specific performance of cl 6(b) ought not to be ordered, because damages
would afford an adequate remedy. I am unable to accept this. It was not suggested that
g there is an active market in shares in the company in which a 44·9% stake in that
company could readily be bought. Counsel for the plaintiff also relied on evidence by the
original vendors that when the sale agreement was made in 1983 they did not want the
shares, and he submitted that the plaintiff as their assignee could be in no better position
than they would be if they were pursuing the claim themselves. I can see nothing in this.
The Rubins sold the shares, so it is not surprising to find that they did not want them.
h They wanted payment, and cl 6(b) was drafted to protect their position and ensure
payment. But that of itself does not afford any sort of reason for the court declining to
order specific performance of cl 6(b). It may also be that if the plaintiff obtains the shares
he will seek to sell them. But, again, this is not a sound answer to a claim for specific
performance.

j *Conclusion*
For these reasons I would make an order in the terms outlined by Dillon LJ. I agree
also with what he says on the irrecoverability of the unpaid instalments if the plaintiff
chooses to take an order for the enforcement of cl 6(b) in the manner discussed above. I
would be disposed to hear counsel on the precise calculation of the plaintiff's actual loss,
in particular with regard to interest and costs.

I regret to find myself differing from Kerr LJ in that I am unable to agree with the alternative course proposed by him. That course would restore the parties, so far as is now possible, to their pre-contract positions. That approach does not accord with the established equitable principle relating to penalty clauses, whereunder equity confines the sum recoverable under a penalty clause to the loss actually suffered by the innocent party by reason of the breach of contract.

KERR LJ. I respectfully differ on one aspect of this puzzling case from the conclusions reached in the judgments of Dillon and Nicholls LJJ, which I have had the great advantage of reading. This concerns the choice of remedies to which the plaintiff should now be entitled.

It is common ground that cl 6(b) is penal in its nature. The reason is of course not that the value of the shares might rise substantially above the agreed price before the end of the period during which the instalments fall to be paid, although in my view, as explained below, this may be relevant to the appropriate order which should now be considered in the unusual circumstances of this case. The reason why cl 6(b) is penal in its nature, as explained by Dillon LJ, is that it subjects the defendant to the same liability irrespective of the gravity and consequences of the breach relied on by the plaintiff in seeking to enforce the clause: see *Dunlop Pneumatic Tyre Co Ltd v New Garage and Motor Co Ltd* [1915] AC 79 at 87, [1914–15] All ER Rep 739 at 742 per Lord Dunedin. This is a question which falls to be decided on the true construction of the clause independently of subsequent events (see [1915] AC 79 at 86–87, [1914–15] All ER Rep 739 at 741–742).

However, it does not follow that a penalty clause is illegal in the same way as, for instance, provisions imposing unlawful restraints of trade. These are simply struck down, or 'blue-pencilled', because they are prohibited on the ground of public policy, unless it is possible to sever the good from the bad. Penalty clauses falling within the principles considered in the *Dunlop Tyre* case are not in the same category. In my view, the combined effect of law and equity on penalty clauses is simply that they will not be enforced in favour of a plaintiff without first giving to the defendant a proper opportunity to obtain relief against their penal consequences.

This is of particular importance in relation to the relevant provision in the present case. I respectfully agree with the analysis of Nicholls LJ in the section of his judgment headed 'A forfeiture clause' that this is the true nature of cl 6(b). Although this classification presents some obvious problems, due to the fact that no property in the shares was retained by the vendor and that the identical shares did not have to be retransferred by the purchaser, taking cl 6(b) in the context of the other provisions to which Nicholls LJ refers it is in my view much closer to what is commonly referred to as a 'forfeiture' than a 'penalty' clause. It follows a fortiori that cl 6(b) is not *necessarily* unenforceable, but merely that the defendant must be given a proper opportunity of seeking appropriate relief before there can be any question of enforcing the provisions.

This analysis is also supported by the course which this action would have taken but for the fact that the defendant's counterclaim for relief came to be struck out due to his own fault, and I did not understand anyone to suggest the contrary. The normal course of events would have been that the defendant would have been granted relief from the obligation to retransfer the shares, but on terms that he must pay the then outstanding instalments in full, together with interest and the plaintiff's costs: see eg per Lord Wilberforce in *Shiloh Spinners Ltd v Harding* [1973] 1 All ER 90 at 100, [1973] AC 691 at 722. However, if it should then have turned out that the defendant was unwilling or unable to abide by these terms, after he had been given every reasonable opportunity to do so, then an order for the retransfer of the shares on the terms of cl 6(b) would have been made. This is an everyday situation in the context of provisions for forfeiture in leases, and it is also the basis on which the law of mortgages and the equity of redemption have developed. It seems to work well in practice and to cause little injustice. Thus, if in

the present case the value of the shares in January 1987 had been greatly in excess of the
a outstanding instalments when Harman J was dealing with the matter, then Mr Johnson,
the defendant, would no doubt have been willing and able to raise the amount of the
outstanding instalments together with interest and costs, if necessary by borrowing on
the security of the shares, in order to obtain relief in the normal way.

However, the defendant chose not to pursue this course. He evidently preferred to let
his counterclaim be struck out. Perhaps he was unwilling to comply with an order which
b would have forced him to reveal his financial circumstances; or it may be that the then
value of the shares made a claim for relief unattractive; or perhaps he had both
considerations in mind. In the result, the stage of considering and formulating the terms
on which relief should be granted was never reached.

In these unusual circumstances, but only with considerable doubt, I respectfully agree
with the judgments of Dillon and Nicholls LJJ that it was at any rate premature to grant
c immediate specific performance of a forfeiture clause which, for the reasons already
stated, was also penal in its nature.

But more than a year has passed since then. Although both parties were somewhat
cagey about explaining the present position, it is clear that circumstances have changed.
On behalf of the defendant, counsel intimated to us, as I understood him, that the shares
were now worth far more than the total outstanding purchase price and that the
d defendant would have no difficulty in raising the necessary sum to be granted relief on
usual terms to obtain their release from escrow. On behalf of the plaintiff, counsel did
not contradict these veiled references to the present value of the shares, but he reminded
us repeatedly that we had no evidence of their value and must not speculate about it. He
also pointed out that counsel for the defendant was careful not to suggest that there was
any way whereby the defendant's struck-out counterclaim for relief could now somehow
e be revived.

If one accepts that the order for specific performance made by Harman J cannot stand,
as I do albeit with doubt, what is the appropriate course which this court should now
take? Two things appear clear. First, the rights of the plaintiff cannot be prejudiced by
the defendant's failure to pursue the offer of relief which the court was bound to, and
f did, grant to him. If this process had run its normal course, then the plaintiff would have
obtained an order for payment by the defendant of all the outstanding instalments,
together with interest and costs, within a reasonable time, or alternatively for the
retransfer of the shares pursuant to cl 6(b) in default of compliance.

Secondly, it is plain that whereas in January 1987 the issue may have been largely
about money, at any rate so far as the defendant was concerned, it is now solely about the
right to the shares. Both sides are clearly most anxious to obtain them and interested in
g little else. That is why counsel for the defendant took pains to let us know, although
perhaps he should not have done so, that the defendant was now willing, able and
extremely keen to comply with any order as to payment if he is permitted to retain the
shares. It is equally the reason why counsel on behalf of the plaintiff not only formally
declined the court's offer of a monetary judgment, but also made no response to counsel
h for the defendant's offer of more or less readily available cash in full.

Quite apart from the fact that the counterclaim for relief has been struck out, I agree
that it is now far too late for the defendant to seek relief in the normal way. I say that,
because in my view the plea in the defence that cl 6(b) is a penal provision obliges the
court to offer relief to the defendant, without the need for any formal counterclaim. It
follows inevitably, once it is clear that the plaintiff is seeking to enforce a penalty clause.
j I also agree that, given that the order of Harman J cannot stand, it is necessary for this
court to reach an appropriate conclusion in equity. To this end the judgments of Dillon
and Nicholls LJJ have offered the choice of two remedies to the plaintiff. The first is an
order for the sale of the shares by the court and payment of the unpaid instalments and
interest out of the proceeds, no doubt together with costs in the ordinary way, and
obviously leaving it open to the plaintiff to sue thereafter for any balance of the price

which may still be outstanding. The second is an inquiry as to the value of the shares, and an order to the effect of cl 6(b) in the event that their present value is less than the *a* total net sum presently due from the defendant; but not otherwise.

In my view neither of these alternatives offers sufficient justice to the plaintiff in the exceptional circumstances of this case. The first alternative differs little from simply granting relief to the defendant in the usual way, save that this would be accompanied by what would in effect be an auction of the shares, in which both parties as well as outsiders could compete. The second alternative is almost certainly unrealistic and not a *b* worthwhile offer in practice, since it is to be suspected that the present value of the shares greatly exceeds all monetary sums to which the plaintiff is now entitled.

In these circumstances it seems to me that, in equity, the plaintiff is entitled to a further alternative. This would be an order giving effect to cl 6(b), but on terms that the plaintiff repays to the defendant, perhaps with interest, the £160,000 which he has received under the agreement. In my view a further option to this effect would do justice *c* to the plaintiff without contravening any principle of equity. It would give effect to the unenforceability of cl 6(b) because of its penal nature, but without simply 'blue-pencilling' it, which would be wrong. Secondly, it would provide some compensation to the plaintiff for having lost the opportunity of obtaining an order in terms of cl 6(b) because the normal process of an application for relief from forfeiture was frustrated by the defendant's decision to allow his counterclaim to be struck out. Above all, it would *d* result in equitable restitution to both parties, without either enforcing or 'blue-pencilling' cl 6(b). There is nothing penal about a provision that, in the event of a failure by the defendant to pay any instalment of the price, the plaintiff is to be entitled to rescind the contract and to recover the goods against a refund of all sums received by him: cf *Alder v Moore* [1961] 1 All ER 1, [1961] 2 QB 57. Clause 6(b) is penal, because its operation takes no account of the sums already received, and to that extent it is unenforceable. But it is *e* enforceable to the extent that it is not a penalty, by requiring full restitution by the plaintiff as a condition of its enforcement. That would not be a case of 'mending men's bargains', but the enforcement of a penal forfeiture clause by the removal of its penal element, and in a situation where relief from forfeiture can no longer be claimed by the defendant.   *f*

Subject to offering this further alternative to the plaintiff I therefore agree that the order of Harman J should be set aside and that the defendant's appeal should be allowed to this extent.

Appeal allowed to extent indicated in judgments of Dillon and Nicholls LJJ.

Solicitors: *Maurice Hackenbroch & Co* (for the defendant); *Jefferies,* Westcliff-on-Sea (for the *g* plaintiff).

Wendy Shockett   Barrister.

a
Atlas Express Ltd v Kafco (Importers and Distributors) Ltd

QUEEN'S BENCH DIVISION (COMMERCIAL COURT)
TUCKER J
12, 13 DECEMBER 1988, 10 JANUARY 1989

b

Contract – Duress – Economic duress – Commercial pressure – Contract to carry goods at agreed consideration – Carriers subsequently seeking to increase charges – Carriers refusing to carry goods unless distributors agreeing to pay increased charges – Distributors agreeing to pay increased charges in order to meet commitments to customers – Whether agreement to pay increased charges valid.

c

The plaintiffs, a national road carrier, entered into a contract with the defendants, a small company which imported and distributed basketware to the retail trade, to deliver cartons of basketware to branches of a national retail chain for the defendants. Before the contract was entered into the plaintiffs' depot manager had inspected the cartons, which were of different sizes, and estimated that each load would contain a minimum of 400
d and possibly as many as 600 cartons and on that basis he agreed a rate of carriage of £1·10 per carton. In fact the first load contained only 200 cartons and the plaintiffs' depot manager told the defendants that the plaintiffs would not carry any more cartons unless the defendants agreed to pay a minimum of £440 per load. The defendants were heavily dependent on the retail chain's contract and were unable at the time to find an alternative carrier. The defendants accordingly agreed to the new terms but later refused to pay the
e new rate. The plaintiffs brought an action to recover the amount owing under the new rate.

Held – Where a party to a contract was forced by the other party to renegotiate the terms of the contract to his disadvantage and had no alternative but to accept the new terms offered, his apparent consent to the new terms was vitiated by economic duress. Applying
f that principle, the pressure applied by the plaintiffs to the defendants to renegotiate the terms of the contract amounted to economic duress which vitiated the contract. In any event, there was no consideration for the new agreement. Accordingly, the plaintiffs could not sue to recover the amount owing under the new rate and the claim would be dismissed (see p 644 g, p 645 b, p 646 h and p 647 a, post).

Dictum of Lord Scarman in *Pao On v Lau Yiu* [1979] 3 All ER 65 at 78–79 applied.

g

Notes
For a contract entered into under duress, see 9 Halsbury's Laws (4th edn) paras 290, 297, and for cases on the subject, see 12 Digest (Reissue) 118–124, 640–679.

h
Cases referred to in judgment
Astley v Reynolds (1731) 2 Stra 915, 93 ER 939.
B & S Contracts and Design Ltd v Victor Green Publications Ltd [1984] ICR 419, CA.
Barton v Armstrong [1975] 2 All ER 465, [1976] AC 104, [1975] 2 WLR 1050, PC.
D & C Builders Ltd v Rees [1965] 3 All ER 837, [1966] 2 QB 617, [1966] 2 WLR 288, CA.
Maskell v Horner [1915] 3 KB 106, [1914–15] All ER Rep 595, CA.
j *North Ocean Shipping Co Ltd v Hyundai Construction Co Ltd, The Atlantic Baron* [1978] 3 All ER 1170, [1979] QB 705, [1978] 3 WLR 419.
Occidental Worldwide Investment Corp v Skibs A/S Avanti, The Siboen and the Sibotre [1976] 1 Lloyd's Rep 293.
Pao On v Lau Yiu [1979] 3 All ER 65, [1980] AC 614, [1979] 3 WLR 435, PC.
Skeate v Beale (1841) 11 Ad & El 983, 113 ER 688.

Universe Tankships Inc of Monrovia v International Transport Workers' Federation [1982] 2
    All ER 67, [1983] 1 AC 366, [1982] 2 WLR 803, HL.

Action
The plaintiffs, Atlas Express Ltd, brought an action against the defendants, Kafco
(Importers and Distributors) Ltd, claiming £10,970·37 and interest being the amount
outstanding under a number of invoices submitted to the defendants for road haulage
services provided to the defendants. The facts are set out in the judgment.

David Fisher for the plaintiffs.
I H Foster for the defendants.

Cur adv vult

10 January. The following judgment was delivered.

TUCKER J. By their statement of claim the plaintiffs, Atlas Express Ltd, claim against
the defendants, Kafco (Importers and Distributors) Ltd, £17,031·83 plus interest, as
outstanding payments due to them under a number of invoices submitted to the
defendants. It is admitted that some of this has since been paid, and the sum now claimed
is £10,970·37.
    The plaintiffs are well-known carriers of goods by road in the United Kingdom. They
offer a parcels delivery service. The defendant company derives its name from the first
letters of the surnames of its three original directors, Messrs King, Armiger and Fox. The
company imports basketware from abroad and supplies it to retailers in the United
Kingdom.
    On 24 June 1986 the plaintiffs entered into a general trading agreement with the
defendants whereby the plaintiffs agreed to deliver cartons of the defendants' basketware
at a rate per carton depending on the number of cartons in the load. By October 1986
the defendants had entered into an agreement to supply their basketware to Woolworth
shops in the United Kingdom. The defendants wished the plaintiffs to make the deliveries
for them, and the plaintiffs agreed to do so. The terms of this agreement were contained
in a trading agreement signed by Mr Armiger on the defendants' behalf on 20 October
1986. The rate agreed was expressed as being £1·10 per carton. There was a minimum
charge of £7·50 per consignment but this referred to the delivery to each branch. The
agreement was silent as to the size of the cartons or as to the number of cartons necessary
to constitute a load. The rate was expressed to be effective from 10 October 1986 to a
review on 31 May 1987. The case proceeded on the basis that this was a concluded
agreement. Neither the plaintiffs' nor the defendants' counsel submitted that it was not
capable of giving effect to the parties' intentions, and this issue was not raised in the
pleadings.
    The rate agreement was that orally agreed between Mr Armiger and Mr Hope, the
manager of the plaintiffs' depot in Wellingborough. They met at the defendants'
warehouse at Tinker's Drove, Wisbech, on 10 October 1986. Mr Hope had gone there to
see a sample of the goods his company were being asked to deliver. He was shown a
range of cartons of the sort the defendants used. He cannot say what size the largest
carton was which he then saw, because he did not take any measurements. The trailers
which the plaintiffs used were 40 feet long. Mr Hope says he calculated the rate per
carton on the basis that the plaintiffs would be transporting a minimum of 400 cartons,
and possibly as many as 600, on each trailer, thus producing a minimum return of £440
per load. In order to achieve this quantity per load, it would be necessary that no carton
should exceed a measurement of 2ft 6in in any dimension. Mr Hope said that to the best
of his memory, he and Mr Armiger discussed the basis on which the rate was calculated,

though later he agreed that he was not sure they had had a conversation about a load of
a 400. Mr Armiger was firmer in his evidence. He said that the sizes of the cartons were
never discussed and nothing was said about the number of cartons which would be
carried, and that he could not have agreed a figure of 400 because he never knew what
revenue the plaintiffs expected, and he did not know how many cartons could be loaded
onto a trailer.

I prefer Mr Armiger's evidence on this point. I think his recollection of the conversation
b is clearer than Mr Hope's, and I believe him. His account is confirmed to some extent by
the telex which he sent to Mr Hope on 13 October, referring simply to the rate per carton
and not to size or number. Further, when Mr Hope drew up the trading agreement, he
made no mention of these matters. As I have already indicated, there was no reference to
this in the written agreement which Mr Armiger signed on 20 October. But when
Mr Hope wrote to Mr Armiger on 17 November about raising a minimum charge, he
c referred to the initial quote of £1·10 per carton but he did not suggest that the basis on
which this figure had been agreed had ever been discussed at the initial meeting.

In any event, the plaintiffs' counsel said that he did not rely on any knowledge by
Mr Armiger of the basis on which the calculation was made. This was not part of his
pleaded case, and he did not submit that this was a term of the contract between the
parties, or that it was a representation made by or on behalf of the defendants.
d
Much more important is the question of the sample or mix of cartons which Mr Hope
saw at the defendants' warehouse at Tinker's Drove, Wisbech. It is agreed that he did not
see any of the goods destined for Woolworth, because they were stored at another
warehouse called Wisbech Roadways. But I accept the evidence of Mr Armiger, supported
to a great extent by that of Mr King, that the cartons which Mr Hope did see included
e three kinds of the same size as those in which the Woolworth goods were contained, and
that the fourth kind of carton used to pack Woolworth's goods was of a smaller size than
the three kinds which Mr Hope saw. I find that the plaintiffs had already carried those
three sizes of cartons for the defendants under their general agreement. I also find that
the largest carton to be carried for Woolworth was a bale measuring 6 feet long by 18
inches diameter, and that bales of that kind and size were present at Mr Hope's inspection.
f I find that Mr Hope saw a fair and representative mix of the kind of cartons which his
company was being asked to deliver, and that he was given every opportunity of
inspecting what was there, so as to enable him to calculate the rate to be quoted. It may
be that Mr Hope mistakenly believed that he could load more cartons on to a trailer than
was physically possible but, in fixing the rate of £1·10 per carton, he was not in any way
misled by the defendants and he should not have been deceived by the sample and mix
g of cartons which he saw.

In pursuance of the written agreement, the plaintiffs proceeded to make the first
delivery. When Mr Hope saw the load from the defendants, he said he was surprised to
see how large the cartons were and how many large cartons were included in the load.
He said they were far larger than the parties had contemplated, and because of this there
were fewer of them, only 200 instead of the 400 he had anticipated. He said he had no
h prior knowledge that cartons of that size would be included. I find that he is wrong
about this. I accept Mr Armiger's evidence that the load was representative of the type of
cartons which Mr Hope had seen at the warehouse, and that the cartons were no larger
than those inspected by him.

However, Mr Hope was convinced that it would not be financially viable to carry such
a load at the rate agreed. He contacted Mr Armiger about it, in an attempt to renegotiate
j the rate. I find that the two of them met to discuss it, and that Mr Hope made it plain to
Mr Armiger that the plaintiffs would not carry any more goods under the Woolworth
agreement unless the defendants agreed to pay at least a minimum rate of £440 per
trailer load. I find that if the defendants had refused, the plaintiffs would not have made
any further deliveries. However, I find that no agreement to renegotiate the terms of the
contract was reached at this stage.

The defendants were a small company and their three directors were personally committed to its success. They had secured a large order from Woolworth and had obtained a large quantity of goods in order to fulfil it. It was essential to the defendants' success and to their commercial survival that they should be in a position to make deliveries. I find that this was obvious to Mr Hope, and was known by him. It was now early November, a time of year when demands on road hauliers and deliverers are heaviest.

It would have been difficult, if not impossible, for the defendants to find alternative carriers in time to meet their delivery dates.

I find that the meeting between Mr Hope and Mr Armiger took place on Friday, 14 November. I derive this date from a letter written by Mr Hope on 17 November, which would have been the following Monday. The letter is in these terms:

'Further to our conversation on Friday 14 November, I would confirm the necessity for Atlas Express Limited to raise a minimum charge of £440 per trailer for distribution to Woolworth Stores. Our initial quote of £1·10 per carton was based purely and simply on our achieving a minimum of 400 cartons per trailer, indeed we were anticipating a far higher figure in some instances. It is unfortunate that this has added considerably to your distribution costs. However, we as a company could not accommodate your operation whilst achieving such a possibly low revenue per movement. I have, therefore, enclosed an updated trading agreement for covering this new aspect of the operation which I will require signing and handing back to my driver by return.'

The following day, 18 November, one of the plaintiffs' drivers arrived at the defendants' premises with an empty trailer. He brought with him a document entitled 'Amended/ Transferred Account Details'. Mr Hope had written in the new rates, which now specified a minimum charge of £400 per trailer. Mr Armiger did not want to agree to this, and he had not done so at the meeting. He queried it with the driver, who said that he had instructions that if the defendants did not sign the agreement he was to take the trailer away unloaded. Mr Armiger had done his best at the meeting to persuade Mr Hope to reduce his demands, but the only concession he had achieved was that the minimum charge would not apply to deliveries within the five counties nearest to the plaintiffs' depot at Wellingborough. Mr Armiger tried to contact Mr Hope on 18 November, but he was unable to do so. Mr Hope was unavailable. I infer that this was deliberate. It prevented the defendants from protesting to him. In these circumstances, Mr Armiger justifiably felt himself to be in a situation of 'take it or leave it'. He could not afford to lose the plaintiffs' services, with all the consequences that would ensue, so he signed the agreement. Before doing so, he wrote in the concession which he had obtained.

I find that when Mr Armiger signed that agreement he did so unwillingly and under compulsion. He believed on reasonable grounds that it would be very difficult, if not impossible, to negotiate with another contractor. He did not regard the fact that he had signed the new agreement as binding the defendants to its terms. He had no bargaining power. He did not regard it as a genuine armslength renegotiation in which he had a free and equal say and, in my judgment, that view was fully justified.

In the words of the co-director, Mr Fox, he felt that he was 'over a barrel'. He tried in vain to contact Mr Hope but, as he said to Mr Armiger, they really had no option but to sign. I accept the evidence of the Woolworth manager, Mr Graham, that if the defendants had told them that they could not supply the goods Woolworth would have sued them for loss of profit and would have ceased trading with them. I find that this was well known to the defendants' directors.

After Mr Armiger signed the agreement, the plaintiffs' driver agreed to load a delivery. Thereafter the plaintiffs carried the defendants' goods and delivered them to Woolworth until 29 December 1986. The plaintiffs knew that the defendants would not be paid by Woolworth until deliveries were completed, and the plaintiffs agreed that they would

not expect payment from the defendants until the defendants had been paid by
Woolworth. Mr Hope recognised that this would not be before 30 January 1987.

a

On 2 February 1987 the defendants sent to the plaintiffs a cheque for £10,000,
expressed as being a payment on account. I do not regard that as an acceptance of the
new terms. The defendants made their position quite clear through their solicitors, who
wrote to the plaintiffs on 2 March 1987, saying that the revised contract was signed under
duress. This was three months before the plaintiffs commenced proceedings.

b

The issue which I have to determine is whether the defendants are bound by the
agreement signed on their behalf on 18 November 1986. The defendants contend that
they are not bound, for two reasons: first, because the agreement was signed under
duress; second, because there was no consideration for it.

The first question raises an interesting point of law, ie whether economic duress is a
concept known to English law.

c

Economic duress must be distinguished from commercial pressure, which on any
view is not sufficient to vitiate consent. The borderline between the two may in some
cases be indistinct. But the authors of *Chitty on Contracts* (25th edn, 1983) and of *Goff and
Jones on the Law of Restitution* (3rd edn, 1986) appear to recognise that in appropriate cases
economic duress may afford a defence, and in my judgment it does. It is clear to me that
in a number of English cases judges have acknowledged the existence of this concept.

d

Thus, in *D & C Builders Ltd v Rees* [1965] 3 All ER 837 at 841, [1966] 2 QB 617 at 625
Lord Denning MR said: 'No person can insist on a settlement procured by intimidation.'
And in *Occidental Worldwide Investment Corp v Skibs A/S Avanti, The Siboen and the Sibotre*
[1976] 1 Lloyd's Rep 293 at 336 Kerr J appeared to accept that economic duress could
operate in appropriate circumstances. A similar conclusion was reached by Mocatta J in
North Ocean Shipping Co Ltd v Hyundai Construction Co Ltd, The Atlantic Baron [1978] 3 All

e

ER 1170 at 1182, [1979] QB 705 at 719.

In particular, there are passages in the judgment of Lord Scarman in *Pao On v Lau Yiu*
[1979] 3 All ER 65 at 78–79, [1980] AC 614 at 635–636, which clearly indicate
recognition of the concept, where Lord Scarman said:

f

'Duress, whatever form it takes, is a coercion of the will so as to vitiate consent.
Their Lordships agree with the observation of Kerr J in *The Siboen and The Sibotre*
[1976] 1 Lloyd's Rep 293 at 336 that in a contractual situation commercial pressure
is not enough. There must be present some factor "which could in law be regarded
as a coercion of his will so as to vitiate his consent". This conception is in line with
what was said in this Board's decision in *Barton v Armstrong* [1975] 2 All ER 465 at
476–477, [1976] AC 104 at 121 by Lord Wilberforce and Lord Simon of Glaisdale,
observations with which the majority judgment appears to be in agreement. In

g

determining whether there was a coercion of will such that there was no true
consent, it is material to enquire whether the person alleged to have been coerced
did or did not protest; whether, at the time he was allegedly coerced into making
the contract, he did or did not have an alternative course open to him such as an
adequate legal remedy; whether he was independently advised; and whether after

h

entering the contract he took steps to avoid it. All these matters are, as was recognised
in *Maskell v Horner* [1915] 3 KB 106, [1914–15] All ER Rep 595, relevant in
determining whether he acted voluntarily or not. In the present case there is
unanimity amongst the judges below that there was no coercion of Lau's will. In
the Court of Appeal the trial judge's finding (already quoted) that Lau considered
the matter thoroughly, chose to avoid litigation, and formed the opinion that the

j

risk in giving the guarantee was more apparent than real was upheld. In short, there
was commercial pressure, but no coercion. Even if this Board was disposed, which
it is not, to take a different view, it would not substitute its opinion for that of the
judges below on this question of fact. It is, therefore, unnecessary for the Board to
embark on an enquiry into the question whether English law recognises a category
of duress known as "economic duress". But, since the question has been fully argued

in this appeal, their Lordships will indicate very briefly the view which they have formed. At common law money paid under economic compulsion could be recovered in an action for money had and received: see *Astley v Reynolds* (1731) 2 Stra 915, 93 ER 939. The compulsion had to be such that the party was deprived of "his freedom of exercising his will" (see 2 Stra 915 at 916 93 ER 939). It is doubtful, however, whether at common law any duress other than duress to the person sufficed to render a contract voidable; see Blackstone's Commentaries (12th edn, 1793) vol 1, pp 130–131 and *Skeate v Beale* (1841) 11 Ad & El 983, 113 ER 688. American law (Williston on Contracts (3rd edn, 1970) ch 47) now recognises that a contract may be avoided on the ground of economic duress. The commercial pressure alleged to constitute such duress must, however, be such that the victim must have entered the contract against his will, must have had no alternative course open to him, and must have been confronted with coercive acts by the party exerting the pressure: see Williston on Contracts ch 47, s 1603. American judges pay great attention to such evidential matters as the effectiveness of the alternative remedy available, the fact or absence of protest, the availability of independent advice, the benefit received, and the speed with which the victim has sought to avoid the contract. Recently two English judges have recognised that commercial pressure may constitute duress the presence of which can render a contract voidable [Lord Scarman then referred to the judgments of Kerr and Mocatta JJ to which I have referred and continued:] Both stressed that the pressure must be such that the victim's consent to the contract was not a voluntary act on his part. In their Lordship's view, there is nothing contrary to principle in recognising economic duress as a factor which may render a contract voidable, provided always that the basis of such recognition is that it must amount to a coercion of will, which vitiates consent. It must be shown that the payment made or the contract entered into was not a voluntary act.'

A further case, which was not cited to me was *B & S Contracts and Design Ltd v Victor Green Publications Ltd* [1984] ICR 419 at 423, where Eveleigh LJ referred to the speech of Lord Diplock in another uncited case, *Universe Tankships Inc of Monrovia v International Transport Workers' Federation* [1982] 2 All ER 67 at 75–76, [1983] AC 366 at 384:

> 'The rationale is that his apparent consent was induced by pressure exercised on him by that other party which the law does not regard as legitimate, with the consequence that the consent is treated in law as revocable unless approbated either expressly or by implication after the illegitimate pressure has ceased to operate on his mind.'

In commenting on this Eveleigh LJ said of the word 'legitimate' ([1984] ICR 419 at 423):

> 'For the purpose of this case it is sufficient to say that if the claimant has been influenced against his will to pay money under the threat of unlawful damage to his economic interest he will be entitled to claim that money back . . .'

Reverting to the case before me, I find that the defendants' apparent consent to the agreement was induced by pressure which was illegitimate and I find that it was not approbated. In my judgment that pressure can properly be described as economic duress, which is a concept recognised by English law, and which in the circumstances of the present case vitiates the defendants' apparent consent to the agreement.

In any event, I find that there was no consideration for the new agreement. The plaintiffs were already obliged to deliver the defendants' goods at the rates agreed under the terms of the original agreement. There was no consideration for the increased minimum charge of £440 per trailer.

Accordingly, I find that the plaintiffs' claim fails, and there will be judgment for the
a defendants with costs.

Action dismissed.

Solicitors: *Shoosmiths & Harrison*, Northampton (for the plaintiffs); *Barlows*, Chertsey (for
the defendants).
b

K Mydeen Esq   Barrister.

R v Secretary of State for Trade and Industry
c   and others, ex parte R

QUEEN'S BENCH DIVISION
MUSTILL LJ AND McCOWAN J
17, 18, 28 NOVEMBER 1988

d
*Company – Investigation by Department of Trade and Industry – Affairs of company –
Investment business – Investigation of past business transactions – Whether powers of investigation
retrospective – Whether business transactions carried out prior to enactment of statutory powers
of investigation constituting 'investment business' – Financial Services Act 1986, s 105.*

e The Secretary of State for Trade and Industry's power under s 105[a] of the Financial
Services Act 1986 to investigate the affairs of an 'investment business' does not entitle
him to investigate business transactions which took place before the date on which the
material provisions of that Act setting out his investigative powers and characterising the
different types of investment business activity that could be investigated came into effect,
ie 18 December 1986, since the investigative scheme created by the Act is not
f retrospective and transactions which took place prior to that date are not 'investment
business' within the meaning of the Act (see p 650 g h and p 651 f to j, post).

Notes
For investigation of any investment business, see Supplement to 32 Halsbury's Laws (4th
edn) para 347.
g   For the Financial Services Act 1986, s 105, see 30 Halsbury's Statutes (4th edn) 360.
As from 19 May 1987 the Secretary of State's powers to investigate investment
businesses were transferred to the Securities and Investments Board Ltd by the Financial
Services Act 1986 (Delegation) Order 1987, SI 1987/942, subject to a reservation that they
were exercisable by the Secretary of State concurrently with the board.

h ### Case cited
Lauri v Renad [1892] 3 Ch 402, CA.

Preliminary issue
A company director applied with leave of Kennedy J given on 12 October 1988 for
judicial review of an order of the Secretary of State for Trade and Industry dated 19 May
j 1988 authorising two inspectors, David Alexander Caruth and John Pitkeathly Percy, to
investigate the applicant's affairs pursuant to s 105 of the Financial Services Act 1986,
seeking, inter alia, a declaration that 'investment business' within the meaning of the
1986 Act did not include business carried on before 18 December 1986, the date when

---

a   Section 105, so far as material, is set out at p 648 *e* to *g*, post

the material provisions of the 1986 Act came into effect. It was agreed that the point of
law raised thereby should be tried as a separate issue. The court held that since the degree   *a*
of confidentiality appropriate to the proceedings had not been determined by the date of
the hearing the applicant should not be identified. The facts are set out in the judgment
of Mustill LJ.

Anthony Arlidge QC, Peter Rook and *David Chivers* for the applicant.
A W H Charles for the Secretary of State.   *b*

Cur adv vult

28 November. The following judgments were delivered.

MUSTILL LJ. The Secretary of State for Trade and Industry, claiming to act in   *c*
pursuance of powers vested in him by s 105(4) of the Financial Services Act 1986, has
called for the disclosure of documents said to be relevant to the affair of a businessman.
The latter challenges this demand by judicial review, raising a number of questions,
some of law, others of mixed law and fact. Only the first of these is before the court
today. Since it turns exclusively on the interpretation of s 105, and since the degree of
confidentiality which should attach to proceedings of this particular kind has been put in   *d*
question but not yet determined, it is convenient for the time being to identify the
businessman only as 'the applicant'.

Although the demand for production is made pursuant to s 105(4), the dispute hinges
on sub-s (1). Section 105(1) and (4) read as follows:

'(1) The powers of the Secretary of State under this section shall be exercisable in   *e*
any case in which it appears to him that there is good reason to do so for the purpose
of investigating the affairs, or any aspect of the affairs, of any person so far as relevant
to any investment business which he is or was carrying on or appears to the Secretary
of State to be or to have been carrying on . . .

(4) The Secretary of State may require the person under investigation or any
other person to produce at a specified time and place any specified documents which   *f*
appear to the Secretary of State to relate to any matter relevant to the investigation;
and—(a) if any such documents are produced, the Secretary of State may take copies
or extracts from them or require the person producing them or any connected
person to provide an explanation of any of them; (b) if any such documents are not
produced, the Secretary of State may require the person who was required to produce
them to state, to the best of his knowledge and belief, where they are.'   *g*

The terminology used in s 105, which is also to be found in many other provisions of the
1986 Act, is established by s 1. So far as material this is in the following terms:

'(1) In this Act, unless the context otherwise requires, "investment" means any
asset, right or interest falling within any paragraph in Part I of Schedule 1 to this
Act.   *h*

(2) In this Act "investment business" means the business of engaging in one or
more of the activities which fall within the paragraphs in Part II of that Schedule
and are not excluded by Part III of that Schedule.'

If one now looks at Sch 1 to the 1986 Act, it is seen to have three relevant parts. The
first contains a list of choses in action which are to rank as 'investments' for the purpose   *j*
of the Act. As one would expect, these included rights under contracts for options,
futures and differences, and long term insurance contracts.

Part II of Sch 1 describes the activities which constitute investment business, subject to
the exceptions in Pt III. These activities comprise dealing in investments, namely buying,
selling, subscribing for or underwriting investments, arranging deals in investments for
others, managing investments for others and giving investment advice. Part III of Sch 1

contains an elaborate statement of activities which are not to constitute investment
a business, even if they fall within the wide scope of Pt II. For present purposes it is
sufficient to note that some of the exclusions are defined by reference to characteristics of
the party with whom the person on whose activities the 1986 Act is focusing does
business. For convenience I will call these the 'counter-party' and the 'primary party'
respectively, although this is not the terminology of the Act. Other exceptions relate to
permissions given or certificates issued by the Secretary of State.

b   The dispute about s 105 arises in this way. Earlier this year, the Secretary of State
appointed two inspectors to exercise the powers conferred on him by s 105. The
inspectors thereupon wrote to the applicant, identifying 14 categories of documents, and
calling on him to produce all documents within these categories emanating from him or
addressed to him or to certain companies which related to the period from 1 January
1984 to date. Although willing to disclose voluntarily certain of the documents comprised
c in this demand, the applicant objected to its validity on the ground that (i) he did not at
any material time carry on 'investment business', within the meaning of the 1986 Act,
(ii) no activities carried on before 18 December 1986, the date on which certain provisions
of the Act, including ss 1, 2 and 105 and Sch 1, came into effect, were capable of
amounting to investment business (see Sch 1 to the Financial Services Act 1986
(Commencement No 3) Order 1986, SI 1986/2246) and (iii) the demands were not for
d 'specified' documents, since they were expressed only in terms of general categories.
Since the inspectors did not accept these objections, the applicant pursued them through
the medium of an application for judicial review. It has been agreed that the point raised
by the second objection shall be determined by the court ahead of the others, in the shape
of the following question: whether activities carried out before 18 December 1986 can
or cannot be investment business within the meaning of the Financial Services Act 1986.

e   Before addressing this question it is necessary to emphasise one important point,
namely that the powers of the inspectors are said to be confined, not by reference to the
dates on the documents whose production is demanded, but to the time when the party
was carrying on the investment business to which the documents called for are said to be
relevant. Thus, it is not in dispute that if on the facts and the law the applicant actually
was, or if it appears to the Secretary of State that he was, carrying on investment business
f after the appointed day, the inspectors have power to call for documents which appear
relevant to the investigation of affairs relating to that business, irrespective of whether
they came into existence before or after the appointed day.

    Returning to the question now before the court, the rival contentions are really very
simple. For the applicant the matter is put in two ways which I believe must be carefully
distinguished. The first is that 'investment business' is a concept which, whatever it
g might mean in ordinary speech, did not exist with this very special connotation until the
1986 Act created it so that it was impossible for anyone to be carrying on investment
business before the appointed day. Second, it is said that even if investment business was
capable of existing before that day Parliament cannot have intended that the powers
under s 105 should be exercised in relation to pre-Act business, and that s 105 should be
h read in a limited sense. In particular, it was contended that the words 'he ... was carrying
on' must be read as subject to the implied qualification 'after the appointed day'.

    To the first limb of this argument the Secretary of State replies that investment
business is not a new species of activity, but simply a new label for an old species of
activity. There is nothing novel or esoteric about the various types of transactions
identified in Pt II of Sch 1, or about carrying them out in relation to the choses in action
j listed in Pt I. They were all going on before the 1986 Act, just as much as afterwards,
even though nobody could at that stage tell that they would later be swept into a
legislative scheme which gave them a special name. The language of s 105(1) can very
well be read as comprising all investment business, even if not currently identified as
such when it was effected; and the fact that s 105 is capable of dealing with the past is
shown by the words 'which he is or was ...' and 'appears ... to be or to have been ...'

    To this argument on the language of s 105(1), the applicant has a response which also depends on the way in which the statute is expressed. As I have said, the definition of investment business involves a qualification expressed partly in terms of the 'Excluded Activities' set out in Pt III of Sch 1. These embrace certain types of transactions where the counter-party falls into the category of 'authorised persons, exempted persons, or persons holding a permission under paragraph 23 below' (see para 17(2)(a)).

Authorised persons are defined in Ch III of the 1986 Act as including members of recognised self-regulatory organisations and persons authorised by recognised professional bodies (see ss 7(1) and 15(1)). Recognition as such an organisation or body has to be applied for, and is granted by the Secretary of State under mechanisms established by the 1986 Act. Other authorised persons include those who hold an authorisation granted by the Secretary of State (s 25). Clearly there could be no authorised persons before the statutory procedures of Ch III had been brought into force.

Again, there are the 'exempted persons' whose presence as counter-parties prevents the principal party's transactions from ranking as investment business. This category includes 'recognised' investment exchanges, clearing houses and money market institutions for the time being included in a list maintained by the Bank of England (see ss 36, 38 and 43). As in the case of authorised persons, the category of exempted persons could not be exhaustively identified before the 1986 Act came into force.

The position is plainly the same with the remaining category of counter-parties referred to in para 17(2)(a), namely persons holding a permission from the Secretary of State under para 23 of Sch 1.

One may now return to the Secretary of State's theory of retrospective labelling. In order to decide whether any pre-Act transaction had those characteristics which would have enabled it to rank as investment business if that concept had then existed as part of English law, it would have been necessary to know two facts: first, whether the transactions concerned investments of a type, and involved dealings of a type, described in Pt I of Sch 1; second, whether the dealing was an excluded activity. Of these, the first fact was objectively ascertainable, its existence being independent of the coming into force of the 1986 Act, and of anything done under the Act. But in many cases the second fact could not be ascertained, for where the primary party dealt as principal it would be necessary to know whether the counter-party fell into one of the three categories referred to in para 17(2)(a), and, as we have seen, these categories could not exist before the mechanisms created by the 1986 Act were available and were utilized.

So far as I can see, the only way to save the idea of retrospective labelling is to hold either that the impossibility of identifying an excepted transaction meant that all pre-Act dealings as principals were automatically excluded from investment business (in which case the category would become larger on the appointed day), or were automatically included (in which case it would shrink). Neither reading conforms with what the 1986 Act says, or with common sense. To my mind, s 105 just will not work if it is read as applying to pre-Act transactions.

Whilst this objection seems unanswerable, I do not find it very satisfying, and would prefer to look at s 105 in a broader context, to see whether a compelling argument to the contrary can be found. We may therefore examine the main provisions of the 1986 Act, not for the purpose of comparing and contrasting their language with that of s 105 (a process which only infrequently yields useful results, and which in my judgment does not yield any here) but in order to see whether the legislature can have intended to confer powers to investigate transactions which were over and done with before the Act came into force.

Following up this line, we see that the 1986 Act begins, in ch II, with a prohibition on the carrying on of investment business, except by authorised or exempted persons. Sanctions are imposed in the shape of penal offences (s 4), unenforceability of bargains (s 5), and injunctions at the suit of the Secretary of State (s 6). Chapters III and IV establish the regimes for the appointment and regulation of the various types of authorised and exempted persons. Disciplinary measures are created in the shape of powers to revoke

authorisations or exemptions, and to issue compliance orders (see ss 12, 20, 28 and 33). It
a may be noted that a person authorised by virtue of establishment in a member state is
guilty of an offence if he begins to carry on investment business in the United Kingdom
without giving seven days notice to the Secretary of State. Chapter V begins by creating
an offence where a misleading statement is made with a view to inducing another to
enter into an investment agreement (ie an agreement relating to business which falls
within Pt II of Sch 1 unless exempted by Pts III and IV). It goes on to render unenforceable
b all investment agreements resulting from unsolicited calls (s 56). These provisions relate
to all persons, but the remainder of the chapter is largely concerned with authorised
persons. Chapters VI and VII confer a wide range of powers relating to the control of
authorised persons, including the restriction of the right to enter into various types of
transactions, the maintenance of assets to secure potential liabilities and the granting of
winding-up orders and administration orders. Chapter IX is concerned with the Financial
c Services Tribunal, which is to hear references concerning the various disciplinary powers
created by the Act. Of the remaining chapters it is necessary to mention only ch XIII,
which permits the Secretary of State to transfer various of his functions to designated
agencies, including Security and Investments Board Ltd.

Looking through the 1986 Act in this way, two things seem to me quite clear. First,
the Act creates an elaborate new structure which is to come into effect for the future, as a
d replacement for the much less ambitious scheme of the Prevention of Fraud (Investments)
Act 1958. This factor is not conclusive in itself, since it would be possible for one isolated
section in the new Act to look backwards, even if the Act as a whole looked forward, but
it does suggest that one should look with care to see what reason the legislature might
have had for giving s 105 this singular effect. Second, and more important, there seems
to be nothing else in the Act which might furnish such a reason. The powers of
e investigation must be there for a purpose. One possible reason for making them work
retrospectively (to use a convenient if not strictly accurate adverb) might have been to
give the Secretary of State means to discover whether an applicant for authorisation is a
fit person to be granted this status. But this is already catered for by s 26(2)(*b*)(ii) and (3),
and in any event there seems no reason why the necessary information should be
restricted, as it would be in s 105, to the applicant's conduct of investment business. I can
f see no other reason why the Secretary of State should have taken the powers created by
s 105 except to enable him to police the proper working of the scheme created by the Act
and to administer the various sanctions conferred by the Act for infractions of that
scheme. These sections, like the scheme itself, are all concerned with events happening
after the appointed day. Plainly, the Secretary of State might in appropriate cases need to
examine what had happened in the past in order to decide what course he should take in
g the future, and this accounts for the words 'was' and 'to have been'. I also accept, as the
parties accept, that a power to look at the past to explain the present must be implicit in
s 105. I do not, however, see any reason why Parliament should have given the Secretary
of State powers to investigate putative investment business before the Act, to underpin
the supervision of a scheme and the application of sanctions to enforce it, when the
scheme only began to come into existence on the first of the appointed days.
h Accordingly, although I recognise that the grammar of s 105 would, if the section
were read out of context, support the Secretary of State's contention, I would, for the two
reasons which I have endeavoured to state, answer the question posed to us in the
negative.

McCOWAN J. I agree.

j
Order accordingly.

Solicitors: *Slaters* (for the applicant); *Solicitor to the Department of Trade and Industry.*

Dilys Tausz   Barrister.

R v Martin

COURT OF APPEAL, CRIMINAL DIVISION
LORD LANE CJ, SIMON BROWN AND ROCH JJ
29 NOVEMBER 1988

Criminal law – Necessity as a defence – Whether necessity a defence recognised in law – What amounts to necessity for purpose of defence – Appropriate direction to jury.

The defence of necessity in extreme circumstances is recognised by English law. The defence arises most commonly as duress, i e pressure put on the accused's will by another's wrongful threats or violence, but it can also arise from other objective dangers threatening the accused or others amounting to duress of circumstances. The defence is available only if, from an objective standpoint, the accused can be said to have acted reasonably and proportionately in order to avoid a threat of death or serious injury. Assuming the defence to be open to the accused on his account of the facts, the defence should be left to the jury with a direction to determine two questions, namely (i) whether the accused was, or might he have been, impelled to act as he did because, as a result of what he reasonably believed to be the situation, he had good cause to fear that otherwise death or serious physical injury would result, and (ii) if so, whether a sober person of reasonable firmness, sharing the characteristics of the accused, would have responded to that situation by acting as the accused had acted, and to acquit if both questions are answered affirmatively since the defence of necessity will then have been established (see p 653 g to p 654 a, post).

R v Conway [1988] 3 All ER 1025 applied.

Notes

For necessity as a defence to a criminal charge, see 11 Halsbury's Laws (4th edn) para 26, and for cases on the subject, see 14(1) Digest (Reissue) 57–59, 266–280.

Cases referred to in judgment

R v Conway [1988] 3 All ER 1025, [1988] 3 WLR 1238, CA.
R v Willer (1986) 83 Cr App R 225, CA.

Case also cited

R v Howe [1987] 1 All ER 771, [1987] AC 417, HL.

Appeal against conviction

Colin Martin appealed against his conviction in the Crown Court at Snaresbrook before his Honour Judge Finney on 2 February on a charge of driving while disqualified, contrary to s 99(b) of the Road Traffic Act 1972, to which he pleaded guilty following a ruling by the judge that he could not plead a defence of necessity to the charge and for which he was sentenced to four months' imprisonment suspended for two years. The grounds of his appeal were that the judge's ruling was erroneous and had deprived him of a valid defence. The facts are set out in the judgment of the court.

Nigel Joseph Ley (assigned by the Registrar of Criminal Appeals) for the appellant.
Samuel Parrish for the Crown.

SIMON BROWN J delivered the following judgment of the court. On 2 February 1988 this appellant pleaded guilty in the Crown Court at Snaresbrook to driving whilst disqualified. He was sentenced by his Honour Judge Finney to four months' imprisonment suspended for two years. In addition, for breach of a sentence of four months' imprisonment suspended for two years, imposed at Waltham Forest Magistrates' Court

on 20 June 1986 for driving whilst unfit through drink or drugs, the operational period
a of the suspension was extended for a further two years.

The appellant now appeals against his conviction as of right on a pure point of law.
The point is whether the defence of necessity is available to a charge of driving whilst
disqualified when that driving occurs in circumstances such as the appellant was
contending arose in his case. To those circumstances I shall come in a moment. In a
private-room hearing before the appellant was arraigned, the judge held not. He
b concluded that, once it was established that the defendant was driving and that he was
disqualified at the time, the offence was established. It was, in short, in those circumstances
an absolute offence.

In consequence of that ruling the appellant pleaded guilty and merely prayed in aid as
mitigation the circumstances on which he relied to establish the necessity of breaking
the law. But for the ruling he would have contested the case.

c The appeal is brought under s 2(1)(*b*) of the Criminal Appeal Act 1968, namely on the
basis that the judgment of the court of trial should be set aside on the ground of a wrong
decision on a question of law.

The circumstances which the appellant desired to advance by way of defence of
necessity were essentially these. His wife has suicidal tendencies. On a number of
occasions before the day in question she had attempted to take her own life. On the day
d in question her son, the appellant's stepson, had overslept. He had done so to the extent
that he was bound to be late for work and at risk of losing his job unless, so it was asserted,
the appellant drove him to work. The appellant's wife was distraught. She was shouting,
screaming, banging her head against a wall. More particularly, it is said she was
threatening suicide unless the appellant drove the boy to work.

The defence had a statement from a doctor which expressed the opinion that 'in view
e of her mental condition it is likely that Mrs. Martin would have attempted suicide if her
husband did not drive her son to work'.

The appellant's case on the facts was that he genuinely, and he would suggest
reasonably, believed that his wife would carry out that threat unless he did as she
demanded. Despite his disqualification he therefore drove the boy. He was in fact
f apprehended by the police within about a quarter of a mile of the house.

Sceptically though one may regard that defence on the facts (and there were, we would
observe, striking difficulties about the detailed evidence when it came finally to be given
before the judge in mitigation), the sole question before this court is whether those facts,
had the jury accepted they were or might be true, amounted in law to a defence. If they
did, then the appellant was entitled to a trial of the issue before the jury. The jury would
of course have had to be directed properly on the precise scope and nature of the defence,
g but the decision on the facts would have been for them. As it was, such a defence was
pre-empted by the ruling. Should it have been?

In our judgment the answer is plainly not. The authorities are now clear. Their effect
is perhaps most conveniently to be found in the judgment of this court in *R v Conway*
[1988] 3 All ER 1025, [1988] 3 WLR 1238. The decision reviews earlier relevant
h authorities.

The principles may be summarised thus: first, English law does, in extreme
circumstances, recognise a defence of necessity. Most commonly this defence arises as
duress, that is pressure on the accused's will from the wrongful threats or violence of
another. Equally however it can arise from other objective dangers threatening the
accused or others. Arising thus it is conveniently called 'duress of circumstances'.

j Second, the defence is available only if, from an objective standpoint, the accused can
be said to be acting reasonably and proportionately in order to avoid a threat of death or
serious injury.

Third, assuming the defence to be open to the accused on his account of the facts, the
issue should be left to the jury, who should be directed to determine these two questions:
first, was the accused, or may he have been, impelled to act as he did because as a result

of what he reasonably believed to be the situation he had good cause to fear that otherwise death or serious physical injury would result; second, if so, would a sober person of reasonable firmness, sharing the characteristics of the accused, have responded to that situation by acting as the accused acted? If the answer to both those questions was Yes, then the jury would acquit; the defence of necessity would have been established.

That the defence is available in cases of reckless driving is established by *R v Conway* itself and indeed by an earlier decision of the court in *R v Willer* (1986) 83 Cr App R 225. *R v Conway* is authority also for the proposition that the scope of the defence is no wider for reckless driving than for other serious offences. As was pointed out in the judgment, 'reckless driving can kill' (see [1988] 3 All ER 1025 at 1029, [1988] 3 WLR 1238 at 1244).

We see no material distinction between offences of reckless driving and driving whilst disqualified so far as the application and scope of this defence is concerned. Equally we can see no distinction in principle between various threats of death; it matters not whether the risk of death is by murder or by suicide or indeed by accident. One can illustrate the latter by considering a disqualified driver being driven by his wife, she suffering a heart attack in remote countryside and he needing instantly to get her to hospital.

It follows from this that the judge quite clearly did come to a wrong decision on the question of law, and the appellant should have been permitted to raise this defence for what it was worth before the jury.

It is in our judgment a great pity that that course was not taken. It is difficult to believe that any jury would have swallowed the improbable story which this appellant desired to advance. There was, it emerged when evidence was given in mitigation, in the house at the time a brother of the boy who was late for work, who was licensed to drive, and available to do so; the suggestion was that he would not take his brother because of 'a lot of aggravation in the house between them'. It is a further striking fact that when apprehended by the police this appellant was wholly silent as to why on this occasion he had felt constrained to drive. But those considerations, in our judgment, were essentially for the jury, and we have concluded, although not without hesitation, that it would be inappropriate here to apply the proviso to s 2(1) of the 1968 Act.

In the result this appeal must be allowed and the conviction quashed.

Appeal allowed. Conviction quashed.

Solicitors: *Crown Prosecution Service*, Snaresbrook.

N P Metcalfe Esq   Barrister.

R v Secretary of State for Foreign and Commonwealth Affairs, ex parte Everett

COURT OF APPEAL, CIVIL DIVISION
O'CONNOR, NICHOLLS AND TAYLOR LJJ
20 OCTOBER 1988

Crown – Prerogative – Passport – Refusal to issue passport to person for whom warrant of arrest issued – Secretary of State refusing to issue passport overseas to applicant for whom warrant of arrest outstanding in United Kingdom – Applicant informed of reason without being given details of warrant or opportunity to challenge accuracy of details or present exceptional circumstances which might justify issue of passport – Whether decision to issue or refuse passport involving exercise of prerogative power – Whether court having jurisdiction to review decision – Whether Secretary of State's decision fair.

The applicant, a British passport holder living in Spain, applied to the British Embassy in Madrid for a new passport to be issued on the expiry of his old one. The Foreign and Commonwealth Office refused to issue a new passport because there was a warrant for the applicant's arrest current in the United Kingdom and it was the Secretary of State's policy not to issue a passport to persons who were wanted by the police on suspicion of a serious crime. No details of the warrant were given. The applicant applied for judicial review by way of an order of certiorari to quash the refusal on the ground, inter alia, that no particulars of the warrant had been made available to him. Two warrants had been issued for the applicant's arrest, one for obtaining a false passport by deception and the other for robbery, and by the date of the hearing the applicant had been given details of the date, place of issue and subject matter of the warrants, neither of which he had sought to challenge. The judge granted the applicant the relief sought, holding that before refusing to issue a passport because of an outstanding warrant of arrest the Secretary of State was required to consider whether his policy should not be applied in the particular case. The Secretary of State appealed, contending that the High Court had no jurisdiction to review a decision to refuse to issue a passport since such a decision involved the exercise of prerogative power.

Held – Although a decision by the Secretary of State to refuse to issue a passport involved the exercise of prerogative power the High Court had jurisdiction to review such a decision and to inquire whether a passport had been wrongly refused. Accordingly, although the Secretary of State's policy of not issuing passports abroad to persons against whom there were warrants of arrest outstanding in the United Kingdom was a valid policy, nevertheless when a passport was refused on that ground the Secretary of State was required to give the reason for the refusal, to provide the applicant with the particulars of the warrant and to inform him that if there were exceptional reasons (e g compassionate grounds) why the policy should not be applied they would be taken into account. However, since the applicant had not suffered any injustice because he had known by the date of the hearing everything which he should have been told by the Secretary of State, and since there were no exceptional reasons in his case, there were no grounds for granting relief. The appeal would therefore be allowed (see p 658 *b c*, p 659 *a* to p 660 *h*, post).

Council of Civil Service Unions v Minister for the Civil Service [1984] 3 All ER 935 applied.

Notes

For the refusal to grant a passport, see 18 Halsbury's Laws (4th edn) para 1412.

Cases referred to in judgments

Council of Civil Service Unions v Minister for the Civil Service [1984] 3 All ER 935, [1985] AC
374, [1984] 3 WLR 1174, HL.
R v Port of London Authority, ex p Kynoch Ltd [1919] 1 KB 176, CA.

Appeal

The Secretary of State for Foreign and Commonwealth Affairs appealed against the
decision of Mann J made on 2 December 1987 whereby on an application of Ronald
James Everett for judicial review he ordered, inter alia, that the decision of the British
Embassy in Madrid made on 12 May 1986 and confirmed by the Foreign and
Commonwealth Office by letter dated 24 July 1986 refusing to grant the applicant a new
passport be quashed. The facts are set out in the judgment of O'Connor LJ.

Roger Ter Haar for the Secretary of State.
Laureen Fleischmann for the applicant.

O'CONNOR LJ. On 2 December 1987 Mann J quashed a decision of the Secretary of
State for Foreign and Commonwealth Affairs given in a letter of 24 July 1986 refusing a
passport to the applicant. The Secretary of State appeals against that decision.

The facts giving rise to this case can be simply stated. The applicant has been living in
Marbella in the south of Spain since June 1984. He was the holder of a British passport
which was due to expire on 20 May 1986. In April of that year he filled in the necessary
form to apply for a new passport with the supporting documents. That can be issued by
a consul in Malaga via the consular department of the British Embassy in Madrid. The
matter went to Madrid, but no passport was forthcoming. On 12 May the applicant sent
a lawyer to the British Embassy to find out why he had not received a new passport and
according to the affidavit of the notary he was told that a passport was not going to be
issued but that a travel document, which was effectively a one-way ticket to England,
could be issued. The report of this interview does not record whether the Spanish lawyer
asked why his client was not getting a passport, nor does it record being told why he was
not given one. In the result solicitors in London on behalf of the applicant wrote to the
Passport Office. It turns out that, when passports are issued abroad, it is handled by the
Foreign Office, as one might expect, from the embassy or consulate as the case may be.
Thus it was that a reply came back on 24 July why no passport had been issued. That
letter reads:

'I refer to your letter of 2 June addressed to the Passport Office. This has been sent
to us for reply as the Foreign and Commonwealth Office are responsible for the
issue of passports overseas. We have noted your comments and the substance of the
notarised declaration made by Mr Luis Bertelli Galvex. However, British passports
are issued overseas at the discretion of the Secretary of State for Foreign and
Commonwealth Affairs and it is a fundamental principle that they should not be
issued to persons for whose arrest a warrant has been issued in the United Kingdom.
Such a warrant has been issued in respect of [the applicant] and it would clearly not
be in the interests of justice if, in these circumstances, a passport were to be issued
to him. We therefore consider that the British Embassy in Madrid were justified in
refusing to issue a standard passport to [the applicant], who has however been
offered an emergency passport to enable him to travel to the United Kingdom only.
I regret that we are not in a position to give you details of the warrant for arrest and
can only advise that you contact the UK police authorities if you wish to have these.'

As a result of that letter these proceedings were launched in October 1986. The relief
sought by way of judicial review was certiorari to quash both the oral decision on 12 May
in Madrid and that contained in the letter on 24 July, together with an order for

mandamus requiring the passport application to be considered in a proper and lawful
a manner.

The grounds which were given for the relief were that no particulars of the warrant
had been made available to the applicant that he was afforded no opportunity for a
hearing before the decision was made in Spain and that therefore the decision was made
in a manner which failed to comply with natural justice. So, too, was the attack on the
letter of 24 July. In addition there was an allegation that the refusal at least had the effect
b of circumventing the extradition rules for Spain, as far as this man is concerned.

An affidavit was sworn by Mr Le Breton, for the Secretary of State, in July 1987, which
was before the judge. By that time leave had been given by Russell J. He had ordered
that inquiries should be made as to the nature of the warrant. The applicant had
information, which we see from correspondence exhibited to an affidavit, including a
letter of 20 February which is not exhibited but referred to, which carried the information
c from Scotland Yard that a warrant had been issued in the Thames Magistrates' Court in
January 1985 for the arrest of this man on a charge of obtaining property by deception,
namely a false passport. There was a further warrant, which had nothing to do with this
refusal because it did not come until December 1986, issued out of the Bow Street
Magistrates' Court on a charge of robbery. The affidavit sworn by Mr Le Breton explained
what had happened. He said:
d

> '2. In April 1986 the Applicant . . . applied through the British Consulate at
> Malaga, Spain for a new passport to replace a passport which was to expire on the
> 20th May 1986. That application was passed to the Consular Section, British
> Embassy, Madrid for processing. It came to the attention of the officers in the
> Consular Section that the Applicant was named on a list which the Director of
e > Public Prosecutions had supplied (through the Embassy) to the Spanish Authorities
> of persons whom the British police wished to question in connection with a robbery.
> 3. The Consular Section therefore raised inquiries with my Department and it
> was established that there was an outstanding Warrant for the arrest of the Applicant
> issued in January 1985 on charges of obtaining property by deception. Those charges
> concern the Applicant having obtained a passport in the false name of Ronald Page
f > in 1983.
> 4. On the basis of long standing practice, which has been brought to Parliament's
> attention on various occasions the issue of a passport is refused to persons for whose
> arrest a Warrant has been issued in the United Kingdom or persons who are wanted
> by the United Kingdom police on suspicion of a serious crime. My Department
> therefore informed the Consular Section in Madrid that a replacement standard
g > passport should not be issued to the Applicant but that he might be offered an
> emergency passport for a single journey to the United Kingdom.'

He then refers to the correspondence.

When the matter came before the judge three matters were taken before him. First,
the Secretary of State objected that judicial review did not lie against the refusal of a
h passport. That forms the first ground of appeal, because the judge rejected the submission.
Once again it can be simply stated. Until the decision of the House of Lords in *Council of
Civil Service Unions v Minister for the Civil Service* [1984] 3 All ER 935, [1985] AC 374 it
was generally assumed that the law was that decisions of the administration taken under
the prerogative were not amenable to judicial review, and so one finds a whole series of
matters which were not amenable to review. In that case it will be remembered that the
j order that employees of GCHQ were not to be union members was taken under an Order
in Council issued under the prerogative by the Minister for the Civil Service. The first
question which had to be decided was whether judicial review of the decision lay at all.

Three of their Lordships, Lord Diplock, Lord Scarman and Lord Roskill, unequivocally
held that judicial review of decisions taken under the prerogative did lie. Lord Scarman
in his speech stated that it was not the origin of the administrative power, but was the

actual factual application which had to be considered (see [1984] 3 All ER 935 at 946–948, [1985] AC 374 at 404–407). It is quite clear since that decision that there are areas of the exercise of the prerogative which the courts can and will review. There are other areas, some of which were identified in that case, which they will not. Obvious examples are the making of treaties, which the court would not entertain by way of judicial review: so, too, policy decisions on foreign affairs and other matters which are to be found in Lord Roskill's speech. I need not refer to them in this judgment.

The judge held that the issue of a passport fell into an entirely different category. That seems common sense. It is a familiar document to all citizens who travel in the world and it would seem obvious to me that the exercise of the prerogative, because there is no doubt that passports are issued under the royal prerogative in the discretion of the Secretary of State, is an area where common sense tells one that, if for some reason a passport is wrongly refused for a bad reason, the court should be able to inquire into it. I would reject the submission made on behalf of the Secretary of State that the judge was wrong to review the case.

I then pass to consider the next ground of appeal, but before I do that I state what the judge decided. He said in his judgment:

'That of course does not conclude the matter. Assuming, as I have held, that the discretion is reviewable, is it here to be flawed? It is apparent that the Secretary of State has a general policy, that is to say that the discretion will not be exercised in favour of a person, at least one who is outside the United Kingdom, who is the subject of a warrant of arrest. The Secretary of State is entitled to have such a general policy, but it must not preclude the exercise of the discretion vested in him. If it does, then, as Bankes LJ said, it amounts to a refusal to exercise any discretion (see *R v Port of London Authority, ex p Kynoch Ltd* [1919] 1 KB 176 at 184–185). What concerns me in this case is that there was not any inquiry of the applicant as to whether or not the policy should here be applied. Indeed, the state of knowledge at the time of refusal was as scant as that contained in the letter of 24 July 1986 and has not subsequently been increased, save by knowledge of the warrant of arrest for robbery issued after any event with which I am concerned.'

I pause there. It seems to me that the judge has fallen into error. By the time the matter came before him there was an advance on the matters contained in the letter of 24 July because by that time it was known when and where and for what the warrant had been issued. The details I have already read in the affidavit of Mr Le Breton. The judge continued:

'I do wish to make it clear that the Secretary of State is entitled to have a policy and that he is entitled to have regard to the fact that warrants of arrest are issued as part of the judicial process. But I do not regard it as satisfactory that he should not inquire as to whether there is any reason why this policy should not be applied in the instant case. What I propose to do is to issue certiorari to quash. The matter will have to be reconsidered. Whether that reconsideration achieves any practically useful consequence, so far as the applicant is concerned, is not for me to say.'

He then went on to deal with the 'veiled extradition' issue, to which I will return in a moment.

It will be seen that the judge was stating that the policy of not issuing passports to persons against whom there was a warrant of arrest outstanding was an intelligible and valid policy, and no appeal is made against that because it is obvious good sense. But the judge came to the conclusion that the fair application of the policy required that if a passport was refused because a warrant was outstanding against the applicant, inquiry had to be made of the applicant before refusing a passport, as to whether he had anything to say.

In my judgment the judge fell into error in concluding that that was required for the

fair exercise of his discretion. It seems to me that the Secretary of State, in the fair exercise
a of his discretion, was entitled to refuse the passport but to give his reason for so doing,
and the fair giving of the reason, if the reason be that there is a warrant for the applicant's
arrest outstanding, was to tell him when the warrant was issued and what offence was
charged. Once he has done that he has all but discharged his duty, but he should, when
notifying the applicant that that was the reason for refusing the passport, tell him that if
there were any exceptional grounds which might call for the issue of a passport he would
b consider them. We have been told very properly by counsel for the Secretary of State that
it is possible that exceptions may arise on compassionate grounds, eg if such a person
were desperately ill in hospital in a foreign country it might be that a passport would be
issued or an exception made. Had that been done, no one could challenge the proper
exercise of the discretion.
   In the present case it has been submitted that the letter of 24 July gives all the
c information, coupled with the visit of a lawyer on behalf of the applicant in Madrid, and
one could assume that the lawyer must have asked why the passport was refused.
   Unfortunately I do not think one can assume if he did ask such a question that he
necessarily got the answer which would be required and it seems to me that the decision
letter of 24 July was not sufficient to give the information which ought to have been
given.
d That is not an end of the matter, because judicial review is a discretionary remedy and
one must look at the position at the time when the application came before the judge.
At that stage the applicant knew everything. He was fully armed with lawyers in this
country, solicitors and counsel, and there is not a word from him of any sort. There is no
suggestion that there are any exceptional circumstances in this case. There is no suggestion
from him that there is anything wrong with the warrant, or that he was not wanted on a
e warrant for an offence of obtaining a false passport or obtaining a passport in the name
of Ronald Page by deception: he knew everything which he ought to have been told. He
certainly knew when he made representations in the launching of the proceedings.
   In those circumstances I cannot see that there are any grounds for thinking that, had
the decision letter contained the information which he got later and contained the offer
f to consider any representations as to exceptional circumstances, any different result
would have come about. Where the court finds itself in that position, namely that the
applicant has suffered no injustice and that to grant the remedy would produce a barren
result there are no grounds for granting relief.
   Finally, I would like to say a few words about extradition. Counsel for the applicant
applied for leave to reopen part of the second ground of the application, namely the
g suggestion that what was happening here was an attempted 'veiled extradition' of this
applicant. In my judgment there is no evidence whatever which could bring that charge
home against the Secretary of State and as it would be quite pointless to raise the matter
here, I would refuse leave to cross-appeal in this case.
   In those circumstances I would allow this appeal and refuse the order for judicial
review.

h
NICHOLLS LJ. I agree and I add a few words only on one aspect of this case.
   The Secretary of State has for some years adopted and followed a policy of refusing to
issue a passport to certain classes of persons. One of these classes comprises persons for
whose arrest a warrant has been issued in the United Kingdom. That the Secretary of
State was entitled to adopt and follow this policy has not been challenged in this case. In
j my view the fair implementation of that policy requires that, when a passport application
is refused on the ground I have mentioned, in general the applicant should be told of
when and where the warrant in question was issued and in respect of what offence or
offences. If he is not given that information the applicant could not, for example, begin
to show that the warrant which has been issued could not in fact relate to him. Of course,
each case must depend on its own particular circumstances and there may be cases where

even those details need not formally be communicated, eg where the applicant already has the substance of the necessary information. Furthermore, in so far as exceptions may *a* be made to the policy in particular cases on some special grounds, such as compassionate grounds, fair implementation of the policy requires that the notification of refusal of a passport should not be in terms which would lead a reasonable applicant to believe that no exceptions were ever made and that his application has inevitably reached the end of the road. Here also each case must depend on its own facts, but it seems to me that in general the fair implementation of the policy also requires that the applicant should be *b* told, when the renewal of the passport is refused, something to the effect that if he wishes to submit that there are compassionate or other special reasons why, despite the policy, a new passport should be issued to him, then he may communicate with the passport issuing authority accordingly, when anything he puts forward will be considered.

Nevertheless I agree, for the reasons given by O'Connor LJ, that the failure by the Secretary of State to follow that approach in this case has not resulted in any prejudice to *c* the applicant. I, too, would allow the appeal.

TAYLOR LJ. I agree and add only a few words on the first ground of appeal of counsel for the Secretary of State concerning the jurisdiction of this court.

I am in no doubt that the court has power to review the withdrawal or refusal to grant or renew a passport. The House of Lords in *Council of Civil Service Unions v Minister for the* *d* *Civil Service* [1984] 3 All ER 935, [1985] AC 374 made it clear that the powers of the court cannot be ousted merely by invoking the word 'prerogative'. The majority of their Lordships indicated that whether judicial review of the exercise of prerogative power is open depends on the subject matter and in particular on whether it is justiciable. At the top of the scale of executive functions under the prerogative are matters of high policy, *e* of which examples were given by their Lordships: making treaties, making law, dissolving Parliament, mobilising the armed forces. Clearly those matters, and no doubt a number of others, are not justiciable. But the grant or refusal of a passport is in a quite different category. It is a matter of administrative decision, affecting the rights of individuals and their freedom of travel. It raises issues which are just as justiciable as, for example, the issues arising in immigration cases. Counsel for the Secretary of State *f* sought to put the grant of passports under the umbrella of foreign affairs and thereby elevate it to that level of high policy which would preclude the intervention of the courts. He says that the grant of a passport involves a request in the name of the Queen to a foreign power to afford the holder free passage and protection. It also extends the protection and assistance of the Crown to the holder whilst he is abroad.

However, those considerations do not, to my mind, render issues arising on the refusal *g* of a passport non-justiciable. The ready issue of a passport is a normal expectation of every citizen, unless there is good reason for making him an exception. The issues arising are no more likely to have foreign policy repercussions than those arising, to take the same analogy as before, in immigration cases. Accordingly, I consider that the judge was right to entertain the application. However, for the reasons given by O'Connor and Nicholls LJJ I agree that his decision on the facts of this case cannot be supported. *h*

Appeal allowed.

Solicitors: *Treasury Solicitor; Hughmans* (for the applicant).

Carolyn Toulmin   Barrister.

Re State of Norway's Application (No 1)

COURT OF APPEAL, CIVIL DIVISION
KERR, GLIDEWELL AND RALPH GIBSON LJJ
3, 4, 5, 6, 9, 10, 11 DECEMBER 1985, 12 FEBRUARY 1986

Evidence – Foreign tribunal – Examination of witnesses in relation to matters pending before foreign tribunal – Evidence for purpose of civil proceedings – Proceedings in civil or commercial matter – Evidence requested by foreign tax tribunal – Whether foreign proceedings civil or commercial matter – Whether proceedings assisting foreign tax-gathering – Evidence (Proceedings in Other Jurisdictions) Act 1975, ss 1, 9(1).

Evidence – Foreign tribunal – Examination of witnesses in relation to matters pending before foreign tribunal – Confidentiality – Confidential information between bank and customer – Whether private interest of confidentiality between banker and customer outweighing duty of disclosure to foreign court – Whether court should compel witnesses to violate duty of confidence.

Evidence – Foreign tribunal – Examination of witnesses in relation to matters pending before foreign tribunal – Evidence for purpose of civil proceedings – Letter of request in nature of 'fishing' operation – Whether terms of request too wide.

J, a wealthy Norwegian shipowner, died in 1982. The county tax committee for that part of Norway in which he had resided decided to raise a retrospective tax assessment against his estate for the years 1972–82 on the ground that he had avoided tax during those years by failing to declare a large part of his assets. The estate commenced proceedings in the court of first instance in Norway to have the assessment declared null and void and appealed to the national tax committee to have it set aside. The Norwegian court, on the application of the State of Norway supported by the estate, issued letters of request addressed to the High Court in England requesting it to summon two named merchant bankers (the witnesses) to attend before an examiner in London to give oral evidence relevant to the issues in the proceedings before the Norwegian court. The bank had acted as bankers for a charitable trust alleged to have been set up and controlled by J and which allegedly held shares for J as beneficial owner. After receiving the letter of request the master made an order under s 2[a] of the Evidence (Proceedings in Other Jurisdictions) Act 1975 granting the application for the oral examination of the witnesses. The witnesses applied to have the order for oral examination set aside. The judge upheld the master's decision subject to certain directions limiting the scope of the questions which could be put to the witnesses. The witnesses appealed to the Court of Appeal, contending, inter alia, (i) that the English court had no jurisdiction to give effect to the letter of request since the legal process pending before the Norwegian court did not constitute 'civil proceedings' within 1[b] of the 1975 Act, which were defined by s 9(1)[c] of that Act as proceedings in a 'civil or commercial matter', (ii) that the letter of request amounted to a request for assistance in the enforcement of a foreign tax law, contrary to public policy, (iii) that the terms of the letter of request were too wide and did not constitute a proper request for evidence and (iv) that, since the giving of testimony by the witnesses would be a breach of their duty of confidentiality as bankers, the judge should have exercised his discretion by refusing the application. The State of Norway and the estate cross-appealed for the removal of the directions limiting the scope of the questions which could be asked.

---

a   Section 2, so far as material, is set out at p 665 h to p 666 c, post
b   Section 1 is set out at p 665 f g, post
c   Section 9(1), so far as material, is set out at p 666 f, post

Held – (1) Where a request was made by a foreign court for the oral examination of
witnesses whose evidence was required for use in foreign proceedings, the English court, *a*
in determining whether the foreign proceedings were 'civil proceedings' within the
meaning of ss 1 and 9(1) of the 1975 Act so as to confer jurisdiction on the court, had to
be satisfied that the proceedings concerned a civil or commercial matter under the law of
the requesting court, and in determining that issue the English court was not bound by
the requesting court's classification if it conflicted with any fundamental principle
recognised by English law regarding the classification of proceedings. Accordingly, even *b*
if the English court concluded that the requirements of the classification had been met
under the law of the requesting court, it could in its discretion refuse to make an order
pursuant to a letter of request if proceedings characterised as proceedings in a civil matter
by the requesting court were nevertheless regarded as criminal or penal proceedings by
English law. Applying that test on the limited evidence of Norwegian law before the
court, although (per Kerr LJ) it was not clear whether the proceedings instituted in the *c*
Norwegian court were public or private law proceedings, it was clear that they would be
characterised as a civil proceeding under English law and therefore that they fell within
the ambit of s 1 of the 1975 Act (see p 676 *b c j* to p 677 *b*, p 678 *g h*, p 679 *j*, p 680 *e g j*,
p 681 *b*, p 689 *h j*, p 690 *b d* and p 692 *b c*, post).
 (2) Although the courts would regard a request by a foreign state to obtain evidence
against a taxpayer of that state as part of the foreign state's tax-gathering process and as a *d*
matter of public policy would not accede to a letter of request issued for such a purpose,
having regard (per Kerr and Ralph Gibson LJJ) to the fact that the taxpayer, ie the estate,
supported the request and had initiated it the court would not decline the request on the
ground that it would assist foreign tax gathering (see p 682 *d* to *g*, p 683 *d e*, p 690 *d* and
p 692 *c*, post); dictum of Lord Somervell in *Government of India Ministry of Finance*
(Revenue Division) v Taylor [1955] 1 All ER 292 at 301–302 considered. *e*
 (3) (Ralph Gibson LJ dissenting) In order to determine whether the witnesses should
be ordered to break their duty of confidentiality by answering the questions raised by the
letter of request, the court had to consider whether the interest in protecting the
confidence reposed in the witnesses was outweighed by the public interest in assisting a
foreign court. In the circumstances the balance was against compelling the witnesses to *f*
violate their duty of confidence. Furthermore, the terms of the letter of request were so
wide that the questions intended to be asked would inevitably include a number which
would elicit information which might lead to a line of inquiry which would disclose
evidence rather than evidence in the proceedings themselves. Since such questions would
be 'fishing', they would be unacceptable. It followed that the court would not order the
witnesses to give evidence on the request as framed. Furthermore, the court was in no *g*
position to bring the request into conformity with what would be permissible. The
witnesses' appeal would accordingly be allowed and the cross-appeal dismissed (see p 684
g j, p 685 *d*, p 686 *f g*, p 688 *b* to *d*, p 689 *d* and p 691 *f h j*, post); *Rio Tinto Zinc Corp v*
Westinghouse Electric Corp [1978] 1 All ER 434 considered.

Notes
For evidence for proceedings in other jurisdictions, see 17 Halsbury's Laws (4th edn) *h*
paras 326–329, and for cases on the subject, see 22 Digest (Reissue) 665–668, 7111–7123.
 For the Evidence (Proceedings in Other Jurisdictions) Act 1975, ss 1, 2, 9, see 17
Halsbury's Statutes (4th edn) 191, 192, 197.

Cases referred to in judgments
A-G of New Zealand v Ortiz [1983] 2 All ER 93, [1984] AC 1, [1983] 2 WLR 809, HL; *affg* *j*
 [1982] 3 All ER 432, [1984] AC 1, [1982] 3 WLR 570, CA.
Ayres v Evans (1981) 39 ALR 129, Aust HC.
Bankers Trust Co v Shapira [1980] 3 All ER 353, [1980] 1 WLR 1274, CA.
Bonalumi v Secretary of State for the Home Dept [1985] 1 All ER 797, [1985] QB 675, [1985]
 2 WLR 722, CA.

British Steel Corp v Granada Television Ltd [1981] 1 All ER 417, [1981] AC 1096, [1980] 3
a   WLR 774, Ch D, CA and HL.
Buchanan (James) & Co Ltd v Babco Forwarding and Shipping (UK) Ltd [1977] 3 All ER 1048,
   [1978] AC 141, [1977] 3 WLR 907, HL.
Buchanan (Peter) Ltd and Macharg v McVey (1951) [1955] AC 516n, Eire HC and SC.
Burchard v Macfarlane, ex p Tindell [1891] 2 QB 241, [1891–94] All ER Rep 137, CA.
Comr of Taxes Federation of Rhodesia v McFarland 1965 (1) SA 470, WLD.
b   *Desilla v Fells & Co* (1879) 40 LT 423, DC.
FDC Co Ltd v Chase Manhattan Bank (29 October 1984, unreported), Hong Kong CA.
Fothergill v Monarch Airlines Ltd [1980] 2 All ER 696, [1981] AC 251, [1980] 3 WLR 209,
   HL.
Hillegom Municipality v Hillenius Case 110/84 [1985] ECR 3947.
India (Government) Ministry of Finance (Revenue Division) v Taylor [1955] 1 All ER 292,
c   [1955] AC 491, [1955] 2 WLR 303, HL.
Morgan v Morgan [1977] 2 All ER 515, [1977] Fam 122, [1977] 2 WLR 712.
Netherlands v Rüffer Case 814/79 [1980] ECR 3807.
O'Reilly v Mackman [1982] 3 All ER 1124, [1983] 2 AC 237, [1982] 3 WLR 1096, HL; *affg*
   [1982] 3 All ER 680, [1983] 2 AC 237, [1982] 3 WLR 1098, QBD and CA.
R v Grossman (1981) 73 Cr App R 302, CA.
d   *Radio Corp of America v Rauland Corp* [1956] 1 All ER 549, [1956] 1 QB 618, [1956] 2
   WLR 612, DC.
*Rio Tinto Zinc Corp v Westinghouse Electric Corp, RTZ Services Ltd v Westinghouse Electric
   Corp* [1978] 1 All ER 434, [1978] AC 547, [1978] 2 WLR 81, HL; *rvsg sub nom Re
   Westinghouse Electric Corp Uranium Contract Litigation MDL Docket No 235* [1977] 3 All
   ER 703, [1978] AC 547, [1977] 3 WLR 492, CA.
e   *Salomon v Customs and Excise Comrs* [1966] 3 All ER 871, [1967] 2 QB 116, [1966] 3 WLR
   1223, CA.
Salvatore v Etat Belge, Ministère des Finances JT, 8 April 1976, p 444, Belgian Cour de
   Cassation.
Senior v Holdsworth [1975] 2 All ER 1009, [1976] QB 23, [1975] 2 WLR 987, CA.
f   *Seyfang v G D Searle & Co* [1973] 1 All ER 290, [1973] QB 148, [1973] 2 WLR 17.
Stag Line Ltd v Foscolo Mango & Co Ltd [1932] AC 328, [1931] All ER Rep 666, HL.
Tournier v National Provincial and Union Bank of England Ltd [1924] 1 KB 461, [1923] All
   ER Rep 550, CA.
Town Investments Ltd v Dept of the Environment [1977] 1 All ER 813, [1978] AC 359, [1977]
   2 WLR 450, HL.
g   *US v Harden* (1963) 41 DLR (2d) 721, Can SC.
Williams & Humbert Ltd v W & H Trade Marks (Jersey) Ltd [1986] 1 All ER 129, [1988]
   AC 368, [1986] 2 WLR 24, HL.
X AG v A bank [1983] 2 All ER 464.

Cases also cited
h   *Asbestos Insurance Coverage Cases, Re* [1985] 1 All ER 716, [1985] 1 WLR 331, HL.
Brokaw v Seatrain UK Ltd [1971] 2 All ER 98, [1971] 2 QB 476, CA.
D v National Society for the Prevention of Cruelty to Children [1977] 1 All ER 589, [1978] AC
   171, HL.
Gourdain v Nadler Case 133/78 [1979] ECR 733.
Gross Re, ex p Treasury Solicitor [1968] 3 All ER 804, [1969] 1 WLR 12.
j   *Huntington v Attrill* [1893] AC 150, PC.
Maliban Biscuit Manufactories Ltd v Subramaniam [1971] AC 988, PC.
S v E [1967] 1 All ER 593, [1967] 1 QB 367.
Settebello Ltd v Banco Totta and Acores [1985] 2 All ER 1025, [1985] 1 WLR 1050, CA.
Stamps Comrs, Straits Settlements v Oei Tjong Swan [1933] AC 378, PC.
Tennekoon v Duraisamy [1958] 2 All ER 479, [1958] AC 334, PC.

Vervaeke v Smith (Messina and A-G intervening) [1982] 2 All ER 144, [1983] 1 AC 145, HL.

Appeal
Lord Kindersley and Mr A J Hardman (the witnesses) appealed, pursuant to leave given by McNeill J, against the decision of the judge on 24 July 1985 whereby he dismissed their application to discharge the order of Master Prebble made on 14 January 1985 for oral examination of the witnesses pursuant to s 2 of the Evidence (Proceedings in Other Jurisdictions) Act 1975, in compliance with a request from the Sandefjord City Court on an application by the State of Norway, supported by the estate of Anders Jahre deceased, and directed that the examination proceed subject to certain directions limiting the scope of the questions which they could by required to answer. The evidence sought by the state and the estate related to information relevant to proceedings brought by the estate of the deceased shipowner against the state concerning a disputed retrospective assessment for tax on the estate for the years 1972–82. The state and the estate cross-appealed seeking the removal of the directions. The facts are set out in the judgment of Kerr LJ.

Michael Crystal QC and *John Higham* for the witnesses.
Anthony Boswood for the state.
Nicolas Bratza for the estate.

Cur adv vult

12 February. The following judgments were delivered.

KERR LJ. This is an appeal from a judgment of McNeill J delivered on 24 July 1985 in open court after a hearing in chambers on appeal from part of an order made by Master Prebble on 14 January 1985. The case raises novel and complex issues of considerable importance, both in this country and internationally, and the hearings below and here occupied some five and seven days respectively. It arises out of a request by the State of Norway, supported by the estate of a deceased Norwegian shipowner Mr Anders Jahre (the estate), for the examination as witnesses pursuant to the Evidence (Proceedings in Other Jurisdictions) Act 1975 of Lord Kindersley, a director of Lazard Bros & Co Ltd (Lazards), and of Mr A J Hardman, a former administration manager (banking division) of Lazards, in aid of proceedings in Norway concerning a disputed retrospective assessment to tax on the estate for the years 1972–82 amounting to just under 338 m Norwegian kroner. The basis for the assessment is that Mr Jahre is alleged to have avoided tax by transferring, and in effect concealing, funds or other assets about which the proposed witnesses from Lazards (the witnesses) are believed to be able to give evidence.

The original request was that the witnesses should be ordered to give oral evidence and to produce certain documents or classes of documents. Lazards and the witnesses take strong objection to this request on a variety of grounds, including the fact that it would involve a breach of their duty of confidentiality as bankers.

On an ex parte application under RSC Ord 70, r 2 Master Prebble granted the application for the oral examination of the witnesses without qualification, but he declined to make any order for the production of documents on the ground that the request appeared too wide and that there was no reason to think that the documentation was in the custody, possession or power of the witnesses. There was no appeal against the latter part of Master Prebble's order, but the witnesses appealed to McNeill J on the part which ordered their oral examination. He heard the matter inter partes supported by a considerable amount of further evidence. Originally only the State of Norway, represented by the Solicitor General, Mr Bjoern Haug, was the party on whose behalf the request was made, but, on the application of the estate, Stuart-Smith J ordered on 25 June 1985 that the estate be joined as a party, on terms, inter alia, that it filed no evidence, since the matter was shortly to come on for hearing. Effectively, therefore, the contest is

a between the State of Norway and the estate, as the applicants on whose behalf the request
is made, and the witnesses, as the respondents who oppose it.

McNeill J dismissed the witnesses' appeal against the order for their oral examination,
but subject to certain directions limiting the scope of the questions which they could be
required to answer, as set out later on in this judgment. The witnesses now appeal to this
court against his decision and ask that the order for their oral examination be set aside,
and the state and the estate cross-appeal for the removal of the judge's directions limiting
b the scope of the examination.

The Evidence (Proceedings in Other Jurisdictions) Act 1975

It is common ground that the 1975 Act was passed mainly in order to give effect to the
accession by the United Kingdom, under the auspices of the Hague Conference on Private
c International Law, to the Hague Convention on the Taking of Evidence abroad in Civil
or Commercial Matters (The Hague, 18 March 1970; TS 20 (1977); Cmnd 6727). This is
nowhere mentioned in the Act but, if authority be required, a number of statements that
this was one of the purposes of the 1975 Act are to be found in the decision of the House
of Lords in the *Westinghouse* case, *Rio Tinto Zinc Corp v Westinghouse Electric Corp, RTZ
Services Ltd v Westinghouse Electric Corp* [1978] 1 All ER 434 at 441, 449, 461, 468, 477,
d [1978] AC 547 at 608, 618, 632, 641, 653 per Lord Wilberforce, Viscount Dilhorne, Lord
Diplock, Lord Fraser and Lord Keith.

It is convenient to begin by setting out the relevant provisions of the 1975 Act, and for
convenience I have emphasised a number of words and phrases which are of particular
importance for present purposes. The 'long title' is in the following terms:

e 'An Act to make new provision for enabling the High Court, the Court of Session
and the High Court of Justice in Northern Ireland to assist in obtaining evidence
required for the purposes of proceedings in other jurisdictions; to extend the powers
of those courts to issue process effective throughout the United Kingdom for
securing the attendance of witnesses; and for purposes connected with those matters.'

The relevant parts of ss 1, 2 and 3 are as follows:
f
'**1.** Where an application is made to the High Court, the Court of Session or the
High Court of Justice in Northern Ireland for an order for *evidence* to be obtained in
the part of the United Kingdom in which it exercises jurisdiction, and the court is
satisfied—(*a*) that the application is made in pursuance of a request issued *by or on
behalf of a court or tribunal* ("the requesting court") exercising jurisdiction in any
other part of the United Kingdom or in a country or territory outside the United
g Kingdom; and (*b*) that the *evidence* to which the application relates is to be obtained
for the purposes of *civil proceedings* which either have been instituted before the
requesting court or whose institution before that court is contemplated, the High
Court, Court of Session or High Court of Justice in Northern Ireland, as the case may
be, shall have the powers conferred on it by the following provisions of this Act.

h **2.**—(1) Subject to the provisions of this section, the High Court, the Court of
Session and the High Court of Justice in Northern Ireland shall each have power, on
any such application as is mentioned in section 1 above, by order to make such
provision for obtaining *evidence* in the part of the United Kingdom in which it
exercises jurisdiction *as may appear to the court to be appropriate for the purpose of
giving effect to the request* in pursuance of which the application is made; and any
j such order may require a person specified therein to take such steps as the court may
consider appropriate for that purpose.

(2) Without prejudice to the generality of subsection (1) above but subject to the
provisions of this section, an order under this section may, in particular, make
provision—(*a*) for the examination of witnesses, either orally or in writing; (*b*) for
the production of documents . . .

(3) An order under this section shall not require any particular steps to be taken unless they are steps which can be required to be taken by way of obtaining evidence *a* for the purposes of *civil proceedings in the court making the order* (whether or not proceedings of the same description as those to which the application for the order relates); but this subsection shall not preclude the making of an order requiring a person to give testimony (either orally or in writing) otherwise than on oath where this is asked for by the requesting court.

(4) An order under this section shall not require a person—(*a*) to state what *b* documents relevant to the proceedings to which the application for the order relates are or have been in his possession, custody or power; or (*b*) to produce any documents other than particular documents specified in the order as being documents appearing to the court making the order to be, or to be likely to be, in his possession, custody or power...

3.—(1) A person shall not be compelled by virtue of an order under section 2 *c* above to give any evidence which he could not be compelled to give—(*a*) in *civil proceedings* in the part of the United Kingdom in which the court that made the order exercises jurisdiction; or (*b*) subject to subsection (2) below, in *civil proceedings* in the country or territory in which the requesting court exercised jurisdiction...

(4) In this section references to giving evidence include references to answering any question and to producing any document...'
d

I need not refer to s 4. Section 5 contains similar provisions for criminal proceedings with certain qualifications; in particular, it only applies to requests made by courts or tribunals outside the United Kingdom and only in relation to criminal proceedings which have already been instituted. Section 6 contains a power to apply the provisions of ss 1 to 3 to certain kinds of 'international proceedings' by Order in Council, but it has no *e* relevance here.

Finally, one comes to the important part of the interpretation provision, s 9, on which much of the argument has turned:

'(1) In this Act—"*civil proceedings*", *in relation to the requesting court, means proceedings in any civil or commercial matter...*'
f

It should also be mentioned that the enactments repealed by Sch 2 to the 1975 Act include the Foreign Tribunals Evidence Act 1856, the Evidence by Commission Act 1859 and the Evidence by Commission Act 1885, to which I will refer later on.

The background facts and allegations
g

Mr Anders Jahre was a wealthy Norwegian shipowner who died in 1982. He had no relevant connection of any kind with this country. On 14 September 1983 the Vestfold County Tax Committee in Norway, in whose area he had resided, decided by four votes to three to raise a supplementary retrospective assessment against his estate in the sum of Nkr337,999,317 for the years 1972–82 on the ground that he had failed to declare, and in effect concealed, a large part of his assets. These are alleged to include the assets of a *h* Panamanian company, Continental Trust Co Inc (CTC), which evidently held large bank accounts, including one in a bank in Stockholm, but it is not alleged that any of the assets are or have ever been in the United Kingdom. The shares of CTC form part of the assets of a charitable foundation (the trust) formed in 1976 in an unknown location. It is alleged that Mr Jahre was the settlor or in control of the trust, directly or indirectly, and accordingly the beneficial owner of the assets of CTC. Mr Jahre was the president or *j* treasurer of CTC from 1970 to 1978, but it is denied that he was a member of the board of directors.

Lord Kindersley is a director of Lazards, a well-known merchant bank in London, and acted as adviser to the trust since its foundation, and Lazards appear to have acted as bankers to the trust at all material times. Mr Hardman, a senior employee of Lazards, *a*   was appointed the assistant secretary of CTC and treasurer in 1978. He retired from the bank in 1977 and from CTC in 1984, when CTC appears to have been dissolved.

Lord Kindersley denies that Mr Jahre or his estate control or have derived any beneficial interest from the trust, but has declined to give any information about its activities or beneficiaries, because this would involve breaches of his duty of confidentiality as its banker and financial adviser. In 1984 he had a meeting with Dr Brunsvig, a Norwegian lawyer acting for the estate, but in correspondence with him, and thereafter between the

b   solicitors, he declined to discuss these matters with Mr Haug, the Solicitor General of Norway. I should quote from three letters which Lord Kindersley wrote to Dr Brunsvig. On 31 October 1980 he wrote:

c   'Dr. Roberto Aleman, Vice-President and Secretary of Continental Trust Co., a Panama corporation, has presented to me a copy of his letter to the Bank of Norway dated 23rd May 1978 [which is not in evidence] and he asked me to confirm to you the following:—(1) I have been an adviser to the Foundation referred to in that letter since its foundation. (2) It is a properly constituted and existing legal entity. (3) The following excerpt from the Trust Deed describes the purpose of the Foundation. "Such income or any part thereof shall be paid to any one or more religious, charitable or educational institution or institutions or any organisations or

d   institutions operating for the public good (and the Trustees shall be the sole and absolute judges of whether any organisation or institution so qualifies as a beneficiary hereunder) the intention being to enable the Trustees to endeavour to act for the good or for the benefit of mankind in general or any section of mankind in particular anywhere in the world or throughout the world. In the case of any question as to the propriety of any distribution or selection by the Trustees the written approval

e   of the advisers to the Trustees, if such exists, shall be an absolute and final determination which shall not be open to question." (4) As stated in Dr. Aleman's letter the advisers to the Foundation are—Lord Kindersley, Thorleif Monsen, John Worsley. (5) The Foundation is the sole owner of the shares of Continental Trust Co. which are registered in the name of the Foundation. I hope this letter will be of some help to you in the discussions which I understand are proceeding with the

f   authorities in your country.'

On 25 April 1984, after the death of Mr Jahre, he wrote:

'I refer to our various telephone conversations over the last weeks during which you asked me whether I would be prepared to receive a visit from you accompanied by the Solicitor-General in my capacity as an adviser to the charitable foundation

g   which holds the shares of Continental Trust Company. The same principles of confidentiality apply here as in the banker to client relationship and I pointed out that I had given you all the information I could in my 1980 letter to you. In particular I was not, and am still not, at liberty to disclose who was the settlor of the foundation since it is obviously undesirable for the donor of substantial funds to have his identity known. In spite of your perfectly sincere promise of confidentiality

h   he is understandably fearful of the publicity which might ensue in today's world where the media seem to have the upper hand. Not only would the flood of requests for help become intolerable, but security risks have become a serious hazard. In my letter I did however describe the settlor to a sufficient extent to make clear that it could not be Mr Anders Jahre. You asked me on the telephone whether I could state categorically that neither Anders Jahre nor his family had benefited in any way

j   from the charitable foundation. I have been an adviser of the foundation since it was formed in 1976 and I can assure you that no donations have been recommended or made which could in any way have benefited Mr. Jahre or his surviving family. I must respect the wishes of the settlor by continuing to refuse to take part in a discussion of the affairs of the foundation. I hope this letter will be of some help to you.'

Finally, on 24 May 1984, after referring to a meeting between him and Mr Hardman
with Dr Brunsvig, Lord Kindersley wrote: *a*

> 'Since our meeting I have been in touch with the settlor who is unwilling to take
> part in any meetings of this sort for reasons with which you are all too familiar.'

In this context there is also an affidavit from Mr Ian Fraser, then joint chairman and a
director of Lazards, sworn in opposition to the present application. He confirmed the
truth of the following extract from an affidavit sworn by a partner in Messrs Linklaters *b*
& Paines on behalf of the witnesses:

> '12. It is important that it should be appreciated that the execution of the letter
> rogatory herein will necessarily involve the involuntary disclosure of confidential
> information which has come into the posession of Lord Kindersley and Mr.
> Hardman purely in their capacities as officers of Lazards and of which both they
> and Lazards as merchant bankers are under a duty owed to Lazards' principals, who *c*
> are not party to the Norwegian legal process, not to disclose. Indeed Lazards'
> principals have specifically indicated to Lazards that information of the nature
> sought by the letter rogatory should not be disclosed by or on behalf of Lazards.'

He went on to say that the matters deposed to in the following two paragraphs of his
own affidavit are matters of concern to Lazards: *d*

> '13. The dispute between the Estate and the Norwegian Government appears to
> have been very widely reported in the Scandinavian press and there has for instance
> been extensive reporting of the evidence given by other witnesses pursuant to the
> Courts of Sweden. Furthermore, the contents of letters written by Lord Kindersley
> to Mr. Brunsvig . . . also appear to have been reported and indeed extracts therefrom *e*
> quoted verbatim in the Norwegian press . . .
> 14. In the circumstances it is clear not only that the execution of the letter
> rogatory herein will certainly lead to the dissemination of confidential information
> presently in the possession of Lazards and their officers to the Revenue Authorities
> of a foreign (albeit in this case friendly) State, but that, on the basis of previous
> experience in this case, it is likely to lead to the dissemination of such confidential *f*
> information to the world at large.'

Mr Fraser concluded his affidavit as follows:

> 'Confidentiality lies at the heart of merchant banking business in the City of
> London and the forced disclosure of confidential information, particularly in a case
> of such notoriety as the present and in particular in a case involving foreign Revenue *g*
> Authorities, is likely to cause damage not only to the reputation and standing of
> Lazards, but also to merchant banking and the ability of merchant bankers to
> conduct business generally in the City of London. I would accordingly submit that
> it would be contrary to the public interest to order the disclosure of such confidential
> information on as broad a basis and in such circumstances as the present save where
> the necessity for such disclosure has been congently and compellingly demonstrated. *h*
> The present case is not in my submission such as to warrant any such disclosure.'

The Norwegian proceedings
The tax assessment made by the Vestfold County Tax Committe is now enforceable
but there are two ways in which an assessment can be discharged. The taxpayer can bring *j*
an action before the appropriate Norwegian court to have it declared null and void and
he can also appeal to a body referred to as the National Tax Committee (the NTC), which
forms part of the Tax Directorate of Norway. There was no evidence that the NTC is a
'court or tribunal' for the purposes of the 1975 Act, and indeed it appears clear from a
letter of 4 November 1985 from the assistant director general of the Tax Directorate to

a   Dr Brunsvig that the NTC acts in an administrative capacity similar to the Inland Revenue Commissioners in this country.

On 3 November 1983 the estate brought an action in the Sandefjord City Court, where Mr Jahre had been resident, to have the assessment set aside, and in view of the importance of the case the Solicitor General took over the defence of these proceedings. The estate did not originally appeal to the NTC, but subsequently decided to do so, and the NTC agreed to consider the appeal although it was out of time. In effect, therefore,

b   the proceedings in the Sandefjord court and the appeal to the NTC are now both pending. If the NTC should decide to set aside the assessment, then that would of course be an end of the matter. It was at one time thought that the NTC would deal with the appeal in the autumn of last year, and therefore before the outcome of the Sandefjord proceedings will be known. However, the position is now that the NTC will not deal with the matter until some time in the future, so that it is uncertain whether the outcome of the court

c   proceedings or the decision of the NTC will come first. But it is clearly to be inferred from the evidence before us that, if the present order stands, then the testimony of the witnesses will be made available not only to the Sandefjord court, but also to the NTC if the appeal before it is then still pending. In effect, to use the phrase of Lord Wilberforce in *Westinghouse* [1978] 1 All ER 434 at 444, [1978] AC 547 at 611, if the examination takes places the testimony of the witnesses will then be 'in the public domain'.

d   As regards the nature of the Sandefjord proceedings, there is an affidavit from the Solicitor General which states the following:

'4. The Norwegian legal system has 4 civil Courts: a Forliksraad (Conciliation Court); a Byrett or a Herredsrett (parallel courts of first instance); the Lagmannsrett (Court of Appeal); and the Hoeyesterett (the final Court of Appeal). Where the

e   Government is a defendant, the plaintiff need not have recourse to the first level, the Conciliation Court. The City Court of Sandefjord is a Byrett.

5. Whilst there are specific tribunals for certain matters (for example, labour disputes), there is no separate system of Courts dealing with civil actions involving the Government. Any civil proceedings brought by or against the Government are brought within the civil system outlined in the preceding paragraph. The Action is,

f   and has to be brought as, a normal civil action, following exactly the same procedure as any other, governed by the Civil Procedure Act of 13th August 1915 No. 6 and the Law Courts Act of 13th August 1915 No. 5. Such an Action will be heard by a normally constituted civil Court, and the same rights of appeal will exist as in any other matter.'

g   The letter of request also referred to the action as a 'civil case'. It is therefore clear that the Sandefjord proceedings are civil proceedings for the purpose of the courts system and the administration of justice in Norway, but there is no evidence whether the subject matter of the proceedings would, under the law of Norway, be regarded as a 'civil or commercial matter' as referred to in s 9(1) of the 1975 Act and discussed below.

h   *The request for letters rogatory*

On 22 June 1984 Dr Brunsvig issued a 'writ of process' in the Sandefjord court stating that 'it is of importance to have the persons examined who have direct knowledge of C.T.C. matters'. He asked for the examination of a Mr Bonde, referred to as a director of CTC, with whom we are not concerned, and of Lord Kindersley, but he made no request

j   in relation to Mr Hardman. The request for the examination of Lord Kindersley was made expressly pursuant to the 1970 convention on the ground that both Norway and the United Kingdom were signatories to it. Dr Brunsvig referred to the 'declarations' which Lord Kindersley had already made in the letters from which I have quoted and concluded as follows: 'It is requested that he be confronted with the declarations and asked to give an explanation of the contents.'

On 5 November 1984 the Solicitor General made a similar request to the Sandefjord court for the examination of Lord Kindersley as well as of Mr Hardman. It is this request with which the present proceedings are directly concerned. The original and the translation of the request were exhibited to an affidavit sworn by a partner in Messrs Freshfields, and formed the basis of the ex parte application before Master Prebble. In connection with this affidavit I should mention one matter in order to get it out of the way. One of the points taken before McNeill J was that the affidavit had failed to make a full disclosure of the material facts, because it made no reference to the possibility that the testimony of the witnesses would also be made available to the NTC. On the hearing of this appeal counsel appearing for the witnesses rightly abandoned this point as such and in my view there was never anything in it. The omission was no doubt regarded as irrelevant and certainly inadvertent, and it is no longer suggested that it has any bearing on the fate of this appeal. But the fact that the testimony may well be made available to the NTC in addition to the Sandefjord court remains a matter for consideration, and I refer to it again later on in this judgment.

The letter of request, as I will call it, had attached to it so-called 'pleadings' dealing with the evidence (used in a purely neutral sense) which was sought from the witnesses. This was set out in Pts (paragraphs) II and III with the following request:

'The witnesses must be confronted with the questions given in paragraph II and ordered to procure and submit original documents, or copies of them, as stated in paragraph III.'

Part II is in the following terms:

'II

The defendant will seek information and evidence from both witnesses respecting the following matters or questions in connection with these:

1. Present and previous owner or owners, direct or indirect, of funds and shares in Continental Trust Company Inc. ("C.T.C.").

2. Information about the trust or foundation (hereinafter "the trust") which is stated to be the owner of all or the majority of the shares in C.T.C., who was settlor, the name of the trust, foundation, structure, object, balance sheet, names of trustees, beneficiaries and who has authority to elect (or remove) trustees and alter the trust deed.

3. Information about C.T.C.'s operations and about Anders Jahre's dealings, direct or indirect, in these operations, also as agent or adviser, and about the administration of C.T.C.'s funds and changes in these both before and after 1976 when Lazard Brothers & Co. Ltd. were entrusted with the adminstration of C.T.C.'s funds in accordance with a resolution by C.T.C.'s board.

4. Information about the trust's funds, including size and investments, and the adminstration of and alterations in these.

5. Further information with regard to which persons, companies or institutions that have exercised control both "de jure" as well as "de facto" of C.T.C.'s funds and shares and the trust's funds and in what way and on what basis such control has been exercised.

6. Relations between Lazard Brothers & Co. Ltd. and the witnesses on the one hand and C.T.C., the trust and Andres Jahre, now his estate, or his companies or representatives on the other hand.

7. If C.T.C. kept accounts, where were these kept, who has kept or keeps these accounts and who has been and is principal in charge of the accounting.

8. Anders Jahre's relations, direct or indirect, both with C.T.C and the trust and his association or relations with any part of the evidence given in connection with questions stated under II.

a
The testimonies of the witnesses respecting the above will be of significance as Lord Kindersley is stated to be adviser for the trust and Mr. A. J. Hardman is stated to have been Treasurer and Assistant Secretary in C.T.C.'

b
Although the request for documents is no longer pursued, it was contended that it remained material to demonstrate the width of the letter of request as a whole, and that it was also relevant to the scope of the oral evidence which it would be sought to elicit from the witnesses. Part III is in the following terms:

'III

The defendant requests that the original documents, or copies of them, mentioned below be submitted:

1. The trust deed, as well as documents respecting possible amendments of the deed, and every document of significance in connection with the foundation of the trust and later statutory meeting.

c
2. Minutes from the trust's meetings.

3. All accounts relating to the trust and its funds.

4. All documents in connection with or giving proof of the administration of or changes in the trust's funds.

d
5. All documents in connection with or giving proof of C.T.C.'s operations or administration of, or changes in C.T.C.'s funds.

6. All correspondence exchanged between the witnesses on their own behalf or on behalf of the companies or institutions these are connected with on the one hand and Anders Jahre, his companies, or any representative on the other hand.'

e
The order of McNeill J

McNeill J did not accept any of the submissions on behalf of the witnesses on the issues with which I deal below, save the one headed 'Fishing', as it was referred to in the argument before us. In that regard he said:

f
'Turning back to the pleadings to which I referred at the outset of this judgment, it is of course clear that in many respects they are seeking the disclosure and contents of documents under the guise of oral testimony, which is impermissible and falls under the same impermissibility as that which affected Pt III of the request which the learned master refused. Indeed, many of the requests not dealing with documents seem to me to have a breadth which is not permissible under this procedure. Accordingly, I have come to the conclusion that I should not strike down the letters rogatory but should make directions to bring them within what is permissible under the statute and the rule and as a matter of discretion.'

g

The directions which he gave 'as to the conduct of the examination', which are sought to be expunged by the cross-appeal, were as follows:

h
'1. No question shall be asked of either witness calculated to elicit the existence or contents of any document; 2. No question shall be asked of Lord Kindersley save as to matters within his direct knowledge as adviser to the charitable foundation and he shall be entitled to decline to answer any question on the ground that the answer is not within his direct knowledge as such adviser; 3. No question shall be asked of Mr. Hardman save as to matters within his knowledge as an officer of C.T.C. and he shall be entitled to decline to answer any question on the ground that the answer is not within his knowledge as such officer.'

j

The issues

These can in the main be summarised under the following headings, without much elaboration at this stage.

A. Civil proceedings: civil or commercial matter
The issue is whether the Sandefjord proceedings fall within the ambit of the 1975 Act.

B. Tax gathering
This phrase is taken from the speech of Lord Somervell in *Government of India Ministry of Finance (Revenue Division) v Taylor* [1955] 1 All ER 292 at 301, [1955] AC 491 at 514. The contention is that compliance with the letter of request would be contrary to public policy and the settled principle that our courts will not lend their assistance to the enforcement, directly or indirectly, of foreign tax liabilities. This issue arises both independently and in the context of issue A.

C. Sovereignty
The contention is that, since the Sandefjord proceedings are concerned with the estate's assessment to tax in Norway, compliance by an English court with the letter of request is precluded by s 4 of the Protection of Trading Interests Act 1980 on the ground that the request, or compliance with it, infringes the jurisdiction of the United Kingdom or is prejudicial to its sovereignty.

D. Dual purpose
The issue concerns the intention to make the testimony of the witnesses available to the NTC, in addition to the Sandefjord court, if the estate's appeal to the NTC will not have been determined by the NTC when the testimony is available.

E. Fishing
The contention is that the terms of the letter of request are far too wide to constitute a proper or acceptable request for evidence under the 1975 Act, irrespective of the limitations contained in the directions given by the judge.

F. Confidentiality
The heading speaks for itself: it is submitted that in all the circumstances the witnesses should not be ordered to break their duty of confidentiality by answering the questions raised by the letter of request. Issues E and F overlap to some extent and fall to be examined in combination.

G. Discretion
Apart from issues as to jurisdiction, issues relating to the proper exercise of the court's discretion inevitably pervade the entire case, and it is convenient at this stage to summarise the issues in that regard.

It was submitted on behalf of the witnesses that, whereas issues A and C go to the jurisdiction of our courts to comply with the letter of request, issues B, D and E go both to jurisdiction and to the court's discretion, whereas issue F clearly goes solely to discretion. In this connection a number of matters were common ground. First, even assuming that the necessary jurisdiction exists, it is ultimately a matter for the discretion of the court, to be exercised judicially whether or not the request should be granted. Second, the court also has a discretionary power to restrict the scope of the request by placing some limitation on it. This is supported by a short passage in the speech of Lord Keith in *Westinghouse* [1978] 1 All ER 434 at 478, [1978] AC 547 at 654 and is also inherent in s 2(1) of the 1975 Act, which provides that the court—

> 'shall ... have power ... to make such provision for obtaining evidence ... as may appear to the court to be appropriate for the purpose of giving effect to the request ...'

But the extent to which the court's discretion should be exercised to use a 'blue pencil' in order to strike out parts of a request which is too wide remains in doubt, although it was referred to in many passages in the judgments and speeches in the *Westinghouse* case in relation to a request for the production of documents, as mentioned later on. Finally, it *a* was common ground that the witnesses were entitled to apply to the court to decline to comply with the letter of request, or, on appeal, to discharge the order made ex parte against them, on the grounds that the request was, inter alia, 'fishing, speculative or oppressive' (see *Senior v Holdsworth* [1975] 2 All ER 1009 at 1016, [1976] QB 23 at 35 per Lord Denning MR and other cases cited in *The Supreme Court Practice 1985* vol 1, para 38/14–19/11) and that this was also a matter for the discretion of the court.

b However, there was inevitably considerable disagreement about the proper exercise of the court's discretion in all the circumstances. Counsel representing the state and the estate respectively relied on two important factors in this connection: first, the principle of international comity, the desirability that the English courts should strive to comply with a request of a foreign court made pursuant to the 1970 convention, to which both Norway and the United Kingdom are parties. (In fact it appears that a bilateral convention concluded in London on 30 January 1931 between the United Kingdom and Norway

c 'regarding legal proceedings in Civil and Commercial Matters' (TS 35 (1931); Cmd 3931) is also still in force; its contents and effects are similar to the 1970 convention, but it was not relied on as such and requires no further mention). Second, and inevitably, they placed in the forefront of their arguments the unprecedented feature of this case that the examination of the witnesses was desired both by the state and the estate, the taxpayer.

d Counsel for the witnesses recognised the weight which was properly to be given to these two factors. But they submitted that they were overcome by the cumulative effect of the matters raised in relation to issues B, D, E and F. As regards the fact that the estate supported the letter of request, they pointed out that Dr Brunsvig's request to the Sandefjord court only related to Lord Kindersley and that it was far narrower than Pt II of the 'pleadings' annexed to the letter of request by the state. They also pointed out that counsel for the estate in effect agreed that the only questions which he would wish to put

e at the examination would be designed to obtain confirmation of the statements made by Lord Kindersley in his letters, as to which he had already waived confidentiality and which had already been published in the Norwegian press.

Apart from these competing general considerations on the balancing exercise which the court has to carry out, there was also disagreement about the course which the proposed examination of the witnesses would and should properly take. This is governed

f by RSC Ords 39 and 70 ('Evidence by deposition: examiners of the court' and 'Obtaining evidence for foreign courts, etc.'). *The Supreme Court Practice 1985* vol 1, para 70/1–6/22, referring to the judgment of Cockburn CJ in *Desilla v Fells & Co* (1879) 40 LT 423 at 423–424, shows that there is considerable latitude about the evidence which may be admitted:

g   'The evidence can only be taken "in the English mode," but that does not mean that it is to be limited to what is admissible in English courts. The foreign Court should be afforded the fullest help it is possible to give. If its rules of evidence are known, effect should be given to them; if not, any questions should be admitted which may be expected to throw light on the matters in issue . . .'

h However, subject to any claim for privilege under s 3(1)(b) of the 1975 Act (see Ord 70, r 6) and any special directions contained in the order, the note points out that examination must be conducted in the manner provided by the relevant provisions of Ord 39. Order 39, r 8 provides for the examination, cross-examination and re-examination of the witnesses 'in like manner as at the trial of a cause or matter'. Rule 10 provides, inter alia, that, if a witness objects to answer any questions put to him, the ground for the objection

j must be set out in the deposition and that the validity of such ground must then be decided by the court and not by the examiner.

There was considerable disagreement between counsel as to how the application of these provisions would and should work out in practice in this case. Prima facie one would expect that the witnesses would be called on behalf of the estate and cross-

examined on behalf of the state. But, when we inquired about this, all counsel were
agreed that the witnesses would and should be called on behalf of the state. This is *a*
understandable, since the relevant part of the letter of request is in the following terms:

'It appears from paragraph II of the pleadings of 24 October 1984 from the
Attorney-General [sic] in Norway which questions will be put to the witnesses. In
this connection reference is also made to pleadings of 22 June 1984 from plaintiff's
counsel [Mr. Brunsvig] in so far as concerns the witness Lord Kindersley [ie 'that he
be confronted with the declarations [his letters, as quoted above] and asked to give *b*
an explanation of the contents'].'

The problems which may result are obvious. Would the state be bound by the answers
given, or could it cross-examine its own witnesses? Objections to many of the questions
covered by Pt II of the 'pleadings' are obviously to be expected. Counsel for the state said
that this should not deter the court from upholding the order. He pointed out that, *c*
although the judge said that he would have declined to allow the witnesses to be
represented by counsel, he was informed that the state subsequently agreed to this, so
that counsel would be present. However, it is to be noted that the judge expressed
reservations about this and said that 'such a course may present very serious practical
difficulties for the examiner'. With respect, it seems to me that this remark in itself
recognises the much more fundamental difficulties which are certain to arise in this case. *d*
Counsel for the state did not accept this. He said that the examination would be
conducted in a friendly and fairly informal manner, and, although counsel for the
witnesses, and the witnesses themselves, could be expected to object to many questions
on the grounds of 'fishing' and confidentiality, these objections would be recorded and,
if necessary, ruled on by the court subsequently. On the other side, counsel for the
witnesses submitted that this approach was far too simplistic. It would clearly involve *e*
further, possibly prolonged, court proceedings. In these, if the present order stands, it
would, inter alia, be submitted on behalf of the state that by upholding the width of the
questions covered by Pt II of the 'pleadings' this court had already impliedly ruled on the
permissible scope of the questions which had to be answered. Further, to the extent that
this submission did not prevail, it would be necessary for the court to consider the
questions and objections in detail. He therefore submitted that if we should conclude *f*
that the scope of Pt II of the 'pleadings' was too wide to be acceptable, and could not
properly be cut down by 'blue pencil' amendments or appropriate directions, then the
judge's order should be reversed and the state and the estate should be invited to
reconsider the position in the light of our judgments.

On this part of the argument I should say at once that I agree with the approach and
submissions of counsel for the witnesses as I have summarised them above. *g*

The final matter to be mentioned, on the various issues which were argued in the
context of the discretion of this court, is that in the circumstances of this case it was not
strongly urged on behalf of the state or the estate that this court was effectively bound by
the way in which the judge had exercised his discretion, having decided that he had
jurisdiction to comply with the letter of request. The importance of giving great weight *h*
to the views which he expressed in this connection requires no emphasis, and I need not
refer to any of the well-known authorities in which it has been laid down that this court
can only interfere if it concludes that the judge has clearly fallen into error in some
relevant respect. But in the present case this conclusion was not seriously challenged in
relation to the 'directions' given by the judge in order to cut down the scope of Pt II of
the 'pleadings' to an acceptable extent. Thus, while contending in general that the judge's *j*
exercise of his discretion should not be overturned, since he had considered and weighed
each of the issues, in support of their cross-appeal counsel for the state and the estate were
themselves highly critical of the judge's directions on the ground that these were
inappropriate and should be deleted, whereas counsel for the witnesses, while seeking to

uphold them if all else failed, had no real answer to these criticisms. I will deal with these
a aspects under issue E, 'fishing'. It was also pointed out on behalf of the witnesses that the
judge may have been under the impression that the submissions under issue F directed
to confidentiality involved a claim for privilege, which would clearly have been
unsustainable. In all these circumstances the thrust of the arguments deployed before us
concerning the court's discretion was primarily directed to the correct solution of the
overall balancing exercise which fell to be performed below and afresh on appeal to this
b court, and this is how I regard the position for the purposes of this judgment.

International comity

Before dealing with issues A to F seriatim, it is right to place this topic in the forefront.
Its importance has been stressed in many cases involving international aspects and
consequences, and the decision of the House of Lords in *Williams & Humbert Ltd v W &*
c *H Trade Marks (Jersey) Ltd* [1986] 1 All ER 129, [1986] AC 368, given shortly after the
conclusion of this appeal, provides the most recent illustration. The relevance of this
topic in the present context is that the court should strive to give effect to the request of
the foreign court unless it is driven to the clear conclusion that it cannot properly do so.
In this connection it is unnecessary to say more than to quote a passage from the
d judgment of McNeill J:

'The general approach of the court should be to assist the requesting court and to
give effect to letters rogatory so far as is proper and practicable and to the extent
permissible under English law: see per Cooke J in *Seyfang v G D Searle & Co* [1973]
1 All ER 290 at 293, [1973] QB 148 at 151: "Judicial and international comity
requires that any request of a foreign court for evidence to be taken under the Act
e [ie the Foreign Tribunals Evidence Act 1856, and the same, I interpolate, applies to
the 1975 Act] should be treated with sympathy and respect and complied with so
far as the principles of English law permit." See also per Lord Denning MR in *Re*
Westinghouse Electric Corp Uranium Contract Litigation MDL Docket No 235 [1977] 3
All ER 703 at 708, [1978] AC 547 at 560: "It is our duty and our pleasure to do all
we can to assist that court", and in the same case in the House of Lords, Lord
f Wilberforce said sub nom *Rio Tinto Zinc Corp v Westinghouse Electric Corp* [1978] 1
All ER 434 at 444, [1978] AC 547 at 611: "This is that, on the whole, I am of opinion
that following the spirit of the 1975 Act which is to enable judicial assistance to be
given to foreign courts, the letters rogatory ought to be given effect to so far as
possible . . ."'

g It should be noted, however, that all counsel were agreed that there appears to be no
precedent for such assistance to have been given internationally in any 'tax gathering'
context, as referred to in issue B (I say 'internationally' to distinguish co-operation by
different courts within one federal system, as also distinguished in *Government of India,*
Ministry of Finance (Revenue Division) v Taylor [1955] 1 All ER 292, [1955] AC 491).
I turn to issues A to F.
h

Issue A: civil proceedings: civil or commercial matter

I have emphasised the various references in the 1975 Act to 'civil proceedings'. This
expression is used both in relation to the courts in the United Kingdom mentioned in s 1
when requests for orders for the obtaining of evidence are addressed to them (to which I
j will refer as 'the court addressed' or generally 'the English courts') and in relation to 'the
requesting court': see s 1(*b*). Thus, in ss 2(3) and 3(1)(*a*) 'civil proceedings' has the meaning
which is to be given to this expression by the court addressed in the United Kingdom.
But in the context of the present issue one is primarily concerned with s 1(*b*): the court
addressed in the United Kingdom must be satisfied—

'that the evidence to which the application relates is to be obtained for the purposes of civil proceedings which either have been instituted before the requesting *a* court or whose institution before that court is contemplated.'

In that context 'civil proceedings' is defined in s 9(1), because it is there defined 'in relation to the requesting court'. It follows that 'civil proceedings' in s 1(*b*) means 'proceedings in any civil or commercial matter'.

Two further consequences follow. First, the issue whether the proceedings in the *b* requesting court are proceedings 'in any civil or commercial matter' goes to the jurisdiction of the court addressed in the United Kingdom, in this case the High Court and this court on appeal from the High Court. Second, the court addressed must somehow reach a conclusion whether or not the proceedings in the requesting court are to be categorised as 'proceedings in any civil or commercial matter'. A great deal of the argument before us revolved on the question how this is to be done. Since this phrase is *c* used in numerous international conventions, both bilateral and multilateral, such as the 1970 convention itself, the problem is clearly of considerable international significance.

Unfortunately, the 1970 convention provides no assistance (in common with all other conventions in which this phrase is used) as to its meaning or scope, or how these are to be determined. These questions have only been determined by the Court of Justice of the European Communities in the decisions referred to below, on the Convention on *d* Jurisdiction and the Enforcement of Judgments in Civil and Commercial Matters (Brussels, 27 September 1968), followed by a 1971 protocol (Luxembourg, 3 June 1971) and the Accession Convention of 1978 (Luxembourg, 9 September 1978) (EC 46 (1978); Cmnd 7395). This added Denmark, the Republic of Ireland and the United Kingdom to what is compendiously known as the European Judgments Convention. Effect has been given to this in the United Kingdom by the Civil Jurisdiction and Judgments Act 1982, *e* in Sch 1 to which the text of the 1968 convention, as amended, is set out. But the relevant parts are not yet in force, and even if the 1982 Act provided any direct assistance, which it does not, it could not be used as a means of interpreting the 1975 Act.

How then is an English court to approach and resolve the problem of categorisation posed by s 9(1) of the 1975 Act? McNeill J said 'it was accepted that reference to the convention could properly be of assistance in construing the statute'. This was not *f* disputed on this appeal, and, since it was pointed out in *Westinghouse* that one of the purposes of the 1975 Act was to implement the convention, this must be the starting point. Where English legislation has been enacted to give effect to a convention, reference to it may, and should where necessary, be made to it to see whether it assists in the interpretation of the legislation, not only where the convention is annexed (see esp Lord Diplock in *Fothergill v Monarch Airlines Ltd* [1980] 2 All ER 696 at 705–707, [1981] AC *g* 251 at 280–283), but even where it is not (see *Salomon v Customs and Excise Comrs* [1966] 3 All ER 871 at 874–876, [1967] 2 QB 130 at 141–145 per Lord Denning MR and Diplock LJ). In statutes giving effect to conventions, an interpretation 'on broad principles of general acceptation' is desirable (see *Stag Line Ltd v Foscolo Mango & Co Ltd* [1932] AC 328 at 350, [1931] All ER Rep 666 at 677 per Lord Macmillan). However, sometimes *h* this may not be possible (see *James Buchanan & Co Ltd v Babco Forwarding and Shipping (UK) Ltd* [1977] 3 All ER 1048 esp at 1052–1053, [1978] AC 141 esp at 152–153 per Lord Wilberforce).

But, having reached the 1970 convention, this provides no assistance whatever. Where then does an English court go next in order to determine whether proceedings in a foreign court, on which a request for assistance under s 2 of the 1975 Act is based, are *j* proceedings 'in a civil or commercial matter'?

Four possible categorisations present themselves: (1) a generally accepted international interpretation; (2) classification under the law of the requesting court; (3) classification under the law of the court addressed; (4) a combination of (2) and (3), ie the court *a* addressed would satisfy itself that the proceedings concern a civil or commercial matter under the law of the requesting court, but would only accept this categorisation for the purposes of assuming jurisdiction if it is not in conflict with any fundamental principle recognised under the laws of the court addressed.

On the evidence and submissions presented on this appeal I have ultimately reached the reluctant conclusion that (4) provides the best answer, because (1) has not been established on the material before us. But it is impossible to express the reasons shortly,
b since many countervailing factors require to be taken into account. I list the main ones below to which reference was made.

(i) 'Civil or commercial matter' is a translation of the French phrase 'matière civile ou commerciale'. Like all Hague conventions since 1961, the 1970 convention was concluded in English and French, and art 42 provides that both texts are equally authentic. This phrase has been used in many previous conventions, but none of them contain any
c definition or other clear guidance as to the meaning or scope of these words. The travaux préparatoires for the 1970 convention (which would be admissible under the decision of the House of Lords in *Fothergill v Monarch Airlines Ltd*) throw no light on it. Counsel for the state told us that the French phrase was first used in a Hague convention in 1896, but we do not know whether its travaux préparatoires would be of any assistance. (Throughout the hearing of this appeal I felt that, if ever there was a case where the
d assistance of an experienced comparative lawyer would have been welcome, this is so here.)

(ii) 'Matière civile ou commerciale' clearly stems from French law and appears to be a concept current in many or all civil law systems and probably others as well. 'Matière' indicates the nature of the litigation, the subject matter of the dispute: see Dalloz *Lexique de Termes Juridiques* (5th edn, 1981). The duality of 'civil' and 'commercial' points away
e from a classification under the common law, since we include commercial cases in ordinary civil cases. But in French law there is a distinction between 'civil' and 'commercial' which is 'rooted in history' (see René David *English Law and French Law* (1980) pp 36 ff), although not in all other civil law countries. The duality of the phrase in Hague conventions and elsewhere was clearly intended to make it clear that no distinction was to be drawn between 'civil' and 'commercial' for international purposes.
f In the present context the issue turns on 'civil'.

(iii) Other passages in *David*, and many untranslated extracts from French treatises which were supplied to us during the hearing, show that civil law countries draw a fundamental distinction between private and public law (droit civil and droit administratif) which is only beginning to emerge in this country. It seems certain that
g this distinction must have been crucially present to the mind of anyone seeking to circumscribe and distinguish 'matières civiles et commerciales' from other, i e 'public law', proceedings. Relations between states and their public authorities on the one hand and private citizens or corporations on the other fall within the sphere of public law. Civil and commercial matters do not, because they are concerned with private disputes. Droit fiscal (or matière fiscale: see the extract quoted below from the speech of Lord
h Somervell in *Government of India Ministry of Finance (Revenue Division) v Taylor* [1955] 1 All ER 292 at 301, [1955] AC 491 at 514) is a recognised part of public law and evidently a special topic which is even separate from the generality of droit administratif. It appears incontestable that no civil law country would ever treat a disputed tax claim as part of 'matière civile ou commerciale'. Droit fiscal is not comprised in 'droits et obligations de caractère civil': see the decision of the Belgian Cour de Cassation in *Salvatore v Etat Belge,*
j *Ministère des Finances* JT, 8 April 1976, p 444.

(iv) International assistance in revenue matters is generally given by double tax conventions, which normally provide for 'exchange of information' (see eg the Double Taxation Relief (Taxes on Income) (Norway) Order 1970, SI 1970/154, giving effect to the Convention (London, 22 January 1969; Cmnd 3954), art 30. As already mentioned, there appears to be no reported instance of an ordinary international convention, whether multi- or bilateral, for evidential judicial assistance being used for this purpose.

(v) For the purposes of the European Judgments Convention it is settled law that the expression 'matière civile ou commerciale' does not include disputes 'between a public authority and a person governed by private law ... if the public authority is acting in the exercise of its public authority powers': see *Netherlands v Rüffer* Case 814/79 [1980] ECR 3807 at 3819 (para 8), following the earlier decisions of the Court of Justice of the European Communities there mentioned. For the purposes of that convention, even in its original form (cf para (vi)(c) below), any dispute concerning liability for taxes could clearly not be a 'civil or commercial matter'.

(vi) But: (a) the subject matter of the European Judgments Convention is the recognition and enforcement of foreign judgments, not merely judicial assistance for the provision of evidence in foreign courts; (b) the European Court is empowered by the EEC Treaty to interpret the European Judgments Convention authoritatively. It does so in a sense which is 'communautaire' within the members of the EEC. There is nothing analogous for the 1970 convention or any other Hague convention, which are open to accession by any country: see eg art 39 of the 1970 convention. The preamble refers to the desirability 'to improve *mutual* judicial co-operation in civil or commercial matters', which may point away from a multilateral or generally international interpretation; (c) the 1978 Accession Convention and our 1982 Act expressly exclude 'in particular ... revenue, customs or administrative matters' from 'civil or commercial matters': see art 1 of the convention as incorporated by Sch 1 to the 1982 Act. This was done to resolve any doubt about the scope of 'civil or commercial matters' in relation to member states which draw no clear distinction between public and private law. But (unfortunately, in my view) it was not done in the 1970 convention or the 1975 Act. In relation to this express exclusion in the 1978 Accession Convention, in *Netherlands v Rüffer* [1980] ECR 3807 at 3831 Mr Advocate General Warner quoted the following passage from the report on the Accession Convention by Professor Dr Peter Schlosser (OJ 1979 C59, p 82), which is an admissible aid to its interpretation by virtue of s 3(1) of the 1982 Act:

> 'The distinction between civil and commercial matters on the one hand and matters of public law on the other is well recognized in the legal systems of the original Member States and is, in spite of some important differences, on the whole arrived at on the basis of similar criteria ... In the United Kingdom and Ireland the distinction commonly made in the original EEC States between private law and public law is hardly known. This meant that the problems of adjustment could not be solved simply by a reference to these classifications ...'

It may well be significant that Professor Schlosser makes no reference to the third acceding state, Denmark, in this connection, whose legal system and jurisprudence may well be similar to that of Norway. But, apart from the extracts from the affidavit of the Norwegian Solicitor General which I have set out, we have no evidence of Norwegian law. All we know is that the action in Sandefjord is 'a normal civil action'. We do not know whether the *substance* of the dispute would be regarded as a 'civil or commercial matter' under the law of Norway or whether Norway recognises a clear distinction between public and private law. I suspect that it does, but unfortunately there is no evidence about it.

(vii) In English law the phrase 'civil or commercial matter' is first to be found in the Foreign Tribunals Evidence Act 1856, the predecessor of the 1975 Act, which was repealed by it. It appears to have been inspired by the Treaty of Paris, with many protocols governing international relations and co-operation, concluded earlier in 1856; and the treaty, its protocols and the 1856 Act are comprised in the state papers for that year. But despite suggestions from the court and the industry of counsel, including a search for 'Notes on Clauses' by the parliamentary draftsman, no further light was shed

on the reasons for the adoption of these words in an English statute. However, s 2 of the
1856 Act is of interest, since it clearly points away from a purely common law
categorisation. This was in the following terms, which find no counterpart in the 1975
Act:

> '*Certificate of Ambassador, &c. sufficient Evidence in support of Application.* A
> Certificate under the Hand of the Ambassador, Minister, or other Diplomatic Agent
> of any Foreign Power, received as such by Her Majesty, or in case there be no such
> Diplomatic Agent, then of the Consul General or Consul of any such Foreign Power
> at *London*, received and admitted as such by Her Majesty, that any Matter in relation
> to which an Application is made under this Act is a Civil or Commercial Matter
> pending before a Court or Tribunal in the Country of which he is the Diplomatic
> Agent or Consul having Jurisdiction in the Matter so pending, and that such Court
> or Tribunal is desirous of obtaining the Testimony of the Witness or Witnesses to
> whom the Application relates, shall be Evidence of the Matters so certified; but
> where no such Certificate is produced other Evidence to that Effect shall be
> admissible.'

Per contra, the Evidence by Commission Acts 1859 and 1885, which were also repealed
by the 1975 Act, do not contain the phrase 'civil or commercial matter', presumably
because they were designed to operate within Her Majesty's dominions, with powers of
extension to other (also mainly common law) territories over which Britain exercised
jurisdiction. The former Act applied to 'any action, suit or proceedings' and the latter,
with differing effect, to any 'civil proceeding' and 'any criminal proceeding'. This
distinction is also adopted in the definition of 'judgment or order' in s 11(1) of the Foreign
Judgments (Reciprocal Enforcement) Act 1933, and in this context, as in the 1978
Accession Convention and the 1982 Act, judgments on tax liabilities are expressly
excluded by s 1(2)(b) of the 1933 Act.

(viii) In the 1975 Act, the 1970 convention is not mentioned at all. The Act clearly
applies to requests for evidential assistance issued by or on behalf of a court or tribunal in
any foreign country, whether or not it has adhered to the 1970 convention. Since the
words 'civil or commercial matter' are wholly unqualified, a wide interpretation was
presumably intended, although in my view one which was clearly designed to exclude
'public law' disputes.

(ix) As Professor Schlosser indicated in his report, the common law does not, or at any
rate not yet, recognise any clear distinction between public and private law. But the
division is beginning to be recognised: see *Town Investments Ltd v Dept of the Environment*
[1977] 1 All ER 813, [1978] AC 359, *A-G of New Zealand v Ortiz* [1982] 3 All ER 432 at
456–460, [1984] AC 1 at 20–24 per Lord Denning MR (decided on a different point in
the House of Lords (see [1983] 2 All ER 93, [1984] AC 1)) and *O'Reilly v Mackman* [1982]
3 All ER 680 at 692, [1983] 2 AC 237 at 255 per Lord Denning MR (CA), [1982] 3 All
ER 1124 at 1128, [1983] 2 AC 237 at 277 per Lord Diplock (HL). Nevertheless, I feel
bound to conclude that the interpretation of the 1975 Act cannot properly be based on
it. Thus, the Act applies between the courts of the different parts of the United Kingdom,
as it does in relation to all foreign countries. But it appears inconceivable that in 1975
Parliament could have intended that inter-UK requests for evidence in civil proceedings
should be based on a categorisation by reference to public and private law. Or, more
realistically, the draftsman of the Act may unfortunately have failed to appreciate that
while this distinction certainly underlay the 1970 convention in using this well-known
phrase, it could not conveniently also be fitted into an inter-UK arrangement, at any rate
without further definition or explanation. However, we must take the Act as we find it.

(x) On the evidence before us the action instituted by the estate in the Sandefjord
court is clearly a civil proceeding, in the sense that it is an action proceeding in the
hierarchy of the ordinary civil courts of Norway. A similar process in this country to

discharge an assessment to tax (before the General or Special Commissioners with an appeal to the High Court, or an application for judicial review before the Divisional Court) would equally be a civil proceeding. McNeill J said:

> 'English law does not recognise any "middle ground" between civil and criminal proceedings: both public and private law matters may be civil matters and dealt with in civil proceedings.'

There is no answer to this, except that the concept of 'civil proceedings' may not be synonymous with 'civil or commercial matter', let alone 'matière civile ou commerciale'.

In all the circumstances, however, contrary to my first, and what would have been my preferred, conclusion, I find it impossible, on the material before us, to give to 'civil or commercial matter' in s 9(1) of the 1975 Act any interpretation which can be seen as being broadly acceptable internationally as well as within the three law districts of the United Kingdom. The approach of the Court of Justice of the European Communities in *Netherlands v Rüffer* [1980] ECR 3807 would in my view undoubtedly provide the best answer, but on the material before us it has not been established in the present context. It is also always important to bear in mind the observation of Lord Wilberforce in *James Buchanan & Co Ltd v Babco Forwarding and Shipping (UK) Ltd* [1977] 3 All ER 1048 at 1053, [1978] AC 141 at 153 dealing with the Convention on the Contract for the International Carriage of Goods by Road (CMR) (Geneva, 19 May 1956; TS 90 (1967); Cmnd 3455):

> 'To base our interpretation of this Convention on some assumed, and unproved, interpretation which other courts are to be supposed likely to adopt is speculative as well as masochistic.'

It follows that I feel constrained to reject category (1). I would also reject each of categories (2) and (3), classifying the proceedings exclusively by reference, respectively, to the law of the requesting court or of the court addressed. There seems no warrant for the latter to the exclusion of the former. The starting point must surely be the law of the requesting court. If it acts in accordance with principles of international comity, it should refrain from making any request under the 1970 convention or the 1975 Act unless the proceedings before it are 'proceedings in a civil or commercial matter' by its own law. But I do not think that the court addressed can be wholly bound by the classification put forward by any requesting court. By s 1 of the 1975 Act the court addressed must be 'satisfied' that the request falls within s 9(1). It is therefore open to it to examine the nature of the proceedings in the requesting court. Accordingly, even if it concludes that the requirements of the classification have been met under the law of the requesting court, I do not think that the court addressed is bound in all cases. If, for instance, proceedings which would clearly be regarded as criminal or penal proceedings by the law of the court addressed are nevertheless characterised as proceedings in a civil matter by the requesting court, then it must be open to the court addressed to decline to accede to the request, if not on jurisdictional grounds, then at least as a matter of discretion. Of the four suggested categories I therefore conclude that (4) is the most acceptable.

Where does that leave the present case? If the *substance* of a dispute is clearly a matter of *public* law in the jurisprudence of the requesting court, then I would not accept that it can properly be regarded as 'matière civile ou commerciale' for the purposes of the 1970 convention or any legislation based on it. But although I regard the evidence on Norwegian law as insufficiently searching, particularly on the characterisation of the substance of these proceedings by reference to the distinction between public and private law which may well be recognised in Norway as in civil law countries, I do not feel able to conclude on the evidence that the Sandefjord action cannot be regarded as a proceeding in a civil matter by the law of Norway.

Counsel for the state offered to produce a further affidavit on this point, but we declined it at this late stage. However, since the Norwegian court was evidently satisfied that the request was a proper one under its own law, and the evidence of the Solicitor a General supports it, I would reluctantly give it the benefit of the doubt, which I nevertheless retain. In any event, in view of my conclusions on issues E and F, in this judgment the matter becomes academic. I would only add that if a similar issue should arise in the future, I hope that our courts will be provided with more satisfactory evidence in the light of the considerations to which I have referred.

So far as concerns the second ingredient of category (4), the characterisation of the Sandefjord action by English law, it is clearly a civil proceeding. Accordingly, although b only with considerable doubt, I would dismiss the appeal on issue A.

Issue B: tax gathering

Since the absence of jurisdiction under s 9(1) of the 1975 Act has not been established, this issue turns on questions of public policy. One could easily write at similar length about this topic, but in the circumstances of this case I can deal with it more shortly. The c witnesses rely on the general principle stated in Dicey and Morris *The Conflict of Laws* (10th edn, 1980) vol 1, pp 89–90:

> 'English courts have no jurisdiction to entertain an action: (1) for the enforcement, either directly or indirectly, of a penal, revenue or other public law of a foreign state ...'

d
This is certainly a principle of general international acceptation: see *Government of India, Ministry of Finance (Revenue Division) v Taylor* [1955] 1 All ER 292 at 295, 301, [1955] AC 491 at 505, 514 per Viscount Simonds and Lord Somervell, the decision of the Irish courts in *Peter Buchanan Ltd and Macharg v McVey* (1951) [1955] AC 516n, the decision of the Supreme Court of Canada in *US v Harden* (1963) 41 DLR (2d) 721, the e South African decision in *Comr of Taxes Federation of Rhodesia v McFarland* 1965 (1) SA 470, the Australian decision in *Ayres v Evans* (1981) 39 ALR 129 and the jurisprudence of the United States.

The passage from the speech of Lord Somervell, on which the appellants relied in particular, especially the second paragraph, is as follows ([1955] 1 All ER 292 at 301–302, [1955] AC 491 at 514):

f > 'There is no decision binding on your Lordships' House and the matter, therefore, falls to be considered in principle. If one state could collect its taxes through the courts of another, it would have arisen through what is described, vaguely perhaps, as comity or the general practice of nations inter se. The appellant was, therefore, in a difficulty from the outset in that, after considerable research, no case of any country could be found in which taxes due to state A had been enforced in the g courts of state B. Apart from the comparatively recently English, Scottish and Irish cases, there is no authority. There are, however, many propositions for which no express authority can be found because they have been regarded as self-evident to all concerned. There must have been many potential defendants.
>
> Tax gathering is an administrative act, though, in settling the quantum, as well h as in the final act of collection, judicial process may be involved. Our courts will apply foreign law if it is the proper law of a contract, the subject of a suit. Tax gathering is not a matter of contract, but of authority and administration as between the state and those within its jurisdiction. If one considers the initial stages of the process, which may, as the records of your Lordships' House show, be intricate and prolonged, it would be remarkable comity if state B allowed the time of its courts to j be expended in assisting in this regard the tax gatherers of state A. Once a judgment has been obtained and it is a question only of its enforcement, the factor of time and expense will normally have disappeared. The principle remains. The claim is one for a tax.
>
> That fact, I think, itself justifies what has been clearly the practice of states. They have not in the past thought it appropriate to seek to use legal process abroad against

debtor taxpayers. They assumed, rightly, that the courts would object to being so
used. The position in the United States of America has been referred to, and I agree   *a*
that the position as between member states of a federation wherever the reserve of
sovereignty may be, does not help.

The following passage from PILLET's TRAITÉ DE DROIT INTERNATIONAL PRIVÉ (1924,
para 674) confirms the negative result of counsel's researches in respect of French
law. "Les jugements rendus en matière criminelle ne sont pas les sculs qui soient
soumis à la loi de la territorialité absolue. Les jugements rendus en matière fiscale   *b*
ne sont eux non plus susceptibles d'aucune exécution à l'étranger, et l'on n'a même
jamais songé à la possibilité de faire exécuter sur le territoire de l'un d'eux une
sentence relative aux droits fiscaux de l'état qui aurait été rendue sur le territoire
d'un autre."

The appellant is asking the English courts to do what the courts of no other
country have done. In some fields this might commend the argument, but here, for   *c*
the reason which I stated at the outset, it is fatal.'

The extract from the French textbook which Viscount Simonds described as 'of high
authority' (see [1955] 1 All ER 292 at 296, [1955] AC 491 at 506) is also of interest since
it refers specifically to 'matière fiscale', as discussed above under issue A in contrast to
'matière civile ou commerciale'.   *d*

However, it is clearly open to argument whether a request for evidential assistance
pursuant to s 2 of the 1975 Act relating to proceedings in a foreign court concerning a
foreign resident's tax liability is properly describable as an action for the enforcement,
directly or indirectly, of a revenue law of a foreign state. The recent decision of the House
of Lords in *Williams & Humbert Ltd v W & H Trade Marks (Jersey) Ltd* [1986] 1 All ER
129, [1986] AC 368 suggests that the principle stated in *Dicey and Morris* is to be   *e*
construed narrowly. It is also important to note that by s 5 of the 1975 Act evidence may
be obtained, albeit to a more limited extent, in relation to criminal, ie penal, proceedings
in foreign countries. Accordingly, despite the references to the various stages of the
process of 'tax gathering' which Lord Somervell mentioned, it must be doubtful whether
the English courts would be wholly debarred from considering a request such as the
present as a matter of public policy. Nevertheless, if this issue had arisen in the present   *f*
case in a different form, ie if a foreign state had sought to enlist the assistance of the
English courts in order to obtain evidence against one of its taxpayers in opposition to
the taxpayer, then I would have regarded such a request as part of the foreign 'tax
gathering' process to which the English courts should not lend their assistance as a matter
of public policy, in keeping with principles which are internationally accepted.

Although this issue is again academic on the basis of my conclusions on issues E and F,   *g*
and partly covered by matters already referred to, it is of sufficient importance to warrant
some additional comments. As already mentioned, despite counsel's researches they were
unable to point to any decision anywhere, or to any published material, suggesting that
the 1970 convention, or any of the many similar bilateral conventions, had been intended
by the participants at the various Hague conventions conferences on private international   *h*
law to be applicable to requests for evidence in aid of fiscal proceedings within the
expression 'civil or commercial matters'. A request for international evidential assistance
by a state against one of its own taxpayers appears to be wholly unprecedented. Many of
the factors mentioned above under issue A point in the opposite direction and suggest
that this would be contrary to comity and the practice of states. Assistance in fiscal
matters is dealt with in special bilateral treaties. Requests for the examination of witnesses   *j*
and the production of documents in relation to such matters are likely to involve
unwilling breaches of confidence on the part of witnesses and the investigation of the
private affairs of persons alleged to be liable for tax in other countries. No such order has
been made in any of the cases referred to below under issue F. The elicitation of evidence

in support of an allegation of fiscal liability involves the consideration of foreign revenue
a laws and therefore their indirect enforcement. The admissibility of such a request on
behalf of a foreign state or revenue authority against the wishes of the person concerned
would certainly not command 'general acceptation' (to quote the expression of Lord
Macmillan in *Stag Line Ltd v Foscolo Mango & Co Ltd* [1932] AC 328 at 350, [1931] All ER
Rep 666 at 677, repeated by Lord Wilberforce in the *Babco* case [1977] 3 All ER 1048 at
1052, [1978] AC 141 at 152) and would probably be rejected out of hand by the courts of
b most countries. Wide powers to compel the disclosure of information relevant to tax
investigations are at the disposal of the Commissioners of Inland Revenue in this country:
see the Taxes Management Act 1970, ss 13, 17, 23, 24, 26 and 28 and the Finance Act
1976, ss 23(3) and (4) and 20A and Sch 6. No doubt similar powers exist in most other
countries. But they appear never to have been applied internationally indirectly, at the
request of a foreign state, as part of the ordinary processes of the civil courts, but only as
c the result of inter-governmental agreement, particularly in connection with criminal
offences going beyond alleged evasion of taxes.

Accordingly, if the request in the present case had been made in opposition to the
estate, I feel no doubt that I should have concluded that it should be refused, whether as
a matter of public policy or of discretion. However, the factual position and the
submissions on this appeal would then have been entirely different. As it is, the estate
d supports the request and indeed initiated it originally, albeit on a far narrower basis. This
is the unprecedented feature of this case which may well remain unique for a long time.
It seems to me that it removes all the objections mentioned above. If the necessary
jurisdiction exists under the 1975 Act, then it cannot be contrary to comity or public
policy to accede to an exceptional request which is in effect being made *jointly* by the state
and the taxpayer.

e Accordingly, on the special facts of this case, I would dismiss the appeal on issue B as
well.

Issue C: sovereignty

Section 4 of the Protection of Trading Interests Act 1980 is in the following terms:

f   'A court in the United Kingdom shall not make an order under section 2 of the
Evidence (Proceedings in Other Jurisdictions) Act 1975 for giving effect to a request
issued by or on behalf of a court or tribunal of an overseas country if it is shown that
the request infringes the jurisdiction of the United Kingdom or is otherwise
prejudicial to the sovereignty of the United Kingdom; and a certificate signed by or
on behalf of the Secretary of State to the effect that it infringes that jurisdiction or is
g   so prejudicial shall be conclusive evidence of that fact.'

The witnesses submitted that the request, or compliance with it, would infringe the
jurisdiction of the United Kingdom or be prejudicial to its sovereignty. They pointed
out, as McNeill J accepted, that a certificate from the Secretary of State was not an essential
prerequisite to this submission. It was based on the fact that the rationalisation of the
h principle against the enforcement of foreign tax liabilities was considered to be founded
on an infringement of sovereignty in some of the authorities referred to under issue B
above. It was also submitted that s 4 echoed the views expressed in *Rio Tinto Zinc Corp v
Westinghouse Electric Corp* [1978] 1 All ER 434 at 447, 460, 466–467, 475, [1978] AC 547
at 615–616, 631, 640, 650–651 per Lord Wilberforce, Viscount Dilhorne, Lord Diplock
and Lord Fraser. But the circumstances to which these passages related were wholly
j different, since the evidence was sought for purposes which could have subjected English
corporations to criminal liability in the United States. We all considered that this
submission was almost unarguable in the context of the present request, and we did not
call on counsel for the state or the estate to deal with it. Accordingly, the appeal on this
issue must equally fail.

Issue D: *dual purpose*

It was submitted, both on jurisdiction and discretion, that compliance with the letter *a* of request should be refused because it is intended that the evidence of the witnesses should be made available to the NTC as well as to the Sandefjord court if the matter is then still pending before the NTC. I have already dealt with the facts in that connection and proceed on the basis that it has not been shown that the NTC is a 'court or tribunal' for the purposes of s 1(a) of the 1975 Act. Nevertheless, I would reject this submission in the circumstances of this case which, in this context also, are quite different from those *b* in the *Westinghouse* case. The primary purpose of the request by the Sandefjord court is clearly to assist its determination of the action before it. This complies with s 1(a) and is in my view sufficient to deal with the submission based on absence of jurisdiction. There remains discretion. Here again the wishes of the estate and the state coincide. Again I cannot find anything to the contrary in the speeches in *Westinghouse* [1978] 1 All ER 434 esp at 444, 450–451, 460, 462, 475–476, [1978] AC 547 esp at 611, 619–620, 631, 634, *c* 651 per Lord Wilberforce, Viscount Dilhorne, Lord Diplock and Lord Fraser. As I read these passages, once it is shown that the primary purpose of the request is bona fide to use the evidence for civil proceedings before a court or tribunal, and not also for some ulterior purpose involving criminal proceedings, let alone a purpose which would infringe the sovereignty of the United Kingdom, the court has a discretion to comply with the request. On this issue I would again give the greatest weight to the common *d* wish of the estate and the state, also bearing in mind that the possible use of the evidence by the NTC cannot by itself conflict with any objection raised in order to protect the witnesses from breaches of confidentiality, since their evidence will by then clearly be in the public domain in any event.

Issue E: *fishing*   *e*

This issue, together with issue F, in my view raises far greater problems. The Solicitor General stated:

> 'Although Freshfields have attempted to explain to me the distinction between a request for evidence which amounts to a "fishing expedition" and one which does not, I confess to having had some difficulty in grasping the concept.'   *f*

This is readily understandable: although 'fishing' has become a term of art for the purposes of many of our procedural rules dealing with applications for particulars of pleadings, interrogatories and discovery, illustrations of the concept are more easily recognised than defined. It arises in cases where what is sought is not evidence as such, but information which may lead to a line of inquiry which would disclose evidence. It is the search for material in the hope of being able to raise allegations of fact, as opposed to *g* the elicitation of evidence to support allegations of fact which have been raised bona fide with adequate particularisation. In the present context, 'fishing' may occur in two ways. First, the 'evidence' may be sought for a preliminary purpose, such as the process of pre-trial discovery in the United States. The fact that this is clearly impermissible for the purposes of the 1975 Act is established in the *Westinghouse* case and was equally so held *h* by this court in relation to the 1856 Act in *Radio Corp of America v Rauland Corp* [1956] 1 All ER 549, [1956] 1 QB 618. This is irrelevant in the present context, since the 'evidence' is required for the trial itself. But 'fishing' is in my view also relevant in another sense in the present context, as the judge rightly indicated. It is perhaps best described as a roving inquiry, by means of the examination and cross-examination of witnesses, which is not designed to establish by means of their evidence allegations of fact which have been *j* raised bona fide with adequate particulars, but to obtain information which may lead to obtaining evidence in general support of a party's case.

In the *Radio Corp* case the court was concerned with the word 'testimony' in the 1856 Act, whose equivalent is now 'evidence' in the 1975 Act. In a passage from the leading

judgment given by Devlin J, which is quoted by Lord Fraser in the *Westinghouse* case
a [1978] 1 All ER 434 at 468, [1978] AC 547 at 642, he said, and I have put in square
brackets the words which do not apply here ([1956] 1 All ER 549 at 552, [1956] 1 QB
618 at 646):

> 'Testimony, if it can be called "testimony", which is mere answers to questions
> [on the discovery proceeding] designed to lead to a train of inquiry, is not
> b   permissible.'

I will give one example which may be relevant to the present case. The state evidently
alleges that Mr Jahre was the settlor and ultimate beneficiary of the trust. Or it may have
alleged (we have not considered the material underlying the Sandefjord action) that X
was the settlor and beneficiary and that he in fact administered the trust and used its
assets for the benefit of Mr Jahre. Under our rules, and presumably equally in Norway,
c such allegations cannot be based on bare assertions, but would have to be adequately
particularised by any facts relied on in support of them. In that event, any questions to
witnesses designed to elicit answers showing whether or not either of these allegations
were true would be requests for 'evidence'. But if these questions were unproductive the
further question 'Who, then, was it?' would in my view be 'fishing'.

The scope of the present request is so wide that I am left in no doubt that it goes far
d beyond the elicitation of 'evidence' and contains a great deal of impermissible 'fishing'. I
am leaving out of account the request for documents in Pt III of the 'pleadings' annexed
to the request, although it is clear, as the judge recognised in the passage already cited,
that Pt II is designed to cover much the same ground. In an affidavit by the Solicitor
General he described the scope of Pt II as follows:

> e   'The questions which it is sought to put to Lord Kindersley and Mr. Hardman are
> directed to ascertain the identities of those who owned or controlled CTC and the
> Foundation at the material times; to whether Anders Jahre had any dealings with
> either of them; to the extent and nature of assets held by CTC and the Foundation;
> and to the nature and location of the accounts and other records kept in relation to
> their activities.'

f This really speaks for itself and is a perfectly fair summary of the effect of Pt II. Indeed, I
do not think that I need go through it in detail to emphasise the width of the scope of the
proposed examination; it also speaks for itself. In particular, it should perhaps be pointed
out that it has never been alleged that Mr Jahre was more than the beneficial owner of
the assets of CTC itself, whereas the scope of the questions comprises the assets and
operations of the trust as a whole, which may of course well go beyond any connection
g with CTC.

McNeill J was clearly of the same opinion, and I have already quoted what he said. It
then remains to consider whether the directions which he gave, or any other limitation
of the scope of Pt II, would be appropriate to remedy the position. As I have already
mentioned, in support of the cross-appeal counsel for the state and the estate submitted
h that the judge's directions 'to bring them [the letters rogatory] within what is permissible
under the statute and the rules and as a matter of discretion' were inappropriate, and
counsel for the witnesses had no real answer to these submissions. Direction 1 appears,
with respect, to have been based on a misunderstanding of s 2(4)(a) of the 1975 Act. This
was virtually common ground and requires no elaboration. Direction 2 seeks to
distinguish between Lord Kindersley's 'direct' and other knowledge as adviser to the
j trust. But how would this work? Inevitably, one supposes, most of his knowledge must
have been derived indirectly from what he was told by the persons from whom he
received his instructions or from documents submitted to him. As regards direction 3,
how is Mr Hardman to distinguish between knowledge which he acquired as an officer
of CTC and knowledge which he obtained as an employee of Lazards, possibly in the

course of assisting Lord Kindersley? I hope that I am not being discourteous to the judge
in these criticisms of his directions. He had no assistance from counsel in regard to them; *a*
we were told that they had not been given on the basis of any submissions put forward
in the course of the hearing, but that it was simply left to the judge to consider whether
any limitations should be imposed on the scope of Pt II. The argument before him was
effectively confined to the question whether Pt II in its present form amounted to 'fishing'
or not, and he clearly concluded that it did.

If the directions are not appropriate, there remains the question whether there should *b*
be some other limitation. The only alternative offered on behalf of the state and the
estate was the deletion of the words 'information and' in the opening paragraph of Pt II
and the omission of 'information', or its substitution by 'evidence', wherever this occurs
in the numbered paragraphs which follow. But this would provide no alteration of
substance whatever. We were also referred to the passages in the speeches in the
Westinghouse case which deal with the possibility of cutting down an excessive request, in *c*
that case for documents, by 'blue pencilling'. This is obviously an easier thing to do in
relation to the production of particular documents or classes of documents than in
relation to the ambit of oral questions, and even in relation to documents it appears to
have been the view of the House of Lords that this court had gone too far in editing the
request (see [1978] 1 All ER 434 at 443–444, 452–454, 454–455, 463, 470–471, 476–477,
[1978] AC 547 at 610–612, 621–625, 625–626, 635–636, 644–645, 652–654 per Lord *d*
Wilberforce, Viscount Dilhorne, Lord Diplock, Lord Fraser and Lord Keith). These
passages undoubtedly show that the court should strive to give effect to letters of request,
if necessary by amendments which may even be substantial, at any rate in relation to the
production of documents. But they are no authority, as I see it, for the proposition that
the court should, in effect, redraft a request in different terms. In the present case I would
not know how to set about doing this, even if it were permissible, and, apart from the *e*
suggestion concerning the word 'information' which I have already mentioned, none of
the parties felt able to make any submissions in this connection or to accept tentative
suggestions offered by the court.

I have accordingly reached the conclusion, ultimately without any hesitation, that this
request is far too wide, that the court is in no position to bring it into conformity with
what would be permissible and, as already mentioned under issue G, ie discretion, that *f*
the state and the estate should be invited to reconsider the position in the light of this
judgment if they wish to pursue their request via the Sandefjord court. In this connection
I have also taken into account the other matters to which I have referred under issue G,
discretion.

Accordingly, I would allow this appeal on these grounds.

g

Issue F: confidentiality

Taken in conjunction with all the other matters already discussed, I would allow this
appeal on this ground as well. I do not think that any of the authorities cited to us are of
direct assistance for present purposes. These included *Tournier v National Provincial and
Union Bank of England Ltd* [1924] 1 KB 461, [1923] All ER Rep 550, *Bankers Trust Co v* *h*
Shapira [1980] 3 All ER 353, [1980] 1 WLR 1274, *R v Grossman* (1981) 73 Cr App R 302,
X AG v A bank [1983] 2 All ER 464, an unreported decision of the Court of Appeal of
Hong Kong in *FDC Co Ltd v Chase Manhattan Bank* (29 October 1984, unreported) and
Bonalumi v Secretary of State for the Home Dept [1985] 1 All ER 797, [1985] QB 675.

In *Tournier v National Provincial and Union Bank of England Ltd* [1924] 1 KB 461 at 473,
[1924] All ER Rep 550 at 554 Bankes LJ said that a banker's obligation not to reveal his *j*
customer's business affairs is subject to four exceptions: (a) where disclosure is under
compulsion by law; (b) where there is a duty to the public to disclose; (c) where the
interests of the bank require disclosure; (d) where the disclosure is made by the express
or implied consent of the customer. Atkin LJ said ([1924] 1 KB 461 at 486, [1924] All ER
Rep 550 at 561):

a
'But I think it safe to say that the obligation not to disclose information such as I have mentioned is subject to the qualification that the bank have the right to disclose such information when, and to the extent to which it is reasonably necessary for the protection of the bank's interests, either as against their customer ... or for protecting the bank, or persons interested, or the public, against fraud or crime.'

b
Exception (a) in the judgment of Bankes LJ merely begs the question in the present context whether or not, in the discretion of the court in all the circumstances, the witnesses should be compelled to submit themselves for examination etc pursuant to RSC Ord 39, r 8. So far as concerns exception (d), I do not think that the estate's joinder in the letter of request gives rise to any express or implied consent by or on behalf of Lazard's customers. Lord Kindersley is one of the advisers of the trust and of the settlor, to whom he referred in his letters of 25 April and 24 May 1984, after Mr Jahre's death.

c
Mr Hardman was an officer of CTC. Lazards were or are bankers of the trust and evidently of CTC. It has not been alleged that any of them ever acted for Mr Jahre. Indeed, the estate contends the contrary and is asserting that Mr Jahre had no connection with the trust. The estate's support for the letter of request can therefore be no relevant consent to the disclosure by the witnesses of the affairs of the trust and CTC, contrary to the duty of confidence which the witnesses owe them. The Solicitor General has

d
recognised throughout, very fairly, that an order complying with the letter of request would compel the witnesses to break the duty of confidence to which they are subject. Finally on this aspect, as regards exception (b), I do not think that any duty of disclosure 'to the public' arises in this case, or, in the words of Atkin LJ, the protection of the public 'against fraud or crime'. The alleged evasion of foreign tax liabilities by a foreigner was obviously not in the mind of the court at all. Nor do I think that one gets much help

e
from the other authorities. All of them recognise the importance of the duty of confidentiality of bankers and the fact that the courts should only intervene to compel disclosure in exceptional circumstances. *Bankers Trust Co v Shapira* [1980] 3 All ER 353, [1980] 1 WLR 1274 was a case of obviously forged cheques for $1m. In ordering disclosure in support of attempts by the defrauded plaintiffs to trace the proceeds Lord Denning MR said ([1980] 3 All ER 353 at 357–358, [1980] 1 WLR 1274 at 1282):

f
'This new jurisdiction must, of course, be carefully exercised. It is a strong thing to order a bank to disclose the state of its customer's account and the documents and correspondence relating to it. It should only be done when there is a good ground for thinking the money in the bank is the plaintiff's money, as for instance when the customer has got the money by fraud, or other wrongdoing, and paid it into his account at the bank. The plaintiff, who has been defrauded, has a right in equity to

g
follow the money ... So the court, in order to give effect to equity, will be prepared in a proper case to make an order on the bank for their discovery.'

Bonalumi v Secretary of State for the Home Dept was also a case involving a criminal offence. The remaining authorities were all concerned with situations in which the courts in one jurisdiction had exercised, or were asked to exercise (in *R v Grossman* in

h
relation to a bank in the Isle of Man), what is nowadays commonly referred to as a 'long-arm' jurisdiction beyond their own frontiers. The fact that the objections of the banks were upheld in all these cases is therefore not a circumstance which is of any direct assistance to Lazards in the present case, which depends on its own circumstances. As Lord Wilberforce said in *British Steel Corp v Granada Television Ltd* [1981] 1 All ER 417 at 455, [1981] AC 1096 at 1168:

j
'Third, as to information obtained in confidence, and the legal duty, which may arise, to disclose it to a court of justice, the position is clear. Courts have an inherent wish to respect this confidence, whether it arises between doctor and patient, priest and penitent, banker and customer, between persons giving testimonials to employees, or in other relationships. A relationship of confidence between a

journalist and his source is in no different category; nothing in this case involves or will involve any principle that such confidence is not something to be respected. But in all these cases the court may have to decide, in particular circumstances, that the interest in preserving this confidence is outweighed by other interests to which the law attaches importance. The only question in this appeal is whether the present is such a case.'

The court must carry out a balancing exercise. In the scales on one side must be placed the desirable policy of assisting a foreign court, in this case supported by both parties to the litigation before it. On the other side there is the opposing principle that the court will give great weight to the desirability of upholding the duty of confidence in relationships in which, as here, it is clearly entitled to recognition and respect. Which way the balance then tilts depends on the weight which is properly to be given to all the other circumstances of the case. In my view it is open to this court to carry out this balancing exercise afresh for the reasons already given, in particular because I do not think that the judge's way of dealing with issue E, ie fishing, can be supported. On this basis I have come to the clear conclusion that the balance is against compelling the witnesses to violate their duty of confidence.

The factors which have cumulatively led me to this conclusion can be summarised as follows, in the order in which they arise under the issues discussed above, without seeking to arrange them in any order of importance.

(i) The subject matter of the letter of request clearly appears to be unprecedented internationally and is almost certainly contrary to the spirit of what the various national delegations who drafted the 1970 convention intended to be covered by a 'civil or commercial matter'. It lies in the field of 'tax gathering' even if it does not constitute an attempt at indirect enforcement of foreign tax liabilities, and it is unlikely that many other countries, if any, would comply with a request for evidential assistance in this field. Indeed, I should be surprised if our revenue authorities would seek to invoke the 1970 or any of the similar bilateral conventions for a similar purpose. The fact that both parties to the litigation exceptionally support the request is irrelevant, since neither is in a position of clients of Lazards whose consent would be relevant (issues A and B).

(ii) The extent to which the witnesses from Lazards would be compelled to disclose banking confidences is very wide indeed. The request is in the nature of a roving investigation which may affect the private financial affairs of unknown persons who were and are entitled to expect that a highly reputable merchant bank in London, whom they entrusted with their affairs, would never be compelled to disclose these by an English court except in circumstances of allegations of fraud or crime on their part, which do not arise. No way has been suggested whereby this consequence can be avoided by means of some more limited investigation, and an attempt to carry it out fairly, under the procedural rules which would be applicable to it, is certain to give rise to further, more specific, problems in the course of the examination of the witnesses and almost certainly to further recourse to the courts (issues D and G).

(iii) There is considerable substance, in all these circumstances, in the matters raised by the affidavit of Mr Ian Fraser on behalf of Lazards and for the protection of banking institutions in the City generally. Confidence in their ability to receive and maintain confidential information, which their clients give to them in confidence, is a crucial part of their stock-in-trade and reputation. This veil of confidentiality should certainly be pierced in cases of bona fide allegations of crime and fraud. But for it to be seen to be pierced in the present context would do great damage, which is not justified by the circumstances.

(iv) Viewed internationally, it should perhaps be noted that since the hearing of this appeal the Court of Justice of the European Communities has recognised a banker's right to rely on his duty of confidentiality in the face of a request for him to give evidence, albeit in a different context: see *Hillegom Municipality v Hillenius* Case 110/84 [1985] ECR

3947. There is no indication that, if the English courts were to order an English bank to
a break its duty of confidentiality merely in order to assist a foreign government to
establish or maintain a claim for tax against one of its own taxpayers, such a precedent
would meet with any international reciprocity whatever. On the contrary, international
practice and jurisprudence point in the opposite direction. There may of course be great
benefit in extending international co-operation to tax evasion, as is already happening in
relation to crime in many fields. But this is a matter for treaties. The framework of the
b Hague conferences on private international law has nothing to do with any such objective,
nor any national legislation which is based on it.

Finally, I would add that, if this judgment reflects the ultimate outcome of this appeal,
then I hope that any renewal of the present letter of request in some more limited and
acceptable form, if this can be devised, should be accompanied by clear evidence as to
what is properly to be regarded as a 'civil or commercial matter' by the law of Norway,
c and in particular whether Norwegian law distinguishes between public and private law.
I feel, frankly, uneasy about my acceptance, dubitante, of the very limited evidence in
this connection on the present application. I would also urge that, at any rate in the
international context, particularly in relation to the concept of 'civil and commercial
matters' in the Hague and similar bilateral conventions, as well as of the 1975 Act, it
would be desirable to recognise a clear-cut distinction between private and public law in
d our jurisprudence, in the same way as in other legal systems.

Accordingly, I would allow this appeal.

GLIDEWELL LJ. Kerr LJ has set out in his judgment the facts relevant to this appeal
and I gratefully adopt his summary. He has also defined the issues before this court, and
e I wish only to comment on some of these, adopting the lettering he has applied.

A. Are the proceedings in the Sandefjord City Court 'civil proceedings' within the
Evidence (Proceedings in Other Jurisdictions) Act 1975?

I agree with Kerr LJ that the phrase has different meanings in different parts of the
1975 Act. As he says 'civil proceedings' in ss 2(3) and 3(1)(*a*) has the meaning which an
English court would give to the expression if there were no statutory definition, ie civil
f as opposed to criminal proceedings. Since, however, the application is made under s 1 of
the 1975 Act, under which the English court has to be satisfied that 'the evidence to
which the application relates is to be obtained for the purpose of *civil proceedings ... before
the requesting court . . .*', it is in my view clear that the English court has to decide whether
the proceedings are properly regarded as civil proceedings by the requesting court. This
question necessarily involves the definition of 'civil proceedings' in s 9(1) of the 1975 Act,
g since this definition applies 'in relation to the requesting court'. So the question is: are
the proceedings in the Sandefjord City Court proceedings in a 'civil or commercial
matter' under the law of Norway?

I also agree with Kerr LJ that, while primarily concerned to inquire whether the
proceedings concern a civil or commercial matter under the law of the requesting court,
the English court would only comply with the application if the proceedings were also
h 'civil proceedings' in the English sense. But this point may be largely, if not entirely,
theoretical. We have no evidence that there is any jurisdiction in which proceedings in a
'civil or commercial matter' would not be regarded as civil proceedings in the English
sense.

If proceedings similar to those in the Sandefjord court were taking place in the High
Court in England, and that court applied for an order for the examination of witnesses to
j a court in a jurisdiction whose relevant statute was in terms identical to those of the 1975
Act, the English High Court would of course say that the proceedings were civil
proceedings. But, if asked to explain its process of reasoning, it might do so in some such
terms as these: 'We do not usually categorise actions which come before our courts in
terms of their subject matter. We do so in order to comply with ss 1 and 9 of your

statute. We say that these proceedings are civil proceedings under English law; therefore they are proceedings in a "civil matter"; therefore they are civil proceedings within the definition in your statute.'

It seems to me that this circular process of reasoning is, in essence, that adopted by the Solicitor General of Norway in his affidavit of 26 June 1985. I therefore do not share the doubts which have troubled Kerr LJ whether the evidence before us should satisfy us that the Sandefjord proceedings are 'in a civil . . . matter'. In my view the evidence makes it clear that they are.

I accept that in a country whose law derives from the 'civil law' the courts adopt a classification of matters coming before them, and that such a classification may categorise the subject of an action such as that in the Sandefjord court as a 'fiscal matter', not as a 'civil or commercial matter'. From the passages read to us from David *English Law and French Law* (1980) it seems clear that this would be the case in France. The argument of counsel for the witnesses is, in effect, that, since some jurisdictions categorise matters in a way which would exclude the subject of this action from the categories 'civil or commercial', a different categorisation may not be adopted for any other jurisdiction. Such an approach must disregard the law and the approach to categorisation of disputes in such other jurisdictions.

In my view, the approach counsel commends, despite the learning with which he supports it, is neither logical nor desirable.

I therefore agree with Kerr LJ that the proceedings in the Sandefjord court are civil proceedings within s 1 of the 1975 Act.

On issue B (tax gathering), I agree with the reasons given by Kerr LJ for dismissing the appeal on this ground, save that I would not myself express any firm view as to what the decision should have been if the application had been opposed by the estate.

On issues C (sovereignty) and D (dual purpose), I agree entirely with Kerr LJ and have nothing to add.

This brings me to issues E (fishing) and F (confidentiality). These issues are inter-related. It is convenient to start by considering confidentiality. I take the view that none of the authorities cited to us relating to the duty of confidence owed by a banker to his customer, to which Kerr LJ refers in his judgment, are of assistance to us except the decision of this court in *Tournier v National Provincial and Union Bank of England Ltd* [1924] 1 KB 461, [1923] All ER Rep 550. The dictum of Bankes LJ does assist by listing the circumstances in which the duty of confidentiality may be held to be qualified, namely:

'(a) where disclosure is under compulsion by law; (b) where there is a duty to the public to disclose; (c) where the interests of the bank require disclosure; (d) where the disclosure is made by the express or implied consent of the customer.'

(See [1924] 1 KB 461 at 473, [1923] All ER Rep 550 at 554.)

In the present case (c) and (d) do not arise. Qualification (a) merely refers to the question we have to decide: should we uphold the order of McNeill J, which may result in overriding the banker's duty of confidence? It is test (b) which, in my judgment, we should apply in making our decision, in the sense that it is in the public interest for our courts to assist a foreign court, and in appropriate circumstances the importance of doing so will outweigh the banker's obligation not to disclose information about his customer's business affairs, so as to justify the court in requiring the disclosure of such information. In this respect the passage from the speech of Lord Wilberforce in *British Steel Corp v Granada Television Ltd* [1981] 1 All ER 417 at 458, [1981] AC 1096 at 1168, quoted by Kerr LJ, is in point.

It is not alleged that Lazards, or Lord Kindersley or Mr Hardman personally, acted for Mr Anders Jahre. If, however, there were some evidence that a person (or persons) who was a customer of Lazards, or for whom Lord Kindersley or Mr Hardman acted, was the nominee or agent of Mr Jahre in relation to any transaction at issue in the proceedings before the Sandefjord court, the importance of assisting that court could, in my judgment,

properly be held to outweigh any duty of confidence owed to such a person. On the
_a_ other hand, the disclosure of information about the affairs of a person who was not
shown to have had such a relationship with, or to have acted for, Mr Jahre would be an
unjustified breach of confidence which the English courts should not require. In the
latter case, if the proceedings were in an English court, the court would not require the
duty of confidence to be overridden and by s 3(1) of the 1975 Act a witness may not be
compelled to give evidence which he could not be compelled to give in English
_b_ proceedings.

I turn to issue E: fishing. I adopt gratefully Kerr LJ's brief definition of a fishing
expedition as one 'where what is sought is not evidence as such, but information which
may lead to a line of inquiry which would disclose evidence'. In _Radio Corp of America v
Rauland Corp_ [1956] 1 All ER 549 at 552, [1956] 1 QB 618 at 646 Devlin J, giving the
leading judgment, in a passage quoted by Lord Fraser in _Rio Tinto Zinc Corp v Westinghouse
c Electric Corp_ [1978] 1 All ER 434 at 468–469, [1978] AC 547 at 642, referred to the
decision of this court in _Burchard v Macfarlane, ex p Tindell_ [1891] 2 QB 241, [1891–94]
All ER Rep 137 and said:

> 'In that authority the distinction is made plain between what I have called
> discovery or indirect material on the one hand, and proof or direct material on the
_d_ > other hand. That is, I think, the true distinction with which one must approach the
> word "testimony" in this Act. Testimony which is in the nature of proof for the
> purpose of the trial is permissible. Testimony, if it can be called "testimony," which
> is mere answers to questions on the discovery proceeding designed to lead to a train
> of inquiry, is not permissible.'

Radio Corp of America v Rauland Corp was a decision on the somewhat different wording
_e_ of s 1 of the Foreign Tribunals Evidence Act 1856, but the principle applies equally to
the 1975 Act, as indeed Lord Fraser said in the _Westinghouse_ case [1978] 1 All ER 434 at
468, [1978] AC 547 at 642.

I agree with Kerr LJ that the scope of the 'matters or questions' about which the state
in the present application is seeking 'information and evidence' is so wide that the
questions intended to be asked will inevitably include a substantial number which will
_f_ elicit information which may lead to a line of inquiry rather than evidence in the
proceedings themselves. Since such questions would be 'fishing', they would be
unacceptable, and it follows that the court should not order the witnesses to give evidence
on the request as at present framed.

Whether some of the questions would also lead to an unacceptable breach of the duty
of confidence I cannot say with certainty, although it is clear that the wider the request
_g_ the more likely it is that the questions would be objectionable on this ground also.

McNeill J also took the view that the request was too wide but decided that he could
by directions confine it within acceptable limits. Kerr LJ has set out these directions in
his judgment, and I need not repeat them. With respect to the judge, I also am of the
view that the directions he gave would not have the effect he intended of limiting the
_h_ questioning of Lord Kindersley and Mr Hardman to questions which would elicit only
relevant evidence. The question thus is: should this court endeavour to impose directions
which would be effective?

Passages in the speeches of all their Lordships in the _Westinghouse_ case make it clear
that, where a court can, by excising inappropriate material, produce a request which is
acceptable and proper, it should adopt this course and make the order sought.

_j_ Nevertheless, I, like Kerr LJ, do not regard the dicta as authority for the proposition
that the court should redraft the request. In the present case the request is so wide that,
to avoid the prospect that questions under it would be objectionable as 'fishing', it would
in my view require to be redrafted. Thus I have reluctantly come to the conclusion that
on this sole ground the order sought by the state and the estate should not be made. I
would therefore allow the appeal.

I must make it clear, however, that in my view a request in much narrower terms could probably be framed which would not fall foul of the 'no fishing' rule, and which *a* would carry little, or a lesser, risk that the answers to the questions could properly be objected to as being in breach of confidence. Whether such a limited request would meet the requirements of either the state or the estate I do not know, but, if it would, the way to an order for the examination of either or both of the witnesses is by no means barred by the decision to allow the present appeal.

b

RALPH GIBSON LJ. I agree that the witnesses, the appellants in this case, have failed to show that the court lacks jurisdiction to order the witnesses to attend before an examiner for oral examination under the Evidence (Proceedings in Other Jurisdictions) Act 1975, and I, too, would dismiss the appeal on issue A (civil or commercial matter), on issue B (tax gathering), on issue C (sovereignity) and on issue D (dual purpose). I agree with the reasons given by Kerr LJ in his judgment for holding that the appeal cannot *c* succeed on issues B (tax gathering), C (sovereignity) and D (dual purpose). On issue A (civil or commercial matter) I would dismiss the appeal on the grounds set out in the judgment of Glidewell LJ, with which I agree, and as to issue B I also would not wish to express any firm view as to what the decision should have been if the application had been opposed by the state.

I have, however, reached a different conclusion on issue E (fishing), and on issue F *d* (confidentiality). I venture to differ from the views of Kerr and Glidewell LJJ only after hesitation and with reluctance, but I would dismiss the appeal.

Kerr LJ has described the background facts and allegations and has set out in full Pt II of the documents attached to the letter of request in which appears the list of questions (the Pt II list) to put to the witnesses. McNeill J referred to many of the requests as having a 'breadth which is not permissible under the procedure'. The judge concluded that he *e* could bring them within what is permissible under the statute and the rules by giving directions. I agree with Kerr LJ that the directions given for this purpose by the judge have been shown on examination to be unsatisfactory and I would not sustain them as part of the court's order. The purpose of the directions was to limit the range of permissible questioning and, in part, to contain that range within our rules of evidence relating to hearsay and to exclude, for example, answers which Lord Kindersley might *f* be able to give based on what he has been told outside his work as adviser to the foundation. If the taking of evidence proceeds as I think that it should, and this is discussed later in this judgment, this difficulty in this particular case can be met without directions of this nature. The admissibility of evidence is a matter for the court in Norway. If their law of evidence should differ from ours, eg, so as to render admissible hearsay evidence generally, that fact would not, in my judgment, widen the scope of the *g* evidence which our courts would consider may be required of a witness under the principles which protect a witness against unreasonably oppressive or intrusive questioning or unjustifiable breach of his obligations of confidence. The parties are agreed that if the witnesses are required to give evidence they will be called on behalf of the state and that the estate would be entitled to cross-examine in the usual way. In *h* considering whether in the court's discretion an order should be made at the request of a foreign court for witnesses to be examined, this court is, I think, entitled to assume, and should assume, that the rules of evidence and of permitted questioning under Norwegian law are the same as ours unless the contrary is proved by evidence. The witnesses would therefore be entitled to refuse to answer if the questioning should be in breach of our rules.

j

It is not in doubt that the evidence which is sought from the witnesses is intended for use at the trial. It was contended for the witnesses that, nevertheless, the letter of request was impermissibly wide in its terms because the categories of questions in the Pt II list raised matters going far beyond the issue in the civil proceedings for which the evidence was requested. That issue was identified as:

a   'whether Mr Jahre was the owner of CTC and accordingly the owner of accounts held by CTC at the SE Bank in Stockholm.'

Such a description is, in my judgment, an incomplete guide to the factual issues in the civil proceedings which could more fully be described as whether Mr Jahre is shown to have exercised such control over CTC and its assets that he is to be treated under Norwegian law in all the circumstances as beneficial owner thereof, and whether, if and

b   when the shares in the assets of CTC passed into the control or nominal ownership of the alleged trust or foundation, there was any real change in the beneficial ownership and control.

It is necessary to look at the pleadings. The estate, as plaintiff, in support of the claim that the supplementary assessment to tax of 14 September 1983 should be nullified, set out its 'principal points' as follows:

c
'The estate of the deceased Anders Jahre has been submitted to supplementary assessment as if Mr Jahre were the owner of the Panamanian limited company CTC ... and accordingly also of the company's accounts with the SE Bank Stockholm. Further the supplementary assessment is based on all deposits which CTC has paid into its account with SEB being regarded as income for Anders Jahre and the balance

d   of all accounts at the end of each year being regarded as his personal assets. Anders Jahre, as well as the individuals who have factual knowledge of CTC in their capacity of "Company Secretary" or member of the Board of Directors or "Adviser" to the foundation which owns the majority of the shares in CTC, have all stated that the shares in CTC during the years 1970 et seq have been owned by others than Anders Jahre ... Anders Jahre was never a member of the Board of Directors of CTC. He

e   has been an officer of the company, being President and for a period of time also Treasurer. In that capacity he has been empowered to make arrangements on behalf of the company within the limits of the instructions issued from time to time by CTC's Board of Directors and general meeting...'

Lord Kindersley is included within the description 'Adviser' and Mr Hardman within

f   the description 'Company Secretary' in the passage cited. The years in respect of which the supplementary assessment applied are 1970 to 1982 inclusive.

It thus appears that the estate was unable to make any assertion as to the identity of the persons who did own the shares during the relevant time in order to demonstrate that those persons were not only ostensibly owners of the shares but also holding them free of any interest or control of Mr Jahre.

g   The defence in the proceedings on behalf of the state sets out relevant principles of law, including the propositions that (i) it is the duty of a taxpayer actively to produce any material he has or may have access to and to contribute towards the clarification of his tax liability and (ii) the tax committee was entitled to disregard the formal structure of the Panamanian company, Pankos/CTC, and to treat the corporate structure as an artificial set-up with no real content or purpose other than to avoid Norwegian taxation if satisfied

h   that Mr Jahre was the direct or indirect owner of the shares with the right of disposal vested in him.

Primary facts asserted in the defence include: (i) a high degree of passivity on the part of the plaintiff, namely, a failure to produce information which could be expected to be provided, and the production of evidence as the case has proceeded which was contradictory; (ii) as to the activities of Pankos/CTC, practically all were conducted from

j   Sandefjord by Mr Jahre or those closest to him. All demonstrable dispositions have practically without exception been for the benefit of Mr Jahre, his wife and properties; (iii) there is negative evidence that Pankos/CTC has not had any funds other than the CTC accounts, including Bergen Bank; (iv) a history of events preceding the relevant period 1970 to 1982 is set out in order to 'illustrate the case', including the role of Mr Jahre in the formation of Pankos/CTC in 1939, the acquisition by that company of a ship in which Mr Jahre had an interest, the transfer in 1940 of practically all the shares in Pankos to one Dalmann of Gothenberg on terms that Mr Jahre could repurchase the shares at par, the transfer of the repurchase right to Jasmin, a Panamanian company in which Mr Jahre was a shareholder until 1955, and the allegation that for the period 1940 to 1954 Dalmann is shown by the documents to have been a 'dummy' for Mr Jahre; (v) Mr Jahre's formal connections with Pankos/CTC were as president or treasurer in the period 1971 to 1978 and he was 'in close connection with Pankos/CTC and its dispositions during the supplementary assessment period 1970–1982'; (vi) in 1972 shares owned by Pankos/CTC in the company Crevettes de Cameroun were sold and funds from the sale were transferred to Mr Jahre to an account with a bank in Paris; (vii) no accounts are available covering the activities carried on by Mr Jahre through CTC.

The defence draws attention to the failure by the estate to produce information: for example, to give adequate explanations of Mr Jahre's relationship with CTC and the funds in the accounts in CTC's name, or to produce documents to give concrete information which shows who was the owner of the shares in the period 1970 to 1982.

It thus appears that under Norwegian law the taxpayer has a duty to clarify his tax liability, and his failure to do so is a fact to which the tax committee can properly have regard in drawing inferences from the primary facts proved before them. The evidence suggesting or proving that Mr Jahre had directed the affairs and use of the assets of Pankos/CTC over a period of many years as if he were the beneficial owner justifies, according to the defence in the proceedings, the conclusions reached by the tax committee. It is clear that the estate, which is trying to persuade the Norwegian court that the inferences of beneficial ownership in Mr Jahre should not on the facts be drawn, has an interest in getting before the Norwegian court evidence to support the out of court statements of Lord Kindersley and any supporting evidence that Mr Hardman can give. Mr Hardman was appointed assistant secretary of CTC in 1977 and treasurer in 1978, retiring from both offices in January 1984. The estate will wish to demonstrate that the shares in CTC were owned beneficially by persons other than Mr Jahre, that those persons were not the nominees or 'dummies' of Mr Jahre, that the shares in CTC, or those not retained by someone else, passed to the charitable foundation as beneficial owner and not as nominee of Mr Jahre and that any apparent control of Mr Jahre at any relevant time over CTC or its assets was consistent with his ostensible position as one working on behalf of CTC as an officer or agent. The out of court statements of Lord Kindersley show that the assets of the foundation included shares in Pankos/CTC. Nothing, I think, asserts positively that the foundation had any other assets of any significance. It would be relevant, so far as I can see, and of assistance to the estate to prove that the foundation did have such further assets derived from sources other than Mr Jahre because it would tend to show that the foundation was exercising real control over its assets independently of Mr Jahre and that, even if any part of its assets had come from or had been passed to it by someone else on the instructions of Mr Jahre, nevertheless Mr Jahre had divested himself of beneficial interest in them and control over them.

The State of Norway, represented in the proceedings by the Ministry of Finance, contends to the court in the pleadings to which I have referred that the tax committee reached a correct or unassailable decision. Mr Haug, the Solicitor General, has stated in his first affidavit before the court that his purpose in seeking the order for the taking of evidence was 'to ascertain the truth relevant to the matter'. It was suggested on behalf of the witnesses that this statement was an indication that the purpose of the application was impermissibly 'fishing' as opposed to an attempt to obtain evidence for the proceedings. I see no force in that suggestion. It is clear to me that evidence available from the witnesses, if found after proper testing and scrutiny to be convincing, as no doubt it would be, might well cause or assist in causing the court to reach a conclusion different from that of the tax committee on all or part of the additional assessment. I am sure that the Solicitor General of Norway does intend, and obviously would intend, to a submit to the court the evidence sought to be obtained by this application as relevant to the factual issues in the proceedings so that it may assist in ascertaining the truth of the matter. It is an attitude to the litigation which I would have assumed the Solicitor General to hold and his statement merely served to confirm it.

It is necessary now to consider the Pt II list, which has been set out in full by Kerr LJ. I take the list as amended by omission of the words 'information and' where they appear in addition to the word 'evidence' and by the substitution of the word 'evidence' for the
b word 'information' wherever it appears. I am confident that nothing of significance turns on the use of the words which have in translation appeared as 'information'.

It seems to me that both witnesses probably have knowledge of some or all of the matters covered by each of the headings, that their evidence of the facts known would probably be relevant in the proceedings and that there is nothing to show that such evidence would be inadmissible under Norwegian law. Paragraph 1 of the Pt II list refers
c to present and previous owners of funds and shares in CTC and the relevance of such evidence is clear in the light of the factual issues set out in the pleadings; in particular the estate will wish to prove that such owners were not Mr Jahre or persons closely connected to him or controlled by him. Evidence about the trust (para 2) is similarly relevant under all headings listed. It might well be that evidence showing that the shares in CTC were received by the trust from a settlor who is not alleged to have been under the control of
d Mr Jahre would render the rest of the heading irrelevant. The witness may know the name of the settlor but not know of his relations with Mr Jahre or from whom or the terms on which that settlor acquired the shares. The other headings may then be relevant: the name of the trust, to identify it, if it appears, in the documents and transactions separately proved; the foundation, structure, object, names of trustees, beneficiaries and powers of election and removal of trustees etc, to demonstrate that any assets once owned
e or controlled by Mr Jahre had effectively passed out of his control; and the balance sheets, both to show (if they exist) assets other than those previously in Pankos/CTC and to explain or disprove the existence of payments to or from the benefit of Mr Jahre. The matters covered by the remaining paragraphs also seem to me to be matters on which the witnesses may well be able to give evidence relevant to the factual issues in the proceedings.
f The witnesses are entitled to the protection of the law at two stages with reference to the attempt by the applicants to obtain their evidence by order of the court: at the first stage (and, as Kerr LJ has pointed out, this was common ground between the parties), the witness cannot be required to comply with the letter of request if it appears to the court that the request is 'irrelevant, or fishing, or speculative, or oppressive': see *Senior v Holdsworth* [1975] 2 All ER 1009 at 1016, [1976] 1 QB 23 at 35 per Lord Denning MR
g and cases cited in *The Supreme Court Practice 1985* vol 1, para 38/14–19/11. That is the test which the court will apply in deciding whether to set aside a subpoena so as to excuse the witness from being required to give any evidence at all. It has been held that the fact that the witness is clearly able to give relevant evidence and that nothing more is sought from him is not decisive: the subpoena may be set aside if, on balancing the value of the
h evidence to the applicant against the burden on the witness, and the degree of intrusiveness of the proposed questioning and all other circumstances, it seems to the court that the request is oppressive: see *Morgan v Morgan* [1977] 2 All ER 515, [1977] Fam 122 at 125 per Watkins J.

The second stage is at the questioning before the examiner if the witness is directed to give evidence. Kerr LJ cited *Desilla v Fells* (1879) 40 LT 423, which shows that the
j evidence can only be taken 'in the English mode' but is not limited to what is admissible in English courts; and he has referred to the provisions of RSC Ord 39. By r 8(1), subject to any directions contained in the order for examination, the witness is to be examined, cross-examined and re-examined 'in like manner as at the trial of a cause or matter'. Rule 10 deals with objections to questions: if the witness objects to answer any question, the

ground for the objection must be set out. The validity of the ground for objection shall be decided by the court and not by the examiner, but the examiner must state his opinion *a* thereon, which must also be recorded. The right of objection in the rules is not limited to any particular grounds.

By s 3(1) of the 1975 Act a person shall not be compelled by virtue of an order under s 2 to give any evidence which he could not be compelled to give either in civil proceedings in this country or in the civil proceedings in Norway. The heading of the section is 'Privilege of witnesses'. The power of the court to decline to compel a witness *b* to attend to give evidence, or to answer particular questions after the witness has been sworn, is not limited to matters of recognised privilege but includes cases where the request for relevant evidence is shown to be oppressive, or where the claim to refuse to answer is based on an obligation of confidence. It was not argued that, if the appeal were dismissed, the witnesses could not claim to refuse to answer particular questions on the grounds of oppressiveness or confidentiality. In my judgment that concession was right *c* and any objection which a witness could make to particular questions, if the examination were proceeding in a court in this country, may be made on the examination of the witness pursuant to an order under the 1975 Act. The argument for the witnesses was that the nature of the request was so impermissibly wide, and so clearly bound to require evidence to be given unreasonably in breach of the duty of confidence, that the request should be rejected. It was argued further that to entrust control of the questioning to the *d* process of objection and ruling by the court was 'simplistic' and would clearly involve further and possibly prolonged court proceedings and that, if the request were upheld, the court would in effect have ruled impliedly on the permissible scope of questions to be answered. In short, the witnesses, having failed on their fundamental opposition to the request on the ground that the court had no jurisdiction to make the order under the 1975 Act, have contended that the order of McNeill J should be set aside in the exercise *e* of this court's discretion and the state and the estate left to consider what new application they should make in more limited terms.

I will deal first with the width of the request. I agree that the terms of the request are wide, but that follows, I think, from the subject matter of the proceedings and the relevant rules of Norwegian law as set out in the defence. I agree, further, that if the *f* order is upheld in the terms which I have proposed it would be possible for questions to be asked which, having regard to answers already given by the witnesses and to the issues in the case as they could then in detail be shown to be, would be impermissible as going beyond what is relevant and necessary.

If it were necessary, in order for the state and the estate to succeed, to demonstrate that the terms of the letter of request are such that no question could be asked outside what *g* will be shown to be relevant and necessary in the proceedings, then the terms of the request set out in the Pt II list would be too wide. I do not think that the law places such a burden on these applicants. In *Re Westinghouse Electric Corp Uranium Contract Litigation MDL Docket No 235* [1977] 3 All ER 703 at 710, [1978] AC 547 at 562 in the Court of Appeal, at the time of the making of the order of 26 May 1977 by which Westinghouse were entitled to proceed to the examination of certain witnesses, Lord Denning MR said: *h*

'So far as evidence is to be given, by word of mouth, the witnesses can, I think, be required to answer any questions which fairly relate to the matters in dispute in the foreign action. Counsel for the appellants asked us to disallow questions of a roving nature, but I do not think the order can or should be so limited. The only practical test of any question is: is it relevant? does it relate to the matters in question? No one would wish the witnesses to be asked about irrelevant matters or to go into *j* other things with which the dispute is not concerned. But it is said there is a difficulty. The witnesses are not conversant with the issues in the case. They do not know what is relevant, and what is not. Any difficulty on that score is readily overcome. By agreement (and I think even without agreeement) these witnesses,

a   when they are asked to give evidence, can and should have legal advisers at their
elbow. There are very reputable and responsible advisers on each side. If a question
is irrelevant the witness will be told and advised not to answer. So the point can and
should be resolved by the responsible lawyers on each side without difficulty.'

Roskill and Shaw LJJ agreed with Lord Denning MR's judgment. In the House of Lords
the majority upheld in general the rightness of the order of 26 May 1977 when made
b   (see sub nom *Rio Tinto Zinc Corp v Westinghouse Electric Corp* [1978] 1 All ER 434 at 444,
463, 471, [1978] AC 547 at 612, 636, 645 per Lord Wilberforce, Lord Diplock and Lord
Fraser). Lord Keith said ([1978] 1 All ER 434 at 478, [1978] AC 547 at 654):

'As regards the oral evidence sought to be obtained under the letters rogatory, I
am of opinion that the Court of Appeal acted rightly in sustaining the order for
examination of the persons named therein as witnesses. On the material made
c   available I consider that there were reasonable grounds for the view that these
persons might be in a position to give evidence relevant to Westinghouse's defence
in the Virginia proceedings. In the face of a statement in letters rogatory that a
certain person is a necessary witness for the applicant, I am of opinion that the court
of request should not be astute to examine the issues in the action and the
circumstances of the case with excessive particularity for the purpose of determining
d   in advance whether the evidence of that person will be relevant and admissible.
That is essentially a matter for the requesting court. Should it appear necessary to
apply some safeguard against an excessively wide-ranging examination, that can be
achieved by making the order for examination subject to a suitably worded
limitation.'

e   Having regard to the words of Lord Denning MR and of Lord Keith in the *Westinghouse*
case, it seems to me that the state and the estate have shown that the witnesses can
probably give evidence relevant to the factual issues in the case pending in Norway and
that the request is not so wide that the court should reject the application. The parties are
agreed that the witnesses may be represented and advised by counsel if they are to be
required to give evidence. This court therefore need not decide whether we could, or
f   should, if otherwise minded to uphold the order of the judge, impose a condition to that
effect. For my part I see no reason why the court could not do so and it is clearly right in
this case that the witnesses should have such advice available to them.
The fact that the witnesses are advised by experienced lawyers and will have their
assistance if required to give evidence should not enable applicants in all cases to obtain
an order which the law should not allow if the witnesses would be without that
protection. Witnesses should not be put to substantial expense to obtain protection which
g   might be provided by a more precise definition of the terms of the request or by the
giving of directions by the court. Allowing, I hope, full weight to these factors it is my
view that the witnesses should, in the circumstances of this case, be required to give
evidence in response to this request. The case is complicated. The extent to which the
witnesses will be required to answer on separate parts of the case will depend on earlier
h   answers given. It seems likely to me that the witnesses would wish to be advised and
represented by lawyers while giving evidence even if the judge's order were set aside and
the state and the estate were left to apply again on a more restricted letter of request.
As to the submission that it is 'simplistic' to rely for proper protection of the witnesses
on advice by counsel, refusal to answer and subsequent ruling by the court, I do not so
regard it. It is to an extent a cumbersome procedure and it may cause delay, in that the
j   examiner before whom witnesses give evidence has no power to rule. But, as in the
Westinghouse case, so here, the parties and the witnesses are advised by responsible and
experienced lawyers. If the appeal is dismissed so that the witnesses are required to give
evidence the judgments in this court would give some, and I think sufficient, indication
as to the extent to which and the principles according to which the court would support

or override any claim by the witnesses to be allowed to refuse to answer a question, whether on the ground that it is 'fishing' and not fairly necessary in the proceedings, or *a* that it is oppressive, or that, and I deal with this issue below, it unreasonably requires the witness to break his obligation of confidence. I would expect the advisers of the parties and of the witnesses to be able to discover without difficulty what evidence the witnesses would be able and willing to give under the headings set out in the Pt II list. The state and the estate could then severally decide what further questions they would ask the witnesses to answer. Evidence given will affect what matter thereafter will be shown to *b* be relevant and necessary. The sanction against seeking more than is relevant and necessary, or evidence on matters which the witnesses will not be required to reveal in breach of confidence, will be an order to pay the costs caused by the further proceedings. That which Kerr LJ has pointed to as deserving the greatest weight on matters of discretion in this case is that the application is pursued at the common wish of the estate and of the state, a special factor capable of removing many of the objections which might *c* otherwise have had great force. If this appeal is dismissed, and when the evidence has been taken to which the witnesses raise no objection in the light of the judgments of this court, it may be that that special factor will no longer be present, or it may be limited to part only of any further contest.

As to the submission that, if this court should uphold the width of the questions covered by the Pt II list, the court would impliedly have ruled on the permissible scope *d* of the questions to be answered, to some extent that is clearly right. To take the example considered by Kerr LJ, I would, for my part, and I am dealing at this point only with the width of the questioning, rule that the witnesses would be required to answer whether to the knowledge of the witnesses Mr Jahre owned or did acts indicating that he owned or controlled the shares in Pankos/CTC, whether those shares were passed to any trust or foundation by or at the direction of Mr Jahre and whether any other named person *e* owned or controlled those shares and the assets of Pankos/CTC and/or the trust and its assets for the benefit of Mr Jahre. It would not be sufficient merely to give a name in order to demonstrate the relevance of the answers sought. It would be necessary also to demonstrate that the person so named is identified in the proceedings as a person so acting on behalf of or under the control of Mr Jahre and that that identification is made by evidence, whether direct or arising by inference, which is available and apparently *f* credible. If either the state or the estate should then wish to ask 'If not Mr Jahre, or any named person, who then was it?', the issue whether the court would regard that question as irrelevant or unnecessary or inadmissibly 'fishing' would have to be decided in the light of the other evidence already given by the witnesses and all necessary information as to the factual issues in the case to which the answer was said to be 'necessary'. It would be for the state and the estate to satisfy the court that the answer was one reasonably *g* necessary to be given. The fact that it is not possible at this stage to be sure of the limits to which the state and the estate may be permitted to go in requiring answers is, in my judgment, no reason to deprive them of the sworn evidence of the witnesses on those matters on which, so far as concerns relevance and necessity, it is clear that the witnesses should be required to answer. It may be that in other cases which will come before the *h* court the utility or importance of what is clearly permissible may be so small, and the ability of the witness to protect himself, either on his own or by any adviser or representative that he can obtain, against the risk of unfairness may be so inadequate, that the order should be refused on the ground that the request is too wide or 'fishing'. I do not regard this as such a case.

As to issue F, confidentiality, Kerr LJ has referred to the principle that the English *j* courts should strive to comply with a request of a foreign court made pursuant to the 1970 convention unless it is driven to the clear conclusion that it cannot properly do so, and to the important feature in this case that the Norwegian court has sought the evidence at the instigation of both parties to the proceedings.

Kerr LJ has demonstrated that the request falls within the terms of the 1975 Act and
a is not excluded by any principle of law, such as tax gathering or sovereignty, subject to
which Parliament must have intended the court to exercise the jurisdiction created by
the Act. The court should, in my judgment, exercise its discretion by applying the
principle that a witness, whose evidence is sought by a foreign court, should be directed
to answer no more and no less than would be required of him in proceedings in the
courts of this country. The witness may be entitled to a special and more extended
b protection under the law of Norway (see s 3(1)(*b*) of the 1975 Act), but that has not so far
been raised in this case. If the order of the judge is upheld, it might be raised hereafter.

Kerr LJ has set out the principle as stated by Lord Wilberforce in *British Steel Corp v
Granada Television Ltd* [1981] 1 All ER 417 at 455, [1981] AC 1096 at 1168: the court
must consider whether the interest in protecting the confidence reposed in the witness is
outweighed by other interests to which the law attaches importance. The factors in
c favour of requiring the witnesses to answer are the importance of assisting the Norwegian
court to obtain evidence which it regards as necessary in the interests of justice and,
further, the great financial importance of the case to the estate of Mr Jahre.

As to the protection of the confidence reposed in the witnesses, for the reasons I have
set out, this court, by upholding the order of the judge, would not be deciding that the
witnesses would hereafter be required to answer all and any questions within the
d headings of the Pt II list; if that were the consequence then I would agree that the
application should be dismissed on this ground. On the material before this court it
would be right, in my judgment, for Lord Kindersley to be required to answer on oath
questions to provide the answers which he has already given in his out of court
statements. There is, in them, no secrecy left to be protected: see the terms of his letter
of 31 October 1980 as set out in the judgment of Kerr LJ. Mr Hardman could rightly be
e asked whether he confirms the answers.

How much further is it possible to say at this stage that the state and the estate should
be allowed to go? In my judgment, if these proceedings were being conducted in a court
in this country on similar issues, the witnesses would be required to answer,
notwithstanding the apparent breach of confidence required of them in so answering, at
least as far as the questioning could properly go, as I have explained above, within the
f limits of relevance and necessity, i e that the witnesses may be required to answer whether
to their knowledge Mr Jahre owned or did acts indicating that he owned or controlled
the shares in Pankos/CTC, whether those shares or any of them were passed to any trust
or foundation by or at the direction of Mr Jahre and whether any other named person
owned or controlled those shares and the assets of Pankos/CTC and /or the trust and its
assets for the benefit of Mr Jahre. And again for these purposes it would not be sufficient
g merely to give a name to found the obligation to answer: it would be necessary also to
demonstrate that the person so named is identified in the proceedings as a person so
acting on behalf of or under the control of Mr Jahre and that identification is made by
evidence which is available and apparently credible. If the state and the estate should
wish to go further they would, as I have said, have to justify their claim.

h My reasons for reaching that conclusion are as follows: the protection which the
banker claimed is for the obligation of confidence which he owes to his customer. It is
important for the banker's business that he be seen to be unswervingly loyal to that
obligation, but the confidence is reposed by the customer and it is his secret which is
revealed if the witness is required to answer. The factual issues and allegations in the
proceedings indicate to me the probability that any person connected with Pankos/CTC
j was also connected with and aware generally of the activities of Mr Jahre down to the
date of his death. Mr Jahre's estate seeks the evidence in order to protect the estate from
what, if their case is right, is a mistaken imposition of a very heavy tax burden based in
part on Jahre's failure to supply information which would rebut inferences otherwise
likely to be drawn. To the extent which I have indicated, it does not seem to me to be

excessively or unfairly intrusive as against any customer of the bank to require of the
witnesses that they answer.

If Pankos/CTC was still in existence a subpoena directed to that company to produce
at the trial specific documents in order to prove, for example, that Mr Jahre was or was
not the owner of shares in the company or of funds held would not, in my judgment, be
set aside on the grounds that the request was unreasonably intrusive or oppressive having
regard to the utility of the evidence and to the demonstrated connection of Mr Jahre with
the company. Evidence which could be required of a company does not become protected
merely by causing the officers of the company to be officers of a bank which has rendered
banking services to the company. The position with reference to the foundation, or trust,
is different: whereas Mr Jahre's connection with Pankos/CTC is, as I have said, sufficiently
indicated in the papers, his connection with the foundation is less clear. The main fact
appears to be that the shares in and the assets of Pankos/CTC became vested in the
foundation. If the identity of the foundation were known it would, I think, be difficult
to justify requiring Lord Kindersley to answer with reference to the connections of Mr
Jahre with the foundation and its assets because the parties could seek such evidence
directly from the foundation and the officers of the foundation could either give the
evidence or state their reasons for claiming the right to refuse. The trust claims to
preserve its anonymity and to direct its adviser to give no evidence at all. The parties can
go nowhere else for the evidence. To the extent which I have indicated, it is right, in my
view, for the witnesses to be required to answer.

I accept that, as Kerr LJ has said, the support of the applications by the estate cannot be
taken as consent to the disclosure by the witnesses of the affairs of the trust and CTC, and
I agree that there is nothing to show that disclosure is required in discharge of any 'duty
to the public'.

As to the submission that the request 'lies in the field of tax gathering', I am unable to
give to that fact any great weight. It is not an attempt to enforce foreign tax liabilities: it
is a request within the jurisdiction established by Parliament. The width of the factual
issues results partly from the proceedings being concerned with the tax affairs of a man
who made much money and controlled, for himself or others, many valuable assets and
partly from the terms of the relevant law. The fact that the liability in issue arises under
a tax law does not seem to me, when the application is supported by both sides, to be of
any particular weight in deciding whether it is fair and reasonable in the interest of those
who seek the evidence to risk intruding into the private financial affairs of as yet
unknown customers of the bank to the extent which I have indicated.

For the reasons I have given, it is my view that the extent of the questioning, and of
any permissible intrusion into the private affairs of the customers of the bank, can be
effectively controlled within the limits laid down by the law of this country. I do not
accept that any difficulty or expense in any further proceedings which may be anticipated
constitute factors of any significant weight in this case in deciding whether to uphold the
order of the judge.

If it were to be finally established by the decisions of the courts of this country that
there is jurisdiction to make the order, and that the witnesses must answer, within the
limits which the law imposes by reference to relevance, necessity, oppressiveness and
confidentiality, the parties would, as I have said, probably be able to arrange quickly for
the evidence to be given on which there would be no further dispute. The state and the
estate, if they wish to go further, would be able to concentrate, in the light of the
judgments of the court, on demonstrating the grounds on which the witnesses may
properly be required to answer further by reference to more precisely defined questions
within the headings covered by the Pt II list and, as I have said, the burden would be on
them to justify their application after refusal by the witnesses. I have in mind the matters
raised by Mr Ian Fraser in his affidavit with reference to the importance to the banking
institutions of their ability to maintain the secrecy of information given to them in
confidence by their clients. If the matter is allowed to proceed in the way which I have

a described there would be no piercing of the veil of secrecy to any greater extent than the law of this country permits or requires. I am uncomfortably aware of the risk of circularity in that statement, but it is my view that, by upholding the order of the judge, varied in the manner suggested, this court would be doing no more than permitting the state and the estate to proceed in accordance with the law of this country. I would dismiss the appeal.

b *Appeal allowed. Witnesses to have one-third of their costs in Court of Appeal and below as against the state. No order as to costs as between the witnesses and estate in Court of Appeal or below. Leave to appeal to the House of Lords refused.*

Solicitors: *Linklaters & Paines* (for the witnesses); *Freshfields* (for the state); *Macfarlanes* (for the estate).

c

Celia Fox   Barrister.

d # Re State of Norway's Application (No 2)

COURT OF APPEAL, CIVIL DIVISION
MAY, BALCOMBE AND WOOLF LJJ
19, 20, 21, 22, 23, 26, 27 OCTOBER, 18 DECEMBER 1987

e *Evidence – Foreign tribunal – Examination of witnesses in relation to matters pending before foreign tribunal – Evidence for purpose of civil proceedings – Proceedings in a civil or commercial matter – Evidence requested by foreign tax tribunal – Whether foreign proceedings civil or commercial matter – Whether proceedings assisting foreign tax gathering – Evidence (Proceedings in Other Jurisdictions) Act 1975, ss 1, 9(1).*

f *Precedent – Court of Appeal – Binding effect of previous decisions of court – Reason which is not essential and necessary to a decision – Dicta – Whether court bound by reason which is not essential and necessary to a decision – Whether court entitled to disregard dicta of court of co-ordinate jurisdiction.*

g *Estoppel – Issue estoppel – Jurisdiction – Evidence to show that court has no jurisdiction – Issue estoppel preventing evidence from being put before court – Whether party can be prevented by issue estoppel from putting evidence to show that court has no jurisdiction.*

Estoppel – Issue estoppel – Appealability – Whether issue estoppel prevented from arising if unsuccessful party unable to appeal.

h

J, a wealthy Norwegian shipowner, died in 1982. The county tax committee for that part of Norway in which he had resided decided to raise a retrospective tax assessment against his estate for the years 1972–1982 on the ground that he had avoided tax during those years by failing to declare a large part of his assets. The estate commenced proceedings in the court of first instance in Norway to have the assessement declared null and void and

j appealed to the national tax committee to have it set aside. The Sandefjord City Court, on the application of the State of Norway supported by the estate, issued letters of request addressed to he High Court in England requesting the court, inter alia, to summon two named merchant bankers (the witnesses) to attend before an examiner in London to give oral evidence relevant to the issues in the proceedings before the Norwegian court. The bank had acted as bankers for a charitable trust alleged to have been set up and controlled

by J and which allegedly held shares for J as beneficial owner. After receiving the letter
of request a Queen's Bench master made an order under s 2ᵃ of the Evidence (Proceedings a
in Other Jurisdictions) Act 1975 granting the application for the oral examination of the
witnesses. The witnesses applied to have the order set aside. The judge upheld the
master's decision subject to certain directions limiting the scope of the questions which
could be put to the witnesses. The witnesses appealed to the Court of Appeal, contending,
inter alia, that the Norwegian proceedings did not constitute 'civil proceedings' under
s 1ᵇ of the 1975 Act, which were defined by s 9(1)ᶜ as proceedings in a 'civil or commercial b
matter', so as to confer jurisdiction on the English court and that the terms of the letter
of request were so wide as to amount to a fishing expedition. The Court of Appeal
allowed the appeal and set aside the order. The court expressed the views that whether
proceedings were a 'civil or commercial matter' depended on their classification under
the law of the requesting court and the law of the court to whom the request was made
and that the Norwegian proceedings would be characterised as a civil proceeding under c
English law and therefore the proceedings fell within the ambit of s 1 of the 1975 Act,
but went on to hold that the terms of the letter of request were too wide for the court to
order the witnesses to give evidence on the request as framed. Following a further
application by the State of Norway, supported by the estate, the Norwegian court issued
a second letter of request for the oral examination of the witnesses on 12 specific issues
and setting out the specific questions to be put to the witnesses. The letter of request d
stated that the Norwegian proceedings were a 'civil action' under Norwegian law and a
'civil matter' under the convention relating to the taking of Evidence Abroad in Civil or
Commercial Matters 1970. The master made an order under s 2 of the 1975 Act for the
examination of the witnesses according to the terms of the letter of request. On appeal
by the witnesses, the judge upheld the order subject to certain limitations on the
testimony which the witnesses could be required to give. The witnesses appealed to e
Court of Appeal. The state contended that the witnesses were prevented by both judicial
precedent and issue estoppel from again contending that the Norwegian proceedings
were not 'civil proceedings' within the meaning of ss 1 and 9(1) of the 1975 Act and that
the English court had no jurisdiction. The state also cross-appealed against the limitations
placed by the judge on the witnesses' testimony.					f

Held – (1) Applying the principle that only matters which were essential and necessary
to the decision of a Court of Appeal were binding on subsequent divisions of that court,
the court was not bound by the views previously expressed by it on the jurisdiction issue
since its decision would have remained the same, having regard to the holding that the
letter of request was too wide, even if the jurisdiction issue had not been discussed or if g
jurisdiction had been assumed to exist. In any event, it was not clear that what was
previously said by the court on the jurisdiction issue was or was intended to be part of
the ratio of its decision. Accordingly, although the views previously expressed by the
court on the jurisdiction issue carried very great weight the court was entitled to depart
from those views if it was satisfied that they were wrong. Similarly, the witnesses were
not estopped from arguing that the Norwegian proceedings were not a 'civil action' h
under Norwegian law, contrary to the previous finding of the Court of Appeal, since that
finding was not fundamental to its decision (see p 710 j to p 711 a j to p 712 a, p 714 g,
p 719 f to p 720 a j to p 721 b, p 723 d e, p 734 g h, p 735 e f and p 736 g h, post); dictum
of Lord Denning MR in *Penn-Texas Corp v Murat Anstalt (No 2)* [1964] 2 All ER at 597
applied; *Leeds Industrial Co-op Society v Slack Ltd* [1924] All ER Rep 259 considered.
(2) (Woolf LJ dissenting) Having regard to the connection between the 1970 Hague j
Convention and the 1975 Act and that fact that there was no distinction between civil or

---

a   Section 2 is set out at p 707 f to p 708 a, post
b   Section 1 is set out at p 707 e f, post
c   Section 9, so far as material, is set out at p 708 c, post

commercial proceedings under the common law, the term proceedings in a 'civil or
a commercial matter' in s 9 of the 1975 Act was to be construed according to its generally
acceptable international interpretation derived from the civil law distinction between
private law (which included civil or commercial proceedings) and public law (which
included fiscal proceedings). Accordingly, jurisdiction under the 1975 Act in respect of
letters of request only arose if the English court was satisfied that the procedings in the
requesting court were either civil or commercial proceedings in a civil law sense and
b since (Woolf LJ concurring) the Norwegian proceedings were clearly fiscal proceedings
they were not proceedings in a 'civil or commercial matter' for the purposes of s 9, with
the result that the court had no jurisdiction to order the examination of the witnesses
according to the terms of the letter of request. The witnesses' appeal would therefore be
allowed (see p 716 c h to p 717 a, p 718 f g, p 719 a, p 721 j, p 724 h j, p 726 e g, p 728 f to
p 729 b, p 730 f g, p 732 e, p 740 f g and p 744 d to f, post); *Re State of Norway's Application*
c *(No 1)* [1989] 1 All ER 661 not followed.

Semble. A party cannot be prevented by issue estoppel from putting before the court
evidence to show that the court has no jurisdiction to make the order sought (see p 715 c,
p 723 f g and p 737b, post).

Per May LJ. An issue estoppel is not prevented from arising merely because the party
against whom the finding was made was unable to appeal against the decision (see
d p 714 g, post).

Notes
For evidence for proceedings in other jurisdictions, see 17 Halsbury's Laws (4th edn)
paras 326–329, and for cases on the subject, see 22 Digest (Reissue) 665–668, 7111–7123.
For the Evidence (Proceedings in Other Jurisdictions) Act 1975, ss 1, 2, 9, see 17
e Halsbury's Statutes (4th edn) 191, 192, 197.

Cases referred to in judgments
Air France v Saks (1985) 84 L Ed 2d 289, US SC.
Badar Bee v Habib Merican Noordin [1909] AC 615, PC.
Bavaria Fluggesellschaft Schwabe & Co KG and Germainair Bedarfsluftfahrt GmbH & Co KG v
f   *Eurocontrol* Joined Cases 9 and 10/77) [1977] ECR 1517.
Block v Cie Nationale Air France (1967) 386 F 2d 323, US Ct of Apps, 5th Cir; cert denied
(1968) 392 US 905.
Bonalumi v Secretary of State for the Home Dept [1985] 1 All ER 797, [1985] QB 675, [1985]
2 WLR 722, CA.
British Steel Corp v Granada Television Ltd [1981] 1 All ER 417, [1981] AC 1096, [1980] 3
g   WLR 774.
Buchanan (James) & Co Ltd v Babco Forwarding and Shipping (UK) Ltd [1977] 3 All ER 1048,
[1978] AC 141, [1977] 3 WLR 907, HL.
Campbell (Donald) & Co Ltd v Pollak [1927] AC 732, [1927] All ER Rep 1, HL.
Carl-Zeiss-Stiftung v Rayner & Keeler Ltd (No 2) [1966] 2 All ER 536, [1967] 1 AC 853,
h   [1966] 3 WLR 125, HL.
Close v Steel Co of Wales Ltd [1961] 2 All ER 953, [1962] AC 367, [1961] 3 WLR 319, HL;
affg [1960] 2 All ER 657, [1960] 2 QB 299, [1960] 3 WLR 401, CA.
Dalmia Dairy Industries Ltd v National Bank of Pakistan [1978] 2 Lloyd's Rep 223, CA.
Deumeland v Germany (1986) 8 EHRR 448, E Ct HR.
Dreyfus v Peruvian Guano Co (1899) 43 Ch D 316, CA.
j *Duedu v Yiboe* [1961] 1 WLR 1040, PC.
Feldbrugge v Netherlands (1986) 8 EHRR 425, E Ct HR.
Fidelitas Shipping Co Ltd v V/O Exportchleb [1965] 2 All ER 4, [1966] 1 QB 630, [1965] 2
WLR 1059, CA.
Fothergill v Monarch Airlines Ltd [1980] 2 All ER 696, [1981] AC 251, [1980] 3 WLR 209,
HL.

Gourdain v Nadler Case 133/78 [1979] ECR 733.
Gross, Re, ex p Treasury Solicitor [1968] 3 All ER 804, [1969] 1 WLR 12.
Huntington v Attrill [1893] AC 150, PC.
India (Government) Ministry of Finance (Revenue Division) v Taylor [1955] 1 All ER 292, [1955] AC 491, [1955] 2 WLR 303, HL.
Khan v Goleccha International Ltd [1980] 2 All ER 259, [1980] 1 WLR 1482, CA.
Kingston's (Duchess) Case (1776) 1 East PC 468, [1775–1802] All ER Rep 623, HL.
Leeds Industrial Co-op Society Ltd v Slack [1924] AC 851, [1924] All ER Rep 259, HL; *rvsg* [1923] Ch 431, CA.
LTU Lufttransportunternehmen GmbH & Co KG v Eurocontrol Case 29/76 [1976] ECR 1541.
Maliban Biscuit Manufactories Ltd v Subramariam [1971] AC 988, [1971] 3 WLR 469, PC.
Netherlands v Rüffer Case 814/79 [1980] ECR 3807.
New Brunswick Rly Co v British and French Trust Corp [1938] 4 All ER 747, [1939] AC 1, HL.
Norway's (State) Application, Re (No 1) [1989] 1 All ER 661, CA.
Penn-Texas Corp v Murat Anstalt [1963] 1 All ER 258, [1964] 1 QB 40, [1963] 2 WLR 111, CA.
Penn-Texas Corp v Murat Anstalt (No 2) [1964] 2 All ER 594, [1964] 2 QB 647, [1964] 3 WLR 131, CA.
R v Hutchings (1880) 6 QBD 300, CA.
R v Southampton Justices, ex p Green [1975] 2 All ER 1073, [1976] QB 11, [1975] 3 WLR 277, CA.
Rio Tinto Zinc Corp v Westinghouse Electric Corp, RTZ Services Ltd v Westinghouse Electric Corp [1978] 1 All ER 434, [1978] AC 547, [1978] 2 WLR 81, HL; *rvsg* sub nom *Westinghouse Electric Corp Urainium Contract Litigation MDL Docket No 235* [1977] 3 All ER 703, [1978] AC 547, [1977] 3 WLR 492.
Salomon v Customs and Excise Comrs [1966] 3 All ER 871, [1967] 2 QB 116, [1966] 3 WLR 1223, CA.
Shoe Machinery Co v Cutlan [1896] 1 Ch 667.
Stag Line Ltd v Foscolo Mango & Co Ltd [1932] AC 328, [1931] All ER 666, HL.
Stamps Comr Straits Settlements v Oei Tjong Swan [1933] AC 378, PC.
Tennekoon (Comr for Registration of Indian and Pakistan Residents) v Duraisamy [1958] 2 All ER 479, [1958] AC 354, [1958] 2 WLR 994, PC.
Thoday v Thoday [1964] 1 All ER 341, [1964] P 181, [1964] 2 WLR 381, CA.
Yat Tung Investment Co v Dao Heng Bank [1975] AC 581, [1975] 2 WLR 690, PC.

Cases also cited

Allsop and Joy's Contracts, Re (1889) 61 LT 213.
Asbestos Insurance Coverage Cases, Re [1985] 1 All ER 716, [1986] 1 WLR 331, HL.
Barham v Lord Huntingfield [1913] 2 KB 193, [1911–13] All ER Rep 663, CA.
Bemberg v Revenue Authorities of the Province of Buenos Aires (24 February 1949, unreported), Cours de Cassation de France.
Bunbury v Fuller (1853) 9 Exch 111, 156 ER 47, Ex Ch.
Connelly v DPP [1964] 2 All ER 401, [1964] AC 1254, HL.
Getty (Sarah C) Trust, Re [1985] 2 All ER 809, [1985] QB 956.
Griffiths v Davies [1943] 2 All ER 209, [1943] KB 618, CA.
Hennessy v Wright (No 2) (1890) 24 QBD 445n.
Hoystead v Taxation Comr [1926] AC 155, [1925] All ER Rep 56, PC.
Jacobs v LCC [1950] 1 All ER 737, [1950] AC 361, HL.
Kok Hoong v Leong Cheong Kweng Mines Ltd [1964] 1 All ER 300, [1964] AC 993, PC.
London Corp v Cox (1867) LR 2 HL 238.
Panthalu v Ramnord Research Laboratories Ltd [1965] 2 All ER 921, [1966] 2 QB 173, CA.
R v Comrs for Special Purposes of the Income Tax (1888) 21 QBD 313, [1886–90] All ER Rep 1139, CA.

R v Hull Prison Board of Visitors, ex p St Germain [1979] 1 All ER 701, [1979] QB 425, CA.

a *R v Lincolnshire Justices, ex p Brett* [1926] 2 KB 192, [1926] All ER Rep 275, CA.

R v Secretary of State for the Environment, ex p Hackney London BC [1984] 1 All ER 956, [1984] 1 WLR 592, CA; *affg* [1983] 3 All ER 358, [1983] 1 WLR 524.

Sebright v Hanbury [1916] 2 Ch 245.

Securities and Exchange Commission v Stockholders of Santa Fe International Corp [1985] ECC 187.

b *Spens v IRC* [1970] 3 All ER 295, [1970] 1 WLR 1173.

Tournier v National Provincial and Union Bank of England [1924] 1 KB 461, [1923] All ER Rep 550, CA.

Waring (decd), Re, Westminster Bank Ltd v Burton-Butler [1948] 1 All ER 257, [1948] Ch 221.

c **Appeal and cross appeal**

Lord Kindersley and Mr A J Hardman (the witnesses) appealed, pursuant to leave given by Kenneth Jones J, against his decision on 20 October 1986 whereby he dismissed the witnesses' application to discharge the order of Master Creightmore made in chambers on 2 April 1986 for oral examination of the witnesses pursuant to s 2 of the Evidence (Proceedings in Other Jurisdictions) Act 1975, in compliance with a request from the
d Sandefjord City Court on an application by the State of Norway, supported by the estate of Anders Jahre deceased, that the witnesses be examined on 12 specified issues, and directed that the examination proceed subject to certain directions limiting the scope of the questions which they could be required to answer. The evidence sought by the applicants related to information relevant to proceedings brought by the estate of the deceased shipowner against the State of Norway concerning a disputed retrospective
e assessment for tax on the estate for the years 1972–82. The state cross-appealed seeking the removal of the directions. The facts are set out in the judgment of May LJ.

Michael Crystal QC, J A Jolowicz and *John Higham* for the witnesses.
Anthony Boswood QC and *Stephen Moriarty* for the state.
f *Nicolas Bratza* for the estate.

Cur adv vult

18 December. The following judgments were delivered.

g **MAY LJ.** This is an appeal against a judgment of Kenneth Jones J of 20 October 1986. He then had before him a summons on behalf of Lord Kindersley and Mr A J Hardman (the witnesses) to set aside an ex parte order of Master Creightmore of 2 April 1986. That summons originally came before Master Prebble who, by consent, adjourned it to the judge in chambers under RSC Ord 32, r 12.

This litigation has had a long history and an application similar to that before the
h judge was before McNeill J in December 1985 and on appeal before the Court of Appeal in February 1986. The decision of this court on that occasion has been fully reported: see *Re State of Norway's Application (No 1)* [1989] 1 All ER 661. In the course of his judgment Kerr LJ set out fully the course which the proceedings had taken until then and all the background facts and allegations (see [1989] 1 All ER 661 at 666–671). As Kenneth Jones J said in his judgment presently under appeal, much of what Kerr LJ said in relation to
j the litigation is relevant to the instant application and appeal and I gratefully incorporate it in this judgment by reference and without unnecessarily repeating it.

Nevertheless, for I hope the easier understanding of this judgment I will briefly set out the background to the case. Mr Anders Jahre was in the 1970s the president of a Panamanian corporation by the name of Continental Trust Co Inc (CTC). In 1976 Lord Kindersley, a director of Lazard Bros & Co Ltd, was appointed one of the advisers to a

charitable foundation formed in that year which became the sole owner of the entire
issued share capital of CTC. In 1977 Mr Hardman, an employee of Lazards, was appointed
assistant secretary of CTC and in 1978 the treasurer of the corporation. In the same year
Mr Jahre retired as the corporation's president. He was a wealthy Norwegian shipowner.
He died domiciled in Norway on 26 February 1982. In the course of the administration
of his estate, on 14 September 1983 the relevant tax authorities raised a supplementary
tax assessment on it retrospectively for the years 1970 to 1982 for the sum of N Kr
337,999,317 on the basis that the deceased had directly or indirectly been the owner of
CTC and that there was reason to disregard the latter's corporate form as a real company.

On 3 November 1983 the estate commenced proceedings in the Sandefjord City Court
in Norway for an order nullifying the supplementary tax assessment. By what is
apparently a parallel procedure, the estate also appealed to the Norwegian National Tax
Committee on 31 January 1984. It was subsequently agreed between the estate and the
state that any evidence given by the proposed witnesses pursuant to the letters of request
to which I shall refer would be presented both to the city court and also to the National
Tax Committee. I interpolate that in January 1984 Mr Hardman retired as the assistant
secretary and treasurer of CTC.

On the estate's application to the Sandefjord City Court, subsequently supported by
the state, the office of the stipendiary magistrate in Sandefjord issued a first letter of
request to the United Kingdom courts on 5 November 1984 for oral testimony to be
given and documents to be produced by the witnesses. The master made the usual ex
parte order. The witnesses then issued a summons to discharge it. This came before
McNeill J who upheld the master's order and effectively granted the joint application of
the estate and the state subject to certain directions which he then gave. The witnesses
then appealed successfully against the judge's order. This was the decision of the first
Court of Appeal to which I have already referred.

There were seven issues in that first appeal which can be listed as follows.

A. *Civil proceedings: 'civil or commercial matter'*
The question was whether the Sandefjord proceedings fell within the ambit of the
Evidence (Proceedings in Other Jurisdictions) Act 1975.

B. *Tax gathering*
A phrase taken from the speech of Lord Somervell in *Government of India Ministry of
Finance (Revenue Division) v Taylor* [1955] 1 All ER 292 at 301, [1955] AC 491 at 514. The
contention was that compliance with the first letter of request would be contrary to
public policy and the settled principles that our courts would not lend their assistance to
the enforcement, directly or indirectly, of foreign tax liabilities.

C. *Sovereignty*
The contention was that since the Sandefjord proceedings were concerned with the
estate's assessment to tax in Norway, compliance by an English court with the letter of
request was precluded by s 4 of the Protection of Trading Interests Act 1980 on the
ground that the request, or compliance with it, would infringe the jurisdiction of the
United Kingdom or be prejudicial to its sovereignty.

D. *Dual purpose*
This concerned the intention to make the testimony of the witnesses available to the
National Tax Committee, in addition to the Sandefjord court.

E. *'Fishing'*
The contention was that the terms of the first letter of request were far too wide to be
an acceptable request for evidence under the 1975 Act, irrespective of certain limitations
contained in directions given by McNeill J.

F. Confidentiality

a   It was submitted that in all the circumstances the witnesses should not be ordered to break their duty of confidentiality to their customers by answering the questions raised by the letter of request.

G. Discretion

It was submitted that whereas issues A and C went to the jurisdiction of our court to
b   comply with the letter of request, issues B, D, and E went to both jurisdiction and to the court's general discretion, whereas issue F went solely to discretion.

In the event the witnesses failed before the first Court of Appeal on issues A, B, C and D but succeeded on issues E and F. The question whether the decision of what I will continue to call the first Court of Appeal created any precedent or issue estoppel binding on us was the first question argued on the hearing of the instant appeal. To this I shall
c   have to return later.

At this point I set out the relevant provisions of the 1975 Act. The long title is in these terms:

'An Act to make new provision for enabling the High Court, the Court of Session and the High Court of Justice in Northern Ireland to assist in obtaining evidence required for the purposes of proceedings in other jurisdictions; to extend the powers
d   of those courts to issue process effective throughout the United Kingdom for securing the attendance of witnesses; and for purposes connected with those matters.'

The relevant parts of ss 1, 2, 3 and 9 are as follows:

'1. Where an application is made to the High Court, the Court of Session or the High Court of Justice in Northern Ireland for an order for evidence to be obtained
e   in the part of the United Kingdom in which it exercises jurisdiction, and the court is satisfied—(a) that the application is made in pursuance of a request issued by or on behalf of a court or tribunal ("the requesting court") exercising jurisdiction in any other part of the United Kingdom or in a country or territory outside the United Kingdom; and (b) that the evidence to which the application relates is to be obtained
f   for the purposes of civil proceedings which either have been instituted before the requesting court or whose institution before that court is contemplated, the High Court, Court of Session or High Court of Justice in Northern Ireland, as the case may be, shall have the powers conferred on it by the following provisions of this Act.

2.—(1) Subject to the provisions of this section, the High Court, the Court of Session and the High Court of Justice in Northern Ireland shall each have power, on
g   any such application as is mentioned in section 1 above, by order to make such provision for obtaining evidence in the part of the United Kingdom in which it exercises jurisdiction as may appear to the court to be appropriate for the purpose of giving effect to the request in pursuance of which the application is made; and any such order may require a person specified therein to take such steps as the court may consider appropriate for that purpose.

h   (2) Without prejudice to the generality of subsection (1) above but subject to the provisions of this section, an order under this section may, in particular, make provision—(a) for the examination of witnesses, either orally or in writing; (b) for the production of documents . . .

(3) An order under this section shall not require any particular steps to be taken unless they are steps which can be required to be taken by way of obtaining evidence
j   for the purposes of civil proceedings in the court making the order (whether or not proceedings of the same description as those to which the application for the order relates); but this subsection shall not preclude the making of an order requiring a person to give testimony (either orally or in writing) otherwise than on oath where this is asked for by the requesting court.

(4) An order under this section shall not require a person—(a) to state what

documents relevant to the proceedings to which the application for the order relates
are or have been in his possession, custody or power; or (*b*) to produce any documents *a*
other than particular documents specified in the order as being documents appearing
to the court making the order to be, or to be likely to be, in his possession, custody
or power . . .

3.—(1) A person shall not be compelled by virtue of an order under section 2
above to give any evidence which he could not be compelled to give—(*a*) in civil
proceedings in the part of the United Kingdom in which the court that made the *b*
order exercises jurisdiction; or (*b*) subject to subsection (2) below, in civil proceedings
in the country or territory in which the requesting court exercises jurisdiction . . .

(4) In this section references to giving evidence include references to answering
any question and to producing any document . . .

9.—(1) In this Act—"civil proceedings", in relation to the requesting court,
means proceedings in any civil or commercial matter . . .'   *c*

Kerr LJ in the first Court of Appeal was critical about the cogency and extent of the
evidence then before the court on what I may describe as the 'international' aspect and
the Norwegian law issue. At the end of his judgment he said ([1989] 1 All ER 661 at
689):

'Finally, I would add that if this judgment reflects the ultimate outcome of this *d*
appeal, then I hope that any renewal of the present letter of request in some more
limited and acceptable form, if this can be devised, should be accompanied by clear
evidence as to what is properly to be regarded as a "civil or commercial matter" by
the law of Norway, and in particular whether Norwegian law distinguishes between
public and private law. I feel, frankly, uneasy about my acceptance, dubitante, of
the very limited evidence in this connection on the present application. I would also *e*
urge that, at any rate in the international context, particularly in relation to the
concept of "civil and commercial matters" in the Hague and similar bilateral
conventions, as well as of the 1975 Act, it would be desirable to recognise a clear-cut
distinction between private and public law in our jurisprudence, in the same way as
in other legal systems.'

As Kenneth Jones J said, this passage was naturally construed first by the state and the *f*
estate as an invitation to make a fresh application for a letter of request in 'some more
limited and acceptable form'. Second, the witnesses read it as an invitation, if a fresh
application were made, to adduce further evidence and material to the court about the
law of Norway and to reopen issue A. Both sides acted swiftly. A second joint application
was made in Norway by the state and the estate on 7 March 1986 and pursuant to it a
second letter of request was issued by the stipendiary magistrate in Sandefjord on *g*
10 March 1986. The topics on which the evidence of the witnesses is now sought are set
out in schedule 1 to the letter of request, but I need not detail them fully at this stage of
this judgment.

Before the judge below and here it was again first argued on behalf of the witnesses
that the underlying proceedings in the Sandefjord court did not fall within the ambit of *h*
the 1975 Act. But on behalf of both the state and the estate the preliminary points were
taken, first, that as a matter of law the judge was bound by way of legal precedent by the
construction placed by the first Court of Appeal on the relevant provisions of that Act
and second, that in so far as the issues raised questions of fact rather than of English law,
particularly questions of the relevant Norwegian law, the witnesses were estopped from
re-opening the issue by the earlier decision of the Court of Appeal.   *j*

When this matter was before the first Court of Appeal Kerr LJ reluctantly found it
impossible to give any 'international' interpretation to the definition of 'civil proceedings'
in s 9(1) of the 1975 Act. He held that the proper approach to the problem required the
court addressed to satisfy itself that the relevant proceedings concerned a civil or
commercial matter under the law of the requesting court, but that the court addressed

would only accept the foreign classification for the purpose of assuming jurisdiction if it
a were not in conflict with any fundamental principle recognised under its own laws. On
the limited material before the court on that occasion Kerr LJ reluctantly concluded that
the Sandefjord proceedings could be regarded as a civil matter by the law of Norway and
that as they were clearly to be so characterised by English law the first letter of request
was within the scope of the 1975 Act and that accordingly the English courts had
jurisdiction to give effect to it, subject to the resolution of the other issues involved. With
b this view both Glidewell and Ralph Gibson LJJ agreed.

In relation to the second letter of request Kenneth Jones J held, firstly, that he was
bound by this decision on the proper construction of s 9(1) in English law by the court.
But on this point he also held, secondly, that the witnesses were not estopped from re-
arguing the question of Norwegian law. Nevertheless, he, thirdly and finally, decided on
the material before him, which he thought was still far from clear, that in Norwegian
c law the proceedings before the Sandefjord court would be categorised as proceedings in a
civil matter for the purposes of the 1975 Act.

Before us the witnesses have once more argued for an international construction of
s 9(1). In any event, and in the alternative, they have contended that the judge's finding
on Norwegian law was wrong. They necessarily submitted that they were bound neither
by precedent nor issue estoppel to prevent them so arguing.
d The state and estate have contended the reverse. First, that the witnesses were bound
by both precedent and issue estoppel. Second, if they were not, that the proper
construction of the 1975 Act did not admit of an international one and further, that the
previous decision of the two judges at first instance and of this court on the question of
Norwegian law had been correct.

Before Kenneth Jones J counsel for the witnesses did not argue issues B (tax gathering),
e C (sovereignty), or D (dual purpose), but reserved his position on them for a higher court.
He has formally argued these issues before us, although more on paper by way of his full
and helpful skeleton argument than orally, but he has recognised the difficulties in his
way posed by the earlier decision of this court on these issues. The state and the estate
have sought to uphold these earlier decisions and have contended that they apply equally
to the second letter of request as to the first. I should add that the decision on these issues
f in the first Court of Appeal was unanimous.

On issue E (fishing), in relation to the first letter of request Kerr and Glidewell LJJ held
in favour of the witnesses. Ralph Gibson LJ took the opposite view. On the second letter
of request, Kenneth Jones J held that, with limited deletions which he ordered, the
questions sought to be asked would not be 'fishing'. As might be expected, on the instant
appeal the witnesses have contended that the judge was wrong, whilst the state and the
g estate have argued the reverse. By a cross-notice the state has further contended that the
judge was wrong even to order the limited deletions which he did.

On issue F, confidentiality, on the previous occasion in this court Kerr LJ again held in
favour of the witnesses and Ralph Gibson LJ in favour of the present state and the estate.
Although I respectfully do not think that Glidewell LJ expressed any final conclusion on
h this issue, on a careful reading of his judgment I think that in general he took the same
view as did Kerr LJ. Before Kenneth Jones J the two issues of 'fishing' and 'confidentiality'
appear to have been argued together. The judge held against the witnesses, who now
appeal. The state and estate have submitted that the judge was correct.

When this matter was before the first Court of Appeal on the first letter of request, in
the light of the majority decision on issues E and F the question of discretion did not
j directly arise. Ralph Gibson LJ would clearly have exercised his discretion in favour of
the witnesses' proposed examination. On the second letter of request, Kenneth Jones J
took the same view as had Ralph Gibson LJ on the first. On this appeal the parties have
taken the appropriate opposing stances.

The first issues which have therefore to be considered in this appeal are first, whether
the decision of the first Court of Appeal created any precedent in law or issue estoppel

binding on us and the witnesses. In so far as the latter are concerned, a subsidiary issue
has been argued, namely that even if otherwise there would be issue estoppel can this *a*
deprive the court of a jurisdiction which it would otherwise possess under the statute? In
addition, we have heard argument on each of the seven issues listed by Kerr LJ (see [1989]
1 All ER 661 at 672).

I turn therefore to the issue of precedent. The question is whether the decision of the
first Court of Appeal on the previous occasion on the question of law of the proper
construction of s 9(1) of the 1975 Act is binding as a legal precedent on us. The general *b*
principles are well known; they are stated in 26 Halsbury's Laws (4th edn) para 573 in
this way:

> 'The use of precedent is an indispensable foundation upon which to decide what
> is the law and its application to individual cases; it provides at least some degree of
> certainty upon which individuals can rely in the conduct of their affairs, as well as a *c*
> basis for orderly development of legal rules. The enunciation of the reason or
> principle upon which a question before a court has been decided is alone binding as
> a precedent.'

In *Close v Steel Co of Wales Ltd* [1961] 2 All ER 953 at 960, [1962] AC 367 at 388 Lord
Denning MR in the course of his speech quoted Sir Frederick Pollock *Progress of* *d*
Continental Law in the Nineteenth Century (Continental Legal History Series) p xliv, on the
same point to this effect:

> 'Judicial authority belongs not to the exact words used in this or that judgment,
> nor even to all the reasons given, but only to the principles accepted and applied as
> necessary grounds of the decision.'

e

Precedents therefore are to be contrasted with dicta, which are statements which are
not necessary to the decision, which go beyond it and lay down a rule that is unnecessary
for the purpose in hand. They have no binding authority on another court, although
they may have some persuasive efficacy.

On the previous occasion that this matter came before the Court of Appeal Kerr LJ
considered the question of the proper construction of s 9(1) of the 1975 Act in detail and *f*
I am respectfully most grateful for the help that I have derived from his judgment. He
ultimately concluded that he could not adopt any 'international' interpretation of the
phrase 'civil or commercial matter' in the relevant subsection. However, at the end of
this part of his judgment he said ([1989] 1 All ER 661 at 681): 'In any event, in view of
my conclusions on issues E and F, in this judgment the matter becomes academic.'

I think that Glidewell LJ in his turn also rejected the international approach to the *g*
question of construction, but not in terms which lead me in any way to think that he
relied on this for his ultimate decision in the case. As I have already said, in my respectful
opinion he expressed no final view on issue F, confidentiality, but expressly agreed with
Kerr LJ in his decision on issue E, 'fishing'. In his judgment Glidewell LJ said ([1989] 1
All ER 661 at 691):

h

> 'Thus I have reluctantly come to the conclusion that on this sole ground the order
> sought by the state and the estate should not be made.'

I think that this makes clear on what basis Glidewell LJ decided that the appeal should be
allowed.

Finally, Ralph Gibson LJ did not specifically refer to the issue of international *j*
construction in the course of his judgment. Nevertheless he agreed generally with the
views of Kerr LJ on issue A as a whole.

On this analysis I do not think that any views expressed by this court on the previous
occasion, that as a matter of law one could not give any international construction to the
relevant phrase in the 1975 Act, formed any part of the ratio for their ultimate decision.

a   Consequently, that which they did say on this particular point is not in my opinion binding on us.

I should, however, refer to an argument put to us attractively by counsel for the estate founded on the decision of the Court of Appeal in *Slack v Leeds Industrial Co-op Society Ltd* [1923] Ch 431. The question in that case was whether on a proper construction of s 2 of the Chancery Amendment Act 1858 (Lord Cairns's Act) a court had any jurisdiction to award damages in substitution for an injunction where the injury to the plaintiff's rights

b   was only apprehended in the future, but no present actionable interference existed. In the earlier case of *Dreyfus v Peruvian Guano Co* (1899) 43 Ch D 316 all three members of the Court of Appeal had expressed the view after full argument that there was no such jurisdiction in those circumstances. However, for two members of the court such a conclusion was not necessary for their decision in that earlier case; the third member of the court in any event dissented. In *Slack v Leeds Industrial Co-op Society Ltd* Lord Sterndale

c   MR and Warrington LJ clearly took a contrary view on the question of construction but, in the light of the earlier dicta, Lord Sterndale MR said (at 452):

> 'It is hardly possible to imagine dicta which are not binding decisions of greater weight, and as I have already pointed out, though they have been referred to on several occasions they have never elicited any expression of disapproval . . . I think

d
> . . . that it is open to us to decide the question contrary to those dicta, and the question is whether we ought to do so. I am of opinion that we ought not, and that if opinions of such weight given after such careful consideration more than thirty years ago, often mentioned and considered during that time and never disapproved, are to be overruled, it should only be done by the final tribunal of appeal and not by a Court of co-ordinate jurisdiction.'

e   Warrington LJ in his turn said (at 456):

> 'In order to get rid of the effect of the opinions deliberately expressed by three judges of this Court it is in my judgment not enough to say "they are mere dicta." They are not views casually expressed on a point not really adequately considered, but they are arrived at and expressed with the same care and deliberation as if they

f
> had been necessary for the decision of the case. Although therefore they are not absolutely binding as would be an actual decision of the Court necessary to its judgment, they are entitled to such weight that we ought to follow them unless we find that they have been overruled or that they are inconsistent with previous decisions.'

Counsel for the estate submitted that following those views so firmly expressed in

g   *Slack's* case, we should not lightly depart from and indeed should follow the considered and reasoned view of Kerr LJ who is extremely experienced in this type of case.

However, when *Slack's* case reached the House of Lords ([1924] AC 851, [1924] All ER Rep 259) the decision of the Court of Appeal was reversed, and in particular for present purposes Lord Dunedin said ([1924] AC 851 at 863–864; [1924] All ER Rep 259 at 265–266):

h
> 'My Lords, I cannot help remarking that I think the judgments in this appeal are in a peculiar position. On the question of construction of the statute all four judges are—so far as their own opinions are concerned—of one mind that the jurisdiction in question is conferred by the words used . . . [Lord Sterndale MR and Warrington LJ] took up a position which personally I cannot quite appreciate. They said that

j
> *Dreyfus* did not bind them, but that the dicta in *Dreyfus* must be followed, and if wrong must be put right by a higher Court, that is, your Lordships' House. My Lords, if a decision is binding, there is an end of it. But if you have only to do with dicta, though such dicta may well serve to help you to form your own opinion, I cannot see that they ought to overrule it.'

I respectfully agree with Lord Dunedin and in my opinion the principle is as I have

quoted from 26 Halsbury's Laws (4th edn) para 573. For this reason I must reject the argument of counsel for the estate. As I have said, I, of course, accord the greatest respect   *a*
to the earlier judgment of Kerr LJ but I do not think that it or any decision of the previous Court of Appeal is binding on us on this question of construction.

Different from their view on the question of law concerning a possible international construction of the relevant section of the 1975 Act, however, I think that each member of the first Court of Appeal did hold that the proceedings in the Sandefjord court were civil proceedings under Norwegian law. This was, of course, a question of fact. In these   *b*
circumstances it was contended both before the judge below and before us that the witnesses were in any event estopped from contending that this was not so. It was submitted that it was a clear case for the application of the principle of issue estoppel.

The principle contended for was that stated in *Thoday v Thoday* [1964] 1 All ER 341 at 352, [1964] P 181 at 198 by Diplock LJ:

c

> 'There are many causes of action which can only be established by proving that two or more different conditions are fulfilled. Such causes of action involve as many separate issues between the parties as there are conditions to be fulfilled by the plaintiff in order to establish his cause of action; and there may be cases where the fulfilment of an identical condition is a requirement common to two or more different causes of action. If in litigation on one such cause of action any of such   *d*
> separate issues whether a particular condition has been fulfilled is determined by a court of competent jurisdiction, either on evidence or on admission by a party to the litigation, neither party can, in subsequent litigation between them on any cause of action which depends on the fulfilment of the identical condition, assert that the condition was fulfilled if the court has in the first litigation determined that it was not, or deny that it was fulfilled if the court in the first litigation determined that it   *e*
> was ... The determination by a court of competent jurisdiction of the existence or non-existence of a fact, the existence of which is not of itself a condition the fulfilment of which is necessary to the cause of action which is being litigated before that court, but which is only relevant to proving the fulfilment of such a condition, does not estop at any rate per rem judicatam either party in subsequent litigation from asserting the existence or non-existence of the same fact contrary to the   *f*
> determination of the first court. It may not always be easy to draw the line between facts which give rise to "issue estoppel" and those which do not, but the distinction is important and must be borne in mind.'

It was submitted that it was a condition precedent to the validity of the first letter of request that the Sandefjord proceedings were indeed civil proceedings under Norwegian   *g*
law; that this point was argued at length on behalf of the witnesses in relation to that first letter of request; that there was no reason at all why the witnesses could not have adduced all the evidence on Norwegian law at that stage which was relevant to the point and which they subsequently sought to introduce in relation to the second letter of request; that after hearing the argument and evidence the issue was fully considered by the Court of Appeal and clearly decided against the witnesses; that whether or not the conclusion   *h*
as to Norwegian law was part of the ratio of the decision on the previous occasion nevertheless the unanimous finding by the members of the court was fundamental to their decision and was clearly not incidental or collateral.

However, it seems clear to me that Kerr LJ did not think that the parties would be precluded from canvassing this particular issue on a later occasion. His inferential invitation to consider a renewal of the first letter of request, accompanied by substantially   *j*
clearer and fuller evidence about Norwegian law, the terms of which I have already quoted, makes this clear. He gave direct expression to his unease about his then acceptance of the very limited evidence on this point that there was before the Court of Appeal on the previous application. I cannot think that the question of possible issue of estoppel was not present to his mind. I think it at least well arguable that he expressly

decided the appeal then before that court on the issues of fishing and confidentiality so
a that the parties should not thereafter be precluded from having the Norwegian law issue
reopened and fully considered on adequate material.

In the court below on the present second occasion the judge was referred to the
decision in *Penn-Texas Corp v Murat Anstalt (No 2)* [1964] 2 All ER 594 esp at 597, [1964]
2 QB 647 esp at 660 per Lord Denning MR:

b   'In my opinion, a previous judgment between the same parties is only conclusive
on matters which were essential and necessary to the decision. It is not conclusive
on other matters which came incidentally into consideration in the course of the
reasoning: see *Duchess of Kingstont's Case* ((1776) 1 East PC 468, [1775–1802] All ER
Rep 623) and *R v Hutchings* ((1881) 6 QBD 300). One of the tests in seeing whether a
matter was necessary to the decision, or only incidental to it, is to ask: could the
c   party have appealed from it? If he could have appealed and did not, he is bound by
it, see *Badar Bee v Habib Merican Noordin* ([1909] AC 615 at 623), per LORD
MACNAGHTEN. If he could not have appealed from it (because it did not affect the
order made), then it is only an incidental matter, not essential to the decision, and
he is not bound.'

d The judge then accepted the submission made on behalf of the witnesses and repeated
before us that they could not have appealed the decision of the previous Court of Appeal
on this Norwegian law point because they had succeeded overall. Consequently there
could be no estoppel.

In challenging this contention in the instant appeal, counsel for the state submitted
that there was no general or absolute rule of law that an issue estoppel is incapable of
e arising merely because the party against whom the finding was made was unable to
appeal against the decision. There is no reference to such a rule in recent authoritative
decisions on the point, such as those of the Privy Council in *Yat Tung Investment Co v Dao
Heng Bank* [1975] AC 581 and the Court of Appeal in *Khan v Goleccha International Ltd*
[1980] 2 All ER 259, [1980] 1 WLR 1482. We were also referred to Spencer-Bower and
Turner *Res Judicata* (2nd edn, 1969) p 144, para 181. In any event, it was contended that
f there was good authority to the contrary. In *Shoe Machinery Co v Cutlan* [1896] 1 Ch 667
there had been an earlier action between the same parties in which a patentee had
claimed damages for an infringement of his patent and an injunction. In answer the
defendant had denied not only the infringement but also the validity of the patent. On
that first occasion the court had upheld the validity of the patent, but had granted no
g injunction or damages on the ground that the evidence of the alleged infringement had
not been admissible. In the second action between the same parties in respect of the same
patent the defendant again denied its validity. The patentee contended that, as the
question of the validity of the patent had been decided on the first occasion, the defendant
was estopped from raising that issue again on the second. Romer J decided this question
in favour of the patentee. Counsel for the state submitted to us that clearly the judge's
h earlier decision that the patent was valid could not have been appealed, and yet he had
held that there had been an issue estoppel. In reply counsel for the witnesses submitted
that Romer J had so decided because he took the view that there could have been an
appeal against his earlier decision, if only against the order for costs. He relied on the
following passage from Romer J's judgment (at 670):

j   'It was because the issue of validity had been found in favour of the plaintiffs that
the Court ordered the defendants to pay the plaintiffs the costs of that issue; and
because the plaintiffs had failed on the issue of infringement that the Court ordered
the plaintiffs to pay the defendants' costs of that issue, and declared that there should
be a set-off. Now clearly, in my judgment, that decision of the Court, so far as
concerns the question of the validity of the patent, and the order which directed the

defendants to pay the costs of that issue, could have been appealed from. It was a
deliberate finding on the question of validity—a question fairly raised for the *a*
decision of the Court as between these two parties and fairly fought out before it;
and I cannot see why the decision given by the Court then on that issue is not to
bind the parties to it.'

Authority for the proposition that in special circumstances an appeal will lie to the
House of Lords on a question issue of costs alone can be found in *Donald Campbell & Co* *b*
Ltd v Pollak [1927] AC 732, [1927] All ER Rep 1.

However, I do not read Romer J's judgment, in so far as it dealt with the contention
that there could be no estoppel because there had been no right of appeal, as being based
on the proposition that there would at least have been a right of appeal on his earlier
order on costs. I think that he took the view that even though the defendant had
succeeded in the action as a whole, he nevertheless could have appealed the determination *c*
of the validity of the patent had he wished to do so. He put the matter again in this way
(at 671):

> 'It appears to me that it sufficiently appears from this judgment that I did not
> dismiss this action so far as concerns this patent, and I found the issue of validity and
> determined it in favour of the plaintiffs, and I ordered the defendants to pay the *d*
> costs of it. I cannot doubt that if the defendants had chosen to appeal from that part
> of the judgment they were entitled to have had that appeal heard by the Court of
> Appeal.'

For present purposes it is unnecessary to decide whether the judge's view was correct.
Even if the case were binding on us, I do not think that it is sufficiently clear authority to *e*
support the argument which was based upon it.

Shoe Machinery Co v Cutlan was referred to in the opinion of the Privy Council in *Duedu*
v Yiboe [1961] 1 WLR 1040. In that case the Ghana Court of Appeal held that in earlier
proceedings between the parties the issue of ownership of a parcel of land had been
decided in the respondent's favour. Consequently in subsequent proceedings seeking a
declaration of title to that land the appellant was estopped by the earlier decision. On a *f*
full reading of the report I think that the Judicial Committee did so hold notwithstanding
the fact that the respondent could not have appealed in the earlier proceedings because
he had succeeded in defeating his opponent's claim for damages for trespass. In my
judgment, this decision of the Privy Council, although not strictly binding on us, is good
persuasive authority for the proposition that there can be an issue estoppel even though
the previous decision could not have been appealed. Nevertheless, this is in no way *g*
inconsistent with the proposition that whether or not an earlier decision could have been
appealed is in many cases a good test of whether it brought into being an issue estoppel.

In my opinion similar considerations arise on this question of issue estoppel as they do
on the question of precedent. I respectfully agree with the statement of the general
principle by Diplock LJ in *Thoday v Thoday* [1964] 1 All ER 341, [1964] P 181. But, as
Lord Denning MR pointed out in *Fidelitas Shipping Co Ltd v V/O Exportchleb* [1965] 2 All *h*
ER 4, [1966] 1 QB 630, the principle is to be applied flexibly. In *Carl-Zeiss-Stiftung v*
Rayner & Keeler Ltd (No 2) [1966] 2 All ER 536 at 573, [1967] AC 853 at 947 Lord Upjohn
said:

> 'All estoppels are not odious but must be applied so as to work justice and not
> injustice, and I think that the principle of issue estoppel must be applied to the *j*
> circumstances of the subsequent case with this overriding consideration in mind.'

As I have already said, in my view whether or not the decision on the previous occasion
was appealable is only one test which may or may not be of help in a given case. The
basic requirement for the operation of the general principle is that the earlier
determination relied on as raising an issue estoppel shall have been fundamental to the

decision first arrived at. The matter is fully dealt with in Spencer-Bower and Turner *Res*
a *Judicata* (2nd edn, 1969) pp 179–182, paras 210–211, of which the opening passage reads:

> 'Even when in one way or another it can be demonstrated that the court has
> *expressly* determined, in the earlier proceedings, the same issue as is now in dispute,
> an issue estoppel will not by any means always be the result. Only determinations
> which are necessary to the decision—which are fundamental to it and without
> which it cannot stand—will found an issue estoppel. Other determinations, without
b> which it would still be possible for the decision to stand, however definite be the
> language in which they are expressed, cannot support an issue estoppel between the
> parties between whom they were pronounced.' (The editor's emphasis.)

In these circumstances it is unnecessary for me to express any decided view on the
question whether the court can be deprived by the operation of the principle of issue
c estoppel of a jurisdiction which it would otherwise possess under the statute. Nevertheless,
having had the question fully argued before us, my present opinion is that it cannot.

Being therefore bound neither by precedent nor by the principle of issue estoppel to
follow without more the conclusions reached on the point by the first Court of Appeal, I
turn to consider afresh the first and fundamental question in this case, namely the proper
construction of the phrase 'proceedings in any civil or commercial matter' in s 9(1) of the
d 1975 Act and whether the Sandefjord proceedings fall within that construction. Three
preliminary comments can be made. First, the answer to this fundamental question will
define the jurisdiction of the court addressed in the United Kingdom, in this case the
High Court and then this court on appeal from the latter. Second, on a first reading of
the phrase in a common law context, the courts are in my view immediately presented
with a patent difficulty. Parliament cannot have intended that the words 'or commercial'
e should be ignored; it is a trite comment that a commercial proceeding in an English
court is in English law a civil proceeding; thus the phrase 'civil or commercial', which ex
hypothesi contrasts the two types of proceedings, has no intelligible common law
meaning. Although, for the reasons which I have already given, we are not bound by the
decision on this point by the first Court of Appeal, the views then expressed of course
carry very considerable persuasive effect and, if I may respectfully say so, I have been
f greatly assisted by them.

I therefore turn to consider the views expressed, first by Kerr LJ ([1989] 1 All ER 661
at 676–678). On the question of how an English court is to approach and resolve the
problem of construction posed by s 9(1) of the 1975 Act it has never been disputed that
reference to the convention can properly be of assistance. As Kerr LJ said ([1989] 1 All
ER 661 at 676):
g

> '... since it was pointed out in *Rio Tinto Zinc Corp v Westinghouse Electric Corp*
> [1978] 1 All ER 434, [1978] AC 547] that one of the purposes of the 1975 Act was to
> implement the convention, this must be the starting point. Where English
> legislation has been enacted to give effect to a convention, reference to it may, and
> should where necessary, be made to it to see whether it assists in the interpretation
h> of the legislation, not only where the convention is annexed (see esp Lord Diplock
> in *Fothergill v Monarch Airlines Ltd* [1980] 2 All ER 696 at 705–707, [1981] AC 251
> at 280–283), but even where it is not (see *Salomon v Customs and Excise Comrs* [1966]
> 3 All ER 871 at 874–876, [1967] 2 QB 130 at 141–145 per Lord Denning MR and
> Diplock LJ). In statutes giving effect to conventions, an interpretation "on broad
> principles of general acceptation" is desirable (see *Stag Line Ltd v Foscolo Mango & Co*
j> *Ltd* [1932] AC 328 at 350, [1931] All ER Rep 666 at 677 per Lord Macmillan).
> However, sometimes this may not be possible (see *James Buchanan & Co Ltd v Babco*
> *Forwarding and Shipping (UK) Ltd* [1977] 3 All ER 1048 esp at 1052–1053, [1978] AC
> 141 esp at 152–153 per Lord Wilberforce).'

But having thus reached the convention, Kerr LJ thought that it itself provided no
assistance on the question at all. In asking where an English court then went, he suggested

that four possible categories presented themselves: (1) a generally accepted international interpretation; (2) classification under the law of the requesting court; (3) classification *a* under the law of the court addressed; (4) a combination of (2) and (3): the court addressed would satisfy itself that the proceedings concern a civil or commercial matter under the law of the requesting court, but would only accept this categorisation for the purposes of assuming jurisdiction if it is not in conflict with any fundamental principle recognised under the laws of the court addressed.

On the material and the submissions presented to the court on that occasion, Kerr LJ *b* reluctantly concluded that (4) provided the best answer. Nevertheless, I think that it is clear that had he felt able so to hold, he would have preferred category (1).

With the help of the substantial additional material and argument which were put before us, I have found myself driven to the conclusion that the generally accepted international interpretation comprised in the first category referred to by Kerr LJ is not only correct but also to be preferred. It is unnecessary to set out or to refer in detail to all *c* the fresh material to which we were referred. I have, however, derived substantial assistance from, and I am especially grateful for, the argument for the witnesses formulated on material assembled by their legal advisers, particularly by Professor J A Jolowicz of the University of Cambridge, and also for the comments of Dr F A Mann in his critical note on the decision of the first Court of Appeal 'Any Civil or Commercial Matter' (1986) 102 LQR 505. *d*

I have already drawn attention to the difficulty, if not impossibility, of attributing an intelligible common law meaning to the phrase in s 9(1) of the 1975 Act, 'civil or commercial'. The combination of 'civil' and 'commercial' points away from a classification under the common law and since that combination is carried over from the 1970 convention into the 1975 Act, I think it right to assume that Parliament intended to point in the same direction. This would not be the first time in this field where *e* Parliament has chosen to do so (see [1989] 1 All ER 661 at 679, per Kerr LJ). As I have, already said, the terms of the 1970 convention are expressed to have the same meaning in each of the two authentic texts and consequently one of those can be looked at to clarify the meaning of the other. The phrase 'civil or commercial matter', which is a translation of the French 'matière civile ou commerciale' clearly directs one's attention to the civil law systems. *f*

Next, the use of the word 'matière' indicates or describes the nature of the litigation, the subject matter of the dispute: see Dalloz *Lexique de Termes Juridiques* (5th edn, 1981) p 270. On such an approach, different from that based on procedural considerations, the duality and indeed the dichotomy between 'civil' and 'commercial' points even more strongly away from a classification under the common law. In French law, however, there exists a clear distinction between 'civil' and 'commercial' which is rooted in history: *g* see David *English Law and French Law* (1980) p 36ff. Whether the distinction should or can be maintained may be a matter of controversy. The authority just referred to shows that in some countries the view has prevailed that the distinction should be repudiated, for instance in Switzerland, Italy and the Netherlands.

However, it is also apparent that civil law countries draw a clear distinction between *h* private and public law, a distinction which, as Kerr LJ remarked, is only beginning to emerge in this country. I respectfully agree with the view also expressed by Kerr LJ that the draftsman of the 1970 convention, when using the phrase 'matière civile ou commerciale' must have had this distinction in mind. Viewed through the eyes of a civil lawyer, the Sandefjord proceedings would be categorised as being concerned with a 'matière fiscale' within the sphere of public law and as such not comprised within the *j* phrase 'matière civile ou commerciale'. Further, as Kerr LJ also said, international assistance in revenue matters is generally given by double tax conventions, which normally provide for the 'exchange of information'.

Against this background, and remembering the widening legal horizons towards which our courts have increasingly to look, it is not difficult in my view to conclude that jurisdiction under the 1975 Act in respect of letters of request only arises if the English court is satisfied that the proceedings in the requesting court are either civil or commercial

a in the sense in which civilian legal systems would understand these words. In other cases this could be a matter of some difficulty and require much further discussion and argument. For the purposes of the instant case, however, it is accepted that if this is the correct approach, then the proceedings in the Sandefjord court are indeed concerned with 'matière fiscale' in a civil law classification and as such are not proceedings sufficient to found the basic jurisdiction.

b   I turn briefly to consider the factors which in the view of Kerr LJ militated against the choice of a generally accepted international interpretation as the proper construction of the phrase used in s 9(1) of the 1975 Act. He first pointed out that the subject matter of the European Judgments Convention of 1968 (set out in Sch 1 to the Civil Jurisdiction and Judgments Act 1982) was the recognition and enforcement of foreign judgments; not merely the more limited one of providing judicial assistance for the provision of

c evidence in foreign courts. Further, the European Court is expressly empowered by the EEC Treaty to interpret the 1968 convention authoritatively. It does so in the sense which is 'communautaire' within the members of the European Economic Community. It is not so empowered with regard to the Hague Convention on the Taking of Evidence abroad in Civil or Commercial Matters (The Hague, 18 March 1970, TS 20 (1977); Cmnd 6727).

d   With respect, I am not persuaded that this makes any difference; each convention is concerned with an aspect of international legal procedures. Unless there is good reason not to do so, I prefer to construe the phrase 'matière civile ou commerciale' and thus its English translation, in the same way in each convention. If this is a correct approach, then the decision in *Netherlands v Rütter* Case 814/79, [1980] ECR 3807 confirms and does not weaken the view I have formed on the 1970 convention and 1975 Act.

e   Kerr LJ then drew attention to the fact that whereas the 1968 convention and the Civil Jurisdiction and Judgments Act 1982 expressly exclude 'in particular . . . revenue, customs or administrative matters' from 'civil or commercial matters', neither the 1970 convention nor the 1975 Act do so. However, he also pointed out that this was done to resolve any doubts about the scope of 'civil or commercial matters' in relation to member states which draw no clear distinction between public and private law. This corresponds

f with the view expressed in other material put before us but which was not before the first Court of Appeal that the phrase or sentence quoted was not an amendment but a clarification of the scope of the 1968 convention (see Kohler 'The Case Law of the European Court on the Judgments Convention—Part II' (1982) 7 EL Rev 104ff). I respectfully agree with Kerr LJ that it is unfortunate that no such clarification was attempted of the 1970 convention and the 1975 Act, but the fact that it was not does not

g lead me to construe the latter differently.

Finally, Kerr LJ pointed out again that the common law does not, at any rate at the present time, recognise any clear distinction between public and private law, although such a distinction is certainly beginning to be recognised. He suggested that it would be wrong to reach any interpretation of the 1975 Act even impliedly on the existence of any

h such distinction. It seemed to him inconceivable that in 1975 Parliament could have intended that inter-United Kingdom requests for evidence in civil proceedings should be based on a categorisation by reference to public and private law. For my part, however, I am not prepared to accept that the draftsman of the 1975 Act did not appreciate that while the distinction inherent in this well-known phrase certainly underlay its use in the 1970 convention, nevertheless it could not conveniently be fitted into an inter-United

j Kingdom arrangement, at any rate without further definition or explanation. The draftsmen were skilled and experienced lawyers whom one might expect to have had more than a nodding acquaintance with the concepts of civil law. It is in my view not difficult to accept that in drafting the 1975 Act based on the international 1970 convention they would have had substantial contact and discussion with lawyers in other relevant countries when drawing up the Act and adhering to the convention and would have been aware of what they were doing.

As to the three other possible categories considered by the first Court of Appeal, it rejected the second and this was not contended for before us. As Balcombe LJ points out in his judgment, which I have had the advantage of reading in draft, if an English court were to be wholly bound by the classification of the requesting court, it might be required to assist in proceedings which were classified by English law as criminal or penal. This would be contrary to the well-established principles of international law reiterated, for instance, in *Huntington v Attrill* [1893] AC 150 at 156.

The third of the possible categories listed by Kerr LJ might appear to have the greatest attraction for an English court in the instant case, and indeed to any court addressed whatever the circumstances. If the proper construction of the convention and, in so far as the United Kingdom is concerned, that of s 9(1) of the 1975 Act, enabled one to prefer this category, then it would enable the courts of this country to accept jurisdiction in those cases in which our law indicated that it was right and proper to do so. However, one's immediate attraction to the third category as keeping the question of jurisdiction to be decided by one's own law is very soon diluted by the difficulty to which I have already referred of resolving the patent dichotomy between 'civil' and 'commercial'.

As to the fourth possible category, I respectfully and gratefully adopt the comments of Balcombe LJ in his judgment on this point, also on the view (which I respectfully agree to have been erroneous) of Dr Mann that categories 2 and 4 must fall together, and on the passage from the judgment of Glidewell LJ in the first Court of Appeal decision (see [1989] 1 All ER 661 at 689–690.

Finally, apart from the purely constructional arguments which I have rehearsed, a substantial attraction for me in the choice of a generally acceptable interpretation of the relevant phrase in the convention and the Act is that it will produce uniformity. That may be based on a civilian law approach rather than on a common law one, but if in a particular instance the one produces certainty and uniformity in a particular context and the other does not, then as a common lawyer I am content. The English courts will now be able to treat letters rogatory under the Act in the same way from whichever country they come if the substance of the proceedings in that other country is the same, however differently they may be viewed under the several legal systems of the requesting countries: cf eg *LTU Lufttransportunternermen GmbH & Co KG v Eurocontrol* Case 29/76 [1976] ECR 1541 at 1551–1553 and *Gourdain v Nadler* Case 133/78 [1979] ECR 733.

In my opinion, therefore, the proper construction of the phrase 'proceedings in any civil or commercial matter' in s 9(1) of the 1975 Act is that which accords with a generally acceptable international interpretation. It is that which a civilian lawyer would give to it and to the corresponding French phrase of which it is the translation. Reverting for a moment to the judgment of Kerr LJ (see [1989] 1 All ER 661 at 680), the question which arose in *James Buchanan & Co Ltd v Babco Forwarding and Shipping (UK) Ltd* [1977] 3 All ER 1048, [1978] AC 141, a decision referred to by the Lord Justice, was the proper measure of damages on the facts of that case based on a detailed construction of a small part of one of the articles of the Convention on the Contract for the International Carriage of Goods by Road (Geneva, 19 May 1956; Cmnd 2260). In that case the interpretation argued for, but held by the House of Lords to be incorrect, may well have been assumed and unproved. That is not the situation in the instant case. The interpretation of 'matière civile ou commerciale' is neither assumed nor unproved. In a civil jurisdiction its interpretation is clear and incapable of dispute. Where the 1975 Act clearly adopted a translation of the phrase and having done so produced a result which is unintelligible at common law, to choose the civil law interpretation in the Act which has the international flavour that it does, is not in my view properly to be described as speculative and in any event it forthwith eases the pain and self humiliation which the very difficult search for an alternative interpretation would involve.

Having reached this conclusion on the fundamental question of construction, it is unnecessary for me to express any detailed views on the remaining issues in this appeal. Equally conscious that anything that I did say would be obiter, I gratefully adopt and *a* agree with the observations on those issues which are contained in the judgment herein of Balcombe LJ.

In these circumstances and for all these reasons I would allow this appeal and discharge the order of Master Creightmore.

BALCOMBE LJ. The facts in this matter are fully set out in the judgment of May LJ and I need not repeat them. The live issues which we have to decide may be summarised *b* as follows.

(1) Has the question whether the Sandefjord City Court proceedings are 'civil proceedings' within the definition of s 9(1) of the Evidence (Proceedings in Other Jurisdictions) Act 1975 been determined as far as we are concerned by the decision of the Court of Appeal on the first letter of request (see *Re State of Norway's Application (No 1)* [1989] 1 All ER 661 and hereafter referred to as 'the first Court of Appeal decision')? This *c* in turn divides into three sub-issues. (A) Are we bound, as a matter of precedent, by the construction given to the 1975 Act in the first Court of Appeal decision? (B) Even if we are not strictly bound, should we not nevertheless follow the first Court of Appeal in their construction of the 1975 Act? (C) In any event, as between the parties to these proceedings, is the question whether the Sandefjord proceedings are qualifying proceedings under the 1975 Act the subject of an issue estoppel arising from the first *d* Court of Appeal decision, by which the appellant witnesses are bound?

(2) If the first Court of Appeal decision is not determinative of this issue, what is the proper meaning of the phrase 'proceedings in any civil or commercial matter' in s 9(1) of the 1975 Act?

(3) If Norwegian law is relevant in determining whether the Sandefjord proceedings are qualifying proceedings under the 1975 Act, are they 'proceedings in any civil or *e* commercial matter' according to the law of Norway?

(4) In any event, should the second letter of request be struck down or amended on the grounds of either (i) 'fishing' or (ii) confidentiality?

Certain other issues were raised by the notice of appeal and the respondents' notice, but as these were not argued before us I need not consider them further. So I turn to consider the issues as set out above.
f

1(A) *Precedent: are we bound by the first Court of Appeal's construction of the 1975 Act?*

The enunciation of the reason or principle on which a question before the court has been decided, the ratio decidendi, is alone binding as a precedent. Statements which are not necessary to the decision, which go beyond the occasion and lay down a rule that is unnecessary for the purpose in hand are generally termed 'dicta': see 26 Halsbury's Laws *g* (4th edn) paras 573–574, *Penn-Texas Corp v Murat Anstalt (No 2)* [1964] 2 All ER 594, [1964] 2 QB 647.

In the first Court of Appeal decision an appeal by the witnesses against an order directing them to attend to give evidence pursuant to the first letter of request was allowed by a majority (Kerr and Glidewell LJJ, Ralph Gibson LJ dissenting). The ratio *h* decidendi of the first Court of Appeal decision was that the first letter of request was too wide, that it was a fishing request (see [1989] 1 All ER 661 at 672, 681, 691 per Kerr and Glidewell LJJ). Kerr LJ would also have allowed the appeal on the ground of confidentiality, that the balancing exercise which the court had to perform came down against the witnesses being compelled to violate their duty of confidence (see [1989] 1 All ER 661 at 686–688. Glidewell LJ would not have allowed the appeal on this ground (see *j* [1989] 1 All ER 661 at 691). All three Lords Justices were of the considered view that the Sandefjord proceedings were 'civil proceedings' as defined by s 9(1) of the 1975 Act. However, that view was not necessary for the decision of the majority, since they decided to reject the first letter of request on grounds not connected with that issue of jurisdiction. The majority need have not dealt with the issue at all, or they could have merely assumed that jurisdiction existed; in either event their decision would have remained the same.

Kerr LJ recognised that his decision on the jurisdiction issue was not part of the ratio decidendi, since he referred to it as 'academic', and he clearly did not consider that any future court would be precluded from considering the matter afresh (see [1989] 1 All ER 661 at 681).

Accordingly I am quite clear in my mind that we are not bound, as a matter of precedent, by the construction given to the 1975 Act in the first Court of Appeal decision.

1(B) *Should we follow the first Court of Appeal in their construction of the 1975 Act?*

Although the judgments of the first Court of Appeal on this question of construction are only technically dicta, nevertheless they are dicta to which great weight must be given since, in the case of Kerr and Glidewell LJJ, they represent their considered views on this issue.

> 'Dicta are of different kinds and of varying degrees of weight. Sometimes they may be called almost casual expressions of opinion upon a point which has not been raised in the case, and is not really present to the judge's mind. Such dicta, though entitled to the respect due to the speaker, may fairly be disregarded by judges before whom the point has been raised and argued in a way to bring it under much fuller consideration. Some dicta however are of a different kind; they are, although not necessary for the decision of the case, deliberate expressions of opinion given after consideration upon a point clearly brought and argued before the Court. It is open no doubt to other judges to give decisions contrary to such dicta, but much greater weight attaches to them than to the former class.'

(See *Slack v Leeds Industrial Co-op Society Ltd* [1923] 1 Ch 431 at 451 per Lord Sterndale MR.)

In the same case Warrington LJ said (at 456):

> 'In order to get rid of the effect of the opinions deliberately expressed by three judges of this Court it is in my judgment not enough to say "they are mere dicta". They are not views casually expressed on a point not really adequately considered, but they are arrived at and expressed with the same care and deliberation as if they had been necessary for the decision of the case. Although therefore they are not absolutely binding as would be an actual decision of the Court necessary to its judgment, they are entitled to such weight that we ought to follow them unless we find that they have been overruled or that they are inconsistent with previous decisions.'

Basing himself on these and other passages from the judgments of Lord Sterndale MR and Warrington LJ in *Slack*'s case, counsel for the estate addressed to us a most persuasive argument that, in the absence of any compelling reasons to the contrary, we should follow the considered dicta of the first Court of Appeal, leaving it to the House of Lords to put matters right, if necessary.

The decision of the Court of Appeal in *Slack*'s case was reversed by the House of Lords on the point of substance, but in the course of his speech Lord Dunedin said ([1924] AC 851, 864):

> 'Lord Blanesburgh, then Younger LJ ... was, however, out-voted by his two colleagues, who took up a position which personally I cannot quite appreciate. They said that *Dreyfus v. Peruvian Guano Co* ((1899) 43 Ch D 316) did not bind them, but that the dicta in *Dreyfus* must be followed, and if wrong must be put right by a higher Court, that is, your Lordships' House. My Lords, if a decision is binding, there is an end of it. But if you have only to do with dicta, though such dicta may well serve to help you to form your own opinion, I cannot see that they ought to overrule it. It is a different question when a practice follows on dicta. A practice it might not be right to disturb, but then it is the practice and not the dicta that forms the binding authority.'

This seems to me to be the answer to counsel's submission. While I would naturally
a wish to give the utmost respect to the views of Kerr and Glidewell LJJ, unless those views
have hardened into a practice which it would be wrong for us to disturb, then we must,
so it seems to me, make up our own minds on this issue and if, after giving all due
weight to those views, we are satisfied that they were wrong, then we both can and
should depart from them.

b 1(C) *Issue estoppel*
In my judgment the same considerations which preclude the judgments of the first
Court of Appeal from constituting a binding precedent also preclude their constituting
an issue estoppel by which the witnesses are bound.

> c 'Even when in one way or another it can be demonstrated that the court has
> *expressly* determined, in the earlier proceeding, the same issue as is now in dispute,
> an issue estoppel will not by any means always be the result. Only determinations
> which are necessary to the decision—which are fundamental to it and without
> which it cannot stand—will found an issue estoppel. Other determinations, without
> which it would still be possible for the decision to stand, however definite be the
> language in which they are expressed, cannot support an issue estoppel between the
> d parties between whom they were pronounced.'

(See Spencer-Bower and Turner *Res Judicata* (2nd edn, 1969) para 210, p 179.)
The editor continues (para 211, pp 181–182):

> 'In order to make this essential distinction [between the fundamental and the
> collateral] one has always to inquire with unrelenting severity—is the determination
> e upon which it is sought to found an estoppel so fundamental to the substantive
> decision that the latter *cannot stand* without the former. Nothing less than this will
> do.' (The editor's emphasis.)

And later he says (para 215, p 186):

> 'Not every finding of fact in a judge's judgment, not every issue of fact determined
> f by a judge or jury, is *res judicata* between the parties in later proceedings. Thus, a
> decision of fact or law *against* the party in whose favour the substantial dispute was
> ultimately decided will not found an estoppel in a later proceeding; and this because
> it cannot have been necessary to the substantive decision. It is merely collateral,
> clearing the way perhaps to the point where a substantive decision can be given, but
> not fundamental or necessary to the decision itself. Moreover, it would be not only
> g illogical but unjust to make it the foundation of a subsequent estoppel; for, the
> substantive decision being in his favour, no appeal is available on such a collateral
> decision to the person against whom it was given.' (The editor's emphasis.)

These statements from this authoritative work are fully supported by the cases there
cited and by the many authorities to which we were referred, and which I do not find it
h necessary to set out in extenso.
Kenneth Jones J in the court below held that the witnesses were not estopped from
arguing that the proceedings in the Sandefjord court were not civil proceedings within
the ambit of the 1975 Act, although he expressed his conclusion as resulting from the
fact that the witnesses could not have appealed against the first Court of Appeal decision
on the jurisdiction issue. I agree with his decision, although I would prefer to base my
j judgment on the wider proposition that the first Court of Appeal decision on the
jurisdiction issue was not fundamental to their substantive decision. I agree with the
editor of *Spencer-Bower and Turner* para 211, p 182 that the question of appealability is
but a useful test to decide whether the determination which is alleged to create an issue
estoppel is fundamental to the substantive decision.
Counsel for the State of Norway placed much reliance on this question of appealability
on the decision of Romer J in *Shoe Machinery Co v Cutlan* [1896] 1 Ch 667. In that case

patentees claimed damages for an infringement and an injunction. The defendants
denied the infringement and also denied the validity of the patent. The court upheld the
validity of the patent, but granted no injunction or damages. The judgment as drawn up
was, so far as relevant, in the following terms (at 667–668):

> 'And the Court not dealing in any way with any alleged infringement of the
> letters patent . . . by the manufacture of machines made subsequent to the date of
> the issue of the writ in this action, and being of opinion that the alleged
> infringements of the said letters patent mentioned in the statement of claim and
> particulars of breaches were not infringements of the said last-mentioned patent,
> doth not think fit to make any order for an injunction in respect of the said letters
> patent . . . and pursuant to s. 31 of the Patents, Designs, and Trade Marks Act, 1883,
> the judge doth certify that the validity of the said patent came into question.'

It was also ordered that it should be referred to the taxing master to tax the plaintiffs'
costs of the action 'so far as it relates to the issue of validity' of the patent and to tax the
defendants' costs of the action so far as they related to the issue of infringement of the
patent and a set-off of costs was ordered.

In a second action between the same parties in respect of the same patent, the
defendants again denied the validity of the patent. The question then arose whether the
defendants were estopped from raising in the second action the question of the validity
of the patent. They argued that they were not so estopped, as on the form of the
judgment as drawn up (there having been no declaration of the validity of the patent)
they could only appeal on two points, costs and the certificate of validity. But the Court
of Appeal, in an earlier case, had held that no appeal lay against the grant of a certificate
of validity. Romer J held that the question of the validity of the patent was res judicata
between the parties. In the course of his judgment he said (at 670–672):

> 'It was because the issue of validity had been found in favour of the plaintiffs that
> the Court ordered the defendants to pay the plaintiffs the costs of that issue; and
> because the plaintiffs had failed on the issue of infringement that the Court ordered
> the plaintiffs to pay the defendants' costs of that issue, and declared that there should
> be a set-off. Now clearly, in my judgment, that decision of the Court, so far as
> concerns the question of the validity of the patent, and the order which directed the
> defendants to pay the costs of that issue, could have been appealed from . . . I desire
> to say emphatically that I dealt with the issues separately, and it was because I came
> to a decision on the issues that I awarded the costs. And further, in my opinion, this
> sufficiently appears from the words of the judgment itself. It is not necessary, in
> considering the question of res judicata, that there should be an express finding in
> terms, if, when you look at the judgment and examine the issues raised before the
> Court, you see that the point came to be decided as a separate issue for decision, and
> was decided between the parties. It was not necessary, in my opinion, therefore, that
> there should be—though I agree that it might have been better if there had been—
> in the judgment in the case a separate declaration stating the validity of the patent:
> a declaration which clearly the Court had jurisdiction to put into the judgment if it
> had thought fit. . . . It appears to me that it sufficiently appears from this judgment
> that I did not dismiss this action so far as concerns this patent, and I found the issue
> of validity and determined it in favour of the plaintiffs, and I ordered the defendants
> to pay the costs of it. I cannot doubt that if the defendants had chosen to appeal
> from that part of the judgment they were entitled to have had that appeal heard by
> the Court of Appeal.'

The industry of counsel has only discovered one reported case in which *Shoe Machinery
Co v Cutlan* has been cited, viz the decision of the Privy Council in *Duedu v Yiboe* [1961] 1
WLR 1040. *Shoe Machinery Co v Cutlan* was there cited without any word of qualification,
but a careful reading of the decision shows that the proposition for which it was cited

(that an express finding in terms in a judgment is not necessary to found an estoppel)
a does not deal with the point whether the finding as to the validity of the patent in *Shoe Machinery Co v Cutlan* was fundamental to the substantive decision in that case and whether it was possible for the defendants to have appealed against a judgment in that particular form.

Shoe Machinery Co v Cutlan was a decision at first instance which is not binding on this court. Although it was decided over ninety years ago, no practice appears to have arisen
b based on it. Since the point was not argued before us, I say nothing as to the validity of the decision on its particular facts, so far as it relates to the issue of the validity of a patent when that is called in question, but I am not prepared to accept it as creating any general exception to the rule as set out in *Spencer-Bower and Turner* and cited above.

Counsel for the state also sought to argue that the witnesses could have appealed to the House of Lords against the order for costs made in the first Court of Appeal decision if
c this order was founded on a wrong view of the law, and in support of this proposition cited *Donald Campbell & Co Ltd v Pollak* [1927] AC 732. Whether or not they could have appealed against the order for costs seems to me to be immaterial: as I have already said, the question of appealability is no more than a test to decide whether a particular issue was fundamental to the substantive decision. I am satisfied that the first Court of Appeal determination on the jurisdiction issue was not fundamental to their substantive decision,
d which was to reject the first letter of request on the grounds of 'fishing' and (in the case of Kerr LJ) confidentiality. So in my judgment the witnesses are not precluded by issue estoppel from again raising the question whether the Sandefjord proceedings are qualifying proceedings under the 1975 Act.

I have some sympathy with the submission of counsel for the state that this decision
e can mean that the jurisdiction issue can in theory be relitigated on each occasion that a fresh letter of request is made, provided that all previous letters of request have been rejected on grounds that do not go to the issue of jurisdiction. However, I do not see why the court should not be asked to include in its order, where appropriate (ie if it considers that the issue has been fully argued and that all relevant evidence has been adduced), a declaration as to jurisdiction. Once such a declaration has been included in the order
f then an estoppel by record will arise; further, it would then be possible for the dissatisfied party (in this case the witnesses) to appeal against the declaration.

In the circumstances I do not find it necessary to reach a decision on the question, which was raised in the course of argument, whether it can ever be possible for jurisdiction to be conferred on the court by estoppel, eg because a party is estopped from denying the existence of a state of affairs necessary to found the court's jurisdiction in the
g particular case. However, I very much doubt whether jurisdiction can be conferred by estoppel: see 10 Halsbury's Laws (4th edn) para 718 and 26 ibid para 1501, note 3.

2. *What is the proper meaning of the phrase 'proceedings in any civil or commercial matter' in s 9(1) of the 1975 Act?*

Section 1 of the 1975 Act provides that, for the High Court to make an order for
h evidence to be obtained pursuant to a request from an overseas court, the High Court must be satisfied that the evidence is to be obtained 'for the purposes of civil proceedings' in the overseas court. Section 9(1) of the 1975 Act provides that '"civil proceedings", in relation to the requesting court, means proceedings in any civil or commercial matter.'

This issue (whether the Sandefjord proceedings fall within the ambit of the 1975 Act) was referred to as issue A in the first Court of Appeal decision. It requires the court to
j construe the phrase 'proceedings in any civil or commercial matter' in the context in which it appears in the 1975 Act. The first Court of Appeal considered that there were four possible categorisations, and no further possibilities were suggested in argument before us. They are: (1) a generally *acceptable* international interpretation (the first Court of Appeal referred to a generally *accepted* international interpretation, but it was never suggested, and cannot have been intended, that the construction adopted should depend

on some sort of international opinion poll); (2) classification under the law of the
requesting court; (3) classification under the law of the court addressed; (4) a combination *a*
of (2) and (3); the English court addressed would satisfy itself that the proceedings
concern a civil or commercial matter under the law of the requesting court, but would
only accept this categorisation for the purposes of assuming jurisdiction if it is not in
conflict with any fundamental principle recognised under English law.

Kerr LJ was evidently much attracted to the international interpretation. He considered
it at great length, but eventually rejected it because— *b*

'contrary to my first, and what would have been my preferred, conclusion, I find
it impossible, on the material before us, to give to "civil or commercial matter" in
s 9(1) of the 1975 Act any interpretation which can be seen as being broadly
acceptable internationally as well as within the three law districts of the United
Kingdom. The approach of the Court of Justice of the European Communities in *c*
Netherlands v Rüffer [1980] ECR 3807 would in my view undoubtedly provide the
best answer, *but on the material before us* it has not been established in the present
context.' (My emphasis.)

(See [1989] 1 All ER 661 at 680.)

So he eventually came down in favour of category (4).

Glidewell LJ had no such hesitation. He categorised the international approach as *d*
'neither logical nor desirable' (see [1989] 1 All ER 661 at 690). He, too, accepted category
(4), whilst acknowledging that this could result in a case in one requesting country being
a 'civil or commercial matter', whereas an identical case in another requesting country
would not, so that the English court would in every case have to consider the law of the
requesting country, and possibly be bound to entertain a request from one country,
whilst having to refuse a request in an identical case from another: see [1989] 1 All ER *e*
661 at 675.

On this issue Ralph Gibson LJ merely expressed his agreement with Glidewell LJ.

At one point in his judgment Kerr LJ said ([1989] 1 All ER 661 at 677):

'Throughout the hearing of this appeal I felt that if ever there was a case where
the assistance of an experienced comparative lawyer would have been welcome, this *f*
is so here.'

The witnesses hearkened to this cri de coeur, and their legal team before us was
augmented by the presence of Professor Jolowicz, who holds the chair of comparative
law at the University of Cambridge, and much new material, some of which is also
mentioned later in this judgment, was presented to us. We were also referred to a note *g*
'"Any Civil or Commercial Matter"' (1986) 102 LQR 505 by the distinguished
jurisprudent Dr F A Mann, expressing strong support for Kerr LJ's preferred international
interpretation.

Before I turn to the four possible categories in detail, I mention certain general matters
which in my judgment are appropriate for the court to consider in its approach to this
question of construction. *h*

(a) To an English lawyer a civil matter, in the context of proceedings in a court of law,
is any matter which is not criminal. Thus to an English lawyer a commercial matter is a
civil matter. The dichotomy 'any civil or commercial matter' has no meaning to an
English lawyer.

(b) It was common ground, both in the first Court of Appeal and before us, that the
1975 Act was passed mainly in order to give effect to the accession by the United *j*
Kingdom to the Hague Convention on the Taking of Evidence abroad in Civil or
Commercial Matters (The Hague, 18 March 1970, TS 20 (1977); Cmnd 6727). That this
was a purpose of the 1975 Act was recognised in the speeches of the House of Lords in *Re
Westinghouse Electric Corp Uranium Contract Litigation MDL Docket No 235 (Nos 1 and 2)*
[1978] 1 All ER 434, [1978] AC 547 (the *Westinghouse* case). It is true that the 1970
convention is not mentioned in the 1975 Act. However—

a   'it is now clear law that where the source of the legislation in question is not the
ordinary parliamentary process, but is an international treaty or convention and the
statute is designed to give effect to that treaty or convention, it is legitimate to look
at that source in order to resolve ambiguities in the legislation which has made those
treaty or convention provisions part of the ordinary municipal law of this country.'

b   (See *Fothergill v Monarch Airlines Ltd* [1980] 2 All ER 696 at 719, [1981] AC 251 at 299 per
Lord Roskill).

(c) The 1970 convention was concluded in the English and French languages, both
texts being equally authentic. In the English text the introduction includes the statement
'Desiring to improve mutual judicial co-operation *in civil or commercial matters*', while
Ch I, art 1 reads: '*In civil or commercial matters* a judicial authority of a Contracting State
may ... request the competent authority of another Contracting State ... to obtain
c   evidence'. In both these passages, and elsewhere in the 1970 convention (see art 15 and
17) the English phrase 'in civil or commercial matters' corresponds to the French phrase
'en matière civile ou commerciale.'

(d) In construing an international treaty (the Warsaw Convention relating to
international transportation by air (12 October 1929; TS 11 (1933); Cmd 4284) the
higher courts of the United States have enunciated certain principles of construction. In
d   *Block v Cie Nationale Air France* (1967) 386 F 2d 323 the US Court of Appeals (Fifth Circuit)
held that a multilateral treaty was like a 'uniform law' within the United States, and the
court had an obligation to keep interpretation as uniform as possible. In that case the
court noted that the underlying concepts of the convention were civilian in origin. The
majority felt (at 336) that—

e   'the determination in an American court of the meaning of an international
convention drawn by continental jurists is hardly possible without considering the
conception, parturition and growth of the convention.'

In *Air France v Saks* (1985) 84 L Ed 2d 289 the United States Supreme Court held that it
was the responsibility of the court to give the specific words of a treaty a meaning
consistent with the shared expectations of the contracting parties. The court said (at 297):
f

'We look to the French legal meaning for guidance as to these expectations
because the Warsaw Convention was drafted in French by continental jurists.'

I appreciate that these cases are concerned with the interpretation of an international
convention itself, but in my judgment we should apply similar principles in construing
g   the 1975 Act, passed to give effect to an international convention, and incorporating
phraseology taken from that convention which has no generally accepted meaning to an
English lawyer.

(e) International comity. As Kerr LJ said in the first Court of Appeal ([1989] 1 All ER
661 at 675): '... the court should strive to give effect to the request of the foreign court
unless it is driven to the clear conclusion that it cannot properly do so.' Whilst I accept
h   that this is a factor which must in any event be taken into account, in my judgment it is
of more significance when considering factors where the court has a discretion to exercise,
than where the court is seeking to construe the enabling Act to see whether or not it has
jurisdiction to accede to the request. In any event, it could point in the opposite direction
to the next factor.

(f) Consistency of interpretation. In my judgment there is much to be said in favour
j   of a construction which leads to the conclusion that what falls within the ambit of the
1975 Act does not depend upon the meaning given to 'civil or commercial matter' by the
law of the requesting court. Such a construction would permit the building up of a series
of precedents as to what does or does not fall within the ambit of the 1975 Act, without
in every case having to consider the law of the requesting court. This would enable the
English courts to deal with individual requests with a measure of certainty as to the
jurisdiction, and a consequent saving of costs to the parties.

With these introductory matters in mind, I turn to consider the four possible categories for the interpretation of 'civil or commercial matter'.   *a*

(1) *The international interpretation*
(i) 'Matière civile ou commerciale' (of which 'civil or commercial matter' is a translation) stems from French law. It is a concept current in many or all civil law systems, based on the Roman jus civile. This system has been categorised as belonging to the Romano-Germanic legal family, as distinct from the common law family and other   *b*
legal systems. A feature of this system is that the law has evolved, primarily for historical reasons, as an essentially private law, as a means of regulating the private relationships between individual citizens: see David and Brierley *Major Legal Systems in the World Today* (3rd edn, 1985) pp 22–24.
(ii) 'Matière' indicates the nature of the litigation, the subject matter of the dispute: see Dalloz *Lexique de Termes Juridiques* (5th edn, 1981) p 270.   *c*
(iii) In French law, and in other systems of law within the Romano-Germanic legal family, there is a distinction between 'civil' and 'commercial' law, which is rooted in history: see René David *English Law and French Law* (1980) at pp 36 ff, and *International Encyclopaedia of Comparative Law* vol 8, ch 2, 'Civil Law and Commercial Law' by D Tallon. From this latter work it appears that whilst those legal systems which recognise openly the autonomy of commercial law all belong to the Romano-Germanic legal   *d*
family, not all systems within that family recognise the autonomy (eg Switzerland), and in others (eg Holland and Italy) there is a movement for the merger of civil and commercial law. However, the Nordic countries (Sweden, Norway, Denmark, Finland and Iceland) have no autonomous system of commercial law. See also *International Encyclopaedia of Comparative Law*, vol 2, ch 2 'The Civil Law System' by C Szladits at pp 70–73.   *e*
(iv) Civil law countries draw a fundamental distinction between private and public law. This fundamental division is considered a basic division, the summa divisio, in all legal systems belonging to the civil law family of laws.

'Public law is that body of law which governs the affairs of the communities (the   *f*
states, municipalities, public corporations, etc.) among themselves and the acts of the authorities to which the individual is subject. Private law regulates legal relations in which persons confront each other as individuals, theoretically, at least, on an equal footing.'

(See *International Encyclopaedia of Comparative Law* vol 2, ch 2, by C Szladits, p 15 and see   *g*
also pp 20, 48.)
Whether fiscal matters are to be treated as part of administrative law, or as a separate category of their own, it is beyond dispute that they are part of public law. Civil or commercial matters are equally incontestably part of private law. 'According to the view held in continental European States, administrative matters (including fiscal matters) . . . fall outside the purview of the term "civil or commercial"' (see *Encyclopaedia of Public*   *h*
International Law vol 9, p 242). Apart from the citations above and those set out by Kerr LJ in [1989] 1 All ER 661 at 677, reference can also be made to Merryman and Clark *Comparative Law: Western European and Latin American Legal Systems* (1978) pp 819–820.
(v) The European Judgments Convention of 1968 (the Brussels convention), to which the United Kingdom acceded in 1978 and to which effect has been given by the Civil Jurisdiction and Judgments Act 1982, also applies in 'civil and commercial matters': see   *j*
art 1. In *Netherlands v Rüffer* Case 814/79 [1980] ECR 3807 the Court of Justice of the European Communities held that an action by a Dutch public authority to recover from the owner of a wrecked vessel the costs of removing the wreck from a public waterway was not a 'civil or commercial matter' within the ambit of the Brussels convention. The European Court followed its own earlier decisions there cited and held (at 3819 (para 7)):

'that the concept "civil and commercial matters" used in Article 1 of the Brussels
Convention must be regarded as an independent concept which must be construed
with reference first to the objectives and scheme of the Convention and secondly to
the general principles which stem from the corpus of the national legal systems.'

And later the court stated (at 3821 (para 14)):

'As the Court has stated in the authorities cited above the Brussels Convention
must be applied in such a way as to ensure, as far as possible, that the rights and
obligations which derive from it for the Contracting States and the persons to whom
it applies are equal and uniform. By that same case-law such a requirement rules
out the possibility of the Convention's being interpreted solely in the light of the
division of jurisdiction between the various types of courts existing in certain States:
on the contrary it implies that the area of application of the Convention is essentially
determined either by reason of the legal relationships between the parties to the
action or of the subject-matter of the action.'

I accept, of course, that this construction of the phrase 'civil or commercial matters' by
the European Court in the context of a different convention and as between members of
the European Economic Community cannot be decisive in the instant case. Nevertheless
the approach of the European Court in that case is one which I find persuasive and to
follow it would lead to a generally acceptable international interpretation of this widely-
used phrase.

Thus far I have followed, with some minor variations, the factors which Kerr LJ in the
first Court of Appeal decision considered as leading towards an international interpretation
(see [1989] 1 All ER 661 at 676). He then changed direction and listed those factors
which persuaded him, reluctantly, to abandon his preferred, international, interpretation
(see [1989] 1 All ER 661 at 676–677). I now consider these seriatim.

(vi) (a) The subject matter of the Brussels convention is the recognition and
enforcement of judgments; not merely judicial assistance for the provision of evidence
in foreign courts. In my judgment this is a distinction without a difference: both matters
are part of an international procedure. At the very least one approaches the question of
construction of a single phrase, 'matière civile ou commerciale', with an inclination to
give it the same meaning in each of the international conventions where it appears.
There is no logic in refusing to recognise a judgment based on a foreign tax claim, but to
be willing to assist in gathering evidence which may lead to an unenforceable judgment.

(b) The judgment of the Court of Justice of the European Communities is
'communautaire' within the EEC. Thus the phrase 'matière civile ou commerciale' has a
definitive interpretation for those countries which are members of the EEC. This
provides the best available guide for what is likely to receive general international
acceptance, what, in the course of argument, was described as 'the lowest common
denominator' as to the meaning of the phrase.

With all respect to Kerr LJ, I do not accept that the use of the words 'mutual judicial co-
operation' in the preamble to the 1970 convention points away from a multilateral, or
general international, interpretation of the convention. This is a phrase commonly used
in international conventions: see eg the 1931 convention between the United Kingdom
and Norway regarding legal proceedings which, incidentally, also applies 'only to civil
and commercial matters'. I do not find that the use of the word 'mutual' points either
towards, or against, an international interpretation.

(c) Article 1 of the Brussels convention, in the form in which it is set out in Sch 1 to
the Civil Jurisdiction and Judgments Act 1982, is in the following terms:

'This Convention shall apply in civil and commercial matters whatever the nature
of the court or tribunal. It shall not extend, in particular, to revenue, customs or
administrative matters.'

The second sentence, which was not part of the original text, and was added on the accession of Denmark, Ireland and the United Kingdom to the Brussels convention, was *a* not an amendment but a clarification of the scope of the convention: see Kohler 'Case Law of the European Court on the Judgments Convention, Part II' (1982) 7 EL Rev 104. Thus, while agreeing with Kerr LJ that it is unfortunate that there was no similar clarification in the 1970 convention or the 1975 Act, I do not accept that this suggests a different interpretation of the phrase 'civil or commercial matter' in the 1970 convention or the 1975 Act: indeed the contrary is the case.   *b*

(vii) As Kerr LJ points out (see [1989] 1 All ER 661 at 678–679), s 2 of the Foreign Tribunals Act 1856 points away from a purely common law categorisation of the phrase 'civil or commercial matter', although it is fair to say that that section points more towards an interpretation according to the law of the requesting court than to an international interpretation. However, the Evidence by Commission Acts 1859 and 1885, since they do not use the phrase at all, throw no light on the question.   *c*

(viii) Since it is common ground that the 1975 Act was passed mainly to give effect to the 1970 convention and that reference could be made to the 1970 convention in construing the 1975 Act the fact that the 1975 Act does not expressly refer to the 1970 convention is irrelevant (see [1989] 1 All ER 661 at 679).

(ix) The fact that the common law does not, yet, recognise any clear distinction between public and private law is, in my judgment, irrelevant, because one cannot *d* approach the construction of the phrase 'civil or commercial matter' in the 1975 Act from a common law standpoint. As I have already said, this phrase to a common lawyer has no sensible meaning. To a civilian it has a very clear meaning. I accept that, as the 1975 Act applies between the courts of the different parts of the United Kingdom, as it does in relation to all foreign countries, the internationalist interpretation will result in inter-United Kingdom requests for evidence in civil proceedings being based upon a *e* categorisation by reference to the civil law. But this is the result of Parliament using a phrase having meaning only to a civilian lawyer, and in my judgment this is a small price to pay for the uniformity and consistency of approach which, as I have said in the introductory para (f) above, is an approach to be favoured.

(x) This point falls to be dealt with more conveniently under classifications (2) to (4). *f*

So, in my judgment, the factors which led Kerr LJ to abandon his preferred international interpretation, when carefully analysed, do not lead to that conclusion.

I can now summarise my reasons for favouring the international interpretation.

(i) The phrase 'civil or commercial matter' has no intelligible meaning at common law. Unless the words 'or commercial' are to be ignored, the use of the phrase points away from a common law interpretation of the word 'civil', ie a purely procedural *g* interpretation. This is reinforced by the use of the word 'matter' as indicating the subject matter of the litigation.

(ii) In the 1970 convention, to give effect to which the 1975 Act was passed, the words 'in civil or commercial matters' correspond to the French phrase 'en matière civile ou commerciale'.

(iii) In civil law countries the dichotomy between civil and commercial law is *h* widespread. In those countries the phrase 'civil matter' would not include a commercial matter: hence the inclusion of the words 'or commercial'.

(iv) So the use of the phrase 'civil or commercial matter' in the 1975 Act points to a civilian meaning for those words.

For the purposes of this judgment I do not find it necessary or desirable to consider what matters are, according to this interpretation, included within, or excluded from, *j* the scope of the phrase 'civil or commercial matters'. It is sufficient to say that no civil law country would ever treat a disputed tax claim as being a civil or commercial matter.

For these reasons I favour the generally acceptable international interpretation, ie an interpretation according to the civil law, of the phrase 'proceedings in any civil or commercial matter' in s 9(1) of the 1975 Act. However, before coming to a final conclusion on this question, it is necessary to consider the other possible categorisations.

(2) Classification under the law of the requesting court

a   This categorisation was rejected by the first Court of Appeal and was not pursued before us. If the English court were to be wholly bound by the classification of the requesting court, it might be required to assist in criminal or penal proceedings (as classified by English law), even though these were classified as 'proceedings in a civil or commercial matter' by the requesting court. This would be contrary to well-established principles of English jurisprudence: see *Huntington v Attrill* [1893] AC 150 at 155, a case

b which was cited to the first Court of Appeal, although not referred to in the judgments.

(3) Classification under the law of the court addressed, ie English law

    Although this categorisation was rejected by the first Court of Appeal and was not pursued before us, it cannot be dismissed out of hand. Although the instinctive reaction

c of a common lawyer is to give the phrase 'civil or commercial matter' a procedural interpretation (see e g *Re Gross, ex p Treasury Solicitor* [1968] 3 All ER 804 at 806, [1969] 1 WLR 12 at 15 per Chapman J) nevertheless English courts can and do draw distinctions as a matter of substance between criminal and civil matters, regardless of the form of the proceedings. Thus in *Bonalumi v Secretary of State for the Home Dept* [1985] 1 All ER 797, [1985] QB 675 this court held that an order made on an application in the High Court by

d the Home Secretary under the Bankers' Books Evidence Act 1879 to inspect the bank accounts of Mr Bonalumi, so that they could be used as evidence in criminal proceedings in Sweden, was an order made in a criminal cause or matter under s 18(1)(*a*) of the Supreme Court Act 1981, so as to exclude an appeal to the Court of Appeal, notwithstanding the civil procedural form of the application. Nevertheless, the obvious difficulty in giving an English interpretation to the phrase is the dichotomy between

e 'civil' and 'commercial' which, as I have already said more than once, has no intelligible meaning to an English lawyer.

(4) The combination of (2) and (3)

    This was the preferred categorisation of the first Court of Appeal: reluctantly on the

f part of Kerr LJ; without hesitation on the part of Glidewell LJ, with whom Ralph Gibson LJ agreed. In the note to which I have already referred, Dr Mann said that if possibility (2) was inapposite, as he held it was for reasons developed in *Huntington v Attrill* [1893] AC 150, 'possibility (4) must necessarily suffer the same fate' (see (1986) 102 LQR 505 at 507). No one before us sought to support the exclusion of possibility (4) on this basis, for the very good reason, as stated by Kerr LJ ([1989] 1 All ER 661 at 680), that the

g combination of English law with the law of the requesting court was for just this purpose: to ensure that the English court would not be precluded from rejecting a classification by the law of the requesting court if this offended fundamental principles of English law.

    Nevertheless, the same problems will arise under this head as arise under classification (3) above, viz where the law of the requesting court, like English law, does not recognise

h the dichotomy between 'civil' and 'commercial'. This would be the case when a request comes from any country with a system of law derived from the common law and, on the evidence before us, is equally the case under Norwegian law, which primarily uses 'civil' in a procedural sense to distinguish it from 'criminal'. But when the law of the requesting court, as with English law, does not normally make a distinction between 'civil' and 'commercial' matters according to subject matter, then a difficulty is bound to arise. That

j difficulty is well exemplified in the present case by the voluminous evidence of Norwegian law, with Professor Fleischer on behalf of the state of Norway stating categorically that the Sandefjord proceedings are civil proceedings under Norwegian law, whereas Professors Huser, Bernt and Haerem, for the witnesses, were equally firm that the Sandefjord proceedings were not proceedings in a civil or commercial matter according to Norwegian law. This difference was not resolved by the cross-examination (at length) of these eminent jurists, and by the nature of things could not have been, for

a perusal of their affidavits and the transcripts of their cross-examination makes it clear
that they were approaching the question from wholly different standpoints; Professor
Fleischer from a procedural standpoint, the others from a substantive one. The dilemma
is well expressed in the following passage from the judgment of Glidewell LJ in the first
Court of Appeal ([1989] 1 All ER 661 at 689–690):

> 'If proceedings similar to those in the Sandefjord court were taking place in the
> High Court in England, and that court applied for an order for the examination of
> witnesses to a court in a jurisdiction whose relevant statute was in terms identical to
> those of the 1975 Act, the English High Court would of course say that the
> proceedings were civil proceedings. But, if asked to explain its process of reasoning,
> it might do so in some such terms as these: "We do not usually categorise actions
> which come before our courts in terms of their subject matter. We do so in order to
> comply with ss 1 and 9 of your statute. We say that these proceedings are civil
> proceedings under English law; therefore they are proceedings in a 'civil matter';
> therefore they are civil proceedings within the definition in your statute." It seems
> to me that this circular process of reasoning is, in essence, that adopted by the
> Solicitor General of Norway in his affidavit of 26 June 1985. I therefore do not share
> the doubts which have troubled Kerr LJ whether the evidence before us should
> satisfy us that the Sandefjord proceedings are "in a civil . . . matter". In my view the
> evidence makes it clear that they are.'

With all respect to Glidewell LJ I do not agree with the reasoning contained in the
following passage: 'We say that these proceedings are civil proceedings under English
law; therefore they are proceedings in a "civil matter".' I do not accept that, because
proceedings may be civil proceedings under English law (classified procedurally), *therefore*
they are proceedings in a 'civil matter' (classified substantively), more especially where
the context requires that a 'civil' matter must be distinguished from a 'commercial'
matter, although both are, by English procedural tests, 'civil' proceedings.

So, although I can understand the reasons which prompted the first Court of Appeal to
choose the fourth categorisation, in my judgment it provides a less satisfactory
interpretation then the international interpretation, ie category (1).

So I answer the main question 2 above: the proper meaning of the phrase 'proceedings
in any civil or commercial matter' in s 9(1) of the 1975 Act is that which accords with a
generally acceptable international interpretation, which is the meaning which a civilian
lawyer would give to the phrase. This necessarily excludes a disputed tax claim, and
therefore excludes the Sandefjord proceedings.

In view of my answer to main question 2, issues 3 and 4 do not arise. However, as it
seems probable that this case will go further, I venture to express an opinion on these
issues recognising, as I do, that my views are necessarily obiter!

3. *The Norwegian law issue*

On the basis (contrary to my view expressed above) that Norwegian law is relevant in
determining whether the Sandefjord proceedings are qualifying proceedings under the
1975 Act, the judge held that these proceedings are 'proceedings in any civil or
commercial matter' according to the law of Norway. His reasons for reaching this
conclusion may be summarised as follows.

(i) This was the conclusion in the first Court of Appeal decision, on the evidence then
before that court. At the very least this threw the evidential burden of proving the
contrary on to the witnesses.

(ii) The evidence before the first Court of Appeal included the affidavit of the Solicitor
General of Norway sworn on the first application. Although there was no affidavit of the
Solicitor General before the judge, he said: 'I regard that as a technicality and I can take
full account of paras 4 and 5 of the Solicitor General's affidavit of 26th June 1985 and
treat its contents as being in evidence before me.' (The effect of those paragraphs was that

the Sandefjord proceedings were civil proceedings for the purpose of the courts' system
a and the administration of justice in Norway, ie applying a procedural test in the same
way that they would be described as 'civil proceedings' if they were being carried on in
an English court.)

(iii) By issuing the letters of request, the Norwegian court was evidently satisfied that
the request was a proper one. (This was a ground on which the first Court of Appeal
relied, and which the judge took as his starting point.)

b   (iv) The evidence of the Norwegian professors before him disclosed a division so deep
that it did not enable him to say with confidence that the evidential burden thrown on
the witnesses had been discharged. However, if he had to make a choice, he preferred
the evidence of Professor Fleischer for the state that the Sandefjord proceedings were
proceedings in a civil matter under Norwegian law.

These findings are attacked by the witnesses on a number of grounds.

c   (a) Before the hearing before Kenneth Jones J, the parties had expressly agreed that
the affidavit of the Solicitor General should not be treated as evidence, expert or otherwise,
on the second application. Neither counsel invited the judge to rely on this affidavit.
This contention is borne out by the correspondence between the parties, and counsel for
the state did not seek to argue the contrary before us. In my judgment, therefore, it is
clear that, in reaching his decision on this issue, the judge took into account material on
d   which he was not entitled to rely.

(b) The issuance of the letters of request, being in a form submitted by the lawyers for
the state of Norway and the estate of Anders Jahre, was no evidence of Norwegian law on
the question which the English court had to decide. In my judgment the fact that the
Norwegian court saw fit to issue the letters of request in their form as drafted, which, in
the case of the second letter of request, asserts that the Sandefjord action 'is a civil action
e   under the law of Norway, and the proceedings are a "civil matter" under the law of
Norway, for the purposes of' the 1970 convention, is a matter which an English court
must take into account on this issue. However, it is not something to which, in the
circumstances in which the letters of request were prepared, the English court should
attach great weight (see the *Westinghouse* case [1978] 1 All ER 434 at 442–443, [1978] AC
f   547 at 609–610 per Lord Wilberforce).

(c) These errors vitiate the judge's conclusions on the Norwegian law issue. We could,
if necessary, order a retrial of the Norwegian law issue before another judge, but since his
decision did not turn on the question of credibility of the expert witnesses, this court is
in as good a position as he was to decide this issue, albeit technically one of fact. I agree:
see *Dalmia Dairy Industries Ltd v National Bank of Pakistan* [1978] 2 Lloyd's Rep 223 at 285–
g   286.

(d) On a proper analysis of the evidence of the four professors, Norwegian law would
not, *as a matter of substance*, characterise the Sandefjord proceedings as a civil matter. As I
have already said, it is clear that the Norwegian lawyers were faced with the same
problem as English lawyers: that the dichotomy between 'civil' and 'commercial' matters
is not one with which Norwegian law is familiar, because Norwegian lawyers, like
h   English lawyers, would normally adopt a procedural approach. However, for the same
reasons that have persuaded me against the adoption of category (4) under issue 2 above,
it seems to me that the evidence given on behalf of the witnesses is to be preferred to that
of Professor Fleischer on behalf of the state of Norway on this issue.

So, had it been material, I would have answered question 3 by saying that the
Sandefjord proceedings are not 'proceedings in any civil or commercial matter' according
j   to the law of Norway.

4. *Fishing/confidentiality*

(a) *Fishing.* I approach this issue with Lord Wilberforce's statement in the *Westinghouse*
case [1978] 1 All ER 434 at 444, [1978] AC 547 at 612 very much in my mind:

'... following the spirit of the 1975 Act which is to enable judicial assistance to be given to foreign courts, the letters rogatory ought to be given effect to so far as possible ...'

Having carefully considered the second letter of request, I am satisfied that, subject to the detailed modifications ordered by Kenneth Jones J to paras 6, 7, 10 and 12 of Sch 1 to the letter, and to one further modification mentioned below, the second letter of request cannot be rejected, as was the first letter of request, as a fishing application. The one further modification to which I refer relates to para 8 of Sch 1. Kenneth Jones J rejected this paragraph in toto. In its original form I am not surprised at that decision, but in the course of the hearing before us the State of Norway put in a modified proposal for para 8. If that paragraph were amended to read:

'If the settlor of the shares and/or assets was Anders Jahre or his nominee or agent, what was or were: the name of the "Foundation", its constitution and objects, and the names of the Trustees and beneficiaries, and who had authority to elect or remove Trustees and to alter the trust deed; were the financial aspects of the "Foundation" including its accounts managed from Norway?'

I would have been prepared to restore the paragraph, thus modified, to the second letter of request.

(b) *Confidentiality.* As the judge said, following Kerr LJ in the first Court of Appeal, the resolution of this issue requires the performance of a balancing exercise by the court. The judge exercised his discretion on this question and I know of no reason why this court should interfere with that exercise.

Conclusion

For the reasons given in my answers to questions 1 and 2 above, I would allow this appeal and discharge the order of Master Creightmore dated 2 April 1986.

WOOLF LJ. I am saved the burden of having to set out the background to the present appeal as this has already been clearly set out in the judgments of May and Balcombe LJJ and the earlier judgments of the other division of the court. The long history of these proceedings does not disclose a happy situation. The Hague Convention on the Taking of Evidence abroad in Civil or Commercial Matters (The Hague, 18 March 1970; TS 20 (1977); Cmnd 6727) was implemented to 'improve mutual judicial co-operation in civil or commercial matters'. The Evidence (Proceedings in other Jurisdictions) Act 1975 was intended to give effect to the United Kingdom's ratification of the convention and, in the terms of its long title, 'to assist in obtaining evidence required for the purpose of proceedings in other jurisdictions'. It is indeed unfortunate that notwithstanding these commendable objectives of the Act and the convention these proceedings should have been so drawn out and expensive. However, this history is explained partly by the difficulty, complexity and importance of the issues involved and partly by the fact that on the previous occasion when the proceedings were before the Court of Appeal (the first appeal), as Kerr LJ made clear in his judgment (see [1989] 1 All ER 661 at 681, 689), the parties did not provide all the assistance and evidence needed to come to an exhaustive determination of the issues involved. In this appeal we certainly cannot complain of too little assistance. It is out of deference to that assistance that I set out my own reasoning even though by doing so I risk dulling the clarity which the judgments of May and Balcombe LJJ have introduced to the issues, since I come to the same conclusion as they do by a route which is mine alone.

The jurisdiction issue

The most important issue before this court is undoubtedly the question as to whether the proceedings which have been brought by the estate of Anders Jahre before the City

Court of Sandefjord are civil proceedings as defined in s 9(1) of the 1975 Act. That is to
a say, are they proceedings in a 'civil or commercial matter'? If they are not proceedings in
a civil or commercial matter then it is quite clear that the High Court has no jurisdiction
to assist the Norwegian court and it is for this reason that it is appropriate to refer to this
issue as being the jurisdiction issue.

If there had not been the previous proceedings in relation to the first letter of request,
in order to determine the jurisdiction issue the court's task would be confined to having
b to determine the proper interpretation of 'proceedings in any civil or commercial matter'
in the context of the 1975 Act and then to apply that interpretation in order to decide
whether the Norwegian proceedings were proceedings in a civil or commercial matter.
However, because of the first appeal in relation to the first letter of request, it is also
necessary to consider whether this court is bound as a matter of legal precedent to follow
the interpretation given on the first appeal and whether issue estoppel operates so as to
c prevent this court in relation to the second letter of request departing from the
determination on the first appeal that the Norwegian proceedings were in fact proceedings
in a civil or commercial matter.

It is preferable to deal with these questions of legal precedent and issue estoppel at the
outset.

d *Precedent*

It is not surprising that before Kenneth Jones J, it was not argued on behalf of the
witnesses that the interpretation of the 1975 Act adopted by the Court of Appeal at the
first hearing should not be followed by him. Obviously, whether or not the interpretation
of the provisions of the Act by the Court of Appeal were strictly binding on him, Kenneth
Jones J would feel most reluctant to adopt a different interpretation. However, before
e this court counsel for the estate sought to reopen the whole question of interpretation
and in doing so had the assistance of a distinguished comparative lawyer, the absence of
whom Kerr LJ had regretted in his judgment in the first appeal. In addition counsel has
relied on a substantial quantity of what I will call additional international material in
support of his argument. With this help, counsel submits an international interpretation
ought to be given to the definition of civil proceedings contained in s 9(1) of the 1975
f Act.

As I read the judgments of this court on the first appeal, there are at least differences in
emphasis between the approach which was adopted to the question of interpretation by
Glidewell LJ (with whom Ralph Gibson LJ agreed on this point) and Kerr LJ. Glidewell
and Kerr LJJ (Kerr LJ reluctantly) did not apply to the definition contained in the Act a
'generally accepted international interpretation' and decided that what was required
g before the court could give effect to an application for assistance by the foreign court was
that the application should relate to proceedings which would be classified both under
the law of the requesting court and under the law of this the addressee court as
proceedings concerning a civil or commercial matter. However, Kerr LJ left open the
question whether or not the view of the court addressed on the question of classification
h went to jurisdiction or discretion and continued ([1989] 1 All ER 661 at 680–681):

'Where does that leave the present case? If the *substance* of a dispute is clearly a
matter of *public* law in the jurisprudence of the requesting court, then I would not
accept that it can properly be regarded as "matière civile ou commerciale" for the
purposes of the 1970 convention or any legislation based on it. But although I regard
the evidence on Norwegian law as insufficiently searching, particularly on the
j characterisation of the substance of these proceedings by reference to the distinction
between public and private law which may well be recognised in Norway as in civil
law countries, I do not feel able to conclude on the evidence that the Sandefjord
action cannot be regarded as a proceeding in a civil matter by the law of Norway.
Counsel for the state offered to produce a further affidavit on this point, but we

declined it at this late stage. However, since the Norwegian court was evidently
satisfied that the request was a proper one under its own law, and the evidence of   *a*
the Solicitor General supports it, I would reluctantly give it the benefit of the doubt,
which I nevertheless retain. In any event, in view of my conclusions on issues E and
F, in this judgment the matter becomes academic. I would only add that if a similar
issue should arise in the future, I hope that our courts will be provided with more
satisfactory evidence in the light of the considerations to which I have referred.'

Glidewell LJ thought it was most unlikely that the need to comply with the English   *b*
classification would cause any difficulty since, as he said ([1989] 1 All ER 661 at 684):

  'We have no evidence that there is any jurisdiction which *proceedings* in a "civil or
  commercial matter" would not be regarded as *civil proceedings* in the English sense.'
  (My emphasis.)

In addition Glidewell LJ took the view that, where under the law of the requesting state   *c*
the classification of the proceedings would not normally be on the basis of their subject
matter but on their procedural characteristics, eg whether they were criminal or civil
proceedings, it was perfectly appropriate to adopt a procedural rather than a substantive
classification. However, both Kerr and Glidewell LJJ, on the evidence before them, came
to the conclusion that under Norwegian law the proceedings would be classified as a civil   *d*
or commercial matter which meant that if the first letter of request was in a satisfactory
form the state and the estate would have succeeded on the appeal. However, both Kerr
and Glidewell LJJ (differing from Ralph Gibson LJ) were of the view that, having regard
to the terms of the request which they regarded as 'fishing', it would not be appropriate
for the court to give effect to the first letter of request and on this ground by a majority
the witnesses' appeal was allowed.   *e*

In these circumstances although counsel for the witnesses did not go so far as to submit
that the views expressed by this court on the first appeal as to interpretation were obiter,
he did submit that they did not form part of the ratio which was binding on this court.
In a powerful, succinct and highly persuasive argument counsel for the estate accepted
that this court was not strictly bound by the previous decision on the question of
interpretation but submitted that as the decision on the first appeal was reached following   *f*
detailed argument and after careful consideration, this court, as a matter of propriety
between two courts of co-ordinate jurisdiction, should not in the absence of the most
compelling circumstances depart from the interpretation adopted.

That the previous decision is not strictly binding upon this court is in my view made
clear by the decision of this court in *Penn-Texas Corp v Murat Anstalt (No 2)* [1964] 2 All
ER 594, [1964] 2 QB 647, a decision which happened to involve the interpretation of the   *g*
predecessor of the 1975 Act, namely the Foreign Tribunals Evidence Act 1856. Lord
Denning MR having indicated that—

  'a previous judgment between the same parties is only conclusive on matters
  which were essential and necessary to the decision. It is not conclusive on other
  matters which came incidentally into consideration in the course of the reasoning . . .'   *h*

made the following statement which would apply equally to these proceedings:

  'The ruling on the second point in *Penn-Texas (No. 1)* ([1963] 1 All ER 258, [1964]
  1 QB 40) was not necessary to the decision. The result would have been the same,
  even if the ruling had been the other way. The ruling is not, therefore, absolutely
  binding, and we are at liberty to depart from it if convinced it is wrong.'   *j*

(See [1964] 2 All ER 594 at 597, [1964] 2 QB 647 at 660–661.)

In support of his submission counsel for the estate referred the court to *Slack v Leeds
Industrial Co-op Society Ltd* [1923] 1 Ch 431. In that case, with regard to dicta which did
not constitute a decision binding on a subsequent court, Lord Sterndale MR said (at 451):

'Dicta are of different kinds and of varying degrees of weight. Sometimes they
may be called almost casual expressions of opinion upon a point which has not been
raised in the case, and is not really present to the judge's mind. Such dicta, though
entitled to the respect due to the speaker, may fairly be disregarded by judges before
whom the point has been raised and argued in a way to bring it under much fuller
consideration. Some dicta however are of a different kind; they are, although not
necessary for the decision of the case, deliberate expressions of opinion given after
consideration upon a point clearly brought and argued before the Court. It is open
no doubt to other judges to give decisions contrary to such dicta, but much greater
weight attaches to them than to the former class.'

At the end of his judgment Lord Sterndale MR added (at 452):

'I am of opinion ... that if opinions of such weight given after such careful
consideration more than thirty years ago, often mentioned and considered during
that time and never disapproved, are to be overruled, it should only be done by the
final tribunal of appeal and not by a Court of co-ordinate jurisdiction.'

Warrington LJ said very much the same thing (at 456).

Counsel for the estate submitted that in this case, having regard to the care with which
the matter was dealt with on the first appeal, the decision of this court in relation to the
nature of the Norwegian proceedings is within the top scale of judicial dicta and should
only be overruled by the House of Lords and not this court.

Counsel for the estate also in the course of his argument examined the submissions
before the other division of this court and the new material relied on by counsel for the
witnesses and contended that the witnesses' case has not materially changed so there was
no compelling reason justifying this court departing from the previous decision. While
there are obviously differing standards of dicta and the previous court's conclusion on the
jurisdiction issue commands the greatest respect, it is material that Kerr LJ regarded the
point as being 'academic' and regretted the absence of the additional assistance which this
court has had. Furthermore, as Balcombe LJ has pointed out, the House of Lords in *Slack's*
case took a very different view from the Court of Appeal. In this situation the appropriate
approach is that indicated by Lord Denning MR to which reference has already been
made. This court should follow the earlier decision unless we are satisfied it is wrong.

Issue estoppel

Although I have dealt with this aspect of the appeal as though the question were one
of judicial precedent, in argument it was also approached on the basis of res judicata.
However, as the previous court's conclusions on the jurisdiction issue were unnecessary
for their decision there can be no question of res judicata. The position is, however,
different with regard to issue estoppel. The previous decision of the Court of Appeal was
unanimous (although Kerr LJ was reluctant and retained doubts as to its correctness) that
the proceedings before the Sandefjord court would be classified under Norwegian law as
proceedings in a civil or commercial matter. This was a decision on an important issue
in the proceedings. However, it is to be noted that while it is a determination of fact as
to the categorisation of the proceedings under foreign law, that finding of fact depends
on the construction which is placed upon the vital phrase 'civil or commercial matter'
and the difference of emphasis as to this, to which I have already drawn attention,
explains why Glidewell LJ found the determination of this issue more straightforward
than did Kerr LJ. Kerr LJ lays more stress on the substance of the proceedings in the
Norwegian court than Glidewell LJ, who considered the Norwegian court would
determine the matter having regard to the nature of the proceedings rather than their
subject matter. Accordingly, if the approach adopted by Glidewell LJ is, in the view of
this court, not the appropriate method of classification, this could affect the premise on
which the argument in favour of issue estoppel is based.

Kenneth Jones J came to the conclusion that there was no issue estoppel because, having regard to the Court of Appeal's conclusions which were in favour of the witnesses, the witnesses were not in a position to appeal on this issue: a test referred to by Lord Denning MR in *Penn-Texas v Murat Anstalt (No 2)* [1964] 2 All ER 594, [1964] 2 QB 647. While counsel for the state accepted that the availability of a right of appeal was a useful rule of thumb, he correctly submitted that the fundamental question was whether a previous finding was 'essential and necessary to the decision', and he also submitted that in fact there was a right of appeal in this case and in any event, if there was not, the absence of a right of appeal did not mean that issue estoppel could not arise.

Having regard to the argument which counsel for the state advanced based on the order for costs which was made by the Court of Appeal on the previous hearing, I would be prepared to accept that technically it would have been possible for the witnesses to have sought leave to appeal in respect of the Court of Appeal's decision in respect of the first letter of request. However, I regard it as quite unrealistic to expect the witnesses to have tried to exercise any such right of appeal and I am certain that if they had sought to do so, they would never have received leave. In these circumstances, in considering whether issue estoppel operates, the only realistic approach is that adopted by the judge. The decision on the first appeal in respect of the issue as to the method of classification which would be adopted under Norwegian law can be treated as not being the subject of a right of appeal. It is relevant here to refer to the speech of Lord Upjohn in *Carl-Zeiss-Stiftung v Rayner & Keeler Ltd (No 2)* [1966] 2 All ER 536 at 573, [1967] 1 AC 853 at 947:

> 'As my noble and learned friend, Lord Reid, has already pointed out there may be many reasons why a litigant in the earlier litigation has not pressed or may even for good reasons have abandoned a particular issue. It may be most unjust to hold him precluded from raising that issue in subsequent litigation (and see Lord Maugham, L.C.'s observations in the *New Brunswick Rly Co v British and French Trust Corp* ([1938] 4 All ER 747, [1939] AC 1)). All estoppels are not odious but must be applied so as to work justice and not injustice, and I think that the principle of issue estoppel must be applied to the circumstances of the subsequent case with this overriding consideration in mind.'

Earlier in his speech Lord Upjohn had also pointed out that with regard to res judicata generally, that issue estoppel—

> 'goes beyond the mere record; it is part of the law of evidence for, to see whether it applies, the facts and reasons given by the judge, his judgement, the pleadings, the evidence and even the history of the matter may be taken into account . . .'

(See [1966] 2 All ER 536 at 572, [1967] 1 AC 853 at 946.)

Adopting this approach to the previous proceedings in this case, I have no doubt that it would be wrong to regard the witnesses as being disentitled from re-opening the question of Norwegian law which inferentially if not expressly Kerr LJ was inviting them to do in any subsequent proceedings. As to *Shoe Machinery Co v Cutlan* [1896] 1 Ch 667 I respectfully adopt the analysis of the effect of that case set out by Balcombe LJ in his judgment.

However, even if I were minded to take a different view, I would not have felt it right on the issue of classification under Norwegian law to have treated the issue as being the subject of issue estoppel. If the witnesses' contention as to Norwegian law was right, then subject to the question as to the proper interpretation of s 9 of the 1975 Act, the proper classification of the Norwegian proceedings would determine whether the English court had jurisdiction to act on the letter of request. The jurisdiction of the High Court to act on the Norwegian court's request is purely statutory and is dependent on the English court being satisfied that the evidence to which the application relates is required for the purposes set out in s 1(b) of the 1975 Act. If there is evidence available to the court which would indicate that the evidence requested was not required for this purpose, then no principle of estoppel can prevent the court investigating the matter. The parties cannot a confer jurisdiction under the 1975 Act on the court by consent and this being so, I cannot see how the failure of one party in previous proceedings to produce evidence or to advance an argument going to the issue of jurisdiction can prevent the court considering that evidence in subsequent proceedings where the same question of jurisdiction arises. Despite the researches of counsel no previous decision was found which in relation to the High Court clearly established that this was the situation. However, it seems to me that the principle is so clear and so obvious that it can be said with confidence that a party

b cannot be prevented by any rule of issue estoppel from putting before the court evidence to establish that the court has no jurisdiction to make the order which is being sought.

Counsel for the state correctly warned the court of the dangers of adopting this view because of the risk of the same issue being constantly relitigated. However, this risk is reduced by the fact that the court can always protect itself against abuse of its process by preventing an issue being raised vexatiously independently of estoppel and what I have

c said as to the question of jurisdiction would not apply where the previous decision constitutes a binding precedent.

Construction of civil or commercial matter

d On this issue I acknowledge at the outset that I have derived considerable assistance from the judgment of Kerr LJ on the first appeal. However, although I accept and gratefully adopt a substantial proportion of Kerr LJ's reasoning, I ultimately differ from his conclusion in a way which is highly significant to the outcome of this appeal.

Before turning to matters of detail which cause me to differ from the conclusions of Kerr LJ, I regard it as necessary to draw attention to certain broad features of the 1975

e Act.

1. Although the 1975 Act was undoubtedly passed in order to give effect to the principles of the 1970 convention, the Act applies to letters of request in respect of civil proceedings pending or contemplated from any country irrespective of whether or not the countries subscribe to the 1970 convention.

2. The 1975 Act clearly draws a distinction between civil and criminal proceedings

f and whatever the context in which the phrase civil proceedings is used in the Act it does not include and is used in contradistinction to criminal proceedings.

3. While the 1970 convention is not expressly referred to in the 1975 Act it is clear (as was accepted by all their Lordships in *Rio Tinto Zinc Corp v Westinghouse Electric Corp, RTZ Services Ltd v Westinghouse Electric Corp* [1978] 1 All ER 434, [1978] AC 547, and by the parties on this appeal) that part of the purpose of the Act was to give effect to the

g 1970 convention. Accordingly, it is appropriate to have regard to the 1970 convention for assistance in interpreting the 1975 Act in so far as its language does not make its meaning clear. However, it should not be forgotten in seeking aid from the convention that the Act also applies to the different jurisdictions within the United Kingdom and therefore it would be less likely that Parliament would intend an international interpretation to be adopted if that international interpretation would lead to difficulties

h in applying the Act within the United Kingdom.

4. Although in the *Westinghouse* case their Lordships did not consider any assistance could be obtained from the legislation which the 1975 Act replaced (see eg [1978] 1 All ER 434 at 461, [1978] AC 547 at 633 per Lord Diplock on this issue) it is relevant to note that the 1975 Act replaced the Foreign Tribunals (Evidence) Act 1856 and the Evidence

j by Commission Acts 1859 and 1885 and while the former Act which applied to requests from foreign courts referred expressly to civil or commercial matters the later Acts which dealt with requests within 'Her Majesty's dominions' did not do so.

5. The definition in s 9(1) of civil proceedings as meaning proceedings in any civil or commercial *matter* indicates that whether the proceedings are civil proceedings in the requesting court is not to be decided by evaluating the procedure adopted but on the

basis of the subject matter of the proceedings. While Glidewell LJ is no doubt right in saying 'we do not usually categorise actions which come before our courts in terms of their subject matter' (see [1989] 1 All ER 661 at 689–690), the English courts can and sometimes have to do so. For example, for the purposes of s 18(1)(a) of the Supreme Court Act 1981 and for the purposes of RSC Ord 53, r 3(4) it is necessary to decide whether proceedings are in a criminal cause or matter and in order to decide whether this is the case it is necessary to examine the substance of the proceedings. Although an application for judicial review procedurally would be classified as civil, it becomes a criminal cause or matter if the application for judicial review is in relation to the decision of a magistrate's court in a criminal matter such as a motoring offence. On the other hand an application for judicial review in respect of a decision by a magistrate's court exercising its criminal jurisdiction to forfeit recognisances entered into by sureties in respect of bail granted to an accused charged with a criminal offence is not a criminal cause or matter. As Lord Denning MR said in *R v Southampton Justices, ex p Green* [1975] 2 All ER 1073 at 1076, [1976] 1 QB 11 at 15:

> 'A recognisance is in the nature of a bond. A failure to fulfil it gives rise to a civil debt. It is different from the ordinary kind of civil debt, because the enforcement is different. It is enforceable like a fine . . . But that method of enforcement does not alter the nature of the debt. It is simply a civil debt on a bond and as such it is not a criminal cause or matter.'

6. Although the definition in s 9(1) relates to civil proceedings in the requesting court, there is nothing in the language used in that section or s 1(b) to indicate that the English court has to adopt the classification which would be adopted by the requesting court if that classification is different from that which would be adopted by the English court. The language is equally consistent with the classification being carried out in accordance with either the classification which would be adopted by the requesting or the English court, though obviously if classifying is being carried out in accordance with the concepts of the assisting court, the concepts may have to be adapted to accommodate any peculiarities of the legal system of the requesting court.

With these preliminary remarks I turn to consider the reasoning of Kerr LJ in order to identify the limited but critical extent to which I differ from his reasoning.

I begin by agreeing that if there was an acceptable international interpretation of civil proceedings as defined by s 9(1) which could be practically applied to requests for assistance within the United Kingdom as well as from abroad then I consider that it would be desirable and appropriate to adopt that interpretation so that this country will deal uniformly with all applications and it is to be hoped that other countries who subscribe to the 1970 convention would do likewise.

In considering whether it is possible to apply an acceptable international interpretation in agreement with Kerr LJ I regard the reference in s 9 to a civil or commercial matter as being derived from matière civile ou commerciale under French law and that the duality of 'civil' and 'commercial' points away from a classification under common law and suggests a classification in accord with that which would be adopted by civil law jurisdictions. I also, of course, accept that Kerr LJ is right to say that—

> 'civil law countries draw a fundamental distinction between private and public law (droit civil and droit administratif) [and that it is to be expected that] this distinction must have been crucially present to the mind of anyone seeking to circumscribe and distinguish "matières civile et commerciales" from other, ie "public law", proceedings. Relations between states and their public authorities on the one hand and private citizens and corporations on the other fall within the sphere of public law. Civil and commercial matters do not, because they are concerned with private disputes.'

(See [1989] 1 All ER 661 at 677.)

However, as Professor Szladits points out, while—

> 'the fundamental division between private law and public law is considered a basic distinction, the *summa divisio* in all legal systems belonging to the civil law families of law the scope of this division differs considerably within the different legal systems, and consequently the theoretical analysis and reasons, as well as the practical effects, of these divisions also differ.'

(See *International Encyclopaedia of Comparative Law* vol 2, ch 2, para 25.)

Although the division is by no means as well developed as in civil jurisdictions, in the majority if not all the common law jurisdictions, the distinction between private and public law is now also well recognised. However, the recognition of the distinction does not solve the problem. It cannot be ignored that in almost every jurisdiction, the line of division between public and private law differs and the range of differences is very substantial. Professor Szladits draws attention to these differences and their historical explanation. Because of these differences it is, in my view, impossible to say that there is some internationally acceptable definition of civil or commercial matters which can be identified by construing that phrase as meaning private law matters as opposed to criminal or public law matters. To do so would not provide an interpretation which is uniform. It would merely alter the problem to what is meant by public and private law unless you can also identify the legal system whose division between public law and private law is to be applied.

If one system was to be chosen, then the obvious candidate would be the French system. Their system recognises not only the difference between public law and private law but also the difference between civil and commercial matters. However, the French classification is so different from our own as well as other common law and civil law jurisdictions that I cannot regard it as being internationally acceptable or as one Parliament could have intended to adopt. Adapting and modifying the language of Kerr LJ (see [1989] 1 All ER 661 at 679) it appears inconceivable that in 1975 Parliament could have intended that inter-United Kingdom requests for evidence of civil proceedings should be based upon a categorisation by reference to the French concept of the distinction between public and private law. To adopt the French classification would result in a wholly unwarranted restriction on the operation of the 1975 Act since many actions which in this country would undoubtedly be regarded as civil proceedings and as having no public or administrative law element would under the French system be excluded from the application of the 1975 Act. I find nothing in the Act or the convention to justify such a consequence.

Regrettably it is not possible to approach the interpretation of the 1970 convention or the 1975 Act in the same way as they could be approached if they formed the subject matter of Community Law. If they were part of community law then it would be possible to give to the expression civil and commercial matters the meaning which would be determined by Community Law and this would unquestionably be a great advantage. However, the decisions of the European Court of the European Communities, in particular in *Netherlands v Rüffer* Case 814/79 [1980] 3 ECR 3807 and in *Bavaria Fluggesellschaft Schwabe & Co KG and Germanair Bedarfsluftfahrt GmbH & Co KG v Eurocontrol* Joined Cases 9 and 10/77 [1977] ECR 1517, make it clear that you cannot adopt the same approach to Community and non-community legislation. The jurisdiction of the European Court in respect of the former is critical. In the *Rüffer* case the concept 'civil or commercial matters' in the Brussels convention was interpreted in a sense communitaire and that interpretation would be recognised by the English courts in applying the Civil Jurisdiction and Judgments Act 1982 which was passed primarily for the implementation of that convention. However, in the *Eurocontrol* case the European Court recognised that even with regard to an area to which the Brussels convention applied, a different interpretation from that which was applicable under the Brussels convention would be given to a bilateral agreement entered into between two members of the community. As the court said (at 1526):

> 'Although this result may lead to the same expression in the Brussels Convention and in a bilateral agreement being interpreted differently, this is due to the different systems in which the concept "civil and commercial matters" is used.'

As Bradley 'Social Security and the Right to a Fair Hearing: The Strasbourg Perspective' [1987] PL 3 makes clear, the recent decisions of the European Court of Human Rights in *Feldbrugge v Netherlands* (1986) 8 EHRR 425 and *Deumeland v Germany* (1986) 8 EHRR 448 also illustrate how difficult it is to find a uniform recognition of the distinction between public and private law. Those cases concerned complaints that the way in which claims for sickness benefit and an industrial widow's pension were dealt with by the appropriate domestic tribunals infringed art 6(1) of the convention in that the claimants had not been granted a fair hearing within a reasonable time in the determination of their civil rights and obligations. 'Previous decisions of the Strasbourg court have assumed that art 6(1) is primarily concerned with the protection of private rather than public law rights' but the majority decisions in these cases confirmed that civil rights and obligations in art 6(1) of the convention was an autonomous concept and were not influenced either by the fact that under both Dutch and German law (as in English law) the claims would be regarded as falling within the public law sphere, or the minority's contention, that the result was inconsistent with the history of the drafting of art 6(1).

While I would not dissent from the approach laid down by Sandra O'Connor J in the United States Supreme Court in *Air France v Saks* (1985) 84 L Ed 2d 289 at 297 that 'it is our responsibility to give the specific words of the treaty a meaning consistent with the shared expectations of the contracting parties' the difficulty of doing this on the basis of a distinction between public law and private law is that there are no identifiable shared expectations as to the distinction between the two categories which can be used as a means of deciding what is meant by public as opposed to civil proceedings.

However, the fact that there is no internationally acceptable interpretation of a civil or commercial matter does not mean that it is necessary to give those words the identical meaning which they would have in a domestic context in this country or in the domestic context of the requesting state. While I cannot identify an acceptable international interpretation of the phrase, I do accept that the material which is before the court is overwhelmingly to the effect that whatever else is or is not included in the concept of a civil or commercial matter, matières fiscales are not within that concept and this can be taken into account in construing the section. Even in common law jurisdictions, so far as enforcement of judgments is concerned it has been recognised that revenue matters come within a different and special category and are subject to rules of public policy which do not apply to other civil proceedings. I here refer to the speech of Lord Somervell in *Government of India v Taylor* [1955] 1 All ER 292 at 301, [1955] AC 491 at 514 cited by Kerr LJ (see [1989] 1 All ER 661 at 681). Taking into account the well-established approach of the courts to assisting in tax gathering by a foreign state, I would regard the proper interpretation of the words 'civil or commercial matter' in the 1975 Act as excluding matières fiscales. I am encouraged to adopt this view by Dr Mann's 'Any Civil or Commercial Matter' (1986) 102 LQR 505 at 509 on the decision on the first appeal and his statement that 'it can be asserted with confidence that very few States (if any) will ever regard a tax claim as a civil or commercial matter.'

The fact that I come to this conclusion is probably sufficient for the purposes of determining this appeal. However, in order to justify my rejection of a general international approach to the phrase 'civil or commercial matter' I should shortly indicate how I believe it is possible to give effect to the wording of the 1975 Act and to do so without creating the difficulties which are inherent in adopting the approach accepted on the first appeal which were dramatically illustrated by the problems which faced a Kenneth Jones J when he sought to ascertain what would be the classification which would be adopted by a Norwegian court.

I have already indicated that I cannot find any indication in the Act that it is necessary to look to the requesting state's classification. As the classification controls the United Kingdom court's jurisdiction, I would regard it as more likely that it is the United Kingdom court's classification which was to prevail and I regard the choice of the United Kingdom court as being preferable to the dual classification suggested on the first appeal.

b The great advantage of adopting a United Kingdom court's classification is that it will only be necessary to look to the requesting court for factual information as to the nature of the proceedings before the requesting court. In the normal case a translation of the pleadings in the requesting court and some limited background information will be ample. There would certainly not be any need to obtain the extensive conflicting expert evidence which has been assembled in this case. Given the material to which I have c referred it should be a relatively easy task for the English court to make up its mind whether on the proper interpretation of a civil or commercial matter the substantive nature of the proceedings before the requesting court falls within the wording of the statute.

This appears to be the predominant approach according to the editors of the *Encyclopaedia of Public International Law* vol 9, p 242 in the chapter dealing with legal d assistance between states in civil matters:

'The substantive nature of a case determines whether a case is civil, criminal or administrative. The branch of the judicial administration handling the case and the type of procedure used for the request are irrelevant. It is not clear, however, whether determination is made according to the law of the requesting State or the e requested State. A special commission on the operation of the Hague Convention on Evidence Abroad (1970) was divided, but the predominant opinion was that with regard to the Convention the characterisation by the law of the *requested* state should prevail.'

In the note to which I have already made reference Dr Mann is also of the view that there is a very great deal of support for this approach and in this connection the passage f in the speech of Lord Watson in *Huntington v Attrill* [1893] AC 150 at 155 which is cited by Dr Mann is not without relevance.

However, although the English court has to perform the act of classifying the nature of the foreign proceedings, it does not do so by adopting any parochial classification of a procedural nature. As the Act requires, the English court has to look at the substantive nature of the matter which is before the foreign court to decide whether it constitutes a g civil or commercial matter as that phrase is interpreted by the English court.

Against this interpretation counsel for the state relied heavily on the decision of Chapman J in *Re Extradition Act 1870* [1968] 3 All ER 804, [1969] 1 WLR 12. That case concerned the application of the Foreign Tribunals Evidence Act 1856. In his judgment Chapman J indicates that 'civil or commercial matter' in s 1 of the 1856 Act did cover all h kinds of suits, petitions, summonses and applications but the learned judge was primarily concerned with the meaning of any criminal matter of a political character. The judge was not concerned with a situation where a contrast was drawn between civil proceedings in general and proceedings in a civil or commercial matter and I do not regard the case as requiring me to take a different view of the interpretation from that which I have indicated above which I believe to be the correct interpretation.

j The other cases on which the state relied were three Privy Council decisions in which public law and fiscal proceedings were regarded as civil proceedings. However in those cases (*Stamps Comr Straights Settlements v Oei Tjong Swan* [1933] AC 378, *Tennekoon (Comr for Registration of Indian and Pakistani Residents) v Duraismy* [1958] 2 All ER 479, [1958] AC 354 and *Maliban Biscuit Manufactories Ltd v Subramaniam* [1971] AC 988) there was no

question of any special meaning being given to the term civil cause or civil action and
the context was quite different. I accordingly find that the cases provide no assistance.   *a*

Finally on this issue I should make it clear that it is possible that there may be other
areas, apart from the fiscal, where there is sufficient unanimity of approach to exclude
what would normally be regarded as a civil or commercial matter under English law
from that phrase as used in the 1975 Act having regard to the intent and purpose of that
Act. However such other areas did not have to be identified and were not identified for
the purposes of the present appeal.   *b*

Norwegian law

Having regard to my view of the proper interpretation of the phrase 'civil or
commercial matter', there can be no doubt that the proceedings before the Norwegian
court are fiscal proceedings and therefore not proceedings in relation to which the 1975
Act is available. Having looked at the pleadings, it appears the proceedings are no   *c*
different (save that they take place before a civil as opposed to an administrative tribunal)
from the proceedings which would take place before the general or special commissioners
in this country if a taxpayer were to appeal against an assessment. This being so I do not
consider that it is possible to treat the proceedings as not being of a fiscal nature because
the application to the Norwegian court is by the estate and the estate as well as the state
require the evidence which they believe the witnesses can give for use in a court.   *d*

If it is wrong to treat a fiscal matter as coming within a special category, then looking
at the substance of the proceedings with English eyes, I would regard them as being a
civil or commercial matter. They would be similar to an application for judicial review
in respect of a tax decision or an appeal in a tax case to the High Court from the decision   *e*
of the commissioners, both of which proceedings I would regard as being civil matters
under the normal English classification. On this approach the Privy Council decisions
relied on by the state of Norway would be relevant.

Finally if, contrary to my view, the classification as a matter of substance has to be
carried out in accordance with Norwegian law, then I would regard the proceedings as
not being a civil or commercial matter. I appreciate that this is contrary to the decision   *f*
of Kenneth Jones J. However, his decision was based upon the approach indicated by
Glidewell LJ on the first appeal. With the assistance of counsel for the witnesses I am
satisfied, on a reading of the expert witnesses' reports and evidence, that if the substance
as opposed to the procedure is looked at under Norwegian law the Norwegian proceedings
are to be regarded as proceedings in a fiscal matter which would not be treated by the
Norwegians as being a civil or commercial matter.   *g*

The factual issues

Under this heading I propose to deal with the remaining issues. I will deal with them
in the same order as they were dealt with by Kerr LJ on the first appeal. They are: B (tax
gathering), C (sovereignty), D (dual purpose), E (Fishing) and F (confidentiality). No   *h*
separate oral argument was advanced before us on issues B, C and D. We did, however,
have the benefit of written submissions. Bearing in mind that having regard to my views
as to jurisdiction these issues do not strictly arise, I will deal with them very briefly. I
have treated them as being factual issues because to a large extent the outcome on the
issues depends upon the facts.

B. and C. Tax gathering: Sovereignty   *j*

I have reservations as to whether our approach to the question of tax gathering should
be the same today as it has been in the past. Having regard to the scale of international
tax avoidance and the undesirable manifestations which are associated with it, a powerful

argument could be advanced for saying it is very much in the interests of this country
and the majority of the other countries in the world that there should be co-operation in
this field. However, it would be wholly inappropriate in this appeal to seek to undermine
the well-established policy identified in the speech of Lord Somerville in *Government of
India v Taylor* [1955] 1 All ER 292, [1955] AC 491. It is sufficient if I say that I agree with
the decision on the first appeal that this case raises special considerations because the
estate are at one with the state in seeking to support the letter of request. The support of
the estate could not make what in my view was not a civil or commercial matter into a
civil or commercial matter. However, it can and does change the situation with regard
to the policy issues from what it would have been otherwise and so the request could not
be rejected because it might provide assistance in foreign tax gathering.

I also agree with the decision of the first Court of Appeal on the question of sovereignty.
Section 4 of the Protection of Trading Interests Act 1980 has no application to the facts of
the present case.

D. *Dual purpose*

The difficulty that I have with regard to this issue is because of the wording of the
1975 Act. I find it difficult to understand why if the proceedings before the National Tax
Committee are not within s 1 why the proceedings before the court should be. However,
assuming the distinction can be drawn between the two sets of proceedings either on the
basis that the tax committee are not a tribunal or otherwise, then I would regard this as a
matter going to discretion and on the basis that the estate supports the letters of request I
would not refuse assistance on this ground.

E. *Fishing*

I have difficulty in applying the concept of fishing to a request that a witness should
be required to give oral evidence. It is in English proceedings commonly used on
applications for interrogatories and it may be said that there is little distinction between
oral cross-examination and written cross-examination and the administering of
interrogatories. However, interrogatories are in my view part of the process of discovery
and so far as the giving of evidence (albeit prior to the trial) is concerned, different
considerations could apply. Questions of privilege are dealt with expressly in s 3. But
subject to the question of privilege, what I would expect normally to concern the court
when considering whether effect should be given to a request, is whether the request is
confined to seeking to obtain evidence which will be relevant to the proceedings in the
foreign court. If it is, then normally that will be the end of the matter. Under the 1975
Act the court does not however have a general discretion and if there are special
circumstances making it important that the examination is confined the court can take
the appropriate action. Here the question of confidentiality can be highly significant.
However, subject to confidentiality I can see no possible objection to the latest request,
which is clearly designed to obtain evidence for use at the hearing. In this connection I
should make it clear that what I have said already, which is of general application, is on
the assumption that the evidence of the witness is required for the hearing. If the
examination of the witness is sought as part of a pre-trial process, in other words as part
of the process of discovery, then different considerations would apply and the principle
of fishing could when appropriate be invoked. Here, therefore, I would regard Ralph
Gibson LJ as indicating the correct approach rather than the majority on the first appeal
who, as I understand their judgments, would extend principles which I would regard as
applicable to discovery to evidence required for the hearing itself.

However, whether the approach is that indicated by the majority on the first appeal or
by Ralph Gibson LJ or in this judgment (in so far as it differs from that adopted by Ralph
Gibson LJ) I am quite satisfied that the letter of request is not flawed on the grounds of
fishing. On the contrary, the letter was designed to elicit evidence which was highly

relevant to the proceedings before the Norwegian court. If this had not been the case, then the court in refusing to give effect to the letter would not ordinarily do so on a jurisdictional basis but as a matter of discretion.

F. *Confidentiality*

The witnesses undoubtedly owe a duty of confidentiality to their clients which the English court will protect so long as this can be done consistently with the duty this court has to assist the Norwegian courts where it is appropriate to do so. As was pointed out on the first appeal and by Kenneth Jones J this involves a balancing exercise. The importance of the evidence which has been requested in the proceedings has to be taken into account in performing the exercise. The court can and should, where this is necessary in order to do justice, give directions or otherwise restrict the request as authorised by the English court to protect a duty of confidence. If the proceedings were taking place before an English court the English court would seek to preserve confidentiality and the broad approach to the request should be the same.

Kenneth Jones J performed the balancing exercise, he directed himself properly when so doing and I can see no reason whatever for interfering with the conclusion to which he came. Criticisms are made as to the directions which Kenneth Jones J made as to the amendment of the letter of request. However, this being a matter for his discretion, I would not interfere with the decision that he made, save in respect of the modified request which was put before this court but was not available to Kenneth Jones J.

I would therefore allow the appeal. I do so on the short ground that on the proper interpretation of the 1975 Act the fiscal proceedings which are now being conducted before the Sandefjord City Court are not capable of being regarded a 'civil or commercial matter' for the purposes of the 1975 Act. I come to this conclusion notwithstanding the fact that it would be my view that if the English court had jurisdiction to assist the Norwegian court it certainly should do so. This would, however, require a further treaty and a statute to implement that treaty which were designed to provide for assistance in relation to proceedings in matières fiscal.

I agree with the order proposed by May and Balcombe LJJ.

Appeal allowed. Order below discharged as to costs, order substituted that there be no order as to costs below. Witnesses to have costs of the appeal. Time extended for applying for leave to appeal against first Court of Appeal decision; leave to appeal to House of Lords in respect of both decisions by Court of Appeal on all issues granted. Leave to cross-appeal granted.

Solicitors: *Linklaters & Paines* (for the witnesses); *Freshfields* (for the state); *Macfarlanes* (for the estate).

Carolyn Toulmin   Barrister.

Re State of Norway's Applications
(Nos 1 and 2)

HOUSE OF LORDS

LORD KEITH OF KINKEL, LORD BRANDON OF OAKBROOK, LORD GRIFFITHS, LORD GOFF OF CHIEVELEY AND LORD LOWRY

17, 18, 19, 20, 24 OCTOBER 1988, 16 FEBRUARY 1989

Evidence – Foreign tribunal – Examination of witnesses in relation to matters pending before foreign tribunal – Evidence for purpose of civil proceedings – Proceedings in civil or commercial matter – Evidence requested by foreign tax tribunal – Whether foreign proceedings civil or commercial matter – Whether proceedings assisting foreign tax gathering – Evidence (Proceedings in Other Jurisdictions) Act 1975, ss 1, 9(1).

J, a wealthy Norwegian shipowner, died in 1982. The county tax committee for that part of Norway in which he had resided decided to raise a retrospective tax assessment against his estate for the years 1972–82 on the ground that he had avoided tax during those years by failing to declare a large part of his assets. The estate commenced proceedings in the court of first instance in Norway to have the assessment declared null and void and appealed to the national tax committee to have it set aside. The Norwegian court, on the application of the State of Norway supported by the estate, issued letters of request addressed to the High Court in England requesting the court, inter alia, to summon two named merchant bankers (the witnesses) to attend before an examiner in London to give oral evidence relevant to the issues in the proceedings before the Norwegian court. The bank had acted as bankers for a charitable trust alleged to have been set up and controlled by J and which allegedly held shares for J as beneficial owner. After receiving the letter of request the master made an order under s 2[a] of the Evidence (Proceedings in Other Jurisdictions) Act 1975 granting the application for the oral examination of the witnesses. The witnesses applied to have the order set aside. The judge upheld the master's decision subject to certain directions limiting the scope of the questions which could be put to the witnesses. The witnesses appealed to the Court of Appeal, contending, inter alia, that the Norwegian proceedings did not constitute 'civil proceedings' under s 1[b] of the 1975 Act, which were defined by s 9(1)[c] of that Act as proceedings in a 'civil or commercial matter', so as to confer jurisdiction on the English court, and that the terms of the letter of request were so wide as to amount to a fishing expedition. In allowing the appeal and setting aside the order the Court of Appeal expressed the view that whether proceedings were a 'civil or commercial matter' depended on their classification under the law of the requesting court and the law of the court to whom the request was made and that the Norwegian proceedings would be characterised as a civil proceeding under English law. The Court of Appeal therefore found that the proceedings fell within the ambit of s 1 of the 1975 Act but went on to hold that the terms of the letter of request were too wide for

---

a Section 2, so far as material, provides:

   '(1) ... the High Court ... shall ... have power ... by order to make such provision for obtaining evidence ... for the purpose of giving effect to [a] request [for evidence for proceedings in other jurisdictions] ...

   (2) ... an order under this section may ... make provision—(*a*) for the examination of witnesses ...

   (3) An order under this section shall not require any particular steps to be taken unless they are steps which can be required to be taken by way of obtaining evidence for the purposes of civil proceedings in the court making the order (whether or not proceedings of the same description as those to which the application for the order relates) ...'

b Section 1 is set out at p 750 *f* to *h*, post

c Section 9(1), so far as material, is set out at p 750 *h*, post

the court to order the witnesses to give evidence on the request as framed. Following a
further application by the State of Norway, supported by the estate, the Norwegian court   *a*
issued a second letter of request for the oral examination of the witnesses on 12 specific
issues and setting out the specific questions to be put to the witnesses. The letter of
request stated that the Norwegian proceedings were a 'civil action' under Norwegian law
and a 'civil matter' under the Convention relating to the Taking of Evidence abroad in
Civil or Commercial Matters of 1970. The master made an order under s 2 of the 1975
Act for the examination of the witnesses according to the terms of the letter of request.   *b*
On appeal by the witnesses, the judge upheld the order subject to certain limitations on
the testimony which the witnesses could be required to give. The witnesses appealed to
Court of Appeal, again contending that the Norwegian proceedings were not 'civil
proceedings' within ss 1 and 9(1) of the 1975 Act and that the English court had no
jurisdiction. The state cross-appealed against the limitations placed by the judge on the
witnesses' testimony. The Court of Appeal held that the witnesses were not prevented by   *c*
either judicial precedent or issue estoppel from again contending that the Norwegian
proceedings were not 'civil proceedings' within ss 1 and 9(1) of the 1975 Act, and held
that, applying a generally acceptable international interpretation derived from the civil
law distinction between private law (which included civil or commercial proceedings)
and public law (which included fiscal proceedings), the Norwegian proceedings, which
were clearly fiscal proceedings, were not proceedings in a 'civil or commercial matter' for   *d*
the purposes of s 9, with the result that the court had no jurisdiction to order the
examination of the witnesses according to the terms of the letter of request. The state
and the estate appealed to the House of Lords against both decisions of the Court of
Appeal.

e

Held – On the true construction of s 9 of the 1975 Act the question whether proceedings
were a 'civil or commercial matter' depended on the classification of those proceedings
according to the law of the requesting court and the law of the court to which the request
was made (ie English law), since the classification could not be made by reference to any
internationally acceptable classification. In answering that question the English court
was required to determine according to the law of the requesting court how the   *f*
proceedings would be classified under the law and practice of that state, having regard to
the manner in which classification was ordinarily made in that country, and then to
determine according to English law whether the proceedings were civil proceedings on
the basis that all proceedings other than criminal proceedings were civil proceedings.
Since under Norwegian law the Norwegian proceedings would be classified as proceedings
in a civil matter and since under English law proceedings in a fiscal matter were civil   *g*
proceedings the court had jurisdiction to order the examination of the witnesses according
to the terms of the letter of request. Furthermore, that jurisdiction was not affected by
the rule that English courts would not entertain an action for the enforcement of a
foreign revenue law, since that rule did not go to jurisdiction and in any event the letter
of request issued by the Norwegian court did not amount to the attempted enforcement,
either directly or indirectly, of Norwegian revenue laws in England but was merely   *h*
seeking the assistance of the English court to obtain evidence to enable Norwegian
revenue laws to be enforced in Norway. The state's appeal would therefore be allowed
(see p 747 *g* to *j*, p 757 *d g* to *j*, p 758 *f h j*, p 759 *g h*, p 760 *h j* and p 761 *g* to p 762 *b*, post).
    Decision of the Court of Appeal [1989] 1 All ER 661 affirmed.
    Decision of the Court of Appeal [1989] 1 All ER 701 reversed.

j

Notes
For evidence for proceedings in other jurisdictions, see 17 Halsbury's Laws (4th edn)
paras 326–329, and for cases on the subject, see 22 Digest (Reissue) 665–668, 7111–7123.
    For the Evidence (Proceedings in Other Jurisdictions) Act 1975, ss 1, 2, 9, see 17
Halsbury's Statutes (4th edn) 191, 192, 197.

Cases referred to in opinions

a   *A-G of New Zealand v Ortiz* [1983] 2 All ER 93, [1984] AC 1, [1983] 2 WLR 809, HL; *affg*
[1982] 3 All ER 432, [1984] AC 1, [1982] 3 WLR 570, CA.
Bemberg v Revenue Authorities of the Province of Buenos Aires (24 February 1949, unreported),
Cours de Cassation de France.
India (Government) Ministry of Finance (Revenue Division) v Taylor [1955] 1 All ER 292,
[1955] AC 491, [1955] 2 WLR 303, HL.

b   *Rio Tinto Zinc Corp v Westinghouse Electric Corp, RTZ Services Ltd v Westinghouse Electric
Corp* [1978] 1 All ER 434, [1978] AC 547, [1978] 2 WLR 81, HL.

Consolidated appeals and cross-appeals

The State of Norway and the estate of Anders Jahre deceased appealed against the decisions
of the Court of Appeal on 12 February 1986 (Kerr and Glidewell LJJ, Ralph Gibson LJ
c   dissenting in part) ([1989] 1 All ER 661) and on 18 December 1987 (May and
Balcombe LJJ, Woolf LJ dissenting in part) ([1989] 1 All ER 701) allowing appeals by
Lord Kindersley and Mr A J Hardman (the witnesses) against the decisions of McNeill J
on 24 July 1985 and Kenneth Jones J on 20 October 1986 respectively dismissing the
witnesses' applications to discharge orders made for the oral examination of the witnesses
pursuant to s 2 of the Evidence (Proceedings in Other Jurisdictions) Act 1975, in
d   compliance with a request from the Sandefjord City Court on an application by the state
supported by the estate. The witnesses cross-appealed against the order of the Court of
Appeal as to costs in *Re State of Norway's Application (No 2)*. The facts are set out in the
opinion of Lord Goff.

The appeals and cross-appeal were consolidated by order of the House of Lords dated 28
e   April 1988.

Anthony Boswood QC and *Stephen Moriarty* for the State of Norway and the estate.
Michael Crystal QC, J A Jolowicz and *David Alexander* for the witnesses.

f   Their Lordships took time for consideration.

16 February. The following opinions were delivered.

LORD KEITH OF KINKEL. My Lords, I have had the opportunity of considering in
draft the speech prepared by my noble and learned friend Lord Goff. I agree with it, and
for the reasons he gives would allow the appeal in *Re State of Norway's Application (No 2)*
g   [1989] 1 All ER 701, and deal with *Re State of Norway's Application (No 1)* [1989] 1 All ER
661 as he proposes.

LORD BRANDON OF OAKBROOK. My Lords, I had the advantage of reading in
draft the speech prepared by my noble and learned friend Lord Goff. I agree with it and
h   for the reasons which he gives I would allow the appeal in *Re State of Norway's Application
(No 2)* [1989] 1 All ER 701 and deal with *Re State of Norway's (No 1)* [1989] 1 All ER 661
in the manner which he proposes.

LORD GRIFFITHS. My Lords, I have had the advantage of reading in draft the speech
of my noble and learned friend Lord Goff. I agree with it, and for the reasons he gives
j   would allow the appeal in *Re State of Norway's Application (No 2)* [1989] 1 All ER 701, and
deal with *Re State of Norway's Application (No 1)* [1989] 1 All ER 661 as he proposes.

LORD GOFF OF CHIEVELEY. My Lords, this appeal is concerned with letters
rogatory issued by a Norwegian court, addressed to the English High Court, requesting
the oral examination of two witnesses in this country, Lord Kindersley and Mr A J
Hardman. The witnesses have opposed any order that they should submit to such oral

examination; their grounds of opposition will appear hereafter, but their principal fear is that, if compelled to give evidence, they will be forced to break their duty of *a* confidentiality as bankers. The result has been extensive litigation in this country, including two hearings before the Court of Appeal; it is the second decision of the Court of Appeal which is, primarily, the subject of the present appeal before your Lordships' House. Before considering the substance of the appeal itself, it is necessary for me to set out, as briefly as I can, the course of the proceedings which have taken place. It will then be possible to identify the issues which arise for decision on this appeal; and so to consider *b* the rival submissions advanced before your Lordships on those issues.

At the heart of the present proceedings lies an assessment to tax raised against the estate of a wealthy Norwegian shipowner, Anders Jahre, who died in 1982. On 14 September 1983 the county tax committee for the area in Norway in which he lived decided to raise a supplementary retrospective tax assessment against his estate in the sum of about 338m Norwegian Kroner for the years 1972–82, on the ground that he had *c* failed to declare a large part of his assets. The undeclared assets are alleged to include the assets of a Panamanian company, Continental Trust Co Inc (CTC). The shares in CTC form part of the assets of a charitable foundation (the trust) founded in 1976; and it is alleged that the deceased was a settlor or in control of the trust, and accordingly the beneficial owner of the assets of CTC. Lord Kindersley is a director of Lazard Bros & Co Ltd who acted as adviser to the trust since its foundation; Lazards appear to have acted as *d* bankers to the trust. Mr Hardman was a senior employee of Lazards who acted as assistant secretary, and subsequently as treasurer, of CTC, until the dissolution of CTC in 1984.

The assessment raised by the county tax committee is enforceable as such, but may be discharged either by an order by the appropriate Norwegian court declaring the assessment null and void, or on an appeal to the National Tax Committee (the NTC). In *e* November 1983 the estate brought an action in the Sandefjord City Court to have the assessment set aside; the Norwegian Solicitor General took over the defence of those' proceedings. Subsequently, the estate also appealed to the NTC. It appears that, if the order for letters rogatory is made, the testimony of the witnesses would be made available not only to the Sandefjord court but also to the NTC.

In June 1984 the lawyer acting for the estate addressed a request to the Sandefjord *f* court for the examination of Lord Kindersley; in the request it was submitted that Lord Kindersley might be asked to give evidence in accordance with the Convention on the Taking of Evidence abroad in Civil or Commercial Matters (The Hague, 18 March 1970, TS 20 (1977); Cmnd 6727), to which both Norway and the United Kingdom are parties. Subsequently, in November 1984, the Solicitor General made a further request for the examination of Lord Kindersley and Mr Hardman. A letter of request from the *g* Sandefjord court, addressed to the competent court in Great Britain, requesting assistance in the examination of both witnesses, formed the basis of the first set of proceedings in this country (which I shall refer to as '*Norway (No 1)*'). The letter of request made no reference to any convention; I do not imagine this to be in any way unusual. Attached to the letter of request were certain pleadings setting out the matters in respect of which *h* evidence was sought from the two witnesses. An order for examination of the witnesses was sought in this country by the State of Norway, and on 14 January 1985, on an ex parte application, Master Prebble made the requested order. The witnesses then applied to discharge that order; the estate was then added as a respondent to the witnesses' summons. On 24 July 1985 McNeill J dismissed the witnesses' application, but directed that the order should take effect subject to certain qualifications which he placed on the *j* matters in respect of which the testimony of the witnesses was sought. The witnesses appealed to the Court of Appeal against the order requiring them to give evidence and the state and the estate cross-appealed against the limitations imposed by McNeill J. By a majority (Kerr and Glidewell LJJ, Ralph Gibson LJ dissenting) the Court of Appeal allowed the appeal (see [1989] 1 All ER 661), on the ground that the letter of request was in such wide terms that it amounted to an impermissible 'fishing expedition', ie that it

was a roving inquiry designed to elicit information which might lead to the obtaining of
a evidence. The majority further concluded that the appeal should also be allowed on the
basis that the order compelled the witnesses to violate their duty of confidence as bankers.

A number of other issues were canvassed before the Court of Appeal in *Norway (No 1)*.
In particular, it considered a submission by the witnesses that the English courts had no
jurisdiction to entertain the application, on the ground that the application was not
concerned with 'proceedings in any civil or commercial matter' and so did not fall within
b the jurisdiction conferred on the English courts by s 1(*b*) of the Evidence (Proceedings in
Other Jurisdictions) Act 1975. The submission was rejected by the Court of Appeal. I
shall have to consider this point in depth at a later stage. At present I need say no more
than that the question was considered in detail by Kerr LJ with whom, on this point,
both Glidewell and Ralph Gibson LJJ agreed (see [1989] 1 All ER 661). With some
reluctance he rejected an argument, advanced on behalf of the witnesses, that the relevant
c words in the 1975 Act, viz 'proceedings in any civil or commercial matter', should be
interpreted as bearing a broadly acceptable international meaning, consistent with that
used in civil law countries, and as such excluding proceedings in public law matters, and
therefore excluding proceedings for the recovery of tax. In particular Kerr LJ (who
considered that the relevant proceedings must be proceedings in a civil or commercial
matter both by the law of the requesting state (here Norway) and by the law of this
d country) felt unable to conclude, on the evidence before him, that the action in the
Sandefjord court could not be regarded as proceedings in a civil matter by the law of
Norway. In the closing paragraph of his judgment he said ([1989] 1 All ER 661 at 689):

'Finally, I would add that if this judgment reflects the ultimate outcome of this
appeal, then I hope that any renewal of the present letter of request in some more
e limited and acceptable form, if this can be devised, should be accompanied by clear
evidence as to what is properly to be regarded as a "civil or commercial matter" by
the law of Norway, and in particular whether Norwegian law distinguishes between
public and private law. I feel, frankly, uneasy about my acceptance, dubitante, of
the very limited evidence in this connection on the present application.'

f Doubtless in response to that invitation, the state and the estate obtained from the
Sandefjord court a second letter of request, addressed to the English High Court, once
again seeking the testimony of Lord Kindersley and Mr Hardman, but limited to 12
specific issues, and setting out the specific questions to be put to the witnesses. The letter
of request contained the statement: 'The action is a civil action under the law of Norway,
and the proceedings are a "civil matter" under the law of Norway, for the purposes of
[the 1970 convention] . . .' It is said that these words were derived from the draft letter
g of request submitted to the court by the parties. No doubt they were; but they were
accepted by the court. At all events, the letter of request led to the proceedings in this
country in *Norway (No 2)*. The application for the order in this country was made by the
State of Norway, though the application was supported by the estate. On an ex parte
application Master Creightmore, on 2 April 1986, made the order requested. The
h witnesses applied to have that order set aside; by judgment on 20 October 1986 and order
dated 18 November 1986 Kenneth Jones J dismissed the witnesses' application, subject to
certain qualifications which he placed on the testimony which the witnesses were
required to give under the master's order. The witnesses appealed to the Court of Appeal
against the judge's order and the state cross-appealed against that part of his order which
imposed limitations on the testimony to be given. The Court of Appeal allowed the
j witnesses' appeal (see [1989] 1 All ER 701). May and Balcombe LJJ did so on the ground
that the words 'proceedings in any civil or commercial matter' in the 1975 Act were to
be construed, in accordance with what they held to be a generally acceptable international
interpretation, in the civil law sense as excluding public law matters and so excluding
fiscal matters, and that therefore the English court had no jurisdiction to entertain the
request of the Sandefjord court. Woolf LJ concluded that there was no internationally
acceptable meaning to be attached to the words 'proceedings in any civil or commercial

matter' in the 1975 Act; he nevertheless held that that expression excluded fiscal matters, and on that basis he also held that the English court had no jurisdiction. The State of *a* Norway and the estate now appeal to your Lordships' House against that decision.

On the appeal before your Lordships' House, four issues emerged in the course of argument. First, the State of Norway challenged the decision of the Court of Appeal that the English court had no jurisdiction to entertain its application. The witnesses, while seeking to uphold the decision of the Court of Appeal on that point, submitted, in the alternative, that the State of Norway's application should in any event be dismissed, either *b* as 'tax-gathering' and as such inconsistent with the well-known principle in *Government of India Ministry of Finance (Revenue Division) v Taylor* [1955] 1 All ER 292, [1955] AC 491 or on the ground that it constituted an illegitimate 'fishing expedition' or because it compelled the witnesses to break their duty of confidentiality as bankers. It is the first two of these issues which raise the matters of principle for decision by your Lordships' House. I shall consider them together, under the heading of jurisdiction. The other two *c* issues I shall consider briefly at the end of this speech.

Jurisdiction

I turn first, therefore, to the central question argued before your Lordships' House, which is whether the proceedings in the Sandefjord court were civil proceedings within s 1(*b*) of the 1975 Act, having regard to the definition of 'civil proceedings' in s 9(1) of the *d* Act, viz that that expression, in relation to the requesting court, means proceedings in any civil or commercial matter.

In order to consider this question, I must set out those parts of the 1975 Act which are of immediate relevance. First, the long title of the Act reads as follows:

> 'An Act to make new provision for enabling the High Court, the Court of Session *e* and the High Court of Justice in Northern Ireland to assist in obtaining evidence required for the purposes of proceedings in other jurisdictions; to extend the powers of those courts to issue process effective throughout the United Kingdom for securing the attendance of witnesses; and for purposes connected with those matters.'

Section 1 of the Act provides as follows: *f*

> 'Where an application is made to the High Court, the Court of Session or the High Court of Justice in Northern Ireland for an order for evidence to be obtained in the part of the United Kingdom in which it exercises jurisdiction, and the court is satisfied—(*a*) that the application is made in pursuance of a request issued by or on behalf of a court or tribunal ("the requesting court") exercising jurisdiction in any other part of the United Kingdom or in a country or territory outside the United *g* Kingdom; and (*b*) that the evidence to which the application relates is to be obtained for the purposes of civil proceedings which either have been instituted before the requesting court or whose institution before that court is contemplated, the High Court, Court of Session or High Court of Justice in Northern Ireland, as the case may be, shall have the powers conferred on it by the following provisions of this Act.'

h

The expression 'civil proceedings' is defined in s 9(1) of the Act as follows:

> 'In this Act—"civil proceedings", in relation to the requesting court, means proceedings in any civil or commercial matter . . .'

It is not in doubt that a major purpose of the 1975 Act was to enable ratification of the 1970 convention. The text of the convention is in the English and French languages, *j* both being authoritative. The convention is entitled 'Convention on the Taking of Evidence abroad in Civil or Commercial Matters'. The first two paragraphs of art 1 of the convention read as follows:

> 'In civil or commercial matters a judicial authority of a Contracting State may, in accordance with the provisions of the law of that State, request the competent

a authority of another Contracting State, by means of a Letter of Request, to obtain evidence, or to perform some other judicial act.

A Letter shall not be used to obtain evidence which is not intended for use in judicial proceedings, commenced or contemplated.'

In the French text, the opening words of art 1 read: 'En matière civile ou commerciale . . .'

The submissions of the witnesses on this point are, in summary, as follows. It was *b* submitted that the main purpose of the 1975 Act was to give effect to the 1970 convention. The words 'civil or commercial matters' in s 9(1) of the Act reflect the same words in art 1 of the convention, and should be given the same meaning. Furthermore, the distinction drawn between 'civil' and 'commercial' matters is inconsistent with the English procedural classification, in which civil matters embrace all matters which are not criminal, and in particular include commercial matters. This suggests that the words *c* 'civil or commercial matters' in s 9(1) should, like the same words in the English text of art 1 of the convention, be regarded as derived from the words 'matière civile ou commerciale' in the French text of art 1. In France, as in other civil law countries, civil matters are categorised as a matter of substance and are regarded as limited to private law matters, excluding public law matters and in particular fiscal matters. This approach was commended as 'internationalist'; and it was suggested that it would achieve uniformity *d* in the construction of art 1 of the convention, and a consistent construction of s 9(1), which is derived from it. In *Norway (No 1)* this approach was rejected, after full and careful consideration, by Kerr LJ, despite the attraction he felt for it; on this point, both Glidewell and Ralph Gibson LJJ agreed with Kerr LJ. However it found favour with the majority of the Court of Appeal in *Norway (No 2)*, who felt free to depart from the conclusion reached on it by the Court of Appeal in *Norway (No 1)*.

e Your Lordships are here concerned with the construction of certain words used in an Act of Parliament (the 1975 Act) which is primarily concerned with conferring jurisdiction on courts in the United Kingdom (in England, the High Court) to obtain evidence pursuant to a request from a court or tribunal outside the jurisdiction of the court (whether elsewhere in the United Kingdom or abroad). The 1975 Act is not the first legislation to be found in the statute book conferring jurisdiction of this kind; and *f* the expression 'civil or commercial matter' is to be found in the earliest Act of Parliament concerned with this subject, the Foreign Tribunals Evidence Act 1856. The question has therefore arisen whether it is legitimate to have recourse to the earlier legislation for the purpose of construing the 1975 Act.

In *Rio Tinto Zinc Corp v Westinghouse Electric Corp, RTZ Services Ltd v Westinghouse Electric Corp* [1978] 1 All ER 434 at 441, [1978] AC 547 at 608 it was said by Lord *g* Wilberforce of the 1975 Act that:

'The 1975 Act is, as I think, clear in its terms so that reference in aid of interpretation to previous statutes is not required.'

Furthermore Lord Diplock said with reference to previous decision of English courts as to the meaning of different words used in the 1856 Act ([1978] 1 All ER 434 at 461, *h* [1978] AC 547 at 633):

'For my part, I do not think that any assistance is to be gained from those decisions. The jurisdiction of English courts to order persons within [their] jurisdiction to provide oral or documentary evidence in aid of proceedings in foreign courts has always been exclusively statutory. There is no presumption that Parliament, in *j* repealing one statute and substituting another in different terms, intended to make the minimum changes in the previous law that it is possible to reconcile with the actual wording of the new statute, particularly where, as in the instant case, the new statute is passed to give effect to a new international convention.'

These observations of course carry much weight. Even so, caution has to be exercised. When it is said that the 1975 Act was passed with, in part, the purpose of giving effect to

the 1970 convention, this is no doubt true; and where words in the Act are derived
directly from the convention, it may well be right that reference to previous Acts of *a*
Parliament in aid of construction would not be appropriate. This is particularly so where,
under the Act, the jurisdiction of the courts in this country is enlarged to accommodate
the convention; though I have to say that only minor provisions were required for this
purpose. But it is not to be forgotten that the 1975 Act was not only passed to ensure that
our domestic law accommodated the 1970 convention and so to enable its ratification by
the United Kingdom. It was also passed to embrace within one Act of Parliament the *b*
relevant powers of superior courts in the United Kingdom, previously contained in a
number of Acts of Parliament; and the 1975 Act confers powers which apply in relation
to other jurisdictions within the United Kingdom and, like its predecessors, enables
courts in the United Kingdom to assist courts in other jurisdictions throughout the
world, whether in convention countries (including not only the 1970 convention but
other conventions to which this country is party) or in non-convention countries (of *c*
which there are still a large number). In these circumstances, in considering the scope of
the jurisdiction conferred by the 1975 Act, it is, in my opinion, both legitimate and
appropriate to have regard to the legislative history of the Act.

I turn therefore to the earlier legislation. As I have already indicated, the first Act of
Parliament concerned with the obtaining of evidence for the assistance of foreign courts
and tribunals is the Foreign Tribunals Evidence Act 1856. The origins of this Act are *d*
obscure; all that we know is that the Act has no direct treaty base. Section 1 of the Act
confers on superior courts in the United Kingdom jurisdiction 'to order the Examination
upon Oath, upon Interrogatories or otherwise, before any Person or Persons named in
such order' of witnesses within the jurisdiction whose testimony 'any Court or Tribunal
of competent Jurisdiction in a Foreign Country, before which any Civil or Commercial
Matter is pending, is desirous of obtaining . . . in relation to such matter . . .' The crucial *e*
point is, of course, the power to compel the witnesses to attend any such examination.

Here we find the first mention in an Act of Parliament, at least in this context, of the
expression 'civil or commercial matter'. It is plain that here the word 'matter' is used as
referring to the relevant proceedings, because in s 1 the 'matter' is required (consistently
with the long title and s 2 of the Act) to be *pending* before the foreign court or tribunal.
This reinforces the natural inference that, in s 1 of the Act, the expression 'civil matter' is *f*
being given no restricted meaning and would be understood in this country as referring
to civil, as opposed to criminal, proceedings. It is true that this gives no weight to the
words 'or commercial' so far as the law of this country is concerned; but it is not
surprising to find these words added in relation to a jurisdiction which will be invoked
by courts or tribunals in foreign countries, many of which differentiate between civil
and commercial matters. *g*

Section 2 of the 1856 Act makes provision for a certification procedure, under which a
certificate of a diplomatic agent or consul of a foreign country—

'that any Matter in relation to which an Application is made under this Act is a
Civil or Commercial Matter pending before a Court or Tribunal in the Country of
which he is the Diplomatic Agent or Consul having Jurisdiction in the Matter so *h*
pending, and that such Court or Tribunal is desirous of obtaining the Testimony of
the Witness or Witnesses to whom the applicant relates . . .'

shall be evidence of the matter so certified. This shows that the general intention of
Parliament in the Act was to provide assistance in respect of any pending matters which,
in the requesting state, would be described as civil or commercial, though it must also *j*
have been intended that the United Kingdom courts (whose jurisdiction was established
under s 1) should not exercise that jurisdiction in matters which would, in the relevant
jurisdiction in this country, be classified as criminal, even though in the requesting state
they are classified as civil or commercial. In any event, there can be no question of the
jurisdiction of the United Kingdom courts being dependent on a 'civil law' classification
of the relevant matter as civil or commercial.

Three years after the 1856 Act there was passed the Evidence by Commission Act 1859
a (subsequently amended by the Evidence by Commission Act 1885), which conferred on
courts or tribunals of competent jurisdiction in Her Majesty's dominions power to obtain
evidence in relation to any action, suit or proceeding pending in or before courts or
tribunals elsewhere in Her Majesty's dominions. The words 'action, suit or proceeding'
are so wide that they must have been intended to embrace all kinds of proceedings, civil
or criminal. Eleven years later, the jurisdiction conferred by the 1856 Act in civil or
b commercial matters was extended by s 24 of the Extradition Act 1870 to apply in relation
to 'any criminal matter pending in a court or tribunal in a foreign state . . .' The 1870
Act provided that all provisions of the 1856 Act should be construed as if the term 'civil
matter' included a criminal matter; it follows that these were to be classified in the same
way as 'civil or commercial' matters under the 1856 Act. Three years later a fresh
provision relating to criminal matters was enacted in s 5 of the Extradition Act 1873,
c which provided that a Secretary of State may, by order under his hand and seal, require a
police magistrate or a justice of the peace to take evidence for the purposes of any criminal
matter pending in any court or tribunal in a foreign state.

These provisions remained in force for many years, until the repeal of all (except s 5 of
the Extradition Act 1873) by the 1975 Act. They were so repealed because, as is evident
from the long title of the 1975 Act, one important purpose of the Act was to make new
d provision, in one statute, for the jurisdiction of superior courts in the United Kingdom
in relation to obtaining evidence for the assistance of courts or tribunals in other
jurisdictions, whether elsewhere in the United Kingdom, or in the few surviving British
dominions (which include the important commercial centre of Hong Kong), or in other
countries (whether or not members of the Commonwealth). The 1873 Act was no doubt
excluded because it did not affect the jurisdiction of the High Court, the Court of Session
e or the High Court of Justice in Northern Ireland.

Such is the legislative history. I turn to the conventions. It appears from the evidence
before your Lordships' House that the first international conventions concerned with
obtaining evidence for the assistance of courts or tribunals in foreign jurisdictions consist
of a series of 23 bilateral conventions entered into between the United Kingdom and
f various foreign countries. The first is a convention with France in 1922; the last before
the 1970 convention was a convention with Israel in 1966. Apart from the convention
with Israel, all the foreign countries concerned can broadly be described as civil law
countries; they include Norway, with which a convention was entered into in 1931
(London, 7 August 1931; TS 35 (1931); Cmd 3934). Each convention has, of course, texts
both in the English language and in the language of the relevant foreign country. In
g each, the convention is stated (in the English text) to apply in civil or commercial matters.

In the convention with France of 1922 (as in that with Belgium in 1924) it is stated in
the French text that the convention applies 'en matière civile ou commerciale'. This
expression is also to be found in an earlier multilateral convention in 1896, to which a
number of European states (though not the United Kingdom) were parties, concerned
with the service of documents (a matter also dealt with in the bilateral conventions and
h now the subject of the 1965 Hague Convention). Doubtless similar expressions were
used, in the various languages, in the other 21 bilateral conventions entered into by the
United Kingdom. In all the circumstances, however, I do not regard it as a legitimate
inference that the English expression 'civil or commercial matters' in these conventions
is a translation from the French 'matière civile ou commerciale,' expecially bearing in
mind that the expression 'any civil or commercial matter' was also to be found in the
j United Kingdom statute conferring the then relevant jurisdiction on our courts, which
had been on the statute book for nearly 70 years before the 1922 convention with France.
Doubtless all states which were parties to these conventions interpreted the expression,
as used in their own languages, in their own ways. Even so, as appears from preparatory
documents relating to the 1970 convention, no difficulty was experienced in practice in
the operation of these conventions. Each provided that any such difficulties as might
arise should be settled through the diplomatic channel. Indeed, the jurisdiction of

national courts, as in this country, is no doubt established by domestic legislation, which may well be (in Norway, as in this country) of wider application, on its face not expressly *a* related to (though no doubt framed to accommodate) any convention to which the country is party.

It is in these circumstances of some interest to have regard to the position relating to Commonwealth countries. In 1859 all the relevant countries were British dominions, and so the courts and tribunals in this country and in the British dominions could, in relation to each other, take advantage of the wide language of the 1859 Act, which *b* referred to 'any action, suit or proceeding'.

Following the Statute of Westminster 1931 and the movement to independence after the 1939–45 war, the great majority of these countries have acquired independent status. Nevertheless, as is normal, much of the old imperial legislation was continued in force in relation to each country on attaining independence, including the 1856 and 1859 Acts. These Acts (repealed by the United Kingdom Parliament by the 1975 Act) have no doubt *c* also been repealed by many Commonwealth countries. I cannot say whether this has invariably been done or, if it has been done, when it was done. Let me however give two examples. In India the two Acts were repealed, together with many other statutes, by the British Statutes (Application to India) Repeal Act 1960, the relevant law then being found in provisions of the Indian Codes of Civil and Criminal Procedure. Under the Code of Civil Procedure 1908, ss 76 and 78 confer jurisdiction on Indian courts relating to the *d* execution and return of commissions and, in the case of commissions issued at the instance of foreign tribunals, Ord 26, r 19, of the relevant rules of court requires only that 'the proceeding is of a civil nature'. In New South Wales it appears that the 1856 and 1859 Acts will shortly be repealed by the Evidence (Evidence on Commission) Amendment Act 1988, which has not yet been brought into force; by that Act they will be replaced (see Pt IX of the 1988 Act, concerned with taking of evidence for foreign and *e* Australian courts) by, inter alia, new provisions applicable in relation to 'proceedings in any civil or commercial matter' which are very similar to ss 1, 2 and 3 of the 1975 Act. Furthermore it appears that, in relation to the few remaining British colonies, the 1856 and 1859 Acts having been repealed, the provisions of the 1975 Act (with appropriate modifications) have been applied to them by various ordinances, in 1975 or later. It follows that, as between many countries in the common law legal family (and, in due *f* course, so far as New South Wales is concerned, as between that state and other Australian states), the relevant jurisdiction is expressed to be in 'proceedings in civil or commercial matters'. But for some years at least in relation to many Commonwealth countries (and, it may be, still today in relation to others), the jurisdiction of the United Kingdom courts has been in proceedings 'in any civil or commercial matter' under the 1975 Act, whereas the jurisdiction of the courts of other Commonwealth countries, in relation to the United *g* Kingdom or in relation to other countries, has been that conferred by the 1856 and 1859 Acts, or (as in the case of India) has otherwise been broadly defined. It is, in my opinion, important to bear in mind, when ascertaining the jurisdiction conferred on the courts of the United Kingdom by the 1975 Act, its impact on the relationship between the courts of this country and the courts of Commonwealth countries, with whom, as fellow *h* members of the largest legal family in the world, we enjoy the closest of legal ties.

It is against this background that I turn to consider the 1975 Act, and in particular the expression 'civil proceedings' in s 1(b) of the Act, as defined in s 9(1), viz "civil proceedings", in relation to the requesting court, means proceedings in any civil or commercial matter . . .'

Now it is true that the words 'proceedings in any civil or commercial matter' in s 9(1) *j* differ from the words 'any civil or commercial matter' in s 1 of the 1856 Act; and it can be argued that, in this slightly different phraseology, it would be tautologous to identify the relevant 'matter' with the proceedings themselves, and that it might therefore be proper to apply a substantive rather than a procedural test for the purpose of characterising the relevant proceedings as civil, and to do so with reference to the French words in the

1970 convention. I cannot however help thinking that this very slight change in wording
a constitutes a slender basis on which to build so substantial a departure from the previous
law. Indeed, it would be remarkable if it were intended to do so, when the relevant
wording in the 1970 convention mirrors that in the 23 bilateral conventions which were
operated without difficulty under the 1856 Act.

But this verbal point pales into insignificance beside the fact that the argument
advanced on behalf of the witnesses would involve a profound departure from the
b established legal practice of conferring a very broad jurisdiction on the courts in the
United Kingdom to enable them to provide assistance for courts in other jurisdictions by
obtaining evidence for them. There is no hint in the statute itself that any such departure
was intended; indeed the long title of the Act makes no reference at all to the 1970
convention. I wish to dwell for a moment on the consequences if the witnesses'
contention were to be accepted, and the expression 'proceedings in any civil or
c commercial matter' in s 9(1) were to be given a restricted construction, derived from the
French text of art 1 of the convention, limited by reference to a civil law meaning to be
derived from the words in the French text.

I first refer to the fact that the jurisdiction under the 1975 Act can be invoked to obtain
evidence for the assistance of a court or tribunal in another jurisdiction in the United
Kingdom. No doubt, within the United Kingdom, it is normal for a court desiring to
d obtain evidence from another jurisdiction in the United Kingdom now to take advantage
(where necessary) of the extended power of subpoena embodied in s 4 of the 1975 Act.
But it may not always be possible to obtain evidence in this way, for example where a
witness is ill and so unable to comply with a subpoena; and the simple fact remains that
the jurisdiction under the Act is not restricted to obtaining evidence in aid of foreign
jurisdictions. It is surely improbable that Parliament should, in these circumstances,
e have legislated that the jurisdiction should be restricted to proceedings in a civil or
commercial matter in a sense understood in civil law countries.

Next, for over a century since 1859, courts or tribunals in British dominions, most of
them now independent members of the Commonwealth, have been able to take
advantage of an unrestricted jurisdiction in all actions, suits or proceedings. It would be
strange indeed if, in relation to these countries, the jurisdiction should not be limited
f with reference to the law of civil law countries, not only in relation to the remaining
Crown colonies, but also in relation to members of the Commonwealth whose courts
continued after independence to enjoy an unrestricted jurisdiction. All (or very nearly
all) of these countries are, as I have said, members of the common law legal family, to
whom the restricted meaning of 'civil or commercial matters', deriving as it does from a
different system of law, is unknown.

g Furthermore the 1975 Act confers, as I have said, a jurisdiction exercisable (like the old
jurisdiction under the 1856 Act) in order to assist courts or tribunals in all countries,
whether or not parties to the 1970 convention. It is understandable that that convention
should have prompted the passage of the 1975 Act; but it is very difficult to see why
Parliament should, for the first time, have here restricted this universal jurisdiction with
reference to the French text of the convention, and most unlikely that it should have
h done so sub silentio, ie without making it express that this was indeed the legislative
purpose.

Lastly the Act provides, consistently with the law as it has stood for over 100 years
(since s 24 of the 1870 Act), for courts in the United Kingdom to have jurisdiction to
assist courts in other countries by obtaining evidence in criminal proceedings. This
j power has nothing to do with private law at all; and it would be surprising if Parliament
was expressly to perpetuate the power in relation to criminal proceedings, which are par
excellence proceedings brought by the foreign state itself, and at the same time be held,
by reference to s 9(1), to have restricted the meaning of the words 'civil or commercial
matter' by excluding from them what are recognised (in varying forms) as public law
cases by the law of certain states. Indeed, the argument for the witnesses leads to the

remarkable conclusion that, if penal proceedings in the requesting court are categorised
as criminal proceedings, the English court can assist under s 5; but if they are not
criminal proceedings, the English court has no jurisdiction to assist.

But the matter does not stop there. Your Lordships' House has, like the courts below,
been provided with a most helpful selection of comparative law material. Study of this
material reveals that it is very difficult to attribute any uniform meaning to 'matière
civile ou commerciale' or 'civil or commercial matter', in civil law countries. There
appears to be little doubt that, in most if not all civil law countries, an important
distinction is drawn between private law and public law, and that public law matters are
generally excluded from civil or commercial matters. But the identification of public
law matters differs from country to country, sometimes in minor respects, sometimes in
major respects. I myself, like Woolf LJ in *Norway (No 2)* [1989] 1 All ER 701, have
derived great assistance from the substantial account, given by Professor Charles Szladits
of the Columbia Law School, of the distinction between public law and private law in
the civil law system, contained in the *International Encyclopaedia of Comparative Law* vol 2.
That volume, entitled 'The Legal Systems of the World: Their Comparison and
Unification', is under the chief editorship of Professor René David; Professor Szladits'
account forms part of ch 2 of the volume, entitled 'Structure and the Divisions of the
Law'. In his introduction, Professor Szladits states (para 25):

> 'The fundamental division between private law and public law is considered a
> basic distinction, the *summa divisio*, in all legal systems belonging to the Civil Law
> family of laws. The scope of this division, however, differs considerably within the
> different legal systems, and consequently the theoretical analysis and the reasons, as
> well as the practical effects, of these divisions also differ. From the point of view of
> comparative law, the description of divisions of law and its explanation is a
> bewildering and difficult task because of their kaleidoscopic nature. Although the
> same categories can be found—more or less—in all the legal systems of the Civil
> Law, the disparity of premises on which they have been established points rather to
> historical accident and practical convenience than to any all-embracing logical or
> structural basis.'

Later he states (para 31):

> 'The dual division of law into public law and private law has been accepted in all
> the Civil Law systems. This uniformity disappears, however, when we consider the
> scope of the division, namely, what branches of law are subsumed under the one or
> the other.'

He then proceeds in this section (and in the following section, concerned with specific
traits of public law) to illustrate by detailed reference the divergences of approach in the
various civil law systems, considering that it is in the French and German legal systems
that the didactic classification of law differs most. It is not necessary for me to go into
detail, but I wish to quote from Professor Szladits on this distinction (para 57):

> 'The distinction between public law and private law "seems to many Continental
> European lawyers to be fundamental, necessary and, on the whole, evident.
> Institutional works, student manuals and treatises contain discussions of the
> dichotomy, often in confidently dogmatic terms that put to rest incipient doubts."
> This is an excellent summary of the situation generally prevailing in the Civil Law
> systems. Yet this division is far from "necessary" and far from "evident." The criteria
> of distinction are established neither in theory nor in the practice of the courts; and,
> in view of the everincreasing interpenetration of public law and private law the
> dichotomy appears to be in process of dissolution, which may indicate that it is not
> even so "fundamental" as it has been hitherto thought to be. Yet in spite of these
> doubts and contradictions, the dichotomy is firmly rooted in the thinking of the
> civilian lawyer.'

In these circumstances, it is scarcely surprising to find, in Preliminary Document No 3
a of August 1968 relating to what became the 1970 convention (Report of the Special
Commission established by M Amram) the statement that:

> 'The opening phrase of Article 1 immediately precipitated a spirited debate on
> the scope of the Convention. There was no disagreement that the Convention
> should be limited to "civil and commercial matters" but there was debate on the
> definition of a "civil and commercial matter"...'
b

However, having ascertained that previous conventions in which this phrase was used
(including the bilateral conventions to which the United Kingdom was party) had
worked effectively without any need for specific definition of the phrase, and having
regard to the historic policy of the Hague Conference to include neither a definition nor
a rule of conflicts to resolve a dispute between the states on such an issue, it was decided
c that art 1 should follow the historic pattern without any definition of 'civil or commercial
matters'.

In these circumstances, it must in any event be very difficult to identify, by reference
to civil law systems, any 'internationally acceptable definition' of the expression 'civil or
commercial matters'. Even if it were appropriate to define the expression in the 1975
Act with reference to the text of the 1970 convention, no internationally acceptable
d definition could be derived from that source. This reinforces my opinion that Parliament
did not intend, by any such means, to make the profound change, now adumbrated by
the witnesses, in the jurisdiction of the courts of the United Kingdom.

I need only add, on this aspect of the case, that I do not feel able to draw any assistance
from the Convention on Jurisdiction and the Enforcement of Judgments in Civil and
Commercial Matters (Brussels, 27 September 1968; EC 46 (1978); Cmnd 7395), to which
e the United Kingdom acceded in 1978, and to which effect was given in the United
Kingdom by the Civil Jurisdiction and Judgments Act 1982. Quite apart from the fact
that the convention excludes certain specific matters, thus delineating the 'civil and
commercial matters' to which it applies, there is a court (the Court of Justice of the
European Communities) which has the power and the duty to impose a uniform
meaning on the convention; and it is scarcely surprising that, bearing in mind that the
f original signatories to the convention were all civil law countries, the meaning so
imposed should be derived from the civil law.

For these reasons, in agreement with the Court of Appeal in *Norway (No 1)* [1989] 1
All ER 661, and with Woolf LJ in *Norway (No 2)* [1989] 1 All ER 701, I have come to the
conclusion that the words 'civil or commercial matters' in the 1975 Act cannot be
construed with reference to any internationally acceptable meaning. There remains
g therefore the question how they should be construed; and to answer that question it is
first necessary to consider by reference to which system of law this question should be
answered.

In the courts below three alternatives were canvassed: (1) the law of the requesting
court; (2) the law of the court addressed (in the present case, the law of this country); and
h (3) a combination of both laws, ie jurisdiction would only be established if the relevant
proceedings were proceedings in a civil or commercial matter under the laws of both
countries. In *Norway (No 1)* the Court of Appeal, having rejected the solution of an
internationally acceptable interpretation, preferred the third solution. In *Norway (No 2)*
the point did not arise for May or Balcombe LJJ; Woolf LJ preferred the second solution.
On this point I find myself to be in agreement with the Court of Appeal in *Norway*
j *(No 1)*. Such a conclusion is consistent with the approach under the 1856 Act. (It is true
that the certification procedure under that Act no longer applies; but that is scarcely
surprising, bearing in mind the improvement in communications.) I can discern, in the
1975 Act, no intention to depart from the former approach, which in any event
introduces a desirable element of comity into the procedure.

It was, of course, because the Court of Appeal in *Norway (No 1)* preferred the third
solution that Kerr LJ regretted that he had insufficient assistance on Norwegian law, with

the consequence that, in *Norway (No 2)*, a substantial body of evidence was made available
to the English court from distinguished Norwegian lawyers. The Norwegian lawyers *a*
provided very full and helpful written opinions on the point. Professor Huser of the
University of Bergen (whose evidence was supported by Professor Haerem and Professor
Bernt) supported the thesis advanced by the witnesses that, by Norwegian law, civil and
commercial matters did not include public law matters and so excluded fiscal matters.
On the other hand Professor Fleischer, of the University of Oslo and the Norwegian
Ministry of Foreign Affairs, supported the thesis that, by Norwegian law as by the law of *b*
this country, it was appropriate to identify civil matters as consisting of all matters other
than criminal matters, and so capable of including fiscal matters. Both Professor Huser
and Professor Fleischer gave oral testimony in addition to their written opinions.

Study of the written opinions of Professor Huser and Professor Fleischer reveals that
the difference of opinion between them stems, to a very substantial degree, from the fact
that they were asking themselves different questions. Professor Huser's opinion was *c*
devoted to an examination of the structure of Norwegian law, and to the division of
Norwegian law into private law and public law; his answer was that the 'subject matter
of the Sandefjord case' should be classified as tax law, which is part of the well-established
category of public law, and so not a civil or commercial matter. Professor Fleischer, on
the other hand, distinguished between classification of the rules of law, and classification
of the cases or matters actually before the courts. He expressed the opinion that, in the *d*
general understanding and common usage of Norwegian lawyers:

> '. . . the term and concept of "civil" refer to "civil" as opposed to "criminal". The
> term "civil" is used to describe both the procedure applied by the courts—in
> conformity with the code on civil procedure as opposed to the code on the procedure
> in criminal cases—and the matters brought before them.'   *e*

It is apparent, therefore, that this difference of opinion could only be resolved by
identifying the correct question which should have been posed for their consideration.

I therefore turn back to the 1975 Act and ask myself: what is the correct question
which should be addressed to experts in the law of the requesting court? The answer is,
in my opinion, a very simple one. It is that it is a matter for the law and practice of the *f*
requesting state, having regard to the manner in which classification is ordinarily made
in that country.

Let me take, as an example, a request by a court in a Commonwealth country. The
court of the requesting state would (like any court in this country) never think that it
was required to delve into a distinction founded only on the substance of the relevant
proceedings. It would simply say to itself: in our country, unlike some other countries,
we do not draw any distinction between civil and commercial matters, and so we can *g*
ignore that; these are plainly civil proceedings, because they are not criminal proceedings;
therefore we can apply for assistance from the English court under s 1 of the 1975 Act. I
have no doubt that the English court would find such an approach entirely acceptable;
and, if it is acceptable in relation to a court in a Commonwealth country, I cannot see
why any different approach should be adopted in relation to a request for assistance from *h*
a Norwegian court.

In the present case Kenneth Jones J concluded, on the evidence before him, that, under
Norwegian law, the proceedings in Norway would be classified as proceedings in a civil
matter. In my opinion, he was entirely justified in reaching that conclusion on the
evidence before him; indeed it seems to me that the evidence of Professor Fleischer, that
this was in accordance with the general understanding and common usage of Norwegian *j*
law, compelled that conclusion, which was also the conclusion reached by the Sandefjord
court itself. In saying this, I intend no disrespect to Professor Huser and his colleagues.
On the contrary, they were in my opinion invited to consider a question restricted to the
substance of the proceedings, irrespective of the ordinary practice in Norway; and indeed
their evidence reveals that the question they were being asked to consider was, in
Norwegian terms, somewhat unreal.

The judge's conclusion is moreover consistent with the view expressed by Lord
a Diplock in the *Westinghouse* case [1978] 1 All ER 434 at 461–462, [1978] AC 547 at 633–
634 that in the ordinary way the English court should be prepared to accept the statement
of the requesting court that the evidence is required for the purpose of civil proceedings.
It is appropriate that the requesting court should have regard to its own ordinary
approach to these matters, without indulging in an analysis which is inappropriate in its
own system. In this way, the 1975 Act can be made to work sensibly in relation to all
b countries in the world, common law countries and civil law countries alike, without
requiring any of them to act in any way which is foreign to its own way of thinking; and
expert evidence will, in the vast majority of cases, be unnecessary. In theory, as under
the 1856 Act, an English court would not treat a matter as civil or commercial which
would, by English law, fall to be classified as criminal, in which event it would treat the
request as falling under s 5 of the Act instead of under s 1. It is however difficult to
c imagine such a case arising in practice.

I turn next to the question whether, as a matter of English law, the jurisdiction of the
High Court under the 1975 Act in respect of civil proceedings is wide enough to embrace
proceedings in fiscal matters. Woolf LJ considered that it was not. He said ([1989] 1 All
ER 701 at 740):

d 'While I cannot identify an acceptable international interpretation of the phrase
['civil or commercial matter'], I do accept that the material which is before the court
is overwhelmingly to the effect that whatever else is or is not included in the concept
of a civil or commercial matter, matières fiscales are not within that concept and
this can be taken into account in construing the section. Even in common law
jurisdictions, so far as enforcement of judgments is concerned it has been recognised
e that revenue matters come within a different and special category and are subject to
rules of public policy which do not apply to other civil proceedings . . . Taking into
account the well-established approach of the courts to assisting in tax gathering by a
foreign state, I would regard the proper interpretation of the words 'civil or
commercial matter' in the 1975 Act as excluding matières fiscales.'

f I feel driven to state, with all respect, that in my opinion the approach of Woolf LJ is, on
this point, not logical. My difficulty with his reasoning is that he appears to conclude
that 'matières fiscales' should be excluded as a matter of general international
interpretation. He has however rejected the existence of any generally acceptable
international interpretation of the expression 'civil or commercial matter', and I do not
see how he can, on any such basis, exclude fiscal matters. The point has, in my opinion,
g to be considered with reference to English law.

I have no doubt that, under English law, the words in s 9(1) should be given their
ordinary meaning, so that proceedings in any civil matter should include all proceedings
other than criminal proceedings, and proceedings in any commercial matter should be
treated as falling within proceedings in civil matters. On this simple approach, I do not
see why the expression should be read as excluding proceedings in a fiscal matter; so that
h the High Court can have jurisdiction in respect of such a matter under the 1975 Act.

In his case note on the Court of Appeal's decision in *Norway (No 1)* entitled 'Any Civil
or Commercial Matter' (1986) 102 LQR 505 at 509 Dr F A Mann stated:

'. . . it can be asserted with confidence that very few States (if any) will ever regard
a tax claim as a civil or commercial matter.'

j
I myself have little doubt that this is broadly true in the case of most civil law countries,
with their classification of law into public law matters (including fiscal matters) and
private law matters (with which alone civil and commercial matters are concerned);
though this does not appear to be true of the law of Norway, having regard to the
evidence of Professor Fleischer and the terms of the relevant parts of the Norwegian Law
Courts Act. But, so far as common law countries are concerned, the matter is, on the

material before your Lordships' House, completely unresolved. The American Law
Institute's Restatement, Third, Foreign Relations Law, §471, comment *f*, §473, *a*
comment *c* indicates that the practice in the United States is to consider any proceeding
which is not criminal as coming within the provisions of the 1970 convention, and that
letters of request may be used in administrative proceedings, including proceedings
concerning fiscal matters. This view appears to be consistent with the Report of the
United States Delegation to the Special Commission on the Operation of the 1970 Hague
Convention, dated June 1978, in which it is stated that the United Kingdom delegates *b*
concurred with the United States interpretation of the convention and stated that the
United Kingdom central authority followed the same practice as the United States. There
appears however to be no decision of any court in the United States on the point; nor has
any relevant decision from any other common law country been drawn to the attention
of your Lordships' House.

It is at this stage necessary to turn to the impact on the jurisdiction conferred on the *c*
courts of this country under the 1975 Act of the principle associated with the decision of
your Lordships' House in *Government of India Ministry of Finance (Revenue Division) v Taylor*
[1955] 1 All ER 292, [1955] AC 491. In *Dicey and Morris on the Conflict of Laws* (11th edn,
1987) p 100, r 3 provides as follows:

> 'English courts have no jurisdiction to entertain an action: (1) for the enforcement, *d*
> either directly or indirectly, of a penal, revenue or other public law of a foreign
> State; or (2) founded upon an act of State.'

In that rule it is stated that the English courts *have no jurisdiction* to entertain such an
action. However, in *Dicey and Morris* p 101 itself it is recognised that the theoretical basis
of the rule is a matter of some controversy. The editors express the opinion that the best
explanation is to be found in the speech of Lord Keith in the *Government of India* case *e*
[1955] 1 All ER 292 at 299, [1955] AC 491 at 511, where he said:

> 'One explanation of the rule . . . may be thought to be that enforcement of a claim
> for taxes is but an extension of the sovereign power which imposed the taxes, and
> that an assertion of sovereign authority by one state within the territory of another,
> as distinct from a patrimonial claim by a foreign sovereign, is (treaty or convention *f*
> apart) contrary to all concepts of independent sovereignties.'

This opinion is consistent with that expressed by Lord Denning MR in *A-G of New
Zealand v Ortiz* [1982] 3 All ER 432 at 457, [1984] AC 1 at 21, where he said:

> 'By international law every sovereign state has no sovereignty beyond its own
> frontiers. The courts of other countries will not allow it to go beyond the bounds. *g*
> They will not enforce any of its laws which purport to exercise sovereignty beyond
> the limits of its authority.'

It is not necessary for the purposes of the present case to decide what is the precise
theoretical basis of the rule, though I am respectfully inclined to agree with Lord Keith's
expression of opinion. At all events the rule cannot, in my view, go to the jurisdiction of *h*
the English court. What the English court does is simply to decline in such cases to
exercise its jurisdiction, and on that basis the relevant proceedings will be either struck
out or dismissed.

The question arises whether, given the fundamental nature of the principle embodied
in r 3 of *Dicey and Morris*, as applied in revenue cases, the jurisdiction conferred by s 1 of
the 1975 Act should be read as qualified by reference to that principle. I myself can see *j*
no basis for concluding that the jurisdiction should be regarded as qualified in this way
as a matter of construction of the Act. The words in the Act are unqualified; and the rule
in *Dicey and Morris* does not, as I see it, go to jurisdiction.

There remains however the further question whether, given that the jurisdiction is
unqualified, the English courts should decline to exercise that jurisdiction in the case of

letters of request for assistance in relation to civil proceedings concerned with the
a enforcement of the revenue laws of the requesting state. It can be argued that they
should decline to do so, as a matter of judicial discretion, on the basis that direct or
indirect enforcement of foreign revenue laws constitutes an invasion of the sovereignty
of this country, and is contrary to a fundamental rule of English law.

It has been suggested that that question can be avoided in the present case because the
letters of request have been issued in response to an application by a taxpayer, seeking
b assistance for the purpose of opposing a claim by a foreign state for tax. In agreement
with the Court of Appeal in *Norway (No 1)*, I am for my part prepared to accept that
submission. I do not see how such letters of request, or their execution, could amount to
the enforcement, direct or indirect, of a foreign revenue law; nor do I see how they could
constitute an invasion of this country's sovereignty. Such a conclusion is, in my opinion,
acceptable, once it is recognised that the rule does not affect the jurisdiction of the court,
c but is concerned rather with circumstances in which the court declines to exercise its
jurisdiction. In the case of an application by a taxpayer, I do not consider that the rule
requires the court to decline to exercise jurisdiction. It is true that in the present case the
request was made by both the state and the estate. But in such a case the English court
could (if necessary) accede to the application of the estate, while rejecting that of the state.

However, since the state, as well as the estate, is applying for the assistance of the
d English courts, it is necessary to consider, in relation to the application of the state, the
broader question whether the execution of letters of request in relation to foreign civil
proceedings in a fiscal matter should, if the request is made on the application not of the
taxpayer but of the taxing authority, be refused by an English court on this ground. I
must confess to having given the most anxious consideration to this question. First, the
rule is deeply embedded not only in the common law but also in the law of civil law
e countries. An eloquent account of it in French law is to be found in the exposition by
Professor Mazeaud of *Bemberg v Revenue Authorities of the Province of Buenos Aires* (24
February 1949, unreported). Second, there appears to exist no case of fiscal proceedings
in relation to which letters of request have been executed in any jurisdiction; and it can
be argued (as indeed it is argued by Mazeaud) that, if a change has to be made, it should
be made by legislation and not by judicial decision.
f
Counsel for the witnesses helpfully placed before your Lordships a most useful bundle
of documents concerned with double taxation conventions, including the text of the
OECD Model Agreement, and also the text of the draft OECD Convention on Mutual
Administrative Assistance in Tax Matters. This last document serves the useful purpose
of demonstrating the range of matters which such a convention might cover, and the
safeguards which might properly be embodied in it. It is right to say, however, that the
g draft convention provides for matters going far beyond simple requests by foreign courts
for assistance in obtaining evidence in relation to pending or contemplated proceedings.

I return to the rule in the *Government of India* case. It is of importance to observe that
that rule is limited to cases of direct or indirect enforcement in this country of the
revenue laws of a foreign state. It is plain that the present case is not concerned with the
h direct enforcement of the revenue laws of the State of Norway. Is it concerned with their
indirect enforcement? I do not think so. It is stated in *Dicey and Morris* p 103 that
indirect enforcement occurs (1) where the foreign state (or its nominee) in form seeks a
remedy which in substance is designed to give the foreign law extra-territorial effect or
(2) where a private party raises a defence based on the foreign law in order to vindicate or
assert the right of the foreign state. I have been unable to discover any case of indirect
j enforcement which goes beyond these two propositions. Even so, since there is no
authority directly in point to guide me, I have to consider whether a case such as the
present should nevertheless be held to fall foul of the rule. For my part, I cannot see that
it should. I cannot see any extra-territorial exercise of sovereign authority in seeking the
assistance of the courts of this country in obtaining evidence which will be used for the
enforcement of the revenue laws of Norway in Norway itself. Let it be supposed, for

example, that in *A-G of New Zealand v Ortiz* [1983] 2 All ER 93, [1984] AC 1 the case was not one of New Zealand seeking to enforce its claim in this country, but of seeking the assistance of the English courts to obtain evidence to enforce its claim in New Zealand. I find it very difficult to imagine that such an application would have been refused. Nor do I consider that refusal of the application of the State of Norway in the present case could easily be reconciled with the power of the courts of this country to exercise their jurisdiction under the 1975 Act in criminal proceedings, for example, criminal proceedings in Norway in a case of tax evasion.

It follows that I am unable to accept the submissions of the witnesses on the first two points argued by them before your Lordships' House.

'Fishing' and confidentiality

I turn then to the two remaining issues, concerned respectively with 'fishing' and confidentiality. These two issues I can deal with very shortly.

On the question of 'fishing', the only issue before your Lordships' House is whether the order made by Kenneth Jones J in *Norway (No 2)*, under which the second letter of request (subject to certain deletions made by him in the list of issues set out in schedule 1 to his order) was held not to constitute an impermissible 'fishing expedition' but to constitute rather a legitimate request for assistance in the obtaining of evidence, should stand. The Court of Appeal in *Norway (No 2)* decided (subject to the restoration of para 8 of schedule 1 in an amended form, as set out in the judgment of Balcombe LJ (see [1989] 1 All ER 701)), to uphold the decision of the judge on this point.

Before your Lordships' House it was submitted on behalf of the witnesses that the second letter of request, taken as a whole, was in substance no more than an exercise in 'fishing' and, as such, should have been rejected in toto without attempting, by editing it, to limit it to a request for assistance in obtaining evidence. Having studied the letter of request, and the limited deletions made by the judge, I am unable to accept this submission. In my opinion, the true position is the reverse. The letter of request was in substance a request for what, by English law, would be regarded as assistance in obtaining evidence. The judge however formed the opinion that some of the issues identified in the letter of request went beyond evidence and deleted them. The Court of Appeal saw no reason to differ from the judge's decision. The witnesses' appeal on this point is concerned only with a matter of judgment, on which your Lordships' House would not normally depart from a concurrent decision by the judge of first instance and the Court of Appeal. I can see no reason to do so in the present case.

I wish, however, to add that, since the state does not appeal against the deletions made by the judge, your Lordships' House does not have to consider any matter of principle on this issue, and in particular does not have to consider the conflict of opinion between Kerr and Glidewell LJJ in *Norway (No 1)* on the one hand and Ralph Gibson LJ in *Norway (No 1)* and Woolf LJ in *Norway (No 2)* on the other hand on the principles to be applied by courts in this country in considering whether or not the matters on which the requesting state seeks assistance do or do not constitute evidence. On this question, I wish to reserve my opinion.

It is accepted on both sides that the question of confidentiality can only be answered by the court undertaking a balancing exercise, weighing on the one hand the public interest in preserving the confidentiality owed by the witnesses as bankers to their customers, and on the other hand the public interest in the English courts assisting the Norwegian court in obtaining evidence in this country. In *Norway (No 2)* that balancing exercise was performed by the judge. He took into account the considerations urged on behalf of the witnesses, and in particular the matters set out in affidavits sworn on behalf of them, stressing the importance of the duty of confidentiality owed by bankers in this country, notably in the City of London. He then said:

'The major consideration is, undoubtedly, that referred to by Lord Kindersley in

his letter to the Norwegian lawyer, acting for the estate, on 15 April 1984 . . .
a namely the identity of the settlor. Lord Kindersley seeks that his identity and
information which might indirectly reveal his identity should remain a matter of
confidence and should not pass into the public domain, as it might do if he were
required to give evidence in the Sandefjord proceedings. On the other hand, if it
could be shown that the settlor in relation to the matters with which the Sandefjord
court is directly concerned, was acting merely as the agent or nominee of Jahre, then
b the public policy of assisting a foreign court to the proper determination of the
matter before it would, in all probability, outweigh the public interest in upholding
the confidential relationship between the witnesses and the settlor.'

On that basis, he decided to reject the submission of the witnesses on the ground of
confidentiality, but made his order subject to a direction:

c   '. . . that the said witnesses shall not be required to reveal the identity of the
Settlor, or to answer any questions under Paragraph 7, 9, 10 or 11, unless the said
witnesses or one of them shall have said in evidence that the Settlor was, in relation
to the CTC shares and/or the assets of CTC held in the name of the Foundation
acting as the nominee or agent for Anders Jahre.'

d The Court of Appeal unanimously decided not to interfere with the judge's exercise of
his discretion on this point. In these circumstances, it would require cogent reasons to
persuade your Lordships to interfere with the judge's decision. For my part, I do not
consider that your Lordships should, in the present case, take that unusual step.

For these reasons, I would allow the appeal in *Norway (No 2)*, and restore the order of
Kenneth Jones J (subject to the restoration of the amended para 8 of schedule 1 to his
e order, to which I have already referred).

If the remainder of your Lordships should be in agreement with the opinion which I
have expressed on the appeal in *Norway (No 2)*, I would suggest that counsel, having
considered your Lordships' conclusion on that appeal, should be given the opportunity
briefly to address your Lordships on the appeal on costs in *Norway (No 1)*.

f **LORD LOWRY.** My Lords, I have had the advantage of reading in draft the speech of
my noble and learned friend Lord Goff. I agree with it and, for the reasons which he
gives, I, too, would allow the appeal in *Re State of Norway's Application (No 2)* [1989] 1 All
ER 701 and restore the order of Kenneth Jones J.

So exactly does the reasoning of that speech represent my view on the jurisdiction
issues that it would be pointless for me to add any observations of my own. I wish,
g however, to take the opportunity of expressly concurring in my noble and learned
friend's interpretation and application of the principle with regard to foreign proceedings
in fiscal matters which was enunciated by Lord Keith in *Government of India Ministry of
Finance (Revenue Division) v Taylor* [1955] 1 All ER 292, [1955] AC 491.

Appeal in Re State of Norway's Application (No 1) dismissed. No order as to costs in House of
h *Lords.*

Appeal in Re Norway's Application (No 2) allowed.

Solicitors: *Freshfields* (for the State of Norway); *Macfarlanes* (for the estate); *Linklaters &*
Paines (for the witnesses).

Mary Rose Plummer   Barrister.

Practice Direction   *a*

(Chancery 1/89)

CHANCERY DIVISION

Practice – Summons for directions – Chancery Division – Exchange of witness statements – Order for exchange normally to be made at hearing of summons for directions – Order to specify day on *b* *which exchange to be made – Objections to order – RSC Ord 3 8, r 2A.*

Practice – Summons for directions – Chancery Division – Pleadings – Complete set of pleadings to be lodged on issuing summons for directions.

1. Henceforward on the hearing of the summons for directions the master will normally *c* make an order under RSC Ord 38, r 2A for the exchange of witness statements of all oral evidence which any party intends to lead at the trial. The order will specify the day on which such exchange is to be made. Any party who objects to the making of such order or desires a modified order for such exchange must specifically raise the point for decision on the summons for directions.

2. Henceforward on issuing the summons for directions a complete set of pleadings *d* must be lodged.

By direction of the Vice-Chancellor.

R D MUNROW

23 January 1989   Chief Master. *e*

Practice Direction   *f*

LORD CHANCELLOR

Mental health – Patient – Legal proceedings involving patient – Appeal – Official Solicitor – Power to appeal to Court of Appeal in cases involving patients – Supreme Court Act 1981, s 90(3)(b) – Mental Health Act 1983 – RSC Ord 80, r 1. *g*

I, the Right Honourable James Peter Hymers, Baron Mackay of Clashfern, do hereby under s 90(3)(b) of the Supreme Court Act 1981 direct that the Official Solicitor to the Supreme Court shall have power to appeal to the Court of Appeal in any case involving a patient within the meaning of RSC Ord 80, r 1[a] which has been heard and determined by the High Court or a county court where (a) the Official Solicitor deems it in the *h* patient's interest that the case should be considered by the Court of Appeal, (b) the case may not otherwise be considered by the Court of Appeal and (c) the Court of Appeal gives leave.

16 January 1989   MACKAY OF CLASHFERN C.

                                                                    j

---

a   Rule 1, so far as material, provides: 'In this Order—"the Act" means the Mental Health Act 1983; "patient" means a person who, by reason of mental disorder within the meaning of the Act, is incapable of managing and administering his property and affairs . . .'

Practice Direction

FAMILY DIVISION

Husband and wife – Maintenance – Address – Disclosure – Address of person against whom order is sought or to be enforced – Disclosure of address by government departments – Disclosure at request of registrar – Particulars to be certified in request – Information to be supplied to registrar by applicant or solicitors prior to request – Maintenance Orders (Facilities for Enforcement) Act 1920 – Maintenance Orders Act 1950 – Army Act 1955, s 153 – Air Force Act 1955, s 153 – Naval Discipline Act 1957, s 101 – Maintenance Orders Act 1958 – Family Law Reform Act 1969, s 6 – Guardianship of Minors Act 1971 – Armed Forces Act 1971, s 62 – Matrimonial Causes Act 1973, ss 23, 24, 24A, 27, 31 – Children Act 1975, s 34 – Matrimonial and Family Proceedings Act 1984, s 17.

Ward of court – Missing ward – Address of ward or of person with whom ward believed to be – Disclosure of address by government departments – Disclosure at request of registrar – Particulars to be certified in request – Information to be supplied to registrar by applicant or solicitors prior to request – Child Abduction and Custody Act 1985 – Family Law Act 1986, Pt I.

The arrangements set out in the Registrar's Direction of 26 April 1988 ([1988] 2 All ER 573, [1988] 1 WLR 648) whereby the court may request the disclosure of addresses by government departments have been further extended. These arrangements will now cover (a) tracing the address of a person in proceedings against whom another person is seeking to obtain or enforce an order for financial provision either for himself or herself or for the children of the former marriage and (b) tracing the whereabouts of a child, or the person with whom the child is said to be, in proceedings under the Child Abduction and Custody Act 1985 or in which a custody order, as defined in Pt I of the Family Law Act 1986, is being sought or enforced. Requests for such information will be made officially by the registrar. The request, in addition to giving the information mentioned below, should certify: (A) *in financial provision applications* either (a) that a financial provision order is in existence, but cannot be enforced because the person against whom the order has been made cannot be traced, or (b) that the applicant has filed or issued a notice, petition or originating summons containing an application for financial provision which cannot be served because the respondent cannot be traced. A 'financial provision order' means any order made under ss 23, 24 24A and 27 of the Matrimonial Causes Act 1973 or the variations of any order made under s 31 of the 1973 Act, and any periodical payments or lump sum order made under s 6 of the Family Law Reform Act 1969, the Guardianship of Minors Act 1971, s 34 of the Children Act 1975 and any order registered in the High Court under the Maintenance Orders (Facilities for Enforcement) Act 1920, the Maintenance Orders Act 1950 and the Maintenance Orders Act 1958 and any order made under s 17 of the Matrimonial and Family Proceedings Act 1984; (B) *in wardship proceedings* that the child is the subject of wardship proceedings and cannot be traced and is believed to be with the person whose address is sought; (C) *in custody proceedings* that that child is the subject of custody proceedings and cannot be traced and is believed to be with the person whose address is sought.

The following notes set out the information required by those departments which are likely to be of the greatest assistance to an applicant.

(1) DEPARTMENT OF SOCIAL SECURITY

The department most likely to be able to assist is the Department of Social Security, whose records are the most comprehensive and complete. The possibility of identifying one person amongst so many will depend on the particulars given. An address will not be supplied by the department unless it is satisfied from the particulars given that the record of the person has been reliably identified.

The applicant or his solicitor should therefore be asked to supply as much as possible of the following information about the person sought: (i) national insurance number; (ii) surname; (iii) forenames in full; (iv) date of birth (or, if not known, approximate age); (v) last known address, with date when living there; (vi) any other known address(es) with dates; (vii) if the person sought is a war pensioner, his war pension and service particulars (if known); and, in applications for financial provision, (viii) the exact date of the marriage and the wife's forenames.

Inquiries should be sent by the registrar to:

Department of Social Security
NICB
Special Section A
Newcastle upon Tyne   NE98 1YX

The department will be prepared to search if given full particulars of the person's name and date of birth, but the chances of accurate identification are increased by the provision of more identifying information. Second requests for records to be searched, provided that a reasonable interval has elapsed, will be met by the Department of Social Security.

Supplementary benefit/income support
Where, in the case of applications for financial provision, the wife is or has been in receipt of supplementary benefit/income support, it would be advisable in the first instance to make inquiries of the manager of the local social security office for the area in which she resides in order to avoid possible duplication of inquiries.

(2) OFFICE OF POPULATION CENSUSES AND SURVEYS NATIONAL HEALTH SERVICE CENTRAL REGISTER
The Office of Population Censuses and Surveys administers the National Health Service Central Register for the Department of Health. The records held in the central register include individuals' names, with dates of birth and national health service number, against a record of the family practitioner committee area where the patient is currently registered with a national health service doctor. The central register does not hold individual patients' addresses, but can advise courts of the last family practitioner committee area registration. Courts can then apply for information about addresses to the appropriate family practitioner committee for independent action.

When application is made for the disclosure of family practitioner committee area registrations from these records the applicant or his solicitor should supply as much as possible of the following information about the person sought: (i) national health service number; (ii) surname; (iii) forenames in full; (iv) date of birth (or, if not known, approximate age); (v) last known address; (vi) mother's maiden name.

Inquiries should be sent by the registrar to:

Office of Population Censuses and Surveys
National Health Service Central Register
Smedley Hydro
Trafalgar Road
Southport
Merseyside   PR8 2HH

(3) PASSPORT OFFICE
If all reasonable inquiries including the aforesaid methods have failed to reveal an address, or if there are strong grounds for believing that the person sought may have made a recent application for a passport, inquiries may be made to the Passport Office. The applicant or his solicitor should provide as much of the following information about the person as possible: (i) surname; (ii) forenames in full; (iii) date of birth (or, if not known, approximate age); (iv) place of birth; (v) occupation; (vi) whether known to have travelled abroad, and, if so, the destination and dates; (vii) last known address, with date living there; (viii) any other known address(es), with dates.

The applicant or his solicitor must also undertake in writing that information given in

response to the inquiry will be used solely for the purpose for which it was requested, ie
a to assist in tracing the husband in connection with the making or enforcement of a
financial provision order or in tracing a child in connection with custody or wardship
proceedings, as the case may be.

Inquiries should be sent to:

The Chief Passport Officer
Passport Department
b   Home Office
Clive House
Petty France
London   SW1H 9HD

c (4) MINISTRY OF DEFENCE

In cases where the person sought is known to be serving or to have recently served in
any branch of HM Forces, the solicitor representing the applicant may obtain the address
for service of financial provision or custody and wardship proceedings direct from the
appropriate service department. In the case of army servicemen the solicitor can obtain a
list of regiments and of the various manning and record offices from the Officer in
d Charge, Central Manning Support Office, Higher Barracks, Exeter EX4 4ND.

The solicitors' request should be accompanied by a written undertaking that the
address will be used for the purpose of service of process in those proceedings and that so
far as is possible the solicitor will disclose the address only to the court and not to the
applicant or any other person, except in the normal course of the proceedings.

Alternatively if the solicitor wishes to serve process on the person's commanding
e officer under the provisions contained in s 101 of the Naval Discipline Act 1957, s 153 of
the Army Act 1955 and s 153 of the Air Force Act 1955 (all of which as amended by s 62
of the Armed Forces Act 1971) he may obtain that officer's address in the same way.

Where the applicant is acting in person the appropriate service department is prepared
to disclose the address of the person sought, or that of his commanding officer, to a
registrar on receipt of an assurance that the applicant has given an undertaking that the
f information will be used solely for the purpose of serving process in the proceedings.

In all cases the request should include details of the person's full name, service number,
rank or rating, and his ship, arm or trade, corps, regiment or unit or as much of this
information as is available. The request should also include details of his date of birth, or,
if not known, his age, his date of entry into the service and, if no longer serving, the date
of discharge, and any other information, such as his last known address. Failure to quote
g the service number and the rank or rating may result in failure to identify the serviceman
or at least in considerable delay.

Inquiries should be addressed as follows:

(a) Officers of Royal Navy and Women's Royal Naval Service	Ministry of Defence (Naval Secretary) Old Admiralty Building Whitehall London SW1A 2BE
Ratings in the Royal Navy, WRNS ratings QARNNS ratings	The Commodore (Naval Drafting Division) HMS Centurion Grange Road Gosport Hants PO13 9XA
Royal Navy medical and dental officers	Ministry of Defence Medical Director General (Naval) First Avenue House High Holborn London WC1V 6HE

h

j

Officers of Queen Alexandra's Royal Naval Nursing Service	Ministry of Defence The Matron-in-Chief QARNNS First Avenue House High Holborn London WC1V 6HE
Naval chaplains	Ministry of Defence Chaplain of the Fleet Lacon House Theobalds Road London WC1X 8RY
(b) Royal Marine officers	The Commandant-General Royal Marines (MS Branch) Old Admiralty Building Whitehall London SW1A 2BE
Royal Marine ranks	The Commodore (DRORM) HMS Centurion Grange Road Gosport Hants PO13 9XA
(c) Army officers (including WRAC and QARANC)	Ministry of Defence Army Officers' Documentation Office Government Buildings (F Block) Stanmore Middlesex HA7 4PZ
Other ranks, army	The manning and record office which is appropriate to the regiment or corps
(d) Royal Air Force and Women's Royal Air Force officers (including PMRAFNS)	Ministry of Defence AR8b (RAF) Eastern Avenue Barnwood Gloucester GL4 7PN
Other ranks, RAF and WRAF	Ministry of Defence RAF Personnel Management Centre RAF Innsworth Gloucester GL3 1EZ

General notes

Records held by other departments are less likely to be of use, either because of their limited scope or because individual records cannot readily be identified. If, however, the circumstances suggest that the address may be known to another department, application may be made to it by the registrar, all relevant particulars available being given.

When any department is able to supply the address of the person sought to the registrar, it will be passed on by him to the applicant's solicitor (or, in proper cases, direct to the applicant if acting in person) on an understanding to use it only for the purpose of the proceedings.

Nothing in this practice direction affects the service in matrimonial causes of petitions which do not contain any application for financial provision etc. The existing arrangements whereby the Department of Social Security will at the request of the solicitor forward a letter by ordinary post to a party's last known address remain in force in such cases.

The Registrar's Direction of 26 April 1988 ([1988] 2 All ER 573, [1988] 1 WLR 648) is hereby revoked.

Issued with the concurrence of the Lord Chancellor.

C F TURNER
Senior Registrar.

13 February 1989

Equal Opportunities Commission v Birmingham City Council

HOUSE OF LORDS

LORD KEITH OF KINKEL, LORD ROSKILL, LORD BRANDON OF OAKBROOK, LORD GRIFFITHS AND LORD GOFF OF CHIEVELEY

I I, I2 JANUARY, 23 FEBRUARY I989

Education – Local education authority – Sex discrimination – Less favourable treatment – Provision of more places for boys than girls at single sex selective secondary schools – Duty of local authority to provide sufficient secondary schools in its area – Duty of local authority not to do any act which constitutes sex discrimination – Whether local education authority unlawfully discriminating against girls by providing more places for boys than girls at selective schools – Education Act 1944, s 8 – Sex Discrimination Act 1975, ss 23(1), 25.

The respondent council, in its capacity as the local education authority, wished to reorganise all selective secondary education in its area on a non-selective basis but had been unable to achieve that, with the result that there were considerably more places available for boys than for girls at selective schools in its area. The council provided 540 places for boys at five single sex grammar schools and 360 places for girls at three equivalent schools and consequently a girl had substantially less chance of obtaining a grammar school education in the council's area than a boy. Local education authorities were required by s 8[a] of the Education Act 1944 to provide sufficient secondary schools having certain specific characteristics in their areas regardless of whether they were selective or non-selective or both. By s 23(1)[b] of the Sex Discrimination Act 1975, in carrying out those functions they were prohibited from doing any act which constituted sex discrimination and by s 25[c] of that Act they were required to see that education facilities were provided without sex discrimination. The council was aware of the disparity in places available for boys and girls at selective schools in its area but took no action to implement the options open to it, such as opening a new selective school for girls, closing two boys schools or changing a boys school to a girls school, because it found those options to be unattractive or difficult to apply. The Equal Opportunities Commission brought an action for judicial review against the council seeking (i) a declaration that the council's arrangements concerning selective education constituted sex discrimination, contrary to s 23(1) of the 1975 Act read with s 8 of the 1944 Act, and (ii) an order of mandamus requiring the council to consider without delay the means by which such discrimination could be removed. The trial judge upheld the commission's complaint and granted the declaration sought. The council appealed to the Court of Appeal, which affirmed the judges decision. The council appealed to the House of Lords, contending (i) that in order to establish that girls had received less favourable treatment than boys the commission had to show that selective education was better than non-selective education, and the commission had produced no evidence to that effect, (ii) that the commission had to show that there was less favourable treatment on grounds of sex because of an intention or motive on the part of the council to discriminate against girls and (iii) that either (a) its failure to provide selective schools was neither an act nor a deliberate omission within s 23(1) of the 1975 Act, since it was not part of the council's duty under s 8 of the 1944 Act to provide selective schools as such because it could perform its functions under s 8 by providing selective or non-selective schools or both,

---

a   Section 8, so far as material, is set out at p 774 j to p 775 b, post
b   Section 23(1) is set out at p 773 g, post
c   Section 25, so far as material, is set out at p 773 h to p 774 a, post

or, alternatively, (b) a breach under s 23(1) only occurred where a local education authority did an act which not only resulted in sex discrimination but itself involved *a* discrimination or arose out of a discriminatory policy.

Held – The appeal would be dismissed for the following reasons—

(1) For the purpose of establishing that there had been less favourable treatment of girls in the council's area on grounds of sex it was not necessary for the commission to show that selective education was 'better' than non-selective education since it was *b* enough for the commission to show that the council had deprived the girls of a choice which was valued by them or their parents (see p 771 *c* to *e*, p 774 *c d* and p 776 *h*, post); *Gill v El Vino Co Ltd* [1983] 1 All ER 398 and *R v Secretary of State for Education and Science, ex p Keating* (1985) 84 LGR 469 applied.

(2) Although the intention or motive of the council to discriminate might be relevant so far as remedies were concerned if sex discrimination was established it was not a *c* necessary condition for liability. Whatever might have been the council's motive, it was because of their sex that girls in the council's area had received less favourable treatment than boys in regard to selective education and so were subject to discrimination under the 1975 Act (see p 771 *c* to *e*, p 774 *e* to *g*, p 776 *h*, post); dicta of Lord Denning MR in *Ministry of Defence v Jeremiah* [1979] 3 All ER 833 at 836, of Browne-Wilkinson J in *Jenkins* *d* *v Kingsgate (Clothing Productions) Ltd* [1981] 1 WLR 1485 at 1494 and of Taylor J in *R v Secretary of State for Education and Science, ex p Keating* (1985) 84 LGR 469 at 475, applied.

(3) A local education authority was in breach of s 23(1) of 1975 Act if its system of selective education was such that fewer places were provided for girls than boys at selective schools, so that girls were required to achieve a higher mark than boys to gain entry to such schools, since a breach of s 23(1) occurred not only where the authority did an act which itself involved sex discrimination but also where it did an act which resulted *e* in sex discrimination. Accordingly, the commission was not required to show that the council was in breach of its duties under s 8 of the 1944 Act but only that in carrying out those duties an act or omission on its part constituted sex discrimination contrary to s 23(1) of the 1975 Act (see p 771 *c* to *e*, p 772 *b c* and p 776 *c* to *e h*, post); *R v Secretary of State for Education and Science, ex p Keating* (1985) 84 LGR 469 applied. *f*

Per curiam. The purpose of s 25 of the 1975 Act is not to outlaw sex discrimination as such but to place on public bodies such as local education authorities a positive role in relation to the elimination of sex discrimination (see p 771 *c* to *e* and p 776 *a*, post).

Notes

For sex discrimination by local education authorities, see 15 Halsbury's Laws (4th edn) *g* para 183.

For the Education Act 1944, s 8, see 15 Halsbury's Statutes (4th edn) 113.

For the Sex Discrimination Act 1975, ss 23, 25, see 6 ibid 716, 717.

Cases referred to in opinions

Gill v El Vino Co Ltd [1983] 1 All ER 398, [1983] QB 425, [1983] 2 WLR 155, CA. *h*

Jenkins v Kingsgate (Clothing Productions) Ltd [1981] 1 WLR 1485, EAT.

Ministry of Defence v Jeremiah [1979] 3 All ER 833, [1980] QB 87, [1979] 3 WLR 857, CA.

R v Secretary of State for Education and Science, ex p Keating (1985) 84 LGR 469.

Appeal

Birmingham City Council appealed, with leave of the Court of Appeal, against the *j* decision of that court (Dillon and Neill LJJ, Woolf LJ dissenting) ([1988] 3 WLR 837) on 13 May 1988 dismissing its appeal from the judgment of McCullough J ([1988] IRLR 96) hearing the Crown Office list on 14 October 1987 whereby, on the application of the Equal Opportunities Commission, he granted judicial review by way of a declaration that the arrangements currently made by the council for the provision of selective *a* secondary education in its area were unlawful pursuant to s 23 of the Sex Discrimination Act 1975 read with s 8 of the Education Act 1944, but refused to make an order of mandamus requiring the council to consider without delay the means by which such unlawful sex discrimination could be removed. The facts are set out in the opinion of Lord Goff.

Michael Beloff QC and *Richard McManus* for the council.
Anthony Lester QC and *David Pannick* for the commission.

b

Their Lordships took time for consideration.

23 February. The following opinions were delivered.

LORD KEITH OF KINKEL My Lords, I have had the opportunity of considering in
c draft the speech to be delivered by my noble and learned friend Lord Goff. I agree with it and for the reasons he gives would dismiss the appeal.

LORD ROSKILL. My Lords, I have had the advantage of reading in draft the speech to be delivered by my noble and learned friend Lord Goff. For the reasons he gives, with which I am in entire agreement, I would dismiss this appeal.

d
LORD BRANDON OF OAKBROOK. My Lords, for the reasons to be given by my noble and learned friend Lord Goff I would dismiss the appeal.

LORD GRIFFITHS. My Lords, I have had the advantage of reading in draft the speech of my noble and learned friend Lord Goff. I entirely agree with it and, for the reasons
e given, I too would dismiss this appeal.

LORD GOFF OF CHIEVELEY. My Lords, this case is concerned with proceedings for judicial review brought by the Equal Opportunities Commission against the Birmingham City Council. The subject matter of these proceedings is the provision by the council for selective education in single-sex secondary schools. At all material times
f there have been available considerably more places for boys at the age of 11 than there have been for girls. As appears from the evidence, there are eight selective schools in the city, all of which are single-sex schools. These are as follows:

	Boys schools	Places
	King Edward's Grammar School for Boys, Aston	90 at age 11
g	King Edward VI Camp Hill School for Boys	90 ,, ,, 11
	King Edward VI Five Ways School	90 ,, ,, 11
	Handsworth Grammar School	120 ,, ,, 11
	Bishop Vesey's Grammar School	150 ,, ,, 12

	Girls schools	
	King Edward VI Camp Hill School for Girls	90 ,, ,, 11
h	King Edward's Grammar School for Girls, Handsworth	120 ,, ,, 11
	Sutton Coldfield County Grammar School for Girls	150 ,, ,, 12

Of these schools, all except Sutton Coldfield County Grammar School for Girls are voluntary-aided secondary schools. It will be seen from the table that there are equal numbers of places available for boys and girls at the age of 12; but at the age of 11,
j whereas there are 390 places available for boys, there are only 210 places available for girls. The total number of places offered for secondary transfer at the age of 11 by selective schools represents only about 5% of the total available secondary places for that age. How this came about is set out in an affidavit sworn in the present proceedings by Mr John Crawford, the director of education of the Birmingham City Council. He has demonstrated how the history of proposals for secondary schools reorganisation in

Birmingham has been a history of changing policies according to the philosophy of the political party in power. I need not rehearse this story. The effect has, however, been that *a* since 1974 when the number of places offered by selective schools represented about 27% of the total number of places available, there has been a substantial reduction in the number of places available in Birmingham. This is the product of a policy to reorganise all selective education in the city on a non-selective basis. But, as a result of successful resistance by voluntary-aided schools and changes in political control (both of the city council and of central government) the voluntary-aided schools I have identified survived *b* as selective schools, with the disparity I have referred to above.

The effect of this disparity is demonstrated in a table, which was placed in evidence, showing the number of places offered by these eight schools to boys and girls respectively over the years 1984 to 1987. The table shows that girls with a test mark near the borderline have a substantially smaller chance of obtaining education at selective schools in Birmingham than do boys with comparable marks. This effect has been known to the *c* council for some years; and since December 1985 the council has known that the Equal Opportunities Commission considered that the arrangements made by the council constitute unlawful sex discrimination contrary to s 23 of the Sex Discrimination Act 1975. Following representations by the commission, a report was prepared by the chief education officer and the city solicitor for the education (policy and finance) sub- committee, in which the whole matter was reviewed in detail. In that report, the options *d* open to the council for remedying the situation were listed as follows:

'(a) to open a new selective school or schools for girls, providing another 180 places per year group [to this option there was later added the alternative of enlarging girls' selective schools by 180 places per year]; (b) to close one (90 place) boys' school and to reopen it as a girls' school; (c) to close two boys' schools; (d) to *e* reorganise two boys' schools as mixed schools; (e) to reorganise all of the selective schools as mixed schools; (f) to cease to maintain any selective schools at all.'

The officers recommended that the sex discrimination in admissions to selective schools should be recognised and that steps should be taken to remove the discrimination at the earliest opportunity; in particular, it was recommended that discussions regarding the *f* steps to be taken should be entered into with the King Edward Foundation and the governors of Handsworth Grammar School. However, the sub-committee resolved, on 17 March 1987, that consideration of the matter should be referred to a later meeting to enable the various options to be further investigated. At a subsequent meeting on 30 June 1987 the sub-committee considered the various courses of action open to them, and decided to deny the allegation of sex descrimination but nevertheless to consult the *g* governing bodies of the schools in question on possible solutions to eliminate sex discrimination. There is no evidence on the question whether such consultations have taken place.

The various options proposed to the sub-committee by the responsible officers were obviously intended to be a list of options theoretically open to the council: it was not being suggested that any one of them constituted a practical or desirable course of action *h* in the circumstances. Furthermore, the council's powers (under s 12 of the Education Act 1980) are subject to several legal restraints. I need not go into detail; it is enough to record that there are important limitations in connection with voluntary schools, and that implementation of proposals by the council is subject always to the overriding attitude of the Secretary of State. In addition, the falling demand for school places in the area creates of itself a major practical constraint. There is no doubt that the council faces *j* great difficulties in the way of solving the problem of disparity between the sexes in selective secondary schools. However, it has to be said that, whatever the difficulties may be, there is no evidence that the council has sought actively to overcome them.

In these circumstances the commission commenced proceedings for judicial review. They sought (1) a declaration that the arrangements currently made by the council for

the provision of selective secondary education were unlawful pursuant to s 23 of the
a 1975 Act, read with s 8 of the Education Act 1944 (as amended), and (2) an order of
mandamus requiring the council to consider without delay the means by which such
unlawful sex discrimination was to be removed. On 14 October 1987 McCullough J
upheld the commission's complaint of sex discrimination. He granted the declaration
asked for but declined to make an order of mandamus. The council appealed to the Court
of Appeal. On 13 May 1988 the Court of Appeal by a majority (Dillon and Neill LJJ,
b Woolf LJ dissenting) ([1988] 3 WLR 837) dismissed the appeal. The council now appeals
to your Lordships' House by leave of the Court of Appeal.

In order to consider the issues in the appeal, it is necessary to set out the terms of the
most relevant statutory provisions of the 1975 Act. Section 1 defines sex discrimination
against women. Subsection (1) provides:

c
'A person discriminates against a woman in any circumstances relevant for the
purposes of any provision of this Act if—(a) on the ground of her sex he treats her
less favourably than he treats or would treat a man, or (b) he applies to her a
requirement or condition which applies or would apply equally to a man but—(i)
which is such that the proportion of women who can comply with it is considerably
smaller than the proportion of men who can comply with it, and (ii) which he
d cannot show to be justifiable irrespective of the sex of the person to whom it is
applied, and (iii) which is to her detriment because she cannot comply with it.'

Sections 22 to 28 are concerned with discrimination in the field of education. Section 22
deals with discrimination by bodies in charge of particular education authorities
(including discrimination in relation to educational establishments maintained by a local
education authority); s 23 deals with other discrimination by local education authorities;
e s 24 with certain designated establishments; and s 25 with a general duty in the public
sector of education. Sections 26 to 28 provide for exceptions in certain cases. In particular,
s 26 provides for an exemption in the case of single-sex establishments, with the effect
that none of the relevant schools in the present case is guilty of unlawful discrimination
by reason of offering places to children of one sex only. Because of that exception, s 22 is
f not relevant in the present case. The two sections which are of direct relevance are ss 23
and 25, it being alleged by the commission that the council is guilty of unlawful
discrimination under s 23. Section 23(1) (as amended by the Education Act 1980, s 33(1)
and the Education Act 1981, Sch 3, para 11) provides as follows:

'It is unlawful for a local education authority, in carrying out such of its functions
under the Education Acts 1944 to 1981 as do not fall under section 22, to do any act
g which constitutes sex discrimination.'

I should add that by s 82(1) an act includes a deliberate omission.
So far as material s 25 provides:

'(1) Without prejudice to its obligation to comply with any other provision of
h this Act, a body to which this subsection applies shall be under a general duty to
secure that facilities for education provided by it, and any ancillary benefits or
services, are provided without sex discrimination.
(2) The following provisions of the Education Act 1944, namely—(a) section 68
(power of Secretary of State of State to require duties under that Act to be exercised
reasonably), and (b) section 99 (powers of Secretary of State where local education
authorities etc. are in default), shall apply to the performance by a body to which
j subsection (1) applies of the duties imposed by sections 22 and 23 and shall also
apply to the performance of the general duty imposed by subsection (1), as they
apply to the performance by a local education authority of a duty imposed by that
Act . . .
(4) The sanctions in subsections (2) and (3) shall be the only sanctions for breach

of the general duty in subsection (1), but without prejudice to the enforcement of
sections 22 and 23 under section 66 or otherwise (where the breach is also a   *a*
contravention of either of those sections) . . .
      (6) Subsection (1) applies to—(*a*) local education authorities in England and Wales
. . .'

      The first argument advanced by the council before your Lordships' House was that
there had not been, in the present case, less favourable treatment of the girls on grounds
of sex. Here two points were taken. It was submitted (1) that it could not be established   *b*
that there was less favourable treatment of the girls by reason of their having been denied
the same opportunities as the boys for selective education unless it was shown that
selective education was better than non-selective education, and that no evidence to that
effect was called before McCullough J, and (2) that, if that burden had been discharged,
it still had to be shown that there was less favourable treatment on grounds of sex, and   *c*
that involved establishing an intention or motive on the part of the council to discriminate
against the girls. In my opinion, neither of these submissions is well founded.
      As to the first, it is not, in my opinion, necessary for the commission to show that
selective education is 'better' than non-selective education. It is enough that, by denying
the girls the same opportunity as the boys, the council is depriving them of a choice
which (as the facts show) is valued by them, or at least by their parents, and which (even   *d*
though others may take a different view) is a choice obviously valued, on reasonable
grounds, by many others. This conclusion has been reached by all the judges involved in
the present case; and it is consistent with previous authority (see, in particular, *Gill v El
Vino Co Ltd* [1983] 1 All ER 398, [1983] QB 425 and *R v Secretary of State for Education
and Science, ex p Keating* (1985) 84 LGR 469). I have no doubt that it is right. As to the
second point, it is, in my opinion, contrary to the terms of the statute. There is   *e*
discrimination under the statute if there is less favourable treatment on the ground of
sex, in other words if the relevant girl or girls would have received the same treatment as
the boys but for their sex. The intention or motive of the defendant to discriminate,
though it may be relevant so far as remedies are concerned (see s 66(3) of the 1975 Act),
is not a necessary condition to liability; it is perfectly possible to envisage cases where the
defendant had no such motive, and yet did in fact discriminate on the grounds of sex.   *f*
Indeed, as counsel for the commission pointed out in the course of his argument, if the
council's submission were correct it would be a good defence for an employer to show
that he discriminated against women not because he intended to do so but (for example)
because of customer preference, or to save money, or even to avoid controversy. In the
present case, whatever may have been the intention or motive of the council, nevertheless
it is because of their sex that the girls in question receive less favourable treatment than   *g*
the boys, and so are the subject of discrimination under the 1975 Act. This is well
established in a long line of authority: see, in particular, *Jenkins v Kingsgate (Clothing
Productions) Ltd* [1981] 1 WLR 1485 at 1494 per Browne-Wilkinson J and *R v Secretary of
State for Education and Science, ex p Keating* (1985) 84 LGR 469 at 475 per Taylor J; see also
Ministry of Defence v Jeremiah [1979] 3 All ER 833 at 836, [1980] QB 87 at 98 per Lord
Denning MR. I can see no reason to depart from this established view.   *h*
      I turn then to the most substantial issue in the case. This turns on the true constructon
of s 23 of the 1975 Act, and its relationship with s 25.
      Counsel for the council fastened on certain words in s 23, which provides that it is
unlawful for a local education authority, *in carrying out such of its functions under* the
Education Acts 1944 to 1981 as do not fall under s 22, to do any act which constitutes sex
discrimination (I have emphasised the words in quesion). The relevant functions of local   *j*
education authorities are to be found in s 8 of the 1944 Act (as amended by the Education
(Miscellaneous Provisions) Act 1948, s 3, the Education Act 1980, Sch 7 and the Education
Act 1981, s 21), which, so far as relevant, provides as follows:

      '(1) It shall be the duty of every local education authority to secure that there will

be available for their area sufficient schools . . . (*b*) for providing secondary education,
that is to say, full-time education suitable to the requirements of senior pupils, other
than such full-time education as may be provided for senior pupils in pursuance of
a scheme made under the provisions of this Act relating to further education and
full-time education suitable to the requirements of junior pupils who have attained
the age of ten years and six months and whom it is expedient to educate together
with senior pupils; and the schools available for an area shall not be deemed to be
sufficient unless they are sufficient in number, character, and equipment to afford
for all pupils opportunities for education offering such variety of instruction and
training as may be desirable in view of their different ages, abilities, and aptitudes,
and of the different periods for which they may be expected to remain at school,
including practical instruction and training appropriate to their respective needs
. . .'

The functions identified in s 8 relate to the provision of a sufficient number of schools
having certain specific characteristics. That function can be performed by the provision
of selective schools or non-selective schools or both; but it is no part of the function of
the authority to supply selective schools as such. It followed, submitted counsel for the
council, that failure to provide selective schools was neither an act nor a deliberate
omission within s 23 of the 1975 Act.

In the alternative, counsel for the council sought to support the conclusion of Woolf
LJ in his dissenting judgment in the Court of Appeal. Woolf LJ was much concerned
with the practical difficulties facing a local education authority when ensuring that
facilities for education are provided without sex discrimination. In this connection he
was concerned not only with the problem facing the Birmingham City Council in the
present case, but also with less important situations, such as, for example, those relating
to size of classes, quality of school buildings, pupil to teacher ratio and, indeed, almost
every aspect of the educational system. He saw the solution to such problems in a proper
identification of the roles of ss 23 and 25 respectively of the 1975 Act. He observed that,
whereas a breach of duty under s 23 led to an action lying in tort against the offending
establishment, a breach of duty under s 25 (assuming that it was not also a breach of s 22
or s 23) led to the result that the breach would only be remedied by the Secretary of State
exercising his powers under s 68 or s 99 of the 1944 Act, whereby he has power to give
appropriate directions to remedy the situation, a much more flexible remedy. Woolf LJ
concluded that, having regard to the wording of s 23, a breach under that section only
occurred where the local education authority did an act which *constituted* sex
discrimination, ie not only resulted in sex discrimination but itself involved sex
discrimination, or where—

'the act complained of amounts to a decision by a local education authority to
implement a policy which is discriminatory or where there is a deliberate failure to
take a decision because of a policy of sex discrimination.'

(See [1988] 3 WLR 837 at 849.)
Only in those circumstances would an act or deliberate omission be unlawful under
s 23. In his opinion, the present was not such a case.

In order to consider these submissions it is necessary to consider the relationship
between ss 22, 23, and 25. As I read them, ss 22 and 23 are concerned with unlawful
discrimination: in s 22, by bodies (including local education authorities) in charge of
particular educational establishments in relation to those establishments, and, in s 23, by
local education authorities in other circumstances. I can see no reason why these two
sections should not, in the field of education, embrace all cases of unlawful discrimination
as such by local education authorities. Section 25, however, is, as I read it, concerned with
something different. It is concerned with a positive duty placed on bodies in the public
sector, including local education authorities, to secure that 'facilities for education

provided by it, and any ancillary benefits or services, are provided without sex discrimination'. That section is therefore intended, not to outlaw acts of discrimination *a* as such, but to place on such bodies a positive role in relation to the elimination of sex discrimination. The idea appears to have been to see that such bodies are, so to speak, put on their toes to ensure that sex discrimination does not occur in areas within their responsibility. It must not be forgotten that, in the field of education, there must be some reluctance on the part of parents to become entangled in disputes with their children's schools, or with the authorities responsible for them, on this subject. Quite *b* apart from fear of prejudicing their children's prospects, the simple fact is that children pass rapidly on to other things, and a complaint of this kind may soon become irrelevant in relation to them.

Bearing the purposes of s 25 in mind, I feel unable to accept either of the submissions of counsel for the council. First of all, I do not think that it can be right to restrict s 23 as he suggests, so as to exclude discrimination in a case such as the present. On this point, I *c* accept the submission of counsel for the commission, that it is not necessary for the commission to show that the council is in breach of its duties under s 8 of the 1944 Act. All that it is necessary for the commission to show is that the council, in carrying out its functions under the section, did an act (or deliberately omitted to do an act) where such act or omission constituted sex discrimination. Were that not so, there would be a serious gap in the legislation. This conclusion is consistent with the decision of Taylor J in *R v* *d* *Secretary of State for Education and Science, ex p Keating* (1985) 84 LGR 469, which appears to me to be correctly decided. Nor, with all respect, is it right, in my opinion, to restrict s 23 as Woolf LJ would do, with reference to the word 'constitutes' in the phrase 'to do any act which constitutes sex discrimination'. I myself do not attach such significance to that word. As I read them, the effect of ss 22 and 23 is to render unlawful all cases of particular acts or (deliberate) omissions by local education authorities which are *e* discriminatory in the sense laid down in s 1 (and s 2) of the 1975 Act. Where there is at the same time a failure by an authority to fulfil its general duty under s 25, a person discriminated against by an act or deliberate omission made unlawful by ss 22 or 23 can still bring proceedings against the local education authority.

For these reasons, I find myself in agreement with the conclusion of McCullough J and with the majority of the Court of Appeal. I agree with the general conclusion expressed *f* by Dillon LJ in the following passage ([1988] 3 WLR 837 at 856):

> 'In truth the council's position really is that they are knowingly continuing their acts of maintaining the various boys' and girls' selective schools, which inevitably results in discrimination against girls in the light of the great disparity in the numbers of places available, because the only alternatives open to the council, even *g* with the consent of the Secretary of State, are unattractive or difficult to apply.'

The time has come for the Birmingham City Council to accept that it is in breach of s 23 of the 1975 Act, and that something has got to be done about it. Its proper course must surely be to respond to the proposal of the commission that it should begin the necessary process of consultation, with a view to finding the most practical solution available which *h* accords with the obligations imposed on it by Parliament.

I would dismiss the appeal.

Appeal dismissed.

Solicitors: *Sharpe Pritchard*, agents for *G W T Pitt*, Birmingham (for the council); *Pattinson* *j* *& Brewer*, agents for *J A Lakin*, Manchester (for the commission).

Mary Rose Plummer   Barrister.

a
R v Secretary of State for the Home Department, ex parte Al-Mehdawi

COURT OF APPEAL, CIVIL DIVISION
O'CONNOR, NICHOLLS AND TAYLOR LJJ
b 25, 26 OCTOBER, 9 NOVEMBER 1988

Natural justice – Hearing – Duty to hear parties etc – Immigration adjudicator – Applicant deprived of hearing through negligence of his own solicitors – Adjudicator not at fault – Whether breach of rules of natural justice – Whether adjudicator's decision subject to judicial review.

c *Precedent – Court of Appeal – Binding effect of previous decisions of court – Power of court to depart from previous decision – House of Lords deciding appeal on different ground from that argued below – Whether Court of Appeal's decision in that case binding on another division of the Court of Appeal.*

The respondent was an Iraqi student who overstayed his leave to remain in the United
d Kingdom. When he was served with a notice of the Secretary of State's decision to deport him he instructed solicitors to lodge an appeal. When a date of hearing for the appeal was fixed the solicitors wrote to notify him of the date but negligently sent the letter to the wrong address and the respondent never received the letter. The adjudicator subsequently dismissed the appeal on the papers since neither the respondent nor his solicitors appeared before him. The respondent applied to have the adjudicator's decision
e quashed. The judge held that he was bound by a previous decision of the Court of Appeal which decided that certiorari ought to be granted where the negligence of an applicant's solicitors deprived him of an oral hearing. The judge accordingly granted certiorari. The Secretary of State appealed, contending (i) that the Court of Appeal was not bound by its previous decision because when that case had gone to the House of Lords on appeal the House had decided the appeal on a different ground and had held that the issue determined below did not arise for decision and (ii) that judicial review was not available
f as a guarantee to a litigant against any perceived unfairness regardless of who was at fault since its purpose was to check procedural impropriety in the decision-making process and control errors by the person making the decision.

Held – (1) Where the House of Lords decided that an issue which was argued in the
g Court of Appeal did not arise for decision on appeal to the House and expressed no view as to the soundness or otherwise of the Court of Appeal's reasoning on that issue, the Court of Appeal's decision on that issue was not binding on another division of the Court of Appeal (see p 780 j, p 781 d and p 784 h, post); *Balabel v Air-India* [1988] 2 All ER 246 applied; *R v Diggines, ex p Rahmani* [1985] 1 All ER 1073 considered.

(2) Since the respondent had been deprived of a hearing by the adjudicator solely
h because of his solicitor's negligence the decision-making process was fundamentally flawed by a breach of the rules of natural justice even though neither the respondent himself nor the adjudicator were at fault. The respondent was therefore entitled to judicial review of the adjudicator's decision dismissing his appeal. The Secretary of State's appeal would accordingly be dismissed (see p 784 b c g h, post); dictum of Stephenson LJ
j in *R v Diggines, ex p Rahmani* [1985] 1 All ER 1073 at 1082 applied.

Notes
For the principles of natural justice and certiorari for breach of those principles, see 1 Halsbury's Laws (4th edn) paras 64, 74, 80, 83, 87, and for cases on the subject, see 1(1) Digest (Reissue) 200–201, 1172–1176 and 16 ibid 388–435, 4237–4797.

For the binding effect of Court of Appeal decisions, see 26 Halsbury's Laws (4th edn) para 578, and for cases on the subject, see 30 Digest (Reissue) 269–273, 763–793.	*a*

Cases referred to in judgments

Balabel v Air-India [1988] 2 All ER 246, [1988] Ch 317, [1988] 2 WLR 1036, CA.
Khan v Secretary of State for the Home Dept, Deen v Secretary of State for the Home Dept [1987] Imm AR 543, CA.
Minter v Priest [1930] AC 558, [1930] All ER Rep 431, HL; *rvsg* [1929] 1 KB 655, CA.	*b*
R v Blundeston Prison Board of Visitors, ex p Fox-Taylor [1982] 1 All ER 646, DC.
R v Diggines, ex p Rahmani [1985] 1 All ER 1073, [1985] QB 1109, [1985] 2 WLR 611, CA; *affd on other grounds* [1986] 1 All ER 921, [1986] AC 475, [1986] 2 WLR 530, HL.
R v Gillyard (1848) 12 QB 527, 116 ER 965.
R v Immigration Appeal Tribunal, ex p Temel [1988] CA Transcript 344.
R v Leicester Recorder, ex p Wood [1947] 1 All ER 928, [1947] KB 726, DC.	*c*
R v Leyland Magistrates, ex p Hawthorn [1979] 1 All ER 209, [1979] QB 283, [1979] 2 WLR 28, DC.
R (Burns) v Tyrone County Court Judge [1961] NI 167, NI DC.
Young v Bristol Aeroplane Co Ltd [1944] 2 All ER 293, [1944] KB 718, CA; *affd* [1946] 1 All ER 98, [1946] AC 163, HL.

d

Cases also cited

Birkett v James [1977] 2 All ER 801, [1978] AC 297, HL.
Council of Civil Service Unions v Minister for the Civil Service [1984] 3 All ER 935, [1985] AC 374, HL.
Davis v Johnson [1978] 1 All ER 1132, [1979] AC 264, HL.
O'Reilly v Mackman [1982] 3 All ER 1124, [1983] 2 AC 237, HL.	*e*
R v Crown Court at Knightsbridge, ex p Goonatilleke [1985] 2 All ER 498, [1986] QB 1, DC.
R v Immigration Appeal Tribunal, ex p Enwia, R v Immigration Appeal Tribunal, ex p AS [1983] 2 All ER 1045, [1984] 1 WLR 117, CA.
R v Secretary of State for the Home Dept, ex p Yeboah, R v Secretary of State for the Home Dept, ex p Dra$z$ [1987] 3 All ER 999, [1987] 1 WLR 1586, CA.	*f*

Appeal

The Secretary of State for the Home Department appealed against the decision of Macpherson J hearing the Crown Office list on 23 November 1987 (i) granting an application by the respondent, Shahib Al-Mehdawi, for judicial review by way of an order of certiorari to quash the determination of an immigration adjudicator dated 5 December 1985 whereby he dismissed an appeal by the respondent against the decision of the Secretary of State issued on 12 March 1985 to deport him pursuant to s 3(5)(a) of the Immigration Act 1971 and (ii) ordering that the matter be remitted to an adjudicator for a further hearing. The facts are set out in the judgment of Taylor LJ.	*g*

John Laws and *David Pannick* for the Secretary of State.	*h*
Sir Charles Fletcher-Cooke QC and *George Warr* for the respondent.

Cur adv vult

9 November. The following judgments were delivered.	*j*

TAYLOR LJ (delivering the first judgment at the invitation of O'Connor LJ). This is an appeal by the Secretary of State for the Home Department from a decision of Macpherson J on 23 November 1987. The judge granted an order of certiorari to quash the determination of an adjudicator dismissing an appeal by Shahib Al-Mehdawi (the respondent) against the Secretary of State's decision to deport him.

The respondent was born in Iraq on 29 April 1956. In August 1977, aged 21, he
a arrived in the United Kingdom as a visitor. Between 1977 and 1984 his leave to remain
was extended from time to time to enable him as a student to pursue various training
courses. He was a conspicuously unsuccessful student and eventually, on 4 May 1984, he
was refused a further extension of time. Despite that refusal, the respondent failed to
leave. Accordingly, on 12 March 1985 the Secretary of State gave notice of his decision to
deport the respondent pursuant to s 3(5)(a) of the Immigration Act 1971. The respondent
b instructed solicitors, Messrs Bowman Ziadie & Co. They lodged a notice of appeal on 28
March 1985. On the same day they wrote to the respondent at his address in Edinburgh
to inform him of the step they had taken.

On 23 September Bowman Ziadie wrote to him again to tell him that the hearing
before an adjudicator was fixed for 21 November. However, most unfortunately and
negligently, their letter was sent, not to the respondent's Edinburgh address, but to his
c former address in Birmingham. The letter did not reach him. It is common ground (a)
that he never knew of the hearing before it was so far passed that he not only missed
attending, but was too late to appeal, and (b) that Bowman Ziadie took no further steps
after their misdirected letter and before the hearing. So, on 21 November neither the
respondent nor anyone from Bowman Ziadie appeared before the adjudicator. A
representative of the Home Secretary was there and invited the adjudicator to determine
d the appeal on the available documents. The adjudicator did so and dismissed the appeal.
On 5 December he sent a copy of his decision to Bowman Ziadie. They wrote to the
respondent telling him that any further appeal had to be lodged by 22 December. But,
again, their letter was wrongly addressed to Birmingham, so no appeal was lodged.

On 28 April 1986 the Secretary of State signed a deportation order directing the
respondent's removal to Iraq. On 23 May he was arrested and detained in Perth prison.
e There followed extended representations and negotiations involving the Home Office
and, on the respondent's behalf, a second firm of solicitors in Scotland and a member of
Parliament. Eventually, via the respondent's third and present firm of solicitors, an
application was made for judicial review on 5 February 1987. The case for the respondent
(the applicant before Macpherson J) was that, owing to the negligence of his solicitors, he
f had been deprived of an oral hearing of his appeal to which he was entitled by the rules
of natural justice and accordingly the decision should be quashed. He relied on the
decision of this court in R v Diggines, ex p Rahmani [1985] 1 All ER 1073, [1985] QB 1109.
Before Macpherson J counsel for the Secretary of State accepted that, unless he could
show fault on the part of the respondent personally, the judge was bound by this court's
decision in Rahmani's case and should grant relief. The judge was not prepared to find the
g respondent had been at fault. Accordingly, he granted certiorari.

On this appeal, counsel's first submission for the Secretary of State is that this court is
not bound by its decision in Rahmani's case in view of the ultimate ruling when the case
went to the House of Lords (see [1986] 1 All ER 921, [1986] AC 475). There it was held
that the issue determined by me at first instance and by the Court of Appeal thereafter
did not arise on a true view of the relevant facts and law.

h Shortly, the facts of Rahmani's case were as follows. The applicant had been refused
leave for herself and her children to remain in the United Kingdom. She appealed to an
adjudicator. She was represented by the United Kingdom Immigrants Advisory Service,
but by the date of the hearing they were unable to contact her since although they had
been given her new address they had failed to record it. By letter to the adjudicator they
said they had no instructions and invited him 'to decide the case in such manner as he
j may deem proper'. In purported exercise of the power in r 12 of the Immigration
Appeals (Procedure) Rules 1972, SI 1972/1684, the adjudicator dismissed the appeal
without a hearing. At first instance I held that there had been a breach of the rules of
natural justice in that the applicant had been denied a hearing. Although that breach was
due to the negligence of her own advisers, she was nevertheless entitled to relief. The
Court of Appeal upheld the decision for the same reasons. Neither before me nor the

Court of Appeal was any criticism made of the adjudicator. However, in the House of
Lords, this important issue of principle was held not to have arisen because the true and   *a*
simple ground for granting the applicant relief was that the adjudicator should not have
determined the case under r 12, there being nothing to justify a finding under para (c) of
that rule that no person was authorised to represent the applicant at the hearing.

In these circumstances, counsel for the Secretary of State contends that the true ratio of
the case was the simple one propounded in the House of Lords. The more general point
of principle decided below did not arise for decision in *Rahmani's* case. He submits the   *b*
case must be considered as one continuous piece of litigation. Therefore, although the
views expressed on the issue of principle in this court are of high persuasive value, they
cannot be regarded as the ratio of the case and thus binding, since they were unnecessary
to its decision.

Counsel referred to *Young v Bristol Aeroplane Co Ltd* [1944] 2 All ER 293, [1944] KB
718, the leading authority on the principle of stare decisis in this court. Lord Greene MR   *c*
stated the principle thus ([1944] 2 All ER 293 at 300, [1944] KB 718 at 729–730):

> 'On a careful examination of the whole matter we have come to the clear
> conclusion that this court is bound to follow previous decisions of its own as well as
> those of courts of co-ordinate jurisdiction. The only exceptions to this rule (two of
> them apparent only) are those already mentioned which for convenience we here   *d*
> summarise: (i) The court is entitled and bound to decide which of two conflicting
> decisions of its own it will follow. (ii) The court is bound to refuse to follow a
> decision of its own which, though not expressly overruled, cannot in its opinion
> stand with a decision of the House of Lords. (iii) The court is not bound to follow a
> decision of its own if it is satisfied that the decision was given *per incuriam*.'

Counsel submits that those exceptions are not exhaustive. In particular, it would seem   *e*
that Lord Greene MR's principles were related to final decisions of the Court of Appeal.
They may well be inapt where the House of Lords, in giving the final decision of a case,
expressly indicates that, on the true facts, the issue resolved by the Court of Appeal did
not require to be decided. Alternatively, such a case may be akin to Lord Greene MR's
exception (ii). In *Rahmani's* case the House of Lords went further than simply to say the
issue below did not arise for decision. Lord Scarman, with whose speech all the other law   *f*
Lords agreed, said ([1986] 1 All ER 921 at 922–923, [1986] AC 475 at 478):

> 'However, the parties and the two courts below proceeded on the basis that r 12
> did apply. At the outset of the hearing before your Lordships it became obvious that
> there must be a serious doubt as to the applicability of r 12 to this case. Your
> Lordships raised the point with counsel for the adjudicator who very fairly said at   *g*
> once that, if your Lordships should be disposed to the view that r 12 does not apply
> in this case, he would not argue for the contrary view. He had come to argue the
> question of principle. Counsel for the immigrants was equally eager to argue the
> question of principle but left the matter in your Lordships' hands. Thereupon and
> with the assistance of counsel, your Lordships examined the terms of the rule and
> the facts of the case and considered that in the circumstances the rule did not apply.   *h*
> Your Lordships have not, therefore, considered, nor have they heard arguments on,
> the point of principle which was the ground of decision in both courts below.
> Accordingly, I express no opinion on the point. I must not be understood to have
> indicated even a provisional view on the soundness or otherwise of the alleged
> principle. Indeed it would be dangerous, in my view, to discuss the point save in a
> case where the circumstances and the facts require it to be decided.'   *j*

It would be strange indeed if, despite those final words, the decision of this court is to
be regarded as binding authority on the point of principle.

Counsel for the respondent referred to *R v Immigration Appeal Tribunal, ex p Temel*
[1988] CA Transcript 344. There, Purchas LJ, referring to *Rahmani's* case, said:

'The matter, we are told, went to the House of Lords, who granted leave to appeal,
a which was refused by this court, presumably because of the important issue of
principle. It is perhaps disappointing that their Lordships did not in the event deal
with this point but disposed of the appeal on a purely procedural technicality. The
position, however, is that the ultimate authority at the moment which binds this
court is *Rahmani's* case and the judgments delivered in it on this particular topic.'

b It would not appear that any argument was addressed to the court as to the precise
effect of the House of Lords' decision on the binding force of this court's ruling. Indeed,
the opening words of the passage I have cited ('The matter, we are told, went to the House
of Lords') suggest that the full report of the House of Lords' decision may not even have
been cited.

Counsel also helpfully referred to an essay contained in Sir Arthur Goodhart's *Essays in
Jurisprudence and the Common Law* (1931) entitled 'Determining the Ratio Decidendi of a
c Case'. He pointed to a number of passages suggesting that the ratio of a court's decision
remained binding even if the facts on which the court based it subsequently turned out
to be wrong. But here it is not merely that knowledge subsequent and extraneous to the
proceedings shows the facts to be wrong: the House of Lords in the very case, giving its
final opinion, has ruled that the issue determined below did not arise for decision.

d In these circumstances I consider that, although the reasoning of the Court of Appeal
in *Rahmani's* case is of powerful persuasive influence, this court is not bound by it.
Support for that view is afforded by a passage from the judgment of this court in *Balabel
v Air-India* [1988] 2 All ER 246, [1988] Ch 317 which, whilst I gave it, is strengthened by
the agreement of Lord Donaldson MR and Parker LJ. The case is concerned with the
extent and scope of legal professional privilege. The relevant passage is ([1988] 2 All ER
e 246 at 250–251, [1988] Ch 317 at 325–326):

'In particular [counsel for the appellant] contends that the decision of the Court
of Appeal in *Minter v Priest* [1929] 1 KB 655 is in his favour and is binding on this
court. That was a defamation case. The respondents' solicitor was approached to
assist in obtaining a loan for the deposit on a contemplated purchase of a house, the
intention being that, if the loan was obtained, the proposed purchasers would
f employ the respondent to complete the purchase. The respondent was alleged to
have defamed the appellant in the course of his interview with the proposed
purchasers and the issue was whether one of the latter was entitled to claim privilege
from disclosing what happened at the interview. The decision of the Court of
Appeal was on the footing that what passed at the interview was between clients and
a solicitor acting in his professional capacity and within the ordinary scope of his
g business as a solicitor. The court upheld the claim to privilege. The House of Lords
reversed the decision on the ground that the respondent was not acting as a solicitor
at the relevant time because, so far from undertaking the duty of a solicitor on the
proposal made to him, the respondent made a counter-proposal involving a
malicious scheme from which he was to profit jointly with the proposed purchasers
h (see [1930] AC 558, [1930] All ER Rep 431). Accordingly, the dicta both in the
Court of Appeal and in the House of Lords touching on the extent of legal
professional privilege where the relationship of solicitor and client does exist were
not essential to the determination of the case, and in my judgment are not binding
on this court. Nevertheless, they are of strong persuasive authority.'

j Should this case go further on the main issue, as seems likely, it may be thought
appropriate for their Lordships to consider stare decisis in the context of cases such as
Balabel's case, the present case and no doubt others in which a decision of their Lordships'
House may neither overrule nor be on all fours with the decision of this court in the
same case.

Before turning to the main issue of principle on this appeal, it is convenient to clear

the ground by dealing with a secondary submission made by counsel for the respondent
in the alternative. It is that, as in *Rahmani*'s case, the adjudicator fell foul of r 12 which   *a*
carries the same number and substance in the 1984 rules applicable here as in those of
1972 which applied in *Rahmani*'s case. Rule 12(1)(c) provides:

> 'An appellate authority may determine an appeal without a hearing if . . . (c) the
> appellate authority is satisfied that the appellant is outside the United Kingdom or
> that it is impracticable to give him notice of a hearing and, in either case, that no   *b*
> person is authorised to represent him at a hearing.'

In *Rahmani*'s case the adjudicator (by chance the same adjudicator as here) expressly
stated in his determination that it was made under r 12, ie without a hearing. Here,
counsel submits that the same situation arose and the same adjudicator dealt with it in
the same way, that is to say without a hearing. The case can therefore, he says, be decided
in the respondent's favour on the same ground as founded the final decision in *Rahmani*'s   *c*
case.

In my judgment, that argument is untenable on the evidence. The determination of
the adjudicator expressly states:

> '3. Although an oral hearing of his appeal against this decision was requested,
> neither the [respondent] nor his representative appeared at the hearing [counsel for   *d*
> the Home Secretary] asked me therefore to determine the appeal on the basis of the
> available documents. Before doing so, however, he drew my attention to paragraph
> 156 of HC 169 [Statement of Changes in Immigration Rules of 9 February 1983
> (HC Paper (1982–83) no 169], which sets out the factors to be taken into account by
> the Secretary of State in considering whether to give effect to a deportation order.
> [Counsel] contended that all these factors had in fact been taken fully into account   *e*
> in this case, and pointed out that the appellant had overstayed his leave to remain
> on no less than 4 occasions during the 8 years he had been here. No compassionate
> circumstances had been advanced in support of the appeal.'

From that, it is clear that there was a hearing, albeit in the absence of the respondent
but physically attended by a representative of the Home Secretary. The adjudicator was   *f*
not acting under r 12, but r 34(2) which permitted him to proceed with the hearing of
an appeal in the absence of the respondent if satisfied that the requisite notice of the time
and place of the hearing had been given and no explanation of the respondent's absence
had been furnished. The provisions as to notice are set out in rr 34(5)(a), 44(1) and 26(1).
It is unnecessary to set them out as it is common ground here that the notice given
complied with them. In my judgment, therefore, there is no substance in this subsidiary
argument on behalf of the respondent.   *g*

This leaves as the main, indeed only, issue the question of principle considered by this
court in *Rahmani*'s case. Counsel for the Secretary of State concedes that if the reasoning
of this court in that case is sound, it is determinative of the present appeal. I confess at
the outset that I adhere to the views I expressed in *Rahmani*'s case which were approved
by this court. Since all three members of the court gave reasoned judgments after   *h*
considering the arguments and the authorities, it is tempting simply to adopt them.
However, counsel for the Secretary of State in this case did not appear in *Rahmani*'s case
and in deference to his forceful submissions, which were not identical with those
advanced there, I set out my reasons for remaining unrepentant.

The respondent's contention, as upheld by this court in *Rahmani*'s case, is formulated
in the Secretary of State's skeleton argument in these terms (at para 2):   *j*

> '. . . a decision of a public authority, which is within the power conferred by
> statute and has been reached without procedural impropriety or irregularity on its
> part, can, nevertheless, be quashed upon judicial review if the exercise of the power
> has—without fault on the part of the complainant—resulted in an infringement of
> natural justice.'

That formulation is, however, not wholly accurate. The respondent contends that *there*

a *was* procedural irregularity in the hearing before the adjudicator although through no fault of his. The question, therefore, is whether judicial review lies only when the public authority, here the adjudicator, is at fault or also when, without his fault, the procedure is, in the event, seriously defective or irregular. Here, the respondent did not have an opportunity to put his case. Is his right to do so to be forfeited without fault on his part simply because there was also no fault by the adjudicator?

b The main submission of counsel for the Secretary of State is that the purpose of judicial review is to impose standards of decision-making and more particularly to control errors and departures from those standards by decision-makers. He submits that the respondent's case involves judicial review being available as a guarantee to a litigant against any form of unfairness in litigation regardless of who, if indeed anyone, is at fault. This would extend judicial review so far, he says, as to leave principles behind, particularly the

c principle requiring finality in litigation.

Referring to the authorities, counsel says that the main exceptions to the requirement of fault by the authority whose decision is impugned are cases of fraud or perjury (see *R v Gillyard* (1848) 12 QB 527, 116 ER 965, *R v Leicester Recorder, ex p Wood* [1947] 1 All ER 928, [1947] KB 726 and *R (Burns) v Tyrone County Court Judge* [1961] NI 167). To these, he concedes there must be added two further exceptional cases which he submits

d are grafted onto the main exception. Those are *R v Leyland Magistrates, ex p Hawthorn* [1979] 1 All ER 209, [1979] QB 283 and *R v Blundeston Prison Board of Visitors, ex p Fox-Taylor* [1982] 1 All ER 646. In the former case, the prosecution failed to disclose to the defence the existence of two material witnesses. In the latter, the prison authority likewise failed to bring possible witnesses to the attention of a prisoner in proceedings against him before the board of visitors. Counsel explains these cases as examples of

e misconduct by a party owing a public duty in the administration of justice. However, in the *Leyland Magistrates* case [1979] 1 All ER 209 at 210–211, [1979] QB 283 at 286 Lord Widgery CJ explained the grant of certiorari in the following terms:

> 'But the problem, and one can put it in a sentence, is that certiorari in respect of
f   breach of the rules of natural justice is primarily a remedy sought on account of an error of the tribunal, and here, of course, we are not concerned with an error of the tribunal, we are concerned with an error of the police prosecutors. Consequently, amongst the arguments to which we have listened an argument has been that this is not a certiorari case at all on any of the accepted grounds. We have given this careful thought over the short adjournment because it is a difficult case in that the consequences of the decision either way have their unattractive features. However,
g   if fraud, collusion, perjury and such like matters not affecting the tribunal themselves justify an application for certiorari to quash the conviction, if all those matters are to have that effect, then we cannot say that the failure of the prosecutor which in this case has prevented the tribunal from giving the defendant a fair trial should not rank in the same category.'

h In *Rahmani's* case [1985] 1 All ER 1073 at 1087, [1985] QB 1109 at 1129 Purchas LJ, after quoting that passage, said:

> 'With respect to Lord Widgery CJ I would venture to comment that the correct approach should have been that the tribunal had failed to try the case according to the rules of natural justice but through no fault of theirs. The fault lay with the
j   prosecution.'

Whichever way it is expressed, the nub of the decision was that since there had been a failure of natural justice in the trial process, certiorari could and should go notwithstanding the absence of fault by the tribunal. Purchas LJ went on to quote with approval the reasoning of Phillips J in *Ex p Fox-Taylor* [1982] 1 All ER 646 at 649–650 to the like effect.

Counsel for the Secretary of State submitted that if negligence of his own advisers could entitle an applicant to a grant of certiorari and a rehearing of his case, Pandora's *a* box would be wide open. He conjured up the possibility of certiorari where the applicant's lawyer failed to call a witness, failed to seek an adjournment, cross-examined incompetently or otherwise left the applicant aggrieved. It was, he said, neither logical nor workable to draw a distinction between a fundamental breach of natural justice which would justify certiorari and any other unfairness which would not. One must go the whole hog. If certiorari lies here, it must lie wherever litigation ends in unfairness *b* however caused.

I cannot accept this argument ad absurdum. It is true, as counsel says, that natural justice cannot be invoked to rectify every perceived unfairness. But, in the present case there was, owing entirely to the solicitors' negligence, a breach of a basic rule of natural justice, audi alteram partem. That was a fundamental flaw in the decision-making process. It is clearly distinguishable from situations within a proper process in which the *c* applicant's case might have been conducted more skilfully or differently. No doubt difficult cases could arise near the borderline between a reviewable defect of process and a grievance without remedy. Where that line should be drawn is perhaps incapable of a universal definition and must depend on the circumstances of each case. The conduct of the applicant himself would clearly be a highly relevant factor. Both in *Ex p Temel* and in *Khan v Secretary of State for the Home Dept* [1987] Imm AR 543 the applicants failed *d* because they were each held to have been responsible for the fact that they did not have a hearing. But in *Khan's* case (at 555) Bingham LJ said:

> 'If a procedural mishap occurs as a result of misunderstanding, confusion, failure of communication, or even perhaps inefficiency, and the result is to deny justice to an applicant, I should be very sorry to hold that the remedy of judicial review was *e* not available.'

In *Rahmani's* case [1985] 1 All ER 1073 at 1082, [1985] QB 1109 at 1122 Stephenson LJ said:

> 'We do not have to consider, and the judge very properly did not consider, whether it is ever permissible to grant judicial review to an applicant who is not *f* wholly innocent. Where the mistake or misunderstanding which leads to the denial of natural justice is the applicant's own, it may seldom, if ever, be right for the court to exercise its discretion in his or her favour; for in most, if not all, cases of that kind there could be no unfairness towards the author and only begetter of the procedural defect. But I would hold, if necessary, that the court has the discretionary power to review and quash a decision reached as a result of an applicant's own fault.' *g*

Whatever may be the position regarding an applicant who is himself at fault, I regard the present case, where no blame attaches to the respondent, as a clear case for relief. I would, accordingly, uphold the decision of Macpherson J and dismiss this appeal.

NICHOLLS LJ. I agree.   *h*

O'CONNOR LJ. I agree that this appeal should be dismissed for the reasons given by Taylor LJ.

Appeal dismissed. Leave to appeal to the House of Lords granted.

Solicitors: *Treasury Solicitor; Burton Woolf & Turk* (for the respondent).

Raina Levy   Barrister.

a

Kleinwort Benson Ltd v Malaysia Mining Corp Bhd

COURT OF APPEAL, CIVIL DIVISION
FOX, RALPH GIBSON AND NICHOLLS LJJ
13, 14 DECEMBER 1988, 2 FEBRUARY 1989

b

Contract – Intention to create legal relationship – Inference of intention from circumstances – Letter of comfort – Plaintiffs making loan to defendants' subsidiary – Defendants furnishing letters of comfort to plaintiffs as part of loan agreement – Loan expressing defendants' policy to ensure that subsidiary's business at all times in a position to meet its liability to plaintiffs – Subsidiary going into liquidation – Plaintiffs suing defendants for subsidiary's debt – Whether letters of comfort having contractual effect.

c

The plaintiff bank agreed with the defendants to make a loan facility of up to £10m available to the defendants' wholly-owned subsidiary, M, which traded in tin on the London Metal Exchange. As part of the facility arrangement the defendants furnished to the plaintiffs two 'letters of comfort', each of which stated in para 3 that 'It is our policy to ensure that the business of [M] is at all times in a position to meet its liabilities to you under the [loan facility] arrangements'. In 1985 the tin market collapsed at a time when M owed the plaintiffs the whole amount of the facility. M went into liquidation and the plaintiffs sought payment of the amount owing from the defendants. When the defendants refused to pay the plaintiffs brought an action against them to recover the amount owing. The judge held that the plaintiffs were entitled to recover. The defendants appealed to the Court of Appeal.

d

e

Held – A letter of comfort from a parent company to a lender stating that it was the policy of the parent company to ensure that its subsidiary was 'at all times in a position to meet its liabilities' in respect of a loan made by the lender to the subsidiary did not have contractual effect if it was merely a statement of present fact regarding the parent company's intentions and was not a contractual promise as to the parent company's future conduct. On the facts, para 3 of the letters of comfort was in terms a statement of present fact and not a promise as to future conduct and in the context in which the letters were written was not intended to be anything other than a representation of fact giving rise to no more than a moral responsibility on the part of the defendants to meet M's debt. The appeal would therefore be allowed (see p 792 *d e*, p 795 *a* to *f*, p 796 *g* to *j* and p 797 *d j* to p 798 *b*, post).

f

g

Edwards v Skyways Ltd [1964] 1 All ER 494 and *Esso Petroleum Co Ltd v Mardon* [1976] 2 All ER 5 considered.

Decision of Hirst J [1988] 1 All ER 714 reversed.

h **Notes**

For intention to create legal relations, see 9 Halsbury's Laws (4th edn) paras 300–304, and for cases on the subject, see 12 Digest (Reissue) 21–26, 2–21.

Cases referred to in judgments

Chemco Leasing SpA v Rediffusion Ltd (19 July 1985, unreported), QBD; *affd* [1987] 1 FTLR
j   201, CA.
Edwards v Skyways Ltd [1964] 1 All ER 494, [1964] 1 WLR 349.
Esso Petroleum Co Ltd v Mardon [1976] 2 All ER 5, [1976] QB 801, [1976] 2 WLR 583, CA.
Hedley Byrne & Co Ltd v Heller & Partners Ltd [1963] 2 All ER 575, [1964] AC 465, [1963]
   3 WLR 101, HL.
Heilbut Symons & Co v Buckleton [1913] AC 30, [1911–13] All ER Rep 83, HL.

Maclaine Watson & Co Ltd v Dept of Trade and Industry [1988] 3 All ER 257, [1988] 3
    WLR 1033, CA.   **a**
Prenn v Simmonds [1971] 3 All ER 237, [1971] 1 WLR 1381, HL.
Rose & Frank Co v J R Crompton & Bros Ltd [1923] 2 KB 261, [1924] All ER Rep 245, CA;
    rvsd [1925] AC 445, [1924] All ER Rep 245, HL.

Appeal
The defendants, Malaysia Mining Corp Bhd, a public limited company incorporated   **b**
under the laws of Malaysia, appealed from the judgment of Hirst J ([1988] 1 All ER 714,
[1988] 1 WLR 799) given on 21 December 1987 whereby he awarded the plaintiffs,
Kleinwort Benson Ltd, damages arising from breach of a warranty and/or representation
contained in an agreement in writing between the plaintiffs and the defendants set out
in letters dated 21 August 1984 and 7 May 1985. The facts are set out in the judgment
of Ralph Gibson LJ.   **c**

S A Stamler QC and *Julian Gibson-Watt* for the defendants.
Mark Waller QC and *Nicholas Padfield* for the plaintiffs.

                                                                            Cur adv vult

2 February. The following judgments were delivered.   **d**

RALPH GIBSON LJ (giving the first judgment at the invitation of Fox LJ). This is an
appeal by the defendants, Malaysian Mining Corp Bhd, from the decision of Hirst J of
21 December 1987 by which the plaintiffs, Kleinwort Benson Ltd, obtained judgment
for damages for breach of contract against the defendants for £12·26m including interest.
The defendants ask that the judgment be set aside and that the plaintiffs' claim be   **e**
dismissed on the ground that the defendants did not enter into any relevant contractual
obligations to the plaintiffs.
    The judgment of Hirst J contains an account of the circumstances in which the
defendants provided to the plaintiffs the comfort letter on the terms of which the
plaintiffs' claim is founded (see [1988] 1 All ER 714 at 716–718, [1988] 1 WLR 799 at
801–803). The description of the document as a comfort letter is that used by the parties   **f**
themselves in the negotiations which preceded the provision of it by the defendants.
    The plaintiffs are merchant bankers of high reputation and long experience. The
defendants are a public limited company incorporated under the laws of Malaysia in
which the Republic of Malaysia has at all material times held a controlling interest. In
1983 the defendants caused to be incorporated under the laws of this country a company
called MMC Metals Ltd (Metals), as a wholly-owned but indirect subsidiary, to operate as   **g**
a ring-dealing member of the London Metal Exchange. The paid up capital of Metals
was £1·5m. To carry out trading on the London Metal Exchange much larger funds
would be required. There were negotiations for the provision of funds by the plaintiffs
to Metals. The plaintiffs sought from the defendants assurances as to the responsibility of
the defendants for the repayment by Metals of any sums lent by the plaintiffs. A 'comfort   **h**
letter' dated 21 August 1984 was provided by the defendants as part of an acceptance
credit/multi-currency cash loan facility granted by the plaintiffs to Metals to a maximum
of £5m. That letter contained, among other statements, the assertion by the defendants
that:

    'It is our policy to ensure that the business of MMC Metals Limited is at all times
    in a position to meet its liabilities to you under the above arrangements.'   **j**

This case turns on the proper construction, in its context, of that assertion by the
defendants. In 1985 the facility was increased by the plaintiffs to a maximum of £10m

a   in reliance on a second comfort letter dated 7 May 1985, which was in substantially identical terms.

In October 1985 the tin market collapsed when the International Tin Council (the ITC) announced that it was unable to meet its liabilities which ran to hundreds of millions of pounds. An account of those events and a list of the sovereign states (including the United Kingdom and Malaysia) which were members of the ITC can be found in the judgment of Kerr LJ in *Maclaine Watson & Co Ltd v Dept of Trade and Industry* [1988] 3

b   All ER 257 at 268–271, [1988] 3 WLR 1033 at 1047–1050. When the tin market collapsed Metals ceased trading. The plaintiffs demanded repayment of all sums outstanding. Nothing was paid, and Metals went into liquidation. The plaintiffs called on the defendants to ensure that the plaintiffs received payment of the sums due.

The defendants refused to pay and said by telex of 3 December 1985:

c   'We have been advised that the statements made in the letter of 7th May [1985] were not intended by either party to impose, and do not impose, any legally binding obligation on us to support Metals. You will appreciate that circumstances are now materially different from those existing at the date of that letter and that although the policy referred to was our policy at that time and in the light of the circumstances then prevailing, no assurance was given that such policy would not be reviewed in

d   the light of changing circumstances. We therefore cannot accept, as you stated in your telex, that we have given any assurances to you that Metals would at all times be kept in a position to meet its liability to you.'

Hirst J described in his judgment the course of the discussions between the defendants and the plaintiffs which led to the provision of the two comfort letters. Before Hirst J and in this court it was accepted by both sides that those events could properly be taken

e   into account as part of the context in which the second comfort letter was sent by the defendants.

I will set out Hirst J's description of those events substantially in his words, which have been accepted as full and accurate by the parties ([1988] 1 All ER 714 at 717–718, [1988] 1 WLR 799 at 802–803):

f   '. . . in the first instance, by letter dated 16 December 1983, [the plaintiffs] offered to both [the defendants] and Metals jointly a facility totalling £5m, on terms that, throughout the currency of the facility, both [the defendants] and Metals should be jointly and severally liable for all amounts due to [the plaintiffs]; on this basis an accepting commission/margin of $\frac{3}{8}$% per annum was proposed. On 9 February 1984 there was a meeting in Singapore, attended on [the plaintiffs'] side by Mr Gordon

g   Irwin, who was the sole witness at the trial. At this stage [the plaintiffs] were proposing a guarantee by [the defendants] rather than joint and several liability, but one of [the defendants'] representatives at the meeting stated that it was [the defendants'] policy not to guarantee their subsidiary's borrowings. At a subsequent meeting in London on 21 June 1984, Mr John Green, who had been newly appointed as the director in charge of Metals' operations, is recorded in [the

h   plaintiffs'] meeting note as having stated as follows: "The original offer was outlined (£5 mn. u.f.n. @ $\frac{3}{8}$% p.a. margin guaranteed by [the defendants]). A facility of this sort appears to fit in with Green's requirements, with the exception of the guarantee. Green said that [the defendants] were now not so keen on issuing guarantees just to keep finance costs down by $\frac{1}{8}$% p.a., and Green himself would be recommending that all MMC Metals' bank lines should be covered by a letter of comfort, rather

j   than by a guarantee. I said that a letter of comfort would not be a problem, but that we would probably have to charge a higher rate." This was reported by Mr Irwin in an internal memorandum dated 3 July 1984 as follows: "Contrary to earlier reports, [the defendants] have now taken a decision not to issue guarantees to cover the banking facilities granted to MMC Metals. As a result, we have been asked to consider a line which would be covered by a letter of comfort from [the defendants]." Mr Irwin in evidence accepted that by this stage he realised that [the plaintiffs] would not be able to obtain either joint and several liability as originally proposed, or a guarantee from [the defendants]. Originally it was proposed that [the defendants] should draft the comfort letter, but eventually on 11 July [the plaintiffs] furnished to Metals a revised facility letter addressed to them only, providing for ½% commission (ie an increase of ⅛%), and accompanied by a draft of a proposed comfort letter, in which the crucial paragraph read as follows: "It is our policy to ensure that the business of MMC Metals Limited is conducted in such a way that MMC Metals Limited is at all times in a position to meet its liabilities to you under the above arrangements." Ie containing at this stage some extra words in the second line. On 10 August 1984 at a board meeting of [the defendants] the following directors' written resolution was passed: "THAT MMC Metals Limited be authorised to accept the above facility on terms and conditions contained in the letter from [the plaintiffs] (KBL) dated July 11, 1984, and that the required Letter of Comfort in the form attached be issued to KBL." Eventually, on 17 September, Metals returned the formal facility letter to [the plaintiffs] accompanied by the first comfort letter, dated 21 August 1984, with the crucial paragraph redrafted by [the defendants]. The full text of the letter is as follows: "We refer to your recent discussion with MMC Metals Limited as a result of which you propose granting MMC Metals Limited: a) banking facilities of up to £5 million; and b) spot and forward foreign exchange facilities with a limitation that total delivery in cash will not on any one day exceed £5 million [1] We hereby confirm that we know and approve of these facilities and are aware of the fact that they have been granted to MMC Metals Limited because we control directly or indirectly MMC Metals Limited. [2] We confirm that we will not reduce our current financial interest in MMC Metals Limited until the above facilities have been repaid or until you have confirmed that you are prepared to continue the facilities with new shareholders. [3] It is our policy to ensure that the business of MMC Metals Limited is at all times in a position to meet its liabilities to you under the above arrangements. Yours faithfully MALAYSIA MINING CORPORATION BERHAD. I have inserted numbers for the three main paragraphs for clarity of reference in this judgment. Paragraph (2) was, as is common ground, contractual.'

Hirst J was referred to four authorities, which in order of date were *Rose & Frank Co v J R Crompton & Bros Ltd* [1923] 2 KB 261, [1924] All ER Rep 245, *Edwards v Skyways Ltd* [1964] 1 All ER 494, [1964] 1 WLR 349, *Prenn v Simmonds* [1971] 3 All ER 237, [1971] 1 WLR 1381 and *Chemco Leasing SpA v Rediffusion Ltd* (19 July 1985, unreported), QBD; affd [1987] 1 FTLR 201.

From those cases and from a passage in *Chitty on Contracts* (25th edn, 1983) para 123 Hirst J accepted the following principles as applicable (I have numbered them separately): (i) an agreement, even though it is supported by consideration, is not binding as a contract if it was made without any intention of creating legal relations; (ii) in the case of an ordinary commercial transaction it is not normally necessary to prove that the parties in fact intended to create legal relations, the onus of proving that there was no such intention 'is on the party who asserts that no legal effect is intended, and the onus is a heavy one': per Megaw J in *Edwards v Skyways Ltd* [1964] 1 All ER 494 at 500, [1964] 1 WLR 349 at 355; (iii) to decide whether legal effect was intended, the courts normally apply an objective test; for example, where the sale of a house is *not* 'subject to contract', either party is likely to be bound even though he subjectively believed that he would not be bound until the usual exchange of contracts had taken place; (iv) the court will, in deciding that question, attach weight (a) to the importance of the agreement of the

parties and (b) to the fact that one of them has acted in reliance on it; (v) in the search for
a agreed terms of a commercial transaction, business men may adopt language of deliberate
equivocation in the hope that all will go well. It may, therefore, be artificial to try to
ascertain the common intention of the parties as to the legal effect of such a claim if in
fact their common intention was that the claim should have such effect as a judge or
arbitrator should decide: see the decision of Staughton J in *Chemco Leasing SpA v Rediffusion
Ltd* cited by Hirst J (see [1988] 1 All ER 714 at 719, [1988] 1 WLR 799 at 805).
b Nevertheless, the court's task is to ascertain what common intentions should be ascribed
to the parties from the terms of the documents and the surrounding circumstances.

Before stating the steps by which, having regard to those principles, Hirst J made his
decision in this case, I must refer to three matters which Hirst J listed as having been
relied on by the defendants as demonstrating that the parties did not intend the words in
para 3 of the comfort letter to have legal effect as a contractual term. They were (i) that
c the comfort letter should be construed against the plaintiffs as the party putting forward
the paragraph in question, ie contra proferentem, (ii) that the language of the paragraph
was not apt to express a legal obligation and was, in that regard, markedly different from
those parts of the comfort letter which did express legal obligation, and in particular the
preceding para 2, and (iii) that the common appreciation by both sides that the defendants
were not willing either to assume joint and several liability, or to enter into a guarantee,
d supported displacement of the presumption.

The steps by which Hirst J reached his conclusion may, I think, be summarised as
follows. (a) The two comfort letters came into existence as part of a commercial banking
transaction and the statement in para 3 of the letter of May 1985 was an important
feature of them. (b) Accordingly, the presumption laid down by *Edwards v Skyways Ltd*
applied and the burden therefore lay on the defendants to show that the parties did not
e intend para 3 in the letter to have legal effect as a contractual term. (c) The three matters
relied on by the defendants were not sufficient to displace that presumption: (i) as to
construction contra proferentem, that principle was not applicable because the wording
was not ambiguous, and, if it was, the paragraph was the product of joint drafting and
was not for this purpose to be regarded as drafted by the plaintiffs; (ii) as to the language
of the paragraph, it was fully apt to express a legal obligation. Hirst J continued ([1988]
f 1 All ER 714 at 722, [1988] 1 WLR 799 at 809):

> 'I see no magic in the opening words "we confirm that we will not . . ." in para
> (2), or their omission from para (3): put another way, I do not think that any greater
> strength would have been added to para (3) if it had begun "We confirm that it is
> our policy . . ."'

g
(iii) as to the common appreciation by both sides that the defendants were not willing
either to assume joint and several liability or to enter into a guarantee, that argument
came 'perilously close to infringing the principle that the course of negotiations cannot
be invoked in order to influence the construction of a written document'. Apart from
h that consideration the argument was unconvincing because the provisions of para 3 are
not to be equated with a guarantee even though, as it happens, the measure of damages
for breach of the term contained in the paragraph would be equivalent to the amount
recoverable on a guarantee. There was, in the judge's view, a very substantial difference
between, on the one hand, a guarantee and, on the other, a paragraph like the one under
consideration in the present case. Further, the underlying premise on which the
j argument was based was unacceptable, namely the suggestion that once a formal
guarantee had been rejected by the defendants, as it was, there was no further scope for
the possibility of any contractually binding obligation of the sort enshrined in para 3.
(d) A number of considerations strongly reinforced the presumption that the parties
intended that the paragraph should have legal effect, namely: (i) the plaintiffs acted in

reliance on the paragraph in agreeing to advance money to Metals; (ii) it was of paramount importance to the plaintiffs that the defendants should ensure that Metals *a* was at all times in a position to meet its liabilities; and (iii) the statement contained in para 3 was also treated as a matter of importance by the defendants, as was shown by their formal board resolution.

Having thus held that the defendants had not demonstrated that the parties did not intend para 3 to have effect as a contractual term, Hirst J considered the interpretation of the words in para 3. The interpretation was, in his view, crystal clear without *b* embellishment. He said ([1988] 1 All ER 714 at 724, [1988] 1 WLR 799 at 811):

> 'It is an undertaking that, now and at all times in future, so long as Metals are under any liability to [the plaintiffs] under the facility arrangements, it is and will be [the defendants'] policy to ensure that Metals is in a position to meet those liabilities.'
>
> *c*

Counsel's submissions in this court for the defendants were as follows. He referred to the use of letters of comfort in banking over recent years, and to the description of that practice in Wood *Law and Practice of International Finance* (1980) para 13.5 from which Staughton J cited passages in the *Chemco* case. He contended that the paragraphs of the comfort letter in this case are typical of a comfort letter, both in substance and in sequence, namely: (i) a statement of the awareness of the parent company of the advances *d* made to the subsidiary; (ii) a promise that the parent will not, without the consent of the bank, relinquish or reduce control of the subsidiary before repayment; and (iii) the words of comfort, stating how far the parent is prepared to go in supporting its subsidiary, often beginning 'it is our intention . . .' or 'it is our policy . . .' Counsel, however, did not contend, as I understood his argument, that the phrase 'comfort letter' was shown to have acquired a precise meaning, in particular as to the limits of any legally enforceable *e* liability which might be assumed by a parent company under such a letter, but he submitted that the phrase was generally understood to include a letter giving comfort only in the sense that the parent company assumed no legally enforceable liability to pay the debts of its subsidiary but did, in order to recognise fully its moral responsibility, acknowledge that the debts had been incurred by the subsidiary with the knowledge and *f* approval of the parent, and state the present policy of the parent as to ensuring repayment.

The defendants have throughout acknowledged that the term in para 2 of the present letter was a contractual promise, ie it was intended to have legal effect as such. The statement in para 3, however, was not, it was submitted, a contractual promise and was not intended to have legal effect as such. It was nevertheless, in counsel's submission, not devoid of legal significance: it was a representation of fact as to the policy of the *g* defendants at the time that the statement was made; and the plaintiffs were entitled to rely on it was a statement of the current policy of the defendants. If it were shown to have been untrue to the knowledge of the defendants at the time when it was made, the plaintiffs would have had a claim in deceit, but there has been no suggestion of that nature.

In addition, the plaintiffs were entitled to rely on the representation as to the current *h* policy of the defendants unless and until they were told that the policy had been changed. If the policy did change, without notice from the defendants so that the representation ceased to be true, and the plaintiffs thereafter relied on it by making further advances to Metals, they would have, it was said, 'a cause of action in misrepresentation', but no cause of action in contract. Since the contract into which the plaintiffs entered in reliance on the representation was not made with the defendants, there could be no claim under s 2 *j* of the Misrepresentation Act 1967, but a claim for negligent misrepresentation might be advanced on the principles stated in *Hedley Byrne & Co Ltd v Heller & Partners Ltd* [1963] 2 All ER 575, [1964] AC 465. No such claim, of course, has been advanced in this case.

The main attack on the analysis and reasoning of the judge, which counsel for the

defendants developed, was directed at the application by Hirst J of the proposition,
illustrated by *Edwards v Skyways Ltd* [1964] 1 All ER 494, [1964] 1 WLR 349, that a
promise, made for consideration in a commercial transaction, will be taken to have been
intended to have contractual effect in law, unless the contrary is clearly shown. The
proposition was not disputed on behalf of the defendants before Hirst J, or this court. It
was, however, submitted that the principle is of no assistance in deciding whether, on
the evidence and on their true construction, the words in question are words of promise
or not.

On that question, it was said, neither *Rose & Frank Co v J R Crompton & Bros Ltd* [1923]
2 KB 261, [1924] All ER Rep 245 nor *Edwards v Skyways Ltd* [1964] 1 All ER 494, [1964]
1 WLR 349 laid down any relevant presumption in favour of the plaintiffs which the
defendants were called on to displace. The judge, it was said, was led into the belief that,
if he took the view that the defendants had failed to displace the presumption laid down
in *Edwards v Skyways Ltd*, it followed that para 3 was to be given effect in law as a
contractual promise.

That approach was demonstrated, it was said, by the passage near the beginning of the
judgment where Hirst J said ([1988] 1 All ER 714 at 716, [1988] 1 WLR 799 at 801):
'The main question . . . is whether . . . the crucial paragraph . . . was contractual in status;
if it is, the subsidiary question arises as to its proper construction.'

It was, counsel for the defendants argued, further demonstrated by the summary
treatment of the question of construction itself where, as set out above, the judge found
the answer to be crystal clear and the meaning to be an undertaking that, 'now and at all
times in future . . . it is and will be [the defendants'] policy to ensure that Metals is in a
position to meet those liabilities' (see [1988] 1 All ER 714 at 724, [1988] 1 WLR 799 at
811).

For the rest, the substance of the submissions advanced by counsel for the defendants,
in which he adopted the comments of Mr Brian Davenport QC in 'A Very Comfortable
Comfort Letter' in [1988] Lloyd's MCLQ 290, was as follows. (i) The words in para 3 are
not words of contractual promise. In that respect they differ markedly from the wording
of para 2: 'We confirm that we will not reduce our current financial interest in MMC
Metals Ltd.' (ii) To give to the words the meaning which the judge held them to have
requires that no force be given to the words 'it is our policy . . .' Further, or in the
alternative, it is necessary to imply, in addition to the statement as to present policy, a
promise that the policy will not be changed and such an implication is not possible on
the evidence in this case. (iii) Therefore, without recourse to any assistance from the
circumstances in which the transaction was conducted, it should be held that by para 3
the defendants did not make the promise which the judge extracted from the words.
(iv) If any doubt could be entertained as to the meaning of para 3 that doubt should be
dispelled by giving due weight to the facts proved, namely that the plaintiffs had sought
to obtain either joint and several liability of the defendants, or a guarantee from the
defendants of the liabilities of Metals to the plaintiffs, and the defendants had refused to
assume either form of obligation; and the plaintiffs knew that, if the transaction was to
proceed, it must be without such security. Further the plaintiffs had, in compensation
for not having that security, stipulated for, and obtained from Metals, the right to an
increased commission of $\frac{1}{8}$%. To put some financial meaning into that point, counsel for
the defendants calculated that if the facility had been revolved four times a year on the
basis of 90-day bills the increase of $\frac{1}{8}$% would be chargeable on £40m, ie £50,000 pa.

The submission in this court for the plaintiffs can be more shortly stated because
counsel adopted and relied on the reasoning of the judge. As to the effect and meaning
to be given to para 3, his main submissions were that: (i) the statement in para 3 was
made in a commercial contractual document and it is to be treated as a contractual
promise if it appears on the evidence to have been so intended: see *Esso Petroleum Co Ltd
v Mardon* [1976] 2 All ER 5, [1976] QB 801; (ii) it is shown to have been so intended

because the statement was made for the purpose of inducing the plaintiffs to enter into the acceptance credit transaction with Metals under the credit facility and it was plainly *a* of decisive commercial importance to the transaction; (iii) the statement as to present policy must be taken as including a promise that that policy will remain in force. This proposition can be tested, it was said, by taking an example remote from banking: suppose a shop, by notice, announced that 'it is our policy to take back all goods purchased and to refund the price, without any questions, on return of the goods in good condition within 14 days of purchase', if a customer should return goods, having bought them in *b* reliance on the notice, the shop could not (said counsel for the plaintiffs) refuse to refund the price on the ground that the notice only stated the shop's policy on the day of purchase so that the shop was free to change its policy within the 14-day period. So in this case it is absurd in commercial terms for the defendants to claim to be free to change their announced policy after money has been advanced in reliance on it. To treat the words of para 3 as no more than a representation of fact is to give no force to the words *c* 'at all times'.

For my part, I am persuaded that the main criticisms of the judgment of Hirst J advanced by counsel for the defendants are well founded and I would, for the reasons which follow, allow this appeal. In my judgment the defendants made a statement as to what their policy was, and did not in para 3 of the comfort letter expressly promise that such policy would be continued in future. It is impossible to make up for the lack of *d* express promise by implying such a promise, and indeed, no such implied promise was pleaded. My conclusion rests on what, in my judgment, is the proper effect and meaning which, on the evidence, is to be given to para 3 of the comfort letters.

Before expressing my reasons for that conclusion, I should refer to the way in which the question of 'intention of creating legal relations' was introduced into this case. The plaintiffs' primary pleaded contention was that by the first letter of 21 August 1984, on *e* its true construction, the defendants warranted that, in consideration of the plaintiffs' granting the loan facility to Metals, the defendants would ensure that Metals was at all times capable of fulfilling its financial obligations to the plaintiffs under the facility. The alternative and secondary contention was that, if the defendants had not given that warranty, the defendants warranted that it was their business policy to ensure that Metals would always have sufficient means to meet its liabilities to the plaintiffs under the terms *f* and conditions of the facility and that, in all the circumstances, the defendants impliedly warranted that they would give to the plaintiffs reasonable notice of their intention to change that business policy.

Those two contentions were repeated with reference to the letter of May 1985. The judge made no findings on the secondary contention, and no alternative claim has been pursued in this court. It is to be noted that the only reliance on implied obligation was in *g* that alternative claim which has not been pursued, no doubt because there is nothing to show that any failure to give notice of the change in policy caused loss to the plaintiffs.

In answer to the plaintiffs' claims, the defendants pleaded that—

> 'the letters of 21 August 1984 and of May 1985 were, and were agreed and understood by both parties to be "letters of comfort" or "letters of awareness" falling *h* short of any legal ... warranty, and that the said statements of policy by the defendants (if given honestly, which they were) were not and were agreed and/or understood by both parties not to be, legally enforceable.'

The defendants added that, if para 3 of the letters constituted any actionable representation, it was only a representation of the defendants' policy or intention at the date of the letter *j* and the defendants' only obligation was to notify the plaintiffs within a reasonable time of any change in such policy or intention.

Particulars were requested and provided of the 'agreement or understanding' on which the defendants relied. In short, the defendants said that, by reference to the course of the

negotiations set out by Hirst J in his judgment, the plaintiffs 'agreed to accept a letter of
a   comfort (rather than any legal liability on the part of the defendants) in consideration of
the increased acceptance commission.'
There were thus included in the pleaded case of the defendants two distinct pleas as to
the intentions of the parties with reference to para 3 of the comfort letters. The first was
that even if, on its true construction, it contained what would have been a contractual
promise, as contrasted with a mere representation of fact, nevertheless it should not be
b   enforced as a contractual promise because there had been a separate agreement or
understanding that it should not be legally enforceable.
The second plea was that, failing proof of that separate agreement or understanding,
the statement in para 3 of the comfort letters was not in its terms a warranty or
contractual promise and was not intended to be such. This second plea is, in this case,
inseparable, in my judgment, from the question of the proper construction of the words
c   of para 3 in their context although, of course, there might be in some cases a separate
issue of construction once it was established that the words, not in express promissory
terms, were intended as a warranty. In this case, if the court is persuaded that the
statement in para 3 as to what the policy of the defendants is, is to be treated as including
a promise as to what that policy would be in future, there was not any real dispute as to
d   what was the extent and meaning of that promise.
In the event, at the trial there was no evidence to support the first plea, i e that there
had been an agreement that the words of the comfort letters should not have legal effect.
The parties had referred to a 'comfort letter', but it was not proved that the parties had
agreed on any specific meaning for that phrase as descriptive of the liabilities to be
undertaken by the defendants. The point was apparently not pursued. The argument
e   concentrated on whether para 3 was to be treated in law as a contractual promise: Hirst J
referred to the main question as being whether para 3 was 'contractual in status', and his
conclusion was, as I have said, that the presumption laid down in *Edwards v Skyways Ltd*
[1964] 1 All ER 494, [1964] 1 WLR 349 applied and that the defendants had failed to
displace the presumption.
Counsel for the plaintiffs before Hirst J had placed strong reliance on *Edwards v*
f   *Skyways Ltd* and his submission was recorded by Hirst J as follows ([1988] 1 All ER 714
at 721, [1988] 1 WLR 799 at 807): '... there was a heavy onus on [the defendants] to
prove that there was no intention to create contractual relations.'
In my judgment counsel for the defendants is right in his submission that the
presumption described in *Edwards v Skyways Ltd* had no application to the issues in this
case once the plea of a separate agreement or understanding to the effect that the comfort
g   letters should have no legal effect had disappeared from the case for want of evidence to
support it. The introduction of that plea into the case appears to have served only to
distract attention from what, if I am right, are the clear merits of the defendants' case as
to the meaning and effect of para 3 of the comfort letters.
To explain why, in my view, the presumption applied by Hirst J had no application to
this case it is necessary to examine in some detail the issues in *Edwards v Skyways Ltd*. In
h   that case Skyways Ltd, the defendants, found it necessary to declare redundant some 15%
of the pilots in their employ. The secretary of Skyways Ltd, at a meeting with
representatives of the airline pilots union, agreed that—

> 'Pilots declared redundant and leaving the company would be given an ex gratia
> payment equivalent to the company's contribution to the Pension Fund [and, in
j   > addition]... a refund of their own contributions to the fund.'

(See [1964] 1 All ER 494 at 497, [1964] 1 WLR 349 at 351.) Edwards, in reliance on that
agreement, left the company and claimed payment under it. The company purported to
rescind its decision to make the ex gratia payment on the ground that it had obligations

to creditors and the promised ex gratia payments were not enforceable in law. The company admitted that a promise had been made to make the payments and that the promise was supported by consideration, but contended (in reliance on *Rose & Frank Co v J R Crompton & Bros Ltd* [1923] 2 KB 261 at 288, [1924] All ER Rep 245 at 249–250) that the promise or agreement had no legal effect because there was no intention to enter into legal relations in respect of the promised payment. It was argued that the mere use of the phrase 'ex gratia', as part of the promise to pay, showed that the parties contemplated that the promise when accepted would have no binding force in law and, further, that there was background knowledge, concerned with the tax consequences of legally enforceable promises to pay, and present to the minds of the representatives of the parties, which gave unambiguous significance to the words 'ex gratia' as excluding legal relationships. Megaw J rejected these arguments on the facts and on his construction of the meaning in the context of the words 'ex gratia'. The company thus failed to show that what was otherwise admittedly a promise, supported by consideration, was to be denied legal effect because of the common intention of the parties that it should not have such effect and, accordingly, the company failed to displace the presumption. Megaw J was not dealing with the sort of question which is raised in this case, namely whether, given that the comfort letter was intended to express the legal relationship between the parties, the language of para 3 does or does not contain a contractual promise (see [1964] 1 All ER 494 at 497–501, [1964] 1 WLR 349 at 354–356).

The central question in this case, in my judgment, is that considered in *Esso Petroleum Co Ltd v Mardon* [1976] 2 All ER 5, [1976] QB 801, on which counsel for the plaintiffs relied in this court but which was not cited to Hirst J. That question is whether the words of para 3, considered in their context, are to be treated as a warranty or contractual promise. Paragraph 3 contains no express words of promise. Paragraph 3 is in its terms a statement of present fact and not a promise as to future conduct. I agree with the submission of counsel for the defendants that, in this regard, the words of para 3 are in sharp contrast with the words of para 2 of the letter: 'We confirm that we will not' etc. The force of this point is not limited, as Hirst J stated it, to the absence from para 3 of the words 'We confirm'. The real contrast is between the words of promise, namely 'We will not' in para 2, and the words of statement of fact, 'It is our policy' in para 3. Hirst J held that, by the words of para 3, the defendants gave an undertaking that now and at all times in the future, so long as Metals should be under any liability to the plaintiffs under the facility arrangements, it is *and will be* the defendants' policy to ensure that Metals is in a position to meet their liabilities. To derive that meaning from the words it is necessary to add the words emphasised, namely 'and will be', which do not appear in para 3. In short, the words of promise as to the future conduct of the defendants were held by Hirst J to be part of the necessary meaning of the words used in para 3. The question is whether that view of the words can be upheld.

The absence of express words of warranty as to present facts or the absence of express words of promise as to future conduct does not conclusively exclude a statement from the status of warranty or promise. According to the well-known dictum of Holt CJ, '... an affirmation can only be a warranty provided it appears on evidence to have been so intended': see Ormrod LJ in *Esso Petroleum Co Ltd v Mardon* [1976] 2 All ER 5 at 19 [1976] QB 801 at 824, citing Viscount Haldane LC in *Heilbut Symons & Co v Buckleton* [1913] AC 30 at 38, [1911–13] All ER Rep 83 at 86. Thus in *Esso Petroleum Co Ltd v Mardon* the statement that Esso 'estimated that the throughput of the Eastbank Street site, in its third year of operation, would amount to 200,000 gallons a year', which had been made as an expert estimate, which was of great commercial importance to a potential tenant of the site, and which induced Mr Mardon to enter into the contract of lease, was held to be a warranty not that such a throughput would be achieved, *but* that, in effect, the estimate had been made with due care on the basis of information in the possession of Esso (see

[1976] 2 All ER 5 at 14, 21, 25, [1976] QB 801 at 818, 827, 832 per Lord Denning MR,
a Ormrod and Shaw LJJ).

Counsel for the plaintiffs in this court placed reliance on the decision in *Esso Petroleum Co Ltd v Mardon*. It is, in my judgment, on the facts of this case, of no assistance to the plaintiffs. The evidence does not show that the words used in para 3 were intended to be a promise as to the future conduct of the defendants but, in my judgment, it shows the contrary.

b The concept of a comfort letter was, as counsel for the defendants acknowledged, not shown to have acquired any particular meaning at the time of the negotiations in this case with reference to the limits of any legal liability to be assumed under its terms by a parent company. A letter, which the parties might have referred to at some stage as a letter of comfort, might, after negotiation, have emerged containing in para 3 in express terms the words used by Hirst J to state the meaning which he gave to para 3. The court *c* would not, merely because the parties had referred to the document as a comfort letter, refuse to give effect to the meaning of the words used. But in this case it is clear, in my judgment, that the concept of a comfort letter, to which the parties had resort when the defendants refused to assume joint and several liability or to give a guarantee, was known by both sides at least to extend to or to include a document under which the defendants would give comfort to the plaintiffs by assuming, not a legal liability to ensure repayment *d* of the liabilities of its subsidiary, but a moral responsibility only. Thus, when the defendants by Mr John Green in June 1984 told the plaintiffs that Mr Green would recommend that credit lines for Metals be covered by a letter of comfort rather than by guarantee, the response of Mr Irwin, before any draft of a comfort letter had been prepared, was '. . . that a letter of comfort would not be a problem, but that [he] would probably have to charge a higher rate'. The comfort letter was drafted in terms which in *e* para 3 do not express any contractual promise and which are consistent with being no more than a representation of fact. If they are treated as no more than a representation of fact, they are in that meaning consistent with the comfort letter containing no more than the assumption of moral responsibility by the defendants in respect of the debts of Metals. There is nothing in the evidence to show that, as a matter of commercial *f* probability or common sense, the parties must have intended para 3 to be a contractual promise, which is not expressly stated, rather than a mere representation of fact which is so stated.

Next, the first draft of the comfort letter was produced by the plaintiffs. Paragraph 1 contained confirmation that the defendants knew of and approved of the granting of the facilities in question by the plaintiffs to Metals, and para 2 contained the express *g* confirmation that the defendants would not reduce their current financial interest in Metals until (in effect) facilities had been paid or the plaintiffs consented. Both are relevant to the present and future moral responsibility of the defendants. If the words of para 3 are to be treated as intended to express a contractual promise by the defendants as to their future policy, which Hirst J held the words to contain, then the recitation of the plaintiffs' approval and the promise not to reduce their current financial interest in *h* Metals, would be of no significance. If the defendants have promised that at all times in the future it will be the defendants' policy to ensure that Metals is in a position to meet its liabilities to the plaintiffs under the facility, it would not matter whether they had approved or disapproved, or whether they had disposed of their shares in Metals. Contracts may, of course, contain statements or promises which are caused to be of no separate commercial importance by the width of a later promise in the same document. *j* Where, however, the court is examining a statement which is by its express words no more than a representation of fact, in order to consider whether it is shown to have been intended to be of the nature of a contractual promise or warranty, it seems to me to be a fact suggesting at least the absence of such intention if, as in this case, to read the statement as a contractual promise is to reduce to no significance two paragraphs included in the plaintiffs' draft, both of which have significance if the statement is read as a *a* representation of fact only.

That point can be made more plainly thus: if para 3 in its original or in its final form was intended to contain a binding legal promise by the defendants to ensure the ability of Metals to pay the sums due under the facility, there was no apparent need or purpose for the plaintiffs, as bankers, to waste ink on paras 1 and 2.

As I have said, the absence of express words of promise does not by itself prevent a *b* statement from being treated as a contractual promise. The example given in argument by counsel for the plaintiffs, namely of the shop stating by a notice that it is its policy to accept, within 14 days of purchase, the return in good condition of any goods bought and to refund the price without question, seems to me to be a case in which a court would be likely to hold that the notice imported a promise that the policy would continue over the 14-day period. It would be difficult on those facts to find any sensible *c* commercial explanation for the notice other than a contractual promise not to change the policy over the 14-day period. It would not be satisfactory or convincing to regard the notice as no more than the assumption of a moral responsibility by the shop giving such a notice to its customers. In such a case, and in the absence of any relevant factual context indicating otherwise, it seems to me that the court would probably hold that the statement was shown to have been intended to be a contractual promise.   *d*

In this case, however, the opposite seems to me to be clear. The context in which the comfort letter was requested and given is before the court without dispute as to the relevance or admissibility of that context. That concession was, in my view, rightly made. The evidence showing the context in which the comfort letters were produced, as set out in the judgment of Hirst J, was evidence of the factual background known to the parties at or before the date of the contract and of the 'genesis' and 'aim' of the transaction *e* (see *Prenn v Simmonds* [1971] 3 All ER 237, [1971] 1 WLR 1381), in short the provision of a comfort letter by the defendants, as the parent company of Metals to which the plaintiffs were intending to provide finance, in circumstances in which the defendants had refused to assume legal liability for the repayment of money lent to Metals by the plaintiffs, whether in the form of joint and several liability or of a guarantee. Those facts are not available to show merely that the defendants did not themselves subjectively *f* intend to assume legal liability and that, therefore, the words eventually included in the comfort letter provided by the defendants should be construed so as to exclude such liability. That, as I understand it, would be misapplying the principles stated in *Prenn v Simmonds*, by which evidence of the factual background is admitted. But the evidence of the refusal by the defendants to assume legal responsibility for the liabilities of Metals to the plaintiffs in the normal form of joint and several liability or of a guarantee, and the *g* consequent resort by the parties to what they described as a comfort letter substantially in the terms submitted by the plaintiffs to the defendants, is, in my judgment, admissible on the question whether, for the purposes of the test applied by this court in *Esso Petroleum Co Ltd v Mardon*, the defendants' affirmation in para 3 appears on the evidence to have been intended as a warranty or contractual promise.   *h*

With that evidence before the court I find it impossible to hold that the words in para 3 were intended to have any effect between the parties other than in accordance with the express words used. For this purpose it seems to me that the onus of demonstrating that the affirmation appears on evidence to have been intended as a contractual promise must lie on the party asserting that it does, but I do not rest my conclusion on failure by the plaintiffs to discharge any onus. I think it is clear that the words of para 3 cannot be *j* regarded as intended to contain a contractual promise as to the future policy of the defendants. If para 3 had been drafted by the plaintiffs and submittted in the form in which Hirst J formulated its meaning (see [1988] 1 All ER 714 at 724, [1988] 1 WLR 799 at 811), namely as—

'an undertaking that, now and at all times in future, so long as Metals are under any liability to [the plaintiffs] under the facility arrangements, it is and will be [the defendants'] policy to ensure that Metals is in a position to meet those liabilities',

it must have appeared to both parties, in the context proved in evidence, as a radically different term from that which was in fact submitted and accepted. Such an undertaking does not fit, as a matter of commercial probability, with the factual background. I do not suggest that people only act in accordance with apparent commercial probability; the plaintiffs might have submitted such an undertaking which, in the light of the prior refusal to give a guarantee, was likely to be rejected and the defendants, contrary to what seemed likely, might have accepted it, but the plaintiffs in fact submitted the words we see in para 3. The plain meaning of those words, without the addition contained in Hirst J's formulation of its meaning, does fit the factual background. Most importantly, that factual background explains, notwithstanding the commercial importance to the plaintiffs of security against failure by Metals to pay and the plaintiffs' reliance on the comfort letter, why the plaintiffs drafted and agreed to proceed on a comfort letter which, on its plain meaning, provided to the plaintiffs no legally enforceable security for the repayment of the liabilities of Metals. I therefore find it impossible to hold that by the words of para 3 the parties must be held to have intended that the plaintiffs be given that security.

I should mention briefly some other points which were argued. As is apparent from what I have said above, the plaintiffs are, in my judgment, to be regarded as the party putting forward the language contained in the comfort letters as a whole. The change in the wording introduced by the defendants made no difference whatever to the meaning. It was not argued that it did. Hirst J held that the principle of construction contra proferentem had no application because there was no ambiguity. I do not agree. The question was whether words, which are not in the form of a contractual promise, are on the evidence to be treated as intended to have been such a promise. Having regard to the defendants' prior refusal to assume joint and several liability or to give a guarantee, and to the resort by the parties to what was referred to as a comfort letter, it seems to me that the defendants are entitled to rely on the fact that, if the plaintiffs required a promise as to the defendants' future policy, it was open to them as experienced bankers to draft para 3 in those terms. I do not, however, regard the point as decisive. If the letter in its final form is to be regarded as the result of joint drafting, my conclusion would not be affected.

Submissions were made to Hirst J, and repeated in this court, as to the differences between the liability of the defendants on a formal guarantee, and the ease of enforcement of that liability, on the one hand, and the liability and attendant problems of enforcement under para 3, on the other hand, according to its meaning and effect as determined by the judge.

I did not find these submissions to be of any assistance in the resolving of the main issue in this case, and I do not propose to deal with them in any detail. I agree with Hirst J that the mere fact that the defendants had refused to give a formal guarantee did not mean that there was a further scope for the subsequent agreement by them to a term having the meaning and effect which Hirst J gave to para 3; but contemplation by either party of the alleged differences in certainty or of the availability of summary judgment seems to me to be wholly improbable.

If my view of this case is correct, the plaintiffs have suffered grave financial loss as a result of the collapse of the tin market and the following decision by the defendant company not to honour a moral responsibility which it assumed in order to gain for its subsidiary the finance necessary for the trading operations which the defendants wished that subsidiary to pursue. The defendants have demonstrated, in my judgment, that they made no relevant contractual promise to the plaintiffs which could support the judgment

in favour of the plaintiffs. The consequences of the decision of the defendants to repudiate
their moral responsibility are not matters for this court.

    I would allow this appeal.

NICHOLLS LJ. I agree.

FOX LJ. I also agree.

Appeal allowed. Leave to appeal to House of Lords refused.

Solicitors: *Freshfields* (for the defendants); *Herbert Smith* (for the plaintiffs).

Frances Rustin   Barrister.

Caparo Industries plc v Dickman and others

COURT OF APPEAL, CIVIL DIVISION
O'CONNOR, BINGHAM AND TAYLOR LJJ
25, 26, 27, 28, 29 APRIL, 3 MAY, 29 JULY 1988

*Negligence – Information or advice – Knowledge third party might rely on information – Auditor
– Preparation of company's accounts – Duty to shareholder – Duty to prospective investor –
Plaintiffs owning shares in public company – Plaintiffs making successful take-over bid for
company in reliance on audited accounts of company – Accounts showing profit instead of loss –
Whether reasonably foreseeable that shareholders and potential investors might rely on auditor's
report when dealing in company's shares – Whether sufficient proximity between auditor and
shareholders or potential investors – Whether just and reasonable to impose duty of care on
auditor – Whether auditor owing duty of care to shareholders or potential investors to carry out
audit with reasonable care and skill.*

The plaintiffs owned shares in a public company, F plc, and were interested in making a
take-over bid for it. As shareholders the plaintiffs were entitled to receive the audited
accounts of F plc and after receipt of the accounts for the year ended 31 March 1984 they
purchased more shares in F plc and later that year made a successful take-over bid.
Following the take-over, the plaintiffs brought an action against, inter alios, the auditors
of F plc, alleging that they had made their bid in reliance on F plc's audited accounts and
that the auditors had been negligent in auditing the accounts, which instead of showing
a reported profit of £1·3m should have shown a loss of £0·46m. On the trial of a
preliminary issue, the judge held that the auditors owed no duty of care to the plaintiffs
either as shareholders or as potential investors. The plaintiffs appealed to the Court of
Appeal.

Held (O'Connor LJ dissenting) – The auditor of a public company owed a duty of care to
individual shareholders to carry out his audit of the company using reasonable care and
skill and, since it was reasonably foreseeable that shareholders and potential investors in
the company might rely on the auditor's report in considering whether and how to deal
in the company's shares, there was sufficient proximity between the auditor and the
shareholders arising out of the close and direct relationship between an auditor and the
shareholders and the fact that the auditor voluntarily assumed direct responsibility to
individual shareholders, and it was just and reasonable to impose a duty of care on the
auditor. However, although such a duty was owed to a shareholder in respect of the
purchase of further shares in the company, it was not owed to potential investors in, or

take-over bidders for, the company, having regard to the lack of proximity between the
a auditor and potential investor and the fact that it would not be just and reasonable to
impose a duty on the auditor to non-shareholding investors. Accordingly, if the plaintiffs
could show that the auditors had failed to exercise the ordinary skill and care of a
reasonable and competent auditor and that they had relied on the audited accounts of F
plc and had suffered damage as a result, they were entitled to succeed in their claim
against them. The appeal would therefore be allowed to that extent (see p 806 *b* to *d*,
b p 807 *h* to p 808 *b*, p 809 *h*, p 811 *j* to p 812 *a f* to *h*, p 813 *a*, p 815 *h*, p 816 *c d*, p 819 *f g*,
p 820 *a* to *d f j*, p 821 *g j* to p 822 *a d e* and p 830 *h j*, post).

Ministry of Housing and Local Government v Sharp [1970] 1 All ER 1009, dicta of Lord
Salmon in *Anns v Merton London Borough* [1977] 2 All ER 492 at 512–513, of Lord Keith
in *Govenors of the Peabody Donation Fund v Sir Lindsay Parkinson & Co Ltd* [1984] 3 All ER
529 at 534 and of Lord Keith *Yuen Kun-yeu v A-G of Hong Kong* [1987] 2 All ER 705 at 710
c applied.

Scott Group Ltd v McFarlane [1978] 1 NZLR 553, *Twomax Ltd v Dickson M'Farlane &
Robinson* 1982 SC 113 and *JEB Fasteners Ltd v Marks Bloom & Co (a firm)* [1983] 1 All ER
583 considered.

Notes

d For auditors' duties and auditors' reports, see 7(1) Halsbury's Laws (4th edn reissue) paras
905, 912–914 and for cases on the subject, see 9 Digest (Reissue) 601–607, *3593–3614*.

For negligence in relation to statements by professional men, see 34 Halsbury's Laws
(4th edn) para 53, and for cases on the subject, see 36(1) Digest (Reissue) 49–50, *149–158*.

Cases referred to in judgments

e *Anns v Merton London Borough* [1977] 2 All ER 492, [1978] AC 728, [1977] 2 WLR 1024,
HL.
Bolam v Friern Hospital Management Committee [1957] 2 All ER 118, [1957] 1 WLR 582.
Candler v Crane Christmas & Co [1951] 1 All ER 426, [1951] 2 KB 164, CA.
Candlewood Navigation Corp Ltd v Mitsui OSK Lines Ltd, The Mineral Transporter, The Ibaraki
f   *Maru* [1985] 2 All ER 935, [1986] AC 1, [1985] 3 WLR 381, PC.
Cann v Willson (1888) 39 Ch D 39.
Citizens State Bank v Timm Schmidt & Co (1983) 113 Wis 2d 376, Wis SC.
Courteen Seed Co v Hong Kong and Shanghai Banking Corp (1927) 245 NY 377, NY Ct of
Apps.
Credit Alliance Corp v Arthur Andersen & Co (1985) 65 NY 2d 536, NY Ct of Apps.
Donoghue (or M'Alister) v Stevenson [1932] AC 562, [1932] All ER Rep 1, HL.
g *Glanzer v Shepard* (1922) 233 NY 236, NY Ct of Apps.
Goldberg v Housing Authority of Newark (1962) 38 NJ 578, NJ SC.
Greater Nottingham Co-op Society Ltd v Cementation Piling and Foundations Ltd [1988] 2 All
ER 971, [1989] QB 71, [1988] 3 WLR 396, CA.
Haig v Bamford (1976) 72 DLR (3d) 68, Can SC.
h *Hedley Byrne & Co Ltd v Heller & Partners Ltd* [1963] 2 All ER 575, [1964] AC 465, [1963]
3 WLR 101, HL.
Hill v Chief Constable of West Yorkshire [1988] 2 All ER 238, [1989] AC 53, [1988] 2 WLR
1049, HL.
Home Office v Dorset Yacht Co Ltd [1970] 2 All ER 294, [1970] AC 1004, [1970] 2 WLR
1140, HL.
j *Ingram Industries Inc v Nowicki* (1981) 527 F Supp 683, ED Ky.
JEB Fasteners Ltd v Marks Bloom & Co (a firm) [1981] 3 All ER 289; *affd* [1983] 1 All ER
583, CA.
Junior Books Ltd v Veitchi Co Ltd [1982] 3 All ER 201, [1983] 1 AC 520, [1982] 3 WLR 477,
HL.
Kingston Cotton Mill Co, Re [1896] 1 Ch 6, CA.
Le Lievre v Gould [1893] 1 QB 491, CA.

London and General Bank, Re (No 2) [1895] 2 Ch 673, [1895–9] All ER Rep 953, CA.
McLoughlin v O'Brian [1982] 2 All ER 298, [1983] 1 AC 410, [1982] 2 WLR 982, HL.   *a*
Ministry of Housing and Local Government v Sharp [1970] 1 All ER 1009, [1970] 2 QB 223,
    [1970] 2 WLR 802, CA.
Muirhead v Industrial Tank Specialities Ltd [1985] 3 All ER 705, [1986] QB 507, [1985] 3
    WLR 993, CA.
Mutual Life and Citizens' Assurance Co Ltd v Evatt [1971] 1 All ER 150, [1971] AC 793,
    [1971] 2 WLR 23, PC.   *b*
Peabody Donation Fund (Governors) v Sir Lindsay Parkinson & Co Ltd [1984] 3 All ER 529,
    [1985] AC 210, [1984] 3 WLR 953, HL.
Rhode Island Hospital Trust National Bank v Swartz Bresenoff Yavner & Jacobs (1972) 455 F
    2d 847, US Ct of Apps, 5th Cir.
Rosenblum (H) Inc v Adler (1983) 93 NJ 324, NJ SC.
Ross v Caunters (a firm) [1979] 3 All ER 580, [1980] Ch 297, [1979] 3 WLR 605.   *c*
Rowling v Takaro Properties Ltd [1988] 1 All ER 163, [1988] AC 473, [1988] 2 WLR 418,
    PC.
Saif Ali v Sydney Mitchell & Co (a firm) [1978] 3 All ER 1033, [1980] AC 198, [1978] 3
    WLR 849, HL.
SCM (UK) Ltd v W J Whittall & Son Ltd [1970] 3 All ER 245, [1971] 1 QB 337, [1970] 3
    WLR 694, CA.   *d*
Scott Group Ltd v McFarlane [1978] 1 NZLR 553, NZ CA; *affg* [1975] 1 NZLR 582, NZ
    SC.
Simaan General Contracting Co v Pilkington Glass Ltd (No 2) [1988] 1 All ER 791, [1988] QB
    758, [1988] 2 WLR 761, CA.
Spartan Steel and Alloys Ltd v Martin & Co (Contractors) Ltd [1972] 3 All ER 557, [1973]
    QB 27, [1972] 3 WLR 502, CA.   *e*
State Street Trust Co v Ernst (1938) 278 NY 104, NY Ct of Apps.
Sutherland Shire Council v Heyman (1985) 60 ALR 1, Aust HC.
Twomax Ltd v Dickson M'Farlane & Robinson 1982 SC 113, Outer House; *rvsd by consent*
    1984 SLT 424, Inner House.
Ultramares Corp v Touche (1931) 255 NY 170, NY Ct of Apps.   *f*
W (an infant), Re [1971] 2 All ER 49, [1971] AC 682, [1971] 2 WLR 1011, HL.
Weller & Co v Foot and Mouth Disease Research Institute [1965] 3 All ER 560, [1966] 1 QB
    569, [1965] 3 WLR 1082.
Yuen Kun-yeu v A-G of Hong Kong [1987] 2 All ER 705, [1988] AC 175, [1987] 3 WLR 776,
    PC.

Cases also cited   *g*
Cattle v Stockton Waterworks Co (1875) LR 10 QB 453, [1874–80] All ER Rep 220, DC.
Clarke v Bruce Lance & Co (a firm) [1988] 1 All ER 364, [1988] 1 WLR 881, CA.
Harris v Wyre Forest DC [1988] 1 All ER 691, [1988] QB 835, CA.
Hickman v Kent or Romney Marsh Sheepbreeders' Association [1915] 1 Ch 881, [1914–15] All
    ER Rep 900.   *h*
Leigh & Sillavan Ltd v Aliakmon Shipping Co Ltd, The Aliakmon [1986] 2 All ER 145, [1986]
    AC 785, HL.
Newton v Birmingham Small Arms Co Ltd [1906] 2 Ch 378.

Interlocutory appeal
The plaintiffs, Caparo Industries plc (Caparo), by writ dated 24 July 1985 brought an   *j*
action against the first and second defendants Stephen Graham Dickman and Robert
Anthony Dickman, who were the directors of Fidelity plc, and the third defendants,
Touche Ross & Co (the auditors), claiming damages against the first and second defendants
for fraud and against the auditors for negligence. The statement of claim alleged that in
July 1983 the directors of Fidelity plc forecast that the company's profits for the year

ended 31 March 1984 would be £2·2m. On 1 March 1984 the company's share price was
a 143p. On 22 May the company announced profits for the year ended 31 March 1984 of
£1·3m and by 1 June the share price had fallen to 63p. Caparo purchased 100,000 shares
in the company at 70p on 8 June and 50,000 shares at 73p on 12 June. On 12 June the
audited accounts for the year ended 31 March 1984 were released to shareholders and in
reliance on the information contained in the accounts Caparo purchased further shares
in the company and by 6 July held 29·9% of the company's stock. On 4 September
b Caparo made a take-over bid for the company at 120p per share which was later increased
to 125p per share at which price the directors of the company, including the first and
second defendants, recommended shareholders to accept the offer. The bid was successful
by 25 October. By para 7 of the statement of claim it was alleged that the accounts
overstated the profits of the company by including non-existent stock, making under-
provision for obsolete stock and making under-provision in respect of after-date sales
c credits. It was alleged that the true position of the comany was that it had made a loss of
at least £465,000 and it was claimed that if Caparo had known the true position it would
not have made its take-over bid for the company at the price it did or at all. It was alleged
that the first and second defendants had forged stock sheets, had included as sales
transactions which were not sales at all and had misrepresented the company's position
to Caparo, and it was further alleged that the auditors had been negligent in failing to
d discover the forgery and other irregularities perpetrated by the first and second defendants
when carrying out the audit of the accounts. Caparo claimed that the auditors knew or
ought to have known that the company required financial assistance and ought to have
foreseen that the company was vulnerable to a take-over and that persons such as Caparo
might well rely on the accounts for the purpose of making a take-over and might well
suffer loss if the accounts were inaccurate. By order of Sir Neil Lawson, sitting as a judge
e of the High Court in the Queen's Bench Division in chambers the question whether on
the facts alleged the auditors owed a duty of care to Caparo as (a) potential investors in
the company or (b) shareholders in the company in respect of the audit of the company's
accounts for the year ended 31 March 1984 was tried as a preliminary issue. On the trial
of that issue Sir Neil Lawson ([1988] BCLC 387) held that the auditors did not owe a duty
of care to Caparo either as potential investors or as shareholders in the company. Caparo
f appealed.

Christopher Bathurst QC and *Michael Brindle* for Caparo.
Peter Goldsmith QC and *Stephen Moriarty* for the auditors.

Cur adv vult
g

29 July. The following judgments were delivered.

BINGHAM LJ (giving the first judgment at the invitation of O'Connor LJ).

'It is not easy, or perhaps possible, to find a single proposition encapsulating a
h   comprehensive rule to determine when persons are brought into a relationship
which creates a duty of care upon those who make statements towards those who
may act upon them and when persons are not brought into such a relationship.'

Thus said the Lord Ordinary (Stewart) in *Twomax Ltd v Dickson M'Farlane & Robinson*
1982 SC 113 at 122. Others have spoken to similar effect. In *Hedley Byrne & Co Ltd v*
j *Heller & Partners Ltd* [1963] 2 All ER 575 at 601, [1964] AC 465 at 514 Lord Hodson
said:

'I do not think that it is possible to catalogue the special features which must be
found to exist before the duty of care will arise in a given case . . .'

and Lord Devlin said ([1963] 2 All ER 575 at 611, [1964] AC 465 at 529–530):

'I do not think it possible to formulate with exactitude all the conditions under which the law will in a specific case imply a voluntary undertaking, any more than a it is possible to formulate those in which the law will imply a contract.'

In *Mutual Life and Citizens' Assurance Co Ltd v Evatt* [1971] 1 All ER 150 at 162, [1971] AC 793 at 810 Lord Reid and Lord Morris said:

'In our judgment it is not possible to lay down hard and fast rules as to when a duty of care arises in this or in any other class of case where negligence is alleged.' b

In *Rowling v Takaro Properties Ltd* [1988] 1 All ER 163 at 172, [1988] AC 473 at 501 Lord Keith, emphasising the need for careful analysis case by case, said:

'It is at this stage that it is necessary, before concluding that a duty of care should be imposed, to consider all the relevant circumstances. One of the considerations underlying certain recent decisions of the House of Lords (*Governors of the Peabody* c *Donation Fund v Sir Lindsay Parkinson & Co Ltd* [1984] 3 All ER 529, [1985] AC 210) and of the Privy Council (*Yuen Kun-yeu v A-G of Hong Kong* [1987] 2 All ER 705, [1988] AC 175) is the fear that a too literal application of the well-known observation of Lord Wilberforce in *Anns v Merton London Borough* [1977] 2 All ER 492 at 498, [1978] AC 728 at 751–752 may be productive of a failure to have regard to, and to d analyse and weigh, all the relevant considerations in considering whether it is appropriate that a duty of care should be imposed. Their Lordships consider that question to be of an intensely pragmatic character, well suited for gradual development but requiring most careful analysis. It is one on which all common law jurisdictions can learn much from each other, because, apart from exceptional cases, no sensible distinction can be drawn in this respect between the various e countries and the social conditions existing in them. It is incumbent on the courts in different jurisdictions to be sensitive to each other's reactions; but what they are all searching for in others, and each of them striving to achieve, is a careful analysis and weighing of the relevant competing considerations.'

The many decided cases on this subject, if providing no simple ready-made solution to the question whether or not a duty of care exists, do indicate the requirements to be f satisfied before a duty is found.

The first is foreseeability. It is not, and could not be, in issue between these parties that reasonable foreseeability of harm is a necessary ingedient of a relationship in which a duty of care will arise: see *Yuen Kun-yeu v A-G of Hong Kong* [1987] 2 All ER 705 at 710, [1988] AC 175 at 192. It is also common ground that reasonable foreseeability, although a necessary, is not a sufficient condition of the existence of a duty. This, as Lord Keith g observed in *Hill v Chief Constable of West Yorkshire* [1988] 2 All ER 238 at 241, [1989] AC 53 at 60, has been said almost too frequently to require repetition.

The second requirement is more elusive. It is usually described as proximity, which means not simple physical proximity but extends to—

'... such close and direct relations that the act complained of directly affects a h person whom the person alleged to be bound to take care would know would be directly affected by his careless act.'

(See *Donoghue v Stevenson* [1932] AC 562 at 581, [1932] All ER Rep 1 at 12 per Lord Atkin.) Sometimes the alternative expression 'neighbourhood' is used, as by Lord Reid in the *Hedley Byrne* case [1963] 2 All ER 575 at 580, [1964] AC 465 at 483 and Lord j Wilberforce in *Anns v Merton London Borough* [1977] 2 All ER 492 at 498, [1978] AC 728 at 751, with more conscious reference to Lord Atkin's speech in the earlier case. Sometimes, as in the *Hedley Byrne* case, attention is concentrated on the existence of a special relationship. Sometimes it is regarded as significant that the parties' relationship is 'equivalent to contract' (see the *Hedley Byrne* case [1963] 2 All ER 575 at 610, [1964] AC

465 at 529 per Lord Devlin) or falls 'only just short of a direct contractual relationship'
a (see *Junior Books Ltd v Veitchi Co Ltd* [1982] 3 All ER 201 at 204, [1983] 1 AC 520 at 533
per Lord Fraser) or is 'as close as it could be short of actual privity of contract' (see the
Junior Books case [1982] 3 All ER 201 at 214, [1983] 1 AC 520 at 546 per Lord Roskill). In
some cases, and increasingly, reference is made to the voluntary assumption of
responsibility: see *Muirhead v Industrial Tank Specialities Ltd* [1985] 3 All ER 705 at 715,
[1986] QB 507 at 528 per Robert Goff LJ, *Yuen Kun-yeu v A-G of Hong Kong* [1987] 2 All
b ER 705 at 711, 714, [1988] AC 175 at 192, 196, *Simaan General Contracting Co v Pilkington
Glass Ltd (No 2)* [1988] 1 All ER 791 at 803, 805, [1988] QB 758 at 781, 784 and *Greater
Nottingham Co-op Society Ltd v Cementation Piling and Foundations Ltd* [1988] 2 All ER 971
at 984, 989, 990, [1989] QB 71 at 100, 106, 107. Both the analogy with contract and the
assumption of responsibility have been relied on as a test of proximity in foreign courts
as well as our own: see *Glanzer v Shepard* (1922) 233 NY 236, *Ultramares Corp v Touche*
c (1931) 255 NY 170 at 182–183, *State Street Trust Co v Ernst* (1938) 278 NY 104 at 111–
112 and *Scott Group Ltd v McFarlane* [1978] 1 NZLR 553 at 566. It may very well be that
in tortious claims based on negligent misstatement these motions are particularly
apposite. The content of the requirement of proximity, whatever language is used, is
not, I think, capable of precise definition. The approach will vary according to the
particular facts of the case, as is reflected in the varied language used. But the focus of the
d inquiry is on the closeness and directness of the relationship between the parties. In
determining this, foreseeability must, I think, play an important part: the more obvious
it is that A's act or omission will cause harm to B, the less likely a court will be to hold
that the relationship of A and B is insufficiently proximate to give rise to a duty of care.

The third requirement to be met before a duty of care will be held to be owed by A to
B is that the court should find it just and reasonable to impose such a duty: see *Governors
e of the Peabody Donation Fund v Sir Lindsay Parkinson & Co Ltd* [1984] 3 All ER 529 at 534,
[1985] AC 210 at 241 per Lord Keith. This requirement, I think, covers very much the
same ground as Lord Wilberforce's second stage test in *Anns's* case [1977] 2 All ER 492 at
498, [1978] AC 728 at 752 and what in cases such as *Spartan Steel and Alloys Ltd v Martin
& Co (Contractors) Ltd* [1972] 3 All ER 557, [1973] QB 27 and *McLoughlin v O'Brian* [1982]
2 All ER 298, [1983] 1 AC 410 was called policy. It was considerations of this kind which
f Lord Fraser had in mind when he said in *Candlewood Navigation Corp Ltd v Mitsui OSK
Lines Ltd, The Mineral Transporter, The Ibaraki Maru* [1985] 2 All ER 935 at 945, [1986]
AC 1 at 25:

> '. . . some limit or control mechanism has to be imposed on the liability of a
> wrongdoer towards those who have suffered economic damage in consequence of
g   > his negligence.'

The requirement cannot, perhaps, be better put than it was by Weintraub CJ in *Goldberg
v Housing Authority of Newark* (1962) 38 NJ 578 at 583:

> 'Whether a *duty* exists is ultimately a question of fairness. The inquiry involves a
> weighing of the relationship of the parties, the nature of the risk, and the public
h   > interest in the proposed solution.' (Weintraub CJ's emphasis.)

If the imposition of a duty on a defendant would be for any reason oppressive, or would
expose him, in Cardozo CJ's famous phrase in *Ultramares Corp v Touche* 255 NY 170 at
179—

> 'to a liability in an indeterminate amount for an indeterminate time to an
j   > indeterminate class . . .'

that will weigh heavily, probably conclusively, against the imposition of a duty (if it has
not already shown a fatal lack of proximity). On the other hand, a duty will be the more
readily found if the defendant is voluntarily exercising a professional skill for reward, if
the victim of his carelessness has (in the absence of a duty) no means of redress, if the

duty contended for (as in *McLoughlin v O'Brian*) arises naturally from a duty which already exists or if the imposition of a duty is thought to promote some socially desirable a objective.

At the heart of this case lies the role of the statutory auditor. That role is, I think, without close analogy. Its peculiar characteristics derive from the nature of the public limited liability company. The members, or shareholders, of the company are its owners. But they are too numerous, and in most cases too unskilled, to undertake the day-to-day management of that which they own. So responsibility for day-to-day management of b the company is delegated to directors. The shareholders, despite their overall powers of control, are in most companies for most of the time investors and little more. But it would, of course, be unsatisfactory and open to abuse if the shareholders received no report on the financial stewardship of their investment save from those to whom the stewardship had been entrusted. So provision is made for the company in general meeting to appoint an auditor (Companies Act 1985, s 384) whose duty is to investigate c and form an opinion on the adequacy of the company's accounting records and returns and the correspondence between the company's accounting records and returns and its accounts (s 237). The auditor has then to report to the company's members (among other things) whether in his opinion the company's accounts give a true and fair view of the company's financial position (s 236). In carrying out his investigation and informing his opinion the auditor necessarily works very closely with the directors and officers of the d company. He receives his remuneration from the company. He naturally, and rightly, regards the company as his client. But he is employed by the company to exercise his professional skill and judgment for the purpose of giving the shareholders an independent report on the reliability of the company's accounts and thus on their investment. Vaughan Williams J said in *Re Kingston Cotton Mill Co* [1896] 1 Ch 6 at 11:

e

'No doubt he is acting antagonistically to the directors in the sense that he is appointed by the shareholders to be a check upon them.'

The auditor's report must be read before the company in general meeting and must be open to inspection by any member of the company (s 241). It is attached to and forms part of the company's accounts (ss 238(3) and 239). A copy of the company's accounts f (including the auditor's report) must be sent to every member (s 240). Any member of the company, even if not entitled to have a copy of the accounts sent to him, is entitled to be furnished with a copy of the company's last accounts on demand and without charge (s 246).

It is pointed out, quite correctly, that the primary duty in and about the preparation of accounts is that of the directors. It is the duty of the company to keep proper g accounting records (s 221). It is the duty of the directors to prepare an annual profit and loss account and balance sheet (s 227) complying with the statutory requirements (s 228). It is the duty of the directors to lay the accounts before the company in general meeting (s 241(1)) and to deliver a copy to the registrar of companies (s 241(3)), who must make them available for inspection by any person (s 709). It is the directors who are criminally liable for breach of the statutory accounting requirements (s 245). The auditor's role is h secondary and accessory. His task is to vet the accounts, not to draw them up in the first place or carry out the detailed accounting work necessary to draw them up.

These provisions show, as I think, a plain parliamentary intention that shareholders in a public company shall receive independent and reliable information on the financial standing of the company (and thus of their investment): see *Re London and General Bank (No 2)* [1895] 2 Ch 673 at 682, [1895–9] All ER Rep 953 at 956 per Lindley LJ. For what j purpose is this required? The company lawyer's answer would, I think, be: to enable the members to make an informed judgment whether, and if so how, they should exercise the powers of control enjoyed by them as members. The commercial man's answer would more probably be: to enable each shareholder to make an informed judgment whether he should retain or reduce or increase his holding of shares in the company. I

see no reason to reject either of these answers. Successive Companies Acts have
a promulgated a detailed code designed to ensure that the ultimate powers of decision are
vested in the members. But it is a truism that possession of adequate information is a
necessary condition of effective decision-making. It would not be realistic to expect
shareholders to exercise their powers of control on the basis only of such information as
the directors chose to give them. But I think these provisions also reflect a wider and
more commercial intention. The growth and development of limited liability companies
b over a relatively very short period have been phenomenal. Their proliferation and
expansion have depended on their acceptance by the investing public as an advantageous
and (on the whole) reliable medium of investment. The statutory requirements that
companies account to their members and that auditors express an independent opinion
to shareholders on the truth and accuracy of company accounts are in my view designed
(in part at least) to fortify confidence in the holding of shares as a medium of investment
c by enabling shareholders to make informed investment decisions. There are obvious
reasons, both economic and social, why this end should be regarded as desirable.

The requirement that a company make its accounts available for inspection by
members of the public who are not shareholders is imposed for reasons which are in part
the same and in part different from those just considered. Submission of accounts to the
registrar could be required for purposes of official supervision and regulation, but this
d would not of itself require the accounts to be available for inspection by the public. This
additional requirement must in my view be imposed (in part at least) for the protection
of those dealing with the company as contracting parties, creditors, lenders and even,
perhaps, defendants in litigation. But again I think that wider commercial considerations
play a part. It would not be conducive to a flourishing and orderly market in company
shares, which is plainly thought to be desirable, if reliable information of a company's
e performance were restricted to its shareholders, directors and employees. The publication
of accounts must limit, if it cannot eliminate, the scope for rumour-inspired speculation
and thus promote an informed and orderly market. It enables prospective investors, like
shareholders, to make informed decisions. For such prospective investors the independent
opinion of the auditor has the same significance as for existing shareholders.

It is common ground between the parties that an auditor owes a duty to the company
f which appoints him to exercise reasonable care and skill in conducting the audit and
making his audit report. Such a duty is plainly to be implied into the contract between
auditor and company. A coincident duty in tort will also arise. If the auditor breaches his
duty he will be liable to the company for any reasonably foreseeable loss the company
suffers as a result of his breach. Helpful examples were given. Thus, for example, the
company may have a good claim if an auditor's negligence allows a dishonest employee
g to continue defrauding it or fails to alert the company to the need to take steps to improve
performance or eliminate losses. But this duty will not of course avail a shareholder or
investor who makes a mistaken investment decision on the strength of a negligent audit
report, because that will cause no loss to and therefore support no claim by the company.

The judge held that the auditor owes no duty of care to the shareholders as a body or
h class. For reasons which will appear when I consider the position of individual
shareholders, I doubt the correctness of this conclusion, unless it be that damage to the
shareholders as a class is not reasonably foreseeable. In almost any situation in which
damage has been suffered by the shareholders as a class, damage will also have been
suffered by the company and in the ordinary way the company will then be the
appropriate plaintiff. Counsel suggested only one case in which damage would be
j suffered by the shareholders as a class but not by the company: where a parent company,
in reliance on a negligent report by the auditor of its subsidiary, sold its shareholding in
the subsidiary at an undervalue. No doubt other examples could be elaborated. But this
example depends on the singularity of the shareholders as a class and it seems clear that a
duty owed to shareholders as a class, if existing at all, would be of minimal practical
significance.

So I turn to consider the first major question arising on this appeal, which is whether the auditor of a public company owes any, and if so what, duty of care to individual *a* shareholders (as distinct from shareholders as a class). This is a question to be answered by applying to the special facts of this relationship the three requirements which I mentioned at the outset.

The judge held that the foreseeability of economic loss to Caparo Industries plc (Caparo) as a shareholder was present when the auditors' report was published. This finding has not been challenged. It was therefore common ground that Caparo could satisfy the first *b* and necessary requirement of foreseeability. I have no doubt this conclusion is correct. The auditors of course knew that their report would be communicated to those who were registered as shareholders when the accounts were sent to members under s 240 or when the report was read in general meeting under s 241. They must have known that some shareholders might rely on the report and accounts in making investment decisions. They must have known that an unqualified report, negligently made, might cause *c* individual shareholders to suffer loss by selling if the accounts undervalued the company's worth or buying if the accounts overvalued the company's worth. These findings are, I think, inherent in the conclusion that economic loss to Caparo as a shareholder was foreseeable by the auditors as a result of any failure to exercise reasonable care in conducting their audit and reporting to the shareholders.

It was on the second requirement of proximity that major battle between the parties *d* was joined. Caparo's case was simple. Auditors are appointed for the important and specific purpose of reporting to the shareholders. A private report to the directors will not suffice (see *Re London and General Bank Ltd (No 2)* [1895] 2 Ch 673, [1895–9] All ER Rep 953). The 1985 Act requires a copy of the report to reach the breakfast table or desk of every shareholder and the report itself to be read before the company in general meeting and to be opened to inspection by any member. Relations between auditor and *e* shareholder are both close and direct. A lack of care will directly affect the very person whose interest the auditor is engaged to protect. *Hedley Byrne & Co Ltd v Heller & Partners Ltd* [1963] 2 All ER 575, [1964] AC 465 shows that the relationship of A and B may be sufficiently proximate if, independently of contract, A assumes the responsibility of giving B deliberate advice; if A engages B contractually to give advice to C, the relationship of B and C is no less proximate, however that expression is interpreted. *f*

Counsel for the auditors sought to rebut Caparo's argument on proximity by a sustained and closely reasoned submission. Most of this was specifically directed to the auditors' relationship with investors who are not shareholders but the principal points applied equally to shareholders. The starting point of the argument was that the law treats negligent words differently from negligent acts. The peculiar character of words has led to insistence on closer proximity between the parties before a duty of care can *g* arise than is required where physical injury or damage is in issue. That this is so emerges, I think, clearly from the *Hedley Byrne* case itself [1963] 2 All ER 575 at 580, 613 [1964] AC 465 at 482, 534 esp per Lord Reid and Lord Pearce. The trend of authority over the last 25 years shows considerable wariness in upholding claims for economic loss divorced from physical injury or damage, although lack of proximity has not usually proved the *h* plaintiff's undoing.

The fundamental submission of counsel for the auditors was that voluntary assumption of direct responsibility to the plaintiff (and thus, here, to Caparo as shareholder) in circumstances equivalent to contract is the touchstone of proximity in cases such as this. This requires that the auditor should deliberately accept a particular responsibility to the shareholder in addition to the responsibility already existing to the company. This also *j* requires that the statement should be made for the very purpose of a particular transaction of which the auditor knows, that the shareholder should be the person (or a member of a small and determinate class) for whom the statement is made and that there should be some communication or conduct linking the auditor to the shareholder so as to show his acceptance of special responsibility to the shareholder. Judged by these tests the

relationship between auditor and shareholder (it was said) lacks the proximity necessary
a before a duty of care can arise.

I think that at this stage of the inquiry it is important to concentrate on the substance
of what one is investigating, which is the degree of closeness between the parties. It is
only too easy to be mesmerised by expressions used in other cases which, however apt in
those cases, provide no universally applicable yardstick. The language used in other cases
guides but does not govern.

b Thus 'voluntary assumption of responsibility', although a very useful expression, does
not provide a single, simple litmus test of proximity. In *Ministry of Housing and Local
Government v Sharp* [1970] 1 All ER 1009 at 1018–1019, [1970] 2 QB 223 at 268–269
Lord Denning MR said:

> 'Counsel for the defendants submitted to us, however, that the correct principle
> did not go to that length. He said that a duty to use due care (where there was no
> *c* contract) only arose when there was a voluntary assumption of responsibility. I do
> not agree. He relied particularly on the words of Lord Reid in *Hedley Byrne & Co Ltd
> v Heller & Partners Ltd* [1963] 2 All ER 575 at 583, [1964] AC 465 at 487, and of
> Lord Devlin ([1963] 2 All ER 575 at 610–611, [1964] AC 465 at 529). I think they
> used those words because of the special circumstances of that case (where the bank
> *d* disclaimed responsibility). But they did not in any way mean to limit the general
> principle. In my opinion the duty to use due care in a statement arises, not from
> any voluntary assumption of responsibility, but from the fact that the person
> making it knows, or ought to know, that others, being his neighbours in this regard,
> would act on the faith of the statement being accurate. That is enough to bring the
> duty into being. It is owed, of course, to the person to whom the certificate is issued
> *e* and who he knows is going to act on it, see the judgment of Cardozo J in *Glanzer v
> Shepard* (1922) 233 NY 236. But it is also owed to any person who he knows or
> ought to know, will be injuriously affected by a mistake, such as the incumbrancer
> here.'

Salmon LJ said ([1970] 1 All ER 1009 at 1027–1028, [1970] 2 QB 223 at 279):

f > 'I do not accept that, in all cases, the obligation to take reasonable care necessarily
> depends on a voluntary assumption of responsibility.'

Cross LJ added ([1970] 1 All ER 1009 at 1038, [1970] 2 QB 223 at 291):

> 'It is true that the phrase "voluntary assumption of risk" occurs frequently in the
> speeches in the *Hedley Byrne* case, but I agree with the judge that that case did not
> *g* purport to lay down any metes and bounds within which legal liability in tort for
> false statements, on which the parties to whom they are made rely, has to be
> confined. (See in particular per Lord Devlin ([1963] 2 All ER 575 at 611, [1964] AC
> 465 at 530–531).) I see no sufficient reason why in an appropriate case the liability
> should not extend to cases in which the defendant is obliged to make the statement
> which proves to be false.'

h
If, however, one asks whether the auditors here voluntarily assumed direct responsibility
to individual shareholders it seems to me inescapable that they did. They did not have to
accept appointment as auditors. Their work was not in reality unrewarded. They
undertook it, no doubt, in the ordinary course of professional practice in order to earn a
fee and, perhaps, obtain additional work from the company. But they knew that the end-
j product of their audit was a report to shareholders on which they knew any shareholder
might rely. It would, I think, be surprising if in those circumstances the auditors were
said not voluntarily to have assumed a responsibility to each shareholder.

There is, of course, no contract between the shareholders (either as a class or
individually) and the auditor. But certainly as between the shareholders as a class and the
auditor the relationship seems to me to be very close indeed to contract. The auditor's

contract is made with the company, but it is a contract made on the company's behalf by
the shareholders; the auditor's fee is paid out of company funds otherwise available (in   *a*
part) for distribution to the shareholders; and the object of the contract is to obtain a
report to shareholders made independently of the company itself. As between the
shareholders individually and the auditor the analogy with contract is less compelling,
but in my view it remains close. If a company engaged a doctor to examine and advise
its senior employees, I would regard the relationship between the doctor and each
individual employee as equivalent to contract for all except strictly legal purposes. The   *b*
relationship between auditor and individual shareholder is less close, but not in my
opinion critically so.

In *Candler v Crane Christmas & Co* [1951] 1 All ER 426 at 435, [1951] 2 KB 164 at 183
Denning LJ confined the duty which he upheld to—

> 'cases where the accountant prepares his accounts and makes his report for the
> guidance of the very person in the very transaction in question.'   *c*

In *Glanzer v Shepard* (1922) 233 NY 236 a buyer who paid his seller on the faith of an
erroneous certificate of weight given by a public weigher succeeded in a claim against
the weigher because use of the certificate by the buyer for the purpose of paying the
seller was, as the weigher knew, 'the end and aim of the transaction'. These cases must be
read in context. Denning LJ was naturally concerned to make his departure from binding   *d*
authority as narrow as possible, and did not wish to be thought to give his blessing to the
foundation of liability on a careless misstatement made to the world at large. Thus
immediately after the words quoted above he continued:

> 'That is sufficient for the decision of this case. I can well understand that it would
> be going too far to make an accountant liable to any person in the land who chooses   *e*
> to rely on the accounts in matters of business, for that would expose him . . . to . . .
> "liability in an indeterminate amount for an indeterminate time to an indeterminate
> class."'

When, in *Ultramares Corp v Touche* (1931) 255 NY 170, Cardozo CJ came to comment on
his earlier decision in *Glanzer v Shepard* he also was at pains to disavow the possibility of
liability at large. But he approved an earlier statement by Pound J in *Courteen Seed Co v*   *f*
Hong Kong and Shanghai Banking Corp (1927) 245 NY 377 at 381 that—

> 'negligent words are not actionable unless they are uttered directly, with
> knowledge or notice that they will be acted on, to one to whom the speaker is bound
> by some relation of duty, arising out of public calling, contract or otherwise, to act
> with care if he acts at all.'   *g*

(See 255 NY 170 at 185.)

This formulation would not exclude the finding of a sufficiently proximate relationship
in the present case if the words 'will be acted on' are replaced, as in English law I think
they should be, by 'may be acted on'.

All these cases are concerned to insist on the need for a clear and close nexus between   *h*
the author and the victim of the allegedly careless misstatement. In cases of physical
injury or damage the nexus rarely causes a problem. It is enough that the plaintiff
chances to be (out of the whole world) the person with whom the defendant collided or :
who purchased the offending ginger beer. Where careless words causing economic loss
are complained of, more is required to establish proximity than the fortuity of suffering
damage. Thus in recent consideration of *Cann v Willson* (1888) 39 Ch D 39, *Le Lievre v*   *j*
Gould [1893] 1 QB 491 and *Candler's* case, and in cases such as those I consider at the end
of this judgment, attention has been concentrated on the author's knowledge of the
victim's intention to rely on the statement complained of in a particular way. But none
of the cases involved relations between a shareholder and a statutory auditor. None was a
case in which the author was subject to a statutory duty to report to the victim in a

capacity in which the victim sues. Even in the absence of a statutory duty, and without
a regard to an accountant's statutory liability (with or without negligence) for
misstatements in a prospectus, Lord Salmon in *Anns v Merton London Borough* [1977] 2 All
ER 492 at 512–513, [1978] AC 728 at 769 plainly regarded the relationship of certifying
accountant and subscriber as sufficiently proximate to give rise ot a duty of care and he
said:

b   'There are a wide variety of instances in which a statement is negligently made by
       a professional man which he knows will be relied on by many people besides his
       client, eg a well-known firm of accountants certifies in a prospectus the annual
       profits of the company issuing it and unfortunately, due to negligence on the part
       of the accountants, the profits are seriously overstated. Those persons who invested
       in the company in reliance on the accuracy of the accountants' certificate would
c   have a claim for damages against the accountants for any money they might have
       lost as a result of the accountants' negligence: see the *Hedley Byrne* case.'

I do not regard the relationship Lord Salmon had in mind as more proximate than the
present. A prospectus, of course, solicits investment whereas an auditor's report appended
to a company's accounts does not. But the recipient of a prospectus (foreseeably) may or
d may not subscribe. The shareholder receiving a company's accounts and auditor's report
(foreseeably) may or may not base an investment decision on them. The greatest
difference is that the class of potential subscribers is in all probability larger and less
determinate than the class of shareholders.
    It is true, as counsel for the auditors argued, that in some of the authorities (as for
example *Haig v Bamford* (1976) 72 DLR (3d) 68 at 75, 80) reference is made to the victim's
e membership of a 'limited class' as a test of proximity. By 'limited', it was said, one should
understand 'small and determinate'. I have little doubt that a victim of a careless misstatement falling within Cardozo CJ's 'indeterminate class' would fail to show sufficient
proximity, as recognised by Lord Wilberforce in *Anns* [1977] 2 All ER 492 at 504, [1978]
AC 728 at 758 when he referred to the possible objection that an endless, indeterminate
class of potential plaintiffs may be called into existence.' Again the emphasis was on the
f need for a clear and close nexus between the author and the victim of the allegedly
careless misstatement. But the class of shareholders to whom an auditor reports is not
indeterminate. The composition of the class changes but the members of it can at any
instant be precisely identified. It cannot be predicted who within that class will rely on
the report, but that does not make indeterminate the class to whose members the duty is
owed but only the identity of the potential claimant. The class may of course, in a large
g public company, be very numerous. That is a relevant consideration when deciding
whether it is just and reasonable and whether as a matter of policy a duty should be
imposed, but I do not think it can deprive of proximity a relationship otherwise having
that quality. Lord Salmon cannot have thought so.
    Weighing the competing submissions on proximity in the light of the many
authorities cited, I am left in no real doubt but that there is a sufficiently proximate
h relationship between the statutory auditor and the shareholder to whom he reports to
sustain a duty of care which it is otherwise right to impose.
    I come, therefore, to the third requirement to be satisfied by Caparo, that it is in all the
circumstances just and reasonable to impose a duty of care on a statutory auditor towards
individual shareholders. Caparo's case was again simple. The duty contended for obliges
j an auditor to do nothing which he is not already obliged to do under his contract with
the company. The existing obligation is one from which the auditor cannot be excused
(see s 310 of the 1985 Act). The duty contended for would simply extend a right of
redress, if the auditor failed to perform his duties with reasonable care and skill, from the
company, which would rarely have a claim, to shareholders, who foreseeably would. It is
just and in principle desirable that those who fail to perform their professional duties in

accordance with professional standards should compensate those foreseeably injured by their failure.

The auditors relied on a number of matters as showing that it would not be just or politic to impose the duty contended for. Where a shareholder suffered loss by relying on misleading accounts, the primary responsibility lay with the directors, who might well be fraudulent. But the directors would usually lack the means to satisfy a large claim against them. So the tendency would be to add the auditor as a party in order to gain the benefit of the auditor's insurance cover, even where no defect in the audit procedure could at the outset be identified. There was, however, already extreme difficulty in obtaining professional indemnity cover. If it could not be obtained, an auditor's personal fortune would be at risk, perhaps through the error of his partner or employee. If it could be obtained, the cost would be high and this would necessarily be reflected in the cost of audit work to the prejudice of the great mass of shareholders. An undesirably defensive and self-protective attitude would moreover be encouraged. Reliance was placed on Lord Keith's observations in *Rowling v Takaro Properties Ltd* [1988] 1 All ER 163 at 173, [1988] AC 473 at 502:

> 'The third is the danger of overkill. It is to be hoped that, as a general rule, imposition of liability in negligence will lead to a higher standard of care in the performance of the relevant type of act; but sometimes not only may this not be so, but the imposition of liability may even lead to harmful consequences. In other words, the cure may be worse than the disease. There are reasons for believing that this may be so in cases where liability is imposed on local authorities whose building inspectors have been negligent in relation to the inspection of foundations, as in the *Anns* case itself, because there is a danger that the building inspectors of some local authorities may react to that decision by simply increasing, unnecessarily, the requisite depth of foundations, thereby imposing a very substantial and unnecessary financial burden on members of the community. A comparable danger may exist in cases such as the present, because, once it became known that liability in negligence may be imposed on the ground that a minister has misconstrued a statute and so acted ultra vires, the cautious civil servant may go to extreme lengths in ensuring that legal advice, or even the opinion of the court, is obtained before decisions are taken, thereby leading to unnecessary delay in a considerable number of cases.'

The duty would, it was said, if imposed, expose auditors to claims indeterminate in number and unquantifiable in amount for periods which could not be calculated. Rather than incur this burden accountants might decline to undertake audit work. It was no answer to say that auditors would usually defeat claims made against them because they would still have the burden and expense of defending themselves, with the inevitable risk of damage to their professional reputation. This was all unnecessary: if shareholders were dissatisfied with the auditor's performance they could remove him.

This argument amounted to much more than a simple submission that a decision in favour of Caparo would open the floodgates to an uncontrollable inrush of claims against auditors. But certain features of the argument, in particular concerning insurance, are hard to assess in the absence of evidence or inquiry. I think that certain conclusions can none the less be reached. (1) The removal of an auditor gives no adequate redress to a shareholder who has suffered loss through his negligence. It is not in any event a remedy open to a minority shareholder or one who has sold his shareholding in reliance on a negligent audit report. (2) Given the duty which already exists, I do not think recognition of a duty to individual shareholders would lead to any significant change in audit practice. (3) Given the duty which already exists, I do not think recognition of a duty to shareholders would lead competent accountants to decline audit work, at any rate unless there were comparable alternative work available which did not expose them to potential liability. (4) I do not think it realistic to envisage auditors being subjected to hundreds or

thousands of claims, as a pharmaceutical manufacturer might be. The reality is that the
a greater the number of claims the smaller each must necessarily be, and the smaller the
claim the smaller the chance that the shareholder will embark on an expensive action.
The probability is that action will be brought, if at all, by one large shareholder, as here,
or by a handful of large shareholders. The quantification of damage would not, I think,
be more problematical than in many tortious situations. The odds are that the auditor's
error, if any, will come to light fairly soon; it is unlikely to lie undiscovered for years, as
b may happen with a negligently designed building or bridge. (5) The shareholder's claim
will in the ordinary way be a very hard claim to establish.

This last point deserves a little elaboration. As in any other claim of professional
negligence the claimant must show that the defendant failed to exercise the ordinary
skill of an ordinary competent man exercising his particular art: see *Bolam v Friern
Hospital Management Committee* [1957] 2 All ER 118, [1957] 1 WLR 582. Lord Diplock
c said in *Saif Ali v Sydney Mitchell & Co (a firm)* [1978] 3 All ER 1033 at 1043, [1980] AC
198 at 220:

> 'No matter what profession it may be, the common law does not impose on those
> who practice it any liability for damage resulting from what in the result turns out
> to have been errors of judgment, unless the error was such as no reasonably well-
> informed and competent member of that profession could have made.'

d

These principles afford special protection to auditors, whose task is not to draw the
accounts nor to turn every stone and open every cupboard but to exercise their very
considerable skill and judgment in carrying out checks and investigations in accordance
with complex but none the less detailed and explicit professional standards. Many entries
in the accounts will depend on the directors' judgment, and here it is for the auditors not
e to satisfy themselves that the judgment is correct but that it is reasonable. Lord Hailsham
LC said in *Re W (an infant)* [1971] 2 All ER 49 at 56, [1971] AC 682 at 700:

> 'Two reasonable parents can perfectly reasonably come to opposite conclusions on
> the same set of facts without forfeiting their title to be regarded as reasonable . . .
> Not every reasonable exercise of judgment is right, and not every mistaken exercise
f > of judgment is unreasonable.'

If, despite these obstacles, the shareholder can show a failure to exercise ordinary skill
and care he must still show that he relied on the auditor's report. Most shareholders will
not do so. Woolf J in *JEB Fasteners Ltd v Marks Bloom & Co (a firm)* [1981] 3 All ER 289 at
297 said:

g > 'The longer the period which elapses prior to the accounts being relied on, from
> the date on which the auditor gave his certificate, the more difficult it will be to
> establish that the auditor ought to have foreseen that his certificate would, in those
> circumstances, be relied on.'

If that obstacle also is overcome, the shareholder must then prove damage. That he can
h do only if the negligence complained of has had a significant effect on the share price. It
is not every oversight or blunder, even if negligent, which will have that effect. Some
error having a real and palpable effect on the value of the company will be called for.

Not many claims by shareholders will, I think, fulfil these stringent requirements. If a
shareholder can prove these things, I think it just and reasonable that he should obtain
redress. I am not persuaded that any compelling consideration of policy should deny
j him. It may be that to begin with auditors will be put to the burden and expense of
defending some bad claims, but the problems facing plaintiffs will be quickly appreciated
and the liability for costs is likely to be an effective deterrent. I simply do not think that
a decision in principle in favour of Caparo will lead to an uncontrollable inrush of claims.

I accordingly conclude that the auditor of a public company does owe individual
shareholders a duty to exercise reasonable care in carrying out his audit and making his

audit report. But that does not conclude even this part of the appeal. For the auditors submitted that if, contrary to their primary contention, an auditor owes a shareholder *a* any duty of care the duty is owed to him as shareholder only, not investor; thus a claim might lie for loss sustained by selling or retaining shares in reliance on a negligent audit report but not for loss sustained by buying, because in buying the shareholder would be acting not as such but as an investor. This distinction is not without a logical basis. The shareholder receives the report by virtue of his existing shareholding and as a report on the stewardship of his existing shareholding. But I have to say (with respect to those who *b* think otherwise) that I do not consider this a sensible place at which to draw the line. There is no distinction to be drawn between selling and retaining on the one hand and buying on the other in terms of foreseeability or proximity. Nor does any consideration of what is just and reasonable or of what policy demands lead me to conclude that a duty imposed in the one situation should be denied in the other. In reality the shareholder is an investor in each situation, whether he is selling, retaining or buying, as the auditor *c* well knows. Nor can it sensibly be said that a duty is owed if a shareholder, in reliance on the audit report, buys a small number of additional shares but not if he buys a large number or seeks to buy all the shares he does not already hold. Any such distinction would in my view deserve Lord Devlin's eloquent denunciation in the *Hedley Byrne* case [1963] 2 All ER 575 at 602–603, [1964] AC 465 at 517.

If I am right so far, the question whether the auditors owed Caparo a duty of care as an *d* investor, irrespective of their capacity as a shareholder, by virtue of the facts pleaded in para 16 of the statement of claim (assumed for purposes of the issue to be true) does not strictly arise. But the question has been very fully argued. It is one of considerable importance. It is appropriate to express a conclusion.

The judge held that a buyer who was not a shareholder could show the foreseeability of economic damage caused by reliance on a negligent audit report. It was, he said, *e* foreseeable that a negligent misstatement in the auditors' report, referring to an annexed account, would cause economic loss to investors. This conclusion was not challenged. So, at any rate on the facts pleaded in para 16, a non-shareholder buyer can satisfy the requirement of foreseeability.

When, however, one turns to the second requirement, of proximity, it is in my view apparent that the relationship between the auditors and Caparo on the facts assumed (but *f* on the assumption that Caparo is not a shareholder) is very much less proximate than that of auditor and shareholder. There is here no statutory duty. The auditor is not engaged by the company to report to such a buyer, even though it is known that the report will be available for his inspection. Such a buyer may be, almost literally, anyone in the world. He may inspect the report and accounts in the public company file. More probably he will obtain a copy from his stockbroker or financial adviser. There is no *g* knowing. Only in a loose sense could the auditor be said to have assumed a responsibility towards him. The relationship falls far short of contract. The nexus or link between the parties is tenuous. If the report were a dangerous chattel likely to cause physical injury the requisite proximity might be found, but the relationship does not in my view satisfy the more stringent standards required of negligent misstatement. In truth, Caparo's case *h* on proximity rests on foreseeability alone and foreseeability alone is not enough.

If, contrary to my view, Caparo can show sufficient proximity I should none the less conclude that it could not on the facts assumed satisfy the third requirement. It is true that the obligation to make the report and accounts available for public inspection, and the general commercial considerations to which I earlier referred, would weigh in favour of a duty not limited to shareholders. It could be said with force to be anomalous that a *j* duty is owed to one who is registered as a shareholder at the date of the general meeting but not to one who becomes a shareholder thereafter and exercises his right to obtain a copy of the accounts under s 246. To extend the duty to non-shareholding investors adds nothing to the substance of what the auditor is in practical terms required to do. It merely increases his potential liability. But this would be a large extension of potential

liability. Time and experience may show such an extension to be desirable or necessary.
a It is, however, preferable that analogical developments of this kind should be gradual
and cautious. I am not at present persuaded that it would be just and reasonable, or
politic, that the law should be extended so as to impose a duty when no more is shown
than the facts Caparo has pleaded.

I consider this conclusion to be broadly consistent with the law as developed in other
common law jurisdictions, to which (in deference to Lord Keith's injunction cited at the
b outset) I should make brief reference.

(1) The most far-reaching statement of principle in this immediate field in any English
case is, I think, that of Woolf J in *JEB Fasteners Ltd v Marks Bloom & Co (a firm)* [1981] 3
All ER 289 at 296. He relied on Lord Wilberforce's oft-quoted statement in *Anns* in
particular and applied what was in substance a foreseeability test. He described (at 293)
the facts before him as in some respects similar to those in *Candler v Crane Christmas &*
c *Co* [1951] 1 All ER 426, [1951] 2 KB 164, but it seems to me that they were in principle
scarcely distinguishable. The plaintiffs on 23 June 1975 acquired the share capital of BG
Fasteners Ltd. The defendants were BG's auditors and (by Mr Marks) its accountant and
financial adviser. Well before the acquisition Mr Marks knew that financial support was
being sought in various forms (at 298). In August 1974 Mr Marks wrote to BG enclosing
draft accounts for the period November 1973 to July 1974, indicating that BG would
d require these for dealing with the plaintiffs. He thought the plaintiffs would want further
information and offered to help (at 298). In April 1975 he sent BG a fair copy of the
(uncertified) accounts for the year ended 31 October 1974 so that BG could visit the bank
with the figures. He also sent a copy to the bank (at 298). After the accounts were
certified a proposal was made that the plaintiffs should take over BG. Mr Marks was fully
aware of the progress of the negotiations thereafter, on which he advised BG. He also
e supplied information to the plaintiffs (at 299). On the day following the acquisition he
submitted a bill which included a charge (albeit modest) for corresponding with the
plaintiffs and advising them on the telephone (at 299). The audited accounts were not,
therefore, certified with the plaintiffs' take-over specifically in view, but the plaintiffs'
interest was known and it was readily to be inferred that after certification the defendants
impliedly represented the accuracy of their report and the accounts which they had (I
f think) themselves prepared. I respectfully doubt whether any extension of *Candler* or
Hedley Byrne principles was called for in order to resolve the duty of care issue in favour
of the plaintiffs.

(2) The facts in *Twomax Ltd v Dickson M'Farlane & Robinson* 1982 SC 113 were less
strong than in *JEB Fasteners* but still stronger than here. The Lord Ordinary (Stewart) said
(at 125):
g

> 'Mr M'Farlane's state of knowledge when he audited the 1973 accounts included
> a number of matters which I consider relevant to an assessment of what he should
> reasonably have foreseen. He was aware that Kintyre was suffering from a shortage
> of capital. He was aware during the summer months of 1973 that a director, Mr
> *h* Anderson, wished to dispose of his shareholding. He was aware that this shareholding
> was substantial, amounting to 10,000 shares. The defenders had in fact advertised
> in the newspaper under a box number on behalf of Mr Anderson. He knew for
> certain that the accounts were being made available to lenders in so far as he knew
> they were lodged with the company's bank. He knew that auditors' certificates,
> when they were "clean" certificates, were commonly relied on by shareholders,
> *j* potential investors, and potential lenders. In the whole circumstances I consider that
> Mr M'Farlane should have foreseen before he certified the 1973 accounts that these
> accounts might be relied on by a potential investor for the purpose of deciding
> whether or not to invest. The situation was such that I would have thought it an
> inevitable inference that Mr M'Farlane should have realised by the time he came to
> grant his audit certificate that there would shortly be some dealings in the issued

shares of Kintyre and might well be fresh shares issued in order to inject new capital into the company.'

In reaching his decision the Lord Ordinary (Stewart) relied on Lord Wilberforce's statement in *Anns* and Woolf J's statement in *JEB Fasteners*. Even so, I think it questionable whether he would have reached a decision in favour of the plaintiffs on the bare facts pleaded here.

(3) In *Haig v Bamford* (1976) 72 DLR (3d) 68 a very similar question was considered by the Supreme Court of Canada. Accountants of a company (who claimed to have carried out an audit but who had not in fact done so) were held to owe a duty of care to an investor in the company who relied on a negligent financial statement. The crucial finding (to which three of the judges in particular attached importance) was (at 70):

'Instructions were issued to the firm of R. L. Bamford & Co. (the accountants), of whom the respondents (defendants) were partners, to prepare the required financial statement and Scholler began a search for an outside investor. He made it known to the accountants that he was seeking an investor. The trial Judge, MacPherson, J., made a crucial finding, not disturbed by the Court of Appeal for Saskatchewan, that the accountants knew, prior to completion of the financial statement, dated June 18, 1965, at the root of the present litigation, that the statement would be used by Sedco, by the bank with whom the Company was doing business, and by a potential investor in equity capital.'

Without that finding, stronger than the facts assumed here, the plaintiffs' claim would, I think, have failed for want of proximity.

(4) The case which perhaps gives Caparo most assistance is *Scott Group Ltd v McFarlane* [1978] 1 NZLR 553. The plaintiffs relied on accounts audited by the defendants to take over John Duthie Holdings Ltd. This company was rich in assets but unimpressive in earnings and thus, as Cooke J put it (at 582), 'a classic case for a takeover or merger'. But when the defendants carried out their audit and signed their report they had no knowledge of any intention by the plaintiffs or anyone else to make a take-over offer. At first instance Quilliam J held that the auditors owed the plaintiffs no duty of care because on the facts there was no special relationship between them (see [1975] 1 NZLR 582). On appeal Richmond P agreed with him, relying in particular on the restrictive statements on principle in the *Hedley Byrne* case and *Candler's* case. But on this point the other two members of the Court of Appeal disagreed. Woodhouse J held that a relationship of sufficient, indeed 'close' (at 575), proximity existed. He attached particular importance (at 575–576) to the publicity requirements in the New Zealand Companies Act 1955 (a point which also caused Richmond P some concern (at 568)). But he limited his decision to the case of a take-over related to the value of shareholders' funds (at 575). The reasoning of Cooke J followed similar lines. He also regarded the publicity requirements as important (at 581), and he also concerned himself with the position of a party taking over a company, reserving his opinion on the position of an ordinary market purchaser who buys in reliance on the audited accounts. Plainly Caparo is assisted by the conclusions of these two distinguished judges. But there was, overall, an equal division of judicial opinion. The majority view may, in the wake of *Anns*, have been unduly coloured by the finding of foreseeability. And I do not, with respect, think the distinction between buying a limited number of shares and buying enough to take the company over is convincing: recognition that a company is ripe for take-over would, after all, be good enough reason for a shrewd investor to buy some shares in the company even if he could not take it over himself. So I am not shaken in my view that English law should not, yet, advance to this position. I am, however, reassured by what I take to be an implicit assumption by all three members of the Court of Appeal that a duty of care is owed by auditors to shareholders (see [1978] 1 NZLR 553 at 555, 568, 575, 581).

(5) The United States cases do not present a consistent picture. In *Ultramares Corp v*

Touche (1931) 255 NY 170 the accountants knew that the accounts when certified would
a be used to raise money and for that purpose supplied 32 certified and serially numbered
copies (at 173–174). On the faith of one of those copies, given to it on its demand, the
plaintiff lent the company money. The audit was found to be negligent. A claim in
negligence failed on the ground that the auditors owed the plaintiff no duty of care, there
being no sufficiently proximate relationship. A requirement of privity, not of contract
but of relationship, was laid down. This rule appears still to be the rule in New York: see
b *Credit Alliance Corp v Arthur Andersen & Co* (1985) 65 NY 2d 536. Other states also adhere
to it. But a much less restrictive rule has been followed elsewhere: see for example
H Rosenblum Inc v Adler (1983) 93 NJ 324 1, in which account was taken of the *Hedley
Byrne* and *JEB Fasteners* cases, and *Citizens State Bank v Timm Schmidt & Co* (1983) 113 Wis
2d 376. In *Rhode Island Hospital Trust National Bank v Swartz Bresenoff Yavner & Jacobs*
(1972) 455 F 2d 847 at 851 the United States Court of Appeals, applying Rhode Island
c law, applied the rule that an accountant should be liable in negligence for careless
financial misrepresentations relied on by actually foreseen and limited classes of persons.
In *Ingram Industries Inc v Nowicki* (1981) 527 F Supp 683 a federal judge applying the law
of Kentucky relied on the American Law Institute's Restatement of the Law, Second,
Torts 2d (1977) §552, pp 126–127. This is perhaps as close as one can come to a concensus
of opinion in the United States. Section 552 provides:

d
'Information Negligently Supplied for the Guidance of Others (1) One who, in
the course of his business, profession or employment, or in any other transaction in
which he has a pecuniary interest, supplies false information for the guidance of
others in their business transactions, is subject to liability for pecuniary loss caused
to them by their justifiable reliance upon the information, if he fails to exercise
e reasonable care or competence in obtaining or communicating the information.
(2) Except as stated in Subsection (3), the liability stated in Subsection (1) is
limited to loss suffered (a) by the person or one of a limited group of persons for
whose benefit and guidance he intends to supply the information or knows that the
recipient intends to supply it; and (b) through reliance upon it in a transaction that
he intends the information to influence or knows that the recipient so intends or in
f a substantially similar transaction.
(3) The liability of one who is under a public duty to give the information
extends to loss suffered by any of the class of persons for whose benefit the duty is
created, in any of the transactions in which it is intended to protect them.'

It would be unprofitable to discuss at length whether this statement accords or should
accord with English law. It would not, I think, support a claim by Caparo otherwise than
g as a shareholder, but subsection (3) would appear to me to cover its claim as shareholder.
The auditors argue that it would be absurd for the important issue of duty or no duty
to turn on the holding of a single share. But that is because, in the ordinary way and
leaving non-commercial considerations aside, it is absurd to hold a single share. The mass
of investors in public companies hold more than a single share, and once one accepts
multiple shareholding as the norm it does not seem to me absurd that the issue of duty
h or no duty should turn on whether a party misled does or does not belong to the specific
class to whom the auditor was engaged to report.
I would allow the appeal against the decision of the judge that the auditors owed no
duty of care to Caparo as a shareholder but dismiss it against his decision that they owed
Caparo no duty of care as a non-shareholding buyer.

j **TAYLOR LJ.** This case raises an important question of principle. To whom do auditors
of a company owe a duty of care in respect of their report made pursuant to s 236 of the
Companies Act 1985 and what is the scope of that duty? The judge dealt with this
question as a preliminary issue. He held that the only duty was to the company itself.
Caparo's case is put on alternative footings. Primarily, they contend that auditors owe

a duty not only to the company but also to individual investors, whether existing
shareholders or potential shareholders and whether the investment relates to a few shares
or to a take-over of the company. Secondly, even if the duty does not extend to all
potential investors, where the company is vulnerable to take-over, it does extend to a
potential 'suitor' (a word used to define a legal entity seeking to take-over the company).
Thirdly, at the very least counsel for Caparo argues that the duty extends to existing
shareholders.

The judge held that three factors must be present to establish a duty of care in the field
of negligent misstatement: firstly, foreseeability of loss; secondly, proximity of the
plaintiff to the defendant; and, thirdly, the court must be satisfied that it is fair, just and
reasonable that the defendant should owe a duty to the plaintiff. The judge incorporated
the element of public policy in his third factor, whereas the auditors treat it as a separate
element. Subject to that, there is no real issue between the parties as to the correctness of
the judge's three-part test.

It is agreed that in the present case the element of foreseeability was present in relation
to both shareholders and potential investors. When the auditors issued their report it was
foreseeable to them that shareholders and potential investors might rely on it in
considering whether and how to deal in the company's shares. Moreover, it is conceded
by counsel for Caparo that proof of such foreseeability although essential is not enough,
even if qualified by the fair, just and reasonable test. There must be present the second
of the judge's three factors, which he called proximity. This is now settled law. The
much-quoted passage from Lord Wilberforce's speech in *Anns v Merton London Borough*
[1977] 2 All ER 492 at 498–499, [1978] AC 728 at 751–752 has been held not to have
laid down any universal rule to the contrary. Thus, in *Governors of the Peabody Donation
Fund v Sir Lindsay Parkinson & Co Ltd* [1984] 3 All ER 529 at 534, [1985] AC 210 at 240
Lord Keith, after quoting Lord Wilberforce, said:

> 'There has been a tendency in some recent cases to treat these passages as being
> themselves of a definitive character. This is a temptation which should be resisted.
> The true question in each case is whether the particular defendant owed to the
> particular plaintiff a duty of care having the scope which is contended for, and
> whether he was in breach of that duty with consequent loss to the plaintiff. A
> relationship of proximity in Lord Atkin's sense must exist before any duty of care
> can arise, but the scope of the duty must depend on all the circumstances of the
> case.'

In *Yuen Kun-yeu v A-G of Hong Kong* [1987] 2 All ER 705 at 710, [1988] AC 175 at 192
Lord Keith, giving the advice of the Privy Council, said:

> 'Foreseeability of harm is a necessary ingredient of such a relationship, but it is
> not the only one. Otherwise there would be a liability in negligence on the part of
> one who sees another about to walk over a cliff with his head in the air, and forbears
> to shout a warning. *Donoghue v Stevenson* [1932] AC 562, [1932] All ER Rep 1
> established that the manufacturer of a consumable product who carried on business
> in such a way that the product reached the consumer in the shape in which it left
> the manufacturer, without any prospect of intermediate examination, owed the
> consumer a duty to take reasonable care that the product was free from defect likely
> to cause injury to health. The speech of Lord Atkin stressed not only the requirement
> of foreseeability of harm but also that of a close and direct relationship of proximity.'

Lord Keith then quoted the famous passage from Lord Atkin's speech in *Donoghue v
Stevenson* [1932] AC 562 at 580, [1932] All ER Rep 1 at 11 beginning: 'Who, then, in law
is my neighbour?...' He continued as follows ([1987] 2 All ER 705 at 711, [1988] AC
175 at 192):

> 'Lord Atkin clearly had in contemplation that all the circumstances of the case,

a
not only the foreseeability of harm, were appropriate to be taken into account in determining whether a duty of care arose.'

The main arguments in the present case have been addressed to the following issues. (1) What amounts to proximity in the context of negligent misstatement? (2) Was the judge right in concluding such proximity did not exist between the auditors and Caparo (a) as shareholders and (b) as investors? (3) Was he right in concluding further that to impose on auditors the duty contended for by Caparo would not be fair, just and
b
reasonable?

1. *Proximity*

Counsel for the auditors in his admirable argument sought to identify the criteria for establishing proximity. His main submission was that there must be by the defendant a
c
voluntary assumption of responsibility towards the individual plaintiff in circumstances akin to contract. That test was propounded in *Hedley Byrne & Co Ltd v Heller & Partners Ltd* [1963] 2 All ER 575, [1964] AC 465. It was applied in *Muirhead v Industrial Tank Specialities Ltd* [1985] 3 All ER 705, [1986] QB 507, in *Simaan General Contracting Co v Pilkington Glass Ltd (No 2)* [1988] 1 All ER 791, [1988] QBD 758 and in *Greater Nottingham Co-op Society Ltd v Cementation Piling and Foundations Ltd* [1988] 2 All ER 971, [1989] QB
d
71. However, in each of those cases there could have been no nexus creating proximity between the parties in the absence of a voluntary assumption of responsibility by the defendant to the plaintiff.

In the *Hedley Byrne* case the plaintiffs and defendants had no reason to know of each other's existence. The plaintiffs, via their bankers, sought a reference for a company which banked with the defendants. The defendants gave the reference negligently
e
knowing that reliance would or might be placed on it by a customer of the inquiring bank and, had they not issued a disclaimer, it was held they would have been liable. That was because they would voluntarily have assumed responsibility to the plaintiff. In that case, proximity could only be established by such a voluntary assumption. There was nothing else.

The other authorities cited above were not negligent misstatement cases. Each was a
f
case in which there was a chain of contracts but no relevant direct contract between the parties. In each case it was sought unsuccessfully to establish liability for economic loss by reliance on the *Hedley Byrne* principle. In the *Simaan* case [1988] 1 All ER 791 at 805, [1988] QB 758 at 784 Dillon LJ said:

'If, however, foreseeability does not automatically lead to a duty of care, the duty
g
in a *Hedley Byrne type of case* must depend on the voluntary assumption of responsibility towards a particular party giving rise to a special relationship, as Lord Keith held in *Yuen Kun-yeu v A-G of Hong Kong* [1987] 2 All ER 705, [1988] AC 175 . . .' (My emphasis.)

The latter case was somewhat closer on its facts to the present one. The Commissioner of
h
Deposit-taking Companies was responsible for registering such companies under an ordinance. One company so registered went into liquidation. The plaintiffs lost money which they had deposited with the company and alleged negligence against the commissioner since he should have known the company was suspect and the plaintiffs had relied on the registration as showing the company to be sound. Lord Keith referred to the *Hedley Byrne* case and *Junior Books Ltd v Veitchi Co Ltd* [1982] 3 All ER 201, [1983] 1
j
AC 520 and continued ([1987] 2 All ER 705 at 714, [1988] AC 175 at 196):

'These decisions turned on the voluntary assumption of responsibility towards a particular party, giving rise to a special relationship. Lord Devlin in the *Hedley Byrne* case [1963] 2 All ER 575 at 611, [1964] AC 465 at 530 proceeded on the proposition that wherever there is a relationship equivalent to a contract, there is a duty of care.

In the present case there was clearly no voluntary assumption by the commissioner
of any responsibility towards the appellants in relation to the affairs of the company.   *a*
It was argued, however, that the effect of the ordinance [Deposit-taking Companies
Ordinance 1976] was to place such a responsibility on him. Their Lordships consider
that the ordinance placed a duty on the commissioner to supervise deposit-taking
companies in the general public interest, but no special responsibility towards
individual members of the public.'

Because in a *Hedley Byrne* type of case a voluntary assumption of responsibility is necessary   *b*
to establish proximity, it does not follow that such an assumption is necessary in every
case. There may be some other nexus sufficient to create proximity. In *Yuen Kun-yeu's*
case Lord Keith considered the argument that the ordinance might suffice. Their
Lordships rejected that argument, not because of any necessity for a voluntary assumption
of responsibility, but because the ordinance did not create a special responsibility to any
individual member of the public. That liability might exist without voluntary   *c*
assumption of risk where the defendant was under an obligation to make a statement
was clearly envisaged by Cross LJ in *Ministry of Housing and Local Government v Sharp*
[1970] 1 All ER 1009 at 1038, 2 QB 223 at 291. He said:

> 'It is true that the phrase "voluntary assumption of risk" occurs frequently in the
> speeches in the *Hedley Byrne* case, but I agree with the judge that that case did not   *d*
> purport to lay down any metes and bounds within which legal liability in tort for
> false statements, on which the parties to whom they are made rely, has to be
> confined. (See in particular per Lord Devlin ([1963] 2 All ER 575 at 611, [1964] AC
> 465 at 530–531).) I see no sufficient reason why in an appropriate case the liability
> should not extend to cases in which the defendant is obliged to make the statement
> which proves to be false.'   *e*

In the same case the other members of the court also indicated that voluntary assumption
of responsibility is not essential to create a duty. Thus, Lord Denning MR said ([1970] 1
All ER 1009 at 1018, [1970] 2 QB 223 at 268):

> '[Counsel for the defendants] said that a duty to use due care (where there was no   *f*
> contract) only arose when there was a voluntary assumption of responsibility. I do
> not agree. He relied particularly on the words of Lord Reid in *Hedley Byrne & Co Ltd
> v Heller & Partners Ltd* [1963] 2 All ER 575 at 583, [1964] AC 465 at 487, and of
> Lord Devlin ([1963] 2 All ER 575 at 610–611, [1964] AC 465 at 529). I think they
> used those words because of the special circumstances of that case (where the bank
> disclaimed responsibility). But they did not in any way mean to limit the general
> principle. In my opinion the duty to use due care in a statement arises, not from   *g*
> any voluntary assumption of responsibility, but from the fact that the person
> making it knows, or ought to know, that others, being his neighbours in this regard,
> would act on the faith of the statement being accurate.'

In using the phrase 'being his neighbours' Lord Denning MR was clearly referring to
'neighbours' in the sense in which the word was used by Lord Atkin, implying proximity   *h*
not merely foreseeability. Salmon LJ said ([1970] 1 All ER 1009 at 1027–1028, [1970] 2
QB 223 at 279):

> 'I do not accept that, in all cases, the obligation to take reasonable care necessarily
> depends on a voluntary assumption of responsibility.'

Counsel for the auditors went on to consider other possible touchstones of proximity.   *j*
He suggested there must be a special relationship between the parties, that the negligent
statement must have been made for the very purpose for which reliance was placed on
it, that the plaintiff must be a member of a small limited class and that there must be
some communing between the plaintiff and the defendant. It is unnecessary to cite the

cases relied on in support of these several tests. Clearly, in appropriate cases it will be
a relevant to have regard to all or some of them. I do not accept, however, that any one or
group of them can be regarded as definitive of the requisite proximity. As Bingham LJ
said in the *Simaan* case [1988] 1 All ER 791 at 803, [1988] QB 758 at 782:

> 'However attractive it may theoretically be to postulate a single principle capable
> of embracing every kind of case, that is not how the law has developed. It would of
b > course be unsatisfactory if (say) doctors and dentists owed their patients a different
> duty of care. I do not, however, think it unsatisfactory or surprising if, as I think, a
> banker's duty towards the recipient of a credit reference and an industrial glass
> manufacturer's duty towards a main contractor, in the absence of any contract
> between them, differ.'

c In my judgment it is not possible to lay down one precise test or set of tests applicable
in every situation to show whether the necessary proximity is established. In each case
the court must inquire how close and direct a relationship exists between the parties and
whether the defendant should have had the plaintiff in contemplation as a person who
would or might rely on the relevant statement.

d **2(a).   *Caparo as shareholders***
Primarily, the duty of auditors is to the company whose accounts they audit. But,
under the Companies Act 1985, they are appointed by the shareholders in general
meeting (s 384). They have a duty to report to the shareholders whether, inter alia, the
company's accounts give a true and fair view of its financial position (s 236). A report
made by auditors to the directors rather than to the shareholders is not a proper
e compliance with that duty (see *Re London and General Bank (No 2)* [1895] 2 Ch 673 at 682,
684–685, [1895–9] All ER Rep 953 at 956–958). By s 240 a copy of the company's
accounts together with the auditor's report must be sent to every shareholder. Further,
the auditor's report must be read at a general meeting of the company's shareholders
(s 241). These provisions show that, although the legal entity which contracts with and
pays the auditors and to which the auditors owe a statutory duty is the company,
f Parliament entrusted the appointment of auditors to the shareholders and required the
auditors to render their report to the shareholders rather than the directors, so that those
owning the company's shares should receive an independent account of its financial state.
Auditors have thus in my judgment a close and direct relationship with the
shareholders. Once auditors accept appointment they know that their report has to be
sent to each shareholder as a named individual who will or may act on it. It is argued
g that the shareholders of a company are a constantly changing body; but, at the relevant
time when the report goes out, their identity is ascertainable and has to be ascertained.
In this context some observations of Megarry V-C in *Ross v Caunters (a firm)* [1979] 3 All
ER 580 at 587, [1980] Ch 297 at 308 are relevant and helpful:

> '. . . the question is whether a solicitor owes a duty of care to a beneficiary under a
h > will that he makes for a client, and, if so, on what basis that duty rests. This is, of
> course, the central core of the case. In considering this, three features of the case
> before me seem to stand out. First, there is the close degree of proximity of the
> plaintiff to the defendants. There is no question of whether the defendants could
> fairly have been expected to contemplate the plaintiff as a person likely to be affected
> by any lack of care on their part, or whether they ought to have done so: there is no
j > "ought" about the case. This is not a case where the only nexus between the plaintiff
> and the defendants is that the plaintiff was the ultimate recipient of a dangerous
> chattel or negligent misstatement which the defendants had put into circulation.
> The plaintiff was named and identified in the will that the defendants drafted for
> the testator. Their contemplation of the plaintiff was actual, nominate and direct. It

was contemplation by contract, though of course, the contract was with a third
party, the testator.'

a

Auditors' contemplation of an individual registered shareholder is also 'actual, nominate
and direct'. They know of the shareholder's actual existence; they know his nominate
identity; and they send directly to that shareholder the report on which his reliance is
foreseeable. Here too one has 'contemplation by contract'. True, the contract is with the
company and not the shareholders but the auditors' appointment by them and duty to
report to them creates a nexus close to contract. Indeed, the only reason there is no
contract with the shareholders derives from the rule giving a limited liability company a
legal identity separate from that of its members.

b

Even if one were to apply the voluntary assumption of responsibility test, it would in
my view be satisfied here. In the *Hedley Byrne* case, the House of Lords clearly indicated
that a voluntary assumption might be implied rather than express (see [1963] 2 All ER
575 esp at 611, [1964] AC 465 esp at 529–530 per Lord Devlin). Auditors are not obliged
to accept appointment. If they do so voluntarily, then they assume (as the statute requires)
the duty to report to each shareholder individually knowing that he may well act in
reliance on the report. In those circumstances, I would hold that a voluntary assumption
of responsibility arises by implication. For these reason, I conclude that there was the
requisite proximity between Caparo as shareholders and the auditors.

c

d

2(b). *Caparo as investors*

The position of a potential investor is very different. He plays no role in the statutory
scheme relating to auditors. He has no part in appointing them; he does not receive their
report directly from them. He may, of course, be shown the accounts and the report by
others. A copy of those documents has to be delivered to the registrar of companies
(s 241(3)) and they must be available for inspection by anyone (s 709). But the right to
inspect them and the option to buy shares are enjoyed by the world at large. Within the
auditors' contemplation there is no focus on any person or class of person who may decide
to invest. All they can foresee is that some unidentified investor or investors may inspect
their report and act on it. By the same token other unascertained persons may also do so,
eg a bank contemplating the grant to the company of a loan or its suppliers or creditors.
In none of these instances is there any close or direct relationship with the auditors.
Foreseeability of reliance is conceded but the element of proximity is in my judgment
lacking.

e

f

Counsel for Caparo argued that where, as pleaded here, a company is vulnerable to
take-over the auditors owe a duty to a suitor in respect of their statutory report. He
submits that especially in the case of an unwelcome suitor the only information available
consists of the published accounts and auditors' report. Ex hypothesi the company will
not itself vouchsafe information. Whereas a duty to investors generally would or could
be owed to vast numbers, there can he submits be only one successful suitor in a take-
over so that liability would be restricted.

g

Apart from the difficulty which would arise from the vague and elusive nature of
vulnerability as a test, I can see no reason in principle to distinguish between a suitor
(welcome or otherwise) and any other investor. Assuming the company was vulnerable
to take-over in the present case, it may have been more readily foreseeable that a suitor
might rely on the auditors' report. However, I do not see how the argument for
proximity is any stronger. I therefore conclude that investors even if they are suitors are
not owed any duty of care by the auditors.

h

j

3. *Fair, just and reasonable?*

The principal concern in this class of case is that casting too wide a duty on a potential
defendant may result in a liability which is intolerably onerous. The courts have therefore
been reluctant to extend the scope of liability for economic loss arising from negligent

misstatement. The fear is well summarised in the much-quoted observation of Cardozo
a CJ in *Ultramares Corp v Touche* (1931) 255 NY 170 at 179:

> '... liability in an indeterminate amount for an indeterminate time to an
> indeterminate class.'

Counsel for the auditors submits that those words would obviously and incontrovertibly
apply if auditors owed a duty to the world of investors at large. But he maintains they
b also apply even if the duty extends no further than to shareholders.

I do not, however, think shareholders can be described as an indeterminate class. The
class may well be very large in the case of a major public company, but its members are
ascertainable. Again, as to time, the period during which reliance could reasonably be
placed on the report would in practice be limited. It is right to say that liability could be
for a large amount. On the other hand, a plaintiff shareholder would have a number of
c hurdles to clear before he could recover damages. He would first have to establish that
the auditors were negligent. It would by no means follow, for example, that failure to
expose deliberate and well concealed fraud on the part of a company's directors would
amount to negligence by the auditors. They are not insurers. They would be judged by
reasonable professional standards. Reliance on the report would have to be proved, as
would damage. These considerations and the risk of having to bear the costs of an
d unsuccessful claim would in my view be sufficient to deter all but the stout-hearted and
seriously aggrieved from bringing proceedings.

It is contended that auditors would find it difficult and cripplingly expensive to obtain
insurance cover. It is even suggested that accountants might decline to be appointed as
auditors. No evidence was adduced on this aspect of the case and if I am right about the
difficulties and disincentives affecting possible claimants the insurance problem should
e not be insurmountable. It would always be open to Parliament to intervene should
limitation of liability be considered necessary.

Counsel for Caparo emphasises that the auditors already have a duty to the company
to prepare their report with proper professional skill and care. No additional work or
different standard would be required of them should their duty extend not merely to the
company but also to the shareholders. It is, he submits, only fair and reasonable that they
f should have a remedy if the auditors they appoint report to them negligently and they
in consequence act to their detriment. The judge said their remedy was to get rid of the
auditors but, as counsel for the auditors accepted, that is no remedy at all. At best the
threat of removal might be some sanction against carelessness. But those shareholders
who have shed their total holdings would have no power to remove the auditors; neither
would a minority. In the unlikely event of a majority of shareholders exercising the
g power, they would merely be shutting the stable door. They would not recoup their
losses.

Balancing the factors urged on both sides, I conclude it is fair, just and reasonable that
an individual shareholder should have a remedy against a negligent auditor. I do not
consider that the reasons advanced against the existence of the duty are of sufficient
h cogency to outweigh those in favour.

But what should be the scope of the duty? Here again fairness and public policy are
the tests. Counsel for the auditors submits that at highest the duty should only apply to
a shareholder in respect of his existing shareholding. It should not extend to his purchase
of further shares in reliance on the report. He submits the only distinction between a
shareholder and any other investor is that the former already owns some shares. In
j respect of any further shares bought he is in no different position from that of any other
investor and should be so treated.

In my view, once proximity to the shareholder is established, the auditor ought prima
facie to be liable for any loss suffered in foreseeable reliance on the report; prima facie,
that is, unless such liability be unfair, unjust or unreasonable. There is no logical basis
for distinguishing between reliance for the purpose of selling shares and reliance in

purchasing more. It is, therefore, necessary to analyse the possible situations which could occur.

A negligent report can result in misrepresentation only of two broad kinds: either an overvalue or an undervalue of the company's shares. A shareholder relying on the report can act only in one of three ways. He may sell; he may retain his holding; or he may buy more shares. If the report undervalues, a shareholder who buys has no complaint. If he retains his shares he has neither lost nor gained by the error. Only if he sells at an undervalue will he have sustained loss. He would then be entitled to claim from the auditors the difference between what he received and the true value. However, since this would involve dealing with his existing shareholding it does not bear on the issue under consideration. Take the converse situation, where the negligent report shows an overvalue. The shareholder who sells will gain and one who simply retains his holding will neither gain nor lose. Only he who buys will suffer damage. This last would therefore be the only instance of liability occurring as a result of extending the duty to all dealings by shareholders and not otherwise. The claim would be for the difference between what the shareholder paid and the true value. I do not consider the liability of the auditors to that extent in that one situation would be unfair, unjust or unreasonable. To exclude it would be illogical and arbitrary. Accordingly, I would hold that the auditors' duty to individual shareholders was not limited to their existing shareholding.

Bingham LJ has considered in detail *JEB Fasteners Ltd v Marks Bloom & Co* [1981] 3 All ER 289 and *Twomax Ltd v Dickson M'Farlane & Robinson* 1982 SC 113 and has also reviewed the American and Commonwealth authorities. I entirely agree with his analysis and cannot usefully add to it.

I, too, would allow this appeal as to the auditors' duty to Caparo qua shareholder and dismiss it against the judge's decision that they owed no duty to Caparo as a non-shareholding investor.

O'CONNOR LJ. In 1984 the plaintiffs (Caparo) made a successful take-over bid for Fidelity plc (Fidelity). At all material times the defendants, Touche Ross & Co (the auditors), were auditors of Fidelity. In July 1985 Caparo commenced this action in which they claim damages for fraud against two directors of Fidelity and damages for negligence against the auditors. Caparo alleged that they made their bid in reliance on the accounts of Fidelity for the year ending 31 March 1984. These were signed by the auditors in May with a clean certificate, sent to shareholders in June, read and approved at the annual general meeting on 4 July. Broadly, Caparo say that so far from giving a true and fair view of the state of affairs of Fidelity the accounts gave a false picture in that the reported profit of £1·3m should have been a loss of £0·46m.

In July 1987 an order was made for the trial of a preliminary issue:

'... whether on the facts set out in paragraphs 4 and 6 and in sub-paragraphs (1) and (2) of paragraph 16 of the Statement of Claim herein, the Third Defendants, Touche Ross & Co., owed a duty of care to the Plaintiffs Caparo Industries PLC...'

That issue was tried by Sir Neil Lawson in December 1987. He decided that the auditors owed no duty of care. Caparo appeal to this court.

I set out para 4 of the statement of claim:

'In June 1984 Caparo began to purchase Fidelity shares in the open market and purchased 100,000 shares at 70 pence each on 8th June 1984. On 12th June 1984, the date on which the Accounts for the period ended 31st March 1984 were issued to shareholders, including Caparo, a further 50,000 shares were purchased at 73 pence each.'

Paragraph 6 sets out the details of the take-over transaction; the material fact averred is that Caparo acted in reliance on the information contained in the accounts.

I set out para 16 in full:

a
'Touche Ross, as auditors of Fidelity carrying out their functions as auditors and certifiers of the Accounts in April and May 1984, owed a duty of care to investors and potential investors, and in particular to Caparo, in respect of the audit and certification of the Accounts. In support of that duty of care Caparo will rely upon the following matters:—(1) Touche Ross knew or ought to have known (a) that in early March 1984 a press release had been issued stating that profits for the financial year would fall significantly short of £2·2m (b) that Fidelity's share price fell from
b
143 pence per share on 1st March 1984 to 75 pence per share on 2nd April 1984 (c) that Fidelity required financial assistance. (2) Touche Ross therefore ought to have foreseen that Fidelity was vulnerable to a take-over bid and that persons such as Caparo might well rely on the Accounts for the purpose of deciding whether to take over Fidelity and might well suffer loss if the Accounts were inaccurate.'

c
Caparo claim to have lost the cost of the take-over, £13m. This may be small in the context of take-over bids ranging up to a billion pounds or more but it is obvious that the decision in this case is of great importance to all accountants who act as auditors.

I must make it clear that the auditors strongly deny that they were negligent in any way and that it is only for the purposes of deciding the point of law that we have to assume that the clean certificate was a negligent misstatement. Once more we have to
d
consider possible liability for economic loss caused by negligent misstatement. The law has developed rapidly since 1963, when the House of Lords opened the door to such liability in *Hedley Byrne & Co Ltd v Heller & Partners Ltd* [1963] 2 All ER 575, [1964] AC 465. What emerges from the cases is that, in a case such as this, in deciding whether a duty of care exists it is also necessary to consider its scope: see *Rowling v Takaro Properties Ltd* [1988] 1 All ER 163 at 172, [1988] AC 473 at 501. In the same case Lord Keith said
e
([1988] 1 All ER 163 at 172, [1988] AC 473 at 501):

'It is at this stage that it is necessary, before concluding that a duty of care should be imposed, to consider all the relevant circumstances. One of the considerations underlying certain recent decisions of the House of Lords (*Governors of the Peabody Donation Fund v Sir Lindsay Parkinson & Co Ltd* [1984] 3 All ER 529, [1985] AC 210)
f
and of the Privy Council (*Yuen Kun-yeu v A-G of Hong Kong* [1987] 2 All ER 705, [1988] AC 175) is the fear that a too literal application of the well-known observation of Lord Wilberforce in *Anns v Merton London Borough* [1977] 2 All ER 492 at 498, [1978] AC 728 at 751–752 may be productive of a failure to have regard to, and to analyse and weigh, all the relevant considerations in considering whether it is appropriate that a duty of care should be imposed. Their Lordships consider that
g
question to be of an intensely pragmatic character, well suited for gradual development but requiring most careful analysis. It is one on which all common law jurisdictions can learn much from each other, because, apart from exceptional cases, no sensible distinction can be drawn in this respect between the various countries and the social conditions existing in them. It is incumbent on the courts in different jurisdictions to be sensitive to each other's reactions; but what they are
h
all searching for in others, and each of them striving to achieve, is a careful analysis and weighing of the relevant competing considerations.'

In *Yuen Kun-yeu v A-G of Hong Kong* [1987] 2 All ER 705 at 710, [1988] AC 175 at 191–192 Lord Keith said:

'Their Lordships venture to think that the two-stage test formulated by Lord
j
Wilberforce for determining the existence of a duty of care in negligence has been elevated to a degree of importance greater than it merits, and greater perhaps than its author intended. Further, the expression of the first stage of the test carries with it a risk of misinterpretation. As Gibbs CJ pointed out in *Sutherland Shire Council v Heyman* (1985) 60 ALR 1 at 13 there are two possible views of what Lord Wilberforce meant. The first view, favoured in a number of cases mentioned by Gibbs CJ, is that

he meant to test the sufficiency of proximity simply by the reasonable contemplation
of likely harm. The second view, favoured by Gibbs CJ himself, is that Lord
Wilberforce meant the expression "proximity or neighbourhood" to be a composite
one, importing the whole concept of necessary relationship between plaintiff and
defendant described by Lord Atkin in *Donoghue v Stevenson* [1932] AC 562 at 580,
[1932] All ER Rep 1 at 11. In their Lordships' opinion the second view is the correct
one. As Lord Wilberforce himself observed in *McLoughlin v O'Brian* [1982] 2 All ER
298 at 303, [1983] 1 AC 410 at 420, it is clear that foreseeability does not of itself,
and automatically, lead to a duty of care. There are many other statements to the
same effect. The truth is that the trilogy of cases referred to by Lord Wilberforce
each demonstrate particular sets of circumstances, differing in character, which were
adjudged to have the effect of bringing into being a relationship apt to give rise to a
duty of care. Foreseeability of harm is a necessary ingredient of such a relationship,
but it is not the only one. Otherwise there would be liability in negligence on the
part of one who sees another about to walk over a cliff with his head in the air, and
forbears to shout a warning.'

In *Hill v Chief Constable of West Yorkshire* [1988] 2 All ER 238 at 241, [1989] AC 53 at
60. Lord Keith said:

'It has been said almost too frequently to require repetition that foreseeability of
likely harm is not in itself a sufficient test of liability in negligence. Some further
ingredient is invariably needed to establish the requisite proximity of relationship
between the plaintiff and defendant, and all the circumstances of the case must be
carefully considered and analysed in order to ascertain whether such an ingredient
is present. The nature of the ingredient will be found to vary in a number of
different categories of decided cases.'

The question in this case is: did the auditors owe a duty of care to someone who, relying
on the certified accounts, bought shares in the company?

The Companies Act 1985 requires every company to appoint auditors at its annual
general meeting to hold office for a year (s 384). The directors are required to lay before
the company in general meeting copies of the accounts (s 241). The accounts must
contain the auditors' report (s 239). The requirements for the auditors' report are found
in s 236:

'(1) A company's auditors shall make a report to its members on the accounts
examined by them, and on every balance sheet and profit and loss account, and on
all group accounts, copies of which are to be laid before the company in general
meeting during the auditors' tenure of office.
(2) The auditors' report shall state—(a) whether in the auditors' opinion the
balance sheet and profit and loss account and (if it is a holding company submitting
group accounts) the group accounts have been properly prepared in accordance with
this Act; and (b) without prejudice to the foregoing, whether in their opinion a true
and fair view is given—(i) in the balance sheet, of the state of the company's affairs
at the end of the financial year, (ii) in the profit and loss account (if not framed as a
consolidated account), of the company's profit or loss for the financial year, and (iii)
in the case of group accounts, of the state of affairs and profit or loss of the company
and its subsidiaries dealt with by those accounts, so far as concerns members of the
company.'

Auditors' duties and powers are set out in s 237:

'(1) It is the duty of the company's auditors, in preparing their report, to carry
out such investigations as will enable them to form an opinion as to the following
matters—(a) whether proper accounting records have been kept by the company
and proper returns adequate for their audit have been received from branches not

a
visited by them, (b) whether the company's balance sheet and (if not consolidated) its profit and loss account are in agreement with the accounting records and returns.

(2) If the auditors are of opinion that proper accounting records have not been kept, or that proper returns adequate for their audit have not been received from branches not visited by them, or if the balance sheet and (if not consolidated) the profit and loss account are not in agreement with the accounting records and returns, the auditors shall state that fact in their report.

b
(3) Every auditor of a company has a right of access at all times to the company's books, accounts and vouchers, and is entitled to require from the company's officers such information and explanations as he thinks necessary for the performance of the auditor's duties.

(4) If the auditors fail to obtain all the information and explanations which, to the best of their knowledge and belief, are necessary for the purposes of their audit,

c
they shall state that fact in their report.

(5) If the requirements of Parts V and VI of Schedule 5 and Parts I to III of Schedule 6 are not complied with in the accounts, it is the auditors' duty to include in their report, so far as they are reasonably able to do so, a statement giving the required particulars.

(6) It is the auditors' duty to consider whether the information given in the

d
directors' report for the financial year for which the accounts are prepared is consistent with those accounts; and if they are of opinion that it is not, they shall state that fact in their report.'

A copy of the accounts must be sent to every member of the company not less than 21 days before the date of the meeting at which they are to be laid (s 240).

e
Section 241(2) provides:

'The auditors' report shall be read before the company in general meeting, and be open to the inspection of any member of the company.'

The result of these statutory provisions is that auditors are employed by the company and it is an implied term of the contract that they will carry out their duties with the

f
care and skill expected from reasonably competent auditors. If they fail to do their audit with the requisite care and skill they may fail to discover some irregularity in the accounts which they ought to have discovered. If the irregularity is such that the auditors ought not to have certified that a true and fair view of the state of the company's affairs is given in the accounts it must follow that the accounts either understate or overstate the true state of affairs. The company itself cannot suffer any loss from the over- or

g
understatement of its affairs, but may suffer loss from the failure of the auditors to discover the irregularity.

Counsel for Caparo submitted that auditors know, or at least must be taken to know, that investors considering buying shares in the company may rely on the accuracy of the accounts certified by the auditors, which are readily available to investors. If the investor was considering a take-over bid he would rely on the certified accounts in making his

h
decision. If as a result of negligent audit the auditors had failed to discover that the accounts overstated the true position of the company, they could foresee that an investor might suffer loss because he would be paying more for the shares than they were really worth.

Counsel for Caparo accepted that foreseeability of damage was not sufficient to impose a duty on the auditors but he submitted that the matters pleaded in para 16 of the

j
statement of claim introduced a sufficient degree of proximity. In support of that contention he relied on the judgment of Woolf J in JEB Fasteners Ltd v Marks Bloom & Co (a firm) [1981] 3 All ER 289. That was a take-over case, as appears from the opening paragraphs of the judgment (at 291):

'. . . the plaintiffs acquired the entire share capital of that company. They contend

that they would not have purchased the company if they had known its true
financial position, but that they did so relying on its audited accounts for the year   *a*
ending 31st October 1974, prepared by the defendants, which did not give a true
and fair view of the state of the company. The plaintiffs allege that they have
suffered substantial loss and damage as a result of the purchase of the company.
Before going into the facts in great detail it is desirable if I indicate my views as to
the legal issues involved which have been in dispute before me. In order to succeed
in this case, the plaintiffs have to establish as a matter of law that the defendants   *b*
owed them a duty of care so as to give rise to liability if they were negligent in the
preparation of the accounts. It is not alleged that at the time the accounts were
audited the defendants knew that the accounts would be relied on by the plaintiffs.
Indeed, no takeover was then contemplated, and counsel for both the plaintiffs and
the defendants agree that there is no direct English authority on the question
whether the defendants owe such a duty in those circumstances.'   *c*

Woolf J then reviewed the authorities and as his decision on them is crucial to the
argument for Caparo in the present case I must look a little more closely at the build up
to his conclusion.

He began with the dissenting judgment of Denning LJ in *Candler v Crane Christmas &*
Co [1951] 1 All ER 426 at 434, [1951] 2 KB 164 at 180–181 approved by the House of   *d*
Lords in *Hedley Byrne & Co Ltd v Heller & Partners Ltd* [1963] 2 All ER 575, [1964] AC
465. In that case the accountants had been asked by the company to prepared accounts
expressly for the purpose of being shown to the plaintiff, who was proposing to invest
money in the company. Denning LJ asked himself to whom accountants owed a duty
and said:

> 'They owe the duty, of course, to their employer or client, and also, I think, to any   *e*
> third person to whom they themselves show the accounts, or to whom they know
> their employer is going to show the accounts so as to induce him to invest money or
> take some other action on them. I do not think, however, the duty can be extended
> still further so as to include strangers of whom they have heard nothing and to
> whom their employer without their knowledge may choose to show their accounts.
> Once the accountants have handed their accounts to their employer, they are not, as   *f*
> a rule, responsible for what he does with them without their knowledge or consent.'

After further citation Woolf J said ([1981] 3 All ER 289 at 293):

> 'In *Candler*, although the facts are in some respects similar to those in the present
> case, it was clear that the accountants concerned had knowledge that the accounts
> were to be supplied to the plaintiffs, and of the specific purpose for which they were   *g*
> required. It is therefore understandable that Denning LJ, having dealt with liability
> of accountants who had such knowledge and the position of strangers to the
> accountants to whom their employer without their knowledge chose to show their
> accounts, did not deal specifically with the position where the accountants had no
> actual knowledge that the accounts would be shown to a particular person, but   *h*
> should reasonably have foreseen that the accounts could be shown to a third person
> who would rely on them.'

Woolf J then referred to the well-known passage from the judgment of Cardozo CJ in
Ultramares Corp v Touche (1931) 255 NY 170 at 179:

> 'If liability for negligence exists, a thoughtless slip or blunder, the failure to detect   *j*
> a theft or forgery beneath the cover of deceptive entries, may expose accountants to
> a liability in an indeterminate amount for an indeterminate time to an indeterminate
> class. The hazards of a business conducted on these terms are so extreme as to
> enkindle doubt whether a flaw may not exist in the implication of a duty that
> exposes to these consequences.'

Woolf J then said that if the law had stood there he would have felt constrained to hold
a that there was no general duty based on foreseeability, but the law had not stood there
and he cited next the oft-cited passage from the speech of Lord Wilberforce in *Anns v
Merton London Borough* [1977] 2 All ER 492 at 498–499, [1978] AC 728 at 751:

'Through the trilogy of cases in this House, *Donoghue v Stevenson* [1932] AC 562,
[1932] All ER Rep 1, *Hedley Byrne & Co Ltd v Heller & Partners Ltd* [1963] 3 All ER
575, [1964] AC 465 and *Home Office v Dorset Yacht Co Ltd* [1970] 2 All ER 294, [1970]
b AC 1004, the position has now been reached that in order to establish that a duty of
care arises in a particular situation, it is not necessary to bring the facts of that
situation within those of previous situations in which a duty of care has been held
to exist. Rather the question has to be approached in two stages. First one has to ask
whether, as between the alleged wrongdoer and the person who has suffered damage
there is a sufficient relationship of proximity or neighbourhood such that, in the
c reasonable contemplation of the former, carelessness on his part may be likely to
cause damage to the latter, in which case a prima facie duty of care arises. Secondly,
if the first question is answered affirmatively, it is necessary to consider whether
there are any considerations which ought to negative, or to reduce or limit the scope
of the duty or the class of person to whom it is owed or the damages to which a
d breach of it may give rise (see the *Dorset Yacht* case [1970] 2 All ER 294 at 297–298,
[1970] AC 1004 at 1027, per Lord Reid). Examples of this are *Hedley Byrne & Co Ltd
v Heller & Partners Ltd* where the class of potential plaintiffs was reduced to those
shown to have relied on the correctness of statements made, and *Weller & Co v Foot
and Mouth Disease Research Institute* [1965] 3 All ER 560, [1960] 1 QB 569 and (I cite
these merely as illustrations, without discussion) cases about "economic loss" where,
e a duty having been held to exist, the nature of the recoverable damages was limited
(see *SCM (United Kingdom) Ltd v W J Whittall & Son Ltd* [1970] 3 All ER 245, [1971]
1 QB 337, *Spartan Steel and Alloys Ltd v Martin & Co (Contractors) Ltd* [1972] 3 All ER
557, [1973] QB 27).'

Woolf J also cited a passage from the speech of Lord Salmon ([1977] 2 All ER 492 at 512–
f 513, [1978] AC 728 at 769):

'There are a wide variety of instances in which a statement is negligently made by
a professional man which he knows will be relied on by many people besides his
client, eg a well-known firm of accountants certifies in a prospectus the annual
profits of the company issuing it and unfortunately, due to negligence on the part
of the accountants, the profits are seriously overstated. Those persons who invested
g in the company in reliance on the accuracy of the accountants' certificate would
have a claim for damages against the accountants for any money they might have
lost as a result of the accountants' negligence: see the *Hedley Byrne* case.'

Next he examined the New Zealand Court of Appeal's decision in *Scott Group Ltd v
McFarlane* [1978] 1 NZLR 553. That was another take-over case; the court was divided
h but Woolf J extracted from the judgments that two members of the court, applying the
foreseeability test from *Anns*, thought that a sufficient degree of proximity existed to
impose liability notwithstanding the fact that the auditors had no direct knowledge of
the plaintiffs or that a take-over from any quarter was contemplated.
Lastly he relied on certain passages in the judgment of Megarry V-C in *Ross v Caunters
(a firm)* [1979] 3 All ER 580, [1980] Ch 297. This is yet another case where the straight
j foreseeability test from *Anns* was used to impose a duty of care on a solicitor to the
beneficiary in a client's will.
After this review of the case law Woolf J said ([1981] 3 All ER 289 at 296–297):

'Without laying down any principle which is intended to be of general application,
on the basis of the authorities which I have cited, the appropriate test for establishing

whether a duty of care exists appears in this case to be whether the defendants knew
or reasonably should have foreseen at the time the accounts were audited that a *a*
person might rely on those accounts for the purpose of deciding whether or not to
take over the company and therefore could suffer loss if the accounts were inaccurate.
Such an approach does place a limitation on those entitled to contend that there has
been a breach of duty owed to them. First of all, they must have relied on the
accounts and, second, they must have done so in circumstances where the auditors
either knew that they would or ought to have known that they might. If the *b*
situation is one where it would not be reasonable for the accounts to be relied on,
then, in the absence of express knowledge, the auditor would be under no duty.
This places a limit on the circumstances in which the audited accounts can be relied
on and the period for which they can be relied on. The longer the period which
elapses prior to the accounts being relied on, from the date on which the auditor
gave his certificate, the more difficult it will be to establish that the auditor ought to *c*
have foreseen that his certificate would, in those circumstances, be relied on.'

The *JEB Fasteners* case was relied on and followed in a case in the Outer House in
Twomax Ltd v Dickson M'Farlane & Robinson 1982 SC 113. In that case the three pursuers
had bought shares in a company relying on the audited accounts. The Lord Ordinary
(Stewart) found as a fact that Mr M'Farlane, the auditor, did not know that any of the *d*
three pursuers were potential investors when he audited the accounts but, applying the
approach suggested by Woolf J, held that the auditors did owe a duty of care. It is
instructive to see how the judge did this. He said (at 125):

'Mr M'Farlane's state of knowledge when he audited the 1973 accounts included
a number of matters which I consider relevant to the assessment of what he should
reasonably have foreseen. He was aware that Kintyre was suffering from a shortage *e*
of capital. He was aware during the summer months of 1973 that a director, Mr
Anderson, wished to dispose of his shareholding. He was aware that this shareholding
was substantial, amounting to 10,000 shares. The defenders had in fact advertised
in the newspaper under a box number on behalf of Mr Anderson. He knew for
certain that the accounts were being made available to lenders in so far as he knew
they were lodged with the company's bank. He knew that auditors' certificates, *f*
when they were "clean" certificates, were commonly relied on by shareholders,
potential investors, and potential lenders. In the whole circumstances I consider that
Mr M'Farlane should have foreseen before he certified the 1973 accounts that these
accounts might be relied on by a potential investor for the purpose of deciding
whether or not to invest. The situation was such that I would have though it an
inevitable inference that Mr M'Farlane should have realised by the time he came to *g*
grant his audit certificate that there would shortly be some dealings in the issued
shares of Kintyre and might well be fresh shares issued in order to inject new capital
into the company. While he did not know then about Twomax and Mr Gordon he
should, in my view, reasonably have foreseen that there would be incorporations or
individuals who would be interested potential investors either in the sense of *h*
purchasing shares already issued or of taking up any fresh issue. To these, the latest
audited accounts of the company would be of very great importance in influencing
them whether or not to invest and at what price. I, therefore, consider that in respect
of Twomax and Mr Gordon, both being in the class of persons who were potential
investors, Mr M'Farlane owed a *prima facie* duty of care in the auditing of the 1973
accounts. That answers affirmatively the first question posed by Lord Wilberforce *j*
in *Anns*.'

I think that the judges in these two cases, *JEB Fasteners* and *Twomax*, understood the
first stage of the test in *Anns* in the first sense referred to by Lord Keith in *Yuen Kun-yeu v
A-G of Hong Kong* [1987] 2 All ER 705 at 710, [1988] AC 175 at 191. They appreciated the
conflict with what I may call 'the *Ultramares* control' and sought to resolve it by confining

foreseeability. Now that the later development of the law has uncoupled proximity from
a foreseeability it is no longer necessary to attempt what I regard as an artificial constriction
of foreseeability. Assume that auditors know, as a result of their professional skill and
experience, that the state of the company is such that a take-over bid may be made, I do
not think that, if a bid is made, that knowledge alone creates a sufficient proximity
between bidder and auditor to impose a duty of care on the auditor. In any given case
the fact that the number of potential take-over bidders is less, or far less if you like, than
b the number of potential share buyers does not produce proximity. In my judgment
there has to be something linking the auditor to the person relying on his certificate
other than knowledge that some person or persons may rely on the certificate. The
linkage which I regard as necessary has sometimes been identified in the cases as
'assumption of responsibility' or 'a special relationship', but I think that it is the same
concept. Obvious examples were given by Denning LJ in *Candler*'s case where it will be
c remembered the accounts had been produced for the express purpose of being shown to
an identified would-be investor. I do not regard it as necessary or desirable to say more as
to what facts may provide the necessary linkage.

In the present case, if one disregards the fact that Caparo were shareholders, I am
satisfied that on the facts pleaded the auditors did not owe any duty of care to Caparo.

Caparo were in fact shareholders: see para 4 of the statement of claim. Counsel for
d Caparo submitted that that fact alone was sufficient to satisfy the requirement of
proximity. I must examine that submission.

Although auditors are employed by the company, the statutory provisions focus on
the report which they are required to make to the shareholders and I have no doubt that
they are under a like duty to exercise care and skill in making their report. Similar
provisions in the Companies Act 1879 were considered in this court in *Re London and*
e *General Bank (No 2)* [1895] 2 Ch 673, [1895–9] All ER Rep 953. In that case the auditors
made a report to the directors pointing out in detail the unsatisfactory nature of the
bank's main asset, 'loans to customers and other securities'. They ended saying that in
their opinion no dividend should be paid for the year. They were persuaded by the
chairman to omit that last sentence from the report before it went to the board. Their
certificate, as laid before shareholders, concluded: 'The value of the assets as shewn on the
f balance-sheet is dependent upon realisation.' As originally drafted it had gone on to say
'And on this point we have reported specifically to the board', but again the chairman
prevailed on them to withdraw that sentence. At the general meeting, on the chairman's
proposal, a dividend was declared. It turned out that the dividend could only be paid and
was paid out of capital. When the bank was wound up the liquidator claimed the sum
paid out as dividend from the auditors. Lindley LJ said ([1895] 2 Ch 673 at 682, [1895–
g 9] All ER Rep 953 at 956–957):

> 'It is impossible to read s. 7 of the Companies Act, 1879, without being struck
> with the importance of the enactment that the auditors are to be appointed by the
> shareholders, and are to report to them directly, and not to or through the directors.
> The object of this enactment is obvious. It evidently is to secure to the shareholders
h > independent and reliable information respecting the true financial position of the
> company at the time of the audit. The articles of this particular company are even
> more explicit on this point than the statute itself, and remove any possible ambiguity
> to which the language of the statute taken alone may be open if very narrowly
> criticised. It is no part of an auditor's duty to give advice, either to directors or
> shareholders, as to what they ought to do. An auditor has nothing to do with the
j > prudence or imprudence of making loans with or without security. It is nothing to
> him whether the business of a company is being conducted prudently or
> imprudently, profitably or unprofitably. It is nothing to him whether dividends are
> properly or improperly declared, provided he discharges his own duty to the
> shareholders. His business is to ascertain and state the true financial position of the
> company at the time of the audit, and his duty is confined to that.'

The court held that the auditors had failed to discharge their duty to the shareholders.

There is a further passage in the judgment of Lindley LJ to which I must refer. He *a* said ([1895] 2 Ch 673 at 688, [1895–9] All ER Rep 953 at 959–960):

> 'A point was made that the form of the order was wrong. But there is nothing in this. Mr. Theobald could obviously be sued alone in an action at law for breach of his statutory duty as auditor, and for damages resulting from the breach of duty, and the measure of damages would be the sum which he has been ordered to pay.'

b

In my judgment the proper analysis of that case is that the shareholders in general meeting took a decision, which but for the breach of duty of the auditors they would not have taken, and that decision caused loss to the company which it could have brought an action to recover. The court was not considering whether any duty was owed by the auditors to the shareholders in their individual capacities. Indeed, in their individual capacities so far from suffering any loss each had gained to the extent of the dividend *c* received.

The statutory duty owed by auditors to shareholders is, I think, a duty owed to them as a body. I appreciate that it is difficult to see how the overstatement of the accounts can cause damage to the shareholders as a body: it will be the underlying reasons for the overstatement which cause damage, for example fraudulent abstraction of assets by directors or servants, but such loss is recoverable by the company. I am anxious to limit *d* the present case to deciding whether the statutory duty operates to protect the individual shareholder as a potential buyer of further shares. If I am wrong in thinking that under the statute no duty is owed to shareholders as individuals, then I think that the duty must be confined to transactions in which the shareholder can only participate because he is a shareholder. The statute imposes a duty to shareholders as a class and the duty should not extend to an individual save as a member of the class in respect of some class activity. *e* Buying shares in a company is not such an activity. Selling shares may be, for only a shareholder can sell shares. (I disregard certain stock exchange short-term gambling practices). We do not have to decide whether in a case where the accounts understate the value of the company a shareholder who sells shares and suffers loss could claim that loss as damages for breach of statutory duty. I say this because, in so far as the statutory duty *f* is relied on as dispensing with other proof of proximity, it can only do so within its confines.

I appreciate that it can be said that it is not sensible to distinguish between a shareholder buying shares and a shareholder selling shares, but I regard it as more sensible than the alternative. Let me give an example. Two friends each have money to invest. One is a shareholder and receives the report with the certified accounts; having read it he hands it to his friend, who also reads it, and both decide individually to buy shares. I find it *g* very difficult to draw any distinction between these two and as I am satisfied that the friend does not establish the required proximity I conclude nor does the shareholder.

I have considered the statutory duty of auditors to shareholders. I see no reason to impose any wider duty at common law.

For these reasons I conclude that the auditors did not owe any duty to Caparo in their *h* capacity as shareholders. Something more was required to create what I regard as the necessary linkage and it is not present in this case.

For these reasons I would dismiss this appeal but, as Bingham and Taylor LJJ take a different view, the order must be that the appeal be allowed.

Appeal allowed. Leave to appeal to House of Lords granted.   *j*

Solicitors: *Berwin Leighton* (for Caparo); *Freshfields* (for the auditors).

Raina Levy Barrister.

Practice Direction

a

CHANCERY DIVISION

Practice – Chancery Division – Hearings by judges outside London – Bristol – New arrangements
– Weekly sittings for motions and other urgent business – Urgent applications at other times –
Commencement of proceedings – Authorised jurisdiction.
b

I am pleased to be able to announce new arrangements for the hearing of cases assigned to the Chancery Division of the High Court. From January 1989 the judge authorised by the Lord Chancellor to hear such cases will sit regularly at the Old Council House, Bristol. He will be available on at least one fixed day each week to hear motions and other urgent business and he will be able to offer fixed and, it is hoped, early dates for trials and other
c longer hearings.

In addition the judge should be available to hear urgent applications, even out of court hours, whenever necessary.

Proceedings will be issued, as at present, in the High Court Registry, Greyfriars, Bristol. When actions commenced in the county court involve issues of Chancery law or
d procedure, these will be heard, if convenient, by the Chancery judge.

The jurisdiction authorised by the Lord Chancellor is unrestricted save as regards particular categories of Chancery business, primarily revenue cases. Nevertheless, if a case arises in any of the excluded categories, or which for any other reason should be heard by a judge of the High Court, and a local hearing is desirable, then I have the authority of the Vice-Chancellor to say that, whenever possible, arrangements will be
e made for a High Court judge to hear the case in Bristol or such other trial centre as may be convenient.

It is hoped that these new arrangements will enable the courts to offer the public in general, and the business and financial communities in particular, a prompt and efficient service for the hearing and resolution of all Chancery disputes.

f
NOLAN J
Presiding Judge
20 December 1988   Western Circuit.

Practice Direction   a

CHANCERY DIVISION

Practice – Chancery Division – Hearings by judges outside London – Cardiff – New arrangements
– Weekly sittings for motions and other urgent business – Urgent applications at other times –
Commencement of proceedings – Authorised jurisdiction.   b

I am pleased to be able to announce new arrangements for the hearing of cases assigned
to the Chancery Division of the High Court. From January 1989 the judge authorised by
the Lord Chancellor to hear such cases will sit regularly at the Law Courts in Cardiff. He
will be available on at least one fixed day each week to hear motions and other urgent
business and he will be able to offer fixed and, it is hoped, early dates for trials and other   c
longer hearings.

In addition the judge should be available in South Wales to hear urgent applications,
even out of court hours, whenever necessary.

Proceedings will be issued, as at present, in the High Court Registry, Westgate Street,
Cardiff. When actions commenced in the county court involve issues of Chancery law or
procedure, these will be heard, if convenient, by the Chancery judge.   d

The jurisidiction authorised by the Lord Chancellor is unrestricted save as regards
particular categories of Chancery business, primarily revenue cases. Nevertheless, if a
case arises in any of the excluded categories, or which for any other reason should be
heard by a judge of the High Court, and a local hearing is desirable, then I have the
authority of the Vice-Chancellor to say that, whenever possible, arrangements will be
made for a High Court judge to hear the case in Cardiff or such other trial centre as may   e
be convenient.

It is hoped that these new arrangements will enable the courts to offer the public in
general, and the business and financial communities in particular, a prompt and efficient
service for the hearing and resolution of all Chancery disputes.

                                                                        EVANS J f
                                                                     Presiding Judge
20 December 1988   Wales and Chester Circuit.

Smith v Stages and another

HOUSE OF LORDS

LORD KEITH OF KINKEL, LORD BRANDON OF OAKBROOK, LORD GRIFFITHS, LORD GOFF OF CHIEVELEY AND LORD LOWRY

26, 27, 31 OCTOBER, 1 NOVEMBER 1988, 23 FEBRUARY 1989

Vicarious liability – Master and servant – Act within course of employment – Journey to temporary job – Employee paid wages while travelling to and from temporary job – Time and mode of travel left to employee's discretion – Whether employee acting within course of employment when travelling to and from temporary job – Whether employer vicariously liable for employee's negligence while travelling to and from temporary job in his own car.

The employee was employed by the employers as a peripatetic lagger to install insulation at power stations. In August 1977 he was working on a power station in the Midlands when he was taken off that job and sent with another employee, the first defendant, to carry out an urgent job on a power station in Wales. The two employees were paid eight hours' pay for the travelling time to Wales and eight hours' pay for the journey back, as well as the equivalent of the rail fare for the journey, although no stipulation was made as to the mode of travel. The two employees travelled to Wales in the first defendant's car and stayed a week in Wales while working on the power station there. At the end of the job, after working for 24 hours without a break in order to finish the job, they decided to drive straight back to the Midlands. On the way back the car, driven by the first defendant, left the road and crashed through a brick wall. The employee was seriously injured and he brought an action against the first defendant, who was uninsured, and against the employers alleging that they were vicariously liable for the first defendant's negligence since he had been acting in the course of his employment while driving the two employees back to the Midlands. The employee subsequently died from unrelated causes and his widow continued the action on behalf of his estate. The judge held that the accident had been caused by the first defendant's negligence but further held that the employers were not liable because he had not been acting in the course of his employment at the time of the accident. On appeal, the Court of Appeal reversed his decision and held that the employers were vicariously liable for the first defendant's negligence. The employers appealed to the House of Lords.

Held – An employee who for a short time was required by his employer to work at a different place of work some distance away from his usual place of work was acting in the course of his employment when returning to his ordinary residence after completing the temporary work if he travelled back to his ordinary residence in the employer's time, which he would be doing if he was paid wages (and not merely a travelling allowance) for the time travelled notwithstanding that the time and mode of travel were left to his discretion. Accordingly, since the employees had been paid while driving back to the Midlands they had been travelling in the employers' time and the employers were vicariously liable for the first defendant's negligence. The appeal would therefore be dismissed (see p 834 h j, p 838 a to d h, p 850 d e and p 851 c to g j, post).

St Helens Colliery Co Ltd v Hewitson [1923] All ER Rep 249, *Canadian Pacific Rly Co v Lockhart* [1942] 2 All ER 464 and dictum of Sir John Donaldson MR in *Nancollas v Insurance Officer* [1985] 1 All ER 833 at 837 applied.

Vandyke v Fender (Sun Insurance Office Ltd, third party) [1970] 2 All ER 335 approved.

Per curiam. An employee travelling on the highway will be acting in the course of his employment if, and only if, he is at the material time going about his employer's business. The duty to turn up for work must not be confused with the concept of already being 'on duty' while travelling to it (see p 834 h j, p 836 c g to p 837 a and p 851 b c, post).

Notes

For accidents arising out of or in the course of employment, see 33 Halsbury's Laws (4th
edn) paras 486–497, and for cases on the subject, see 35 Digest (Reissue) 6863–707, 6723–
6840.

Cases referred to in opinions

Alderman v Great Western Rly Co [1937] 2 All ER 408, [1937] AC 454, HL.
Barras v Aberdeen Steam Trawling and Fishing Co Ltd [1933] AC 402, [1933] All ER Rep 52,
   HL.
Blee v London and North Eastern Rly Co [1937] 4 All ER 270, [1938] AC 126, HL.
Canadian Pacific Rly Co v Lockhart [1942] 2 All ER 464, [1942] AC 591, PC.
Elleanor v Cavendish Woodhouse Ltd [1973] 1 Lloyd's Rep 313, CA.
Harvey v R G O'Dell Ltd (Galway, third party) [1958] 1 All ER 657, [1958] 2 QB 78, [1958]
   2 WLR 473.
Nancollas v Insurance Officer [1985] 1 All ER 833, CA.
Netherton v Coles [1945] 1 All ER 227, CA.
Nottingham v Aldridge (Prudential Assurance Co Ltd, third party) [1971] 2 All ER 751, [1971]
   2 QB 739, [1971] 3 WLR 1.
R v Industrial Injury Benefits Tribunal, ex p Fieldhouse (1974) 17 KIR 63, DC.
St Helens Colliery Co Ltd v Hewitson [1924] AC 59, [1923] All ER Rep 249, HL.
Vandyke v Fender (Sun Insurance Office Ltd, third party) [1970] 2 All ER 335, [1970] 2 QB
   292, [1970] 2 WLR 929, CA.
Weaver v Tredegar Iron and Coal Co Ltd [1940] 3 All ER 157, [1940] AC 955, HL.

Appeal

The second defendants, Darlington Insulation Co Ltd (the employers), appealed with the
leave of the Appeal Committee of the House of Lords given on 12 April 1988 against the
decision of the Court of Appeal (Lord Donaldson MR, Glidewell LJ and Sir Denys
Buckley) ([1988] ICR 201) on 1 December 1987 allowing the appeal of the plaintiff, Mary
Smith, the widow and administratrix of Ronald George Machin, against the decision of
his Honour Judge Wilson Mellor QC, sitting as a judge of the High Court in the Queen's
Bench Division at Birmingham, upholding the claim brought by Mr Machin and
continued by the plaintiff after his death against the first defendant, George Stages, for
damages for personal injury but dismissing Mr Machin's claim against the employers
that they were vicariously liable for the first defendant's negligence as his employers.
The facts are set out in the opinion of Lord Goff.

Piers Ashworth QC and *Peter Bowers* for the employers.
D H Stembridge for the plaintiff.
The first defendant did not appear.

Their Lordships took time for consideration.

23 February. The following opinions were delivered.

LORD KEITH OF KINKEL. My Lords, I have had the opportunity of considering in
draft the speech to be delivered by my noble and learned friend Lord Lowry. I agree
with it, and for the reasons he gives would dismiss the appeal.

LORD BRANDON OF OAKBROOK. My Lords, for the reasons given by my noble
and learned friends Lord Goff and Lord Lowry I would dismiss the appeal.

LORD GRIFFITHS. My Lords, I agree that this appeal should be dismissed for the
reasons given in the speech of my noble and learned friend Lord Lowry.

LORD GOFF OF CHIEVELEY. My Lords, Mr Machin and the first defendant, Mr
a Stages, were employed by the second defendants, Darlington Insulation Co Ltd (the
employers). The employers specialise in the insulation of pipes, boilers and power
stations. Mr Machin and Mr Stages worked for them as laggers at powers stations; they
had both worked for the employers in that capacity for many years. In August 1977 they
were members of a group of about 20 laggers, employed by the employers, working at
Drakelow power station at Burton-on-Trent. At that time, Mr Machin appears to have
b been living in Burton-on-Trent; it is not clear where Mr Stages was living. There was
another job to be done at Pembroke power station. Mr Pye, the employers' contract
manager, visited the power station at Pembroke to assess the job. It was urgent, and had
to be completed by 29 August 1977. So it was decided to withdraw Mr Machin and Mr
Stages from Drakelow to do the job at Pembroke. They went down to Pembroke on
Monday, 22 August, travelling in Mr Stages's car. They started work there on Tuesday,
c 23 August; they worked right through the rest of the week and the following weekend,
working long hours, and, by working straight through Sunday and Sunday night,
finished the job by 8.30 am on Monday, 29 August, which was the August bank holiday.
Shortly after finishing work on the Monday morning, they drove back home in Mr
Stages's car. On the way there was a serious accident. Mr Stages's car left the road; it
crashed through a brick wall into a field, and both men were seriously injured. No other
d vehicle was involved. Mr Stages, the driver, was plainly at fault. Mr Machin survived the
accident, but he died about two years later from lung cancer unconnected with the
accident.

In December 1978, before his death, Mr Machin commenced proceedings against Mr
Stages for damages for his personal injuries arising out of the accident. In the following
March the employers were joined as second defendants; this was no doubt because Mr
e Stages proved to be uninsured. Mr Machin alleged that the employers were vicariously
liable for the negligence of Mr Stages. This allegation raised the crucial question in the
case, which was whether, at the time of the accident, Mr Stages was acting in the course
of his employment with the employers.

After Mr Machin's death in August 1979, his widow continued the action on behalf of
her husband's estate. In the action, the employers alleged contributory negligence on the
f part of Mr Machin, in allowing himself to be driven by Mr Stages when he knew that he
had not had enough sleep. The action came on for trial in October 1986 before his
Honour Judge Wilson Mellor QC, sitting as a judge of the High Court. The judge held
that Mr Stages (who took no part in the trial) had been negligent, and dismissed the
employers' allegation of contributory negligence against Mr Machin; but he dismissed
the action against the employers on the grounds that Mr Stages was at the relevant time
g acting neither as agent for the employers nor in the course of his employment with
them. In December 1987 the Court of Appeal reversed that decision, holding that Mr
Stages had been acting in the course of his employment (see [1988] ICR 201). It is against
that decision that the employers now appeal to your Lordships' House.

The present case can be seen as one of those cases, which have troubled the courts in
h the past, in which the question has arisen whether an employee, travelling to or from a
place of work, is acting in the course of his employment. In order to consider the question
in the present case, it is necessary first to examine the facts of the case in a little detail.
The full facts are set out in that speech of my noble and learned friend Lord Lowry, on
whose account I gratefully rely.

The employers set aside a normal working day (Monday, 22 August) for the two men's
j journey to Pembroke; they were paid as for an eight-hour day for the journey. In
addition, each received the equivalent of their rail fare as travelling expenses. The
employers made no direction as to the means by which the men travelled. The two men
were however expected to start work at 8 am on Tuesday, 23 August, and to finish the
job by 8.30 am on Monday, 29 August, which, to their great credit, they did. After that,

they were expected to report for work at Drakelow at 8 am on Wednesday, 31 August. While they were working at Pembroke, they were paid for the actual hours worked by them, the usual premium rate being paid for overtime. An allowance was paid for their lodgings in Pembroke. At the end of the job they were also paid eight hours' sleeping time, because they had worked for one day and one night consecutively (on Sunday, 28 August). Although the men were expected to sleep on the next day, Monday, there was no way in which the employers could compel them to sleep on that day. Since Monday was the August bank holiday, they were also paid holiday time for that day. Another normal working day (Tuesday, 30 August) was made available for the journey back. The two men were again paid as for an eight-hour day for the journey; they were also given the same allowance for travelling expenses as on the way out. Once again, it is plain that they could travel by any means they liked; their duty was to report for work at Drakelow on the Wednesday morning.

I now turn to the applicable principles of law. The fundamental principle is that an employee is acting in the course of his employment when he is doing what he is employed to do, to which it is sufficient for present purposes to add, or anything which is reasonably incidental to his employment. In *Canadian Pacific Rly Co v Lockhart* [1942] 2 All ER 464 at 468, [1942] AC 591 at 600 (a case concerned with vicarious liability) Lord Thankerton said: 'In these cases the first consideration is the ascertainment of what the servant was employed to do.' This statement reflects a statement of principle by Lord Atkinson in an earlier case, *St Helens Colliery Co Ltd v Hewitson* [1924] AC 59 at 70–71, [1923] All ER Rep 249 at 256 (a workmen's compensation case), in which he said:

'I myself have been rash enough to suggest a test—namely, that a workman is acting in the course of his employment when he is engaged "in doing something he was employed to do." Or what is, in other and I think better words, in effect the same thing—namely, when he is doing something in discharge of a duty to his employer, directly or indirectly, imposed upon him by his contract of service. The true ground upon which the test should be based is a duty to the employer arising out of the contract of employment, but it is to be borne in mind that the word "employment" as here used covers and includes things belonging to or arising out of it.'

As usual, it is comparatively easy to state the principle; but it is more difficult to apply it to the facts of individual cases. Even so, it is important always to keep the principle in mind.

As I have already observed, we are here concerned with a case which may be seen as one of those cases concerned with travelling to or from work. I have used guarded language in so describing it, because (as will appear) I do not consider the present case to fall strictly within that category of case. Even so, it is helpful to use the cases in that category as a starting point. We can begin with the simple proposition that, in ordinary circumstances, when a man is travelling to or from his place of work, he is not acting in the course of his employment. So a bank clerk who commutes to the City of London every day from Sevenoaks is not acting in the course of his employment when he walks across London Bridge from the station to his bank in the City. This is because he is not employed to travel from his home to the bank: he is employed to work at the bank, his place of work, and so his duty is to arrive there in time for his working day. Nice points can arise about the precise time, or place, at which he may be held to have arrived at work; but these do not trouble us in the present case. Likewise, of course, he is not acting in the course of his employment when he is travelling home after his day's work is over. If, however, a man is obliged by his employer to travel to work by means of transport provided by his employer, he may be held to be acting in the course of his employment when so doing.

These are the normal cases. There are, however, circumstances in which, when a man is travelling to (or from) a place where he is doing a job for his employer, he will be held

to be acting in the course of his employment. Some of these are listed by Lord Atkin in
Blee v London and North Eastern Rly Co [1937] 4 All ER 270 at 273, [1938] AC 126 at 131–
132. So, if a man is employed to do jobs for his employer at various places during the
day, such as a man who goes from door to door canvassing for business, or who distributes
goods to customers, or who services equipment like washing machines or dishwashers,
he will ordinarily be held to be acting in the course of his employment when travelling
from one destination to another, and may also be held to do so when travelling from his
home to his first destination and home again after his last. Again, it has been held that,
in certain circumstances, a man who is called out from his home at night to deal with an
emergency may be acting in the course of his employment when travelling from his
home to his place of work to deal with the emergency: see _Blee v London and North Eastern
Rly Co_. There are many other cases.

But how do we distinguish the cases in this category in which a man is acting in the
course of his employment from those in which he is not? The answer is, I fear, that
everything depends on the circumstances. As Sir John Donaldson MR said in _Nancollas v
Insurance Officer_ [1985] 1 All ER 833 at 836, the authorities—

> 'approve an approach which requires the court to have regard to and to weigh in
> the balance every factor which can be said in any way to point towards or away from
> a finding that the claimant was in the course of his employment. In the context of
> the present appeals, there are a number of such factors to which we must have
> regard, but none is of itself decisive.'

For example, the fact that a man is being paid by his employer in respect of the relevant
period of time is often important, but cannot of itself be decisive. A man is usually paid
nowadays during his holidays; and it often happens that an employer may allow a man
to take the afternoon off, or even a whole day off, without affecting his wages. In such
circumstances, he will ordinarily not be acting in the course of his employment despite
the fact that he is being paid. Indeed, any rule that payment at the relevant time is
decisive would be very difficult to apply in the case of a salaried man. Let me, however,
give an example concerned with travelling to work. Suppose that a man is applying for a
job, and it turns out that he would have a pretty arduous journey between his home and
his new place of work, lasting about an hour each way, which is deterring him from
taking the job. His prospective employer may want to employ him, and may entice him
by offering him an extra hour's pay at each end of the day, say ten hours' pay a day
instead of eight. In those circumstances he would not, I think, be acting in the course of
his employment when travelling to or from work. This is because he would not be
employed to make the journey: the extra pay would simply be given to him in
recognition of the fact that his journey to and from work was an arduous one.

That example serves, I think, to point up the two alternative solutions under
consideration in the present case. For to me, the question is this. Was Mr Stages employed
to travel to and from Pembroke? Or was the pay given to him simply in recognition of
the fact that he had lost two days' work at Drakelow because, in order to work at the
power station at Pembroke, he would have to make his own way to Pembroke and back
again to the Midlands? If we can solve that problem, we can answer the question whether
Mr Stages was acting in the course of his employment when, worn out, he crashed his
car on the A40 near Llandeilo.

I propose first to consider the problem not in relation to his journey back from
Pembroke when the accident in fact happened, but in relation to his journey out to
Pembroke. I shall do so because I find it easier to consider the problem uncomplicated by
the fact that Monday, 29 August, was a bank holiday or by the fact that Mr Stages was
being paid eight hours' sleeping time because he had worked through the night of
Sunday, 28 August, although, as will appear, I consider both facts to be irrelevant. I
should add that Mr Stages's contract of service was not apparently in evidence before the
judge; and so, although that is normally a material document, sometimes a highly

material document, in these cases, your Lordships' House has (like the courts below) to reach a conclusion unassisted by the terms of the relevant contract.

I approach the matter as follows. I do not regard this case as an ordinary case of travelling to work. It would be more accurate to describe it as a case where an employee, who has for a short time to work for his employers at a different place of work some distance away from his usual place of work, has to move from his ordinary base to a temporary base (here lodgings in Pembroke) from which he will travel to work at the temporary place of work each day. For the purpose of moving base, a normal working day was set aside for Mr Stages's journey, for which he was paid as for an eight-hour day. In addition to his day's pay he was given a travel allowance for his journey, and an allowance for his lodgings at his temporary base in Pembroke. In my opinion, in all the circumstances of the case, Mr Stages was required by the employers to make this journey, so as to make himself available to do his work at the Pembroke power station, and it would be proper to describe him as having been employed to do so. The fact that he was not required by his employer to make the journey by any particular means, nor even required to make it on the particular working day made available to him, does not detract from the proposition that he was employed to make the journey. Had Mr Stages wished, he could have driven down on the afternoon of Sunday, 21 August, and have devoted the Monday to (for example) visiting friends near Pembroke. In such circumstances it could, I suppose, be said that Stages was not travelling 'in his employers' time'. But this would not matter; for the fact remains that the Monday, a normal working day, was made available for the journey, with full pay for that day to perform a task which he was required by the employers to perform.

I have it very much in mind that Mr Machin and Mr Stages were described by counsel for the employers as peripatetic laggers working at such sites as were available. This may well be an accurate description of their work. If so, their contracts of service may have provided at least an indication as to how far they would be acting in the course of their employment when changing from one power station to another. Indeed, accepting the description as correct, it is difficult to know how much weight to give to it in the absence of their contracts of service. However, the present case can in any event be differentiated on the basis that it was a departure from the norm in that it was concerned with a move to a temporary base to deal with an emergency, on the terms I have described.

I turn to Mr Stages's journey back. Another ordinary working day, Tuesday, 30 August, was made available for the journey, with the same pay, to enable him to return to his base in the Midlands to be ready to travel to work on the Wednesday morning. In my opinion, he was employed to make the journey back, just as he was employed to make the journey out to Pembroke. If he had chosen to go to sleep on the Monday morning and afternoon for eight hours or so, and then to drive home on the Monday evening so that he could have Tuesday free (as indeed Mr Pye expected him to do), that would not have detracted from the proposition that his journey was in the course of his employment. For this purpose, it was irrelevant that Monday was a bank holiday. Of course, it was wrong for him to succumb to the temptation of driving home on the Monday morning, just after he had completed so long a spell of work; but once again that cannot alter the fact that his journey was made in the course of his employment.

For these reasons, I would dismiss the appeal.

LORD LOWRY. My Lords, the plaintiff and respondent is the widow and administratrix of Ronald George Machin deceased (the deceased). He and the first defendant, George Stages, were employed as laggers by the second defendants and appellants, Darlington Insulation Co Ltd (the employers), and on 29 August 1977, having finished a lagging job at Pembroke power station, they were returning to the Midlands in Mr Stages's motor car when, by reason of Mr Stages's negligent driving, the car left the road and crashed and both men were seriously injured. The deceased died on 30 August

1979 from lung cancer which was unrelated to the 1977 accident but was caused by
a asbestosis for which the employers admitted liability.

On 11 December 1978 the deceased had sued Mr Stages for damages for personal
injuries, loss and damage sustained, as alleged, by reason of Mr Stages's negligence and
on 26 March 1979 (no doubt because Mr Stages proved to be uninsured and the Motor
Insurers' Bureau was by then out of reach) he had joined the employers as defendants
under RSC Ord 20, r 1, alleging that, as the employers of Mr Stages, they were vicariously
b liable for his negligence. The plaintiff continued this action for the benefit of the
deceased's estate under the Law Reform (Miscellaneous Provisions) Act 1934 and also
sued the employers under the Fatal Accidents Act 1976 for damages occasioned by the
deceased's death from lung cancer.

In the first action Mr Stages by his defence denied negligence but did not appear, nor
was he represented, at the trial or subsequently. The employers by their defence and at
c the trial denied that the accident to the deceased was caused by Mr Stages's negligence
and that either the deceased or Mr Stages was in the course of his employment at the
time of the accident and alleged that the accident was caused wholly or partly by the
negligence of the deceased in travelling with Mr Stages when the latter, to the knowledge
of the deceased, had not had sufficient rest.

Both actions were tried in October 1986 at Birmingham by his Honour Judge Wilson
d Mellor QC sitting as a judge of the High Court. In the first action he found Mr Stages to
have been negligent and rejected the allegation of contributory negligence, but gave
judgment for the employers against the plaintiff on the ground that Mr Stages was not
the agent of the employers or acting in the course of his employment at the time of the
accident. The judge then assessed the damages in both actions and stated his reasons on
10 November in a carefully considered judgment.

e Your Lordships have no further concern with the Fatal Accidents Act claim, but the
plaintiff appealed against the judgment in favour of the employers in the first action.
They in turn cross-appealed against the negative finding on contributory negligence. The
Court of Appeal (Sir John Donaldson MR, Glidewell LJ and Sir Denys Buckley) by their
judgment on 1 December 1987 allowed the plaintiff's appeal and dismissed the cross-
appeal (see [1988] ICR 201). From that judgment, in so far as it allowed the plaintiff's
f appeal, the employers have appealed by leave of this House. Thus the question whether
Mr Stages was acting in the course of his employment when driving his car at the time
of the accident is the sole question for your Lordships to decide. I turn first to the
evidence.

At the trial the plaintiff put in form BI 76, a questionnaire relating to an industrial
injuries claim by the deceased, which was issued by the Department of Health and Social
g Security at Burton-on-Trent and answered on 16 September 1977 by Mr William
Wilkinson, the office manager of the employers' Birmingham branch. The form
contained the erroneous statement that at the time of the accident the deceased was
travelling from one site to another, but nothing now turns on this.

The plaintiff also relied on interrogatories which had been administered to the
h employers, but the information contained in the answers appears from the employers'
evidence. The address of the deceased was given as 4 Short Street, Stapenhill, Burton-on-
Trent in the writ of summons when it was first issued.

As part of their evidence, the employers read a statement which Mr Wilkinson, who
had died in 1983, made to their solicitors in Birmingham in May 1981. It showed that
the employers had a Birmingham branch, of which the witness had been the office
j manager for 31 years, and that they applied insulation to a number of power stations
'throughout the southern area'. In August 1977 they had 20 or 30 men engaged at
Drakelow power station, Burton-on-Trent and also had a contract to carry out thermal
insulation at Pembroke power station. Mr Pye, the contracts manager, went to Pembroke
to price the job and assess the time required. It was urgent and had to be completed by
8.30 am on 29 August. The deceased and Mr Stages, both experienced men, were
'withdrawn' from Drakelow power station and sent to Pembroke power station. The

deceased was with the employers for nearly 23 years and Mr Stages for 12. Before they
went to Pembroke they were 'instructed by Mr Pye', who told them what had to be done,   *a*
when the job had to be completed and the number of hours involved.

The remainder of the statement reads as follows:

'They travelled down to Pembroke on Monday, 22 August 1977 and on that day
they were paid eight hours' travelling time. They were to be paid eight hours'
travelling time each way. They were given the equivalent of rail fare each as
travelling expenses. No stipulation was made as to how they travelled. We raised no   *b*
objection if they travelled by car. In fact we had no way of knowing how they
travelled. No stipulation was made when they travelled. They were given eight
hours' travelling on Monday, 22 August 1977 and we expected them to start work
at 8 am on Tuesday, 23 August 1977. They worked from Tuesday, 23 August 1977
through to the following Sunday night and Monday morning. They worked 11
hours on Tuesday, Wednesday and Thursday, and 9 hours on Friday. 13 hours on   *c*
the Saturday and 19 hours on Sunday into Monday morning. On the Sunday they
worked from 8.30 am to 6.30 pm and had a one-hour break in that time for meals.
They then recommenced at 9 pm and worked until 8.30 am the following morning
with a 1½-hour break in that spell. They were the actual working hours they were
paid for. The usual premium rate was paid on overtime hours. At Pembroke power   *d*
station the men clocked in and out but that was for the purpose of security at the
power station. It was not for our purposes. The men could clock in and rest if they
wished. We would not have known of the clocking in and out hours if it had not
been thought necessary to obtain them because of the accident. The men finished
their physical work at 8.30 am. That was the time they were paid until. They
clocked out at 8.37 am. On top of the hours they worked they were paid eight   *e*
hours' sleeping time. That was in accordance with our usual procedures. They were
aware of that and had each been paid that on several occasions before. The sleeping
time was given because they worked one day and one night consecutively and it
enabled them to rest before making their journey home and be paid for it. It was
accepted that the men required rest before returning home because they had been
deprived of their sleep by virtue of the work done. Although the men were paid to   *f*
rest there was no way we could enforce that. They could rest for as long or as little
as they liked without our knowledge. Monday, 29 August 1977 was a bank holiday.
That was the day they were paid sleeping time. On Tuesday, 30 August 1977 they
were paid eight hours' travelling time. They were expected to return to work at
Drakelow power station at 8 am on Wednesday, 31 August 1977. The men did not
ask us if they could travel back on the Monday and I would not have expected them   *g*
to. We had no jurisdiction over them after they clocked out because the moneys
they were paid after that time were allowances not for the work done. They would
have known that if they had asked us if they could travel on the Monday we would
have had to say no. It would not only have been unsafe but it was against the
regulations. We would in fact have forbidden them to travel by road without first
having their proper rest. The position was that we were not paying them to work   *h*
but were paying them an allowance in accordance with r 3(ii)(e) of the national
agreement between the Thermal Insulation Contracting Industry and the General
and Municipal Workers Union and the Transport and General Workers' Union.'

Only r 3 (overtime) of the national agreement was in evidence and only r 3(ii)(e) is
germane to this case: *j*

'Any operative working one day and one night consecutively shall not work for
the ensuing day of 8 hours which shall be paid at plain time rates.'

It must perforce be assumed that the national agreement contains nothing about
sleeping or travelling time, pay or allowances which sheds light on the question.

a Mr Pye then gave evidence. He had since 1977 moved to Darlington as technical representative. Examining him, counsel for the employers said: 'As I understand the position the men are paid the rail fare between their home base and wherever they are going to work?' The witness confirmed this and stated that the men received the fare (in each direction) in cash. He also confirmed that the employers had no control over how the men travelled to the site, except where company transport was supplied. He would know how the men travelled, but would not have to give permission. He added: 'I am

b not concerned how they travel. I am concerned that they get on the job and get it completed on time.' It did not matter, he said, in which direction the men went or how long they took. I give the next passage verbatim:

'Q. In order to get to Pembroke are they given any time paid? A. Yes, they are paid travelling time.

Q. Is that based on an eight-hour day? A. For Pembroke it was eight hours
c travelling. Normally it is the travelling time plus time to find accommodation, and we thought eight hours is an appropriate time.

Q. So they received payment for that? A. Yes.

Q. Did they receive a day off whilst they were being paid that?

Counsel for the plaintiff: Do not lead the witness, please.

d A. No, no. They don't receive a day off. The day they are travelling down there they are receiving time.

Q. So they are paid a day to travel? A. Yes.

Q. Does it matter if they travel during that day or not? A. No, they are given time when they should report to the job, and normally they travel the day previous because they have got to find accommodation as well, you see.'

e Asked when the two men were expected to report for work again, Mr Pye said: 'At 8 am Wednesday at Drakelow.' He had no control from 8.30 am on Monday until then. The employers had to pay 'eight hours' sleeping time' to men who worked a day and a night consecutively, and, in this case, 'eight hours' travelling time' as well. It did not matter to the employers what the men did between finishing the job and reporting for work on the Wednesday. When asked if he would have expected the men to travel

f straight after finishing work, the witness replied: 'Not really, no, but I have got to be truthful; it does go on, or it did go on at that time, you know.'

I shall refer to just one passage in the cross-examination of counsel for the plaintiff:

'Q. You knew they were travelling by motor car? A. Yes.

Q. In Mr Stages's motor car? A. Yes.

g Q. You knew that Mr Machin would be travelling as his passenger? A. Yes.

Q. You or the company was paying them wages during the time they spent travelling from the Midlands to this power station, and again back from the power station to the Midlands, were you not? A. Yes.'

Mr Pye also clarified the point that the men (like other employees) received ten and
h two-thirds hours' pay (time and a third) in respect of Monday, 29 August because it was a public holiday, as well as eight hours' travelling time in each direction and eight hours' sleeping time.

The last defence witness was Mr Bostock. I refer to his cross-examination on the question of sleeping time:

j 'Q. They are not doing physical work (we know that), but they were regarded as being employed by you on that Monday, were they not, and you were paying them? A. They were using the allowance for sleeping time, yes.

Q. It was not an allowance; it was a wage, was it not? A. It was a wage for sleeping time, yes, which was paid to them in respect of the eight hours they would spend sleeping.'

I have devoted some time to the evidence because in this case, as in most others, the facts constitute the essential basis for the legal inquiry into the question at issue. The picture may be regarded as incomplete, since your Lordships do not know the terms of Mr Stages's contract of service or the arrangements which the employers may customarily have made with regard to the pay and allowances of their men when travelling from home or from a place of employment to undertake various jobs. It is, of course, possible that nothing of consequence has been omitted, but it all too frequently happens that, only when the legal principles have been analysed in depth, is the significance recognised of facts which are not in evidence and cannot then be ascertained. In such a situation it becomes necessary to assume that everything relevant has been ascertained and to hope that nothing is missing which could have led to a different conclusion.

The trial judge found that the deceased and Mr Stages were employed at Drakelow power station and were sent by Mr Pye to Pembroke power station to do the lagging on a job which he had assessed. They were paid for a standard eight-hour day for the journey and for the time spent finding themselves accommodation in Pembroke. The employers knew that the men travelled in Mr Stages's car but they neither required nor specifically authorised them to do so. Each man was paid the equivalent of the railway fare and allowed to travel in any way he chose. As a result of working a whole night the men became entitled to a day's wages for sleeping. They also were entitled to a day for travelling back to the Midlands. The men were not supervised at Pembroke and there was no evidence of any instructions being given to them there. He also referred to r 3(ii)(e) of the national agreement, cited above.

The employers argued that it necessarily followed from this rule that the men could not be working when travelling on Monday, because pursuant to the rules Monday was to be the day paid for as sleeping time. The judge rejected this point but, after summarising the facts, he found 'no basis for the suggestion that Mr Stages drove his car as agent for the defendants'.

Then, after reviewing a number of decided cases to which, so far as may be necessary, I shall return, the trial judge further concluded—

'that the claim by the plaintiff in the first action on the footing that the [employers] are vicariously liable for the negligence of Mr Stages must fail.'

The plaintiff appealed against the decision that Mr Stages was not driving during and in the course of his employment on the grounds that (a) the accident occurred during normal working hours at a time when Mr Stages and the deceased were being paid for their services, (b) the employers knew that and had approved of the fact that Mr Stages was using his motor car and taking the deceased with him as a passenger to travel to and from Pembroke power station where they were required to carry out work on behalf of the employers. The plaintiff also averred that the judge misdirected himself in holding that Mr Stages was not driving his motor car 'incidental to his work as a lagger.'

The Court of Appeal allowed the appeal, and I now come to the judgment of Glidewell LJ, in which the other members of the court concurred. Glidewell LJ, after stating the facts, noted the trial judge's first main finding (see [1988] ICR 201 at 207):

'I find no evidence that those rules were ever brought to the attention of the deceased, or, indeed, Stages. They seem designed as much for the protection of an employee as for the protection of the employer ... I regard the attempt before me to allocate the Monday as a sleeping day and Tuesday as a travelling day as an ex post facto rationalisation designed to exonerate the [employers] from liability for Stages' conduct. I conclude that the facts, in summary, were these: the [employers] were aware that the deceased had travelled in Stages' car to Pembroke and would probably travel back in the same way on the Monday. Having paid each man his travelling allowance his mode of travel was left by the [employers] to his discretion. The travelling day was paid for as a working day and the [employers] were entitled to *a* direct how the deceased and Stages should act during that day. The [employers], however, issued no instructions in the manner of travel. Stages drove his car and neither sought nor received any authority from the [employers] to do so. In these circumstances I can find no basis for the suggestion that Stages drove his own car as agent for the [employers].'

Glidewell LJ then said (at 207):

b 'I should say that in that passage the judge was finding that what Mr. Wilkinson said—that the [employers] had no control over Stages and Machin during the time between 8.30 on the Monday morning and the time when they were due to arrive at Drakelow—was inaccurate. If indeed at the relevant times, when they should or might have been sleeping and were in fact travelling home, these men were acting in the course of their employment (i.e. both activities took place during the *c* company's time), I respectfully agree with the judge that the company could have directed the deceased and Stages and told them how to act. They could have ordered them not to travel, certainly by car, on the day on which they were being paid for resting. That is contingent upon both periods, the rest period and the travelling period, being periods when they were acting or expected to act within the scope of their employment.'

d
He noted without surprise, as I do, that the judge had concluded that Mr Stages was not acting as the employers' agent; the plaintiff's real case was that Mr Stages was driving the car in the course of his employment so as to render the employers vicariously liable for his negligence. On that issue the judge had found against the plaintiff (at 207–208):

e 'Nevertheless, he was not paid to drive; he was not instructed or obliged to drive; no control was exercised or claimed by the [employers] as to how he should travel; and no allowance was paid. [As to that, Glidewell LJ said: 'That last remark is a little difficult to understand in the light of the evidence.' The trial judge continued:] Although these men were travelling by car they were equally entitled to travel by train or coach or howsoever they pleased. The allowance in working hours and pay for such hours for travelling does not, in my view, necessarily bring such travel *f* within the ambit of a man's work. I therefore conclude that the claim by the plaintiff in the first action on the footing that the [employers] are vicariously liable for the negligence of Stages must fail.'

Glidewell LJ then reviewed that conclusion in the light of a number of authorities, which he summarised to good effect. For the moment I shall be content merely to list *g* them. They were *Canadian Pacific Rly Co v Lockhart* [1942] 2 All ER 464, [1942] AC 591, *Harvey v R G O'Dell Ltd (Galway, third party)* [1958] 1 All ER 657, [1958] 2 QB 78, *Vandyke v Fender (Sun Insurance Office Ltd, third party)* [1970] 2 All ER 335, [1970] 2 QB 292 (in which reference was made to *St Helens Colliery Co Ltd v Hewitson* [1924] AC 59, [1923] All ER Rep 249 and *Weaver v Tredegar Iron and Coal Co Ltd* [1940] 3 All ER 157, [1940] AC 955) and *Nottingham v Aldridge (Prudential Assurance Co Ltd, third party)* [1971] *h* 2 All ER 751, [1971] 2 QB 739. All these cases had been mentioned by the trial judge; Glidewell LJ cited two more: *Elleanor v Cavendish Woodhouse Ltd* [1973] 1 Lloyd's Rep 313 and *Nancollas v Insurance Officer* [1985] 1 All ER 833. From these cases he derived four principles which he set out (at 211):

j 'First, where an employee is driving solely between his home and his normal place of work or vice versa, it may well be that he is not in the course of his employment unless the test laid down by Lord Denning M.R. in *Vandyke v. Fender* ([1970] 2 All ER 335, [1970] 2 QB 292) is satisfied, that is to say that it is an obligation to travel in the way in which he is travelling. Secondly, when he is travelling between two places of work—for example, as here, if the employee is travelling between a main base and a distant place at which he is engaged to work

temporarily, particularly if the second place is premises not occupied by the
employers but premises at which he is to work, generally the journey will be within
the course of his employment. Thirdly, if he makes such a journey—that is to say
in the employers' time and in order to carry out his employment at a place distant
from his main base—but for convenience he actually starts off in the morning from
his own home instead of leaving from his home base, so to speak, or returns in the
evening to his own home rather than going via his base, it may well be that such a
journey too will be within the course of his employment. It is a question of whether,
within the contract of his employment, he was required to make that particular
journey, even though the beginning or end of it may be his home rather than the
base. Finally, if no other transport is available, and for convenience sake he travels
in his own car and the employers know that and approve of it and permit him to do
so—in other words authorise him to travel by car rather than in some other way—
that may well mean that the journey in his own car will be in the course of his
employment.'

He then disposed, conclusively in my opinion, of an attempt by the employers' counsel
to distinguish the present case from those in which an employee who had left his base in
the morning and come back the same day had been held to have been travelling in the
course of his employment. This is an unsound distinction: it should not matter whether
a travelling salesman, for example, completes his rounds on one day (or a succession of
days on each of which he returns to base) or stays away for a night or several nights in the
course of his peripatetic employment. And the mere fact that he is not acting in the
course of his employment while sitting in his hotel or lodgings or while going out in the
evening does not alter the character of his journey while he is travelling on his employer's
business. Similarly, the plaintiff has no need to show that the deceased and Mr Stages
were in the course of their employment while relaxing at Pembroke during the evenings
of their stay there. They were in the same position there as the ticket collector in
Alderman v Great Western Rly Co [1937] 2 All ER 408, [1937] AC 454.

The employers argued secondly that on the Monday, 'when, according to the evidence,
they were being paid to rest and not to travel,' the men were not acting in the course of
their employment and that, if they chose to travel on that day, it was not within the
course of their employment. Glidewell LJ met that submission (convincingly, in my
opinion) with the following observations (at 212–213):

'The difficulty which faces that argument which to my mind is in the end
conclusive—I must say that it was an argument which greatly attracted me at first—
is the finding of the judge to which I have already referred but to which I return
that the travelling day was paid as a working day and the employers were entitled
to direct how the deceased and Stages should act during that day. I have already said
that this can only be correct if prima facie Stages' journey, if made at some other
time—for instance, if it had been made on the Tuesday—would have been in the
course of his employment. That is I think what the judge had in mind. Then the
employers would have been entitled to direct that he should not drive on the
Monday. But they did not do so. If it is right that they were entitled to direct that
Stages should not drive on the Monday and should drive on the Tuesday—or
certainly should not travel by car on the Monday because he would be so exhausted—
the fact that the employers did not take the opportunity to give such directions
means in my view that, whenever Stages embarked on the journey back, which
itself was to be made in the employers' time and was regarded as part of Stages' and
Machin's job that week and thus was a part of the course of their employment, that
journey took place during the course of their employment. It was left to them to
decide when to drive to Staffordshire. Whenever they chose to do it, if the employers
did not take the opportunity to direct them, the journey was made during the
course of their employment. Since the employers had authorised Stages to drive,

a and to drive Machin, not merely was the journey made during the course of their employment but Stages was driving in the course of his employment. Therefore in my view, based upon the conclusion to which the judge came to which I have just referred, the eventual conclusion to which he came was, with respect to him, wrong. I would hold that this journey, on the facts of this particular case, was made during the course of Stages' employment and thus that the [employers] were vicariously liable for his negligent driving.'

b At an earlier point in his judgment Glidewell LJ adverted to a passage in the judgment of Sir John Donaldson MR in *Nancollas v Insurance Officer* [1985] 1 All ER 833 at 840 in which he said:

'We cannot overemphasise the importance of looking at the factual picture as a whole and rejecting any approach based on the fallacious concept that any one factor *c* is conclusive. The addition or subtraction of one factor in a given situation may well tip the balance. In another, the addition or subtraction of the same factor may well make no difference. We appreciate that it would assist if we could lay down rules or even guidelines. However, there are no rules, other than that which is contained in the statute: if, looking at the whole factual picture, the claimant suffered the accident whilst in the course of his employment, he is eligible for benefit, assuming all other *d* conditions are satisfied. As to guidelines, it would be possible to point to material factors: was he being paid for what he was doing? Was it the employer's car? If not, was he paid mileage allowance? Was it of any concern to the employer that he was where he was? Had he a fixed place of work and was he going to it? Had he more than one fixed place of work and was he travelling between them? But any such list would mislead, if, as is almost inevitable, it was once thought to be comprehensive. *e* We could list factors which are irrelevant, but again any examples would have to be so extreme as to be unhelpful, because otherwise we might be dismissing a factor which, in exceptional circumstances which we had not envisaged, might nevertheless have had some weight.'

These observations on the crucial importance of the facts teach a valuable lesson, but I *f* would be reluctant to see them as indicating that there are no principles in the light of which to resolve the question your Lordships have had to consider.

The trial judge's conclusion was one of mixed fact and law. Was it susceptible of attack and, if so, on what grounds? I agree with Glidewell LJ that the judge was right (or was at least justified) in regarding 'the attempt . . . to allocate the Monday as a sleeping day and Tuesday as a travelling day as an ex post facto rationalisation designed to exonerate the *g* [employers]' (see [1988] ICR 201 at 207). Once he had gone that length in the plaintiff's favour, with the men having been paid their wages while travelling to Pembroke and back, it could well be thought that the case had been decided in the plaintiff's favour. But he found against the plaintiff on the course of employment issue. I am, however, satisfied that the Court of Appeal was right and I consider that the judge misdirected himself in point of law by drawing faulty conclusions from cases decided on different *h* facts. In a passage already quoted above the judge said:

'[1] Nevertheless, he was not paid to drive; [2] he was not instructed or obliged to drive; [3] no control was exercised or claimed by the [employers] as to how he should travel; [4] and no allowance was paid.'

j (I have inserted the figures for ease of reference.)

My observations are as follows. (1) This point would be relevant to answer the claim based on agency, but it does not prevent Mr Stages from having been in the course of his employment; the fact that he was driving is incidental. The deceased was a passenger but that fact was consistent with the deceased's being in the course of his employment; both men were employed to go to Pembroke, do the lagging job and come back. Both their

travelling, by car or other means, and their work at Pembroke were to be paid for by the
employers and done in the employers' time. (2) It was up to the deceased and Mr Stages *a*
how they reached Pembroke and how they returned; a travelling salesman with no
special directions or orders as to his mode of transport would have been in the same
position. The question of obligation to use a particular means arises only where the
employee prima facie is not making a paid journey in his employer's time on his
employer's business, e g when he is going from his home to his main place of work. (3) In
this case the employers had the right of control, although they did not exercise it. (4) This *b*
is wrong; quite apart from the travelling allowance, the important thing is that the men
were paid their wages to travel there and back.

The next sentence in the judgment adds nothing which has not been covered by what
I have said: 'Although these men were travelling by car, they were equally entitled to
travel by train or coach or howsoever they pleased.' The judge went on: 'The allowance
in working hours and pay for such hours for travelling does not, in my view, necessarily *c*
bring such travel within the ambit of a man's work.' Not *necessarily*, it may be, but the
payment of wages makes a prima facie case which is uncontradicted. It is, moreover,
important that the employers (who had 20 or 30 men engaged at Drakelow) 'withdrew'
the deceased and Mr Stages from there and 'sent them to Pembroke'. They were paid
eight hours' travelling time there and back as well as eight hours' sleeping time. They
were not regarded as having a day off when travelling but were 'receiving time'. The *d*
employers knew that they were travelling in Mr Stages's car and were paying their wages
during the time spent travelling to Pembroke and back. All this is taken directly from
the employers' evidence.

The first case to which the trial judge looked for assistance was *Nottingham v Aldridge*
[1971] 2 All ER 751, [1971] 2 QB 739. The plaintiff and the first defendant were
apprentices attending a residential training school as part of their employment with the *e*
second defendants. They were returning from a weekend spent at home in a van driven
by the first defendant and owned by his father when the plaintiff was injured in an
accident caused by the first defendant's negligence. Eveleigh J held that the employers
were not liable for the driver's negligence because at the relevant time he was not acting
as either their servant or their agent. Although he was given both a mileage and a
passenger allowance and had a duty to present himself at the detached place of work, the *f*
first defendant was under no duty to drive himself or the plaintiff there: the mode and
time of travel and the route were at his discretion and the employers had no right of
control. Many of these points coincided with the circumstances of the present case, but
in *Nottingham v Aldridge* the occupants of the car were travelling in their own time (that
is unpaid time) and not in the employers' time and were not on duty but merely
returning to duty after a weekend off. The driver was receiving allowances but neither *g*
he nor his passengers were being paid wages to cover the time of their journey. That
case, as well as others, exemplifies the danger of picking out features and treating them
as decisive in a different context. With respect, this is what I think the trial judge did
when he relied on *Nottingham v Aldridge* to defeat the plaintiff on the course of
employment issue. The judge further relied on a passage from the judgment of Lord *h*
Denning MR in *Vandyke v Fender* [1970] 2 All ER 335 at 340, [1970] 2 QB 292 at 305,
which Eveleigh J had cited in *Nottingham v Aldridge* [1971] 2 All ER 751 at 756, [1971] 2
QB 739 at 747. Referring to the words 'arising out of and in the course of his
employment', Lord Denning MR said:

'The selfsame words have been used in the Road Traffic Acts 1930 and 1960. They *j*
have also been used in employers' liability policies. In my opinion they should
receive the same interpretation in all three places for they are all so closely connected
that they ought, as a matter of common sense, to receive the same interpretation in
each. The words were construed and applied in thousands of cases under the
Workmen's Compensation Acts and I think we should follow those cases. The two

leading cases, most apposite for present purposes, are *St Helens Colliery Co Ltd v Hewitson* [1924] AC 59, [1923] All ER Rep 249 and *Weaver v Tredegar Iron Coal Co Ltd* [1940] 3 All ER 157, [1940] AC 955. They show, to my mind quite conclusively, that when a man is going to or coming from work, along a public road, as a passenger in a vehicle provided by his employer, he is not then in the course of his employment—unless he is *obliged* by the terms of his employment to travel in that vehicle. It is not enough that he should have the right to travel in the vehicle, or be permitted to travel in it. He must have an *obligation* to travel in it. Else he is not in the course of his employment. That distinction must be maintained, for otherwise there would be no certainty in this branch of the law.' (Lord Denning MR's emphasis.)

What was here said about the passenger in relation to the course of his employment was also apposite to the driver, as Eveleigh J pointed out.

My Lords, let me say at once that I entirely agree with all of Lord Denning MR's general observations on the consistently continuing meaning of the specified words and also with his answer to the particular questions which arose for decision in *Vandyke v Fender* [1970] 2 All ER 335, [1970] 2 QB 292. Both the plaintiff and Fender (who was driving) were undertaking their customary journey from their homes to their regular place of work. The employers provided a car and a travelling allowance, no doubt as an inducement to the men to accept their employment, but the men *were not paid for the time during which they were travelling to work*; they were not on duty and not in the course of their employment. Fender was, however, by virtue of his arrangements with the employers held to have been their agent, although not acting as their employee, while driving, with the result that they were liable to the plaintiff but had a right of indemnity against Fender (which in practice meant the insurers nominated by the Motor Insurers' Bureau). The real contest was between the Motor Insurers' Bureau and the company insuring the employer's liability risk, which would arise only if the plaintiff, while a passenger in the car, was in the course of his employment. Accordingly, my Lords, to hold that *Vandyke v Fender* is of no help to the employers does not weaken its authority in any way.

The judge, rightly observing that 'Cases where the servant is driving in his own time out of working hours fall on one side of the line', included among them, as I would, *Nottingham v Aldridge* and *Vandyke v Fender*. He then adverted to *Canadian Pacific Rly Co v Lockhart* [1942] 2 All ER 464, [1942] AC 591 and *Harvey v R G O'Dell Ltd* [1958] 1 All ER 657, [1958] 2 QB 78, which fell on the other side. In *Lockhart's* case the railway company employed a handyman called Stinson whose duties took him away from his base at Toronto to places which could be reached by rail. He was paid for the time needed to reach those places and was sometimes instructed or permitted to go by tram, and given a ticket. Men could use their own cars but there was a strict prohibition against doing this if the cars were not insured. Stinson had already been reprimanded for disregarding this rule. Despite this, he used his car (other means being available) while uninsured and negligently injured the plaintiff on the highway. The Privy Council, affirming the Supreme Court of Canada, which had reversed the trial judge and the Court of Appeal for Ontario, held that the company was liable for the negligence of Stinson because, although not paid to drive, he was acting in the course of his employment. It is noteworthy that the only argument before the Judicial Committee, and the only judicial opinions in the courts below, to the contrary effect were based on Stinson's disobedience in failing to have his car insured. *Lockhart's* case is therefore not only distinguishable from the cases already cited but strongly supportive of the plaintiff here.

A number of interesting motor insurance questions arose in *Harvey v R G O'Dell Ltd*. For present purposes your Lordships are concerned only with whether a workman driving his own motor cycle combination was acting in the course of his employment when driving a fellow employee on a five-mile return journey from a lunch break during

which the men had collected tools. McNair J held that both when going out to the job in
the morning in the employer's paid time and when returning from the break the a
workman was acting in the course of his employment and further stated that he would
have so held, even if tools had not been involved. I draw attention to what he said (see
[1958] 1 All ER 657 at 665, [1958] 2 QB 78 at 102). The judge here cited that passage,
and made no attempt to distinguish the present case on its facts. *Harvey v R G O'Dell Ltd*
primarily exemplifies incidental deviation or interruption. It is also in general terms in
favour of the plaintiff in this case and gives no support to the employers.   b

The judge also referred to *Netherton v Coles* [1945] 1 All ER 227, where the question
was whether a painter who had to work at a hospital was in the course of his employment
when travelling from there to his home. The Court of Appeal, reversing the county
court judge, decided against the claimant: by the general rule a workman was not in the
course of his employment between his home and his workplace; the employer had for
the time being appointed the hospital as the workplace and the workman, though paid a c
travelling allowance equivalent to half-an-hour's pay per day, received no pay and was
regarded as being outside working hours when coming and going. The general
observations of Finlay LJ are helpful to the plaintiff in the present case and were cited by
the judge without comment.

Glidewell LJ reviewed the judge's cases (except *Netherton v Coles*) and mentioned in
addition *Elleanor v Cavendish Woodhouse Ltd* [1973] 1 Lloyd's Rep 313 and *Nancollas v* d
Insurance Officer [1985] 1 All ER 833. In *Elleanor's* case the Court of Appeal affirmed
Ormrod J's finding that a salesman, who worked during the day at his employer's
showroom and who canvassed for orders with a fellow employee in the evening (while
receiving commission on orders, expenses and free petrol), was acting in the course of his
employment while driving the fellow employee to the latter's home after a canvassing
trip. In the course of his judgment Lawton LJ put the matter with both wisdom and e
brevity ([1973] 1 Lloyd's Rep 313 at 314–315):

'At one stage of this case it looked as if the Court would have to consider and
review a long line of authorities relating to what is meant by the phrase "in the
course of employment". Mr. Justice Ormrod had had to consider some of the
authorities and he described them as "a nightmare". Perhaps they are, if one tries to f
distinguish the very many reported cases on their facts. But in my judgment it is
unnecessary to review the law in any detail at all, because ever since 1924, the
principles applicable in this class of case have been established by the decision of the
House of Lords in *St. Helens Colliery Co. Ltd. v. Hewitson* ([1924] AC 59, [1923] All ER
Rep 249). What is required in this case (and it may be a difficult task) is to apply
those principles to the facts of this case as established by the evidence.'   g

Nancollas v Insurance Officer [1985] 1 All ER 833 was concerned with a claim for
industrial injury benefit by a disablement resettlement officer who lived at West
Worthing, whose main office was at Worthing and whose duties took him to other job
centres in his area and to the homes of disabled persons. He adjusted his working hours
to the duties he had to perform. One morning he was driving from home to keep an h
appointment to see a disabled person in Aldershot when he was involved in an accident
and injured. The Court of Appeal, reversing the Social Security Commissioners, held that
at the time of the accident the claimant was in the course of his employment. There is an
important passage in Sir John Donaldson MR's judgment (at 837):

'The reasoning which led them to reject the claim is long and detailed but the
substance sufficiently appears from what follows in this judgment. The starting j
point is a proposition of law which the commissioners derived from the judgment
of Lord Denning MR in *Vandyke v Fender* [1970] 2 All ER 335, [1970] 2 QB 292 that
"The journey to and from work is not a journey in the course of employment unless
the claimant is fulfilling a duty to his employer in undertaking it at the time or in

the manner in which he is doing so", coupled with references to the *St Helens Colliery*
a and *Weaver* cases. With the greatest respect to the commissioners, this discloses
what may be a misreading and certainly a misapplication of the authorities. In all
three cases the employees concerned each had only one regular work place, a mine
or a factory, and the courts proceeded on the basis that the journeys were between
home and the work place. They then considered whether any and, in the *St Helens*
and *Weaver* cases, how much of that journey could properly be said to be in the
b course of the employment. In Mr Nancollas's case, the issue was different. He had
indeed a regular work place in his Worthing office, but on the day in question he
was going somewhere else for the purposes of his work. The issue was whether the
journey was not only in the course of, but part of, his work: whether at the material
time the road was his work place. More specifically, it was whether Mr Nancollas
was employed, inter alia, to drive to places in his area at which disabled persons
c could be interviewed and there interview them or whether he had a number of
work places which he had to reach in order to work at them. Mr Nancollas lived in
Worthing. He had his main base office in Worthing. He was sufficiently senior to
decide for himself when and in what manner to travel to outstations and, if he had
set out for Aldershot from his Worthing office instead of from his home, there can
be no doubt that the whole of his journey from that office would have been
d undertaken in the course of his employment. It cannot, in principle, make any
difference that, no doubt for sensible reasons such as that there would be no time to
undertake any worthwhile work at the Worthing base office, he drove straight to
Aldershot from his home. This was not a case of a man who one day worked at a
Guildford office, on another at an Aldershot office and on a third at a Worthing
office, travelling by car from home to the relevant "work place" each day. He was
e an itinerant officer who, in the course of his employment, had to roam his area
calling at appropriate offices and, no doubt, private homes to attend case conferences
and to interview disabled people. In driving to Aldershot, Mr Nancollas was not
going to work. That was part of his work.'

The point I would stress before parting with *Nancollas*'s case is that the decisions of the
f commissioners which were reversed were founded not on *Vandyke v Fender* [1970] 2 All
ER 335, [1970] 2 QB 292 but on a misreading of that authority. It cannot be supposed
that Lord Denning MR, when he laid down the *general* rule about travel between home
and place of work, intended to treat as if they had never existed authorities such as
Canadian Pacific Rly Co v Lockhart [1942] 2 All ER 464, [1942] AC 591 and *Blee v London*
and North Eastern Rly Co [1937] 4 All ER 270, [1938] AC 126 (in which a railway worker
g was by his contract obliged to turn out from his home in emergencies and was to be paid
from the time he left home in answer to the summons).

The only other case of this kind which I wish to mention is *R v Industrial Injury Benefits*
Tribunal, ex p Fieldhouse (1974) 17 KIR 63, which culminated in an application for an
order of certiorari and in which a peripatetic petrol station manager who had been
injured in a traffic accident while travelling on the direct route between two petrol
h stations, intending to spend the night at his home on the way, failed in his claim for
industrial injury benefit. Lord Widgery CJ stated in his judgment that the claimant was
travelling in off duty hours; furthermore, it was common ground between the parties
that the commissioners had not erred in law. Not surprisingly, the commissioners'
finding that the claimant had not been at the material time in the course of his
employment was not disturbed.

j Accordingly, in agreement with the Court of Appeal, I conclude that the judge went
wrong in the way I have described. I would add that, in my clear opinion, the decisions
which are typified at the highest level by *St Helens Colliery Co Ltd v Hewitson* [1924] AC
59, [1923] All ER Rep 249 are correct and remain of binding authority. Parliament has
continuously indorsed the effect of those decisions by its repeated use in various statutes

of the phrase 'in the course of his employment', and the application of the principle so clearly enunciated in *Barras v Aberdeen Steam Trawling and Fishing Co Ltd* [1933] AC 402, a [1933] All ER Rep 52 can rarely have been more obviously justified than in relation to those words. But the facts of each particular case are crucial and new social and economic factors, though not in any way undermining or detracting from the guiding principles to be deduced from the cases relied on by the present employers, have created some new situations to which the older authorities, though binding as to principle, do not always furnish a cut and dried solution.

In their printed case and before your Lordships the employers described the issues as:

'(a) What are the correct principles to be applied in determining whether an employee travelling to or from work along a public highway is acting in the course of his employment? (b) Whether the test laid down by the Court of Appeal in *Vandyke v. Fender* ([1970] 2 All ER 335, [1970] 2 QB 292) is the correct test, and whether that case was correctly decided. (c) Whether the payment of an agreed allowance for working exceptional hours and/or for travelling time and/or the payment of travelling expenses affect the general principles and have the result that an employee travelling home is deemed to be travelling in the course of his employment whenever and by whatever means he chooses to make the journey.'

The answer to question (b) is that the test in *Vandyke v Fender* is the correct test in situations to which it applies and that that case *was* correctly decided. This conclusion, however, does not lead to the further conclusion that the Court of Appeal went wrong in the case now before your Lordships. The answer to question (c) is No, but that question appears to have been designed to sidestep or to render irrelevant the fact, which was clearly demonstrated by the employers' evidence, that the men were paid not merely allowances but wages for travelling to Pembroke and back *in their employers' time*. My Lords, I am not impressed by the employers' counter-argument to the effect that the payment (expressly stated by the employers' witnesses to be a payment of wages) was in reality an allowance in addition to the travelling expenses already allowed, a recompense to the workmen for missing two days' employment at Drakelow. As to that I would make two points. There appears to be no justification for thus interpreting what the employers' witnesses described as wages. Secondly, if there had been any further evidence on this important issue to contradict or explain the evidence already given, it would have been within the power of the employers, as well as in their interest, to produce it. A much simpler interpretation, wholly consistent with the authorities, is that the men, so far from being compensated for not working, were being paid their wages for performing a duty, that is for going to Pembroke, carrying out the lagging job and coming back, as directed.

Again, the employers in their printed case described the deceased and Stages as 'peripatetic laggers working at such sites and on such contracts as were from time to time available', suggesting that the work at Drakelow was 'simply a longer and larger contract than that at Pembroke' and that the fact that they were to return to work at Drakelow rather than at Pembroke '[did] not and [could] not affect the nature of their journey home from Pembroke'. This concept seems to me quite inconsistent with arranging to pay the men wages (or even compensation) when instructing them to stop work at Drakelow, go to Pembroke to carry out an urgent job and then resume work at Drakelow. As Mr Wilkinson put it in his statement, the men were 'withdrawn from Drakelow' and 'sent to Pembroke'. There was no reason why their employment should not include going to and returning from Pembroke and being treated as on their employers' payroll while doing so; as Glidewell LJ put it in the passage from his judgment which I have already cited ([1988] ICR 201 at 212):

'... whenever Stages embarked on the journey back, which itself was to be made in the employers' time and was regarded as part of Stages' and Machin's job that

a week and thus was a part of the course of their employment, that journey took place during the course of their employment.'

If the employers cannot succeed, they seek in the alternative as much certainty as the common law and your Lordships' House can give them in a field which can too easily provide wasteful and expensive opportunities for conflict between the insurers, on the one hand, of motorists alleged to have caused damage by negligence and, on the other, of employers who are sought, by reason of someone's allegedly negligent driving, to be
b rendered vicariously liable for (and sometimes to) one of their employees.

The paramount rule is that an employee travelling on the highway will be acting in the course of his employment if, and only if, he is at the material time going about his employer's business. One must not confuse the duty to turn up for one's work with the concept of already being 'on duty' while travelling to it.

c It is impossible to provide for every eventuality and foolish, without the benefit of argument, to make the attempt, but some prima facie propositions may be stated with reasonable confidence. (1) An employee travelling from his ordinary residence to his regular place of work, whatever the means of transport and even if it is provided by the employer, is not on duty and is not acting in the course of his employment, but, if he is obliged by his contract of service to use the employer's transport, he will normally, in the absence of an express condition to the contrary, be regarded as acting in the course of his
d employment while doing so. (2) Travelling in the employer's time between workplaces (one of which may be the regular workplace) or in the course of a peripatetic occupation, whether accompanied by goods or tools or simply in order to reach a succession of workplaces (as an inspector of gas meters might do), will be in the course of the employment. (3) Receipt of wages (though not receipt of a travelling allowance) will
e indicate that the employee is travelling in the employer's time and for his benefit and is acting in the course of his employment, and in such a case the fact that the employee may have discretion as to the mode and time of travelling will not take the journey out of the course of his employment. (4) An employee travelling *in the employer's time* from his ordinary residence to a workplace other than this regular workplace or in the course of a peripatetic occupation or to the scene of an emergency (such as a fire, an accident or
f a mechanical breakdown of plant) will be acting in the course of his employment. (5) A deviation from or interruption of a journey undertaken in the course of employment (unless the deviation or interruption is merely incidental to the journey) will for the time being (which may include an overnight interruption) take the employee out of the course of his employment. (6) Return journeys are to be treated on the same footing as outward journeys.

g All the foregoing propositions are subject to any express arrangements between the employer and the employee or those representing his interests. They are not, I would add, intended to define the position of salaried employees, with regard to whom the touchstone of payment made in the employer's time is not generally significant.

In framing these propositions I acknowledge my debt to Glidewell LJ's statement of principles in the Court of Appeal (see [1988] ICR 201 at 211). I would, however,
h respectfully suggest that some of the conditions laid down in the fourth principle are a little too restrictive.

My Lords, for the reasons I have already given, I would dismiss this appeal and affirm the order of the Court of Appeal.

Appeal dismissed.
j

Solicitors: *Turner Kenneth Brown*, agents for *Jacksons Monk & Rowe*, Middlesbrough (for the employers); *Sharpe Pritchard*, agents for *F A Greenwood & Co*, Birmingham (for the plaintiff).

Mary Rose Plummer   Barrister.

Holmes v Bangladesh Biman Corp

HOUSE OF LORDS

LORD BRIDGE OF HARWICH, LORD GRIFFITHS, LORD ACKNER, LORD JAUNCEY OF TULLICHETTLE AND LORD LOWRY

30 NOVEMBER, 5, 6, 7 DECEMBER 1988, 16 FEBRUARY 1989

Carriage by air – Carriage of passengers – Domestic carriage – Foreign domestic carriage – Limitation of carrier's liability – Death of passenger in air crash in Bangladesh – Claim by widow of passenger against carrier for damages – Carrier admitting liability – Bangladesh not party to international conventions governing contracts of carriage by air – Whether United Kingdom legislation governing non-convention carriage by air applicable – Whether amount of damages determinable by reference to Bangladesh law or United Kingdom rules – Whether United Kingdom rules to be given extra-territorial effect – Carriage by Air Act 1961, s 10 – Carriage by Air Acts (Application of Provisions) Order 1967, art 3, Sch 1.

In 1984 an aircraft operated by the appellants crashed on an internal domestic flight in Bangladesh. The respondent's husband, who was a passenger, was killed. The respondent brought an action against the appellants in England claiming damages on behalf of herself and her children under the Fatal Accidents Act 1976 and on behalf of her deceased husband's estate under the Law Reform (Miscellaneous Provisions) Act 1934, s 1. The appellants admitted liability and the only issue between the parties was the amount of damages recoverable. Under Bangladesh law, which governed the contract of carriage, the damages recoverable were limited to £913, whereas if the law to be applied was British law, which governed carriage by air under Sch 1 to the Carriage by Air Acts (Application of Provisions) Order 1967, the damages recoverable would be £83,763. The 1967 order was made under s 10(1)[a] of the Carriage by Air Act 1961, which conferred power by Order in Council to apply Sch 1 to that Act (which gave the force of law in England to the provisions of the Hague Convention) 'to carriage by air, not being carriage by air to which the Convention applies, of such description as may be specified in the Order'. Article 3[b] and Sch 1 to the 1967 order provided rules for 'all carriage by air, not being carriage to which [the Warsaw and Hague conventions] applies'. The question whether the rules contained in Sch 1 to the 1967 order applied to foreign domestic carriage, ie carriage within the territory of a foreign state, was ordered to be tried as a preliminary issue. The judge and the Court of Appeal held that the rules were so applicable. The appellants appealed to the House of Lords.

Held – The 1967 order could have no wider scope and effect than was duly authorised by the power conferred by s 10 of 1961 Act to legislate by Order in Council and, in conformity with the rule against giving extra-territorial effect to legislation, s 10 was to be construed as authorising legislation limited to carriage wholly within the United Kingdom or non-convention carriage involving a place of departure or destination or an agreed stopping place in a foreign state and a place of departure or destination or an agreed stopping place in the United Kingdom or other British territory. Accordingly, a contract of carriage made and to be performed wholly within the territory of a single foreign state or between two foreign states was excluded from the scope of the 1967 order. It followed that the rules contained in Sch 1 to the 1967 order did not apply to the contract of carriage between the deceased and the appellants and the respondent was therefore not entitled to rely on those rules. The appeal would therefore be allowed (see p 855 j to p 856 a, p 860 f to p 861 d, p 862 g, p 863 b, p 864 f g, p 865 d to j, p 875 e, p 876 a d to g and p 877 c to f, post).

---

a   Section 10(1) is set out at p 855 d e, post
b   Article 3 is set out at p 869 d e, post

a   *The Zollverein* (1856) Sw 96, *Cope v Doherty* (1858) 2 De G & J 614, *Re Sawers, ex p Blain* [1874–80] All ER Rep 708 and *Grein v Imperial Airways Ltd* [1936] 2 All ER 1258 applied.

Notes
For rules as to liability in non-international air carriage and death or injury to passengers, see 2 Halsbury's Laws (4th edn) paras 1397, 1402–1405.

b   For the Law Reform (Miscellaneous Provisions) Act 1934, s 1, see 17 Halsbury's Statutes (4th edn) 312.

For the Carriage by Air Act 1961, s 10, Sch 1, see 4 ibid 26, 28.

For the Fatal Accidents Act 1976, see 31 ibid 202.

For the Carriage by Air Acts (Application of Provisions) Order 1967, art 3, Sch 1, see 3 Halsbury's Statutory Instruments (Grey Volume) 23, 24.

c   As from a day to be appointed Sch 1 to the 1961 Act is to be substituted by s 1 of and Sch 1 to the Carriage by Air and Road Act 1979.

Cases referred to in opinions
AB & Co, Re [1900] 1 QB 541, CA.
Air-India v Wiggins [1980] 2 All ER 593, [1980] 1 WLR 815, HL.
d   *Blain, Ex p, re Sawers* (1879) 12 Ch D 522, [1874–80] All ER Rep 708, CA.
Clark (Inspector of Taxes) v Oceanic Contractors Inc [1983] 1 All ER 133, [1983] 2 AC 130, [1983] 2 WLR 94, HL.
Cope v Doherty (1858) 2 De G & J 614, 44 ER 1127, LJJ.
Cox v Army Council [1962] 1 All ER 880, [1963] AC 48, [1962] 2 WLR 126, HL.
Cox v Hakes (1890) 15 App Cas 506, HL.
e   *Goldman v Thai Airways International Ltd* [1983] 3 All ER 693, [1983] 1 WLR 1186, CA.
Grein v Imperial Airways Ltd [1936] 2 All ER 1258, [1937] 1 KB 50, CA.
Hawkins v Gathercole (1854) 6 De GM & G 1, 43 ER 1129, LJJ.
Hollandia, The [1982] 3 All ER 1141, [1983] 1 AC 565, [1982] 3 WLR 1111, HL.
Pearson, Re, ex p Pearson [1892] 2 QB 263, [1891–4] All ER Rep 1066, CA.
R v Jameson [1896] 2 QB 425.
f   *Zollverein, The* (1856) Sw 96, 166 ER 1038.

Appeal
Bangladesh Biman Corp, a Bangladesh airline, appealed with the leave of the Appeal Committee of the House of Lords given on 7 July 1988 against the decision of the Court of Appeal (Lord Donaldson MR, Dillon and Bingham LJJ) ([1988] 2 Lloyd's Rep 120) on
g   26 February 1988 dismissing their appeal against the judgment of Leggatt J ([1987] 2 Lloyd's Rep 192) given on 29 January 1987 on the hearing of a preliminary issue in the action brought by the respondent, Keiko Holmes, suing as the widow and executrix of the will of Geoffrey Paul Mervyn Holmes, otherwise known as Paul Holmes, deceased, against the appellants claiming damages under the Fatal Accidents Act 1976 on behalf of
h   herself and her children and under the Law Reform (Miscellaneous Provisions) Act 1934 on behalf of the estate of her deceased husband who died in an air accident in Bangladesh while a passenger on an internal domestic flight in an aircraft operated by the appellants. The preliminary issue was whether the relevant carriage by air was one in respect of which Sch 1 to the Carriage by Air Acts (Application of Provisions) Order 1967, SI 1967/480, had effect. Leggatt J and the Court of Appeal held that the 1967 order was applicable.
j   The facts are set out in the opinion of Lord Bridge.

Charles Sparrow QC and *Robert Webb QC* for the appellants.
Timothy Walker QC and *Simon Browne-Wilkinson* for the respondent.

Their Lordships took time for consideration.

16 February. The following opinions were delivered.

a

LORD BRIDGE OF HARWICH. My Lords, the respondent is the widow of Geoffrey Paul Mervyn Holmes who was killed in an air crash in August 1984. He was a passenger in an aircraft operated by the appellant airline flying from Chittagong to Dhaka in Bangladesh. The plane crashed as it approached Zia International Airport. This was a purely internal Bangladesh flight.

The widow sues the airline for damages under the Fatal Accidents Act 1976 on behalf b
of herself and her children and under the Law Reform (Miscellaneous Provisions) Act 1934 on behalf of the estate of her deceased husband. Liability not being in dispute, the only issue between the parties is as to the amount of damages recoverable. Under the terms of the contract between Mr Holmes and the airline and in accordance with the relevant Bangladesh legislation applicable to carriage by air in Bangladesh the damages the widow could recover would be limited to £913. But if the law to be applied is that c
which governs carriage by air under Sch 1 to the Carriage by Air Acts (Application of Provisions) Order 1967, SI 1967/480, damages would be recoverable up to a limit of £83,763. A preliminary issue in the action was ordered to be tried, namely:

> 'Whether or not the carriage by air referred to in the Statement of Claim was
> carriage by air in respect of which Schedule 1 to the Carriage by Air Acts (Application d
> of Provisions) Order 1967 had effect.'

Before the issue came to be tried the parties had agreed that the damages suffered exceeded the limit imposed by Sch 1 to the 1967 order. Accordingly, the final outcome of the action will now be governed by the determination of the issue. If it is determined in the widow's favour, she will be entitled to judgment for £83,763; if not, for £913 only. Leggatt J determined the issue in the widow's favour (see [1987] 2 Lloyd's Rep e
192). His judgment was affirmed by the Court of Appeal (Lord Donaldson MR, Dillon and Bingham LJJ) ([1988] 2 Lloyd's Rep 120). The airline now appeals by leave of your Lordships' House.

There are now two international conventions in force, each providing a uniform set of rules governing contracts of international carriage by air to which the convention applies. The first is the Warsaw Convention agreed in 1929. The second is an amended version of f
the Warsaw Convention agreed at The Hague in 1955, which it will be convenient to refer to as 'the Hague Convention'. The United Kingdom is a party to both conventions. The Warsaw Convention was enacted into United Kingdom law by the Carriage by Air Act 1932. This came into force in the United Kingdom, the Channel Islands and the Isle of Man on 13 May 1933 and in all other dependent British territories on 3 March 1935. For brevity I shall hereafter refer to the Channel Islands, the Isle of Man and all other g
dependent British territories collectively as 'other British territory'. The Hague Convention was enacted into United Kingdom law by the Carriage by Air Act 1961 and was brought into force in the United Kingdom and other British territory on 1 June 1967.

The scope of the Hague Convention appears from art 1, which provides: h

> '(1) This Convention applies to all international carriage of persons, baggage or
> cargo performed by aircraft for reward. It applies equally to gratuitous carriage by
> aircraft performed by an air transport undertaking.
> (2) For the purposes of this Convention, the expression *international carriage*
> means any carriage in which, according to the agreement between the parties, the
> place of departure and the place of destination, whether or not there be a break in j
> the carriage or a transhipment, are situated either within the territories of two High
> Contracting Parties or within the territory of a single High Contracting Party if
> there is an agreed stopping place within the territory of another State, even if that
> State is not a High Contracting Party. Carriage between two points within the

a
territory of a single High Contracting Party without an agreed stopping place within
the territory of another State is not international carriage for the purposes of this
Convention . . .'

Article 1(1) of the Hague Convention repeats art 1(1) of the Warsaw Convention and
the definition of 'international carriage' in art 1(2) repeats with immaterial drafting
amendments that contained in art 1(2) of the Warsaw Convention. But a number of
b
countries, notably the United States of America, which are party to the Warsaw
Convention have never adopted the Hague Convention. Hence the scope of the
'international carriage' to which each convention applies is quite different.

Section 1 of the 1961 Act enacts that the provisions of the Hague Convention—

c
'as set out in the First Schedule to this Act shall, so far as they relate to the rights
and liabilities of carriers, carriers' servants and agents, passengers, consignors,
consignees and other persons, and subject to the provisions of this Act, have the
force of law in the United Kingdom in relation to any carriage by air to which the
Convention applies, irrespective of the nationality of the aircraft performing that
carriage; and the Carriage by Air Act, 1932 (which gives effect to the Warsaw
Convention in its original form), shall cease to have effect.'

d Section 10(1) of the Act enacts:

'Her Majesty may by Order in Council apply the First Schedule to this Act,
together with any other provisions of this Act, to carriage by air, not being carriage
by air to which the Convention applies, of such descriptions as may be specified in
the Order, subject to such exceptions, adaptations and modifications, if any, as may
be so specified.'

e
Section 10(2) provides a corresponding power to legislate by Order in Council for other
British territory. Section 10 of the 1961 Act is a re-enactment with immaterial drafting
amendments of s 4 of the 1932 Act which had been exercised by the Carriage by Air
(Non-international Carriage) (United Kingdom) Order 1952, SI 1952/158, to impose a
modified version of the Warsaw Convention providing a set of rules to govern all carriage
f by air not governed by the Warsaw Convention. When the 1961 Act was brought into
force, it was necessary to give continuing force in United Kingdom law to the provisions
of the Warsaw Convention in relation to 'international carriage' to which it still applied.
The enabling power conferred by s 10 was exercised by the Carriage by Air Acts
(Application of Provisions) Order 1967 both for this purpose and for the purpose of
enacting a modified version of the Hague Convention providing a set of rules governing
g all carriage by air not falling within the definition of 'international carriage' in either of
the two conventions. Thus there are now three sets of rules in the law of the United
Kingdom and other British territory which govern different categories of carriage by air
to which I shall refer for convenience as 'the Hague rules' (Sch 1 to the 1961 Act), 'the
Warsaw rules' (Sch 2 to the 1967 order) and 'the United Kingdom rules' (Sch 1 to the
1967 order). The question is whether the United Kingdom rules apply to carriage by air
h which, according to the agreement between the parties, is to be performed wholly within
the territory of a foreign state.

With so much by way of introduction, I have to say at once, with all respect, that, in
my opinion, the judge and the Court of Appeal never applied their minds to the right
question. They concentrated their attention exclusively on the language, structure and
drafting technique of the 1967 order and found that it led them to a conclusion in favour
j of the widow which both Dillon and Bingham LJJ described as 'startling'. But the 1967
order can have no wider scope and effect than is duly authorised by the power conferred
by s 10 of the 1961 Act to legislate by Order in Council. If that power is unlimited, the
scope of its exercise by the order will be a matter to be determined on the true
construction of the order. But if on the true construction of s 10 the enabling power is

itself limited, then it is axiomatic that the order cannot exceed that limit. Accordingly, it seems to me that the essential prior question to be answered, before attempting to construe the order, is whether the words in s 10, 'carriage by air . . . of such descriptions as may be specified', ought to be read as subject to any limitation.

At the heart of the issue lies a principle embodied in a line of authority which I shall have to examine and which certainly establishes a presumption limiting the scope which should be given to general words in a United Kingdom statute in their application to the persons, property, rights and liabilities of the subjects of other sovereign states who do not come within the jurisdiction of the United Kingdom Parliament. This presumption is often described, and has been referred to throughout the argument of this case at all levels, as 'the presumption against extra-territorial legislation'. This may be a convenient shorthand expression, but if it is understood as accurately and comprehensively expressing the principle involved it is potentially misleading. I cannot help thinking that it has led to some confusion of thought in discussion of the issue arising in this appeal. In one sense all legislation enacted in the United Kingdom to give effect to international conventions, long familiar in the field of maritime law, is extra-territorial in effect. But it would be absurd to suggest that in legislating to embody the terms of such internationally agreed conventions in our municipal law Parliament is in any sense usurping an illegitimate authority over the subjects of foreign states. But it is precisely such illegitimate usurpation which Parliament is presumed not to intend and it is against such usurpation that the so-called presumption against extra-territorial legislation is directed. There can be no difficulty in construing s 10 of the 1961 Act as enabling provision to be made by Order in Council, as it was by the 1967 order, for continuing the Warsaw rules in effect. The question we should ask in considering how far s 10 gave power to legislate in relation to carriage by air not within the scope of either the Warsaw or the Hague conventions is not simply whether such legislation may take effect in relation to extra-territorial carriage by air, but whether it is subject to any limitation arising from the presumption that Parliament is not to be taken, by the use of general words, to legislate in the affairs of foreign nationals who do nothing to bring themselves within its jurisdiction.

An early statement of the relevant principle which underlies the presumption is found in the judgment of Dr Lushington in *The Zollverein* (1856) Sw 96 at 98, 166 ER 1038 at 1040:

'In endeavouring to put a construction on a statute, it must be borne in mind how far the power of the British legislature extends, for unless the words are so clear that a contrary construction can in no way be avoided, I must presume that the legislature did not intend to go beyond this power. The laws of Great Britain affect her own subjects everywhere—foreigners only when within her own jurisdiction.'

In *Cope v Doherty* (1858) 2 De G & J 614, 44 ER 1127 the question at issue was whether the provisions of ss 503 and 504 of the Merchant Shipping Act 1854 limiting the liability of the owner of 'any sea-going ship' could be invoked by the American owners of an American ship in litigation in the English courts arising out of a collision between that ship and another American ship on the high seas. Turner LJ said (2 De G & J 614 at 623–624, 44 ER 1127 at 1131):

'The words of these sections are no doubt wide and extensive. The words "any sea-going ship," construed with reference to the interpretation clause, would embrace every vessel navigating the sea, which is not propelled by oars, but it is not because general words are used in an Act of Parliament every case which falls within the words is to be governed by the Act. It is the duty of the Courts of justice so to construe the words as to carry into effect the meaning and intention of the legislature. We had occasion very much to consider this point in *Hawkins* v. *Gathercole* ((1854) 6 De GM & G 1, 43 ER 1129), in which case we restrained the effect of general words in the Act on which the case depended, and there are many cases in the books to the same effect, some of which are referred to in that case, and others not, but are to be found in *Viner's Abridgment*, title *"Statutes."* Was it then the intention of the legislature that the general words contained in the sections to which I have referred should extend to the case of a collision between foreign ships owned by foreigners? I think it was not. This is a British Act of Parliament, and it is not, I think, to be presumed that the British Parliament could intend to legislate as to the rights and liabilities of foreigners. In order to warrant such a conclusion, I think that either the words of the Act ought to be express or the context of it to be very clear.'

The fullest discussion of the relevant principle of statutory construction is found in the judgments in *Ex p Blain, re Sawers* (1879) 12 Ch D 522, [1874–80] All ER Rep 708. The issue in the case was whether a foreigner, domiciled and resident abroad, who had never been to England but was a partner in a firm which traded in England and had defaulted, could be made bankrupt here. The context was thus far removed from the subject matter with which we are now concerned, but the statements of principle in the judgments are comprehensive and illuminating. James LJ said (12 Ch D 522 at 526, [1874–80] All ER Rep 708 at 709–710):

'It appears to me that the whole question is governed by the broad, general, universal principle that English legislation, unless the contrary is expressly enacted or so plainly implied as to make it the duty of an English court to give effect to an English statute, is applicable only to English subjects or to foreigners who by coming into this country, whether for a long or a short time, have made themselves during that time subject to English jurisdiction. Every foreigner who comes into this country, for however limited a time, is, during his residence here within the allegiance of the sovereign, entitled to the protection of the sovereign and subject to all the laws of the sovereign. But, if a foreigner remains abroad, if he has never come into this country at all, it seems to me impossible to imagine that the English legislature could have ever intended to make such a man subject to particular English legislation.'

Brett LJ said (12 Ch D 522 at 528, [1874–80] All ER Rep 708 at 711):

'It is said that the case is literally within the words of the statute, and so, no doubt, it is. But does it follow that, because a case is literally within the words of a statute of any country, therefore it is within the jurisdiction of the courts of that country? Certainly not. The governing principle is that all legislation is *prima facie* territorial, that is to say, that the legislation of any country binds its own subjects and the subjects of other countries who for the time being bring themselves within the allegiance of the legislating power.'

And finally, Cotton LJ said (12 Ch D 522 at 531–532, [1874–80] All ER Rep 708 at 713):

'All we have to do is to interpret an Act of Parliament which uses a general word, and we have to say how that word is to be limited, when of necessity there must be some limitation. I take it the limitation is this, that all laws of the English Parliament must be territorial—territorial in this sense, that they apply to and bind all subjects of the Crown who come within the fair interpretation of them, and also all aliens who come to this country, and who, during the time they are here, do any act which, on a fair interpretation of the statute as regards them, comes within its provisions.'

In order to determine what, if any, application the principle of statutory construction discussed in these authorities may have in limiting the ambit of the power to legislate by Order in Council conferred originally by s 4 of the 1932 Act, now by s 10 of the 1961 Act, in relation to carriage by air which is not subject to either the Warsaw or the Hague

conventions, it is first necessary to consider the general character and purposes of the
Warsaw and the Hague rules, which are authorised to be applied by Order in Council to *a*
non-convention carriage by air with or without exceptions, adaptations and modifications.
The rules have these features in common. They impose liability on the carrier without
proof of fault in respect of the death of or injury to passengers and damage to or loss of
baggage or cargo which the carrier, however, may rebut by proving certain matters in
relation to the relevant causative event. They impose limits on the amount recoverable
in respect of the relevant death, injury, loss or damage. They nullify contractual *b*
provisions tending to relieve the carrier of liability or to lower the applicable limits of
liability. They allow, however, recovery against the carrier of an amount in excess of the
relevant limit if the claimant can prove certain matters in relation to the relevant
causative event. Actions for damages pursuant to the rights given by the rules can only
be brought subject to the rules and are to the exclusion of other remedies. Such actions
must be brought within a time limit. Perhaps most important of all, each set of rules *c*
contains a provision to prevent avoidance of the rules by any contractual term 'deciding
the law to be applied'. Thus, if a carrier undertakes carriage by air to which the rules
apply, he cannot contract out of the rules by a choice of law clause.

The philosophy underlying the Warsaw Convention is expounded in what I find a
most illuminating judgment of Greene LJ in *Grein v Imperial Airways Ltd* [1936] 2 All
ER 1258 at 1278–1279, [1937] 1 KB 50 at 74–77. He said: *d*

> 'The rules laid down are in effect an international code declaring the rights and
> liabilities of the parties to contracts of international carriage by air; and when by the
> appropriate machinery they are given the force of law in the territory of a High
> Contracting Party they govern (so far as regards the courts of that party) the
> contractual relations of the parties to the contract of carriage of which (to use *e*
> language appropriate to the legal systems of the United Kingdom) they become
> statutory terms. The desirability of such an international code for air carriage is
> apparent. Without it, questions of great difficulty as to the law applicable to a
> contract of international carriage by air would constantly arise. Our courts are
> familiar with similar questions arising under contracts of through carriage otherwise
> than by air; and it is easy to imagine cases where questions of the greatest difficulty *f*
> might arise as to which law or laws governed the contract and whether different
> laws might not apply to different stages of the journey ... Thus different laws
> might be held to apply according as a ticket (to take a simple case) was taken in Paris
> for a flight to London or in London for a flight to Paris, according as the carrier was
> a French or an English company, according as an accident took place in England or
> in France. Where the carriage is effected by stages covering several countries and *g*
> involving aeroplanes belonging to companies incorporated in several countries, the
> difficulties increase as well as the unlikelihood of finding in the various countries in
> which actions might be brought any uniformity of legal principles for their decision.
> It is, I think, apparent from the subject matter with which the convention deals and
> from its contents that the removal of these difficulties by means of a uniform
> international code, to be applied by the courts of the various countries adopting the *h*
> convention, is one, at any rate, of the main objects at which the convention aims;
> and it is in my judgment essential to approach it with a proper appreciation of this
> circumstance in mind. The convention is limited to international carriage. There
> was no necessity for any agreement as to carriage performed within the territory of
> one state; nor was it thought necessary to deal with the case where an aeroplane
> performing the contract of carriage began and ended its journey in the territory of *j*
> the same state without coming to earth, even if during its flight it passed over the
> territory of another state. In such a case difficulties as to the law applicable would
> not be likely to arise; in this country at any rate it could scarcely be said, for instance,
> that a contract to carry a passenger direct from London to Gibraltar without an

a intermediate landing (were such a flight possible) would be affected in any way by French law by reason of the fact that the machine in the course of its flight passed over French territory or made a forced landing therein. It was not considered useful to class as international carriage cases where the carriage begins in the territory of a state adopting the convention and ends in one which does not adopt it or *vice versa*. The reason, I think, is that the courts of the non-adopting state would not be bound by the convention and there would accordingly be no possibility of uniformity of

b decision. The fact that in cases such as this the convention does not apply, is in my judgment no argument in favour of the view that the present case is not one of international carriage. On the other hand, where the contract of carriage provides for a descent in foreign territory, the fact that the carriage begins and ends in territory belonging to the same state, would not necessarily prevent questions from arising in the courts of that state as to the law applicable to that part of the flight

c which took place over the foreign territory in question. Accordingly the convention makes express provision for this case. To take an example, any one who takes a ticket for a flight from Berlin to (say) Konigsberg in East Prussia under terms of carriage providing for an intermediate descent upon Polish territory in the Corridor will know that his contract with the carrier will be held by German courts to be governed by the code and that no question of Polish law will arise; and this would

d be so whether or not Poland was a party to the convention. The reason for confining the application of the convention where the carriage begins and ends in the territory of the same state to cases where descent in the territory of another state is provided for by the contract of carriage is sufficiently obvious. It is, I think, that where the descent in the territory of another state was involuntary, no question of the applicability of the law of that state to the contract of carriage would be likely to

e arise.'

It is to be noted that the scope of 'international carriage' within the convention definition is in no way dependent on the nationality of the carrier. There are now very few countries which are not party to one or other or both of the conventions. One, frequently referred to in the course of the argument as a source of illustrative examples,

f is Thailand. When Thai Airways carry a passenger or a cargo pursuant to a single contract from Bangkok to London or from London to Bangkok the carriage is not subject to either convention. But it was decided in *Grein v Imperial Airways Ltd* and appears never to have been doubted since that carriage of a passenger pursuant to the single contract embodied in a return ticket from a place of departure in a convention country to a destination in a non-convention country and back to the original place of departure is

g 'international carriage' within the convention definition. Thus, if Thai Airways carry a passenger on a return ticket London–Bangkok–London, this is 'international carriage' subject to the Hague Convention. This was accepted without argument in *Goldman v Thai Airways International Ltd* [1983] 3 All ER 693, [1983] 1 WLR 1186.

The United Kingdom rules have the same common features as those to which I have drawn attention in the Warsaw and Hague rules. In authorising the application of such

h rules, based on or adapted from the Hague rules, to non-convention carriage by air, what categories of such carriage may Parliament have reasonably had in contemplation as the proper subject matter of United Kingdom legislation? Just as the character of 'international carriage' in the convention definition is determined by reference to the places of departure and destination and agreed stopping places 'according to the agreement between the parties', so may the potential categories of non-convention carriage to which the United

j Kingdom rules might apply be similarly distinguished. It seems to me that four distinct categories fall for consideration. (1) Carriage in which the places of departure and destination and any agreed stopping places are all within the United Kingdom or other British territory. (2) Non-convention carriage involving a place of departure or destination or an agreed stopping place in a foreign state and a place of departure or destination or an agreed stopping place in the United Kingdom or other British territory. (3) Non-convention carriage between places of departure and destination in two foreign states *a* with no agreed stopping place in the United Kingdom or other British territory. (4) Carriage in which the places of departure and destination and any agreed stopping places are all within the territory of a single foreign state, being either a convention or a non-convention country.

Carriage in category (1) is clearly within the proper scope of the United Kingdom legislation and is covered by the United Kingdom rules. The main argument before your *b* Lordships was addressed to the classification of carriage in category (2) and the primary thrust of the submissions made on behalf of the appellant airline was directed to showing that this category of carriage by air was excluded from the proper scope of the legislation authorised by s 10 of the 1961 Act because such legislation would be 'extra-territorial' and must therefore be presumed not to be authorised by the general words of the section. In refuting this argument, counsel for the respondent widow cogently pointed out that, *c* like the conventions themselves, the United Kingdom rules had as one of their primary objectives the elimination of conflict of laws problems and that such problems would be just as likely to arise, if not excluded by uniform rules, from non-convention as from convention carriage. This proposition certainly holds good in relation to carriage in category (2). On this basis counsel for the respondent further contended that the presumption against extra-territorial legislation is effectively rebutted in relation to the *d* construction of s 10 which must therefore be construed without limitation as authorising legislation by Order in Council regulating *all* extra-territorial carriage by air.

It is precisely here that concentration on an imprecisely defined concept of extra-territoriality has, as it seems to me, confused the issue. If I may say so with respect, I believe that much of the argument addressed to your Lordships on both sides was really directed at the wrong target. All carriage by air which is, in the colloquial sense, *e* international, whether or not it falls within the definition of 'international carriage' in either of the conventions, is, again in the colloquial sense, extra-territorial. But we are here concerned with legislation governing the rights and liabilities of parties to international contracts of carriage. If contracts for international carriage by air, as in the case of carriage within category (2), provide for carriage from or to a place of departure or destination or via an agreed stopping place in the United Kingdom or other British *f* territory, British legislation imposing certain compulsory terms on such contracts does not seem to me to involve any usurpation of an illegitimate authority over foreign subjects of the kind which Parliament is presumed not to intend. It is right to emphasise again the obvious desirability, in relation to carriage in category (2), as in relation to 'international carriage' within the convention definition, of uniform rules applicable by British courts for the avoidance of the kind of conflict of laws problems discussed by *g* Greene LJ in the passage from his judgment in *Grein v Imperial Airways Ltd* [1936] 2 All ER 1258 at 1278–1279, [1937] 1 KB 50 at 74–77 which I have quoted. For relevant purposes, carriers, passengers, consignors, consignees and others who enter into contracts with such a British connection as is presupposed in relation to carriage by air in category (2) may fairly be regarded, in my opinion, as coming within the jurisdiction of the *h* British legislature in relation to their contractual rights and obligations. In relation to carriage in category (2), I conclude that the so-called presumption against extra-territorial legislation has no relevance and s 10 is to be construed as duly authorising the United Kingdom rules imposed by Sch 1 to the 1967 order in relation to that category of carriage.

But when I turn to consider contracts of carriage by air in categories (3) and (4) it seems to me that a wholly different question arises from that raised by carriage in category (2). *j* Contracts of carriage by air in direct flights between two non-convention countries can be of no legitimate concern to the United Kingdom legislature and if Parliament claimed to regulate the rights and liabilities of the parties to such contracts, it would indeed be asserting a jurisdiction over foreign subjects who have done nothing to bring themselves within that jurisdiction. If this applies to carriage in category (3), it applies a fortiori to

carriage in category (4), which is strictly the only category of carriage in relation to which
a your Lordships have to decide whether the United Kingdom rules apply. Carriage in
category (3) may give rise to conflict of laws problems, albeit problems with which it is
unlikely in the extreme that British courts need ever be concerned. But carriage in
category (4) could only exceptionally give rise to any such problems at all. A contract
made and to be performed wholly within the territory of a foreign state will normally be
subject to the laws of that state and to no other. That the United Kingdom Parliament
b should exercise a power to regulate the terms of such contracts would seem to me to
present an extreme example of the legislature doing precisely that which the relevant
authorities tell us it is presumed not to intend. To illustrate the proposition graphically
by a concrete example, it is surely inconceivable that Parliament by s 10 of the 1961 Act
intended to authorise the imposition by Order in Council of the Hague rules or any
modified version of them on contracts of carriage to be performed wholly within the
c United States of America, notwithstanding that in relation to international carriage the
United States of America had chosen to retain the Warsaw rules in preference to the
Hague rules.
   For these reasons I have reached the conclusion that the words of s 10 'carriage by air
. . . of such descriptions as may be specified' should be construed as limited to carriage in
categories (1) and (2), which are appropriate subjects of United Kingdom legislation, but
d as excluding carriage in categories (3) and (4), which are not.
   In reaching this conclusion I have not overlooked the fact that two current legal
textbooks which address the point favour the conclusion reached by the judge and Court
of Appeal: see Shawcross and Beaumont *Air Law* (4th edn, 1977) para 401 and *Dicey and
Morris on The Conflict of Laws* (11th edn, 1987) vol 2, p 1272. But in assessing the weight
to be attributed to this textbook consensus it is necessary to consider its evolution.
e   The question at issue could not have arisen before the coming into force of the Carriage
by Air (Non-international Carriage) (United Kingdom) Order 1952. The first edition of
Shawcross and Beaumont published after 1952 was the third edition in 1966. The view was
there expressed that the words of the order itself applying the provisions of Sch 3 to the
order to *all carriage by air* meant no less than they said (see p 362). The fourth edition,
published in 1977 after the coming into force of the 1967 order, enlarges on the point in
f the following passage (pp 388–389):

> 'In cases coming before the English courts, almost all such carriage [ie non-
> convention carriage] (the exceptional cases being those of gratuitous carriage other
> than by the Crown or by an air transport undertaking) is governed by the First
> Schedule to the Carriage by Air Acts (Application of Provisions) Order 1967, and so
> *g* far as the issues are regulated by provisions of that Schedule further choice-of-law
> questions cannot arise. At first sight, the proposition just advanced may seem
> surprising. It ill accords with the common law rules of the conflict of laws to find,
> for example, that an action in the English courts arising out of the injury of a
> Nigerian passenger travelling on a domestic Nigerian flight operated by a Nigerian
> carrier and under a contract the proper law of which was Nigerian should be
> *h* governed by the provisions of an English statutory instrument, without any
> reference to the law of Nigeria. The proposition is, however, in accordance with
> article 3 of the 1967 Order, made under section 10 of the Carriage by Air Act
> 1961:"This Order shall apply to all carriage by air, not being carriage to which the
> amended Convention applies". Some of the provisions of the Order, that is the
> Second Schedule, expressly apply to international carriage, and are not limited to
> *j* examples of such carriage linked in some way to England. Accordingly the normal
> presumption, in interpreting a statute, against giving it extra-territorial effect cannot
> apply.'

   The editions of *Dicey and Morris* published since 1952 are the seventh (1958), eighth
(1967), ninth (1973), tenth (1980) and eleventh (1987). The view expressed in each

edition up to the ninth is sufficiently indicated in the following short passage from that
edition (pp 829–830):

> 'Not all contracts for through carriage by air are "international" contracts as
> defined by the Warsaw Convention. If the Convention does not apply and if the
> parties have failed to determine the proper law either expressly or by implication,
> an English court will perhaps be inclined to apply the law of the country from
> which the aircraft took off for the first portion of its flight. This will often be the *lex
> loci contractus*. There does not appear to be any English or Scottish authority on the
> point. Where the law to be applied is that of England, Scotland or Northern Ireland,
> the substantive provisions of the Conventions (with some modifications) will apply
> to non-international carriage by virtue of the Carriage by Air Acts (Application of
> Provisions) Order 1967.'

But by the time of publication of the tenth edition Dr Morris (at p 844) had adopted the
view expressed in the fourth edition of *Shawcross and Beaumont*.

It seems to me, with respect to the learned authors, that, like the judge and the Court
of Appeal, they never addressed the basic question whether the enabling power conferred
by s 10 of the 1961 Act in relation to non-convention carriage by air should be construed
as subject to any limitation, and moreover they proceeded on the fallacious assumption
that because Sch 2 to the 1967 order, continuing to give legal effect to the Warsaw rules
in United Kingdom law, was 'extra-territorial' in effect, Sch 1 must necessarily be given
an unlimited extra-territorial operation.

It remains only to notice that an important component, perhaps even the cornerstone,
of the argument for the respondent widow was that Sch 1 to the 1967 order could safely
be held to apply in British courts to contracts of carriage by air made and to be performed
wholly within a foreign state because in the overwhelming majority of such cases,
notwithstanding that the plaintiff had succeeded in effecting service on the carrier here,
the carrier would be able to obtain a stay of execution on the ground that the courts of
the relevant foreign state would provide the only convenient forum for the litigation and
would thus escape the application of the United Kingdom rules. But the doctrine of
forum non conveniens cannot possibly provide any effective counterweight to the
presumption that Parliament does not intend by general words to legislate in relation to
the affairs of foreign subjects beyond its jurisdiction in circumstances where that
presumption properly applies. If the presumption applies, it must enable a foreigner
beyond the jurisdiction, though duly served in a British court, to claim that the legislation
has no application to him rather than being forced to rely on the doctrine of forum non
conveniens to escape its application.

For these reasons I would allow the appeal. Leave to appeal was given on terms that
the appellants would not seek to disturb the orders for costs below and would pay the
respondent's costs of the appeal in any event. I would accordingly propose that the orders
of the judge and the Court of Appeal be set aside, save as to costs, that the preliminary
issue be answered to the effect that the carriage by air referred to in the statement of
claim was not carriage by air in respect of which Sch 1 to the Carriage by Air Acts
(Application of Provisions) Order 1967 had effect and that the appellants pay the
respondent's costs in this House.

LORD GRIFFITHS. My Lords, the question in this appeal is whether the Carriage by
Air Act 1961 and the Carriage by Air Acts (Application of Provisions) Order 1967, SI
1967/480, were intended by Parliament to apply to an air accident in Bangladesh on an
internal domestic flight which was not governed by any international convention. The
history of the English legislation and the background, content and primary purpose of
the Warsaw Convention and the amended Warsaw Convention known as the Hague
Convention are reviewed in the speeches of my noble and learned friends Lord Bridge
and Lord Jauncey. I gratefully adopt what they have said and will not repeat it. Although

the judge and the Court of Appeal recognised that it was a surprising result, they felt
a compelled by the wording of the Carriage by Air Acts (Application of Provisions) Order
1967 to conclude that it was intended to apply to such a flight. That the language of the
order is wide enough to embrace this result is beyond argument. But the language of
many statutes and orders read literally is of sufficient width to apply to situations in other
countries. It is, however, unnecessary for the draftsman to insert language specifically
limiting the effect of statutes to this country because of the well-recognised rule that the
b statute will be construed to apply only to matters that fall properly to be legislated by our
own Parliament and that, in the absence of clear and compelling words, they will not be
given extra-territorial effect.

In the field of air law a recent example of the application of this rule is to be found in
Air-India v Wiggins [1980] 2 All ER 593, [1980] 1 WLR 815. In that case Air-India carried
a cargo of live birds consigned from India to Heathrow Airport. Owing to lack of
c ventilation most of the birds died on the journey before the aircraft entered British
airspace. The defendant airline was charged with contravening art 5(2) of the Transit of
Animals (General) Order 1973, SI 1973/1377, made under s 23(b) and (c) of the Diseases
of Animals Act 1950 (as adapted to air transport by s 11 of and Sch 2 to the Agriculture
(Miscellaneous Provisions) Act 1954), by carrying the birds in a way likely to cause them
injury or unnecessary suffering. The statute and the order were drafted in the widest
d terms. Section 23 of the 1950 Act provided:

> 'The Minister may make such orders as he thinks fit . . . (b) for ensuring for
> animals carried by sea or by air a proper supply of food and water and proper
> ventilation during the passage and on landing; (c) for protecting them from
> unnecessary suffering during the passage and on landing.'

e Article 3(3) of the 1973 order provided:

> 'In relation to carriage by sea or air, the provisions of this order shall apply to
> animals carried on any vessel or aircraft to or from a port or airport in Great Britain,
> whether or not such animals are loaded or unloaded at such port or airport.'

f Article 5(2) provided:

> 'No person shall carry any animal by sea, air, road or rail, or cause or permit any
> animal to be so carried, in a way which is likely to cause injury or unnecessary
> suffering to the said animal.'

The justices convicted the airline holding that, by virtue of art 3(3), proceedings could
g be brought against foreign nationals for offences committed abroad. The Crown Court
and the Divisional Court upheld the decision of the magistrates. This House allowed an
appeal by the airline holding that s 23 and the order made thereunder were to be
construed as limited by the presumption against extra-territorial effect and that the
statute was confined to incidents occurring in British airspace. In his speech Lord Diplock
explained the application of the principle in the following passage ([1980] 2 All ER 593
h at 596, [1980] 1 WLR 815 at 819):

> 'My Lords, in construing Acts of Parliament there is a well-established presumption
> that, in the absence of clear and specific words to the contrary, an "offence-creating
> section" of an Act of Parliament (to borrow an expression used by this House in *Cox
> v Army Council* ([1962] 1 All ER 880 at 882, [1963] AC 48 at 67) was not intended to
> **j** make conduct taking place outside the territorial jurisdiction of the Crown an
> offence triable in an English criminal court. As Viscount Simonds put it ([1962] 1
> All ER 880 at 882, [1963] AC 48 at 67): ". . . apart from those exceptional cases in
> which specific provision is made in regard to acts committed abroad, the whole
> body of the criminal law of England deals with acts committed in England." *Cox v
> Army Council* was concerned with a statute which in the plainest possible words

made acts committed abroad by serving members of the British army offences
triable by court-martial. The presumption against a parliamentary intention to   *a*
make acts *done by foreigners abroad* offences triable by English criminal courts is even
stronger. As Lord Russell CJ said in *R v Jameson* [1896] 2 QB 425 at 430: "One other
general canon of construction is this—that if any construction otherwise be possible,
an Act will not be construed as applying to foreigners in respect to acts done by
them outside the dominions of the sovereign power enacting." Two consequences
follow from these principles of statutory construction: the first is that if the minister   *b*
had power to make an order under the statute, making acts done by foreigners
abroad offences triable in English criminal courts, such power must have been
conferred on him by words in the statute so clear and specific as to be incapable of
any other meaning; the second is that the words of the order must themselves be
explicable only as a clear and unambiguous exercise of that power. If either the
empowering words of s 23(*b*) of the Act or the enacting words of art 3(3) of the order   *c*
would have a sensible content if restricted to acts done within the territorial
jurisdiction of the Crown, they must be so construed.'

That was, of course, a case dealing with a criminal offence; the line of authority cited
by Lord Bridge shows that the presumption or rule applies equally to statutes that affect
civil liability. I can see no reason, in principle, why it should be any more the concern of   *d*
our Parliament to legislate to create civil rights in foreign countries triable in our courts
than it would be to create criminal offences in a foreign country triable in our courts. I
can discern no legitimate purpose for this country to seek to impose either its own
criminal law or its own civil law on foreigners in their own countries. It is, of course,
true that Mr Holmes was a visitor to Bangladesh and not a native of that country; but
that can make no difference. If a foreigner comes to this country he must conduct   *e*
himself in accordance with our laws and, by the same token, if one of our citizens goes
to a foreign country, he must conduct himself in accordance with the laws of that country
and, if misfortune there befalls him, be it of a civil or criminal nature, it is by the laws of
that country that he should be judged. If Mr Holmes had been killed in Bangladesh in a
car or railway accident and his widow was permitted, under the principles of forum
conveniens to bring a claim for his death in this country, it would be judged by the law   *f*
of Bangladesh. I can see no reason why our Parliament should wish to legislate to provide
for domestic air law in Bangladesh any more than it would wish to legislate on road
traffic or railway safety in Bangladesh, and I do not believe that it intended to do so.

The basis of the rule that statutes do not have extra-territorial effect is the presumption
that our own Parliament will not seek to intervene in matters that are legitimately the
concern of another country. Countries respect one another's sovereignty and the right of   *g*
each country to legislate for matters within their own boundaries. If as a result of
international co-operation a number of countries agree to adopt the same law, the
domestic legislation that gives effect to this international agreement in this country is
not extra-territorial within the meaning of the rule. In such circumstances our domestic
legislation is not an interference with the sovereignty of the other countries but the
recognition of their wish that we should alter our own law to accord with the common   *h*
will. The Warsaw and Hague conventions dealt with international carriage by air as
therein defined. It is significant, however, that they did not deal with domestic carriage
by air which did not involve another country. If before the conventions were entered
into Parliament had enacted a statute giving power to Her Majesty in Council to make
orders 'in respect of such carriage by air as may be specified in the order' I do not believe
that anyone would have supposed that Parliament intended to authorise the making of   *j*
orders to govern carriage by air on domestic airlines within, say, the United States of
America. It would be no legitimate concern of Parliament to do so and the rule against
the extra-territorial effect of our legislation would apply.

After we had entered into the first Warsaw Convention, s 4 of the Carriage by Air Act
1932 provided:

a
'His Majesty may by Order in Council apply the provisions of the First Schedule to this Act and any provision of section one of this Act to such carriage by air, not being international carriage by air as defined in the said First Schedule, as may be specified in the Order, subject however to such exceptions, adaptations and modifications, if any, as may be so specified. Any such order may extend to the United Kingdom, and to all or any of the territories mentioned in the last preceding section.'

b
In my view the rule applies to this wording with equal force to prevent the power being construed to apply to domestic carriage by air in the United States. It is not legitimate to say that because this country and the United States have agreed to adopt the same rules for certain types of international carriage by air, our Parliament should now be free to legislate for the domestic affairs of the United States. The very fact that the Warsaw
c Convention did not apply to purely domestic carriage shows that it was the intention of the signatories to retain the right to legislate for carriage by air within their own boundaries, and we should apply a construction to our own legislation that does not violate that right.

The same argument applies to the power contained in s 10 of the Carriage by Air Act 1961 which must bear the same construction as s 4 of the Carriage by Air Act 1932.

d The construction adopted by the courts below fails, in my view, to give sufficient weight to the presumption against the intention of Parliament to legislate for matters that are properly the concern of other countries. It was referred to as a 'tentative assumption that it was not intended to subject transactions taking place abroad to British statutory rules overriding the proper law of the transaction'. In my view, the rule of construction is far more deeply entrenched than a 'tentative assumption'. The Court of
e Appeal concentrated its attention on the construction of the Carriage by Air Acts (Application of Provisions) Order 1967, but the crucial question in this case is to decide whether Parliament ever intended to give the power to make orders governing domestic air law in other countries, and this depends on the construction to be given to 'carriage by air' in the 1932 and 1961 Acts. I can think of no reason why Parliament should have thought it right to take on itself to legislate for matters which are no concern of ours.
f The limit of recovery for a fatal accident in Bangladesh is set at £913 by their domestic law. This seems a pitifully inadequate sum by European standards but may have a wholly different significance in the context of that country's economy. It surely cannot be the concern of this country to substitute for that limit of £913 the sum of £83,763 which would be the result of giving extra-territorial effect to our legislation.

In my view the phrase 'carriage by air . . . of such descriptions as may be specified' in
g s 10 of the Carriage by Air Act 1961, in conformity with the rule against the extra-territorial effect of our legislation, cannot have been intended to apply to the circumstances of this accident, and I agree that the phrase should receive the limited construction proposed by my noble and learned friend Lord Bridge. Naturally, I feel the greatest sympathy with the widow but, for these reasons and those contained in the speeches of my noble and learned friends Lord Bridge and Lord Jauncey, with which I am in full
h agreement, I would allow this appeal.

LORD ACKNER. My Lords, I have had the advantage of reading in draft the speeches of my noble and learned friends Lord Bridge, Lord Griffiths and Lord Jauncey. For the reasons they give I would allow the appeal and would make the order which my noble
j and learned friend Lord Bridge proposes.

LORD JAUNCEY OF TULLICHETTLE. My Lords, in August 1984 the respondent's husband, a British citizen, was killed when one of the appellant's aircraft in which he was travelling crashed during the course of an internal scheduled flight between the two Bangladeshi cities of Chittagong and Dhaka. The contract of carriage was made

in Bangladesh to be wholly performed within that country and it is not in dispute that
the proper law applicable thereto was that of Bangladesh. The question raised by this *a*
appeal is whether notwithstanding the admitted proper law of contract the respondent,
having sued the appellants in England, is entitled to rely on the provisions of the Carriage
by Air Acts (Application of Provisions) Order 1967, SI 1967/480, rather than on the law
of Bangladesh in relation to the contract of carriage. If Bangladeshi law applies the
respondent can recover no more than £913, whereas if United Kingdom law applies she
can, under the above order, recover £83,763, which sum is agreed to be less than that *b*
which she would otherwise have been able to recover if no limit of liability existed.

In order to understand the issues involved it is necessary to examine in some detail the
relevant United Kingdom legislation and the historical background thereto. On 12
October 1929 the United Kingdom government became a signatory at Warsaw to a
convention for the unification of certain rules relating to international carriage by air
(the Warsaw Convention). On 15 May 1933 there came into force the Carriage by Air *c*
Act 1932, of which the long title was in the following terms:

> 'An Act to give effect to a Convention for the unification of certain rules relating
> to international carriage by air, to make provision for applying the rules contained
> in the said Convention, subject to exceptions, adaptations and modifications, to
> carriage by air which is not international carriage within the meaning of the *d*
> Convention, and for purposes connected with the purposes aforesaid.'

Section 1(1) of the 1932 Act was in the following terms:

> 'As from such day as His Majesty may by Order in Council certify to be the day
> on which the Convention comes into force as regards the United Kingdom, the
> provisions thereof as set out in the First Schedule to this Act shall, so far as they *e*
> relate to the rights and liabilities of carriers, passengers, consignors, consignees and
> other persons and subject to the provisions of this section, have the force of law in
> the United Kingdom in relation to any carriage by air to which the Convention
> applies, irrespective of the nationality of the aircraft performing that carriage.'

Section 1(4) provided that any liability imposed on a carrier by the Warsaw Convention *f*
in respect of the death of a passenger should be in substitution for any liability under
statute or at common law. Section 4 of the 1932 Act provided that any provisions of the
Warsaw Convention, which were set out in Sch 1 could by Order in Council be applied
'to such carriage by air, not being international carriage by air as defined in the said First
Schedule, as may be specified in the Order ...' The Warsaw Convention applies to
'international carriage' which was defined in art 1(2) thereof as meaning: *g*

> 'any carriage in which, according to the contract made by the parties, the place of
> departure and the place of destination, whether or not there be a break in the
> carriage or a transhipment, are situated either within the territories of two High
> Contracting Parties or, within the territory of a single High Contracting Party, if
> there is an agreed stopping place within a territory subject to the sovereignty, *h*
> suzerainty, mandate or authority of another Power, even though that Power is not a
> party to the Convention ...'

In summary, the Warsaw Convention (1) imposes liability on an air carrier for damage
sustained in the event of death or injury of a passenger arising out of an accident on
board the aircraft or in the course of embarking or disembarking. This liability can be
avoided if the carrier proves that he and his servants or agents have taken all necessary *j*
measures to avoid the damage or that it was impossible for him or them so to do, (2)
limits the liability of a carrier for each passenger to a fixed sum and makes null and void
any provision tending to reduce or exclude the carrier's liability, (3) removes the carrier's
right to limit his liability if the damage is caused by his wilful misconduct, (4) specifies a

number of forums in the territory of high contracting parties to the convention, in one
a of which the plaintiff must elect to sue the carrier, (5) imposes a time limit on the raising
of actions and (6) provides that any clause in the contract whereby the parties purport to
infringe the rules in the convention whether by deciding the law to be applied or by
altering the rules as to jurisdiction shall be null and void.

The object of the convention was stated to be 'the Unification of Certain Rules relating
to International Carriage by Air', and in relation thereto I cannot do better than quote
b the words of Greene LJ in *Grein v Imperial Airways Ltd* [1936] 2 All ER 1258 at 1277–
1278, [1937] 1 KB 50 at 74–75:

> 'By "unification of certain rules" is clearly meant, "the adoption of certain uniform
> rules," that is to say, rules which will be applied by the courts of the High
> Contracting Parties in all matters where contracts of international carriage by air
> *c* come into question. The rules laid down are in effect an international code declaring
> the rights and liabilities of the parties to contracts of international carriage by air;
> and when by the appropriate machinery they are given the force of law in the
> territory of a High Contracting Party they govern (so far as regards the courts of that
> party) the contractual relations of the parties to the contract of carriage of which (to
> use language appropriate to the legal systems of the United Kingdom) they become
> *d* statutory terms. The desirability of such an international code for air carriage is
> apparent. Without it, questions of great difficulty as to the law applicable to a
> contract of international carriage by air would constantly arise. Our courts are
> familiar with similar questions arising under contracts of through carriage otherwise
> than by air; and it is easy to imagine cases where questions of the greatest difficulty
> might arise as to which law or laws governed the contract and whether different
> *e* laws might not apply to different stages of the journey.'

The Carriage by Air (Non-international Carriage) (United Kingdom) Order 1952, SI
1952/158, which came into operation on 1 April 1952 and which was made in exercise
of the powers contained in s 4 of the 1932 Act applied the Warsaw Convention with
certain modifications 'to all carriage by air, not being international carriage by air as
f defined in the [convention].' Although there appears to have been no decision in the
courts of the United Kingdom on the meaning of these words in the 1952 order, the
authors of Shawcross and Beaumont *Air Law* (3rd edn, 1966) submit at the beginning of
ch 21 that it would apply to cases coming before the English courts whether or not the
damage occurred outside the United Kingdom and whether or not the proper law of the
contract of carriage was the law of a country outside the United Kingdom. The reference
to 'English courts' must of course be read as a reference to United Kingdom courts. If this
g submission which was repeated in subsequent editions of the above work were correct it
would follow that, so long as the 1952 order was in force, in any action of damages at the
instance of a passenger against an air carrier the United Kingdom courts would, with one
or two very limited exceptions, be bound to apply either the rules of the Warsaw
Convention where appropriate, or those rules as modified by the 1952 order irrespective
h of the terms of the contract of carriage or the places between which that contract took
effect.

In September 1955 a number of states including the United Kingdom signed at The
Hague a convention amending the Warsaw Convention, to which for convenience I shall
refer as the Hague Convention. On 22 June 1961 there was passed the Carriage by Air
Act 1961, whose long title was:

j
> 'An Act to give effect to the Convention concerning international carriage by air
> known as "the Warsaw Convention as amended at The Hague 1955," to enable the
> rules contained in that Convention to be applied, with or without modification, in
> other cases and, in particular, to non-international carriage by air; and for connected
> purposes.'

Section 1(1) of the 1961 Act, which came into force on 1 June 1967, is in the following terms:

'Subject to this section, the provisions of the Convention known as "the Warsaw Convention as amended at The Hague, 1955" as set out in the First Schedule to this Act shall, so far as they relate to the rights and liabilities of carriers, carriers' servants and agents, passengers, consignors, consignees and other persons, and subject to the provisions of this Act, have the force of law in the United Kingdom in relation to any carriage by air to which the Convention applies, irrespective of the nationality of the aircraft performing that carriage; and the Carriage by Air Act, 1932 (which gives effect to the Warsaw Convention in its original form), shall cease to have effect.'

Section 9 provides that the 1961 Act with or without modification may be extended by Order in Council to the Isle of Man, any of the Channel Islands and any colony or protectorate, protected state or United Kingdom trust territory. Section 10(1) is in the following terms:

'Her Majesty may by Order in Council apply the First Schedule to this Act, together with any other provisions of this Act, to carriage by air, not being carriage by air to which the Convention applies, of such descriptions as may be specified in the Order, subject to such exceptions, adaptations and modifications, if any, as may be so specified.'

Schedule 1 to the 1961 Act contains the English and French texts of the Hague Convention of which the following articles have relevance to this appeal. Article 1 is in the following, inter alia, terms:

'(1) This Convention applies to all international carriage of persons, baggage or cargo performed by aircraft for reward. It applies equally to gratuitous carriage by aircraft performed by an air transport undertaking.

(2) For the purposes of this Convention, the expression *international carriage* means any carriage in which, according to the agreement between the parties, the place of departure and the place of destination, whether or not there be a break in the carriage or a transhipment, are situated either within the territories of two High Contracting Parties or within the territory of a single High Contracting Party if there is an agreed stopping place within the territory of another State, even if that State is not a High Contracting Party. Carriage between two points within the territory of a single High Contracting Party without an agreed stopping place within the territory of another State is not international carriage for the purposes of this Convention . . .'

Article 2(2) excludes the carriage of mail and postal packages from the application of the convention. Article 17 imposes liability on the carrier for physical damage sustained by a passenger. Article 20 sets out what the carrier must prove in order to avoid liability. Article 22(1) specifies the limit of the carrier's liability for each passenger. Article 23(1) provides:

'Any provision tending to relieve the carrier of liability or to fix a lower limit than that which is laid down in this Convention shall be null and void, but the nullity of any such provision does not involve the nullity of the whole contract, which shall remain subject to the provisions of this Convention.'

Article 28(1) provides:

'An action for damages must be brought, at the option of the plaintiff, in the territory of one of the High Contracting Parties, either before the court having jurisdiction where the carrier is ordinarily resident, or has his principal place of

business, or has an establishment by which the contract has been made or before the
court having jurisdiction at the place of destination.'

Article 32 provides, inter alia:

'Any clause contained in the contract and all special agreements entered into
before the damage occurred by which the parties purport to infringe the rules laid
down by this Convention, whether by deciding the law to be applied, or by altering
the rules as to jurisdiction, shall be null and void . . .'

The principal differences between the Warsaw and the Hague conventions are that in
the latter (1) the limit of liability of the carrier is doubled and (2) the circumstances are
extended in which the carrier is disabled from relying on limitation of liability.

At present 35 states are parties to the Warsaw Convention and over 100 are parties to
the Hague Convention. A number of states including the United Kingdom are parties to
both conventions whereas the United States is a party only to the Warsaw Convention.
With the notable exception of Thailand almost every state in the world of any significance
is a party to one or other of the conventions. Since international carriage in each
convention is defined by reference to the high contracting parties thereto, it follows that
carriage from the territory of a state which is a party only to one convention to the
territory of a state which is a party only to the other is not covered by the rules of either
convention.

On 1 June 1967 there also came into operation the Carriage by Air Acts (Application
of Provisions) Order 1967, SI 1967/480, of which art 3 is in the following terms: 'This
Order shall apply to all carriage by air, not being carriage to which the amended
Convention applies.' The 1967 order has two principal purposes, namely (1) to apply the
Hague Convention with modification to carriage which is not international carriage as
defined in the Warsaw Convention, and (2) to re-enact the Warsaw Convention as part of
the law of the United Kingdom consequent on the repeal of the 1932 Act. The first
purpose is achieved by art 4 and Sch 1. Article 4 is headed 'Non-international carriage,
and carriage of mail and postal packages' and is in the following terms:

'Schedule 1 to this Order shall have effect in respect of carriage to which this
Order applies, being either—(a) carriage which is not international carriage as
defined in Schedule 2 to this Order, or (b) carriage of mail or postal packages.'

Schedule 1 sets out the exceptions, adaptations and modifications to the Hague Convention
which are effected by the order. For the purposes of this appeal two modifications are
important, namely (1) an increase in the limit of liability in art 22(1) from 250,000 to
875,000 francs for each passenger and (2) the omission of art 28.

The second purpose is achieved by art 5 and Sch 2 which together give effect in the
law of the United Kingdom to the Hague Convention amended to the extent that it has
assumed the original Warsaw form.

Further orders applying the 1961 Act and the 1967 order to the Channel Islands, the
Isle of Man and to specified overseas territories came into operation on 1 June 1967. For
convenience I shall hereafter refer to all territories to which the 1961 Act and the 1967
order apply and have been applied as 'United Kingdom territory'.

The combined effect of the 1961 Act and the 1967 order is to create three different
categories of carriage by air to which the legislation applies, namely (1) international
carriage as defined in the Hague Convention, (2) international carriage as defined in the
Warsaw Convention and (3) carriage to which art 4 of and Sch 1 to the 1967 order are
applicable.

The issue between the parties to this appeal is whether the contract of carriage between
the deceased and the appellants was subject to the provisions of art 4 and Sch 1 and hence
within the third category. The question was tried as a preliminary issue before Leggatt J,
who found in favour of the respondent that these provisions did apply (see [1987] 2

Lloyd's Rep 192). The Court of Appeal affirmed his judgment (see [1988] 2 Lloyd's Rep
120). Bingham LJ considered that Sch 2 to the 1967 order was—   *a*

> 'of crucial importance in construing the 1967 Order for two reasons. First, it is
> inescapable that schedule 2 has the force of law in the United Kingdom in cases to
> which it applies. This the appellant airline rightly acknowledged. Secondly, as again
> the appellant airline rightly acknowledged, schedule 2 must be understood as having
> extra-territorial effect. If a claim is brought here against an airline over which the *b*
> English Court has jurisdiction under art 28, schedule 2 would be applied even
> though the carriage in question was between the territories of two foreign states
> (parties to the unamended Convention) not touching the United Kingdom at any
> point.'

(See [1988] 2 Lloyd's Rep 120 at 122–123.)   *c*
   He continued:

> 'The question whether a statutory enactment is intended to have extra-territorial
> effect is, however, one to be decided on the language of the enactment in question
> having regard to the subject-matter and other relevant circumstances. Here, it is
> accepted that the amended Convention scheduled to the 1961 Act and the *d*
> unamended Convention in schedule 2 to the 1967 order have the force of law and
> have extra-territorial effect. Schedule 1, as I have suggested, plainly has the force of
> law. The language used in the order and in schedule 1 could not have been more
> comprehensive. The draftsman could not have failed to appreciate that this language
> was broad enough to embrace international travel not covered by the amended or
> unamended Conventions and not touching the United Kingdom, domestic flights *e*
> abroad and domestic flights at home. If he intended to differentiate, it seems to me
> inconceivable that he would not have done so, or that he would have relied on a
> presumption which in the context of this legislation read as a whole would have
> been quite inappropriate. No presumption against extra-territoriality can in my
> view survive a straightfoward reading of these provisions.'
>   *f*

Dillon LJ considered that the judgment of Leggatt J produced a startling result but was
unable to see any escape from the conclusion that he was right (at 124).
   The arguments before your Lordships ranged a good deal wider than they appear to
have done in the courts below. The appellants maintained that Sch 1 to the 1967 order
applied only to contracts of carriage where the proper law of the carriage was that of a
United Kingdom country, and they relied heavily on the presumption that a statute will *g*
not be construed as having extra-territorial effect unless it plainly so provides. The
respondent on the other hand submitted that the 1961 Act and the 1967 order read
together produced a comprehensive code which embraced all actions in the United
Kingdom arising out of carriage by air anywhere. Any presumption against extra-
territoriality was ousted by the unambiguous terms of the Act and the order. The effect *h*
of the respondent's argument is to treat art 4 of the 1967 order as a residue clause
applicable to all carriage by air wheresoever it may take place which does not fall within
the scope of either the Hague or the Warsaw convention.
   The words 'such carriage by air, not being . . . as may be specified' and 'carriage by air,
not being . . . as may be specified' occurring respectively in ss 4 and 10 of the 1932 and
1961 Acts are very general. So also are the words 'all carriage by air, not being . . .' which *j*
occur in arts 1 and 3 respectively of the 1952 and 1967 orders. However, in construing
such general words regard must be had to the object of the statute, to the powers of the
legislature and to the context in which the words appear. Frequently have the courts
refused to give unlimited meaning to general words because of one or more of the above
factors. Indeed, as Lord Halsbury LC in *Cox v Hakes* (1890) 15 App Cas 506 at 517 said:

a

'. . . it is impossible to contend that the mere fact of a general word being used in a statute precludes all inquiry into the object of the statute or the mischief which it was intended to remedy.'

Lord Halsbury LC's words are particularly apposite when considering whether or not general words were intended to operate extra-territorially because there is a long line of authority to the effect that English legislation is presumed to be territorial in its effect, that is to say is presumed not to try and regulate matters which are primarily the concern

b of another state, unless the contrary is expressed or so clearly implied as to be inescapable. This presumption, which has been described as a rule of construction, is critical to the issue raised in this appeal. Before turning to the authorities in which the principle is enunciated I should add that although they are all English it must follow that the presumption as to territoriality would apply equally to the United Kingdom as a whole where the statute applied to the United Kingdom rather than to England alone.

c In *The Zollverein* (1856) Sw 96 at 98, 166 ER 1038 at 1040 Dr Lushington, in considering the applicability of a section of the Merchant Shipping Act 1854 to a foreign ship, said:

d

'In endeavouring to put a construction on a statute, it must be borne in mind how far the power of the British legislature extends, for unless the words are so clear that a contrary intention can in no way be avoided, I must presume that the legislature did not intend to go beyond this power. The laws of Great Britain affect her own subjects everywhere—foreigners only when within her own jurisdiction. Attempts have been made, as in trying to enforce customs' laws, to bind foreigners out of our own jurisdiction, and great inconvenience has resulted therefrom.'

e In *Cope v Doherty* (1858) 2 De G & J 614, 44 ER 1127 the question of the applicability of other sections of the Merchant Shipping Act 1854 to two foreign ships on the high seas was considered. Turner LJ said (2 De G & J 614 at 623–624, 44 ER 1127 at 1131):

f

g

h

'The words of these sections are no doubt wide and extensive. The words "any sea-going ship," construed with reference to the interpretation clause, would embrace every vessel navigating the sea, which is not propelled by oars, but it is not because general words are used in an Act of Parliament every case which falls within the words is to be governed by the Act. It is the duty of the Courts of justice so to construe the words as to carry into effect the meaning and intention of the legislature. We had occasion very much to consider this point in *Hawkins* v. *Gathercole* ((1854) 6 De GM & G 1, 43 ER 1129), in which case we restrained the effect of general words in the Act on which the case depended, and there are many cases in the books to the same effect, some of which are referred to in that case, and others not, but are to be found in *Viner's Abridgment*, title "*Statutes.*" Was it then the intention of the legislature that the general words contained in the sections to which I have referred should extend to the case of a collision between foreign ships owned by foreigners? I think it was not. This is a British Act of Parliament, and it is not, I think, to be presumed that the British Parliament could intend to legislate as to the rights and liabilities of foreigners. In order to warrant such a conclusion, I think that either the words of the Act ought to be express or the context of it to be very clear.'

Later, he said (2 De G & J 614 at 625, 44 ER 1127 at 1131):

j

'But what seems to me to be more decisive upon the subject, is the context of the Act. If the 504th section reaches the case of a collision between foreign vessels owned by foreigners, the 503rd section must also reach that case, and then we must suppose that the British Parliament meant by this Act to legislate upon the questions what should be inserted in the bills of lading of foreign shippers, and what should be declared by them to the masters of the vessels on board which their goods were shipped.'

In *Ex p Blain, re Sawers* (1879) 12 Ch D 522, [1874–80] All ER Rep 708 the Court of
Appeal refused to apply the provisions of the Bankruptcy Act 1869 to two foreigners *a*
domiciled and permanently resident in Chile. James LJ said (12 Ch D 522 at 526, [1874–
80] All ER Rep 708 at 709):

> 'It appears to me that the whole question is governed by the broad, general,
> universal principle that English legislation, unless the contrary is expressly enacted
> or so plainly implied as to make it the duty of an English Court to give effect to an *b*
> English statute, is applicable only to English subjects or to foreigners who by coming
> into this country, whether for a long or a short time, have made themselves during
> that time subject to English jurisdiction.'

Brett LJ said (12 Ch D 522 at 528, [1874–80] All ER Rep 708 at 711):

> 'It is said that the case is literally within the words of the statute, and so, no doubt, *c*
> it is. But does it follow that, because a case is literally within the words of a statute
> of any country, therefore it is within the jurisdiction of the Courts of that country?
> Certainly not. The governing principle is that all legislation is *primâ facie* territorial,
> that is to say, that the legislation of any country binds its own subjects and the
> subjects of other countries who for the time being bring themselves within the *d*
> allegiance of the legislating power.'

Cotton LJ said (12 Ch D 522 at 531–532, [1874–80] All ER Rep 708 at 713):

> 'All we have to do is to interpret an Act of Parliament which uses a general word,
> and we have to say how that word is to be limited, when of necessity there must be
> some limitation. I take it the limitation is this, that all laws of the English Parliament *e*
> must be territorial—territorial in this sense, that they apply to and bind all subjects
> of the Crown who come within the fair interpretation of them, and also all aliens
> who come to this country, and who, during the time they are here, do any act
> which, on a fair interpretation of the statute as regards them, comes within its
> provisions.'
> *f*

Cotton LJ's reference to 'the English Parliament', an institution which ceased to exist
more than 170 years prior to 1879, must have been intended to be a reference to the
Parliament of the United Kingdom.

Ex p Blain was followed in *Re AB & Co* [1900] 1 QB 541, another bankruptcy case, in
which Lindley MR said (at 544–545):
g

> 'What authority or right has the Court to alter in this way the status of foreigners
> who are not subject to our jurisdiction? If Parliament had conferred this power in
> express words, then, of course, the Court would be bound to exercise it. But the
> decisions go to this extent, and rightly, I think, in principle, that, unless Parliament
> has conferred upon the Court that power in language which is unmistakable, the
> Court is not to assume that Parliament intended to do that which might so seriously *h*
> affect foreigners who are not resident here, and might give offence to foreign
> Governments. Unless Parliament has used such plain terms as shew that they really
> intended us to do that, we ought not to do it. That is the principle which underlies
> the decisions in *Ex parte Blain* and *In re Pearson* ([1892] 2 QB 263, [1891–4] All ER
> Rep 1066).'
> *j*

Finally, in *Clark (Inspector of Taxes) v Oceanic Contractors Inc* [1983] 1 All ER 133 at
143, [1983] 2 AC 130 at 151 Lord Wilberforce referred to the general principle that
'English legislation is primarily territorial' and cited with approval the passage in the
judgment of James LJ in *Ex p Blain* to which I have already referred. He observed with
reference to the territorial principle ([1983] 1 All ER 133 at 144, [1983] 2 AC 130 at 152):

'That principle, which is really a rule of construction of statutes expressed in
general terms and which, as James LJ said, a "broad principle", requires an inquiry
to be made as to the person with respect to whom Parliament is presumed, in the
particular case, to be legislating.'

My Lords, it is clear from the foregoing authorities that the presumption proceeds on
the basis that Parliament is unlikely to seek to interfere and has no interest to interfere in
matters which are properly the concern of the legislature of another state. In all these
authorities the relevant legislation was unilateral in the sense that it did not seek to
implement an international agreement. Where, however, Parliament incorporates into
domestic legislation an international convention which necessarily gives to that domestic
legislation extra-territorial effect in the broadest sense an entirely different situation
arises. The extra-territorial effect of such legislation is not within the presumption at all
since the basis for the presumption no longer exists. Even if the principle does apply to
all legislation whether unilateral or not all the necessary conditions for its rebuttal would
exist in the case of convention legislation. With these important distinctions in mind I
turn to consider in more detail the statutory provisions which are relevant to this appeal.

I take as a starting point the 1932 Act, of which the primary object was to give effect
to the Warsaw Convention. The respondent argued that the words 'irrespective of the
nationality of the aircraft' occurring in s 1(1) of that Act and of the 1961 Act demonstrated
that Parliament intended the Acts to have unilateral extra-territorial effect inasmuch as
owners of aircraft who were nationals of states which were not high contracting parties
to the convention (non-HCP owners) would be subject to the provisions if their aircraft
were engaged to any extent in international carriage within the meaning of the
convention. There are, in my view, two answers to this argument. In the first place it is
reasonable to assume that the existence and terms of the convention were widely known
among persons undertaking international carriage by air as therein defined. Such persons
could be expected to know what would be the consequences of performing such
international carriage. Per contra there would be no reason why a carrier operating on
one side of the world should consider or even be aware of the carriage by air laws of a
state situated on the other side with which his operations had no connection. To bring a
foreign carrier within the ambit of a widely publicised international convention because
he chooses to operate within the territory of parties to the convention is far removed
from bringing such carrier within the ambit of the municipal law of a state with which
his operations may have no connection. In the second place, and in any event, non-HCP
owners would only be affected by s 1(1) if a United Kingdom court satisfied one of the
four alternatives set out in art 28 of the convention. The first two alternatives are not
relevant to extra-territoriality since they presuppose that the carrier is ordinarily resident
or has his principal place of business within the jurisdiction of the United Kingdom
courts. If the contract were neither made in the United Kingdom nor was the United
Kingdom the destination of the carriage, a United Kingdom court would satisfy neither
of the second alternatives and s 1(1) would not apply to the non-HCP owner. In my view
the words to which I have referred at the beginning of this paragraph do no more than
emphasise what is implicit in art 1 of the Warsaw and Hague conventions that it is the
contract of carriage and not the nationality of the carrier which brings them into
operation.

If s 4 of the 1932 Act reserved power by Order in Council to apply the Warsaw
Convention to any carriage by air other than that to which the convention applied, the
exercise of such power could have produced surprising results. For example, the United
Kingdom legislature could unilaterally have applied the convention in whole or in an
adapted form to domestic carriage taking place wholly within the territory of any one or
more of the high contracting parties. Thus, international carriage affecting high
contracting parties would have been brought within the ambit of United Kingdom
legislation because the high contracting parties had so agreed, but purely domestic
carriage affecting them would have become subject to the law of the United Kingdom

because the legislature at its own hand and without reference to them had so decided. This would have been a very remarkable result indeed and one which hardly accorded with the ordinary principles of comity of nations. A further example would have been the unilateral application of the convention by the United Kingdom legislature to international carriage between two states which were not high contracting parties. Thus states which had not signed the convention could have found themselves treated by the United Kingdom legislature as though they had. This would also have been a somewhat startling result. Both these examples would apply equally to the exercise of the power reserved in s 10(1) of the 1961 Act, which is, for practical purposes, in terms identical to those of s 4 of the 1932 Act. However, by virtue of the number of states which are high contracting parties to one or both of the Warsaw and Hague conventions, a more appropriate second example would be the unilateral application of the Hague Convention to contracts of carriage where the place of departure was within the territory of a state which was a party only to the Warsaw Convention and the place of destination was within the territory of a state which was a party only to the Hague Convention or vice versa.

My Lords, I have referred to the two Acts in the first place because I consider that it is essential to construe the 1967 order in the light of the provisions of ss 1 and 10 of the 1961 Act. To look at the order alone without regard to the purpose and provisions of the Act is an illegitimate approach and one likely to lead to a wrong conclusion. The Act rules and the scope of the order are limited by the extent of the powers in the Act. In *Grein v Imperial Airways Ltd* [1936] 2 All ER 1258 at 1278–1279, [1937] 1 KB 50 at 76 Greene LJ, after referring to difficulties created by the different laws which might be applicable where an accident took place in the country of departure or in the country of destination or where the carriage was effected by stages covering several countries, observed:

'It is, I think, apparent from the subject matter with which the convention deals and from its contents that the removal of these difficulties by means of a uniform international code, to be applied by the courts of the various countries adopting the convention, is one, at any rate, of the main objects at which the convention aims; and it is in my judgment essential to approach it with a proper appreciation of this circumstance in mind. The convention is limited to international carriage. There was no necessity for any agreement as to carriage performed within the territory of one state; nor was it thought necessary to deal with the case where an aeroplane performing the contract of carriage began and ended its journey in the territory of the same state without coming to earth, even if during its flight it passed over the territory of another state. In such a case difficulties as to the law applicable would not be likely to arise . . .'

If international agreement was not needed to regulate conditions of domestic carriage within one state it is difficult to see why the United Kingdom legislature should seek unilaterally to apply United Kingdom law to such contracts of carriage whose proper law is not in doubt and in relation to which no question of conflict of laws could otherwise arise. Indeed, such unilateral application of United Kingdom law, far from resolving difficult questions of conflict of laws would appear to create them in situations where they would not otherwise exist. It may be said that because the 1952 and 1967 orders have applied parts of the relevant conventions to domestic carriage within the United Kingdom and its dependencies where otherwise no conflict of law would arise they could equally apply the conventions to foreign domestic carriage. That is, in my view, nothing to the point since there is a yawning gap between the application by a state of an international convention in modified terms to its own domestic carriage by air, a convenient method of providing a suitable domestic code, and the unilateral application of that convention to foreign domestic carriage where the proper law of the contract is not in doubt.

a Turning to the 1967 order, there can be no doubt that the words in art 3 'all carriage by air, not being carriage to which the amended Convention applies' are capable of comprehending all carriage throughout the world which is not within the Hague Convention. Parliament by s 1 of the 1961 Act having repealed the 1932 Act thereby deprived the Warsaw Convention of the force of law in the United Kingdom. Since that convention still subsisted Parliament clearly had to reclothe it by some other means with the force of law. This was done by the process to which I have already referred. In his

b judgment Leggatt J said ([1987] 2 Lloyd's Rep 192 at 196):

> 'By virtue of art. 3, schedule 2 applies the unamended Warsaw Convention to international carriage, and schedule 1 applies the amended Warsaw Convention to non-international carriage. Since schedule 2 is undeniably extra-territorial in its effect, so must schedule 1 be extra-territorial also.'

c Bingham LJ, in the passage to which I have already referred, considered that Sch 2 to the 1967 order was of crucial importance in construing the order because (i) it had the force of law in the United Kingdom and (ii) Sch 2 must be construed as having extra-territorial effect (see [1988] 2 Lloyd's Rep 120 at 122).

My Lords, with all respect to the reasoning of Leggatt J and Bingham LJ, I think that they have overlooked the fundamental difference, to which I have already referred,

d between legislation which has extra-territorial effect unilaterally and in pursuance of an international convention. When the 1961 Act came into force the Warsaw Convention was still operative and it was incumbent on the United Kingdom as a party thereto to continue to give it legal effect. This is precisely what art 5 of and Sch 2 to the 1967 order did. I do not therefore consider that the extra-territorial effect of Sch 2 in pursuance of the Warsaw Convention affords any support for the view that art 4 and Sch 1 have

e unilateral extra-territorial effect.

It is clear from the long title of the 1961 Act that its primary purpose was to give effect in the law of the United Kingdom to the Hague Convention. An equally important purpose was to enable the Warsaw Convention to be reincorporated in the law of the United Kingdom on the repeal of the 1932 Act. These purposes are effected by s 1 and exercise of the powers conferred in s 10 of the 1961 Act. Do its other purposes include

f legislation relating to foreign domestic travel wholly unconnected with the United Kingdom in relation to which no question of conflict of law arises? I do not consider that they do and that for a number of reasons.

In the first place, if one looks at the events in relation to which Parliament is presumed to be legislating one might as an example ask what interest Parliament has in legislating for the terms of the carriage by air of two Russians in a Russian owned aircraft from

g Omsk to Tomsk. The commonsense answer would be none, just as Parliament would have had no interest had the two Russians chosen instead to make the same journey by the Trans-Siberian Railway. In the second place, the fact that Parliament has, by giving effect in the law of the United Kingdom to the Warsaw and Hague conventions, legislated in relation to certain matters which are likely to affect high contracting parties suggests

h that Parliament would be unlikely to legislate in relation to other similar matters without the agreement of those same high contracting parties who were likely to be affected. In the third place, there is nothing in the 1932 or 1961 Acts which expressly enacts that foreign carriage by air of any description other than convention 'international carriage' falls within their ambit. In relation to such latter carriage Parliament had no difficulty in making its intentions clear and unambiguous. Similarly, in s 1(2) and (3) of the Carriage

j of Goods by Sea Act 1971 Parliament had no difficulty in providing unambiguously that the Hague Visby Rules should have the force of law in the United Kingdom and should apply to carriage where the port of shipment was a port in the United Kingdom. The rules accordingly were held to apply to an incident occurring at a foreign port of transhipment for onward carriage to the agreed port of destination: see *The Hollandia* [1982] 3 All ER 1141, [1983] 1 AC 565. Furthermore, for the reasons which I have just given, far from there being a plain implication in the Acts that foreign carriage by air of any description was intended to be brought within their scope all the circumstances *a* point in the opposite direction. I therefore conclude that the 1961 Act and the 1967 order did not apply to the contract of carriage between the deceased and the appellants. In reaching this conclusion I am fortified by the knowledge that it is more likely to produce a degree of certainty between carriers and their passengers than would the result sought by the respondent. It must be a matter of importance to both carriers and passengers that they should be aware of the extent of their rights and liabilities at the time when the *b* contract of carriage is entered into. If the law applicable to the contract limits the carrier's liability to a small amount the passenger can, if so advised, readily effect further insurance to cover accident during the carriage. Equally the carrier having limited his liability in accordance with the proper law of the contract can make appropriate insurance arrangements. Both parties know where they stand. If, on the other hand, the respondent's argument were correct, a foreign domestic carrier would never know at the time when *c* he entered into a contract of carriage what his ultimate liability might be because the passenger in question or his representatives might at some future date be able to invoke the jurisdiction of the United Kingdom courts and resist any attempt by the carrier to plead forum non conveniens. If the Warsaw and Hague conventions were intended to produce the adoption of certain uniform rules whereby parties to contracts of carriage by air knew where they stood the results contended for by the respondent would produce *d* precisely the opposite result.

My Lords, although I am in favour of the appellants' general submissions, I reject their contention that art 4 of and Sch 1 to the 1967 order applies only to contracts of carriage whose proper law is that of the United Kingdom. While it is sufficient for the disposal of this appeal that these provisions did not extend to the deceased's contract of carriage I think it right to express a positive rather than a purely negative view as to the scope of *e* the schedule. The flaw in the appellants' contention is that it gives no content to art 32 of the amended convention which has been retained in Sch 1. If the schedule only applied to contracts whose proper law was that of the United Kingdom the words in art 32 'whether by deciding the law to be applied' would be otiose. Any contractual attempt to remove or reduce a carrier's liability below the limits provided in the schedule is already struck at by art 23. The above words, in my view, relate to contracts of carriage which *f* provide for the application thereto of a system of law other than that of the United Kingdom. I have already concluded that the 1961 Act and the 1967 order do not apply to foreign domestic carriage. My reasons for reaching that conclusion apply equally to carriage between the territories of two or more states, where that carriage (1) does not fall within the definition of 'international carriage' in either of the conventions, and (2) involves neither departure, stopping place nor destination within United Kingdom *g* territory.

There is no doubt that Sch 1 to the 1967 order applies to domestic carriage wholly within or between parts of the United Kingdom territory. The more difficult question is how much further it extends. I was at first minded to conclude that it extended to any contract of carriage which did not fall within the ambit of either of the conventions and *h* which involved entry into United Kingdom air space even for purposes of passage only. On further reflection, however, I do not think that it extends so far. In *Grein v Imperial Airways Ltd* [1936] 2 All ER 1258 at 1278–1279, [1937] 1 KB 50 at 76 Greene LJ pointed out that no difficulties as to the law applicable would arise where the contract related to non-stop carriage between two points within the territory of one state albeit passage over the territory of another state was involved. Per contra carriage between two such points *j* which involved an agreed stopping place within the territory of another state is covered by both conventions for the obvious reason that difficulties as to the law applicable to the contract could in such circumstances arise. Both the original and amended conventions are concerned solely with carriage which is defined by reference to places of departure

and destination and agreed stopping places. The airspace through which the aircraft
a passes is irrelevant to the definition. Thus, carriage from the territory of one high
contracting party to that of another is within the convention definition whether in the
case of that carriage the aircraft passes over the territory of a third high contracting party
or over that of a state which is not a party to the convention. Why then should Parliament
seek to apply United Kingdom law to a contract of carriage which involves a purely
ephemeral contact with United Kingdom airspace but none with United Kingdom
b territory? To take an extreme example, a foreign aircraft flying from America to
Scandinavia might spend a fraction of a second passing through United Kingdom airspace
over Rockall and perhaps one or two seconds passing over the Shetland Islands. It is
difficult to see what interest Parliament could have in applying United Kingdom law to
the contracts of carriage of the passengers. I am satisfied that Parliament never intended
to legislate in relation to contracts of carriage which merely involved passage through
c United Kingdom airspace for varying degrees of time. Some more positive connection
with United Kingdom territory must have been intended. In my view Sch 1 to the 1967
order applies to (1) carriage wholly within or between parts of United Kingdom territory
and (2) carriage which, in terms of the contract, has either a place of departure, a place of
destination or an agreed stopping place within United Kingdom territory and is not
included within the definition of international carriage in either of the conventions.
d Such carriage would, for example, include (i) carriage by single ticket from London to
Bangkok or return ticket Bangkok–London–Bangkok and (ii) carriage from a Warsaw
point of origin to a Hague point of destination with an agreed stopping place in the
United Kingdom where neither the Warsaw state nor the Hague state were parties to the
other convention.

e My Lords, for the foregoing reasons I would allow the appeal.

LORD LOWRY. My Lords, I have had the advantage of reading in draft the speeches
of my noble and learned friends Lord Bridge, Lord Griffiths and Lord Jauncey. I agree
with them and would, in particular, express my respectful and complete acceptance of
the reasoning in the course of which they have explained and applied the principle which
f is commonly referred to as the presumption against extra-territorial legislation.

Accordingly, for the reasons given by my noble and learned friends, I, too, would
allow the appeal and would make the order which my noble and learned friend Lord
Bridge proposes.

*Appeal allowed. Orders of judge and Court of Appeal set aside save as to costs. Appellants to pay
g respondent's costs in House of Lords.*

Solicitors: *Beaumont & Son* (for the appellants); *Clifford Chance* (for the respondent).

Mary Rose Plummer   Barrister.

Robbins v Secretary of State for the Environment and another

a

HOUSE OF LORDS

LORD BRIDGE OF HARWICH, LORD BRANDON OF OAKBROOK, LORD TEMPLEMAN, LORD ACKNER
AND LORD LOWRY

23, 24 JANUARY, 2 MARCH 1989

b

Town and country planning – Building of special architectural or historic interest – Repairs notice – Compulsory acquisition of listed building requiring repair – Service of notice specifying works 'reasonably necessary for proper preservation' of building – Whether 'preservation' including restoration – Whether inclusion in notice of excessive items invalidating notice – Whether *c* *'preservation' referring to features existing when building first listed or features existing at date of notice – Town and Country Planning Act 1971, ss 114, 115.*

The appellant was the owner of a windmill which had been built in 1868 and included in a list of buildings of special architectural or historic interest in 1951. The appellant had acquired the windmill in 1969 and had converted it into a dwelling house. The appellant allowed the windmill to deteriorate and in 1983 the local council served a *d* repairs notice on him under s 115^a of the Town and Country Planning Act 1971 specifying the works which they considered were 'reasonably necessary for the proper preservation of the building'. The appellant failed to comply with the notice and the council, in their capacity of local planning authority, made a compulsory purchase order under s 114^b of the 1971 Act. The appellant objected to the confirmation of the order, claiming that the repairs notice was invalid because it included items which amounted *e* to restoration and were outside the scope of a repairs notice. After a public inquiry the Secretary of State for the Environment confirmed the order. The appellant applied to the High Court to quash the Secretary of State's decision but his application was dismissed by the judge, whose decision was upheld by the Court of Appeal. The appellant appealed to the House of Lords. The questions arose (i) as to what was the scope of the 'proper preservation' of a listed building in the context of ss 114 and 115 of the 1971 Act which *f* the works specified in a repairs notice under s 115 might be directed to achieve and whether 'preservation' of a listed building referred to the preservation of the building in the state it was in when it was listed or when the repairs notice was served and (ii) whether the repairs notice was invalid because it specified some works which fell outside the proper scope of such a notice.

g

Held – (1) On its true construction the word 'preservation' in s 115(1)(*a*) of the 1971 Act was to be given its ordinary meaning and did not extend to restoration work. However, having regard to the policy of the 1971 Act and the public interest in preserving buildings of special architectural or historic interest, the 'preservation' of a listed building referred to it being kept in the state it was in when first listed and not when the repairs notice was *h* served (see p 883 *j*, p 884 *h*, p 885 *b*, p 886 *j*, p 887 *a*, p 889 *c* and p 890 *g h*, post).

(2) A repairs notice served on the owner of a listed building under s 115 of the 1971 Act which specified works considered reasonably necessary for the proper preservation of the building was an effective notice for the purpose of the compulsory purchase procedure under s 114 of that Act even if the list of works specified included a number of items which went beyond the scope of s 115. It followed that the Secretary of State had been *j* entitled to confirm the compulsory purchase order. The appeal would therefore be dismissed (see p 886 *h j*, p 887 *a* and p 890 *f* to *h*, post).

---

a   Section 115, so far as material, is set out at p 882 *j* to p 883 *b*, post
b   Section 114, so far as material, is set out at p 882 *e* to *j*, post

Notes

a For compulsory acquisition of a listed building needing repair, see 34 Halsbury's Laws (4th edn) paras 677–678.

For the Town and Country Planning Act 1971, ss 114, 115, see 46 Halsbury's Statutes (4th edn) 394, 396.

Appeal

b Tom Robbins appealed with the leave of the Appeal Committee of the House of Lords given on 26 October 1988 against the decision of the Court of Appeal (Slade, Glidewell and Russell LJJ) on 17 May 1988 dismissing his appeal against the decision of Mr Malcolm Pill QC, sitting as a deputy judge of the High Court in the Queen's Bench Division on 13 November 1987, dismissing his application under s 23 of the Acquisition of Land Act 1981 for an order quashing the decision of the first respondent, the Secretary of State for *c* the Environment, on 16 December 1986 confirming a compulsory purchase order made by the second respondent, Ashford Borough Council, on 15 October 1984 under s 114 of the Town and Country Planning Act 1971 relating to Willesborough Windmill, Mill Lane, Willesborough, Ashford, Kent, which was a listed building owned by the appellant. The facts are set out in the opinion of Lord Bridge.

d *Michael Barnes QC* and *Richard Hayward* for the appellant.
Jeremy M Sullivan QC and *Mark Lowe* for the respondents.

Their Lordships took time for consideration.

e 2 March. The following opinions were delivered.

LORD BRIDGE OF HARWICH. My Lords, the appellant challenges a compulsory purchase order made by Ashford Borough Council on 15 October 1984 and confirmed by the Secretary of State on 16 December 1986 which authorises the council to acquire compulsorily the Willesborough Windmill. The authorisation was given pursuant to *f* s 114 of the Town and Country Planning Act 1971 on the ground that it appeared to the Secretary of State that 'reasonable steps are not being taken for properly preserving' the windmill, which is a listed building. It is a condition precedent to a compulsory acquisition under s 114 that at least two months before initiating the compulsory purchase proceedings the acquiring authority should serve on the owner of the building a notice under s 115 'specifying the works which they consider reasonably necessary for *g* the proper preservation of the building'. The notice is referred to in the section as a 'repairs notice'. The ground of the appellant's challenge is that the repairs notice which was served on him by the council on 7 October 1983 did not satisfy the condition precedent in that some of the works specified as considered by the council to be reasonably necessary for the proper preservation of the windmill were incapable, on the true *h* construction of s 115, of being so considered and that the inclusion of these excessive items invalidated the notice. The challenge thus raises two distinct questions of statutory construction. First, what, in the context of ss 114 and 115, is the scope of the 'proper preservation' of a listed building which the works specified in a repairs notice under s 115 may be directed to achieve? Second, if the notice specifies some works falling within that scope but also others which exceed it, is the statutory condition precedent to *j* compulsory acquisition satisfied or is the notice ineffective for that purpose?

The appellant applied to the High Court pursuant to s 23 of the Acquisition of Land Act 1981 for the quashing of the compulsory purchase order. The application was dismissed by Mr Malcolm Pill QC, sitting as a deputy judge of the High Court in the Queen's Bench Division. His decision was affirmed by the Court of Appeal (Slade, Glidewell and Russell LJJ). The appellant now appeals by leave of your Lordships' House.

For the purpose of deciding the appeal the relevant facts may be quite shortly stated. The windmill was built in 1868. It continued in operation as a windmill until 1938. In September 1951 it was included in a list of buildings of special architectural and historic interest pursuant to s 30(1) of the Town and Country Planning Act 1947. The notes entered in the list descriptive of the building read as follows:

'Built in 1868 by John Hill of Ashford, Mill-wright. Rect. brick base of 2 s. Above this an octagonal smock mill of white weather-boarding with a platform and railing round above the base. Sash ws. with gl. bars intact. Hooded cap. Fantail and sweeps partly missing. The Windmill is still worked as a mill but not by wind. Unusually good condition.'

In 1969 the windmill was acquired by the appellant and converted to a dwelling house. Over the years the condition of the windmill deteriorated greatly. In particular, by the time the council served the repairs notice in October 1983 the platform and railing round the base of the mill (the catwalk) had mostly decayed or been removed, parts of the fantail had been removed and what remained was in danger of collapse, and very little was left of the sweeps.

The repairs notice served under s 115 specified 20 items of works which the council considered reasonably necessary for the proper preservation of the building. It is now accepted that 14 of those items, those numbered 1 to 12, 14 and 18 in the list, specified either works of an emergency nature (dismantling the dangerous remains of the fantail) or works in the nature of repairs required to prevent further deterioration of the structure or of parts of the windmill which were subsisting at the date of service of the notice. The remaining items, however, went beyond this. They included, inter alia, the complete reconstruction of the catwalk and the fantail and the renewal of the stocks and whips (but not the framework or shutters) of the sweeps. The work specified for the catwalk and the sweeps was to be 'to the original standard or to a standard approved by the council'. I shall for convenience refer to items 13, 15, 16, 17, 19 and 20 collectively as 'the restoration items'.

When the compulsory purchase order was made the appellant duly objected to its confirmation and a public inquiry was held in December 1985 by an inspector appointed by the Secretary of State. In a lengthy report, dated 10 January 1986, the inspector records the submissions made to him and sets out his findings of fact. Objection was taken on behalf of the appellant that the inclusion in the repairs notice of the restoration items was unlawful. Since service of the repairs notice the ruinous remains of the fantail had been dismantled, but apart from that it is clear that very little work had been done in response to the notice. The inspector found that—

'the steps taken can in my opinion only be described as preliminaries for the eventual preservation of the building rather than as substantial works for its proper preservation.'

The inspector concluded—

'that no reasonable steps are being taken for properly preserving the building and that it is expedient to make provision for its preservation and to authorise compulsory acquisition for that purpose.'

The crucial paragraphs of the Secretary of State's decision letter, dated 16 December 1986, read, so far as presently material, as follows:

'5. Careful consideration has been given to the legal points set out by the Inspector at paragraphs 27 to 44 of his report and his opinion at paragraph 45 that they are for the Secretary of State to decide. Representations were made to the effect that:—(i) some of the works included in the repairs notice were appropriate to the restoration of the building rather than to its preservation. The Secretary of State takes the view that the question whether works are properly considered to be reasonably necessary for the proper preservation of a building is bound, to a certain extent, to be one of fact and degree. He agrees with the inspector's view that in certain instances works which might normally be considered more appropriate to restoration can, in other circumstances, be regarded as necessary for the proper preservation of a building. In the Secretary of State's view, the repairs required to preserve the building contained in the Council's repairs notice do not include such items as would invalidate the notice although the Secretary of State accepts that had all, or most, or even a substantial amount of the works required by items 1–12, 14 and 18 of the schedule to the notice been carried out, he would have been satisfied that reasonable steps were being taken for properly preserving the building . . .

6. The Secretary of State, having considered the legal points raised on behalf of the owners of the mill, considers that there is no legal impediment to prevent him from reaching a decision on the compulsory purchase order on the merits of the case.

7. The Inspector's findings of fact and conclusions have been carefully considered. The Inspector's conclusion that the building is a particularly important one which warrants every effort being made to preserve it is accepted, as is also his conclusion that no reasonable steps are being taken for properly preserving it . . .

9. The Secretary of State accepts the Inspector's findings of fact and his recommendation and he is satisfied that it is expedient to make provision for the preservation of the building and to authorise its compulsory purchase for that purpose. He has accordingly decided to confirm the order without modification.'

Before examining the rival submissions of the parties it is essential to consider the general scheme of the 1971 Act in relation to the preservation of buildings of special architectural or historic interest. Lists of such buildings are compiled or approved by the Secretary of State under s 54(1). Section 54(2) provides:

'In considering whether to include a building in a list compiled or approved under this section, the Secretary of State may take into account not only the building itself but also . . . (b) the desirability of preserving, on the ground of its architectural or historic interest, any feature of the building consisting of a man-made object or structure fixed to the building or forming part of the land and comprised within the curtilage of the building.'

As soon as may be after listing the local authority are notified and they in turn notify the owner of the building (see sub-ss (4) and (7)). A copy of the entry in the list is registered as a local land charge (see sub-s (6)). Thus every subsequent owner will acquire with knowledge that the building is listed. Once a building has been listed under s 54, s 55 makes it a criminal offence to demolish the building or to alter or extend it in any manner which would affect its character as a building of special architectural interest, unless permission, referred to in the Act as 'listed building consent', has been granted by the local planning authority or the Secretary of State. The owner of a listed building is not consulted and has no right of objection before the building is listed. However, if he applies for listed building consent and it is not granted by the local planning authority, he has, on appeal to the Secretary of State, a full opportunity to canvass the merits of the listing and it is at that stage that the Secretary of State will have to reach a decision for or against the merits of preserving the building. If listed building consent is refused or granted subject to conditions, compensation is, in appropriate circumstances, payable to the owner pursuant to s 171.

The machinery the Act provides to secure the preservation of a listed building may be considered under three headings: first, sanctions for unlawful demolition or alteration; second, provision for preservation work to be undertaken by the local authority or the Secretary of State; third, provision for compulsory acquisition when reasonable steps are not being taken by the owner for properly preserving the building.

The offence created by s 55(1) is punishable by a fine or imprisonment (see sub-s (5)). In addition, when works have been carried out in contravention of s 55(1), ss 96 to 100 of the Act provide an elaborate procedure initiated by the service of a listed building enforcement notice, analogous to the enforcement notice procedure applicable to ordinary breaches of planning control, to secure the restoration of the listed building. In particular, by s 96(1)(*b*)(i) (as substituted by the Local Government and Planning (Amendment) Act 1981, s 1 and Sch, para 9), a listed building enforcement notice may require such steps as may be specified to be taken 'for restoring the building to its former state'. One of the grounds of appeal available against such a notice under s 97(1)(*g*) (as substituted) is that 'the requirements of the notice exceed what is necessary for restoring the building to its condition before the works were carried out'. Non-compliance with a valid listed building enforcement notice attracts further criminal penalties under s 98 and the ultimate sanction to secure restoration of the listed building is provided by s 99, which allows the local planning authority to take the steps required to be taken by the enforcement notice and to recover the expenses of so doing from the owner.

Subject to certain limitations, s 101 provides that when it appears to the local authority or the Secretary of State that works are urgently necessary for the preservation of a listed building they may execute the works. Since 1 April 1987 the significance of this provision, as an encouragement to the owner of a listed building to keep it in proper repair, has been strengthened by the addition of s 101A, introduced by the Housing and Planning Act 1986 (s 40 and Sch 9, para 7), which enables the expenses of works executed under s 101 to be recovered from the owner. I mention this as a recent enhancement of the statutory machinery for the preservation of listed buildings, but I recognise, of course, that it cannot affect the construction of ss 114 and 115.

Turning now to the machinery for compulsory acquisition, I first set out so much of ss 114 and 115 (as amended) as seems to me material as follows:

'**114.**—(1) Where it appears to the Secretary of State, in the case of a building to which this section applies, that reasonable steps are not being taken for properly preserving it, the Secretary of State may authorise the council of the county or county district in which the building is situated . . . to acquire compulsorily under this section the building and any land comprising or contiguous or adjacent to it which appears to the Secretary of State to be required for preserving the building or its amenities, or for affording access to it, or for its proper control or management . . .

(3) This section applies to any listed building . . .

(4) The Secretary of State shall not make or confirm a compulsory purchase order for the acquisition of any building by virtue of this section unless he is satisfied that it is expedient to make provision for the preservation of the building and to authorise its compulsory acquisition for that purpose.

(5) The Acquisition of Land Act 1981 shall apply to the compulsory acquisition of land under this section.

(6) Any person having an interest in a building which it is proposed to acquire compulsorily under this section may, within twenty-eight days after the service of the notice required by section 12 of the Acquisition of Land Act 1981, apply to a magistrates' court acting for the petty sessions area within which the building is situated for an order staying further proceedings on the compulsory purchase order; and, if the court is satisfied that reasonable steps have been taken for properly preserving the building, the court shall make an order accordingly.

(7) Any person aggrieved by the decision of a magistrates' court on an application under subsection (6) of this section may appeal against the decision to the Crown Court.

115.—(1) The compulsory purchase of a building under section 114 of this Act shall not be started by a council . . . unless at least two months previously they have served on the owner of the building, and not withdrawn, a notice under this section

a
(in this section referred to as a "repairs notice")—(a) specifying the works which they consider reasonably necessary for the proper preservation of the building; and (b) explaining the effect of sections 114 to 117 of this Act . . .

(4) For the purposes of this section a compulsory acquisition is started when the council . . . serve the notice required by section 12 of the Acquisition of Land Act 1981.'

b
Section 116 provides that the measure of compensation on compulsory acquisition of a listed building, unless compensation has already become payable under s 171 on refusal of listed building consent or grant of such consent subject to conditions, shall be assessed on the assumption that listed building consent for demolition, alteration or extension of the building would be granted. This ensures that the open market value on which compensation is assessed is not to be depreciated by the restriction inherent in the listing.

c
Section 117 provides for a reduced level of compensation in a case where the building has been deliberately allowed to fall into disrepair for the purpose of justifying its demolition. It is not suggested that this is such a case.

Counsel, who has presented the case for the appellant with conspicuous skill and cogency, submits that a line must be drawn between preservation and restoration and that, on the true construction of ss 114 and 115, works cannot be considered necessary

d
for the proper preservation of a listed building which are not directed to the preservation of the building as it subsists at the date when the repairs notice is served. He accepts, of course, that the concept of preservation in these sections cannot be limited to keeping the building in the exact condition in which it is when the notice is served since this would frustrate the whole procedure. But he submits that no more can ever be considered necessary for preservation than such repairs as are required to secure whatever remains

e
of the building from further deterioration. Thus, for example, if part of the roof is missing or a wall has become unstable, it is accepted that works to repair the roof or stabilise the wall would properly be directed to preservation of the building. But, on the other hand, if some distinct part of the building, some decorative feature of the building without structural significance or some free-standing object included in the listing under s 54(2)(b) has been accidentally destroyed, works to repair or replace those items would

f
exceed the ambit of preservation and could not properly be included in a repairs notice. This construction, counsel for the appellant submits, accords with the ordinary meaning of the word 'preservation' in contrast with the word 'restoration' found in the provisions relating to the enforcement notice procedure in ss 96 and 97. On the basis of this construction the restoration items specified in the repairs notice in this case were beyond the scope of s 115.

g
Counsel for the respondents submits that the phrase 'reasonably necessary for the proper preservation of the building' must be construed as a whole and establishes the criterion to be applied by the acquiring authority when they serve the repairs notice and the Secretary of State when deciding whether to confirm the compulsory purchase order in the circumstances of any particular case, which is partly a matter of fact and degree and partly a matter of discretion. Their decisions in the application of that criterion, he

h
submits, are only susceptible to review by the courts on the ground of irrationality. I readily accept, as did counsel for the appellant in argument, that the use of the words 'reasonably' and 'proper' in the phrase under consideration call for value judgments, weighing such matters as the cost and the benefit of works required for the preservation of a listed building, and that such judgments are entrusted to the acquiring authority under s 115 and to the Secretary of State under s 114. But I think that the word

j
'preservation' has to be given its ordinary meaning in contrast with 'restoration' and that this does impose an objective limitation which must be applied in considering what the works specified in a repairs notice may be directed to achieve.

The more difficult question is whether 'preservation' of the listed building in these sections refers to the preservation of the building as it was when listed or of the building as it is when the repairs notice is served. I think the language of the sections is capable of either construction. Indeed, both counsel adopted the proposition that the sections refer *a* to preservation of the building as it subsisted at the date of listing as an alternative to their primary submissions, albeit with very different emphasis. Counsel for the appellant's bottom line, if I may use that colloquialism, is that the preservation envisaged by ss 114 and 115 must at least exclude the restoration of features of a building which ceased to exist before the building was listed. Counsel for the respondents' bottom line is that it must at least include anything designed to preserve the building as it subsisted when first *b* listed and that this would include, in the case of a building in disrepair at the time of listing, works designed to remedy the disrepair and secure the building against further deterioration.

I accept that the legislature cannot have intended that immediately following the listing of a building it should be liable to compulsory purchase on the ground that steps were not being taken for properly preserving it because the owner was unwilling to *c* restore features of the building which had ceased to exist before listing. I accept, on the other hand, that if what I will call the date of listing construction is to be preferred to the date of notice construction, a building in disrepair when listed may be the subject of a repairs notice under s 114 specifying works necessary to prevent further deterioration. The line between repair and restoration may not be an easy one to draw with precision, but in practice I doubt if any great difficulty will be found in saying whether any *d* particular works fall on one side of the line or the other. The important issue is whether the date of listing or the date of notice construction is correct.

Counsel for the appellant naturally places much emphasis on the specific references to restoration which can be required to be undertaken by or at the expense of the owner under the listed building enforcement notice procedure in ss 96 to 100. He also contends, I think rightly, that the works urgently necessary for the preservation of a listed building, *e* which may be undertaken by the local authority or the Secretary of State under s 101 and the expenses of which since 1 April 1987 may be recovered from the owner under s 101A, can only refer to works urgently necessary to preserve the building as it subsists when the works are undertaken. These indications, he submits, point strongly in favour of the date of notice construction. I am conscious of the force of counsel's submission but I cannot accept that the considerations on which he relies are decisive. An enforcement *f* notice under s 96 is both penal and coercive: it compels the owner to restore the building or to bear the cost of restoration. A repairs notice is in no way either penal or coercive: it is a procedural preliminary to compulsory acquisition designed to give the owner the opportunity, if he chooses, to undertake the works reasonably necessary for the proper preservation of the building as an alternative to selling it at its market value to the acquiring authority. Again, it is clear that works can only be urgently necessary for the *g* preservation of a building so as to justify works being undertaken pursuant to s 101 if they are necessary for the preservation of the building as it subsists when the works are carried out. Thus there is no ambiguity in s 101. I do not think it follows that the proper preservation of a listed building, which is the objective of the compulsory acquisition procedure under ss 114 and 115, is limited in the same way.

I believe that the question whether the date of listing or the date of notice construction *h* is correct is to be resolved purposively by considering the underlying policy of the legislation. The public interest in the preservation of buildings of special architectural or historic interest needs no emphasis. Once a building has been listed, that public interest has been declared. If the owner seeks and is denied unconditional listed building consent he will recover any compensation payable under s 171. If a listed building falls into *j* disrepair and that disrepair becomes apparent before the building or part of it collapses, the character of the building can be preserved, if necessary, by emergency works under s 101. But, if part of a building collapses without warning or is destroyed by fire or storm damage, the character of the building as a building of special architectural historic interest can only be preserved if the damage is made good. If the date of notice

construction is correct, the compulsory purchase machinery is ineffective to serve the
a   public interest in such cases and ss 114 and 115 are of very limited utility. On the other
hand, if the date of listing construction is correct, compulsory purchase is available in
such cases as the only means, if the owner is unwilling to make good the damage, of
preserving the character of the building from which its special architectural and historic
interest derives. I have no hesitation in concluding that the date of listing construction is
to be preferred. Sections 114 and 115, given this more generous construction, do no
b   more than to enable the building as listed to be acquired and preserved at the public
expense. The interest of the owner, if he is unwilling to undertake the necessary works,
in retaining his property has to yield to the public interest in the same way and on the
same terms as the interest of any other property owner whose property is acquired for
some necessary public purpose.

I have felt it appropriate to examine this issue of construction at some length since it
c   was fully argued and is of obvious importance. At the end of the day, however, I do not
think the result of the appeal turns on it. I accept the submission of counsel for the
appellant that even on the date of listing construction the repairs notice served by the
council specified works exceeding what could be considered reasonably necessary for the
proper preservation of the windmill. The notes entered in the 1951 list recorded that the
fantail and sweeps were then partly missing. The restoration items in the repairs notice
d   specified works for the full restoration of the fantail and partial restoration of the sweeps.
The former clearly are, and the latter, in the absence of evidence as to which parts of the
sweeps were missing in 1951, must be taken to be, works for the restoration of the
building to the condition that it was in before it was listed.

The Secretary of State, however, clearly did not rely on the fact that none of the works
specified in relation to the restoration items had been carried out in reaching his
e   conclusion that reasonable steps were not being taken for preserving the windmill. There
was ample material on which he could reach that conclusion in reliance on the failure to
carry out works specified as reasonably necessary for the preservation of the windmill in
relation to the other 14 items listed in the repairs notice. His confirmation of the
compulsory purchase order, therefore, was perfectly lawful under s 114 unless, as counsel
for the appellant contends, the inclusion in the repairs notice of the restoration items
f   relating to the fantail and the sweeps invalidated the remainder of the notice so that the
condition precedent to compulsory purchase under s 115 was not satisfied.

Before turning to that issue I should observe that the statutory code relating to the
preservation of listed buildings on which I have based the opinion expressed as to the
proper construction of ss 114 and 115 is the 1971 consolidating Act. A large part of that
code, including the provisions now found in ss 114 and 115, was first enacted by the
g   Town and Country Planning Act 1968 amending the original code under the Town and
Country Planning Act 1947. I leave open for future consideration, if the question should
ever arise, whether works specified for the restoration of some feature of a building first
listed under s 30 of the 1947 Act which had disappeared before the 1968 Act came into
force could properly be regarded as necessary for the preservation of the listed building
within the meaning of ss 114 and 115. The point does not arise here and no argument
h   was addressed to it. It is very unlikely, I would think, to arise in the future and I express
no opinion on it.

The remaining and crucial question on which the appeal depends is whether a repairs
notice which specifies a list of works considered reasonably necessary for the proper
preservation of a listed building which includes a number of items within the scope of
the section (valid items) and also a number of items beyond the scope of the section
j   (invalid items) effectively satisfies the condition precedent to compulsory purchase
imposed by s 115. This is a pure question of the construction of the section and I do not
think that any assistance is to be derived from authorities on severance in very different
legal contexts. On the face of the language of s 115 a notice listing a number of valid
items is a notice 'specifying the works which they consider reasonably necessary for the

proper preservation of the building' notwithstanding that it also includes invalid items. Provided that the list of valid items is sufficiently substantial to support a conclusion by the Secretary of State, in the event that the specified works are not carried out, that reasonable steps are not being taken for properly preserving the building, it is difficult to see why the invalid items should not simply be disregarded. Counsel for the appellant submits, however, that the purpose of a repairs notice is to give the owner of a listed building the opportunity to avoid compulsory purchase by undertaking the works which are reasonably necessary for the proper preservation of the building and that a notice which is excessive puts him in a dilemma: he does not know whether to carry out all the specified works or to omit those works which he considers to be excessive at the risk of having his property acquired if he is held to have been wrong. Such a dilemma may arise whenever the owner of a listed building wishes to challenge any items of works specified in the repairs notice as excessive. The ground of a challenge may be that the disputed items are excessive in fact, ie that valid items exceed what is in fact reasonably necessary for the proper preservation of the building, or it may be that the disputed items are excessive in law, ie that they are invalid items. Counsel for the appellant rightly concedes that a notice containing valid items which are excessive in fact satisfies the condition precedent to compulsory purchase imposed by s 115. It is otherwise, he submits, if invalid items are included because the acquiring authority, in serving the notice, has erred in law.

The dilemma of the owners is the same whether he wishes to challenge certain items in the repairs notice as being excessive in fact or excessive in law. It seems to me that recourse to the magistrates' court under s 114(6) is tailor-made to provide a solution to the dilemma in either case. This unusual provision empowers the magistrates' court to override the opinion of the acquiring authority and to pre-empt the decision of the Secretary of State in determining what works are reasonably necessary for the proper preservation of the listed building. The procedure will operate in the following way. The owner who wishes to retain his property in the listed building will put in hand the works specified in the repairs notice which he admits to be necessary for its proper preservation, but not the works specified in the items listed which he wishes to dispute. On receipt of notice under s 12 of the 1981 Act initiating the compulsory purchase proceedings, he will then apply to the magistrates' court under s 114 for an order staying those proceedings. If the magistrates' court is satisfied that he has taken reasonable steps for properly preserving the listed building by the works he has already put in hand and that the disputed items are excessive, the owner will be entitled to an order staying further proceedings on the compulsory purchase order. In relation to the disputed items, the proceedings initiated in the magistrates' court will in due course resolve all issues of both fact and law and can, if necessary, be taken on appeal to the Crown Court or on a point of law to the High Court. If at the conclusion of the proceedings it is held against the owner that some of the disputed items are reasonably necessary for the proper preservation of the listed building, he will then be able to put in hand the works specified in relation to those items, and it is inconceivable that the acquiring authority would proceed with the acquisition. If they were to do so, the owner could make a fresh application to the magistrates' courts under s 114(6) which would be bound to succeed.

Being satisfied that this procedure is available to protect the owner of a listed building who is willing to carry out such works as are reasonably necessary for its proper preservation from any prejudice by the inclusion in a repairs notice of invalid items, I am equally satisfied that the inclusion of such items does not invalidate the remainder of the notice.

I would accordingly dismiss this appeal.

LORD BRANDON OF OAKBROOK. My Lords, for the reasons given in the speeches of my noble and learned friends Lord Bridge and Lord Ackner, I would dismiss the appeal.

LORD TEMPLEMAN. My Lords, for the reasons given by my noble and learned friend Lord Bridge I would dismiss this appeal.

LORD ACKNER. My Lords, I have had the advantage of reading in draft the speech of my noble and learned friend Lord Bridge. I gratefully adopt and therefore need not repeat his recital of the facts which led to this appeal.

The central issue in this appeal is the meaning of the phrase 'works . . . reasonably necessary for the proper preservation' of a listed building in s 115(1)(a) of the Town and Country Planning Act 1971.

The purpose of 'listing' buildings and how this is achieved

Before considering the rival contentions of the parties, the provisions of the 1971 Act, in so far as they relate to listed buildings, must first be considered. The purpose of 'listing' buildings is to ensure the protection and enhancement of the local heritage of buildings. The Secretary of State, pursuant to his statutory obligation under s 54 of the Act, compiles lists of buildings of special architectural or historic interest or approves such lists compiled by the Historic Buildings and Monuments Commission for England or by other persons or bodies of persons as appear to him appropriate as having special knowledge of, or interest in, buildings of architectural or historic interest.

Under s 54(2), in considering whether to include a building in a list compiled or approved under the section, the Secretary of State may take into account not only the building itself, but also any respect in which its exterior contributes to the architectural or historic interest of any group of buildings of which it forms part, and the desirability of preserving on grounds of its architectural or historic interest any feature of the building. Moreover, s 54(9) contains an extended definition of 'listed building' to include any object or structure fixed to the building and any object or structure within the curtilage of the building which, although not fixed to the building, forms part of the land and has done so since before 1 July 1948.

The purpose of 'listing' buildings, to which I have referred earlier, is achieved in the first place by making it a criminal offence for a person to execute—

'any works for the demolition of a listed building or for its alteration or extension in any manner which would affect its character as a building of special architectural or historic interest . . .'

(See s 55(1).) Quite apart from the penalties that may be incurred in carrying out unauthorised work to a listed building, power is given to the local authority to issue a notice (a building enforcement notice) to restore the building to its former state or to the state in which it would have been if the terms and conditions of any listed building consent which had been granted had been complied with (see s 96). If such a notice is not complied with not only does the owner commit a further offence (see s 98), but provision is made for the local authority to carry out the necessary work and recover the expenses reasonably incurred (see s 99).

Those sections relate to acts of commission. To cater for acts of *omission* s 101 makes provision where urgent works are necessary to preserve the listed building. In such a case the owner is given notice in writing of the intention to carry out the works, and under s 101A the expense of executing those works are recovered by the authority who carries them out.

Where the works required to preserve the building are not urgently necessary, a notice under s 115 (referred to as a 'repairs notice') may be served by a local authority 'specifying the works which they consider reasonably necessary for the proper preservation of the building'. Such a notice, unlike a notice under the Housing Acts, does not require the *execution* of any work and places no statutory obligation on the owner to carry out any work. It is a warning shot, a preliminary to compulsory acquisition of that listed building if not complied with. The notice has to explain that the local authority consider that reasonable steps are not being taken for the proper preserving of the building and that the works which they specify in the notice are reasonably necessary for its proper preservation. It warns the owner that, if the works are not carried out within two months from service of the notice, they may exercise their powers under s 114 of the Act to begin proceedings for the compulsory purchase of the building. The notice also has to point out that, if (which was not the case in respect of this property) it appears that the building has been deliberately allowed to fall into disrepair for the purpose of justifying its demolition and the development or redevelopment of the site, a compulsory purchase order may include a direction under s 117 for 'minimum compensation' the effect of which will be to limit the compensation otherwise payable on compulsory acquisition by requiring it to be assessed on the assumption that neither planning permission nor listed building consent under the Act would be granted for any works except to restore the building to a proper state of repair and to maintain it in such a state. In cases where the building has not been deliberately left derelict, compensation is based on the assumption that listed building consent would be granted for any works for the alteration or extension of the building or for its demolition, other than works in respect of which such consent has been applied for before the date of the order and refused or granted subject to conditions.

If the repairs notice is not complied with and the Secretary of State is satisfied that reasonable steps are not being taken properly to preserve the building, he will authorise the local authority to acquire the building compulsorily under s 114. However, he may not make or confirm a compulsory purchase order under this section unless he is satisfied that it is expedient to make provision for the preservation of the building and to authorise its compulsory acquisition for that purpose.

Thus, it will be seen that, although the owner may disregard the repairs notice, he does so at his peril since thereby he renders the building liable to be compulsorily acquired. Thus, given that works are reasonably necessary for the proper preservation of the building, their execution is achieved either at the owner's expense (aided by such grants as may be available) or at the public expense after the public has compulsorily acquired the building. Thus, Parliament's purpose to ensure the protection and enhancement of the local heritage of buildings is fulfilled.

The construction of the words 'works . . . reasonably necessary for the proper preservation of the building'

'Works' within the meaning of s 115(1)(a) must be works (1) for the preservation of the building and (2) which the local authority consider reasonably necessary for its proper preservation.

There is no dispute that the works specified in the repairs notice prepared by the second respondents satisfied (2) above. The essential issue is whether they were works for the 'proper preservation of the building'. This raises two questions, namely (i) the correct construction, in its context, of the word 'preservation' and (ii) by reference to what date is the condition of the building to be preserved, and, in particular, is the condition in which it is to be preserved to be that which existed as at the date of the repairs notice *or* the date of its listing?

Counsel, who has argued the case for the appellant with very great skill, has submitted that the works of preservation are confined to works necessary to prevent deterioration or further deterioration of the building from the condition in which it was at the time of the notice. Accordingly, features of the building, which on account of their architectural or historic interest had occasioned the listing of the building but which before the service of the repairs notice had been destroyed or seriously damaged, cannot properly be the subject of the repairs notice. Its preservation in its condition as at the date of the notice is all that can be required. According to this submission, it would matter not whether it

was the owner's omissions or an act of nature or a combination of both which had
a brought about the destruction or damage.

Counsel's argument can be well illustrated by a particular feature of this windmill. In
the brief description in the list dated 24 September 1951 there is a specific reference to 'a
platform and railing round above the base', that is the rectangular brick base of two
storeys. This is the 'catwalk' and is clearly shown in the photograph of the mill taken not
long before the listing. As at the date of the repairs notice (7 October 1983) the catwalk
b was in a very poor condition, with very little if any of the handrail intact. It would follow
from counsel's submission that although, no doubt, some work would be necessary to
prevent further deterioration of the catwalk there would be no need to replace any of the
handrail, clearly a feature at the time the building was listed. Indeed, counsel for the
appellant readily accepted that it would follow, if his submissions were valid, that if
important features of this or any building were blown or burnt down the day before the
c notice was served, the repairs notice could not extend to such features.

In my judgment the submissions of counsel for the appellant would clearly produce
results contrary to the underlying policy of the Act, which is to preserve the building, i e
to keep it and its features as they existed at the date of listing in sound condition.

Did the inclusion in the repairs notice of works which went beyond what was reasonably
d *necessary for the proper preservation of the windmill render the notice invalid?*

Counsel for the appellant accepted that if the notice included works which went
beyond what was reasonably necessary for the proper preservation of the building,
because the notice required an unreasonable amount of preservation work to be carried
out, this did not render the notice invalid. For instance, where a roof was in a state of
disrepair because there were a dozen or more tiles missing, to require the roof to be
e completely stripped and retiled would clearly be excessive. However, he submitted that
where the requirement was excessive, because works specified were not works of
preservation at all but were works involving restoring the building to a condition it did
not enjoy at the material date, be it the date of listing or the date of the repairs notice,
whichever be the correct date, the notice became an invalid notice, albeit that it contained
a substantial amount of work reasonably necessary for the proper preservation of the
f building. This was so because, so he submitted, the excessive demands in the notice were
not due to the incorrect assessment of the amount of preservation work which was
needed, but to a wrong construction by the authority of the meaning of the word
'preservation'.

I am prepared to accept that certain of the works specified in the repairs notice went
beyond works reasonably necessary for the preservation of the building in the state in
g which it was when listed since they were works of restoration to a pre-existing state. In
the notes in the list there is a reference to 'fantail and sweeps partly missing'. In the
repairs notice the appellant was required to *renew* the fantail and the sweeps. Counsel for
the appellant submits that that is an indication that the respondents wrongly construed
the word 'preserve' as including restoration to a pre-existing state. For the purpose of his
argument I am prepared to accept that he may well be right, particularly when one has
h regard to the fact that work which was described as 'long-term restoration work' in the
report of the engineers and millwrights retained by the council was in part incorporated
in the repairs notice.

I am unable, however, to understand why one category of excessive work can be
properly excised or severed from the notice, whereas another category attributable to an
j erroneous interpretation should not be excisable or severable and thus renders the entire
notice bad. I of course accept that a notice which requires excessive work, whatever the
reason may be for the excess, places the owner of a property in a dilemma. He can either,
without further ado, comply with the unjustifiable requirement and thereby avoid any
risk of an application compulsorily to acquire his property or he can take the following

alternative steps. Under s 114(6) he may, within 28 days after the service of the compulsory purchase order, of which the authority seeks confirmation from the Secretary *a* of State, apply to a magistrates' court for an order staying further proceedings on the compulsory purchase order. If the court is satisfied that reasonable steps have been taken for properly preserving the building, the court shall make an order accordingly. Additionally or alternatively the owner, after service of the compulsory purchase order for which confirmation is sought, may enter an objection to the Secretary of State, who will then hold an inquiry. The compulsory purchase order may then be confirmed if the *b* Secretary of State is satisfied that reasonable steps are not being taken for properly preserving the building. Even then, as stated above, he will not make or confirm a compulsory purchase order unless satisfied that it is expedient to make provision for the preservation of the building and to authorise its compulsory acquisition for that purpose (see s 114(4)). Both counsel for the appellant and counsel for the respondents accepted that before the magistrates or at the inquiry it was not essential for the owner to have *c* actually carried out any work, so long as he could establish that he had taken reasonable steps with a view to carrying out such work. For example, he may have instructed surveyors to advise him as to which of the items in the repairs notice could fairly be said to be reasonably necessary for the proper preservation of the building and, having received their report and found that only certain items fell within that category, instructed them to carry out such work after the proceedings before the magistrates or *d* the inquiry had terminated.

Whichever is the reason for the owner's quandary, these options are open to him. Moreover, where his contention is that neither the local authority nor the minister is entitled in law to construe 'works . . . reasonably necessary for the proper preservation of the building' in the manner in which they have done, he has the additional right of appeal from the Crown Court to the Divisional Court by way of case stated, and from the *e* decision of the Secretary of State to the High Court under s 23 of the Acquisition of Land Act 1981.

I therefore conclude that, so long as there is not inextricably mingled in the repairs notice works which have not the character of work of preservation, such works can properly be excised from the repairs notice, leaving the notice valid as respects those works which are reasonably necessary for proper preservation of the building. *f*

Since it is common ground that the appellant had not carried out even those 14 out of the 20 items in the repairs list which were undoubtedly reasonably necessary for the proper preservation of the building, the minister was entitled to confirm the compulsory purchase. It is also common ground that he was entitled to conclude that it was expedient to make provision for the preservation of the building and to authorise its compulsory purchase for that purpose. Accordingly, for the above reasons and those given by my *g* noble and learned friend Lord Bridge I would dismiss this appeal with costs.

LORD LOWRY. My Lords, I have had the advantage of reading in draft the speech of my noble and learned friend Lord Bridge. I agree with it and, for the reasons which he gives, I, too, would dismiss the appeal.

h

Appeal dismissed.

Solicitors: *Edwin Coe*, agents for *Roderick O'Driscoll & Partners*, Maidstone (for the appellant); *Treasury Solicitor*; *Sharpe Pritchard*, agents for *A E Drew*, Ashford, Kent (for the second respondent).

Mary Rose Plummer   Barrister.

Practice Note

COURT OF APPEAL, CIVIL DIVISION
LORD DONALDSON OF LYMINGTON MR, BINGHAM AND MANN LJJ
1 MARCH 1989

Court of Appeal – Practice – Civil Division – Presentation of appeals – Skeleton argument – Content of skeleton argument – Chronology of events – Reference to law reports – Timetable for exchange and submission of skeleton arguments – Supplementary skeleton arguments – Listing changes – Time estimates – Oral hearing

LORD DONALDSON OF LYMINGTON MR made the following statement at the sitting of the court. The purpose of the Practice Direction which is being handed down this morning is to give advance notice of some important changes which the Civil Division of the Court of Appeal will be introducing with effect from 6 June 1989.

The principal changes relate to skeleton arguments, presentation of oral argument in court and Court of Appeal listing.

Our objective is to reduce the amount of time spent in court whilst at the same time adhering to our long-established tradition of oral argument in open court. Time spent in court is costly both to the nation and to the parties. It is therefore vital that it is used economically and effectively.

The time lag between the date of lodging and the date of hearing of appeals is still far too long, particularly in the case of appeals against final orders made in the High Court. The average time lag in the case of such appeals (other than cases involving children and other urgent appeals) is still about 12 months. It is not right that a successful party to a High Court action, for instance a plaintiff who has been injured in a road or factory accident, should have to wait a year before knowing whether the award of damages in his or her favour is going to be upheld. This is particularly so bearing in mind the fact that the case is likely to have taken a considerable time to come to trial. Likewise a defendant who has a decision against him or her which is erroneous should not have to wait a year before having that judgment varied or set aside. Justice delayed is always unsatisfactory and it can amount to justice denied.

It is for those reasons that we have been giving thought to ways of reducing the amount of time spent in court and increasing the court's 'productivity' without detracting from the quality of our appellate system.

A working party was set up under the chairmanship of Purchas LJ. A number of proposals were made as a result of the deliberations of that working party and there were very helpful discussions with the representatives of the solicitors' and barristers' professions. The proposals included the establishment of a team of lawyers to assist the Civil Division, along the lines of the system of office lawyers which has obtained in the Criminal Division for some time. The need for such a team has been accepted by the Lord Chancellor and it is in the course of being established.

A very important element in the working party's strategy, which has been indorsed by all the judges of the court, is that time spent in court will be shortened if the members of the court who are going to hear the appeal are able to do effective prereading. This can only be done if, well in advance of the hearing, the court has details of the points which are going to be argued and the authorities which are going to be cited. For that reason the keystone of the new system is that skeleton arguments will no longer be optional, but will be required for all civil appeals (other than appeals heard with exceptional urgency). So far as timing is concerned, in all cases (other than those assigned to the short warned list, to which a different timetable will apply) skeleton arguments must be lodged not less that four weeks before the date on which the hearing is scheduled to begin.

Requiring the skeleton arguments to be lodged well before the appeal hearing has three main advantages. First and foremost, the judges can do really effective prereading *a* and thus save a considerable amount of time which would otherwise be spent reading aloud in court. Second, they can consider whether the time estimate is realistic, and, if not, the court can direct that the necessary adjustments to the listing be made well in advance. Third, it brings forward the point of time at which the parties, particularly the appellant's side, have to make a firm decision whether or not to proceed to a hearing before the Court of Appeal or whether to settle the case. Accelerating this point of *b* decision should help to reduce the number of cases where the appeal is settled a matter of hours, or even minutes, before the hearing is due to commence or where an appeal is pursued simply because a true appreciation of the prospects of success was only reached so late that a settlement could save little or no expense. Settlements of appeals the night before or at the door of the court usually result in a court day being wasted, because it is then too late to call another appeal on from the short warned list. This is a hardship to *c* the parties to appeals waiting to be heard.

There is an important point which I want to make clear at this stage. When the practice of inviting counsel to put in skeleton arguments for the use of the Court of Appeal was first introduced about five years ago, word filtered back to us that some lawyers took the view that this was a first step towards adopting the system which is operated by the appellate courts in the United States of having very full arguments *d* submitted in writing and then limiting oral argument in court to a very short period. That is not the case. I cannot emphasise too strongly that the English Court of Appeal remains firmly wedded to its long-established tradition of oral argument in open court. For that reason, as the Practice Direction makes clear, skeleton arguments should be confined to identifying the points, not arguing them.

The court recognises that calling for skeleton arguments to be lodged four weeks *e* before the hearing date will involve counsel preparing the appeal well in advance of the hearing and then inevitably doing further work by way of recapitulation shortly before the hearing. For that reason and with a view to ensuring that counsel are entitled to appropriate remuneration for any *extra* work involved, the court is directing the taxing masters to tax the costs of preparing a skeleton argument separately from brief fees, but with due regard to the fact that more work may be involved in preparing the oral *f* argument if the counsel presenting that argument has not been involved in the preparation of the skeleton.

The point was rightly made by the representatives of the two branches of the profession in our discussions about these new proposals that, if counsel are going to have to 'get the case up' twice, that would make all concerned even more anxious to have counsel of their first choice to argue the appeal. We recognise that, and we are changing the arrangements *g* relating to appeals which qualify for a fixture with a view to achieving greater certainty in relation to hearing dates. We are also giving directions designed to ensure that counsel's estimates of the length of hearing, which are a key factor in listing, are monitored and kept up to date.

I should make it clear, however, that it will still be necessary for the Court of Appeal *h* to have a short warned list to which relatively short appeals will continue to be assigned and put 'on call' from a specified date.

So that there are no misconceptions about our reasons for having a short warned list, I should perhaps say something about this. We do not maintain a short warned list on the basis of the notion, which may have obtained in earlier times, that the judge is such an important figure that not a moment of his time must be wasted and therefore there must *j* always be cases on call to fill any gaps. In the modern Court of Appeal the short warned list is not based on the dignitas of the judiciary. It is there to ensure that we make full use of the courtrooms and judicial resources at our disposal. However, there is reason to hope that improved listing and increased flexibility consequent on judges devoting more

of their time to prereading in their rooms may reduce, even if it is unlikely to eliminate,
a the need for appeals to be included in this list.

We recognise that in the case of appeals which are put into the short warned list a
party's counsel of first choice may not be available on the day for which the appeal is
called on and that in such circumstances the brief will have to change hands. This is an
inevitable consequence of putting cases into a short warned list, but we have to maintain
one for the reasons I have given. We also recognise that, in such a situation, equity
b requires that each counsel should be properly remunerated for the part which he or she
has played in the whole process of preparing and presenting the appeal. We believe that
our direction to the taxing masters will achieve that result.

The Practice Direction sets out changes in the way in which oral argument is to be
presented in future in cases where skeleton arguments have been lodged in advance and
prereading has been done by the judges with the aid of the skeleton. For the benefit of
c those appearing in the case, and particularly their clients, it is important that the
documents and authorities which have been preread should be identified, and the
presiding Lord Justice will do so at the commencement of the hearing. The rest of the
directions dealing with oral argument are designed to achieve what we consider to be the
proper and legitimate objective of ensuring that oral argument is devoted to making the
relevant points, not working up to making them.
d It is important that members of the legal profession should explain to their clients in
advance of the appeal hearing what the Court of Appeal's practice is in relation to oral
argument. Without such an explanation, the clients might jump to the mistaken
conclusion that insufficient time has been allowed for their case to be put before the
court. If it is explained to them that the appeal bundles and the cases which bear on the
branches of the law concerned have been studied by the members of the Court of Appeal,
e together with skeleton arguments, it will not come as a shock to the parties to find that
the court then expects counsel to proceed to deal straight away with the grounds of
appeal.

These new arrangements represent the most fundamental change that has been made
since October 1982, when the parts of the Supreme Court Act 1981 dealing with the
Court of Appeal and the rules made in that connection came into force. When I
f introduced my Practice Statement in October 1982 explaining that new system, I said
that we would need the co-operation of both branches of the profession (see *Practice Note*
[1982] 3 All ER 376 at 377). We have enjoyed that co-operation over the past six years,
we have had it in the fullest measure in considering the changes which are now being
introduced and I am sure that we shall continue to enjoy it in the future.
g We recognise that so substantial a change in the practice of the court is bound to give
rise to teething troubles, but are confident that, with assistance from both branches of
the profession, they can be quickly overcome. We also recognise that as a result of lessons
learnt in what might be described as the 'running-in period', it may be desirable to
introduce modifications. In this context, as in all others, we shall welcome constructive
criticisms from both branches of the profession and from users generally.

h
CHANGES IN THE PRACTICE AND PROCEDURE OF THE COURT OF APPEAL

1. The changes announced in this Practice Direction will apply to all appeals to the Civil
Division of the Court of Appeal which have a hearing date commencing on or after 6
June 1989.

j
Skeleton arguments
2. With effect from that date skeleton arguments will be compulsory in the case of all
appeals to the Civil Division of the Court of Appeal, except in the case of appeals which
are heard as a matter of great urgency and any individual case where the court otherwise

directs. If counsel consider that a skeleton argument is unnecessary, application should be made to the registrar for a special order.   *a*

Content of skeleton arguments

3. The purpose of a skeleton argument is to identify not to argue the points. A skeleton argument should therefore be as succinct as possible. In the case of points of law, it should state the point and cite the principal authority or authorities in support, with references to the particular page(s) where the principle concerned is enunciated. In *b* the case of questions of fact, the skeleton argument should state briefly the basis on which it is contended that the Court of Appeal can interfere with the finding of fact concerned, with cross-references to the passages in the transcript or notes of evidence which bear on the point.

In the case of respondents whose arguments will be simply that the judgment of the court below is correct for the reasons given, counsel for the respondent can send in a *c* letter to that effect in lieu of a skeleton argument. Where, however, the respondent is going to rely on any authority or refer to any evidence which is not dealt with in the judgment of the court below, a respondent's skeleton argument must be lodged. The respondent's side must always lodge a skeleton argument in any case where there is a respondent's notice.

Skeleton arguments are *not* pleadings and, save in exceptional cases (see para 8 below), *d* need not answer the skeleton arguments of the other side.

Chronology of events

4. The appellant's skeleton argument must be accompanied by a written chronology of events relevant to the appeal. This must be a separate document in order that it can easily be consulted in conjunction with other papers.   *e*

Specialist law reports

5. There is no objection to counsel referring to specialist law reports, whether or not the decision is also reported in the Law Reports, if doing so would assist the court. However, it must be appreciated that such reports may not be readily available to the *f* judges and photostat copies should be provided of any such authorities relied on in the skeleton argument. The Law Reports are to be preferred both by reason of their nature and their general availability. Accordingly, where a decision is reported in that series of reports, the need to refer to specialist reports should be explained.

Timetable for exchange and submission of skeleton arguments

6. *Appeals with fixed dates*   In the case of appeals which are given any form of fixture *g* (ie all appeals, other than appeals assigned to the short warned list and appeals which are heard as a matter of urgency) the skeleton arguments must be sent or delivered to the other side and three copies lodged with the Civil Appeals Office not less than four weeks before the date on which the hearing is due to commence.

7.   *Short warned list cases*   In the case of appeals assigned to the short warned list the *h* skeleton arguments must be sent to the other side and three copies lodged with the Civil Appeals Office ten days before the date from which the short warned list appeal is 'on call'.

Supplementary skeleton arguments

8. Either side may lodge a supplementary skeleton argument if exceptional *j* circumstances give rise to a need for one. This will only occur if (a) one side raised a point which could not have been anticipated on a reading of the notice of appeal or any respondent's notice *and* (b) it called for an answer, e g confession and avoidance. Wherever a supplementary skeleton argument is called for, a copy of it must be sent to the other side and three copies lodged with the Civil Appeals Office at the earliest possible moment.

Listing changes

a   9. Consequent on the new arrangements for compulsory skeleton arguments, some changes will be made to the Court of Appeal listing arrangements.

10. *Fixtures* The present system of giving fixtures to appeals estimated to last five days or more and a 'flexible fixture' (ie a hearing date within a band) to appeals estimated at four days or less (see generally *The Supreme Court Practice 1988* vol 1, para 59/1/10) will be replaced by a single form of fixture.

b   In the case of all appeals (other than those assigned to the short warned list) which have a hearing due to commence on or after 6 June 1989 (whenever fixed) the present system of 'banded dates' will be replaced by a single form of flexible fixture which will apply to all such appeals, namely that the appeal will be booked to commence on a specified date, or on the next following sitting day.

If it does not prove to be possible for the court concerned to take the appeal on the
c   specified date or on the following sitting day, and the listing office are unable to transfer the appeal to another court, the hearing date will have to be rearranged.

The purpose of providing this new system is to assist both counsel and solicitors by providing greater certainty.

11. *Short warned list* Unless the court otherwise directs, three weeks' notice will be given of the entry of an appeal into the short warned list. This will allow time for the
d   skeleton argument to be prepared, sent to the other side and lodged within the ten-day time limit prescribed above (see para 7).

The court appreciates that, in the case of appeals assigned to the short warned list, counsel who has prepared the skeleton argument may not always be available on the date on which the appeal is called on, with the result that the brief will have to change hands. In order to ensure that the original counsel who prepared the skeleton argument is
e   appropriately remunerated for that work, and that the brief fee is suitably adjusted to take account of the fact that the skeleton has already been done, a general instruction is being given to taxing masters to tax the cost of preparing skeleton arguments separately from brief fees in all appeals.

f   *Time estimates*

12. The system to be adopted in relation to counsel's certified time estimates of the length of the appeal hearing is that set out in the Practice Statement of 2 October 1987 (see *Practice Note* [1987] 3 All ER 434, [1987] 1 WLR 1422; see also para 59/1/9A in the current cumulative supplement to *The Supreme Court Practice 1988*). From 4 April 1989 it will be subject to this additional requirement, namely that a copy of the certified estimate must be placed and kept with counsel's papers. Each time counsel is asked to
g   give any advice or to deal with anything in connection with the appeal he or she must look at the estimate and check whether it is still correct. It is particularly important that, when preparing the skeleton argument, counsel should check the certified time estimate to ensure that it is as realistic and accurate as possible. Efficient listing, which is in everyone's interests, is heavily dependent on the accuracy of time estimates.

h   *Oral hearing*

13. The following procedure will be adopted in the case of all appeals to the Civil Division, unless the court announces in any individual case that some other course should be adopted.

(a) The judges will already have read the notice of appeal, any respondent's notice, the
j   judgment under appeal and the skeleton arguments. At the commencement of the hearing the presiding Lord Justice will state what other documents and authorities have also been read.

(b) It will not normally be necessary to open the facts and, unless otherwise directed, counsel for the appellant will be expected to proceed immediately to the ground of appeal which is in the forefront of the appellant's case. Likewise, the respondent's counsel will be expected to proceed immediately with his or her submissions on the issues in the appeal without any preamble. In an exceptional case, such as where there is technical *a* evidence which will need to be explained by counsel and to this extent some opening is necessary, the presiding Lord Justice will notify counsel in advance of the hearing.

(c) When citing an authority which has been preread, counsel should not read the case at length, but go immediately to the passage in the judgment where the principle relied on in the skeleton argument is to be found.

(d) When dealing with issues of fact, the passages in the transcripts or notes of evidence *b* relied on will have been listed in the skeleton argument (see para 3 above) and accordingly counsel should so far as possible avoid reading from them in extenso.

14. It will be the duty of solicitors and counsel to ensure that their lay clients have had explained to them before the appeal hearing what the procedure will be and how the Court of Appeal now deals with oral argument. It is important that both appellants and respondents should be made aware of the new procedure, particularly the extent to *c* which the court relies on prereading, so that the parties do not infer that, because the appeal hearing has been shorter than has hitherto been customary, their case has not been just as fully considered.

Frances Rustin   Barrister.

d

Practice Direction

(Chancery 2/89)

e

CHANCERY DIVISION

Practice – Chancery Division – Administrative arrangements – Chancery Chambers – Official referees' business – Location.

1. The following arrangements have been directed by the Vice-Chancellor and approved *f* by the Lord Chancellor with a view to the better dispatch of business and the convenience of the public.

2. From 4 April 1989 such parts of Chancery Chambers as deal with all aspects of business which is to be heard by the official referees will be relocated in St Dunstan's House, Fetter Lane, London EC4. This will include the issue of writs and summonses and the payment of fees thereon, the entry of and searching of acknowledgments of *g* service, the drawing up and filing of orders and documents, default judgments and the issue of fieri facias and payment of fees thereon.

3. The Practice Direction of 29 July 1982 ([1982] 3 All ER 124, [1982] 1 WLR 1189) is to be read subject to this direction, which amends the room numbers set out therein in so far as they relate to official referees' business.

h

By direction of the Vice-Chancellor and with the concurrence of the Lord Chancellor.

R D MUNROW
Chief Master.

13 March 1989

a
Department of Transport v Chris Smaller (Transport) Ltd

HOUSE OF LORDS

LORD KEITH OF KINKEL, LORD ROSKILL, LORD GRIFFITHS, LORD OLIVER OF AYLMERTON AND LORD GOFF OF CHIEVELEY

b
23, 24 JANUARY, 2 MARCH 1989

Practice – Dismissal of action for want of prosecution – Inordinate delay without excuse – Delay before and after issue of writ – Writ issued six months before expiration of six-year limitation period – Writ not served until three months after expiration of limitation period – Fair trial of action still possible despite delay – Defendants suffering no prejudice from post-writ delay –
c
Whether plaintiff should be penalised for delay occurring between accrual of cause of action and date of issue of writ within limitation period – Whether post-writ delay sufficient ground for striking out action – Whether prejudice justifying striking out confined to prejudice affecting conduct of trial or extending to prejudice to defendant's business interests – Whether anxiety accompanying litigation sufficient ground of prejudice justifying striking out action.

d
In December 1978 a lorry owned by the defendants and driven by their employee crashed into a motorway bridge killing the driver and badly damaging the bridge. Early in 1979 the plaintiff department, who owned the bridge, notified the defendants that they intended making a claim in respect of the damage to the bridge if it had been caused by the negligence of the defendants' driver. In June 1982 the plaintiffs presented their claim
e
for £334,885, being the cost of the repairs. The defendants' insurers instructed a consulting engineer to advise on the plaintiffs' claim but he was unable to arrange a meeting to agree the value of the claim. On 30 May 1984, five and a half years after the accident and six months before the expiry of the six-year limitation period, the plaintiffs issued a writ against the defendants; six months later, on 19 March 1985, the writ was served on the defendants. The statement of claim was delivered on 23 September 1985
f
and the defendants filed a defence denying liability. Pleadings closed on 20 December 1985. The plaintiffs failed to issue a summons for directions and instead the defendants did so on 24 June 1986. The summons was heard on 8 July 1986, when the plaintiffs were ordered to give further and better particulars, to answer interrogatories and to set the action down for trial, all within 28 days. The plaintiffs provided further and better particulars and answered interrogatories within that period but failed to set the action
g
down for trial. On 28 April 1987 the defendants applied to have the action struck out for want of prosecution. The master struck out the plaintiffs' claim but the judge reversed his decision on the ground that although the plaintiffs had been guilty of inordinate and inexcusable delay for 13 months in the period following the issue of the writ there was no real risk that there could not be a fair trial of the action and the defendants had failed to show that they would suffer more than minimal prejudice as a result of the post-writ
h
delay. On appeal by the defendants the Court of Appeal affirmed the judge's decision. The defendants appealed to the House of Lords, contending that inordinate and inexcusable delay in the conduct of the litigation after the expiry of the limitation period ought to be a ground for striking out even though there could be a fair trial and the defendant would suffer no prejudice. The defendants further contended that they had in fact been prejudiced by the delay because their insurance cover was less than the amount
j
claimed by the plaintiffs and the contingent liability for the balance had hindered them in raising finance for their business.

Held – (1) A plaintiff could not be penalised for any delay occurring between the accrual of the cause of action and the issue of the writ if the writ was issued within the limitation period (see p 899 *a b*, p 900 *h*, p 903 *a* to *c* and p 905 *d* to *h*, post).

(2) Inordinate and inexcusable delay by the plaintiff in prosecuting an action after the limitation period had expired was not a ground for striking out the action for want of *a* prosecution unless the defendant had suffered prejudice from the delay or a fair trial of the issues was impossible. However, where a long delay before the issue of the writ had caused the defendant prejudice he only had to show something more than minimal additional prejudice as the result of post-writ delay to justify the action being struck out. On the facts, the 13-month delay after the issue of the writ had only caused the defendants minimal prejudice because any difficulties arising from the contingent liability hanging *b* over them as the result of the action were attributable to the statutory limitation period of six years and not to the post-writ delay. The appeal would therefore be dismissed (see p 899 *a b*, p 903 *d e j*, p 904 *b* and p 905 *h*, post); *Allen v Sir Alfred McAlpine & Sons Ltd* [1968] 1 All ER 543 and *Birkett v James* [1977] 2 All ER 801 applied.

Per curiam. (1) Prejudice entitling a defendant to strike out an action is not confined to prejudice affecting the actual conduct of the trial but includes, inter alia, prejudice to *c* the defendant's business interests (see p 899 *a b*, p 904 *j* and p 905 *a b*, post).

(2) The court should be cautious about allowing the mere fact of the anxiety that accompanies any litigation to be regarded as a sufficient ground of prejudice which by itself would justify striking out an action (see p 899 *a b* and p 905 *b h*, post); dictum of Griffiths LJ in *Eagil Trust Co Ltd v Pigott-Brown* [1985] 3 All ER 119 at 124 approved.

d

Notes
For dismissal of actions for want of prosecution, see 37 Halsbury's Laws (4th edn) paras 447–450, and for cases on the subject, see 37(3) Digest (Reissue) 67–78, 3293–3341.

Cases referred to in opinions
Allen v Sir Alfred McAlpine & Sons Ltd, Bostic v Bermondsey and Southwark Group Hospital *e* *Management Committee, Sternberg v Hammond* [1968] 1 All ER 543, [1968] 2 QB 229, [1968] 2 WLR 366, CA.
Birkett v James [1977] 2 All ER 801, [1978] AC 297, [1977] 3 WLR 38, HL.
Biss v Lambeth Southwark and Lewisham Health Authority [1978] 2 All ER 125, [1978] 1 WLR 382, CA.
Bridgnorth DC v Henry Willcock & Co Ltd [1983] CA Transcript 958. *f*
Eagil Trust Co Ltd v Pigott-Brown [1985] 3 All ER 119, CA.
Electricity Supply Nominees Ltd v Longstaff & Shaw Ltd [1986] CA Transcript 1063.
Haynes v Atkins (1983) Times, 12 October, CA.
Note [1966] 3 All ER 77, [1966] 1 WLR 1234, HL.
President of India and Union of India v John Shaw & Sons (Salford) Ltd (1977) Times, 27 October, CA. *g*
Tolley v Morris [1979] 2 All ER 561, [1979] 1 WLR 592, HL.
Westminster City Council v Clifford Culpin & Partners (a firm) (1987) 137 NLJ 736, CA.

Appeal
The defendants, Chris Smaller (Transport) Ltd, appealed with the leave of the Appeal *h* Committee of the House of Lords given on 7 July 1988 against the order of the Court of Appeal (Nicholls and Staughton LJJ) dated 4 March 1988 dismissing their appeal from the order of Sir Neil Lawson sitting as a judge of the High Court in the Queen's Bench Division in chambers on 26 October 1987 whereby he allowed an appeal by the plaintiffs, the Department of Transport, from the order of Master Lubbock dated 5 May 1987 dismissing the plaintiffs' action for want of prosecution. The facts are set out in the *j* opinion of Lord Griffiths.

Michael Connell QC, Sean Overend and *Michael Pooles* for the defendants.
John Laws and *Guy Sankey* for the plaintiffs.

Their Lordships took time for consideration.

March 2. The following opinions were delivered.

a
LORD KEITH OF KINKEL. My Lords, I have had the opportunity of considering in draft the speech prepared by my noble and learned friend Lord Griffiths. I agree with it, and for the reasons he gives would dismiss this appeal.

LORD ROSKILL. My Lords, I have had the advantage of reading in draft the speech
b about to be delivered by my noble and learned friend Lord Griffiths. I agree with it, and for the reasons he gives I would dismiss this appeal.

LORD GRIFFITHS. My Lords, over ten years ago, on 8 December 1978, a lorry, owned by the defendants and driven by a lorry driver in their employment, crashed into a bridge on the M50 motorway. The lorry driver was killed and the bridge was badly
c damaged. The Department of Transport, the plaintiffs, who owned the bridge, wrote promptly, on 24 January 1979, to the defendants saying that they would consider making a claim for the cost of repairing the bridge if it appeared that the accident was due to negligence of the defendants or their driver. As no other vehicle had been involved in the accident, the plaintiffs clearly had a strong prima facie case that the accident was caused by the negligence of the defendants or their driver. Thereafter, however, matters
d proceeded at a snail's pace.

The contract for the repair of the bridge was made in May 1980 but it was not until 24 June 1982 that the plaintiffs first wrote to present their claim for the sum of £334,885. The defendants' insurers had instructed a Mr Parkinson Hill, a consulting engineer, to investigate the claim in 1979 but he had been unable to advise on the value of the claim until it was formulated in June 1982. Thereafter, he sought particulars of the claim from
e the plaintiffs, which were finally delivered to him on 8 March 1983. In July and August 1983 Mr Parkinson Hill wrote trying to arrange a meeting with the plaintiffs to agree the value of the claim, subject to liability. The plaintiffs responded to the second of these letters, asking to see his calculations and ending 'we will contact you thereafter as requested'. Mr Parkinson Hill sent his calculations but nothing more was heard about the claim until a writ was served on the defendants on 19 March 1985, over 18 months
f after he had last written to the plaintiffs with his calculations. The writ had been issued on 30 May 1984, five and a half years after the accident and six months before the expiration of the six-year limitation period. It was not served until three months after the limitation period had expired.

It is difficult to see any justification for a government department to be so tardy in attempting to recover money due to public funds, and one would have at least expected
g that the action, once commenced, would be pursued as swiftly as possible; but that was not to be. The statement of claim was not delivered until 23 September 1985. The defence denied negligence on the part of the lorry driver alleging a sudden loss of consciousness from natural causes. It also alleged design and construction faults in the structure of the bridge and the safety barrier in the road and a failure to mitigate damage.
h The pleadings closed on 20 December 1985 but the plaintiffs failed to take out the summons for directions, which they should have done by 20 January 1986. Eventually, it was the defendants who took the initiative and issued the summons for directions on 24 June 1986, five months after the date on which it should have been issued by the plaintiffs.

The summons for directions was heard on 8 July 1986. The plaintiffs were ordered to
j give further and better particulars, to answer interrogatories and to set down the action, all within 28 days. The plaintiffs failed to comply with any of these directions. The defendants took out a summons for a peremptory order for further and better particulars and answers to the interrogatories returnable on 20 October. This appears to have galvanised the plaintiffs into action: the further and better particulars were served on 15 October and the answers to interrogatories on 19 October, therefore on the summons on 20 October the only order made was for the defendants to have their costs. The

plaintiffs still failed to set down the action for trial and on 28 April 1987 the defendants took out a summons to strike the action out for want of prosecution. This summons was taken out nine months after the date on which the plaintiffs should have set the action down for trial.

The master struck out the plaintiffs' claim. The judge allowed the plaintiffs' appeal. He held, applying the principles in *Birkett v James* [1977] 2 All ER 801, [1978] AC 297, that the plaintiffs had been guilty of inordinate and inexcusable delay for a period of 13 months but that there was no real risk that there could not be a fair trial of the issues and the defendants had failed to show that they would suffer more than minimal prejudice as a result of the post-writ delay.

The Court of Appeal dismissed the defendants' appeal and your Lordships gave leave to appeal so that they might re-examine the principles that have governed applications to strike out for want of prosecution since the decision of this House in *Birkett v James* in the light of criticisms as to the effectiveness of those principles expressed in certain judgments in the Court of Appeal.

The principles on which the jurisdiction to strike out for want of prosecution is exercised were settled by the Court of Appeal in *Allen v Sir Alfred McAlpine & Sons Ltd* [1968] 1 All ER 543, [1968] 2 QB 229, and approved by the decision of this House is *Birkett v James*. The power should be exercised only where the court is satisfied either (1) that the default has been intentional and contumelious, e g disobedience to a peremptory order of the court or conduct amounting to an abuse of the process of the court, or (2)(a) that there has been inordinate and inexcusable delay on the part of the plaintiff or his lawyers and (b) that such delay will give rise to a substantial risk that it is not possible to have a fair trial of the issues in the action or is such as is likely to cause or to have caused serious prejudice to the defendants, either as between themselves and the plaintiffs, or between each other, or between them and a third party.

These principles left unresolved three further questions on which divergent views had been expressed in the Court of Appeal. They were (1) the relevance of the fact that the limitation period had not expired by the time the application to dismiss for want of prosecution was heard, (2) the relevance of the period which the plaintiff had allowed to lapse before action was brought, when this was done within the limitation period, and (3) whether the judge ought to weigh up the plaintiff's prospects of success in any remedy he might have against his solicitor if the action were dismissed, and, if so, how his estimate should affect the exercise of his discretion.

It was to resolve these questions that leave to appeal was given in *Birkett v James*. The answers given were (1) that only in 'wholly exceptional circumstances' should an action be struck out within the relevant limitation period, because the plaintiff would be able to issue a fresh writ which would result in the action being heard at an even later date as a result of the striking out. 'Wholly exceptional circumstances' were discussed in the speeches of Lord Diplock and Lord Edmund-Davies but do not fall for further consideration in this appeal. (2) Time that has elapsed between the accrual of the cause of action and the issue of a writ within the limitation period cannot constitute inordinate and inexcusable delay. Although a defendant may well have been prejudiced by this delay and in some cases it may even make it difficult to have a fair trial, these considerations do not justify striking out an action which a plaintiff has commenced within the period of limitation set by Parliament. The plaintiff must have been guilty of inordinate and inexcusable delay in the prosecution of the action after the issue of the writ and the defendant must show prejudice flowing directly from the post-writ delay which must be additional to any prejudice suffered because the plaintiff did not commence his action as soon as he could have done. (3) The fact that the plaintiff may or may not have an alternative remedy against his solicitor is not a relevant consideration in deciding whether or not to dismiss an action for want of prosecution.

It was hoped that the initiative taken by the Court of Appeal in *Allen v McAlpine* to strike out actions for want of prosecution and the indorsement of those principles by this House in *Birkett v James* would be a sufficient deterrent to ensure that all plaintiffs'

solicitors would in future pursue litigation with reasonable dispatch rather than face an
a action against them by their clients when the action was struck out. Unfortunately, this
has not proved to be the case. There are still far too many applications to strike out
actions for want of prosecution. In a postscript to his judgment in *Westminster City Council
v Clifford Culpin & Partners (a firm)* (1987) 137 NLJ 736 at 737–738 Kerr LJ expressed the
frustration of the court at the present state of affairs. He said:

b
'Although more complex than most, and of course unusual to the extent that the
plaintiffs were represented by their own legal department during the relevant years,
this case is typical of the large numbers of applications to strike out claims for want
of prosecution which are constantly before our courts. These are only the tip of the
iceberg. For every contested case there are no doubt dozens which are settled or not
pursued. Their causes and consequences are pernicious. They are caused by
c inexcusable dilatoriness or inefficiency on the part of lawyers and sometimes others,
such as insurers. This then leads to extensive further delays and wasted costs
involved in contesting the resulting striking-out applications. Apart from the delays
between 1973 and early 1986 when the summonses to strike out were issued in this
case, one should reflect on the time and effort, and the thousands of pounds spent
on lawyers' fees and other costs, which have been expended over the last 18 months
d without any relevance or benefit for the subject-matter of the proceedings. This
period has been taken up with numerous complex fresh pleadings and applications
to amend or to appeal and three court hearings until now, involving three firms of
solicitors and four barristers on each occasion. The proceedings involved in killing a
claim on the one hand, and trying to keep it alive on the other, can take far longer
and cost far more than its trial. And such proceedings are necessarily entirely sterile
e and unproductive in relation to the substantive issues. There are constant complaints
about delays in our legal processes and suggestions for reforms, such as the current
'Civil Justice Review' by the Lord Chancellor's Department. But no changes in the
organisation or administration of the courts would make any material difference to
cases such as the present. By far the major part of all delays stems solely from the
way in which litigation is conducted. In this connection our law needs to be
f changed, both in substance and procedurally. The principles laid down in *Birkett v
James* are unsatisfactory and inadequate. They are far too lenient to deal effectively
with excessive delays. Moreover they then breed excessive further delays and costs
in their application. The long line of decisions concerned with striking out
applications, both reported and unreported, demonstrate that the regime of *Birkett v
James* should be replaced by a system of rules which are much stricter, more effective
g and simple to apply. And it is highly questionable whether plaintiffs should be
allowed the benefit of the full periods of limitation, with virtual impunity, where
the facts are known and there is no obstacle to the speedy institution and prosecution
of claims. The present system provides insufficient sanctions for those responsible
for the dilatory and inefficient conduct of litigation, and it is frequently unfair to
litigants.'

h
Sir John Megaw, who was sitting with him, gave his support to these comments. In
Electricity Supply Nominees Ltd v Longstaff & Shaw Ltd [1986] CA Transcript 1063 Mustill
LJ expressed similar misgivings. The court was dealing with an action in which the first
intimation of claim received by one of the defendants was the service of the writ almost
seven years after the cause of action arose. Thereafter, the plaintiff was guilty of inordinate
j and inexcusable delay for a period of ten months in the conduct of the action before the
application to strike out for want of prosecution. The court was driven to the conclusion
that, although the defendants had obviously been prejudiced by the seven years' delay,
the additional delay of a period of ten months could not have added any further
significant prejudice to their position or to the prospect of a fair trial. The official referee
had struck the action out on the ground that there would be further prejudice caused by
the ten months' delay. But after reviewing and rejecting this conclusion Mustill LJ said:

'I accordingly feel constrained to hold that these appeals should be allowed. I say *a* "constrained" because I differ with great hesitation from the official referee on a matter lying so particularly within his special field of experience, the more so since the conclusion at which he arrived accords with what I believe to be the instinctive reaction of many (and it was certainly mine) that this stale, old claim should not through the culpable delay of the plaintiffs be allowed to become even older and more stale. But I cannot find that the clear and well-established authorities binding on this court leave any room for such a blunt approach to the present problem.'   *b*

His reference to the blunt approach is, I believe, a reference to a suggestion he made at an earlier stage in the judgment where he said:

'One possible avenue of escape from this renewed dilemma would be to open up the discretion by enabling the court to dismiss an action for culpable delay in those cases where the commencement of proceedings has been long postponed, regardless *c* of any specific extra detriment. This was, I believe, the solution preferred by Lord Denning MR in *Biss v Lambeth Southwark and Lewisham Health Authority* [1978] 2 All ER 125, [1978] 1 WLR 382, but despite its attraction it must, I believe, be rejected as inconsistent with the clear tenor of the authorities.'

The defendants, relying on these passages, have invited your Lordships to depart from *d* *Birkett v James* and to hold that inordinate and inexcusable delay occurring after the expiration of the limitation period should be a sufficient ground to strike out an action even if there can still be a fair trial of the issues and even if the defendant has suffered no prejudice as a result of the delay. Counsel for the defendants submits that, as *Birkett v James* was in fact dealing with a case in which the delay had occurred before the expiration of the limitation period, your Lordships are free to regard as obiter all that was said about *e* inordinate and inexcusable delay arising outside the limitation period. This would in my view be altogether too narrow a view of the effect of the decision, which clearly intended to lay down principles to govern questions of delay and prejudice arising both before and after the expiration of the limitation period. If your Lordships are to depart from the principles in *Birkett v James* it must be because you are convinced that time has shown that the principles are flawed and that it is now right to adopt a different approach in *f* accordance with the 1966 practice statement (see *Note* [1966] 3 All ER 77, [1966] 1 WLR 1234).

This case is due to be tried in November 1989, that is 11 years after the accident. This is a totally unnecessary delay, but it is principally due to the fact that the plaintiffs did not commence the action for five and a half years and then did not serve the writ until nine months later. Under the present law of limitation, the plaintiffs were allowed six *g* years in which to commence their action and, under the present rules of practice, were allowed a further 12 months in which to serve the writ. Kerr LJ in the *Westminster City Council* case (1987) 137 NLJ 736 at 738, in the passage I have cited, said:

'... it is highly questionable whether plaintiffs should be allowed the benefit of the full periods of limitation, with virtual impunity, where the facts are known and *h* there is no obstacle to the speedy institution and prosecution of claims.'

I see the force of this observation, particularly in a case like the present, when there is no good reason why the action should not have been started much earlier than it was. But limitation periods are set by Parliament and not by the courts. The six-year period of limitation for actions in tort other than for personal injury was considered in the Twenty-first Report of the Law Reform Committee, Final Report on Limitation of Actions *j* (Cmnd 6923 (1977)). No change was recommended and that period is now provided for in an Act as recent as the Limitation Act 1980. It may be thought that six years is too long in the vast majority of cases, but it must be remembered that most people who suffer injury will wish to recover damages and will not wait until the limitation period is almost due to expire before commencing their action, and the limitation period has to

cover the unusual as well as the usual case. In the unusual case there may be special
a   circumstances that make it impossible or inadvisable to commence proceedings shortly
after the cause of action arises. It would, I think, introduce intolerable uncertainty into
the litigation process if litigants were at risk of being penalised even if they commenced
their actions within the limitation period and thereafter pursued them expeditiously.
The effect would be to push people into precipitate litigation for fear that the court might
eventually rule that they had not started their action soon enough. The vast majority of
b   claims are settled without resort to litigation and it would place an insupportable burden
on our already overloaded system to push these claims unnecessarily into the litigation
process. The courts must respect the limitation periods set by Parliament; if they are too
long then it is for Parliament to reduce them. I therefore commence my assessment of
the present regime by concluding that the plaintiff cannot be penalised for any delay that
occurs between the accrual of the cause of action and the issue of the writ provided it is
c   issued within the limitation period. Counsel for the defendants, I think, accepted this
conclusion, for he did not seek to persuade your Lordships that, save possibly in case of
deliberate breach of a peremptory order, it would be right to strike out an action within
the limitation period when the plaintiff would be able to start a fresh action.

However, counsel for the defendants submits that, once the limitation period has
expired so that the plaintiff cannot commence a fresh action, inordinate and inexcusable
d   delay in the conduct of the litigation should be a ground for striking out even though
there can be a fair trial of the issues and the defendant has suffered no prejudice from the
delay. What would be the purpose of striking out in such circumstances? If there can be
a fair trial and the defendant has suffered no prejudice, it clearly cannot be to do justice
between the parties before the court; as between the plaintiff and defendant such an
order is manifestly an injustice to the plaintiff. The only possible purpose of such an
e   order would be as a disciplinary measure which by punishing the plaintiff will have a
beneficent effect on the administration of justice by deterring others from similar delays.
I have no faith that the exercise of the power in these circumstances would produce any
greater impact on delay in litigation than the present principles. There are still many
cases that are struck out for want of prosecution, which shows that the deterrent effect of
Allen v Sir Alfred McAlpine & Sons Ltd [1968] 1 All ER 543, [1968] 2 QB 229 has not been
f   as successful as was hoped for, and I see no reason to suppose that the deterrent effect of
extending the principle to cover this new situation would be likely to be any more
successful. At least it can be said that under the present principle such limited success as
has been achieved has been with a view to protection of the defendant. To extend the
principle purely to punish the plaintiff in the illusory hope of transforming the habits of
other plaintiffs' solicitors would, in my view, be an unjustified way of attacking a very
g   intractable problem. I believe that a far more radical approach is required to tackle the
problems of delay in the litigation process than driving an individual plaintiff away from
the courts when his culpable delay has caused no injustice to his opponent. I, for my part,
recommend a radical overhaul of the whole civil procedural process and the introduction
of court controlled case management techniques designed to ensure that once a litigant
h   has entered the litigation process his case proceeds in accordance with a timetable as
prescribed by rules of court or as modified by a judge: see Civil Justice Review, Report of
the Review Body on Civil Justice (Cm 394 (1988)).

The principles in *Allen v Sir Alfred McAlpine & Sons Ltd* and *Birkett v James* are now well
understood and I have not been persuaded that a case has been made out to abandon the
need to show that the post-writ delay will either make a fair trial impossible or prejudice
j   the defendant. Furthermore, it should not be forgotten that long delay before issue of
the writ will have the effect of any post-writ delay being looked at critically by the court
and more readily being regarded as inordinate and inexcusable than would be the case if
the action had been commenced soon after the accrual of the cause of action. And that if
the defendant has suffered prejudice as a result of such delay before issue of the writ he
will only have to show something more than minimal additional prejudice as a result of
the post-writ delay to justify striking out the action.

Alternatively, counsel for the defendants submits that at least the burden should be on the plaintiff guilty of inordinate post-writ delay to prove that the defendant will not *a* suffer prejudice as a result of the delay. I regard this as a wholly impractical suggestion. It would put an unrealistic burden on the plaintiff. The plaintiff will not know the defendant's difficulties in meeting the case, such as the availability of witnesses and documents nor will the plaintiff know of other collateral matters that may have prejudiced the defendant such as the effect of delay on the defendant's business activities. The defendant, on the other hand, has no difficulty in explaining his position to the court *b* and establishing prejudice if he has in fact suffered it. I must, therefore, reject this second limb of the argument of counsel for the defendants.

Finally, counsel for the defendants submitted that even applying the principles in *Birkett v James* your Lordships should allow this appeal. Although this action will be tried 11 years after the accident, there is no suggestion that there cannot be a fair trial of the issues. There is no medical evidence to support the suggestion that the lorry driver was *c* overcome by sudden unconsciousness and the faith in such a plea receives little support from the fact that the defendants paid into court £90,000 on 6 December 1985, almost immediately after the commencement of the action. In so far as criticisms are aimed at the design and construction of the bridge and safety barrier, there is no reason to suppose that all the necessary drawings and other documents will not be available to debate these issues even 11 years after the accident. Indeed, counsel for the defendants did not seek to *d* persuade your Lordships that there could not be a fair trial of the action.

The defendants, however, submit that the delay has prejudiced them because it has hindered them in raising finance to expand their business. The plaintiffs' claim is for £335,000 plus interest. The defendants' insurance cover is limited to £250,000 plus interest, leaving a potential liability on the defendants of £85,000 plus interest. The defendants maintain that this contingent liability in their accounts prevented them from *e* raising the finance with which they wished to expand their business.

Counsel for the plaintiffs submitted that the prejudice that entitled a defendant to strike out an action should be limited to proof of prejudice in the conduct of the litigation. This seems to me to be but another way of saying that delay has prevented a fair trial of the action; but in both *Allen v Sir Alfred McAlpine & Sons Ltd* and *Birkett v* *f* *James* reference is made to the risk both that there could not be a fair trial of the action and of prejudice to the defendants, which, one would suppose, was intended to mean some prejudice other than the mere inability to have a fair trial. Counsel for the plaintiffs frankly conceded that the weight of authority was against his submission. In *Biss v Lambeth Southwark and Lewisham Health Authority* [1978] 2 All ER 125, [1978] 1 WLR 382 Lord Denning MR and Geoffrey Lane LJ considered that the anxiety suffered by nurses whose professional competence was in question was a sufficient prejudice in that case to *g* justify striking out the action, and they also instanced the prejudice that might be caused to a small business with a huge claim hanging over it as another example of prejudice that would justify making a striking out order. In *Tolley v Morris* [1979] 2 All ER 561 at 568, [1979] 1 WLR 592 at 600 Lord Diplock said:

'*Biss*'s case was concerned with the nature of the prejudice that must be shown, a *h* matter that it was not necessary to discuss in *Birkett v James*. I see no reason for disagreeing with the actual decision in *Biss*'s case . . .'

The decisions of the Court of Appeal in *President of India and Union of India v John Shaw & Sons (Salford) Ltd* (1977) Times, 27 October and *Bridgnorth DC v Henry Willcock & Co Ltd* [1983] CA Transcript 958 are further examples of the court taking business prejudice *j* into account as a ground for striking out, and *Haynes v Atkins* (1983) Times, 12 October is an example of delay hanging over a professional man being taken into account as a ground of prejudice. In the face of this powerful line of authority, I cannot accept the submission of counsel for the plaintiffs. These authorities clearly establish that prejudice may be of varying kinds and it is not confined to prejudice affecting the actual conduct

of the trial. It would be foolish to attempt to define or categorise the type of prejudice
a justifying striking out an action, but there can be no doubt that if the defendants had
been able to establish significant damage to their business interests, flowing directly from
the culpable delay of 13 months after the issue of the writ, a judge would have been
entitled to regard it as prejudice justifying striking out the action. I would, however,
express a note of caution against allowing the mere fact of the anxiety that accompanies
any litigation being regarded as of itself a sufficient prejudice to justify striking out an
b action. Counsel for the defendants did not seek to argue that the anxiety occasioned by
the extra 13 months in this case should be regarded as a sufficient ground of prejudice to
justify making a striking out order. There are, however, passages in some of the
judgments that suggest that the mere sword of Damocles, hanging for an unnecessary
period, might be a sufficient reason of itself to strike out. On this aspect I repeat the note
of caution I expressed in the Court of Appeal in *Eagil Trust Co Ltd v Pigott-Brown* [1985] 3
c All ER 119 at 124, where I said:

> 'Any action is bound to cause anxiety, but it would as a general rule be an
> exceptional case where that sort of anxiety alone would found a sufficient ground
> for striking out in the absence of evidence of any particular prejudice. *Biss's* case is
> an example of such an exceptional case, the action hanging over for $11\frac{1}{2}$ years, with
d > professional reputations at stake.'

In the event, the defendants failed to satisfy either the judge or the Court of Appeal
that the additional 13 months delay had caused more than minimal prejudice to them.
The reasons for this conclusion are cogently set out in the judgment of Nicholls LJ. They
may be briefly summarised by saying that such difficulties as the defendants may have
had in raising finance in 1986 because of the contingent liability hanging over them
e were not attributable to delay after the issue of the writ because it would have existed
even if the claim had been pursued diligently after the issue of the writ. The truth is that
the defendants' embarrassment flowed from the statutory limitation period of six years
and not from the delay subsequent to the writ. The judge and the Court of Appeal
concluded that the fact that this contingent liability will not be quantified until 18
months later than the date it would have been quantified if the action had proceeded
f expeditiously did not cause the defendants' business more than minimal prejudice. It is
well established that your Lordships will only re-examine the exercise of a discretion in
exceptional circumstances. Such circumstances do not exist in this case. The judge and
the Court of Appeal respectively exercised and reviewed the discretion on the principles
established in *Birkett v James* [1977] 2 All ER 801, [1978] AC 297 and no grounds have
been shown for interfering with their conclusions.
g For these reasons I would dismiss the appeal.

LORD OLIVER OF AYLMERTON. My Lords, I have had the advantage of reading
in draft the speech delivered by my noble and learned friend Lord Griffiths, with which
I entirely agree. I too would dismiss the appeal.

h
LORD GOFF OF CHIEVELEY. My Lords, I have had the advantage of reading in
draft the speech delivered by my noble and learned friend Lord Griffiths, with which I
agree. I too would dismiss the appeal.

Appeal dismissed.

j
Solicitors: *Gregory Rowcliffe & Milners*, agents for *John Stallard & Co*, Worcester (for the
defendants); *Treasury Solicitor*.

Mary Rose Plummer   Barrister.

R v Inland Revenue Commissioners, ex parte Taylor

QUEEN'S BENCH DIVISION (CROWN OFFICE LIST)
FARQUHARSON J
25 MAY 1988

COURT OF APPEAL, CIVIL DIVISION
O'CONNOR, NICHOLLS AND TAYLOR LJJ
24, 25, 26 OCTOBER 1988

Discovery – Legal professional privilege – Document prepared with a view to litigation – Written request for legal advice – Investigation of taxpayer's affairs – Inspector issuing notice for delivery up of documents – Inspector anticipating that notice likely to be challenged in proceedings – Inspector seeking advice from Revenue solicitor before issuing notice – Whether request for advice privileged.

Discovery – Judicial review proceedings – Affidavit filed in connection with judicial review proceedings – Discovery of documents referred to in affidavit – Notice requiring applicant to deliver documents relevant to his liability to tax – Affidavit sworn on behalf of Revenue referring to report from inspector leading to issue of notice – Whether applicant entitled to discovery of documents referred to in affidavit – Taxes Management Act 1970, s 20(2) – RSC Ord 24, rr 10(1), 13(1), 17

The applicant was a solicitor who advised clients on tax matters. During the course of investigation into his own tax affairs by an inspector, the Board of Inland Revenue, acting through R, served on him a notice under s 20(2)[a] of the Taxes Management Act 1970 requiring him to deliver to the inspector all the documents in his possession or power as specified in a schedule attached to the notice. The applicant applied for leave to bring judicial review proceedings, seeking an order of certiorari to quash the notice or, alternatively, a declaration that the notice was ultra vires, on the grounds, inter alia, that the notice was not in accordance with s 20(2) of the 1970 Act and that it was oppressive in that it required him to give up documents in breach his duty of confidentiality to his clients. Leave was given in February 1987. In the course of those proceedings R filed an affidavit which stated his authority for issuing the notice and referred to two documents. The first was a request dated 8 May 1986 written by the inspector to the Revenue's solicitor seeking legal advice because, from past experience of the applicant, he anticipated that if a s 20(2) notice was issued the applicant would be likely to challenge it in legal proceedings. The second document was a report from the inspector dated 8 September 1986 which led to the issue of the s 20(2) notice. The applicant requested the production for inspection of the two documents under RSC Ord 24, r 10(1)[b] but that request was refused. In interlocutory proceedings the applicant applied to the court for an order for discovery of the two documents. The judge refused the application, holding that there were no grounds on which R's decision to issue the notice could be challenged, and that therefore disclosure of the documents which helped him arrive at that decision could not properly be ordered. The applicant appealed.

Held – The appeal would be dismissed for the following reasons—
(1) On the facts there was ample evidence that the Revenue had anticipated litigation if a s 20(2) notice was served. It followed therefore that the written request for a legal opinion on 8 May 1986 was protected by legal professional privilege (see p 915 *b c*, p 917 *d* and p 918 *a b*, post).

---

a   Section 20(2) is set out at p 912 *d*, post
b   Rule 10(1) is set out at p 910 *h*, post

a (2) Where a party sought the production of documents for inspection under RSC Ord
24, r 13(1)^c, prima facie it was for that party to show that it was necessary for disposing
fairly of the case. On the facts, the applicant had failed to show that production of the
documents was necessary for the fair disposal of the issues raised in the application for
judicial review. The court, however, had power under Ord 24, r 17^d to reopen the matter
and on the substantive hearing the court would have unfettered discretion to decide
whether the report of 8 September 1986 should be disclosed (see p 916 a and p 917 a b d
b to f j to p 918 a, post).

Notes

For production for inspection of documents referred to in pleadings and affidavits or of
other relevant documents and for ordering their production for inspection, see 13
Halsbury's Laws (4th edn) paras 58–59, 62–64, and for cases on the subject, see 18 Digest
c (Reissue) 77–85, 548–611.
For the Taxes Management Act 1970, s 20, see 42 Halsbury's Statutes (4th edn) 286.

Cases referred to in judgments

IRC v National Federation of Self-Employed and Small Businesses Ltd [1981] 2 All ER 93,
   [1982] AC 617, [1981] 2 WLR 722, HL.
d O'Reilly v Mackman [1982] 3 All ER 1124, [1983] 2 AC 237, [1982] 3 WLR 1096, HL.
R v IRC, ex p J Rothschild Holdings plc [1986] STC 410; affd [1987] STC 163, CA.
R v Secretary of State for the Home Dept, ex p Harrison [1987] CA Transcript 1246.

Cases also cited

Preston v IRC [1985] 2 All ER 327, [1985] AC 835, HL.
R v Lancashire CC, ex p Huddleston [1986] 2 All ER 941, CA.
e R v Secretary of State for the Home Dept, ex p Herbage (No 2) [1987] 1 All ER 324, [1987] QB
   1077, CA.

Application

Thomas Patrick Denton Taylor applied by notice of motion dated 24 February 1988 for
discovery of two documents dated 8 May 1986 and 8 September 1986 compiled by John
f Christopher Ward, an inspector of taxes, and referred to by John Herbert Roberts, an
under secretary appointed by the Commissioners of Inland Revenue, in an affidavit
sworn in connection with an application by the applicant for judicial review, leave to
apply for which had been given by Nolan J on 20 February 1987, of a notice issued
against the applicant by the commissioners on 23 September 1986 under s 20(2) of the
Taxes Management Act 1970. The facts are set out in the judgment.
g

Michael Ashe for Mr Taylor.
Roy Lemon for the Crown.

FARQUHARSON J. This is an application for discovery arising out of a motion for
h judicial review which has yet to be heard. On 23 September 1986 the Commissioners of
Inland Revenue issued a notice against the applicant, Mr Taylor, under s 20(2) of the
Taxes Management Act 1970. It will be helpful if I cite that particular statutory provision
straight away:

      'Subject to this section, the Board may by notice in writing require a person to
      deliver, to a named officer of theirs, such documents as are in the person's possession
j   or power and as (in the Board's reasonable opinion) contain, or may contain,
      information relevant to any tax liability to which he is or may be subject, or to the
      amount of any such liability.'

c Rule 13(1) is set out at p 911 c, post
d Rule 17 is set out at p 911 d, post

The notice contained a schedule with an extensive list of documents which the commissioners were asking Mr Taylor to produce. Mr Taylor on a number of grounds *a* objected to the form and content of that document, and it is that notice which is the subject, as I have just said, of his application for judicial review.

The grounds on which his application is based spell out his objections. He says the notice was wrong in law and was not in accordance with s 20(2) of the Taxes Management Act 1970, there were no grounds or alternatively insufficient grounds for its issue, the notice was oppressive in relation to the range of documents which he was called on to *b* produce, there were no or insufficient reasons given for the demand, the documents required related to matters that were the subject of an appeal by him in relation to certain assessments, and there was a risk that if he complied with the notice he would have to surrender documents which would breach his duty of confidentiality to his clients, Mr Taylor being a solicitor who advises clients on revenue matters. It was Mr Taylor's case that the object of this exercise was to get information in relation to the tax affairs not *c* only of himself but of his clients as well.

On 22 December 1986 Mr Taylor initiated this application for leave to apply for judicial review, and supported it by an affidavit.

The case seems to have drifted on through the year 1987, for reasons that have not been satisfactorily explained to me, but in January 1988 at long last the Revenue filed an affidavit from an under secretary in the Inland Revenue, a Mr John Herbert Roberts. He *d* was the person to whom Mr Ward, the inspector, was responsible, Mr Ward being the person who had been delegated to serve the notice.

That affidavit set out the history of the circumstances in which the notice under s 20(2) came to be issued. Mr Roberts deals, during the course of that affidavit, with the reasons why he was of the opinion that the notice was properly issued, and he deals at some considerable length with the grounds on which it was decided that the Board, through *e* Mr Ward, should serve the notice on Mr Taylor. Those grounds are extensive. They go in particular into matters which were the subject of inquiry by the Board relating to the tax affairs of Mr Taylor.

Further, in that affidavit there were references to certain documents of which Mr Ward was the author. One of them was a document dated 8 May 1986, which of course *f* was before the service of the s 20 notice, in which Mr Ward had sought legal advice from the legal department of the Inland Revenue. It was of course in relation to the projected service of this notice that he sought that advice, in anticipation, on his former experience of Mr Taylor, that legal questions would be raised as a result of that notice, the substance and form of which would be likely to be challenged, whether in judicial review proceedings or otherwise.

There was a further document referred to by Mr Roberts in his affidavit, also *g* emanating from Mr Ward. That was a report dated 8 September 1986, in which Mr Ward set out the reasons why he was submitting that a notice should be authorised to be served on Mr Taylor. The latter document, that is to say the report of 8 September 1986, is the subject of extensive quotation by Mr Roberts in his affidavit. Indeed, it was necessary that it should be, as it was setting out the basis of the reasoning why he *h* authorised the service of the notice. It is as a result of the service of that document that Mr Taylor now comes before the court to seek the discovery of documents. The items in respect of which he seeks discovery are, first of all, the order of the Crown going back to 3 May 1979, whereby Mr Roberts was delegated by the Board to issue notices under s 20(2). This is not an application, at any rate in relation to that particular document, on which counsel for Mr Taylor places much reliance. He says that once the authority has *j* been challenged there would be no difficulty in the document being produced for examination.

I have been referred by counsel for the Crown to the provisions of the Inland Revenue Regulation Act 1890, by which the power to grant that kind of authority is vested in the Board by virtue of s 4A, and indeed that as well as other delegations of power are a presumed as a matter of form to be regularly given by the provisions of s 24 of the same Act. For my part I do not think this is a serious argument, and in the circumstances of those statutory provisions I do not find that an order for discovery should be made in respect of that document.

The second and third documents are of course the two reports to which I have already alluded emanating from Mr Ward: first, that of 8 May 1986; second, that of 8 September 1986. Some reference has been made to the law applicable to the rules of discovery in

b relation to judicial review proceedings. It is, I think, common ground that the procedure with regard to discovery is different in judicial review matters from that which obtains in ordinary actions which are begun by writ.

I have been referred to some very helpful comments in the authorities as to the basis on which the court should approach an application of this nature. Without wishing to go through them I think it would be most helpful to turn to the judgment of Simon

c Brown J in *R v IRC, ex p J Rothschild Holdings plc* [1986] STC 410. There the judge considered the approach which should be made when this question comes before the court and cited a number of authorities, including *O'Reilly v Mackman* [1982] 3 All ER 1124, [1983] 2 AC 237 and *IRC v National Federation of Self-Employed and Small Businesses Ltd* [1981] 2 All ER 93, [1982] AC 617, where various speeches were made in the House of Lords on this question. They are summarised by the judge in this way (at 413):

d

> 'In my judgment, this is a case where discovery is required in order that the justice of the case may be advanced and likewise a case where it is, within the meaning of Ord 24, r 8, necessary for disposing fairly of the matter.'

Counsel for Mr Taylor, in his submissions to me, suggested that he comes within that rule, certainly in relation to the two memoranda or reports to which I have referred. He

e pointed out that as a matter of general practice in ordinary actions where a document is referred to in an affidavit normally the other side is entitled to call for it. The answer which is given by counsel for the Crown is this: he said the distinction which has to be made, as of course is well known, is not whether the decision made by the Board through their agent Mr Roberts is correct, but whether the procedure or the manner in which he came to that decision can be challenged. He said that within the context of this case the

f affidavit which has been filed on behalf of the Crown, and which has been made by Mr Roberts, sets out that reasoning in detail. Furthermore, it makes reference, in the context of the reports, to the basis on which that reasoning rested. In those circumstances he said that the present application is simply directed to seeing whether, by the production of the documents, there is any material there to be discovered which could question or challenge that reasoning.

g It is conceded by counsel for Mr Taylor that the truth of Mr Roberts's affidavit is not in dispute, although I say at once that counsel for Mr Taylor goes on to contend that that of course is not the end of the matter.

My decision in this case, which is that this application should not succeed, is based on the fact that there is no material before me which can be relied on which tends to show

h that Mr Roberts's process of reasoning was defective or unreasonable or open to challenge. If there was some material to which Mr Taylor could point which showed that the affidavit is not to be relied on, however truthful it may be, because of other features which show that the process of reasoning was suspect or open to challenge in the normal way in this type of proceeding, then it would be appropriate to order that the report should be disclosed in full, but if the purpose of the application is to study that report to

j see if there is any flaw in the manner of Mr Roberts's decision-making process it seems to me that it goes to the other side of the line, and it is not a case where the court can properly order disclosure. For those reasons, as I have already indicated, I dismiss this application.

Application dismissed. Leave to appeal granted.

Interlocutory appeal

Mr Taylor appealed to the Court of Appeal.

a

Leolin Price QC and *Penelope Reed* for Mr Taylor.
Timothy Brennan for the Crown.

O'CONNOR LJ. The applicant (Mr Taylor) appeals against the refusal of Farquharson J
to order the Commissioners of Inland Revenue to give inspection of documents referred *b*
to in an affidavit filed as their evidence in judicial review proceedings brought by the
applicant with leave. Counsel for Mr Taylor referred us at once to RSC Ord 24, which is
applied to judicial review proceedings by Ord 53, r 8. He reminded us of what Lord
Diplock had said on this topic in *O'Reilly v Mackman* [1982] 3 All ER 1124 at 1131–1132,
[1983] 2 AC 237 at 282, where he said:

> 'Those disadvantages, which formerly might have resulted in an applicant being *c*
> unable to obtain justice in an application for certiorari under Ord 53, have all been
> removed by the new rules introduced in 1977. There is express provision in the
> new r 8 for interlocutory applications for discovery of documents, the administration
> of interrogatories and the cross-examination of deponents to affidavits. Discovery of
> documents (which may often be a time-consuming process) is not automatic as in *d*
> an action begun by writ, but otherwise Ord 24 applies to it and discovery is
> obtainable on application whenever, and to the extent that, the justice of the case
> requires . . .'

For my part, I am content to look at Ord 24 in the light of what Lord Diplock said in
O'Reilly v Mackman and also to bear in mind what was said in *IRC v National Federation of
Self-Employed and Small Businesses Ltd* [1981] 2 All ER 93, [1982] AC 617, in two short *e*
passages. Lord Wilberforce, dealing with discovery, said ([1981] 2 All ER 93 at 100,
[1982] AC 617 at 635):

> 'Finally, if as I think, the case against the Revenue does not, on the evidence, leave
> the ground, no court, in my opinion, would consider ordering discovery against the
> Revenue in the hope of eliciting some impropriety.'   *f*

Lord Scarman and Lord Roskill pronounced to the same effect (see [1981] 2 All ER 93 at
114, 121, [1982] AC 617 at 654, 664).

Discovery in our procedure is a two-pronged device. The first part of Ord 24, rr 1 to 8,
deals with the discovery of documents in the sense of requiring the party to state what
documents relevant to the issues raised in the proceedings are or have been in his
possession, and, if they have left his possession, what has happened to them, and, in *g*
making a list or affidavit, as the case may be, that is the time for claiming privilege
against production to the other side of any of the documents which are disclosed. Rules
9 and 10 (which is the vital one here) relate to inspection of documents. Rule 9 deals
with the inspection of documents referred to in the list. Rule 10 provides:

> '(1) Any party to a cause or matter shall be entitled at any time to serve a notice *h*
> on any other party in whose pleadings or affidavits reference is made to any
> document requiring him to produce that document for the inspection of the party
> giving the notice and to permit him to take copies thereof.
> (2) The party on whom a notice is served under paragraph (1) must, within 4
> days after service of the notice, serve on the party giving the notice a notice stating a
> time within 7 days after the service thereof at which the documents, or such of *j*
> them as he does not object to produce, may be inspected at a place specified in the
> notice, and stating which (if any) of the documents he objects to produce and on
> what grounds.'

So it will be seen that there is special provision for documents referred to in the pleadings a and in affidavits, because in the nature of things, if objection to production is to be taken, it has to be taken subsequent to referring to the documents in the pleadings or affidavits.

Rule 11 provides:

b '(1) If a party . . . who is served with a notice under rule 10(1)—(a) fails to serve a notice under . . . rule 10(2), or (b) objects to produce any document for inspection, or (c) offers inspection at a time or place such that, in the opinion of the Court, it is unreasonable to offer inspection then or, as the case may be, there, then, subject to rule 13(1), the Court may, on the application of the party entitled to inspection, make an order for production of the documents in question for inspection at such time and place, and in such manner, as it thinks fit.'

Rule 13 provides:

c '(1) No order for the production of any documents for inspection or to the Court shall be made under any of the foregoing rules unless the Court is of opinion that the order is necessary either for disposing fairly of the cause or matter or for saving costs . . .'

d Those are the provisions with which we are primarily concerned, but for completeness, as it will be relevant later in my judgment, r 17 provides:

'Any order made under this Order (including an order made on appeal) may, on sufficient cause being shown, be revoked or varied by a subsequent order or direction of the Court made or given at or before the trial of the cause or matter in connection with which the original order was made.'

e It follows, as I read r 17, that an order made at any time before that can be varied on good grounds at a later stage.

Counsel for Mr Taylor submitted that here was an affidavit filed in these proceedings referring to two documents, that proper request had been made under r 10(1) and that there were no grounds for not ordering inspection of the two documents. To put it quite simply, if in judicial review proceedings in the affidavits a party refers to documents,
f prima facie he should be ordered to produce them to the other side on request. It is against that background that it is necessary to look in some detail (I fear in more detail than the judge, perfectly properly, found it necessary to do) to see what has happened in this case.

Mr Taylor is a solicitor who specialises in tax avoidance. He has been at loggerheads with the Revenue over his own tax affairs since 1983. The evidence for the Revenue is
g found in an affidavit sworn on 25 January 1988 by Mr Roberts, an under secretary in the Inland Revenue, and I must refer to some paragraphs in that affidavit. He starts (at para 1):

'I am the Director of Technical Division 2, and have held this post since 1985. The post entails overall responsibility for all the specialist investigation units of the
h Inland Revenue which are directly controlled from Head Office, which include Special Investigations Section.'

He then says that he is the person duly authorised to issue notices under s 20(2) of the Taxes Management Act 1970. He says:

j '3. On 8 September 1986, Mr J C Ward submitted to me a detailed report concerning the tax affairs of Mr Taylor which he (Mr Ward) has had under investigation since 1983, the purpose of which was to recommend the issue to Mr Taylor of a notice under Section 20(2), Taxes Management Act 1970. Mr Ward is one of the Inspectors in the Special Investigations Section within my Division: a large part of their work is concerned with the investigation of substantial cases of suspected tax avoidance (many of them involving pre-planned schemes). As well as his investigation into Mr Taylor's own tax affairs, Mr Ward's duties since he joined the section in 1982 have also included investigation of a number of tax avoidance *a* schemes entered into by taxpayers, both corporate and individual, on advice given by Mr Taylor.

4. Mr Ward's report drew my attention to his earlier report, dated 8 May 1986, to the Inland Revenue Solicitor's Office in which he had asked for legal advice on a number of points, including the form and content of the proposed notice, which (on the basis of his experience of similar cases) he anticipated might be taken by Mr *b* Taylor in the event of the service on him of a notice under Section 20(2), Taxes Management Act 1970. This report, and the advice of the Solicitors' Office were available to me with Mr Ward's report to me (dated 8 September 1986), for it was on the same file. In his report dated 8 September 1986 Mr Ward mentioned that in his view any notice issued to Mr Taylor under Section 20(2), Taxes Management Act 1970 was likely to be challenged in legal proceedings (and possibly by application *c* for judicial review).'

I shall return to Mr Roberts's affidavit later.

Section 20(2) of the Taxes Management Act 1970 provides:

'Subject to this section, the Board may by notice in writing require a person to deliver, to a named officer of theirs, such documents as are in the person's possession *d* or power and as (in the Board's reasonable opinion) contain, or may contain, information relevant to any tax liability to which he is or may be subject, or to the amount of any such liability.'

It will be seen that it is a blanket provision requiring the taxpayer to make documents available to the Revenue which, in the Board's reasonable opinion, contain information *e* which may be relevant to his tax liability.

The notice which was served on 23 September 1986 required the delivery up of a large number of classes of documents. For example, in para 2 of the schedule, Mr Taylor was required to produce and deliver up:

'Books of account including inter alia cash books, ledgers, journals, expense *f* vouchers, invoices, fee notes, work-in-progress valuations and business correspondence and all other records relating to your practice as a Solicitor for the period from 1 May 1979 to 30 April 1984.'

And in para 4:

'All agreements, contracts, business correspondence, accounting records in respect *g* of any trade, profession or vocation carried on by yourself in partnership either in the United Kingdom or abroad during the period from 6 April 1980 to 5 April 1985, for the period during which such trade, profession or vocation was carried on in that period.'

The other four categories, which I need not cite, were also very broadly based.

As Mr Roberts and Mr Ward had anticipated, on the last day of the three months *h* available to Mr Taylor he applied for judicial review on 22 December 1986, and the relief sought was to quash the notice. He listed no less than nine grounds on which relief was sought:

'1. That the Board of Inland Revenue was wrong in law to issue the aforesaid Notice. 2. That the aforesaid Notice was not in accordance with Section 20(2) of the *j* Taxes Management Act 1970. 3. That there were no or alternatively insufficient grounds for the issue of the aforesaid Notice. 4. That the aforesaid Notice is oppressive in relation to the amount of documents which it requires and/or the time which it gives for those documents to be delivered. 5. That no or insufficient reason has been given for the demand for documents to which the aforsaid notice relates.

6. That the documents required by the aforesaid Notice relate to the conduct of
pending appeals by the Applicant and that if the documents were to be sought an
order should have been obtained from The Special Commissioners under Section 51
of the Taxes Management Act. 7. That the aforesaid Notice requires documents
which if given up pursuant to its terms would breach the duty of confidentiality
which the Applicant has as a Solicitor to his clients. 8. That the aforesaid Notice is
wholly or partly designed to get information not about the tax affairs of the
Applicant but about the Applicant's clients. 9. That the aforesaid Notice was issued
in bad faith.'

Those were the grounds on which leave was duly given.

In his affidavit in support Mr Taylor said, on the matters which are relevant to this
appeal:

'19. It may be said that I have been unco-operative with the Inland Revenue but
in the face of the kind of approach exhibited by the tax inspector in this case I regard
it as my right to require The Board of Inland Revenue to act in accordance with the
law. I do not regard their actions as being well founded in law. It strikes me as
extraordinary that without any allegation of fraud or even any expressed suspicions
the Revenue can, without any independent sanction, require not only the immediate
background information supporting my audited accounts but also details of my
clients and of my practice to such an extent that in effect substantially all my practice
papers should be looked at. In these circumstances I find it difficult to accept that
either Mr. Ward or the Board have acted in good faith.

20. Many of the details requested will necessarily breach my duty of
confidentiality to my clients. I dispute whether the Board of Inland Revenue has the
power to do this but even if they have I contend that the exercise of their power was
unreasonable as they should not use their powers to breach professional confidences
without substantial grounds—none of which have been shown. I have been
concerned that this is an indiscriminate fishing expedition which the Inland
Revenue [has] embarked on with the hope of gaining information on my clients
affairs. My practice is concerned with tax matters and many of my clients are or
have been themselves under investigation by the Inland Revenue in relation to
schemes for tax mitigation or tax avoidance in which they engaged. In some cases I
was partly or wholly responsible for these schemes, in others I have been instructed
in relation to litigation arising out of schemes devised and implemented by others.
In recent years judicial attitudes to the efficacy of pre-planned or pre-ordained tax
saving schemes has altered. I am concerned that, notwithstanding the denials of the
Inspector of Taxes in correspondence, the investigation into my affairs is wholly or
partly motivated by a desire to ascertain the identity of my clients, their affairs and
in particular any schemes for tax mitigation or tax avoidance about which they have
been advised but which have not been subjected to tax litigation. Mr. Ward is the
Inspector who since he became an Inspector at Special Investigation Section on or
about 1st October 1983 is or has been dealing with all except two of the cases in
which I am or have been acting professionally. The Special Investigations Section to
which Mr. Ward is attached is the Inland Revenue unit concerned with investigating
and challenging tax avoidance schemes.'

So there we find that, apart from the earlier paragraphs in the grounds which I have
read, Mr Taylor was putting forward two main grounds, namely that the s 20 notice had
been served on him with the avowed object of a fishing expedition through his papers in
order to get information about his clients who were engaged in tax avoidance or tax
mitigation schemes, and that, if that were so, it was bad faith on the part of the Revenue
and it vitiated and flawed the decision-making process for the issue of the notice.

It is not therefore surprising that Mr Roberts in his affidavit dealt with these allegations.
I turn back to his affidavit:

'8. There was, in addition, another aspect of the case which concerned me. This was the fact that Mr Ward was—and had for some time been—engaged in *a* investigating a number of transactions or schemes carried out by some of Mr Taylor's clients, and that Mr Taylor (in his letter dated 31 July 1986) had suggested that Mr Ward's wish to see documents relating to some of his clients was an illegitimate and unreasonable exercise of his duties in investigating his (Mr Taylor's) affairs. Mr Taylor had suggested that Mr Ward's main purpose, or one of his main purposes, was to obtain information from him for use in connection with his *b* investigations into the affairs of his (Mr Taylor's) clients which Mr Taylor had described as "a declared fishing investigation into the affairs of persons who are, or who have been, clients of mine". As regards this aspect of the case, I was well aware that if the Revenue wish to require a person to make available documents in connection with an investigation into another person's tax affairs the appropriate power is that conferred by Section 20(3) of that Act, and that it is a statutory *c* requirement that in such a "third party" notice the name of the taxpayer under investigation shall be stated in the notice (see the closing words of Section 20(8) of the Act).

9. Accordingly, I directed my mind to the question whether (as Mr Taylor had suggested) Mr Ward was in reality proposing to use a Board's notice to Mr Taylor under Section 20(2) of the Act as a "fishing investigation" as part of his investigations *d* into transactions carried out by or involving clients of Mr Taylor. I concluded that this was not the case, although at the same time I recognised that in the circumstances—if Mr Taylor complied with the notice—Mr Ward might well obtain information which would also be relevant to those other investigations. It seemed to me that if in the event a part of the information in the documents made available by Mr Taylor under the proposed notice were to be of some use to Mr *e* Ward in his other investigations, this would be no more than an incidental consequence of Mr Taylor making available documents considered to be of relevance to his own tax affairs. I considered therefore that this was not a reason for concluding that the issue of the notice was not in all the circumstances justified, or for excluding from the notice documents which might fall into that category.

10. In reaching the conclusion that the issue of a notice was justified, I took into *f* account the following features of the case to which Mr Ward drew attention in his report dated 8 September 1986, having noted that in Mr Ward's view there were aspects of Mr Taylor's returns, accounts and tax computations which required further consideraion (and further information) before they could be agreed . . .'

And he set out five major areas of investigation which I need not further refer to. Then *g* he said that he was satisfied that Mr Taylor was not prepared to make a voluntary disclosure of his documents, and he concluded:

'I was not persuaded that Mr Ward was acting in bad faith, and I noted that Mr Ward had denied the allegation in his letter [to Mr Taylor] dated 6 August 1986 . . .'

And he denied that it was a fishing expedition. *h*

It was in that state of affairs, when that affidavit was received, that on 27 January 1988 (two days after the affidavit was sworn) Mr Taylor's solicitors applied by letter under Ord 24, r 10(1) for production of the two reports from Mr Ward dated 8 May and 8 September 1986. They asked also for the document by which the board had delegated power to Mr Roberts to issue the notice. The judge refused all three requests.

In this court counsel for Mr Taylor has not pursued any request for the authority *j* giving Mr Roberts power to issue the notice. The appeal is confined to the two reports of Mr Ward dated 8 May and 8 September.

In refusing production, the solicitor for the Inland Revenue replied on 29 January 1988 to the letter of 27 January 1988. He said:

'The purpose of Mr Ward's report of 8 May 1986, which was addressed to the
a Solicitor's Office, Inland Revenue (and not to Mr Roberts) was to seek legal advice,
so that it is subject to legal professional privilege; and I must decline to produce it
on that ground.'

I pause there for one moment. Counsel for Mr Taylor submitted that no litigation had
been in anticipation at the time when Mr Ward produced his report for consideration by
the Solicitor's Department in May 1986. I have already referred to the paragraph in Mr
b Roberts's affidavit, and it seems to me that there was ample evidence that the Revenue
anticipated that if a s 20 notice was served on this taxpayer litigation was bound to ensue.
In my judgment Mr Ward was fully entitled to take the solicitor's opinion on any matter
which might be arising out of such a notice, and I can see no grounds for ordering the
production of the report of 8 May 1986 because, on the face of it, it is plainly protected
by legal professional privilege.
c The second paragraph of the letter of 29 January 1988 reads as follows:

'Mr Ward's report of 8 September 1986 was addressed to Mr Roberts, and its
purpose was to ask him to issue the Section 20(2) notice. As I explained in my letter
of 21 January, we are advised that there is some doubt as to whether the applicant
taxpayer in this type of case is entitled to discovery of such a report; and, as I have
d already indicated, we consider that it should only be made available to you if the
Court so directs.'

When the matter came before Farquharson J, he said (p 909, ante):

'It is conceded by counsel for Mr Taylor that the truth of Mr Roberts's affidavit is
not in dispute, although I say at once that counsel for Mr Taylor goes on to contend
e that that of course is not the end of the matter. My decision in this case, which is
that this application should not succeed, is based on the fact that there is no material
before me which can be relied on which tends to show that Mr Roberts's process of
reasoning was defective or unreasonable or open to challenge. If there was some
material to which Mr Taylor could point which showed that the affidavit is not to
be relied on, however truthful it may be, because of other features which show that
f the process of reasoning was suspect or open to challenge in the normal way in this
type of proceedings, then it seems to me that it would be appropriate to order that
the report should be disclosed in full, but if the purpose of the application is to study
that report to see if there is any flaw in the manner of Mr Roberts's decision-making
process it seems to me that it goes to the other side of the line, and it is not a case
where the court can properly order disclosure. For those reasons . . . I dismiss this
g application.'

It is said that the judge fell into error in so deciding. Counsel for Mr Taylor submitted
that on the face of it this report formed part of the decision-making process undertaken
by Mr Roberts and would throw a clear light on whether he was acting in abuse of power
and issuing the notice with the ulterior motive of getting information about the tax
h affairs of Mr Taylor's clients.

At first sight that may seem a powerful argument, but the problem is that before the
judge, counsel who then appeared for Mr Taylor said in terms that he was not challenging
the truth of Mr Roberts's affidavit, and in this court counsel for Mr Taylor has adopted
exactly the same stance. He says that at this stage he is not challenging it because he
cannot. If that be the state of affairs, one asks oneself how stands this case when it goes
j for trial on the grounds in the notice of motion that the Revenue acted in bad faith and
in order to collect material in respect of other taxpayers and not this one? Those grounds
have not been abandoned; they still stand; but at this stage, if one asks oneself the
question which in my judgment one is bound to ask oneself under Ord 24, r 13, 'Is it
necessary for disposing fairly of this cause that the report of 8 September 1986 should be

produced?', on the state of the case as it stands today and as it stood before the judge, in
my judgment, the right answer to that is: 'I don't know.' It seems to me that prima facie
it is for Mr Taylor to show that it is necessary for the fair disposal of the case, and at the
present time he has not done so.

In so far as the judge came to the conclusion that he could not go behind Mr Roberts's
affidavit unless there was other material available to show that it might be in error (and I
deliberately do not say untruthful), reliance was placed by counsel for the Crown on an
unreported decision of this court in *R v Secretary of State for the Home Dept, ex p Harrison*
[1987] CA Transcript 1246. That was a case arising out of the refusal of the Home Office
to pay compensation to a man who had been convicted of crime and imprisoned, and
who had later had his appeal allowed because the Court of Appeal, Criminal Division,
held that the trial judge had fallen into error in directing the jury. The question in the
case was whether such an ex-prisoner qualified for compensation. Compensation having
been refused, judicial review proceedings were commenced in order to bring into
question that decision. In the course of those proceedings, not only was there a request
for discovery of documents against the Secretary of State, but also for production of
documents referred to in the affidavit sworn by the department in that case. So both
matters were before the court. Glidewell LJ, who gave the first judgment, dealt shortly
with the cases. He then turned to Ord 24 (it will be remembered that the court was
dealing with both those things) and, having gone through the provisions of the order
and having dealt with the affidavit in that case, he said:

'The question of whether or not there should be judicial review at all and, if so,
whether, for instance, the Home Secretary owed to Mr Harrison a duty of fairness
which would oblige him to disclose to Mr Harrison any material of which he had
possession which contained comment adverse to the applicant are both questions
which are in issue in these proceedings themselves. If the arguments for the Home
Office succeed there will be no question of discovery, because there will be nothing
to be disclosed. If there is no duty of fairness there is no need to disclose the
documents which were not disclosed to Mr Harrison. If on the other hand the Home
Office are wrong in their arguments and if these proceedings succeed, then, says
[counsel for the Home Secretary], and says accurately, the Home Secretary's decision
not to make an ex gratia payment will have to be quashed, the application will have
to be reconsidered and at that stage, if it is not granted, another attack by way of
judicial review could no doubt be mounted. It may be that at that time, if it is ever
reached, an application for discovery might be appropriate, but not at this stage in
these proceedings. That argument also is one which I find convincing. I therefore
do not find it necessary to say much about [counsel for the Home Secretary's] wider
argument as to the nature and ambit of discovery generally in judicial review, but I
would comment on one other submission which he made as part of this wider
submission. He suggests that to a not immaterial extent what is being sought here
is material which it is hoped by the applicant will, at least in part, contradict matter
contained in Mr Caffarey's affidavit. In other words what is being sought is
documents which can be used to check the accuracy of what Mr Caffarey asserts in
his affidavit. [Counsel for the Home Secretary] submits that an applicant is not
entitled to go behind an affidavit in order to seek to ascertain whether it is correct
or not unless there is some material available outside that contained in the affidavit
to suggest that in some material respect the affidavit is not accurate. If there is such
material it may be right to order discovery to follow that up. But without some
prima facie case for suggesting that the affidavit is in some respects incorrect it is
improper to allow discovery of documents the only purpose of which, as I have said,
would be to act as a challenge to the accuracy of the affidavit. With that submission
also, which is of general application, I agree.'

When one applies what Glidewell LJ says to the present case, one sees that counsel for *a*   Mr Taylor both here and below said in terms that they are not impugning the truth of Mr Roberts's affidavit. He is the decision-maker for the purposes of this case. While that state of affairs lasts, the time for seeking to go behind it by calling for production of Mr Ward's report of 8 September simply has not arrived. It is for those reasons that, in my judgment, at the present time and before the judge it could not be said that the production of the document is necessary for the fair disposal of the issues raised in these proceedings. Whether that will prevail at the trial I know not. As I have already said, the

b   rules themselves give power to reopen the matter. I do not regard this as being the appropriate time to make any order. It is not a question of refusing to order production except in the sense that, in my judgment, the application simply cannot stand with the attitude adopted on behalf of Mr Taylor up to this time. I do not know whether bad faith is going to be persisted in when it comes to the trial. I would say that in order to try and deal with the other part of the case, namely that the notice is intended to investigate the

c   affairs of other taxpayers, we invited counsel for the Crown to say, if he was able, how widely the Crown intended to argue that the notice applied. He took instructions on the matter and came to the conclusion that the only help that he could give the court is to say that of course documents which had nothing to do with Mr Taylor's tax affairs would not be within the net which had been cast. It may well be that, when the case comes to trial, the judge in the exercise of his discretion, when he sees exactly how the issues are

d   put before him, will order production of this report, and nothing which I have said must be taken in any way as fettering his discretion so to do.

       For those reasons, which are a little different from those given by the judge, I would dismiss this appeal and refuse the order for production of any documents.

NICHOLLS LJ. I agree, and I add only some brief observations of my own.

e   The decision being impugned in these judicial review proceedings was made by Mr Roberts. He has made an affidavit setting out with a fair degree of particularity what were the matters that he had in mind and took into account when reaching his decision. Mr Taylor has disclaimed any attack on Mr Roberts's truthfulness. In those circumstances I see no answer to the contention of counsel for the Crown that the issue to be determined at the hearing of the judicial review application is whether the reasons for which Mr

f   Roberts made his decision, set out in an admittedly truthful affidavit, are adequate to support his decision.

       Perusal of the contents of Mr Ward's reports is, therefore, not necessary for disposing fairly of the proceedings. It is not necessary because, having regard to the contents of the affidavit, the reports are not material to the issue before the court.

       However, although Mr Taylor has, very fairly, accepted the honesty of Mr Roberts's

g   affidavit, he still seeks to challenge Mr Roberts's decision on the ground of bad faith. Quite how these two attitudes can lie together in this case, having regard to the contents of Mr Roberts's affidavit, is a matter which I find puzzling. As I understand it, Mr Taylor does not accept Mr Ward's good faith. But where that leaves matters is far from clear. Suffice it to say that nothing which was submitted to this court had persuaded me of the relevance of Mr Ward's state of mind. Quite rightly, however, on this interlocutory

h   application counsel have not fully developed their arguments on this point. Moreover, the question of what on its proper construction is the scope of the notice and, if relevant, the question of what Mr Roberts understood to be the scope of the notice when he made his decision are matters which remain to be considered.

       Whilst, therefore, as matters stand at present I am not satisfied that production of the September report is necessary for fairly disposing of these proceedings, I can envisage

j   circumstances in which, when these matters are considered fully at the substantive hearing and the mass of documentary material not considered by us has been looked into, things may appear different. What is not now apparent, namely that production of the September report is necessary for disposing fairly of the matter, may become apparent in the clearer light that there will then be. I too would not say anything which might be thought to tie the hands of the judge or to preclude Mr Taylor from renewing his application for production of the September report if such an eventuality should arise.

    I refer only to the September report because I agree that the earlier report made in May 1986 is privileged from production on the ground of legal professional privilege.

    I too would dismiss this appeal whilst none the less leaving the door open to the extent I have mentioned.

TAYLOR LJ. I agree with both the judgments that have been delivered.

Appeal dismissed. Leave to appeal to the House of Lords refused.

30 January 1989. The Appeal Committee of the House of Lords (Lord Bridge of Harwich, Lord Templeman and Lord Goff of Chieveley) refused a petition for leave to appeal.

Solicitors: *Gregory Rowcliffe & Milners* (for Mr Taylor); *Solicitor of Inland Revenue.*

Heather Whicher   Barrister.

Lombard Tricity Finance Ltd v Paton

COURT OF APPEAL, CIVIL DIVISION

SLADE, STOCKER AND STAUGHTON LJJ

6, 27 OCTOBER 1988

Consumer credit – Agreement – Form and content of agreement – Statement of circumstances in which variation of terms of agreement may occur – Increase in rate of interest – Lender's discretion to raise rate of interest – Consumer credit agreement providing that lender could increase rate of interest in its absolute discretion – Whether provision lawful – Consumer Credit (Agreements) Regulations 1983, reg 2, Sch 1, para 19.

By an agreement dated 10 October 1985 the defendant borrower entered into a credit agreement with the plaintiff credit company to finance the purchase of a computer on a credit charge account. The agreement was a regulated agreement under the Consumer Credit Act 1974. A box on the face of the agreement stated that the interest payable on the credit balance was 'Subject to variation by the creditor from time to time on notification as required by law', while cl 2(a) on the reverse of the agreement referred to variations in the interest charged 'as may from time to time be notified'. While the account was still running the credit company increased the rate of interest from 2·3% per month to 2·45% and when the defendant fell into arrears the interest rate rose to 2·95%. When the defendant continued to default in his monthly payments the credit company brought proceedings in the county court claiming the amount due. The registrar dismissed the claim and the judge upheld his decision on the ground that the agreement did not comply with reg 2[a] of and para 19[b] of Sch 1 to the Consumer Credit (Agreements) Regulations 1983 since it did not indicate 'the circumstances in which [a] variation [sc in

---

a   Regulation 2, so far as material, provides:

    '(1) ... documents embodying regulated consumer credit agreements ... shall contain the information set out in ... Schedule 1 to these Regulations ...

    (4) ... the information about financial and related particulars set out in ... Schedule 1 to these Regulations ... shall be shown together as a whole in documents embodying regulated consumer credit agreements ...'

b   Paragraph 19 is set out at p 922 *c d, post*

a the rate of interest] may occur' and was therefore not properly executed by virtue of s 61(1)[c] of the 1974 Act. The credit company appealed to the Court of Appeal.

Held – It was lawful for a consumer credit contract to provide that the lender could unilaterally vary the rate of interest in its absolute discretion subject to notice to the borrower as required by law. Such a provision did not conflict with para 19 of Sch 1 to the 1983 regulations, since 'the circumstances in which any variation . . . may occur' did
b not refer to external factors such as changes in the market rates of interest which might cause a variation, and neither the 1974 Act nor the 1983 regulations made such a provision unlawful. Accordingly, the lender was not obliged to set out the factors which could cause him to exercise his contractual power to increase the rate of interest. Nor was it necessary for such an agreement to state specifically that the lender had an absolute discretion or that it could raise the interest rate for any reason whatsoever. It followed
c that, since the agreement between the credit company and the defendant did not infringe para 19 of Sch 1 to the 1983 regulations, the appeal would be allowed (see p 923 g to j and p 924 b c g, post).

Notes
For the variation of consumer credit agreements, see 22 Halsbury's Laws (4th end) para
d 111.
For the Consumer Credit Act 1974, s 61, see 11 Halsbury's Statutes (4th edn) 57.

Case referred to in judgment
May & Butcher Ltd v R [1934] 2 KB 17, [1929] All ER Rep 679, HL.

e **Appeal**
The plaintiffs, Lombard Tricity Finance Ltd (Lombard), appealed with the leave of the judge against the decision of his Honour Judge Heald given in the Nottingham County Court on 29 March 1988 whereby he held that the agreement dated 10 October 1985 made between Lombard and the defendant, Martin Shaun Paton, did not comply with
f the requirements of paras 18 and 19 of Sch 1 to the Consumer Credit (Agreements) Regulations 1983, SI 1983/1553, and was thereby not properly executed within the meaning of s 61(1) of the Consumer Credit Act 1974. The facts are set out in the judgment of the court.

Michael Beloff QC and *Stephen Morris* for Lombard.
Alexander Hill-Smith for Mr Paton.
g
Cur adv vult

27 October. The following judgment of the court was delivered.

STAUGHTON LJ. Martin Paton, the defendant in an action in the Nottingham
h County Court and respondent to this appeal, was in September 1985 minded to buy an Amstrad computer from Currys Ltd. The price, including an extended warranty insurance policy, was £244·98. Mr Paton decided to borrow the money, or rather the greater part of it, from Lombard Tricity Finance Ltd (Lombard), the plaintiffs in the action and appellants in this appeal. Instead of a credit sale agreement, he was offered a credit charge account, which was a species of running-account credit as defined in s 10 of
j the Consumer Credit Act 1974. But there was no other transaction after the purchase of the computer, for which the initial loan was £218.

---

c Section 61(1), so far as material, provides: 'A regulated agreement is not properly executed unless— (a) a document in the prescribed form itself containing all the prescribed terms and conforming to regulations under section 60(1) is signed in the prescribed manner both by the debtor . . . and by or on behalf of the creditor . . . and (b) the document embodies all the terms of the agreement . . .'

The agreement, dated 10 October 1985, was thus a regulated agreement within s 8 of the 1974 Act. It is suggested that there was a failure to comply with the provisions of the Act in one important respect. In a box on its face there were these provisions:

'Interest charge (per month) 2·3%
Annual Percentage Rate 31·3%
Interest is payable on credit balance. Subject to variation by the creditor from time to time on notification as required by law. In calculating the APR no account has been taken of any variation of it which may occur under this Agreement.'

That information was evidently intended to comply with reg 2 of the Consumer Credit (Agreements) Regulations 1983, SI 1983/1553. By para (4) of that regulation certain financial and related particulars must be 'shown . . . as a whole . . . and not interspersed with other information . . .' We are told that in the trade the part of the agreement which contains those particulars is called 'the holy ground', because no other material may trespass on it. For our part we would describe it, with equal inaccuracy, as 'the child's guide', since it is intended to set out succinctly the principal effect of the agreement for those untrained in reading such documents.

Since it is compliance with reg 2 that is in question, it is not to the point to quote any other terms of the document. But for completeness we set out cl 2(a) on the reverse:

'If the sum payable monthly by me under Clause 1 above is paid by banker's Direct Debiting Mandate, I shall pay an interest charge of 2·3% per month (equivalent to AN ANNUAL PERCENTAGE RATE OF 31·3%) or such other percentage as may from time to time be notified to me by you on the total amount, if any, outstanding on my Creditcharge Account immediately after the expiration of each month during which such Account is in existence. If such sum is paid in any other way, I shall pay an interest charge of 2·7% per month (equivalent to AN ANNUAL PERCENTAGE RATE OF 37·6%) or such other percentage as may from time to time be notified to me by you on such total amount, if any, outstanding immediately after the expiration of each month during which my Creditcharge Account is in existence. In all cases such interest charge will be debited to my said Account and will run after as well as before any judgment obtained against me.'

Payments of £10 or £20 were duly made by Mr Paton from time to time. These were credited to his account. There was debited in each month an interest charge at 2·3% on the outstanding balance. There was also a charge calculated at 0·3% for credit protection insurance, but nothing turns on that.

Then on 9 March 1986 the interest rate was increased to 2·45%. There is an issue whether due notice of that increase was given. This may well not have been investigated in the county court, for reasons which will appear later. When it was raised before us, counsel for Lombard observed that it could only affect quantum, and only to the extent of £10 (being the difference between the sum that would be due if the original interest rate had continued in force throughout and the sum in fact claimed). He was prepared to waive that amount. So the issue as to notice disappears.

Shortly afterwards Mr Paton defaulted on his obligations; his direct debit payments ceased. The interest rate charged thereupon rose to 2·95%. Four further payments of £10 were made; but then there was again default, and by 9 November 1986 the amount outstanding was £203·62.

Lombard on 22 December 1986 commenced an action in the Nottingham County Court, claiming that amount together with interest and costs. Mr Paton filed a defence saying that he disputed the claim as to £100 for reasons which are not material. The case came before the deputy registrar as an arbitration on 6 October 1987. He dismissed the claim entirely. Lombard appealed to his Honour Judge Heald, who on 29 March 1988 upheld the decision of the deputy registrar, but gave Lombard leave to appeal to this court.

The only issue before the registrar and the judge was whether the credit charge agreement complied with the provisions of the 1974 Act and the regulations made under it. Section 60 of the 1974 Act provides:

'(1) The Secretary of State shall make regulations as to the form and content of documents embodying regulated agreements, and the regulations shall contain such provisions as appear to him appropriate with a view to ensuring that the debtor or hirer is made aware of—(a) the rights and duties conferred or imposed on him by the agreement, (b) the amount and rate of the total charge for credit (in the case of a consumer credit agreement), (c) the protection and remedies available to him under this Act, and (d) any other matters which, in the opinion of the Secretary of State, it is desirable for him to know about in connection with the agreement.

(2) Regulations under subsection (1) may in particular—(a) require specified information to be included in the prescribed manner in documents, and other specified material to be excluded; (b) contain requirements to ensure that specified information is clearly brought to the attention of the debtor or hirer, and that one part of a document is not given insufficient or excessive prominence compared with another . . .'

By s 61(1) a regulated agreement is not properly executed if it does not conform with regulations made under s 60. The consequence is set out in s 65(1):

'An improperly-executed regulated agreement is enforceable against the debtor or hirer on an order of the court only.'

Before turning to the section which deals with enforcement orders, we should mention s 82(1). This provides that regulations may be made as to how notice shall be given of any variation made under a power contained in a regulated agreement. Under that section the Consumer Credit (Notice of Variation of Agreements) Regulations 1977, SI 1977/328, provide:

'Notice valid for any variation
    2. Subject to regulation 3 below, notice of variation of any regulated agreement shall—(a) set out particulars of the variation; and (b) be served on the debtor or hirer not less than seven days before the variation takes effect.

Notice valid for special variations
    3.—(1) This regulation applies to a variation of a regulated consumer credit agreement where—(a) the amount of the payments of interest charged under the agreement is determined, both before and after the variation takes effect, by reference to the amount of the balance outstanding, established as at daily intervals; and (b) the variation is a variation of the rate of interest payable under the agreement.
    (2) In the case of a variation to which this regulation applies, the requirements of regulation 2(b) above shall be treated as satisfied where—(a) the notice of variation—(i) is published in at least three national daily newspapers, in each case being printed in a type not less than 3 mm in height and occupying a space of not less than 100 sq cm, or (ii) if it is not reasonably practicable so to publish it, is published in the Gazette, and (b) if it is reasonably practicable to do so, the notice of variation is prominently displayed, so that it may easily be read, in a part (if any) open to the public of the premises of the creditor where the agreement to which the variation relates is maintained.'

Section 127 provides, among other things, that on any application for an enforcement order the court may reduce any sum payable by the debtor 'so as to compensate him for prejudice suffered as a result of the contravention in question'. That is a most important feature of the 1974 Act. Under the old law as to moneylenders it was in general all or nothing, sudden death. Failure by the moneylender to comply with the law meant that he could recover nothing, however large the sum involved and however trivial his default. Now the court has power to make an equitable adjustment. But CCR Ord 49, r 4(9)(*a*) provides that application for an enforcement order must be made by originating application. None has been made by Lombard. So for the present the only question is whether the credit charge agreement complied with the regulations prescribing the form and content of regulated agreements. These are to be found in the Consumer Credit (Agreements) Regulations 1983. The material provisions are Sch 1, paras 18 and 19, as follows:

TYPE OF AGREEMENT (1)	INFORMATION (2)
. . .	
18. Agreements under which the rate or amount of any item included in the total charge for credit will or may be varied (other than a variation in consequence of an event which is certain to occur).	A statement indicating that in calculating the APR no account has been taken of any variation which may occur under the agreement of the rate or amount of any item entering into that calculation.
19. Agreements falling within paragraph 18.	A statement indicating the circumstances in which any variation referred to in paragraph 18 above may occur and, where that information is ascertainable at the time at which the document referred to in section 61(1) of the Act is presented or sent to the debtor for signature, the time at which any such variation may occur.
. . .	

It is said that there was a failure to comply with para 19, and thus a breach of s 61(1), on the ground that the agreement did not state the circumstances in which a variation in the interest rate might occur. The case for Lombard was that they were entitled to alter the interest rate from time to time at their absolute discretion, and that the only circumstance required was notice by them to the debtor, which was stated in the agreement. The judge rejected that argument. He said:

'To my mind the words "a statement of circumstances" require a reference to external factors by which the debtor can judge whether the variation is being properly exercised, e g by a reference to base rates, retail price indices or such other guidelines as the creditor may care to choose. I take the view that notice is something essentially different from the change in circumstances which gives rise to the variation. Likewise I take the view that the mere whim or desire of the creditor is not a circumstance. The relevant clause does not comply with para 19 of Sch 1 to the regulations.'

The implications of that decision are considerable. It is of course possible to borrow and lend money at a fixed rate of interest for a fixed period. The government does it habitually, and the discount market does little else. But it is very common indeed for private individuals to agree to a rate of interest which may fluctuate. Borrowers on a mortgage or real property are presently finding to their cost that interest rates have increased.

No doubt it would be possible for lenders to comply with the judge's requirements, and state the considerations which will induce them to increase or reduce their interest rate; there is nothing which a draftsman cannot achieve if he has clear instructions and enough ink in his pen. But it could well be a cumbersome procedure. It might also tend to defeat the purpose of 'the child guide', by cluttering up that part of the agreement with a mass of detail. The alternative solution, for the lender to apply in every case for an enforcement order in the county court because his agreement did not state the circumstances in which the interest rate could be varied, as defined by the judge, would cause grave disruption in the business of the courts.

On two potential issues there has been no dispute before us. The first is whether the
a contract does, as a matter of construction, provide that Lombard may vary the interest
rate in their absolute discretion, subject only to due notice. The second, whether such a
contract, if made, is lawful. Counsel for Mr Paton concedes that the answer is Yes to both
questions. But as the case is of some general importance, and as his concessions mean that
he is, to some extent at any rate, unable to support the reasoning of Judge Heald in the
county court, we think it right to explain why in our view they were rightly made.

b In general it is no doubt unusual for a contract to provide that its terms may be varied
unilaterally by one party, in his absolute discretion, to the detriment of the other; in
general one would require clear words to achieve that result. But in this particular case it
is, we think, part of the background, matrix or surrounding circumstances that market
rates of interest are known to vary from time to time and that some variation was very
likely to occur during the lifetime of this agreement. There is also provision that the
c borrower may bring it to an end at any time by repaying the amount outstanding. In
theory he could thus avoid the effect of an increase in the interest rate, if he found it
unattractive. But we recognise that in practice this remedy is unlikely to be available,
since he is unlikely to have the money, or to be able to borrow it from some other lender
at less than the prevailing market rate.

Counsel for Lombard observed that the provision of credit is a competitive industry,
d and that the effect of competition is likely to restrain Lombard from a capricious increase
in their interest rate. That is no doubt true if they increase rates by the same amount and
at the same time for both new and old borrowers, as he tells us they do. Indeed if a
provider of credit capriciously treated old borrowers unfavourably, one would hope that
the Director General of Fair Trading would consider whether he should still have a
licence under the 1974 Act. It was also suggested that the provisions of the Act relating
e to extortionate credit bargains might provide protection for the borrower. But counsel
for Mr Paton suggested that ss 137 and 138 may apply only to the original credit
agreement, and not to how it is subsequently operated. It is unnecessary to express any
view on that point.

Bearing all those considerations in mind, we consider that on a fair reading of the
agreement it does provide, as counsel for Mr Paton accepts, that Lombard may increase
f the interest rate at their absolute discretion subject only to notice. A power to vary the
rate is conferred in plain terms, there is no other express restriction on it and we can see
no sufficient basis for any implied restriction.

The second question is whether such an agreement is lawful. At common law it is.
One can compare a contract for the sale of goods, of which Viscount Dunedin said in
May & Butcher Ltd v R [1934] 2 KB 17 at 21, [1929] All ER Rep 679 at 684: '... with
g regard to price it is a perfectly good contract to say that the price is to be settled by the
buyer.' If that be the law where the other party is locked into the contract with no means
of escape, we do not see that it can be different in a contract of loan, where the borrower
has (in theory at any rate) the opportunity to repay the whole outstanding balance.

Is there anything in the statute or regulations which renders such a contract unlawful?
h Apart from para 19 of Sch 1 to the 1983 regulations, it has not been suggested that any
legislative provision has this effect. Indeed para 9 of the schedule points in the opposite
direction, since it refers to:

> 'Agreements for fixed-sum credit except agreements ... (c) which provide for a
> variation of, or permit the creditor to vary, (whether or not by reference to any
> index) the amount or rate of any item included in the total charge for credit after
j the relevant date ...'

So the question is whether para 19, with its reference to 'circumstances', requires as a
matter of law that a power to increase the interest rate can be provided by contract only
if justified by external factors such as an increase in the general level of rates prevailing
in the money market. We are not sure whether Judge Heald thought that it did, but if
that was the judge's view we agree that it cannot be supported. There may well be reasons

of policy why Parliament might itself have enacted such a law, or given the Secretary of
State power to do so. But s 60 of the 1974 Act confers powers to make regulations 'as to
the form and content of documents embodying regulated agreements', and provides that
they shall contain provisions 'with a view to ensuring that the debtor is made aware of'
certain matters. It is by no means clear that the regulations may affect the substance of
such agreements, or render unlawful a term which would otherwise be lawful. This
restriction is reflected in reg 2 itself, which provides that documents 'shall contain the
information set out in Column 2 of Schedule 1'. And the schedule is headed 'Information
to be Contained in Documents Embodying Regulated Consumer Credit Agreements...'
Accordingly, if it was the judge's view that an agreement cannot lawfully confer on the
lender a power to increase the interest rate in his absolute discretion, we agree that this
view cannot be supported. That conclusion would seem to have the support of Professor
Guest and Mr Michael Lloyd in *Encyclopaedia of Consumer Credit Law* para 3–224 and
indeed of counsel for Mr Paton in his capacity of author of *Consumer Credit: Law and
Practice* (1985) p 96.

So we turn at last to the one point that was ultimately in issue in this appeal, which
was formally raised only by a respondent's notice at the conclusion of the argument. This
was that the true effect of the contract was not stated with sufficient clarity in the box (or
child's guide) on the front, so as to comply with para 19 of Sch 1. It used the words:
'Subject to variation by the creditor from time to time on notification as required by law.'
It was accepted by both counsel, and we agree, that, where para 19 requires a statement
'indicating the circumstances in which any variation ... may occur', this refers to a
variation which the contract permits, rather than to the circumstances in which a
contractual power may in practice happen to be exercised. But counsel for Mr Paton
argues that the statement, in order to reflect accurately the power conferred by the
contract, should have contained words such as 'for any reason whatsoever' or 'in its
absolute discretion'. In other words counsel for Mr Paton argues that, although cl 2(a) of
the contract is clear enough to achieve the result which Lombard contend for, very much
the same language, when used in the box on the front of the agreement, is not a sufficient
statement of 'the circumstances' required by para 19. That is not necessarily an
implausible result. Lawyer's language in the body of the contract will not necessarily
serve equally well in the child's guide. What is needed there is language which is succinct
and plain, so that the reader will not become weary or impatient and will readily
understand what is said.

In our judgment the words on the face of the contract here are sufficient to convey, to
the average reader of modest intelligence, that Lombard have the right to vary the
interest rate at will if they choose to do so, subject only to proper notification. There is
nothing to suggest that their right is otherwise fettered or limited in any way, and we do
not think that the reader would assume that there is any limitation. There was no failure
to comply with para 19. Accordingly, we would allow the appeal, remit the case to the
deputy registrar and direct that there be an award in favour of Lombard for £192·75.
(That figure results from the concession of counsel for Lombard that he does not seek the
increased rate of interest.) The deputy registrar may be asked to exercise his discretion
over interest and costs.

In conclusion we would mention that 'the child's guide' on the face of the agreement
made no mention of the fact that the interest rate would be increased, under cl 2(a), if
the borrower ceased to pay by direct debit. No reliance was placed on that point before
us, and we express no view on it.

Appeal allowed. Judgment for Lombard for £192·75.

Solicitors: *Mishcon de Reya*, agents for *I M Harding*, Enfield (for Lombard); *Cruickshanks*,
Long Eaton (for Mr Paton).

Celia Fox   Barrister.

Bank Mellat v Kazmi and others (Secretary of State for Social Services intervening)

COURT OF APPEAL, CIVIL DIVISION

PURCHAS, NOURSE AND STUART-SMITH LJJ

22 NOVEMBER, 21 DECEMBER 1988

Practice – Pre-trial or post-judgment relief – Mareva injunction – Assets – Supplementary benefit arrears – Benefit arrears owed to defendant whose assets frozen by injunction – Crown having notice of injunction – Probability that defendant would dispose of payment of arrears in breach of injunction – Crown applying to court for directions as to payment – Whether payment should be made directly to defendant or into bank account frozen by injunction – Crown Proceedings Act 1947, s 25(4) – Supplementary Benefits Act 1976, s 16(1).

Social security – Supplementary benefit – Payment – Mareva injunction – Benefit arrears owing to defendant with assets frozen by injunction – Whether order for payment into bank account frozen by injunction an 'assignment of, or charge on, any supplementary benefit' – Whether court prevented from making order – Supplementary Benefits Act 1976, s 16(1).

The defendant, while employed by the plaintiff bank, obtained an employee's mortgage on his house. Following his conviction and imprisonment for fraud committed during his employment, the bank issued a writ against him claiming damages for conversion and obtained a Mareva injunction over the defendant's assets including sums of money held in certain named bank accounts. After realising the defendant's assets, including the house, the bank was still owed some £123,000. The defendant was subsequently found to be owed £8,480·15 by the Secretary of State for Social Services in arrears of supplementary benefit for mortgage interest relief on the house. The Secretary of State became aware of the Mareva injunction against the defendant and applied to the court for directions whether payment of the £8,480·15 should be made direct to the defendant, having regard to the provisions of s 25(4)[a] of the Crown Proceedings Act 1947, which prohibited garnishee proceedings against the Crown, or s 16(1)[b] of the Supplementary Benefits Act 1976, which made any 'assignment of, or charge on, any supplementary benefit' or 'agreement to assign or charge any such benefit' void. The judge rejected the bank's request for an order for payment into one of the bank accounts named in the injunction and ordered that the arrears of supplementary benefit be paid directly to the defendant, even though his evidence demonstrated a probability that he would dispose of the money in breach of the terms of the injunction. The bank appealed, contending that an order for payment into a named bank account would not be contrary to either s 25(4) of the 1947 Act or s 16(1) of the 1976 Act.

Held – Where the court had notice of the probability that a defendant would dispose of money owed to him in breach of the terms of a Mareva injunction, the court ought not to assist the defendant in flouting its previous order and accordingly it could, with the debtor's assent, order the money to be paid into the defendant's account at a bank that had notice of the injunction, unless prevented by statute from doing so. In the circumstances, an order requiring the Secretary of State to pay arrears of supplementary benefit into a named account would not be prohibited by s 25(4) of the 1947 Act or s 16(1) of the 1976 Act, since (a) even if the order was a process in the nature of an attachment, the Crown was not being forced to pay the arrears but rather was ready and

---

a Section 25(4), so far as material, is set out at p 929 *g h*, post

b Section 16(1) is set out at p 930 *a b*, post

willing to follow the court's directions for payment and (b) the order would have the same effect as the injunction to which it would be subordinate and, as such, would operate only in personam without creating any assignment, or charge on, the payment of arrears. Accordingly, the bank's appeal would be allowed and an order would be made directing that the £8,480·15 be paid into a named bank account (see p 929 c to f, p 930 c to g and p 932 a to d g h, post).

Dictum of Buckley LJ in *Cretanor Maritime Co Ltd v Irish Marine Management Ltd* [1978] 3 All ER 164 at 170 applied.

Walker v Walker [1983] 2 All ER 909 distinguished.

Notes

For orders made in respect of money due from the Crown, see 11 Halsbury's Laws (4th edn) para 1436.

For the Crown Proceedings Act 1947, s 25, see 13 Halsbury's Statutes (4th edn) 33.

For the Supplementary Benefits Act 1976, s 16, see 46 Halsbury's Statutes (3rd edn) 1060.

Cases referred to in judgments

Cretanor Maritime Co Ltd v Irish Marine Management Ltd [1978] 3 All ER 164, [1978] 1 WLR 966, CA.

Law Society v Shanks (1987) 131 SJ 1626, CA.

Walker v Walker [1983] 2 All ER 909, [1983] Fam 68, [1983] 3 WLR 421, CA.

Z Ltd v A [1982] 1 All ER 556, [1982] QB 558, [1982] 2 WLR 288, CA.

Cases also cited

Avant Petroleum Inc v Gatoil Overseas Inc [1986] 2 Lloyd's Rep 236, CA.

Ranson v Ranson [1988] 1 WLR 183, CA.

Roberts v Roberts [1986] 2 All ER 483, [1986] 1 WLR 437.

Appeal

The plaintiff, Bank Mellat, a bank incorporated under the laws of the Islamic Republic of Iran, appealed with the leave of the judge against the decision of Sir Neil Lawson sitting as a judge of the High Court in the Queen's Bench Division in chambers on 20 April 1988 whereby on the hearing of an application made to the court for directions by the Secretary of State for Social Services, as intervener, the judge ordered, inter alia, that the Secretary of State pay the sum of £8,480·15, being arrears of supplementary benefit for mortgage relief, directly to the first defendant, Sibtal Hassan Kazmi, whose assets (including sums of money held in named bank accounts) were subject to a Mareva injunction which had been granted by Parker J on 13 July 1981 and continued by Robert Goff J on 28 July 1981 in respect of an action for damages for fraud and conversion brought by the bank against Mr Kazmi, its former employee. The facts are set out in the judgment of Nourse LJ.

Hazel Williamson QC for the bank.
John Mummery for the Secretary of State.
Mr Kazmi appeared in person.

Cur adv vult

21 December. The following judgments were delivered.

NOURSE LJ (giving the first judgment at the invitation of Purchas LJ). The question in this case is whether, with the approval of the debtor, the court can direct moneys to a defendant who is restrained from disposing of or dealing with them by a Mareva injunction to be paid into an account of the defendant at a bank which has notice of the

injunction. So stated, the question is one which is capable of arising in any case where a
a Mareva injunction is in force. But here there is a further complication in that the moneys
are owed by the Crown for arrears of supplementary benefit. It has been argued that the
order would offend s 25(4) of the Crown Proceedings Act 1947 and s 16(1) of the
Supplementary Benefits Act 1976, as amended by the Social Security Act 1980.

The first defendant, Sibtal Hassan Kazmi, was formerly employed by Bank Pars, which
on 9 November 1979 granted him an employee's mortgage and took from him an all
b moneys legal charge over 41 Milton Road, London E17. In 1980 Bank Pars merged with
Bank of Tehran to form the plaintiff bank, Bank Mellat (the bank). In or about July 1981
Mr Kazmi, who was then an internal auditor with the bank, was arrested on charges of
obtaining money belonging to the bank by deception. On 13 July 1981 the writ in this
action was issued against Mr Kazmi and other defendants, with a claim for damages for
fraud and conversion against Mr Kazmi. On the same day the bank applied ex parte and
c obtained Mareva relief. On 28 July 1981 Robert Goff J made a consent order continuing
that relief in the following terms, so far as material:

> '... the Injunction granted herein on 13th July 1981 restraining the First
> Defendant ... from disposing, pledging, transferring or otherwise dealing with any
> assets he may have within the jurisdiction of this Court including and in particular
d > the sums of money standing to the credit of the Bank Accounts particularised in the
> first Schedule hereto or removing or taking any steps to remove the same out of the
> jurisdiction be continued until further order.'

Although much has happened in the mean time, that injunction is still running
against Mr Kazmi. He has never applied for a modification so as to allow the defrayment
of living expenses and so forth. It is unnecessary to recount the intervening events except
e to say, first, that in March 1983 Mr Kazmi was convicted on three counts of obtaining
money by deception and received concurrent sentences of three years' imprisonment on
each count, second, that judgment in this action was subsequently entered against him
for damages assessed at £96,681·40 plus costs and, third, that extensive realisations were
made by the bank both before and after judgment, including the sale of 41 Milton Road
for about £60,750 net. The bank claims that as at 22 November 1988 the amount
f outstanding under the judgment (including interest) was about £61,400 and that a
further sum of about £62,320 was owing to it in respect of principal and interest on Mr
Kazmi's loan account.

Between 1981 and 1984 Mr Kazmi claimed supplementary benefit in respect of
mortgage interest payable by him under the bank's legal charge over 41 Milton Road.
On 16 November 1987 an adjudication officer determined that he was entitled to receive
g an aggregate sum of £8,480·15 in respect of those claims. The effect of the determination
was to render the Crown, in the person of the Secretary of State for Social Services, a
debtor to Mr Kazmi in that amount. It is also believed that a further sum of about £2,000
may become due in respect of the same liability after further calculations have been
made.

h Early in November 1987 it came to the attention of the Secretary of State that the bank
had obtained a Mareva injunction against Mr Kazmi and that that injunction remained
in full force and effect. The Department of Health and Social Security's solicitor
accordingly communicated with both the bank and Mr Kazmi, as a result of which it
became clear that the Secretary of State was faced with a dilemma. On one side the bank,
maintaining that payment to Mr Kazmi direct would or might constitute an aiding and
j abetting of a breach of the injunction by Mr Kazmi and thus a contempt of court by the
Secretary of State, requested that payment should be made into one of the bank accounts
particularised in the order of Robert Goff J, none of which is held with the bank itself.
On the other side, Mr Kazmi maintained that payment should be made to him direct.
He indicated that if that could not be done he would withdraw the claim altogether.

The practical result of all this was that the Secretary of State had no alternative but to
seek to intervene in the proceedings, for the purpose of being given directions—

'under the injunction herein granted to the Plaintifffs on 28 July 1981 or otherwise as to whom and in what manner the Proposed Intervener might make payment of all sums awarded to the First Defendant by way of arrears of supplementary benefit in respect of mortgage payments.'   *a*

That application came before Sir Neil Lawson, sitting as a judge of the High Court in the Queen's Bench Division, on 20 April 1988, when he ordered that all sums awarded to Mr Kazmi by way of arrears of supplementary benefit in respect of mortgage payments should be paid direct to Mr Kazmi or to his order. He gave the bank leave to appeal and   *b* granted a stay of execution on his order pending an appeal. The bank has now appealed to this court.

Both here and below the Secretary of State and the bank have appeared by counsel. Mr Kazmi has appeared in person. The Secretary of State, being in much the same position as an interpleader, has correctly adopted a neutral stance. To him it is a matter of indifference whether the money is paid into the designated bank account or to Mr Kazmi   *c* direct. His only interest in the matter is to comply with the directions of the court. But at the invitation of the court and with the approval of Mr Kazmi, counsel for the Secretary of State was good enough to address to us the principal arguments which would have been advanced on Mr Kazmi's behalf, if he had appeared here by counsel. Having heard those arguments, Mr Kazmi was content to adopt them for himself and, except on one   *d* point (see below), did not add anything of his own. Counsel's assistance in arriving at a sound decision of the matter has proved invaluable.

Although they were argued in the reverse order, I find it both logical and convenient to begin with the general question and then to go on to that which arises by virtue of the special position of the Secretary of State.

In *Z Ltd v A* [1982] 1 All ER 556 at 563, [1982] QB 558 at 574 Lord Denning MR, after   *e* considering the effect of a Mareva injunction on banks and bank accounts, said:

'But the same applies to any specific asset held by a bank for safe custody on behalf of the defendants, be it jewellery, stamps, or anything else, and to any other person who holds any other asset of the defendant. If the asset is covered by the terms of the Mareva injunction, that other person must not hand it over to the defendant or do anything to enable him to dispose of it. He must hold it pending further order.'   *f*

In *Law Society v Shanks* (1987) 131 SJ 1626 (a transcript of which was before us) Sir John Donaldson MR (with whose judgment Neill LJ and Sir Roualeyn Cumming-Bruce ageeed), after reading an earlier passage from Lord Denning MR's judgment in *Z Ltd v A* [1982] 1 All ER 556 at 562, [1982] QB 558 at 572 and then the passage quoted above, said: *g*

'It is generally accepted that a Mareva injunction prevents banks or other people who hold assets to the order of the defendant from assisting the defendant to dispose of those assets to third parties or to dissipate them, but I know of no authority other than this particular passage for the proposition that it prevents anybody handing the asset over to the owner of the asset, in this case the defendant. That does not of itself   *h* amount to a dissipation or a disposal of any kind whatsoever. In special circumstances, where it is known that the sole purpose of requiring the asset to be handed over to the defendant is to facilitate a dissipation of that asset, different considerations may arise, but that is not suggested in this case. That would be a very peculiar case indeed.'

j

He added that the two passages from Lord Denning MR's judgment did not represent a general statement of the law which is applicable in any ordinary case.

I respectfully agree that mere notice of the existence of a Mareva injunction cannot render it a contempt of court for a third party to make over an asset to the defendant direct. Otherwise it might be impossible, for example, for a debtor with notice to pay over to the defendant even the most trivial sum without seeking the directions of the

court. A distinction must be drawn between notice of the injunction on the one hand
a and notice of a probability that the asset will be disposed of or dealt with in breach of it
on the other. It is only in the latter case that the third party can be guilty of a contempt
of court. No general test can be propounded for the latter class of case, although the facts
here suggest that it may not be quite as peculiar as Sir John Donaldson MR thought. In a
letter to the Department of Health and Social Security's solicitor of 10 December 1987,
Mr Kazmi gave this reason for withdrawing the claim, if the money could not be paid to
b him direct: '... as the Bank Mellat got £70,000 house back and further you will pay
them arrears that will be the injustice. Now you will decide who is the big looser.' Mr
Kazmi's evident resolve to prevent the money getting into the hands of the bank at any
cost demonstrated a probability that he would, if he could, dispose of it in breach of the
injunction. The Secretary of State's decision to seek the directions of the court was
entirely appropriate.
c   What then ought the attitude of the court to be when asked to decide to whom and in
what manner the money available to satisfy the debt should be paid? This question
admits of only one answer. If the debtor has notice of a probability that the money will,
if paid to the defendant direct, be disposed of in breach of the injunction, so has the
court. And the court has no choice, nor, I will add, any inclination in the matter, except
to come to the aid of its previous order. It must take some course which will effectively
d subject the money to the operation of the Mareva injunction. On a conventional
approach, the correct course might be to order it to be paid into court. But in a case
where there is already a bank account with one of the major clearing banks whose
balance from time to time is frozen by the injunction it is preferable in practice, and
unobjectionable in theory, for it to be paid into that account. That will not give the
creditor any better right to receive the money than if it had been paid into court. He will
e still have to take garnishee proceedings against the bank under RSC Ord 49.
    Applying these general considerations to the facts of the present case, I am in no doubt
that, unless prevented by the fact that the debtor here is the Secretary of State, we ought
to accede to the bank's appeal and order the sums in question to be paid into one of the
bank accounts maintained with a major clearing bank which are particularised in the
order of Robert Goff J. I now turn to consider whether the material legislation prevents
f us from taking that course.
    Part III of the Crown Proceedings Act 1947 is headed 'Judgments and Execution' and
consists of ss 24 to 27. Sections 24 and 26 are not material to the present inquiry.
Subsections (1) to (3) of s 25 provide, shortly stated, for the issuing and service of
certificates of orders made against the Crown and, in the case of an order for the payment
of any money by way of damages or otherwise or of any costs, for the payment by the
g appropriate government department of the amount so certified. The first part of sub-s
(4) of s 25 is in these terms:

> 'Save as aforesaid no execution or attachment or process in the nature thereof shall
> be issued out of any court for enforcing payment by the Crown of any such money
> or costs as aforesaid . . .'

h Thus the effect of s 25(4) is, amongst other things, to prohibit garnishee proceedings
against the Crown, being the process by which a debt owing to a judgment debtor by a
third party can be attached by the judgment creditor. But then s 27 goes on to provide
for a process analogous to garnishee proceedings, by which money payable by the Crown
can, except in certain cases, be attached. The substantive provisions are contained in
j s 27(1). They need not be quoted in full, because it is clear that the bank would prima
facie be able to obtain an order under the subsection, were it not for the proviso, which
is in these terms:

> 'Provided that no such order shall be made in respect of:—(a) any wages or salary
> payable to any officer of the Crown as such; (b) any money which is subject to the
> provisions of any enactment prohibiting or restricting assignment or charging or
> taking in execution.'

Those are the material provisions of the 1947 Act. Also material is s 16(1) of the
Supplementary Benefits Act 1976, as amended by the Social Security Act 1980, which is
in these terms:

> 'Every assignment of, or charge on, any supplementary benefit, and every
> agreement to assign or charge any such benefit, shall be void; and, on the bankruptcy
> of a person entitled to any supplementary benefit, no rights in respect of the benefit
> shall pass to any trustee or other person acting on behalf of his creditors.'

Counsel for the bank accepts, correctly, that, by virtue of s 16(1), Mr Kazmi's arrears of
supplementary benefit are 'money which is subject to the provisions of [an] enactment
prohibiting or restricting assignment or charging or taking in execution' within para (b)
of the proviso to s 27(1) of the 1947 Act. She accordingly accepts that the bank cannot
obtain an order in its own favour under s 27. But she nevertheless submits that an order
for payment into a bank account particularised in the order of Robert Goff J would not
offend either s 25(4) of the 1947 Act or s 16(1) of the 1976 Act.

Counsel for the Secretary of State has submitted that the order sought by the bank is a
process in the nature of attachment within s 25(4). I am not sure whether that submission
is correct or not. Certainly it is a process preliminary to attachment, in the sense that
without it garnishee proceedings cannot be taken. But it lacks essential features of a
garnishee order, in that it neither divests the judgment debtor of his title to the debt nor
gives it to the judgment creditor. Moreover, in *Cretanor Maritime Co Ltd v Irish Marine
Management Ltd* [1978] 3 All ER 164 at 170, [1978] 1 WLR 966 at 974 Buckley LJ thought
it manifest that a Mareva injunction could not operate as an attachment. And so it might
well be said that an order whose effect is to subject money to such an injunction cannot
be a process in the nature of attachment. It is, however, unnecessary to resolve this
problem, because a simpler answer to counsel's submission was suggested in argument
by Stuart-Smith LJ. Even if the order sought by the bank is a process in the nature of
attachment, it is not one, in the circumstances of this case, 'for enforcing payment by the
Crown'. Not only is the Crown not being forced to pay the arrears, it is ready, willing
and able to pay them to whomsoever and in whatsoever manner the court shall direct.
The order sought by the bank offends neither the letter nor the spirit of s 25(4).

I turn then to s 16(1), which, so far as material, avoids any assignment of, or charge on,
any supplementary benefit and any agreement to assign or charge any such benefit. As a
matter of principle it cannot be doubted that a Mareva injunction, which, like any other
injunction, operates only in personam, does not create any assignment of, or charge on,
the assets in respect of which it is granted, or any agreement to assign or charge those
assets. If authority be needed for that proposition, reference can again be made to the
judgment of Buckley LJ in the *Cretanor Maritime* case [1978] 3 All ER 164 at 170, [1978]
1 WLR 966 at 974. Accordingly, had it not been for the decision of this court in *Walker
v Walker* [1983] 2 All ER 909, [1983] Fam 68, the submission by counsel for the bank
that the order sought by the bank would not offend s 16(1) could have been accepted
without more ado.

In *Walker v Walker* the husband, who was discharged from the army before decree
absolute, was entitled to a resettlement grant from the Ministry of Defence. On an
application by the wife under s 37 of the Matrimonial Causes Act 1973 the county court
registrar ordered the Paymaster General to pay the amount of the grant into court
pending trial of the issues relating to ancillary relief for the wife and the children of the
family. Objection having been taken by the Ministry of Defence, the proceedings were
transferred to the High Court, where Sheldon J discharged the registrar's order as being
in contravention of s 203 of the Army Act 1955. His decision was affirmed by this court.

Section 203 of the 1955 Act is in these terms:

> '(1) Every assignment of or charge on, and every agreement to assign or charge,
> any pay, military award, grant, pension or allowance, payable to any person in
> respect of his or any other person's service in Her Majesty's military forces shall be
> void.

a
> (2) Save as expressly provided by this Act, no order shall be made by any court the effect of which would be to restrain any person from receiving anything which by virtue of this section he is precluded from assigning and to direct payment thereof to another person . . .'

It will be observed that sub-s (1) of that section is for all practical purposes to the same effect as s 16(1) of the Supplementary Benefits Act 1976, which does not, however, contain any provision equivalent to sub-s (2) of s 203. Counsel for the Secretary of State
b
told us that similar provisions, in one form or the other, are to be found in other Acts, so that the problem is one which may arise in other contexts also.

It seems that in *Walker v Walker* Sheldon J, although he did not think that payment into court would be payment 'to another person', nevertheless based his decision on s 203(2): see the reference to his views in the judgment of Cumming-Bruce LJ in the
c
Court of Appeal ([1983] 2 All ER 909 at 911, [1983] Fam 68 at 73). However, it is clear from the following passage that Cumming-Bruce LJ based his decision on both subsections of s 203 ([1983] 2 All ER 909 at 913–914, [1983] Fam 68 at 76):

> 'Either a cheque payable by the Ministry of Defence to Her Majesty's Accountant General by way of payment into court of the sum representing the entitlement of the former soldier to his resettlement grant was payable to another person pursuant
d
> to the order of the court that the money be paid into court, in which case such order for payment into court would be contrary to the express terms of s 203(2) of the 1955 Act, or alternatively, if that is wrong, the order for payment into court is itself bad, because the only explanation or reason for such an order would be to circumvent the prohibition in s 203(1) which prohibits any charge on the grant in question. I am content to hold that the order for payment into court made by the county court,
e
> making the order against Her Majesty's Paymaster General, was bad, either because the Paymaster General, on paying this cheque to the Accountant General was paying to another person, which is prohibited, or if he was not, then what he was ordered to do was to take the step which, to have any valid or useful effect for the benefit of the petitioner, must involve at some stage a restraint or charge on the grant, which
f
> itself is prohibited by sub-ss (1) and (2).'

Griffiths LJ rested his decision on s 203(2), primarily because he thought that an order directing payment into court would be an order directing payment to another person. He continued ([1983] 2 All ER 909 at 914, [1983] Fam 68 at 77):

> 'If I were wrong in this view, I would still follow the judge's line of reasoning. It is manifest that the judge could not, under sub-s (2), make an order that this money
g
> should be paid direct to the wife because on any view that would be an order directing payment to another person, which he is not entitled to do. It seems to me that it would be quite wrong to construe the subsection as enabling him to achieve this same end in two steps, namely by first ordering the money to be brought into court and then, by a further order, seeing that it fell into the hands of the wife.'

h Griffiths LJ did not therefore rely on s 203(1). Sir Roger Ormrod agreed in terms with both the other judgments and did not add anything of his own on s 203.

On a strict view, by virtue of Sir Roger Ormrod's agreement with the judgment of Cumming-Bruce LJ, we are thus faced with a decision of this court to the effect that an order for payment into court of an army resettlement grant pending trial of ancillary relief proceedings offends not only sub-s (2), but also sub-s (1), of s 203 of the 1955 Act.
j
Counsel for the Secretary of State has accordingly submitted that the order sought by the bank in this case would likewise offend s 16(1) of the 1976 Act. My reasons for thinking that we ought not to accede to that submission are these. First, the view of Cumming-Bruce LJ was based on his belief that the only explanation or reason for an order for payment into court would be to circumvent the prohibition in s 203(1), and that it was a step which, to have any valid or useful effect for the benefit of the wife, must involve at some stage a restraint or charge on the grant. That no doubt is an entirely realistic view

of the effect of an order for payment into court made at the suit of a wife in ancillary
relief proceedings. But I do not think that the same can be said of the order proposed in
the present case. True it is that it will enable the bank to take garnishee proceedings but,
unless and until it obtains a garnishee order, the money will still be held to the account
of Mr Kazmi and it will still, in theory at any rate, be available to satisfy the claims of all
creditors and not just one of them. Secondly, I do not see that we can disregard the
proposition, established both in principle and on authority, that a Mareva injunction
does not create any assignment of, or charge on, the assets in respect of which it is
granted, or any agreement to assign or charge those assets. A subsequent order which
ensures that a specific asset will not be disposed of or dealt with in breach of the
injunction cannot have any different effect. Thirdly and perhaps most important, if the
money were to be paid to Mr Kazmi direct, admittedly there would be no offence to
s 16(1). But in that event he would come under an immediate obligation, by virtue of an
injunction which is already in force, to preserve it. On the general principles already
stated, the court would be bound to come to the aid of its previous order by directing Mr
Kazmi to pay the money into the designated bank account. And so the court is only
achieving by one order that which it could achieve by two.

For these reasons I conclude that we are not prevented by the decision in *Walker v
Walker* from making the order sought by the bank. I express no opinion as to what the
position might have been if the 1976 Act had contained a provision equivalent to s 203(2)
of the 1955 Act. That question is better left for decision in a case in which it directly
arises.

Counsel for the Secretary of State referred us to s 1(1) of the 1976 Act, which gives an
absolute right to benefit where resources are insufficient to meet requirements. There is
no obligation on the recipient to apply it for some special purpose, in this case, for
example, in discharge of the mortgage interest payments. Counsel also referred us to
para 6 of the Supplementary Benefit (Claims and Payments) Regulations 1981, SI 1981/
1525, which provides in effect that Mr Kazmi is entitled to be paid his arrears of benefit
by means of an instrument of payment, unless the Secretary of State makes other
arrangements for payment. I do not think that these provisions have any inhibiting
effect on the order sought by the bank. The objection, if there was one, could again be
met by ordering the Secretary of State to pay the money to Mr Kazmi direct, with a
further order directing Mr Kazmi to pay it into the designated bank account.

Having held that the court has jurisdiction to make the order sought by the bank, I
am in no doubt that, as a matter of discretion, the order should be made. Mr Kazmi
submitted that the discretion should be exercised by not making the order, but it is
obvious that that submission must be rejected. Finally, it must be said that it would be
of no avail to Mr Kazmi to seek to withdraw his claim for supplementary benefit, more
accurately to forgive the debt which is owed to him by the Crown, because that would in
itself constitute the disposal of an asset in breach of the Mareva injunction.

For these reasons I would allow this appeal and make the order sought by the bank.

STUART-SMITH LJ. I agree.

PURCHAS LJ. I also agree.

*Appeal allowed. Order in respect of costs in court below to stand; no order in respect of costs of
appeal.*

Solicitors: *Stephenson Harwood* (for the bank); *Treasury Solicitor.*

Dilys Tausz   Barrister.

a
R v Secretary of State for Transport and others, ex parte de Rothschild and another

COURT OF APPEAL, CIVIL DIVISION
SLADE, CROOM-JOHNSON AND RALPH GIBSON LJJ
11, 12 JULY 1988

b

Compulsory purchase – Compulsory purchase order – Application to quash order – Grounds on which order may be challenged – Acquisition of land for bypass – Alternative routes proposed by objectors – Objectors willing to sell land for alternative routes – Whether Secretary of State entitled to impose route on landowner willing to sell other land which would serve same purpose equally well taking all relevant considerations into account – Test to be applied.

c

A highway authority made a compulsory purchase order to acquire land owned by the appellants for the construction of a bypass. The appellants objected to the order and an inquiry was held at which they put forward four alternative routes for the bypass on other land which they owned and were prepared to sell to the highway authority. The inspector found that the disadvantages of extra cost and delay positively outweighed the
d advantages of the appellants' alternative routes. The Secretary of State confirmed the order, stating in his decision letter that he did not believe that any of the suggested alternatives had sufficient advantages or benefits which would justify its adoption in place of the scheme proposed by the highway authority. The appellants applied for judicial review of the Secretary of State's decision by way of an order of certiorari
e quashing it. The judge dismissed the application and the appellants appealed, contending, inter alia, that the onus was on the highway authority to justify the compulsory purchase order and that the Secretary of State had applied a test which was wrong in law, because a compulsory purchase order should only be confirmed if it was decisively in the public interest to do so.

Held – There were no special rules beyond the ordinary rules relating to unreasonableness
f which fell to be applied by the court when considering a challenge to the confirmation by the Secretary of State of a compulsory purchase order. However, given the draconian nature of such an order, no reasonable Secretary of State would be likely to confirm such an order in the absence of what he perceived to be a sufficient justification for his decision on its merits or to impose such an order on an unwilling landowner if the owner was willing to sell other land which would serve the same purpose equally well taking all
g relevant considerations, including delay and cost, into account. On a fair reading of the decision letter, however, the Secretary of State was intending to indorse all the inspector's conclusions including his conclusion that, on the facts, the highway authority had shown unequivocally that the route in the compulsory purchase order was a better route in the public interest than any of the alternative routes proposed by the appellants. Accordingly, there were no grounds for challenging the decision of the Secretary of State as being
h wrong in law and the appeal would be dismissed (see p 938 j to p 939 a, p 942 a b e to h, p 943 c to f and p 944 c d, post).

Associated Provincial Picture Houses Ltd v Wednesbury Corp [1947] 2 All ER 680 and *Ashbridge Investments Ltd v Minister of Housing and Local Government* [1965] 3 All ER 371 applied.

j **Notes**
For the right to apply to quash a compulsory purchase order, see 8 Halsbury's Laws (4th edn) paras 35–37.

Cases referred to in judgments
A-G v De Keyser's Royal Hotel Ltd [1920] AC 508, [1920] All ER Rep 80, HL.

Ashbridge Investments Ltd v Minister of Housing and Local Government [1965] 3 All ER 371,
  [1965] 1 WLR 1320, CA.
Associated Provincial Picture Houses Ltd v Wednesbury Corp [1947] 2 All ER 680, [1948] 1
  KB 223, CA.
Brown v Secretary of State for the Environment (1978) 40 P & CR 285.
Chilton v Telford Development Corp [1987] 3 All ER 992, [1987] 1 WLR 872, CA.
Prest v Secretary of State for Wales (1982) 81 LGR 193, CA.
R v Secretary of State for the Environment, ex p Melton BC (1985) 52 P & CR 318.

Appeal

Evelyn de Rothschild and Eranda Herds Ltd appealed against the decision of Mann J
hearing the Crown Office list on 12 November 1987 dismissing their application for
judicial review by way of an order of certiorari quashing the decision of the Secretary of
State for Transport contained in a letter dated 26 November 1986 confirming the
Bedfordshire County Council (Leighton Linslade Southern Bypass) Compulsory Purchase
(No 2) Order 1985 made by the Bedfordshire County Council as the local highway
authority. The facts are set out in the judgment of Slade LJ.

Jeremy M Sullivan QC and *Brian Ash* for the appellants.
John Laws for the Secretary of State.
Charles George for the council.

SLADE LJ. This is an appeal by Mr Evelyn de Rothschild and Eranda Herds Ltd from a
judgment of Mann J given on 12 November 1987 whereby he dismissed an application
by the appellants, who were seeking to quash a compulsory purchase order.

The appellants are the owners and occupiers of certain land in Bedfordshire which the
Bedfordshire County Council, who are the second respondents to this appeal, have sought
to acquire compulsorily for the construction of a southern bypass to the town of Leighton
Linslade. For this purpose the council made a compulsory purchase order relating to part
of the appellants' land, namely the Bedfordshire County Council (Leighton Linslade
Southern Bypass) Compulsory Purchase (No 2) Order 1985. The order was made by the
council in its capacity as highway authority and in exercise of the powers conferred on it
by ss 239, 240, 246 and 250 of the Highways Act 1980 and s 2 of the Acquisition of Land
Act 1981. The confirming authority in regard to the order was the Secretary of State for
Transport, who is the first respondent to this appeal.

While it was not disputed that the order fell within the letter of the council's statutory
powers, the appellants objected to it on its merits. Accordingly, pursuant to s 13(2) of the
1981 Act the Secretary of State, before confirming the order, caused a public local inquiry
to be held before an inspector appointed for the purpose. Section 13(2) reads as follows:

> 'If any objection duly made as aforesaid is not withdrawn, the confirming
> authority shall, before confirming the order, either cause a public local inquiry to
> be held or afford to any person by whom any objection has been duly made as
> aforesaid and not withdrawn an opportunity of appearing before and being heard
> by a person appointed by the confirming authority for the purpose, and, after
> considering the objection and the report of the person who held the inquiry or the
> person appointed as aforesaid, may confirm the order either with or without
> modifications.'

The subsection by its terms appears to confer on the Secretary of State a very wide
discretion as to whether or not to confirm a compulsory purchase order, and we have
heard a good deal of argument on this appeal concerning the proper principles to be
applied by him in exercising this function. It is convenient to deal with this aspect of the
case at this point.

It has been common ground that the exercise of this power of the Secretary of State
a may be challenged, at least on any of the grounds set out by Lord Denning MR in his
judgment in *Ashbridge Investments Ltd v Minister of Housing and Local Government* [1965]
3 All ER 371 at 374, [1965] 1 WLR 1320 at 1326, where he said:

> 'The court can only interfere on the ground that the Minister has gone outside
> the powers of the Act or that any requirement of the Act has not been complied
> with. Under this paragraph, it seems to me that the court can interfere with the
b > Minister's decision if he has acted on no evidence; or if he has come to a conclusion
> to which, on the evidence, he could not reasonably come; or if he has given a wrong
> interpretation to the words of the statute; or if he has taken into consideration
> matters which he ought not to have taken into account, or vice versa; or has
> otherwise gone wrong in law. It is identical with the position when the court has
> power to interfere with the decision of a lower tribunal which has erred in point of
c > law.'

These, as Mann J said in his judgment in the present case, are the conventional grounds
of challenge and, in particular, the grounds which derive from the decision of this court
in *Associated Provincial Picture Houses Ltd v Wednesbury Corp* [1947] 2 All ER 680, [1948]
1 KB 223. I will for brevity refer to these grounds as 'the *Wednesbury/Ashbridge* grounds'.
d However, it has to be recognised that the compulsory purchase of land involves a serious
invasion of the private proprietary rights of citizens. As Purchas LJ described them in
Chilton v Telford Development Corp [1987] 3 All ER 992 at 997, [1987] 1 WLR 872 at 878,
the powers of compulsory purchase of an acquiring authority are of a draconian nature.
The power to dispossess a citizen of his land against his will is clearly not one to be
exercised lightly and without good and sufficient cause.
e   On behalf of the appellants counsel have submitted that there are to be derived from
the authorities what they call 'special rules', beyond the *Wednesbury/Ashbridge* grounds
which are applicable whenever the court is considering a challenge to a compulsory
purchase order. They summarise these so-called special rules in five propositions as
follows (I am quoting from their skeleton argument):

f   '(i) The onus is upon the acquiring authority to justify a compulsory purchase
order and upon the Secretary of State to justify his decision to confirm such an order.
(ii) A compulsory purchase order should only be confirmed if it is decisively in the
public interest to do so, or if there is a "compelling case" in the public interest. (iii)
Any reasonable doubt as to the justification for a compulsory purchase order is to be
resolved in favour of the owner of the affected land. (iv) If alternative land is
g   available that is equally suitable for the purposes of the acquiring authority but
which can be acquired without the use of compulsory purchase powers, the use of
such powers cannot be justified. (v) At the very least it is for the acquiring authority
to demonstrate that compulsory acquisition is necessary, and not for the landowner
to demonstrate the converse.'

h   By way of support for these five propositions, counsel referred to general principles of
our constitutional law, including the Magna Carta and art 1 of the First Protocol to the
European Convention for the Protection of Human Rights and Fundamental Freedoms
(Paris, 20 March 1952; TS 46 (1954); Cmd 9221). More specifically, he relied on three
reported cases.
    The first was the decision of Forbes J in *Brown v Secretary of State for the Environment*
j   (1978) 40 P & CR 285. In that case a local authority, with a view to providing a site for
gipsies in pursuance of their duty under s 6 of the Caravan Sites Act 1968, made a
compulsory purchase order in respect of land owned by the applicants. The applicants
objected to the order and an inquiry was held. The inspector found that there were other
sites available to the local authority, including one owned by them. He went so far as to
say that the applicants' site was probably the worst. Nevertheless, the Secretary of State

confirmed the order. In his decision letter he expressly stated that he was solely concerned with the merits or otherwise of the order land and did not think it material to his decision *a* whether or not the local authority would have chosen the applicants' land if they had considered all the possible locations at the same time. As Forbes J pointed out, the Secretary of State disagreed with the inspector's conclusion—

> 'not because he disagrees with the inspector on a value judgment about the suitability of these sites but because he has directed himself that the suitability of *b* these sites is an immaterial matter for consideration in forming his decision.'

(See 40 P & CR 285 at 291.)

On an application for judicial review, Forbes J considered that the Secretary of State had misdirected himself. He said the letter set out no adequate reasons for the disagreement with the inspector's conclusions. In a passage relied on by counsel for the appellants he went on to say (at 291):   *c*

> 'It must also, it seems to me, be a matter of supreme importance, in considering whether or not to confirm a compulsory purchase order, that not only is there another suitable site available but that that very site happens to be in the ownership of the authority that is seeking to exercise compulsory purchase powers. It seems to me that there is a very long and respectable tradition for the view that an authority *d* that seeks to dispossess a citizen of his land must do so by showing that it is necessary, in order to exercise the powers for the purposes of the Act under which the compulsory purchase order is made, that the acquiring authority should have authorisation to acquire the land in question. If, in fact, the acquiring authority is itself in possession of other suitable land—other land that is wholly suitable for that purpose—then it seems to me that no reasonable Secretary of State faced with that *e* fact could come to the conclusion that it was necessary for the authority to acquire other land compulsorily for precisely the same purpose'.

Though in this passage Forbes J used words which could be read as indicating that an onus of proof fell on the authority to show that acquisition was 'necessary', I do not read his judgment as indicating that he regarded any special principle other than ordinary *Wednesbury/Ashbridge* principles as applicable, or that he founded his ratio decidendi on *f* any question of onus of proof. In what seems to me to be the ratio of his judgment he summarised the grounds for quashing the decision as being (at 292):

> '... first, that the Secretary of State has wrongly directed himself that the suitability of alternative sites is a matter that is immaterial to his decision, and, secondly, that he has not anywhere considered, so far as I can see, the fact that this *g* acquiring authority seeking compulsory purchase powers had already in its hand land of its own found by the inspector to be more suitable for the purpose of the Act than the applicants' land. In those circumstance, it seems to me that the Secretary of State ignored that factor, which was a material consideration ...'

The *Brown* decision, therefore, in my judgment illustrates a conventional application *h* of *Wednesbury/Ashbridge* principles, namely on the grounds that the Secretary of State had failed to take into consideration a matter which he ought to have taken into account.

The second of the authorities on which counsel for the appellants relied in support of his contention that special rules apply where the court is considering a challenge to a compulsory purchase order was the decision of this court in *Prest v Secretary of State for Wales* (1982) 81 LGR 193. In that case a water authority needed to make a new sewage *j* works on land owned by the applicants. A compulsory purchase order was made in respect of a site forming part of that land. At a public inquiry the applicants offered to convey to the authority either of two alternative sites at 'existing use value' as agricultural land. The inspector recommended that the order be confirmed and the Secretary of State in due course confirmed it. However, the Secretary of State, in writing his decision letter,

failed to take into account the cost of acquiring the compulsory purchase order site as
against the cost of acquiring the alternative sites offered by the applicants. When the case
reached this court, fresh evidence was available showing that it was highly probable that
the owners of the land would obtain planning permission for development of the site
proposed by the water authority for industrial purposes. This court held that the
compulsory purchase order should be set aside. In the course of their judgments, the
members of the court made some broad observations which have been strongly relied on
by counsel for the appellants in the course of their argument. Lord Denning MR said (81
LGR 193 at 198):

> 'To what extent is the Secretary of State entitled to use compulsory powers to
> acquire the land of a private individual? It is clear that no Minister or public
> authority can acquire any land compulsorily except that power to do so be given by
> Parliament: and Parliament only grants it, or should only grant it, when it is
> necessary in the public interest. In any case, therefore, where the scales are evenly
> balanced—for or against compulsory acquisition—the decision—by whomsoever it
> is made—should come down against compulsory acquisition. I regard it as a
> principle of our constitutional law that no citizen is to be deprived of his land by
> any public authority against his will, unless it is expressly authorised by Parliament
> and the public interest decisively so demands: and then only on the condition that
> proper compensation is paid: see *Attorney-General v De Keyser's Royal Hotel Ltd*
> ([1920] AC 508, [1920] All ER Rep 80). If there is any reasonable doubt on the
> matter, the balance must be resolved in favour of the citizen.'

Then Lord Denning MR cited with approval the first of the two passages from the
judgment of Forbes J in *Brown's* case I have already quoted. However, later in his
judgment, Lord Denning MR, in referring to the power of the court to intervene in cases
of this nature, specifically referred to the passage from his own judgment in the *Ashbridge*
case which I have already quoted. Furthermore, he ultimately expressed the two grounds
of his decision in terms which seem to me to echo the conventional *Wednesbury/Ashbridge*
grounds. He said (81 LGR 193 at 202):

> 'In view of the fresh evidence it would be quite unreasonable for the acquiring
> authority to proceed with the compulsory purchase order. Yet on 18 May 1981 they
> gave notice to treat and have only held their hand pending these proceedings. In the
> second place, even if the fresh evidence be disregarded, when the Secretary of State
> wrote the decision letter confirming the compulsory purchase order, he failed to
> take into account the cost of acquiring the CPO site as against the cost of acquiring
> the alternative site offered by Sir Brandon. This was a most relevant consideration.'

In other words, as I read it, Lord Denning MR's judgment was ultimately founded on
the grounds of unreasonableness and of failure to take into account a material
consideration.

Watkins LJ, in the course of his judgment in the same case, made some general
observations, again strongly relied on by counsel for the appellants. He said (at 211):

> 'In the sphere of compulsory land acquisition, the onus of showing that a
> compulsory purchase order has been properly confirmed rests squarely on the
> acquiring authority and, if he seeks to support his own decision, on the Secretary of
> State. The taking of a person's land against his will is a serious invasion of his
> proprietary rights. The use of statutory authority for the destruction of those rights
> requires to be most carefully scrutinised. The courts must be vigilant to see to it that
> that authority is not abused. It must not be used unless it is clear that the Secretary
> of State has allowed those rights to be violated by a decision based upon the right
> legal principles, adequate evidence and proper consideration of the factor which
> sways his mind into confirmation of the order sought.'

As I read his judgment, however, its ratio is to be found in the immediately succeeding paragraph where he said (at 212):

> 'I have come to the conclusion that his decision should not be upheld. A vital consideration was not inquired into, in my view. It was, therefore, left out of account in the exercise of the Secretary of State's discretion. The hope value of parts of the Miskin lands should not have been disregarded as it was, especially seeing that there was evidence of its possible existence. An inquiry into it would not, it seems to me, have delayed the decision by much time, if any. To fail to make that inquiry was a glaring omission going to a fundamental consideration.'

In other words, the Secretary of State had failed to take into account a material consideration.

Fox LJ's judgment contains a passage, also relied on by the appellants in this case, which I think is to the same effect. He said (at 216):

> 'I can only conclude that, in a case where the Secretary of State decided to confirm the compulsory purchase order primarily on considerations of cost, and where shortly before his decision he was asked to take account of land acquisition costs, he confirmed the order without material as to what the latter costs were. Accordingly, I do not think that he can have given the proper degree of consideration to the overall question of cost. The onus of establishing that a compulsory purchase order has been properly made must be on the acquiring authority. The question of cost was a material issue.'

Having considered the judgments of this court in *Prest v Secretary of State for Wales* and of Forbes J in *Brown v Secretary of State for the Environment*, I conclude that both of them were merely examples of challenges to the Secretary of State's decision on conventional *Wednesbury/Ashbridge* grounds. Though all the judgments in *Prest's* case contained observations regarding onus, I, for my part, read them as doing no more than giving a warning that, in cases where a compulsory purchase order is under challenge, the draconian nature of the order will itself render it more vulnerable to successful challenge on *Wednesbury/Ashbridge* grounds unless sufficient reasons are adduced affirmatively to justify it on its merits.

In *R v Secretary of State for the Environment, ex p Melton BC* (1985) 52 P & CR 318 Forbes J summarised what he understood to be the effect of the *Prest* decision in a passage on which counsel for the appellants also relied. He said (at 326):

> 'Throughout that case it is quite plain that the Court of Appeal was deciding that the duty of the Secretary of State to look, if necessary, for other sources of information before coming to his conclusion, arose when he was minded to confirm a compulsory purchase order. The reason for that was, quite simply, that he must satisfy himself that the compulsory purchase order is necessary before he can confirm the order so that a private citizen's land is compulsorily acquired.'

I have already stated my own understanding of the *Prest* decision. I think that the word 'necessary' itself carried with it an element of ambiguity and uncertainty and I would prefer to avoid it in this context. It does not appear in s 13(2) of the 1981 Act and counsel for the appellants expressly disclaimed any submission that it should be read into the subsection by a process of implication.

In answer to counsel's submissions as to 'special rules', I summarise my conclusions thus. First, I do not accept that any special rules beyond the ordinary *Wednesbury/Ashbridge* rules fall to be applied when the court is considering a challenge to the Secretary of State's confirmation of a compulsory purchase order. Second, however, the Secretary of State, as counsel on his behalf accepted and submitted, must be satisfied that the compulsory purchase order is justified on its merits before he can properly confirm it.

He must not exercise his powers capriciously. Given the obvious importance and value
_a_ to land owners of their property rights, the abrogation of those rights in the exercise of
his discretionary power to confirm a compulsory purchase order would, in the absence
of what he perceived to be a sufficient justification on the merits, be a course which
surely no reasonable Secretary of State would take.

I think that this approach to the matter reconciles the judgments in _Prest v Secretary of_
State for Wales with the ordinary principles of our law applicable to claims for judicial
_b_ review. Furthermore, it has the merit of avoiding any reference to onus of proof, which
is an expression more appropriate, as counsel for the Secretary of State pointed out, to a
lis inter partes. As Lord Denning MR observed in _Prest_ itself, the Secretary of State's
decision certainly is not a lis inter partes. As he said (81 LGR 193 at 200):

> 'It is a public inquiry—at which the acquiring authority and the objectors are
_c_ > present and put forward their cases—but there is an unseen party who is vitally
> interested and is not represented. It is the public at large. It is the duty of the
> Secretary of State to have regard to the public interest.'

In making his decision, there are a multitude of different factors which the Secretary of
State has to take into account. To mention only a few: questions of landscape and other
amenity, feasibility, cost and delay. To talk of questions of onus of proof when so many
_d_ competing factors have to be taken into the balance seems to me not only inappropriate
but a somewhat difficult concept.

While, in response to the invitation of all counsel, I have thought it right to state fully
my understanding of the principles which fall to be applied by the court in this class of
case, I believe that ultimately, on the particular facts of this appeal, the question which
we will have to decide will be quite a short one, depending on the construction of one
_e_ sentence in the inspector's letter of decision. I will explain why later in this judgment.
Meantime, I revert to the facts.

The inquiry was held in April and June 1986 before an inspector. At the inquiry, as
the inspector recorded in para 177 of his report, there was no objection in principle to
the need for the southern bypass of Leighton Linslade and all the evidence supported the
_f_ need both to relieve traffic in Leighton Linslade and neighbouring villages and to
improve access to the industrial area of the town. The appellants, however, objected to
the proposed route for the bypass and the order affecting their own land. They put
forward four alternative schemes which they said were better on engineering, agricultural
and environmental grounds. All four were on land which they owned and offered to sell
to the council at a valuation. By inference they accepted that some of their land would
be needed for the making of a new bypass. The question was what land and what scheme
_g_ were the appropriate ones.

The four schemes are to be found summarised in para 70 of the inspector's report
where he referred to them as options 2B, 3B, 4B and 5B. In para 69 of his report he had
referred to a submission made on behalf of the appellants that the onus of proof was on
the acquiring authority to show there were compelling reasons for compulsory purchase
_h_ of land which belonged to them other than that which they had offered to sell. In para
90 the inspector recorded the acceptance by the council that it was their responsibility to
show that the order route was superior to other proposals on the balance of factors
involved.

The inspector gave a very full and very careful report. Having summarised the parties'
respective submissions, in paras 120 to 175 he set out his findings of fact. Then in the
_j_ remaining paragraphs he set out his conclusions. In paras 185 to 197 he dealt very fully
with the appellants' four alternative schemes. In para 185 he said that the route across
the land owned by the appellants had been considered in considerable depth, since the
objectors' alternative proposals were presented in some detail with the evidence of a
number of expert witnesses. He recorded that option 2B was stated to be the preferred
option, but in presentation and evidence option 3B was given more prominence. Then,

after further observations on these alternative schemes, he stated his ultimate conclusions
as to options 2B and 4B in para 191, where he stated his firm conclusion that they should   *a*
be rejected on grounds of extra cost, the unsuitability of a proposed grade separated
junction as a permanent junction and doubts about its design suitability and because of
landscape disadvantages. Similarly, in para 193 he rejected option 5B on the ground of
cost; and in paras 194–195 he rejected option 3B on the grounds both of extra cost and of
substantial delay, pointing out that the council's scheme was one which virtually had
universal approval and support. He clearly regarded delay as being a very significant   *b*
factor. In para 196 he summarised his conclusions in regard to the alternative proposals
thus:

> 'I am of the opinion that there are no factors, including the offer to sell alternative
> land at Ascott Farm, which individually or together outweigh the disadvantages of
> extra cost and exceptional delay which would result from the adoption of the
> objectors' alternative route and I believe that the Bedfordshire County Council has   *c*
> shown unequivocally that the Order route is the best in the public interest under
> the circumstances.'

Counsel for the appellants, as I understood him, submitted, inter alia, that this para
196, when properly read, did not amount to a finding by the inspector that the
disadvantages of extra cost and delay positively outweighed the advantages of the   *d*
appellants' alternatives. Reading para 196 in conjunction with the earlier paragraphs to
which I have referred, I have no hesitation in rejecting this particular submission. I do
not think it indicates any misdirection on his part. However, as counsel for the appellants
correctly pointed out, it is the Secretary of State's decision as recorded in his letter and not
that of the inspector which is under challenge on this appeal.

The inspector in due course submitted his report to the Secretary of State,   *e*
recommending that the compulsory purchase order, together with certain other orders
of the same nature, should be confirmed. By a letter of 26 November 1986 the Secretary
of State gave his decision to confirm the order. In para 14 he summarised the effect of
the inspector's report as follows:

> 'Having considered the four alternative options of [the appellants'] the Inspector   *f*
> believes that the Council's route and the alternatives are comparable in environmental
> terms and marginally in the objectors' favour if there were a railway underbridge.
> Considering the alignment between the A418 and the railway line on its own, the
> Inspector says the agricultural advantage probably lies with the objectors' route since
> it uses pasture rather than arable land, but in engineering terms, there is a little
> more certainty that the Council's alignment is more soundly based. The Inspector   *g*
> does not believe there is much to choose between the locations for the bypass
> junction on the A418 but says that a grade separated junction would take more land,
> cost extra, does not appear to be justified in traffic terms and the proposed design is
> open to question. For these reasons he does not believe a grade separated junction
> should be pursued, and says the junction with the A418 should be a roundabout.
> The Inspector considers, given that the access to the northern part of Mentmore   *h*
> Road is not required, the only advantage of an underbridge for the railway crossing
> is from a landscaping point of view and while he accepts the proposed embankment
> and bridge would be more visible he does not consider that, with the proposed
> landscaping, they would detract unacceptably from the existing landscape. The
> Inspector believes the costs and potential delay outweigh the environmental
> advantages of an underbridge compared with the proposed overbridge and believes   *j*
> it would be preferable to maintain the published vertical alignment of the bypass
> between the canal and the A4146. On the assumption that the bypass junction with
> the A418 is a roundabout, and allowing for differences in estimates, the Inspector
> notes that the railway underbridge and overbridge on the objectors' alignment

a would cost extra,, in terms of money and delay. The Inspector is of the opinion that there are no factors which individually or together outweigh the disadvantages of extra cost and delay which would result from the adoption of the objectors' alternative route. He believes the County Council has shown unequivocally that the Order route is the best in the public interest under the circumstances.'

b Counsel for the appellants accepted that this was a full and fair summary of the reasons given by the inspector for his recommendation in regard to the route of the proposed bypass. It is, I think, quite clear that the Secretary of State had fully understood and digested the effect of what the inspector had found and recommended in this context.

In para 16 the Secretary of State said:

c 'The Inspector notes that there was no objection in principle to the need for a bypass and all the evidence supports that need. He says the Council's scheme has been carefully worked out and in paying due regard to environmental and agricultural circumstances it achieves a reasonable balance between all the factors involved. The Inspector concludes that the objections to the Orders cannot be supported and recommends that the Orders and bridge scheme should be confirmed, with minor amendments to the Side Roads Order.'

d There then followed in the Secretary of State's letter a section headed 'SECRETARY OF STATE'S DECISION', of which the first paragraph, para 17, read as follows:

e 'The Secretary of State has carefully considered the report and recommendations of the Inspector together with all matters raised by the objectors both at the Public Inquiries and in writing. He notes that the need for the bypass to relieve traffic in Leighton Linslade and neighbouring villages and to improve access to the industrial area of the town is not in dispute, and that there is a large measure of support from the public both for the bypass and for work to start on it as soon as possible. From the evidence the Secretary of State does not believe that any of the suggested alternatives has sufficient advantages or benefits which would justify its adoption in place of the scheme as proposed by the County Council.'

f It is the effect of the last sentence of this paragraph, which I will call 'the crucial sentence', on which ultimately the whole of this appeal turns.

The only other paragraph of the Secretary of State's letter to which I need refer is para 20, which began with the words: 'Accordingly, the Secretary of State agrees with the Inspector's conclusions and recommendations . . .' He went on to express his decision to confirm the three compulsory purchase orders under consideration.

g A notice of motion was issued by the appellants on 29 December 1986 challenging the Secretary of State's decision. In its original form the notice was, or may have been, defective for reasons explained at the end of the judge's judgment. However, the judge permitted an amendment of it and, by its amended form, the notice of motion sought an order that the relevant orders and scheme made by the council be quashed on the grounds that the decision of the Secretary of State contained in the letter of 26 November confirming the compulsory purchase order was not 'within the powers of the said Acts' in that:

h

j 'In concluding in paragraph 17 of his said letter that: "from the evidence the Secretary of State does not believe that any of the suggested alternatives has sufficient advantages or benefits which would justify its adoption in place of the scheme as proposed by the County Council", the First Respondent applied a test which is wrong in law. The question was not whether the Applicants' alternative alignment for the proposed road had advantages or benefits when compared with the scheme proposed by the Second Respondent but whether the advantages or benefits of the latter so outweighed those of the former that there was a "compelling" or "decisive"

case for compulsory acquisition of land in the public interest, any reasonable doubt
on the matter being reseolved in favour of the Applicants.'   *a*

In a variety of attractive guises this is substantially the point which counsel for the
appellants have urged on us in support of this appeal. For reasons which I have already
explained, I do not think that any special rules fall to be applied by us beyond the
Wednesbury/Ashbridge rules when the court is considering a challenge to the confirmation
by the Secretary of State of a compulsory purchase order. However, I have also already   *b*
accepted that, given the draconian nature of such an order, no reasonable Secretary of
State would be likely to confirm such an order in the absence of what he perceived to be
a sufficient justification of his decision on its merits.

Now, on the facts of the present case, counsel for the appellants have accepted, as was
accepted on behalf of the appellants at the inquiry, that a southern bypass to the town of
Leighton Linslade is required in the public interest. They have further accepted that, if   *c*
such a bypass is to be constructed at all, part of it must inevitably pass over *some* part of
the appellants' land. If, therefore, the Secretary of State had explicitly said that he
considered that the route proposed by the council was better than those proposed by the
appellants under options 2B, 3B, 4B or 5B, I do not believe that this appeal could have got
off the ground, or indeed that it would have been brought. However, in the crucial
sentence in para 17 of his decision letter quoted above, the Secretary of State did not say   *d*
this in terms. He merely said that he did not believe that any of the suggested alternatives
had sufficient advantages or benefits which would justify its adoption in place of the
schemes proposed by the council.

I would accept that, if the ultimate conclusion of the Secretary of State as expressed in
his letter, when properly read as a whole, was merely that, after taking all the
circumstances into account, the appellants had not shown that any of their schemes were   *e*
better than the council's scheme, his decision would be impeachable on *Wednesbury*
grounds. For it seems to me that no reasonable Secretary of State would confirm a
compulsory purchase order, imposing a purchase on an unwilling landowner, if that
same landowner was willing to sell to the acquiring authority land which would be seen
to serve equally well for the same purpose after all relevant considerations, including, of
course, cost and delay, have been taken into account. This is essentially the way in which   *f*
counsel for the appellants has invited us to read the crucial sentence in the Secretary of
State's letter. This is why earlier in this judgment I have described the issue on this appeal
as ultimately depending on a short question of construction.

However, I, for my part, cannot accept counsel's construction of this sentence. If the
crucial sentence in para 17 were wrenched out of its context and read in isolation, I
suppose it might be understood as indicating the Secretary of State's view that the onus   *g*
was on the appellants to show that their alternative schemes, or any of them, had positive
advantages over the routes proposed in the order and that the appellants had failed to
discharge this onus. However, in my judgment, the crucial sentence cannot properly be
read in isolation and out of its context; and, when read in its context, it does not bear this
meaning.

In para 17 of his letter the Secretary of State was clearly echoing and indorsing in   *h*
abbreviated form the report and recommendations of the inspector which he had already
fully and fairly summarised in para 14. In particular there can be no doubt that in the
crucial sentence the Secretary of State was echoing and indorsing, at the very least, the
inspector's conclusion that 'there are no factors which individually or together outweigh
the disadvantages of extra cost and delay which would result from the adoption of the
objectors' alternative route'. At the very least, therefore, the Secretary of State was saying   *j*
that the suggested alternatives were no better than the council's route. He quite clearly
had in mind the factors of delay and expense which had weighed so heavily with the
inspector. However, the submission is that the Secretary of State by his letter was not
going so far as to indorse or accept the inspector's conclusion that the council had
affirmatively shown that the order route was the best route, simply because, in the crucial

sentence in para 17, he did not expressly echo the words of para 196 of the inspector's
a report stating what the council had 'unequivocally' shown.

In my judgment, it could not be right to analyse and pick to pieces each sentence of
the Secretary of State's letter as if it were a subsection in a taxing statute. To accept the
appellants' submission would, in my judgment, involve an altogether too analytical,
indeed I would say perverse, construction of the language by which the Secretary of State
expressed himself, when his letter is read as a whole. In para 14 he fully and fairly
b summarised the inspector's conclusions, including his crucial final conclusion that the
council had shown 'unequivocally' that the order route was the best in the public interest.
In the last sentence of para 16, which led in to para 17, he referred to the inspector's
conclusion that the objections to the order could not be supported. On a fair reading of
the letter as a whole, it is in my opinion clear that the Secretary of State was intending to
indorse the whole of the inspector's conclusions. And, indeed, in para 20 he stated
c without qualification that he agreed with the inspector's conclusions.

Counsel for the appellants submitted that para 20 of the decision letter was of no
assistance to the Secretary of State's argument, essentially on the grounds that the
inspector himself had proceeded under an error of law as regards the burden of proof,
similar to that which he had attributed to the Secretary of State. I have already stated in
my view that the inspector did not misdirect himself in any respect.

d Some reliance was placed on the phrase used by Lord Denning MR in *Prest v Secretary
of State for Wales* (1982) 81 LGR 193 at 198 that no citizen is to be deprived of his land by
any public authority against his will unless the public interest 'decisively so demands'. As
I read the inspector's report and the Secretary of State's decision, both of them considered
that the public interest did decisively so demand. The bypass was needed. *Some* land of
the appellants had to be acquired for the purpose. They both took the view that the
e council had shown unequivocally that the order route was better in the public interest
than any of the alternative routes over other land of the appellants which they had
proposed.

For the reasons which I have stated, the alleged error of law on the part of the Secretary
of State has not, in my judgment, been substantiated and I agree with the judge that
there are no grounds for challenging his decision. I would accordingly dismiss this
f appeal.

CROOM-JOHNSON LJ. I agree. I have prepared a judgment which I was intending
to give, but the matters in it have so comprehensively been covered by Slade LJ in his
judgment that there is no purpose in my going over the same ground again.

g I would like to add only one very short matter and it is this. In the suggestion that in
what is a special rule in compulsory purchase order cases there has to be some form of
discharge of an onus of proof, I entirely agree that the form of the inquiry and the form
of the decision which has to be taken by the Secretary of State is hardly appropriate for
the discharge of a burden of proof in such a form. At the end what the minister has to do
is to investigate all the facts, the arguments and so forth and ultimately perform a
h balancing exercise. At the end he has to balance things against each other which are not
at all compatible; they are not like each other and cannot be the subject of direct
comparison.

In various cases, though not necessarily in this one, he may have to balance, for
example, the effect on traffic flow, the requirement of the road in particular form and in
a particular place, the question whether it is arable or pasture land which is being taken
j in the course of the compulsory purchase order, the effect on amenity and the
environment and, of course, very importantly, the question of cost and the question of
the time factor which has to be regarded in the carrying out of the work. In the end he
comes out with what must be a value judgment that to confirm the order is justified in
the public interest, and in my view it is not right to turn this value judgment into a legal
formula.

The law was very succinctly stated by Watkins LJ in *Prest v Secretary of State for Wales* (1982) 81 LGR 193 at 211:

> 'The use of statutory authority for the destruction of those rights requires to be most carefully scrutinised. The courts must be vigilant to see to it that that authority is not abused. It must not be used unless it is clear that the Secretary of State has allowed those rights to be violated by a decision based upon the right legal principles, adequate evidence and proper consideration of the factor which sways his mind into confirmation of the order sought.'

It is true that that passage follows immediately on another passage in which Watkins LJ dealt with the seriousness of taking a man's land against his will; but that was the context in which the later passage came, and in my view there is no such special rule as has been urged on us by counsel for the appellants in compulsory purchase order cases.

I would like to add I entirely agree also with the construction which has been put on the Secretary of State's letter by Slade LJ and I would agree that the appeal should be dismissed.

RALPH GIBSON LJ. I agree that this appeal should be dismissed for the reasons given by Slade LJ in his judgment.

Appeal dismissed. Leave to appeal to the House of Lords refused.

Solicitors: *Horwood & James*, Aylesbury (for the appellants); *Treasury Solicitor*; R C *Wilkinson*, Bedford (for the council).

Celia Fox.   Barrister.

Gatewhite Ltd and another v Iberia Lineas Aereas de España SA

QUEEN'S BENCH DIVISION (COMMERCIAL COURT)
GATEHOUSE J
18, 24 MARCH, 3 MAY, 29 JULY 1988

Considered in Sidhu v British Airways plc
[1997] 1 All ER 193

Carriage by air – Carriage of goods – International carriage – Right of action – Goods damaged in transit – Owner of goods not named as consignor or consignee in air waybill – Owner of goods named as party to be notified – Whether right of action dependent on plaintiff being a party to contract of carriage as consignor or consignee – Whether owner of goods entitled to sue for damages – Carriage by Air Act 1961, Sch 1, arts 24(1), 30(3).

The purpose of arts 24(1)[a] and 30(3)[b] of Sch 1 to the Carriage by Air Act 1961, which confer on the consignor and consignee named in the air waybill evidencing the contract of carriage a right of action against an international air carrier, is not to deprive the owner of goods damaged in transit of his common law right to sue the carrier but to enable a party to the contract with no proprietary interest in the goods, such as the owner's customs clearing agent or a forwarding agent, to maintain an action against the carrier. Accordingly, an owner who was neither the consignor nor the consignee of goods which were damaged in transit has a right of action against the carrier, particularly where his name appears on the air waybill as the party to be notified, which should put the carrier

---

a   Article 24(1) is set out at p 947 j, post.

b   Article 30(3), so far as material, provides: 'As regards . . . cargo, the . . . consignor will have a right of action against the first carrier, and the . . . consignee who is entitled to delivery will have a right of action against the last carrier, and further, each may take action against the carrier who performed the carriage during which the destruction, loss, damage, or delay took place. These carriers will be jointly and severally liable . . . to the consignor or consignee.'

a   on notice that the owner is the party with an interest in the goods as opposed to one of
the parties to the contract of carriage (see p 950 d to g, post).

Parke Davis & Co v British Overseas Airways Corp (1958) 170 NYS 2d 385 and Tasman
Pulp and Paper Co Ltd v Brambles J B O'Loghlen Ltd [1981] 2 NZLR 225 applied.

Manhattan Novelty Corp v Seaboard and Western Airlines Inc (1957) 5 Avi Cas 17229,
Holzer Watch Co Inc v Seaboard and Western Airlines Inc (1957) 5 Avi Cas 17854 and Pilgrim
Apparel Inc v National Union Fire Insurance Co (1959) 6 Avi Cas 17733 not followed.

b

Notes

For actions against an international air carrier for loss of or damage to goods, see 2
Halsbury's Laws (4th edn) paras 1379, 1383.

For the Carriage by Air Act 1961, Sch 1, see 4 Halsbury's Statutes (4th edn) 28.

As from a day to be appointed arts 24 and 30 of Sch 1 to the 1961 Act are to be replaced
c   by arts 24 and 30 of Sch 1 to the Carriage by Air and Road Act 1979.

Cases referred to in judgment

Bart v British West Indian Airways Ltd [1967] 1 Lloyd's Rep 239, Guyana CA.
Cordial Manufacturing Co Ltd v Hong Kong–America Air Transport [1976] HKLR 555, Hong
Kong HC.
d   Corocraft Ltd v Pan American Airways Inc [1969] 1 All ER 82, [1969] 1 QB 616, [1968] 3
WLR 1273, CA.
El Al Israel Airlines Ltd v Oram Electrical Industries Ltd (1974) IATA ACLR No 468, Tel
Aviv Ct.
Foscolo Mango & Co Ltd v Stag Line [1932] AC 328, [1931] All ER Rep 666, HL.
Holzer Watch Co Inc v Seaboard and Western Airlines Inc (1957) 5 Avi Cas 17854, NY City
e   Ct.
Manhattan Novelty Corp v Seaboard and Western Airlines Inc (1957) 5 Avi Cas 17229, NY
SC.
Pan American World Airways Inc v SA Fire and Accident Insurance Co Ltd 1965 (3) SA 150,
SA SC (App Div).
f   Parke Davis & Co v British Overseas Airways Corp (1958) 170 NYS 2d 385, NY City Ct.
Pilgrim Apparel Inc v National Union Fire Insurance Co (1959) 6 Avi Cas 17733, NY City Ct.
Scruttons v Midland Silicones Ltd [1962] 1 All ER 1, [1961] AC 446, [1962] 2 WLR 186,
HL.
Tasman Pulp and Paper Co Ltd v Brambles J B O'Loghlen Ltd [1981] 2 NZLR 225, NZ HC.

g   **Action**

The first plaintiff, Gatewhite Ltd, issued a writ on 14 December 1987 against the
defendant, Iberia Lineas Aereas de España SA, who had contracted to transport by air a
consignment of chrysanthemums owned by the plaintiff from Las Palmas, Gran Canaria
to London via Madrid on 27 and 28 February 1987, claiming, inter alia, damages of
£17,000 for the total loss of the flowers which had perished as a result of an unaccountable
h   delay in transportation, that amount being the sound arrived market value of the flowers
in London. The second plaintiff, Cultivos de Primor SA, the grower of the flowers, took
no part in the action. The action was heard in chambers but judgment was given by
Gatehouse J in open court. The facts are set out in the judgment.

Geoffrey Kinley for the plaintiff.
j   Simon Browne-Wilkinson for the defendant.

Cur adv vult

29 July. The following judgment was delivered.

GATEHOUSE J. At all material times the first plaintiff, who is an English wholesaler,
was the owner of a consignment of chrysanthemums which was carried by the defendant
from Las Palmas airport via Madrid to Heathrow.

The second plaintiff, who has taken no part in this summons, was the grower of the flowers in Grand Canary. It is not in dispute that ownership passed from the second *a* plaintiff to the first plaintiff on delivery of the consignment to the defendant and that in the course of discharging a running account between the two plaintiffs, who have been doing regular business with each other, the second plaintiff has been paid for the goods.

It is also not in dispute that the goods arrived at Heathrow some four or five days late and in a damaged condition; they were in fact valueless and were destroyed. There has been no suggestion that the defendant was not responsible for the damage. The sole issue *b* before me is whether the first plaintiff is entitled to sue.

To someone brought up in the principles of English common law, the argument that the owner of goods damaged by a carrier is not entitled to sue the latter in respect of the damage is, to say the least, somewhat startling. But the defendant says that this being a case of international carrriage by air, it is governed by the Carriage by Air Act 1961 and the Warsaw Convention as amended at The Hague 1955 which is contained in Sch 1 to *c* the Act, and that under the convention, only the consignor or the consignee has a right of action against the carrier. The first plaintiff was not the consignor nor was it the consignee in the air waybill issued by the defendant; accordingly it has no claim.

The writ in the action was issued on 14 December 1987 and the points of claim served the following day. This matter came before the court on the plaintiffs' summons for RSC Ord 14 judgment. It was clear from an early stage that the defendant was raising this *d* substantial defence in law entitling it to unconditional leave to defend but, as both counsel were fully prepared to deal with the issue, it was sensibly agreed that the hearing of the summons should be treated as the trial of the action. I have accordingly heard full argument and, at the request of both counsel, I agreed to deliver judgment in open court. Although the issue has arisen on a number of occasions in other jurisdictions where the convention applies, this is the first occasion it has arisen for decision in our courts. *e*

To deal briefly with the undisputed facts, the goods were delivered to the defendant at Las Palmas airport on 27 February 1987 and an air waybill of that date was issued by it. The shipper was the second plaintiff. The goods were described as chrysanthemums, Canary Island produce, 'per' which presumably indicates perishable. The carriage was to be by successive Iberian Airways flights, to Madrid on 27 February and on to London on *f* 28 February. The consignees were named as Perishables Transport Co Ltd, who are the first plaintiff's customs clearing agents. The first plaintiff's name appeared as the 'notify party'. Although the insured value of the goods was stated as 1·5m pesetas (the price at which the shippers had sold to the first plaintiff) no value was inserted in the box entitled 'Declared value for Carriage' and the claim was based on the sound arrived market value on the relevant date, namely £17,000. The goods were unaccountably delayed, arriving *g* in two lots on 2 and 3 March and on survey were found to have been damaged or to have deteriorated through heating in the course of transit to such an extent as to be valueless.

Before reviewing the various decisions in other jurisdictions, I turn to the 1961 Act and the convention itself. Section 1(1) of the 1961 Act, on which counsel for the first plaintiff naturally placed much emphasis, provides that—

> 'Subject to this section, the provisions of the Convention known as "The Warsaw *h* Convention as amended at The Hague, 1955" . . . shall, so far as they relate to the rights and liabilities of carriers, carriers' servants and agents, passengers, consignors, consignees and other persons . . .'

have the force of law in the United Kingdom in relation to international air carriage. Counsel points, of course, to the addition of the words 'and other persons' after the *j* specific words 'consignors, consignees'. I need not refer to any of the other sections of the Act and I go at once to the convention set out in Sch 1. It is divided into five chapters, but only Chs II and III require any detailed consideration.

Chapter II is headed 'Documents of Carriage' and is divided into three sections: s 1 dealing with the passenger ticket, s 2 with the baggage check, neither of which is relevant, and s 3 with the air waybill.

The air waybill evidences the contract of carriage entered into between the consignor
a and the carrier, and arts 5 to 11 provide the procedural requirements as to the making
out and the contents of the air waybill. The only parties concerned in the production of
the document are the consignor and the carrier (although one of the three original parts
is to be marked 'for the consignee' and is to accompany the cargo). It may, however, be
relevant to note that art 10(2) provides:

b
'The consignor shall indemnify the carrier against all damage suffered by him, or
by any other person to whom the carrier is liable, by reason of the irregularity,
incorrectness or incompleteness of the particulars and statements furnished by the
consignor.'

So the convention does not in terms limit the carrier's liability, as a result of some defect
in the information furnished by the consignor, to the consignee alone. Damages suffered
c by the owner of the goods would therefore appear to fall within the words 'any other
person to whom the carrier is liable' and thus be included within the indemnity.

Article 12 is of importance because it has been relied on by other courts concerned
with the present issue. It gives to the consignor a right of disposal up to the moment
when the consignee's right begins under art 13. Article 12 is concerned solely with the
right of disposal; it has nothing to do with any right of action against the carrier for loss
d of or damage to the goods. The carrier's liability in this latter respect is dealt with in the
next chapter headed 'Liability of the Carrier' and, in the case of cargo, arts 18 and 19,
subject to the qualifications contained in the remaining articles in Ch III.

Article 13(1) and (2) give rights to the consignee to require delivery of the cargo to
him, provided the consignor has not exercised or resumed his right of disposal under
art 12.

e
Article 13(3) seems somewhat anomalous in its context. All the preceding paragraphs
of arts 12 and 13 are limited to dealing with the consignor's right of disposal, and
thereafter the consignee's right to delivery, of the cargo. Yet art 13(3) provides that in the
two specified events 'the consignee is entitled to put into force against the carrier the
rights which flow from the contract of carriage'. This wide form of wording appears to
refer to all rights, including rights of action for loss of or damage to the cargo. But the
f latter rights would be quite out of place in Ch II and in my view the framers of the
convention intended that art 13(3) should be limited to enforcing the rights given to the
consignee by the preceding paragraphs of the article.

If that is right art 14 is likewise limited. I mention the point at this stage because some
of the reported decisions holding that only the consignor and consignee are entitled to
sue the carrier for damage to cargo are based in part on the provisions of arts 12, 13 and
g 14. In my respectful view, the authority of those decisions is to that extent weakened.

Article 15(2) provides for variation of the provisions of the three preceding arts by
means of express provision in the air waybill. Article 15(3) was added by amendment as
a result of the Hague Protocol in 1955. The plaintiff relies strongly on this provision
permitting the issue of negotiable air waybills as indicating that the carrier must
h contemplate that ownership of cargo may change in the course of the contract of carriage
and may thus become vested in persons of whose identity he is unaware.

Chapter III is the self-contained part of the convention dealing with the liability of the
carrier for (i) death or personal injury suffered by a passenger (art 17), (ii) damages arising
out of the destruction or loss of or damage to baggage or cargo (art 18). Article 19 imposes
liability on the carrier for damage caused by delay. Articles 20 to 23 provide qualifications
j and limitations to the carrier's liability.

Article 24 is important. By para (1) it provides: 'In the case covered by Articles 18 and
19 any action for damages, however founded, can only be brought subject to the
conditions and limits set out in this Convention.' By contrast para (2) provides:

'In the cases covered by Article 17 the provisions of the preceding paragraph also
apply, without prejudice to the questions as to who are the persons who have the
right to bring suit and what are their respective rights.'

The defendant naturally relies on these provisions as a clear indication that whereas, in the case of death or personal injury, the category of possible plaintiffs is not limited, in cases of loss of or damage to cargo the conditions and limits set out in the convention do restrict the possible plaintiffs to (in the defendant's contention) the parties named as parties to the contract of carriage, ie consignor and consignee alone.

The last article I need refer to is art 30, dealing with carriage performed by successive carriers. Its third paragraph confers rights of action, in the case of cargo, on the consignor and consignee in the various circumstances set out. It does not confer rights of action on any other person. The defendant relies strongly on its limited wording in support of its contention.

In considering the construction of the convention one needs to beware of adopting too parochial an approach. Representatives of many different countries took part in its drafting, not only from common law countries but also from countries whose legal system was based on the civil law and, it may well be, countries with systems of law even less familiar to English lawyers.

Having said that, it is nevertheless remarkable that nowhere does the convention expressly exclude the right of the owner of goods to sue the carrier for damage to or loss of the goods. The limitation of this right to consignor or consignee alone, for which the defendant contends, arises if at all by implication, principally, in my view, from the wording of arts 24 and 30.

I was asked by the plaintiff to look at the traveaux préparatoires which preceded the amendments of the convention agreed in 1955, and I did so despite the defendant's formal objection to my use of such an aid to construction. I have to say that I derived no assistance from this source. I was also referred to the standard textbooks, *Shawcross and Beaumount on Air Law* (3rd edn, 1966; 4th edn, 1977) and *Chitty on Contract* (25th edn, 1983), and to an interesting extract from Miller *Liability in International Air Transport* (1977) ch 14, 'The Warsaw Plaintiff'.

But principally the parties referred me to the various decisions from other jurisdictions, and to these I now turn. It is right to say that most of these are in favour of the defendants' argument limiting the right to sue to consignor or consignee alone. There are two decisions the other way, and some powerful dissenting judgments.

Taking them chronologically, the first is a decision of the New York Supreme Court in January 1957, *Manhattan Novelty Corp v Seaboard and Western Airlines Inc* 5 Avi Cas 17229 at 17230, where, in a case involving loss of cargo, Benvenga J said:

'The convention gives the right of action to the consignee (articles 12, 13, 14, 15, 30) who may sue in his own name "whether he is acting in his own interest or in the interest of another" (Article 14). These provisions are intended to be exclusive. The plaintiff has no right of action, even though he has a proprietary interest in the goods shipped and even though the consignee may have been the plaintiff's custom broker.'

This was followed by a judge of the City Court of the City of New York in September 1957 in *Holzer Watch Co Inc v Seaboard and Western Airlines Inc* 5 Avi Cas 17854. Rivers J said that he could not agree that the result reached on the authority of the *Manhattan Novelty* case was unreasonable, adding (at 17855):

'It is reasonable that the carrier be subject to suit only by those whom it knowingly dealt with, that is, by the consignor or consignee named in the air waybill. It is not unreasonable that the identities of consignor and consignee be disclosed in the air waybill and that others be not permitted to sue.'

The reports of both cases available to me are brief in the extreme, and not convincing in so far as the reasoning is based in part on arts 12 to 15 of the convention. Nor do I follow the point that it is reasonable that the carrier should only be liable to parties with whom it 'knowingly' dealt. The carrier by sea is not so protected. The cargo is the same cargo, whoever may be the owner. What magic is there in the name on an air waybill?

a   In January 1958 in *Parke Davis & Co v British Overseas Airways Corp* 170 NYS 2d 385 another judge of the City Court of the City of New York, Baer J, distinguished both those cases because, it appears, the named consignee was in each case the plaintiff's customs broker and the plaintiff's name did not appear on the air waybill. In the case before him, Baer J pointed out that after the name of the customs broker there appeared the words 'a/ c Parke Davis & Company, Detroit, Michigan'. It was also necessary, said the judge, that the 'real party in interest' (ie the plaintiff) should procure its customs broker to arrange

b   the details. The decision turned on the failure to file the claim within the time limit provided by the convention, but it does appear that the judge considered that the owner of the cargo was entitled to sue although it was not the named consignee, apparently on the ground that its name appeared on the air waybill and thus the carrier was on notice that the plaintiff was the real party in interest. Later in the short judgment, however, he appears to have regarded the plaintiff as the consignee.

c   The last of the US decisions cited to me was *Pilgrim Apparel Inc v National Union Fire Insurance Co* 6 Avi Cas 17733, another case in the City Court of the City of New York decided in November 1959. The judge followed the previous *Manhattan Novelty* and *Holzer Watch* cases in holding that only the consignor or consignee named in the air waybill was entitled to sue the carrier. Again, the reasoning is brief in the extreme and is unsatisfactory as being expressly based on arts 13, 14 and 15.

d   Turning to other jurisdictions where the issue has arisen, the next authority is a case in the Appellate Division of the Supreme Court of South Africa in 1965, *Pan American World Airways Inc v SA Fire and Accident Insurance Co Ltd* 1965 (3) SA 150. Four of the judges of appeal concurred in the view that only the consignor or consignee had a right of action under the convention. There is a strong dissenting judgment by Steyn CJ (though in fact obiter as he decided the appeal on another ground). Of the majority,

e   Ogilvie Thompson JA relied on the 'cumulative effect of the various relevant articles of the Convention' without being more precise, and added that the majority view seemed to be 'uniformly supported by the American decisions—see particularly *Parke Davis and Co. v. B.O.A.C. and Others* (1958) 170 NYS 2d 385) and *Pilgrim Apparel Inc. v. National Union Fire Insurance Co* ((1959) 6 Avi Cas 17733) . . .' (see 1965 (3) SA 150 at 167). In my view

f   the *Parke Davis* case supports the opposite conclusion and *Pilgrim Apparel* is the least satisfactory of the other three American authorities.

Holmes JA (with whom Potgieter AJA simply agreed without adding reasons) does not carry the matter further, except that he disagreed with Steyn CJ's judgment on this issue. The principal judgment dealing with the issue is clearly that of Rumpff JA (see 1965 (3) SA 150 at 176–179).

g   In 1967 the Guyana Court of Appeal divided two to one on the point in *Bart v British West Indian Airways Ltd* [1967] 1 Lloyd's Rep 239. Stoby C agreed with the dissenting judgment of Steyn CJ in the *Pan American* case. The contrary view was developed by Luckhoo JA, with whom Bollers CJ agreed without giving separate reasons.

Luckhoo JA expressed himself as 'deeply conscious of the serious and grievous consequences in restricting the rights of an affected party to have redress for a wrong by

h   raising a prohibition on a doubtful premise' but nevertheless he came to the conclusion that, despite the strong dissenting judgment of Steyn CJ in the *Pan American* case, the restrictive construction of the convention was correct (see [1967] 1 Lloyd's Rep 239 at 286–287). He relied in part on the terms of the articles in Ch II of the convention and the correlative rights and duties of the carrier, consignor and consignee; in part on arts 24 and 30, and in part on the three American decisions, *Manhattan Novelty*, *Holzer Watch*

j   and *Pilgrim Apparel*.

In 1974 the magistrate's court in Tel Aviv in *El Al Israel Airlines Ltd v Oram Electrical Industries Ltd* (1974) IATA ACLR No 468, a case involving delay in delivery, appears to have decided that the carrier was under no liability to anyone other than the consignee under art 13(2), following the reasoning in a Dutch case on art 13. But the decision seems to have turned on the particular provision of the local statute adopting the convention and replacing the carrier's liability under any other law. The report was not available.

A further decision in favour of the restrictive approach contended for by the defendants is that of Trainor J in the Hong Kong High Court in *Cordial Manufacturing Co Ltd v Hong Kong–America Air Transport Ltd* [1976] HKLR 555. Most of the judgment, so far as the convention is concerned, revolved around arts 12 to 15 and the judge found support for his view in the three American cases referred to in *Bart*, and in the majority judgments in *Bart* itself. The case carries the argument no further.

Finally, in 1981 there comes the most recent decision, that of Prichard J in the New Zealand High Court in *Tasman Pulp and Paper Co Ltd v Brambles J B O'Loghlen Ltd* [1981] 2 NZLR 225. Not only is this the latest reported decision on the point at issue, I find in it, with respect, the most convincing reasoning. Counsel for the defendant is entitled to say that its persuasive effect is lessened by the fact that the actual case before the court was merely an application by the carrier to strike out the statement of claim against it, that the decision refusing the application was therefore limited in reality to a decision that the owner of the goods had an arguable case under the convention against the carrier, and that this was not, therefore, an authority against him of much weight even as a persuasive authority.

But the fact is that the judge, while acknowledging that he was not coming to a final conclusion, clearly indicated his view that he 'took his stand' with Stoby C in *Bart's* case and Steyn CJ in the *Pan American* case (see [1981] 2 NZLR 225 at 235). Apart from a mistaken reference to art 24 of the convention, where the judge must clearly mean art 13(3), I find myself in respectful agreement with his reasoning (see [1981] 2 NZLR 225 at 231). In my view the owner of goods damaged or lost by the carrier is entitled to sue in his own name and there is nothing in the convention which deprives him of that right. As the convention does not expressly deal with the position by excluding the owner's right of action (though it could so easily have done so) the lex fori, as it seems to me, can fill the gap. While bearing in mind the need to guard against the parochial view of the common lawyer, I see no good reason why the civil lawyer's approach to the construction of the convention, based on the importance of contract, should be of overriding importance. The fact is that the convention is silent where it could easily have made simple and clear provision excluding the rights of the 'real party in interest', had that been the framers' intention.

It would be a curious and unfortunate situation if the right to sue had to depend on the ability and willingness of the consignee alone to take action against the carrier, when the consignee may be (and no doubt frequently is) merely a customs clearing agent, a forwarding agent or the buyer's bank. It would seem artificial in the extreme to require a special contract in the air waybill itself under art 15(2) to provide the goods owner with a remedy in such a normal situation.

I have also borne in mind the desirability of uniform construction of international conventions: see *Scruttons Ltd v Midland Silicones Ltd* [1962] 1 All ER 1 at 9, [1962] AC 446 at 471–472, *Foscolo Mango & Co Ltd v Stag Line* [1932] AC 328 at 350, [1931] All ER Rep 666 at 677 and *Corocraft Ltd v Pan American Airways Inc* [1969] 1 All ER 82 at 88, [1969] 1 QB 616 at 655. But it seems to me that there is already a division of opinion on the issue, to be found not only in dissenting judgments but in actual decisions.

If I am wrong in principle, nevertheless the facts of this case seem to me to bring it within the ratio of the *Parke Davis* case. The first plaintiff was the notify party named in the air waybill and there appears to me to be no real distinction between that and the added words 'a/c Parke Davis . . .' etc.

The first plaintiff is entitled to judgment for damages to be assessed.

Judgment for first plaintiff for damages to be assessed.

Solicitors: *Clyde & Co* (for the plaintiff); *Lavington Thatcher & Taylor* (for the defendant).

K Mydeen Esq   Barrister.

a
Mitsui & Co Ltd and another v Flota Mercante Grancolombiana SA The Ciudad de Pasto, The Ciudad de Neiva

COURT OF APPEAL, CIVIL DIVISION

b PURCHAS, STAUGHTON LJJ AND SIR GEORGE WALLER
19, 20 APRIL 1988

Sale of goods – Passing of property – Reservation of right of disposal – Fob contract – Payment by instalments – Bill of lading stating that goods deliverable to sellers' order – Part payment by buyers – Goods found to be damaged on discharge – Whether property passing to buyers on
c *shipment – Whether buyers having title to sue for damage – Sale of Goods Act 1979, s 19.*

The second plaintiffs, a Japanese company, agreed to buy from the sellers in Colombia cartons of prawns which were to be shipped fob by the sellers on board the defendants' ships to Japan. Under the bills of lading the goods were deliverable to the order of the sellers. Payment of 80% of the purchase price was made before shipment by a letter of
d credit. On discharge the prawns were found to be damaged and the second plaintiffs brought an action against the shipowners claiming damages. The issue arose whether the plaintiffs had title to sue, having regard to the prima facie presumption under s 19ᵃ of the Sale of Goods Act 1979 that where by the bills of lading shipped goods were deliverable to the order of the seller the seller reserved the right of disposal and the property in the goods did not pass to the buyer until the conditions imposed by the seller
e had been fulfilled. The judge held that that presumption had been displaced and that the second plaintiffs had become owners of the goods on shipment and were therefore entitled to sue in tort for such damage as had occurred while the goods were in the shipowners' custody. The shipowners appealed, contending that the second plaintiffs had no title to sue since the property in the goods only passed to them when the balance of
f 20% was paid and there was no evidence that the damage had occurred before that payment was made.

Held – Arising out of the presumption in s 19ᵃ of the 1979 Act that where by the bills of lading shipped goods were deliverable to the order of the seller the seller reserved the right of disposal and the property in the goods did not pass to the buyer until the conditions imposed by the seller had been fulfilled, it was to be presumed that where
g only part of the purchase price had been paid the condition imposed by the seller for the passing of the property in the goods was payment of the balance of the purchase price, since in the ordinary way a seller would not wish to part with the property in his goods if they were shipped overseas until he had been paid in full. On the facts, that presumption had not been displaced since the sellers took the bills of lading to their own
h order and consequently retained the property in the goods until the balance of the purchase price had been paid. Since the second plaintiffs had been unable to show that their claim failed. The appeal would therefore be allowed (see p 955 h, p 957 f g, p 958 b to d and p 960 c to g, post).

Notes
j For the passing of property and reservation of rights of disposal under a contract for the sale of goods, see 41 Halsbury's Laws (4th edn) para 926, and for cases on the subject, see 39(2) Digest (Reissue) 300–303, 2390–2404.
  For the Sale of Goods Act 1979, s 19, see 39 Halsbury's Statutes (4th edn) 124.

---

a   Section 19, so far as material, is set out at p 955 f g, post

Cases referred to in judgments

Brandt & Co v Liverpool Brazil and River Plate Steam Navigation Co Ltd [1924] 1 KB 575, **a**
   [1923] All ER Rep 656, CA.
Karberg (Arnhold) & Co v Blythe Green Jourdain & Co [1915] 2 KB 379; *affd* [1916] 1 KB
   495, CA.
Leigh & Sillavan Ltd v Aliakmon Shipping Co Ltd, The Aliakmon [1986] 2 All ER 145, [1986]
   AC 785, [1986] 2 WLR 902, HL.
Parchim, The [1918] AC 157, PC.   **b**
Smyth (Ross T) & Co Ltd v T D Bailey Son & Co [1940] 3 All ER 60, HL.
Sorfareren, The (1915) 85 LJP 121; *on appeal* (1917) 117 LT 259, PC.
Stein Forbes & Co v County Tailoring Co (1916) 115 LT 215.
Wait v Baker (1848) 2 Exch 1, 154 ER 380.

Cases also cited   **c**

Karlshamns Oljefabriker v Eastport Navigation Corp, The Elafi [1982] 1 All ER 208.
London Joint Stock Bank Ltd v British Amsterdam Maritime Agency Ltd (1910) 16 Com Cas
   102.
South African Reserve Bank v Samuel & Co Ltd (1931) 40 Ll L Rep 291, CA.

d

Appeal
The defendants, Flota Mercante Grancolombiana SA (the shipowners), appealed against
the decision of Hobhouse J ([1987] 2 Lloyd's Rep 392) on 6 April 1987 giving judgment
for the first plaintiffs, Mitsui & Co Ltd, who were the parent company of the second
plaintiffs, Colombia Fisheries Ltd, in their claim for damages against the shipowners in
respect of damage caused to a consignment of frozen prawns which had been carried on **e**
the shipowners' ships Ciudad de Pasto and Cuidad de Neiva from Colombia to Japan.
The facts are set out in the judgment of Staughton LJ.

R D Jacobs for the shipowners.
M S Howard for the plaintiffs.

f

STAUGHTON LJ (giving the first judgment at the invitation of Purchas LJ). Colombia
Fisheries Ltd, a Japanese company and the second plaintiffs in this action, operate a fleet
of trawlers, which are registered in Japan, in the Caribbean Sea. They catch prawns,
which are a popular food in Japan, particularly because prawns caught on a Japanese
vessel may not have to bear import duty. Colombia Fisheries sell the prawns to a
Colombian company, Cia Pesquera Vikingos de Colombia SA (Vikingos), who have a **g**
processing and packaging plant in Colombia. This arrangement gives some advantage to
Colombia Fisheries because it enables them to obtain a licence to fish off the Colombian
coast. After processing and packaging the goods are shipped by Vikingos to Cartagena
for carriage to Japan. They are sold back to Colombian Fisheries by Vikingos. In turn,
Colombia Fisheries sell the prawns to Mitsui & Co Ltd, another Japanese company, the **h**
parent of Colombia Fisheries and the first plaintiffs in this action. But that last sale is
expressed to take place 'upon clearance of custom declaration', in other words after the
goods have reached Japan.
      Another company, Mitsui USA, had a part to play in the resale contract between
Vikingos and Colombia Fisheries, apparently because Mitsui USA were best placed to
open a letter of credit in favour of Vikingos in the terms which the parties had agreed. **j**
But nothing turns on the intervention of Mitsui USA.
      This appeal is concerned with a parcel of 2,426 cartons of prawns that were shipped by
Vikingos on board the vessel Ciudad de Pasto on 29 August 1980 at Cartagena. Part of
the prawns had been caught by a Colombia Fisheries vessel but part had not. The Ciudad
de Pasto belonged to the defendants, who were shipowners carrying on business in

Colombia. The goods were transhipped at Buenaventura to the Ciudad de Neiva, also
a   owned by the defendants; and thence they were carried via San Francisco to Yokohama.
They were discharged there on 7 October 1980.

On discharge the prawns were found to be damaged: some heavily, some to a medium
extent and some lightly. Mitsui & Co Ltd were paid for the damage by their insurers,
who bring this action in the names of Colombia Fisheries and Mitsui & Co Ltd as
plaintiffs. The trial did not start until March 1987. One reason for that may have been
b   that the parties took three and a half years to complete the pleadings. Another may have
been that the parties and their legal advisers expected, as the judge found, that the claim
would be settled, like a very high proportion of all cargo actions started in the Commercial
Court. Indeed, one issue was whether the claim had in fact been settled. The judge held
that it had not. Hobhouse J said in his judgment ([1987] 2 Lloyd's Rep 392 at 394):

c   'The state of the evidence both oral and documentary before me at the trial can
only be described as woefully inadequate. Relevant documents had not been
preserved. The oral evidence had to rely upon the manifestly unreliable recollection
of witnesses about events which had occurred over six years before.'

The principal issue at the trial appears to have been whether the damage to the prawns,
apparently caused by lack of refrigeration, occurred while they were in the custody of
d   the shipowners, or before shipment at Cartagena. The judge found that the heavy
damage was not proved to have occurred during the voyage, but that one-third of the
light damage and of the medium damage was caused by matters for which the shipowners
were responsible during the second stage of the voyage. The cost of that came to 3·6m
yen, as opposed to the sum of 15·5m yen which the plaintiffs had claimed.

There was another issue, which is the only one that arises on this appeal. It is whether
e   the plaintiffs have title to sue, in contract or in tort. In general, there are four means by
which a claim can be made for damage to goods on board a ship. First, the shipper may
sue in contract, assuming that he has not divested himself of his rights by indorsement
of the bill of lading. Second, a consignee named in the bill of lading or an indorsee of the
bill of lading can sue in contract under s 1 of the Bills of Lading Act 1855. Third, an
implied contract can arise out of the circumstances in any particular case in which
f   delivery is taken at the port of discharge: see *Brandt & Co v Liverpool Brazil and River Plate
Steam Navigation Co Ltd* [1924] 1 KB 575, [1923] All ER Rep 656. Fourth, the person who
was owner of the goods at the time when the damage occurred can sue in tort. (I leave
out the case of a charterparty.) The House of Lords has held in *Leigh & Sillavan Ltd v
Aliakmon Shipping Co Ltd, The Aliakmon* [1986] 2 All ER 145, [1986] AC 785 that a person
who is not the owner at the time that the damage occurred can not sue in tort.
g   The plaintiffs did not seek to proceed by the first of those routes. The goods were
shipped by Vikingos and it was not alleged at the trial that they were agents of either of
the plaintiffs for that purpose. It is too late for Colombia Fisheries to suggest now, as they
do in their outline argument at any rate, that Vikingos may have been agents for
Colombia Fisheries to ship the goods.
h   As to the second route, Colombia Fisheries were not named in the bills of lading as
consignees; nor was there any evidence of an indorsement of the bills of lading to them.
Nor as to the third route, was there any evidence which might establish an implied
contract when delivery was taken at the port of discharge. So the judge held that there
was no right to sue in contract. There has been no respondent's notice contesting that
conclusion.
j   As to tort, Mitsui & Co Ltd, the first plaintiffs, only became the owners of the goods
on discharge in Japan. Again, that is not challenged by respondent's notice. However,
the judge did hold that Colombia Fisheries, the second plaintiffs, became owners of the
goods on shipment. Hence their claim succeeded in tort to the extent that the damage
was found to have occurred while the goods were in the custody of the shipowners. It is
that conclusion which alone is in issue in this appeal.

The remaining facts are very short. Colombia Fisheries agreed to buy the prawns from Vikingos. No copy of the contract is available, but the judge was able to find that it *a* contained the term fob; that conclusion is again not challenged. Payment of 80% of the price was made before shipment by means of a letter of credit which had been opened by, or at the instance of, Mitsui USA. The judge found ([1987] 2 Lloyd's Rep 392 at 400) that: 'Mitsui U.S.A. were interposed between Colombia Fisheries and Vikingos but again in each case on f.o.b. terms.' Whether or not it be strictly accurate, it is for all material purposes sufficient to treat the contract of sale as one between Colombia Fisheries and *b* Vikingos, with Mitsui USA providing the letter of credit on behalf of Colombia Fisheries.

No copy of the letter of credit is available. Apparently it provided that 80% of the price was payable 'when the goods were made available for consignment but before shipment'. It is entirely a matter of speculation whether any documents had to be presented in order to obtain that payment under the letter of credit, and whether those documents (if any) provided any security to Mitsui USA or the bank which issued the credit. For my part, I *c* find it difficult to see how they could have provided any effective security; but I may be wrong about that.

The remaining 20% of the price no doubt had to be paid somehow. There is no evidence as to how it should have been paid or was paid. I would be inclined to assume that it was payable as a second instalment of the letter of credit, against the presentation of bills of lading. But that again is speculative. What is important is that there is no *d* evidence as to *when* it was paid, whether before or after the damage to the prawns occurred on the voyage. Neither party has invited the court to consider which is more likely to have occurred first, the damage to the prawns on the voyage or the payment of the remaining 20% of the price.

The goods were shipped by Vikingos, who obtained five bills of lading. In the box marked 'Shipper/Exporter' the name of Vikingos was inserted; in that marked 'Consignee' *e* the words 'to order'. So the shipowners undertook to deliver the goods to Vikingos or to the party whom they should designate by an indorsement, general or special, of the bills of lading. There is no evidence that there were any indorsements. In the box marked 'Notify Party' there was inserted the name and address of Mitsui & Co Ltd. There is evidence that in fact Colombia Fisheries suffered no loss because they were paid in full by their buyers, Mitsui & Co Ltd. That is not relied on by counsel for the shipowners as *f* a reason why this appeal should be allowed. Indeed, it does not feature in his notice of appeal; but he desires to keep the point open in case this case goes further.

Colombia Fisheries contend that the property in the prawns passed to them on shipment. As a variant of that argument counsel on their behalf said that it passed to them no later than the date of shipment, and so advanced the possibility that this may have happened earlier, for example when the 80% was paid. Without any detailed *g* knowledge of the sale contract or of the letter of credit I can find no evidence that the property passed to Colombia Fisheries before shipment. It is not even proved that the goods agreed to be sold had been ascertained, in terms of the Sale of Goods Act 1979, before shipment. In my judgment, counsel can only argue that the property passed on shipment, the point on which Hobhouse J found in his favour.

Counsel for the shipowners argues that the property passed to Colombia Fisheries only *h* when the remaining 20% of the price was paid. As there is no evidence that this occurred before the damage, he submits that the claim in tort must fail.

The Sale of Goods Act 1979 supplies part of the answer. Section 16 provides:

'Where there is a contract for the sale of unascertained goods no property in the goods is transferred to the buyer unless and until the goods are ascertained.' *j*

There is no evidence that the goods in this case were ascertained when the contract of sale was made, or as I think at any time before shipment. But on shipment they were ascertained.

Section 17 provides:

'(1) Where there is a contract for the sale of specific or ascertained goods the property in them is transferred to the buyer at such time as the parties to the contract intend it to be transferred.

(2) For the purpose of ascertaining the intention of the parties regard shall be had to the terms of the contract, the conduct of the parties and the circumstances of the case.'

Although the contract in this case was, in all probability, for a sale of unascertained goods, it is agreed that s 17 applied once the goods had been ascertained. The court accordingly has to resolve the problem by the means set out in s 17(2).

However, various presumptions are supplied by ss 18 and 19. Section 18 begins:

'Unless a different intention appears, the following are rules for ascertaining the intention of the parties as to the time at which the property in the goods is to pass to the buyer.'

The relevant rule in this case is r 5:

'(1) Where there is a contract for the sale of unascertained or future goods by description, and goods of that description and in a deliverable state are unconditionally appropriated to the contract, either by the seller with the assent of the buyer or by the buyer with the assent of the seller, the property in the goods then passes to the buyer; and the assent may be express or implied, and may be given either before or after the appropriation is made.

(2) Where, in pursuance of the contract, the seller delivers the goods to the buyer or to a carrier or other bailee or custodier (whether named by the buyer or not) for the purpose of transmission to the buyer, and does not reserve the right of disposal, he is to be taken to have unconditionally appropriated the goods to the contract.'

In this case prima facie Vikingos did not unconditionally appropriate the goods to the contract, but reserved a right of disposal. That appears from s 19, which provides:

'(1) Where there is a contract for the sale of specific goods or where goods are subsequently appropriated to the contract, the seller may, by the terms of the contract or appropriation, reserve the right of disposal of the goods until certain conditions are fulfilled; and in such a case, notwithstanding the delivery of the goods to the buyer, or to a carrier or other bailee or custodier for the purpose of transmission to the buyer, the property in the goods does not pass to the buyer until the conditions imposed by the seller are fulfilled.

(2) Where goods are shipped, and by the bill of lading the goods are deliverable to the order of the seller or his agent, the seller is prima facie to be taken to reserve the right of disposal . . .'

Here by the bills of lading the goods were deliverable to the order of the sellers; consequently the prima facie presumption is that they reserved the right of disposal. Unless the presumption is displaced, that has the result that the property did not pass to the buyers until the condition imposed by the sellers was fulfilled. That condition was, presumably, that the balance of the price be paid.

The question then is whether that presumption is displaced. The judge, when dealing with the issue, said ([1987] 2 Lloyd's Rep 392 at 399–400):

'The clear inference is that Colombia Fisheries brought the goods on f.o.b. terms. Therefore unless there was a breach of the agreement, or some failure on the part of their sellers to perform their agreement, the title in the goods should have been passed to Colombia Fisheries at the time of shipment . . . In the present case I do not consider that I should conclude that Vikingos were intending not to perform their obligation to pass the property in the goods on shipment.'

Counsel for the plaintiffs has not sought to support the proposition that appears to
emerge from those passages in the judgment. He acknowledges that it would not be a
breach of contract for an fob seller to reserve the right of disposal when the goods are
shipped. With that concession I agree, at all events unless there is provision to the
contrary in the contract. *Benjamin's Sale of Goods* (3rd edn, 1987) para 1861 states:

> 'By section 19(2) of the Sale of Goods Act 1979, a seller is prima facie taken to
> reserve a right of disposal "where goods are shipped, and by the bill of lading the
> goods are deliverable to the order of the seller or his agent." This subsection is based
> on a number of nineteenth century cases, some of which were concerned with f.o.b.
> contracts, in which the taking of a bill of lading in this form was regarded as
> evidence of intention on the part of the seller to reserve a right of disposal. The
> suggestion that section 19(2) does not apply to an f.o.b. contract would therefore
> seem to be historically unsound. It appears to be based on the view that a seller who
> reserves a right of disposal acts "contrary to the contract" and not "in performance
> of his contract to place them [the goods] 'free on board.'" But if this view is (as has
> been submitted) incorrect, there is no good reason why section 19(2) should not be
> capable of applying to an f.o.b. contract. Under such a contract the seller is not
> bound to pass the property in the goods at any particular time. It is submitted that
> he can perfectly well ship the goods "in performance of his contract" and so perform
> his duty to deliver without simultaneously making an *unconditional* appropriation
> so as to pass the property. If this were not the case, considerable difficulties would
> arise in financing f.o.b. sales.'

See also *Wait v Baker* (1848) 2 Exch 1, 154 ER 380. That was one of the cases on which
s 19(2) appears to have been based. The expression 'fob' determines how the goods shall
be delivered, how much of the expense shall be borne by the sellers and when the risk of
loss or damage shall pass to the buyers. It does not necessarily decide when the property
is to pass.

Counsel for the plaintiffs argued that the passages which I have quoted formed no part
of the judge's reasons for deciding that the property passed on shipment. In my
judgment, they did form a significant part of his reasons. But there are other grounds on
which the judge also relied.

The intention of the parties that the property passed on shipment is, according to
counsel for the plaintiffs, to be derived from the facts that 80% of the price had been paid
and a letter of credit was available which (as I have assumed) secured payment of the
remaining 20%. In *Ross T Smyth & Co Ltd v T D Bailey Son and Co* [1940] 3 All ER 60 at 67
Lord Wright said:

> 'It is true that all these rules, both under sect. 18 and under sect. 19, are *prima facie*
> rules, and depend on intention, but the intention in this regard by the parties is
> seldom or never capable of proof. It is to be ascertained, as already stated here, by
> having regard to the terms of the contract, the conduct of the parties and the
> circumstances of the case.'

We have been referred to a number of cases in which it has been held that the property
did or did not pass on shipment, as a guide to what the intention of the parties is likely to
have been in this case.

Counsel for the shipowners relied on the *Ross T Smyth* case (which was concerned with
a cif contract), *Wait's* case, *Arnhold Karberg & Co v Blythe Green Jourdain & Co* [1915] 2 KB
379 at first instance and *Stein Forbes & Co v County Tailoring Co* (1916) 115 LT 215. While
those cases provide powerful support for the presumption in s 19 (which in any case is
statutory), in none of them had there been any prepayment of the price. Counsel for
Vikingos relied on *The Sorfareren* (1915) 85 LJP 121. There the buyers had paid half the
price in advance, but the sellers had taken a bill of lading to their own order. It was held
that the property had passed to the buyers.

Counsel for the shipowners seeks to distinguish that case on the ground that the sale
a contract there did not provide that the payment of the balance of the price would be
against presentation of the bill of lading. The balance was to be paid (see 85 LJP 121 at
126) after discharge of the goods. That, as it seems to me, would make it less likely that
the property would pass on shipment rather than more likely. So I cannot see that that is
a valid ground of distinction. But it is to be observed that Evans P did not in that case
make any mention of s 19 of the Sale of Goods Act 1893. He found that there had been
b no reservation of the right of disposal (at 125), but he reached that conclusion without, as
I have said, adverting to the presumption that s 19 provides.
     There is a comment on that case in *Benjamin* para 1863, where the editors say:

     'The decision is best explained on the ground that the sellers had shown that they
         did not intend to reserve a right of disposal; for in making their claim they had
         described themselves not as owners of the cargo, but as persons "interested in the
c   cargo to the extent of the unpaid balance."'

I can only treat that case as a decision on its own facts.
     Counsel for the plaintiffs also relied on *The Parchim* [1918] AC 157, where it was held
on other grounds that the presumption in s 19 had been rebutted and that the property
passed on shipment. One of the factors to which importance was attached by Lord Parker
d in delivering the advice of the board was that the risk of loss or damage had passed to the
buyers and that, in his Lordship's opinion, was a factor indicating that the property had
passed also (at 171). Counsel in this case acknowledges that he cannot wholeheartedly
support that reasoning. The case is again commented on in *Benjamin* para 1864, where
the editors say: 'With respect, it is submitted that this reasoning is no longer acceptable
as a general rule.' There is then a considerable discussion on the case. It is again to be
e noted that many factors were taken into account by the Privy Council in reaching its
decision which were special to that case.
     For my part, I do not find other decisions, many of them reached 70 years ago or more
when commercial conditions may well have been different, of much assistance. Nor do I
derive any help from cases which say that a seller would be unlikely to part with property
and then be content to rely on a lien; those seem to be matched by other cases where it
f was held that the sellers had done exactly that, as the judge held that Vikingos did in this
case.
     It seems to me that in the ordinary way a seller will not wish to part with the property
in his goods if they are shipped overseas until he has been paid in full. There is support
for that view again in *Benjamin* para 1484:

g   'In overseas sales, there is, therefore, a fairly strong presumption that the seller
         does not intend to part with property until he has either been paid or been given an
         adequate assurance of payment. Of course the presumption may be rebutted: for
         example, by the fact that buyer and seller are associated companies (so that the seller
         does not need security for payment) or by the fact that the contract expressly
         provides for credit.'

h
Of course, the seller may choose to give credit, but I would not readily infer that he
intended to do so. I find it difficult to draw any distinction for this purpose between a
seller who has received 80% of the price in advance and one who has received, say, 40%,
or none.
     Nor can I attach much weight to the fact that the balance of the price was (as I assume)
j payable by letter of credit. Even the most copper-bottomed letter of credit sometimes
fails to produce payment for one reason or another; and the seller who has a letter of
credit for 100% of the price will nevertheless often retain the property in his goods until
he has presented the documents and obtained payment. If only 20% is outstanding his
worries will be less, but they may not have disappeared altogether.
     One must, of course, pay attention to the position of Colombia Fisheries, since it is the

common intention of the parties which must be ascertained. They had paid 80% of the
price and would be anxious to obtain some security. But it seems to me that they had *a*
already been content to assume that risk. They had advanced the 80% as a matter of trust,
with no security so far as the evidence goes, or none that I can discern, up to the time of
shipment. I can see no very powerful argument that, between the time of shipment and
the presentation of the bills of lading under the letter of credit for payment of the
remaining 20%, they intended to acquire the property in the goods to safeguard their
advance.   *b*

Looking at the case as a whole I consider that the presumption in s 19 is not displaced.
As counsel for the shipowners observed in the course of his reply this morning, if the
parties wanted it to be displaced all they had to do was arrange that Vikingos should
insert the name of Colombia Fisheries as consignee in the bills of lading. Vikingos did
not do that. They took bills of lading to their own order and, therefore, in accordance
with the presumption they retained the property in the goods until the balance of the *c*
price was paid. It is not proved that this occurred before the goods were damaged.
Consequently the claim fails. Like the judge, I consider this a most unsatisfactory case.
But, if plaintiffs or their insurers delay until the evidence which they need is lost, they
cannot complain.

I would allow this appeal and enter judgment for the defendants.
                                                                                         d
PURCHAS LJ. I agree that this appeal should be allowed. As we are differing from a
judge with great experience in this field, however, I shall add a few words of my own.

The circumstances have already fully been set out in the judgment of Staughton LJ.
The judge was faced with a well-nigh impossible task on the evidence before him, which
he justifiably described as woefully inadequate and continued to criticise in the terms
which have already been quoted by Staughton LJ.   *e*

For the purposes of this appeal the missing documents, which were clearly of crucial
importance, included the letter of credit with the so-called 'red clause', the contractual
documents as between Vikingos and Mitsui and other evidence which would normally
be available in an action of this kind. The main evidence which was led to the contractual
aspect of the case was restricted to two statements admitted under the Civil Evidence Act *f*
1968 from persons employed respectively by each of the plaintiffs.

After a skilful and meticulous consideration of this wholly inadequate evidence, which
might well have been thought by some judges to fall short of discharging the onus of
proof placed on any plaintiff in establishing the cause of action of damage to the cargo at
all, the judge managed to draw inferences on this aspect of the case which, very properly,
have not been attacked on appeal. However, the effect of the inadequacy of the evidence
does not end there and, as the judge commented in relation to the evidence as to the   *g*
cause of damage, where evidence was wholly inadequate the impact of the burden of
proof assumed critical importance (see [1987] 2 Lloyd's Rep 392 at 394). The same can
be said when it comes to the consideration of the question where the property in the
goods lies and whether that property has passed to the buyer. Parliament has provided a
statutory, if prima facie, presumption as to how the intention of the parties as to the   *h*
passing of property should be resolved.

The relevant sections of the Sale of Goods Act 1979 have already been cited in the
judgment of Staughton LJ and it is unnecessary for me to repeat them here. The vital
section, however, is sub-s (2) of s 19 and, purely for the sake of reference, I refer to that
only:

> 'Where goods are shipped, and by the bill of lading the goods are deliverable to the *j*
> order of the seller or his agent, the seller is prima facie to be taken to reserve the
> right of disposal.'

The question which faced the judge was whether that prima facie position had been
disturbed by the inadequate evidence placed before him.

In addition, the authority of the speech of Lord Wright in *Ross T Smyth & Co Ltd v T D*
a *Bailey Son & Co* [1940] 3 All ER 60 at 67 already cited by Staughton LJ lends support to
this presumption where the seller reserves or retains for himself the right of payment by
cash against documents.

The judge approached this problem in this way ([1987] 2 Lloyd's Rep 392 at 399):

b
> 'The next issue I have to consider is the issue of title to sue. The plaintiffs have
> alleged that they have the title to sue both in tort and in contract. I will take tort
> first. This is based upon the allegation that the plaintiffs, or one or other of them,
> was the owner of the goods at all material times while they were in the care and
> custody of the defendants. The burden of proof is upon the plaintiffs to establish
> this title and the evidence which they have placed before the Court is most
> unsatisfactory. As I have already commented the material documents, or at any rate
c
> a large proportion of them, although they will have been at one time in the
> possession and power of the plaintiffs are no longer available and their case has to
> depend in substance upon two statements put in under the Civil Evidence Act.
> Despite the unsatisfactory nature of the plaintiffs' evidence I am prepared to find on
> the balance of probabilities that the title in the relevant goods passed to Colombia
> Fisheries on shipment and remained in them until after the completion of discharge
d
> at Yokohama.'

It is at this point of the judge's judgment, like Staughton LJ, that regretfully I find myself
unable to follow him in drawing that inference. I therefore direct by attention to see
where the difference has arisen. The judge said (at 399–400):

e
> 'The relevant dispute before me centered upon whether it was right to conclude
> that title had passed to Colombia Fisheries at the time of shipment at Cartagena or
> only at some later, unidentified time. The clear inference is that Colombia Fisheries
> bought the goods on f.o.b. terms. Therefore unless there was a breach of the
> agreement, or some failure on the part of their sellers to perform their agreement,
> the title in the goods should have been passed to Colombia Fisheries at the time of
> shipment.'
f

The inference which the judge has drawn from the statements before him under the
Civil Evidence Act 1968 that the goods were bought on fob terms has not been
challenged on appeal. In citing that as one of the leading inferences on which the judge
inferred that the property passed on shipment, it is difficult not to conclude that at this
point in his judgment Homer must have nodded in overlooking the fact that in an fob
g contract it is still open to the seller to reserve to himself the right of disposal of the goods
the subject matter of the contract. If it were otherwise it is unlikely that the judge would
have referred to that particular aspect of the case at that point in his judgment.

I now turn to the judgment again where reference is made to s 19(2) of the 1979 Act
(at 400):

h
> 'I was asked by the [shipowners] to infer that Vikingos had not passed the title to
> Mitsui U.S.A. on shipment because of the terms in which Vikingos took the bills of
> lading, which were to their own order. Prima facie taking bills of lading in such a
> form is an indication that the shipper wishes to reserve the right of disposal of the
> goods and not at that time to pass the property in the goods to any other person. No
> reliance before me was placed upon any difference between any foreign legal system
j
> and English law and the parties among other things referred me to the Sale of Goods
> Act and the well known passage in Lord Wright's speech in *Ross T. Smyth v. T. Bailey*
> *Son & Co.* ([1940] 3 All ER 60). However in each case it is a question of evaluating
> all the evidence of the parties' conduct including the contracts which they have
> made in order to see whether they have intended that the general property should
> not pass on shipment. In the present case I do not consider that I should conclude

that Vikingos were intending not to perform their obligation to pass the property in the goods on shipment.'

There again, with respect to the judge, he has returned to the error which, in my judgment, he made in the application of the accepted fact that the contract was on fob terms to the problem of deciding when the property in the goods should pass. He continued then to this finding, which was based on that erroneous inference:

'The correct inference is in my judgment that they were at most merely reserving a special property in order to facilitate the operation of the letter of credit mechanism for payment. Vikingos would have a lien on the bills of lading until they were paid and thereafter the bankers would have a lien. But there is no reason why the general property should not pass down the line to Colombia Fisheries. Further it would be extravagant that the general property should not pass seeing that Vikingos had already been paid 80 per cent. of the value of the goods prior to shipment and were only interested in collecting the balance of 20 per cent.'

In my judgment, there was simply no evidence from which secondary inferences could be drawn which would entitle the departure from the prima facie presumption arising from the form in which the bills of lading were drawn. The only authority to which I wish to refer, since the cases have been fully discussed by Staughton LJ and I wholly agree with his analysis of the authorities, is *The Parchim* [1918] AC 157. In that case, notwithstanding that the form of the bills of lading pointed to the opposite, their Lordships came to the conclusion that property passed on shipment. The significance of that authority, in my judgment, is not that distinction but the considerable detail into which their Lordship saw fit to go before they were prepared to depart from the prima facie presumption to be found in s 19(2).

So far as counsel for the plaintiffs' courageous attempt to take the path of avoiding the impact of s 19(2) is concerned, while accepting that the inference apparently drawn by the judge from the fact that the contract was on fob terms was not one that he was entitled to draw, I find myself in agreement with Staughton LJ that I cannot follow counsel's able and attractive submissions along that path. In particular, I adopt with gratitude the analysis that Staughton LJ has given of the point based on the so-called 'red clause', that Vikingos had already been paid 80% of the value of the goods prior to shipment. In my judgment, that is an aspect which has little or no impact on the general evidence necessary if a party is to avoid the prima facie presumption contained in s 19(2).

For those reasons and for the reasons already given by Staughton LJ I agree that this appeal should be allowed.

SIR GEORGE WALLER. I agree with both judgments that have been delivered and do not wish to add anything.

Appeal allowed.

Solicitors: *Sinclair Roche & Temperley* (for the shipowners); *Clyde & Co*, Guildford (for the plaintiffs).

Celia Fox   Barrister.

a   # Bradley v Eagle Star Insurance Co Ltd

HOUSE OF LORDS
LORD KEITH OF KINKEL, LORD BRANDON OF OAKBROOK, LORD TEMPLEMAN, LORD OLIVER OF
AYLMERTON AND LORD JAUNCEY OF TULLICHETTLE
30, 31 JANUARY, 2 MARCH 1989

b
*Insurance – Employers' liability insurance – Third party's rights against insurers – Action by
third party against insurers – Employee contracting respiratory disease through inhalation of
cotton dust in course of employment – Employee alleging disease caused by negligence of employer
company – Company insured against liability for personal injuries to employees – Company
dissolved twelve years before action brought – Amount or existence of liability of company to*
c   *employee not established before company dissolved – Whether employee entitled to indemnity from
insurers in respect of company's liability – Third Parties (Rights against Insurers) Act 1930,
s 1(1)(b).*

Between 1933 and 1970 the appellant was employed in a textile company's cotton mill
for three periods totalling 24 years. In 1970 she was certified as suffering from byssinosis,
d   a respiratory disease caused by the inhalation of cotton dust. The textile company was
voluntarily wound up in 1975 and dissolved in 1976. In 1984 the appellant decided to
bring an action against the respondent insurers under s 1(1)(b)[a] of the Third Parties
(Rights against Insurers) Act 1930 on the basis that her injuries were caused by the
negligence or breach of statutory duty of her former employer, which had insured
against those risks with the respondents during the relevant period. In order to obtain
e   the necessary material on which to found the proposed action the appellant applied in
1986 for pre-action discovery of the relevant insurance policies issued by the respondents
to the company. The district registrar made an order for disclosure but on appeal the
judge set it aside. The appellant appealed to the Court of Appeal, which dismissed her
appeal. The appellant appealed to the House of Lords.

f   **Held** (Lord Templeman dissenting) – An insured person's right of indemnity under a
policy of insurance against liability to third parties did not arise until the existence and
amount of his liability to the third party had first been established either by action,
arbitration or agreement. Accordingly, since the appellant's former employer was a
company which had been wound up and dissolved the existence and amount of the
employer's liability to the appellant had never been established while the employer
g   existed and there was now no longer any means whereby that liability could be
established; that being so, there was now no longer any right of indemnity of the
employer against the respondents in respect of any such liability which could be
transferred to and vested in the appellant under s 1(1) of the 1930 Act. Since the
appellant's proposed action against the respondents could not succeed, pre-action discovery
in support of that action could not be ordered. The appeal would therefore be dismissed
h   (see p 962 f, p 963 g to p 964 a, p 965 g h, p 966 f g, p 967 g and p 969 a b, post).
Post Office v Norwich Union Fire Insurance Society Ltd [1967] 1 All ER 577 approved.

Notes
For statutory subrogation of rights under an insurance policy, see 25 Halsbury's Laws
j   (4th edn) para 708, and for cases on the subject, see 29 Digest (Reissue) 586–590, 5167–
5184.
    For the Third Parties (Rights against Insurers) Act 1930, s 1, see 4 Halsbury's Statutes
(4th edn) 688.

a   Section 1(1) is set out at p 963 *d* to *f*, post

Cases referred to in opinions

Harrington Motor Co Ltd, Re, ex p Chaplin [1928] Ch 105, CA.

Hood's Trustees v Southern Union General Insurance Co of Australasia Ltd [1928] Ch 793, CA.

Post Office v Norwich Union Fire Insurance Society Ltd [1967] 1 All ER 577, [1967] 2 QB 363, [1967] 2 WLR 709, CA.

West Wake Price & Co v Ching [1956] 3 All ER 821, [1957] 1 WLR 45.

Appeal

Doris Bradley appealed, with the leave of the Appeal Committee of the House of Lords given on 14 July 1988, against the decision of the Court of Appeal (Purchas, Lloyd and Staughton LJJ) ([1988] 2 Lloyd's Rep 233) on 25 March 1988 dismissing her appeal against the order of Macpherson J in chambers dated 9 April 1987 allowing the appeal of the respondents, Eagle Star Insurance Co Ltd, against the order of Mr District Registrar Burton in chambers dated 30 January 1987 whereby, pursuant to RSC Ord 24, r 7A, he granted the appellant pre-action discovery of the terms and particulars of all contracts of insurance issued by the respondents to the Federation of Master Cotton Spinners Association Ltd relating to the liability of the appellant's former employer, Dart Mill Ltd, to its employees for personal injuries sustained by the employees at work during the periods 1933 to 1934, 1940 to 1946 and 1953 to 1970. The facts are set out in the opinion of Lord Brandon.

David Clarke QC and *David Allan* for the appellant.
Stephen Grime QC and *Patrick Field* for the respondents.

Their Lordships took time for consideration.

2 March. The following opinions were delivered.

LORD KEITH OF KINKEL. My Lords, I have had the opportunity of considering in draft the speech to be delivered by my noble and learned friend Lord Brandon. I agree with it, and for the reasons he gives would dismiss this appeal.

LORD BRANDON OF OAKBROOK. My Lords, the appellant, Mrs Doris Bradley, was employed by Dart Mill Ltd in the cardroom of its cotton mill at Bolton from 1933 to 1934, 1940 to 1946 and 1953 to 1970. In August 1970 she was certified by the pneumoconiosis medical panel to be suffering from byssinosis and her disability caused by it was assessed at 30%. Byssinosis is a respiratory disease caused by the inhalation of cotton dust. It is the appellant's case, first, that in the course of her employment by Dart Mill Ltd the conditions in which she worked necessarily involved her in the inhalation of substantial quantities of cotton dust, second, that the byssinosis from which she suffers was caused by such inhallation, third, that the exposure to such inhalation was caused by the negligence and breach of statutory duty of Dart Mill Ltd and, fourth, that Dart Mill Ltd was, during the periods when she was employed by that company, insured in respect of liability for personal injuries to its employees by the respondents, Eagle Star Insurance Co Ltd.

Dart Mill Ltd was voluntarily wound up in 1975 and dissolved in 1976. Under s 651 of the Companies Act 1985 the company could not be restored to the register more than two years after it was dissolved. In the result the company no longer exists and is incapable by any means of being restored to existence.

In 1984 the appellant's solicitor decided to bring an action on her behalf against the respondents under s 1(1) of the Third Parties (Rights against Insurers) Act 1930. In order to enable him to have the necessary material on which to found the action, the appellant's solicitor required to have prior discovery of the relevant insurance policies issued by the respondents to Dart Mill Ltd. Accordingly, on 26 September 1986 he applied on behalf of the appellant, under s 33(2) of the Supreme Court Act 1981 and RSC Ord 24, r 7A, in

a
the Oldham District Registry of the High Court, Queen's Bench Division, for an order
that the respondents should disclose to the appellant the terms and particulars of all
contracts of insurance issued by the respondents to Dart Mill Ltd in respect of that
company's liability to its employees for personal injuries sustained at work during the
periods 1933 to 1934, 1940 to 1946 and 1953 to 1970.

The originating summons came first before Mr District Registrar Burton, who on 30
January 1987 ordered the respondents to make substantially the disclosure applied for on
b behalf of the appellant. The respondents appealed to Macpherson J, who on 9 April 1987
allowed the appeal and set aside the order of the district registrar. Macpherson J refused
the appellant leave to appeal to the Court of Appeal, but such leave was subsequently
given by that court. On 25 March 1988 the Court of Appeal (Purchas, Lloyd and
Staughton LJJ) ([1988] 2 Lloyd's Rep 233) unanimously dismissed the appeal.

In order to understand the basis of the substantive claim which the appellant seeks to
c bring against the respondents, and the grounds on which the Court of Appeal decided
her application for pre-action discovery against her, it is necessary to refer to the relevant
provisions of the Third Parties (Rights against Insurers) Act 1930. That Act provides:

'**1.**—(1) Where under any contract of insurance a person (hereinafter referred to
as the insured) is insured against liabilities to third parties which he may incur,
d then—(a) in the event of the insured becoming bankrupt or making a composition
or arrangement with his creditors; or (b) in the case of the insured being a company,
in the event of a winding-up order being made, or a resolution for a voluntary
winding-up being passed, with respect to the company, or of a receiver or manager
of the company's business or undertaking being duly appointed, or of possession
being taken, by or on behalf of the holders of any debentures secured by a floating
e charge, of any property comprised in or subject to the charge; if, either before or
after that event, any such liability as aforesaid is incurred by the insured, his rights
against the insurer under the contract in respect of the liability shall, notwithstanding
anything in any Act or rule of law to the contrary, be transferred to and vest in the
third party to whom the liability was so incurred.

(2) Where an order is made under section one hundred and thirty of the
f Bankruptcy Act, 1914, for the administration of the estate of a deceased debtor
according to the law of bankruptcy, then, if any debt provable in bankruptcy is
owing by the deceased in respect of a liability against which he was insured under a
contract of insurance as being a liability to a third party, the deceased debtor's rights
against the insurer under the contract in respect of that liability shall, notwithstanding
anything in the said Act, be transferred to and vest in the person to whom the debt
g is owing . . .'

The grounds on which the Court of Appeal decided against the appellant on her
application for pre-action discovery can be stated as follows. First, under s 1(1) of the
1930 Act the appellant only had transferred to and vested in her such rights against the
respondents as Dart Mill Ltd itself would have had under the relevant contracts of
h insurance. Second, Dart Mill Ltd would only have been entitled, under such contracts of
insurance, to be indemnified by the respondents in respect of any liability incurred by it
to the appellant if the existence and amount of that liability had first been established
either by a judgment of a court, or by an award in an arbitration, or by an agreement
between Dart Mill Ltd and the appellant. Third, the existence and amount of any liability
incurred by Dart Mill Ltd to the appellant had never been established in any of those
j three ways while Dart Mill Ltd existed or was capable of being restored to existence, and
there was now therefore no longer any means by which the existence and amount of any
such liability could be established. Fourth, that being so, there was not, and could not
now ever be, any right of indemnity of Dart Mill Ltd against the respondents in respect
of any such liability which could be transferred to and vested in the appellant under
s 1(1) of the 1930 Act. Fifth, that being so, the appellant's proposed action against the

respondents could not succeed, and it would therefore serve no useful purpose to make the order for pre-action discovery sought by her.

The Court of Appeal, rightly in my view, considered itself bound to reach the conclusion which it did by an earlier decision of that court in *Post Office v Norwich Union Fire Insurance Society Ltd* [1967] 1 All ER 577, [1967] 2 QB 363. It follows that this appeal requires your Lordships to consider whether that earlier case was rightly decided.

The facts in the *Post Office* case, as they appear mainly from the headnote of the report ([1967] 2 QB 363), were these. In May 1963 a company of contractors called Potters damaged a Post Office cable. The Post Office by letter claimed £839 10s 3d for its repair. The contractors denied liability. Before any proceedings had been begun to determine liability and quantum, the contractors in June 1964 went into compulsory liquidation. The contractors were insured under a public liability policy in the usual terms which provided that the insurers 'will indemnify the insured against all sums which the insured shall become legally liable to pay ... in respect of ... damage to property'. On 17 June 1965 the Post Office issued a writ against the contractors' insurance company claiming that under s 1 of the 1930 Act they were entitled, once the contractors had gone into liquidation, to claim against the insurance company direct the sum of £839 10s 3d. The trial judge gave judgment for the Post Office, against which the insurers appealed to the Court of Appeal (Lord Denning MR, Harman and Salmon LJJ).

That court allowed the appeal and dismissed the Post Office's claim on two grounds. The first ground, which was unanimous, turned on a particular condition of the contract of insurance, to which it is not necessary to refer futher. The second ground, which was relied on by Lord Denning MR and Salmon LJ but not by Harman LJ, was that the contractors could not have claimed to be indemnified by the insurance company until the existence and amount of their liability to the Post Office had been properly established, and the Post Office could not be in any better position as against the insurance company in this respect than the contractors.

Referring to s 1(1) of the 1930 Act, Lord Denning MR said ([1967] 1 All ER 577 at 579–580, [1967] 2 QB 363 at 373–374):

'Under that section the injured person steps into the shoes of the wrongdoer. There are transferred to him the wrongdoer's "rights against the insurers under the contract". What are those rights? When do they arise? So far as the "liability" of the insured is concerned, there is no doubt that his liability to the injured person arises at the time of the accident, when negligence and damage coincide; but the "rights" of the insured person against the insurers do not arise at that time. The policy in the present case provides that "the [defendants] will indemnify the insured against all sums which the insured shall become legally liable to pay as compensation in respect of loss of or damage to property." It seems to me that [Potters] acquire only a right to sue for the money when their liability to the injured person has been established so as to give rise to a right of indemnity. Their liability to the injured person must be ascertained and determined to exist, either by judgment of the court or by an award in arbitration or by agreement. Until that is done, the right to an indemnity does not arise. I agree with the statement by DEVLIN, J., in *West Wake Price & Co.* v. *Ching* ([1956] 3 All ER 821 at 825, [1957] 1 WLR 45 at 49): "The assured cannot recover anything under the main indemnity clause or make any claim against the underwriters until they have been found liable and so sustained a loss." Under s. 1 of the Act of 1930 the injured person cannot sue the insurance company except in such circumstances as the insured himself could have sued the insurance company. Potters could only have sued for an indemnity when their liability to the third person was established and the amount of the loss ascertained. In some circumstances an insured might sue earlier for a declaration, e.g., if the insurance company were repudiating the policy for some reason; but where the policy is admittedly good, the insured cannot sue for an indemnity until his own liability to the third person is ascertained.'

Lord Denning MR continued ([1967] 1 All ER 577 at 580, [1967] 2 QB 363 at 375):

a

> 'In these circumstances I think the right to sue for these moneys does not arise until the liability is established and the amount ascertained. How is this to be done? If there is an unascertained claim for damages in tort, it cannot be proved in the bankruptcy, nor in the liquidation of the company; but the injured person can bring an action against the wrongdoer. In the case of a company, he must get the leave of the court. No doubt leave would automatically be given. The insurance company can fight that action in the name of the wrongdoer. In that way liability can be established and the loss ascertained. Then the injured person can go against the insurance company.'

b

Salmon LJ agreed with Lord Denning MR. He said ([1967] 1 All ER 577 at 582, [1967] 2 QB 363 at 377–378):

c

> 'The case really resolves itself into this simple question: could Potters on June 17, 1965, have successfully sued their insurers for the sum of £839 10s. 3d. which they were denying they were under any obligation to pay to the Post Office? Stated in that way, I should have thought the question admits of only one answer. Obviously Potters could not have claimed that money from their insurers. It is quite true that
>
> d
>
> if Potters in the end are shown to have been legally liable for the damage resulting from the accident to the cable, their liability in law dates from the moment when the accident occurred and the damage was suffered. Whether or not there is any legal liability, however, and, if so, the amount due from Potters to the Post Office can, in my view, only be finally ascertained either by agreement between Potters and the Post Office or by an action or arbitration between Potters and the Post
>
> e
>
> Office. It is quite unheard of in practice for any assured to sue his insurers in a money claim when the actual loss against which he wishes to be indemnified has not been ascertained. I have never heard of such an action, and there is nothing in law that makes such an action possible. I agree with the statement of DEVLIN, J., in *West Wake Price & Co. v. Ching* ([1956] 3 All ER 821 at 825, [1957] 1 WLR 45 at 49), to which LORD DENNING, M.R., has already referred. This statement is obiter, but I
>
> f
>
> think it correctly states the legal position, although it does not expressly point out that liability and quantum can be ascertained not only by action but also by arbitration or agreement.'

In my opinion the reasoning of Lord Denning MR and Salmon LJ contained in the passages from their respective judgments in the *Post Office* case set out above, on the basis

g

of which they concluded that, under a policy of insurance against liability to third parties, the insured person cannot sue for an indemnity from the insurers unless and until the existence and amount of his liability to a third party has been established by action, arbitration or agreement, is unassailably correct. I would, therefore, hold that the *Post Office* case was rightly decided, and that the principle laid down in it is applicable to the present case.

h

There is, however, a vital difference between the *Post Office* case and the present case. In the *Post Office* case the wrongdoing company, although in compulsory liquidation, was still in existence. It was, therefore, still open to the Post Office, as Lord Denning MR explained, to bring an action, with the leave of the Companies Court, against that company, in order to establish the existence and amount of the liability in issue. By contrast, in the present case, because Dart Mill Ltd no longer exists and can no longer be

j

resurrected, the same solution to the problem is not available, with the result arrived at by the Court of Appeal.

Counsel for the appellant accepted that it was necessary, in order to enable her to recover in an action against the respondents under s 1(1) of the 1930 Act, for her to establish the existence and amount of the liability which Dart Mill Ltd incurred to her in the past. He contended, however, that these matters could be established in the action proposed to be brought by the appellant against the respondents. In support of this contention he made two forceful points which deserve careful consideration.

The first point was that, in certain kinds of cases, such as an action against a solicitor for negligence in failing to bring an action within a relevant period of limitation, the court was accustomed, in order to assess the damages recoverable, to put a value on the lost claim, and that process necessarily involved consideration of the existence and amount of the liability of a third party who was not a party to the action. The second point was that, even if Dart Mill Ltd were still in existence or capable of being resurrected, so as to make it possible for the appellant, with the leave of the Companies Court, to bring an action against that company in order to establish the existence and amount of its liability to her, such action would in practice be defended by the respondents in the company's name, so that in substance, though not in form, the dispute would be between the appellant on one side and the respondents on the other. That being so, it made no difference to the substance of the matter that Dart Mill Ltd itself could no longer be sued.

The first point, though superficially attractive is, in my view, unsound. In the case of an action of the kind suggested, namely an action against a solicitor for negligence in failing to bring proceedings in time, what the court has to do is not to establish that the lost claim would have succeeded and what the amount of damages recovered would have been. All that the court has to do is to make an assessment of the value of the claim as between the plaintiff and the defendant solicitor, which is in no way binding on the person against whom the plaintiff's action, if it had not been lost due to the solicitor's negligence, would have been brought. That assessment of value will take account of all contingencies, including where appropriate the contingency of complete or partial failure in the lost action. In these circumstances I do not consider that the kind of case suggested provides any real analogy to the kind of case with which your Lordships are here concerned.

The second point illustrates the fact that the difficulty which the appellant faces is, to a large extent at any rate, a procedural difficulty rather than a substantive one. But this difficulty, however it may be categorised, is a necessary consequence of two matters: first, the nature of the rights given to an insured person under a policy of insurance against liability to third parties; and, second, the terms of s 1(1) of the 1930 Act relating to the transfer of rights, in certain events, from an insured person to a third party.

For the reasons which I have given I am of opinion that neither of the two points relied on by counsel for the appellant, though fully deserving of consideration, is sustainable in law.

The complaint may be made, and has been forcefully made on behalf of the appellant in this appeal, that the decision reached by the Court of Appeal, with which it is apparent that I fully agree, depends really on procedural technicalities and produces a result which is unfair to the appellant and gives an unmerited bonus to the respondents. In answer to that complaint I think that it is right to draw attention to two matters: first, the historical reason for the passing of the 1930 Act; and, second, the inference to be drawn from the terms of s 1(2) of that Act, which I set out earlier above with s 1(1).

The historical reason for the passing of the 1930 Act was to remedy a particular form of injustice which had become apparent from two then recent decisions of the Court of Appeal. The first of these two decisions was *Re Harrington Motor Co Ltd, ex p Chaplin* [1928] Ch 105. In that case a person injured in a road accident had obtained a judgment for damages against a company, but had been unable to enforce the judgment before the company went into liquidation. The company's motor insurers paid the amount of the judgment to the liquidator, who then treated the injured person as an unsecured creditor with no special interest in the insurance moneys. It was held by the Court of Appeal that the liquidator had been right to deal with the matter in that way.

The second decision was *Hood's Trustees v Southern Union General Insurance Co of Australasia Ltd* [1928] Ch 793. In that case H, being insured by the defendant company against liability to third parties, negligently injured C in a road accident. C subsequently

brought an action against H for damages but, before he could obtain judgment, H was
a made bankrupt and the official receiver was appointed trustee in the bankruptcy. The
trustee informed the defendant company in reply to a question that he did not propose
to take any part in C's action against H. H later purported, for an agreed sum much
below the value of the claim, to release the defendant company from its obligation under
the policy to indemnify him in respect of any judgment obtained against him by C.
Shortly afterwards C obtained judgment against H for damages for the personal injuries
b sustained by him. Subsequently H was made bankrupt a second time and another trustee
in bankruptcy was appointed. It was held by Tomlin J that the benefit of the indemnity
under H's policy of insurance vested in the trustee in the first bankruptcy, notwithstanding
that C's claim, being one in respect of tort for which judgment was not obtained until
after the commencement of the first bankruptcy, was not itself provable in bankruptcy.
That decision was subsequently affirmed by the Court of Appeal.

c   These two decisions showed that, even where an injured person obtained a judgment
for damages against a wrongdoer, if the wrongdoer being a company went into
liquidation, or being an individual became bankrupt, and the judgment had not by then
been enforced by execution, the moneys payable by way of indemnity under any policy
of insurance by which the wrongdoer was insured against liability to third parties did
not go solely to benefit the injured person but were payable to the liquidator or trustee
d in bankruptcy of the wrongdoer for distribution pari passu among all the unsecured
creditors. This was recognised to be plainly unjust, and the 1930 Act was passed to
remedy that injustice. It was not passed to remedy any injustice arising from other
matters; in particular, it was not passed to remedy any injustice which might arise as a
result of the dissolution of a company making it impossible to establish the existence and
amount of the liability of such company to a third party. That kind of situation was not,
e in my view, contemplated by the legislature at all.

The significance of s 1(2) of the 1930 Act is this. In that subsection the legislature dealt
expressly with the situation where a deceased's estate was ordered to be administered in
bankruptcy, and provided that, if any debt provable in bankruptcy was owing to the
deceased in respect of a liability against which he was insured as being a liability to a
third party, the deceased debtor's rights against the insurer should be transferred to and
f vest in the person to whom the debt was owing. While the legislature dealt expressly in
this way with the case of a deceased debtor's estate being administered in bankruptcy, it
made no provision of any kind with regard to the case of a company dissolved after being
wound up. This action leads to the inference that the legislature, in enacting the 1930
Act, did not have a situation of that kind in contemplation at all.

My Lords, for the reasons which I have given, and despite the natural sympathy which
g one is bound to feel for the difficulty in which the appellant finds herself, I would dismiss
this appeal. I would only add that, even if the appeal had succeeded, the appellant would
still have had other serious difficulties to surmount with regard to limitation of actions
under the Limitation Act 1980.

h **LORD TEMPLEMAN.** My Lords, the appellant, Mrs Bradley, was employed by Dart
Mill Ltd at its cotton mill at times between 1933 and 1970. For present purposes it must
be assumed that the Dart Mill company was insured with the respondents, Eagle Star
Insurance Co Ltd, against claims by employees, including the appellant, for injuries
suffered as a result of the negligence or breach of statutory duty by the Dart Mill
company. The appellant asserts that she contracted byssinosis because she was exposed to
j cotton dust while she was working for the Dart Mill company and that she is entitled to
damages for negligence and breach of statutory duty which are risks covered by the Eagle
Star insured policy. At some stage, the court must consider whether the appellant is
entitled to proceed with her claim because of the delay which has occurred. For present
purposes the delay is irrelevant. At some time after 1970, the Dart Mill company passed
a resolution for voluntary winding up and, in 1976, the Dart Mill company was dissolved.

Section 1 of the Third Parties (Rights against Insurers) Act 1930 applies—

'(1) Where under any contract of insurance a person (hereinafter referred to as *a* the insured) is insured against liabilities to third parties which he may incur . . .'

In the present case, under a contract of insurance, the insured, the Dart Mill company, was insured by the respondents against liabilities to a third party, the appellant, which the Dart Mill company may have incurred.

Where s 1 of the 1930 Act applies, then—   *b*

'(1) . . . (b) in the case of the insured being a company, in the event of a winding-up order being made, or a resolution for a voluntary winding-up being passed . . . if, either before or after that event, any such liability as aforesaid is incurred by the insured, his rights against the insurer under the contract in respect of the liability shall, notwithstanding anything in any Act or rule of law to the contrary, be *c* transferred to and vest in the third party to whom the liability was so incurred.'

In the present case a resolution for the voluntary winding up of the Dart Mill company was passed, and, if liability to the appellant was incurred, the rights of the Dart Mill company against the insurers, the respondents, in respect of the liability to the appellant were transferred to and are now vested in the appellant. The appellant seeks to enforce *d* against the respondents the rights she claims are vested in her in respect of the policy. Of course, any proceedings by the appellant will fail if she cannot prove that the Dart Mill company by its negligence or breach of duty incurred a liability to her and that the Dart Mill company was insured against that liability with the respondents. But the respondents contend that, even if the Dart Mill company became liable to the appellant and even if that liability was covered by an insurance policy effected by the Dart Mill company with *e* the respondents, nevertheless the appellant is not entitled to exercise the rights under insurance policy transferred to her by the 1930 Act.

It is said on behalf of the respondents that the 1930 Act does not avail the appellant because, following the resolution to wind up, the Dart Mill company was dissolved in 1976 and no longer exists. But it seems to me that the existence or non-existence of the *f* Dart Mill company at present is irrelevant. The Dart Mill company did exist and, if it insured with the respondents against liability to the appellant, if the Dart Mill company incurred liability to the appellant its rights under the Eagle Star insurance policy are vested in the appellant. The 1930 Act was intended to protect a person who suffers an insured loss at the hands of a company which goes into liquidation. That protection was afforded by transferring the benefit of the insurance policy from the company to the injured person. In my opinion, Parliament cannot have intended that the protection *g* afforded against a company in liquidation should cease as soon as the company in liquidation reaches its predestined and inevitable determination in the dissolution of the company. It is conceded that within two years (now 12 years) after the date of dissolution, the appellant could have obtained an order of the court reviving the defunct Dart Mill company for the sole purpose of enabling the appellant to recover against the respondents. *h* But there would be no point in restoring the Dart Mill company for that limited purpose. The Dart Mill company would have no interest in a quarrel over an insurance policy between the insurance company, the respondents, and the person, the appellant, in whom the benefit of the insurance policy is claimed to be already vested by virtue of the 1930 Act. To restore the Dart Mill company in these circumstances would do no more than authorise the appellant to make use of a name carved on a tombstone. The use of *j* the name could not restore life to the skeleton.

The dissolution of the Dart Mill company has no significance in the present case save that it enables the respondents to argue that they are not bound to pay in respect of a liability which they accepted and for which they were paid premiums. I would allow this appeal and enable the appellant to proceed with her action against the respondents.

LORD OLIVER OF AYLMERTON. My Lords, I have had the advantage of reading
a in draft the speech delivered by my noble and learned friend Lord Brandon, with which
I entirely agree. I too would dismiss the appeal.

LORD JAUNCEY OF TULLICHETTLE. My Lords, I have had the advantage of
reading in draft the speech prepared by my noble and learned friend Lord Brandon. I
agree with it and for the reasons given therein I would dismiss the appeal.
b   I would only add a further word about s 1(2) of the Third Parties (Rights against
Insurers) Act 1930. That subsection only applies where a debt provable in bankruptcy is
owing by the deceased in respect of insured liability. In terms of s 30(1) of the Bankruptcy
Act 1914 a claim for unliquidated damages arising in tort is not provable in bankruptcy.
It follows that no rights which the deceased may have had against insurers in respect of
such a claim are transferred to the person to whom he had incurred liability. If the
c appellant's argument were correct it would follow that the third party to whom an
individual had incurred insured liability would be able to proceed direct against his
insurers on his becoming bankrupt but would be unable to to proceed if after his death
an order were made under s 130 of the 1914 Act. This would be a curious result which
has no apparent logic. Far more likely is it that the legislature intended that in both
subsections the type of rights capable of being transferred to third parties should be the
d same.

Appeal dismissed.

Solicitors: *Field Fisher & Martineau*, agents for *John Pickering*, Oldham (for the appellant);
Davies Arnold Cooper, agents for *T Unsworth*, Urmston (for the respondents).
e

Mary Rose Plummer   Barrister.

Bray (Inspector of Taxes) v Best

f HOUSE OF LORDS
LORD MACKAY OF CLASHFERN LC, LORD KEITH OF KINKEL, LORD BRANDON OF OAKBROOK, LORD
OLIVER OF AYLMERTON AND LORD GOFF OF CHIEVELEY
28, 29, 30 NOVEMBER 1988, 23 FEBRUARY 1989

Income tax – Emoluments from office or employment – Receipts 'from' employment – Receipts
g *after employment has ceased – Distribution of assets of trusts for benefit of employees – Employing*
company taken over – Employment transferred to parent company – Trusts wound up and assets
distributed among all employees after transfer of employment to parent company – Whether
receipts attributable to any employment or year of assessment – Income and Corporation Taxes
Act 1970, s 181.

h *Practice – Citation of cases – Reports – Revenue cases – Law Reports series or Reports of Tax*
Cases – Tax Cases may be used if counsel think it more convenient – References to Law Reports
also to be given.

The taxpayer was employed by a company from 1958–59 to 1978–79. In anticipation of
the transfer on 1 April 1979 of all the employees of the company to employment by its
j parent company, the trustees of two trusts for the benefit of the company's employees
exercised their powers to bring into effect provisions leading to the winding up of the
trusts and the distribution of the net assets. In 1979–80 the taxpayer was allocated two
sums totalling £18,111. He was assessed to income tax under s 181(1), Sch E[a], Case I of

---

a   Schedule E, so far as material, is set out at p 974 *e f*, post

the Income and Corporation Taxes Act 1970. He appealed against the assessment
contending that the allocations were not emoluments from his employment. The *a*
Revenue contended that the allocations were emoluments and that it was appropriate to
attribute the allocations over the whole period of the taxpayer's employment or,
alternatively, that the whole allocation should be attributed to 1978–79, the taxpayer's
final year of employment with the company. A Special Commissioner determined that
the allocations were emoluments from the taxpayer's employment and were attributable
to the year in which they were paid but they could not be attributed to any one or more *b*
of the relevant years of assessment during which the taxpayer had been employed by the
company and there was accordingly no chargeable period. The judge allowed an appeal
by the Crown, holding that the allocations were emoluments and as such had to be paid
in respect of some period of service and that that period was either a definable special
period or the whole of the period of employment. The judge accordingly ordered that
the case be remitted to the commissioner to determine, as a question of fact, over what *c*
period the emoluments should be deemed to have been earned and how they should be
apportioned over the tax years in that period. On appeal, the Court of Appeal upheld the
commissioner's decision and allowed the taxpayer's appeal. The Crown appealed to the
House of Lords.

Held – Income tax was a tax of an annual nature and for an emolument to be chargeable *d*
to income tax under Sch E it had to be not only an emolument from an employment but
also an emolument for the year of assessment in respect of which the charge was sought
to be raised. The period to which any given payment was to be attributed was a question
to be determined as one of fact in each case, depending on all the circumstances, including
its source and the intention of the payer so far as it could be gathered either from direct
evidence or from the surrounding circumstances. Since the Special Commissioner could *e*
find no feature of any significance which would indicate that the payment made to the
taxpayer fell to be attributed either to the last year or to all or any of the previous years
during which he was employed by the company, it followed that there was no period to
which the payment of the sums could be attributed. The appeal would therefore be
dismissed (see p 971 *e g h*, p 974 *j* to p 975 *a* and p 978 *b c g h*, post).

Per Lord Mackay LC. If counsel appearing in the House of Lords think it more *f*
convenient to do so, they may refer to the report of a case in Tax Cases, even though the
case is also reported in the Law Reports, but if they decide to do so references to the case
in the Law Reports should also be given (see p 971 *f*, post).

Decision of the Court of Appeal [1988] 2 All ER 105 affirmed.

Notes *g*

For voluntary payments to a holder of an office or employment, see 23 Halsbury's Laws
(4th edn) para 644, and for cases on the subject, see 28(1) Digest (Reissue) 335–337, *1211–
1218*.

For citation of reports of decisions as authorities, see 26 Halsbury's Laws (4th edn) para
587, and for cases on the subject, see 30 Digest (Reissue) 285–289, *931–1005*. *h*

In relation to taxation for the year 1988–89 and subsequent years of assessment s 181
of the Income and Corporation Taxes Act 1970 was replaced by ss 19 and 192(1) of the
Income and Corporation Taxes Act 1988. For ss 19 and 192 of the 1988 Act, see 44
Halsbury's Statutes (4th edn) 57, 240.

Cases referred to in opinions *j*

Board of Inland Revenue v Suite [1986] 2 All ER 577, [1986] AC 657, [1986] 2 WLR 1042,
PC.
Bridges (Inspector of Taxes) v Hewitt [1957] 2 All ER 281, [1957] 1 WLR 674, CA.
Brown v National Provident Institution [1921] 2 AC 222, HL.
Brumby (Inspector of Taxes) v Milner [1976] 3 All ER 636, [1976] 1 WLR 1096, HL; *affg*
[1975] 3 All ER 1004, [1976] 1 WLR 29, CA; *affg* [1975] 2 All ER 773, [1975] 1 WLR
958.

Hamblett v Godfrey (Inspector of Taxes) [1987] 1 All ER 916, [1987] 1 WLR 357, CA.
Heasman v Jordan (Inspector of Taxes) [1954] 3 All ER 101, [1954] Ch 744, [1954] 3 WLR 432.
Hochstrasser (Inspector of Taxes) v Mayes [1959] 3 All ER 817, [1960] AC 376, [1960] 2 WLR 63, HL; *affg* [1958] 3 All ER 285, [1959] Ch 22, [1958] 3 WLR 215, CA; *affg* [1958] 1 All ER 369, [1959] Ch 22, [1958] 2 WLR 982.
Hunter (Inspector of Taxes) v Dewhurst (1932) 16 TC 605, [1932] All ER Rep 753, HL.
b *Laidler v Perry (Inspector of Taxes)* [1965] 2 All ER 121, [1966] AC 16, [1965] 2 WLR 1171, HL.
Seymour v Reed [1927] AC 554, [1927] All ER Rep 294, HL.

Appeal
The Crown appealed with the leave of the House of Lords given on 21 March 1988
c against the decision of the Court of Appeal (May, Balcombe and Woolf LJJ) ([1988] 2 All ER 105, [1988] 1 WLR 784) on 30 October 1987 allowing an appeal by Peter Maurice Best (the taxpayer) against the decision of Walton J ([1986] STC 96) on 20 January 1986 whereby on a case stated (set out at [1986] STC 97–108) the judge reversed the decision of a Commissioner for the Special Purposes of the Income Tax Acts discharging assessments made on the taxpayer for the years 1958–59 to 1977–79 inclusive and
d reducing the assessment for the year 1978–79 to the agreed figure of £8,111. The facts are set out in the opinion of Lord Oliver.

J M Chadwick QC and *Alan Moses* for the Crown.
Andrew Park QC and *Richard Bramwell* for the taxpayer.

e Their Lordships took time for consideration.

23 February. The following opinions were delivered.

LORD MACKAY OF CLASHFERN LC. My Lords, I have had the advantage of reading in draft the speech about to be delivered by my noble and learned friend Lord
f Oliver. I agree with his reasoning and conclusion that this appeal should be dismissed.
In the course of the hearing of this appeal their Lordships found that on occasion the report of a case in Tax Cases may appropriately be referred to even when the case is also reported in the Law Reports. Accordingly, I consider that for the future in this House counsel should be entitled, if they think that the more convenient course, to use the report of such a case in Tax Cases rather than in the Law Reports but if they decide to do
g so the references to the case in the Law Reports should also be given.

LORD KEITH OF KINKEL. My Lords, I have had the opportunity of considering in draft the speech to be delivered by my noble and learned friend Lord Oliver. I agree with it, and for the reasons given by him would dismiss the appeal.

h **LORD BRANDON OF OAKBROOK.** My Lords, for the reasons given in the speech of my noble and learned friend Lord Oliver, I would dismiss the appeal.

LORD OLIVER OF AYLMERTON. My Lords, this appeal is concerned with the assessability to income tax under Sch E of distributions made by the trustees of two trust funds established for the benefit of the employees of a trading company which was taken
j over by a larger organisation, such distributions having been determined on and made after the cessation of the relevant employment. The company, A Gallenkamp & Co Ltd, was an old established family company carrying on the business of manufacturing laboratory equipment. Towards the latter part of the 1950s the directors, partly with a view to making the company less vulnerable to take-over and partly to provide additional incentive for its employees, established a trust fund for the benefit of employees. By a trust deed dated 3 December 1957 and made between the company of the one part and three trustees (the company's chairman, its solicitor and its accountant) of the other part,

it was provided that during a lengthy trust period, defined by reference to the life of the
survivor of all descendants then living of His late Majesty King George V the trustees *a*
should hold the trust fund (being such sums as should from time to time be advanced by
the company for the purposes of the deed) on trust to raise thereout and apply such sums
as should be necessary for the subscription or purchase of such fully-paid shares in the
company as the company should direct. It is unnecessary to recite the trusts of the deed
in any detail beyond saying that the beneficiaries were confined to employees who had
not themselves sold or transferred shares to the trustees and that provision was made for *b*
shares purchased by the trustees to be offered to employees of the company, for the
income in each year to be divided at the company's discretion among such qualified
employees as the company should determine and, in so far as not so applied, for it to be
invested as an accretion to capital and for the trustees in their discretion at any time to
determine the trust. There was also reserved to the company a wide power in its
discretion to alter or modify the trusts or provisions of the deed. *c*

In 1961 the trustees purchased from a Mrs Jarrom, the widow of a former managing
director, a substantial parcel of shares which were segregated and made the subject of a
separate trust which closely followed the pattern of the 1957 deed, save that income was
distributable at the trustees' rather than the company's discretion and that the employees
and directors eligible to benefit were limited to those with ten or more years' service.
The reason for this, it appears, was that Mrs Jarrom had expressed a wish that a separate *d*
fund should be established in memory of her late husband, Harry Jarrom, and that it
should be for the benefit of long-serving members of the company's staff.

On 25 August 1977 the company became a wholly-owned subsidiary of Fisons plc and
following this the trustees anticipated that there might come a time in the future when
the company's workforce would be absorbed by the parent company and they might
either find themselves with no beneficiaries or find themselves unable effectively to *e*
restrict the beneficiaries to employees who had given service to the company. They
accordingly set about making arrangements to wind up the trusts, arrangements which,
in 1979, were accelerated by the knowledge that the parent company planned to transfer
all the employees of the company to its own employment on 1 April 1979. By deeds
dated 15 March 1979 both the trusts were varied, the material alterations for present
purposes being (1) the insertion, for the protection of the trustees on any distribution, of *f*
a clause enabling them to rely conclusively on a signed statement of the secretary of
company containing particulars of the employees on any particular date and containing
information regarding length of service, salary and other data relating to any employee
and (2) the substitution, by way of a schedule, of new trusts to take effect on the
termination of the trust period. So far as material the provisions in the schedule of the
1957 deed were as follows: *g*

'1. In this Schedule . . . (2) "the Termination Date" means the date of expiration
or earlier termination of the Trust Period. (3) "Eligible Employee" means a person
who was at the 31st December 1977 and is at the Termination Date an employee of
the Company (including a director holding salaried employment or office with the
Company) but who has not at any time before the Termination Date sold or *h*
transferred any share in the Company to the Trustees for the time being of the
Principal Deed . . . (5) "the Terminal Fund" means the net monies remaining held
by the Trustees . . . after payment of or provision for . . . liabilities . . .
2. The Trustees shall within the nine months immediately following the
Termination Date pay or provide for all liabilities mentioned in the definition of
the Terminal Fund and apply the Terminal Fund by allocating thereout in respect *j*
of each Eligible Employee such a sum as the Trustees shall in their absolute and
unfettered discretion think fit but so that A. No Eligible Employee shall be entitled
to receive as of right any sum allocated to him B. The Trustees shall apply all sums
allocated to Eligible Employees in one or more of the following ways and such
application shall be made within three months of the allocation in question (the

choice of application to be in the absolute and unfettered discretion of the Trustees)
namely:—(i) by paying the same to the Eligible Employee in each case or where the
Eligible Employee is dead, to his personal representative as an accretion to his Estate;
(ii) by purchasing from an insurance company ... a non-commutable non-
assignable annuity policy in his name the annuity whereunder is payable as from
his attainment of age 65 (or in the case of a woman, age 60) or, if such age has
already been attained at the date of purchase, is payable as an immediate annuity.
    3. Every allocation and application shall be made in writing and pursuant to a
unanimous resolution of the Trustees.
    4. The Trustees before making any payment shall be entitled to deduct or make
provision for all taxation payable by the Trustees in respect thereof.
    5. Subject to the trusts aforesaid, the Trustees shall hold the Terminal Fund upon
trust to divide and pay the same to and amongst all the Eligible Employees in shares
proportional to their salaries for the year ended 31st December 1978 ... and any
payment so falling to be made to an Eligible Employee who has died before it has
been made shall be paid to his legal personal representatives.'

The schedule to the amended deed regulating the Harry Jarrom Trust was in similar
terms save that eligible employees were limited to those who had been in the service of
the company on 31 December 1975.

These alterations having been effected, the trustees, by deeds dated 29 March 1979,
directed that the trust period in relation to each fund should thereupon terminate in
relation to the whole of the trust property. It thus became necessary, unless the ultimate
trust in default was to take effect, for the trustees to allocate the funds among the eligible
employees before the end of December 1979. On 1 April 1979 all the company's
employees were transferred to the employment of the parent company and their
employment by the company ceased. On the previous day a notice had been posted on
the company's notice board informing employees of the existence of the trusts,
announcing their winding up and outlining the procedure which would be followed.
For many employees this may well have been the first occasion on which they were
aware of the existence of trusts.

The trustees were concerned that the division of the funds should be conducted as
fairly as possible and various computer print-outs were obtained showing the effect of
applying various formulae which attached different weights to length of service and
salary scales. None of these was actually adopted, but they were used to form the basis for
ultimate allocation, although, by adopting a lower cut-off point to reduce differentials,
there was a substantial departure from the figures yielded by the print-outs. By written
resolutions dated 21 December 1979 the trustees of both funds resolved on the allocation
of the funds among some 770 employees (633 in the case of the Harry Jarrom Trust
fund) in accordance with the decision at which they had ultimately arrived. As a result
there became payable to the taxpayer an aggregate sum of £18,111 from the two funds,
being as to the major part capital before provision for tax and as to the balance interest
after provision for tax at 45%. On 22 February 1980 letters were dispatched to each
qualified employee stating the amount allotted and on 18 March 1980 the trustees passed
formal resolutions for the application of the funds in accordance with the allocation. A
small number of allocations were made in the form of annuity purchases but the majority
were applications of cash, including those to the taxpayer, Mr Best, who was a senior
employee who had been in the service of the company continuously since 23 April 1957.

On 4 March 1983 the inspector of taxes raised assessments on the taxpayer in respect
of each year from the year 1958–59 to the year 1978–79 (inclusive) in sums which
represented the inspector's calculation of an appropriate proportion of the taxpayer's total
allocation from the funds for each year of his service, the assessment for the year 1978–
79 being in a sum of £13,728, which was intended as an alternative assessment raised on
the footing that the whole allocation was chargeable for that year and to be reduced
appropriately if the remaining assessments were confirmed on appeal to the

commissioners. The taxpayer appealed to the Special Commissioner, who, on 16 February 1984, allowed the appeal and, at the request of the Crown, stated a case for the High   *a* Court (set out at [1986] STC 97–108). The underlying basis of the Special Commissioner's conclusion was that, although the sums allocated to the taxpayer constituted an emolument from his employment which would otherwise be taxable under Case I of Sch E, they escaped the charge to tax because they could not be attributed to any year of assessment other than the year 1979–80 in which the taxpayer's entitlement arose, and that, since in that year there was no employment of the taxpayer and consequently no   *b* source from which the emolument arose, there could be no charge to tax under Case I of Sch E, although it was not disputed and had never been disputed that there was a liability under s 187 of the Income and Corporation Taxes Act 1970 but subject to the exemption provided in s 188 of that Act. On 20 January 1986 Walton J ([1986] STC 96) allowed the Crown's appeal, holding that emoluments from an employment must be paid in respect of some period of service which must either be a definable period or, failing that, the   *c* whole period of the employment. He accordingly remitted the matter to the commissioner to determine, as a question of fact, over what period the sums allocated should be deemed to have been earned and how they should be apportioned. From this decision the taxpayer appealed to the Court of Appeal ([1988] 2 All ER 105, [1988] 1 WLR 784), which unanimously allowed the appeal and upheld the conclusion of the Special Commissioner.   *d*

My Lords, the relevant statutory provisions fall within a small compass. Section 181 of the Income and Corporation Taxes Act 1970 provides (so far as material) as follows:

'(1) The Schedule referred to as Schedule E is as follows:—

SCHEDULE E

1. Tax under this Schedule shall be charged in respect of any office or employment   *e* on emoluments therefrom which fall under one, or more than one, of the following Cases—Case I: where the person holding the office or employment is resident and ordinarily resident in the United Kingdom, any emoluments for the chargeable period ... and tax shall not be chargeable in respect of emoluments of an office or employment under any other paragraph of this Schedule ...'

Section 183(1) provides that the expression 'emoluments' shall 'include all salaries, fees,   *f* wages, perquisites and profits whatsoever'. 'Chargeable period' is defined in s 526(5) as 'an accounting period of a company or a year of assessment' and 'year of assessment' is defined by the same section as meaning 'with reference to any income tax, the year for which such tax was granted by any Act granting income tax'.

The only other provisions which ought to be mentioned, since they form the   *g* foundation of one of the Crown's submissions, are ss 29 and 50 of the Taxes Management Act 1970. Sections 7 and 8 of that Act contain machinery for the making of returns by persons chargeable to income tax for any year of assessment and s 29(1) provides for an assessment to be made by a tax inspector. If it appears to the inspector that there are chargeable profits which have not been included in a return 'he may make an assessment to tax to the best of his judgment' (s 29(1)(b)). Alternatively, if an inspector 'discovers'   *h* either that profits which ought to have been assessed to tax have not been so assessed or that an assessment to tax is insufficient, he may make an assessment 'in the amount, or the further amount, which ought in his ... opinion to be charged' (s 29(3)). Section 50 regulates the procedure on an appeal to the commissioners of income tax and sub-s (6) provides that if on such an appeal it appears to the majority of the commissioners present at the hearing 'by examination of the appellant ... or by other lawful evidence, that the   *j* appellant is overcharged by any assessment, the assessment shall be reduced accordingly, but otherwise every such assessment shall stand good'.

The provisions of the Income and Corporation Taxes Act 1970 to which I have referred underline the annual nature of income tax. For an emolument to be chargeable to income tax under Sch E, not only must it be an emolument *from* an employment but it must be an emolument *for* the year of assessment in respect of which the charge is sought

to be raised. The argument for the taxpayer is a very simple one. Granted, it is said, that
a the payment to which the taxpayer became entitled out of the trust funds was a profit
which derived from his previous employment with the company and thus an emolument
from that employment, the only chargeable period *for* which it could possibly be said to
have been paid is the year of assessment, 1979–80. It is a well-established principle,
deriving from the nature of income tax as an annual tax, that a receipt or entitlement
arising in a year of assessment is not chargeable to tax unless there exists during that year
b a source from which it arises (see, for instance, *Brown v National Provident Institution*
[1921] 2 AC 222). The principle is conveniently expressed in *Whiteman and Wheatcroft on
Income Tax* (2nd edn, 1976) p 21 as follows:

> '. . . most types of income are classified by reference to the source from which
> they come. From this it was held to follow that if a taxpayer ceased to possess a
c > particular source of income, he could not be taxed on delayed receipts from that
> source unless they were referable to, and could be assessed in respect of, a period
> during which he possessed the source.'

There is, it is argued, no ground for attributing the payment in the instant case to any
period other than that in which the taxpayer became entitled to and received it, and,
since in that period he had ceased to be employed and thus to possess the source from
d which the entitlement arose, the sum cannot be taxable under Sch E for that period,
although it is not contested that the payment was one made in connection with the
termination of his employment and so taxable under the provisions of s 187 of the Act.
The argument of the Crown can, I think, be fairly summarised in the following five
propositions. (1) The trusts were instituted as a reward for the services of employees of
the company and the payments made to the taxpayer and other ex-employees were found
e as a fact by the Special Commissioner to be a 'reward for their services' (see [1986] STC
96 at 107). (2) A reward for services is the same as remuneration and can only be
remuneration for a period during which services are being performed under the contract
of services. (3) It follows that the emolument must be for a chargeable period during
which the employment continued and in the absence of any clear ascription to any
particular year or years of the employment it can only be 'for' the whole period of the
f employment. (4) The inspector was accordingly entitled to apportion the payment to the
best of his ability in the exercise of the judgment which he is called on to exercise under
s 29(1)(*b*) of the Taxes Management Act 1970 or the opinion which he has to form under
s 29(3) of that Act. (5) Having regard to the provisions of s 50(6) of the Act, the assessment
must stand unless the taxpayer can point conclusively to some other period of
apportionment or some more appropriate period of attribution.
g In effect, the submission of the Crown amounts to this: that it is in the very nature of
an emolument from an employment that it cannot be otherwise than 'for' a chargeable
period during which the employment continued and it is this that is at the root of the
argument, although counsel for the Crown would, I think, say that he does not have to
go this far because he has a finding of fact in his favour which necessarily entails the
h consequence that the payment to the taxpayer was made for some chargeable period
during which the taxpayer's contract of employment was in being.
Although before the Special Commissioner and in the High Court the taxpayer had
contested that the sum paid constituted an emolument from his employment, the
decision of this House in *Brumby (Inspector of Taxes) v Milner* [1976] 3 All ER 636, [1976]
1 WLR 1096 effectively precludes further argument on this point and the question has
j not been pursued either before the Court of Appeal or before your Lordships. Thus the
only question which has now to be determined is whether the payments made to the
taxpayer comprised or included emoluments for all or any of the chargeable periods
1958–59 to 1978–79 inclusive for which he has been assessed. Nevertheless, although
the payment to the taxpayer is accepted to be an emolument from his employment, it is
still necessary for the purposes of answering the only remaining question to determine
the nature of the emolument, particularly in the light of the Special Commissioner's

finding of fact on which the Crown relies. I turn therefore to that finding. In *Brumby v Milner* [1975] 3 All ER 1004 at 1010, [1976] 1 WLR 29 at 36 in the Court of Appeal, *a* Lord Russell in delivering the judgment of the court said:

'We do not consider that the provision for terminal payments can be considered as, so to speak, a throwaway provision bearing no colour of reward for services; the very existence of the discretion to allocate is against this inference. It appears to us that the scheme is one scheme based fundamentally on reward for services by employees, and the fact that after the final payment there is no more by way of *b* bonus to look for does not relevantly distinguish that final payment.'

That was a case the facts of which were very similar to those of the instant case save that there was no question but that the employment was continuing when the payment was made.

So far as material for present purposes the commissioner's finding was expressed in a *c* passage in which, after quoting the excerpt from the Court of Appeal's judgment just referred to, he continued ([1986] STC 96 at 107):

'After careful consideration I find that those words summarise also my view of the facts of the present case, so far as the source of the payment is concerned.'

A little later he observed: *d*

'The company was obviously very prosperous and its support for any application for shares amounted in my view to a reward for services.'

Counsel for the Crown argues that this amounts to a distinct finding of fact that the payments made to the taxpayer were remuneration for the services which he rendered to the company and a finding that, since there were no such services rendered in the year *e* in which the taxpayer's entitlement arose, they were remuneration for previous years of service and assessable as such.

My Lords, for my part I find myself unpersuaded that it is possible to deduce from the commissioner's reference to a 'reward for services' a finding that the payment either was or was intended to be, as it were, additional remuneration for services rendered to the *f* company in respect of the previous years in which the taxpayer was employed. The expression 'reward for services' in this context probably derives from the decision of this House in *Hochstrasser (Inspector of Taxes) v Mayes* [1959] 3 All ER 817 at 821, [1960] AC 376 at 388, where Viscount Simonds cited with approval the judgment of Upjohn J in the same case where he said ([1958] 1 All ER 369 at 375, [1959] Ch 22 at 33):

'... payment must be made in reference to the service the employee renders by *g* virtue of his office, and it must be something in the nature of a reward for services past, present or future.'

This was merely restating in slightly different terms a test propounded by Viscount Cave LC in *Seymour v Reed* [1927] AC 554 at 559, [1927] All ER Rep 294 at 297, where he spoke of an emolument as including 'all payments made to the holder of an office or *h* employment as such, that is to say, by way of remuneration for his services'. It has, however, to be remembered that in *Hochstrasser v Mayes* both Upjohn J and Viscount Simonds were speaking in the context of a case in which the only question in issue was whether an indemnity given by an employer formed in effect additional remuneration for the employee's services in the year in question. Lord Radcliffe in the same case *j* pointed out that all the various expressions which had been used to test whether particular payments arose 'from' an employment (such as payments 'made to an employee as such' or 'in his capacity as an employee' or 'by way of remuneration for his services') were no more than glosses on the statutory language which might be illustrative but could not be treated as definitive (see [1959] 3 All ER 817 at 823, [1960] AC 376 at 391). He observed ([1959] 3 All ER 817 at 823, [1960] AC 376 at 391–392):

a
'For my part, I think that their meaning is adequately conveyed by saying that, while it is not sufficient to render a payment assessable that an employee would not have received it unless he had been an employee, it is assessable if it has been paid to him in return for acting as or being an employee.'

In an earlier case, *Bridges (Inspector of Taxes) v Hewitt* [1957] 2 All ER 281 at 296, [1957] 1 WLR 674 at 691, Morris LJ referred to an emolument as embracing the 'conception . . . that some taxable remuneration may accrue to a person by reason of his having or

b
exercising an office or employment of profit'. Again, in *Laidler v Perry (Inspector of Taxes)* [1965] 2 All ER 121 at 125, [1966] AC 16 at 31 Lord Reid observed that, although the word 'reward' had been used in many cases, it was not apt to include all the cases which can fall within the statutory words, and he gave as an example a gift made to an employee in the hope or expectation that it would produce good service in the future. Lord Morris in the same case said that the facts showed that the employee had received the taxable

c
benefit only 'because he was a staff employee . . . the reasons for the distribution are to be found in the employer-employee relationship' (see [1965] 2 All ER 121 at 126–127, [1960] AC 16 at 33–34). Similarly Lord Hodson referred to the employment as being the 'causa causans' of the receipt in question (see [1965] 2 All ER 121 at 127, [1960] AC 16 at 34). It is perhaps worth mentioning that in that case, although the extent of the benefits

d
conferred on employees was directly related to the length of their respective periods of employment, there was no question but that they were taxable as emoluments for the year of receipt.

Of course, emoluments include, and indeed normally consist primarily of, sums paid by way of periodic remuneration for services, but it is, I think, clear that that concept is not an essential ingredient of the term. It is worth mentioning that in *Brumby v Milner*

e
[1975] 2 All ER 773, [1975] 1 WLR 958 Walton J, whose decision was affirmed both in the Court of Appeal and in this House, adopted Lord Radcliffe's test in *Hochstrasser v Mayes* and expressly rejected the submission that, in order to qualify as an emolument, the sum had to be paid 'in respect of services rendered by' the employee. 'In return for . . . being an employee' meant, he observed, exactly what it said, although, as he went on to point out, the distinction may seem a semantic one. An employee renders services so

f
that, in some circumstances at least, 'in return for being an employee' may be expanded into 'in return for being a person who renders services' and then contracted again into 'in return for rendering services' (see [1975] 2 All ER 773 at 788, [1975] 1 WLR 958 at 969). In this House, the test adopted both by Lord Simon and Lord Kilbrandon was whether the profit arose 'from the employment or from something else', quoting Lord Reid in *Laidler v Perry*. But perhaps the most striking example, which really conclusively

g
negatives the notion of periodic remuneration as an essential ingredient of an emolument, is the recent case of *Hamblett v Godfrey (Inspector of Taxes)* [1987] 1 All ER 916, [1987] 1 WLR 357, where a sum paid to an employee at the Government Communications Headquarters for relinquishing his right to remain a member of a trade union was held to be a taxable emolument from his employment. In the light of these authorities, I cannot read the phrase 'reward for services' as anything more than a conventional

h
expression of the notion that a particular payment arises from the existence of the employer-employee relationship and not, to use Lord Reid's words in *Laidler v Perry* [1965] 2 All ER 121 at 124, [1966] AC 16 at 30, from 'something else'. I cannot attribute to the commissioner in the instant case the distinct finding of fact for which the Crown has contended and indeed the commissioner's inability to find any ground for attributing the payment to any year of the taxpayer's service is inconsistent with the suggestion that

j
he regarded himself as having made any such finding. It is, in addition, to be noted that the commissioner adopted Lord Russell's reasoning 'so far as the source of the payment is concerned' (see [1986] STC 96 at 107). He was at that stage considering only the question of whether the payment was an emolument, not the nature of the emolument.

That, however, is not the end of the case, for the question remains whether, finding of fact or no finding of fact, there is necessarily subsumed in the concession that the payment constituted an emolument from the employment a conclusion that it must therefore be 'for' a chargeable period within the aggregate period during which the *a* employment subsisted, so that the commissioner should, in any event, either have upheld the assessment or reallocated the payment in some other manner. My Lords, I can see no reason in logic or authority why it should be nor does such a concept emerge from the various paraphrases of the statutory language to which I have already referred. In the Court of Appeal it was said that there is a prima facie presumption that an emolument is paid 'for' the year of assessment in which the payee becomes entitled to receive it. I *b* would prefer, however, to say simply that the period to which any given payment is to be attributed is a question to be determined as one of fact in each case, depending on all the circumstances, including its source and the intention of the payer so far as it can be gathered either from direct evidence or from the surrounding circumstances. In the course of his judgment in the Court of Appeal, May LJ conducted a careful review of the relevant authorities and it would be a work of supererogation to repeat it here. Suffice it *c* to say that *Hunter (Inspector of Taxes) v Dewhurst* (1932) 16 TC 605, [1932] All ER Rep 753 is an example of a case where, although the payment was calculated by reference to a specified length of past service, it was clearly shown on the facts to be referable to the year in which the payee became entitled to it, whilst *Heasman v Jordan (Inspector of Taxes)* [1954] 3 All ER 101, [1954] Ch 744 and *Board of Inland Revenue v Suite* [1986] 2 All ER 577, [1986] AC 657 are examples of cases in which the facts clearly established the *d* payment in question to be referable to a period other than the year of assessment in which the entitlement arose. I gratefully accept and adopt the conclusion expressed by May LJ in his judgment when he said ([1988] 2 All ER 105 at 112, [1988] 1 WLR 784 at 792):

'In my respectful opinion, therefore, the judge's conclusion that an emolument *e* from an employment must of necessity and as a matter of law be attributed to a period or periods of that employment is erroneous. I think that the year or years of assessment to which to attribute such an emolument is a question of fact to be decided in the light of all the circumstances of the particular case. From the very nature of an emolument from an employment it may well be that in most cases this has indeed to be attributed to a year or particular years of the employment. But this *f* does not necessarily follow.'

In the instant case, the commissioner could, on the facts, find no feature of any significance which would indicate that the payment made to the taxpayer fell to be attributed either to the last year in which he was employed or to all or any of the previous years during his employment by the company. The Court of Appeal could find none and, for my part, I can find none. The mere fact that the seniority of the taxpayer as an *g* employee was a matter taken into account in arriving at the amount of the distribution does not appear to me to be any indication that the payment determined on and made in the year of assessment 1979–80 (because that was the only period within which, in accordance with the trusts declared, it had to be resolved on) can properly be treated as made for or in respect of any other period. I would accordingly dismiss the appeal. *h*

LORD GOFF OF CHIEVELEY. My Lords, I have had the advantage of reading in draft the speech delivered by my noble and learned friend Lord Oliver, and for the reasons he gives I would dismiss the appeal.

Appeal dismissed. *j*

Solicitors: *Solicitor of Inland Revenue*; *Rawlison & Butler*, Crawley (for the taxpayer).

Rengan Krishnan Esq   Barrister.

a Coronation Street Industrial Properties Ltd v Ingall Industries plc

HOUSE OF LORDS

LORD KEITH OF KINKEL, LORD BRANDON OF OAKBROOK, LORD TEMPLEMAN, LORD JAUNCEY OF TULLICHETTLE AND LORD LOWRY

b 22, 23 FEBRUARY, 16 MARCH 1989

Landlord and tenant – Covenant – Covenant running with land – Covenant by surety to accept new lease if tenant becoming insolvent and disclaiming lease – Whether surety's covenant running with land – Whether covenant enforceable by landlord against surety if tenant becoming insolvent and disclaiming lease.

c

By a lease dated 30 August 1972 the tenant was granted the lease of industrial premises for a term of 21 years. Performance of the tenant's covenants was guaranteed by the surety. The lease further provided that in the event of the tenant going into liquidation and the lease being disclaimed the surety 'hereby covenants with the Lessor that it will accept from the Lessor a Lease of the Demised Premises' for the unexpired residue and d on the same terms and conditions of the tenant's lease except for the surety provisions. In 1984 the tenant went into voluntary liquidation and the liquidators disclaimed the lease. The landlord gave notice to the surety calling on it to take a lease of the unexpired term. The surety refused to enter into a new lease and the landlord brought proceedings to enforce the surety's covenant to accept a new lease. The master granted the landlord specific performance and, on appeal by the surety, his decision was upheld by the judge. e A further appeal by the surety to the Court of Appeal was dismissed. The surety appealed to the House of Lords, contending that a covenant to renew a lease only touched and concerned the demised land in the case of a renewal by the tenant and did not cover an option given to the landlord to create a new lease with a different party.

f **Held** – A covenant by the surety of a tenant to accept a lease replacing the lease granted to the tenant if the tenant became insolvent and disclaimed his lease was a covenant which ran with the land and was therefore enforceable by the landlord against the surety. The appeal would therefore be dismissed (see p 980 c d, p 983 b to e h to p 984 a, post).

P & A Swift Investments (a firm) v Combined English Stores Group plc [1988] 2 All ER 885 applied.

g **Notes**

For the passing of the burden of the tenant's covenants in a lease, see 27 Halsbury's Laws (4th edn) para 391, and for cases on the subject, see 31(1) Digest (Reissue) 371–379, 2967–3028.

h **Cases referred to in opinions**

Hunter's Lease, Re, Giles v Hutchings [1942] 1 All ER 27, [1942] Ch 124.
Muller v Trafford [1901] 1 Ch 54.
Swift (P & A) Investments (a firm) v Combined English Stores Group plc [1988] 2 All ER 885, [1988] 3 WLR 313, HL.
Vyvyan v Arthur (1823) 1 B & C 410, [1814–23] All ER Rep 349, 107 ER 152.
j *Woodall v Clifton* [1905] 2 Ch 257, [1904–7] All ER Rep 268, CA.

Appeal

Ingall Industries plc (the surety) appealed with leave of the Court of Appeal against the decision of the Court of Appeal (Croom-Johnson LJ and Sir Denys Buckley) on 30 March 1988 dismissing the surety's appeal from the decision of Rose J on 16 July 1987 dismissing the surety's appeal from the order of Master Turner dated 8 May 1987 granting the plaintiff, Coronation Street Industrial Properties Ltd (the landlord), specific performance *a* of a covenant to take a lease of premises at Ashmore Lake Road, Willenhall, Walsall. The facts are set out in the opinion of Lord Templeman.

Gavin Lightman QC and *Elizabeth Weaver* for the surety.
Roger Ellis for the landlord.

b

Their Lordships took time for consideration.

16 March. The following opinions were delivered.

LORD KEITH OF KINKEL. My Lords, I have had the opportunity of reading in draft the speech to be delivered by my noble and learned friend Lord Templeman. I *c* agree with it, and for the reasons he gives would dismiss this appeal.

LORD BRANDON OF OAKBROOK. My Lords, for the reasons given in the speech of my noble and learned friend Lord Templeman, I would dismiss the appeal.

LORD TEMPLEMAN. My Lords, the question raised by this appeal is whether a *d* covenant by a surety to accept a lease replacing a lease disclaimed on behalf of an insolvent tenant is a covenant which touches and concerns the land so that the benefit of the covenant runs with the reversion.

By a lease dated 30 August 1972 made between the original landlords, Griffiths Bentley & Co Ltd, of the first part, the tenant, Griffiths Bentley (Engineers) Ltd, of the second part, and the appellant surety, Ingall Industries plc (then Ingall Industries Ltd), of the *e* third part, premises at Willenhall, Walsall, were demised to the tenant for the term of 21 years from 30 August 1972 at a rent and subject to covenants on the part of the tenant to pay the rent, to repair and decorate and to perform and observe other obligations which touched and concerned the land so as to be enforceable by assignees and successors in title of the original landlords against the tenant and the successors in title of the tenant without express assignment of the benefit of the tenant's covenants. Clause 5 of the lease *f* was in these terms:

'THE Surety at the request of the Lessee and in consideration of the demise hereinbefore contained hereby covenants and guarantees with and to the Lessor that the Lessee or the Surety will at all times hereafter duly pay the rents and other sums hereby reserved . . . and duly perform and observe all the covenants on the part of *g* the Lessee and conditions herein contained and also that the Surety will at all times hereafter pay and make good to the Lessor on demand all losses costs, damages and expenses occasioned to it by the non-payment of the rent and other sums or any part thereof or the breach or non-observance of any of the said covenants and conditions . . . and in the event of the tenant (being a Company) going into liquidation or (being an individual) becoming bankrupt and this Lease being disclaimed by a *h* Liquidator or a Trustee in Bankruptcy . . . the Surety hereby covenants with the Lessor that it will accept from the Lessor a Lease of the Demised Premises for a term commencing on the date of such disclaimer and continuing for the residue then unexpired of the term hereby granted such Lease to be at the cost of the Surety and to contain the like Lessee's and Lessor's covenants respectively and the like provisoes and conditions in all respects (including the proviso for re-entry but excluding any *j* provisions for a Surety) and to reserve the like rents and other sums as are herein reserved and made payable provided always that the Surety shall not be bound to accept any such Lease unless the Lessor within the period of three months after such disclaimer serves upon the Surety a Notice in writing so to do . . .'

On 4 August 1981 the original landlords conveyed to the respondent landlord,
a Coronation Street Industrial Properties Ltd, the freehold reversion of the premises
demised by the lease subject to and with the benefit of the lease. The benefit of the
covenant by the surety contained in the lease was not expressly assigned.

On 18 May 1984 the tenant went into voluntary liquidation. Pursuant to an order of
the Companies Court made on 4 February 1986 the liquidators of the tenant on 11 March
1986 disclaimed all the interests of the tenant in the lease. On 5 June 1986 the landlord
b gave notice to the surety requiring the surety to take a lease of the demised premises in
conformity with the covenant on the part of the surety contained in the lease. In these
proceedings the landlord sought and obtained an order requiring the surety to take a
lease accordingly. The surety appeals on the grounds that the covenant on the part of the
surety to take a lease did not touch and concern the land. Therefore the benefit of the
surety's covenant does not run with the reversion and, in the absence of an express
c assignment of the benefit of the covenant, the landlord cannot enforce the covenant.

In *P & A Swift Investments (a firm) v Combined English Stores Group Plc* [1988] 2 All ER
885, [1988] 3 WLR 313 this House considered the covenant by a surety in a form set out
and indistinguishable from the present covenant by the surety (see [1988] 2 All ER 885
at 888, [1988] 3 WLR 313 at 317). In that case the tenant defaulted in payment of rent,
went into voluntary liquidation and disclaimed the lease. An assignee of the reversion
d sought and was held entitled to be paid rent on the grounds that covenant by the surety
to pay the rent touched and concerned the land and the benefit of the covenant ran with
the reversion without express assignment of the benefit of the covenant. Lord Oliver
reaffirmed ([1988] 2 All ER 885 at 889, [1988] 3 WLR 313 at 318) the validity of the
pronouncement by Best J in *Vyvyan v Arthur* (1823) 1 B & C 410 at 417, [1814–23] All
ER Rep 349 at 352 to the following effect:
e
'The general principle is, that if the performance of the covenant be beneficial to
the reversioner, in respect of the lessor's demand, and to no other person, his assignee
may sue upon it; but if it be beneficial to the lessor, without regard to his continuing
owner of the estate, it is a mere collateral covenant, upon which the assignee cannot
sue.'

f Lord Oliver made the following observations ([1988] 2 All ER 885 at 890–891, [1988] 3
WLR 313 at 320):

'Formulations of definitive tests are always dangerous, but it seems to me that,
without claiming to expound an exhaustive guide, the following provides a
satisfactory working test for whether, in any given case, a covenant touches and
g concerns the land. (1) The covenant benefits only the reversioner for the time being,
and if separated from the reversion ceases to be of benefit to the covenantee. (2) The
covenant affects the nature, quality, mode of user or value of the land of the
reversioner. (3) The covenant is not expressed to be personal (that is to say neither
being given only to a specific reversioner nor in respect of the obligations only of a
specific tenant). (4) The fact that a covenant is to pay a sum of money will not
h prevent it from touching and concerning the land so long as the three foregoing
conditions are satisfied and the covenant is connected with something to be done
on, to or in relation to the land.'

The surety's obligation to take a new lease after a disclaimer gives effect to the surety's
obligation to procure compliance with the terms of the old lease. In these circumstances,
j it seems to me that the considerations which led this House in the *Swift Investments* case
to hold that the covenant by the surety touched and concerned the land apply in equal
measure to the whole covenant including the covenant to take a new lease after
disclaimer. Counsel for the surety, however, in the course of an ingenious and painstaking
submission, argued that the decision of this House in the *Swift Investments* case only

applied to that part of the surety's covenant which deals with the payment of rent and performance and observance of the tenant's covenant and did not deal with the second *a* part of the covenant by the surety which obliges the surety to accept a lease after disclaimer.

Counsel submits that the covenant by the surety to take a lease conferred an option on the landlords to create a new lease. A provision in a lease which provides for the creation of a new lease only touches and concerns the land, he submitted, in the case of a covenant to renew the lease and that exception to the general rule is anomalous and should not be *b* extended.

The rule against perpetuities does not apply to a covenant which touches and concerns the land; the courts, anxious to limit the grant of estates in the future to a perpetuity period, will not extend the anomalous rule that a covenant to renew is a covenant which touches and concerns the land demised. In *Muller v Trafford* [1901] 1 Ch 54 a covenant by a mesne landlord to grant a further term to a subtenant, if the mesne landlord *c* acquired a further term from the head landlord, was held not to be a covenant for renewal and therefore not to run with the land. Farwell J said (at 60–61):

'It is said that this is a covenant running with the land. If so, then no question of perpetuity would arise. A covenant to renew has been held for at least two centuries to be a covenant running with the land ... Now, if, as has been argued, the rule *d* that covenants for renewal run with the land, and are not, therefore, within the rule of perpetuity, is a mere technical rule, resting on authority and not on any rational principle, then I answer technicality with technicality, and say that this is not a covenant for renewal at all; and I should not be prepared to extend what has been stated in the arguments to be an anomaly, without any reason underlying it, to a case which is not strictly a covenant for renewal.' *e*

Similarly, in *Woodall v Clifton* [1905] 2 Ch 257, [1904–7] All ER Rep 268 an option conferred on a tenant to purchase the fee simple was held not to touch and concern the land demised. Romer LJ said ([1905] 2 Ch 257 at 279, [1904–7] All ER Rep 268 at 271– 272):

'The covenant is aimed at creating, at a future time, the position of vendor and *f* purchaser of the reversion between the owner and the tenant for the time being. It is in reality not a covenant concerning the tenancy or its terms. Properly regarded, it cannot in our opinion, be said to directly affect or concern the land, regarded as the subject-matter of the lease, any more than a covenant with the tenant for the sale of the reversion to a stranger to the lease could be said to do so. It is not a provision for the continuance of the term, like a covenant to renew, which has been *g* held to run with the reversion, though the fact that a covenant to renew should be held to run with the land has by many been considered as an anomaly, which it is too late now to question, though it is difficult to justify.'

In *Re Hunter's Lease, Giles v Hutchings* [1942] 1 All ER 27, [1942] Ch 124 a covenant by a landlord to pay a sum to the tenant on the expiration or sooner determination of the lease *h* was held not to touch and concern the interest which was the subject matter of the lease and Uthwatt J said ([1942] 1 All ER 27 at 30, [1942] Ch 124 at 131):

'To hold that the burden of the covenant which is here in question runs with the reversion would be to extend the operation of the rule, stated by the Court of Appeal to be anomalous that a covenant to renew touches and concerns the thing demised.'

j

It does not seem to me that the option cases on which counsel for the surety relies were concerned with the position where a new lease is substituted for an old lease which, through no fault of the landlord, ceases to be effective. It is true that the covenant by the surety in the present case involves the creation of a new tenancy and the creation of a new landlord and tenant relationship, but the new tenancy which replaces the old

tenancy is no more perpetuitous than the old. For the benefit of the creditors of an
a insolvent tenant company and in order to enable the assets of the insolvent company to
be distributed, the Companies Acts enable the liquidator to disclaim a lease with the
consent of the court. Such consent must have been given in the present instance in the
belief that the landlords would not be prejudicially affected by the disclaimer. The new
tenancy is substituted for the old disclaimed tenancy with the substitution of the surety
for the tenant because the surety covenanted in the first place to ensure that the tenant's
b obligations under the old tenancy would be performed and observed throughout the
term granted by the old tenancy. The original landlords insisted on a covenant by a
surety in the old lease in order to provide against the very possibility which happened,
namely the insolvency of the tenant. In these circumstances I adhere to the views which
were expressed in the *Swift Investments* case [1988] 2 All ER 885 at 887, [1988] 3 WLR
313 at 316:

c
     'A surety for a tenant is a quasi tenant who volunteers to be a substitute or twelfth
     man for the tenant's team and is subject to the same rules and regulations as the
     player he replaces.'

As a result of the disclaimer the tenant retires mortally wounded and the surety is the
substitute. The covenants by the surety in the old lease touch and concern the land
d demised and the benefit of and the right to enforce that covenant ran with the reversion
and became vested in the landlord when the old tenancy was assigned to it.
    Accordingly, I would dismiss this appeal.

LORD JAUNCEY OF TULLICHETTLE. My Lords, I have had the advantage of
reading in draft the speech of my noble and learned friend Lord Templeman with which
e I entirely agree, and I wish to add only a few words of my own. The gravamen of the
argument of counsel for the surety was that, with the single anomalous exception of an
option to the tenant to renew his lease options in leases did not touch and concern the
land and consequently did not run with the land. The provision with which this appeal
was concerned was an option in favour of the lessor. I very much doubt whether it is
correct so to describe the provision. I would prefer to describe it as a contingent obligation
f by the surety on the lease being disclaimed on behalf of the lessee to accept a lease of the
premises for the unexpired portion of the lease. The contingency is a timeous demand
being made by the lessor.
    Counsel for the landlord was, in my view, well founded in submitting that the second
part of the covenant was analogous to the first part. Indeed I would go further and say
that it was both analogous and complementary thereto. The first part protects the lessors'
g interest by guaranteeing performance of the lessee's obligations to the lessors while the
lease subsists. The second part protects that interest by covenanting to accept a lease for
the residue of the term on the same conditions in the event of the lease being disclaimed
on behalf of the lessee. The second covenant satisfies the working test suggested by Lord
Oliver in *P & A Swift Investments (a firm) v Combined English Stores Group plc* [1988] 2 All
h ER 885 at 890–891, [1988] 3 WLR 313 at 320. If the lessors had not conveyed the
reversion to the landlord the surety would have been bound on a disclaimer by the
lessee's liquidator to accept a lease if called on timeously to do so. He would have been
similarly bound if the lessors had previously conveyed the reversion and had expressly
assigned the benefit of the surety's covenant. Why then should he be able to avoid the
performance of his covenant because events have occurred which affect neither the extent
j of the obligations of the lessee nor of himself and over which neither of them had any
control? So far as the surety is concerned, the only effect of the conveyance of the
reversion is that he receives a lease from, pays rent to and otherwise performs his
obligations as tenant to someone other than the original lessor. In my view neither justice
nor common sense require that he shall be relieved of his obligations in these
circumstances.

LORD LOWRY. My Lords, I have had the advantage of reading in draft the speeches of my noble and learned friends Lord Templeman and Lord Jauncey and, for the reasons given by my noble and learned friends, I, too, would dismiss this appeal.

Appeal dismissed.

Solicitors: *George Carter & Co* (for the surety); *Wigram & Co* (for the landlord).

Mary Rose Plummer   Barrister.

British Medical Association v Greater Glasgow Health Board

HOUSE OF LORDS
LORD KEITH OF KINKEL, LORD BRANDON OF OAKBROOK, LORD TEMPLEMAN, LORD JAUNCEY OF TULLICHETTLE AND LORD LOWRY
20, 21, 22 FEBRUARY, 16 MARCH 1989

Crown – Proceedings against – Health authority – Scottish health board – Relief against Crown – Interdict proceedings against Scottish health board – Whether action against health board a proceeding against Crown – Whether health board entitled to immunity from suit – Crown Proceedings Act 1947, ss 17(3), 21 – National Health Service (Scotland) Act 1978, s 2.

An action against a health board constituted under s 2[a] of the National Health Service (Scotland) Act 1978 is not a proceeding against the Crown for the purposes of s 21[b] of the Crown Proceedings Act 1947, read with s 17(3)[c] of that Act and s 2(8)[d] of the 1978 Act, and accordingly such boards are not entitled to immunity from interdict proceedings by virtue of s 21 of the 1947 Act (see p 985 e to g, p 990 h j and p 991 b to d f, post).

Notes

For limitation of proceedings against the Crown, see 8 Halsbury's Laws (4th edn) para 969 and 11 ibid para 1435.

For the Crown Proceedings Act 1947, ss 17, 21, see 13 Halsbury's Statutes (4th edn) 28, 30.

The functions of health boards constituted in Scotland under s 2 of the National Health Service (Scotland) Act 1978 are performed in England and Wales by health authorities established under s 8 of the National Health Service Act 1977. For s 8 of the 1977 Act, see 30 Halsbury's Statutes (4th edn) 815.

Cases referred to in opinions

BBC v Johns (Inspector of Taxes) [1964] 1 All ER 923, [1965] Ch 32, [1964] 2 WLR 1071, CA.

Feather v R (1865) 6 B & S 257, 122 ER 1191.

---

a   Section 2, so far as material, is set out at p 986 e, post
b   Section 21, so far as material, is set out at p 987 d to f, post
c   Section 17(3) is set out at p 990 f g, post
d   Section 2(8) provides: 'A Health Board shall, notwithstanding that it is exercising functions on behalf of the Secretary of State, be entitled to enforce any rights acquired, and shall be liable in respect of any liabilities incurred (including liability in damages for wrongful or negligent acts or omissions), in the exercise of those functions in all respects as if the Health Board were acting as a principal; and all proceedings for the enforcement of such rights or liabilities shall be brought by or against the Health Board in its own name.'

Pfizer Corp v Ministry of Health [1963] 3 All ER 779, [1964] Ch 614, [1963] 3 WLR 999,
a   CA; *affd* [1965] 1 All ER 450, [1965] AC 512, [1965] 2 WLR 387, HL.
Raleigh v Goschen [1898] 1 Ch 73.
Town Investments Ltd v Dept of the Environment [1977] 1 All ER 813, [1978] AC 359, [1977]
     2 WLR 450, HL.
Wood v Leeds Area Health Authority (Training) [1974] ICR 535, NIRC.

b **Appeal**
The Greater Glasgow Health Board appealed with leave of the Inner House of the Second
Division of the Court of Session in Scotland against an interlocutor of that court (the Lord
Justice Clerk (Ross), Lord Dunpark and Lord Mayfield) (1988 SCLR 403) dated 10 March
1988 refusing a reclaiming motion by the appellants against an interlocutor of the Lord
Ordinary (Prosser) (1988 SCLR 1) dated 26 February 1987 granting the respondents, the
c British Medical Association, interim interdict against the appellants from interviewing
candidates for the position of Director of the Plastic and Oral Surgery Unit, Canniesburn
Hospital, Glasgow unless and until the grievance of the consultants in the unit had been
determined in accordance with the procedures in the agreement between the appellants
and organisations represented on the Whitley Council, including, inter alia, the
respondents. The facts are set out in the opinion of Lord Jauncey.
d

R N M MacLean QC and *M G Clarke* (both of the Scottish Bar) for the appellants.
M S R Bruce QC and *C M Campbell* (both of the Scottish Bar) for the respondents.

Their Lordships took time for consideration.

e 16 March. The following opinions were delivered.

LORD KEITH OF KINKEL. My Lords, I have had the opportunity of considering in
draft the speech to be delivered by my noble and learned friend Lord Jauncey. I agree
with it, and would dismiss the appeal for the reasons he gives.

f **LORD BRANDON OF OAKBROOK.** My Lords, for the reasons set out in the
speech to be delivered by my noble and learned friend Lord Jauncey, I would dismiss the
appeal.

LORD TEMPLEMAN. My Lords, for the reasons to be given by my noble and learned
g friend Lord Jauncey, I would dismiss the appeal.

LORD JAUNCEY OF TULLICHETTLE. My Lords, this appeal arises out of a
dispute between consultants at the West of Scotland Regional Plastic and Oral Surgery
Unit at Canniesburn Hospital, Glasgow, and the Greater Glasgow Health Board. The sole
issue raised by the appeal is whether a health board constituted under the National Health
h Service (Scotland) Act 1978 is entitled to immunity from interdict proceedings by virtue
of s 21 of the Crown Proceedings Act 1947. It is necessary to say no more about the
dispute than that it concerned the appointment of a director of the unit. The Lord
Ordinary (Prosser) granted interim interdict against the health board 'from interviewing
candidates for the position of Director of the Plastic and Oral Surgery Unit, Canniesburn
Hospital, Glasgow' (see 1988 SCLR 1). The interdict sought was at the instance of the
j British Medical Association, who represent the consultants in dispute, and extended also
to the appointment of a director, but in view of an undertaking by the health board to
make no appointment until certain agreed disputes procedures had been exhausted,
interdict against appointment became unnecessary. The health board reclaimed the Lord
Ordinary's interlocutor but the Second Division refused the reclaiming motion (see 1988
SCLR 403).

The health board has now appealed. However, in the interval which elapsed between the interlocutor of the Second Division of 10 March 1988 and the hearing of the appeal in this House the disputes procedures were exhausted and a director was appointed. It followed that the question of whether interim interdict should stand or be recalled had become academic. Nevertheless counsel for the appellants moved your Lordships to hear the appeal for two reasons, namely (1) that a live issue still existed between the parties in relation to expenses in the courts below and costs in this House and (2) that the question raised by the appeal was one of general importance which would be likely to arise again in disputes between the British Medical Association and its members on the one hand and the health boards on the other. Counsel for the respondents did not oppose this motion. Your Lordships took the view that as there was still a lis between the parties it would be proper to hear the appeal.

In addressing the question of whether a health board is entitled to immunity from interdict proceedings it is necessary in the first place to look at the relevant statutory provisions. Section 36(1) of the National Health Service (Scotland) Act 1978 provides:

'It shall be the duty of the Secretary of State to provide throughout Scotland, to such extent as he considers necessary to meet all reasonable requirements, accommodation and services of the following descriptions—(a) hospital accommodation, including accommodation at state hospitals; (b) premises other than hospitals at which facilities are available for any of the services provided under this Act; (c) medical, nursing and other services, whether in such accommodation or premises, in the home of the patient or elsewhere.'

Section 2(1) of the 1978 Act (as amended by para 1 of Sch 7 to the Health and Social Services and Social Security Adjudications Act 1983) provides, inter alia:

'The Secretary of State shall by order constitute in accordance with Part I of Schedule 1 boards for such areas as he may by order determine, for the purpose of exercising such of his functions under this Act as he may so determine . . .'

Paragraph 1 of Sch 1 to the 1978 Act provides that a health board shall be a body corporate and shall have a common seal. Subsections (8) and (9) of s 2 are in the following terms:

'(8) A Health Board shall, notwithstanding that it is exercising functions on behalf of the Secretary of State, be entitled to enforce any rights acquired, and shall be liable in respect of any liabilities incurred (including liability in damages for wrongful or negligent acts or omissions), in the exercise of those functions in all respects as if the Health Board were acting as a principal; and all proceedings for the enforcement of such rights or liabilities shall be brought by or against the Health Board in its own name.

(9) A Health Board shall not be entitled to claim in any proceedings any privilege of the Crown in respect of the recovery or production of documents; but this subsection shall be without prejudice to any right of the Crown to withhold, or procure the withholding from production of, any document on the ground that its disclosure would be contrary to the public interest.'

Although health boards are creatures of the 1978 Act the functions which they perform were previously carried out by regional hospital boards and boards of management under the National Health Service (Scotland) Act 1947. That Act imposed on the Secretary of State duties similar to those imposed on him by s 36(1) of the 1978 Act. Section 13 of the 1947 Act was in the following terms:

'(1) A Regional Hospital Board shall, notwithstanding that they are exercising functions on behalf of the Secretary of State and a Board of Management shall, notwithstanding that they are exercising functions on behalf of the Regional a   Hospital Board be entitled to enforce any rights acquired, and shall be liable in respect of any liabilities incurred (including liability in damages for wrongful or negligent acts or omissions), in the exercise of those functions, in all respects as if the Regional Hospital Board or Board of Management, as the case may be, were acting as a principal, and all proceedings for the enforcement of such rights or liabilities shall be brought by or against the Regional Hospital Board or Board of Management, as the case may be, in their own name.

b   (2) A Regional Hospital Board or Board of Management shall not be entitled to claim in any proceedings any privilege of the Crown in respect of the recovery or production of documents, but this subsection shall be without prejudice to any right of the Crown to withhold or procure the withholding from production of any document on the ground that its disclosure would be contrary to the public interest.'

c   Section 13 of the comparable English Act, the National Health Service Act 1946, was in virtually identical terms. Section 21 of the Crown Proceedings Act 1947, which was later in time than the National Health Service (Scotland) Act 1947 is, so far as relevant, in the following terms:

d   '(1) In any civil proceedings by or against the Crown the court shall, subject to the provisions of this Act, have power to make all such orders as it has power to make in proceedings between subjects, and otherwise to give such appropriate relief as the case may require: Provided that:—(a) where in any proceedings against the Crown any such relief is sought as might in proceedings between subjects be granted by way of injunction or specific performance, the court shall not grant an injunction or make an order for specific performance, but may in lieu thereof make an order declaratory of the rights of the parties . . .

e   (2) The court shall not in any civil proceedings grant any injunction or make any order against an officer of the Crown if the effect of granting the injunction or making the order would be to give any relief against the Crown which could not have been obtained in proceedings against the Crown.'

Against this statutory background counsel for the appellants propounded two
f   alternative tests for determining whether a body fell to be treated as the Crown for the purposes of s 21. In the *first* place the Crown extended to Her Majesty's government in the United Kingdom and those persons and bodies which are appointed or created to carry out exclusively the functions of the executive government. In the *second* place the Crown included a body, person or corporation whose essential activities were carried out exclusively in the performance of a duty or the exercise of a power which is imposed on
g   or vested in the executive government by statute or prerogative. Such a body might be a government agency. A health board, it was said, satisfied both these tests. In support of this argument counsel referred to a number of authorities as showing that the Crown embraces agencies which carry out the executive functions of government on its behalf. In *BBC v Johns (Inspector of Taxes)* [1964] 1 All ER 923 at 941, [1965] Ch 32 at 79 Diplock LJ, in considering whether the BBC were entitled to Crown immunity from payment of
h   taxes, said:

'But to use the expression "the Crown" as personifying the executive government of the country tends to conceal the fact that the executive functions of sovereignty are of necessity performed through the agency of persons other than the Queen herself. Such persons may be natural persons or, as has been increasingly the
j   tendency over the last hundred years, fictitious persons—corporations. The question here is whether the B.B.C. carries on all or any of its activities as agent for the executive government. Are they carried out in the performance of a duty or in the exercise of a power which is imposed on or vested in the executive government of the United Kingdom by statute or by the prerogative? (cf. *Pfizer Corpn. v. Ministry of Health* ([1963] 3 All ER 779 at 788, [1964] Ch 614 at 645)).'

In *Town Investments Ltd v Dept of the Environment* [1977] 1 All ER 813 at 818, [1978] AC
359 at 381 Lord Diplock said: *a*

'Where, as in the instant case, we are concerned with the legal nature of the
exercise of executive powers of government, I believe that some of the more
Athanasian-like features of the debate in your Lordships' House could have been
eliminated if instead of speaking of "the Crown" we were to speak of "the
government"—a term appropriate to embrace both collectively and individually all
of the Ministers of the Crown and Parliamentary Secretaries under whose direction   *b*
the administrative work of government is carried on by the civil servants employed
in the various government departments. It is through them that the executive
powers of Her Majesty's Government in the United Kingdom are exercised,
sometimes in the more important administrative matters in Her Majesty's name,
but most often under their own official designation. Executive acts of government
that are done by any of them are acts done by "the Crown" in the fictional sense in   *c*
which that expression is now used in English public law.'

Both these cases were concerned with Crown immunity and necessarily involved
consideration of whether for general purposes a particular individual or body was the
Crown.

Perhaps more germane to the present appeal is *Pfizer Corp v Ministry of Health* [1963] 3   *d*
All ER 779, [1964] Ch 614, which was concerned with whether the use of drugs by the
National Health Service was 'for the services of the Crown' for the purposes of s 46(1) of
the Patents Act 1949. In the Court of Appeal Willmer LJ, after reference to certain
sections of the National Health Service Act 1946, said ([1963] 3 All ER 779 at 786, [1964]
Ch 614 at 642):
                                                                                               e
'These provisions of the Act of 1946 to which I have referred seem to me to lead
inexorably to the conclusion that regional hospital boards, hospital management
committees and hospital officers, in exercising their respective functions, are acting
on behalf of the minister for the purpose of discharging the duties laid by the statute
on him, and are therefore carrying on services of the Crown.'

Diplock LJ said ([1963] 3 All ER 779 at 792–793, [1964] Ch 614 at 652–653):   *f*

'The duty to provide hospital and specialist services is imposed on the Minister. It
is in its nature a duty which he can only perform vicariously through agents acting
on his behalf. The Act requires him to do so through the immediate agency of the
regional hospital boards. The regional hospital boards, being corporations, can
themselves only do the physical acts involved in the provision of the services on   *g*
behalf of the Minister, vicariously through their officers and servants. Any act done
by an officer or servant of a regional hospital board for the purpose of providing
hospital or specialist services is accordingly done on behalf of the Minister in
performance of the statutory duty which is imposed on him. Their acts are acts of a
government department. Counsel for [Pfizer Corp] placed considerable reliance on
s. 13 of the Act of 1946, as showing that the regional hospital boards exercise their   *h*
functions as principals and not as agents of the Minister. But the section seems to
me to be directed to quite a different matter. The National Health Service Act, 1946,
was passed before the Crown Proceedings Act, 1947. At that date the fact that a
regional hospital board was acting on behalf of a minister of the Crown would have
entitled it to shelter behind the immunity of the crown from suit except by petition
of right: (see *Feather* v. *R.* ((1865) 6 B & S 257, 122 ER 1191)); *Raleigh* v. *Goschen*   *j*
([1898] 1 Ch 73). All that s. 13 does is to re-assert that a regional hospital board is
acting on behalf of the Minister (i.e., on behalf of the Crown) but to provide that,
for the purpose of legal proceedings for the enforcement of rights and liabilities, it
shall be treated, notwithstanding that it is an agent of the Crown, as if it were acting

as principal and shall sue and be sued in its own name. Such a provision would have
a   been unnecessary unless a regional hospital board, in exercising its functions under
the Act, was acting on behalf of the Crown. It is not, in my view, necessary to
determine whether the officers and servants of a regional hospital board are strictly
"servants of the Crown". It is sufficient for the decision of the present appeal that, in
administering or supplying drugs to in-patients or out-patients for the purpose of
their treatment at National Health Service hospitals, such officers and servants are
b   acting on behalf of the Minister in fulfilment of his statutory duty to provide
medical, nursing and other services required at or for the purposes of hospitals. The
use of patented drugs for this purpose is thus, in my view, a use by a government
department.'

The Court of Appeal's decision that supply of patented drugs to hospital patients was
c for the service of the Crown was upheld by this House, where Pfizer Corp conceded that
doctors and nurses in National Health hospitals were to be treated as servants or agents of
the Crown (see [1965] 1 All ER 450 at 453, [1965] AC 512 at 533 per Lord Reid). Counsel
for the appellants relied strongly on the dictum of Diplock LJ that acts of an officer or
servant of a regional hospital board 'are acts of a government department' in support of
the proposition that health boards were the Crown or, in any event, agents of the Crown
d in a sense which identified them much more closely with the Crown than would a
private agent be identified with his principal (see [1963] 3 All ER 779 at 792, [1964] Ch
614 at 653). He also referred to *Wood v Leeds Area Health Authority (Training)* [1974] ICR
535 at 538, in which Donaldson P, in the National Industrial Relations Court, having
posed the question of whether national health service employees were servants of the
Crown, referred to the National Health Service Act 1946 and to the passage from the
e judgment of Willmer LJ in *Pfizer Corp v Ministry of Health* [1963] 3 All ER 779 at 786,
[1964] Ch 614 at 642 which I have quoted above, and concluded that the plaintiff, who
was a national health service employee, was in fact a Crown servant. If, it was argued, a
national health service employee engaged and paid by a health authority was a Crown
servant it must follow that the authority was itself the Crown or an agent thereof.
Accordingly, proceedings against the health authority were proceedings against the
f Crown. Reliance was also placed on (1) s 138(5) of and Sch 5 to the Employment
Protection (Consolidation) Act 1978, which provided that for the purposes of certain
parts of that Act health boards should not be regarded as performing functions on behalf
of the Crown so that employment by them would not be Crown employment, and (2)
s 1(1)(a) of the National Health Service (Amendment) Act 1986, which is in the following
terms:

g
> 'For the purposes of food legislation—(a) a health authority shall not be regarded
> as a servant or agent of the Crown, or as enjoying any status, immunity or privilege
> of the Crown . . .'

These two statutory provisions, it was said, showed that for all purposes other than
those therein referred to, health authorities were the Crown.
h   My Lords, these arguments were attractive, but I consider that they failed to address
directly the critical question which is not whether health boards perform functions on
behalf of the Crown, a matter which was not disputed by counsel for the respondents,
nor whether health boards for the purposes of statutory immunity or other purposes fall
to be treated as the Crown or as agents so clearly identified with the Crown that they are
for all practical purposes indistinguishable therefrom, but whether the respondents'
j petition amounted to 'proceedings against the Crown' within the meaning of s 21(1) of
the Crown Proceedings Act 1947. The four authorities to which I have referred were not
concerned with this point. That Act, as counsel for the respondents pointed out, is not
concerned with Crown immunity and who qualifies therefor, but in the words of the
long title with 'the civil liabilities and rights of the Crown' and 'civil proceedings by and

against the Crown'. Indeed, s 40(2)(*f*) specifically provides that the presumption of Crown immunity from statutory liability is not to be affected. The two primary objects of the Act were (1) to enable a plaintiff in England to proceed against the Crown as of right instead of by petition of right and (2) to subject the Crown in both England and Scotland to actions founded in tort and delict in the same way as other defendants and defenders.

Historically the position of the private litigant vis-à-vis the Crown differed in Scotland and England. While actions founded in tort and delict could be brought against the Crown in neither country, other actions could be brought as of right in Scotland, whereas in England it was necessary to proceed by petition of right. Indeed, interdict was available against the Crown in Scotland although such a remedy was, I understand, inconceivable in England. It could be said that Scots law took a more robust view of the individual's rights against the Crown than did the law of England. Had the present interdict proceedings been instituted against a regional hospital board after the passing of the National Health Service (Scotland) Act 1947 but before the coming into force of the Crown Proceedings Act 1947, no one could have suggested that they were incompetent. I refer briefly to this historical background because the Crown Proceedings Act 1947 is selective in its application to Scotland, and the historical background must be relevant to this selectivity.

My Lords, s 21(1) of the Crown Proceedings Act 1947 provides that in any proceedings against the Crown the court shall not grant injunction or interdict but shall instead make a declaratory order. Section 21(2) is designed to ensure that sub-s (1) is not circumvented by a litigant obtaining an injunction or interdict against an officer of the Crown which would have the effect of enjoining or interdicting the Crown. Officer in relation to the Crown is defined by s 38(2) as including 'any servant of His Majesty, and accordingly (but without prejudice to the generality of the foregoing provision) includes a Minister of the Crown'. It was not and in my view could not have been contended that a health board was an officer of the Crown for the purposes of s 21(2). However, the appellants' argument produces the curious result that whereas the Secretary of State is an officer of the Crown for the purposes of s 21, a health board which carries out functions on his behalf is not an officer of the Crown but the Crown itself. In considering the scope of the proceedings to which s 21 applies, regard must be had to s 17(3) which provides:

> 'Civil proceedings against the Crown shall be instituted against the appropriate authorised Government department, or, if none of the authorised Government departments is appropriate or the person instituting the proceedings has any reasonable doubt whether any and if so which of those departments is appropriate, against the Attorney General.'

This section applies only to England, no doubt because provision already existed for suing the Lord Advocate as representing government departments by virtue of the Crown Suits (Scotland) Act 1857. However, although this is a Scottish case, s 17(3) is important as showing the sort of proceedings which Parliament had in mind in s 21, namely proceedings against the appropriate government department or the Attorney General. It is, in my view, inconceivable that Parliament should have intended to fetter the right of the subject to obtain a prohibitory order more strictly in Scotland than in England, particularly when the historical background is remembered. Counsel for the respondents was, in my view, well founded in contending that the underlying approach in s 17(3) and in the 1857 Act was similar. Thus looking at the Crown Proceedings Act 1947 alone, it appears that Parliament intended that relief from prohibitory orders should only be available to the Crown in such proceedings as were instituted in accordance with s 17(3) or with the 1857 Act.

However, this appeal does not turn solely on the provisions of the Crown Proceedings Act 1947 because s 2(8) of the 1978 Act provides that health boards should be liable in respect of any liabilities incurred in the exercise of their functions as if they were

principals and should be sued in their own name. As I mentioned earlier, a similar
a provision appeared in the English and the Scottish National Health Service Acts prior to
the Crown Proceedings Act, and if Parliament had intended that actions against regional
hospital boards and hospital management committees should be treated as civil
proceedings against the Crown, it would have been very simple to have so provided in
s 17(3) of the Crown Proceedings Act. Section 2(8) of the 1978 Act is prima facie
inconsistent with the view that an action against the health board is a proceeding against
b the Crown for the purposes of s 21 of the Crown Proceedings Act. Counsel for the
appellants sought to argue that s 2(9) of the 1978 Act demonstrated that but for its
provisions a health board would be entitled to claim Crown privilege in relation to
recovery of documents. Even if that is the proper inference to be drawn, of which I am
by no means certain, the mere fact that a health board, in exercising the functions
imposed on the Secretary of State, could claim Crown privilege in relation to a document,
c cannot convert it into the Crown for the purposes of proceedings against it. When s 2(8)
of the 1978 Act and ss 17(3) and 21 of the Crown Proceedings Act are read together, the
inference is inescapable that s 21 was never intended to apply to proceedings against a
regional hospital board or its successor, a health board. I am fortified in reaching this
conclusion by the fact that the general purpose of the Crown Proceedings Act was to
make it easier rather than more difficult for a subject to sue the Crown. To hold that the
d Act had clothed with immunity from prohibitory proceedings a body which prior to its
passing would have enjoyed no such immunity would be to run wholly counter to its
spirit. Furthermore, neither principle nor logic would appear to require that a body such
as a health board should be granted such a privilege.

All three judges in the Second Division concluded that, although a health board
performed certain functions on behalf of the Secretary of State, it was not the Crown and
e therefore not entitled to protection under the Crown Proceedings Act 1947 (see 1988
SCLR 403). I do not in any way criticise these conclusions, but I do not find it necessary
to decide this case on so broad a basis, preferring to rely on a construction of the sections
above referred to. I would therefore dismiss the appeal.

f **LORD LOWRY.** My Lords, I have had the advantage of reading in draft the speech
prepared by my noble and learned friend Lord Jauncey.

I agree with it and, for the reasons given by my noble and learned friend I, too, would
dismiss this appeal.

Appeal dismissed.

g Solicitors: *Lawrence Graham,* agents for *James I McCubbin,* Edinburgh (for the appellants);
S J Berwin & Co, agents for *Morton Fraser & Milligan WS,* Edinburgh (for the respondents).

Mary Rose Plummer   Barrister.

R v Lombardi

COURT OF APPEAL, CRIMINAL DIVISION
LORD LANE CJ, SIMON BROWN AND ROCH JJ
15, 21 NOVEMBER 1988

Indictment – Addition of new counts – Count founded on facts or evidence before examining justices – Count based on evidence before examining justices but in respect of which defendant not committed – Whether permissible to add or substitute count based on evidence before examining justices but not founded on same facts or forming part of series of same or similar offences as counts in existing indictment – Administration of Justice (Miscellaneous Provisions) Act 1933, s 2(2) proviso – Indictment Rules 1971, r 9.

Additional counts based on evidence which was before the examining justices but in respect of which there has been no committal may only be preferred under the proviso to s 2(2)[a] of the Administration of Justice (Miscellaneous Provisions) Act 1933 in substitution for or in addition to counts in an indictment in respect of which the defendant has been committed if the new counts can properly be joined in that indictment under r 9[b] of the Indictment Rules 1971 because they are founded on the same facts or form or are a part of a series of offences of the same or a similar character (see p 995 b to e, post).

Notes

For the joinder of offences on the same indictment, see 11 Halsbury's Laws (4th edn) para 213, and for cases on the subject, see 14(1) Digest (Reissue) 284–285, 2148–2164.

For defective indictments, see 11 Halsbury's Laws (4th edn) para 216, and for cases on the subject, see 14(1) Digest (Reissue) 304–305, 2327–2336.

For the Administration of Justice (Miscellaneous Provisions) Act 1933, s 2, see 12 Halsbury's Statutes (4th edn) 225.

For the Indictment Rules 1971, r 9, see 6 Halsbury's Statutory Instruments (Grey Volume) 13.

Case referred to in judgment

R v Newland [1988] 2 All ER 891, [1988] QB 402, [1988] 2 WLR 382, CA.

Cases also cited

R v Cairns (1983) 87 Cr App R 287, CA.
R v Roe [1967] 1 All ER 492, [1967] 1 WLR 634, CA.

Appeal against conviction

Raymond Alexander Lombardi appealed with the leave of the single judge against his conviction in the Crown Court at Southwark before Mr T Maher sitting as an assistant recorder on four charges under the Bankruptcy Act 1914 to which he pleaded guilty following the rejection of a submission on his behalf that the indictment containing the counts charging the offences should not be preferred or signed because he had not been committed for trial on those offences. The appellant was sentenced to three months imprisonment to run consecutively with a sentence of 30 months' imprisonment imposed for counterfeiting offences on which the appellant had been found guilty after trial on another indictment. The facts are set out in the judgment of the court.

---

a   Section 2(2), so far as material, is set out at p 993 f to j, post
b   Rule 9 is set out at p 994 b, post

G A Pringle (assigned by the Registrar of Criminal Appeals) for the appellant.

a   *John Blair-Gould* for the Crown.

Cur adv vult

21 November. The following judgment of the court was delivered.

b   **LORD LANE CJ.** On 9 February 1988 in the Crown Court at Southwark the appellant faced two indictments. The first indictment charged him with four offences under the Forgery and Counterfeiting Act 1981. He was convicted on three of those counts and sentenced to a total of 30 months' imprisonment. His appeal against that sentence was dismissed on 15 November 1988.

On the second indictment he faced four charges under the Bankruptcy Act 1914.

c   Before arraignment on those charges counsel moved to quash the indictment. The assistant recorder heard argument on both sides and then in a judgment which was admirably succinct and clear he ruled against the application. The appellant then pleaded guilty and was sentenced to a total of three months' imprisonment to run consecutively to the 30 months in respect of the first indictment.

The history of events, so far as it is material, was as follows. On 6 March 1987 the

d   appellant was committed for trial by the Horseferry Road justices on a number of charges under the 1981 Act. In early June 1987 there appeared two indictments, one in relation to the counterfeiting offences (on which the appellant had been committed for trial) and the other (the second indictment) in relation to bankruptcy offences, in respect of which there was, so it happened, ample evidence before the justices but no charge and no committal.

e   It was submitted, unsuccessfully, on behalf of the appellant to the assistant recorder at the trial that the second indictment did not comply with the provisions of the Administration of Justice (Miscellaneous Provisions) Act 1933. On this appeal, which comes by leave of the single judge, it is submitted that the ruling of the assistant recorder was wrong, the indictment was bad and the conviction on the bankruptcy charges should accordingly be quashed.

f   Section 2(2) of the 1933 Act provides as follows:

'Subject as hereinafter provided no bill of indictment charging any person with an indictable offence shall be preferred unless either—(a) the person charged has been committed for trial for the offence; or (b) the bill is preferred by the direction of the criminal division of the Court of Appeal or by the direction or with the

g   consent of a judge of the High Court . . .'

The provisions of para (b) have no application in the present case. The justices did not commit the appellant for trial on these charges. Therefore the provisions of para (a) were not applicable. Accordingly the Crown was thrown back onto the proviso to that section, which read as follows:

h   'Provided that—(i) where the person charged has been committed for trial, the bill of indictment against him may include, either in substitution for or in addition to counts charging the offence for which he was committed, any counts founded on facts or evidence disclosed in any examination or deposition taken before a justice in his presence, being counts which may lawfully be joined in the same indictment . . .'

j   There is no dispute that there was the necessary evidence before the justices which disclosed the commission of the bankruptcy offences.

What counsel for the appellant submits in short is that the proviso only allows the prosecution to add or substitute charges to those in the bill of indictment against the defendant, and does not permit the prosecution to prefer another indictment containing

charges on which he was not committed for trial, even though they may be amply
supported by evidence which was before the justices.

a

Why then, one asks rhetorically, did the prosecution not simply add these bankruptcy
counts to the indictment charging the counterfeiting offences? The answer to that is that
those counts could not lawfully be included in the same indictment because of the
provisions of r 9 of the Indictment Rules 1971, SI 1971/1253, which read as follows:

> 'Charges for any offences may be joined in the same indictment if those charges
> are founded on the same facts, or form or are a part of a series of offences of the same
> or a similar character.'

b

The counterfeiting charges and the bankruptcy offences do not fall within that
description.

Why then, one asks again, should the prosecution not add the fresh charges to the
original indictment and then apply to sever the charges and thus make two indictments?

c

The answer to that question again is to be found in r 9, which, as already pointed out,
prohibits the first step of that exercise. That is emphasised, if emphasis is required, by
the decision of another division of this court in *R v Newland* [1988] 2 All ER 891, [1988]
QB 402. In that case it was held that the power to sever an indictment within s 5(3) of
the Indictments Act 1915 was applicable only to a valid indictment. Since the indictment
in that case charged the appellant with three counts of drug offences and three counts of
assault occasioning actual bodily harm, which were not connected with the drug offences,
the indictment was invalid and accordingly the power to sever did not exist.

d

Thus, if the submission of the appellant is correct, one reaches this situation. If the
justices had committed for trial on both sets of charges, the prosecution could then
legitimately have preferred two separate indictments, one charging the counterfeiting
and the other the bankruptcy offences. Since they did not commit on both (although
they might have done), the prosecution cannot add the counts because of the terms of
r 9, nor can they prefer a second different indictment because s 2 of the 1933 Act only
permits addition or substitution to the existing indictment and makes no provision for
the preferring of an altogether fresh indictment. The only way, it is suggested, that the
prosecution can legitimately proceed on the fresh charges is to obtain a voluntary bill or
else to charge the defendant and apply to have him committed for trial by the justices on
the fresh charge.

e

f

It is tolerably clear that this situation was not present to the minds of those who were
responsible for the wording of the proviso to s 2(2) of the 1933 Act. The question is
whether the words of the proviso are apt to cover the present situation, namely where
the fresh charges are contained in a separate indictment.

Counsel for the Crown puts his case in this way. There is nothing to prevent more
than one indictment based on one committal. Therefore the words 'the bill of indictment'
in the section must mean any bill of indictment, or the bill of indictment which is under
consideration at that particular time. The second indictment here contains charges
admittedly based on evidence which was before the justices; these charges, he suggests,
were 'in substitution' for the charges on which the defendant was committed, and they,
being all charges under the Bankruptcy Act 1914 of a similar nature to each other, could
lawfully be joined in the same indictment. Therefore the second indictment falls within
the terms of the proviso.

g

h

Section 2(2) is clearly restrictive. Its primary purpose is to prevent indictments being
preferred save after committal or alternative judicial leave. The proviso allows some
relaxation, which is itself restricted by the final words 'being counts which may lawfully
be joined in the same indictment'.

j

It would, in our judgment, be contrary to the whole tenor of the section to allow the
prosecution to prefer indictments in the way they here suggest without any reference to
justices, judge or appellate court. This is particularly so where, under the present day
committal proceedings, there may be much evidence on paper, perhaps only marginally

relevant to the charges on which committal is being sought, but providing evidence of
a the commission of other criminal offences, and therefore also providing ample scope for
further charges and further potential indictments.

It is true that the words 'bill of indictment' are apt to include more than one bill of
indictment. Thus, as already noted, where the justices have committed on more than
one charge, the prosecution are at liberty, in the appropriate case, to prefer a separate
indictment in respect of each. However, charges in respect of which there has been no
b committal, even though based on evidence which was before the justices, can only be the
proper subject of indictment where two conditions are satisfied. First, they must be in
'substitution' for, or in addition to, the counts in respect of which the defendant was
committed. The contentions advanced by the prosecution involve the necessity, so it
seems to us, of treating this provision as otiose, or, even worse, of allowing the prosecution
to prefer two indictments to create a notional 'substitution'.
c   The second condition which has to be satisfied is that the new counts 'may lawfully be
joined in the same indictment'. That must, in our judgment, mean the same indictment
as that containing the charges on which the defendant was committed. That is clear from
the whole context and also from the use of the word 'include'. The prosecution
contentions require that those words should mean simply that no indictment must
contain counts which cannot lawfully be joined, which scarcely needs stating. If
d Parliament had intended the law to be as the prosecution claim it to be, it would have
been easy in plain terms to say so.

In short, in the judgment of this court, the words of s 2(2) and its proviso are not apt
to entitle the prosecution to prefer the second indictment. The assistant recorder should
have acceded to the motion to quash that indictment. We therefore allow this appeal and
quash these convictions.
e

Appeal allowed. Convictions quashed.

Solicitors: *Crown Prosecution Service*, Southwark.

N P Metcalfe Esq   Barrister.
f

R v Follett

COURT OF APPEAL, CRIMINAL DIVISION
g LORD LANE CJ, SIMON BROWN AND ROCH JJ
21 NOVEMBER, 9 DECEMBER 1988

*Indictment – Second indictment – Second indictment preferred to cure earlier defective indictment
– Earlier indictment charging defendant and others with disparate offences not arising out of
same facts – Judge giving leave to prefer three further bills of indictment – Original indictment
h stayed – Fresh indictment containing two counts against accused – One count same as in original
indictment – Second count based on evidence given at committal proceedings – Whether new
indictment valid – Indictment Rules 1971, r 9.*

The appellant was committed for trial for theft and burglary under a single indictment
which charged the appellant and others with disparate offences of theft, burglary, cheque
j and credit card offences, handling stolen property and drug offences. The indictment
contravened r 9[a] of the Indictment Rules 1971 because the charges were not founded on
the same facts and they did not form nor were they part of a series of offences of the same
or a similar character. The trial judge gave the prosecution leave to prefer three voluntary

---

a   Rule 9 is set out at p 997 *d e*, post

bills out of time splitting up the offences so that each indictment complied with r 9.
Proceedings on the original indictment were stayed. The new indictment contained two
counts of theft, the first of which had not appeared in the original indictment but was
based on the evidence given at the committal proceedings and could thus properly be
included in the new indictment and the second of which was the same as a count in the
original indictment. The appellant pleaded guilty to the second count and his trial on the
first count proceeded. The appellant was found guilty on the first count. He appealed,
contending that the prosecution were not entitled to prefer a fresh series of indictments
in order to cure an original indictment which was defective.

Held – Where an indictment was invalid because it was not drawn according to r 9 of
the 1971 rules the court was entitled to give leave to the prosecution to prefer out of time
fresh indictments which conformed to the 1971 rules, notwithstanding the existence of
the original invalid indictment, and then stay proceedings on the original indictment
and proceed to trial on the fresh indictments. The appeal would therefore be dismissed
(see p 999 d e and p 1001 g h, post).

R v Thompson [1975] 2 All ER 1028 explained.

R v Newland [1988] 2 All ER 891 distinguished.

Notes

For the joinder of offences on the same indictment, see 11 Halsbury's Laws (4th edn)
paras 213, and for cases on the subject, see 14(1) Digest (Reissue) 284–285, 2148–2164.

For defective indictments, see 11 Halsbury's Laws (4th edn) para 216, and for cases on
the subject, see 14(1) Digest (Reissue) 304–305, 2327–2336.

For the Indictment Rules 1971, r 9, see 6 Halsbury's Statutory Instruments (Grey
Volume) 13.

Cases referred to in judgment

Poole v R [1960] 3 All ER 398, [1961] AC 223, [1960] 2 WLR 770, PC.
Practice Note [1976] 2 All ER 326, [1976] 1 WLR 409, CA.
R v Bell (1984) 78 Cr App R 305, CA.
R v Groom [1976] 2 All ER 321, [1977] QB 6, [1976] 2 WLR 618, CA.
R v Newland [1988] 2 All ER 891, [1988] QB 402, [1988] 2 WLR 382, CA.
R v Thompson, R v Clein [1975] 2 All ER 1028, [1975] 1 WLR 1425, CA.

Case also cited

R v Cairns (1983) 87 Cr App R287, CA.

Appeal against conviction

Gary Follett appealed with the leave of the single judge against his conviction in the
Crown Court at Stoke-on-Trent before Mr J H B Saunders sitting as an assistant recorder
and a jury on a charge of theft for which, together with another charge of theft to which
he pleaded guilty, he was sentenced to four months' imprisonment. The grounds of the
appeal were that the conviction arose out of a defective indictment. The facts are set out
in the judgment of the court.

A Nadim (assigned by the Registrar of Criminal Appeals) for the appellant.
J Goldring QC for the Crown.

Cur adv vult

9 December. The following judgment of the court was delivered.

LORD LANE CJ. On 29 February 1988 in the Crown Court at Stoke-on-Trent the
appellant was arraigned on an indictment dated 29 February 1988 which contained two

counts. He pleaded guilty to a charge of theft in count 2 and two days later, after a trial,
a he was convicted of the theft charged against him in count 1, and on that he was
sentenced to four months' imprisonment. No separate penalty was imposed on count 2.
He now appeals against conviction on a point of law.

Nothing turns on the facts of the offences, but the chronology of events is important.
Five defendants were charged on an indictment, which was dated 1 February 1988.
Angela Salmon pleaded guilty to count 4, which was the only count affecting her. One
b defendant, Shaun Smith, did not appear. The other defendants, including the appellant,
all pleaded not guilty to the various counts and the matter was then adjourned for trial.
The judge on that occasion expressed doubts about the propriety of the indictment in the
form in which it stood, but no action was taken. On 29 February 1988 the case was listed
again, this time before Mr J H B Saunders sitting as an assistant recorder. Three defendants
were before the court for trial: Barry Chevin, John David Chevin and the appellant.
c Shaun Smith was present on this occasion and pleaded guilty.

The original indictment dated 1 February 1988 contained nine counts. Counts 1 to 3
charged the Chevins and in one count the appellant as well with thefts and burglary.
Counts 4 to 5 were charges of credit card and cheque offences against the Chevins. Counts
6, 7 and 8 charged Smith with drug offences and count 9 charged Smith with handling.
It is clear that this indictment was not drawn according to the rules. Indeed, whoever
d was responsible for drafting it had not paid any attention to r 9 of the Indictment Rules
1971, SI 1971/1253, which provides:

> 'Charges for any offences may be joined in the same indictment if those charges
> are founded on the same facts, or form or are part of a series of offences of the same
> or a similar character.'

e There was no such nexus between the various groups of charges in that indictment.

Counsel for the prosecution on 29 February conceded the breach of r 9 of the 1971
rules, and he in the first instance applied to the assistant recorder to quash the indictment
and for leave to prefer further bills out of time. Doubt was felt however by both the
assistant recorder and counsel as to the propriety of that course. In the upshot the assistant
f recorder gave leave to prefer three further bills of indictment splitting up the offences
into their proper compartments (as should have been done originally), so that each
indictment prima facie complied with r 9. These indictments ((a), (b) and (c)) were
accordingly settled and dated 29 February. The assistant recorder then ordered that all
proceedings on the original indictment should be stayed as against the appellant and the
two Chevins. The original indictment was not quashed nor were any of the counts in the
g original indictment amended out of that indictment.

Overnight the full report of *R v Newland* [1988] 2 All ER 891, [1988] QB 402 was
obtained. Up to that time the court had only been provided with The Times newspaper
report of the judgment in that case. The assistant recorder discovered that he had (so he
thought) done what in *R v Newland* it was held a court should not do.

The assistant recorder was faced with a difficult situation. Due to no fault of his own
h he had apparently, so to speak, burnt his boats. He had been left with this situation. The
original indictment was still in existence, although proceedings on it had been stayed.
There were now three fresh indictments founded on the same committal proceedings
which he had given leave to prefer out of time covering most of the ground of the
original indictment with a trial in prospect on one of the fresh indictments. That
indictment contained two counts. Count 1 on which he was tried was based on count 2
j in the original indictment. There was a fresh count 2, to which the appellant pleaded
guilty. That was an additional count not appearing in the original indictment but based
on evidence which was before the justices on committal. It was a charge which could
properly be joined in the same indictment as the offence on which the justices had
committed him for trial.

In *R v Newland* [1988] 2 All ER 891, [1988] QB 402, where the indictment had been
drawn in breach of r 9 of the 1971 rules, the recorder had simply ordered severance of

the two disparate sets of counts so that they could be tried separately. It was there held
by another division of this court that that course was not permissible. It was contended   *a*
by the prosecution in that case that severance was permissible by virtue of s 5(3) of the
Indictments Act 1915, which provides as follows:

> 'Where, before trial, or at any stage of a trial, the court is of opinion that a person
> accused may be prejudiced or embarrassed in his defence by reason of being charged
> with more than one offence in the same indictment, or that for any other reason it
> is desirable to direct that the person should be tried separately for any one or more   *b*
> offences charged in an indictment, the court may order a separate trial of any count
> or counts of such indictment.'

That argument was rejected. Watkins LJ said ([1988] 2 All ER 891 at 894, [1988] QB 402
at 406):

> '. . . that subsection can only apply to a valid indictment. It states what the court   *c*
> may do by way of ordering separate trials of counts in a valid indictment in the
> interests of a fair trial for a defendant or defendants.'

What the court could and should have done was, as Watkins LJ went on to say, to take
advantage of the provisions of s 5(1) of the 1915 Act:
                                                                                            d
> 'Where, before trial, or at any stage of a trial, it appears to the court that the
> indictment is defective, the court shall make such order for the amendment of the
> indictment as the court thinks necessary to meet the circumstances of the case . . .'

Then Watkins LJ continued ([1988] 2 All ER 891 at 894, [1988] QB 402 at 406):

> 'It was clearly open therefore to the assistant recorder to amend the indictment.   *e*
> He could have done that simply by ordering that the drugs counts or the assault
> counts be deleted from the indictment, and that the trial of the indictment take
> place in its amended form. If he had so ordered, then a perfectly lawful trial would
> have ensued.'

Thus in the present case there could have been no objection if all the counts save those
on which the appellant and his co-defendants stood charged had been deleted from the   *f*
indictment and the trial of these three men had continued on the surviving counts. This
is not what happened, as already described. The original indictment stood unamended.
Three fresh indictments, (a), (b) and (c), were with leave preferred, proceedings on the
first indictment were stayed and the trial took place on one of the counts in fresh
indictment (c). The leave which was granted was (as already explained) leave to prefer
the indictment after the time set by the 1971 rules had expired.   *g*
    The appellant criticises that course on two main grounds. They are these. First, it does
what the court in *R v Newland* [1988] 2 All ER 891 at 894, [1988] QB 402 at 406 (albeit
in an obiter dictum) seems to suggest should not be done. This is the passage:

> 'What the prosecution could have done, if anything, about the counts which had
> been amended out of the indictment is altogether a different matter. But that was   *h*
> for the prosecution to concern itself with and not the court. What the prosecution
> could not have done in the circumstances, nor could the court have ordered that to
> be done, was to draft a fresh indictment to include the counts amended out of the
> original indictment. There is no such power known to us. In order to proceed on
> the counts amended out, it would have been necessary for the prosecution to seek a
> voluntary bill.'   *j*

Second, it is contended that in any event there is no power to prefer a fresh series of
indictments in order to cure a defective original indictment.
    So far as the first point is concerned, namely the impact of the decision in *R v Newland*,
it seems to us that that case was dealing with a different situation from that which faces

us. The ratio decidendi there was that it is not permissible to amend an indictment
a invalid by reason of misjoinder of counts by severing the disparate parts and trying each
separately. That was not done here. What could be done was to amend the invalid
indictment by deleting one of the disparate parts and to conduct the trial on the basis of
what remained. The obiter dictum simply said that, having 'deleted' one set of counts,
that deleted portion could not properly be the subject of a fresh indictment without the
assistance of a voluntary bill. That would seem to flow from the provisions of s 2(2) of
b the Administration of Justice (Miscellaneous Provisions) Act 1933, which provides in
effect that an indictment must be founded on charges on which the justices have
committed or else on a voluntary bill. Once the counts have been deleted, the effect of
the justices' committal is, so to speak, spent. No counts were deleted in the instant case.
The stay was only ordered after the new bills of indictment had been preferred.

It follows that the problem in the present case comes down to this. Where an
c indictment is invalid by reason of a misjoinder of counts as here, is the prosecution
entitled to prefer two or more fresh indictments drawn in accordance with r 9 and
covering the same ground as the original indictment, providing that they thereafter elect
which of the indictments they will proceed on?

Counsel for the Crown submits that there is nothing in the 1915 Act or the 1971 rules
to render such a course improper.
d The first step is to ask whether, under the terms of s 2(2) of the 1933 Act and the
proviso thereto, the defendant was committed for trial for the offence, or alternatively
whether the count in question was founded on facts or evidence disclosed in any
examination or deposition taken before a justice in his presence. The answer to that is
Yes. One of the counts was in respect of an offence on which the justices had committed
him for trial; the other was founded on evidence which was before the justices.
e Next, is there anything to prevent there being in existence at the same time two
indictments against the same person for the same offence? Counsel for the Crown
submits to us that the answer to that question is to be found in the practice direction
issued by Lord Widgery CJ on 9 March 1976 (*Practice Note* [1976] 2 All ER 326, [1976] 1
WLR 409), which stated as follows:

f   'There is no rule of law or practice which prohibits two indictments being in
      existence at the same time for the same offence against the same person on the same
      facts. But the court will not allow the prosecution to proceed on both such
      indictments. They cannot in law be tried together and the court will insist that the
      prosecution elect the one on which the trial shall proceed.'

g It is true that the case on which that practice note was based, namely *R v Groom* [1976] 2
All ER 321, [1977] QB 6, was not concerned with two indictments based on the same
committal, but the words of the practice note, it is submitted, cover the present situation
fully.

As against that, counsel for the appellant submits that the decision in *R v Thompson, R
v Clein* [1975] 2 All ER 1028, [1975] 1 WLR 1425 shows that the course adopted by the
h prosecution and court in the present case is not permissible. In *R v Thompson* the
indictment consisted solely of counts which did not follow the committal charges. The
circuit judge quashed the indictment and then gave leave to prefer a fresh indictment
based on the committal charges. If the fresh charges had been by way of amendment and
the old charges had thereafter been quashed, no harm would have been done. That
would have been in accordance with s 5(1) of the 1915 Act. The submission of the
j appellant in that case was that, once an indictment is preferred on the basis of a valid
committal, that committal has served its purpose. It has brought the accused person
before that court. If that indictment is quashed, unless there is some other reason
independent of those proceedings for keeping him in custody, the accused is entitled to
be discharged, the commital having been spent.

There was another wider way of putting the argument. That is that the prosecution are not entitled to prefer more than one indictment based on one committal for trial; that they are not entitled to prefer indictment after indictment if one, then another and then another fails on a motion to quash; that, having elected the form of indictment to be put before the trial court on the authority of the committal, if it is found that the election results in the quashing of that indictment, the only course open to the prosecution is to obtain leave to prefer a new bill from a High Court judge or this court.

James LJ delivering the judgment of the court in that case said ([1975] 2 All ER 1028 at 1032, [1975] 1 WLR 1425 at 1430):

> 'As indicated earlier we do not think that the decision of these appeals depends on the view that once the indictment based on the committal is quashed the committal itself is a dead letter, rather than on the principle that the Crown can only once prefer an indictment as a result of one committal ... I would prefer to base the decision on the latter principle, that it is only once that an indictment can be preferred on the basis of one committal. If that indictment fails in toto, the remedy for the Crown if it is desired to pursue the prosecution is to obtain leave in accordance with the provisions of the 1933 Act.'

If the wider ratio in *R v Thompson* is correct, then there is no valid distinction to take the present case outside the principle and the appeal would accordingly succeed. The position is quite different if the true ratio in that case is the narrower principle stated in the report, namely ([1975] 2 All ER 1028 at 1031, [1973] 1 WLR 1425 at 1429):

> '... that the Crown is not entitled to prefer indictment after indictment if one indictment, then another and then another fails on a motion to quash; that, having elected the form of indictment to be put before the trial court on the authority of the committal, if it is found that the election results in the quashing of that indictment the only course open to the Crown is to obtain leave to prefer a new bill and that leave can only be obtained from a High Court judge or the Court of Appeal Criminal Division'.

If that is the correct ratio, it applies only in cases where the first indictment has been quashed. On that basis, once the first indictment has been quashed, the prosecution cannot then produce a second indictment based on the same committal containing the same matters as those which were covered by the first. On the other hand, if the defects in the first indictment are appreciated before that indictment is quashed, then, subject to limitations as to time and to any questions which may arise under the terms of s 2(2) of the 1933 Act, a second indictment based on the same committal can be preferred.

The reasons are these. A single committal can result in a defendant being committed for trial for offences which may not all be legitimately joined in a single indictment because of the provisions of r 9 of the 1971 rules. There can be more than one indictment based on a single committal: see *R v Groom* [1976] 2 All ER 321, [1977] QB 6 and *Practice Note* [1976] 2 All ER 326, [1976] 1 WLR 409.

There can be in existence at the same time two indictments against the same person for the same offence or for offences based on the same facts: see *Poole v R* [1960] 3 All ER 398, [1961] AC 223. This was a Privy Council case. Their Lordships' reasons for dismissing the appeal were delivered by Lord Tucker, who said ([1960] 3 All ER 398 at 407, [1961] AC 223 at 244):

> 'Their Lordships are, therefore, satisfied that a second indictment or information is not inherently bad by reason of the pendency of an earlier one for the same offence against the same person on the same facts. In the present case, whether or not there were at any moment of time two such informations in existence depends on the proper construction of s. 250 and s. 255 of the Criminal Procedure Code [of Kenya]. Section 255 provides that the indictment "... when so signed shall be as valid and effectual in all respect, as an indictment in England which has been signed by the

a proper officer of the court in accordance with the Administration of Justice (Miscellaneous Provisions) Act, 1933."'

The only limitations on indictments based on a single committal are these. First, the indictment or indictments should be preferred in the time laid down by the rules, or such further time in respect of which the trial judge gives leave. Second, the offences in the indictment must be offences in respect of which the accused has been committed for

b trial or be offences in respect of which he may be charged in addition to or in substitution for those offences for which he has been committed for trial (see the proviso to s 2(2) of the 1933 Act). Third, the offences charged in a single indictment must be properly joined in that single indictment.

In our judgment the decision in R v Thompson [1975] 2 All ER 1025, [1975] 1 WLR 1425 should be restricted to the narrower principle for these reasons. The wider principle

c in that case was a point raised by the court itself, and not by the appellant. It was not fully argued (see [1975] 2 All ER 1028 at 1031, [1975] 1 WLR 1425 at 1429, where this passage occurs):

'Counsel for the Crown has referred us to such authorities he has found in the very limited time available for him to do any research.'

d In particular the decision in Poole v R [1965] 3 All ER 398, [1961] AC 223 was not cited to the court.

In R v Bell (1984) 78 Cr App R 305 this court did so confine the decision in R v Thompson. In that case appears the following passage in the judgment of the court (at 310):

e 'The Court in THOMPSON AND CLEIN was not dealing with a case where the Crown had preferred two separate indictments—one alleging charge A upon which the appellant had been properly committed for trial and the other alleging charges B, C and D upon which also he had been properly committed, neither of which had been quashed. It does not seem to us that, read against the facts of that case, the judgment of James L.J. in THOMPSON AND CLEIN is any authority for saying that the Crown's composite indictment in the present case should not have been preferred. The

f Practice Direction ([1976] 2 All ER 326, [1976] 1 WLR 409) already referred to is not, on this analysis, in conflict with the decision in THOMPSON AND CLEIN. It would indeed be surprising had that been so for a number of reasons, not least the fact that the Direction was given at the conclusion of GROOM ([1976] 2 All ER 321, [1977] QB 6), in which the reserved judgment of the five-judge Court was given by James L.J., as was the judgment in THOMPSON AND CLEIN.'

g In our judgment there was nothing to prevent the court in this case taking the course which it did, that is to say giving leave to the prosecution to prefer out of time fresh indictments which conformed with the rules, despite the existence of the original invalid indictment, and then staying proceedings on the invalid indictment and proceeding to trial on the others.

h We only pause to add that this situation would not arise if those responsible for drawing the indictment in the first place were to have proper regard to the 1971 rules.

The appeal accordingly is dismissed.

Appeal dismissed.

j Solicitors: *Crown Prosecution Service*, Stafford.

N P Metcalfe Esq   Barrister.

Derby & Co Ltd and others v Weldon and others (No 2)

COURT OF APPEAL, CIVIL DIVISION
LORD DONALDSON OF LYMINGTON MR, NEILL AND BUTLER-SLOSS LJJ
28, 29, 30 NOVEMBER, I, 16 DECEMBER 1988

Practice – Pre-trial or post-judgment relief – Mareva injunction – Worldwide Mareva injunction – Pre-trial injunction – Extra-territorial effect of injunction – Protection of third parties – Injunction restraining foreign defendants from disposing of assets outside jurisdiction – Defendants having no assets within jurisdiction and likely to dissipate their assets to frustrate judgment or order against them – Whether pre-trial Mareva injunction should be granted against foreign defendant with no assets within jurisdiction – Whether receiver of foreign assets should be appointed – Whether defendants should be ordered to reveal the nature, value and whereabouts of foreign assets – Whether order should be made subject to proviso that third parties indirectly affected by it not bound by it until it is recognised or registered or enforced by foreign court.

The plaintiffs were seven associated companies which were all part of a United States banking group. The first and second defendants were the directors of a London company, CML, a commodity dealer which specialised in trading internationally in cocoa. CML was owned by the third defendant, a Panamanian company, and the fourth defendant, a Luxembourg company, both of which were under the control of the first and second defendants. In 1981 the plaintiff group purchased CML, which continued to be managed by the first and second defendants. While under their management CML offered very extensive credit to a Far Eastern commodity dealer which in 1984 became insolvent owing over £35m to CML. The plaintiff group recovered less than £1½m in the insolvency and brought an action against the defendants alleging breach of contract, conspiracy and fraudulent breach of fiduciary duty. The plaintiffs applied for and were granted a Mareva injunction restricting the first and second defendants from dealing with their assets worldwide until judgment in the action. The plaintiffs later sought similar relief against the third and fourth defendants and also the appointment of a receiver of their assets and an order for disclosure of their assets. The judge granted the plaintiffs a worldwide Mareva injunction against the fourth defendant, appointed a receiver of its assets and made a disclosure order but he refused to grant similar relief against the third defendant because of the difficulty of enforcing such orders in Panama. The fourth defendant appealed, contending that the court had no jurisdiction to grant the Mareva injunction because it was a necessary precondition for granting a Mareva injunction that the defendant had some assets within the jurisdiction of the court and the fourth defendant had no such assets. The plaintiffs cross-appealed against the judge's refusal to grant a Mareva injunction and other relief against the third defendant. It was conceded for the purposes of the appeal that the first and second defendants might dissipate their assets so that they would not be available to satisfy any judgment which might be given against them in the action and might cause the third and fourth defendants to do the same and that the third and fourth defendants might be found liable to the plaintiffs for sums in excess of £25m.

Held – The appeal would be dismissed and the cross-appeal would be allowed for the following reasons—

(1) The court had jurisdiction in an appropriate case to grant a pre-judgment Mareva injunction over a defendant's foreign assets, notwithstanding that he had no assets within the jurisdiction, if such an order was necessary to prevent the defendant from taking action to frustrate subsequent orders of the court. However, where there were sufficient assets within the jurisdiction the injunction should be confined to those assets. The court accordingly had jurisdiction to grant a worldwide Mareva injunction against both the

third and fourth defendants (see p 1009 *b* to *f*, p 1010 *b c*, p 1015 *d e*, p 1018 *j*, p 1020 *c e*,
a p 1022 *a* and p 1023 *c*, post); *Derby & Co Ltd v Weldon (No 1)* [1989] 1 All ER 469
followed.

(2) Although the court would refrain from making an order even where the justice of
the case required it if it was doubtful whether the order would be obeyed and there was
no real sanction to enforce compliance with the order, in the context of the grant of a
Mareva injunction a sufficient sanction existed in the fact that the court could bar the
b defendant's right to defend in the event of disobedience of the order. It followed that no
distinction should have been made between the third and fourth defendants in relation
to the grant of a Mareva injunction (see p 1010 *g j*, p 1011 *c d*, p 1015 *d e*, p 1021 *g*,
p 1022 *a* and p 1023 *c h*, post).

(3) Furthermore, when granting a Mareva injunction against a foreign defendant who
had no assets within the jurisdiction the court should protect the position of third parties
c outside the jurisdiction who were indirectly affected by the order by including a proviso
that, in so far as the order purported to have extra-territorial effect, no person, whether
natural or juridical, should be affected by it or concerned with its terms until it was
declared enforceable or recognised or enforced by an appropriate foreign court (see
p 1012 *f*, p 1013 *b c*, p 1015 *a* to *d*, p 1020 *g* to *j*, p 1022 *a* and p 1023 *a h*, post).

(4) Since a Mareva injunction operated in personam and did not normally offend the
d principle that English courts would refrain from making orders which infringed the
exclusive jurisdiction of foreign courts, the court had jurisdiction to make an order
appointing a receiver of foreign assets in support of a Mareva injunction. In the
circumstances the court had rightly appointed a receiver of the assets of the fourth
defendant and since Luxembourg was a party to the European Judgments Convention
and the fourth defendant was a party to the action the order should take effect regardless
e of whether it was recognised and enforced in Luxembourg. Moreover, the third
defendant should not be treated any differently from the fourth defendant, because the
fact that Panama was not a party to the convention or to any agreement to which effect
could be given under the Foreign Judgments (Reciprocal Enforcement) Act 1933 was not
an absolute bar to the appointment of a receiver of its assets since the task of the receiver
would be to preserve the third defendant's assets, assisted by the sanction that if the third
f defendant did not co-operate it would not be allowed to defend the action. Furthermore,
the third defendant should be required to reveal the nature, value and whereabouts of
those assets (see pp 1011 *g*, p 1014 *d* to *j*, p 1015 *a* to *d*, p 1021 *a e*, p 1022 *a* and p 1023 *h*,
post).

Notes
g For Mareva injunctions, see 37 Halsbury's Laws (4th edn) para 362, and for cases on the
subject, see 37(2) Digest (Reissue) 474–476, 2947–2962.

For power of court to appoint a receiver, see 37 Halsbury's Laws (4th edn) para 381,
and for cases on the subject, see 37(2) Digest (Reissue) 484–485, 3002–3007.

For the Foreign Judgments (Reciprocal Enforcement) Act 1933, see 22 Halsbury's
h Statutes (4th edn) 283.

Cases referred to in judgments
Ashtiani v Kashi [1986] 2 All ER 970, [1987] QB 888, [1986] 3 WLR 647, CA.
Babanaft International Co SA v Bassatne [1989] 1 All ER 433, [1989] 2 WLR 232, CA.
Beddow v Beddow (1878) 9 Ch D 89.
j *Bekhor (A J) & Co Ltd v Bilton* [1981] 2 All ER 565, [1981] QB 923, [1981] 2 WLR 601, CA.
Blunt v Blunt [1943] 2 All ER 76, [1943] AC 517, HL.
Chartered Bank v Daklouche [1980] 1 All ER 205, [1980] 1 WLR 107, CA.
Derby & Co Ltd v Weldon (No 1) [1989] 1 All ER 469, [1989] 2 WLR 276, CA.
Faith Panton Property Plan Ltd v Hodgetts [1981] 2 All ER 877, [1981] 1 WLR 927, CA.
Haiti (Republic) v Duvalier [1989] 1 All ER 456, [1989] 2 WLR 261, CA.
Hamlin v Hamlin [1985] 2 All ER 1037, [1986] Fam 11, [1985] 3 WLR 629, CA.

Intraco Shipping Corp v Notis Shipping Corp, The Bhoja Trader [1981] 2 Lloyd's Rep 256, CA.
Jagger v Jagger [1926] P 93, [1926] All ER Rep 613, CA.
Liddell's Settlement Trusts, Re, Liddell v Liddell [1936] 1 All ER 239, [1936] Ch 365, CA.
Lister & Co v Stubbs (1890) 45 Ch D 1, [1886–90] All ER Rep 797, CA.
Locabail International Finance Ltd v Agroexport [1986] 1 All ER 901, [1986] 1 WLR 657, CA.
Mareva Cia Naviera SA v International Bulkcarriers SA, The Mareva (1975) [1980] 1 All ER 213, CA.
MBPXL Corp v Intercontinental Banking Corp Ltd [1975] CA Transcript 411.
Newton v Newton (1885) 11 PD 11.
Ninemia Maritime Corp v Trave Schiffahrtsgesellschaft mbH & Co KG, The Niedersachsen [1984] 1 All ER 398, [1983] 1 WLR 1412, CA.
Nippon Yusen Kaisha v Karageorgis [1975] 3 All ER 282, [1975] 1 WLR 1093, CA.
Ownbey v Morgan (1921) 256 US 94, US SC.
Prince Abdul Rahman Bin Turki Al Sudairy v Abu-Taha [1980] 3 All ER 409, [1980] 1 WLR 1268, CA.
Rasu Maritima SA v Perusahaan Pertambangan Minyak Dan Gas Bumi Negara (Pertamina) and Government of Indonesia (as interveners) [1977] 3 All ER 324, [1978] QB 644, [1977] 3 WLR 518, CA.
Robinson v Pickering (1881) 16 Ch D 660, CA.
South Carolina Insurance Co v Assurantie Maatschappij 'de Zeven Provincien' NV [1986] 3 All ER 487, [1987] AC 24, [1986] 3 WLR 398, HL.
Third Chandris Shipping Corp v Unimarine SA, The Pythia, The Angelic Wings, The Genie [1979] 2 All ER 972, [1979] QB 645, [1979] 3 WLR 122, CA.
Ward v James [1965] 1 All ER 563, [1966] 1 QB 273, [1965] 2 WLR 455, CA.
Wickins v Wickins (Goode, party cited) [1918] P 265, CA.

Cases also cited
Allied Arab Bank Ltd v Hajjar [1987] 3 All ER 739, [1988] QB 787.
Altertext Inc v Advanced Data Communications Ltd [1985] 1 All ER 395, [1985] 1 WLR 457.
Ballabil Holdings Pty Ltd v Hospital Products Ltd [1985] 1 NSWLR 155, NSW CA.
Bayer AG v Winter [1986] 1 All ER 733, [1986] 1 WLR 497, CA.
Chellaram v Chellaram [1985] 1 All ER 1043, [1985] Ch 409.
de Cavel v de Cavel Case 143/78 [1979] ECR 1055.
Denilauler v Snc Couchet Frères Case 125/79 [1980] ECR 1553.
Duder v Amsterdamsch Trustees Kantoor [1902] 2 Ch 132.
Ebrahimi v Westbourne Galleries Ltd [1972] 2 All ER 492, [1973] AC 360, HL.
Evans v Clayhope Properties Ltd [1988] 1 All ER 444, [1988] 1 WLR 358, CA.
Hart v Emelkirk Ltd, Howroyd v Emelkirk Ltd [1983] 3 All ER 15, [1983] 1 WLR 1289.
Interpool Ltd v Galani [1987] 2 All ER 981, [1988] QB 738, CA.
Mediterranea Raffineria Siciliana Petroli SpA v Mabanaft GmbH [1978] CA Transcript 816.
'Morocco Bound' Syndicate Ltd v Harris [1895] 1 Ch 534.
National Bank of Greece v Constantinos Dimitriou (1987) Times, 16 November, CA.
Schemmer v Property Resources Ltd [1974] 3 All ER 451, [1975] Ch 273.
Siskina (cargo owners) v Distos Cia Naviera SA, The Siskina [1977] 3 All ER 803, [1979] AC 210, HL.
Vocalion (Foreign) Ltd, Re [1932] 2 Ch 196, [1932] All ER Rep 519.

Interlocutory appeal and cross-appeal
The plaintiffs, Derby & Co Ltd, Cocoa Merchants Ltd (CML), Phibro-Salomon Finance AG, Phibro-Salomon Ltd, Philipp Bros Inc, Philipp Bros Ltd and Salomon Inc of the

a   United States (the holding company of the other plaintiff companies), by a writ issued on
      25 June 1987 brought an action against (1) Anthony Henry David Weldon, (2) Ian Jay,
      (3) Milco Corp, a Panamanian company, and (4) CML Holding SA of Luxembourg (CMI),
      claiming damages for breach of contract, misrepresentation, negligence, deceit, conspiracy
      to defraud and fraudulent breach of fiduciary duty arising out of the trading activities of
      CML between February 1981 and June 1984 while under the management of the first
      and second defendants as executive directors of CML after it had been purchased by
b   Salomon Inc from the liquidator of a subsidiary of Milco, which was itself a subsidiary of
      CMI. In particular, the plaintiffs alleged that between June 1981 and February 1984 the
      first and second defendants caused CML to suffer losses of £35m on unauthorised
      advances and credit made available to the Allied Group of companies of Hong Kong
      when the first and second defendants were owed large sums in their personal capacity by
      the persons who controlled Allied. The plaintiffs further alleged that when Allied
c   collapsed in 1984 the plaintiffs were owed £35,580,424, of which they were only able to
      recover £1,485,148 in the insolvency. On 4 December 1987 the plaintiffs applied ex
      parte to Sir Nicolas Browne-Wilkinson V-C and were granted Mareva injunctions against
      the first and second defendants restraining them from removing their assets out of the
      United Kingdom or those countries which were parties to the Convention on Jurisdiction
      and the Enforcement of Civil and Commercial Judgments 1968 or from dealing in any
d   way with those assets except to the extent that they exceeded £25m and requiring the
      first and second defendants to file an affidavit disclosing the full value of their assets. By
      a notice of motion dated 8 December the plaintiffs sought an order freezing the first and
      second defendants' assets up to £25m wheresoever in the world situated and disclosure
      of particulars of bank accounts, nominees etc. On 27 June 1988 Mervyn Davies J granted,
      inter alia, a Mareva injunction restricted to the first and second defendants' assets in the
e   United Kingdom but on appeal by the plaintiffs the Court of Appeal ([1989] 1 All ER
      469, [1989] 2 WLR 276) granted a worldwide Mareva injunction against the first and
      second defendants. By notices of motion dated 16 August and 4 November 1988 the
      plaintiffs sought worldwide Mareva injunctions and receivership and discovery orders
      against CMI and Milco. On 4 November 1988 Sir Nicolas Browne-Wilkinson V-C
      ordered, inter alia, (1) that CMI be restrained until after judgment in the action or further
f   order from disposing of or transferring, charging, diminishing or in any way howsoever
      dealing with any of its assets wheresoever the same might be situated, except in so far as
      the value of such assets exceeded £25m, and on 7 November 1988 he ordered, inter alia,
      (2) (as varied by order dated 11 November 1988) (a) that Christopher Morris be appointed
      until further order receiver without security of all the assets of CMI 'including without
      limitation . . . any interest whether direct or indirect legal or beneficial of [CMI] in any
g   asset' and (b) that CMI procure, so far as it lay within its power, that its assets be forthwith
      delivered to the receiver (provided, however, that no steps be taken to enforce that part
      of the order until after the courts of Luxembourg had declared the order enforceable or
      otherwise enforced the same) and that none of the assets held by or in the name of or to
      the order of Domaine Investment Corp of Panama (Domaine), a subsidiary company of
      CMI, or any direct or indirect subsidiary or associated company of Domaine or CMI or
h   any asset held by trustees or nominees in whole or in part for CMI, Domaine or any other
      subsidiary or associated company should be disposed of by Domaine or any other person
      or company until after judgment or further order except with the consent of the receiver
      or leave of the court, and (3) that CMI by a responsible officer make and serve within
      seven days an affidavit disclosing the full value of all the assets of CMI of any description.
j   CMI appealed with leave of Sir Nicolas Browne-Wilkinson V-C against those orders. The
      plaintiffs cross-appealed against the order of Sir Nicolas Browne-Wilkinson V-C made on
      4 November 1988 refusing to continue the worldwide Mareva injunction granted ex
      parte against Milco by Mervyn Davies J on 11 August 1988 and refusing to appoint a
      receiver of Milco's assets. The facts are set out in the judgment of Lord Donaldson MR.

A G Bompas and *Rosalind Nicholson* for CMI and Milco.
Michael Lyndon-Stanford QC, Charles Purle and *J Stephen Smith* for the plaintiffs.
Leslie Kosmin for the receiver.

a

Cur adv vult

16 December. The following judgments were delivered.

LORD DONALDSON OF LYMINGTON MR. The complexity of the issues   *b*
involved in this action is only matched by the size of the sums in dispute, not less than
£25m and probably more. However, the issues in the appeal and cross-appeal which
concern protective interlocutory measures, Mareva injunctions, the appointment of
receivers and disclosure of the nature, amount and whereabouts of assets, are much more
confined. So far as the action as a whole is concerned, it is sufficient to say that the
plaintiffs complain that they have been defrauded by the defendants by or in connection   *c*
with dealings in the cocoa market.

The action first came before this court in July 1988 when the plaintiffs successfully
appealed against the refusal of Mervyn Davies J to grant Mareva relief on a worldwide
basis against the first two defendants (Mr Weldon and Mr Jay) (see *Derby & Co Ltd v
Weldon (No 1)* [1989] 1 All ER 469, [1989] 2 WLR 276). In so far as this court then
decided any matters of law, its decision of course binds us. The present appeal is by the   *d*
fourth defendant, CML Holding SA of Luxembourg (referred to in argument and
hereafter in this judgment as 'CMI' in order to distinguish it from the plaintiff, Cocoa
Merchants Ltd). CMI appeals against orders by Sir Nicolas Browne-Wilkinson V-C on 4
and 7 November 1988, as amended by a further order on 11 November 1988, granting a
worldwide Mareva injunction, appointing a receiver of the assets of CMI and a disclosure
order. The plaintiffs cross-appeal against the refusal of Sir Nicolas Browne-Wilkinson V-C   *e*
to continue a worldwide Mareva injunction granted ex parte against the third defendant,
Milco Corp of Panama (Milco), and his refusal to appoint a receiver of its assets and to
order disclosure of its assets. The plaintiffs also seek modification of the orders against
CMI.

The issues confronting this court have been simplified, but by no means resolved, by   *f*
four concessions which have very sensibly been made (for the purposes of the appeal
only) on behalf of CMI and Milco following the hearings before Sir Nicolas Browne-
Wilkinson V-C. They are: (a) that the first defendant (Mr Weldon) and the second
defendant (Mr Jay) might be likely to dissipate their own assets so as not to be available
to satisfy any judgment against them in this action; (b) that Mr Weldon and Mr Jay are
to be assumed to exercise a high degree of control over CMI and Milco; (c) that, in view   *g*
of (a) and (b) above, CMI and Milco might be likely to dissipate their assets so as not to be
available to satisfy any judgment against them or either of them in this action, and
(d) that CMI and Milco might at trial be found liable to some one or other of the plaintiffs
in respect of the claims (referred to in specified paragraphs of the amended statement of
claim) and that the approximate amount of the judgment against CMI or Milco could
with interest be as much as £25m. Three issues arise: (1) whether, and if so in what   *h*
circumstances and on what terms, a pre-judgment Mareva injunction should be granted
against a foreign defendant who has no assets within the jurisdiction of the court;
(2) whether, and if so in what circumstances and on what terms, a receiver of the assets
of such a foreign defendant should be appointed before judgment for purposes similar to
those served by a Mareva injunction; (3) whether, and if so in what circumstances and
on what terms, such a foreign defendant should be required to disclose the nature, value   *j*
and whereabouts of his assets.

THE MAREVA JURISDICTION GENERALLY

The fundamental principle underlying this jurisdiction is that, within the limits of its
powers, no court should permit a defendant to take action designed to ensure that

subsequent orders of the court are rendered less effective than would otherwise be the

a case. On the other hand, it is not its purpose to prevent a defendant carrying on business in the ordinary way or, if an individual, living his life normally pending the determination of the dispute, nor to impede him in any way in defending himself against the claim. Nor is it its purpose to place the plaintiff in the position of a secured creditor. In a word, whilst one of the hazards facing a plaintiff in litigation is that, come the day of judgment it may not be possible for him to obtain satisfaction of that judgment fully or at all, the

b court should not permit the defendant artificially to create such a situation.

The jurisdictional basis of the Mareva injunction is to be found in s 37(1) to (3) of the Supreme Court Act 1981, which, in sub-s (1), is the lineal successor of s 45 of the Supreme Court of Judicature (Consolidation) Act 1925 and s 25(8) of the Supreme Court of Judicature Act 1873. Those subsections provide as follows:

c '(1) The High Court may by order (whether interlocutory or final) grant an injunction or appoint a receiver in all cases in which it appears to the court to be just and convenient to do so.

(2) Any such order may be made either unconditionally or on such terms and conditions as the court thinks just.

(3) The power of the High Court under subsection (1) to grant an interlocutory

d injunction restraining a party to any proceedings from removing from the jurisdiction of the High Court, or otherwise dealing with, assets located within that jurisdiction shall be exercisable in cases where that party is, as well as in cases where he is not, domiciled, resident or present within that jurisdiction.'

In *Beddow v Beddow* (1878) 9 Ch D 89 at 93 Jessel MR said:

e '... I have unlimited power to grant an injunction in any case where it would be right or just to do so: and what is right or just must be decided, not by the caprice of the Judge, but according to sufficient legal reasons or on settled legal principles.'

That remains the position to this day, the only issue being whether in particular circumstances the grant is 'right or just'. What changes is not the power or the principles but the circumstances, both special and general, in which courts are asked to exercise this

f jurisdiction. This can and does call for changes in the practice of the courts. We live in a time of rapidly growing commercial and financial sophistication and it behoves the courts to adapt their practices to meet the current wiles of those defendants who are prepared to devote as much energy to making themselves immune to the courts' orders as to resisting the making of such orders on the merits of their case. Hence it comes about that, as was pointed out by Neill LJ in *Babanaft International Co SA v Bassatne* [1989]

g 1 All ER 433 at 448, [1989] 2 WLR 232 at 251–252 and by May LJ in *Derby & Co Ltd v Weldon (No 1)* [1989] 1 All ER 469 at 472–473, [1989] 2 WLR 276 at 280, this is a developing branch of the law. To that I would add that a failure or refusal to grant an injunction in any particular case is an exercise of discretion which cannot, as such, provide a precedent binding on another court concerned with another case, save in so far

h as that refusal is based on basic principle applicable in both such cases.

THE RELEVANCE OF AN ABSENCE OF ASSETS WITHIN THE JURISDICTION

When the matter was before Sir Nicolas Browne-Wilkinson V-C there was no evidence showing, or giving rise to any inference, that CMI, which is a Luxembourg company,

j had any assets within the jurisdiction. That remains the position to this day, although as a result of the compulsory disclosure of information it now appears that a company within the group of companies of which CMI is the holding company may have such assets. In this situation the first submission on behalf of CMI is that a necessary precondition for granting a Mareva injunction is that the defendant has some assets within the jurisdiction. The significance of this submission is that, if correct, it would distinguish this appeal from *Derby & Co Ltd v Weldon (No 1)*, where the relevant defendants had assets within the jurisdiction.

Counsel for CMI submitted that this was the ratio of the decision of this court in *Intraco Shipping Corp v Notis Shipping Corp, The Bohja Trader* [1981] 2 Lloyd's Rep 256. In that case Staughton J had been asked to restrain the defendants from claiming under a guarantee given by the London branch of a French bank and had refused to do so on the well-established principle that the courts will not grant such an injunction unless fraud is involved. Instead, he looked to the proceeds of the guarantee and enjoined the defendants from removing such proceeds from the jurisdiction. On appeal the plaintiffs unsuccessfully appealed against the refusal to prevent the defendants claiming under the guarantee. The defendants, however, successfully appealed against the Mareva injunction on the grounds that any moneys payable under the guarantee were payable in Greece, a matter which had never been pointed out to Staughton J, and that accordingly these moneys would never be within the jurisdiction and capable of being removed from it. No one suggested that there were any other assets within the jurisdiction or that the injunction should be extended to cover the dissipation of Greek assets. This decision accordingly neither supports nor detracts from CMI's contention.

When a similar submission was made to Sir Nicolas Browne-Wilkinson V-C he was also referred to the decisions of this court in *Third Chandris Shipping Corp v Unimarine SA, The Pythia, The Angelic Wings, The Genie* [1979] 2 All ER 972 at 984–985, 988, [1979] QB 645 at 668, 673, *A J Bekhor & Co Ltd v Bilton* [1981] 2 All ER 565, [1981] QB 923 and *Ashtiani v Kashi* [1986] 2 All ER 970, [1987] QB 888. He concluded that it might just be possible to say that in these three cases the statements as to the need for local assets were obiter, but that in the *Intraco* case it was plainly the ratio decidendi. For the reasons which I have given, I think that in this later respect he was mistaken. This is not of great significance because it now appears that in *MBPXL Corp v Intercontinental Banking Corp Ltd* [1975] CA Transcript 411 this court (Stephenson and Scarman LJJ) held in terms and as the ratio of the court's decision that a Mareva injunction is an exceptional remedy—

'which will only be granted by the court where there is clear evidence that there are assets in this country, not immovable but movable assets, in the possession of the defendant.'

Sir Nicolas Browne-Wilkinson V-C said:

'It has been said many times that Mareva relief is a developing field. There is no doubt that as a matter of English law this court has jurisdiction to grant relief against any party properly before it in relation to assets wherever situate. However, the circumstances under which such jurisdiction should be exercised must depend on and vary with the circumstances of every case. The rationale of the earlier decisions was plain: the court was seeking to freeze assets against which an eventual judgment in the English court could be enforced. In my judgment the earlier decisions merely show what was a settled practice in the ordinary case; that is to say in a case where there was no question of extending the order beyond local assets. For myself, I believe that the practice of requiring some grounds for believing there are local assets is still applicable in such case. But the three recent Court of Appeal cases were not the normal case [see *Babanaft International Co SA v Bassatne* [1989] 1 All ER 433, [1989] 2 WLR 232, *Republic of Haiti v Duvalier* [1989] 1 All ER 456, [1989] 2 WLR 261 and *Derby & Co Ltd v Weldon (No 1)* [1989] 1 All ER 469, [1989] 2 WLR 276]. In each judgment the Court of Appeal stressed they were very special cases. They involved a claim for Mareva relief over assets not situate here. If the case of *Derby & Co Ltd v Weldon (No 1)* before the Court of Appeal was a very special case, so is this application, which is intimately linked with exactly the same matter. In my judgment, I am free to exercise the undoubted jurisdiction to make the orders sought in the particular circumstances of this case. But, to my mind, three requirements ought to be satisfied before the court takes the extreme step that is asked for in this case. The first requirement is that the special circumstances of the case justify such an exceptional order. Second, that the order is in accordance with the rationale on which Mareva relief has been based in the past. Third, that the order does not conflict with the ordinary principles of international law.'

In substance I agree. The normal form of order should indeed be confined to assets within the jurisdiction, although the practice has changed since the decision in the MBPXL case and such an order could well extend to the disposition of a freehold interest in a house. The reason for that change is that, whereas initially the courts focused on assets being removed from the jurisdiction in an attempt to make the defendant 'judgment proof', later experience suggested that there were other ways of achieving this object and at least as much attention was then paid to that part of the common form order which forbade the disposal of assets as to that which prohibited their removal from the jurisdiction. The reason why at present the normal form of order should be so confined is that most defendants operate nationally rather than internationally. But, once the court is concerned with an international operator, the position may well be different.

In my judgment, the key requirement for any Mareva injunction, whether or not it extends to foreign assets, is that it shall accord with the rationale on which Mareva relief has been based in the past. That rationale, legitimate purpose and fundamental principle I have already stated, namely that no court should permit a defendant to take action designed to frustrate subsequent orders of the court. If for the achievement of this purpose it is necessary to make orders concerning foreign assets, such orders should be made, subject, of course, to ordinary principles of international law. When Sir Nicolas Browne-Wilkinson V-C said that special circumstances had to be present to justify such an exceptional order, I do not understand him to have been saying more than that the court should not go further than necessity dictates, that in the first instance it should look to assets within the jurisdiction and that in the majority of cases there will be no justification for looking to foreign assets.

Returning to the submission of counsel for CMI, I can see neither rhyme nor reason in regarding the existence of some asset within the jurisdiction of however little value as a precondition for granting a Mareva injunction in respect of assets outside the jurisdiction. The existence of *sufficient* assets within the jurisdiction is an excellent reason for confining the jurisdiction to such assets, but, other considerations apart, the fewer the assets within the jurisdiction the greater the necessity for taking protective measures in relation to those outside it.

The reality is, I think, that it is only recently that litigants have sought extra-territorial relief and that the courts have had to consider whether to grant it and on what conditions. During the last year it has been granted in the three cases to which Sir Nicolas Browne-Wilkinson V-C referred, namely the *Babanaft* case [1989] 1 All ER 433, [1989] 2 WLR 232, *Republic of Haiti v Duvalier* [1989] 1 All ER 456, [1989] 2 WLR 261 and *Derby & Co Ltd v Weldon (No 1)* [1989] 1 All ER 469, [1989] 2 WLR 276. Counsel for CMI seeks to distinguish the *Babanaft* case on the grounds that the injunction was granted in aid of execution of an existing judgment. This I accept as a distinction in that the court will have less hesitation in taking measures in support of a judgment creditor than it would in support of a *potential* judgment creditor. The decision in *Republic of Haiti v Duvalier* he seeks to distinguish on the grounds that it was a tracing case and that the funds were under the control of an agent resident within the jurisdiction. This is certainly a distinction in fact, although I am not sure that it is one of principle. In *Derby & Co Ltd v Weldon (No 1)* he seeks to distinguish on the ground that the defendants had assets within the jurisdiction, but, for the reasons which I have already given, I do not consider this to be a distinction in principle.

There remains one other authority to which I should refer. This is the decision of the House of Lords in *South Carolina Insurance Co v Assurantie Maatschappij 'de Zeven Provincien' NV* [1986] 3 All ER 487, [1987] AC 24. Counsel for CMI relied on it for the general proposition that the jurisdiction of the court under s 37(1) of the 1981 Act was 'circumscribed by judicial authority dating back many years' (see [1986] 3 All ER 487 at *a* 495, [1987] AC 24 at 40 per Lord Brandon). It followed, so he said, that there was no scope for a new and extended use of the power. I do not accept this submission for at least two reasons. First, Lord Brandon said in terms that the jurisdiction in relation to Mareva injunctions was an exception to the principle that its exercise was circumscribed by judicial authority (see [1986] 3 All ER 487 at 496, [1987] AC 24 at 40). Second, the House was not considering a case which involved Mareva injunctions. *b*

Once the suggested distinction based on the absence of *any* assets within the jurisdiction is rejected, the short answer to the submission that the court cannot, or alternatively should not, grant a Mareva injunction extending to the overseas assets of CMI is provided by *Derby & Co Ltd v Weldon (No 1)*. That case is binding authority for the proposition that the court *can* grant such an injunction in the circumstances of this case and persuasive authority for doing so. *c*

Sir Nicolas Browne-Wilkinson V-C then went on to consider other aspects stemming from the fact that CMI and Milco differ from Mr Weldon and Mr Jay in that they are juridical and not natural persons and are incorporated abroad, CMI in Luxembourg and Milco in Panama.

ENFORCEABILITY OF THE INJUNCTIONS *d*

First amongst these considerations was that, as Sir Nicolas Browne-Wilkinson V-C said, 'nothing brings the law into greater disrepute than the making of orders which cannot be enforced. The maxim "equity does not act in vain" is a very sound one'. It was suggested in argument that, on the authorities, the maxim referred not to enforceability but to the making of orders with which it was impossible to comply, eg to fell a tree which had already been blown down or which lawfully could at once be nullified, eg to *e* grant the plaintiff a tenancy at will. However that may be, Sir Nicolas Browne-Wilkinson V-C was plainly right in his general proposition, although it requires careful examination in the context of particular circumstances.

I find it difficult to believe that, in using the words 'cannot be enforced', he meant 'cannot be specifically enforced'. That that is not the true test is clear, because it is not uncommon for a court to order the disclosure of information which exists only in the *f* mind of an individual. If he is unusually obdurate the order is unenforceable in the sense that the information will not be disclosed. Courts assume, rightly, that those who are subject to its jurisdiction will obey its orders: see *Re Liddell's Settlement Trusts, Liddell v Liddell* [1936] 1 All ER 239 at 248, [1936] Ch 365 at 374, which, although said in relation to an order affecting wards of court normally resident in this country against a mother normally so resident, is I think of general application. It is only if there is doubt about *g* whether the order will be obeyed and if, should that occur, no real sanction would exist, that the court should refrain from making an order which the justice of the case requires.

This consideration led Sir Nicolas Browne-Wilkinson V-C to examine the extent to which a Mareva injunction could be enforced against CMI in Luxembourg, which is a party to the European Convention on Jurisdiction and the Enforcement of Judgments in *h* Civil and Commercial Matters to which this country gave effect by the Civil Jurisdiction and Judgments Act 1982, to which the convention is scheduled. This certainly is deserving of examination but, in the context of the grant of the Mareva injunction, I think that a sufficient sanction exists in the fact that, in the event of disobedience, the court could bar the defendants' right to defend. This is not a consequence which they could contemplate lightly as they would become fugitives from a final judgment given *j* against them without their explanations having been heard and which might well be enforced against them by other courts. It may be that CMI is inherently law-abiding or that some such consideration has occured to it, but it is certainly the fact that it has co-operated fully with the receiver appointed by Sir Nicolas Browne-Wilkinson V-C, has made some disclosure of its assets and began to do so before the Luxembourg court made an order enforcing that of the Vice-Chancellor.

a When it came to Milco, which is incorporated in Panama, but no doubt like most Panamanian companies has its base of operations elsewhere, Sir Nicolas Browne-Wilkinson V-C said that 'there is no evidence before me that either a Mareva order or any eventual judgment can be enforced against Milco in Panama even if it has any assets'. This involves two considerations: lack of assets and Panamanian enforcement.

So far as lack of assets is concerned, there was evidence that, until recently Milco had very considerable assets. Whether they have indeed gone elsewhere and how and why *b* they have disappeared will be a matter of some interest to the plaintiffs if they become judgment creditors of Milco, and I do not think that any alleged and unproved lack of assets should be regarded as a bar to the making of the order.

So far as enforcement is concerned, I have already indicated that the ordinary sanction of being debarred from defending should suffice, but in any event I think that it is a mistake to spend time considering whether English orders and judgments can be *c* enforced against Panamanian companies in Panama. Whilst that is not perhaps the last forum to be considered in the context of such enforcement, it is certainly not the first. If in due time the plaintiffs are concerned to enforce a judgment against Milco, they will be resorting to the jurisdiction where its assets, if any, happen to be.

In the event Sir Nicolas Browne-Wilkinson V-C refused to make any order against Milco, but made an order against CMI calling for the disclosure of assets of its subsidiary *d* Domaine and subsidiaries of that subsidiary, which includes Milco.

For my part, for the reasons which I have given, I would make no distinction between CMI and Milco in relation to the grant of a Mareva injunction.

THE IMPACT OF INTERNATIONAL LAW

e The third requirement examined by Sir Nicolas Browne-Wilkinson V-C was that the Mareva injunction, and indeed any other order of the court, should not conflict with the ordinary principles of international law. This has two aspects. The first is the nature or content of the order itself. The second is its effect on third parties.

f *The nature and content of the order*

Considerations of comity require the courts of this country to refrain from making orders which infringe the exclusive jurisdiction of the courts of other countries. For present purposes it suffices to refer to s 5, art 16 of the convention set out in the schedule to the Civil Jurisdiction and Judgments Act 1982, under the heading of 'Exclusive Jurisdiction', as indicating the scope of this impediment.

g A Mareva injunction operates solely in personam and does not normally offend this principle in any way. I will revert to this aspect when considering the appointment of a receiver.

The effect on third parties

h Here there is a real problem. Court orders only bind those to whom they are addressed. However, it is a serious contempt of court, punishable as such, for anyone to interfere with or impede the administration of justice. This occurs if someone, knowing of the terms of the court order, assists in the breach of that order by the person to whom it is addressed. All this is common sense and works well so long as the 'aider and abettor' is wholly within the jurisdiction of the court or wholly outside it. If he is wholly within *j* the jurisdiction of the court there is no problem whatsoever. If he is wholly outside the jurisdiction of the court, he is either not to be regarded as being in contempt or it would involve an excess of jurisdiction to seek to punish him for that contempt. Unfortunately, juridical persons, notably banks, operate across frontiers. A foreign bank may have a branch within the jurisdiction and so be subject to the English courts. An English bank may have branches abroad and be asked by a defendant to take action at such a branch which will constitute a breach by the defendant of the court's order. Is action by the

foreign bank to be regarded as contempt, although it would not be so regarded but for
the probably irrelevant fact that it happens to have an English branch? Is action by the
foreign branch of an English bank to be regarded as contempt, when other banks in the
area are free to comply with the defendant's instructions?

   All this was considered in the *Babanaft* appeal and gave rise to what is known as the
'*Babanaft* proviso' which was included in the order made by Sir Nicolas Browne-Wilkinson
V-C. That is not in fact the proviso adopted by the Court of Appeal in the *Babanaft* case
itself, but was its preferred solution. As applied by Sir Nicolas Browne-Wilkinson V-C to
the circumstances of the application before him, it read:

   '(a) No person other than Rea Bros plc, Walsa Nominees Ltd and the fourth
   defendant and any officer and any agent appointed by power of attorney of the
   fourth defendant and any individual resident in England and Wales who has notice
   of this paragraph shall as regards acts done or to be done outside England and Wales
   be affected by the terms of this paragraph or concerned to inquire whether any
   instruction given by or on behalf of the fourth defendant or anyone else, whether
   acting on behalf of the fourth defendant or otherwise, is or may be a breach of this
   paragraph save to the extent that this paragraph is delcared enforceable by or is
   otherwise enforced by an order of a court outside England and Wales and then only
   within the jurisdiction of that other court . . .'

   The express reason for including such a proviso was that Mareva injunctions 'have an
in rem effect on third parties' and that 'Mareva injunctions have a direct effect on third
parties who are notified of them and hold assets comprised in the order' (per Kerr LJ in
the *Babanaft* case [1989] 1 All ER 433 at 438, [1989] 2 WLR 232 at 240). I know what
was meant, but I am not sure that it is possible to have an 'in rem effect' on persons
whether natural or juridical and a Mareva injunction does not have any in rem effect on
the assets themselves or the defendant's title to them. Nor does such an injunction have
a *direct* effect on third parties. The injunction (a) restrains those to whom it is directed
from exercising what would otherwise be their rights and (b) indirectly affects the rights
of some, but not all, third parties to give effect to instructions from those directly bound
by the order to do or concur in the doing of acts which are prohibited by the order.
Whether any particular third party is indirectly affected, depends on whether that person
is subject to the jurisdiction of the English courts.

   I have no doubt of the practical need for some proviso, because in its absence banks
operating abroad do not know where they stand and foreign banks without any branch
in England who are thus outside the jurisdiction of the English courts may take, and
have indeed taken, offence at being, as they see it, 'ordered about' by the English courts.
All this is recorded in the judgment of Kerr LJ in the *Babanaft* case [1989] 1 All ER 433 at
438–439, [1989] 2 WLR 232 at 240–241. However, I am not sure that the *Babanaft*
proviso is the right answer to this dilemma.

   The first objection is that it treats natural persons differently from juridical persons.
Why should an English merchant bank which is a partnership, if such there still be, and
carries on business abroad as well as in this country be treated differently from a company,
yet the proviso does not apply to 'any individual resident in England'.

   The second objection is that it places an English corporate bank in a very difficult
position. It may know of the injunction and wish to support the court in its efforts to
prevent the defendant from frustrating the due course of justice, but the proviso deprives
it of the one justification which it would otherwise have for refusing to comply with his
instructions.

   The third objection I record without expressing any view on its validity. It is that an
order which includes this proviso has ex facie no extra-territorial effect and so is not of a
character enabling it to be recognised under the European Judgments Convention and
enforced abroad thereunder. In other words, the proviso has a circular effect. This is
apparently being argued in the Luxembourg Court of Appeal following an order for the

recognition and enforcement of Sir Nicolas Browne-Wilkinson V-C's order by the
a Luxembourg Court of first instance.

What should be done? I should prefer a proviso on the following lines:

> 'PROVIDED THAT, in so far as this order purports to have any extra-territorial effect,
> no person shall be affected thereby or concerned with the terms thereof until it shall
> be declared enforceable or be enforced by a foreign court and then it shall only affect
> them to the extent of such declaration or enforcement UNLESS they are (a) a person to
> *b* whom this order is addressed or an officer of or an agent appointed by a power of
> attorney of such a person or (b) persons who are subject to the jurisdiction of this
> court and (i) have been given written notice of this order at their residence or place
> of business within the jurisdiction, and (ii) are able to prevent acts or omissions
> outside the jurisdiction of this court which assist in the breach of the terms of this
> order.'
c

This seems to me to meet any charge that the court is seeking to exercise an exorbitant
jurisdiction, to be even-handed as between natural and juridical persons and to avoid any
argument based on circularity.

THE RECEIVERSHIP

d By an order made on 7 November 1988 as amended by a further order made on
11 November, Sir Nicolas Browne-Wilkinson V-C appointed a receiver of the assets of
CMI and ordered the two individual defendants and CMI to do all in their power to vest
these assets in the receiver. This order was subject to a *Babanaft* proviso covering the
position of third parties and to a special proviso that no steps should be taken to enforce
the vesting of the assets until after the courts of Luxembourg should have declared his
e order enforceable or otherwise enforced it. Finally, the receiver was instructed to allow
CMI to defend this action independently of him.

EXTRA-TERRITORIALITY

Sir Nicolas Browne-Wilkinson V-C posed the question of whether it was right for the
f court to appoint a receiver of assets outside the jursdiction belonging to a company which
had no residence in this country. He answered it by saying:

> 'I have grave doubts whether, in the absence of proper evidence of Luxembourg
> law, I would have been prepared to appoint a receiver. It seems to me that the court
> should not appoint receivers over non-residents in relation to assets which are not
> within the jurisdiction of this court, unless satisfied that the local court either of
> *g* residence or of the situation of the assets will act in aid of the English court in
> enforcing it. That is why the evidence of Luxembourg law is, to my mind,
> important in this case. The evidence of Luxembourg law is not in any way full at
> this stage but, broadly, it appears to be this. Under the 1968 European Judgments
> Convention which is incorporated in English law in the Civil Jurisdiction and
> *h* Judgments Act 1982, art 24 provides under the rubric "Provisional, including
> protective, measures" as follows: "Application may be made to the courts of a
> Contracting State for such provisional, including protective, measures as may be
> available under the law of that State, even if, under this Convention, the courts of
> another Contracting State have jurisdiction as to the substance of the matter." Under
> art 24, therefore, it is proper for this court to make protective orders of the kind
> *j* such as in Mareva relief or in aid of Mareva relief, which can be enforced under the
> convention in the other convention countries including Luxembourg. The evidence
> before me suggests that the Luxembourg court will probably enforce any order that
> I make for the appointment of a receiver. The exact working out of such order and
> the manner in which the effect of the English order is reproduced under
> Luxembourg law may give rise to trouble. But the basic position, as I understand

the evidence before me, is that if the order properly falls within art 24 (as it does), the Luxembourg court will enforce it. I am not seeking by this order in any way to make an order encroaching on the jurisdiction of the Luxembourg court. I will require the insertion in the order of a proviso modelled on the proviso in the *Babanaft* case . . . Accordingly, the order I propose to make today will not be directly enforceable within Luxembourg save to the extent that the Luxembourg court itself thinks it proper so to do in a case falling within art 24.'

I think that there may have been some confusion between the objects and effect of art 24 on the one hand and arts 25 to 45 on the other.

The convention in no way affects the powers of the courts of state A which is properly seised of the substance of the dispute. However, it provides for the courts of another contracting state, state B, to assist in two quite different ways. First, in arts 25 to 45 it provides a code for the recognition and enforcement of the orders of the courts of state A by the courts of state B. Second, in art 24, it authorises the courts of state B to entertain a direct application for protective orders in support of the primary proceedings before the courts of state A. In the instant case Sir Nicolas Browne-Wilkinson V-C seems, rightly as events have shown, to have contemplated that the Luxembourg courts would be invited to recognise and enforce his orders, ie would act under arts 25 to 45 and not under art 24.

In this situation I do not understand why the order that the assets vest in the receiver should only take effect if and when the order was recognised by the Luxembourg courts. True it is that CMI is a Luxembourg company, but it is a party to the action and can properly be ordered to deal with its assets in accordance with the orders of this court, regardless of whether the order is recognised and enforced in Luxembourg. The only effect of non-recognition would be to remove one of the potential sanctions for disobedience.

CMI

I would affirm the orders of Sir Nicolas Browne-Wilkinson V-C in relation to the receivership of the assets of CMI, subject only to (a) amending the *Babanaft* proviso in the terms which I have already indicated and (b) deleting the proviso that the order requiring CMI and the two individual defendants to vest the assets in the receiver should only take effect if the order was recognised by the Luxembourg courts.

MILCO

Panama is not a party to the European Judgments Convention or to any agreement to which effect would be given under the Foreign Judgments (Reciprocal Enforcement) Act 1933. There would therefore be problems in enforcing the orders of the English courts in Panama. However, I do not think that this should be regarded as an absolute bar to the appointment of a receiver of its assets. What really matters is the extent to which the receiver could effectively carry out his task, whatever that might be. In the instant case it would be to preserve any assets of Milco. He would be assisted by the sanction that, absent co-operation, Milco would not be allowed to defend the action. He would also be able to make use of the European Judgments Convention if, as seems not unlikely, any assets of Milco were situated in countries which were parties to that convention. In the circumstances I see no reason why Milco should be treated differently from CMI.

DISCLOSURE OF ASSETS

Once it is decided that a receiver should be appointed of all Milco's assets, it follows that Milco should be required to reveal the nature, value and whereabouts of those assets. It is not therefore necessary to consider whether it would be right to order such disclosure if no other relief were to be granted against Milco.

CONCLUSION

a   I would vary the orders in relation to CMI by deleting the proviso in the Mareva injunction (order of 4 November) and the proviso in para (2) of the receivership order (order of 7 November) substituting in each case the following proviso:

b   'PROVIDED THAT, in so far as this order purports to have any effect outside England and Wales, no person shall be affected by it or concerned with the terms of it until it shall have been declared enforceable or shall have been recognised or registered or enforced by a foreign court (and then it shall only affect such person to the extent of such declaration or recognition or registration or enforcement) UNLESS that person is (a) a person to whom this order is addressed or an officer or an agent appointed by power of attorney of such a person or (b) a person who is subject to the jurisdiction of this court and who (i) has been given written notice of this order at his or its residence or place of business within the jurisdiction and (ii) is able to prevent acts
c   or omissions outside the jurisdiction of this court which assist in the breach of the terms of this order.'

I would make orders in relation to Milco in the same terms mutatis mutandis as those in relation to CMI.

d   **NEILL LJ.** I have had the advantage of reading in draft the judgment of Lord Donaldson MR. I agree with it and with the orders which Lord Donaldson MR proposes. Nevertheless I think it right to deal with some of the issues which arise in this appeal in my own words. In particular, I intend to consider the questions whether the court has power to grant a Mareva injunction in respect of assets overseas or in cases where the defendant has no assets within the jurisdiction.

e

THE MAREVA INJUNCTION

By his order dated 4 November 1988 Sir Nicolas Browne-Wilkinson V-C granted an injunction against the fourth defendant CML Holding SA of Luxembourg (CMI), restraining CMI until after judgment in the action—

f   'from disposing of or transferring charging or diminishing or in any way howsoever dealing with any of its assets wheresoever the same might be situate save insofar as the value of such assets exceeds the sum of [£25m].'

CMI has appealed against this order. It was argued in support of the appeal (a) that the court was precluded by binding authority from granting a Mareva injunction against a foreign defendant who had no assets within the jurisdiction and (b) that, even if the court
g   had such jurisdiction in an exceptional case, the judge erred in principle in granting an injunction in the present case.

In order to consider these arguments it is necessary to examine the history of the Mareva jurisdiction and to try to discover the basis on which it is founded.

Before the decisions of the Court of Appeal in 1975 in *Nippon Yusen Kaisha v Karageorgis*
h   [1975] 3 All ER 282, [1975] 1 WLR 1093 and in *Mareva Cia Naviera SA v International Bulkcarriers Ltd, The Mareva* (1975) [1980] 1 All ER 213 it was generally thought that any order preventing a defendant from dealing freely with his assets would infringe the principle recognised by the Court of Appeal in *Lister & Co v Stubbs* (1890) 45 Ch D 1, [1886–90] All ER Rep 797.

Indeed, in the *Mareva* case [1980] 1 All ER 213 at 215, which came before the Court
j   of Appeal ex parte, Roskill LJ drew attention to the fact that in the Commercial Court an injunction of the kind sought had from time to time been asked for but had been consistently refused.

In *Lister & Co v Stubbs* the defendant was employed by the plaintiffs to buy materials on their behalf. It was alleged that by a corrupt bargain Stubbs had obtained commissions

or bribes from a firm who supplied goods to the plaintiffs and that he had used the
money in purchasing houses and property and in making deposits in banks. Before the   *a*
judge the plaintiffs sought an interlocutory injunction to restrain Stubbs from dealing
with the real estate on which part of the money had been spent and an order directing
him to bring the other investments and the cash into court. The judge rejected the
argument that the plaintiffs could follow the money as trust money and refused any
relief. The plaintiffs appealed.

It seems clear, however, that in the Court of Appeal the plaintiffs' argument was to the   *b*
effect that, if the money could not be followed as trust money, at any rate the money in
cash, or in investments which could be so dealt with, should be paid or brought into
court. This argument was rejected. Cotton LJ pointed out that it was not a case where
payment in was asked for as a term of the grant of leave to defend under RSC Ord 14.
He said (45 Ch D 1 at 13, [1886–90] All ER 797 at 799):

> 'I know of no case where, because it was highly probable that if the action were   *c*
> brought to a hearing the plaintiff could establish that a debt was due to him from
> the defendant, the defendant has been ordered to give security until that has been
> established by the judgment or decree.'

In the light of the argument advanced in the Court of Appeal in *Lister & Co v Stubbs* it
can be said that the Mareva cases are distinguishable because a Mareva injunction does   *d*
not constitute the plaintiff a secured creditor. That may be a valid point of distinction as
far as *Lister & Co v Stubbs* itself is concerned, but it seems to me that, in order to determine
how far the *Mareva* decision represented a departure from the pre-1975 practice, it is
helpful to look shortly at some of the other earlier authorities.

These earlier authorities were considered by the Court of Appeal when the new
phenomenon of the Mareva injunction was examined inter partes in *Rasu Maritima SA v*   *e*
Perusahaan Pertambangan Minyak Dan Gas Bumi Negara (Pertamina) and Government of
Indonesia (as interveners) [1977] 3 All ER 324, [1978] QB 644. Lord Denning MR drew
attention to the old process of foreign attachment, which had fallen into desuetude in
England though it had survived in the United States (*Ownbey v Morgan* (1921) 256 US 94)
(see [1977] 3 All ER 324 at 331, [1978] QB 644 at 657–658). Lord Denning MR stated   *f*
what he believed to be the practice at that time relating to defendants who were within
the jurisdiction and who had assets here. He said ([1977] 3 All ER 324 at 332, [1978] QB
644 at 659):

> 'So far as concerns defendants who are within the jurisdiction of the court and
> have assets here, it is well established that the court should not, in advance of any
> order or judgment, allow the creditor to seize any of the money or goods of the   *g*
> debtor or to use any legal process to do so.'

Lord Denning MR then referred to earlier dicta. It is sufficient to take three examples.
(a) In *Robinson v Pickering* (1881) 16 Ch D 660 at 661 James LJ said in the course of
argument: 'You cannot get an injunction to restrain a man who is alleged to be a debtor
from parting with his property.' (b) In *Newton v Newton* (1885) 11 PD 11 at 13 Hannen P   *h*
said: '. . . it is not competent for a Court, merely quia timet, to restrain a respondent from
dealing with his property.' (c) In *Jagger v Jagger* [1926] P 93 at 102, [1926] All ER Rep
613 at 618 Scrutton LJ said: 'I am not aware of any statutory or other power in the court
to restrain a person from dealing with his property . . .'

Pausing there, it seems to me to be clear that 30 years ago an injunction on the lines of
a Mareva injunction would not have been available in any division of the High Court.   *j*

In 1973, however, the court was given a statutory power to grant injunctions to stop
transactions intended to prevent or reduce financial relief in matrimonial proceedings.
Section 37(2) of the Matrimonial Causes Act 1973 is in these terms:

> 'Where proceedings for financial relief are brought by one person against another,

a
the court may, on the application of the first-mentioned person—(a) if it is satisfied that the other party to the proceedings is, with the intention of defeating the claim for financial relief, about to make any disposition or to transfer out of the jurisdiction or otherwise deal with any property, make such order as it thinks fit for restraining the other party from so doing or otherwise for protecting the claim . . .'

b
It is not necessary for the purpose of the present judgment to make any further detailed reference to the 1973 Act. It may be observed, however, that in *Hamlin v Hamlin* [1985] 2 All ER 1037, [1986] Fam 11 the Court of Appeal held that the court had power under s 37(2) of the 1973 Act to restrain the respondent from disposing of a house in Spain.

The early Mareva injunctions had three limiting characteristics: (a) they were only granted against persons resident outside the jurisdiction; (b) they were only granted against persons who had property within the jurisdiction; and (c) they were only granted
c
to restrain the removal of property from the jurisdiction. In order to obtain an injunction all these elements had to be shown to be present.

In the course of time a number of developments took place. I should refer to some of these.

In *Chartered Bank v Daklouche* [1980] 1 All ER 205, [1980] 1 WLR 107, and in other cases decided at about the same time, it was held that Mareva injunctions could be
d
granted whether the defendant was resident inside or outside the jurisdiction and whatever his domicile or nationality might be.

Next, in *Prince Abdul Rahman Bin Turki Al Sudairy v Abu-Taha* [1980] 3 All ER 409 at 412, [1980] 1 WLR 1268 at 1273 Lord Denning MR expressed the opinion obiter that a Mareva injunction could be obtained if the plaintiff established that there was a danger that the defendant would dispose of his assets within the jurisdiction. This dictum of
e
Lord Denning MR was doubted by some other members of the Court of Appeal in *Faith Panton Property Plan Ltd v Hodgetts* [1981] 2 All ER 877, [1981] 1 WLR 927 and in *A J Bekhor & Co Ltd v Bilton* [1981] 2 All ER 565, [1981] QB 923. But later authorities, including *Ninemia Maritime Corp v Trave Schiffahrtsgesellschaft mbH & Co KG, The Niedersachsen* [1984] 1 All ER 398, [1983] 1 WLR 1412, have clearly established that a Mareva injunction may be granted if it is shown that there is a risk that the defendant
f
may dispose of his assets within the jurisdiction.

It is to be noted, however, that in reaching this conclusion the courts have placed some reliance on the wording of s 37(3) of the Supreme Court Act 1981. That subsection provides as follows:

g
'The power of the High Court under subsection (1) to grant an interlocutory injunction restraining a party to any proceedings from removing from the jurisdiction of the High Court, or otherwise dealing with, assets located within that jurisdiction shall be exercisable in cases where that party is, as well as in cases where he is not, domiciled, resident or present within that jurisdiction.'

Finally, in the summer of 1988, the previous practice in regard to Mareva injunctions was extended in three cases which reached the Court of Appeal by the grant of an
h
injunction relating to the assets of the defendant wherever they might be situated: see *Babanaft International Co SA v Bassatne* [1989] 1 All ER 433, [1989] 2 WLR 232, *Republic of Haiti v Duvalier* [1989] 1 All ER 456, [1989] 2 WLR 261 and *Derby & Co Ltd v Weldon (No 1)* [1989] 1 All ER 469, [1989] 2 WLR 276.

In support of the present appeal it was submitted: (a) that the worldwide injunction granted in *Babanaft* could be explained and justified on the basis that it was granted post-
j
judgment by which time the defendants had become judgment debtors; (b) that *Duvalier* and *Derby (No 1)*, which were pre-judgment cases, involved an impermissible extension of the Mareva jurisdiction and of the recognised practice which had become established over the past 13 years; (c) that in any event the injunction which was granted in the present case could not be supported because it involved the grant of an injunction against

a defendant who had no assets within the jurisdiction and was therefore contrary to the
decision of the Court of Appeal in *Intraco Shipping Corp v Notis Shipping Corp, The Bhoja* *a*
Trader [1981] 2 Lloyd's Rep 256.

In the course of his careful and persuasive argument counsel referred us to a number
of the earlier authorities, and to the words of Jessel MR in *Beddow v Beddow* (1878) 9 Ch D
89 at 93 where, having drawn attention to the width of the discretion given by s 25(8) of
the Supreme Court of Judicature Act 1873 (now s 37(1) of the Supreme Court Act 1981),
he emphasised that the discretion had to be exercised 'according to sufficient legal reasons *b*
and on settled legal principles'.

He also referred us to the speech of Lord Brandon in *South Carolina Insurance Co v
Assurantie Maatschappij 'de Zeven Provincien' NV* [1986] 3 All ER 487 at 495–496, [1987]
AC 24 at 39–40, where he set out the basic principles governing the grant of injunctions
under the statutory powers contained in s 37 of the 1981 Act. Counsel placed particular
emphasis on the following passages in Lord Brandon's speech, where he said: *c*

> 'The second basic principle is that, although the terms of s 37(1) of the 1981 Act
> and its predecessors are very wide, the power conferred by them has been
> circumscribed by judicial authority dating back many years. The nature of the
> limitations to which the power is subject has been considered in a number of recent
> cases in your Lordships' House . . . The effect of these authorities, so far as material *d*
> to the present case, can be summarised by saying that the power of the High Court
> to grant injunctions is, subject to two exceptions to which I shall refer shortly,
> limited to two situations. Situation (1) is when one party to an action can show that
> the other party has either invaded, or threatens to invade, a legal or equitable right
> of the former for the enforcement of which the latter is amenable to the jurisdiction
> of the court. Situation (2) is where one party to an action has behaved, or threatens *e*
> to behave, in a manner which is unconscionable . . . The power of the court to grant
> Mareva injunctions may also, before it was statutorily recognised, have been a
> further exception to the second basic principle stated above. That power, however,
> has now been expressly recognised by s 37(3) of the Supreme Court Act 1981, and
> again the present case is in no way concerned with it.'   *f*

In addition, counsel drew our attention to the decision of the Court of Appeal in
Ashtiani v Kashi [1986] 2 All ER 970, [1987] QB 888, in which it was recognised that it
was the established practice of the courts not to grant Mareva injunctions over assets
which were situated outside the jurisdiction.

I do not find it necessary for the purpose of the present appeal to come to a final
conclusion whether the decision in the *Intraco* case can be relied on as authority for the *g*
proposition that a Mareva injunction can only be granted where there is clear evidence
that there are assets within the jurisdiction. The matter is academic because, as Lord
Donaldson MR has already pointed out, in *MBPXL Corp v International Continental Banking
Corp Ltd* [1975] CA Transcript 411 the Court of Appeal held in terms that a Mareva
injunction could only be granted if there was evidence that there were movable assets in *h*
the possession of the defendant within the jurisdiction of the court.

In these circumstances it is necessary to consider two questions: (a) whether the court
is prevented by binding authority from granting a Mareva injunction in the circumstances
of the present case and on a worldwide basis; (b) whether the grant of such an injunction
can be reconciled with the basic principles enunciated by Lord Brandon in the *South
Carolina* case.   *j*

I have come to the conclusion that the court is entitled to grant an injunction in the
circumstances of the present case against CMI and to grant such an injunction on a
worldwide basis. I can state the reasons for my conclusion as follows.

(1) One starts with the wording of s 37(1) of the 1981 Act, which provides as follows:

a 'The High Court may by order (whether interlocutory or final) grant an injunction or appoint a receiver in all cases in which it appears to the court to be just and convenient to do so.'

(2) In *Blunt v Blunt* [1943] 2 All ER 76 at 78, [1943] AC 517 at 525 Viscount Simon LC adopted the view of the Court of Appeal in *Wickins v Wickins* (*Goode, party cited*) [1918] P 265 at 272:

b '... where Parliament has invested the court with a discretion which has to be exercised in an almost inexhaustible variety of delicate and difficult circumstances, and where Parliament has not thought fit to define or specify any cases or classes of cases fit for its application, this court ought not to limit or restrict that discretion by laying down rules within which alone the discretion is to be exercised...'

c This principle was applied by the Court of Appeal in *Ward v James* [1965] 1 All ER 563 at 571, [1966] 1 QB 273 at 295, where Lord Denning MR gave his guidance as to the way in which a discretion is to be exercised:

'... the courts can lay down the considerations which should be borne in mind in exercising the discretion ... From time to time the considerations may change as public policy changes, and so the pattern of decision may change. This is all part of
d the evolutionary process.'

The principle was further considered by the Court of Appeal in the context of Mareva injunctions in the *Rasu Maritima* case.

(3) As I ventured to suggest in the course of my judgment in the *Babanaft* case, the practice as to the grant of Mareva injunctions is still in the course of development.
e Having regard to the changes in the practice which have already taken place since 1975, I see no good reason for saying that a practice which has so recently come into existence has already become ossified. Circumstances change. It is to be remembered that exchange control was withdrawn in the United Kingdom as recently as 1979. The transfer of funds from one jurisdiction to another grows ever more speedy and the methods of transfer more sophisticated.

f (4) The true basis for the grant of a Mareva injunction is that which was stated in the *Mareva* case (1975) [1980] 1 All ER 213 at 215 itself by Lord Denning MR in these words:

'If it appears that the debt is due and owing, and there is a danger that the debtor may dispose of his assets so as to defeat it before judgment, the court has jurisdiction in a proper case to grant an interlocutory judgment so as to prevent him from
g disposing of those assets.'

To the same effect were the words used by Kerr LJ in *The Niedersachsen* [1984] 1 All ER 398 at 419, [1983] 1 WLR 1412 at 1422 where he said:

'In our view the test is whether, on the assumption that the plaintiff has shown at
h least "a good arguable case", the court concludes, on the whole of the evidence then before it, that the refusal of a Mareva injunction would involve a real risk that a judgment or award in favour of the plaintiff would remain unsatisfied.'

(5) It is to be noted that in the *Mareva* case [1980] 1 All ER 213 at 214 Lord Denning MR referred to a passage in 21 Halsbury's Laws (3rd edn) para 729 (now 24 Halsbury's
j Laws (4th edn) para 918) to the effect that—

'whenever a right, which can be asserted either at law or in equity, does exist, then, whatever the previous practice may have been, the Court is enabled by virtue of this provision, in a proper case, to grant an injunction to protect that right.'

The plaintiff has to show a good arguable case that money is due to him and that he needs
the protection of an injunction to ensure that any judgment which he obtains from the
court is not rendered nugatory by the actions of the defendant. Lord Denning MR
applied the principle which he had cited from Halsbury's Laws to the case of a creditor
who was seeking judgment for payment of a debt and who wanted to protect the right
to enforce that judgment. On this analysis it seems to me possible to fit the grant of
Mareva injunctions within the first of the two situations considered by Lord Brandon in
his examination of the basic principles in the *South Carolina* case.The injunction is an
ancillary power which is required for the enforcement of the plaintiff's right.

(6) It seems to me that the time has come to state unequivocally that in an appropriate
case the court has power to grant an interlocutory injunction even on a worldwide basis
against any person who is properly before the court, so as to prevent that person by the
transfer of his property frustrating a future judgment of the court. The jurisdiction to
grant such injunctions is one which the court requires and it seems to me that it is
consistent with the wide words of s 37(1) of the 1981 Act.

In matters of this kind it is essential that the court should adapt the guidelines for the
exercise of a discretion to meet changing circumstances and new conditions, provided
always the court does not exceed the jurisdiction which is conferred on it by Parliament
or by subordinate legislation. It remains true, of course, that the jurisdiction must be
exercised with care.

The legitimate interests of the defendant must be respected and he must be allowed to
continue his normal business and to have funds to meet his reasonable living expenses. I
anticipate that orders against a defendant's foreign assets or in cases where the defendant
has no assets within the jurisdiction will be unusual. In such cases it will be necessary to
safeguard the position of third parties outside this country. But I see no reason in
principle to reject the existence of the jurisdiction to grant a Mareva injunction in these
cases or why fetters should be placed on the exercise of the wide discretion given by
statute if the purpose of the injunction is to enable the court to protect the effectiveness
of its own procedures. Moreover, it seems to me that this approach is consistent with the
policy underlying s 37(2)(a) of the Matrimonial Causes Act 1973 which is designed to
protect the rights of those seeking financial relief in matrimonial proceedings from being
defeated by deliberate transfers of property by the other party.

I can turn now to consider some of the other matters which have been argued in the
course of this appeal.

THE BABANAFT PROVISO

I have already drawn attention to the fact that, where an injunction is granted which
affects the transfer or other disposition of property which is situated outside the
jurisdiction of the court, steps must be taken to safeguard the position of third parties
who are themselves outside the jurisdiction. This question arose for consideration in the
Babanaft case and led to the incorporation in the order in that case of a proviso designed
to protect overseas banks and other persons over whom the court was not seeking to
assert any direct control.

I have now been able to read that part of the judgment of Lord Donaldson MR in
which he deals in some detail with this aspect of the case. I agree with the revised form
of proviso which he suggests. It may be that in some future case a further refinement
may be developed, but at this stage it seems to me that the wording proposed by Lord
Donaldson MR gives the right degree of protection to the third parties whom it is
intended to assist.

THE APPOINTMENT OF A RECEIVER

Section 37(1) of the 1981 Act gives the High Court a similar jurisdiction to appoint a
receiver to that conferred for the grant of an injunction. The remedies are of course

separate remedies and in some cases it may be appropriate to grant only one of these
a remedies rather than both. I am quite satisfied, however, that in this case the judge was
right to appoint a receiver of the assets of CMI as well as granting an injunction.

I agree with Lord Donaldson MR that the precise form of order should be modified in
the manner which he proposes.

THE DISCOVERY OF ASSETS
b It may be open to argument in some future case that in certain circumstances a
discovery order can be made with a wider ambit than the Mareva injunction to which it
is ancillary. As at present advised, however, I remain of the opinion which I expressed in
Ashtiani v Kashi [1986] 2 All ER 970 at 980, [1987] QB 888 at 905 that the discovery order,
if made at all, should not go further than the injunction. The basis of the jurisdiction to
c make an order for discovery was examined by this court in A J Bekhor & Co Ltd v Bilton
[1981] 2 All ER 565, [1981] QB 923.

It was there held by the majority of the court that the order for discovery, being
ancillary to the Mareva injunction, should not go beyond the ambit of the injunction. I
do not find it necessary in this case to consider further whether, and, if so, in what
circumstances, there may be exceptions to this general rule. I would only urge that in
d this field the court should scrutinise very carefully any submission that its powers are
circumscribed more narrowly than the justice of the case demands.

In the course of this appeal some reference was made to the fact that assets, like the
Cheshire cat, may disappear unexpectedly. It is also to be remembered that modern
technology and the ingenuity of its beneficiaries may enable assets to depart at a speed
which can make any feline powers of evanescence appear to be sluggish by comparison.
e To return to the facts of the present case.

I am satisfied that Sir Nicolas Browne-Wilkinson V-C was fully justified in making the
order for discovery against CMI which he made in this case.

THE RELEVANCE OF ENFORCEABILITY
It was argued on behalf of CMI that one of the strongest reasons against the grant of
f worldwide Mareva injunctions was the difficulty of enforcement. We were referred to a
number of authorities including Locabail International Finance Ltd v Agroexport [1986] 1
All ER 901, [1986] 1 WLR 657 in support of the proposition that it is a general principle
of the law relating to injunctions not to make orders which cannot be enforced.

This aspect of the matter has, however, already been dealt with by Lord Donaldson
MR in the section of his judgment headed 'Enforceability of the injunctions'.
g I agree with his analysis of the position. I also agree that there is no adequate reason to
make any distinction between CMI and Milco. The same relief should be granted against
both companies.

THE RELEVANCE OF THE EUROPEAN JUDGMENTS CONVENTION
h The main action is proceeding in this country. We are therefore not concerned with
the powers referred to in art 24 of the European Convention on Jurisdiction and the
Enforcement of Judgments in Civil and Commercial Matters (Brussels, 27 September
1968; EC 46 (1978); Cmnd 7395) which enable the courts in one convention country to
make interlocutory orders in aid of actions which are proceeding in another convention
country.
j At a later stage of the action, however, it may be necessary to look further at the way
the present orders are enforced by registration or otherwise both in convention countries
and elsewhere. It is to be remembered that a Mareva injunction is a remedy which takes
effect in personam and may have characteristics which are unfamiliar in some
jurisdictions overseas.

CONCLUSION

I too would dismiss the appeal by CMI and allow the cross-appeal by the plaintiffs *a* against Milco on the terms proposed by Lord Donaldson MR.

BUTLER-SLOSS LJ. I agree with the judgments of Lord Donaldson MR and Neill LJ.

I would venture to summarise the present position. The jurisdiction to grant Mareva injunctions is now to be found in the Supreme Court Act 1981, s 37(1). The practice has considerably developed since Roskill LJ in *Mareva Cia Naviera SA v International* *b* *Bulkcarriers SA, The Mareva* (1975) [1980] 1 All ER 213 at 215 said:

'Indeed it is right to say that, as far as my own experience in the Commercial Court is concerned, an injunction in this form has in the past from time to time been applied for but has been consistently refused.'

It is adapting to meet changing circumstances and the increased mobility of assets and *c* interchangeability of international companies. The developing practice was referred to by Kerr LJ in *Babanaft International Co SA v Bassatne* [1989] 1 All ER 433 at 440, [1989] 2 WLR 232 at 242 and by Nicholls LJ in *Derby & Co Ltd v Weldon (No 1)* [1989] 1 All ER 469 at 476, [1989] 2 WLR 276 at 284. Neill LJ in the *Babanaft* case [1989] 1 All ER 433 at 448, [1989] 2 WLR 232 at 251 said:

d

'We are concerned in this appeal with a branch of the law which is in a stage of development and where the court will be asked to exercise its discretion to grant injunctive relief in many differing sets of circumstances. It seems to me therefore that any guidelines which are laid down by this court should be expressed in general terms.'

The Mareva injunction is an equitable remedy which operates 'in personam', in *e* circumstances in which the plaintiffs show a good arguable case and that it is likely that the defendants will dissipate their assets so as not to be available to satisfy a judgment against them. It may be granted either pre-judgment or post-judgment. If there are insufficient or no assets within the jurisdiction the relief may be granted against assets held outside the jurisdiction, either within the countries which are party to the European Convention on Jurisdiction and the Enforcement of Judgments in Civil and Commercial *f* Matters (Brussels, 27 September 1968; EC 46 (1978); Cmnd 7395) or worldwide. It has been granted to support an action brought in another convention country (see *Republic of Haiti v Duvalier* [1989] 1 All ER 456, [1989] 2 WLR 261). In analogous proceedings for an injunction under the provisions of s 37(2)(a) of the Matrimonial Causes Act 1973 relief has been granted to restrain a husband from disposing of real property owned by him in Spain (see *Hamlin v Hamlin* [1985] 2 All ER 1037, [1986] Fam 11). *g*

It is a matter of discretion for the judge whether in the circumstances it appears to be just and convenient to grant the relief sought. The court may be more willing to restrain a defendant from dealing with his assets after than before judgment has been given against him. It is only in an unusual case that the court will make a worldwide pre-judgment Mareva order. Factors such as the impossibility of compliance with or *h* enforcement of the equitable remedy are relevant considerations in the exercise of discretion.

To assist the effectiveness of the pre-judgment Mareva an order for disclosure of assets may within the ambit of the injunction be granted. An order for a receiver may either be made independently under s 37(1) or in support of the Mareva.

The grant of such remedies against defendants must not be oppressive in its outcome. *j* Specific terms or undertakings should therefore generally be part of any worldwide pre-judgment Mareva. The conditions imposed in the wording of the order must balance on the one side the need to freeze the assets in question and gain the information required against restrictions to protect the defendants, inter alia, from unjustified results in other jurisdictions, a misuse of the information gained or an unwarranted invasion of privacy *a* and to permit them to have funds to continue business and to meet reasonable living expenses. They should also contain qualifications to safeguard the position of third parties under the English order, leaving it open for orders to be sought in the courts of the country asked to enforce the English order. I would therefore respectfully indorse the form of order set out in the judgment of Lord Donaldson MR.

Turning to this appeal, in *Derby & Co Ltd v Weldon (No 1)* the Court of Appeal was satisfied that the first and second defendants were 'well used to moving funds worldwide'.

b May LJ said in respect of the first two defendants [1989] 1 All ER 469 at 473, [1989] 2 WLR 276 at 280):

'... for my part I think that this case also is one which cries out for a worldwide Mareva injunction even though it is being sought before judgment.'

Lord Donaldson MR has set out in his judgment the concessions of the plaintiffs in
c their skeleton argument on behalf of CMI (the holding company) which include that the first and second defendants 'are to be assumed to exercise a high degree of control over CMI' and the likelihood of dissipation of the assets of CMI. In the circumstances of this case the relief granted was entirely justified. I would dismiss the appeal.

In considering the cross-appeal in respect of Milco, this company is to be deemed a creature of the first and second defendants against whom Mareva injunctions have been
d granted outside the jursidiction. It is a Panamanian company with no assets within the jurisdiction. If, as I consider it is, it is proper to grant a Mareva injunction outside the jurisdiction against the holding company, I cannot see in principle why such an order should not be made against the subsidiary. It had at one time in the recent past very substantial assets. We are now told it has no assets anywhere. The companies of the group have now been restructured so that Milco is now a subsidiary of Domaine, itself a
e subsidiary of CMI. The ability of CMI as the holding company to control Milco under the existing order is therefore at one remove. There are separate claims in the pleadings against Milco in addition to joint and several claims with the other three defendants.

Sir Nicolas Browne-Wilkinson V-C declined to make an order against Milco on the ground that—

f   'there is no evidence before me that either a Mareva order or any eventual judgment in this action can be enforced against Milco in Panama even if it has any assets. On that basis, I decline to make an order directly against Milco.'

I, for my part, would prefer to turn the proposition round. Although Milco is registered in Panama there is no evidence of assets held in Panama. On the contrary, the assets at one time held by Milco were likely to have been held elsewhere. If there are
g assets there is at present no evidence that the order would be unenforceable and the granting of an order for a receiver may greatly assist in understanding the position of Milco. Sir Nicolas Browne-Wilkinson V-C may have been unduly pessimistic as to the effect of an order which subject to unenforceability it appears he would have been prepared to make. To make or refuse to make the order against Milco is a matter of
h discretion, not of jurisdiction. I would allow the cross-appeal and grant the relief sought in the terms set out by Lord Donaldson MR.

Appeal dismissed and cross-appeal allowed. Leave to appeal to the House of Lords refused.

Solicitors: *Theodore Goddard* (for CMI and Milco); *Lovell White Durrant* (for the plaintiffs); *Cameron Markby* (for the receiver).

Mary Rose Plummer   Barrister.

Practice Note

a

QUEEN'S BENCH DIVISION
WATKINS LJ AND PHILLIPS J
7 MARCH 1989

Judicial review – Leave to apply for judicial review – Practice – Affidavit in reply – Time for
filing affidavit – Increase in time for filing – Extension of time only to be granted in exceptional
circumstances – Hearing applications for extension of time – Abridgment of time where expedited
hearing ordered – RSC Ord 3, r 5, Ord 53, r 6(1)(4) – RSC (Amendment) 1989.

b

WATKINS LJ gave the following direction at the sitting of the court. With effect from
7 March 1989 and by virtue of RSC (Amendment) 1989, SI 1989/177, the period allowed
to a respondent in judicial review proceedings for filing an affidavit in reply under RSC
Ord 53, r 6(4) will be increased from 21 days to 56 days.

c

This follows a general acceptance that the period of 21 days was unrealistically short
and therefore, in many cases, unenforceable. The period substituted cannot be so
characterised. It has been set realistically, having regard to the interests of both applicants
and respondents, and as such must be strictly adhered to. Although there is provision for
extending this period (see Ord 3, r 5) it must be clearly understood that extensions of
time will be granted only in circumstances which are wholly exceptional and for the
most compelling reasons. For all practical purposes respondents would be well advised to
treat the period of 56 days as absolute.

d

Thus, in any case in which the notice of motion and other documents referred to in
Ord 53, r 6(1) are served on a respondent on or after 7 March, that respondent has 56
days in which to file in the Crown Office any affidavit in reply.

e

The Crown Office will not accept respondents' affidavits outside the 56-day period
unless an extension of time has first been obtained.

Applications for extension of time will be considered in the first instance by the Master
of the Crown Office. An appeal against his decision will lie to a judge hearing cases in the
Crown Office list.

f

Where a judge directs an expedited hearing by entering a case in Part D of the Crown
Office list (see the Lord Chief Justice's practice direction of 3 February 1987 (*Practice Note*
[1987] 1 All ER 368, [1987] 1 WLR 232)) applicants should have in mind the need to
invite the judge to abridge the 56-day period where the circumstances of the case so
require.

Delays in lodging respondents' affidavits have hitherto caused severe prejudice to
applicants and consequent damage to the administration of justice. The amendment to
Ord 53, r 6(4) and the procedure set out in this practice note will prevent the continuance
of this difficulty.

g

Raina Levy   Barrister.

Calveley and others v Chief Constable of the Merseyside Police and other appeals

HOUSE OF LORDS

LORD BRIDGE OF HARWICH, LORD ACKNER, LORD OLIVER OF AYLMERTON, LORD GOFF OF CHIEVELEY AND LORD LOWRY

6, 7, 8 FEBRUARY, 16 MARCH 1989

Police – Discipline – Disciplinary proceedings – Investigation – Conduct of proceedings – Duty of care – Police officer under investigation alleging that investigation carried out in breach of statutory duty and negligently – Whether chief constable and investigating officer owing common law duty of care to police officer under investigation – Whether police officer having right of action for damages for breach of duty of care – Whether breach of statutory duty under Police Acts and regulations giving rise to right of action – Whether investigating officer guilty of misfeasance in public office – Police Act 1964 – Police (Discipline) Regulations 1977, reg 7.

Public office – Abuse of – Misfeasance by a public officer – Ingredients of tort – Whether necessary to prove that public officer acted in bad faith or without reasonable excuse in exercise of official power – Whether suspect in criminal or disciplinary proceedings having cause of action in tort for misfeasance in public office where investigating police officer making false and defamatory report to superior officer.

The plaintiffs in three actions were police officers who had been the subject of police disciplinary proceedings under the Police (Discipline) Regulations 1977. They had been suspended on full pay and allowances pending the outcome of the investigation into the complaints made against them. The complaints had either been dismissed, quashed on appeal or discontinued because the officer concerned was discharged on medical grounds, but the plaintiffs alleged that the disciplinary proceedings had been misconducted and that they had thereby suffered loss. The plaintiffs brought actions against their chief constables claiming special damages for lost overtime pay and general damages for anxiety, vexation and injury to reputation. In the first two actions the plaintiffs alleged that the chief constable and other officers for whom he was vicariously liable had been in breach of statutory duty and/or negligent in failing to proceed expeditiously with the investigation, in failing to give the officers written notice of the complaints made against them as soon as practicable as required by reg 7[a] of the 1977 regulations and in misconducting the investigation. A similar allegation of misconduct was the basis of the complaint in the third action. The judge struck out the claims, holding that no action lay for damages against the police for the way in which they conducted a disciplinary inquiry and that the plaintiffs' remedy was confined to seeking damages in proceedings for judicial review. The plaintiffs appealed, contending that the investigating officer owed a duty of care at common law to conduct the investigation properly and expeditiously and that they had a right of action for breach of that duty and for breach of statutory duty under the Police Act 1964 and the 1977 regulations. The Court of Appeal rejected those contentions and dismissed their appeals. The plaintiffs appealed to the House of Lords. At the hearing of the appeal one of the plaintiffs raised for the first time an allegation that the investigating officer had been guilty of misfeasance in public office.

Held – The appeals would be dismissed for the following reasons—

(1) A police officer whose conduct had been the subject of a disciplinary investigation and who alleged that those proceedings had been misconducted had no cause of action

---

a   Regulation 7 is set out at p 1027 *j* to p 1028 *b*, post

against his chief constable or the investigating officer for breach of statutory duty arising out of the 1964 Act or the 1977 regulations since the duty under reg 7 of the 1977 *a* regulations to give notice of the matters alleged to the police officer under investigation as soon as practicable was a procedural step designed to protect the officer's position in relation to proceedings which might be brought against him and was not intended to protect him from injury of a kind for which he would be entitled to compensation. If he was prejudiced by any failure to perform that duty the appropriate remedy was to seek judicial review to quash any conviction and nullify its consequences (see p 1029 *g* to *j*, *b* p 1030 *a b* and p 1032 *f* to *j*, post).

(2) Similarly, a police officer who alleged that disciplinary proceedings brought against him had been misconducted had no cause of action against his chief constable or the investigating officer in negligence since the suspension from duty while the disciplinary investigation was carried out was not in itself, and did not involve, any foreseeable injury of a kind capable of sustaining a cause of action in negligence (see p 1030 *a* to *j*, p 1031 *b* *c* and p 1032 *f* to *j*, post).

(3) For the tort of misfeasance in public office to be proved it had to be shown at least that a public officer had done in bad faith or, possibly, without reasonable cause an act in the exercise or purported exercise of some power or authority with which he was clothed by virtue of the office he held. Since no such act was identified by the pleading the allegation in the third action that the investigating officer had been guilty of misfeasance *d* in public office could not be substantiated (see p 1031 *e j* to p 1032 *b f* to *j*, post).

Per curiam. If a police officer investigating suspected criminal or disciplinary offences maliciously makes a false report to his superior officer which is defamatory of the suspect so that the report loses its status of qualified privilege, the suspect has a cause of action in tort against the author of the report in defamation, not misfeasance in public office (see p 1032 *e* to *j*, post). *e*

Decision of the Court of Appeal [1988] 3 All ER 385 affirmed.

Notes

For negligence in relation to statutory functions, see 34 Halsbury's Laws (4th edn) para 4.

For judicial review generally, see 37 ibid paras 567–583.

For the Police Act 1964, see 33 Halsbury's Statutes (4th edn) 597. *f*

For the Police (Discipline) Regulations 1977, see 17 Halsbury's Statutory Instruments (4th reissue) 254.

Cases referred to in opinions

Donoghue (or M'Alister) v Stevenson [1932] AC 562, [1932] All ER Rep 1, HL.

R v Chief Constable of the Merseyside Police, ex p Calveley [1986] 1 All ER 257, [1986] QB *g* 424, [1986] 2 WLR 144, CA.

Consolidated appeals

The plaintiffs, (1) William Kenneth Calveley and others, (2) Terence Richard Worrall and others and (3) John Bernard Park, in three actions appealed with leave of the Court of Appeal against the decision of that court (Lord Donaldson of Lymington MR, Glidewell and Staughton LJJ) ([1988] 3 All ER 385, [1989] QB 136) on 7 July 1988 dismissing *h* appeals by the plaintiffs against orders of Sir Neil Lawson sitting as a judge of the High Court in chambers dated 2 June 1987 striking out the plaintiffs' claims against the defendants, the Chief Constable of the Merseyside Police in the first two actions, and the Chief Constable of the Greater Manchester Police in the third action, for damages for negligence and breach of statutory duty in the conduct of police disciplinary proceedings. *j* The facts are set out in the opinion of Lord Bridge.

The appeals were consolidated by order of the House of Lords dated 8 November 1988.

John E A Samuels QC, Charles Pugh and *Benedict Patten* for the plaintiffs.
Alan Rawley QC and *Frederick James Maugham Marr-Johnson* for the defendants.

Their Lordships took time for consideration.

a

16 March. The following opinions were delivered.

LORD BRIDGE OF HARWICH. My Lords, the three actions in which these appeals arise are brought by police officers or former police officers against the chief constables of their respective forces. I shall refer to them as 'the Calveley action', 'the Worrall action'
b and 'the Park action'. Save for certain paragraphs of the statement of claim in the Park action which assert a claim to damages for malicious procurement of a search warrant, the plaintiffs' claims have been struck out as disclosing no reasonable cause of action. The order to strike out in the Park action was made by Master Hodgson. An appeal from that order came before Sir Neil Lawson, sitting as judge of the High Court in the Queen's Bench Division, and was heard together with applications by the defendant to strike out
c in the other two actions. Sir Neil Lawson dismissed the Park appeal and ordered that the writs and statements of claim be struck out in the Calveley and Worrall actions. Appeals in all three cases were heard together by the Court of Appeal (Lord Donaldson MR, Glidewell and Staughton LJJ) ([1988] 3 All ER 385, [1989] QB 136), which affirmed Sir Neil Lawson but gave leave to appeal to your Lordships' House.

The appeals now brought raise issues whether certain provisions of the Police Act 1964
d and the Police (Discipline) Regulations 1977, SI 1977/580, create a civil cause of action for breach of statutory duty and whether officers performing certain functions under the Act and regulations owe a duty of care at common law to those in the position of the plaintiffs which founds a cause of action in negligence. These issues arise in all three appeals. In the Park action a separate issue arises whether the facts pleaded are capable of founding the tort of misfeasance in public office.

e   It will be convenient, before referring to the facts, to set out the provisions of the 1964 Act and 1977 regulations which are primarily in question. Sections 48(1) and 49(1) of the 1964 Act provide as follows:

> '**48.**—(1) The chief officer of police for any police area shall be liable in respect of torts committed by constables under his direction and control in the performance
f   or purported performance of their functions in like manner as a master is liable in respect of torts committed by his servants in the course of their employment, and accordingly shall in respect of any such tort be treated for all purposes as a joint tortfeasor.
> **49.**—(1) Where the chief officer of police for any police area receives a complaint from a member of the public against a member of the police force for that area he
g   shall (unless the complaint alleges an offence with which the member of the police force has then been charged) forthwith record the complaint and cause it to be investigated and for that purpose may, and shall if directed by the Secretary of State, request the chief officer of police for any other police area to provide an officer of the police force for that area to carry out the investigation.'

h The 1977 regulations, which were in force at the material time, but have now been superseded by the Police (Discipline) Regulations 1985, SI 1985/518, set out in Sch 2 the provisions of the discipline code to which members of police forces are subject and provide for the formulation, hearing and determination of charges alleging offences against discipline under that code and punishment of such offences. Regulations 6, 7 and 24 provide, so far as material, as follows:

j
> '**6.**—(1) Where a report, allegation or complaint is received from which it appears that an offence may have been committed by a member of a police force (hereinafter referred to as "the member subject to investigation"), the matter shall be referred to an investigating officer who shall cause it to be investigated . . .
> **7.** The investigating officer shall, as soon as is practicable (without prejudicing

his or any other investigation of the matter), in writing inform the member subject
to investigation of the report, allegation or complaint and give him a written *a*
notice—(*a*) informing him that he is not obliged to say anything concerning the
matter, but that he may, if he so desires, make a written or oral statement concerning
the matter to the investigating officer or to the chief officer concerned, and (*b*)
warning him that if he makes such a statement it may be used in any subsequent
disciplinary proceedings.

   24.—(1) Where a report, allegation or complaint is received from which it *b*
appears that a member of a police force may have committed a disciplinary or
criminal offence the chief officer concerned may suspend that member from
membership of the force and from his office as constable, whether or not the matter
has then been investigated, and in such case he shall be suspended until—(*a*) the
chief officer decides otherwise; (*b*) it is decided that the member shall not be charged
with a disciplinary offence; or (*c*) the member has been so charged and either all the *c*
charges have been dismissed or ... punishments have been imposed, whichever
first occurs ...'

We must, of course, assume the facts as pleaded to be true. But it is unnecessary for
the purpose of resolving the issue in the appeals to set out more than a very brief
summary of the facts in each action on which the claims for damages for breach of *d*
statutory duty and negligence depend.

The Calveley action

   On 21 June 1981 the five plaintiffs in this action were concerned in the arrest of five
men. The men arrested made complaints about the conduct of the plaintiffs. The
complainants were prosecuted and tried by the magistrates' court. The plaintiffs gave *e*
evidence for the prosecution. The complainants were acquitted on 23 December 1981.
The formal notices to the plaintiffs, required to be given by reg 7 of the 1977 regulations,
of the original complaints and of other matters alleged against them arising from the
incident on 21 June 1981 and the subsequent prosecution and trial of the complainants
were not given until dates between 28 November and 12 December 1983. The plaintiffs
were later charged with offences against the discipline code of abuse of authority, *f*
falsehood and prevarication. On 26 September 1984 they were found guilty at a hearing
before the chief constable and dismissed from the force. They instituted proceedings for
judicial review of the chief constable's decision. They succeeded before the Court of
Appeal (Sir John Donaldson MR, May and Glidewell LJJ) who, in judgments delivered
on 27 November 1985, quashed the decision of the chief constable on the ground that
the plaintiffs had been irremediably prejudiced by the delay in giving them notice of the *g*
matters alleged against them: see *R v Chief Constable of the Merseyside Police, ex p Calveley*
[1986] 1 All ER 257, [1986] QB 424. On 2 December 1985 the plaintiffs were reinstated
and received their back pay and allowances for the period since their dismissal. The
plaintiffs now claim damages for 'anxiety, vexation and injury to reputation' and special
damages for loss of overtime earnings in the period from dismissal to reinstatement on
the basis that these were caused by breaches of statutory duty under the Act and *h*
regulations or negligent conduct of the investigation.

The Worrall action

   The three plaintiffs in this action were concerned in an incident on 12 September 1981
in which a man named Forwood was arrested. Forwood and other members of the public
made complaints about the conduct of the plaintiffs. On 19 July 1982 Forwood was tried *j*
and convicted by the magistrates' court of assaulting the plaintiff Worrall. On 10 January
1983 this conviction was affirmed by the Crown Court. The plaintiffs gave evidence for
the prosecution in these proceedings. On 7 July 1983 Forwood's conviction was quashed
by the Divisional Court on the ground that he had not been informed of the relevant
complaints made about the plaintiffs' conduct by other members of the public or given

the names and addresses of those complainants. On 25 November 1983 the plaintiffs

a were suspended from duty under reg 24. Pursuant to regs 35 and 69 and para 2 of Sch 6 to the Police Regulations 1979, SI 1979/1470, they received their pay and certain allowances whilst suspended. Following an investigation the plaintiff Worrall was charged with assaulting Forwood and all three plaintiffs were charged with conspiracy to pervert the course of justice and perjury. They were tried and acquitted of all charges by the Crown Court on 3 December 1984 and returned to duty on the following day. On

b return to duty they were entitled under para 3 of Sch 6 to the 1979 regulations to receive any relevant allowances which had been withheld during the period of their suspension. The plaintiffs in this action also claimed damages for 'anxiety, vexation and injury to reputation' and special damages for loss of overtime earnings during the period of suspension on the basis that these were caused by breaches of statutory duty under the Act and regulations or by negligent conduct of the investigation.

c

The Park action

The plaintiff in this action was the subject of an investigation into complaints by certain members of the public that he was guilty of corruption. On 22 June 1983 he was suspended from duty. On 7 June 1984 the plaintiff was given notice pursuant to reg 7 of

d the 1977 regulations of 41 charges against him. The nature of these charges is not specified in the statement of claim. In the event he was not prosecuted. On 11 January 1985, before any disciplinary proceedings had been commenced, the plaintiff was discharged from the force on medical grounds. He claims to have suffered injury, particularised as 'depressive illness and anxiety state' which is attributed in the pleading to breaches of statutory duty or negligence in the conduct of the investigation. He

e further claims special damages for loss of overtime earnings from the date of his suspension to the date of his discharge on medical grounds and loss of earnings and promotion prospects thereafter. The same damages are claimed on the basis of misfeasance in public office, but this issue will require separate consideration.

Breach of statutory duty

f It has not been, nor could it be, seriously argued that the duty imposed by s 49 of the 1964 Act and reg 6 of the 1977 regulations to investigate a complaint by a member of the public against a member of a police force was intended to give a cause of action in damages to the member of the police force who is the subject of the complaint if the duty is not performed. Whether the officer conducting the investigation owes a duty of care at common law to the person under investigation is quite a different question. It

g was, however, submitted that the duty under reg 7 to give notice to the member subject to investigation as soon as is practicable of the matters alleged against him was intended to give the member a cause of action in damages if not performed. That the duty is imposed for the benefit of the police officer subject to investigation is plain. But it seems to me equally plain that the legislature cannot have contemplated that the object of the duty was to protect the officer from any injury of a kind attracting compensation and

h cannot therefore have been intended to give him a right to damages for breach of the duty. The duty is imposed as a procedural step to protect the position of the officer subject to investigation in relation to any proceedings which may be brought against him. If he is not prejudiced in any such proceedings by failure to perform the duty, he has no ground of complaint. If, as in the case of the plaintiffs in the Calveley action, the delay in giving notice under reg 7 coupled with other factors causes irremediable

j prejudice to the officer in disciplinary proceedings which result in his conviction of an offence against the discipline code, he has his remedy by way of judicial review to quash that conviction and nullify its consequences. The proposition that the legislature should have intended to give a cause of action in contemplation of the remoter economic consequences of any delay in giving notice under reg 7 is really too fanciful to call for serious consideration. I shall examine the question what, if any, foreseeable damage may

result from delay in the conduct of an investigation in connection with the alleged
common law duty of care.   *a*

It was also submitted that reg 24 of the 1977 regulations imposes a duty, once a
member of a police force has been suspended, to review that suspension 'periodically'. I
can find nothing, express or implied, in the language of reg 24 which points to the
existence of such a duty, let alone to an intention to give an action for damages for its
breach.
                                                                                      b

Negligence

Leading counsel for the plaintiffs submitted that a police officer investigating any
crime suspected to have been committed, whether by a civilian or by a member of a
police force, owes to the suspect a duty of care at common law. It follows, he submits,
that the like duty is owed by an officer investigating a suspected offence against discipline
by a fellow officer. It seems to me that this startling proposition founders on the rocks of *c*
elementary principle. The first question that arises is: what injury to the suspect ought
reasonably to be foreseen by the investigator as likely to be suffered by the suspect if the
investigation is not conducted with due care which is sufficient to establish the
relationship of legal neighbourhood or proximity in the sense explained by Lord Atkin
in *Donoghue (or M'Alister) v Stevenson* [1932] AC 562 at 580–582, [1932] All ER Rep 1 at
11–12 as the essential foundation of the tort of negligence? The submission that anxiety, *d*
vexation and injury to reputation may constitute such an injury needs only to be stated
to be seen to be unsustainable. Likewise, it is not reasonably foreseeable that the negligent
conduct of a criminal investigation would cause injury to the health of the suspect,
whether in the form of depressive illness or otherwise. If the allegedly negligent
investigation is followed by the suspect's conviction, it is obvious that an indirect
challenge to that conviction by an action for damages for negligent conduct of the *e*
investigation cannot be permitted. One must therefore ask the question whether
foreseeable injury to the suspect may be caused on the hypothesis either that he has never
been charged or, if charged, that he has been acquitted at trial or on appeal, or that his
conviction has been quashed on an application for judicial review. It is, I accept,
foreseeable that in these situations the suspect may be put to expense, or may conceivably
suffer some other economic loss, which might have been avoided had a more careful *f*
investigation established his innocence at some earlier stage. However, any suggestion
that there should be liability in negligence in such circumstances runs up against the
formidable obstacles in the way of liability in negligence for purely economic loss.
Where no action for malicious prosecution would lie, it would be strange indeed if an
acquitted defendant could recover damages for negligent investigation. Finally, all other
considerations apart, it would plainly be contrary to public policy, in my opinion, to *g*
prejudice the fearless and efficient discharge by police officers of their vitally important
public duty of investigating crime by requiring them to act under the shadow of a
potential action for damages for negligence by the suspect.

If no duty of care is owed by a police officer investigating a suspected crime to a civilian
suspect, it is difficult to see any conceivable reason why a police officer who is subject to *h*
investigation under the 1977 regulations should be in any better position. Junior counsel
for the plaintiffs, following, put the case in negligence on a very much narrower basis.
He submitted that in the case of a police officer subject to investigation a specific duty of
care is owed to him to avoid any unnecessary delay in the investigation precisely because
the officer is, or is liable to be, suspended from duty until the investigation is concluded.
The short answer to this submission is that suspension from duty is not in itself and does *j*
not involve any foreseeable injury of a kind capable of sustaining a cause of action in
negligence. The effect of regs 35 and 69 of and Sch 6 to the 1979 regulations is that an
officer who is suspended, unless either he has been convicted of a criminal offence and is
held in custody or he has absented himself and his whereabouts are unknown, is entitled
during suspension to receive his full pay and rent allowance, supplementary rent
allowance or compensatory grant. On return to duty he receives any other appropriate

allowances to which he would have been entitled during the period of suspension. It is
a true that while suspended he cannot earn overtime as a police officer. As against this, the
effect of reg 12 of the 1979 regulations is that, subject to giving notice to the chief
constable, the suspended officer is at liberty during the suspension to engage in any
gainful employment which is not incompatible with his membership of the police force.
The question of compatibility is determined in the first instance by the chief constable
with a right in the officer to appeal from an adverse decision to the police authority and,
b if they affirm the decision, to require a reference to the Secretary of State. In the light of
these considerations, suspension is not a foreseeable cause of even economic loss.

Misfeasance in public office

It is contended that paras 22 and 24 of the statement of claim in the Park action disclose
a reasonable cause of action in that they allege, in effect, the essential ingredients of the
c tort of misfeasance in public office. The Court of Appeal did not address this point, and
there is some difference in recollection between counsel as to how far it was canvassed in
argument.

The investigation of the matters alleged against the plaintiff Park was carried out by
an officer named Grant. Paragraphs 22 and 24 of the statement of claim read as follows:

d   '22. In carrying out the said investigation pursuant to Regulation 6 the Defendant
        through his sevant or agent, Grant, and other investigating officers, acted maliciously
        and/or negligently . . .
        24. Further, the decision to suspend the Plaintiff, alternatively the failure to
        make a decision to reinstate the Plaintiff between June, 1983 and November, 1984,
        amounted to a malicious abuse of power, alternatively negligence on the Defendant's
e   part . . .'

The particulars given under para 22 do not, it is now rightly conceded, contain any
allegation of an act done by Grant or any other officer concerned in the investigation
which could itself amount to the tort of misfeasance in public office. What the pleader
has done is to summarise under the heading 'Particulars of Malice and/or Negligence' the
f matters proposed to be proved as to the manner in which Grant conducted the
investigation, as to various omissions in its conduct and as to Grant's state of mind, from
all of which it is alleged that malice, in the sense of an improper motive on the part of
Grant, is to be inferred.

The particulars given under para 24 are headed 'Particulars of Malicious Abuse of
Power/Negligence' and read as follows:

g   '(a) The suspension, and the continuance of the same, amounts to the procuring
        of the execution of a ministerial act. (b) There was absence of reasonable and
        probable cause: Grant and other members of the investigating team knew or
        believed from an early stage that the corruption allegations were probably unfounded
        and that other disciplinary complaints were of relatively minor importance.
        (c) Malice: The plaintiff will rely upon the matters hereinbefore set out in paragraph
h   22 above. (d) As to damage, the plaintiff has suffered damage to his fame since the
        matter whereof the plaintiff was accused was scandalous and the suspension, and the
        continuance of the suspension for 18 months, damaged the plaintiff's standing both
        within and without the force by tending to imply that there was a good prima facie
        case of corruption, when the contrary was true. Accordingly, by reason of the
        suspension and continuation of it the plaintiff was injured in his calling.'

j
I do not regard this as an occasion where it is necessary to explore, still less to attempt
to define, the precise limits of the tort of misfeasance in public office. It suffices for
present purposes to say that it must at least involve an act done in the exercise or
purported exercise by the public officer of some power or authority with which he is
clothed by virtue of the office he holds and which is done in bad faith or (possibly)
without reasonable cause. The decision to suspend the plaintiff Park under reg 24 was

taken by the deputy chief constable. If this had been done maliciously in the sense indicated, this would certainly be capable of constituting the tort of misfeasance in public office. But it was conceded that no malice is alleged against the deputy chief constable and that malice on the part of Grant cannot be imputed to him. The pleaded case must therefore stand or fall according as to whether it identifies any act done by Grant in the exercise or purported exercise of a power or authority vested in him as investigating officer which was infected by the malice pleaded against him. I can find no such act identified by the pleading.

No formal application to amend the pleading was made in the course of the argument, but at a late stage a document was placed before your Lordships indicating a pleading of additional particulars under paras 22 and 24 which the plaintiff might seek leave to add by way of amendment if those two paragraphs in the statement of claim were allowed to stand. The particulars which it is suggested might be added under para 24 would read as follows:

'From an early stage (the date whereof the plaintiff cannot further particularise until after discovery and/or interrogatories herein) Grant knew or believed that there were no proper grounds for suspending the plaintiff yet procured the imposition of and/or the continuation of the suspension by continuing the investigation and giving misleading and/or incomplete reports concerning the same.'

It is evident that if a police officer investigating suspected criminal or disciplinary offences makes a false report to his superior officer which is defamatory of the suspect and that report is made maliciously so as to lose its status of qualified privilege, the suspect has a cause of action in tort against the author of the report. But the tort is defamation not misfeasance in public office, since the mere making of a report is not a relevant exercise of power or authority by the investigating officer. I express no opinion whether in those circumstances the chief constable would be vicariously liable under s 48(1) of the 1964 Act. However that may be, the suggested additional particulars under para 24 of the statement of claim would do nothing to validate the pleading of misfeasance in public office and obviously fall far short of disclosing a reasonable cause of action in defamation.

I would accordingly dismiss the appeals.

LORD ACKNER. My Lords, I have had the advantage of reading in draft the speech delivered by my noble and learned friend Lord Bridge. I agree with it and would accordingly dismiss all three appeals for the reasons which he has given.

LORD OLIVER OF AYLMERTON. My Lords, I have had the advantage of reading in draft the speech delivered by my noble and learned friend Lord Bridge. I agree with it and would accordingly dismiss all three appeals for the reasons which he has given.

LORD GOFF OF CHIEVELEY. My Lords, I have had the advantage of reading in draft the speech delivered by my noble and learned friend Lord Bridge. I agree with it and would dismiss all three appeals for the reasons which he has given.

LORD LOWRY. My Lords, I have had the advantage of reading in draft the speech delivered by my noble and learned friend Lord Bridge. I agree with it and would accordingly dismiss all three appeals for the reasons which he has given.

Appeals dismissed.

Solicitors: *Russell Jones & Walker* (for the plaintiffs); *Sharpe Pritchard*, agents for *Helen M Mercer*, Kirkby and *Roger C Rees*, Swinton (for the defendants).

Mary Rose Plummer   Barrister.

a
R v Commissioner for Local Administration, ex parte Croydon London Borough Council and another

QUEEN'S BENCH DIVISION
b WOOLF LJ AND HUTCHISON J
3, 4, 27 MAY 1988

Local government – Maladministration – Complaint to local commissioner – Jurisdiction of commissioner – Exclusion of jurisdiction – Action taken in exercise of administrative functions – Action in respect of which aggrieved person has remedy by way of proceedings in any court of law
c *– Decision of education appeal committee – Complaint to local commissioner regarding committee's decision – Finding of injustice by reason of maladministration – Whether committee's decision administrative or judicial function – Whether persons aggrieved having legal remedy by way of judicial review of committee's decision – Whether commissioner having jurisdiction to investigate complaint – Whether findings of maladministration justified – Local Government Act 1974, s 26(1)(6).*

d
The parents of a child who was due to start her secondary education indicated to the local education authority their preference for three particular schools. The authority instead allocated the child to a fourth school. The parents appealed to the authority's education appeal committee against the authority's refusal to allow the child to attend the school of the parents' choice. The committee decided that the child's allocation to the fourth school
e should stand. The parents made a complaint to the commissioner for local administration, who conducted an inquiry into the complaint and concluded that there had been maladministration in the way the committee had dealt with the appeal. In particular, the commissioner found that the committee had not properly determined (i) whether there would be prejudice to efficient education if the child was admitted to the school of the parents' choice, but had instead accepted the council's policy that any increase above
f a given number of places would cause prejudice, or (ii) whether if there was prejudice it outweighed parental considerations. The authority applied for judicial review of the commissioner's decision, contending that the commissioner's jurisdiction to investigate the complaint was excluded either by s 26(1)[a] of the Local Government Act 1974, because the committee had not been exercising 'administrative functions' but a judicial function, or by s 26(6) of that Act, because the persons aggrieved, viz the parents, had a remedy by
g way of legal proceedings, in that they could have applied for judicial review of the committee's decision.

Held – (1) The commissioner's findings that the committee had acted on inadequate evidence and had reached its decision by applying the council's policy without considering
h the merits of the particular case related to the manner in which the committee had reached its decision and therefore the commissioner had jurisdiction under s 26(1) of the 1974 Act to investigate the complaint (see p 1043 *h* to p 1044 *a* and p 1046 *j*, post).

(2) In deciding whether his jurisdiction to investigate a complaint was excluded by s 26(1) of the 1974 Act on the grounds that the person aggrieved had a remedy by way of legal proceedings, the commissioner had to determine whether that person might be
j entitled to obtain some form of remedy if he commenced proceedings within the time limit laid down and his complaint was justified. In declining to investigate on the ground that the person aggrieved had a remedy by way of legal proceedings the commissioner merely had to be satisfied that the courts were the appropriate forum for investigating

---

a Section 26, so far as material, is set out at p 1037 *j* and p 1038 *c d*, post

the subject matter of the complaint and not whether in fact the legal proceedings would
succeed. Moreover, having regard to the commissioner's discretion to discontinue an *a*
investigation at any stage, he was under a continuing duty to consider whether he should
carry on with an investigation if it became apparent during the course of the investigation
that the issues were appropriate to be resolved in the courts. Although the commissioner
could still investigate a complaint where the courts had jurisdiction, he ought to have
regard to the fact that if there was a specialist tribunal set up to deal specifically with the
issue raised in the complaint and if the relief recommended by him was the same as *b*
could be provided by judicial review his jurisdiction was not subject to the same
safeguards and protection for public bodies. On the facts, there had been ample material
before the committee from which it could conclude that the admission of the child to
the school of the parents' choice would be prejudicial to efficient education and,
furthermore, the commissioner's criticism of the committee's reasoning was not justified
since it had not decided the matter on policy grounds alone. It followed that there was *c*
no foundation for the commissioner's finding of maladministration. The authority
would accordingly be granted a declaration that his report was void and of no effect (see
p 1044 *e* to p 1045 *d g j* and p 1046 *b h j*, post).

Notes
For the investigation of complaints by a commissioner for local administration, see 28 *d*
Halsbury's Laws (4th edn) paras 1394–1400.
    For the Local Government Act 1974, s 26, see 25 Halsbury's Statutes (4th edn) 519.

Cases referred to in judgments
Associated Provincial Picture Houses Ltd v Wednesbury Corp [1947] 2 All ER 680, [1948] 1 *e*
    KB 223, CA.
R v Comr for Local Administration, ex p Eastleigh BC [1988] 3 All ER 151, [1988] QB 855,
    [1988] 3 WLR 113, CA.
*R v Local Comr for Administration for the North and East Area of England, ex p Bradford
    Metropolitan City Council* [1979] 2 All ER 881, [1979] QB 287, [1979] 2 WLR 1, CA.
R v South Glamorgan Appeals Committee, ex p Evans (10 May 1984, unreported), QBD. *f*

Cases also cited
Malloch v Aberdeen Corp [1971] 2 All ER 1278, [1971] 1 WLR 1578, HL.
Maxwell v Dept of Trade and Industry [1974] 2 All ER 122, [1974] QB 523, CA.
R v Stratford-on-Avon DC, ex p Jackson [1985] 3 All ER 769, [1985] 1 WLR 1319, CA.
                                                         g

Application for judicial review
Croydon London Borough Council and an education appeal committee set up by the
council pursuant of s 7 of and Sch 2 to the Education Act 1980 to consider an appeal by
the parents of a child living in the London borough of Sutton applied, with leave of
Webster J given on 17 February 1987, for judicial review of a report made on 27 October *h*
1986 by the chairman of the Commission for Local Administration (the commissioner)
on an investigation into a complaint in which he found that the complainant had suffered
injustice by reason of maladministration by the education committee. The relief sought
by the council was (1) an order of certiorari to quash the report of the commissioner and
(2) a declaration that the report and/or the findings of maladministration made therein
were void and/or of no effect and/or made without jurisdiction. The facts are set out in *j*
the judgment of Woolf LJ.

Elizabeth Appleby QC and *G Caws* for Croydon.
Michael Beloff QC and *John Hobson* for the commissioner.

                                                                 Cur adv vult

27 May. The following judgments were delivered.

a

WOOLF LJ. This is an application for judicial review by Croydon London Borough Council (Croydon) in respect of a report which was made by Dr Yardley (the commissioner), who is chairman of the Commission for Local Administration in England. In the report the commissioner concluded that there had been maladministration by an education appeal committee (the committee) set up by Croydon in the course

b of considering an appeal by parents who lived in the adjoining borough of Sutton against the refusal of Croydon to allow their daughter to attend a secondary school in Croydon in accordance with the preference which they had expressed. The application raises a general issue as to the extent of the jurisdiction of a local commissioner and education appeal committees. In addition it raises specific issues as to the manner in which the committee came to its decision to dismiss the appeal and the basis for the commissioner's

c conclusion that there had been maladministration by the committee.

The facts

For the purposes of the application the facts can be briefly summarised. In October 1984 the parents indicated that they would prefer their daughter to commence her secondary education the following year at one of three schools which they named. One

d of those schools, the school with which this application is concerned, was Woodcote High School, which was the school which the daughter's elder sister attended. The daughter was in fact allocated to none of the schools for which the parents had expressed a preference and instead she was allocated to a fourth school. On 6 June 1985 the parents appealed against the decision of Croydon in relation to the Woodcote High School. The appeal was heard by the committee and the appeal was dismissed. On 20 June 1985 a

e complaint was referred by a councillor to the commissioner in relation to dismissal of that appeal and the other appeals which were heard as a result of the refusal to admit the daughter to any of the preferred schools. In October 1985 the commissioner wrote to Croydon notifying them of the complaint and asking for certain information so that the commissioner could decide the extent to which there should be further investigation of the complaint.

f

In due course the information was supplied, but it did not satisfy the commissioner. He decided to embark on an inquiry during which his investigating officer interviewed members of the committee and Croydon's officers and on 27 October 1986, having completed his investigation, the commissioner made a report.

In that report the commissioner set out the results of his inquiries, and his reasons for coming to the conclusion that there was maladministration in the way the committee

g dealt with the appeal and the injustice which he concluded had occurred as a result. He also expressed the opinion that the only fair way to remedy the maladministration was for the appeal to be reheard by a fresh committee with all the available evidence before them. He also made certain general recommendations as to how appeal committees should perform their functions in the future. There was then a meeting between officers

h of the council and the commissioner and subsequently the commissioner wrote a letter on 20 November 1986 clarifying his conclusions and recommendations.

On 16 January 1987 Croydon authorised the institution of these proceedings and on 26 January 1987 the application was lodged and leave was granted by Webster J on 17 February 1987.

Notwithstanding Croydon's criticisms of the commissioner's conduct made in these

j proceedings, Croydon did in fact offer the parents a fresh appeal but this was not accepted by the parents because their daughter had started her secondary education at the allocated school where she was making satisfactory progress.

In order to consider the issues raised on the application, it will be necessary to examine the commissioner's report in some detail but before doing this, it is necessary to refer to the relevant legislation and a decision of Forbes J in *R v South Glamorgan Appeals Committee, ex p Evans* (10 May 1984, unreported).

The legislation

I refer first of all to the Education Act 1980, which deals with the right of parents to   *a*
express a preference, the obligations on an education authority to comply with the
parents' preference and the parents' right of appeal against admission decisions to which
they object. Section 6 of the 1980 Act deals with parental preference. It provides:

> '(1) Every local education authority shall make arrangements for enabling the
> parent of a child in the area of the authority to express a preference as to the school   *b*
> at which he wishes education to be provided for his child in the exercise of the
> authority's functions and to give reasons for his preference.
> (2) Subject to subsection (3) below, it shall be the duty of a local education
> authority and of the governors of a county or voluntary school to comply with any
> preference expressed in accordance with the arrangements.
> (3) The duty imposed by subsection (2) above does not apply—(*a*) if compliance   *c*
> with the preference would prejudice the provision of efficient education or the
> efficient use of resources . . .'

The right of appeal is contained in s 7 of the 1980 Act. That section provides:

> '(1) Every local education authority shall make arrangements for enabling the
> parent of a child to appeal against—(*a*) any decision made by or on behalf of the   *d*
> authority as to the school at which education is to be provided for the child in the
> exercise of the authority's functions . . .
> (4) Any appeal by virtue of this section shall be to an appeal committee constituted
> in accordance with Part I of Schedule 2 to this Act; and Part II of that Schedule shall
> have effect in relation to the procedure on any such appeal.
> (5) The decision of an appeal committee on any such appeal shall be binding on   *e*
> the local education authority or governors by or on whose behalf the decision under
> appeal was made and, in the case of a decision made by or on behalf of a local
> education authority, on the governors of any county or controlled school at which
> the committee determines that a place should be offered to the child in question . . .'

Section 7 also amended the Tribunals and Inquiries Act 1971 and the Local Government   *f*
Act 1974 so as to make appeal committees subject to the Council on Tribunals and subject
to investigation by the local commissioner.

The relevant provisions of Sch 2 referred to in s 7(4) are important since they indicate
the nature of appeal committees and the procedure which they are required to follow.
Those provisions of the schedule are as follows:

g

'PART I

CONSTITUTION OF APPEAL COMMITTEES

1.—(1) An appeal pursuant to arrangements made by a local education authority
under section 7(1) of this Act shall be to an appeal committee constituted in   *h*
accordance with this paragraph.
(2) An appeal committee shall consist of three, five or seven members nominated
by the authority from among persons appointed by the authority under this
paragraph; and sufficient persons may be appointed to enable two or more appeal
committees to sit at the same time.
(3) The persons appointed shall comprise—(*a*) members of the authority or of   *j*
any education committee of the authority; and (*b*) persons who are not members of
the authority or of any education committee of the authority but who have
experience in education, are acquainted with the educational conditions in the area
of the authority or are parents of registered pupils at a school . . .

PART II

PROCEDURE

5. An appeal shall be by notice in writing setting out the grounds on which it is made.

6. An appeal committee shall afford the appellant an opportunity of appearing and making oral representations and may allow the appellant to be accompanied by a friend or to be represented.

7. The matters to be taken into account by an appeal committee in considering an appeal shall include—(a) any preference expressed by the appellant in respect of the child as mentioned in section 6 of this Act; and (b) the arrangements for the admission of pupils published by the local education authority or the governors under section 8 of this Act . . .

10. Appeals pursuant to arrangements made under section 7 of this Act shall be heard in private except when otherwise directed by the authority or governors by whom the arrangements are made but, without prejudice to paragraph 6 above, a member of the local education authority may attend as an observer any hearing of an appeal by an appeal committee constituted in accordance with paragraph 1 above and a member of the Council on Tribunals may attend as an observer any meeting of any appeal committee at which an appeal is considered.

11. Subject to paragraphs 5 to 10 above, all matters relating to the procedure on appeals pursuant to arrangements made under section 7 of this Act, including the time within which they are to be brought, shall be determined by the authority or governors by whom the arrangements are made; and neither section 106 of the Local Government Act 1972 nor paragraph 44 of Schedule 12 to that Act (procedure of committees of local authorities) shall apply to an appeal committee constituted in accordance with paragraph 1 above.'

Paragraph 7 refers to s 8 of the Act. That section provides:

'(1) Every local education authority shall, for each school year, publish particulars of—(a) the arrangements for the admission of pupils to schools maintained by the authority, other than aided or special agreement schools . . . (c) the arrangements made by the authority under sections 6(1) and 7(1) above . . .

(3) The particulars to be published under subsections (1)(a) and (2)(a) above shall include particulars of—(a) the number of pupils that it is intended to admit in each school year to each school to which the arrangements relate, being pupils in the age group in which pupils are normally admitted or, if there is more than one such group, in each such group; (b) the respective admission functions of the local education authority and the governors; (c) the policy followed in deciding admissions; (d) the arrangements made in respect of pupils not belonging to the area of the local education authority . . .'

The powers of the commissioner are contained in the Local Government Act 1974. As already indicated that Act, as amended, expressly includes education appeal committees as being among the authorities subject to investigation (see s 25(5)). Section 26 of the 1974 Act is important because it deals with the jurisdiction of the commissioner. It provides:

'(1) Subject to the provisions of this Part of this Act where a written complaint is made by or on behalf of a member of the public who claims to have sustained injustice in consequence of maladministration in connection with action taken by or on behalf of an authority to which this Part of this Act applies, being action taken in the exercise of administrative functions of that authority, a Local Commissioner may investigate that complaint . . .'

I draw attention to the requirement in this subsection of a claim to have sustained injustice 'in consequence of maladministration' with a reference to the exercise of an *a* 'administrative function'. Section 26 continues:

'(2) A complaint shall not be entertained under this Part of this Act unless—(*a*) it is made in writing to a member of the authority, or of any other authority concerned, specifying the action alleged to constitute maladministration, and (*b*) it is referred to the Local Commissioner, with the consent of the person aggrieved, or of a person acting on his behalf, by that member, or by any other person who is a *b* member of any authority concerned, with a request to investigate the complaint . . .

(6) A Local Commissioner shall not conduct an investigation under this Part of this Act in respect of any of the following matters, that is to say,—(*a*) any action in respect of which the person aggrieved has or had a right of appeal, reference or review to or before a tribunal constituted by or under any enactment; (*b*) any action in respect of which the person aggrieved has or had a right of appeal to a Minister of *c* the Crown; or (*c*) any action in respect of which the person aggrieved has or had a remedy by way of proceedings in any court of law: Provided that a Local Commissioner may conduct an investigation notwithstanding the existence of such a right or remedy if satisfied that in the particular circumstances it is not reasonable to expect the person aggrieved to resort or have resorted to it . . . *d*

(10) In determining whether to initiate, continue or discontinue an investigation, a Local Commissioner shall, subject to the preceding provisions of this section, act at discretion; and any question whether a complaint is duly made under this Part of this Act shall be determined by the Local Commissioner . . .'

Section 26(6) is important because it indicates the limits that Parliament intended should apply to the jurisdiction of the commissioner subject to his exercising his *e* discretion under the proviso to that subsection. In particular it makes clear that the general rule is that, inter alia, in relation to a complaint in respect of which the parents have or had a remedy in the courts by way of an application for judicial review they should resort to that remedy rather than apply to the commissioner and the commissioner should only exercise his discretion to investigate such a complaint 'in the particular *f* circumstances'.

Where the commissioner decides to conduct an investigation, he has wide powers as indicated by s 29(1) and (2), which provides as follows:

'(1) For the purposes of an investigation under this Part of this Act a Local Commissioner may require any member or officer of the authority concerned, or any other person who in his opinion is able to furnish information or produce *g* documents relevant to the investigation, to furnish any such information or produce any such documents.

(2) For the purposes of any such investigation a Local Commissioner shall have the same powers as the High Court in respect of the attendance and examination of witnesses, and in respect of the production of documents.'

h

The final provision to which I should refer is s 34(3), which again deals with the extent of the commissioner's jurisdiction and states as follows:

'It is hereby declared that nothing in this Part of this Act authorises or requires a Local Commissioner to question the merits of a decision taken without maladministration by an authority in the exercise of a discretion vested in that authority.' *j*

It is not necessary for me to refer to s 31(8) of the London Government Act 1963 since, while Croydon initially thought that the commissioner was alleging that Croydon were improperly discriminating against parents from Sutton who wanted to send their children to Croydon schools, this was not in fact the case and there has been no suggestion

on the hearing of this application that Croydon have contravened the provisions of that
a subsection.

Many of the statutory provisions dealing with the local government commissioner are
mirrored by the provisions of the Parliamentary Commissioner Act 1967. I do not
propose to make express reference to the relevant provisions of that Act. However, I have
well in mind that our decision on this application could have implications in respect of
the important jurisdiction exercised by the Parliamentary Commissioner.

b Although the decision of Forbes J in *R v South Glamorgan Appeals Committee, ex p Evans*
(10 May 1984) is unreported, it is regarded as being of considerable significance by those
concerned with pupil admissions. In particular the guidance which he gave as to the
application of s 6 of the 1980 Act resulted in the Association of County Councils, in
consultation with other local authority associations and the Council on Tribunals, issuing
a revised code of practice in February 1985 which has been followed by appeal committees
c up and down the country including the appeal committee constituted by Croydon. It
has also resulted in guidance being given from time to time to education authorities by
the commissioner. However, counsel on behalf of Croydon explained how that decision,
particularly as it has been interpreted by the commissioner, has given rise to difficulties
for large education authorities such as Croydon.

It is not necessary to refer to the facts of the *Glamorgan* case: it is sufficient to refer to
d those passages of Forbes J's judgment in which he gave general guidance as to the
application of the 1980 Act:

'In practical terms it seems to me that, because the appeal is only by a parent,
appeals are only likely to arise because parental choice has not been followed and,
therefore, the necessary background is that the education authority has decided to
e reject the parental choice on the grounds that one of the matters set out in s 6(3) [of
the 1980 Act] applies. The only one with which we are concerned, of course, is
under para (*a*), that is, prejudice to efficient education ... So the question of the
efficient use of resources does not really arise. That is the necessary factual
background, it seems to me, to the appeal. Against that, if an appeal committee
were not satisfied that there had been prejudice, it seems to me they would be
f bound to allow the appeal because of the existence of the statutory duty under s 6(2).
It follows inevitably, it seems to me, that the first task of an appeal committee under
this statute is to decide whether the case of prejudice is made out. Paragraph 7 of
Sch 2 makes clear that that is not an end of the matter because the committee must
have regard to parental preference in the arrangements for the admission of pupils.
g Curiously enough, the paragraph does not mention the question of prejudice but it
seems clear to me that in embarking on an appeal the appeal committee has not
merely to decide whether there would be prejudice; it has to embark, if it decides
there is prejudice, on the balancing exercise of whether the degree of prejudice is
sufficient to outweigh what I will call the parental considerations, including such
matters as the priority factors set out in the passage in the arrangements I have read
h and those arrangements themselves. The procedure adopted by these committees is
one agreed with the Council on Tribunals as applicable to all county educational
authorities ... It might be helpful, therefore, if the procedure were looked at again,
particularly to indicate to these committees that it is indeed a two-stage exercise on
which they embark: the first being to decide what is really a question of fact, is there
or would there be prejudice to the efficient education etc if this child were admitted
j and the second, the question of discretion, balancing between the degree of prejudice
and the extent of applicability of the parental factors. The onus seems to me to be
clearly on the education authority in stage 1. As the Act can be read as indicating
that its primary object is to support parental choice, it may be that it should be
considered that the onus remains on the education authority to demonstrate that
the prejudice is of sufficiently serious degree to outweigh the parental factor, and

that therefore the procedure at present adopted should be reversed so that the
education authority should make its case to the committee first rather than after the *a*
parent as at present. I merely throw this suggestion out. What I am really suggesting
is that the procedure should be looked at again in order to offer more assistance to
the appeal committees in the discharge of their functions and to give some guidance
as to the order in which the parties should be heard . . . Turning to the remaining
points, [counsel for the applicant's] first submission was that in the circumstances
and on the evidence before it no reasonable committee, addressing itself to the *b*
relevant considerations, could have come to the conclusion that the admission of
this child would have prejudiced the provision of efficient education at that school.
That is a plea to that part of the well-known case of *Associated Provincial Picture
Houses Ltd v Wednesbury Corp* [1947] 2 All ER 680, [1948] 1 KB 223, which is often
referred to as being "*Wednesbury* perverse". It seems to me that there was clear
evidence in this case that the presence of six children over the maximum of 30 did *c*
in fact prejudice efficient education. If you look at the evidence of Mr Pearce and
Mrs Jones, who were the two witnesses called before the appeal committee by the
education authority, the effect of their evidence was to show, and seems to have
been designed to show, that 36 was a figure which already prejudiced efficient
education. The point to which the committee should address itself, it seems to me,
is not whether there already was prejudice but whether compliance with parental *d*
preference would prejudice the provision of efficient education. Compliance with
parental preference in this case would be limited to the one child under
consideration; in other words, the question before the appeal committee would be
whether the addition of this one child would aggravate an existing prejudiced
situation. There was no evidence called to justify that assertion at all. The evidence
which was called was merely to show that with a class of 36 prejudice existed. If that *e*
were all, it might, it seems to me, be possible to say that this was a perverse decision
under the doctrine of *Wednesbury* because there was no adequate evidence led before
the committee to indicate that the addition of this one child would itself aggravate
an already prejudiced situation. But, and I think it is a big but, one must look at the
composition of this committee. I find it impossible to say that a tribunal whose *f*
members were chosen, and quite clearly chosen, for their connection, with and
presumably their knowledge of, educational matters would be perverse if they took
the view that, despite the absence of any direct evidence, the addition of one child
might well aggravate an already prejudiced situation. That seems to me to be a
matter which, if I can use a compendious expression, an especially knowledgeable
committee might be prepared and entitled to take into account of their own
knowledge and not necessarily on the evidence before them. The evidence, of *g*
course, would give them the picture that here were 36 children in a class in which
the maximum should have been 30 and so on. Without any evidence of that kind,
of course, it might be different; but once they had got the basic facts it seems to me
it is impossible to say that they had been *Wednesbury* perverse, if with their
knowledge of these matters, they took the view that an addition of one child might *h*
well prejudice or aggravate what was already a prejudiced situation.'

I have no doubt that Forbes J was perfectly right to take the view that there should be
a two-stage exercise. Unless an appeal committee comes to the conclusion that compliance
with the parents' preference would prejudice the provision of efficient education or the
efficient use of resources, the local education authority remains under a duty to comply *j*
with the expressed preference and if they fail to do so they are in breach of duty.
Accordingly, an appeal will automatically be allowed if an appeal committee do not
consider that to give effect to the preference would result in such prejudice. If, however,
an appeal committee comes to the conclusion that efficiency would be prejudiced by
complying with the preference, then the appeal committee will have to proceed to the

second stage and decide how to exercise its discretion, by weighing up the advantages
a which would be achieved by complying with the preference as against the prejudice this
would cause. In general therefore I indorse Forbes J's approach.

Counsel on behalf of Croydon also criticises the views expressed by Forbes J as to the
onus resting on the education authority 'to demonstrate that the prejudice is of
sufficiently serious degree to outweigh the parental factor' (that is on the second stage).
Clearly in so far as it is appropriate to talk of onus, the onus is on the education authority
b at stage one. With regard to stage two the position is not as clear but as the education
authority are relying on the prejudice, in the normal way it is only from the education
authority that the appeal committee is going to obtain evidence which is relevant as to
prejudice. However, as Hutchison J pointed out in the course of argument, it is really
not helpful in the case of proceedings of this sort to talk about onus. It has been the
practice since the *Glamorgan* case for the education authority to present its case first and
c this is clearly sensible. However, once all the material is before the committee,
particularly on stage two, when the committee is going to have to perform a balancing
act, the decision in practice will not depend on the onus of proof. The committee has to
come to its decision on the basis of all the material which it has available and by applying
its expertise to that material it should decide where the balance lies.

The only other procedural issue to which I should draw attention is the difference in
d view between the commissioner and Croydon whether all the appeals in relation to the
admissions to a particular school should be heard before the committee reaches its
decision on any of those appeals. There is clearly an advantage in adopting this course if
it is practical because children whose appeals are heard last could otherwise be prejudiced
because of decisions which had been reached already by an appeal committee to send
children to a particular school. However, Croydon points out that because they are one
e of the largest, if not the largest, education authority, they have to conduct a great many
appeals. During June and July 1985, for example, Croydon were involved in appeals in
respect of decisions made in 158 cases, of which 30 were in respect of the school with
which we are concerned. Mr Hemmings, the controller of administration and solicitor
to Croydon, in his affidavit sums up the position as follows:

f   'In fact, it is quite impractical for Croydon (and I believe many other authorities)
          in view of the number of appeals, the constraints on the time of individual members
          of Appeal Committees, the need to arrange appeals at times and on dates to suit
          parental convenience, the need to notify the decisions as quickly as possible and the
          staggered nature of appeals that I have explained, to so group appeals that all appeals
          in relation to one particular school are heard at the same time by the same members
g   of the Appeal Committee.'

The answer to this situation is provided by the fact that an appeal committee like any
other administrative tribunal (in the absence, as here, of statutory constraints) is the
master of its own procedure and having regard to the evidence of Mr Hemmings it is not
possible to criticise the committee for coming to a decision not to adopt the course
h preferred by the local commissioner.

The commissioner's report

The commissioner is an academic lawyer of great distinction who personally has
considerable experience of administrative tribunals and is the author of a well-known
book on administrative law. It is not surprising therefore that his report sets out the legal
j and administrative background to the investigation and the information which was
obtained during the course of the investigation with admirable clarity. The criticisms
which are made of the report are based on his conclusions and so far as relevant these are
as follows:

          '42. The judgement in the *South Glamorgan* case held that the Appeal Committee's task is in two stages. First they must decide whether the local education authority have proved (and in his judgement Forbes J states that the onus of proof is clearly on *a* the authority) that compliance with parental preference by admitting one particular child would prejudice the provision of efficient education or the efficient use of resources. If they find against the authority on this issue the Appeal must succeed, but if they conclude that the case of prejudice has been made out, then they must embark on the second stage of considering the merits of the case before them in order to determine whether the degree of prejudice is outweighed by the "parental *b* considerations".

43. This investigation has been concerned not with the way the Council presented their case but with the way the Appeal Committee Members considered the evidence before them. It would appear that the Members did not ask for further information to support the statement made by the education officer. Certainly from the outset they simply accepted that it would follow from the Council's decision on the *c* number of first year places at the School that an increase above the 210 figure would cause prejudice. In the circumstances I cannot see that the Appeal Committee Members were in any position objectively to decide whether the admission of Victoria to the School would be prejudicial.

44. In short, the Appeal Committee Members would appear to me virtually to have missed out the first required stage of their deliberations; and I am not satisfied *d* that the majority of the Members properly approached the second stage. I accept that the Council are entitled to make a policy that priority should be given to children from the Council's area, just as they are entitled to decide what the planned admissions limits should be, but I do not consider that Appeal Committee Members should regard that policy as constituting a good reason for failing to consider an appeal from an out-borough child on his/her merits. Yet that is what three of the *e* five Members considering Victoria's appeal appear to have done.

45. For the reasons given in paragraphs 43 and 44, I find that there was maladministration in the way the Appeal Committee dealt with this Appeal, and it is inevitable that injustice to Mrs Brown has flowed from it. The only fair way to remedy this is for the Appeal to be reheard by a fresh Committee with all the *f* available evidence before them, and by making sure that the two-stage procedure is properly followed. The Council should also ensure that future Appeal Committee Members are clear about their procedures and functions. The Chairman's Aide-Memoire could usefully be more explicit about the two-stage process required. The Notes of Guidance for appellants make only a brief mention of the concept of "prejudice", and I feel it would be helpful for appellants if this were strengthened *g* (although I note that Mr Jones did raise the point on Mrs Brown's behalf).'

There is a further paragraph of conclusions, para 46, but this deals with the preferred procedure with regard to announcing the outcome of appeals to which I have already made reference and as this is only a recommendation by the commissioner which does not go to the substance of this application, I need not make any further reference to it.

So far as para 45 is concerned, apart from repeating that in practice there is no necessity *h* to lay stress on the onus of proof, I need make no further comment.

The jurisdiction issue

It is on para 43 that counsel for Croydon bases her submissions that the commissioner had no jurisdiction. She submits that the committee when considering the evidence and deliberating on its decision is performing a quasi-judicial or a judicial function and in *j* these circumstances is not subject to the scrutiny of the commissioner. She submits that the committee is not exercising 'administrative functions' within the meaning of that term in s 26(1) and that you cannot have 'maladministration' in connection with activities of this sort. Furthermore, she relies on the terms of s 34(3) as supporting her contentions.

In her submission administrative functions have to be contrasted with judicial or
a legislative functions and here, having regard to the statutory provisions, the functions
were judicial.

There is only limited previous judicial authority as to what is meant by
maladministration and administrative functions. Their meaning was considered in *R v
Local Comr for Administration for the North and East Area of England, ex p Bradford
Metropolitan City Council* [1979] 2 All ER 881, [1979] QB 287 and recently has again been
b considered by the Court of Appeal in *R v Comr for Local Administration, ex p Eastleigh BC*
[1988] 3 All ER 151, [1988] QB 855. As the words 'administrative functions' also appear
in the Parliamentary Commissioner Act 1957, s 51, their interpretation is important. In
the *Eastleigh* case [1988] 3 All ER 151 at 155, [1988] QB 855 at 863 Lord Donaldson MR,
having referred to the *Bradford* case, said:

c   'All three judges (Lord Denning MR, Eveleigh LJ and Sir David Cairns) expressed
        themselves differently, but in substance each was saying the same thing, namely
        that administration and maladministration, in the context of the work of a local
        authority, is concerned with the *manner* in which decisions by the authority are
        reached and the *manner* in which they are or are not implemented (see [1979] 2 All
        ER 881 at 897–898, 900, 903, [1979] QB 287 at 311, 314, 318). Administration and
d   maladministration have nothing to do with the nature, quality or reasonableness of
        the decision itself.' (Lord Donaldson MR's emphasis.)

Parker LJ in the *Eastleigh* case [1988] 3 All ER 151 at 158, [1988] QB 855 at 868 cited
with approval a passage from the judgment of Eveleigh LJ in the *Bradford* case ([1979] 2
All ER 881 at 902, [1979] QB 287 at 316) in which Eveleigh LJ said:

e   'If the local commissioner carries out his investigation and in the course of it
        comes personally to the conclusion that a decision was wrongly taken, but is unable
        to point to any maladministration other than the decision itself, he is prevented by
        s 34(3) from questioning the decision.'

Counsel for the commissioner, on the other hand, submits that an administrative
f function in the context of s 26(1) is only to be contrasted with a legislative function. He
submits that, as the appeal committees are expressly made subject to the jurisdiction of
the commissioner, he must be entitled to carry out investigations and it cannot have
been intended that his investigations should be confined to activities such as the arranging
of the listing of cases and peripheral matters of that nature. He points out that when the
education authority deals with admissions it is clearly exercising an administrative
g function and this being so he questions why the position should be different merely
because the decision is taken by an appeal committee.

On this issue I find s 34(3) of the 1974 Act of negligible assistance since that subsection
only applies to the merits of a decision where it is 'taken without maladministration',
and to ascertain whether or not there is maladministration is the very object of an
investigation.
h   However, in relation to s 26(1), while I obtain assistance from the guidance given by
Lord Donaldson MR, I accept also that there is force in the submissions of counsel for the
commissioner and I do not find it at all easy to define precisely the limits of the
commissioner's jurisdiction. I do not therefore propose to do more than express a
conclusion as to jurisdiction in relation to the particular matters of which the
commissioner has made complaint in paras 43 and 44 of his report. In so far as it is
j possible to categorise the complaints I regard them as relating to the manner in which
the decision was reached although I recognise that this can also affect the quality of the
decision. In short, the specific criticisms are, first, that the committee acted on inadequate
evidence and did not seek, as it should have done, further evidence; and, second, that the
committee in reaching its decision applied its policy to the exclusion of the merits of the

particular case which was before it. These are matters of complaint which I regard the commissioner as having jurisdiction to consider within the terms of s 26(1).   *a*

Counsel for Croydon next argued that the subject of the investigation related to action in respect of which 'the person aggrieved has or had a remedy by way of proceedings in any court of law', and that prima facie the jurisdiction of the commissioner was excluded by s 26(6). The commissioner in his evidence indicates that when the complaint was referred to him, on the facts available to him at that time, there was no basis on which any view could be taken as to whether a remedy was then, or would at an earlier time *b* have been, available to the complainant by way of judicial review. He adds that at the time when he decided to proceed with the investigation in detail the possibility that there might be, or might have been, a remedy to the complainant in law was so remote as to be more theoretical than real. He also points out that by the time he had completed his investigation the normal time limits for making an application for judicial review had long since expired and there was no more than a remote possibility that the facts *c* provided a foundation for an application for judicial review and that leave to pursue such an application out of time would be granted. He therefore did not consider at any material time whether the proviso to s 26(6) of the 1974 Act should be applied.

However, in his second affidavit he makes it clear that if he had considered whether to operate the proviso, he would have regarded it as unreasonable to expect the complainant to take on the burden of litigation and would not have discontinued his involvement.   *d*

In considering this issue, it is first necessary to decide in what sense the words 'remedy by way of proceedings in any court of law' are used in s 26(6). Counsel for the commissioner submits that what is meant is that if proceedings are brought they will succeed and result in a remedy being granted. Counsel for Croydon on the other hand submits that all that is required is that the issue is one which could be the subject of proceedings in a court of law irrespective of whether or not those proceedings would be *e* successful. In my view, when sub-s (6) is looked at as a whole, it is reasonably clear that what is being dealt with is a situation where if the complaint was justified the person concerned might be entitled to obtain some form of remedy in respect of the subject matter of the complaint if he had commenced proceedings within the appropriate time limits. The commissioner is not concerned to consider whether in fact the proceedings *f* would succeed. He merely has to be satisfied that the court of law is an appropriate forum for investigating the subject matter of the complaint.

The other important feature to observe with regard to s 26(6) is that it is not clear from its language whether it is only a threshold requirement or whether it applies at any stage of an investigation. Counsel for the commissioner submits that it only applies at the stage when the commissioner is deciding whether or not to conduct an investigation and *g* once he has embarked on an investigation it has no application. On balance I agree that s 26(6) is directed to the threshold requirement. However, I do not regard this as being significant, because the commissioner has a continuing discretion not to continue, and to discontinue an investigation. Therefore, even if s 26(6) does not expressly deal with the subsequent stages after the commencement of an investigation, in exercising his discretion under s 26(10) whether to discontinue an investigation the commissioner *h* should approach the matter very much in the same way as he would if s 26(6) did apply. If it becomes apparent during the course of an investigation that the issues being investigated are appropriate to be resolved in a court of law, then giving effect to the general intent of s 26, the commissioner is required to consider whether, notwithstanding this, it is appropriate to continue with the investigation broadly on the lines indicated in the proviso to s 26(6). When performing this exercise the extent to which the *j* investigation has proceeded is a relevant consideration for the commissioner to take into account in deciding whether or not to discontinue the investigation.

Section 26(6) makes it clear that where there is a remedy in the sense which I have indicated, inter alia, in a court of law, the courts do not have the sole jurisdiction and the commissioner may still intervene. On the other hand the general tenor of s 26(6) is that,

if there is a tribunal (whether it be an appeal tribunal, a minister of the Crown or a court
a of law) which is specifically designed to deal with the issue, that is the body to whom the
complainant should normally resort.

I suggest this approach is particularly important in the case of issues which are capable
of being resolved on judicial review. Parliament, by s 31(6) of the Supreme Court Act
1981 and by the Rules of the Supreme Court, made it clear that in respect of applications
for judicial review there should be protection for public bodies and if, as in this case, the
b commissioner is going to recommend the very same relief as could be provided on
judicial review he should take into account before doing so the fact that his jurisdiction
is not subject to the same safeguards.

The commissioner should also have well in mind, even when the holder of the office
is a distinguished lawyer as is the case here, that his expertise is not the same as that of a
court of law. Issues whether an administrative tribunal has properly understood the
c relevant law and the legal obligations which it is under when conducting an inquiry are
more appropriate for resolution by the High Court than by a commissioner, however
eminent.

On the facts of this case, having regard to his evidence, I am not prepared to find that
the commissioner should have appreciated at the outset that the investigation was one in
relation to which the complainant had a remedy by way of judicial review. However, in
d the course of the investigation it should have been appreciated that the complainant had
had such a remedy, particularly bearing in mind the nature of the conclusions to which
the commissioner came.

Counsel for the commissioner contends that this approach cannot be right because it
has the effect, in practice, of preventing the commissioner from ever being able to
investigate the activities of an education appeal committee (in relation to which he has
e express statutory jurisdiction) unless he applies the proviso, since any matter of
maladministration by such a body would be the subject of judicial review. If this is the
result, then I am not convinced that it is unsatisfactory. The commissioner retains his
discretion whether to apply the proviso and unless he exercises this discretion unlawfully
the courts will not and cannot interfere with his decision.

f The problem in this case is that the commissioner apparently never appreciated that
there was a conflict between his jurisdiction and that of the court. In my view he should
have done so at least before he concluded his investigation and then he should have
exercised his discretion whether to discontinue his investigation. However, as he indicates
that if he had considered the question of discretion he would undoubtedly have decided
to proceed, I would not be prepared to grant relief solely on this basis.

g However, counsel for Croydon also complains about the two grounds on which the
commissioner found maladministration. She says that his own report makes it clear that
there was no justification for either finding. I accept that this submission is well founded.

The commissioner apparently has taken the view in para 43 that the committee was
not entitled, on the basis that the daughter's admission would result in an increase above
the 210 figure which was the planned admission limit for the school, to conclude that to
h allow the appeal of the parents would cause prejudice. However, as the report makes
clear, this limit was part of Croydon's transitional arrangements to establish a new sixth
form entry under a reorganisation scheme approved in December 1982 by the Secretary
of State. The committee had the statement of Croydon which explained the circumstances
in which that limit had been determined. The committee was aware that it was Croydon's
policy that apart from 30 pupils from a specific area in Sutton, all the places at the school
j had to be offered to children who, unlike the daughter, were resident in Croydon. 272
children living in Croydon had in fact given the school as a first preference and in
consequence 97 parents from Croydon still had their names on the school's waiting list.
In these circumstances there was ample material available which entitled the committee
to come to the conclusion that admission of the daughter would be prejudicial.

The substance of the second criticism made by the commissioner was that the committee not only took into account the policy but in the case of three out of five of the members regarded that policy as constituting good cause for not considering the appeal *a* at all. However, the commissioner in his report carefully sets out the reasoning of the five members and the contents of his own report make it clear that this criticism is just not justified. The members of the committee, as they were entitled to, took different views of the importance of the policy, but in no case did any member decide the case on policy considerations alone. It follows that as criticisms are unjustified there is no foundation for the commissioner's finding of maladministration.   *b*

I am also concerned about the recommendation which the commissioner made, which Croydon honoured, that the parents should be offered a further appeal. The commissioner made his report a year after the complainants' daughter would have been admitted to the school if her appeal had been successful. By then she was established in another school. If at that time she was to consider moving, it would not be sensible for the merits of the case to be dealt with on a fresh appeal relating to the previous year. The commissioner *c* was proposing that the previous decision of the committee should be treated as a nullity and that there should be a rehearing of the appeal a year after the proper date for admission. I have some reservations as to the legal status of such an appeal, but quite apart from this it does create problems in practice. Fortunately, however, Croydon's offer of a fresh appeal was not taken up by the parents.

d

Delay

Counsel for the commissioner vehemently submitted that if Croydon were otherwise entitled to relief, they should not obtain relief on the grounds of delay. He submits that instead of waiting until the report became available, Croydon should have applied to the court as soon as the commissioner's jurisdiction to conduct an investigation was disputed in December 1985. While I fully recognise the importance of applications for judicial *e* review being made promptly, I would not criticise in any way Croydon's decision in this case. If Croydon had applied at the time the commissioner was embarking on his investigation, I have little doubt that they would have been faced with an argument that their application was premature. Certainly the application could at that stage have proved to be wholly unnecessary and at best would have merely resulted in the commissioner *f* having the opportunity to decide whether to exercise his discretion under the proviso to s 26(6). It would then still have been necessary for a second application to be made to challenge the commissioner's findings of maladministration. Such a duplication of proceedings would not have been in anyone's interests.

While in the public law field, it is essential that the courts should scrutinise with care any delay in making an application and a litigant who does delay in making an application *g* is always at risk, the provisions of RSC Ord 53, r 4 and s 31(6) of the Supreme Court Act 1981 are not intended to be applied in a technical manner. As long as no prejudice is caused, which is my view of the position here, the courts will not rely on those provisions to deprive a litigant who has behaved sensibly and reasonably of relief to which he is otherwise entitled.

My conclusion therefore is that the applicants are entitled to declaratory relief in *h* respect of this report by the commissioner.

HUTCHISON J. I agree that this application succeeds for the reasons which Woolf LJ has given.

Declaration accordingly.   *j*

Solicitors: *Sharpe Pritchard*, agents for *R G Hemmings*, Croydon (for Croydon); *Thornton Lynne & Lawson*, agents for *J J Bash* (for the commissioner).

Sophie Craven   Barrister.

R v Secretary of State for Social Services and another, ex parte Child Poverty Action Group and others

COURT OF APPEAL, CIVIL DIVISION

BALCOMBE, WOOLF AND RUSSELL LJJ

13, 14 SEPTEMBER, 7 OCTOBER 1988

Social security – Supplementary benefit – Administration of claims – Statutory requirements for administration – Delay in determination of claims – Duties of adjudication officers – Time limit for consideration and determination of claims – Duty of Secretary of State to submit claims to adjudication officers 'forthwith' – Forthwith – Duty of adjudication officer to consider claim and so far as practicable dispose of it within 14 days – Whether Secretary of State under duty to ensure claims considered immediately on receipt – Social Security Act 1975, ss 98, 99(1).

Practice – Parties – Locus standi – Locus standi going to jurisdiction of court – Whether parties can consent to court hearing party with no locus standi.

The Secretary of State's duty under s 98[a] of the Social Security Act 1975 to ensure that any claim for income support, contributory benefit, industrial injury benefit or family credit 'shall be submitted forthwith to an adjudication officer for determination' is a duty to submit the claim to an adjudication officer as soon as reasonably possible once the Department of Health and Social Security is satisfied that it is in possession of the basic information required to enable the claim to be determined, but until that information is received the duty does not arise. Furthermore, although it might be reasonable for there to be verification of that information, the need for verification does not of itself justify delay in submitting the claim. Accordingly, there is no duty on the Secretary of State to have an adjudication officer available to consider a claim immediately it is received. Moreover, the requirement in s 99(1)[b] that an adjudication officer 'take [the claim] into consideration and, so far as practicable, dispose of it ... within 14 days' does not impose a duty on the Secretary of State to ensure that all claims be considered within 14 days and then disposed of within that time or as soon as practicable thereafter; instead, since the length of time available for determination of a claim sets the length of time available for its consideration it is sufficient if consideration of the claim enables it to be disposed of within 14 days or as soon as reasonably practicable thereafter and, accordingly, matters independent of the claim, such as the volume of claims awaiting determination or the number of investigating officers available to deal with claims, can be relevant in determining whether a claim has been disposed of within 14 days or as soon as reasonably practicable thereafter (see p 1053 a b e to j and p 1054 d to f, post); dictum of Diplock LJ in *R v Deputy Industrial Comr, ex p Moore* [1965] 1 All ER 81 at 93 applied.

The question of locus standi of parties to proceedings goes to the jurisdiction of the court, and where the court has no such jurisdiction the parties are not entitled to confer such jurisdiction on the court by consent (see p 1056 b, post).

Notes

For the meaning of 'forthwith', see 10 Halsbury's Laws (4th edn) para 410 and 26 ibid para 542.

For the Social Security Act 1975, ss 98, 99, see 45 Halsbury's Statutes (3rd edn) 1196.

---

a   Section 98, so far as material, is set out at p 1051 e f, post

b   Section 99(1) is set out at p 1051 g h, post

Cases referred to in judgment

Associated Provincial Picture Houses Ltd v Wednesbury Corp [1947] 2 All ER 680, [1948] 1 *a*
     KB 223, CA.

R v Deputy Industrial Injuries Comr, ex p Moore [1965] 1 All ER 81, [1965] 1 QB 456,
     [1965] 2 WLR 89, CA.

Scottish Old Peoples Welfare Council 1987 SLT 179, Outer House.

Cases also cited   *b*

Hillingdon London Borough v Cutler [1967] 2 All ER 361, [1968] 1 QB 124, CA.

Knight v Demolition and Construction Co Ltd [1953] 2 All ER 508, [1953] 1 WLR 981; *affd*
     [1954] 1 All ER 711, [1954] 1 WLR 563, CA.

Appeal

The Child Poverty Action Group, Islington London Borough Council, Hackney London *c*
Borough Council and the National Association of Citizens Advice Bureaux appealed
against the decision of Schiemann J, hearing the Crown Office list on 5 February 1988,
whereby he dismissed their application for judicial review by way of, inter alia, a
declaration that the duties imposed on the Secretary of State by ss 98 and 99 of the Social
Security Act 1975 involved (i) that the duty to refer a claim to an adjudication officer
arose as soon as a claim for benefit was received by the Secretary of State, (ii) that the duty *d*
was to refer the claim for determination in accordance with s 99 and involved referring
the claim to an adjudication officer who was in a position to take the claim into
consideration and (iii) that the adjudication officer to whom a case had been validly
submitted had to dispose of it within 14 days if practicable and that in deciding what was
practicable regard could be had to matters internal to the claim but not to extrinsic
factors. The respondents to the appeal were the Secretary of State for Social Services and *e*
the chief adjudication officer. The facts are set out in the judgment of the court.

Richard Drabble for the appellants.

Michael Beloff QC, Duncan Ouseley and *Jonathan McManus* for the respondents.

                                                           Cur adv vult *f*

7 October. The following judgment of the court was delivered.

WOOLF LJ. This appeal is from a decision of Schiemann J dismissing the appellants'
application for judicial review. The appeal raises issues as to the proper construction of
ss 98 and 99 of the Social Security Act 1975 as amended. The appellants contend that *g*
those statutory provisions have been wrongly interpreted by the Secretary of State and
the chief adjudication officer and in consequence claims for supplementary benefit,
particularly in London, have not been administered in accordance with the duties placed
on the Secretary of State and the chief adjudication officer.

If the appellants' contentions are correct, it is the individual claimants for supplementary *h*
benefit whose claims have been delayed who were directly affected as a result of the
Secretary of State and the chief adjudication officer misinterpreting their responsibilities.
However, the application for judicial review has been made by the appellants because the
issues raised are agreed to be important in the field of social welfare and not ones which
individual claimants for supplementary benefit could be expected to raise. Furthermore,
the Child Poverty Action Group and the National Association of Citizens Advice Bureaux *j*
play a prominent role in giving advice, guidance and assistance to such claimants. In
addition, many claimants live within the boroughs of Islington and Hackney and those
boroughs contend that the way the supplementary benefit scheme has been administered
has adversely affected the boroughs in their carrying out of their responsibilities as well
as adversely affecting their residents who are individual claimants for benefit.

a Since the date of Schiemann J's judgment supplementary benefit has been replaced by income support but the outcome of this appeal is still a matter of importance since ss 98 and 99 of the Social Security Act 1975 apply to income support as well as to contributory benefits, industrial injury benefits and family credit.

On the application for judicial review declarations were sought also as to the proper interpretation of two paragraphs, namely paras 13002 and 13052, of the Supplementary Benefits Manual (the 'S' Manual). The purpose of the manual is to provide detailed

b guidance to adjudication officers on the determination of questions and entitlement to supplementary benefit and to the staff of the department on the administration of the supplementary benefit scheme. The way in which the manual is printed distinguishes between advice given by the chief adjudication officer and procedural instructions of the Secretary of State. However, on the introduction of income support, the paragraphs of the 'S' Manual in respect of which declaratory relief was sought ceased to have effect and

c accordingly, when opening this appeal, counsel for the appellants abandoned any claim for the first two declarations set out in his application for judicial review. It is not necessary, therefore, for us to refer to those declarations, but we should refer to the third declaration since that sets out clearly the manner in which the appellants contend claims both under the previous regime and the new regime should be dealt with if the Secretary of State and the adjudication officers are to comply with the law. The declaration reads as

d follows:

'A declaration that the duties imposed by ss. 98 and 99 of the Social Security Act 1975 involve on the true construction of the relevant provisions the following propositions (i) The duty to refer a claim to an Adjudication Officer arises as soon as a claim for benefit is received by the Secretary of State (ii) That duty is to refer the

e claim for determination in accordance with s. 99 and involves referring the claim to an Adjudication Officer who is in a position to take the claim into consideration (iii) That the Adjudication Officer to whom a case has been validly submitted must dispose of it within 14 days if practicable and that in deciding what is practicable regard can be had to matters internal to the claim but not to extrinsic factors.'

f The Secretary of State and the chief adjudication officer do not accept that this declaration accurately sets out their statutory duties. They contend the Secretary of State is entitled, in accordance with the practice which he adopted previously in respect of claims for supplementary benefit or single payments, to carry out certain administrative tasks before a claim is referred to an adjudication officer, that there is no duty to have an adjudication officer available immediately to consider the claim and that a decision can

g be lawfully reached after 14 days if it is not practicable for a decision to be reached earlier, for example because of a sudden influx of claims or because of the non-availability of adjudication officers because of sickness or some other reason.

As to the handling of claims for supplementary benefit, the practice adopted by the department appears clearly in para 10 of the affidavit sworn on the department's behalf

h by Brian Taylor. Mr Taylor explains that most claims for supplementary benefit are made by post. The claimant is asked to provide on the claim form detailed information about his circumstances which is relevant to the assessment of his claim. When the claim form is received in the office it is associated with any existing papers of the claimant (the case papers) and passed for action to an administrative officer, acting on behalf of the Secretary of State. Some of the information on the form needs to be checked for accuracy

j and sometimes further information has to be sought either from the claimant or, for example, from his former employer before the claim can be determined. Most of these further inquiries are handled by post or on the telephone but occasionally an office interview or a home visit is required.

Mr Platt, the chief adjudication officer, confirms this evidence from Mr Taylor and in para 7 of his affidavit Mr Platt summarises the position in this way:

'The adjudication function is quite separate from the receipt and preliminary investigation of claims which is for the Secretary of State. Adjudication Officers can call for more evidence and can review their own decisions if new evidence comes to light.'

The paragraphs of the 'S' Manual to which we have referred were in terms which reflected the approach of the Secretary of State and the chief adjudication officer.

Schiemann J accepted the Secretary of State's and the chief adjudication officer's view of their statutory requirements. He rejected the appellants' submissions and he refused to grant any declaratory relief and dismissed the application for judicial review.

Having outlined the rival contentions of the parties it is convenient to turn to the relevant statutory provisions and we begin with the Supplementary Benefits Act 1976 in its finally amended form.

Section 2(1) provides:

'The question whether any person is entitled to supplementary benefit and the amount of any such benefit and any other question relating to supplementary benefit which arises under this Act or section 6 of the Social Security (No. 2) Act 1980 shall be determined by an adjudication officer appointed under section 97 of the Social Security Act 1975 ... in accordance with regulations made for the purposes of this section ...'

The power to make the regulations is contained in s 14, which provides:

'(1) Regulations may make provision for carrying into effect this Part of this Act ... and nothing in any other provision of this Act shall be construed as prejudicing the generality of this subsection.

(2) Regulations may make provision—(a) for requiring claims for supplementary benefit to be made in such manner and within such time as may be specified in the regulations ... (c) for prescribing the evidence which is to be provided in support of claims for supplementary benefit ...'

Regulations were made under s 14 and these were the Supplementary Benefits (Claims and Payments) Regulations 1981, SI 1981/1525, as amended. Regulations 3 and 4 are relevant. Regulation 3 provides:

'(1) Subject to the following provisions of this regulation, every claim for benefit shall be made in writing to the Secretary of State either—(a) in the case of a claim for a pension or allowance, on a form approved for the purpose by him and supplied without charge by such persons as he may appoint or authorise for the purpose; or (b) in the case of any claim, in such manner as he may accept as sufficient in the circumstances of any particular case or class of cases.

(2) A claim for benefit—(a) in the case of a claim for an allowance by a claimant required to ... be available for employment pursuant to section 5, shall be delivered or sent (for forwarding to an office of the Department) to the relevant unemployment benefit office, unless in any case or class of cases the Secretary of State directs that sub-paragraph (b) shall apply; (b) in any other case, shall be delivered or sent to an office of the Department.

(3) The date on which a claim for benefit is made shall be—(a) in a case to which paragraph (2)(a) applies, the date on which it is received at the relevant unemployment benefit office; (b) in any other case, the date on which it is received at an office of the Department.

(4) Where—(a) a claim for benefit made in writing is defective on the day on which it is received, but is subsequently amended; or (b) a claim for a pension or allowance is made other than in writing, but is subsequently made in writing, the Secretary of State may treat the claim as if it had been duly made in the first instance.

(5) The Secretary of State may in any particular case or class of cases accept—(a) a

a claim for benefit under section 3 (single payment to meet an exceptional need) other than in writing . . .'

Regulation 4 provides:

b 'Every person who makes a claim for benefit shall furnish such certificates, documents, information and evidence for the purpose of determining the claim or of determining the question which partner of a married or unmarried couple satisfies the conditions of regulation 1A of the Aggregation Regulations as may be required by the Secretary of State and, if reasonably so required, shall for that purpose attend at any office or place as the Secretary of State may direct.'

c It will be observed that for the purpose of the regulations a claim for benefit is 'made' on the date it is received at the relevant office and in the normal circumstances consists of the document submitted by the claimant.

Turning to the sections of the 1975 Act which are relevant:

d '**97.**—(1) Adjudication officers shall be appointed by the Secretary of State, subject to the consent of the Treasury as to number, and may include officers of the Department of Employment appointed with the concurrence of the Secretary of State in charge of that Department . . .

(1C) It shall be the duty of the Chief Adjudication Officer to advise adjudication officers on the performance of their functions under this or any other Act.

(1D) The Chief Adjudication Officer shall keep under review the operation of the system of adjudication by adjudication officers under this and any other Act and matters connected with the operation of that system . . .

e **98.**—(1) There shall be submitted forthwith to an adjudication officer for determination in accordance with sections 99 to 104 below—(*a*) any claim for benefit; (*b*) subject to subsection (2) below, any question arising in connection with a claim for, or award of, benefit; and (*c*) any question whether a person would by reason of the provisions of, or of any regulations under, section 20(1) or (2) of this Act have been disqualified for receiving unemployment benefit, sickness benefit or invalidity benefit if he had otherwise had a right thereto . . .

f (3) Different aspects of the same claim or question may be submitted to different adjudication officers under the foregoing provisions of this section; and for that purpose those provisions and the other provisions of this Part of this Act with respect to the determination of claims and questions shall apply with any necessary modifications.'

g It is also necessary to refer to s 99(1), which provides:

'An adjudication officer to whom a claim or question is submitted under section 98 shall take it into consideration and, so far as practicable, dispose of it in accordance with this section, and with procedure regulations under section 115, within 14 days of its submission to him.'

h The subsequent provisions of the 1975 Act deal with appeals to social security appeal tribunals and appeals from the tribunals to commissioners. It is not necessary to refer to those provisions but, before turning to consider the three issues which counsel for the appellants identifies as dividing the parties, it is relevant to point out that, although an adjudication officer is under statutory duty to dispose of claims, he is acting administratively when doing so. It is therefore not surprising that the evidence discloses

j that most adjudication officers do not spend all their time on adjudicating functions but are also engaged on other departmental duties including supervising other staff, paying benefits and interviewing and visiting claimants. However, when acting as adjudication officers, they are acting independently of the department and, while they will no doubt take into account advice offered by the chief adjudication officer and any relevant

decisions of the social security commissioners, they are required to come to their
independent decision as to the merits of any particular claim and, once they have come   *a*
to a decision, that decision is binding on the Secretary of State subject to the statutory
provisions as to appeal etc. Furthermore, like immigration officers, they are under an
obligation to carry out their adjudicating role fairly.

In *R v Deputy Industrial Injuries Comr, ex parte Moore* [1965] 1 All ER 81 at 93, [1965] 1
QB 456 at 486 Diplock LJ accurately described the adjudicator's role when dealing with
his statutory predecessor, who was called an insurance officer. Diplock LJ said: *b*

> 'His duties are administrative only; he exercises no quasi-judicial functions for
> there is, at this stage, no other person between whose contentions and those of the
> claimant he can adjudicate. He must form his own opinion as to the validity of the
> claim, and for this purpose he may make whatever inquiries he thinks fit.'

We will deal with the three issues identified by counsel for the appellants.   *c*

Issue 1 : when a claim should be submitted to an adjudication officer
The language of ss 98(1) and 99(1) of the 1975 Act makes it clear that it was intended
by Parliament that claims for benefits should be dealt with expeditiously. Counsel for
the appellants submits, with force, that the time limit contained in s 99(1) of 14 days
would be less effective if the department was entitled to carry out extensive investigations   *d*
before the claim was submitted since it is only from the claim being submitted that the
14-day period starts to run. Counsel for the respondents, on the other hand, submits (and
this submission was accepted by the judge) that whether the investigations are carried
out before the claim is submitted or thereafter in practice makes no difference. If the
investigations are necessary they will need to be carried out in any event and the time
required for a decision will certainly be no longer and could be shorter if they are carried   *e*
out at the outset since this avoids the adjudication officer having to refer the papers back
to those responsible for the investigation. While this may be true in many cases, we do
not regard it as being a complete answer to counsel's contention for the appellants. If the
investigations are carried out after submission then the adjudication officer will decide
on what investigations are necessary and this, in some cases at any rate, will avoid
successive investigations (investigations directed by the department followed by   *f*
investigations directed by an adjudication officer). More importantly, once the claim is
submitted to the adjudication officer, and the 14-day period begins to run, there will be
a breach of duty unless the decision is reached within the 14-day period unless it is shown
that it was not practicable to reach a decision within that period. If, however, the
investigations take place before submission, they are not the subject of the time limit.

However, the answer to the first issue has to be decided primarily on the language   *g*
used in the relevant sections and not by asking which result will produce the best
administrative solution. As to the language counsel for the appellants relies on the
distinction drawn in the statutory scheme and the regulations made thereunder between
the making of a claim and 'the evidence which is to be provided in support of claims for
supplementary benefit' (see s 14 of the 1976 Act and regs 3 and 4 of the 1981 regulations).   *h*
It is to be noted that the regulations could have specified a later time for identifying
when claims are to be treated as having been made but they do not do so.

However, as counsel for the appellants is prepared to concede, before submission to
the adjudication officer some administrative tasks may have to be performed by the staff
of the department. For example, it is not in dispute that, if a claim form was inadequately
completed so that it could not be regarded as a claim at all, the claimant could be required   *j*
to provide additional information. In addition, as there is a power contained in s 98(3) to
refer different aspects of the claim to different officers, the claim would have to be
considered to ascertain whether this would be appropriate. What counsel really complains
about is the department investigating a claim before it is submitted.

In deciding what, if any, investigation is permitted, we would stress that s 98 provides

that the claim is to be submitted forthwith to an adjudication officer for '*determination*'.
As was pointed out by Russell LJ in the course of argument, those words provide the key
to the resolution of this question. In our view, they indicate that what the department is
required to do is to submit the claim when it is in a fit state for determination albeit this
is after the date on which it is treated as being made for the purpose of the regulations.
The fact that a claim is to be submitted 'forthwith' does not require a claim to be
submitted for determination when it is incapable of being determined. To ascertain
whether it is in a fit state for determination will often require no more than an
examination of the claim form completed by the applicant and the attaching to that
form of the necessary file so that the two can be transmitted together to the adjudication
officer. However, in the course of argument there was put before us a sample of the
claim form for supplementary benefit and the claim form for income support and, on
examination of those forms, it is apparent that there could be cases, perhaps a minority
of cases, where, although a claim form was properly filled in, because of the circumstances
of the claimant or the specific benefit being claimed it would not be possible to start on
the process of determining whether a claimant is entitled to benefit on the basis of the
information contained in the claim form and the file. We draw attention to the fact that
the form used for claiming supplementary benefit invites the claimant, at the beginning
of the form, to write down 'don't know' if the claimant is not sure of the answer to a
question and goes on to state 'we may visit you later or ask you to call to see us at the
Social Security Office'. There is also the example, cited by Balcombe LJ in the course of
argument, of the complicated position of a person affected by a trade dispute which is
dealt with in s 8 of the Supplementary Benefits Act 1976. It could well be impossible on
the basis of the information contained in a claim form to start on the determination of a
claim by such a person.

We conclude that the duty to submit the claim 'forthwith' does not arise until the
department is in possession of not only the claim form but the basic information which
is required to enable a claim to be determined, and it is therefore in order for the
department to take the steps which are necessary to obtain that information before
submitting the claim. The department is not, however, entitled to delay submitting a
claim once that information is available. In particular, in the course of argument, counsel
for the respondents drew attention to the need in some cases to verify information.
While it might be reasonable for there to be verification, the need for verification by
itself does not justify delay in the submission of the claim. If verification is to delay the
determination, it is the responsibility of the adjudication officer to put in motion such
further inquiries as are required for that purpose.

The distinction between the basic material required for a claim to be determined and
verification would have been particularly important in claims for single payments since
claims were advanced by claimants in an informal manner. Single payments do not,
however, exist under the new regime.

So far we have not separately considered the sense in which the word 'forthwith' is
used in s 98(1). It can have many meanings according to the context. However, as
already pointed out, none of those meanings in the present context could require the
department to submit to the adjudication officer a claim form which did not provide the
material needed for a determination. In the context of s 98 the presence of the word
'forthwith' indicates that the department is required, once that material is available, to
submit the claim to the adjudicator as soon as reasonably possible. Because of the
requirement to deliver the claim forthwith the department, in deciding what steps it
should take in order to make the claim suitable for submission and in carrying out those
steps, is under an obligation to bear in mind the need for expedition.

Issue 2: the construction of s 99

Counsel for the appellants contended that the statutory scheme involved there being
two stages after a claim was submitted to the adjudication officer, the first being the

consideration of the claim and then the disposal of the claim. He was anxious to maintain the distinction between these two stages because he submitted that the words 'so far as *a* practicable' only governed the disposal stage and accordingly the consideration stage should have taken place before it was necessary to decide whether it was a situation where there should be any extension of the 14 days for reasons of practicability. He submitted that, once the claim had been taken into consideration, the only matters which could render it impracticable to dispose of the claim in 14 days are internal matters arising from the process of consideration. For example, there could be a need for further *b* investigation or supporting evidence. He argued that the need for an extension of time could not depend on matters which had nothing to do with the consideration stage since, once the consideration stage was completed, the adjudication officer should be in a position to make a decision and therefore there could not be circumstances making it impracticable for the decision to be taken.

That it is possible to identify counsel's two stages we do not doubt. In this connection *c* we noted with interest that the National Insurance (Industrial Injuries) Act 1965 (s 44) and its predecessor, the National Insurance (Industrial Injuries) Act 1946 (s 45), both specifically require both the submission of the claim and the consideration of the claim to take place forthwith. However, we do not accept that the two stages produce the results for which counsel for the appellants contends. The length of time available for determination, in practice, sets the limit on the time available for consideration. Because *d* the decision is required to be taken within 14 days where this is practicable, the consideration stage must also be completed within 14 days where this is practicable. However, as long as the consideration stage enables disposal to take place within 14 days or, where disposal is not practicable within 14 days, as early as is reasonably practicable thereafter, the time requirements of s 99(1) are complied with. The fact that there are two stages, only one of which is expressly made subject to the time limit, does not alter *e* the factors which can be taken into account in deciding what is practicable. There is nothing in the language of s 99(1) which means that it is not permissible to look at factors other than those involved in an individual claim in deciding whether it was practicable to come to a decision within 14 days. Section 99(1) does not require matters independent of the claim to be ignored in deciding what is practical. The volume of claims awaiting *f* determination and the number of investigating officers available to deal with the claims are examples of matters which can be relevant to the decision whether or not it was practicable to come to a determination within the 14-day period. Counsel for the appellants argues that this construction makes the statutory code meaningless. He points out that, if there was a drastic shortage in the number of officers available, the officers would be unable to process claims no matter how simple and urgent they were within *g* 14 days. The answer to this argument is to be found from considering the answer to the third issue, to which we must now turn and which is closely related to the second issue.

Issue 3: the Secretary of State's duty under s 98

Counsel's argument for the appellants here, as we understand it, is that, because the claim has to be submitted for determination forthwith to an adjudication officer and he *h* has to take the claim into consideration so that it can be determined within 14 days, the Secretary of State is under a duty to appoint such number of adjudication officers as will enable an officer to be available to consider a claim promptly as soon as it is submitted.

The power of the Secretary of State to appoint adjudication officers under s 97(1) is expressly made subject to the consent of the Treasury as to numbers. This requirement of consent is wholly inconsistent with the Secretary of State being under some open- *j* ended commitment to ensure that there is always an adjudication officer available to deal immediately with any claim submitted. However, quite apart from this requirement of the consent of the Treasury, we would not regard the statutory scheme as creating the duty for which counsel contends. It would clearly lead to an absurd situation if the number of adjudication officers who had to be appointed was to be dictated by the largest

conceivable number of difficult claims which could arise for consideration at any one
a time. For no good reason Parliament would have placed a duty on the Secretary of State
which would inevitably in practice be breached if there was some emergency which
could not be anticipated.

The fact that we have rejected counsel's submission does not mean that the Secretary
of State is under no obligation as to numbers of adjudication officers whom he should
appoint and this is a discretion to be exercised reasonably, taking into account the
b legislative scheme requiring the expeditious disposal of claims within 14 days where this
is practicable. If, for reasons other than the refusal of the Treasury to give its consent, the
Secretary of State were to exercise this discretion unreasonably or, to use another word,
irrationally, then a *Wednesbury* challenge could be mounted (see *Associated Provincial
Picture Houses Ltd v Wednesbury Corp* [1947] 2 All ER 680, [1948] 1 KB 223). There is,
however, nothing in the evidence which is before the court to indicate that the Secretary
c of State has acted or is acting in a way which would justify an application for judicial
review on this basis. Indeed, the evidence is that the Secretary of State is concerned about
the present position and steps have been taken and further steps are to be taken to
improve the position.

We would, therefore, reject the appellants' argument on the third issue as well.
However, the fact that we have not accepted counsel's argument does not mean that we
d do not recognise that the appellants had cause for concern about the time which was
being taken to dispose of claims for supplementary benefit and in particular single
payments. There have clearly been difficulties in disposing of these claims as quickly as
the department would like and this difficulty has been particularly acute in the London
area. The degree of difficulty is not in issue on this appeal and it is not necessary for this
court to come to any conclusion about it. The object of the proceedings from the
e appellants' point of view was to require the Secretary of State to approach the complex
question as to the proportion of the available resources which should be allocated to the
administration of social security in accordance with the requirements of the legislation.
If the decision of this court assists in clarifying what those requirements are it will have
served a useful purpose. With regard to the first issue in particular the requirements
were far from clear and, while we have rejected counsel's argument on this issue, we do
f not accept the argument of counsel for the respondents in so far as he was contending
that it was open to the department to delay submitting a claim to the adjudication officer
to enable the claim to be verified by the department's staff. Although we have sought to
clarify this issue, we emphasise that it is not possible to draw a precise line as to what is
permissible and what is not permissible. This makes it difficult, if not impossible, to
frame declaratory relief satisfactorily except in relation to what occurred in the handling
g of a particular claim. However, the appellants accepted that, whatever the outcome of
this appeal, it is not necessary for there to be declaratory relief and the judgments of this
court are all that is required.

This concession on the part of the appellants makes it unnecessary for us to deal with
the argument of counsel for the respondents as to why the court should, in any event,
h reject the declaratory relief in its discretion, particularly having regard to the change
which has taken place in the legislation. We would, however, indicate that, were it not
for the difficulty with regard to framing the declaration, we would not have regarded
this case as being one in which declaratory relief should be refused if the appellants were
otherwise entitled to such a relief. There is clearly an issue between the parties as to the
proper interpretation of the law and that issue is only likely to be decided in declaratory
j proceedings of this sort.

The fact that the court is not required to give declaratory relief also means that it is
unnecessary for the court to deal with the question of the appellants' locus standi to make
their application for judicial review. In the court below Schiemann J's judgment records
that, because of the importance of the issue, the respondents did not dispute the issue of
locus standi while making it plain that they reserved their right to argue the point of

locus standi in analogous cases in the future. Before this court the respondents wished to
adopt the same position but indicated that, if this court required argument, they were *a*
prepared to advance the argument. Counsel indicated that he would have relied on the
decision in the Scottish case of *Scottish Old People's Welfare Council* 1987 SLT 179. This
court did not require counsel to advance the argument which he wished to reserve.
However, we make it clear that in our view the question of locus standi goes to
jurisdiction of the court and therefore the approach adopted by the department in this
case, while understandable, is not appropriate. The parties are not entitled to confer *b*
jurisdiction, which the court does not have, on the court by consent and, if this court had
been minded to grant declaratory relief, the respondents would have had to advance any
arguments which were available to them or to accept the consequences of not doing so.
Having regard to the outcome of this appeal we can content ourselves by indicating that,
on the evidence but without the advantage of argument, we have no doubt that it was in
order for this court and Schiemann J to treat the application for judicial review as being *c*
one which the court had jurisdiction to hear.
    We dismiss this appeal.

Appeal dismissed. Leave to appeal to the House of Lords refused.

Solicitors: *Penny Wood* (for the appellants); *Solicitor to the Department of Health and Social* *d*
Security.

                                                    Carolyn Toulmin   Barrister.

                                                                                    e

Shearson Lehman Hutton Inc and another v Maclaine Watson & Co Ltd and others

QUEEN'S BENCH DIVISION (COMMERCIAL COURT)
WEBSTER J   *f*
8 JUNE 1988

Discovery – Privilege – Confidential documents – Documents obtained for purposes of legal
proceedings – Arbitration proceedings – Documents obtained for purposes of arbitration
proceedings between defendant and third party – Plaintiff bringing action against defendant –
Plaintiff applying for disclosure of arbitration documents in defendant's possession – Whether *g*
arbitration documents privileged from disclosure in subsequent public litigation between different
parties.

In 1985 the plaintiffs sold large quantities of tin to the defendant company under
contracts which incorporated the rules of the London Metal Exchange. Following the
collapse of the International Tin Council (the ITC) and the consequent ruling by the *h*
exchange that outstanding tin contracts, including that between the plaintiffs and the
defendant, be settled at a fixed price, which was substantially lower than the contract
price at which the plaintiffs had sold to the defendants, the plaintiffs brought an action
against the defendants claiming either the full contract price or damages. In the course
of the litigation the plaintiffs issued a summons against the defendant for an order that
the defendant disclose to the plaintiffs all documents in its possession, custody or power *j*
relating proceedings in which a claim by the defendant against the ITC had been referred
to arbitration. The documents in issue included the pleadings in the arbitration, any
documents produced by way of evidence in the course of the arbitration, a transcript of
the evidence and the award. The judge granted the order. The defendant then claimed
privilege for all the documents on the ground that documents used in a private arbitration

were privileged from production in subsequent proceedings between different parties.
a On the hearing of the defendant's claim for privilege,

Held – Documents produced voluntarily in a private arbitration were not privileged
from disclosure in subsequent public litigation between different parties, since, in view
of the fact that such documents had been disclosed voluntarily and not compulsorily
pursuant to a court order, there was no significant risk that parties to an arbitration
b would, contrary to the interests of justice, be discouraged from making full and frank
disclosure of confidential documents used in the arbitration by their possible use in
subsequent litigation between different parties. Accordingly, there was no policy reason
which would justify the court in protecting the documents from further disclosure. The
defendant's claim to privilege therefore failed (see p 1059 *b d g h*, post).

Distillers Co (Biochemicals) Ltd v Times Newspapers Ltd [1975] 1 All ER 41 and Crest Homes
c plc v Marks [1987] 2 All ER 1074 considered.

Notes
For documents protected from production, see 13 Halsbury's Laws (4th edn) para 69.

Cases referred to in judgment
d Buccleuch (Duke) v Metropolitan Board of Works (1872) LR 5 HL 418, [1861–73] All ER Rep
654.
Crest Homes plc v Marks [1987] 2 All ER 1074, [1987] AC 829, [1987] 3 WLR 293, HL.
D v National Society for the Prevention of Cruelty to Children [1977] 1 All ER 589, [1978] AC
171, [1977] 2 WLR 201, HL.
Distillers Co (Biochemicals) Ltd v Times Newspapers Ltd [1975] 1 All ER 41, [1975] QB 613,
e [1974] 3 WLR 728.
Home Office v Harman [1982] 1 All ER 532, [1983] 1 AC 280, [1982] 2 WLR 338, HL.
Rawstone v Preston Corp (1885) 30 Ch D 116.
Riddick v Thames Board Mills Ltd [1977] 3 All ER 677, [1977] QB 881, [1977] 3 WLR 63,
CA.
f Wheeler v Le Marchant (1881) 17 Ch D 675, CA.

Application
The plaintiffs, Shearson Lehman Hutton Inc and Shearson Lehman Hutton Commodities
Ltd, issued a summons on 9 May 1988 against the first defendant, Maclaine Watson &
Co Ltd, against whom they were conducting litigation arising out of the collapse of the
International Tin Council (the ITC), seeking, inter alia, an order requiring the first
g defendant to disclose to the plaintiffs all documents in its possession, custody or power
relating to its arbitration proceedings against the ITC. On 12 May 1988 Webster J ordered
the first defendant to disclose to the plaintiffs by list all such documents and verify on
affidavit the documents which it claimed were privileged and the nature of the privilege
relied on. The first defendant, by an affidavit sworn on 26 May 1988, claimed privilege
h in respect of all the documents in issue on the ground that they were produced during
confidential arbitration proceedings between different parties. The first defendant's claim
of privilege was then heard inter partes. The facts are set out in the judgment.

Ian Glick QC for the plaintiffs.
Richard Aikens QC and Adrian Hughes for the first defendant.

j

WEBSTER J. On 9 May 1988 the plaintiffs issued a summons against the first defendant
in which, inter alia, they applied for an order that:

'The defendants do forthwith disclose to the plaintiffs all the documents in their
possession, custody or power which relate to those arbitration proceedings.'

On 12 May 1988 I made orders in this action which included an order that:

> 'The first defendants do disclose to the plaintiffs by list all the documents which *a*
> are or have been in their possession, custody or power relating to their arbitration
> proceedings against the ITC and verify on affidavit which documents they claim are
> privileged and the nature of the privilege relied on.'

Miss George, on behalf of the first defendant, swore an affidavit on 26 May. She
deposed to the fact, inter alia, that she was advised that privilege had been claimed in *b*
respect of the documents which are the subject matter of this application on the ground
that documents used in proceedings with different parties are privileged from production
in other proceedings, particularly where the documents of which discovery is sought
were produced for or during confidential arbitration proceedings and any one party to
the current proceedings was a party to the previous arbitration proceedings.

The documents which are in those circumstances in issue on this application are (and I *c*
am perhaps not being exhaustive when I list them) the pleadings in the arbitration, any
documents produced by way of evidence in the course of the arbitration, evidence given,
as shown in the transcript of the proceedings, and the award itself.

Counsel for the plaintiffs does not pursue any claim for the discovery of any of the
documents disclosed to the first defendants by the International Tin Council in the
arbitration. There is no issue about the relevance to this action of the documents which I *d*
have listed, and nor is there any issue relating to legal professional privilege, that is to say
counsel for the first defendant accepts that documents which were once protected by
legal professional privilege but which have subsequently lost their privilege are no longer
protected by that privilege.

Counsel for the plaintiffs on his part concedes, for the purpose of this application at
least, that the privacy of arbitration proceedings confers confidentiality on those *e*
proceedings. But he relies on the decisions of the court in *Wheeler v Le Marchant* (1881)
17 Ch D 675 and of the House of Lords in *D v National Society for the Prevention of Cruelty
to Children* [1977] 1 All ER 589, [1978] AC 171. Those decisions clearly establish in my
view that there is no principle that every confidential communication is protected from
discovery. The decision of the House of Lords in *D v NSPCC* also establishes, first, that
the principle involved in a question such as this is one which extends not only to *f*
discovery but also to the admissibility of evidence and, second, that documents or
evidence are protected if the public interest in protecting them overrides the public
interest that at a trial in this country the truth will out.

It is not necessary for me for present purposes to decide whether that is a clear-cut
question of law which has to be decided in the light of authority, or whether it involves
carrying out a balancing exercise as between the one interest and the other. For present *g*
purposes, I will assume that I am not fettered by authority and that I can and should
carry out the balancing exercise. I accept in principle, and for the purposes of argument
at this stage, that the categories of documents protected for this reason are not closed, and
that the question is, therefore, whether the court should as a matter of policy hold that
documents produced in the course of a private arbitration cannot be inspected in *h*
subsequent public litigation between different parties in the absence of the consent of
the parties to the arbitration.

It is common ground that there is no authority directly in point. Counsel for the first
defendant relies, however, on the principle to be derived, he submits, from *Distillers Co
(Biochemicals) Ltd v Times Newspapers Ltd* [1975] 1 All ER 41, [1975] QB 613, *Riddick v
Thames Board Mills Ltd* [1977] 3 All ER 677, [1977] QB 881, *Home Office v Harman* [1982] *j*
1 All ER 532, [1983] 1 AC 280 and *Crest Homes plc v Marks* [1987] 2 All ER 1074, [1987]
AC 829. But in all those cases the document or information which the court held should
be protected was a document which had been disclosed, and which had to be disclosed,
in the process of discovery or of complying with an Anton Piller order or was information
derived from such a document. The clear reasoning, sometimes expressed and sometimes

implicit, in the judgments and speeches in those decisions was that it would be contrary
a to the interests of justice if parties were to be discouraged from making full and frank
discovery in an action because of their apprehension that documents disclosed might be
used by or for the purposes of persons not parties to the litigation in question.

Counsel's submission therefore, as I understand it (and I am sure I understand it right),
is that the same principle should be applied so as to protect the privacy and confidentiality
of an arbitration. But in my view the considerations are very different. Discovery is a
b process of involuntary disclosure. Parties to litigation are obliged to give discovery of
relevant documents in their possession. But documents adduced or evidence given in an
arbitration are in no sense adduced or given involuntarily, and I see no significant risk
that parties to arbitrations would be inhibited in their conduct of them by apprehension
about the possible subsequent use of documents or evidence relied on by them in those
arbitrations by other parties.
c In coming to that conclusion, I take into account what I have no doubt is the case, that
these courts would not wish to do anything which might discourage parties from overseas
using our English arbitration procedure. All discovery represents an invasion of privacy.
Sometimes it requires the production of a private and possibly confidential file of
correspondence, and sometimes of a memorandum of a private and possibly confidential
meeting. Arbitrations are also private and confidential, but I can find no special privacy
d or confidentiality in them which entitles parties to them to the protection which counsel
on behalf of the first defendant seeks to assert.

I would come to the same conclusion in the absence of the two principal authorities
on which counsel for the plaintiffs relies as being closest, he submits, to the facts of the
present case. I refer to *Duke of Buccleuch v Metropolitan Board of Works* (1872) LR 5 HL
418, [1861–73] All ER Rep 654, and the opinions of the judges summoned to advise
e their Lordships' House in their decision on that case, and the decision in *Rawstone v
Preston Corp* (1885) 30 Ch D 116. Neither of those decisions deter me from the conclusion
that I have already reached, and I think I can say that they are more consistent with that
conclusion than inconsistent with it.

I recognise that neither of those cases are by any means on all fours with the
circumstances of the present case. The question that arose in the first of them was
f whether an arbitrator could be called to give evidence in an action to enforce an award.
In the second case both the action and arbitration were between the same parties,
although the issues were not the same. So neither of those cases in any sense bind me,
nor are they in any sense determinant of the decision which I have reached. But for the
reasons that I have expressed I conclude that the plaintiffs are entitled to the discovery
which they seek.
g If I have a discretion in the matter, which I very much doubt, it would only be a
discretion to examine the documents in order to assess their probative value and to
balance that against the two public interest considerations which I have mentioned. But
at this stage in a complicated action of this kind I would not exercise my discretion and
examine the documents even if I had such a discretion which, as I have said, I very much
h doubt if I have.

Consequently, I grant this application for discovery.

Order accordingly.

Solicitors: *Simmons & Simmons* (for the plaintiffs); *Allen & Overy* (for the first defendant).

K Mydeen Esq   Barrister.

Director of Public Prosecutions v Hutchinson and another

R v Secretary of State for Defence, ex parte Parker

R v Secretary of State for Defence, ex parte Hayman

QUEEN'S BENCH DIVISION

MANN LJ AND SCHIEMANN J

19, 20, 21, 25, 26 JULY, 21 OCTOBER 1988

Byelaw – Validity – Byelaw wider than authorised by statute – Prohibited action within scope of byelaw if byelaw properly made – Military land byelaws prejudicially affecting rights of common – Statute authorising Secretary of State to make byelaws regulating use of military land providing they did not take away or prejudicially affect rights of common – Secretary of State making byelaws which prejudicially affected rights of common – Applicants entering prohibited area – Applicants not exercising rights of common – Applicants convicted under byelaws – Whether convictions lawful – Military Lands Act 1892, s 14(1).

In two separate cases the question arose whether a person could be lawfully convicted under byelaws which appeared on their face to be wider than was authorised by the enabling Act. The byelaws had been made in 1985 and 1987 under s 14(1)[a] of the Military Lands Act 1892, which authorised the Secretary of State for Defence to make byelaws regulating the use of land appropriated for military purposes provided that such byelaws did not 'take away or prejudicially affect any right of common'. In the first case, H and S were convicted of entering a protected area without authority or permission contrary to the 1985 byelaws. H and S appealed to the Crown Court, contending that, although they had entered the protected area, which was an act forbidden by the byelaws, the convictions should be quashed on the ground that the byelaws were invalid since they prejudicially affected rights of common. Their appeals were allowed and the Director of Public Prosecutions appealed. In the second case, P was arrested and charged with contravening the 1987 byelaws, which provided, inter alia, that 'No person shall remain in the Controlled Area after having been directed to leave . . .' P did not dispute that he had been in the relevant controlled area and that he had been asked to leave by a constable but he applied for judicial review to challenge the validity of the byelaws on the ground that they prejudicially affected rights of common and were therefore ultra vires. H, S and P did not claim that they themselves had any rights of common, nor did they claim to have been attempting to exercise such rights on behalf of anyone else.

Held – Where an administrative decision had a wider ambit than was permitted by the enabling Act the court would, in certain circumstances, reduce the ambit of the decision so as to preserve those parts of it which were intra vires. That would only be done where the court was sure that the altered decision represented that which the decision-maker would have made had he appreciated the limitation on his powers. Therefore, a person could be lawfully convicted of an offence against a byelaw which was wider than was permitted by the enabling statute where, had the byelaws been drawn only as widely as the enabling Act authorised, the person charged would still have been properly convicted. Accordingly, although the 1985 and 1987 byelaws prejudicially affected rights of common contrary to the proviso to s 14(1) of the 1892 Act, H, S and P had been lawfully convicted of offences against the byelaws since they had not been exercising rights of

a   Section 14(1) is set out at p 1063 *b c*, post

common when they entered onto the land in question and would therefore have been
_a_ properly convicted if the byelaws had not prejudicially affected rights of common. The
appeal in the first case would therefore be allowed and the application for judicial review
in the second case dismissed (see p 1064 *c d*, p 1070 *g h*, p 1072 *f g*, p 1073 *h* and p 1074
c, post).

Dunkley v Evans [1981] 3 All ER 285 and *Thames Water Authority v Elmbridge BC* [1983]
1 All ER 836 applied.
_b_

Notes
For the severance of partly invalid instruments, see 1 Halsbury's Laws (4th edn) para 26.
For the Military Lands Act 1892, s 14, see 3 Halsbury's Statutes (4th edn) 1140.

_c_ **Cases referred to in judgments**
A-G (ex rel Thornbury RDC) v Brock Bros Ltd [1972] CA Transcript 30.
Alexander v Alexander (1755) 2 Ves Sen 640, 28 ER 408.
Associated Provincial Picture Houses v Wednesbury Corp [1947] 2 All ER 680, [1948] 1 KB
223, CA.
Dunkley v Evans [1981] 3 All ER 285, [1981] 1 WLR 1522, DC.
_d_ *Dyson v A-G* [1912] 1 Ch 158, CA.
Dyson v London and North Western Rly Co (1881) 7 QBD 32, DC.
Kruse v Johnson [1898] 2 QB 91, [1895–9] All ER Rep 105, DC.
Olsen v Camberwell City Corp [1926] VLR 58, Vict SC.
R v North Hertfordshire DC, ex p Cobbold [1985] 3 All ER 486.
Sydney Municipal Council, v A-G for New South Wales [1894] AC 444, PC.
_e_ *Thames Water Authority v Elmbridge BC* [1983] 1 All ER 836, [1983] QB 570, [1983] 2
WLR 743, CA.
Turner, Re, Hudson v Turner [1932] 1 Ch 31, [1931] All ER Rep 782.
United City Merchants (Investments) Ltd v Royal Bank of Canada [1982] 2 All ER 720, [1983]
AC 168, [1982] 2 WLR 1039, HL.

_f_ **Cases also cited**
Agricultural Horticultural and Forestry Industry Training Board v Aylesbury Mushrooms Ltd
[1972] 1 All ER 280, [1972] 1 WLR 190.
Alty v Farrell [1896] 1 QB 636, DC.
Champlin Refining Co v Corporation Commission of Oklahoma (1931) 286 US 210, US SC.
Cinnamond v British Airports Authority [1980] 2 All ER 368, [1980] 1 WLR 582, CA.
_g_ *Daganayasi v Minister of Immigration* [1980] 2 NZLR 130, NZ CA.
Dunlop v Woollahra Municipal Council [1981] 1 All ER 1202, [1982] AC 158, PC.
Findlay v Secretary of State for the Home Dept [1984] 3 All ER 801, [1985] AC 318, HL.
MacFisheries (Wholesale and Retail) Ltd v Coventry Corp [1957] 3 All ER 299, [1957] 1 WLR
1066, DC.
_h_ *Mixnam's Properties Ltd v Chertsey UDC* [1964] 2 All ER 627, [1965] AC 735, HL.
Newbury DC v Secretary of State for the Environment [1980] 1 All ER 731, [1981] AC 578,
HL.
Powell v May [1946] 1 All ER 444, [1946] KB 330, DC.
R v Hillingdon Health Authority, ex p Goodwin [1984] ICR 800.
R v London Residuary Body, ex p Inner London Education Authority (1987) Times, 24 July,
DC.
_j_
R v Secretary of State for the Home Dept, ex p Khan [1985] 1 All ER 40, [1984] 1 WLR 1337,
CA.
Baird (Robert) Ltd v Glasgow Corp [1936] AC 32, HL.
Rossi v Edinburgh Corp [1905] AC 21, HL.
Secretary of State for Education and Science v Tameside Metropolitan Borough [1976] 3 All ER
665, [1977] AC 1014, HL.
Strickland v Hayes [1896] 1 QB 290, [1895–9] All ER Rep 201, DC.

Case stated and applications for judicial review

DPP v Hutchinson and anor a

The Director of Public Prosecutions appealed by way of a case stated by the Crown Court at Reading (his Honour Judge Lait and two lay justices) in respect of its decision on 25 February 1988 to allow appeals by Jean Emily Hutchinson and Georgina Smith against their conviction by the Newbury justices on 23 July 1986 of entering a protected area without authority or permission, contrary to para 2(b) of the Royal Air Force Greenham Common Byelaws 1985, SI 1985/485, and s 17(2) of the Military Lands Act 1892. The b question for the opinion of the High Court was whether the Crown Court was correct in law in holding (i) that byelaws 2(a), (b), (c), (d), (g), (h) and (l) were ultra vires and invalid on the grounds that they took away all rights of common and prejudicially affected such rights and/or that, in making the said byelaws, the Secretary of State had failed to take account of the existing rights of common and (ii) that the byelaws were not invalid on any of the other grounds relied on by Hutchinson and Smith. The facts are set out in the c judgment of Schiemann J.

R v Secretary of State for Defence, ex p Parker

Jonathan Parker applied, with the leave of Mann J given on 7 October 1987, for judicial review of the Royal Air Force Fylingdales Byelaws 1987, SI 1987/1069, made by the Secretary of State for Defence on 18 June 1987 in exercise of his powers under Pt II of the d Military Lands Act 1892, seeking a declaration that byelaw 3(k) was ultra vires and of no legal effect on the ground, inter alia, that the byelaw had prejudicially affected rights of common contrary to the proviso to s 14(1) of the 1892 Act. The facts are set out in the judgment of Schiemann J.

R v Secretary of State for Defence, ex p Hayman e

Margaret Hayman applied, with the leave of Mann J given on 7 October 1987, for judicial review of the Royal Air Force Fylingdales Byelaws 1987, SI 1987/1069, made by the Secretary of State for Defence on 18 June 1987 in exercise of his powers under Pt II of the Military Lands Act 1892, seeking declarations that byelaws 3(a), (k) and 4 were ultra vires and of no legal effect on the ground that they prejudicially affected rights of common f contrary to the proviso to s 14(1) of the 1892 Act. The facts are set out in the judgment of Schiemann J.

John Laws and David Pannick for the Director of Public Prosecutions.
Miss Hutchinson appeared in person.
Beverley Lang for Miss Smith.
Stephen Sedley QC and Beverley Lang for Mr Parker and Miss Hayman. g
David Pannick for the Secretary of State.

Cur adv vult

21 October. The following judgments were delivered. h

SCHIEMANN J (giving the first judgment at the invitation of Mann LJ). There are before the court two applications for judicial review and one case stated from the Crown Court. The cases have been heard together because they appeared to raise a common point: the efficacy of certain byelaws made under the Military Lands Act 1892 and, in particular, the question whether if those byelaws go beyond the powers in the enabling j Act they may nevertheless be enforced in so far as they do not go beyond the enabling Act. During the course of the hearing it became clear that the issues raised in one of them, the Hayman case, were no longer live and therefore the court indicated that it would as a matter of discretion not grant the relief sought. I deal with that case at the end of this judgment.

The Hutchinson case concerned the Royal Air Force Greenham Common Byelaws
a 1985, SI 1985/485. The Parker and Hayman cases both concern the Royal Air Force
Fylingdales Byelaws 1987, SI 1987/1069. Each set of byelaws was made in purported
exercise of powers contained in s 14 of the 1892 Act. That section reads as follows:

> '(1) Where any land belonging to a Secretary of State or to a volunteer corps is for
> the time being appropriated by or with the consent of a Secretary of State for any
> *b* military purpose, a Secretary of State may make byelaws for regulating the use of
> the land for the purposes to which it is appropriated, and for securing the public
> against danger arising from that use, with power to prohibit all intrusion on the
> land and all obstruction of the use thereof. Provided that no byelaws promulgated
> under this section shall authorise the Secretary of State to take away or prejudicially
> affect any right of common.
> *c* (2) Where any such byelaws permit the public to use the land for any purpose
> when not used for the military purpose to which it is appropriated, those byelaws
> may also provide for the government of the land when so used by the public, and
> the preservation of order and good conduct thereon . . . and for the prevention of
> anything interfering with the orderly use thereof by the public for the purpose
> permitted by the byelaws . . .'

d RAF Greenham Common belongs to the Secretary of State for Defence. It is subject to
the 1985 byelaws made under the 1892 Act. The area so subject is defined in the byelaws
as 'the Protected Area'. The byelaws contain the following:

> '2. No person shall . . . (b) enter, pass through or over or remain in or over the
> Protected Area without authority or permission given by or on behalf of one of the
> *e* persons mentioned in byelaw 5(1) . . .
> 3. Subject to the provisions of byelaw 5 any person contravening byelaw 2 in any
> way thereby commits an offence . . .
> 5. (1) Nothing done by a person acting under and in accordance with any
> authority or permission given by or on behalf of the Secretary of State, the Air
> Officer Commanding-in-Chief RAF Support Command, or the RAF commander
> *f* RAF Greenham Common shall be an offence against any of these byelaws . . .'

On 18 June 1986 the Misses Hutchinson and Smith entered the protected area without
authority. They were charged with the offence and found guilty by the magistrates.
They appealed to the Crown Court. They admitted that they had done that which, on
the face of it, was forbidden by the byelaws but contended that the byelaws were ultra
vires and that therefore they ought to be acquitted. That contention found favour with
g the Crown Court. The Director of Public Prosecution appeals by way of case stated to this
court.

The argument which succeeded in the court below went as follows: (1) the byelaws
were made under s 14(1) of the 1892 Act; (2) the byelaw under which they were charged
prejudicially affects rights of common; (3) therefore it is ultra vires; (4) therefore the
h ladies ought to be acquitted.

The 1987 byelaws also on their face prejudicially affect rights of common. They apply
to what is described therein as 'the Controlled Area', which comprises the air force
establishment known as RAF Fylingdales. The byelaws also provide in byelaw 3(k) that:

> 'No person shall . . . (k) remain in the Controlled Area after having been directed
> to leave by any of the persons mentioned in byelaw 6.'

j
Byelaw 6 provides:

> 'The following persons are hereby authorised to remove from the Controlled Area
> and to take into custody without warrant any person committing an offence against
> any of the preceding byelaws . . . (a) The Air Officer Commanding in Chief RAF
> Strike Command; (b) The Air Officer Commanding No 11 Group; (c) The Officer

Commanding RAF Fylingdales; (d) Any officer, any warrant officer, or non-commissioned officer in uniform and being for the time being under the command *a* of any of the officers mentioned in sub-paragraphs (a) to (c) of this byelaw; (e) Any public officer being a Crown servant authorised in writing by or on behalf of any of the officers mentioned in sub-paragraphs (a) to (c) of this byelaw; (f) Any constable.'

On 4 July 1987 Mr Parker was arrested and charged with contravening byelaw 3(k) of the 1987 byelaws and s 17(2) of the 1892 Act 1892. It was alleged that he remained in *b* the controlled area after being directed to leave by a constable. He does not dispute that he was in the controlled area as defined in the byelaws and that he was asked to leave by a constable and failed to do so. However, he challenges the validity of byelaw 3(k) both on the basis that it is invalid in itself and on the basis that the byelaws in their entirety are invalid in that some of them prejudicially affect rights of common and that therefore all the byelaws, including byelaw 3(k), are invalid.   *c*

I pause to note that neither of the ladies nor Mr Parker claims that they themselves had any rights of common nor do they claim to have been attempting to exercise them on behalf of anyone else. It follows that had the byelaws been drafted more narrowly so as not prejudicially to affect any rights of common then the ladies and Mr Parker would have been unable to run this argument. However, they were not so drafted.

I look, firstly, at the various points which arose in relation to the failure of the byelaws *d* to make provision for commoners' rights.

The first question I address is: what is meant by 'any right of common' in s 14(1) of the 1892 Act? Counsel for Mr Parker and Miss Hayman submitted that this phrase as used in the 1892 Act was not confined to rights of common properly so called but was wide enough to embrace any general practice of taking air and exercise over common land. Clearly, if that submission be right, then the restriction on the byelaw-making *e* power contained in the proviso to the subsection is greater than at first sight would appear.

In support of this submission, he pointed to the following factors.

1. The statutory forerunner of s 14 of the 1892 Act was s 2 of the Artillery and Rifle Ranges Act 1885. That section contained no equivalent to the proviso to s 14(1) of the *f* 1892 Act.

2. The 1885 Act, however, did, by s 3, in relation to land by the seaside, enact that byelaws under the Act 'shall not injuriously affect any public right within the meaning of this section'. Subsection (3) of the section goes on to provide: 'For the purposes of this section "public right" means any right of navigation, anchoring, grounding, fishing, bathing, walking or recreation.'

3. This provision was re-enacted in s 2(4) of the Military Lands Act 1900.   *g*

4. The concept of public rights there referred to is wider than rights enforceable as between individuals in the courts.

5. Similarly, in *Sydney Municipal Council v A-G for New South Wales* [1894] AC 444 the Privy Council construed the words 'permanent common' in a dedication made by the Crown of certain land as being wide enough to comprise a dedication of that land for *h* public enjoyment notwithstanding the technical meaning of the word 'common' in normal legal parlance.

6. A similar desire in the legislature to recognise the de facto public usage of commons is evidenced in s 93 of the Law of Property Act 1925, which gives the public certain 'rights of access for air and exercise' on various commons.

In my judgment, while these factors do indicate that in certain circumstances *j* Parliament and the courts have taken cognisance of the widespread public habit of walking over commons, they do not lead to the conclusion that in s 14(1) of the 1892 Act the phrase 'right of common' has any other than its ordinary meaning. To construe the proviso as covering more than legal rights would make it impossible in practice for the

Secretary of State to use for military purposes any common land; even if he reaches an
a accommodation with those with rights of common, or removes their rights through the
statutory procedures on paying compensation, the freedom of the public to pass over the
land would still exist. If s 14(1) meant that no common land might be used for military
purposes it would have said so.

The next question which I address is: what is the proper construction of the proviso to
s 14 of the 1892 Act? There are a number of possible constructions of the proviso to s 14.
b First, that it provides (a) that byelaws should not authorise the Secretary of State to take
away rights of common and (b) that byelaws should not prejudicially affect rights of
common.

This construction has a lot of grammatical merit but it involves what seems to me to
be an absurdity, namely that Parliament, while enacting the foregoing limitations of the
Secretary of State's power in making byelaws, left him free to make byelaws which might
c authorise him prejudicially to affect rights of common, albeit that they could not
authorise him to take such rights away. If that were permissible, the Secretary of State
could do indirectly what he could not do directly by byelaw and moreover could
indirectly deprive commoners of rights without compensation. I am conscious that one
could argue that a byelaw containing such a provision for authorising the Secretary of
State to direct matters which would prejudicially affect common rights could itself be
d regarded as prejudicially affecting the rights of commoners albeit only indirectly.
However, while that argument, if successful, would meet the absurdity point, it would
leave the byelaw as one directly infringing the proviso and so would not avail the
Secretary of State.

A second possible construction is that it provides that no byelaw shall authorise the
Secretary of State to (a) take away a right of common or (b) prejudicially affect a right of
e common, but that the byelaws can do so directly. That was the submission of counsel for
the Secretary of State. That would permit the Secretary of State to do directly by making
a byelaw what he could not do indirectly and again would involve taking away rights
without compensation. In my judgment, in circumstances where there is no provision
for laying the byelaws before Parliament, such a distinction would serve no purpose and
f if that were the effect of the proviso the result would again be an absurdity.

A third possible construction is that Parliament's intention was to secure that the
Secretary of State should not by the use of the byelaw-making power given to him take
away or prejudicially affect rights of common. This accords with my instinctive grasp of
the purpose of the proviso and in my judgment is its correct construction.

Counsel for the Secretary of State recognised that, if this be the proper approach to the
meaning of the proviso, the byelaws as made do on the face of them prejudicially affect
g rights of common. He also recognised that this was not permitted by the legislation. I
deal later in this judgment with a submission by counsel that where a byelaw covers a
larger area than is permitted by statute it may none the less have force within the smaller
area which is permitted by statute, provided that the smaller area is within the larger
area. I shall refer to this as the *Dunkley* submission: see *Dunkley v Evans* [1981] 3 All ER
285, [1981] 1 WLR 1522. Counsel made, however, a further submission, namely that
h the byelaws must be read so that their only field of application is consistent with the
proviso because the proviso forbids any other field of application. This latter submission,
in so far as it is separate from the *Dunkley* submission, I reject. Of course I accept that in
cases of doubtful meaning in a byelaw one can look at the enabling statute in order to
clarify the doubt left by the wording of the byelaw. However, that is not this case. The
j instant byelaws are perfectly clear and in my judgment go further than the enabling Act
permits.

In the light of the foregoing findings, the position in relation to the byelaws is
essentially as follows. (1) The byelaws on their face prejudicially affect rights of common.
(2) This is not authorised by the empowering Act. (3) The ladies and Mr Parker have no

right to exercise any right of common. (4) What they did is on the fact of it prohibited by or under the byelaws.

The essential and important questions before the court are: (1) whether, and if so in what circumstances, a person can lawfully be convicted of an offence against a byelaw when the byelaw on the face of it is wider in its field of application than is permitted by the empowering Act and yet had the byelaw been drawn only as widely as the empowering Act authorises the person convicted would undoubtedly have been rightly convicted; (2) whether, and if so in what circumstances, a person can be convicted of an offence against a byelaw when the byelaw-maker must have failed to take into account a relevant consideration, namely that he had no power to make a byelaw of the breadth of application which the relevant byelaw had.

The court is thus faced with subordinate legislation which covers more than is permitted by the empowering legislation. In such circumstances, the courts could adopt a number of possible approches: (1) never to enforce any part of the subordinate legislation; (2) always to enforce those parts of the subordinate legislation which are permitted by the empowering legislation; or (3) in some but not all circumstances to enforce those parts of the subordinate legislation which are permitted by the empowering legislation.

The first of these courses has the merit of simplicity and of encouraging the subordinate legislator to keep within his powers. The disadvantage of such a course is that much to which no objection can be taken is then unenforceable. In any event, whatever the theoretical merits of such a course, it is clear that it does not represent the law as it has been developed: see *Dunkley v Evans* [1981] 3 All ER 285, [1981] 1 WLR 1522 and *Thames Water Authority v Elmbridge BC* [1983] 1 All ER 836, [1983] QB 570.

It is equally clear that on occasions the court will strike down the whole of the instrument under attack, even though all of it is not outwith the empowering legislation: see *Dyson v London and North Western Rly Co* (1881) 7 QBD 32, *Dyson v A-G* [1912] 1 Ch 158 and *R v North Hertfordshire DC, ex p Cobbold* [1985] 3 All ER 486.

So much is common ground between the parties, who all agree that in some circumstances the courts will enforce an instrument which is bad in parts. Where they differ is the formulation of the test to be applied to identify the circumstances in which the court will enforce such an instrument.

There are two recent cases in which the English courts have considered similar questions: the *Dunkley* case and the *Thames Water Authority* case just referred to.

The background to the former case was that under the Seafish (Conservation) Act 1967 ministers concerned might make orders prohibiting fishing within a certain area as defined in the Act. They made an order which covered the area referred to in the 1967 Act but also covered an area in respect of which the Act did not permit them to make an order. Mr Evans was fishing inside the area referred to in the Act. The prosecutor submitted that the fact that the order was ultra vires in so far as a small area was concerned did not render the whole order ultra vires. The defence contended that the whole order was rendered invalid by including this area of the sea. Ormrod LJ, reading the judgment of the court, stated as follows ([1981] 3 All ER 285 at 287, [1981] 1 WLR 1522 at 1524):

'The offending area represents 0·8% of the area covered by the order. The only question, therefore, is whether it is possible to sever the invalid part from the valid part of the order, or whether the whole order is invalidated by the inclusion of this small area. The general principle is stated in 1 Halsbury's Laws (4th Edn) para 26 thus: "Unless the invalid part is inextricably interconnected with the valid, a court is entitled to set aside or disregard the invalid part, leaving the rest intact." The principle is more fully formulated in the judgment of Cussen J in the Supreme Court of Victoria in *Olsen v City of Camberwell Corpn* [1926] VLR 58 at 68, where he said: "If the enactment with the invalid portion omitted is so radically or substantially different a law as to the subject matter dealt with by what remains from what it

a   would be with the omitted portions forming part of it as to warrant the belief that
the legislative body intended it as a whole only, or in other words, to warrant belief
that if all could not be carried into effect, the legislative body would not have enacted
the remainder independently, then the whole must fail." We respectfully agree
with and adopt this statement of the law. It would be difficult to imagine a clearer
example than the present case of a law which the legislative body would have
enacted independently of the offending portion and which is so little affected by
b   eliminating the invalid portion. This is clearly, therefore, an order which the court
should not strive officiously to kill to any greater extent than it is compelled to do.'

Ormrod LJ then indicated that the defendant's main point was that the court could
not sever the invalid portion of this order from the remainder because it was not possible
to excise from the text of the order the words which rendered part of it invalid. He
c   rejected this submission, saying ([1981] 3 All ER 285 at 288, [1981] 1 WLR 1522 at
1525):

'We can see no reason why the powers of the court to sever the invalid portion of
a piece of subordinate legislation from the valid should be restricted to cases where
the text of the legislation lends itself to judicial surgery, or textual emendation by
excision. It would have been competent for the court in an action for a declaration
d   that the provisions of the order in this case did not apply to the area of the sea off
Northern Ireland . . . to make the declaration sought, without in any way affecting
the validity of the order in relation to the remaining 99·2% of the area referred to in
the schedule to the order.'

The court certified the following points of law of general public importance namely
e   ([1981] 3 All ER 285 at 288, [1981] 1 WLR 1522 at 1526):

'1. Whether where a statutory instrument (on the true construction of which
criminal liability depends) has been made partly ultra vires, the court can construe
it and give effect to it in so far as it would probably have applied had it been made
intra vires; 2. if so, in what circumstances and on what principles should the court
act in deciding whether so to construe and give effect to it? In particular, is the
f   doctrine of severance applicable? If so, should the court apply the "blue pencil test"
or some other, and if so what, test?'

However, the case went no further.
In the *Thames Water Authority* case an urban district council prior to its dissolution had
passed resolutions appropriating some land, 'the blue land', for planning purposes.
g   Within the blue land was a small area shown edged green, 'the green land'. There was no
power to appropriate the green land, although there was power to appropriate the rest of
the blue land. The reason there was no power to appropriate the green land was because
at the appropriate date its use for sewerage purposes had not ceased. The water authority
contended that, since the appropriation was bad in part, the whole appropriation was
invalid. The borough council submitted that the appropriation was valid save and in so
h   far as it included the green land. Dunn LJ said ([1983] 1 All ER 836 at 841, [1983] QB
570 at 576):

'Counsel for the water authority submitted that the court can only sever when
the authors of the document have themselves so framed the document that the part
to be discarded is already segregated on the face of the document. The question of
j   severance only arises if there is something which, on a perusal of the document
itself, is capable of severance; and the court is not entitled to look at the factual
situation on the ground, but is confined to the four corners of the document. He
submitted that there was no case, whether concerned with contracts in restraint of
trade, statutory orders, byelaws or planning permission subject to conditions, in
which the court has severed the bad provisions from the good unless the bad

provisions appear in the documents themselves. He said that the court would not consider severance until the severable or exciseable part had been identified in the *a* document itself. This is known as the "blue pencil test".'

Dunn LJ then referred to *Dunkley*'s case and said that it was not possible to distinguish it from the instant case ([1983] 1 All ER 836 at 843, [1983] QB 570 at 579):

> 'In *Dunkley v Evans*, in order to find the invalidity, the court had to look outside the order at the principal Act. So here; in order to find the invalidity, the court has *b* to look outside the resolution at the factual situation on the ground, namely that the green land is still being used for sewage disposal.'

After having cited *United City Merchants (Investments) Ltd v Royal Bank of Canada* [1982] 2 All ER 720, [1983] AC 168, where the courts were concerned with enforcing part of a contract but not the remainder on the basis that the remainder was illegal as being *c* contrary to exchange control regulations, he went on to say ([1983] 1 All ER 836 at 844, [1983] QB 570 at 580–581):

> 'That was admittedly a contract case but the principle seems to me to apply a fortiori to public law. The question in the instant case is not as to the true construction of the resolution but whether, and to what extent, the urban district council had power to give effect to it. For that purpose the court is entitled, and *d* indeed bound, to look outside the document itself to see whether the urban district council, in fact and in law, had power to do what the resolution on the face of it purports to authorise. In this case it finds an easily identifiable part, namely the green land, which the urban district council had no power to appropriate. There is no more difficulty in deciding whether the resolution was invalid in respect of that part and valid in respect of the remainder than if the green land had been identified *e* in the resolution itself, and no difficulty in the court declaring that the resolution is invalid in respect of the green land and valid in respect of the remainder. It does not seem to me to matter whether one calls that process severance or whether one calls it modification of the resolution, or whether one uses some other word, or expression, to describe it. In the realm of judicial review it could be dealt with by declarations that the purported appropriation of the green land was ultra vires and *f* the remainder intra vires . . . I would echo the words of Ormrod LJ in *Dunkley v Evans* [1981] 3 All ER 285 at 287, [1981] 1 WLR 1522 at 1524, that the court should not strive officiously to kill to any extent greater than it is compelled to do. If, as here, it is perfectly plain that the urban district council had no power to do what it purported to do in respect of an easily identifiable parcel of land, it would not be conducive to good public administration for the court officiously to hold that the *g* whole document, including that part which was within the power of the council, was invalid.'

Dillon LJ said ([1983] 1 All ER 836 at 846–847, [1983] QB 570 at 583–584):

> 'It is apparent, therefore, that the council's resolution represents an excessive *h* exercise of the council's power of appropriation. But examination of the underlying facts shows also that there is no difficulty at all in identifying the extent of the excess . . . In private law the effect of excessive exercise of a power is not in doubt. As Maugham J said in *Re Turner, Hudson v Turner* [1932] 1 Ch 31 at 37, [1931] All ER Rep 782 at 785: "When the donee of a power of appointment has purported to exercise the power for an amount greater than that over which it was given, the *j* appointment is good with regard to the correct amount." Nearly two hundred years before, Clarke MR had adopted much the same approach when he said in *Alexander v Alexander* (1755) 2 Ves Sen 640 at 644, 28 ER 408 at 411: "If the court can see the boundaries it will be good for the execution of the power, and void as to the excess." This is the sensible approach and I see no reason why there should not be a similar

a approach in public law. None the less, counsel for the water authority submits that there is in public law, though not in private law, an overriding requirement that an excessive exercise of a power will be wholly void, and not merely void as to the excess, unless the document exercising the power is so worded as to include words describing the permitted exercise of the power as well as further words describing the excess in such a way that the excess can be excised by the use of a blue pencil, leaving unaltered the wording in the document expressly covering the permitted

b exercise of the power. I fail to see the sense or logic of such a requirement. Any excessive exercise of a power, whether in public or private law, is likely to be the result of a mistake on the part of the person exercising the power, ie an erroneous belief that the power extends further than it in truth does. But it is in the highest degree unlikely that that person will realise that he is making such a mistake and yet will not correct it. Therefore it is unlikely to happen, and if it does happen it

c will be purely fortuitous, that the wording of the exercise of the power will describe in express terms the extent of the permitted exercise of the power as part of the wording used to achieve a wider, and in truth excessive, execution of it. Therefore, if counsel for the water authority's overriding blue pencil requirements is in truth a requirement of public law, it would depend on chance, and not on any actual or presumed intention of the person exercising the power, or on any rational process

d of construction of the relevant document, whether the purported exercise of the power is wholly void or pro tanto valid.'

Stephenson LJ started his judgment as follows ([1983] 1 All ER 836 at 847–848, [1983] QB 570 at 585–586):

e 'For some centuries our courts have been applying to the benevolent interpretation of written instruments of all kinds, including statutes, the commonsense principle preserved in latin as ut res magis valeat quam pereat: Co Litt 36A; Broom's Select Legal Maxims (10th edn, 1939) p 361. By applying that principle they have been able not only to make sense of near nonsense but also to give effect to what is good and enforce what is valid, while refusing to enforce what is bad and giving no effect to

f what is invalid. This latter exercise can be carried out, and can, of course, be carried out only, where the good and bad parts are clearly identifiable and the bad part can be separated from the good and rejected without affecting the validity of the remaining part. But this ought to be done whenever the good and bad parts can be so identified and separated and what remains is clearly valid in the sense that there is nothing inherently unenforceable about it and all the surrounding circumstances indicate that common sense and the intention of the maker of any document which

g includes both good and bad parts would give effect to it. There will be cases where no such identification and separation of good from bad is possible and the invalidity of one part will taint and invalidate the whole. (The curate's egg was such a tainted whole, whatever its deferential consumer may have intended to hint to the contrary.) But I cannot see why this should be so in every case where the document which

h confronts the court does not itself identify the invalid part. To treat every such document as the egg of the curate would disable the court, by a matter of form only, from dividing what is clearly divisible into its component parts . . . where what is alleged to be invalid and unenforceable can be isolated and identified with precision, the court should not refuse to enforce the rest . . . That is so when there is nothing in the document to isolate and identify the unenforceable, but outside circumstances

j supply the identification and reveal the true nature of the transaction . . . Though it may be easier to apply the principle where the contract or resolution intrinsically identifies the illegal or ultra vires matter, it is in my judgment equally applicable where, as here, the thing is extrinsic and identifiable by looking outside. There may also be cases where the court cannot be certain what the author of a written contract, for example, would have intended if he had known the facts which made part performance impossible, or the law which made part performance unlawful or beyond his powers. Then the court cannot enforce what remains.'

    Counsel on behalf of those challenging the validity of the byelaws made the following submissions. 1. The court's power of modification or of severance can only be used (i) negatively and (ii) restrictively. This means that the court is confined to (a) finding a discreet element in an instrument to be ultra vires and (b) then reducing the ambit of the instrument to correspond with the power. He described this process as one of subtraction.

    2. Even so, the power of subtraction cannot be used (a) if when the exercise is performed what is left would probably not have been enacted or it cannot be shown that what is left would have been enacted and (b) if the severance alters the character of what is left (see *R v North Hertfordshire DC, ex p Cobbold* [1985] 3 All ER 486).

    3. The underlying reason for these close restrictions is not pedantry; it is that to go any further would breach the separation of powers and would thrust the court into the role of lawmaker.

    4. For these reasons one particular application of the restriction on the process of modification is that there must be no feasible alternative for the modification for which the rule-maker contends. The modification must be uniquely appropriate. If there is more than one possible modification then the court has to cast itself into the role of legislator in order to make the choice.

    5. Independently of the statutory vires question the omission of any saving or exception for rights of common is consistent only with the Secretary of State having failed, in making the byelaws, to pay regard to a matter made expressly relevant by statute, namely the preservation of rights of common. The byelaws are consequently unlawful and void on *Wednesbury* grounds (see *Associated Provincial Picture Houses v Wednesbury Corp* [1947] 2 All ER 680, [1948] 1 KB 223).

    I accept that in such a modification exercise the court, as a matter of substance, can only cut down the ambit of the decision so as to reflect the limitations of the empowering statute. The court cannot make the decision cover cases which, although within the ambit of the empowering statute, were not in fact covered by the decision under review. However, it is in my judgment clear that the drafting technique used by the court in modifying the decision (striking out words, altering a plan to which reference is made, adding words or making a declaration that the decision does not cover certain cases) is in itself not of importance.

    For my part, I accept that, when the court is performing an exercise which is essentially the alteration of a decision made by another under statutory powers given to that other and not to the court, the court should only do so when sure that the altered decision represents that which the decision-maker would have enacted had he appreciated the limitation on his powers. For the court to go further would be to assume the function of the decision-maker. If, however, the court thus restricts itself in performing the modification exercise then it also overcomes the difficulty that the decision-maker failed to take into account the fact that he did not have such wide powers as he thought he had or was labouring under some mistake of fact. If the court is in any doubt then in my judgment it should quash the decision and leave the decision-maker to decide afresh.

    It is arguable that the legal approach which I have adopted is stricter, as against the byelaw-maker, than that warranted by some of the words in the *Dunkley* case and the *Thames Water Authority* case and that we are bound by authority to adopt a laxer approach to modification. Since such a laxer approach would only weaken the position of those challenging the byelaws I need not trouble to consider it further. If I have erred, I have erred in their favour.

    I accept that there are several techniques, whether of byelaw drafting or of buying out, which the Secretary of State might have adopted for dealing with any commoners, but this uncertainty does not matter in the present case for we are not dealing with commoners. What we must be certain of is not what would have happened to the a commoners but what would have happened to the rest of the world. Applying the approach which I have indicated, it seems to me abundantly clear that the byelaw-maker, if he had appreciated the limitation on his powers, would both at Greenham Common and at Fylingdales nevertheless have gone on to make the byelaws in such a way that the proviso to s 14(1) was given effect but that all the world save commoners would still have been within their ambit.

Before disposing of the Greenham case I turn to consider some submissions made by
b Miss Hutchinson.

Miss Hutchinson, at the beginning of the hearing before us, withdrew her instructions from counsel and thereafter appeared in person. She made three submissions not made by counsel.

First, there is an overlap between the matters covered by the byelaws and matters covered by the Official Secrets Act 1911 in that the latter makes it a crime to be in the
c neighbourhood of or enter any prohibited place within the meaning of that Act. She submitted that in consequence the byelaws were necessarily invalid. Assuming that the area covered by the byelaws included a prohibited place, in my judgment there is no necessary invalidity in a byelaw creating a summary offence punishable by a fine when there is in existence a statute under which proof of the same facts will render the offender liable to a much greater penalty. It is to be noted that prosecutions under the Official
d Secrets Act 1911 cannot be instituted except by or with the consent of the Attorney General, but it does not follow that prosecutions for offences under the byelaws cannot be instituted by others. Such byelaws are commonplace.

Second, she raises points on procedural impropriety as to which I need say no more than to adopt the following passage of the judgment of his Honour Judge Lait in the court below as my own:
e

'. . . it was submitted by the appellants [Miss Hutchinson and Miss Smith] that there had been insufficient time for consideration by the Secretary of State of objections to the proposed byelaws. Section 17 of the enabling Act provides, inter alia, that "A Secretary of State, before making any byelaws under this Act . . . shall
f receive and consider all objections made . . ." The last date for receipt of objections, it is agreed, was 18 March 1985. The byelaws were made on 22 March 1985. The appellants expressed themselves as "astonished at such undue haste". We consider that there was, albeit a short period, a none the less adequate period of time for consideration of objections . . . it was submitted by the appellants that the Secretary of State had not considered all the objections which had been made. In support of
g this submission they relied on the contents of a letter which was handed in to us. The letter is on Ministry of Defence notepaper from A M Boardman and is dated 25 March 1985. At the start of the body of the letter is typed the heading "Proposed Byelaws RAF Greenham Common". It then continues: "Thank you for your letter dated 18 March 1985 addressed to the Secretary of State for Defence. The points you raise will be brought to the attention of the Secretary of State, who will consider
h them before he decides whether to make the byelaws. I have been asked however to respond to the matters you have raised." The writer then goes on to refer to various matters. The point taken by the appellants is that, three days after the byelaws were made, this letter is stating that the points raised will be considered by the Secretary of State. Assuming that the objections in the letter were received in time, that is not later than 18 March, it is none the less our view that the highly probable explanation
j is that a letter dictated by A M Boardman was duly typed, and on the following Monday (as 25 March would have been) was then signed and dated. We are of that view because the letter is typed, but the addressee's name is written in, as is the 25 March date, and as is the signature followed by "pp A M Boardman". Suffice it to say that on the evidence of that letter we are very far from satisfied that the Secretary

of State did not consider the matters raised by the person being written to before
deciding to make the byelaws.'   *a*

I note that the heading of the letter refers to 'proposed' byelaws.

Third, Miss Hutchinson drew our attention to byelaw 1 of the 1985 byelaws, which
provides:

> '(1) The area to which these byelaws apply consists of land . . . the boundary of
> which is marked by, and includes, the outer perimeter fence and gates of RAF   *b*
> Greenham Common . . .'

She also drew our attention to s 194 of the Law of Property Act 1925, which reads:

> '(1) The erection of any building or fence . . . whereby access to land to which
> this section applies is prevented or impeded, shall not be lawful unless the consent
> of the Minister thereto is obtained . . .   *c*
> (2) Where any building or fence is erected . . . without such consent as is required
> by this section, the county court within whose jurisdiction the land is situated, shall,
> on an application being made by the council of any county or district concerned, or
> by the lord of the manor or any other person interested in the common, have power
> to make an order for the removal of the work . . .'   *d*

While there may be an argument for maintaining that fences and buildings erected at
Greenham Common have been erected in contravention of s 194 of the 1925 Act, and I
make no finding on this point, that would not affect in itself the validity of the byelaws.
I note that no one has made application under s 194(2) for an order for the removal of
the allegedly illegal erections which have been up for many years. It is to say the least
doubtful whether such an order would now be made on the application of anyone let   *e*
alone Miss Hutchinson: see *A-G (ex rel Thornbury RDC) v Brock Bros Ltd* [1972] CA
Transcript 30.

In the light of the foregoing, in my judgment the magistrates' court were right in
convicting the ladies. The Crown Court, rightly in my judgment, concluded that the
byelaws went beyond the powers of the enabling Act but no sustained argument was
addressed to the Crown Court such as we have had over a number of days to the effect *f*
that it is possible to have a valid conviction under a byelaw, even if the byelaw is wider
in its application than permitted by the enabling Act. In those circumstances, it is not
surprising that the Crown Court came to the judgment to which it came.

The foregoing disposes of the Hutchinson (Greenham Common) case and of the
commons side of the Parker (Fylingdales) case. There remains the question of byelaw
3(k) of the 1987 byelaws.   *g*

Counsel for Mr Parker and Miss Hayman submitted that the powers of the Secretary
of State under s 14, in addition to the general byelaw-making power, are of two sorts: (a)
a power vested in the Secretary of State directly to prohibit all intrusion on the land and
all obstruction of the use of it (s 14(1)); and (b) a secondary or conditional power, where
advantage is not being taken of the first power of blanket exclusion, to make provision   *h*
in the byelaws to regulate public use of the land (s 14(2)). He submitted that byelaw 3(k)
was ultra vires (a) because it purports to permit the exercise by others of a power which
can only be exercised by the Secretary of State and (b) because the only point at which the
Secretary of State can exercise it is at the time of making the byelaws, at which time the
Secretary of State elected not to exercise it but instead to permit the public to use the land
subject to provisions regulating its use.   *j*

In reply to this, counsel for the Secretary of State submitted that s 14(1) empowered
the Secretary of State to make byelaws for two purposes, for regulating the use of the
land for the purposes to which it is appropriated and for securing the public against
dangers arising from that use, and in furtherance of either of those objectives it gives a
very broad 'power to prohibit all intrusion on the land and all obstruction of the use

a thereof'. He submitted that if, as the language used by Parliament states, byelaws may prohibit all intrusion then there is no reason why they should not empower an authorised person to direct persons to leave on pain of criminal sanctions for disobedience. There is nothing in s 14(1) to suggest that Parliament intended to confine the very broad powers conferred to the Secretary of State himself or to the time when he originally made the byelaws. In my judgment, counsel's submission is manifestly correct.

b Further, counsel for Mr Parker and Miss Hayman submitted that there was no limitation in the byelaw on the ground on which a direction to leave might be given. Thus it might be given (a) without any reason at all, (b) without any reason lying within the purposes of the statute, (c) therefore without the possibility of any subsequent examination of the validity of the direction and (d) without conveying the supposed reason to the person affected and therefore affording that person an opportunity to say why he or she should not be directed to leave the controlled area. He submitted that it *c* followed that byelaw 3(k) (a) permits arbitrary, capricious or mistaken directions to cut down elementary civic rights on pain of criminal sanctions, (b) offends against elementary fairness by giving no opportunity to disabuse an official of whatever reason he may have for contemplating giving a direction to leave, (c) exceeds the purposes prescribed by s 14(2) inasmuch as it allows on its face any exclusion for any purpose and (d) goes beyond the general law in restricting individual rights to an extent which is both intrinsically *d* unreasonable and not fairly or reasonably related to the purpose either of the statute or of the byelaws themselves.

Counsel for the Secretary of State submitted as follows.

1. The military purpose for which the land is being used strongly suggests that Parliament intended to give a very broad discretion to the Secretary of State to decide what byelaws were appropriate. In the military context, it should not be assumed in the *e* absence of express words that Parliament intended to confer power to make directions only if reasons were given and the person concerned is offered an opportunity to debate the matter. Parliament did not so confine the power because in the military context it considered that it might be appropriate to make byelaws requiring persons to leave after receiving a direction from an authorised person as a matter of urgency without debate. Parliament intended to give a broad discretion to the Secretary of State as to the removal *f* of persons on the land in the special circumstances of dealing with land used for military purposes.

2. In so far as counsel for Mr Parker and Miss Hayman asserted that the broad scope of byelaw 3(k) allowed for arbitrary direction, counsel for the Secretary of State submitted that it was not the law that any delegated power is bad in law if its terms are sufficiently wide to allow as a matter of construction for arbitrary application. Judicial review would *g* lie if there was an arbitrary exercise of the power. In any event, it was difficult to see the scope for arbitrariness in the context of the present case given that Mr Parker was where he was prohibited from going under byelaw 2 and where he had no right to be anyhow.

3. He relied on the general principle as stated in *Kruse v Johnson* [1898] 2 QB 91 at 99–100, [1895–9] All ER Rep 105 at 110: a court should be slow to find unreasonable a byelaw made by a public representative body.
h For my part, I accept these submissions by counsel for the Secretary of State and do not find byelaw 3(k) to be invalid. I would therefore refuse any relief to Mr Parker, who asks the court to declare that byelaw 3(k) is ultra vires.

I turn, lastly, to the Hayman case. This case also concerns the Fylingdales byelaws. The applicant is not threatened with prosecution, still less has she been prosecuted. She does, *j* however, regularly walk along a path known as Lyke Wake Walk, which runs along the northern boundary of the controlled area. A notice was put up stating 'Walkers on the Lyke Wake Walk are not to leave the track'. She saw no reason for this notice and had some fear that some military policeman would inhibit her from walking along the public right of way. However, early in these proceedings the following was made clear on behalf of the Secretary of State: 1. with regard to the Lyke Wake Walk (i) it is accepted that the Lyke Wake Walk is a public right of way, (ii) it is accepted that by reason of byelaw 8 of the 1987 byelaws nothing in the byelaws affects the lawful exercise by any person of a public right of way, (iii) it is therefore accepted that nothing in or done under the byelaws prevents the applicant from exercising her lawful right to pass and repass along the Lyke Wake Walk. 2. With regard to the notice prohibiting access to the land to the north of Lyke Wake Walk (i) that notice has been removed, (ii) there is no other notice prohibiting access on foot to the land to the north of the Lyke Wake Walk, (iii) the Secretary of State has no present intention to prohibit access on foot to the land to the north of Lyke Wake Walk.

In view of that statement, and its acceptance on behalf of Miss Hayman, the court indicated that we were not minded to make any declaration and so we heard no prolonged argument on the point.

MANN LJ. I agree.

Appeal in DPP v Hutchinson allowed. Case remitted to Crown Court with direction to dismiss appeals from conviction. Applications for judicial review refused. The court refused leave to appeal to the House of Lords but certified, under s 1(2) of the Administration of Justice Act 1960, that the following points of law of general public importance were involved in the decision: (1) whether, and if so in what circumstances, a person could lawfully be convicted of an offence against a byelaw when the byelaw on the face of it was wider in its field of application than was permitted by the empowering Act and yet, had the byelaw been drawn only as widely as the empowering Act authorised, the person convicted would undoubtedly have been rightly convicted; (2) whether, and if so in what circumstances, a person could be convicted of an offence against a byelaw when the byelaw-maker must have failed to take into account a relevant consideration, namely that he had no power to make a byelaw of the breadth of application which the relevant byelaws had.

27 February 1989. The Appeal Committee of the House of Lords gave leave to appeal.

Solicitors: *Crown Prosecution Service*; *Hodge Jones & Allen* (for Miss Smith); *Paul Hunt* (for the Mr Parker and Miss Hayman); *Treasury Solicitor*.

Dilys Tausz   Barrister.

Department of the Environment v Thomas Bates & Son Ltd (New Towns Commission, third party)

COURT OF APPEAL, CIVIL DIVISION

O'CONNOR, NICHOLLS AND TAYLOR LJJ

1, 2, 3, 24 NOVEMBER 1988

Negligence – Duty to take care – Economic loss – Building – Defect in building – Cost of repair – Building unfit for intended use – No imminent threat of physical injury to occupants – Remedial works required to render building fit for intended use – Whether builder liable for cost of repair.

The plaintiffs were the underlessees of an 11-storey office building constructed by the defendant builders in 1970 and 1971. For seven years the plaintiffs used the building without trouble but in 1981 and 1982, while other remedial works were being carried out by the plaintiffs, it was discovered that low strength concrete had been used by the defendants in pillars supporting the various floors of the building and, on expert advice, the plaintiffs carried out remedial work to strengthen nine pillars, which, although sufficient to support the existing load, were insufficient to support the design load. The plaintiffs were warned not to increase the loading of the building until the pillars were strengthened, but the weakness in the concrete did not give rise to any imminent danger to the health or safety of persons using the building provided the existing loading was not exceeded. After carrying out the remedial work to strengthen the pillars the plaintiffs claimed the cost of the work from the defendants. The judge accepted the need to strengthen eight of the pillars but dismissed the claim on the ground that the weakness of the concrete in the pillars was not physical damage which gave rise to imminent danger to the health or safety of either the plaintiffs' employees or the public but a defect which restricted the plaintiffs' full use of the building. The plaintiffs appealed, contending that an occupier was entitled to recover against a negligent builder the cost of remedial work undertaken in advance of any physical damage to the building in order to avert imminent risk of physical injury to persons.

Held – A builder was not liable in tort for the cost of remedying defects in a building constructed by him if the defects did not pose an imminent threat of physical injury to the building's occupants and the only purpose of the remedial works was to render the building fit for its intended use. Since on the judge's findings of fact the remedial works had been carried out to restore the building to the full capacity for which the plaintiffs had bargained in taking their underlease and not to avert an otherwise inevitable danger, the appeal would be dismissed (see p 1085 *b* to *d j*, p 1086 *d e h* and p 1088 *e g*, post).

D & F Estates Ltd v Church Comrs for England [1988] 2 All ER 992 applied.

Notes

For liability of builders and contractors, see 34 Halsbury's Laws (4th edn) paras 31, 33.

For the duty of care and standard of care, see 34 ibid paras 5–12, and for cases on the subject, see 36(1) Digest (Reissue) 17–55, 34–177.

Cases referred to in judgments

Anns v Merton London Borough [1977] 2 All ER 492, [1978] AC 728, [1977] 2 WLR 1024, HL.

Batty v Metropolitan Property Realizations Ltd [1978] 2 All ER 445, [1978] QB 554, [1978] 2 WLR 500, CA.

Bottomley v Bannister [1932] 1 KB 458, [1931] All ER Rep 99, CA.

Bowen v Paramount Builders (Hamilton) Ltd [1977] 1 NZLR 394, NZ CA.
Clay v A J Crump & Sons Ltd [1963] 3 All ER 687, [1964] 1 QB 533, [1963] 3 WLR 866,   *a*
     CA.
Clayton v Woodman & Son (Builders) Ltd [1962] 2 All ER 33, [1962] 1 WLR 585, CA.
D & F Estates Ltd v Church Comrs for England [1988] 2 All ER 992, [1988] 3 WLR 368,
     HL.
Donoghue (or M'Alister) v Stevenson [1932] AC 562, [1932] All ER Rep 1, HL.
Dutton v Bognor Regis United Building Co Ltd [1972] 1 All ER 462, [1972] 1 QB 373, [1972]   *b*
     2 WLR 299, CA.
Gallagher v N McDowell Ltd [1961] NI 26, NI CA.
Greater Nottingham Co-op Society Ltd v Cementation Piling and Foundations Ltd [1988] 2 All
     ER 971, [1988] 3 WLR 396, CA.
Hedley Byrne & Co Ltd v Heller & Partners Ltd [1963] 2 All ER 575, [1964] AC 465, [1963]
     3 WLR 101, HL.   *c*
Junior Books Ltd v Veitchi Co Ltd [1982] 3 All ER 201, [1983] 1 AC 520, [1982] 3 WLR 477,
     HL.
Ketteman v Hansel Properties Ltd [1988] 1 All ER 38, [1987] AC 189, [1987] 2 WLR 312,
     HL; *affg* [1985] 1 All ER 352, [1984] 1 WLR 1274, CA.
London Congregational Union Inc v Harriss & Harriss (a firm) [1988] 1 All ER 15, CA.
Pirelli General Cable Works Ltd v Oscar Faber & Partners (a firm) [1983] 1 All ER 65, [1983]   *d*
     2 AC 1, [1983] 2 WLR 6, HL.
Rivtow Marine Ltd v Washington Iron Works [1974] SCR 1189, Can SC.
Robbins v Jones (1863) 15 CBNS 221, [1861–73] All ER Rep 544, 143 ER 768.
Simaan General Contracting Co v Pilkington Glass Ltd (No 2) [1988] 1 All ER 791, [1988] QB
     758, [1988] 2 WLR 761, CA.
Sparham-Souter v Town and Country Developments (Essex) Ltd [1976] 2 All ER 65, [1976]   *e*
     QB 858, [1976] 2 WLR 493, CA.
Ultramares Corp v Touche (1931) 255 NY 170, NY Ct of Apps.
Voli v Inglewood Shire Council (1963) 110 CLR 74, Aust HC.

Cases also cited
Aswan Engineering Establishment Co v Lupdine Ltd (Thurgar Bolle Ltd, third party) [1987] 1   *f*
     All ER 135, [1987] 1 WLR 1, CA.
Peabody Donation Fund (Governors) v Sir Lindsay Parkinson & Co Ltd [1984] 3 All ER 529,
     [1985] AC 210, HL.
Tozer Kemsley & Milbourn (Holdings) Ltd v J Jarvis & Sons Ltd (1983) 1 Const LJ 79.

Appeal   *g*
The plaintiffs, the Department of the Environment, appealed against that part of the
order made on 28 April 1987 by his Honour Judge David Smout QC, hearing official
referees' business, whereby he ordered that the plaintiffs had no cause of action against
the defendants, Thomas Bates & Son Ltd, for damages for repairs undertaken to
strengthen supporting pillars in the tower block at Great Oaks House, Basildon, Essex.
The defendants issued a respondent's notice in which they contended that, if the plaintiffs   *h*
did have a cause of action, it was statute-barred. The third party, the New Towns
Commission (as successor to the Basildon Department Corp), took no part in the appeal.
The facts are set out in the judgment of Taylor LJ.

John Laws and *Michael Lerego* for the plaintiffs.
David Hunt QC and *Terence Mowschenson* for the defendants.   *j*

Cur adv vult

24 November. The following judgments were delivered.

TAYLOR LJ (giving the first judgment at the invitation of O'Connor LJ). This case
a raises yet another variant of a vexed question: what is the liability of a builder in tort for
economic loss? The plaintiffs are underlessees of parts of a building complex. They sued
the defendants who built the complex alleging negligence. Two separate complaints
were made. The first related to leakage through a defective flat roof; the second concerned
weakness of the concrete used to construct supporting pillars. The action was tried by his
Honour Judge David Smout QC as official referee. After a lengthy hearing, the judge
b gave his judgment on 26 January 1987. He found for the plaintiffs, although not to the
full extent of their claim, in respect of the flat roof. There is no appeal against that part
of his judgment. However, he found for the defendants in respect of the defective pillars,
ruling that the plaintiffs had no cause of action. They now appeal against that finding.
There is a cross-appeal by which the builders contend that, if the plaintiffs did have a
cause of action, it was statute-barred.
c   The building complex is known as Great Oaks House at Basildon in Essex. The
freeholder, Basildon Corporation, granted a lease to EMI Development Holdings Ltd
(EMI). EMI engaged the defendants as builders, under a JCT contract, to construct the
building complex. This they did during 1970 and 1971. On 15 October 1971, prior to
the completion of the works, EMI agreed to grant the plaintiffs an underlease of part of
the complex. The plaintiffs went into occupation on 30 December 1971 in accordance
d with the terms of the underlease, which was for 42 years and was dated 6 March 1972.
EMI's reversion in the property, less a day, was acquired by the Church Commissioners
on 14 April 1972. At the centre of the complex was a low-rise, two-storey building with
a flat roof consisting of offices, a job centre and a supermarket with ancillary
accommodation. One end of this low-rise building abuts on an eleven-storey tower block,
the upper nine storeys of which comprise offices. There are other buildings in the
e complex not concerned in these proceedings. By their underlease the plaintiffs occupied
parts of the low-rise building but the reversioner retained the main structure of the
building including the roof. The plaintiffs also occupy the upper nine storeys of the
tower block.
    For over seven years the plaintiffs occupied and used the premises without trouble.
But in March 1979 water began to drip through the ceiling of the job centre from the
f flat roof. Leakages continued in 1980 and 1981. Alternative accommodation for the
plaintiffs' staff had to be found. Eventually, remedial work was done between September
1981 and August 1982. In 1982 and 1983 there was litigation about these matters. The
cases were settled, but in the present proceedings the plaintiffs sought to recover from
the defendants what they had paid towards the remedial works, together with the costs
of the alternative accommodation. The judge found that the condition of the roof—
g
        'presented imminent danger to the health of the plaintiffs' employees and was
        likely if not remedied to cause further damage to the plaintiffs' premises.'

After reviewing the authorities the judge held that the plaintiffs were entitled to recover
the cost of remedying the defects of the roof, ie averting the danger, but they were not
entitled to recover any other loss, eg the cost of alternative accommodation.
h   I turn now to the defective pillars, the subject of the finding under appeal. While the
defective roof was being remedied it was discovered that some of the concrete beams
there were soft. This led to a wider investigation which revealed that low strength
concrete had been used by the defendants in pillars supporting the various floors in the
eleven-storey tower block. The plaintiffs' expert concluded that nine of those pillars,
while sufficient to support the existing load, were insufficient to support the design load.
j Accordingly in 1985, on his advice, the pillars were strengthened. Again, the plaintiffs
sought to recover in tort from the defendant builders what they had paid in respect of
the remedial works in accordance with their underlease. Although the judge accepted
the need to strengthen eight of the nine pillars, he held that the plaintiffs had no cause of
action against the defendant builders. It will be necessary to examine closely his findings

of fact and the reasons for his decision. First, however, it is convenient to consider the law presently applicable in this field.

The problems facing the courts have been threefold. Firstly, liability in tort for negligence on the principles of *Donoghue (or M'Alister) v Stevenson* [1932] AC 562, [1932] All ER Rep 1 required proof of physical injury to persons or their property. How, if at all, can such liability attach in respect of a defective building which has not yet caused injury to persons or damaged other property? Secondly, if such liability can exist, what is its touchstone, short of equating tortious liability to a breach of warranty of fitness appropriate only in contract? Thirdly, what damages are to be recoverable having regard to the courts' reluctance to allow claims for pure economic loss which might lead, in the words of Cardozo CJ in *Ultramares Corp v Touche* (1931) 255 NY 170 at 179—

> 'to a liability in an indeterminate amount for an indeterminate time to an indeterminate class.'

Counsel on both sides have helpfully referred to the relevant authorities, English, Commonwealth and American. They begin with *Dutton v Bognor Regis United Building Co Ltd* [1972] 1 All ER 462, [1972] 1 QB 373 in which, for the first time, *Donoghue (or M'Alister) v Stevenson* was applied to real property. There followed a long series of cases, including the landmark decision of the House of Lords in *Anns v Merton London Borough* [1977] 2 All ER 492, [1978] AC 728 and culminating in the most recent House of Lords authority, *D & F Estates Ltd v Church Comrs for England* [1988] 2 All ER 992, [1988] 3 WLR 368. I propose to refer only to those two decisions of the House of Lords, since the authorities cited by counsel were fully reviewed and considered in the latter case by Lord Bridge and Lord Oliver.

Anns v Merton London Borough was a case in which the foundations of a block of maisonettes were too shallow, so that some eight years after they were built, structural damage was caused. The appellant council was alleged to have passed the plans negligently and in breach of building byelaws made under statute and to have failed to make proper inspections. The case was argued on a preliminary issue as to whether on assumed facts any action lay against the council and if so whether it was statute-barred. The case did not therefore directly concern the tortious liability of the builder. However Lord Wilberforce said ([1977] 2 All ER 492 at 504–505, [1978] AC 728 at 758–760):

> '*The position of the builder.* I agree with the majority in the Court of Appeal in thinking that it would be unreasonable to impose liability in respect of defective foundations on the council, if the builder, whose primary fault it was, should be immune from liability. So it is necessary to consider this point, although it does not directly arise in the present appeal. If there was at one time a supposed rule that the doctrine of *Donoghue v Stevenson* did not apply to realty, there is no doubt under modern authority that a builder of defective premises may be liable in negligence to persons who thereby suffer injury: see *Gallagher v N McDowell Ltd* [1961] NI 26, per Lord MacDermott CJ, a case of personal injury. Similar decisions have been given in regard to architects (*Clayton v Woodman & Son (Builders) Ltd* [1962] 2 All ER 33, [1962] 1 WLR 585, *Clay v A J Crump & Sons Ltd* [1963] 3 All ER 687, [1964] 1 QB 533. *Gallagher's* case expressly leaves open the question whether the immunity against action of builder-owners, established by older authorities (e g *Bottomley v Bannister* [1932] 1 KB 458, [1931] All ER Rep 99) still survives. That immunity, as I understand it, rests partly on a distinction being made between chattels and real property, partly on the principle of "caveat emptor" or, in the case where the owner leases the property, on the proposition that (fraud apart) there is no law against letting a "tumbledown house" (*Robbins v Jones* (1863) 15 CBNS 221 at 240, [1861–73] All ER Rep 544 at 547, per Erle CJ). But leaving aside such cases as arise between contracting parties, when the terms of the contract have to be considered (see *Voli v Inglewood Shire Council* (1963) 110 CLR 74 at 85, per Windeyer J), I am unable to

understand why this principle or proposition should prevent recovery in a suitable case by a person, who has subsequently acquired the house, on the principle of *Donoghue v Stevenson*: the same rules should apply to all careless acts of a builder: whether he happens also to own the land or not. I agree generally with the conclusions of Lord Denning MR on this point (*Dutton's* case [1972] 1 All ER 462 at 471–472, [1972] 1 QB 373 at 392–394). In the alternative, since it is the duty of the builder (owner or not) to comply with the byelaws, I would be of opinion that an action could be brought against him, in effect, for breach of statutory duty by any person for whose benefit or protection the byelaw was made. So I do not think that there is any basis here for arguing from a supposed immunity of the builder to immunity of the council.

Nature of the damages recoverable and arising out of the cause of action. There are many questions here which do not directly arise at this stage and which may never arise if the actions are tried. But some conclusions are necessary if we are to deal with the issue as to limitation. The damages recoverable include all those which foreseeably arise from the breach of the duty of care which, as regards the council, I have held to be a duty to take reasonable care to secure compliance with the byelaws. Subject always to adequate proof of causation, these damages may include damages for personal injury and damage to property. In my opinion they may also include damage to the dwelling-house itself; for the whole purpose of the byelaws in requiring foundations to be of certain standard is to prevent damage arising from weakness of the foundations which is certain to endanger the health or safety of occupants. To allow recovery for such damage to the house follows, in my opinion, from normal principle. If classification is required, the relevant damage is in my opinion material, physical damage, and what is recoverable is the amount of expenditure necessary to restore the dwelling to a condition in which it is no longer a danger to the health or safety of persons occupying and possibly (depending on the circumstances) expenses arising from necessary displacement. On the question of damages generally I have derived much assistance from the judgment (dissenting on this point, but of strong persuasive force) of Laskin J in the Canadian Supreme Court case of *Rivtow Marine Ltd v Washington Iron Works* [1974] SCR 1189 at 1220–1222 and from the judgments of the New Zealand Court of Appeal (furnished by courtesy of that court) in *Bowen v Paramount Builders (Hamilton) Ltd* [1977] 1 NZLR 394.

When does the cause of action arise? We can leave aside cases of personal injury or damage to other property as presenting no difficulty. It is only the damage for the house which required consideration. In my respectful opinion the Court of Appeal was right when, in *Sparham-Souter v Town and Country Developments (Essex) Ltd* [1976] 2 All ER 65, [1976] QB 858, it abjured the view that the cause of action arose immediately on delivery, ie conveyance of the defective house. It can only arise when the state of the building is such that there is present or imminent danger to the health or safety of persons occupying it. We are not concerned at this stage with any issue relating to remedial action nor are we called on to decide on what the measure of the damages should be; such questions, possibly very difficult in some cases, will be for the court to decide. It is sufficient to say that a cause of action arises at the point I have indicated.'

In *D & F Estates Ltd v Church Comrs for England* the third defendants, a building company, were the main contractors for the construction of a block of flats owned by the first defendant. The builders engaged a sub-contractor for the plasterwork reasonably believing him to be skilled and competent. In fact the sub-contractor carried out the work negligently. The plaintiffs were the lessees and occupiers of a flat in the block. Some 15 years after the flats were built and again some three years later, the plaintiffs found that plaster in their flat was loose. They brought an action against, inter alia, the

builders claiming the cost of remedial work already done and the estimated cost of future
remedial work. The plaintiffs succeeded at first instance, but the Court of Appeal reversed   *a*
the decision on two grounds. Firstly, the builders owed no further duty of care to the
plaintiffs having employed a competent sub-contractor; and secondly, the cost of
replacing the defective plaster was not recoverable in tort because it was pure economic
loss. The House of Lords unanimously upheld that decision on both grounds. It is
necessary to refer in some detail to the speeches of Lord Bridge and Lord Oliver with
which all their Lordships agreed. After considering the provisions of the Defective   *b*
Premises Act 1972, which was based on the recommendations of a Law Commission
report on *Civil Liability of Vendors and Lessors for Defective Premises* (Law Com no 40), Lord
Bridge reviewed the authorities prior to *Anns*'s case. He then set out the passage from
Lord Wilberforce's speech, quoted above, with which Lord Diplock, Lord Simon and
Lord Russell had agreed. He said ([1988] 2 All ER 992 at 1002, [1988] 3 WLR 368 at
380–381):   *c*

> 'It is particularly to be noted that Lord Wilberforce founded his view of the
> builder's liability on the alternative grounds of negligence and breach of statutory
> duty and that his opinion as to the nature of the damages recoverable is strictly
> applicable to the liability of the local authority, and perhaps also to the liability of
> the builder for breach of duty under the byelaws, but is obiter in relation to the   *d*
> builder's liability for the common law tort of negligence. It is, moreover, difficult
> to understand how a builder's liability, whatever its scope, in respect of a dangerous
> defect in a building can arise only when there is imminent danger to the health and
> safety of occupiers. In any event, the last sentence in the passage quoted leaves open
> the critical question as to the measure of damages in relation to remedial action.'

e

Lord Bridge went on to consider later authorities and summarised the principles
applicable first to chattels and then to real property as follows ([1988] 2 All ER 992 at
1006, [1988] 3 WLR 368 at 385–386):

> '. . . if the hidden defect is discovered before any such damage is caused, there is
> no longer any room for the application of the *Donoghue v Stevenson* principle. The   *f*
> chattel is now defective in quality, but is no longer dangerous. It may be valueless
> or it may be capable of economic repair. In either case the economic loss is
> recoverable in contract by a buyer or hirer of the chattel entitled to the benefit of a
> relevant warranty of quality, but is not recoverable in tort by a remote buyer or
> hirer of the chattel. If the same principle applies in the field of real property to the
> liability of the builder of a permanent structure which is dangerously defective, that *g*
> liability can only arise if the defect remains hidden until the defective structure
> causes personal injury or damage to property other than the structure itself. If the
> defect is discovered before any damage is done, the loss sustained by the owner of
> the structure, who has to repair or demolish it to avoid a potential source of danger
> to third parties, would seem to be purely economic. Thus, if I acquire a property
> with a dangerously defective garden wall which is attributable to the bad   *h*
> workmanship of the original builder, it is difficult to see any basis in principle on
> which I can sustain an action in tort against the builder for the cost of either
> repairing or demolishing the wall. No physical damage has been caused. All that
> has happened is that the defect in the wall has been discovered in time to prevent
> damage occurring. I do not find it necessary for the purpose of deciding the present
> appeal to express any concluded view as to how far, if at all, the ratio decidendi of   *j*
> *Anns v Merton London Borough* [1977] 2 All ER 492, [1978] AC 728 involves a
> departure from this principle establishing a new cause of action in negligence
> against a builder when the only damage alleged to have been suffered by the plaintiff
> is the discovery of a defect in the very structure which the builder erected.'

Lord Bridge then considered the argument that in a complex structure, a defect in one
a part causing damage in another might be said to have caused damage to 'other property',
but he held that could not apply to the defective plaster on the ceiling in that case. The
relevant part of the speech concluded with these words ([1988] 2 All ER 992 at 1007,
[1988] 3 WLR 368 at 386–387):

> 'It seems to me clear that the cost of replacing the defective plaster itself, either as
> carried out in 1980 or as intended to be carried out in future, was not an item of
b > damage for which the builder of Chelwood House could possibly be made liable in
> negligence under the principle of *Donoghue v Stevenson* or any legitimate development
> of that principle. To make him so liable would be to impose on him for the benefit
> of those with whom he had no contractual relationship the obligation of one who
> warranted the quality of the plaster as regards materials, workmanship and fitness
c > for purpose. I am glad to reach the conclusion that this is not the law, if only for the
> reason that a conclusion to the opposite effect would mean that the courts, in
> developing the common law, had gone much further than the legislature were
> prepared to go in 1972, after comprehensive examination of the subject by the Law
> Commission, in making builders liable for defects in the quality of their work to all
> who subsequently acquire interests in buildings they have erected. The statutory
d > duty imposed by the 1972 Act was confined to dwelling houses and limited to
> defects appearing within six years. The common law duty, if it existed, could not
> be so confined or so limited. I cannot help feeling that consumer protection is an
> area of law where legislation is much better left to the legislators.'

Lord Oliver began with the quoted passage from Lord Wilberforce's speech in *Anns*'s case
from which he distilled a number of points. He continued ([1988] 2 All ER 992 at 1010,
e [1988] 3 WLR 368 at 390):

> 'These propositions involve a number of entirely novel concepts. In the first place,
> in no other context has it previously been suggested that a cause of action in tort
> arises in English law for the defective manufacture of an article which causes no
> injury other than injury to the defective article itself.'

f Lord Oliver drew attention to a number of anomalies arising from these propositions,
pointing out more than once that they involved an entirely new concept of the law of
negligence in relation to building cases. He said ([1988] 2 All ER 992 at 1011–1012,
[1988] 3 WLR 368 at 392):

> 'Moreover, it is, I think now entirely clear that the vendor of a defective building
g > who is also the builder enjoys no immunity from the ordinary consequences of his
> negligence in the course of constructing the building, but beyond this and so far as
> the case was concerned with the extent of or limitations on his liability for common
> law negligence divorced from statutory duty, Lord Wilberforce's observations were,
> I think, strictly obiter. My Lords, so far as they concern such liability in respect of
> damage which has actually been caused by the defective structure other than by
h > direct physical damage to persons or to other property, I am bound to say that, with
> the greatest respect to their source, I find them difficult to reconcile with any
> conventional analysis of the underlying basis of liability in tort for negligence. A
> cause of action in negligence at common law which arises only when the sole
> damage is the mere existence of the defect giving rise to the possibility of damage
> in the future, which crystallises only when that damage is imminent, and the
j > damages for which are measured, not by the full amount of the loss attributable to
> the defect but by the cost of remedying it only to the extent necessary to avert a risk
> of physical injury, is a novel concept . . . For my part, therefore, I think the correct
> analysis, in principle, to be simply that, in a case where no question of breach of
> statutory duty arises, the builder of a house or other structure is liable at common

law for negligence only where actual damage, either to a person or to property, results from carelessness on his part in the course of construction.'

Lord Oliver concluded ([1988] 2 All ER 992 at 1014, [1988] 3 WLR 368 at 395):

'My Lords, I have to confess that the underlying logical basis for and the boundaries of the doctrine emerging from *Anns v Merton London Borough* are not entirely clear to me and it is in any event unnecessary for the purposes of the instant appeal to attempt a definitive exposition. This much at least seems clear: that in so far as the case is authority for the proposition that a builder responsible for the construction of the building is liable in tort at common law for damage occuring through his negligence to the very thing which he had constructed, such liability is limited directly to cases where the defect is one which threatens the health or safety of occupants or of third parties and (possibly) other property. In such a case, however, the damages recoverable are limited to expenses necessarily incurred in averting that danger.'

In summary, the effect of their Lordships' speeches in the *D & F Estates* case can be stated thus: (1) the propositions as to the tortious liability of a builder contained in Lord Wilberforce's speech represent a departure from the established principles of the law of tort; (2) they were obiter; (3) (per Lord Oliver) in so far as they are authoritative, such liability is limited directly to the cost of averting danger where the defect in the building imminently threatens the health or safety of occupants or of third parties and (possibly) other property.

I now return to the judge's findings of fact which he set out very clearly in his judgment. He heard evidence from experts from both sides; Mr Heggie for the plaintiffs and Mr Ham for the defendants. He quoted two paragraphs from Mr Heggie's report as follows:

'6.02. Although this structure shows no signs of distress in the critically loaded members, the compressive failure mode of a reinforced concrete column is sudden and not progressive. No noticeable increasing deformation would be expected as a failure approached. It is clear that existing factors of safety in the eight members noted above are much lower than those provided in any properly designed structure. As a result the probability of collapse is at an unacceptable level. 6.03. Since the situation has persisted for a number of years, we do not consider evacuation to be essential. It is important that alterations in internal layout are minimized and any potential build-up of loading prevented (e.g., new filing room). Remedial works should be carried out as soon as practicable so that the building can be used without restriction and its occupants can enjoy the level of safety normally expected.'

The judge then commented as follows:

'Taking the evidence as a whole I do not accept, nor do I think Heggie intended to convey, that the probability of collapse was at an unacceptable level on the actual loading then imposed on the tower bock. Nor do I accept that the occupants had not at all times enjoyed a satisfactory level of safety. Had it been otherwise Heggie would have ordered immediate evacuation. But it was Heggie's view that in due course danger would arise if, as might be expected in an office building, the actual load were to increase over the years and were to approach the design load. That view was challenged by Ham and must be examined.'

He then considered the rival arguments and, for the reasons given by Mr Heggie, accepted the need to strengthen all eight pillars. He summarised his findings of fact as follows:

'(1) Until late 1982 or thereabouts, the plaintiff had no knowledge of any need for any limitation on use of the tower block. Until that time the plaintiff had used

the tower block as freely as it wished but had not in fact loaded to design capacity.
a   (2) In or about late 1982 the plaintiff was warned by the consultants not to increase
the then loading on the tower block. The warning was heeded. No other restriction
was placed on its use. (3) The offices in the tower block included that of the
Department of Health and Social Security to which the public had regular access.
(4) At no time did the weakness of the concrete in the pillars of the tower block give
rise to imminent danger to health or safety of either the plaintiff's employees or of
b   the public. However, had the tower block been loaded to design capacity at any
time prior to strengthening of the pillars in January 1985 imminent danger would
have resulted. (5) There is no evidence that there was at any time cracking of the
tower block occasioned by the weakness of the concrete. (6) The strengthening of
the pillars by the plaintiff was not with the intention of averting imminent danger
to health or safety for it was recognised that there was no such imminent danger.
c   The purpose was to cure a defect which otherwise prevented the plaintiff from
making full use of the building to the extent for which it was designed.'

On these findings there was in the judge's words 'no injury threatened by the mere
use of the tower block: rather there was a restriction on the full extent of future use'. The
judge did not have the advantage of reading the decision in the *D & F Estates* case which
d   was given 18 months later. He relied, in rejecting the plaintiffs' claim, on the decision of
the House of Lords in *Pirelli General Cable Works Ltd v Oscar Faber & Partners (a firm)*
[1983] 1 All ER 65, [1983] 2 AC 1. The issue in that case was when a cause of action arose
in tort against engineers in respect of a defective building. A factory chimney had been
lined with unsuitable material when built in 1969. Cracks developed by April 1970. The
plaintiff occupiers could not have discovered the damage until October 1972 and did not
e   do so until November 1977. Extensive remedial work was carried out. In October 1978,
the plaintiffs issued their writ against the defendant engineers who had designed the
chimney. It was held that the cause of action in tort arose when the damage came into
existence, not when it was discovered or ought to have been discovered. The claim was
therefore barred. In the present case the judge relied on the *Pirelli* case as showing that
the cause of action was only complete when physical damage occurred, not when the
f   defect causing the damage (ie the use of the unsuitable lining) occurred or was discovered.
He said:

'In the instant case the constitution of the concrete was likewise the defect: no
cracks occurred because on discovery of the defect sensible precautions were taken
to ensure that the concrete was not loaded beyond its bearing capacity. The
subsequent remedial work has enabled the concrete pillars to be reconstructed so as
g   to be capable of bearing the intended load as designed. There has thus been no
physical damage in the sense of cracks of any significance at any time. Nor has there
been any other form of physical damage. The weak concrete was not physical
damage, that was the defect. The discovery of the defect cannot convert the defect
into physical damage for physical damage is objective not subjective.'

h   Anticipating the decision of the House of Lords in the *D & F Estates* case, the judge
referred to a dictum of Ralph Gibson LJ in *London Congregatational Union Inc v Harriss &
Harriss (a firm)* [1988] 1 All ER 15. That case also concerned limitation and the court
again drew a distinction between a defect and resultant physical damage, only the latter
of which gave a cause of action. Ralph Gibson LJ said (at 24):

j   'For my part, I am not impressed by the prophecy of unjust denial of relief to
plaintiffs who have discovered a negligent defect but are not entitled to relief in
contract and are faced by the prospect of physical damage which has not yet been
caused but is likely to result from the defect. Firstly, of course, the concept of
negligence is not intended to offord to owners of buildings rights equivalent to
contractual rights. Justice does not require that a defendant pay damages in tort for

a defect in design which, in Lord Fraser's words, "may never lead to any damage at
all to the building" (see the *Pirelli* case [1983] 1 All ER 65 at 70, [1983] 2 AC 1 at 16). **a**
Secondly, if a negligent defect is discovered and the building owner can prove an
immediate duty or clear need, in protection of himself or of others or of the
building, to carry out repairs to remove the defect so as to avoid physical damage
which is shown to be impending, ie likely to occur in the immediate future, it
seems to me that the law would accept such a situation as proof of damage . . .'

b

The judge considered that the second of these observations was irreconcilable with the
ratio of the *Pirelli* case. This conflict is essentially the same as that with which the House
of Lords wrestled in the *D & F Estates* case when considering the impact of *Anns's* case on
the established principles of the law of negligence.

Counsel for the plaintiffs submits that the judge was wrong to regard this case as
governed by the *Pirelli* case, a limitation case not specifically concerned with the problem **c**
of a present defect and only anticipated damage. He submits that an occupier can recover
against a negligent builder in tort the cost of remedial work undertaken in advance of
any physical damage to the building in order to avert imminent risk of physical injury
to persons. That proposition is, he says, supported by the dictum of Ralph Gibson LJ in
the *London Congregational Union* case, by *Anns's* case and by the dissenting speech of Lord
Brandon in *Junior Books Ltd v Veitchi Co Ltd* [1982] 3 All ER 201 at 215–218, [1983] 1 AC **d**
520 at 549–552, approved in *D & F Estates*. It is even supported he submits by Lord
Oliver in *D & F Estates* itself, although, as already demonstrated, that support might be
described as at most lukewarm. Even assuming counsel's proposition is right and
supported by authority, however, the question remains whether, on the judge's findings,
the plaintiffs can succeed here. Crucially, the question is whether the remedial works
were 'to avert imminent risk of physical injury to persons'. The judge found that there **e**
had been no danger. Danger would have arisen only if the loading in the tower block
had increased towards the design load. Once the warning was given there was no
question of that happening. So, the remedial works were not to avert imminent danger;
they were to enable the building to be used to the full extent of the design load.

Counsel for the plaintiffs says this *was* to avert imminent danger because (a) the word **f**
'imminent' should not be interpreted too restrictively as to time and (b) there would be
danger if the building were to be used as it was intended or might be expected to be
used.

As to (a) he submitted that 'imminent' means no more in this context than soon. The
danger does not have to be immediate. In support of this, he cited a passage from the
judgment of Lawton LJ in *Ketteman v Hansel Properties Ltd* [1985] 1 All ER 352 at 364– **g**
365, [1984] 1 WLR 1274 at 1290. That was a case in which faulty foundations caused
cracks in the walls of five houses. In an action against the builders, the local authority
and the architects, the test of 'imminent danger to health and safety of the plaintiffs'
derived from *Anns* was applied. Lawton LJ said:

'An absurd situation, said counsel for the plaintiiffs, would arise if the occupiers **h**
of a building which was structurally unsound due to a local authority's negligence
and which was likely to become a danger to health or safety unless remedial action
were taken had to wait until it was about to collapse before his right of action against
the local authority was accrued. Counsel for the second defendants submitted that
the occupier did have to wait until there was a present or imminent danger to health
or safety because that is what Lord Wilberforce had said . . . Having regard to the **j**
absurdity to which counsel for the plaintiffs invited our attention, it seems to me
that Lord Wilberforce's use of the word "imminent" should be understood to mean
a danger which was likely to arise soon, and how long soon was in any case would
depend on the facts and would be a matter of degree . . . Having regard to the nature
and extent of the cracks and the likelihood that the damage would be progressive, I

a would adjudge that there was an imminent danger to the safety of the occupiers of all five houses.'

In that case there was no doubt that damage was going to occur at some stage unless remedial underpinning was done. Here, once the weakness was detected in the eight pillars and warning was given, the danger was eliminated. It was not going to occur immediately, soon or at all.

b As to (b), the building could continue to be used as it had been in safety providing the load was not increased. The remedial works were done, therefore, not to avert otherwise inevitable danger, but to restore to the plaintiffs the full capacity of the building for which they bargained by their underlease. To allow recovery in tort if defective building makes remedial work necessary to avoid injury, but not if it is necessary only to render the building fit for its intended use, may seem a dismal distinction to an aggrieved occupier. But it is a necessary distinction if, as at present, the law declines to allow an action in tort equivalent to the enforcement in contract of a warranty of fitness.

c In my judgment therefore, on the facts of this case, counsel for the plaintiffs is unable to bring his claim within the proposition on which he relies. For these reasons, which differ slightly from those of the trial judge, I would agree with him that the plaintiffs have failed to establish a cause of action in tort against the defendants.

d Counsel for the defendants, to whose lucid argument I pay tribute, submitted in support of his cross-appeal that even if there were a cause of action it was statute-barred. In view of the conclusion I have reached on the main issue, it is unnecessary to consider this issue raised by the defendants' notice. I would dismiss this appeal.

NICHOLLS LJ. This appeal is concerned with an area of the law which is currently in a state of considerable uncertainty. In *D & F Estates Ltd v Church Comrs for England* [1988] e 2 All ER 992 at 1002, 1011, [1988] 3 WLR 368 at 380, 392 both Lord Bridge and Lord Oliver noted that the observations made in *Anns v Merton London Borough* [1977] 2 All ER 492, [1978] AC 728 regarding the liability of the builder for the common law tort of negligence were obiter. Both of them evinced concern, for reasons stated by them and which I would respectfully echo, regarding the rationale and ambit of this head of f liability. Neither of them, however, expressed any concluded view. Furthermore both Lord Bridge and Lord Oliver doubted the correctness of the decision of this court in *Batty v Metropolitan Property Realizations Ltd* [1978] 2 All ER 445, [1978] QB 554 so far as it related to the liability of the builder (see [1988] 2 All ER 992 at 1002, 1006, 1014, [1988] 3 WLR 368 at 381, 386, 395). The House of Lords, however, did not overrule that decision.

g For my part I have difficulty in distinguishing the present case from *Batty*'s case. There, the builder's negligence consisted of failing to appreciate the unsuitability of the site. At the time the action was heard the house, as distinct from the garden, had not yet suffered any physical damage such as cracking. Likewise in the present case, no physical damage was sustained by the building as a result of the defectively-prepared cement used in the structural pillars. If, therefore, *Batty*'s case was wrongly decided as to the builder, and the h builder was under no liability in negligence in that case even though the house was doomed, it must surely follow that the builders were under no liability in negligence in the present case. I cannot see that the different form which the builders' negligence took in the two cases represents an acceptable ground of distinction.

In my view, however, this court is not required to decide what is the present status of the decision in *Batty*'s case, for the following reason. Let it be assumed, in favour of the j plaintiffs in the present action, that *Batty*'s case was correctly decided against the builder. Even so, in order to succeed the plaintiffs must, at the very least, show that the weakness in the concrete threatened the safety of occupants or users of the building. That is a question of fact. On that question the judge found that at no time did the weakness of the pillars give rise to 'imminent danger' to the health or safety either of the plaintiffs' employees or of the public. The occupants at all times enjoyed a satisfactory level of safety. He also found that the plaintiffs' purpose in strengthening the pillars early in 1985 was to cure a defect which otherwise prevented the plaintiffs from making use of *a* the building to the full extent for which it was designed.

In my view the effect of these findings is tolerably clear. Those who used the building were never in danger. Nor would users have been in danger if the existing manner of use of the tower block had continued without any strengthening of the pillars. Danger would have arisen if, but only if, the loading of the building had been increased up to its design capacity. It there were any doubt that this is what the judge meant, the doubt *b* would be removed by a later passage in his judgment where the judge said that 'there was no injury threatened by the mere use of the tower block: rather there was a restriction on the full extent of future use'.

In fact, as the judge also found, the plaintiffs always enjoyed substantial and effective use of the tower block after taking occupation in 1972. Precisely what were the activities likely to be undertaken in this office block in the future which could not have been *c* pursued safely without strengthening of the pillars was not a matter explored by the judge, beyond a reference by him to a passage in the report of Mr Heggie, the plaintiffs' expert, which mentions the 'build-up of loading . . . (e.g. new filing room)'. Given the extent to which the plaintiffs enjoyed and, more importantly, could have continued to enjoy this office block without danger, I do not think that the defective pillars can be said to have given rise to a danger, imminent or otherwise, to the safety of the occupants. *d* True, the pillars could not safely support the design load. But the claim in this action against the contractors is in negligence, not in contract. If, despite inability to support the design load, the building was fit for the purpose for which it would normally be used, viz as offices, then the claim in negligence must fail. In my view the judge's findings of fact are fatal to the plaintiffs' claim. Apart from any other difficulties confronting the plaintiffs in this action, their claim must fail on this narrow point. *e*

I add only one further comment. One of the arguments advanced by counsel for the defendants concerned limitation. He submitted that if the plaintiffs had a cause of action in this case it arose when the building was handed over, in which event the plaintiffs' claim was time-barred long before the writ was issued in October 1982. He pointed out that there was no physical damage to the building. He submitted that the cause of action *f* could not have accrued when the plaintiffs discovered the defect, because that would be contrary to the decision in *Pirelli General Cable Works Ltd v Oscar Faber & Partners (a firm)* [1983] 1 All ER 65, [1983] 2 AC 1. Nor, he further submitted, could the cause of action have accrued when the plaintiffs incurred expenditure in remedying the defect in the pillars, because that would enable a plaintiff to postpone the actual accrual of the cause of action until such time as he might choose to carry out remedial works. This conundrum *g* does not need to be solved on this appeal; but it is another difficulty which will need to be faced when the correctness of the decision in *Batty's* case as against the builder falls to be decided.

O'CONNOR LJ. I have had the advantage of reading the judgment prepared by Taylor LJ and I agree that this appeal should be dismissed for the reasons given by him. I add a *h* few words of my own out of deference to the arguments addressed to us by counsel for the plaintiffs.

The facts have been set out in the judgment of Taylor LJ and I need not repeat them.

There is a formidable body of judicial opinion that no cause of action in tort arises against a party as a result of whose negligence a latent defect is present in a building, unless and until the building suffers some physical damage. As I pointed out in *London* *j* *Congregational Union Inc v Harriss & Harriss (a firm)* [1988] 1 All ER 15 at 35–37, numerous attempts have been made to produce a cause of action before damage founding on the speech of Lord Fraser in *Pirelli General Cable Works Ltd v Oscar Faber & Partners (a firm)* [1983] 1 All ER 65 at 70, [1983] 2 AC 1 at 16:

a   'There may perhaps be cases where the defect is so gross that the building is doomed from the start, and where the owner's cause of action will accrue as soon as it is built, but it seems unlikely that such a defect would not be discovered within the limitation period. Such cases, if they exist, would be exceptional.'

    In *Ketteman v Hansel Properties Ltd* [1988] 1 All ER 38 at 50–51, [1987] AC 189 at 205–206 Lord Keith finally disposed of the doomed from the start argument. He said:

b   'The architects' presentation of this argument involved two aspects. In the first place it was maintained that the plaintiffs' respective causes of action accrued, not when the physical damage to their houses occurred, but when they became the owners of houses with defective foundations. It was argued that they then suffered economic loss because the houses were less valuable than they would have been if the foundations had been sound. The proposition that a cause of action in tort

c accrued out of negligence resulting in pure economic loss was sought to be vouched by reference to *Junior Books Ltd v Veitchi Co Ltd* [1982] 3 All ER 201, [1983] 1 AC 520. That case was also cited in the *Pirelli* case [1983] 1 All ER 65, [1983] 2 AC 1 in support of the argument that, since in that case there was economic loss when the chimney was built, the cause of action arose then. The argument was clearly rejected in the speech of Lord Fraser concurred in by all the others of their Lordships who

d participated in the decision. He expressed the opinion that a latent defect in a building does not give rise to a cause of action until damage occurs (see [1983] 1 All ER 65 at 70, [1983] 2 AC 1 at 16). In the present case there can be no doubt that the defects in the houses were latent. No one knew of their existence until damage occurred in the summer of 1976. This branch of the argument for the architects is, in my opinion, inconsistent with the decision of the *Pirelli* case, and must be rejected.

e In the second branch of the argument it was maintained that a distinction fell to be drawn between the case where the defect in a building was such that damage must inevitably eventuate at some time and the case of a defect such that damage might or might not evenuate. The former case was that of a building "doomed from the start" such as was in the contemplation of Lord Fraser when he made reference to that concept in his dicta in the *Pirelli* case. In the present case the houses were

f doomed from the start because the event showed that damage was bound to occur eventually. My Lords, whatever Lord Fraser may have had in mind in uttering the dicta in question, it cannot, in my opinion, have been a building with a latent defect which must inevitably result in damage at some stage. That is precisely the kind of building that the *Pirelli* case was concerned with, and in relation to which it was held that the cause of action accrued when the damage occurred. This case is

g indistinguishable from the *Pirelli* case and must be decided similarly. The second branch of the architects' argument fails. I understand that all your Lordships agree.'

    Alongside this line of authority there has been a stream of authority where attempts have been made to recover economic loss arising from negligence in the construction of a building: *Simaan General Contracting Co v Pilkington Glass Ltd (No 2)* [1988] 1 All ER 791,

h [1988] QB 758, *Greater Nottingham Co-op Society Ltd v Cementation Piling and Foundations Ltd* [1988] 2 All ER 971, [1988] 3 WLR 396 and finally *D & F Estates Ltd v Church Comrs for England* [1988] 2 All ER 992, [1988] 3 WLR 368 in the House of Lords.

    Counsel for the plaintiffs attempted a Houdini escape from the chains by which they were bound. Armed with the approval given to it by Lord Bridge in the *D & F Estates* case he turned to two passages in the speech of Lord Brandon in *Junior Books Ltd v Veitch*

j *Co Ltd* [1982] 3 All ER 201 at 216–218, [1983] 1 AC 520 at 550–551:

       'My Lords, a good deal of the argument presented to your Lordships during the hearing of the appeal was directed to the question whether a person can recover, in an action founded on delict alone, purely pecuniary loss which is independent of any physical damage to persons or their property. If that were the question to be decided in the present case, I should have no hesitation in holding that, in principle *a* and depending on the facts of a particular case, purely pecuniary loss may be recoverable in an action founded on delict alone. Two examples can be given of such case. First, there is the type of a case where a person suffers purely pecuniary loss as a result of relying on another person's negligent misstatements: see *Hedley Byrne & Co Ltd v Heller & Partners Ltd* [1963] 2 All ER 575, [1964] AC 465. Second, *b* there may be a type of case where a person, who has a cause of action based on *Donoghue v Stevenson*, reasonably incurs pecuniary loss in order to prevent or mitigate imminent danger of damage to the persons or property exposed to that danger: see the dissenting judgment of Laskin J in the Canadian Supreme Court case of *Rivtow Marine Ltd v Washington Iron Works* [1974] SCR 1189, referred to with approval in the speech of Lord Wilberforce in *Anns v Merton London Borough* [1977] 2 All ER 492 at 505, [1978] AC 728 at 760 ... The first consideration is that, in *Donoghue v c Stevenson* itself and in all the numerous cases in which the principle of that decision has been applied to different but analogous factual situations, it has always been either stated expressly, or taken for granted, that an essential ingredient in the cause of action relied on was the existence of danger, or the threat of danger, of physical damage to persons or their property, excluding for this purpose the very piece of property from the defective condition of which such danger, or threat of danger, *d* arises. To dispense with that essential ingredient in a cause of action of the kind concerned in the present case would, in my view, involve a radicial departure from long-established authority.'

Counsel for the plaintiffs submitted that as soon as the defect in the pillars was discovered there was a 'threat' of danger of physical damage to persons sufficient to *e* produce 'an imminent danger' which justified the incurring of pecuniary loss.

I would reject this argument on two grounds: firstly, on the facts I do not think it right to say that there was any imminent danger of damage to persons; secondly, the eight pillars were 'the very piece of property from the defective condition of which' any threat of danger arose and were thus excluded by Lord Brandon.

Counsel for the plaintiffs submitted that to allow this claim would not be to transfer a *f* warranty of fitness from the sphere of contract to the sphere of tort, but properly be looked at as a warranty of safety which public policy might dictate as having a proper place in tort. This is an attractive argument, but I do not think that it can prevail in the face of the authorities.

I too would dismiss this appeal.

g

Appeal dismissed. Leave to appeal to the House of Lords granted.

Solicitors: *Treasury Solicitor*; *Tolhurst & Fisher*, Southend-on-Sea (for the defendants).

Raina Levy   Barrister.

W v Egdell and others

CHANCERY DIVISION
SCOTT J SITTING AS VICE-CHANCELLOR OF THE COUNTY PALATINE OF LANCASTER
22, 23, 24, 25, 28 NOVEMBER, 9 DECEMBER 1988

Medical practitioner – Doctor and patient – Disclosure of confidential information – Public interest – Doctor's duty to patient and to public – Disclosure of report on patient in public interest – Psychiatrist instructed by patient detained in secure hospital to prepare independent report on patient's mental condition – Psychiatrist disclosing report to hospital charged with patient's care and encouraging hospital to disclose report to public authorities responsible for making decisions about patient's future – Whether psychiatrist barred by duty of confidence owed to patient from disclosing contents of report – Whether duty of confidence subordinate to duty owed to public – Whether doctor's public duty requiring him to disclose report to public authorities responsible for patient's treatment and future – Mental Health Act 1983, s 71(2).

W, who had shot and killed five people and wounded two others, was detained as a patient in a secure hospital without limit of time as a potential threat to public safety. Ten years after he had been detained he applied to a mental health review tribunal to be discharged or transferred to a regional secure unit with a view to his eventual discharge. His solicitors instructed a consultant psychiatrist, E, to examine W and report on his mental condition with a view to using the report to support W's application to the tribunal. In his report E opposed W's transfer and recommended that further tests and treatment of W would be advisable, and drew attention to W's long-standing interest in firearms and explosives and the possibility that W might have a 'psychopathic deviant personality'. E sent the report to W's solicitors in the belief that it would be placed before the tribunal, but, in view of the contents of the report, W's solicitors withdrew his application. When E learnt that the application had been withdrawn and that neither the tribunal nor the hospital charged with W's clinical management had received a copy of his report he contacted the medical director of the hospital, who, having discussed the W's case with E, agreed that the hospital should receive a copy of the report in the interests of W's further treatment. As E had also stressed the importance of sending a copy of his report to the Home Secretary because of its relevance to the exercise of his discretionary power to refer W's case to a mental health review tribunal under s 71ᵃ of the Mental Health Act 1983, the hospital forwarded a copy to the Home Office and another copy to the Department of Health and Social Security. The Home Secretary, in turn, forwarded the report to the tribunal when referring W's case to them for consideration, as he was required to do every three years under s 71(2). When W discovered that the report had been disclosed he issued writs against E and also against the Secretary of State for Health, the Home Secretary, the hospital board and the mental health review tribunal seeking (i) an injunction to restrain the respective defendants from using or disclosing the report, (ii) delivery up of all copies of the report and (iii) damages against W, the Home Secretary and the hospital board for breach of the duty of confidence.

Held – The duty of confidence owed by a doctor to a patient detained in a secure hospital in the interest of public safety who had instructed him to prepare a report for the patient was subordinate to his public duty to disclose the results of his examination to the authorities responsible for the patient if, in his opinion, such disclosure was necessary to ensure that the authorities were fully informed about the patient's condition. Accordingly, the duty of confidence owed by E to W did not bar E from disclosing his report on W's mental condition to the hospital charged with W's clinical care, since it was relevant to his treatment, or to the Home Secretary and the mental health review tribunal, since

---

a   Section 71, so far as material, is set out at p 1093 f g, post

they needed to be fully informed about W's mental condition when making decisions
concerning his future. It followed that W's claims against E and the other defendants *a*
failed and would be dismissed (see p 1104 *d e h j*, p 1105 *b* to *g*, p 1108 *b*, p 1109 *c* and
p 1110 *c* to *g*, post).

Notes

For a medical practitioner's obligation to give evidence, see 30 Halsbury's Laws (4th edn)
para 19, and for cases on the subject, see 33 Digest (Reissue) 256, *2109–2111*.   *b*
    For the Mental Health Act 1983, s 71, see 28 Halsbury's Statutes (4th edn) 711.

Cases referred to in judgment

A-G v Guardian Newspapers Ltd (No 2) [1988] 3 All ER 545, [1988] 3 WLR 776, HL; *affg*
    [1988] 3 All ER 545, [1988] 2 WLR 805, CA.
Addis v Gramophone Co Ltd [1909] AC 488, [1908–10] All ER Rep 1, HL.   *c*
Bliss v South East Thames Regional Health Authority [1987] ICR 700, CA.
Cox v Philips Industries Ltd [1976] 3 All ER 161, [1976] 1 WLR 638.
Harmony Shipping Co SA v Davis [1979] 3 All ER 177, sub nom *Harmony Shipping Co SA v
    Saudi Europe Line Ltd* [1979] 1 WLR 1380, CA.
Heywood v Wellers [1976] 1 All ER 300, [1976] QB 446, [1976] 2 WLR 101, CA.
Hunter v Mann [1974] 2 All ER 414, [1974] QB 767, [1974] 2 WLR 742, DC.   *d*
Jarvis v Swans Tours Ltd [1973] 1 All ER 71, [1973] QB 233, [1973] 3 WLR 954, CA.
Parry-Jones v Law Society [1968] 1 All ER 177, [1969] 1 Ch 1, [1968] 2 WLR 397, CA.
R v King [1983] 1 All ER 929, [1983] 1 WLR 411, CA.
X v Y [1988] 2 All ER 648.

Cases also cited   *e*

AB v CD (1851) 14 D 177, Ct of Sess.
A-G v Associated Newspapers Group plc [1989] 1 All ER 604, DC.
Albert (Prince) v Strange (1849) 1 Mac & G 25, 41 ER 1171, LC.
Archer v Brown [1984] 2 All ER 267, [1985] QB 401.
Argyll (Margaret), Duchess of v Duke of Argyll [1965] 1 All ER 611, [1967] Ch 302.   *f*
Ashburton (Lord) v Pape [1913] 2 Ch 469, [1911–13] All ER Rep 708, CA.
Ashingdane v Secretary of State for Social Services [1980] CA Transcript 47.
Calcraft v Guest [1898] 1 QB 759, [1895–9] All ER Rep 346, CA.
Comfort Hotels Ltd v Wembley Stadium Ltd [1988] 3 All ER 53, [1988] 1 WLR 872.
D v National Society for the Prevention of Cruelty to Children [1977] 1 All ER 589, [1978] AC
    171, HL.   *g*
Distillers Co (Biochmicals) Ltd v Times Newspapers Ltd [1975] 1 All ER 41, [1975] QB 613.
Francome v Mirror Group Newspapers Ltd [1984] 2 All ER 408, [1984] 1 WLR 892, CA.
Fraser v Evans [1969] 1 All ER 8, [1969] 1 QB 349, CA.
Gartside v Outram (1856) 26 LJ Ch 113.
Hubbard v Vosper [1972] 1 All ER 1023, [1972] 2 QB 84, CA.
ITC Film Distributors Ltd v Video Exchange Ltd [1982] 2 All ER 241, [1982] Ch 431.   *h*
Lion Laboratories Ltd v Evans [1984] 2 All ER 417, [1985] QB 526, CA.
R v Board of Inland Revenue, ex p Goldberg [1988] 3 All ER 248, [1988] 3 WLR 522, DC.
R v Bracknell Justices, ex p Griffiths [1975] 2 All ER 881, [1976] AC 314, HL.
*R v Licensing Authority, ex p Smith Kline & French Laboratories Ltd (Generics (UK) Ltd
    intervening)* [1989] 1 All ER 175, [1988] 3 WLR 896, CA.
R v Statutory Visitors to St Lawrence's Hospital, Caterham, ex p Pritchard [1953] 2 All ER *j*
    766, [1953] 1 WLR 1158, DC.
R v Tompkins (1977) 67 Cr App R 181, CA.
R v Uljee [1982] 1 NZLR 561, NZ CA.
Saltman Engineering Co Ltd v Campbell Engineering Co Ltd (1948) [1963] 3 All ER 413, CA.
Schering Chemicals Ltd v Falkman Ltd [1981] 2 All ER 321, [1982] QB 1, CA.
Tarasoff v Regents of the University of California (1976) 17 Cal 3d 358, Cal SC.
W, Re [1970] 2 All ER 502, [1971] Ch 123.

a   *Waldron, Ex p* [1986] QB 824, CA.
     Waugh v British Rlys Board [1979] 2 All ER 1169, [1980] AC 521, HL.
     Weld-Blundell v Stephens [1919] 1 KB 520, CA; *affd* [1920] AC 956, [1920] All ER Rep 32,
        HL.
     White v Wilson (1806) 13 Ves 87, 33 ER 227, LC.
     Winch v Jones [1985] 3 All ER 97, [1986] QB 296, CA.
     X v UK (1981) 4 EHRR 188, E Ct HR.

b

Consolidated actions
W, a patient who had been detained in a secure hospital as a potential danger to public
safety, issued a writ on 22 December 1987 against Dr Henry George Egdell, an
independent psychiatrist whom W's solicitors had instructed to report on his mental
condition, seeking, inter alia, an injunction restraining Dr Egdell from disclosing the
c   contents of his report on W dated 29 July 1987, delivery up of all copies of the report and
damages for breach of the duty of confidentiality arising out of Dr Egdell's disclosure of
the report to the hospital charged with W's clinical management, copies of which were
then sent by the hospital to the Home Office and the Department of Health and Social
Security. On the same day as the writ was issued his Honour Judge O'Donoghue sitting
as a judge of the High Court granted an ex parte injunction restraining Dr Egdell from
d   any further disclosure of his report, which, by consent, was continued until trial. W
issued a second writ on 19 July 1988 against the Secretary of State for Social Services, the
Home Secretary, Moss Side and Park Lane Hospitals Board and the Mersey Mental Health
Review Tribunal, who had received a copy of the report when the Home Secretary
referred W's case to them for consideration under s 71(2) of the Mental Health Act 1983,
seeking an injunction to restrain the respective defendants from disclosing the contents
e   of Dr Egdell's report, delivery up of all copies of the report and, as against the Home
Secretary and the hospital board, damages for breach of the duty of confidentiality. W's
case against each defendant was based on the confidential nature of his interview with Dr
Egdell and of the report. On 27 July 1988 Scott J consolidated the actions and at the
beginning of the trial made an order under s 11 of the Contempt of Court Act 1981
prohibiting the publication of W's name. On 28 November 1988 the relevant functions
f   and liabilities of the Secretary of State for Social Services were transferred to the Secretary
of State for Health. The writs in the actions were issued out of the Liverpool District
Registry but the actions were heard and judgment was given in London. The facts are
set out in the judgment.

g   *Geoffrey Robertson QC* and *Nicholas Orr* for W.
     Kieran Coonan for Dr Egdell.
     John Laws and *Philip Havers* for the Secretary of State for Health, the Home Secretary and
        the hospital board.
     Nigel Pleming for the tribunal.

                                                                          Cur adv vult
h
     9 December. The following judgment was delivered.

     SCOTT J. This case has required an examination in an unusual context of the breadth
     of the duty of confidentiality owed by a doctor to his patient. The patient is the plaintiff,
     to whom I will refer as W. The first defendant, Dr Egdell, is the doctor. At the beginning
j   of the trial I made an order under s 11 of the Contempt of Court Act 1981 prohibiting
     the publication of the name of the plaintiff. I propose to continue that order. It may be
     that the details given in this judgment of the background to the case will enable those
     who are minded to do so to identify the plaintiff. That possibility is unfortunate but, in
     my view, unavoidable if this judgment is to be made public. No one has suggested it
     should not be made public.
         About ten years ago W shot the four members of a neighbouring family. He shot
     another neighbour who had come to investigate the shooting. He then drove off in his

car, throwing handmade bombs as he did so. Later the same day he shot two more
people, not neighbours, but strangers to him. Five of his victims died of their injuries.
The other two needed major surgery for serious bullet wounds. W was diagnosed as
suffering from paranoid schizophrenia. It was believed by the doctors who examined
him that he had been suffering from this illness for about two years before the offences.
The illness involved delusions that he was being persecuted by his neighbours. In the
circumstances W's plea of guilty to manslaughter on the grounds of diminished
responsibility was accepted by the Crown and he was convicted accordingly. Orders were
made under ss 60 and 65 of the Mental Health Act 1959, now ss 37 and 41 of the Mental
Health Act 1983, providing for his detention without limit of time. He was at first
detained at Broadmoor Hospital. In 1981 he was transferred, in accordance with a
transfer direction given by the Home Secretary, to a secure hospital in the north of
England. References hereafter in this judgment to 'the hospital' will be references to this
hospital where W is still detained.

I must describe in some detail the statutory scheme under which W, and persons like
him, are detained. Section 37 of the 1983 Act enables a hospital order to be made if, inter
alia, 'the court is satisfied ... that the offender is suffering from mental illness,
psychopathic disorder, severe mental impairment or mental impairment' (see s 37(2)(a)).
Section 41(1) provides:

> 'Where a hospital order is made in respect of an offender by the Crown Court,
> and it appears to the court, having regard to the nature of the offence, the antecedents
> of the offender and the risk of his committing further offences if set at large, that it
> is necessary for the protection of the public from serious harm so to do, the court
> may, subject to the provisions of this section, further order that the offender shall be
> subject to the special restrictions set out in this section, either without limit of time
> or during such period as may be specified in the order; and an order under this
> section shall be known as "a restriction order".'

Section 41(3) sets out the restrictions that apply to a person subject to a restriction
order. These include the requirement that the transfer of the patient to another hospital
can only be carried out with the consent of the Home Secretary (see sub-s (3)(c)(ii)). W is
subject to a hospital order and a restriction order; both orders were made by the Crown
Court on his conviction. Section 41(6) provides:

> 'While a person is subject to a restriction order the responsible medical officer
> shall at such intervals (not exceeding one year) as the Secretary of State may direct
> examine and report to the Secretary of State on that person; and every report shall
> contain such particulars as the Secretary of State may require.'

The responsible medical officer is the registered medical practitioner in charge of the
patient (see s 55(1)). The Secretary of State referred to in sub-s (6) is the Home Secretary.

From March 1984 to January 1988 W's responsible medical officer was Dr Ghosh. Dr
Ghosh was transferred to Broadmoor Hospital in January 1988. Since then W's responsible
medical officer has been Dr Coorey. Both Dr Ghosh and Dr Coorey are consultant
psychiatrists.

The Home Secretary has extensive powers over, and in connection with, persons
subject to restriction orders. These powers are set out in s 42 of the 1983 Act. There is
power under sub-s (1) to direct that the special restrictions set out in s 41(3) shall cease to
apply to the patient. The power is exercisable if the Home Secretary 'is satisfied that . . . a
restriction order is no longer required for the protection of the public from serious harm'.
Under sub-s (2) the Home Secretary may, either absolutely or subject to conditions,
discharge the patient from the secure hospital where he is held. And sub-s (3) gives power
to the Home Secretary to recall a patient who has been conditionally discharged under
sub-s (2).

These statutory powers are discretionary powers and the Home Secretary is, in the
a exercise of his discretion, the guardian of the public interest. It is easy to conclude that
the safety and protection of members of the public will be in the forefront of the Home
Secretary's mind when contemplating the exercise of any of these discretions. And it
may reasonably be expected that the Home Secretary will expect to be kept informed of
all relevant matters and views concerning the patient in question. The contents of the
patient's hospital file, including the reports from time to time submitted pursuant to
b s 41(6) and also the patient's case notes, will be available to the Home Secretary.

A patient subject to a restriction order has an alternative avenue by means of which to
seek to be relieved from the restrictions imposed by the order. The Mental Health Act
1959 provided for the setting up of mental health review tribunals to review the cases of
patients detained under the provisions of the Act. The system was continued by the 1983
Act (see s 65). Four such tribunals have been established. The Mersey Mental Health
c Review Tribunal covers the area in which the hospital is situated. The constitution of
mental health review tribunals is provided for in Sch 2 to the 1983 Act. The members
are nominated by the Lord Chancellor, who also appoints a chairman. The members
who constitute the tribunal for the purposes of a particular case will usually be three in
number and will be nominated by the chairman. One will be a lawyer, another will have
a medical, usually a psychiatric, qualification. The procedure of tribunals is provided for
d in the Mental Health Review Tribunal Rules 1983, SI 1983/942, made pursuant to s 78
of the 1983 Act.

I must read some of the provisions of the 1983 Act that relate to applications by or in
respect of patients subject to restriction orders. Section 70 provides:

'A patient who is a restricted patient . . . and is detained in a hospital may apply
e to a Mental Health Review Tribunal—(*a*) in the period between the expiration of
six months and the expiration of 12 months beginning with the date of the relevant
hospital order or transfer direction; and (*b*) in any subsequent period of 12 months.'

Section 71 provides, so far as material:

'(1) The Secretary of State may at any time refer the case of a restricted patient to
f a Mental Health Review Tribunal.
(2) The Secretary of State shall refer to a Mental Health Review Tribunal the case
of any restricted patient detained in a hospital whose case has not been considered
by such a tribunal, whether on his own application or otherwise, within the last
three years . . .
(6) For the purposes of subsection (5) above a person who applies to a tribunal
g but subsequently withdraws his application shall be treated as not having exercised
his right to apply, and where a patient withdraws his application on a date after the
expiration of the period there mentioned the Secretary of State shall refer his case as
soon as possible after that date.'

Section 72(1) provides:

h
'Where application is made to a Mental Health Review Tribunal by or in respect
of a patient who is liable to be detained under this Act, the tribunal may in any case
direct that the patient be discharged, and . . . (*b*) the tribunal shall direct the discharge
of a patient liable to be detained . . . if they are satisfied—(i) that he is not then
suffering from mental illness, psychopathic disorder, severe mental impairment or
j mental impairment or from any of those forms of disorder of a nature or degree
which makes it appropriate for him to be liable to be detained in a hospital for
medical treatment; or (ii) that it is not necessary for the health or safety of the
patient or for the protection of other persons that he should receive such treatment
. . .'

Section 73 provides:

'(1) Where an application to a Mental Health Review Tribunal is made by a *a* restricted patient who is subject to a restriction order, or where the case of such a patient is referred to such a tribunal, the tribunal shall direct the absolute discharge of the patient if satisfied—(*a*) as to the matters mentioned in paragraph (*b*)(i) or (ii) of section 72(1) above; and (*b*) that it is not appropriate for the patient to remain liable to be recalled to hospital for further treatment.

(2) Where in the case of any such patient as is mentioned in subsection (1) above *b* the tribunal are satisfied as to the matters referred to in paragraph (*a*) of that subsection but not as to the matter referred to in paragraph (*b*) of that subsection the tribunal shall direct the conditional discharge of the patient.

(3) Where a patient is absolutely discharged under this section he shall thereupon cease to be liable to be detained by virtue of the relevant hospital order, and the *c* restriction order shall cease to have effect accordingly . . .'

The effect of these statutory provisions in relation to a patient subject to a restriction order is that a tribunal has, strictly, three courses open to it on a review of the patient's case. The tribunal can make no order. It can direct the absolute discharge of the patient. Or it can direct the conditional discharge of the patient. The tribunal is obliged to direct the discharge of the patient, absolutely or conditionally as the case may be, if it is satisfied *d* that the statutory criteria have been established. In cases where a tribunal is not so satisfied and, therefore, does not direct the discharge of the patient, it has become a common practice for the tribunal to make recommendations in relation to the patient. These recommendations do not have binding force.

I should refer also to s 76. Subsection (1) provides as follows:

'For the purpose of advising whether an application to a Mental Health Review Tribunal should be made by or in respect of a patient who is liable to be detained . . . or of furnishing information as to the condition of a patient for the purposes of such an application, any registered medical practitioner authorised by or on behalf of the patient or other person who is entitled to make or has made the application— (*a*) may at any reasonable time visit the patient and examine him in private, and (*b*) *f* may require the production of and inspect any records relating to the detention or treatment of the patient in any hospital.'

Rule 6 of the 1983 rules provides as follows:

'(1) The responsible authority shall send a statement to the tribunal and, in the case of a restricted patient, the Secretary of State, as soon as practicable and in any *g* case within 3 weeks of its receipt of the notice of application; and such statement shall contain—(*a*) the information specified in Part A of Schedule 1 to these Rules, in so far as it is within the knowledge of the responsible authority; and (*b*) the report specified in paragraph 1 of Part B of that Schedule; and (*c*) the other reports specified in Part B of that Schedule, in so far as it is reasonably practicable to provide them.

(2) Where the patient is a restricted patient, the Secretary of State shall send to *h* the tribunal, as soon as practicable and in any case within 3 weeks of receipt by him of the authority's statement, a statement of such further information relevant to the application as may be available to him . . .

(4) Any part of the authority's statement or the Secretary of State's statement which, in the opinion of—(*a*) (in the case of the authority's statement) the responsible authority; or (*b*) (in the case of the Secretary of State's statement) the Secretary of *j* State, should be withheld from the applicant or (where he is not the applicant) the patient on the ground that its disclosure would adversely affect the health or welfare of the patient or others, shall be made in a separate document in which shall be set out the reasons for believing that its disclosure would have that effect.

(5) On receipt of any statement provided in accordance with paragraph (1), (2) or (3), the tribunal shall send a copy to the applicant and (where he is not the applicant)

a   the patient, excluding any part of any statement which is contained in a separate
document in accordance with paragraph (4).'

I need not read the rest of r 6. The reference in r 6 to the 'responsible authority' is a
reference to the Secretary of State for Health (see r 2, s 145 of the 1983 Act and s 4 of the
National Health Service Act 1977). The reference to the Secretary of State is in the rules,
as in the 1983 Act, a reference to the Home Secretary.

b   Under Pt A of Sch 1 to the 1983 rules basic information regarding the patient and his
history must be given. Under Pt B the following information is required to be given:

'1. An up-to-date medical report, prepared for the tribunal, including the relevant
medical history and a full report on the patient's mental condition.

2. An up-to-date social circumstances report prepared for the tribunal including
reports on the following—(a) the patient's home and family circumstances, including
c   the attitude of the patient's nearest relative or the person so acting; (b) the
opportunities for employment or occupation and the housing facilities which would
be available to the patient if discharged; (c) the availability of community support
and relevant medical facilities; (d) the financial circumstances of the patient.

3. The views of the authority on the suitability of the patient for discharge.

4. Any other information or observations on the application which the authority
d   wishes to make.'

It is to be noted that the obligations imposed on the Secretary of State for Health under
r 6(1) and on the Home Secretary under r 6(2) to provide the tribunal with information
are mandatory statutory obligations.

It is important also to notice that the nature of a hearing before a mental health review
e   tribunal is inquisitorial, not adversarial. This appears particularly from the following
rules in the 1983 rules:

'*Medical examination*

11. At any time before the hearing of the application, the medical member or,
where the tribunal includes more than one, at least one of them shall examine the
f   patient and take such other steps as he considers necessary to form an opinion of the
patient's mental condition; and for this purpose the patient may be seen in private
and all his medical records may be examined by the medical member, who may
take such notes and copies of them as he may require, for use in connection with
the application. . .

g   *Evidence*

14.—(1) For the purpose of obtaining information, the tribunal may take evidence
on oath and subpoena any witness to appear before it or to produce documents, and
the president of the tribunal shall have the powers of an arbitrator under section
12(3) of the Arbitration Act 1950 . . . but no person shall be compelled to give any
evidence or produce any document which he could not be compelled to give or
h   produce on the trial of an action.

(2) The tribunal may receive in evidence any document or information
notwithstanding that such document or information would be inadmissible in a
court of law.

Further information

j   15.—(1) Before or during any hearing the tribunal may call for such further
information or reports as it may think desirable, and may give directions as to the
manner in which and the persons by whom such material is to be furnished . . .

Hearing procedure

22 . . . (2) At any time before the application is determined, the tribunal or any
one or more of its members may interview the patient, and shall interview him if

he so requests, and the interview may, and shall if the patient so requests, take place in the absence of any other person . . .'

There are therefore, two avenues by means of which a patient subject to a restriction order may seek to be discharged. He can apply to the Home Secretary and rely on the Home Secretary's discretionary powers. Or he may apply to a tribunal and endeavour to satisfy the statutory criteria which, if satisfied, will oblige the tribunal to order his discharge, either absolutely or conditionally.

Having described the statutory scheme regulating the detention of persons such as W, I must now turn to outline the history of W's detention at the hospital.

[His Lordship then described the history of W's detention at the hospital and stated that in 1987 the Home Secretary had refused to accept a recommendation by Dr Ghosh that W be transferred to a regional secure unit. His Lordship continued:] In the face of the Home Secretary's unwillingness to accept Dr Ghosh's recommendation for a transfer to a regional secure unit, W decided to pursue the alternative avenue, namely, to make an application to the mental health review tribunal. The gist of Dr Ghosh's reports had been that W's offences were attributable to the paranoid schizophrenia from which he had been suffering at the time, that he had been cured of that illness and that, provided he remained on suitable medication, he no longer represented a danger to the public. In the light of these reports W was hoping to obtain from the tribunal a conditional discharge. So, on 1 April 1987, W's then solicitors, Messrs E Rex Makin & Co, sent to the tribunal W's application for a review of his case. The tribunal notified the Department of Health and Social Security (the DHSS) and the Home Office of the application (see r 4 of the 1983 rules).

On 2 April 1987 W was granted legal aid for the purposes of his application. The legal aid certificate authorised 'an application to the Mental Health Review Tribunal under the Mental Health Act 1983 and to include an independent Psychiatric Report . . .'

The statement required by r 6(1) to be sent by the Secretary of State for Health to the tribunal was made by Dr Ghosh and dated 19 May 1987. The statement said:

'[W] has been diagnosed as suffering from schizophrenia. His mental illness is now controlled by medication and he has been stable for the past 5 years. He has considerable insight into his mental state and accepts the need for continuing on medication. He also realises that he requires close and careful monitoring of his mental state. It is my opinion that [W] requires to move gradually through graded security with maximum and intermediate supervision being available in the early stages. [W] was recommended for transfer on 20 March 1985. He has been accepted by Doctor R Cope for the Birmingham Secure Unit at Barnsley Hall Hospital on 20 June 1986. His previous Mental Health Review Tribunal supported a recommendation of transfer to a Regional Secure Unit. We are still awaiting Home Office permission for such a move.'

A copy of this statement was provided to W and his solicitors.

The Home Office's statement, made pursuant to r 6(2), was dated June 1987. It, too, was disclosed to W and his solicitors. The statement set out the circumstances of W's offences, referred to Dr Ghosh's statement of 19 May 1987 and reiterated the Home Secretary's refusal to consent to W's transfer to a regional secure unit. The penultimate sentence of the Home Office statement said:

'Furthermore, [the Home Secretary] would feel more confident towards [W's] removal from conditions of maximum security when his interest in weapons has been more fully explored and explained and he would be prepared to consider the case for [W] to move to a secure unit in perhaps 18 months' time in the light of these findings.'

Notwithstanding that authority for an independent psychiatric report had been given by the legal aid certificate of 2 April 1987, the report was not bespoken until after W and

his solicitors had seen both Dr Ghosh's statement of 19 May 1987 and the Home Office's
statement of June 1987.

a

The independent psychiatrist instructed to give the report was Dr Egdell. He is a
distinguished consultant psychiatrist and a member of the Mersey Mental Health Review
Tribunal. His instructions were contained in a letter dated 2 July 1987 from E Rex
Makin & Co. The first paragraph of the letter asked Dr Egdell to 'attend upon our client
and complete a report for use at his forthcoming Mental Health Review Tribunal'. For

b the purposes of the report Dr Egdell reviewed the case records held at the hospital. These
included the reports to which I have already referred and no doubt others as well. He
had discussions about the case with Dr Ghosh. He had brief interviews with some of the
nurses at the hospital. And on 23 July he had a long interview with W himself. Based on
this material he made a ten-page report dated 29 July 1987. The report contained two
main sections. The first section summarised the information about W that Dr Egdell had

c obtained from the sources I have mentioned. The contents are set out under various
subheadings: personal background; work and interests; interest in guns; interest in
'fireworks'; alcohol history; attitude to medication; attitude to the victims and relatives
in the index offence; reports of nursing staff; attitude to future problems. The subheading
'Interest in "fireworks"' is of particular importance partly because the preparation and
use by W of homemade bombs had been part of the index offence and also because,

d although some reference to W's interest in explosives is to be found in the records on file
at the hospital, Dr Ghosh had not dealt with this aspect of W's history in any of her
reports. The information given by W to Dr Egdell and recorded under this subheading
seems, at least in its detail, not to have been previously disclosed. The references in
previous reports to W's interests in bombs and explosives had been cursory, lacking in
detail and had not indicated anything unusual that predated the onset of the mental

e illness from which W was suffering when the index offences were committed. Dr
Egdell's report on the other hand, records a long-standing interest by W in making what
W seems euphemistically to have described as 'fireworks'. These so-called fireworks
included sections of steel piping packed with explosive chemicals. The subsection under
the heading 'Interest in Guns' contains considerable detail of W's long-standing interest
in guns. This interest had, unlike W's interest in explosives, been well documented in

f previous reports on W made by others.

The second section of Dr Egdell's report is headed 'Psychiatric Opinion and
Recommendation'. This too is divided into subsections. Under the subheading 'Illness'
Dr Egdell agreed that at the time of the index offences W was suffering from a mental
illness, but Dr Egdell referred to the possibility, first raised by Dr Boyd, an independent
psychiatrist engaged by W, in a report dated 30 July 1984, that the illness might be a

g paranoid psychosis rather than paranoid schizophrenia. The relevance of the distinction,
according to Dr Egdell, was that medication would be less effective in the former case
than in the latter in protecting against a relapse. In the second paragraph under this
subheading Dr Egdell said: 'I was not convinced that he really had insight into his illness
. . .' This paragraph is in disagreement with the first paragraph of Dr Ghosh's statement
of 19 May 1987.

h

Under the subheading 'Personality' Dr Egdell said:

'He has difficulty accepting or even listening to the views of others and would not
even consider psychological treatment to explore or influence his former interest in
fire-arms and explosives.'

j This conclusion is obviously relevant to the recommendation in the report of 18 April
1986 prepared by Dr Tulloch, who wrote his report after having seven sessions with W
at the request of Dr Cope, the consultant forensic psychiatrist at Barnsley Hall Hospital.
Later under the same subheading Dr Egdell said:

'My overall opinion would be that [W] has a clearly abnormal personality,
particularly in regard to his relationships, to the management of his feelings and

dealing with frustration and an unwillingness to look at his own personal problems *a*
in the past and in the future and to review the motivation lying behind the killings.
I am reluctant at this stage to say that [W] suffers from a psychopathic personality,
as my contacts with him were confined to one interview, and [there is] also the
report of the clinical psychologist, Mr. R Tulloch of 18th April 1986. There does
seem to be a serious conflict between the findings of Mr. Tulloch and my overall
impression culled from various sources. I think it would be important for this
conflict to be resolved before a decision is made on [W's] departure from [the *b*
hospital].'

This passage seems to me important. It reflects the possibility that underlying the mental
illness from which W was suffering at the time of the index offences, there might be a
psychopathic deviant personality.

Under the subheading 'Attitude to fire-arms' Dr Egdell expressed this opinion: *c*

'. . . his interests in guns was profound, very prolonged and, in the last years
before the offence, clearly abnormal. In discussions with him of his current interests
I found him totally unconvincing that he had in the past a passing interest in guns
which has no relevance for the future.'

Under the subheading 'Home made bombs' Dr Egdell said: *d*

'My view would be that this all points to a seriously abnormal interest in the
making of home made bombs. He euphemistically calls them "fireworks". They are
clearly much more dangerous than that.'

Finally, under the subheading 'Fitness for transfer to a Regional Secure Unit' Dr Egdell
said: *e*

'In my view this should be considered after there has been clarification of [W's]
personality as recommended above, as well as further exploration of [W's] interests
in guns and explosives . . . In summary, I would strongly recommend that [W] is
not considered for transfer to an RSU until the above recommendations are fulfilled.
Even when these are completed there may be indications for further prolonged stay *f*
under the present secure conditions.'

In the first paragraph under the last subheading Dr Egdell expressed views about
regional secure units that Dr Kay, an experienced forensic psychiatrist, in his affidavit,
sworn on 16 November 1988, has disputed. Dr Kay has considerable experience of
regional secure units and Dr Egdell, having read Dr Kay's affidavit, has deferred to that
experience. Dr Egdell's misgivings about the suitability of the transfer of W to a regional *g*
secure unit have, therefore, to some extent been shown to be unfounded.

There are several important features of Dr Egdell's report for present purposes. First,
it opposed Dr Ghosh's recommendation for a transfer to a regional secure unit. Second,
it expressed reservations about, if not disagreement with, Dr Ghosh's opinion that W,
now that his schizophrenic illness was cured or under control, was no longer a danger to *h*
the public. Third, it explored in greater detail than any other report the significance of
W's interests in explosives.

Dr Egdell sent his report to W's solicitors. It was his belief when he did so that the
report would be placed before the tribunal at the forthcoming hearing. That belief was
justified by the opening paragraph of the letter of 7 July 1987, as well as by a letter dated
6 July 1987 from W's solicitors advising Dr Egdell that the tribunal would sit on 25 *j*
August 1987 and adding: 'We shall be pleased to see your report not less than two weeks
before that date.'

Counsel for W argued that Dr Egdell was not entitled to have assumed that his report
would be placed before the tribunal. The report was, he suggested, intended simply for
the assistance of W and his solicitors. I agree that it was open to W and his solicitors,

having received the report, to decide not to use it. But Dr Egdell was, in my view, when
a he examined W, wrote his report and sent it to W's solicitors, reasonable in assuming
that the report would be placed before the tribunal. It was, according to his letter of
instructions, for that purpose that the report had been bespoken.

By a letter dated 18 August 1987, received by the tribunal on 19 August, W's solicitors
withdrew his application to the tribunal. This was done in view of the contents of Dr
Egdell's report. On the same day, 19 August, Dr Egdell telephoned the tribunal to ask
b whether the tribunal had received a copy of his report. Dr Egdell was informed by the
tribunal that a copy of his report had not been received and that W's application had been
withdrawn.

Dr Egdell knew from a telephone conversation he had had with Dr Ghosh on a date
between 24 and 27 July 1987, ie after his interview with W on 23 July, that his views
regarding W were not accepted by Dr Ghosh (see para 4 of Dr Egdell's fourth affidavit).
c So, after learning that W's application to the tribunal had been withdrawn and that a
copy of his report was not on W's file at the hospital, Dr Egdell telephoned Dr Hunter,
the acting medical director at the hospital.

I can best explain how matters proceeded by reference to passages from the evidence.
In para 4 of his affidavit sworn on 1 October 1988 Dr Egdell said:

d 'On learning that my report was not available to the Mental Health Review
Tribunal I telephoned Dr Hunter at [the hospital] for advice in this matter. This was
the first occasion on which I spoke to Dr Hunter about this patient. I explained my
concern that my views were so different from those expressed by Dr Ghosh (W's
Responsible Medical Officer) and also my belief that two important matters relating
to W's interests in firearms and explosives had not been properly explored or even
e appreciated. Dr Hunter indicated that additional information about his patient was
always helpful and indeed welcome. He asked me to contact W's solicitors as a
matter of courtesy to see if they would agree to disclosure of my report of 29th July
to Dr Hunter. They declined to agree.'

Dr Egdell's terse 'They declined to agree' is amplified by para 9 of the affidavit of Mr
f Ronald, W's solicitor, sworn on 5 September 1988. Mr Ronald said:

'Following the 19th August and prior to the 24th August the First Defendant
[that is Dr Egdell] telephoned Mr Brian Canavan to discuss the Plaintiff's case. In
the course of this conversation he was advised that the tribunal application had been
withdrawn and he queried what would happen to his report. It was explained to
him by Mr Canavan that his reports would be on their files and would not be drawn
g to anyone's attention. The First Defendant expressed a wish that the reports be
forwarded to [the hospital] so that they were aware of his findings, however, Mr
Canavan declined to do this in view of the clear instructions that he had received
from the Plaintiff.'

What passed between Dr Egdell and Dr Hunter in their telephone conversation on 24
h August 1987 is set out in a letter dated 25 April 1988 written by Dr Hunter to Messrs
Irwin Mitchell, W's present solicitors. The letter said:

'Dr Egdell expressed the view that the material which he felt had been revealed
from his examination cast a new light upon the patient's dangerousness and ought
to be known to those responsible for his care and for the formulation of any
recommendations for discharge. During this conversation I asked Dr Egdell to
j forward to me a report in writing of his concerns about the patient and this report
to me, dated 25 August 1987, was received in the hospital shortly thereafter.'

Following that telephone conversation and in accordance with Dr Hunter's request,
recorded by Dr Hunter in his letter, Dr Egdell sent Dr Hunter a report dated 25 August
1987. Dr Egdell substituted the name and address of Dr Hunter for the name and address

of E Rex Makin & Co, and he altered the opening paragraph so as to read: 'The following report is provided at your formal verbal request to me on the 24th August 1987.' That apart, the report sent to Dr Hunter was identical with that dated 19 July 1987 that had been sent to W's solicitors.

It was Dr Egdell's opinion that a copy of his report ought also to be supplied to the Home Office. Dr Egdell pressed this opinion on Dr Hunter and on 18 November 1987 wrote to Dr Hunter in these terms:

'I am sorry I have not yet received formal confirmation from you that the report prepared on [W] dated the 29th July 1987 has been made available in his case notes. I regret to have to say this but without this I shall feel obliged to send a copy directly to the Home Office. I would prefer to avoid this.'

By letter dated 20 November 1987, signed by Dr Ghosh, Dr Egdell was informed that 'a copy of your report on the above patient was forwarded to the Home Office and a further copy is on our case notes'.

Consistently with that a copy of the report was received by the Home Office on 25 November 1987. On the same day a copy was received at the DHSS. There seems to be some mystery as to by whom, or on whose authority, these copies were sent. I do not, however, think that the mystery is one that needs to be solved. There is no doubt that the Home Office and the DHSS did receive copies, nor that the copies were sent by someone at the hospital, nor that this was in accordance, at least so far as the Home Office is concerned (and nothing turns on the fact that a copy was sent to the DHSS), with Dr Egdell's expressed wishes.

Another significant event took place on 25 November 1987. The Home Secretary referred W's case to the Mersey Mental Health Review Tribunal under s 71(2) of the 1983 Act. He was obliged to do so because W's case had not been before the tribunal within the last three years.

On 10 December 1987 the tribunal informed W and the hospital of this referral of W's case. A statement pursuant to r 6(1) was requested of the hospital.

The news of the referral of W's case to the tribunal seems to have prompted Dr Ghosh to communicate with W's solicitors and express misgivings about the use that might be made of Dr Egdell's report. But the solicitors were not told by Dr Ghosh that the Home Office already had a copy of the report. They were told that a copy was held by the hospital and that Dr Egdell was pressing for a copy to be sent to the Home Office. This information prompted the issue of a writ against Dr Egdell. The writ sought an injunction in these terms:

'An injunction restraining the Defendant whether by himself, his servants or agents or otherwise from communicating the contents of a report dated 29th July 1987, made by the Defendant concerning the Plaintiff or any other further report whether written or oral, prepared by the Defendant concerning the Plaintiff, to any person or persons and further from expressing any opinion whether written or oral concerning the Plaintiff to any person or persons.'

Paragraph 2 of the prayer sought delivery up of any copies of the report held by Dr Egdell and para 3 claimed damages for breach by Dr Egdell of his duty of confidentiality. On the same day his Honour Judge O'Donoghue sitting as a judge of the High Court granted an ex parte injunction restraining Dr Egdell from communicating to anyone the contents of the report. The ex parte injunction was by consent continued until trial.

[His Lordship described the events which followed the referral of W's case to the tribunal and continued:] There is a reference in the minutes of a case conference on W, which was held at the hospital on 23 June 1988, to the possibility that a court order requiring copies of Dr Egdell's report to be removed from W's file might be sought by W against, presumably, the hospital. This possibility became a reality with the issue, on 19 July 1988, of a second writ, this time accompanied by a statement of claim. W was again the plaintiff. The defendants were the Secretary of State for Health, the Home

a Secretary, Moss Side and Park Lane Hospitals Board and the Mersey Mental Health Review Tribunal. The main relief sought was an injunction to restrain the respective defendants from using or disclosing to anyone Dr Egdell's report. Delivery up of all copies of the report was sought. Damages, including aggravated damages, for breach of the duty of confidentiality were sought against the Home Secretary and the hospital board.

b On 19 July 1988 the statement of claim in the first action, the action against Dr Egdell, was served. On 27 July 1988 I made an order consolidating the two actions. It was at some stage, perhaps on 27 July, agreed that further pleadings would be dispensed with and that evidence would be given by affidavit. There have been a number of deponents. No cross-examination has been requested. These steps have enabled the action to come on for trial very quickly. The pending review by the tribunal of W's case has been

c adjourned sine die until the conclusion of the litigation.

The basis of W's case is that his interview with Dr Egdell on 23 July 1987 and the report written by Dr Egdell on the basis of that interview is, or ought to have been, protected from disclosure by the duty of confidence resting on Dr Egdell as W's doctor. It is claimed that Dr Egdell was in breach of his duty of confidence in telling Dr Hunter about the report, in sending a copy of the report to Dr Hunter and in urging the despatch

d of a copy to the Home Office. The hospital, represented by the hospital board (the fourth defendant), ought, it is contended, to have recognised the confidential character of the report, that it came under a duty not to disclose it and that it broke that duty by sending a copy to the Home Office. The Home Office likewise came under a duty to respect the confidential character of the report and broke that duty by sending a copy thereof to the tribunal. The claim against the Secretary of State for Health and against the tribunal is

e for an order that each be required to deliver up or destroy the copies of the report that each holds.

The case against each defendant is therefore based on the confidential character, first, of the communication between W and Dr Egdell on 23 July 1987 and, second, of Dr Egdell's report. The doctor/patient relationship is relied on. The cases against the

f respective defendants are not, however, identical. The breadth and nature of the duty of confidence, if any, that affects each defendant must be separately assessed. In *A-G v Guardian Newspapers Ltd (No 2)* [1988] 3 All ER 545 at 600, [1988] 2 WLR 805 at 873 (the *Spycatcher* case) in the Court of Appeal Sir John Donaldson MR said:

'In an earlier passage in his judgment Scott J had considered whether the duty to maintain confidentiality was in all circumstances the same in relation to third parties

g who became possessed of confidential information as it was in relation to the primary confidant ... His conclusion was that it was not necessarily the same. I agree. The reason is that the third party recipient may be subject to some additional and conflicting duty which does not affect the primary confidant or may not be subject to some special duty which does affect that confidant. In such situations the equation is not the same in the case of the confidant and that of the third party and

h accordingly the result may be different.'

No disagreement with this statement of principle is to be found in the judgments in the House of Lords ([1988] 3 All ER 545, [1988] 3 WLR 776).

I propose therefore to start with the case against Dr Egdell.

Counsel for W relies on two sources for the obligation of confidence or of non-

j disclosure on which W's action against Dr Egdell is based. One source is implied contract, the other is equity. The two sources will in most cases cover the same ground.

It is convenient for me first to ask myself what duty of confidence a court of equity ought to regard as imposed on Dr Egdell by the circumstances in which he obtained information from and about W and prepared his report. It is in my judgment plain, and the contrary has not been suggested, that the circumstances did impose on Dr Egdell a duty of confidence. If, for instance Dr Egdell had sold the contents of his report to a newspaper, I do not think any court of equity would hesitate for a moment before *a* concluding that his conduct had been a breach of his duty of confidence. The question in the present case is not whether Dr Egdell was under a duty of confidence; he plainly was. The question is as to the breadth of that duty. Did the duty extend so as to bar disclosure of the report to the medical director of the hospital? Did it bar disclosure to the Home Office? In the *Spycatcher* case [1988] 3 All ER 545 at 658–659, [1988] 3 WLR 776 at 805, 807 in the House of Lords Lord Goff, after accepting 'the broad general principle . . . that *b* a duty of confidence arises when confidential information comes to the knowledge of a person (the confidant) in circumstances where he has notice, or is held to have agreed, that the information is confidential, with the effect that it would be just in all the circumstances that he should be precluded from disclosing the information to others', formulated three limiting principles. He said:

c

'The third limiting principle is of far greater importance. It is that, although the basis of the law's protection of confidence is that there is a public interest that confidences should be preserved and protected by the law, nevertheless that public interest may be outweighed by some other countervailing public interest which favours disclosure. This limitation may apply, as the learned judge pointed out, to all types of confidential information. It is this limiting principle which may require *d* a court to carry out a balancing operation, weighing the public interest in maintaining confidence against a countervailing public interest favouring disclosure.'

In *X v Y* [1988] 2 All ER 648 at 653, a case which concerned doctors who were believed to be continuing to practise despite having contracted AIDS, Rose J said:
e

'In the long run, preservation of confidentiality is the only way of securing public health; otherwise doctors will be discredited as a source of education, for future individual patients "will not come forward if doctors are going to squeal on them". Consequently, confidentiality is vital to secure public as well as private health, for unless those infected come forward they cannot be counselled and self-treatment *f* does not provide the best care . . .'

The question in a particular case whether a duty of confidentiality extends to bar particular disclosures that the confidant has made or wants to make requires the court to balance the interest to be served by non-disclosure against the interest served by disclosure. Rose J struck that balance. It came down, he held, in favour of non-disclosure. *g* In the *Spycatcher* case that balance too was struck. In that case the balance did not come down in favour of non-disclosure. I must endeavour to strike the balance in the present case.

A convenient starting point is the guidance given to doctors by the General Medical Council. The council publishes rules entitled 'Advice on Standards of Professional Conduct and of Medical Ethics'. Rules 79 and 80 provide as follows: *h*

'79. The following guidance is given on the principles which should govern the confidentiality of information relating to patients.
80. It is the doctor's duty, except in the cases mentioned below, strictly to observe the rule of professional secrecy by refraining from disclosing voluntarily to any third party information about the patient which he has learnt directly or indirectly *j* in his professional capacity as a registered medical practitioner. The death of the patient does not absolve the doctor from this obligation.'

Rule 81 sets out circumstances where exceptions to r 80 may be permitted. The exceptions include the following:

'(a) If the patient or his legal adviser gives written and valid consent, information to which the consent refers may be disclosed.

(b) Confidential information may be shared with other registered medical practitioners who participate in or assume responsibility for clinical management of the patient . . .

(f) If the doctor is directed to disclose information by a judge or other presiding officer of a court before whom he is appearing to give evidence, information may at that stage be disclosed . . . But where litigation is in prospect, unless the patient has consented to disclosure or a formal court order has been made for disclosure, information should not be disclosed merely in response to demands from other persons, such as another party's solicitor or an official of the court.

(g) Rarely, disclosure may be justified on the ground that it is in the public interest which, in certain circumstances such as, for example, investigation by the police of a grave or very serious crime, will override the doctor's duty to maintain his patient's confidence.'

These rules do not provide a definitive answer to the question raised in the present case as to the breadth of the duty of confidence owed by Dr Egdell. They seem to me valuable, however, in showing the approach of the General Medical Council to the breadth of the doctor/patient duty of confidence. Rule 80 underlines the importance attached by the council to that duty. Rule 81 shows that the duty is not absolute. Paragraphs (b) and (g) of r 81 seem to me particularly relevant for present purposes. The duty of confidence does not prevent a doctor from disclosing confidential information to other doctors charged with the care or treatment of the patient (para (b)). And para (g) preserves the propriety of a doctor disclosing confidential information in the rare cases where the public interest overrides this duty to his patient.

The duty of confidence owed by Dr Egdell to W in the present case was both created and circumscribed by the particular circumstances of the case. So what were those particular circumstances as at June 1987? They were, in my view, these. W was a person who had killed five people and seriously wounded two others. He had been diagnosed as suffering from mental illness and, not as a punishment, but for the public safety, had been ordered to be detained without limit of time. He was subject to a restriction order. Dr Ghosh, the psychiatrist who, from 1984 to 1987 had been responsible for W's treatment, regarded him as no longer a danger to the public provided he remained on suitable medication. She regarded the index offences as having been occasioned by mental illness from which he had been cured. W was being detained at the hospital. While he remained there the authorities at the hospital were responsible for his treatment and care, for his 'clinical management' to borrow the expression used in r 81(b). A proposal was on foot for W's transfer to a regional secure unit. The Home Secretary had a discretion whether or not to allow the transfer. Public safety would be a paramount consideration for the Home Secretary in deciding how to exercise his discretion. W had applied for his case to be reviewed by a tribunal. The tribunal had power to discharge him absolutely or conditionally. The tribunal could not discharge him unless satisfied that it was 'not necessary for the health or safety of the patient or for the protection of other persons that he should receive medical treatment' (see s 72(1)(b)(ii) of the 1983 Act). But if the tribunal was so satisfied it would be bound to discharge him. Dr Egdell was instructed to examine W and to make a report 'for use at the forthcoming Mental Health Review Tribunal'. Facilities were provided at the hospital for Dr Egdell to examine W in private and to peruse W's hospital file (see s 76(1) of the 1983 Act). Dr Egdell discussed W with Dr Ghosh before making his report. So the facts of Dr Egdell's examination and that he was making a report were known to the hospital authorities.

These, in summary, seem to me to be the relevant circumstances pertaining at the time when Dr Egdell examined W and made his report.

Having examined W, Dr Egdell formed the opinion that there was a possibility that W had a psychopathic personality. He formed the opinion that insufficient significance might have been attached to W's interests in guns and explosives. He formed the opinion that further tests on and treatment of W were advisable before a decision was taken to transfer W to a regional secure unit, let alone to discharge him, conditionally or otherwise. Then, having formed these opinions and having written his report, Dr Egdell learnt that the application to the tribunal had been withdrawn, that his report was not on file at the hospital, and that W and W's solicitors proposed to suppress it.

Did these circumstances impose on Dr Egdell a duty not to disclose his opinions and his report to Dr Hunter, the medical director at the hospital? In my judgment they did not. Dr Egdell was expressing opinions which were relevant to the nature of the treatement and care to be accorded to W at the hospital. Dr Egdell was, in effect, recommending a change from the approach to treatment and care that Dr Ghosh was following. He was expressing reservations about Dr Ghosh's diagnosis. The case seems to me to fall squarely within para (b) of r 81.

But I would base my conclusion on broader considerations than that. I decline to overlook the background to Dr Egdell's examination of W. True it is that Dr Egdell was engaged by W. He was the doctor of W's choice. None the less, in my opinion, the duty he owed to W was not his only duty. W was not an ordinary member of the public. He was, consequent on the killings he had perpetrated, held in a secure hospital subject to a regime whereby decisions concerning his future were to be taken by public authorities, the Home Secretary or the tribunal. W's own interests would not be the only nor the main criterion in the taking of those decisions. The safety of the public would be the main criterion. In my view, a doctor called on, as Dr Edgell was, to examine a patient such as W owes a duty not only to his patient but also a duty to the public. His duty to the public would require him, in my opinion, to place before the proper authorities the result of his examination if, in his opinion, the public interest so required. This would be so, in my opinion, whether nor not the patient instructed him not to do so.

Counsel for W argued that the dominant public interest was the public interest in patients being able to make full and frank disclosure to their doctors, and in particular to their psychiatrists, without fear that the doctors would disclose information to others. I accept the general importance in the public interest that this should be so. It justifies the General Medical Council's r 80.

But counsel's route from the general to the particular was not, to my mind, convincing. W was not short of psychiatrists. A succession of them had attended him since the time when he committed the index offences. He had disclosed confidential information about himself to each of them. Each of them owed him a duty of confidence. None would have been entitled to sell the information to a newspaper or to make general disclosure of it. But the reports of each of these psychiatrists had been placed in W's file and were available to his responsible medical officer and to the Home Office. It was not suggested that this feature had inhibited W in his dealings with these psychiatrists. Why should W's relationship with Dr Egdell and the report of Dr Egdell be differently treated? Counsel's answer would be, I think, that Dr Egdell, (like Dr Boyd in 1984) was an independent psychiatrist employed by W for the purpose of the examination in private referred to in s 76(1). The other psychiatrists were psychiatrists within the hospital regime. So Dr Egdell owed a duty of confidence more extensive than that owed by the hospital psychiatrists. But this answer, in my opinion, confuses private interest with public interest. I readily accept that W had a strong private interest in barring disclosure of the Egdell report to the Home Office and, probably, to the hospital authorities as well. But what public interest is served by imposing on Dr Egdell a duty of confidence more extensive than that owed by the hospital psychiatrists? Counsel's answer to that question was this. Independent psychiatric reports were, he said, of great assistance to tribunals. In about 80% of the cases reviewed by mental health review tribunals independent psychiatric reports were submitted. If patients were held to be unable to suppress unfavourable reports, they would in future be unwilling to take the chance of commissioning such reports; alternatively they might not be wholly frank when being a examined and the value of the independent reports would be reduced. I do not think that this answer has much weight. The possibility of a lack of frankness must always be present when a psychiatric examination takes place. An experienced psychiatrist would, I think, expect to be able to detect it. And the lack of frankness itself would constitute material of interest to the psychiatrist. As to the suggestion that the commissioning of independent reports will be reduced unless unfavourable ones can be suppressed, that likelihood does not seem to me in the least self-evident.

b In truth, as it seems to me, the interest to be served by the duty of confidence for which counsel for W contends is the private interest of W and not any broader public interest. If I set the private interest of W in the balance against the public interest served by disclosure of the report to Dr Hunter and the Home Office, I find the weight of the public interest prevails.

I do not reach this conclusion in reliance on the importance of the information about c W's interest in explosives, nor on the extent to which Dr Egdell's fears about W's personality reveal some relevant risk to public safety, nor on any other specific part of the contents of the Egdell report. Rather, I base my conclusion on the particular circumstances in which the report was commissioned. If a patient in the position of W commissions an independent psychiatrist's report, the duty of confidence that undoubtedly lies on the doctor who makes the report does not, in my judgment, bar the doctor from disclosing d the report to the hospital that is charged with the care of the patient if the doctor judges the report to be relevant to the care and treatment of the patient, nor from disclosing the report to the Home Secretary if the doctor judges the report to be relevant to the exercise of the Home Secretarys' discretionary powers in relation to that patient.

I accept that this conclusion places W and persons like him in a position in which the duty of confidence owed by their psychiatrists is less extensive than the duty that would e be owed by psychiatrists to ordinary members of the public. But this, in my view, is an inevitable result of the circumstances that have led to W being subjected to a restriction order under the 1983 Act. This limitation of W's rights is, in my judgment, justified by the need that, first, the hospital in charge of his clinical management, second, the Home Secretary, in whom very important discretionary powers are reposed and, third, the tribunal on whom the obligation in certain circumstances to order his discharge is placed f should be fully informed about W.

In my judgment, therefore, the circumstances of this case did not impose on Dr Egdell an obligation of conscience, an equitable obligation, to refrain from disclosing his report to Dr Hunter, or to refrain from encouraging its disclosure to the Home Office. It follows also that that obligation cannot be imposed on Dr Egdell by implied contract. If the officious bystander had asked the usual question, Dr Egdell's answer would not have g been the testy 'Of course'. He would, I believe, have said that the question required very careful consideration. And after consideration he would, I think, have said that he would regard himself as entitled to disclose his report to the relevant authorities if, in his judgment, the public interest so required. If he had given that answer he would, in my judgment, have been right.

h Counsel for W had an alternative to the equitable or contractual duty of confidence on which to base the obligation of non-disclosure for which he contended. He relied on legal privilege. The report was obtained for the purposes of the forthcoming tribunal hearing, that is to say for forthcoming legal proceedings. Accordingly, he submitted, it was covered by legal professional privilege.

There are two authorities to which I should refer in dealing with this submission. j *Harmony Shipping Co SA v Davis* [1979] 3 All ER 177, [1979] 1 WLR 1380 concerned a handwriting expert who had given the plaintiff his opinion on the genuineness of a certain document. Subsequently he was asked by the defendant's solicitors to advise on the same point. He inadvertently forgot that he had already advised the plaintiff and gave an opinion to the defendant. His opinion must have been favourable to the defendant, for the defendant sought to call him as a witness at the trial and the plaintiff objected. Lord Denning MR said ([1979] 3 All ER 177 at 180–181, [1979] 1 WLR 1380 at 1384–1385):

> 'So far as witnesses of fact are concerned, the law is as plain as can be. There is no property in a witness. The reason is because the court has a right to every man's evidence. Its primary duty is to ascertain the truth. Neither one side nor the other can debar the court from ascertaining the truth either by seeing a witness beforehand or by purchasing his evidence or by making communication to him. In no way can one side prohibit the other side from seeing a witness of fact, from getting the facts from him and from calling him to give evidence or from issuing him with a subpoena . . . The question in this case is whether or not that principle applies to expert witnesses. They may have been told the substance of a party's case. They may have been given a great deal of confidential information. On it they may have given advice to the party. Does the rule apply to such a case? Many of the communications between the solicitor and the expert witness will be privileged. They are protected by legal professional privilege. They cannot be communicated to the court except with the consent of the party concerned. That means that a great deal of the communications between the expert witness and the lawyer cannot be given in evidence to the court. If questions were asked about it, then it would be the duty of the judge to protect the witness (and he would) by disallowing any questions which infringed the rule about legal professional privilege or the rule protecting information given in confidence, unless, of course, it was one of those rare cases which come before the courts from time to time where in spite of privilege or confidence the court does order a witness to give further evidence. Subject to that qualification, it seems to me that an expert witness falls into the same position as a witness of fact. The court is entitled, in order to ascertain the truth, to have the actual facts which he has observed adduced before it and to have his independent opinion on those facts.'

The other case to which I would refer is *R v King* [1983] 1 All ER 929, [1983] 1 WLR 411. In that case the defendant was charged with conspiracy to defraud. His solicitors sent to a handwriting expert certain documents for examination. The prosecution desired to put in evidence the expert's opinion on these documents and served subpoenas on the expert for that purpose. It was contended for the defendant that the expert's opinion on these documents was protected by privilege. Dunn LJ, who gave the judgment of the court, said ([1983] 1 All ER 929 at 930–931, [1983] 1 WLR 411 at 413–414):

> 'Counsel on behalf of the [defendant] submitted in this court that any communication passing between a solicitor and a third party for the purpose of taking advice was privileged. He relied on a passage in *Cross on Evidence* (5th edn, 1979) p 286 in the following terms: "The rationale of the head of legal professional privilege under consideration was succinctly stated by the Law Reform Committee to be "to facilitate the obtaining and preparation of evidence by a party to an action in support of his case". The privilege is essential to the adversary system of procedure which would be unworkable if parties were obliged to disclose communications with prospective witnesses." While accepting that there is no property in a witness, counsel for the [defendant] submitted that at common law an expert who had been consulted by solicitors for one party should not be called as a witness by the other party to give evidence as to any communication sent to him by the solicitors. Counsel submitted that exhibit 257 formed part of the communication from the defendant's solicitors to the expert [exhibit 257 was the document sent for examination] . . . Dealing first with the general position, the rule is that in the case of expert witnesses legal professional privilege attaches to confidential communications between the solicitor and the expert, but it does not attach to the chattels or documents on which the expert based his opinion, or to the independent opinion of

the expert himself: see *Harmony Shipping Co v Davis* [1979] 3 All ER 177 at 181,
[1979] 1 WLR 1380 at 1385 per Lord Denning MR. The reasons for that are that
there is no property in an expert witness any more than in any other witness and
the court is entitled, in order to ascertain the truth, to have the actual facts which
the expert has observed adduced before it in considering his opinion. In general
then no privilege will attach to exhibit 257. It was one of the documents examined
by [the expert], on which he based his opinion, and the court was entitled to have it
adduced in evidence. Is there any difference because the document was examined
in criminal proceedings rather than in civil proceedings? On principle we can see
no reason why that should be so.'

Exhibit 257 in that case was a document which was in existence before proceedings
commenced. It had not been brought into existence for the purpose of the proceedings
themselves. So the question arises whether that would have made any difference to the
result. Suppose the genuineness of a cheque is in question. If the cheque is submitted by
one side to a handwriting expert for his opinion on the signature, the other side can call
the expert to give evidence of that opinion. The *Harmony Shipping* case and *R v King*
establish that that is so. If a document already in existence before proceedings were
contemplated had been, for purposes of comparison, submitted to the expert together
with the cheque, the other side could put in evidence the expert's opinion not simply on
the cheque but also on the other document, the 'control' document: see *R v King* [1983]
1 All ER 929 at 930, [1983] 1 WLR 411 at 412. But suppose the control document had
been brought into existence, after proceedings had commenced, for the purpose of being
submitted with the cheque to the handwriting expert. Counsel for W submitted that the
other side could not call the expert to give opinion evidence on the comparision between
the cheque and *that* control document. The reason, he said, is that *that* control document
had been brought into existence for the purposes of the proceedings and so would be
covered by legal privilege.

I do not accept that this distinction is a sound one. If a document is submitted to an
expert witness for examination and if the opinion of the expert is relevant to an issue in
the case, the expert is, in my judgment, in civil cases at least, a competent and compellable
witness to give evidence of what has been put before him and of his opinion on it. Legal
professional privilege attaches to documents brought into existence for the purpose of
legal proceedings; but, if such a document is placed before an expert witness for his
opinion, it becomes, in my judgment, part of the facts on which the opinion is based.
The expert cannot be barred when giving evidence of his opinion from referring to the
facts on which the opinion is based, including, if it be the case, documents which, in the
hands of solicitors, would be covered by legal professional privilege.

There is, in my judgment, a clear and important distinction to be drawn between, on
the one hand, instructions given to an expert witness and, on the other hand, the expert's
opinion given pursuant to those instructions. The instructions are covered by legal
professional privilege. The opinion is not. This distinction I take to be established by, in
particular, the passage in Dunn LJ's judgment in *R v King* [1983] 1 All ER 929 at 931,
[1983] 1 WLR 411 at 414.

In the present case the letter of instructions dated 2 July 1987 was covered by legal
privilege. But Dr Egdell did not disclose that letter. So far as I know neither the hospital
nor the Home Office has ever had a copy of it.

For the purposes of the examination itself, Dr Egdell no doubt encouraged W to be
forthcoming about himself. W communicated a great deal of information to Dr Egdell,
some of it information that does not seem previously to have been revealed. Counsel for
W categorised all this information as information given for the purpose of legal
proceedings, ie the tribunal hearing. The information was, he said, tantamount to
instructions being given to Dr Egdell by W. The information was therefore covered by
legal professional privilege. I disagree. The more accurate analysis, in my judgment, is

that the information acquired from W formed part of the facts on which Dr Egdell's opinion expressed in the report was based. Neither the opinion, nor the facts on which it *a* was based, whether obtained from W or from Dr Egdell's perusal of the records, were, in my judgment, protected by legal professional privilege.

There is also, I think, a further answer to counsel's reliance on legal professional privilege. The function of privilege is to protect material from being produced on discovery or being placed in evidence in legal proceedings. What is complained of in the present case is that Dr Egdell supplied a copy of his report to the hospital and, indirectly, *b* to the Home Secretary. Legal professional privilege is not a basis on which this complaint can be constructed.

In the result, in my judgment, the case against Dr Egdell fails.

If I had found Dr Egdell liable for breach of his duty of confidentiality I would have had to consider the issue on damages. It has, rightly in my opinion, not been argued by counsel that W's continued detention subject to a restriction order, or continued detention *c* at the hospital rather than at a regional secure unit, whether or not those things are to any extent attributable to the disclosure of the report, can sound in damages. It has been argued, however, that W was caused shock and distress by Dr Egdell's disclosure of the report and that that shock and distress should be reflected in an award of damages. An enquiry as to the amount of the damages is suggested.

The evidence that W was caused shock or distress by Dr Egdell's disclosure of the *d* report is unconvincing. The affidavit sworn on 5 September 1988 by Mr Ronald refers, at para 8 to W's 'shock that the First Defendant did not support his application for discharge or transfer'. A note of an interview that Mr Ronald had with W on 18 August 1987 records that W 'was absolutely shocked to find that Dr. Egdell did not back up his Application for discharge or transfer'. The absence of any evidence that W was caused shock by the disclosure of the report, as opposed to shock by its contents, was the subject *e* of comment in the course of counsel's submission for Dr Egdell. The comment led to counsel for W seeking leave to file an affidavit sworn by W on 24 November 1988, the third day of the hearing. In para 4 W says: 'I was extremely upset that this report had been disclosed because I thought it was factually wrong in a number of ways.' In para 5 W says: 'I now feel very shocked and upset at what has happened, and I feel my record has been unfairly damaged by disclosure of this inaccurate report on me.' *f*

I gave leave for this affidavit to be filed but the circumstances of its late arrival deprived it of much cogency.

Further, it is, I think, open to question whether shock and distress caused by the unauthorised disclosure of confidential information can, in any event, properly be reflected in an award of damages.

In *Bliss v South East Thames Regional Health Authority* [1987] ICR 700 at 717–718 Dillon *g* LJ said:

> 'The general rule laid down by the House of Lords in *Addis v. Gramophone Co. Ltd.* ([1909] AC 488, [1908–10] All ER Rep 1) is that where damages fall to be assessed for breach of contract rather than in tort it is not permissible to award general damages for frustration, mental distress, injured feelings or annoyance occasioned *h* by the breach. Modern thinking tends to be that the amount of damages recoverable for a wrong should be the same whether the cause of action is laid in contract or in tort. But in the *Addis* case Lord Loreburn regarded the rule that damages for injured feelings cannot be recovered in contract for wrongful dismissal as too inveterate to be altered, and Lord James of Hereford supported his concurrence in the speech of Lord Loreburn by reference to his own experience at the Bar. There are exceptions *j* now recognised where the contract which has been broken was itself a contract to provide peace of mind or freedom from distress: see *Jarvis v. Swans Tours Ltd* ([1973] 1 All ER 71, [1973] QB 233) and *Heywood v. Wellers* ([1976] 1 All ER 300, [1976] QB 446). Those decisions, do not however cover this present case. In *Cox v. Philips*

Industries Ltd ([1976] 3 All ER 161, [1976] 1 WLR 638) Lawson J. took the view that
damages for distress, vexation and frustration, including consequent ill-health, could
be recovered for breach of a contract of employment if it could be said to have been
in the contemplation of the parties that the breach would cause such distress etc.
For my part, I do not think that that general approach is open to this court unless
and until the House of Lords has reconsidered its decision in the *Addis* case.'

This Court of Appeal authority seems to me to preclude W from recovering damages
(save nominal damages) to the extent that his claim is based on breach of an implied
contractual term. I do not see any reason, on this point, why equity should not follow
the law.

Accordingly, in my judgment, W would not, even if I had found Dr Egdell to be
liable, have been entitled to damages. He would have had to be content with a declaration
and an injunction.

I must now consider the position of the other defendants. If I am right in concluding
that the case against Dr Egdell fails, the case against the other defendants must also fail.
But this case may go further and I ought, I think, to consider the position of the other
defendants in case it should subsequently be held that Dr Egdell was in breach of duty in
disclosing his report to Dr Hunter.

The hospital, acting by an unidentified person or persons, sent a copy of the report to
the Home Office. The Home Office still holds a copy of the report and sent a copy to the
tribunal. I must consider these matters on the hypothesis that the disclosure of the report
to the hospital was a breach by Dr Egdell of the duty of confidence he owed to W.

There are two authorities which seem to me to be relevant. The first is *Parry-Jones v
Law Society* [1968] 1 All ER 177, [1969] 1 Ch 1. The plaintiff was a solicitor on whom the
Law Society had served a notice to produce for inspection his books of account and other
documents. The notice was served pursuant to the rules made by the Law Society under
s 29 of the Solicitors Act 1957. The rules have statutory force. The plaintiff objected on
the ground that the documents to be produced contained confidential information about
his clients and that he owed his clients a duty not to disclose this information to others.
Lord Denning MR said ([1968] 1 All ER 177 at 179, [1969] 1 Ch 1 at 8):

> 'In my opinion that rule is a valid rule which overrides any privilege or confidence
> which otherwise might subsist between solicitor and client. It enables the Law
> Society for the public good to hold an investigation, even if it involves getting
> information as to clients' affairs; but they and their accountant must themselves
> respect the obligation of confidence. They must not use it for any purpose except
> the investigation, and any consequential proceedings.'

Diplock LJ said ([1968] 1 All ER 177 at 180, [1969] 1 Ch 1 at 9):

> 'What we are concerned with here is the contractual duty of confidence, generally
> implied though sometimes expressed, between a solicitor and client. Such a duty
> exists not only between solicitor and client, but, for example, between banker and
> customer, doctor and patient and accountant and client. Such a duty of confidence
> is subject to, and overriden by, the duty of any party to that contract to comply with
> the law of the land. If it is the duty of such a party to a contract, whether at common
> law or under statute, to disclose in defined circumstances confidential information,
> then he must do so . . .'

The other case is *Hunter v Mann* [1974] 2 All ER 414, [1974] QB 767, which concerned
the statutory obligation imposed by s 168 of the Road Traffic Act 1972. A doctor was
asked by a police officer to divulge the identity of the driver of a vehicle that had been
involved in an accident. The doctor refused on the ground that he had obtained the
information from a patient, namely the driver, and that to divulge his identity would be
in breach of his obligation of professional confidence. The doctor was convicted of

contravening s 168(3). He appealed. The Divisional Court dismissed his appeal. The
statutory duty to disclose the information overrode the doctor's duty of confidence to his *a*
patient.

The scheme set up by the 1983 Act for dealing with patients subject to restriction
orders requires co-operation between the hospitals in which patients are held and the
Home Secretary. The Home Secretary when deciding whether or not to exercise any of
his discretionary powers under s 41(3) is dependent on information from the hospital in
which the patient in question is held to supply him with relevant information about that *b*
patient. It could not, in my view, ever be right for the authorities of such a hospital to
withhold from the Home Secretary relevant information about a patient subject to a
restriction order. The importance for public safety that the Home Secretary should be
fully informed requires that that be so. Accordingly, even if Dr Egdell were in breach of
duty in disclosing his report to Dr Hunter, the decision, by whoever took it, to send a
copy of the report to the Home Secretary was not, in my judgment, a breach of any duty *c*
lying on the hospital. On the contrary, in my opinion, the hospital had a duty to send a
copy to the Home Secretary. A fortiori, the Home Secretary was under a duty to send a
copy of the report to the tribunal. Rule 6(2) of the 1983 rules places a statutory obligation
on the Home Secretary to send to the tribunal for the purpose of cases being reviewed by
the tribunal 'a statement of such further information relevant to the application as may
be available to him'. The Egdell report was further information available to the Home *d*
Secretary. The Home Secretary's statutory duty under r 6(2) overrode, in my judgment,
any confidentiality attaching to the report.

Finally, I must consider the position of the tribunal. The tribunal holds copies of the
Egdell report. It is, in my judgment, entitled to retain these copies and to make such use
of them as it thinks fit on the hearing or the adjourned review of W's case. Both the
public interest in the tribunal being fully informed and the inquisitorial nature of the *e*
tribunal's proceedings override any confidentiality attaching to the report.

In the result W's action fails, in my judgment, against each of the defendants. It does
not fail because Dr Egdell's conclusions are necessarily to be preferred to those of Dr
Ghosh, or of Dr Coorey, or of Dr Kay. I must emphasise that I have formed no opinion
in favour of Dr Egdell's views as opposed to those of the others. The action fails because *f*
Dr Egdell's report is, in my view, relevant material to be taken into account by the
hospital, by the Home Office and by the tribunal in the discharge of their respective
functions regarding W and because in the very special circumstances of this case the duty
of confidence owed by Dr Egdell to his patient W does not bar disclosure of the report to
those recipients. It is for those recipients of the report to attribute to it such weight as
they think it merits. The consolidated action is therefore dismissed.

  g

Actions dismissed.

Solicitors: *Irwin Mitchell*, Sheffield (for W); *Hempsons* (for Dr Egdell); *Treasury Solicitor*.

Jacqueline Metcalfe   Barrister.

a

Lester and another v Ridd

COURT OF APPEAL, CIVIL DIVISION
SLADE, DILLON AND STAUGHTON LJJ
5, 20 DECEMBER 1988

b   *Landlord and tenant – Leasehold enfranchisement – House – Lease of house comprised in agricultural holding – Partition and severance of leasehold interest of agricultural holding between several assignees – Partition of house from agricultural land – Landlord's consent to partition and severance not obtained – Assignee of house applying to purchase freehold – Whether partition creating two separate tenancies of two separate holdings in absence of landlord's consent – Whether house still comprised in agicultural holding – Whether assignee having right of leasehold*
c   *enfranchisement – Leasehold Reform Act 1967, s 1(3)(b).*

By a lease dated 17 January 1902 the landlord's predecessor in title demised a house (the glebe house) and some 23 acres of land to L for a term of 99 years from 25 December 1901 at a yearly rent of £9. In 1955 all the lands and premises comprised in the lease were assigned for the full unexpired residue of the term of the lease to a father and son
d   who carried on farming in partnership together until 1963. It was common ground that until 1963 the demised premises were used for agriculture by way of trade or business. By a deed of partition dated 16 December 1963 the lease of the glebe house and two acres of surrounding land (the glebe house property) was assigned to the father for the unexpired residue at a yearly rent of £5 while the rest of the land comprised in the lease was assigned to the son for the unexpired residue of the term at a yearly rent of £4. On
e   13 December 1982 the appellants purchased the leasehold interest in the glebe house property. However, it was not until after the assignment to the appellants that the landlord learnt of the deed of partition. On 23 December 1985 the appellants gave notice of their desire to purchase the freehold of the glebe house property and when the landlord refused to sell they sought a declaration that they were entitled to acquire the freehold under the Leasehold Reform Act 1967. The judge found that no part of the property
f   assigned to the appellants had been used as agricultural land since December 1982 but that the remainder of the land comprised in the 1901 lease had continued to be used as agricultural land. The judge dismissed the application on the ground that the appellants were not entitled to acquire the freehold because the house was 'comprised in an agricultural holding' and therefore excluded by s 1(3)(b)[a] of the 1967 Act from the provisions relating to leasehold enfranchisement contained in that Act. The appellants
g   appealed.

Held – Partition of a leasehold interest without the landlord's consent and the subsequent severance of the leasehold interest between several assignees did not create two separate holdings with separate tenants for each holding. Furthermore, since an 'agricultural holding' was defined as meaning the aggregate of the land (whether agricultural or not)
h   comprised in a contract of tenancy which was a contract for an agricultural tenancy, it followed that when considering whether a leasehold tenant's house was comprised in an agricultural holding the land comprised in the original contract of tenancy had to be looked at as a whole. Accordingly, the glebe house property was still comprised in an agricultural holding (consisting of the whole of the premises demised by the 1902 lease) when the appellants gave notice of their desire to purchase the freehold on 23 December
j   1985. It followed that s 1(3)(b) of the 1967 Act deprived the appellants of any right of enfranchisement which they might otherwise have enjoyed. The appeal would therefore be dismissed (see p 1115 d e, p 1116 j to p 1117 a e f and p 1118 j to p 1119 a e to h, post).
Jelley v Buckman [1973] 3 All ER 853 applied.

---

a   Section 1(3), so far as material, is set out at p 1112 j, post

Notes

For what constitutes an agricultural holding, see 1 Halsbury's Laws (4th edn) paras 1001–1002, and for cases on the subject, see 2 Digest (Reissue) 4–6, 3–10.

For the Leasehold Reform Act 1967, s 1, see 23 Halsbury's Statutes (4th edn) 198.

Cases referred to in judgments

Curtis v Spitty (1835) 1 Bing NC 756, 131 ER 1309.
Gamon v Vernon (1678) 2 Lev 231, 83 ER 532.
Hare v Cator (1778) 2 Cowp 766, 98 ER 1350.
Howkins v Jardine [1951] 1 All ER 320, [1951] 1 KB 614, CA.
Jelley v Buckman [1973] 3 All ER 853, [1974] QB 488, [1973] 3 WLR 585, CA.
Stevenson v Lambard (1802) 2 East 575, 102 ER 490.
Wetherall v Smith [1980] 2 All ER 530, [1980] 1 WLR 1290, CA.
Whitham v Bullock [1939] 2 All ER 310, [1939] 2 KB 81, CA.

Case also cited

Blackmore v Butler [1954] 2 All ER 403, [1954] 2 QB 171, CA.

Appeal

Ronald Arthur Lester and Gloria Ann Lester appealed against the decision of Mr L P Laity, sitting as an assistant recorder in the Taunton County Court on 7 December 1987, whereby he dismissed their application for a declaration under s 20(2) of the Leasehold Reform Act 1967 that they were entitled to acquire the freehold of the house and premises known as Glebe House, Oare, Somerset owned by the respondent, John Ridd. The facts are set out in the judgment of Dillon LJ.

Sir Ashley Bramall for the appellants.
Stephen Lowry for the respondent.

Cur adv vult

20 December. The following judgments were delivered.

DILLON LJ (giving the first judgment at the invitation of Slade LJ). This appeal from a decision of Mr L P Laity sitting as an assistant recorder, given in the Taunton County Court on 7 December 1987, raises a novel point which, despite the admirably clear reserved judgment of the recorder, I have found very difficult.

On 13 December 1982 the appellants, Mr and Mrs Lester, purchased the leasehold interest in a house now known as Glebe House at Oare in Somerset, and two acres of surrounding land. From the date of purchase they occupied the house as their residence, and by the originating application in these proceedings issued on 25 February 1986 they claimed a declaration that they were entitled to acquire the freehold of the house and land thus assigned to them, under the Leasehold Reform Act 1967, as amended. The requisite notice of their desire to have the freehold had been given on 23 December 1985 to the respondent, Mr John Ridd, who is the owner of the freehold.

Section 1(1) of the 1967 Act, as amended, confers the right to acquire the freehold, subject to certain conditions which are not in issue in the present case, when at the time he gives notice of his desire to have the freehold the tenant has been 'occupying the house as his residence' for the last three years. That is qualified, however, by s 1(3), which provides, so far as material:

'This Part of this Act shall not confer on the tenant of a house any right by reference to his occupation of it as his residence (but shall apply as if he were not so occupying it) at any time when ... (b) it is comprised in an agricultural holding within the meaning of the Agricultural Holdings Act 1948.'

a The question, therefore, in the present case is whether, during the time from the assignment of the leasehold interest in it to the appellants to the time when they gave their notice of their desire to have the freehold, Glebe House was comprised in an agricultural holding. The recorder held that it was so comprised, and that the appellants were therefore not entitled to acquire the freehold (because as a result of s 1(3) they were to be treated as not having occupied Glebe House as their residence for the three years' qualifying period); that is the decision against which the appellants now appeal.

b The Agricultural Holdings Act 1948, which is referred to in s 1(3)(b) of the 1967 Act, was amended by the Agricultural Holdings Act 1984, and both have since been repealed by the present Act, the Agricultural Holdings Act 1986, which is a consolidating Act, but was only enacted after these proceedings had been commenced. Counsel were agreed, however, and we accept, that it is convenient to look at the provisions of the 1986 Act since in relation to what is 'comprised in an agricultural holding' these provisions
c concisely set out the effect of the corresponding provisions of the 1948 Act as interpreted by the courts. Before I turn, however, to the provisions of the 1986 Act, it is convenient to set out the facts.

By a lease of 17 January 1902 Glebe House and the two acres subsequently assigned to the appellants were demised as part of a larger area of some 23 acres of former glebe land by the then owner Thomas Ridd (a lineal ancestor of the present respondent) to one
d Lethaby for a term of 99 years from 25 December 1901 at a yearly rent of £9 payable quarterly. Glebe House is described as a house in the course of erection on the land. The lease seems to have been a building lease, and, not surprisingly in the case of a lease for a long term at a ground rent (though contrary to the modern practice with agricultural tenancies), it did not contain any restriction on assignment. It merely contained a covenant that, on any assignment of the demised premises or any part thereof, notice of
e the assignment would be given to the lessor.

The lease also includes a covenant by the lessee not without the consent in writing of the lessor to carry on any trade or business on any part of the demised premises. It is, however, common ground that, notwithstanding this covenant, the demised premises were for very many years up to at least 1963 used for agriculture by way of trade or business.
f It is sufficient to pick up the devolution of the leasehold title under the lease in 1955, when by a deed of 7 December 1955 all the lands and premises comprised in the lease were assigned for the full unexpired residue of the term of the lease to Alfred John Burge and William John Burge. They were father and son, and both were farmers; they carried on farming in partnership together under the style of A J Burge & Son, and the lands and premises so assigned to them were to be held as part of their partnership property. Their
g partnership was dissolved, however, on 16 December 1963, with effect from 5 April 1962, and by a deed of partition of 16 December 1963 Glebe House and the two acres subsequently assigned to the appellants were assigned to A J Burge for the unexpired residue of the term of the lease at a yearly rent of £5 while the rest of the land comprised in the lease, viz appriximately 18 acres, was assigned to W J Burge for the unexpired
h residue of the term at the yearly rent of £4. The assignment to the appellants on 13 December 1982 of Glebe House and the two acres was made by the executors of A J Burge, who had died on 1 August 1981.

In fact it was not until after the assignment to the appellants that the respondent learnt of the partition effected between A J Burge and W J Burge in December 1963. The ground rent had presumably continued to be paid by some member of the Burge family
j without anyone particularly worrying which. It seems that A J Burge occupied Glebe House from 1955 or thereabouts until soon after 1963, when he moved elsewhere. Glebe House and the two acres were then let to a Mr Stevens, who farmed other lands; at this stage Glebe House was known as Glebe Farm. Mr Stevens died in May 1979, and Glebe House and the two acres were then let to Philip Burge, a grandson of A J Burge and one of the two sons of W J Burge. Philip Burge was also a farmer and, like his brother, in partnership with W J Burge in farming various Burge farming lands.

Against this background, the relevant provisions of the Agricultural Holdings Act 1986, which are all contained in s 1, are as follows: *a*

'(1) In this Act "agricultural holding" means the aggregate of the land (whether agricultural land or not) comprised in a contract of tenancy which is a contract for an agricultural tenancy . . .
(2) For the purposes of this section, a contract of tenancy relating to any land is a contract for an agricultural tenancy if, having regard to—(*a*) the terms of the tenancy, (*b*) the actual or contemplated use of the land at the time of the conclusion   *b* of the contract and subsequently, and (*c*) any other relevant circumstances, the whole of the land comprised in the contract, subject to such exceptions only as do not substantially affect the character of the tenancy, is let for use as agricultural land.
(3) A change in user of the land concerned subsequent to the conclusion of a contract of tenancy which involves any breach of the terms of the tenancy shall be   *c* disregarded for the purpose of determining whether a contract which was not originally a contract for an agricultural tenancy has subsequently become one unless it is effected with the landlord's permission, consent or acquiescence.
(4) In this Act "agricultural land" means—(*a*) land used for agriculture which is so used for the purposes of a trade or business . . .
(5) In this Act "contract of tenancy" means a letting of land, or agreement for   *d* letting land, for a term of years or from year to year . . .'

Since, despite the covenant against trade or business use in the 1902 lease, the use of the land comprised in that lease as 'agricultural land' as defined in sub-s (4) was plainly acquiesced in by the landlord, it must follow, in the light of sub-s (3), that, even if the letting of the land under the 1902 lease was not originally a contract for an agricultural tenancy, it had become one well before the 1963 partition.   *e*

The wording used in sub-s (2), '. . . if . . . the whole of the land comprised in the contract, subject to such exceptions only as do not substantially affect the character of the tenancy, is let for use as agricultural land', reflects the interpretation put on the wording of the 1948 Act by this court in *Howkins v Jardine* [1951] 1 All ER 320 at 329, [1951] 1 KB 614 at 628, where Jenkins LJ said: *f*

'. . . the substance of the matter must be looked at to see whether as a matter of substance the land comprised in the tenancy, taken as a whole, is an agricultural holding. If it is, then the whole of it is entitled to the protection of the Act. If it is not, then none of it is so entitled.'

In that case there had been an agricultural tenancy of some land and three cottages but   *g* the cottages were subsequently sublet to persons not engaged in agriculture. It was argued that for the purposes of the 1948 Act there must be deemed to have been a partition of the tenancy as between agricultural and non-agricultural property, so that the protection of the tenant under the 1948 Act would only apply to the agricultural land, and not the cottages as the cottages were not used for agriculture. That argument was, however, rejected by this court, because there was no relevant provision in the Act   *h* for the partition or severance of an agricultural tenancy. Somervell LJ commented ([1951] 1 All ER 320 at 326, [1951] 1 KB 614 at 623):

'A cottage . . . may at any time change hands. An agricultural worker may succeed to someone not engaged in agriculture. To treat such cottages, covered in what is in substance an agricultural tenancy, as coming within and going out of the Act according to the occupation of the tenants at the moment would be a result so   *j* absurd that only the clearest words would make me come to such a conclusion.'

It is established law that the protection of the Agricultural Holdings Act will be lost if agricultural activity is wholly or substantially abandoned during the course of the tenancy: see *Wetherall v Smith* [1980] 2 All ER 530, [1980] 1 WLR 1290. That would

apply, for instance, if the use of the land was changed to business activities which do not
a fall within statutory definition of 'agriculture' (now in s 96 of the 1986 Act). If part only
of the land comprised in an agricultural tenancy ceases to be used for agriculture and is
used instead for some other business, then on the *Howkins v Jardine* approach the court
would have to consider the land comprised in the tenancy, taken as a whole, to see
whether, as a matter of substance, the land as a whole is an agricultural holding. The
correctness of that approach is underlined by the wording used in s 1 of the 1986 Act,
b since the term 'agricultural holding' (which is the term used in s 1(3)(b) of the Leasehold
Reform Act 1967 and therefore the term which is crucial to this case) is defined as
meaning the aggregate of the land (whether agricultural land or not) comprised in a
contract of tenancy which is a contract for an agricultural tenancy and the key to
determining whether a contract of tenancy is a contract for an agricultural tenancy is
whether the whole of the land comprised in the contract, subject to such exceptions only
c as do not substantially affect the character of the tenancy, is let as agricultural land.

In the present case the recorder has found as a fact that no part of the property assigned
to the appellants has been used as agricultural land since the assignment to the appellants
in December 1982. But the rest of the land comprised in the 1902 lease, viz the land
assigned to W J Burge on the 1963 partition, has continued to be used as agricultural
land.
d   One question to be considered is whether the effect of the partition, or of the partition
and the subsequent assignment to the appellants of their part of the land, is to create two
separate tenancies of two separate holdings, each of which has to be looked at on its own.
But, if that is not the effect, it is still necessary, despite the partition, to look at the land
comprised in the 1902 lease as a whole. If the land is looked at as a whole, the answer, in
my judgment, must be, as on its own facts was the case in *Howkins v Jardine*, that the
e whole of the land, with an exception only which does not substantially affect the character
of the tenancy, is still let for use as agricultural land. If the land comprised in the 1902
lease has to be looked at as a whole the appellants must fail because, on that approach, the
house and the land assigned to them, of which they desire to have the freehold, is still
comprised in an agricultural holding. If it were to be held, on looking at the land as a
f whole, that the house and land assigned to the appellants is not comprised in an
agricultural tenancy, it would necessarily have to be held as a corollary that the 18 acres
allocated to W J Burge on the partition and still used as agricultural land are also not
comprised in any agricultural tenancy, and do not constitute or form part of an
agricultural holding.

Is it, then, possible to conclude that, as a result, direct or indirect, of the partition two
g separate tenancies have been created of two separate holdings, each of which has to be
looked at on its own?

The effect in law of the partition of the demised premises in 1963 by the assignment
of part to A J Burge and the remainder to W J Burge for the residue then unexpired, in
each case, of the term of the 1902 lease was, notwithstanding that the landlord did not
concur in the partition, to sever the covenants of the lease so as to follow the land. Thus
h after comparable assignments of parts to separate assignees an action on the covenant
would lie against each assignee of part for not repairing his part: see *Stevenson v Lambard*
(1802) 2 East 575 at 580, 102 ER 490 at 492 per Lord Ellenborough CJ. Moreover,
established authority shows that under the covenant for payment of rent the landlord
could only sue an assignee of part only of the premises for an apportioned part of the
rent: see *Gamon v Vernon* (1678) 2 Lev 231, 83 ER 532, *Hare v Cator* (1778) 2 Cowp 766,
j 98 ER 1350, a decision of Lord Mansfield CJ, and *Stevenson v Lambard*. Some doubts as to
these authorities were expressed by Tindal CJ in *Curtis v Spitty* (1835) 1 Bing NC 756, 131
ER 1309, but he none the less followed the earlier authorities; his doubts are recorded in
the judgment of this court in *Whitham v Bullock* [1939] 2 All ER 310, [1939] 2 KB 81, but
it was not necessary to resolve them. The law has continued to be stated in the textbooks
on the subject as being that an assignee of part of the land cannot be sued for the whole

of the rent, but only for a proportionate part thereof. However, the proportionate part which the landlord could recover from an assignee of part only of the land would be the *a* part of the whole rent which the court thought fairly attributable to the part of the land in question, and not necessarily the part of the rent which the several assignees had agreed among themselves, without the concurrence of the landlord, to be attributable to that part of the land. More importantly, however, it is clear and undoubted law that, after assignments of separate parts of the land demised to separate assignees, the landlord can still distrain on any part for the rent which accrues due for the whole, because the *b* rent for the whole is considered to become due out of each and every part of the land: see *Curtis v Spitty* and *Whitham v Bullock*.

Is that enough to achieve the position that as a result of the partition two separate tenancies have been created of two separate holdings, each of which has to be looked at on its own?

In *Jelley v Buckman* [1973] 3 All ER 853, [1974] QB 488 this court had to consider the *c* converse position where there had been a severance of the reversion. In that case the common owner had granted a weekly tenancy of a dwelling house and land. A successor in title of the original landlord sold to a third party the reversion on the land, but not the reversion on the dwelling house, and the rent payable by the tenant had consequently to be apportioned between the two reversioners. The reversioner on the land claimed that the original tenancy had thereby been divided into two separate tenancies, one of the *d* dwelling house and one of the land and that consequently the tenant no longer enjoyed the protection of the Rent Acts in respect of the land. But this court rejected that contention. Stamp LJ in giving the judgment of the court said, after setting out the terms of s 140 of the Law of Property Act 1925 which is concerned with the severance of the reversionary estate in any land composed in a lease ([1973] 3 All ER 853 at 856–857, [1974] QB 488 at 497–498): *e*

> 'Now it is no doubt correct that the effect of the legislation is that each reversioner has rights and remedies similar to those which he would have if he had granted a separate tenancy of the land in respect of which he is the owner. But it is one thing to say that each reversioner has rights and remedies similar to or even indistinguishable from the rights and remedies which he would have had if there *f* had been two separate tenancies and quite another thing to say that this operates against the tenant and that he therefore has two tenacies; and we cannot read s 140 as producing the latter result. We can find nothing in the section to suggest for a moment that the legislature intended that following a severance to which the lessee was not a party, he should find himself holding part of his land under one tenancy and part under another. In relation to a lease for years as opposed to a weekly *g* tenancy the change in the law would be dramatic and had the legislature intended to create that result one would expect to find some clear expression of that intention.'

Where, as in the present case, there has been severance of the leasehold interest between several assignees, rather than a severance of the reversion, there is no relevant statutory provision comparable to s 140. The reasoning of Stamp LJ is, however, none *h* the less cogent. The injustice that there would have been to the tenant in *Jelley v Buckman* if by a transaction to which he was not a party he had thrust on him the two tenancies, one of the dwelling house and the other of the land, of which the latter would not carry Rent Act protection, would be paralleled by injustice to the landlord in the present case if by a transaction to which he was not a party he had thrust on him a separate tenancy of Glebe House and the two acres since assigned to the appellants which carried with it *j* the potential right to enfranchisement under the Leasehold Reform Act 1967 as amended. Moreover, the notion that two separate tenancies were created by the partition of the leasehold interest between two separate assignees is wholly inconsistent with the recognised position in law that the whole of the rent under the original 1902 lease can, despite the separate assignments, be recovered by distress levied on any part of the land originally comprised in that lease.

I am therefore constrained to reject the argument that what has happened here is that
a a separate contract of tenancy has come about in relation to Glebe House and the two
acres assigned to the appellants, which is not a contract for an agricultural tenancy or a
tenancy of an agricultural holding.

It follows for the reasons given that I would, albeit with some reluctance, dismiss this
appeal.

Counsel for the appellants has urged, with his accustomed skill, an alternative
b argument that a conclusion that there is a single contract for an agricultural tenancy
when one part of the land is vested in one assignee of the term and the rest is vested in a
separate assignee for the remainder of the term is wholly inconsistent with the scheme
of the Agricultural Holdings Act. He refers to the provisions of ss 8, 12, 13 and 28 of the
1986 Act, and submits that these do not fit at all where separate parts of the land are held
by separate assignees for the residue of the tenancy unless each such separate assignee is
c to be treated, at any rate for the purposes of the Act, as holding under a separate tenancy
agreement relating to a separate holding. I see the force of this, but am unable to find
enough in the point to get over the appellants' other difficulties, to which I have already
referred. An assignment of separate parts of leasehold property to separate assignees for
the residue of the term is nowadays tolerably rare, and it would not surprise me if this
possibility had been overlooked by the draftsmen of the successive Agricultural Holdings
d Acts, including the 1986 Act.

Counsel for the appellants is, of course, right in saying that on the facts *Howkins v
Jardine* [1951] 1 All ER 320, [1951] 1 KB 614 is distinguishable in that the cottages in
that case had been sublet and not assigned for the residue of the tenancy. But I am
concerned with the principle of the decision, which I find reflected in the wording of s 1
of the 1986 Act.
e As indicated, I would dismiss this appeal.

STAUGHTON LJ. I agree with both judgments.

SLADE LJ. I too have found this case very difficult, but I agree that the appeal must fail
f for the reasons given by Dillon LJ. I will add something of my own out of deference to
the argument of counsel for the appellants, particularly having regard to his submission
that a number of the sections of the Agricultural Holdings Act 1986 are not intended or
apt to deal with a situation where there are two or more separate tenants of a single
holding.

In the present case all the affirmative conditions which have to be satisfied, if the right
to enfranchisement conferred by s 1 of the Leasehold Reform Act 1967 (as amended) is
g to be exercisable by the appellants in respect of Glebe House and the two acres of
surrounding land (the Glebe House property), are satisfied. The only question is whether
the negative condition imposed by s 1(3)(*b*) is also satisfied, so as to deprive them of this
right. At the time when they gave notice of their desire to purchase the freehold of the
Glebe House property on 23 December 1985, were the premises 'comprised in an
h agricultural holding within the meaning of the Agricultural Holdings Act 1948'? If so,
s 1 of the 1967 Act does not avail them.

It is indisputable (and common ground) that immediately before the execution of the
deed of partition of 16 December 1963 the Glebe House property was comprised in one
'agricultural holding', consisting of the aggregate of the land comprised in the 'contract
for an agricultural tenancy' embodied in the lease of 17 January 1902.
j By the deed of partition the lease of the Glebe House property was assigned to Alfred
Burge and the lease of the rest of the premises comprised in the 1902 lease was assigned
to William Burge. Clause 3 provided that the yearly rent of £9 reserved by that lease
should be apportioned, so that the yearly rent of £5 should be exclusively payable in
respect of the Glebe House property, in exoneration of the rest of the premises comprised
in the lease, and the yearly rent of £4 should be exclusively payable in respect of the rest
of the premises, in exoneration of the Glebe House property.

If the landlord had concurred in the apportionment of rent provided for by the 1963 deed of partition, this might well have given rise to the emergence of two new 'contracts   *a* of tenancy', by way of novation, to each of which the landlord was a party, the first contract relating to the Glebe House property and providing for the payment of £5 annual rent to the landlord, the second contract relating to the rest of the premises comprised in the 1902 lease and providing for the payment of £4 annual rent. Whether or not the landlord's concurrence had this effect would have depended on the manner and terms of his concurrence. If two new contracts of tenancy had emerged, so too would   *b* two new and separate 'agricultural holdings'. (At that stage, it would appear, the contemplated use of both units was still for the purpose of the trade or business of agriculture.)

However, the parties to the 1963 deed of partition did not obtain the landlord's consent to any apportionment of the rent. The evidence of Mr Henry John Ridd, who became the landlord after the death of his father in 1960, was that Mr A J Burge paid him the full   *c* rent of £9 per annum and that after his death (which occurred in 1981) his widow paid this entire rent. A letter dated 27 April 1983 from the landlord's solicitors to the appellants' solicitors records the rejection by the landlord of a tender by the appellants of an apportioned £5 rent.

Section 190(3) of the Law of Property Act 1925 (so far as material) provides:
d

'Where in a conveyance for valuable consideration, other than a mortgage, of part of land comprised in a lease, for the residue of the term or interest created by the lease, the rent reserved by such lease or a part thereof is, without the consent of the lessor, expressed to be ... (*c*) apportioned between the land conveyed or any part thereof and the land retained by the assignor or any part thereof; then, without prejudice to the rights of the lessor, such ... apportionment shall be binding as   *e* between the assignor and the assignee under the conveyance and their respective successors in title'.

Section 190(6) provides that the section applies only if and so far as a contrary intention is not expressed in the conveyance. Section 190(7) provides, inter alia, that the remedies conferred by the section do not apply where 'the rent is ... legally apportioned with the   *f* consent of the owner or lessor'.

As the words 'without prejudice to the rights of the lessor' in s 190(3) implicitly recognise, an apportionment of rent effected without the landlord's consent on an assignment of part of the demised premises is not, at least in all respects, binding on the lessor. It does not affect the landlord's right to distrain on that part for the rent of the whole: see *Witham v Bullock* [1939] 2 All ER 310 at 315, [1939] 2 KB 81 at 86 per Clauson   *g* LJ. On the authorities it is not entirely clear whether the landlord ceases to be in a position to sue any one except the original lessee (whom he can sue in contract) for the whole rent and can only sue the tenants of the severed parts in respect of a proportion of the rent. This court expressly left this question open in *Whitham v Bullock*. Nevertheless, I think it is clear that if the landlord can only sue the tenants of the severed parts in respect of a proportion of the rent, such proportion is a fair proportion to be determined by the   *h* court. It is not necessarily the proportion which the assignor and assignee may have agreed between themselves. The proportion thus agreed is not as such binding on the landlord.

Throughout, it has to be remembered that the definition of a 'contract for an agricultural tenancy' in s 1(2) of the 1986 Act directs attention to 'the whole of the land comprised in the contract'. In the circumstances of this case there has been only one   *j* relevant 'contract of tenancy', that is to say the contract embodied in the 1902 lease. So far as the landlord is concerned, a second contract has never been made and no part of the premises comprised in the original contract has ever been removed from it.

With all these points in mind, I cannot accept the submission that the execution of the 1963 deed of partition, without the landlord's consent, had the effect of imposing on him

a the creation of two new and distinct 'agricultural holdings' with separate tenants of each
holding and with all the other consequences attendant on the creation of two new distinct
holdings. In my judgment, if he had known about the execution of the deed of partition,
he would have been entitled to say that, so far as he was concerned, the relevant
'agricultural holding' was the same as it always had been, namely the whole of the
premises comprised in the 1902 lease.

b I recognise that, as counsel for the appellants cogently pointed out, this view of the
matter gives rise to potential problems in applying certain provisions of the 1986 Act,
for example ss 8, 12, 13 and 14, which do not appear to contemplate or cater adequately
for the case where there are separate tenants of separate parts of one agricultural holding.
Nevertheless, the existence of such problems does not, in my judgment, compel or justify
the acceptance of the submission referred to in the immediately preceding paragraph.

c I would add these observations. Section 6 of the 1986 Act now contains provisions
which, if invoked, may effectively enable the landlord of an agricultural holding to
prevent future assignments of all or part of the tenancy without his written consent,
even though the original tenancy agreement contains no such restriction: see particularly
s 6(1) and (5) of and para 9 of Sch 1 to the 1986 Act. Having regard to para 9, I do not
think the legislature in the 1986 Act entirely overlooked the possibility of assignments
of separate parts of leasehold property to separate assignees for the residue of the term.
d However, it may well have considered that such assignments would be rare in practice.
Equally, in drafting ss 8, 12, 13 and 14, it may well have overlooked the possibility of
such assignments taking place without the landlord's consent. For the reasons given
above, assignments of parts of the demised premises *with* the landlord's consent are much
less likely to raise problems in practice.

e Be this as it may, I am satisfied that after the execution of the 1963 deed of partition
the entirety of the premises demised by the 1902 lease remained one single 'agricultural
holding' for the purpose of the Agricultural Holdings Acts. The assignment of 13
December 1982 relating to the Glebe House property made by the executors of Alfred
Burge in favour of the appellants, again without the landlord's consent, did not, in my
judgment, alter the situation. Thereafter, the Glebe House property, which up to that
f time, on the recorder's findings of fact, had been used for the purposes of a trade or
business of agriculture, ceased to be so used. In my judgment, however, also on the
recorder's findings of fact, if the land comprised in the 1902 lease is looked at as a whole
(which I think it must be), that land, with an exception which does not substantially
affect the character of the tenancy (viz the Glebe House property), has still continued to
be 'let for use as agricultural land' within the meaning of s 1(2) of the 1986 Act.

g It follows that, in my judgment, on 23 December 1985, (1) the Glebe House property
was still comprised in an agricultural holding within the meaning of the 1948 Act,
consisting of the whole of the premises demised by the 1902 lease, (2) s 1(3)(b) of the
1967 Act accordingly operated so as to deprive the appellants of any right of
enfranchisement which they might otherwise have enjoyed.

For these reasons, and the other reasons given by Dillon LJ I too would dismiss this
h appeal.

Appeal dismissed.

Solicitors: *Clarke Willmott & Clarke,* Taunton (for the appellants); *Hole & Pugsley,* Tiverton
(for the respondent).

Celia Fox   Barrister.

Practice Note

QUEEN'S BENCH DIVISION
LORD LANE CJ, KENNEDY AND HUTCHISON JJ
10 MARCH 1989

Practice – Chambers proceedings – Queen's Bench Division – Chambers applications and appeals – Inter partes applications and appeals – Listing – General list – Chambers appeals list – Special appointments – Estimate of length of hearing – Papers for perusal by judge – Skeleton argument or chronology.

LORD LANE CJ gave the following direction at the sitting of the court. In order to expedite the hearing of work listed to be heard by the Queen's Bench judge in chambers the inter partes procedure has been reorganised. Part A of the existing Practice Direction (see *Practice Note* [1983] 1 All ER 1119, [1983] 1 WLR 433) is replaced by the following.

Queen's Bench judge in chambers: inter partes applications and appeals.

1. All inter partes applications and appeals to the Queen's Bench judge in chambers will initially be entered in a general list. They will be listed for hearing in room 98 or some other room at the Royal Courts of Justice on Tuesdays or Thursdays.

Whenever it appears or is agreed that any application or appeal is likely to last more than 30 minutes it will immediately and automatically be transferred to either (1) the chambers appeals list or (2) for all cases other than appeals to the special appointments list.

2. Cases in the special appointments list will usually be heard on a date fixed after application to fix has been made by the parties. The application to fix must be accompanied by an estimate of the length of the hearing signed by the applicant's counsel or solicitor who is to appear on the application.

3. Cases in the chambers appeals list will be listed in the Daily Cause List. This will be done by the clerk of the lists when he prepares the following day's list at 2 pm. They may be listed on any day of the week but particularly on Fridays, when there is often a need for short cases. They may be listed as floaters when, because no experts or other witnesses are involved, they seem particularly well suited as such. Fixtures will only be given in exceptional circumstances.

4. In order to ensure that a complete set of papers in proper order is available for perusal by the judge before hearing such applications and appeals, the parties must in advance of the hearing lodge in room 119 a bundle properly paged in order of date and indexed, containing copies of the following documents: (i) the notice of appeal or, as the case may be, the application; (ii) the pleadings (if any); (iii) copies of all affidavits (together with exhibits thereto) on which any party intends to rely; and (iv) any relevant order made in the action. The bundle should be agreed. The originals of all affidavits intended to be relied on should be bespoken or produced at the hearing and all exhibits thereto should be available.

Where a date for the hearing has been fixed (which will normally be the case for special appointments) the bundle must be lodged *not later than five clear days before the fixed date.*

For appeals and other cases where there is no fixed date for hearing the bundle must be lodged not later than 48 hours after the parties have been notified that the case is to appear in the warned list.

Except with leave of the judge, no document may be adduced in evidence or relied on unless a copy of it has been lodged and the original bespoken as aforesaid.

In cases of complexity a skeleton argument or, where that would be helpful, a chronology should be lodged in room 119 at the same time as the bundle.

N P Metcalfe Esq   Barrister.

a

J v J (C intervening)

COURT OF APPEAL, CIVIL DIVISION
O'CONNOR LJ AND BOOTH J
13 DECEMBER 1988, 25 JANUARY 1989

b
Divorce – Financial provision – Child – Maintenance – Matters to be considered by court when making order – Financial resources – Interest under discretionary will trust – Father ordered to pay maintenance for children of marriage following divorce – Mother subsequently dying and leaving estate to children – Discretionary will trust established for benefit of children – Whether children's interest under discretionary will trust a 'financial resource' – Whether children's interest under will trust to be taken into account in determining amount of maintenance payable by father – Matrimonial Causes Act 1973, s 25(3)(b).

c

Following the divorce of the parents, custody of the two children of the marriage was given to the mother in 1978 and the father was ordered to make periodical payments to the mother and the children. In 1982 the periodical payments were increased to £45 per week for the mother and £15 and £12 per week for each child respectively. In 1986 the
d father transferred his half share in the former matrimonial home to the mother in satisfaction of her claim for arrears of maintenance. In 1987 the mother died leaving an estate of £17,525 to the two children. The trustees were empowered in their discretion to pay the whole or any part of the income or capital from the trust for the benefit of either of the children until they reached the age of 18, when they would become entitled to the trust fund absolutely, but the trustees' stated aim was to preserve the fund until
e the children reached the age of 18 and not to advance funds for their maintenance unless they were compelled to do so. Following their mother's death the children went to live with their maternal grandmother, who applied for an increase in the maintenance paid by the father. The registrar and, on appeal, the judge refused to order any increase on the ground that the children's interest in the trust fund was a 'financial resource' within s 25(3)(b)[a] of the Matrimonial Causes Act 1973 and that taking that interest into account
f there was no reason to vary the father's maintenance payments. The grandmother appealed to the Court of Appeal.

Held – The children's interest under the discretionary trust was a 'financial resource' within s 25(3)(b) of the 1973 Act and had correctly been taken into account by the judge when determining the amount of maintenance payable by the father in respect of the
g children, but in assessing the value of their interest under the trust the court had to balance the necessity to ensure that the children's needs were properly met without the father being required to pay more than he could properly afford against placing improper pressure on the trustees to exercise their discretion to make payments for the children which they would not otherwise make. In particular, the court had to have regard to the trustees' intentions, the nature of the trust fund and the father's duty to maintain the
h children in accordance with his means. Since the judge had assumed the trust fund was available for the maintenance of the children without considering the father's duty to maintain them the appeal would be allowed and the case remitted to the judge for further consideration (see p 1123 j, p 1124 c d h j and p 1125 c e to h, post).

B v B (financial provision) (1982) 3 FLR 298 followed.
Howard v Howard [1945] 1 All ER 91 applied.
j *Lord Lilford v Glynn* [1979] 1 All ER 441 distinguished.

---

a   Section 25(3), so far as material, provides: 'As regards the exercise of the powers of the court [with respect to financial provision in connection with divorce proceedings etc] . . . in relation to a child of the family, the court shall in particular have regard to . . . (b) the income, earning capacity (if any), property and other financial resources of the child . . .'

Notes

For the principles of assessment to which the court must have regard when making *a*
orders for financial provision, see 13 Halsbury's Laws (4th edn) paras 1060–1066, and for
cases on the subject, see 27(3) Digest (2nd reissue) 167–186, 10243–10293.

For the Matrimonial Causes Act 1973, s 25, see 27 Halsbury's Statutes (4th edn) 729.

Cases referred to in judgments

B v B (*financial provision*) (1982) 3 FLR 298, CA.
Howard v Howard [1945] 1 All ER 91, [1945] P 1, CA.   *b*
Lilford (Lord) v Glynn [1979] 1 All ER 441, [1979] 1 WLR 78, CA.

Cases also cited

Douglas v Andrews (1849) 12 Beav 310, 50 ER 1080.
Peel, Re, Tattersall v Peel [1936] Ch 161, [1935] All ER Rep 179.
Saunders v Vautier (1841) Cr & Ph 240, [1835–42] All ER Rep 58, 41 ER 482, LC.   *c*
Wilson v Turner (1883) 22 Ch D 521 CA.

Interlocutory appeal

The grandmother of two children, having been given leave to intervene in divorce
proceedings on the death of her daughter and having had vested in her by consent the
custody, care and control of the children with reasonable access to the respondent, the   *d*
father, appealed against the order of his Honour Judge Kellock QC sitting in chambers at
Chesterfield on 5 August 1988, whereby he dismissed her appeal from the order of Mr
Registrar Hibbert sitting in chambers at Chesterfield on 25 May 1988 dismissing her
application on behalf of the children for an increase in the amount of periodical payments
paid by the father. The grandmother sought an order that he pay to the children such
sum by way of periodical payments as appeared just. The facts are set out in the judgment *e*
of Booth J.

Graham Robinson for the grandmother.
The father did not appear.

Cur adv vult
f
25 January. The following judgments were delivered.

BOOTH J (giving the first judgment at the invitation of O'Connor LJ). This appeal
from an order of his Honour Judge Kellock QC raises an important issue as to what
extent, if any, in assessing the quantum of maintenance to be paid by a father for his
children the court should have regard to the children's financial interests under a
discretionary will trust.   *g*

The material facts can be briefly stated. The two children are A, born on 27 December
1972, and S, born on 29 October 1977. Their father is the respondent to this appeal,
although he has not been represented or appeared before us. Their mother died in August
1987. The appellant is the children's maternal grandmother, who now has the custody
of both children.

The parents were married but subsequently divorced. In May 1978 custody of the   *h*
children was vested in the mother and the father was ordered to make periodical
payments for them and for her. Quantum of maintenance was varied on 1 February
1982, when the father was ordered to pay £45 per week for the mother, £15 per week
for A and £12 per week for S. On 12 June 1986 a consent order was made by which the
father transferred his half interest in the former matrimonial home to the mother subject
to the then existing mortgage, her claim for periodical payments for herself was dismissed *j*
and arrears of maintenance which had accrued both in respect of her and the children
were remitted. The order for the children's periodical payments continued unchanged.

Following the mother's sudden death in August 1987 the children went to the home
of their maternal grandmother, where they have since remained. Leave was given to her

to intervene in the divorce proceedings and on 6 April 1988, by consent, the custody,
a care and control of the children were vested in her with reasonable access to the father.
Immediately prior to that, on 29 March 1988, the grandmother had issued an application
to vary by increasing the periodical payments for the children. That application was
dismissed by Mr Registrar Hibbert and the appeal from that order was in turn dismissed
by Judge Kellock on 5 August 1988. It is her further appeal from the order of Judge
Kellock which has brought the grandmother to this court.

b   The grandmother, who is a widow and a housewife, derives her income from her state
pension, in addition to which she receives child benefit and the single parent allowance.
The father is a coal miner who, when the matter was before Judge Kellock, had an
income of approximately £14,200 gross per annum. Although he had remarried and has
a son by that marriage, it was common ground between the parties that he could afford
to pay more for the two children of his first marriage if he was ordered to do so. The
c reason why both the registrar and the judge declined to increase the periodical payments
for the children was the fact that they are both beneficiaries of their mother's estate under
the terms of her will.

By her will, dated 1 May 1980, the mother appointed two solicitors, John Blakesley
and Clifford William Bellamy, to be her joint executors and trustees. She left the whole
of her estate to those trustees on trust either to retain or to sell it and, after paying all
d debts, taxes and executorship expenses, to pay the residue equally to A and S. The will
empowered the trustees, in their discretion, to pay the whole or any part of the income
or capital for the benefit of either child until each became of age and absolutely entitled
to his and her share.

Following the mother's death, the former matrimonial home, which had been
transferred into her sole name, was sold and thereupon her net estate amounted to
e £17,525. This money has been invested and it is again common ground that, if the
whole of the income derived from the trust fund was to be advanced by the trustees for
the children's maintenance, then their needs would be met and it would not be necessary
for the father to have to pay more by way of periodical payments.

In concluding that the order against the father should not be varied, the judge held
f that s 25(3)(b) of the Matrimonial Causes Act 1973, as amended, required him to take
into account the trust fund for the benefit of the children and, although the power on
the part of the trustees to advance income and capital was discretionary, it was nevertheless
a financial resource within the meaning of that section. The judge expressed the view
that it was not unfair to take the fund into consideration inasmuch as it was the
equivalent of the mother contributing to the children's upbringing and on that ground
g he held that there was no case to vary the payments made by the father.

Counsel for the grandmother first submitted that, since the children cannot call for
neither the income or the capital of the trust fund until Pmthey come of age, they have
no present financial resource within the meaning of s 25(3) of the 1973 Act. He supported
that submission by pointing to the difference in wording between s 25(2)(a) and s 25(3)(b).
When dealing with the financial position of the parties to a marriage, the court is required
h to have regard not only to the income, earning capacity, property and other financial
resources which each of the parties has, but also to that which he or she is likely to have
in the foreseeable future, whereas in the case of a child the court's attention is directed
only to the income, earning capacity (if any), property and other financial resources
which the child presently has without being required to have regard to what the future
may hold in that respect. Counsel for the grandmother argued that as the children are
j unable to require the trustees to pay them capital or income from the fund then it must
follow that they have no present financial resource in respect of that fund, which will not
come under their absolute control until they respectively attain their majorities. Thus,
he says, the judge was wrong in holding their present interests to be a financial resource
within the meaning of the 1973 Act.

I cannot accept that argument. I do not think that the position of the children in this

case can be distinguished from that of the wife in B v B (*financial provision*) (1982) 3 FLR
298. In that case the wife was a beneficiary under two settlements. Under the first, made   *a*
by her father, the trustees had power in their absolute discretion to vest the whole or any
part of the trust capital in the wife absolutely. Under the second, of which she herself
was the settlor, she was permitted to withdraw all or any part of the trust fund with the
consent of the trustees. The Court of Appeal held that both settlements were potential
sources of capital for the wife and were, therefore, 'other financial resources' within the
meaning of s 25(2)(a) of the 1973 Act although neither fund was under her absolute   *b*
control. The court further held that, in assessing her means for the purpose of an ancillary
relief application by the husband, some assessment must be made of the worth of those
potential sources of capital to the wife in terms of the practical realities of life or in terms
of reasonable expectations. Similarly, in my view, in this case the mother's will trust
provides a potential source of income for the children at the present time, and, following
the decision in B v B, it must constitute a financial resource to which the court must have   *c*
regard even though neither child is absolutely entitled to the fund. I therefore agree with
the approach of the judge when he said that he was compelled to have regard to the
children's interests under their mother's will. But, that being so, it then becomes
necessary for some assessment to be made of the realities of the situation and what each
child may reasonably expect to receive by way of income or capital until he or she attains
the age of 18.   *d*

The means by which the court can make such an assessment is not likely to be easy.
Section 31(1)(i) of the Trustee Act 1925 generally empowers trustees in their sole
discretion to advance such income from a trust as may be reasonable to a parent or
guardian of a minor beneficiary for his maintenance, education or benefit having regard
to his age and requirements and generally to all the circumstances of the case. That
general power is specifically contained in the trust created by the mother's will, so that it   *e*
is clear that the children, during their respective minorities, will receive only such capital
or income from the fund as the trustees think fit to advance. Although it is not clear
what evidence the judge had as to the policy to be followed by the trustees, counsel for
the grandmother has told us that it is not their intention to advance funds for the purpose
of maintaining the children unless they are compelled to do so and to date they have only
advanced one modest sum of £140 with which to buy gifts for them as a small   *f*
consolation for the death of their mother. In the light of that stated intention and of the
trustees' absolute discretion under the terms of the trust, counsel for the grandmother
submitted that the judge was wrong to assume that the whole of the trust income would
nevertheless be available for the children's maintenance and that assumption led him to
overlook the fact that the primary duty to maintain the children continues to rest on the
father and to overlook his ability to pay more for them. Counsel for the grandmother   *g*
concedes, however, that despite their stated intention to preserve the funds the trustees
may nevertheless be willing to advance moneys to provide things for the children which
could not otherwise be afforded.

When faced with such a situation as this, the court has to perform a careful balancing
exercise to ensure that the children's needs are met without requiring the father to pay   *h*
more than he can properly afford while at the same time not placing improper pressure
on the trustees to exercise their discretion in such a way that they would not otherwise
have thought it right to exercise it: see Howard v Howard [1945] 1 All ER 91, [1945] P 1.
In performing this exercise, it seems to me to be helpful for the court to consider a
number of matters. Any statement made by a trustee as to the future exercise by him of
his discretion under the trustees needs to be evaluated, a task which in this case may be   *j*
made the more difficult since those same solicitors who are the trustees for the children's
fund also act for the grandmother in this application.

It is also necessary for the court to have regard to the nature of the trust under which
the child is a beneficiary. In this case, the trust fund represents an inheritance which in
the normal course of events the children would not have received until a much later

stage in their lives. The fund was not established for the purpose of providing for the
a children's maintenance and education, as was the situation in *Lord Lilford v Glynn* [1979]
1 All ER 441, [1979] 1 WLR 78. This is a family from a modest financial background
and the fund which is now held in trust for the children is likely to be their only major
capital asset, which, had the mother lived, would have continued to have been invested
in the bricks and mortar of her home, yielding no income, but appreciating in value
with the rise in property prices. Had it not been for the mother's untimely death, there
b would have been no question of the children deriving any benefit from the property
other than the fact that it provided a roof over their heads. Further, the court should not
lose sight of the fact that the mother's death in no way alters the duty of the father to
maintain the children in accordance with his means. It would, therefore, be wrong to
treat the trust fund which has come about as a result of the mother's death as representing
something of a windfall for the father absolving him to a great extent from the burden
c he would otherwise have to bear in maintaining the children.

Those are all factors which, in my view, are relevant for the court to consider in
assessing how best the needs of the children can be met. No one can imagine that the
current order, made as long ago as 1982, of £15 per week for a 16-year-old boy and £12
per week for an 11-year-old girl, could come anywhere near paying for their essential
requirements. There is no evidence before us that the children's needs have in fact been
d fully quantified, but I venture to think it unlikely that any order which could reasonably
be made against this father could do more than contribute towards the maintenance of
the children, leaving the grandmother, with or without the assistance of the trust fund,
to do the rest.

For the reasons I have given, I have come to the conclusion that the judge correctly
decided that he must have regard for the trust fund as a financial resource, but misdirected
e himself in simply assuming that the whole income should be available for the children
without carrying out the balancing exercise to which I have referred. We have been told
that the means of the parties have changed since the matter was heard by the judge, so
that, in my judgment, it is necessary to remit the matter back to him for further
consideration. I would, therefore, allow this appeal.

f **O'CONNOR LJ.** I agree with the judgment of Booth J and I agree that the case must
go back to the judge.

I have no doubt, for the reasons given by Booth J, that the interest of the children in
their mother's will is 'a financial resource' within the meaning of s 25(3)(*b*) of the
Matrimonial Causes Act 1973. The difficulty comes in assessing its worth when deciding
what it is fair to order the father to pay. No pressure is to be put on the trustees, but, in
g my judgment, the court is entitled to assume that they will act reasonably in all the
circumstances of the case. Each case must depend on its own facts. The financial position
of the father and the size of the trust are quite obviously very important considerations.
In this balancing exercise, common sense should prevail so that rich fathers should not
expect much relief whereas poor father should not have the last drop of money extracted
h from them.

The appeal must be allowed and the case sent back to the judge.

Appeal allowed. Case remitted to judge for further consideration.

Solicitors: *Blakesley & Rooth*, Chesterfield (for the grandmother).

Raina Levy   Barrister.

Director of Public Prosecutions v Watkins   *a*

QUEEN'S BENCH DIVISION
TAYLOR LJ AND HENRY J
23, 24 JANUARY, 1 MARCH 1989

Road traffic – Being in charge of vehicle when unfit to drive through drink or drugs – In charge – *b*
Defendant in car holding ignition key – Defendant's blood-alcohol level above prescribed limit –
Defendant not owner of vehicle – Engine not running – No evidence that ignition key capable of
starting car – Whether defendant 'in charge' of motor vehicle – Road Traffic Act 1972, ss 5, 6.

The defendant was found by two police officers sitting in a car which he did not own
holding a key which bore the name of a different make of car but which could be inserted *c*
into the car's ignition. The car was stationary and the engine was not running. The
defendant had a blood-alcohol level above the prescribed limit and he was charged with
being in charge of a motor vehicle while unfit to drive, contrary to s 5[a] of the Road
Traffic Act 1972, and being in charge of a motor vehicle while his blood-alcohol level
exceeded the prescribed limit, contrary to s 6[b] of that Act. There was no evidence that
the defendant had been in the car with the owner's permission or that the ignition key *d*
which he had been holding was capable of starting the car. The magistrates held that
there was no case to answer because the prosecution had not shown that the defendant
had been 'in charge' of the motor vehicle and they dismissed the charges. The prosecution
appealed.

Held – Although there was no hard and fast all-embracing test of what constituted being *e*
'in charge' of a motor vehicle for the purposes of drink-driving charges under ss 5 and 6
of the 1972 Act, there had to be a close connection between the defendant and control of
the vehicle before the charge could be proved. That connection could be evidenced by
the defendant's position in relation to the car, his actions, possession of a key which fitted
the ignition, his intentions as regards control of the vehicle and the position of anyone
else in, at or near the vehicle. Proof of the likelihood of the defendant driving the vehicle *f*
was not necessary and once a prima facie case of being in charge had been made out
against him the burden was on him to prove that there was no likelihood of him driving
the vehicle. The question in every case was (i) whether, if the defendant had been in
charge of the vehicle by virtue of being the owner, lawful possessor or recent driver of it,
he was still in charge or had relinquished charge or (ii) whether, if he was not the owner,
lawful possessor or recent driver of it but was sitting in it or was otherwise involved with *g*
it at the relevant time, he had assumed charge. Since the defendant's presence in the
driving seat holding an ignition key supported an inference that he intended to take
control of the car by starting it, the magistrates had been premature to conclude that he
was not in charge of the vehicle. The appeal would therefore be allowed and the case
remitted to the magistrates to continue the hearing (see p 1131 *ef*, p 1132 *h* to p 1133 *c g*
to p 1134 *c*, post).   *h*
Haines v Roberts [1953] 1 All ER 344 not followed.

---

a   Section 5, so far as material, is set out at p 1130 *a* to p 1131 *c*, post
b   Section 6, so far as material, provides:
       '(1) If a person . . . (*b*) is in charge of a motor vehicle on a road or other public place after
       consuming so much alcohol that the proportion of it in his breath, blood or urine exceeds the *j*
       prescribed limit he shall be guilty of an offence.'
       (2) It is a defence for a person charged with an offence under subsection (1)(*b*) above to prove
       that at the time he is alleged to have committed the offence the circumstances were such that there
       was no likelihood of his driving the vehicle whilst the proportion of alcohol in his breath, blood or
       urine remained likely to exceed the prescribed limit; but in determining whether there was such
       a likelihood the court may disregard any injury to him and any damage to the vehicle.'

Notes

a For being in charge of a motor vehicle while unfit to drive or with a blood-alcohol level which exceeds the prescribed limit, see 40 Halsbury's Laws (4th edn) paras 482, 487, and for cases on the subject, see 39(1) Digest (Reissue) 490, 3665–3667.

For the Road Traffic Act 1972, s 5, see 42 Halsbury's Statutes (3rd edn) 1646, and for s 6 of that Act (as substituted by the Transport Act 1981, s 25(3), Sch 8), see 51 ibid 1427.

As from 15 May 1989 ss 5 and 6 of the 1972 Act have been replaced by ss 4 and 5 of
b the Road Traffic Act 1988.

Cases referred to in judgments

Blayney v Knight (1975) 60 Cr App R 269, DC.
Crichton v Burrell 1951 JC 107, HC of Just.
DPP v Webb [1988] RTR 374, DC.
c *Fisher v Keaton* (1964) 108 SJ 258, DC.
Haines v Roberts [1953] 1 All ER 344, [1953] 1 WLR 309, DC.
Morton v Confer [1963] 2 All ER 765, [1963] 1 WLR 763, DC.
Northfield v Pinder [1968] 3 All ER 854, [1969] 2 QB 7, [1969] 2 WLR 50, DC.
Woodage v Jones (No 2) (1975) 60 Cr App R 260, DC.

d
Cases also cited

Dawson v Procurator Fiscal (25 February 1976, unreported), HC of Just.
Dean v Wishart 1952 JC 9, HC of Just.
Hooper v Stansfield (1950) 114 JP 368, DC.
Jowett-Shooter v Franklin [1949] 2 All ER 730, DC.
e *Kelly v Hogan* [1982] RTR 352, DC.
R v Hawkes (1931) 22 Cr App R 172, CCA.
Sheldon v Jones [1970] RTR 38, DC.
Walker v Rountree [1963] NI 23, NI CA.

Case stated

f The Director of Public Prosecutions appealed by way of case stated by the justices acting in and for the petty sessional division of North Westminster in respect of their adjudication as a magistrates' court sitting at Wells Street on 25 April 1988 whereby they dismissed an information laid by the appellant charging the respondent, Steven Watkins, with (i) being in charge of a motor vehicle on a road while unfit through drink or drugs, contrary to s 5 of and Sch 4 to the Road Traffic Act 1972, and (ii) being in charge of a
g motor vehicle on a road or other public place when the proportion of alcohol in his blood exceeded the prescribed limit, contrary to s 6 of and Sch 4 to the 1972 Act. The questions for the opinion of the High Court were (i) whether the magistrates were correct in finding no case to answer at the conclusion of the prosecution case on the grounds that there was insufficient evidence that the defendant was in charge of a motor vehicle, (ii) whether in determining at the conclusion of the prosecution case that there was
h insufficient evidence that the defendant was in charge of a motor vehicle, the magistrates were right to take into account (a) evidence that the car did not belong to the defendant and (b) doubts whether car keys found in his possession could, in fact, start the car, and (iii) whether the meaning of the phrase 'in charge' necessitated a close connection between a defendant and the control of, or likelihood of driving, a motor vehicle. The facts are set out in the judgment of Taylor LJ.

j
Michael Birnbaum for the appellant.
Nigel Pleming as amicus curiae.
The respondent did not appear.

Cur adv vult

1 March. The following judgments were delivered.

TAYLOR LJ. In this case the Crown Prosecution Service appeal by way of case stated   *a*
from a decision of the North Westminster magistrates sitting as a magistrates' court at
Wells Street on 25 April 1988.

The justices had before them two informations alleging that the respondent (1) on the
13 February 1988 at Noel Street, London W1, was in charge of a motor vehicle on a road
whilst unfit through drink or drugs, contrary to s 5 of and Sch 4 to the Road Traffic Act   *b*
1972, as substituted by s 25 of and Sch 8 to the Transport Act 1981, and (2) on the same
date at the same place was in charge of a motor vehicle on a road or other public place
when the the proportion of alcohol in his blood exceeded the prescribed limit, contrary
to s 6 of and Sch 4 to the 1972 Act, as substituted by s 25 of and Sch 8 to the 1981 Act.

The justices found the following facts:

> '(i) On 13th February 1988 at 12.10 a.m. two uniformed Police Officers found   *c*
> the defendant seated in the driver's seat of a Mini motor vehicle registration EKO
> 539Y. The defendant was drunk.
> (ii) The Mini motor vehicle EKO 539Y was not owned by the defendant and
> there was no evidence that he was in that car with the owner's permission. The
> police did not trace or contact the owner of the vehicle.   *d*
> (iii) The defendant was holding a bunch of keys in his right hand, with one key
> marked "Honda" held between his thumb and forefinger. The key could be inserted
> into the ignition of the Mini motor vehicle, but there was no evidence it was capable
> of starting the engine. The lights of the car were not switched on and the engine
> was not running.
> (iv) The defendant was arrested and taken to West End Central Police Station   *e*
> where he was required to give a specimen of blood which on analysis, was shown to
> contain not less than 188 milligrammes of alcohol in 100 millilitres of blood.'

On those facts the appellant contended that a prima facie case had been raised in
support of the two informations. The appellant relied on the fact that the respondent was
seated in the car, he was drunk and he had a key in his possession which fitted the
ignition. There was no evidence that the key would not start the car.   *f*

The respondent relied on the fact that the car did not belong to him. Although the
key fitted the ignition, it bore the name of a different make of car, and the appellant had
failed to prove that the key would start the engine. In those circumstances it was argued
that there was no likelihood of the respondent driving the car away. Therefore there was
no case to answer and the charges should be dismissed.

The justices upheld the respondent's submission that there was no case to answer.   *g*
They were of the opinion that the prosecution had failed to establish that the defendant
was in charge of the vehicle and accordingly dismissed both charges.

The questions posed by the justices for the opinion of this court are:

> '(i) Whether we were correct in finding no case to answer at the conclusion of the
> prosecution case on the grounds that there was insufficient evidence that the   *h*
> defendant was in charge of a motor vehicle. (ii) Whether in determining at the
> conclusion of the prosecution case that there was insufficient evidence that the
> defendant was in charge of a motor vehicle, we were right to take into account:—
> (a) evidence that the car did not belong to the defendant and (b) doubts as to whether
> the car keys found in his possession could in fact start the car. (iii) Whether the
> meaning of the phrase "in charge" necessitates a close connection between a   *j*
> defendant and the control of, [or a] likelihood of driving, a motor vehicle.'

Those last words are taken verbatim from *Wilkinson's Road Traffic Offences* (13th edn,
1987) vol 1, p 1/203.

There were two regrettable omissions by the police. First, they failed to discover from
the owner whether the defendant had his permission to be in the car and for what

purpose. Second, they failed to test whether the key in the defendant's had would in fact
turn on the engine.

a

The result is that the facts of this case have the unreality of a student examination
problem. They raise in acute form the question: what must the prosecution prove to
establish that a defendant is 'in charge of a motor vehicle'.

That phrase has appeared in successive statutes since the Road Traffic Act 1930. There
have been many reported cases in which differing, and often bizarre facts, have been said

b to fall on one or other side of the line, but no exhaustive definition has been given as to
the scope of the phrase. Probably it cannot be. In a number of the cases the court has said
that whether a person is 'in charge' is a matter of fact and degree (see eg *Fisher v Keaton*
(1964) 108 SJ 258, *Woodage v Jones (No 2)* (1975) 60 Cr App R 260 at 263 and most
recently *DPP v Webb* [1988] RTR 374 at 379).

Nevertheless, we have been invited to give what guidance we can as to the relevant
c criteria and considerations on the issue, 'in charge' or no. In my judgment it would not
be profitable to embark on an exhaustive review of the many decided cases, most of
which turn on their special facts. But it may be helpful to examine such principles as
have been applied in the light of statutory changes.

Even before the 1930 Act the phrase had been used in the Intoxicating Liquor
(Licensing) Act 1872, s 12 of which provided, so far as is relevant, as follows:

d

> 'Every person . . . who is drunk while in charge on any highway or other public
> place of any carriage, horse, cattle or steam engine . . . shall be liable to a penalty . . .'

The words 'drunk while in charge on any highway', and the application of the phrase
to livestock as well as to carriages and steam engines, seems to have required physical
proximity of the defendant on the highway sufficient to exercise control.

e Section 15(1) of the 1930 Act defined an offence committed by any person who—

> 'when in charge of, a motor vehicle on a road or other public place is under the
> influence of drink or a drug to such an extent as to be incapable of having proper
> control of the vehicle . . .'

Thus the geographical emphasis was put on the position of the vehicle rather than of
f the defendant (see *DPP v Webb*).

The effect of that provision was held by the English courts to be that, if a motor vehicle
was on a road, he who had put it there was in charge of it unless and until he put it in the
charge of someone else. In *Haines v Roberts* [1953] 1 All ER 344, [1953] 1 WLR 309 a
motor cyclist became drunk and incapable. His friends were in process of arranging for
someone else to ride the motor cycle and for its drunken owner to be taken home.
g Nevertheless the owner, who was near the cycle, was held to be in charge.

Lord Goddard CJ said ([1953] 1 All ER 344 at 345, [1953] 1 WLR 309 at 311):

> 'How can it be said that in those circumstances the respondent was not in charge
> of the motor cycle? He had not put it into anybody else's charge. It may be that, if a
> man goes to a public house and leaves his car outside or in the car park and, getting
h > drunk, asks a friend to go and look after the car for him or take the car home, he has
> put it in charge of somebody else, but if he does not put the vehicle in charge of
> somebody else he is in charge of it until he does so. His car is away from home . . .
> and he is in charge.'

That is a simple robust statement of principle but it can hardly be complete. For
j example, if a stranger were to take and drive the car away without the owner's consent
and were then to stop the car temporarily, remaining in the driving seat, he would
doubtless be in charge of it even though the owner had not put him in charge.

In Scotland the approach has been different. In *Crichton v Burrell* 1951 JC 107 the
defendant was arrested while standing beside his motor car under the influence of drink.
The driving door of the car was open and the defendant possessed an effective ignition
key. He had been driven earlier in the evening by a chauffeur who had a duplicate key

and was waiting for the chauffeur to return to drive him home when arrested. He was convicted under s 15(1) of the 1930 Act and appealed. Allowing the appeal the Lord Justice General (Cooper) said (at 110–111):

> 'On these facts the only fair and just inference which I find it possible to draw is that for the whole of that evening and, in particular, at the time when the apprehension was effected, the person truly "in charge of" that car within the meaning of section 15 of the Act was the chauffeur ... The appellant cannot be convicted because he might in strict legal theory have taken action which he is not proved to have intended to take, much less to have put into operation, the proved facts pointing plainly to the conclusion that he meant to do nothing of the kind. On a fair consideration of section 15 we know quite well what is meant by referring to a person who is driving or attempting to drive a car, and when the section goes on to refer also to a person "in charge of" a car the reference must be to the person in de facto control, even though he may not be at the time actually driving or attempting to drive. Any other reading and any attempt to include the owner merely because he was present, or because he had possession of a removable ignition key of a car which he had arranged should be driven by a chauffeur, would lead to extravagant results, some of which were instanced in the course of debate.'

Lord Keith said (at 111):

> 'In my view, the words "in charge of" in section 15 of the Act mean being responsible for the control or driving of the car. They do not mean necessarily that the person concerned is driving or is attempting to drive. That is specially provided for in the section. A person may be convicted under this section if he is doing neither of these things, if, in fact, he is the person who is for the time being in control of the vehicle.'

These rival views are summarised as follows in *Wilkinson's Road Traffic Offences* (13th edn, 1987) vol 1, p 1/203:

> 'In general, the Scottish courts have required a close connection between the defendant and the control of, or likelihood of driving, the motor vehicle. The English courts have tended to work from the presumption that someone must be "in charge" of any motor vehicle which is parked on a road or public place, and, prima facie, that person will be the person with the keys.'

Since the 1930 Act there have been a number of statutes affecting this branch of the law. It is not necessary to set out their provisions in detail. For the purposes of this case they may be summarised as follows.

The provisions of s 15(1) of the 1930 Act were in effect repeated in the Road Traffic Act 1956 by s 9. However, for the first time that section provided a defence where the person charged could prove that at the material time the circumstances were such that there was no likelihood of his driving the vehicle so long as he remained unfit to drive. Both the English and Scottish cases cited above were decided when no such defence was available.

Section 6(2) of the Road Traffic Act 1960 re-enacted the provisions as in the 1956 Act. The Road Traffic Act 1962 by s 1 altered the wording as to the test of unfitness through drink. The Road Safety Act 1967 introduced for the first time offences of driving, attempting to drive or being in charge of a motor vehicle with alcohol in the blood above a specified limit.

The present law is contained in the Road Traffic Act 1972, as amended by the Transport Act 1981. Section 5 of that Act deals with driving or being 'in charge' when under the influence of drink or drugs. Section 6, re-enacting s 1 of the 1967 Act, deals with offences involving a blood-alcohol level above the prescribed limit.

The relevant terms of s 5 are as follows:

> '(1) A person who, when driving or attempting to drive a motor vehicle on a road

or other public place, is unfit to drive through drink or drugs shall be guilty of an
offence.

(2) Without prejudice to subsection (1) above, a person who, when in charge of a
motor vehicle which is on a road or other public place, is unfit to drive through
drink or drugs shall be guilty of an offence.

(3) For the purposes of subsection (2) above a person shall be deemed not to have
been in charge of a motor vehicle if he proves that at the material time the
circumstances were such that there was no likelihood of his driving it so long as he
remained unfit to drive through drink or drugs but in determining whether there
was such a likelihood the court may disregard any injury to him and any damage to
the vehicle . . .'

In regard to that section two broad propositions are clear. First, the offence of being 'in
charge' is the lowest in the scale of three charges relating to driving and drink. The two
higher in the scale are driving and attempting to drive. Therefore a defendant can be 'in
charge' although neither driving nor attempting to drive. Clearly, however, the mischief
aimed at is to prevent driving when unfit through drink. The offence of being 'in charge'
must therefore be intended to convict those who are not driving and have not yet done
more than a preparatory act towards driving, but who in all the circumstances have
already formed or may yet form the intention to drive the vehicle, and may try to drive
it whilst still unfit.

Second, Parliament has thought it necessary, by a deeming provision, to provide that
proof of no likelihood of driving whilst still unfit negatives being 'in charge'. It must
follow that but for that defence a person could be 'in charge' notwithstanding there is no
likelihood of his driving. Thus to establish that a person is prima facie 'in charge' of a
vehicle does not require proof of likelihood to drive it while still unfit. The burden is on
him, once there is a prima facie case, to show there was no such likelihood. If he
discharges that burden, he is deemed not to have been 'in charge'.

Accordingly, to raise a prima facie case, the prosecution have to prove some connection,
which can be less than attempting to drive, between a person in the proscribed condition
and a motor vehicle on a road or public place. The nature of that connection is the elusive
element.

The test laid down in Haines v Roberts [1953] 1 All ER 344, [1953] 1 WLR 309 has been
criticised as being too strict. In Woodage v Jones (No 2) (1975) 60 Cr App R 260 the
defendant had driven erratically, stopped his car and, when told the police were coming,
walked away without locking the car. He was arrested at a phone box over half a mile
away. He was unfit through drink. The issue in the case was the lawfulness of his arrest
and the statutory defence under s 5(3) of the 1972 Act was not raised. James LJ cited the
passage already quoted from the judgment of Lord Goddard CJ in Haines v Roberts and
continued (at 263):

'Those words express the view expressed in many cases that once a person takes a
vehicle on to the public road he remains in charge of that vehicle until he has taken
it off the road again unless some intervening act occurs whereby he puts it in the
charge of someone else. [Counsel for the appellant] frankly concedes that in the
present day when circumstances are such that persons frequently have no option
but to leave their vehicles on the public road parked at night, for example because
they have no means of taking it off the road to park it in a garage, some relaxation
of the former rigid principle ought to be adopted. But there are limits to the
relaxation and in every case it must be a matter of fact and degree as to whether a
person is in charge of the vehicle.'

It would seem that the court agreed with counsel's concession that some relaxation of
the rigid rule should be allowed. In my judgment that must be so. Otherwise the owner
of a vehicle who parks it on the road near his home, drinks to excess and is later fast
asleep in bed for the night would still be 'in charge' of the vehicle and prima facie guilty

of an offence. Even more absurdly, he would be 'in charge' if he parked it at an airport or railway station, took the keys and was drunk whilst away on holiday. No doubt since the *a* statutory defence became available, he would be able in either of those instances to invoke it. But in my judgment the phrase is not so wide as to import even prima facie liability on those facts.

As to the statutory defence, two decisions should be mentioned. In *Morton v Confer* [1963] 2 All ER 765, [1963] 1 WLR 763 the defendant was found by a constable at 10.50 pm slumped over the wheel of his car asleep. The constable woke the defendant, who *b* immediately switched on the ignition. He was unfit through drink. In evidence he stated he had drunk a great deal at a club which he left at 10 pm. About a mile from home 'the drinks hit him'. He immediately stopped and his intention was not to continue until he was fit. The justices accepted his evidence and dismissed the charge. The prosecutor's appeal was allowed. Lord Parker CJ, said ([1963] 2 All ER 765 at 767, [1963] 1 WLR 763 at 765–766):   *c*

> 'In my judgment, the justices were not entitled to find that defence proved merely by an acceptance of what the respondent said. They would have to be satisfied further that not only was that his intention, but that there was no likelihood that that intention would be departed from . . . the fact that the respondent, when awakened, automatically used the ignition key and switched on the ignition showed *d* the danger of the justices accepting the intention . . .'

In *Northfield v Pinder* [1968] 3 All ER 854, [1969] 2 QB 7 justices dismissed an information alleging the defendant was in charge of a motor vehicle having consumed alcohol above the prescribed limit. They found that between 9.10 pm, when he was first seen, and 9.15 pm, when he was arrested, the defendant was so drunk that he could not even find his vehicle or indeed stand up. They held there was therefore no likelihood of *e* his driving while he remained unfit. Allowing the prosecutor's appeal, Lord Parker CJ said ([1968] 3 All ER 854 at 857, [1969] 2 QB 7 at 12):

> 'It seems to me perfectly clear that, if one is judging the likelihood of his driving between 9.10 and 9.15 p.m., quite clearly there was no probability of his driving then because at that time, in that five minutes, he was hopelessly drunk, so incapable *f* that he could not find his own car, get into it or do anything. But, in my judgment, that is not the end of the case, because he has to prove that, at the material time, the circumstances were such that there was no likelihood of his driving it, that is, in the future, so long as there was any probability of his having alcohol in his blood in a proportion exceeding the prescribed limit . . . The most normal way of proving that would be for him to prove that he had handed over the keys to somebody else, or *g* that he had taken a room for the night realising that he was drunk . . . but there was really no evidence here from which the justices could say that they were satisfied that, even if the worst effects of the alcohol wore off, he still would not drive it until it had come down to the prescribed limit.'

We have been greatly assisted by counsel for the appellant and counsel who has *h* appeared as amicus curiae. They both accept that no hard and fast all-embracing test can be propounded as to the meaning of the phrase 'in charge'.

Broadly there are two distinct classes of case. (1) If the defendant is the owner or lawful possessor of the vehicle or has recently driven it, he will have been in charge of it, and the question for the court will be whether he is still in charge or whether he has relinquished his charge. That is the class of case to which the *Haines v Roberts* rule was *j* directed. Usually such a defendant will be prima facie in charge unless he has put the vehicle in someone else's charge. However, he would not be so if in all the circumstances he has ceased to be in actual control and there is no realistic possibility of his resuming actual control while unfit, eg if he is at home in bed for the night, if he is a great distance from the car or if it is taken by another. (2) If the defendant is not the owner, the lawful possessor or recent driver but is sitting in the vehicle or is otherwise involved with it, the

question for the court is, as here, whether he has assumed being in charge of it. In this
a class of case the defendant will be in charge if, whilst unfit, he is voluntarily in de facto
control of the vehicle or if, in the circumstances, including his position, his intentions
and his actions, he may be expected imminently to assume control. Usually this will
involve his having gained entry to the car and evinced an intention to take control of it.
But gaining entry may not be necessary if he has manifested that intention some other
way, eg by stealing the keys of a car in circumstances which show he means presently to
b drive it.

The circumstances to be taken into account will vary infinitely, but the following will
be relevant: (i) whether and where he is in the vehicle or how far he is from it; (ii) what
he is doing at the relevant time; (iii) whether he is in possession of a key that fits the
ignition; (iv) whether there is evidence of an intention to take or assert control of the car
by driving or otherwise; (v) whether any other person is in, at or near the vehicle and, if
c so, the like particulars in respect of that person.

It will be for the court to consider all the above factors with any others which may be
relevant and reach its decision as a question of fact and degree.

It has been held that a person does not become in charge of a car merely because he sits
himself in the driving seat against the will of the owner: see *Blayney v Knight* (1975) 60
Cr App R 269. That case turned, however, on its very special facts. The defendant was
d one of three wishing to hire a taxi at a disco. A taxi arrived for someone else and the
driver got out leaving his engine running and the driver's door open. The defendant's
two friends got into the back of the taxi. The defendant tried to join them, but could not
open the rear door, so he got into the driver's seat. The door was still open. The taxi
driver returned and sought to eject the defendant. In the struggle the defendant's foot
accidentally operated the accelerator pedal and the car went forward injuring the taxi
e driver. The justices acquitted the defendant both of driving and of being in charge with
excess alcohol. The Divisional Court upheld their decision. Lord Widgery CJ said (at
271):

> 'I do not think that a person becomes in charge of a car merely because he seats
> himself in the driving seat against the will of the owner. Something very much
f > more than that is required before one can properly attribute to an individual all the
> responsibility which nowadays attaches to someone in charge of a motor car. I think
> this is an exceptional case, perhaps because the facts are so unusual . . .'

Apart from sitting in the driving seat, none of the criteria (i) to (iv) above pointed to
the defendant in that case being in charge. Moreover, under (v) the taxi driver was clearly
g in charge of the vehicle when he stopped it with its engine running and in common
sense remained so throughout.

In the present case the respondent was not only in the driving seat: he was holding one
of a bunch of keys between his thumb and forefinger. Those facts support an inference
that he intended to take control of the car by starting it. There was no evidence of any
other person at or near the car. In my judgment there was sufficient to show either he
h was voluntarily in de facto control of the car or that he could be expected imminently to
take such control. In those circumstances it was open to a reasonable bench of justices to
conclude that he was in charge.

The justices stated that the appellant had failed to prove the key would start the car.
Therefore they held there was no likelihood of the defendant driving and the prosecution
had failed to establish a prima facie case.

j But there was no burden of proof on the prosecution in regard to the likelihood of the
respondent driving. The burden was on him to establish that defence once a prima facie
case of being in charge was made out against him. If he were to prove that the key in his
hand would not turn on the engine, the justices might conclude he had proved the
defence under s 5(3), and should therefore be deemed not to be in charge. So the justices'
approach to the uncertainty regarding the efficacy of the key put the burden of proof on
the wrong party and their conclusion was premature.

I would therefore answer the questions posed by the justices as follows. (i) No. (ii) In considering at the conclusion of the prosecution case whether there was sufficient *a* evidence that the defendant was in charge of a motor vehicle, the justices were right to take into account evidence that the car did not belong to the defendant. They would have been right to take into account the presence of the key in the defendant's hand as that would go to his intention. However, they were wrong to take into account doubts whether the car keys found in his possession could in fact start the car, ie the absence of proof of the likelihood of his driving. (iii) The meaning of the phrase 'in charge' does *b* necessitate a close connection between the defendant and the control of a motor vehicle in the way I have endeavoured to indicate in this judgment. It does not necessitate proof of a likelihood of the defendant driving the vehicle.

I would therefore allow the appeal and remit the case to the justices to continue the hearing.

c

HENRY J. I agree.

Appeal allowed. Case remitted to justices to continue the hearing.

Solicitors: *Crown Prosecution Service*, Inner London (for the appellant); *Treasury Solicitor.*

d

Dilys Tausz   Barrister.

Litster and others v Forth Dry Dock and Engineering Co Ltd and another

e

HOUSE OF LORDS

LORD KEITH OF KINKEL, LORD BRANDON OF OAKBROOK, LORD TEMPLEMAN, LORD OLIVER OF AYLMERTON AND LORD JAUNCEY OF TULLICHETTLE

1, 2 FEBRUARY, 16 MARCH 1989

f

Employment – Continuity – Transfer of trade, business or undertaking – Employment by transferor immediately before transfer – Immediately before – Receivers of company dismissing employees at 3.30 pm and selling company to new owners at 4.30 pm – Whether new owners liable to pay compensation for unfair dismissal – Whether employees employed in company's business 'immediately before the transfer' of the business – Transfer of Undertakings (Protection of *g* *Employment) Regulations 1981, reg 5(1)(3)*

The applicant employees were employed by a ship repairing company (the old owners), which was one of a group of companies which became insolvent and went into receivership. On 6 February 1984 the receivers agreed to sell the assets of the company to another company (the new owners) which wished to replace the workforce with workers *h* from another shipyard who had been made redundant when that yard closed and who were prepared to work for lower wages than the applicants and their fellow employees. At 3.30 pm on 6 February the receivers dismissed the employees with immediate effect stating that there was no money to pay the statutory period of notice or accrued holiday pay. At 4.30 pm the transfer to the new owners took effect. Under reg 5(1)[a] and (3)[b] of the Transfer of Undertakings (Protection of Employment) Regulations 1981 the transfer *j* of a business did not operate so as to terminate the contracts of employment of employees who were employed in the business 'immediately before the transfer' of the business and, relying on reg 5, the applicants made a complaint to an industrial tribunal that they had

---

a   Regulation 5(1) is set out at p 1142 *b c*, post
b   Regulation 5(3) is set out at p 1142 *d e*, post

been unfairly dismissed. The tribunal upheld their complaint and held that the new
a owners were liable to pay compensation to the applicants based on 26 weeks' loss of
employment. On appeal by the new owners the Employment Appeal Tribunal upheld
the industrial tribunal's decision on the complaint of unfair dismissal but a further appeal
by the new owners to the Court of Session was allowed on the ground that the applicants
and their fellow employees were not employed in the business 'immediately before the
transfer' of the business, and the new owners were ordered to be dismissed from the
b proceedings. The applicants appealed to the House of Lords.

Held – Applying a purposive construction to reg 5 of the 1981 regulations, read in
conjunction with reg 8(1)^c, reg 5 applied not only to employees who were employed in
the business immediately before the transfer in point of time but also to employees who
would have been so employed but for being unfairly dismissed before the transfer for a
c reason connected with the transfer. Such a construction was in accordance with art 3^d of
EC Council Directive 77/187, the object of which was to protect the rights of employees
in the event of a change of employer. Accordingly, it was not open to the seller and buyer
of a business to arrange for the seller to dismiss the employees of the business shortly
before the transfer became operative so that the buyer could avoid the liability in respect
of unfair dismissal or redundancy claims which would accrue if the dismissals were made
d after the transfer. The appeal would accordingly be allowed (see p 1136 *c j* to p 1137 *a*,
p 1139 *g* to *j*, p 1142 *g* to p 1143 *a*, p 1147 *h j*, p 1152 *e f*, p 1153 *c* to *g* and p 1154 *b* to *d*,
post).

>   *Pickstone v Freemans plc* [1988] 2 All ER 803 applied.
>   *Secretary of State for Employment v Spence* [1986] 3 All ER 616 distinguished.
>   *Alphafield Ltd v Barratt* [1984] 3 All ER 795 disapproved.
e

Notes

For the protection of employees on the transfer of undertakings, see 52 Halsbury's Laws
(4th edn) para 21–20 and Supplement to 16 ibid para 606A.

f ## Cases referred to in opinions

Alphafield Ltd v Barratt [1984] 3 All ER 795, [1984] 1 WLR 1062, EAT.
Bork (P) International A/S (in liq) v Foreningen af Arbejdsledere i Danmark Case 101/87 [1989]
  IRLR 41, CJEC.
Foreningen af Arbejdsledere i Danmark v A/S Danmols Inventar (in liq) Case 105/84 [1985]
  ECR 2369.
g *Foreningen af Arbejdsledere i Danmark v Daddy's Dance Hall A/S* Case 324/86 [1988] IRLR
  315, CJEC.
Landsorganisationen i Danmark v Ny Molle Kro Case 287/86 [1989] IRLR 37, CJEC.
Pickstone v Freemans plc [1988] 2 All ER 803, [1989] AC 66, [1988] 3 WLR 265, HL.
Premier Motors (Medway) Ltd v Total Oil GB Ltd [1984] 1 WLR 377, EAT.
Secretary of State for Employment v Anchor Hotel (Kippford) Ltd [1985] ICR 724, EAT.
h *Secretary of State for Employment v Spence* [1986] 3 All ER 616, [1987] QB 179, [1986] 3
  WLR 380, CA.
von Colson v Land Nordrhein-Westfalen Case 14/83 [1984] ECR 1891.
Wendelboe v L J Music ApS (in liq) Case 19/83 [1985] ECR 457.

Appeal

j William Forsyth Litster and 11 other appellants, all former employees of the first
respondents, Forth Dry Dock and Engineering Co Ltd, appealed against the decision of
the Second Division of the Court of Session (the Lord Justice Clerk (Ross), Lord Dunpark
and Lord Wyllie) dismissing the second respondents, Forth Estuary Engineering Ltd,

---

c Regulation 8(1) is set out at p 1142 *e*, post
d Article 3 is set out, so far as material, at p 1140 *j*, post

from proceedings brought by the appellants against the respondents for unfair dismissal and allowing the second respondents' appeal against the decision of the Employment Appeal Tribunal ([1986] IRLR 59) dismissing the second respondents' appeal against the decision of an industrial tribunal on 27 February 1985 awarding the appellants compensation payable by the second respondents in respect of their unfair dismissal by the first respondents. The facts are set out in the opinion of Lord Oliver.

D A O Edward QC and *Paul B Cullen* (both of the Scottish Bar) for the applicants.
K H Osborne QC and *Ian D Truscott* (both of the Scottish Bar) for the second respondents.

Their Lordships took time for consideration.

16 March. The following opinions were delivered.

LORD KEITH OF KINKEL. My Lords, I agree with the speeches of my noble and learned friends Lord Oliver and Lord Templeman, which I have had the opportunity of reading in draft, and will add only a few observations of my own.

In *Pickstone v Freemans plc* [1988] 2 All ER 803, [1989] AC 66 there had been laid before Parliament under para 2(2) of Sch 2 to the European Communities Act 1972 the draft of certain regulations designed, and presented by the responsible ministers as designed, to fill a lacuna in the equal pay legislation of the United Kingdom which had been identified by a decision of the Court of Justice of the European Communities. On a literal reading the regulation particularly relevant did not succeed in completely filling the lacuna. Your Lordships' House, however, held that in order that the manifest purpose of the regulations might be achieved and effect given to the clear but inadequately expressed intention of Parliament certain words must be read in by necessary implication.

In the present case the Transfer of Undertakings (Protection of Employment) Regulations 1981, SI 1981/1794, were similarly laid before Parliament in draft and approved by resolutions of both Houses. They were so laid as designed to give effect to EC Council Directive 77/187 dated 14 February 1977. It is plain that if the words in reg 5(3) of the 1981 Regulations 'a person so employed immediately before the transfer' are read literally, as contended for by the second respondents, Forth Estuary Engineering Ltd, the provisions of reg 5(1) will be capable of ready evasion through the transferee arranging with the transferor for the latter to dismiss its employees a short time before the transfer becomes operative. In the event that the transferor is insolvent, a situation commonly forming the occasion for the transfer of an undertaking, the employees would be left with worthless claims for unfair dismissal against the transferor. In any event, whether or not the transferor is insolvent, the employees would be deprived of the remedy of reinstatement or re-engagement. The transferee would be under no liability towards the employees and a coach and four would have been driven through the provisions of reg 5(1).

A number of decisions of the European Court, in particular *P Bork International A/S (in liq) v Foreningen af Arbejdsledere i Danmark* Case 101/87 [1989] IRLR 41, have had the result that where employees have been dismissed by the transferor for a reason connected with the transfer, at a time before the transfer takes effect, then for purposes of art 3(1) of EC Council Directive 77/187 (which corresponds to reg 5(1)) the employees are to be treated as still employed by the undertaking at the time of the transfer.

In these circumstances it is the duty of the court to give to reg 5 a construction which accords with the decisions of the European Court on the corresponding provisions of the directive to which the regulation was intended by Parliament to give effect. The precedent established by *Pickstone v Freemans plc* indicates that this is to be done by implying the words necessary to achieve that result. So there must be implied in reg 5(3) words indicating that where a person has been unfairly dismissed in the circumstances described in reg 8(1) he is to be deemed to have been employed in the undertaking immediately before the transfer or any of a series of transactions whereby it was effected.

My Lords, I would allow the appeal.

LORD BRANDON OF OAKBROOK. My Lords, for the reasons given in the
a speeches of my noble and learned friends Lord Keith, Lord Templeman and Lord Oliver,
I would allow the appeal.

LORD TEMPLEMAN. My Lords, by art 3 of EC Council Directive 77/187 dated 14
February 1977 the Council of the European Communities directed that on the transfer
of a business from one employer to another, the benefit and burden of a contract of
b employment between the transferor (the old owner) and a worker in the business should
devolve on the transferee (the new owner). The directive thus imposed on the new owner
liability for the workers in the business, although the member states were authorised by
art 3 to continue the liability of the old owner to the workers in the business 'in addition
to the transferee'. The object of the directive was expressed to be—

c   'to provide for the protection of employees in the event of a change of employer,
         in particular, to ensure that their rights are safeguarded . . .'

Article 4(1) of the directive provided:

         'The transfer of an undertaking, business or part of a business shall not in itself
         constitute grounds for dismissal by the transferor or the transferee. This provision
d   shall not stand in the way of dismissals that may take place for economic, technical
         or oranisational reasons entailing changes in the workforce . . .'

The result of art 4(1) is that the new owner intending to dismiss the workers cannot
achieve his purpose by asking the old owner to dismiss the workers immediately prior to
the transfer taking place. The new owner cannot dismiss the workers himself after the
transfer has taken place. Any such dismissal, whether by the old owner or the new
e owner, would be inconsistent with the object of protecting the rights of the workers and
is prohibited by art 4(1).

The Transfer of Undertakings (Protection of Employment) Regulations 1981, SI 1981/
1794, were approved by a resolution of each House of Parliament in pursuance of para
2(2) of Sch 2 to the European Communities Act 1972 for the express purpose of
f implementing EC Council Directive 77/187. Regulation 5(1) provides, in conformity
with art 3 of the directive:

         'A relevant transfer shall not operate so as to terminate the contract of employment
         of any person employed by the transferor in the undertaking or part transferred but
         any such contract which would otherwise have been terminated by the transfer shall
         have effect after the transfer as if originally made between the person so employed
g   and the transferee.'

Thus on the transfer of a business from one employer to another the benefit and
burden of a contract of employment between the old owner and a worker in the business
devolves on the new owner.

Regulation 8 provides, in conformity with art 4:

h   '(1) Where either before or after a relevant transfer, any employee of the transferor
         or transferee is dismissed, that employee shall be treated . . . as unfairly dismissed if
         the transfer or a reason connected with it is the reason or principal reason for his
         dismissal . . .'

The result of reg 8(1) is the same as art 4(1), namely that if the new owner wishes to
j dismiss the workers he cannot achieve his purpose either by procuring the old owner to
dismiss the workers prior to the transfer taking place, or by himself dismissing the
workers after the date of the transfer.

In the present case, the old owners agreed with the new owners to dismiss the workers.
The old owners were the Forth Dry Dock and Engineering Co Ltd (Forth Dry Dock).
Forth Dry Dock was the subsidiary and a member of a group of companies headed by a
parent company which defaulted in payments under a debenture issued to Lloyd's Bank

plc. On 28 September 1983 Lloyd's Bank appointed receivers to all the companies in the group. The business of Forth Dry Dock, namely the business of ship repairers, was *a* carried on under a lease of the Edinburgh dock at Leith, and this business was continued after the appointment of receivers by 25 workers including 12 who are the present appellants. A consultant to the parent company in the group, on financial and personnel matters, a Mr Brooshooft, was minded to purchase the business of Forth Dry Dock from the receivers. He acted in conjunction with a Mr Hughes, the manager of Forth Dry Dock, and a Mr Paterson who had formerly been a manager of another ship-repairing *b* company, Robb Caledon. The workforce of Robb Caledon had been made redundant and were sufficiently chastened by unemployment to be offered lower wages than the wages of the workers of Forth Dry Dock. Mr Brooshooft formed a new company which became Forth Estuary Engineering Ltd (Forth Estuary). Forth Estuary declined to purchase the lease of the Edinburgh dock vested in Forth Dry Dock but took a new lease from the landlords. Forth Estuary declined to purchase the goodwill of Forth Dry Dock *c* and was only prepared to purchase the tangible assets of Forth Dry Dock but of course possession of these assets, plus possession of a lease replacing the lease to Forth Dry Dock, conferred on Forth Estuary the goodwill of Forth Dry Dock. The object of taking a new lease and of declining to take the goodwill expressly, was to make it appear that the directive and the regulations did not apply because the whole of the business of the Forth Dry Dock company had not been transferred or because a third party, the landlords, were *d* involved. These arguments have rightly been rejected at all stages of this litigation. The workers of Forth Dry Dock were given the impression that their employment would be continued by a new owner. On 6 February 1984 the receivers appointed by Lloyds Bank agreed in writing to sell to Forth Estuary 'the business assets' defined as the plant, machinery, equipment, furniture and office equipment detailed in the schedule, 'as the same shall exist at the close of business' on 6 February 1984 in consideration of £33,500 *e* paid by Forth Estuary to the receivers when the agreement was executed in the morning or early afternoon of that day. At 3.30 pm the receivers appointed by Lloyds Bank informed the workforce of Forth Dry Dock in writing that 'no further funds can be made available to pay your wages with effect from the close of business today' and that no payments would be made for accrued holiday pay or damages for failure to give the *f* statutory period of notice. Thereafter Forth Estuary continued the business of Forth Dry Dock, employed the former dockmaster and two other employees of Forth Dry Dock, but replaced the remainder of the workforce with former employees of Robb Caledon at lower wages. Thus Lloyds Bank, acting for the receiver transferred the business at 4.30 pm on 6 February 1984, that being the time of close of business and one hour after the Forth Dry Dock workers had been dismissed. The assets of Forth Dry Dock were *g* taken by Lloyds Bank as debenture holders so that nothing was available to pay the workers of Forth Dry Dock either their holiday entitlement or damages for dismissal without notice, or damages for unfair dismissal.

It is argued that Forth Estuary, which is solvent, is not liable to the workers because they were dismissed one hour before the transfer of the business. Article 3 of the directive and reg 5(1) of the 1981 Regulations were plainly intended to prevent an insolvent old *h* owner from dismissing a workforce at the behest of a solvent new owner so as to deprive the workforce effectively of their rights. Forth Estuary appear to deny that they are liable to the appellants for compensation for unfair dismissal pursuant to reg 8. The Court of Session found in favour of Forth Estuary.

The appellants were dismissed at 3.30 pm on 6 February by Forth Dry Dock and the business was transferred to Forth Estuary at 4.30 pm on the same day. It is argued on *j* behalf of Forth Estuary that despite the directive and the regulations they are not liable to the appellants in respect of their unfair dismissal because reg 5(3) provides:

'Any reference in paragraph (1) . . . above to a person employed in an undertaking or part of one transferred by a relevant transfer is a reference to a person so employed immediately before the transfer, including, where the transfer is effected by a series of two or more transactions, a person so employed immediately before any of those

a   transactions.'

Thus, it is said, since the workforce of Forth Dry Dock were dismissed at 3.30 pm, they were not employed 'immediately before the transfer' at 4.30 pm and therefore reg 5(1) did not transfer any liability for the workforce from Forth Dry Dock to Forth Estuary. The argument is inconsistent with the directive. In *P Bork International A/S (in*

b   *liq) v Foreningen af Arbejdsledere i Danmark* Case 101/87 [1989] IRLR 41 at 44 (paras 17–18) the Court of Justice of the European Communities ruled:

'. . . the only workers who may invoke Directive 77/187 are those who have current employment relations or a contract of employment at the date of the transfer. The question whether or not a contract of employment or employment relationship exists at that date must be assessed under national law, subject, however,

c   to the observance of the mandatory rules of the Directive concerning the protection of workers against dismissal by reason of the transfer. It follows that the workers employed by the undertaking whose contract of employment or employment relationship has been terminated with effect on a date before that of the transfer, in breach of Article 4(1) of the Directive, must be considered as still employed by the undertaking on the date of the transfer with the consequence, in particular, that the

d   obligations of an employer towards them are fully transferred from the transferor to the transferee, in accordance with Article 3(1) of the Directive . . .'

In *von Colson v Land Nordrhein-Westfalen* Case 14/83 [1984] ECR 1891 at 1909 (para 26) the European Court, dealing with EC Council Directive 76/207 forbidding discrimination on grounds of sex regarding access to employment, ruled:

e
'. . . the Member States' obligation arising from a directive to achieve the result envisaged by the directive and their duty under Article 5 of the Treaty to take all appropriate measures, whether general or particular, to ensure the fulfilment of that obligation, is binding on all the authorities of Member States including, for matters within their jurisdiction, the courts. It follows that, in applying the national law

f   and in particular the provisions of a national law specifically introduced in order to implement Directive No 76/207, national courts are required to interpret their national law in the light of the wording and the purpose of the directive in order to achieve the result referred to in the third paragraph of Article 189.'

Thus the courts of the United Kingdom are under a duty to follow the practice of the European Court by giving a purposive construction to directives and to regulations issued

g   for the purpose of complying with directives. In *Pickstone v Freemans plc* [1988] 2 All ER 803, [1989] AC 66 this House implied words in a regulation designed to give effect to EC Council Directive 75/117 dealing with equal pay for women doing work of equal value. If this House had not been able to make the necessary implication the Equal Pay (Amendment) Regulations 1983, SI 1983/1794, would have failed in their object and the United Kingdom would have been in breach of its treaty obligations to give effect to

h   directives. In the present case, in the light of EC Council Directive 77/187 and in the light of the ruling of the European Court in *Bork's* case [1989] IRLR 41, it seems to me, following the suggestion of my noble and learned friend Lord Keith, that reg 5(3) of the 1981 Regulations was not intended and ought not to be construed so as to limit the operation of reg 5 to persons employed immediately before the transfer in point of time.

j   Regulation 5(3) must be construed on the footing that it applies to a person employed immediately before the transfer or who would have been so employed if he had not been unfairly dismissed before the transfer for a reason connected with the transfer. It would, of course, still be open for a new owner to show that the employee had been dismissed for an 'economic, technical or organisational reason entailing changes in the workforce', but no such reason could be advanced in the present case where there was no complaint against the workers, they were not redundant and there were no relevant reasons

entailing changes in the workforce. I would therefore allow the appeal and make the
order proposed by my noble and learned friend Lord Oliver.   *a*

LORD OLIVER OF AYLMERTON. My Lords, this appeal raises, not for the first
time, the broad question of the approach to be adopted by courts in the United Kingdom
to domestic legislation enacted in order to give effect to this country's obligations under
the EEC Treaty. The legislation with which the appeal is concerned is a statutory
instrument made on 14 December 1981 pursuant to para 2(2) of Sch 2 to the European   *b*
Communities Act 1972 and entitled the Transfer of Undertakings (Protection of
Employment) Regulations 1981, SI 1981/1794. The regulations were made by the
Secretary of State, and this is common ground, in order to give effect to EC Council
Directive 77/187 adopted by the Council of the European Communities on 14 February
1977 to provide for the approximation of the laws of the member states relating to the
safeguarding of employees' rights in the event of transfers of undertakings, businesses or *c*
parts of businesses. The question which arises is whether it has achieved this object.
    The approach to the construction of primary and subordinate legislation enacted to
give effect to the United Kingdom's obligations under the EEC Treaty have been the
subject matter of recent authority in this House (see *Pickstone v Freemans plc* [1988] 2 All
ER 803, [1989] AC 66) and is not in doubt. If the legislation can reasonably be construed
so as to conform with those obligations, obligations which are to be ascertained not only *d*
from the wording of the relevant directive but from the interpretation placed on it by
the Court of Justice of the European Communities, such a purposive construction will be
applied even though, perhaps, it may involve some departure from the strict and literal
application of the words which the legislature has elected to use.
    It will, I think, be convenient to consider the terms of the directive and the regulations
before outlining the circumstances in which the instant appeal arises. The broad scope of *e*
the directive appears from the following two recitals:

> 'Whereas economic trends are bringing in their wake, at both national and
> Community level, changes in the structure of undertakings, through transfers of
> undertakings, businesses or parts of businesses to other employers as a result of legal
> transfers or mergers; Whereas it is necessary to provide for the protection of   *f*
> employees in the event of a change of employer, in particular, to ensure that their
> rights are safeguarded . . .'

By art 1 it is provided that the directive shall apply to the transfer of an undertaking,
business or part of a business to another employer. Article 2 contains definitions, the
relevant ones for present purposes being: *g*

> '(a) "transferor" means any natural or legal person who, by reason of a transfer
> within the meaning of Article 1(1), ceases to be the employer in respect of the
> undertaking, business or part of the business; (b) "transferee" means any natural or
> legal person who, by reason of a transfer within the meaning of Article 1(1), becomes
> the employer in respect of the undertaking, business or part of the business . . .'   *h*

Section II is headed '*Safeguarding of employees' rights*' and contains three articles of which
the relevant ones for present purposes are arts 3 and 4. Article 3 provides (so far as
material):

> 1. The transferor's rights and obligations arising from a contract of employment   *j*
> or from an employment relationship existing on the date of a transfer within the
> meaning of Article 1(1) shall, by reason of such transfer, be transferred to the
> transferee . . .'

Paragraph (2) deals with the continuation of collective agreements and para (3) excepts
from the preceding paragraphs employees' rights to old-age, invalidity or survivors'

benefits under company pension schemes outside the member states' social security
a schemes. The latter part of the paragraph may, however, have a peripheral relevance in
the present context, as indicating that the expressions 'on the date of the transfer' and 'at
the time of the transfer' are used interchangeably in the directive. It provides:

> 'Member States shall adopt the measures necessary to protect the interests of
> employees and of persons no longer employed in the transferor's business at the
> time of the transfer within the meaning of Article 1(1) in respect of rights conferring
b > on them . . . entitlement to old-age benefits . . . under supplementary schemes
> referred to in the first subparagraph.'

Article 4 is, so far as material, in the following terms:

> '1. The transfer of an undertaking, business or part of a business shall not in itself
> constitute grounds for dismissal by the transferor or the transferee. This provision
c > shall not stand in the way of dismissals that may take place for economic, technical
> or organisational reasons entailing changes in the workforce . . .
> 2. If the contract of employment or the employment relationship is terminated
> because the transfer within the meaning of Article 1(1) involves a substantial change
> in working conditions to the detriment of the employee, the employer shall be
> regarded as having been responsible for termination of the contract of employment
d > or of the employment relationship.'

Section III (art 6) contains requirements for providing information to representatives
of employees which do not need to be recited in any detail. The provisions of para (1) of
art 6, however, ought to be referred to in the context of the overall purpose of the
directive of ensuring that the interests of employees are to be safeguarded on any transfer
e of the undertaking in which they are employed. It provides as follows:

> 'The transferor and the transferee shall be required to inform the representatives
> of their respective employees affected by a transfer within the meaning of Article
> 1(1) of the following: the reasons for the transfer, the legal, economic and social
> implications of the transfer for the employees, measures envisaged in relation to the
f > employees. The transferor must give such information to the representatives of his
> employees in good time before the transfer is carried out.'

Finally, art 7, which provides that the directive shall not affect the rights of member
states to apply or introduce measures more favourable to employees, contains the clear
implication that the protection envisaged by the directive is the minimum requirement
for which the member states are obliged to give effect.
g Turning now to the 1981 regulations, which came into operation in 1982 and which
represent the British government's perception at that time of its obligations under the
directive, these provide for relevant purposes as follows:

> '2.—(1) In these Regulations . . . "employee" means any individual who works
> for another person whether under a contract of service or apprenticeship or otherwise
h > but does not include anyone who provides services under a contract for services and
> references to a person's employer shall be construed accordingly . . . "the 1978 Act"
> and "the 1976 Order" mean, respectively . . . the Employment Protection
> (Consolidation) Act 1978 and the Industrial Relations (Northern Ireland) Order 1976
> . . . "relevant transfer" means a transfer to which these Regulations apply and
> "transferor" and "transferee" shall be construed accordingly; and "undertaking"
j > includes any trade or business but does not include any undertaking or part of an
> undertaking which is not in the nature of a commercial venture . . .
> 3.—(1) Subject to the provisions of these Regulations, these Regulations apply to
> a transfer fom one person to another of an undertaking situated immediately before
> the transfer in the United Kingdom or a part of one which is so situated.
> (2) Subject as aforesaid, these Regulations so apply whether the transfer is effected
> by sale or by some other disposition or by operation of law . . .

(4) It is hereby declared that a transfer of an undertaking or part of one may be effected by a series of two or more transactions between the same parties, but in determining whether or not such a series constitutes a single transfer regard shall be had to the extent to which the undertaking or part was controlled by the transferor and transferee respectively before the last transaction, to the lapse of time between each of the transactions, to the intention of the parties and to all the other circumstances. . . .

5.—(1) A relevant transfer shall not operate so as to terminate the contract of employment of any person employed by the transferor in the undertaking or part transferred but any such contract which would otherwise have been terminated by the transfer shall have effect after the transfer as if originally made between the person so employed and the transferee.

(2) Without prejudice to paragraph (1) above, on the completion of a relevant transfer—(a) all the transferor's rights, powers, duties and liabilities under or in connection with any such contract, shall be transferred by virtue of this Regulation to the transferee; and (b) anything done before the transfer is completed by or in relation to the transferor in respect of that contract or a person employed in that undertaking or part shall be deemed to have been done by or in relation to the transferee.

(3) Any reference in paragraph (1) or (2) above to a person employed in an undertaking or part of one transferred by a relevant transfer is a reference to a person so employed immediately before the transfer, including, where the transfer is effected by a series of two or more transactions, a person so employed immediately before any of those transactions . . .

8.—(1) Where either before or after a relevant transfer, any employee of the transferor or transferee is dismissed, that employee shall be treated for the purposes of Part V of the 1978 Act and Articles 20 to 41 of the 1976 Order (unfair dismissal) as unfairly dismissed if the transfer or a reason connected with it is the reason or principal reason for his dismissal.

(2) Where an economic, technical or organisational reason entailing changes in the workforce of either the transferor or the transferee before or after a relevant transfer is the reason or principal reason for dismissing an employee—(a) paragraph (1) above shall not apply to his dismissal . . .

12. Any provision of any agreement (whether a contract of employment or not) shall be void in so far as it purports to exclude or limit the operation of Regulation 5, 8 or 10 above . . .'

It will be seen that, as is to be expected, the scope and purpose of both the directive and the regulations are the same, that is to ensure that on any transfer of an undertaking or part of an undertaking, the employment of the existing workers in the undertaking is preserved or, if their employment terminates solely by reason of the transfer, that their rights arising out of that determination are effectively safeguarded. It may, I think, be assumed that those who drafted both the directive and the regulations were sufficiently acquainted with the realities of life to appreciate that a frequent, indeed, possibly the most frequent, occasion on which a business or part of a business is transferred is when the original employer is insolvent, so that an employee whose employment is terminated on the transfer will have no effective remedy for unfair dismissal unless it is capable of being exerted against the transferee. It can hardly have been contemplated that, where the only reason for determination of the employment is the transfer of the undertaking or the relevant part of it, the parties to the transfer would be at liberty to avoid the manifest purpose of the directive by the simple expedient of wrongfully dismissing the workforce a few minutes before the completion of the transfer. The European Court has expressed, in the clearest terms, the opinion that so transparent a device would not avoid the operation of the directive, and if the effect of the regulations is that under the law of

the United Kingdom it has that effect, then your Lordships are compelled to conclude
a that the regulations are gravely defective and the government of the United Kingdom
has failed to comply with its mandatory obligations under the directive. If your Lordships
are in fact compelled to that conclusion, so be it; but it is not, I venture to think, a
conclusion which any of your Lordships would willingly embrace in the absence of the
most compulsive context rendering any other conclusion impossible.

My Lords, the circumstances in which the question has arisen for decision in the
b instant case are these. The first respondents, Forth Dry Dock and Engineering Co Ltd,
carried on a business of ship repairers at the Edinburgh dry dock, premises which they
held under a lease from the Forth Ports Authority. At the material time, the 12 appellants
were tradesmen employed in that business. They were part of a permanent workforce of
skilled shipworkers of various trades who had been continuously employed by the first
respondents since 1981 or 1982. In the year 1983 the group of companies of which the
c first respondents formed part was in financial difficulties and the receiver of the various
companies in the group (including the first respondents) was appointed by the debenture
holder, Lloyd's Bank, on 28 September 1983. The workforce was then told by the
receiver's representative, a Mr Page, that the intention was to sell the business as a going
concern and that their jobs would be safe. That belief may have been genuinely
entertained at the time, but it was falsified in the event.

d On 23 November 1983 the second respondents, Forth Estuary Engineering Ltd (Forth
Estuary) was incorporated. A few days before the transfer of the first respondents' assets,
which took place on 6 February 1984, the capital of Forth Estuary was increased from
£1,000 to £20,000: 85% of the issued capital became vested in a Mr Brooshooft, who had
been a financial adviser to the first respondents' company, and 10% in a Mr Hughes, who
had been a director of and had managed the business of the first respondents. On 6
e February 1984 an agreement was entered into between the first respondents, the receivers
and Forth Estuary under which (a) all the first respondents' business assets, consisting of
plant, machinery, equipment, furniture and office equipment specified in a schedule,
were acquired by Forth Estuary at a price of £33,500 payable on execution of the
agreement, (b) the first respondents undertook to cease business at close of business on
f that day (at which time the sale and purchase was to be carried into effect) and (c) the first
respondents undertook forthwith to relinquish their rights under the lease of the dry
dock which they held from the ports authority. Before this, it is not clear exactly when,
Forth Estuary had obtained from the Forth Ports Authority a new lease of the property
previously let to the first respondents (with the exception of one shed). It is interesting to
note that under cl 14 of this agreement, its construction, validity and performance were
g to be governed by English law and the courts of England were given exclusive
jurisdiction. As a matter of English law, therefore, the ownership of the assets transferred
passed in equity to Forth Estuary on the execution of the agreement and those assets
were, assuming, as we must assume, that the consideration was then paid as provided by
the agreement, then held by the transferor as a bare trustee for the transferee. Up to this
point the appellants had continued to be employed by the first respondents. It had,
h however, clearly been determined by the receivers, and, one infers, by Forth Estuary,
that that situation was not to be permitted to continue and it is difficult, if not impossible,
to resist the inference that the reason why it was not to be permitted to continue was that
both parties were very well aware of the provisions of the regulations to which I have
already referred. It can hardly have been merely a fortunate coincidence that officers
from the redundancy payments section of the Department of Employment were already
j at the dock on that afternoon when Mr Hughes and Mr Page arrived at approximately
3 pm having come straight from the office of Messrs Brodies, where the agreement had
been signed. They addressed the workforce and told them that the business was to close
down at 4.30 pm that day and that they were dismissed 'with immediate effect'. Each of
the appellants was given a letter from the receivers under the first respondents' letterhead
which was dated 6 February 1984 and was, so far as material, in the following terms:

'We would advise you that no further funds can be made available to pay your
wages with effect from the close of business today and accordingly we have to *a*
inform you that your employment with the company is terminated with immediate
effect. No payments will be made in respect of your accrued holiday pay, or the
failure to give you your statutory period of notice. Under the Insolvency provisions
of the Employment Protection Act, any claim you may have for the above will,
subject to certain limitations, be paid to you by the Department of Employment
out of the Redundancy Fund . . . Your wages up to the date of dismissal will be paid *b*
in the normal way and you will be issued with a P45 from the company's head
office.'

One of the less creditable aspects of the matter is that one of the appellants, Mr Walker,
who was the union shop steward, asked specifically whether the business was being taken
over by Forth Estuary, and was told by Mr Hughes that he knew nothing about a new
company taking over, while Mr Page said that he knew nothing about a company called *c*
Forth Estuary Engineering. This indicates a calculated disregard for the obligations
imposed by reg 10 of the 1981 regulations. Within 48 hours of their dismissal, the
appellants learned, at the local job centre, that Forth Estuary was recruiting labour and a
group of them went to fill in application forms for employment. None was successful
and indeed only three former employees of the first respondents were taken on. Work *d*
which was in progress on the vessels on 6 February was subsequently continued and
completed by Forth Estuary, which very soon had a workforce of similar size to that of
the first repondents, embracing the same trade but recruited at lower rates of pay
elsewhere than from the existing employees. The industrial tribunal, in their reasons for
decision, commented:

'The fact that Forth Estuary, apart from the three exceptions, has not retained or *e*
employed the former employees of Forth Dry Dock is consistent with Mr
Brooshooft's decision (which he referred to in his evidence) not to employ the
existing employees as he wanted to start "with a clean sheet", although he had no
criticism of them.'

It is difficult to resist the inference that Mr Brooshooft was not unmindful of the *f*
disadvantages which might flow under the regulations from the continuance of the
employment of the existing workforce as compared with the advantages to be derived
from the pool of unemployed tradesmen anxious for work on any available terms.
Although the industrial tribunal made no finding as to this, the sequence of events and
the secrecy with which they were enshrouded are such that they cannot rationally be *g*
accounted for otherwise than by the hypothesis that the dismissal of the existing
workforce was engineered specifically with a view to preventing any liability for the
obligations incidental to their contracts of employment from attaching to Forth Estuary,
so as to leave them with nothing but a claim for redundancy on the redundancy fund
under s 106 of the Employment Protection Act 1978 and an illusory claim for unfair
dismissal against an insolvent company. *h*

The appellants applied to an industrial tribunal complaining that they had been
unfairly dismissed and by an order of 28 September 1984 Forth Estuary was sisted as an
additional and second-named respondent to that application. On 27 February 1985 the
industrial tribunal determined that the appellants had been unfairly dismissed by the
first repondents and that Forth Estuary was liable to pay monetary compensation which
was assessed on the basis of 26 weeks' loss of employment. From that decision Forth *j*
Estuary appealed to the Employment Appeal Tribunal on the grounds, first that there
had been no relevant transfer of the business within the terms of the regulations; second
that the appellants were not employees employed in the business immediately before the
transfer and that, accordingly, the obligations under their respective contracts of
employment were not transferred to Forth Estuary; third that the appellants had not
been unfairly dismissed; and, fourth, that in any event there was no justification for the

assessment of compensation on the basis of 26 weeks' loss of employment. The appellants
a cross-appealed against the decision so far as it restricted the compensation to a figure
based on 26 weeks' loss of employment. On 5 December 1985 the Employment Appeal
Tribunal ([1986] IRLR 59) affirmed the decision on the industrial tribunal, save that it
concluded that the onus of establishing that if the appellants had been employed by Forth
Estuary that company would have dismissed them in the future for some proper reason
other than for the mere transfer of the business rested with Forth Estuary. There was, on
b the evidence, no ground for limiting the appellants' claim to the period assumed by the
industrial tribunal. They accordingly remitted the case to the industrial tribunal to
reconsider the basis for assessment of compensation.

    One of the curiosities of the appeal is that the principal and, substantially, the only
question argued before this House on behalf of the respondents, that is to say, that
adumbrated in the second ground mentioned in the notice of appeal to the Employment
c Appeal Tribunal, was not in fact relied on there, the principal arguments being that there
had been no relevant transfer so as to enable the appellants to invoke the regulations at
all and that, in any event, the appellants had not been unfairly dismissed for the reason
specified in reg 8(1). In my view, the latter point is really unarguable on the facts. It was
entirely unsupported by any evidence on the part of the first respondent and was rightly
rejected both by the industrial tribunal and the Employment Appeal Tribunal. Since,
d however, counsel for the Forth Estuary has sought, as he did before the Court of Session,
to keep the first point alive, it may be convenient to deal with it at this point. It has not
been contested, nor could it easily be with any conviction, that the business of the first
respondents was not transferred to Forth Estuary; but what is said is that the transfer was
not a 'relevant transfer' within the regulations, inasmuch as one of the steps involved the
concurrence of a third party, that is to say the Forth Ports Authority, which was involved
e to the extent of accepting the relinquishment of the first respondents' lease and granting
a new lease to Forth Estuary. What is said is that reg 3(4), which declares, ex abundanti
cautela, that a transfer may be effected by a series of 'two or more transactions between
the same parties' rules out, by implication, as a relevant element in the transfer, a
transaction between one of the parties and a third party. In fairness to counsel for the
Forth Estuary, I should say that he was the first to acknowledge that this argument hardly
f qualified for the description of the jewel in his crown. In my judgment there is no
substance in it. I do not, for a start, consider that any such implication can be legitimately
drawn from the words of the regulation, but in any event, reg 3(4) does not purport to
be anything more than declaratory and cannot be properly construed as in any sense an
exclusive defintiion of what can constitute a transfer.

    To continue with the history, the respondents appealed to the Court of Session ([1988]
g IRLR 289) which, by an interlocutor of the Second Division of the Inner House dated
18 March 1988, sustained the appeal and ordered that the cases of all the appellants
should be remitted to the industrial tribunal with a direction that Forth Estuary should
be dismissed from the proceedings and that the industrial tribunal should proceed to
consider the cases against the first respondents. It is against that interlocutor that the
h appellants now appeal to this House.

    The ground on which the Second Division of the Inner House sustained the appeal was
that although the dismissal occurred on the same day as the transfer, reg 5 did not apply
to continue the employment of the appellants by Forth Estuary because the dismissal,
having been effected before, albeit only shortly before, the transfer took effect, there was,
at that point of time, no longer any contract of employment in existence and the
j appellants were not therefore employed by the first respondents at the time of the
transfer. Accordingly, reg 5(1) and (2) never operated to transfer the appellants to the
employment of Forth Estuary or to impose on that company any of the obligations of
the first respondents as employers. In so deciding, the Second Division followed the
decision of the Court of Appeal in England in *Secretary of State for Employment v Spence*
[1986] 3 All ER 616, [1987] QB 179, which was decided on 15 May 1986, that is to say,
after the date of the decision of the Employment Appeal Tribunal. At the date of that

decision the point was generally thought to be concluded against the respondents by two
decisions of the Employment Appeal Tribunal in England in *Alphafield Ltd v Barratt*   *a*
[1984] 3 All ER 795, [1984] 1 WLR 1062 and *Secretary of State for Employment v Anchor
Hotel (Kippford) Ltd* [1985] ICR 724. In *Spence's* case the Court of Appeal overruled those
decisions. Your Lordships are now invited to overrule *Spence's* case.

There is, I think, a serious question whether, on the facts of the instant case, the
question of the correctness of the decision in *Spence's* case arises at all. Having regard both
to the terms of the agreement to which I have referred and to those of the letters of   *b*
dismissal received by the appellants, there appear to be respectable arguments in favour
of a contention that the appellants' employment was not, in fact, determined until after,
or eo instante with, the transfer of the business. The point has, however, not been fully
argued and your Lordships have been invited to approach the appeal on the footing that
the dismissals took effect at about 3.30 pm on 6 February and that the transfer did not
take place until 4.30 pm on that day. I therefore make that assumption.   *c*

Two questions then arise. First, was the time which elapsed between the dismissals
and the transfer of so short a duration that, on the true construction of reg 5, the
appellants were 'employed immediately before' the transfer, as required by para (3) of
that regulation? Second, if the answer to that question is in the negative, what difference
(if any) does it make that the reason, or the principal reason, for the dismissals was, as it
clearly was, the imminent occurrence of the transfer so that the dismissals were, by   *d*
reg 8(1), deemed to be unfair dismissals?

The expression 'immediately before' is one which takes its meaning from its context,
but in its ordinary signification it involves the notion that there is, between two relevant
events, no intervening space, lapse of time or event of any significance. If, for instance,
the question is whether a deceased person was seized of property immediately before his
death, attention is focussed on the very instant at which the death occured. In construing   *e*
the regulations with which this appeal is concerned, one gets little help from the terms
of the directive to which they were intended to give effect. Article 3, as has been seen
already, refers to an employment relationship existing 'on the date of the transfer', but
this expression seems to be used interchangeably with the expression 'at the time of the
transfer' (in the French text 'au moment du transfert') which appears to embrace the
notion that what has to be regarded is the status of the employee vis-à-vis his employer at   *f*
the very instant at which the employer's business is transferred.

As will already have become apparent, there have been a number of decisions in which
the provisions of reg 5 have fallen to be construed and your Lordships' attention has, in
addition, been drawn to a number of decisions in which arts 3 and 4 of the directive have
fallen to be interpreted by the European Court. Before referring to these, however, it
may be helpful to consider the regulations without the assistance of authority, but   *g*
bearing in mind their overall purpose of giving effect to the provisions of the directive.
To begin with, it is to be noted that the reference in reg 5(1) to a 'contract which would
otherwise have been terminated by the transfer' is, strictly speaking, a misdescription.
The reason why a contract of employment is said to 'terminate' on a transfer of the
employer's business is simply that such a transfer operates as a unilateral repudiation by   *h*
the employer of his obligations under the contract and thus as a dismissal of the employee
from his service. Because the relationship between employer and employee is of an
essentially personal nature, the repudiation severs the factual relationship resulting from
the contract, since the primary obligations on both sides are no longer capable of being
performed. The contract itself, however, is not, strictly speaking, terminated but remains
in being and undischarged so far as the enforcement of secondary obligations is concerned.   *j*
This may seem a truism but it has, I believe, an importance in the analysis, in particular
in relation to the meaning to be ascribed to the words 'terminated by the transfer' in
reg 5(1) and the words 'immediately before the transfer' in reg 5(3). The necessary
assumption in para (1) of the regulation is that the contract of employment to which the
consquence stated in the paragraph is to attach, is one which, apart from the transfer,

would have continued in force and that what 'terminates' it, or would, apart from the
a regulation, have terminated it, is the repudiatory breach constituted by the transfer. That
paragraph can, therefore, operate only on a subsisting contract. There is nothing in the
terms of para (2), if it stood alone, which necessarily involves the same restriction. It is,
however, clearly intended merely to supplement the provisions of para (1), and para (3)
supplies the connection by expressly limiting the operation of both paras (1) and (2) to
the case where the relevant employee is employed in the undertaking 'immediately
b before the transfer', that is to say, to the circumstances envisaged in para (1) in which,
apart from the regulation, the event producing the termination is the transfer. The
crucial question, therefore, is what is meant by the reference to a contract being
terminated '*by*' a transfer.

This could embrace a number of different possibilities. If nothing at all occurs to
disturb the relationship of master and servant apart from the simple unannounced fact
c of the transfer of business by the employer, it is the transfer itself which constitutes the
repudiatory breach which, apart from reg 5(1) 'terminates' the contract. If, however, the
employer, contemporaneously with the transfer, announces to his workforce that he is
transferring the business and that they are therefore dismissed without notice, it is,
strictly, the oral notification which terminates the contract; yet it could not, as a matter
of common sense, be denied that the contract has been 'terminated by the transfer' of the
d business, particularly when reference is made to the supplementary provisions of para (2)
of reg 5 when read in conjunction with para (3). Similarly, if the employer, a week, or it
may be a day, before the actual transfer, hands to each employee a letter announcing that
he is proposing to transfer his undertaking at the close of business on the transfer date, at
which time the employees are to consider themselves as forthwith dismissed, it could
hardly be contended under the regulations that their employment had not been
e terminated by the transfer, even though, at the date of the notice, the dismissal might be
capable of taking effect independently, in the event, for instance, of the actual transfer of
the business being postponed to a date or time later than the expiry of the notice. In each
hypothetical case the employer's repudiation of the contract of service is differently
communicated but its essential quality of a repudiation by the transfer of the undertaking
f remains the same and the contract can quite properly be described as having been
terminated by the transfer. If, by contrast, the employer announces to his workforce that
he is transferring his business to another person at 5 pm on the following Friday and that
they are to consider themselves dismissed from his employment at 4.59 pm on that day,
it is difficult to see any reason why the interposition of a one-minute interval between
the express repudiation becoming effective and the transfer which would, in any event,
have operated as a repudiation if nothing had been said, should invest the breach of
g contract by the employer with some different quality. In each case the effective cause of
the dismissal is the transfer of the business, whether it be announced in advance or
contemporaneously, or whether it be unannounced, and it would be no misuse of
ordinary language in each case to speak of the termination of the contracts of the
workforce as having been effected by the transfer. It is absurd to suggest that there is any
h distinction in substance between any of the hypothetical cases which I have envisaged.
Can it then, one asks, possibly have been the intention of the Secretary of State in framing
legislation expressly directed to safeguarding the rights of employees when an
undertaking is transferred, to make its effectiveness depend on whether the transferor, as
a result perhaps of a collusive bargain with the transferee, allows a scintilla temporis to
elapse between the operation of a notice dismissing his workforce and the completion of
j the legal formalities of the transfer which is the true cause of their dismissal, particularly
having regard to the provisions of reg 8, which were clearly intended to have the same
effect as art 4 of the directive? My Lords, I should be reluctant so to construe the
regulations, quite apart from any authority. When, however, they are considered in the
light of the interpretation placed by the European Court on the provisions of the
directive, it becomes, I think, clear that your Lordships are not compelled to do so.

In *Wendelboe v L J Music ApS (in liq)* Case 19/83 [1985] ECR 457 the original employer company was on the brink of insolvency. So far as appears, no transfer of their *a* undertaking was in contemplation when financial stringency compelled closure of the business and the dismissal of the major part of the workforce with immediate effect. That occurred on 28 February 1980. On 4 March 1980 the company was declared insolvent and a little over three weeks later an agreement was concluded transferring the business to a purchaser with effect from 4 March, the court having conduct of the insolvency having authorised the (then prospective) purchaser to use the company's *b* premises and equipment from 5 March onwards. The three plaintiffs were part of the original workforce and had in fact been engaged by the purchaser on 6 March but on terms that they lost their rights to seniority. They sued the original employer for damages for wrongful dismissal and arrears of holiday pay and were met with the defence that under the Danish legislation, which had been passed to give effect to the directive, all liabilities in respect of their employment had been transferred to the purchaser. The *c* question submitted by the Danish court to the European Court, pursuant to art 177 of the EEC Treaty, was whether the directive required member states to enact provisions under which the transferee of an undertaking became liable in respect of obligations concerning holiday pay and compensation to former employees who were not employed in the undertaking on the date of the transfer. That question was answered in the negative, as might indeed have been surmised purely from a textual interpretation of *d* art 3(1) of the directive. The following extract from the judgment of the court (at 466–467 (paras 15–16)) is, however, of interest in relation to the question of the relationship between arts 3 and 4 of the directive (which are reflected substantially in regs 5 and 8 of the regulations):

> 'That interpretation of the scope of Article 3(1) is also in conformity with the *e* scheme and the purposes of the directive, which is intended to ensure, as far as possible, that the employment relationship continues unchanged with the transferee, in particular by obliging the transferee to continue to observe the terms and conditions of any collective agreement (Article 3(2)) and by protecting workers against dismissals motivated solely by the fact of the transfer (Article 4(1)). Those *f* provisions relate only to employees in the service of the undertaking on the date of the transfer, to the exclusion of those who have already left the undertaking on that date. The existence or otherwise of a contract of employment or an employment relationship on the date of the transfer within the meaning of Article 3(1) of the directive must be established on the basis of the rules of national law, subject however to observance of the mandatory provisions of the directive and, more *g* particularly, Article 4(1) thereof, concerning the protection of employees against dismissal by the transferor or the transferee by reason of the transfer. It is for the national court to decide, on the basis of those factors, whether or not, on the date of the transfer, the employees in question were linked to the undertaking by virtue of a contract of employment or employment relationship.'

h
What is of particular interest here in relation to the questions raised by this appeal, is the statement that art 4(1), as well as art 3(1), apply 'only to employees in the service of the undertaking on the date of the transfer' and the observation that the determination according to the rules of national law is 'subject . . . to observance of the mandatory provisions of . . . Article 4(1)'. There is clearly scope here for the view that where the employment has been determined by the transferor solely on the ground of the transfer, *j* which art 4(1) states is not to 'constitute grounds for dismissal *by the transferor or the transferee*' (emphasis added) the employee is to be treated as if he had continued to be employed at the date of the transfer. That was a point which did not in fact arise in the *Wendelboe* case but which is reflected in the following passage from the opinion of the Advocate General, Sir Gordon Slynn (at 460–461):

'Whether or not a contract of employment or an employment relationship has
terminated at the time of transfer is of course for national law to determine.
However, the first sentence of Article 4(1) provides that "the transfer of an
undertaking, business or part of a business shall not in itself constitute grounds for
dismissal by the transferor or the transferee" . . . Where employees are dismissed,
with a view to and before, a transfer falling within the Directive and are re-engaged
immediately by the transferee thereafter, their dismissal must be regarded as
contrary to Article 4(1), subject to the exceptions specified in that paragraph.
Whether the remedy for such unlawful dismissal consists in a court order declaring
that dismissal to be a nullity or the award of damages or some other effective remedy
is for the Member States to determine. In any event, the Member States are required
to provide for a remedy which is effective and not merely symbolic . . . If the
remedy consists in treating the dismissal as a nullity, then it would follow that the
rights and obligations of the employee concerned are transferred to the transferee.'

The proposition that art 4(1) operates, in effect, to prohibit the exclusion of the rights
conferred by art 3 by dismissal of the employee immediately before the transfer, except
for one of the reasons specified in the second sentence of the article, receives some further
support from the opinion of the Advocate General, Sir Gordon Slynn, in the later case of
Foreningen af Arbejdsledere i Danmark v A/S Danmols Inventar (in liq) Case 105/84 [1985]
ECR 2639 at 2641, in which he commented on the *Wendelboe* case and observed:

'In *Wendelboe v LJ Music* it was held that only persons employed by the transferor
at the moment of the transfer fall within the provision; it was also pointed out that
Article 4(1) prohibits an employee from being dismissed by reason solely of such a
transfer, subject however to certain exceptions. The effect of the Directive, in my
opinion, is that an employee of the transferor at the time of transfer is entitled to
insist, as against the transferee, on all the rights under his existing employment
relationship. By virtue of Article 3, he can thus claim to continue to be employed
by the transferee on the same terms as he was employed with the transferor, or if
the transferee refuses or fails to observe those terms, he can bring a claim for breach
of contract or the relationship, against the transferee. Under Article 4, the transfer
does not by itself justify his dismissal by the transferor or the transferee unless such
dismissal is for economic, technical or organisational reasons entailing changes in
the work force . . . The employer who dismisses an employee for one of the reasons
specified in Article 4(1) can thus justify the dismissal. Otherwise if the dismissal or
purported dismissal is based on the transfer of the undertaking or business, the
employee can insist on his rights under Article 3.'

The prohibitory nature of art 4 was emphasised again in *Foreningen af Arbejdsledere i
Danmark v Daddy's Dance Hall A/S* Case 324/86 [1988] IRLR 315 at 317 (para 14), where
the court in the course of its judgment observed:

'. . . Directive 77/187 aims at ensuring for workers affected by a transfer of
undertaking the safeguarding of their rights arising from the employment contract
or relationship. As this protection is a matter of public policy and, as such, outside
the control of the parties to the employment contract, the provisions of the Directive,
in particular those relating to the protection of workers against dismissal because of
transfer, must be considered as mandatory, meaning that it is not permissable to
derogate from them in a manner detrimental to the workers.'

(See also *Landsorganisationen i Denmark v Ny Molle Kro* Case 287/86 [1989] IRLR 37.)
In a subsequent case, *P Bork International A/S v Foreningen af Arbejdsledere i Danmark*
Case 101/87 [1989] IRLR 41, the question arose whether the directive applied to a

situation where the workforce had been dismissed on the termination by the employer
of the lease of the premises on which the undertaking was carried on, the assets of the *a*
business having been purchased shortly afterwards by the new lessee of the premises,
which re-engaged over half the original workforce. The court held that the directive
applied and, in relation to the question of whether workers dismissed before the transfer
could claim the benefit of the directive as against the transferee, said (at 44 (paras 17–
19)):

> '... the only workers who may invoke Directive 77/187 are those who have *b*
> current employment relations or a contract of employment at the date of the
> transfer. The question whether or not a contract of employment or employment
> relationship exists at that date must be assessed under national law, subject, however,
> to the observance of the mandatory rules of the Directive concerning the protection
> of workers against dismissal by reason of the transfer. It follows that the workers *c*
> employed by the undertaking whose contract of employment or employment
> relationship has been terminated with effect on a date before that of the transfer, in
> breach of Article 4(1) of the Directive, must be considered as still employed by the
> undertaking on the date of the transfer with the consequence, in particular, that the
> obligations of an employer towards them are fully transferred from the transferor
> to the transferee, in accordance with Article 3(1) of the Directive. In order to *d*
> determine whether the only reason for dismissal was the transfer itself, account
> must be taken of the objective circumstances in which the dismissal occurred and,
> in particular, in a case like the present one, the fact that it took place on a date close
> to that of the transfer and that the workers concerned were re-engaged by the
> transferee. The factual assessment needed in order to determine the applicability of
> the Directive is a matter for the national courts, *having regard to the interpretative* *e*
> *criteria laid down by the court*.' (My emphasis.)

It does not appear that the impact of art 4 (and thus of reg 8) on the construction and
effect of art 3 (or reg 5) in relation to the employee's rights has previously fallen to be
considered in any of the reported cases in the United Kingdom. In *Alphafield Ltd v Barratt*
[1984] 3 All ER 795, [1984] 1 WLR 1062 the receiver of an undertaking, having *f*
negotiated a transfer of the undertaking to be completed on Monday, 17 January 1983,
dismissed the workforce at the close of business on the previous Friday, 14 January, at
the same time requesting them to report for work on the following Monday with a view
to re-engagement by the transferee. On the afternoon of 17 January the applicant was
told that his services would not be required. He claimed that the effect of reg 5 was that
his employment had been continued with the transferee and that he had, therefore, been *g*
unfairly dismissed by the transferee as a result of the latter's refusal to employ him. The
principal question argued was whether he had been employed 'immediately before' the
transfer. Both the industrial tribunal and the Employment Appeal Tribunal held that he
was. The decision of the Employment Appeal Tribunal was delivered by Tudor Evans J,
who said ([1984] 3 All ER 795 at 799, [1984] 1 WLR 1062 at 1066–1067):

> '... it seems to us to be a question of fact in each case dependent on the particular *h*
> circumstances whether or not a person was employed "immediately before" the
> transfer. It seems to us quite impossible, however desirable and helpful it might be,
> to say what period does and what period does not qualify. It must depend on the
> circumstances of each particular case whether dismissal is sufficiently proximate to
> the transfer. We think that, apart from analysis of the words used, it has to be
> remembered that if the words are construed in the strictest sense, as contended by *j*
> the employers, it would be very easy for a transferor without funds to agree with a
> transferee, for reasons convenient to them both, that employees should be dismissed
> a short time before transfer, thus leaving them with a worthless remedy and so
> defeating the protection afforded by the Regulations.'

In *Secretary of State for Employment v Anchor Hotel (Kippford) Ltd* [1985] ICR 724 the
a question was whether the original employer, who had given his employees a notice to
terminate their employment which expired on the same date as that on which the
transfer of the business took effect and who had made redundancy payments to them
following the transfer, was entitled to claim a rebate from the redundancy fund pursuant
to s 104 of the 1978 Act. The argument on behalf of the Secretary of State, which was
accepted by the Employment Appeal Tribunal, was that no rebate was due inasmuch as
b the claimant was never liable to make the redundancy payments, since his liability had
been transfered to the transferee of the business pursuant to reg 5, the employees having
been employed 'immediately before' the transfer. In giving the decision of the tribunal,
Waite J observed that it would serve no purpose to remit the case to the industrial
tribunal for a determination of the precise order in which the relevant events took place
since that was irrelevant, adding (at 729–730):
c

> 'We hold that when a dismissal notice given by the transferor expires on the same
> day as the transfer date, then it matters not for the purposes of the Regulations in
> precisely which order on that day the two events have occurred or whether they
> have occurred exactly simultaneously. The result will in every case be the same—a
> substitution of the transferee for the transferor as the party responsible for the
d dismissal and so liable to make a redundancy payment to the employee.'

The decisions in both the *Alphafield* and *Anchor Hotel* cases were, however, disapproved
by the Court of Appeal in England in *Secretary of State for Employment v Spence* [1986] 3
All ER 616, [1987] QB 179, which was followed and applied by the Second Division of
e the Inner House in the instant case. In that case the transferor company was in
receivership and the receivers had been negotiating a transfer of the business under a
threat by the company's major customer to withdraw its work unless a transfer of the
business had been agreed by 24 November 1983. No sale had been agreed by that date
and although on 28 November 1983 the negotiations were continuing, the receivers had
to decide whether it was proper in the interests of the debenture holders to continue to
f employ the workforce and to continue trading. Since there was no guarantee that the
negotiations would be successful, the decision was taken to cease trading immediately
and, at 11 am on that morning the employees were notified that they were dismissed
with immediate effect. In fact, the negotiations were successful and an agreement for the
sale of the undertaking was signed at 2 pm on that day. The employees were in fact re-
employed by the transferee but claimed redundancy payments from the Redundancy
g Fund under s 106 of the 1978 Act. The claim was resisted on the ground that, since the
claimants were employed 'immediately before the transfer' their employment was
continued with the transferee of the business by reg 5(1), following the decision in the
Anchor Hotel case [1985] ICR 724. It is worth noting that it was found as a fact by the
industrial tribunal first, that the sequence of events was the result of independent action
by the receivers and the transferees and that there was no collusion between them and
h second, that the reason why the receivers decided to dismiss the workforce was that, until
a contract could be renegotiated with the company's principal customer, there was no
prospect of any work for the business. It follows from these findings that the reason for
the dismissal was not one connected with the transfer but was due to economic
considerations, with the result that reg 8(1) did not render the dismissals unfair. The
only question for decision, therefore, was whether, having regard to the very short time
j which in fact elapsed between the dismissals taking effect and the conclusion of the
transfer agreement, the workforce was employed 'immediately before the transfer'. After
a careful analysis of the cases, the Court of Appeal rejected the approach of the
Employment Appeal Tribunal in *Alphafield Ltd v Barratt* and *Secretary of State for
Employment v Anchor Hotel (Kippford) Ltd* and held that reg 5(1) can apply only where, at

the very moment of transfer, the contract of employment (in the sense of the existing relationship of employer and employee) is still subsisting. If it is not, then there is *a* nothing on which the regulation can bite, even though the employment has been determined only a matter of minutes (or, it may be, seconds) before the transfer. My Lords, for my part, I can detect no flaw in the reasoning by which Balcombe LJ, who delivered the leading judgment in the Court of Appeal, reached the conclusion on the facts of that case that reg 5(1) did not operate to transfer the obligations of the original employer to the transferee. Where, before the actual transfer takes place, the employment *b* of an employee is terminated for a reason unconnected with the transfer, I agree that the question of whether he was employed 'immediately' before the transfer cannot sensibly be made to depend on the degree of temporal proximity between the two events, except possibly in a case where they are so closely connected in point of time that it is, for practical purposes, impossible realistically to say that they are not precisely contempora-neous. Either the contract of employment is subsisting at the moment of the transfer or *c* it is not, and if it is not, then, on the pure textual construction of reg 5, neither para (1) nor para (2) (which is clearly subsidiary to and complementary with para (1)) can have any operation. But *Spence's* case was decided, and quite properly decided, entirely without reference to the effect of reg 8(1) and in the context of the two important findings of fact by the industrial tribunal to which I have drawn attention. The Court of Appeal did not consider, and was not called on to consider, a position where, whether under a collusive *d* bargain or otherwise, an employee is dismissed from his employment solely or principally because of the prospective transfer of the undertaking in which he is employed, so that his dismissal is statutorily deemed to be unfair; and, of course, the case was decided without reference to the important *Bork* case [1989] IRLR 41 already referred to, which had not been decided at the date of the Court of Appeal judgment and which had not been reported at the time when the instant case was argued before the Court of Session. *e*

It is, I think, now clear that under art 4 of the directive, as construed by the European Court, a dismissal effected before the transfer and solely because of the transfer of the business is, in effect, prohibited and is, for the purpose of considering the application of art 3(1), required to be treated as ineffective. The question is whether the regulations are so framed as to be capable of being construed in conformity with that interpretation of *f* the directive.

This cannot, I think, be effected by adopting the flexible construction of the words 'immediately before' suggested in *Alphafield Ltd v Barratt* , for the meaning to be given to those words, taken alone, cannot sensibly be made to depend on whether the reason for the determination of the employment was the transfer or something else. Such an approach would involve the conclusion that the obligations of the transferor would be transferred to the transferee even in the case where, as in *Spence's* case, the employment *g* had been terminated for economic, technical or organisational reasons. That cannot, I think, have been intended, and I, for my part, agree with the rejection by the Court of Appeal in *Spence's* case of the reasoning of the Employment Appeal Tribunal in *Alphafield Ltd v Barratt* and *Secretary of State for Employment v Anchor Hotel (Kippford) Ltd*. Nor do I find a solution in the suggestion canvassed by counsel for the applicants that a dismissal *h* accepted by the transferee solely because of the impending transfer is to be treated as ineffective by some form of estoppel on the ground that the parties to the transfer cannot be permitted to take advantage of their own wrong. A termination for economic reasons, for instance, if effected without proper notice, would be as much a 'wrong' as a termination by reason of the transfer and, in any event, a termination effected without the collusion of the transferee could not be a 'wrong' on the part of the transferee, to *j* whose benefit the termination of the employment would enure.

The critical question, it seems to me, is whether, even allowing for the greater latitude in construction permissible in the case of legislation introduced to give effect to this country's Community obligations, it is possible to attribute to reg 8(1), when read in conjunction with reg 5, the same result as that attributed to art 4 in the *Bork* case [1989] IRLR 41. Purely as a matter of language, it clearly is not. Regulation 8(1) does not follow literally the wording of art 4(1). It provides only that if the reason for the dismissal of the employee is the transfer of the business, he has to be treated 'for the purposes of Part V of the 1978 Act' as unfairly dismissed so as to confer on him the remedies provided by ss 69–79 of the Act (including, where it is considered appropriate, an order for reinstatement or re-engagement). If this provision fell to be construed by reference to the ordinary rules of construction applicable to a purely domestic statute and without reference to treaty obligations, it would, I think, be quite impermissible to regard it as having the same prohibitory effect as that attributed by the European Court to art 4 of the directive. But it has always to be borne in mind that the purpose of the directive and of the regulations was and is to 'safeguard' the rights of employees on a transfer and that there is a mandatory obligation to provide remedies which are effective and not merely symbolic to which the regulations were intended to give effect. The remedies provided by the 1978 Act in the case of an insolvent transferor are largely illusory unless they can be exerted against the transferee as the directive contemplates and I do not find it conceivable that, in framing regulations intending to give effect to the directive, the Secretary of State could have envisaged that its purpose should be capable of being avoided by the transparent device to which resort was had in the instant case. *Pickstone v Freemans plc* [1988] 2 All ER 803, [1989] AC 66 has established that the greater flexibility available to the court in applying a purposive construction to legislation designed to give effect to the United Kingdom's treaty obligations to the Community enables the court, where necessary, to supply by implication words appropriate to comply with those obligations: see particularly the speech of Lord Templeman ([1988] 2 All ER 803 at 813–814, [1989] AC 66 at 120–121). Having regard to the manifest purpose of the regulations, I do not, for my part, feel inhibited from making such an implication in the instant case. The provision in reg 8(1) that a dismissal by reason of transfer is to be treated as an unfair dismissal, is merely a different way of saying that the transfer is not to 'constitute a ground for dismissal' as contemplated by art 4 of the directive and there is no good reason for denying to it the same effect as that attributed to that article. In effect this involves reading reg 5(3) as if there were inserted after the words 'immediately before the transfer' the words 'or would have been so employed if he had not been unfairly dismissed in the circumstances described in reg 8(1)'. For my part, I would make such an implication which is entirely consistent with the general scheme of the regulations and which is necessary if they are effectively to fulfil the purpose for which they were made of giving effect to the provisions of the directive. This does not involve any disapproval of the reasoning of the Court of Appeal in *Spence*'s case which, on the facts there found by the industrial tribunal, did not involve a dismissal attracting the consequences provided in reg 8(1).

The only reservation that I have with regard to that case is in relation to the approval by the Court of Appeal of a passage from the judgment of the Employment Appeal Tribunal in *Premier Motors (Medway) Ltd v Total Oil GB Ltd* [1984] 1 WLR 377, in which, after correctly pointing out that where an employee's contract is continued by virtue of reg 5, the transferee who plans to employ him, will be liable for a redundancy payment, Browne-Wilkinson J observed (at 382):

'To protect himself, the transferee must agree with the transferor either that the transferor will dismiss the employee before the transfer or will indemnify the transferee against redundancy payments and other employment liabilities.'

It follows from the construction that I attach to reg 5(3) that where an employee is dismissed before and by reason of the transfer the employment is statutorily continued with the transferee by virtue of the regulations and the first of the two options referred to in the passage quoted above is not, therefore, one which will effectively protect the transferee from the employee's claim for a redundancy payment. It also follows that both *Alphafield Ltd v Barratt* and *Secretary of State for Employment v Anchor Hotel (Kippford) Ltd*, in each of which the employment was clearly terminated by reason of the impending transfer, were correctly decided on their respective facts albeit not for the reasons given.

In the instant case it is quite clear that the reason for the dismissal of the appellants was the transfer of the business which had just been agreed and was going to take place almost at once. The effect of reg 5, construed as I have suggested that it should be, is that their employment continued with Forth Estuary. I would therefore allow the appeal. Counsel for Forth Estuary has submitted that in the event of the appeal being allowed, the order of the Employment Appeal Tribunal should be varied so as to remit back to the industrial tribunal the question whether the receivers had acted reasonably in dismissing the workforce in the context of s 57(3) of the 1978 Act. The respondents had the opportunity before the industrial tribunal of demonstrating, if they could, that there were some economic, technical or organisational reasons for the appellants' dismissals and it was therefore reasonable. They did not do so and I see no grounds now for allowing that question to be reopened. I would accordingly reverse the interlocutor of the Second Division of the Inner House and restore the order of the Employment Appeal Tribunal.

LORD JAUNCEY OF TULLICHETTLE. My Lords, I have had the advantage of reading in draft the speeches prepared by my noble and learned friends Lord Keith, Lord Templeman and Lord Oliver. I agree with them and for the reasons given therein I would allow the appeal and make the order which they propose.

Appeal allowed.

Solicitors: *Robin Thompson & Partners* (for the applicants); *Simmons & Simmons*, agents for *Brodies* WS, Edinburgh (for the new owners).

Mary Rose Plummer   Barrister.

a   # Re F (a minor)

COURT OF APPEAL, CIVIL DIVISION
RALPH GIBSON, BUTLER-SLOSS LJJ AND SIR EDWARD EVELEIGH
23 JUNE, I JULY 1988

b   *Ward of court – Jurisdiction – Child subject to immigration legislation – Child brought to United*
Kingdom and placed with foster parents – Child overstaying leave to enter – Child liable to
removal under immigration legislation – Foster parents applying to make child ward of court –
Whether wardship jurisdiction exercisable if it would fetter immigration authorities' discretion –
Whether court having jurisdiction to make child ward of court.

c   F, a minor, was born in Nigeria on 27 April 1981. His father died in July 1982 and
nothing was known for certain about his mother. In August 1982 he was brought to
England by his aunt on her passport and they were granted leave to enter as visitors for
six months. While in England F was placed with foster parents under an informal
fostering arrangement with the knowledge of the local social services department. His
uncle sent monthly payments to the foster parents for F's maintenance. F lived with the
d   foster parents until December 1986, when, on his own passport, he was taken to Nigeria
to visit his uncle. When he returned on 21 January 1987 it was discovered that he had
overstayed the six months' leave originally granted. He was granted temporary admission
while inquiries were made, and returned to his foster parents, who had been unaware of
any restriction on F's entry into or residence in the United Kingdom. The foster parents
issued an originating summons to make F a ward of court but on the application of the
e   Secretary of State the wardship summons was struck out as an abuse of process. The
foster parents appealed. Before the hearing of the appeal the Secretary of State agreed not
to take any steps to remove the child until adoption proceedings commenced by the
foster parents had been determined.

f   **Held** – It was an abuse of process to use the wardship jurisdiction to keep within the
jurisdiction a child who had overstayed his leave to enter thereby impeding the
immigration authorities in exercising their statutory power to remove the child, since if
the court were to make the child a ward of court in such circumstances it would be
putting a fetter or a clog on the discretion given by Parliament to the immigration
authorities and would frustrate the immigration legislation. However, there could be
rare and exceptional cases where the use of the wardship jurisdiction could be necessary
g   for the welfare of the child pending consideration of his position. On the facts, and
having regard to the Secretary of State's decision not to take further action pending the
outcome of the adoption proceedings, the court would make F a ward of court while he
remained in the country or until further order and to that extent the appeal would be
allowed (see p 1158 c to g, p 1159 g to j and p 1160 e f, post).
h   *Re A (an infant), Hanif v Secretary of State for Home Affairs* [1968] 2 All ER 145
considered.

Notes
For the wardship jurisdiction of the court over a child who is subject to immigration
control, see 24 Halsbury's Laws (4th edn) para 577.

j   ### Cases referred to in judgments
A (an infant), Re, Hanif v Secretary of State for Home Affairs [1968] 2 All ER 145, sub nom
    Re Mohamed Arif (an infant) [1968] Ch 643, [1968] 2 WLR 1290, CA.
H (a minor) (adoption: non-patrial), Re [1982] 3 All ER 84, [1982] Fam 121, [1982] 3 WLR
    501.

W (a minor), Re [1985] 3 All ER 449, [1986] Fam 54, [1985] 3 WLR 945, CA.

Appeal

The foster parents of F, a 7-year-old boy, appealed against the order of Hollings J on 22 January 1988 striking out as an abuse of the process of the court an originating summons issued by them on 22 April 1987 to make the child a ward of court. The respondents to the application were the child's guardian and the Secretary of State for the Home Department. The respondent to the appeal was the Secretary of State. The facts are set out in the judgment of Butler-Sloss LJ.

Charles Howard for the appellants.
Guy Sankey for the Secretary of State.

Cur adv vult

1 July. The following judgments were delivered.

BUTLER-SLOSS LJ (giving the first judgment at the invitation of Ralph Gibson LJ). This is an appeal from the decision of Hollings J whereby on 22 January 1988 he struck out an originating summons in wardship as an abuse of the wardship process and thereby dewarded the child.

The short facts are that the child concerned, F, whom I shall refer to as Tony, is seven, having been born on 27 April 1981 in Lagos, Nigeria. His father died on 7 July 1982. It is uncertain whether his mother is alive or dead. On 28 August 1982 Tony came to England with his aunt, Mrs Farinu, and a friend, Mrs Abedeyo. Tony's name was included on his aunt's passport. They were given leave to enter as visitors for six months. Mrs Farinu placed Tony with the appellants in an informal fostering arrangement, with the knowledge of the social services, who had approved informal fostering by this couple on previous occasions.

The appellants were unaware of any restriction on Tony's entry into, or residence in, the United Kingdom. They received monthly payments from Chief Farinu, who said he was the child's uncle and guardian. Infrequent visits were made to see the child, but in December 1986 the foster parents were told that Tony was to be returned to Lagos for Christmas. Mrs Abedeyo took him on 20 December to Nigeria and returned with him on 21 January 1987. At that time Tony had acquired his own passport.

Mrs Abedeyo was interviewed by an immigration official on her return and it was discovered that Tony had overstayed his welcome by some three years and ten months. The immigration official gave him temporary admission to the United Kingdom while inquiries were made in Nigeria and he was returned to the care of the foster parents.

The exact circumstances of his parentage, the whereabouts of his mother, if still alive, the exact relationship to Chief Farinu or Mrs Farinu were and remain unclear. From a telegram sent from Nigeria it was said that Chief Farinu was the eldest uncle and guardian of the boy and that he was financially responsible for the boy. It also said that the decision to send the boy to England was a family decision and they intended to bring the child back to Nigeria when he was about ten years old. The senior uncle, Chief Farinu, has his own house in London.

While the matter was under consideration, on 22 April 1987 the appellants issued an originating summons in wardship and made Chief Farinu the first defendant and the Secretary of State was joined as the second defendant on 8 July 1987.

In October 1987 the Secretary of State issued a summons to strike out the originating summons and it was that issue which was heard by Hollings J in January 1988.

The effect of the issue of a wardship originating summons is to make the child a ward of court on the making of the application: see the Supreme Court Act 1981, s 41(2). A child ceases to be a ward of court either, if an application for an appointment for the

hearing of the summons is not made within 21 days after issue of the summons, at the
a expiry of that period, or by order of the court to deward: see RSC Ord 90, r 4. A further
effect of the wardship is to prevent the removal of the ward from the jurisdiction without
the leave of the court.

The consequences of the wardship jurisdiction invoked in respect of a foreign child
entering the United Kingdom and subject to the immigration legislation was considered
in *Re A (an infant), Hanif v Secretary of State for Home Affairs* [1968] 2 All ER 145, [1968]
b Ch 643. In the two cases concerned the immigration officials refused the children
admission and the applicants for their entry made them wards of court. During the
argument it was conceded by counsel for the Secretary of State that a child of any
nationality who is lawfully, albeit temporarily, in England may be made a ward of court.
The purpose of the wardship proceedings in those cases, however, was to prevent the
removal of the child from the country. Lord Denning MR said ([1968] 2 All ER 145 at
c 151–152, [1968] Ch 643 at 660–662):

'First, it is said that once a child has been ordered to be removed, there is no
jurisdiction to make him a ward of court. I do not think it necessary to determine
that point. I can well see that there may be exceptional cases where such a
jurisdiction may be desirable. Second, it is said that at any rate, even if there is
d jurisdiction, it ought not to be exercised in cases like the present one. I think that
this second submission is correct. It seems to me . . . Parliament laid down a full and
complete code to govern the entry or removal of immigrants from the
Commonwealth and has entrusted the administration of it to the immigration
officers. So much so that the courts ought not to interfere with their decisions save
in the most exceptional circumstances . . . The court will not exercise its jurisdiction
e so as to interfere with the statutory machinery set up by Parliament. The wardship
process is not to be used so as to put a clog on the decisions of the immigration
officers or as a means of reviewing them.'

Russell LJ said ([1968] 2 All ER 145 at 153, [1968] Ch 643 at 663):

f 'The wardship of the infants, in my judgment, has not, and could not in law have,
any effect on the powers and duties of the immigration authorities so as to hamper
them in any way in removing the infants from the jurisdiction under the
[Commonwealth Immigrants Act 1962].'

At the hearing before Hollings J in January the argument on behalf of the Secretary of
State was that the issue of the wardship proceedings was an abuse of the process of the
g court, and he relied on *Re A (an infant)*. Counsel for the appellants sought to distinguish
Re A and pointed to the period that Tony had lived in this country, that the home was
the only home he knew, the credentials of the appellants, their desire to adopt the child
and their fear that the uncle might move him pending any decision, and there was no
way, other than wardship, to prevent him doing so.

The judge found that the main thrust of the submission for the wardship to continue
h was that, once an adoption application was lodged, different considerations would apply
to whether the child should remain in England and he said:

'But of course such a situation has not yet been created in the present case and I
do not consider that it would be a legitimate use of wardship proceedings to hold
the status quo until that situation has been potentially created by the institution of
j adoption proceedings. The court would otherwise indeed be exercising its
jurisdiction so as to interfere with the statutory machinery set up by Parliament,
and be putting a clog on the decision of immigration officers or on the Secretary of
State. I agree that the situation of the ward in the present case is vastly different
from what it was in *Re A (an infant)*. If the wardship jurisdiction exists, or should be
exercised, then there would be strong grounds for awarding care and control to the

plaintiffs and continuing the wardship. But that begs the question, which is whether such exercise of jurisdiction, however justified in itself, is a clog or fetter on the statutory machinery of immigration control. To that there can only be one answer.' (Hollings J's emphasis.)

Counsel for the appellants in his submissions to us relied on distinguishing the present case from *Re A (an infant)*, in particular that since no decision had been made by the Secretary of State there was no interference with any decision made under the Immigration Act 1971, and that the wardship proceedings were not being used to review decisions of immigration officers. He conceded, however, that his main submission to us is that the presence of the child in this country pending any application for adoption and until the determination of any adoption proceedings should be at the direction of the court and not by the grace of the Secretary of State. He did also put before us, as he put before the judge, the need to safeguard the child's well-being independently of the immigration issue, and that there are good prospects of success in the adoption application.

There can be little doubt, however, that the main purpose of the appellants in invoking the wardship jurisdiction was to impede the Secretary of State from exercising his discretion to remove the child from the jurisdiction and to require the Secretary of State to apply to the court for leave. The court, according to counsel for the appellants, should decide on grounds analogous to those considered in adoption cases, to which I shall refer later. I do not agree with that submission. The use of the wardship jurisdiction to keep the child within the jurisdiction until further proceedings can be initiated and to frustrate the immigration legislation for a short or long period is in my judgment a fetter or clog on the discretion given by Parliament to the immigration officials and to the Secretary of State and is an abuse of the process of the court. Indeed the issue of the originating summons itself with the automatic warding of the child impedes the Secretary of State from removing the child from the jurisdiction.

This is not to say, however, that wardship may never be instituted in cases where the position of the child concerned is being considered or has been considered under the immigration legislation. I do not think that Hollings J was saying that there is no jurisdiction to continue wardship proceedings in any circumstances where immigration officials may wish to act. That position was left open by Lord Denning MR in *Re A (an infant)* and in my judgment there are cases in which the use of wardship may be necessary for the welfare of the child, bearing always in mind that those occasions are likely to be exceptional and that the jurisdiction must not be invoked or continued in such a manner as to clog the discretion of, or implementation of the decision of, the Secretary of State. It would seem to me desirable that if wardship is to be instituted in the rare cases where it might be appropriate, the plaintiff's claim should indicate on the face of the originating summons that the purpose of the issue of the wardship is to safeguard the welfare of the child while the Secretary of State is considering the immigration implications. If it is intended to be a challenge to the overriding discretion of the Secretary of State, then that issue should equally be made clear in the originating summons.

Since, however, the primary purpose of invoking wardship in this case was to circumscribe the powers of the Secretary of State, I entirely agree with the conclusions of the judge on the facts before him in January.

We are here considering the problems associated with the arrival in this country of a little boy of seven who, through no fault of his own, overstayed his welcome and whose future is being considered by the Secretary of State. There is no reason to assume, as the judge did not, that the Secretary of State in arriving at his decision will not have regard to the welfare of Tony as well as other considerations.

At the time that this matter came before Hollings J no adoption application had been made and after the issue of the wardship summons could not have been properly made without leave of the court. But subsequent to the hearing in January and after the child was dewarded the foster parents issued the application in adoption on 8 May 1988.

a Different considerations apply in adoption applications. Section 6 of the Adoption Act 1976 requires the court to 'have regard to all the circumstances, first consideration being given to the need to safeguard and promote the welfare of the child throughout his childhood.' Where the proceedings concern a foreign national the court is required to balance the factors in favour of adoption against the factors relating to immigration and the refusal of admission. In *Re H (a minor) (adoption: non-patrial)* [1982] 3 All ER 84 at 94, [1982] Fam 121 at 133 Hollings J said that the court—

b 'must pay great regard to the "immigration decision" and in particular considerations of public policy and where relevant national security. It must be on its guard against the possibility of abuse; but the mere fact that nationality or patriality would result is not conclusive. It must treat welfare as the first consideration, outweighing any one other factor but not all factors.'

c The Court of Appeal in *Re W (a minor)* [1985] 3 All ER 449, [1986] Fam 54 approved the decision in *Re H*. Balcombe LJ indicated the considerations which should apply and said ([1985] 3 All ER 449 at 454, [1986] Fam 54 at 63):

d '(3) The court should also consider whether the welfare of the child would be better, or as well, promoted by another type of order which does not have the same effect on nationality and immigration as an adoption order, eg a custodianship order ...'

Before the judge counsel for the Secretary of State declined to give an undertaking not to arrive at or implement a decision until the issue of the adoption proceedings. The situation is now different. The Secretary of State, freed from the constraints of pressure e from the wardship proceedings, has indicated in correspondence, about which we were told, that he will not take any steps to remove the child until the adoption proceedings have been determined on certain wholly reasonable conditions, including the hearing of the adoption application within a reasonable time.

There will now be no conflict between the child's status as a ward and the exercise of the discretion of the Secretary of State during the period up to the hearing of the adoption f application. The child will, with the agreement of all present, remain in this country and with the appellants. The only matter which remains is whether pending the hearing of the adoption application, a period which with all reasonable diligence may still take months or more, the child should have his position regularised. Counsel for the appellants says with some force that no one within the jurisdiction has any right to take decisions over this child, unless Chief Farinu is present in this country. He has not attended the g appeal and has taken no part in these proceedings. Nevertheless, the foster parents fear that he may decide to remove the child. He has not up to now done so, but he has not yet been served with the adoption proceedings. For my part I see some force in the suggestion that for a limited purpose, unconnected with the issue of immigration, the child's position in England should be regularised and his de facto caretakers should have the right during that period to assume responsibility for him subject to the direction of h the court, to provide protection for him in the widest sense against any eventuality, including any disaster which might befall him or his caretakers. This case does seem to me to fall within the category of exceptional cases to which I referred earlier where wardship can properly be invoked.

In the knowledge that this court is now looking at circumstances which had not arisen before the judge, in my view this court should exercise its discretion to ward the child j for such period as the child may remain in this country or until further order. The wardship should run to the determination of the adoption application or until the decision of the Secretary of State that the child be not permitted to enter the United Kingdom. I have phrased it in that way since technically the child has only been permitted to enter on a temporary basis. On either of those two eventualities taking place, the child should be dewarded. If the judge hearing the adoption application decides on some other order, such as custodianship, then no doubt the whole matter would have to be reconsidered before him. In the event that the Secretary of State decides that the *a* child be not permitted to enter the United Kingdom, the child should be dewarded and the originating summons dismissed at the moment that the child leaves the jurisdiction of this court.

There are some other matters on which I should like to make some comments. The point of this appeal and the two elements of the argument before this court were clear to counsel on both sides and did not include any argument as to where the welfare of the *b* child lay. In his judgment Hollings J set out that counsel for the Secretary of State conceded that Tony's welfare may be better served if he remains in England. For my part I cannot see the need to reproduce at public expense all the affidavits (ten in all), and other evidence as to the suitability of the foster parents' care long-term for Tony. In my view it is an expensive exercise unnecessary for the decision at which we had to arrive.

It was clearly wrong that the Secretary of State had not been informed of the adoption *c* application until the day of the appeal and that equally no directions hearing in the Principal Registry had been sought. We were told of certain difficulties, but they should not be allowed to impede the involvement as soon as possible of the Official Solicitor, whom I am assuming will be invited in the adoption proceedings to represent the child.

It will be necessary to hear counsel on details of the order to be made. But consideration will have to be given to warding the child immediately, granting care and control to the *d* foster parents and giving leave to continue the adoption proceedings. This might be a case where it would be appropriate to make the child a party to the wardship proceedings as third defendant and to invite the Official Solicitor to act for him and thereby gain the assistance of the Official Solicitor at the earliest possible stage. I would allow the appeal to the limited extent that I have already indicated.

e

SIR EDWARD EVELEIGH. I agree.

RALPH GIBSON LJ. I also agree.

Appeal allowed in part.

f

Solicitors: *Hilliers,* Baldock (for the appellants); *Treasury Solicitor.*

Sophie Craven   Barrister.

a Rhodes and another v Allied Dunbar Pension Services Ltd and others
Re Offshore Ventilation Ltd

COURT OF APPEAL, CIVIL DIVISION
b O'CONNOR, NICHOLLS AND TAYLOR LJJ
17, 18, 19 OCTOBER, 9 NOVEMBER 1988

Distress – Distress for rent – Competing claims – Claims by landlords and debenture holder – Debenture holder of tenant appointing receivers of tenant's property – Landlords serving notice on subtenants to pay to landlords rent owing to tenant – Receivers levying distress on subtenants *c* *to collect rent owing to tenant – Whether sum raised by distraint on subtenants payable to debenture holder or to landlords – Law of Distress Amendment Act 1908, ss 3, 6.*

In 1984 the landlords granted three 20-year leases of parts of a freehold factory to a company. The company sublet parts of the factory to subtenants. In March 1986 the company entered into a deed of debenture in favour of its bank to secure all moneys *d* owed to the bank from time to time. From June neither the company nor the subtenants paid the rent due and in July 1986 the bank, which was owed over £150,000, appointed receivers and managers of the company in accordance with its powers under the debenture. The landlords, who were aware of the receivers' appointment, served notices on the subtenants under s 6[a] of the Law of Distress Amendment Act 1908 seeking to obtain from them the rent due from the company. Shortly thereafter the receivers levied *e* distress at the factory in respect of the arrears of rent owing by the subtenants and obtained about £16,000 from them. The receivers applied to the court for directions whether the sum raised by the distraint could be retained by the receivers or was payable to the landlords. The question arose whether the statutory assignment effected by the s 6 notices had priority over the previous equitable assignment effected by the appointment of the receivers. The landlords contended that by virtue of s 3[b] of the 1908 Act, under *f* which an underlessee was 'deemed to be the immediate tenant of the superior landlord' for the purposes of rent payable by an underlessee under a s 6 notice, they were entitled to the rent due from the subtenants after service of the notices. The judge held that the notices were ineffective to assign to the landlords the right to receive the subtenants' rent because the landlords were aware of the prior assignment to the bank at the time the notices were served, and therefore the receivers were entitled to retain the sum raised by *g* the distraint. The landlords appealed.

Held – On the proper analysis of the deed of debenture it did not have the effect of an equitable assignment to the bank of the right to future payments of rent by the subtenants but merely created a charge by way of a legal mortgage over the company's *h* leases. Moreover, since the bank had not taken possession of the premises under the debenture by requiring the subtenants to pay their rent direct to the bank but had instead allowed the company to remain in possession and receive the subtenants' rent and since the receivers were deemed by the debenture to be the company's agents, the receivers had obtained the sum raised by the distraint as agents of the company and, in the absence of an assignment by the company, they were required to pay it to the landlords when the *j* s 6 notices were served. Accordingly, the question of competing assignments to the landlords and to the bank did not arise. The appeal would therefore be allowed (see p 1166 *g*, p 1167 *b* to *d j* to p 1168 *b h*, post).
Decision of Harman J [1988] 1 All ER 524 reversed.

---

a   Section 6 is set out at p 1165 *c* to *e*, post
b   Section 3 is set out at pp 1164 *h* to p 1165 *a*, post

Notes

For the recovery by a superior landlord of rent from an undertenant, see 13 Halsbury's   *a*
Laws (4th edn) paras 260–261, and for a case on the subject, see 18 Digest (Reissue) 317,
425.

For the Law of Distress Amendment Act 1908, ss 3, 6, see 13 Halsbury's Statutes (4th
edn) 586, 588.

Cases referred to in judgments   *b*
Challoner v Robinson [1908] 1 Ch 49.
Dearle v Hall (1828) 3 Russ 1, [1824–34] All ER Rep 28, 38 ER 475, LC.
Gaskell v Gosling [1897] AC 575, [1895–9] All ER Rep 300, HL; *rvsg* [1896] 1 QB 669, CA.
Ind Coope & Co Ltd, Re [1911] 2 Ch 223.
Knill v Prowse (1884) 33 WR 163.
Ratford v Northavon DC [1986] 3 All ER 193, [1987] QB 357, [1986] 3 WLR 771, CA.   *c*
Turner v Walsh [1909] 2 KB 484, CA.
Wallrock v Equity and Law Life Assurance Society [1942] 1 All ER 510, [1942] 2 KB 82, CA.

Cases also cited
Druce & Co Ltd v Beaumont Property Trust Co Ltd [1935] 2 KB 257, [1935] All ER Rep 404.
Fulham v McCarthy (1848) 1 HL Cas 703, 9 ER 937.   *d*
Liverpool Corp v Hope [1939] 1 All ER 492, [1938] 1 KB 751, CA.
Nicholl v Cutts [1985] BCLC 322, CA.
Pfeiffer (E) Weinkellerei-Weineinkauf GmbH & Co v Arbuthnott Factors Ltd [1987] BCLC 522,
    [1988] 1 WLR 150.
Walton, Ex p, re Levy (1881) 17 Ch D 746, [1881–5] All ER Rep 548, CA.
Williams v Hayward (1859) 1 E & E 1040, 120 ER 1200.   *e*
Willment (John) (Ashford) Ltd [1979] 2 All ER 615, [1980] 1 WLR 73.
Woolston v Ross [1900] 1 Ch 788.

Appeal

Terence Peter Sims and Stephen Paul Tarrant, who were the trustees of a pension fund   *f*
known as the 'OSV (Self-administered) Pension Plan' and landlords of premises at 44A
Gloucester Road, Croydon, Surrey, let to Offshore Ventilation Ltd (the company),
appealed against the decision of Harman J ([1988] 1 All ER 524, [1987] 1 WLR 1703) on
19 June 1987 declaring that Geoffrey William Rhodes and Ian David Holland, the
receivers of the company appointed by the Royal Bank of Scotland plc under a debenture
dated 3 March 1986, were entitled to sums recovered or recoverable from underlessees
of the premises in respect of rent owed to the company. The facts are set out in the   *g*
judgment of Nicholls LJ

William Goodhart QC for the trustees.
Christopher Pymont for the receivers.

h

Cur adv vult

9 November. The following judgments were delivered.

NICHOLLS LJ (giving the first judgment at the invitation of O'Connor LJ). This appeal   *j*
concerns the effectiveness of four notices served by a superior landlord on four
undertenants under s 6 of the Law of Distress Amendment Act 1908. Under that section
a superior landlord may serve a notice on an undertenant requiring the undertenant to
make all future payments of rent directly to him until the arrears of rent due from the
intermediate landlord to the superior landlord have been paid.

The notices were served in the following circumstances. The appellants are the trustees
a of a pension fund known as the 'OSV (Self-administered) Pension Plan'. One of the assets
of that fund was the freehold of a factory at 44A Gloucester Road, Croydon. On 9 May
1984 the trustees granted three 20-year leases, each of a different part of the factory, to
Offshore Ventilation Ltd (the company). The company subsequently sublet parts of the
factory to four individual undertenants, by four underleases for periods varying from
five years to almost twenty years.

b   On 3 March 1986 the company entered into a debenture deed in favour of its bankers,
the Royal Bank of Scotland plc, to secure all money from time to time owing. By that
deed the company granted to the bank a first fixed legal charge over the factory. The
deed also created, in the usual way, a fixed charge over all the book debts and other debts
of the company, present and future, and a floating charge on all the undertakings and
property of the company. Shortly thereafter on 31 July 1986 the bank (which was owed
c more than £150,000 by the company) appointed the respondents to this appeal to be
joint receivers and managers of the company, under a power in that behalf contained in
the debenture. The rent due from the company to the superior landlords in June 1986
was not paid, nor did the receivers pay the rents falling due from the company under the
headleases in September and December 1986. These rents totalled about £17,200.
Furthermore, the undertenants did not pay rents due from them in December 1986
d totalling £16,897.

On 2 February 1987 the trustees, who were aware of the appointment of the receivers,
served the notices in dispute on the undertenants. Thereupon the receivers, two or three
days later, proceeded to levy distress at the factory in respect of the arrears of rent due
from the undertenants. The warrants were executed on 9 and 10 February. The outcome
was that the bailiffs received from the four undertenants sums amounting in the
e aggregate to about £16,000.

The receivers then applied to the court for directions regarding that sum. In short, the
issue was whether the s 6 notices were, in the circumstances outlined above, effective to
assign to the trustees as superior landlords the right to receive the undertenants' rents. If
they were, the receivers were not entitled to recover those rents, the distress authorised
by them was unlawful, and the money received by them under that distress ought not to
f be retained by them but must be paid to the trustees. Conversely, if the notices were
ineffective to assign that right to the trustees, then the distraints were lawful and the
receivers were entitled to retain the money. On 19 June 1987 Harman J held that the
notices were ineffective (see [1988] 1 All ER 524, [1987] 1 WLR 1703). From that
decision the trustees have appealed.

g *Law of Distress Amendment Act 1908*

Distress for rent is a remedy which enables landlords to recover arrears of rent, without
going to the court, by taking goods from the demised property and selling them. Its
origin is the common law, but over the centuries the scope of the remedy has been
modified and extended and, more recently, restricted by Parliament. The basic rule of
h common law is that any goods physically on the property for which rent is due are liable
to be taken by the distraining landlord, even though they belong to an undertenant or
other third party and even though the distraining landlord knows that the goods are not
the property of the tenant (see 13 Halsbury's Laws (4th edn) para 227). Exceptions were
grafted onto this rule, for example in the interests of trade, husbandry and public
convenience, and in some circumstances a landlord might be estopped by his own
j conduct from asserting his right to seize the property of a third party. Nevertheless, the
basic rule still stood at the beginning of this century.

In 1907 *Challoner v Robinson* [1908] 1 Ch 49 came before the court. A superior landlord
levied distress on some paintings belonging to various artists which were in the possession
of an underlessee for the purposes of exhibition and sale on part of the premises. Neville
J, and subsequently the Court of Appeal, held that the pictures did not fall within any of

the exceptions. Accordingly, the basic common law rule applied and the superior
landlord was entitled to seize and sell the pictures.   *a*

When giving judgment Neville J delivered himself of a trenchant observation on the
state of the law. He said (at 55):

> 'Now this is the year 1907, and it seems to me extraordinary that it should be
> possible in a country which boasts of civilization, which purports to protect the
> property of the law-abiding citizen, to raise such a question. But so it is. The rule   *b*
> that the landlord is entitled to distrain on the property of third persons upon the
> premises, subject to certain exceptions, has up to the present day escaped the zeal of
> the legal reformer, and therefore I have to deal with the law as I find it . . .'

In following year, the Law of Distress Amendment Act 1908 was passed. In short, s 1
protects from distress goods of certain undertenants, lodgers and other persons who are
not tenants and have no beneficial interest in any tenancy if the person in question makes   *c*
a declaration that the goods are not the goods of the immediate tenant but are his goods
or in his possession and, in the case of an undertenant or lodger, if he undertakes in
future to pay his rent directly to the superior landlord until the arrears of rent in respect
of which the distress is being levied have been paid. Shorn of words immaterial for
present purposes, s 1 provides:
                                                                                          d
> 'If any superior landlord shall levy . . . a distress on any . . . goods . . . of—(a) any
> under tenant liable to pay . . . a rent which would return in any whole year the full
> annual value of the premises or of such part thereof as is comprised in the under
> tenancy, or (b) any lodger, or (c) any other person whatsoever not being a tenant of
> the premises or of any part thereof, and not having any beneficial interest in any
> tenancy of the premises or of any part thereof, for arrears of rent due to such superior   *e*
> landlord by his immediate tenant, such under tenant, lodger, or other person
> aforesaid may serve such superior landlord . . . with a declaration in writing made
> by such under tenant, lodger, or other person aforesaid, setting forth that such
> immediate tenant has no right of property or beneficial interest in the . . . goods . . .
> so distrained or threatened to be distrained upon, and that such . . . goods . . . are the
> property or in the lawful possession of such . . . under tenant or lodger, setting forth   *f*
> the amount of rent (if any) then due to his immediate landlord, and the times at
> which future instalments of rent will become due, and the amount thereof, and
> containing an undertaking to pay to the superior landlord any rent so due or to
> become due to his immediate landlord, until the arrears of rent in respect of which
> the distress was levied or authorised to be levied have been paid off, and to such
> declaration shall be annexed a correct inventory . . . of the . . . goods . . . referred to   *g*
> in the declaration . . .'

Section 2 provides that it is unlawful to proceed with a distress on the goods of the
undertenant or lodger or other person after the requirements of s 1 have been met.

Section 3 is a consequential provision. It provides: *h*

> 'For the purposes of the recovery of any sums payable by an under tenant or
> lodger to a superior landlord under such an undertaking as aforesaid, or under a
> notice served in accordance with section six of this Act, the under tenant or lodger
> shall be deemed to be the immediate tenant of the superior landlord, and the sums
> payable shall be deemed to be rent; but, where the under tenant or lodger has, in
> pursuance of any such undertaking or notice as aforesaid, paid any sums to the   *j*
> superior landlord, he may deduct the amount thereof from any rent due or which
> may become due from him to his immediate landlord, and any person (other than
> the tenant for whose rent the distress is levied or authorised to be levied) from
> whose rent a deduction has been made in respect of such a payment may make the

a like deductions from any rent due or which may become due from him to his immediate landlord.'

It will be noted that the latter part of this section envisages that the undertenant who has paid rent direct to a superior landlord pursuant to a s 1 undertaking or a s 6 notice may not be the immediate tenant of the person in respect of whose rent the superior landlord has levied distress.

b Sections 4 and 5 exclude from the Act certain goods, and certain undertenancies, such as those created in breach of covenant. Thus far, the Act operates to restrict superior landlords' rights to distrain when an undertenant or lodger or other person takes the steps prescribed by s 1. Section 6, however, enables the superior landlord to short-circuit this procedure in the case of undertenants and lodgers. Instead of having first to levy a distress, which is then rendered abortive by the service of the necessary declaration and undertaking, s 6 empowers the superior landlord, where the rent of his immediate tenant
c is in arrears, to serve a notice on any undertenant or lodger requiring all future payments of rent to be made direct to him. Section 6 provides:

'In cases where the rent of the immediate tenant of the superior landlord is in arrear it shall be lawful for such superior landlord to serve upon any under tenant or lodger a notice (by registered post addressed to such under tenant or lodger upon
d the premises) stating the amount of such arrears of rent, and requiring all future payments of rent, whether the same has already accrued due or not, by such under tenant or lodger to be made direct to the superior landlord giving such notice until such arrears shall have been duly paid, and such notice shall operate to transfer to the superior landlord the right to recover, receive, and give a discharge for such rent.'

e It was pursuant to this section that the trustees served the notices which are in contention in this case.

Successive assignments
Prima facie these notices fall within s 6. The rent payable by the company, which was
f the immediate tenant of the trustees, was in arrears. The trustees, as the superior landlord, served notices in due form on the four undertenants. Prima facie, therefore, the consequence prescribed by the section follows: the notices operated to transfer to the trustees the right to recover, receive and give a discharge for all future payments of rent by the undertenants until the arrears of rent due to the trustees had been paid.

Counsel for the receivers contended otherwise. He submitted that the s 6 notices were
g not effectual *against the bank*. He developed an argument to the following effect. This is a case of successive assignments of the same chose in action, viz the right to be paid the undertenants' rents. The s 6 notices, as observed by Lord Greene MR in *Wallrock v Equity and Law Life Assurance Society* [1942] 1 All ER 510 at 511, [1942] 2 KB 82 at 84, brought about a statutory assignment of that chose in action. But that was not the only assignment of that right in the present case. On the contrary, here there had been a prior assignment
h of the same right. When the receivers were appointed the floating charge created by the debenture crystallised, and by reason thereof, even if the fixed charge over book debts had not already achieved that result, the right to future payments of rent was assigned in equity to the bank. Priority as between those two successive assignments is governed by the rule in *Dearle v Hall* (1828) 3 Russ 1, [1824–34] All ER Rep 28. In the instant case, each s 6 notice operated as the assignment itself and also as notice thereof to the debtor,
j viz the undertenant. But this did not give the trustees priority, because when the assignments to the trustees were made the trustees already knew of the appointment of the receivers and, hence, of the prior assignment to the bank. That knowledge prevented the trustees from acquiring priority, in accordance with the principle and authorities summarised in *Snell's Principles of Equity* (28th edn, 1982) pp 65–66.

Counsel for the receivers next pointed out that the 1908 Act contemplates only the relationships of landlord, tenant, undertenant and lodger. No mention is made of *a* assignees of the rent payable by undertenants, even though in law there can be an assignment of the right to recover rent simpliciter (see e g *Knill v Prowse* (1884) 33 WR 163). The 1908 Act, it was submitted, cannot have been intended to strip a legal or equitable assignee of the benefit of such an assignment even if he has given valuable consideration for it, and to do so without giving him any compensation. The Act should be construed so as to avoid such an injustice and, therefore, as not overriding the rights *b* of prior assignees who would have priority under the rule in *Dearle v Hall*.

This argument found favour with the judge. However, it is important to note that before the judge the starting point of the contention of counsel for the receivers seems to have been common ground between the parties. By 'the starting point,' I mean counsel's contention that the crystallisation of the floating charge by the appointment of the receiver had the effect of assigning to the bank in equity the right to future payments of *c* the undertenants' rent. In this court, counsel for the trustees disputed that this was the proper analysis of the debenture.

I turn, therefore, to the terms of the debenture deed. Clause 4(i) reads:

'For the purpose of securing all such moneys and/or the discharge of all such liabilities as aforesaid the Company as Beneficial Owner hereby charges its *d* undertaking and all its property and other assets of whatsoever nature both present and future including its uncalled capital for the time being and the charge hereby created shall rank as:—(a) a first fixed charge by way of legal mortgage of all (if any) the freehold and leasehold property now vested in the Company (including land of which the Company is registered as proprietor at H.M. Land Registry details of which are set out in the Schedule hereto) together with all fixtures and fittings *e* (including trade fixtures and fittings) and fixed plant and machinery from time to time therein or thereon; (b) a first fixed charge on all the goodwill and uncalled capital for the time being of the Company and all other (if any) the freehold and leasehold property hereafter vested from time to time in the future in the Company; (c) a first fixed charge on all the book debts and other debts of the Company both present and future; and (d) a first floating charge on all the undertaking and all the *f* property and assets of the Company both present and future not subject to a fixed charge hereunder.'

At the date of this deed the company owned the three leases of the factory at 44A Gloucester Road. Clause 4(i)(a) of the debenture, therefore, created in favour of the bank a charge by way of legal mortgage over those leases. I shall consider first what was the effect of this fixed charge in relation to the undertenants' rents and, second, whether this *g* position was affected by cl 4(i)(c) or (d) of the debenture.

The charge by way of legal mortgage

As a chargee by way of legal mortgage the bank obtained, by virtue of s 87 of the Law of Property Act 1925, the same protection, powers and remedies, including the right to *h* take proceedings to obtain possession from the occupiers and the persons in receipt of rents and profits, as if a sub-term less by one day than the term vested in the company had been thereby created in favour of the bank. Had such a sub-term been created, the bank would have been entitled to take possession. In this case, where the property was leasehold and was occupied by undertenants under subsisting underleases, possession would have taken the form of requiring the undertenants to pay their rent to the bank. *j* The legal mortgagee of a lease is the reversioner expectant on the underleases (see *Re Ind Coope & Co Ltd* [1911] 2 Ch 223 at 231–232), and a legal chargee is placed in a similar position by s 87.

However, a mortgagee may permit the mortgagor to remain in possession. If he does so, even though the mortgagor remains in possession only by leave and licence of the

mortgagee, the mortgagor remains entitled to receive and retain the income of the
a mortgaged property without any liability to account at law or in equity. That means,
where the mortgaged property is leasehold and subject to underleases, that so long as he
is so entitled to the income of the mortgaged property, the mortgagor may recover the
rent payable by the undertenants despite the existence of the mortgagee's reversionary
interest (see s 141(2) of the Law of Property Act 1925 and the observations of Farwell LJ
in *Turner v Walsh* [1909] 2 KB 484 at 494, [1908–10] All ER Rep 822 at 825). In the
b present case, the bank never went into possession of the property and thus, in accordance
with these established principles, the company remained entitled to receive the rents
from the undertenants notwithstanding the charge by way of legal mortgage.

In this regard, in my view, the appointment of the receivers made no material
difference. Although the receivers were appointed by the bank they were, pursuant to
cl 10 of the debenture, deemed to be the agents of the company. As Slade LJ observed in
c *Ratford v Northavon DC* [1986] 3 All ER 193 at 203, [1987] QB 357 at 371, citing passages
from the classical exposition of the status of receivers given by Rigby LJ in *Gaskell v
Gosling* [1896] 1 QB 669 at 685, subsequently approved by the House of Lords ([1897] AC
575, [1895–9] All ER Rep 300), this agency of receivers is a real one, even though it has
some peculiar incidents. Thus although, after their appointment, it was the receivers
who were entitled to payment of the undertenants' rents, their entitlement was as agents
d of the company. This was so even though, when they received the rents, they were
obliged to deal with the money, as with other money coming to their hands as receivers,
in accordance with the terms of the debenture.

The floating charge

I turn next to consider whether the presence in the debenture of paras (c) and (d) of
e cl 4(i) alters the position regarding the undertenants' rents in any way. In my view, it
does not. The opening words of cl 4(i) create a charge on all the property of the company.
The nature of this charge is then further defined: '. . . and the charge hereby created shall
rank as . . .'. Paragraph (a) deals explicitly and unambiguously with land currently owned
by the company. In my view, para (a) was intended to state, and it was effective to state,
what was to be the nature of the bank's charge over such land. It was to be a charge by
f way of legal mortgage, with all the incidents which would flow from that (save as
expressly provided elsewhere in the deed, as, for example, in cl 6). Those incidents, as
mentioned above, covered what was to happen to the rents of the undertenants.

Given the existence of that charge by way of legal mortgage, I can see no scope for the
operation, in relation to the same property, of the fixed charge created by para (c) or the
floating charge created by para (d), nor do I see any reason to think that para (c) or para
g (d) was intended to apply, in some way or other, to property or rights in property in
respect of which a fixed charge by way of legal mortgage had been created. Indeed, in
the case of para (d), the closing words make it abundantly plain that the floating charge
was intended to be a residual provision, operating only in the absence of a fixed charge.

In my view, the rights of the bank in respect of the receipt of rents from the
h undertenants were governed by para (a) and those rights were not enlarged or altered by
para (c) or para (d).

The s 6 notices

If the debenture is thus construed, the present case does not seem to me to give rise to
any particular difficulty. The spectre of successive assignments of the same chose in
j action vanishes. Instead, the case presents a comparatively straightforward picture. The
company, as the undertenants' immediate landlord, was entitled to their rent payments
before the debenture was executed on 3 March 1986; the company continued to be so
entitled after the execution of the debenture, the bank not having exercised its right to
take possession; and the company, in the persons of the receivers who were its agents,
continued to be so entitled after the appointment of the receivers on 31 July 1986.

That remained the position when the s 6 notices were served on 2 February 1987. *a*
Thus there is no question of competing assignments; there is no question of some person
other than the company having become entitled, in place of the company and by reason
of an assignment from the company, to receive the undertenants' rents which fell due in
and after December 1986.

On that short ground, which seems not to have been argued in front of the judge, I
would allow this appeal.

I do not find the result surprising or, even less, unconscionable. Quite the contrary. If *b*
the company had never executed the debenture but had failed to pay its rent, s 6 plainly
would have been available to the trustees.

Conversely, if the bank had gone into possession of the property under the debenture
and had not paid rent to the trustees as freeholders, s 6 would have been available to the
trustees. Section 6 is as much available where the defaulting tenant is an assignee of the
lease as it is available where he is the original lessee. The statutory right of the superior *c*
landlord to serve a s 6 notice and divert to himself rent payable by an undertenant, where
the intermediate lessor has failed to pay his rent, and also the statutory right of an
undertenant to undertake to pay his rent direct to the superior landlord under s 1 and
thereby preclude the superior landlord from levying distress on the undertenant's goods
in respect of arrears of rent due to the superior landlord, are now incidents of the superior
landlord/intermediate landlord/undertenant relationship. A person who takes an *d*
assignment of a headlease does so subject to the possibility that if the rent due to the
superior landlord is not paid, the superior landlord may garnishee, so to speak, the rent
due from undertenants. He takes, subject to that possibility, in the same way as he takes
subject to the possibility that if there is default in payment of the rent under the
headlease, the superior landlord may forfeit the headlease, with the consequence that
(unless relief is granted) any undertenancies will automatically be brought to an end. *e*
Likewise, in my view, in the case of a person, including a mortgagee, who takes not an
assignment of a headlease, but a sub-term carved out of the headlease. Such a person
acquires an estate which from its inception is subject to the rights conferred on superior
landlords and undertenants by ss 6 and 1.

If that is right, and the s 6 notices would have been effectual according to their tenor if *f*
no legal charge in favour of the bank had been created, and if also the notices would
equally have been effectual if the bank had gone into possession under the legal charge, I
think it would be surprising to find that such notices were ineffectual if a receiver were
appointed under the legal charge. I can see no rhyme or reason in that.

Other points *g*
In the light of the conclusion stated above, it is not appropriate or necessary for me to
express any view on what would be the position under s 6 of the 1908 Act, or under s 1,
if there were any assignment of a right to receive rent from an undertenant
unaccompanied by an assignment of the reversion. That point can be decided if and
when it arises.

h
TAYLOR LJ. I agree.

O'CONNOR LJ. I also agree.

Appeal allowed. Leave to appeal to the House of Lords refused.

j
Solicitors: *A R Drummond & Co*, Epsom (for the trustees); *Nabarro Nathanson* (for the
receivers).

　　　　　　　　　　　　　　　　　　　　　　　　Carolyn Toulmin　Barrister.

Bookbinder v Tebbit

COURT OF APPEAL, CIVIL DIVISION
RALPH GIBSON AND RUSSELL LJJ
8 DECEMBER 1988

Libel and slander – Justification – Wider meaning – Justification of wider meaning than that pleaded by plaintiff – Plaintiff pleading particular and general charges of squandering public funds – Defendant pleading justification of specific issue and wider meaning – Plaintiff withdrawing general charge – Whether defendant entitled to continue to rely on general charge to support plea of justification.

In 1984 the Labour-controlled Derbyshire County Council decided to overprint the caption 'Support Nuclear Free Zones' on all school stationary in its area. In 1986 at a by-election meeting in the West Derbyshire constituency the defendant, who was chairman of the Conservative Party, stated that the overprinting had cost £50,000 and described it as a 'damn fool idea'. The plaintiff, who was leader of the county council, issued a writ alleging, inter alia, that the natural and ordinary meaning of the words complained of were that the plaintiff had acted irresponsibly in causing large-scale squandering of public funds. The defendant by his defence pleaded, inter alia, justification relying on (i) the specific issue of the overprinting and (ii) other occasions of alleged squandering of public money by the council under the plaintiff's leadership. The plaintiff subsequently amended his statement of claim by withdrawing the general charge of squandering public funds and substituting a particular charge of squandering £50,000 on the overprinting and then applied to have the defence of justification based on the general charge of squandering public funds struck out. The judge dismissed the application and the plaintiff appealed to the Court of Appeal.

Held – A defendant was not entitled to rely on a general charge of wrongdoing unless a wider meaning or a more general charge could fairly be gathered from the words used, notwithstanding that the plaintiff had originally alleged in his statement of claim that the words used bore the general charge of wrongdoing and had later amended his statement of claim to withdraw that general charge leaving only an allegation that a particular charge of wrongdoing was defamatory. On the facts, once the plaintiff withdrew the general charge of squandering public funds the wider meaning was not a meaning which a jury could properly apply to the words used by the defendant and accordingly the defamatory charge in the words used was limited to the specific issue of the overprinting. It followed that the appeal would be allowed and the defence of justification based on the general charge of squandering public funds would be struck out (see p 1175 g to j, p 1177 j to p 1178 c e to h and p 1179 d e, post).

London Computer Operators Training Ltd v BBC [1973] 2 All ER 170, *Williams v Reason* (1983) [1988] 1 All ER 262 and *Khashoggi v IPC Magazines Ltd* [1986] 3 All ER 577 considered.

Notes

For justification in defamation actions, see 28 Halsbury's Laws (4th edn) paras 185–186, and for cases on the subject, see 32 Digest (Reissue) 201–216, 1722–1839.

Cases referred to in judgments

Bonnard v Perryman [1891] 2 Ch 269, [1891–4] All ER Rep 965, CA.
Davey v Harrow Corp [1957] 2 All ER 305, [1958] 1 QB 60, [1957] 1 WLR 941, CA.
Hollis v Burton [1892] 3 Ch 226, CA.
Khashoggi v IPC Magazines Ltd [1986] 3 All ER 577, [1986] 1 WLR 1412, CA.

Lewis v Daily Telegraph Ltd [1963] 2 All ER 151 [1964] AC 234, [1963] 2 WLR 1063, HL.
London Computer Operators Training Ltd v BBC [1973] 2 All ER 170, [1973] 1 WLR 424, a
  CA.
Lucas-Box v News Group Newspapers Ltd [1986] 1 All ER 177, [1986] 1 WLR 147, CA.
Maisel v Financial Times (No 1) (1915) 84 LJKB 2145, HL.
Polly Peck (Holdings) plc v Trelford [1986] 2 All ER 84, [1986] QB 1000, [1986] 2 WLR
  845, CA.
Speidel v Plato Films Ltd [1961] 1 All ER 876, [1961] AC 1090, [1961] 2 WLR 470, HL.   b
Warner v Sampson [1959] 1 All ER 120, [1959] 1 QB 297, [1959] 2 WLR 109, CA.
Williams v Reason (1983) [1988] 1 All ER 262, [1988] 1 WLR 96, CA.

Interlocutory appeal
The plaintiff, David Melvyn Bookbinder, appealed against the decision of Caulfield J
dated 26 April 1988 whereby he refused the plaintiff's application to strike out para 6 of c
the defence in an action for defamation against the defendant, the Rt Hon Norman
Tebbit MP. The facts are set out in the judgment of Ralph Gibson LJ.

Alan Newman for the plaintiff.
Geoffrey Shaw and *Stephen Suttle* for the defendant.   d

Cur adv vult

8 December. The following judgments were delivered.   e

RALPH GIBSON LJ. This is an interlocutory appeal in an action for damages for
allegedly defamatory words brought by the plaintiff, Mr David Melvin Bookbinder, who
at the material time was the leader of the Labour majority which controls the Derbyshire
County Council. The defendant is the Rt Hon Norman Tebbit, MP, chairman of the
Conservative Party. The plaintiff applied for part of the particulars of justification set out f
in the defence to be struck out on the ground that the allegations contained in them
disclose no reasonable defence and are vexatious and/or are an abuse of the process of the
court. Caulfield J on 26 April 1988 dismissed the application and the plaintiff has
appealed to this court.
    The history of the dispute began in 1984 when the council decided that the caption
'Support Nuclear Free Zones' should be printed on its stationery including the stationery g
of the county's schools and educational institutions. Existing stationery stocks were
overprinted. It seems that there were suggestions that this exercise had cost much money
and a sum of £50,000 was mentioned in a newspaper. In May 1986 there was a by-
election for the West Derbyshire constituency. On the evening of 6 May 1986, at a public
meeting in Matlock Bath, held in support of the Conservative candidate, the defendant h
referred to the matter. It is common ground between the parties that the defendant,
speaking at the public meeting, said the following words:

   'The £50,000 spent on printing anti-nuclear statements on county schools
   stationery was a damn fool idea. I hope that Councillor David Bookbinder has also
   told the Russians of Derbyshire's nuclear free policy. If not, it is arguable that he has
   lost £50,000 on this damn fool idea on school notepaper.'   j

    It is to be noted that the words he used state as a fact that £50,000 had been spent on
printing the anti-nuclear message on the school stationery. The opinion is then expressed
that that was a damn fool idea; and there is then what might be thought to be a sarcastic
reference to telling the Russians of Derby's nuclear free policy and the suggestion that, if
the Russians had not been told, the £50,000 might have been lost.

The plaintiff's action was commenced by writ on 11 March 1987 after the lapse of
a some eight months available for reflection. The plaintiff's statement of claim alleged that
the task of overprinting stationery was undertaken by the council without the
employment of any extra staff, without making any special collections or deliveries, and
by using spare printing time at the county's printing department; so that the cost of that
form of advertising of the council's policy was minimal. The plaintiff thus asserts that
the fact alleged in the defendant's statement was untrue; but that assertion is denied by
b the defendant and the real cost of the overprinting is disputed.

Next the statement of claim alleged that the words, in their natural and ordinary
meaning, meant and were understood to mean that the plaintiff, as leader of the
Derbyshire County Council, had acted irresponsibly in causing large scale squandering
of public funds. Thus, in its first form, the statement of claim alleged a general charge of
squandering and did not merely allege that the words meant that the plaintiff had caused
c a sum of about £50,000 to be squandered on overprinting school stationery.

The defence was served on 29 April 1987. It denied that the words were or were
capable of bearing any defamatory meaning. The defendant next relied, in the alternative,
on the defence of fair comment on a matter of public interest, namely the expenditure
by the council of money collected as rates. The viability of the defence of fair comment,
of course, depends on proof of the substantial truth of the facts stated. In addition, the
d defence pleaded justification: the defendant said that, if the words which he used had the
meaning which the plaintiff alleged, that is to say that the plaintiff had been guilty of
irresponsible squandering of public funds, then the defendant would show that the
charge was true and in para 6 he gave particulars of the facts and matters on which he
relied. These particulars fall into two categories: the first part, sub-paras (1) to (6) are
directed to the specific issue of overprinting. The second part of the particulars, namely
e sub-paras (7) to (19) deal with other occasions of alleged squandering of public money by
the council under the leadership of the plaintiff. Examples are as follows: in sub-paras
(7), (8) and (9), the publication from 1983 by the council of a free quarterly newspaper at
an alleged annual cost of £76,000 and containing allegedly political propaganda; in sub-
para (10), the employment in 1985 of an advertising agency to launch an advertising
campaign on behalf of the council, the cost of the campaign being estimated at £660,000;
f in sub-para (11), the sending in 1986 of councillors abroad in furtherance of 'twinning'
arrangements; in sub-para (13), the giving in March 1985 of £33,000 to a college outside
Derbyshire; in sub-para (14), the organising in about 1983 of a 'peace conference' at
Matlock in 1983; in sub-para (15), the cost in 1982 of early retirement of a council
surveyor; in sub-para (17), the spending in 1985 of £20,000 on sponsorship of a relay
run by young people to the Russian border; in sub-para (18), the allegation that in March
g 1987 Derbyshire was the highest rated county in England. The last, sub-para (19), reads
as follows:

> 'By reason of [those] facts and matters . . . the defendant will contend that the
> plaintiff as leader of the Derbyshire County Council has indeed acted irresponsibly
> in causing large scale squandering of public funds.'

h
The plaintiff, who, it is submitted, wishes to have tried the issue on which he started
his action and not all the other issues which the defendant has raised, repented of the
form of his pleading and amended it. Paragraph 5 of his statement of claim now reads
(with the amendment shown in italics):

> 'The said words in their natural and ordinary meaning meant and were understood
j > to mean that the plaintiff as Leader of the Derbyshire County Council had acted
> irresponsibly in squandering £50,000 of public money *on printing statements
> supportive of nuclear free zones on its stationery.*'

The plaintiff invited the defendant to amend his defence accordingly and to delete sub-
paras (7) to (19) of para 6 but the defendant declined. Hence the application to strike out
those sub-paragraphs.

Caulfield J dismissed the plaintiff's application because, in his judgment, the wider meaning was one which a jury might conceivably attach to the words used: the defendant *a* was saying that 'the plaintiff was irresponsible in squandering public money and was giving an example in the overprinting of the school stationery'. He added:

'There is a common sting here between the words used by the defendant and complained of by the plaintiff and the point of justification made by the defendant and the common sting is a waste of ratepayers' money.'

b

The submission to this court for the plaintiff by counsel for the plaintiff in summary form was as follows. (i) The wider meaning of the words, as first alleged by the plaintiff in the statement of claim settled by counsel, was not a meaning of which the words were reasonably capable and, if the defendant had made application, the court must have struck out the allegation on that ground. (ii) The plaintiff is entitled to correct the error in his pleading. There is no estoppel. Now that the words have been removed by *c* amendment the action proceeds as if they had never been there: *Warner v Sampson* [1959] 1 All ER 120 at 129, [1959] 1 QB 297 at 321. (iii) The matters alleged in sub-paras (7) to (19) of para 6 of the defence may be regarded as having been relevant and permissible while the plaintiff's pleading contained the alleged wider meaning. (There are matters of dispute as to the state of the pleading even if the wider meaning should be upheld as a meaning which the jury might reasonably attach to the words but those matters will, if *d* necessary, be left for resolution by requests for particulars.) On amendment of the statement of claim, since the wider meaning is not a conceivable meaning which the jury could properly attach to the words, sub-paras (7) to (19) should be struck out since they allege irrelevant matters which do not justify the charge contained in the words used and therefore constitute allegations designed to reduce the damage and as such are impermissible: *Spiedel v Plato Films Ltd* [1961] 1 All ER 876, 1090. (iv) The wider *e* meaning is not a reasonably conceivable meaning of the words used because the words allege one specific 'damn fool idea' in the spending of a named sum, £50,000 on one particular exercise, namely the overprinting of stationery. (v) The defendant's attempt to adhere to the wider meaning, and thereby to introduce the other issues into the trial, will greatly prolong the trial and increase the expense of it. The result would be oppressive to the plaintiff. *f*

The contentions in answer put forward by counsel for the defendant went as follows. (i) Where the plaintiff has pleaded a wide meaning, the defendant is entitled to justify that meaning: see *Maisel v Financial Times (No 1)* (1915) 85 LJKB 2145. The plaintiff ought not to be allowed to circumvent that principle after service of the defence by an amendment. Counsel referred to 'moving the goal posts'. (ii) Although the plaintiff can by amendment remove his original allegation from his pleading, the fact is that the *g* plaintiff, of whom the words were spoken, considered that, as applied to him, they had the wider meaning; the jury may well agree with his first view; and the court should not say that such a view is not reasonably conceivable. (iii) The defendant is entitled to justify any meaning which the words can conceivably bear: *London Computer Operators Training Ltd v BBC* [1973] 2 All ER 170, [1973] 1 WLR 424; and, for the purposes of an *h* interlocutory application to strike out, the test is whether the wider meaning sought to be justified by the defendant is 'reasonably arguable' as the meaning of the words complained of: see *Williams v Reason* [1988] 1 All ER 262 at 270, [1988] 1 WLR 96 at 102 per Stephenson LJ. (iv) Right-minded persons on hearing the words used would think the worse of the plaintiff not because of any particular frolic on which he has wasted public money but because he wasted public money; and the defendant ought to be *j* allowed to prove, if he can, the fact that the plaintiff had wasted public money by reference to other items of expenditure.

It is first necessary, in my judgment, to decide what effect must be given to the original pleading of the plaintiff. Counsel for the plaintiff has contended that the first form of pleading was a mistake. It was not put forward for any tactical purpose. When the

consequence of the error was seen there was a prompt attempt to correct it: the statement
a of claim was served on 11 March 1987; the defence was served on 29 April 1987; and
notice of intention to amend the statement of claim was given on 22 July 1987. It has
not been argued on behalf of the defendant that, irrespective of the merits of the point as
to the proper meaning of the alleged libel, the plaintiff could be prevented from
amending the statement of claim by reason of any disadvantage to the defendant, arising
from the original form of the pleading, which could not be put right by an order for
b costs.

A party is normally entitled to correct by amendment a bona fide error in his pleading
where the other side is not unfairly disadvantaged if the error is corrected. That principle
is plain where, for example, an incorrect admission of fact is made by mistake: see *Hollis
v Burton* [1892] 3 Ch 226 at 231. This case is concerned with a contention as to the
meaning of an alleged libel and by it notice is given of what claim will be made by the
c plaintiff at the trial. It may sometimes be wrong to permit a party to resile from the
position adopted and maintained for a considerable period of time in his pleading with
reference to some issue in the case: see *Davey v Harrow Corp* [1957] 2 All ER 305 at 307,
[1958] 1 QB 60 at 69 per Lord Goddard CJ. There is nothing, in my judgment, in *Maisel
v Financial Times* cited by counsel for the defendant which establishes any principle which
might deny to this plaintiff the right to amend in due time such an allegation made by
d him in his pleading. According to the construction which the plaintiff in that case had in
his pleading placed on the libel the defendants were sued for a general charge that the
plaintiff was a dishonest person. It was, therefore, obvious that they were entitled to give
particulars showing why they said he was a dishonest person; but there was no question
there of the plaintiff amending his allegation so as to withdraw the wider charge.

If, in a defamation case, the plaintiff were not free by amendment, made in due time,
e to correct an error in his pleading the plaintiff might, by such an error, be caused to have
to fight a case on issues which the law would otherwise have excluded. In my judgment,
the only force of the wider allegation originally made by the plaintiff is, as counsel for
the defendant pointed out, that the plaintiff, with the assistance of advice, considered
that, as applied to him, the words had that wider meaning.

The question for this court, therefore, is whether the words used could reasonably be
f regarded by the jury as meaning that the plaintiff was in 1986 a councillor who had acted
irresponsibly in causing large scale squandering of public funds generally, and not only
that he had squandered £50,000 of public funds on a particular 'damn fool idea', namely
the overprinting of stationery. That question is, of course, not to be answered by deciding
whether the jury could in fact in probability be persuaded to accept that the words had
the wider meaning. It is a question of law whether the words are capable of having the
g wider meaning for which the defendant now contends: see per Lord Reid in *Lewis v Daily
Telegraph Ltd* [1963] 2 All ER 151 at 155, [1964] AC 234 at 260. In that case the jury had
found the words to have the wider meaning for which, in that case, the plaintiff
contended, but the Court of Appeal set aside the verdict and judgment on the ground of
misdirection and the House of Lords, by a majority of four to one, upheld the decision of
h the Court of Appeal. As to the approach of the court in considering what meaning the
jury might properly infer from the words used, Lord Reid in that case said ([1963] 2 All
ER 151 at 155, [1964] AC 234 at 259):

'Ordinary men and women have different temperaments and outlooks. Some are
unusually suspicious and some are unusually naïve. One must try to envisage people
j between these two extremes and see what is the most damaging meaning they
would put on the words.'

That passage is cited in *Duncan and Neill on Defamation* (2nd edn) para 4.15.
The question with reference to these words might have been raised, and in my view
can usefully be considered, in a different context, as counsel for the plaintiff pointed out,

if the case had gone to trial on the issue as first pleaded by the plaintiff and with a plea of justification directed to the sole issue of spending or squandering public funds, to the *a* extent of £50,000, or some smaller amount, on overprinting stationery. If the judge had directed the jury that they could, if they saw fit, find that the words in their natural meaning were not limited to a charge of squandering public funds on publicising the council's anti-nuclear policy by printing a caption on stationery but extended to a general charge of having caused large scale squandering of public funds while a councillor, and if the jury had found for the plaintiff and awarded damages appropriate to that general *b* charge, would this court have been obliged to uphold the verdict and judgment on the ground that the wider meaning was one which the jury could properly attach to the words?

It has not been, and could not be, suggested that a particular charge of wrongdoing necessarily may be regarded by the jury in all cases as including a general charge of that sort of wrongdoing. Even where a defendant has published two distinct libels about a *c* plaintiff the law permits the plaintiff to complain of one only, and to have that issue decided, and the law does not permit the defendant to justify the one of which complaint is made by proving the truth of the other. Nor does the law permit a defendant to lead evidence of particular acts of misconduct on the part of the plaintiff in mitigation of damages where the defendant has failed to justify the libel complained of (see *Speidel v Plato Films Ltd* [1961] 1 All ER 876, [1961] AC 1090) but the two libels must be distinctly *d* severable into distinct parts and, if they are not, the plaintiff cannot pick and choose between them: see *Polly Peck (Holdings) plc v Trelford* [1986] 2 All ER 84 at 97, [1986] QB 1000 at 1025.

The question whether a particular charge of wrongdoing carries a general charge may depend on the context in which the words appear. Where the words are published in written form the writing conveys the context and the defendant is normally entitled to *e* insist that the jury see the whole of the context. In this case the words were spoken in the course of a public meeting. It is common ground that the meaning which the jury might properly attach to the words might be affected by the context, for example by the form of a question to which the words were given in answer, or the general course of a speech in which the words formed a passage; but neither the plaintiff nor the defendant has pleaded reliance on any such context and counsel for the defendant stated in this court *f* that the defendant did not rely on any unpleaded context.

Whether the words complained of were spoken, or were written, a party who alleges that the meaning of the words is affected by the context in which they were written or spoken must, in my judgment, give notice by his pleading of that fact and must state what the relevant context was. Where the words were spoken there may be a conflict of evidence as to what was said before and after the words complained of and, therefore, as *g* to what the context was in which the words were said. The obligation to plead the context, if reliance is to be placed on it for the purposes of supporting a contention as to what the meaning of the words was, is imposed, in my view, by RSC Ord 18, r 7(1):

> 'Subject to the provisions of this rule, and rules 7A, 10, 11 and 12, every pleading must contain, and contain only, a statement in a summary form of the material *h* facts on which the party pleading relies for his claim or defence, as the case may be, but not the evidence by which those facts are to be proved, and the statement must be as brief as the nature of the cases admits.'

The requirement is also covered, so far as concerns the defence of a defendant, by the provision in Ord 18, r 8(1): *j*

> 'A party must in any pleading subsequent to a statement of claim plead specifically any matter . . . (*b*) which, if not specifically pleaded, might take the opposite party by surprise . . .'

It therefore seems to me that the court on this application cannot speculate as to what the

context might be shown to have been in which the words in question were used beyond
a the matters to which reference is made in the pleading.

Reference, however, should be made to the manner in which this matter of the context
arose in the course of this appeal. I did not understand from counsel for the defendant
that consideration on behalf of the defendant had been given to the known context in
which the words were used or that the defendant was intending expressly to abandon
any question of reliance on such context. Indeed, I got the impression that until the
b matter was raised by Russell LJ in the course of argument direct attention had not been
given to the context. It appeared that the parties were not in possession of a transcript of
the meeting, if any recording existed from which a transcript might be made. I am not,
of course, suggesting that there was some relevant context to which either side could
usefully refer but, just as the plaintiff has amended his pleading, so the defendant might
on his part, provided the application was made in due time, seek leave to amend his
c defence in order to allege what the context was if the evidence to justify such an
application were available. In other words, the decision which I think this court should
make on this appeal is based on the material contained in the pleading as it now stands.

The question as to the width of the conceivably proper meaning of the words used is
therefore to be answered on the material before this court by reference to the words
themselves spoken at a public meeting in support of a candidate in a by-election and
d spoken of a councillor, who was the leader of the controlling majority of the council. If
the court is to say that these words, by their own force and in that context, may properly
be held to contain a general charge of squandering public money, then it seems to me
that we would be very close to holding that it is open to a jury, at least with reference to
a person holding elective office and of known political views, to find that any specific
charge against him of wrongdoing, based on stated specific facts, imports a general charge
e of preceding similar wrongdoing which may be justified by different specific facts. To
take an example from the other side of the political debate, a specific charge of cruel and
damaging cuts in public spending, based upon a stated reduction of funds to a particular
cause or body, could, without support from the context, and by the force of the particular
words alone, be held to contain a charge of other preceding allegedly cruel and damaging
cuts, based on other reductions of funds to other causes and bodies.
f For my part, I consider that the law should not, and does not, permit such wide
discretion to a jury in selecting the meaning of words used. I do not, of course, assume
or suggest that in this case any charge or allegation has been made on a false factual basis.
The question of the cost of the overprinting is in issue and will be decided by the jury
together with the primary question whether the words used were defamatory at all. But
if in such a case as this a defamatory charge has been made on a false factual basis then,
g unless a wider meaning or a more general charge can fairly be gathered from the words
used, or from the context, it is important to the even-handed conduct of such trials that
it should not be open to a defendant, who has mistakenly charged the plaintiff with some
form of alleged misconduct, be it squandering of public money or the making of
damaging cuts, when there has been in fact no such squandering or no such cuts in
h funds, to defend the specific claim in defamation by reference to any other alleged
examples of squandering or of cuts, merely on the ground that they are allegedly true
examples in the past conduct of the plaintiff of the alleged kind of wrongdoing of which
a specific charge has been made. A plaintiff ought to be able, if he can, to prove the
untruth of a specific mistaken or false charge without having to face the burden of a trial
directed to any number of preceding incidents of expenditure or of cutting expenditure
j in which he was concerned.

Counsel for the defendant argued that to hold that the words cannot properly bear the
wider meaning would be to prevent ventilation at the trial of the real issue, namely
whether or not there had been squandering of money left, right and centre by the council
under the leadership of the plaintiff. He said that assistance could be found in support of
the plaintiff's contention that the words import a sting of a general nature from the

decision of the court in *Khashoggi v IPC Magazines Ltd* [1986] 3 All ER 577, [1986] 1 WLR
1412; and that two cases, *London Computer Operators Training Ltd v BBC* [1973] 2 All ER   *a*
170, [1973] 1 WLR 424 and *Williams v Reason* (1983) [1988] 1 All ER 262, [1988] 1 WLR
96, were 'on all fours with this case'.

In my view, on the essential question as to the possible meanings of the words used in
this case, those cases relied on by counsel for the defendant provide little if any assistance,
and that is not surprising because the relevant principle applicable in this case is not in
issue between the parties and the application of the principle by the court to one set of   *b*
facts can rarely be of direct assistance in applying it to different facts. A brief examination
of these cases will be sufficient. In *Khashoggi's* case the publication contained various
express allegations about the sexual behaviour of the plaintiff but she complained in her
proceedings of one allegation only of an affair with a named man. It was contended for
the defendants that they could properly claim to justify the sting of the libel, for the
purposes of the principle in *Bonnard v Perryman* [1891] 2 Ch 269, [1891–4] All ER Rep   *c*
965, so as to prevent the grant of an interlocutory injunction, by proof of conduct
showing sexual promiscuity although they could not prove the allegation with reference
to the named man. This court upheld that submission and thereby held, as I understand
it, that it would be open to the jury on the facts of that case to find that the meaning of
the words used in the publication as a whole was that contended for by the defendants.
The application of the principle by the court to the facts of that case seems to me to be of   *d*
no assistance in answering the question in this case. There was here no allegation of
wrongdoing, additional to the specific charge in issue, capable of supporting a wider
meaning.

Next, as to *London Computer Operator's Training Ltd v BBC*, the proprietors of an
establishment which claimed to train computer operators claimed damages for libel
contained in a radio programme, broadcast by the defendants, which was an exposé of   *e*
the training provided, and included comments that it was a financial racket; that the
aptitude test and final certificate were bogus; and it referred to the founder of the school,
who was not a plaintiff in the action, with the words: 'Is this the sort of man to run a
computer school?' The defendants, who had pleaded justification and fair comment,
applied for leave to amend their defence by adding to the particulars of justification   *f*
details of previous convictions of the founder of the school for offences of dishonesty not
connected with the running of the school. The defendants were held by this court to be
entitled to plead those convictions on the ground that the programme was capable of
being interpreted by a reasonable jury as meaning that the company was being run by
people of questionable honesty; and, as that was a conceivable meaning, evidence of the
convictions should be before the jury. That case is another example of the application of
the principle that any facts may be proved which are relevant to justify the sting of the   *g*
libel according to any meaning which the jury may properly attach to it; but there is, I
think, no particular assistance to be derived as to the factors by reference to which the
court is to decide whether, in the absence of a relevant context, it is properly open to a
jury to hold that a specific allegation of wrongdoing contains for these purposes a general
charge of such wrongdoing.

Finally, as to *Williams v Reason*, which was decided by this court (Stephenson, O'Connor   *h*
and Purchas LJJ) in November 1983 the libels were published in two articles in the Daily
Telegraph in 1979. They alleged that the plaintiff had infringed his amateur status by
writing a book for money. One article contained the heading 'Board should act now to
halt Shamateurism'; and, in addition to references to the writing of the book, the article
said: *j*

'I have not met anyone who does not believe that the [plaintiff's] case has infringed
at least three of the intentions of the International Board's amateur principles. I have
no doubt that Rugby Union football in Britain and in at least two other countries in

a
Europe is rapidly approaching the state of shamateurism which so disfigured the top level of so-called English soccer for many years.'

The plaintiff by his statement of claim alleged that the words in the article meant that the plaintiff had (i) infringed his amateur status by writing a book, (ii) was guilty of 'shamateurism', (iii) had played an international match against England though he knew that he was a professional and (iv) had by his conduct brought disgrace and disrepute on the game of rugby and his country. There was a dispute of fact at the trial as to whether

b the plaintiff had or had not written the book for money, intending to keep the money which was paid to him, or whether he had always intended to give the money to charity and had not changed his intention about keeping the money after publication of the first article in the Daily Telegraph. The jury held the publications to have been defamatory and awarded damages. The judgment and verdict were set aside and a new trial ordered for reasons not relevant to this case. The defendants were given leave to amend the

c defence to allege, as particulars of justification, not new facts relevant to the alleged writing of a book for money but facts relevant to the taking of money for wearing the boots of a named boot manufacturer; and leave was granted on the grounds set out in a passage in Stephenson LJ's judgment on which counsel for the defendant placed particular reliance ([1988] 1 All ER 262 at 269, [1988] 1 WLR 96 at 103):

d
'...I conclude that [it] is right ... that the sting of the libel here is "shamateurism", the charge, still tied to his book but nevertheless carrying with it a charge of hypocrisy and deviousness, that the plaintiff was a professional while claiming to be an amateur, that the evidence that alleges that the plaintiff regularly took boot money, if accepted, would prove that he had by reason of reg 5 of the board's regulations no amateur status to infringe or lose at the time when he wrote the book

e because he had already lost it by taking boot money and that a jury which heard evidence that he had accepted boot money might have been influenced into finding that he had, on any interpretation of the regulations, infringed them by writing a book for money that he never intended to give to charity until the publication of the first of Mr Reason's articles in the Daily Telegraph.'

f   Again, in my view, that case was an example of the application of established principle to the widely varying circumstances of particular cases; and, again, I can derive little assistance from the case in the decision of the central question to this case. I note, however, that Stephenson LJ, with whose judgment both O'Connor and Purchas LJJ in substance agreed, said ([1988] 1 All ER 262 at 269, [1988] 1 WLR 96 at 103):

g
'... I have not found it easy to decide whether the evidence of boot money is relevant to the words that Mr Reason wrote of the plaintiff, understood in any meaning that they are reasonable capable of bearing.'

For my part I regard that case as far stronger than this for the purpose of finding in the words used a general charge, in that case of 'shamateurism', by reference to a particular example, namely the writing of a book for money.

h
As I have said, it is not to be expected that much assistance will be capable of being derived from the decision as to the reasonably possible meaning of one set of words for the purpose of deciding the meaning of another set of words. As Lord Reid said in Lewis v Daily Telegraph Ltd [1963] 2 All ER 151 at 155, [1984] AC 234 at 250:

j
'What the ordinary man, not avid for scandal, would read into the words complained of must be a matter of impression.'

I have reached the clear conclusion that the wider meaning, now abandoned by the plaintiff but put forward by the defendant, is not a meaning which the jury could properly apply to the words used. I have had very much in mind the view of Caulfield J, who has wide experience in defamation cases, and I have been slow to reach a conclusion *a* different from that expressed by him. But, in the end, I have found myself unable to share his view.

The clear impression which I have formed of these words, in their context as now before us, is that the ordinary man envisaged by Lord Reid would regard the defamatory charge in the words used, if there was any, as limited to the spending of stated sums on the stated project. Next, the defamatory charge, if there was any, was not of a stated *b* crime or of a form of moral turpitude but was, by no means unimportant or trivial but of a different order, in my view, of causing the spending of public money to such an extent and for such a purpose that the spending was wholly unjustified. The fact that a person is by his social judgment moved to cause to be made an unjustified expenditure, if that should be proved, on publicising an anti-nuclear policy does not, in my view, suggest that he has in the past been moved to make unjustified expenditure on different *c* projects or for different social purposes, or is of such a character that he is likely to have so acted.

Further, I have tested the point in the way suggested by counsel for the plaintiff. If it should have been proved that the defendant had incorrectly asserted that £50,000 had been spent on the idea of printing the anti-nuclear caption on council stationery, and if the jury should have found that the words used were defamatory in their context, *d* including therein the assertion that the expenditure was a damn fool idea, it would in my view have been unjust for the jury to have awarded damages on the basis that by the words used the defendant had generally charged the plaintiff with the squandering of public money in the plaintiff's prior direction of expenditure of public money by the council in all or any part of its functions. The fact that the defendant now asserts the wider meaning, in order to be allowed the opportunity to try to prove other distinct *e* items of public expenditure which he wishes to try to prove to have amounted to squandering of public money, does not, in my judgment, alter the case or widen the possible meaning of the words used.

For my part, therefore, I would allow this appeal and direct that sub-paras (7) to (19) of para 6 of the defence be struck out.
f

RUSSELL LJ. I agree. As Ralph Gibson LJ has pointed out, I was concerned during the submissions of counsel that the context in which the words were spoken by the defendant might well have a bearing on the conceivable meanings that the words are capable of bearing. On the one hand, the allegation might have been an isolated and self-contained one, confined to the assertion that £50,000 had been spent on the overprinting on school stationery, with the derisive comments about that activity. If such were the reality it is *g* impossible, in my judgment, to give the words a meaning wider than that now contended for by the plaintiff. On the other hand, the offending words might well have formed a part or illustration of a much broader based political attack on alleged maladministration at the expense of ratepayers by the local authority of which the plaintiff was the leader. If this were the true context in which the words were spoken, then I think it is plain that *h* a conceivable meaning of the words used could be as is now contended for by the defendant. This seemed to be the view of Caulfield J when he said in his judgment that a conceivable meaning was 'that the plaintiff was irresponsible in squandering public money and [*the defendant*] *was giving an example in the over-printing of the school stationery*' (my emphasis).

Unfortunately neither counsel could assist as to the context in which the words were *j* spoken, and we are left with the pleadings. They are silent as to the context.

In these circumstances I am satisfied that, in the absence of a pleaded context, the court should not speculate, where to do so might lead to a defendant being permitted to prolong the hearing and to adduce a welter of evidence not relevant to the real issue for the jury's determination. Whilst recognising that the striking out of a pleading, or part

of it, is a draconian step, I do not shrink from it in this case so long as the pleadings do
a not assist in ascribing to the words a broader meaning than that which they bear when
looked at in isolation.

In *Lucas-Box v News Group Newspapers Ltd* [1986] 1 All ER 177 at 181 [1986] 1 WLR
147 at 161 Ackner LJ said:

> 'It is axiomatic that the function of pleadings is to define the issues between the
> parties, so that both the plaintiff and the defendant know what is the other side's
b > case, and then everyone, counsel, judge and jury are able to focus on the real nature
> of the dispute. Although to some it may seem a startling observation, we can see no
> reason why libel litigation should be immune from the ordinary pleading rules.'

Counsel for the defendant told us that in libel the context was normally pleaded by a
reference to the full material passage where a defence of justification and/or fair comment
c was raised. However, in his wide experience he could not recall the context being pleaded
in slander proceedings: certainly not as a matter of practice or convention by those
practising extensively in this field.

For my part I can see no reason why slander should be different from libel, and the
words of Ackner LJ cited above seem to me to be entirely appropriate to both forms of
defamation.

d Like Ralph Gibson LJ I must not be taken as suggesting that a context which would
permit of a wider meaning than that pleaded by the plaintiff was present, but in my view
if such is to be alleged it should be pleaded, and provided that the defendant makes his
application to amend timeously in order to allege the appropriate context, the order of
this court on this interlocutory appeal should in no way preclude the amendment being
made.

e I too, therefore, would allow this appeal and make the order proposed by Ralph Gibson
LJ.

Appeal allowed. Leave to appeal refused.

f Solicitors: *Cooper Sons Hartley & Williams*, Manchester (for the plaintiff); *Peter Carter-Ruck & Partners* (for the defendant).

Radhika Edwards   Barrister.

Norwich City Council v Harvey and others

COURT OF APPEAL, CIVIL DIVISION

MAY, CROOM-JOHNSON AND GLIDEWELL LJJ

15, 16 NOVEMBER, 21 DECEMBER 1988

Building contract – Sub-contractors – Liability for loss or damage – Limitation of liability – Standard form contract between employer and main contractor – Contract providing that damage by fire at sole risk of employer – Fire damage caused by sub-contractor's employee – Whether sub-contractor protected by exemption clause in main contract – Whether just and reasonable to hold sub-contractor liable – Whether sub-contractor owing duty of care to employer – JCT Standard Form of Building Contract (Local Authorities' Edition with Quantities, 1963 edn (July 1977 revision)), cl 20[C].

The plaintiff building owners entered into a contract for the extension of a swimming pool complex under a contract in the JCT standard form of local authority building contract (1963 edition, revised in 1977), cl 20[C] of which provided that 'The existing structures . . . owned by him or for which he is responsible and the Works . . . shall be at the sole risk of the Employer [ie the building owners] as regards loss or damage by fire . . . and the Employer shall maintain adequate insurance against those risks'. The contractor sub-contracted certain roofing work to the defendant sub-contractors, one of whose employees, while using a blowtorch, set fire to both the existing buildings and the new extension. The building owners brought an action against the sub-contractors and their employee claiming damages for negligence. The trial judge dismissed the action and the building owners appealed to the Court of Appeal.

Held – Where a contract for the erection of a building contained a provision that the building owner was to bear the risk of loss or damage caused to the building by fire thereby reflecting the intention of the building owner and the contractor that the former would accept the risk of damage by fire to his premises, and a sub-contractor had contracted with the contractor on that basis, it would not be just and reasonable to exclude the sub-contractor from the protection of that provision in the main contract if the building was damaged by fire as the result of the negligence of the sub-contractor, even though there was no privity of contract between him and the building owner. Furthermore, in such circumstances there was not such a close and direct relationship between the building owner and the sub-contractor for the latter to owe a duty of care to the former. It followed that the sub-contractors were entitled to the benefit of the exemption from liability contained in cl 20[C] of the main contract in respect of the claim brought against them by the building owners in respect of their employee's negligence. The appeal would accordingly be dismissed (see p 1184 g, p 1187 b f and p 1188 f g, post).

James Archdale & Co Ltd v Comservices Ltd [1954] 1 All ER 210 and *Scottish Special Housing Association v Wimpey Construction UK Ltd* [1986] 2 All ER 957 considered.

Notes

For negligence and the duty to take care, see 34 Halsbury's Laws (4th edn) para 5, and for cases on the subject, see 36(1) Digest (Reissue) 17–55, 34–177.

Cases referred to in judgments

Aberdeen Harbour Board v Heating Enterprises (Aberdeen) Ltd (1988) Times, 25 March, Ct of Sess.

Anns v Merton London Borough [1977] 2 All ER 492, [1978] AC 728, [1977] 2 WLR 1024, HL.

Archdale (James) & Co Ltd v Comservices Ltd [1954] 1 All ER 210, [1954] 1 WLR 459, CA.

a *Curran v Northern Ireland Co-ownership Housing Association Ltd (Stewart, third party)* [1987] 2 All ER 13, [1987] AC 718, [1987] 2 WLR 1043, HL.

Davis Contractors Ltd v Fareham UDC [1956] 2 All ER 145, [1956] AC 696, [1956] 3 WLR 37, HL.

Donoghue (or M'Alister) v Stevenson [1932] AC 562, [1932] All ER Rep 1, HL.

Hedley Byrne & Co Ltd v Heller & Partners Ltd [1963] 2 All ER 575, [1964] AC 465, [1963]
b 3 WLR 101, HL.

Home Office v Dorset Yacht Co Ltd [1970] 2 All ER 294, [1970] AC 1004, [1970] 2 WLR 1140, HL.

Leigh & Sillavan Ltd v Aliakmon Shipping Co Ltd, The Aliakmon [1986] 2 All ER 145, [1986] AC 785, [1986] 2 WLR 902, HL.

Peabody Donation Fund (Governors) v Sir Lindsay Parkinson & Co Ltd [1984] 3 All ER 529,
c [1985] AC 210, [1984] 3 WLR 953, HL.

Rowlands (Mark) Ltd v Berni Inns Ltd [1985] 3 All ER 473, [1986] QB 211, [1985] 3 WLR 964, CA.

Rumbelows Ltd v AMK (a firm) (1982) 19 Build LR 25.

SCM (UK) Ltd v W J Whittall & Son Ltd [1970] 3 All ER 245, [1971] 1 QB 337, [1970] 3 WLR 694, CA.

d *Scottish Special Housing Association v Wimpey Construction UK Ltd* [1986] 2 All ER 957, [1986] 1 WLR 995, HL.

Southern Water Authority v Carey [1985] 2 All ER 1077.

Spartan Steel and Alloys Ltd v Martin & Co (Contractors) Ltd [1972] 3 All ER 557, [1973] QB 27, [1972] 3 WLR 502, CA.

e *Sutherland Shire Council v Heyman* (1985) 60 ALR 1, Aust HC.

Twins Transport Ltd v Patrick (1984) 25 Build LR 65.

Weller & Co v Foot and Mouth Disease Research Institute [1965] 3 All ER 560, [1966] 1 QB 569, [1965] 3 WLR 1082.

Welsh Health Technical Services Organisation v Haden Young (IDC, third party) (1987) 37 Build LR 130.

f *Yuen Kun-yeu v A-G of Hong Kong* [1987] 2 All ER 705, [1988] AC 175, [1987] 3 WLR 776, PC.

Cases also cited

Johnson Matthey & Co Ltd v Constantine Terminals Ltd [1976] 2 Lloyd's Rep 215.

g *Junior Books Ltd v Veitchi Co Ltd* [1982] 3 All ER 201, [1983] 1 AC 520, HL; *affg* 1982 SLT 333, Ct of Sess.

New Zealand Shipping Co Ltd v A M Satterthwaite & Co Ltd [1974] 1 All ER 1015, [1975] AC 154, PC.

Petrofina (UK) Ltd v Magnaload Ltd [1983] 3 All ER 35, [1984] QB 127.

Raymond v Honey [1982] 1 All ER 756, [1983] 1 AC 1, HL.

h *Scruttons Ltd v Midland Silicones Ltd* [1962] 1 All ER 1, [1962] AC 446, HL.

Simaan General Contracting Co v Pilkington Glass Ltd (No 2) [1988] 1 All ER 791, [1988] QB 758, CA.

Tai Hing Cotton Mill Ltd v Liu Chong Hing Bank Ltd [1985] 2 All ER 947, [1986] AC 80, PC.

j **Appeal**

The plaintiffs, Norwich City Council, appealed from the judgment of Garland J (39 Build LR 75) given on 2 November 1987 dismissing their claim against the first defendant, Paul Clarke Harvey, and the second defendants, Briggs Amasco Ltd, for £56,362·17 being damages for negligence in respect of fire damage caused by the first defendant while employed by the second defendants, who were sub-contractors on the building of an extension of a swimming pool complex owned by the plaintiffs. The facts are set out in the judgment of May LJ.

Robert Akenhead for the plaintiffs.
Nicholas Dennys for the defendants.

Cur adv vult

21 December 1988. The following judgments were delivered.

MAY LJ. This is an appeal by the plaintiffs from a judgment of Garland J of 2 November 1987 (see 39 Build LR 75). The judge then had before him a claim for damages for negligence against both defendants which he dismissed. The plaintiffs now appeal asking that that order should be set aside and that judgment should be entered for them for damages of £56,362·17.

The case concerns a building contract and a sub-contract. I take the facts of the case from the judge's judgment in which they are clearly set out. The plaintiffs, the building owners, own and operate a swimming pool complex at St Augustines in Norwich. In March 1981 they entered into a contract with main contractors, called Bush Buildings (Norwich) Ltd, for an extension to the complex. The latter sub-contracted certain felt roofing work to the second defendants. Unfortunately one of the latter's employees, the first defendant, while using a gas blowtorch, set fire to both the existing buildings and the new extension causing damage, which gave rise to the claim in these proceedings.

The judge held that any duty of care which would otherwise have been owed by the defendants to the plaintiffs had been qualified by the terms of the respective contracts between the parties, whereby the plaintiffs accepted the risk of damage by fire and other perils to their property and that consequently it would not be just and reasonable to hold that the defendants owed any duty to the plaintiffs to take reasonable care to avoid such damage. This is the fundamental issue in this case.

The contract between the plaintiffs and Bush Builders, to which I shall refer as the 'main contract', was in the familiar JCT Standard Form of Building Contract, Local Authorities' Edition with Quantities, 1963 edn (July 1977 revision). The material clauses of that contract for present purposes are cll 17, 18, 19 and 20[C] of which the relevant parts are as follows:

'17 The Contractor shall not without the written consent of the Employer assign this Contract, and shall not without the written consent of the Architect/Supervising Officer (which consent shall not be unreasonably withheld to the prejudice of the Contractor) sub-let any portion of the Works . . .

18(2) Except for such loss or damage as is at the risk of the Employer under clause 20[B] or clause 20[C] of these Conditions (if applicable) the Contractor shall be liable for, and shall indemnify the Employer against, any expense, liability, loss, claim or proceedings in respect of any injury or damage whatsoever to any property real or personal in so far as such injury or damage arises out of or in the course of or by reason of carrying out of the Works, and provided always that the same is due to any negligence, omission or default of the Contractor, his servants or agents or of any sub-contractor his servants or agents.

19(1)(a) Without prejudice to his liability to indemnify the Employer under clause 18 of these conditions the Contractor shall maintain and shall cause any sub-contractor to maintain such insurances as are necessary to cover the liability of the Contractor or, as the case may be, of such sub-contractor in respect of personal injury or death arising out of or in the course of or caused by the carrying out of the Works not due to any act or neglect of the Employer or of any person for whom the Employer is responsible and in respect of injury or damage to property, real or personal, arising out of or in the course of or by reason of the carrying out of the

Works and caused by any negligence, omission or default of the Contractor, his
servants or agents or, as the case may be, of such sub-contractor, his servants or
agents...

20[C] The existing structures together with the contents thereof owned by him
or for which he is responsible and the Works and all unfixed materials and goods,
delivered to, placed on or adjacent to the Works and intended therefor ... shall be
at the sole risk of the Employer as regards loss or damage by fire [and other listed
risks] and the employer shall maintain adequate insurance against those risks...'

Clearly therefore, as between the employer and the main contractor, the former was
solely liable in respect of any loss or damage to his premises caused by, inter alia, fire.

In so far as the second defendants, as sub-contractors, were concerned, they were
invited to tender by the main contractor. The document doing so identified the form of
the main contract and in attached extracts from the relevant bill of quantities the main
contractor expressly stated that cl 20[C] (employer's risk) would apply. In their own
additional conditions they also provided inter alia:

'The work is to be carried out in accordance with the contract which exists
between Bush Builders (Norwich) Ltd. (hereinafter called the Main Contractor) and
the Employer, and the acceptance of this order binds the Sub-contractors and
Suppliers to the same terms and conditions as those of the Main Contract. It is not
however the intention of the Main Contractor to issue formal Sub-Contract
Documents unless specifically required.'

The sub-contractors duly tendered on 20 January 1981. Their tender was accepted on
17 March 1981 by the main contractor by a document containing the following
conditions:

'1. The work is to be carried out in accordance with the contract which exists
between Bush Builders (Norwich) Limited (hereinafter called the Main Contractor)
and the employer, and the acceptance of this order binds the sub-contractors and
suppliers to the same terms and conditions as those of the main contract ...

5. No exclusions or limitations of liabilities of suppliers or sub-contractors are
accepted unless agreed separately in writing by the Main Contractor and all suppliers
and sub-contractors will be held responsible for any increased costs due to their
actions together with any consequential loss.

6. The suppliers or sub-contractors shall take out and maintain, to the satisfaction
of the Main Contractor, all necessary insurance policies as required by law and the
contract and shall produce evidence of the same if required to do so ...'

On the facts of this case it is not disputed that, if the sub-contractors owed any duty to
take care to avoid damage to the employers' property by fire, then they were in breach of
that duty and the employers are entitled to recover.

The judge held that there was no privity of contract between the employer and the
sub-contractors, and also that there was no question of the main contractor acting either
as the agent or trustee for the sub-contractors (see his Honour Judge David Smout QC in
Southern Water Authority v Carey [1985] 2 All ER 1077). The judge further declined to act
on any analogy with the bailment cases where, as in *Leigh & Sillavan Ltd v Aliakmon
Shipping Co Ltd, The Aliakmon* [1986] 2 All ER 145, [1986] AC 785, the contractual
exemption is in the defendant sub-bailee's contract with the bailee. Having considered a
number of recent authorities relating to the existence and extent of a duty of care he
concluded (39 Build LR 75 at 87–88):

'The matter must be approached as one of principle: is the duty owed by the
defendant to the plaintiff qualified by the plaintiffs' contract with the main
contractor, or to put it more broadly, by the plaintiffs propounding a scheme
whereby they accepted the risk of damage by fire and other perils to their own

property—existing structures and contents—and some property which does not belong to them—unfixed materials and goods, the value of which has not been *a* included in any certificate—while requiring the contractor to indemnify them against liabilities arising from the omission or default of both the contractor and of any sub-contractor; then requiring the contractor to insure and to cause any sub-contractor to insure against the liabilities included in the indemnity? I am left in no doubt that the duty in tort owed by the sub-contractor to the employer is so qualified. This appears to me to follow from the passage to which I have referred in *b* *Peabody v Parkinson* ([1984] 3 All ER 529 at 534, [1985] AC 210 at 240–241), and to be consistent with the approach, albeit on different facts in *Scottish Housing v Wimpey* ([1986] 2 All ER 957, [1986] 1 WLR 995) and *Mark Rowlands v Berni Inns* ([1985] 3 All ER 473, [1986] QB 211) . . . Each case must turn both on its own facts, and on the authority of *Peabody v Parkinson*, what is just and reasonable.'

c

I trust I do no injustice to the plaintiffs argument in this appeal if I put it shortly in this way. There is no dispute between the employer and the main contractor that the former accepted the risk of fire damage: see *James Archdale & Co Ltd v Comservices Ltd* [1954] 1 All ER 210, [1954] 1 WLR 459 and *Scottish Special Housing Association v Wimpey Construction UK Ltd* [1986] 2 All ER 957, [1986] 1 WLR 995. However cl 20[C] does not give rise to any obligation on the employer to indemnify the sub-contractor. That clause *d* is primarily concerned to see that the works were completed. It was intended to operate only for the mutual benefit of the employer and the main contractor. If the judge and the sub-contractors are right, the latter obtain protection which the rules of privity do not provide. Undoubtedly the sub-contractors owed duties of care in respect of damage by fire to other persons and in respect of other property (for instance the lawful visitor, employees of the employer or other buildings outside the site); in those circumstances it *e* is impracticable juridically to draw a sensible line between the plaintiffs on the one hand and others on the other to whom a duty of care was owed. The employer had no effective control over the terms on which the relevant sub-contract was let and no direct contractual control over either the sub-contractors or any employee of theirs.

In addition, the plaintiffs pointed to the position of the first defendant, the sub-contractors' employee. Ex hypothesi he was careless and, even if his employers are held *f* to have owed no duty to the building employers, on what grounds can it be said that the employee himself owed no such duty? In my opinion, however, this particular point does not take the matter very much further. If in principle the sub-contractors owed no specific duty to the building owners in respect of damage by fire, then neither in my opinion can any of their employees have done so.

In reply the defendants contend that the judge was right to hold that in all the *g* circumstances there was no duty of care on the sub-contractors in this case. Alternatively they submit that the employers' insurers have no right of subrogation to entitle them to maintain this litigation against the sub-contractors.

The law relevant to the question whether or not a duty of care arises in given circumstances has been considered by the House of Lords and the Privy Council in a number of recent decisions. For present purposes one can start with the dictum from the *h* speech of Lord Wilberforce in *Anns v Merton London Borough* [1977] 2 All ER 492 at 498–499, [1978] AC 728 at 751–752:

'Through the trilogy of cases in this House, *Donoghue v Stevenson* [1932] AC 562, [1932] All ER Rep 1, *Hedley Byrne & Co Ltd v Heller & Partners Ltd* [1963] 2 All ER 575, [1964] AC 465 and *Home Office v Dorset Yacht Co Ltd* [1970] 2 All ER 294, [1970] *j* AC 1004, the position has now been reached that in order to establish that a duty of care arises in a particular situation, it is not necessary to bring the facts of that situation within those of previous situations in which a duty of care has been held to exist. Rather the question has to be approached in two stages. First one has to ask whether, as between the alleged wrongdoer and the person who has suffered damage a there is a sufficient relationship of proximity or neighbourhood such that, in the reasonable contemplation of the former, carelessness on his part may be likely to cause damage to the latter, in which case a prima facie duty of care arises. Secondly, if the first question is answered affirmatively, it is necessary to consider whether there are any considerations which ought to negative, or to reduce or limit the scope of the duty or the class of person to whom it is owed or the damages to which a breach of it may give rise (see the *Dorset Yacht* case [1970] 2 All ER 294 at 297–298,

b [1970] AC 1004 at 1027, per Lord Reid). Examples of this are *Hedley Byrne & Co Ltd v Heller & Partners Ltd* where the class of potential plaintiffs was reduced to those shown to have relied on the correctness of statements made, and *Weller & Co v Foot and Mouth Disease Research Institute* [1965] 3 All ER 560, [1966] 1 QB 569 and (I cite these merely as illustrations, without discussion) cases about "economic loss" where, a duty having been held to exist, the nature of the recoverable damages was limited

c (see *SCM (United Kingdom) Ltd v W J Whittall & Son Ltd* [1970] 3 All ER 245, [1971] 1 QB 337, *Spartan Steel and Alloys Ltd v Martin & Co (Contractors) Ltd* [1972] 3 All ER 557, [1973] QB 27).'

However, in *Governors of the Peabody Donation Fund v Sir Lindsay Parkinson & Co Ltd* [1984] 3 All ER 529 at 534, [1985] AC 210 at 240–241 Lord Keith commented on Lord
d Wilberforce's dictum in these terms:

'There has been a tendency in some recent cases to treat these passages as being themselves of a definitive character. This is a temptation which should be resisted. The true question in each case is whether the particular defendant owed the particular plaintiff a duty of care having the scope which is contended for, and
e whether he was in breach of that duty with consequent loss to the plaintiff. A relationship of proximity in Lord Atkin's sense must exist before any duty of care can arise, but the scope of the duty must depend on all the circumstances of the case. In *Home Office v Dorset Yacht Co Ltd* [1970] 2 All ER 294 at 307–308, [1970] AC 1004 at 1038–1039 Lord Morris, after observing that at the conclusion of his speech in *Donoghue v Stevenson* [1932] AC 562 at 599, [1932] All ER Rep 1 at 20 Lord Atkin
f said that it was advantageous if the law "is in accordance with sound common sense" and expressing the view that a special relation existed between the prison officers and the yacht company which give rise to a duty on the former to control their charges so as to prevent them doing damage, continued: "Apart from this I would conclude that in the situation stipulated in the present case it would not only be fair and reasonable that a duty of care should exist but that it would be contrary to the
g fitness of things were it not so. I doubt whether it is necessary to say, in cases where the court is asked whether in a particular situation a duty existed, that the court is called on to make a decision as to policy. Policy need not be invoked where reasons and good sense will at once point that way. If the test whether in some particular situation a duty of care arises may in some cases have to be whether it is fair and reasonable that it should so arise the court must not shrink from being the arbiter.
h As Lord Radcliffe said in his speech in *Davis Contractors Ltd v Fareham Urban District Council* [1956] 2 All ER 145 at 160, [1956] AC 696 at 728, the court is 'the spokesman of the fair and reasonable man'." So in determining whether or not a duty of care of particular scope was incumbent on a defendant it is material to take into consideration whether it is just and reasonable that it should be so.'

j In *Curran v Northern Ireland Co-ownership Housing Association Ltd (Stewart, third party)* [1987] 2 All ER 13, [1987] AC 718 the House of Lords held that a statutory authority responsible for the provision of housing accommodation had no powers of control of building operations when paying an improvement grant. Accordingly, it did not owe subsequent occupiers a duty to take care not to make payment in respect of defective work. Lord Bridge said ([1987] 2 All ER 13 at 17, [1987] AC 718 at 724):

'My Lords, *Anns v Merton London Borough* may be said to represent the high-water mark of a trend in the development of the law of negligence by your Lordships' House towards the elevation of the "neighbourhood" principle derived from the speech of Lord Atkin in *Donoghue v Stevenson* into one of general application from which a duty of care may always be derived unless there are clear countervailing considerations to exclude it.'

Lord Bridge then quoted a longer passage from the speech of Lord Keith in the *Peabody* case, including the passage which I have already quoted, and went on to consider in particular the extent to which a duty of care should be imposed on a statutory authority exercising a statutory power given to it. Such considerations are of course not directly relevant in the instant case, but Lord Bridge concluded ([1987] 2 All ER 13 at 20, [1987] AC 718 at 729):

'Here, in my opinion, the dictate of good sense and the consideration of what is fair and reasonable point clearly against the imposition of any duty of care owed by the executive to the plaintiffs and it would be contrary to the fitness of things to hold it to be under any such duty.'

In *Yuen Kun-yeu v A-G of Hong Kong* [1987] 2 All ER 705, [1988] AC 175, the question arose whether the Commissioner of Deposit-taking Companies owed any duty to persons who deposited moneys with a company which he had registered to take reasonable care to ensure that that company's affairs were not being conducted fraudulently, speculatively or to the detriment of its depositors. The opinion of the Privy Council was delivered by Lord Keith. He quoted the familiar passage to which I have already referred from the speech of Lord Wilberforce in *Anns*'s case and after referring to other cases in which the passage had been treated with some reservation, he said ([1987] 2 All ER 705 at 710, [1988] AC 175 at 191):

'Their Lordships venture to think that the two-stage test formulated by Lord Wilberforce for determining the existence of a duty of care in negligence has been elevated to a degree of importance greater than it merits, and greater perhaps than its author intended.'

He then went on to express the approval of their Lordships of the view favoured by Gibbs CJ in the High Court of Australia in *Sutherland Shire Council v Heyman* (1985) 60 ALR 1 at 13 that Lord Wilberforce meant the expression 'proximity or neighbourhood' to be a composite one importing the whole concept of necessary relationship between the plaintiff and the defendant described by Lord Atkin in *Donoghue v Stevenson* [1932] AC 562, [1932] All ER Rep 1. Lord Keith pointed out that although the foreseeability of harm is a necessary ingredient of such a relationship, it is not the only one and, having quoted from passages from the speech of Lord Atkin in *Donoghue v Stevenson*, he said ([1987] 2 All ER 705 at 711, [1988] AC 175 at 192):

'Lord Atkin clearly had in contemplation that all the circumstances of the case, not only the foreseeability of harm, were appropriate to be taken into account in determining whether a duty of care arose.'

Subsequently he expressed the opinion that the second stage of Lord Wilberforce's test in *Anns v Merton London Borough* [1977] 2 All ER 492, [1978] AC 728 was one which would rarely have to be applied. It can arise only in a limited category of cases where, notwithstanding that a case of negligence is made out on a proximity basis, public policy requires that there should be no liability.

In my opinion the present state of the law on the question whether or not a duty of care exists is that, save where there is already good authority that in the circumstances there is such a duty, it will only exist in novel situations where not only is there foreseeability of harm, but also such a close and direct relation between the parties

concerned, not confined to mere physical proximity, to the extent contemplated by Lord
a Atkin in his speech in *Donoghue v Stevenson* [1932] AC 562, [1932] All ER Rep 1. Further,
a court should also have regard to what it considers just and reasonable in all the
circumstances and facts of the case.

In the instant case it is clear that as between the employer and the main contractor the
former accepted the risk of damage by fire to its premises arising out of and in the course
of the building works. Further, although there was no privity between the employer and
b the sub-contractor, it is equally clear from the documents passing between the main
contractors and the sub-contractors to which I have already referred that the sub-
contractors contracted on a like basis. In *Scottish Special Housing Association v Wimpey
Construction UK Ltd* [1986] 2 All ER 957, [1986] 1 WLR 995 the House of Lords had to
consider whether, as between the employer and main contractors under a contract in
precisely the same terms as those of the instant case, it was in truth intended that the
c employer should bear the whole risk of damage by fire, even fire caused by the
contractor's negligence. The position of sub-contractors was not strictly in issue in the
Scottish Housing case, which I cannot think the House did not appreciate, but having
considered the terms of cll 18, 19 and 20[C] of the same standard form as was used in the
instant case Lord Keith, in a speech with which the remainder of their Lordships agreed,
said ([1986] 2 All ER 957 at 959, [1986] 1 WLR 995 at 999):

d
'I have found it impossible to resist the conclusion that it is intended that the
employer shall bear the whole risk of damage by fire, including fire caused by the
negligence of the contractor or that of sub-contractors.'

As Lord Keith went on to point out, a similar conclusion was arrived at by the Court of
Appeal in England in *James Archdale & Co Ltd v Comservices Ltd* [1954] 1 All ER 210,
e [1954] 1 WLR 459 on the construction of similarly but not identically worded
corresponding clauses in a predecessor of the standard form used in the *Scottish Housing*
and instant cases. Again the issue only arose in the earlier case as between employer and
main contractor, but approaching the question on the basis of what is just and reasonable
I do not think that the mere fact that there is no strict privity between the employer and
the sub-contractor should prevent the latter from relying on the clear basis on which all
f the parties contracted in relation to damage to the employer's building caused by fire,
even when due to the negligence of the contractors or sub-contractors.

We were also referred to the decision of Macpherson J in *Welsh Health Technical Services
Organisation v Haden Young (IDC, third party)* (1987) 37 Build LR 130. That again was a
case concerning a building contract and damage caused by fire due to the negligence of a
plumbing sub-contractor. On the facts of that particular case the judge concluded that
g there had been a direct contractual relationship between the employer and the sub-
contractor which excused the latter from any liability in respect of the negligence of their
servants. As he said (at 141):

'Primarily, I base my decision upon acceptance of the argument that there was
indeed here a contract between [the employers] and [the sub-contractors] at the
h   outset and on acceptance of the tender.'

Nevertheless he went on to consider the situation if he were wrong that any such contract
had been made. It is true that in considering whether the sub-contractors were under
any liability to the employers the judge applied in favour of the latter the second part of
Lord Wilberforce's dictum in *Anns v Merton London Borough* [1977] 2 All ER 492 at 498,
j [1978] AC 728 at 752 in a way which the recent decisions of the House of Lords to which
I have referred indicate may be impermissible. Nevertheless, he did conclude that in
principle the situation comprising the general contractual arrangements between the
three parties was a 'consideration which ought to negative, or to reduce, or limit the
scope of the duty ... or the damages to which a breach of it may give rise' (see 37 Build
LR 130 at 142). A little later in his judgment he said (at 143):

'My conclusion is simply that in the light of all that [the main contractor] put forward and insisted on by way of conditions of tender, and in view of the whole "contractual setting", it would indeed be right to negative their *prima facie* right to damages. Such matters being ideally "considerations" within the second part of Lord Wilberforce's words. I am at least heartened to some extent by the approach of the three official referees whose experience and wisdom in these fields is much greater than mine, even if these cases are not directly parallel to the present case.'

The judge was there referring to *Twins Transport Ltd v Patrick* (1984) 25 Build LR 65, *Rumbelows Ltd v AMK (a firm)* (1982) 19 Build LR 25 and the extremely helpful judgment of Judge David Smout in *Southern Water Authority v Carey* [1985] 2 All ER 1077 to which I have already referred.

Finally, we were also referred to *Aberdeen Harbour Board v Heating Enterprises (Aberdeen) Ltd* (1988) Times, 25 March, a decision of the Outer House of the Court of Session. Once again the case concerned the same standard form of building contract as is involved in the instant appeal. The claim was by the proprietors of premises in Aberdeen against the sub-contractors of tenants of part of the premises in respect of the negligence of those sub-contractors in the use of blowtorches in the course of their work. Having regard to the terms of the contracts between the building employer, the main contractors and the defendant sub-contractors the latter contended that if they were liable to the owners of the premises they were nevertheless entitled to be indemnified by the building employer tenants. Towards the end of this judgment (a transcript of which was before us), having held that they were entitled to no such indemnity, Lord Clyde added:

'The problem in the present case appears to have arisen because of the fact that the employer was the occupier of only part of larger premises and indeed was not even the proprietor of that part. When the employer owns and occupies the whole premises the whole interest in the property will be his and the clause [cl 20[C] of the standard form] should operate without difficulty. No question of indemnity would arise. The loss would be that of the employer and he having undertaken the whole risk there is no liability on the contractor or the sub-contractor even for their own negligence.'

In these circumstances the overall burden of the authorities to which our attention was drawn in my opinion supports the view taken by the judge below and, accordingly, I do not think it necessary to consider the question of the insurance position and subrogation rights as between the parties and their respective insurers.

For the reasons that I have given I would dismiss this appeal.

CROOM-JOHNSON LJ. I agree.

GLIDEWELL LJ. I also agree.

Appeal dismissed. Leave to appeal to House of Lords refused.

Solicitors: *Daynes Hill & Perks*, Norwich (for the plaintiffs); *Mills & Reeve Francis*, Norwich (for the defendants).

Carolyn Toulmin   Barrister.

a Attock Cement Co Ltd v Romanian Bank for Foreign Trade

COURT OF APPEAL, CIVIL DIVISION
SIR NICOLAS BROWNE-WILKINSON V-C, WOOLF AND STAUGHTON LJJ
b 30 NOVEMBER, 1, 2, 21 DECEMBER 1988

Practice – Service out of the jurisdiction – Action on contract governed by English law – Disputed issue of fact – Standard of proof – Contract for construction of cement plant in Pakistan by Romanian contractors for Cayman Island plaintiffs – Contract governed by English law – Contract containing obligation that contractors provide plaintiffs with performance bond – Plaintiffs bringing action against bank providing bond to enforce bond – Disputed oral agreement
c that performance bond subject to English law – Whether plaintiffs having good arguable case that performance bond subject to English law – Whether plaintiffs entitled to leave to serve writ out of jurisdiction – RSC Ord 11, r 1(1).

Bank – Documentary credit – Performance bond – Proper law of performance bond – Performance
d bond given by contractor pursuant to contractual obligation – Contract for construction of cement plant in Pakistan by Romanian contractors for Cayman Islands company – Contract governed by English law – Whether performance bond impliedly subject to English law.

The plaintiffs, a Cayman Islands company, concluded a contract with the contractors, a Romanian state trading organisation, for the construction of a cement plant in Pakistan at a price of $US66m. The contract was expressly made subject to English law and
e contained an obligation on the part of the contractors to provide the plaintiffs with a performance bond in the sum of $US6·6m to cover faithful performance of the contract. Pursuant to that obligation, a bank which was another Romanian state trading organisation issued a performance bond at the contractors' request. In February 1987 the plaintiffs gave notice to the contractors terminating the contract and in July 1987 the
f plaintiffs made a demand on the performance bond. The demand was not complied with and the plaintiffs brought an action against the bank claiming $6·6m. The plaintiffs obtained leave under RSC Ord 11, r 1(1)(d)[a] to serve a writ on the bank out of the jurisdiction on the ground that the performance bond was governed by English law and subject to English jurisdiction. The bank applied to set aside the grant of leave. The judge granted the application and set aside the service of the writ. The plaintiffs appealed,
g claiming that there was a good arguable case that there was a collateral oral agreement that the performance bond was subject to English law and jurisdiction or alternatively that it was by implication governed by English law.

Held – Where the defendant applied to set aside leave granted ex parte under RSC Ord 11, r 1 to serve a writ out of the jurisdiction and there was a disputed question of fact
h essential to determining whether the action fell within the provisions of Ord 11, r 1, the standard of proof required was that the plaintiff had to establish a good arguable case, ie the judge had to reach a provisional or tentative conclusion on all the admissible material before him that the plaintiff was probably right on the disputed question of fact, before allowing service to stand. Applying that test, it had not been established on a provisional

---

j *a* Rule 1(1), so far as material provides: '. . . service of a writ out of the jurisdiction is permissible with the leave of the Court if in the action begun by the writ . . . (d) the claim is brought to enforce, rescind, dissolve, annul or otherwise affect a contract, or to recover damages or obtain other relief in respect of the breach of a contract, being (in either case) a contract which . . . (iii) is by its terms, or by implication, governed by English law, or (iv) contains a term to the effect that the High Court shall have jurisdiction to hear and determine any action in respect of the contract . . .'

or tentative view that there was an oral agreement that the performance bond was subject to English law and jurisdiction. Furthermore, it could not be implied that the *a* performance bond was governed by English law since a letter of credit or performance bond was intended to be a separate transaction and was therefore not affected by the proper law of the underlying commercial transaction but rather was ordinarily governed by the law of the place where payment was to be made under it. Accordingly, the plaintiffs did not have a good arguable case that the performance bond was governed by English law. The appeal would therefore be dismissed (see p 1196 *j* to p 1197 *a*, p 1198 *e* *b* to *g*, p 1199 *j*, p 1200 *c* and p 1201 *fg*, post).

Tyne Improvement Comrs v Armement Anversois SA, The Brabo [1949] 1 All ER 294 and *Vitkovice Horni a Hutni Te\u017eirstvo v Korner* [1951] 2 All ER 334 considered.

Notes

For service of a writ out the jurisdiction with leave in an action for breach of contract, see *c* 37 Halsbury's Laws (4th edn) paras 172, 178, and for cases on the subject, see 37(2) Digest (Reissue) 279–282, 285–291, *1801–1813, 1831–1849.*

For commercial letters of credit, see 3 Halsbury's Laws (4th edn) paras 131–137, and for cases on the subject, see 3 Digest (Reissue) 665–670, *4121–4136.*

Cases referred to in judgments   *d*

Bremen, The v Zapata Off-Shore Co (1972) 407 US 1, US SC.
Broken Hill Pty Co Ltd v Xenakis [1982] 2 Lloyd's Rep 304.
Chemische Fabrik vormals Sandoz v Badische Anilin und Soda Fabriks (1904) 90 LT 733, [1904–7] All ER Rep 234, HL.
First Line (Liberia) Ltd v Minister for Finance of Ireland (11 December 1986, unreported), QBD.   *e*
Libyan Arab Foreign Bank v Manufacturers Hanover Trust Co [1988] 2 Lloyd's Rep 494.
Mackender v Feldia AG [1966] 3 All ER 847, [1967] 2 QB 590, [1967] 2 WLR 119, CA.
Offshore International SA v Banco Central SA [1976] 3 All ER 749, [1977] 1 WLR 399.
Owen (Edward) Engineering Ltd v Barclays Bank International Ltd [1978] 1 All ER 976, [1978] QB 159, [1977] 3 WLR 764, CA.
Power Curber International Ltd v National Bank of Kuwait SAK [1981] 3 All ER 607, [1981] *f* 1 WLR 1233, CA.
Spiliada Maritime Corp v Cansulex Ltd, The Spiliada [1986] 3 All ER 843, [1987] AC 460, [1986] 3 WLR 972, HL.
Tyne Improvement Comrs v Armement Anversois SA, The Brabo [1949] 1 All ER 294, [1949] AC 326, HL.
Vitkovice Horni a Hutni Te\u017eirstvo v Korner [1951] 2 All ER 334, [1951] AC 869, HL. *g*

Cases also cited

GKN Contractors Ltd v Lloyds Bank plc (1985) 30 Build LR 48, CA.
United Trading Corp SA v Allied Arab Bank Ltd [1985] 2 Lloyd's Rep 554, CA.

Application for leave to appeal   *h*

The plaintiffs, Attock Cement Co Ltd (the owners), a company incorporated under the laws of the Cayman Islands, applied for leave to appeal against the order of Leggatt J made on 23 June 1988 setting aside service of the writ on the defendants, the Romanian Bank for Foreign Trade (the bank), a Romanian central bank concerned with payments, credits and exchange control in connection with the foreign operations of Romanian *j* state trading corporations, and dismissing the owners' application for summary judgment against the bank in their action against the bank for $US6·6m alleged to be due to the owners under a performance bond entered into by the bank as security for the performance by Uzinexportimport Enterprise for Foreign Trade of Romania of its obligations under a contract to construct a cement plant in Pakistan for the owners. On

2 November 1988 Kerr LJ adjourned the application to the full court. The facts are set
a out in the judgment of Staughton LJ.

Kenneth Rokison QC and *Peter Roth* for the owners.
Michael Burton QC, Roger Ter Haar and *Emma Griffiths* for the bank.

b At the conclusion of the argument the court announced that it would grant leave to
appeal and, by consent of the parties, treat the hearing of the application as the hearing
of the appeal, judgment in which would be given later.

21 December. The following judgments were delivered.

c **STAUGHTON LJ** (giving the first judgment at the invitation of Sir Nicolas Browne-
Wilkinson V-C). On 23 June 1988 Leggatt J in the Commercial Court had to consider
two summonses. The first, by the defendants in this action, was to set aside service of
proceedings out of the jurisdiction in Romania, on two grounds: that the case was not
within RSC Ord 11, r 1, so that leave to serve out of the jurisdiction should not have been
given, and that as a matter of discretion the case was not a proper one for service out of
d the jurisdiction within Ord 11, r 4(2). On the first point, the grounds put forward for
service out were those in Ord 11, r 1(1)(*d*)(iii) and (iv), viz that the contract sued on was
governed by English law and contained a term that the High Court should have
jurisdiction.
   The other summons, taken out by the plaintiffs, was for summary judgment under
Ord 14.
e   The judge held (a) that the contract was governed by English law, (b) that it contained
a term that the High Court should have jurisdiction, but (c) that the case was not a proper
one for service out of the jurisdiction as a matter of discretion and (d) that he would not
have granted summary judgment. Consequently the proceedings were set aside. From
this decision the plaintiffs applied for leave to appeal, seeking to challenge conclusions (c)
and (d). The defendants resisted that challenge and also, by a draft respondent's notice,
f disputed conclusions (a) and (b). Kerr LJ adjourned the plaintiffs' application for leave to
appeal to the full court. After hearing full argument we granted leave to appeal, and by
consent of the parties treated this as the hearing of the appeal.

Outline facts
g   On 11 May 1981 the plaintiffs, whom I shall call 'the owners', concluded a contract
with Uzinexportimport Enterprise for Foreign Trade (the contractors) for the construction
of a cement plant at Lasbella in Pakistan at a price of $US66m. It was to be successfully
completed by 10 February 1984. Article 19.1 provided:

   'The CONTRACTOR shall provide to the OWNER a Performance Bond of 10% (ten
   percent) of the TURNKEY CONTRACT price, to cover and secure the CONTRACTORS faithful
h   performance and execution of this TURNKEY CONTRACT ... The wording of this
   Performance Bond shall be agreed upon between the OWNER and the CONTRACTOR.'

By art 25.1 all disputes arising out of the contract or in connection with it—

   'may be submitted by either party to arbitration in accordance with the Rules
   of Conciliation and Arbitration of the International Chamber of Commerce in
j   Paris...'

The arbitration court was to be 'seated in Paris or at a place to be mutually agreed' (see art
25.5). By art 26 the construction contract was to be governed by the laws of England.
The owners are a Cayman Islands company, with connections in England, Pakistan and
Saudi Arabia. The contractors are a Romanian state trading organisation.

On 16 March 1982, no doubt at the request of the contractors, the Romanian Bank for Foreign Trade, the defendants in this action, issued a performance bond. They are a Romanian central bank concerned in the foreign operations of Romanian state trading organisations and I shall call them 'the bank'. It is the contract contained in or evidenced by that performance bond which is sued on in this action. Its written terms were as follows:

'Whereas, UZINEXPORTIMPORT Bucharest, foreign trade company, established under the laws of the Socialist Republic of Romania (the Contractor) and ATTOCK CEMENT LTD., incorporated under the laws of the Cayman Islands (the Owner) have executed a United States Dollars Sixty Six Million fixed price Turnkey Contract signed on 11.05.1981, for engineering, supply and construction of a 2·000 mtpd cement plant in Pakistan, on basis of successful operation and completion no later than February 10, 1984. Whereas, in accordance with Article 19 of the above Turnkey Contract, UZINEXPORTIMPORT (the Contractor) has to furnish a Performance Bond of 10 (ten/ percent) of the Turnkey Contract price for its obligations stipulated in the said contract. At the request of UZINEXPORTIMPORT (the Contractor), the Romanian Bank for Foreign Trade Bucharest hereby open our unconditional and irrevocable performance bond for an amount of United States Dollars 6.600.000 (six point six million). Now, therefore, we, the Romanian Bank for Foreign Trade, do hereby expressly and unconditionally agree and undertake to pay, in favor of ATTOCK CEMENT LTD. in United States Dollars, within 30 days from its first demand without any other formality of whatever nature or without recourse to the Contractor, such sum or sums as may be demanded by ATTOCK CEMENT LTD. against the simple demand accompanied by its declaration that UZINEXPORTIMPORT (the Contractor) has failed to fulfill any of its obligations under Articles 3; 15; 16 and 17 of the above contract. This Performance Bond shall come into force immediately and remain in full force and effect and be operative and binding on us for a period of twelve months after the completion date of the Turnkey Contract i.e. up to 10 February 1985. Providing that the contracting parties agree to one or several extensions of the validity of this Performance Bond, the liability herein shall be automatically extended accordingly, without any other formality.'

Those, as I say, were the written terms. The case for the owners is that there was a collateral oral agreement as to proper law and jurisdiction. This is put forward in the affidavit of Munawar Ahmed Akhtar, a solicitor acting for the owners.

'8. Following the signing of the said Contract in Paris on 11th May 1981 there were negotiations between the Plaintiff's lawyer Amer Lodhi and the UEI's legal Adviser Georgou Marenescu who also represented the Defendant about the Performance Bond and about advance payments bank guarantees to be issued pursuant to the Contract. At these negotiations it was specifically agreed that since the Performance Bond was a creature of the main Contract it would be governed by English Law and that it was unnecessary to repeat the Appropriate Law Clause in the Performance Bond. Further it was expressly said on behalf of the Defendant that as London is the centre of international trade and commerce and the Defendant had an office in London (which at the time it probably did) and its officers regularly visited London, English Law should be the appropriate law and English Courts the appropriate forum . . .

10. Negotiations continued on various other aspects of the project culminating in meetings in Bucharest, Romania, between 25th October 1981 and 1st November 1981, attended by Taltif Ahmed Tausif Lodhi, Amer Lodhi and Mahmood Ahmad on behalf of the Plaintiff, Rapanu Toader, Radu Traian and Petra Valer of UEI. At those meetings Radu Traian acted for the Defendant having authority to make decisions about the form of the Performance Bond on their behalf. At this meeting it was inter alia stressed that delivery of the Performance Bond to the Plaintiff was

overdue. In the light of the previous negotiations it was again agreed by all parties

a that the Performance Bond would be governed by English law and that English Courts would be the appropriate forum for any dispute. A final draft for the Performance Bond was initialled on 2nd November 1981 . . .'

That evidence is firmly denied in evidence from the bank and the contractors. Subsequently there were by agreement various extensions of the expiry date in the

b performance bond, the latest being to 2 August 1987.

Meanwhile all had not gone well in the performance of the building contract. The completion date of 10 February 1984 was not achieved. An inauguration ceremony was held on 1 October 1986 and some cement was produced, but there is still a dispute whether the contract was properly performed. Finally on 8 February 1987 the owners gave notice to the contractors stating that, in the light of the contractors' substantial

c breaches of their obligations, the contract was terminated. On the following day armed security guards of the owners prevented the contractors' employees from entering the plant.

It is said that the owners have paid sums totalling $13m towards the total purchase price of $66m. Further sums totalling $35m would be accruing due from the owners to the contractors, under the terms of the building contract, if some documents called

d sectional protocols had been signed by the parties. These were, in effect, certificates of completion up to a certain stage of each production department in the plant. The sum of $35m was to be paid in 20 half-yearly instalments, the first falling due 12 months from the date of the last sectional protocol. It is said by the contractors that the owners have wrongfully failed to sign the sectional protocols.

On 24 (or 25) July 1987 the owners made a demand on the performance bond. It was

e in these terms:

'Attock Cement Limited hereby declares that Uzinexportimport (the contractor) has failed to fulfil its obligations under articles 3, 15, 16 and 17 of the turnkey contract including in particular but without limitation the obligation to complete the cement plant by the dates specified in the turnkey contract. Attock Cement

f Limited therefore demands that the Romanian Bank for Foreign Trade pay in favour of Attock Cement Limited the amount of U.S.dlrs. 6,600,000·00 pursuant to your unconditional and irrevocable performance bond no 45/1/1153/82 within 30 days after this demand by transfer to our foreign currency term deposit account no. 030-5903-8 with Bank of Credit N Commerce International (Overseas) Limited, BCC House, 1.1 Chundrigar Road, Karachi, Pakistan.'

g The demand was not complied with. Consequently this action was brought, by writ issued by the owners against the bank on 22 September 1987, claiming $6·6m.

In addition a flurry of litigation has occurred elsewhere. The contractors have commenced an action in the High Court of Sind at Karachi against an associated company of the owners registered in Pakistan. They have also commenced an arbitration under

h the auspices of the International Chamber of Commerce in Paris against the owners and others. The owners for their part have commenced legal proceedings against the bank in Zurich and Paris. More significantly for present purposes, the contractors on 27 March 1987 obtained an ex parte order from the Law Court of the Third Ward, Bucharest, in proceedings against the bank and the owners. That order granted an injunction of preventive sequester and a ban on the execution of the performance bond, until the

j pronouncement of a final decision in the arbitration between the contractors and owners in Paris. The court fixed a date for the validation of this injunction, which has been extended from time to time and is presently, on the evidence, 13 December 1988. Neither the bank nor the contractors, who are both defendants in that action, have yet made any application to set aside the ex parte order of 27 March 1987. I should mention, since the owners attach importance to the fact, that notice of the ex parte order was given

to them only on 9 July 1987, three and a half months after it was made, apparently in
response to a telex from the owners of 28 June 1987 requiring the bank either to grant a *a*
further extension of the expiry date of the bond or to pay $6·6m to the owners.

A further aspect of the Romanian litigation is that it now comprises a claim for
damages by the bank against the owners, 'temporarily evaluated at the amount of
1,200,000 dollars', for 'the abusive institution of proceedings for an inexistent debt'. It
seems that part at any rate of the grounds for that claim are that the owners have frozen
funds of the bank in Zurich and in Paris, although the French restraint is no longer *b*
effective.

A good arguable case

The standard of proof that an action falls within the provisions of Ord 11, r 1 is a topic
which frequently arises in practice. At the ex parte stage the master or judge looks to see
whether the facts deposed to in the plaintiff's affidavit, if true, bring the case within the *c*
rule. At that stage he has only the plaintiff's evidence, although it should include by
virtue of the plaintiff's duty of disclosure such information or documents as are available
to the plaintiff and demonstrate what may be the defendant's case. No doubt the master
or judge will refuse leave ex parte if the plaintiff's evidence is, in a word, incredible.
Otherwise he will grant leave if the facts deposed to satisfy Ord 11, r 1. Nothing that I
say touches on the practice at that stage.   *d*

It is when the defendant applies to set aside service that the problem is more likely to
arise. The court may then have conflicting evidence or arguments. Traditionally, masters
and judges have directed themselves in accordance with the note now found in *The
Supreme Court Practice 1988* vol 1, para 11/1/6:

> 'The degree of proof required was discussed in *The Brabo* ([1949] 1 All ER 294, *e*
> [1949] AC 326) and *Vitkovice Horni* v. *Korner* ([1951] 2 All ER 334, [1951] AC 869).
> The expression "good arguable case" is probably the best way of summarising the
> effect of these authorities; it indicates that, though the Court will not, at this stage,
> require proof of the plaintiff's case to its satisfaction, it will expect something better
> than a mere prima facie case. The practice, where questions of fact are concerned, is
> to look primarily at the plaintiff's case and not to attempt to try disputes of fact on *f*
> affidavit; it is, of course, open to the defendant to show that the evidence of the
> plaintiff is incomplete or plainly wrong. On questions of law, however, the Court
> may go fully into the issues and will refuse leave if it concludes that the plaintiff's
> case is bound to fail. Even if the Court does not reach so adverse a view, if the
> plaintiff's case is weak, this may be a relevant consideration on the exercise of the
> Court's discretion.'   *g*

The present case raises in an acute form the question as to the proper standard of proof.
The owners allege an oral agreement that the performance bond was governed by English
law and subject to English jurisdiction. The bank deny that there was any such oral
agreement, or that if there was it was made by anyone acting on their behalf. Is the court
then required, in terms of *The Supreme Court Practice*, 'to look primarily at the plaintiff's *h*
case and not to attempt to try disputes of fact on affidavit'? Counsel for the owners
submits that this is indeed the law. He acknowledges that the court may decide against
the owners if it finds their evidence 'incredible', for there is not then a good arguable
case. Otherwise, he submits, the court must accept the owners' evidence.

It may well be that the problem is even more difficult when the issue as to jurisdiction
is not one which will occur again at trial in connection with liability. For example, if *j*
service in the present case is allowed to stand, it is unlikely that there will be any issue at
the trial as to the proper law of the performance bond. The affidavit of Mr Maier, a
solicitor acting for the bank, states:

> 'So far as Romanian law is concerned as to any defence to a claim under a Bond of
> this nature, I believe that the situation is very similar to English law.'

a   Counsel in argument for the bank, no doubt for tactical reasons, wished to preserve the possibility that Romanian law may be different. But we can only go by what is said in the bank's affidavit. So there is unlikely to be any issue at the trial as to the proper law of the contract; and there will almost certainly be no issue at the trial whether the parties agreed to English jurisdiction. This can be contrasted with the case where the very existence of the contract sued on is in dispute: the issue then has to be determined once under Ord 11, and a second time (if service is allowed to stand) at the trial. The plaintiff

b   may succeed at the first stage but fail at the second. Here, on the other hand, if the owners succeed in the Ord 11 proceedings on English proper law or an agreement to English jurisdiction, it is probable that those issues will never fall to be considered at the trial. The House of Lords in *Vitkovice Horni a Hutni Tezirstvo v Korner* [1951] 2 All ER 334, [1951] AC 869 considered that a form of order which would allow the defendant to raise at the trial an issue as to *where* the contract was to be performed was undesirable.

c   That was an issue which went to the jurisdiction under Ord 11 only, and would not appear to have been relevant to liability. In such a case the House of Lords evidently considered that the court must make up its mind, once and for all, at the Ord 11 stage.

In the light of those difficulties I consider that some re-examination of the authorities is necessary, and I start with the *Vitkovice* case although it is not first in time. Lord Simonds (with whom Lord Normand agree) considered the problem (see [1951] 2 All ER

d   334 at 337–338, [1951] AC 869 at 878–880). I think that I can fairly summarise his opinion as follows.

(i) He adopted an earlier observation of Lord Davey that a mere statement by a deponent in an affidavit may not be sufficient, but—

'the court is not ... called upon to try the action or express a premature opinion
e   on its merits.'

(See *Chemische Fabrik Vormals Sandoz v Badische Anilin und Soda Fabriks* (1904) 90 LT 733 at 735, [1904–7] All ER Rep 234 at 236.)

(ii) He observed that the plaintiff's case could not possibly be said to be 'on the face of it false or frivolous'.

(iii) The judge had been wrong to say that he was not 'satisfied', since that meant that
f   the fact in issue had not been proved 'beyond all reasonable doubt'.

(iv) He said in the very next sentence:

'... a plaintiff can make it sufficiently appear that the case is a proper one for service out of the jurisdiction while falling short of the standard of proof which must be attained at the trial.'

g   (v) He concluded:

'... the question is not so much whether a *prima facie* case has been made out as whether, on all the materials then before him, the judge is of the opinion that the case—I can find no better word—is a proper one to be heard in our courts. The description "a good arguable case" has been suggested and I do not quarrel with it.
h   For the purpose of this appeal, however, it is sufficient to say negatively that the learned judge fell into error in thinking that the court had no jurisdiction to grant leave because he was not "satisfied" that there had been a breach within the jurisdiction.'

Lord Oaksey took the view that the standard of proof required could be affected by
j   other matters which were relevant to the court's discretion. He said ([1951] 2 All ER 334 at 339, [1951] AC 869 at 881–882):

'Even if there were only the slightest evidence as to the breach of the pensions agreement having been committed within the jurisdiction, the evidence as to *forum conveniens* is, in my opinion, such as to make it sufficiently to appear that the case is a proper one for service out of the jurisdiction.'

Lord Radcliffe did not wish to chop the meaning of words overfine (see [1951] 2 All ER 334 at 339–341, [1951] AC 869 at 882–885), a sentiment which I would echo in this *a* case. He rejected the extremes of—

    'asking no more of the applicant than his assertion that the action which he desires to bring involves one or more of the qualifying conditions'

on the one hand and asking him to establish it 'beyond reasonable doubt' on the other. The judge was in his view 'expected to exercise some more critical function' than merely *b* accepting the plaintiff's statement on affidavit. In Lord Radcliffe's view:

    '. . . a case does not sufficiently appear to be a proper case for the purposes of this order unless, on consideration of all admissible material, there remains a strong argument for the opinion that the qualifying conditions are, indeed, satisfied.'

He observed: *c*

    '. . . the existence of the conditions . . . cannot be ascertained with the same finality as would be appropriate at a trial . . .'

And he concluded:

    'What determines me is that, when the evidence is weighed, there remains a *d* strong argument for the respondent's contention that in respect of each of his heads of claim there had been a breach within the jurisdiction.'

Lord Tucker was influenced by a point which I have already mentioned, that the relevant condition under Ord 11 in that case was not one which would fall to be reconsidered at the trial (see [1951] 2 All ER 334 at 334, [1951] AC 869 at 889–890). He said, of a collision case, that the court—   *e*

    'should, in my opinion, receive cogent evidence pointing to a strong probability that the collision occurred within the jurisdiction before it will allow service out of the jurisdiction, this being an issue which may never arise at the trial and which, if it does arise, and if it be proved that the collision took place outside the jurisdiction, will not divest the court of the jurisdiction it has wrongly assumed.'   *f*

In his view the judge was—

    'concerned to inquire and to satisfy himself that the probabilities of the case were strongly in favour of the plaintiff's contention that the contracts contained a term providing for payment in England.'

    g

I have also considered *Tyne Improvement Comrs v Armement Anversois SA, The Brabo* [1949] 1 All ER 294, [1949] AC 326. That, as it seems to me, was almost entirely concerned with the question whether an action was 'properly brought against some other person duly served within the jurisdiction' under Ord 11, r 1(*g*), as it then was. To the extent that there are observations in the speeches on the general question of the standard of proof under Ord 11, I would regard them as superseded by the much fuller *h* consideration of that topic in the *Vitkovice* case.

It is to my mind plain from the *Vitkovice* case that a master or judge may on some occasions find himself obliged to assess the relative strength of the plaintiff's and the defendant's cases. In doing so, he does not try the case on affidavits, because he reaches only a provisional conclusion: the stage for trial and for final decision has not been reached. But he must have regard to all the admissible material before him, as Lord *j* Simonds and Lord Radcliffe said, not just the plaintiff's case. He must conclude that there is a good arguable case (Lord Simonds), not just a case that can be argued, or a strong argument (Lord Radcliffe). What need not be shown is that the plaintiff is right beyond all reasonable doubt.

Save in the speech of Lord Tucker, which deals with a special problem, I cannot find in the decision any express consideration of the balance of probability. Nevertheless I

a conclude that, where there is a disputed question of fact which is essential to the application of Ord 11, r 1, the judge must reach a provisional or tentative conclusion that the plaintiff is probably right on it before he allows service to stand. The nettle must be grasped, and that is what I take to be meant by a good arguable case.

In the light of my later conclusions it is unnecessary to decide whether some additional burden should, as Lord Tucker suggests, be laid on a plaintiff who invokes Ord 11, r 1 on

b some ground which will not, if leave is granted, arise for re-examination at the trial. I can understand the motive for imposing such an additional burden; as Woolf LJ said in the course of the argument, unless one adopts that approach grave injustice could be involved. But I find difficulty in seeing how, logically, Ord 11, r 4(2) can be read as imposing a heavier burden in that case than any other.

Having described the test which in my view should be applied, I would add that the

c master or judge should do his best to discourage voluminous evidence or prolonged argument whether it is fulfilled. In those cases where there is a critical dispute of fact, the decision which he has to make will necessarily be of a provisional or tentative nature. It would be a disservice to the law if the process of determination were treated as a trial in all but name. In particular we were referred to Ord 12, r 8(5):

d   'Upon hearing an application under paragraph (1) the Court, if it does not dispose of the matter in dispute, may give such directions for its disposal as may be appropriate, including directions for the trial thereof as a preliminary issue.'

Paragraph (1) of the rule deals with many kinds of application besides one to set aside leave to serve a writ out of the jurisdiction. I know of no case where on such an application the trial of a preliminary issue has been ordered, or even cross-examination

e on affidavits. And I find it hard to imagine that such a case could arise, except perhaps at the suggestion of the defendant. He should not be compelled to come to trial in our courts on a preliminary issue whether he can be compelled to come to trial.

Thus far I have not mentioned what I regard as the most difficult aspect of the *Vitkovice* decision. This is the suggestion that, in applying the appropriate standard of proof to

f determine whether one of the conditions laid down by Ord 11, r 1 is fulfilled, the court is exercising a discretion. This features from time to time in the speeches. See, for example, Lord Simonds ([1951] 2 All ER 334 at 336, [1951] AC 869 at 877): 'My Lords, to me it appears that the crux of the matter lies in the question whether the learned judge did exercise his discretion, and did so on right principles . . .' See also the passage I have quoted from the speech of Lord Oaksey, which suggests that deficiency in the

g standard of proof can be made up by the strength of the arguments in favour of trial here.

These dicta are of high authority but it is not easy to reconcile them with the modern treatment of Ord 11 cases. This divides the question into (i) jurisdiction, that is whether one of the conditions of Ord 11, r 1 is made out by the appropriate standard of proof, and (ii) discretion, whether it is shown that England is the more appropriate forum for the

h ends of justice and the interests of the parties. That was how the case was argued in the court below and before us, how it was treated by Leggatt J, and how all Ord 11 cases are now considered. In particular the speech of Lord Goff in *Spiliada Maritime Corp v Cansulex Ltd, The Spiliada* [1986] 3 All ER 843, [1987] AC 460 contains no hint, from beginning to end, that application of the appropriate standard of proof to Ord 11, r 1 is itself part of the discretion conferred by the opening words of Ord 11, rr 1 and 4(2), although it is

j sometimes said (no doubt correctly) that the strength of the plaintiff's case is something which the court can consider in exercising its discretion.

There was no argument before us on the point, and I hesitate to express a concluded view on it. But I do think it right to say that, in my provisional opinion, the assessment by a master or judge of whether the standard of proof required under Ord 11, r 1, that one of the required conditions is fulfilled, is not the exercise of a discretion. It is a judgment as to past or existing facts. Nevertheless, the decision is, from its very nature, one with which this court will be slow to disagree.   *a*

The oral agreement

I have already set out the affidavit evidence on the side of the owners as to an oral agreement that the performance bond was subject to English law and jurisdiction, which is denied in the bank's evidence. On this dispute Leggatt J concluded: *b*

'... I am not prepared to say that the [owners] have not made out a good arguable case that the contract and indeed the jurisdiction was to be under English law, and that the dispute was to be submitted to the jurisdiction of the English court. That, so far as the heading of Ord 11 is concerned, resolves the issue of service out in favour of the [owners]. The [owners] must also show that the case is a proper one for service out of the jurisdiction, which is where the discretion of the court comes *c* in.'

There was a good deal of argument in this court on the question whether any such oral agreement as the owners contend for was ever concluded, and if so whether it was made on behalf of the bank by persons in the employ of the contractors. Criticism was made of the statements that witnesses would make, and also of their failure in some instances *d* to deal with matters relied on by the other side. I do not think it desirable to discuss those points, since the case will still have to be tried somewhere and it is conceivable (although unlikely) that an oral agreement as to proper law may then be raised.

Two points alone are in my view sufficient for finding that the oral agreement, on a provisional or tentative view at this stage, is not established. The first is that, according to the affidavit of Mr Akhtar, the agreement was that proper law and jurisdiction need *e* not be mentioned in the performance bond for a number of reasons, including the fact that proper law was to be found in the building contract. But the building contract contained nothing about English jurisdiction; it provided for disputes to be determined by arbitration in Paris. The suggestion of an oral agreement as to jurisdiction is one that I find inherently implausible; if it is unfounded, there must be doubt as to the effect of the same evidence in establishing an oral agreement as to proper law.   *f*

Secondly, if representatives of the owners and the contractors had reached an oral agreement as to proper law and jurisdiction, I would have expected them to insert it in the performance bond. There had been discussions as to the wording of the bond, and a draft was initialled by those parties at the conclusion of the meeting in Bucharest which the owners rely on. It said nothing about proper law or jurisdiction.

My provisional or tentative conclusion is thus that an oral agreement for proper law *g* and jurisdiction is not made out. Of course, that conclusion is based only on the written evidence presently before us, and is open to review in other proceedings elsewhere.

Proper law apart from express agreement

In the alternative the owners argued that the performance bond was by implication governed by English law. This argument was founded on the principle stated in Dicey *h* and Morris *Conflict of Laws* (11th edn, 1987) p 1185:

'The legal or commercial connection between one contract and another may enable a court to say that the parties must be held implicitly to have submitted both contracts to the same law.'

As an example of the application of that principle there was cited a judgment of my own *j* in chambers at first instance some two years ago (see *First Line (Liberia) Ltd v Minister for Finance of Ireland* (11 December 1986, unreported)). The principle is not confined to contracts between the same parties. It is classified in *Dicey and Morris* as an example of an implied choice of law. While I do not quarrel with that classification, I wonder whether it may not equally be an example of the rule that, in the absence of an express or implied

choice, the proper law of a contract is that system of law with which the contact has the
a closest and most real connection.

Another example is provided by the decision of Bingham J in *Broken Hill Pty Co Ltd v
Xenakis* [1982] 2 Lloyd's Rep 304. In that case a charterparty provided for arbitration in
London, and was held to be by implication governed by English law. After an arbitration
had been started here the defendant, who was not himself a party to the principal
contract, gave a guarantee of any sum found payable in the arbitration by the owners of
b the vessel. The judge said (at 306):

'It seems to me quite plain that in the context of a primary obligation, admittedly
governed and being resolved according to English law, the most likely implication
would be that the guarantee was to be governed by the same law... The
overwhelming inference in my judgment is that the guarantee was to be governed
c by the same law that was governing the charter-party and the conduct of the
arbitration.'

By contrast we were referred to two cases concerned with the proper law of a letter of
credit. In *Offshore International SA v Banco Central SA* [1976] 3 All ER 749, [1977] 1 WLR
399 Ackner J held that a letter of credit opened by a Spanish bank, and payable at
(although not confirmed by) a bank in New York, was governed by the law of New York.
d In reaching that conclusion the judge relied on Gutteridge and Megrah *Law of Bankers'
Commercial Credits* (5th edn 1976) p 198:

'... the presumption must be that matters connected with the performance by
the banker of his contract under a commercial credit are to be regulated by the law
prevailing at the place of performance ...'

e It does not appear what system of law governed the underlying commercial transaction,
which was for the construction of an oil rig.

That decision was approved by the Court of Appeal in *Power Curber International Ltd v
National Bank of Kuwait SAK* [1981] 3 All ER 607, [1981] 1 WLR 1233. It was there held
that a letter of credit was governed by the law of the place where payment was to be
f made under it. Once again it does not appear that the proper law of the underlying
commercial transaction was thought to be relevant. Indeed Lord Denning MR quoted
from the Uniform Customs and Practice for Documentary Credits (1974 revision):

'(c) Credits, by their nature, are separate transactions from the sales or other
contracts on which they may be based and banks are in no way concerned with or
bound by such contracts.'

g
(See [1981] 3 All ER 607 at 611, [1981] 1 WLR 1233 at 1239.) In that case the uniform
customs were expressly incorporated in the letter of credit, whereas they are not here
incorporated in the performance bond. Despite the claim made by their title, I would
not hold that all aspects of the uniform customs are incorporated by custom into a letter
of credit or performance bond; in some respects they are no more than a series of
h exceptions or limitations on liability which banks commonly choose to incorporate. But
I do hold that art (c), quoted by Lord Denning MR, does not more than restate the
common law applicable to all letters of credit and performance bonds unless otherwise
agreed. That appears from a number of recent cases: see for example *Edward Owen
Engineering Ltd v Barclays Bank International Ltd* [1978] 1 All ER 976, [1978] QB 159.

Almost every letter of credit or performance bond is issued pursuant to some
j underlying commercial transaction. Yet we were referred to no case where it had even
been argued that one was affected by the proper law of the other. Seeing that the letter of
credit or performance bond is intended to be a separate transaction, I would hold that it
is not so affected, and is ordinarily governed by the law of the place where payment is to
be made under it. That is in general accord with the rule applicable to the banker-
customer relationship arising from a current or deposit account, which is ordinarily

governed by the law of the place where the account is kept: see *Libyan Arab Foreign Bank v Manufacturers Hanover Trust Co* [1988] 2 Lloyd's Rep 494. The *Broken Hill* case is in my opinion readily distinguishable: a guarantee is often intended to be governed by the same law as the principal obligation, but it is of the essence of performance bonds and letters of credit that they are not, in law, guarantees.

Counsel for the owners relies on art 26 of the building contract, which provided:

> '26.1   Regardless of the place of signing this TURNKEY CONTRACT the place of performance, or otherwise, this TURNKEY CONTRACT and all Annexures, amendments, modifications, alterations or supplements hereto, shall be construed under governed by, and the legal relations between the Parties hereto determined in accordance with, the laws of ENGLAND.'

I do not find that of any assistance, since I would not regard the performance bond as an annexure or a supplement to the building contract.

Accordingly I do not find there to be a good arguable case, at this stage, that the performance bond was by implication governed by English law. In reaching that conclusion I have not had regard to one aspect of the evidence which counsel for the bank relied on. This related to the advance payment guarantee, another document which under the building contract was to be provided by the bank. At one stage in the negotiations as to the form of that document it contained an express provision that it should be governed by English law, but that was later deleted. This was relied on to show that the performance bond was not governed by English law. The evidence had initially been introduced in connection with the allegation of an express oral agreement as to proper law and jurisdiction, which in my judgment fails. I am by no means convinced that it is admissible for or against the alternative case that the performance bond is by implication governed by English law, any more than the statement of the bank that they never contract by any law other than Romanian.

Discretion

Since in my judgment it is not shown that the case is within Ord 11, r 1, I would in any event uphold the order of Leggatt J, although not on the same grounds as he relied on. There was extensive argument before us as to discretion, that is to say whether it is clearly shown that an English forum is more appropriate for the ends of justice and the interests of the parties. It is unnecessary to say much about that topic, but there are two points which ought to be considered.

The first concerns fraud on the part of the owners. In point of form that arose in the judge's consideration of their application for summary judgment under Ord 14. If they were able to make out a case for summary judgment, that would be relevant to the exercise of the discretion under Ord 11, since it might mean that the convenience of witnesses did not need to be taken into account, or that delay would be less in one forum than another.

There was no dispute before us as to the substantive rule of English law applicable to a claim such as this on a performance bond. The beneficiary who makes a demand in the form required by the bond is entitled to payment, and the bank has no defence, unless (as it was put in the owners' outline argument) there is (i) a clear and obvious inference of fraud (ii) to the knowledge of the bank from which payment is sought. Counsel for the bank was prepared to accept, in broad terms, that statement of the law. The first of those requirements appears to be derived from the judgment of Geoffrey Lane LJ in *Edward Owen Engineering Ltd v Barclays Bank International Ltd* [1978] 1 All ER 976 at 986, [1978] QB 159 at 175. It is to be noted that the knowledge required of the bank is at the time when payment is demanded; the bank may not refuse to pay out of suspicion or caprice, and seek to justify its conduct later by proof of fraud.

Leggatt J in his consideration of the application under Ord 14 held that the bank had an arguable defence to the owners' claim. He must therefore have held that there was an

arguable case that the owners' claim was fraudulent to the knowledge of the bank. We
a have considered a substantial amount of evidence on that topic. The owners point in
particular to a formal admission by the contractors during performance of the building
contract that they were liable for damages, and to evidence of independent consultants
that the finished plant had to be shut down and was deteriorating. The bank point to the
fact that the plant was completed so that it could produce cement, while the owners have
paid only $13m out of a total price of $66m and have failed to sign the sectional protocols
b which would cause later instalments to accrue due. How then, the bank ask, can the
owners have an honest claim to recover $6·6m under the bond?

I do not consider that it would be right, in the circumstances, to express any view on
this point, one way or the other. The issue of fraud will remain to be tried elsewhere,
and neither party at that trial should be assisted or hampered by any view which this
court may express on it.

c The second aspect of discretion on which I wish to say something is the effect of a
contractual choice of a neutral forum. If the owners had succeeded on their case that
there was an oral agreement that disputes under the performance bond should be tried
in England, it would certainly be a possible view that this was a deliberate choice of a
neutral forum. In such a case many of the factors to be considered, under the decision in
d The Spiliada [1986] 3 All ER 843, [1987] AC 460, will not point to the place which the
parties have chosen; it will *not* be a place where one or the other party is resident, and it
will *not* be the place which is convenient for witnesses, any more than Paris is likely to be
convenient for witnesses in the dispute under the building contract. But the parties to
large commercial contracts sometimes prefer what they perceive as impartiality to
convenience, and if they do there is much to be said for respecting their choice. True
there is still a discretion, since Ord 11, r 4(2) applies to cases where there is a contractual
e choice of English jurisdiction as to other cases within Ord 11, r 1. But the choice of a
neutral forum is surely a factor to be taken into account. Both English and United States
courts tend to favour the enforcement of such an agreement in favour of a foreign
jurisdiction: see *Mackender v Feldia AG* [1966] 3 All ER 847, [1967] 2 QB 590 and the
judgment of Burger CJ in *The Bremen v Zapata Off-Shore Co* (1972) 407 US 1. For my part
f I think that we should also look with favour on a choice of our own jurisdiction, when it
appears to have been made in order to find a court which is neutral rather than one that
is convenient. But that consideration does not now apply in the present case.

I would dismiss this appeal.

SIR NICOLAS BROWNE-WILKINSON V-C. I agree.

g **WOOLF LJ.** I agree.

Appeal dismissed.

Solicitors: *Amhurst Brown Colombotti* (for the owners); *Simon Olswang & Co* (for the bank).

Celia Fox   Barrister.

R v Kensington and Chelsea Royal London Borough Council, ex parte Hammell

a

COURT OF APPEAL, CIVIL DIVISION

FOX, PARKER AND CROOM-JOHNSON LJJ

2, 3, 4 AUGUST 1988

b

Housing – Homeless person – Duty of housing authority to provide accommodation – Duty to provide accommodation to person they have reason to believe may be homeless and have a priority need – Duty to provide accommodation pending inquiries – Person to be treated as homeless if unreasonable for him to continue to occupy accommodation – Applicant occupying council flat in Scotland – Applicant leaving Scotland because of husband's harassment – Applicant applying to London council for accommodation as homeless person – Council disregarding husband's *c* *harassment because it occurred outside applicant's flat – Council deciding applicant not homeless – Applicant seeking judicial review and interim mandatory injunction requiring council to house applicant pending hearing of judicial review application – Whether court having jurisdiction to grant interim mandatory injunction pending hearing of judicial review application – Whether unreasonable for applicant to continue to occupy flat in Scotland – Whether injunction should be* *d* *granted – Supreme Court Act 1981, s 37 – Housing Act 1985, ss 58(2A), 62, 63, 64 – RSC Ord 53, r 3(10).*

The applicant, who was separated from her husband, was the tenant of a council flat in Scotland. Following violence and harassment by the husband, who lived nearby, the applicant moved with her three children to London and stayed with her sister in the sister's one-bedroom flat until the sister asked her to leave. The applicant then applied to *e* the council in whose area the sister's flat was situated for accommodation as a homeless person. Under s 62[a] of the Housing Act 1985 the council was required to make such inquiries as were necessary to satisfy itself that the applicant was homeless or threatened with homelessness and if it had reason to believe that the applicant was homeless and had a priority need it was required by s 63[b] of that Act to provide accommodation to the *f* applicant pending the outcome of its inquiries and the making of a final decision under s 64[c] of the Act whether the applicant was homeless or threatened with homelessness and entitled to accommodation as a homeless person. Under s 58(2A)[d] of the 1985 Act a person was not to be treated as having accommodation unless it was reasonable for him to continue to occupy it. The council interviewed the applicant and after making some inquiries in Scotland, from which it learnt that the applicant still held the tenancy of the *g* council flat and that she had obtained an injunction against her husband and had taken no steps to commit him for breach of it, decided that it was not satisfied that the applicant was homeless or threatened with homelessness because she was still entitled to occupy the council flat in Scotland. In arriving at that decision the council ignored the fact of the husband's violence because it had taken place outside the flat. The applicant applied for judicial review of the council's decision by way of an order of certiorari to quash the *h* decision and an interim mandatory injunction requiring the council to house her and her children pending the hearing of the application for judicial review. The judge granted the injunction ex parte, but on the council's application set it aside on the ground that although he had jurisdiction to grant such an injunction the case did not fall into the highly exceptional category which warranted such an injunction. The applicant appealed. *j*

---

a   Section 62 is set out at p 1205 *b* to *d*, post

b   Section 63 is set out at p 1205 *d e*, post

c   Section 64, so far as material, is set out at p 1205 *g h*, post

d   Section 58(2A) is set out at p 1209 *h*, post

Held – The appeal would be allowed for the following reasons—

a   (1) Having regard to the court's wide power under s 37[e] of the Supreme Court Act 1981 to grant injunctive relief and its power under RSC Ord 53, r 3(10)[f] to grant on an application for judicial review such interim relief as could be granted on an action begun by writ, the court had jurisdiction to grant an interim mandatory injunction requiring a local housing authority to house an applicant who had been granted leave to apply for judicial review pending the hearing of his application, since in such a case the applicant

b   was asserting that a public law right (viz to have the right decision made by the local authority) which he was entitled to have protected had been invaded by reason of the wrong decision (see p 1208 *f* to *j*, p 1209 *b* to *d*, p 1213 *a b* and p 1216 *f h*, post); *De Falco v Crawley BC* [1980] 1 All ER 913, *O'Reilly v Mackman* [1982] 3 All ER 1124 and *South Carolina Insurance Co v Assurantie Maatschappij 'de Zeven Provincien' NV* [1986] 3 All ER 487 applied.

c   (2) When the court was exercising its jurisdiction to grant an interim mandatory injunction against a local housing authority requiring it to house an applicant pending the hearing of his application for judicial review, the appropriate test was whether the applicant had shown a strong prima facie case of breach of duty by the housing authority rather than whether the case was so highly exceptional as to warrant the grant of such an injunction. The court was also required to balance the injustice which the applicant

d   would suffer if he was not housed pending the hearing of his application for judicial review against the public interest in not requiring the housing authority to provide accommodation to applicants ahead of others waiting to be rehoused. By her application for judicial review the applicant was asserting not only an invasion of her public law right under s 62 of the 1985 Act that the council would make proper inquiries and reach a proper decision on whether she was homeless but also an invasion of her private law

e   right under s 63 to be provided with temporary accommodation. Since, contrary to s 58(2A) of the 1985 Act, the council had not considered whether it was unreasonable for the applicant to continue to occupy the council flat in Scotland and had wrongly disregarded the husband's violence because it had taken place outside the home, and since the council's inquiries were, on the facts, inadequate, there was a very strong prima facie case that the council was in breach of its duty and that its decision was bad in law.

f   Furthermore, the balance of convenience came down in the applicant's favour since the injustice which would be caused to her if she was not rehoused but was right would be immense whereas the council would only be required to provide housing for a temporary period if at the hearing of the application for judicial review it was held that the council had been right (see p 1212 *a* to *e j* to p 1213 *e*, p 1214 *h* to p 1215 *a* and p 1216 *e* to *h*, post).

g

Notes

For a housing authority's duties to homeless persons, see 22 Halsbury's Laws (4th edn) para 513, and for cases on the subject, see 26 Digest (Reissue) 797–800, 5325–5338.

For the grant of an injunction on judicial review, see 37 Halsbury's Laws (4th edn) para 577.

h   For the Supreme Court Act 1981, s 37, see 11 Halsbury's Statutes (4th edn) 792.

For the Housing Act 1985, ss 58, 62, 63, 64, see 21 ibid 86, 90, 91, 92.

Cases referred to in judgments

A-G (ex rel Tilley) v Wandsworth London Borough [1981] 1 All ER 1162, [1981] 1 WLR 854, CA.

j   *e*   Section 37, so far as material, provides:
     '(1) The High Court may by order (whether interlocutory or final) grant an injunction . . . in all cases in which it appears to the court to be just and convenient to do so.
     (2) Any such order may be made either unconditionally or on such terms and conditions as the court thinks just . . .'
     f   Rule 3(10) is set out at p 1208 *h j*, post

American Cyanamid Co v Ethicon Ltd [1975] 1 All ER 504, [1975] AC 396, [1975] 2 WLR 316, HL.

Associated Provincial Picture Houses Ltd v Wednesbury Corp [1947] 2 All ER 680, [1948] 1 KB 223, CA.

Cocks v Thanet DC [1982] 3 All ER 1135, [1983] 2 AC 286, [1982] 3 WLR 1121, HL.

De Falco v Crawley BC [1980] 1 All ER 913, [1980] QB 460, [1980] 2 WLR 664, CA.

London and Clydeside Estates Ltd v Aberdeen DC [1979] 3 All ER 876, [1980] 1 WLR 182, HL.

O'Reilly v Mackman [1982] 3 All ER 1124, [1983] 2 AC 237, [1982] 3 WLR 1096, HL.

Puhlhofer v Hillingdon London BC [1986] 1 All ER 467, [1986] AC 484, [1986] 2 WLR 259, HL.

Sierbien v Westminster City Council (1987) 151 LG Rev 888, CA.

South Carolina Insurance Co v Assurantie Maatschappij 'de Zeven Provincien' NV [1986] 3 All ER 487, [1987] AC 24, [1986] 3 WLR 398, HL.

Wandsworth London BC v Winder [1984] 3 All ER 976, [1985] AC 461, [1984] 3 WLR 1254, HL.

Cases also cited

Chief Constable of Kent v V [1982] 3 All ER 36, [1983] QB 34, CA.

Films Rover International Ltd v Cannon Film Sales Ltd [1986] 3 All ER 772, [1987] 1 WLR 670.

Parker v Camden London BC [1985] 2 All ER 141, [1986] Ch 162, CA.

R v Wandsworth London Borough, ex p Henderson (1986) 18 HLR 522.

Appeal

By a notice dated 18 April 1988 Mrs Agnes Cross Hammell applied for judicial review by way of (i) an order of certiorari to quash the decisions of Kensington and Chelsea Royal London Borough Council made on 13 April 1988 that it was not satisfied that she was homeless and on 14 April not to review that decision, (ii) an order of mandamus requiring the council to secure that accommodation became available for occupation by Mrs Hammell and her family, (iii) a declaration that Mrs Hammell was homeless within the Housing Act 1985 and (iv) interim relief, namely an interlocutory injunction requiring the council to secure that accommodation was made available for occupation by Mrs Hammell and her family until the hearing of the application for judicial review. On 20 April 1988 Nolan J granted Mrs Hammell leave to apply for judicial review and made an interim mandatory injunction directing the council to secure that accommodation was made available for her and her family by 25 April, but gave the council liberty to apply to set aside the interim injunction. On 17 May 1988, on the council's application, Nolan J set aside the injunction. Mrs Hammell appealed, seeking reinstatement of the injunction. The facts are set out in the judgment of Parker LJ.

Robin Allen and *Martin Westgate* for Mrs Hammell.
Timothy Straker for the council.

PARKER LJ (giving the first judgment at the invitation of Fox LJ). On 12 April 1988 the applicant, Mrs Hammell, a divorced woman with custody of the three children of her former marriage, two boys aged 11 and 9 and a girl aged 7, applied in person to the respondent housing authority (the council) for accommodation. She was seen by a Mr Ashton. Put in its shortest form the basis of her application was that although she had a tenancy of a council house or flat in Alloa, Scotland, provided by the Clackmannan District Council, she had, in January 1988, been forced to flee therefrom due to violence and harassment on the part of her ex-husband and others instigated by him. He was living with a woman, who had at least one child, only a matter of some 50 yards away. Since coming to London in January 1988 she has been staying with her sister in a one-a bedroomed flat in the council's area, but her sister had, not surprisingly, had enough of sharing a small flat with her and her three children and required her to leave.

Not unnaturally the account which she gave to Mr Ashton resulted in him having reason to believe that she might (1) be homeless or threatened with homelessness and (2) have a priority need within the meaning of ss 58 and 59 of the Housing Act 1985 as amended by the Housing and Planning Act 1986.

b The consequences of Mr Ashton forming the view that he had reason to believe as aforesaid are set out in ss 62 and 63 of the 1985 Act. Section 62 provides as follows:

'(1) If a person (an "applicant") applies to a local housing authority for accommodation, or for assistance in obtaining accommodation, and the authority have reason to believe that he may be homeless or threatened with homelessness, they shall make such inquiries as are necessary to satisfy themselves as to whether he is homeless or threatened with homelessness.

c (2) If they are so satisfied, they shall make any further inquiries necessary to satisfy themselves as to—(a) whether he has a priority need, and (b) whether he became homeless or threatened with homelessness intentionally; and if they think fit they may also make inquiries as to whether he has a local connection with the district of another local housing authority in England, Wales or Scotland.'

d Section 63 provides:

'(1) If the local housing authority have reason to believe that an applicant may be homeless and have a priority need, they shall secure that accommodation is made available for his occupation pending a decision as a result of their inquiries under section 62.

e (2) This duty arises irrespective of any local connection which the applicant may have with the district of another local housing authority.'

The council had therefore, first, a duty under s 62 to make such inquiries as were necessary to enable them to satisfy themselves whether Mrs Hammell was homeless or threatened with homelessness and, second, a duty under s 63 to secure that accommodation

f was made available to her and her children pending a decision as a result of the necessary inquiries under s 62.

The council did make some inquiries on the following day, to which I shall revert hereafter, but later on the following day they issued a written notice under or purporting to be under s 64 of the 1985 Act. That section, so far as immediately material, provides as follows:

g '(1) On completing their inquiries under section 62, the local housing authority shall notify the applicant of their decision on the question whether he is homeless or threatened with homelessness.

(2) If they notify him that their decision is that he is homeless or threatened with homelessness, they shall at the same time notify him of their decision on the question whether he has a priority need . . .

h (4) If the local housing authority notify the applicant—(a) that they are not satisfied that he is homeless or threatened with homelessness . . .'

The notice which was given is in these terms:

'Dear M/S Hammell

j *Housing Act 1985*

Under the terms of Section 64 of the above Act, I write to inform you of my decision concerning your application for assistance. This Authority is *not* satisfied that you are homeless or threatened with homelessness. This Authoirty is satisfied that you have a priority need. This decision has been reached for the following reason:—You have accommodation at 24 Menteith Court Alloa which you are entitled to occupy. Travel warrants are available for you and your children to enable you to return.

Yours sincerely . . .'

It is signed by the director of housing and property services of the respondent council.

The issue of that notice was followed by some fruitless discussion between Mrs Hammell's solicitor and the council in an endeavour to secure a change of mind on their part. On 18 April 1988 a written application for leave to move for judicial review was lodged. It sought, inter alia, judicial review and quashing of the decision communicated by the notice which I have read and also interim relief by way of interlocutory injunction pending the hearing, the injunction sought being a mandatory injunction that the council should accommodate her pending such hearing.

The council were notified of the intention to make the application for an injunction and that the written application for leave requested an oral hearing. On 20 April the oral hearing took place before Nolan J who ex parte, the council not having elected to appear due to some muddle in the offices, granted interim relief and leave to move. The order so far as interim relief was concerned was in the following terms:

'AND IT IS FURTHER ORDERED that the Respondents by themselves their agents or servants or otherwise howsoever do secure that accommodation is made avilable for the occupation by the Applicant and her family by the 25th day of April 1988 until the hearing of their application for Judicial Review or further order and that the Respondents do have liberty to apply to vary or set aside this interlocutory injunction on an 24 hours notice to the applicant or her representatives.'

The council, as one might have expected, duly complied with the order of the court, but also applied to set aside the interim injunction. The application in that behalf was heard also by Nolan J on 17 May. He then set aside the order. In substance he held, contrary to the council's submission, that there was jurisdiction to grant relief by way of interim mandatory injunction, but that the case did not in his view fall into what he described as the highly exceptional category in which such relief could be granted. Against the discharge of the injunction, Mrs Hammell now appeals.

I deal first with the question of jurisdiction. That point arose in *De Falco v Crawley BC* [1980] 1 All ER 913, [1980] QB 460. The headnote accurately summarises the effect of the judgments and I begin by reading part of it ([1980] QB 460 at 462):

'*Per curiam.* Though the [Housing (Homeless Persons) Act 1977] itself provides no remedy for a person adversely affected by a breach of statutory duty, it has already been decided that such person could bring an ordinary action for damages in the county court, and there is no reason why in such an action, whether in the county court or the High Court, he could not also claim declarations that a decision was invalid, and an injunction; that, alternatively, he could bring proceedings for judicial review under R.S.C., Order 53, and in either case could apply for interim relief by way of mandatory injunction ordering the provision of accommodation; but such relief should only be granted where a strong prima facie case of breach of duty is made out at the interlocutory stage.'

I refer also to passages in the judgments in that case. First, Lord Denning MR under the heading 'The granting of an interlocutory injunction' said ([1980] 1 All ER 913 at 922, [1980] QB 460 at 478):

'This is not the same sort of case as *American Cyanamid Co v Ethicon Ltd* [1975] 1 All ER 504, [1975] AC 396 because the plaintiffs here cannot give any worthwhile undertaking in damages. No injunction should be granted against the council unless the plaintiffs made out a strong prima facie case that the council's finding of "intentional homelessness" was invalid. I would go further. It should not be granted unless it is a case in which, on an application for judicial review, certiorari would be granted to quash their decision: and mandamus issued to command them to consider the case afresh.'

Bridge LJ said ([1980] 1 All ER 913 at 924, [1980] QB 460 at 481):

'I have no doubt therefore that the court may properly exercise its discretion to grant a mandatory injunction on an interlocutory application in an appropriate case. In considering what principles should govern the exercise of this discretion, I do not think much assistance is to be derived from authority. In particular I am satisfied that the principles expounded by Lord Diplock in *American Cyanamid Co v Ethicon Ltd* governing the grant of prohibitory injunctions on interlocutory applications have no relevance to the case we are considering. A dispute between an applicant who claims entitlement to be provided with accommodation, and a local authority who dispute that entitlement, exhibits sufficiently unusual features to make a comparison even with other types of litigation where a mandatory injunction may be granted on an interim application difficult and possibly misleading. I think the appropriate principles can only be derived from a consideration of the likely consequences to the parties to such a dispute of granting or withholding relief. In a case where the applicant is entitled to relief but it is withheld, he will be rendered homeless when he should have been housed. This is an injury which is sufficiently traumatic and hardly compensable in damages. On the other hand, if the local authority are required to provide accommodation to which the applicant is not entitled, this may, as the figures we have been given in the present case show, impose a heavy financial burden on the ratepayers with no prospect of recompense by way of a cross-undertaking in damages. What is perhaps more important, a mandatory injunction to provide accommodation for a particular applicant who ought not to enjoy priority may operate to the detriment of others on the local authority's housing list by interfering with the local authority's own system of priorities for the fair distribution of limited housing resources. In the light of these considerations, I think the court inevitably must make the best assessment it can, on an interim application for a mandatory injunction, of the strength of the applicant's claim to impugn the local authority's decision adverse to him and should only grant the relief sought if a strong prima facie case is made out.'

That case is clear authority that there is jurisdiction in this court to grant such an injunction, whether the application is made in an action commenced by writ or by way of judicial review under RSC Ord 53. It is contended, however, that the decision can no longer stand in the light of decisions of the House of Lords in *O'Reilly v Mackman* [1982] 3 All ER 1124, [1983] 2 AC 237, *Cocks v Thanet DC* [1982] 3 All ER 1135, [1983] 2 AC 286, *Puhlhofer v Hillingdon London BC* [1986] 1 All ER 467, [1986] AC 484 and *South Carolina Insurance Co v Assurantie Maatschappij 'de Zeven Provincien' NV* [1986] 3 All ER 487, [1987] AC 24. The last of these cases does not appear to have been cited to the judge.

As to the first three I am, for my part, unable, as was the judge, to see that anything stated in those cases affects the *De Falco* decision on the particular point. It is true that since that time *O'Reilly v Mackman* and *Cocks v Thanet DC* have made it clear that if it is desired to take the positive step of initiating the court to quash a decision on such a matter, the route by which that must be done is by Ord 53, but I have found nothing in any of the three cases which indicates that the court's view that there was power to grant a mandatory injunction is regarded by the House of Lords as having been wrong, the more particularly since the case was itself referred to without any observation to that effect. It was observed that the position might have gone differently had it been realised that procedurally it was wrong. But that is a wholly different matter. Indeed *O'Reilly v Mackman* appears to me to afford strong ground for saying that the decision was entirely right and has full force and effect. In that case Lord Diplock said ([1982] 3 All ER 1124 at 1133–1134, [1983] 2 AC 237 at 283–285):

'So Ord 53 since 1977 has provided a procedure by which every type of remedy for infringement of the rights of individuals that are entitled to protection in public *a* law can be obtained in one and the same proceeding by way of an application for judicial review, and whichever remedy is found to be the most appropriate in the light of what has emerged on the hearing of the application, can be granted to him. If what should emerge is that his complaint is not of an infringement of any of his rights that are entitled to protection in public law, but may be an infringement of his rights in private law and thus not a proper subject for judicial review, the court *b* has power under r 9(5), instead of refusing the application, to order the proceedings to continue as if they had begun by writ. There is no such converse power under the Rules of the Supreme Court to permit an action begun by writ to continue as if it were an application for judicial review; and I respectfully disagree with that part of the judgment of Lord Denning MR in the instant case which suggests that such a power may exist; not do I see the need to amend the rules in order to create one . . . *c* The position of applicants for judicial review has been drastically ameliorated by the new Ord 53. It has removed all those disadvantages, particularly in relation to discovery, that were manifestly unfair to them and had, in many cases, made applications for prerogative orders an inadequate remedy if justice was to be done. This it was that justified the courts in not treating as an abuse of their powers resort to an alternative procedure by way of action for a declaration or injunction (not then *d* obtainable on an application under Ord 53), despite the fact that this procedure had the effect of depriving the defendants of the protection to statutory tribunals and public authorities for which for public policy reasons Ord 53 provided. Now that those disadvantages to applications have been removed and all remedies for infringements of rights protected by public law can be obtained on an application for judicial review, as can also remedies for infringements of rights under private *e* law if such infringements should also be involved, it would in my view as a general rule be contrary to public policy, and as such an abuse of the process of the court, to permit a person seeking to establish that a decision of public authority infringed rights to which he was entitled to protection under public law to proceed by way of an ordinary action and by this means to evade the provisions of Ord 53 for the *f* protection of such authorities.'

That appears to me to be saying in the plainest terms that, whatever you could have got by either route prior to the decision in *O'Reilly v Mackman*, you can now get by the one route which you must proceed along, namely Ord 53, and the *De Falco* decision [1980] 1 All ER 913, [1980] QB 460 therefore appears to me to be reinforced rather than weakened by *O'Reilly v Mackman*. When one adds to this the general terms of s 37 of the Supreme *g* Court Act 1981, which confers a wide power to grant such interlocutory relief, and the terms of Ord 53, r 3(10), it appears to me that the jurisdiction is made plain. I do not read again s 37 of the 1981 Act, but I do read r 3(10) of Ord 53, which is in these terms:

'Where leave to apply for judicial review is granted, then—(*a*) if the relief sought is an order of prohibition or certiorari and the Court so directs, the grant shall *h* operate as a stay of the proceedings to which the application relates until the determination of the application or until the court otherwise orders; (*b*) if any other relief is sought, the Court may at any time grant in the proceedings such interim relief as could be granted in an action begun by writ.'

In an action begun by writ it is beyond doubt that a mandatory injunction could, in appropriate cases, be granted. The matter is dealt with by Ord 29, r 1. *j*

As to the last of the cases which is said to affect the matter, the decision of the House of Lords in *South Carolina Insurance Co v Assurantie Maatschappij 'de Zeven Provincien' NV* [1986] 3 All ER 487, [1987] AC 24, the effect of the decision was adequately stated in the headnote, which is in these terms ([1987] AC 24 at 25):

a '... although the power of the High Court to grant injunctions, which was a statutory power conferred by section 37(1) of the Supreme Court Act 1981, was very wide it was limited, save for two exceptions irrelevant to the present proceedings, to the situations (Lord Mackay of Clashfern and Lord Goff of Chieveley dubitante) (i) where one party to an action could show that the other party had either invaded, or threatened to invade, a legal or equitable right of the former for the enforcement of which the latter was amenable to the jurisdiction of the court ...'

b In cases such as this the application for judicial review is in effect asserting that a public law right which is entitled to protection (see Lord Diplock in the passages I have quoted) has been invaded in that a wrong decision has been made. It may be that as a matter of discretion the court on the hearing of the application for judicial review, while accepting the submission, will not grant the relief claimed, but that the applicant is asserting that a *c* right in public law has been invaded I regard for myself as being beyond all argument.

In my view there is clearly jurisdiction to grant relief whenever leave to move for judicial review is given and it is clear from *Puhlhofer v Hillingdon London BC* [1986] 1 All ER 467, [1986] AC 484 that leave will only be given in limited circumstances. Those circumstances, I entirely accept, must involve the applicant in showing a strong prima facie case; that is said in clear terms in *De Falco v Crawley BC* [1980] 1 All ER 913, [1980] *d* QB 460. I accept also that, unlike in the ordinary case where the balancing on the matter of convenience is between the two parties directly concerned, in all, or most, cases where the application is for judicial reivew, a very important consideration will be the public interest involved; that matter is dealt with in *Sierbien v Westminster City Council* (1987) 151 LG Rev 888.

With these matters in mind it is now necessary to examine in some detail the events *e* which occurred on 12 and 13 April 1988 and the consequences of such events. But first I refer to s 58 of the Housing Act 1985. So far as relevant s 58 reads:

'(1) A person is homeless if he has no accommodation in England, Wales or Scotland.

(2) A person shall be treated as having no accommodation if there is no *f* accommodation which he, together with any other person who normally resides with him as a member of his family or in circumstances in which it is reasonable for that person to reside with him—(a) is entitled to occupy by virtue of an interest in it or by virtue of an order of a court ...

(3) A person is also homeless if he has accommodation but ... (b) it is probable that occupation of it will lead to violence from some other person residing in it or to threats of violence from some other person residing in it and likely to carry out *g* the threats ...'

To that section there was added by s 14 of the Housing and Planning Act 1986 the following subsections:

'(2A) A person shall not be treated as having accommodation unless it is *h* accommodation which it would be reasonable for him to continue to occupy.

(2B) Regard may be had, in determining whether it would be reasonable for a person to continue to occupy accommodation, to the general circumstances prevailing in relation to housing in the district of the local housing authority to whom he has applied for accommodation or for assistance in obtaining accommodation.'

j In the present instance the duty of the council, it being plain that there was accommodation which Mrs Hammell and her children were entitled to occupy, was as follows: (1) to make inquiries necessary to satisfy themselves that 24 Menteith Court was accommodation which it would be reasonable for Mrs Hammell to continue to occupy and (2) to house her and her children until they had completed such inquiries and so

decided. It is to be noted that the section requires a positive decision to be made by the
council that the accommodation is accommodation which it would be reasonable for her *a*
to continue to occupy.

I go now to the council's documents to see in more detail what happened. The formal
form of application signed by Mrs Hammell is followed by internal notes by the council's
officers. The form filled in by Mrs Hammell reveals her present address, which is her
sister's address. It reveals the names and dates of birth of her three children. It reveals the
name of her tenanted property in Scotland, 24 Menteith Court, Alloa and her previous *b*
address, which had been the matrimonial home which had had to be sold during the
course of the proceedings leading to the divorce and as a result of which sale she was
granted a tenancy of 24 Menteith Court. There is a page which refers to medical details,
but I find nothing on that of significance.

I come now to the notes of what happened when Mrs Hammell came for interview
and thereafter. The notes relating to the day on which she came for interview are headed *c*
with the date, 12 April 1988, and are in these terms:

> 'Is at present living with sister at Adair Tower for 10 weeks—she is now asking
> her to leave. She has got a council tenancy in Alloa but has left there because of
> violence & harassment from ex-husband. M/S Hammell separated from her husband
> & was rehoused by Alloa. Unfortunately he has now moved in with someone else *d*
> opposite where M/S Hammell lives. Her ex-husband not only harasses her himself
> [but sends] friends around to do the same. She has not got a telephone & cannot
> raise the alarm when he comes around. When she came to England she went to
> SHAC [the Shelter Housing Action Centre] & they advised her to go to
> [Hammersmith and Fulham housing authority] or [Royal Borough of Kensington
> and Chelsea housing authority] & seek NMS transfer.'   *e*

NMS refers to a national mobility scheme, which is of no statutory force but which is
operated by many of the councils in England, Wales and Scotland, enabling council
tenants for various reasons to be transferred from one area to another. The notes continue,
setting out the name of Mrs Hammell's solicitor in Alloa and reporting the facts that she
had told Mr Ashton that she had been advised by her solicitor that in order to obtain an *f*
injunction she would need a witness; that she apparently went to Hammersmith and
Fulham, who suggested the emergency national mobility scheme and that she should
not give up the tenancy but should go to Scotland to fill up the forms. She in fact went
to Scotland for the day pursuant to that advice, filled in forms and then returned. The
note continues:

> 'Came back & saw [Hammersmith and Fulham] & they said no connection (NMS *g*
> for them suggested [Royal Borough of Kensington and Chelsea housing authority])
> as staying there. Came here checked nothing had come to us. Discovered
> Clackmannan [District Council] had lost papers. Served notice.'

That requires a word of explanation. On her arrival in this country on 26 January 1988
Mrs Hammell very sensibly went to the shelter housing action centre. They advised her *h*
immediately to go to Scotland and apply for a transfer under the national mobility
scheme. She did so. Having done so she lodged her papers with them and returned to
London. That was a day trip which took place on 28 January. Thereafter, while waiting
for a communication, nothing occurred until on 31 March, addressed to her sister's flat,
she received a notice of abandonment relating to the tenancy at 24 Menteith Court. That
no doubt surprised her. She sought again assistance from the housing action centre. They *j*
communicated with Clackmannan District Council and explained to them that they
must have had the application, or they would not otherwise have known that the proper
place to find her was at her sister's address, whereupon they suspended the operation of
the abandonment notice.

There is recorded at the bottom of the first page of these notes the following by Mr
a Ashton:

> 'Spoke to Sue [that is a Mrs or Miss Sue Lucking] about case. She said violence was
> from outside the home & she considered it reasonable for her to return & [seek]
> legal assistance to protect herself and her interests.'

That concludes the notes of 12 April and it is not surprising that, on the basis of what
b he there recorded, Mr Ashton concluded that there was reason to believe that she might
be homeless and have a priority need. Indeed had he not so concluded, the decision
would, as it seems to me, have been wholly irrational or *Wednesbury* unreasonable (see
Associated Provincial Picture Houses Ltd v Wednesbury Corp [1947] 2 All ER 680, [1948] 1
KB 223), but it is accepted that the conclusion was so reached. Thereupon it became the
council's duty to make the inquiries and to provide accommodation.
c   The position is exactly the same as was referred to by Sir David Cairns in *De Falco v
Crawley BC* [1980] 1 All ER 913 at 926, [1980] QB 460 at 483 where he says:

> 'Once a housing authority have reason to believe that an applicant for housing
> accommodation may be homeless and may have a priority need they are obliged, if
> they consider that he may be intentionally homeless, to secure accommodation for
d > him while they make enquiries about the matter (s 3(4) of the Housing (Homeless
> Persons) Act 1977). Then they must not thereafter deprive him of accommodation
> on the ground of intentional homelessness unless (a) they are satisfied that he is
> intentionally homeless (s 4(2)), and (b) he has had such time as they consider will
> give him a reasonable opportunity of finding accommodation for himself (s 4(3)).'

That deals with a different problem because it was in that case intentional homelessness
e which arose. But the principle there stated is clearly right; once the conclusion has been
reached which imposes the duty to make the inquiries and to procure accommodation,
the applicant cannot be deprived of that right unless and until the inquiries have been
made and the appropriate decision reached.
    On 13 April the notes continue as follows:

f > 'Rang Clackmannan District Council. Spoke to Mr M'Andrew estate office. He
> confirmed property was still available to her. They had cancelled abandonment
> procedure after receiving letter from H.A.C [the housing action centre]. They were
> investigating problems with harassment & then they will decide to put through a
> N.M.S. Asked if they were aware of any damage caused by ex-husband or anyone
> else. He said No. Rang solicitor Mr Adams of I Allen Grant & Co. He said he hadn't
g > seen Ms Hammell for over 6 months (at least). He knew she had problems in the
> past with her ex-husband & [there] was an injunction in 1986–1987. He did not
> have to go back to courts at any time because of any breach by her ex-husband. He
> did confirm that [an] injunction in Scotland did need witness before they can
> proceed. He also added that he thought she had come down to England earlier than
> 10 weeks ago. When I told him that we were likely to say she was not homeless—
h > he replied "I am not surprised, but I cannot lie". Spoke to Ian Mitchell NMS cannot
> help family units no point in nominating. *Graham* Section 64 prepared Not homeless
> Violence is from outside the home and it is Sue's opinion it will be reasonable.'

There somewhat surprisingly the notes end.
    There is, in addition to the notes I have already read, a note signed by the same person
j who signed the notice, in the following terms:

> 'Sec 64 issued No Duty—not homeless violence occurs outside home. I appreciate
> the situation will be difficult for her but would suggest that she takes legal advice
> regarding non-molestation order if necessary with power of arrest. Also she should

approach Alloa council regarding possibility of urgent management transfer. She
also be offered travel warrant.'

The notice itself can be attacked on a number of grounds. In the first place the reason
given was on its face bad in law. It would have been good in law until the enactment of
s 58(2A) by s 14 of the Housing and Planning Act 1986, but the result of that was that
before the council could determine that she was not homeless, they had to reach a positive
decision that it would be reasonable for her and her children to continue to occupy 24
Menteith Court, Alloa.

Secondly it can be attacked because there was material to show that the background
reason was that violence was outside the home and therefore did not matter. That again
would no doubt have been a sufficient reason had it not been for the enactment of sub-s
(2A) of s 58, because under s 58(3)(b) of the 1985 Act there is provision that a person is
homeless is he has accommodation but it is probable that occupation of it will lead to
violence from some other person residing in it. But since it is now the position that the
test is reasonableness of occupation, it cannot be right in law to suggest, as the council
appear to believe, that violence outside the home is not at least a very important factor
going to the question of whether it is reasonable to occupy. There used to be, and indeed
may still be among the many complications of the criminal law, an offence known as
watching and besetting, which is something quite sufficient to render life intolerable to
somebody, albeit nothing takes place within the premises themselves.

Thirdly, it can be attacked on the ground that the real reason, albeit a bad one, was
that the violence was outside the home and not the reason stated.

Fourthly, it can be attacked on the ground that the inquiries that the council were
obliged to make were insufficient to fulfil their statutory duty and that no reasonable
council could, on the result of those inquiries, have supposed either (a) that the inquiries
were sufficient, or (b) that they justify a conclusion that it would be reasonable for Mrs
Hammell and her family to go back to 24 Menteith Court. As to this last matter, one
asks: what did they know? They knew that Clackmannan District Council had confirmed
that the house was available. They knew that there had been an injunction. They knew
that Clackmannan District Council were going to investigate the matter of harassment.
They had from a solicitor the observation that he was not surprised that the council were
likely to reject the suggestion that Mrs Hammell was homeless. But they also knew that
the solicitor had not seen her for at least six months. For my part I cannot regard anything
which the solicitor said, other than confirmation of the legal position that she could not
get an injunction without a witness and that there had been no application for breach of
the earlier injunction, as being of the slightest significance.

On the basis of those notes, one would perhaps have expected that the council, having
initiated quite properly, and very speedily, as they are encouraged to do, the inquiries
which the statute obliges them to make would have pursued them. Instead the council
stopped at a point when everything indicated the necessity of obtaining from
Clackmannan District Council the result of their inquiries into the matter of harassment.
But that did not occur either before or after issue of the s 64 purported notice. Since
14 April it appears that the council have not inquired of Clackmannan District Council
how their inquiries are going and what they have found. It was submitted by counsel for
the council that the respondent council are not obliged to make CID-type inquiries. I
would readily accept that. But this is not a case of CID-type inquiries. Having properly
approached the people who could most readily ascertain whether Mrs Hammell's account
was right and whether the degree of harassment was such as she described, they then
took no further action, save that they ascertained just before the hearing before us began
that nothing further had occurred since 13 April.

The position may now be analysed. Mrs Hammell had on 12 April acquired a private
right. That was a private right to be provided with accommodation on a temporary basis.
It was accepted by counsel for the council, quite rightly, that that right, so long as it
existed, could be enforced by a mandatory injunction. That injunction would, albeit

limited in point of time, have been a final rather than an interim injunction. The duty
a of the council was plain at that point of time. Mrs Hammell could, in my view, only be
deprived of the right that she had then acquired by a decision validly taken by the council
after they had fulfilled their duty to make necessary inquiries that it was reasonable for
her to go back to Scotland and occupy the accommodation in Alloa. She had a public
right to have that decision properly taken. Until that time, had the council originally
provided accommodation and then purported to take it away, she could in my view have
b set up the invalidity of the purported s 64 decision as an answer to any attempt to remove
her. She has to have a strong prima facie case that the council's duty was not fulfilled and
that their decision was bad in law. In my view she succeeds. She has raised not only a
serious question to be tried within *American Cyanamid Co v Ethicon Ltd* [1975] 1 All ER
504, [1975] AC 396, not only a strong prima facie case, which, on the basis of *De Falco v
Crawley BC* [1980] 1 All ER 913, [1980] QB 460, is enough, but in my view a very strong
c prima facie case. She is entitled to protection with regard to her public law right to have
the necessary inquiries made and the decision thereon properly made and also in the
meantime to protection of her private right on the basis that she may show, when the
case comes to trial, that it has been sought wrongly to take it away from her.

As to the respective injustice and the public interest, the injustice to Mrs Hammell, if
she is not housed but is right, is clearly immense, as Bridge LJ pointed out in the *De Falco*
d case [1980] 1 All ER 913 at 924, [1980] QB 460 at 481. If she is housed, but it turns out
in the end that the council were right, they will have been obliged to house her
temporarily, but there can be no question of permanent queue-jumping. This is no more
than interim protection for as long as it takes to decide the substantive matter of judicial
review.

As to the public interest involved, it is plain that under s 22 of the 1985 Act the council
e is under a positive duty to give preference to those people, among others, who are
homeless. It is also clear that under s 1 of the Child Care Act 1980 the council have a duty
to promote the welfare of children. That duty under s 1 was previously imposed by s 1
of the Children and Young Persons Act 1963 and under that Act it was held in *A-G (ex rel
Tilley) v Wandsworth London Borough* [1981] 1 All ER 1162, [1981] 1 WLR 854 that the
duty under the section and the power under the section to provide assistance included a
f power in the local authority to provide or pay for accommodation and that that power
might be exercised, notwithstanding that the parents of the children in question had
been found to be intentionally homeless.

The council's position is that they are, of course, at liberty to try to cure the position
and it is worthwhile referring in relation to that and also in relation to the use of so-called
terms of art, to the speech of Lord Hailsham LC in *London and Clydeside Estates Ltd v
g Aberdeen DC* [1979] 3 All ER 876 at 883, [1980] 1 WLR 182 at 189, where he said:

'In the reported decisions there is much language presupposing the existence of
stark categories such as "mandatory" and "directory", "void" and "voidable", a
"nullity", and "purely regulatory". Such language is useful; indeed, in the course of
this opinion I have used some of it myself. But I wish to say that I am not at all clear
h that the language itself may not be misleading in so far as it may be supposed to
present a court with the necessity of fitting a particular case into one or other of
mutually exclusive and starkly contrasted compartments, compartments which in
some cases (eg "void" and "voidable") are borrowed from the language of contract
or status, and are not easily fitted to the requirements of administrative law. When
Parliament lays down a statutory requirement for the exercise of legal authority it
j expects its authority to be obeyed down to the minutest detail. But what the courts
have to decide in a particular case is the legal consequence of non compliance on the
rights of the subject viewed in the light of a concrete state of facts and a continuing
chain of events. It may be that what the courts are faced with is not so much a stark
choice of alternatives but a spectrum of possibilities in which one compartment or
description fades gradually into another. At one end of this spectrum there may be

cases in which a fundamental obligation may have been so outrageously and
flagrantly ignored or defied that the subject may safely ignore what has been done   *a*
and treat it as having no legal consequences on himself. In such a case if the
defaulting authority seeks to rely on its action it may be that the subject is entitled
to use the defect in procedure simply as a shield or defence without having taken
any positive action of his own.'

I pause there to observe that Lord Hailsham LC there foreshadowed a later decision in
Wandsworth London BC v Winder [1984] 3 All ER 976, [1985] AC 461. Lord Hailsham LC   *b*
continued ([1979] 3 All ER 876 at 883, [1980] 1 WLR 182 at 189–190):

'At the other end of the spectrum the defect in procedure may be so nugatory or
trivial that the authority can safely proceed without remedial action, confident that,
if the subject is so misguided as to rely on the fault, the courts will decline to listen
to his complaint. But in a very great number of cases, it may be in a majority of   *c*
them, it may be necessary for a subject, in order to safeguard himself, to go to the
court for declaration of his rights, the grant of which may well be discretionary, and
by the like token it may be wise for an authority (as it certainly would have been
here) to do anything in its power to remedy the fault in its procedure so as not to
deprive the subject of his due or themselves of their power to act. In such cases,
though language like "mandatory", "directory", "void", "voidable", "nullity" and so   *d*
forth may be helpful in argument, it may be misleading in effect if relied on to
show that the courts, in deciding the consequences of a defect in the exercise of
power, are necessarily bound to fit the facts of a particular case and a developing
chain of events into rigid legal categories or to stretch or cramp them on a bed of
Procrustes invented by lawyers for the purposes of convenient exposition.'
                                                                                       e
In the light of that elegant statement of the difficulties, I do not propose to try and
state any formula for the exercise of the discretion to grant a mandatory injunction in
the case of applications under Ord 53. Attempts in the past have led to no more than
explanations in subsequent decisions. The case was clearly stated by this court in *De Falco
v Crawley BC* [1980] 1 All ER 913, [1980] QB 460, which, as I have said, is in my view
still good law.   *f*
I would therefore reverse the decision of Nolan J. He dealt with the matter as a matter
of discretion, but it is to be noted, first, that of course he had far less developed argument
than has been available to this court and it is also to be observed that he dealt with the
matter very shortly. He said:

'I say nothing more about the merits of this case which seems to me, as it did   *g*
when I granted leave, to be an arguable case save that, in the light of all the
information now disclosed to me [which was basically the council's internal
documents], I can no longer regard it as such an exceptional case as to justify the
exceptional relief of an interim injunction for the provision of accommodation. On
the applicant's evidence it is undoubtedly an extremely sad case but I cannot, as a
matter of law, regard it as falling into the highly exceptional category to which the   *h*
authorities now relegate relief of this sort.'

The reference to 'exceptional' I take to be something which comes from the last page
of the speech of Lord Brightman in *Puhlhofer v Hillingdon London BC* [1986] 1 All ER 467
at 474, [1986] AC 484 at 518, which was a speech in which the remaining members of
the Appellate Committee concurred. It is perfectly true that the word 'exceptional' is   *j*
there used, but it is not in my view used as a term of art, as is perfectly plain from what
follows. Lord Brightman was merely rehearsing the grounds on which courts will review
the exercise of administrative discretion and although stated in terms which could
possibly mean that there had been a radical alteration, do not appear to me to produce
that result. I am satisfied that in the present case this court is entitled to interfere on the

grounds that the legal significance of s 58(2A) of the 1985 Act was not appreciated and
a that as a result the decision was plainly wrong.

There remains a matter of procedure which was canvassed by counsel for the council,
namely the question whether, assuming an application, as I hold it can, can be made for
interim relief of this sort, it can be made made ex parte or must be made on notice to the
other side. The position under Ord 53 is that every application for leave to move must
be made ex parte in the first instance (r 3(2)) and it is on the grant of leave, which may be
b made on such ex parte application, that the alternative powers under Ord 53, r 3(10)
arise. The judge, when considering whether or not to grant an application for interim
relief, having decided that he would grant leave and therefore given himself jurisdiction
to grant relief of either of the types mentioned in the paragraph, will no doubt consider
whether the case is sufficiently urgent to warrant his dealing with it at that time, or
whether he should put it over to be heard inter partes. In so doing he would be reflecting
c the procedure under Ord 29 that would apply in the case of an action, for there it is
provided that except in urgent cases the application for interim relief must be made by
motion or on summons (see Ord 29, r 1(2)). It is therefore impossible to rule that all such
applications must be on notice. I would, however, for my part observe that where an
application for interim relief is intended to be made, the applicant would be well advised
to give notice to the other party that such an application is being made in order that the
d other party may, if he so wishes, attend and assist the court by filling in any gaps in the
information which may be available and thereby enable the matter to be dealt with
properly at a first hearing and dispense with the necessity of having a second hearing. I
can therefore say no more than that notice that an ex parte application for interim relief
is going to be made would be an advisable step in all cases.

For the reasons which, I fear at great length, I have endeavoured to give, I would allow
e this appeal. I would conclude only by thanking counsel for their assistance, which I have
found to be invaluable.

CROOM-JOHNSON LJ. The duties of the local housing authority with respect to
homelessness begin with the Housing Act 1985, s 62(1). It is for the authority to decide
as a question of fact whether it has reason to believe that an applicant may be homeless.
f In the present case it is common ground that the respondent housing authority (the
council) did have such reason. The authority then has a duty under s 62(1) to 'make such
inquiries as are necessary to satisfy themselves as to whether [the applicant] is homeless'.
It is not until the authority is satisfied whether the applicant is homeless that the duty
arises to satisfy themselves whether the applicant has a priority need: see s 62(2). In the
present case there never was any doubt that the applicant, Mrs Hammell, if she was
g homeless, had a priority need. The right to be accommodated under s 63 does not have
to await the result of the inquiries to be made under s 62. That right comes into existence
immediately the authority decides that it has reason to believe the applicant may be
homeless and may have a priority need. It is a right which subsists until the inquiries are
complete and lasts while the decision to be made as a result of its inquiries is pending. It
h is when the inquiries are complete that the authority comes to its so-called s 64 decision
whether the applicant is homeless and then if the decision is adverse to the applicant the
right to be accommodated would normally come to an end.

Counsel for the council submitted that, subject to any later challenge by way of a
judicial review or to a decision which is obviously irregular, the decision is final. Counsel
further submitted that when the decision is made, the applicant's rights are restricted to
j whatever disposal is authorised by the later sections of the Act, but that if the decision is
adverse, his rights are restricted to whatever remedies would be available to him on an
application under RSC Ord 53. If he applies for judicial review, he says the decision
stands until it is quashed and an order similar to a mandamus is made that the authority
shall come to a proper decision. For that he relies on the speech of Lord Bridge in *Cocks v
Thanet DC* [1982] 3 All ER 1135 esp at 1140, [1983] 2 AC 286 esp at 295, where he said:

'But it will be otherwise where the housing authority's decision is successfully impugned on other grounds, as for instance that the applicant was not fairly heard or that irrelevant factors have been taken into account. In such cases certiorari to quash and mandamus to re-determine will, in strictness, be the appropriate remedies and the only appropriate remedies.'

I say nothing about the validity of those submissions, but in any event they would depend on certain previous requirements having been met. In the first place the inquiries made under s 62 must be such as are necessary. In the present case I do not think that the two telephone calls to Scotland without any follow-up fulfilled that test. One has great sympathy with the council. They are deluged with these applications. We have been told that throughout the country they number about 200,000 a year. The authorities have to work at speed in reliance on uncertain and possibly unsafe sources of information. But there was that about this case which clearly needed further investigation.

I do not wish to prejudge what may hereafter turn out to be the proper decision as to whether Mrs Hammell really is homeless and therefore whether the decision of 13 April 1988 was a proper decision. But it does appear possible that her right to be accommodated under s 63 may not have been properly determined.

There is another point which arises on counsel's argument for the council. It is that under s 64 the decision reached by the authority should be notified to the applicant. The council did tell Mrs Hammell that in their view she was not homeless and s 64 requires that if they were not so satisfied they should notify her of their reason. In this case Mrs Hammell's homelessness was entirely dependent on whether she could claim the benefit of s 58(2A) of the 1985 Act to which Parker LJ has already referred. The notification given to her on 13 April made no mention of whether it was reasonable for her to occupy 24 Menteith Court, Alloa. All it said was 'you are entitled to occupy', and as a legal fact that was correct. The notification, and thus the document embodying the decision, was in my view bad on the face of it. There was at least uncertainty as to whether the decision was properly reached, as to which I make no pronouncement. But if it was not properly reached, then Mrs Hammell's right to interim accommodation under s 63 did not come to an end. The judicial review in this case has not yet taken place, but until these matters have been resolved, Mrs Hammell is entitled, in my opinion, to an injunction to protect her s 63 right. The test to be applied in seeing whether she should have an injunction is not whether the case is exceptional, which is what Nolan J appeared to be considering in his judgment. When Lord Brightman used that word in *Puhlhofer v Hillingdon London BC* [1986] 1 All ER 467 at 474, [1986] AC 484 at 518 he was referring to whether leave for judicial review should be given. He was not referring to the circumstances in which an injunction should be given. Leave has already been given for judicial review. The decision whether to grant the injunction has to be made on what I concede to be the ordinary lines as outlined by Parker LJ.

In my view there is an arguable case of sufficient seriousness here for the court to grant the injunction and if one looks at the balance of convenience it comes down clearly in Mrs Hammell's favour. I too would allow the appeal from the decision of Nolan J.

FOX LJ. I agree with the judgment of Parker LJ and I would allow the appeal accordingly.

Appeal allowed. Leave to appeal to the House of Lords refused.

Solicitors: *Brocklesby & Co* (for Mrs Hammell); *A J Colvin* (for the council).

Wendy Shockett   Barrister.

End of volume 1